S0-AYF-489

'06

THROUGH MY EYES

THROUGH MY EYES

The Story of a Surgeon Who Dared to Take on the Medical World

by Charles D. Kelman, M.D.

Crown Publishers, Inc.
New York

HES

Dedicated to the aspiring struggling hungry underdogs of the world

This story is true. Some of the names and places have been changed—what was done is important, who did it is not. In some cases, two or more characters have been compressed into one for the sake of clarity and brevity. Certain scenes have been dramatized for the sake of continuity. The story is, as stated, the truth, as seen through my eyes.

Copyright © 1985 by Dr. Charles Kelman
All rights reserved. No part of this book may be reproduced or transmitted in any form or by any means, electronic or mechanical, including photocopying, recording, or by any information storage and retrieval system, without permission in writing from the publisher.
Published by Crown Publishers, Inc., One Park Avenue, New York, New York 10016 and simultaneously in Canada by General Publishing Company Limited
Manufactured in the United States of America
Crown is a trademark of Crown Publishers, Inc.

Library of Congress Cataloging in Publication Data
Kelman, Charles D.
Through my eyes.
1. Kelman, Charles D. 2. Ophthalmologists—United States—Biography. 3. Surgeons—United States—Biography. I. Title.
RE36.K45A38 1985 617.7′092′4 [B] 84-21446
ISBN 0-517-55600-6

Book design by Lenny Henderson

10 9 8 7 6 5 4 3 2 1

First Edition

Contents

Acknowledgments

Writing a book is basically a lonely job, but yet it can not be done alone. Few are clever enough to be objective about their own words; we need the feedback, the encouragement and yes, the cries of dismay which our true friends, critics, and editors give us. So, although I have written this book myself, I am greatly beholden to the many who helped me along the way. To Sam Wisgord who first suggested I write it, to Debbie Gasparri who listened, and read each paragraph and gave me the confidence in the value of the story, to Annette Annechild who helped structure and edit the manuscript.

But putting the book aside for a moment, I must acknowledge those who had a profound effect on my life: my father who said, "First be a doctor;" Sid Miller who, with his skill and compassion, inspired me to go into Ophthalmology; Pete Roy who believed enough in me to support my work with Hartford Foundation Funds; Buddy Kaye who led me to the book on PsychoCybernetics; Joan Kelman who, in spite of our differences, was a caring mother to our children David, Lesley and Jennifer; my sister Ruth and brother-in-law Bob who always had a sensitive ear for my problems; and finally my mother who, after each new adventure of mine says with a sigh, "Charlie, I don't know if you'll ever grow up," and then adds, "But I hope you never will."

I hold a doctrine to which I owe
not much, but indeed all the little
I ever had—namely that with ordinary
talent and extraordinary perseverance,
all things are attainable.

T. F. Buxton

Prologue

I was awakened by a clap of winter thunder, like a tympani roll, ominously heralding the day. I opened my eyes to the gray beginnings of dawn, and as my mind erased a dream, a feeling of dread surged through me. I knew that they would soon come for me. Dread turned to panic, as I sank back against the starched pillowcase, fighting the nausea.

I studied the room: a wooden chair, a worn dresser, a sink in the corner, a window with bars. It was like a prison cell, maybe like the cell that was waiting for me if I failed.

Why me? Millions of others would wake today to their usual routines. For me, it was a day of life or death. I wanted to run, or to push open the dull silver windows and fly away. But there was nowhere to run, and the dull silver windows were barred. There was no escape.

"Dr. Kelman, Dr. Kelman." The night nurse loomed over the bed. "Time to get up now. You're due in surgery in less than an hour." She looked at me somewhat disdainfully, but I didn't know why till I splashed some water on my face, and looked at myself in the mirror.

I had a two-day beard over a sickly complexion. There were deep morning bags under my eyes accentuating the bags I had inadvertently created by ripping off my mask after each operation, sometimes six a day. I had once seen a movie where the hero, a doctor, had stripped his mask off in a macho gesture after saving a life, and without realizing it I had been imitating that gesture for years. I looked at my thirty-six-year-old face in the mirror and saw a tired old man. What had I done to myself, to my body, to my mind? Was it worth it?

If I succeeded today, it might just be *worth it. I might affect the sight and the lives of millions of people, some of them now destined to go blind. I might be a hero; I might be famous, with a place in medical history, a professorship at some prestigious medical school. But if I failed . . .*

Someone once told me when I was worried all I had to do was imagine the worst, be prepared for it, and then I would no longer be worried. Well, the worst thing I could imagine was failure, and on that gray morning, in that small, ground-floor room with bars on the window, a room reserved for the occasional doctor who had to sleep at the hospital, failure and disgrace seemed distinct possibilities. Maybe even loss of my license to practice medicine.

The years of secret research, of scrounging for funds, of hopeless days and endless nights, all would have been suffered for nothing. All the years just to get to this one operation which would prove my idea was not crazy, the years of fighting off those doctors who would either try to claim credit for my idea or try to suppress it, would become a bitter memory. I would be the failure that my high school principal had predicted I would be years ago. Thinking of the worst in no way made me feel better.

"Get hold of yourself," I commanded. "It's going to work. You are going to pull this thing off." I heard the thunder again, and the lights flickered. An omen! But for good or evil? I didn't know.

I had been up most of the night trying to get the damn machine to work, and finally had fallen into the hospital bed, exhausted. I had no comb, no razor, no toothbrush.

I called my wife. "I had to stay at the hospital last night."

"You always have to stay at the hospital," she answered. "Especially when one of the kids is sick."

"Who is sick?" I asked, knowing that I mustn't get upset today. Not today.

"Lesley. Lesley Kelman. Your daughter. Remember her? And me? And David, and Jennifer. Remember us?" She gave a little laugh.

"What is the matter with her?" I tried to speak calmly.

"She has a temperature," she said.

"How high, damn it. Why do I have to pull it out of you?" I knew Joan had her right to be angry at me for not calling. But she really didn't know what agony I was going through, and I wasn't able to put myself in her place either, at that moment.

"One hundred and four. I'm taking her to the doctor now."

"It's probably her tonsils again," I said. "Maybe we should have them removed."

"Maybe when you give us some time, we'll discuss it," she said, and hung up. If I lived through the day, I would try to make it up to her, I vowed. She deserved more than I was giving her.

I went to the doctor's dressing room, trying to be invisible, knowing that I looked like anything but a surgeon. Knowing that I felt like anything but a surgeon.

A group of doctors were changing clothes in the narrow room lined with gray metal lockers on each side. "Hey, Kelman, what are you going to freeze today?" one of the senior doctors joked. I wanted to say "your ass," but I didn't. I merely smiled and turned away, but not before he had gotten a good look at me.

"Looks like you had a rough night there, Mr. Playboy. Why didn't you invite your friends along for the ride?" The other doctors laughed. It irritated me to see grown men standing around in their wrinkled underwear laughing at a stupid joke.

I quickly got into my green pants and shirt, pulled my boot covers over my shoes, ripped a mask and hat from the box, and fled from the room toward the operating theater. Behind the door of the dressing room I heard laughter.

With the mask on, at least my beard was covered. Suddenly a plan came to my mind. I would wait until the doctors left the dressing room, go back, change into my street clothes, and call in sick. I would cancel the operation. Maybe I could say my daughter was sick. That was it. Perfect. I would forget this whole crazy idea. But in spite of my plan, my feet kept going toward the operating room. And then I was there.

The smell of antiseptic, of anesthesia fumes and ether, made me really sick. A nurse pulled on my arm.

"They're running late in there, doctor. They had to pull the nurse out for an emergency. Your case will be delayed about an hour."

I hid in a little anteroom piled with old anesthesia machines, the convoluted black tubes hanging off the shelves like a Martian's lung in a bad movie. Taking a long, deep breath, I could feel my heartbeat pounding at my temples. I thought about my family and my friends and how they had been gradually pushed back by my obsession. As the wall clock mercilessly ticked the time toward the operation, my mind slid back, and I remembered. . . .

1

First Be a Doctor

It was Christmas. I was about four years old and standing in a crowded room. It was the first time I had seen a decorated Christmas tree; I was fascinated with the tinsel and lights. I asked my mother why *we* didn't have such a tree and she whispered that it was only for Christians, telling me in hushed tones that except for my father, my sister, herself, and me, everyone else in the room was a Christian. I remember feeling inadequate, and deprived. If I wasn't a Christian, what was I? Not much if I couldn't have a tinseled Christmas tree.

The hostess arrived with a plate of fruit. She was a big Irish lady, with a round smiling face and very blue eyes. When she spied me standing next to the forbidden tree, her eyes lit up. "Charley! Charley!" She was practically screaming my name and now all the Christians were looking. "Would you like a pear?" she asked. I smiled and looked around the room and then back to her. I needed a line. A good one. I knew full well she was offering me a piece of fruit, but I answered, "A pair of what?"

The laughter broke—they shook their heads and roared—and they kept laughing! I had made them happy. They were amazed at me, and so was I amazed. All that happiness for what? A little original thinking. From that moment on, the essence of my life became: "A pair of what?" I learned to seek an original spelling of life, because I loved the feeling I had when I amazed other people and made them happy. I also learned something else about myself. I learned that I wanted to be a star. Actually, I learned that I needed to be a star.

I set off in that direction at the age of six. I wore short pants and a bow tie. Filled with stage excitement but no stage fright, I played the hamonica on "The Horn & Hardart Children's Radio Hour." The live audience loved me. They really loved me. What was really important was that *I* loved me. I was making them happy with my playing, and they were making me happy with their reaction. Unfortunately, however, the radio judges loved the kid who tapdanced even more. He won. Can you imagine? The judges couldn't even *see* this kid dancing. This was *radio*. They only heard him and he beat me. Although I didn't win, the sense of a real audience, of real applause left me with the gnawing need for more. I was hooked.

My parents must have realized that there was no future in a harmonica, so they bought me a saxophone and a clarinet. I studied with the best: Bennie Bonacio, the sweet little man who played the glissando with Paul Whiteman's band on "Rhapsody in Blue"; Hymie Schertzer, the lead alto with Benny Goodman who played the solo on "Sing, Sing, Sing"; and Joe Allard, who was considered the finest studio musician in the business. I even took a few lessons from Jimmy Dorsey, who normally did not give anybody lessons. They all said that I would be the best! The very best! Someday!

In high school I *was* the best. I played first clarinet with the Forest Hills High School orchestra and also first clarinet in the highly competitive All City Orchestra, in which the most accomplished players from the whole city played. Being the best helped me overcome some of the other problems of growing up. I thought I was ugly. I felt like I was scrawny, pimply, and short. Looking back at my high school pictures, I can see that I was wrong. I wasn't scrawny or pimply. Maybe a little short. But playing that saxophone in front of an audience made me comfortable and secure. It was my old "pair of what?"

* * *

My saxophone and clarinet sustained me when other joys in life eluded me. And then, one day, it was over. How I remember that day when I went up to the room where the high school orchestra rehearsed and heard him. The sounds from his clarinet soared and tumbled, like a bird in flight. The notes cascaded across the room with purity and elegance. My heartbeat matched the rhythm of the cadenza he was playing as I raced into the room. There he was. Sitting in *my* chair. First clarinet. Perry. The kid who just transferred over from Jamaica High, the kid I had just become friends with. The kid who I had never heard play, but whom I had advised to try out for the orchestra.

The conductor let me down gently. "Kelman, you're on the second chair from now on. That's it."

My dad saw how depressed I was that evening. "It's not fair," I whimpered. "He's the best looking guy in school. He gets good grades without trying, and he plays the clarinet like a pro without even practicing. Look at me, I have to try so damn hard for everything."

My father was understanding and wise. "Listen, son," he said, soothingly, "that's precisely why someone like you will be successful later on, and maybe someone like him won't. By having to try hard, you are preparing yourself for the real world out there. Perry isn't. Things come too easily to him. When he gets into real life competition, maybe he'll fold. You won't."

Needless to say, I didn't believe him. Not then. But so much of what my father told me proved to be true later on. He was a tremendously gifted man with an enormous heart. His life personified the American dream. Born in Greece, he arrived in the United States at the age of two, one of four children. He was forced to quit school at fifteen to help support his family. His first job was driving a butcher wagon through the streets of New York City. By twenty-four, he owned and operated his own manufacturing company and had the equivalent of three hundred thousand dollars in today's money in the bank. He hired all his family and friends, and they manufactured the fruits of his imagination. He invented the cellophane Christmas wreaths still popular today, built crystal radios as a hobby, and developed a method of removing tar from his hand-rolled cigarettes in the 1930s. In his early twenties, he met my mother, Eva, at a local dance. It was love at first sight and they were married five months later. They had two girls soon after, but one died at a young age. It was then they decided to have another child, who turned out to be me.

My dad was pleased when I formed my own band in high school. We played for dances and parties. He bought us one of the first home recording units sold, and my band and I would make records in my basement. One day, our piano player quit. "You all play well," he explained, "but I am great. I have to play with great players like myself." (We called him "Happy," since he almost never smiled. He was really serious about his music.) So Happy went off to other pastures. I often wondered what happened to him. One day I learned. He dropped the nickname, and went by his given name, Burt. Burt Bachrach. I still have all of the old, scratchy recordings we made. My band folded shortly after Happy quit.

And then one day, at the age of sixteen, after ten years of saxophone lessons, and fourteen thousand six hundred hours of practice in the basement, my father summoned me and my saxophone upstairs to the living room.

"Play," he commanded.

"What?"

"Play the best thing you can!"

I put my horn in my mouth, puffed up my cheeks, and blew into the mouthpiece; out came a somewhat twangy but fairly credible rendition of a saxophone virtuoso piece entitled "Beautiful Colorado." I waited for his pronouncement. It wasn't given so easily.

"Do you play that better than Jimmy Dorsey?" he asked.

"Jimmy Dorsey doesn't play that piece," I said defensively.

"If he did play it, would he play it better than you?" Dad asked patiently.

"I guess he would play it better," I mumbled.

It was then he made his famous pronouncement.

"Son," he began benignly, "it's your life. You can do with it whatever you like." His tone was warming up now. It was soothing. "You can be a songwriter, a singer, a saxophone player, or any other kind of bum you want." He paused for a moment, and then his voice became tough. "Any kind of bum you want. But first, you'll be a doctor."

In those days, kids listened to their parents. He was my father, he wanted me to be a doctor, and that was that. End of discussion. In my mind, however, I was sure that, although I would be a doctor, I would fulfill the rest of his prophecy. As soon as I got my degree in medicine, I would swing right back into "Beautiful Colorado" and a career as a bandleader.

The next day, I went to Mr. Ryan's office. I had only been in the principal's office once before, when I had played hookey to hear Artie Shaw at the Paramount.

"Kelman," Ryan said, shaking his head slowly from side to side as he perused my somewhat less than brilliant record at Forest Hills High School, "I'm going to do you a favor. I'm *not* going to give you a recommendation for college, because you're just not college material. I *will* give you a recommendation, however, to a trade school."

"They don't graduate doctors from trade school, Mr. Ryan," I said plainly. "I need to go to college."

"You'd never make it in college," he decreed.

"I'm going to make it, Mr. Ryan. I'm going to be a surgeon."

It's funny how sounds stay with you. I could hear Ryan laughing almost hysterically as I walked out of his office. I could hear him all the way down the hall, and I could hear that damn laugh years later, every time I had the slightest doubt about my abilities. There were times I couldn't tell whether it was Ryan laughing, or the whole world, or whether I was laughing at myself. Maybe, instead of him being an idiot, he was really a genius. Maybe when I was out of earshot that day, he suddenly stopped laughing and said to himself, "Well, Ryan, old fellow, I hope you succeeded in giving that kid some motivation." I really don't think it happened that way, but it makes a nice fantasy.

Somehow, without Leo Ryan's recommendation, I got into college. During my first year, my dad became ill. Cancer of the thyroid. I doubled up my courses so that I could graduate six months early. I eased up on music and devoted myself to my schoolwork. I wanted to go as fast as I could, so that perhaps my dad could see his dream come true: his son, a doctor. Tufts was a blur as I plunged ahead and graduated in two-and-a-half years. I occasionally played a job, a wedding or bar mitzvah, but I didn't have much time to pursue my music. Then I discovered I could not get accepted to an American medical school for at least another year. I did, however, get accepted to the University of Geneva in Switzerland. Racing the time clock ticking in my dad, I decided to attend. . . . One month later I was on my way to Geneva.

There is a festive quality to an ocean voyage that can never be matched by airline travel. The departure of the ship is a great event with thousands of laughing, shouting people kissing and hugging and giving last-minute advice before the great belch of the ship's stacks signals the race to the gangplank to disembark. On board the ship there is also a keen appreciation of the distance to be traveled, since it is measured in days and not hours.

As I watched the crane hoist my steamer trunk onto *La Liberté*, I was filled with great joy and expectation, as well as with great sadness. Though it was an incredible challenge to face studying in a country where I did not speak the language—a giant step into the unknown—it also put a great distance between my parents and myself at a time when I knew that my father's years were short. We never spoke about that. We spoke instead of my great future as a doctor. At this point, I didn't mind the idea of studying medicine. I was even looking forward to it. My childhood experience with making people happy could well be repeated by making them healthy. I instinctively knew it would be a satisfying career. I just wanted to be a musician as well. I swore to myself I would never give that up.

My folks left the ship and stood on the dock. The smokestacks bellowed forth, vibrating the marrow of my bones. The flashbulbs went off for the final pictures, and the figures on the dock slowly receded, becoming undistinguishable specks. I was on my own.

2

Mon Petit Charley

I was not used to the violent pitching and rolling of the giant ocean liner and so I spent the entire five days of my trip vomiting. It began coming up as we passed the Statue of Liberty and continued intermittently until we reached Le Havre, France. When I arrived in Paris, it was raining and cold. The streets of Paris reflected the lights under the red awnings in front of the sidewalk cafés, and the sounds of the rapid-fire French language ricocheted between the buildings. There were wonderful vendors on the streets hawking magazines, rain hats, and some unmentionables. And there was excitement and life in the air and in the people. You could actually feel the spirit of the city: Paris immediately made herself known not only as a city, but as a personality. And yet, I had the feeling I had seen it all before, and then realized that I had—on Third Avenue in New York, in the wholesale "art" galleries devoted to imitations of the works of Toulouse-Lautrec.

I began literally pinching myself to make certain I wasn't dreaming. The immensity of being so far from home, so alone, embarking on such a fantastic adventure clung to my person like a lovely cologne. It was, however, difficult for me to completely enjoy the wonders of the city on that first night. I didn't speak the language and I had a bad flu. The hotel, recommended by my travel agent, was a fleabag. With real fleas. You could actually see them jumping on the bed in the dingy room. From my window I had an excellent view of brassieres and drawers flapping helplessly in the rain from a clothesline, waiting for better weather. I threw my suitcase up on the highest closet shelf I could find and went out into the streets, searching for penicillin for my flu and powder for my acrobatic roommates. The thin raincoat I wore was no match for the October chill and rain. In less than a block, my coat was soaked and I could feel water between my toes. I could not find an open drugstore. Not on the main street nor on the side streets. Not anywhere.

In desperation, I decided to ask someone. In French, of course. Only I didn't speak French. But I had my little dictionary, and I looked up the words. Where are . . . *ou sont* . . . all the . . . *toutes les* . . . drugstores . . . *pharmacies*? There was a man selling socks and handkerchiefs from a little box on a street corner, under an awning. He looked like he might know. I rehearsed my line as I walked over to him.

"Ou sont toutes les pharmacies?" I tried to say.

He got very excited, and started talking animatedly. Then he snapped his case shut, and tucked it under my arm. He motioned for me to watch it for him, then he was gone. I was left to reflect on how wonderful the French were. Where in America would someone go through all that trouble, just to find a drugstore for a foreigner? But something was wrong—he was returning with a statuesque blonde. He was beaming at me, and pointing to her for my approval. Actually, she *was* attractive, but I was ill. I tried to explain that I had a bad cold by holding my nose. They misinterpreted my gesture. I tried to explain that I was nauseated—by holding my stomach. They continued to misinterpret. By now, they were cursing at me, attracting a small crowd. Everyone was glaring at me as if I had committed some heinous crime. Crazy thoughts of being lynched at the Arc de Triomphe entered my head. I did exactly the correct thing, at exactly the correct moment. I ran as fast as my wet shoes would carry me—back to my hotel, where I jumped into bed, shivering, happy now to be threatened only by the fleas. I stayed in bed for three days, drinking only water and soup. I obtained the soup by picking up the phone and hollering "soup" into it as loudly as I could in English.

When I recovered enough to go down to the lobby, the concierge greeted me in perfect English. How was I to know that almost everyone in Paris spoke English? The concierge explained my mistake on the street corner. *Pharmacie* meant drugstore. I had said *"femme ici."* Not much of a difference, you will admit, but that meant "women here." What I had said to the man on the street was, "Where are all the women around here?"

The next evening I left for my new home in Geneva, an overnight train ride spent trying to sleep in a crowded third-class compartment. The man on my left smelled, the woman on my right snored, and the baby opposite me squealed. I would have been better off on a New York subway, I thought. I envied the immaculate Swiss who were traveling first class in sleeping compartments. I had looked at the price of this kind of ticket and realized it was not for me. I remember wondering if it ever would be.

Morning and our arrival in Geneva finally came. Almost immediately on exiting the train station one is on the rue de Mont Blanc, and there, off in the distance, true to its name, was that majestic white mountain, Mont Blanc, the morning sun shining off the snowcapped peak. I stook there looking at it with my bloodshot eyes, still pinching myself.

My father had arranged for a boardinghouse, called a pensione, for me to live in, and a taxi dropped me at the door to a ten-story building on a dark, narrow street. It looked somewhat forbidding. I would be living with eight other students from different parts of the world, and we all would speak in French, even though I, of course, didn't know any. I was greeted at the door by an elderly spinster in her mid-eighties. We rode up to my room in a tiny elevator with me making friendly conversation—in English, naturally. She glared at me and said, *"Ici, Monsieur Kelman, on parle français."* Three floors up, she left me at my door.

It was a small room but neat and comfortable enough. I unpacked my tape recorder first, selected my favorite tape, plugged the machine in, and immediately plunged the whole building into darkness by blowing the main fuse. How was I to know that Switzerland was 220 volts and that my tape recorder was 110? I heard screams in the hall and rushed to my door. The screams were coming from the elevator where the mistress of the house was now trapped between floors in a little iron cage. It took forty minutes for the electricians to free her. From that day on our relationship deteriorated. I don't think she ever forgave me. I don't blame her.

In those first months, I spent much of my spare time away from the pensione, busy with my preoccupation: looking for girls. In the early fifties in the States, Victorian morals still held sway. In Europe the girls were supposed to be refreshingly loose. I was anxious to test that hypothesis. Someone said that the Palais d'Hiver was *the* place to go. It was a monstrous dance hall, packed with *vendeuses* (salesgirls) and *écoliers* (schoolgirls), and all other types of girls. I went there with my little dictionary safely hidden from view in my breast pocket. I was more than a little bit nervous. Even back home, where I spoke the language, I was far from a Don Juan. I expected to get rejected, and usually I was. What could I expect in a foreign country? I put myself to the test.

"Mademoiselle, voulez-vous danser?" My God, it worked. I was dancing with a lovely little lady from Lausanne. Now that I had her safely locked in my arms, I pulled out my dictionary and started talking to my captive. It was absolutely the best way to learn French. Other Americans were taking night courses, but I had not learned French taking courses in the States, and I didn't think I would learn French taking courses in Switzerland either. Battlefield action was what was needed. In six months I had not only tested the "loose" hypothesis, but I spoke better Fench than most of the guys who had been there for five years.

Studying in French those first months was not easy. I sat through a lecture which I thought was on comparative anatomy, because the professor kept talking about *la rat.* Since *rat* was the only word I understood, I was pretty confident that I at least knew about what he was talking, even though I didn't know what he was talking about. Bored with the subject of rats, I leaned over to an American who had already been there a year and asked when we were ever going to get away from animals and on to humans. *Rat,* he explained, was a *French* word. It meant spleen. It was a lecture on human histology.

I was told exactly how it would happen, and although I hadn't believed it, it was exactly as described: One day, about three months into the semester, after listening to lectures where I did not understand a single word, suddenly I understood everything—like a jigsaw puzzle that the mind puts together, where only the last piece tells you what the picture means. There it was, as if the professor were talking in English. The rest was easy.

The Palais d'Hiver offered something else as well—the possibility of becoming involved in the music scene in Switzerland. There was a contest being held there. The winner would get a chance to audition for the Swiss broadcasting system. Or so they claimed. Of course, I entered. I had the music with me to good old "Beautiful Colorado." I didn't even have to look at it. Playing that thing was like breathing to me. I just stood there holding the saxophone, and out came "Beautiful Colorado" every time. During the rehearsals, I had seen all the other acts, and only one worried me: a pair of Spanish dancers. The night of the performance, the male dancer dropped his partner on her head. "Beautiful Colorado" was a shoo-in.

I waited for the call from the radio station, and when it was not forthcoming, I called them. I could never get past the secretary, who kept telling me that they didn't need any saxophone players. She promised that the program producer would call me. I was really annoyed, and so I just kept calling the station daily, sometimes twice a day. *"Je vous demande quand je peux venir auditioner."* At that point, I never expected to get an audition, but for some reason I persisted. Finally, one day, "This is Mr. Rey's secretary. Your audition is next Thursday afternoon." I had gotten my audition, but I had gotten much more than that. I had learned an invaluable lesson: Persist! Persist! Persist some more! That bit of wisdom would continue to help me throughout my life.

The audition went well. They needed a saxophone player for a new radio show called "Hotel Melodie," where the live audience would call out song titles to the band and try to stump them. They needed a saxophone player who knew every song. For the audition, the producer would call out a song and Achille Scotti, the station's blind pianist, would play it. He had a brain like a musical computer. When he would play it, the producer would ask, "Well, Kelman, do you know that one?" I didn't know any of the songs, but it didn't matter. I had a really good ear and a good musical memory. Once I heard it, I could play it. They actually believed I knew all of those songs, and I got the job. On the air, Achille would play the first chorus, and then I would join in. We were called the Swiss Jazz Quartet. There was one Swiss in the group, the drummer. The others were a Frenchman, an Italian, and an American. I was the only American medical student to get a work permit in Switzerland. You had to be able to do something that no Swiss could do. No Swiss could play every song ever published, including "Beautiful Colorado."

I was becoming proficient in handling two careers—at least, most of the time. One day I was making ward rounds in the hospital with a group of students and our venerable, lovable Professor Roche, a white-haired, white-bearded, white-skinned old patriarch, whose frail body looked as if it had suffered every disease he discussed. All of the students were crowded around the patient's bedside, the professor at the head. There was a hush in the room due to the seriousness of the illness. I was the farthest away from the professor, almost out of earshot of his thin voice. Everyone was intent on the patient and his symptoms . . . everyone except me. I couldn't hear, or see, what was going on. My mind began to drift to the radio special I was to do that evening. There was a tricky musical passage I had to play that was giving me some trouble. I began to go over the phrasing in my mind. A few moments later, I realized that the professor had stopped talking. All was quiet in the room. All heads were turned in my direction, where I was standing, eyes closed, humming, "Da-dooda da doo da, da doo da da doo." I opened my eyes. "May we continue?" the old man asked, a twinkle in his tone.

In addition to my serious medical pursuits, I found time to write a song with a French composer, François Charpin, a musician I had befriended in an after-hours club. We wrote "Le Petit Dejeuner," which was recorded by the then-famous singer Jean Sablon. The record sold well, and to this day I still receive an occasional small royalty check as a souvenir of my days and nights in Geneva. In my mind, medicine and music were always closely connected, perhaps as closely associated as medicine and surgery were for other people. Studying the anatomy of the arm while thinking of a rhyme for *"chaussette"* was natural and easy.

While our main hospital for learning was in Geneva, we were encouraged to work for a few months in other cities. Now, two years after my first disastrous encounter with the French in Paris, with the language fairly well mastered, I was anxious to return. There were some excellent hospitals and some important music publishers in Paris—two good reasons to go. When I learned that there was a one-month internship available at the Hôpital Saint Louis, I accepted without even knowing what the job would be. Probably because I was the only one who *didn't* request the job, I got what all the young medical students came to Paris hoping for—the official French stamp. I would apply the stamp to the cards of the prostitutes who came in weekly for their inspection. I was the inspector. Some job! Legs up . . . mm hm . . . roll over . . . mm hm. Draw some blood. Look at it under the microscope for spirochetes. A slap on the ass. A stamp on the card. Another job well done.

The girls were terrific. I was only twenty-one and had a lot to learn. They all wanted to be my teacher. Not sex, but life. They all had fantastic stories to tell about their children, who thought they were madonnas, and their aged mothers, who thought they were executives. There were stories about their boyfriends and pimps, whips and chains, pain and pleasure. I couldn't get enough of an "education" during the brief examination. I would go to sleep at five in the afternoon so that I could go to their after-work meeting place each night. A huge café in Les Halles was where all these girls would congregate at 4:00 A.M. to exchange stories about their lives, their customers, and their dreams of escape. I became their darling "*petit* Charley," the hookers' mascot. I didn't mind. I was indeed learning about life. The girls would vie with each other to invite me to dinner on Sunday, or to a movie on nights when they weren't working. Within a few weeks, there was not a pro in Paris who didn't know me by name.

Toward the end of the month, my parents came to Paris on their first trip to Europe. I met them at their hotel and we went for a walk on the Champs-Elysées. On every street corner there was a girl with a dog, waving madly, calling out "*Bonjour, mon petit Charley.*" My father feigned anger. "You seem to know every whore in Paris," he whispered, so that my mother wouldn't hear him. "Is this the way you've been studying?" My mother remarked only that I seemed to know a lot of people in the city. I knew my dad was really impressed by the whole thing, so I just shrugged and gave him a knowing wink. A few weeks later, when my parents returned home, my father increased my allowance.

3

Choosing a Path

My reverie was disturbed by the chatter of passing nurses beyond my door. Nurses, like doctors, are only people. A patient might be lying on the table in the operating room, undergoing a procedure which might restore his sight, or cure his cancer, but a few feet away the nurses gossiped about restaurants, boyfriends, and the Pill.

It was hot in the anteroom. And stuffy. The hospital radiators clanged out a desert-dry heat that parched my nose and lungs, the kind of heat that dries you out so that the germs can get in. Hospitals promote disease, I thought. I knew that it was cooler in the hall, but I was afraid to move; afraid of being seen, afraid of the probing questions I was used to, afraid of the casual observer who might want to watch my surgery.

I was drifting back deep into my memories when the door jerked open. I almost jumped out of my chair. It was Joe.

"Sirotka's in the hospital," he blurted out. His eyes were wide with fear. My heart stopped beating, and then started again, catching up with the lost beats in a crazy flurry. Sirotka. My nemesis. Head of the eye department. I had deliberately scheduled this case on a day when he was supposed to be in his office, deluged with patients. This was not one of his days for surgery.

One look at my machine, one question or a suspicion on his part, and it was over before it began.

"What the hell is he doing here today?" I gasped.

"Emergency case. Some kid stuck a nail file into his eye," Joe said, and then hesitated for a moment. "He'll be operating in O.R. 5—the room right next to yours."

While still a medical student, I was sitting in with a band on one of the ocean liners returning to Europe. A man, in his forties, approached the bandstand and asked me if he could play my saxophone. Well, a saxophone is a very personal thing. The mouthpiece goes deep into your mouth and is bathed in saliva. It's not the kind of thing you lend to a casual stranger, since when he's done, you either quit playing, or you stick it back in your own mouth again.

This gentleman was very well dressed, clean-shaven, and evenly tanned. He looked not only clean, but immaculate. I said okay, and let him play my horn. He was a good player. His feel was a little more Dixieland than mine, but that went along with him being some twenty years older than I. When he finished, the band took a break to drink the bottle of champagne this gentleman had offered them. He and I and his wife, Gertrude, sat down together to drink the other bottle of champagne he had ordered for me.

His name was Sid Miller. He was an ophthalmologist. He practiced upstate in New York and had a son who didn't want to be a doctor. And he loved the way I played the saxophone. It all sounded just right. Perhaps I would become an ophthalmologist. I figured I still had plenty of time to decide, but the seed was planted.

I returned to Paris and resumed life as "*mon petit* Charley." Many of the girls had become close friends by now, especially one in particular. Her name was Monique. We would meet late at night at Les Halles and Monique would tell me all of her dreams. Her grand plan was to work ten more years and then retire to a villa in Corsica. She would send her children to the best boarding schools and she herself would live like faded royalty, sleeping until noon and then doing a little gardening if she so desired. She would entertain lavishly and go to bed only with handsome young men. I listened to all this, rapt and attentive, collecting her dreams and sharing my own.

One day, when I got back to my apartment after the coffee and brioche that had become my daily morning meal, the phone was ringing. It was a friend of Monique, and she wanted me to come immediately. When I arrived at the house, there was a commotion in the streets. I pushed through the crowd and found several of the girls crying hysterically. They poured out the story. Apparently, a drunken foreign sailor had approached Monique in the early morning hours and flashed a large roll of bills. He promised her he'd be generous if she added a few "specialties." Monique complied, but not before arguing hotly about the price. A few hours later, the next-door neighbor heard shouting. She rushed across the corridor and was nearly toppled over by a man who ran from the room, covered with blood. When she got inside, she found Monique unconscious, her right eye dangling from its socket. She had called the police, who had taken Monique to the hospital some hours ago.

I got to the Hospital St. Louis in ten minutes, not quite aware of how I did it. The admitting nurse in emergency told me that Monique had lost her eye; the sailor had used a switchblade. But she had already regained consciousness and, apparently, her sense of rage at the entire world. "Don't go fawning over her," the nurse cautioned me. "She'll just bite your head off."

I donned my white coat and joined my group for the day's rounds. Our professor was the opposite of Professor Roche in Geneva. Dr. Prieffer was a small tyrant with piglike eyes who told the patients far too much—things they generally didn't need to hear about their conditions. First we covered the heart patients, then the cancer floor, and finally ophthalmology. As we entered the long ward, I spotted Monique down near the end. She was attempting to remove the bandage over her right eye.

"Mademoiselle!" Dr. Prieffer shrieked, breaking into a run. The rest of us hastened to accompany him to Monique's bedside. "Leave that dressing alone!" he screamed at her. "Do you understand why you are here?"

"Because some insane son of a bitch sliced me up," she sniffed, readjusting the gauze. She had seen me, but looked away.

"And do you understand why you must wear this patch now?"

"Because *you,* you incompetent son of a bitch, were not able to repair my eye properly," she snapped.

My sweet Monique with the tongue of a hacksaw. A ripple of appreciation went through the group, and I noticed a few of my colleagues did not have their attention glued to her dressing. I dutifully completed rounds, but came back to her bedside as soon as I was free.

"Eh bien." She nodded, sitting up and patting her disheveled hair into place. "This is the end of my career, *mon petit* Charley. You know this?"

"Sweetie, it's only your eye. Your ass still works fine."

She took my hands in hers and gazed at me with her good eye. "I'm frightened, Charley. What will I do if I cannot feed the children now?" I held her then, and I let her cry, not knowing what I could say to ease the pain. She had no illusions about herself or her street worth. It was going to be hard for her from now on, and there would be no retirement villa at the end of her career. For the next three months I spent a good deal of time with her and her kids, and I read everything I could find about the field of ophthalmology.

Then, six months before I graduated from medical school, I lost the race with time for my father. When he said good-bye to me as I left New York for my last year at school, we both knew it might be the last time we saw each other. He'd been getting weaker from the disease and from the cobalt radiation treatments, but he never lost his dignity. He faced death as he had lived life, fully and with great courage. When he died we found a list of people he had been supporting for years, both family and friends. None of us had ever known.

That summer, when I went home, I visited Sid Miller, and watched him operate. He was doing muscle surgery for crossed eyes on the first few cases, and I was almost turned off. I was really never too comfortable with bleeding, and there seemed to be quite a bit going on in the eye. And then Sid did a few cataracts. I knew in a minute that I could do that. He made it look so easy. A clean sweeping incision across the cornea of the eye, halfway round, and then a delicate little forceps to pull the darkened lens, the cataract, out. The longest part was the stitching up at the end. Sid placed ten stitches in the eye before he was done.

That night, after a dinner at his home, we went out with our saxophones looking for places to play. At two o'clock in the morning, full of admiration for the man who could do such beautiful surgery and still play a mean horn, I was sold. Sid Miller was going to get a follower after all.

4

Tin Pan Alley

I left Europe in 1956 with an honors degree in medicine, a good deal of savvy about life, but no great success in music. I had written a lot of songs, composed lyrics for radio and television specials, and even coauthored a musical for the locally renowned Casino de Geneve. I had come close with my "hit" in Paris. Close, but no cigar.

In New York, I disembarked from the same pier from which I had left, some five years earlier. I was soon going to be twenty-six years old, and I was supposed to know what I wanted in life. Medicine? Music? My father had said, "First be a doctor." Okay, so I was a doctor. Now what? I didn't know. I remembered my departure from that dock, the excitement, the gaiety, the champagne, and most of all my father who was no longer alive. His absence from that pier and from my life weighed me down suddenly. In Switzerland there were few memories of him, but here in New York it was different. My mother was unable to come to the pier, because she was recuperating from minor abdominal surgery. There was no one to meet me, and the loneliness of my arrival was in sharp contrast to the excitement of living in Europe. I felt that everyone on the pier was looking at me, feeling sorry that I was the only one without a welcoming party, without hugs, without kisses. I wanted to get back on the boat and return to the shores of Lac Leman.

I hailed a taxi at the end of the pier. "Where to, buddy?" the driver asked. He was wearing jeans and a filthy undershirt, and was swallowing a slice of pizza held in his fingers, like a sword swallower in a carnival. "The Edison Hotel," I said. It was an inexpensive, unimpressive building around the corner from the music publishers row on Broadway. My dad had left me enough money to get started in life, but not enough to live in high style. One day I would be thankful for that. The Edison fit my budget. I just hoped there were no fleas.

Although I had a medical degree, it really served no purpose unless I could pass my New York State license examination, and for that I was required to do an internship. Since it was the middle of the year, openings were scarce in New York, but there was a hospital in Baltimore that I heard needed a few interns. I applied, and was immediately accepted. I drove to Baltimore and saw the building. It was a rundown gray stone structure that had been obsolete for at least twenty years. The steps were littered, and the windows were covered with a century of grime.

I was put on OB-GYN. Obstetrics and gynecology. I was to be the only intern on the service. I was told the resident doctor, the one who was supposed to instruct me, was away for a while, and that I was on my own. Didn't they realize I was just out of school? Sure, I had some theoretical knowlege—I knew where the uterus was, I knew the arteries and veins that supplied it, and the nerves, and I knew the names of some of the diseases that it was susceptible to—but what if an emergency came up? What if, my God, what if surgery had to be done? I wanted to run to the administrator and tell him, "Look, I'm really a saxophone player. I don't know what to do if someone gets sick. Let me out of here."

It only took a few minutes for my fears to be realized. A black woman was brought in bleeding. She was having a miscarriage. The nurses were calm, as if this was a routine occurrence. I learned it *was* a routine occurrence. I learned that in that depressed area, when a woman already had several children she could ill afford, a coat hanger inserted into the uterus would start the bleeding. Then it would be legal to do an abortion. In 1956, doing an abortion was illegal unless there was a need to save the mother's life. If she were bleeding heavily, that was a good reason.

Only I didn't know how to do an abortion, called a "D & C," dilation and curetage. I trembled when the nurse showed me how to scrub, how to wash my hands properly so that the drippings would flow toward my elbows away from my fingers, and finally how to hold the curette. It looked like a teaspoon with a very long handle. One side of the spoon was sharp, and was used to scrape off the bleeding lining of the uterus. But first the opening, the cervix, had to be dilated. Long round rods were inserted into the opening, starting with a very thin one, and ending with a rod of about an inch in diameter. The woman was on the table, her massive legs up in stirrups. "C'mon, doc," the nurse urged. "You can do it." Thank God for the nurses. Most of them were understanding and had held many a young doctor's hands guiding him through his first surgical experience. They had seen and probably done this procedure a thousand times.

The patient was wide awake, unafraid, and unimpressed with the seriousness of the situation. I imagined that she had already been a frequent occupant of that surgical table and felt quite at home. I began working, the nurse instructing me as I went. I was very embarrassed that the patient obviously heard everything and had to know that this was my first experience.

"You have a good touch, doctor," the nurse encouraged me.

"I bet you say that to all the boys," I answered. I couldn't really believe that I was doing this. It was totally foreign to my desires, my talents, my whole being. And it was unpleasant. I was not used to the blood, the sweat, the smell, and the brutality of what I was doing. When it was over, I went to my room and, for the first time since my father died, there were tears in my eyes. I couldn't cry for too long, however. There were already three more "bleeders" downstairs, all waiting to be relieved of their unwanted pregnancies.

I worked straight through the day, and straight through the night. That is all I did, that is all that was expected of me, and I learned that had I not been there, the surgical residents would have taken turns doing this "menial" work. To me, it wasn't menial. It was ghastly. I never even let myself think about taking a life, because that had already been done outside of the hospital with the coat hangers. I was just cleaning up the mess. At the end of thirty-six hours, I was off duty. For eight hours of sleep. And then, I was to report back for more of the same. I couldn't believe the number of hours I was expected to work. Since that time the interns and residents have banded together and have obtained more reasonable conditions of work. In those days, many a doctor's life was shortened by the years of having to destroy his own body in order to save another's.

I had been living in comfort and affluence in Geneva, earning enough from my radio and television shows for a lovely apartment overlooking the park, and a Fiat sports car at my door. I was used to sipping aperitifs at sidewalk cafés. In Baltimore, I had a closet-size room with no air conditioning, and my car was rotting in the parking lot, since I worked practically without stop, except for sleep. Even eating was done in between cases. Instead of sipping aperitifs on Lake Geneva, I was gulping down Pepto-Bismol in hospital dispensaries. I weighed 110 pounds when I started the internship, and after one month I was below 100 and had developed an ominous cough. When I learned that two interns from the previous year were still recuperating in the tuberculosis sanitarium, it was good-bye Baltimore. Good-bye medicine. Hello music.

For six months I traveled across the country with pickup bands, playing theaters, studio recording dates, and whatever else I could find. I didn't like it. Actually, I hated it. Playing someone else's music, when I wanted to be creating my own, was the worst punishment I could imagine. I had been spoiled by the utopian existence I had found in Geneva and I longed to go back, knowing full well that it would be impossible. I was a foreigner there. My mother, my family, and all my ties were in the States. I knew I had to find a place for myself. I didn't feel much like a doctor, but I certainly didn't feel like a band musician either. I felt out of touch in Geneva, and out of place in New York. At twenty-six, I was a man without a home, and without a profession.

I tried another internship, this time in Brooklyn, at Kings County Hospital. The hours were long, and the work was hard, but it was survivable. I was close to New York, close to the Brill Building where hundreds of publishers had their tiny offices. It was Tin Pan Alley. This name was given to the building in the thirties when everyone was selling ragtime songs. The sound of hundreds of badly tuned pianos plunking syncopated tunes was likened to the sound of banging pans in an alley.

I had my routine down cold. Every other Thursday I was off duty. I would pull up to the Brill Building, my automobile replete with M.D. license plates, step out with my black doctor's bag, dressed in my white intern's suit, and enter the building. There wasn't even a stethoscope in that black bag; it was full of demo records, songs I had written and recorded in my free time.

I became a familiar character in the building. But only one of hundreds of characters, prowling the halls, looking for a publisher's door enough ajar to get a foot in. One who would maybe listen to a few bars of a song before saying, "Sorry, fella, that's not what we're looking for." In my case, they never said that. They said, "Sorry, doc, that's not what we're looking for." Not that I was a bad songwriter. I was okay. Even good. But getting a song into the market is a question of style and timing. My songs were just a little behind the time of the moment. I was "late." I was able to imitate successful songs, but by the time I was there the market had gone somewhere else. At the end of that year, after hundreds of trips to the Brill Building, all I had to show for it was a certificate of completed internship in medicine.

It was now time to apply for my residency. At this point, I knew I wanted it in ophthalmology. What I didn't know was that ophthalmology was a very popular field. It encompassed medicine, surgery, and optics; the hours were good; and the emergencies were few. It was almost impossible to find a residency in that specialty that was not full for two or three years. I had taken a year of graduate work in ophthalmology after my internship, but did not have a place to go for my residency. New York was totally out of the question. Someone mentioned that Wills Eye Hospital in Philadelphia had an opening. I telephoned, but was told there was no opening. I took a chance and drove to Philadelphia. In spite of the discouragement I had received on the telephone I was allowed to speak to the hospital administrator for a moment: No openings! Not next year either. Nor the year after. Sorry, good-bye.

I imagine I looked depressed and discouraged as I stood waiting for the elevator. A fine looking man came up next to me.

"And why do we look so sad, my boy?" he crooned in a bit of an Irish brogue.

I told him my story, although I had no idea who he was. Something told me that this was an important person. He listened, then questioned me about my background and training, about my aspirations, and then he finally introduced himself: Patrick J. Kennedy, M.D., in charge of resident selection. I guess he liked the romance of finding a resident practically on the street, or he liked the things I said, but he told me, "Not to worry, my boy. Not to worry." He expected an opening and when it materialized, he assured me I would have the job. I thanked him as best I could. I didn't really believe in miracles. A few days later I got the telegram: "YOU HAVE BEEN SELECTED FOR THE RESIDENCY PROGRAM AT WILLS. REPORT FOR DUTY ON JULY FIRST."

I reported, happy to be accepted at one of the finest eye hospitals in the country. I knew it was luck, but I believed in my luck. I have always lived with the philosophy that my mother instilled in us: Everything happens for the best. But while she used this phrase to placate us after a disappointment, my interpretation was that something better was going to come along. While I was somewhat disappointed that I was still in medicine; while I still had the urge to be a "star"; while I still envied every singer, actor, and personality, I knew somehow that what was happening *was* for the best, that there was a grand design somewhere for me. I thought more in terms of a lucky star than in terms of religion, but I wonder if there really is any difference.

Ophthalmology was interesting. In the morning we would fit glasses, later on we would measure the amount of cross to the eyes of a strabismic child, and in the afternoon we would attend lectures and demonstrations on surgery. Once in a while we would be called on to assist in surgery. The first operation that I observed was a cataract removal. I watched as my benefactor, Patrick Kennedy, passed a thin, exquisitely sharp knife across the eye, in one side and out the other, and then in a flourish of the hand connected the two incisions to complete a half circle. The eye was laid open, like lifting a watch glass off the face of a watch. This was beautiful and delicate. He then took a tiny forceps, like a tweezer, and grasped what seemed to be like a cellophane wrapper around the cataract. He then lifted it out of the eye. When he handed me the needle and thread to sew up the eye, I was greatly honored. Usually this was reserved for the second-year residents. I placed twelves stitches in the eye. The patient would be confined to the hospital, lying on his back for almost two weeks. Kennedy told me I had "good hands." I was beginning to like medicine.

My lucky star guided me to the neighborhood playhouse. Here amateur performers acted in musicals and plays. I was taking a walk in the neighborhood of the hospital after a long day. I had never walked on that street before, and knew nothing of the existence of the playhouse. As I passed by, I saw the sign taped to the front door: "COMPOSER NEEDED FOR A NEW MUSICAL." Two days later, after having played some of my old songs for the producer, I was writing the music and lyrics to *Tongue in Cheek,* the musical revue which was to be performed first in Philadelphia, then Atlantic City, and then who knows? Having made the first contact, it was easy to meet other people in show business. One of them was Pete D'Angeles, one of the owners of Chancellor Records. This company had created and developed Frankie Avalon and Fabian, and they were riding high on back-to-back hit records with each of these artists.

"I wrote a terrific song for Frankie," I said to Pete.

"Bring it around some time," he said lackadaisically. But that was all I needed. I went home and wrote the song I had just told Pete about. I modeled it after Frankie's then-current hit, "Venus," and in two days made a "demo." In less than a week I was on Pete's doorstep with the recording. I had been on many other doorsteps with songs, and I knew that the odds were against me. But this felt different, and it was. Pete loved the song, and called Avalon to come over to hear it, at last. At last!

Frankie Avalon didn't like it. He thought it was okay, but he had four other songs ready for release that he liked better. But it didn't end there. The bosses at Chancellor called me aside.

"We like the song, doc. Let's record it with the kid who sang it on the demo," Pete said. I gulped.

"I'm the kid," I said hopefully. This was too good to be true. My voice was passable, but I never considered myself a singer.

"So, you're the kid! Okay. We'll record you next week. Do you want to use your own name?"

I couldn't believe it. Here I had waited all of my life for The Big Break, and now it was being handed to me. Casually. As if it were perfectly natural for me to be singing on a major company's label. I was, however, concerned about using my own name. I was afraid that the medical society would think it unprofessional for a doctor to be singing on a pop record. I called him back the next day with the name I had chosen, Kerry Adams. No one would ever identify me with that name.

I had dinner that night with Bill, the stage manager from the neighborhood playhouse. We were interested in many of the same things, and had become good friends. The only fault

I found in our friendship was that I had to sit and listen for hours as he described his girl friend, Ellen.

"She sings with a band . . . she was a ski instructor in Austria . . . she is a top fashion designer . . . she is a gourmet prize-winning cook . . . she is a model . . . she is . . . she is . . ."

"Knock it off, Bill. No one like that exists." I didn't know what a prophet I was.

"Okay, Charley, you'll see. I'll bring her around next weekend."

After hearing about her for a year I didn't think there was much chance that Bill would actually produce her. And even if he did, I didn't expect to be impressed. When someone is as talked up as she had been, there is no way, absolutely no way that the person can be anything but a big disappointment. No way.

"Ellen, this is Charley."

"HOLY SHIT . . . HOLY, HOLY SHIT." I couldn't stop repeating the words in my mind.

I had been sitting at the piano, going over a number with the cast of *Tongue in Cheek,* which was now playing in Atlantic City.

"Charley, this is Ellen."

"How are you?" I said, "Holy shit" still in my mind.

Bill had lied to me. Lied about her for a year. She wasn't anything at all like he described. She was better, much better. She walked into that room, full of pretty young actresses, and she *owned* them. She overpowered them. Not with anything she said, but just by the way she carried herself. You looked at her and you knew she was *someone.* Sure, she had a handsome, Germanic face with clear blue eyes, and she tossed her head slightly every now and again to nudge the hair from her eyes. Sure, she had a sturdy but feminine body with nice breasts nestled into the folds of her soft wool sweater. Yet, there was something more, something I couldn't define. Like the last thought in your head before you succumb to general anesthesia. She was a bridge between reality and fantasy, and it was hard to know which of the two worlds you were in when you met her. She seemed to belong to a fantastic world of friendship, fellowship, playful sex, and great depths of emotion reserved for one person. I was sure as soon as I saw her that she had been reserving the latter for me. Her eyes seemed to say "I've been waiting all of my life for you. I've made a lot of good friends, and made a lot of good love, but now, thank God, you're here." Her eyes really said all that to me in the very first few seconds that we looked at each other. I assumed that Bill had given me the same buildup that he had given her, and that she was ready for me . . . waiting for me . . . there for me. For me only. I automatically relegated her relationship to Bill to that of mere friendship. It had to be—she didn't look at him that way. It was easy to make myself believe Bill wouldn't care.

"It's really nice to meet you," she said. It was a symphony. She touched my arm when she said it, letting her fingers linger on my bare skin long enough for me to feel the heat in her. When she took her hand away, my arm felt naked, wanting her touch, waiting for it.

"So, you're the composing, singing doctor," she teased. She tossed her hair. My tongue stuck to the roof of my mouth. I couldn't pry it loose. "C'mon, doc, sing us a song." Oh God, she was touching me again. She had me by the shoulders and was turning me around, sitting me down at the piano. I felt like a child. Whatever she wanted, I would do. Just let her keep her hands on my shoulders. She did. All through the first song, and the second. At one point she leaned close to me, her hair flirting with my ear, and whispered, "You're so talented." I was certain her lips brushed against my cheek. If I could have prolonged the sensation I felt at that moment for forty or fifty years, or for whatever time I had left on this earth, I would gladly have remained there, content to the end of my days, feeling her presence, her scent, her mystery.

Bill was getting restless. Angry, I suppose. For some reason he felt left out. Of course, he was left out. She was mine. Her eyes, her hands, her body, they all said so. But she was his date, and he dragged her away with some lame excuse. Her smile flashed at me as she looked over her shoulder in the doorway. Although her lips never moved, her message was clear. "Call me tomorrow," she said with her mind and body.

I couldn't call her the next day, as much as I wanted to. It was my big day. Kerry Adams was going to record "Telephone Numbers." I drove from Philadelphia to New York for the recording session. It was a dream come true: a studio full of musicians, sound engineers, and photographers, coupled with the thrill of hearing my song come to life. The musical arrangements for that song and two of my others had been prepared, and we were planning to record all three—with me, Kerry Adams, singing. The name was on the studio as Gerry Adams. I was going to tell them that it was Kerry, not Gerry, but they would find out soon enough when the record was a hit.

The orchestra played, laying down the tracks. The backup girls sang. I sang. They mixed it all together. It sounded great. They had added some reverberation and echo to my voice. I hardly recognized myself. I savored the sounds and the words each time they played it back.

Telephone numbers, I got so many numbers
of pretty girls I knew
last summer at the shore

Telephone numbers, of just the cutest numbers
and more than just a few
a fella could adore

Barbara and Jean were kind of fun
Ann was the warmest one
Linda was cute, and so was Penny
Oo Oo Oo, I got so many

Numbers, a whole darn book of numbers
but I would gladly toss them in the sea
if you loved me, if you loved me.

It was incredible. Although I had written the song before I'd ever met Ellen, it fit her perfectly. I would have gladly tossed everything into the sea if she loved me.

Suddenly the session was over, the musicians gone, and the studio empty. I sat in the dark, with only the dim red lights from the mixing board faintly glimmering, and I stared into the future. Was this going to be it? A hit? The big one? What I had chased for so many years? I might even have the most wonderful girl in the whole world standing beside me. I pinched myself as I used to do so frequently in Europe. It had been a long time in between pinches.

Bill called me the next morning. "How did it go, star?" he joked.

"I'm in love with her, Bill. I mean, it's the real thing. I've never felt this way about anyone before. Bill listen. Let me have her number."

"What in hell are you talking about? Whose number?" Bill asked. I could tell from his voice that he knew.

"Ellen's number," I said as gently as I could.

"Get lost," he said.

"Bill, I'm serious. I've got to see her again. I know you like her, but she's just a good friend to you. Bill, she's in love with me. C'mon," I pleaded. "Where can I reach her?"

"She wouldn't be good for you," he answered. "She would only get you crazy."

"I'll find her anyway. You might as well give me her number."

"If you want to commit suicide, I won't help you," he said emphatically. Then he hung up. I guess I couldn't expect anything else. He was about to lose what I was about to gain. The girl of a lifetime.

I knew she worked for a fashion design company in Reading, Pennsylvania, and after a few tries with the Yellow Pages, I had her on the line.

"Charley who?"

I panicked. "You know, we met last weekend in Atlantic City. The singing eye doctor. Remember?"

"Oh yes, I think I remember now."

She *thinks* she remembers? Was I going crazy? Was this the same girl whose eyes had said "I love you" to me the day before? Did I have the wrong number? The wrong Ellen?

"Why are you calling me?" she asked.

"Jesus, Ellen, I'm calling because I thought we had something going. I want to see you. How about dinner tonight?" My whole world was falling apart. This was far from the conversation I had imagined in my mind a hundred times before I got her on the phone. Nothing like the enthusiasm and excitement I had anticipated.

"Thursday night would be fine." She said it so matter-of-factly, it sounded like I was a shipment of pickles she was having delivered. "Pick me up at eight. I've got to run now. I've created a whole new line of bathing suits for Givenchy. I'm in a meeting with some guys who just flew in from Paris to see me about it."

The day arrived. On the road to Reading, my mind alternated from her warm hands on my shoulders to her cold voice on the phone to visions of myself as a singing star. The mixing session for the recording was in a week. That's when they add the echo, and balance out the sound between the lead vocal, the orchestra, and the backup girl singers. I had to keep reminding myself to slow down—I had the car going as fast as my mind. Suddenly, I pulled up in front of her building.

I took a quick look at my hair in the rear-view mirror, sprayed some mouth freshener on my neck and some cologne in my mouth, spit on the curb, and rang the buzzer to her first-floor apartment in a brownstone on a quiet street. She opened the door. Holy shit! When I had first seen her, she had been in jeans and a little white sweater, and wasn't wearing any makeup. Now she was in some kind of designer dress, and whatever girls do to their face to make it pretty, she had done with such artistry that I was no longer able to separate my brain from my mouth.

"Holy shit," I blurted out.

"That's the nicest greeting anyone ever gave me." She laughed. She really meant it. That look, that "you're-the-one" look was back in her eyes. She had a warm, deep voice, with a touch of hoarseness that added to her intrigue, and hinted of beautiful people at beautiful parties. Her "hello" was more than just a word . . . it was an invitation, and was accompanied by her hands holding mine as she drew me into her apartment. It was modestly decorated. I noticed there were several bouquets of flowers around the room, each one with its card neatly tucked among the petals. The significance of the flowers and cards escaped me, but even had I known what it all meant, I would have been powerless at that point to change what fate had already ordained.

We had a drink and talked. I don't remember a word that was said. When we left, the phone was ringing, but she didn't answer it. I was flattered by this, but once again I had an uneasy premonition. *Something* was wrong, but I didn't really care.

The restaurant she chose was on top of a mountain overlooking the city. It would have been impossible for me to have planned a more romantic setting if I had spent years getting it all together. The huge harvest moon was an orange balloon hanging on the horizon below our feet, splashing gold onto the rooftops, turning the humble dwellings in town into glittering mosques in Mecca. A warm, fragrant breeze visited among the tables set on the terrace for dining by candlelight, and the sound of a sweet gypsy violin floated out from inside the restaurant. When we walked to our table, conversation in the room stopped, and I could see and feel the heads turn to look at her. All during the meal, I could catch glimpses of men looking at her with appreciation and desire, and the women looking at her with admiration and envy. Ellen seemed not to notice any of it. Her eyes were on me, telling me that only I existed, only I mattered, there was no room for anyone else.

No one had ever been able to touch me so deeply, or to convey such feeling. Yet she never said a word about what was in her heart. The conversation was light, mostly about the things she had done. She was slightly reluctant to talk about herself, but I found it easy to open her up, to get her to tell about her many talents and accomplishments. I had been told myself, many times, that I was well rounded, that I was a Renaissance Man, but she put me to shame. She had sung with a band, had taught skiing in Austria, and had won awards for her designing and cooking.

Late in the evening, just before they were ready to close up the place, she and I went into the empty bar where I played the piano and composed a song for her. I guess it must have been obvious to everyone in the place that we were madly in love. The owner finally came over to the piano with a bottle of Scotch and a key. He smiled knowingly as he said, "I'm leaving, but you don't have to. Just lock the front door and put the key under the mat. Enjoy it." And that was that. The place was ours. The terrace, the piano, and the rest of that summer night. There was never any question as to whether I would stay with her that evening, and when I took her home it was natural for me to follow her in, it was natural for me to have a drink with her, and it was natural for me to make love to her. The phone rang a few times without her answering it, and finally when she saw that it bothered me, she took it off the hook. In the middle of that night, we decided that we had each found what we wanted.

Sleep finally overtook us at five o'clock in the morning. The alarm went off two hours later. I was barely able to unglue my eyelids. When I did, I saw that Ellen was already out of bed, had showered, and looked as fresh and bright as though she had just returned from a vacation in the Bahamas. She stood in front of me, dressed and made up for her day. My head pounded from the lack of sleep and the drinks, and my tongue had a crust of dried chopped liver on it. She kissed me and let me know there was coffee on the stove, and eggs warming in the oven.

I called Bill that night. "We're going to get married, Bill," I said jubilantly.

"Yeah, sure, Charley. Tell me another one."

"C'mon Bill, be happy for me. I've never met anyone like her."

"She's not right for you. She's going to mess up your life. She's not . . ."

"Knock it off, Bill," I said roughly. "I love her." I knew he was going to say things I already sensed, but I didn't want to hear any of them. I didn't want to ruin my rapture.

"Okay, pal. You're going to have to learn the hard way."

I called her at work late that afternoon. She must have been in another meeting, because she couldn't talk much. She told me she couldn't see me until Sunday. Something about a designer's meeting on Friday, a "private" reception in New York on Saturday with some old friends, and then a luncheon on Sunday. After that she would drive back to Reading and meet me at her apartment. The key was in the milk box.

I was starving for her. I felt like a man dying of thirst, bound hand and foot in front of a glass of water. If I tried to get the water to my lips, I was certain to spill it. I wrote a few songs, played "Telephone Numbers" a few hundred times, tried to read a book on ocular physiology, and relived that night on the mountain. Sunday finally came, and I was back on the road to Reading.

It was even better than the last time, she was more beautiful, and we were even more in love. And yet, when I left her at six that morning, I again learned that I couldn't see her until Friday. More meetings, more receptions, more "private dinners." We had, however, set a tentative date for the wedding. Six weeks from that day. She would tell her parents "soon," and they would fly in from Colorado. I was totally happy—almost! But somehow I knew something was wrong.

Things started to come together, or come apart, depending on how you looked at it, the following Saturday morning.

I was back in her apartment, back in her bed after another long and loving night, and she was again dressed, fresh as the morning air, ready to leave. No, she couldn't see me that night. Some friends were throwing a party in her honor in New York. She had to go. I couldn't come. She didn't want her friends to know about me. Not yet. They wouldn't understand. Not yet. She hadn't told her parents. Not yet.

I drifted off into a troubled sleep. I dreamed about our wedding. Her mother wore black, and so did Ellen. Her father was dressed as a clown, with a big red nose which he kept blowing during the ceremony. The man who was marrying us was neither a priest nor a rabbi. He was the chief resident at my hospital. Leo Ryan, my high school principal, was among those in the pews. He was smiling, and I prayed that he wasn't going to laugh. I was wearing roller skates, but I still couldn't keep pace with her, and she arrived at the altar before I did. She instructed the chief resident to start the ceremony without me. Her father blew his clown nose. Her mother told him to shut up. I was crying. I woke up.

I was going to wait for her to come back on Sunday and tell her about the dream. In the meantime, I would get some work done. I needed some paper and some pencils. I called her at work. She was pleasant on the phone, and told me to make myself comfortable. The paper and pencils were in the bottom drawer of the dresser, on the right side. I thanked her, told her to have a good time, that I would see her Sunday night when she returned from New York.

I went to the drawer and opened it. Paper and pencils on the right side. I took what I needed and started to close the drawer. My eye caught a few printed announcements on the left side of the drawer. Her name was engraved on the cards. I picked one up and started to read. For a moment I thought I was back in my dreams. But this was worse. I was going to throw up. I could feel my muscles contracting, starting to heave, but there was nothing in my stomach. The printed cards were invitations—invitations to an engagement party for that evening. Ellen was going to New York that night to become engaged to Richard Spencer Rosenman. I was in her bed and she was supposed to marry *me* in six weeks.

I ran to the bathroom to splash cold water on my face. I hardly recognized myself in the mirror. My skin was gray, my face was lined, and I looked how I imagined I would look when I was sixty-five. I took a cold shower, still feeling sick to my stomach.

After two cups of black coffee, I was able to think more clearly. Like a detective. My mind raced to the flowers, and the cards. She had also gotten a bunch of telegrams over the last couple of weeks. Whatever her talents were, they did not include hiding things. The top drawer of the dresser was the first place I looked. They were all there, neatly piled. I grabbed them and started to read:

"Darling Ellen . . . Please let me see you again. On your terms. Whenever you want. Please. Love, Roger."

And another:

"Sweetheart . . . Please let's get together. I know you love me. It will be however you want it. No more questions. No more jealousy. I love you. . . . Ted."

All the cards said basically the same thing. They pleaded, they begged, they promised not to question her. There were six different names among the twenty-odd cards and telegrams. Her fiancé was not represented. Not yet, I thought. Neither was I. I sat there with the cards and telegrams strewn around me, like feathers from a plucked chicken.

It must have been her intuition that made her stop by her apartment at lunchtime, on her way to New York. I was still sitting there with everything around me. I heard her come in, but I couldn't bring myself to look up at her. She was carefully picking everything up, carefully folding the telegrams, and stacking her cards. Then she came over to me, cradling my head against her.

"They mean nothing to me. None of them. Only you."

I felt like a man in pain who had just been given a heavy shot of morphine. I looked up at her. "Ellen, is that true?"

"Silly," she cajoled. "We're getting married, aren't we?"

Those eyes! How could I have doubted her? "What about that engagement party? How was it possible?"

She explained. Easily. Naturally. Credibly. She had been planning this engagement for a year. He was a nice guy, but she didn't really love him. She kind of felt sorry for him, what with his ailing mother and all that. And he hardly knew how to manage his affairs, what with his father dying and leaving all that money. She didn't know if she could ever really love anyone, so she was willing to get married to him. But then I came along. And she knew what love really was. But she couldn't hurt his feelings that way. And his ailing mother would die if she broke off the engagement so suddenly. She was going to get engaged, and then later, gradually, easily, break it off. The announcements were left there on purpose. It was easier for her if I found them; it made it easier to explain. She wanted me to see them. The telegrams and flowers were from people she had only casually met. It wasn't her fault if they fell in love with her.

When you want to believe something, when you need to believe something, when your own self-esteem cries out for you to believe it, then you believe. And I did. Almost. Somewhere, deep inside my brain, in some deeply tucked away nerve cells, an alarm was ringing. I knew that someone else in her position would have been more straightforward, would have found the right moment to explain, and would have done so. But the relief was so great hearing her explanation that I snuffed out the signal being sent to those sentinel brain cells.

"I understand. It's okay."

She was late. She had to go. She was gone. There was no trace of her, or the cards or the telegrams. They were no longer in the drawer. Had I hallucinated? Was that part of the dream? I didn't have long to wonder about that. The doorbell rang. I signed for the flowers. They were from someone named Ted.

Two weeks later, I sat in the car in front of an East Side apartment, while she went up to return Richard Spencer Rosenman's engagement ring.

"Well, that's done," she said. "Now let's forget it."

To her it was yesterday's linen. Washed, dried, folded neatly, and put away.

Tuesday and Thursday of that week she had meetings. Private meetings. I knew that she wasn't in New York, and I wondered if perhaps Richard had come to Reading to see her. I found his number and dialed. He sounded like a nice guy with a knife in his chest. I understood the feeling. I didn't answer his hello. I just hung up. . . .

Something told me to postpone the date of our wedding. Instead, we would go to Europe for a week since I had vacation coming up, and there was nothing further to do until the recordings were pressed and ready for distribution. To this change in plans she simply said, "Okay." No question as to why the postponement, no argument or even discussion. Europe would be fine with her. She would take her vacation also.

My passport needed renewing, and I asked her about hers. I didn't know exactly when she had taught skiing in Austria. She always claimed a poor memory for dates, and I could understand, having the same problem myself. I thought I would take care of her renewal, if it was necessary. She was evasive. Yes, she'd had a passport at one time, but she didn't know where it was. I was suspicious.

"I can't get you a new one unless I know the number on your old one," I lied. "I'll have them look it up at the passport office."

"I never actually had a passport when I went to Europe." She smiled. "I was taken there on a private jet, and we never had to go through customs."

I had been to Europe enough times to know this couldn't happen. I remember seeing Adlai Stevenson standing in line having his passport checked, just like everyone else. There was no way she could have gotten in and out of the country without a passport.

"You've never been to Europe, have you?" I gambled.

"If you don't believe me, I won't discuss this any further," she said tersely. "Just get me a new one." I knew I had guessed correctly.

We went to Europe. She couldn't ski worth a damn. Other lies surfaced. I tried to find out when and where she sang with a band. I had never even heard her hum while we danced. I was still crazy for her, but that little alarm in my brain had turned into a wailing siren which I couldn't shut off. Many nights when she had "private meetings," I saw her being accompanied to the door by different men, giving each one a more than friendly good-night kiss.

"They are just business acquaintances." She shrugged at my questions. "Why can't you learn to trust me?"

At that point, I trusted her as much as I trusted a scorpion in my bed. Yet, I didn't walk out. I couldn't walk out. I kept hoping against hope that each lie would be her last. What bothered me the most was that many of her lies were meaningless. They were trivial. There was absolutely no need for the lie.

One night when I had been studying for a few hours in her apartment, I was going out to the delicatessen to buy some sandwiches. She asked for a bologna on rye. Okay. Bologna on rye. When I came back she was on the phone, and didn't hear me enter. I knew she was talking about me but I couldn't believe what I was hearing.

"Charley went to Chinatown to get my dish. That's right. It's the one I taught the chef to make in that little Cantonese place. They call it Ellen Foo Yung. They say it's the most popular dish in the place. He should be back any minute. Bye now."

I had her dead to rights. There was no way even the cleverest liar could get out of this one. She would once and for all see how blatant her lies were.

"What in hell was all that about—Ellen Foo Yung? You know damn well I went to the delicatessen. Why do you have to tell these crazy lies?" I had her. There was no way out.

Ellen never even hesitated. "For once, just once, I thought you were going to surprise me. You know how I hate delicatessen. Maybe it was wishful thinking, that 'Ellen Foo Yung.' Maybe a real man would have known I wouldn't eat this shit." She flung the sandwich across the room and tears began to flow. "How can you be so inconsiderate of me?"

That was it. I knew, all at once, the "diagnosis." A pathological liar. Someone who had to invent everything. The inability to tell the truth. I had heard about the condition, I had learned how convincing these people could be. And yet, I had fallen in love with one of the worst. Or best.

"I'm sorry," I heard myself saying. "I should have known better." Twenty minutes later we were at the Chinese restaurant. She didn't order "Ellen Foo Yung." Neither did I.

The record was pressed and released in five weeks, which was, I think, a record in the recording industry. To me it felt like an eternity. I must have played my copy of "Telephone Numbers" a thousand times. We all waited for the reviews. *Cashbox* would listen to the releases from the big companies and rate them. Four stars were the best rating, no stars the lowest. *Billboard* had the same system. Both publications appeared on the same day.

Four stars in *Cashbox.* The same in *Billboard.* Furthermore, the song was "pick of the week" in about thirty cities across the country! I called Ellen, but she was in a meeting and couldn't come to the phone.

My imagination raced ahead to concerts, Hollywood, personal appearances. The thrill of hearing my song on the radio was indescribable. I spent days twisting the dials, listening for that familiar sound. I started to get asked to perform at record hops. Far from Hollywood, these were gymnasium dances where the disc jockey would spin records while the kids danced. Once in a while, they would produce a real live star who would do his own song. This meant moving your lips in time to the record, to make believe you were singing it. Sometimes at an important hop there would be several performers. At one such hop I sat on a bench with one sixteen-year-old and two thirteen-year-old sisters. I was the fourth, Kerry Adams, the thirty-year-old doctor incognito. I must admit I was more than a little uncomfortable. But the end justified the means. I was going to be a star.

After the record hop, the disc jockey was buying us kids sodas. I was more in the mood for a Scotch on the rocks, but I took what he offered. He was really a kind man, and was quite concerned for his aging performer.

"Kerry," he began cautiously, "have you ever thought what you would do with your life if you didn't make it as a singer?"

"Sure, Paul," I said, the tone of my voice trying to convey to him that I didn't want to discuss that. He was not to be stopped. I saw the inevitable coming.

"You really should finish school, if you haven't," he fished around.

"Yeah, Paul. I did." I was hoping one of the sisters would drop some ice cream in her lap to distract him. No luck.

"High school?" He shook his head as if to answer the question for me.

"Right." I tried to make it sound final.

"Kerry, how about college? You really can't get anywhere today without that college education. Did you go?"

"Yeah, Paul. I went to college."

He was surprised. "Well, Kerry, you really should finish. It's not too late to go back."

"Yeah, Paul. I finished." There was no way to prevent the rest of my story from being uncovered now.

"Finished college!" he was impressed. "Well, how about some postgraduate school?" he persisted. I could see what hopes he held out for me as a singer.

"Yeah, I did that too, Paul."

"Did what?" his eyes bulged a little.

"Medical school." I nodded my head affirmatively. "I finished medical school," I added, to save him the next question.

"Well, what are you doing to do with all of that education?" He seemed overwhelmed by the possibility that someone who had been through all of that schooling would be sitting there with teeny-boppers after a record hop.

"I'm going to open my practice of ophthalmology," I stated matter-of-factly.

"Ofthal what?"

"Ophthalmology. Eye surgery."

It all caught up to him. He leaned back his head and laughed. At first I thought he was laughing at me, but he wasn't. He thought I had deliberately led him down that path.

"You son of a bitch." He laughed good-naturedly. "Why didn't you tell me you were a doctor?"

"I was really trying to avoid the subject." I laughed with him. His look told me that he understood my whole story, without further comment. He knew the power of the show-biz magnet. He turned to the other kids sipping their sodas, and began lecturing them on how they should continue their education, "just like old Kerry, here." The kids looked at me blankly, ice cream spread over their faces, as if I were from another planet. I guess I was.

Ellen had told me she was going to a reunion at the Fashion Institute of Technology. I had offered to accompany her, but no, it was restricted to graduates. I didn't insist. Instead, I rented a car.

I wanted a plain black car that would not be easily noticed. I had never followed anyone before in my life, and in a way it was exciting. In another way, it was degrading. When I got to my apartment, I put on a blue demin jacket and jeans, and walked three blocks to Hertz Rent a Car.

Once I was safely behind the wheel, I peeled off the backing of the moustache I had purchased in a joke store and pressed the disguise to my face. Not too bad. I drove away quickly, not wanting anyone from the neighborhood coming over to say, "Hey, doc, what are ya doin' with the black car and a moustache?"

I parked by the East River to kill a few hours. I knew she would be leaving FIT at about eleven. I had really come prepared: sandwiches, a thermos of coffee, and a bagful of doughnuts. At the appointed time, I put the car in gear, feeling like Perry Mason, and slithered over to the entrance of her school.

In twenty minutes, she appeared. It looked like she had been telling the truth. God, what an idiot I was for not trusting her. *Hold on.* There were two guys coming with her. Each one took an arm, and she certainly didn't seem to be protesting. They walked to her station wagon. She reached in and pulled out her overnight bag. Then they all got into a Chrysler, all three in front, with her, of course, in the middle. I pulled into traffic behind them, checking my moustache in the mirror. God, this was exciting. Like waiting for the jury to come back with a verdict of guilty or not, and *you* are the defendant.

A ten-minute ride took them to a Second Avenue restaurant, and they sauntered in laughing, still arm in arm, the three goddamn musketeers. I sat in the car for an hour. This was stupid. It was all innocent, although I didn't see why I couldn't have been invited. I almost felt like pulling away and going home. I didn't. They came out and moved quickly away in traffic. They seemed in a rush on the F.D.R. Drive. Me behind them. Moving downtown now. Very fast. Too fast. Almost as if they knew they were being followed. Don't lose them now . . . 60 mph . . . 70 mph. Damn. Damn. Damn. A police car was coming up fast behind me, obviously in pursuit. I could just imagine him stopping both cars, all of us getting out, Ellen looking accusingly at me, while the cops ripped my moustache off my lip and handcuffed me. Oh God! The cop swerved around me and went after the Chrysler, siren wailing. About a quarter of a mile ahead, he pulled them off the road. There was no exit between us. I had to keep going. Please, don't stop me. Please.

I passed them doing about forty. The cop ignored me. Oh, thank you, thank you. I caught a glimpse of Ellen sweet talking the cop. But I didn't want to lose them. I raced to the next exit, got off, and then got back on again going uptown. As I passed them again, they were getting back in the car. I had to get to the next exit and turn around again to catch them. I was doing eighty-five now, but I had no choice. If I got stopped by a cop, I would peel off the moustache and take my summons. At least she wouldn't be there. I made it. I screamed downtown again, and caught sight of them just as they got off the Drive to go to Brooklyn. It all ended in front of a motel. All three of them. In the same room. I sat outside for a long time.

The next few weeks helped me ease the pain. Chancellor Records was having me photographed and fitted for glittering dinner jackets for personal appearances as the record continued to pick up momentum. One night at a record hop, I opened my mouth to move my lips with the record but had to stop short. They were playing the wrong record. When they finally got the correct one on the turntable, the crowd was still laughing. It was an omen.

A few days later, something happened which forever

LIBRARY OF
UNIVERSITY CLUB
WINTER PARK, FLA.

changed the direction of pop music in the world. Chubby Checker's recording of "The Twist" was released. Twist fever spread across the country like an infectious plague. Pop music would never be the same. The soft sound was, at least temporarily, out. Twist songs hit the airwaves from morning until late at night. "Telephone Numbers" was now the wrong number; it had had its last play on the radio.

A few days later I called Pete at Chancellor, trying to keep it light. "Hey, Pete, I've written a terrific twist for Kerry Adams."

Pete didn't answer right away. Finally, he said four words—"Kerry Adams is dead!"—and hung up. The following week I opened my office in New York for the practice of ophthalmology.

5

The Practice

I jumped out of the chair, and opened the door a crack. In my mind, I saw the elevator door open and Sirotka walk out. It was a clear picture. And then, as a self-fulfilling prophecy, it happened: the elevator door opened, and Sirotka walked out. It was like instant replay. For a moment his face was just inches from mine. Then his massive frame glided by me as he headed for O.R. 5.

Sirotka was aggressive, forceful, and tough—a bully. He intimidated every doctor, every nurse, and every employee on the staff. The crazy thing was that he thought everyone loved him. He had a huge square face with silver-rimmed glasses, and a heavy-set body which nevertheless moved gracefully, almost in a shuffle. On his feet, he always wore space shoes—with the big round toes and flat heels. His hands reminded me of paws; they were large and flabby. But they were, I hated to admit, the best hands in surgery at the hospital, maybe in New York. He had trained himself to move his fingers as delicately as if each were a miniature ballet dancer. His surgery was beautiful to watch, and its speed and economy of movement were envied by all the other surgeons.

Because of his bully image, he was somewhat of a father figure to many at the hospital. As he had once been to me. But I had disobeyed his rules. I was making a name for myself; I was crawling out from under his shadow. He didn't like that at all, and he hated me. When you got on Sirotka's shit list, your days at the hospital were miserable, since no one dared to befriend Sirotka's enemy. I knew that if I succeeded today, I would never again have to walk in his shadow. He might, just might, have to walk in mine.

I watched him disappear into O.R. 5. He would be intent on his case now—deciding whether to take out the injured lens of the eye, to sew it up, or to remove the entire eye if it was too hopelessly destroyed. Now he would have no thoughts as to what was going on in the next room. But when he finished . . . He had a habit of poking his head into every operating room, giving advice, or a huff if he didn't like what he saw, or a pontifical tap on the shoulder if he favored you on that day. When Sirotka finished his own case, that's when I would be in danger. That's when he would look into O.R. 6, down at the end of the corridor. That's when he would see me with my machine.

It was a spring day, but filled with darkness. I had been in practice four months.

"You're not *listening*, doctor."

From out on the street, muffled laughter. "I heard you, you said your eyes itch in the morning." Air, I needed air.

"No-o-o, I said they *burn* in the morning. They *itch* at night."

Itch, burn. "Can you see better with this lens, or this one? Number o-n-e or number t-w-o?" While she described how the letters looked *lighter* with number one but somehow *clearer* with number two, my mind drifted out through the heavy curtain, and my depression deepened. Ellen and "Telephone Numbers" played a funeral march in my head. What in hell was I doing in a dark room on such a beautiful day?

". . . and I use my eyes a great deal, doctor." She leaned forward and said confidentially, "One thing I must tell you about myself is that I *need* my eyes."

Who in hell doesn't need their eyes, for Christ's sake, I thought. "Madam, you do not have glaucoma, or cataracts, or retinal detachments. You have healthy eyes. I think you worry too much about your eyes." As soon as I said it, I knew it was a mistake.

"Too worried about my eyes? Too worried? My eyes? Don't

you think eyes are important, doctor? I pay my dues every month to the Health Insurance Plan. Every month. And I'm supposed to have a doctor who is interested in my condition. You *are* paid by the health plan, aren't you, doctor?'' She hit hard on the word doctor.

I didn't even get angry. I was used to this. One of the ways to pay expenses when you first open an office is to join this HIP plan. The patients pay a few, a very few, dollars a month to the plan, and I got paid a small, a very small, salary. The patients can come to you as often as they want, without it costing them an additional nickel. So I was used to being scolded and threatened. If I was not a good boy, if I didn't listen to the same complaint ten times, I would be reported. I would be thrown out.

Not that I lacked compassion. I had my share. There were patients with real eye problems, and when they got me, they got the very best I had to give. But most of the patients in this group were just killing time. They had neuroses. They needed a friend, or psychiatrist, or a priest. Not an ophthalmologist.

''This is a prescription for some new glasses,'' I said, ignoring her tirade. ''I think you will see better and feel better when you use them.''

I knew that patients often focused their neuroses on their eyes. To the patient, the problem *was* a real problem. Maybe it was really a lack of affection, or a lack of sex, or a fear of dying, but what the patient *felt* was a pain or an itch in the eye. I could usually understand their problem and sympathize with them. Usually. But not on this spring day, not when the whole world was out in the sun and I was in the dark. On this kind of day it was much easier to sympathize with myself.

I was a Gemini . . . an air sign . . . a songwriter . . . a poet and a musician. Sure, I was also a doctor, but that was practically an accident.

The next patient of that day was a precocious six-year-old kid accompanied by his permissive mother. He had to touch everything within reach. While this might be the sign of superior intelligence, to me, in my office on that spring day, it was the sign that a monstrous brat wanted to destroy my still-unpaid-for equipment.

"Tommy, mustn't touch," his mother purred. "No, Tommy. Oh, Tommy, now Tommy has let that nice man's flashlight fall. Mommy hopes that Tommy has learned his lesson. No, Tommy. Tommy musn't play with the nice man's stick. . . ."

It wasn't a flashlight and it wasn't a stick. It was a three-hundred-dollar retinoscope which lay in pieces on the floor, and a six-hundred-dollar ophthalmoscope which was now clutched in Tommy's precocious little fist. I wrenched it from his little hand, noting with some pleasure that in so doing, I had twisted little Tommy's arm. Tommy was looking at me and his eyes showed that he somehow understood all of the psychological forces at work, which made us covert adversaries. Tommy's little foot lashed out unexpectedly, catching me on the shin. It was obviously a highly practiced maneuver.

"Tommy musn't squirm," his mother oiled. "Tommy must sit quietly like a gentleman."

Pain flashed through my shin to my kneecap as I nonchalantly reached for the necessary drops to dilate his pupils. It gave me a secret twinge of pleasure to know that they would sting little Tommy's eyeballs. But I was no match for him. While I leaned over to drop the harmless but fiery drops into his eyes, his arm flicked out with the speed of a striking cobra, and the colored solution tumbled to the floor, making yellow stains on my white loafers. Later that day, I would be ridiculed by my friends for having urinated on my shoes.

There was no question in my mind. I was not cut out for this kind of work. What hurt the most was that although these patients came willingly to see me for their glasses and other minor complaints, when they needed surgery, they would thank me for my diagnosis and run as quickly as they could to someone with a "big name." A professor. Someone who would charge them a lot, make them wait weeks for an appointment and then hours in the waiting room. Me, I could be had at a moment's notice, and surgery was included in the monthly peanut payment to the group. How could my surgery be any good if it was free?

Surgery is the most respected, most coveted, and most highly paid activity in any specialty. It is glamorized in the movies and on television: the romantic intensity of heads bent over a trusting, helpless form, with nurses brow mopping the famed surgeon while he devises instant solutions to life-threatening emboli and infarcts, which the human body endlessly supplies to the willing hands and ego of the man behind the mask. What power, to be able to change someone's entire life with a few words like, "We did all we could" or "It's a boy" or "Thank God, we got it in time."

Even in the relatively unfrenetic atmosphere of an eye surgeon's operating room, the ability to make the blind see again is about as close to saving a life as one can get. I had visited the great eye surgeons from all over the world . . . Switzerland, Spain, France, New York, and California, and the mystique around these gifted men with gifted hands was overwhelming—and crushing to the novice surgeon. The delicacy of the human eye made surgery upon it the most magical feat, surpassing even the mystery of surgery on the brain. These great eye surgeons were superstars, and were therefore permitted, even encouraged, eccentricity in their personal lives.

One famous cataract surgeon allowed himself the luxury of smoking cigars while plucking out cataracts, and when ashes would drop onto the surgical field, would remark that, after all, ashes were quite sterile. Another great would swill down half a bottle of bourbon on the morning of surgery, and then proceed to practically anesthetize his patients by merely breathing on them. Another would inject cow's milk into the buttocks of young ladies with uveitis, an eye allergy-infection. These men were revered. They became legends, having reached that heady pinnacle of success where their adulators would laud their most ludicrous idiosyncracies. In my case, if I were to examine a HIP patient without wearing a tie, word would come thundering down from above that I should be more dignified. What the hell . . . I wanted to "smoke my own cigars" in my own way, and yet there I was, having to obey the most banal ordinances.

Ten minutes later, little Tommy left my office with his mother and a new prescription for glasses. She had already warned me that the prescription would be checked by "her brother, the optician." Little Tommy made an obscene gesture to me behind his mother's back, as they walked out on me, my broken ophthalmoscope, and yellow shoes. I looked at my schedule. Forty-four more people, eighty-eight eyeballs, and I would be done for the day. I wasn't at all certain that I would survive.

The days passed slowly. Almost all my friends and colleagues were married and I was filled with the emptiness of a life alone. I tried to throw myself into my work and to bury all thoughts of Ellen. Unfortunately, since I had given up the HIP clinic and had just opened my own private practice, business was slow, to say the least. I didn't really even have an office. I had a room I rented for three hours a day on Fifth Avenue and Sixty-seventh Street. It was a nice building with a pretty receptionist in the lobby. All of us who rented there carried our nameplates in our black bags. There were two little hooks on every office door, and when you arrived for your rented time, your name was allowed to hang there. I went there diligently every day. I greeted the receptionist warmly, walked a flight up to "my" office, attached my nameplate to the door, and waited. Day after day I sat there waiting, reading my mail, straightening my books, mostly going crazy wondering what I was going to do for the rest of my life. All of my friends had said they would send me patients. The way they talked I should have had a line out the door. But no. Each day I kept my vigil alone.

And then one day the phone rang. It was the receptionist. She was sending up a patient. The blood rushed to my head—a real patient! Then my heart sank as a beautiful young woman, obviously an actress or model, appeared. My friends, I thought. My crazy, wonderful, show-business buddies. What a great joke to play on their struggling doctor friend. But I played along. So did she. She gave me her name and sat down pretending to be interested in an eye exam. I maintained my doctor's composure and calmly told her to step into the examining room and take off all her clothes. She seemed surprised but she went into the adjacent room. She was in there five minutes or so, when it dawned on me that maybe, just maybe, it wasn't a joke. Maybe I had a real patient taking all of her clothes off in my eye examining room. I tapped gingerly at the door. I asked her who'd sent her. She said Mid-Cities Hospital had given her the name of three doctors—the other two were busy. My first patient! Luckily, she had a good sense of humor. After she quickly dressed, we laughed as I explained the story. I examined her eyes for free, and sent her on her way. Then all too quickly I resumed my dark routine.

Early one Sunday morning, two of my friends called, inviting me out for a game of golf. I had been a recluse for months and decided a day in the sun would be a good idea. Off we went to the country. We played eighteen holes of golf and then relaxed over lunch. We had just sat down when my attention was drawn back to the entrance. Three young women had just arrived: two petite brunettes and a tall blond. I couldn't keep my eyes off the blond. Soft blond hair framed a face that was pretty without a trace of makeup. Her clothes were simple but classic. Not since Ellen had I been interested in meeting a woman. This one I *had* to meet. I looked over to signal my friends but their eyes were glued to the doorway already.

We ate lunch totally distracted by the ladies' presence. At the end of our meal, I signaled the waiter and gave him a note for them. The two brunettes responded with waves and laughter; the blond was shaking her head negatively. One of the brunettes waved us over, and moments later we were ordering dessert and coffee. The blond was Joan, and she was everything Ellen was not. Simple, direct, honest—I liked her immediately. Unfortunately, so did my friend—Elliot. By the end of our coffee, he had her phone number. As we were walking away, I turned back and said softly, "If he doesn't call you, I will." I knew Elliot lived far into New Jersey and that Joan lived in Queens. I hoped he would tire quickly of the two-hour commute.

I went back to my practice that Monday but my mind constantly wandered back to Joan. She was the kind of woman I *should* marry. It wasn't a fantasy girl I needed; it was one rooted in reality—a woman I could trust and depend on. Joan was such a person. I could feel it.

By the time Elliot stopped seeing her, I was mentally ready to marry her. Her reaction to my first call was, however, aloof. Yes, she remembered me. Yes, I could see her next Saturday night; but there was no warmth, no enthusiasm.

So what if she wasn't terribly excited, I told myself. I would really impress her on Saturday night. Unfortunately, Saturday turned out to be a difficult day. An emergency at the office, trouble with my car—by the time I reached Queens I was forty minutes late.

Joan's mother greeted me at the door. After Ellen, I was delighted to meet a girl with a real mother. We sat and had coffee. We ate doughnuts. I entertained her with stories of my work. A half hour passed with no sign of Joan. Forty minutes later, she finally emerged. Cool and calm, she looked beautiful in a loose gray sweater and khaki jeans. A few minutes later, we were off. The first thing she did was to inform me that (a) I had been forty minutes late, and (b) not *everyone* thought I was so great. Now, this was a woman who spoke her mind! I liked it. I loved it. The difference was so striking between her and Ellen, I laughed out loud. Here was a real challenge and I took up the chase with glee. By our third date, I was convinced I would marry her. I plied her with flowers, presents, and promises. I worked on her mother and her whole family as well. Six months later she was my wife.

6

The Goddess of Tomorrow

Those of us who grow up with show business in our blood develop a peculiar sense of tomorrow. Everything is going to happen, Tomorrow. The play being written by the aspiring playwright will be a smash, the song being recorded is going to be a hit, the world will give the deserved acclaim, all . . . Tomorrow. If religion is the opiate of the masses, then Tomorrow is the opiate of show business. We worship the Goddess of Tomorrow.

It matters not that Tomorrow usually never comes. The novel is rejected, the song is a flop, the part is given to someone else. That all happened yesterday, or at worst today, but Tomorrow—just wait until Tomorrow. This implausible optimism is one of the most important attributes required for show business. Without this, no one can endure a career for very long, because there are virtually no instant successes. Every star is the product of smashed dreams and jagged edges of failure. We all live with the dream that someday our Tomorrow will catch up with today, and that they will meet and embrace in a blinding flash of success.

The hard part is that even when, against all odds, the incredible becomes credible, the impossible becomes possible, the dream becomes reality, and the success longed for with such passion is achieved, we are still stuck with Tomorrow.

What in hell are we going to do to maintain or surpass that success Tomorrow? I don't think there is any other profession in the world that has such a tantalizing and wicked mistress as the Tomorrow goddess of show business. Yet she imparts to her subjects a special ability that ordinary, non-show-business persons do not possess—the ability to handle failure. In spite of the crushing defeats I was about to suffer in life, my battlefield training on the shores of show business enabled me to handle failure, rejection, and scorn without waving the white flag of surrender.

I was still optimistic, still hopeful that the next venture, whatever it might be, would be my salvation. I had a peculiar advantage over everyone else I knew in medicine: I had hope. Death occurs not when a person's heart stops beating, but when, having reaped failure after failure, that person no longer believes there will be a future success. With that belief gone, all further movements of the body are merely spastic twitches of a corpse. I was still very much alive, and my antennae were alert to the slightest radiation from a possible source of fulfillment. Joan and I were just settling into married life and I was pushed to succeed for both our sakes.

One of the friends I had made along the way was a well-known songwriter, Buddy Kaye, who had written the lyrics to "Till the End of Time," "Quiet Nights," "A You're Adorable," and hundreds of other published songs. Although he and I became fast friends, I could never get him to help with my musical career. Maybe he thought being a doctor was enough, maybe he didn't want me to be distracted, or maybe he thought I didn't have enough talent.

We did share many deep discussions about life. In one of these discussions, he advised me to read a book, *Psychocybernetics.* The technique of visualizing what you wanted, as if it were already your own, was new to me and I devoured the book. Another friend gave me a tiny book entitled *It Works.* This book described the mind as a cybernetic missile. If you programmed the mind by accurately listing your goals, and then visualized them as if in your grasp, they would somehow magically come to you. I read these books over and over again during the first months of my marriage. My difficulty was not knowing exactly what I wanted from life, but reading the books prepared my mind for what was to come.

One evening, as I slowly climbed the stairs to our apartment, I was expecting nothing out of the ordinary—and that, of course, is precisely when the extraordinary occurred. I was thumbing through my mail and, just as in a well-constructed murder mystery when one clue suddenly and dramatically points you to the perpetrator, one glance at the cover of *Look* magazine triggered that sudden flash of insight in me.

On the cover of the magazine was a picture of a man in a surgeon's mask. The story inside said the man—Dr. Irving S. Cooper—had found a way to cure victims of certain neurological diseases, such as Parkinson's, by freezing a tiny part of their brain. He had invented the technique and developed an apparatus which, at his command, would create a small ice ball at the tip of a slender probe placed deep inside the skull.

There were photographs of children walking who had been paralyzed, old men drinking from cups who had not been able to hold anything in their shaking hands, and young mothers caressing the infants they had never been able to touch. He had cured the incurable and he had made a deep niche for himself in the history of surgery. What fulfillment he must feel! There were also pictures of him standing proudly in front of his mansion, lounging on his yacht, and enjoying the material wealth which had been a by-product of his contribution to humanity.

My reaction was not that of jealousy—it was that of anxiousness. I was anxious to do in my field what he had done in his. What he had, I wanted, and what he had done, I wanted to do. I knew in one micro-millisecond exactly how I would use his freezing technique and his apparatus in my own field. Invention is really the synthesis of information in a novel form. The invention of the automobile was the synthesis of the wheel, the gasoline engine, a transmission, and everything else that goes into a vehicle. Not only did I know exactly what I wanted to do with Cooper's machine, I knew, without any question of a doubt, that it would work. I also imagined what it would bring. The contribution to humanity, the medical acclaim, the wealth and power. And, I knew I could be even more comfortable with this kind of success than with the success I had been chasing as Kerry Adams.

What I didn't know was that it was almost impossible even to speak to this great surgeon on the telephone. All I wanted was to use his laboratory a few days a week until I too could make my breakthrough and become famous. I just needed his help until Tomorrow . . . but I couldn't get it. After ten unreturned phone calls, I got the idea. He was too busy and not interested in some young guy who wanted to annoy him. But I had learned my lesson in persistence back in Switzerland to gain an audition for the radio show. Since he wasn't interested in my phone calls, perhaps a few telegrams would work. They produced the same result—nothing.

I wanted to freeze the retina of the eye, creating an irritation there, which would make it form a firm scar to the underlying tissue. The retina in the eye is similar to the film in a camera: The sensitive layer of nerve cells picks up the images focused upon it. Occasionally, this thin layer detaches from the tissue supporting it, and when this happens the nerve cells lose their nourishment and die. The current method of surgical treatment involved creating a scar at the area of detachment so that the retina would stick back on and be held by the scar, just as a rivet holds two pieces of metal together. Methods of retinal detachment surgery involved a hot needle, and while this was successful in a fair number of cases, the heat of the needle destroyed the outer supportive shell of the eye, the sclera. I knew instinctively that freezing, rather than burning with a needle, would create the same scar and would spare the sclera from damage. It would be a revolutionary breakthrough in the treatment of retinal detachment. With that, my place in the inner circle of medicine would be assured. At least this was the dream, this was the plan, this was the true motivation.

I considered buying one of those ice machines, but learned that the price was sixty thousand dollars. I *had* to find a way to gain access to the man from *Look*. I was haunted by the image of an ice ball, deep inside of the eye. So, I tracked Irving S. Cooper, M.D. I parked myself on his doorstep. Actually, I sat endlessly in his waiting room. All around me were victims of neurologic disease. Their heads had been shaved where they had been, or were going to be, operated on. It seemed to me that his waiting room was divided into two halves: On one side were those who were not yet operated and who shook; on the other side of the room were those who had been operated on and who shook not. On a long couch was sitting such a group who had not yet undergone surgery. It was as if a massive vibrator had been turned loose under them.

"Kelman, you are the most persistent son of a bitch I ever met." It was Cooper. He had appeared from his inner sanctum, looking very much as if he belonged on a magazine cover. He was tall, with curly blond hair and steel-blue hard eyes that held just a very faint trace of humor in them. He carried himself with an arrogance that defied description. I had come prepared to try to convince him to allow me to use his laboratory by reciting some of the exciting possibilities I had dreamed up for his machine. I had a folder with me of all the projects I wanted to try. I had letters of recommendation. Now I shook in his presence.

"Come on in," he commanded, as he disappeared into his office. I followed, rehearsing mentally the approach I would take.

Before I could say anything, Cooper looked at me, shaking his head as if to say, "So this is the pain in the ass that has been bugging me." Then, he turned his back to me and spoke, as he looked out of the window.

"Okay, Kelman, you can use my lab, my animals, and my technician two days a week. You are now on my staff at one hundred dollars a week. Don't bug me, but keep me posted." He turned around to face me, pointed to the door, and said, "Now I have bigger fish to fry. Get lost."

That was it. I got lost. As a matter of fact, I almost got killed. I was so excited, I drove like a maniac back to Joan in Manhattan. I knew I had just gotten my first real chance, my Big Break, and I was ready to go for it all.

The next day I flew to a meeting of the American Academy of Ophthalmology in Chicago; 6,000 eye surgeons at their yearly convention. The group consisted really of two divisions: 5,950 attendees and about 50 honchos, who presented their reports to the rest of us commoners. Of the 50, there were only about 10 who were really big names. When these men walked by, everyone greeted them deferentially, practically bowing. These were the men who not only had the highest academic rank, but, because of that rank, were doing most of the major eye surgery in the country. They had established a virtual monopoly in the most lucrative aspect of ophthalmology. Some of these men had instruments named after them, and some of them even had surgical procedures bearing their names. The McClean suture, the Troutman microscope, the Scheie operation. These men were the giants, looming over the rest of us. Theirs was a private club, defying admittance to anyone but one of their chosen heirs. If you wanted in, you put yourself in the shadow of one of these giants and you obsequiously did all of the office work, research work, and whatever other kind of work he commanded you to do. Then, if you lived long enough, if you were lucky, if you had not stepped on any toes, *and* if you had ability, you might, just might, make it into that club. Actually, I guess it was no different from any other field of endeavor. People protect their positions of power. They resist young upstarts who want to come in to replace them. It is the way of the world.

Whereas the crowd would part for these princes and kings who walked among them, I, of course, was anonymous. No one knew me or even cared to. I was a dues-paying cog in the wheel that permitted these giants to exist. I sat in back of the auditorium and listened to the lectures. The speakers joked with each other on the podium with great ease and repartee. The crowd laughed with them, applauded them, admired and worshipped them. I hated it. I hated being a nobody. I was at the bottom of the barrel, and I was suffocating. But I did have my direction now: freezing. Cryosurgery. It was a term none of these men had even heard of. Few specialists are actually aware of what is going on in other specialties. I was certain that either no one there knew about Cooper's work or else no one had seen fit to look into its possible applications. No one but me. I was going to be first. I was going to make it in one giant flying leap from the back of the auditorium to the podium. I became restless and couldn't concentrate on what was being presented. I left the meeting after only a day, four days early, so that I could get to work on my project. On the plane, I read about the effects of freezing on brain tissue and began to prepare for my first experiment.

Cooper's freezing machine was a monster. It looked like a refrigerator on a thick, giant stilt: a white box up in the air, with a thick silver hose ending in a long slender needle. A technician worked the dial that allowed more or less liquid nitrogen into the tip of the probe. Depending on how much nitrogen came in, the tip could go down to absolute zero. Cold enough to make an ice ball that would destroy everything in its interior.

I watched Cooper operate. The patient was awake, but anesthetized so that he couldn't feel the hole being drilled into his skull. Once an opening had been made, Cooper would slowly insert the needle, monitoring the position with X-rays. When he got to the part of the brain he wanted to freeze, he would call out temperatures: "Minus ten degrees. Minus fifteen. Hold at minus eighteen." As he chilled the correct area of the brain, the low temperature would temporarily paralyze the cells. Upon observing that the tremors had ceased, he would call for still lower temperatures to kill the offending, irritable nerve cells causing the tremors. "Minus twenty. Minus forty. Minus one hundred." The lower the temperature he called out, the more impressed the crowd of ever-present observers became. I almost expected him to bow to the audience after each case, but he hardly ever acknowledged the presence of visitors or observers. He seemed only aware of the machine, the patient's tremors, and then the lack of tremors. He was the greatest and most awesome performer I had ever seen.

There was one of these freezing machines in the laboratory

for use with experimental animals. I had never operated on live cats or dogs. To me they were pets, not guinea pigs. Even guinea pigs were not guinea pigs to me; they, too, were pets. I would later be plagued by a recurring dream: I would be trying to climb up the side of a very slippery, rocky slope. Behind me would be hundreds of vicious, angry cats chasing me up the wall of the slope. I would awaken either as I fell off the cliff, or as the cats caught up to me. . . .

I drilled a hole in an anesthetized cat's skull, alongside of its eyeball, so that I could get this long probe into the back of the eye. I knew that if my theory held true, I would have to design my own curved probe that would fit around the side of the eye and not require drilling into the bone. The drill ground through the bone like wood, except it smelled like burning flesh. I was nauseated, but I kept going. The cat was under deep anesthesia, of course, and felt nothing. I touched the probe to the back of the eyeball, pushing it through the opening in the skull I had made with the drill. I called out the numbers and, as the temperature dropped, with my eye pressed to the ophthalmoscope one inch from the cat's eye, saw to my amazement the retina turning bright red, like a fiery sunball setting in the sea, and then white. Snow white. Freezing, frozen white. A perfect, tiny circle of ice inside the eye. Exactly as I had imagined. I let the probe warm up and the blood flowed again around the frozen area, but in the center was an exudate, an outpouring of fluid. That meant a scar would form. I could hardly believe it. One try, one success. I had changed the treatment of retinal detachment surgery forever. Could it really be this easy? I froze a few other areas in the retina with exactly the same result and photographed everything. Where was the heartbreak of research? The failure, the effort? I knew I had succeeded on the first try. I left the laboratory elated and four days later I examined the cat again. The scar was forming, the retina was firmly adherent. Retinal detachment surgery would never be the same. I repeated the experiment on other animals, sacrificed them, and wrote my first scientific paper, which I submitted to several journals.

Back in the lab, I was also trying other experiments. The thing that surprised me most was my passion. I had stumbled onto something that stimulated me more than anything else I had known. The desire for success in music seemed to have been something *learned,* something *acquired* at an early age. The thrill of, and love for, research on the other hand seemed *instinctive.* It was part of my body and brain. I knew what to do from intuition. I had practiced "Beautiful Colorado" for a thousand hours, and I still couldn't play the damn thing perfectly. In the research laboratory, for the first time in my life, I felt confident and at home. I cut into a cat's eye that had been sacrificed for some brain experiment of Cooper's. I wanted to observe the effect of freezing on the tissues inside the eye. The first thing I froze, the very first thing I touched, was the lens of the cat. And the very first observation I made was that the ice ball bonded the probe to the lens. There was no way to detach the probe from the lens without defrosting the probe—like sticking your tongue on freezing metal and not being able to remove it, but a thousand times stronger. I realized immediately that I had just unearthed my second discovery. I had stumbled onto a new way of removing cataracts. Just like that! I had spent a total of eight hours in the laboratory and here was my *second* major breakthrough.

Cataract surgery at that time was successful in about 90 percent of cases, but that still left one case out of ten with serious problems. A cataract is a lens that has turned cloudy. The lens of the eye is deep in the pupil of the eye, behind the iris, which is the colored portion. It is not on the surface as most people think, nor can it be peeled off. To remove it, you have to open the eye in a complete semicircle with a knife, reach behind the iris into the black hole of the pupil, and grasp the slippery cataract with a forceps, which is a small tweezer. The cataract is held in place by ligaments. In order to remove the cataract you have to pull on it so that the ligaments rupture, releasing the cataract. Usually, this works out well, but in about one out of ten cases, the slippery *capsule* tears—rather than the ligaments—spilling the contents of the cataract, a toxic protein, into the eye, usually setting up a severe inflammation that results in either blindness or at least greatly reduced vision. The problem was holding onto that capsule, a thin, plastic wraplike layer around the cataract, without that capsule breaking. The ice ball that I had observed in the second cat's eye went deep into the substance of the cataract, solidifying the tissue as it went, making rupture of the capsule almost impossible.

I admitted a patient to the hospital who needed a cataract operation. There was never a question in my mind as to the safety of this procedure. Cold cannot be transmitted to distant tissue as X rays can. This would be safe, simple, and effective. No doubt. No need for further experimentation.

And then, there I was, in Cooper's operating room, my patient covered by surgical drapes, except for her eye. The pupil had been widely dilated with drops so that the white cataract was visible from across the room. I had explained to her that I would be using a freezing probe to take out her cataract, and that this was a new type of surgery I had developed. She did not seem apprehensive. Neither was I. I had the old familiar stage excitement, without stage fright, though Cooper was in the room observing me, with about a dozen of his staff. I prepared the eye, opening the cornea in a wide smooth semicircle. Years of practicing intricate passages on the saxophone helped to keep my hands calm and steady as I took the long silver hose, draped it over my shoulder, and approached the cataract. I knew that the needle would freeze at minus twenty degrees, but I had learned my lesson well—the lesson of operating-room showmanship. I had had the best teacher and he was in the room.

"Minus five," I called. The technician set the dial and the tip cooled slightly. "Minus ten." Nothing yet. No ice ball. I wasn't surprised. But the tension was building. It seemed as if everyone was holding his breath, not daring to move. "Minus fifteen." Still nothing. The probe was just touching the cataract. Now I began to get excited. I knew the next number I called would freeze the tip of the instrument to the lens. I knew that I would then be able to pull out the cataract.

I knew it would work. I would have bet my life on it. I would also have bet anything that I was the first to try it. "Minus twenty." My voice was steady. A tiny ice ball sprang from the end of the tip and jumped onto the lens. "Steady at minus twenty," I called, as I gently lifted the cataract from the eye. Jesus, I had done it! Everyone in the room exhaled together. The incredible tension was relieved in that brief instant when they could all see the cataract, about the size of a small bean, frozen firmly to the end of the probe. I held it up briefly for them to examine. I had time, in that moment of triumph, to see the door close behind Cooper, who had exited just as soon as he saw that I had been successful. His departure detracted only a bit from my elation. I had visions of my own face on the cover of *Look*.

7

Out in the Cold

The six operating rooms at Mid-Cities Hospital are lined up on the north side of the seventh floor of the building. They all connect, except for O.R. 6, at the east end of the corridor, which is separated from the others by a double door, opposite the elevator. There, tucked away in the corner, is O.R. 6 and the adjacent anteroom where I was waiting. Reserved for "dirty" cases, those highly infectious or contaminated, or for surgeons of low prestige in the hospital pecking order. It usually irked me to be stuck down there. It meant that few visiting doctors would see my surgery, that the least experienced nurses would be assigned there, and that if an emergency came up for one of the honchos, personnel would be pulled from that room. But today I was happy to be there, hoping to remain unnoticed until it was over.

Joe was forty-five years old, but he had a round baby face without a wrinkle. He looked like a young boy on his first job. Now his face was white, and his lip held a quiver, almost as if he was going to break into tears.

"Where is Cheryl?" I asked.

"She's in the prep room with Banko, sterilizing the handpiece."

"Tell them both not to go out in the hall. I don't want Sirotka to spot them."

"Joe," I called after him, "hang that sign on the door." Joe

looked behind him and then saw the sign. A smile started to spread across his face. CONTAMINATED ROOM, *the sign read. The thing that most surgeons fear most is an uncontrollable infection. It can turn an eye into a blind bag of pus in a matter of a few hours. It can turn a perfect case into a hopeless disaster. When surgeons see that sign on a room, they run the other way. I hoped that Sirotka would be the fastest runner in the bunch.*

The news of my sensational success spread throughout the hospital in a matter of hours. Those who had witnessed the operation carried the tale back to every department. To the observer, it was even more dramatic than Cooper's surgery. When Cooper finished a case, there was nothing to see. A great service had been rendered, and yet all the observer could see when it was over was a patient lying quietly on a table—certainly not an unusual sight for the hospital staff. The observer might have a feeling of awe for the surgeon, but the surgery itself, especially that of boring a hole into the patient's skull, was bloody. The actual freezing took place deep in the invisible crevices of the brain's convolutions. In no part of the operation was there any intrinsic beauty.

My cataract surgery, on the other hand, allowed the visitor to witness a lily yellow jewel, with a frozen miniature flower of snow in its center, as it clung magically to the slender probe while being gently lifted from the interior of the eye. Aesthetically, it was gorgeous. There was no blood. There was no mess. Only the jewel!

By the time I left for the day, there were already a few deferential "Hello, Dr. Kelmans" from the staff. As I walked down the corridors, I saw nurses looking my way, whispering to each other behind their charts, their eyes shining in my direction. And even the elevator operator who, heretofore, had closed his gate twice on my foot, stood proudly aside with a gracious *"Buenos días, señor"* as I entered.

Days later, Cooper announced the success of my operation in his report to the John A. Hartford Foundation, the group that supported his medical research. A picture of the ice ball was printed in their monthly newsletter. The fact that he reported this to the Hartford Foundation would be of major importance to me later on, although I was unaware of it at the time.

As I continued to perform the cataract operation, it became obvious that a smaller instrument would be needed, both for retinal and cataract surgery. Having that heavy hose, like that from a gasoline pump, draped over my shoulder, was not the most ideal situation for delicate surgery on the eye. I visited the Linde Corporation, the branch of the giant, Union Carbide, that made Cooper's machine. The office was on Park Avenue, in a steel, chrome, and glass temple of opulence. I had an attaché case with my sketches inside, and as I took the elevator I felt a strange twinge of déjà vu. It seemed I had done this before. Then I remembered: It had not been more than a few years back when I had prowled the Brill Building with my black bag, trying to sell my songs. That seemed like another me, in another life.

I was ushered into a small office. Not that of the president certainly. Not that of the vice-president either. There were two men there. They said they weren't certain if there was enough of a market in eye surgery for them to recommend the development of a special probe. I was told they would check it out with their "consultants." I left the office feeling mildly depressed. I had expected a hero's welcome.

Soon after, I had to take a two-week break from my work in the laboratory. It was time to take my specialty board examinations in ophthalmology. Unless I passed these exams, I would never be allowed to operate in a first-class eye hospital.

Without passing these examinations you have to have a "certified board man" assisting you on every case. Certainly not a high-prestige situation. The ordeal took place in Baltimore, Maryland. One week of intensive, round-the-clock study, followed by a week of oral examinations. These examinations were given by the elite. The professors were the inquisitors, who would evaluate your knowledge and see if you were worthy of the certificate. I was not at all opposed to the concept.

Medicine should supervise itself and doctors should evaluate each other. This was a necessary ordeal, and although I didn't resent it, I certainly had not been looking forward to it. At each examination you were putting all of the years of college, medical school, and post-graduate training in the hands of someone you didn't know, who would decide whether or not you were worthy.

I hoped that none of the professors who were to examine me had heard of my work. If they had, they might make it more difficult for me to pass. I had been around long enough to know that they would not be overjoyed with a smart New York kid trying to change the whole concept of eye surgery. As it turned out, I had nothing to fear. I was still, very much, anonymous. I did have one rough moment during my examination with a southern gentleman who looked at my name tag, saw that I was from New York, and immediately affected an expression which said "I've seen your kind before."

"Well now, doctah, what's yaw diagnosis of this here patient's condition?"

"Sjögren's syndrome," I answered confidently.

He smiled deprecatingly. "Don't give me none o' them fancy New York names now, doctah. What do most of us *common* doctahs call this here condition?"

I gave him the simplest name I could think of for the condition. "Dry eyes, sir."

His eyes bulged with scorn. "Give me the medical name, doctah. We are *medical* people and we have *medical* words, you know."

I felt I was being whipsawed. First, I was too technical, then I was too common. There was only one other term for the condition. It had to be what he wanted. "Keratoconjunctivitis sicca," I said quickly, with a halfhearted smile.

He drew closer, speaking at first in a whisper. "Doctah, are you trying to make me look foolish?" His face was now one inch from mine and he shouted, "What is the name of this here condition? Do you or don't you know, suh?"

I paled. There was no other name. "I don't think I know of any other name, sir." I had an impulse to bite the wart on his nose, only an inch from my teeth. He turned suddenly triumphant, as if to face an imaginary audience. He looked at "them," as if asking them to attest to my stupidity while he phrased the next, and most devastating question. "Doctah," he doled out the words slowly, "did you ever hear of Sjögren's syndrome?"

I almost fainted. I was torn between telling that bastard that it was my first answer, or just saying something noncommittal, like "Oh yes, now I remember." I chose the truth.

"Sir, that was the first answer I gave you. Sjögren's syndrome."

He shared his feelings of incredulousness with his "audience" for a moment, and then hanging his head sadly, he turned back to me. "If you had said that, suh, would I not have heard it? Which are you calling me, suh, deaf or a liar?"

That was it, I thought. The end of my brilliant career. "Neither, sir. Perhaps I gave you the answer too softly because I was nervous and you didn't hear me say Sjögren's syndrome." It was a fair try, but it didn't work.

"Ah kin see that your specialty is Park Avenue answers, suh," he said slowly, fixing me with his gaze. "Those kinds of answers won't get you very far in this profession. You are dismissed, suh."

That was, fortunately, my last examination. I never thought I would pass, but miraculously, a month later the letter came. I had passed all of the subjects and was now board certified. I still don't know whether that was just a game he played with me, or whether he had been forced to raise my mark in that subject, since I did well in all of the others. In any case, I could now perform surgery on my own, without someone being required to stand by.

When I walked into my apartment, after my four-hour train ride from Baltimore, the last examination was still playing in my head, like a song you can't stop singing in your mind. The ending was the same, always the same. "You are dismissed, suh." What I needed was a lift. Something to cheer me up. Out of habit, I glanced over at the table to see if there was any mail. There it was, on top of the pile, from the ophthalmology journal. At last! They were writing to accept my article on freezing. I tore open the letter, my heart racing. There was a lot of writing on the page, but my eye caught the one word that told it all. *"Rejected."* "Not enough details." "Need corroboration."

Corroboration, my ass. I had shown the adhesion between the retina and the underlying tissue after freezing. I had shown it in pictures and slides. The only thing that remained to be done was to prove it in human beings. A tissue that you burn in animals, burns exactly the same way in humans. The same is true of freezing. If it worked on animals, it would work on humans. I knew it, and they knew it. Proving it in humans would involve a clinical trial on patients with retinal detachment. Such patients went to super-specialists in ophthalmology, not to little guys with big ideas. I didn't care if someone else did the clinical work, I wanted credit for the *idea.* I went to see Cooper the next day. He handed me a few other surprises.

"I think you should drop the study on the retina," he said when I told him about the journal's rejection. When Cooper said "I think" the translation was "I'm telling you exactly what I want you to do."

I was amazed at his reaction. I knew he had not gotten to where he was by quitting. "Coop"—I allowed myself to call him the way his other associates did—"I think it is really important. It's going to totally change the treatment of detachments."

"Look, Charles"—as soon as he said Charles I knew it was trouble . . . he had only called me Kelman up until then—"retina is a special field. Leave it to the retinal men."

This didn't make sense to me. "But I want to get the credit for having done it. I just want to prove it on animals, and then I will work together with a retinal surgeon." I was pleading, but somehow I knew there was more to his story. I was right. He then dropped the bomb.

"Curt Driscut, at Eastern Medical School, is interested in

the project," he said. "He became interested in what I was doing in brain surgery and wants to start a retinal project with me."

It was as if he had kicked me in the head. My stomach turned over. I knew that idea was mine. I was certain that someone at Eastern had reviewed my article and had become interested. Otherwise, Cooper would have mentioned the Eastern group to me when I first told him about my ideas of freezing the retina for detachment. Now the explanation of the rejection from the ophthalmology journal became clear.

Cooper actually looked sorry, I will say that. I had seen him look at terminal patients, dying of brain tumors, and not seen him exhibit the expression he showed. That made him, in my eyes, more culpable. He had helped to take away my idea. "Eastern has the facilities, the prestige, the money . . ." he went on, rationalizing, explaining, and trying to placate me. "Besides, your work in cataracts is so important. My advice to you, Charles, is to continue with the cataract investigation. Don't try to hog it all."

My interview with him was over. He stood up to indicate my dismissal. And if I had any doubts about the conversation being terminated, he added, "Well, I have other fish to fry." I passed the cat lab on my way out. Cooper's lab technician called out to me, "Hey, doc, you wanna examine the cats today?"

Screw the cats. I didn't say it, but I thought it.

I finally gave the rejected article to the *Eye, Ear, Nose, and Throat Monthly,* where I knew it would get published. I also knew that publication in this journal was practically meaningless, since their circulation was extremely small, and it was not on the list of "university publications." In order for an article to have scientific impact, it must appear in one of the major journals and have its title inscribed on the massive volume of important articles compiled every year. My published article on freezing the retina would never be listed with other major papers. If in the future one went to research the literature to find out if an article on freezing of the retina had been already written, my article would not be found.

When the article did appear, I only got one call about it from a doctor in Ohio who wanted to know if I could donate such a machine to his research foundation. I did show it to my mother. When I had been an intern and had come home once a week to her house for dinner, I would always sit down and play her my latest song. She would stand at the sink, drying the dishes, listening grudgingly, and when I was finished she would always say the same thing, "So what about your medicine?" That's a mother for you. Now, when I showed her the article in the *Eye, Ear, Nose, and Throat Monthly,* she looked at it and said, "So what about your music?" Now that's a *Jewish* mother for you.

I was starting to walk around with a pretty sour expression on my face. Nothing really seemed to be working out for me. The challenge that I had enjoyed so much in the beginning with Joan had grown old fast. With Joan, it became quickly apparent that it was a challenge to even win a kind word or a smile. She worked hard as a housekeeper, but rarely expressed warmth as a wife. Whenever I told her of my career problems, she somehow found a way to take my opposition's side. Nothing I did impressed or delighted her.

I was also beginning to feel the power and the weight of organized ophthalmology. The Establishment. I had trained in Europe and had been more interested in music than medicine during my residency. I had not made any powerful friends, and had no university appointment or position. I was basically a loner in the profession. As a resident, I had not kept it a secret that my goal was in music, and I remember at one particular American Academy of Ophthalmology meeting in Chicago several other ophthalmologists were baiting me regarding my plans for the next year. At that time, my musical career as Kerry Adams had just ended. "I am going to open an office in New York and just practice ophthalmology," I said defensively. "As an ophthalmologist you make a terrific musician," one of them wisecracked. Everyone in the group laughed, except me. I was familiar with that laughter. I had heard it in Leo Ryan's office.

So now, with almost no hope of getting any credit for the

freezing operation on the retina, I had two chances to break through.

One was the cataract operation, which at that time was still going well. Several of the other physicians at Cooper's hospital were sending me occasional patients for cataract surgery. When I had a series of twenty-five cases without rupturing the capsule, I would submit it for publication. I had already made up my mind that if it was rejected, I would announce my technique to the press. Although that would bring the wrath of organized medicine down on my head, at least I would be able to keep the credit. No one would dare to publish "first" what had already been written up in the *Wall Street Journal.*

The other area I had great hope for was in the development of a small probe. If Union Carbide's Linde Division would make a probe and put my name on it, the way they had done for Cooper, even if it was used for retinal surgery, I would still get some credit for it.

One day I was walking to the laboratory where I was investigating the effects of freezing on other tissues inside the eye. In the hall I saw a familiar face. I knew I had seen this man before but I didn't know immediately when or where.

"Hello, Dr. Kelman," he said, but he seemed embarrassed, almost as if he were trying not to be seen.

"Refresh my memory," I said. "I know you, but from where?"

"I'm with the Linde Company. We met the day you came to see us about the small probe."

I knew the answer to the question I was going to ask. Just by the way things had been going for me, I knew it. Goddamn it. I knew it! "What's happening?" I tried to sound casual.

"We are working on a probe for Eastern." He wanted to be somewhere else. Anywhere else. I could see it in his eyes. "I'm sure they'll let you use it once it's developed," he said lamely.

Sure. Once they get it built, reported, and take all the credit. Why not?

"I'll be seeing you," I said. I didn't want him to see a doctor cry.

So far, it looked like all of my efforts were really for nothing. No credit, no papers published. Just another guy fighting the establishment and losing. I knew this much about myself: I was not the classical model of a doctor. I had that overwhelming need to be successful. Not that other researchers didn't claw, scrape, and wheedle to get credit. They all did. It's the credit that really matters in medical research—not the money, but the name. The spotlight. The applause. Even to the guys who had never been on a stage. Even to them it was a need. To me, it was my life. I was fighting for my life, and I was losing every battle at every turn.

Now, my last hope was credit for the freezing cataract operation. I applied to the American Academy of Ophthalmology to give a paper on freezing. I included the retina work as well as cataracts. Even more prestigious than publication in a journal, reading a paper at the academy meeting in front of five thousand participants was perhaps the acme of acceptance. At my very first academy meeting, I had been imbued with that desire to emulate Cooper's success.

The reply to my application came back rather quickly. I was informed that Eastern University was already on the program and they would cover freezing of the retina. I wasn't surprised, but I was angry—very angry. So angry, I sat down and immediately composed my reply. I told my story from the beginning of my freezing research. I named names, verified dates, and sent it off certified, by return mail. A week later there was a second letter from the American Academy. I tore it open. I was to be allowed a few minutes following Eastern's presentation to discuss my cataract operation. I read the letter at least five times before I believed it. I had done it. I had really done it. I was on the program. The Kelman operation was here. Visions of standing ovations rocketed through my head. My God, it had been worth it after all. My only concern was that while the surgical team from Eastern discussed the retina they would also claim priority for the cataract operation. I was really concerned that at the last minute they would take it away from me. But I was wrong. The surgical team from Eastern did not take the credit away from me at the meeting. It was never mine to begin with.

The *Medical Tribune,* although not a high-priority scientific journal, is widely read by almost everyone in the profession. It often had feature stories on new developments in the field. It was on my desk. A front-page story with a large picture. His name was Krawicz—Dr. Theodorus Krawicz. From Warsaw. There was a picture of his probe, cooled by dry ice and alcohol, frozen to a cataract he had removed. He had published this in the *Polish Journal* at about the same time I had started my freezing research. It was the Krawicz cataract operation, using freezing. The cataract looked like a lily yellow jewel, with its frozen white flower in the center, clinging magically to the slender probe. I had been struck by a tidal wave, and I was going under.

Cooper saw the article and said nothing for a few days. When he finally called me into his office, he simply told me that he thought I should continue my work at an eye hospital and that he had helped me all that he could. I was off the staff at the hospital. I was totally alone and out in the cold.

8

Back Home in the Last Row

It was a wet and windy October day. As I drove to the American Academy meeting, the pain and disappointment of the past two years flooded through me. I had made that giant leap from the back of the audience to the podium, but the entrenched giants had stolen my applause. Sure, I would get my five minutes, but only after Sanders spoke for twenty. What was worse was that my cataract research, my big second chance, was gone too. Krawicz, the Polish researcher, who wouldn't even be there, had managed to upstage my second act. Sure, I could present it, but he had *published* it before me. I arrived and sat gloomily on the podium. Looking out at the sea of faces, I tried to see who was sitting in the last row where I had sat so miserably two years before. I wondered what I had really accomplished since then.

Sanders was at the microphone describing everything I had surmised from my initial experiments, substantiating the work with a series of successful patients. As I had predicted, freezing did not affect the sclera. It did not destroy it as burning did. It was a safer and more effective method of treating retinal detachments. It was everything I had hoped it would be except for one thing: It was not the Kelman operation.

When Sanders was finished speaking, the crowd applauded him warmly and appreciatively. I walked to the podium as they announced my name. I began with some films of freezing the retina, but no one was particularly impressed since Sanders had just demonstrated the same subject. I moved into my work on cataracts. I showed the frozen lens being lifted out of the eye. There seemed to be some interest. One can sense a crowd's reaction. It is like a single person with a single response. Almost as if the crowd is one living entity. For a brief moment, I had that living entity interested and with me. Then I showed the machine. Cooper's sixty-thousand-dollar machine. Someone said something in the audience and someone else laughed. The laughter was contagious. I was talking about the machine over the sound of audience laughter. I read the rest of my paper as fast as I could to hasten my departure from the podium. Later, someone explained that a doctor had shouted out that he could do the same thing with a two-dollar forceps. In the eyes of that crowd that is what I had done. I had replaced a two-dollar forceps with a sixty-thousand-dollar machine, and it was laughable to them. Sanders was treated as a hero with his retinal treatment, and I was ridiculed as an idiot with a gimmick. The fact that the gimmick made cataract surgery safer did not occur to anyone. Only the size and cost of the machine seemed to matter. I spent the next few days avoiding my colleagues and left the meeting bruised and bewildered.

"Is it better with this lens . . . or this one? Number one or number two?"

"Could you try that just one more time, doctor, and not so fast, please?"

There I was. Back in the anonymity of the black hole, fitting glasses on my patients. I thought I would now abandon my research plans, since I was an unaffiliated maverick who had no patron to help me retain credit for my ideas. It seemed hopeless to struggle against the powerful institutions. I would just have to learn to be one of the little guys. One of the regular boys. I could be happy being just a regular doctor, attending an occasional meeting and listening to the big guns shoot off. I could do my twenty or thirty operations a year; that's not a bad life. The satisfaction is great and the money is good. A nice house in the suburbs, a country club, civic groups, conventions in foreign places, private school for the kids. Not a bad life at all.

Bullshit. I couldn't buy it even when I tried to sell it to myself. I had to keep going, trying to achieve something. Okay. I was on my own. What I needed was a laboratory. There was a mystique around that damn ball of ice that wouldn't let go of me. I wanted to learn what happened to every tissue when it was frozen. I was certain that there were many good applications of freezing techniques in ophthalmology. I wanted to find them. Not only for the fame. I was really becoming hooked on the pure joy of coming up with new ideas. It was very much like the old days, writing lyrics to songs. I was obsessed.

The liquid that Cooper used in his machine to get the cooling was nitrogen. Liquid nitrogen. It had to be kept in special containers, since it was always boiling away. If you peeked into one of the giant containers you felt a blast of cold air against your face, as if you had opened the front door on a bitter winter day. The temperature is minus 196 degrees Fahrenheit. Close to absolute zero. Colder than the most frozen iceberg in the North Pole. Colder than the surface of the dark side of the moon. So cold that if you immersed your finger in the liquid for a few seconds, it would never survive. It would fall off. If you took a goldfish and dropped it into the liquid for a few seconds, it became frozen so solid that it was brittle. Brittle enough to smash into pieces if you dropped it onto the floor. It was fascinating stuff. Naturally, for the cataract and retinal work we never allowed the temperature to get that low. Just low enough to freeze the tissue—about minus 30 degrees. The temperature on a cold day in North Dakota. The kind of cold that gives frostbite.

I wanted to know what would happen when the frozen cornea thawed. The cornea is the transparent layer that covers the pupil. Would freezing destroy the cornea? Could cold be used to preserve corneal transplants? Each question that came to mind opened the door to a thousand other questions. To do these things, I needed money. Money for equipment, laboratory rent, animals, and personnel. I estimated that I would need about fourteen thousand dollars as a minimum for the first three years. Instead of using Cooper's expensive machine, I would use pure liquid nitrogen; otherwise I would have needed forty or fifty thousand dollars more. I knew there was no way I could get that kind of money.

I applied to the National Institutes of Health for a grant. I listed all the things I wanted to learn and pretty much how I intended to go about my investigations. I was very detailed and very explicit.

The grant application required a coinvestigator. I went to a well-respected surgeon and explained my project. Would he be willing to put his name down as coinvestigator? It was simply an endorsement.

Seymour Anderson said yes, he would like to. The night before I sent out the application, I brought it to Anderson to sign.

"Sorry, Charles, I have been advised that my own career would suffer if I associate with you."

"But why didn't you tell me sooner?" I said, dismayed. "This has to be in by tomorrow."

"Sorry, Charles," he said, but his tone belied the words.

Bob Coles was in the clinic. He had been one of my instructors in ophthalmology. We shared a love of the French language. "You bet," he said when I asked him. With his signature on the page, I sent off the application.

They came from Washington that month to interview me. The consultants sat me down in an office at Mid-Cities Hospital and began to ask me questions.

"What effect does freezing have, Dr. Kelman, on the ciliary body?"

"Sir, I don't know. That is what I want the money for—to find out."

"Dr. Kelman, what effect does freezing have on the endothelial cells of the cornea?"

"I don't know. That's what I need the money for. To find out."

"What effect does freezing have on the optic nerve, Dr. Kelman?"

"Sir, these are the very things I wish to investigate. I don't know the answers, nor does anybody else. That's why I am making a request." I felt like I was taking my board examinations again. Only this time I really failed.

The answer came in a few days. The National Institutes of Health felt that my project was unworthy of fourteen thousand dollars. It was no great shock to me when I later learned that Eastern did receive a grant for the very same studies. I was becoming a seasoned boxer, learning how to take the punches. I had already spent two years doing research instead of building a practice. Cooper's hundred dollars a week, plus the money I made from my small practice, was just enough to keep Joan and me alive.

Still looking for a way to make a smaller cataract probe, I made the rounds of the great corporations—Westinghouse, General Electric, and some surgical companies—trying to interest someone in its manufacture. Cooper's probe was too complicated and expensive and Krawicz's probe was too simplistic. He merely dipped his probe into a mixture of dry ice and alcohol so that it would chill enough to stick to the cataract. But dry ice could not be sterilized, and if the probe accidently touched another tissue, and had to be thawed, the rechilling process would have to be restarted, delaying the operation. This was not the type of instrument that would be accepted in the American operating room. But all of the companies I went to were uninterested, saying there was no market for freezing of the lens. They had checked with their "consultants."

That could have been the end had it not been for a chance meeting and an offhand remark. I sat with Bob Dorfman, my brother-in-law, at a cousin's wedding, telling him about my trials and tribulations. He mentioned a small company he had read about in a trade magazine that had used thermoelectric energy to create freezing. That sounded exciting. With Cooper's machine, a constant supply of liquid nitrogen had to be delivered daily, since it was always boiling away. If there could be a technique of generating freezing with an electrical device, it might be a superior method. I called the president of the company in Connecticut the next day.

"I think you are too late, Dr. Kelman. We're going out of business. There doesn't seem to be much of a demand for our products in the thermoelectric field."

"Just tell me a little how thermoelectricity creates cold," I asked him.

"Simple. An electric current passes across two dissimilar metals. One gets hot, the other gets cold."

"Listen, before you go out of business, why don't you come down and visit. I have an idea which may be good for both of us."

Ralph Crump, the president, came from Connecticut that night. He had short hair, a baby face, and wore a bow tie. After speaking with him for fifteen minutes, I was convinced he was a mathematical genius. But he was more than that—he seemed to be a consummate businessman. He listened while I told him of a possible market for cryoextractors, the instrument I would use to extract cataracts with. Ralph was beaming, and in less than a week he was back in my apartment, carrying a large box of plastic tubing, wires, and electrical conductors, all of which looked like the hidden insides of a complicated telephone switchboard. I couldn't imagine how this mess could help me.

Ralph saw my dismay and chuckled. "Don't worry, Charley. When I get this finished, it will all fit inside of a pencil." He assembled the mass of wires and tubing that led to a small blunt tip. Ralph plugged his instrument into the wall. For fifteen minutes, while we stared at the damn thing, nothing happened. There were no sounds, there was no movement, and there certainly was no freezing. I was convinced that I had invited a lunatic into my apartment. I looked at his face but he didn't seem worried.

"Give it time, Charley. Give it time."

I was discouraged. I knew that in an operating room we didn't have all of this time to wait between freezing and defrosting. It was sometimes necessary to defrost the probe once it touched the cataract, in order to reposition it. If it was going to take fifteen minutes to refreeze again, there was no way this electric probe would work. And then, there it was. My old friend the ice ball. When I touched the probe to an egg yolk it froze to it and held it firm. I asked Ralph if he could make it freeze quicker.

"Thermoelectric freezing produces two things, Charley, heat on one side and cold on the other. I can make it get colder faster if I take away the heat with a water pump through some tubing. Then it will freeze in only a couple of seconds."

Ralph was back in a week. The box he carried was half the size of the previous one. He connected two long tubes up to the sink, we broke open another egg, and the tip froze to it in five seconds. Ralph and I did a little jig around the apartment. Here was a guy who had total commitment. When he spoke, his bow tie bobbed on his Adam's apple, punctuating his remarks with its gyrations. Ralph seemed so sure of his own abilities; I wondered whether he had the same secret doubts about himself that I always had.

In just four months the Kelman Cryostylet was advertised in the ophthalmology journals. After all that time and all that work there was finally an instrument bearing my name. Not only that, it worked incredibly well. The cataracts I removed with it almost never ruptured. The incidence of capsule rupture and serious post-operative problems following cataract surgery would be greatly reduced if others would adopt this instrument. It still was a little too large, looking more like a harmonica than a pencil. But once a surgeon got accustomed to holding it in the palm of his hand, and just maneuvering the delicate tip with his fingers, it was not difficult. It had two tubes for the cooling water and one small wire for electricity. These had to be placed on the surgeon's shoulder while he was removing the cataract.

Medical World News, a publication describing what is new in medicine, did a feature story, "Surgeon Freezes Out the Lens." There it was, my picture in a medical magazine. The elation and joy that I might have had were tempered by my knowledge that this type of publication was not a true scientific journal. I was certainly not in the inner circle of my profession by any stretch of the imagination. I was still an outsider—one of the millions of sperm dancing around an egg, attacking it, one of the millions who might never get in.

From the start, there was tremendous resistance from the profession in accepting the freezing technique for cataracts. "Too cumbersome," they said. "Who needs it?" "I can do just as well with my old forceps," they lied. I spent three years traveling from one end of the country to the other talking at small ophthalmology meetings. Wherever I went, my ideas were met with skepticism, laughter, and rejection. But in every group, there was usually one doctor who would wait until everyone else had left, and then come over to me. He would say, "I think you have something really good here. How can I get one?"

I was beginning to become quite controversial in the profession because of persistence. I was also starting to have a small following of ophthalmologists who had purchased the Kelman Cryostylet, and who had substantiated my findings. They too agreed that the freezing technique reduced the incidence of disasters following cataract surgery.

I thought it was time for me to get back on the American Academy program and present the new instrument. With the statistics of my followers and the small handheld instrument, there wouldn't be laughter. I sensed a small grassroots movement toward the freezing technique for cataracts. I, and the others who used the instrument, had also learned that it worked superbly for especially difficult cases. Cataracts whose capsules had been ruptured by injury could be removed, since the freezing probe would seal the tear in the capsule. Cataracts that had fallen from their normal place, back into the deep portion of the jelly of the eye, could be retrieved with the freezing probe. Cataracts in young individuals could more easily and safely be removed because of the greater adhesion of the probe. I applied to the American Academy of Ophthalmology for another chance on the program.

What is it about human nature that makes some of us rejoice at the misfortune of others? There was definitely joy in the voice of my "friend" who called me one morning. Hidden joy, but joy nevertheless.

"Well, Charley, it looks like you've been screwed again."

That kind of remark could produce a physical reaction on my part. I could feel the heat going up and down my back and heard a ringing in my ears as I said, "Okay, what are you talking about?"

"Did you see the program for the American Academy of Ophthalmology?"

I hadn't seen it, but I knew what he was going to say, just from his manner. I was not to be on the American Academy program. I knew I had been walking a very narrow path from which I could easily be dislodged. What I had done did not compare to what Cooper had done. He had been able to take a disease that no one else could cure and found a way to cure it. There was no other treatment, no other alternative to Cooper's operation at that time.

In my case, all I had done was to make an already good operation somewhat better, somewhat safer. I had not cured the incurable.

"The program is on page 471. Look at it for yourself," my friend said.

I dressed quickly and went to the office. There was the journal in the mail. I opened to the page. It seemed like my life was to be one heartache after another. It was so unfair, so goddamn unfair. There was going to be a symposium on cryosurgery in ophthalmology. A blue-ribbon panel of those from the inner sanctum was going to discuss the merits of the freezing technique.

There it was. The use of freezing for the removal of cataracts was highlighted on the program. It was to be given by that famous professor, Al Perkins. When I read that, I knew what it must be like to have emphysema. I knew what it must feel like to see your infant child being swept away by a stranger, never to be seen again. And I knew what a murderer must feel like in his heart.

Those bastards. I had done all of the work. I had traveled

back and forth across the country describing the advantages of the technique to the profession. I had dreamed, I had schemed, I had worked diligently, and now my ideas were being formally introduced to the profession by the members of "the private club." They were in, I was out. Freezing of the retina—I had lost that one a couple of years before. And now the use of freezing for cataracts was to be presented by one of the very men who had belittled the idea, one who had ridiculed me when I first presented it.

I swore I wouldn't go to the meeting. I knew what it would feel like, how I would suffer if I went. I didn't think I could survive sitting in that room, listening to that program . . . and yet I couldn't stay away. Perhaps I thought that maybe somewhere in his talk, Perkins, who was a fair man with an impeccable reputation, would refer to the work I had done.

The room was packed. There was an electricity in the air. Until now, ophthalmologists had argued at meetings about which was a better needle, or which was a better suture, and about how deep an incision should be. These were all minute details, and were really not terribly interesting, but now there was something new and exciting and everyone felt it. I sat down, masochistically, where I had sat years before, in the back of the auditorium. No one recognized or noticed me. I was still anonymous.

Sanders spoke first about the treatment of the retina. It was an established fact by now, proven by years of his work. He deserved the credit and, had I been in his place, had I had a strong patron to help me, I would have done exactly as he did—I would have taken the credit. I just might have mentioned that there was someone else who started on the same subject before me. But I don't blame Sanders. His work was well documented, highly scientific, and he deserved the ovation he got.

Perkins was next. Professor at one of the most important eye institutes in the country. The most important man in ophthalmology. He was the spokesman, and when he spoke everyone listened, and usually everyone agreed. The slides he showed were similar to the ones that I had been showing for two years. I remember how I felt, sitting in back listening to my work being described by someone else. The two emotions I remember are anger and resolve. I was mostly angry at them, but also at myself, for having let it happen. I was resolved it would never happen again. I knew I would have other ideas, I would make other discoveries, and I knew I had learned a great deal from my encounters.

Perkins was now talking about instrumentation. He mentioned the Linde Corporation and another company. The Kelman Cryostylet was never mentioned. To this day I don't remember where I went or what I did following that meeting. I do remember walking out during the thunderous applause that was given to the professor for his discussion of freezing of cataracts, wondering what I had to do to win.

9

E. Pierre Roy

Joe went out with the CONTAMINATED *sign, leaving me alone again. I sank back into my chair and put my feet up. Calm! Stay calm. Relax! Tick tock, tick tock, tick tock . . .*

I was no longer affiliated with Cooper. I had lost the freezing of the retina operation to Sanders. Krawicz had beat me on freezing of cataracts, and Perkins had stolen my thunder at the American Academy meeting. I had been turned down for a grant by the National Institutes of Health. And now a doctor at Mid-Cities Hospital had just developed a small pencil-like freezing probe using freon gas which was smaller than my Kelman Cryostylet, and would, I knew, replace it. The only bright spot in my life was Joan's announcement: She was pregnant. Somehow I was able to keep going. Somehow, I was able to handle it all. "There is always Tomorrow," I kept telling myself. I was learning to be my own best friend, to treat myself with good-natured compassion. I really had no one else to turn to for that kind of support. I lived for Tomorrow!

I knew there must be dozens of other applications of freezing in ophthalmology. In order to explore this I had to have money, research money. I remembered that Cooper had applied to the John A. Hartford Foundation, and that they had supported him. The Hartford Foundation was giving away thirteen million dollars a year for medical research. All I needed was a paltry fourteen thousand dollars. I took out my old grant application, the one that had been turned down by the National Institutes of Health, and looked at it. Seven pages long, it described my proposal to freeze various tissues in the eye and to observe the effects. How boring! I read through it again and again: same reaction. "So what? Who cares? Why bother?" I kept asking myself. Was this important enough to interest the Hartford Foundation?

I went to bed filled with these doubts, and spent the night rolling from one side of the bed to the other. I knew my application would get turned down again—the Hartford Foundation was only interested in the dramatic, and I couldn't cure brain disease or cancer. My field was cataracts. What could I do in cataract surgery that would drastically change the operation? It was already considered a perfect operation. Hadn't one of the well-known professors, I think it was Troutman, stated that the operation currently being performed for cataracts was the end of the line in the development of the surgical technique? It *was* quasi-perfect. It didn't need any change. Almost everyone agreed. But if I was going to intrigue the Hartford people, I had to identify and reach the next step.

Freezing out cataracts did not really change the operation. A patient who had a successful operation with an expensive cryoprobe was no better off than the patient who had a successful operation with a simple tweezer. I knew that the freezing operation for cataracts was in no way on a par with the dramatic work of Salk, Sabin, or Cooper. I knew that now I had to come up with something of such importance that the Hartford Foundation would have to give me money. How could they get excited with this old grant application of mine if I wasn't?

I wish I could trace my thoughts up to the exact moment in which the idea was born. If only I could recapture that creative synapse in my brain, if only I could identify it and nurture it for future use. But there it was. Like a sudden spark, the idea burst into my consciousness. I sat up in bed.

Cataract surgery, by any means, involved a semicircular cut into the eye, large enough to allow for the passage of the cataract out of the eye. Because of this large incision, the stardard recuperation period was eight to ten days in the hospital, followed by four to six weeks at home. After that the patient could return to gentle activities. For young patients this represented a significant loss of productive time. For old patients it sometimes was even worse. Elderly people fare poorly away from their familiar surroundings, and when bedridden, as is usual after cataract surgery, the elderly disintegrate rapidly. Many elderly cataract patients are never the same physically after the surgery. The general anesthesia for over an hour is difficult enough to recover from. But being inactive for ten days weakens the muscles considerably. Once these patients were hospitalized, many of them were apathetic or weakened for the rest of their lives. For this reason, cataract surgery in elderly patients was often not even considered.

Sometime during that night a flash of insight into the patient's problem and into my own core as an investigator came to me. I got out of bed as if in a trance, and at the end of that grant application typed in the following: *In addition to investigating the effects of freezing on the ocular tissue, another investigation will be begun. A method of removing a cataract through a needle puncture, rather than a semicircular incision, will be investigated; the cataract will be removed through a minute needle puncture, rather than by cutting the eye in half. There will be no need for hospitalization and the patient will be able to return immediately to his or her occupation. The savings to the hospital, insurance carriers, and to the patient, would be billions of dollars a year and the morbidity of cataract surgery will be greatly reduced."*

I outlined some of the methods I envisioned for this needle puncture removal: "disruptive energy," which might liquefy the cataract, and "chemicals," which might dissolve the cataract, although I didn't know which chemicals might work. It was a short paragraph, obviously added at the last minute. I mailed it on Monday and waited.

Three days later, the call came—from the head man himself. Pete Roy was the man in charge; he alone decided who would get research money from the Hartford Foundation. With an office on the hundredth floor of the Chrysler Building, and with thirteen million dollars a year to give away, Mr.

E. P. Roy was literally and figuratively sitting on top of the world. I learned something about him before my appointment. He had been an accountant for the Atlantic and Pacific food chain. He had no medical background, but apparently he had no need of one. Pete Roy picked winners: hyperbaric oxygenation, cryosurgery, vascular surgery, and heart transplantation—to name a few. I was told he could spot a phony in a second. I didn't think I was a phony. I hoped he didn't either.

High in the sky, in a huge office with a great mahogany desk set against the East River one hundred floors below, was where Mr. Roy greeted me. I was prepared to be terrified of this man, expecting him to be a mirror image of Cooper, but I was dead wrong. Pete Roy was ever so slightly portly, about fifty-five years old, with a kindly, understanding face and perceptive, intelligent eyes. I thought they had a twinkle in them as he motioned me to sit down.

"Kelman, this application is a bunch of dull crap." He was holding the application by one corner, dangling it over his wastebasket, letting it swing back and forth. "This is the kind of stuff the National Institutes of Health will fund. Not us." (Maybe he knows they turned me down . . . maybe he's testing me . . . maybe I should tell him . . .)

"Mr. Roy—"

He interrupted me with a signal from his hand. Then he let the application drop into the wastebasket. I didn't understand, but I knew that wasn't the end of it; Pete Roy had a broad grin on his face. He reached over to his desk and took a single sheet of paper in his hand. My God! It was the last paragraph of my application. Roy tapped it with the back of his hand.

"This part intrigues me, Kelman. This could get you the grant." His smile was broader now. "We're really not interested in supporting any more research on freezing."

My intuition had paid off. I wanted to jump out of my chair and throw my arms around him. "Thank you, sir. Thank you," I said.

He continued, "I love the idea of making cataract surgery

an office procedure. I think that would be of great importance to everyone. Just think what it would do in the undeveloped countries of the world."

My God, he was selling me my own idea. He was mentioning things I hadn't even thought of. Mr. Roy stood up. I knew that meant it was time for me to go, but he hadn't told me anything yet.

"The only problem is fourteen thousand dollars, Kelman," he said. "We don't give grants for that amount." He handed me a bulletin. "Take this home and look through it. If you can tailor your needs to the amount of money we are able to give, call me and we will speak some more about your idea."

He shook my hand, still smiling. I was crushed. I didn't feel much like smiling since I knew I couldn't do anything for less than fourteen thousand dollars. That was the minimum. I had already eliminated most of the expensive equipment that I would need even for the cryosurgery investigation. If I was now going to look into a whole new field, if I was going to have to develop chemicals and machines to dissolve the cataract, if I was going to make a real breakthrough in surgery, I knew there was no way I could do it even for fourteen thousand dollars. Damn it. I shook his hand and took the brochure. I was tempted to throw it into the wastebasket as I walked out of his office, but I didn't.

That night, after dinner, I glumly perused it. No wonder they had all that money, those cheap bastards—they doled it out so slowly.

I opened to the page where there was a list of all of the institutions that had received money from the Hartford Foundation over the last several years. Next to the name of each institution was the amount it received. My fingers turned the pages rapidly as I started to chuckle, and then laugh, and then roar. The *smallest* grant the Hartford Foundation had given in the last five years was for $240,000. And I had asked for $14,000. No wonder Mr. Roy had said he couldn't give that type of grant. It was way too *small* for the Hartford Foundation. They wanted a really significant project.

Two hundred forty thousand dollars! My mind ticked off

the equipment I could buy, the people I could hire, and the laboratory I could equip. Life had just gone from the pits to the top of the Chrysler Building. I pulled out my typewriter and started typing. Lab equipment $20,000—no, make that $40,000. Laboratory technicians $6,000—wait a minute, I could use two technicians, $12,000. Instrument supplies $10,000 . . . maybe $20,000 would be better. When I was done putting in everything I could think of, it only added up to $210,000 for three years. I dreamed some more and came up with other things I could use.

When I walked into Mr. Roy's office three days later I had a grant application in my hand for $299,000 over a three-year period. The application described with a little more detail some of my ideas, relative to removing a cataract through a tiny incision. Mr. Roy looked more serious this time and asked me to sit down. It was a fifteen-page application. The first thing he did was to look at the last page, the bottom line, $299,000.

"That's more like it, Kelman. This is an application I can handle."

"I'm going to make it work, Mr. Roy. I'm going to accomplish everything in there."

He motioned for me to be still while he took the application and read it. I sat there while he read every word.

When he finished he looked at me. "There are a lot of things in here I question, Kelman. A lot of breakthroughs will be needed before you could do this type of operation through a small puncture. Isn't that so?"

"Yes, sir, a lot of breakthroughs would be required. But I intend to devote every minute of the day, and every day of the week, and every week of the month, and every month of the year to solving this problem. I'm going to do it."

Mr. Roy had heard all of that before, I guess. He took the application and drew it closer to him, ready to put it into his drawer. He stood up. "Well, Kelman, we'll show it to our consultants. If they feel you can do it, you will have our support."

An alarm went off inside of my head. The consultants. *Bullshit!* Not again. I was not going to lose this one. I was not going to let *this* idea be stolen. I had already struck out after two times at bat. This was my last chance. I didn't care if it never got done, I was not going to give it away to someone else. I reached across his desk quickly and snatched the application away from him. He was startled.

"Sorry, Mr. Roy, I don't want any consultants looking at this work. I would rather not get the money. With all due respect, sir, if you turn down this grant and one of your consultants begins to work on my project, it will be lost to me forever. I would rather try to go somewhere else for the money." I took the application, shook his hand, and strode toward the door, leaving him surprised.

It happened like in a Hollywood movie. If I had written the script myself, I could not have changed a single detail to improve on it. My hand was on the doorknob, the door was open, and I had one foot out of the door. Mr. Roy said softly, "Kelman." I stopped, turned around, and faced him. He was standing at his desk looking out the window, just as Cooper had once done. Only when Mr. Roy turned around to look at me again there was an expression on his face that I would remember for the rest of my life. It was an expression of trust and belief.

"I've never given funds without consultants before," he said. "I don't know why, but I believe in you. I think you are going to succeed." He came around the desk to shake my hand. "Congratulations," he said. "You have our support."

Two days later, the check came—$299,000!

10

Bright Eyes

Tomorrow had finally collided with today. I had obtained the largest grant ever given to a private ophthalmologist: an amount equal to that given to Cooper. It was even more than most large universities had gotten from the Hartford Foundation. If a secret observer had started to follow me just a week ago, knowing nothing of what had gone on before, he would have observed a very lucky person with an "overnight" success. It was a beautiful day and I walked the twenty blocks back to my office with a feeling of warmth and expansiveness. I wanted to shake everyone's hand that I passed on the street. I wanted to tell them all that I had just gotten a huge grant and on top of that I was going to be a *father*.

In the grant application I had budgeted a salary for myself of twelve thousand dollars a year. This, with the income from my practice, would allow Joan and me to live on the upper East Side of New York, closer to Mid-Cities Hospital. The success of my project was, in my mind, a foregone conclusion. How could I fail? Had I not spent only eight hours in Cooper's laboratory before discovering freezing of the retina and of cataracts? Certainly one of the simple ideas I had outlined would work. Certainly I could accomplish what I envisioned in six months or a year, and then go on to other projects. Certainly I was going to change the future of cataract surgery.

My only concern was secrecy. It was imperative for me to

keep the details and the objectives of my work from the eyes and ears of others, who might then be inspired to start a crash research program of their own. This one was going to be mine! I had learned a great deal over the past few years, and I vowed I would not let this idea get away.

I was given ample space on the research floor at Mid-Cities Hospital where the walls were smashed down, a laboratory to house my cats was built, and instruments and machines were installed. Because of the grant—from which the hospital was entitled to 15 percent—I was given the title Director of Cataract Research at Mid-Cities Hospital. The title had been created especially for me, since there was no director of cataract research before me. As far as anyone in the hospital knew, including the administrator, and the attending surgeons who reviewed my grant, I would be investigating freezing techniques in ophthalmology. Other than Mr. Roy at the Hartford Foundation, no one saw the paragraphs devoted to "project X."

While my laboratory was being equipped, I engaged a firm in New Jersey to make the first experimental device for small incision cataract surgery. It was a collapsible, miniature butterfly net, with the net made of rubber. The concept was to make a tiny incision, insert this net into the eye, trap the cataract in the rubber net, mash it up, and then withdraw the net with the mashed up cataract inside of it. My medical artist, Ron Lotozo, made drawings of the operation before the instrument was even made, before I even tried it. It looked perfectly simple in the drawings. It looked perfectly beautiful.

Ron Lotozo had been a friend of mine from my days in Philadelphia. He sang in several of the shows I had written and had a strong baritone voice. He worked as a draftsman for an architectural firm in Philadelphia, but when I needed a medical artist to work for me—Cooper had an artist, so I needed an artist—I convinced Ron to come to New York and learn the techniques. Today, he is one of the very best in the field and works independently.

My feelings of confidence stemmed from my two easy successes. What I didn't realize was that my other successes started with an *observation* of a phenomenon, the freezing of the retina or the cataract, and ended with a *conclusion* as to what use this observation might have. Now, I was starting at the opposite end, the finished product in my mind—the removal of a cataract through a small incision—and going backwards to look for the correct method. It would have been the same had I given myself the project of finding a better way to adhere to a cataract, then having had to invent Cooper's machine. The difference was enormous. The time and energy it would take could not be imagined. Yet I was completely oblivious to even the slightest possibility that I could fail.

Otto Richter, a young man in his early seventies, was an engineer, a scientist, and a very fine human being. He had been working part time for an ophthalmologist friend, Al Rizzutti, at Brooklyn Eye and Ear. One day when Al and I were discussing my new grant, he suggested Otto to me, to actually create the new instrument I thought up. I met him, liked him, and hired him. Later, Otto would provide me with many instruments and ideas, but his biggest value to me was his ability, whenever I was discouraged, to pick me up, brush me off, and practically order me, in his Germanic way, to keep going.

At this point in time I was jubilant, I had been immensely successful in just obtaining this grant, and I could not imagine what the future held.

News of the grant appeared in several ophthalmology journals, and I began to notice a different attitude in my colleagues. First of all, many of them realized that I had done cryoextraction of cataracts (freezing) first in the United States, and that I was really responsible for its success—and a huge success it was. After Perkins's presentation at the American Academy, most of the detractors—those who had called my operation and my instrument gimmicks, those who had belittled me both openly and behind my back—now, without acknowledgment that they had been wrong, bought cryoprobes and began doing the freezing operation. Within a year more than three quarters of all the cataracts in the United States were taken out with some type of freezing probe. Although I had been denied the honor of being on that American Academy panel, a certain amount of the credit and credibility did remain with me.

News had somehow gotten around that I was working on a new operation. I merely tightened the secrecy around my laboratory. Everyone who worked for me knew that their job was on the line if they were in any way responsible for the release of information regarding my investigations.

The first of the three years passed rapidly. Early in that first year, our son David was born and Joan delighted in her new role as mother. My research got underway in the laboratory, and at home we underwent the transition from being a couple to being a family. Setting up the laboratory took several months. And then it seemed to take forever to get the delivery on my little rubber butterfly nets. I kept looking at Lotozo's drawings, certain that the idea was sound. Finally, they arrived; they were the wrong size. More weeks of waiting, and then I got the new delivery. I tried the nets on cadaver eyes. The rubber was too stiff, and it broke off at the hinge. There was a thinner rubber, available from Belgium. More weeks of waiting. Now the rubber tore at another spot. The weeks flew by. The money flew by. My patience flew out the window. This was not the way it had been in Cooper's lab.

Then, one year after the grant had begun, much to my confusion, embarrassment, and ignorance of how I could have possibly failed, I discarded the idea of the rubber bag. It was too traumatic to the eye; the bags would break and there was no way to sufficiently miniaturize the device, so that it could go through a small incision. I had spent one whole year, $140,000, and had nothing, absolutely nothing, to show for it.

The second year of the grant started less optimistically than the first. The specter of spending all of this Hartford money, and not succeeding, reared its head. Now I felt anxiety and an urgency to find the solution quickly. I had sent in my yearly report to Mr. Roy, with no success to report in our important project. I had investigated other aspects of freezing, having hired Helen Chi, a research ophthalmologist, to undertake that part of the program. She did come up with some important discoveries, which were published under her name and mine. That was small potatoes. The meat on the plate was still missing.

The look of confidence that Pete Roy gave me as I walked out of his office haunted me. I told him I would do it, he knew I could do it, and now I just would *have* to do it. What had started out as a research project had become an obsession. I was now into it seven days a week, sometimes ten or twelve hours a day, and was, at the same time, attempting to run my small, but growing, practice in ophthalmology.

Some of the older ophthalmologists, who had come to observe my freezing operation, were starting to send me their cataract patients. Other ophthalmologists were starting to send me their difficult cases, those who required a special knowledge of the freezing technique. The results of my years of lecturing were being felt in practice. Yet, as rewarding as this was, I had another mission, and I had to succeed. It was as simple as that. My days were filled with surgery and research, my evenings with David and Joan. Then Joan had a surprise for me—she was pregnant again.

Even in a perfect marriage, children can sometimes so alter the relationship that the marriage falters. The husband, who was the sole recipient of his wife's attention and affection, finds that he has been replaced—he is relegated to second place. And to make matters worse, he can't even complain about it; his wife is, after all, only being a good mother.

In my case, I had hoped that a child would strengthen our marriage, would give us something to share, would give us a common purpose. I was wrong; it seemed to separate us even more. Joan, being a perfectionist, devoted every ounce of energy, every moment in time, to her son, David. He never had dirt on his face or clothes, there was never a speck of dirt in the house, and our toilets sparkled like diamonds.

David was great fun for me to play with. We took rides in the car, him in his little car seat, and I took him with me everywhere I could—to the hospital, to the laboratory, and yes, even to the zoo. But with Joan's compulsions driving in opposite direction to my compulsion, she and I were like two ships sailing slowly away from each other.

The second year of the grant might be called the year of the drills. I theorized that if a dentist could drill a tooth, I could drill a cataract. In fact, if you held a cataract between your thumb and index finger, a dental drill would destroy it. It would pulverize and liquefy it in a matter of seconds. It seemed to be a logical approach: make a tiny hole, put a tiny dental drill in, liquefy the hard cataract, and suck it out. Why, that was easy! Why hadn't I thought of that before? Why hadn't anyone else thought of that before? This *was* going to be easy.

Lotozo's drawings of the proposed operation were beautiful. With the grant money, I went out and purchased a high-speed dental drill and got to work. Now I was on the right track. Finally.

I have a film of that—my first try with the high-speed drill, holding the cataract between my fingers and seeing it literally disappear in seconds. I tried it on cadaver eyes. There was some difficulty holding the cataract in one place, so I devised various instruments to hold it securely during my second try. The difficulty seemed to be overcome, and I prepared for my first experiment on a laboratory animal.

The cat was anesthetized, my small staff was in attendance; I placed the high-speed dental probe inside the cat's eye. It started to disintegrage the cataract—working just like in Lotozo's drawing—and then . . . I watched in horror as the eye filled with blood as the cat's iris, the colored portion of the eye, wound itself around the rotating drill.

I devised several instruments to protect the iris and a couple of weeks later tried again. This time the iris was spared, and the cataract was finally removed, after about fifteen minutes. Whereas a tooth is held firmly in place by its roots during drilling, the cataract, once the sac or capsule has been opened, is free to slosh around inside the eye and must be chased with the rotating drill.

The next day, the cat's eye was totally destroyed: white, blistered, and opaque, instead of clear like a watch-glass crystal. I wasn't sure why. It was very disturbing, but I was sure that I would find the cause. The next months were spent finding more and more sophisticated ways of holding onto the cataract with a second instrument while I drilled it with the first. Days, weeks, and months went by while Otto made one instrument after another. Many times I would get an inspiration for an instrument late in the day, and I would show the sketch to Otto. "I must have this tomorrow," I'd tell him. "This is the instrument that is going to work. I just know it. Please do it tonight . . ."

Otto would then take my drawing and walk away muttering in German. Of course he had heard it all before. "This is the one that is going to work. Ya. Ya." But Otto was faithful and Otto was loyal and Otto was ever optimistic. The next morning he would come in, bleary eyed from having spent a sleepless night, and in his hand would be the instrument I had designed. And then—how many times? a few hundred?—I would try that instrument, and then frustrated when it didn't work, fling it across the room in despair. Only a year and a half left, and I was still nowhere.

Finally I succeeded in devising a really good instrument for holding the cataract while it was being drilled. I did an operation where I was certain that the cataract never moved away from the drill and never bounced up against the inner lining of the cornea, the endothelium. It is this delicate layer of cells on the inside of the cornea that keeps that tissue free from water, thereby assuring its transparency. The cornea, the watch-glass crystal of the eye, turns white and opaque if water is not constantly pumped out of it. The endothelial cells lining the cornea do the pumping. All my attempts with the cats failed because the cataract was bouncing up against this delicate layer and killing the cells—cells that do not regenerate. Like nerve cells, once they are destroyed, they are gone forever. But that day, I had done an operation where I *knew* that there was no bouncing of the cataract up against these cells. I couldn't wait to examine the cat the next day.

The eye was destroyed. I couldn't explain why.

I called in a photographer who had a special high-speed camera. This camera would take over one thousand pictures every second, and one second of action could be shown back in super-slow-motion for several minutes. I had a photograph taken of the inside of the eye while I was using my dental drill. Looking at the pictures, I could see what was happening. Tiny lens particles, as they were being drilled off the lens, were being flung up against the endothelium, like a sandblasting, destroying it. I had spent these many months trying to hold the cataract in place, but that had not been the only problem. The problem had been inherent in the rotation of that high-speed drill. The fine particles of cataract acted as an abrasive, and destroyed the cornea. They destroyed the eye. And the whole problem was destroying me.

How could it be so difficult? Had I just been lucky in Cooper's lab? I tried drills which turned slower, but they didn't work. Time passed. I tried drills which rotated in opposite directions, trying to neutralize these high-speed currents inside the eye; they didn't work either. More time passed. I tried oscillating drills, those which instead of going in a complete circle went back and forth, but they didn't work. Everything that I used in one way or another destroyed that delicate lining of the cornea. Time was running out.

My report to the Hartford Foundation at the end of two years was short. I described only the few investigations in freezing. The last line of the report read, "Work continues in an attempt to find a small incision cataract operation." By now, I had become sophisticated enough to know what the problem was. Every instrument that I touched to the cataract caused the cataract to move. In so moving it would destroy the endothelium. Even if the cataract did not move, tiny particles would be flung up against that delicate lining in an eddy current. There seemed to be no solution. There was nothing that could act on that cataract without the cataract jiggling, bouncing, or having tiny pieces flung away by the energy. I was stymied. In the midst of my dilemma, my second child, Lesley, was born. A few months later, a third child was on the way.

I went back to my investigation into the use of chemicals to soften the cataract, but any chemical that worked on the cataract also destroyed the endothelium. With six months left to the grant, I walked around with my eyes red from lack of sleep and my spirits destroyed by a sense of my own failure. *This* failure I couldn't blame on anyone stealing anything from me. It was mine. Strictly mine.

I had had every chance to succeed. I had the money. I had the facilities. I had my choice of people to hire. And I had now spent $250,000, a quarter of a million dollars, with nothing to show for it. I avoided looking at myself in the mirror. Love, music, and laughter were foreign to my life. I envisioned the end of the grant, my sad regrets to Mr. Roy, his look of disappointment, and my public acknowledgment of failure. I had no more ideas. For centuries ophthalmologists have had a dream: to dissolve cataracts. How stupid, how presumptuous of me to think I could do it. It was over.

I had to prepare myself now to face the world: to return to the reality of being with my family, my patients, my friends. I had neglected my appearance for about a year, and I studied my reflection in the mirror. A tired old man with long, unkempt hair, a pasty complexion, and yellowing teeth with matching nicotine fingers looked back at me with disgust. I thought I might face defeat better if I looked better, and so I prepared. The haircut came first, then a shoeshine, and finally, the dentist. My teeth were covered with tar and nicotine from the smoke of the endless cigarettes I inhaled daily.

Larry Kuhn was the dentist Joan was working for when I met her. When she introduced me to Larry, I immediately liked his sense of humor and his joie de vivre, and when I called him for an appointment, he made room for me that same day.

I sat in his chair, as he reached over, took a long silver instrument out of its cradle, and turned it on. A fine mist came off the tip but the tip didn't seem to be moving. He applied the tip to my teeth, and I felt an exquisite vibration and heard a high-pitched sound. I pushed his hand away. Larry thought he had hurt me. I jumped out of the chair.

"What is that thing, Larry? What kind of an instrument is it?" I asked.

Larry smiled at my lack of knowledge. He explained: "This is an ultrasonic probe, which vibrates twenty-five thousand times a second. That's how it can clean your teeth, picking off those particles of tartar, without you feeling it. It's a question of *acceleration.*"

I threw my arms around his neck and kissed him on the cheek. And then on the other cheek.

He pushed me away. "What the hell is the matter with you?" he shouted, his eyes wide with fear.

"I love you, Larry, I love you. You just saved my life."

"Nurse, nurse," Larry called out. A round little nurse hurried into the room. I grabbed her.

"I love you, too," I sputtered, laughing as I kissed her on the neck. Larry was reaching for the phone, probably to call the police, or the psycho ward. The more concerned he got, the funnier it seemed to me, and the harder I laughed. It was like an explosion—two years' worth of laughter had been bottled up for the right moment. And I knew this was the moment.

Just as I had known about freezing of the retina, and freezing of the cataract, I knew it. I had made my observation! I *knew* it. I still had the dental gown around my neck as I ran, laughing, through the waiting room and out to my car. I could see them all at the window, watching me in amazement as I burned rubber and pulled away with a squeal of the tires. I had to wipe the tears from my eyes—tears of laughter and tears of relief—to see where I was going.

In twenty minutes I was back in his office. One of the patients who had seen me run through the waiting room, an elderly lady, was now in Larry's chair. Neither she nor Larry seemed glad to see me.

"Please get out of that chair," I said to her, looking as crazy as I could. I didn't have to coax her. She shot off that seat as if it had suddenly turned red hot, then she bolted from the room.

"Charley," Larry said in a soothing voice, "just sit down and stay calm. I'm going to give you a little injection."

"Don't worry, I'm not crazy. I think you just solved my biggest problem. Let's see."

I took a jar from my pocket. In it was a cataract that had just been extracted at Mid-Cities Hospital. I held the cataract under the bright dental light and applied the ultrasonic probe to it. I knew it was going to work, and yet . . . I had been sure so many times before; I'd thought I'd had it so many times before. But now, with practically no pressure, the probe was making tiny grooves in the cataract. Just as a speeding bullet can penetrate a standing plank without it falling over, because of the velocity, so too this probe could penetrate the cataract without the cataract moving. I knew that it wouldn't be quite that easy, that the instrument would have to be modified, perhaps a hundred times, but I also knew that I had found, finally, in the eleventh hour, the road that would lead to small incision cataract surgery. I sat back in the treatment chair and let Larry finish his work on me. I reveled in the delicious sensation of that ultrasonic probe against my teeth.

Now I had to hurry; only a few months remained. I had to prove it would work on an animal before the grant ran out: otherwise, no renewal. I was sure of that.

I contacted Cavitron, the firm that made the ultrasonic dental probe. No, they didn't think it would work; no, they didn't think there was a market for an ultrasonic cataract probe; no, they weren't interested. I tried other ultrasonic companies, but they, too, turned me down. I went back to Cavitron, and asked them to build an instrument for me, at my expense. (I could not use grant money to develop what might become a commercial product.)

After I badgered Bob Navin, the president, much as I had badgered Cooper, Cavitron finally agreed to build me a small handpiece with some of the necessary features; but they said it would take them a year. I pleaded. I begged. I wheedled . . . and I got it. A month later I had a modification of the dental unit with a small hole for suction. That's what I needed, a way to remove the sludge, the waste, the liquefied cataract from the eye.

As I prepared for surgery one more time, my hands trembled as I felt the urgency of the hour. Only a few months left. I *had* to be successful this time. The operation on the cat took about forty-five minutes.

When I had examined my cats the day after each of the other unsuccessful operations, the corneas had been totally white and cloudy the next morning. With this cat I decided to keep an all-night vigil over the cornea, which, like all of the others, was clear immediately at the end of the surgery. I took the sleeping cat back to the house, where we were now living. With the birth of my third child, Jennifer, an apartment was no longer adequate and we had moved to the suburbs of New York. My basement seemed like a good place for a vigil; I installed myself there for the night with the cat, a flashlight, a magnifying glass, and a bottle of champagne. I set an alarm to go off every hour, but I didn't need to—I never slept.

The cornea started to turn cloudy at three in the morning. By four, I knew I had failed again. I was devastated. I took a walk outside to watch the sun rise and see some of the normal people going about their normal activities: going to work, earning a living, being happy. I looked at myself. What had happened to the Gemini? What had happened to the musician? What had happened to the guy who wanted to be outside, free as the air? I had become a recluse, an obsessed recluse. I had become everything I didn't want to be. And yet something inside told me to keep going. I felt I was so close. There was only one more link. One more problem. I knew it. I felt it. . . .

Larry was waiting for a call to hear how things had gone. I thought of what a fool I had been in his office. I couldn't bring myself to make that call. I went back to the lab, taking the unopened champagne and my half-blind cat along for the ride. I had proven with motion pictures that this ultrasonic probe did *not* sandblast the cornea. The particles that came off the tip were immediately sucked into the hollow probe.

Also the probe was not turning in a circular motion and there were no eddy currents set up, no whirlpool currents to fling these particles against the cornea. Having proven to my own satisfaction that this ultrasonic probe did not allow the particles of lens to damage the cornea, I wondered where I had gone wrong. What was the missing link?

I sat in a chair and thought about the operation. By now I knew what my strength was. It was observation and conclusion. I tried to recall all of my impressions, all of my inputs. Many things passed through my mind, but one sensation kept trying to surface from my subconscious: While the probe was in the eye, I would put a gloved finger against the eye to steady it. There was a sensation at my fingertip—not of vibration, not of movement, but of something else. And then I remembered. My finger inside of the glove felt warm during the surgery. Very warm. I slowly got out of my chair, almost in a trance, and anesthetized the cat. When it was sleeping, I placed it on the operating table and readied the ultrasonic probe. I took a tiny thermometer, and placed it on the cat's eye. The temperature was normal, 97 degrees. I put the ultrasonic emulsifier in the eye, touching it to the cataract . . . 97, 99, 110 degrees!

My God! That was it. I had been cooking the eyeball! The ultrasonic vibration was causing friction. Friction caused heat. I had been burning the cornea. That's why it had turned white. Like a cooked egg. All I would have to do was to cool the probe and I would have a normal eye. It would be simple to add a flow of salt solution dripping from a bottle. When Otto came in I operated on another cat, keeping the eye cool with a flow of fluid; this time my gloved finger stayed cool.

I took the cat home for my all-night watch.

"Must you bring those smelly cats in here?" Joan complained.

I really didn't blame her. These cats really were aromatic. "This one's a winner, honey. This one will do it." I put the cat in the little bed I had made for it in the basement, and went to play with the children.

"Daddy, why do you have to bring those smelly cats

home?" Lesley asked, unconsciously imitating her mother.

"They're sick, sweetheart, and I'm making them better," I lied.

I installed myself in the basement with my flashlight, my magnifying glass, and my cat. At 3:00 A.M. the eye appeared normal; 4:00 A.M. the same. Five, six, seven, eight, nine o'clock in the morning, the eye looked perfect. I had done it. I had actually done it. The cat's eye was now without its lens.

Where was the champagne? I had removed the cataract, the cat's eye had remained normal, and I had done it through an opening *one tenth the size* of that required for standard surgery. I petted the cat and hugged it to my chest. "Bright eyes, you're gonna live forever." My report to the Hartford Foundation was due in two weeks.

When I finally emerged from the basement that morning, bleary eyed but elated, Joan was in the kitchen. What a moment to share with her. I took the stairs three at a time.

"Kelly! [my nickname for her] It's finished. We did it! The eye is clear. It worked!" I panted from my race up the stairs and from my excitement. I waited for her enthusiasm.

"Well, maybe now you can clear those stinking cats out of here."

I could never seem to interest Joan in my work. Usually I ignored her lack of enthusiasm, but this time I desperately needed someone to share my excitement. "But it worked. It finally worked," I persisted. "It's really important. The cornea stayed clear."

"It's always important," she yawned.

I stood there, wanting to be hugged, wanting to be kissed. Wanting to celebrate and share the triumph with her, needing and begging for her enthusiasm. Instead, I found myself saying, "I'll get the cats out of here today." . . . "And I won't be home until late. I have a meeting tonight." I didn't know yet with whom, but I'd find somebody.

One of the nurses who had helped in the lab was delighted to have dinner with me that night. Her eyes reflected my rekindled enthusiasm as I described the details of my all-night vigil. Her exuberance, her empathy, her desire to understand what I had gone through, were perfect. It was all perfect except for one small thing—she was the wrong person.

I had married Joan, coming off Ellen. Ellen was a liar and a cheat; Joan was straightforward and honest. When I married Joan, I was still suffering withdrawal pangs from the disastrous year I had spent chasing Ellen. But I should have realized that Joan's inability to provide me with warmth and tenderness would eventually destroy our marriage. I should have realized that I needed even more love than the average person. I should have realized that I was too involved with my research to work out our problems when they were still solvable. I should have. But at that time, with the pain of Ellen still a stabbing recollection, I was able to convince myself that Joan's virtues overshadowed that "small" shortcoming.

There is a theory that if we have had an unsuccessful relationship with a parent, we seek out a mate with whom we can continue that very same struggle. In my case, it certainly seemed to work that way. My mother still reminds me about how, as a child, I would ask her dozens of times a day, "Ma, do you love me? Ma, do you love me?" My mother to this day thinks it's funny. She doesn't realize that I was pleading for a demonstration of her love. I'm sure she gave me the normal amount, but obviously I needed more.

When I married Joan, perhaps I was really continuing the struggle I had had with my mother. It is an appealing theory, and makes it easier to understand why I chose to marry Joan, knowing that what I wanted most from her would be withheld. It also explains why Ellen was so appealing: She would occasionally let me win my lifelong struggle, giving me a great deal of warmth and tenderness. But no sooner did I get it, than she was off with another, leaving me with an even greater ache, having known the pleasure of satisfied inner need.

With Joan I did not have the anguish of wondering whether she was unfaithful. But I missed terribly the little things . . . a touch on the cheek . . . a kiss on the head . . . a conspiratorial smile. These were the missing ministrations that made me lie awake nights with a dull desire for something I couldn't define.

And yet, there is another side to all of this. Suppose I was to have married a girl who would have given me the warmth I needed—someone to whom I could have poured my heart out, who would have listened sympathetically, and then with her love have made everything all right, made the pain of defeat go away. What would my reaction have been as things started to sour with my research? Might I not have let myself be comforted, and have forsaken research in favor of her loving and caring person? Is it not possible that I persisted in my work, in spite of the difficulties, precisely because I found no solace in my own home? I think, with Krawicz beating me to the freezing operation, with Perkins speaking in my place at the academy, with Cooper kicking me out of his hospital, that with the "right" woman, I might have retreated to the safety and comfort of her consolations and found a way to be happy without success. Maybe I would have picked up my marbles and gone home to Mother complaining how rotten the world was. But I had no one to complain to. And so I tried harder. I persisted.

11

Chow

Time crept forward, while my mind raced backward, tracing the events that led me to my hiding place. Joe was inside with Cheryl and Banko. I was alone. That's the way it had to be. There was no way that I could confide in any of them without causing them to lose confidence. And if they had doubts, it would affect me. It would be a vicious cycle. I had to appear sure. I realized then a basic truth about human nature: Whistling in the dark is not a cliché, but a truism. The act of whistling stifles fear.

Making believe that I was confident made me actually feel confident—but only as long as I was acting. So as long as they were there, I felt strong. But it's harder to act when you are alone. And now, in the anteroom before John Martin's operation, I was alone. Discovery was inches away. There was no whistling going on.

After several more successful cat operations, I had to try the procedure on another type of animal; I had to be certain there wasn't something special about the eye of a cat that allowed the operation to be successful. I had to operate on a dog with the same good results. I was now starting to plan for my first human surgery. But now I felt it was time to publish my animal work. I was concerned that others might be on the same track and publish before me. The thought of being second again, the thought of reading a report by someone else, the thought of the wasted effort and time and energy kept me on the razor's edge of anxiety. I had to publish.

My new neighbor had actually been asking me to operate on his dog Chow for a few months. Chow had cataracts and was unaccustomed to the new house he found himself living in when his "family" moved. He was forever falling down the stairs or walking into the walls. Until now, I had not wanted to bother with treating a neighbor's dog, but now. . . .

"I guess I could do your dog now," I told them. "I'll take him to the lab tomorrow."

"Will he be able to see?" my neighbor asked concernedly.

"I'll have to make up some special glasses to fit over his eyes," I said. "But, don't worry, I'll work something out."

Chow was a good patient. He went to sleep with one injection and both cataracts were out in less than half an hour. I had made a hood with two lenses sewn into the holes over the eyes and Chow looked like a visitor from a far-off planet when the next day he tentatively padded his way around the lab. If it were not such an important success it would have been funny. Actually, it was funny anyway. Whoever saw us (taking a walk in the park that afternoon, waiting for a taxi later on) without knowing what had transpired, broke out into good-natured laughter. One guy came up to me and said, "See that your son gets a seat up front in the classroom," before he giggled his way back to his group of hilarious friends.

Somehow Chow knew he was a star and walked with a certain arrogance as he looked at the world through his Coke bottle glasses.

I was very concerned about leaks; now there were too many people who knew about my work. Even though I had shrouded it in secrecy and disguised the reports so as not to include any important details, I was afraid that someone else, with more political clout, would pick up where I had left off and beat me to the credit.

Sending the work into one of the journals seemed to invite

just what I was afraid of—someone else reading it, then having my paper rejected, and then . . . and then . . . being second again. It was time to find a "patron," someone who was well-known, highly respected, who would be willing to help. If my manuscript were sent in for publication with an introductory letter from such a patron, there would be less chance for foul play.

Such a man was Dr. Irving Leopold. When I was a resident at Wills Eye Hospital, he was the head man—surgeon director. He had written several hundred scientific papers, was an acknowledged genius in pharmacological ophthalmology, and was now in New York as professor and chairman of Ophthalmology at Mount Sinai Hospital. He was a man of integrity, and would, I hoped, be willing to help an ex-resident and alumnus of Wills.

I telephoned his secretary for an appointment, and was told I could not see him for six weeks. He was booked solid until then. "It's an emergency," I told her. Leopold was on the line a minute later.

"What is it, Charles?" he asked politely.

"I can't tell you on the phone, Dr. Leopold. It is really urgent."

"Okay, C'mon over. I'll find the time."

I went to my laboratory and put a leash on Chow. Although I had just removed both of his cataracts, his eyes looked almost normal. Had I used conventional surgery on him, they would have been red, tearing, and the dog would have been trying to scratch at them without interruption. I did not want to attract undue attention at Leopold's Clinic, so I removed his hood with the glasses. Chow walked slightly unsteadily, not being able to focus clearly, but other than that he was fine.

Leopold's office at Mount Sinai looked like a national convention for the blind and partially sighted. Patients from all over the world stood vigil, waiting for their name to be called, so that they could get the final opinion. If Leopold said there was nothing that could be done, they would resign themselves to their fate. He was the court of last appeal for those losing their sight from a malicious eye disease called uveitis—a slow inflammation that eats away at the vision, sometimes with smoldering pain, sometimes with no other symptoms than the loss of central vision. Leopold wrote the book on that subject.

It was really not one disease, but many, each requiring a specific diagnosis and treatment. The wrong medication would not only be ineffective, it could worsen the condition with a more rapid onset of blindness. One could feel the urgency in the room, the importance of the day for these poor souls, some of whom had waited six weeks or more, some of whom had traveled across the globe for a precious few minutes with this man.

A battery of assistants worked several examining rooms off the main waiting room, calling patients for preliminary examinations. Names were being called, patients answering, nurses scurrying back and forth with reports, and every few moments, the large double door to Leopold's office would open a few degrees, a patient would emerge, and everything would stop. No noise, no movement, nothing. A nurse would appear at the double door and call out the name of the next patient, who would answer excitedly, as if he had just won the lottery: "Yes, yes I'm here! I'm here!"

I stood in the midst of all of this with Chow, and wondered if I had done the right thing, intruding on this scene with my own comparatively inconsequential problems. A nurse tapped me on the shoulder and led me to a small darkened office, where Chow and I waited for some ten minutes.

"Well, Charley, how are you?" I could hardly believe the composure of the man. With all of this going on, he was cool, unharassed, and by his manner seemed to say, "Relax, I have all the time in the world." He was tall and trim with a long, handsome face and had brown hair that was thinning at the top.

"I'm okay, Dr. Leopold," I began nervously. I noticed that in the dark he had not seen Chow at first, but he was now looking at the dog suspiciously.

"That's Chow." I smiled at him. "Would you please take a look at his eyes?"

The composure I had seen evaporated like a flash of gunpowder.

"Son of a bitch!" he exploded. "With all of these poor devils waiting for me, you want me to examine your goddamn dog? Are you out of your mind, Kelman? Get the hell out of here!" He turned to leave.

I had to get his attention now—or never. I was quietly insistent. "Irv," I gambled, using his first name, "I wanted you to be the first to see this." I was on target.

"See what?" he asked angrily, one foot out the door.

I continued my gamble. "I'm not going to tell you. Take a look for yourself." I spoke slowly and calmly, nodding my head up and down in an imperceptible "yes" movement. He shut the door and took a small flashlight out of his pocket, grudgingly shining it into Chow's eyes. Chow licked at his fingers. Leopold was perplexed. He looked at one eye, and then the other, going back and forth several times. Then he put the light back into his white smock and turned to me. "This dog has no lenses."

"He had them yesterday," I said. I knew I was home. I could feel my heart beating wildly and hoped Leopold couldn't hear it.

He took out his light and looked again. Then he pressed a buzzer on the wall, and in a second, a nurse appeared. "Tell the other doctors to get in here, right away," he ordered. He was beginning to relax and enjoy the break from his usual routine. I relaxed also.

They all came in, about ten of them, and examined the dog. At first no one noticed the missing lenses in the eyes, until one of the resident doctors made the observation. Then they all looked again.

"What . . . is . . . story . . . here?" a Chinese doctor asked Leopold.

"I'll let you know when I find out." He laughed. "Now all of you had better get back to work."

"What is story here?" Leopold mimicked.

I told him what I had done and how I had done it. I described the machine and all of my failures.

When I finished, he said, "What can I do for you?"

"I want you to help get it published," I said, and then I told him about my fears of losing the credit for the work.

He sat down at a desk and picked up the phone. "Get me Frank Newell," he said.

My heart jumped. Frank Newell was the editor of one of the most prestigious journals of ophthalmology.

"Frank?" Leopold said a moment later. "How are you? . . . and the family? . . . Good. Good . . . Listen, Frank, I want you to consider an article which will be sent in tomorrow. It's something very special. Original work by Kelman . . . No, not Spellman. Kelman. Please, get it in as soon as possible. I've seen some of the results . . . No, I'm not a coauthor. Wish I was. Thanks, Frank."

Leopold put down the receiver. "Now will you get *out* of here and let me get back to work?"

That was all there was to it. Chow and I went to Burger King to celebrate. He loved the burger, but spit out the lettuce. I ate the pickle.

12

John Martin

The paper was entitled "Phacoemulsification and Aspiration: Preliminary Study." In medicine, we generally use Greek and Latin words to describe techniques. *Phaco,* in Greek, means lens. Emulsification is from the root *emulsi,* which means fine particles suspended in a solution, and *aspiris* adds the final descriptive term, *aspiration.* So the name means chopping up the lens of the eye into fine particles in a fluid, and sucking them out of the eye.

With the paper's acceptance in the journal several weeks after Leopold's telephone call, I still had about nine months to wait for it to be printed and actually released. Although I felt more secure knowing that it would be in print, I really wouldn't feel comfortable until the article appeared. My next job was to get the instrument to perform reliably enough to be able to use it on a patient. Up until this time, the instrument used had been a modified dental unit. No large sums had been spent on the equipment, since we weren't even sure that the technique would work. Navin said it would take about *half a million dollars* to perfect the machine: a staggering expense that he could not justify.

Where was this money to come from? I could not use Hartford funds for this purpose, because that amount had not been budgeted. And also if Hartford funds were used to make a commercial instrument, the rights to the instrument could not be protected or patented, which would discourage any company from trying to develop the instrument. I had to convince Navin to *invest* the money.

I met with Navin that week; he was a hard man to sell. I told him how much I personally needed this piece of equipment to be built—no sale. I explained the benefits of such a machine to humanity—mild interest, no sale. I described what it could do for Cavitron—faint skepticism, no sale. I was running out of arguments. Desperately I outlined how a farsighted decision on his part would effect his reputation in the entire industry, how he would become a legend—*sold!*

I truly believed it would, and so did he. Three months later I had a handpiece just adequate for a clinical trial on a patient. The handpiece was so large and so heavy, however, that I had to build a special device, like a miniature crane, to hold it over the operating field. It was Rube Goldberg, but it was a start.

Now, I needed a low-risk patient. Someone who not only had a cataract, but who had some other condition that prevented him from seeing—if possible, a patient who was in need of having his eye removed. This type of patient is rare. No matter how blind the eye, or how disfigured it is, we can usually control pain enough so that the eye can remain. Only in desperate cases of late glaucoma, where everything else has failed, where there is constant pain in a blind eye, is the eye in need of removal. That operation is called an enucleation; it is the operation we as eye surgeons detest, since it is a sign of our impotence in the face of disease. Such a patient, even if my operation didn't work, would not lose anything since he would never see out of the eye, cataract or no cataract. Where was I going to find such a patient?

He appeared on my doorstep, so to speak, almost as soon as I identified the type of eye I was seeking. It really seemed that Somebody up there was looking out for me. John Martin was the man. He had severe glaucoma, which had blinded him entirely in one eye and which had reduced his vision considerably in the other. The blind eye, furthermore, had a cataract. On top of all of this, the blind eye was painful, and would probably, sooner or later, have to be removed. The patient actually was requesting that I remove this painful eye. He was a fine gentleman, seventy-nine years old, from the West Indies.

"John, before I remove your eye, I want to do another operation on it."

"Will this other operation make me see a little from it?"

"No, John."

"Then I guess I don't want it."

"John, I want to do an experimental operation on the eye. If it works, it will help a lot of other people. If it doesn't work, then nothing was lost."

John looked at me for a moment. I knew what was on his mind. I anticipated his question: "This can't affect the other eye, John. It will not take away any vision from the other eye."

"I want to help you, doc. Go ahead and do your operation."

My chief engineer, Anton Banko, and a few assistants, started to get the machine in condition for the operation at six o'clock in the evening on the night before surgery. John Martin was relaxed and happy in his room. I had told him that one way or another, the pain would be over. Either he would feel better after this operation, or the eye would be removed. Banko said it would take a few hours to check everything out, and that I should stop by at about nine o'clock that night for a final check. I had a quick dinner and returned at eight-thirty.

"Problems, doc." Banko never used too many words. The machine was in pieces on the floor. I could see how crude the wiring was, how flimsy the connectors, how unsuitable this machine was to be used commercially.

"What kind of problems?" I asked.

"Electronic problems. I'll fix them."

"How long will it take?" I asked nervously.

"It will be ready before the operation."

Banko worked all that night. I left him at one o'clock in the morning so that I could get some sleep. I wanted to be as rested as possible for the operation. I fell into an empty hospital bed and asked the night nurse to wake me at 6:30 A.M. A few brief hours of sleep, and then there I was—at the beginning of that gray dawn, wishing I could run away or jump out the dull silver windows that didn't even open.

* * *

All the years of struggling rolled through my mind. It was a long, hard movie. I knew I was destined to be judged a pioneer or a madman, that this operation would push me down one of those paths. With a deep breath, I pushed myself out of my chair and went into the operating room. Banko had dark circles and a heavy stubble.

"It's okay . . . I think," he said gravely. He always had a sad, middle-European look on his face, but now it was funereal.

"But will it hold together long enough for the whole procedure?" I knew that I would have to go slower in a human eye than in a cat, where the actual emulsification, the breaking up of the lens, took about eight minutes. I figured about fifteen minutes for John Martin's cataract.

"I think it will hold together," he said.

A fresh wave of panic hit me like a slap in the face when I saw them wheeling John Martin into the operating room. It was what a soldier must feel the first time he has to engage in hand-to-hand combat. Fear. Anxiety. Helplessness in the face of events. Wanting to run. Shame of wanting to run. Talking to yourself to get courage, knowing courage can kill. Better to run. Coward, stand and fight.

Oh shit, it was time to scrub. Banko was already dressed in white and was turning the dials. His black circles and twenty-four-hour beard stood out starkly against the whiteness of his cap and operating gown. I scrubbed my hands while Dr. Angelo, the anesthesiologist, put John to sleep.

The case was scheduled as a cataract removal. Nothing more. I knew that the operating-room staff would think that this machine was some new freezing machine I was testing. I had done that many times, with many engineers present. For them this was nothing new. For me, it was madness.

What I was doing was not really illegal—a doctor can perform any operation he sees fit for the benefit of the patient—yet this operation, on the other hand, could not really benefit John Martin. It was an experiment. True, the patient understood that, but nevertheless it was *an experiment. I felt a great compassion for John. He had a sweet disposition and a long, expressive face. Glaucoma, if untreated, can wreck the nerves of the eye without the patient realizing it until it is too late.*

I couldn't stop thinking about the risk I was taking also. Maybe my name would be in the papers: DOCTOR BLINDS UNFORTUNATE MAN IN EXPERIMENT. *I could see not only the headline, but the whole article. I looked down at my hands as I washed them; miraculously they were steady—somehow my nerves did not seem to be connected to them. I took another deep breath and walked back into the operating room.*

A black tube poured out of John Martin's mouth and was attached to a shiny bag which the anesthesiologist pumped from time to time. "He's all yours," he said. I took a long needle on the end of a syringe and gave John an injection just below the eye, pushing the needle all the way into the back of the socket. This would not only anesthetize the eye but would help to dilate the pupil so as to provide a better view of the cataract while operating. The cornea, normally clear as glass, was in John's case like ground glass due to his disease. It was going to be difficult to see in there.

"That's a funny-looking machine, Charley," the anesthesiologist said with some suspicion.

"It's funny, all right," I said. "It's one big joke." I wanted to cut off his questions.

"What the hell does that thing do?" he persisted.

"Look," I said, stopping what I was doing, "I have to concentrate on this operation. Give me a break will you?" He did. If I had told him, he would have been as liable medico-legally as I was, since he would have known about it. I think he understood all of this without it being said. In any case, he shut up.

I made the first tiny incision into the eye. The pupil, which had dilated somewhat from the drops and injection, became smaller. I injected pure Neo-Synephrine directly into the eye, to try to dilate the pupil again, but it worked poorly since this patient had been taking drops for years to do the opposite . . .

constrict the pupil. That was the treatment for glaucoma. It was hard to reverse the effect of these constricting drops with a few doses of dilating drops in the operating room.

I put a tiny hook into the eye to open the capsule of the cataract to expose it. My hands were steady. About one half hour had gone by since I had entered the operating room. I called for the emulsifier—not by name, but by just saying, "I'm ready for the instrument." Banko handed it to me with a little prayer on his lips.

The handpiece was a monster; it had heavy black wires and tubes coming around the sides. Unlike the delicate eye instruments I was used to, this was long and thick, like a four-cell-battery flashlight. And heavy. So heavy, that I had to use the ceiling support I had constructed, hooks and wires suspended over John Martin's head. It was about as delicate an eye instrument as a shovel. I supported the front of this handpiece with my left hand, while my right hand guided the needle into John Martin's eye.

Under the microscope the needle's tip looked much larger than what I was used to seeing—then I realized with dismay that the human eye was *smaller* than the cat or dog eye. There was four times the volume of space inside the animal eye. I had hardly started the case and perspiration was pouring off my forehead, into my eyes, and running down my cheeks. A nurse wiped my forehead, but the sweat continued to pour. She wrapped a sterile towel around my neck, and I kept going.

I stepped on the foot switch, activating the vibration of the needle as it touched John's cataract. *Buzz . . . buzz . . . buzz.* The needle bore into the cataract just the way it was supposed to. There was so little room to maneuver the tip inside the eye. I had to be careful not to rub off the inner layer of the cornea. After a few moments, I was totally convinced that no other surgeon in his right mind would want to subject himself to performing this operation. The standard operation, opening the eye in a semicircle, was so easy compared to this madness, *Buzz, buzz, buzz.* The needle was slowly eating away the cataract.

Then something happened which had never happened in an animal eye. I could feel my coronary arteries constrict, almost as if I wished to stop my own heart from beating—to end it all right then. Goddamn it to hell! The cornea had collapsed against the vibrating tip. Like a parachute collapses when it hits the ground, the cornea had suddenly been sucked down against the emulsifying needle. I was sure that I had partially emulsified the cornea. In any case, I had certainly rubbed off a large number of the delicate endothelial cells lining it. Those were the same cells I had destroyed in the cat by cooking them. Damn, damn, damn.

My foot jerked spastically off the pedal, and the eye filled slowly with fluid running in from an infusion bottle, restoring its shape. I took the probe out of the eye and tried to calm myself. My hands were now shaking, as if I had Parkinson's disease. The anesthesiologist and Banko looked at me questioningly, wondering perhaps if I had gotten an electric shock from the instrument, since I had jerked away so quickly. This was no time to go into explanations. I had to get control of myself and control of the situation, or I was finished.

I looked carefully at the cornea, but couldn't see any gross signs of burn. That was a small consolation. With the cats there had been no sign of burn either, until the next day. What could I do? I could open the eye at this time, making a large incision, and spoon out the cataract. But I knew for sure that if I gave it up now, I would give it up forever. This was one horse from which, should I get thrown, I would never be able to remount. Too much anguish, too much preparation, too much intrigue had gone into this. I had to go on. . . .

I put the probe back into the eye. The pupil was getting smaller, and now wouldn't react at all, even to pure Neo-Synephrine. I carefully buzzed away at that part of the cataract visible in the small pupil. Oh, no! No! The cornea collapsed again. This time I didn't remove the probe from the eye. With dogged determination, I kept going. I was torn; I was ripped apart in my mind. Quit. Stop! Pull out. . . ! Keep going, don't give up, full speed ahead.

In the final analysis, the decision I made in my head was to stop. The machine had to be malfunctioning. There had never been these collapses in the animal eye. Something had to be wrong. Okay. Stop!

Stop! Stop! Stop! My head was giving orders, but my hands were not obeying. *Buzz, buzz, buzz.* The operation continued. I was obsessed. I was like a madman with a fiendish, gruesome task. There it was, another collapse. But the emulsifier kept grinding away at the cataract, which was slowly yielding. Slowly being dissolved and absorbed. My left foot activated the emulsifier, my right foot the movie camera that was filming the operation through the microscope. Later I would have the opportunity to view this film, for hours on end, trying to see where I had gone wrong.

I continued until all of the cataract visible through the pupil had been removed, but there was still a large mass of it behind the pupil. In the cat, the pupil had remained widely dilated, so that I could see the cataract until it had all been emulsified. Here I had only removed the center of it. I had only made a hole in the doughnut. I looked up at the clock. I could hardly believe the time. I had been working for two and one half hours.

I placed the tip behind the iris where I could *not* see it, and activated it. A small piece was removed, and then another. And another. We were three hours into the operation. The anesthesiologist was getting concerned. Cataract operations generally take, at most, one hour. I felt his concern. Four or five hours of anesthesia gives an elderly patient quite a hangover. He was anxious to finish the case. So was I. Too anxious. I pushed a little too hard with the tip, and I ruptured the back layer of the cataract. This meant that part of the cataract could fall deep into the eye, and set up an inflammation.

There was no longer an intact barrier between the anterior chamber and the posterior chamber. My breathing became shallow, the sweat poured from every part of my body. I felt hopelessly committed to a road I no longer had any desire to be on. I kept going, sucking out cataract and vitreous—the jelly that fills the posterior part of the eye—until I felt I had gotten all that I could. And that was it. It was finished. So was I.

I took the emulsifier from the eye and put in one stitch. I looked at the eye. It was horrible. The cornea had deep white lines etched onto it. The iris had been touched several times by the emulsifier and was ragged and chewed away. I injected some cortisone around the eye and patched it.

When I got up from the chair, I again looked at the clock. Four and a half hours, seventy-nine minutes of which were emulsification time. I had been sitting in one position for so long I had cut off the circulation to my legs. I swayed as I stood, holding onto the table. My clothes and the operating gown were drenched. The anesthesiologist looked at me as if I were insane. I dragged myself to an adjacent, unused operating room where I stretched out on the table, telling myself that everything was going to be all right. . . . Everything was going to be all right. . . .

I sat in the visitor's chair in John Martin's room all that day, and all that night. He slept during the whole time, from his anesthesia. I examined his eye every hour.

I woke up, sitting in the visitor's chair, at 6:00 A.M., when the nurse came to take his temperature. I took one last look at the eye before I left. It had not changed since late evening. It was a bag of pus—ugly yellow, green, and white pus. I took out John Martin's eye in the afternoon, as an emergency procedure. The movie of my life which had played in my head as I waited for the case to start, now seemed to be rushing toward a lousy ending.

13

Pushing On

The vertical blinds allowed thin slits of sunlight to burst through the cracks between the slats; I stared at the diagonal lines which had slowly crept along the far wall of the den. I had followed the progress of the lighted comb across the wall since sunrise. Stretched out on the couch, fully clothed, I had lain there all night trying to figure out what had gone wrong in surgery, and what had gone wrong with my life.

When I had returned home after removing John Martin's eye the day before, I'd wanted to talk about what had happened. I hadn't needed to be told that I had lost my first eye in surgery. I hadn't needed to be reminded that I had wasted years of my life on an operation that didn't work. I hadn't needed to be threatened that there could be very serious consequences for me. I hadn't needed any of that, but that's exactly what I'd got. I had ended up slamming the bedroom door. With a tightness in my chest and with tears for John Martin and for myself, I had gone to the den to try to sleep.

I couldn't! I had to watch the film of the operation which had come back from the developer that afternoon. Alone in the den I'd watched. After the first few collapses of the cornea, I couldn't bear to relive the agony of those hours. I had to shut off the projector—but by the time I'd shut it off, I knew what the problem was.

In the animal eye, except for Chow, the lenses had not

really been cataracts; they had not been that hard, so that the suction had never built up to any great extent. Also, the animal eye was larger and there was more fluid, so that Chow's eye never collapsed. John Martin's eye had had a real cataract. While the instrument was chiseling away at this rock-hard lens, the suction had been building up in the line. When the needle finally perforated through, the suction was enough not only to suck in pieces of the cataract, but to suck out all of the fluid in the front part of the eye, causing it to collapse.

I knew then that I had only developed half an operation. I had found a way to dissolve and break up the cataract. Now I needed a way to suck it out with a gentle, controlled suction, which would prevent these collapses of the cornea. My heart ached because of John Martin's eye and because of my own personal situation. Worst of all, I did not see any way of solving that suction problem.

It seemed that I had foolishly undertaken a project that was beyond me. I had ignored the advice of wiser heads who had told me *this* one wouldn't work. I had gambled and I had lost.

When I went up to see John Martin in his room, he was surprisingly cheerful. More so than I. I looked at the empty socket where his eye had been and assured him that everything was fine. There was no infection. There was no bleeding. There was no swelling. There was no eye.

He had recovered sufficiently from the anesthesia and was ready to be discharged. I didn't have to tell him that the experimental operation didn't work, he knew. When I was leaving his room, he came over to me, shook my hand, and told me not to be discouraged, not to quit. I think if he had put his arm around me and hugged me, I would have cried.

I wanted to get away for a few days, play some golf and relax. Joan really didn't want to go, so I ended up alone in a motel in Florida, watching the rain pour down outside my window. I knew a few people in Florida whom I could have called, but I preferred to remain by myself, going over my failure again and again.

The first day, as I walked in the rain, feeling as if the drops were washing away my tension, I thought, there is *no* way to control that damn suction. On the second day, the rain had stopped, but the sky was a sullen gray. I sat on the dunes and thought, *maybe,* just maybe there is a way.

When I woke on the third day, it was the kind of day that people came to Florida in the winter to experience. There was a bright sun in the sky, and a peculiar softness in the air, a vague scent of grass and flowers and life that I have only experienced in Florida. On that day, as I jogged along the beach, I knew there *was* a way, and I knew I was going to find it. I was not going to quit now, not after all I had been through.

I went to Bob Navin at Cavitron on my return to New York.

"We need a flow control, Bob. Something that will shut off the suction before the eye collapses."

"Banko quit," Navin said. He looked at me squarely. "He quit when he learned you took out your first patient's eye." His tone was accusing.

I was stunned. I knew that Banko had taken the failure personally.

Navin stood up to indicate that the meeting was over. "Besides, we are an ultrasonic company; we do not make suction-control devices. You'll have to solve your problem somewhere else," he concluded, showing me the door.

The problem was very much like trying to vacuum a marble with a long-handled vacuum cleaner. But what I had to do was shut off the vacuum when the marble was halfway up the handle. There had to be something to sense the rush of a tiny drop of fluid in a tiny tube and shut the pump off just as the fluid started to move. I discussed the problem with anyone and everyone I could think of. Engineers, physicists, and washroom attendants. For three months I immersed myself in engineering journals and haunted the stacks at the library looking for some solution. I had a year and a half left on the second grant, and I knew that if I couldn't perform a successful human case, it was all over. There were times when I almost wanted to return the unused money and go back to playing the saxophone with a road band—almost!

And then I found it in an advertisement in a scientific journal: Carolina Medical Electronics. They described a flow meter that they had developed for measuring the rate of flow in small arteries in the body. If I could measure the rate of flow in the suction line, and when that rate of flow exceeded a critical amount, automatically shut off the pump and open the line to kill the suction, I would have it.

I was on the plane that same day to North Carolina. After going through the laboratories with the engineers, I was convinced it could be done. It would mean developing equipment, testing it, and adding it to Cavitron's machine, but I knew it could be done.

Six months and dozens of trips to North Carolina later, I was testing it in my laboratory. I had a tiny balloon, the size of a small lollipop, attached to the suction needle. The balloon was filled with fluid. When I pinched off the suction line, the pump kept pumping, building up suction. This was the same thing that happened when the tip got buried in John Martin's cataract. When I released the suction line suddenly, the needle shot up to a high value, but as the needle moved you could hear a click. A beautiful, wonderful click, which sensed the surge in the suction line. Through a computerlike process, it stopped the pump and killed the suction. *The little bag did not collapse.* That was the ultimate test. I kissed that little bag, I must have kissed it fifty times after fifty tries when it didn't collapse.

Cavitron's enthusiasm was rekindled, and a new man was brought in to head the project. He would put the suction control unit on the phacoemulsifier, and we would be ready for another patient. The thought of it made me weak from anxiety. I tested the machine over and over trying to make that little bag collapse, almost hoping that it would, so I wouldn't have to do another patient. It never collapsed; it worked every time.

I began looking for my next patient.

14

Anna

After John Martin's operation, I made myself scarce around the operating room. When Chuck Titone, a friend from my internship days, asked me to join him on a charter ski trip to Europe, I agreed.

A few days later, I was thousands of miles away from everything that was familiar, surrounded only by snow-covered mountains and blue-black sky: a sky, at twelve thousand feet above the sea, so devoid of air, with so few atoms to reflect the light, that it appeared almost black. At that altitude, the snow, reflecting the brilliant mountain sun, can temporarily blind a person in just a few moments—if one looks directly into the reflection. Snow blindness! The eye receives so much excess stimulation that the nerves are paralyzed and can no longer transmit images to the brain.

The town of Davos is nestled at the foot of the mountains in the Swiss Alps. Chuck and I were on top of the mountain, looking down at the town in the valley below, our dark ski goggles in place, ready for the descent. My trials and tribulations in New York were fading from my mind in the brisk, biting, beautiful rarefied air. It was heaven.

"This way, Chuck," I said. "Let's take this shortcut and go over to Wolfgang for lunch."

"Hey, there's no trail over there. You're crossing over the front of the mountain," he said skeptically.

"Look at the map," I argued. "It looks flat and easy. C'mon." I pushed off across the virgin snow, directly into the face of the blazing sun. Chuck followed.

Your ability to ski depends on the feel of the snow beneath your feet, as well as your vision of the contour of the snow. In a few moments, I lost both. Skiing in untracked deep powder is like walking on air; there is no sensation at all from the skis, just smoothness. Not used to skiing in this type of snow, I soon fell, and then in horror, watched as my ski goggles flippity-flopped down the mountain, disappearing into the snow. I called out for Chuck, but he was gone. I was alone. And then in a moment I was blind, totally blind: snow blind. I got back on my feet, but with a flash of terror I realized I was moving. Fast! There was practically no sensation, except for the wind against my face. I tried to squint, to see where I was going, but the ultraviolet light had burned my eyes. I didn't know whether the tears were from pain or from fear—or both.

I tried to stop by making a wedge with my skis, a snowplow, when suddenly I felt myself flying in midair. Oh, God! I was tumbling head over heels, my skis flying off my feet, my arms flailing wildly. I was falling off the mountain to my death.

And then, I don't know how—God?—there was a branch of a small pine tree, and it was in my hand. I felt the yank on my body as I suddenly jerked to a stop. And there I hung—over a precipice. I was hanging off a sheer drop on the side of the mountain, and between my feet, as I looked down away from the sun, I could see the church steeple of Davos, some eight thousand feet below. Then my vision went again, as I swung gently in the wind, suspended by one arm holding onto my pine tree. God's pine tree!

Instinctively, I dug my boots into the side of the mountain; they penetrated into the soft powder, giving me a footing. This took some weight off my aching arm. I reached up and brought my other arm up, now holding the tree with both. I closed my eyes for a moment to let them recover. I coaxed the terror from my mind. I tried to assess my situation—it was not good—and when I forced my eyes open, I saw that I was on a sheer cliff, about twenty yards away from a flat, safe plateau. If I could get over there, I would be all right until the ski patrol came to get me. Surely Chuck would start looking for me soon. But I couldn't stay where I was much longer. My arms were getting tired and my body was getting stiff from the lack of motion and the cold. I had to move.

Anger. That was my only emotion. Anger at myself. I was furious that on a stupid whim, I had violated one of the most important rules of mountain skiing: Stay on the trails. And now I was going to die for that careless, irresponsible mistake. "Good-bye, Joan. Good-bye, David, Lesley, and Jennifer," I said, anger ripping at my throat.

I had to do something. Staying where I was was certain death. I pulled my left foot out of the deep crevice I had made and moved it twelve inches farther to the left, digging the toe into the snow. And then the right foot. And then I let go of the branch with my left arm and dug that into the snow, up to my armpit. My right arm was still holding the branch. "Let go," I commanded myself. But I couldn't. I prayed for a moment, apologizing to God for only calling on Him when I was in trouble. I tried to assure Him that I had always believed. I hoped He was convinced. Then I let go of the branch, expecting to fall off the cliff and impale myself on the church steeple. Somehow, I held my position.

I dug my right arm into the snow now, also up to my armpit. I was now like a fly on flypaper, with all four limbs dug into the side of the mountain. Now the left leg, left arm, right leg, right arm, inching over to the left. Only nineteen yards to go. I tried not to think, just developing a rhythm. Left arm, left leg, right arm . . . I don't know how long it took. Maybe a half hour or more. I was almost there. Only a few yards to go. But then when I dug my left foot in, I knew something was different. There was no support, no solidity. When my left arm went in, I knew. There was only a three-inch layer of snow, under which there was air. I was now on a sheet of snow suspended over a hollow in the face of the cliff. I looked into the hole my arm had made and saw inside the tent of snow, the gray rock, four feet away. I moved faster now, only a few more moves and I would be there.

"I made it!" I screamed. "Thank you, God."

I was lying on my back, sobbing hysterically, when Chuck reappeared. He stayed with me for a few moments, and then went off to get the ski patrol. They came with skis and goggles, and led me back to the trail.

The next day, I forced myself to ski again. This time I stayed on the trail.

When I came home, my schedule at the hospital resumed, but I was amazed that there was no aftermath following the removal of John Martin's eye. True, it had been a glaucomatous, painful eye, requiring removal in any case, but I had expected some kind of inquiry into the operation I had performed prior to the removal. There had been none. I soon learned why; the anesthesiologist on the case had moved out of state, the scrub nurse had transferred to another hospital, and the circulating nurse had taken a maternity leave of absence.

Back in the operating room—doing routine cases—I was surprised by the attitudes of two of my most vociferous detractors; they had become downright friendly. Previously they had snubbed me academically; now they invited me to lecture at the university. Previously they had snubbed me socially; now they invited me to their homes for dinner. Previously they had snubbed me professionally; now they began to appear unexpectedly in the operating room, ostensibly to say hello, to discuss a case, or to offer pearls of wisdom. I cautiously rejoiced at this acceptance, but avoided giving them answers to their oblique questions about the nature of my research. Indeed, their presence in the operating room made me nervous—nervous about the next operation with my phacoemulsifier. I had found the perfect patient and had scheduled her for surgery.

Anna Swetze was a woman in her early seventies. She had been a patient for more than five years, and I had watched helplessly while the ravages of diabetes had blinded her. After twenty years, or more, of diabetes, there are often severe changes in the blood vessels in the eye which lead to hemorrhages; these hemorrhages destroy the nerves of vision. Anna was one of these patients. She was fortunate because she had maintained fairly good vision until the age of seventy, at which time a large hemorrhage had eliminated the vision in her right eye. There was nothing I could do to help her, nor was there anything to prevent this dreaded complication of diabetes. She still had a modest amount of vision in one eye. In the blind eye, she had a cataract. That was the eye I wanted to operate on. But this was different from John Martin's case; this was not a painful eye. It did not *have* to be removed. Moreover, with diabetes, Anna suffered more of a chance of infection than the average person; there was more of a risk.

I explained everything in great detail to Anna; I described my research, I described the operation, I described the problems and the failures. Finally, I told her about John Martin. When I finished my story, I stopped and looked at her. Anna's face was wrinkled like a prune, and there were deep expression lines etched between those wrinkles. Anna had laughed and cried a lot in her life, it was all written there, easy to see. Now her face was puckered in deep thought. But her eyes were smiling. "So you want my eye, you want to try your operation on my eye, is that it?"

"Anna, I think it will work now. I think I've solved the problems."

"It won't make me see? You can't give me my sight back, can you?"

"No, Anna, it will not make you see. I'm not doing this operation for you. I'm doing it only for me."

"Not for you," she said. "You would be doing it for all of the others. All of those who will see later on."

"There is a chance you could lose your eye, Anna."

She sat back in her chair and closed her eyes. Her lips trembled. "I'm an old lady," she finally said. "I don't have anyone now, and I still wouldn't have anyone if I lost an eye. It's okay. . . . I'll take your operation, doctor."

With my two new "friends" spying on me, I had to do the surgery on a day when neither of them was in the hospital. One of them traveled a great deal, lecturing all over the country; he was away for weeks at a time. With the other I had to be more careful. I had to schedule the operation on a day when I knew he would be busy—very busy—in his office. On Tuesdays he was swamped with patients. Tuesday—that would be the day.

As the day approached for Anna's operation, I experienced the same anxiety that I'd had with John Martin. I had the same problems with the malfunctioning machine. And I even had the same fight with Joan. But one thing was different: These were no longer uncharted waters for me. I had navigated them before. True, I had shipwrecked, but at least I had learned where some of the rocks were.

Tuesday. When I arrived in the operating room, Banko's replacement, a tough, aggressive engineer from Brooklyn, was there, having worked on the machine all night. My knees became weak when they wheeled Anna into the room, weaker when she smiled at me, and weaker still when she beckoned me to come to her side. The anesthesiologist—thank God, a new man on the staff who would not even understand what I was doing—was about to put Anna to sleep. I went to her and she reached out to me.

"Doctor darling . . . let me kiss your hands." Then she let the anesthesiologist put her to sleep. I fought back emotion—any emotion that could destroy my composure for her sake, for my sake, for everybody's sake. I went in to scrub and returned to the operating room. I was ready. Anna was asleep. The machine was there, waiting. . . .

The operation took three hours. There were no collapses, but the pupil constricted again, as it had in John Martin's case, making visualization of the cataract difficult. I was sweating profusely, feeling nauseous, and I wanted to stop. But I kept going.

At last it was finished; Anna's eye looked almost as bad as John Martin's. Although there had been no collapses, I had been emulsifying for more than one hour. Her diabetes-ridden cornea had not tolerated the procedure well. I had touched the iris several times with the emulsifier, leaving ugly areas of scar tissue. I left the operating room in a daze. I swore to myself that if I had to remove Anna's eye, it would be the end. I would give up. I would have no choice.

I sat with Anna all that day and sat with her all that night, just as I had with John Martin. When morning came, I was tired, my skin was gray, my eyes were bloodshot, but I had reason for a glimmer of hope: Anna's eye had not become infected. It had not been burned. It did not look any worse than it had immediately after the operation. Anna's eye had survived the first twenty-four hours. In the animals, any eye that survived the first twenty-four hours had finally recovered.

I left Anna with a dozen roses, and went home, finally able to sleep. I examined her eye every day. After only two weeks I knew her eye would heal perfectly. Her sick, diabetic eye had tolerated the operation. It was a success.

And I had movies of the operation and could show them to the Hartford Foundation; my grant would be renewed! During the next six months, I operated on four other patients with blind eyes—eyes that would have no chance of seeing after the cataract operation—on which I could improve my technique. All of the eyes tolerated the procedure. The last one only took two hours. It looked like I was on my way.

15

On Trial

Without great warmth or wars (except for the usual skirmishes) life with Joan continued. The children—David and Lesley just out of diapers, Jennifer still in—demanded all of Joan's attention, as well as her affection. I loved rollicking and rolling on the floor with my children until they, exhausted, were sent to bed, and I, filled with their love, returned to my work in the laboratory. In the evening after dinner, Joan liked her reading time, her quiet time, which I guess she needed after a day with three infants. I do know that I could never have succeeded in her job. In spite of the au pair helpers, the mother's helpers, and the day workers, it all had to be a tremendous responsibility for her—she was a perfectionist—and I suppose that she, at age twenty-six, was as overwhelmed with her responsibilities as was I, then thirty-seven.

With referrals now coming in from other eye surgeons—they were starting to send me their complicated cases—my practice and my staff were increasing. I was lucky to have found Cheryl. One of Joan's great abilities was picking people. She picked Cheryl, who was working as a baby-sitter. Joan was impressed with Cheryl's intelligence and diligence and suggested I give her a job in the office; I did. Receptionist, secretary, office manager, and finally registered ophthalmic technician, Cheryl progressed from one to the other with speed and grace and assisted me in surgery.

With Cheryl so occupied, I needed someone else in the office, and after interviewing many, chose Marcia to take on some of Cheryl's duties, including typing up my confidential operative reports on the phacoemulsification patients.

Marcia, who had a warm, southern drawl; Marcia who had a wonderful sense of humor; Marcia who would soon nearly be responsible for my downfall. . . .

One evening, with Cheryl and Marcia gone for the day, the phone rang; it was a patient requesting a receipt. I remembered examining him that day, but when I looked at Marcia's daily sheet, his name was not there. He said that he had paid in cash. It could mean only one thing: Marcia had pocketed the sixty dollars and had made the records correspond to the theft by omitting his name. There was no way of knowing how much she had taken prior to that day. The next day I confronted her. She admitted the theft, pleading dire financial straits because of an ailing mother. But I had no choice, I had to let her go. I told her to leave as soon as Cheryl came back from the lab; I left her alone in the office.

My remaining staff consisted of Otto, my German engineer, and Joe, my office administrator.

Joe Lizerbram and I had become friends during my Philadelphia days as Kerry Adams; he'd had a record company and was distributing my song, "Telephone Numbers." He was about ten years older than I, looked half his age, and after a few minutes with him he'd have his arm around you. When you needed to talk, Joe, with his earnest look of sincerity, concern, and interest, had you babbling the darkest secrets of your life within moments. During my affair with Ellen, Joe's eyes had glistened with admiration and concern—admiration for the adventure, concern that it might hurt. His wife, Esther, was a perfect complement to him. Attractive, happy, and warm, she was also a wonderful friend. When I had a story to tell, or a song to sing, Joe and Esther listened.

Shortly after my residency, Joe's business was destroyed in the famous Philadelphia riots, and although I had never thought of hiring an administrator, I hired him. He soon became my right arm, befriending those I had no time to befriend, entertaining those I couldn't, and speaking to patients and their families as a fatherly advisor. And best of all, Joe also had music in his blood. While I had let that interest wither—how far I had strayed from the musician-singer-songwriter I had been—he now encouraged me to pursue it. We had come full circle, Joe and I. Earlier, in Philadelphia, when I was engrossed with being Kerry Adams, Joe was sitting on my couch, and felt a piece of paper under his feet. He bent down and picked it up; it was my medical diploma, which had been languishing in the dust under the couch. A few days later he brought it back, appropriately framed. His forehead was wrinkled with despair. "Don't ever lose your interest in medicine," he admonished me then.

Now, ten years later, he was telling me not to forget about music, and I started to play the saxophone on Friday afternoons with a group called "Jazz at Noon." Doctors, lawyers, janitors, men from all walks of life would play old songs at a restaurant, where the patrons paid to lunch and listen. It was good getting the saxophone back in my mouth, it was good hearing the crowd applaud, and it was good releasing the pressures of surgery and of my home life.

One Friday, as I was returning from a lunchtime musical break, Abe Levin was led into my office. Abe was in his early seventies, a bright, philosophical, and personable man who, until he had lost his vision from macular degeneration and cataracts, had been a tailor. Macular degeneration is best explained as a crumbling of the retina usually associated with old age, a disease that burns away the critical area for vision, the area used for reading. His left eye had had a cataract removed years before, but now the ravages of the degenerative process had eliminated almost all vision in it.

Abe's right eye had a cataract and was also practically blind, and it was reasonable to assume that the degenerative process had affected this eye too. It was a subcapsular cataract, different from the others I had worked on, with only a thin layer of clouded cells on the back of the lens, the rest of the lens remaining clear. This meant that Abe's cataract was soft and would be easier to emulsify than any of the others.

It was a near-blind eye, and I discussed my operation with him. He was a well-read man, highly intelligent, and looked more like a senator than a tailor. He agreed to the surgery, and I scheduled him; the operation went well. Since the lens was soft (the ultrasonic time was below thirty minutes), the cornea looked perfect at the end of the operation.

It was the first time I didn't sit with the patient all day and night; I didn't have to. I knew that although Abe Levin wouldn't see, the operation worked. Soon I would schedule a patient who had the potential for vision. Then I would *really* prove the value of the operation. I had deliberately postponed doing a useful eye until I was absolutely sure of the outcome. After Abe Levin, I was ready. Things were going well for me at last. At last! Maybe Joan and I could get our lives together, now that the pressure was off; maybe we would celebrate that evening. . . .

I left the hospital and returned to my office to find Joe anxiously waiting for me. Anguish, like a silk-stocking mask, deformed his face. It had been two weeks since I'd fired Marcia.

"Charley, Tom Wurtz telephoned," Joe said, as if announcing a funeral. "We got a problem, buddy; we got a real problem." Joe shook his head up and down, as if to impress me with the gravity of the situation.

Wurtz was head of anesthesia at Mid-Cities and chairman of the medical board. He had always been friendly to me since we shared a common love, flying. He and his son owned an airplane, and I had always been interested in piloting and even took some lessons. I called him on the telephone.

"Dr. Kelman"—he was now formal—"someone has informed the hospital directors that you are doing experimental surgery and that you have blinded four people." I was stunned. "The board is going to hold an inquiry. If the charges are true, if this experimental surgery has caused patients to lose their vision, you must be dropped from the staff of the hospital." He said all of this as if hoping the accusations were false but believing that they were true.

The hearing was to be in two days; I could, if I wished,

bring a lawyer, he told me. My worst fears, my most horrible nightmares, were coming true. I desperately hoped, however, that when I proved these patients were already near blind before the surgery without any hope of recovering vision, when I would show the directors the signed consent forms acknowledging that the patients understood all of this, then the charges would be dropped. No one, after all, had the right to dictate to me what type of operation I could do—as long as I was getting good results.

I rushed to my files for the records of those four patients. The first one I sought was missing—probably misfiled, I thought. The second file I sought was missing; the third and the fourth were not there either. My records were gone. Oh my God! Marcia! I had left her alone in the office after I'd fired her. The pieces suddenly fell into place.

Lying on my back in the lonely den that night, watching the reflections of passing headlights bounce off the ceiling, I had a lot to think about. Abe Levin's operation that day had been a triumph: When I had examined him before I came home, his eye looked really good, better, in fact, than any cataract operation I had ever done by the usual method. His cornea had no swelling, his eye had no redness, and there was no sign of infection. Looking at him from two feet away, it was impossible to tell that Abe had had surgery. Had I not had to worry about the inquest, I would have been drinking champagne.

The phone rang in the middle of the night. I was still dressed, asleep on the couch in the den. I looked at my watch. It was four o'clock in the morning.

"Don't ask who this is," a muffled voice rasped. "Just let me say, it's a friend." I thought I recognized the voice of Tom Wurtz, but I couldn't be sure. The man with the disguised voice spoke for thirty seconds, and then stopped. The phone went dead.

Sirotka and Driscoll, the voice had told me, were the ones who had demanded the inquiry; they were the ones who were going to "put Kelman out of business"; they were the ones who knew—how did they know?—that I had no records on these patients. There was one bit of good news: They were not going to claim that I was doing experimental surgery—only that none of the four patients who had had my operation could see. This intrigued me as much as how they knew I had lost my records. Yes, surely Marcia had gone to them with those records she had taken. But why were they not prepared to open the Pandora's box of experimental surgery? Probably because they too were performing certain procedures not on the list of standard operations.

So all I had to do was prove that these patients were blind or near blind before the surgery, that my surgery neither helped nor worsened their condition, and that they were well informed of all of the facts. But without my records it would be impossible. Could I bring in the four of them to testify for me? Not likely. It would be embarrassing. It might lead to the initiation of a lawsuit (if the patients were given the impression that I had done something wrong), and my opponents might even try to convince the patients to sue. No, there was no way I could bring them in to help me.

The next day, in the lab, in the clinic, in the halls, I heard the whispering: some if it intended for my ears. Sirotka had been collaring every surgeon in his path, jubilantly gossiping about my predicament. Word spread that I was finished. Perhaps in his own mind he was acting in the interest of the hospital, perhaps he truly believed that I had committed some heinous crime. Perhaps all of his motives were pure—but I doubted it. More likely, he simply considered me a threat. Because of the success of the freezing operation, my surgical practice had grown. My little office, directly opposite the hospital, often had a line of waiting patients at nine o'clock in the morning. My detractors, on their way into the hospital, could not fail to take notice of this popularity.

As I began to perform more patient surgery—as well as hundreds of hours of animal surgery—I became highly skilled: more skilled, according to the residents, than Sirotka. I was the one to whom the resident doctors sent their relatives. I was the one called in by other doctors for their problem patients. I was the one who was the biggest threat to Sirotka's reputation as number one.

My other nemesis, Driscoll, was still smoldering because of my success with the freezing operation, an operation he had publicly belittled and ridiculed as a gimmick for so many years. The other doctors on the staff would also shed no tears if I was chastised and removed. My success had not endeared me to them either. Of all the professionals, I think doctors are the most jealous; they feel the most threatened when a colleague in the same specialty does well. Legendary is the competition and hatred between giants: Salk-Sabin, Cooley-De Bakey, Pasteur-Lister. I was aware of this frailty of human nature, I was aware of it in ophthalmologists, and, I was aware of it in myself—but that made it no easier to bear the resentment of my colleagues.

They now had a perfect hammer with which they could smash me. I stood practically alone. Yet I did have a feeling that Tom Wurtz would be fair, as well as Robert Snyder, who was head of the eye department. Snyder and I had always gotten on well, and since his specialty was retina, not cataracts, I thought I could depend on him to be just. That left eight members on the board, including Sirotka and Driscoll.

Timing is so important in life. One month more and I could have had one or even two patients who would have been able to see. With that, the board of surgeons would have had nothing of which to accuse me.

Joe had been calling the other doctors who would attend the meeting, trying to drum up some support for me. There was none to be found. I was a condemned prisoner before his execution. I tossed and turned in my bed that night, trying to decide if I should bring a lawyer.

On the appointed day, at the appointed time, I appeared at the meeting, accompanied by a distinguished pinstripe-suited, elderly gentleman, carrying an attaché case. He sat next to me on one side of a long table—the other doctors were already seated on the other side. The air was charged with an excitement reminiscent of a bullfight I had seen in Spain. Only, I was the bull! I braced myself for the picadors. My heart raced, my throat was dry; I didn't know if I had any chance at all, but I was going to gamble everything on the success of a plan I had formulated the day before.

Sirotka, the matador, described in detail the operations I had performed; it was now clear to me from where he had gotten his information—from my missing private diary! He knew about the collapses, he knew about the pupils becoming smaller during surgery, he knew about the corneas being cloudy for some time after the operations. A few of the other doctors asked questions. They were asked accusingly. Wurtz and Snyder made halfhearted attempts to stem the tide of emotion running strongly against me, but desisted when they saw that it was to no avail.

They concentrated heavily on the "evidence" that none of the patients could see after surgery. And what was that evidence? Telephone calls had been made to the patients asking them to describe their vision. "Practically none," they had answered.

Wasn't it possible, Sirotka asked, that the operation damaged the optic nerve? That the eye was blinded by ultrasonic waves? Wasn't it possible that all of the animals I had operated on were left blind? What proof did I have that these animals could see? Of course I had none. One cannot get a cat to read a chart. But I knew they could see, I had seen the animals patter around the room perfectly well after both eyes had been operated on.

Then it was my turn to speak. I described in detail the animal work, and the conditions of the patients' eyes prior to the surgery; conditions which would make them sightless even with a successful cataract operation. No, I did not have the records on these patients, they had disappeared. I saw them shake their heads in disbelief, in scorn. I spoke for ten minutes, but I knew, by looking at their solemn faces, that they had made up their minds. I was running out of time. I signaled my companion in the pinstriped suit and he opened his attaché case. Ceremoniously, he reached into his pocket, put on his glasses, took out a typewritten paper, and began reading slowly, picking up his pace as he went along.

"Gentlemen, it is the surgeon's right and duty to perform what he considers to be the best procedure for his patient. That Dr. Kelman chose *not* to inform you of the type of operation he was doing is his right. He did what he and his patients thought best." He paused, while he poured himself a glass of water from a pitcher, and then continued with a slight smile. "Let me now address myself to the success or failure of Dr. Kelman's technique." I looked at the others in the room: they seemed unimpressed. But they were listening.

"Dr. Kelman has stated that until now, all the operations have been on eyes that had no ability to see." He paused. "Two days ago, however, Dr. Kelman did, most definitely operate on a patient with useful vision: the first of many such patients who will benefit by his technique. I will now prove to you the success of the operation."

He carefully folded the paper, returned it to the attaché case, and closed it. The snap of the lock was a rifle shot in the quiet of the room. He took off his glasses, put them in his pocket, and looked for a second into the eyes of each man after the other, sitting opposite him. They looked at him, waiting for his "proof."

He opened the attaché case again—another rifle shot—and took out a black patch, which he slipped in front of his left eye. "A, E, X, D, R." He was reading the eye chart on the wall. They were perplexed.

"The operation Dr. Kelman performed two days ago was on a certain Abe Levin," he continued, now smiling broadly at them. "I am Abe Levin . . . and . . . I can see perfectly with that eye."

I saw them all lean across the table in disbelief. The man sitting opposite them did in no way look like a patient who had just had surgery on his eye. His eyes, from the time he walked into that room, had appeared normal—not red; they were white and widely open all of the time. There was no tearing, there was no glassy look to them; and at least one of them had vision, since he had just read the chart, and before that, the printed statement. Then, the surgeon directors on the board all examined his eyes and checked his sight.

* * *

Joe was waiting outside of that room. I had not even told him of my plan. Now I explained that macular degeneration, the condition that blinded Abe's first eye, is *usually* found in both eyes. Usually. Although there was no way to know at the time of his surgery, Abe Levin *did* have useful vision behind that cataract. When I had visited him the day after surgery, using glasses borrowed from the patient in the next bed, Abe Levin had been *reading* the newspaper. "Good boy," Joe said, a broad smile on his face.

Somehow the degenerative process had spared enough vision in the eye I had operated on to permit him a small island of sight, enough for Abe to read. Enough to take the wind from the sails of my detractors. Enough vision to allow me to continue to perform the operation. More than that, I had been spared the anguish of knowing I was operating on a sighted eye. God had given me a present. There was now no question in my mind, or in anybody else's in that room, that the operation had restored Abe Levin's vision. There was no way the other doctors could prevent me from continuing my work.

Abe Levin left the hospital that day in the pinstriped suit I had bought him at Bloomingdale's. He planned to go back to work at a tailor shop. I promised him all of my business.

16

The Smutters

Victory! I knew I had won a victory, albeit a temporary one. The board of surgeon directors had so emphasized my not having a *seeing* patient, that when I produced Abe I startled and confused them, and they became, at least for that moment, impotent. From that moment on, however, my operating-room door would be wide open; no more secret surgery for me. My results would be carefully scrutinized, my reports verified. But the timing *had* been right. I *was* ready. I had a long list of patients waiting for cataract surgery, many of whom agreed to the operation even knowing that it was still "under investigation." I wished I had more time to perfect the technique and the instrument before being obliged to operate in front of critical observers, but I was thankful to be able to continue at all. I chose the next few patients with great care, those with softer cataracts, which would be easier to emulsify. The operating time was down to an hour and one half with only fifteen minutes for emulsification.

I had one chronic problem that I could not understand: The pupils would not remain dilated during surgery. Since the inquest, in every case the pupil not only dilated poorly initially, but during surgery it also became smaller, making the operation infinitely more difficult. Before beginning one operation I asked the patient if he had gotten all of his drops, referring to his dilating drops, given an hour before surgery. His answer chilled my blood.

"I got all of the drops, doc, even the ones in the middle of the night. They burned the most."

Drops in the middle of the night? I hadn't ordered any drops in the middle of the night! "Are you *sure* you got eye drops in the middle of the night?" I asked.

"Yeah, doc. I asked the doctor what the drops were for but he didn't answer."

"Did you get a look at him?" I asked hopefully.

"No, he never turned the light on. He just stood behind me with a little flashlight. He seemed to be in a big hurry."

Had someone, in the middle of the night, been putting constricting drops in my patients' eyes? I was repulsed at the thought. I questioned other patients who had had surgery; some remembered getting drops during the night—always in the dark. If, in fact, somebody had been trying to sabotage my surgery, I was never to learn who it was. For the next month I insisted that a relative stay with the patient all during the night. From then on, the pupils dilated better.

I photographed and videotaped every operation. Each night I would watch my cases for hours, looking for ways to simplify the procedure. Otto was still working in the lab, Cheryl was at my side in surgery, and Joe was managing the office and the rest of my affairs. I raced from the laboratory, to my home, to the operating room, to my lectures—I was now being asked to lecture on phacoemulsification—in a frenzy of activity. I never had time to think about it, but I was happy. It never even dawned on me then that I was coming close to the realization of my dream: creating something that would enhance the lives of many others. I was just too busy.

During that six-month period I was relatively free from major problems. That state of affairs did not last very long, though; the next hurdle was just around the corner.

Sheldon Smutter was a plumber, a mild-mannered man in his fifties, anxious to return to work as soon as possible after his cataract surgery. He was a pleasant man; he was a reasonably good-looking human being. His wife was another story. To say she was obese would be an understatement—sloppy, would be charitable; vicious, would be kind. Her voice was as shrill as a parrot's, and she waved her finger in your face when she spoke. She tried to dissuade her husband from any type of surgery, even though he was legally blind in one eye and losing vision rapidly in the other. Whenever she came into my office the staff would run for cover.

I suppose I should have had better sense. I should not have scheduled him for a phacoemulsification, in case there was a surgical problem. But he was such a perfect candidate—his cataract was soft and he needed a rapid rehabilitation. I explained my operation to him, and over his wife's strident objections, he agreed to have it performed. When they left, Joe said, "I hope everything goes well on *his* operation."

Things did not go well. Halfway through Sheldon Smutter's operation, part of the cataract fell back into the deeper portion of the eye, the vitreous. (This had occurred also in John Martin's case.) I worked unsuccessfully for three hours trying to suck it back up toward the tip. At the end of the procedure, a small piece of cataract remained in Sheldon Smutter's eye. This piece would either be slowly absorbed or, if not, the eye might be lost. I was crushed. My antagonists at the hospital were just waiting for this type of catastrophe.

I was due to go to a meeting in Puerto Rico the following day. Prior to boarding the plane, I stopped by to see Smutter; his eye looked worse. I departed, leaving him in the hands of my friend, the doctor who had, eight years before, cosigned my grant application to the National Institutes of Health, Robert Coles. Coles called me the next day in Puerto Rico. "It doesn't look good, Charley. It may be a lost eye."

I knew there was nothing I could do that Coles couldn't, but I wondered, should I go back to New York? Any doubts were dispelled by the next call. It was Sally Smutter.

"You rotten son of a bitch. Get your ass back here." That's the way she started the conversation. After that, she became impolite and vulgar. She ended by saying, "If you're not back here tonight, I'll raise a fuss that will put you out of practice. Forever." She clicked off. I called the airline.

When I got to New York that night, Smutter's eye was worse. It was an angry, violent red, with yellow streaks across the cornea. I wanted to cry—for him, for me, for the operation. I could not afford a lost eye; especially this one, with Sally Smutter waiting to pounce on me like an overfed cat. This case, if a failure, would mean the end.

Bob Coles and I gave the patient every medication we could—cortisone; antibiotics; anti-inflammatory drugs, drops, and injections. A week later his eye looked still worse. The cornea was beginning to develop blisters—an ominous sign.

No matter how many times you are threatened by a firing squad, no matter how many times you survive, each time brings new terror. It seems I had been living and would be living forever in the shadow of catastrophe. I was in a cauldron. Every time I got close to success, it got hotter. And every time I thought it couldn't get any hotter, it always did. That night, the temperature in the cauldron went off the thermometer.

"I want to talk to you, you bastard." It was Sally Smutter on the phone again. "Get your ass over here or you'll be sorry," she screamed into my ear. "I've had enough of this whole thing and I've decided to do something about it."

Do something about it? What did that mean? A lawsuit? A formal complaint to the medical society? I didn't know. I stopped off at the hospital to see Smutter and then I drove to the address she had given me on Long Island.

When she opened the door she seemed surprisingly cordial, and was dressed better than I had ever seen her. "I want to talk about my husband," she said.

I sat and waited for her to go on.

"I want you to know that I hate that prick. He's mean, he's rotten, and I don't give a shit what happens to his eye. He's not my kind of guy at all."

I couldn't believe what I had just heard. And then, oh God, I knew what was coming.

"You're my kind of guy . . . Charley," she said with a little quiver in her lip. "You're the kind of guy I could really go for." She leaned toward me, a beefy arm beginning an encircling maneuver on my neck.

I would have done many things to save my operation: I would have borrowed money, given up my other interests in life, sold my soul—but not this! I jumped back as if stung by a hornet, mumbled something about devotion to my wife, and invented a chronic infection of my genitals. I ran out of the house moments later, tripping my way down the front stairs.

Thank God, the next day Sheldon Smutter's eye improved. A week later he was out of the hospital, his eye saved. So was the operation.

17

"*Overnight*" *Success*

Eleven years had gone by since I had left Geneva as a mixed-up kid, not knowing whether to treat the blind, sing a song, or blow a saxophone. I often thought nostalgically about those days, and the people I knew, especially about the blind pianist, Achille Scotti, with whom I had worked at the radio station. Then, as a student, I hadn't known enough about eyes to even inquire about his blindness; now I was often haunted by the thought that maybe, just maybe, I could help him to see. When I got an invitation to come to Geneva for an anniversary party, and to play the saxophone on a radio broadcast, I jumped at the chance. I also knew I might get the opportunity to examine my friend's eyes.

What a thrill to be back in the studio with my old cronies, playing the old songs, reliving the old stories—but there was a difference now. I was a doctor. I had another profession. I was given a certain respect that I never could have gotten as a musician. How right my father had been with his "first be a doctor" lecture. After the broadcast, a remake of my old show "Hotel Melodie," we had a reception; that's when I got my chance with Achille. He was by the punch bowl, pouring himself a drink. Achille did not like other people doing things for him. I once saw him fall in the street, and then practically beat people away with his cane when they tried to help him. Now he had a glass in his left hand, with two fingers inside of the glass so that he would know when it was full, as he ladled with his right hand. He didn't spill a drop.

I came up behind him and put my hand on his shoulder. He had an uncanny knack of knowing who was there just by the touch.

"Hi, Kelman," he said. "How do you like being back in Geneva?"

"I'd like to take a quick look at your eyes as long as I'm here," I said as offhandedly as I could.

"Go to hell," he said. "No one has examined my eyes since I was six years old, and no one is going to."

"C'mon, Achille, I'm a doctor and your friend. It's not for you, it's for me. You probably have some weirdo musician's condition that I might never get a chance to see again. Just let me run you over to the clinic for a quick look." I knew I had to make it seem that he was doing *me* the favor.

"There's nothing you can do for me—nothing you can do to help me—you know that?"

"I don't want to help *you.*" I laughed. "I want to help *me.* I need the experience. C'mon."

In the clinic, one look with the ophthalmoscope and I knew. Both optic nerves were pure white—there were no blood vessels on them. Achille was hopelessly blind.

"Pretty bad?" Achille asked, a catch in his voice.

"Well, you're a bum." I tried joking. "I've seen this condition before. You're not so unusual after all, old pal."

"That's it?" he asked.

"That's it," I said, maybe a little too sadly.

There was a little café across the street from the hospital and we went there for a sandwich. We were both deep in thought; conversation was hard to come by. It was Achille who broke the silence.

"Kelman, I want to tell you a funny story. Would you like to hear it?"

I didn't think it was going to be funny, but I said, "Yes, why not?"

Achille stopped eating, put his hands in his lap, and stared at me with his unseeing eyes as he spoke: "Once upon a time there was a little blind girl,'' he recited, ''who, in spite of her condition, was always smiling and happy. One day her mother said to her, 'Sweetie, would you like to see your mommy's face?' The little girl answered, 'Yes, Mommy. Oh yes I would.' 'And would you like to see your friends, and be able to run and play with them?' The little girl answered, 'Oh, yes, Mommy. Yes. Yes.' 'And would you like to see the sun turn red in the evening, and see the trees, and see your little doggie?' The answer was the same. 'Yes, Mommy. Oh yes I would.' Then the mother put her hand on the little girl's head and said, 'Well, just close your eyes, and I'm going to count to three. When you open them, you'll be able to see all of that. So close your eyes'—and the little girl did—'and I'll count. One . . . two . . . three. Open your eyes.' 'Mommy, mommy,' the little girl said, 'I don't see anything. I'm still blind.' 'April fool, April fool,' the mother laughed.''

Achille stood up, his chair scraping against the floor. ''Please take me home now,'' he said.

I left for New York that evening, depressed by the incident, but knowing that what I did had had to be done. I *had* to be certain that there was no chance for vision. I also knew that if I ever had another blind friend, I would want to do the same thing, in spite of the pain it caused. I never saw Achille again.

When I arrived back in New York it was on my desk. Finally, in the May issue of the *American Journal of Ophthalmology,* 1967, it appeared—complete with color photographs: my article on phacoemulsification. It described all of my animal surgery, as well as my first twelve human cases. (I had not included John Martin's case, largely because the instrument I was describing employed *controlled* suction; there had been no control in his case, the lack of which caused the cornea to collapse.)

There it was, ''The Kelman Procedure,'' *finally.* I wish I could say I was thrilled when I saw it. I wish I could say I was elated as I held it in my hands. I wish I could say I was proud of what I had accomplished; but I wasn't. At least not as much as I would have expected to be. So much had happened, so many battles had been fought, that the article was anticlimactic. The recognition had been so long in coming, I was almost too numb to appreciate it.

Perhaps only "instant success" carries complete naïve elation. Winning a lottery, having your first song recorded by Sinatra, having a beautiful woman fall in love with you on sight—maybe that brings elation. Perhaps elation is tied up somehow with the secret knowledge that the success is undeserved—that it is illicit or illegal. That kind of success that I had was hard fought; I felt I had earned it; I deserved it. It was an outcome of so much labor that it was impossible to get overly excited.

What was exciting was that after the article appeared, Cavitron started to get calls from doctors wanting to buy the equipment. That meant that the makeshift apparatus I had been using would be refined and perfected, making my surgery much easier. Cavitron now wanted to make a royalty deal with me. I couldn't foresee much of a market for this machine; the operation was difficult to perform, more difficult for other surgeons to learn, and the machine would cost about fifty thousand dollars. But Herb Roth, my attorney, advised me: "You never know how far this thing can go, Charley. I'm going to try to make as good a deal for you as I can."

"It's academic, Herb. They'll never sell enough machines to make any money. And besides, I don't think it's ethical for a doctor to accept royalties."

"How many do you think they can sell in the next five years?" Herb asked.

"Maybe ten machines, if they're lucky."

"I'm still going to make the best deal I can for you," Herb said. "And later, if there are any royalties, and if we get a decision that it is unethical to accept them, you can always donate the money to research." He negotiated with the president of Cavitron for three days. The agreement was twenty-seven pages long. I never thought anything would come of it.

"Ethical?" Mike shouted at me. Mike Temkin, my accountant and close friend, was advising me as to the royalty problem. "There is absolutely no law against accepting money for an invention, even if a doctor is the inventor." Mike blew his cigar smoke toward the ceiling. "Take my advice. You handle the inventions, I'll handle the other issues. In the meantime, just sign the contract."

The first week after the publication of the article, much to my surprise, twenty-eight surgeons called, requesting a course on the technique: Several of them were prominent men in the field. My technique was still quite primitive, the instrument was still unreliable, the procedure was still vulnerable to instant cut-off if a disaster case occurred, but I had to sail with the tide, as the saying goes, or perhaps be forever stranded, losing everything I had fought for. Since the article was now published, others would surely try to copy what I had done and improve on it. I had absolutely no choice. Ready or not, here they come, I thought. I scheduled the first course.

It was a bright, cold New York morning. I was out of bed before dawn. That day eight eye surgeons from different parts of the country would arrive at my lab. I knew their reasons for coming ranged from true interest in the procedure to hope of finding proof of my incompetence. I didn't care. I'd greet them all with enthusiasm. They might love or detest me but this operation was bigger than all of us and I wanted to share it with them.

Many patients previously inoperable until their cataract "ripened" would now be able to see again. Surgery on children's cataracts would be safer and more successful. Maybe, because of the tiny incision, cataract surgery could be routinely performed in a doctor's office, sparing the patient the expense and especially the anguish of going into a hospital. Feeling like one of King Arthur's knights, I pulled on my clothes and stepped out onto Sixty-fourth Street, filled with excitement.

The company of strangers on the street heightened my awareness. I was jostled by people in the crowd, insulted by a wino, and almost run down by a delivery boy on a bicycle, but I loved them all. They contributed to the reality of the moment. Some of them looked so preoccupied, so blank, so far away from the moment, as though they were living for some future world. Looking at them, I saw myself better. That is how I must have been for the past ten years: always living for the future. Perhaps that is the price you have to pay for accomplishment. But having realized that, I understood a basic truth: Reality is *now*. Not yesterday or tomorrow. I was at that moment in time savoring that moment in time, and I was intensely happy. Could that be what happiness was all about? Enjoying the present—taking time to smell the flowers? It was something to think about.

That night, they began to arrive, from all over the country. Some looked skeptical, some embarrassed, some pleased and excited. Tomorrow there would be a brief orientation, and then I would perform four operations while they observed on closed-circuit TV. A three-hour lecture explaining the procedure would follow. I went to bed that night wired with the tension of the moment. And the anticipation. I could hear the future knocking at my door. *Now.*

Five-thirty in the morning: I took the thermometer from under my tongue. I was burning with 102 degrees and it felt like I had a throat abcess. This had been building for a week. I was overworked and underfed—and the pressure had taken its toll. At 8:00 A.M., looking more like a patient than a doctor, I staggered into the operating room.

Joe was there waiting. When he saw me, he rushed to my side, as if to hold me up. "What the hell is the matter?" he gasped.

I assured him it was nothing. "I'm not contagious, Joe, and this course is just too important. I can't cancel it now."

The very person I least wanted to see at that particular moment came gliding down the hall, his massive frame blocking the light from the window like a solar eclipse. He stopped about one foot away from me and glared.

"Kelman, you're gonna make yourself and this hospital the laughingstock of medical science," Sirotka puffed directly into my face. "And now you're giving courses to surgeons who are ten times better than you?" He lifted a short stub of a finger to my nose. "I'll get you kicked out of here yet," he sneered, turning his heel and gliding away, the light from the window returning. I knew he was deliberately trying to rattle me before I did my cases. Whatever color I had, drained away; he had succeeded. Down the hall I saw the group of distinguished surgeons, my "students," waiting for me in the observer's room. I went in and introduced myself. They all appeared very grim—like a jury before an important trial. They were here to judge me, as well as the operation.

Weak and feverish, I scrubbed carefully, taping my mask tightly to my face so none of my germs would fall on the operating field. One infection now, and the operation would be forever ridiculed throughout the country. Two infections, and I might just as well get a job driving a taxi. Normally, with a fever, I might have cancelled the cases. To do so today, however, might send the doctors back home convinced that I had been misleading the medical community with my report. I taped the mask on even tighter, and then sprayed antiseptic on it, the fumes almost choking me. Then I went into the operating room and performed four absolutely perfect cases: There were no collapses, there were no machine failures, there were no complications of any sort. God had answered the prayer I had offered before beginning the surgery.

When I finished, I was exhausted; but I still had a three-hour lecture to give that day, so that on the following day the visitors could begin to learn how to handle the instrument.

I checked into a hospital room as a patient. Joe set up a microphone by my bedside and a loudspeaker down in the laboratory. From my bed, I gave my lecture, and when I finished, I slept for fourteen hours. The next day I was back on my feet.

When the doctors examined the patients with me, one day after surgery, all the corneas were crystal clear, all the eyes were wide open, and all of the eyes were white and without irritation. With two of the patients, it was almost impossible to tell which eye had been operated on.

All of this was in contrast with what was normal for cataract surgery at that time, where the eyes normally showed somewhat cloudy corneas, slitlike lid openings, and bloody-red irritated eyes. The eyes of most cataract patients operated on at that time had to be practically pried open for the surgeon to examine them, there was so much photophobia. Here there was none.

I examined the surgeons' faces as much as I examined the patients' eyes. There was a new look there, a look of astonishment. A look that said: Could this be true? I saw one surgeon secretly look at the hospital chart, checking to see that it was one of the patients done the day before. I was proud that day.

For the remainder of the week, the visiting surgeons worked on model plastic eyes and animal eyes. They learned how to set up the machine and break it down, and how to troubleshoot. Many of those who had come with an eyebrow raised in skepticism now were enthusiastically emulsifying lenses, and were, I could see, dreaming of doing the procedure in their own practice.

The procedure *was* intricate and difficult to perform, but the results were amazing. As they became more practiced with the technique, enthusiasm and confidence filled them. One of those attending, a Dr. Callahan, was particularly impressed. A refined southern gentleman with a long kindly face, he shook my hand vigorously before departing for his home.

"I must say, Dr. Kelman, that when I first saw you perform that intricate work, I doubted that I would be capable of it. But now I do believe that with practice I shall be able to accomplish this difficult surgery. My son is an intern and we intend to practice together. I would be pleased if he could learn this procedure directly from you when the time comes."

Neither of us knew at the time that in a few years, I would be removing *his* cataracts (Dr. Callahan senior) by phacoemulsification.

Soon, with handshakes and goodwill, all the doctors were on their way home. I sat alone, exhausted but exhilarated. I paused to savor the moment. Acceptance of phacoemulsification had begun; there were four orders for Kelman Phaco-Emulsifiers on Bob Navin's desk.

Just when things seemed to be inching forward, Navin asked me to come and see him. His face was ashen and his fingers tapped—uncontrollably, I thought—on his desk.

"Foxx has outfoxed us," he said, trying to lighten the darkness that had descended on him, but not succeeding.

"What do you mean?" I asked. Foxx, the engineer who had replaced Banko, was brilliant, if a somewhat abrasive fellow. And he'd built a machine that I had some confidence in. It worked well enough to start making a few production models. Banko had helped create the pieces, but Foxx had really put them together in a neat package. The entire console was about the size of a street hot-dog stand, and it was sturdy and reliable.

"Blackmail," Navin said flatly. "He wants to be made a vice-president with a long contract or he'll quit." He anticipated my "so what?" "All of the specs on the machine are in his notebook. *In code.* None of the suppliers are named. We would have to start from scratch building this thing."

"What are you gonna do?" I asked, knowing the answer.

"Fire the bastard and start from scratch," he said. It was then decided that the machine would be built in California.

Cavitron had just acquired a company there, and its president, Alan McMillen, would be given the job. Much to his and general manager Bill Freeman's credit, in a few months they had it—smaller, more effective, and ready for the market. Foxx tried to start his own company to make a competing phacoemulsifier but apparently couldn't get the financing. He disappeared from view, proving again that no one is indispensable.

Within two weeks, I had fifty surgeons on a waiting list for the next training session. As the list grew, I realized the need for some sort of screening mechanism to test the surgical skills of those I taught. As much as I longed for widespread use of phaco, it was a difficult procedure. A mishandled operation would be as bad for the procedure as it would be for the patient. To effectively screen the physicians, I developed the "dextrometer," a testing device that measured hand-eye coordination, depth perception, and performance under pressure.

I planned to present the instrument to every doctor at the opening of each session. If a doctor failed the test, I would refund his course fee and send him home. I could not allow phacoemulsification to be attempted by someone with less than the required skill.

I was in the midst of preparing for my second seminar, when my world as I knew it exploded. First, *Medical World News* published an article about phaco, then Frank Field did an in-depth segment on his NBC show, "Research Project." When *Newsweek* arrived for a feature story, I knew my life was changed forever. Phaco had become a message of the media and I, its flamboyant creator. It seemed that the press delighted in the fact that I played the saxophone.

In one week, my face was all over the press; phaco was not only accepted, but my Hartford grant was renewed, bringing the total of grant money I'd been awarded for research to more than $900,000! My practice was booming; the phones rang nonstop. Everyone wanted their cataract removed the new, modern way. I bought Joan a fur coat, took the kids on a camping trip, and pinched myself as I used to do when I lived in Switzerland. One of the biggest thrills was thinking that I had been able to do what so many people had said was impossible.

It was all more than I had ever dreamed of. Or was it? Wasn't this what I had envisioned for myself when I saw Cooper's picture in *Look:* an operation that would radically change the course of surgery for the better, personal acceptance by the profession, and appreciation by the public? It seemed like I had it all.

18

Can a Saxophone Player Find Happiness as an Eye Surgeon?

One of my most interesting cases began with a phone call at two o'clock in the morning. It was eight o'clock in Belgium where the call originated, but what did some Chasidic Jews over there know about time changes? I took the call when the operator said it was from the head rabbi of that sect, Jacob Mendelowitz. These highly orthodox people are the ones who wear the long black robes and long curled sideburns (*peyes*) and who have other, difficult-to-understand traditions. But the leader's name I knew: Jacob Mendelowitz was truly world renowned. The call actually was being placed by his doctor, who asked me if I would be willing to operate on this ninety-three-year-old, near-blind rabbi. After some discussion about his general condition, I said I would.

Good. Could I come to Belgium and operate there? I said it would be better if he came to New York, where an operating room at my hospital was fully equipped with the special instruments I needed, including a large and heavy machine to produce the ultrasonic vibrations. I also had a technician to operate the machine and an operating-room nurse, both of whom had been specially trained for the operation. To bring the equipment and people to Europe would cost a great deal more than to bring the rabbi to New York. The caller said he would talk to other people and call me back.

While waiting for the call, I did some research on the rabbi.

He was the leader of a close-knit, fiercely devoted group: On a previous trip to New York, so many of his American followers had turned out to greet him that they tied up Kennedy Airport. It was also said that some of the things that had occurred while he was here verged on the miraculous. I'll skip those stories because I want to tell you only about what I myself saw and heard.

Now, I'm not supposed to believe in miracles. I'm a doctor of medicine, and so my whole professional education and training have taught me to be skeptical of anything that cannot be proven by the most rigorous scientific evidence. And yet . . .

I'll just tell you what happened. Judge for yourself whether or not there was anything miraculous about it.

The call came. The old gentleman's followers wanted to spare him the discomfort of travel and separation from home. They would bear the extra cost of transporting the machine, nurse, and technician. I agreed to come. This all sounded like a delightful challenge.

I went to Antwerp where I met and examined my new patient. He looked the way I thought an Old Testament prophet should look, with a halo of white hair and a full snowy beard surrounding a beatific old man's face. There was what I can only call—the rabbi should forgive me—a look of saintliness about him.

"It's a pity you aren't operating on someone younger who can enjoy the result longer," he said through an interpreter. "But you will bring the gift of sight to an old man for a couple of years. That will be a great comfort to me."

He explained that he wanted to reach the age of ninety-five and then he wanted to die on Yom Kippur. That is the Day of Atonement when Jews are supposed to atone for all the sins committed in the preceding year. It is the holiest of all days in the Jewish religious calendar. I patted his hand and told him that I hoped he would live a good deal longer than that. He gave me a sweet smile.

Ironically, the only hospital in Belgium where I had already operated and where I had operating privileges was a first-class

Roman Catholic hospital. They agreed to give me an operating room. I called the rabbi's aide to ask if the holy man would mind being operated on in a hospital where, more than likely, there would be statues of Jesus behind his bed. Through the interpreter, the answer came back: "God is God."

The rabbi appeared there for his operation. The nuns were enchanted by him and went out of their way to make him feel welcome. The operation itself went smoothly and a couple of hours later I visited my patient in his hospital room. He was sitting up in bed beaming, surrounded by several of his followers. We were both pleased by the outcome of the surgery. In fact, he wanted to go home that very afternoon, and I said he could.

It seemed to me that the rabbi had some strange kind of tumor in his chest. His dressing gown bulged as though there was a brick under it. It wasn't a brick. It was a very thick wad of U.S. hundred-dollar bills that he pulled from his breast pocket.

"It's our custom to pay for medical services when they are rendered," the interpreter said. The rabbi counted out the bills in his lap, something more than twelve thousand dollars worth, as I remember. I thanked him, and the "tumor" was transferred from his chest to mine.

"You have done a good thing," he said, "and this money is blessed. It will bring good luck."

"I can use all the luck I can get," I joked, and asked that it be translated for the rabbi.

He didn't laugh. He said something in Hebrew in a voice that sounded like he was reciting one of the Ten Commandments. The translation came to me with the same tone. "I said that the money would bring good luck. I didn't say that it would bring *you* good luck." Knowing of the rabbi's ability to predict the future, I left him feeling a little sick to my stomach.

I didn't want to carry all that cash around, so I immediately started to get rid of it by paying my assistants and all the other expenses I could. I decided to take a skiing holiday in the

Swiss Alps before going home. I bought my ski equipment, went to Gstaad, and paid my hotel bill in advance.

That still left me with more than nine thousand dollars, part of it for me and part to pay for my trip back to the States. I stuffed the bankroll into a shoulder bag and carried it with me wherever I went. My first evening at the ski resort, I went to a movie and parked the bag—I now referred to it as the "rabbi's bag"—in my lap. Several hours later when I got back to my hotel room I suddenly realized that it was missing.

Panic-stricken, I tried to remember how I could have lost it. I remembered taking it from under the seat at the end of the movie, but that was all. I had run into someone I knew as I was leaving and had stopped to chat for a moment. Possibly the shoulder strap had slipped off and I had dropped it somewhere—maybe on the floor of the theater? The place was closed now, of course. Perhaps in the morning the police could find the manager's home telephone number and get him to open the theater so I could look. It was a slim hope, but the best I could think of.

Early the next morning, I went to the police station. Behind the desk was a grizzled, hard-looking officer who reminded me of one of those tough French cops played in the movies by Jean Gabin. A cigarette dangled from a corner of his mouth, and he was writing something. He did not look up as I stood before him.

"M'sieu," I said in my best French. *"M'sieu, j'ai un problème."* He continued to write.

"M'sieu, j'ai un problème très serieux."

As though I did not exist, he continued to write. At last he finished what he was doing, put the paper aside, and looked at me for the first time, with a long, thoughtful gaze. He then reached down to the floor beside him and came up with—my bag. "Is this your problem, *m'sieu?*"

I don't remember what I said, but it was to the effect of, "Whoopee!"

His craggy face split into a smile. Maybe it was only my overwhelming relief that made it seem like a miracle.

"How did you know it was mine?" I asked.

"The band on the cigar you are smoking tells me it is a Don Diego. There are several Don Diegos in this bag. There was also a thick wad of hundred-dollar bills, *monsieur.* And if you wish to claim it, you must tell me exactly how many such bills there are."

I told him, and he smiled. "Who found it?" I asked. "I must reward him."

"Unnecessary. It is already done. It is our custom to reward an honest finder with ten percent of the value of the find. You will see that an amount has been deducted from your money."

"Tell me who he is anyway. I must at least thank him."

"He is a Swedish student named Lars Peterson who was also on holiday in the town," the officer said. "Very late last night he had been walking home to his room when he felt the natural effect of the excellent Swiss beer he had taken on. He stepped off the path to relieve himself and there in the snow he saw the bag."

It couldn't have been a miracle that made him leave the path at precisely that place. It must have been a coincidence, mustn't it?

Back in his room, Lars Peterson opened the bag and his eyes popped. How much that money could do for a poor student! Sitting on his bed he counted it out. Then he sorted it into piles. This pile would enable him to finish his education. This one would buy his mother the new sewing machine she so badly needed. This one would get him the shiny new motorbike he'd dreamed of.

All through the rest of the night, he stared at the money—more than he had ever seen in his life. When the sky brightened, and the sun began to climb on the mountain, he scooped it back into the bag and took it to the police station.

I went in search of young Mr. Peterson. At the modest guest house where he was staying, the landlady said it would be very unlikely that I would find him there. He spent all day on the ski slopes, she said, and all evening in the local discos and beer cellars. "He only comes here very late for a few hours' sleep,'' she said, adding with a sly smile, ''if he comes at all.'' Everywhere I went, I asked for Lars Peterson and explained why I wanted to see him. Many people knew him, but he and I were never in the same place at the same time. Three fruitless days and nights passed. Although I skied, and felt exhilarated with the clean biting air of the Alps in my throat and lungs, I was sad that I couldn't find this honest boy.

It was not until my last night in Switzerland that I found him. Yes, they knew him in one disco. As a matter of fact, he was the tall fellow over there in the corner talking to a stunning girl.

I ran to him. ''Lars. Lars Peterson. Is that you? I'm the one whose bag you found. I have to thank you for what you did.''

He looked at me and laughed. ''Are you crazy?'' he said. ''You want to thank me? I have to thank you. I can never thank you enough,'' he exclaimed, and reached as if to hug me.

I backed away. ''I don't understand,'' I said. ''You found *my* bag, and returned nine thousand dollars, and you want to thank me? Have I gone mad?''

''It is I who must thank you,'' he insisted, still laughing. ''You've been telling this story all over town. Everybody has heard it. Not only do people keep talking to me about it, but some who left must be telling it back home too, because I've even gotten telegrams from abroad about it. Several of these people have offered me jobs,'' Lars said. ''Good jobs, better than a poor student with no influence could ever have expected to get. You have helped my career more than you can imagine, and it is I who should thank you.''

''I didn't say it would bring *you* good luck!'' The words rang in my head.

''Not me,'' I said, ''thank the rabbi.''

''What?''

''Nothing,'' I said. ''It's a long story. Now that you are going to be rich with all these job offers, come buy me a beer.''

When I left Lars that night he had an additional reward in his pocket and a big smile on his face, and I went home thinking about the miracles of the rabbi.

Some time later I heard that the rabbi had died in his ninety-sixth year. He slipped away peacefully in his sleep on Yom Kippur.

When I arrived back in New York, a copy of the *Saturday Review* was on my desk. In it there was a cover story on me. This type of article had never been written about an ophthalmologist before. At that time it was heresy to allow a lay publication to extoll the virtues of any particular doctor. Cooper had gotten into difficulty because of his many appearances in magazines, and I was on my way with this article.

From *Saturday Review,* April 15, 1972, CATARACT SURGERY: A DIFFERENT TUNE, "Can a Saxophone Player Find Happiness as an Eye Surgeon?":

"The occasion is something called Jazz at Noon, and it happens every Friday in the appropriately named Rough Rider Room of New York's Roosevelt Hotel. The crowd is noisy and appreciative, lustily acknowledging any solo that lasts more than four bars—two, in the case of drums—while the musicians trundle on and off the bandstands, energetically trying to recapture something they may once have had. It's the city's most incongruous jazz band; twenty or so men, wielding assorted instruments and dressed for Wall Street or Madison Avenue; twenty or so ex-musicians who, every Friday at noon, give it another shot.

" 'Okay, now we got something special,' announces Les Lieber, the public relations–executive emcee, gilding the enthusiasm lily. 'A real treat, Dr. Charles Kelman is here. Charley's an eminent eye surgeon and, as many of you know, a great baritone sax player. Come on up here, Charley.'

"Charley the eminent eye surgeon. Like Harry the eminent account executive on guitar and Frank the eminent broker on trumpet. If there is a typical eye surgeon, Charley is certainly not it. He's wearing an expensive suit that comes close to being mod, a shirt with a flowered pattern, and a wide tie with a different flowered pattern. He has Sammy Glick good looks, and he's the only one on the bandstand with a tan. When the rhythm section cranks out the opening chords of 'Out of Nowhere,' Charley closes his eyes, brings the mouthpiece of his huge saxophone to his lips and looks as if he belongs on the bandstand. He also looks as though he knows what to do with the horn in his hands, and those Rough Rider Room patrons who know the difference between kind of good and awfully good start listening seriously. Charley is awfully good.

"But at one table at the side of the room, eight men are staring up at Charley in amazement. They have just spent a week at Mid-Cities Hospital, taking an intensive course in *Phacoemulsification and Aspiration*—a relatively new and totally revolutionary technique of cataract removal. The men are eye surgeons themselves, and their teacher during the week has been Dr. Charles Kelman, who has been rapidly developing a reputation as one of the nation's leading eye surgeons and medical researchers. When he invited them to lunch to mark the unofficial conclusion of the one-week course in the technique he invented, they had no idea he was going to be part of the entertainment.

"But that's Charley's style. He spent the first few months of his life in Brooklyn, and he never quite got over it. He spent the first few decades of his life thinking of himself primarily as a musician. It has been only in the last few years, and only with reluctance, that he has been accepting the fact that he is an ophthalmologist.

"Charley is also a songwriter, and when you hear one of his songs, the lyric has Charley written all over it. Charley Kelman the eminent eye surgeon and, for those who care about such things, one hell of a sax player."

There was a picture of me sitting expansively in my office, and another, blowing a big, baritone saxophone.

With all of the publicity coming my way, patients were lining up outside of the door to my small office, which was now inadequate to handle that kind of volume. The operation definitely had public appeal. Not only did patients read about it and hear about it on the radio and television, but those patients who had undergone the operation took great pleasure in lauding it over their friends who'd had the standard six-week recuperation procedure. My patients delighted in teasing their friends who were using "old-fashioned doctors." While this was good for the practice, it was very bad for my relations with the rest of the profession.

One of my patients shared a room with a patient of Sirotka's. They had been admitted on the same day. *My* patient was discharged the following day, and four days later came to visit his roommate, who was still in the hospital. He came with a bouquet of flowers to chide his new friend for being an invalid. When Sirotka heard about this, a meeting of the board at the hospital was called. A notice went out shortly thereafter to all the doctors on the staff. A formula had been developed that limited the amount of cases a surgeon could perform at Mid-Cities Hospital depending on his length of service at the hospital. I had been doing fourteen operations a week there, but with this edict, I was cut down to five. I was the only one affected by the new rule. The hospital also ruled that cataract patients must stay in the hospital for at least three days.

The publicity also made it difficult for me at medical meetings where I had been invited to lecture. My "overnight success" irritated most of my colleagues. Often when I lectured on phacoemulsification it was to a hostile audience. The emotion prevented the doctors from judging the operation objectively. At that time it was still a difficult operation and many doctors thought that they would never be able to perform it. They were also concerned that perhaps someone else in their town would. My lectures, therefore, were met with stone-faced silence, followed by hostile questioning.

The questions were always the same: "Why do we need this operation? The one we have works fine. What makes you think that patients want to leave the hospital in one day?"

In city after city where I'd been invited to lecture, there were often only disgruntled mumblings and hostile remarks after I spoke. At first this was demoralizing; I felt small, demeaned, and discouraged. After several dozen of these encounters, I was able to shrug off the barbs and maintain my dignity. Since the hostile questions were always the same, I became more practiced with the answers. I found that usually a funny remark or story was better than an angry retort, and I became fairly skilled at medical repartee. Humor served me well. But there was one time when things went beyond the humorous stage.

It happened in Houston, at a meeting of the Pan American Society of Ophthalmology. It was a broiling day in that city and the air conditioning in the auditorium was out of order. There were no windows, and the room was steamy. It was about to get more so.

I was scheduled to deliver a paper explaining the methods of teaching my operation. The large hall was filled with more than one thousand eye surgeons. I was so controversial that my name on the program was enough to fill the hall. Not with admirers, but with skeptics who came to see "that nut from New York" who was trying to put something over on the poor surgeons who were doing a good job with the standard operation. They came to see the fun, to chuckle, and to revel in ridicule. On the podium, forming the panel of experts, were several of my avowed antagonists.

My paper was low key and brief, and I was at ease on the podium, in spite of the undercurrent of antagonism, having had my skin thickened at smaller meetings. My seven-year-old son was with me, seated in the front of the auditorium. I smiled at him from time to time, hoping he was impressed enough to want to be a doctor one day. I finished my talk and was about to leave the podium. Suddenly, the chairman rose and asked me to remain in place. I thought that perhaps—it *was* possible—he had some congratulatory remarks he wished to address to me.

The chairman called on Sergi Amandoresca, one of the world's most celebrated eye surgeons, a man close to seventy-five years old, who limped to the podium. This was wonderful, I thought; with his praise and blessing there would be less antagonism toward me, and the operation.

Amandoresca called for his first slide, never even looking at me, as I stood shoulder to shoulder with him. I wondered what slide he would show—and then it flashed on the screen: It was a picture of me, taken from the *Saturday Review* article, with my eyes closed, blowing a baritone saxophone. "He's going to congratulate me for being competent in two professions," I naïvely told myself. But at the same time, an alarm began sounding somewhere in my brain. It had good reason to.

Amandoresca's shrill voice screamed into the microphone, making me jump. "This is the kind of unethical publicity this man engages in!" His arm stretched out, pointing first to my face on the screen, and then to me, and then back to the screen. He avoided looking directly at me. "This is where he belongs," he shrieked, "in a bar . . . not at a medical meeting. . . . He is in flagrant disregard of medical ethics . . ." He went on and on, showing slides of other articles about me and about other doctors using my technique. Blood drained from my face, my fists clenched, and my breathing grew labored, but I looked straight ahead, expressionless, motionless, trying to make myself think of something else. Every minute he spoke lasted a full sixty seconds. I couldn't bring myself to glance at my son in the front row.

Each word stung like the lash of the whip. What was most ridiculous was that this man, this Amandoresca, had in his time been the most widely written about eye surgeon in history. He himself had been a pioneer in corneal grafts. He had been virtually in every newspaper and magazine in the country, and had supposedly placed advertisements in foreign newspapers looking for "customers."

When Amandoresca finished ten minutes later, I was still standing tall. I refused to be bowed. I looked straight ahead out into the audience and managed a sardonic smile. Every eye in that room scrutinized me. I could see compassion in the faces of a few, but glee on the faces of most. How quickly these men had forgotten their prior jealousy of Amandoresca. But he was an old man and no longer a threat to them. I was.

"Do you have anything to say for yourself?" Amandoresca said finally, when he had finished in an orgasmic crescendo.

"Yes, I do," I said, half turning toward him, but keeping

my face toward the audience. My flair for theatrics was coming to my aid. "I am surprised that the very person who makes me look like a shy wallflower was chosen to deliver that hypocritical tirade." It was his turn to turn red. I continued. "While I do not in any way invite comparison of myself to Jesus Christ, permit me to quote him." I turned fully toward him now and pointed my finger at him, waiting for a brief second, just long enough for most people to guess what I was going to say: "Let he who hath never sinned, cast the first stone."

I stepped off the podium and to my surprise found I had gained some support from the audience. There was a burst of applause, and a few men in the room actually stood up while applauding. I grabbed David's hand as I went down the aisle, and we went to the pool for the rest of the morning.

I was cold white with fury. I was drained of all energy and could only lie in the chair, trying to regain my strength. But whatever I was, I was not sorry. I would have done the same thing all over again. The publicity, none of which I had sought out, had assured me rightful credit to an operation I still felt was destined to become an important factor in treating blindness. Perkins and Duggan were sitting on that panel. I had no doubt in my mind; it was they who had instigated Amandoresca in order to dissuade me from making future presentations. Probably, Amandoresca had promised that whenever I spoke, wherever I spoke, someone would be there to do what he had done: show "publicity" slides.

But I had gone too far with my rebuttal to turn back. I had committed myself to a fight, and the years of frustration in show business and in research had equipped me for this battle. I contacted one of the leading newspaper clipping services and engaged them to prepare a file on Amandoresca, Perkins, and many of my other opponents in the field. In a short time I had a huge collection of slides which I had made from the clippings I had received. Amandoresca, of course, was the subject of most of them. His headlines made mine look like the fine print in the phone book. Perkins himself was well represented. There were several front-page pictures of him shaking hands with various notables, including the president of the United States. That's not too bad a job of publicity. Some of the most revered names in ophthalmology, even the professors at the untouchable universities, were represented in my collection. I hoped I would never have to use this weapon and in that regard, but I made it known to a few key people that the collection existed.

I prominently labeled the box of slides PUBLICITY SLIDES OF OTHER DOCTORS, and I carried it with me to every meeting. There was never a repeat of the Houston incident. No one knew whether he was represented or not in my box of slides. There was no doubt that the higher up you got, the heavier was the fighting.

Since the number of cases I could do at Mid-Cities Hospital had been limited by the new regulation, I had found other places where I could perform additional surgery. One of them was St. Barnabas Hospital in New Jersey, a beautiful modern facility, where they were anxious for the increased hospital business. Since I had a large number of patients from New Jersey, I decided to begin performing surgery at that institution. The problem was that it took two hours in traffic to drive from my home to St. Barnabas. One day, as I sat in a traffic jam, a helicopter flew over my head. I stared at it longingly. It was like a bird flying over some worms. I was a worm. I wanted to be the bird.

I took three weeks off from my practice and enrolled in a school. I had always been sensitive to motion; on the sea I got seasick, on the land I got carsick—and so, naturally, in a helicopter I got airsick. The kind of airsick that requires a paper bag. Only on my first flight, there was no paper bag. When I felt it coming, I looked around frantically for some receptacle, but in the cockpit of a helicopter one does not find empty jars. At the last second I reached for the only thing remotely able to receive my offering—the pilot's hat. Needless to say, he never wore that hat again. Needless to say, for my next lesson I had a different instructor, as well as a supply of paper bags, which I used on my first four or five flights. I was really wondering whether or not I could ever get over the sickness, but I persisted. Finally, for no apparent reason except perhaps habituation, it went away.

One day, while I was still pretty shaky on the controls and having difficulty making a soft landing, my instructor and I set down on a little island of sand on the south shore of Long Island. It was one of my worst landings, and I thought the pilot would wash me up. Suddenly, he opened his door and got out. I should take it around myself, he said. Maybe I would do better. He bent over to avoid a rotor blade haircut, and disappeared. I was on my own. With a do-or-die scream in my throat, I lifted off, circled around, and made my best landing.

The instructor grinned when he climbed back inside. "I didn't think you could do it," he said. I still don't know if he meant that. Soon after that, I had a helicopter pilot's license, as well as a helicopter, which I parked on my front lawn. Now I could be at my hospital in New Jersey in less than fifteen minutes. Now, I was the bird.

The thrill of racing at 140 mph over snarled traffic is extraordinary. My energy knew no bounds. In the evening, after doing battle, the ride home in the sunset, or starlight, was ethereal, millions of lights floated under me like a sea of stars. Joe wanted me to get a pilot, but since flying that machine demanded concentration and perfection, I wanted to know what the pilot had done the night before. Since I was the pilot, I knew. If I was tired, I didn't fly.

I occasionally used the helicopter for recreational activities. Joan and I were invited to a wedding in upstate New York. I got directions and we took off, Joan in a beautiful dress, and me in a white suit, white hat, and white shoes. When we got to a golf course in the area, I was supposed to be able to see the awning and tent where the wedding was being held. There was no awning or tent to be seen. I circled and circled, but obviously I had the wrong golf course.

One of the wonderful things about a helicopter is that you can land it anywhere. I did! I landed it in a potato patch, next to a small farmhouse.

An old man with wrinkled skin and dark Mediterranean eyes emerged from the bushes, wide eyed with fear, as I stepped out of my vehicle.

"Do you have a telephone?" I asked.

"Momma mia. Momma mia," he called, wringing his hands as he bowed and led me into the house, continuing to bow. "Rosa, Rosa," he cried excitedly. "Bring some provalone, make some pasta. Rosa, Rosa, quick."

While I telephoned for further instructions, I heard a great commotion in the house. I got my new directions, hung up, and walked into the living room to thank him. There they were, the whole family: Papa, Momma, and six or seven children, all holding platters of food, all staring incredulously at the man in the white suit who had dropped out of the sky. They must have thought the Messiah had come, like a miracle, to their humble home. Joan and I stayed long enough to taste everything and then we disappeared into the sky.

During this period, I continued to lecture. After the crowd of hostile ophthalmologists left the room, there would sometimes be one who remained. He would come up to me and say, "I would like to learn that technique." Little by little, small pockets of support appeared.

Some well-known personalities were beginning to find their way to my office. One of the very colorful ladies who appeared was Hedy Lamarr. I don't know how many films I've seen of Hedy Lamarr, but I remember best when she was in *Ecstasy,* wearing nothing at all. I believe she was the first to be seen in a major motion picture with nothing but the trees in the forest covering her. Although it had been many years since then, I easily saw her beauty shining through her surgically tightened skin. She was still exciting, not only to look at, but to talk to. She spoke with an enthusiasm usually reserved for the young ingenue on the set. Plans for the future were her greatest stock in trade.

That such a beauty should end up with cataracts was a sad commentary on the dirty tricks that life plays on our bodies. Hedy sat in my examining chair, squinting to get a better view of me, obviously sizing me up. She knew what she needed, having been to many other ophthalmologists. I suppose that she was afraid of the surgery, but I think I knew what most worried her.

"Miss Lamarr, the operation will be totally invisible. No one will be able to see any scar. Your eyes will remain as they are—beautiful." A look of relief came over her. I think that being afraid of the answer, she had never put that question to any other ophthalmologist. With that, she was mine.

I went over the details of the surgery and the recuperative period with her and then casually mentioned the fee. I suppose she was used to getting free surgery, the surgeon gaining only the notoriety and reputation of operating on the famous Hedy.

At the mention of the fee, with great surprise and hurt, she reached down to her hem, and neatly showed me her tan, trim body in white bikini underwear. I was startled.

"With a body like this, you cannot charge me?" she questioned, fire in her eyes.

I said, "Hedy, with a body like that, you should charge me." She laughed, I laughed, and she agreed to pay the normal fee. I eventually operated on both her eyes, and then, a few years later, when they were perfected, placed implants in her eyes, so that she wouldn't have to wear contact lenses or thick glasses. To this day we are still friends, and have a glass of wine at the Friars Club when she comes to town.

I soon had the pleasure of examining another famous lady. I was really excited when I got a call from the Israeli secret service in New York. I immediately envisioned a secret mission or doing something intriguing for the Israeli government: maybe a request that I become a helicopter rescue pilot for some upcoming war. As romantic as all that sounded, when they explained what they wanted, I was even more excited. The prime minister of Israel, Golda Meir, wanted to see me in her suite at the Regency Hotel, where she was living during a meeting at the United Nations.

I arrived at the appointed hour, and went through a vigorous and very serious security check—including a body search. With pants down. The prime minister had requested that we be alone during our conversation, and I guess that meant extra precautions. When the three tough guards were convinced that I had no knives in any bodily crevices, I was ushered into her suite. Or rather, up to her floor. For security reasons, it was necessary to have the whole floor for her and her immediate aides.

My guard discreetly knocked on her apartment door, which promptly was opened by the great lady herself. I had been warned that my interview was for ten minutes only, since there were many others scheduled to see her. She was surrounded by a heavy veil of cigarette smoke, which prompted her first words to me, "Come in, Dr. Kelman, and please excuse me. I smoke too much."

Rarely at a loss for words, I answered, "Ms. Meir, if I had your responsibilities, I would smoke too much also." She laughed heartily and motioned for me to sit down. Tea and crackers were on the table. As she told me what she had heard about me, we poured each other cups of tea. And she smoked.

I supposed she wanted to talk about her eyes, but I was not pretentious enough to appear with a black bag of instruments. We spoke about life in the United States compared to Israel, about her successful career as a politician in Israel, about her life as a housewife in the United States, and a little about my career. The ten minutes were long gone, and we were into a half hour. At last the question came: If one had a cataract, what would the chance of success be in Israel compared to the United States? I explained that the operation was about 98 percent successful in both countries.

What were the serious complications? I explained them. Hemorrhage, infection, glaucoma, retinal swelling and detachment. She seemed well versed in the subject, as if she had heard the answers before. And then finally, what would the difference be if I operated with phacoemulsification? I explained that the recuperation would be more rapid, days instead of weeks. But she wanted to know whether, if she had the usual surgery in Israel, she would still be able to read and function. I told her yes.

The sum and substance of our discussion revolved around the image of Israeli medicine, and whether it would suffer if I did the surgery; she was fiercely chauvinistic. When I left her, almost an hour after I arrived, I knew her decision had been made. She would have the operation in Israel. If anything went wrong, she would come to me for the second eye. She called in her official photographer to take pictures of our meeting, and we said good-bye.

Two weeks later she was operated on in Jerusalem, and everything went well. I had mixed emotions about not doing her eyes. On the one hand, I would have been greatly honored had I been able to do the surgery, but on the other I would have been resented by the many fine ophthalmologists in Israel.

There was a great interest in my courses for learning the operation. I formed the David J. Kelman Research and Teaching Foundation, named for my father, the man who had said "first be a doctor."

After a year, we had our first meeting—at midnight, for a late supper. Eggs and champagne. All the attendees had been recipients of some of the same jealousy and resentment that I had experienced. We spoke in hushed tones of our surgical and political problems. I was proud of these men who had risked their own careers on my operation. I was beginning to feel the tide coming in at last. It had taken a long time.

In 1969 I was invited to give an important speech at the Japanese Ophthalmology Society in Tokyo. It was a four-day meeting. My lecture was scheduled for the last day. There were a few other Americans on the program, and I assumed that the Japanese understood English. Sitting in the huge auditorium, I observed that when the Americans spoke, the Japanese nodded politely, but stopped taking notes. They weren't writing anything, because they did not understand anything. I left the lecture hall, went back to the hotel, found a translator, and had him write out my lecture in phonetic Japanese. Then I had him record it on my tape recorder. For three days I studied the words and listened to his voice, *"wataka kushi wa . . ."* My musical background made it easy for me to imitate his sounds.

I wanted to know if the Japanese were understanding me, so on page 3 I had inserted an appropriately humorous story.

When I began speaking on the day of my lecture, the room suddenly became enveloped in silence. While I spoke I could imagine the translator's voice in my ear, as I mimicked the sounds and read the words. I was anxious to get to page 3 to see if they would laugh at my joke, I didn't know exactly where on the page the joke was, since I didn't understand, word for word, what I was reading. I was at the middle of the third page, and then down at the bottom. The Japanese didn't smile. God, they didn't understand a word I was saying. I had to go on. I began page 4, and on the fifth word, laughter rocked the audience. The punch line had been put on that page. At the end of an hour, I stepped down to a very hearty round of thunderous applause. A professor from the Midwest was to follow me on the program, in English of course. As I walked down the steps from the podium, he walked up. As we crossed, he smiled at me, and out of the corner of his mouth hissed, "You son of a bitch."

Some time later, I received a telegram from Russia. Krasnov, one of the leading Russian ophthalmologists, wanted to purchase a phacoemulsifier. I called Cavitron, but Navin felt the machine still required too much service, and he was also afraid that if he sent one behind the Iron Curtain, it would be dismantled so that the Russians could then invent it. Cavitron wanted more time before going international. I discussed this rather amusing chain of events with Joan one evening, and she had a brilliant idea. I put her plan into action.

I wrote to Krasnov, telling him the company could not yet sell him a machine. I added that there was a way I could get him one immediately, but I did not wish to discuss it by letter. I ended by saying, "If you plan a trip to the United States, I would be happy to discuss this." I had baited the hook.

I soon received a telegram that Krasnov was coming to America, and confirmed by return cable a luncheon meeting with him. He arrived at the appointed time with an "interpreter."

Krasnov spoke perfect English, and was dressed in a fashionable British suit. His interpreter was probably a secret agent, appointed to stay with Krasnov and prevent his defection. With his ruddy cheeks, large roughened hands, and ill-fitting clothes, the agent appeared as a farmhand dressed for church. On one occasion when the "interpreter" lost sight of Krasnov for just a few seconds, I saw a look of panic on his face. From that time on, the two of them were glued together.

The three of us had lunch. I spoke about life in the United States, ophthalmology, music, and dance. I never mentioned the instrument. Nor did he. At the end of an hour I looked at my watch. "Well, Professor Krasnov, it's time for me to leave," I said.

He looked shaken. "But what about the machine?" he said. "You wrote that you could get me a machine."

"Oh that," I said. "Yes, of course I can get you a machine delivered to you in Russia at no cost to you. The machine will be donated by Hadassah, in return for one thousand exit visas for Jews from Russia."

Krasnov turned the color of the white tablecloth. His "interpreter" looked menacingly at him, and then stood up. "Ve must be going," the interpreter said brusquely. Then, they were gone.

It was a good try, but it didn't work. Two years later the Russians purchased twelve machines at fifty-thousand dollars each. They wanted an American to come to Russia to teach them the technique, but they stipulated that it should not be Kelman. Interestingly enough, about six months after my conversation with Krasnov, Russia began allowing certain Jews to emigrate. I expected to hear from him, demanding his free machine, but I suppose he had nothing to do with that temporary softening of Russian policy.

I personally had not suffered because of anti-Semitism. I admit that the road to success would have been easier to navigate, starting with access to medical school, had I been from some inner-sanctum WASP family, but actually I enjoyed coming up the hard way, and I think that I can appreciate my success even more because of it. And so I was not upset or too proud to accept an invitation by one of my few early supporters, Professor of Ophthalmology Murray McCaslin. Murray had sent me many patients for cataract surgery with my Roto-Rooter technique, as he called it—patients from some of the most prominent families of Pittsburgh.

Murray was a member of a very exclusive, very private hunting and fishing club, to which people with names like Mellon, Rockefeller, and Carnegie belonged. He had convinced the reluctant members of the guest committee—one had to be approved as a guest—that I could conduct myself appropriately in spite of my less than blue-blooded background.

Murray was a sweet old gentleman on the verge of retiring. He had taken a liking to me when he first visited my surgery, and had tried to help me whenever he could. I spent the night in his home in the hills of Pennsylvania, and at four o'clock in the morning we began dressing. Long-sleeved green shirts—to discourage mosquitoes—with many pockets to hold the paraphernalia of the fisherman, hip boots, fisherman's hat, the whole works. I had never gone trout fishing before and I was very excited. We arrived at The Sanctuary, a mansion set back a few miles from the main road, with hundreds of acres of streams and fields. I was impressed. I was also just a little bothered by the knowledge that no matter what I ever achieved in life, I would never be welcome as a member of this club. Not that the members were all that terrific. In the great room of the club, in their great armchairs, they were a pretty stuffy bunch, even to each other.

We went to our assigned spot on the stream, a quarter of a mile of frontage exclusively ours to fish, upsteam and downstream. And on the other side were other twosomes. It was really paradise. Other than the sounds of the forest, there were no intrusions—it wouldn't surprise me if jets were diverted from this area so as not to disturb the serenity.

Murray showed me how to tie a fly on the line, and I flicked it into the water. The little cork bobbed up and down gently, serenely, like the surroundings, and for a moment I was hypnotized by the beauty of it all. Murray then bent down to tie his own fly, when the cork on my line took a dive, and I felt a jerk. I whispered excitedly, "Murray, Murray, I've got a bite."

I was told to reel it in, and I did. Suddenly we could see the fish beneath the surface; it was really big. Murray's eyes bulged, and his face reddened.

"Cut the line," he said quickly. "Let it go, Charley." He was fumbling in his box for a knife.

"Murray, what the hell . . . ? It's a beauty. Why do you want me to let it go?"

Murray had the line in his hand now, and was approaching it with the knife. I watched in complete confusion as he prepared to cut. And then . . . he let go of the line and said, "No, Charley, let's not cut the line. What's meant to be will be. Reel it in."

I reeled it in, babbling a mixture of excitement and confusion. There it was, at the end of my line. I held it over the water, all three feet of trout, while Murray held a net under the wiggling, squirming beauty. And then from downstream I heard the call, and I knew in a flash what the story was.

"They got Big George, they got Big George," the voice cried. And then from farther downstream, but fainter now, the same cry. "They got Big George." It was like a wave, going upstream and downstream.

"Murray, what the hell is Big George?" I asked, as if I didn't know.

"The prize fish, Charley. The one they've all been trying to catch for two seasons now." I didn't know whether to laugh or cry.

"Shall I throw it back?" I offered.

"No. If you did, they'd probably be trying *not* to catch it again." We both laughed.

"They let one like me in here for ten minutes and he grabs the biggest fish." I laughed. "I guess I'll be the last one they'll ever let in."

"More than that," Murray said. "You'll definitely be *my* last guest."

I know how the members must have felt, and yet, in spite of that, the congratulatory remarks back in the clubhouse, where I stayed for one quick drink, were, I think, sincere.

19

Still Another Battle

As time went by, the number of doctors performing my operation increased beyond my wildest dreams. At the sixth meeting of the Kelman Alumni Association there were six hundred doctors in the audience, most of whom were performing phacoemulsification. At that meeting, a motion was made by Alston Callahan, M.D., one of the first to become interested in my work, that the operation officially be called the "Kelman Procedure." At that time Cavitron had sold more than five hundred instruments: one hundred times more than I had predicted when making a royalty agreement with them. Herb Roth's negotiations were paying off. I was now walking around with a truly positive feeling of contentment. The knowledge that every day, somewhere, someone's vision was being restored by my operation and by my apparatus was, by then, a constant source of pride and pleasure.

There were many cataracts which could not be safely removed by the older, more conventional methods. Fortuitously, the more difficult the operation was by conventional means, the easier it was by phacoemulsification. Many people who would have been destined for blindness could be operated on successfully with this technique.

In infants and young children, it was extremely simple, whereas the standard method was hazardous and often did not give good results. Every day children were being given the wonderful gift of vision. Starting in 1970, more and more practitioners accepted the method, and as the controversy died down, my life became more productive.

Except at home. Now that I was less involved with research, I had more time at home. It seemed, however, that the more time I spent there, the less Joan and I could enjoy each other's company. The children were wonderful, and watching them grow and become real people was rewarding. I know I tried hard to make our marriage work, and Joan tried too. There was no other woman in my life—I still loved Joan—but now that I had time to think, I was beginning to miss whatever it was that I was missing, even more.

In 1972 I moved into a spacious new suite of offices in a modern building on a high floor in Manhattan, designed to be relaxing and pleasing to the patients who came there. The first day the office was open I slept there on the couch. It was so beautiful, I couldn't bring myself to leave. The next morning when Joe came in, he found me standing at the window, looking at the city.

"Joe, it's a crazy thing, but I'm depressed. It feels like I've done it all. Everything has worked out, and there's nothing more to fight for. I'm only forty-two, and it seems like it's all over."

Joe always knew the right thing to say. He came over and looked out the window with me. "You know, Charley, this is only the thirty-fourth floor. You can't even begin to see how many floors there are above you." Joe was a prophet.

One of the remaining problems I had was that the technique, being a departure from the standard, required learning. No one can deny that with age the ability to learn new skills decreases. That meant that the older ophthalmologists had more difficulty learning the procedure than the younger men. The problem was that the older ophthalmologists were the ones who were politically important. They were the elder statesmen, they were the spokesmen. They controlled the official position of the profession on all issues. These elder statesmen made one last try to repress the operation.

I was informed that the American Academy of Ophthalmology was going to select a committee to investigate the effectiveness of phacoemulsification. They had never done anything like this before; it was going to be an inquisition. With a little imagination, I could easily guess who they would appoint as their chairman—John Driscoll, M.D. My guess was correct. He was to prepare a lengthy questionnaire to be sent to all ophthalmologists to fill in, describing their results and complications with phacoemulsification. He was going to tabulate these results with a computer and compare them to standard surgery, at which time the American Academy of Ophthalmology would make an official statement as to the effectiveness of the operation.

Although my name was officially put on the committee, I was never invited to a meeting until months after its formation. Driscoll then called to inform me that the results had been tabulated. If I had the time, I might drop by for a conference before these results were submitted. I was furious that I had not been included in the project itself. At the conference, Driscoll's results came out: "Phacoemulsification statistics were far inferior to the standard. *Case Closed.*"

Through the efforts of hundreds of my followers, I got the American Academy of Ophthalmology to agree to an independent statistical analysis by someone who would work closely with Driscoll and monitor his findings. I chose a professor of mathematics at Columbia in New York, Gus Gramus.

Gus was a little hesitant at first: "If you hire me, Dr. Kelman, I will tell it the way it is. If I agree with Driscoll's method of procedure and his findings, I will say so."

"Dr. Gramus, that's why I am hiring you—for your reputation and for your integrity. . . . I want the statistics to speak for themselves. But you know as well as I do that statistics can be made to say whatever you want them to. I just want them to be fair." Under those circumstances, Gus Gramus took the job and reviewed and collaborated with Driscoll.

Shortly before the results were going to be tabulated, there was a large, well-attended ophthalmology meeting in Bermuda, where many doctors liked to get away from the cold climate and relax a little in the sun. The meeting was headed by Hubert Stoor, M.D., one of the most outspoken opponents of phacoemulsification. Stoor had sent out letters to every ophthalmologist in the country requesting information about phacoemulsification disasters—the theme of his meeting. I was not invited. I learned later that at the entrance to that meeting stood a patient wearing a sign which read: I WAS BLINDED BY PHACOEMULSIFICATION.

Fortunately, there were many surgeons there who had performed phaco. For every misstatement that was made by my detractors, a corresponding rebuttal was made. My friend Alston Callahan sat in the front row with a bull horn on his lap, prepared to shout down any unfair remarks. Stoor could not come up with his series of disasters. His attempt to influence the academy failed.

When the American Academy finally read its announcement, prepared with Gus Gramus's help, it read, "We find that phacoemulsification is *as* effective as other means for removing cataracts." A great victory!

What this statement did not say was that, *with* phacoemulsification, the patient was rehabilitated immediately, whereas with other methods recovery was much slower. But what it said was enough. That battle was finally over.

At about that time, Jan Peerce, the great tenor, was referred to me. He had had one eye operated on elsewhere, and complications had developed, which unfortunately occurs in a certain number of cases, though it is no one's fault. There is a saying that the only surgeons who do not have complications are the surgeons who never operate. Jan Peerce had had a cataract removed, had a hemorrhage, and had to have the eye removed.

Naturally, when he developed a cataract in his other eye, he was terrified of having a similar occurrence. As a matter of fact, when a patient has a hemorrhage in one eye, the likelihood of having a similar occurrence in the second eye is exceptionally high; it has to do with the type of circulation that the patient has. Jan had been told that he might lose his second eye if it ever was operated on.

And so he delayed surgery; his vision got dimmer and dimmer until he could barely see the stage. The bright footlights made him totally blind, and he was helpless without his wife Alice at his side. One night in the middle of a performance of "Laugh a Little, Cry a Little," at the Westbury Music Fair, he fell off the stage into the orchestra pit.

With his leg in a cast up to his hip, Jan knew that he had to make a decision: either to go blind slowly, or take a chance with another operation—risking a hemorrhage.

He had heard about my technique from several sources: Friends had told him, some of my patients had told him, and his family had read articles about the technique of phacoemulsification. Being a thorough man, he had researched the subject himself and had learned that it was not universally accepted—there were doctors who said it was not as safe as the standard method. What was he to do? Being a deeply religious man, he consulted his rabbi.

"Go to three well-known ophthalmologists and ask their opinion about Dr. Kelman and his operation. If two out of the three recommend him, then have him do the surgery," he was told.

The first doctor he went to said "no," and the other two "yes." He came to see me.

Operating on someone's eye is a major responsibility. If the patient is well known, perhaps the responsibility is even greater. But when the patient has only one eye *and* is internationally renowned, it becomes a heavy responsibility indeed. Failure in a case like this means a white cane for the patient—and ignominy for the surgeon.

Stories in the newspapers had already appeared about Jan Peerce falling off the stage; and now he had announced to the press that he was going to have another operation, this time by Kelman. By the day his surgery appointment was upon us, it had become anything but a secret. . . .

Most cataract operations that I perform are done under local anesthesia. The soft music playing in the operating room, the preoperative sedation—an injection of Valium—

are enough to relax most patients. But in a case like this, I thought, only general anesthesia would do. And yet when they wheeled Jan Peerce into the operating room, I could see no sign of anxiety on his face.

"How are you, Mr. Peerce?" I asked.

"In God's hands . . . and yours." He smiled.

The injection put him out, and the black mask and tubing from the anesthesia machine completed the sedation—and the rest was up to me.

He was extremely nearsighted. This makes certain post-operative complications more frequent, but on the other hand, the surgery itself becomes easier, especially for phacoemulsification. The eye is large and there is more room to maneuver instruments inside it. Jan Peerce's case was extremely easy. In less than ten minutes his cataract was emulsified, the cornea was beautifully clear, and he was on his way to the recovery room. Normally, I do not put a patch on the eye; in this case I wanted to be certain that he didn't rub it. There had been no hemorrhage on the operating table, and I didn't want one later.

I thanked God for giving us both a break, and went on to the rest of that morning's cases.

The next day I went in to examine Jan Peerce. It was the typical Hollywood scene: the anxious family hovering over the patched patient, the quiet hushed tones, a prayer book by the bedside, and the unspoken question uppermost in everyone's mind—Will he see?

"Well, let's take a look at what we have here," I said in a cool professional manner as I removed the patch. The eye looked beautiful—absolutely beautiful—as if it had never been operated on. "Can you see, Mr. Peerce?" I asked expectantly.

"Yes, I can see," he answered roughly.

I was taken aback; I expected jubilation and I was getting animosity. "Can you count my fingers?" I asked, holding two fingers in front of him.

"Yes," he said. "Two."

He definitely sounded angry. "Can you see your family behind me?" I asked, hoping the sight of them would warm his heart. I was perplexed and vexed at his reaction.

"I can see them," he said flatly.

I was exasperated. "Mr. Peerce, yesterday you were blind; today you can see perfectly well. And yet you sound angry."

"I am."

"Can you please tell me why?" I asked.

"I'll tell you why," he said. "Yesterday when they wheeled me into the operating room, you had music playing. You had Tony Bennett singing. Tony Bennett! I make records, too, you know." He paused, and then to my surprise it was his joke, his way of relieving his tension. He pulled me down to him, kissing my face and hands, laughing and crying at the same time. "Thank you, Dr. Kelman," he said. "And thank God."

"You're welcome, from both of us," I said, "but you got the order wrong."

When Jan Peerce wrote his book *Bluebird of Happiness,* he devoted a chapter to his cataract operation.

On the same day that I'd operated on Jan Peerce, I operated on another well-known personality, New York's favorite disc jockey, William B. Williams. His inimitable greeting, "Hello, world," is heard daily by millions. I had jokingly asked him, when I first examined him, if he could play my record of "Telephone Numbers" on his show. His answer had been that he did not decide what was played, that that was the job of the program director. On the day when he was in my operating room, lying helpless on the table, I said, "Willie, this is a very sharp knife in my hand, right next to your eye."

"So what does that mean, doc?" he asked, knowing full well what was coming.

"It means you'll play my record, Willie, that's what it means. Right?"

"Night and day, doc, I'll play it. Night and day," he answered. His operation went just fine, in spite of the kidding.

Willie loved flying, and the day after the operation I invited him and Jan Peerce to fly back to New York with me in the helicopter. Willie accepted, Jan declined. When we landed in New York, Willie and I went for some lunch before going back to my office. When we arrived at my office, there was Jan Peerce, beaming. He thought he had beaten us with the limousine. I never had the heart to tell him.

A week later, I got a call from the radio station WNEW that Willie was on the air and that I should tune in. I did.

"This record is being played as a promise to Doc Kelman," Willie said to his "world." I waited, expecting to hear my old song "Telephone Numbers" again. Instead, he played, as promised, "Night and Day."

20

Surgeon by Day

In 1974, I gave a paper at the American Academy of Ophthalmology meeting in Las Vegas. Many other well-known ophthalmologists were on the program describing the results, benefits, and problems of my operation. So many were performing it at this time, that it was no longer controversial. By those that performed it, it was acknowledged as an important adjunct to the technique of cataract surgery. Some used it all the time, some used it part of the time, and those who never used it at least accepted it.

The doctors who didn't or couldn't do the operation had learned to live with it. They found that there were still patients who accepted the standard technique of large-incision surgery. They did not lose their surgical practice or their patients. Implants, a plastic lens inserted into the eye, had since come onto the scene. All the controversy within the profession was now focused there. I had been too busy fighting my battle to get involved with implants at that time.

At any rate, there I was, finally in front of the auditorium, finally with some credibility, finally on the inside. I remember sitting on that podium that day and looking out at the sea of faces. How many Charley Kelmans were out there desperate to do something important in the profession? Would I now try to help them, or would I fall into the trap of trying to protect my own position? I resolved that I would never have a closed mind to new ideas, never try to prevent anyone else from succeeding, never do to others what was done to me.

What was strange was that I was a little bored. Was I a masochist? Now that I had it all, why was I less than ecstatic? Sure, there was an occasional challenge in surgery, there was an occasional kudo thrown my way, and I was accepted in the ophthalmic community; but something was missing.

I had grown accustomed to the challenge, to the fight against overwhelming odds. Now that it was gone I felt as if I had lost a friend. I realized then why I had been depressed the day I had opened my new office. I had foreseen this moment, when I would move from a sideshow tent to the main arena. It was the deserved reward for all the struggle, yet subconsciously I was not able to accept it.

That evening, I sat in the nightclub at Caesar's Palace with Joe and Cheryl. Vic Damone was on stage. He was singing, loose and easy, joking with the audience, having one hell of a good time. It looked so natural. Vic didn't have a big voice, just a pleasant one. What the hell was that feeling inside of me?

I couldn't believe it! I had succeeded beyond my wildest dreams in ophthalmology and yet I was *jealous* of Vic Damone. I wanted to be on that stage, and what is more ridiculous, I had never sung before a live audience. I had this crazy idea that, at age forty-four, I wanted to become a singer. My blood raced through my body as my tired bones vibrated to the thought of a new challenge. I wanted to be able to perform like Vic did. With a big band behind me, a swinging microphone in my hand, I wanted to make people laugh at my jokes and cry at my sad songs.

Just at a time when I should have been able to relax and enjoy it, to reap the harvest of twelve years of frustration, sacrifice, and hard labor, here I was feeling jealous of a performer, who, given the opportunity, might have gladly changed places with me.

I left Las Vegas the next day to go back to my practice, my family, the magical life I had created. It occurred to me that I had done what I had set out to do when I saw that magazine

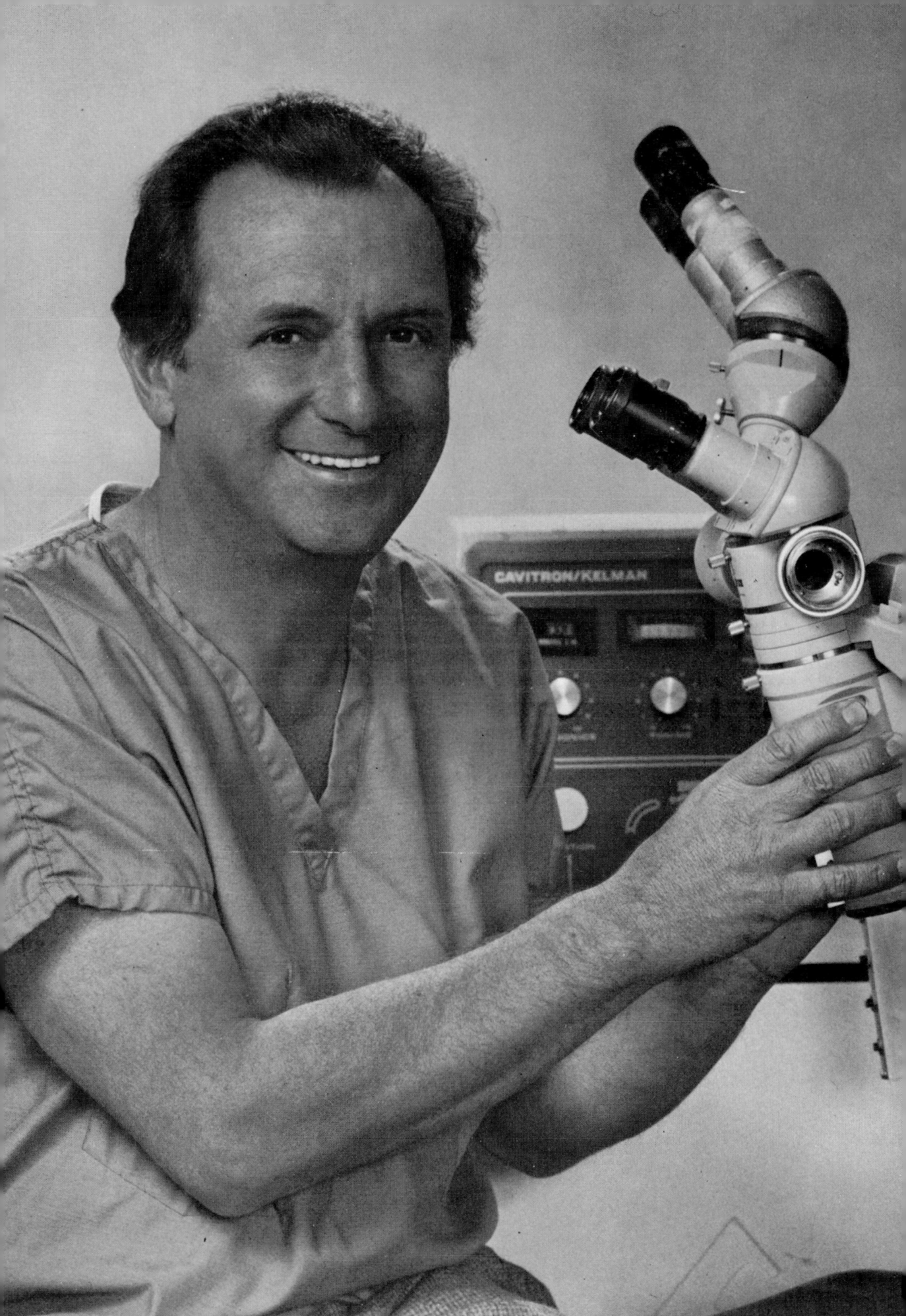

Setting up microscope

Marty Fox

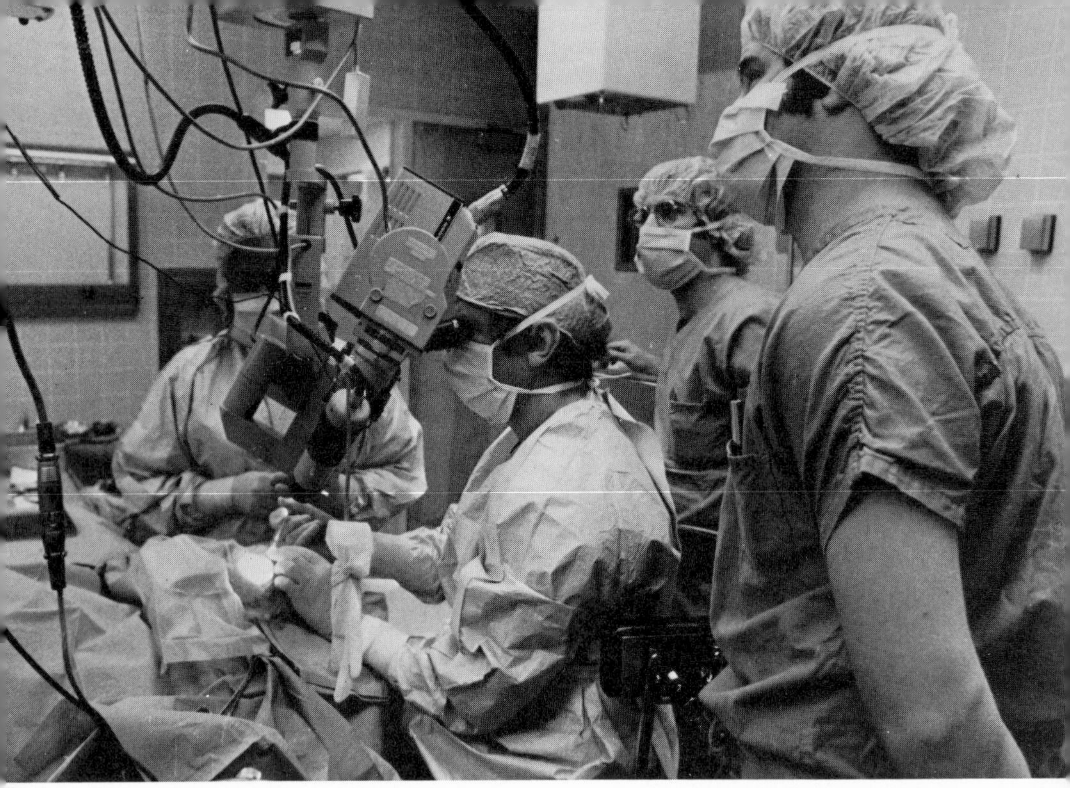

Performing Phacoemulsification *Kelman Research Foundation*

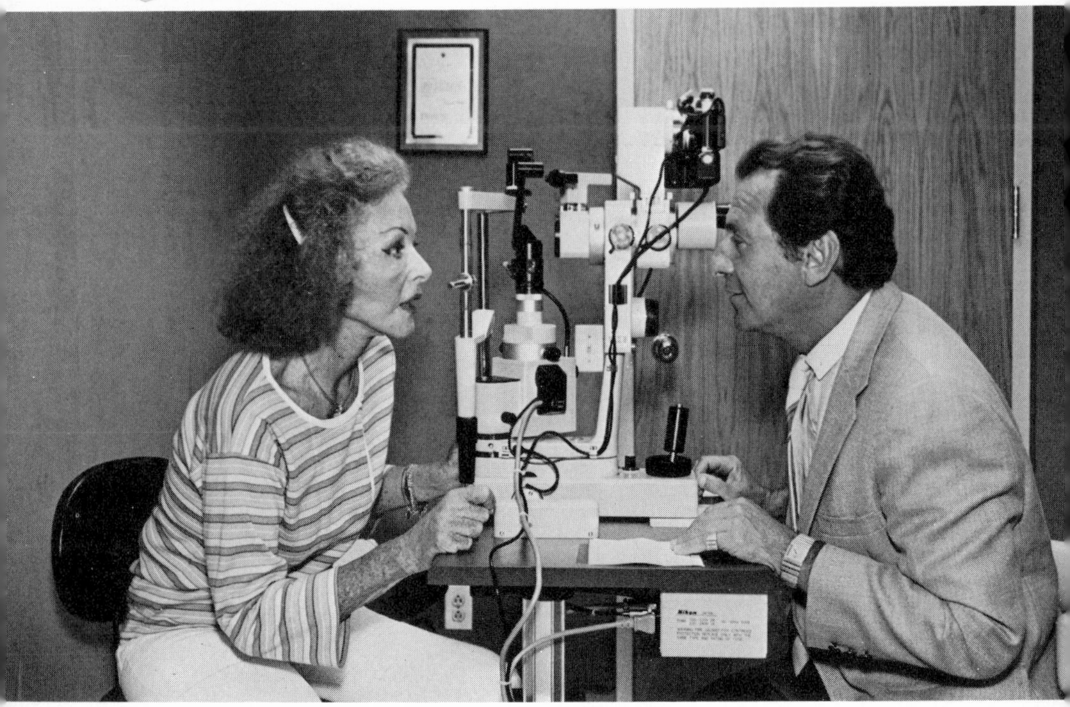

Examining Hedy Lamarr, 1984 *Marty Fox*

At the Regency Hotel in New York with Golda Meir, 1975

Visiting Senator Robert Packwood in Washington, D.C.
Office of Senator Robert Packwood

Jan Peerce and William B. Williams one day after surgery

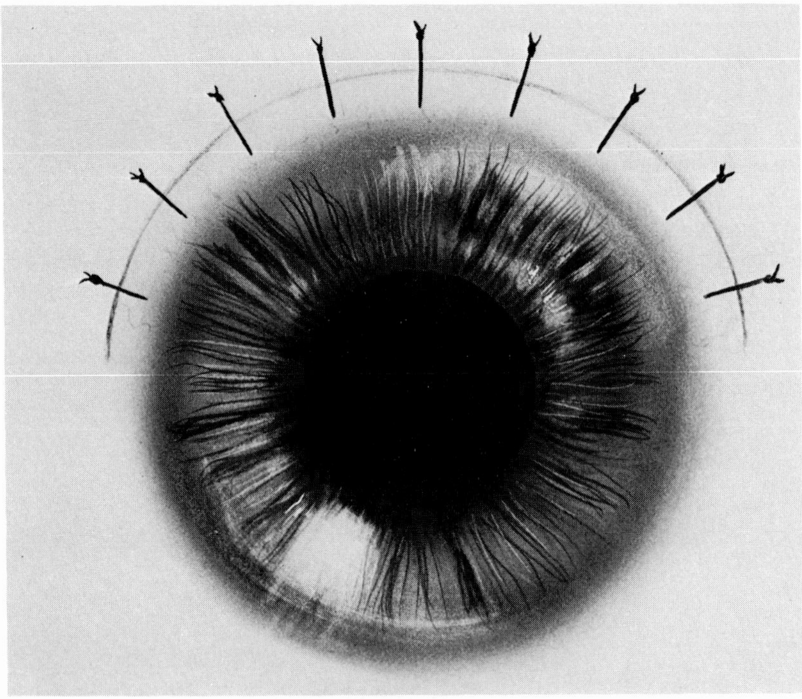
Drawing by Ron Lotozo

Large incision for standard or Cryo extraction cataract (freezing)

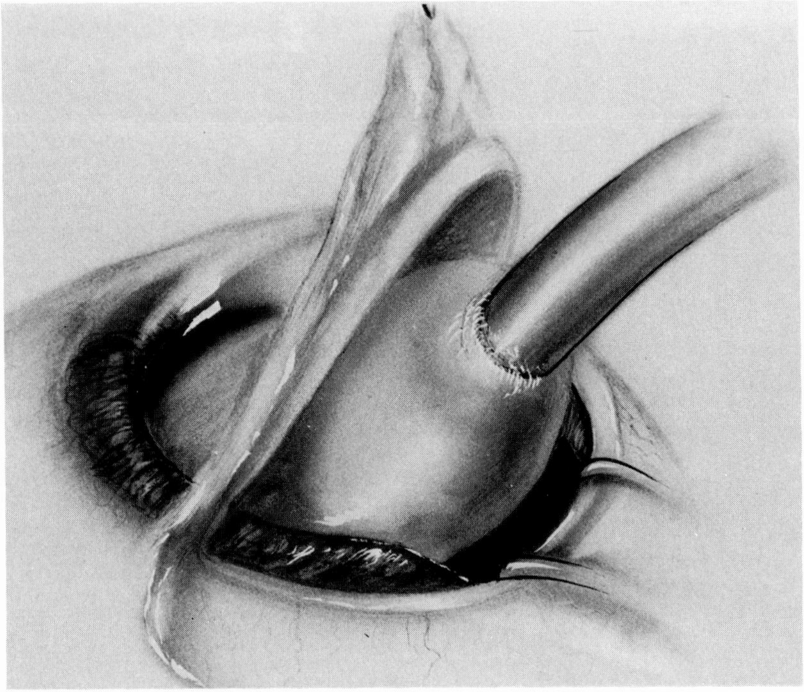
Drawing by Ron Lotozo

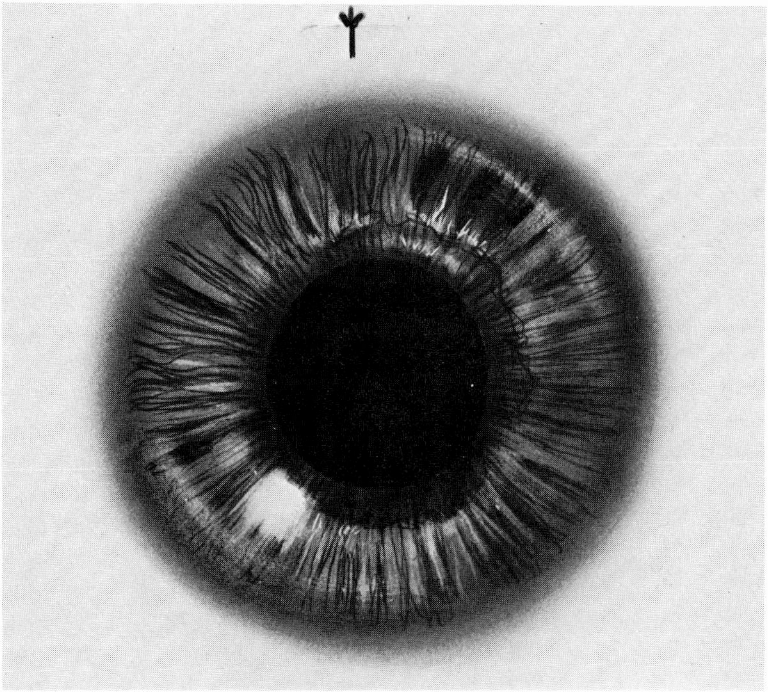

Drawing by Ron Lotozo

Small incision for Phacoemulsification cataract

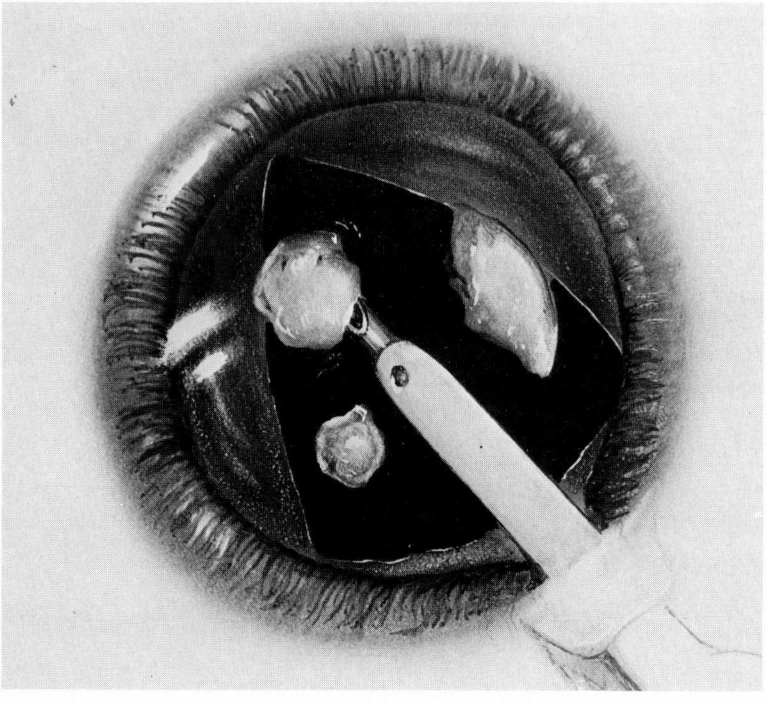

Drawing by Ron Lotozo

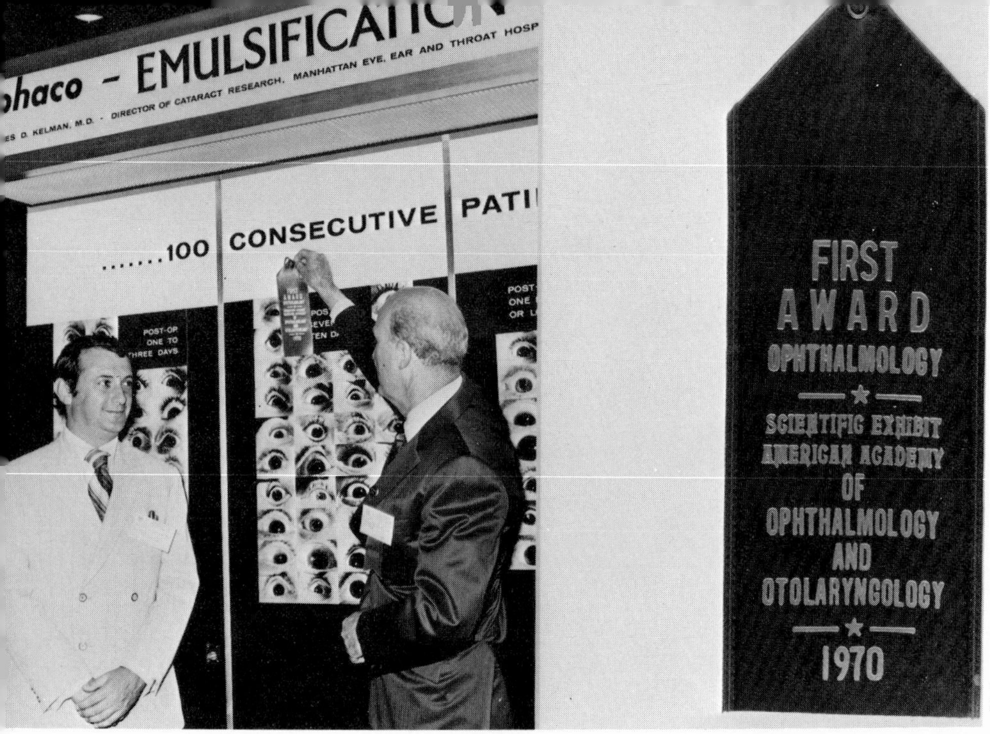

Kelman Research Foundation

Recognition of the American Academy of Ophthalmology, 1970

Kelman Research Foundation

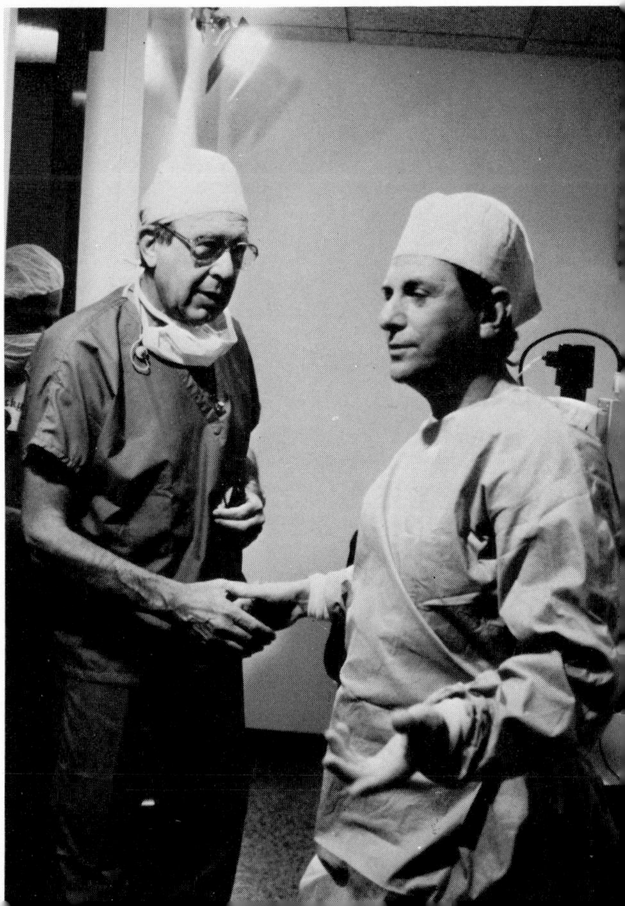

After performing a live Phacoemulsification and lens implant on the *Today* show with Frank Fields as commentator

With Joey Heatherton prior to Carnegie Hall concert, 1976 *Courtesy Bob Perilla*

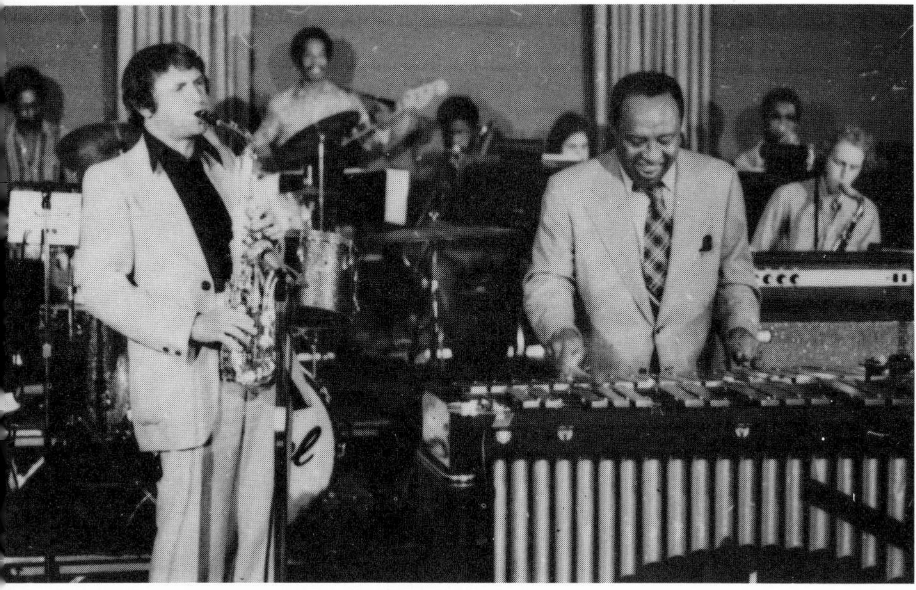

Jazz concert with Lionel Hampton, 1978

Courtesy Charles Kelman

Performing with Lester Lanin on a cruise ship, 1979

Courtesy Charles Kelman

Commuting by helicopter. No traffic jams up here.

article on Irving Cooper. I wondered if he was satisfied with *his* life. . . .

It came to me in a taxi driving from the heliport to my office. We passed an advertisement for Carnegie Hall. It seemed like such a good idea at the time. Why shouldn't *I* sing at Carnegie Hall? The fact that I didn't know how to sing didn't bother me. I had perfect pitch and could carry a tune. Certainly I could learn to improve the quality of my voice. I would give a benefit performance at Carnegie Hall to raise funds for a hospital. It was a natural.

I got back to the office and simply told Joe, "Book Carnegie Hall, I'm going to give a benefit there." Joe somehow knew when not to question me. Then as I became immersed again in my practice, in my teaching, in my flying, I forgot about the whole thing.

A week later, Joe came into my office. "Well, Charley, I signed the contract today.

"What contract?" I asked absently, thinking he was talking about some new piece of equipment that was to be delivered to the office.

"The contract for Carnegie Hall. You have a date! May 5. Signed, sealed, and delivered."

How could I have let him do such a stupid thing? It was one of those ideas that seemed great in the middle of the night, but in the light of morning, it was ridiculous! But here it was, signed, sealed, and delivered. Carnegie Hall. I had one year to get ready for it.

I was incredibly excited. I had a great new challenge, probably an even more impossible one than the others I had undertaken. I was still lecturing, operating, and doing my work in ophthalmology, but I was back where I belonged. I was trying to make it again in show business. It was a disease, but I loved it.

Carlo Menotti was one of the best-known voice teachers in New York, and when I first sang scales for him he gave me the old joke: "Hey, doc, don-a give up-a your day job." He was kidding, but he was serious. When the other students got their lessons, he left his studio open so that those of us in the waiting room could hear the quality of the voice, the soaring vibrato coming from his students' throats. When I sang, he closed the door. I understood, but I was undaunted. I had been told that my "operation" wouldn't work many times in the past. I would make it work.

After six months of lessons, I had progressed one inch. I only had one hundred miles to go. But Carnegie Hall was waiting. It was time to get some experience on stage. I had performed with a saxophone in my mouth many times. But that was not the same. Standing in *front* of the band, with a microphone in my hand, *singing,* was to be a totally different experience.

I decided to give myself some experience. I had joined a tennis club some years before in order to get some exercise. The chairman of the entertainment committee knew that I had written some songs and asked me if I would perform for the club. It was the perfect opportunity.

I hired an arranger. I hired an orchestra. I began taking lessons in performing live on stage, from Bobby Kroll, a well-known coach for Las Vegas people. He was kind and he was patient, and he understood that we were on a crash program. Many nights we worked together in front of my faithful videotape machine, the same one I had used to develop phacoemulsification, until neither one of us could go on. Joan's enthusiasm for my new "career" was less than encouraging.

"You're going to embarrass me," she said. "You can't sing, you can't tell stories, and you're going to make an ass of yourself."

Good! I worked harder. I invited a few of the people in New York that I had operated on to help me do the show. There was "Willie B.," William B. Williams. He would be delighted to introduce me. Lionel Hampton, on whom I had done two cataract operations, was also free that evening and came with his vibraphone.

Shelter Rock Tennis Club was full. Not only did almost every club member attend, but most of them brought guests. It was "Charley Kelman Night." Complete with a large picture on the marquee. One hour before the show, I was still trying to polish my act with Bobby Kroll. I raced over to the club in time to dress in my spangled tuxedo. The band was sensational. The overture I had written was literally and figuratively music to my ears. God, this was fun. It was going to be easy. I was going to be "a Star." I ambled up on stage as William B. Williams introduced me, snapping my fingers just the way Vic had done in Vegas. Here I go! . . .

Halfway through the first song I knew it: I was awful. The expression of those who watched was a mixture of pity and disgust, and I had a full hour to go on stage. I developed "flop sweat," the acute and embarrassing perspiration that plagues performers who know they are bombing out. There was no doubt about it—*I* was bombing out. As a matter of fact, I had already bombed out. But the funeral was going to last another hour. Oh God. I felt like I was back in the operating room with John Martin. I bumbled through the show, wanting to die, and only later, by playing the saxophone with Lionel Hampton, did we save the evening. He is such a great performer that he could save even *that* evening; and I was still pretty good on the sax.

We went out on a twenty-minute chorus of "Flying Home," and everyone left happy. Everyone except me. I had six months to go before Carnegie Hall. We had already sold most of the tickets to patients and their relatives, and I would have a full house. It was a desperate situation. There didn't seem any way that I could overcome it. But it was familiar ground, and I loved it. I was home again—behind the proverbial eight ball.

At about that time, I got a call from an ophthalmologist in Philadelphia. One of his patients, a heavyweight champion boxer, had developed a traumatic cataract. Did I think my operation would be safer for a boxer than the standard operation with a large incision? Did I? It was like asking if I thought the sun was warmer than the moon.

Joe Frazier was big, and when he sat in my examining chair, looking into the slit lamp, it was like being face to face with a Sherman tank. He did have a cataract. After the surgery it would take about six months before his eye could withstand a blow; that was exactly the time he had before meeting Ali in the ring for the heavyweight title. But the operation had to be a secret, I was told.

I admitted him to Lydia Hall Hospital, a small private institution on Long Island, where there would be less of a chance of his being traced. Joe Smith was the name he chose to use. The surgery was easy. He was a young man, and with the phaco operation, only a tiny slit had to be made, only slightly wider than a toothpick. If Joe had had the standard operation, he would not have been able to fight for at least a year, and maybe more. The case went very smoothly, with no complications. He had shaved his head at that time, but in spite of that, I think a few of the orderlies recognized him.

I got an urgent message to see him, about an hour after the case. I rushed to his room.

"Howard Cosell got wind of something, doc. He may be sending someone over to check it out. Doc, get me out of here."

"Don't worry," I said. "I'll take you to my house."

Joe packed his things quickly, and we went out the back way. I stopped on the way to telephone Joan. "Guess who's coming to dinner?" I said.

With five months to go before Carnegie Hall, my opponents played one more card. They were able to get my operation classified as experimental by the United States government. That meant patients could not get reimbursed by Medicare. That meant doctors would not get reimbursed by Medicare. That meant from one day to the next, in hundreds of hospitals all over the country, the use of my technique and my instrument was discontinued. Stopped cold!

For every inch I had advanced, I was pushed back a half inch. But still, there was a half inch of progress. I remembered reading something which stuck in my mind: "No man, or organization, is strong enough to resist an idea whose time has come." The time had come for phacoemulsification. Thousands of cases were being done every month, by more than a thousand eye surgeons. Many "greats," from all walks of life, had had their cataracts removed by this technique, and had been able to return to their activities immediately.

Many of these patients, scheduled to have their second eye operated on, were told that the government had declared the operation experimental. There was an uproar in every city and town. For the first time since I began the development of the operation I was not alone. I had hundreds upon hundreds of ophthalmologists, and thousands upon thousands of patients to stand beside me, all of us exerting pressure on whatever political figures we could find. The friend I had made a few years back, my accountant, now handled all my financial affairs. Mike Temkin recommended a major law firm in Washington. The efforts of that office, combined with the efforts of my colleagues and their patients, succeeded in having the decision of the government reversed. Two months later, phacoemulsification was once again accepted as a bona-fide method of cataract removal.

It had only taken two months, but they were two *precious* months. Although I was still able to take my singing, dancing, and performing lessons, plus do ten to twenty cataract operations per week, I had had to spend a great deal of time mustering the forces to effect that turnabout decision. Now I only had three months to go before I was to step onto the stage at Carnegie Hall.

The pace of my efforts increased; I would wake at six in the morning and jog for a half hour. This was supposed to be good not only for the heart, but for the lungs. It would make my voice stronger, Carlo Menotti said, so I ran. After that, I would start singing scales, first singing in the shower, and then singing right through breakfast, and then still singing during the commute into New York, whether by helicopter or automobile.

I once neglected to shut off my microphone in the helicopter after talking to the tower at La Guardia Airport; for ten minutes all small aircraft had to be delayed because of my singing. No messages could get through to the air controllers from other private pilots. Fortunately, the airlines were on a different frequency. When I got a complaint from the controllers, I sent them tickets to my show at Carnegie Hall.

After seeing my patients in the office, I would hurry to Menotti's studio for a voice lesson, and then on to Bobby Kroll for "interpretation" lessons. Bobby taught me to feel every word, experience every emotion, suffer or rejoice as each song might dictate.

After returning to the office and finally back home, I would practice my saxophone and also the guitar. And then, in my studio, which I dubbed the "war room," I would perform a song while recording it on videotape. I watched the tape after that, looking for ways to improve. It was crazy, it was frantic—it was wonderful.

In New York there are several nightclubs where young performers can try out their acts. I had learned one important thing from my first appearance at Shelter Rock Tennis Club: People want to be entertained. If someone has an incredibly great voice, that voice alone can be entertaining. I did not have an incredibly great voice, not even an incredibly good one—not even good—just passable. But it wasn't enough to entertain. I needed an act.

I canceled all but the most urgent surgical cases for the next two months, and I haunted the clubs around New York, looking for style. Looking for material. Getting up on the stage myself and trying out the things I had written. During the day, I worked in front of the videotape machine, trying to polish my delivery.

As immersed as I was, I still kept up with what was happening in my field. The big news was intraocular lenses. Implants. No one was talking about my operation anymore because of all the excitement about these implants.

When I thought about it, I felt my gut tighten. Damn. I had missed the boat on this one. In spite of all the excitement with Carnegie Hall, I still didn't want to be a has-been in my field. I spent a night, a precious night away from my rehearsals, reading everything I could about these tiny little plastic lenses that were put into the patient's eye after cataract surgery. Instead of having to wear thick glasses, or to bother with a contact lens, the patient was able to see in most cases perfectly with no glasses, thanks to this marvelous advance from England.

A Dr. Ridley had observed that World War Two fighter pilots who had had plexiglass windshields shattered by bullets, often had splinters of plexiglass inside the eye. After observing that these plexiglass splinters created no problems, that they were well tolerated by the eye, he made some tiny lenses and started putting them in cataract patients after the surgery. In some cases the results were spectacular; in other cases, the eyes did poorly. It seemed to me, to be a question not of the material—not the plexiglass—but more of the design used. The crucial question seemed to be how the implant was held inside of the patient's eye.

I started looking at the designs in the literature, and I didn't like what I read. They seemed to be all wrong from a mechanical standpoint. If they moved about inside the eye, they created an irritation, just the way a loose shoe would irritate the foot. The ones being used were stiff, and they were shaped in such a way that they seemed to be either unstable or else very thick and cumbersome. The worst part of it all was that in order to insert these lenses inside the eye, a large incision had to be made. That meant the benefits of the small incision, the benefits of my operation of phacoemulsification, would be lost. I had to admit to myself that a rapid recovery after cataract surgery was in no way as important as the final result. With my operation through the small incision, the patient had to wear thick glasses or a contact lens. There didn't seem to be any way to get a really stable lens inside the eye through a small incision. Everything I had worked for was going up in smoke. While I had been frittering away my time in frivolous pursuits, my profession was passing me by.

It seemed to me the ideal shape for an implant would be a large triangle with widespread fixation of the three feet, sort of like a tripod that's used for photography. I drew that shape on a piece of paper.

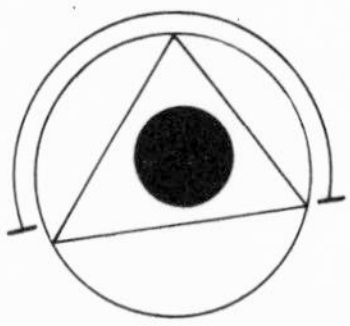

Since the material wasn't soft enough to fold or bend, it seemed as if I had painted myself into a corner. There would be no way to get a large triangle, with the sides measuring a half an inch, inside an incision which measured a quarter of an inch.

I went to sleep with my mind vacillating between lyrics for songs and triangles in eyes.

When I awoke in the morning, I had the answer. I called my friend Ralph Crump, the engineer who had developed the freezing probe with me. "There's no way you can get a large triangle inside of a tiny slit, Kelman," he said. "If you can show me how you do it, we'll make it for you. But I'd be willing to bet you can't."

He was in my office the next day, and I showed him my sketch.

"God, that's so simple. I think we're in business, Charley."

I had Joe sign me up to give some lectures after Carnegie Hall on the use of this implant. I had never tried it, I had never had it in my hands, but I knew it would work.

I put it out of my mind and dove back into the routine of my rehearsals.

A month before Carnegie Hall, Carlo Menotti started leaving the door open when I sang. At first just a crack, and then all the way. My performances at small clubs were much improved, and I was even asked to return. Charlie Grean, my musical director and conductor, was preparing musical arrangements for a complete orchestra: sax section, trumpet and trombone section, rhythm section, and a full string section.

I was, of course, still practicing ophthalmology at the same time, and one day I was surprised when Diane, my administrative secretary, announced that Barbara Walters was there to see me. In she came—a dynamo—with her entourage: a medical doctor, an optometrist, and a psychologist. They had decided that Barbara's father, Lou Walters (who owned the Latin Quarter, one of New York's landmark nightclubs), would be operated on by me in Florida. He was in a nursing home there, had only one eye, and couldn't be moved to New York City for the surgery.

I had no license to operate in Florida, but between Barbara and myself, we were able to get a temporary license for me—for a day—to operate.

During the days just before and after surgery I got to know Barbara. Underneath her tough exterior was a warm and even slightly vulnerable lady. When it was all over and Lou Walters was reading the newspaper again, Barbara said, "I never asked what your fee is, Charles. Now I'm afraid to ask. What do I owe you?"

"A favor," I said. "I will be performing in Carnegie Hall soon for a charity, and I would like you to help me publicize the event so that we can raise some real money. I'd like to be on the 'Today' show."

Barbara brushed that request aside with "It's really not up to me. My producer decides who will appear on the show. You would have to see him."

I looked her in the eye and said, "Call him, now." She did.

He arranged for an audition. When it was over, he said, "Doc, you're not the greatest singer."

"I know that," I replied.

"You're only a fair comedian," he continued.

"I know that too," I persisted.

"But you do play a hell of a saxophone."

"So?" I smiled.

"So—you're on the show."

At the start of the interview, Barbara Walters held the microphone in front of me in a typical interviewer style for me to reply to a question. In a not-so-typical response, I firmly took the microphone from her—much to her surprise—and, a not-so-great singer sang, a fair comedian told jokes, and a jazz saxophonist played on the "Today" show, in New York City.

Some months later, I operated on her mother—both eyes.

The first rehearsal for Carnegie Hall with the orchestra, one week prior to the event, was one of the biggest thrills of my life. Most of the songs I was doing were original ones, and to hear them come to life in a studio, being played by the finest musicians in New York, was an unimaginable fantasy come true. I was never happier in my life than during those final days before Carnegie Hall.

Charlie Grean was an old pro. He had written many songs himself, including "The Thing," and had conducted for Jack Paar in the height of Paar's career. He had reluctantly agreed to conduct in Carnegie Hall as a favor, probably out of friendship for Irv Siders, a mutual friend and a theatrical producer, to whom I had gone for advice when I needed a conductor. Now, I was excited because even Grean was getting excited. I could see his face light up when I was belting out a note with that great orchestra behind me.

Many people suggested that this concert, because it was being done for charity, and because it was so unusual, deserved to get promotion on Johnny Carson's "Tonight" show. Many people, some well placed in the business, said that they would arrange for me to appear on the show. They did not realize that for every person who appears on the Carson show, hundreds were rejected.

Irv Siders came to me about a week before Carnegie Hall. "Why don't you get on the Carson show, Charley?"

"Are you kidding? Everyone says they can get me on, but no one has done it."

"You want to get on? I'll get you on."

Irv went to the phone and dialed California. After a few secretaries transferred the call, he was saying, "Hello, Johnny! Listen, I've got this crazy doctor friend who is going to do a benefit. . . ."

Within minutes I was rushing to pack my bag to go to the Coast. I was to audition and then the talent managers would decide whether they wanted me. Irv had done what he could. The rest was up to me.

The talent director who interviewed me loved some of the crazy stories I told about my life and my profession. He liked the way I played and sang—and that was it! I was on the show! It was to be for Thursday night. I was going to be on the "Tonight" show. Was this really happening?

With just about everybody in the world I knew alerted to watch me that Thursday night, I dressed in the hotel to go to the studio. Irv Siders and Charlie Grean had come with me to California. We were all as excited as we could possibly be. Just before I left for the studio, the call came: My appearance had been cancelled! There had been a holdover from the night before, and Johnny was very sorry. I would, however, probably be on the next evening. *Probably!*

We called as many people as we could in New York to let them know that it had been cancelled. After a couple of hours, all the calls were made. We were down, but we were not out. Tomorrow was another day. If I did not get on the show on Friday, though, I would not get on. The following week Carson was to be in Las Vegas. And I had to be back in New York preparing for Carnegie Hall.

I sat in the Green Room, watching the early part of the Carson show. George Segal was the first guest. He was good. He was funny. He was too good. He was too funny. Carson was keeping him on too long. He had occupied two slots. Damn, damn. I blew air into my saxophone to keep it warm, and wondered whether I would get to play it.

David Brenner was next. He was too good. He was too funny. Time was running out. There was room for only *one more act.* Los Trabajeros, or me. They sat on one side of the

Green Room strumming their guitars, looking menacingly at me. I sat on the other side blowing air into my saxophone, looking menacingly at them. I had a sinking feeling about the whole thing. Any moment the producer would come into the Green Room and call either them or me. The door opened and he walked in. "Dr. Kelman," he began.

I shot up. "Yes, here I am."

"I'm sorry, doc. Johnny wants the Los Trabajeros on next. There won't be time for you. I'm really sorry."

I was most concerned about all the people who would be watching and waiting for me to appear and then having a good laugh at my expense. No one liked being laughed at, and I was no exception. Los Trabajeros flashed triumphant gold smiles as they left the room preparing to go in the wings. I put my horn away, and closed the saxophone case.

Then, suddenly, the producer was back. "Doc, doc, you're on! You're on. Johnny changed his mind. He wants *you.*"

It's about a hundred yards from the Green Room to the backstage entrance leading to the stage. I ran the hundred yards while trying to put my horn together. I was halfway there when I heard Johnny announcing me. I ran faster.

"Yes, that's what I said," Johnny chuckled. "We have a singing ophthalmologist. Here he is"—I wasn't quite there yet—"Dr. Charles Kelman."

I just made it to the back of the curtain. I jammed my saxophone into the hands of a stagehand, stopped short, and stepped out as casually as I could in front of twelve million people. I was just a little out of breath.

Johnny had been given a few notes, taken during the talent interview. He had never seen me before, but he knew the subjects we would talk about. He is a master at what he does, and puts his guests in a situation where they are shown off to their best advantage. Not only can Johnny provoke you to say funny things, but when you do, he can top them. He led into a question that allowed me to tell my story—the one the talent agent had liked the most. The one about the monkey.

Several years before, I had been in Bologna, Italy, at an

international conference, where I lectured and performed surgery, which was televised for five hundred Italian ophthalmologists. That afternoon a professor at Bologna cornered me and asked if I would do him a favor.

It seemed that a very important Sicilian (he didn't say Mafia, but I got the message) had been married for many years. He and his wife had never had children, but they did have a pet monkey—a very intelligent monkey. A monkey they loved and cherished. I was told that this monkey was able to perform many amazing feats, such as using the telephone and being able to dial a simple number. At dinner parties, to show off his monkey, the host would have the monkey dial a number. The monkey never missed. It was always the Sicilian's mother on the phone. Johnny and the audience were laughing pretty hard at this point.

I said to Johnny, "This is a true story, Johnny!"

"Well, you couldn't be making this up," he said. The audience roared.

I continued my story. Lately, the monkey had been dialing the wrong number. It seems the monkey had cataracts. The professor wanted me and only me to remove them. I explained to him that the operation would be easy, but that anesthesia on monkeys is very delicate. I had had enough experience with monkeys during my laboratory days. The anesthesiologist must be a specialist in veterinary medicine, I told him. He assured me that such a man would be available and I agreed to do the case.

That night many notables in the field of ophthalmology came to watch the surgery. Phaco was still a great novelty in Europe in those days. The Sicilian and his wife arrived, tenderly carrying the baby-blue blanket with a tiny creature inside of it.

In the operating room the monkey was very cute, pinching the nurses and jabbering away excitedly, as if he were at a cocktail party. While I prepared my instruments and the machine, I saw the anesthesiologist, Dr. Lasagna, take an enormous syringe and swiftly inject every drop of it into the monkey. The monkey, who had been chattering excitedly, suddenly stopped, his head lolling to the side. I looked at the professor alongside of me, and nudged him with my elbow.

"That monkey's dead," I said. "Lasagna just killed the monkey."

"No. No. Start the operation. Start the operation."

I started the operation. I'm not an expert on monkeys, after all, and I thought perhaps the monkey was under deep anesthesia. It wasn't. A few minutes into the operation Dr. Lasagna threw up his hands and loudly cried, *"Morto! Morto!"*

"He's been *morto* for twenty minutes," I said.

I just wanted to get the hell out of there. I dressed as quickly as I could and had no intention of stopping to speak to the "family." I was now running toward my car in the parking lot. I thought I was moving fast, but Dr. Lasagna made me look like I was standing still.

When I finished the story, Johnny asked me to sing and play with the band. I thought of my dad, wishing he could see me now—hoping that he somehow could.

After the show, Johnny put his hand on my shoulder and said, "Doc, if I had known you were going to be that funny, I would have put you on *first.*" Twelve million people knew my monkey story. I was on my way to Carnegie Hall.

Soon, Irv Siders was wearing a gold watch, which I had inscribed: OTHERS BUZZ, IRV DOES.

21

Here's Charley!

The seats that remained to be sold went quickly after the Carson show. After telling Carson my monkey story, the song I did was "To See a Butterfly." I wrote it about a little blind girl who, one day in my office, told me about the things she would like to see someday.

How I'd love to see . . . a butterfly
a butterfly fly away
And I'd love to see the flowers blooming
and to watch the sun turn red each day

How I'd love to see my daddy smile
when I sit on his knee
and someday when I have my own children
how I pray that they'll see me.

I can hear a world of laughter—
lovely sounds, they seem enchanted
Yet I miss the only thing, the very thing
you take for granted

Open up your eyes and you'll see me
that's all you have to do
And someday if I am really lucky,
I'll see butterflies . . . and you.

I got more than a hundred requests after that program for copies of the song. I was planning to perform it in Carnegie Hall.

After a blur of rehearsals, tuxedo fittings, appearances on the "Today" show with the incredible Barbara Walters, and then more rehearsals, that Saturday arrived. I was ready. I knew it. I walked into Carnegie Hall at 6:00 P.M. and stood on the empty stage, wondering how I would feel in just two and a half hours. I imagined the applause, I imagined the laughter, I imagined the tears.

I went upstairs to dress, to put on makeup, and to do all the other things a performer has to do before his show. My invited guest performers on that program were William B. Williams as master of ceremonies, Jan Peerce, and Lionel Hampton. They had all been operated on by me. They all were happy to devote their time. I was going to do the first forty-five minutes and after the intermission, Jan Peerce and Lionel Hampton would each do twenty. Then I was going to close the show with the orchestra.

I peeked out of the small opening in the dressing room provided to allow the performer to see the size of the house. It was full. I saw Joan and my children in the front row. No matter how she tried to dissuade me from starting a second "career," when the time actually came, she was of great help. She sold tickets to her friends from various organizations, and now before the show, she was gaily, if somewhat nervously, greeting those in the audience whom she knew.

My mother, whom I would later introduce during the show, was about to burst with pleasure. My sister, Ruth, and brother-in-law, Bob, and the rest of my family were all there down front in the one-hundred-dollar seats.

I could feel the electricity in the air. For many of the patients who had come it was their first time in Carnegie Hall. One doctor, Moshe Lazar, flew over from Israel, just for the show. Another doctor and his wife, Eric and Veronica Arnott, came from London. Patients came from as far away as California. I have often thought about the emotion I experienced before that show, sitting up in that dressing room. I had wanted to be alone before the performance, and except for Joan and the kids, who only stayed a minute, no one had been allowed to come up.

As many times as I have thought about it, the feeling that I remember having was a religious one. I was so thankful to have been given the gifts that I had—the gift of invention, of music, of friendship, of perseverance, and above all the love of so many people—that I did something that I hadn't done since I was hanging from a cliff in Switzerland: I prayed. But it was not a prayer of supplication, rather it was one of thanks. I finished my prayer by saying, "I'm not going to let you down tonight, God. Don't worry."

Then it was time for me to go downstairs. The band was tuning up softly and the overture was about to begin. Joe was backstage handling a million details. Charlie Grean, in his tails, said casually, "Give 'em hell." Hymie Schertzer, the man who had played the alto solo in Benny Goodman's "Sing, Sing, Sing," and who had been one of my saxophone teachers when I was a boy, was playing lead alto sax. Ron Odrich, another special and good friend, was playing sax and clarinet. Ron, in addition to being a professional musician, also happens to be one of the best periodontists in New York.

The sound of the audience from behind the curtain was deafening. People were calling to each other from across the aisles, patients who hadn't seen each other since their operation, others who hadn't spoken to each other for years—doctors, family, friends—all playing an important part in this happening. And a happening it was. Then the lights dimmed. . . .

The overture was being played on a simple piano, in front of the curtain. The audience did not even know that there was a full orchestra behind that curtain. Lanny Myers, one of New York's finest pianists, arpeggio-ed his way through the songs I had written for the show. My heart was racing with excitement. I was not afraid. I was just nervous.

And then William B. Williams was out there. I could hear the audience laughing at his jokes. He was poking good-natured fun at me as a singer and as an entertainer, thanking me for having saved his sight. It must have been very easy for many people in the audience to identify with him. If anyone was going to step out onto a stage with the dice loaded in his favor, it was me.

And then the curtain opened, and the orchestra filled the hall with sound. I was on stage, making the moves I had rehearsed, flipping the microphone cord the way I had learned, looking down into the faces of my wife—who seemed happier than I had ever seen her—my children, and my friends. The lyric I wrote for my opening number told the story.

I've done a lot of things all through the years
crazy and wild things in many careers,
but in my book here's the craziest of all
WHAT AM I DOING IN CARNEGIE HALL?

I'm not a singer, my voice might just crack
For fancy dancing I don't have the knack
I'm not really handsome, and certainly not tall
so WHAT AM I DOING IN CARNEGIE HALL?

It's a silly thing for me to be up here
there's no way to disguise it
it's insane, who denies it?
but I did realize it

Let's set the record straight once and for all
If you think I'm nuts, and "over the wall"
You bought the tickets . . . just think about that
You paid to hear me sing flat . . . IN CARNEGIE HALL.

It was all there. The applause, the laughter, the love. And then the band was moving into the next number, which was a hit at the time, "You're the Best Thing That Ever Happened to Me."

During the intermission, the dressing room was swamped. No one could believe that I had done it, least of all myself. I still had the second part of the second act to do, but the first part had gone so well that I was more confident now.

Jan Peerce was warm and wonderful. He, too, referred to his operation and how it had changed his life. And then he sang. Jan Peerce did not need jokes to carry his act. He had an incredibly great voice. He finished "Blue Bird of Happiness" to an ovation.

Lionel Hampton, an habitué of Carnegie Hall, having returned many times with his own band, came on stage like he was walking into his own living room. When, after half an hour, he finished with his famous "Flying Home," the reaction from the crowd was that accorded any rock star. They were screaming, they were whistling, they were jumping up and down. I came out and did an original number with him and then I was back alone on stage again.

I closed the show by thanking them for coming. By thanking my family for their patience with me, by singing the song about the little blind girl, "To See a Butterfly." I didn't think the crowd had any energy left to applaud and to react after Lionel's performance, but they did. They had saved something for me . . . plenty. I must have taken a dozen bows before it was over.

Sunday, the day after Carnegie Hall, was spent with my family, reliving those golden moments until finally Joan said to me, "Well, at last that's over. I hope now you have this out of your system." I never told her about my own doubts.

I had begun to wonder: Would I give up ophthalmology for show business if I had the chance? Now that I had a taste of performing again, it would be hard to resist a bona-fide offer to continue as a professional. I knew that many people in show business had seen the Carnegie Hall performance and wondered if anything would come of it. I also wondered how I would respond to any offer. I didn't have long to wait for the answer.

Monday morning the first call came. It was from a producer who had seen me on the Carson show. The opening act at a large Miami hotel had cancelled because of illness and if I could get down to Miami that night, I would have my shot in the real world of show biz. Was this really happening? He had to know immediately so that if I couldn't do it he could get someone else. He said that it didn't pay much, but that it would be a nice way for me to start. Little did he know I would gladly have paid *him* at that point. I had given myself a few days off after Carnegie Hall to recuperate from all the excitement and so I was free and I was able to do it.

"I'll be there for rehearsal this afternoon." I hung up the phone and started singing my scales again. God, it was Kerry Adams, boy singer, all over again. I started to pack a suitcase. I was on my way. It was funny that I didn't even have to think twice about it.

About an hour later the next call came. "Dr. Kelman, this is Dr. Robert Stillben," the voice said. "Please excuse me for calling you at home, but this is urgent."

"Go ahead," I said impatiently. I often got calls from doctors wanting information about my operation, or from doctors actually doing it who wanted advice. I always did my best to accommodate them. But of all days, this was not one when I wanted to spend time on the telephone.

"Your machine works on cataracts," Stillben said. "Does it work on any other tissue?" I was intrigued. I put down the shirts I was holding.

"Yes, I tried it on liver, kidney, fatty tissues and it works fine. You need a different power for the different types of tissues, of course," I said.

"How about the brain?" he asked.

"Yeah, sure. It will eat out any soft tissue like that. I always wanted to find a brain surgeon and have him try it on some difficult case."

"You just found one," he said. "I'm a neurosurgeon and I have a case that can't be done any other way. It is virtually inoperable. It's a tumor right on the nerve fibers, at the base of the brain. Will your machine be able to dissect off the tumor without destroying the underlying nerves and blood vessels?"

"Yes, if you use a lower power, it will. Nerve cells and tumor cells are softer than the nerve fibers," I explained.

"I want to try it," he said.

"O.K., but right now I'm on my way to Miami. I should be back in a week."

"We don't have a week," he said. "The tumor is choking off the nerve and will destroy the function at the base of the brain. This kid could be dead by the end of the week or at least paralyzed."

"What kid?" I asked for no reason, just to give myself time to think.

"My patient. He's a seven-year-old boy." He paused. "He's a real nice kid, Dr. Kelman. How long would it take me to learn how to use your machine?"

"About a day," I said. I was being torn in half.

"Could you teach me tomorrow, please," he begged. "Could you postpone your trip?"

"Let me have your number, I'll call you back in less than an hour."

"Please try, Dr. Kelman. It's his only hope."

I hung up and stared out the window for a few minutes. I could have one of my associates teach this brain surgeon. But then I had a flash of me singing on a stage in Florida while a brain operation was being performed with my machine. Even for a Gemini, this seemed incongruous. Then I heard a voice as if he were standing there next to me. I guess he really was. "Be anything you want, Charlie—but first be a doctor."

"Thanks, Dad," I said aloud, suddenly finding myself with tears on my cheek.

It wasn't such a hard decision after all. I worked with Still-ben all the next day, and Wednesday I watched as he removed a tumor from the base of the brain, easy as pie.

22

People, Now

Many things happened after Carnegie Hall.

Joe, my administrator, went back to his home in Philadelphia. He is now working for one of my students.

Cheryl, my faithful first assistant, got married and lives in Florida.

Otto, the master machinist who not only made instruments but gave encouragement, at age ninety is living in Germany.

Ralph Crump, the man who built my first cryo instrument while on the verge of bankruptcy, developed Frigitronics into a multimillion-dollar public corporation. One of the most successful ventures of this corporation was the branch that made intraocular lenses. The lens that I had given to Ralph Crump to manufacture just before Carnegie Hall, and its successors which I designed, became one of the largest factors in the company's success. Since then I have designed other lenses for other companies, and the Kelman Intraocular Lenses are among the world's most widely used today.

Sirotka, the chief of the Eye Department at Mid-Cities Hospital, spent a fortune trying to develop a better way of removing cataracts—with a modified water pick—and failed.

Joan and I were divorced in 1979.

Leo Ryan, the principal who would not give me a recommendation to college, came out of retirement to preside at the twenty-fifth reunion of Forest Hills High School. After reading a list of the illustrious alumni from that school, Leo Ryan presented *me* with the award for the most distinguished alumnus in the history of the high school. I did not remind him about our prior encounter decades before that, but I think he knew.

Cavitron modified the Kelman PhacoEmulsifier for brain surgery, and according to Dr. Samuel Kasoff, Director of Neurosurgery at the Westchester County Medical Center, this equipment has been instrumental in saving the lives of dozens of children. Whenever I get to feeling blue, I only have to think about that.

Driscoll bought a Kelman PhacoEmulsifier, but I understand he rarely uses it. Our paths crossed one day in Florence, Italy, where we were both on a medical program. I was seated in the great hall of the Excelsior Hotel having breakfast when I spied Driscoll coming into the room. Although our eyes never met, I was aware of his presence, and I am sure he was aware of mine. He chose to take a table by himself behind me, away from my line of vision. It was time to have some fun.

I was wearing a beeper watch, the kind that if you press a small button, a beeping sound is emitted. The room was appropriately hushed and still except for the occasional clinking of forks against plates. I casually pressed the button and a loud shrill beep could be heard throughout the dining room. I let it beep a couple of times and then put the watch directly in front of my mouth.

"Hello," I shouted into the watch as if it were a telephone. "How are you, Diane? How's the weather in New York?"

I then put the watch to my ear as if listening. During the next three minutes I had a nice conversation with my secretary in New York over my imaginary telephone.

At the end of the conversation, I named the street in Florence where I had purchased this new electronic marvel.

I understand that Driscoll wandered for hours up and down the street looking for it.

I've performed at the Concord Hotel, appeared on many television programs, traveled about the country being a surgeon by day and a performer by night, given dozens of benefit performances for various charitable organizations. In 1976 I was back in Carnegie Hall with a new show for another charity. This time I had *two* singing coaches, having added Marty Lawrence to the fold. Those who saw both said they enjoyed the second even more than the first.

My children, David, Lesley, and Jennifer, all attend college now, and we spend their vacation time together.

I won the American Academy of Achievement award, given to leaders in each field. Salk, Sabin, and Cooley were some of the prior recipients in medicine. I've developed other new surgical ideas and devices. One of them, an intraocular implant used after cataract surgery, is one of the most widely used in the world.

I've become a clinical professor of ophthalmology, and the American Academy of Ophthalmology has made the Kelman Foundation an official part of the program. I've operated on many persons who have become my friends.

Senator Robert Packwood from Oregon and Congressman Guy Vander Jagt from Michigan both came for surgery at around the same time. Meeting these men gave me tremendous respect for the caliber of our elected representatives. Bob Packwood was confident, immensely knowledgeable, and shared with Guy Vander Jagt the gift of doing a lot of active listening. Each man seemed to be intent on learning what *I* knew, and feeling what *I* felt. Guy Vander Jagt's case became an adventure.

He had come to me for several reasons: He had little time for recuperation; Congress was in session; he was concerned about disfigurement; he often spoke in public; and he had been chosen to give the keynote address at the Republican convention. He had a cataract in one eye.

Guy, like Bob Packwood, had that elusive quality, that mysterious ingredient, that indefinable spice called charisma. I had operated on many political figures before him—some of them constantly in the news and prominently known—who'd fly in for a quick operation under an assumed name to avoid the "stigma" of having cataract surgery. To many persons, cataracts unfortunately, ridiculously, equate to old age. Some other Washington patients, concerned that cataracts might signal to their constituents that they were failing, required that secrecy. (Neither Vander Jagt nor Packwood required that.) And so it was not the fact that Guy was a congressman, but rather that he was himself—an ebullient, warm, friendly, and concerned human being—that attracted me to him, and made me want him to be my friend. He, for his part, like most patients, felt a warmth toward his physician and surgeon, and we started our mutual admiration society and friendship.

Guy was excited and proud to be giving the keynote address, and of course expected his eye to be perfectly healed in the three months between the surgery and the address. His other eye was normal, with no sign of a cataract, making me think that perhaps the cataract he had was from some injury so mild that he didn't remember it.

When I operated on his eye, there was the usual heightened awareness that someone very special was on the table. The operation was letter perfect and only took about fourteen minutes. At that time, I was not enthusiastic about placing an implant in his eye, since he was a young man, and could easily, I assumed, handle a contact lens.

My assumption was incorrect. For a brilliant, sophisticated, agile human being, when it came to his contact lens, Guy Vander Jagt was a klutz. I told him that if he ever became president, the Russians would be perfectly safe from a retaliatory attack. Guy's finger would probably miss the missile button.

I spent hours with him, at first trying to teach him to place the lens gently on his eye, and then, when he finally mastered that, teaching him to gently press the lens down toward the bottom of the eye, and then pinch it to lift it off. This was the worst part. Poor Guy would practically gouge his eye out, trying to remove the lens. When he left New York to return to Washington he had a perfect eye, into which he could place a contact lens every morning. But he needed his wife or daughter to remove the lens every evening.

It was exciting to watch the convention on television, and

then to see my friend and patient take the podium and deliver a stirring address. When the camera zoomed in on him, I saw that it was impossible to tell that he had had an operation. Both eyes looked perfect. But wait a minute . . . something was happening. Guy's operated eye was tearing now, and was partially closing. One hundred or more million people watching, and something was going wrong with his eye in front of the whole damn world.

And then it seemed as if Guy looked directly at me, through the television screen, almost giving me an enigmatic smile, while he, in a flash of a second, reached up and deftly plucked the irritating lens from his eye. To anyone else, it probably looked as if he momentarily brushed his eyelashes—no one else would have paid the slightest attention to the gesture. But to me, it was a miracle. Here with most of the civilized world watching, he had succeeded in doing the very thing he had failed to do in the privacy of my office. He then continued his address, which fortunately he had memorized, without interruption.

I couldn't help wonder what he had done with his lens. I didn't find out until later, when I spoke with him on the phone: The next speaker had been George Bush. While the camera stayed zoomed in on Bush's head, two stagehands crept along the floor to the podium, out of sight of the camera, their fingers searching the podium, until one of them felt the slippery lens. With Guy Vander Jagt's lens resting safely in its case, the camera zoomed back and the Republican convention continued without further ado. Sometime later, the New York State senator Al D'Amato read into the *Congressional Record* a description of my work with cataracts.

Recently, a young marine was being honored at the White House. He had lost an arm and one eye in Vietnam. His other eye was badly damaged: He had a traumatic cataract that was mixed with shrapnel, and it was dislocated, the clear jelly (vitreous) having come in front of the cataract. His vision was so poor that he had to hold his head all the way back in an effort to see under his cataract—and with that he was barely able to function. An operation on this eye would be extremely risky, since it could easily lead to the loss of this young man's only eye.

At the White House, after presenting the marine, Wayne Hanby, with a plaque for bravery, the president asked him if there was any service *he* could do for the marine, since Hanby had done so much for the country. Hanby answered "yes." He wanted his eye to be operated on by a surgeon recommended by the president. The president told him that he would recommend a doctor in New York. The marine was given my name.

The operation was extremely difficult. Without the phacoemulsifier, there would have been no way to do this surgery. When it was over, Wayne Hanby was able to see 20/20. He had perfect vision. I wrote to the president, thanking him for giving me the opportunity of serving someone who had given so much to his country.

When I ask myself whether everything I went through was worth it, I have only to read the letter from the White House.

> *Dear Dr. Kelman,*
>
> *I only received your letter today, but let me tell you that it brightened my day. It was wonderful to get the word on Wayne Hanby, and I will spread that word in the West Wing. Thank you for what you did for him and for us. May God bless you.*
>
> *Sincerely yours,*
> *Ronald Reagan*
> *President of the United States of America*

Epilogue

There are many reasons why people write autobiographies. Some do it because they are very famous, and there is a great public demand for information about their private lives. That is not the case with me. Some do it as an ego trip, thinking their lives are so important that everyone should know about them; I don't think that reason applies to me either. Some do it because they think that what has happened to them may be inspirational to others, may help others to succeed, may provide others with useful information. That was my motivation.

Writing an autobiography gives a unique opportunity to review one's life, to evaluate the weaknesses and strengths, to pinpoint the lessons learned, and to make the rest of one's life more meaningful and successful. And so, in reviewing my life, through my eyes, I have had a wonderful chance to reflect on it.

I admit that I may have certain talents as an inventor, musician, and surgeon, but they are nothing compared to my ability to persevere, to keep going in the face of discouragement, to take the blows and stand up again; the ability to be my own best friend. These are certainly key factors in any success story.

One must also have the ability to evaluate the real possibility of success of any given venture, aspiration, or dream. Had my dream been to be an opera star, no matter how hard I tried, I probably would not have made it. It becomes a matter of selecting the *possible* impossible dream. This is really the key to great success—evaluating your own aspirations—not setting them too low, but rather too high . . . just a little too high.

I have often wondered whether this operation could have been developed in today's government-controlled environment. All new machines and devices must be carefully reported to the Food and Drug Administration, with careful controls and safeguards for the patient. After much thought and experience with the FDA, I must conclude that it definitely could have been developed, although it would have taken longer.

The safeguards and controls that the government imposes are no less strict than the ones I impose on myself: never to experiment on any patient except when that patient was a) completely informed of the nature of the new technique, b) informed as to what alternate methods of treatment were available, and c) informed of the risks involved and the probable chance of success. I therefore welcome the "over-the-shoulder" approach to research that the government is taking, although I think this could just as easily (and less expensively) be performed by the medical profession itself. In my case, no patient ended up with less vision than he or she would have had with the more conventional technique, and all were properly informed.

Am I bitter because of the reluctance of the medical profession to accept new ideas? Absolutely not. For every bonafide investigator and idea, there are dozens of quacks and entrepreneurs who might, save for this medical conservatism, foist their dangerous "cures" on the unsuspecting public. If one is to do research in medicine, one must learn that skepticism and restraint are a necessary part of the process.

Do I believe in wholesale slaughter of domestic animals for the sake of research? Reading about the cats in this book might give the reader the impression that I'm all for it. But that would be wrong. I am an animal lover, and have been from childhood, and have always had pets. The animals used in my research were already scheduled to be "put to sleep"—they were homeless and unwanted and would have been destroyed in any case. Those "animal lovers" who have pets and allow them to multiply uncontrollably create the condition of pet surplus.

Cruelty was never part of my research. The animals were properly anesthetized for surgery, and when they were sacrificed, it was done with an injection of a barbiturate: painlessly and humanely. The reader may wonder why "pets" such as cats are used, rather than mice, rats, or guinea pigs. The answer lies in the size of the eye of these animals: the eyes of such rodents are not only too small to deal with surgically, they are too far distant from the structure of the human eye for conclusions to be drawn.

The hundreds, perhaps thousands of infants, children, and adults who can see today owe their vision to the research done on these animals. Certainly none of them would object to having gained their vision at the cost of the life of a cat. Unfortunately, after all the trials on dead tissue, any new technique must pass the test on live tissue. So, better a cat than an infant.

Through my eyes, it was all worth it. I began this book at the age of fifty, and consider myself lucky to have lived the life that I've had. I hope there are more good experiences coming. In any case I take great satisfaction in knowing that now there are many who I have never met, who have never heard of me, but who can see today, because of the work that I was privileged to do.

Recently, I operated on Lee Solomon, a hard-hitting, good-looking, fast-talking agent of the William Morris Agency. "King of Atlantic City" is his nickname, since he books most of the talent for the casinos there. He came into my examining room and told me that I was *going* to operate on his eye, *when* I was going to operate on his eye, and that I had better get a *perfect* result. That was his style. Since he hinted at a "booking" for me in Atlantic City, I operated when he wanted and got the result that he wanted. When it was over, the "booking" turned out to be a table at the show to see Frank Sinatra in Atlantic City—not bad, but not quite the booking I was half hoping for. What the hell. I didn't get mad. I knew I'd get even. I got my chance a few months later.

Lee barged into my office. "Walter Matthau is coming to town and tomorrow you're going to fly him in your chopper up to Connecticut to look at a school for his son."

"Lee," I protested. "I have patients to see all day. I can't do it."

"Cancel the patients. He'll meet you at the heliport at 8:00 A.M." With that he turned and walked out of my office.

The next morning, Walter Matthau and his son were waiting for me at the heliport. After a few pleasantries, we climbed into the helicopter and I took them for a ten-minute sight-seeing ride around Manhattan, finishing up with a breathtaking view of the Statue of Liberty, fifty feet away from her crown. I then flew back to the heliport, where a professional pilot I had hired took over the controls to fly them to Connecticut. I went back to the office.

I arrived just as Lee was telephoning to see if everything had gone off as planned. I signaled my secretary to put him on hold, and then I told her what to say.

"I'll put you through directly to Dr. Kelman in the helicopter," she said sweetly.

"I didn't know he had a phone in the helicopter," Lee said.

"Oh yes," she lied. "He's coming on the line now."

I picked up the phone, turned on my electric razor, and pressed it to the mouthpiece. "Hello, Lee," I shouted into the phone.

"Hey, doc, it's great talking to you up there. How's it going?" Solomon asked gaily.

"Lee, I got a problem," I screamed over the sound of the "motor."

"A problem? How's Walter? How's Walter?"

"He's in the back seat throwing up," I said. "But that's not the real problem."

"Walter? In the back seat throwing up? My God. What the hell's the real problem then?" he cried.

Sitting there on the edge of my desk, I was digging a letter opener into my hand to control my laughter. I was choking on it as I said the words, and he must have thought I was crying. "Lee, I can't find the school . . . and I'm running out of gas."

"What? What? You're running out of gas?"

That's when I shut off the razor. Ten seconds of silence followed.

"Doc?" he whispered into the phone. It was a prayer.

"Lee?" I answered, no longer able to control myself. I exploded with convulsions of laughter.

"You son of a bitch!" he yelled, and then he too started laughing. For a full minute we held onto the phones, unable to speak, listening to each other laugh ourselves silly.

Finally he said, "No one ever put one over on me like that. No one."

"I owed it to you for that 'booking' in Atlantic City," I answered, and the laughter started all over again.

It must really have been a first, because Lee told the story to everyone in the William Morris Agency. Even to the president, Sam Weisbord, who having heard it wanted to meet me. We spent an hour in my office, while Sam drew my life story out of me. When I finished, he got up from his chair and came over to me. "Dr. Kelman, everyone has a book inside of him." He put his arm around me then. "Your book, you should write." I thanked him, shook his hand, and our meeting ended. But my work had just begun. I had a book to write.

Maybe they will make a movie from it.

Maybe I'll write the title song for the movie.

Maybe the song will be a hit!

Maybe Tomorrow . . .

But right now, they're waiting for me in the operating room.

	insulin (regular)	isoproterenol	lactated Ringer's	lidocaine	methylprednisolone sodium succinate	mezlocillin	midazolam	morphine sulfate	nafcillin	norepinephrine	normal saline solution	ondansetron	oxacillin	oxytocin	penicillin G potassium	phenylephrine	phenytoin	phytonadione	piperacillin	potassium chloride	procainamide	ranitidine	sodium bicarbonate	ticarcillin	tobramycin	vancomycin	verapamil
acyclovir			4		4			4	4				4		4				4	4		4	4	4	4	4	
albumin																											
amikacin			24				24	4		24	24	4	8		8			24		4		24	24			24	24
aminophylline			24	24	?				24		24									4		24	24				
amiodarone	24	24		24			24	24		24	24				4	24				24	24				4	4	24
ampicillin	2							4			8							3		4		?	?			?	
calcium gluconate			24	24			24				24									4					1		48
cefazolin	2		24				24	4			24	4										?				?	24
cefoxitin	24		24					4			24	4											24		24		24
ceftazidime								4			24	4										?	6				
cimetidine	24	24		24	24		24				48	4			24			24		24						24	24
ciprofloxacin			48	24			24												24	24		24			24		24
clindamycin			24		24		24	4			24	4			24				48	24		?	24		48		24
dexamethasone sodium phosphate								4				4								4		24	4				24
dextrose 5% in water (D_5W)		24		24	?	24			24	24		48	6	6	24				24	24	24	48	24	24	24	24	24
D_5W in lactated Ringer's		24		24									24		24					24							24
D_5W in normal saline solution		24		24	?				24			48	?		24				24	24			24		48		24
diazepam																						?					24
diphenhydramine							4	¼				4			24					4		1					
dobutamine		24	24	24			4	4		24	24					24				?	24	48					24
dopamine			48	24	18		4	4			48		24							24		48					24
epinephrine			24				4	4		4	24							3		4		24					24
erythromycin lactobionate			18				24	4			22											24	24				24
esmolol			24				24	8	24	24	24				24		24		24	24		24			24	24	24
gentamicin	2		24				24	1			24	4			1							24					24
heparin sodium	2	24		24	?		24	1				4	4	4	?			4	6	24	4	24	24	6			24
hydrocortisone sodium succinate	4	4	24		?			4			24	4	4					4	24		4		24				24
insulin (regular)				24			24	1						2						4		24	3	2	2	2	48
isoproterenol			24								24											24					24
lactated Ringer's		24		24	?	72			24				24		24				24	24				24	24		24
lidocaine	24		24					4	48		24										24	24	24				48
methylprednisolone sodium succinate			?				24	4			?				24					?		48	2				24
mezlocillin			72								48																
midazolam	24				24			24		24		24							24	24					24	24	
morphine sulfate	1			4	4		24		4	4		4	4	1	4				4	4		1	3	4	1	4	24
nafcillin			24	48				4			24									24			24				
norepinephrine							24	4			24											4					24
normal saline solution		24		24	?	48			24	24		48	24		24				24	24	24	48	24	24	48	24	24
ondansetron							24	4			48									4		4		4		4	
oxacillin			24					4			24																
oxytocin	2							1												4			24				24
penicillin G potassium			24		24			4			24											24					24
phenylephrine																				24			24				
phenytoin																							24				48
phytonadione																				4			24				
piperacillin			24				24	4			24									24		4					24
potassium chloride	4		24		?		24	4	24		24	4		4		24		4	24		4	48	24				24
procainamide				24							24									4		24					48
ranitidine	24	24		24	48			1		4	48	4			24				4	48	24			24	24	24	
sodium bicarbonate	3			24	2			3	24		24			24		24	24	24		24							
ticarcillin	2		24								24	4										24					24
tobramycin	2		24				24	1			48											24					24
vancomycin	2						24	4			24	4										24					24
verapamil	48	24	24	48	24			24		24	24			24	24		48		24	24	48			24	24	24	

Springhouse Nurse's Drug Guide 2004

FIFTH EDITION

Springhouse Nurse's Drug Guide 2004

FIFTH EDITION

LIPPINCOTT WILLIAMS & WILKINS
A Wolters Kluwer Company
Philadelphia • Baltimore • New York • London
Buenos Aires • Hong Kong • Sydney • Tokyo

Staff

Publisher
Judy Schilling McCann, RN, MSN

Editorial Director
William J. Kelly

Senior Art Director
Arlene Putterman

Art Director
Elaine Kasmer

Clinical Manager
Eileen Cassin Gallen, RN, BSN

Drug Information Editor
Melissa M. Devlin, PharmD

Project Editor
Christiane L. Brownell

Clinical Project Editor
Minh N. Luu, RN, BSN, JD

Clinical Editors
Lisa Bonsall, RN, MSN, CRNP;
Shari Cammon, RN, MSN;
Christine M. Damico, RN, MSN, CPNP
JoAnne C. Fante, RN, BSN;
Kimberly Zalewski, RN, MSN;

Editors
Lynne Christensen, Patricia Nale, Karla Schroeder

Copy Editors
Kelly Falcheck, Tom Groff, Anne Jacko, Caryl Knutsen, Beth Pitcher, Mary Pendergraft

Digital Composition Services
Diane Paluba (manager),
Donald G. Knauss (project manager),
Joyce Rossi Biletz (senior desktop assistant)

Manufacturing
Patricia K. Dorshaw (manager),
Beth Janae Orr (book production manager)

Editorial Assistants
Danielle J. Barsky, Carol A. Caputo, Arlene P. Claffee

Indexer
Barbara Hodgson

The clinical procedures described and recommended in this publication are based on research and consultation with nursing, medical, pharmaceutical, and legal authorities. To the best of our knowledge, these procedures reflect currently accepted practice; nevertheless, they can't be considered absolute and universal recommendations. For individual application, all recommendations must be considered in light of the patient's clinical condition and, before the administration of new or infrequently used drugs, in light of the latest package-insert information. The authors and publisher disclaim responsibility for adverse effects resulting directly or indirectly from the suggested procedures, from undetected errors, or from the reader's misunderstanding of the text.

©2004 by Lippincott Williams & Wilkins. All rights reserved. This book is protected by copyright. No part of it may be reproduced, stored in a retrieval system, or transmitted, in any form or by any means—electronic, mechanical, photocopy, recording, or otherwise—without prior written permission of the publisher, except for brief quotations embodied in critical articles and reviews and testing and evaluation materials provided by the publisher to instructors whose schools have adopted its accompanying textbook. Printed in the United States of America. For information, write Lippincott Williams & Wilkins, 1111 Bethlehem Pike, P.O. Box 908, Springhouse, PA 19477-0908.

Visit our Web site at eDrugInfo.com

SNDG5–D N O S A J
05 04 03 10 9 8 7 6 5 4 3 2
ISSN 1088-8063
ISBN 1-58255-262-2

Contents

Consultants and contributors

At the time of publication, the consultants and contributors held the following positions.

Cheryl L. Brady, RN, MSN
Adjunct Faculty
Kent State University
East Liverpool, Ohio

James M. Camamo, PharmD
Clinical Pharmacist
University Medical Center
Tucson, Ariz.

S. Kim Genovese, RNC, MSN, MSA, CARN
Associate Professor of Nursing
Acting Director of Nursing Section
Purdue University, North Central
Westville, Ind.

Jennifer J. Gorrell, PharmD
Clinical Coordinator
Pharmacy Management & Consulting Services
Madison, W. Va.

Tatyana Gurvich, PharmD
Clinical Pharmacologist
Glendale Adventist Family Practice Residency Program
Glendale, Calif.

Connie S. Heflin, RN, MSN
Professor
Paducah Community College
Paducah, Ky.

Erin P. Jaynes, RN, MSN
Administrative Nurse Specialist
Medical College of Ohio
Toledo, Ohio

Yun Lu, RPh, MS, PharmD, BCPS
Clinical Pharmacy Specialist
Hennepin County Medical Center
Minneapolis, Minn.

Randall A. Lynch, PharmD
Assistant Director, Pharmacy Services
Presbyterian Medical Center
University of Pennsylvania Health System
Philadelphia, Pa.

William O'Hara, RPh, BS, PharmD
Clinical Coordinator
Thomas Jefferson University Hospital
Philadelphia, Pa.

Robert Lee Page II, PharmD, BCPS
Assistant Professor
University of Colorado Health Sciences Center
School of Pharmacy
Denver, Colo.

Larry A. Pfeifer, RPh, M.Ap.St.
Chief, Pharmacy Services
National Hansen's Disease Program
Baton Rouge, La.

Christine Price, PharmD
Clinical Coordinator
Department of Pharmacy
Morton Plant Mease Health Care
Clearwater, Fla.

Ruthie Robinson, RN, MSN, CCRN, CEN
Nursing Faculty
Lamar University
Beaumont, Tex.

Susan Sard, PharmD
Clinical Pharmacist
Anne Arundel Medical Center
Annapolis, Md.

Maria A. Summa, RPh, PharmD, BCPS
Clinical Pharmacist, Ambulatory Care
St. Francis Hospital and Medical Center
Hartford, Conn.

Catherine Ultrino, RN, MS, OCN
Staff Nurse
Kindred Hospital Central Tampa
Tampa, Fla.

Barbara S. Wiggins, PharmD
Pharmacy Clinical Specialist
University of Virginia Health System
Charlottesville, Va.

Foreword

Countless times during my nearly 30 years of teaching pharmacology to undergraduate and graduate nursing students, I have been asked to suggest a drug reference that is complete and user-friendly. Taking into account the needs of prospective and practicing nurses for a drug reference that provides instructional as well as clinically practical information about the vast array of drugs available today, I think of only one name. *Springhouse Nurse's Drug Guide* provides that information, and much more, in a clearly organized, easily readable, and compact portable format. Compiled, written, and thoroughly reviewed by a geographically diverse array of nurses, pharmacists, and university professors, this impressive resource of concise, accurate, topical, and complete drug information enables nurses to administer and monitor drugs safely and effectively.

The extent of practical information in *Springhouse Nurse's Drug Guide* is impressive. An I.V. drug compatibility chart on the inside front cover provides crucial information to nurses administering these drugs in an acute care setting. The first chapters of the book are devoted to important aspects of nursing pharmacology, such as proper drug administration, prevention of medication errors, and a review of dosage calculations. The drug classifications section enables the reader to place commonly used drugs into their appropriate classifications to better understand how the drugs share similar actions and characteristics, an important perspective for the undergraduate student.

The drug monographs provide extensive information on each drug, including not only relevant pharmacologic data but also many nursing considerations using the nursing process model. The detailed information for each drug has been updated and expanded continually through the earlier editions of the book. This fifth edition continues this tradition with some new sections in each monograph. Contraindications and precautions relevant to specific populations, including pregnant, breast-feeding, pediatric, and geriatric patients have been added under a new Lifespan logo. A particularly useful feature of each drug monograph is the listing of adverse reactions in different typefaces to signify either common, uncommon, life-threatening, or common and life-threatening reactions. With multiple drug therapies being so common today, the likelihood of drug interactions has greatly increased; accordingly, comprehensive drug-drug interactions are listed in each monograph for ready reference. In addition, *Springhouse Nurse's Drug Guide* provides information on drug-herb, drug-food, and drug-lifestyle interactions. This information is especially important in the outpatient setting where patient behavior in a largely uncontrolled environment is frequently a significant factor in altered drug responses. Information about the effects of drugs on laboratory test results is an equally informative new feature.

Photographs of many of the most widely prescribed tablet and capsule medications, shown in actual size for accurate identification, are cross-referenced to the page on which the drug is discussed. Patients often present a prescription vial containing two or more different medications and are sometimes uncertain as to which drug is properly indicated on the label. Accurate identification of the contents, with the aid of the photoguide, can frequently prevent complications resulting from improper drug administration.

Over-the-counter herbal medications have an expanding role in alternative drug therapy and patient self-help health care. Although widely used, many herbs may interact dangerously with prescription drugs. Thus, anyone prescribing or monitoring drug therapy today should know about herbal pharmacology. *Springhouse Nurse's Drug Guide* provides one of the most complete reviews of herbal medicine available in a guidebook format.

A wealth of important information for students and practicing nurses can also be found in the appendices. Of particular note is a listing of look-alike and sound-alike drug names. With the growing availability of new drugs, some of which have been given brand names that sound or appear quite similar to existing drugs, this feature is particularly helpful in preventing medication error.

The index is extensive, listing all drugs by both generic (all small letters) and brand (first letter capitalized) names. Also, drugs shown in the photoguide are highlighted with boldface. An added feature, a mini CD-ROM, contains a pharmacology review and self-test, a game to match photos of pills with their drug classes, and an Internet link to a Web site that provides drug news and updates.

While many drug guidebooks are currently available, none approaches the scope and depth of detail of *Springhouse Nurse's Drug Guide.* This new 5th edition contains detailed monographs of over 60 recently approved drugs and vital new information on many aspects of drug therapy, while retaining all of the features of the well-received previous editions. Endorsed by the National Student Nurses' Association (NSNA), the *Springhouse Nurse's Drug Guide* provides students with a wide range of practical information, such as essentials of drug calculations and an illustrated overview of drug administration techniques. Additional useful features include common medical abbreviations, a glossary of important medical terminology, pregnancy risk categories, schedules of controlled substances, standardized laboratory test values, and even an English–Spanish drug phrase section.

As a professor of pharmacology for nursing students for nearly 30 years and as an author of several nursing pharmacology textbooks, I am very aware of the need for nursing students to have a sound foundation in pharmacology. In today's increasingly time-stressed health care environment, practicing nurses also need to have a readily accessible source of drug information that is both complete and easily accessible. *Springhouse Nurse's Drug Guide* is able to fulfill both of these needs. Not only does it serve as an indispensable drug reference for student nurses learning about drugs for the first time, it likewise provides a convenient, comprehensive, and accurate drug compilation for the practicing nurse. Its scope, detail, and completeness make it an invaluable addition to the library of every nurse who must dispense and monitor the assortment of drugs that make up our current therapeutic arsenal.

Roger T. Malseed, PhD
Adjunct Associate Professor
University of Pennsylvania
School of Nursing
Philadelphia, Pennsylvania

How to use *Springhouse Nurse's Drug Guide 2004*

Springhouse Nurse's Drug Guide is the premier drug reference for all nursing students—beginning to advanced. Tightly organized entries offer consistent, practical pharmacologic information about more than 750 common generic drugs, presented in a clear writing style that beginning students can understand. The book is a must-have for advanced students as well; it includes comprehensive pharmacokinetic and pharmacodynamic information and route-onset-peak-duration tables that give readers a clear understanding of drug actions. Because each entry also follows a nursing process organization, the book even helps students formulate accurate care plans. Students of all levels will find that *Springhouse Nurse's Drug Guide* offers a comprehensive, convenient resource for all aspects of drug information.

The book begins with introductory material crucial to safe, accurate drug administration. Chapter 1 discusses drug therapy as it relates to the nursing process. Chapter 2 explains how to calculate dosages and provides examples for each step in the calculations. Chapter 3 discusses how to administer drugs by commonly used routes and includes illustrations to guide students through the steps of each procedure. Chapter 4 focuses on common medication errors and explains how to avoid them.

Drug classifications

Springhouse Nurse's Drug Guide provides complete overviews of 40 pharmacologic and therapeutic drug classifications, from alkylating drugs to xanthine derivatives. Following the class name is an alphabetical list of examples of drugs in that class; the drug highlighted in color represents the prototype drug for the class. The text then provides class-specific information on indications, actions, adverse reactions, contraindications, and precautions. Look for the special Lifespan logo for contraindications and precautions for specific populations including children, pregnant and breast-feeding women, and elderly patients.

Alphabetical listing of drugs

Drug entries in this text appear alphabetically by generic name for quick reference. The generic name is followed by a pronunciation guide and an alphabetical list of brand (trade) names. Brands that don't need a prescription are designated with a dagger (†); those available only in Canada with a closed diamond (♦); those available only in Australia with an open diamond (◊); those that contain alcohol with a single asterisk (*); and those that contain tartrazine with a double asterisk (**). The mention of a brand name in no way implies endorsement of that product or guarantees its legality.

Each entry then identifies the drug's pharmacologic and therapeutic classifications; that is, its chemical category and its major clinical use. Listing both classifications helps you grasp the multiple, varying, and sometimes overlapping uses of drugs within a single pharmacologic class and among different classes. Each entry then lists the drug's pregnancy risk category and, if appropriate, its controlled substance schedule.

Indications and dosages

The next section lists the drug's indications and provides dosage information for adults, children, and elderly patients, as applicable. Off-label indications (uses that are clinically accepted but not approved by the FDA) are designated with a double dagger (‡). Dosage instructions reflect current clinical trends in therapeutics and can't be considered as absolute or universal recommendations. For individual application, dosage instructions must be considered in light of the patient's clinical condition.

Contraindications and precautions

This section specifies conditions in which the drug should not be used and details recommendations for cautious use. The Lifespan logo draws your attention to contraindications and precautions for special populations, such as children, pregnant and breast-feeding women, and elderly patients.

Adverse reactions

This section lists adverse reactions to each drug by body system. The most common adverse reactions (those experienced by at least 10% of people taking the drug in clinical trials) are in *italic* type; less common reactions are in roman type; life-threatening reactions are in ***bold italic*** type; and reactions that are common *and* life-threatening are in **BOLD CAPITAL** letters.

Interactions

This section lists each drug's confirmed, clinically significant interactions with other drugs (additive effects, potentiated effects, and antagonistic effects), herbs, foods, and lifestyle (such as alcohol use or smoking).

Drug interactions are listed under the drug that is adversely affected. For example, antacids that contain magnesium may decrease absorption of tetracycline. Therefore, this interaction is listed under tetracycline. To determine the possible effects of using two or more drugs simultaneously, check the interactions section for each of the drugs in question.

Effects on lab test results

This section lists increased and decreased levels, counts, and other laboratory test results that may be caused by the drug's systemic effects.

Pharmacokinetics

This section describes absorption, distribution, metabolism, and excretion, along with the drug's half-life when known. It also provides a quick reference table highlighting onset, peak, and duration for each route of administration. Values for half-life, onset, peak, and duration are for patients with normal renal function, unless specified otherwise.

Pharmacodynamics

This section explains the drug's chemical and therapeutic actions. For example, although all antihypertensives lower blood pressure, they don't all do so by the same pharmacologic process.

Available forms

This section lists all available preparations for each drug (for example, tablets, capsules, solutions for injection) and all available dosage forms and strengths. As with the brand names discussed above, over-the-counter dosage forms and strengths are marked with a dagger (†); those available only in Canada with a closed diamond (♦); those available only in Australia with an open diamond (◊); and those that contain alcohol with an asterisk (*).

Nursing Process

This section uses the nursing process as its organizational framework. It also contains an Alert logo to call your attention to vital, need-to-know information or serve as a warning about a common drug error.

- Assessment focuses on observation and monitoring of key patient data, such as vital signs, weight, intake and output, and laboratory values.
- Nursing diagnoses represent those most commonly applied to drug therapy. In actual use, nursing diagnoses must be relevant to an individual patient; therefore, they may not include the listed examples and may include others not listed.
- Planning and implementation offers detailed recommendations for drug administration, including full coverage of P.O., I.V., I.M., S.C., and other routes.
- Patient teaching focuses on explaining the drug's purpose, promoting compliance, and ensuring proper use and storage of the drug. It also includes instructions for preventing or minimizing adverse reactions.
- Evaluation identifies the expected patient outcomes for the listed nursing diagnoses.

Because nursing considerations in this text emphasize drug-specific recommendations, they don't include standard recommendations that apply to all drugs, such as "assess the five rights of drug therapy before administration" or "teach the patient the name, dose, frequency, route, and strength of the prescribed drug."

Photoguide to tablets and capsules

To make drug identification easier and to enhance patient safety, *Springhouse Nurse's Drug Guide* offers a full-color photoguide to the most commonly prescribed tablets and capsules. Shown in their actual sizes, the drugs are arranged alphabetically by generic names. Trade names and most common dosage strengths are included. Page references appear under each drug name so you can turn quickly to information about the drug.

Herbal medicines

Herbal medicine entries appear alphabetically by name, followed by a phonetic spelling and an alphabetical list of common names.

Reported uses

This section lists reported uses of the herbal medicine. Some of these uses are based on anecdotal claims; other uses have been studied. However, a listing in this section should not be considered as a recommendation.

Dosages

This section lists the routes and general dosage information for each form of the herb and, where available, in accordance with its reported use. This information has been gathered from the herbal literature, anecdotal reports, and available clinical data. However, not all uses have specific dosage information; often, no consensus exists. Dosage notations reflect current clinical trends and should not be considered as recommendations by the publisher.

Cautions

This section lists any condition, especially a disease, in which use of the herbal remedy is undesirable. It also provides recommendations for cautious use, as appropriate.

Adverse reactions

This section lists undesirable effects that may follow use of an herbal supplement. Some of these effects have not been reported but are theoretically possible, given the chemical composition or action of the herb.

Interactions

This section lists each herb's clinically significant interactions, actual or potential, with other herbs, drugs, foods, or lifestyle choices. Each statement describes the effect of the interaction and then offers a specific suggestion for avoiding the interaction. As with adverse reactions, some interactions have not been proven but are theoretically possible.

Actions

This section describes the herb's chemical and therapeutic actions.

Common forms

This section lists the available preparations for each herbal medicine as well as dosage forms and strengths.

Nursing considerations

This section offers helpful information, such as monitoring techniques and methods for the prevention and treatment of adverse reactions. Patient teaching tips that focus on educating the patient about the herb's purpose, preparation, administration, and storage are also included, as are suggestions for promoting patient compliance with the therapeutic regimen and steps the patient can take to prevent or minimize the risk or severity of adverse reactions.

Appendices and index

The appendices include a list of look-alike and sound-alike drug names for use in preventing drug errors, a listing of narcotic and nonnarcotic analgesic combination products detailing the components of each product, a list of dialyzable drugs, a glossary explaining medical words and phrases found in the book, a list of drugs that shouldn't be crushed, and a list of normal laboratory test values.

The comprehensive index lists drug classifications, all generic drugs, brand names, indications, and herbal medicines included in this book.

PharmDisk 5.0

The CD-ROM included with this book (inside the back cover) offers two exciting Windows-based software programs. "Pharmacology Self-test" tests your knowledge with 300 multiple-choice questions. And a challenging interactive game helps you learn drug classifications. *PharmDisk 5.0* also provides a link to eDrugInfo.com.

eDrugInfo.com

This Web site keeps *Springhouse Nurse's Drug Guide 2004* current by providing the following features:

- updates on new drugs, new indications, and new warnings
- patient teaching aids on new drugs
- news summaries of pertinent drug information.

The Web site also gives you:

- information on herbs
- links to pharmaceutical companies, government agencies, and other drug information sites
- a bookstore full of nursing books, software, and more.

Plus, registering with eDrugInfo.com entitles you to e-mail notifications when new drug updates are posted.

Guide to abbreviations

ACE	angiotensin-converting enzyme
ACT	activated clotting time
ADH	antidiuretic hormone
AIDS	acquired immunodeficiency syndrome
ALT	alanine transaminase
APTT	activated partial thromboplastin time
AST	aspartate transaminase
AV	atrioventricular
b.i.d.	twice daily
BPH	benign prostatic hyperplasia
BUN	blood urea nitrogen
cAMP	cyclic adenosine monophosphate
CBC	complete blood count
CK	creatine kinase
CMV	cytomegalovirus
CNS	central nervous system
COPD	chronic obstructive pulmonary disease
CSF	cerebrospinal fluid
CV	cardiovascular
CVA	cerebrovascular accident
DIC	disseminated intravascular coagulation
D_5NS	dextrose 5% in normal saline
D_5W	dextrose 5% in water
dl	deciliter
DNA	deoxyribonucleic acid
ECG	electrocardiogram
EEG	electroencephalogram
EENT	eyes, ears, nose, throat
FDA	Food and Drug Administration
g	gram
G	gauge
GABA	gamma-aminobutyric acid
GFR	glomerular filtration rate
GGT	gamma-glutamyltransferase
GI	gastrointestinal
gtt	drops
GU	genitourinary
G6PD	glucose-6-phosphate dehydrogenase
H	histamine
HDL	high-density lipoprotein
HIV	human immunodeficiency virus
hr	hour
h.s.	at bedtime
ICU	intensive care unit
I.D.	intradermal
I.M.	intramuscular
INR	international normalized ratio
IPPB	intermittent positive-pressure breathing
IU	international unit
I.V.	intravenous
kg	kilogram
L	liter
lb	pound
LD	lactate dehydrogenase
LDL	low-density lipoprotein
M	molar

m^2	square meter
MAO	monoamine oxidase
mcg	microgram
mEq	milliequivalent
mg	milligram
MI	myocardial infarction
min	minute
ml	milliliter
mm^3	cubic millimeter
Na	sodium
NG	nasogastric
NSAID	nonsteroidal anti-inflammatory drug
OTC	over-the-counter
oz	ounce
PABA	para-aminobenzoic acid
$Paco_2$	carbon dioxide partial pressure
Pao_2	oxygen partial pressure
PCA	patient-controlled analgesia
P.O.	by mouth
P.R.	by rectum
p.r.n.	as needed
PT	prothrombin time
PTT	partial thromboplastin time
PVC	premature ventricular contraction
q	every
q.i.d.	four times daily
RBC	red blood cell
RDA	recommended daily allowance
REM	rapid eye movement
RNA	ribonucleic acid
RSV	respiratory syncytial virus
SA	sinoatrial
S.C.	subcutaneous
SIADH	syndrome of inappropriate antidiuretic hormone
S.L.	sublingual
T_3	triiodothyronine
T_4	thyroxine
tbs	tablespoon
tsp	teaspoon
t.i.d.	three times daily
USP	United States Pharmacopeia
UTI	urinary tract infection
WBC	white blood cell

1

Drug therapy and the nursing process

Springhouse Nurse's Drug Guide uses the nursing process in its organizational framework for good reason. The nursing process guides nursing decisions about drug administration to ensure the patient's safety and to meet medical and legal standards. This process provides thorough assessment, appropriate nursing diagnoses, effective planning and implementation, and consistent evaluation.

Assessment

Data collection begins with a patient history. After taking the patient's history, perform a thorough physical examination. Also, evaluate the patient's knowledge and understanding of the drug therapy he's about to receive.

History

When taking a history, investigate the patient's allergies, use of drugs and herbs, medical history, lifestyle and beliefs, and socioeconomic status.

Allergies

Specify the drug or food to which the patient is allergic. Describe the reaction he has; its situation, time, and setting; and any contributing factors, such as a significant change in eating habits or the simultaneous use of stimulants, tobacco, alcohol, or illegal drugs. Don't forget to place an allergy label conspicuously on the patient's chart and place an allergy band on the patient.

Drugs and herbs

Take a complete drug history that includes both prescription and over-the-counter drugs. Also, find out which herbs, if any, the patient takes. Investigate the patient's reasons for using a drug or herb and his knowledge of its use. Explore the patient's thoughts and attitudes about drug use to see if he may encounter problems with drug therapy. Note any special procedures he'll need to perform, such as monitoring his glucose level or checking his heart rate, and make sure he can perform them correctly.

After the patient starts taking the drug, discuss the effects of therapy to determine whether new symptoms or adverse drug reactions have developed. Also, talk about measures the patient has taken to recognize, minimize, or avoid adverse drug reactions or accidental overdose. Ask the patient where he stores his medication and what system he uses to help himself remember to take it as prescribed.

Medical history

Note any chronic disorders the patient has, and record date of diagnosis, the prescribed treatment, and the name of the prescriber. Careful attention during this part of the history can uncover one of the most important problems with drug therapy: conflicting and incompatible drug regimens.

Lifestyle and beliefs

Ask about the patient's support systems, marital status, childbearing status, attitudes toward health and health care, and daily patterns of activity. They all affect patient compliance and, therefore, the plan of care.

Also, ask about the patient's diet. Certain foods can influence the efficacy of many drugs. Also, inquire about the patient's use of alcohol, tobacco, caffeine, and illegal drugs, such as marijuana, cocaine, and heroin. Note the substance used and the amount and frequency of use.

Socioeconomic status

Note the patient's age, educational level, occupation, and insurance coverage. These characteristics help determine the plan of care, the likelihood of compliance, and the possible need for financial assistance, counseling, or other social services.

Physical examination

Examine the patient closely for expected drug effects and for adverse reactions. Every drug has a desired effect on one body system, but it may also have one or more undesired effects on that or another body system. For example, chemotherapeutic drugs destroy cancer cells, but they also affect normal cells and typically cause hair loss, diarrhea, or nausea. Besides looking for adverse drug effects, investigate whether the patient has any sensory impairments or changes in mental state.

Sensory impairment

Assess the patient for sensory impairments that could influence the plan of care. For example, impaired vision or paralysis can hinder the patient's ability to give himself a subcutaneous injection, break a scored tablet, or open a medication container. Hearing impairment can complicate effective patient instruction.

Mental state

Note whether the patient is alert, oriented, and able to interact appropriately. Assess whether he can think clearly and converse appropriately. Check his short-term and long-term memory; he needs both to follow a prescribed regimen correctly. Also, determine whether the patient can read and at what level.

Understanding drug therapy

A patient is more likely to comply if he understands the reason for drug therapy. During your assessment, evaluate your patient's understanding of his therapy and the reason for it. Pay particular attention to his emotional acceptance of the need for the drug treatment plan. For instance, a young patient being prescribed an antihypertensive may need more education than an older patient to ensure compliance.

Nursing diagnosis

Using the information you gathered during assessment, define drug-related problems by formulating each problem into a relevant nursing diagnosis. The most common problem statements related to drug therapy are "Deficient knowledge," "Ineffective health maintenance," and "Noncompliance." Nursing diagnoses provide the framework for planning interventions and outcome criteria (patient goals).

Planning and implementation

Make sure that your outcome criteria state the desired patient behaviors or responses that should result from nursing care. Such criteria should have the following characteristics:

- measurable
- objective
- concise
- realistic for the patient
- attainable by nursing management.

Express patient behavior in terms of expectations, and specify a time frame. An example of a good outcome statement is "Before discharge, the patient verbalizes major adverse effects related to his chemotherapy."

After developing outcome criteria, determine the interventions needed to help the patient reach the desired goals. Appropriate interventions may include administration procedures and techniques, legal and ethical concerns, patient teaching, and concerns related to pregnant, breast-feeding, pediatric, and geriatric patients. Interventions also may be independent nursing actions, such as turning a bedridden patient every 2 hours, or actions that require a prescriber's order.

Evaluation

The final component of the nursing process is a formal and systematic process for determining the effectiveness of nursing care. This evaluation process lets you determine whether outcome criteria were met, which then helps you make informed decisions about subsequent interventions. If you stated the outcome criteria in measurable terms, then you can evaluate easily the extent to which they were met.

For example, if a patient experiences relief from headache pain within 1 hour after receiving an analgesic, the outcome criterion was met. If the headache was the same or worse, the outcome criterion wasn't met. In that case, you'll need to reassess the patient, which may yield a new plan, new data that might invalidate the initial nursing diagnosis, or new nursing interventions that are more specific or more appropriate for the patient. For instance, this reassessment could lead to a higher dosage, a different analgesic, or finding the underlying cause of the headache pain.

Evaluation enables you to design and implement a revised plan of care, to continuously reevaluate the effectiveness of your interventions for each outcome, and to provide the highest quality of care to your patient.

2

Essentials of dosage calculations

Nurses perform drug and intravenous (I.V.) fluid calculations frequently. That's why you need to know and understand drug weights and measures, how to convert between systems and measures, how to compute drug dosages, and how to make adjustments, particularly for children.

Systems of drug weights and measures

Prescribers use several systems of measurement when ordering drugs. The three most commonly used are the metric, household, and apothecaries' systems. The metric and household systems are so widely used that most brands of medication cups for liquid measurements are calibrated in both systems. The apothecaries' system isn't as widely used as the first two but still may be encountered in clinical practice. A fourth system, the avoirdupois system, uses solid units of measure, such as the ounce and the pound, and isn't used as often in the clinical setting.

Metric system

The metric system is the international system of measurement, the most widely used system, and the system used by the U.S. Pharmacopoeia. It has units for both liquid and solid measures. Among its many advantages, the metric system enables accuracy in calculating small drug dosages. It uses Arabic numerals, which are commonly used by health care professionals worldwide. And most manufacturers calibrate newly developed drugs using the metric system.

Liquid measures

In the metric system, one liter (L) is about equal to 1 quart in the apothecaries' system. Liters are often used when ordering and administering I.V. solutions. Milliliters are frequently used to administer parenteral drugs (drugs administered by means other than the GI tract, such as injection or infusion) and some oral drugs. One milliliter (ml) equals $\frac{1}{1,000}$ of a liter.

Solid measures

The gram (g) is the basis for solid measures or units of weight in the metric system. One milligram (mg) equals $\frac{1}{1,000}$ of a gram. Drugs are frequently ordered in grams, milligrams, or an even smaller unit, the microgram (mcg), depending on the drug. One microgram equals $\frac{1}{1,000}$ of a milligram. Body weight is usually recorded in kilograms (kg). One kilogram equals 1,000 g.

The following are examples of drug orders using the metric system:

- 30 ml milk of magnesia P.O. h.s.
- Ancef 1 g I.V. q 6 hr.
- Lanoxin 0.125 mg P.O. daily.

Household system

Most foods, recipes, over-the-counter drugs, and home remedies use the household system. Health care professionals seldom use this system for drug administration; however, knowledge of household measures may be useful in some clinical situations, such as patient teaching.

Liquid measures

Liquid measurements in the household system include teaspoons (tsp) and tablespoons (tbs). For clinical purposes, these measurements have been standardized to 5 milliliters and 15 milliliters, respectively. Using these standardized amounts, 3 teaspoons equal 1 tablespoon, 6 teaspoons equal 1 ounce, and so forth. Patients who need to measure doses by teaspoon or tablespoon should do so using calibrated clinical devices to make sure they receive exactly the prescribed amount. Advise against using an ordinary household spoon to measure a teaspoonful of a medication because the amount will most likely be inaccurate. Spoon sizes may vary from 4 to 6 milliliters or more.

The following are examples of drug orders using the household system:

- 2 teaspoons Bactrim P.O. b.i.d.
- Riopan 2 tablespoons P.O. 1 hour before meals and h.s.

Apothecaries' system

Two unique features distinguish the apothecaries' system from other systems: the use of Roman numerals and the placement of the unit of measurement before the Roman numeral. For example, a measurement of 5 grains would be written as *grains V.*

In the apothecaries' system, equivalents among the various units of measure are close approximations of one another. By contrast, equivalents in the metric system are exact. When using apothecaries' equivalents for calculations and conversions, the calculations, although not precise, must fall within acceptable standards.

The apothecaries' system is the only system of measurement that uses both symbols and abbreviations to represent units of measure. Although the use of the apothecaries' system is becoming less common in health care, you must still be able to read dosages that have been written in the apothecaries' system and convert them to the metric system.

Liquid measures

The smallest unit of liquid measurement in the apothecaries' system is the minim (♏) , which is about the size of a drop of water. Fifteen to 16 minims equal about 1 ml.

Solid measures

The grain (gr) is the smallest solid measure or unit of weight in the apothecaries' system. It equals about 60 milligrams. One dram equals about 60 grains.

The following are examples of drug orders using the apothecaries' system:

- Robitussin fʒ (fluidrams) IV P.O. q 6 hr.
- Mylanta f℥ (fluidounce) I P.O. 1 hour after meals
- Tylenol gr (grains) X P.O. q 4 hr p.r.n. for headache.

Units, international units, and milliequivalents

For some drugs, you'll need to use a measuring system developed by drug manufacturers. Three of the most common special systems of measurement are units, international units, and milliequivalents.

Units

Insulin is one of several drugs measured in units. The international standard of U-100 insulin means that 1 ml of insulin solution contains 100 units of insulin, regardless of type. Heparin, an anticoagulant, is also measured in units, as are several antibiotics, available in liquid, solid, and powder forms for oral or parenteral use. Each manufacturer of drugs made available in units provides specific information about the measurement of each drug.

The following are examples of drug orders using units:

- Inject 14 units NPH insulin S.C. this a.m.
- Heparin 5,000 units S.C. q 12 hr
- Nystatin 200,000 units P.O. q 6 hr.

The unit is not a standard measure. Thus, different drugs, although each measured in units, may have no relationship to one another in quality or activity. It was once common practice to see the abbreviation U for units, but growing concern for the potential to misread the U as a "zero," thus causing a tenfold overdose, has many prescribers spelling out the word "units." You may still come across this abbreviation in practice. Always double-check your orders.

International units

International units (IU) are used to measure biologicals, such as vitamins, enzymes, and hormones. For instance, the activity of calcitonin, a synthetic hormone used in calcium regulation, is expressed in international units. As with the U abbreviation, the IU abbreviation can easily be misread; for instance, it may be read as I.V. Thus, it is better to spell out "international units" but be aware that IU is still used in practice.

The following are examples of drug orders using international units:

- 100 IU calcitonin S.C. daily
- 8 IU somatropin S.C. three times a week.

Milliequivalents

Electrolytes may be measured in milliequivalents (mEq). Drug manufacturers provide information about the number of metric units needed to provide a prescribed number of milliequivalents. Potassium chloride (KCl), for example, is usually ordered in milliequivalents.

The following are examples of drug orders using milliequivalents:

- 30 mEq KCl P.O. b.i.d.
- 1 L D_5NS with 40 mEq KCl to be run at 125 ml/hr.

Conversions between measurement systems

Sometimes you may need to convert from one measurement system to another, particularly when a drug is ordered in one system but available only in another system. To perform conversion calculations, you need to know the equivalent measurements for the different systems of measurement. One of the most commonly used methods for converting drug measurements is the fraction method.

Fraction method

The fraction method for converting between measurement systems involves an equation consisting of two fractions. Set up the first fraction by placing the ordered dose over x units of the available dose.

For example, say a prescriber orders 7.5 ml of acetaminophen elixir to be given by mouth. To find the equivalent in teaspoons (tsp), first set up a fraction in which the milliliter dose represents the ordered dose and the teaspoon dose represents the unknown (x) available dose:

$$\frac{7.5 \text{ ml}}{x \text{ tsp}}$$

Then, set up the second fraction, which appears on the right side of the equation. This fraction consists of the standard equivalents between the ordered and the available measures. Because milliliters must be converted to teaspoons, the right side of the equation appears as:

$$\frac{5 \text{ ml}}{1 \text{ tsp}}$$

The same unit of measure should appear in the numerator of both fractions. Likewise, the same unit of measure should appear in both denominators. The entire equation should appear as:

$$\frac{7.5 \text{ ml}}{x \text{ tsp}} = \frac{5 \text{ ml}}{1 \text{ tsp}}$$

To solve for x, cross multiply.

$$x \text{ tsp} \times 5 \text{ ml} = 7.5 \text{ ml} \times 1 \text{ tsp}$$

$$x \text{ tsp} = \frac{7.5 \cancel{\text{ml}} \times 1 \text{ tsp}}{5 \cancel{\text{ml}}}$$

$$x \text{ tsp} = \frac{7.5 \times 1 \text{ tsp}}{5}$$

$$x \text{ tsp} = 1.5 \text{ tsp}$$

The patient should receive 1.5 teaspoons of acetaminophen elixir.

Computing drug dosages

Computing a drug dosage is a two-step process that you complete after verifying the drug order. First, determine whether the ordered drug is available in units in the same system of measurement. If not, then convert the measurement for the ordered drug to the system used for the available drug.

If the ordered units of measurement are available, calculate how much of the available dosage form should be administered. For example, if the prescribed dose is 250 mg, determine the quantity of tablets (tab), powder, or liquid that would equal 250 mg. To determine that quantity, use one of the methods described below.

Fraction method

When using the fraction method to compute a drug dosage, write an equation consisting of two fractions. First, set up a fraction showing the number of units to be given over *x*, which represents the quantity of the dosage form.

On the other side of the equation, set up a fraction showing the number of units of the drug in its dosage form over the quantity of dosage forms that supply that number of units. The number of units and the quantity of dosage forms are specific for each drug. In most cases, the stated quantity equals 1. Information provided on the drug label should supply the details needed to form the second fraction.

For example, if the number of units to be administered equals 250 mg, the first fraction in the equation would appear as:

$$\frac{250 \text{ mg}}{x \text{ tab}}$$

The drug label states that each tablet contains 125 mg, so the second fraction would appear as:

$$\frac{125 \text{ mg}}{1 \text{ tab}}$$

Note that the same units of measure appear in the numerators and the same units appear in the denominators. Note also that the units of measure in the denominators differ from the units in the numerators.

The entire equation would appear as:

$$\frac{250 \text{ mg}}{x \text{ tab}} = \frac{125 \text{ mg}}{1 \text{ tab}}$$

Solving for *x* determines the quantity of the dosage form—2 tablets, in this example.

Ratio method

To use the ratio method, write the amount of the drug to be given and the quantity of the dose (*x*) as a ratio. Using the example shown above, you'd write:

$$250 \text{ mg} : x \text{ tab}$$

Next, complete the equation by forming a second ratio from the number of units in each tablet (or whatever form the drug comes in). The manufacturer's label provides this information. Again using the preceding example, the entire equation is:

$$250 \text{ mg} : x \text{ tab} :: 125 \text{ mg} : 1 \text{ tab}$$

Solve for *x* by multiplying the means (inner portions) and extremes (outer portions) of the equation. The patient should receive 2 tablets.

Desired-available method

You can also use the desired-available method, also known as the dose-over-on-hand method. This method converts ordered units into available units and computes the drug dosage all in one step. The desired-available equation appears as:

$$x \text{ quantity to give} = \frac{\text{ordered units}}{1} \times \text{conversion fraction} \times \frac{\text{quantity of dosage form}}{\text{stated quantity of drug within each dosage form}}$$

For example, say you receive an order for gr X (10 gr) of a drug. The drug is available only in 300-mg tablets. To determine the number of tablets to give the patient, substitute gr X (the ordered number of units) for the first element of the equation. Then use the conversion fraction as the second portion of the formula. The conversion factor is:

$$\frac{60 \text{ mg}}{1 \text{ gr}}$$

The measure in the denominator must be the same as the measure in the ordered units. In this case, the order specified gr X. As a result, grains appears in the denominator of the conversion fraction.

The third element of the equation shows the dosage form over the stated drug quantity for that dosage form. Because the drug is available in 300-mg tablets, the fraction appears as:

$$\frac{1 \text{ tab}}{300 \text{ mg}}$$

The dosage form—tablets—should always appear in the numerator, and the quantity of drug in each dosage form should always appear in the denominator. The completed equation is:

$$x \text{ tab} = 10 \text{ gr} \times \frac{60 \text{ mg}}{1 \text{ gr}} \times \frac{1 \text{ tab}}{300 \text{ mg}}$$

Solving for x shows that the patient should receive 2 tablets.

The desired-available method has the advantage of using only one equation. However, you need to memorize an equation more elaborate than the one used in the fraction method or the ratio method. Relying on your memorization of a more complicated equation may increase the chances of an error.

Dimensional analysis

A variation of the ratio method, dimensional analysis (also known as factor analysis or factor labeling) eliminates the need to memorize formulas and requires only one equation to determine the answer. To compare the two methods at a glance, read the following problem and solutions.

A physician prescribes 0.25 g of streptomycin sulfate I.M. The vial reads 2 ml = 1 g. How many milliliters should you give?

Dimensional analysis

$$\frac{0.25 \text{ g}}{1} \times \frac{2 \text{ ml}}{1 \text{ g}} = 0.5 \text{ ml}$$

Ratio method

$$1 \text{ g} : 2 \text{ ml} :: 0.25 \text{ g} : x \text{ ml}$$

$$x = 2 \times 0.25$$

$$x = 0.5 \text{ ml}$$

When using dimensional analysis, you arrange a series of ratios, called factors, in a single (although sometimes lengthy) fractional equation. Each factor, written as a fraction, consists of two quantities and their related units of measurement. For instance, if 1,000 ml of a drug should be given over 8 hours, the relationship between 1,000 and 8 hours is expressed by the fraction

$$\frac{1{,}000 \text{ ml}}{8 \text{ hr}}$$

When a problem includes a quantity and a unit of measurement that are unrelated to any other factor in the problem, they serve as the numerator of the fraction, and 1 (implied) becomes the denominator.

Some mathematical problems contain all of the information needed to identify the factors, set up the equation, and find the solution. Other problems require the use of a conversion factor. Conversion factors are equivalents (for example, 1 g = 1,000 mg) that you can memorize or obtain from a conversion chart. Because the two quantities and units of measurement are equivalent, they can serve as the numerator or the denominator; thus, the conversion factor 1 g = 1,000 mg can be written in fraction form as:

$$\frac{1{,}000 \text{ mg}}{1 \text{ g}} \text{ or } \frac{1 \text{ g}}{1{,}000 \text{ mg}}$$

The factors given in the problem plus any conversion factors needed to solve the problem are called *knowns*. The quantity of the answer, of course, is *unknown*. When setting up an equation in dimensional analysis, work backward, beginning with the unit of measurement of the answer. After plotting all the knowns, find the solution by following this sequence:

- Cancel similar quantities and units of measurement.
- Multiply the numerators.
- Multiply the denominators.
- Divide the numerator by the denominator.

Mastering dimensional analysis can take practice, but you may find your efforts well rewarded. To understand more fully how dimensional analysis works, review the following problem and the steps taken to solve it.

A physician prescribes grains (gr) X of a drug. The pharmacy supplies the drug in 300-mg tablets (tab). How many tablets should you administer?

- Write down the unit of measurement of the answer, followed by an "equal to" symbol.

$$\text{tab} =$$

- Search the problem for the quantity with the same unit of measurement (if one doesn't exist, use a conversion factor); place this in the numerator and its related quantity and unit of measurement in the denominator.

$$\text{tab} = \frac{1\ \text{tab}}{300\ \text{mg}}$$

• Separate the first factor from the next with a multiplication symbol.

$$\text{tab} = \frac{1\ \text{tab}}{300\ \text{mg}} \times$$

• Place the unit of measurement of the denominator of the first factor in the numerator of the second factor; search the problem for the quantity with the same unit of measurement (if one doesn't exist, as in this example, use a conversion factor); place this in the numerator and its related quantity and unit of measurement in the denominator, and follow with a multiplication symbol. Repeat this step until all known factors are included in the equation.

$$\text{tab} = \frac{1\ \text{tab}}{300\ \text{mg}} \times \frac{60\ \text{mg}}{1\ \text{gr}} \times \frac{10\ \text{gr}}{1}$$

• Treat the equation as a large fraction. First, cancel similar units of measurement in the numerator and the denominator (what remains should be what you began with—the unit of measurement of the answer; if not, recheck your equation to find and correct the error). Next, multiply the numerators and then the denominators. Finally, divide the numerator by the denominator.

$$\text{tab} = \frac{1\ \text{tab}}{300\ \cancel{\text{mg}}} \times \frac{60\ \cancel{\text{mg}}}{1\ \cancel{\text{gr}}} \times \frac{10\ \cancel{\text{gr}}}{1}$$

$$= \frac{60 \times 10\ \text{tab}}{300}$$

$$= \frac{600\ \text{tab}}{300}$$

$$= 2\ \text{tab}$$

For more practice, study the following examples, which use dimensional analysis to solve various mathematical problems common to dosage calculations and drug administration.

1. *A patient weighs 140 lb. What is his weight in kilograms (kg)?*

Unit of measurement of the answer: kg

$$\text{1st factor (conversion factor): } \frac{1\ \text{kg}}{2.2\ \text{lb}}$$

$$\text{2nd factor: } \frac{140\ \text{lb}}{1}$$

$$\text{kg} = \frac{1\ \text{kg}}{2.2\ \cancel{\text{lb}}} \times 140\ \cancel{\text{lb}}$$

$$= \frac{140\ \text{lb}}{2.2\ \text{lb}}$$

$$= 63.6\ \text{kg}$$

2. *A physician prescribes 75 mg of a drug. The pharmacy stocks a multidose vial containing 100 mg/ml. How many milliliters should you administer?*

Unit of measurement of the answer: ml

$$\text{1st factor: } \frac{1\ \text{ml}}{100\ \text{mg}}$$

$$\text{2nd factor: } \frac{75\ \text{mg}}{1}$$

$$\text{ml} = \frac{1\ \text{ml}}{100\ \cancel{\text{mg}}} \times \frac{75\ \cancel{\text{mg}}}{1}$$

$$= \frac{75\ \text{ml}}{100}$$

$$= 0.75\ \text{ml}$$

3. *A nurse practitioner prescribes 1 teaspoon (tsp) of a cough elixir. The pharmacist sends up a bottle whose label reads 1 ml = 50 mg. How many milligrams should you administer?*

Unit of measurement of the answer: mg

$$\text{1st factor: } \frac{50\ \text{mg}}{1\ \text{ml}}$$

$$\text{2nd factor (conversion factor): } \frac{5\ \text{ml}}{1\ \text{tsp}}$$

$$\text{3rd factor: } \frac{1\ \text{tsp}}{1}$$

$$\text{mg} = \frac{50\ \text{mg}}{1\ \cancel{\text{ml}}} \times \frac{5\ \cancel{\text{ml}}}{1\ \cancel{\text{tsp}}} \times \frac{1\ \cancel{\text{tsp}}}{1}$$

$$= 50 \times \frac{50\ \text{mg}}{1}$$

$$= 250\ \text{mg}$$

4. *A physician prescribes 1,000 ml of an I.V. solution to be administered over 8 hours. The I.V. tubing delivers 15 gtt/ml per minute. What is the infusion rate in gtt/minute?*

Unit of measurement of the answer: gtt/minute

1st factor: $\frac{15 \text{ gtt}}{1 \text{ ml}}$

2nd factor: $\frac{1{,}000 \text{ ml}}{8 \text{ hr}}$

3rd factor (conversion factor): $\frac{1 \text{ hr}}{60 \text{ min}}$

$$\text{gtt/minute} = \frac{15 \text{ gtt}}{1 \cancel{\text{ml}}} \times \frac{1{,}000 \cancel{\text{ml}}}{8 \cancel{\text{hr}}} \times \frac{1 \cancel{\text{hr}}}{60 \text{ min}}$$

$$= \frac{15 \text{ gtt} \times 1{,}000 \times 1}{8 \times 60 \text{ min}}$$

$$= \frac{15{,}000 \text{ gtt}}{480 \text{ min}}$$

$$= 31.3 \text{ or } 31 \text{ gtt/min}$$

5. *A physician prescribes 10,000 units of heparin added to 500 ml of D_5W at 1,200 units/hour. How many drops per minute should you administer if the I.V. tubing delivers 10 gtt/ml?*
Unit of measurement of the answer: gtt/minute

1st factor: $\frac{10 \text{ gtt}}{1 \text{ ml}}$

2nd factor: $\frac{500 \text{ ml}}{10{,}000 \text{ units}}$

3rd factor: $\frac{1{,}200 \text{ units}}{1 \text{ hr}}$

4th factor (conversion factor): $\frac{1 \text{ hr}}{60 \text{ min}}$

$$\text{gtt/minute} = \frac{10 \text{ gtt}}{1 \cancel{\text{ml}}} \times \frac{500 \cancel{\text{ml}}}{10{,}000 \cancel{\text{units}}} \times \frac{1{,}200 \cancel{\text{units}}}{1 \cancel{\text{hr}}} \times \frac{1 \cancel{\text{hr}}}{60 \text{ min}}$$

$$= \frac{10 \times 500 \times 1{,}200 \text{ gtt}}{10{,}000 \times 60 \text{ min}}$$

$$= \frac{6{,}000{,}000 \text{ gtt}}{600{,}000 \text{ min}}$$

$$= 10 \text{ gtt/min}$$

Special computations

The fraction, ratio, and desired-available methods and dimensional analysis can be used to compute drug dosages when the ordered drug and the available form of the drug occur in the same unit of measure. These methods also can be used when the quantity of a particular dosage form differs from the unit in which the dosage form is administered.

For example, if a patient is to receive 1,000 mg of a drug available in liquid form and measured in milligrams, with 100 mg contained in 6 ml, how many milliliters should the patient receive? Because the ordered and the available dosages are in milligrams, no initial conversions are needed. The fraction method would be used to determine the number of milliliters the patient should receive—in this case, 60 ml.

If the drug must be given in ounces (oz), the number of ounces should be determined using a conversion method. For the fraction method of conversion, the equation would appear as:

$$\frac{60 \text{ ml}}{x \text{ oz}} = \frac{30 \text{ ml}}{1 \text{ oz}}$$

Solving for x shows that the patient should receive 2 ounces of the drug.

To use the desired-available method, change the order of the elements in the equation to correspond with the situation. The revised equation should appear as:

$$x \text{ quantity to give} = \frac{\text{ordered units}}{1} \times \frac{\text{quantity of dosage form}}{\text{stated quantity of drug within each dosage form}} \times \text{conversion fraction}$$

Placing the given information into the equation results in:

$$x \text{ oz} = \frac{1{,}000 \text{ mg}}{1} \times \frac{6 \text{ ml}}{100 \text{ mg}} \times \frac{1 \text{ oz}}{30 \text{ ml}}$$

Solving for x shows that the patient should receive 2 ounces of the drug.

Inexact nature of dosage computations

Converting drug measurements from one system to another and then determining the amount of a dosage form to give can easily produce inexact dosages. A rounding error made during computation or discrepancies in the dosage may occur, depending on the conversion standard used in calculation. Or, you may determine a precise amount to be given, only to find that administering that amount is impossible. For example, precise computations may indicate that a patient should receive 0.97 tablet. Administering such an amount is impossible.

The following general rule helps avoid calculation errors and discrepancies between theoretical and real dosages: *No more than a 10% variation should exist between the dosage ordered and the dosage to be given.* Following this simple rule, if you determine that a patient should receive 0.97 tablet, you can safely give 1 tablet.

Computing parenteral dosages

The methods for computing drug dosages can be used not just for oral but also for parenteral routes. The following example shows how to determine a parenteral drug dosage. Say a prescriber orders 75 mg of Demerol. The package label reads: meperidine (Demerol), 100 mg/ml. Using the fraction method to determine the number of milliliters the patient should receive, the equation should appear as:

$$\frac{75 \text{ mg}}{x \text{ ml}} = \frac{100 \text{ mg}}{1 \text{ ml}}$$

To solve for x, cross multiply:

$$x \text{ ml} \times 100 \text{ mg} = 75 \text{ mg} \times 1 \text{ ml}$$

$$x \text{ ml} = \frac{75 \text{ mg} \times 1 \text{ ml}}{100 \text{ mg}}$$

$$x \text{ ml} = \frac{75}{100}$$

$$x \text{ ml} = 0.75 \text{ ml}$$

The patient should receive 0.75 ml.

Reconstituting powders for injection

Although a pharmacist usually reconstitutes powders for parenteral use, nurses sometimes perform this function by following the directions on the drug label. The label gives the total quantity of drug in the vial or ampule, the amount and type of diluent to be added to the powder, and the strength and expiration date of the resulting solution.

When you add diluent to a powder, the powder increases the fluid volume. That's why the label calls for less diluent than the total volume of the prepared solution. For example, a label may tell you to add 1.7 ml of diluent to a vial of powdered drug to obtain a 2-ml total volume of prepared solution.

To determine the amount of solution to administer, use the manufacturer's information about the concentration of the solution. For example, if you want to administer 500 mg of a drug and the concentration of the prepared solution is 1 g (1,000 mg)/10 ml, use the following equation:

$$\frac{500 \text{ mg}}{x \text{ ml}} = \frac{1{,}000 \text{ mg}}{10 \text{ ml}}$$

The patient would receive 5 ml of the prepared solution.

Intravenous rates and flow rates

Make sure you know the difference between I.V. drip rate and flow rate and also how to calculate each rate. I.V. drip rate refers to the number of drops of solution to be infused per minute. Flow rate refers to the number of milliliters of fluid to be infused over 1 hour.

To calculate an I.V. drip rate, first set up a fraction showing the volume of solution to be delivered over the number of minutes in which that volume should be infused. For example, if a patient should receive 100 ml of solution in 1 hour, the fraction would be written as:

$$\frac{100 \text{ ml}}{60 \text{ min}}$$

Multiply the fraction by the drip factor (the number of drops contained in 1 ml) to determine the number of drops per minute to be infused, or the drip rate. The drip factor varies among different I.V. sets and should appear on the package that contains the I.V. tubing administration set.

Following the manufacturer's directions for drip factor is a crucial step. Standard I.V. administration sets have drip factors of 10, 15, or 20 gtt/ml. A microdrip, or minidrip, set has a drip factor of 60 gtt/ml.

Use the following equation to determine the drip rate of an I.V. solution:

$$\text{gtt/min} = \frac{\text{total no. of ml}}{\text{total no. of min}} \times \text{drip factor}$$

The equation applies to I.V. solutions that infuse over many hours or to small-volume infusions such as those used for antibiotics, usually administered in less than 1 hour. For example, if an order requires 1,000 ml of 5% dextrose in normal saline solution to infuse over 12 hours and the administration set delivers 15 gtt/ml, what should the drip rate be?

$$x \text{ gtt/min} = \frac{1{,}000 \text{ ml}}{720 \text{ min}} \times 15 \text{ gtt/ml}$$

$$x \text{ gtt/min} = 20.83 \text{ gtt/min}$$

The drip rate would be rounded to 21 gtt/minute.

You'll use flow rate calculations when working with I.V. infusion pumps to set the number of milliliters to be delivered in 1 hour. To perform this calculation, you should know the total volume in milliliters to be infused and the amount of time for the infusion. Use the following equation:

$$\text{flow rate} = \frac{\text{total volume ordered}}{\text{number of hours}}$$

Quick methods for calculating drip rates

Keep in mind that quicker methods exist for computing I.V. solution administration rates. To administer an I.V. solution through a microdrip set, adjust the flow rate (number of milliliters per hour) to equal the drip rate (gtt/minute).

Using this method, the flow rate would be divided by 60 minutes and then multiplied by the drip factor, which also equals 60. Because the flow rate and the drip factor are equal, the two arithmetic operations cancel each other out. For example, if 125 ml/hour represented the ordered flow rate, the equation would be:

$$\text{drip rate (125)} = \frac{125 \text{ ml}}{60 \text{ min}} \times 60$$

Rather than spend time calculating the equation, you can use the number assigned to the flow rate as the drip rate.

For I.V. administration sets that deliver 15 gtt/ml, the flow rate divided by 4 equals the drip rate. For sets with a drip factor of 10, the flow rate divided by 6 equals the drip rate.

Critical care calculations

Many drugs given on the critical care unit are used to treat life-threatening problems; you must be able to perform calculations swiftly and accurately, prepare the drug for infusion, administer it, and then observe the patient closely to evaluate the drug's effectiveness. Three calculations must be performed before administering critical care drugs:

- Calculate the concentration of the drug in the I.V. solution.
- Figure the flow rate needed to deliver the desired dose.
- Determine the needed dosage.

Calculating concentration

To calculate the drug's concentration, use the following formula:

$$\text{concentration in mg/ml} = \text{mg of drug/ml of fluid}$$

To express the concentration in mcg/ml, multiply the answer by 1,000.

Figuring flow rate

To determine the I.V. flow rate per minute, use the following formula:

$$\frac{\text{dose/min}}{x \text{ ml/min}} = \frac{\text{concentration of solution}}{1 \text{ ml of fluid}}$$

To calculate the hourly flow rate, first multiply the ordered dose, given in milligrams or micrograms per minute, by 60 minutes to determine the hourly dose. Then use the following equation to compute the hourly flow rate:

$$\frac{\text{hourly dose}}{x \text{ ml/hr}} = \frac{\text{concentration of solution}}{1 \text{ ml of fluid}}$$

Determining dosage

To determine the dosage in milligrams per kilogram of body weight per minute, first determine the concentration of the solution in milligrams per milliliter. (If a drug is ordered in micrograms, convert milligrams to micrograms by multiplying by 1,000.) To determine the dose in milligrams per hour, multiply the hourly flow rate by the concentration using the formula:

$$\text{dose in mg/hr} = \text{hourly flow rate} \times \text{concentration}$$

Then calculate the dose in milligrams per minute. Divide the hourly dose by 60 minutes:

$$\text{dose in mg/min} = \frac{\text{dose in mg/hr}}{\text{60 min}}$$

Divide the dose per minute by the patient's weight, using the following formula:

$$\text{mg/kg/min} = \frac{\text{mg/min}}{\text{patient's weight in kg}}$$

Finally, make sure that the drug is being given within a safe and therapeutic range. Compare the amount in milligrams per kilogram per minute to the safe range shown in a drug reference book.

The following examples show how to calculate an I.V. flow rate using the different formulas.

Example 1

A patient has frequent runs of ventricular tachycardia that subside after 10 to 12 beats. The prescriber orders 2 g (2,000 mg) of lidocaine in 500 ml of D_5W to infuse at 2 mg/minute. What's the flow rate in milliliters per minute? Milliliters per hour?

First, find the concentration of the solution by setting up a proportion with the unknown concentration in one fraction and the ordered dose in the other fraction:

$$\frac{x \text{ mg}}{1 \text{ ml}} = \frac{2{,}000 \text{ mg}}{500 \text{ ml}}$$

Cross multiply the fractions:

$$x \text{ mg} \times 500 \text{ ml} = 2{,}000 \text{ mg} \times 1 \text{ ml}$$

Solve for x by dividing each side of the equation by 500 ml and canceling units that appear in both the numerator and denominator:

$$\frac{x \text{ mg} \times \cancel{500 \text{ ml}}}{\cancel{500 \text{ ml}}} = \frac{2{,}000 \text{ mg} \times 1 \cancel{\text{ml}}}{500 \cancel{\text{ml}}}$$

$$x = \frac{2{,}000 \text{ mg}}{500}$$

$$x = 4 \text{ mg}$$

The concentration of the solution is 4 mg/ml. Next, calculate the flow rate per minute needed to deliver the ordered dose of 2 mg/minute. To do this, set up a proportion with the unknown flow rate per minute in one fraction and the concentration of the solution in the other fraction:

$$\frac{2 \text{ mg}}{x \text{ ml}} = \frac{4 \text{ mg}}{1 \text{ ml}}$$

Cross multiply the fractions:

$$x \text{ ml} \times 4 \text{ mg} = 1 \text{ ml} \times 2 \text{ mg}$$

Solve for x by dividing each side of the equation by 4 mg and canceling units that appear in both the numerator and denominator:

$$\frac{x \text{ ml} \times \cancel{4 \text{ mg}}}{\cancel{4 \text{ mg}}} = \frac{1 \text{ ml} \times 2 \cancel{\text{mg}}}{4 \cancel{\text{mg}}}$$

$$x = \frac{2 \text{ ml}}{4}$$

$$x = 0.5 \text{ ml}$$

The patient should receive 0.5 ml/minute of lidocaine. Because lidocaine must be given with an infusion pump, compute the hourly flow rate. Set up a proportion with the unknown flow rate per hour in one fraction and the flow rate per minute in the other fraction:

$$\frac{x \text{ ml}}{60 \text{ min}} = \frac{0.5 \text{ ml}}{1 \text{ min}}$$

Cross multiply the fractions:

$$x \text{ ml} \times 1 \text{ min} = 0.5 \text{ ml} \times 60 \text{ min}$$

Solve for x by dividing each side of the equation by 1 minute and canceling units that appear in both the numerator and denominator:

$$\frac{x \text{ ml} \times \cancel{1 \text{ min}}}{\cancel{1 \text{ min}}} = \frac{0.5 \text{ ml} \times 60 \cancel{\text{min}}}{1 \cancel{\text{min}}}$$

$$x = 30 \text{ ml}$$

Set the infusion pump to deliver 30 ml/hour.

Example 2

A 200-pound patient is scheduled to receive an I.V. infusion of dobutamine at 10 mcg/kg/min. The package insert says to dilute 250 mg of the drug in 50 ml of D_5W. Because the drug vial contains 20 ml of solution, the total to be infused is 70 ml (50 ml of D_5W plus 20 ml of solution). How many micrograms of the drug should the patient receive each minute? Each hour?

First, compute the patient's weight in kilograms. To do this, set up a proportion with the weight in pounds and the unknown weight in kilograms in one fraction and the number of pounds per kilogram in the other fraction:

$$\frac{200 \text{ lb}}{x \text{ kg}} = \frac{2.2 \text{ lb}}{1 \text{ kg}}$$

Cross multiply the fractions:

$$x \text{ kg} \times 2.2 \text{ lb} = 1 \text{ kg} \times 200 \text{ lb}$$

Solve for x by dividing each side of the equation by 2.2 lb and canceling units that appear in both the numerator and denominator.

$$\frac{x \text{ kg} \times 2.2 \cancel{\text{lb}}}{2.2 \cancel{\text{lb}}} = \frac{1 \text{ kg} \times 200 \cancel{\text{lb}}}{2.2 \cancel{\text{lb}}}$$

$$x = \frac{200 \text{ kg}}{2.2}$$

$$x = 90.9 \text{ kg}$$

The patient weighs 90.9 kg. Next, determine the dose in micrograms per minute by setting up a proportion with the patient's weight in kilograms and the unknown dose in micrograms per minute in one fraction and the known dose in micrograms per kilogram per minute in the other fraction:

$$\frac{90.9 \text{ kg}}{x \text{ mcg/min}} = \frac{1 \text{ kg}}{10 \text{ mcg/min}}$$

Cross multiply the fractions:

$$x \text{ mcg/min} \times 1 \text{ kg} = 10 \text{ mcg/min} \times 90.9 \text{ kg}$$

Solve for x by dividing each side of the equation by 1 kg and canceling units that appear in both the numerator and denominator:

$$\frac{x \text{ mcg/min} \times 1 \cancel{\text{kg}}}{1 \cancel{\text{kg}}} = \frac{10 \text{ mcg/min} \times 90.9 \cancel{\text{kg}}}{1 \cancel{\text{kg}}}$$

$$x = 909 \text{ mcg/min}$$

The patient should receive 909 mcg of dobutamine every minute. Finally, determine the hourly dose by multiplying the dose per minute by 60:

$$909 \text{ mcg/min} \times 60 \text{ min/hr} = 54{,}540 \text{ mcg/hr}$$

The patient should receive 54,540 mcg of dobutamine every hour.

Pediatric dosage considerations

To determine the correct pediatric dosage of a drug, prescribers, pharmacists, and nurses usually use two computation methods. One is based on weight in kilograms; the other uses the child's body surface area. Other methods are less accurate and not recommended.

Dosage range per kilogram of body weight

Currently, many pharmaceutical companies provide information on the safe dosage ranges for drugs given to children. The companies usually provide the dosage ranges in milligrams per kilogram of body weight and, in many cases, give similar information for adult dosage ranges. The following example and explanation show how to calculate the safe pediatric dosage range for a drug, using the company's suggested safe dosage range provided in milligrams per kilogram.

For a child, a prescriber orders a drug with a suggested dosage range of 10 to 12 mg/kg of body weight/day. The child weighs 12 kg. What is the safe daily dosage range for the child?

You must calculate the lower and upper limits of the dosage range provided by the manufacturer. First, calculate the dosage based on 10 mg/kg of body weight. Then, calculate the dosage based on 12 mg/kg of body weight. The answers, 120 mg and 144 mg, represent the lower and upper limits, respectively, of the daily dosage range, expressed in mg/kg of the child's weight.

Body surface area

A second method for calculating safe pediatric dosages uses the child's body surface area. This method may provide a more accurate calculation because the child's body surface area is thought to parallel the child's organ growth and maturation and metabolic rate.

You can determine the body surface area of a child by using a three-column chart called a nomogram. Mark the child's height in the first column and weight in the third column. Then draw a line between the two marks. The point at which the line intersects the vertical scale in the second column is the child's estimated body surface area in square meters. To calculate the child's approximate dose, use the body surface area measurement in the following equation:

$$\frac{\text{body surface area of child}}{\text{average adult body surface area } (1.73\text{m}^2)} \times \text{average adult dose} = \text{child's dose}$$

The following example illustrates the use of the equation. The nomogram shows that a 25-lb (11.3-kg) child who is 33 inches (84 cm) tall has a body surface area of 0.52 m². To determine the child's dose of a drug with an average adult dose of 100 mg, the equation would appear as:

$$\frac{0.52\text{ m}^2}{1.73\text{ m}^2} \times 100\text{ mg} = \begin{matrix}30.06\text{ mg}\\ \text{(child's dose)}\end{matrix}$$

The child should receive 30 mg of the drug. Keep in mind that many facilities have guidelines that determine acceptable calculation methods for pediatric dosages. If you work in a pediatric setting, make sure to familiarize yourself with your facility's policies about pediatric dosages.

3

Drug administration

You may administer drugs by many routes, including topical, oral, buccal, sublingual (S.L.), ophthalmic, otic, respiratory, nasogastric (NG), vaginal, rectal, subcutaneous (S.C.), intramuscular (I.M.), and intravenous (I.V.) routes. No matter which route you use, however, you'll need to follow established precautions to make sure you give the right drug in the right dose to the right patient at the right time and by the right route. These precautions include checking the order, medication record, and label; confirming the patient's identity; following standard safety procedures; and addressing any patient's questions.

Check the order

Make sure that you have a written order for every drug given. Verbal orders should be used only in emergencies and should be signed by the prescriber within the time period specified by your facility. If your facility has a computerized order system, it may allow prescribers to order drugs electronically from the pharmacy. The computer may indicate whether the pharmacy has the drug and triggers the pharmacy staff to fill the prescription. A computerized order also may generate a patient record on which you can document medication administration. In fact, you may be able to document administration right on the computer.

Computer systems offer several advantages over paper systems. For instance, drugs may arrive on the unit or floor more quickly. Documentation is quicker and easier. Prescribers can see at a glance which drugs have been administered. Errors won't result from poor handwriting (although typing mistakes may occur). Finally, computerized records are easier to store than paper records.

Check the medication record

Check the order on the patient's medication record against the prescriber's order.

Check the label

Before administering a drug, check its label three times to make sure you're giving the prescribed drug and the prescribed dose. First, check the label when you take the container from the shelf or drawer. Next, check the label right before pouring the drug into the medication cup or drawing it into the syringe. Finally, check the label again before returning the container to the shelf or drawer. If you're giving a unit-dose drug, you'll be opening the container at the patient's bedside. Check the label for the third time immediately after pouring the drug and again before discarding the wrapper.

Don't administer a drug from a poorly labeled or unlabeled container. Also, don't attempt to label a drug or to reinforce a label that is falling off or improperly placed. Instead return the drug to the pharmacist for verification and proper labeling.

Confirm the patient's identity

Before giving the drug, ask the patient his full name, and confirm his identity by checking his name and medical record number on his patient identification wristband against the medication administration record. Don't rely on information that can vary during a hospital stay, such as a room or bed number. Check again that you have the correct drug, and make sure the patient has no allergy to it.

If the patient has any drug allergies, check to make sure the chart and medication administration record are labeled accordingly and that the patient is wearing an allergy wristband identifying the allergen.

Follow safety procedures

Whenever you administer a drug, follow these safety procedures:

- Never give a drug poured or prepared by someone else.
- Never allow the medication cart or tray out of your sight once you've prepared a dose.
- Never leave a drug at a patient's bedside.

• Never return unwrapped or prepared drugs to stock containers; instead, dispose of them, and notify the pharmacy.
• Keep the medication cart locked at all times.
• Follow standard precautions, as appropriate.

Respond to questions

If the patient questions you about his drug or dosage, check his medication record again. If the drug you're giving is correct, reassure the patient. Explain any changes in his drug or dosage. Instruct him, as appropriate, about possible adverse reactions, and ask him to report anything that he feels may be an adverse reaction.

Topical administration

Topical drugs, such as patches, lotions, and ointments, are applied directly to the skin. They're commonly used for local, rather than systemic, effects. Keep in mind, however, that certain types of topical drugs—known as transdermal drugs—are meant to enter the patient's bloodstream, and therefore, exert a systemic effect after you apply them.

Equipment and preparation

• Check the chart and the medication administration record.
• Gather the prescribed drug, sterile tongue blades, gloves, sterile gloves for open lesions, sterile 4″ × 4″ gauze pads, transparent semipermeable dressing, adhesive tape, normal saline solution, cotton-tipped applicators, gloves, and linen savers, if necessary.

Implementation

• Confirm the patient's identity by asking his full name and checking the name and medical record number on his wristband.
• Explain the procedure to the patient because, after discharge, he may have to apply the drug by himself.
• Premedicate the patient with an analgesic if the procedure is uncomfortable. Give the medication time to take effect.
• Wash your hands to reduce the risk of cross-contamination, and glove your dominant hand.
• Help the patient to a comfortable position, and expose the area to be treated. Make sure the skin or mucous membrane is intact (unless the drug has been ordered to treat a skin lesion). Application of drug to broken or abraded skin may cause unwanted systemic absorption and further irritation.
• If necessary, clean debris from the skin. You may have to change your gloves if they become soiled.

To apply paste, cream, or ointment

• Open the container. Place the cap upside down to avoid contaminating its inner surface.
• Remove a tongue blade from its sterile wrapper, and cover one end of it with drug from the tube or jar. Then transfer the drug from the tongue blade to your gloved hand.
• Apply the drug to the affected area with long, smooth strokes that follow the direction of hair growth. This technique avoids forcing the drug into hair follicles, which can cause irritation and lead to folliculitis. Avoid excessive pressure when applying the drug because it could abrade the skin or cause the patient discomfort.
• When applying a drug to the patient's face, use cotton-tipped applicators for small areas, such as under the eyes. For larger areas, use a sterile gauze pad.
• To prevent contamination of the drug, use a new sterile tongue blade each time you remove a drug from its container.
• Remove and discard your gloves, and wash your hands.

To apply transdermal ointment

• Choose the application site—usually a dry, hairless spot on the patient's chest or upper arm.
• To promote absorption, wash the site with soap and warm water. Dry it thoroughly.
• Put on gloves.
• If the patient has a previously applied medication strip at another site, remove it and wash this area to clear away any drug residue.
• If the area you choose is hairy, clip excess hair rather than shaving it; shaving causes irritation, which the drug may worsen.

• Squeeze the prescribed amount of ointment onto the application strip or measuring paper. Don't get the ointment on your skin.
• Apply the strip, drug side down, directly to the patient's skin.
• Maneuver the strip slightly to spread a thin layer of the ointment over a 3″ (8-cm) area, but don't rub the ointment into the skin.
• Secure the application strip to the patient's skin by covering it with a semipermeable dressing or plastic wrap.
• Tape the covering securely in place.
• If required by your facility's policy, label the strip with the date, time, and your initials.
• Remove your gloves and wash your hands.

To apply a transdermal patch

• Remove the old patch.
• Choose a dry, hairless application site.
• As with the transdermal ointment, clip (don't shave) hair from the chosen site. Wash the area with warm water and soap, and dry it thoroughly.
• Open the drug package and remove the patch.
• Without touching the adhesive surface, remove the clear plastic backing.
• Apply the patch to the site without touching the adhesive.
• If required by your facility's policy, label the patch with the date, time, and your initials.

To remove ointment

• Wash your hands and put on gloves.
• Gently swab ointment from the patient's skin using a sterile 4″ × 4″ gauze pad saturated with normal saline solution.
• Don't wipe too hard because you could irritate the skin.
• Remove and discard your gloves, and wash your hands.

Nursing considerations

• To prevent skin irritation from drug accumulation, never apply a drug without first removing previous applications.
• Always wear gloves to prevent absorption by your skin.
• Never apply ointment to the eyelids or ear canal unless ordered. The ointment may congeal and occlude the tear duct or ear canal.
• Inspect the treated area frequently for allergic or other adverse reactions.
• Don't apply a topical drug to scarred or callused skin because this may impair absorption.
• Don't place a defibrillator paddle on a transdermal patch. The aluminum on the patch can cause electrical arcing during defibrillation, resulting in smoke and thermal burns. If a patient has a patch on a standard paddle site, remove the patch before applying the paddle.

Oral administration

Because oral drug administration is usually the safest, most convenient, and least expensive, most drugs are administered by this method. Drugs for oral administration are available in many forms: tablets, enteric-coated tablets, capsules, syrups, elixirs, oils, liquids, suspensions, powders, and granules. Some require special preparation before administration, such as mixing with juice to make them more palatable.

Oral drugs are sometimes prescribed in higher dosages than their parenteral equivalents because, after absorption through the gastrointestinal (GI) system, they're broken down by the liver before they reach the systemic circulation.

Equipment and preparation

• Check the chart and the medication administration record.
• Gather the prescribed drug and medication cup.
• If necessary, gather a mortar and pestle for crushing pills and an appropriate vehicle, such as jelly or applesauce for crushed pills or juice, water, or milk for liquid drugs. These variations are commonly used for children or elderly patients.

Implementation

• Wash your hands.
• Confirm the patient's identity by asking his full name and checking the name and medical record number on his wristband.
• Assess the patient's condition, including level of consciousness and vital signs, as needed.

Changes in the patient's condition may warrant withholding the drug.

- Give the patient the drug. If appropriate, crush the drug to facilitate swallowing or mix it with an appropriate vehicle or liquid to aid swallowing, minimize adverse effects, or promote absorption.
- Stay with the patient until he has swallowed the drug. If he seems confused or disoriented, check his mouth to make sure he has swallowed it. Return and reassess the patient's response within 1 hour after giving the drug.

Nursing considerations

- To avoid damaging or staining the patient's teeth, give acid or iron preparations through a straw. An unpleasant-tasting liquid can usually be made more palatable if taken through a straw because the liquid contacts fewer taste buds.
- If the patient can't swallow a whole tablet or capsule, ask the pharmacist if the drug is available in liquid form or if it can be administered by another route. If not, ask the pharmacist if the tablet can be crushed or if capsules can be opened and mixed with food.
- Don't crush sustained-action drugs, buccal tablets, S.L. tablets, or enteric-coated drugs because these drugs may become ineffective if crushed.

Buccal and sublingual administration

Certain drugs are given buccally (between the cheek and teeth) or S.L. (under the tongue) to bypass the digestive tract and facilitate absorption into the bloodstream. Erythrityl tetranitrate is an example of a drug given buccally. Drugs given S.L. include ergotamine tartrate, erythrityl tetranitrate, isoproterenol hydrochloride, isosorbide dinitrate, and nitroglycerin. When using either administration method, observe the patient carefully to make sure he doesn't swallow the drug or develop mucosal irritation.

Equipment and preparation

- Check the chart and the medication administration record.
- Gather the prescribed drug, medication cup, and gloves.

Implementation

- Wash your hands. Put on gloves if you'll be placing the drug into the patient's mouth.
- Confirm the patient's identity by asking his full name and checking the name and medical record number on his wristband.
- For buccal administration, place the tablet in the patient's buccal pouch, between the cheek and teeth, as shown below.

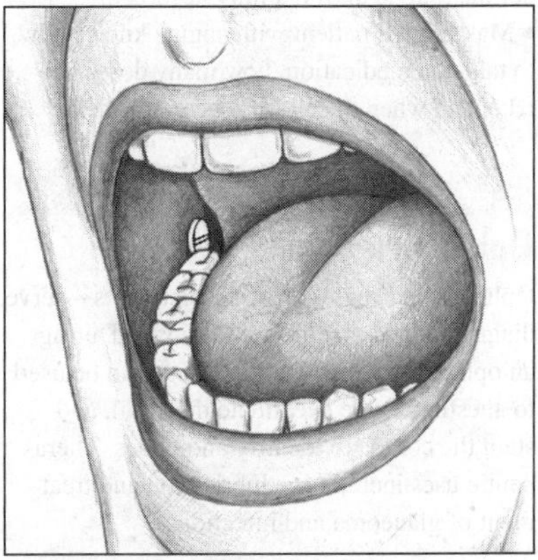

- For S.L. administration, place the tablet under the patient's tongue, as shown below.

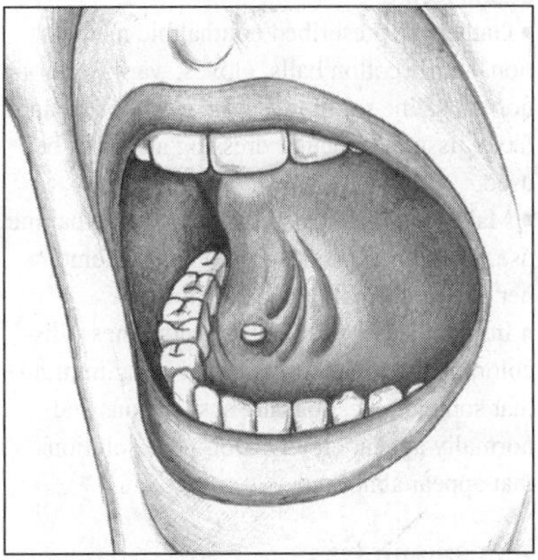

- Remove and discard your gloves, and wash your hands.
- Instruct the patient to keep the drug in place until it dissolves completely to ensure absorp-

tion. Caution the patient against chewing the tablet or touching it with his tongue to prevent accidental swallowing.
- Tell the patient not to smoke before the drug has dissolved because the vasoconstrictive effects of nicotine slow drug absorption.

Nursing considerations

- Don't give liquids until a buccal tablet is absorbed, in some cases up to 1 hour.
- If the patient has angina, tell him to wet the nitroglycerin tablet with saliva and keep it under his tongue until it's fully absorbed.
- Make sure a patient with angina knows how to take the medication, how many doses to take, and when to call for emergency help.

Ophthalmic administration

Ophthalmic drugs—drops or ointments—serve diagnostic and therapeutic purposes. During an ophthalmic examination, drugs can be used to anesthetize the eye, dilate the pupil, and stain the cornea to identify anomalies. Therapeutic uses include eye lubrication and treatment of glaucoma and infections.

Equipment and preparation

- Check the chart and the medication administration record.
- Gather the prescribed ophthalmic medication, sterile cotton balls, gloves, warm water or normal saline solution, sterile gauze pads, and facial tissue. An ocular dressing also may be used.
- Make sure the drug is labeled for ophthalmic use. Then check the expiration date. Remember to date the container after first use.
- Inspect ocular solutions for cloudiness, discoloration, and precipitation, keeping in mind that some medications are suspensions and normally appear cloudy. Don't use solutions that appear abnormal.

Implementation

- Make sure you know which eye to treat because different drugs or doses may be ordered for each eye.
- Confirm the patient's identity by asking his full name and checking the name and medical record number on his wristband.
- Put on gloves.
- If the patient has an eye dressing, remove it by pulling it down and away from his forehead. Avoid contaminating your hands. Don't apply pressure to the area around the eyes.
- To remove exudates or meibomian gland secretions, clean around the eye with sterile cotton balls or sterile gauze pads moistened with warm water or normal saline solution. Have the patient close his eye; then gently wipe the eyelids from the inner to the outer canthus. Use a fresh cotton ball or gauze pad for each stroke, and use a different cotton ball or pad for each eye.
- Have the patient sit or lie in the supine position. Instruct him to tilt his head back and toward his affected eye so that any excess drug can flow away from the tear duct, minimizing systemic absorption through the nasal mucosa.
- Remove the dropper cap from the drug container, and draw the drug into the dropper. Or, if the bottle has a dropper tip, remove the cap and hold or place it upside down to prevent contamination.
- Before instilling eyedrops, instruct the patient to look up and away. This moves the cornea away from the lower lid and minimizes the risk of touching it with the dropper.

To instill eyedrops

- Steady the hand that's holding the dropper by resting it against the patient's forehead. With your other hand, gently pull down the lower lid of the affected eye, and instill the drops in the conjunctival sac. Never instill eyedrops directly onto the eyeball.
- When teaching elderly patients how to instill eyedrops, keep in mind that they may have difficulty sensing drops in the eye. Suggest chilling the drug slightly because the cold drops will be easier to feel when they enter the eye.

To apply eye ointment

- Squeeze a small ribbon of drug on the edge of the conjunctival sac from the inner to the outer canthus. Cut off the ribbon by turning the tube. Don't touch the eye with the tip of the tube.

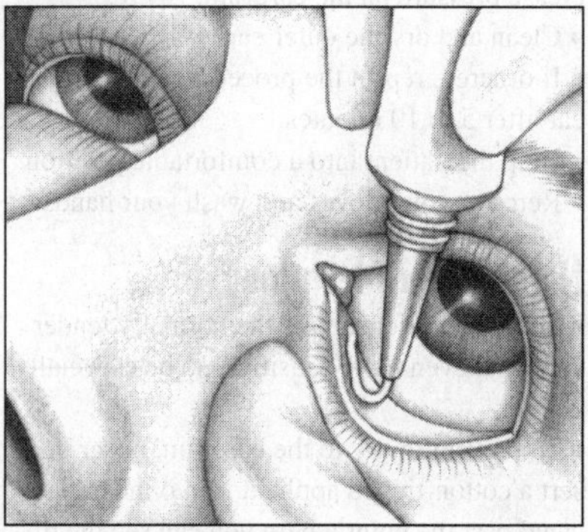

• After instilling eyedrops or applying ointment, instruct the patient to close his eyes gently, without squeezing the lids shut. If you instilled drops, tell the patient to blink. If you applied ointment, tell him to roll his eyes behind closed lids to help distribute the drug over the eyeball.
• Use a clean tissue to remove any excess drug that leaks from the eye. Use a fresh tissue for each eye to prevent cross-contamination.
• Apply a new eye dressing, if necessary.
• Remove and discard your gloves. Wash your hands.

Nursing considerations

• When administering an eye medication that may be absorbed systemically, gently press your thumb on the inner canthus for 1 to 2 minutes after instillation while the patient closes his eyes. Avoid applying pressure around the eye.
• Urge the patient not to rub his eyes.
• To maintain the drug container's sterility, don't put the cap down after opening the container, and never touch the tip of the dropper or bottle to the eye area. Discard any solution remaining in the dropper before returning it to the bottle. If the dropper or bottle tip has become contaminated, discard it and use another sterile dropper. Never share eyedrops between patients.

Otic administration

Eardrops may be instilled to treat infection and inflammation, to soften cerumen for later removal, to produce local anesthesia, or to facilitate removal of an insect trapped in the ear.

Equipment and preparation

• Check the chart and the medication administration record.
• Gather the prescribed eardrops, gloves, a light, and facial tissue or cotton-tipped applicators. Cotton balls and a bowl of warm water may be needed, as well.
• First, warm the drug to body temperature in the bowl of warm water, or carry the drug in your pocket for 30 minutes before administration. If necessary, test the temperature of the drug by placing a drop on your wrist. (If the drug is too hot, it may burn the patient's eardrum.)
• To avoid injuring the ear canal, check the dropper before use to make sure it's not chipped or cracked.

Implementation

• Wash your hands and put on clean gloves.
• Confirm the patient's identity by asking his full name and checking the name and medical record number on his wristband.
• Have the patient lie on the side opposite the affected ear.

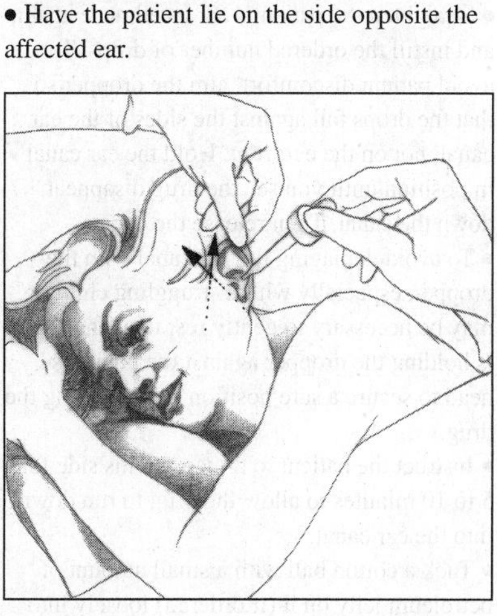

• Straighten the patient's ear canal. For an adult, pull the auricle up and back. For an infant or child under age 3, gently pull the auricle down and back because the ear canal is straighter at this age.

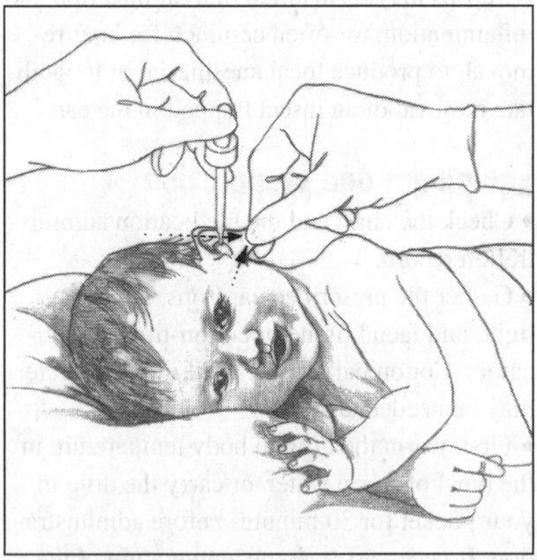

• Using a light, examine the ear canal for drainage. If you see drainage, gently clean the canal with the tissue or cotton-tipped applicators because drainage can reduce the effectiveness of the drug. Never insert an applicator past the point where you can see it.
• Compare the label on the eardrops to the order on the patient's medication record. Check the label again while drawing the drug into the dropper. Check the label for the final time before administering the eardrops into the patient's ear.
• Straighten the patient's ear canal once again, and instill the ordered number of drops. To avoid patient discomfort, aim the dropper so that the drops fall against the sides of the ear canal, not on the eardrum. Hold the ear canal in position until you see the drug disappear down the canal. Then release the ear.
• To avoid damaging the ear canal with the dropper, especially with a struggling child, it may be necessary to gently rest the hand that is holding the dropper against the patient's head to secure a safe position before giving the drug.
• Instruct the patient to remain on his side for 5 to 10 minutes to allow the drug to run down into the ear canal.
• Tuck a cotton ball with a small amount of petroleum jelly on it (if ordered) loosely into the opening of the ear canal to prevent the drug from leaking out. Be careful not to insert it too deeply into the canal because doing so may prevent drainage of secretions and increase pressure on the eardrum.
• Clean and dry the outer ear.
• If ordered, repeat the procedure in the other ear after 5 to 10 minutes.
• Help the patient into a comfortable position.
• Remove your gloves and wash your hands.

Nursing considerations

• Some conditions make the normally tender ear canal even more sensitive, so be especially gentle.
• To prevent injury to the eardrum, never insert a cotton-tipped applicator into the ear canal past the point where you can see the tip.
• After instilling eardrops to soften cerumen, irrigate the ear as ordered to facilitate its removal. If the patient has vertigo, keep the side rails of his bed up and assist him as needed during the procedure. Also, move slowly to avoid worsening his vertigo.
• If necessary, teach the patient to instill the eardrops correctly so that he can continue treatment at home. Review the procedure, and let the patient try it himself while you observe.

Respiratory administration

Hand-held oropharyngeal inhalers include the metered-dose inhaler and the turbo-inhaler. These devices deliver topical drugs to the respiratory tract, producing local and systemic effects. The mucosal lining of the respiratory tract absorbs the inhalant almost immediately. Examples of inhalants are bronchodilators, which improve airway patency and facilitate mucous drainage, and mucolytics, which liquefy tenacious bronchial secretions.

Equipment and preparation

• Check the chart and the medication administration record.
• Gather the metered-dose inhaler or turbo-inhaler, prescribed drug, and normal saline solution.

To use a metered-dose inhaler

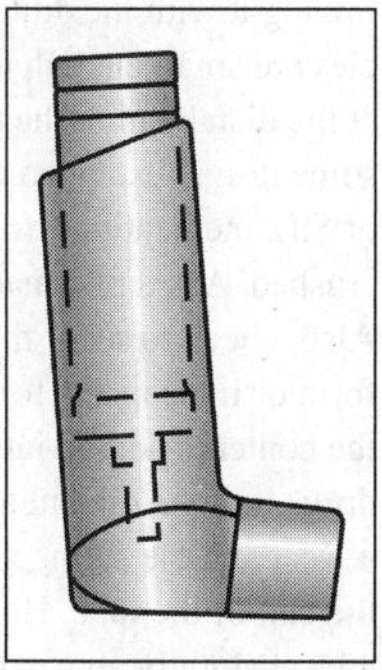

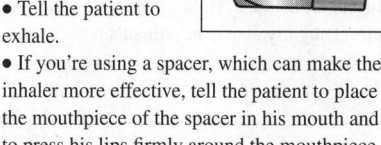

- Shake the inhaler bottle. Remove the cap and insert the stem into the small hole on the flattened portion of the mouthpiece, as shown.
- Place the inhaler about 1″ (2.5 cm) in front of the patient's open mouth.
- Tell the patient to exhale.
- If you're using a spacer, which can make the inhaler more effective, tell the patient to place the mouthpiece of the spacer in his mouth and to press his lips firmly around the mouthpiece.
- As you push the bottle down against the mouthpiece, instruct the patient to inhale slowly through his mouth and to continue inhaling until his lungs feel full. Compress the bottle against the mouthpiece only once.
- Remove the inhaler and tell the patient to hold his breath for several seconds. Then instruct him to exhale slowly through pursed lips to keep distal bronchioles open and allow increased absorption and diffusion of the drug.
- Have the patient gargle with normal saline solution or water to remove the drug from his mouth and the back of his throat. This step helps prevent oral fungal infections. Warn the patient not to swallow after gargling, but rather to spit out the liquid.

To use a turbo-inhaler

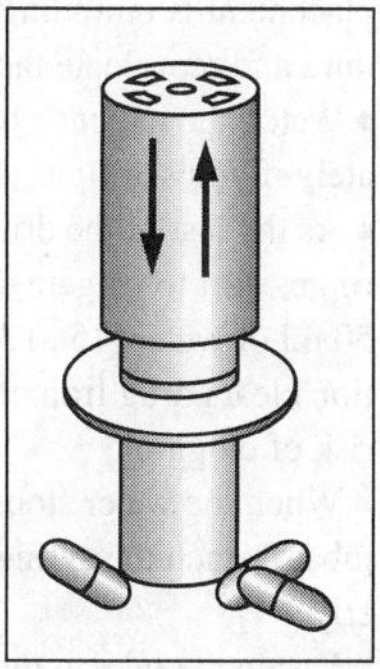

- Hold the mouthpiece in one hand. With the other hand, slide the sleeve away from the mouthpiece as far as possible, as shown.
- Unscrew the tip of the mouthpiece by turning it counterclockwise.
- Press the colored portion of the drug capsule into the propeller stem of the mouthpiece.
- Screw the inhaler together again.
- Holding the inhaler with the mouthpiece at the bottom, slide the sleeve all the way down and then up again to puncture the capsule and release the drug. Do this only once.
- Have the patient exhale completely and tilt his head back. Instruct him to place the mouthpiece in his mouth, close his lips around it, and inhale once. Tell him to hold his breath for several seconds.
- Remove the inhaler from the patient's mouth, and tell him to exhale as much air as possible.
- Repeat the procedure until all the drug in the device is inhaled.
- Have the patient gargle and spit with normal saline solution or water, if desired, to remove the drug from his mouth and the back of his throat.

Nursing considerations

- Teach the patient how to use the inhaler so he can continue treatments after discharge, if needed. Explain that overdose can cause the drug to lose its effectiveness. Tell him to record the date and time of each inhalation and his response.
- Be aware that some oral respiratory drugs may cause restlessness, palpitations, nervousness, and other systemic effects. They also can cause hypersensitivity reactions, such as rash, urticaria, or bronchospasm.
- Administer oral respiratory drugs cautiously to patients with heart disease because these drugs may potentiate coronary insufficiency, cardiac arrhythmias, or hypertension. If paradoxical bronchospasm occurs, discontinue the drug and call the prescriber to prescribe another drug.
- If the patient is prescribed a bronchodilator and a corticosteroid, give the bronchodilator first so the air passages can open fully before the patient uses the corticosteroid.
- Instruct the patient to keep an extra inhaler handy.
- Instruct the patient to discard the inhaler after taking the prescribed number of doses and to then start a new inhaler.
- Urge the patient to notify his clinician if he notices an increased use of or need for an inhaler or his symptoms are not relieved with the prescribed regimen.

Nasogastric administration

Besides providing an alternative means of nourishment for patients who can't eat normally, a nasogastric (NG) tube allows direct instillation of drugs into the GI system.

Equipment and preparation

- Check the chart and the medication administration record.
- Gather equipment for use at the bedside, including prescribed drug, towel or linen-saver pad, 50- or 60-ml piston-type catheter-tip syringe, feeding tubing, two 4″ × 4″ gauze pads, stethoscope, gloves, diluent (juice, water, or a nutritional supplement); cup for mixing drug and fluid, spoon, 50-ml cup of water, and rubber band. Pill-crushing equipment and a clamp (if not already attached to the tube) also may be needed.
- Make sure that liquids are at room temperature to avoid abdominal cramping and that the cup, syringe, spoon, and gauze are clean.

Implementation

- Wash your hands and put on gloves.
- Confirm the patient's identity by asking his full name and checking the name and medical record number on his wristband.
- Unpin the tube from the patient's gown. To avoid soiling the sheets during the procedure, fold back the bed linens and drape the patient's chest with a towel or linen-saver pad.
- Help the patient into Fowler's position, if his condition allows.
- After unclamping the tube, auscultate the patient's abdomen about 3″ (8 cm) below the sternum as you gently insert 10 ml of air into the tube with the 50- or 60-ml syringe. You should hear the air bubble entering the stomach. Gently draw back on the piston of the syringe. The appearance of gastric contents indicates that the tube is patent and is properly placed in the stomach.
- If no gastric contents appear or if you meet resistance, the tube may be lying against the gastric mucosa. Withdraw the tube slightly or turn the patient to free it.
- Clamp the tube, detach the syringe, and lay the end of the tube on the 4″ × 4″ gauze pad.
- If the drug is in tablet form, crush it before mixing it with the diluent. Make sure the particles are small enough to pass through the eyes at the distal end of the tube. Keep in mind that some drugs (extended release, enteric-coated, or S.L. medications, for example) shouldn't be crushed. Ask a pharmacist if you aren't sure. Also, check to see if the drug comes in liquid form or if a capsule form may be opened and the contents poured into a diluent. Pour liquid drugs into the diluent and stir well.
- Reattach the syringe, without the piston, to the end of the tube. Holding the tube upright at a level slightly above the patient's nose, open the clamp and pour the drug in slowly and steadily, as shown below.

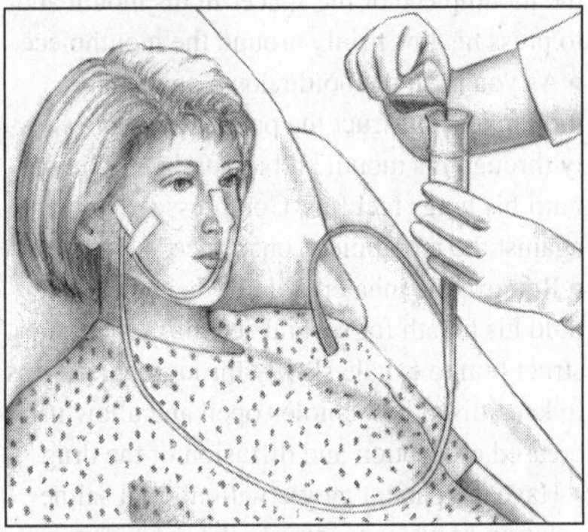

- To keep air from entering the patient's stomach, hold the tube at a slight angle and add more drug before the syringe empties. If the drug flows smoothly, slowly give the entire dose. If it doesn't flow, it may be too thick. If so, dilute it with water. If you suspect that tube placement is inhibiting flow, stop the procedure and reevaluate the placement.
- Watch the patient's reaction. Stop immediately if you see signs of discomfort.
- As the last of the drug flows out of the syringe, start to irrigate the tube by adding 30 to 50 ml of water (15 to 30 ml for a child). Irrigation clears drug from the tube and reduces the risk of clogging.
- When the water stops flowing, clamp the tube. Detach the syringe, and discard it properly.
- Fasten the tube to the patient's gown, and make the patient comfortable.

• Leave the patient in Fowler's position or on his right side with his head partially elevated for at least 30 minutes to facilitate flow and prevent esophageal reflux.
• Remove and discard your gloves, and wash your hands.

Nursing considerations

• If you must give a tube feeding as well as instill a drug, give the drug first to make sure the patient receives it all.
• Certain drugs—such as dilantin—bind with tube feedings, decreasing the availability of the drug. Stop the tube feeding for 2 hours before and after the dose, according to your facility's policy.
• If residual stomach contents exceed 150 ml, withhold the drug and feeding, and notify the prescriber. Excessive stomach contents may indicate intestinal obstruction or paralytic ileus.
• Never crush enteric-coated, buccal, S.L., or sustained-release drugs.
• If the NG tube is on suction, turn it off for 20 to 30 minutes after giving a drug.

Vaginal administration

Vaginal drugs can be inserted as topical treatment for infection, particularly *Trichomonas vaginalis* and vaginal candidiasis or inflammation. Suppositories melt when they contact the vaginal mucosa, and the drug diffuses topically.

Vaginal drugs usually come with a disposable applicator that enables placement of drug in the anterior and posterior fornices. Vaginal administration is most effective when the patient can remain lying down afterward to retain the drug.

Equipment and preparation

• Check the chart and the medication administration record.
• Gather the prescribed drug and applicator (if needed), gloves, water-soluble lubricant, and a small sanitary pad.

Implementation

• If possible, give vaginal drugs at bedtime when the patient is recumbent.
• Confirm the patient's identity by asking her full name and checking the name and medical record number on her wristband.
• Wash your hands, explain the procedure to the patient, and provide privacy.
• Ask the patient to void.
• Ask the patient if she would rather insert the drug herself. If so, provide appropriate instructions. If not, proceed with the following steps.
• Help her into the lithotomy position. Drape the patient, exposing only the perineum.
• Remove the suppository from the wrapper and lubricate it with water-soluble lubricant.
• Put on gloves, and expose the vagina by spreading the labia. If you see discharge, wash the area with several cotton balls soaked in warm, soapy water. Clean each side of the perineum and then the center, using a fresh cotton ball for each stroke. While the labia are still separated, insert the suppository or vaginal applicator about 3″ to 4″ (7.6 to 10 cm) into the vagina.

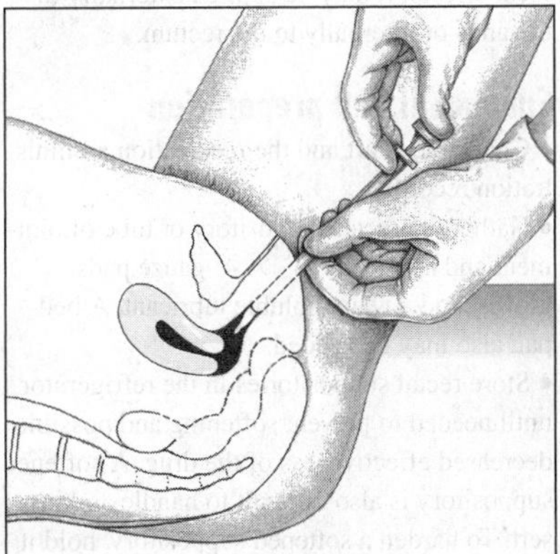

• After insertion, wash the applicator with soap and warm water, and store or discard it, as appropriate. Label it so it will be used only for one patient.
• Remove and discard your gloves.
• To keep the drug from soiling the patient's clothing and bedding, provide a sanitary pad.

• Help the patient return to a comfortable position, and tell her to stay in bed as much as possible for the next several hours.
• Wash your hands thoroughly.

Nursing considerations

• Refrigerate vaginal suppositories that melt at room temperature.
• If possible, teach the patient how to insert the vaginal drug because she may have to administer it herself after discharge. Give her instructions in writing if possible.
• Instruct the patient not to insert a tampon after inserting a vaginal drug because the tampon will absorb the drug and decrease its effectiveness.

Rectal administration

A rectal suppository is a small, solid, medicated mass, usually cone shaped, with a cocoa butter or glycerin base. It may be inserted to stimulate peristalsis and defecation or to relieve pain, vomiting, and local irritation. An ointment is a semisolid drug used to produce local effects. It may be applied externally to the anus or internally to the rectum.

Equipment and preparation

• Check the chart and the medication administration record.
• Gather the rectal suppository or tube of ointment and applicator, 4″ × 4″ gauze pads, gloves, and a water-soluble lubricant. A bedpan also may be needed.
• Store rectal suppositories in the refrigerator until needed to prevent softening and possible decreased effectiveness of the drug. A softened suppository is also difficult to handle and insert. To harden a softened suppository, hold it (in its wrapper) under cold running water.

Implementation

• Confirm the patient's identity by asking his full name and checking the name and medical record number on his wristband.
• Wash your hands.

To insert a rectal suppository

• Place the patient on his left side in Sims' position. Drape him with the bedcovers, exposing only his buttocks.
• Put on gloves. Unwrap the suppository, and lubricate it with water-soluble lubricant.
• Lift the patient's upper buttock with your nondominant hand to expose the anus.
• Instruct the patient to take several deep breaths through his mouth to relax the anal sphincter and reduce anxiety during drug insertion.
• Using the index finger of your dominant hand, insert the suppository—tapered end first—about 3″ (8 cm) until you feel it pass the internal anal sphincter, as shown.

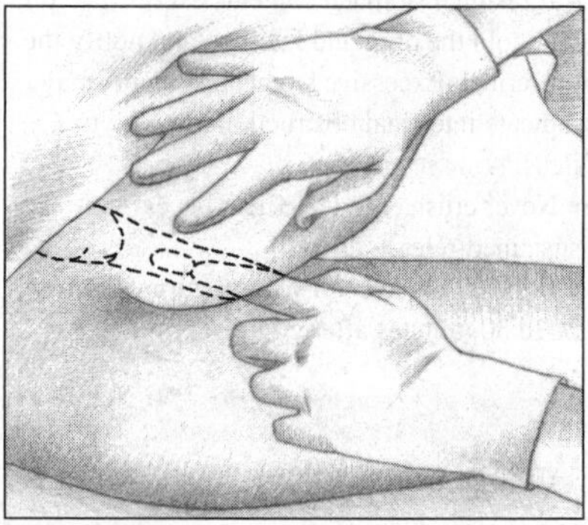

• Direct the tapered end of the suppository toward the side of the rectum so it contacts the membranes.
• Encourage the patient to lie quietly and, if possible, to contract his anal sphincter and buttocks together to retain the suppository for the correct length of time. Press on the patient's anus with a gauze pad, if necessary, until the urge to defecate passes.
• Discard the used equipment and gloves. Wash your hands.

To apply an ointment

• For external application, put on gloves and use a gauze pad to spread the drug over the anal area. For internal application, attach the end of the applicator to the tube of ointment, and coat the applicator with water-soluble lubricant.
• Expect to use about 1″ (2.5 cm) of ointment. To gauge how much pressure to use during ap-

plication, try squeezing a small amount from the tube before you attach the applicator.

- Lift the patient's upper buttock with your nondominant hand to expose the anus.
- Tell the patient to take several deep breaths through his mouth to relax the anal sphincter and reduce discomfort during insertion. Then gently insert the applicator, directing it toward the umbilicus.
- Squeeze the tube to eject drug.
- Remove the applicator, and place a folded 4″ × 4″ gauze pad between the patient's buttocks to absorb excess ointment.
- Disassemble the tube and applicator, and recap the tube. Clean the applicator with soap and warm water and store or discard it. Remove and discard your gloves. Then wash your hands thoroughly.

Nursing considerations

- Because the intake of food and fluid stimulates peristalsis, a suppository for relieving constipation should be inserted about 30 minutes before mealtime to help soften the stool and facilitate defecation. A medicated retention suppository should be inserted between meals.
- Tell the patient not to expel the suppository. If retaining it is difficult, place the patient on a bedpan.
- Make sure that the patient's call button is handy, and watch for his signal because he may be unable to suppress the urge to defecate.
- Inform the patient that the suppository may discolor his next bowel movement.

Subcutaneous administration

Injection of drug into subcutaneous (S.C.) tissue allows slower, more sustained administration than intramuscular (I.M.) injection. Drugs and solutions delivered by the S.C. route are injected through a relatively short needle using sterile technique.

Equipment and preparation

- Check the chart and the medication administration record.
- Gather gloves, prescribed drug, needle of appropriate gauge and length, 1- to 3-ml syringe, and alcohol sponges. Other materials may include antiseptic cleanser, filter needle, insulin syringe, and insulin pump.
- Inspect the drug to make sure it's not cloudy and is free of precipitates.

For single-dose ampules

- Wrap the neck of the ampule in an alcohol sponge and snap off the top, directing it away from you.
- If desired, attach a filter needle to the needle and withdraw the drug.
- Tap the syringe to clear air from it.
- Cover the needle with the needle sheath by placing the sheath on the counter or medication cart and sliding the needle into the sheath.
- Before discarding the ampule, check the label against the patient's medication record.
- Discard the filter needle and the ampule.
- Attach the appropriate-sized needle to the syringe.

For single-dose and multidose vials

- Reconstitute powdered drugs according to the instructions on the label.
- Clean the rubber stopper on the vial with an alcohol sponge.
- Pull the syringe plunger back until the volume of air in the syringe equals the volume of drug to be withdrawn from the vial.
- Insert the needle into the vial.
- Inject the air, invert the vial, and keep the bevel tip of the needle below the level of the solution as you withdraw the prescribed amount of drug.
- Tap the syringe to clear air from it.
- Cover the needle with the needle sheath by placing the sheath on the counter or medication cart and sliding the needle into the sheath.
- Check the drug label against the patient's medication record before returning the multidose vial to the shelf or drawer or before discarding the single-dose vial.

Implementation

- Confirm the patient's identity by asking his full name and checking the name and medical record number on his wristband.

• Select the injection site from those shown, and tell the patient where you'll be giving the injection.

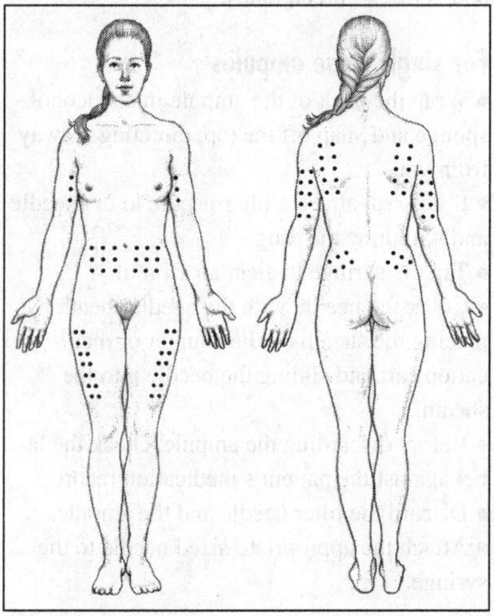

• Put on gloves. Position and drape the patient if necessary.
• Clean the injection site with an alcohol sponge. Loosen the protective needle sheath.
• With your nondominant hand, pinch the skin around the injection site firmly to elevate the S.C. tissue, forming a 1″ (2.5 cm) fat fold, as shown.

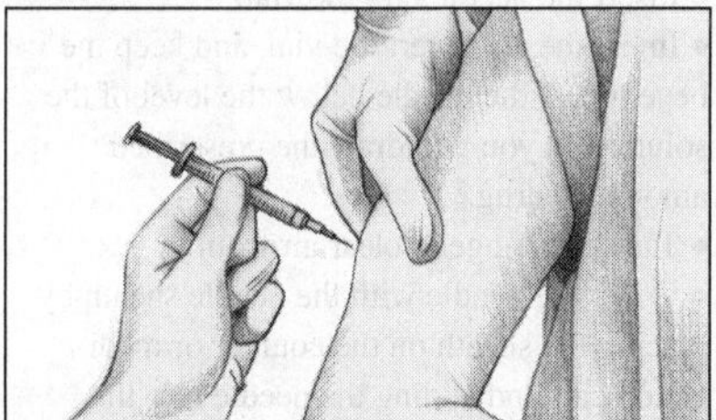

• Holding the syringe in your dominant hand, grip the needle sheath between the fourth and fifth fingers of your nondominant hand (while continuing to pinch the skin around the injection site with the index finger and thumb of your nondominant hand). Pull the sheath back to uncover the needle. Don't touch the needle.
• Position the needle with its bevel up.
• Tell the patient she'll feel a prick as you insert the needle. Do so quickly, in one motion, at a 45-degree or 90-degree angle, as shown below. The needle length and the angle you use depend on the amount of S.C. tissue at the site. Some drugs, such as heparin, should always be injected at a 90-degree angle.

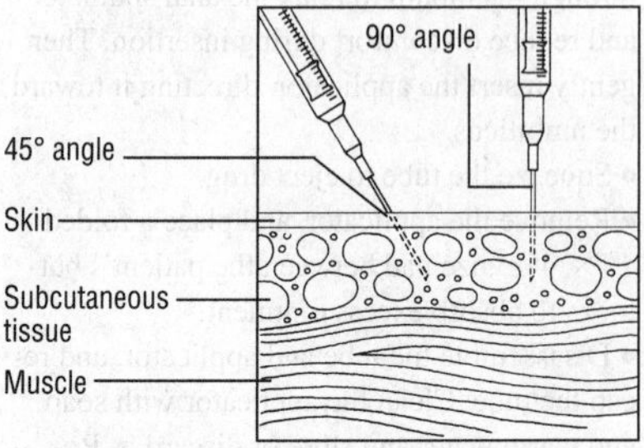

• Release the skin to avoid injecting the drug into compressed tissue and irritating the nerves. Pull the plunger back slightly to check for blood return. If blood appears, withdraw the needle, prepare another syringe, and repeat the procedure. If no blood appears, slowly inject the drug.
• After injection, remove the needle at the same angle you used to insert it. Cover the site with an alcohol sponge, and massage the site gently.
• Remove the alcohol sponge, and check the injection site for bleeding or bruising.
• Don't recap the needle. Follow your facility's policy to dispose of the injection equipment.
• Remove and discard your gloves. Wash your hands.

Nursing considerations

ALERT: Don't aspirate for blood return when giving insulin or heparin. It's not necessary with insulin and may cause a hematoma with heparin.
• Don't massage the site after giving heparin.
ALERT: Repeated injections in the same site can cause lipodystrophy, a natural immune response. This complication can be minimized by rotating injection sites.

Intramuscular administration

You'll use I.M. injections to deposit up to 5 ml of drug deep into well-vascularized muscle for rapid systemic action and absorption.

Equipment and preparation

• Check the chart and the medication administration record.

• Gather the prescribed drug, diluent or filter needle (if needed), 3- to 5-ml syringe, 20G to 25G 1″ to 3″ needle, gloves, and alcohol sponges.

• The prescribed drug must be sterile. The needle may be packaged separately or already attached to the syringe. Needles used for I.M. injections are longer than those used for S.C. injections because they reach deep into the muscle. Needle length also depends on the injection site, the patient's size, and the amount of S.C. fat covering the muscle. A larger needle gauge accommodates viscous solutions and suspensions.

• Check the drug for abnormal changes in color and clarity. If in doubt, ask the pharmacist.

• Use alcohol to wipe the stopper that tops the drug vial, and draw up the prescribed amount of drug.

• Provide privacy, and explain the procedure to the patient.

• Position and drape him appropriately, making sure that the site is well lit and exposed.

Implementation

• Wash your hands.

• Confirm the patient's identity by asking his full name and checking the name and medical record number on his wristband.

• Select an appropriate injection site. Avoid any site that looks inflamed, edematous, or irritated. Also, avoid using injection sites that contain moles, birthmarks, scar tissue, or other lesions. The dorsogluteal and ventrogluteal muscles are used most commonly for I.M. injections.

Dorsogluteal muscle

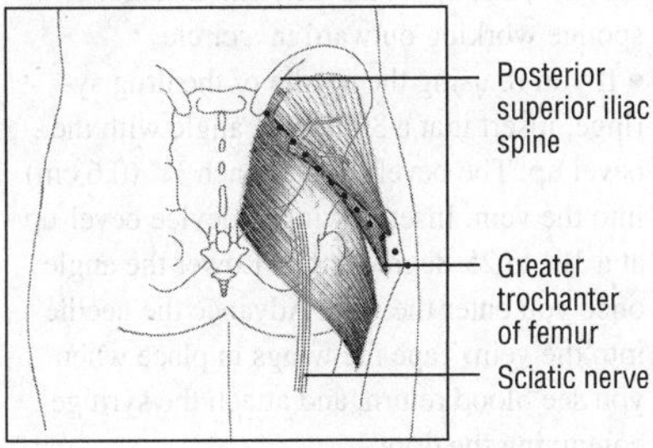

Ventrogluteal muscle

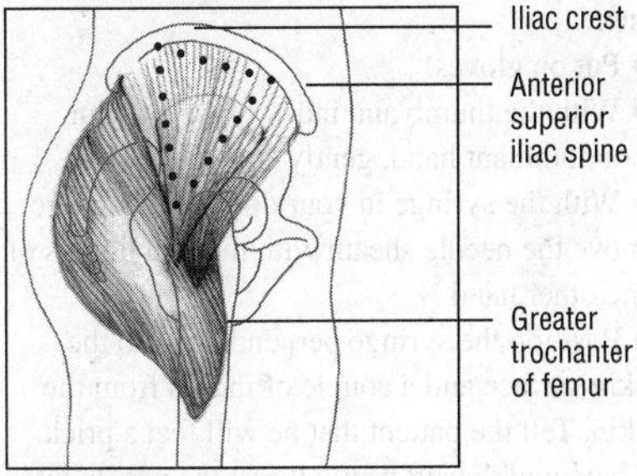

• The deltoid muscle may be used for injections of 2 ml or less.

Deltoid muscle

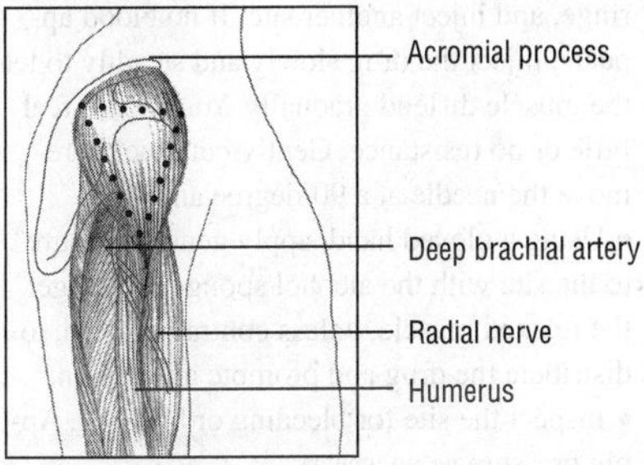

• The vastus lateralis muscle is used most often in children; the rectus femoris may be used in infants.

Vastus lateralis and rectus femoris muscles

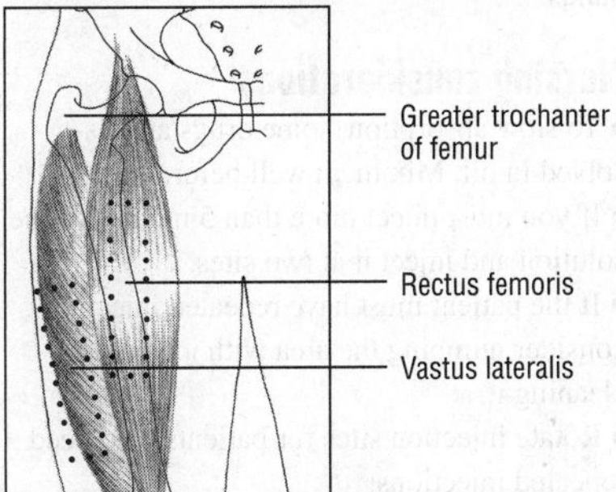

• Loosen, but don't remove, the needle sheath.

• Gently tap the site to stimulate nerve endings and minimize pain.

• Clean the site with an alcohol sponge, starting at the site and moving outward in expanding circles to about 2″ (5 cm). Allow the skin

to dry because wet alcohol stings in the puncture.
- Put on gloves.
- With the thumb and index finger of your nondominant hand, gently stretch the skin.
- With the syringe in your dominant hand, remove the needle sheath with the free fingers of the other hand.
- Position the syringe perpendicular to the skin surface and a couple of inches from the skin. Tell the patient that he will feel a prick. Then quickly and firmly thrust the needle into the muscle.
- Pull back slightly on the plunger to aspirate for blood. If blood appears, the needle is in a blood vessel. Withdraw it, prepare a fresh syringe, and inject another site. If no blood appears, inject the drug slowly and steadily to let the muscle distend gradually. You should feel little or no resistance. Gently but quickly remove the needle at a 90-degree angle.
- Using a gloved hand, apply gentle pressure to the site with the alcohol sponge. Massage the relaxed muscle, unless contraindicated, to distribute the drug and promote absorption.
- Inspect the site for bleeding or bruising. Apply pressure as necessary.
- Discard all equipment properly. Don't recap needles; put them in an appropriate biohazard container to avoid needle-stick injuries.
- Remove and discard your gloves. Wash your hands.

Nursing considerations

- To slow absorption, some drugs are dissolved in oil. Mix them well before use.
- If you must inject more than 5 ml, divide the solution and inject it at two sites.
- If the patient must have repeated injections, consider numbing the area with ice before cleaning it.
- Rotate injection sites for patients who need repeated injections.
- Urge the patient to relax the muscle to reduce pain and bleeding.
- Never inject into the gluteal muscles of a child who has been walking for less than 1 year.
- Keep in mind that I.M. injections can damage local muscle cells and elevate serum creatine kinase levels, which can be confused with elevated levels caused by myocardial infarction. Diagnostic tests can be used to differentiate between them.

Intravenous bolus administration

In this method, rapid I.V. administration allows drug levels to quickly peak in the bloodstream. This method also may be used for drugs that can't be given I.M. because they're toxic or because the patient has a reduced ability to absorb them. And it may be used to deliver drugs that can't be diluted. Bolus doses may be injected directly into a vein or through an existing I.V. line.

Equipment and preparation

- Check the chart and the medication administration record. Gather the prescribed drug, 20G needle and syringe, diluent (if needed), tourniquet, alcohol sponge, sterile 2″ × 2″ gauze pad, gloves, adhesive bandage, and tape. Other materials may include a winged device primed with normal saline solution and a second syringe (and needle) filled with normal saline solution.
- Draw the drug into the syringe and dilute it if needed.

Implementation

- Confirm the patient's identity by asking his full name and checking the name and medical record number on his wristband.
- Wash your hands and put on gloves.

To give a direct injection

- Select the largest vein suitable to dilute the drug and minimize irritation.
- Apply a tourniquet above the site to distend the vein, and clean the site with an alcohol sponge working outward in a circle.
- If you're using the needle of the drug syringe, insert it at a 30-degree angle with the bevel up. The bevel should reach ¼″ (0.6 cm) into the vein. Insert a winged device bevel-up at a 10- to 25-degree angle. Lower the angle once you enter the vein. Advance the needle into the vein. Tape the wings in place when you see blood return, and attach the syringe containing the drug.

• Check for blood backflow.
• Remove the tourniquet, and inject the drug at the ordered rate.
• Check for blood backflow to ensure that the needle remained in place and all of the injected drug entered the vein.
• For a winged device, flush the line with normal saline solution from the second syringe to ensure complete delivery.
• Withdraw the needle, and apply pressure to the site with the sterile gauze pad for at least 3 minutes to prevent hematoma.
• Apply an adhesive bandage when the bleeding stops.
• Remove and discard your gloves. Wash your hands.

To inject through an existing line

• Wash your hands, and put on gloves.
• Check the compatibility of the drug.
• Close the flow clamp, wipe the injection port with an alcohol sponge, and inject the drug as you would a direct injection.
• Open the flow clamp and readjust the flow rate.
• Remove and discard your gloves. Wash your hands.
• If the drug isn't compatible with the I.V. solution, flush the line with normal saline solution before and after the injection.

Nursing considerations

• If the existing I.V. line is capped, making it an intermittent infusion device, verify patency and placement of the device before injecting the drug. Then flush the device with normal saline solution, administer the drug, and follow with the appropriate flush.
• Immediately report signs of acute allergic reaction or anaphylaxis. If extravasation occurs, stop the injection, estimate the amount of infiltration, and notify the prescriber.
• When giving diazepam or chlordiazepoxide hydrochloride through a steel needle winged device or an I.V. line, flush with bacteriostatic water to prevent precipitation.

Intravenous administration through a secondary line

A secondary I.V. line is a complete I.V. set connected to the lower Y-port (secondary port) of a primary line instead of to the I.V. catheter or needle. It features an I.V. container, long tubing, and either a microdrip or a macrodrip system, and it can be used for continuous or intermittent drug infusion. When used continuously, it permits drug infusion and titration while the primary line maintains a constant total infusion rate.

A secondary I.V. line used only for intermittent drug administration is called a piggyback set. In this case, the primary line maintains venous access between drug doses. A piggyback set includes a small I.V. container, short tubing, and usually a macrodrip system, and it connects to the primary line's upper Y-port (piggyback port).

Equipment and preparation

• Check the chart and the medication administration record.
• Gather the prescribed I.V. drug, diluent (if needed), prescribed I.V. solution, administration set with secondary injection port, 22G 1″ needle or a needleless system, alcohol sponges, 1″ (2.5 cm) adhesive tape, time tape, labels, infusion pump, extension hook, and solution for intermittent piggyback infusion.
• Wash your hands.
• Inspect the I.V. container for cracks, leaks, or contamination.
• Check the expiration date.
• Check compatibility with the primary solution.
• Determine whether the primary line has a secondary injection port.
• If necessary, add the drug to the secondary I.V. solution (usually 50- to 100-ml "minibags" of normal saline solution or D_5W). To do so, remove any seals from the secondary container and wipe the main port with an alcohol sponge.
• Inject the prescribed drug and agitate the solution to mix the drug.
• Label the I.V. mixture.

• Insert the administration set spike, and attach the needle or needleless system.
• Open the flow clamp and prime the line. Then close the flow clamp.
• Some drugs come in vials that can hang directly on an I.V. pole. In this case, inject diluent directly into the drug vial. Then spike the vial, prime the tubing, and hang the set.

Implementation

• If the drug is incompatible with the primary I.V. solution, replace the primary solution with a fluid that's compatible with both solutions, and flush the line before starting the drug infusion.
• Hang the container of the secondary set and wipe the injection port of the primary line with an alcohol sponge.
• Insert the needle or needleless system from the secondary line into the injection port, and tape it securely to the primary line.
• To run the container of the secondary set by itself, lower the primary set's container with an extension hook. To run both containers simultaneously, place them at the same height.
• Open the clamp and adjust the drip rate.
• For continuous infusion, set the secondary solution to the desired drip rate; then adjust the primary solution to the desired total infusion rate.
• For intermittent infusion, wait until the secondary solution has completely infused; then adjust the primary drip rate, as required.
• If the secondary solution tubing is being reused, close the clamp on the tubing and follow your facility's policy: Either remove the needle or needleless system and replace it with a new one, or leave it taped in the injection port and label it with the time it was first used.
• Leave the empty container in place until you replace it with a new dose of drug at the prescribed time. If the tubing won't be reused, discard it appropriately with the I.V. container.

Nursing considerations

• If institutional policy allows, use a pump for drug infusion. Place a time tape on the secondary container to help prevent an inaccurate administration rate.
• When reusing secondary tubing, change it according to your facility's policy, usually every 48 to 72 hours. Inspect the injection port for leakage with each use; change it more often if needed.
• Except for lipids, don't piggyback a secondary I.V. line to a total parenteral nutrition line because it risks contamination.

4

Avoiding medication errors

In the state where you practice nursing, a number of different health care professionals may be legally permitted to prescribe, dispense, and administer medications—such as doctors, nurse practitioners, dentists, podiatrists, and optometrists. Most often, however, doctors prescribe medications, pharmacists dispense them, and nurses administer them.

That means you're almost always on the front line when it comes to patients and their medications. It also means that you bear a major share of the responsibility for avoiding medication errors. Besides faithfully following your facility's drug administration policies, you can help prevent medication errors by studying and avoiding the common slip-ups that allow them to happen. This chapter outlines some common causes of medication errors.

Name game

Drugs with similar-sounding names can be easy to confuse. Even different-sounding names can look similar when written out rapidly by hand on a medication order: Soriatane and Loxitane, for example, both of which are capsules. If the patient's drug order doesn't seem right for his diagnosis, call the prescriber to clarify the order.

ALERT: Many nurses have confused an order for morphine with one for hydromorphone (Dilaudid). Both drugs come in 4-mg prefilled syringes. If you give morphine when the prescriber really ordered hydromorphone, the patient could develop respiratory depression or even arrest. Consider posting a prominent notice in your medication room that warns the staff about this common mix-up. Or, try attaching a fluorescent sticker printed with NOT MORPHINE to each hydromorphone syringe.

Drug names aren't the only words you can confuse. Patient names can cause trouble as well if you fail to verify each person's identity. This problem can be especially troublesome if two patients have the same first name.

Consider this clinical scenario. Robert Brewer, age 5, was hospitalized for measles. Robert Brinson, also age 5, was admitted after a severe asthma attack. The boys were assigned to adjacent rooms on a small pediatric unit. Each had a nonproductive cough. When Robert Brewer's nurse came to give him an expectorant, the child's mother told her that Robert had already inhaled a medication through a mask.

The nurse quickly figured out that another nurse, new to the unit, had given Robert Brinson's medication (acetylcysteine, a mucolytic) to Robert Brewer in error. Fortunately, no harmful adverse effects ensued. Had the nurse checked her patient's identity more carefully, however, the error wouldn't have occurred.

Always check each patient's full name. Also, teach each patient (or parent) to offer an identification bracelet for inspection and to state his full name when anyone enters the room with the intention of giving a medication. (See *Reducing medication errors through patient teaching*, page 34). Also, urge patients to tell you if an identification bracelet falls off, is removed, or gets lost. Replace it right away.

Allergy alert

Once you've verified your patient's full name, take time to check whether he has any drug allergies—even if he's in distress. Consider this real-life example.

A doctor issued a stat order for chlorpromazine (Thorazine) for a distressed patient. By the time the nurse arrived with the drug, the patient had grown more distressed and was demanding relief. Unnerved by the patient's demeanor, the nurse gave the drug without checking the patient's medication administration record or documenting the order—and the patient had an allergic reaction to it.

Any time you're in a tense situation with a patient who needs or wants medication fast, resist the temptation to act first and document

Reducing medication errors through patient teaching

You aren't the only one who's at risk for making medication errors. Patients are at an even higher risk because they know so much less about medications than you do. Although inpatient deaths from medication errors rose more than twofold from 1983 to 1993, outpatient deaths rose more than eightfold. Clearly, patient teaching is a crucial aspect of your responsibility in minimizing medication errors and their consequences—especially as more patients receive outpatient rather than inpatient care.

To help minimize medication errors, teach your patient about his diagnosis and the purpose of his drug therapy. Make sure he knows the name of each drug in his regimen, how much of each drug he's supposed to take, and when and how he's supposed to take it. Use an interpreter if he doesn't understand English. Ideally, the patient should go home with his drug information in clear and legible writing. Explaining the drug therapy regimen to the patient's family and others closely involved with his care and drug administration also helps to reduce medication errors.

Remember that some types of drug therapy can be quite confusing for patients. One patient who went home with a warfarin prescription took the 2.5 and 5 mg tablets at the same time rather than 2.5 and 5 mg on alternating days. He eventually was hospitalized with GI bleeding—a problem that might have been avoided had he better understood his dosage regimen. Likewise, any regimen that requires a patient to take more than one drug greatly increases the complexity of the therapy and the chance of confusion and medication errors. The patient may need special help to establish a practical, workable dosing schedule.

Also, ask if your patient takes over-the-counter medications at home in addition to his prescribed drugs. Make a special point of asking about herbal remedies and other nutritional supplements. Some herbal remedies have druglike effects and can cause or contribute to a drug-related problem. What's more, because these preparations aren't regulated as drugs, government assurance standards don't apply to their labeling or manufacturing, and their ingredients can be misrepresented, substituted, or contaminated.

Finally, tell your patient which kinds of drug-related problems warrant a call to his prescriber. Encourage him to report anything about his drug therapy that concerns or worries him.

later. Skipping that crucial assessment step could easily lead to a medication error.

ALERT: A patient who is severely allergic to peanuts could have an anaphylactic reaction to ipratropium bromide (Atrovent) aerosol given by metered-dose inhaler. Ask your patient or his parents whether he's allergic to peanuts before you administer this drug. If you find that he has such an allergy, you'll need to use the nasal spray and inhalation solution form of the drug. Because it doesn't contain soy lecithin, it's safe for patients who are allergic to peanuts.

Compound errors

Many medication errors stem from compound problems—a mistake that could have been caught at any of several steps along the way. For a medication to be administered correctly, each member of the health care team must fulfill the appropriate role. The prescriber must write the order correctly and legibly. The pharmacist must evaluate whether the order is appropriate and then fill it correctly. And the nurse must evaluate whether the order is appropriate and then administer it correctly.

A breakdown anywhere along this chain of events easily can lead to a medication error. That's why it's so important for members of the health care team to act as a real team, checking each other and catching any problems that arise before those problems affect the patient's health. Do your best to foster an environment in which professionals can double-check each other.

For instance, the pharmacist can help clarify the number of times a drug should be given each day. He can help you label drugs in the most appropriate way. He can remind you to always return unused or discontinued medications to the pharmacy.

You can—indeed, you must—clarify any prescriber's order that doesn't seem clear or correct. You also must correctly handle and store any multidose vials obtained from the pharmacist. Only administer drugs that you've prepared personally. And never give a drug that has an ambiguous label or no label at all. Here's an actual example of what could happen if you do:

A nurse placed an unlabeled cup of phenol (used in neurolytic procedures) next to a cup of guanethidine (a postganglionic-blocking drug). The doctor accidentally injected the phenol instead of the guanethidine, causing severe tissue damage to a patient's arm. The patient needed emergency surgery and later developed neurologic complications as a result of receiving the wrong and unlabeled injection.

Obviously, this was a compound problem. The nurse should have labeled each cup clearly, and the doctor shouldn't have given an unlabeled substance to a patient.

Here's another example of a compound problem: In the neonatal intensive care unit, a nurse prepared and administered a dose of aminophylline for an infant. He didn't have anyone else check his work. After receiving the drug, the infant developed tachycardia and other signs of theophylline toxicity. She later died. The nurse thought the order read 7.4 ml of aminophylline; instead, it read 7.4 mg.

This tragedy might have been avoided if the doctor had written a clearer order, if the nurse had clarified the order, if a pharmacist had prepared and dispensed the drug, or if another nurse had checked the dose calculation. To help prevent such problems, many facilities prefer or require that a pharmacist prepare and dispense nonemergency parenteral doses whenever commercial unit doses aren't available.

Here's another example: A container of 5% acetic acid, used to clean tracheostomy tubing, was left near nebulization equipment in the room of a 10-month-old infant. A respiratory therapist mistook the liquid for normal saline solution and used it to dilute albuterol for the child's nebulizer treatment. During treatment, the child experienced bronchospasm, hypercapnic dyspnea, tachypnea, and tachycardia.

Leaving dangerous chemicals near patients is extremely risky, especially when the container labels don't warn of toxicity. To prevent such problems, read the label on every drug you prepare, and never administer anything that isn't labeled or is labeled poorly.

Route trouble

Many medication errors stem at least in part from problems related to the route of administration. The risk of error increases when a patient has several lines running for different purposes. Consider this example:

A nurse prepared a dose of digoxin elixir for a patient who had both a central intravenous (I.V.) line and a jejunostomy tube—and she mistakenly administered the drug into the central I.V. line. Fortunately, the patient had no adverse reaction. To help prevent such mix-ups in route of administration, prepare all oral medications in a syringe that has a tip small enough to fit an abdominal tube but too big to fit a central line.

Here's another error that could have been avoided: To clear air bubbles from a 9-year-old patient's insulin infusion, a nurse disconnected the tubing and raised the pump rate to 200 ml/hour to flush the bubbles through quickly. She then reconnected the tubing and restarted the infusion, but she forgot to reset the drip rate back to 2 units/hour. The child received 50 units of insulin before the error was detected. To prevent this kind of error, never increase a drip rate to clear bubbles from a line. Instead, remove the tubing from the pump, disconnect it from the patient, and use the flow-control clamp to establish gravity flow.

Risky abbreviations

Abbreviating drug names is risky, as in this example. Cancer patients with anemia may receive epoetin alfa, commonly abbreviated EPO, to stimulate red blood cell production. In one case, when a cancer patient was admitted to a hospital, the doctor wrote, "May take own supply of EPO." However, the patient wasn't anemic. Sensing that something was wrong, the pharmacist interviewed the patient, who confirmed that he was taking "EPO"—evening primrose oil—to lower his cholesterol level. Ask all prescribers to spell out drug names.

Unclear orders

A patient was supposed to receive one dose of the antineoplastic lomustine to treat brain cancer. (Lomustine is typically given as a single oral dose once every 6 weeks.) The doctor's order read "Administer h.s." Because a nurse misinterpreted the order to mean every night, the patient received nine daily doses, developed severe thrombocytopenia and leukopenia, and died.

If you're unfamiliar with a drug, check a drug book before administering it. If a prescriber uses "h.s." but doesn't specify the frequency of administration, ask him to clarify the order. When documenting orders, note "h.s. nightly" or "h.s. one dose today."

Color changes

In two reports, alert nurses noticed that antineoplastics prepared in the pharmacy didn't look the way they should. The first error involved a 6-year-old child who was to receive 12 mg of methotrexate intrathecally. In the pharmacy, a 1-g vial was mistakenly selected instead of a 20-mg vial, and the drug was reconstituted with 10 ml of normal saline. The vial containing 100 mg/ml was incorrectly labeled as containing 2 mg/ml, and 6 ml of the solution was drawn into a syringe. Although the syringe label indicated 12 mg of drug, the syringe actually contained 600 mg of drug.

When the nurse received the syringe and noted that the drug's color didn't appear right, she returned it to the pharmacy for verification. The pharmacist retrieved the vial used to prepare the dose and drew the remaining solution into another syringe. The solutions in both syringes matched, and no one noticed the vial's 1-g label. The pharmacist concluded that a manufacturing change caused the color difference.

The child received the 600-mg dose and experienced seizures 45 minutes later. A pharmacist responding to the emergency detected the error. The child received an antidote and recovered.

A similar case involved a 20-year-old patient with leukemia who received mitomycin instead of mitoxantrone. The nurse had questioned the drug's unusual bluish tint, but the pharmacist assured her that the color difference was due to a change in manufacturer. Fortunately, the patient didn't suffer any harm.

If a familiar drug seems to have an unfamiliar appearance, investigate the cause. If the pharmacist cites a manufacturing change, ask him to double-check whether he has received verification from the manufacturer. Always document the appearance discrepancy, your actions, and the pharmacist's response in the patient record.

Stress levels

A nurse-anesthetist administered the sedative midazolam (Versed) to the wrong patient. When she discovered the error, she reached for what she thought was a vial of the antidote flumazenil (Romazicon), withdrew 2.5 ml of the drug, and administered it. When the patient didn't respond, she realized she'd reached for a vial of ondansetron (Zofran), an antiemetic, instead. Another practitioner assisted with proper I.V. administration of flumazenil, and the patient recovered without harm.

Committing a serious error can cause enormous stress and cloud your judgment. If you're involved in a drug error, ask another professional to administer the antidote.

Clearly, you carry a great deal of responsibility for making sure that the right patient gets the right drug in the right concentration at the right time by the right route. By staying aware of potential trouble spots, you can minimize your risk of making medication errors and maximize the therapeutic effects of your patients' drug regimens.

Drug Classifications

Alkylating drugs

altretamine
busulfan
carboplatin
carmustine
chlorambucil
cisplatin
cyclophosphamide
dacarbazine
ifosfamide
lomustine
mechlorethamine hydrochloride
melphalan
temozolomide
thiotepa

Indications

▶ Treatment of various tumors, especially those having large volume and slow cell-turnover rate. See individual drugs for specific uses.

Actions

Alkylating drugs appear to act independently of a specific cell-cycle phase. They are polyfunctional compounds that can be divided chemically into five groups: nitrogen mustards, ethylenimines, alkyl sulfonates, triazines, and nitrosoureas. Highly reactive, they primarily target nucleic acids and form covalent links with nucleophilic centers in many different kinds of molecules. This allows the drugs to cross-link double-stranded DNA and to prevent strands from separating for replication, which appears to contribute to the cytotoxic effects of these drugs.

Adverse reactions

The most common adverse reactions are bone marrow depression, leukopenia, thrombocytopenia, fever, chills, sore throat, nausea, vomiting, diarrhea, flank or joint pain, anxiety, swelling of feet or lower legs, hair loss, and redness or pain at injection site.

Contraindications and precautions

- Contraindicated in patients hypersensitive to drug.
- Use cautiously in patients receiving other cytotoxic drugs or radiation therapy.

Lifespan: Alkylating drugs appear in breast milk. To avoid possible adverse effects in infants, instruct patient to discontinue breast-feeding during therapy. In children, safety and efficacy of many alkylating drugs haven't been established. Geriatric patients have an increased risk of adverse reactions; monitor them closely.

NURSING PROCESS

Assessment

- Perform a complete assessment before therapy begins.
- Monitor patient for adverse reactions throughout therapy.
- Monitor hematocrit, platelet and total and differential leukocyte counts, and BUN, ALT, AST, LDH, serum bilirubin, serum creatinine, uric acid, and other levels as needed.
- Monitor vital signs and patency of catheter or I.V. line throughout administration.

Key nursing diagnoses

- Ineffective protection related to thrombocytopenia
- Risk for infection related to immunosuppression
- Risk for deficient fluid volume related to adverse GI effects

Planning and implementation

- Follow established procedures for safe and proper handling, administration, and disposal of chemotherapeutic drugs.
- Treat extravasation promptly.
- Keep epinephrine, corticosteroids, and antihistamines available during carboplatin or cisplatin administration. Anaphylactoid reactions may occur.
- Administer ifosfamide with mesna, as prescribed, to prevent hemorrhagic cystitis.
- Give lomustine 2 to 4 hours after meals. Nausea and vomiting usually last less than 24 hours, although loss of appetite may last for several days.
- Administer adequate hydration before and for 24 hours after cisplatin treatment.
- Be aware that allopurinol may be prescribed to prevent drug-induced hyperuricemia.

Prototype drug

Patient teaching

- Caution patient to avoid people with bacterial or viral infections because chemotherapy can increase susceptibility. Urge him to report signs of infection promptly.
- Review proper oral hygiene, including cautious use of toothbrush, dental floss, and toothpicks.
- Advise patient to complete dental work before therapy begins or to delay it until blood counts are normal.
- Warn patient that he may bruise easily because of drug's effect on blood count.

Evaluation

- Patient develops no serious bleeding complications.
- Patient remains free from infection.
- Patient maintains adequate hydration.

Alpha-adrenergic blockers

doxazosin mesylate
ergotamine tartrate
prazosin hydrochloride
tamsulosin hydrochloride
terazosin hydrochloride

Indications

▶ Peripheral vascular disorders (Raynaud's disease, acrocyanosis, frostbite, acute atrial occlusion, phlebitis, diabetic gangrene), vascular headaches, dermal necrosis, mild-to-moderate urinary obstruction in men with BPH, hypertension, pheochromocytoma.

Actions

Selective alpha-adrenergic blockers (doxazosin, prazosin, and terazosin) have readily observable effects. They decrease vascular resistance and increase venous capacity, thereby lowering blood pressure and causing pink warm skin, nasal and scleroconjunctival congestion, ptosis, orthostatic and exercise hypotension, mild-to-moderate miosis, and interference with ejaculation. They also relax nonvascular smooth muscle, notably in the prostate capsule, thereby reducing urinary symptoms in men with BPH. Because $alpha_1$ blockers don't block $alpha_2$ receptors, they don't cause transmitter overflow.

Nonselective alpha-adrenergic blockers (ergotamine and tolazoline) antagonize both $alpha_1$ and $alpha_2$ receptors. Generally, alpha-adrenergic blockade results in tachycardia, palpitations, and increased renin secretion because of abnormally large amounts of norepinephrine (transmitter overflow) released from adrenergic nerve endings as a result of the concurrent blockade of $alpha_1$ and $alpha_2$ receptors. Norepinephrine's effects are clinically counterproductive to the major uses of nonselective alpha-adrenergic blockers.

Adverse reactions

Selective alpha-adrenergic blockers may cause severe orthostatic hypotension and syncope, especially with the first dose. The most common adverse effects of $alpha_1$ blockade are dizziness, headache, and malaise.

Nonselective alpha-adrenergic blockers typically cause orthostatic hypotension, tachycardia, palpitations, fluid retention (from excess renin secretion), nasal and ocular congestion, and aggravation of respiratory tract infection.

Contraindications and precautions

- Contraindicated in patients with MI, coronary insufficiency, or angina.

Lifespan: In pregnant or breast-feeding women, use cautiously. In children, safety and efficacy of many alpha-adrenergic blockers haven't been established; use cautiously. In elderly patients, hypotensive effects may be more pronounced.

NURSING PROCESS

Assessment

- Monitor vital signs, especially blood pressure.
- Monitor patient closely for adverse reactions.

Key nursing diagnoses

- Decreased cardiac output related to hypotension
- Acute pain related to headache
- Excessive fluid volume related to fluid retention

Planning and implementation

- Give at bedtime to minimize dizziness or light-headedness.

• Begin therapy with small dose to avoid first-dose syncope.

Patient teaching

• Warn patient not to rise suddenly from a lying or sitting position.
• Urge patient to avoid hazardous tasks that require mental alertness until the full effects of drug are known.
• Advise patient that alcohol, excessive exercise, prolonged standing, and heat exposure will intensify adverse effects.
• Tell patient to promptly report dizziness or irregular heartbeat.

Evaluation

• Patient maintains adequate cardiac output.
• Patient's headache is relieved.
• Patient has no edema.

Aminoglycosides

amikacin sulfate
gentamicin sulfate
kanamycin sulfate
neomycin sulfate
streptomycin sulfate
tobramycin sulfate

Indications

▶ Septicemia; postoperative, pulmonary, intra-abdominal, and urinary tract infections; skin, soft tissue, bone, and joint infections; aerobic gram-negative bacillary meningitis (not susceptible to other antibiotics); serious staphylococcal, *Pseudomonas aeruginosa*, and *Klebsiella* infections; enterococcal infections; nosocomial pneumonia; anaerobic infections involving *Bacteroides fragilis;* tuberculosis; initial empiric therapy in febrile, leukopenic patient.

Actions

Aminoglycosides are bactericidal. They bind directly and irreversibly to 30S ribosomal subunits, inhibiting bacterial protein synthesis. They're active against many aerobic gram-negative and some aerobic gram-positive organisms.

Susceptible gram-negative organisms include *Acinetobacter, Citrobacter, Enterobacter, Escherichia coli, Klebsiella,* indole-positive and indole-negative *Proteus, Providencia, P. aeruginosa, Salmonella, Serratia,* and *Shigella.* Streptomycin is also active against *Brucella, Calymmatobacterium granulomatis, Pasteurella multocida,* and *Yersinia pestis.*

Susceptible gram-positive organisms include *Staphylococcus aureus* and *S. epidermidis.* Streptomycin is also active against *Nocardia, Erysipelothrix,* and some mycobacteria, including *Mycobacterium tuberculosis, M. marinum,* and certain strains of *M. kansasii* and *M. leprae.*

Adverse reactions

Ototoxicity and nephrotoxicity are the most serious complications. Neuromuscular blockade also may occur. Oral forms most commonly cause nausea, vomiting, and diarrhea. Parenteral drugs may cause vein irritation, phlebitis, and sterile abscess.

Contraindications and precautions

• Contraindicated in patients hypersensitive to aminoglycosides.
• Use cautiously in patients with neuromuscular disorder or renal impairment.

Lifespan: In pregnant women, use cautiously. In breast-feeding women, safety hasn't been established. In neonates and premature infants, the half-life of aminoglycosides is prolonged because of their immature renal systems. In infants and children, dosage adjustment may be needed. Geriatric patients have an increased risk of nephrotoxicity and commonly need reduced dosages and longer dosing intervals; they're also susceptible to ototoxicity and superinfection.

NURSING PROCESS

Assessment

• Obtain patient's history of allergies.
• Monitor patient for adverse reactions.
• Obtain results of culture and sensitivity tests before first dose, and check tests periodically to assess drug efficacy.
• Monitor vital signs, electrolyte levels, hearing ability, and renal function studies before and during therapy.
• Draw blood for peak level 1 hour after I.M. injection (30 minutes to 1 hour after I.V. infusion); for trough level, draw sample just before

Prototype drug

next dose. Time and date all blood samples. Don't use heparinized tube to collect blood samples because it interferes with results.

Key nursing diagnoses

- Risk for injury related to nephrotoxicity and ototoxicity
- Risk for infection related to drug-induced superinfection
- Risk for deficient fluid volume related to adverse GI reactions

Planning and implementation

- Keep patient well hydrated to minimize chemical irritation of renal tubules.
- Don't add or mix other drugs with I.V. infusions, particularly penicillins, which inactivate aminoglycosides. If other drugs must be given I.V., temporarily stop infusion of primary drug.
- Follow manufacturer's instructions for reconstitution, dilution, and storage of drugs; check expiration dates.
- Shake oral suspensions well before administering.
- Administer I.M. dose deep into large muscle mass (gluteal or midlateral thigh); rotate injection sites to minimize tissue injury. Apply ice to injection site to relieve pain.
- Too rapid I.V. administration may cause neuromuscular blockade. Infuse I.V. drug continuously or intermittently over 30 to 60 minutes for adults, 1 to 2 hours for infants; dilution volume for children is determined individually.

Patient teaching

- Teach signs and symptoms of hypersensitivity and other adverse reactions. Urge patient to report unusual effects promptly.
- Emphasize importance of adequate fluid intake.

Evaluation

- Patient maintains pretreatment renal and hearing functions.
- Patient is free from infection.
- Patient maintains adequate hydration.

Angiotensin-converting enzyme inhibitors

benazepril hydrochloride
captopril
enalapril maleate
fosinopril sodium
lisinopril
moexipril hydrochloride
perindopril erbumine
quinapril hydrochloride
ramipril
trandolapril

Indications

▶ Hypertension, heart failure.

Actions

Angiotensin-converting enzyme (ACE) inhibitors prevent conversion of angiotensin I to angiotensin II, a potent vasoconstrictor. Besides decreasing vasoconstriction and thus reducing peripheral arterial resistance, inhibition of angiotensin II decreases adrenocortical secretion of aldosterone. This reduces sodium and water retention and extracellular fluid volume. ACE inhibition also causes increased levels of bradykinin, resulting in vasodilation. This decreases heart rate and systemic vascular resistance.

Adverse reactions

The most common adverse effects of therapeutic doses are headache, fatigue, hypotension, tachycardia, dysgeusia, proteinuria, hyperkalemia, rash, cough, and angioedema of face and limbs. Severe hypotension may occur at toxic drug levels.

Contraindications and precautions

- Contraindicated in patients hypersensitive to ACE inhibitors.
- Use cautiously in patients with impaired renal function or serious autoimmune disease and in those taking other drugs known to depress WBC count or immune response.
- **Lifespan:** Women of childbearing age receiving ACE inhibitor therapy should report suspected pregnancy immediately to prescriber. High risks of fetal morbidity and mortality are linked to ACE inhibitor exposure,

especially in the second and third trimesters. Some ACE inhibitors appear in breast milk. To avoid adverse effects in infants, instruct patient to discontinue breast-feeding during therapy. In children, safety and efficacy haven't been established; give drug only if potential benefit outweighs risk. Geriatric patients may need lower doses because of impaired drug clearance.

NURSING PROCESS

Assessment
- Observe patient for adverse reactions.
- Monitor vital signs regularly and WBC counts and serum electrolyte levels periodically.

Key nursing diagnoses
- Risk for trauma related to orthostatic hypotension
- Ineffective protection related to hyperkalemia
- Acute pain related to headache

Planning and implementation
- Stop diuretic therapy 2 to 3 days before beginning ACE inhibitor therapy to reduce risk of hypotension. If drug doesn't adequately control blood pressure, diuretics may be reinstated.
- Give a reduced dosage if the patient has impaired renal function.
- Give potassium supplements, potassium-containing salt substitutes, and potassium-sparing diuretics cautiously because ACE inhibitors may cause potassium retention.
- Stop ACE inhibitors if patient becomes pregnant. These drugs can cause birth defects or fetal death in the second and third trimesters.

Patient teaching
- Tell patient that drugs may cause a dry, persistent, tickling cough that stops when therapy stops.
- Urge patient to report light-headedness, especially in the first few days of therapy, so the dosage can be adjusted. Also, tell him to report signs of infection (such as sore throat and fever) because these drugs may decrease WBC count; facial swelling or difficulty breathing because these drugs may cause angioedema; and loss of taste, for which therapy may stop.
- Caution patient to avoid sudden position changes to minimize orthostatic hypotension.
- Warn patient to seek medical approval before taking self-prescribed cold preparations.
- Tell women to report pregnancy at once.

Evaluation
- Patient sustains no injury from orthostatic hypotension.
- Patient's WBC counts remain normal throughout therapy.
- Patient's headache is relieved by mild analgesic.

Antacids
aluminum carbonate
aluminum hydroxide
calcium carbonate
magaldrate
magnesium hydroxide
magnesium oxide
sodium bicarbonate

Indications
▶ Ulcer pain.

Actions
Antacids reduce the total acid load in the GI tract and elevate gastric pH to reduce pepsin activity. They also strengthen the gastric mucosal barrier and increase esophageal sphincter tone.

Adverse reactions
Antacids containing aluminum may cause aluminum intoxication, constipation, hypophosphatemia, intestinal obstruction, and osteomalacia. Antacids containing magnesium may cause diarrhea or hypermagnesemia (in renal failure). Calcium carbonate, magaldrate, magnesium oxide, and sodium bicarbonate may cause milk-alkali syndrome or rebound hyperacidity.

Contraindications and precautions
- Calcium carbonate, magaldrate, and magnesium oxide are contraindicated in patients with severe renal disease. Sodium bicarbonate is contraindicated in patients with hypertension, renal disease, edema, or vomiting; patients re-

Prototype drug

ceiving diuretics or continuous GI suction; and patients on sodium-restricted diets.
- In patients with mild renal impairment, give magnesium oxide cautiously
- Give aluminum preparations, calcium carbonate, and magaldrate cautiously in elderly patients; in those receiving antidiarrheals, antispasmodics, or anticholinergics; and in those with dehydration, fluid restriction, chronic renal disease, or suspected intestinal absorption.

Lifespan: Breast-feeding women may take antacids. In infants, serious adverse effects are more likely from changes in fluid and electrolyte balance; monitor them closely. Geriatric patients have an increased risk of adverse reactions; monitor them closely. In elderly patients, give magnesium oxide cautiously.

NURSING PROCESS

Assessment
- Assess patient's condition before therapy and regularly thereafter.
- Record number and consistency of stools.
- Observe patient for adverse reactions.
- Monitor patient receiving long-term, high-dose aluminum carbonate and hydroxide for fluid and electrolyte imbalance, especially if patient is on a sodium-restricted diet.
- Monitor serum phosphate levels in a patient receiving aluminum carbonate or hydroxide.
- Watch for signs of hypercalcemia in a patient receiving calcium carbonate.
- Monitor serum magnesium levels in a patient with mild renal impairment who takes magaldrate.

Key nursing diagnoses
- Constipation related to adverse effects of aluminum-containing antacid
- Diarrhea related to adverse effects of magnesium-containing antacid
- Ineffective protection related to drug-induced electrolyte imbalance

Planning and implementation
- Manage constipation with laxatives or stool softeners, or ask prescriber about switching patient to a magnesium preparation.
- If patient suffers from diarrhea, obtain an order for an antidiarrheal, as needed, and ask prescriber about switching patient to an antacid containing aluminum.
- Shake container well, and give with small amount of water or juice to facilitate passage. When giving through an NG tube, make sure the tube is patent and placed correctly. After instilling the drug, flush the tube with water to ensure passage to the stomach and to clear the tube.

Patient teaching
- Warn patient not to take antacids indiscriminately or to switch antacids without prescriber's consent.
- Tell patient not to take calcium carbonate with milk or other foods high in vitamin D.
- Warn patient not to take sodium bicarbonate with milk because doing so could cause hypercalcemia.

Evaluation
- Patient regains normal bowel pattern.
- Patient states that diarrhea is relieved.
- Patient maintains normal electrolyte balance.

Antianginals

Beta blockers
atenolol
metoprolol
nadolol
propranolol hydrochloride

Calcium channel blockers
amlodipine besylate
bepridil hydrochloride
diltiazem hydrochloride
nicardipine hydrochloride
nifedipine
verapamil hydrochloride

Nitrates
isosorbide dinitrate
isosorbide mononitrate
nitroglycerin

Indications

▶ Moderate-to-severe angina (beta blockers); classic, effort-induced angina and Prinzmetal's angina (calcium channel blockers); recurrent angina (long-acting nitrates and topical, transdermal, transmucosal, and oral extended-release nitroglycerin); acute angina (S.L. nitroglycerin and S.L. or chewable isosorbide dinitrate); unstable angina (I.V. nitroglycerin).

Prototype drug

Actions

Beta blockers block catecholamine-induced increases in heart rate, blood pressure, and myocardial contraction. Calcium channel blockers inhibit influx of calcium through muscle cells, which dilates coronary arteries and decreases afterload. Nitrates decrease left ventricular end-diastolic pressure (preload) and systemic vascular resistance (afterload) and increase blood flow through collateral coronary vessels.

Adverse reactions

Beta blockers may cause bradycardia, heart failure, cough, diarrhea, disturbing dreams, dizziness, dyspnea, fatigue, fever, hypotension, lethargy, nausea, peripheral edema, and wheezing. Calcium channel blockers may cause bradycardia, confusion, constipation, depression, diarrhea, dizziness, edema, elevated liver enzyme levels (transient), fatigue, flushing, headache, hypotension, insomnia, nervousness, and rash. Nitrates may cause alcohol intoxication (from I.V. preparations containing alcohol), flushing, headache, orthostatic hypotension, reflex tachycardia, rash, syncope, and vomiting.

Contraindications and precautions

- Beta blockers are contraindicated in patients hypersensitive to them and in patients with cardiogenic shock, sinus bradycardia, heart block greater than first degree, bronchial asthma, or heart failure unless failure results from tachyarrhythmia that is treatable with propranolol. Calcium channel blockers are contraindicated in patients with severe hypotension or heart block greater than first degree (except with functioning pacemaker). Nitrates are contraindicated in patients with severe anemia, cerebral hemorrhage, head trauma, glaucoma, or hyperthyroidism.
- Use beta blockers cautiously in patients with nonallergic bronchospastic disorders, diabetes mellitus, or impaired hepatic or renal function. Use calcium channel blockers cautiously in patients with hepatic or renal impairment, bradycardia, heart failure, or cardiogenic shock. Use nitrates cautiously in patients with hypotension or recent MI.

Lifespan: In pregnant women, use beta blockers cautiously. Recommendations for breast-feeding vary by drug; use beta blockers and calcium channel blockers cautiously. In children, safety and efficacy haven't been established. Check with prescriber before giving these drugs to children. Geriatric patients have an increased risk of adverse reactions; use cautiously.

NURSING PROCESS

Assessment

- Monitor vital signs. With I.V. nitroglycerin, monitor blood pressure and pulse rate every 5 to 15 minutes while adjusting dosage and every hour thereafter.
- Monitor effectiveness of prescribed drug.
- Observe for adverse reactions.

Key nursing diagnoses

- Risk for injury related to adverse reactions
- Excessive fluid volume related to adverse CV effects of beta blockers or calcium channel blockers
- Acute pain related to headache

Planning and implementation

- Have patient sit or lie down when receiving the first nitrate dose; take his pulse and blood pressure before giving dose and when drug action starts.
- Don't give a beta-blocker or calcium channel blocker to relieve acute angina.
- Withhold the dose and notify prescriber if patient's heart rate is below 60 beats/minute or systolic blood pressure is below 90 mm Hg.

Patient teaching

- Warn patient not to discontinue drug abruptly without prescriber's approval.
- Teach patient to take his pulse before taking a beta blocker or calcium channel blocker. Tell him to withhold the dose and alert the prescriber if his pulse rate is below 60 beats/minute.
- Instruct patient taking nitroglycerin S.L. to go to the emergency department if three tablets taken 5 minutes apart don't relieve anginal pain.
- Tell patient to report serious or persistent adverse reactions.

Evaluation

- Patient sustains no injury from adverse reactions.
- Patient maintains normal fluid balance.

• Patient's headache is relieved with mild analgesic.

Antiarrhythmics

Class I
moricizine hydrochloride
Class Ia
disopyramide
procainamide hydrochloride
quinidine bisulfate
quinidine gluconate
quinidine polygalacturonate
quinidine sulfate
Class Ib
lidocaine hydrochloride
mexiletine hydrochloride
phenytoin
phenytoin sodium
tocainide hydrochloride
Class Ic
flecainide acetate
propafenone hydrochloride
Class II (beta blockers)
acebutolol
esmolol hydrochloride
propranolol hydrochloride
sotalol hydrochloride
Class III
amiodarone hydrochloride
bretylium tosylate
dofetilide
ibutilide fumarate
Class IV (calcium channel blocker)
verapamil hydrochloride

Indications

▶ Atrial and ventricular arrhythmias.

Actions

Class I drugs reduce the inward current carried by sodium ions, stabilizing neuronal cardiac membranes. Class Ia drugs depress phase 0, prolong the action potential, and have cardiac membrane–stabilizing effects. Class Ib drugs depress phase 0, shorten the action potential, and have cardiac membrane–stabilizing effects. Class Ic drugs block the transport of sodium ions, decreasing conduction velocity but not repolarization rate. Class II drugs decrease heart rate, myocardial contractility, blood pressure, and AV node conduction. Class III drugs prolong the action potential and refractory period. Class IV drugs decrease myocardial contractility and oxygen demand by inhibiting calcium ion influx; they also dilate coronary arteries and arterioles.

Adverse reactions

Most antiarrhythmics can aggravate existing arrhythmias or cause new ones. They also may produce hypersensitivity reactions; hypotension; GI problems, such as nausea, vomiting, or altered bowel elimination; and CNS disturbances, such as dizziness or fatigue. Some antiarrhythmics may worsen heart failure. Class II drugs may cause bronchoconstriction.

Contraindications and precautions

• Contraindicated in patients hypersensitive to drug.
• Many antiarrhythmics are contraindicated or require cautious use in patients with cardiogenic shock, digitalis toxicity, and second- or third-degree heart block (unless patient has a pacemaker).
Lifespan: Many antiarrhythmics appear in breast milk. Children have an increased risk of adverse reactions; monitor them closely. Geriatric patients exhibit physiologic alterations in CV system; use these drugs cautiously.

NURSING PROCESS

Assessment

• Monitor ECG continuously when therapy starts and dosage is adjusted.
• Monitor patient's vital signs frequently and assess for signs of toxicity and adverse reactions.
• Measure apical pulse rate before giving drug.
• Monitor serum drug levels as indicated.

Key nursing diagnoses

• Decreased cardiac output related to arrhythmias or myocardial depression
• Ineffective protection related to adverse reactions
• Noncompliance related to long-term therapy

Planning and implementation

• Don't crush sustained-release tablets.

• Take safety precautions if adverse CNS reactions occur.
• Notify prescriber about adverse reactions.

Patient teaching
• Stress the importance of taking drug exactly as prescribed.
• Teach patient to take his pulse before each dose. Tell him to notify prescriber if his pulse is irregular or below 60 beats/minute.
• Instruct patient to avoid hazardous activities that require mental alertness if adverse CNS reactions occur.
• Tell patient to limit fluid and salt intake if his prescribed drug causes fluid retention.

Evaluation
• Patient maintains adequate cardiac output, as evidenced by normal vital signs and adequate tissue perfusion.
• Patient has no serious adverse reactions.
• Patient states importance of compliance with therapy.

Antibiotic antineoplastics

bleomycin sulfate
dactinomycin
daunorubicin hydrochloride
doxorubicin hydrochloride
epirubicin hydrochloride
idarubicin hydrochloride
mitomycin
mitoxantrone hydrochloride
plicamycin
procarbazine hydrochloride
valrubicin

Indications

▶ Treatment of various tumors.

Actions

Although classified as antibiotics, these drugs produce cytotoxic effects that rule out their use as antimicrobials alone. They interfere with proliferation of malignant cells through several mechanisms. Their action may be cell-cycle-phase nonspecific, cell-cycle-phase specific, or both. Some exhibit activity resembling alkylating drugs or antimetabolites. By binding to or complexing with DNA, antibiotic antineoplastics directly or indirectly inhibit DNA, RNA, and protein synthesis.

Adverse reactions

The most common adverse reactions include nausea, vomiting, diarrhea, fever, chills, sore throat, anxiety, confusion, flank or joint pain, swelling of the feet or lower legs, hair loss, redness or pain at the injection site, bone marrow depression, and leukopenia.

Contraindications and precautions

• Contraindicated in patients hypersensitive to drug.
Lifespan: Instruct breast-feeding patient to stop breast-feeding during therapy to avoid adverse effects in infants. In children, safety and efficacy of some drugs haven't been established. Geriatric patients have an increased risk of adverse reactions; monitor them closely.

NURSING PROCESS

Assessment
• Perform a complete assessment before therapy begins.
• Monitor patient for adverse reactions.
• Monitor vital signs and patency of catheter or I.V. line.
• Monitor hemoglobin, hematocrit, platelet and total and differential leukocyte counts, ALT, AST, LDH, bilirubin, creatinine, uric acid, and BUN levels.
• Monitor pulmonary function tests in a patient receiving bleomycin. Assess lung function regularly.
• Monitor ECG before and during treatment with daunorubicin and doxorubicin.

Key nursing diagnoses
• Ineffective protection related to thrombocytopenia
• Risk for infection related to immunosuppression
• Risk for deficient fluid volume related to adverse GI effects

Planning and implementation
• Follow established procedures for safe and proper handling, administration, and disposal of chemotherapeutic drugs.

• Try to ease anxiety in patient and his family before treatment.
• Keep epinephrine, corticosteroids, and antihistamines available during bleomycin therapy. Anaphylactoid reactions may occur.
• Treat extravasation promptly.
• Ensure adequate hydration during idarubicin therapy.
• Discontinue procarbazine and notify prescriber if patient becomes confused or neuropathies develop.

Patient teaching
• Warn patient to avoid close contact with persons who have received the oral poliovirus vaccine.
• Caution patient to avoid exposure to persons with bacterial or viral infections because chemotherapy increases susceptibility. Urge him to report signs of infection immediately.
• Review proper oral hygiene, including cautious use of toothbrush, dental floss, and toothpicks. Chemotherapy can increase the risk of microbial infection, delayed healing, and bleeding gums.
• Urge patient to complete dental work before therapy begins or to delay it until blood counts are normal.
• Warn patient that he may bruise easily.
• Tell patient to report redness, pain, or swelling at injection site immediately. Local tissue injury and scarring may result if I.V. infiltration occurs.
• Warn patient taking procarbazine to avoid hazardous activities that require alertness until drug's CNS effects are known. Also advise him to take procarbazine at bedtime and in divided doses to reduce nausea and vomiting.
• Advise patient taking daunorubicin, doxorubicin, or idarubicin that his urine may turn orange or red for 1 to 2 days after therapy begins.

☑ Evaluation
• No serious bleeding complications develop.
• Patient remains free from infection.
• Patient maintains adequate hydration.

Anticholinergics
atropine sulfate
benztropine mesylate
dicyclomine hydrochloride
glycopyrrolate
scopolamine
scopolamine butylbromide
scopolamine hydrobromide

Indications
▶ Prevention of motion sickness, preoperative reduction of secretions and blockage of cardiac reflexes, adjunct treatment of peptic ulcers and other GI disorders, blockage of cholinomimetic effects of cholinesterase inhibitors or other drugs, and (for benztropine) various spastic conditions, including acute dystonic reactions, muscle rigidity, parkinsonism, and extrapyramidal disorders.

Actions
Anticholinergics competitively antagonize the actions of acetylcholine and other cholinergic agonists at muscarinic receptors.

Adverse reactions
Therapeutic doses commonly cause dry mouth, decreased sweating or anhidrosis, headache, mydriasis, blurred vision, cycloplegia, urinary hesitancy and retention, constipation, palpitations, and tachycardia. These reactions usually disappear when therapy stops. Toxicity can cause signs and symptoms resembling psychosis (disorientation, confusion, hallucinations, delusions, anxiety, agitation, and restlessness); dilated, nonreactive pupils; blurred vision; hot, dry, flushed skin; dry mucous membranes; dysphagia; decreased or absent bowel sounds; urine retention; hyperthermia; tachycardia; hypertension; and increased respirations.

Contraindications and precautions
• Contraindicated in patients hypersensitive to drug and in those with angle-closure glaucoma, renal or GI obstructive disease, reflux esophagitis, or myasthenia gravis.
• Use cautiously in patients with heart disease, GI infection, open-angle glaucoma, prostatic hypertrophy, hypertension, hyperthyroidism,

ulcerative colitis, autonomic neuropathy, or hiatal hernia with reflux esophagitis.

Lifespan: Breast-feeding women should avoid anticholinergics because these drugs may decrease milk production, and some may appear in breast milk, possibly causing infant toxicity. In children, safety and efficacy haven't been established. Patients older than age 40 may be more sensitive to these drugs. In geriatric patients, use cautiously and give a reduced dosage as indicated.

NURSING PROCESS

Assessment

- Monitor patient regularly for adverse reactions.
- Check vital signs at least every 4 hours.
- Measure urine output; check for urine retention.
- Assess patient for changes in vision and for signs of impending toxicity.

Key nursing diagnoses

- Urinary retention related to adverse effect on bladder
- Constipation related to adverse effect on GI tract
- Acute pain related to headache

Planning and implementation

- Give drug 30 minutes to 1 hour before meals and at bedtime to maximize therapeutic effects. In some instances, drug should be administered with meals; follow dosage recommendations.
- Provide ice chips, cool drinks, or hard candy to relieve dry mouth.
- Relieve constipation with stool softeners or bulk laxatives.
- Give a mild analgesic for headache.
- Notify prescriber of urine retention, and be prepared for catheterization.

Patient teaching

- Teach patient how and when to take the drug; caution him not to take other drugs unless prescribed.
- Warn patient to avoid hazardous tasks if he experiences dizziness, drowsiness, or blurred vision. Inform him that the drug may increase his sensitivity to or intolerance of high temperatures, resulting in dizziness.
- Advise patient to avoid alcohol because it may cause additive CNS effects.
- Urge patient to drink plenty of fluids and to eat a high-fiber diet to prevent constipation.
- Tell patient to notify prescriber promptly if he experiences confusion, rapid or pounding heartbeat, dry mouth, blurred vision, rash, eye pain, significant change in urine volume, or pain or difficulty on urination.
- Advise women to report planned or known pregnancy.

Evaluation

- Patient maintains normal voiding pattern.
- Patient regains normal bowel patterns.
- Patient is free from pain.

Anticoagulants

Coumarin derivative

warfarin sodium

Heparin derivatives

argatroban
bivalirudin
dalteparin sodium
danaparoid sodium
enoxaparin sodium
fondaparinux sodium
heparin sodium
tinzaparin sodium

Indications

▶ Pulmonary emboli, deep vein thrombosis, thrombus, blood clotting, disseminated intravascular coagulation.

Actions

Heparin derivatives accelerate formation of an antithrombin III-thrombin complex. It inactivates thrombin and prevents conversion of fibrinogen to fibrin. The coumarin derivative, warfarin, inhibits vitamin-K–dependent activation of clotting factors II, VII, IX, and X, which are formed in the liver.

Adverse reactions

Anticoagulants commonly cause bleeding and may cause hypersensitivity reactions. Warfarin may cause agranulocytosis, alopecia (long-term use), anorexia, dermatitis, fever, nausea, tissue necrosis or gangrene, urticaria, and vomiting. Heparin derivatives may cause thrombocytopenia and may increase liver enzyme levels.

Contraindications and precautions

- Contraindicated in patients with aneurysm, active bleeding, CV hemorrhage, hemorrhagic blood dyscrasias, hemophilia, severe hypertension, pericardial effusions, or pericarditis; and in patients undergoing major surgery, neurosurgery, or ophthalmic surgery.
- Use cautiously in patients with severe diabetes, renal impairment, severe trauma, ulcerations, or vasculitis.

Lifespan: In pregnant women and in women who have just had a threatened or complete spontaneous abortion, drug is contraindicated. Women should avoid breastfeeding during therapy, if possible. Infants, especially neonates, may be more susceptible to anticoagulants because of vitamin K deficiency. Geriatric patients are at greater risk for hemorrhage because of altered hemostatic mechanisms or age-related deterioration of hepatic and renal functions.

NURSING PROCESS

Assessment

- Monitor patient closely for bleeding and other adverse reactions.
- Check PT, INR, PTT, or activated PTT.
- Monitor vital signs, hemoglobin level, and hematocrit value.
- Assess patient's urine, stools, and emesis for blood.

Key nursing diagnoses

- Ineffective protection related to drug's effects on body's normal clotting and bleeding mechanisms
- Risk for deficient fluid volume related to bleeding
- Noncompliance related to long-term warfarin therapy

Planning and implementation

- Don't administer heparin I.M., and avoid I.M. injections of any anticoagulant, if possible.
- Keep protamine sulfate available to treat severe bleeding caused by heparin. Keep vitamin K available to treat frank bleeding caused by warfarin.
- Notify prescriber about serious or persistent adverse reactions.
- Maintain bleeding precautions throughout therapy.

Patient teaching

- Urge patient to take drug exactly as prescribed. If he's taking warfarin, tell him to take it at night and to have blood drawn for PT or INR in the morning for accurate results.
- Advise patient to consult his prescriber before taking any other drug, including OTC medications or herbal remedies.
- Review bleeding-prevention precautions to take in everyday living. Urge patient to make repairs and to remove safety hazards from home to reduce risk of injury.
- Caution patient not to increase his intake of green, leafy vegetables because vitamin K may antagonize anticoagulant effects.
- Instruct patient to report bleeding or other adverse reactions promptly.
- Encourage patient to keep appointments for blood tests and follow-up examinations.
- Advise women to report planned or known pregnancy.

Evaluation

- Patient has no adverse change in health status.
- Patient has no evidence of bleeding or hemorrhaging.
- Patient demonstrates compliance with therapy, as evidenced by normal bleeding and clotting values.

Anticonvulsants

acetazolamide sodium
carbamazepine
clonazepam
clorazepate dipotassium
diazepam
divalproex sodium
fosphenytoin sodium
gabapentin
lamotrigine
levetiracetam
magnesium sulfate

oxcarbazepine
phenobarbital
phenobarbital sodium
phenytoin
phenytoin sodium
phenytoin sodium (extended)
primidone
tiagabine hydrochloride
topiramate
valproate sodium
valproic acid

Indications

▶ Seizure disorders; acute, isolated seizures not caused by seizure disorders; status epilepticus; prevention of seizures after trauma or craniotomy.

Actions

Anticonvulsants comprise six classes of drugs: selected hydantoin derivatives, barbiturates, benzodiazepines, succinimides, iminostilbene derivatives (carbamazepine), and carboxylic acid derivatives. Two miscellaneous anticonvulsants are acetazolamide and magnesium sulfate. Some hydantoin derivatives and carbamazepine inhibit the spread of seizure activity in the motor cortex. Some barbiturates and succinimides limit seizure activity by increasing the threshold for motor cortex stimuli. Selected benzodiazepines and carboxylic acid derivatives are thought to increase the inhibiting action of gamma-aminobutyric acid in brain neurons. Acetazolamide inhibits carbonic anhydrase. Magnesium sulfate interferes with the release of acetylcholine at the myoneural junction.

Adverse reactions

Anticonvulsants can cause adverse CNS effects, such as confusion, somnolence, tremor, and ataxia. Many anticonvulsants also cause GI effects, such as vomiting; CV disorders, such as arrhythmias and hypotension; and hematologic disorders, such as leukopenia and thrombocytopenia.

Contraindications and precautions

• Contraindicated in patients hypersensitive to anticonvulsants.

Lifespan: In breast-feeding women, the safety of many anticonvulsants hasn't been established. Children, especially young ones, are sensitive to CNS depressant effects of some anticonvulsants; use cautiously. Geriatric patients are sensitive to CNS effects and may require lower doses. Also, elimination of some anticonvulsants may be prolonged because of decreased renal function, and parenteral use is more likely to cause apnea, hypotension, bradycardia, and cardiac arrest.

NURSING PROCESS

Assessment

• Monitor patient's response to prescribed drug and serum levels as indicated.
• Monitor patient for adverse reactions.
• Assess patient's compliance with therapy at each follow-up visit.

Key nursing diagnoses

• Risk for trauma related to adverse reactions
• Impaired physical mobility related to sedation
• Noncompliance related to long-term therapy

Planning and implementation

• Administer oral forms with food to reduce GI irritation.
• Phenytoin binds with tube feedings, thus decreasing absorption of drug. Turn off tube feedings for 2 hours before and after giving phenytoin, according to your facility's policy.
• Expect to adjust dosage according to patient's response.
• Take safety precautions if patient has adverse CNS reactions.

Patient teaching

• Instruct patient to take drug exactly as prescribed and not to stop drug without medical supervision.
• Urge patient to avoid hazardous activities that require mental alertness if adverse CNS reactions occur.
• Advise patient to wear or carry medical identification at all times.

Evaluation

• Patient sustains no trauma from adverse reactions.

Prototype drug

• Patient maintains physical mobility.
• Patient complies with therapy and has no seizures.

Antidepressants, tricyclic

amitriptyline hydrochloride
amitriptyline pamoate
amoxapine
clomipramine hydrochloride
desipramine hydrochloride
doxepin hydrochloride
imipramine hydrochloride
imipramine pamoate
nortriptyline hydrochloride

Indications

▶ Depression, anxiety (doxepin hydrochloride), obsessive-compulsive disorder (clomipramine), enuresis in children older than age 6 (imipramine).

Actions

Tricyclic antidepressants (TCAs) may inhibit reuptake of norepinephrine and serotonin in CNS nerve terminals (presynaptic neurons), thus enhancing the concentration and activity of neurotransmitters in the synaptic cleft. TCAs also exert antihistaminic, sedative, anticholinergic, vasodilatory, and quinidine-like effects.

Adverse reactions

Adverse reactions include sedation, anticholinergic effects, and orthostatic hypotension. Tertiary amines (amitriptyline, doxepin, and imipramine) exert the strongest sedative effects; tolerance usually develops in a few weeks. Amoxapine is most likely to cause seizures, especially with overdose.

Contraindications and precautions

• Contraindicated in patients with urine retention, angle-closure glaucoma, or hypersensitivity to TCAs.
• Use cautiously in patients with suicidal tendencies, CV disease, or impaired hepatic function.

Lifespan: In breast-feeding women, safety hasn't been established; use cautiously. For children under age 12, TCAs aren't recommended. Geriatric patients are more sensitive to therapeutic and adverse effects; they need lower dosages.

NURSING PROCESS

Assessment

• Observe patient for mood changes to monitor drug effectiveness; benefits may not appear for 3 to 6 weeks.
• Check vital signs regularly for decreased blood pressure or tachycardia; observe patient carefully for other adverse reactions and report changes. Check ECG in patients older than age 40 before starting therapy.
• Monitor patient for anticholinergic adverse reactions (urine retention or constipation), which may require dosage reduction.

Key nursing diagnoses

• Disturbed thought processes related to adverse effects
• Risk for injury related to sedation and orthostatic hypotension
• Noncompliance related to long-term therapy

Planning and implementation

• Make sure patient swallows each dose; depressed patient may hoard pills for suicide attempt, especially when symptoms begin to improve.
• Don't withdraw drug abruptly; gradually reduce dosage over several weeks to avoid rebound effect or other adverse reactions.
• Follow manufacturer's instructions for reconstitution, dilution, and storage of drugs.

Patient teaching

• Explain to patient the rationale for therapy and its anticipated risks and benefits. Inform patient that full therapeutic effect may not occur for several weeks.
• Teach patient how and when to take his drug. Warn him not to increase his dosage, discontinue the drug, or take any other drug (including OTC medicines and herbal remedies) without medical approval.
• Because overdose with TCAs commonly is fatal, entrust a reliable family member with the medication, and warn him to store drug safely away from children.
• Advise patient not to take drug with milk or food to minimize GI distress. Suggest taking

full dose at bedtime if daytime sedation is troublesome.
- Tell patient to avoid alcohol.
- Advise patient to avoid hazardous tasks that require mental alertness until full effects of drug are known.
- Warn patient that excessive exposure to sunlight, heat lamps, or tanning beds may cause burns and abnormal hyperpigmentation.
- Urge diabetic patient to monitor his glucose level carefully because drug may alter it.
- Recommend sugarless gum or hard candy, artificial saliva, or ice chips to relieve dry mouth.
- Advise patient to report adverse reactions promptly.

Evaluation
- Patient regains normal thought processes.
- Patient sustains no injury from adverse reactions.
- Patient complies with therapy, and his depression is alleviated.

Antidiarrheals

bismuth subgallate
bismuth subsalicylate
calcium polycarbophil
diphenoxylate hydrochloride and atropine sulfate
kaolin and pectin mixtures
loperamide
octreotide acetate
opium tincture
opium tincture, camphorated

Indications

▶ Mild, acute, or chronic diarrhea.

Actions

Bismuth preparations may have a mild water-binding capacity, may absorb toxins, and provide a protective coating for the intestinal mucosa. Kaolin and pectin mixtures decrease fluid in the stool by absorbing bacteria and toxins that cause diarrhea. Opium preparations increase smooth muscle tone in the GI tract, inhibit motility and propulsion, and decrease digestive secretions.

Adverse reactions

Bismuth preparations may cause salicylism (with high doses) or temporary darkening of tongue and stools. Kaolin and pectin mixtures may cause constipation and fecal impaction or ulceration. Opium preparations may cause dizziness, light-headedness, nausea, physical dependence (with long-term use), and vomiting.

Contraindications and precautions

- Contraindicated in patients hypersensitive to drug.

Lifespan: Some antidiarrheals may appear in breast milk; check individual drugs for specific recommendations. For infants younger than age 2, don't give kaolin and pectin mixtures. For children or teenagers recovering from flu or chickenpox, consult prescriber before giving bismuth subsalicylate. For geriatric patients, use caution when giving antidiarrheal drugs, especially opium preparations.

NURSING PROCESS

Assessment
- Assess patient's condition before therapy and regularly thereafter.
- Monitor fluid and electrolyte balance.
- Observe patient for adverse reactions.

Key nursing diagnoses
- Constipation related to adverse effect of bismuth preparations on GI tract
- Risk for injury related to adverse CNS reactions
- Risk for deficient fluid volume related to GI upset

Planning and implementation
- Administer drug exactly as prescribed.
- Take safety precautions if patient experiences adverse CNS reactions.
- Don't substitute opium tincture for paregoric.
- Notify prescriber about serious or persistent adverse reactions.

Patient teaching
- Instruct patient to take drug exactly as prescribed; caution him that excessive use of opium preparations can lead to dependence.

• Instruct patient to notify prescriber if diarrhea lasts for more than 2 days and to report adverse reactions.
• Warn patient to avoid hazardous activities that require alertness if CNS depression occurs.

Evaluation
• Patient doesn't develop constipation.
• Patient remains free from injury.
• Patient maintains adequate hydration.

Antihistamines
azelastine hydrochloride
brompheniramine maleate
chlorpheniramine maleate
clemastine fumarate
cyproheptadine hydrochloride
desloratadine
dimenhydrinate
diphenhydramine hydrochloride
fexofenadine hydrochloride
loratadine
meclizine hydrochloride
promethazine hydrochloride
promethazine theoclate
triprolidine hydrochloride

Indications
▶ Rhinitis, urticaria, pruritus, vertigo, nausea and vomiting, sedation, dyskinesia, parkinsonism.

Actions
Antihistamines are structurally related chemicals that compete with histamine for histamine H_1-receptor sites on smooth muscle of bronchi, GI tract, uterus, and large blood vessels, binding to cellular receptors and preventing access to and subsequent activity of histamine. They don't directly alter histamine or prevent its release.

Adverse reactions
Most antihistamines cause drowsiness and impaired motor function early in therapy. They also can cause dry mouth and throat, blurred vision, and constipation. Some antihistamines, such as promethazine, may cause cholestatic jaundice (thought to be a hypersensitivity reaction) and may predispose patients to photosensitivity.

Contraindications and precautions
• Contraindicated in patients hypersensitive to drug.
• Use cautiously in patients with angle-closure glaucoma, stenosing peptic ulcer, pyloroduodenal obstruction, or bladder neck obstruction.
Lifespan: During breast-feeding, antihistamines shouldn't be used; many of these drugs appear in breast milk. As a result, infants may experience unusual excitability. Neonates, especially premature infants, may experience seizures. Children, especially those younger than age 6, may experience paradoxical hyperexcitability with restlessness, insomnia, nervousness, euphoria, tremors, and seizures; administer cautiously. Geriatric patients usually are more sensitive to the adverse effects of antihistamines, especially dizziness, sedation, hypotension, and urine retention; use cautiously and monitor patient closely.

NURSING PROCESS

Assessment
• Monitor patient for adverse reactions.
• Monitor blood counts during long-term therapy; watch for signs of blood dyscrasia.

Key nursing diagnoses
• Risk for injury related to sedation
• Impaired oral mucous membrane related to dry mouth
• Constipation related to anticholinergic effect of antihistamines

Planning and implementation
• Reduce GI distress by giving antihistamines with food.
• Provide sugarless gum, hard candy, or ice chips to relieve dry mouth.
• Increase fluid intake (if allowed) or humidify air to decrease adverse effect of thickened secretions.

Patient teaching
• Advise patient to take drug with meals or snacks to prevent GI upset.
• Suggest that patient use warm water rinses, artificial saliva, ice chips, or sugarless gum or

candy to relieve dry mouth. Tell him to avoid overusing mouthwash, which may worsen dryness and destroy normal flora.

• Warn patient to avoid hazardous activities until full CNS effects of drug are known.
• Caution patient to seek medical approval before using alcohol, tranquilizers, sedatives, pain relievers, or sleeping medications.
• Advise patient to stop taking antihistamines 4 days before diagnostic skin tests to preserve accuracy of test results.

Evaluation

• Patient sustains no injury from sedation.
• Patient maintains normal mucous membranes by using preventive measures throughout therapy.
• Patient maintains normal bowel function.

Antihypertensives

ACE inhibitors
benazepril hydrochloride
captopril
enalaprilat
enalapril maleate
fosinopril sodium
lisinopril
moexipril hydrochloride
perindopril erbumine
quinapril hydrochloride
ramipril
trandolapril
Alpha-adrenergic blockers
doxazosin mesylate
prazosin hydrochloride
terazosin hydrochloride
Angiotensin II receptor blockers
candesartan cilexetil
eprosartan mesylate
irbesartan
losartan potassium
telmisartan
valsartan
Beta blockers
acebutolol
atenolol
betaxolol hydrochloride
bisoprolol fumarate
carvedilol
labetalol hydrochloride
metoprolol tartrate
nadolol
pindolol
propranolol hydrochloride
timolol maleate
Calcium channel blockers
amlodipine besylate
diltiazem hydrochloride
felodipine
isradipine
nicardipine hydrochloride
nifedipine
nisoldipine
verapamil hydrochloride
Centrally acting sympatholytics
clonidine hydrochloride
guanfacine hydrochloride
methyldopa
Rauwolfia alkaloid
reserpine
Vasodilators
diazoxide
hydralazine hydrochloride
minoxidil
nitroprusside sodium

Indications

▶ Essential and secondary hypertension.

Actions

Antihypertensives reduce blood pressure through various mechanisms. For information on the action of ACE inhibitors, alpha-adrenergic blockers, angiotensin II receptor blockers, beta blockers, calcium channel blockers, and diuretics, see their individual drug class entries. Centrally acting sympatholytics stimulate central alpha-adrenergic receptors, reducing cerebral sympathetic outflow, thereby decreasing peripheral vascular resistance and blood pressure. Rauwolfia alkaloids bind to and gradually destroy the norepinephrine-containing storage vesicles in central and peripheral adrenergic neurons. Vasodilators act directly on smooth muscle to reduce blood pressure.

Adverse reactions

Most antihypertensives commonly cause orthostatic hypotension, changes in heart rate, headache, nausea, and vomiting. Other reactions vary greatly among different drug types. Centrally acting sympatholytics may cause constipation, depression, dizziness, drowsiness, dry mouth, headache, palpitations, severe rebound hypertension, and sexual dysfunction; methyldopa also may cause aplastic anemia and thrombocytopenia. Rauwolfia alkaloids may cause anxiety, depression, drowsiness, dry mouth, hyperacidity, impotence, nasal stuffiness, and weight gain. Vasodilators may cause heart failure, ECG changes, diarrhea, dizziness, palpitations, pruritus, and rash.

Contraindications and precautions

• Contraindicated in patients hypersensitive to drug and in those with hypotension.
• Use cautiously in patients with hepatic or renal dysfunction.
Lifespan: Some antihypertensives appear in breast milk; use cautiously. In children, safety and efficacy of many antihypertensives haven't been established; give these drugs cautiously and monitor patients closely. Geriatric patients are more susceptible to adverse reactions and may need lower maintenance doses; monitor them closely.

NURSING PROCESS

Assessment

• Obtain baseline blood pressure and pulse rate and rhythm; recheck regularly.
• Monitor patient for adverse reactions.
• Monitor patient's weight and fluid and electrolyte status.
• Monitor patient's compliance with treatment.

Key nursing diagnoses

• Risk for trauma related to orthostatic hypotension
• Risk for deficient fluid volume related to GI upset
• Noncompliance related to long-term therapy or adverse reactions

Planning and implementation

• Administer drug with food or at bedtime, as indicated.
• Follow manufacturer's guidelines when mixing and administering parenteral drugs.
• Take steps to prevent or minimize orthostatic hypotension.
• Maintain patient's nonpharmacologic therapy, such as sodium restriction, calorie reduction, stress management, and exercise program.

Patient teaching

• Instruct patient to take drug exactly as prescribed. Warn him not to stop drug abruptly.
• Review adverse reactions caused by drug, and urge patient to notify prescriber of serious or persistent reactions.
• Advise patient to avoid sudden changes in position to prevent dizziness, light-headedness, or fainting.
• Caution patient to avoid hazardous activities until full effects of drug are known. Also, warn patient to avoid physical exertion, especially in hot weather.
• Advise patient to consult prescriber before taking any OTC medications or herbal remedies; serious drug interactions can occur.
• Encourage patient to comply with therapy.

Evaluation

• Patient sustains no trauma from orthostatic hypotension.
• Patient maintains adequate hydration.
• Patient complies with therapy, as evidenced by normal blood pressure.

Antilipemics

atorvastatin calcium
cholestyramine
clofibrate
colesevelam hydrochloride
fenofibrate
fluvastatin sodium
gemfibrozil
lovastatin
pravastatin sodium
simvastatin

Indications

▶ Hyperlipidemia, hypercholesterolemia.

Actions

Antilipemics lower elevated blood levels of lipids. Bile-sequestering drugs (cholestyramine and colesevelam) lower blood levels of low-density lipoproteins by forming insoluble

Prototype drug

complexes with bile salts, triggering cholesterol to leave the bloodstream and other storage areas to make new bile acids. Fibric acid derivatives (clofibrate, gemfibrozil) reduce cholesterol formation, increase sterol excretion, and decrease lipoprotein and triglyceride synthesis. Cholesterol synthesis inhibitors (fluvastatin, lovastatin, pravastatin, simvastatin) interfere with enzymatic activity that generates cholesterol in the liver.

Adverse reactions

Antilipemics commonly cause GI upset. Bile-sequestering drugs may cause cholelithiasis, constipation, bloating, and steatorrhea. Fibric acid derivatives may cause cholelithiasis and GI or CNS effects. Use of gemfibrozil with lovastatin may cause myopathy. Cholesterol synthesis inhibitors may affect liver function or cause rash, pruritus, increased CK levels, and myopathy.

Contraindications and precautions

- Contraindicated in patients hypersensitive to drug. Also, bile-sequestering drugs are contraindicated in patients with complete biliary obstruction. Fibric acid derivatives are contraindicated in patients with primary biliary cirrhosis or significant hepatic or renal dysfunction. Cholesterol synthesis inhibitors are contraindicated in patients with active liver disease or persistently elevated serum transaminase levels.
- Use bile-sequestering drugs cautiously in constipated patients. Use fibric acid derivatives cautiously in patients with peptic ulcer. Use cholesterol synthesis inhibitors cautiously in patients who consume large amounts of alcohol or who have a history of liver disease.

Lifespan: In pregnant women, use bile-sequestering drugs and fibric acid derivatives cautiously and avoid giving cholesterol synthesis inhibitors. In breast-feeding women, avoid giving fibric acid derivatives and cholesterol synthesis inhibitors; give bile-sequestering drugs cautiously. In children ages 10 to 17, certain antilipemics have been approved to treat heterozygous familial hypercholesterolemia. Geriatric patients have an increased risk of severe constipation; use bile-sequestering drugs cautiously and monitor patients closely.

NURSING PROCESS

Assessment

- Monitor blood cholesterol and lipid levels before and periodically during therapy.
- Monitor CK levels when therapy begins and every 6 months thereafter. Also, check CK levels if a patient who takes a cholesterol synthesis inhibitor complains of muscle pain.
- Monitor patient for adverse reactions.

Key nursing diagnoses

- Risk for deficient fluid volume related to adverse GI reactions
- Constipation related to adverse effect on bowel
- Noncompliance related to long-term therapy

Planning and implementation

- Mix powder form of bile-sequestering drugs with 120 to 180 ml of liquid. Never administer dry powder alone because patient may inhale it accidentally.
- Administer daily fibric acid derivative at prescribed times.
- Give lovastatin with evening meal, simvastatin in the evening, and fluvastatin and pravastatin at bedtime.

Patient teaching

- Instruct patient to take drug exactly as prescribed. If he takes a bile-sequestering drug, warn him never to take the dry form.
- Stress importance of diet in controlling serum lipid levels.
- Advise patient to drink 2 to 3 L of fluid daily and to report persistent or severe constipation.

Evaluation

- Patient maintains adequate fluid volume.
- Patient doesn't experience severe or persistent constipation.
- Patient complies with therapy, as evidenced by normal serum lipid and cholesterol levels.

Prototype drug

Antimetabolite antineoplastics

capecitabine
cytarabine
cytarabine liposomal
fludarabine phosphate
fluorouracil
hydroxyurea
mercaptopurine
methotrexate
pentostatin
thioguanine

Indications

▶ Treatment of various tumors.

Actions

Antimetabolites are structural analogues of normally occurring metabolites and can be divided into three subcategories: purine analogues, pyrimidine analogues, and folinic acid analogues. Most of these drugs interrupt cell reproduction at a specific phase of the cell cycle. Purine analogues are incorporated into DNA and RNA, interfering with nucleic acid synthesis (via miscoding) and replication. They also may inhibit synthesis of purine bases through pseudo-feedback mechanisms. Pyrimidine analogues inhibit enzymes in metabolic pathways that interfere with biosynthesis of uridine and thymine. Folic acid antagonists prevent conversion of folic acid to tetrahydrofolate by inhibiting the enzyme dihydrofolic acid reductase.

Adverse reactions

The most common adverse effects include nausea, vomiting, diarrhea, fever, chills, hair loss, flank or joint pain, redness or pain at injection site, anxiety, bone marrow depression, leukopenia, and swelling of the feet or lower legs.

Contraindications and precautions

- Contraindicated in patients hypersensitive to drug.

Lifespan: Pregnant women should be informed of the risks to the fetus. Breast-feeding is contraindicated in women receiving chemotherapy drugs, including antimetabolite antineoplastics. In children, safety and efficacy of some drugs haven't been established. Geriatric patients have an increased risk of adverse reactions; monitor them closely.

NURSING PROCESS

Assessment

- Perform a complete assessment before therapy begins.
- Monitor patient for adverse reactions.
- Monitor vital signs and patency of catheter or I.V. line throughout administration.
- Monitor hematocrit; ALT, AST, LDH, serum bilirubin, serum creatinine, uric acid, and BUN levels; platelet and total and differential leukocyte counts; and other values as required.

Key nursing diagnoses

- Ineffective protection related to thrombocytopenia
- Risk for infection related to immunosuppression
- Risk for deficient fluid volume related to adverse GI effects

Planning and implementation

- Follow established procedures for safe and proper handling, administration, and disposal of drugs.
- Try to ease anxiety in patient and his family before treatment.
- Give an antiemetic before giving drug to lessen nausea.
- Give cytarabine with allopurinol to decrease the risk of hyperuricemia. Promote a high fluid intake.
- Provide diligent mouth care to prevent stomatitis with cytarabine, fluorouracil, or methotrexate therapy.
- Anticipate the need for leucovorin rescue with high-dose methotrexate therapy.
- Treat extravasation promptly.
- Tell patient to defer immunizations if possible until hematologic stability is confirmed.
- Anticipate diarrhea, possibly severe, with prolonged fluorouracil therapy.

Patient teaching

- Teach patient proper oral hygiene, including cautious use of toothbrush, dental floss, and toothpicks. Chemotherapy can increase the risk of microbial infection, delayed healing, and bleeding gums.

• Advise patient to complete dental work before therapy begins or to delay it until blood counts are normal.
• Warn patient that he may bruise easily because of drug's effect on platelets.
• Advise patient to avoid close contact with persons who have taken oral poliovirus vaccine and who have been exposed to persons with bacterial or viral infection because chemotherapy may increase susceptibility. Urge patient to notify prescriber promptly if he develops signs or symptoms of infection.
• Instruct patient to report redness, pain, or swelling at injection site. Local tissue injury and scarring may result from tissue infiltration at infusion site.

Evaluation

• Patient develops no serious bleeding complications.
• Patient remains free from infection.
• Patient maintains adequate hydration.

Antiparkinsonians

amantadine hydrochloride
benztropine mesylate
bromocriptine mesylate
entacapone
carbidopa and levodopa
levodopa
pergolide mesylate
pramipexole dihydrochloride
ropinirole hydrochloride
selegiline hydrochloride
tolcapone
trihexyphenidyl hydrochloride

Indications

▶ Parkinson's disease.

Actions

Antiparkinsonians include synthetic anticholinergic and dopaminergic drugs and the antiviral drug amantadine. Anticholinergics probably prolong the action of dopamine by blocking its reuptake into presynaptic neurons in the CNS and by suppressing central cholinergic activity. Dopaminergic drugs act in the brain by increasing dopamine availability, thus improving motor function. Entacapone is a reversible inhibitor of peripheral catechol-*O*-methyltransferase, which is responsible for elimination of various catecholamines, including dopamine. Blocking this pathway when administering carbidopa and levodopa should result in higher serum levels of levodopa, thereby allowing greater dopaminergic stimulation in the CNS and leading to a greater clinical effect in treating parkinsonian symptoms. Amantadine is thought to increase dopamine release in the substantia nigra.

Adverse reactions

Anticholinergic drugs typically cause decreased sweating or anhidrosis, dry mouth, headache, mydriasis, blurred vision, cycloplegia, urinary hesitancy and urine retention, constipation, palpitations, and tachycardia. Dopaminergic drugs may cause vomiting, orthostatic hypotension, confusion, arrhythmias, and disturbing dreams. Amantadine commonly causes irritability, insomnia, and livedo reticularis (with prolonged use).

Contraindications and precautions

• Contraindicated in patients hypersensitive to drug.
• Use cautiously in patients with prostatic hyperplasia or tardive dyskinesia and in debilitated patients.
Lifespan: Antiparkinsonians may appear in breast milk; a decision should be made to stop the drug or stop breast-feeding, taking into account the importance of the drug to the mother. In children, safety and efficacy haven't been established. Geriatric patients have an increased risk for adverse reactions; monitor them closely.

NURSING PROCESS

Assessment

• Obtain baseline assessment of patient's impairment, and reassess regularly to monitor drug effectiveness.
• Monitor patient for adverse reactions.
• Monitor vital signs, especially during dosage adjustments.

Key nursing diagnoses

• Risk for injury related to adverse CNS effects

Prototype drug

• Urine retention related to anticholinergic effect on bladder
• Disturbed sleep pattern related to amantadine-induced insomnia

Planning and implementation

• Administer drug with food to prevent GI irritation.
• Adjust dosage according to patient's response and tolerance.
• Never withdraw drug abruptly.
• Institute safety precautions.
• Provide ice chips, drinks, or sugarless hard candy or gum to relieve dry mouth. Increase fluid and fiber intake to prevent constipation, as appropriate.
• Notify prescriber about urine retention, and be prepared to catheterize patient, if necessary.

Patient teaching

• Instruct patient to take drug exactly as prescribed, and warn him not to stop drug suddenly.
• Advise patient to take drug with food to prevent GI upset.
• Teach patient how to manage anticholinergic effects, if appropriate.
• Caution patient to avoid hazardous tasks if adverse CNS effects occur. Tell him to avoid alcohol during therapy.
• Encourage patient to report severe or persistent adverse reactions.

Evaluation

• Patient remains free from injury.
• Patient has no change in voiding pattern.
• Patient's sleep pattern isn't altered during amantadine therapy.

Antivirals

abacavir sulfate
acyclovir sodium
amantadine hydrochloride
amprenavir
cidofovir
delavirdine mesylate
didanosine
efavirenz
famciclovir
foscarnet sodium
ganciclovir
indinavir sulfate
lamivudine
lamivudine/zidovudine
lopinavir/ritonavir
nelfinavir mesylate
nevirapine
oseltamivir phosphate
ribavirin
rimantadine hydrochloride
ritonavir
saquinavir mesylate
stavudine
valacyclovir hydrochloride
valganciclovir
zalcitabine
zanamivir
zidovudine

Indications

▶ Viral infections.

Actions

Acyclovir, cidofovir, didanosine, famciclovir, ganciclovir, valacyclovir, valganciclovir, and zalcitabine interfere with DNA synthesis and replication. Amantadine prevents the release of infectious viral nucleic acid into the host cell and possibly interferes with viral penetration into the cells. Foscarnet blocks the pyrophosphate-binding site. Ribavirin's mechanism of action is unknown. Rimantadine prevents viral uncoating. Abacavir, amprenavir, indinavir, ritonavir, saquinavir, and stavudine inhibit the activity of HIV protease. Delavirdine, efavirenz, lamivudine, nevirapine, and zidovudine inhibit reverse transcriptase.

Adverse reactions

Antiviral drugs may cause anorexia, chills, confusion, depression, diarrhea, dry mouth, edema, fatigue, hallucinations, headache, nausea, and vomiting.

Contraindications and precautions

• Contraindicated in patients hypersensitive to drug.
Lifespan: In breast-feeding women, some antivirals are contraindicated, but others require cautious use. For infants and children, recommendations vary with the antiviral pre-

scribed. Geriatric patients have an increased risk of adverse reactions; monitor them closely.

NURSING PROCESS

Assessment
- Obtain baseline assessment of patient's viral infection, and reassess regularly to monitor drug's effectiveness.
- Monitor renal and hepatic function, CBC, and platelet count regularly. Monitor electrolytes (calcium, phosphate, magnesium, potassium) in patients receiving foscarnet.
- Inspect patient's I.V. site regularly for signs of irritation, phlebitis, inflammation, or extravasation.
- If patient has a history of heart failure, watch closely for exacerbation or recurrence during amantadine therapy.
- Monitor patient's cardiac status during ribavirin therapy.

Key nursing diagnoses
- Ineffective protection related to adverse hematologic reactions
- Risk for deficient fluid volume related to GI upset
- Noncompliance related to long-term therapy

Planning and implementation
- Adjust dosage of selected antiviral drugs for patient with decreased renal function, especially during parenteral therapy.
- Follow manufacturer's guidelines for reconstituting and administering antiviral drugs.
- Obtain an order for an antiemetic or antidiarrheal drug, if needed.
- Take safety precautions if patient has adverse CNS reactions. For example, place bed in low position, raise bed rails, and supervise ambulation and other activities.
- Notify prescriber about serious or persistent adverse reactions.

Patient teaching
- Instruct patient to take drug exactly as prescribed, even if he feels better.
- Urge patient to notify prescriber promptly about severe or persistent adverse reactions.
- Encourage patient to keep appointments for follow-up care.
- Provide additional teaching as indicated by individual drug.

Evaluation
- Patient has no serious adverse hematologic effects.
- Patient maintains adequate hydration.
- Patient complies with therapy, and viral infection is eradicated.

Barbiturates
amobarbital
amobarbital sodium
pentobarbital sodium
phenobarbital
phenobarbital sodium
primidone
secobarbital sodium

Indications
▶ Insomnia, seizure disorders.

Actions
Barbiturates act throughout the CNS, especially in the mesencephalic reticular activating system, which controls the CNS arousal mechanism. The main mechanisms of anticonvulsant action are reduction of nerve transmission and decreased excitability of the nerve cell. Barbiturates decrease presynaptic and postsynaptic membrane excitability by facilitating the actions of GABA. They also depress respiration and GI motility and raise the seizure threshold.

Adverse reactions
Drowsiness, lethargy, vertigo, headache, and CNS depression are common with barbiturates. After hypnotic doses, a hangover effect, subtle distortion of mood, and impaired judgment and motor skills may continue for many hours. After dosage reduction or discontinuation, rebound insomnia or increased dreaming or nightmares may occur. Barbiturates cause hyperalgesia in subhypnotic doses. They also can cause paradoxical excitement at low doses, confusion in elderly patients, and hyperactivity in children. High fever, severe headache, stomatitis, conjunctivitis, or rhinitis may precede potentially fatal skin eruptions. Withdrawal symptoms may occur after as little as 2 weeks of uninterrupted therapy.

Contraindications and precautions

- Contraindicated in patients hypersensitive to drug and in those with bronchopneumonia or other severe pulmonary insufficiency.
- Use cautiously in patients with blood pressure alterations, pulmonary disease, or CV dysfunction.

Lifespan: During pregnancy, use of barbiturates can cause fetal abnormalities; avoid use. Barbiturates appear in breast milk and may result in infant CNS depression; use cautiously. Premature infants are more susceptible to depressant effects of barbiturates because of their immature hepatic metabolism. Children may experience hyperactivity, excitement, or hyperalgesia. Use cautiously and monitor children carefully. Geriatric patients may experience hyperactivity, excitement, or hyperalgesia; use cautiously.

NURSING PROCESS

Assessment

- Assess patient's level of consciousness and sleeping patterns before and during therapy to evaluate drug effectiveness. Monitor neurologic status for alteration or deterioration.
- Assess vital signs frequently, especially during I.V. administration.
- Monitor seizure character, frequency, and duration for changes, as indicated.
- Observe patient to prevent hoarding or self-dosing, especially if patient is depressed, suicidal, or drug dependent.

Key nursing diagnoses

- Risk for injury related to sedation
- Disturbed thought processes related to confusion
- Impaired adjustment related to drug dependence

Planning and implementation

- When giving parenteral drug, avoid extravasation, which may cause local tissue damage and tissue necrosis; inject I.V. or deep I.M. only. Don't exceed 5 ml for any I.M. injection site to avoid tissue damage.
- Keep resuscitative measures available. Too rapid I.V. administration may cause respiratory depression, apnea, laryngospasm, or hypotension.
- Take seizure precautions, as necessary.
- Institute safety measures to prevent falls and injury. Raise side rails, assist patient out of bed, and keep call light within easy reach.
- Stop drug slowly. Abrupt discontinuation may cause withdrawal symptoms.

Patient teaching

- Explain that barbiturates can cause physical or psychological dependence.
- Instruct patient to take drug exactly as prescribed. Caution him not to change the dosage or take other drugs, including OTC medications or herbal remedies, without prescriber's approval.
- Reassure patient that a morning hangover is common after therapeutic use of barbiturates.
- Advise patient to avoid hazardous tasks, driving a motor vehicle, or operating machinery while taking drug and to review other safety measures to prevent injury.
- Instruct patient to report skin eruption or other significant adverse effects.

Evaluation

- Patient sustains no injury from sedation.
- Patient maintains normal thought processes.
- Patient doesn't develop physical or psychological dependence.

Beta blockers

$Beta_1$ blockers
acebutolol
atenolol
betaxolol hydrochloride
bisoprolol fumarate
esmolol hydrochloride
metoprolol tartrate

$Beta_1$ and $beta_2$ blockers
carvedilol
labetalol hydrochloride
nadolol
pindolol
propranolol hydrochloride
sotalol hydrochloride
timolol maleate

Indications

▶ Hypertension (most drugs), angina pectoris (atenolol, metoprolol, nadolol, and propranolol), arrhythmias (acebutolol, esmolol, pro-

Prototype drug

pranolol, and sotalol), glaucoma (betaxolol and timolol), prevention of MI (atenolol, metoprolol, propranolol, and timolol), prevention of recurrent migraine and other vascular headaches (propranolol and timolol), pheochromocytomas or essential tremors (selected drugs), heart failure (atenolol, bisoprolol, carvedilol, metoprolol).

Actions

Beta blockers are chemicals that compete with beta agonists for available beta-receptor sites; individual drugs differ in their ability to affect beta-receptors. Some drugs are considered nonselective: they block $beta_1$ receptors in cardiac muscle and $beta_2$ receptors in bronchial and vascular smooth muscle. Several drugs are cardioselective and, in lower doses, primarily inhibit $beta_1$ receptors. Some beta blockers have intrinsic sympathomimetic activity and stimulate and block beta-receptors, thereby decreasing cardiac output. Others have a membrane-stabilizing activity that affects cardiac action potential.

Adverse reactions

Therapeutic doses may cause bradycardia, fatigue, and dizziness; some may cause other CNS disturbances, such as nightmares, depression, memory loss, and hallucinations. Toxic doses can produce severe hypotension, bradycardia, heart failure, or bronchospasm.

Contraindications and precautions

- Contraindicated in patients hypersensitive to drug and in patients with cardiogenic shock, sinus bradycardia, heart block greater than first degree, bronchial asthma, and heart failure unless failure is caused by tachyarrhythmia treatable with propranolol.
- Use cautiously in patients with nonallergic bronchospastic disorders, diabetes mellitus, or impaired hepatic or renal function.

Lifespan: In pregnant women, use cautiously. Beta blockers appear in breast milk. In children, safety and efficacy of beta blockers haven't been established; use only if the potential benefits outweigh the potential risks. Geriatric patients may need reduced maintenance doses because of increased bioavailability or delayed metabolism and may also have increased adverse effects; use cautiously.

NURSING PROCESS

Assessment

- Check apical pulse rate daily; alert prescriber about extremes, such as a pulse rate below 60 beats/minute.
- Monitor blood pressure, ECG, and heart rate and rhythm frequently; be alert for progression of AV block or bradycardia.
- If patient has heart failure, weigh him regularly; watch for weight gain of more than 2.25 kg (5 lb) per week.
- Observe diabetic patients for sweating, fatigue, and hunger. Signs of hypoglycemic shock are masked.

Key nursing diagnoses

- Risk for injury related to adverse CNS effects
- Excessive fluid volume related to edema
- Decreased cardiac output related to bradycardia or hypotension

Planning and implementation

- Discontinue a beta blocker before surgery for pheochromocytoma. Before any surgical procedure, notify anesthesiologist that patient is taking a beta blocker.
- Keep glucagon nearby in case prescriber prescribes it to reverse beta blocker overdose.

Patient teaching

- Teach patient to take drug exactly as prescribed, even when he feels better.
- Warn patient not to stop drug suddenly. Abrupt discontinuation can worsen angina or precipitate MI.
- Tell patient not to take OTC medications or herbal remedies without medical consent.
- Explain potential adverse reactions, and stress importance of reporting unusual effects.

Evaluation

- Patient remains free from injury.
- Patient has no signs of edema.
- Patient maintains normal blood pressure and heart rate.

Prototype drug

Calcium channel blockers

amlodipine besylate
bepridil hydrochloride
diltiazem hydrochloride
felodipine
isradipine
nicardipine hydrochloride
nifedipine
nisoldipine
verapamil hydrochloride

Indications

▶ Prinzmetal's variant angina, chronic stable angina, unstable angina, mild-to-moderate hypertension, arrhythmias.

Actions

The main physiologic action of calcium channel blockers is to inhibit calcium influx across the slow channels of myocardial and vascular smooth muscle cells. By inhibiting calcium influx into these cells, calcium channel blockers reduce intracellular calcium concentrations. This, in turn, dilates coronary arteries, peripheral arteries, and arterioles and slows cardiac conduction.

When used to treat Prinzmetal's variant angina, calcium channel blockers inhibit coronary spasm, which then increases oxygen delivery to the heart. Peripheral artery dilation decreases total peripheral resistance, which reduces afterload. This, in turn, decreases myocardial oxygen consumption. Inhibiting calcium influx into the specialized cardiac conduction cells (specifically, those in the SA and AV nodes) slows conduction through the heart. Of the calcium channel blockers, verapamil and diltiazem have the greatest effect on the AV node, which slows the ventricular rate in atrial fibrillation or flutter and converts supraventricular tachycardia to normal sinus rhythm.

Adverse reactions

Adverse reactions vary with the drug used. Verapamil, for instance, may cause bradycardia, various degrees of heart block, worsening of heart failure, and hypotension after rapid I.V. administration. Prolonged oral verapamil therapy may cause constipation. Nifedipine may cause hypotension, peripheral edema, flushing, light-headedness, and headache. Diltiazem most commonly causes anorexia and nausea and also may induce various degrees of heart block, bradycardia, heart failure, and peripheral edema.

Contraindications and precautions

- Contraindicated in patients hypersensitive to drug.

Lifespan: In pregnant women, use cautiously. Calcium channel blockers may appear in breast milk; instruct patient to discontinue breast-feeding during therapy. In neonates and infants, adverse hemodynamic effects of parenteral verapamil are possible, but safety and efficacy of other calcium channel blockers haven't been established; avoid use, if possible. In geriatric patients, the half-life of calcium channel blockers may be increased as a result of decreased clearance; use cautiously.

NURSING PROCESS

Assessment

- Monitor cardiac rate and rhythm and blood pressure carefully when therapy starts or dosage increases.
- Monitor fluid and electrolyte status.
- Monitor patient for adverse reactions.

Key nursing diagnoses

- Decreased cardiac output related to adverse CV reactions
- Constipation related to oral verapamil therapy
- Noncompliance related to long-term therapy

Planning and implementation

- Don't give calcium supplements while patient takes a calcium channel blocker; they may decrease the drug's effectiveness.
- Expect to decrease dosage gradually; don't stop calcium channel blockers abruptly.

Patient teaching

- Teach patient to take drug exactly as prescribed, even if he feels better.
- Instruct patient to take a missed dose as soon as possible, unless it's almost time for his next dose. Warn him never to take a double dose.
- Caution patient not to stop drug suddenly; abrupt discontinuation can produce serious adverse effects.

Prototype drug

• Urge patient to report irregular heartbeat, shortness of breath, swelling of hands and feet, pronounced dizziness, constipation, nausea, or hypotension.

☑ Evaluation

• Patient maintains adequate cardiac output throughout therapy, as evidenced by normal blood pressure and pulse rate.
• Patient regains normal bowel pattern.
• Patient complies with therapy, as evidenced by absence of symptoms related to underlying disorder.

Cephalosporins

First generation
cefadroxil monohydrate
cefazolin sodium
cephalexin monohydrate
Second generation
cefaclor
cefmetazole sodium
cefonicid sodium
cefotetan disodium
cefoxitin sodium
cefprozil
cefuroxime axetil
cefuroxime sodium
loracarbef
Third generation
cefdinir
cefditoren pivoxil
cefoperazone sodium
cefotaxime sodium
cefpodoxime proxetil
ceftazidime
ceftibuten
ceftizoxime sodium
ceftriaxone sodium

Indications

▶ Infections of the lungs, skin, soft tissue, bones, joints, urinary and respiratory tracts, blood, abdomen, and heart; CNS infections caused by susceptible strains of *Neisseria meningitidis, Haemophilus influenzae,* and *Streptococcus pneumoniae;* meningitis caused by *Escherichia coli* or *Klebsiella;* infections that develop after surgical procedures classified as contaminated or potentially contaminated; penicillinase-producing *N. gonorrhoeae;* otitis media and ampicillin-resistant middle ear infection caused by *H. influenzae.*

Actions

Cephalosporins are chemically and pharmacologically similar to penicillin; they act by inhibiting bacterial cell wall synthesis, causing rapid cell lysis. Their sites of action are enzymes known as penicillin-binding proteins. The affinity of certain cephalosporins for these proteins in various microorganisms helps explain the differing spectra of activity in this class of antibiotics. Cephalosporins are bactericidal; they act against many aerobic gram-positive and gram-negative bacteria and some anaerobic bacteria but don't kill fungi or viruses.

First-generation cephalosporins act against many gram-positive cocci, including penicillinase-producing Staphylococcus aureus and *S. epidermidis; S. pneumoniae,* group B streptococci, and group A beta-hemolytic streptococci; susceptible gram-negative organisms include *Klebsiella pneumoniae, E. coli, Proteus mirabilis,* and *Shigella.*

Second-generation cephalosporins are effective against all organisms attacked by first-generation drugs and have additional activity against *Moraxella catarrhalis, H. influenzae, Enterobacter, Citrobacter, Providencia, Acinetobacter, Serratia,* and *Neisseria. Bacteroides fragilis* is susceptible to cefotetan and cefoxitin.

Third-generation cephalosporins are less active than first- and second-generation drugs against gram-positive bacteria, but are more active against gram-negative organisms, including those resistant to first- and second-generation drugs. They have the greatest stability against beta-lactamases produced by gram-negative bacteria. Susceptible gram-negative organisms include *E. coli, Klebsiella, Enterobacter, Providencia, Acinetobacter, Serratia, Proteus, Morganella,* and *Neisseria.* Some third-generation drugs are active against *B. fragilis* and *Pseudomonas.*

Adverse reactions

Many cephalosporins share a similar profile of adverse effects. Hypersensitivity reactions range from mild rashes, fever, and eosinophilia to fatal anaphylaxis and are more common in

Prototype drug

patients with penicillin allergy. Adverse GI reactions include nausea, vomiting, diarrhea, abdominal pain, glossitis, dyspepsia, and tenesmus. Hematologic reactions include positive direct and indirect antiglobulin (Coombs' test), thrombocytopenia or thrombocythemia, transient neutropenia, and reversible leukopenia. Minimal elevation of liver function test results occurs occasionally. Adverse renal effects may occur with any cephalosporin; they are most common in older patients, those with decreased renal function, and those taking other nephrotoxic drugs.

Local venous pain and irritation are common after I.M. injection; these reactions occur more often with higher doses and long-term therapy. Disulfiram-type reactions occur when cefoperazone or cefotetan are administered within 72 hours of alcohol ingestion. Bacterial and fungal superinfections result from suppression of normal flora.

Contraindications and precautions

- Contraindicated in patients hypersensitive to drug.
- Use cautiously in patients with renal or hepatic impairment, history of GI disease, or allergy to penicillins.

Lifespan: In breast-feeding women, use cautiously; cephalosporins appear in breast milk. In neonates and infants, serum half-life is prolonged; use cautiously. Geriatric patients are susceptible to superinfection and coagulopathies, commonly have renal impairment, and may need a lower dosage; use cautiously.

NURSING PROCESS

Assessment

- Review patient's history of allergies. Try to determine whether previous reactions were true hypersensitivity reactions or adverse effects (such as GI distress) that patient interpreted as allergy.
- Monitor patient continuously for possible hypersensitivity reactions or other adverse effects.
- Obtain culture and sensitivity specimen before administering first dose; check test results periodically to assess drug's effectiveness.
- Monitor renal function studies; dosages of certain cephalosporins must be lowered in patients with severe renal impairment. In patients with decreased renal function, monitor BUN and creatinine levels, and urine output for significant changes.
- Monitor PT and platelet counts, and assess patient for signs of hypoprothrombinemia, which may occur (with or without bleeding) during therapy with cefoperazone, cefonicid, cefotetan, or ceftriaxone. It usually occurs in elderly, debilitated, malnourished, and immunocompromised patients and in patients with renal impairment or impaired vitamin K synthesis.
- Monitor patients on long-term therapy for possible bacterial and fungal superinfection, especially elderly and debilitated patients and those receiving immunosuppressants or radiation therapy.
- Monitor susceptible patients receiving sodium salts of cephalosporins for possible fluid retention.

Key nursing diagnoses

- Ineffective protection related to hypersensitivity
- Risk for infection related to superinfection
- Risk for deficient fluid volume related to adverse GI reactions

Planning and implementation

- Administer cephalosporins at least 1 hour before bacteriostatic antibiotics (tetracyclines, erythromycins, and chloramphenicol); by decreasing cephalosporin uptake by bacterial cell walls, the antibiotics inhibit bacterial cell growth.
- Refrigerate oral suspensions (stable for 14 days); shake well before administering to ensure correct dosage.
- Follow manufacturer's directions for reconstitution, dilution, and storage of drugs; check expiration dates.
- Administer I.M. dose deep into large muscle mass (gluteal or midlateral thigh); rotate injection sites to minimize tissue injury.
- Don't add or mix other drugs with I.V. infusions, particularly aminoglycosides, which will be inactivated if mixed with cephalosporins. If other drugs must be given I.V., temporarily stop infusion of primary drug.
- Ensure adequate dilution of I.V. infusion and rotate site every 48 hours to help minimize lo-

cal vein irritation; using a small-gauge needle in a larger available vein may be helpful.

Patient teaching

- Make sure patient understands how and when to take drug. Urge him to comply with instructions for around-the-clock dosage and to complete the prescribed regimen.
- Advise patient to take oral drug with food if GI irritation occurs.
- Review proper storage and disposal of drug, and remind him to check drug's expiration date.
- Teach signs and symptoms of hypersensitivity and other adverse reactions, and emphasize importance of reporting unusual effects.
- Teach signs and symptoms of bacterial and fungal superinfection, especially if patient is elderly or debilitated or has low resistance from immunosuppressants or irradiation. Emphasize importance of reporting signs and symptoms promptly.
- Warn patient not to ingest alcohol in any form within 72 hours of treatment with cefoperazone or cefotetan.
- Advise patient to add yogurt or buttermilk to diet to prevent intestinal superinfection resulting from suppression of normal intestinal flora.
- Advise diabetic patient to monitor urine glucose level with Diastix and not to use Clinitest.
- Urge patient to keep follow-up appointments.

☑ Evaluation

- Patient has no evidence of hypersensitivity.
- Patient is free from infection.
- Patient maintains adequate hydration.

Corticosteroids

betamethasone
betamethasone sodium phosphate
cortisone acetate
dexamethasone
dexamethasone acetate
dexamethasone sodium phosphate
fludrocortisone acetate
hydrocortisone
hydrocortisone acetate
hydrocortisone cypionate
hydrocortisone sodium phosphate
hydrocortisone sodium succinate
methylprednisolone
methylprednisolone acetate
methylprednisolone sodium succinate
prednisolone
prednisolone acetate
prednisolone sodium phosphate
prednisolone steaglate
prednisolone tebutate
prednisone
triamcinolone
triamcinolone acetonide
triamcinolone diacetate
triamcinolone hexacetonide

Indications

▶ Hypersensitivity; inflammation, particularly of eye, nose, and respiratory tract; induction of immunosuppression; replacement therapy in adrenocortical insufficiency.

Actions

Corticosteroids suppress cell-mediated and humoral immunity in three ways: by reducing levels of leukocytes, monocytes, and eosinophils; by decreasing immunoglobulin binding to cell-surface receptors; and by inhibiting interleukin synthesis. They reduce inflammation by preventing hydrolytic enzyme release into the cells, preventing plasma exudation, suppressing polymorphonuclear leukocyte migration, and disrupting other inflammatory processes.

Adverse reactions

Systemic corticosteroid therapy may suppress the hypothalamic-pituitary-adrenal (HPA) axis. Excessive use may cause cushingoid symptoms and various systemic disorders, such as diabetes and osteoporosis. Other effects may include euphoria, insomnia, edema, hypertension, peptic ulcer, increased appetite, fluid and electrolyte imbalances, dermatologic disorders, and immunosuppression.

Contraindications and precautions

- Contraindicated in patients with systemic fungal infection or hypersensitivity to drug or its components.
- Use cautiously in patients with GI ulceration, renal disease, hypertension, osteoporosis, varicella, vaccinia, exanthema, diabetes melli-

tus, hypothyroidism, thromboembolic disorder, seizures, myasthenia gravis, heart failure, tuberculosis, ocular herpes simplex, hypoalbuminemia, emotional instability, or psychosis.

Lifespan: In pregnant women, avoid use, if possible, because of risk to fetus. Women who need corticosteroid therapy should stop breast-feeding because drugs appear in breast milk and could cause serious adverse effects in infants. In children, long-term use should be avoided, if possible, because stunted growth may result. Geriatric patients may have an increased risk of adverse reactions; monitor them closely.

NURSING PROCESS

Assessment

- Establish baseline blood pressure, fluid and electrolyte status, and weight; reassess regularly.
- Monitor patient closely for adverse reactions.
- Evaluate drug effectiveness at regular intervals.

Key nursing diagnoses

- Ineffective protection related to suppression of HPA axis with long-term therapy
- Risk for injury related to severe adverse reactions
- Risk for infection related to immunosuppression

Planning and implementation

- Give drug early in the day to mimic circadian rhythm.
- Give drug with food to prevent GI irritation.
- Take precautions to avoid exposing patient to infection.
- Don't stop drug abruptly.
- Notify prescriber of severe or persistent adverse reactions.
- Avoid prolonged use of corticosteroids, especially in children.

Patient teaching

- Teach patient to take drug exactly as prescribed, and warn him never to stop the drug suddenly.
- Tell patient to notify prescriber if stress level increases; dosage may need to be temporarily increased.
- Instruct patient to take oral drug with food.
- Urge patient to report black tarry stools, bleeding, bruising, blurred vision, emotional changes, or other unusual effects.
- Encourage patient to wear or carry medical identification at all times.

Evaluation

- Patient has no evidence of adrenal insufficiency.
- Patient remains free from injury.
- Patient is free from infection.

Diuretics, loop

bumetanide
ethacrynate sodium
ethacrynic acid
furosemide
torsemide

Indications

▶ Edema from heart failure, hepatic cirrhosis, or nephrotic syndrome; mild-to-moderate hypertension; adjunct treatment in acute pulmonary edema or hypertensive crisis.

Actions

Loop diuretics inhibit sodium and chloride reabsorption in the ascending loop of Henle, thus increasing renal excretion of sodium, chloride, and water. Like thiazide diuretics, loop diuretics increase excretion of potassium. Loop diuretics produce more diuresis and electrolyte loss than thiazide diuretics.

Adverse reactions

Therapeutic doses commonly cause metabolic and electrolyte disturbances, particularly potassium depletion. They also may cause hypochloremic alkalosis, hyperglycemia, hyperuricemia, and hypomagnesemia. Rapid parenteral administration may cause hearing loss (including deafness) and tinnitus. High doses can produce profound diuresis, leading to hypovolemia and CV collapse.

Contraindications and precautions

- Contraindicated in patients hypersensitive to drug and in patients with anuria, hepatic coma, or severe electrolyte depletion.

Prototype drug

• Use cautiously in patients with severe renal disease.

Lifespan: In pregnant women, use cautiously. In breast-feeding women, don't use. In neonates, use cautiously; the usual pediatric dose can be used, but dosage intervals should be extended. Geriatric patients are more susceptible to drug-induced diuresis, and reduced dosages may be indicated; monitor these patients closely.

NURSING PROCESS

Assessment

• Monitor blood pressure and pulse rate (especially during rapid diuresis). Establish baseline values before therapy begins, and watch for significant changes.
• Establish baseline CBC (including WBC count), liver function test results, and levels of serum electrolytes, carbon dioxide, magnesium, BUN, and creatinine. Review periodically.
• Assess patient for evidence of excessive diuresis: hypotension, tachycardia, poor skin turgor, excessive thirst, or dry and cracked mucous membranes.
• Monitor patient for edema and ascites. Observe the legs of ambulatory patients and the sacral area of patients on bed rest.
• Weigh patient each morning immediately after voiding and before breakfast, in the same type of clothing, and on the same scale. Weight provides a reliable indicator of patient's response to diuretic therapy.
• Monitor and record patient's intake and output carefully every 24 hours.

Key nursing diagnoses

• Risk for deficient fluid volume related to excessive diuresis
• Impaired urine elimination related to change in diuresis pattern
• Ineffective protection related to electrolyte imbalance

Planning and implementation

• Give diuretics in morning to ensure that major diuresis occurs before bedtime. To prevent nocturia, administer diuretics before 6 p.m.
• If ordered, reduce dosage for patient with hepatic dysfunction, and increase dosage for patient with renal impairment, oliguria, or decreased diuresis. (Inadequate urine output may result in circulatory overload, causing water intoxication, pulmonary edema, and heart failure). If ordered, increase dosage of insulin or oral hypoglycemic in diabetic patient, and reduce dosage of other antihypertensive drugs.
• Take safety measures for all ambulatory patients until response to diuretic is known.
• Consult dietitian about need for potassium supplements.
• Keep urinal or commode readily available to patient.

Patient teaching

• Explain rationale for therapy and importance of following prescribed regimen.
• Review adverse effects, and urge patient to report symptoms promptly, especially chest, back, or leg pain; shortness of breath; dyspnea; increased edema or weight; or excess diuresis (weight loss of more than 0.9 kg [2 lb] daily).
• Advise patient to eat potassium-rich foods and to avoid high-sodium foods (lunch meat, smoked meats, processed cheeses). Caution him not to add table salt to foods.
• Encourage patient to keep follow-up appointments to monitor effectiveness of therapy.

Evaluation

• Patient maintains adequate hydration.
• Patient states importance of taking diuretic early in the day to prevent nocturia.
• Patient complies with therapy, as evidenced by improvement in underlying condition.

Diuretics, thiazide and thiazide-like

Thiazide
chlorothiazide
hydrochlorothiazide
Thiazide-like
indapamide
metolazone

Indications

▶ Edema from right-sided heart failure, mild-to-moderate left-sided heart failure, or nephrotic syndrome; edema and ascites caused by hepatic cirrhosis; hypertension; diabetes in-

Prototype drug

sipidus, particularly nephrogenic diabetes insipidus.

Actions

Thiazide and thiazide-like diuretics interfere with sodium transport across the tubules of the cortical diluting segment in the nephron, thereby increasing renal excretion of sodium, chloride, water, potassium, and calcium.

Thiazide diuretics also exert an antihypertensive effect. Although the exact mechanism is unknown, direct arteriolar dilation may be partially responsible. In diabetes insipidus, thiazides cause a paradoxical decrease in urine volume and an increase in renal concentration of urine, possibly because of sodium depletion and decreased plasma volume. This increases water and sodium reabsorption in the kidneys.

Adverse reactions

Therapeutic doses cause electrolyte and metabolic disturbances, most commonly potassium depletion. Other abnormalities include hypochloremic alkalosis, hypomagnesemia, hyponatremia, hypercalcemia, hyperuricemia, hyperglycemia, and elevated cholesterol levels.

Contraindications and precautions

- Contraindicated in patients hypersensitive to drug and in those with anuria.
- Use cautiously in patients with severe renal disease, impaired hepatic function, or progressive liver disease.

Lifespan: In pregnant women, use cautiously. In breast-feeding women, thiazides are contraindicated because they appear in breast milk. In children, safety and efficacy haven't been established. Geriatric patients are more susceptible to drug-induced diuresis, and reduced dosages may be needed; monitor patient closely.

NURSING PROCESS

Assessment

- Monitor patient's intake, output, and serum electrolyte levels regularly.
- Weigh patient each morning immediately after voiding and before breakfast, in the same type of clothing, and on the same scale. Weight provides a reliable indicator of patient's response to diuretic therapy.
- Monitor blood glucose level in a diabetic patient. Diuretics may cause hyperglycemia.
- Monitor serum creatinine and BUN levels regularly. Drug isn't as effective if these levels are more than twice normal. Also monitor blood uric acid level.

Key nursing diagnoses

- Risk for deficient fluid volume related to excessive diuresis
- Impaired urine elimination related to change in diuresis pattern
- Ineffective protection related to electrolyte imbalance

Planning and implementation

- Give drug in the morning to prevent nocturia.
- Consult a dietitian to provide a high-potassium diet.
- Administer potassium supplements as prescribed to maintain acceptable serum potassium level.
- Keep urinal or commode readily available to patient.

Patient teaching

- Explain the rationale for therapy and the importance of following the prescribed regimen.
- Tell patient to take drug at the same time each day to prevent nocturia. Suggest taking drug with food to minimize GI irritation.
- Urge patient to seek prescriber's approval before taking any other drug, including OTC medications and herbal remedies.
- Advise patient to record his weight each morning after voiding and before breakfast, in the same type of clothing, and on the same scale.
- Review adverse effects, and urge the patient to report symptoms promptly, especially chest, back, or leg pain; shortness of breath; dyspnea; increased edema or weight; or excess diuresis (weight loss of more than 0.9 kg [2 lb] daily). Warn him about photosensitivity reactions that usually occur 10 to 14 days after initial sun exposure.
- Advise patient to eat potassium-rich foods and to avoid high-sodium foods (lunch meat, smoked meats, processed cheeses). Caution him not to add table salt to foods.
- Encourage patient to keep follow-up appointments to monitor effectiveness of therapy.

☑ Evaluation
• Patient maintains adequate hydration.
• Patient states importance of taking diuretic early in the day to prevent nocturia.
• Patient complies with therapy, as evidenced by improvement in underlying condition.

Estrogens
diethylstilbestrol
diethylstilbestrol diphosphate
esterified estrogens
estradiol
estradiol cypionate
estradiol valerate
estrogenic substances, conjugated
estrone
estropipate
ethinyl estradiol

Indications
▶ Prevention of vasomotor symptoms, such as hot flushes and dizziness; stimulation of vaginal tissue development, cornification, and secretory activity; inhibition of hormone-sensitive cancer growth; prevention of bone decalcification; ovulation control; prevention of conception.

Actions
Estrogens promote the development and maintenance of the female reproductive system and secondary sexual characteristics. They inhibit the release of pituitary gonadotropins and have various metabolic effects, including retention of fluid and electrolytes, retention and deposition in bone of calcium and phosphorus, and mild anabolic activity. Of the six naturally occurring estrogens in humans, three (estradiol, estrone, and estriol) are present in significant quantities.

Estrogens and estrogenic substances administered as drugs have effects related to endogenous estrogen's mechanism of action. They can mimic the action of endogenous estrogen when used as replacement therapy and can inhibit ovulation or the growth of certain hormone-sensitive cancers. Conjugated estrogens and estrogenic substances are normally obtained from the urine of pregnant mares. Other estrogens are manufactured synthetically.

Adverse reactions
Acute adverse reactions include changes in menstrual bleeding patterns (spotting, prolongation or absence of bleeding), abdominal cramps, swollen feet or ankles, bloating (fluid and electrolyte retention), breast swelling and tenderness, weight gain, nausea, loss of appetite, headache, photosensitivity, and loss of libido.

Long-term effects include elevated blood pressure (sometimes into the hypertensive range), cholestatic jaundice, benign hepatomas, endometrial carcinoma (rare), and thromboembolic disease (risk increases markedly with cigarette smoking, especially in women older than age 35).

Contraindications and precautions
• Contraindicated in women with thrombophlebitis or thromboembolic disorders, unexplained abnormal genital bleeding, or estrogen-dependent neoplasia.
• Use cautiously in patients with hypertension; metabolic bone disease; migraines; seizures; asthma; cardiac, renal, or hepatic impairment; blood dyscrasia; diabetes; family history of breast cancer; or fibrocystic disease.
Lifespan: In pregnant or breast-feeding women, use is contraindicated. In adolescents whose bone growth isn't complete, use cautiously because of effects on epiphyseal closure. Postmenopausal women with long-term estrogen use have an increased risk of endometrial cancer.

NURSING PROCESS

Assessment
• Monitor patient regularly to detect improvement or worsening of symptoms; observe patient for adverse reactions.
• If patient has diabetes mellitus, watch closely for loss of diabetes control.
• Monitor PT of patient receiving warfarin-type anticoagulant. If ordered, adjust anticoagulant dosage.

Key nursing diagnoses
• Excessive fluid volume related to drug-induced fluid retention
• Risk of injury related to adverse effects
• Noncompliance related to long-term therapy

Planning and implementation

• Notify pathologist of patient's estrogen therapy when sending specimens for evaluation.

• Keep in mind that estrogens usually are given cyclically (once daily for 3 weeks, followed by 1 week without drugs; repeated as needed).

Patient teaching

• Urge patient to read the package insert describing adverse reactions. Follow this with a verbal explanation. Tell patient to keep the package insert for later reference.

• Advise patient to take drug with meals or at bedtime to relieve nausea. Reassure her that nausea usually disappears with continued therapy.

• Teach patient how to apply estrogen ointments or transdermal estrogen. Review symptoms that accompany a systemic reaction to ointments.

• Teach patient how to insert intravaginal estrogen suppository. Advise her to use sanitary pads instead of tampons when using suppository.

• Teach patient how to perform routine monthly breast self-examination.

• Tell patient to stop taking drug immediately if she becomes pregnant because estrogens can harm fetus.

• Remind patient not to breast-feed during estrogen therapy.

• If patient is receiving cyclic therapy for postmenopausal symptoms, explain that withdrawal bleeding may occur during the week off, but that fertility hasn't been restored and ovulation doesn't occur.

• Explain that medical supervision is essential during prolonged therapy.

• Tell man on long-term therapy about possible temporary gynecomastia and impotence, which will disappear when therapy ends.

• Instruct patient to notify prescriber immediately if she experiences abdominal pain; pain, numbness, or stiffness in legs or buttocks; pressure or pain in chest; shortness of breath; severe headaches; visual disturbances, such as blind spots, flashing lights, or blurriness; vaginal bleeding or discharge; breast lumps; swelling of hands or feet; yellow skin and sclera; dark urine; or light-colored stools.

• Urge diabetic patient to report symptoms of hyperglycemia or glycosuria.

Evaluation

• Patient experiences only minimal fluid retention.

• Serious complications of estrogen therapy don't develop.

• Patient complies with therapy, as evidenced by improvement in underlying condition or absence of pregnancy.

Hematinics, oral

ferrous fumarate
ferrous gluconate
ferrous sulfate

Indications

▶ Prevention and treatment of iron-deficiency anemia.

Actions

Iron is an essential component of hemoglobin. It's needed in adequate amounts for erythropoiesis and for efficient oxygen transport in the blood. After absorption into the blood, iron is immediately bound to transferrin, a plasma protein that transports iron to bone marrow, where it's used during hemoglobin synthesis. Some iron is also used during synthesis of myoglobin and other nonhemoglobin heme units.

Adverse reactions

Because iron is corrosive, GI intolerance is common (5% to 20% of patients); symptoms include nausea, vomiting, anorexia, constipation, and dark stools. Liquid forms may stain teeth.

Contraindications and precautions

• Contraindicated in patients with hemochromatosis, hemolytic anemia, or hemosiderosis.

• Use cautiously in patients with peptic ulcer disease, regional enteritis, ulcerative colitis, or sensitivity to sulfites or tartrazine.

Lifespan: In breast-feeding women, iron supplements are commonly recommended; no adverse effects are known. With children, caution parents about possible lethal effects of iron overdose. In elderly patients, iron-induced constipation is common; stress proper diet high in fiber to minimize this effect. Elderly patients also may need higher doses because reduced gastric secretions and achlorhydria may lower their capacity for iron absorption.

NURSING PROCESS

Assessment

• Monitor patient for adverse reactions, especially those related to bowel function.
• Monitor hemoglobin and reticulocyte counts during therapy.

Key nursing diagnoses

• Risk for deficient fluid volume related to GI upset
• Constipation related to adverse effect on bowel function
• Noncompliance related to adverse effects or long-term use

Planning and implementation

• Dilute liquid forms in juice (preferably orange juice, which promotes iron absorption) or water, but not in milk or antacids. To avoid staining teeth, give liquid preparations through a straw. Don't give antacids within 1 hour before or 2 hours after an iron product, if possible, to prevent interference with absorption.
• Don't crush tablets or capsules; if patient has trouble swallowing, use a liquid form.

Patient teaching

• Explain rationale for therapy, and urge patient to follow the prescribed regimen.
• Tell patient to continue his regular dosage schedule if he misses a dose, and warn him not to take double doses.
• Advise patient to dilute liquid form in juice (preferably orange juice) or water. Suggest that he use a straw to avoid staining his teeth.
• Review possible adverse effects. Tell patient that oral iron may turn stools black, and reassure him that this is harmless. Teach dietary measures to help prevent constipation.
• Explain the toxicity of iron, and emphasize importance of keeping iron away from children to prevent poisoning. As few as three or four tablets can cause serious iron poisoning.
• Urge patient to report diarrhea or constipation because prescriber may want to adjust dosage, modify diet, or order further tests.
• Explain that iron therapy may be required for 4 to 6 months after anemia resolves. Encourage compliance.

Evaluation

• Patient maintains adequate hydration.
• Patient regains normal bowel pattern.
• Patient complies with therapy, as evidenced by return of normal hemoglobin levels and resolution of iron deficiency anemia.

Histamine$_2$-receptor antagonists

cimetidine
famotidine
nizatidine
ranitidine hydrochloride

Indications

▶ Acute duodenal or gastric ulcer, Zollinger-Ellison syndrome, gastroesophageal reflux.

Actions

All H_2-receptor antagonists inhibit the action of H_2 receptors in gastric parietal cells, reducing gastric acid output and concentration, regardless of the stimulant (histamine, food, insulin, caffeine) or basal conditions.

Adverse reactions

H_2-receptor antagonists rarely cause adverse reactions. Mild and transient diarrhea, neutropenia, dizziness, fatigue, cardiac arrhythmias, and gynecomastia are possible.

Contraindications and precautions

• Contraindicated in patients hypersensitive to drug.
• Use cautiously in patients with impaired renal or hepatic function.
Lifespan: In pregnant women, use cautiously. In breast-feeding women, H_2-receptor antagonists are contraindicated because they may appear in breast milk. In children, safety and efficacy haven't been established. Geriatric patients have increased risk of adverse reactions, particularly those affecting the CNS; use cautiously.

NURSING PROCESS

Assessment

- Monitor patient for adverse reactions, especially hypotension and arrhythmias.
- Periodically monitor laboratory tests, such as CBC and renal and hepatic studies.

Key nursing diagnoses

- Risk for infection related to drug-induced neutropenia
- Decreased cardiac output related to adverse CV effects (cimetidine)
- Fatigue related to drug's CNS effects

Planning and implementation

- Administer once-daily dose at bedtime, twice-daily doses in morning and evening, and multiple doses with meals and at bedtime. Most clinicians prefer once-daily dose at bedtime to promote compliance.
- Don't exceed recommended infusion rates when administering drugs I.V.; doing so increases risk of adverse CV effects. Continuous I.V. infusion may suppress acid secretion more effectively.
- Administer antacids at least 1 hour before or after H_2-receptor antagonists. Antacids can decrease drug absorption.
- Anticipate dosage adjustment for patient with renal disease.
- Avoid discontinuing drug abruptly.

Patient teaching

- Teach patient how and when to take drug, and warn him not to stop drug suddenly.
- Review possible adverse reactions, and urge him to report unusual effects.
- Caution patient to avoid smoking during therapy; smoking stimulates gastric acid secretion and worsens the disease.

Evaluation

- Patient is free from infection.
- Patient maintains a normal heart rhythm.
- Patient states appropriate management plan for combating fatigue.

Hypoglycemics, oral

acarbose
chlorpropamide
glimepiride
glipizide
glyburide
metformin hydrochloride
miglitol
nateglinide
pioglitazone hydrochloride
repaglinide
rosiglitazone maleate

Indications

▶ Mild to moderately severe, stable, nonketotic non-insulin-dependent diabetes mellitus that cannot be controlled by diet alone.

Actions

Oral hypoglycemics come in several types. Sulfonylureas are sulfonamide derivatives that exert no antibacterial activity. They lower glucose levels by stimulating insulin release from the pancreas. These drugs work only in the presence of functioning beta cells in the islet tissue of the pancreas. After prolonged administration, they produce hypoglycemia through significant extrapancreatic effects, including reduction of hepatic glucose production and enhanced peripheral sensitivity to insulin. The latter may result from an increased number of insulin receptors or from changes in events after insulin binding. Sulfonylureas are divided into first-generation drugs, such as chlorpropamide, and second-generation drugs, such as glyburide, glimepiride, and glipizide. Although their mechanisms of action are similar, the second-generation drugs carry a more lipophilic side chain, are more potent, and cause fewer adverse reactions. Clinically, their most important difference is their duration of action.

Meglitinides, such as nateglinide and repaglinide, are non-sulfonylurea hypoglycemics that stimulate the release of insulin from the pancreas.

Metformin decreases hepatic glucose production, reduces intestinal glucose absorption, and improves insulin sensitivity (increases peripheral glucose uptake and utilization). With metformin therapy, insulin secretion remains unchanged, and fasting insulin levels and day-long plasma insulin response may decrease.

Alpha-glucosidase inhibitors, such as acarbose and miglitol, delay digestion of carbohydrates, resulting in a smaller rise in blood glucose levels.

Rosiglitazone and pioglitazone are thiazolidinediones, which lower blood glucose levels by improving insulin sensitivity. These drugs are potent and highly selective agonists for receptors found in insulin-sensitive tissues, such as adipose tissue, skeletal muscle, and liver.

Adverse reactions

Sulfonylureas cause dose-related reactions that usually respond to decreased dosage: headache, nausea, vomiting, anorexia, heartburn, weakness, and paresthesia. Hypoglycemia may follow excessive dosage, increased exercise, decreased food intake, or alcohol consumption.

The most serious adverse reaction linked to metformin is lactic acidosis. It's rare and most likely to occur in patients with renal dysfunction. Other reactions to metformin include GI upset, megaloblastic anemia, rash, dermatitis, and unpleasant or metallic taste.

Contraindications and precautions

- Contraindicated in patients hypersensitive to drug and in patients with diabetic ketoacidosis with or without coma. Metformin is also contraindicated in patients with renal disease or metabolic acidosis and generally should be avoided in patients with hepatic disease.
- Use sulfonylureas cautiously in patients with renal or hepatic disease. Use metformin cautiously in patients with adrenal or pituitary insufficiency and in debilitated and malnourished patients. Alpha-glucosidase inhibitors should be used cautiously in patients with mild-to-moderate renal insufficiency. Use thiazolidinediones cautiously in patients with edema or heart failure.

Lifespan: In pregnant or breast-feeding women, use is contraindicated; oral hypoglycemics appear in small amounts in breast milk and may cause hypoglycemia in the breast-feeding infant. In children, oral hypoglycemics aren't effective in type 1 diabetes mellitus.

Geriatric patients may be more sensitive to these drugs, usually need lower dosages, and are more likely to develop neurologic symptoms of hypoglycemia; monitor these patients closely. In geriatric patients, avoid chlorpropamide use because of its longer duration of action.

NURSING PROCESS

Assessment

- Monitor patient's blood glucose level regularly. Increase monitoring during periods of increased stress (infection, fever, surgery, or trauma).
- Monitor patient for adverse reactions.
- Assess patient's compliance with drug therapy and other aspects of diabetic treatment.

Key nursing diagnoses

- Risk for injury related to hypoglycemia
- Risk for deficient fluid volume related to adverse GI effects
- Noncompliance related to long-term therapy

Planning and implementation

- Give sulfonylurea 30 minutes before morning meal (once-daily dosing) or 30 minutes before morning and evening meals (twice-daily dosing). Give metformin with morning and evening meals. Alpha-glucosidase inhibitors should be taken with the first bite of each main meal three times daily.
- Patients who take a thiazolidinedione should have liver enzyme levels measured at the start of therapy, every 2 months for the first year of therapy, and periodically thereafter.
- Keep in mind that a patient transferring from one oral hypoglycemic to another (except chlorpropamide) usually needs no transition period.
- Anticipate patient's need for insulin during periods of increased stress.

Patient teaching

- Emphasize importance of following the prescribed regimen. Urge patient to adhere to diet, weight reduction, exercise, and personal hygiene recommendations.
- Explain that therapy relieves symptoms but doesn't cure the disease.

• Teach patient how to recognize and treat hypoglycemia.

Evaluation
• Patient sustains no injury.
• Patient maintains adequate hydration.
• Patient complies with therapy, as evidenced by normal or near-normal glucose level.

Laxatives

Bulk-forming
calcium polycarbophil
methylcellulose
psyllium
Emollient
docusate calcium
docusate potassium
docusate sodium
Hyperosmolar
glycerin
lactulose
magnesium citrate
magnesium hydroxide
magnesium sulfate
sodium phosphates
Lubricant
mineral oil
Stimulant
bisacodyl
castor oil
senna

Indications
▶ Constipation, irritable bowel syndrome, diverticulosis.

Actions
Laxatives promote movement of intestinal contents through the colon and rectum via several modes of action: bulk-forming, emollient, hyperosmolar, lubricant, and stimulant.

Adverse reactions
All laxatives may cause flatulence, diarrhea, abdominal discomfort, weakness, and dependence. Bulk-forming laxatives may cause intestinal obstruction, impaction, or (rarely) esophageal obstruction. Emollient laxatives may cause a bitter taste or throat irritation. Hyperosmolar laxatives may cause fluid and electrolyte imbalances. Lubricant laxatives may cause impaired absorption of fat-soluble vitamins or anal irritation if given rectally. Stimulant laxatives may cause urine discoloration, malabsorption, and weight loss.

Contraindications and precautions
• Contraindicated in patients with GI obstruction or perforation, toxic colitis, megacolon, nausea and vomiting, or acute surgical abdomen.
• Use cautiously in patients with rectal or anal conditions, such as rectal bleeding or large hemorrhoids.
Lifespan: For use in breast-feeding women, recommendations vary for individual drugs. Infants and children have an increased risk of fluid and electrolyte disturbances; use cautiously. In elderly patients, dependence is more likely to develop because of age-related changes in GI function; monitor these patients closely.

NURSING PROCESS

Assessment
• Obtain baseline assessment of patient's bowel patterns and GI history before giving laxative.
• Monitor patient for adverse reactions.
• Monitor bowel pattern throughout therapy. Assess bowel sounds and color and consistency of stools.
• Monitor patient's fluid and electrolyte status during administration.

Key nursing diagnoses
• Diarrhea related to adverse GI effects
• Acute pain related to abdominal discomfort
• Impaired health maintenance related to laxative dependence

Planning and implementation
• Don't crush enteric-coated tablets.
• Time administration so that bowel evacuation doesn't interfere with sleep.
• Make sure patient has easy access to bedpan or bathroom.
• Institute measures to prevent constipation.

Prototype drug

Patient teaching

- Advise patient that therapy should be short-term. Point out that abuse or prolonged use can cause nutritional imbalances.
- Tell patient that stool softeners and bulk-forming laxatives may take several days to achieve results.
- Encourage patient to remain active and to drink plenty of fluids if he's taking a bulk-forming laxative.
- Explain that stimulant laxatives may cause harmless urine discoloration.
- Teach patient about including foods high in fiber into diet.

Evaluation

- Patient regains normal bowel pattern.
- Patient states that pain is relieved with stool evacuation.
- Patient discusses dangers of laxative abuse and importance of limiting laxative use.

Nonsteroidal anti-inflammatory drugs

celecoxib
diclofenac potassium
diclofenac sodium
diflunisal
etodolac
ibuprofen
indomethacin
indomethacin sodium trihydrate
ketoprofen
ketorolac tromethamine
mefenamic acid
meloxicam
nabumetone
naproxen
naproxen sodium
oxaprozin
piroxicam
rofecoxib
sulindac
valdecoxib

Indications

▶ Mild-to-moderate pain, inflammation, stiffness, swelling, or tenderness caused by headache, arthralgia, myalgia, neuralgia, dysmenorrhea, rheumatoid arthritis, juvenile arthritis, osteoarthritis, or dental or surgical procedures.

Actions

The analgesic effect of NSAIDs may result from interference with the prostaglandins involved in pain. Prostaglandins appear to sensitize pain receptors to mechanical stimulation or to other chemical mediators. NSAIDs inhibit synthesis of prostaglandins peripherally and possibly centrally.

Like salicylates, NSAIDs exert an anti-inflammatory effect that may result in part from inhibition of prostaglandin synthesis and release during inflammation. The exact mechanism hasn't been clearly established.

Adverse reactions

Adverse reactions chiefly involve the GI tract, particularly erosion of the gastric mucosa. The most common symptoms are dyspepsia, heartburn, epigastric distress, nausea, and abdominal pain. CNS reactions also may occur. Flank pain with other evidence of nephrotoxicity occurs occasionally. Fluid retention may aggravate hypertension or heart failure.

Contraindications and precautions

- Contraindicated in patients with GI lesions or GI bleeding and in patients hypersensitive to drug.
- Use cautiously in patients with cardiac decompensation, hypertension, fluid retention, or coagulation defects.

Lifespan: For breast-feeding women, NSAIDs aren't recommended. In children younger than age 14, safety of long-term therapy hasn't been established. Geriatric patients older than age 60 may be more susceptible to toxic effects of NSAIDs because of decreased renal function.

NURSING PROCESS

Assessment

- Assess patient's level of pain and inflammation before therapy begins, and evaluate drug effectiveness after administration.
- Monitor patient for signs and symptoms of bleeding. Assess bleeding time if patient needs surgery.

▶ Prototype drug

• Monitor ophthalmic and auditory function before and periodically during therapy to detect toxicity.
• Monitor CBC, platelet count, PT, and hepatic and renal function studies periodically to detect abnormalities.
• Watch for bronchospasm in patients with aspirin hypersensitivity, rhinitis or nasal polyps, and asthma.

Key nursing diagnoses

• Risk for injury related to adverse reactions
• Excessive fluid volume related to fluid retention
• Disturbed sensory perception (visual and auditory) related to toxicity

Planning and implementation

• Administer oral NSAIDs with 8 oz (240 ml) of water to ensure adequate passage into the stomach. Have patient sit up for 15 to 30 minutes after taking drug to prevent lodging in esophagus.
• As needed, crush tablets or mix with food or fluid to aid swallowing. Administer with antacids to minimize GI upset.

Patient teaching

• Encourage patient to take drug as directed to achieve desired effect. Explain that he may not notice benefits of drug for 2 to 4 weeks.
• Review methods to prevent or minimize GI upset.
• Work with patient on long-term therapy to arrange for monitoring of laboratory values, especially BUN and creatinine levels, liver function test results, and CBC.
• Instruct patient to notify prescriber about severe or persistent adverse reactions.

Evaluation

• Patient remains free from injury.
• Patient shows no signs of edema.
• Patient maintains normal visual and auditory function.

Opioids

alfentanil hydrochloride
codeine phosphate
codeine sulfate
difenoxin
diphenoxylate
fentanyl citrate
hydromorphone hydrochloride
meperidine hydrochloride
methadone hydrochloride
morphine sulfate
oxycodone hydrochloride
oxymorphone hydrochloride
propoxyphene hydrochloride
propoxyphene napsylate
sufentanil citrate

Indications

▶ Moderate-to-severe pain from acute and some chronic disorders; diarrhea; dry, nonproductive cough; management of opiate dependence.

Actions

Opioids act as agonists at specific opiate-receptor binding sites in the CNS and other tissues, altering the patient's perception of and emotional response to pain.

Adverse reactions

Respiratory and circulatory depression (including orthostatic hypotension) are the major hazards of opioids. Other adverse CNS effects include dizziness, visual disturbances, mental clouding, depression, sedation, coma, euphoria, dysphoria, weakness, faintness, agitation, restlessness, nervousness, and seizures. Adverse GI effects include nausea, vomiting, constipation, and biliary colic. Urine retention or hypersensitivity also may occur. Tolerance to the drug and psychological or physical dependence may follow prolonged therapy.

Contraindications and precautions

• Contraindicated in patients hypersensitive to drug and in those who have recently taken an MAO inhibitor.
• Use cautiously in patients with head injury, increased intracranial or intraocular pressure, and hepatic or renal dysfunction.

• Use cautiously in patients with mental illnesses and emotional disturbances, and in patients exhibiting drug-seeking behaviors.

Lifespan: In pregnant or breast-feeding women, use cautiously; codeine, meperidine, methadone, morphine, and propoxyphene appear in breast milk. Breast-feeding infants of women receiving methadone therapy may develop physical dependence. In children, safety and efficacy haven't been established. Geriatric patients may be more sensitive to opioids; lower doses are usually indicated.

NURSING PROCESS

Assessment

- Obtain baseline assessment of patient's pain, and reassess frequently to determine drug effectiveness.
- Evaluate patient's respiratory status before each dose; watch for respiratory rate below patient's baseline level and for restlessness, which may be compensatory signs of hypoxia. Respiratory depression may last longer than the analgesic effect.
- Monitor patient for other adverse reactions.
- Monitor patient for tolerance and dependence. The first sign of tolerance to opioids is usually a shortened duration of effect.

Key nursing diagnoses

- Ineffective breathing pattern related to respiratory depression
- Risk for injury related to orthostatic hypotension
- Ineffective individual coping related to drug dependence

Planning and implementation

- Keep resuscitative equipment and a narcotic antagonist (naloxone) available.
- Give I.V. drug by slow injection, preferably in diluted solution. Rapid I.V. injection increases the risk of adverse effects.
- Give I.M. or S.C. injections cautiously to patients with decreased platelet counts and to patients who are chilled, hypovolemic, or in shock; decreased perfusion may lead to drug accumulation and toxicity. Rotate injection sites to avoid induration.
- Carefully note the strength of solution when measuring a dose. Oral solutions of varying concentrations are available.
- For maximum effectiveness, give on a regular dosage schedule rather than p.r.n.
- Institute safety precautions.
- Encourage postoperative patients to turn, cough, and breathe deeply every 2 hours to avoid atelectasis.
- Give oral forms with food if GI irritation occurs.
- Withdrawal symptoms, including tremors, agitation, nausea, and vomiting, may occur if drug is stopped abruptly. Monitor patients with these symptoms carefully and provide supportive therapy.

Patient teaching

- Teach patient to take drug exactly as prescribed. Urge him to call prescriber if he isn't experiencing desired effect or is experiencing significant adverse reactions.
- Warn patient to avoid hazardous activities until drug's effects are known.
- Advise patient to avoid alcohol while taking opioids; it will cause additive CNS depression.
- Suggest measures to prevent constipation, such as increasing fiber in diet and using a stool softener.
- Instruct patient to breathe deeply, cough, and change position every 2 hours to avoid respiratory complications.

Evaluation

- Patient maintains adequate ventilation, as evidenced by normal respiratory rate and rhythm and pink color.
- Patient remains free from injury.
- Tolerance to therapy doesn't develop.

Penicillins

Natural penicillins
penicillin G benzathine
penicillin G potassium
penicillin G procaine
penicillin G sodium
penicillin V potassium
Aminopenicillins
amoxicillin and clavulanate potassium
amoxicillin trihydrate
ampicillin
ampicillin sodium and sulbactam sodium
ampicillin trihydrate

Penicillinase-resistant penicillins
dicloxacillin sodium
nafcillin sodium
oxacillin sodium
Extended-spectrum penicillins
carbenicillin indanyl sodium
mezlocillin sodium
piperacillin sodium
piperacillin sodium and tazobactam sodium
ticarcillin disodium
ticarcillin disodium and clavulanate potassium

Indications

▶ Streptococcal pneumonia; enterococcal and nonenterococcal Group D endocarditis; diphtheria; anthrax; meningitis; tetanus; botulism; actinomycosis; syphilis; relapsing fever; Lyme disease; pneumococcal infections; rheumatic fever; bacterial endocarditis; neonatal Group B streptococcal disease; septicemia; gynecologic infections; infections of urinary, respiratory, and GI tracts; infections of skin, soft tissue, bones, and joints.

Actions

Penicillins are generally bactericidal. They inhibit synthesis of the bacterial cell wall, causing rapid cell lysis. They're most effective against fast-growing susceptible bacteria. Their sites of action are enzymes known as penicillin-binding proteins (PBPs). The affinity of certain penicillins for PBPs in various microorganisms helps explain differing spectra of activity in this class of antibiotics.

Susceptible aerobic gram-positive cocci include *Staphylococcus aureus;* nonenterococcal Group D streptococci; Groups A, B, D, G, H, K, L, and M *streptococci; S. viridans;* and enterococcus (usually with an aminoglycoside). Susceptible aerobic gram-negative cocci include *Neisseria meningitidis* and non-penicillinase-producing *N. gonorrhoeae.*

Susceptible aerobic gram-positive bacilli include *Corynebacterium, Listeria,* and *Bacillus anthracis.* Susceptible anaerobes include *Peptococcus, Peptostreptococcus, Actinomyces, Clostridium, Fusobacterium, Veillonella,* and non-beta-lactamase–producing strains of *S. pneumoniae.* Susceptible spirochetes include *Treponema pallidum, T. pertenue, Leptospira, Borrelia recurrentis,* and, possibly, *B. burgdorferi.*

Aminopenicillins have uses against more organisms, including many gram-negative organisms. Like natural penicillins, aminopenicillins are vulnerable to inactivation by penicillinase. Susceptible organisms include *Escherichia coli, Proteus mirabilis, Shigella, Salmonella, S. pneumoniae, N. gonorrhoeae, Haemophilus influenzae, Staphylococcus aureus, Staphylococcus epidermidis* (non-penicillinase-producing Staphylococcus), and *Listeria monocytogenes.*

Penicillinase-resistant penicillins are semisynthetic penicillins designed to remain stable against hydrolysis by most staphylococcal penicillinases and thus are the drugs of choice against susceptible penicillinase-producing staphylococci. They also act against most organisms susceptible to natural penicillins.

Extended-spectrum penicillins offer a wider range of bactericidal action than the other three classes and usually are given in combination with aminoglycosides. Susceptible strains include *Enterobacter, Klebsiella, Citrobacter, Serratia, Bacteroides fragilis, Pseudomonas aeruginosa, Proteus vulgaris, Providencia rettgeri,* and *Morganella morganii.* These penicillins are also vulnerable to beta-lactamase and penicillinases.

Adverse reactions

With all penicillins, hypersensitivity reactions range from mild rash, fever, and eosinophilia to fatal anaphylaxis. Hematologic reactions include hemolytic anemia, transient neutropenia, leukopenia, and thrombocytopenia.

Certain adverse reactions are more common with specific classes: For example, bleeding episodes are usually seen with high doses of extended-spectrum penicillins whereas GI adverse effects are most common with ampicillin. In patients with renal disease, high doses, especially of penicillin G, irritate the CNS by causing confusion, twitching, lethargy, dysphagia, seizures, and coma. Hepatotoxicity is common with penicillinase-resistant penicillins; hyperkalemia and hypernatremia are common with extended-spectrum penicillins.

Local irritation from parenteral therapy may be severe enough to warrant administration by subclavian or centrally placed catheter or discontinuation of therapy.

Contraindications and precautions

• Contraindicated in patients hypersensitive to drug.
• Use cautiously in patients with history of asthma or drug allergy, mononucleosis, hemorrhagic condition, or electrolyte imbalance.
Lifespan: In pregnant women, use cautiously. For breast-feeding patients, recommendations vary depending on the drug. For children, dosage recommendations have been established for most penicillins. Geriatric patients are susceptible to superinfection and renal impairment, which decreases excretion of penicillins; use cautiously and at a lower dosage.

NURSING PROCESS

Assessment

• Assess patient's history of allergies. Try to find out whether previous reactions were true hypersensitivity reactions or adverse reactions (such as GI distress) that patient interpreted as allergy.
• Keep in mind that a patient who has never had a penicillin hypersensitivity reaction may still have future allergic reactions; monitor patient continuously for possible allergic reactions or other adverse effects.
• Obtain culture and sensitivity tests before giving first dose; repeat tests periodically to assess drug's effectiveness.
• Monitor vital signs, electrolytes, and renal function studies.
• Assess patient's consciousness and neurologic status when giving high doses; CNS toxicity can occur.
• Coagulation abnormalities, even frank bleeding, can follow high doses, especially of extended-spectrum penicillins. Monitor PT, INR, and platelet counts. Assess patient for signs of occult or frank bleeding.
• Monitor patients (especially elderly patients, debilitated patients, and patients receiving immunosuppressants or radiation) receiving long-term therapy for possible superinfection.

Key nursing diagnoses

• Ineffective protection related to hypersensitivity
• Risk for infection related to superinfection
• Risk for deficient fluid volume related to adverse GI reactions

Planning and implementation

• Give penicillin at least 1 hour before bacteriostatic antibiotics (tetracyclines, erythromycins, and chloramphenicol); these drugs inhibit bacterial cell growth and decrease rate of penicillin uptake by bacterial cell walls.
• Follow manufacturer's directions for reconstituting, diluting, and storing drugs; check expiration dates.
• Give oral penicillin at least 1 hour before or 2 hours after meals to enhance GI absorption.
• Refrigerate oral suspensions (stable for 14 days); shake well before administering to ensure correct dosage.
• Give I.M. dose deep into large muscle mass (gluteal or midlateral thigh), rotate injection sites to minimize tissue injury, and apply ice to injection site to relieve pain. Don't inject more than 2 g of drug per injection site.
• With I.V. infusions, don't add or mix another drug, especially an aminoglycoside, which will become inactive if mixed with a penicillin. If other drugs must be given I.V., temporarily stop infusion of primary drug.
• Infuse I.V. drug continuously or intermittently (over 30 minutes). Rotate infusion site every 48 hours. Intermittent I.V. infusion may be diluted in 50 to 100 ml sterile water, normal saline solution, D_5W, D_5W and half-normal saline, or lactated Ringer's solution.

Patient teaching

• Make sure patient understands how and when to take drug. Urge him to complete the prescribed regimen, comply with instructions for around-the-clock scheduling, and keep follow-up appointments.
• Teach patient signs and symptoms of hypersensitivity and other adverse reactions. Urge him to report unusual reactions.
• Tell patient to check drug's expiration date and to discard unused drug. Warn him not to share drug with family or friends.

Evaluation

• Patient shows no signs of hypersensitivity.
• Patient is free from infection.
• Patient maintains adequate hydration.

Prototype drug

Phenothiazines

chlorpromazine hydrochloride
fluphenazine
mesoridazine besylate
perphenazine
prochlorperazine
promazine hydrochloride
promethazine
thioridazine hydrochloride
thiothixene
trifluoperazine hydrochloride

Indications

▶ Agitated psychotic states, hallucinations, manic-depressive illness, excessive motor and autonomic activity, severe nausea and vomiting induced by CNS disturbances, moderate anxiety, behavioral problems caused by chronic organic mental syndrome, tetanus, acute intermittent porphyria, intractable hiccups, itching, symptomatic rhinitis.

Actions

Phenothiazines are believed to function as dopamine antagonists, blocking postsynaptic dopamine receptors in various parts of the CNS. Their antiemetic effects result from blockage of the chemoreceptor trigger zone. They also produce varying degrees of anticholinergic and alpha-adrenergic receptor blocking actions.

Adverse reactions

Phenothiazines may produce extrapyramidal symptoms (dystonic movements, torticollis, oculogyric crises, parkinsonian symptoms) ranging from akathisia during early treatment to tardive dyskinesia after long-term use. A neuroleptic malignant syndrome resembling severe parkinsonism may occur (most often in young men taking fluphenazine). The progression of elevated liver enzyme levels to obstructive jaundice usually indicates an allergic reaction. Other adverse reactions include orthostatic hypotension with reflex tachycardia, fainting, dizziness, arrhythmias, anorexia, nausea, vomiting, abdominal pain, local gastric irritation, seizures, endocrine effects, hematologic disorders, visual disturbances, skin eruptions, and photosensitivity.

Contraindications and precautions

- Contraindicated in patients with CNS depression, bone marrow suppression, heart failure, circulatory collapse, coronary artery or cerebrovascular disorders, subcortical damage, or coma. Contraindicated with use of spinal and epidural anesthetics and adrenergic blockers.
- Use cautiously in debilitated patients and in those with hepatic, renal, or CV disease; respiratory disorders; hypocalcemia; seizure disorders; suspected brain tumor or intestinal obstruction; glaucoma; and prostatic hyperplasia.

Lifespan: Women shouldn't breast-feed during therapy, if feasible, because most phenothiazines appear in breast milk and directly affect prolactin levels. For children younger than age 12, phenothiazines aren't recommended unless otherwise specified; use cautiously for nausea and vomiting. Acutely ill children (chickenpox, measles, CNS infections, dehydration) have a greatly increased risk of dystonic reactions. Geriatric patients are more sensitive to therapeutic and adverse effects, especially cardiac toxicity, tardive dyskinesia, and other extrapyramidal effects; use cautiously, and give reduced doses as indicated, adjusting dosage to patient response.

NURSING PROCESS

Assessment

- Check vital signs regularly for decreased blood pressure (especially before and after parenteral therapy) or tachycardia; observe patient carefully for other adverse reactions.
- Check intake and output for urine retention or constipation, which may require dosage reduction.
- Monitor bilirubin levels weekly for the first 4 weeks. Establish baseline CBC, ECG (for quinidine-like effects), liver and renal function test results, electrolyte levels (especially potassium), and eye examination findings. Monitor these findings periodically thereafter, especially in patients receiving long-term therapy.
- Observe patient for mood changes monitor progress.
- Monitor patient for involuntary movements. Check patient receiving prolonged treatment at least once every 6 months.

Prototype drug

Key nursing diagnoses
• Risk for injury related to adverse reactions
• Impaired mobility related to extrapyramidal symptoms
• Noncompliance related to long-term therapy

Planning and implementation
• Don't withdraw drug abruptly. Although physical dependence doesn't occur with antipsychotic drugs, rebound worsening of psychotic symptoms may occur, and many drug effects may persist.
• Follow manufacturer's guidelines for reconstitution, dilution, administration, and storage of drugs; slightly discolored liquids may or may not be acceptable for use. Check with pharmacist.

Patient teaching
• Teach patient how and when to take drug. Caution him not to increase the dosage or discontinue the drug without prescriber's approval. Suggest taking the full dose at bedtime if daytime sedation occurs.
• Explain that full therapeutic effect may not occur for several weeks.
• Teach signs and symptoms of adverse reactions, and urge patient to report unusual effects, especially involuntary movements.
• Instruct patient to avoid beverages and drugs containing alcohol, and warn him not to take other drugs, including OTC or herbal products, without prescriber's approval.
• Advise patient to avoid hazardous tasks until full effects of drug are established. Explain that sedative effects will lessen after several weeks.
• Inform patient that excessive exposure to sunlight, heat lamps, or tanning beds may cause photosensitivity reactions. Advise him to avoid exposure to extreme heat or cold.
• Explain that phenothiazines may cause pink or brown discoloration of urine.

Evaluation
• Patient remains free from injury.
• Extrapyramidal symptoms don't develop.
• Patient complies with therapy, as evidenced by improved thought processes.

Skeletal muscle relaxants
baclofen
carisoprodol
chlorzoxazone
cyclobenzaprine hydrochloride
methocarbamol

Indications
▶ Painful musculoskeletal disorders, spasticity of multiple sclerosis.

Actions
All skeletal muscle relaxants, except baclofen, reduce impulse transmission from the spinal cord to skeletal muscle. Baclofen's mechanism of action is unclear.

Adverse reactions
Skeletal muscle relaxants may cause ataxia, confusion, depressed mood, dizziness, drowsiness, dry mouth, hallucinations, headache, hypotension, nervousness, tachycardia, tremor, and vertigo. Baclofen also may cause seizures.

Contraindications and precautions
• Contraindicated in patients hypersensitive to drug.
• Use cautiously in patients with impaired renal or hepatic function.
Lifespan: In breast-feeding women and in children, recommendations vary for use. Geriatric patients have an increased risk of adverse reactions; monitor them carefully.

NURSING PROCESS

Assessment
• Monitor patient for hypersensitivity reactions.
• Assess degree of relief obtained to help prescriber determine when dosage can be reduced.
• Watch for increased seizures in epileptic patient receiving baclofen.
• Monitor CBC results closely.
• In patient receiving cyclobenzaprine, monitor platelet counts.
• In patient receiving methocarbamol, watch for orthostatic hypotension.

• In patient receiving long-term baclofen or chlorzoxazone therapy, monitor hepatic function and urinalysis results.
• In patient receiving long-term therapy, assess compliance.

Key nursing diagnoses
• Risk for trauma related to baclofen-induced seizures
• Disturbed thought processes related to confusion
• Noncompliance related to long-term therapy

Planning and implementation
• After long-term therapy and unless patient has severe adverse reactions, don't stop baclofen or carisoprodol abruptly to avoid withdrawal symptoms, such as insomnia, headache, nausea, and abdominal pain.
• Institute safety precautions as needed.
• To prevent GI distress, give oral forms of drug with meals or milk.
• Obtain an order for a mild analgesic to relieve drug-induced headache.

Patient teaching
• Tell patient to take drug exactly as prescribed. Caution him not to stop baclofen or carisoprodol suddenly after long-term therapy to avoid withdrawal symptoms.
• Instruct patient to avoid hazardous activities that require mental alertness until CNS effects of drug are known.
• Advise patient to avoid alcohol during therapy.
• Advise patient to follow prescriber's advice regarding rest and physical therapy.
• Instruct patient receiving cyclobenzaprine or baclofen to report urinary hesitancy.
• Inform patient taking methocarbamol or chlorzoxazone that urine may be discolored.

Evaluation
• Patient remains free from seizures.
• Patient exhibits normal thought processes.
• Patient complies with therapy, as evidenced by pain relief or improvement of spasticity.

Sulfonamides
co-trimoxazole (trimethoprim and sulfamethoxazole)
sulfadiazine
sulfasalazine

Indications
▶ Bacterial infections, nocardiosis, toxoplasmosis, chloroquine-resistant *Plasmodium falciparum* malaria, inflammatory bowel disease.

Actions
Sulfonamides are bacteriostatic. They inhibit biosynthesis of tetrahydrofolic acid, which is needed for bacterial cell growth. They're active against some strains of staphylococci, streptococci, *Nocardia asteroides* and *brasiliensis, Clostridium tetani* and *perfringens, Bacillus anthracis, Escherichia coli,* and *Neisseria gonorrhoeae* and *meningitidis.* Sulfonamides are also active against organisms that cause urinary tract infections, such as *E. coli, Proteus mirabilis* and *vulgaris, Klebsiella, Enterobacter,* and *Staphylococcus aureus,* and genital lesions caused by *Haemophilus ducreyi* (chancroid).

Adverse reactions
Many adverse reactions stem from hypersensitivity, including rash, fever, pruritus, erythema multiforme, erythema nodosum, Stevens-Johnson syndrome, toxic epidermal necrolysis, Lyell's syndrome, exfoliative dermatitis, photosensitivity, joint pain, conjunctivitis, leukopenia, and bronchospasm. GI reactions include nausea, vomiting, anorexia, stomatitis, pancreatitis, diarrhea, and folic acid malabsorption. Hematologic reactions include granulocytopenia, thrombocytopenia, agranulocytosis, hypoprothrombinemia and, in G6PD deficiency, hemolytic anemia. Renal effects usually result from crystalluria (precipitation of sulfonamide in renal system).

Contraindications and precautions
• Contraindicated in patients hypersensitive to drug.
• Use cautiously in patients with impaired renal or hepatic function, bronchial asthma, severe allergy, or G6PD deficiency.

Lifespan: In pregnant women at term and in breast-feeding women, use is contraindicated; sulfonamides appear in breast milk. In infants younger than age 2 months, sulfonamides are contraindicated unless there is no therapeutic alternative. In children with fragile X chromosome and mental retardation, use cautiously. Geriatric patients are susceptible to bacterial and fungal superinfection and have an increased risk of folate deficiency anemia and adverse renal and hematologic effects.

NURSING PROCESS

Assessment

- Assess patient's history of allergies, especially to sulfonamides or to any drug containing sulfur (such as thiazides, furosemide, and oral sulfonylureas).
- Monitor patient for adverse reactions; patients with AIDS have a much higher risk of adverse reactions.
- Obtain culture and sensitivity tests before first dose; check test results periodically to assess drug effectiveness.
- Monitor urine cultures, CBC, and urinalysis before and during therapy.
- During long-term therapy, monitor patient for possible superinfection.

Key nursing diagnoses

- Ineffective protection related to hypersensitivity
- Risk for infection related to superinfection
- Risk for deficient fluid volume related to adverse GI reactions

Planning and implementation

- Give oral dose with 8 oz (240 ml) of water. Give 3 to 4 L of fluids daily, depending on drug; patient's urine output should be at least 1,500 ml daily.
- Follow manufacturer's directions for reconstituting, diluting, and storing drugs; check expiration dates.
- Shake oral suspensions well before administering to ensure correct dosage.

Patient teaching

- Urge patient to take drug exactly as prescribed, to complete the prescribed regimen, and to keep follow-up appointments.
- Advise patient to take oral drug with full glass of water and to drink plenty of fluids; explain that tablet may be crushed and swallowed with water to ensure maximal absorption.
- Teach signs and symptoms of hypersensitivity and other adverse reactions. Urge patient to report bloody urine, difficulty breathing, rash, fever, chills, or severe fatigue.
- Advise patient to avoid direct sun exposure and to use a sunscreen to help prevent photosensitivity reactions.
- Tell diabetic patient that sulfonamides may increase effects of oral hypoglycemic drugs. Tell him not to use Clinitest to monitor urine glucose levels.
- Inform patient taking sulfasalazine that it may cause an orange-yellow discoloration of urine or skin and may permanently stain soft contact lenses yellow.

Evaluation

- Patient exhibits no signs of hypersensitivity.
- Patient is free from infection.
- Patient maintains adequate hydration.

Tetracyclines

doxycycline
doxycycline hyclate
doxycycline hydrochloride
minocycline hydrochloride
oxytetracycline hydrochloride
tetracycline hydrochloride

Indications

▶ Bacterial, protozoal, rickettsial, and fungal infections.

Actions

Tetracyclines are bacteriostatic but may be bactericidal against certain organisms. They bind reversibly to 30S and 50S ribosomal subunits, which inhibits bacterial protein synthesis.

Susceptible gram-positive organisms include *Bacillus anthracis, Actinomyces israelii, Clostridium perfringens, C. tetani, Listeria monocytogenes,* and *Nocardia.*

Susceptible gram-negative organisms include *Neisseria meningitidis, Pasteurella multocida, Legionella pneumophila, Brucella, Vib-*

rio cholerae, Yersinia enterocolitica, Y. pestis, Bordetella pertussis, Haemophilus influenzae, H. ducreyi, Campylobacter fetus, Shigella, and many other common pathogens.

Other susceptible organisms include *Rickettsia akari, R. typhi, R. prowazekii, R. tsutsugamushi, Coxiella burnetii, Chlamydia trachomatis, C. psittaci, Mycoplasma pneumoniae, M. hominis, Leptospira, Treponema pallidum, T. pertenue,* and *Borrelia recurrentis.*

Adverse reactions

The most common adverse effects involve the GI tract and are dose-related; they include anorexia; flatulence; nausea; vomiting; bulky, loose stools; epigastric burning; and abdominal discomfort. Superinfections also are common. Photosensitivity reactions may be severe. Renal failure has been attributed to Fanconi's syndrome after use of outdated tetracycline. Permanent discoloration of teeth occurs if drug is administered during tooth formation (in children younger than age 8).

Contraindications and precautions

- Contraindicated in patients hypersensitive to tetracyclines.
- Use cautiously in patients with impaired renal or hepatic function.

Lifespan: In pregnant or breast-feeding women, use is contraindicated; tetracyclines appear in breast milk. Children under age 8 shouldn't receive tetracyclines; these drugs can cause permanent tooth discoloration, enamel hypoplasia, and a reversible decrease in bone calcification. Some elderly patients have decreased esophageal motility; use these drugs cautiously and monitor patients for local irritation from slow passage of oral forms. Elderly patients are also more susceptible to superinfection.

NURSING PROCESS

Assessment

- Assess patient's allergic history.
- Monitor patient for adverse reactions.
- Obtain culture and sensitivity tests before first dose; check cultures periodically to assess drug effectiveness.
- Check expiration dates before administration. Outdated tetracyclines may cause nephrotoxicity.
- Monitor patient for bacterial and fungal superinfection, especially if patient is elderly, debilitated, or receiving immunosuppressants or radiation therapy; watch especially for oral candidiasis.

Key nursing diagnoses

- Ineffective protection related to hypersensitivity
- Risk for infection related to superinfection
- Risk for deficient fluid volume related to adverse GI reactions

Planning and implementation

- Give all oral tetracyclines except doxycycline and minocycline 1 hour before or 2 hours after meals for maximum absorption; don't give drug with food, milk or other dairy products, sodium bicarbonate, iron compounds, or antacids, which may impair absorption.
- Give water with and after oral drug to facilitate passage to stomach because incomplete swallowing can cause severe esophageal irritation. Don't give drug within 1 hour of bedtime to prevent esophageal reflux.
- Follow manufacturer's directions for reconstituting and storing; keep drug refrigerated and away from light.
- Monitor I.V. injection sites and rotate routinely to minimize local irritation. I.V. administration may cause severe phlebitis.

Patient teaching

- Urge patient to take drug exactly as prescribed, to complete the prescribed regimen, and to keep follow-up appointments.
- Warn patient not to take drug with food, milk or other dairy products, sodium bicarbonate, or iron compounds because they may interfere with absorption. Advise him to wait 3 hours after taking tetracycline before taking an antacid.
- Instruct patient to check expiration dates and to discard any expired drug.
- Teach signs and symptoms of adverse reactions, and urge patient to report them promptly.
- Advise patient to avoid direct exposure to sunlight and to use a sunscreen to help prevent photosensitivity reactions.

Evaluation

- Patient shows no signs of hypersensitivity.
- Patient is free from infection.
- Patient maintains adequate hydration.

Thyroid hormones

levothyroxine sodium
liothyronine sodium
thyroid

Indications

▶ Hypothyroidism, simple goiter, goitrogenesis.

Actions

Thyroid hormones have catabolic and anabolic effects and influence normal metabolism, growth, and development. Affecting every organ system, these hormones are vital to normal CNS function. Thyroid-stimulating hormone increases iodine uptake by the thyroid, increases formation and release of thyroid hormone, and is produced from bovine anterior pituitary glands.

Adverse reactions

Adverse reactions include nervousness, insomnia, tremor, tachycardia, palpitations, nausea, headache, fever, and sweating.

Contraindications and precautions

- Contraindicated in patients with MI, thyrotoxicosis, or uncorrected adrenal insufficiency.
- Use with extreme caution in patients with angina pectoris, hypertension or other CV disorders, renal insufficiency, or ischemia. Use cautiously in patients with myxedema.

Lifespan: Minimal amounts of exogenous thyroid hormones appear in breast milk. However, problems haven't been reported in breast-feeding infants. Children may have partial hair loss during first few months of therapy; reassure child and parents that this is temporary. In patients older than age 60, initial hormone replacement dosage should be 25% less than the usual recommended starting dosage.

NURSING PROCESS

Assessment

- Assess patient's thyroid function test results regularly.
- Monitor pulse rate and blood pressure.
- Monitor patient for signs of thyrotoxicosis or inadequate dosage, including diarrhea, fever, irritability, listlessness, rapid heartbeat, vomiting, and weakness.
- Monitor PT and INR; patients taking anticoagulants usually need lower doses.

Key nursing diagnoses

- Risk for injury related to adverse CV reactions
- Disturbed sleep pattern related to insomnia
- Noncompliance related to long-term therapy

Planning and implementation

- Thyroid hormone dosage varies widely. Begin treatment at lowest level, adjusting to higher doses according to patient's symptoms and laboratory data, until euthyroid state is reached.
- Give thyroid hormones at same time each day, preferably in the morning to prevent insomnia.
- Thyroid medications may be supplied either in micrograms (mcg) or in milligrams (mg). Don't confuse these dose measurements.

Patient teaching

- Instruct patient to take drug exactly as prescribed. Suggest taking dose in morning to prevent insomnia.
- Advise patient to report signs and symptoms of overdose (chest pain, palpitations, sweating, nervousness) or aggravated CV disease (chest pain, dyspnea, tachycardia).
- Tell patient who has achieved a stable response not to change brands.
- Inform parents that child may lose hair during first months of therapy, but reassure them that this is temporary.
- Urge patient to keep follow-up appointments and have regular laboratory testing of thyroid levels.

Evaluation

- Patient sustains no injury from adverse reactions.
- Patient gets adequate sleep during the night.
- Patient complies with therapy, as evidenced by normal thyroid hormone levels and resolution of underlying disorder.

Xanthine derivatives

aminophylline
theophylline

Indications

▶ Asthma and bronchospasm from emphysema and chronic bronchitis.

Actions

Xanthine derivatives are structurally related; they directly relax smooth muscle, stimulate the CNS, induce diuresis, increase gastric acid secretion, inhibit uterine contractions, and exert weak inotropic and chronotropic effects on the heart. Of these drugs, theophylline exerts the greatest effect on smooth muscle.

The action of xanthine derivatives isn't completely caused by inhibition of phosphodiesterase. Current data suggest that inhibition of adenosine receptors or unidentified mechanisms may be responsible for therapeutic effects. By relaxing smooth muscle of the respiratory tract, they increase airflow and vital capacity. They also slow onset of diaphragmatic fatigue and stimulate the respiratory center in the CNS.

Adverse reactions

Adverse effects are dose-related, except for hypersensitivity, and can be controlled by dosage adjustment. Common reactions include hypotension, palpitations, arrhythmias, restlessness, irritability, nausea, vomiting, urine retention, and headache.

Contraindications and precautions

- Contraindicated in patients hypersensitive to xanthines.
- Use cautiously in patients with arrhythmias, cardiac or circulatory impairment, cor pulmonale, hepatic or renal disease, active peptic ulcers, hyperthyroidism, or diabetes mellitus.

Lifespan: Breast-feeding women shouldn't be given xanthines because they appear in breast milk, and infants may have serious adverse reactions. Small children may have excessive CNS stimulation; monitor them closely. In geriatric patients, use cautiously.

NURSING PROCESS

Assessment

- Monitor theophylline levels closely; therapeutic levels range from 10 to 20 mcg/ml.
- Monitor patient closely for adverse reactions, especially toxicity.
- Monitor vital signs.

Key nursing diagnoses

- Disturbed sleep pattern related to CNS effects
- Urine retention related to adverse effects on bladder
- Noncompliance related to long-term therapy

Planning and implementation

- Don't crush or allow patient to chew timed-release preparations.
- Expect prescriber to calculate dosage from lean body weight because theophylline doesn't distribute into fatty tissue.
- Anticipate adjustment of daily dosage in elderly patients and in those with heart failure or hepatic disease.
- Provide patient with nondrug sleep aids, such as a back rub or milk-based beverage.

Patient teaching

- Tell patient to take drug exactly as prescribed.
- Caution patient to check with prescriber before using any other drug, including OTC medications or herbal remedies, or before switching brands.
- If patient smokes, tell him that doing so may decrease theophylline levels. Urge him to notify prescriber if he quits smoking because the dosage will need adjustment to avoid toxicity.

Evaluation

- Patient sleeps usual number of hours without interruption.
- Patient has no change in voiding pattern.
- Patient complies with therapy, as evidenced by maintenance of therapeutic levels.

Prototype drug

Alphabetical listing of drugs

A

abacavir sulfate

(uh-BACK-ah-veer SUL-fayt)
Ziagen

Pharmacologic class: nucleoside analogue reverse transcriptase inhibitor
Therapeutic class: antiviral
Pregnancy risk category: C

Indications and dosages

▶ **HIV-1 infection.** *Adults:* 300 mg P.O. b.i.d. with other antiretrovirals.
Children ages 3 months to 16 years: 8 mg/kg P.O. b.i.d. (maximum of 300 mg P.O. b.i.d.) with other antiretrovirals.

Contraindications and precautions

- Contraindicated in patients hypersensitive to abacavir or its components. Abacavir therapy can cause fatal hypersensitivity reactions. If a patient develops evidence of hypersensitivity—such as fever, rash, fatigue, nausea, vomiting, diarrhea, or abdominal pain—he should stop therapy and seek medical attention immediately.
- Give drug cautiously to patient with risk factors for liver disease. Lactic acidosis and severe hepatomegaly with steatosis have occurred in patients (women more often than men) taking nucleoside analogues, such as abacavir and other antiretrovirals. Obesity and prolonged nucleoside exposure may be risk factors.

Lifespan: Use during pregnancy only if potential benefits outweigh risk. No adequate studies of drug effect on pregnancy exist.

Adverse reactions

CNS: insomnia, sleep disorders, headache, fever.
GI: *nausea, vomiting,* diarrhea, loss of appetite, anorexia.
Skin: rash.
Other: ***hypersensitivity reaction.***

Interactions

Drug-lifestyle. *Alcohol use:* Decreases elimination of abacavir, increasing overall exposure to drug. Discourage using together.

Effects on lab test results

- May increase GGT and triglyceride levels.

Pharmacokinetics

Absorption: Rapid and extensive; the mean absolute bioavailability of the tablet is 83%. Systemic exposure is comparable for oral solution and tablets; they may be used interchangeably.
Distribution: Distributed into extravascular space; about 50% binds to plasma proteins.
Metabolism: In the liver, alcohol dehydrogenase and glucuronyl transferase metabolize the drug to form two inactive metabolites. Cytochrome P-450 enzymes don't significantly metabolize the drug.
Excretion: Mainly excreted in urine, with 1.2% unchanged. About 16% of a dose is eliminated in feces. *Half-life (elimination):* 1 to 2 hours.

Route	Onset	Peak	Duration
P.O.	Unknown	Unknown	Unknown

Pharmacodynamics

Chemical effect: Inhibits the activity of HIV-1 reverse transcriptase after being converted intracellularly to the active metabolite carbovir triphosphate, thereby terminating viral DNA growth.
Therapeutic effect: Reduces the symptoms of HIV-1 infection.

Available forms

Oral solution: 20 mg/ml
Tablets: 300 mg

NURSING PROCESS

Assessment

- Assess patient's condition before therapy and regularly thereafter.
- Watch for hypersensitivity reaction.
- Assess patient for risk factors of liver disease. Lactic acidosis and severe hepatomegaly with steatosis may occur, especially in woman or patient who is obese or has prolonged exposure to nucleosides. Stop treatment if patient

develops evidence of lactic acidosis or pronounced hepatotoxicity, which may include hepatomegaly and steatosis, even without elevated transaminase levels.
• Evaluate patient's and family's knowledge of drug therapy.

Nursing diagnoses
• Risk for infection secondary to presence of HIV
• Ineffective individual coping related to HIV infection
• Deficient knowledge related to drug therapy

Planning and implementation
• Drug should always be given with other antiretrovirals, never alone.
• Register pregnant woman taking abacavir with the Antiretroviral Pregnancy Registry at 1-800-258-4263.
• Don't restart drug after a hypersensitivity reaction because more severe signs and symptoms will recur within hours and may include life-threatening hypotension. To aid in reporting of hypersensitivity reactions, register patient with the Abacavir Hypersensitivity Registry at 1-800-270-0425.
• Drug may cause mildly elevated glucose level. Monitor glucose during therapy.
• Lactic acidosis and hepatomegaly with steatosis may occur in patient taking nucleoside analogues alone or in combination. Monitor patient.

Patient teaching
• Inform patient that abacavir can cause a life-threatening hypersensitivity reaction. Tell patient to stop drug and notify prescriber immediately if evidence of hypersensitivity develops—such as fever, rash, severe fatigue, achiness, a generally ill feeling, or GI signs or symptoms, such as nausea, vomiting, diarrhea, or stomach pain.
• Give written information about drug with each new prescription and refill. Patient also should receive—and be instructed to carry—a warning card summarizing abacavir hypersensitivity reaction.
• Explain that the drug neither cures HIV infection nor reduces the risk of transmitting HIV to others. Its long-term effects are unknown.
• Tell patient to take drug exactly as prescribed.
• Inform patient that drug can be taken with or without food.

Evaluation
• Patient has reduced signs and symptoms of infection.
• Patient demonstrates adequate coping mechanisms.
• Patient and family state understanding of drug therapy.

abciximab
(ab-SIKS-ih-mahb)
ReoPro

Pharmacologic class: fab fragment of chimeric human-murine monoclonal antibody 7E3
Therapeutic class: platelet aggregation inhibitor
Pregnancy risk category: C

Indications and dosages
▶ **Adjunct to percutaneous transluminal coronary angioplasty (PTCA) or atherectomy for prevention of acute cardiac ischemic complications in patients at high risk for abrupt closure of treated coronary vessel.** *Adults:* 0.25 mg/kg as I.V. bolus 10 to 60 minutes before PTCA or atherectomy, followed by continuous I.V. infusion of 0.125 mcg/kg per minute (maximum of 10 mcg/minute) for 12 hours.
▶ **Patients with unstable angina not responding to conventional medical therapy who are to undergo percutaneous coronary intervention within 24 hours.** *Adults:* 0.25 mg/kg as I.V. bolus; then an 18- to 24-hour infusion of 10 mcg/minute, concluding 1 hour after percutaneous coronary intervention.

Contraindications and precautions
• Contraindicated in patient hypersensitive to a drug component or to murine proteins and in patient with active internal bleeding, a history of CVA within 2 years or with significant residual neurologic deficit, bleeding diathesis, thrombocytopenia (platelets less than 100,000/mm^3), intracranial neoplasm, intracranial arteriovenous malformation, intracranial aneurysm, severe uncontrolled hypertension, or a history of vas-

culitis. Also contraindicated within 6 weeks of major surgery, trauma, or GI or GU bleeding; when oral anticoagulants have been given within 7 days unless PT is less than or equal to 1.2 times control; and when I.V. dextran is used before or during PTCA.

• Use cautiously in patient at increased risk for bleeding (patient who weighs less than 165 lb [75 kg], is older than age 65, has history of GI disease, or is receiving thrombolytic drugs). Conditions that increase risk of bleeding include PTCA within 12 hours of onset of symptoms for acute MI, prolonged PTCA (lasting more than 70 minutes), failed PTCA, and use of heparin with abciximab.

Lifespan: In pregnant or breast-feeding women, use cautiously. In children, safety and efficacy of drug haven't been established.

Adverse reactions

CNS: hypoesthesia, confusion, headache, pain.
CV: *hypotension, chest pain, **bradycardia,*** peripheral edema.
EENT: abnormal vision.
GI: *nausea, vomiting, abdominal pain.*
Hematologic: bleeding, ***thrombocytopenia,*** anemia, leukocytosis.
Musculoskeletal: *back pain.*
Respiratory: pleural effusion, pleurisy, pneumonia.

Interactions

Drug-drug. *Antiplatelet drugs, heparin, NSAIDs, other anticoagulants, thrombolytics:* May increase risk of bleeding. Monitor patient closely.

Effects on lab test results

• May increase WBC count. May decrease hemoglobin, hematocrit, and platelet count.

Pharmacokinetics

Absorption: Administered I.V.
Distribution: Rapidly binds to platelet GPIIb/IIIa receptors.
Metabolism: Unknown.
Excretion: Unknown. *Half-life:* Initially, less than 10 minutes; second phase, about 30 minutes.

Route	Onset	Peak	Duration
I.V.	Almost immediate	Almost immediate	About 24 hr

Pharmacodynamics

Chemical effect: Prevents binding of fibrinogen, von Willebrand factor, and other adhesive molecules to GPIIb/IIIa receptor sites on activated platelets.
Therapeutic effect: Inhibits platelet aggregation.

Available forms

Injection: 2 mg/ml

NURSING PROCESS

Assessment

• Note patient's history. Patients at risk for abrupt closure (candidates for abciximab) include those undergoing PTCA with at least one of the following: unstable angina, non-Q wave MI, acute Q wave MI within 12 hours of onset of symptoms, two type B lesions in artery to be dilated, one type B lesion in artery to be dilated in a woman older than age 65 or a patient with diabetes, one type C lesion in artery to be dilated, and angioplasty of infarct-related lesion within 7 days of MI.
• Assess vital signs and evaluate bleeding studies before therapy.
• Monitor patient closely for bleeding. Bleeding caused by therapy falls into two categories: that observed at arterial access site used for cardiac catheterization and internal bleeding involving GI or GU tract or retroperitoneal sites.
• Be alert for adverse reactions and drug interactions.
• Evaluate patient's and family's knowledge of drug therapy.

Nursing diagnoses

• Ineffective cerebral or cardiopulmonary tissue perfusion related to patient's underlying condition
• Risk for deficient fluid volume related to drug-induced bleeding
• Deficient knowledge related to drug therapy

Planning and implementation

• Inspect solution for particulate matter before administering it. If you see opaque particles, discard solution and obtain new vial. Withdraw drug for I.V. bolus injection through sterile, nonpyrogenic, low–protein-binding 0.2- or

0.22-micron filter into syringe. Give I.V. bolus 10 to 60 minutes before procedure.
• Withdraw 4.5 ml of drug for continuous I.V. infusion through sterile, nonpyrogenic, low-protein-binding 0.2- or 0.22-micron filter into syringe. Inject into 250 ml of sterile normal saline solution or D_5W, and infuse at 17 ml/hour for 12 hours via continuous infusion pump equipped with in-line filter. Discard unused portion.
• Give drug in separate I.V. line; don't add other drug to infusion solution.
• Institute bleeding precautions. Keep patient on bed rest for 6 to 8 hours after removing sheath or stopping abciximab infusion, whichever is later.
ALERT: Keep epinephrine, dopamine, theophylline, antihistamines, and corticosteroids available in case of anaphylaxis.
• Drug is intended for use with aspirin and heparin.
ALERT: Don't confuse abciximab with arcitumomab.

Patient teaching
• Teach patient about his disease and therapy.
• Stress the importance of reporting adverse reactions.

Evaluation
• Patient maintains adequate tissue perfusion.
• Patient maintains adequate hydration.
• Patient and family state understanding of drug therapy.

acarbose
(ay-KAR-bohs)
Precose

Pharmacologic class: alpha-glucosidase inhibitor
Therapeutic class: antidiabetic
Pregnancy risk category: B

Indications and dosages
▶ **Adjunct to diet to lower glucose level in patients with type 2 (non–insulin-dependent) diabetes mellitus whose hyperglycemia can't be managed by diet alone or by diet and a sulfonylurea.** *Adults:* Initially, 25 mg P.O. t.i.d. at start of each main meal. Subsequent dosage adjustment made q 4 to 8 weeks, based on glucose level and tolerance 1 hour after a meal. Maintenance dosage is 50 to 100 mg P.O. t.i.d.
▶ **Adjunct to insulin or metformin therapy in patients with type 2 (non–insulin-dependent) diabetes mellitus whose hyperglycemia can't be managed by diet, exercise, and insulin or metformin alone.** *Adults:* Initially, 25 mg P.O. t.i.d. with first bite of each main meal. Adjust dosage at 4- to 8-week intervals based on glucose level and tolerance 1 hour after meals to determine minimum effective dosage of each drug. Maintenance dosage is 50 to 100 mg P.O. t.i.d. based on patient's weight. Maximum dosage for patients weighing 60 kg (132 lb) or less is 50 mg P.O. t.i.d.; for patients weighing more than 60 kg, maximum dosage is 100 mg P.O. t.i.d.

Contraindications and precautions
• Contraindicated in patient hypersensitive to drug and in patient with diabetic ketoacidosis, cirrhosis, inflammatory bowel disease, colonic ulceration, partial intestinal obstruction, predisposition to intestinal obstruction, chronic intestinal disease with marked disorder of digestion or absorption, and conditions that may deteriorate because of increased intestinal gas formation.
• Drug isn't recommended in renally impaired patient.
• Use cautiously in patient receiving sulfonylurea or insulin. Drug may increase the hypoglycemic potential of sulfonylurea.
Lifespan: In pregnant or breast-feeding women, drug isn't recommended. In children, safety and efficacy haven't been established.

Adverse reactions
GI: *abdominal pain, diarrhea, flatulence.*

Interactions
Drug-drug. *Calcium channel blockers, corticosteroids, estrogens, isoniazid, nicotinic acid, oral contraceptives, phenothiazines, phenytoin, sympathomimetics, thiazides and other diuretics, thyroid products:* May cause hyperglycemia and loss of glucose control during use or hypoglycemia when withdrawn. Monitor glucose level.
Digestive enzyme preparations containing carbohydrate-splitting enzymes (such as amy-

lase, pancreatin), intestinal adsorbents (such as activated charcoal): May reduce effect of acarbose. Don't give together.
Digoxin: May decrease digoxin level. Monitor digoxin level.
Drug-herb. *Aloe, bilberry leaf, bitter melon, burdock, dandelion, fenugreek, garlic, ginseng:* May improve glucose control and allow reduced antidiabetic dosage. Urge patient to discuss herbal products with prescriber before use.

Effects on lab test results

- May increase ALT and AST levels. May decrease calcium and vitamin B_6 levels.

Pharmacokinetics

Absorption: Minimal.
Distribution: Acts locally within GI tract.
Metabolism: Metabolized exclusively in the GI tract, primarily by intestinal bacteria and to a lesser extent by digestive enzymes.
Excretion: Almost completely excreted by the kidneys. *Half-life:* 2 hours.

Route	Onset	Peak	Duration
P.O.	Unknown	1 hr	2-4 hr

Pharmacodynamics

Chemical effect: An alpha-glucosidase inhibitor that delays digestion of carbohydrates.
Therapeutic effect: Delays glucose absorption and lowers postprandial hyperglycemia.

Available Forms

Tablets: 25 mg, 50 mg, 100 mg

NURSING PROCESS

Assessment

- Monitor glucose level 1 hour after a meal to determine therapeutic effectiveness of acarbose and to identify appropriate dose. Report hyperglycemia to prescriber.
- Monitor glycosylated hemoglobin every 3 months.
- Monitor transaminase level every 3 months in first year of therapy and periodically thereafter in patient receiving doses in excess of 50 mg t.i.d. Report abnormalities to prescriber.
- Obtain baseline creatinine level; drug isn't recommended in patient with a creatinine clearance greater than 2 mg/dl.
- Evaluate patient's and family's knowledge of drug therapy.

Nursing diagnoses

- Risk for imbalanced fluid volume related to adverse GI effect
- Imbalanced nutrition: less than body requirements related to patient's underlying condition
- Deficient knowledge related to drug therapy

Planning and implementation

- In patient weighing less than 60 kg (132 lb), don't exceed 50 mg t.i.d.
- Watch for elevated transaminase and bilirubin levels and low calcium and vitamin B_6 levels with doses exceeding 50 mg t.i.d.
- Acarbose may increase hypoglycemic potential of sulfonylureas. Closely monitor patient receiving both drugs. If hypoglycemia occurs, treat with oral glucose (dextrose), I.V. glucose infusion, or glucagon. Report hypoglycemia to prescriber.
- Insulin therapy may be needed during increased stress (such as infection, fever, surgery, or trauma).

Patient teaching

- Tell patient to take drug daily with first bite of each of three main meals.
- Explain that therapy relieves symptoms but doesn't cure the disease.
- Stress importance of adhering to specific diet, weight reduction, exercise, and hygiene programs. Show patient how to monitor blood glucose level and to recognize and treat hyperglycemia.
- Teach patient to recognize hypoglycemia and to treat symptoms with a form of dextrose rather than with a product containing table sugar.
- Urge patient to carry medical identification at all times.

Evaluation

- Patient maintains adequate fluid volume balance.
- Patient doesn't experience hypoglycemic episodes.
- Patient and family state understanding of drug therapy.

acebutolol

(as-ih-BYOO-tuh-lol)
Monitan, Sectral

Pharmacologic class: beta blocker
Therapeutic class: antihypertensive, antiarrhythmic
Pregnancy risk category: B

Indications and dosages

▶ **Hypertension.** *Adults:* 400 mg P.O. as single daily dose or in divided doses b.i.d. Patients may receive as much as 1,200 mg daily.
▶ **Suppression of PVCs.** *Adults:* 400 mg P.O. in divided doses b.i.d. Dosage increased to provide adequate clinical response. Usual dosage is 600 to 1,200 mg daily. In patients with impaired renal function, dosage is reduced. Elderly patients may require lower dosage; dosage shouldn't exceed 800 mg daily.
▶ **Stable angina‡.** *Adults:* Initially, 200 mg P.O. b.i.d. Increase dose up to 800 mg daily until angina is controlled. Patients with severe stable angina may require higher doses.
Patients with renal impairment: decrease dose by 50% if creatinine clearance in less than 50 ml/minute; decrease dose by 75% if creatinine clearance in less than 25 ml/minute. Reduce dose in geriatric patients to less than 800 mg daily.

Contraindications and precautions

• Contraindicated in patient with persistently severe bradycardia, second- or third-degree heart block, overt heart failure, or cardiogenic shock.
• Use cautiously in patient with heart failure, peripheral vascular disease, bronchospastic disease, diabetes, or impaired hepatic function.
Lifespan: In pregnant woman, use cautiously. In breast-feeding woman, use is contraindicated. In children, safety of drug hasn't been established.

Adverse reactions

CNS: *fatigue,* headache, dizziness, fever, insomnia.
CV: chest pain, edema, ***bradycardia, heart failure,*** hypotension.
GI: nausea, constipation, diarrhea, dyspepsia, flatulence, vomiting, ***mesenteric arterial thrombosis.***
Metabolic: *hypoglycemia,* increased risk of developing type 2 diabetes mellitus.
Musculoskeletal: arthralgia, myalgia.
Respiratory: dyspnea, cough, ***bronchospasm.***
Skin: rash.
Other: impotence.

Interactions

Drug-drug. *Alpha-adrenergic stimulants:* Increases hypertensive response. Use together cautiously.
Cardiac glycosides, diltiazem, verapamil: May cause excessive bradycardia and increased depressant effect on myocardium. Use together cautiously.
Insulin, oral antidiabetics: May alter dosage requirements in previously stabilized patient with diabetes. Observe patient carefully.
NSAIDs: Decreases antihypertensive effect. Monitor blood pressure. Dosage may require adjustment.
Reserpine: Additive effect. Monitor patient closely.

Effects on lab test results

• May increase AST and ALT levels.
• May cause positive antinuclear antibody test result.

Pharmacokinetics

Absorption: Well absorbed after oral administration.
Distribution: About 25% protein-bound; minimal quantities detected in CSF.
Metabolism: Undergoes extensive first-pass metabolism in liver.
Excretion: From 30% to 40% of dose is excreted in urine; remainder, in feces and bile. *Half-life:* 3 to 4 hours.

Route	Onset	Peak	Duration
P.O.	1-1.5 hr	2.5 hr	Up to 24 hr

Pharmacodynamics

Chemical effect: Antihypertensive action unknown. Possible mechanisms include reduced cardiac output, decreased sympathetic outflow to peripheral vasculature, and inhibited renin release. Antiarrhythmic action decreases myocardial contractility and heart rate and has mild intrinsic sympathomimetic activity.
Therapeutic effect: Lowers blood pressure and heart rate and restores normal sinus rhythm.

Available forms

Capsules: 200 mg, 400 mg

NURSING PROCESS

Assessment

- Assess patient's blood pressure and heart rate and rhythm before and during therapy.
- Monitor patient's energy level.
- Be alert for adverse reactions and drug interactions.
- Evaluate patient's and family's knowledge of drug therapy.

Nursing diagnoses

- Risk for injury related to patient's underlying condition
- Fatigue related to drug-induced CNS adverse reactions
- Deficient knowledge related to drug therapy

Planning and implementation

- Acebutolol may be removed by hemodialysis.
- Dosage should be reduced in elderly patient and patient with decreased renal function.
- Check apical pulse before giving drug; if slower than 60 beats/minute, withhold drug and call prescriber.

ALERT: Don't stop drug abruptly; doing so may worsen angina and MI.

- Before surgery, notify anesthesiologist about patient's drug therapy.

ALERT: Don't confuse Sectral with Factrel or Septra.

Patient teaching

- Teach patient how to take his pulse, and instruct him to withhold dose and notify prescriber if pulse rate is less than 60 beats/minute.
- Warn patient that drug may cause dizziness. Instruct him to avoid sudden position changes and to sit down immediately if he feels dizzy.
- Explain the importance of taking drug as prescribed, even when feeling well.

Evaluation

- Patient's blood pressure and heart rate and rhythm are normal.
- Patient effectively combats fatigue.
- Patient and family state understanding of drug therapy.

acetaminophen (APAP, paracetamol)

(as-ee-tuh-MIH-nuh-fin)

Abenol; Aceta Elixir*†; Acetaminophen Uniserts†; Aceta Tablets†; Actamin†; Actimol†; Aminofen†; Anacin-3†; Anacin-3 Children's Elixir*†; Anacin-3 Children's Tablets†; Anacin-3 Extra Strength†; Anacin-3 Infants'†; Apacet Capsules†; Apacet Elixir*†; Apacet Extra Strength Caplets†; Apacet Infants'†; Apo-Acetaminophen♦†; Arthritis Pain Formula Aspirin Free†; Atasol Caplets♦†; Atasol Drops♦†; Atasol Elixir*†; Atasol Tablets♦†; Banesin†; Dapa†; Dapa X-S†; Datril Extra-Strength; Dorcol Children's Fever and Pain Reducer†; Dymadon◊†; Exdol†; Feverall, Children's◊; Feverall Junior Strength◊; Feverall Sprinkle Caps◊; Genapap Children's Elixir†; Genapap Children's Tablets†; Genapap Extra Strength Caplets†; Genapap, Infants'†; Genapap Regular Strength Tablets†; Genebs Extra Strength Caplets†; Genebs Regular Strength Tablets†; Genebs X-Tra†; Halenol Elixir*†; Liquiprin Infants' Drops†; Meda Cap†; Neopap†; Oraphen-PD†; Panadol†; Panadol, Children's†; Panadol Extra Strength†; Panadol, Infants'†; Panadol Maximum Strength Caplets†; Redutemp†; Ridenol Caplets†; Robigesic†; Rounox†; Snaplets-FR†; St. Joseph Aspirin-Free Fever Reducer for Children†; Suppap-120†; Suppap-325†; Suppap-650†; Tapanol Extra Strength Caplets†; Tapanol Extra Strength Tablets†; Tempra†; Tempra D.S.†; Tempra, Infants'†; Tempra Syrup†; Tylenol Children's Elixir†; Tylenol Children's Tablets†; Tylenol Extended Relief†; Tylenol Extra Strength Caplets†; Tylenol Infants' Drops†; Tylenol Junior Strength Caplets†; Valorin†; Valorin Extra†

Pharmacologic class: para-aminophenol derivative
Therapeutic class: nonnarcotic analgesic, antipyretic
Pregnancy risk category: B

Indications and dosages

▶ **Mild pain or fever.** *Adults and childen older than age 12:* 325 to 650 mg P.O. or P.R. q 4 hours, p.r.n.; or 1 g P.O. t.i.d. or q.i.d., p.r.n.

Alternatively, 2 extended-release caplets P.O. q 8 hours. Maximum, 4 g daily. Dosage for long-term therapy shouldn't exceed 2.6 g daily unless monitored by prescriber.
Children ages 11 to 12: 480 mg P.O. or P.R. q 4 to 6 hours p.r.n.
Children ages 9 to 10: 400 mg P.O. or P.R. q 4 to 6 hours p.r.n.
Children ages 6 to 8: 320 mg P.O. or P.R. q 4 to 6 hours p.r.n.
Children ages 4 to 5: 240 mg P.O. or P.R. q 4 to 6 hours p.r.n.
Children ages 2 to 3: 160 mg P.O. or P.R. q 4 to 6 hours p.r.n.
Children ages 12 to 23 months: 120 mg P.O. q 4 to 6 hours p.r.n.
Infants ages 4 to 11 months: 80 mg P.O. q 4 to 6 hours p.r.n.
Infants age 3 months or younger: 40 mg P.O. q 4 to 6 hours p.r.n.
▶ **Osteoarthritis.** *Adults:* Up to 1,000 mg P.O. q.i.d.

Contraindications and precautions

- No known contraindications.
- Use cautiously in patient with history of chronic alcohol abuse; hepatotoxicity may occur after therapeutic doses.

Lifespan: In pregnant or breast-feeding woman, use cautiously.

Adverse reactions

Hematologic: hemolytic anemia, ***neutropenia, leukopenia, pancytopenia, thrombocytopenia.***
Hepatic: *liver damage* (with toxic doses), jaundice.
Metabolic: ***hypoglycemia.***
Skin: rash, urticaria.

Interactions

Drug-drug. *Barbiturates, carbamazepine, hydantoins, rifampin, sulfinpyrazone, isoniazid:* High doses or long-term use of these drugs may reduce therapeutic effects and enhance hepatotoxic effects of acetaminophen. Avoid use together.
Warfarin: May increase hypoprothrombinemic effects with long-term use with high doses of acetaminophen. Monitor PT and INR closely.
Zidovudine: May increase risk of bone marrow suppression because of impaired zidovudine metabolism. Monitor patient closely.
Drug-food. *Caffeine:* May enhance analgesic effects of acetaminophen. Monitor patient for effect.
Drug-lifestyle. *Alcohol use:* May increase risk of hepatic damage. Discourage using together.

Effects on lab test results

- May decrease hemoglobin, hematocrit, and neutrophil, WBC, RBC, and platelet counts.
- May produce false-positive decrease in glucose level. May alter laboratory tests for urinary 5-hydroxyindoleacetic acid.

Pharmacokinetics

Absorption: Absorbed rapidly and completely via GI tract.
Distribution: 25% protein-bound. Plasma levels don't correlate well with analgesic effect but do correlate with toxicity.
Metabolism: 90% to 95% metabolized in liver.
Excretion: Excreted in urine. *Half-life:* 1 to 4 hours.

Route	Onset	Peak	Duration
P.O., P.R.	Unknown	1-3 hr	1-3 hr

Pharmacodynamics

Chemical effect: Believed to produce analgesic effect by blocking pain impulses, probably by inhibiting prostaglandin or other substances that sensitize pain receptors. May relieve fever by action in hypothalamic heat-regulating center.
Therapeutic effect: Relieves pain and reduces fever.

Available forms

Caplets (extended-release): 650 mg
Capsules: 500 mg†
Elixir: 120 mg/5 ml, 130 mg/5 ml*†, 160 mg/5 ml*†, 325 mg/5 ml*†
Granules: 80 mg/packet†, 325 mg/capful†
Infant drops: 100 mg/ml†
Oral liquid: 160 mg/5 ml†, 500 mg/15 ml†
Oral solution: 48 mg/ml†, 100 mg/ml†
Oral suspension: 120 mg/5 ml ◇, 100 mg/ml†, 160 mg/ml†
Powder for solution: 1 g/packet
Sprinkles: 80 mg/capsule, 160 mg/capsule
Suppositories: 120 mg†, 125 mg†, 300 mg†, 325 mg†, 650 mg†
Tablets: 160 mg†, 325 mg†, 500 mg†, 650 mg†
Tablets (chewable): 80 mg†, 160 mg†

Tablets for solution: 325 mg
Wafers: 120 mg†

NURSING PROCESS

Assessment
- Assess patient's pain or temperature before and during therapy.
- Assess patient's medication history. Many OTC products and combination prescription pain products contain acetaminophen; be aware of this when calculating total daily dosage.
- Be alert for adverse reactions and drug interactions.
- Evaluate patient's and family's knowledge of drug therapy.

Nursing diagnoses
- Acute pain related to patient's underlying condition
- Risk for injury related to drug-induced liver damage with toxic doses
- Deficient knowledge related to drug therapy

Planning and implementation
- **P.O. use:** Administer liquid form to children and other patients who have trouble swallowing.

ALERT: When giving oral preparation, calculate dosage based on level of drug because drops and elixir have different concentrations.
- **P.R. use:** Use this route in small child and other patients for whom oral administration isn't feasible.

Patient teaching
- Tell parents to consult prescriber before giving drug to children younger than age 2.
- Tell patient that drug is for short-term use only. Prescriber should be consulted if administering to children for more than 5 days or to adults for more than 10 days.
- Tell patient not to use drug for marked fever (over 103.1° F [39.5° C]), fever persisting longer than 3 days, or recurrent fever unless directed by prescriber.
- Warn patient that high doses or unsupervised long-term use can cause hepatic damage. Excessive ingestion of alcoholic beverages may increase risk of hepatotoxicity.
- Tell patient to keep track of daily acetaminophen intake, including OTC and prescription medications. Warn patient not to exceed total recommended dose of acetaminophen per day because of risk of hepatotoxicity.
- Tell breast-feeding patient that drug is found in breast milk in low levels (less than 1% of dose). Patient may use drug safely if therapy is short-term and doesn't exceed recommended doses.

Evaluation
- Patient reports pain relief with drug.
- Patient's liver function test results remain normal.
- Patient and family state understanding of drug therapy.

acetazolamide
(ah-see-tuh-ZOH-luh-mighd)
Acetazolam, Apo-Acetazolamide, Diamox, Diamox Sequels

acetazolamide sodium
Diamox

Pharmacologic class: carbonic anhydrase inhibitor
Therapeutic class: adjunct therapy for open-angle glaucoma, agent for perioperative treatment of acute angle-closure glaucoma, anticonvulsant, agent for management of edema and prevention and treatment of acute mountain sickness
Pregnancy risk category: C

Indications and dosages

▶ **Secondary glaucoma and preoperative management of acute angle-closure glaucoma.** *Adults:* 250 mg P.O. q 4 hours, or 250 mg P.O. or I.V. b.i.d. for short-term therapy. For some acute glaucomas, 500 mg P.O., then 125 mg to 250 mg P.O. q 4 hours. I.V. administration (100 to 500 mg/minute) is preferred.
▶ **Edema in heart failure.** *Adults:* 250 to 375 mg (5 mg/kg) P.O. daily in a.m.
▶ **Chronic open-angle glaucoma.** *Adults:* 250 mg to 1 g P.O. daily in divided doses q.i.d., or 500 mg (extended-release) P.O. b.i.d.
▶ **Prevention or amelioration of acute mountain sickness.** *Adults:* 500 mg to 1 g P.O. daily in divided doses q 8 to 12 hours, or 500 mg (extended-release) P.O. b.i.d. Treat-

ment started 24 to 48 hours before ascent and continued for 48 hours while at high altitude.

▶ **Adjunct treatment of myoclonic, refractory generalized tonic-clonic, absence, or mixed seizures.** *Adults and children:* 8 to 30 mg/kg P.O. daily in divided doses. The optimum dosage is 375 mg to 1 g daily. When given with other anticonvulsants, the initial dose is 250 mg daily.

▶ **Drug-induced edema.** *Adults:* 250 to 375 mg (5 mg/kg) P.O. as a single dose for 1 to 2 days with one drug-free day.

▶ **Periodic paralysis.** *Adults:* 250 mg P.O. b.i.d. or t.i.d., not to exceed 1.5 g daily.

Contraindications and precautions

- Contraindicated in patients hypersensitive to drug; in those undergoing long-term therapy for chronic noncongestive angle-closure glaucoma; and in those with hyponatremia, hypokalemia, renal or hepatic disease or dysfunction, adrenal gland failure, and hyperchloremic acidosis.
- Use cautiously in patients with respiratory acidosis, emphysema, or chronic pulmonary disease, and in patients receiving other diuretics.

Lifespan: In pregnant woman, use cautiously. In breast-feeding woman, drug is contraindicated. In children, safety and efficacy of drug haven't been established.

Adverse reactions

CNS: drowsiness, paresthesia, confusion.
EENT: transient myopia.
GI: nausea, vomiting, anorexia, altered taste.
GU: crystalluria, renal calculi, hematuria, asymptomatic hyperuricemia.
Hematologic: ***aplastic anemia,*** hemolytic anemia, ***leukopenia.***
Metabolic: hyperchloremic acidosis, hypokalemia.
Skin: rash.
Other: *pain at injection site,* sterile abscesses.

Interactions

Drug-drug. *Amphetamines, anticholinergics, mecamylamine, quinidine, tricyclic antidepressants, procainamide:* May decrease renal clearance of these drugs, increasing toxicity. Monitor patient closely.
Lithium: May increase lithium secretion. Monitor patient.
Methenamine: May reduce effectiveness of acetazolamide. Avoid using together.
Salicylates: May cause accumulation and toxicity of acetazolamide, including CNS depression and metabolic acidosis. Monitor patient closely.

Effects on lab test results

- May increase uric acid level. May decrease potassium level.
- May decrease WBC count, thyroid iodine uptake, hemoglobin, and hematocrit.
- May cause false-positive urine protein test results.

Pharmacokinetics

Absorption: Well absorbed from GI tract after oral administration.
Distribution: Distributed throughout body tissues.
Metabolism: None.
Excretion: Excreted primarily in urine through tubular secretion and passive reabsorption. *Half-life:* 10 to 15 hours.

Route	Onset	Peak	Duration
P.O.			
tablets	1-1.5 hr	2-4 hr	8-12 hr
capsules	2 hr	8-12 hr	18-24 hr
I.V.	2 min	15 min	4-5 hr

Pharmacodynamics

Chemical effect: Blocks action of carbonic anhydrase, promoting renal excretion of sodium, potassium, bicarbonate, and water, and decreases secretion of aqueous humor in eye. As anticonvulsant, may inhibit carbonic anhydrase in CNS and decrease abnormal paroxysmal or excessive neuronal discharge. In acute mountain sickness, carbonic anhydrase inhibitors produce respiratory and metabolic acidosis that may stimulate ventilation, increase cerebral blood flow, and promote release of oxygen from hemoglobin.
Therapeutic effect: Lowers intraocular pressure, controls seizure activity, and may improve respiratory function.

Available forms

Capsules (extended-release): 500 mg
Injection: 500 mg/vial
Tablets: 125 mg, 250 mg

NURSING PROCESS

Assessment
- Assess patient's underlying condition before and during therapy, including, as appropriate, eye discomfort and intraocular pressure in those with glaucoma; edema in those with heart failure; and neurologic status in those with seizures. Also monitor intake and output.
- Be alert for adverse reactions and drug interactions.
- Evaluate patient's and family's knowledge of drug therapy.

Nursing diagnoses
- Excessive fluid volume related to patient's underlying condition
- Impaired urine elimination related to diuretic action of drug
- Deficient knowledge related to drug therapy

Planning and implementation
- **P.O. use:** Give oral preparation early in morning to avoid nocturia. Give second dose early in afternoon.

– Check with pharmacist if patient can't swallow oral forms. He may make suspension using crushed tablets in highly flavored syrup, such as cherry, raspberry, or chocolate. Although concentrations up to 500 mg/5 ml are feasible, concentrations of 250 mg/5 ml are more palatable. Refrigeration improves palatability but doesn't improve stability. Suspensions are stable for 1 week.
- **I.V. use:** Reconstitute 500-mg vial with at least 5 ml of sterile water for injection. Use within 24 hours. Inject 100 to 500 mg/minute into large vein, using 21G or 23G needle. Intermittent or continuous infusion isn't recommended.
- Diuretic effect decreases with acidosis but is reestablished by withdrawing drug for several days and then restarting it or by using intermittent administration.

ALERT: Don't confuse acetazolamide with acetohexamide. Also don't confuse acetazolamide sodium (Diamox) with acyclovir sodium (Zovirax); these vials may appear similar.
- Withhold drug and notify prescriber if hypersensitivity or adverse reactions occur.

Patient teaching
- Advise patient to take drug early in day to avoid interruption of sleep caused by nocturia.
- Teach patient to monitor fluid volume by measuring weight, intake, and output daily.
- Encourage patient to avoid high-sodium foods and to choose high-potassium foods.
- Teach patient to recognize and report signs and symptoms of fluid and electrolyte imbalance.

Evaluation
- Patient is free from edema.
- Patient adjusts lifestyle to accommodate altered patterns of urine elimination.
- Patient and family state understanding of drug therapy.

acetylcysteine
(as-ee-til-SIS-teen)

Airbron♦, Mucomyst, Mucomyst 10, Mucosil-10, Mucosil-20, Parvolex◊

Pharmacologic class: amino acid (L-cysteine) derivative
Therapeutic class: mucolytic, antidote for acetaminophen overdose
Pregnancy risk category: B

Indications and dosages
▶ **Pneumonia, bronchitis, tuberculosis, cystic fibrosis, emphysema, atelectasis (adjunct), complications of thoracic and CV surgery.** *Adults and children:* 1 to 2 ml of 10% or 20% solution by direct instillation into trachea as often as hourly; or 3 to 5 ml of 20% solution or 6 to 10 ml of 10% solution by nebulization q 2 to 3 hours p.r.n.

▶ **Acetaminophen toxicity.** *Adults and children:* Initially, 140 mg/kg P.O., followed by 70 mg/kg P.O. q 4 hours for 17 doses; or, where available, 300 mg/kg by I.V. infusion.

▶ **Prevention of acute renal failure related to radiographic contrast media‡.** *Adults:* 600 mg P.O. b.i.d. given the day before and on the day of contrast media administration for a total of four doses. Or, if for hydration, give with half-normal saline solution injection for I.V. infusion at 1 ml/kg per hr for 12 hours before and 12 hours after contrast media administration.

Contraindications and precautions
- Contraindicated in patients hypersensitive to drug.

• Use cautiously in debilitated patients with severe respiratory insufficiency.
Lifespan: In pregnant and breast-feeding women and in elderly patients with severe respiratory insufficiency, use cautiously.

Adverse reactions

EENT: *rhinorrhea, hemoptysis.*
GI: *stomatitis, nausea, vomiting.*
Respiratory: BRONCHOSPASM.

Interactions

Drug-drug. *Activated charcoal:* Limits acetylcysteine's effectiveness. Avoid using together in treating drug toxicity.

Effects on lab test results

None reported.

Pharmacokinetics

Absorption: Most inhaled acetylcysteine acts directly on mucus in lungs; remainder is absorbed by pulmonary epithelium. After oral administration, drug is absorbed from GI tract.
Distribution: Unknown.
Metabolism: Metabolized in liver.
Excretion: Unknown.

Route	Onset	Peak	Duration
P.O., I.V., inhalation	Unknown	Unknown	Unknown

Pharmacodynamics

Chemical effect: Increases production of respiratory tract fluids to help liquefy and reduce viscosity of tenacious secretions. Also, restores glutathione in liver to treat acetaminophen toxicity.
Therapeutic effect: Thins respiratory secretions and reverses toxic effects of acetaminophen.

Available forms

Injection: 200 mg/ml ♦ ◇
Solution: 10%, 20%

NURSING PROCESS

Assessment

• Assess patient's respiratory secretions before and frequently during therapy.
• Be alert for adverse reactions and drug interactions.
• Evaluate patient's and family's knowledge of drug therapy.

Nursing diagnoses

• Ineffective airway clearance related to patient's underlying condition
• Impaired oral mucous membrane related to drug-induced stomatitis
• Deficient knowledge related to drug therapy

Planning and implementation

• **P.O. use:** Dilute oral doses with cola, fruit juice, or water before administering to treat acetaminophen overdose. Dilute 20% solution to a concentration of 5% (add 3 ml of diluent to each ml of acetylcysteine). If patient vomits within 1 hour of initial or maintenance dose, repeat dose.
• **I.V. use:** To prepare I.V. infusion, dilute calculated dose in D_5W. Dilute initial dose (150 mg/kg) in 200 ml of D_5W and infuse over 15 minutes. Dilute second dose (50 mg/kg) in 500 ml of D_5W and infuse over 4 hours. Dilute final dose (100 mg/kg) in 1,000 ml of D_5W and infuse over 16 hours.
• **Nebulization use:** Use plastic, glass, stainless steel, or another nonreactive metal when giving by nebulization.
– Hand-bulb nebulizers aren't recommended because output is too small and particle size is too large.
– Before aerosol administration, have patient clear airway by coughing.
• After opening, store in refrigerator, and use within 96 hours.
• Drug is physically or chemically incompatible with tetracyclines, erythromycin lactobionate, amphotericin B, and ampicillin sodium. If administered by aerosol inhalation, these drugs should be nebulized separately. Iodized oil, trypsin, and hydrogen peroxide are physically incompatible with acetylcysteine; don't add to nebulizer.
• Have suction equipment available in case patient can't effectively clear his air passages.
• Alert prescriber if patient's respiratory secretions thicken or become purulent or if bronchospasm occurs.
ALERT: Acetylcysteine is given to treat acetaminophen overdose within 24 hours after ingestion. Start treatment immediately; don't wait for drug level determinations.

ALERT: Don't confuse acetylcysteine with acetylcholine.

Patient teaching

- Instruct patient to follow directions on drug label exactly. Explain importance of using drug as directed.
- If patient's condition doesn't improve within 10 days, tell him to notify prescriber. Drug shouldn't be used for prolonged period without direct medical supervision.
- Teach patient how to use and clean nebulizer.
- Inform patient that drug may have foul taste or smell.
- Instruct patient to clear his airway by coughing before aerosol administration to achieve maximum effect.
- Instruct patient to rinse mouth with water after nebulizer treatment because it may leave sticky coating on oral cavity.

Evaluation

- Patient has clear lung sounds, decreased respiratory secretions, and reduced frequency and severity of cough.
- Patient's oral mucous membranes remain unchanged.
- Patient and family state understanding of drug therapy.

activated charcoal

(AK-tih-vay-ted CHAR-kohl)

Actidose†, Actidose-Aqua†, CharcoAid†, CharcoCaps†, Liqui-Char†, Superchar†, Insta-Char Pediatric†

Pharmacologic class: adsorbent
Therapeutic class: antidote
Pregnancy risk category: C

Indications and dosages

▶ **Flatulence, dyspepsia.** *Adults:* 600 mg to 5 g P.O. t.i.d. after meals.

▶ **Poisoning.** *Adults:* Initially, 1 g/kg (30 to 100 g) P.O. or five to ten times amount of poison ingested as suspension in 180 to 240 ml of water.
Children: Five to ten times estimated weight of drug or chemical ingested, with minimum dose being 30 g P.O. in 240 ml of water to make a slurry, preferably within 30 minutes of poisoning. Larger dose is necessary if food is in stomach. Commonly used for treating poisoning or overdose with acetaminophen, aspirin, atropine, barbiturates, cardiac glycosides, poisonous mushrooms, oxalic acid, parathion, phenol, phenytoin, propantheline, propoxyphene, strychnine, or tricyclic antidepressants. Check with poison control center for use in other types of poisonings or overdoses.

▶ **To relieve GI disturbances (such as halitosis, anorexia, nausea, and vomiting) in uremic patients‡.** *Adults:* 20 to 50 g P.O. daily.

Contraindications and precautions

- No known contraindications.

Adverse reactions

GI: black stools, nausea, constipation.

Interactions

Drug-drug. *Acetylcysteine, ipecac:* Render charcoal ineffective. Don't give together, and don't perform gastric lavage until all charcoal is removed.

Effects on lab test results

None reported.

Pharmacokinetics

Absorption: None.
Distribution: None.
Metabolism: None.
Excretion: In feces.

Route	Onset	Peak	Duration
P.O.	Immediate	Unknown	Unknown

Pharmacodynamics

Chemical effect: Adheres to many drugs and chemicals, inhibiting their absorption from GI tract.
Therapeutic effect: Used as antidote for selected poisons and overdoses.

Available forms

Capsules: 260 mg†
Oral suspension: 0.625 g/5 ml†, 0.83 g/5 ml†, 1 g/5 ml†, 1.25 g/5 ml†
Powder: 30 g†, 50 g†
Tablets: 200 mg ◇ †, 300 mg ◇ †, 325 mg†, 650 mg†

NURSING PROCESS

Assessment
- Obtain history of substance reportedly ingested, including time of ingestion, if possible. Drug isn't effective for all drugs and toxic substances.
- Be alert for adverse reactions and drug interactions.
- Evaluate patient's and family's knowledge of drug therapy.

Nursing diagnoses
- Risk for injury related to ingestion of toxic substance or overdose
- Risk for deficient fluid volume related to drug-induced vomiting
- Deficient knowledge related to drug therapy

Planning and implementation
- Give after emesis is complete because drug absorbs and inactivates syrup of ipecac.
- Don't give to semiconscious or unconscious persons unless airway is protected and NG tube is in place for instillation.
- Mix powder form (most effective) with tap water to form consistency of thick syrup. Add small amount of fruit juice or flavoring to make mix more palatable.
- Give by NG tube after lavage, if needed.
- Don't give in ice cream, milk, or sherbet, which may reduce absorption.
- Repeat dose if patient vomits shortly after administration.
- Keep airway, oxygen, and suction equipment nearby.
- Follow treatment with stool softener or laxative to prevent constipation.

ALERT: Don't confuse Actidose with Actos.

Patient teaching
- Warn patient that feces will be black.
- Instruct patient to report respiratory difficulty immediately.

Evaluation
- Patient doesn't experience injury from ingesting toxic substance or from overdose.
- Patient exhibits no signs of deficient fluid volume.
- Patient or family states understanding of drug therapy.

acyclovir sodium
(ay-SIGH-kloh-veer SOH-dee-um)
Acihexal ◇, Acyclo-V ◇, Avirax ♦, Zovirax

Pharmacologic class: synthetic purine nucleoside
Therapeutic class: antiviral
Pregnancy risk category: C

Indications and dosages
▶ **Initial and recurrent episodes of mucocutaneous herpes simplex virus (HSV-1 and HSV-2) infections in immunocompromised patients; severe initial episodes of herpes genitalis in nonimmunocompromised patients.** *Adults and children age 12 and older:* 5 mg/kg I.V. at constant rate over 1 hour q 8 hours for 7 days (5 days for herpes genitalis). *Children younger than age 12:* 250 mg/m^2 I.V. at constant rate over 1 hour q 8 hours for 7 days (5 days for herpes genitalis).

▶ **Initial genital herpes.** *Adults:* 200 mg P.O. q 4 hours during waking hours (total of 5 capsules daily) for 10 days.

▶ **Genital herpes in immunocompromised patients‡.** *Adults:* 400 mg P.O. three to five times daily.

▶ **Intermittent therapy for recurrent genital herpes.** *Adults:* 200 mg P.O. q 4 hours during waking hours (total of 5 capsules daily) for 5 days. Start therapy at first sign of recurrence.

▶ **Long-term suppressive therapy for recurrent genital herpes.** *Adults:* 400 mg P.O. b.i.d. for up to 12 months.

▶ **Long-term suppressive or maintenance therapy for recurrent HSV infections in patients with HIV‡.** *Adults and adolescents:* 200 mg P.O. t.i.d. or 400 mg P.O. b.i.d. *Infants and children:* 600 to 1,000 mg P.O. daily in three to five divided doses.

▶ **Chickenpox.** *Adults and children age 2 and older weighing more than 40 kg (88 lb):* 800 mg P.O. q.i.d. for 5 days.

▶ **Acute herpes zoster.** *Adults:* 800 mg P.O. q 4 hours, five times daily for 7 to 10 days. Give within 48 hours of rash onset.

▶ **Disseminated herpes zoster‡.** *Adults:* 5 to 10 mg/kg I.V. q 8 hours for 7 to 10 days. Infuse over at least 1 hour.

▶ **Herpes simplex encephalitis.** *Adults:* 10 mg/kg infused at a constant rate over 1 hour, q 8 hours for 10 days.
Children ages 6 months to 12 years: 500 mg/m^2 at a constant rate over at least 1 hour, q 8 hours for 10 days.
▶ **Varicella zoster in immunocompromised patients:** *Adults:* 10 mg/kg infused at a constant rate over 1 hour, q 8 hours for 7 days.
Children younger than age 12: 20 mg/kg q 8 hours for 7 days, or 500 mg/m^2 at a constant rate over at least 1 hour, q 8 hours for 7 days. Obese patients should be given 10 mg/kg (ideal body weight). Maximum dose equivalent to 500 mg/m^2 q 8 hours shouldn't be exceeded.
▶ **Acute herpes zoster ophthalmicus‡.** *Adults:* 600 mg P.O. q 4 hours five times daily for 10 days, preferably within 72 hours of rash onset, but no longer than 7 days.
▶ **Rectal herpes infection‡.** *Adults:* 400 mg P.O. five times daily for 10 days or until resolution; alternatively, give 800 mg P.O. q 8 hours for 7 to 10 days.
Patients with renal impairment: If creatinine clearance is less than 10 ml/minute, decrease the normal oral dose (200 to 400 mg) to 200 mg q 12 hours. For normal oral doses more than 400 mg, consult package insert. In patients with renal failure, give 100% of the I.V. dose q 8 hours if creatinine clearance exceeds 50 ml/minute; 100% of the dose q 12 hours if creatinine clearance falls between 25 and 50 ml/minute; 100% of the dose q 24 hours if the creatinine clearance ranges from 10 to 25 ml/minute; and 50% of the dose q 24 hours if it falls below 10 ml/minute.

Contraindications and precautions

- Contraindicated in patients hypersensitive to drug.
- Use cautiously in patients with underlying neurologic problems, renal disease, or dehydration and in those receiving other nephrotoxic drugs.

Lifespan: In pregnant and breast-feeding women, use cautiously. In children younger than age 2, safety and efficacy haven't been established.

Adverse reactions

CNS: *encephalopathic changes including lethargy, obtundation, tremor, confusion, hallucinations, agitation, seizures, coma, headache* (with I.V. dosage).
CV: hypotension.
GI: *nausea, vomiting,* diarrhea.
GU: hematuria.
Skin: rash, itching, *vesicular eruptions.*
Other: *inflammation, phlebitis at injection site.*

Interactions

Drug-drug. *Phenytoin:* May decrease phenytoin level. Monitor patient closely.
Probenecid: Increases acyclovir level. Monitor patient for possible toxicity.
Valproic acid: Decreases valproic acid level. Monitor patient closely.
Zidovudine: May cause drowsiness or lethargy. Use together cautiously.

Effects on lab test results

- May increase BUN, creatinine, and liver enzyme levels.
- May decrease hemoglobin and hematocrit. May increase or decrease platelet, neutrophil, and WBC counts.

Pharmacokinetics

Absorption: Slow and incomplete (15% to 30%). Not affected by food.
Distribution: Widely distributed to organ tissues and body fluids. CSF levels equal about 50% of serum levels. From 9% to 33% of dose binds to plasma proteins.
Metabolism: Metabolized primarily inside viral cell to its active form. About 10% of dose is metabolized extracellularly.
Excretion: Up to 92% of systemically absorbed acyclovir is excreted unchanged by kidneys via glomerular filtration and tubular secretion. *Half-life:* 2 to 3½ hours with normal renal function; up to 19 hours with renal failure.

Route	Onset	Peak	Duration
P.O.	Unknown	Unknown	Unknown
I.V.	Immediate	Immediate	Unknown

Pharmacodynamics

Chemical effect: Becomes incorporated into viral DNA and inhibits viral multiplication.
Therapeutic effect: Kills susceptible viruses.

Available forms

Capsules: 200 mg
Injection: 500 mg/vial, 1 g/vial

Suspension: 200 mg/5 ml
Tablets: 400 mg, 800 mg

NURSING PROCESS

Assessment

- Assess infection before and regularly during therapy.
- Be alert for adverse reactions and drug interactions.
- Monitor patient for renal toxicity. Bolus injection, dehydration, renal disease, and use of other nephrotoxic drugs increase risk.
- Monitor patient's mental status when giving drug I.V. Encephalopathic changes are more likely in patients with neurologic disorders or in those who have had neurologic reactions to cytotoxic drugs.
- Monitor patient's hydration status if adverse GI reactions occur with oral administration.
- Evaluate patient's and family's knowledge of drug therapy.

Nursing diagnoses

- Infection related to presence of virus
- Risk for deficient fluid volume related to adverse GI reactions to oral drug
- Deficient knowledge related to drug therapy

Planning and implementation

- **P.O. use:** Follow normal protocol.
- **I.V. use:** Give I.V. infusion over at least 1 hour to prevent renal tubular damage. Also, ensure I.V. infusion is accompanied by adequate hydration.

ALERT: Don't give I.M., S.C., or by bolus injection.

ALERT: Concentrated solutions (10 mg/ml or more) increase the risk of phlebitis.

Patient teaching

- Tell patient that drug effectively manages herpes infection but doesn't eliminate or cure it.
- Warn patient that drug won't prevent spread of infection to others.
- Help patient to recognize early symptoms of herpes infection (tingling, itching, pain) so he can take drug before infection fully develops.
- Tell patient to alert nurse if he has pain or discomfort at I.V. injection site.

Evaluation

- Patient's infection is eradicated.
- Patient maintains adequate hydration.
- Patient and family state understanding of drug therapy.

adenosine

(uh-DEN-oh-seen)
Adenocard

Pharmacologic class: nucleoside
Therapeutic class: antiarrhythmic
Pregnancy risk category: C

Indications and dosages

▶ **Conversion of paroxysmal supraventricular tachycardia (PSVT) to sinus rhythm.** *Adults:* 6 mg I.V. by rapid bolus injection over 1 to 2 seconds. If PSVT isn't eliminated in 1 to 2 minutes, 12 mg by rapid I.V. bolus may be given and repeated (if needed). Single doses larger than 12 mg aren't recommended.

Contraindications and precautions

- Contraindicated in patients hypersensitive to drug and in those with second- or third-degree heart block or sick-sinus syndrome unless artificial pacemaker is present. Adenosine decreases conduction through AV node and may produce transient first-, second-, or third-degree heart block. Patients in whom significant heart block develops shouldn't receive additional doses.
- Use cautiously in patients with asthma because bronchoconstriction may occur.

Lifespan: In pregnant and breast-feeding women and in children, safety of drug hasn't been established

Adverse reactions

CNS: apprehension, burning sensation, dizziness, heaviness in arms, light-headedness, numbness, tingling in arms.
CV: chest pain, *facial flushing,* headache, hypotension, palpitations.
EENT: metallic taste, blurred vision.
GI: nausea.
Musculoskeletal: back pain, neck pain.
Respiratory: *chest pressure, dyspnea, shortness of breath,* hyperventilation.
Skin: diaphoresis.
Other: *tightness in throat, groin pressure.*

Interactions

Drug-drug. *Carbamazepine:* Higher degrees of heart block may occur. Monitor patient.
Digoxin, verapamil: In rare cases, combined use causes ventricular fibrillation. Use cautiously.
Dipyridamole: May potentiate adenosine's effects. Smaller doses may be needed.
Methylxanthines: May antagonize adenosine's effects. Patients receiving theophylline or caffeine may require higher doses or may not respond to adenosine therapy.
Drug-herb. *Guarana:* May decrease therapeutic response. Discourage using together.
Drug-food. *Caffeine:* May antagonize adenosine's effects. May require higher doses.

Effects on lab test results

None reported.

Pharmacokinetics

Absorption: Administered I.V.
Distribution: Rapidly taken up by erythrocytes and vascular endothelial cells.
Metabolism: Metabolized within tissues to inosine and adenosine monophosphate.
Excretion: Unknown. *Half-life:* Less than 10 seconds.

Route	Onset	Peak	Duration
I.V.	Immediate	Immediate	Extremely short

Pharmacodynamics

Chemical effect: Acts on AV node to slow conduction and inhibit reentry pathways. Drug also is useful in treating PSVT with accessory bypass tracts (Wolff-Parkinson-White syndrome).
Therapeutic effect: Restores normal sinus rhythm.

Available forms

Injection: 3 mg/ml in 2-ml vials, 2-ml and 5-ml syringes

NURSING PROCESS

Assessment

- Monitor patient's heart rate and rhythm before and during therapy.
- Be alert for adverse reactions and drug interactions.
- Evaluate patient's and family's knowledge of drug therapy.

Nursing diagnoses

- Decreased cardiac output related to arrhythmias
- Ineffective protection related to drug-induced proarrhythmias
- Deficient knowledge related to drug therapy

Planning and implementation

- Check solution for crystals that may form if solution is cold. If crystals are visible, gently warm solution to room temperature. Don't use unclear solutions.
- Give rapidly for effective drug action. Give directly into vein if possible; if I.V. line is used, inject drug into most proximal port and follow with rapid saline flush to ensure that drug reaches systemic circulation quickly.
- Discard unused drug; it contains no preservatives.
- If ECG disturbances occur, withhold drug, obtain rhythm strip, and notify prescriber immediately.

ALERT: Have emergency equipment and drugs on hand to treat new arrhythmias.

Patient teaching

- Teach patient and family about his disease and therapy.
- Stress importance of alerting nurse if chest pain or dyspnea occurs.
- Advise patient to avoid caffeine.

Evaluation

- Patient's arrhythmias are corrected and his heart maintains normal sinus rhythm.
- Patient doesn't experience proarrhythmias.
- Patient and family state understanding of drug therapy.

albumin 5%
(al-BYOO-min)
Albuminar-5, Albutein 5%, Buminate 5%, Plasbumin-5

albumin 25%
Albuminar-25, Albutein 25%, Buminate 25%, Plasbumin-25

Pharmacologic class: blood derivative
Therapeutic class: plasma volume expander
Pregnancy risk category: C

Indications and dosages

▶ **Hypovolemic shock.** *Adults:* Initially, 500 ml 5% solution by I.V. infusion, repeated p.r.n. Dosage varies with patient's condition and response. Don't give more than 250 g in 48 hours.
Children: 10 to 20 ml/kg 5% solution by I.V. infusion, repeated in 15 to 30 minutes if response isn't adequate. Alternatively, 2.5 to 5 ml/kg 25% solution I.V., repeated after 10 to 30 minutes, if needed.

▶ **Hypoproteinemia.** *Adults:* 1,000 to 1,500 ml 5% solution by I.V. infusion daily, with maximum rate of 5 to 10 ml/minute; or 200 to 300 ml 25% solution by I.V. infusion daily, with maximum rate of 3 ml/minute. Dosage varies with patient's condition and response.

▶ **Hyperbilirubinemia.** *Infants:* 1 g albumin (4 ml 25%)/kg I.V. 1 to 2 hours before transfusion.

Contraindications and precautions

- Contraindicated in patients hypersensitive to drug.
- Use with extreme caution in patients with hypertension, cardiac disease, severe pulmonary infection, severe chronic anemia, or hypoalbuminemia with peripheral edema.

Lifespan: In pregnant women, use cautiously.

Adverse reactions

CNS: fever.
CV: ***vascular overload,*** hypotension, altered pulse rate.
GI: increased salivation, nausea, vomiting.
Respiratory: altered respiration.
Skin: urticaria, rash.
Other: chills.

Interactions

None significant.

Effects on lab test results

- May increase albumin level.

Pharmacokinetics

Absorption: Administered I.V.
Distribution: Albumin accounts for about 50% of plasma proteins; it is distributed into intravascular space and extravascular sites, including skin, muscle, and lungs.
Metabolism: Unknown.
Excretion: Unknown, although liver, kidneys, or intestines may provide elimination mechanisms for albumin. *Half-life:* 15 to 20 days.

Route	Onset	Peak	Duration
I.V.	15 min for hydrated patient	15 min for hydrated patient	Up to several hr with reduced blood volume

Pharmacodynamics

Chemical effect: Albumin 5% supplies colloid to blood and expands plasma volume. Albumin 25% provides intravascular oncotic pressure in 5:1 ratio, causing fluid shift from interstitial spaces to circulation and slightly increasing plasma protein level.
Therapeutic effect: Relieves shock by increasing plasma volume and corrects plasma protein deficiency.

Available forms

Injection: 50-ml, 250-ml, 500-ml, 1,000-ml vials (albumin 5%); 10-ml, 20-ml, 50-ml, 100-ml vials (albumin 25%)

NURSING PROCESS

Assessment

- Assess patient's underlying condition.
- Be alert for adverse reactions.
- Monitor fluid intake and output, hemoglobin, hematocrit, and protein and electrolyte levels.
- Evaluate patient's and family's knowledge of drug therapy.

Nursing diagnoses

- Deficient fluid volume related to patient's underlying condition
- Excessive fluid volume related to adverse effects of drug
- Deficient knowledge related to drug therapy

Planning and implementation

- Minimize waste when preparing and administering drug. This product is expensive, and random shortages are common.
- Avoid rapid I.V. infusion. Infusion rate is individualized according to patient's age, condition, and diagnosis. Dilute with normal saline solution or D_5W. Use solution promptly and discard any unused solution because it contains

no preservatives. Don't use cloudy solutions or those containing sediment. Solution should be clear amber.
ALERT: Don't give more than 250 g in 48 hours.
- One volume of 25% albumin is equivalent to five volumes of 5% albumin in producing hemodilution and relative anemia.
- Follow storage instructions on bottle. Freezing may cause bottle to break.
- Withhold fluids in patient with cerebral edema for 8 hours after infusion to avoid fluid overload.

Patient teaching
- Explain how and why albumin is given.
- Tell patient to report chills, fever, dyspnea, nausea, or rash immediately; normal serum albumin can cause allergic reaction.

Evaluation
- Patient's deficient fluid volume is resolved.
- Patient doesn't experience fluid overload.
- Patient and family state understanding of drug therapy.

albuterol (salbutamol)
(al-BYOO-ter-ohl)
Proventil, Ventolin

albuterol sulfate (salbutamol sulfate)
Proventil, Proventil HFA, Proventil Repetabs, Ventolin, Ventolin HFA, Volmax

Pharmacologic class: adrenergic
Therapeutic class: bronchodilator
Pregnancy risk category: C

Indications and dosages
▶ **Prevention of exercise-induced bronchospasm.** *Adults and children age 4 and older:* Two aerosol inhalations 15 to 30 minutes before exercise.
▶ **To prevent or treat bronchospasm in patients with reversible obstructive airway disease.** ***Aerosol inhalation.*** *Adults and children age 4 and older:* One or two inhalations q 4 to 6 hours. More frequent administration and more inhalations aren't recommended. Proventil isn't indicated for use in children younger than age 12.
Solution for inhalation. *Adults and children age 12 and older:* 2.5 mg t.i.d. or q.i.d. by nebulizer. To prepare solution, use 0.5 ml of 0.5% solution diluted with 2.5 ml normal saline solution. Or, use 3 ml of 0.083% solution.
Children ages 2 to 12: Initially, 0.1 to 0.15 mg/kg by nebulizer, with subsequent dosing adjusted to response. Don't exceed 2.5 mg t.i.d. or q.i.d. by nebulization.
Syrup. *Adults and adolescents age 15 and older:* 2 to 4 mg (1 to 2 tsp) P.O. t.i.d. or q.i.d. Maximum, 8 mg P.O. q.i.d.
Children ages 6 to 14: 2 mg (1 tsp) P.O. t.i.d. or q.i.d. Maximum, 24 mg daily in divided doses.
Children ages 2 to 5: Initially, 0.1 mg/kg P.O. t.i.d. Starting dose shouldn't exceed 2 mg (1 tsp) t.i.d. Maximum, 4 mg (2 tsp) t.i.d.
Tablets. *Adults and children older than age 12:* 2 to 4 mg P.O. t.i.d. or q.i.d. Maximum, 8 mg q.i.d.
Children ages 6 to 12: 2 mg P.O. t.i.d. or q.i.d. Maximum, 6 mg q.i.d.
Elderly patients and patients sensitive to beta stimulators: 2 mg P.O. t.i.d. or q.i.d. tablets or syrup. Maximum, 8 mg t.i.d. or q.i.d.
Extended-release tablets. *Adults and children older than age 12:* 4 to 8 mg P.O. q 12 hours. Maximum, 16 mg b.i.d.
Children ages 6 to 12: 4 mg P.O. q 12 hours. Maximum, 12 mg b.i.d.

Contraindications and precautions
- Contraindicated in patients hypersensitive to drug or its components.
- Use cautiously in patients with CV disorders (including coronary insufficiency and hypertension), hyperthyroidism, or diabetes mellitus and in those unusually responsive to adrenergics.
- Use extended-release tablets cautiously in patients with GI narrowing.

Lifespan: With pregnant women, use cautiously. Advise breast-feeding women against taking drug. Safety of drug hasn't been established in children younger than age 6 for tablets and Repetabs, younger than age 4 for aerosol and capsules for inhalation, and younger than age 2 for inhalation solution and syrup.

Adverse reactions

CNS: *tremor, nervousness,* dizziness, insomnia, headache.
CV: tachycardia, palpitations, hypertension.
EENT: drying and irritation of nose and throat.
GI: heartburn, nausea, vomiting.
Metabolic: hypokalemia, weight loss.
Musculoskeletal: muscle cramps.
Respiratory: ***bronchospasm.***

Interactions

Drug-drug. *CNS stimulants:* Increases CNS stimulation. Avoid using together.
Levodopa: Increases risk of arrhythmias. Monitor patient closely.
MAO inhibitors, tricyclic antidepressants: Increases adverse CV effects. Monitor patient closely.
Propranolol, other beta blockers: Mutual antagonism. Monitor patient carefully.
Drug-herb. *Herbs containing caffeine:* Additive adverse effects. Discourage using together.
Drug-food. *Foods and beverages containing caffeine:* Increases CNS stimulation. Discourage using together.

Effects on lab test results

- May decrease potassium level.

Pharmacokinetics

Absorption: After inhalation, drug appears to be absorbed over several hours from respiratory tract; however, most of dose is swallowed and absorbed through GI tract. After oral administration, drug is well absorbed through GI tract.
Distribution: Doesn't cross blood-brain barrier.
Metabolism: Extensively metabolized in liver to inactive compounds.
Excretion: Rapidly excreted in urine and feces. *Half-life:* About 4 hours.

Route	Onset	Peak	Duration
P.O.	15-30 min	2-3 hr	6-12 hr
Inhalation	5-15 min	1-1.5 hr	3-6 hr

Pharmacodynamics

Chemical effect: Relaxes bronchial and uterine smooth muscle by acting on $beta_2$-adrenergic receptors.
Therapeutic effect: Improves ventilation.

Available forms

Aerosol inhaler: 90 mcg/metered spray, 100 mcg/metered spray
Solution for inhalation: 0.083%, 0.5%
Syrup: 2 mg/5 ml
Tablets: 2 mg, 4 mg
Tablets (extended-release): 4 mg, 8 mg

NURSING PROCESS

Assessment

- Obtain baseline assessment of patient's respiratory status, and assess frequently throughout therapy.
- Be alert for adverse reactions and drug interactions.
- Evaluate patient's and family's knowledge of drug therapy.

Nursing diagnoses

- Impaired gas exchange related to underlying respiratory condition
- Risk for injury related to drug-induced adverse reactions
- Deficient knowledge related to drug therapy

Planning and implementation

- **P.O. use:** Pleasant-tasting syrup may be taken by children as young as age 2. Syrup contains no alcohol or sugar.
- **Inhalation use:** Wait at least 2 minutes between doses if more than one dose is ordered. If corticosteroid inhaler also is used, first have patient use bronchodilator, wait 5 minutes, and then have patient use corticosteroid inhaler. This permits bronchodilator to open air passages for maximum corticosteroid effectiveness.
  – Aerosol form may be prescribed for use 15 minutes before exercise to prevent exercise-induced bronchospasm.
- Patients may use tablets and aerosol together.

ALERT: Don't confuse albuterol with atenolol or Albutein.

Patient teaching

- Warn patient to stop drug immediately if paradoxical bronchospasm occurs.
- Give patient correct instructions for using metered-dose inhaler: Clear nasal passages and throat. Breathe out, expelling as much air from lungs as possible. Place mouthpiece well into

mouth and inhale deeply as dose is released. Hold breath for several seconds, remove mouthpiece, and exhale slowly.
- Advise patient to wait at least 2 minutes before repeating procedure if more than one inhalation is ordered.
- Warn patient to avoid accidentally spraying inhalant form into eyes, which may blur vision temporarily.
- Tell patient to reduce intake of foods and herbs containing caffeine, such as coffee, cola, and chocolate, when using a bronchodilator.
- Show patient how to check his pulse rate. Instruct him to check pulse before and after using bronchodilator and to call prescriber if pulse rate increases more than 20 to 30 beats/minute.

Evaluation
- Patient's respiratory signs and symptoms improve.
- Patient has no injury from adverse drug reactions.
- Patient and family state understanding of drug therapy.

alemtuzumab
(ah-lem-TOO-zeh-mab)
Campath

Pharmacologic classification: monoclonal antibody
Therapeutic classification: antineoplastic
Pregnancy risk category: C

Indications and dosages
▶ **B-cell chronic lymphocytic leukemia in patients treated with alkylating drugs, and in whom fludarabine therapy has failed.**
Adults: Initially, 3 mg I.V. infusion over 2 hours daily; if tolerated, increase dose to 10 mg daily, as tolerated; then increase to 30 mg daily. Escalation to 30 mg usually can be accomplished in 3 to 7 days. As maintenance, give 30 mg I.V three times weekly on nonconsecutive days (such as Monday, Wednesday, Friday) for up to 12 weeks. Don't give single doses greater than 30 mg or weekly doses greater than 90 mg.

For patients with hematologic toxicity, see table for dosage adjustments.

Hematologic toxicity	Dosage adjustment
1st occurrence of absolute neutrophil count (ANC) $\leq 250/mm^3$ or platelets $\leq 25{,}000/mm^3$	Stop therapy; resume at same dose when ANC $\geq 500/mm^3$ or platelets $\geq 50{,}000/mm^3$. If delay between doses is ≥ 7 days, start therapy at 3 mg; increase to 10 mg then 30 mg as tolerated.
2nd occurrence of ANC $\leq 250/mm^3$ or platelets $\leq 25{,}000/mm^3$	Stop therapy; when ANC returns to $\geq 500/mm^3$ or platelets to $\geq 50{,}000/mm^3$, resume at 10 mg; if delay between doses is ≥ 7 days, start therapy at 3 mg; increase to 10 mg only.
3rd occurrence of ANC $\leq 250/mm^3$ or platelets $\leq 25{,}000/mm^3$	Stop therapy.
For a decrease of ANC or platelet count $\leq 50\%$ of the baseline value in patients starting therapy with a baseline ANC $\leq 500/mm^3$ or baseline platelet count $\leq 25{,}000/mm^3$	Stop therapy; when ANC or platelet count returns to baseline, resume therapy. If the delay between dosing is ≥ 7 days, start therapy at 3 mg and increase to 10 mg, then 30 mg as tolerated.

Contraindications and precautions
- Contraindicated in patients with active systemic infections, underlying immunodeficiency (such as HIV), or type I hypersensitivity or anaphylactic reactions to drug or its components.

Lifespan: In pregnant women, benefits of drug should be weighed against risks to the fetus because immunoglobolin G crosses the placental barrier and causes fetal B and T lymphocyte depletion. Advise breast-feeding women to stop breast-feeding during treatment and for at least 3 months after taking last dose of drug. In children, safety and efficacy of drug haven't been established.

Adverse reactions
CNS: *fever, insomnia,* depression, somnolence, *asthenia, headache, dysthenias, dizziness, fatigue,* malaise, tremor.
CV: *edema, peripheral edema, hypotension, hypertension, tachycardia,* **SUPRAVENTRICULAR TACHYCARDIA.**
EENT: epistaxis, rhinitis, *pharyngitis.*

GI: *anorexia, nausea, vomiting, diarrhea, stomatitis, ulcerative stomatitis, mucositis, abdominal pain, dyspepsia,* constipation.
Hematologic: NEUTROPENIA, *anemia, **pancytopenia,*** THROMBOCYTOPENIA, purpura.
Musculoskeletal: *pain, skeletal pain, back pain, myalgias.*
Respiratory: *dyspnea, cough, bronchitis, pneumonitis, **bronchospasm.***
Skin: *rash, urticaria, pruritus, increased sweating.*
Other: SEPSIS, *infection, herpes simplex, rigors,* chills, candidiasis.

Interactions

None reported.

Effects on lab test results

- May decrease hemoglobin, hematocrit, and CD4+, lymphocyte, neutrophil, WBC, RBC, and platelet counts.
- May interfere with diagnostic tests that use antibodies.

Pharmacokinetics

Absorption: Administered I.V.
Distribution: Binds to various tissues.
Metabolism: Unknown.
Excretion: Unknown. *Half-life:* 12 days.

Route	Onset	Peak	Duration
I.V.	Unknown	Unknown	Unknown

Pharmacodynamics

Chemical effect: Binds to CD_{52} and causes antibody-dependent lysis of leukemic cells following cell-surface binding.
Therapeutic effect: Destroys leukemic cells.

Available forms

Ampules: 10 mg/ml, in 3-ml ampules

NURSING PROCESS

Assessment

- Assess patient's underlying condition before therapy for signs or symptoms of active infection or immunocompromise.
- Obtain baseline CBC and platelet count before starting therapy.
- Monitor blood pressure and be alert for hypotensive symptoms during drug administration.

ALERT: Monitor hematologic studies carefully during therapy. Even with normal dosages, patients may experience signs and symptoms of hematologic toxicity, including myelosuppression, bone marrow dysplasia, and thrombocytopenia. Initial doses of greater than 3 mg aren't well tolerated. Extremely high doses can cause acute bronchospasm, cough, shortness of breath, anuria, and death. Treatment consists of stopping drug and providing supportive treatment.
- Monitor CBC and platelet counts weekly during therapy and more frequently if anemia, neutropenia, or thrombocytopenia worsens.
- After treatment, monitor CD4+ count until it reaches 200 cells/mm^3 or more.

Nursing diagnoses

- Risk for infection related to immunocompromised state.
- Fatigue due to drug therapy.
- Deficient knowledge related to alemtuzumab therapy.

Planning and implementation

- Don't give as I.V. push or bolus. Infuse over 2 hours.
- Premedicate with 50 mg diphenhydramine and 650 mg acetaminophen 30 minutes before initial infusion and before each dose increase. May give 200 mg hydrocortisone to decrease severe infusion-related adverse events. Give anti-infective prophylaxis while patient is receiving therapy, such as TMP-sulfa DS b.i.d. three times weekly and 250 mg famciclovir (or equivalent) b.i.d. Prophylaxis should continue for 2 months, or until CD4+ count is 200 cells/mm^3 or more, whichever occurs later.
- Don't use solution if discolored or contains precipitate. Don't shake ampule before use. Filter with a sterile, low–protein-binding, 5-micron filter before dilution. Add to 100 ml normal saline solution or D_5W. Gently invert bag to mix solution. Use within 8 hours of dilution.

ALERT: Don't confuse alemtuzumab with trastuzumab.
- Irradiate blood if transfusions are needed to protect against graft vs. host disease.
- Don't immunize with live viral vaccines.
- If therapy is stopped for more than 7 days, restart with gradual dose increase.

Patient teaching

- Tell patient to report immediately infusion reactions, such as rigors, chills, fever, nausea, or vomiting.
- Advise patient to report immediately signs or symptoms of infection.
- Advise patient that blood tests will be done frequently during therapy to observe for adverse effects.
- Tell women of childbearing age and men to use effective contraceptive methods during therapy and for at least 6 months following completion of therapy.

☑ Evaluation

- Patient remains free from infection.
- Patient doesn't suffer any harmful drug-induced adverse reactions.
- Patient and family state understanding of drug therapy.

alendronate sodium

(ah-LEN-droh-nayt SOH-dee-um)
Fosamax

Pharmacologic class: inhibitor of osteoclast-mediated bone resorption
Therapeutic class: antiosteoporotic
Pregnancy risk category: C

Indications and dosages

▶ **Osteoporosis in postmenopausal women; to increase bone mass in men with osteoporosis.** *Adults:* 10 mg P.O. daily or 70-mg tablet P.O. once weekly with water at least 30 minutes before first food, beverage, or medication of the day.

▶ **Prevention of osteoporosis in postmenopausal women.** *Women:* 5 mg P.O. daily or 35-mg tablet P.O. once weekly taken with water at least 30 minutes before first food, beverage, or medication of the day.

▶ **With calcium and vitamin D supplementation in the treatment of corticosteroid-induced osteoporosis.** *Adults:* 5 mg P.O. daily. *Postmenopausal women not receiving estrogen replacement therapy:* 10 mg P.O. daily.

▶ **Paget's disease of bone.** *Adults:* 40 mg P.O. daily for 6 months taken with water at least 30 minutes before first food, beverage, or drug of the day.

Contraindications and precautions

- Contraindicated in patients with hypocalcemia, severe renal insufficiency, or hypersensitivity to drug or its components.
- Use cautiously in patients with dysphagia, esophageal diseases, gastritis, duodenitis, ulcers, or mild-to-moderate renal insufficiency.

Lifespan: In breast-feeding women and in children, safety of drug hasn't been established.

Adverse reactions

CNS: headache.
GI: abdominal pain, nausea, dyspepsia, constipation, diarrhea, flatulence, acid regurgitation, esophageal ulcer, vomiting, dysphagia, abdominal distention, gastritis, taste perversion.
Musculoskeletal: musculoskeletal pain.

Interactions

Drug-drug. *Antacids, calcium supplements, and many other oral medications:* Interferes with alendronate absorption. Have patient wait 30 minutes after alendronate dose before taking other drugs.
Aspirin, NSAIDs: May increase risk of upper GI reactions with alendronate doses greater than 10 mg daily. Monitor patient closely.
Drug-food. *Any food:* May decrease absorption of drug. Don't give drug with food.

Effects on lab test results

None reported.

Pharmacokinetics

Absorption: Absorbed from GI tract; food or beverages can significantly decrease bioavailability.
Distribution: Distributed to soft tissues but rapidly redistributed to bone or excreted in urine; about 78% protein-bound.
Metabolism: Doesn't appear to be metabolized.
Excretion: Excreted in urine. *Terminal half-life:* More than 10 years.

Route	Onset	Peak	Duration
P.O.	1 mo	3-6 mo	3 wk (after therapy)

Pharmacodynamics

Chemical effect: Suppresses osteoclast activity on newly formed resorption surfaces, reducing bone turnover.
Therapeutic effect: Increases bone mass.

Available forms

Tablets: 5 mg, 10 mg, 35 mg, 40 mg, 70 mg

NURSING PROCESS

Assessment

- Obtain history of patient's underlying disorder before therapy.
- Monitor calcium and phosphate levels throughout therapy.
- Be alert for adverse reactions and drug interactions.
- Evaluate patient's and family's knowledge of drug therapy.

Nursing diagnoses

- Risk for injury related to decreased bone mass
- Risk for deficient fluid volume related to drug-induced GI upset
- Deficient knowledge related to drug therapy

Planning and implementation

- Hypocalcemia and other disturbances of mineral metabolism (such as vitamin D deficiency) should be corrected before therapy begins.
- Give drug in the morning at least 30 minutes before first meal, fluid, or other oral drug administration.

ALERT: Don't confuse Fosamax with Flomax.

Patient teaching

- Advise patient to take drug with 6 to 8 ounces of water upon rising. Drug is absorbed better when taken on an empty stomach.

ALERT: Warn patient not to lie down for at least 30 minutes after taking drug to facilitate delivery to stomach and reduce potential for esophageal irritation.

- Tell patient to take supplemental calcium and vitamin D, if daily dietary intake is inadequate.
- Show patient how to perform weight-bearing exercises, which help increase bone mass.
- Urge patient to limit or restrict smoking and alcohol use, if appropriate.

Evaluation

- Patient remains free from bone fracture.
- Patient maintains adequate hydration.
- Patient and family state understanding of drug therapy.

alfentanil hydrochloride

(al-FEN-tah-nil high-droh-KLOR-ighd)
Alfenta

Pharmacologic class: opioid
Therapeutic class: analgesic, adjunct to anesthesia, anesthetic
Pregnancy risk category: C
Controlled substance schedule: II

Indications and dosages

▶ **Adjunct to general anesthetic.** *Adults:* Initially, 8 to 50 mcg/kg I.V.; then increments of 3 to 15 mcg/kg I.V. q 5 to 20 minutes. Reduced dosage needed for elderly and debilitated patients.

▶ **Primary anesthetic.** *Adults:* Initially, 130 to 245 mcg/kg I.V.; then 0.5 to 1.5 mcg/kg per minute I.V. Reduced dosage needed for elderly and debilitated patients.

Contraindications and precautions

- Contraindicated in patients hypersensitive to drug.
- Use cautiously in patients with head injury, pulmonary disease, decreased respiratory reserve, or hepatic or renal impairment.

Lifespan: With pregnant and breast-feeding women, use cautiously. In children younger than age 12, safety of drug hasn't been established.

Adverse reactions

CNS: blurred vision, agitation, anxiety, headache, confusion.
CV: hypotension, hypertension, ***bradycardia,*** tachycardia, palpitations, orthostatic hypotension.
GI: nausea, vomiting.
Musculoskeletal: intraoperative muscle movement.
Respiratory: ***chest wall rigidity, bronchospasm, respiratory depression, hypercapnia.***
Skin: itching.

Interactions

Drug-drug. *Cimetidine:* May cause CNS toxicity. Monitor patient.
CNS depressants: May have additive effects. Use together cautiously.

Diazepam: With high doses of alfentanil, may cause CV depression and decrease blood pressure. Use together cautiously.

Effects on lab test results

• May increase amylase and lipase levels.

Pharmacokinetics

Absorption: Administered I.V.
Distribution: More than 90% is protein-bound.
Metabolism: Metabolized in liver.
Excretion: Excreted in urine. *Half-life:* About 1½ hours.

Route	Onset	Peak	Duration
I.V.	1 min	1½-2 min	5-10 min

Pharmacodynamics

Chemical effect: Binds with opiate receptors in CNS, altering perception of and emotional response to pain through unknown mechanism.
Therapeutic effect: Enhances anesthetic effect and relieves pain.

Available forms

Injection: 500 mcg/ml

NURSING PROCESS

Assessment

• Assess patient's CV and respiratory status before and during therapy.
• Drug decreases rate and depth of respirations. Monitoring arterial oxygen saturation may aid in assessing effects of respiratory depression.
• Be alert for adverse reactions and drug interactions.
• Evaluate patient's and family's knowledge of drug therapy.

Nursing diagnoses

• Ineffective health maintenance related to need for surgery
• Ineffective breathing pattern related to drug-induced respiratory depression
• Deficient knowledge related to drug therapy

Planning and implementation

• Drug should be administered only by those specifically trained in use of I.V. anesthetics.
• Drug is compatible with D_5W, D_5W in lactated Ringer's solution, and normal saline solution. Most clinicians use infusions containing 25 to 80 mcg/ml.
• Stop infusion no less than 10 to 15 minutes before surgery ends.
• Use tuberculin syringe to administer small volumes of drug accurately.
• Keep narcotic antagonist (naloxone) and resuscitation equipment available.
• Notify prescriber immediately if assessment findings deviate from expected norm. Patient who has developed tolerance to other opioids may become tolerant to alfentanil as well.
ALERT: Don't confuse alfentanil with Anafranil, fentanyl, or sufentanil; or Alfenta with Sufenta.

Patient teaching

• Explain anesthetic effect of drug.
• Inform patient that another analgesic will be available after effects of drug have worn off.

Evaluation

• Patient regains previous health after alfentanil administration and recovers from surgery.
• Patient's respiratory status returns to normal after effects of drug wear off.
• Patient and family state understanding of drug therapy.

allopurinol

(al-oh-PYOOR-ih-nol)
Alloremed ◇, Capurate ◇, Lopurin, Zyloprim

Pharmacologic class: xanthine oxidase inhibitor
Therapeutic class: antigout drug
Pregnancy risk category: C

Indications and dosages

▶ **Gout, primary or secondary to hyperuricemia.** Dosage varies with severity of disease; can be given as single dose or in divided doses, but doses larger than 300 mg should be divided. *Adults:* Mild gout, 200 to 300 mg P.O. daily; severe gout with large tophi, 400 to 600 mg P.O. daily. Same dosage for maintenance in gout secondary to hyperuricemia.

▶ **Hyperuricemia secondary to malignancies.** *Children ages 6 to 10:* 300 mg P.O. daily or divided t.i.d.
Children younger than age 6: 50 mg P.O. t.i.d.
▶ **Prevention of acute gouty attacks.** *Adults:* 100 mg P.O. daily; increase at weekly intervals by 100 mg without exceeding maximum dose (800 mg), until uric acid level falls to 6 mg/100 ml or less.
▶ **Prevention of uric acid nephropathy during cancer chemotherapy.** *Adults:* 600 to 800 mg P.O. daily for 2 to 3 days, with high fluid intake.
▶ **Recurrent calcium oxalate calculi.** *Adults:* 200 to 300 mg P.O. daily in single or divided doses.
Patients with renal impairment: 100 mg q 3 days if creatinine clearance is up to 9 ml/minute; 100 mg q 2 days, 10 to 19 ml/minute; 100 mg daily, 20 to 39 ml/minute; 150 mg daily, 40 to 59 ml/minute; 200 mg daily, 60 to 79 ml/minute; 250 mg daily, 80 ml/minute.

Contraindications and precautions

• Contraindicated in patients with idiopathic hemochromatosis or hypersensitivity to drug.
Lifespan: In pregnant or breast-feeding women, use cautiously.

Adverse reactions

CNS: drowsiness, headache.
EENT: cataracts, retinopathy.
GI: nausea, vomiting, diarrhea, abdominal pain.
GU: ***renal failure,*** uremia.
Hematologic: ***agranulocytosis,*** anemia, ***aplastic anemia, thrombocytopenia.***
Hepatic: ***hepatitis.***
Skin: *rash, usually maculopapular;* ***exfoliative lesions;*** urticarial and purpuric lesions; ***erythema multiforme;*** severe furunculosis of nose; ichthyosis; ***toxic epidermal necrolysis.***

Interactions

Drug-drug. *ACE inhibitors:* Higher risk of hypersensitivity reaction. Monitor patient closely.
Amoxicillin, ampicillin, bacampicillin: Increases possibility of rash. Avoid using together.
Anticoagulants, dicumarol: Potentiates anticoagulant effect. Dosage adjustments may be needed.
Antineoplastics: May increase potential for bone marrow suppression. Monitor patient carefully.
Azathioprine, mercaptopurine (purinethol): May increase levels of these drugs. Dosage adjustments may be needed.
Chlorpropamide: May increase hypoglycemic effect. Avoid using together.
Diazoxide, diuretics, mecamylamine, pyrazinamide: May increase uric acid level. Allopurinol dosage adjustment may be needed.
Ethacrynic acid, thiazide diuretics: May increase risk of allopurinol toxicity. Reduce dosage of allopurinol and closely monitor renal function.
Uricosuric drugs: Additive effect. May be used to therapeutic advantage.
Urine-acidifying drugs: May increase possibility of kidney stone formation. Monitor patient carefully.
Xanthines: May increase theophylline level. Adjust dosage of theophylline.
Drug-lifestyle. *Alcohol use:* May increase uric acid level. Discourage using together.

Effects on lab test results

• May increase alkaline phosphatase, AST, ALT, BUN, and creatinine levels.
• May decrease hemoglobin, hematocrit, granulocyte and platelet counts.

Pharmacokinetics

Absorption: From 80% to 90% of dose is absorbed.
Distribution: Distributed widely throughout body except brain, where levels are 50% of those found elsewhere. Allopurinol and oxypurinol aren't bound to plasma proteins.
Metabolism: Metabolized to oxypurinol by xanthine oxidase.
Excretion: Excreted primarily in urine, with minute amount excreted in feces. *Half-life:* Allopurinol, 1 to 2 hours; oxypurinol, about 15 hours.

Route	Onset	Peak	Duration
P.O.			
allopurinol	2-3 days	0.5-2 hr	1-2 wk
oxypurinol	4.5-5 hr		

Pharmacodynamics

Chemical effect: Reduces uric acid production by inhibiting biochemical reactions preceding its formation.
Therapeutic effect: Alleviates gout symptoms.

Available forms

Capsules: 100 mg, 300 mg
Tablets (scored): 100 mg, 300 mg

NURSING PROCESS

Assessment

- Assess patient's history. Gout may be secondary to such diseases as acute or chronic leukemia, polycythemia vera, multiple myeloma, and psoriasis.
- Assess patient's uric acid level, joint stiffness, and pain before and during therapy. Optimal benefits may require 2 to 6 weeks of therapy.
- Monitor fluid intake and output. Daily urine output of at least 2 L and maintenance of neutral or slightly alkaline urine are desirable.
- Monitor CBC and hepatic and renal function at start of therapy and periodically during therapy.
- Be alert for adverse reactions and drug interactions.
- Evaluate patient's and family's knowledge of drug therapy.

Nursing diagnoses

- Acute pain (joint) related to patient's underlying condition
- Risk for infection related to drug-induced agranulocytosis
- Deficient knowledge related to drug therapy

Planning and implementation

- Give drug with or immediately after meals to minimize adverse GI reactions.
- Have patient drink plenty of fluids while taking drug, unless contraindicated.
- Notify prescriber if renal insufficiency occurs during treatment; this usually warrants dosage reduction.

ALERT: Don't confuse Zyloprim with Zorprin.

- Give colchicine with allopurinol, if ordered. This combination prophylactically treats acute gout attacks that may occur in first 6 weeks of therapy.

Patient teaching

- Advise patient to refrain from driving or performing hazardous tasks requiring mental alertness until CNS effects of drug are known.
- Advise patient taking allopurinol for treatment of recurrent calcium oxalate stones to reduce intake of animal protein, sodium, refined sugars, oxalate-rich foods, and calcium.
- Tell patient to stop drug at first sign of rash, which may precede severe hypersensitivity or other adverse reaction. Rash is more common in patients taking diuretics and in those with renal disorders. Tell patient to report all adverse reactions immediately.
- Advise patient to avoid alcohol consumption during drug therapy.

Evaluation

- Patient expresses relief of joint pain.
- Patient is free from infection.
- Patient and family state understanding of drug therapy.

almotriptan malate

(AL-moh-trip-tan MAH-layt)
Axert

Pharmacologic classification: serotonin 5-HT_1 receptor agonist
Therapeutic classification: antimigraine drug
Pregnancy risk category: C

Indications and dosages

▶ **Acute migraine with or without aura.**
Adults: 6.25-mg or 12.5-mg tablet P.O., with one additional dose after 2 hours if headache is unresolved or recurs. Maximum, two doses within 24 hours.
Patients with hepatic or renal impairment: Initially, 6.25 mg P.O. daily, with a maximum daily dose of 12.5 mg.

Contraindications and precautions

- Contraindicated in patients hypersensitive to almotriptan or its components. Also contraindicated in those with angina pectoris, history of MI, silent ischemia, uncontrolled hypertension, coronary artery vasospasm (for example,

Prinzmetal's variant angina), other CV disease, or hemiplegic or basilar migraine.

- Don't give within 24 hours after treatment with other serotonin agonists or ergotamine drugs.
- Use cautiously in patients with renal or hepatic impairment and in those with cataracts because of the potential for corneal opacities.
- Use cautiously in patients with risk factors for coronary artery disease (CAD), such as obesity, diabetes, and family history of CAD.

Lifespan: In breast-feeding women, use cautiously because it isn't known whether drug appears in breast milk. No drug studies on children are available; therefore, drug isn't recommended for use in children.

Adverse reactions

CNS: paresthesia, headache, *dizziness, somnolence.*

GI: nausea, dry mouth.

Interactions

Drug-drug. *CYP2D6 inhibitors, MAO inhibitors:* May increase level of almotriptan. Although no adverse clinical effects are reported, monitor patient for potential adverse reaction. May need to reduce dosage.

CYP3A4 inhibitors such as ketoconazole: May increase level of almotriptan. Monitor patient for potential adverse reaction. May need to reduce dosage.

Ergot-containing drugs, serotonin$_{1B/1D}$ agonists: May cause additive effects. Avoid using together.

Selective serotonin reuptake inhibitors: May cause additive serotonin effects, resulting in weakness, hyperreflexia, or incoordination. Monitor patient closely if given together.

Effects on lab test results

None reported.

Pharmacokinetics

Absorption: Rapid and extensive; reaches peak level in 1 to 3 hours. Food doesn't affect absorption.

Distribution: Protein-binding is minimal and volume of distribution is high.

Metabolism: No active metabolites. Monoamine oxidase-A and P-450 3A4 and 2D6 are responsible for the majority of metabolism.

Excretion: 75% is eliminated through renal excretion. *Half-life:* 3 to 4 hours.

Route	Onset	Peak	Duration
P.O.	1-3 hr	1-3 hr	3-4 hr

Pharmacodynamics

Chemical effect: Binds selectively to various serotonin receptors. Its primary agonistic effect occurs on serotonin$_{1B/1D}$ receptors resulting in cranial vessel constriction, which inhibits the subsequent cascade of events that causes migraine headache.

Therapeutic effect: Blocks neuropeptide release to the pain pathways to prevent migraine headaches.

Available forms

Tablets: 6.25 mg, 12.5 mg

NURSING PROCESS

Assessment

- Assess patient's condition before and during drug therapy. The drug isn't intended for patient with ischemic heart disease or hemiplegic or basilar migraine.
- Obtain list of patient's medication intake within 24 hours to prevent drug-drug interactions. Use caution when giving drug to patient who is taking an MAO inhibitor or a CYP-450 3A4 or 2D6 inhibitor. Don't give drug with other serotonin agonist or ergotamine derivatives.
- Be alert for any adverse reactions.
- Monitor ECG in patients with risk factors for CAD or with symptoms similar to those of CAD, such as chest or throat tightness, pain, and heaviness.
- Evaluate patient's and family's knowledge of drug therapy.

Nursing diagnoses

- Acute pain related to presence of acute migraine attack.
- Risk for injury related to drug-induced interactions.
- Deficient knowledge related to almotriptan therapy.

Planning and implementation

- Give dose as soon as patient complains of migraine symptoms.

• Reduce dosage in patients with poor renal or hepatic function.
• Repeat dose after 2 hours if needed.
• Don't give more than two doses within 24 hours.

Patient teaching
• Advise patient to take drug only when he is having a migraine.
• Teach patient to avoid possible migraine triggers, such as cheese, chocolate, citrus fruits, caffeine, and alcohol.
• Advise patient to repeat dose only once within 24 hours and no sooner than 2 hours after initial dose.
• Advise patient that other commonly prescribed migraine medications may interact with almotriptan.
• Advise patient to report chest, throat, jaw, or neck tightness, pain, or heaviness immediately and to discontinue use of drug until further notice from prescriber.
• Advise patient to use caution while driving or operating machinery while receiving drug therapy.

Evaluation
• Patient's symptoms are alleviated and patient is free from pain.
• Serious complications from drug interactions don't develop.
• Patient and family state understanding of drug therapy.

alosetron hydrochloride
(a-LOE-se-tron high-droh-KLOR-ighd)
Lotronex

Pharmacologic classification: selective 5-HT_3 receptor antagonist
Therapeutic classification: GI agent
Pregnancy risk category: B

Indications and dosages
▶ **Treatment of irritable bowel syndrome (IBS) in women with severe diarrhea.**
Women: 1 mg P.O. b.i.d. with or without food.

Contraindications and precautions
• Contraindicated in patients hypersensitive to alosetron or its components and in patients with a history of chronic or severe constipation, sequelae from constipation, intestinal obstruction, stricture, toxic megacolon, GI perforation, GI adhesions, ischemic colitis, impaired intestinal circulation, thrombophlebitis, or hypercoagulable state. Also contraindicated in patients with current or history of Crohn's disease, ulcerative colitis, or diverticulitis. Patients shouldn't take alosetron if they are constipated or if their chief bowel symptom is constipation.
Lifespan: In breast-feeding women, use cautiously because it's unknown whether alosetron or its metabolites appear in breast milk. Use in children hasn't been studied and, therefore, isn't recommended. In elderly patients, use cautiously because they may be at greater risk for complications of constipation.

Adverse reactions
CNS: headache, sedation, abnormal dreams, anxiety, sleep and depressive disorders.
CV: ***arrhythmias,*** *hypertension.*
EENT: *photophobia, allergic rhinitis, throat and tonsil discomfort and pain, bacterial ear, nose, and throat infections.*
GI: *constipation,* nausea, GI discomfort and pain, abdominal discomfort and pain, abdominal distention, gaseous symptoms, viral gastrointestinal infections, proctitis, hemorrhoids, dyspeptic symptoms, ***ileus, perforation, ischemic colitis, small bowel mesenteric ischemia.***
GU: UTI, polyuria, diuresis.
Respiratory: *cough.*
Skin: rash, acne, folliculitis.

Interactions
Drug-drug. *Hydralazine, isoniazid, procainamide:* May slow metabolism and increase level of these drugs because of inhibition of N-acetyltransferase. Monitor patient for toxicity.

Effects on lab test results
• May increase ALT, AST, alkaline phosphatase, and bilirubin levels.

Pharmacokinetics
Absorption: Rapid. Mean absolute bioavailability is 50% to 60%. Food decreases rate of absorption by 25%.

Distribution: Alosetron is 82% bound to plasma proteins.
Metabolism: Extensively metabolized in the liver by cytochrome P-450 enzymes (2C9, 3A4, 1A2) and other hepatic mechanisms (11%).
Excretion: Excreted 7% unchanged in urine. Radiolabeled dose 73% eliminated in urine and 24% in feces. *Half-life:* 90 minutes.

Route	Onset	Peak	Duration
P.O.	Unknown	1 hr	Variable

Pharmacodynamics

Chemical effect: Alosetron selectively inhibits 5-HT_3 receptors on enteric neurons in the GI tract. By inhibiting activation of these cation channels, neuronal depolarization is blocked, resulting in decreased visceral pain, colonic transit, and GI secretions, which usually contribute to the symptoms of IBS.
Therapeutic effect: Relieves pain and decreases frequency of loose stools caused by IBS.

Available forms

Tablets: 1 mg

NURSING PROCESS

Assessment

ALERT: Not indicated for use in men.
- Don't use in patient whose main symptom is constipation.
- Assess patient before and during drug therapy.

Nursing diagnoses

- Diarrhea related to underlying IBS condition.
- Acute pain related to underlying IBS condition.
- Deficient knowledge related to drug therapy.

Planning and implementation

ALERT: Explain to patient that she must be enrolled in the GlaxoSmithKline Prescribing Program. Counsel the patient about the risks and benefits of the drug, give instruction, answer questions, and give her a medication guide. The patient must review and sign a patient-physician agreement. A special program sticker must be affixed to all written prescriptions; no telephone, facsimile, or computerized prescriptions are permitted.
- If patients develop constipation while on this drug, therapy should be suspended and the usual care of laxatives and fiber should be prescribed until the constipation resolves.

ALERT: Fatalities have occurred when patient has developed ischemic colitis and serious complications of constipation. If patient complains of rectal bleeding or sudden worsening of abdominal pain, therapy should be discontinued and acute ischemic colitis should be ruled out.
- Acute symptoms of toxicity include labored respiration, ataxia, subdued behavior, tremors, and seizures. No antidote exists for alosetron overdose. Treatment for overdose includes supportive care.

Patient teaching
- Instruct patient not to start alosetron if she is constipated.

ALERT: Urge patient to be alert for constipation or signs and symptoms of ischemic colitis, such as rectal bleeding, bloody diarrhea, or worsened abdominal pain or cramping. Tell patient to discontinue drug and consult prescriber immediately if symptoms occur.
- Explain that this drug isn't a cure but may alleviate some of the symptoms of IBS. If the drug doesn't adequately control symptoms after twice-daily therapy, advise patient to discontinue and contact prescriber.
- Inform patient that most women notice their symptoms improving after about 1 week of therapy, but some may take up to 4 weeks to experience relief of abdominal pain, discomfort, and diarrhea. Symptoms usually return within 1 week of stopping therapy.

Evaluation

- Patient's symptoms, including pain and frequency of loose stools, related to IBS are relieved.
- Patient and family state understanding of drug therapy.

alprazolam

(al-PRAH-zoh-lam)
Apo-Alpraz ◇, Novo-Alprazol ◇, Nu-Alpraz ◇, Xanax

Pharmacologic class: benzodiazepine
Therapeutic class: anxiolytic

Pregnancy risk category: D
Controlled substance schedule: IV

Indications and dosages

▶ **Anxiety.** *Adults:* Usual initial dose, 0.25 to 0.5 mg P.O. t.i.d. Maximum, 4 mg daily in divided doses.
Elderly or debilitated patients or those with advanced liver disease: Usual initial dose, 0.25 mg P.O. b.i.d. or t.i.d. Maximum, 4 mg daily in divided doses.
▶ **Panic disorders.** *Adults:* 0.5 mg P.O. t.i.d., increased q 3 to 4 days in increments of no more than 1 mg. Maximum, 10 mg daily in divided doses.

Contraindications and precautions

- Contraindicated in patients with acute angle-closure glaucoma or hypersensitivity to drug or other benzodiazepines.
- Use cautiously in patients with hepatic, renal, or pulmonary disease.

Lifespan: In pregnant women, use with extreme caution because infant could be at risk for withdrawal symptoms. In breast-feeding women, drug therapy isn't recommended. In children, safety of drug hasn't been established.

Adverse reactions

CNS: drowsiness, light-headedness, headache, confusion, hostility, anterograde amnesia, restlessness, psychosis.
CV: transient hypotension, tachycardia.
EENT: vision disturbances.
GI: dry mouth, nausea, vomiting, constipation, discomfort.
GU: incontinence, urine retention, menstrual irregularities.

Interactions

Drug-drug. *Antihistamines, antipsychotics, CNS depressants:* May increase CNS depression. Avoid using together.
Cimetidine: May increase sedation. Monitor patient carefully.
Digoxin: May increase digoxin level, increasing toxicity. Monitor patient closely.
Fluoxetine, oral contraceptives: May increase alprazolam level. Watch for toxicity.
Tricyclic antidepressants: May increase tricyclic antidepressant level. Watch for toxicity.
Drug-herb. *Calendula, hops, lemon balm, skullcap, valerian:* May enhance sedative effects. Discourage using together.
Kava: May enhance CNS sedation. Discourage using together.
Drug-lifestyle. *Alcohol use:* May increase CNS depression. Discourage using together.
Smoking: May decrease effectiveness of benzodiazepine. Help patient to quit smoking.

Effects on lab test results

- May increase ALT and AST levels.

Pharmacokinetics

Absorption: Well absorbed.
Distribution: Distributed widely throughout body; 80% to 90% of dose is bound to plasma protein.
Metabolism: Metabolized in liver equally to alpha-hydroxyalprazolam and inactive metabolites.
Excretion: Alpha-hydroxyalprazolam and other metabolites are excreted in urine. *Half-life:* 6.3 to 26.9 hours.

Route	Onset	Peak	Duration
P.O.	Unknown	1-2 hr	Unknown

Pharmacodynamics

Chemical effect: Unknown. Probably potentiates effects of GABA, an inhibitory neurotransmitter, and depresses CNS at limbic and subcortical levels of brain.
Therapeutic effect: Decreases anxiety.

Available forms

Oral solution: 0.5 mg/5 ml, 1 mg/ml (concentrate)
Tablets: 0.25 mg, 0.5 mg, 1 mg, 2 mg

NURSING PROCESS

Assessment

- Assess patient's anxiety before and frequently after therapy.
- In patient receiving repeated or prolonged therapy, monitor liver, renal, and hematopoietic function test results periodically.
- Be alert for adverse reactions and drug interactions.
- Evaluate patient's and family's knowledge of drug therapy.

Nursing diagnoses
- Anxiety related to patient's underlying condition
- Risk for injury related to drug-induced CNS reactions
- Deficient knowledge related to drug therapy

Planning and implementation
- Drug shouldn't be given for everyday stress or for long-term use (more than 4 months).
- When giving drug, check to see that patient has swallowed tablets before leaving.
- Expect to give lower doses at longer intervals in elderly or debilitated patients.

ALERT: Don't withdraw drug abruptly after long-term use; withdrawal symptoms may occur. Abuse or addiction is possible.

ALERT: Don't confuse alprazolam with alprostadil or Xanax with Zantac or Tenex.

Patient teaching
- Warn patient to avoid hazardous activities that require alertness and psychomotor coordination until CNS effects of drug are known.
- Tell patient to avoid alcohol consumption and smoking while taking drug.
- Caution patient to take drug as prescribed and not to stop without prescriber's approval. Inform him of potential for dependence if taken longer than directed.
- Teach patient how to manage or avoid adverse reactions, such as constipation and drowsiness.

Evaluation
- Patient is less anxious.
- Patient doesn't experience injury from adverse CNS reactions.
- Patient and family state understanding of drug therapy.

alprostadil
(al-PROS-tuh-dil)
Prostin VR Pediatric

Pharmacologic class: prostaglandin
Therapeutic class: ductus arteriosus patency adjunct
Pregnancy risk category: NR

Indications and dosages
▶ **Palliative therapy for temporary maintenance of patent ductus arteriosus until surgery can be performed.** *Infants:* 0.05 to 0.1 mcg/kg per minute by I.V. infusion. When therapeutic response is achieved, reduce infusion rate to lowest dosage that will maintain response. Maximum dosage is 0.4 mcg/kg per minute. Alternatively, drug can be given through umbilical artery catheter placed at ductal opening.

Contraindications and precautions
Lifespan: In neonates with bleeding tendencies, use cautiously because drug inhibits platelet aggregation. In neonates with respiratory distress syndrome or in premature infants with a patent ductus arteriosus, drug is contraindicated.

Adverse reactions
CNS: fever, *seizures.*
CV: flushing, ***bradycardia, cardiac arrest,*** hypotension, tachycardia.
GI: diarrhea.
Hematologic: ***DIC.***
Respiratory: **APNEA.**
Other: ***sepsis.***

Interactions
None significant.

Effects on lab test results
- May decrease potassium level.

Pharmacokinetics
Absorption: Administered I.V.
Distribution: Distributed rapidly throughout body.
Metabolism: About 68% of dose is metabolized in one pass through lung, primarily by oxidation; 100% is metabolized within 24 hours.
Excretion: All metabolites are excreted in urine within 24 hours. *Half-life:* About 5 to 10 minutes.

Route	Onset	Peak	Duration
I.V.	5-10 min	20 min	1-3 hr

Pharmacodynamics
Chemical effect: Relaxes smooth muscle of ductus arteriosus.

Therapeutic effect: Improves cardiac circulation.

Available forms

Injection: 500 mcg/ml

NURSING PROCESS

Assessment

- Obtain baseline assessment of infant's cardiopulmonary status before therapy.
- Measure drug's effectiveness by monitoring blood oxygenation of infants with restricted pulmonary blood flow and by systemic blood pressure and blood pH of infants with restricted systemic blood flow.
- Be alert for adverse reactions throughout therapy.
- Evaluate parent's knowledge of drug therapy.

Nursing diagnoses

- Ineffective cardiopulmonary tissue perfusion related to underlying condition
- Risk for injury related to drug-induced adverse reactions
- Deficient knowledge related to drug therapy

Planning and implementation

- A differential diagnosis should be made between respiratory distress syndrome and cyanotic heart disease before drug is given. Don't use drug in neonates with respiratory distress syndrome.
- Dilute drug before administering. Prepare fresh solution daily; discard solution after 24 hours.

ALERT: Don't use diluents that contain benzyl alcohol. Fatal toxic syndrome may occur.

- Drug isn't recommended for direct injection or intermittent infusion. Give by continuous infusion using constant-rate pump. Infuse through large peripheral or central vein or through umbilical artery catheter placed at level of ductus arteriosus. If flushing occurs as a result of peripheral vasodilation, reposition catheter.
- Reduce infusion rate if fever or significant hypotension develops in infant.
- If apnea and bradycardia develop, stop infusion immediately. This may reflect drug overdose.
- Keep respiratory and emergency equipment available.
- In prolonged infusions, infant may develop gastric outlet obstruction, morphologic changes in pulmonary arteries, and proliferation of long bones.

ALERT: Don't confuse alprostadil with alprazolam.

Patient teaching

- Keep parents informed of infant's status.
- Explain that parents will be allowed as much time and physical contact with infant as feasible.

Evaluation

- Patient demonstrates stable and effective cardiopulmonary status as indicated by adequate cardiac and pulmonary parameters and peripheral systemic perfusion.
- Patient has no injury from adverse drug reactions.
- Parents state understanding of drug therapy.

alteplase (tissue plasminogen activator, recombinant; tPA)

(AL-teh-plays)

Actilyse ◇, Activase, Cathflo Activase

Pharmacologic class: enzyme
Therapeutic class: thrombolytic enzyme
Pregnancy risk category: C

Indications and dosages

▶ **Lysis of thrombi obstructing coronary arteries in acute MI.** *Adults:* 100 mg I.V. infusion over 3 hours as follows: 60 mg in first hour, of which 6 to 10 mg is given as bolus over first 1 to 2 minutes. Then, 20 mg/hour infusion for 2 hours. Smaller adults (less than 65 kg [143 lb]) should receive 1.25 mg/kg in similar fashion (60% in first hour with 10% as bolus, then 20% of total dose per hour for 2 hours). Don't exceed 100-mg dose. Higher doses may increase risk of intracranial bleeding.

▶ **Management of acute massive pulmonary embolism.** *Adults:* 100 mg I.V. infusion over 2 hours. Heparin begun at end of infusion when PTT or PT returns to twice normal or less. Don't exceed 100-mg dose. Higher doses may increase risk of intracranial bleeding.

Also,‡ may infuse 30 or 50 mg intrapulmonary artery over 1½ or 2 hours, respectively, in conjunction with heparin therapy.

▶ **Management of acute ischemic CVA.** *Adults:* 0.9 mg/kg (maximum 90 mg) I.V. over 60 minutes with 10% of the total dose given as initial bolus over 1 minute.

▶ **Restoration of function to central venous access devices as assessed by the ability to withdraw blood.** ***Cathflo Activase.*** *Adults and children older than age 2 and weighing more than 30 kg (66 lbs):* Instill 2 mg in 2 ml sterile water into catheter.

Adults and children older than age 2 and weighing 10 kg (22 lbs) to 30 kg (66 lbs): Instill 110% of the internal lumen volume of the catheter, not to exceed 2 mg. After 30 minutes of dwell time, assess catheter function by aspirating blood. If function is restored, aspirate 4 to 5 ml of blood to remove Cathflo Activase and residual clot, and gently irrigate the catheter with normal saline solution. If catheter function not restored after 2 hours, instill a second dose.

▶ **Prevention of reocclusion after thrombolysis for acute MI‡.** *Adults:* 3.3 mcg/kg per minute by I.V. infusion for 4 hours with heparin therapy immediately following initial thrombolytic infusion.

▶ **Lysis of arterial occlusion in a peripheral vessel or bypass graft.** *Adults:* 0.05 to 0.1 mg/kg per hour infused via the intrapulmonary artery for 1 to 8 hours.

Contraindications and precautions

- Contraindicated in patients with active internal bleeding, intracranial neoplasm, arteriovenous malformation, aneurysm, severe uncontrolled hypertension, history of CVA, known bleeding diathesis, or intraspinal or intracranial trauma or surgery within past 2 months.
- Use cautiously in patients who had major surgery within past 10 days; in those with organ biopsy; trauma (including cardiopulmonary resuscitation); GI or GU bleeding; cerebrovascular disease; hypertension; mitral stenosis, atrial fibrillation, or other condition that may lead to left-sided heart thrombus; acute pericarditis or subacute bacterial endocarditis; septic thrombophlebitis; or diabetic hemorrhagic retinopathy; and in patients receiving anticoagulants.

Lifespan: During pregnancy, the first 10 days postpartum, and lactation, use cautiously. In children, safety of drug hasn't been established. In patients age 75 and older, use cautiously.

Adverse reactions

CNS: ***cerebral hemorrhage,*** fever.
CV: hypotension, ***arrhythmias,*** edema.
GI: nausea, vomiting.
Hematologic: ***severe, spontaneous bleeding.***
Musculoskeletal: arthralgia.
Skin: urticaria.
Other: bleeding at puncture sites, hypersensitivity reactions, ***anaphylaxis.***

Interactions

Drug-drug. *Aspirin, coumarin anticoagulants, dipyridamole, heparin:* May increase risk of bleeding. Monitor patient carefully.
Drug-herb. *Dong quai, garlic, ginkgo:* May increase risk of bleeding. Discourage using together.

Effects on lab test results

None reported.

Pharmacokinetics

Absorption: Administered I.V.
Distribution: Rapidly cleared from plasma by liver (about 80% cleared within 10 minutes after infusion stops).
Metabolism: Primarily hepatic.
Excretion: Over 85% excreted in urine, 5% in feces. *Half-life:* Less than 10 minutes.

Route	Onset	Peak	Duration
I.V.	Immediate	About 45 min	About 4 hr

Pharmacodynamics

Chemical effect: Binds to fibrin in thrombus and locally converts plasminogen to plasmin, which initiates local fibrinolysis.
Therapeutic effect: Dissolves blood clots in coronary arteries and lungs.

Available forms

Injection: 50-mg (29 million IU), 100-mg (58 million IU) vials
Solution for intracatheter clearance: 2-mg single-use vials

NURSING PROCESS

Assessment
- Assess patient's cardiopulmonary status (including ECG, vital signs, and coagulation studies) before and during therapy.
- Be alert for adverse reactions and drug interactions.
- Monitor patient for internal bleeding, and check puncture site frequently.
- Assess the cause of catheter dysfunction before using Cathflo Activase. Conditions that can occlude the catheter include catheter malposition, mechanical failure, constriction by a suture, and lipid deposits or drug precipitates within the catheter lumen. Don't attempt to suction because of the risk of damage to the vascular wall or collapse of soft-walled catheters.
- Evaluate patient's and family's knowledge of drug therapy.

Nursing diagnoses
- Ineffective cardiopulmonary tissue perfusion related to patient's underlying condition
- Risk for injury related to adverse effects of drug therapy
- Deficient knowledge related to drug therapy

Planning and implementation
Actilyse ◇, Activase
- Recanalization of occluded coronary arteries and improvement of heart function require starting alteplase as soon as possible after onset of symptoms.
- Reconstitute drug with sterile water (without preservatives) for injection only. Check manufacturer's label for specific information. Don't use vial if vacuum seal isn't present. Reconstitute with large-bore (18G) needle, directing stream of sterile water at lyophilized cake. Don't shake, but make sure that drug is dissolved completely. Slight foaming is common, and solution should be clear or pale yellow.
- Drug may be given as reconstituted (1 mg/ml) or diluted with equal volume of normal saline solution or D_5W to make 0.5 mg/ml solution. Adding other drugs to infusion isn't recommended.
- Reconstitute alteplase solution immediately before use, and give within 8 hours because it contains no preservatives. Drug may be stored temporarily at 35° to 86° F (2° to 30° C), but it's stable for only 8 hours at room temperature. Discard unused solution.
- Heparin is frequently started after treatment with alteplase to reduce risk of rethrombosis.
- For arterial puncture, select site on arm and apply pressure for 30 minutes afterward. Also use pressure dressings, sand bags, or ice packs on recent puncture sites to prevent bleeding.
- Notify prescriber if severe bleeding occurs and doesn't stop with intervention; alteplase and heparin infusions will need to be discontinued.

ALERT: Have antiarrhythmics available. Coronary thrombolysis is linked to arrhythmias induced by reperfusion of ischemic myocardium.
- Avoid invasive procedures during thrombolytic therapy.

Cathflo Activase
- Reconstitute Cathflo Activase with 2.2 ml sterile water. Dissolve completely into a colorless to pale yellow solution that yields a concentration of 1 mg/ml. Solutions are stable for up to 8 hours at room temperature.
- Don't use excessive pressure while instilling Cathflo Activase into the catheter because it could cause catheter rupture or expulsion of the clot into the circulation.

Patient teaching
- Tell patient to report immediately chest pain, dyspnea, changes in heart rate or rhythm, nausea, and bleeding.

Evaluation
- Patient's cardiopulmonary assessment findings demonstrate improved perfusion.
- Patient has no serious adverse drug reactions.
- Patient and family state understanding of drug therapy.

aluminum carbonate
(uh-LOO-mih-num KAR-buh-nayt)
Basaljel†

Pharmacologic class: inorganic aluminum salt
Therapeutic class: antacid, hypophosphatemic drug
Pregnancy risk category: B

Indications and dosages

▶ **Antacid; relief of peptic ulcer symptoms.** *Adults:* Two tablets or capsules, or 10 ml suspension (in water or fruit juice) q 2 hours p.r.n. up to 12 times daily.

▶ **Hyperphosphatemia and prevention of urinary phosphate stones (with low-phophate diet).** *Adults:* 1 g P.O. t.i.d. or q.i.d. After monitoring diet and phosphate level, adjust to lowest possible dosage after therapy begins.

Contraindications and precautions

- No known contraindications.
- Use cautiously in patients with chronic renal disease.

Lifespan: No known contraindications.

Adverse reactions

GI: anorexia, constipation, intestinal obstruction.
Metabolic: hypophosphatemia.

Interactions

Drug-drug. *Allopurinol, antibiotics (including quinolones and tetracyclines), corticosteroids, diflunisal, digoxin, ethambutol, H_2-receptor antagonists, iron, isoniazid, penicillamine, phenothiazines, thyroid hormones:* May decrease pharmacologic effect because of possible impaired absorption. Give aluminum carbonate separately.
Enteric-coated drugs: May release prematurely in stomach. Separate doses by at least 1 hour.

Effects on lab test results

- May increase gastrin level. May decrease phosphate level.

Pharmacokinetics

Absorption: Small amounts absorbed.
Distribution: None.
Metabolism: None.
Excretion: In feces.

Route	Onset	Peak	Duration
P.O.	Unknown	Unknown	20-40 min if fasting; up to 3 hr if taken 1 hr after meals

Pharmacodynamics

Chemical effect: Relieves GI discomfort and prevents phosphate stone formation in urinary tract.
Therapeutic effect: Relieves GI discomfort and prevents phosphate stone formation in urinary tract.

Available forms

Oral suspension: aluminum hydroxide equivalent 400 mg/5ml†
Tablets or capsules: aluminum hydroxide equivalent 500 mg†

NURSING PROCESS

Assessment

- Assess patient's discomfort before therapy and regularly thereafter.
- In patients with restricted sodium intake, monitor long-term, high-dose use. Each tablet, capsule, or 5 ml of suspension contains about 3 mg of sodium.
- Be alert for adverse reactions and drug interactions.
- Evaluate patient's and family's knowledge of drug therapy.

Nursing diagnoses

- Acute pain related to gastric hyperacidity
- Constipation related to drug's adverse effects
- Deficient knowledge related to drug therapy

Planning and implementation

- Shake suspension well; give with small amount of water or fruit juice to ease passage.
- When administering through NG tube, make sure tube is patent and placed correctly; after instilling, flush tube with water to ensure passage to stomach and to clear tube.
- Don't give other oral medications within 2 hours of antacid administration. This may cause premature release of enteric-coated drugs in stomach.

Patient teaching

- Caution patient to take aluminum carbonate only as directed, to shake suspension well, and to follow with sips of water or juice.
- Warn patient not to switch antacids without prescriber's advice.
- Warn patient that drug may color stool white or cause white streaks.

• Teach patient how to prevent constipation.

Evaluation
• Patient's pain is relieved.
• Patient maintains normal bowel function.
• Patient and family state understanding of drug therapy.

aluminum hydroxide
(uh-LOO-mih-num high-DROKS-ighd)
AlternaGEL†, Alu-Cap†, Alu-Tab†, Amphojel†, Dialume†, Nephrox†

Pharmacologic class: aluminum salt
Therapeutic class: antacid
Pregnancy risk category: C

Indications and dosages
▶ **Antacid; relief of peptic ulcer or gastric symptoms; hyperphosphatemia.** *Adults:* 500 to 1,500 mg P.O. (tablet or capsule) 1 hour after meals and h.s.; or 5 to 30 ml (suspension) as needed 1 hour after meals and h.s.

Contraindications and precautions
• No known contraindications.
• Use cautiously in patients with chronic renal disease.
Lifespan: In pregnant women, consult prescriber before giving.

Adverse reactions
GI: anorexia, constipation, intestinal obstruction.
Other: hypophosphatemia.

Interactions
Drug-drug. *Allopurinol, antibiotics (including quinolones and tetracyclines), corticosteroids, diflunisal, digoxin, ethambutol, H_2-receptor antagonists, iron, isoniazid, penicillamine, phenothiazines, thyroid hormones:* May decrease pharmacologic effect because of possible impaired absorption. Give aluminum hydroxide separately.
Enteric-coated drugs: May release prematurely in stomach. Separate doses by at least 1 hour.

Effects on lab test results
• May increase gastrin level. May decrease phosphate level.

Pharmacokinetics
Absorption: Small amounts absorbed.
Distribution: None.
Metabolism: None.
Excretion: Excreted in feces.

Route	Onset	Peak	Duration
P.O.	Varies: liquids more rapid than tablets or capsules	Unknown	20-60 min if fasting; 3 hr if taken 1 hr after meal

Pharmacodynamics
Chemical effect: Reduces total acid load in GI tract, elevates gastric pH to reduce pepsin activity, strengthens gastric mucosal barrier, and increases esophageal sphincter tone.
Therapeutic effect: Relieves GI discomfort.

Available forms
Capsules: 400 mg†, 500 mg†
Liquid: 600 mg/5 ml†
Suspension: 320 mg/5 ml†, 450 mg/5 ml†, 675 mg/5 ml†
Tablets: 300 mg†, 500 mg†, 600 mg†

NURSING PROCESS

Assessment
• Assess patient's discomfort before therapy and regularly thereafter.
• In patient with restricted sodium intake, monitor long-term, high-dose use. Each tablet, capsule, or 5 ml of suspension contains 2 to 3 mg of sodium.
• Be alert for adverse reactions and drug interactions.
• Evaluate patient's and family's knowledge of drug therapy.

Nursing diagnoses
• Acute pain related to gastric hyperacidity
• Constipation related to drug's adverse effects
• Deficient knowledge related to drug therapy

Planning and implementation
• Shake suspension well; give with small amount of milk or water to ease passage.
• When administering through NG tube, make sure tube is patent and placed correctly; after instilling, flush tube with water to ensure passage to stomach and to clear tube.

• Don't give other oral medications within 2 hours of antacid administration. This may cause premature release of enteric-coated drugs in stomach.

Patient teaching

• Advise patient not to take aluminum hydroxide indiscriminately or to switch antacids without prescriber's advice.
• Instruct patient to shake suspension well and to follow with sips of water or juice.
• Warn patient that drug may color stool white or cause white streaks.
• Teach patient how to prevent constipation.

Evaluation

• Patient's pain is relieved.
• Patient maintains normal bowel function.
• Patient and family state understanding of drug therapy.

amantadine hydrochloride

(uh-MAN-tah-deen high-droh-KLOR-ighd)

Antadine ◇, Symadine, Symmetrel

Pharmacologic class: synthetic cyclic primary amine
Therapeutic class: antiviral, antiparkinsonian
Pregnancy risk category: C

Indications and dosages

▶ **Prophylactic or symptomatic treatment of influenza type A virus; respiratory tract illnesses in geriatric or debilitated patients.** *Adults age 64 and younger and children age 10 and older:* 200 mg P.O. daily in single dose or divided b.i.d.
Children ages 1 to 9: 4.4 to 8.8 mg/kg P.O. daily in single dose or divided b.i.d. Maximum, 150 mg daily.
Adults older than age 64: 100 mg P.O. once daily. Treatment should continue for 24 to 48 hours after symptoms disappear. Prophylaxis should start as soon as possible after initial exposure and continue for at least 10 days. When inactivated influenza A vaccine is unavailable, may continue prophylactic treatment for the duration of known influenza A in the community because of repeated or suspected exposures. If used with influenza vaccine, dose is continued for 2 to 4 weeks until protection develops from vaccine.

▶ **Drug-induced extrapyramidal reactions.** *Adults:* 100 mg P.O. b.i.d. Occasionally, patients whose responses aren't optimal may benefit from an increase to 300 mg P.O. daily in divided doses.

▶ **Idiopathic parkinsonism, parkinsonian syndrome.** *Adults:* 100 mg P.O. b.i.d.; in patients who are seriously ill or receiving other antiparkinsonians, 100 mg daily for at least 1 week, then 100 mg b.i.d., p.r.n.

Contraindications and precautions

• Contraindicated in patients hypersensitive to drug.
• Use cautiously in patients with seizure disorders, heart failure, peripheral edema, hepatic disease, mental illness, eczematoid rash, renal impairment, orthostatic hypotension, or CV disease. Dosage may need adjustment in patients with renal failure.

Lifespan: In pregnant and breast-feeding women, use cautiously. In children younger than age 1, safety of drug hasn't been established. In elderly patients, use cautiously.

Adverse reactions

CNS: depression, fatigue, confusion, dizziness, psychosis, hallucinations, anxiety, irritability, ataxia, insomnia, weakness, headache, lightheadedness, difficulty concentrating.
CV: peripheral edema, orthostatic hypotension, ***heart failure.***
GI: anorexia, nausea, constipation, vomiting, dry mouth.
GU: urine retention.
Skin: livedo reticularis.

Interactions

Drug-drug. *Anticholinergics:* May increase adverse anticholinergic effects. Use together cautiously.
CNS stimulants: May cause additive CNS stimulation. Use together cautiously.
Hydrochlorothiazide, sulfamethoxazole, triamterene, trimethoprim: May increase amantadine levels. Use together cautiously.
Quinidine, quinine: May reduce renal clearance of amantadine. Use together cautiously.
Thioridazine: May worsen tremor in elderly patients. Monitor these patients closely.

Drug-herb. *Jimsonweed:* May adversely affect CV function. Discourage using together.

Effects on lab test results

None reported.

Pharmacokinetics

Absorption: Well absorbed from GI tract.
Distribution: Distributed widely throughout body; crosses blood-brain barrier.
Metabolism: About 10% of drug is metabolized.
Excretion: About 90% is excreted unchanged in urine, primarily by tubular secretion. Portion of drug may be excreted in breast milk. Excretion rate depends on urine pH. *Half-life:* About 24 hours; with renal dysfunction, may be prolonged to 10 days.

Route	Onset	Peak	Duration
P.O.			
antidyskinetic	48 hr	2-4 hr	Unknown
antiviral	Unknown	Unknown	Unknown

Pharmacodynamics

Chemical effect: May interfere with influenza A virus penetration into susceptible cells. In parkinsonism, action unknown.
Therapeutic effect: Protects against and reduces symptoms of influenza A viral infection and extrapyramidal symptoms.

Available forms

Capsules: 100 mg
Syrup: 50 mg/5 ml

NURSING PROCESS

Assessment

- Obtain baseline assessment of patient's exposure to influenza A virus or history of Parkinson's disease, as appropriate.
- Be alert for adverse reactions and drug interactions.
- Monitor patient's hydration status if adverse GI reactions occur.
- Evaluate patient's and family's knowledge of drug therapy.

Nursing diagnoses

- Ineffective health maintenance related to patient's underlying condition
- Risk for deficient fluid volume related to adverse GI reactions
- Deficient knowledge related to drug therapy

Planning and implementation

- Elderly patients are more susceptible to neurologic adverse effects. Giving drug in two daily doses rather than as single dose may reduce these effects.
- Give drug after meals for best absorption.

ALERT: Don't confuse amantadine with rimantadine.

Patient teaching

- Advise patient to take drug several hours before bedtime to prevent insomnia.
- Advise patient not to stand or change positions too quickly to prevent orthostatic hypotension.
- Instruct patient to report adverse reactions, especially dizziness, depression, anxiety, nausea, and urine retention.
- Warn patient with parkinsonism not to stop drug abruptly because doing so could cause a parkinsonian crisis.

Evaluation

- Patient exhibits improved health.
- Patient maintains adequate hydration.
- Patient and family state understanding of drug therapy.

amifostine

(am-eh-FOS-teen)
Ethyol

Pharmacologic class: organic thiophosphate cytoprotective drug
Therapeutic class: antimetabolite
Pregnancy risk category: C

Indications and dosages

▶ **Reduction of cumulative renal toxicity from repeated administration of cisplatin in patients with advanced ovarian cancer or non–small-cell lung cancer.** *Adults:* 910 mg/m² daily as a 15-minute I.V. infusion, starting 30 minutes before chemotherapy. If hypotension occurs and blood pressure doesn't return to normal within 5 minutes after stopping treatment, subsequent cycles should use 740 mg/m².

▶ **Reduction of moderate-to-severe xerostomia in patients undergoing postoperative radiation treatment for head or neck cancer.** *Adults:* 200 mg/m^2 daily as a 3-minute I.V. infusion, starting 15 to 30 minutes before standard fraction radiation therapy. Hydrate patient adequately before infusion. Give antiemetic before and with amifostine infusion. Monitor patient's blood pressure before and immediately after infusion, and periodically thereafter as indicated.

Contraindications and precautions

• Contraindicated in patients hypersensitive to aminothiol compounds or mannitol.
• Don't use drug in patients receiving chemotherapy for potentially curable malignancies (including certain malignancies of germ cell origin), except for patients involved in clinical studies. Also contraindicated in hypotensive or dehydrated patients and in those receiving antihypertensives that can't be stopped during the 24 hours preceding amifostine administration.
• Use cautiously in patients with ischemic heart disease, arrhythmias, heart failure, or history of CVA or transient ischemic attacks.
• Use cautiously in patients for whom common adverse effects (nausea, vomiting, and hypotension) are likely to have serious consequences.
Lifespan: Breast-feeding women shouldn't be given drug because it's unknown whether drug or its metabolites appear in breast milk. Use cautiously in children and in elderly patients because safety hasn't been established in these patients.

Adverse reactions

CNS: dizziness, somnolence, flushing or feeling of warmth, chills or feeling of coldness.
CV: hypotension.
EENT: sneezing.
GI: nausea, vomiting.
Metabolic: hypocalcemia.
Respiratory: hiccups.
Other: allergic reactions ranging from rash to rigors.

Interactions

Drug-drug. *Antihypertensives, other drugs that could potentiate hypotension:* May potentiate hypotension. Consider giving amifostine to patients taking these drugs.

Effects on lab test results

• May decrease calcium level.

Pharmacokinetics

Absorption: Administered I.V.
Distribution: Less than 10% remains in plasma 6 minutes after administration.
Metabolism: Metabolized to an active free thiol metabolite.
Excretion: Renally excreted. *Half-life (elimination):* 8 minutes.

Route	Onset	Peak	Duration
I.V.	5-8 min	Unknown	Unknown

Pharmacodynamics

Chemical effect: Dephosphorylated by alkaline phosphatase to pharmacologically active free thiol metabolite. Free thiol in normal tissues is available to bind to and detoxify reactive metabolites of cisplatin.
Therapeutic effect: Reduces toxic effects of cisplatin on renal tissue.

Available forms

Injection: 500 mg anhydrous base and 500 mg mannitol in 10-ml vial

NURSING PROCESS

Assessment

• Patients who receive amifostine should be adequately hydrated before administration. Keep patient supine during infusion.
• Monitor blood pressure every 5 minutes during infusion. If hypotension occurs and requires interrupting therapy, notify prescriber and place patient in Trendelenburg's position. Then give an infusion of normal saline solution, using a separate I.V. line. If blood pressure returns to normal within 5 minutes and patient is asymptomatic, restart infusion so full dose of drug can be given. If full dose can't be given, subsequent doses should be limited to 740 mg/m^2.
• Antiemetics, including dexamethasone 20 mg I.V. and a serotonin 5-HT_3 receptor antagonist, should be given before and with amifostine. Additional antiemetics may be needed

based on chemotherapeutic drugs administered.
• Monitor patient's fluid balance when drug is given with highly emetogenic chemotherapy.
• Monitor calcium level in patients at risk for hypocalcemia, such as those with nephrotic syndrome. Give calcium supplements if needed.
• Evaluate patient's and family's knowledge of drug therapy.

Nursing diagnoses

• Ineffective health maintenance related to neoplastic disease
• Deficient knowledge related to drug therapy

Planning and implementation

• Reconstitute each single-dose vial with 9.5 ml of sterile normal saline solution. Don't use other solutions to reconstitute drug. Reconstituted solution (500 mg amifostine/10 ml) is chemically stable for up to 5 hours at room temperature (about 77° F [25° C]) or up to 24 hours under refrigeration (35° to 46° F [2° to 8° C]).
• Drug can be prepared in polyvinyl chloride bags in concentrations of 5 to 40 mg/ml and has the same stability as when it is reconstituted in single-use vial.
• Inspect vial for particulate matter and discoloration before use. Don't use if cloudy or precipitate has formed.
• If possible, stop antihypertensive therapy 24 hours before giving drug. If antihypertensive therapy can't be stopped, don't use amifostine because severe hypotension may occur.
• Don't infuse for more than 15 minutes; longer infusion raises the risk of adverse reactions.

Patient teaching

• Instruct patient to remain in supine position throughout infusion.

Evaluation

• Patient shows positive response to drug.
• Patient and family state understanding of drug therapy.

amikacin sulfate

(am-eh-KAY-sin SUL-fayt)
Amikin

Pharmacologic class: aminoglycoside
Therapeutic class: antibiotic
Pregnancy risk category: D

Indications and dosages

▶ **Serious infections caused by sensitive strains of *Pseudomonas aeruginosa, Escherichia coli, Proteus, Klebsiella, Serratia, Enterobacter, Acinetobacter, Providencia, Citrobacter, Staphylococcus;* meningitis.** *Adults and children:* 15 mg/kg daily divided q 8 to 12 hours I.M. or I.V. infusion.
Neonates: Initially, loading dose of 10 mg/kg I.V., followed by 7.5 mg/kg q 12 hours.
Patients with impaired renal function: Initially, 7.5 mg/kg I.M. or I.V. Subsequent doses and frequency determined by drug level and renal function test results.
▶ **Uncomplicated UTI.** *Adults:* 250 mg I.M. or I.V. b.i.d.
▶ ***Mycobacterium avium* complex, with other drugs‡.** *Adults:* 15 mg/kg I.V. daily, in divided doses q 8 to 12 hours.
Patients with renal impairment: Initially, 7.5 mg/kg I.M or I.V. Subsequent doses and frequency determined by amikacin level. Keep peak level between 15 and 35 mcg/ml; trough level shouldn't exceed 10 mcg/ml.

Contraindications and precautions

• Contraindicated in patients hypersensitive to drug or other aminoglycosides.
• Use cautiously in patients with impaired renal function or neuromuscular disorders.
Lifespan: In pregnant women, use with extreme caution and only if benefit outweighs risk to fetus. In breast-feeding women, don't give drug. In neonates and infants, use cautiously. In elderly patients, use cautiously.

Adverse reactions

CNS: headache, lethargy, ***neuromuscular blockade.***
EENT: ototoxicity.
GU: ***nephrotoxicity.***
Hepatic: ***hepatic necrosis.***
Other: hypersensitivity reactions, ***anaphylaxis.***

Interactions

Drug-drug. *Acyclovir, amphotericin B, cephalothin, cisplatin, methoxyflurane, other aminoglycosides, vancomycin:* May increase nephrotoxicity. Use together cautiously.
Dimenhydrinate: May mask symptoms of ototoxicity. Use cautiously.
General anesthetics, neuromuscular blockers: May potentiate neuromuscular blockade. Monitor patient.
Indomethacin: May increase trough and peak levels of amikacin. Monitor amikacin level closely.
I.V. loop diuretics (such as furosemide): May increase ototoxicity. Use together cautiously.
Parenteral penicillins (such as ticarcillin): May cause amikacin inactivation in vitro. Don't mix.

Effects on lab test results

- May increase BUN, creatinine, nonprotein nitrogen, and urine urea levels.

Pharmacokinetics

Absorption: Rapidly absorbed after I.M. administration.
Distribution: Distributed widely; protein binding is minimal; drug crosses placenta.
Metabolism: None.
Excretion: Excreted primarily in urine by glomerular filtration. *Half-life:* 2 to 3 hours (adults); 30 to 86 hours (patients with severe renal damage).

Route	Onset	Peak	Duration
I.V.	Immediate	Immediate	8-12 hr
I.M.	Unknown	1 hr	8-12 hr

Pharmacodynamics

Chemical effect: Inhibits protein synthesis by binding directly to 30S ribosomal subunit. Generally bactericidal.
Therapeutic effect: Kills susceptible bacteria and many aerobic gram-negative organisms (including most strains of *Pseudomonas aeruginosa*) and some aerobic gram-positive organisms. Ineffective against anaerobes.

Available forms

Injection: 50 mg/ml, 250 mg/ml

NURSING PROCESS

Assessment

- Assess patient's infection, hearing, weight, and renal function test values before therapy and regularly thereafter.
- Watch for signs of ototoxicity, including tinnitus, vertigo, and hearing loss.
- Monitor amikacin level. Obtain blood for peak amikacin level 1 hour after I.M. injection and 30 minutes to 1 hour after infusion ends; for trough level, draw blood just before next dose. Don't collect blood in heparinized tube because heparin is incompatible with aminoglycosides. Peak level above 35 mcg/ml and trough level above 10 mcg/ml may raise the risk of toxicity.
- Be alert for signs of nephrotoxicity, including cells or casts in urine, oliguria, proteinuria, decreased creatinine clearance, and increased BUN and creatinine levels.
- Evaluate patient's and family's knowledge of drug therapy.

Nursing diagnoses

- Risk for infection related to bacteria
- Impaired urine elimination related to amikacin-induced nephrotoxicity
- Deficient knowledge related to drug therapy

Planning and implementation

- Obtain specimen for culture and sensitivity tests before first dose. Therapy may begin before receiving results.
- **I.V. use:** For adults, dilute in 100 to 200 ml of D_5W or normal saline solution and infuse over 30 to 60 minutes. Volume for children depends on dose. Infants should receive a 1- to 2-hour infusion.
– After I.V. infusion, flush line with normal saline solution or D_5W.
- **I.M. use:** Follow normal protocol.
- Therapy usually lasts 7 to 10 days.
- Drug potency isn't affected if solution turns light yellow.
- Patient should be well hydrated while taking drug to minimize renal tubule irritation.
- If no response occurs after 5 days, therapy may be stopped and new specimens obtained for culture and sensitivity testing.

ALERT: Don't confuse Amikin with Amicar or amikacin with anakinra.

Patient teaching
- Tell patient to immediately report changes in hearing or in appearance or elimination pattern of urine. Teach patient how to measure intake and output.
- Emphasize importance of drinking 2 L of fluid daily, unless contraindicated.
- Teach patient to watch for and promptly report signs of superinfection (continued fever and other signs of new infections, especially of upper respiratory tract).

☑ Evaluation
- Patient's infection is eradicated.
- Patient's renal function test values remain unchanged.
- Patient and family state understanding of drug therapy.

amiloride hydrochloride
(uh-MIL-uh-righd high-droh-KLOR-ighd)
Kaluril, Midamor

Pharmacologic class: potassium-sparing diuretic
Therapeutic class: diuretic, antihypertensive
Pregnancy risk category: B

Indications and dosages
▶ **Hypertension; edema caused by heart failure, usually in patients also taking thiazide or other potassium-wasting diuretics.** *Adults:* 5 mg P.O. daily. Increase to 10 mg daily, if necessary. Maximum, 20 mg daily.
▶ **Lithium-induced polyuria‡.** *Adults:* 5 to 10 mg P.O. b.i.d.

Contraindications and precautions
- Contraindicated in patients with potassium level higher than 5.5 mEq/L; in those receiving other potassium-sparing diuretics, such as spironolactone; in those with anuria, acute or chronic renal insufficiency, diabetic nephropathy, or hypersensitivity to drug.
- Use with extreme caution, if at all, in patients with diabetes mellitus.
- Use cautiously in patients with severe hepatic insufficiency and in debilitated patients.

Lifespan: In pregnant women, use cautiously. In breast-feeding women, drug is contraindicated. In neonates and infants, use cautiously. In children, safety of drug hasn't been established. In elderly patients, use cautiously.

Adverse reactions
CNS: headache, weakness, dizziness.
CV: orthostatic hypotension.
GI: nausea, anorexia, diarrhea, vomiting, abdominal pain, constipation.
GU: impotence.
Hematologic: ***aplastic anemia.***
Metabolic: ***hyperkalemia.***

Interactions
Drug-drug. *ACE inhibitors, potassium-containing salt substitutes, potassium-sparing diuretics, potassium supplements:* May cause hyperkalemia. Monitor potassium level closely.
Lithium: May decrease lithium clearance, increasing risk of lithium toxicity. Monitor lithium level.
NSAIDs: May decrease diuretic's effectiveness. Monitor patient for lack of therapeutic effect.
Drug-food. *Foods high in potassium, potassium-containing salt substitutes:* May cause hyperkalemia. Monitor potassium level closely.

Effects on lab test results
- May increase BUN and potassium levels. May decrease sodium level.
- May decrease hemoglobin, hematocrit, and neutrophil count. May cause abnormal liver function test values.

Pharmacokinetics
Absorption: About 50% of dose is absorbed from GI tract; food decreases absorption to 30%.
Distribution: Wide extravascular distribution.
Metabolism: Insignificant.
Excretion: Excreted primarily in urine. *Half-life:* 6 to 9 hours.

Route	Onset	Peak	Duration
P.O.	2 hr	6-10 hr	24 hr

Pharmacodynamics
Chemical effect: Inhibits sodium reabsorption and potassium excretion in distal tubule.
Therapeutic effect: Reduces blood pressure; promotes sodium and water excretion while blocking potassium excretion.

Available forms

Tablets: 5 mg

NURSING PROCESS

Assessment

- Assess patient's blood pressure, urine output, weight, electrolyte levels, and degree of edema before therapy and regularly thereafter.
- Be alert for adverse reactions and drug interactions.
- Evaluate patient's and family's knowledge of drug therapy.

Nursing diagnoses

- Excessive fluid volume related to fluid retention
- Risk for injury related to potential for drug-induced hyperkalemia
- Deficient knowledge related to drug therapy

Planning and implementation

- Give with meals to prevent nausea.
- Give early in the day to prevent nocturia.
- Alert prescriber immediately if potassium level exceeds 6.5 mEq/L, and expect drug to be discontinued.
- Choose diet with caution.

ALERT: Don't confuse amiloride with amiodarone.

Patient teaching

- Advise patient to avoid sudden posture changes and to rise slowly to avoid orthostatic hypotension.
- Warn patient to limit potassium-rich foods (such as oranges and bananas), potassium-containing salt substitutes, and potassium supplements to prevent serious hyperkalemia.
- Teach patient and family to identify and report signs of hyperkalemia.
- Teach patient and family to monitor patient's fluid volume by recording daily weight and intake and output.

Evaluation

- Patient's fluid retention is relieved.
- Patient's potassium level remains normal.
- Patient and family state understanding of drug therapy.

amino acid infusions, crystalline

(uh-MEEN-oh AS-id in-FYOO-zhuns)

Aminosyn, Aminosyn II, Aminosyn-PF, FreAmine III, Novamine, Travasol, TrophAmine

amino acid infusions in dextrose

Aminosyn II with Dextrose

amino acid infusions with electrolytes

Aminosyn with Electrolytes, Aminosyn II with Electrolytes, FreAmine III with Electrolytes, ProcalAmine with Electrolytes, Travasol with Electrolytes

amino acid infusions with electrolytes in dextrose

Aminosyn II with Electrolytes in Dextrose

amino acid infusions for hepatic failure

HepatAmine

amino acid infusions for high metabolic stress

Aminosyn-HBC, BranchAmin, FreAmine HBC

amino acid infusions for renal failure

Aminess, Aminosyn-RF, NephrAmine, RenAmin

Pharmacologic class: protein substrate
Therapeutic class: parenteral nutritional therapy and caloric
Pregnancy risk category: C

Indications and dosages

▶ **Total parenteral nutrition in patients who can't or won't eat.** *Adults:* 1 to 1.7 g/kg I.V. daily.
Children: 2 to 3 g/kg I.V. daily.

▶ **Nutritional support in patients with cirrhosis, hepatitis, or hepatic encephalopathy.** *Adults:* 80 to 120 g of amino acids (12 to 18 g of nitrogen) I.V. daily using formulation for hepatic failure.

▶ **Nutritional support in patients with high metabolic stress.** *Adults:* 1.7 g/kg I.V. daily using formulation for high metabolic stress.

Contraindications and precautions

• Contraindicated in patients with anuria; inborn errors of amino acid metabolism, such as maple syrup urine disease and isovaleric acidemia; severe uncorrected electrolyte or acid-base imbalances; hyperammonemia; or decreased circulating blood volume.
• Use cautiously in patients with renal insufficiency or failure, cardiac disease, or hepatic impairment.
• Use with caution in diabetic patients; insulin may be needed to prevent hyperglycemia. Give cautiously to patients with cardiac insufficiency because it may cause circulatory overload. Patients with fluid restriction may tolerate only 1 to 2 L.
Lifespan: In children and neonates, especially those of low birth weight, use with extreme caution.

Adverse reactions

CNS: confusion, unconsciousness, headache, dizziness.
CV: flushing, hypervolemia, ***heart failure*** (in susceptible patients), pulmonary edema, worsening of hypertension (in predisposed patients), thrombophlebitis, thrombosis.
GI: nausea, vomiting.
GU: glycosuria, osmotic diuresis.
Hepatic: fatty liver.
Metabolic: ***rebound hypoglycemia,*** hyperglycemia, metabolic acidosis, alkalosis, hypophosphatemia, ***hyperosmolar hyperglycemic nonketotic syndrome,*** hyperammonemia, electrolyte imbalances.
Skin: feeling of warmth.
Other: chills, hypersensitivity reactions, tissue sloughing at infusion site caused by extravasation, catheter sepsis, dehydration (if hyperosmolar solutions are used).

Interactions

Drug-drug. *Tetracycline:* May reduce protein-sparing effects of infused amino acids because of its antianabolic activity. Monitor patient.

Effects on lab test results

• May increase ammonia and liver enzyme levels. May decrease phosphate, magnesium, and potassium levels. May increase or decrease glucose level.

Pharmacokinetics

Absorption: Administered I.V.
Distribution: Unknown.
Metabolism: Unknown.
Excretion: Unknown.

Route	Onset	Peak	Duration
I.V.	Immediate	Immediate	Unknown

Pharmacodynamics

Chemical effect: Provides substrate for protein synthesis or enhances conservation of existing body protein. Formulations for hepatic failure and high metabolic stress contain essential and nonessential amino acids, with high levels of branched chain amino acids isoleucine, leucine, and valine. Formulations for renal failure contain histidine and minimal amounts of essential amino acids; nonessential amino acids are synthesized from excess ammonia in blood of uremic patient, thus lowering azotemia.
Therapeutic effect: Provides body with needed calories and protein.

Available forms

Injection: 250 ml, 500 ml, 1,000 ml, 2,000 ml containing amino acids in varying concentrations.
Crystalline: Aminosyn, 3.5%, 5%, 7%, 8.5%, 10%. Aminosyn II, 3.5%, 5%, 7%, 8.5%, 10%. Aminosyn-PF, 7%, 10%. FreAmine III, 8.5%, 10%. Novamine, 11.4%, 15%. Travasol, 5.5%, 8.5%, 10%. TrophAmine, 6%, 10%.
In dextrose: Aminosyn II, 3.5% in 5% dextrose, 3.5% in 25% dextrose, 4.25% in 10% dextrose, 4.25% in 20% dextrose, 4.25% in 25% dextrose, 5% in 25% dextrose.
With electrolytes: Aminosyn, 3.5%, 7%, 8.5%. Aminosyn II, 3.5%, 7%, 8.5%, 10%. FreAmine III, 3%, 8.5%. ProcalAmine, 3%. Travasol, 3.5%, 5.5%, 8.5%.
With electrolytes in dextrose: Aminosyn II, 3.5% with electrolytes in 5% dextrose, 4.25% with electrolytes in 10% dextrose.
For hepatic failure: HepatAmine, 8%.
For high metabolic stress: Aminosyn-HBC, 7%. BranchAmin, 4%. FreAmine HBC, 6.9%.

For renal failure: Aminess, 5.2%. Aminosyn-RF, 5.2%. NephrAmine, 5.4%. RenAmin, 6.5%.

NURSING PROCESS

Assessment

- Assess electrolyte, glucose, BUN, calcium, and phosphate levels before therapy and regularly thereafter.
- Be alert for adverse reactions and drug interactions.
- Check infusion site frequently for erythema, inflammation, irritation, tissue sloughing, necrosis, and phlebitis.
- Evaluate patient's and family's knowledge of drug therapy.

Nursing diagnoses

- Altered nutrition (less than body requirements) related to patient's underlying condition
- Risk for deficient fluid volume related to adverse drug reactions
- Deficient knowledge related to drug therapy

Planning and implementation

- Control infusion rate carefully with infusion pump. If infusion rate falls behind, notify prescriber; don't increase rate to catch up.
- Peripheral infusions should be limited to 2.5% amino acids and dextrose 10%.
- Prescriber will individualize dosage according to patient's metabolic and clinical response as determined by nitrogen balance and body weight corrected for fluid balance.
- If patient has chills, fever, or other signs of sepsis, replace I.V. tubing and bottle and send them to laboratory so a culture can be taken.

ALERT: Don't confuse Aminosyn with Amikacin.

Patient teaching

- Tell patient to report discomfort at injection site or unusual symptoms.

Evaluation

- Patient's nutritional status improves.
- Patient maintains adequate hydration.
- Patient and family state understanding of drug therapy.

aminocaproic acid

(uh-mee-noh-kah-PROH-ik AS-id)

Amicar

Pharmacologic class: carboxylic acid derivative
Therapeutic class: fibrinolysis inhibitor
Pregnancy risk category: C

Indications and dosages

▶ **Excessive bleeding from hyperfibrinolysis.** *Adults:* 4 to 5 g I.V. over first hour, followed with constant infusion of 1 g/hour for about 8 hours or until bleeding is controlled. Maximum, 30 g/24 hours. Or, 5 g (10 tablets or 4 tsp of syrup) P.O. during the first hour of treatment; then, 1 g (2 tablets) or 1.25 g (1 tsp of syrup) per hour for about 8 hours or until bleeding is controlled.

▶ **Chronic bleeding tendency.** *Adults:* 5 to 30 g P.O. daily in divided doses at 3- to 6-hour intervals.

▶ **Antidote for excessive thrombolysis from administration of streptokinase or urokinase‡.** *Adults:* 4 to 5 g I.V. in first hour, followed by continuous I.V. infusion of g/hour. Continue treatment for 8 hours or until hemorrhaging is controlled.

▶ **Secondary ocular hemorrhaging in nonperforating traumatic hyphema‡.** *Adults:* 100 mg/kg P.O. q 4 hours for 5 days; maximum, 5 g/dose and 30 g daily.

▶ **Hereditary hemorrhagic telangiectasia‡.** *Adults:* 1 to 1.5 g P.O. b.i.d. for 1 to 2 months, followed by 1 to 2 g daily.

Contraindications and precautions

- Contraindicated in patients with active intravascular clotting or DIC unless heparin is used at the same time.
- Use cautiously in patients with cardiac, hepatic, or renal disease.

Lifespan: In pregnant and breast-feeding women, use cautiously. In newborns, injectable form is contraindicated. In children, safety of drug hasn't been established.

Adverse reactions

CNS: dizziness, headache, delirium, ***seizures***, weakness, malaise.
CV: hypotension, ***bradycardia, arrhythmias.***

EENT: tinnitus, nasal stuffiness, conjunctival suffusion.
GI: nausea, cramps, diarrhea.
GU: ***acute renal failure.***
Hematologic: generalized thrombosis.
Musculoskeletal: myopathy.
Skin: rash.

Interactions

None reported.

Effects on lab test results

- May increase BUN, creatinine, CK, AST, and ALT levels.

Pharmacokinetics

Absorption: Rapidly and completely absorbed from GI tract.
Distribution: Readily permeates human blood cells and other body cells. It isn't protein-bound.
Metabolism: Insignificant.
Excretion: 65% of single oral dose is excreted unchanged in urine.

Route	Onset	Peak	Duration
P.O.	1 hr	2 hr	Unknown
I.V.	< 1 hr	1-2 hr	< 3 hr

Pharmacodynamics

Chemical effect: Inhibits plasminogen activator substances and blocks antiplasmin activity.
Therapeutic effect: Promotes blood-clotting activity.

Available forms

Injection: 250 mg/ml
Syrup: 250 mg/ml
Tablets: 500 mg

NURSING PROCESS

Assessment

- Assess history of blood loss, coagulation studies, blood pressure, and heart rhythm before therapy.
- Monitor coagulation studies throughout therapy.
- Muscle weakness and rhabdomyolysis have been reported. Monitor patient carefully for symptoms.
- Observe heart rhythm, especially when giving I.V. dose.
- Be alert for adverse reactions and drug interactions.
- Evaluate patient's and family's knowledge of drug therapy.

Nursing diagnoses

- Deficient fluid volume related to excessive bleeding
- Altered venous tissue perfusion related to drug-induced generalized thrombosis
- Deficient knowledge related to drug therapy

Planning and implementation

- Dilute solution with sterile water for injection, normal saline solution, D_5W, or Ringer's injection. Infuse slowly. Don't give by direct or intermittent injection.
- Keep oxygen and resuscitation equipment nearby.

ALERT: Don't confuse Amicar with Amikin.

Patient teaching

- Explain all procedures to patient and family.
- Instruct patient and family to report respiratory difficulty, pain, or changes in mental status immediately.

Evaluation

- Patient regains normal fluid volume status.
- Patient shows no signs of impaired venous tissue perfusion.
- Patient and family state understanding of drug therapy.

aminoglutethimide

(uh-mee-noh-gloo-TETH-ih-mighd)
Cytadren

Pharmacologic class: antiadrenal hormone
Therapeutic class: antineoplastic
Pregnancy risk category: D

Indications and dosages

▶ **Suppression of adrenal function in Cushing's syndrome, treatment of postmenopausal women with advanced breast carcinoma and patients with metastatic prostate carcinoma‡.** *Adults:* 250 mg P.O. q.i.d. at 6-hour intervals. Increase dosage in increments of 250 mg daily q 1 to 2 weeks to maximum of 2 g daily.

Contraindications and precautions

- Contraindicated in patients hypersensitive to drug or to glutethimide.

Lifespan: In pregnant patients, use with extreme caution because drug can harm fetus. In breast-feeding women, drug is contraindicated. In children, safety of drug hasn't been established.

Adverse reactions

CNS: fever, drowsiness, headache, dizziness.
CV: hypotension, tachycardia.
GI: nausea, anorexia.
GU: masculinization.
Hematologic: ***transient leukopenia, agranulocytosis, thrombocytopenia.***
Metabolic: hypothyroidism.
Musculoskeletal: myalgia.
Skin: morbilliform rash, pruritus, urticaria, hirsutism.
Other: adrenal insufficiency.

Interactions

Drug-drug. *Dexamethasone, medroxyprogesterone:* May increase hepatic metabolism of these drugs. Monitor patient closely.
Digoxin: May increase drug clearance. Monitor patient closely.
Oral anticoagulants: May decrease anticoagulant effect. Monitor PT and INR.
Theophylline: Reduces action of theophylline. Monitor patient closely.
Drug-lifestyle. *Alcohol use:* May potentiate effects of aminoglutethimide. Discourage using together.

Effects on lab test results

- May increase AST, alkaline phosphatase, and bilirubin levels.
- May decrease WBC, granulocyte, and platelet counts. May alter thyroid function test results.

Pharmacokinetics

Absorption: Well absorbed through GI tract.
Distribution: Distributed widely into body tissues. Drug is minimally protein-bound.
Metabolism: Metabolized extensively in liver.
Excretion: Excreted primarily through kidneys; half of the drug is excreted unchanged and 20% to 50% as metabolites. *Half-life:* 11 to 16 hours (5 to 9 hours after 1 to 2 weeks).

Route	Onset	Peak	Duration
P.O.	Unknown	1.5 hr	1.5–3 days

Pharmacodynamics

Chemical effect: Blocks conversion of cholesterol to delta-5-pregnenolone in adrenal cortex, inhibiting synthesis of adrenal steroids.
Therapeutic effect: May decrease adrenocortical hormone levels.

Available forms

Tablets: 250 mg

NURSING PROCESS

Assessment

- Assess patient's underlying condition before therapy, and note improvement.
- Watch for adrenal hypofunction, especially under stressful conditions, such as surgery, trauma, or acute illness.
- Be alert for adverse reactions and drug interactions.
- Evaluate patient's and family's knowledge of drug therapy.

Nursing diagnoses

- Ineffective health maintenance related to patient's underlying condition
- Ineffective protection related to drug-induced adrenal suppression
- Deficient knowledge related to drug therapy

Planning and implementation

- Give drug on schedule, and alert prescriber if dose is delayed or missed.
- Patient may need more supplements during stress, such as a mineralocorticoid supplement to treat hyponatremia and orthostatic hypotension. Glucocorticoid replacement also may be needed.

Patient teaching

- Instruct patient to notify prescriber of increased stress; patient may need additional therapy.
- Caution patient to watch for signs of infection (fever, sore throat, fatigue) and bleeding (easy bruising, nosebleeds, bleeding gums, melena). Tell patient to take temperature daily.

• Warn patient to avoid hazardous activities until full CNS effects of drug are known.
• Advise patient to stand up slowly to minimize orthostatic hypotension.
• Tell patient to report rash that lasts more than 8 days. Reassure patient that drowsiness, nausea, and loss of appetite usually diminish within 2 weeks after start of therapy, but advise him to notify prescriber if symptoms persist.
• Advise patient to avoid alcohol consumption during drug therapy.

☑ Evaluation

• Patient's health is maintained.
• Patient has no hypoadrenalism.
• Patient and family state understanding of drug therapy.

aminophylline (theophylline and ethylenediamine)

(uh-mih-NOF-il-in)

Aminophyllin, Cardophyllin ◇, Corophyllin ♦, Phyllocontin, Phyllocontin-350, Somophyllin, Somophyllin-DF, Truphylline

Pharmacologic class: xanthine derivative
Therapeutic class: bronchodilator
Pregnancy risk category: C

Indications and dosages

▶ **Symptomatic relief of bronchospasm.** *Patients currently receiving theophylline products who require rapid relief of symptoms:* Loading dose is 6 mg/kg (equivalent to 4.7 mg/kg anhydrous theophylline) I.V. (25 mg/minute or less), then maintenance infusion.
Adults (nonsmokers): 0.7 mg/kg per hour I.V. for 12 hours; then 0.5 mg/kg per hour.
Otherwise healthy adult smokers: 1 mg/kg per hour I.V. for 12 hours; then 0.8 mg/kg per hour.
Older patients and adults with cor pulmonale: 0.6 mg/kg per hour I.V. for 12 hours; then 0.3 mg/kg per hour.
Adults with heart failure or liver disease: 0.5 mg/kg per hour I.V. for 12 hours; then 0.1 to 0.2 mg/kg per hour.
Children ages 9 to 16: 1 mg/kg per hour I.V. for 12 hours; then 0.8 mg/kg per hour.
Children ages 6 months to 8 years: 1.2 mg/kg/hour for 12 hours; then 1 mg/kg/hour.
Patients currently receiving theophylline products: Aminophylline infusion of 0.63 mg/kg (0.5 mg/kg anhydrous theophylline) increases plasma level of theophylline by 1 mcg/ml. Some clinicians recommend dose of 3.1 mg/kg (2.5 mg/kg anhydrous theophylline) with no obvious signs of theophylline toxicity.
▶ **Chronic bronchial asthma.** Dosage is highly individualized. Rectal dosage is same as oral dosage.
Adults: 600 to 1,600 mg P.O. daily in divided doses t.i.d. or q.i.d.
Children: 12 mg/kg P.O. daily in divided doses t.i.d. or q.i.d.
▶ **Periodic apnea related to Cheyne-Stokes respirations, promote diuresis, paroxysmal nocturnal dyspnea‡.** *Adults:* 200 to 400 mg I.V. bolus.
▶ **Reduction of severe bronchospasm in infants with cystic fibrosis‡.** *Infants:* 10 to 12 mg/kg I.V. daily.

Contraindications and precautions

• Contraindicated in patients with active peptic ulcer disease, seizure disorders (unless anticonvulsant therapy is given), and hypersensitivity to xanthine compounds (caffeine, theobromine) or ethylenediamine.
• Use cautiously in patients with heart failure or other cardiac or circulatory impairment, COPD, cor pulmonale, renal or hepatic disease, hyperthyroidism, diabetes mellitus, peptic ulcer, severe hypoxemia, or hypertension.
Lifespan: In pregnant or breast-feeding women, neonates, infants, young children, and elderly patients, use cautiously.

Adverse reactions

CNS: nervousness, restlessness, dizziness, headache, insomnia, light-headedness, ***seizures***, muscle twitching.
CV: palpitations, tachycardia, extrasystole, flushing, hypotension, ***arrhythmias.***
GI: nausea, vomiting, anorexia, dyspepsia, heavy feeling in stomach, diarrhea, bitter aftertaste.
Respiratory: increased respiratory rate, ***respiratory arrest.***
Skin: urticaria, local irritation with rectal suppositories.

Interactions

Drug-drug. *Adenosine:* May decrease antiarrhythmic effectiveness. Higher doses of adenosine may be needed.
Alkali-sensitive drugs: May reduce drug's activity. Don't add to I.V. fluids containing aminophylline.
Allopurinol (high doses), cimetidine, influenza virus vaccine, macrolide antibiotics (such as erythromycin), oral contraceptives, quinolone antibiotics (such as ciprofloxacin): May decrease hepatic clearance of theophylline and elevate theophylline level. Monitor patient for toxicity.
Amiodarone, ticlopidine, verapamil: May increase theophylline level. Use together cautiously.
Barbiturates, carbamazepine, nicotine, phenytoin, rifampin: May enhance metabolism and decrease theophylline level. Monitor patient for decreased aminophylline effect.
Beta blockers: May cause antagonism. In particular, propranolol and nadolol may cause bronchospasm in sensitive patients. Use together cautiously.
Ephedrine, other sympathomimetics: Theophylline may exhibit synergistic toxicity with these drugs, predisposing patient to arrhythmias. Monitor patient closely.
Isoniazid, ketoconazole: May decrease theophylline absorption.
Lithium: Theophylline may increase lithium level. Monitor patient closely.
Drug-herb. *Caffeine-containing herbs (such as guarana):* May increase adverse effects. Discourage using together.
St. John's wort: May lower level of drug, making it less effective. Monitor patient for lack of therapeutic effect. Discourage using together.
Drug-food. *Caffeinated foods, colas:* May increase CNS adverse effects. Advise patient to monitor caffeine intake.
Drug-lifestyle. *Smoking:* May increase clearance and decrease half-life of theophylline. Higher doses may be needed to achieve desired effect.

Effects on lab test results

- May increase glucose and free fatty acid levels.

Pharmacokinetics

Absorption: Well absorbed except for suppository form, which is unreliable and slow. Food may alter rate but not extent of absorption of oral doses.
Distribution: Distributed in all tissues and extracellular fluids except fatty tissue.
Metabolism: Converted to theophylline, then metabolized to inactive compounds.
Excretion: Excreted in urine as theophylline (10%). *Half-life:* depends on many variables, including smoking status, concurrent illness, age, and formulation used.

Route	Onset	Peak	Duration
P.O.			
tablets	15-60 min	2 hr	Varies
extended-release	Unknown	4-7 hr	Varies
solution	15-60 min	1 hr	Varies
I.V.	15 min	Immediate	Varies
P.R.	Varies	Varies	Varies

Pharmacodynamics

Chemical effect: Inhibits phosphodiesterase, the enzyme that degrades cAMP, thereby relaxing smooth muscle of bronchial airways and pulmonary blood vessels.
Therapeutic effect: Eases breathing.

Available forms

Injection: 250 mg/10 ml, 500 mg/20 ml, 500 mg/2 ml, 100 mg/100 ml in half-normal saline solution, 200 mg/100 ml in half-normal saline solution
Oral liquid: 105 mg/5 ml
Rectal suppositories: 250 mg, 500 mg
Tablets: 100 mg, 200 mg
Tablets (extended-release): 225 mg, 350 mg ♦

NURSING PROCESS

Assessment

- Assess patient's underlying respiratory condition.
- Monitor drug effectiveness by regularly auscultating lungs and noting respiratory rate and results of laboratory studies, such as arterial blood gas analysis.
- Monitor patient's hydration status if adverse GI reactions occur.

• Be alert for adverse reactions and drug interactions.
• Evaluate patient's and family's knowledge of drug therapy.

Nursing diagnoses

• Impaired gas exchange related to bronchospasm
• Risk for deficient fluid volume related to drug-induced adverse GI reactions
• Deficient knowledge related to drug therapy

Planning and implementation

• Make sure that patient hasn't had recent theophylline therapy before giving loading dose.
• **P.O. use:** Give drug with full glass of water at meals. Food in stomach delays absorption. Enteric-coated tablets may delay and impair absorption.
• **I.V. use:** Because I.V. drug can burn, dilute with compatible I.V. solution and inject at no more than 25 mg/minute. Exceeding recommended I.V. infusion rates increases the risk of adverse reactions. Drug is compatible with most I.V. solutions except invert sugar, fructose, and fat emulsions.
• **P.R. use:** Suppositories are slowly and erratically absorbed. Give suppository only if patient can't take drug orally. Schedule after evacuation, if possible; may be retained better if given before meal. Have patient remain recumbent for 15 to 20 minutes after insertion.
• Aminophylline is a soluble salt of theophylline. Dosage is adjusted by monitoring response, tolerance, pulmonary function, and theophylline level. Theophylline concentration should range from 10 to 20 mcg/ml; toxicity may occur with level above 20 mcg/ml.
ALERT: Don't confuse aminophylline with amitriptyline or ampicillin.

Patient teaching

• Supply instructions for home care and dosage schedule. Some patients may need an around-the-clock schedule.
• Warn elderly patients that dizziness is common at start of therapy.
• Warn patient to check with prescriber or pharmacist before combining aminophylline with other drugs; OTC products and herbal remedies may contain ephedrine. Excessive CNS stimulation may result.
• Advise patient to avoid switching brands without consulting prescriber.
• Tell patient to notify prescriber if he quits smoking. Dosage may need to be reduced.

Evaluation

• Patient's appearance, vital signs, and laboratory test results demonstrate improved gas exchange.
• Patient remains hydrated throughout therapy.
• Patient and family state understanding of drug therapy.

amiodarone hydrochloride

(am-ee-OH-dah-rohn high-droh-KLOR-ighd)
Aratac♦, Cordarone, Cordarone X♦, Pacerone

Pharmacologic class: benzofuran derivative
Therapeutic class: ventricular antiarrhythmic
Pregnancy risk category: D

Indications and dosages

▶ **Recurrent ventricular fibrillation, unstable ventricular tachycardia, atrial fibrillation‡, angina‡, and hypertrophic cardiomyopathy‡.** *Adults:* Loading dose of 800 to 1,600 mg P.O. daily for 1 to 3 weeks until initial therapeutic response occurs, then 650 to 800 mg P.O. daily for 1 month, then 200 to 600 mg P.O. daily as maintenance dosage. Or, for first 24 hours, 150 mg I.V. over 10 minutes (mixed in 100 ml D_5W); then 360 mg I.V. over 6 hours (mix 900 mg in 500 ml D_5W); then maintenance dose of 540 mg I.V. over 18 hours at 0.5 mg/minute. After first 24 hours, continue a maintenance infusion of 0.5 mg/minute in a concentration of 1 to 6 mg/ml. For infusions longer than 1 hour, concentrations shouldn't exceed 2 mg/ml unless you use a central venous catheter. Don't use for more than 3 weeks.
▶ **Conversion from I.V. to P.O.** *Adults:* After daily dose of 720 mg I.V. (assuming rate of 0.5 mg/min) for less than 1 week, start 800 to 1,600 mg P.O. daily; for 1 to 3 weeks, give 600 to 800 mg P.O. daily; and for more than 3 weeks, give 400 mg P.O. daily.
▶ **Supraventricular arrhythmias‡.** *Adults:* 600 to 800 mg P.O. for 1 to 4 weeks or until

supraventricular tachycardia is controlled. Maintenance dose is 100 to 400 mg P.O. daily.

Contraindications and precautions

- Contraindicated in patients hypersensitive to drug, and in those with severe sinus node disease, bradycardia, second- or third-degree AV block (unless artificial pacemaker is present), and bradycardia-induced syncope.
- Use with extreme caution in patients receiving other antiarrhythmics.
- Use cautiously in patients with pulmonary or thyroid disease.

Lifespan: In pregnant women, use with extreme caution. In breast-feeding women, drug is contraindicated. In children, safety of drug hasn't been established. In fetuses, infants, and toddlers, Cordarone (I.V.) has been known to leach out plasticizers such as DEHP, which can adversely affect male reproductive tract development.

Adverse reactions

CNS: peripheral neuropathy, extrapyramidal symptoms, headache, malaise, fatigue.
CV: ***bradycardia,*** hypotension, ***arrhythmias, heart failure, heart block, sinus arrest.***
EENT: corneal microdeposits, vision disturbances.
GI: nausea, vomiting, constipation.
Hepatic: hepatic dysfunction.
Metabolic: hypothyroidism, hyperthyroidism.
Musculoskeletal: muscle weakness.
Respiratory: SEVERE PULMONARY TOXICITY (PNEUMONITIS, ALVEOLITIS).
Skin: photosensitivity, blue-gray skin.
Other: gynecomastia.

Interactions

Drug-drug. *Antiarrhythmics:* Amiodarone may reduce hepatic or renal clearance of certain antiarrhythmics (especially flecainide, procainamide, or quinidine); use of amiodarone with other antiarrhythmics (especially disopyramide, mexiletine, procainamide, propafenone, or quinidine) may induce torsades de pointes. Monitor ECG closely.
Antihypertensives: May increase hypotensive effect. Use together cautiously.
Beta blockers, calcium channel blockers: May increase cardiac depressant effects and potentiate slowing of sinus node and AV conduction. Use together cautiously.
Cardiac glycosides: May increase digoxin level (average of 70% to 100%). Monitor digoxin level closely.
Cholestyramine: May decrease amiodarone level and half-life. Avoid using together.
Cimetidine: May increase amiodarone level. Avoid using together.
Cyclosporine: May increase cyclosporine level. Monitor creatinine level.
Phenytoin: May decrease phenytoin metabolism. Monitor phenytoin level.
Theophylline: May increase theophylline level and lead to toxicity. Monitor theophylline level.
Warfarin: May increase INR (average of 100% within 1 to 4 weeks of therapy). Warfarin dosage should be decreased 33% to 50% when amiodarone is started. Monitor patient closely.
Drug-herb. *Pennyroyal:* May change the rate at which toxic metabolites of pennyroyal form. Discourage using together.
Drug-lifestyle. *Sun exposure:* May cause photosensitivity reaction. Advise against prolonged or unprotected sun exposure.

Effects on lab test results

- May increase ALT, AST, alkaline phosphatase, and GGT levels.
- May increase PT and INR. May alter thyroid function test results.

Pharmacokinetics

Absorption: Slow and variable.
Distribution: Distributed widely, accumulating in adipose tissue and in organs with marked perfusion, such as lungs, liver, and spleen. It is highly protein-bound (96%).
Metabolism: Metabolized extensively in liver to active metabolite, desethyl amiodarone.
Excretion: Main excretory route is hepatic through biliary tree. *Half-life:* 25 to 110 days (usually 40 to 50 days).

Route	Onset	Peak	Duration
P.O.	2-21 days	3-7 hr	Varies
I.V.	Unknown	Unknown	Unknown

Pharmacodynamics

Chemical effect: Unknown; thought to prolong refractory period and duration of action potential and decrease repolarization.
Therapeutic effect: Abolishes ventricular arrhythmia.

Available forms

Injection: 50 mg/ml
Tablets: 100 mg, 200 mg, 400 mg

NURSING PROCESS

Assessment

- Assess CV status before therapy.
- Review pulmonary, liver, and thyroid function test results before and regularly during therapy.
- Continuously monitor cardiac status of patient receiving I.V. amiodarone to evaluate its effectiveness.
- Be alert for adverse reactions and drug interactions.
- Monitor patient carefully for pulmonary toxicity, which can be fatal. Risk increases in patients receiving more than 400 mg daily.
- Monitor electrolytes, particularly potassium and magnesium levels.
- Evaluate patient's and family's knowledge of drug therapy.

Nursing diagnoses

- Decreased cardiac output related to ventricular arrhythmia
- Risk for injury related to drug-induced adverse reactions
- Deficient knowledge related to drug therapy

Planning and implementation

- Adverse reactions commonly limit drug's use.

ALERT: Drug poses major and potentially life-threatening management problems in patients at risk for sudden death and should be used only in patients with documented, life-threatening, recurrent ventricular arrhythmias nonresponsive to documented adequate doses of other antiarrhythmics or when alternative drugs can't be tolerated. Amiodarone can cause fatal toxicities, including hepatic and pulmonary toxicity. In addition to treatment of recurrent ventricular tachycardia and ventricular fibrillation, amiodarone has been used to treat atrial fibrillation, atrial flutter, paroxysmal supraventricular tachycardia (PSVT), and, at low doses, heart failure.

- **P.O. use:** Divide oral loading dose into three equal doses and give with meals to decrease GI intolerance. Maintenance dosage may be given once daily or divided into two doses taken with meals if GI intolerance occurs.
- **I.V. use:** Amiodarone may be given I.V. where facilities for close monitoring of cardiac function and resuscitation are available. Initial dosage of 5 mg/kg should be mixed in 250 ml of D_5W. Repeat doses should be given through central venous catheter. Patient should receive maximum of 1.2 g in up to 500 ml of D_5W daily.
- Maintain ECG monitoring during start and alteration of dosage. Notify prescriber of significant change.
- Recommend instillation of methylcellulose ophthalmic solution during amiodarone therapy to minimize corneal microdeposits.
- Cordarone I.V. contains benzyl alcohol, which has caused gasping syndrome in neonates. Monitor neonates for symptoms of sudden onset of gasping respiration, hypotension, bradycardia, and cardiovascular collapse.

ALERT: Don't confuse amiodarone with amiloride.

Patient teaching

- Stress importance of taking medication exactly as prescribed.
- Emphasize importance of close follow-up and regular diagnostic studies to monitor drug action and assess for adverse reactions.
- Warn patient that drug may cause blue-gray skin pigmentation.
- Advise patient to use sunscreen to prevent photosensitivity reaction (burning or tingling skin followed by erythema and possible blistering).
- Inform patient that adverse effects are more prevalent at high doses but are generally reversible when therapy stops. Resolution of adverse reactions may take up to 4 months.

Evaluation

- Patient's arrhythmia is corrected.
- Patient has no injury from adverse reactions.
- Patient and family state understanding of drug therapy.

amitriptyline hydrochloride

(am-ih-TRIP-tuh-leen high-droh-KLOR-ighd)
Apo-Amitriptyline ♦, Elavil, Emitrip, Endep, Enovil, Levate ♦, Novotriptyn ♦, PMS-Amitriptyline ♦, Tryptanol ◊

amitriptyline pamoate

Elavil ♦

Pharmacologic class: tricyclic antidepressant
Therapeutic class: antidepressant
Pregnancy risk category: C

Indications and dosages

▶ **Depression.** *Adults:* 50 to 100 mg P.O. h.s., gradually increasing to 150 mg daily; maximum dosage is 300 mg daily, if needed. Or, 20 to 30 mg I.M. q.i.d., which should be changed to oral route as soon as possible. *Elderly patients and adolescents:* 10 mg P.O. t.i.d. and 20 mg h.s. daily.

▶ **Anorexia or bulimia related to depression or as adjunctive therapy for neurogenic pain‡.** *Adults:* If outpatient, initially 75 to 100 mg P.O. in divided doses daily. If inpatient, 100 to 300 mg P.O. in divided doses daily. After maximum effect is achieved, gradually lower dose to maintenance dose of 50 to 100 mg or less P.O. daily for a minimum of 3 months.

Contraindications and precautions

- Contraindicated during acute recovery phase of MI, in patients hypersensitive to drug, and in patients who received an MAO inhibitor within past 14 days.
- Use cautiously in patients with history of seizures, urine retention, prostatic hypertrophy, angle-closure glaucoma, or increased intraocular pressure; in those with hyperthyroidism, CV disease, diabetes, or impaired liver function; and in those receiving thyroid medications.

Lifespan: In pregnant women, use cautiously. In breast-feeding women, drug is contraindicated. In children younger than age 12, don't use drug. In elderly patients, who may experience increased falls and increased anticholinergic effects while taking this drug, use cautiously.

Adverse reactions

CNS: drowsiness, dizziness, excitation, tremors, weakness, confusion, headache, ***CVA,*** nervousness, EEG alterations, ***seizures,*** extrapyramidal reactions.
CV: orthostatic hypotension, tachycardia, ECG changes, hypertension, ***MI, arrhythmias.***
EENT: blurred vision, tinnitus, mydriasis.
GI: dry mouth, constipation, nausea, vomiting, anorexia, paralytic ileus.
GU: urine retention.
Hematologic: ***agranulocytosis, thrombocytopenia.***
Skin: diaphoresis, rash, urticaria, photosensitivity reaction.
Other: hypersensitivity reactions.

Interactions

Drug-drug. *Barbiturates, CNS depressants:* May enhance CNS depression. Avoid using together.
Cimetidine, methylphenidate: May increase tricyclic antidepressant level. Monitor patient for enhanced antidepressant effect.
Clonidine: May cause hypertensive crisis. Avoid using together.
Epinephrine, norepinephrine: May increase hypertensive effect. Use cautiously.
Guanethidine: May antagonize antihypertensive action of guanethidine. Monitor patient.
MAO inhibitors: Especially at high dosage, may cause severe excitation, hyperpyrexia, or seizures. Use cautiously.
Drug-herb. *St. John's wort, SAMe, yohimbe:* May cause serotonin level to become too high. Discourage using together.
Drug-lifestyle. *Alcohol use:* May enhance CNS depression. Discourage using together.
Smoking: May lower drug level. Monitor patient for lack of effect.
Sun exposure: May increase risk of photosensitivity reactions. Advise against prolonged or unprotected sun exposure.

Effects on lab test results

- May increase or decrease glucose level.
- May increase liver function test values and eosinophil count. May decrease granulocyte, platelet, and WBC counts.

Pharmacokinetics

Absorption: Absorbed rapidly from GI tract after oral administration and from muscle tissue after I.M. administration.
Distribution: Distributed widely into body, including CNS and breast milk. Drug is 96% protein-bound.
Metabolism: Metabolized by liver to active metabolite nortriptyline; significant first-pass effect may account for variable levels in different patients taking same dosage.
Excretion: Most of drug is excreted in urine.

Route	Onset	Peak	Duration
P.O., I.M.	Unknown	2-12 hr	Unknown

Pharmacodynamics

Chemical effect: Unknown, but tricyclic antidepressant increases norepinephrine, serotonin, or both in CNS by blocking their reuptake by presynaptic neurons.
Therapeutic effect: Relieves depression.

Available forms

Injection: 10 mg/ml
Syrup: 10 mg/5 ml
Tablets: 10 mg, 25 mg, 50 mg, 75 mg, 100 mg, 150 mg

NURSING PROCESS

Assessment

- Assess patient's depression before therapy.
- Be alert for adverse reactions and drug interactions.
- Evaluate patient's and family's knowledge of drug therapy.

Nursing diagnoses

- Ineffective individual coping related to depression
- Risk for injury related to adverse CNS reactions
- Deficient knowledge related to drug therapy

Planning and implementation

- **P.O. use:** Oral therapy should replace injection as soon as possible.
- **I.M. use:** Follow normal protocol. Effects may appear more rapidly than with oral administration.
- Administer full dose h.s. when possible.
- Expect reduced dosage in adolescents and elderly or debilitated patients.
- Don't withdraw drug abruptly.
- Expect prescriber to reduce dosage if signs of psychosis occur or increase. Allow patient only minimum supply of drug.
- Because hypertensive episodes have occurred during surgery in patients receiving tricyclic antidepressants, drug should be gradually stopped several days before surgery.

ALERT: Don't confuse amitriptyline with nortriptyline or aminophylline, Elavil with Equanil or Mellaril, or Endep with Depen.

Patient teaching

- Advise patient to take full dose h.s., but warn him of possible morning orthostatic hypotension.
- Tell patient to avoid using alcohol and smoking while taking drug.
- Warn patient to avoid hazardous activities until full CNS effects of drug are known. Drowsiness and dizziness usually subside after a few weeks.
- Advise patient to consult prescriber before taking other prescription drugs, OTC medications, or herbal remedies.
- Teach patient to relieve dry mouth with sugarless hard candy or gum. Saliva substitutes may be needed.
- Advise patient to use sunblock, wear protective clothing, and avoid prolonged exposure to strong sunlight.
- Warn patient not to stop drug therapy abruptly. After abrupt withdrawal of long-term therapy, patient may experience nausea, headache, and malaise. These symptoms don't indicate addiction.
- Tell patient to watch for urine retention and constipation. Instruct him to increase fluids and suggest stool softener or high-fiber diet as needed.
- Advise patient that effects of drug may be apparent for 2 to 3 weeks.

Evaluation

- Patient's behavior and communication indicate improvement of depression.
- Patient doesn't experience injury from CNS adverse reactions.
- Patient and family state understanding of drug therapy.

amlodipine besylate
(am-LOH-dih-peen BES-eh-layt)
Norvasc

Pharmacologic class: dihydropyridine calcium channel blocker
Therapeutic class: antianginal, antihypertensive
Pregnancy risk category: C

Indications and dosages

▶ **Chronic stable angina; vasospastic angina (Prinzmetal's [variant] angina).** *Adults:* Initially, 10 mg P.O. daily.
Small, frail, or elderly patients or patients with hepatic insufficiency: Begin therapy at 5 mg daily. Most patients need 10 mg daily for adequate results.

▶ **Hypertension.** *Adults:* Initially, 5 mg P.O. daily.
Small, frail, or elderly patients, patients currently receiving other antihypertensives, and patients with hepatic insufficiency: Begin therapy at 2.5 mg daily. Dosage adjusted based on patient response and tolerance. Maximum, 10 mg daily.

Contraindications and precautions

• Contraindicated in patients hypersensitive to drug.
• Use cautiously in patients receiving other peripheral vasodilators (especially those with severe aortic stenosis) and in those with heart failure.
• In patients with severe hepatic disease, use cautiously and in reduced dosage because drug is metabolized by liver.
Lifespan: In pregnant women, use cautiously. In breast-feeding women, drug is contraindicated. In children, safety of drug hasn't been established.

Adverse reactions

CNS: headache, fatigue, somnolence.
CV: edema, dizziness, flushing, palpitations.
GI: nausea, abdominal pain, dyspepsia.

Interactions

None reported.

Effects on lab test results

None reported.

Pharmacokinetics

Absorption: Absolute bioavailability from 64% to 90%.
Distribution: About 93% of circulating drug is bound to plasma proteins.
Metabolism: About 90% of drug is converted to inactive metabolites in liver.
Excretion: Excreted primarily in urine. *Half-life:* 30 to 50 hours.

Route	Onset	Peak	Duration
P.O.	Unknown	6-9 hr	24 hr

Pharmacodynamics

Chemical effect: Inhibits calcium ion influx across cardiac and smooth-muscle cells, thus decreasing myocardial contractility and oxygen demand. Also dilates coronary arteries and arterioles.
Therapeutic effect: Reduces blood pressure and prevents angina.

Available forms

Tablets: 2.5 mg, 5 mg, 10 mg

NURSING PROCESS

Assessment

• Assess patient's blood pressure or angina before therapy and regularly thereafter.
• Monitor patient carefully for pain. In some patients, especially those with severe obstructive coronary artery disease, increased frequency, duration, or severity of angina or even acute MI has developed after start of calcium channel blocker therapy or at time of dosage increase.
• Be alert for adverse reactions.
• Evaluate patient's and family's knowledge of drug therapy.

Nursing diagnoses

• Acute pain related to increased oxygen demand in cardiac tissue
• Risk for injury related to hypertension
• Deficient knowledge related to drug therapy

Planning and implementation

• Prescriber should adjust dosage based on patient response and tolerance.

• Administer S.L. nitroglycerin as needed for acute angina.

ALERT: Don't confuse amlodipine with amiloride.

Patient teaching

• Tell patient that S.L. nitroglycerin may be taken as needed for acute angina. If patient continues nitrate therapy during adjustment of amlodipine dosage, urge continued compliance.

• Caution patient to continue taking drug even when feeling better.

Evaluation

• Patient's blood pressure is normal.

• Patient states anginal pain occurs with less frequency and severity.

• Patient and family state understanding of drug therapy.

amoxicillin and clavulanate potassium

(uh-moks-uh-SIL-in and KLAV-yoo-lan-ayt poh-TAH-see-um)

Augmentin, Augmentin ES-600, Clavulin ♦

Pharmacologic class: aminopenicillin, beta-lactamase inhibitor
Therapeutic class: antibiotic
Pregnancy risk category: B

Indications and dosages

▶ **Lower respiratory tract infections, otitis media, sinusitis, skin and skin-structure infections, and UTI caused by susceptible strains of gram-positive and gram-negative organisms.** *Adults:* 250 mg (based on amoxicillin component) P.O. q 8 hours. For more severe infections, 500 mg q 8 hours, or 875 mg P.O. q 12 hours.

Children: 20 to 40 mg/kg (based on amoxicillin component) P.O. daily in divided doses q 8 hours.

Neonates and infants younger than age 12 weeks: 30 mg/kg P.O. daily in divided doses q 12 hours.

▶ **Recurrent or persistent acute otitis media caused by *Streptococcus pneumoniae, Haemophilus influenzae, or Moraxella catarrhalis,* in children with antibiotic exposure within the last 3 months and who either are age 2 years or younger or attend daycare.** *Infants and children ages 3 months to 12 years:* 90 mg/kg daily Augmentin ES-600 (based on amoxicillin component) P.O. q 12 hours for 10 days. Experience with this medication in patients weighing 40 kg or more is unavailable.

Contraindications and precautions

• Contraindicated in patients hypersensitive to drug or other penicillins and in those with a history of amoxicillin-related cholestatic jaundice or hepatic dysfunction.

• Use cautiously in patients with other drug allergies, especially to cephalosporins (possible cross-sensitivity), and in those with mononucleosis (high risk of maculopapular rash).

Lifespan: In pregnant and breast-feeding women, use cautiously.

Adverse reactions

GI: nausea, vomiting, diarrhea.
Hematologic: anemia, ***thrombocytopenia, thrombocytopenic purpura,*** eosinophilia, ***leukopenia, agranulocytopenia.***
Other: hypersensitivity reactions (erythematous maculopapular rash, urticaria, ***anaphylaxis***), overgrowth of nonsusceptible organisms.

Interactions

Drug-drug. *Allopurinol:* May cause rash. Monitor patient.
Probenecid: May increase level of amoxicillin and other penicillins. Probenecid may be used for this purpose.

Effects on lab test results

• May increase eosinophil count. May decrease hemoglobin, hematocrit, and granulocyte, platelet, and WBC counts.

• Urine glucose determinations may be false-positive with copper sulfate tests (Benedict's solution, Clinitest).

Pharmacokinetics

Absorption: Well absorbed.
Distribution: Both drugs are distributed into pleural fluid, lungs, and peritoneal fluid; high urine levels are attained. Amoxicillin also is distributed into synovial fluid, liver, prostate, muscle, and gallbladder and penetrates into middle ear effusions, maxillary sinus secre-

tions, tonsils, sputum, and bronchial secretions. Both drugs have minimal protein binding.
Metabolism: Amoxicillin is metabolized only partially; clavulanate potassium appears to undergo extensive metabolism.
Excretion: Amoxicillin is excreted principally in urine by renal tubular secretion and glomerular filtration; clavulanate potassium is excreted by glomerular filtration. *Half-life:* Amoxicillin, 1 to 1½ hours (7½ hours in severe renal impairment); clavulanate, about 1 to 1½ hours (4½ hours in severe renal impairment).

Route	Onset	Peak	Duration
P.O.	Unknown	1-2.5 hr	6-8 hr
P.O. Augmentin ES-600	Unknown	1-4 hr	Unknown

Pharmacodynamics

Chemical effect: Prevents bacterial cell-wall synthesis during replication. Clavulanic acid increases amoxicillin's effectiveness by inactivating beta lactamases, which destroy amoxicillin.
Therapeutic effect: Kills susceptible bacteria. Active against penicillinase-producing gram-positive bacteria, *Neisseria gonorrhoeae, N. meningitidis, Haemophilus influenzae, Escherichia coli, Proteus mirabilis, Citrobacter diversus, Klebsiella pneumoniae, P. vulgaris, Salmonella,* and *Shigella.*

Available forms

Oral suspension: 125 mg amoxicillin trihydrate and 31.25 mg clavulanic acid/5 ml (after reconstitution); 200 mg amoxicillin trihydrate and 28.5 mg clavulanic acid/5 ml (after reconstitution); 250 mg amoxicillin trihydrate and 62.5 mg clavulanic acid/5 ml (after reconstitution); 400 mg amoxicillin trihydrate and 57 mg clavulanic acid/5 ml (after reconstitution); 600 mg amoxicillin trihydrate and 42.9 mg clavulanic acid/5 ml (after reconstitution)
Tablets: 875 mg amoxicillin trihydrate, 125 mg clavulanic acid
Tablets (chewable): 125 mg amoxicillin trihydrate, 31.25 mg clavulanic acid; 200 mg amoxicillin trihydrate, 28.5 mg clavulanic acid; 250 mg amoxicillin trihydrate, 62.5 mg clavulanic acid; 400 mg amoxicillin trihydrate, 57 mg clavulanic acid
Tablets (film-coated): 250 mg amoxicillin trihydrate, 125 mg clavulanic acid; 500 mg amoxicillin trihydrate, 125 mg clavulanic acid

NURSING PROCESS

Assessment

- Before therapy begins, assess patient's infection, ask him about past allergic reactions to penicillin (although negative history is no guarantee against allergic reaction), and obtain specimen for culture and sensitivity tests. Therapy may begin pending results.
- Be alert for adverse reactions and drug interactions.
- Monitor hydration status if adverse GI reactions occur.
- Evaluate patient's and family's knowledge of drug therapy.

Nursing diagnoses

- Infection related to susceptible bacteria
- Risk for deficient fluid volume related to drug-induced adverse GI reactions
- Deficient knowledge related to drug therapy

Planning and implementation

- Give drug with food to prevent GI distress. Adverse effects, especially diarrhea, are more common than with amoxicillin alone.
- Give drug at least 1 hour before bacteriostatic antibiotics.
- Both 250-mg and 500-mg film-coated tablets contain same amount of clavulanic acid (125 mg). Therefore, two 250-mg film-coated tablets don't equal one 500-mg film-coated tablet. Also, do not interchange the oral suspensions because of clavulanic aid content.

ALERT: Augmentin ES-600 is intended for children only. There is no experience with this drug in adults.
- This drug combination is particularly useful with amoxicillin-resistant organisms.
- After reconstitution, refrigerate oral suspension and discard after 10 days.

ALERT: Don't confuse amoxicillin with amoxapine.

Patient teaching

- Tell patient to take entire quantity of drug exactly as prescribed, even after he feels better.
- Tell patient to call prescriber if rash develops (sign of allergic reaction).

• Instruct patient to take drug with food to prevent GI distress.

Evaluation
• Patient is free from infection.
• Patient maintains adequate hydration.
• Patient and family state understanding of drug therapy.

amoxicillin trihydrate (amoxycillin trihydrate)

(uh-moks-uh-SIL-in trigh-HIGH-drayt)
Alphamox ◇, Amoxil, Apo-Amoxi ♦, Cilamox ◇, Moxacin ◇, Novamoxin ♦, Nu-Amoxi ♦, Trimox

Pharmacologic class: aminopenicillin
Therapeutic class: antibiotic
Pregnancy risk category: B

Indications and dosages

▶ **Systemic infections, acute and chronic UTI caused by susceptible strains of gram-positive and gram-negative organisms.** *Adults:* 250 mg P.O. q 8 hours.
Children: 20 to 40 mg/kg P.O. daily, divided into doses given q 8 hours.
Adults and children weighing more than 20 kg (44 lb) who have severe infections or infections caused by susceptible organisms: 500 mg P.O. q 8 hours or 875 mg P.O. q 12 hours may be needed.
▶ **Uncomplicated gonorrhea.** *Adults:* 3 g P.O. as a single dose.
Children older than age 2: 50 mg/kg given with 25 mg/kg probenecid as a single dose.
▶ **Endocarditis prophylaxis for dental procedures.** *Adults:* Initially, 3 g P.O. 1 hour before procedure; then 1.5 g 6 hours later.
Children: Initially, 50 mg/kg P.O. 1 hour before procedure; then half of initial dose 6 hours later.
▶ ***H. pylori*** **eradication to reduce the risk of duodenal ulcer with clarithromycin or lansoprazole.** ***Dual therapy.*** *Adults:* Amoxicillin 1 g P.O. and lansoprazole 30 mg P.O., each q 8 hours for 14 days.
Triple therapy. *Adults:* Amoxicillin 1 g P.O., clarithromycin 500 mg P.O., lansoprazole 30 mg P.O.; each q 12 hours for 14 days.
▶ **Postexposure prophylaxis to penicillin-susceptible anthrax.** *Adults and children older than age 9:* 500 mg P.O. t.i.d. for 60 days.
Children younger than age 9: 80 mg/kg daily P.O., divided t.i.d. for 60 days.
▶ **Lyme disease‡.** *Adults:* 250 to 500 mg P.O. t.i.d. or q.i.d. for 10 to 30 days.
Children: 25 to 50 mg/kg daily (maximum, 1 to 2 g daily) P.O. in three divided doses for 10 to 30 days.
▶ **Acute complicated UTI in nonpregnant women‡.** *Adults:* 3 g P.O. as a single dose.

Contraindications and precautions

• Contraindicated in patients hypersensitive to drug or other penicillins.
• Use cautiously in patients with other drug allergies, especially to cephalosporins (possible cross-sensitivity), and in those with mononucleosis (high risk of maculopapular rash).
Lifespan: In pregnant or breast-feeding women, use cautiously.

Adverse reactions

CNS: *seizures.*
GI: nausea, vomiting, diarrhea.
Hematologic: anemia, ***thrombocytopenia, thrombocytopenic purpura,*** eosinophilia, ***leukopenia, agranulocytosis.***
Other: hypersensitivity reactions (erythematous maculopapular rash, urticaria, ***anaphylaxis***), overgrowth of nonsusceptible organisms.

Interactions

Drug-drug. *Allopurinol:* May increase risk of rash. Monitor patient.
Probenecid: May increase level of amoxicillin and other penicillins. Probenecid may be used for this purpose.

Effects on lab test results

• May increase eosinophil count. May decrease hemoglobin, hematocrit, and granulocyte, platelet, and WBC counts.
• May cause false-positive urine glucose determinations with copper sulfate tests (Clinitest).

Pharmacokinetics

Absorption: About 80%.
Distribution: Distributed into pleural, peritoneal, and synovial fluids; lungs; prostate; muscle; liver; and gallbladder. Also penetrates middle ear, maxillary sinus and bronchial secretions,

tonsils, and sputum. Amoxicillin readily crosses placenta and is 17% to 20% protein-bound.
Metabolism: Only partially metabolized.
Excretion: Excreted principally in urine by renal tubular secretion and glomerular filtration; also excreted in breast milk. *Half-life:* 1 to 1½ hours (7½ hours in severe renal impairment).

Route	Onset	Peak	Duration
P.O.	Unknown	1-2 hr	6-8 hr

Pharmacodynamics

Chemical effect: Inhibits cell-wall synthesis during bacterial multiplication.
Therapeutic effect: Kills *Streptococcus, Pneumococcus, Enterococcus, Haemophilus influenzae, Escherichia coli, Proteus mirabilis, Neisseria meningitidis, N. gonorrhoeae, Shigella, Salmonella, and Borrelia burgdorferi.*

Available forms

Capsules: 250 mg, 500 mg
Oral suspension: 50 mg/ml (pediatric drops), 125 mg/5 ml, 200mg/5 ml; 400 mg/5 ml; 250 mg/5 ml (after reconstitution)
Tablets (film coated): 500 mg, 875 mg
Tablets (chewable): 200 mg, 250 mg, 400 mg

NURSING PROCESS

Assessment
- Before therapy, assess patient's infection, ask him about allergic reactions to drug or other forms of penicillin (although negative history doesn't guarantee future safety), and obtain specimen for culture and sensitivity tests. Therapy may begin pending test results.
- Be alert for adverse reactions and drug interactions.
- Monitor patient's hydration status if adverse GI reactions occur.
- Evaluate patient's and family's knowledge of drug therapy.

Nursing diagnoses
- Infection related to susceptible bacteria
- Risk for deficient fluid volume related to drug-induced adverse GI reactions
- Deficient knowledge related to drug therapy

Planning and implementation
- Give amoxicillin at least 1 hour before bacteriostatic antibiotics.
- Give with food to prevent GI distress.
- Trimox oral suspension may be stored at room temperature for up to 2 weeks. Check individual product labels for storage information.

ALERT: Don't confuse amoxicillin with amoxapine.

Patient teaching
- If drug allergy develops, advise patient to wear or carry medical identification stating penicillin allergy.
- Tell patient to take entire quantity of drug exactly as prescribed, even after he feels better.
- Tell patient to call prescriber if rash (most common), fever, or chills develop.
- Instruct patient to take drug with food to prevent GI distress.
- Warn patient never to use leftover amoxicillin for a new illness or to share it with others.

Evaluation
- Patient is free from infection.
- Patient maintains adequate hydration.
- Patient and family state understanding of drug therapy.

amphotericin B
(am-foh-TER-ah-sin bee)
Fungilin Oral◇, Fungizone Intravenous

Pharmacologic class: polyene macrolide
Therapeutic class: antifungal
Pregnancy risk category: B

Indications and dosages

▶ **Systemic fungal infections (histoplasmosis, coccidioidomycosis, blastomycosis, cryptococcosis, disseminated candidiasis, aspergillosis, mucormycosis).** *Adults:* Test dose of 1 mg I.V. in 20 ml of D_5W infused over 20 to 30 minutes may be recommended. If tolerated, start daily dosage at 0.25 to 0.3 mg/kg by slow I.V. infusion (0.1 mg/ml) over 2 to 6 hours. Increase dose gradually, as patient develops tolerance, to maximum of 1 mg/kg daily. Do not exceed 1.5 mg/kg daily. Alternate-day dosing is recommended for total daily doses of 1.5 mg/kg. If drug is discontinued for

1 week or more, resume with initial dose and increase gradually.

▶ **Fungal endocarditis, fungal septicemia‡.** *Adults and children:* Test dose of 1 mg I.V. in 20 ml of D_5W infused over 20 minutes. If patient tolerates initial test dose, then give daily dose of 0.25 to 0.3 mg/kg, gradually increasing by 5 to 10 mg daily until daily dose is 1 mg/kg or 1.5 mg/kg q alternate day. Duration of therapy depends on severity and nature of infection.

▶ **Infections of GI tract caused by *Candida albicans*.** *Adults:* 100 mg P.O. q.i.d. for 2 weeks.

▶ **Oral and perioral candidal infections.** *Adults:* 1 lozenge q.i.d. for 7 to 14 days. Lozenge should be allowed to dissolve slowly.

▶ **Candidal cystitis‡.** *Adults:* Bladder irrigation in levels of 5 to 50 mcg/ml instilled periodically or continuously for 5 to 7 days.

▶ **Prophylaxis of fungal infection in bone marrow transplant recipients‡.** *Adults:* 0.1 mg/kg/day as I.V. infusion.

Contraindications and precautions

• Contraindicated in patients hypersensitive to drug.

• Use cautiously in patients with impaired renal function.

Lifespan: In pregnant women, use cautiously. In breast-feeding women, drug is contraindicated. In children, safety of drug hasn't been fully established, but therapy has been successful.

Adverse reactions

CNS: fever, malaise, headache, peripheral neuropathy, ***seizures,*** peripheral nerve pain, paresthesia (with I.V. use).

CV: hypotension, ***arrhythmias, asystole,*** phlebitis, thrombophlebitis.

GI: anorexia, weight loss, nausea, vomiting, dyspepsia, diarrhea, epigastric cramps, ***hemorrhagic gastroenteritis.***

GU: abnormal renal function with hypokalemia, azotemia, hyposthenuria, hypomagnesemia, renal tubular acidosis, nephrocalcinosis, ***permanent renal impairment,*** anuria, oliguria.

Hematologic: normochromic normocytic anemia, ***thrombocytopenia, agranulocytosis.***

Hepatic: ***acute liver failure.***

Metabolic: hypokalemia.

Musculoskeletal: arthralgia, myalgia.

Skin: burning, stinging, irritation, tissue damage with extravasation, pain at injection site.

Other: chills, generalized pain; ***anaphylactoid reactions.***

Interactions

Drug-drug. *Cardiac glycosides:* May increase risk of digitalis toxicity in potassium-depleted patients. Monitor patient closely.

Corticosteroids: May cause potassium depletion. Monitor potassium level.

Flucytosine: May increase flucytosine toxicity. Monitor patient closely.

Other nephrotoxic drugs (such as antibiotics, antineoplastics): May increase risk of nephrotoxicity. Give cautiously.

Skeletal muscle relaxants: May increase effects of muscle relaxants. Monitor patient for increased effects.

Thiazide diuretics: May increase potassium loss. Monitor patient for signs of hypokalemia; monitor potassium level.

Effects on lab test results

• May increase urine urea, uric acid, BUN, creatinine, alkaline phosphatase, ALT, AST, GGT, LDH, and bilirubin levels. May decrease potassium and magnesium levels. May increase or decrease glucose level.

• May decrease platelet and granulocyte counts, hemoglobin, and hematocrit. May increase or decrease WBC and eosinophil counts.

Pharmacokinetics

Absorption: Poor.

Distribution: Distributed well into pleural cavities and joints; less so into aqueous humor, bronchial secretions, pancreas, bone, muscle, and parotid gland. Drug is 90% to 95% bound to plasma proteins.

Metabolism: Not well defined.

Excretion: Up to 5% excreted unchanged in urine. *Half-life:* Initially, 24 hours; second phase, about 15 days.

Route	Onset	Peak	Duration
P.O.	Unknown	Unknown	Unknown
I.V.	Immediate	Immediate	Unknown

Pharmacodynamics

Chemical effect: May bind to sterol in fungal cell membrane and alter cell permeability, allowing leakage of intracellular components.

Therapeutic effect: Decreases activity of or kills susceptible fungi, such as *Histoplasma*

*Liquid form contains alcohol. **May contain tartrazine. ♦Canada ◊Australia †OTC ‡Off-label use

capsulatum, Coccidioides immitis, Blastomyces dermatitidis, Cryptococcus neoformans, Candida, Aspergillus fumigatus, Mucor, Rhizopus, Absidia, Entomophthora, Basidiobolus, Paracoccidioides brasiliensis, Sporothrix schenckii, and *Rhodotorula.*

Available forms

Lozenges: 10 mg ◇
Oral suspension: 100 mg/ml ◇
Powder for injection: 50-mg lyophilized cake

NURSING PROCESS

Assessment

- Obtain history of fungal infection and samples for culture and sensitivity tests before first dose. Reevaluate condition during therapy.
- Be alert for adverse reactions and drug interactions.
- Monitor patient's pulse, respiratory rate, temperature, and blood pressure every 30 minutes for at least 4 hours after giving drug I.V.; fever, shaking chills, anorexia, nausea, vomiting, headache, tachypnea, and hypotension may appear 1 to 3 hours after start of I.V. infusion. Symptoms are usually more severe with initial doses.
- Monitor BUN, creatinine (or creatinine clearance), and electrolyte levels; CBC; and liver function test results at least weekly.
- Use of amphotericin is linked to rhinocerebral phycomycosis, especially in patients with uncontrolled diabetes. Leukoencephalopathy also may occur. Monitor pulmonary function. Acute reactions are characterized by dyspnea, hypoxemia, and infiltrates.
- Evaluate patient's and family's knowledge of drug therapy.

Nursing diagnoses

- Infection related to presence of susceptible fungal infection
- Risk for injury related to drug-induced adverse reactions
- Deficient knowledge related to drug therapy

Planning and implementation

- **P.O. use:** Lozenge form of drug should be dissolved slowly.
- **I.V. use:** Give drug parenterally only in hospitalized patients, under close supervision, after diagnosis of potentially fatal fungal infection is confirmed. Be prepared to give an initial test dose; 1 mg is added to 20 ml of D_5W and infused over 20 to 30 minutes.

– Use an infusion pump and in-line filter with a mean pore diameter larger than 1 micron. Infuse over 2 to 6 hours; rapid infusion may cause CV collapse.
– Use I.V. sites in distal veins. If thrombosis occurs, alternate sites.
– Reconstituted solution is stable for 1 week in refrigerator, 24 hours at room temperature, and 8 hours in room light.
– Give antibiotics separately; don't mix or piggyback with amphotericin B.
– Amphotericin B appears to be compatible with limited amounts of heparin sodium, hydrocortisone sodium succinate, and methylprednisolone sodium succinate.
– Store dry form at 36° to 46° F (2° to 8° C). Protect from light. Reconstitute with 10 ml sterile water only. To avoid precipitation, don't mix with solutions containing sodium chloride, other electrolytes, or bacteriostatic drugs (such as benzyl alcohol). Don't use if solution contains precipitate or foreign matter.

ALERT: Different amphotericin B preparations aren't interchangable, and dosages vary.

- If BUN level exceeds 40 mg/dl, or if creatinine level exceeds 3 mg/dl, prescriber may reduce or stop drug until renal function improves. Drug may be stopped if alkaline phosphatase or bilirubin level increases.

ALERT: If patient has severe adverse infusion reactions to initial dose, stop infusion and notify prescriber, who may prescribe antipyretics, antihistamines, antiemetics, or small doses of corticosteroids. To prevent reactions during subsequent infusions, premedicate with these drugs or give amphotericin B on an alternate-day schedule.

Patient teaching

- Teach patient signs and symptoms of hypersensitivity, and stress importance of reporting them immediately.
- Warn patient that therapy may take several months; teach personal hygiene and other measures to prevent spread and recurrence of lesions.
- Urge patient to comply with prescribed regimen and recommended follow-up.
- With oral form, instruct patient to let lozenges dissolve slowly.

• With I.V. therapy, warn patient that discomfort at injection site and adverse reactions may occur during therapy, which may last several months.

Evaluation

• Patient is free from fungal infection.
• Patient doesn't experience injury as a result of drug-induced adverse reactions.
• Patient and family state understanding of drug therapy.

amphotericin B lipid complex

(am-foe-TER-ah-sin bee LIP-id KOM-pleks)
Abelcet

Pharmacologic class: polyene antibiotic
Therapeutic class: antifungal
Pregnancy risk category: B

Indications and dosages

▶ **Treatment of invasive fungal infections including *Aspergillus fumigatus, Candida albicans, C. guillermondii, C. stellatoideae,* and *C. tropicalis, Coccidioidomyces* sp., *Cryptococcus* sp., *Histoplasma* sp., and *Blastomyces* sp. in patients refractory to or intolerant of conventional amphotericin B therapy.** *Adults and children:* 5 mg/kg daily as a single I.V. infusion. Give by continuous I.V. infusion at 2.5 mg/kg/hour.

Contraindications and precautions

• Contraindicated in patients hypersensitive to amphotericin B or its components.
• Use cautiously in patients with renal impairment.
Lifespan: In pregnant women, safety hasn't been established; use only if benefits outweigh the risks to the fetus. In breast-feeding women, a decision must be made to stop breast-feeding or stop drug.

Adverse reactions

CNS: fever, headache, pain.
CV: chest pain, ***cardiac arrest,*** hypertension, hypotension.
GI: abdominal pain, diarrhea, ***hemorrhage,*** nausea, vomiting.
GU: ***kidney failure.***
Hematologic: anemia, ***leukopenia, thrombocytopenia.***
Hepatic: bilirubinemia.
Metabolic: hypokalemia.
Respiratory: dyspnea, respiratory disorder, ***respiratory failure.***
Skin: rash.
Other: chills, infection, **MULTIPLE ORGAN FAILURE, *sepsis.***

Interactions

Drug-drug: *Antineoplastics:* May increase risk of renal toxicity, bronchospasm, and hypotension. Use cautiously.
Corticosteroids, corticotropin: May enhance hypokalemia, which may lead to cardiac dysfunction. Monitor electrolytes and cardiac function.
Cyclosporin A: May increase renal toxicity. Monitor patient closely.
Cardiac glycosides: May increase risk of digitalis toxicity and induced hypokalemia. Monitor potassium level closely.
Flucytosine: May increase risk of flucytosine toxicity due to increased cellular uptake or impaired renal excretion. Use cautiously.
Imidazoles (clotrimazole, fluconazole, itraconazole, ketoconazole, miconazole): May decrease efficacy of amphotericin B because of inhibition of ergosterol synthesis. Clinical significance is unknown.
Leukocyte transfusions: May cause acute pulmonary toxicity. Avoid use together.
Nephrotoxic drugs (aminoglycosides, pentamidine): May increase risk of renal toxicity. Use cautiously. Monitor renal function closely.
Skeletal muscle relaxants: May enhance effects of skeletal muscle relaxants because of drug-induced hypokalemia. Monitor potassium level closely.
Zidovudine: May increase myelotoxicity and nephrotoxicity. Monitor renal and hematologic function.

Effects on lab test results

• May increase BUN, creatinine, alkaline phosphatase, ALT, AST, bilirubin, GGT, and LDH levels. May decrease potassium level.
• May decrease hemoglobin, hematocrit, and WBC and platelet counts.

Pharmacokinetics

Absorption: Administered I.V.

Distribution: Well distributed. Volume increases with dose. Amphotericin B lipid complex yields measurable amphotericin B levels in spleen, lung, liver, lymph nodes, kidney, heart, and brain.
Metabolism: Unknown.
Excretion: Although rapidly cleared from blood, amphotericin B lipid complex has a terminal half-life of about a week, probably because of slow elimination from tissues.

Route	Onset	Peak	Duration
I.V.	Unknown	Unknown	Unknown

Pharmacodynamics

Chemical effect: Amphotericin B binds to sterols in fungal cell membranes, resulting in enhanced cellular permeability and cell damage. It has fungistatic or fungicidal effects, depending on fungal susceptibility.
Therapeutic effect: Decreases activity of or kills susceptible fungi, including *Aspergillus fumigatus, Candida albicans, C. guillermondii, C. stellatoideae, and C. tropicalis, Cryptococcus* sp., *Coccidioidomyces* sp., *Histoplasma* sp., and *Blastomyces* sp.

Available forms

Suspension for injection: 50 mg/10-ml vial; 100 mg/20-ml vial

NURSING PROCESS

Assessment

- Obtain history of fungal infection and samples for culture and sensitivity tests before therapy. Reevaluate condition during therapy.
- Be alert for adverse reactions and drug interactions.
- Assess renal function before therapy starts.
- Monitor liver function, creatinine, and electrolyte levels (especially magnesium and potassium), and CBC during therapy.
- Evaluate patient's and family's knowledge of drug therapy.

Nursing diagnoses

- Risk for infection related to presence of susceptible fungal infection
- Risk for injury related to drug-induced adverse reactions
- Deficient knowledge related to drug therapy

Planning and implementation

- To prepare, shake the vial gently until you see no yellow sediment. Using aseptic technique, draw the calculated dose into one or more 20-ml syringes, using an 18G needle. You'll need more than one vial. Attach a 5-micron filter needle to the syringe and inject the dose into an I.V. bag of D_5W. One filter needle can be used for up to four vials of drug. The volume of D_5W should be sufficient to yield a final concentration of 1 mg/ml.
- For children and patients with CV disease, the recommended final concentration is 2 mg/ml.
- Shake the bag and check the contents for foreign matter. Discard unused drug; it contains no preservatives.
- Don't mix with saline solution or infuse in the same I.V. line as other drugs. Don't use an in-line filter.
- If infusing through an existing I.V. line, flush first with D_5W.
- Infusions are stable for up to 48 hours when refrigerated at 36° to 46° F (2° to 8° C) and for up to 6 hours at room temperature.
- Refrigerate and protect from light. Don't freeze.

ALERT: Different amphotericin B preparations aren't interchangable, and dosages vary.

- Premedicate patient with acetaminophen, antihistamines, and corticosteroids to prevent or lessen the severity of infusion-related reactions, such as fever, chills, nausea, and vomiting, which occur 1 to 2 hours after the start of infusion.
- Slowing the infusion rate also may decrease the risk of infusion-related reactions.
- For infusions lasting more than 2 hours, shake the I.V. bag every 2 hours to ensure an even suspension.
- If severe respiratory distress develops, stop the infusion, provide supportive therapy for anaphylaxis, and notify the prescriber. Don't resume the infusion.

Patient teaching

- Inform patient that fever, chills, nausea, and vomiting may occur during the infusion and that these reactions usually subside with subsequent doses.
- Instruct patient to report any redness or pain at the infusion site.

• Teach patient to recognize and report any symptoms of acute hypersensitivity, such as respiratory distress.
• Tell patient to expect frequent laboratory testing to monitor kidney and liver function.

Evaluation
• Patient is free from fungal infection.
• Patient has no injury from adverse drug reactions.
• Patient and family state understanding of drug therapy.

amphotericin B liposomal
(am-foh-TER-ah-sin bee lye-po-SO-mal)
AmBisome

Pharmacologic class: polyene antibiotic
Therapeutic class: antifungal
Pregnancy risk category: B

Indications and dosages

▶ **Empirical therapy for presumed fungal infection in febrile, neutropenic patients.** *Adults and children:* 3 mg/kg I.V. infusion daily.
▶ **Treatment of systemic fungal infections caused by *Aspergillus* sp., *Candida* sp., or *Cryptococcus* sp. refractory to amphotericin B deoxycholate or in patients with renal impairment or unacceptable toxicity that precludes the use of amphotericin B deoxycholate.** *Adults and children:* 3 to 5 mg/kg I.V. infusion daily.
▶ **Treatment of visceral leishmaniasis in immunocompetent patients.** *Adults and children:* 3 mg/kg I.V. infusion daily on days 1 to 5, 14, and 21. A repeat course of therapy may be beneficial if initial treatment fails to achieve parasitic clearance.
▶ **Treatment of visceral leishmaniasis in immunocompromised patients.** *Adults and children:* 4 mg/kg I.V. infusion daily on days 1 to 5, 10, 17, 24, 31, and 38. Expert advice regarding further treatment is recommended if initial therapy fails or relapse occurs.
▶ **Cryptococcal meningitis in HIV-infected patients.** *Adults and children:* 6 mg/kg daily I.V. infusion over 2 hours. Infusion time may be reduced to 1 hour if well tolerated or increased if discomfort occurs.

Contraindications and precautions

• Contraindicated in patients hypersensitive to drug or its components. Use cautiously in patients with impaired renal function.
Lifespan: In pregnant women and elderly patients, use cautiously.

Adverse reactions

CNS: *anxiety, confusion, fever, headache, insomnia, asthenia, pain.*
CV: *chest pain, hypotension, tachycardia,* hypertension, *edema,* vasodilation.
EENT: *epistaxis,* rhinitis.
GI: *nausea, vomiting, abdominal pain, diarrhea,* ***hemorrhage.***
GU: *hematuria.*
Hepatic: *hepatomegaly.*
Metabolic: *hyperglycemia,* hypernatremia, *hypocalcemia, hypokalemia, hypomagnesemia.*
Musculoskeletal: *back pain.*
Respiratory: *cough, dyspnea,* hypoxia, *pleural effusion, lung disorder,* hyperventilation.
Skin: *pruritus, rash,* sweating.
Other: *chills, infection,* ***anaphylaxis, sepsis, blood product infusion reaction.***

Interactions

Drug-drug. *Antineoplastics:* May enhance potential for renal toxicity, bronchospasm, and hypotension. Use cautiously.
Cardiac glycosides: May increase risk of digitalis toxicity in potassium-depleted patients. Monitor potassium level closely.
Corticosteroids, corticotropin: May potentiate hypokalemia, which could result in cardiac dysfunction. Monitor potassium level and cardiac function.
Flucytosine: May increase flucytosine toxicity by increasing cellular uptake or impairing renal excretion of flucytosine. Monitor renal function closely.
Imidazole antifungals (clotrimazole, ketoconazole, miconazole): May induce fungal resistance to amphotericin B. Use combination therapy with caution.
Leukocyte transfusions: May increase risk of acute pulmonary toxicity. Avoid using together.
Other nephrotoxic drugs (antibiotics, antineoplastics): May increase risk of nephrotoxicity. Give cautiously. Monitor renal function closely.
Skeletal muscle relaxants: May enhance effects of skeletal muscle relaxants because of

amphotericin-induced hypokalemia. Monitor potassium level.

Effects on lab test results

- May increase BUN, creatinine, glucose, sodium, alkaline phosphatase, ALT, AST, bilirubin, GGT, and LDH levels. May decrease potassium, calcium, and magnesium levels.

Pharmacokinetics

Absorption: Administered I.V.
Distribution: Unknown.
Metabolism: Unknown.
Excretion: *Initial half-life:* 7 to10 hours with 24 hour dosing; *terminal elimination half-life:* about 4 to 6 days.

Route	Onset	Peak	Duration
I.V.	Unknown	Unknown	Unknown

Pharmacodynamics

Chemical effect: Amphotericin B binds to the sterol component of a fungal cell membrane, leading to alterations in cell permeability and to cell death.
Therapeutic effect: Decreases activity of or kills susceptible fungi, including *Aspergillus* sp., *Candida* sp., or *Cryptococcus* sp. refractory to amphotericin B deoxycholate or in patients with renal impairment or unacceptable toxicity that precludes the use of amphotericin B deoxycholate. Treats visceral protozoal infections caused by *Leishmania sp.*

Available forms

Injection: 50-mg vial

NURSING PROCESS

Assessment

- Obtain history of fungal infection and samples for culture and sensitivity tests before therapy. Reevaluate condition during therapy.
- Carefully assess patients who are also receiving chemotherapy or bone marrow transplantation because they are at greater risk for additional adverse reactions, including seizures, arrhythmias, thrombocytopenia, and respiratory failure.
- Monitor CBC, liver function test results, and creatinine, BUN, and CBC and electrolyte levels, particularly magnesium and potassium.
- Monitor patient for signs of hypokalemia, such as ECG changes, muscle weakness, cramping, and drowsiness.
- Watch for adverse reactions. Patients who receive drug may have fewer chills, decreased BUN level, a lower risk of hypokalemia, and less vomiting than patients who receive regular amphotericin B.
- Evaluate patient's and family's knowledge of drug therapy.

Nursing diagnoses

- Risk for infection related to presence of susceptible fungal or parasite infections
- Risk for injury related to drug-induced adverse reactions
- Deficient knowledge related to drug therapy

Planning and implementation

ALERT: Different amphotericin B preparations aren't interchangeable, and dosages vary.
- Reconstitute each 50-mg vial of amphotericin B liposomal with 12 ml of sterile water for injection to yield a solution of 4 mg amphotericin B per ml. Don't reconstitute with bacteriostatic water for injection, and don't allow bacteriostatic drug into the solution. Don't reconstitute with saline solution; instead, add saline solution to the reconstituted concentration, or mix with other drugs. After reconstitution, shake vial vigorously for 30 seconds or until particulate matter disappears. Withdraw calculated amount of reconstituted solution into a sterile syringe and inject through a 5-micron filter into the appropriate amount of D_5W to a final concentration of 1 to 2 mg/ml. Lower concentrations (0.2 to 0.5 mg/ml) may be appropriate for children to provide sufficient volume for infusion.
- Flush existing I.V. line with D_5W before infusing drug. If this isn't feasible, give drug through a separate line.
- Use a controlled infusion device and an inline filter with a mean pore diameter larger than 1 micron. Initially, infuse drug over at least 2 hours. Infusion time may be reduced to 1 hour if the treatment is well tolerated. If the patient has discomfort during infusion, the duration of infusion may be increased.
- Observe patient closely for adverse reactions during infusion. If anaphylaxis occurs, stop the infusion immediately, provide supportive therapy, and notify the prescriber.

• Refrigerate unopened drug at 36° to 46° F (2° to 8° C). Once reconstituted, the product may be stored for up to 24 hours at 36° to 46° F (2° to 8° C). Don't freeze.
• To lessen the risk or severity of adverse reactions, premedicate patient with antipyretics, antihistamines, antiemetics, or corticosteroids.
• Therapy may take several weeks to months.

Patient teaching
• Teach patient signs and symptoms of hypersensitivity, and stress importance of reporting them immediately.
• Warn patient that therapy may take several months; teach personal hygiene and other measures to prevent spread and recurrence of lesions.
• Instruct patient to report adverse reactions.
• Instruct patient to watch for and report signs of hypokalemia, such as muscle weakness, cramping, and drowsiness.
• Advise patient that frequent laboratory testing will be performed.

Evaluation
• Patient is free from fungal or parasite infection.
• Patient doesn't experience injury as a result of drug-induced adverse reactions.
• Patient and family state understanding of drug therapy.

ampicillin
(am-pih-SIL-in)
Apo-Ampi♦, Novo-Ampicillin♦, Nu-Ampi♦, Omnipen, Principen

ampicillin sodium
Ampicin♦, Ampicyn Injection◇, Omnipen-N, Penbritin♦, Polycillin-N, Totacillin-N

ampicillin trihydrate
Ampicyn Oral◇, D-Amp, Omnipen, Penbritin◇, Polycillin, Principen-250, Principen-500, Totacillin

Pharmacologic class: aminopenicillin
Therapeutic class: antibiotic
Pregnancy risk category: B

Indications and dosages
▶ **Systemic infections and acute and chronic UTI caused by susceptible gram-positive and gram-negative organisms.** *Adults and children weighing 20 kg (44 lb) or more:* 250 to 500 mg P.O. q 6 hours; or 2 to 12 g I.M. or I.V. daily in divided doses q 4 to 6 hours.
Children weighing less than 20 kg: 50 to 100 mg/kg P.O. daily in divided doses q 6 hours; or 100 to 200 mg/kg I.M. or I.V. daily in divided doses q 6 hours.
Neonates older than 1 week: 50 mg/kg I.V. q 8 hours (if weight is under 2 kg) or q 6 hours (if weight is over 2 kg).
Neonates younger than 1 week: 50 to 75 mg/kg I.V. q 12 hours (if weight is under 2 kg) or q 8 hours (if weight is over 2 kg).
▶ **Prophylaxis of neonatal group B streptococcus infections‡.** *Adults:* 2 g I.V. given to the mother 4 hours before delivery, then 1 to 2 g I.V q 4 to 6 hours until delivery.
▶ **Meningitis.** *Adults:* 8 to 14 g (or 150 mg to 200 mg/kg) I.V. daily in divided doses q 3 to 4 hours.
Children ages 2 months to 12 years: Up to 400 mg/kg I.V. daily for 3 days; then up to 300 mg/kg I.M. divided q 4 hours.
▶ **Uncomplicated gonorrhea.** *Adults and children weighing more than 45 kg (99 lb):* 3.5 g P.O. with 1 g probenecid in a single dose.
▶ **Endocarditis prophylaxis for dental procedures.** *Adults:* 2 g I.V. or I.M. 30 minutes before procedure.
Children: 50 mg/kg I.V. or I.M. 30 minutes before procedure.
▶ **Treatment of enterococcal endocarditis.** *Adults:* 12 g daily by continuous I.V. infusion or in six equally divided doses in conjunction with gentamicin for 4 to 6 weeks.

Contraindications and precautions
• Contraindicated in patients hypersensitive to drug or other penicillins.
• Use cautiously in patients with other drug allergies, especially to cephalosporins (possible cross-sensitivity), and in those with mononucleosis (high risk of maculopapular rash).
Lifespan: In pregnant and breast-feeding women, use cautiously.

Adverse reactions
CNS: *seizures.*
CV: vein irritation, thrombophlebitis.

GI: *nausea,* vomiting, *diarrhea,* glossitis, stomatitis.
Hematologic: anemia, ***thrombocytopenia, thrombocytopenic purpura***, eosinophilia, ***leukopenia, agranulocytosis.***
Other: hypersensitivity reactions (maculopapular rash, urticaria, ***anaphylaxis***), overgrowth of nonsusceptible organisms, pain at injection site.

Interactions

Drug-drug. *Allopurinol:* May increase risk of rash. Monitor patient.
Probenecid: May increase level of ampicillin and other penicillins. Probenecid may be used for this purpose.

Effects on lab test results

- May increase eosinophil count. May decrease hemoglobin, hematocrit, and platelet, WBC, and granulocyte counts.
- May cause false-positive urine glucose determinations with copper sulfate tests (Clinitest).

Pharmacokinetics

Absorption: About 42% is absorbed after an oral dose; unknown after I.M. administration.
Distribution: Distributed into pleural, peritoneal, and synovial fluids; lungs; prostate; liver; and gallbladder. Also penetrates middle ear effusions, maxillary sinus and bronchial secretions, tonsils, and sputum. Ampicillin is minimally protein-bound at 15% to 25%.
Metabolism: Only partially.
Excretion: Excreted in urine by renal tubular secretion and glomerular filtration. *Half-life:* About 1 to 1½ hours (10 to 24 hours in severe renal impairment).

Route	Onset	Peak	Duration
P.O.	Unknown	2 hr	6-8 hr
I.V.	Immediate	Immediate	Unknown
I.M.	Unknown	1 hr	Unknown

Pharmacodynamics

Chemical effect: Inhibits cell-wall synthesis during microorganism multiplication.
Therapeutic effect: Kills susceptible bacteria, including non-penicillinase-producing gram-positive bacteria and many gram-negative organisms, such as *Neisseria gonorrhoeae, N. meningitidis, Haemophilus influenzae, Escherichia coli, Proteus mirabilis, Salmonella,* and *Shigella.*

Available forms

Capsules: 250 mg, 500 mg
Infusion: 500 mg, 1 g, 2 g
Injection: 125 mg, 250 mg, 500 mg, 1 g, 2 g, 10-g bulk package
Oral suspension: 125 mg/5 ml, 250 mg/5 ml (after reconstitution)

NURSING PROCESS

Assessment

- Obtain history of patient's infection before therapy, and reassess for improvement regularly thereafter.
- Before giving drug, ask patient about previous allergic reaction to penicillin. A negative history of penicillin allergy doesn't rule out future reaction.
- Obtain specimen for culture and sensitivity tests before giving first dose.
- Be alert for adverse reactions and drug interactions.
- Monitor patient's hydration status if adverse GI reactions occur.
- Evaluate patient's and family's knowledge of drug therapy.

Nursing diagnoses

- Risk for infection related to presence of susceptible bacterial infection
- Risk for deficient fluid volume related to drug-induced adverse GI reactions
- Deficient knowledge related to drug therapy

Planning and implementation

- **P.O. use:** Give 1 hour before or 2 hours after meals. When given orally, drug may cause adverse GI reactions. Food may interfere with absorption.
- **I.V. use:** Reconstitute with bacteriostatic water for injection. Use 5 ml for 125-mg, 250-mg, or 500-mg vials; 7.4 ml for 1-g vials; and 14.8 ml for 2-g vials. Give direct I.V. injections over 3 to 5 minutes for doses of 500 mg or less; over 10 to 15 minutes for larger doses. Don't exceed 100 mg/minute. Alternatively, dilute in 50 to 100 ml of normal saline solution and give by intermittent infusion over 15 to 30 minutes. Don't mix with solutions containing dextrose or fructose because

these solutions promote rapid breakdown of ampicillin.
– Use initial dilution within 1 hour. Follow manufacturer's directions for stability data when ampicillin is further diluted for I.V. infusion.
– Give intermittently to prevent vein irritation. Change site every 48 hours.
– Don't give I.V. unless prescribed and infection is severe or patient can't take oral dose.
- **I.M. use:** Don't give I.M. unless prescribed and infection is severe or patient can't take oral dose.
- Dosage should be altered in patients with impaired renal function.
- Give ampicillin at least 1 hour before bacteriostatic antibiotics.
- In pediatric meningitis, ampicillin may be given with parenteral chloramphenicol for 24 hours pending culture results.
- Stop drug immediately if anaphylaxis occurs. Notify prescriber and prepare to administer immediate treatment, such as epinephrine, corticosteroids, antihistamines, and other resuscitative measures.

Patient teaching
- Tell patient to take entire quantity of drug exactly as prescribed, even after he feels better.
- Tell patient to call prescriber if a rash (most common), fever, or chills develop.
- Warn patient never to use leftover ampicillin for a new illness or to share it with others.
- Tell patient to take oral ampicillin 1 hour before or 2 hours after meals for best absorption.

Evaluation
- Patient is free from infection.
- Patient maintains adequate hydration.
- Patient and family state understanding of drug therapy.

ampicillin sodium and sulbactam sodium
(am-pih-SIL-in SOH-dee-um and sul-BAC-tam SOH-dee-um)
Unasyn

Pharmacologic class: aminopenicillin/beta-lactamase inhibitor combination
Therapeutic class: antibiotic
Pregnancy risk category: B

Indications and dosages
▶ **Intra-abdominal, gynecologic, and skin and skin-structure infections caused by susceptible gram-positive, gram-negative, and beta-lactamase-producing strains.** *Adults:* Dosage expressed as total drug (each 1.5-g vial contains 1 g ampicillin sodium and 0.5 g sulbactam sodium)—1.5 to 3 g I.M. or I.V. q 6 hours. Maximum daily dosage is 4 g sulbactam (12 g of combined drugs).
▶ **Skin and skin-structure infections caused by susceptible organisms.** *Children older than age 1:* 300 mg/kg I.V. daily in equally divided doses q 6 hours. Children should receive a maximum of 14 days of therapy. Children weighing 40 kg (88 lb) or more may receive the usual adult dosage.
▶ **Pelvic inflammatory disease.** *Adults and children:* 3 g (2 g ampicillin and 1 g sulbactam) I.V. or I.M. q 6 hours, given with doxycycline 100 mg P.O. q 12 hours. Continue parenteral therapy for 24 hours after clinical improvement. Continue with oral doxycycline 100 mg P.O. b.i.d. to complete the 14-day cycle.

Contraindications and precautions
- Contraindicated in patients hypersensitive to drug or other penicillins.
- Use cautiously in patients with other drug allergies, especially to cephalosporins (possible cross-sensitivity), and in those with mononucleosis (high risk of maculopapular rash).

Lifespan: In pregnant and breast-feeding women, use cautiously. In children younger than age 1, safety of drug hasn't been established. In children age 1 and older, drug can be used I.V. for skin and skin-structure infections. Children shouldn't receive the drug I.M.

Adverse reactions
CV: vein irritation, thrombophlebitis.
GI: *nausea,* vomiting, *diarrhea,* glossitis, stomatitis.
Hematologic: anemia, ***thrombocytopenia, thrombocytopenic purpura,*** eosinophilia, ***leukopenia, agranulocytosis.***
Other: hypersensitivity reactions (erythematous maculopapular rash, urticaria, ***anaphylax-***

is), overgrowth of nonsusceptible organisms, pain at injection site.

Interactions

Drug-drug. *Allopurinol:* May increase risk of rash. Monitor patient.
Oral contraceptives: May decrease efficacy of oral contraceptives. Advise patient to use barrier contraception until course of therapy is complete.
Probenecid: May increase ampicillin level. Probenecid may be used for this purpose.

Effects on lab test results

- May increase BUN, creatinine, ALT, AST, alkaline phosphatase, bilirubin, LDH, CK, and GGT levels.
- May increase eosinophil count. May decrease hemoglobin, hematocrit, and platelet, WBC, and granulocyte counts.
- May cause false-positive urine glucose determinations with copper sulfate tests (Clinitest).

Pharmacokinetics

Absorption: Unknown.
Distribution: Both drugs are distributed into pleural, peritoneal, and synovial fluids; lungs; prostate; liver; and gallbladder. They also penetrate middle ear effusions, maxillary sinus and bronchial secretions, tonsils, and sputum. Ampicillin is minimally protein-bound at 15% to 25%; sulbactam is about 38% protein-bound.
Metabolism: Both drugs are metabolized only partially.
Excretion: Both drugs are excreted in urine by renal tubular secretion and glomerular filtration. *Half-life:* 1 to 1½ hours (10 to 24 hours in severe renal impairment).

Route	Onset	Peak	Duration
I.V.	Immediate	Immediate	Unknown
I.M.	Unknown	Unknown	Unknown

Pharmacodynamics

Chemical effect: Ampicillin inhibits cell-wall synthesis during microorganism multiplication; sulbactam inactivates bacterial beta-lactamase, the enzyme that inactivates ampicillin and provides bacterial resistance to it.
Therapeutic effect: Kills susceptible bacteria, such as beta-lactamase-producing strains of *Staphylococcus aureus, Escherichia coli, Klebsiella, Proteus mirabilis, Bacteroides, Enterobacter,* and *Acinetobacter calcoaceticus.*

Available forms

Injection: vials and piggyback vials containing 1.5 g (1 g ampicillin sodium with 0.5 g sulbactam sodium); 3 g (2 g ampicillin sodium with 1 g sulbactam sodium); pharmacy bulk package containing 15 g (10 g ampicillin sodium with 5 g sulbactam sodium)

NURSING PROCESS

Assessment

- Obtain history of patient's infection before therapy and observe for improvement in condition throughout therapy.
- Before giving drug, ask patient about previous allergic reaction to penicillin. A negative history of penicillin allergy doesn't rule out future reaction.
- Obtain specimen for culture and sensitivity tests before administering first dose.
- Be alert for adverse reactions and drug interactions.
- Monitor patient's hydration status if adverse GI reactions occur.
- Evaluate patient's and family's knowledge of drug therapy.

Nursing diagnoses

- Risk for infection related to presence of susceptible bacterial infection
- Risk for deficient fluid volume related to drug-induced adverse GI reactions
- Deficient knowledge related to drug therapy

Planning and implementation

- **I.V. use:** When preparing injection, reconstitute powder with any of the following diluents: normal saline solution, D_5W, lactated Ringer's solution, 1/6 M sodium lactate, dextrose 5% in half-normal saline solution for injection, and 10% inert sugar. Stability varies with diluent, temperature, and concentration of solution.
– After reconstitution, allow vials to stand for a few minutes to allow foam to dissipate to permit visual inspection of contents for particles.
– Give dose by slow injection (over 10 to 15 minutes), or dilute in 50 to 100 ml of a compatible diluent and infuse over 15 to 30 minutes. If permitted, give intermittently to prevent vein irritation. Change site every 48 hours.

– Don't add or mix with other drugs because they might be physically or chemically incompatible.
• **I.M. use:** Reconstitute with sterile water for injection or with 0.5% or 2% lidocaine hydrochloride. Add 3.2 ml to a 1.5-g vial (or 6.4 ml to a 3-g vial) to yield a concentration of 375 mg/ml. Administer deeply.
• Dosage should be altered in patients with impaired renal function.
• Give drug at least 1 hour before bacteriostatic antibiotics.
• Stop drug immediately if anaphylaxis occurs. Notify prescriber and prepare to give immediate treatment, such as epinephrine, corticosteroids, antihistamines; and other resuscitative measures.

Patient teaching
• Tell patient to call prescriber if rash (most common), fever, or chills develop.
• Advise women taking oral contraceptives to use an additional form of contraception during drug therapy.

☑ Evaluation
• Patient is free from infection.
• Patient maintains adequate hydration.
• Patient and family state understanding of drug therapy.

amprenavir
(am-PREH-nah-veer)
Agenerase

Pharmacologic class: HIV protease inhibitor
Therapeutic class: antiviral
Pregnancy risk category: C

Indications and dosages
▶ **Treatment of HIV-1 infection with other antiretrovirals.** *Adults and adolescents ages 13 to 16 weighing 50 kg (110 lb) or more:* 1,200 mg (eight 150-mg capsules) P.O. b.i.d. with other antiretrovirals.
Children ages 4 to 16 weighing less than 50 kg: For capsules, give 20 mg/kg P.O. b.i.d. or 15 mg/kg P.O. t.i.d. (maximum, 2,400 mg daily) with other antiretrovirals. For oral solution, give 22.5 mg/kg (1.5 ml/kg) P.O. b.i.d. or 17 mg/kg (1.1 ml/kg) P.O. t.i.d. (maximum, 2,800 mg daily) with other antiretrovirals.
Patients with hepatic impairment and a Child-Pugh score of 5 to 8: For capsule, reduce dosage to 450 mg P.O. b.i.d.
Patients with hepatic impairment and a Child-Pugh score of 9 to 12: For capsules, reduce dosage to 300 mg P.O. b.i.d.

Contraindications and precautions
• Contraindicated in patients hypersensitive to amprenavir or its components.
• Use cautiously in patients with moderate or severe hepatic impairment, diabetes mellitus, sulfonamide allergy, or hemophilia A or B.
• Drug can cause severe or life-threatening rash, including Stevens-Johnson syndrome. Therapy should be stopped if patient develops a severe or life-threatening rash or a moderate rash with systemic signs and symptoms.
Lifespan: In pregnant women, use cautiously. In children age 4 and younger, drug is contraindicated because of risk of toxicity.

Adverse reactions
CNS: *paresthesia,* depressive or mood disorders.
GI: *nausea, vomiting, diarrhea or loose stools,* taste disorders.
Hepatic: *hypertriglyceridemia,* hypercholesterolemia.
Metabolic: *hyperglycemia.*
Skin: *rash,* ***Stevens-Johnson syndrome.***

Interactions
Drug-drug. *Antacids:* Interferes with absorption. Separate doses by at least 1 hour.
Antiarrhythmics, such as amiodarone; lidocaine (systemic); quinidine; anticoagulants, such as warfarin; tricyclic antidepressants: May affect amprenavir level. Monitor amprenavir level closely.
Bepridil and other calcium channel blockers, dihydroergotamine, midazolam, rifampin, triazolam: May cause serious and life-threatening interactions. Avoid using together.
Cimetidine, indinavir, nelfinavir, ritonavir: May increase amprenavir level. Monitor patient closely for increased adverse effects.
Efavirenz: May decrease exposure of amprenavir to the body. Increase dose accordingly.
Ethinyl estradiol and norethindrone: Loss of virologic response and possible resistance to

amprenavir. Tell patient to use alternative method of birth control.
Ketoconazole: May increase levels of both drugs. Monitor patient closely for adverse reactions.
HMG-CoA reductase inhibitors, such as atorvastatin, lovastatin, and simvastatin: May increase levels of these drugs; therefore, may increase risk of myopathy, including rhabdomyolysis. Avoid using together.
Macrolides: May increase amprenavir level. No adjustment necessary.
Psychotherapeutic agents: May increase CNS effects. Monitor patient closely.
Rifabutin: May decrease exposure of amprenavir to the body and increase rifabutin level by 200%. Decrease rifabutin dose to 150 mg daily or 300 mg two to three times weekly.
Saquinavir: May decrease exposure of amprenavir to the body. Monitor patient closely.
Sildenafil: May substantially increase sildenafil levels, causing an increase in sildenafil-associated effects, including hypotension, and priapism. Don't exceed 25 mg of sildenafil in a 48-hour period.
Drug-herb. *St. John's wort:* May decrease amprenavir level. Discourage using together.
Drug-food. *Grapefruit juice:* May affect blood levels of amprenavir. Monitor patient closely.
High-fat meals: May reduce drug absorption. Discourage taking drug with a high-fat meal.

Effects on lab test results

- May increase glucose, triglyceride, and cholesterol levels.

Pharmacokinetics

Absorption: Rapid.
Distribution: Apparent volume of distribution is about 430 L. In vitro, about 90% of drug binds to plasma proteins.
Metabolism: Cytochrome P-450 CYP3A4 enzyme system metabolizes the drug in the liver.
Excretion: Minimal excretion of unchanged drug in urine and feces. *Half-life (plasma elimination):* 7 to 10½ hours.

Route	Onset	Peak	Duration
P.O.	Unknown	1-2 hr	Unknown

Pharmacodynamics

Chemical effect: Inhibits HIV-1 protease by binding to the active site of HIV-1 protease, which causes immature noninfectious viral particles to form.
Therapeutic effect: Reduces symptoms of HIV-1 infection.

Available forms

Capsules: 50 mg, 150 mg
Oral solution: 15 mg/ml

NURSING PROCESS

Assessment

- Assess patient for appropriateness of drug therapy.
- Because drug may interact with other drugs, obtain patient's complete drug history. Ask patient to show you the drugs he takes.
- Patients with moderate or severe hepatic impairment, diabetes mellitus, known sulfonamide allergy, or hemophilia A or B must be monitored very closely while taking this drug.
- Determine whether patient is pregnant or plans to become pregnant. No adequate studies exist regarding effects of amprenavir given during pregnancy. Use during pregnancy only if potential benefits outweigh risks.
- Monitor patient for adverse reactions. A patient taking a protease inhibitor may experience a redistribution of body fat, including central obesity, dorsocervical fat enlargement (buffalo hump), peripheral wasting, breast enlargement, and cushingoid appearance.
- Evaluate patient's and family's knowledge about drug therapy.

Nursing diagnoses

- Risk for infection secondary to presence of HIV
- Ineffective individual coping related to HIV infection
- Deficient knowledge related to drug therapy

Planning and implementation

- Don't give patient high-fat foods because they may decrease absorption of oral drug.

ALERT: Amprenavir capsules aren't interchangeable with amprenavir oral solution on a milligram-per-milligram basis.

- Monitor coagulation studies. Drug provides high daily doses of vitamin E.
- Protease inhibitors cause spontaneous bleeding in some patients with hemophilia A or B. In some patients, additional factor VIII may be

required. Often, treatment with protease inhibitors is continued or restarted.

Patient teaching

- Inform patient that drug doesn't cure HIV infection and that opportunistic infections and other complications may develop. Also, explain that drug doesn't reduce the risk of transmitting HIV to others.
- Tell patient that drug can be taken with or without food, but that he shouldn't take it with a high-fat meal because doing so may decrease drug absorption.
- Urge patient to report adverse reactions, especially rash.
- Advise patient to take drug every day as prescribed, always with other antiretrovirals. Warn against changing the dosage or stopping the drug without prescriber's approval.
- If patient takes an antacid or didanosine, tell him to do so 1 hour before or after amprenavir to avoid interfering with amprenavir absorption.
- If patient misses a dose by more than 4 hours, tell him to wait and take the next dose at the regularly scheduled time. If he misses a dose by less than 4 hours, tell him to take the dose as soon as possible and then take the next dose at the regularly scheduled time. Caution against doubling the dose.
- Caution patient not to take supplemental vitamin E because high levels of this vitamin may worsen the blood coagulation defect of vitamin K deficiency caused by anticoagulant therapy or malabsorption.
- If patient uses a hormonal contraceptive, warn her to use another contraceptive during therapy with amprenavir.
- Urge patient to notify prescriber about planned, suspected, or known pregnancy during therapy.
- Advise patients receiving sildenafil of the increased risk of sildenafil-associated adverse events with one dose, including hypotension, visual changes, and priapism. These patients should promptly report symptoms to their prescribers and shouldn't exceed 25 mg of sildenafil in a 48-hour period.

☑ Evaluation

- Patient exhibits reduced signs and symptoms of infection.
- Patient demonstrates adequate coping mechanisms.
- Patient and family state understanding of drug therapy.

anakinra
(ann-u-KIN-ruh)
Kineret

Pharmacologic classification: lymphokine
Therapeutic classification: immunoregulatory drug; antirheumatic
Pregnancy risk category: B

Indications and dosages

▶ **Moderate-to-severe active rheumatoid arthritis (RA) after one failure with disease-modifying antirheumatics.** *Adults:* 100 mg S.C. daily.

Contraindications and precautions

- Contraindicated in patients hypersensitive to *Escherichia coli*–derived proteins or components of the product. Don't use in immunosuppressed patients or in patients with chronic or active infection. Use extreme caution with other tumor necrosis factor (TNF) blockers because of the increased risk of neutropenia.

Lifespan: In pregnant women, no adequate, well-controlled studies exist. Use only if necessary. In breast-feeding women, use cautiously because it's unknown whether drug appears in breast milk. In patients with juvenile RA, safety and efficacy haven't been established. In elderly patients, use drug cautiously because they have a greater risk of infection and are more likely to have renal impairment.

Adverse reactions

CNS: *headache.*
EENT: sinusitis.
GI: abdominal pain, diarrhea, nausea.
Hematologic: ***neutropenia.***
Respiratory: *upper respiratory tract infection.*
Skin: *injection site reactions (erythema, ecchymosis, inflammation, pain).*
Other: *infection (cellulitis, pneumonia, bone and joint),* flu-like symptoms.

Interactions

Drug-drug. No drug-drug interaction studies have been conducted.
Etanercept, other TNF blockers: May increase risk of severe infection. Use together with extreme caution.
Vaccines: May decrease effectiveness of vaccines or increase risk of secondary transmission of infection with live vaccines. Avoid using together.

Effects on lab test results

• May increase differential percentage of eosinophils. May decrease neutrophil, WBC, and platelet counts.

Pharmacokinetics

Absorption: Plasma levels peak 3 to 7 hours after S.C. administration (1 to 2 mg/kg).
Distribution: Absolute bioavailability is 95% after a 70-mg S.C. injection.
Metabolism: Unknown.
Excretion: Renal. Clearance increases with increasing creatinine clearance and body weight. Mean plasma clearance decreases 70% to 75% in patients with severe or end-stage renal disease (creatinine clearance less than 30 ml/minute). *Half-life:* 4 to 6 hours.

Route	Onset	Peak	Duration
S.C.	Unknown	3-7 hr	Unknown

Pharmacodynamics

Chemical effect: A recombinant, nonglycosylated form of the human interleukin-1 receptor antagonist (IL-1Ra). The level of naturally occurring IL-1Ra in synovium and synovial fluid from patients with RA isn't enough to compete with the elevated level of locally produced IL-1. Anakinra blocks the biological activity of IL-1 by competitively inhibiting IL-1 from binding to the interleukin-1–type receptor, which is found in a wide variety of tissues and organs.
Therapeutic effect: Decreases inflammation and cartilage degradation.

Available forms

Injection: 100 mg/ml in prefilled glass syringe.

NURSING PROCESS

Assessment

• Assess patient's condition before starting drug therapy.
• Assess patient for signs and symptoms of chronic or active infection. Don't start treatment if patient has active infection.
• Obtain neutrophil count before treatment, monthly for the first 3 months of treatment, and then quarterly for up to 1 year.
• Monitor patient for infections and injection site reactions.

Nursing diagnoses

• Risk of infection related to anakinra therapy.
• Risk of pain due to underlying rheumatoid arthritis.
• Risk of impaired skin integrity due to injection site reaction.

Planning and implementation

• Inject the entire contents of the prefilled syringe S.C.
• Discontinue drug if patient develops a serious infection.
ALERT: Don't confuse anakinra with amikacin.

Patient teaching

• Tell patient to store drug in refrigerator and not to freeze or expose to excessive heat. Tell patient to allow drug to come to room temperature before injecting.
• Teach patient proper technique for S.C. administration and disposal of syringes in a puncture-resistant container. Also, caution patient not to reuse needles.
• Urge patient to rotate injection sites.
• Review with patient the signs and symptoms of allergic and other adverse reactions and the symptoms of infection. Urge patient to contact prescriber immediately if they arise. Inform patient that injection site reactions are common, are usually mild, and typically last 14 to 28 days.
• Tell patient to avoid live-virus vaccines while taking anakinra.

Evaluation

• Patient is free from infection or adverse reactions during drug therapy.
• Patient's symptoms of RA are relieved.

• Patient and family state understanding of drug therapy and give drug properly.

anastrozole

(uh-NAS-truh-zohl)

Arimidex

Pharmacologic class: nonsteroidal aromatase inhibitor
Therapeutic class: antineoplastic
Pregnancy risk category: D

Indications and dosages

▶ **First-line treatment of postmenopausal women with hormone receptor positive or hormone receptor unknown locally advanced or metastatic breast cancer; treatment of advanced breast cancer in postmenopausal women with disease progression following tamoxifen therapy; adjuvant treatment of postmenopausal women with hormone receptor positive early breast cancer.**
Adults: 1 mg P.O. daily.

Contraindications and precautions

Lifespan: In pregnant women, drug isn't recommended. In breast-feeding women, use cautiously. In children, safety of drug hasn't been established.

Adverse reactions

CNS: pain, asthenia, headache, dizziness, depression, paresthesia.
CV: chest pain, edema, thromboembolic disease, peripheral edema, *vasodilation.*
EENT: pharyngitis.
GI: nausea, vomiting, diarrhea, constipation, dry mouth, abdominal pain, anorexia.
GU: pelvic pain, ***vaginal hemorrhage,*** vaginal dryness.
Metabolic: weight gain, increased appetite.
Musculoskeletal: back pain, bone pain.
Respiratory: dyspnea, increased cough.
Skin: *hot flashes,* rash, sweating.

Interactions

None reported.

Effects on lab test results

• May increase liver enzyme levels.

Pharmacokinetics

Absorption: Absorbed from GI tract. Food affects extent of absorption.
Distribution: 40% bound to plasma proteins.
Metabolism: Metabolized in liver.
Excretion: Excreted in urine. *Half-life:* About 50 hours.

Route	Onset	Peak	Duration
P.O.	Unknown	Unknown	Unknown

Pharmacodynamics

Chemical effect: Significantly lowers estradiol level.
Therapeutic effect: Hinders cancer cell growth.

Available forms

Tablets: 1 mg

NURSING PROCESS

Assessment

• Obtain history of patient's neoplastic disease before therapy.
• Be alert for adverse reactions.
• Evaluate patient's and family's knowledge of drug therapy.

Nursing diagnoses

• Ineffective health maintenance related to neoplastic disease
• Risk for deficient fluid volume related to drug-induced adverse GI reactions
• Deficient knowledge related to drug therapy

Planning and implementation

• Rule out pregnancy before treatment begins.
• Give drug under supervision of a clinician experienced in using antineoplastics.
• Patients with advanced breast cancer should continue therapy until tumor progression is evident.

Patient teaching

• Instruct patient to report adverse reactions.
• Stress importance of follow-up care.

Evaluation

• Patient has positive response to therapy.
• Patient maintains adequate hydration.
• Patient and family state understanding of drug therapy.

anistreplase (anisoylated plasminogen-streptokinase activator complex; APSAC)
(an-ih-STREP-layz)
Eminase

Pharmacologic class: thrombolytic enzyme
Therapeutic class: thrombolytic enzyme
Pregnancy risk category: C

Indications and dosages

▶ **Lysis of coronary artery thrombi after acute MI.** *Adults:* 30 units I.V. over 2 to 5 minutes by direct injection.

Contraindications and precautions

• Contraindicated in patients with history of severe allergic reaction to anistreplase or streptokinase and in those with active internal bleeding, CVA, intraspinal or intracranial surgery or trauma within past 2 months, aneurysm, arteriovenous malformation, intracranial neoplasm, uncontrolled hypertension, or known bleeding diathesis.
• Use cautiously in patients with major surgery within 10 days; trauma (including cardiopulmonary resuscitation); GI or GU bleeding; cerebrovascular disease; hypertension; mitral stenosis, atrial fibrillation, or other conditions that may lead to left-sided heart thrombus; acute pericarditis or subacute bacterial endocarditis; septic thrombophlebitis; diabetic hemorrhagic retinopathy; and in patients receiving anticoagulants.
Lifespan: During pregnancy, first 10 days postpartum, and breast-feeding, use cautiously. In children, safety of drug hasn't been established. In patients age 75 and older, use cautiously.

Adverse reactions

CNS: ***intracranial hemorrhage.***
CV: **ARRHYTHMIAS,** conduction disorders, hypotension, edema.
GI: ***bleeding,*** gum or mouth hemorrhage.
GU: hematuria.
Hematologic: ***bleeding tendency,*** eosinophilia.
Musculoskeletal: arthralgia.
Respiratory: hemoptysis.
Skin: hematomas, urticaria, itching, flushing.
Other: bleeding at puncture sites, ***anaphylaxis or anaphylactoid reactions.***

Interactions

Drug-drug. *Heparin, oral anticoagulants, drugs that alter platelet function (including aspirin, dipyridamole):* May increase risk of bleeding. Use together cautiously.
Drug-herb. *Ginger, ginkgo, St. John's wort:* May increase risk of bleeding. Discourage using together.

Effects on lab test results

• May cause transient increase of liver enzyme levels. May decrease plasminogen and fibrinogen levels.
• May increase eosinophil count and PTT, APTT, and PT. May affect in vitro coagulation tests.

Pharmacokinetics

Absorption: Administered I.V.
Distribution: Unkown.
Metabolism: Immediately after injection, drug is catalyzed by a nonenzymatic process to form active streptokinase-plasminogen complex.
Excretion: Unknown. *Half-life:* 70 to 120 minutes.

Route	Onset	Peak	Duration
I.V.	Immediate	About 45 min	6 hr-2 days

Pharmacodynamics

Chemical effect: Anistreplase, derived from lys-plasminogen and streptokinase, is formulated into a fibrinolytic enzyme plus activator complex with activator temporarily blocked by an anisoyl group. Drug is activated in vivo by a nonenzymatic process that removes the anisoyl group. The active lys-plasminogen–streptokinase activator complex is progressively formed in bloodstream or within thrombus.
Therapeutic effect: Dissolves blood clots in coronary arteries.

Available forms

Injection: 30 units/vial

NURSING PROCESS

Assessment
- Obtain history of patient's underlying cardiac condition before therapy.
- Monitor drug's effectiveness by carefully checking ECG and vital signs.
- Drug's efficacy may be limited if antistreptokinase antibodies are present. Antibody levels may be elevated if more than 5 days have elapsed since treatment with anistreplase or streptokinase or if patient has recently had a streptococcal infection.
- Be alert for adverse reactions and drug interactions.
- Evaluate patient's and family's knowledge of drug therapy.

Nursing diagnoses
- Ineffective tissue perfusion related to presence of coronary thrombosis
- Risk for injury related to drug-induced adverse reactions
- Deficient knowledge related to drug therapy

Planning and implementation
- Reconstitute drug by slowly adding 5 ml of sterile water for injection. Direct stream against side of vial, not at drug powder. Gently roll vial to mix dry powder and water. To avoid excessive foaming, don't shake vial. Reconstituted solution should be colorless to pale yellow. Inspect for precipitate. If drug isn't administered within 30 minutes of reconstituting, discard vial.

ALERT: Unlike other thrombolytics that must be infused, anistreplase should be given by direct injection over 2 to 5 minutes.
- Don't mix anistreplase with other drugs; don't dilute solution after reconstitution.
- Be prepared to treat bradycardia or ventricular irritability. Thrombolytic therapy is linked with reperfusion arrhythmias that may signify successful thrombolysis.
- Avoid I.M. injections and nonessential handling or moving of patient.
- If arterial puncture is necessary, select a compressible site (such as an arm), and apply pressure for 30 minutes afterward. Also, use pressure dressings, sandbags, or ice packs on recent puncture sites to prevent bleeding.
- Heparin therapy is frequently started after treatment with anistreplase to decrease risk of rethrombosis.

ALERT: Don't confuse anistreplase with alteplase.

Patient teaching
- Teach patient to recognize signs of internal bleeding, and tell him to report them immediately.
- Advise patient about proper dental care to avoid excessive gum trauma.
- Advise patient to report shortness of breath or palpitations.

Evaluation
- Patient's ECG and vital signs reflect improvement in cardiopulmonary perfusion.
- Patient has no injury from anistreplase therapy.
- Patient and family state understanding of drug therapy.

antihemophilic factor (AHF)

(an-tigh-hee-moh-FIL-ik FAK-tor)

Bioclate, Helixate, Helixate FS, Hemofil M, Humate-P, Hyate:C, Koate-HP, Koate-DVI, Kogenate, Kogenate FS, Monarc-M, Monoclate-P, Recombinate

Pharmacologic class: blood derivative
Therapeutic class: antihemophilic
Pregnancy risk category: C

Indications and dosages

▶ **Hemophilia A (factor VIII deficiency).** *Adults and children:* Dosage is highly individualized and depends on patient's weight, severity of deficiency, severity of hemorrhage, presence of inhibitors, and level of factor VIII desired.

Contraindications and precautions

- Contraindicated in patients hypersensitive to murine (mouse) protein or to drug.
- Use cautiously in patients with hepatic disease because of susceptibility to hepatitis, which may be transmitted in AHF.

Lifespan: In pregnant women, use cautiously. In breast-feeding women, safety of drug hasn't been established. In neonates and infants, use cautiously.

Adverse reactions

CNS: *fever,* headache, paresthesia, flushing, clouding or loss of consciousness, somnolence, lethargy.
CV: tachycardia, hypotension, tightness in chest.
EENT: visual disturbances.
GI: nausea, vomiting.
Hematologic: hemolysis (in patients with blood type A, B, or AB).
Respiratory: wheezing.
Skin: *erythema,* urticaria.
Other: *chills,* backache, hypersensitivity reactions, rigor, stinging at injection site, ***hepatitis B, HIV.***

Interactions

None significant.

Effects on lab test results

- May increase fibrinogen level.
- May decrease hemoglobin and hematocrit.

Pharmacokinetics

Absorption: Administered I.V.
Distribution: Unknown.
Metabolism: Cleared rapidly from plasma.
Excretion: Consumed during blood clotting.
Half-life: 4 to 24 hours (average, 12 hours).

Route	Onset	Peak	Duration
I.V.	Immediate	1-2 hr	Unknown

Pharmacodynamics

Chemical effect: Directly replaces deficient clotting factor that converts prothrombin to thrombin.
Therapeutic effect: Causes blood clotting.

Available forms

Injection: vials, with diluent. Units specified on label.

NURSING PROCESS

Assessment

- Obtain thorough history of patient's underlying condition (including hematocrit, results of coagulation studies, and vital signs) before therapy begins and regularly throughout therapy.
- Inhibitors to factor VIII develop in some patients, leading to decreased response to drug.
- Assess patient for adverse reactions to drug.
- Evaluate patient's and family's knowledge of drug therapy.

Nursing diagnoses

- Ineffective health maintenance related to bleeding caused by underlying condition
- Risk for injury related to drug-induced adverse reactions
- Deficient knowledge related to drug therapy

Planning and implementation

- Give hepatitis B vaccine before giving drug.

ALERT: One AHF unit equals the activity present in 1 ml normal pooled plasma less than 1 hour old. Don't confuse commercial product with blood-bank–produced cryoprecipitated factor VIII from individual donors. Drug is designed for I.V. use only; use plastic syringe because solution adheres to glass surfaces.

- Take baseline pulse before giving drug. If pulse rate increases significantly, flow rate should be reduced or administration stopped.
- Refrigerate concentrate until ready to use. Warm concentrate and diluent bottles to room temperature before reconstituting. To mix drug, gently roll vial between your hands.
- Use reconstituted solution within 3 hours. Store away from heat, and don't refrigerate. Refrigeration after reconstitution may cause active ingredient to precipitate. Don't shake or mix with other I.V. solutions.

ALERT: Kogenate FS and Helixate FS should be refrigerated at all times at temperatures of 36° to 46° F (2° to 8° C) (NOT room temperature) to ensure potency through the expiration date. Previously, manufacturers of Kogenate FS and Helixate FS allowed for storage at room temperature for up to 2 months as an alternative to refrigeration.

- Don't give S.C. or I.M.
- A porcine product is available for patients with congenital hemophilia A who have antibodies to human factor VIII:C.

Patient teaching

- Educate patient about drug therapy.
- Inform patient about risks of drug therapy, such as contracting hepatitis or HIV.

• Instruct patient to call prescriber if adverse reactions develop.

Evaluation
• Patient's vital signs and blood studies are within normal parameters with no bleeding.
• Patient doesn't experience injury as a result of drug therapy.
• Patient and family state understanding of drug therapy.

anti-inhibitor coagulant complex
(an-tigh-in-HIB-eh-tor koh-AG-yoo-lant KOM-pleks)
Autoplex T, Feiba VH Immuno

Pharmacologic class: blood derivative
Therapeutic class: antihemophilic
Pregnancy risk category: C

Indications and dosages
▶ **Prevention and control of hemorrhagic episodes in certain patients with hemophilia A in whom inhibitor antibodies to antihemophilic factor have developed; management of bleeding in patients with acquired hemophilia who have spontaneously acquired inhibitors to factor VIII; management of bleeding in patients with factor IX inhibitors.** *Adults and children:* Highly individualized and varies among manufacturers. For Autoplex T, 25 to 100 units/kg I.V., depending on severity of hemorrhage. If no hemostatic improvement occurs within 6 hours after administration, dose is repeated. For Feiba VH Immuno, 50 to 100 units/kg I.V. q 6 or 12 hours until clear signs of improvement.

Contraindications and precautions
• Contraindicated in patients with signs of fibrinolysis, in those with DIC, and in those with a normal coagulation mechanism.
• Use cautiously in patients with liver disease.
Lifespan: In pregnant women, use cautiously. In breast-feeding women, safety of drug hasn't been established.

Adverse reactions
CNS: fever, dizziness, headache, lethargy, drowsiness.
CV: flushing, hypotension, transient chest discomfort, changes in pulse rate, ***acute MI, thromboembolic events.***
GI: nausea.
Hematologic: *DIC.*
Respiratory: dyspnea.
Skin: rash, urticaria.
Other: chills, hypersensitivity reactions, ***risk of hepatitis B and HIV.***

Interactions
Drug-drug. *Antifibrinolytic drugs:* May alter effects of anti-inhibitor coagulant complex. Don't use together.

Effects on lab test results
None reported.

Pharmacokinetics
Absorption: Administered I.V.
Distribution: Unknown.
Metabolism: Unknown.
Excretion: Unknown.

Route	Onset	Peak	Duration
I.V.	10-30 min	Unknown	Unknown

Pharmacodynamics
Chemical effect: Unknown. Efficacy may be related to presence of activated factors, which leads to more complete activation of factor X in conjunction with tissue factor, phospholipid, and ionic calcium, and allows coagulation to proceed beyond those stages that require factor VIII.
Therapeutic effect: Causes blood clotting.

Available forms
Injection: Number of units of factor VIII correctional activity indicated on label of vial

NURSING PROCESS

Assessment
• Obtain history of patient's underlying condition (including hematocrit, results of coagulation studies, and vital signs) before therapy and regularly throughout therapy.
• Be alert for adverse reactions and drug interactions.
• Evaluate patient's and family's knowledge of drug therapy.

Nursing diagnoses

- Ineffective health maintenance related to bleeding caused by underlying condition
- Risk for injury related to drug-induced adverse reactions
- Deficient knowledge related to drug therapy

Planning and implementation

- Give hepatitis B vaccine before giving drug.
- Warm drug and diluent to room temperature before reconstitution. Reconstitute according to manufacturer's directions. Use filter needle provided by manufacturer to withdraw reconstituted solution from vial into syringe; filter needle should then be replaced with a sterile injection needle for administration. Administer as soon as possible. Autoplex T infusions should be completed within 1 hour after reconstitution; Feiba VH Immuno infusions, within 3 hours.
- The rate of administration should be individualized according to patient's response. Autoplex T infusions may begin at 1 ml/minute; if well tolerated, infusion rate may be increased gradually to 10 ml/minute. Feiba VH Immuno infusion rate shouldn't exceed 2 units/kg.
- Keep epinephrine readily available to treat anaphylaxis.
- If flushing, lethargy, headache, transient chest discomfort, or changes in blood pressure or pulse rate develop because of rapid infusion, stop drug and notify prescriber. These symptoms usually disappear when infusion stops. Infusion then may be resumed at a slower rate.

Patient teaching

- Teach patient about anti-inhibitor coagulant complex therapy.
- Reassure patient that because of the manufacturing process used, risk of HIV transmission is extremely low.

Evaluation

- Patient's vital signs and blood studies are within normal parameters with no bleeding.
- Patient doesn't experience injury as a result of anti-inhibitor coagulant complex therapy.
- Patient and family state understanding of drug therapy.

antithrombin III, human (ATIII, heparin cofactor I)

(an-tigh-THROM-bin three, HYOO-mun)
ATnativ, Thrombate III

Pharmacologic class: glycoprotein
Therapeutic class: anticoagulant, antithrombotic
Pregnancy risk category: C

Indications and dosages

▶ **Thromboembolism from hereditary ATIII deficiency.** *Adults and children:* Initial dose is quantity needed to increase ATIII activity to 120% of normal activity 30 minutes after administration. Usual dose is 50 to 100 IU/minute I.V., not to exceed 100 IU/minute. Dose based on anticipated 1% increase in ATIII activity produced by 1 IU/kg of body weight using the formula: Dose (IU) is equal to desired activity (%) minus baseline activity (%) times weight (kg) divided by 1.4 (IU/kg). Maintenance dosage is quantity required to increase ATIII activity to 80% of normal activity and is given at 24-hour intervals. To calculate dosage, multiply desired ATIII activity (as % of normal) minus baseline ATIII activity (as % of normal) by body weight (kg). Divide by actual increase in ATIII activity (%) produced by 1 IU/kg as determined 30 minutes after administration of initial dose. Treatment usually continues for 2 to 8 days but may be prolonged in pregnancy or during surgery or immobilization.

Contraindications and precautions

- No known contraindications.

Lifespan: In children and neonates, safety and efficacy haven't been established; use with extreme caution.

Adverse reactions

CV: vasodilation, lowered blood pressure.
GU: diuresis.

Interactions

Drug-drug. *Heparin:* May increase anticoagulant effect of both drugs. Reduced heparin dose may be needed.

Effects on lab test results

None reported.

Pharmacokinetics

Absorption: Administered I.V.
Distribution: Binding to epithelium and redistribution into extravascular compartment removes ATIII from blood. Special receptors on hepatocytes bind ATIII clotting factor complexes, rapidly removing them from circulation.
Metabolism: Unknown.
Excretion: Unknown. *Half-life:* 2 to 3 days.

Route	Onset	Peak	Duration
I.V.	Immediate	Unknown	About 4 days

Pharmacodynamics

Chemical effect: Replaces ATIII in patients with hereditary ATIII deficiency, normalizing coagulation inhibition and inhibiting thromboembolism. Also deactivates plasmin but to a lesser extent than clotting factor.
Therapeutic effect: Prevents or decreases blood clotting.

Available forms

Injection: 500 IU/vial, 1,000 IU/vial

NURSING PROCESS

Assessment

- Obtain history of patient's underlying condition before therapy, and reassess regularly throughout therapy.
- Because of risk of fatality from neonatal thromboembolism in children of parents with hereditary ATIII deficiency, be ready to determine neonate's ATIII levels immediately after birth.
- Obtain ATIII activity levels twice daily until dosage requirement stabilizes, then daily immediately before dose. Functional assays are preferred because quantitative immunologic test results may be normal despite decreased ATIII activity.
- Be alert for adverse reactions and drug interactions.
- Watch for dyspnea and increased blood pressure, which may occur if administration is too rapid.
- Evaluate patient's and family's understanding of drug therapy.

Nursing diagnoses

- Ineffective tissue perfusion related to underlying condition
- Deficient knowledge related to drug therapy

Planning and implementation

- Reconstitute drug using 10 ml of sterile water (provided), normal saline solution, or D_5W. Don't shake vial. Dilute further in same diluent solution, if desired.
- Drug isn't recommended for long-term prophylaxis of thrombotic episodes.
- Store drug at 36° to 46° F (2° to 8° C).

Patient teaching

- Tell patient to report difficulty breathing and any other sudden symptoms immediately while drug is being given; rate adjustment may be needed.
- Inform patient that risk of contracting hepatitis or HIV is minimal.

Evaluation

- Patient has adequate tissue perfusion.
- Patient and family state understanding of drug therapy.

aprotinin

(uh-proh-TIN-in)
Trasylol

Pharmacologic class: naturally occurring protease inhibitor
Therapeutic class: systemic hemostatic drug
Pregnancy risk category: B

Indications and dosages

▶ **To reduce blood loss or need for transfusion in patients undergoing coronary artery bypass grafts.** *Adults:* Start with 10,000 kallikrein inactivator units (KIU) test dose at least 10 minutes before loading dose. If no allergic reaction is evident, anesthesia may be induced while loading dose of 2 million KIU is given slowly over 20 to 30 minutes. When loading dose is complete, sternotomy may be performed. Before bypass, cardiopulmonary bypass circuit is primed with 2 million KIU of drug by replacing an aliquot of priming fluid with drug. A continuous infusion at 500,000 KIU/hour is then given until patient leaves operating room. This is known as regimen A. A second regimen, called regimen B, may be given, which is half the dosage of regimen A (except for test dose).

Contraindications and precautions

• Contraindicated in patients hypersensitive to beef because drug is prepared from bovine lung.
Lifespan: In pregnant women, use cautiously. In breast-feeding women and in children, safety of drug hasn't been established.

Adverse reactions

CNS: fever, ***cerebral embolism, CVA.***
CV: ***cardiac arrest, heart failure, MI, ventricular tachycardia,*** atrial fibrillation, atrial flutter, hypotension, ***supraventricular tachycardia.***
GU: ***nephrotoxicity, renal failure.***
Respiratory: pneumonia, respiratory disorder, ***bronchospasm,*** pulmonary edema.
Other: hypersensitivity reactions, ***anaphylaxis.***

Interactions

Drug-Drug. *Captopril:* May decrease hypotensive effects of captopril. Monitor blood pressure.
Fibrinolytics: May inhibit fibrinolytics. Monitor patient for clinical effects.
Heparin: May prolong activated clotting time (ACT) when determined by the celite surface activation method. Kaolin-based ACTs should be used while patient is taking both drugs.

Effects on lab test results

• May increase AST, ALT, creatinine, and glucose levels. May decrease potassium level.
• May prolong ACT and PTT and may falsely prolong whole blood clotting times when determined by surface activation methods.

Pharmacokinetics

Absorption: Administered I.V.
Distribution: Rapidly distributed into total extracellular space, leading to a rapid initial decrease in plasma levels.
Metabolism: Unknown.
Excretion: 25% to 40% excreted in urine over 48 hours. *Half-life:* About 10 hours.

Route	Onset	Peak	Duration
I.V.	Unknown	Unknown	Unknown

Pharmacodynamics

Chemical effect: Acts as systemic hemostatic drug, decreasing bleeding and turnover of coagulation factors. Drug inhibits fibrinolysis by affecting kallikrein and plasmin, prevents triggering of contact phase of coagulation pathway, and increases resistance of platelets to damage from mechanical injury and high plasmin levels that occur during cardiopulmonary bypass.
Therapeutic effect: Decreases bleeding.

Available forms

Injection: 10,000 KIU/ml (1.4 mg/ml) in 100-ml and 200-ml vials

NURSING PROCESS

Assessment

• Obtain history of allergies. Patients with a history of allergic reactions to drugs or other substances may be at higher risk for developing an allergic reaction to aprotinin.
• Obtain history of patient's bleeding status before therapy and reassess regularly thereafter.
• Be alert for adverse reactions.
• Monitor laboratory studies.
• Evaluate patient's and family's understanding of drug therapy.

Nursing diagnoses

• Risk for deficient fluid volume related to potential bleeding during surgery
• Risk for injury related to drug-induced adverse reactions
• Deficient knowledge related to drug therapy

Planning and implementation

• Be prepared to give a test dose, particularly in patients who have previously received drug. They have a higher risk of anaphylaxis. In these patients, pretreat with an antihistamine.
• Aprotinin is incompatible with amino acids, corticosteroids, fat emulsions, heparin, and tetracyclines. Don't add any drugs to I.V. container, and use a separate I.V. line.
• Administer all doses through a central line.
• To avoid hypotension, make sure patient is lying down during loading dose.
• Store drug between 36° and 77° F (2° and 25° C). Protect from freezing.

• If symptoms of hypersensitivity (such as skin eruptions, itching, dyspnea, nausea, or tachycardia) occur, stop infusion immediately, call prescriber, and provide supportive treatment.

Patient teaching
• Inform patient and family about aprotinin's use with cardiopulmonary bypass surgery and its adverse reactions.

☑ Evaluation
• Patient's bleeding during surgery is minimal.
• Patient doesn't experience injury as a result of aprotinin therapy.
• Patient and family state understanding of drug therapy.

argatroban
(are-GA-troe-ban)
Argatroban

Pharmacologic classification: direct thrombin inhibitor
Therapeutic classification: anticoagulant
Pregnancy risk category: B

Indications and dosages
▶ **Prevention or treatment of thrombosis in patients with heparin-induced thrombocytopenia.** *Adults:* 2 mcg/kg per minute, given as a continuous I.V. infusion; adjust dose until steady state PTT is one and a half to three times the initial baseline value, not to exceed 100 seconds; maximum dose is 10 mcg/kg/minute.

The standard infusion rates for 2 mcg/kg per minute are shown below.

Body weight (kg)	Infusion rate (ml/hr)
50	6
60	7
70	8
80	10
90	11
100	12
110	13
120	14
130	16
140	17

Patients with moderate hepatic impairment: Initially, reduce dose to 0.5 mcg/kg per minute, given as a continuous infusion. Monitor PTT closely; dosage should be adjusted as indicated.

▶ **Anticoagulation in patients at risk for heparin-induced thrombocytopenia during percutaneous coronary interventions.** *Adults:* 350 mcg/kg I.V. bolus over 3 to 5 minutes. Start a continuous I.V. infusion at 25 mcg/kg per minute. Check activated clotting time (ACT) 5 to 10 minutes after the bolus dose is completed.

If ACT is less than 300 seconds, give an additional I.V. bolus dose of 150 mcg/kg increase infusion dose to 30 mcg/kg, and check ACT 5 to 10 minutes later. If the ACT is greater than 450 seconds, decrease infusion rate to 15 mcg/kg per minute, and check ACT 5 to 10 minutes later. Once an ACT (between 300 and 450 seconds) is achieved, continue this infusion dose for duration of procedure.

In case of dissection, impending abrupt closure, thrombus formation during the procedure, or inability to achieve or maintain an ACT longer than 300 seconds, give an additional bolus of 150 mcg/kg and increase infusion rate to 40 mcg/kg per minute. Check ACT 5 to 10 minutes after each bolus or change in infusion rate and at the end of the procedure. Additional ACT should be drawn about every 20 to 30 minutes during a prolonged procedure.

Contraindications and precautions
• Contraindicated in patients hypersensitive to drug or its components and in patients with active bleeding.
• Use cautiously in patients with hepatic disease; disease states that create an increased risk of hemorrhage, such as severe hypertension; very recent lumbar puncture, spinal anesthesia, or major surgery, especially involving the brain, spinal cord, or eye; and hematologic conditions linked to increased bleeding tendencies, such as congenital or acquired bleeding disorders and GI lesions and ulcerations.
Lifespan: In breast-feeding women, a decision should be made to stop breast-feeding or drug because it's unknown if drug appears in

breast milk. In children, safety and efficacy haven't been established.

Interactions

Drug-drug. *Oral anticoagulants, antiplatelet drugs:* May prolong PT and INR and increase risk of bleeding. Discontinue all parenteral anticoagulants and antiplatelet drugs before giving argatroban.
Thrombolytics: May increase risk of intracranial bleeding. Avoid using together.

Adverse reactions

CV: ***atrial fibrillation, cardiac arrest, cerebrovascular disorder, hemorrhage,*** hypotension, ***ventricular tachycardia,*** *vasodilation.*
GI: abdominal pain, diarrhea, ***GI bleeding,*** hemoptysis, nausea, vomiting.
GU: abnormal renal function, groin bleeding, *hematuria,* urinary tract infection.
Hematologic: anemia.
Respiratory: *cough, dyspnea, pneumonia.*
Skin: *rash, bullous eruptions*
Other: brachial bleeding, fever, infection, pain, ***sepsis,*** *allergic reactions (in patients concomitantly receiving thrombolytic therapy for acute MI).*

Effects on lab test results

- May increase APTT, ACT, INR, and WBC and platelet counts. May decrease hemoglobin and hematocrit.

Pharmacokinetics

Absorption: Administered I.V.
Distribution: Mainly in the extracellular fluid. Drug is 54% bound to human proteins, of which 34% is bound to a_1-acid glycoprotein and 20% to albumin.
Metabolism: Metabolized mainly in the liver by hydroxylation. The formation of four metabolites is catalyzed in the liver by the cytochrome P-450 enzymes CYP3A4/5. The primary metabolite is 20% weaker than that of the parent drug. The other metabolites are detected in low levels in urine.
Excretion: Primary excretion in the feces, presumably through the biliary tract. *Half-life:* 39 to 51 minutes.

Route	Onset	Peak	Duration
I.V.	Rapid	1-3 hr	Until infusion stops

Pharmacodynamics

Chemical effect: Reversibly binds to the thrombin active site and inhibits reactions catalyzed or induced by thrombin, including fibrin formation, activation of coagulation factors V, VIII, and XIII and protein C, and platelet aggregation. Argatroban can inhibit the action of both free and clot-related thrombin.
Therapeutic effect: Prevents clot formation.

Available forms

Injection: 100 mg/ml.

NURSING PROCESS

Assessment

- Assess patient for increased risk of bleeding or overt bleeding before starting argatroban therapy.
- Obtain baseline coagulation tests, platelet counts, hemoglobin, and hematocrit before therapy. Note abnormalities and notify prescriber.
- Discontinue all parenteral anticoagulants before giving argatroban.
- Check APTT 2 hours after giving argatroban; dosage adjustments may be needed to attain a targeted APTT (one and a half to three times the baseline, not to exceed 100 seconds).
- Additional ACT should be drawn about every 20 to 30 minutes during a prolonged procedure.
- Determine patient's and family's understanding of argatroban therapy.

Nursing diagnoses

- Ineffective tissue perfusion due to blood clots
- Increased risk for injury related to increased APTT and increased risk of bleeding from drug therapy.
- Deficient knowledge related to argatroban therapy and anticoagulant safety precautions.

Planning and implementation

- Dilute in normal saline solution, D_5W, or lactated Ringer's injection to a final concentration of 1 mg/ml.
- Each 2.5-ml vial should be diluted 1:100 by mixing it with 250 ml of diluent.
- Mix the constituted solution by repeatedly turning over the diluent bag for 1 minute.
- Don't mix other medications with argatroban infusion.

• Prepared solutions are stable for up to 24 hours at 77° F (25° C).
• Hemorrhage can occur in patients receiving argatroban. If an unexplained drop in hematocrit or blood pressure or another unexplained symptom occurs, suspect a hemorrhagic event.
• Excessive anticoagulation, with or without bleeding, may occur in overdose. Symptoms of acute toxicity include loss of reflex, tremors, clonic seizures, limb paralysis, and coma. No specific antidote is available. Discontinue immediately and monitor APTT and other coagulation tests. Provide symptomatic and supportive therapy.
• To convert to oral anticoagulant therapy, give warfarin with argatroban at doses of up to 2 mcg/kg per minute until the INR is above 4. After argatroban is discontinued, repeat the INR in 4 to 6 hours. If the repeat INR is below the desired therapeutic range, resume argatroban infusion. Repeat the procedure daily until the desired therapeutic range is reached on warfarin alone.
ALERT: Don't confuse Aggrastat (tirofiban) with argatroban.

Patient teaching
• Advise patient that argatroban can cause bleeding, and urge him to report immediately any unusual bruising, bleeding (nosebleeds, bleeding gums, ecchymosis, or hematuria), or tarry or bloody stools.
• Advise patient to avoid activities that carry a risk of injury or cuts, and instruct him to use soft toothbrush and electric razor while taking argatroban.
• Tell patient to notify prescriber if she is pregnant or breast-feeding, or recently had a baby.
• Tell patient to notify prescriber if he has stomach ulcers or liver disease; if he's had recent surgery, radiation treatments, falls, or other injury; or if wheezing, difficulty breathing, or rash occurs.

Evaluation
• Patient doesn't have any unnecessary bruising or bleeding.
• Patient doesn't develop blood clots while on argatroban.
• Patient and family state understanding of argatroban therapy.

arsenic trioxide
(AR-sen-ik try-OX-ide)
Trisenox

Pharmacologic classification: antineoplastic
Therapeutic classification: antileukemic drug
Pregnancy risk category: D

Indications and dosages
▶ **Acute promyelocytic leukemia (APL) in patients who have relapsed from or are refractory to retinoid and anthracycline chemotherapy.** *Adults and children age 5 and older:* ***Induction phase.*** 0.15 mg/kg I.V. daily until bone marrow remission. Maximum 60 doses. ***Consolidation phase.*** 0.15 mg/kg I.V. daily for 25 doses over a period of up to 5 weeks, beginning 3 to 6 weeks after completion of induction therapy.

Contraindications and precautions
• Contraindicated in patients hypersensitive to arsenic. Use cautiously in patients with heart failure, renal failure, a history of torsades de pointes, prolonged QT interval, or conditions that result in hypokalemia or hypomagnesemia.
Lifespan: Caution women of childbearing age to avoid becoming pregnant during therapy. In breast-feeding women, avoid use; arsenic appears in breast milk and may cause fetal harm. In children younger than age 5, safety and efficacy haven't been established.

Adverse reactions
CNS: *headache, insomnia, paresthesia, dizziness, tremor,* ***seizures,*** somnolence, ***coma,*** *anxiety, depression,* agitation, confusion, *fatigue, weakness.*
CV: *tachycardia,* PROLONGED QT INTERVAL, *palpitations, edema, chest pain,* ***ECG abnormalities,*** *hypotension, flushing, hypertension.*
EENT: *eye irritation, epistaxis, blurred vision,* dry eye, earache, tinnitus, *sore throat, postnasal drip,* facial and eyelid edema, *sinusitis,* nasopharyngitis, painful red eye.
GI: *nausea, vomiting, diarrhea, anorexia, abdominal pain, constipation, loose stools, dyspepsia,* oral blistering, fecal incontinence, ***GI hemorrhage,*** dry mouth, abdominal tenderness or distension, bloody diarrhea, oral candidiasis.

GU: ***renal failure,*** renal impairment, oliguria, incontinence, ***vaginal hemorrhage,*** intermenstrual bleeding.
Hematologic: *leukocytosis, anemia,* **THROMBOCYTOPENIA, NEUTROPENIA,** ***DIC, hemorrhage,*** lymphadenopathy.
Metabolic: *hypokalemia, hypomagnesemia, hyperglycemia, hypocalcemia,* ***hypoglycemia,*** acidosis, *weight gain,* weight loss, **HYPERKALEMIA.**
Musculoskeletal: *arthralgia, myalgia, bone pain, back pain, neck pain, limb pain.*
Respiratory: *cough, dyspnea, hypoxia, pleural effusion, wheezing, decreased breath sounds, crepitations, rales,* hemoptysis, tachypnea, rhonchi, *upper respiratory tract infection.*
Skin: *dermatitis, pruritus, dry skin, erythema, increased sweating,* night sweats, petechiae, hyperpigmentation, urticaria, skin lesions, local exfoliation, *pallor,* ecchymosis.
Other: *fever;* drug hypersensitivity; *pain, erythema, or edema at injection site; rigors;* lymphadenopathy; facial edema; *herpes simplex infection;* bacterial infection; herpes zoster; ***sepsis.***

Interactions

Drug-drug. *Drugs that can lead to electrolyte abnormalities (diuretics or amphotericin B):* May increase risk of electrolyte abnormalities. Use cautiously.
Drugs that can prolong QT interval (antiarrhythmics or thioridazine): May further prolong QT interval. Use cautiously.

Effects on lab test results

- May increase AST, ALT, BUN, magnesium, calcium, and creatinine levels. May decrease sodium level. May increase or decrease glucose and potassium levels.
- May decrease hemoglobin, hematocrit, and RBC, WBC, neutrophil, and platelet counts.

Pharmacokinetics

Absorption: Administered I.V.
Distribution: Stored mainly in the liver, kidneys, heart, lungs, hair, and nails.
Metabolism: Metabolized in the liver.
Excretion: Excreted in urine in the methylated form.

Route	Onset	Peak	Duration
I.V.	Unknown	Unknown	Unknown

Pharmacodynamics

Chemical effect: Arsenic trioxide causes morphologic changes and DNA fragmentation resulting in death of promyelocytic leukemic cells.
Therapeutic effect: Destroys promyelocytic leukemic cells.

Available forms

Injection: 1 mg/ml

NURSING PROCESS

Assessment

ALERT: Arsenic trioxide can cause fatal arrhythmias and complete atrioventricular block.
ALERT: Arsenic trioxide has been linked to APL differentiation syndrome, characterized by fever, dyspnea, weight gain, pulmonary infiltrates, and pleural or pericardial effusions with or without leukocytosis. This syndrome can be fatal and requires treatment with high-dose steroids.

- Arsenic trioxide may alter blood pressure. Monitor patient closely.
- Perform ECG; obtain potassium, calcium, magnesium, and creatinine levels; and correct electrolyte abnormalities before starting therapy.
- Monitor electrolyte levels and hematologic and coagulation profiles at least twice weekly during treatment. Keep potassium levels above 4 mEq/dL and magnesium levels above 1.8 mg/dL.
- Monitor patient for syncope and rapid or irregular heart rate. If these occur, discontinue drug, hospitalize patient, and monitor serum electrolyte levels and QTc interval. Drug may be restarted when electrolyte abnormalities are corrected and QTc interval falls below 460 msec.
- Monitor ECG at least weekly during therapy. Prolonged QTc interval commonly occurs between 1 and 5 weeks after infusion and returns to baseline about 8 weeks after infusion. If QTc interval is longer than 500 msec at any time during therapy, assess patient carefully and consider discontinuing drug.
- Assess patient's and family's knowledge of drug therapy.

Nursing diagnoses
- Risk of decreased cardiac output due to drug-induced toxicity.
- Risk for infection related to drug-induced thrombocytopenia or neutropenia.
- Deficient knowledge related to arsenic trioxide therapy.

Planning and implementation
- Follow facility policy for preparation and handling of antineoplastics. The active ingredient is a carcinogen.
- Dilute with 100 to 250 ml of D_5W or normal saline solution. After dilution, drug is stable for 24 hours at room temperature and for 48 hours if refrigerated.
- Administer I.V. over 1 to 2 hours. Infusion time may be extended up to 4 hours if vasomotor reactions occur.
- Monitor patient carefully for adverse reactions or drug toxicity. Symptoms of acute arsenic toxicity include confusion, muscle weakness, and seizures. If overdose occurs, discontinue immediately. Treatment may include 3 mg/kg dimercaprol I.M. q 4 hours until life-threatening toxicity subsides; then give 250 mg penicillamine P.O. up to q.i.d.

Patient teaching
- Tell patient to report immediately fever, shortness of breath, bloody stools, or weight gain.
- Instruct patient to tell prescriber about all drugs currently being taken and to check with prescriber before staring any new drug.
- Inform patient with diabetes that drug may cause hyperglycemia or hypoglycemia, and instruct him to monitor glucose level closely.
- Caution woman of childbearing age to avoid becoming pregnant during therapy.

Evaluation
- Patient tolerates therapy and responds positively to drug therapy.
- Patient doesn't have infection or life-threatening adverse events.
- Patient and family state understanding of arsenic trioxide therapy.

asparaginase (L-asparaginase)
(as-PAR-ah-jin-ays)
Elspar, Kidrolase ♦

Pharmacologic class: enzyme (L-asparagine amidohydrolase), cell-cycle–phase specific, G1 phase
Therapeutic class: antineoplastic
Pregnancy risk category: C

Indications and dosages
▶ **Acute lymphocytic leukemia (ALL) (with other drugs).** *Adults and children:* For ALL Regimen I treatment period, on day 22 of treatment, give 1,000 IU/kg I.V. daily for 10 days, injected over 30 minutes or by slow I.V. push; or for ALL Regimen II treatment protocol, give 6,000 IU/m^2 I.M. at intervals specified in protocol.
▶ **Sole induction drug for remission of ALL.** *Adults and children:* 200 IU/kg I.V. daily for 28 days.

Contraindications and precautions
- Contraindicated in patients with pancreatitis or history of pancreatitis and previous hypersensitivity unless desensitized.
- Use cautiously in patients with hepatic dysfunction.

Lifespan: In pregnant women, use cautiously. In breast-feeding women, drug shouldn't be used.

Adverse reactions
CNS: fever, confusion, drowsiness, depression, hallucinations, nervousness, lethargy, somnolence.
GI: *vomiting, anorexia, nausea,* cramps, weight loss, **HEMMORHAGIC PANCREATITIS.**
GU: azotemia, ***renal failure,*** uric acid nephropathy, glycosuria, polyuria, *increased blood ammonia level.*
Hematologic: *anemia,* ***hypofibrinogenemia, thrombocytopenia, leukopenia.***
Hepatic: ***hepatotoxicity.***
Metabolic: *hyperuricemia, hyperglycemia.*
Skin: rash, urticaria.
Other: **ANAPHYLAXIS,** chills, ***fatal hyperthermia.***

Interactions

Drug-drug. *Methotrexate:* May decrease methotrexate's effectiveness when given immediately before or with methotrexate. Monitor levels of methotrexate. Watch patient for signs of decreased effect.
Prednisone, vincristine: May increase toxicity. Monitor patient closely.

Effects on lab test results

- May increase BUN, AST, ALT, bilirubin, glucose, uric acid, and ammonia levels. May decrease calcium, fibrinogen, and albumin levels, and levels of other clotting factors. May increase or decrease total lipid level.
- May decrease hemoglobin, hematocrit, thyroid function test values, and WBC and platelet counts.

Pharmacokinetics

Absorption: Unknown.
Distribution: Primarily distributed within intravascular space, with detectable levels in thoracic and cervical lymph. Minimal amount crosses blood-brain barrier.
Metabolism: Hepatic sequestration by reticuloendothelial system may occur.
Excretion: Unknown. *Half-life:* 8 to 30 hours.

Route	Onset	Peak	Duration
I.V.	Almost immediate	Almost immediate	23-33 days after stopping drug
I.M.	Almost immediate	4-24 hr after stopping drug	23-33 days

Pharmacodynamics

Chemical effect: Destroys amino acid asparagine, which is needed for protein synthesis in acute lymphocytic leukemia. This leads to death of leukemic cell.
Therapeutic effect: Kills leukemic cells.

Available forms

Injection: 10,000 IU vial

NURSING PROCESS

Assessment

- Obtain history of patient's leukemic condition.
- Monitor effectiveness of treatment by evaluating CBC and bone marrow function test results. Bone marrow regeneration may take 5 to 6 weeks.
- Be alert for adverse reactions and drug interactions.
- Evaluate patient's and family's knowledge of drug therapy.

Nursing diagnoses

- Ineffective health maintenance related to leukemic condition
- Ineffective protection related to drug-induced adverse reactions
- Deficient knowledge related to drug therapy

Planning and implementation

- Give drug in a hospital under close supervision.
- Follow facility policy to reduce risks. Preparation and administration of parenteral form is linked with carcinogenic, mutagenic, and teratogenic risks for personnel.
- Prevent tumor lysis, which can result in uric acid nephropathy, by increasing fluid intake. Allopurinol should be started before therapy begins.

ALERT: The risk of hypersensitivity reaction increases with repeated doses. An I.D. skin test should be performed before initial dose and repeated after an interval of a week or more, between doses. To perform skin test, give 2 IU of drug I.D. Observe site for at least 1 hour for erythema or a wheal, which indicates a positive response. An allergic reaction to the drug may still develop in a patient with a negative skin test.

- A desensitization dose of 1 IU I.V. may be ordered. Dose is doubled q 10 minutes if no reaction occurs, until total amount given equals patient's total dose for that day.
- **I.V. use:** Give injection over 30 minutes through a running infusion of normal saline solution for injection or D_5W injection.
- **I.M. use:** Limit dose at single injection site to 2 ml.
- Reconstitute with 2 to 5 ml of either sterile water or normal saline solution for injection. Don't shake vial. Don't use cloudy solutions.
- Drug shouldn't be used alone to induce remission unless combination therapy is inappropriate. Not recommended for maintenance therapy.
- Refrigerate unopened dry powder. Reconstituted solution is stable for 8 hours if refrigerated.

• If drug contacts skin or mucous membranes, wash with copious amounts of water for at least 15 minutes.
• Keep epinephrine, diphenhydramine, and I.V. corticosteroids available for treating anaphylaxis.
• Because of vomiting, administer parenteral fluids for 24 hours or until patient can tolerate oral fluids.

Patient teaching
• Tell patient to watch for signs of infection (fever, sore throat, fatigue) and bleeding (easy bruising, nosebleeds, bleeding gums, melena). Instruct patient to take temperature daily.
• Encourage patient to maintain an adequate fluid intake to increase urine output and facilitate excretion of uric acid.
• Tell patient that drowsiness may occur during therapy or for several weeks after treatment ends. Warn patient to avoid hazardous activities requiring mental alertness.

☑ Evaluation
• Patient is free of leukemic cells after asparaginase therapy.
• Patient doesn't experience injury as a result of drug-induced adverse reactions.
• Patient and family state understanding of drug therapy.

aspirin (acetylsalicylic acid)
(AS-prin)
Ancasal♦†, Arthrinol♦†, Artria S.R.†, ASA†, ASA Enseals†, Aspergum†, Aspro◇, Astrin♦†, Bayer Aspirin†, Bex Powders◇, Coryphen♦†, Easprin†, Ecotrin†, Empirin†, Entrophen♦†, Halfprin, Measurin♦†, Norwich Aspirin Extra Strength†, Novasen♦†, Riphen-10♦†, Sal-Adult♦†, Sal-Infant♦†, Sloprin◇, Supasa♦†, Triaphen-10♦†, Vincent's Powders◇, ZORprin†

Pharmacologic class: salicylate
Therapeutic class: nonnarcotic analgesic, antipyretic, anti-inflammatory, antiplatelet drug
Pregnancy risk category: C (D in third trimester)

Indications and dosages
▶ **Arthritis.** *Adults:* Initially, 2.4 to 3.6 g P.O. daily in divided doses. Maintenance dosage is 3.6 to 5.4 g P.O. daily in divided doses. *Children:* 60 to 130 mg/kg P.O. daily in divided doses.
▶ **Mild pain or fever.** *Adults:* 325 to 650 mg P.O. or P.R. q 4 hours, p.r.n.
Children: For mild pain only, 65 mg/kg P.O. or P.R. daily in four to six divided doses.
▶ **Prevention of thrombosis.** *Adults:* 1.3 g P.O. daily in two to four divided doses.
▶ **Reduction of risk of MI in patients with previous MI or unstable angina.** *Adults:* 160 to 325 mg P.O. daily.
▶ **Kawasaki syndrome (mucocutaneous lymph node syndrome).** *Adults:* 80 to 100 mg/kg P.O. daily in four divided doses during febrile phase. Some patients may need up to 120 mg/kg. When fever subsides, decrease dosage to 3 to 8 mg/kg once daily, adjusted according to salicylate level.
▶ **Prophylaxis for TIA.** *Adults:* 50 to 325 mg P.O. daily.
▶ **Treatment of TIA.** *Adults:* 160 to 325 mg P.O. immediately within 48 hours of onset of CVA.
▶ **Prevention of reocclusion in coronary revascularization procedures.** *Adults:* 325 mg P.O. q 6 hours after surgery and for 1 year.
▶ **Rheumatic fever‡.** *Adults:* 4.9 to 7.8 g P.O. daily in divided doses q 4 to 6 hours for 1 to 2 weeks. Decrease to 60 to 70 mg/kg daily for 1 to 6 weeks, then gradually withdraw over 1 to 2 weeks. *Children:* 90 to 130 mg/kg P.O. daily in divided doses q 4 to 6 hours.
▶ **Pericarditis after acute MI‡.** *Adults:* 160 to 325 mg P.O. daily.
▶ **Stent implantation‡.** *Adults:* 160 to 325 mg P.O. q 2 hours before stent placement and continued indefinitely.

Contraindications and precautions
• Contraindicated in patients with G6PD deficiency; bleeding disorders such as hemophilia, von Willebrand's disease, and telangiectasia; NSAID-induced sensitivity reactions; and hypersensitivity to drug.
• Use cautiously in patients with GI lesions, impaired renal function, hypoprothrombinemia, vitamin K deficiency, thrombocytopenia, thrombotic thrombocytopenic purpura, or severe hepatic impairment.

Lifespan: In pregnant women, use cautiously. In breast-feeding women, safety hasn't been established.
ALERT: Because of the link with Reye's syndrome, the Centers for Disease Control and Prevention recommend not giving salicylates to children or teenagers with chickenpox or flu-like illness. In elderly patients, use cautiously because GI and renal adverse effects may be exacerbated.

Adverse reactions

EENT: *tinnitus, hearing loss.*
GI: *nausea, vomiting, GI distress, occult bleeding,* dyspepsia, ***GI bleeding.***
GU: transient renal insufficiency.
Hematologic: *prolonged bleeding time,* ***thrombocytopenia.***
Hepatic: ***hepatitis.***
Skin: *rash,* bruising, urticaria.
Other: ***angioedema,*** hypersensitivity reactions, (***anaphylaxis,*** asthma), ***Reye's syndrome.***

Interactions

Drug-drug. *Ammonium chloride, other urine acidifiers:* May increase levels of aspirin products. Watch for aspirin toxicity.
Antacids in high doses (and other urine alkalinizers): May decrease levels of aspirin products. Watch for decreased aspirin effect.
Beta blockers: May decrease antihypertensive effect. Avoid long-term aspirin use if patient is taking antihypertensives.
Corticosteroids: May enhance salicylate elimination. Watch for decreased salicylate effect.
Heparin, oral anticoagulants: May increase risk of bleeding. Monitor patient for signs of bleeding.
Methotrexate: May increase risk of methotrexate toxicity. Monitor patient closely.
NSAIDs, steroids: May increase risk of GI bleeding. Monitor patient closely.
NSAIDs, including diflunisal, fenoprofen, ibuprofen, indomethacin, meclofenamate, naproxen, piroxicam: May alter pharmacokinetics of these drugs, leading to lower levels and decreased effectiveness. Avoid using together.
Oral antidiabetics: May increase hypoglycemic effect. Monitor patient closely.
Probenecid, sulfinpyrazone: May decrease uricosuric effect. Avoid aspirin during therapy with these drugs.
Drug-herb. *Dong quai, feverfew, garlic, ginger, horse chestnut, red clover:* May increase risk of bleeding. Monitor patient for increased effects, and discourage using together.
Drug-food. *Caffeine:* May increase the absorption of aspirin. Monitor patient for increased effects.
Drug-lifestyle. *Alcohol use:* May increase risk of GI bleeding. Discourage using together.

Effects on lab test results

- May increase liver function test values. May decrease WBC and platelet counts.

Pharmacokinetics

Absorption: Absorbed rapidly and completely from GI tract.
Distribution: Distributed widely into most body tissues and fluids. Protein-binding to albumin is concentration-dependent; it ranges from 75% to 90%, and decreases as level increases.
Metabolism: Hydrolyzed partially in GI tract to salicylic acid, with almost complete metabolism in liver.
Excretion: Excreted in urine as salicylate and its metabolites. *Half-life:* 15 to 20 minutes.

Route	Onset	Peak	Duration
P.O.			
solution	5-30 min	15-60 min	1-4 hr
regular	5-30 min	25-40 min	1-4 hr
buffered	5-30 min	1-2 hr	1-4 hr
extended-release	5-30 min	1-2 hr	1-4 hr
enteric-coated	5-30 min	4-8 hr	1-4 hr
P.R.	5-30 min	3-4 hr	1-4 hr

Pharmacodynamics

Chemical effect: Produces analgesia by blocking prostaglandin synthesis (peripheral action). Aspirin and other salicylates may prevent lowering of pain threshold that occurs when prostaglandins sensitize pain receptors to mechanical and chemical stimulation. Exerts its anti-inflammatory effect by inhibiting prostaglandin synthesis; also may inhibit synthesis or action of other mediators of inflammatory response. Relieves fever by acting on hypothalamic heat-regulating center to cause peripheral vasodilation. This increases peripheral blood supply and promotes sweating, which leads to

heat loss and to cooling by evaporation. In low doses, aspirin also appears to impede clotting by blocking prostaglandin synthesis, which prevents formation of platelet-aggregating substance thromboxane A_2.
Therapeutic effect: Relieves pain, reduces fever and inflammation, and decreases risk of transient ischemic attacks and MI.

Available forms

Capsules: 325 mg†, 500 mg†
Chewing gum: 227.5 mg†
Suppositories: 60 mg†, 65 mg†, 120 mg†, 125 mg†, 130 mg†, 195 mg†, 200 mg†, 300 mg†, 325 mg†, 600 mg†, 650 mg†
Tablets†: 325 mg, 500 mg, 600 mg, 650 mg
Tablets (chewable): 81 mg†
Tablets (enteric-coated): 165 mg, 325 mg†, 500 mg†, 650 mg†, 975 mg
Tablets (extended-release): 800 mg
Tablets (timed-release): 650 mg†

NURSING PROCESS

Assessment

- Obtain history of patient's pain or fever before therapy, and monitor patient throughout therapy.
- Be alert for adverse reactions and drug interactions.
- During long-term therapy, monitor serum salicylate level. Therapeutic level in arthritis is 10 to 30 mg/dl. With long-term therapy, mild toxicity may occur at plasma levels of 20 mg/dl. Tinnitus may occur at plasma levels of 30 mg/dl and above but doesn't reliably indicate toxicity, especially in very young patients and those older than age 60.
- Evaluate patient's and family's knowledge of drug therapy.

Nursing diagnoses

- Acute pain related to underlying condition.
- Risk for injury related to drug-induced adverse GI reactions
- Deficient knowledge related to drug therapy

Planning and implementation

- **P.O. use:** Give aspirin with food, milk, antacid, or large glass of water to reduce adverse GI reactions.
- If patient has trouble swallowing, crush aspirin, combine it with soft food, or dissolve it in liquid. Give immediately after mixing with liquid because drug doesn't stay in solution. Don't crush enteric-coated aspirin.
- Enteric-coated products are slowly absorbed and not suitable for acute effects. They cause less GI bleeding and may be more suited for long-term therapy, such as for arthritis.
- **P.R. use:** Absorption after P.R. administration is slow and variable, depending on how long suppository is retained. If retained for 2 to 4 hours, absorption of dose is 20% to 60%; if retained for at least 10 hours, absorption is 70% to 100%.
- Hold dose and notify prescriber if bleeding, salicylism (tinnitus, hearing loss), or adverse GI reactions develop.
- Stop aspirin 5 to 7 days before elective surgery.

ALERT: Don't confuse aspirin with Asendin or Afrin.

Patient teaching

- Advise patient receiving high-dose prolonged treatment to watch for petechiae, bleeding gums, and signs of GI bleeding and to maintain adequate fluid intake. Encourage use of a soft toothbrush.
- Because of many possible drug interactions involving aspirin, warn patient who takes prescription form to check with prescriber or pharmacist before taking OTC combinations containing aspirin or herbal preparations.
- Explain that various OTC preparations contain aspirin. Warn patient to read labels carefully to avoid overdose.
- Advise patient to avoid alcohol consumption during drug therapy.
- Advise patient to restrict intake of caffeine during drug therapy.
- Instruct patient to take aspirin with food or milk.
- Instruct patient not to chew enteric-coated products.
- Emphasize safe storage of medications in the home. Teach patient to keep aspirin and other drugs out of children's reach. Aspirin is a leading cause of poisoning in children. Encourage use of child-resistant containers in households with children, even if only as occasional visitors.

Evaluation

- Patient states that aspirin has relieved pain.
- Patient remains free of adverse GI effects throughout drug therapy.
- Patient and family state understanding of drug therapy.

atenolol

(uh-TEN-uh-lol)

Apo-Atenolol◆, Noten◇, Nu-Atenol◆, Tenormin

Pharmacologic class: beta blocker
Therapeutic class: antihypertensive, antianginal
Pregnancy risk category: D

Indications and dosages

▶ **Hypertension.** *Adults:* Initially, 50 mg P.O. daily as a single dose. Dosage increased to 100 mg once daily after 7 to 14 days. Doses over 100 mg are unlikely to produce further benefit. Dosage adjustment required in patients with creatinine clearance below 35 ml/minute. *Older adults:* Initially 25 mg P.O. daily and increase slowly until desired response.

▶ **Angina pectoris.** *Adults:* 50 mg P.O. once daily. Increase as needed to 100 mg daily after 7 days for optimal effect. Maximum dosage is 200 mg daily.

▶ **Reduction of CV mortality rate and risk of reinfarction in patients with acute MI.** *Adults:* 5 mg I.V. over 5 minutes, followed by another 5 mg 10 minutes later. After another 10 minutes, 50 mg P.O., followed by 50 mg P.O. in 12 hours. Thereafter, 100 mg P.O. daily (as a single dose or 50 mg b.i.d.) for at least 7 days.

▶ **To slow rapid ventricular response to atrial tachyarrhythmias after acute MI without left ventricular dysfunction and AV block‡.** *Adults:* 2.5 to 5 mg I.V. over 2 to 5 minutes, p.r.n. to control rate. Maximum, 10 mg over a 10- to 15-minute period.

Contraindications and precautions

- Contraindicated in patients with sinus bradycardia, greater than first-degree heart block, overt cardiac failure, or cardiogenic shock.
- Use cautiously in patients at risk for heart failure and in those with bronchospastic disease, diabetes, and hyperthyroidism.

Lifespan: In pregnant women, don't use unless absolutely necessary because fetal harm can occur. In breast-feeding women, use cautiously. In children, safety of drug hasn't been established.

Adverse reactions

CNS: fever, fatigue, lethargy.
CV: ***BRADYCARDIA, PROFOUND HYPOTENSION***, ***heart failure,*** intermittent claudication, ***second- or third-degree AV block.***
GI: nausea, vomiting, diarrhea, dry mouth.
Metabolic: increased risk of type 2 diabetes.
Respiratory: dyspnea, ***bronchospasm.***
Skin: rash.

Interactions

Drug-drug. *Antihypertensives:* May enhance hypotensive effect. Use together cautiously.
Cardiac glycosides, diltiazem, verapamil: May cause excessive bradycardia and may increase depressant effect on myocardium. Use together cautiously.
Insulin, oral antidiabetics: May alter dosage requirements in previously stabilized patient with diabetes. Observe patient carefully.
Reserpine: May cause hypotension. Use with caution.

Effects on lab test results

- May increase BUN, creatinine, potassium, uric acid, glucose, transaminase, alkaline phosphatase, and LDH levels. May decrease glucose level.
- May increase platelet count.

Pharmacokinetics

Absorption: About 50% to 60%.
Distribution: Distributed into most tissues and fluids except brain and CSF. About 5% to 15% protein-bound.
Metabolism: Minimal.
Excretion: From 40% to 50% of dose is excreted unchanged in urine; remainder is excreted as unchanged drug and metabolites in feces. *Half-life:* 6 to 7 hours (increases as renal function decreases).

Route	Onset	Peak	Duration
P.O.	1 hr	2-4 hr	24 hr
I.V.	5 min	5 min	12 hr

Pharmacodynamics

Chemical effect: Selectively blocks $beta_1$-adrenergic receptors; decreases cardiac output, peripheral resistance, and cardiac oxygen consumption; and depresses renin secretion.
Therapeutic effect: Decreases blood pressure, relieves angina, and reduces CV mortality rate and risk of reinfarction after acute MI.

Available forms

Injection: 5 mg/10 ml
Tablets: 25 mg, 50 mg, 100 mg

NURSING PROCESS

Assessment

• Obtain history of patient's underlying condition.
• If prescribed for hypertension, monitor drug's effectiveness by frequently checking patient's blood pressure. Full antihypertensive effect may not appear for 1 to 2 weeks after therapy starts. If prescribed for angina pectoris, monitor frequency and severity of anginal pain, and if prescribed to reduce CV mortality rate and risk of reinfarction after acute MI, monitor signs of reinfarction.
• Be alert for adverse reactions and drug interactions.
• Evaluate patient's and family's understanding of drug therapy.

Nursing diagnoses

• Risk for injury related to underlying condition
• Decreased cardiac output related to drug-induced adverse CV reactions
• Deficient knowledge related to drug therapy

Planning and implementation

• Patients with renal insufficiency and those receiving hemodialysis require a dosage adjustment.
• Check patient's apical pulse before giving drug; if slower than 60 beats/minute, withhold drug and call prescriber.
• **P.O. use:** Give as a single daily dose.
• **I.V. use:** Give by slow injection, not to exceed 1 mg/minute. Doses may be mixed with D_5W, normal saline solution, or dextrose and sodium chloride solutions. Solution is stable for 48 hours after mixing.
• Be prepared to treat shock or hypoglycemia because this drug masks common signs of these conditions.
• Notify prescriber immediately if patient shows signs of decreased cardiac output.
ALERT: Withdraw drug gradually over 1 to 2 weeks to avoid serious adverse reactions.
ALERT: Don't confuse atenolol with timolol or albuterol.

Patient teaching

• Caution patient that stopping drug abruptly can worsen angina and MI. Drug should be withdrawn gradually over a 2-week period.
• Counsel patient to take drug at same time every day.
• Tell woman to notify prescriber if pregnancy occurs. Drug will need to be discontinued.
• Teach patient how to take his pulse. Tell patient to withhold drug and call prescriber if pulse rate is below 60 beats/minute.

Evaluation

• Patient's underlying condition improves with drug therapy.
• Patient's cardiac output remains unchanged throughout drug therapy.
• Patient and family state understanding of drug therapy.

atorvastatin calcium

(uh-TOR-vah-stah-tin KAL-see-um)
Lipitor

Pharmacologic class: 3-hydroxy-3-methylglutaryl-coenzyme A (HMG-CoA) reductase inhibitor
Therapeutic class: antilipemic
Pregnancy risk category: X

Indications and dosages

▶ Adjunct to diet to reduce elevated low-density lipoprotein (LDL), total cholesterol, apo B, and triglyceride levels and to increase high-density lipoprotein (HDL) in patients with primary hypercholesterolemia (heterozygous familial and nonfamilial) and mixed dyslipidemia (Fredrickson Types IIa and IIb); adjunct to diet for the treatment of patients with elevated serum triglyceride levels (Fredrickson Type IV); primary dys-

betalipoproteinemia (Fredrickson Type III) in patients who do not respond adequately to diet. *Adults:* Initially, 10 or 20 mg P.O. once daily. Patients who require a large reduction in LDL cholesterol (more than 45%) may be started at 40 mg once daily. Increase dose, p.r.n., to maximum of 80 mg daily as single dose. Dosage based on lipid levels drawn within 2 to 4 weeks after starting therapy.

▶ **Alone or as an adjunct to lipid-lowering treatments such as LDL apheresis to reduce total cholesterol and LDL cholesterol in patients with homozygous familial hypercholesterolemia.** *Adults:* 10 to 80 mg P.O. once daily.

▶ **Heterozygous familial hypercholesterolemia.** *Children ages 10 to 17:* 10 mg P.O. once daily. May adjust dose after 4 weeks to 20 mg daily.

Contraindications and precautions

• Contraindicated in patients with active liver disease, conditions linked with unexplained persistent increases in serum transaminase levels, or hypersensitivity to drug.

Lifespan: In pregnant and breast-feeding women and in women who have the potential to become pregnant, drug is contraindicated.

Adverse reactions

CNS: *headache,* asthenia, fever, malaise.
EENT: sinusitis, pharyngitis.
GI: abdominal pain, constipation, diarrhea, dyspepsia, flatulence.
Musculoskeletal: back pain, arthralgia, myalgia.
Skin: rash.
Other: *infection,* accidental injury, flulike syndrome, hypersensitivity reaction.

Interactions

Drug-drug. *Antacids:* May decrease bioavailability. Give separately.
Azole antifungals, cyclosporine, erythromycin, fibric acid derivatives, niacin: May cause rhabdomyolysis. Avoid using together.
Colestipol and other bile-acid sequestrants: May decrease atorvastatin level; however, these drugs may be used together for therapeutic effect. Monitor patient.
Digoxin: May increase digoxin level. Monitor digoxin levels.
Erythromycin: May increase drug level. Monitor patient.
Oral contraceptives: May increase hormone levels. Consider when selecting an oral contraceptive.
Warfarin: May increase anticoagulant effect. Monitor INR and patient for bleeding.

Effects on lab test results

• May increase ALT and AST levels.

Pharmacokinetics

Absorption: Rapid.
Distribution: 98% bound to plasma proteins.
Metabolism: Metabolized by liver.
Excretion: Eliminated in bile.

Route	Onset	Peak	Duration
P.O.	Unknown	1-2 hr	Unknown

Pharmacodynamics

Chemical effect: Selectively inhibits HMG-CoA reductase, which converts HMG-CoA to mevalonate, a precursor of sterols.
Therapeutic effect: Lowers plasma cholesterol and lipoprotein levels.

Available forms

Tablets: 10 mg, 20 mg, 40 mg, 80 mg

NURSING PROCESS

Assessment

• Withhold drug in patients with serious, acute conditions that suggest myopathy and in those at risk for renal failure caused by rhabdomyolysis from trauma; major surgery; severe metabolic, endocrine, and electrolyte disorders; severe acute infection; hypotension; or uncontrolled seizures.
• Evaluate patient's and family's understanding of drug therapy.

Nursing diagnoses

• Risk for injury related to elevated cholesterol levels
• Deficient knowledge related to drug therapy

Planning and implementation

• Use drug only after diet and other nonpharmacologic treatments prove ineffective. Patient should follow a standard low-cholesterol diet before and during therapy.

• Before starting treatment, perform a baseline lipid profile to exclude secondary causes of hypercholesterolemia. Liver function test results and lipid levels should be obtained before therapy, after 6 and 12 weeks, or following a dosage increase and periodically thereafter.
ALERT: Don't confuse Lipitor with Levatol.

Patient teaching
• Teach patient about proper dietary management, weight control, and exercise and explain their role in controlling elevated lipid levels.
• Warn patient to avoid alcohol.
• Tell patient to inform prescriber of adverse reactions such as muscle pain, tenderness, or weakness, especially if accompanied by fever or malaise.
• Urge woman to notify prescriber immediately if pregnancy is suspected.

Evaluation
• Patient's cholesterol level is within normal limits.
• Patient and family state understanding of drug therapy.

atovaquone
(uh-TOH-vuh-kwohn)
Mepron

Pharmacologic class: ubiquinone analogue
Therapeutic class: antiprotozoal
Pregnancy risk category: C

Indications and dosages
▶ **Prevention of *Pneumocystis carinii* pneumonia in patients who are intolerant to co-trimoxazole, including HIV-infected individuals.** *Adults and children age 13 and older:* 1,500 mg (10 ml) P.O. daily with a meal.
Children older than 24 months‡: 30 mg/kg P.O. once daily.
Infants 4 to 24 months: 45 mg/kg P.O. daily‡.
▶ **Treatment of mild-to-moderate *P. carinii* pnuemonia in patients who can't tolerate co-trimoxazole.** *Adults and children age 13 and older:* 750 mg P.O. b.i.d. for 21 days.
Children‡: 40 mg/kg P.O. daily in two divided doses.
▶ **Prevention of toxoplasmosis in HIV-infected patients‡.** *Adults and children age 13 and older:* 1,500 mg P.O. daily.

Contraindications and precautions
• Contraindicated in patients hypersensitive to drug.
• Use cautiously with other highly protein-bound drugs because drug is highly bound to plasma protein (greater than 99.9%).
Lifespan: In pregnant and breast-feeding women, use cautiously. In children, safety of drug hasn't been established.

Adverse reactions
CNS: dreams, *headache, insomnia,* asthenia, dizziness.
EENT: visual difficulties
GI: *nausea,* diarrhea, *vomiting,* oral ulcers, *abdominal pain,* anorexia, dyspepsia, gastritis.
Respiratory: cough.
Skin: pruritus.

Interactions
Drug-drug. *Highly protein-bound drugs:* May compete for receptor sites affecting drug levels. Use cautiously.
Rifabutin, rifampin: May decrease atovaquone's steady-state levels. Avoid using together.

Effects on lab test results
• May increase alkaline phosphatase, ALT, and AST levels.
• May decrease hemoglobin, hematocrit, and WBC counts.

Pharmacokinetics
Absorption: Limited absorption. Bioavailability is increased twofold when administered with meals. Fat enhances absorption significantly.
Distribution: 99.9% bound to plasma proteins.
Metabolism: Not metabolized.
Excretion: Undergoes enterohepatic cycling and is primarily excreted in feces. Less than 0.6% is excreted in urine. *Half-life:* 2 to 3 days.

Route	Onset	Peak	Duration
P.O.	Unknown	1-8 hr (1st peak); 1-4 days (2nd peak)	Unknown

Pharmacodynamics

Chemical effect: Unknown; appears to interfere with electron transport in protozoal mitochondria, inhibiting enzymes needed for synthesis of nucleic acids and adenosine triphosphate.

Therapeutic effect: Kills *Pneumocystis carinii* protozoa.

Available forms

Suspension: 750 mg/5 ml

NURSING PROCESS

Assessment

- Obtain history of patient's protozoal respiratory infection and reassess regularly.
- Be alert for adverse reactions.
- Monitor patient's hydration if adverse GI reactions occur.
- Evaluate patient's and family's knowledge of drug therapy.

Nursing diagnoses

- Infection related to presence of susceptible protozoal organisms
- Risk for deficient fluid volume related to drug-induced adverse GI reactions
- Deficient knowledge related to drug therapy

Planning and implementation

- Give drug with food to improve bioavailability.

Patient teaching

- Instruct patient to take drug with meals because food enhances absorption significantly.
- Warn patient not to perform hazardous activities if dizziness occurs.
- Emphasize importance of taking drug as prescribed, even if patient is feeling better.
- Tell patient to notify prescriber if serious adverse reactions occur.

Evaluation

- Patient's infection is eradicated.
- Patient remains adequately hydrated throughout therapy.
- Patient and family state understanding of drug therapy.

atovaquone and proguanil hydrochloride

(uh-TOH-vuh-kwohn and pro-GWAN-ill high-droh-KLOR-ighd)

Malarone

Pharmacologic classification: hydroxynapthalenedione and biguanide hydrochloride

Therapeutic classification: antimalarial

Pregnancy risk category: C

Indications and dosages

▶ **Prevention of *Plasmodium falciparum* malaria, including areas where chloroquine resistance has been reported.** *Adults and children weighing more than 40 kg (88 lb):* One adult-strength tablet (250 mg atovaquone and 100 mg proguanil) P.O. once daily with food or milk. Begin 1 or 2 days before entering a malaria-endemic area. Continue prophylactic treatment during stay and for 7 days after return.

Children weighing 31 to 40 kg (68 to 88 lb): Three pediatric-strength tablets P.O. once daily with food or milk, beginning 1 or 2 days before entering endemic area. Total daily dose is 187.5 mg atovaquone and 75 mg proguanil. Treatment should continue during stay and for 7 days after return.

Children weighing 21 to 30 kg (46 to 68 lb): Two pediatric-strength tablets P.O. once daily with food or milk, beginning 1 or 2 days before entering endemic area. Total daily dose is 125 mg atovaquone and 50 mg proguanil. Treatment should continue during stay and for 7 days after return.

Children weighing 11 to 20 kg (24 to 45 lb): One pediatric-strength tablet P.O. daily with food or milk, beginning 1 or 2 days before entering endemic area. Continue treatment during stay and for 7 days after return.

▶ **Treatment of acute, uncomplicated *P. falciparum* malaria.** *Adults and children weighing more than 40 kg:* Four adult-strength tablets, with food or milk, P.O. once daily for 3 consecutive days. Total daily dose is 1 g atovaquone and 400 mg proguanil.

Children weighing 31 to 40 kg: Three adult-strength tablets P.O. once daily, with food or milk, for 3 consecutive days. Total daily dose is 750 mg atovaquone and 300 mg proguanil.

Children weighing 21 to 30 kg: Two adult-strength tablets P.O. once daily, with food or milk, for 3 consecutive days. Total daily dose is 500 mg atovaquone and 200 mg proguanil.
Children weighing 11 to 20 kg: One adult-strength tablet P.O. once daily, with food or milk, for 3 consecutive days.

Contraindications and precautions

• Contraindicated in patients hypersensitive to atovaquone, proguanil, or any component of the formulation. Use cautiously in patients with severe renal failure because proguanil is renally eliminated. Use cautiously in vomiting patients. Not intended for those with severe malaria, or for patients with recrudescent *P. falciparum* infection after treatment with Malarone or failure of chemoprophylaxis with Malarone.
Lifespan: In breast-feeding women, use cautiously because drug appears in breast milk in small amounts. In children weighing less than 11 kg, safety and efficacy haven't been established. In elderly patients, use cautiously because they may respond differently than younger patients and are more likely to have decreased renal function.

Adverse reactions

CNS: asthenia, dizziness, fever, *headache.*
GI: *abdominal pain,* diarrhea, anorexia, dyspepsia, gastritis, *nausea, vomiting.*
Musculoskeletal: back pain, *myalgia.*
Respiratory: cough, upper respiratory tract infection.
Skin: pruritus.
Other: ***anaphylaxis,*** flu syndrome.

Interactions

Drug-drug. *Metoclopramide:* May decrease atovaquone bioavailability. Consider alternative antiemetics.
Proguanil-containing drugs: Proguanil is eliminated by renal excretion. Avoid using together.
Rifampin: May reduce atovaquone level by about 50%. Avoid using together.
Tetracycline: May reduce atovaquone levels by about 40%. Monitor patient closely for signs and symptoms of parasitemia.

Effects on lab test results

• May increase ALT, AST, and serum creatinine levels.
• May decrease hemoglobin, hematocrit, and neutrophil count.

Pharmacokinetics

Absorption: Bioavailability of atovaquone is 23% when tablet formulation is taken with food. Atovaquone bioavailability varies considerably. Dietary fat increases the rate and extent of atovaquone absorption compared with fasting. Proguanil is well absorbed without regard to food. Absorption is decreased in patients with diarrhea and vomiting.
Distribution: Atovaquone is more than 99% protein-bound; proguanil, 75%.
Metabolism: Atovaquone undergoes virtually no metabolism. Proguanil is metabolized in the liver to cycloguanil (primarily via cytochrome P-450 2C19) and 4-chlorophenylbiguanide.
Excretion: More than 94% of atovaquone is eliminated unchanged in the feces over 21 days. The kidneys eliminate 40% to 60% of proguanil and its metabolites. Half-life in children is decreased. *Atovaquone half-life:* 2 to 3 days in adults. *Proguanil half-life:* 12 to 21 hours in adults and children.

Route	Onset	Peak	Duration
P.O.	Unknown	Unknown	Unknown

Pharmacodynamics

Chemical effect: Thought to interfere with nucleic acid replication in the malarial parasite by inhibiting biosynthesis of pyrimidine compounds in two different pathways. Atovaquone selectively inhibits parasitic mitochondrial electron transport. Proguanil disrupts deoxythymidilate synthesis through inhibition of dihydrofolate reductase.
Therapeutic effect: Prevents and treats symptoms of malaria.

Available forms

Tablets: 250 mg atovaquone and 100 mg proguanil (adult-strength); 62.5 mg atovaquone and 25 mg proguanil (pediatric-strength)

NURSING PROCESS

Assessment

• Assess patient for signs and symptoms of malaria.
• Assess patient and travel plans for need for antimalarial prophylaxis.

• Be alert for drug-induced adverse reactions.
• Monitor patient's liver and renal function during drug therapy.

Nursing diagnoses

• Risk of infection related to exposure to *P. falciparum* in malaria-endemic areas
• Deficient knowledge related to drug therapy

Planning and implementation

• Atovaquone absorption may be decreased by persistent diarrhea or vomiting. Alternative antimalarial therapy may be needed in patients with persistent diarrhea or vomiting. Antiemetics are recommended.
• If treatment or prophylaxis fails, an alternative antimalarial is indicated.
• Give atovaquone and proguanil at the same time each day with food or milk.
• Store tablets at controlled room temperature 59° to 86° F (15° to 30° C).

Patient teaching

• Tell patient to take dose at the same time each day.
• Advise patient to take drug with food or milk.
• If patient vomits within 1 hour after taking a dose, tell him to take a repeat dose.
• Advise patient to contact prescriber if he can't complete the course of therapy as prescribed.
• Instruct patient that, in addition to drug therapy, malaria prophylaxis should include the use of protective clothing, bed nets, and insect repellents.

Evaluation

• Patient doesn't have malaria.
• Patient and family state understanding of antimalarial drug therapy.

atracurium besylate

(uh-trah-KYOO-ree-um BES-eh-layt)
Tracrium

Pharmacologic class: nondepolarizing neuromuscular blocker
Therapeutic class: skeletal muscle relaxant
Pregnancy risk category: C

Indications and dosages

▶ **Adjunct to general anesthesia, to facilitate endotracheal intubation and cause skeletal muscle relaxation during surgery or mechanical ventilation.** Dosage depends on anesthetic used, individual needs, and response. Dosages given here are representative and must be adjusted.
Adults and children older than age 2: 0.4 to 0.5 mg/kg by I.V. bolus. Maintenance dosage of 0.08 to 0.1 mg/kg within 20 to 45 minutes of initial dose should be given during prolonged surgical procedures. Maintenance dosages may be given q 15 to 25 minutes in patients receiving balanced anesthesia. For prolonged surgical procedures, a constant infusion of 5 to 9 mcg/kg/minute may be used after initial bolus.
Children ages 1 month to 2 years: Initial dose, 0.3 to 0.4 mg/kg. Frequent maintenance doses may be needed.

Contraindications and precautions

• Contraindicated in patients hypersensitive to drug.
• Use cautiously in patients with CV disease; severe electrolyte disorders; bronchogenic carcinoma; hepatic, renal, or pulmonary impairment; neuromuscular diseases; myasthenia gravis; and in debilitated patients.
Lifespan: In pregnant women, breastfeeding women, and elderly patients, use cautiously.

Adverse reactions

CV: increased heart rate, ***bradycardia,*** hypotension.
Respiratory: ***prolonged dose-related apnea,*** wheezing, increased bronchial secretions.
Skin: *flushing,* erythema, pruritus, urticaria.
Other: ***anaphylaxis.***

Interactions

Drug-drug. *Aminoglycoside antibiotics (including amikacin, gentamicin, kanamycin, neomycin, streptomycin); polymyxin antibiotics (colistin, polymyxin B sulfate); clindamycin; general anesthetics (such as enflurane, halothane, isoflurane); quinidine:* May potentiate neuromuscular blockade, leading to increased skeletal muscle relaxation and prolongation of effect. Use cautiously during surgical and postoperative periods.

Lithium, magnesium salts, opioid analgesics: May potentiate neuromuscular blockade, leading to increased skeletal muscle relaxation and, possibly, respiratory paralysis. Reduce dose of atracurium.

Effects on lab test results

None reported.

Pharmacokinetics

Absorption: Administered I.V.
Distribution: Distributed into extracellular space. About 82% protein-bound.
Metabolism: Rapidly metabolized by Hofmann elimination and by nonspecific enzymatic ester hydrolysis. The liver doesn't appear to play a major role.
Excretion: Atracurium and its metabolites are excreted in urine and feces. *Half-life:* 20 minutes.

Route	Onset	Peak	Duration
I.V.	2 min	3-5 min	35-70 min

Pharmacodynamics

Chemical effect: Prevents acetylcholine from binding to receptors on muscle end plate, thus blocking depolarization and resulting in skeletal muscle paralysis.
Therapeutic effect: Relaxes skeletal muscles.

Available forms

Injection: 10 mg/ml

NURSING PROCESS

Assessment

- Obtain history of patient's neuromuscular status before therapy and reassess regularly.
- Be alert for adverse reactions and interactions.
- Monitor respirations closely until patient fully recovers from neuromuscular blockade, as evidenced by tests of muscle strength (hand grip, head lift, and ability to cough).
- A nerve stimulator and train-of-four monitoring are recommended to confirm antagonism of neuromuscular blockade and recovery of muscle strength. Before attempting pharmacologic reversal with neostigmine, some evidence of spontaneous recovery should be seen.
- Evaluate patient's and family's understanding of drug therapy.

Nursing diagnoses

- Risk for injury related to underlying condition
- Impaired spontaneous ventilation related to drug-induced respiratory paralysis
- Deficient knowledge related to drug therapy

Planning and implementation

- Give sedatives or general anesthetics before neuromuscular blockers. Neuromuscular blockers don't decrease consciousness or alter pain threshold.

ALERT: Use this drug only under direct medical supervision by personnel skilled in use of neuromuscular blockers and techniques for maintaining a patent airway. Don't use unless facilities and equipment for mechanical ventilation, oxygen therapy, and intubation as well as an antagonist are immediately available.

- Drug usually is given by rapid I.V. bolus injection but may be given by intermittent or continuous infusion. At 0.2 to 0.5 mg/ml, drug is compatible for 24 hours in D_5W, normal saline solution injection, or dextrose 5% in normal saline solution injection.
- Don't use lactated Ringer's solution. In lactated Ringer's solution for injection, atracurium is stable for 8 hours at a concentration of 0.5 mg/ml. Because of increased drug degradation in this solution, it isn't recommended.
- Don't give by I.M. injection.
- Don't mix with acidic or alkaline solution; precipitate may form.
- Prior administration of succinylcholine doesn't prolong duration of action but quickens onset and may deepen neuromuscular blockade.
- Explain all events to patient because he can still hear.
- Give analgesics for pain. Patient may have pain but be unable to express it.
- Keep airway clear. Have emergency equipment and drugs immediately available.
- After spontaneous recovery starts, be prepared to reverse atracurium-induced neuromuscular blockade with an anticholinesterase (such as neostigmine or edrophonium). These drugs usually are given with an anticholinergic (such as atropine).

Patient teaching

- Instruct patient and family about drug therapy.

• Reassure patient and family that patient will be monitored at all times and that respiratory life support will be used during paralysis.
• Reassure patient that pain medication will be given as needed.

☑ Evaluation
• Patient's underlying condition is resolved without causing injury.
• Patient sustains spontaneous ventilation after effects of atracurium besylate wear off.
• Patient and family state understanding of drug therapy.

atropine sulfate
(AH-troh-peen SUL-fayt)
AtroPen Auto-Injector, Sal-Tropine

Pharmacologic class: anticholinergic, belladonna alkaloid
Therapeutic class: antiarrhythmic, vagolytic
Pregnancy risk category: C

Indications and dosages

▶ **Symptomatic bradycardia, bradyarrhythmia (junctional or escape rhythm).** *Adults:* Usually 0.5 to 1 mg I.V. push; repeat q 3 to 5 minutes to maximum of 2 mg, p.r.n. Lower doses (less than 0.5 mg) can cause bradycardia.
Children: 0.02 mg/kg I.V. to a maximum of 1 mg; or 0.3 mg/m^2; may repeat q 5 minutes.
▶ **Antidote for anticholinesterase insecticide poisoning.** *Adults and children:* 1 to 2 mg I.M. or I.V. repeated q 20 to 30 minutes until muscarinic symptoms disappear or signs of atropine toxicity appear. Patient with severe poisoning may require up to 6 mg q hour.
▶ **Preoperatively for decreasing secretions and blocking cardiac vagal reflexes.** *Adults and children weighing 20 kg (44 lb) or more:* 0.4 mg I.M. or S.C. 30 to 60 minutes before anesthesia.
Children weighing less than 20 kg: 0.1 mg I.M. for 3 kg, 0.2 mg I.M. for 4 to 9 kg, 0.3 mg I.M. for 10 to 20 kg 30 to 60 minutes before anesthesia.
▶ **Adjunct treatment of peptic ulcer disease; treatment of functional GI disorders such as irritable bowel syndrome.** *Adults:* 0.4 to 0.6 mg P.O. q 4 to 6 hours.
Children: 0.01 mg/kg or 0.3 mg/m^2 (not to exceed 0.4 mg) q 4 to 6 hours.

Contraindications and precautions

• Contraindicated in patients with acute angle-closure glaucoma, obstructive uropathy, obstructive disease of GI tract, paralytic ileus, toxic megacolon, intestinal atony, unstable CV status in acute hemorrhage, asthma, myasthenia gravis, or hypersensitivity to drug.
• Use cautiously in patients with Down syndrome.
Lifespan: In pregnant women, use cautiously. Use in breast-feeding women isn't recommended. Children and elderly patients may have increased adverse effects.

Adverse reactions

CNS: *headache, restlessness,* ataxia, disorientation, hallucinations, delirium, ***coma,*** *insomnia, dizziness,* excitement, agitation, confusion.
CV: *tachycardia, palpitations, angina,* ***arrhythmias,*** flushing.
EENT: photophobia, *blurred vision, mydriasis.*
GI: *dry mouth,* thirst, *constipation,* nausea, vomiting.
GU: urine retention.
Hematologic: leukocytosis.
Other: ***anaphylaxis.***

Interactions

Drug-drug. *Antacids:* May decrease absorption of anticholinergics. Give at least 1 hour apart.
Anticholinergics, drugs with anticholinergic effects (such as amantadine, antiarrhythmics, antiparkinsonians, glutethimide, meperidine, phenothiazines, tricyclic antidepressants): May cause additive anticholinergic effects. Use together cautiously.
Ketoconazole, levodopa: May decrease absorption. Avoid using together.
Methotrimeprazine: May produce extrapyramidal symptoms. Monitor patient carefully.
Potassium chloride wax matrix tablets: May increase risk of mucosal lesions. Use cautiously.

Effects on lab test results

• May increase WBC count.

Pharmacokinetics

Absorption: Well absorbed after P.O. and I.M. administration; unknown for S.C. administration.
Distribution: Distributed throughout the body, including CNS. Only 18% binds with plasma protein.
Metabolism: Metabolized in liver to several metabolites.
Excretion: Excreted primarily through kidneys; small amount may be excreted in feces and expired air. *Half-life:* Initial, 2 hours; second phase, 12½ hours.

Route	Onset	Peak	Duration
P.O.	0.5-1 hr	2 hr	4 hr
I.V.	Immediate	2-4 min	4 hr
I.M.	30 min	1-1.6 hr	4 hr
S.C.	Unknown	Unknown	4 hr

Pharmacodynamics

Chemical effect: Inhibits acetylcholine at parasympathetic neuroeffector junction, blocking vagal effects on SA node. This enhances conduction through AV node and speeds heart rate.
Therapeutic effect: Increases heart rate, decreases secretions preoperatively, and slows GI motility. Antidote for anticholinesterase insecticide poisoning.

Available forms

Injection: 0.05 mg/ml, 0.1 mg/ml, 0.3 mg/ml, 0.4 mg/ml, 0.5 mg/ml, 0.6 mg/ml, 0.8 mg/ml, 1 mg/ml, 1.2 mg/ml
Tablets: 0.4 mg, 0.6 mg

NURSING PROCESS

Assessment

- Obtain history of patient's underlying condition and reassess regularly.
- Be alert for adverse reactions and drug interactions.
- Monitor patients, especially those receiving small doses (0.4 to 0.6 mg), for paradoxical initial bradycardia, which is caused by a drug effect in CNS and usually disappears within 2 minutes.

ALERT: Watch for tachycardia in cardiac patients because it may cause ventricular fibrillation.

- Evaluate patient's and family's knowledge of drug therapy.

Nursing diagnoses

- Ineffective health maintenance related to underlying condition
- Risk for injury related to drug-induced adverse reactions
- Deficient knowledge related to drug therapy

Planning and implementation

- **P.O. use:** May be taken with or without food.
- **I.V. use:** Give by direct I.V. into a large vein or I.V. tubing over 1 to 2 minutes.
- **I.M. and S.C. use:** Follow normal protocol.
- If ECG disturbances occur, withhold drug, obtain a rhythm strip, and notify prescriber immediately.
- Have emergency equipment and drugs on hand to treat new arrhythmias. Other anticholinergic drugs may increase vagal blockage.
- Use physostigmine salicylate as antidote for atropine overdose.

Patient teaching

- Teach patient about atropine sulfate therapy.
- Instruct patient to ask for assistance with activities if adverse CNS reactions occur.
- Teach patient how to handle distressing anticholinergic effects.

Evaluation

- Patient's underlying condition improves.
- Patient has no injury as a result of therapy.
- Patient and family state understanding of drug therapy.

auranofin

(or-AN-uh-fin)
Ridaura

Pharmacologic class: gold salt
Therapeutic class: antiarthritic
Pregnancy risk category: C

Indications and dosages

▶ **Rheumatoid arthritis, psoriatic arthritis‡, active systemic lupus erythematosus‡, Felty's syndrome‡.** *Adults:* 6 mg P.O. daily, either as 3 mg b.i.d. or 6 mg once daily. After 4 to 6 months, dosage may be increased to 9 mg daily. Discontinue drug if no response at 9 mg daily for 3 months.

Contraindications and precautions

• Contraindicated in patients with history of severe gold toxicity, necrotizing enterocolitis, pulmonary fibrosis, exfoliative dermatitis, bone marrow aplasia, severe hematologic disorders, or history of severe toxicity resulting from previous exposure to other heavy metals. Also contraindicated in patients with urticaria, eczema, colitis, severe debilitation, hemorrhagic conditions, or systemic lupus erythematosus and in patients who recently received radiation therapy.

• Use cautiously with other drugs that cause blood dyscrasia. Also use cautiously in patients who have renal, hepatic, or inflammatory bowel disease; rash; or a history of bone marrow depression.

Lifespan: In breast-feeding women, use isn't recommended. In children, safety of drug hasn't been established.

Adverse reactions

CNS: confusion, ***seizures.***
EENT: metallic taste.
GI: *diarrhea, abdominal pain, nausea, vomiting,* stomatitis, enterocolitis, anorexia, dyspepsia, flatulence.
GU: proteinuria, hematuria, glomerulonephritis, ***acute renal failure,*** nephrotic syndrome.
Hematologic: ***thrombocytopenia, aplastic anemia, agranulocytosis, leukopenia,*** eosinophilia.
Hepatic: jaundice.
Respiratory: interstitial pneumonitis.
Skin: *rash, pruritus, dermatitis,* exfoliative dermatitis.

Interactions

Drug-drug. *Phenytoin:* May raise phenytoin blood levels. Watch for toxicity.

Effects on lab test results

• May increase BUN, creatinine, ALT, AST, and alkaline phosphatase levels.

• May increase eosinophil count. May decrease hemoglobin, hematocrit, and platelet, granulocyte, and WBC counts.

Pharmacokinetics

Absorption: 25% absorbed through GI tract.
Distribution: Distributed widely in body tissues. Synovial fluid levels are about 50% of blood levels. Drug is 60% protein-bound.
Metabolism: Unknown.
Excretion: 60% of absorbed drug is excreted in urine and remainder in feces. *Half-life:* 26 days.

Route	Onset	Peak	Duration
P.O.	1-3 mo	2 hr	Unknown

Pharmacodynamics

Chemical effect: Unknown. Anti-inflammatory effects in rheumatoid arthritis are probably caused by inhibition of sulfhydryl systems, which alters cellular metabolism. Auranofin also may alter enzyme function and immune response and suppress phagocytic activity.
Therapeutic effect: Relieves symptoms of rheumatoid arthritis.

Available forms

Capsules: 3 mg

NURSING PROCESS

Assessment

• Obtain history of patient's joint pain and stiffness before therapy and reassess regularly.
• Be alert for adverse reactions and drug interactions.
• Monitor patient's hydration status if adverse GI reactions occur.
• Monitor patient's platelet count and CBC regularly.
• Evaluate patient's and family's knowledge of drug therapy.

Nursing diagnoses

• Acute pain related to presence of rheumatoid arthritis
• Risk for deficient fluid volume related to drug-induced adverse GI reactions
• Deficient knowledge related to drug therapy

Planning and implementation

• Store at controlled room temperature and in a light-resistant container.
• Continue to give other drug therapies, such as NSAIDs.
• Notify prescriber and expect to stop drug if patient's platelet count falls below 100,000/mm^3, if hemoglobin drops suddenly, if granu-

locyte count is less than 1,500/mm^3, if leukopenia (WBC count less than 4,000/mm^3) or eosinophilia (eosinophil count greater than 75%) occurs.

Patient teaching

- Encourage patient to take drug as prescribed and not to alter dosage schedule.
- Tell patient to continue taking other drug therapy, such as NSAIDs, if prescribed.
- Remind patient to see prescriber monthly to monitor platelet counts. Auranofin should be stopped if platelet count falls below 100,000/mm^3, if hemoglobin drops suddenly, if granulocyte count is less than 1,500/mm^3, or if leukopenia (WBC count less than 4,000/mm^3) or eosinophilia (eosinophil count greater than 75%) occurs.
- Advise patient to have regular urinalysis. If proteinuria or hematuria is detected, notify prescriber and stop drug because nephrotic syndrome or glomerulonephritis may occur.
- Tell patient to continue taking drug if he experiences mild diarrhea and to contact prescriber immediately if he notices blood in stool. Diarrhea is the most common adverse reaction.
- Advise patient to report rashes or other skin problems immediately. Pruritus often precedes dermatitis; any pruritic skin eruption that occurs while patient is receiving auranofin should be considered a reaction to the drug until proven otherwise. Advise patient to stop therapy until reaction subsides and to notify prescriber.
- Advise patient that stomatitis is often preceded by a metallic taste, which should be reported to prescriber immediately. Promote careful oral hygiene during therapy.
- Reassure patient that beneficial drug effect may be delayed as long as 3 months. If response is inadequate and maximum dosage has been reached, expect prescriber to stop drug.
- Warn patient not to give drug to others. Auranofin, like injectable gold preparations, should be prescribed only for selected rheumatoid arthritis patients.

☑ Evaluation

- Patient expresses that arthritic pain has been relieved.
- Patient maintains fluid volume balance throughout therapy.
- Patient and family state understanding of drug therapy.

aurothioglucose

(or-oh-thigh-oh-GLOO-kohs)
Gold-50 ◇, Solganal

gold sodium thiomalate

(gohld SOH-dee-um thee-oh-MAH-layt)
Myochrysine

Pharmacologic class: gold salt
Therapeutic class: antiarthritic
Pregnancy risk category: C

Indications and dosages

▶ **Rheumatoid arthritis.** ***aurothioglucose.*** *Adults:* Initially, 10 mg I.M., followed by 25 mg for second and third doses at weekly intervals. Then, 50 mg weekly until 0.8 to 1 g has been given. If improvement occurs without toxicity, 50 mg is continued at 3- to 4-week intervals indefinitely as maintenance therapy. *Children ages 6 to 12:* One-fourth usual adult dosage, not to exceed 25 mg per dose.
gold sodium thiomalate. *Adults:* Initially, 10 mg I.M., followed by 25 mg in 1 week. Then 25 to 50 mg weekly until 14 to 20 doses have been given. If improvement occurs without toxicity, 25 to 50 mg is continued q 2 weeks for four doses; then 25 to 50 mg q 3 weeks for four doses; then 25 to 50 mg every month indefinitely as maintenance therapy. If relapse occurs during maintenance therapy, injections are resumed at weekly intervals.
Children: 1 mg/kg I.M. weekly for 20 weeks. The maximum single dose for children younger than age12 is 50 mg. If response is good, may be given q 3 to 4 weeks indefinitely.
▶ **Palindromic rheumatism‡.** ***gold sodium thiomalate.*** *Adults:* 10 to 50 mg I.M. weekly dose until a total of 1 g.
▶ **Pemphigus‡.** *Adults:* Initial dose of 10 mg I.M. for the first week, 25 mg I.M for the second week, then 50 mg I.M. weekly until corticosteroids are eliminated from the drug regimen. Maintenance dosage of 25 to 50 mg I.M. q 2 weeks.

Contraindications and precautions

- Contraindicated in patients hypersensitive to drug or with a history of severe toxicity from exposure to gold or other heavy metals, hepatitis, or exfoliative dermatitis; severe, uncontrollable diabetes; renal disease; hepatic dysfunction; uncontrolled heart failure; systemic lupus erythematosus; colitis; Sjögren's syndrome; urticaria; eczema; hemorrhagic conditions; severe hematologic disorders; or recent radiation therapy.

• Use with extreme caution, if at all, in patients with rash, marked hypertension, compromised cerebral or CV circulation, or history of renal or hepatic disease, drug allergies, or blood dyscrasia.

Lifespan: In pregnant women, use cautiously. In breast-feeding women, drug isn't recommended. In children younger than age 6, safety of drug hasn't been established.

Adverse reactions

CNS: *dizziness,* syncope, ***seizures.***
CV: ***bradycardia,*** hypotension.
EENT: corneal gold deposition, corneal ulcers.
GI: *stomatitis,* difficulty swallowing, nausea, vomiting, metallic taste.
GU: albuminuria, proteinuria, nephrotic syndrome, nephritis, ***acute tubular necrosis, acute renal failure.***
Hematologic: ***thrombocytopenia, aplastic anemia, agranulocytosis, leukopenia,*** eosinophilia.
Hepatic: ***hepatitis,*** jaundice.
Skin: diaphoresis, photosensitivity reaction, *rash, dermatitis.*
Other: ***anaphylaxis, angioedema.***

Interactions

None significant.

Effects on lab test results

• May increase BUN, creatinine, ALT, AST, and alkaline phosphatase levels.
• May increase eosinophil count. May decrease hemoglobin, hematocrit, and platelet, granulocyte, and WBC counts.

Pharmacokinetics

Absorption: Slow and erratic because drug is in oil suspension.
Distribution: Distributed widely throughout body in lymph nodes, bone marrow, kidneys, liver, spleen, and tissues. About 85% to 90% is protein-bound.
Metabolism: Not broken down into elemental form.
Excretion: About 70% in urine; 30% in feces. *Half-life:* 14 to 40 days.

Route	Onset	Peak	Duration
I.M.	Unknown	3-6 hr	Unknown

Pharmacodynamics

Chemical effect: Unknown. Anti-inflammatory effects in rheumatoid arthritis are probably caused by inhibition of sulfhydryl systems, which alters cellular metabolism. Gold salts also may alter enzyme function and immune response and suppress phagocytic activity.
Therapeutic effect: Relieves signs and symptoms of rheumatoid arthritis.

Available forms

Injection: 50 mg/ml with benzyl alcohol (gold sodium thiomalate)
Injection (suspension): 50 mg/ml in sesame oil with aluminum monostearate 2% and propylparaben 0.1% in 10-ml container (aurothioglucose)

NURSING PROCESS

Assessment

• Obtain history of patient's rheumatoid arthritis before therapy and reassess regularly.
• Be alert for adverse reactions.
• Analyze urine for protein and sediment changes before each injection.
• Monitor CBC, including platelet count, before every second injection.
• Evaluate patient's and family's knowledge of drug therapy.

Nursing diagnoses

• Acute joint pain related to presence of rheumatoid arthritis
• Risk for injury related to drug-induced adverse reactions
• Deficient knowledge related to drug therapy

Planning and implementation

• Give only under constant supervision of prescriber who is thoroughly familiar with drug's toxicities and benefits.

ALERT: Rash and dermatitis occur in 20% of patients and may lead to fatal exfoliative dermatitis if drug isn't stopped.

• Gold compounds are typically used only in active rheumatoid arthritis that hasn't respond-

ed adequately to salicylates, rest, and physical therapy. Some clinicians advocate earlier use before disease progresses.
- Give all gold salts I.M., preferably intragluteally. Drug is pale yellow; don't use if it darkens.
- Immerse vial of aurothioglucose suspension in warm water, and shake vigorously before injecting.
- When giving gold sodium thiomalate, have patient lie down and remain recumbent for 10 to 20 minutes after injection to minimize hypotension.
- Observe patient for 30 minutes after administration because of possible anaphylactoid reaction.
- If adverse reactions develop and are mild, some rheumatologists resume gold therapy after 2 to 3 weeks' rest.
- Monitor platelet count if patient develops purpura or ecchymoses.
- Keep dimercaprol on hand to treat acute toxicity.

Patient teaching
- Inform patient that benefits of therapy may not appear for 3 to 4 months or longer.
- Advise patient that increased joint pain may occur for 1 to 2 days after injection but usually subsides after a few injections.
- Advise patient to report rashes or skin problems immediately. Pruritus often precedes dermatitis; pruritic skin eruptions that develop while patient is receiving gold salt therapy should be considered a reaction to therapy until proven otherwise. Advise patient to stop therapy until reaction subsides and to notify prescriber.
- Advise patient that stomatitis is often preceded by metallic taste, which should be reported to prescriber immediately. Promote careful oral hygiene during therapy.
- Tell patient to avoid sunlight and artificial ultraviolet light to minimize risk of photosensitivity.
- Stress need for medical follow-up and frequent blood and urine tests during therapy.

☑ Evaluation
- Patient's joint stiffness and pain are relieved.
- Patient doesn't experience injury as a result of drug-induced adverse reactions.
- Patient and family state understanding of drug therapy.

azathioprine
(ay-zuh-THIGH-oh-preen)
Imuran, Thioprine ◇

Pharmacologic class: purine antagonist
Therapeutic class: immunosuppressant
Pregnancy risk category: D

Indications and dosages

▶ **Immunosuppression in kidney transplantation.** *Adults and children:* Initially, 3 to 5 mg/kg P.O. or I.V. daily, usually beginning on day of transplantation. Maintained at 1 to 3 mg/kg daily (dosage varies considerably according to patient response).

▶ **Severe, refractory rheumatoid arthritis.** *Adults:* Initially, 1 mg/kg (about 50 mg to 100 mg) P.O. daily as single dose or as two doses. If patient response isn't satisfactory after 6 to 8 weeks, dosage may be increased by 0.5 mg/kg daily (up to maximum of 2.5 mg/kg daily) at 4-week intervals.

Contraindications and precautions
- Contraindicated in patients hypersensitive to drug.
- Use cautiously in patients with hepatic or renal dysfunction.

Lifespan: In pregnant women, don't use drug to treat rheumatoid arthritis. In breast-feeding women, drug isn't recommended.

Adverse reactions
EENT: esophagitis.
GI: nausea, vomiting, anorexia, ***pancreatitis,*** steatorrhea, mouth ulceration.
Hematologic: LEUKOPENIA, ***bone marrow suppression,*** anemia, ***pancytopenia,*** THROMBOCYTOPENIA.
Hepatic: ***hepatotoxicity,*** jaundice.
Musculoskeletal: arthralgia, muscle wasting.
Skin: rash, alopecia, pruritus.
Other: ***immunosuppression,*** infections, ***neoplasia.***

Interactions
Drug-drug. *ACE inhibitors:* May cause severe leukopenia. Monitor patient closely.

*Liquid form contains alcohol. **May contain tartrazine. ♦ Canada ◇ Australia †OTC ‡Off-label use

Allopurinol: May impair inactivation of azathioprine. Decrease azathioprine dose to one-fourth or one-third normal dose.
Cyclosporine: May decrease cyclosporine level. Monitor level.
Methotrexate: May increase 6-MP metabolite level. Monitor patient for increased adverse effects.
Nondepolarizing neuromuscular blockers: May decrease or reverse effects of these agents. Monitor patient for clinical effects.
Vaccines: May decrease immune response. Postpone routine immunization.
Warfarin: May inhibit anticoagulant effect of warfarin. Monitor PT and INR.

Effects on lab test results

- May increase AST, ALT, alkaline phosphatase, and bilirubin levels. May decrease uric acid levels.
- May decrease hemoglobin, hematocrit, and WBC, RBC, and platelet counts.

Pharmacokinetics

Absorption: Well absorbed from the GI tract.
Distribution: Distributed throughout body; I.V. and P.O. forms are 30% protein-bound.
Metabolism: Primarily metabolized to mercaptopurine.
Excretion: Small amounts of azathioprine and mercaptopurine are excreted intact in urine; most of given dose is excreted in urine as secondary metabolites. *Half-life:* About 5 hours.

Route	Onset	Peak	Duration
P.O., I.V.	4-8 wk	1-2 hr	Unknown

Pharmacodynamics

Chemical effect: Unknown.
Therapeutic effect: Suppresses immune system activity.

Available forms

Injection: 100 mg
Tablets: 50 mg

NURSING PROCESS

Assessment

- Obtain history of patient's immune status before therapy.
- Monitor effectiveness by observing patient for signs of organ rejection. Therapeutic response usually occurs within 8 weeks.
- Be alert for adverse reactions and drug interactions.
- Monitor hemoglobin, hematocrit, and WBC and platelet counts at least once monthly—more often at beginning of treatment.
- Evaluate patient's and family's knowledge of drug therapy.

Nursing diagnoses

- Ineffective protection related to threat of organ rejection
- Risk for infection related to drug-induced immunosuppression
- Deficient knowledge related to drug therapy

Planning and implementation

- **P.O. use:** Give in divided doses or after meals to minimize adverse GI effects.
- **I.V. use:** Reconstitute 100-mg vial with 10 ml of sterile water for injection. Visually inspect for particles before giving. Drug may be given by direct I.V. injection or further diluted in normal saline solution or D_5W and infused over 30 to 60 minutes. Use only for patient who can't tolerate P.O. medications.
- Benefits must be weighed against risks with systemic viral infections, such as chickenpox and herpes zoster.
- Patients with rheumatoid arthritis previously treated with alkylating drugs, such as cyclophosphamide, chlorambucil, and melphalan, may have prohibitive risk of neoplasia if treated with azathioprine.
- To prevent irreversible bone marrow suppression, drug should be stopped immediately when WBC count is less than 3,000/mm³. Notify prescriber.
- To prevent bleeding, avoid I.M. injections when platelet count is below 100,000/mm³.

ALERT: Don't confuse azathioprine with azidothymidine, Azulfidine, or azatadine. Don't confuse Imuran with Inderal.

Patient teaching

- Warn patient to report even mild infections (colds, fever, sore throat, and malaise) because drug is a potent immunosuppressant.
- Instruct woman to avoid conception during therapy and for 4 months after stopping therapy.
- Warn patient that thinning of hair is possible.

• Tell patient taking this drug for refractory rheumatoid arthritis that it may take up to 12 weeks to be effective.

Evaluation
• Patient exhibits no signs of organ rejection.
• Patient demonstrates no signs and symptoms of infection.
• Patient and family state understanding of drug therapy.

azelastine hydrochloride
(ah-zuh-LAST-een high-droh-KLOR-ighd)
Astelin, Optivar

Pharmacologic class: H_1-receptor agonist
Therapeutic class: antihistamine
Pregnancy risk category: C

Indications and dosages

▶ **Treatment of the symptoms of seasonal allergic rhinitis, such as rhinorrhea, sneezing, and nasal pruritus.** *Adults and children age 12 and older:* 2 sprays (274 mcg/2 sprays) per nostril b.i.d.
Children ages 5 to 11 years: 1 spray (137 mcg/spray) per nostril b.i.d.
▶ **Treatment of the symptoms of vasomotor rhinitis, such as rhinorrhea, nasal congestion and postnasal drip.** *Adults and children age 12 and older:* 2 sprays (274 mcg/2 sprays) per nostril b.i.d.
▶ **Treatment of itching of eye related to allergic conjunctivitis.** *Adults and children older than age 3:* Give 1 drop into affected eye b.i.d.

Contraindications and precautions

• Contraindicated in patients hypersensitive to drug.
Lifespan: In pregnant women, drug should be used only if benefit justifies risk to fetus. Breast-feeding women shouldn't take drug. In children younger than age 5, safety and effectiveness haven't been established for treatment of seasonal allergic rhinitis. In children younger than age 12, don't use drug for vasomotor rhinitis.

Adverse reactions

CNS: fatigue, *headache, somnolence,* dizziness.
EENT: transient eye burning, stinging, nasal burning, conjunctivitis, eye pain, pharyngitis, rhinitis, paroxysmal sneezing, temporary blurring of vision, epistaxis, sinusitis.
GI: *bitter taste,* dry mouth, nausea.
Metabolic: weight gain.
Musculoskeletal: myalgia.
Respiratory: asthma, dyspnea.
Skin: pruritus.
Other: flulike symptoms, dysesthesia.

Interactions

Drug-drug. *Cimetidine:* May increase plasma levels of azelastine. Avoid using together.
CNS depressants: May reduce alertness and impair CNS performance. Avoid using together.
Drug lifestyle. *Alcohol use:* May reduce alertness and cause impairment of CNS if using the nasal spray. Discourage using together.

Effects on lab test results

None reported.

Pharmacokinetics

Absorption: Not absorbed.
Distribution: Systemic bioavailability is 40%.
Metabolism: After dosing to a steady state, level ranges from 20% to 50%.
Excretion: Based on I.V. and oral administration, drug was shown to be excreted in feces. *Half-life:* 22 hours.

Route	Onset	Peak	Duration
Nasal	Unknown	2-3 hr	12 hr
Eye drops	3 min	Unknown	8 hr

Pharmacodynamics

Chemical effect: Exhibits histamine H_1-receptor agonist activity.
Therapeutic effect: Relieves seasonal allergic rhinitis.

Available forms

Nasal solution: 1 mg/ml (137 mcg/spray)
Ophthalmic solution: 0.05%

NURSING PROCESS

Assessment
• Obtain history of patient's allergy condition before therapy begins and reassess regularly thereafter.

• Be alert for adverse reactions and drug interactions.
• Evaluate patient's and family's knowledge of drug therapy.

Nursing diagnoses

• Ineffective health maintenance related to underlying allergic condition
• Deficient knowledge related to drug therapy

Planning and implementation

• Don't contaminate eye dropper tip or solution.
• Make sure patient removes contact lenses before giving eyedrops. Tell patient to wait at least 10 minutes before reinserting them.
• When using nasal spray, avoid spraying into patient's eyes.

Patient teaching

• Warn patient not to drive or perform hazardous activities if somnolence occurs.
• Advise patient not to use alcohol, CNS depressants, or other antihistamines while taking drug.
• Teach patient proper use of nasal spray. Instruct patient to replace child-resistant screw top on bottle with pump unit. Prime delivery system with four sprays or until a fine mist appears. If 3 or more days have elapsed since last use, reprime system with two sprays or until a fine mist appears. Store bottle upright at room temperature with pump closed tightly. Keep unit away from children.
• Tell patient to avoid getting spray in eyes.

Evaluation

• Patient's allergic symptoms are relieved with drug therapy.
• Patient and family state understanding of drug therapy.

azithromycin

(uh-zith-roh-MIGH-sin)
Zithromax

Pharmacologic class: azalide macrolide
Therapeutic class: antibiotic
Pregnancy risk category: B

Indications and dosages

▶ **Acute bacterial exacerbations of chronic obstructive pulmonary disease caused by *Haemophilus influenzae, Moraxella (Branhamella) catarrhalis,* or *Streptococcus pneumoniae;* uncomplicated skin and skin-structure infections caused by *Staphylococcus aureus, Streptococcus pyogenes,* or *Streptococcus agalactiae;* and second-line therapy for pharyngitis or tonsillitis caused by *S. pyogenes.*** *Adults and adolescents age 16 and older:* Initially, 500 mg P.O. as a single dose on day 1, followed by 250 mg daily on days 2 through 5. Total cumulative dose is 1.5 g. Alternatively, for COPD exacerbations, 500 mg P.O. daily for 3 days.

▶ **Community-acquired pneumonia caused by *Chlamydia pneumoniae, H. influenzae, Mycoplasma pneumoniae, S. pneumoniae;* I.V. form is also used for *Legionella pneumophila, M. catarrhalis,* and *S. aureus.*** *Adults and adolescents age 16 and older:* 500 mg P.O. as a single dose on day 1, followed by 250 mg P.O. daily on days 2 through 5. Total dose is 1.5 g. For patients requiring initial I.V. therapy, 500 mg I.V. as a single daily dose for 2 days, followed by 500 mg P.O. as a single daily dose to complete a 7- to 10-day course of therapy. Switch from I.V. to P.O. therapy should be done at prescriber's discretion and based on patient's clinical response.

▶ **Nongonococcal urethritis or cervicitis caused by *Chlamydia trachomatis.*** *Adults and adolescents age 16 and older:* 1 g P.O. as a single dose.

▶ **Prevention of disseminated *Mycobacterium avium* complex disease in patients with advanced HIV infection.** *Adults:* 1,200 mg P.O. once weekly, as indicated.
Children‡: 20 mg/kg P.O. (maximum dose of 1.2 g) weekly or 5 mg/kg (maximum dose of 250 mg) can be given P.O. daily.

▶ **Urethritis and cervicitis caused by *Neisseria gonorrhoeae.*** *Adults:* 2 g P.O. as a single dose.

▶ **Pelvic inflammatory disease caused by *C. trachomatis, N. gonorrhoeae,* or *Mycoplasma hominis* in patients who require initial I.V. therapy.** *Adults:* 500 mg I.V. as a single daily dose for 1 to 2 days, followed by 250 mg P.O. daily to complete a 7-day course of therapy. Switch from I.V. to P.O. therapy should be done at prescriber's discretion and based on patient's clinical response.

▶ **Prophylaxis for sexual assault victims‡.** *Adults:* 1 g P.O. as a single dose with metronidazole and ceftriaxone.

▶ **Genital ulcer disease caused by *Haemophilus ducreyi* (chancroid) in men.** *Adults:* 1 g P.O. as a single dose.

▶ **Acute otitis media.** *Children older than age 6 months:* 30 mg/kg P.O. as a single dose. Or, 10 mg/kg P.O. once daily for 3 days. Or 10 mg/kg P.O. on day 1; then 5 mg/kg once daily on days 2 to 5.

▶ **Pharyngitis, tonsillitis.** *Children older than age 2:* 12 mg/kg (maximum, 500 mg) P.O. daily for 5 days.

▶ **Chancroid‡.** *Adults:* 1 g P.O. as a single dose.
Children and infants: 20 mg/kg (maximum, 1 g) as a single dose.

▶ **Prophylaxis of bacterial endocarditis in penicillin-allergic adults at moderate-to-high risk‡.** *Adults:* 500 mg I.V. 1 hour before injection.

▶ **Chlamydial ophthalmia neonatorum‡.** *Infants:* 20 mg/kg once daily P.O. for 3 days.

Contraindications and precautions

- Contraindicated in patients hypersensitive to erythromycin or other macrolides.
- Use cautiously in patients with impaired hepatic function.

Lifespan: In pregnant or breast-feeding women, use cautiously.

Adverse reactions

CNS: dizziness, vertigo, headache, fatigue, somnolence.
CV: palpitations, chest pain.
GI: *nausea, vomiting, diarrhea, abdominal pain,* dyspepsia, flatulence, melena, cholestatic jaundice, ***pseudomembranous colitis.***
GU: candidiasis, vaginitis, nephritis.
Skin: rash, photosensitivity.
Other: ***angioedema.***

Interactions

Drug-drug. *Antacids containing aluminum and magnesium:* May lower peak azithromycin level. Separate administration times by at least 2 hours.
Digoxin: May elevate digoxin level. Monitor patient closely.
Dihydroergotamine, ergotamine: May cause acute ergot toxicity. Avoid using together.
Drugs metabolized by cytochrome P-450 system: May elevate carbamazepine, cyclosporine, hexobarbital, and phenytoin levels. Monitor patient closely.
Theophylline: May increase theophylline level with other macrolides; effect of azithromycin is unknown. Monitor theophylline levels carefully.
Triazolam: May increase pharmacologic effect of triazolam. Use cautiously.
Warfarin: May increase PT with other macrolides; effect of azithromycin is unknown. Monitor PT and INR carefully.
Drug-food. *Any food:* May decrease absorption. Give at least 1 hour before or 2 hours after a meal.
Drug-lifestyle. *Sun exposure:* May cause photosensitivity reactions. Advise against prolonged or unprotected sun exposure.

Effects on lab test results

None reported.

Pharmacokinetics

Absorption: Rapidly absorbed from GI tract; food decreases both maximum level and amount of drug absorbed.
Distribution: Distributed rapidly throughout body and readily penetrates cells; it doesn't readily enter CNS. Drug concentrates in fibroblasts and phagocytes. Significantly higher levels are reached in tissues compared with plasma.
Metabolism: None.
Excretion: Excreted mostly in feces after excretion into bile. Less than 10% in urine. *Terminal elimination half-life:* 68 hours.

Route	Onset	Peak	Duration
P.O.	Unknown	2.5-4.4 hr	Unknown
I.V.	Unknown	Unknown	Unknown

Pharmacodynamics

Chemical effect: Binds to 50S subunit of bacterial ribosomes, blocking protein synthesis; bacteriostatic or bactericidal, depending on concentration.
Therapeutic effect: Hinders or kills susceptible bacteria, including many gram-positive and gram-negative aerobic and anaerobic bacteria, such as *Haemophilus influenzae, Moraxella ca-*

tarrhalis, Staphylococcus aureus, Streptococcus agalactiae, Streptococcus pneumoniae, Streptococcus pyogenes, and *Chlamydia trachomatis.*

Available forms

Injection: 500 mg
Powder for oral suspension: 100 mg/5 ml, 200 mg/5 ml; 1,000 mg/packet
Tablets: 250 mg, 500 mg, 600 mg

NURSING PROCESS

Assessment

- Obtain history of patient's infection before therapy and reassess regularly thereafter.
- Obtain specimen for culture and sensitivity tests before first dose. Therapy may begin pending test results.
- Be alert for adverse reactions and drug interactions.
- Evaluate patient's and family's knowledge of drug therapy.

Nursing diagnoses

- Infection related to presence of susceptible bacteria
- Ineffective protection related to drug-induced superinfection
- Deficient knowledge related to drug therapy

Planning and implementation

- **P.O. use:** Give 1 hour before or 2 hours after meals; don't administer with antacids.
- **I.V. use:** Reconstitute drug by adding 4.8 ml sterile water for injection to 500-mg vial and shake until all the drug is dissolved. Further dilute in 250 to 500 ml D_5W, normal saline solution, or other compatible solution. Infuse over 1 to 3 hours. Reconstituted solution is stable for 7 days if stored in refrigerator (41° F [5° C]).

Patient teaching

- Tell patient that drug should always be taken on an empty stomach because food or antacids decrease absorption.
- Tell patient to take all medication as prescribed, even after he feels better.
- Instruct patient to use sunblock and avoid prolonged exposure to the sun to decrease risk of photosensitivity reactions.

Evaluation

- Patient's infection is eliminated.
- Patient doesn't experience superinfection during therapy.
- Patient and family state understanding of drug therapy.

aztreonam

(az-TREE-oh-nam)
Azactam

Pharmacologic class: monobactam
Therapeutic class: antibiotic
Pregnancy risk category: B

Indications and dosages

▶ **UTI, lower respiratory tract infections, septicemia, skin and skin-structure infections, intra-abdominal infections, surgical infections, gynecologic infections caused by various aerobic organisms; or as adjunct therapy to pelvic inflammatory disease‡ or gonorrhea‡.** *Adults:* 500 mg to 2 g I.V. or I.M. q 8 to 12 hours. For severe systemic or life-threatening infection, 2 g q 6 to 8 hours. Maximum dosage is 8 g daily.

Contraindications and precautions

- Contraindicated in patients hypersensitive to drug.
- Use cautiously in elderly patients and in those with impaired renal function. Dosage adjustment may be needed.

Lifespan: In breast-feeding women, drug isn't recommended. In children, safety of drug hasn't been established.

Adverse reactions

CNS: *seizures,* headache, insomnia, confusion.
CV: hypotension.
EENT: halitosis, altered taste.
GI: diarrhea, nausea, vomiting.
Hematologic: ***neutropenia,*** anemia, ***thrombocytopenia, pancytopenia.***
Other: hypersensitivity reactions (rash, ***anaphylaxis***); rash, thrombophlebitis at I.V. site; discomfort, swelling at I.M. injection site.

Interactions

Drug-drug. *Aminoglycosides, beta-lactam antibiotics, other anti-infectives:* May have synergistic effect. Monitor patient closely.
Cefoxitin, imipenem: May have antagonistic effect. Avoid using together.
Furosemide, probenecid: May increase aztreonam levels. Avoid using together.

Effects on lab test results

- May increase BUN, creatinine, ALT, AST, and LDH levels.
- May increase PT, PTT, and INR. May decrease neutrophil and RBC counts, hemoglobin, and hematocrit. May increase or decrease WBC and platelet counts.

Pharmacokinetics

Absorption: Rapid and complete.
Distribution: Distributed rapidly and widely to all body fluids and tissues, including bile, breast milk, and CSF.
Metabolism: From 6% to 16% metabolized to inactive metabolites by nonspecific hydrolysis of beta-lactam ring; 56% to 60% protein-bound, less if renal impairment is present.
Excretion: Excreted primarily unchanged in urine by glomerular filtration and tubular secretion; 1.5% to 3.5% excreted unchanged in feces. *Half-life:* average 1.7 hours.

Route	Onset	Peak	Duration
I.V.	Immediate	Immediate	Unknown
I.M.	Unknown	0.6-1.3 hr	Unknown

Pharmacodynamics

Chemical effect: Inhibits bacterial cell-wall synthesis, ultimately causing cell-wall destruction; bactericidal.
Therapeutic effect: Kills susceptible bacteria, including *Enterobacter, Escherichia coli, Klebsiella pneumoniae, Proteus mirabilis,* and *Pseudomonas aeruginosa.* Limited activity against *Citrobacter, Haemophilus influenzae, Hafnia, Klebsiella oxytoca, Moraxella catarrhalis, Neisseria gonorrhoeae, Providencia,* and *Serratia margaris.*

Available forms

Injection: 500-mg, 1-g, 2-g vials

NURSING PROCESS

Assessment

- Obtain history of patient's infection before therapy, and reassess regularly thereafter.
- Obtain urine specimen for culture and sensitivity tests before giving first dose. Therapy may begin pending test results.
- Be aware of adverse reactions and drug interactions.
- Patients who are allergic to penicillins or cephalosporins may not be allergic to aztreonam. However, closely monitor patients who have had an immediate hypersensitivity reaction to these antibiotics.
- Evaluate patient's and family's understanding of drug therapy.

Nursing diagnoses

- Infection related to presence of susceptible bacteria
- Ineffective protection related to drug-induced superinfection
- Deficient knowledge related to drug therapy

Planning and implementation

- **I.V. use:** To give bolus dose, inject drug slowly (over 3 to 5 minutes) directly into vein or I.V. tubing. Give infusion over 20 minutes to 1 hour.
- **I.M. use:** Give I.M. injection deep into large muscle mass, such as upper, outer quadrant of gluteus maximus or lateral aspect of thigh. Give doses larger than 1 g by I.V. route.

Patient teaching

- Tell patient to report pain or discomfort at I.V. site.
- Warn patient receiving drug I.M. that pain and swelling may develop at injection site.
- Instruct patient to report signs or symptoms that suggest superinfection.

Evaluation

- Patient is free of infection.
- Patient doesn't develop superinfection as a result of therapy.
- Patient and family state understanding of drug therapy.

B

bacillus Calmette-Guérin (BCG), live intravesical

(bah-SIL-us kal-MET geh-RAN, in-trah-VES-ih-kal)

ImmuCyst♦, TheraCys, TICE BCG

Pharmacologic class: bacterial agent, biological response modifier
Therapeutic class: antineoplastic, antituberculotic
Pregnancy risk category: C

Indications and dosages

▶ **In situ carcinoma of urinary bladder (primary and relapsed).** *Adults:* Consult published protocols, specialized references, and manufacturer's recommendations.

▶ **Tuberculosis prevention (TICE BCG only).** *Adults and children older than age 1 month:* 0.2 to 0.3 ml injected percutaneously using a multiple-puncture device.
Neonates younger than age 1 month: Decrease dose by 50% by reconstituting the vaccine with 2 ml instead of 1 ml sterile water for injection without preservatives.

Contraindications and precautions

- Contraindicated in immunocompromised patients, in those receiving immunosuppressive therapy (because of risk of bacterial infection), in those with urinary tract infection (because of risk of increased bladder irritation or disseminated BCG infection), and in those with fever of unknown origin. If fever is caused by an infection, withhold drug until patient has recovered.

Lifespan: Pregnant or breast-feeding women should use with caution. In children, safety of drug hasn't been established.

Adverse reactions

CNS: fever above 101° F (38.3° C), *malaise,* headache, dizziness, fatigue.
GI: *nausea, vomiting,* anorexia, diarrhea, mild abdominal pain, constipation.
GU: *dysuria, urinary frequency, hematuria, cystitis, urinary urgency,* urinary incontinence, *urinary tract infection,* cramps, pain, decreased bladder capacity, tissue in urine, local infection, ***nephrotoxicity,*** *genital pain.*
Hematologic: *anemia,* ***leukopenia, thrombocytopenia, DIC.***
Metabolic: ***renal toxicity.***
Musculoskeletal: myalgia, arthralgia.
Skin: ulceration, scarring, and lymphangitis at injection site; rash.
Other: hypersensitivity reaction, *chills,* flulike symptoms, systemic infection, ***disseminated sepsis.***

Interactions

Drug-drug. *Antibiotics:* May attenuate response to BCG intravesical. Avoid use together.
Bone marrow suppressants, immunosuppressants, radiation therapy: May impair response to BCG intravesical by decreasing immune response; also may increase risk of osteomyelitis or disseminated BCG infection. Avoid use together.

Effects on lab test results

- May increase liver enzyme levels.
- May decrease hemoglobin, hematocrit, and WBC and platelet counts.

Pharmacokinetics

Absorption: Unknown.
Distribution: Unknown.
Metabolism: Unknown.
Excretion: Unknown.

Route	Onset	Peak	Duration
Intravesical, percutaneous	Unknown	Unknown	Unknown

Pharmacodynamics

Chemical effect: *Antineoplastic action:* Instillation of live bacterial suspension causes local inflammatory response. Local infiltration of histiocytes and leukocytes is followed by decrease in superficial tumors in bladder. *Antituberculotic action: Mycobacterium bovis* present in the vaccine is immunologically similar to *M. tuberculosis.* Vaccination stimulates natural infection with *M. tuberculosis* and promotes cell-mediated immunity.

Therapeutic effect: *Antineoplastic action:* Decreases risk of superficial bladder tumors. *Antituberculotic action:* Immunizes against *M. tuberculosis.*

Available forms

Powder for suspension: 50-mg vial, 81-mg vial, 120-mg single-dose ampule

NURSING PROCESS

Assessment

- Obtain history of patient's bladder cancer.
- Monitor drug's effectiveness by regularly checking tumor size and growth rate through appropriate studies and by noting results of follow-up diagnostic tests and overall physical status.
- Be alert for adverse reactions and drug interactions.
- Closely monitor patient for evidence of systemic BCG infection. Such infections are seldom detected by positive cultures.
- Evaluate patient's and family's understanding of drug therapy.

Nursing diagnoses

- Risk for injury related to underlying condition
- Risk for trauma related to instillation procedure for drug therapy
- Deficient knowledge related to drug therapy

Planning and implementation

- Drug isn't used as an immunizing agent to prevent cancer or tuberculosis; drug shouldn't be confused with BCG vaccine.
- Drug shouldn't be handled or administered by caregiver with known immunologic deficiency.

ALERT: Don't give BCG intravesical within 7 to 14 days of transurethral resection or biopsy. Fatal disseminated BCG infection has occurred after traumatic catheterization.

- To give TheraCys or ImmuCyst, reconstitute with 1 ml of provided diluent per vial, just before use. Don't remove rubber stopper to prepare solution. Use immediately. Add contents of three reconstituted vials to 50 ml of sterile, preservative-free saline solution (final volume, 53 ml). Instill urethral catheter into bladder under aseptic conditions, drain bladder, and infuse 53 ml of prepared solution by gravity feed. Remove catheter and properly dispose of unused drug.
- To give TICE BCG, use thermosetting plastic or sterile glass containers and syringes. Draw 1 ml of sterile, preservative-free saline solution into 3-ml syringe. Add to 1 ampule of drug; gently expel back into ampule three times to mix thoroughly. Use immediately. Dispense cloudy suspension into top end of catheter-tipped syringe that contains 49 ml of saline solution. Gently rotate syringe. Don't shake to avoid producing foam. Give the vaccine using a multiple-puncture disc. Keep the puncture area dry for at least 24 hours after administration. Properly dispose of unused drug.
- Following percutaneous administration, the skin lesion usually appears at the site within 10 to 14 days. Quicker results occur if the patient has tuberculosis.
- Handle drug and all materials used for instillation of drug as biohazardous material because they contain live attenuated mycobacteria. Dispose of all materials (syringes, catheters, and containers) as biohazardous waste.
- Use strict aseptic technique when giving drug to minimize trauma to GU tract and to prevent introduction of other contaminants.
- If patient has evidence of traumatic catheterization, don't give drug, and alert prescriber. Treatment may resume after 1 week.
- Therapy should be withheld if systemic infection is suspected (short-term fever above 103° F [39.4° C], persistent fever above 101° F [38.3° C] over 2 days, or severe malaise). Prescriber may contact an infectious disease specialist for starting fast-acting antituberculosis therapy.
- Be prepared to treat symptoms of bladder irritation with phenazopyridine, acetaminophen, and propantheline. Systemic hypersensitivity can be treated with diphenhydramine. To minimize risk of systemic infection, give isoniazid for 3 days starting on first day of treatment.

Patient teaching

- Tell patient to retain drug in bladder for 2 hours after instillation (if possible). For the first hour, have patient lie prone for 15 minutes, supine for 15 minutes, and on each side for 15 minutes; the second hour may be spent in sitting position.

- Instruct patient to sit when voiding to avoid splashing of urine.
- Instruct patient to disinfect urine for 6 hours after instillation of drug. Tell him to add undiluted household bleach (5% sodium hypochlorite solution) in equal volume to voided urine in toilet and let stand for 15 minutes before flushing.
- Tell patient to call prescriber if symptoms worsen or if the following symptoms develop: blood in urine, frequent urge to urinate, painful urination, fever and chills, nausea, vomiting, joint pain, or rash.
- Tell patient to notify prescriber immediately if cough develops after therapy because it may indicate life-threatening BCG infection.

☑ Evaluation

- Patient exhibits no further evidence of superficial bladder tumors.
- Patient doesn't experience trauma as result of drug use.
- Patient and family state understanding of drug therapy.

baclofen

(BAH-kloh-fen)

Clofen ◇, Lioresal, Lioresal Intrathecal

Pharmacologic class: chlorophenyl derivative [GABA derivative]
Therapeutic class: skeletal muscle relaxant
Pregnancy risk category: C

Indications and dosages

▶ **Spasticity in multiple sclerosis, spinal cord injury.** *Adults:* Initially, 5 mg P.O. t.i.d. for 3 days. Dosage may be increased based on response at 3-day intervals by 15 mg (5 mg/dose) daily up to maximum of 80 mg daily (20 mg q.i.d.).

▶ **Management of severe spasticity in patients who don't respond to or cannot tolerate oral baclofen therapy.** *Adults (screening phase):* After test dose, give drug by an implantable infusion pump. The test dose is 50 mcg in 1 ml dilution administered into intrathecal space by barbotage over 1 minute or more. Significantly decreased severity or frequency of muscle spasm or reduced muscle tone should be evident in 4 to 8 hours. If response is inadequate, give second test dose of 75 mcg/1.5 ml 24 hours after the first. If response is still inadequate, give final test dose of 100 mcg/2 ml 24 hours later. Patients unresponsive to 100-mcg dose shouldn't be considered candidates for implantable pump. *Children younger than age 12:* Testing dose is the same as for adults (50 mcg); but for very small children, an initial dose of 25 mcg may be given.
Adults (maintenance therapy): Initial dose adjusted based on screening dose that elicited an adequate response. This effective dose is doubled and given over 24 hours. If screening-dose efficacy is maintained for 8 hours or more, dosage isn't doubled. After first 24 hours, increase dose slowly, as needed and tolerated, by 10% to 30% daily until desired clinical effects are obtained.

Contraindications and precautions

- Contraindicated in patients hypersensitive to drug.
- Use cautiously in patients with impaired renal function or seizure disorder or when spasticity is used to maintain motor function.

Lifespan: In pregnant or breast-feeding women, use cautiously. In children younger than age 12, safety of oral use of drug hasn't been established. In children younger than age 4, safety of intrathecal drug hasn't been established.

Adverse reactions

CNS: drowsiness, dizziness, headache, weakness, fatigue, *hypotonia,* confusion, insomnia, dysarthria, ***paresthesias,*** SEIZURES.
CV: ankle edema, hypotension.
EENT: nasal congestion, blurred vision.
GI: nausea, constipation, vomiting.
GU: urinary frequency, urinary incontinence.
Metabolic: hyperglycemia, weight gain.
Musculoskeletal: ***muscle rigidity or spasticity, rhabdomyolysis.***
Respiratory: dyspnea.
Skin: rash, pruritus, excessive perspiration.
Other: sexual dysfunction, impotence, ***high fever, multiple organ-system failure.***

Interactions

Drug-drug. *CNS depressants:* Increases CNS depression. Avoid use together.
MAO inhibitors, tricyclic antidepressants: CNS and respiratory depression, hypotension may occur. Avoid use together.
Drug-lifestyle. *Alcohol use:* Increases CNS depression. Discourage use together.

Effects on lab test results

- May increase AST, alkaline phosphatase, and glucose levels.

Pharmacokinetics

Absorption: Rapid and extensive with P.O. administration; may vary.
Distribution: Widely distributed throughout body, with small amounts crossing blood-brain barrier. It's about 30% plasma protein–bound.
Metabolism: About 15% metabolized in liver via deamination.
Excretion: 70% to 80% excreted in urine unchanged or as metabolites; remainder excreted in feces. Half-life: 2½ to 4 hours.

Route	Onset	Peak	Duration
P.O.	Hr-wk	2-3 hr	Unknown
Intrathecal	0.5-1 hr	4 hr	4-8 hr

Pharmacodynamics

Chemical effect: Unknown; appears to reduce transmission of impulses from spinal cord to skeletal muscle.
Therapeutic effect: Relieves muscle spasms.

Available forms

Intrathecal injection: 500 mcg/ml, 2,000 mcg/ml
Tablets: 10 mg, 20 mg, 25 mg

NURSING PROCESS

Assessment

- Obtain history of patient's pain and muscle spasms from underlying condition before therapy, and reassess regularly thereafter.
- Be alert for adverse reactions and drug interactions.
- Watch for increased risk of seizures in patient with seizure disorder. Seizures have been reported during overdose and withdrawal of intrathecal baclofen as well as in patients maintained on therapeutic doses of intrathecal baclofen. Monitor patients carefully and institute seizure precautions.
- Evaluate patient's and family's understanding of drug therapy.

Nursing diagnoses

- Acute pain related to spasticity
- Risk for injury related to drug-induced adverse CNS reactions
- Deficient knowledge related to drug therapy

Planning and implementation

- **P.O. use:** Give with meals or milk to prevent GI distress.

– Drug shouldn't be given orally to treat muscle spasm caused by rheumatic disorders, cerebral palsy, Parkinson's disease, or CVA because efficacy hasn't been established.
– Treatment for oral overdose is supportive; emesis shouldn't be induced and respiratory stimulant shouldn't be used in obtunded patient.

- **Intrathecal use:** Implantable pump or catheter failure can result in sudden loss of effectiveness of intrathecal baclofen.

ALERT: Don't administer intrathecal injection by I.V., I.M., S.C., or epidural route.

- The amount of relief determines whether dose (and drowsiness) can be reduced.
- Avoid abrupt discontinuation of intrathecal baclofen. Early symptoms of baclofen withdrawal may include return of baseline spasticity, pruritus, hypotension, and paresthesias. Symptoms that have occurred include high fever, altered mental status, exaggerated rebound spasticity, and muscle rigidity that in rare cases has advanced to rhabdomyolysis, multiple organ-system failure, and death. The treatment of intrathecal baclofen withdrawal is the restoration of intrathecal baclofen at or near the same dosage as before therapy was interrupted. However, if restoration of intrathecal baclofen is delayed, treatment with GABAergic agonist or I.V. benzodiazepines may prevent potentially fatal sequelae. P.O. or enteral baclofen alone shouldn't be relied upon to halt the progression of intrathecal baclofen withdrawal.
- About 10% of patients may develop tolerance to drug. In some cases, this may be treated by hospitalizing patient and by slowly withdrawing drug over 2-week period.

Patient teaching
- Tell patient to avoid activities that require alertness until drug's CNS effects are known. Drowsiness usually is transient.
- Tell patient to avoid alcohol while taking drug.
- Advise patient to follow prescriber's orders about rest and physical therapy.
- Advise patient to take drug with food or milk to prevent GI distress.

Evaluation
- Patient reports that pain and muscle spasms have ceased with drug therapy.
- Patient doesn't experience injury as a result of drug-induced drowsiness.
- Patient and family state understanding of drug therapy.

balsalazide disodium
(bal-SAL-a-zide digh-SOH-dee-um)
Colazal

Pharmacologic classification: gastrointestinal agent
Therapeutic classification: anti-inflammatory
Pregnancy risk category: B

Indications and dosages
▶ **Ulcerative colitis.** *Adults:* 2.25 g P.O. (three 750-mg capsules) t.i.d for a total of 6.75 g daily for 8 weeks.

Contraindications and precautions
- Contraindicated in patients hypersensitive to salicylates or to any component of balsalazide metabolites.
- Use cautiously in patients with history of renal disease or renal dysfunction.
- Use judiciously in patients with pyloric stenosis because of prolonged retention of drug. Safety and effectiveness beyond 12 weeks haven't been established.

Lifespan: In breast-feeding women, use cautiously because it's unknown whether balsalazide appears in breast milk. In children, safety and effectiveness haven't been established.

Adverse reactions
CNS: fever, dizziness, fatigue, headache, insomnia.
EENT: pharyngitis, rhinitis, sinusitis.
GI: abdominal pain, anorexia, constipation, cramps, diarrhea, dyspepsia, flatulence, frequent stools, nausea, rectal bleeding, vomiting, dry mouth, ***hepatotoxicity.***
GU: urinary tract infection.
Musculoskeletal: arthralgia, back pain, myalgia.
Respiratory: cough, respiratory infection.
Other: flu-like symptoms.

Interactions
Drug-drug. *Oral antibiotics and anti-infectives:* May interfere with release of mesalamine in the colon. Monitor patient for worsening of symptoms.
Azathioprine and 6 mercaptopurine: Balsalazide may interfere with the metabolism of these drugs. Use with caution.

Effects on lab test results
- May increase AST, ALT, LDH, alkaline phosphatase, and bilirubin levels.

Pharmacokinetics
Absorption: Very low and variable in healthy patients. 60 times greater in patients with ulcerative colitis.
Distribution: 99% or more binding to plasma proteins.
Metabolism: Metabolized to mesalamine (5-aminosalicylic acid), the active component of the drug.
Excretion: Excreted by the kidneys. Less than 1% recovered in urine. *Half-life:* Unknown.

Route	Onset	Peak	Duration
P.O.	Unknown	Unknown	Unknown

Pharmacodynamics
Chemical effect: Balsalazide is converted in the colon to mesalamine, which is then converted to 5-aminosalicylic acid. The mechanism of action is unknown, but it appears to be local rather than systemic. In patients with chronic inflammatory bowel disease, the production of arachidonic acid metabolites is increased. Balsalazide likely blocks the production of arachidonic acid metabolites in the colon.

Therapeutic effect: Decreases inflammation in the colon.

Available forms

Capsules: 750 mg

NURSING PROCESS

Assessment

- Assess patient's underlying condition and note frequency of bowel movements before starting drug therapy.
- Hepatotoxicity, including elevated liver function test results, jaundice, cirrhosis, liver necrosis, and liver failure, has occurred with other products containing or metabolized to mesalamine. Although no signs of hepatotoxicity have been reported with balsalazide disodium, monitor patient closely for evidence of hepatic dysfunction.
- Evaluate patient's and family's knowledge of balsalazide disodium therapy and ulcerative colitis.

Nursing diagnoses

- Diarrhea related to underlying disease process
- Risk of imbalanced nutrition: less than body requirements related to frequent bowel movements due to ulcerative colitis
- Deficient knowledge related to balsalazide disodium therapy

Planning and implementation

- Give drug as prescribed.
- Notify prescriber if drug has been given for 8 to 12 weeks or longer.

Patient teaching

- Advise patient not to take drug if allergic to aspirin or salicylate derivatives.
- Advise patient to report adverse reactions promptly to the prescriber.

Evaluation

- Patient states that diarrhea has improved.
- Due to decreasing symptoms of ulcerative colitis, patient is able to tolerate and absorb a balanced diet.
- Patient and family state understanding of balsalazide disodium therapy.

basiliximab

(ba-sil-IK-si-mab)
Simulect

Pharmacologic class: recombinant chimeric human monoclonal antibody IgG_{1k}
Therapeutic class: immunosuppressant
Pregnancy risk category: B

Indications and dosages

▶ **Prevention of acute organ rejection in patients receiving renal transplant when used as part of immunosuppressive regimen including cyclosporine and corticosteroids.**
Adults and children weighing more than 35 kg (77 lb): 20 mg I.V. given within 2 hours before transplant surgery and 20 mg I.V. given 4 days after transplantation.
Children weighing less than 35 kg (77 lb): 10 mg I.V. given within 2 hours before transplant surgery and 10 mg I.V. given 4 days after transplantation.

Contraindications and precautions

- Contraindicated in patients hypersensitive to drug or its components.
- **Lifespan:** Breast-feeding women should discontinue nursing or the drug because of potential for adverse effects; it's unknown whether the drug appears in breast milk. In elderly patients, use cautiously.

Adverse reactions

CNS: *fever,* agitation, anxiety, asthenia, depression, *dizziness, headache,* hypoesthesia, *insomnia,* neuropathy, paresthesia, *tremor,* fatigue.
CV: angina pectoris, ***arrhythmias,*** atrial fibrillation, ***heart failure,*** chest pain, abnormal heart sounds, aggravated hypertension, *hypertension,* hypotension, tachycardia.
EENT: abnormal vision, cataract, conjunctivitis, *rhinitis,* sinusitis, *pharyngitis.*
GI: *abdominal pain, candidiasis, constipation, diarrhea, dyspepsia,* esophagitis, enlarged abdomen, flatulence, gastroenteritis, GI disorder, ***GI hemorrhage,*** gum hyperplasia, melena, *nausea,* ulcerative stomatitis, *vomiting.*
GU: abnormal renal function, albuminuria, bladder disorder, *dysuria,* frequent micturition, genital edema, hematuria, *increased nonpro-*

tein nitrogen, oliguria, renal tubular necrosis, ureteral disorder, *urinary tract infection,* urine retention, impotence.
Hematologic: ***anemia,*** hematoma, ***hemorrhage,*** *polycythemia,* purpura, ***thrombocytopenia,*** thrombosis.
Metabolic: ***acidosis,*** dehydration, diabetes mellitus, fluid overload, hypercalcemia, *hypercholesterolemia, hyperglycemia,* **HYPERKALEMIA,** hyperlipemia, *hyperuricemia, hypocalcemia, hypokalemia,* hypomagnesemia, *hypophosphatemia,* hypoproteinemia, *weight gain.*
Musculoskeletal: arthralgia, arthropathy, *back pain,* bone fracture, cramps, hernia, *leg pain,* myalgia.
Respiratory: abnormal chest sounds, bronchitis, ***bronchospasm,*** *cough, dyspnea,* pneumonia, pulmonary disorder, ***pulmonary edema,*** *upper respiratory tract infection.*
Skin: *acne,* cyst, herpes simplex, herpes zoster, hypertrichosis, pruritus, rash, skin disorder or ulceration.
Other: accidental trauma, *viral infection, leg or peripheral edema,* general edema, infection, ***sepsis,*** *surgical wound complications.*

Interactions

None significant.

Effects on lab test results

- May increase calcium, cholesterol, glucose, lipid, and uric acid levels. May decrease magnesium, phosphorus, and protein levels. May increase or decrease potassium level.
- May increase RBC count. May decrease hemoglobin, hematocrit, and platelet count.

Pharmacokinetics

Absorption: Administered I.V.
Distribution: Unknown.
Metabolism: Unknown.
Excretion: Unknown. *Half-life:* About 7.2 days in adults, 9.5 days in children, 9.1 days in adolescents.

Route	Onset	Peak	Duration
I.V.	Unknown	Immediate	Unknown

Pharmacodynamics

Chemical effect: Binds specifically to and blocks the interleukin (IL)-2 receptor alpha chain on the surface of activated T lymphocytes, inhibiting IL-2–mediated activation of lymphocytes, a critical pathway in the cellular immune response involved in allograft rejection.
Therapeutic effect: Prevents organ rejection.

Available forms

Injection: 20-mg vials

NURSING PROCESS

Assessment

- Monitor patient for anaphylactoid reactions. Be sure that drugs for treating severe hypersensitivity reactions are available for immediate use.
- Check for electrolyte imbalances and acidosis during drug therapy.
- Monitor patient's intake and output, vital signs, hemoglobin, and hematocrit during therapy.
- Be alert for signs and symptoms of opportunistic infections during drug therapy.
- Evaluate patient's and family's knowledge of drug therapy.

Nursing diagnoses

- Risk for injury related to potential for organ rejection
- Ineffective protection related to drug-induced immunosuppression
- Deficient knowledge related to drug therapy

Planning and implementation

- Reconstitute with 5 ml sterile water for injection. Shake vial gently to dissolve powder. Dilute reconstituted solution to volume of 50 ml with normal saline solution or D_5W for infusion. When mixing solution, gently invert bag to avoid foaming. Don't shake.
- Infuse over 20 to 30 minutes via a central or peripheral vein. Don't add or infuse other drugs simultaneously through same I.V. line.
- Use reconstituted solution immediately; may be refrigerated between 36° and 46° F (2° and 8° C) for up to 24 hours or kept at room temperature for 4 hours.
- Drug must be used only under supervision of prescriber qualified and experienced in immunosuppressive therapy and management of organ transplantation.

Patient teaching

• Inform patient of potential benefits and risks of immunosuppressive therapy, including decreased risk of graft loss or acute rejection. Advise patient that immunosuppressive therapy increases risks of developing lymphoproliferative disorders and opportunistic infections. Tell him to report signs and symptoms of infection promptly.

• Tell women of childbearing age to use effective contraception before therapy starts and for 2 months after therapy ends.

• Instruct patient to report adverse effects to prescriber immediately.

• Explain that drug is used with cyclosporine and corticosteroids.

Evaluation

• Patient doesn't experience organ rejection while taking this drug.

• Patient is free from infection and serious bleeding episodes throughout drug therapy.

• Patient and family state understanding of drug therapy.

becaplermin

(be-KAP-ler-min)

Regranex

Pharmacologic class: recombinant human platelet-derived growth factor (rh-PDGF-BB)
Therapeutic class: wound repair agent
Pregnancy risk category: C

Indications and dosages

▶ **Diabetic neuropathic leg ulcers that extend into the subcutaneous tissue or beyond and have adequate blood supply.** *Adults:* Apply daily in 1/16-inch even thickness to entire surface of wound and cover with a saline solution–moistened dressing for 12 hours. Use the following table to calculate the length of gel to apply in inches or centimeters, which depends on wound size and tube size.

Tube size	Inches	Centimeters
2 g	Ulcer length × ulcer width × 1.3	(Ulcer length × ulcer width) ÷ 2
7.5 g, 15 g	Ulcer length × ulcer width × 0.6	(Ulcer length × ulcer width) ÷ 4

Contraindications and precautions

• Contraindicated in patients hypersensitive to drug or its components (such as parabens or m-cresol) and in those with neoplasms at application site.

Lifespan: In breast-feeding women, use cautiously. In children younger than age 16, safety and efficacy haven't been established.

Adverse reactions

Musculoskeletal: osteomyelitis.
Skin: erythematous rash.
Other: cellulitis, infection.

Interactions

None significant.

Effects on lab test results

None reported.

Pharmacokinetics

Absorption: Minimal systemic absorption.
Distribution: Unknown.
Metabolism: Unknown.
Excretion: Unknown.

Route	Onset	Peak	Duration
Topical	Unknown	Unknown	Unknown

Pharmacodynamics

Chemical effect: Thought to promote chemotactic recruitment and proliferation of cells involved in wound repair and formation of new granulation tissue.
Therapeutic effect: Wound repair.

Available forms

Gel: 100 mcg/g in tubes of 2 g, 7.5 g, 15 g

NURSING PROCESS

Assessment

• Obtain history of patient's underlying condition before therapy, and reassess regularly thereafter.

• Ask woman if she's breast-feeding; use cautiously in breast-feeding women.

• Monitor wound size and healing; recalculate amount of drug to be applied at least once weekly. If ulcer doesn't decrease in size by about one-third after 10 weeks, or if complete healing hasn't occurred within 20 weeks, reassess treatment.

- Watch for application site reactions. Sensitization or irritation caused by parabens or m-cresol should be considered.
- Evaluate patient's and family's knowledge of drug therapy.

Nursing diagnoses

- Impaired skin integrity related to leg ulcer
- Acute pain related to presence of skin wound
- Deficient knowledge related to drug therapy

Planning and implementation

- When using the dosage formula, measure ulcer at its greatest length and width. Squeeze the gel onto clean measuring surface such as waxed paper. Use cotton swab or other application aid to transfer and spread drug over entire ulcer area in a ¹⁄₁₆-inch continuous layer. Place a saline solution–moistened dressing over site and leave in place for about 12 hours. After 12 hours, remove dressing and rinse away residual gel with normal saline solution or water, and apply a fresh moist dressing, without becaplermin, for rest of day.
- Drug is for external use only.

ALERT: Don't use drug in wounds that close by primary intention.

- Treatment efficacy hasn't been evaluated for diabetic neuropathic ulcers that don't extend through the dermis into subcutaneous tissue or for ischemic diabetic ulcers.
- Drug facilitates complete healing of diabetic ulcers when used as an adjunct to good ulcer care practices, which include initial sharp debridement, infection control, and pressure relief.

Patient teaching

- Instruct patient to wash hands thoroughly before applying gel.
- Advise patient not to touch tip of tube against ulcer or any other surfaces.
- Instruct patient on proper procedure for wound care, including applying gel and changing dressings.
- Stress need to keep area covered with a wet dressing at all times.
- Tell patient to store drug in refrigerator (36° to 46° F [2° to 8° C]).
- Instruct patient not to use drug after expiration date.

Evaluation

- Patient's ulcer heals.
- Patient doesn't experience pain.
- Patient and family state understanding of drug therapy.

beclomethasone dipropionate

(bek-loh-METH-eh-sohn digh-proh-PIGH-uh-nayt)

Aldecin Aqueous Nasal Spray◇, Beclodisk◇, Becloforte Inhaler◇, QVAR, Vanceril, Vanceril Double Strength

Pharmacologic class: glucocorticoid
Therapeutic class: anti-inflammatory, antiasthmatic
Pregnancy risk category: C

Indications and dosages

▶ **Asthma.** *Adults and children age 12 and older:* Oral inhalation. For regular strength, 2 inhalations t.i.d. or q.i.d. or 4 inhalations b.i.d.; for patients with severe asthma, start with 12 to 16 sprays per day and then reduce the dosage to the lowest effective level. For double strength, 2 inhalations b.i.d.; for severe asthma, start with 6 to 8 inhalations per day and adjust down. Maximum dosage is 10 inhalations (840 mcg) daily. For QVAR, when used with bronchodilators alone, 40 to 80 mcg twice daily, initially. When used with inhaled corticosteroids, 40 to 160 mcg twice daily, initially. Adjust dosage as needed up to a maximum dose of 320 mcg twice daily.
Children ages 5 to 11: For regular strength, 1 to 2 inhalations t.i.d. or q.i.d; maximum dosage is 10 inhalations per day. For double strength, 2 inhalations b.i.d. Maximum dosage is 5 inhalations per day. For QVAR, safety and efficacy in children younger than age 12 haven't been established.

Contraindications and precautions

- Contraindicated in patients hypersensitive to drug or its components (fluorocarbons, oleic acid) and in those with status asthmaticus.
- Don't use in patients with asthma controlled by bronchodilators or other noncorticosteroids alone or in those with nonasthmatic bronchial diseases.

• Use with extreme caution, if at all, in patients with tuberculosis, fungal or bacterial infections, ocular herpes simplex, or systemic viral infections.
• Use with caution in patients receiving systemic corticosteroid therapy.
Lifespan: In pregnant or breast-feeding women, use cautiously.

Adverse reactions

EENT: hoarseness, fungal infections of throat, throat irritation, irritation of nasal mucosa.
GI: dry mouth, fungal infections of mouth.
Respiratory: ***bronchospasm.***
Other: ***angioedema, adrenal insufficiency.***

Interactions

None significant.

Effects on lab test results

None reported.

Pharmacokinetics

Absorption: Rapid from lungs and GI tract.
Distribution: No evidence of tissue storage of beclomethasone or its metabolites. About 10% to 25% of an orally inhaled dose is deposited in respiratory tract. The remainder, deposited in mouth and oropharynx, is swallowed. When absorbed, it's 87% bound to plasma proteins.
Metabolism: Most of drug is metabolized in liver.
Excretion: Unknown, although when drug is given systemically, its metabolites are excreted mainly in feces and, to a lesser extent, in urine. *Half-life:* Average 15 hours.

Route	Onset	Peak	Duration
Inhalation	1-4 wk	Unknown	Unknown

Pharmacodynamics

Chemical effect: Decreases inflammation, mainly by stabilizing leukocyte lysosomal membranes.
Therapeutic effect: Helps alleviate asthma symptoms.

Available forms

Oral inhalation aerosol: 40 mcg/metered spray, 50 mcg /metered spray ◇, 80 mcg/metered spray

NURSING PROCESS

Assessment

• Obtain history of patient's asthma before therapy and reassess regularly thereafter.
• Be alert for adverse reactions.
• Monitor patient closely during times of stress (trauma, surgery, or infection) because systemic corticosteroids may be needed to prevent adrenal insufficiency in previously steroid-dependent patients.
• Periodic measurement of growth and development may be necessary during high-dose or prolonged therapy in children.
• Check for irritation of nasal mucosa.
• Evaluate patient's and family's understanding of drug therapy.

Nursing diagnoses

• Impaired gas exchange related to asthma
• Impaired oral mucous membranes related to drug-induced fungal infections
• Deficient knowledge related to drug therapy

Planning and implementation

ALERT: Never give drug to relieve an emergency asthma attack because onset of action is too slow.
• Give prescribed bronchodilators several minutes before beclomethasone.
• Have patient hold breath for a few seconds after each puff and rest 1 minute between puffs to enhance drug action.
• Spacer device may help ensure delivery of proper dose, although use of such a device with Becloforte Inhaler isn't recommended.
• Taper oral glucocorticoid therapy slowly. Acute adrenal insufficiency and death have occurred in patients with asthma who changed abruptly from oral corticosteroids to beclomethasone.
• Notify prescriber if decreased response is noted after giving drug.
• Have patient gargle and rinse mouth with water after inhalations to help prevent oral fungal infections.
• Keep inhaler clean and unobstructed by washing it with warm water and drying it thoroughly after each use.

Patient teaching

• Inform patient that drug doesn't relieve acute asthma attacks.

• Tell patient who needs a bronchodilator to use it several minutes before drug.
• Instruct patient to wear or carry medical identification indicating need for supplemental systemic glucocorticoid during stress.
• Instruct patient to contact prescriber if response to therapy decreases or if symptoms don't improve within 3 weeks; dosage may need to be adjusted. Tell patient not to exceed recommended dose on his own.
• Tell patient to keep inhaler clean and unobstructed by washing it with warm water and drying it thoroughly.
• Tell patient to prevent oral fungal infections by gargling or rinsing mouth with water after each use but not to swallow water.
• Tell patient to report symptoms of corticosteroid withdrawal, including fatigue, weakness, arthralgia, orthostatic hypotension, and dyspnea.
• Instruct patient to store drug between 36° and 86° F (2° and 30° C). Advise him to ensure delivery of proper dose by gently warming canister to room temperature before using. He may carry canister in pocket to keep it warm.

☑ Evaluation

• Patient's lungs are clear, and breathing and skin color are normal.
• Patient doesn't exhibit an oral fungal infection during therapy.
• Patient and family state understanding of drug therapy.

beclomethasone dipropionate monohydrate

(bek-loh-METH-eh-sohn digh-proh-PIGH-uh-nayt mon-oh-HIGH-drayt)

Beconase AQ Nasal Spray, Vancenase AQ 84 mcg, Vancenase Pockethaler

Pharmacologic class: glucocorticoid
Therapeutic class: anti-inflammatory
Pregnancy risk category: C

Indications and dosages

▶ **Relief of symptoms of seasonal or perennial rhinitis; prevention of recurrence of nasal polyps after surgical removal.** *Adults and children older than age 6:* For 42 mcg/metered spray, usual dosage is 1 or 2 sprays in each nostril, b.i.d. Maximum dosage is 336 mcg daily. For 84 mcg/metered spray, usual dosage is 1 to 2 inhalations daily. Maximum dosage is 336 mcg daily.
Children ages 6 to 12: 1 spray in each nostril t.i.d. (252 mcg daily).

Contraindications and precautions

• Contraindicated in patients hypersensitive to drug and in those experiencing status asthmaticus or other acute episodes of asthma.
• Use cautiously, if at all, in patients with active or quiescent respiratory tract tubercular infections or untreated fungal, bacterial, systemic viral, or ocular herpes simplex infections. Also use cautiously in patients who've recently had nasal septal ulcers, nasal surgery, or trauma.
Lifespan: In pregnant or breast-feeding women, use cautiously. In children younger than age 6, safety of drug hasn't been established.

Adverse reactions

CNS: headache.
EENT: *mild, transient nasal burning and stinging;* nasal congestion; sneezing; epistaxis; watery eyes; nasopharyngeal fungal infections; irritation of nasal mucosa.
GI: nausea, vomiting.

Interactions

None significant.

Effects on lab test results

None reported.

Pharmacokinetics

Absorption: Primarily through nasal mucosa with minimal systemic absorption.
Distribution: Unknown.
Metabolism: Most of drug is metabolized in liver.
Excretion: Unknown, although when drug is administered systemically, its metabolites are excreted mainly in feces and, to a lesser extent, in urine. *Biological half-life:* Average 15 hours.

Route	Onset	Peak	Duration
Inhalation	5-7 days	≤ 3 wk	Unknown

Pharmacodynamics

Chemical effect: Decreases nasal inflammation, mainly by stabilizing leukocyte lysosomal membranes.
Therapeutic effect: Helps relieve nasal allergy symptoms.

Available forms

Nasal aerosol: 42 mcg/metered spray
Nasal spray: 42 mcg/metered spray, 84 mcg/ metered spray

NURSING PROCESS

Assessment

- Obtain history of patient's allergy symptoms and nasal congestion before therapy, and reassess regularly thereafter.
- Be alert for adverse reactions.
- Monitor patient's hydration status if adverse GI reactions occur.
- Check for irritation of nasal mucosa.
- Evaluate patient's and family's understanding of drug therapy.

Nursing diagnoses

- Ineffective health maintenance related to allergy-induced nasal congestion
- Risk for deficient fluid volume related to drug-induced adverse GI reactions
- Deficient knowledge related to drug therapy

Planning and implementation

- Drug isn't effective for acute exacerbations of rhinitis. Decongestants or antihistamines may be needed.
- Shake container and invert. Have patient clear his nasal passages and then tilt his head backward. Insert nozzle into nostril (pointed away from septum), holding other nostril closed. Deliver spray while patient inhales. Shake container and repeat in other nostril.
- Notify prescriber if relief isn't obtained or signs of infection appear.

Patient teaching

- Instruct patient to shake container before using, to blow nose to clear nasal passages, and to tilt head slightly backward and insert nozzle into nostril, pointing away from septum. Tell him to hold other nostril closed and then to inhale gently and spray. Next, have him shake container again and repeat in other nostril.
- Advise patient to pump new nasal spray three or four times before first use and then once or twice before first use each day thereafter. Also tell patient to clean cap and nosepiece of activator in warm water every day and then air-dry them.
- Advise patient to use drug regularly, as prescribed, because its effectiveness depends on regular use.
- Explain that drug's therapeutic effects, unlike those of decongestants, aren't immediate. Most patients achieve benefit within a few days, but some may require 2 to 3 weeks.
- Warn patient not to exceed recommended doses because of risk of hypothalamic-pituitary-adrenal function suppression.
- Tell patient to notify prescriber if symptoms don't improve within 3 weeks or if nasal irritation persists.
- Teach patient good nasal and oral hygiene.

Evaluation

- Patient's nasal congestion subsides with therapy.
- Patient maintains adequate hydration throughout therapy.
- Patient and family state understanding of drug therapy.

benazepril hydrochloride

(ben-AY-zuh-pril high-droh-KLOR-ighd)
Lotensin

Pharmacologic class: ACE inhibitor
Therapeutic class: antihypertensive
Pregnancy risk category: C (D in second and third trimesters)

Indications and dosages

▶ **Hypertension.** *Adults not taking diuretics:* Initially, 10 mg P.O. daily. Dose adjusted, as needed and tolerated; most patients take 20 to 40 mg daily, equally divided into one or two doses. Maximum dose is 80 mg daily.
Adults taking diuretics: Discontinue diuretic 2 to 3 days before starting benazepril hydrochloride to minimize hypotension. If unable to discontinue diuretic, starting dose should be 5 mg daily.
Patients with renal insufficiency and a creatinine clearance below 20 mg/minute: The start-

ing dose is 5 mg daily. Don't exceed 40 mg P.O. daily.

Contraindications and precautions

- Contraindicated in patients hypersensitive to ACE inhibitors.
- Use cautiously in patients with impaired hepatic or renal function.

Lifespan: In pregnant women, use only if absolutely necessary and then with extreme caution. Drug is usually discontinued during pregnancy. With breast-feeding women, use cautiously. In children, safety of drug hasn't been established.

Adverse reactions

CNS: asthenia, headache, dizziness, lightheadedness, anxiety, amnesia, depression, insomnia, nervousness, neuralgia, neuropathy, paresthesia, somnolence.
CV: symptomatic hypotension, syncope, angina, ***arrhythmias,*** palpitations, edema.
GI: nausea, vomiting, abdominal pain, constipation, dyspepsia, gastritis, dysphagia, increased salivation.
GU: impotence.
Metabolic: ***hyperkalemia,*** weight gain.
Musculoskeletal: arthralgia, arthritis, myalgia.
Respiratory: dry, persistent, tickling, nonproductive cough; dyspnea.
Skin: rash, dermatitis, increased diaphoresis, pruritus, photosensitivity, purpura.
Other: ***angioedema,*** hypersensitivity reactions.

Interactions

Drug-drug. *ACE inhibitors, diuretics, other antihypertensives:* Risk of excessive hypotension. Discontinue diuretic or lower dose of benazepril, as directed.
Digoxin: May increase digoxin level. Monitor patient for toxicity.
Indomethacin: May reduce hypotensive effects. Monitor blood pressure.
Lithium: Increases lithium level and lithium toxicity. Avoid using together.
Potassium-sparing diuretics, potassium supplements: Risk of hyperkalemia. Monitor patient closely.
Drug-herb. *Capsicum:* May aggravate or cause ACE-induced cough. Discourage using together.
Licorice: May cause sodium retention, thus decreasing ACE effects. Discourage using together.
Drug-food. *Foods, especially those high in fat:* May impair drug absorption. Instruct patient to take drug on an empty stomach.
Sodium substitutes containing potassium: Risk of hyperkalemia. Monitor patient closely.

Effects on lab test results

- May increase BUN, creatinine, and potassium levels.

Pharmacokinetics

Absorption: At least 37%.
Distribution: Protein binding of benazepril is about 96.7%; that of benazeprilat, 95.3%.
Metabolism: Almost completely metabolized in liver to benazeprilat, which has much greater ACE inhibitory activity than benazepril, and to glucuronide conjugates of benazepril and benazeprilat.
Excretion: Primarily in urine. *Half-life:* Benazepril, 0.6 hours; benazeprilat, 10 to 12 hours.

Route	Onset	Peak	Duration
P.O.	≤ 1 hr	2-4 hr	24 hr

Pharmacodynamics

Chemical effect: Inhibits ACE, preventing conversion of angiotensin I to angiotensin II, a potent vasoconstrictor. Reduced formation of angiotensin II decreases peripheral arterial resistance, thus decreasing aldosterone secretion. This reduces sodium and water retention and lowers blood pressure. Benazepril also has antihypertensive activity in patients with low-renin hypertension.
Therapeutic effect: Lowers blood pressure.

Available forms

Tablets: 5 mg, 10 mg, 20 mg, 40 mg

NURSING PROCESS

Assessment

- Obtain history of patient's blood pressure before therapy and reassess regularly thereafter. Measure blood pressure when drug levels are at peak (2 to 6 hours after dose) and at trough (just before dose) to verify adequate blood pressure control.

- Be alert for adverse reactions and drug interactions.
- Monitor patient's ECG.
- Monitor renal and hepatic function periodically. Also monitor potassium levels.
- Monitor patient's CBC with differential every 2 weeks for first 3 months of therapy and periodically thereafter. Other ACE inhibitors have been linked to agranulocytosis and neutropenia.
- Evaluate patient's and family's understanding of drug therapy.

Nursing diagnoses
- Risk for injury related to hypertension
- Decreased cardiac output related to drug-induced arrhythmias
- Deficient knowledge related to drug therapy

Planning and implementation
- If patient is taking a diuretic, dose should be lower than if patient isn't taking a diuretic; excessive hypotension can occur when drug is given with diuretics.
- Dosage adjustment may be necessary in patients with renal impairment.
- Give drug at about the same time every day to maintain consistent effect on blood pressure.
- Give drug when patient's stomach is empty.

Patient teaching
- Instruct patient to take drug on an empty stomach; meals, particularly those high in fat, can impair absorption.
- Tell patient to avoid sodium substitutes; such products may contain potassium, which can cause hyperkalemia in patients taking drug.
- Tell patient to rise slowly to minimize risk of dizziness, which may occur during first few weeks of therapy. If dizziness does occur, patient should stop taking drug and call prescriber immediately.
- Tell patient to use caution in hot weather and during exercise. Inadequate fluid intake, vomiting, diarrhea, and excessive perspiration can lead to light-headedness and syncope.
- Urge patient to report signs of infection, such as fever and sore throat. Also tell him to call prescriber if the following signs or symptoms occur: easy bruising or bleeding; swelling of tongue, lips, face, eyes, mucous membranes, or limbs; difficulty swallowing or breathing; and hoarseness.
- Tell women to notify prescriber if pregnancy occurs. Drug will need to be discontinued.

Evaluation
- Patient's blood pressure is normal.
- Patient maintains adequate cardiac output during drug therapy.
- Patient and family state understanding of drug therapy.

benztropine mesylate
(BENZ-troh-peen MES-ih-layt)
Apo-Benztropine ♦, Cogentin

Pharmacologic class: anticholinergic
Therapeutic class: antiparkinsonian
Pregnancy risk category: NR

Indications and dosages
▶ **Drug-induced extrapyramidal disorders (except tardive dyskinesia).** *Adults:* 1 to 4 mg P.O. or I.M. once or twice daily.
▶ **Acute dystonic reaction.** *Adults:* 1 to 2 mg I.V. or I.M., followed by 1 to 2 mg P.O. b.i.d. to prevent recurrence.
▶ **Parkinsonism.** *Adults:* 0.5 to 6 mg P.O. daily. Initial dose is 0.5 to 1 mg. I.M. or P.O. Because of cumulative action, initiate at a low dose and increase by 0.5 mg q 5 to 6 days. Adjust dosage to meet individual requirements. Maximum daily dose is 6 mg.

Contraindications and precautions
- Contraindicated in patients with acute angle-closure glaucoma and in patients hypersensitive to drug or its components.
- Use cautiously in patients exposed to hot weather and in those with mental disorders.

Lifespan: In pregnant women, use cautiously. In breast-feeding women and children younger than age 3, drug is contraindicated. In children age 3 and older and patients older than age 60, use cautiously.

Adverse reactions
CNS: disorientation, restlessness, irritability, incoherence, hallucinations, headache, sedation, depression, nervousness, confusion.
CV: palpitations, tachycardia, ***paradoxical bradycardia,*** flushing.

EENT: dilated pupils, blurred vision, photophobia, difficulty swallowing.
GI: dry mouth, *constipation,* nausea, vomiting, epigastric distress.
GU: urinary hesitancy, urine retention.
Musculoskeletal: muscle weakness.

Interactions

Drug-drug. *Amantadine, phenothiazines, tricyclic antidepressants:* May cause additive anticholinergic adverse reactions, such as confusion and hallucinations. Reduce dose before administering.
Anticholinergics and other antiparkisonians: May increase anticholinergic effects and may be fatal. Use extreme caution.

Effects on lab test results

None reported.

Pharmacokinetics

Absorption: Absorbed from GI tract when administered P.O.
Distribution: Largely unknown; however, drug crosses blood-brain barrier.
Metabolism: Unknown.
Excretion: Excreted in urine as unchanged drug and metabolites. After P.O. therapy, small amounts may be excreted in feces as unabsorbed drug.

Route	Onset	Peak	Duration
P.O.	1-2 hr	Unknown	24 hr
I.V., I.M.	≤ 15 min	Unknown	24 hr

Pharmacodynamics

Chemical effect: Unknown; thought to block central cholinergic receptors, helping to balance cholinergic activity in basal ganglia.
Therapeutic effect: Improves capability for voluntary movement.

Available forms

Injection: 1 mg/ml in 2-ml ampules
Tablets: 0.5 mg, 1 mg, 2 mg

NURSING PROCESS

Assessment

- Obtain history of patient's dyskinetic movements and underlying condition before therapy.
- Monitor effectiveness by regularly checking body movements for signs of improvement; full effect of drug may take 2 to 3 days.
- Be alert for adverse reactions and drug interactions. Some adverse reactions may result from atropine-like toxicity and are dose-related.
- Evaluate patient's and family's understanding of drug therapy.

Nursing diagnoses

- Impaired physical mobility related to dyskinetic movements
- Risk for injury related to drug-induced adverse CNS reactions
- Deficient knowledge related to drug therapy

Planning and implementation

- **P.O. use:** Give drug after meals to help prevent GI distress.
- **I.V. use:** Drug is seldom used I.V. because of small difference in onset compared with I.M. route.
- **I.M. use:** The I.M. route is preferred for parenteral administration.
- Give drug at bedtime if patient is to receive single daily dose.

ALERT: Never discontinue drug abruptly; reduce dose gradually.

Patient teaching

- Warn patient to avoid activities requiring alertness until CNS effects of drug are known.
- If patient is to receive single daily dose, tell him to take it at bedtime.
- If patient is to receive drug orally, tell him to take it after meals.
- Advise patient to report signs of urinary hesitancy or urine retention.
- Tell patient to relieve dry mouth with cool drinks, ice chips, sugarless gum, or hard candy.
- Advise patient to limit activities during hot weather because drug-induced anhidrosis may result in hyperthermia.

Evaluation

- Patient exhibits improved mobility with reduction in muscle rigidity, akinesia, and tremors.
- Patient doesn't experience injury as a result of drug-induced adverse CNS reactions.
- Patient and family state understanding of drug therapy.

bepridil hydrochloride

(BEH-prih-dil high-droh-KLOR-ighd)
Vascor

Pharmacologic class: calcium channel blocker
Therapeutic class: antianginal
Pregnancy risk category: C

Indications and dosages

▶ **Chronic stable angina in patients who can't tolerate or who fail to respond to other drugs.** *Adults:* Initially, 200 mg P.O. daily. After 10 days, increase dosage based on patient's tolerance and response. Maintenance dosage in most patients is 300 mg daily. Maximum daily dosage is 400 mg.

Contraindications and precautions

- Contraindicated in patients hypersensitive to drug and in those with uncompensated cardiac insufficiency, sick sinus syndrome, or second- or third-degree AV block unless patient has pacemaker; hypotension; congenital QT interval prolongation; or history of serious ventricular arrhythmias. Also contraindicated in those receiving other drugs that prolong QT interval.
- Use cautiously in patients with left bundle branch block, sinus bradycardia (less than 50 beats/minute), impaired renal or hepatic function, or heart failure.

Lifespan: In pregnant women, use cautiously. For breast-feeding women, risk-benefit ratio must be assessed because of risk of serious adverse reactions in infants. In children, safety of drug hasn't been established.

Adverse reactions

CNS: dizziness, confusion, headache.
CV: edema; flushing; palpitations; tachycardia; ***ventricular arrhythmias, including torsades de pointes, ventricular tachycardia, and ventricular fibrillation.***
GI: nausea, diarrhea, constipation.
Hematologic: ***agranulocytosis.***
Respiratory: dyspnea.
Skin: rash.

Interactions

Drug-drug. *Antiarrhythmics, tricyclic antidepressants:* Could prolong QT interval. Use together cautiously.
Beta blockers: May increase adverse effects due to depressant effects on myocardial contractility or AV conduction. Use together cautiously.
Cardiac glycosides: Could exaggerate AV nodal conduction. Use together cautiously.

Effects on lab test results

- May increase ALT level.
- May decrease granulocyte count.

Pharmacokinetics

Absorption: Rapid and complete.
Distribution: More than 99% is plasma protein–bound.
Metabolism: Metabolized in the liver.
Excretion: Over 10 days, 70% is excreted in urine, 22% in feces as metabolites. *Half-life:* After multiple doses, averages 24 hours.

Route	Onset	Peak	Duration
P.O.	Unknown	2-3 hr	24 hr

Pharmacodynamics

Chemical effect: Inhibits calcium ion influx across cardiac and smooth muscle cells. This action dilates coronary arteries, peripheral arteries, and arterioles; it may reduce heart rate, decrease myocardial contractility, and slow AV node conduction.
Therapeutic effect: Prevents anginal pain.

Available forms

Tablets: 200 mg, 300 mg, 400 mg

NURSING PROCESS

Assessment

- Obtain history of patient's angina before therapy; reassess regularly thereafter.
- Be alert for adverse reactions and drug interactions.
- Monitor patient's ECG, heart rate, and rhythm regularly; use of bepridil may cause severe ventricular arrhythmias, including torsades de pointes.
- Monitor patient's CBC and differential; use of drug is linked to agranulocytosis.
- Elderly patients don't need a reduced dosage but do need frequent monitoring for hepatic impairment.
- Evaluate patient's and family's understanding of drug therapy.

Nursing diagnoses

- Acute pain related to presence of angina
- Ineffective protection related to drug-induced ventricular arrhythmias
- Deficient knowledge related to drug therapy

Planning and implementation

- Give drug following usual protocol for P.O. administration.
- Consult prescriber if patient doesn't experience pain relief.

Patient teaching

- Tell patient to report promptly unusual bruising, bleeding, or signs of persistent infection.
- Stress the importance of taking drug exactly as prescribed, even when feeling well.
- Tell patient to schedule activities to allow adequate rest.
- Encourage patient to restrict fluid and sodium intake to minimize edema.

Evaluation

- Patient states that angina is relieved.
- Patient's ECG, heart rate, and rhythm are unchanged with therapy.
- Patient and family state understanding of drug therapy.

beractant (natural lung surfactant)

(beh-RAK-tant)
Survanta

Pharmacologic class: bovine lung extract
Therapeutic class: lung surfactant
Pregnancy risk category: NR

Indications and dosages

▶ **Prevention and rescue treatment of respiratory distress syndrome (RDS) or hyaline membrane disease in premature infants weighing 1,250 g (2.75 lb) or less at birth or having symptoms of surfactant deficiency.**
Infants: 4 ml/kg administered by intratracheal instillation through a #5 French end-hole catheter inserted into the neonate's endotracheal tube with the tip of the catheter protruding just beyond the end of the tube above the carina. Length of catheter should be shortened before inserting it through the tube. Drug shouldn't be instilled into a mainstem bronchus. Four doses can be given in the first 48 hours of life, but no more frequently than q 6 hours. Use the following dosing table.

BERACTANT DOSING TABLE

Weight (g)	Total dose (ml)
600 to 650	2.6
651 to 700	2.8
701 to 750	3
751 to 800	3.2
801 to 850	3.4
851 to 900	3.6
901 to 950	3.8
951 to 1,000	4
1,001 to 1,050	4.2
1,051 to 1,100	4.4
1,101 to 1,150	4.6
1,151 to 1,200	4.8
1,201 to 1,250	5
1,251 to 1,300	5.2
1,301 to 1,350	5.4
1,351 to 1,400	5.6
1,401 to 1,450	5.8
1,451 to 1,500	6
1,501 to 1,550	6.2
1,551 to 1,600	6.4
1,601 to 1,650	6.6
1,651 to 1,700	6.8
1,701 to 1,750	7
1,751 to 1,800	7.2
1,801 to 1,850	7.4
1,851 to 1,900	7.6
1,901 to 1,950	7.8
1,951 to 2,000	8

Contraindications and precautions

- No contraindications reported.

Lifespan: For use in premature infants only.

Adverse reactions

CV: ***bradycardia,*** vasoconstriction, hypotension.
Respiratory: ***endotracheal tube reflux or blockage, apnea,*** decreased oxygen saturation, hypocapnia, hypercapnia.
Other: pallor.

Interactions

None significant.

Effects on lab test results

• May decrease oxygen saturation levels. May increase or decrease carbon dioxide levels.

Pharmacokinetics

Absorption: Most of dose becomes lung-associated within hours.
Distribution: Across alveolar surface.
Metabolism: Lipids enter endogenous surfactant pathway of recycling and reutilization.
Excretion: Alveolar clearance of lipid components is rapid.

Route	Onset	Peak	Duration
Intratracheal	0.5-2 hr	Unknown	2-3 days

Pharmacodynamics

Chemical effect: Lowers surface tension of alveoli during respiration and stabilizes alveoli against collapse. An extract of bovine lung containing neutral lipids, fatty acids, surfactant-associated proteins, and phospholipids that mimics naturally occurring surfactant; palmitic acid, tripalmitin, and colfosceril palmitate are added to standardize solution's composition.
Therapeutic effect: Prevents RDS in premature neonates with specific characteristics.

Available forms

Suspension for intratracheal instillation: 25 mg/ml

NURSING PROCESS

Assessment

• Obtain history of neonate's respiratory status before therapy.
• Continuously monitor neonate before, during, and after beractant administration for effectiveness.
• Continuously monitor ECG and transcutaneous oxygen saturation; also, frequently monitor arterial blood pressure and sample arterial blood gas. Transient bradycardia and oxygen desaturation are common after dosing.
• Evaluate parents' understanding of drug therapy.

Nursing diagnoses

• Risk for injury related to potential for RDS
• Deficient knowledge related to drug therapy

Planning and implementation

ALERT: Beractant should be given only by personnel experienced in care of clinically unstable premature neonates. Such personnel should have knowledge of neonatal intubation and airway management.
• Accurate determination of weight is essential to ensure proper measurement of dose.
• Endotracheal tube may be suctioned before giving drug.
• Allow neonate to stabilize before proceeding with administration; however, it's preferable to give drug within 15 minutes of birth to prevent RDS.
• Refrigerate drug at 36° to 46° F (2° to 8° C). Warm before giving by allowing drug to stand at room temperature for at least 20 minutes or by holding in hand for at least 8 minutes. Don't use artificial warming methods. Unopened vials that have been warmed to room temperature may be returned to refrigerator within 8 hours; warm and return drug to refrigerator only once. Vials are for single use only; discard unused drug once vial has been opened.
• Beractant doesn't need sonication or reconstitution before use. Inspect contents before giving; ensure that color is off-white to light brown and that contents are uniform. If settling occurs, swirl vial gently; don't shake. Some foaming is normal.
• Homogeneous distribution of drug is important. In clinical trials, each dose of drug was given in four quarter-doses, with patient positioned differently after each administration. Each quarter-dose was given over 2 to 3 seconds; the catheter was removed and patient ventilated between quarter-doses. With head and body inclined slightly downward, first quarter-dose was given with head turned to right; second quarter-dose with head turned to left. Then head and body were inclined slightly upward; third quarter-dose was given with head turned to right; fourth quarter-dose with head turned to left.
• Moist breath sounds and crackles can occur immediately after administration. Don't suction neonate for 1 hour unless other signs of airway obstruction are evident.
• Audiovisual materials that describe dose and administration procedures are available from manufacturer.
• Beractant can rapidly affect oxygenation and lung compliance. Peak ventilator inspiratory

pressures may need to be adjusted if chest expansion improves substantially with therapy. Notify prescriber and adjust immediately, as directed, because lung overdistention and fatal pulmonary air leakage may result.
- For active rescue treatment, give first dose within 8 hours of birth.

Patient teaching
- Teach parents about beractant therapy.
- Reassure parents that neonate will be monitored at all times.

☑ Evaluation
- Patient doesn't develop RDS.
- Parents state understanding of drug therapy.

17 beta-estradiol and norgestimate
(17 bay-ta-eh-stray-DYE-ol nor-JES-ti-mate)
Ortho-Prefest

Pharmacologic class: combined synthetic estrogen and progestin
Therapeutic class: hormone replacement
Pregnancy risk category: X

Indications and dosages
▶ **Treatment of moderate-to-severe vasomotor symptoms and vulvar and vaginal atrophy caused by menopause; prevention of osteoporosis in women with an intact uterus.** *Adults:* 1 mg estradiol (pink tablet) P.O. daily for 3 days; then 1 mg estradiol/0.09 mg norgestimate (white tablet) P.O. daily for 3 days. Repeat cycle until blister card is empty.

Contraindications and precautions
- Contraindicated in patients hypersensitive to any component of Ortho-Prefest and in patients with cancer of the breast, estrogen-dependent neoplasia, undiagnosed abnormal vaginal bleeding, or active or previous thrombophlebitis or thromboembolic disorders.
- Use cautiously in women who have had a hysterectomy, who are overweight, who have abnormal lipid profiles, or who have impaired liver function.

Lifespan: In patients who are or may be pregnant, drug is contraindicated.

Adverse reactions
CNS: depression, dizziness, fatigue, pain, *headache.*
EENT: pharyngitis, sinusitis.
GI: flatulence, nausea, *abdominal pain.*
GU: dysmenorrhea, vaginal bleeding, vaginitis.
Musculoskeletal: arthralgia, myalgia, *back pain.*
Respiratory: cough, *upper respiratory tract infection.*
Other: *flulike symptoms,* viral infection, *breast pain,* tooth disorder.

Interactions
None reported.

Effects on lab test results
- May increase thyroid-binding globulin; factors II, VII antigen, VIII antigen, VIII coagulant activity, IX, X, XII, VII-X complex, and II-VII-X complex; beta-thromboglobulin; HDL, triglyceride, corticosteroid, sex steroid, angiotensin and renin substrate, $alpha_1$-antitrypsin, ceruloplasmin, fibrinogen, and plasminogen antigen levels. May decrease folate, metyrapone, LDL, anti-factor Xa, and antithrombin III levels.
- May increase PT, PTT, platelet aggregation time, and platelet count. May decrease T_3 resin uptake and glucose tolerance.

Pharmacokinetics
Absorption: Estradiol reaches peak levels about 7 hours after a dose. The metabolite of norgestimate, 17-deacetylnorgestimate, reaches peak levels about 2 hours after a dose. When given with a high-fat meal, peak levels of estrone and estrone sulfate were increased by 14% and 24% respectively; peak level of 17-deacetylnorgestimate was decreased by 16%.
Distribution: Estrogens are widely distributed throughout the body. Estradiol is bound mainly to sex hormone–binding globulin, and to albumin. The primary active metabolite of norgestimate, 17-deacetylnorgestimate, is about 99% protein-bound.
Metabolism: Estrogens are mainly metabolized in the liver. Estradiol is converted reversibly to estrone, and both can be converted to estriol, which is the major urinary metabolite. Estrogens also undergo enterohepatic recirculation via sulfate and glucuronide conju-

gation in the liver, biliary secretion of conjugates in the intestine, and hydrolysis in the gut followed by reabsorption. Norgestimate is extensively metabolized by first-pass metabolism to 17-deacetylnorgestimate in the GI tract or liver.
Excretion: Estradiol, estrone, and estriol are excreted in the urine. Norgestimate metabolites are eliminated in the urine or feces. *Half-life:* About 16 hours for estradiol and 37 hours for 17-deacetylnorgestimate in postmenopausal women.

Route	Onset	Peak	Duration
P.O.	Unknown	7 hr (estradiol), 2 hr (norgestimate)	Unknown

Pharmacodynamics

Chemical effect: Mimics the action of endogenous estrogen and natural progesterone. Circulating estrogens modulate pituitary secretion of gonadotropins, luteinizing hormone, and follicle-stimulating hormone through a negative feedback mechanism. They also contribute to the shaping of the skeleton. Estrogen replacement therapy reduces elevated levels of these hormones in postmenopausal women. Estradiol is more potent than its metabolites estrone and estriol.

Norgestimate mimics the natural hormone progesterone. Progestins counter estrogenic effects by decreasing the number of nuclear estradiol receptors and suppressing epithelial DNA synthesis in endometrial tissue.
Therapeutic effect: Relieves menopausal vasomotor symptoms and vaginal dryness; reduces the severity of osteoporosis.

Available forms

Tablets: Blister card of 15 pink and 15 white tablets, for a total of 30 tablets
Pink tablets: 1 mg estradiol
White tablets: 1 mg estradiol and 0.09 mg norgestimate

NURSING PROCESS

Assessment

- Obtain history of patient's underlying condition before therapy and reassess regularly thereafter.
- Make sure patient has a thorough physical examination before starting drug therapy.
- Assess patient's risks for venous thromboembolism.
- Assess patient's risk for cancer; hormone replacement therapy may increase the risk of breast cancer in postmenopausal women.
- Be alert for adverse reactions.
- Evaluate patient's and family's knowledge of drug therapy.

Nursing diagnoses

- Ineffective peripheral tissue perfusion related to drug-induced thromboembolism
- Ineffective health maintenance related to underlying condition
- Deficient knowledge related to drug therapy

Planning and implementation

- Reassess patient at 6-month intervals to make sure treatment is still needed.
- Estrogens may induce malignant neoplasms. Combining progestin therapy with estrogen therapy significantly reduces this risk.
- Monitor patient for hypercalcemia if she has breast cancer and bone metastases. If severe hypercalcemia occurs, notify the prescriber and stop the drug; take the appropriate measures to reduce calcium level.

Patient teaching

- Explain the risks of taking estrogen therapy, including breast cancer, cancer of the uterus, abnormal blood clotting, and gallbladder disease.
- Tell patient to immediately report any undiagnosed, persistent, or recurring abnormal vaginal bleeding.
- Instruct women taking this drug to perform monthly breast examinations. Also, recommend a mammogram if patient is older than age 50.
- Tell patient to immediately report pain in the calves or chest, sudden shortness of breath, coughing blood, severe headache, vomiting, dizziness, faintness, changes in vision or speech, and weakness or numbness in arms or legs. These are warning signals of blood clots.
- Urge patient to report evidence of liver problems, such as yellowing of skin or eyes and upper right quadrant pain.
- Instruct patient to report pain, swelling, or tenderness in abdomen, which may indicate gallbladder problems.

• Tell patient to store drug at room temperature away from excessive heat and moisture. It remains stable for 18 months.

Evaluation

• Patient has no thromboembolic event during therapy.
• Patient's underlying condition improves.
• Patient and family state understanding of drug therapy.

betamethasone

(bay-tuh-METH-uh-sohn)
Betnesol ♦, Celestone*

betamethasone acetate and betamethasone sodium phosphate

Celestone Chronodose ◇, Celestone Soluspan

betamethasone sodium phosphate

Celestone Phosphate, Selestoject

Pharmacologic class: glucocorticoid
Therapeutic class: anti-inflammatory
Pregnancy risk category: NR

Indications and dosages

▶ **Conditions of severe inflammation or that need immunosuppression.** ***betamethasone.*** *Adults:* 0.6 to 7.2 mg P.O. daily. *Children:* 0.0175 to 0.25 mg/kg P.O. daily. ***betamethasone acetate and sodium phosphate.*** *Adults:* 0.25 to 2 ml of sodium phosphate-acetate suspension injected into joint or soft tissue q 1 to 2 weeks, p.r.n. ***betamethasone sodium phosphate.*** *Adults:* 0.5 to 9 mg I.V., I.M., or injected into joint or soft tissue daily.

▶ **Hyaline membrane disease‡.** *Adults:* Give 2 ml I.M. daily to expectant mothers for 2 to 3 days before delivery.

Contraindications and precautions

• Contraindicated in patients hypersensitive to drug and in those with viral or bacterial infections (except in life-threatening situations) or systemic fungal infections.
• Use with extreme caution, and only in life-threatening situations, in patients with recent MI or peptic ulcer.
• Use cautiously in patients with renal disease, hypertension, osteoporosis, diabetes mellitus, hypothyroidism, cirrhosis, diverticulitis, nonspecific ulcerative colitis, recent intestinal anastomoses, thromboembolic disorders, seizures, myasthenia gravis, heart failure, tuberculosis, ocular herpes simplex, emotional instability, or psychotic tendencies. Because some formulations contain sulfite preservatives, use cautiously in patients sensitive to sulfites.

Lifespan: In pregnant women, use cautiously. Breast-feeding women should discontinue breast-feeding if taking drug. In children younger than age 12, safety of drug hasn't been established.

Adverse reactions

CNS: *euphoria, insomnia,* psychotic behavior, pseudotumor cerebri, ***seizures.***
CV: ***heart failure,*** hypertension, edema, ***thromboembolism.***
EENT: cataracts, glaucoma.
GI: *peptic ulceration,* GI irritation, increased appetite, ***pancreatitis.***
Metabolic: hypokalemia, hyperglycemia, carbohydrate intolerance.
Musculoskeletal: muscle weakness, osteoporosis, growth suppression in children.
Skin: hirsutism, delayed wound healing, acne, various skin eruptions.
Other: susceptibility to infections, ***acute adrenal insufficiency*** after stress (infection, surgery, or trauma) or abrupt withdrawal after long-term therapy.

Interactions

Drug-drug. *Aspirin, indomethacin, other NSAIDs:* May increase risk of GI distress and bleeding. Give together cautiously.
Barbiturates, phenytoin, rifampin: Decreases corticosteroid effect. Corticosteroid dosage may need to be increased.
Oral anticoagulants: Alters dosage requirements. Monitor PT and INR closely.
Potassium-depleting drugs (such as thiazide diuretics): Enhances potassium-depleting effects of betamethasone. Monitor potassium levels.
Skin test antigens: Decreases response. Defer skin testing until therapy is completed.

Toxoids, vaccines: Decreases antibody response and increases risk of neurologic complications. Avoid using together. Delay vaccines, if possible.

Effects on lab test results

- May increase glucose and cholesterol levels. May decrease potassium and calcium levels.

Pharmacokinetics

Absorption: Absorbed readily after P.O. administration. Systemic absorption occurs slowly after intra-articular injections.
Distribution: Removed rapidly from blood and distributed to muscle, liver, skin, intestines, and kidneys. Bound weakly to plasma proteins. Only unbound portion is active.
Metabolism: Metabolized in liver to inactive glucuronide and sulfate metabolites.
Excretion: Inactive metabolites and small amounts of unmetabolized drug are excreted in urine. Insignificant quantities of drug are also excreted in feces. *Half-life:* 36 to 54 hours.

Route	Onset	Peak	Duration
P.O.	Unknown	1-2 hr	3.25 days
I.V., I.M., intra-articular	Rapid	Unknown	7-14 days

Pharmacodynamics

Chemical effect: Not completely defined. Decreases inflammation, mainly by stabilizing leukocyte lysosomal membranes; suppresses immune response; stimulates bone marrow; and influences protein, fat, and carbohydrate metabolism.
Therapeutic effect: Causes immunosuppression.

Available forms

betamethasone
Syrup: 600 mcg/5 ml
Tablets: 600 mcg
Tablets (effervescent): 500 mcg
betamethasone acetate and betamethasone sodium phosphate
Injection (suspension): betamethasone acetate 3 mg and betamethasone sodium phosphate (equivalent to 3-mg base) per ml
betamethasone sodium phosphate
Injection: 4 mg (equivalent to 3-mg base)/ml in 5-ml vials

NURSING PROCESS

Assessment

- Obtain history of patient's underlying condition and current health status, including vital signs and weight.
- Be alert for adverse reactions and drug interactions. Most adverse reactions are dose- or duration-dependent.
- Monitor patient's weight, blood pressure, and glucose and potassium levels regularly.
- Monitor patient for early signs of adrenal insufficiency or cushingoid symptoms. Adrenal suppression may last up to 1 year after drug is stopped.
- Monitor patient's stress level. Stress (fever, trauma, surgery, or emotional problems) may increase adrenal insufficiency.
- Evaluate patient's and family's understanding of drug therapy.

Nursing diagnoses

- Ineffective health maintenance related to underlying condition
- Risk for injury related to drug-induced adverse reactions
- Deficient knowledge related to drug therapy

Planning and implementation

- **P.O. use:** Give drug with milk or food to reduce GI irritation.
- **I.V. use:** Drug is compatible with normal saline solution, D_5W, lactated Ringer's injection, dextrose 5% in lactated Ringer's injection, and dextrose 5% in Ringer's injection. Suspension for injection isn't for I.V. use.
- **I.M. use:** Give I.M. injection deeply to prevent muscle atrophy. Rotate injection sites.
- **Intra-articular use:** Prepare drug for prescriber to give.
- Drug shouldn't be used for alternate-day therapy.
- Give once-daily dose in the morning for best results and least toxicity.
- Drug should always be adjusted to lowest effective dose.

ALERT: Gradually reduce drug dosage after long-term therapy. After abrupt withdrawal, patient may experience rebound inflammation, fatigue, weakness, arthralgia, fever, dizziness, lethargy, depression, fainting, orthostatic hypotension, dyspnea, anorexia, and hypoglycemia.

After prolonged use, sudden withdrawal may be fatal.

- Expect to increase dose during times of physiologic stress (surgery, trauma, or infection).
- Potassium supplements may be necessary for patients receiving long-term therapy.

Patient teaching

- Tell patient not to stop drug abruptly or without prescriber's consent.
- Tell patient using effervescent tablets to dissolve them in water immediately before ingestion.
- Teach patient about drug's effects. Warn patient receiving long-term therapy about cushingoid symptoms; instruct him to report sudden weight gain or swelling to prescriber.
- Instruct patient to report symptoms of corticosteroid withdrawal, including fatigue, weakness, arthralgia, orthostatic hypotension, and dyspnea.
- Tell patient to contact prescriber if symptoms worsen or drug is no longer effective. Also tell him not to increase dose without prescriber's consent.
- Advise elderly patient receiving long-term therapy to consider exercise or physical therapy. Tell him to ask prescriber about vitamin D or calcium supplements.
- Advise patient receiving prolonged therapy to have periodic ophthalmic examinations.
- Tell patient to report slow healing.
- Instruct patient to wear or carry medical identification indicating his need for supplemental corticosteroids during stress.

Evaluation

- Patient's underlying condition improves.
- Patient doesn't experience injury as a result of drug-induced adverse reactions.
- Patient and family state understanding of drug therapy.

betaxolol hydrochloride

(beh-TAKS-oh-lol high-droh-KLOR-ighd)

Betoptic, Betoptic S, Kerlone

Pharmacologic class: beta blocker
Therapeutic class: antihypertensive
Pregnancy risk category: C

Indications and dosages

▶ **Hypertension.** *Adults:* Initially, 10 mg P.O. once daily. If desired response not achieved in 7 to 14 days, may increase dose to 20 mg P.O. once daily.

▶ **Elevated intraocular pressure, ocular hypertension, chronic open-angle glaucoma.** *Adults:* 1 to 2 drops in affected eye(s) b.i.d.

Patients with renal impairment and geriatric patients: Initial dose is 5 mg P.O. daily. May increase by 5-mg/day increments q 2 weeks to a maximum of 20 mg P.O. daily.

Contraindications and precautions

- Contraindicated in patients hypersensitive to drug and in those with severe bradycardia, greater than first-degree heart block, cardiogenic shock, or uncontrolled heart failure.
- Use cautiously in patient with heart failure controlled by cardiac glycosides and diuretics because he may show signs of cardiac decompensation with beta blocker therapy.

Lifespan: In pregnant or breast-feeding women, use cautiously. In children, safety of drug hasn't been established.

Adverse reactions

CNS: dizziness, syncope, fatigue, headache, lethargy, anxiety.
CV: ***bradycardia,*** chest pain, hypotension, worsening of angina, peripheral vascular insufficiency, ***heart failure,*** edema, orthostatic hypotension, conduction disturbances.
GI: flatulence, constipation, nausea, diarrhea, vomiting, anorexia, dry mouth.
Respiratory: ***bronchospasm,*** dyspnea, wheezing.
Skin: rash.

Interactions

Drug-drug. *Calcium channel blockers:* Increased risk of hypotension, left ventricular failure, and AV conduction disturbances. Use I.V. calcium channel blockers with caution.
Catecholamine-depleting drugs, reserpine: May have an additive effect. Monitor patient closely.
General anesthetics: Increased hypotensive effects. Watch patient carefully for excessive hypotension, bradycardia, and orthostatic hypotension.
Lidocaine: May increase the effects of lidocaine. Monitor patient closely.

Effects on lab test results

None reported.

Pharmacokinetics

Absorption: Complete. Small first-pass effect reduces bioavailability by about 10%.
Distribution: About 50% bound to plasma proteins.
Metabolism: Metabolized in liver.
Excretion: Excreted primarily in urine (about 80%) as metabolites. *Half-life:* 14 to 22 hours.

Route	Onset	Peak	Duration
P.O.	≤ 3 hr	2-4 hr (antihypertensive effects peak in 7-14 days)	24-48 hr

Pharmacodynamics

Chemical effect: Unknown.
Therapeutic effect: Reduces blood pressure.

Available forms

Tablets: 10 mg, 20 mg

NURSING PROCESS

Assessment

- Obtain history of patient's blood pressure before therapy and reassess regularly thereafter.
- Be alert for adverse reactions and drug interactions.
- Monitor glucose level regularly in patient with diabetes. Beta blockade may inhibit glycogenolysis and signs and symptoms of hypoglycemia (such as tachycardia and blood pressure changes).
- Evaluate patient's and family's understanding of drug therapy.

Nursing diagnoses

- Risk for injury related to presence of hypertension
- Decreased cardiac output related to drug-induced adverse CV reactions
- Deficient knowledge related to drug therapy

Planning and implementation

ALERT: Never discontinue drug abruptly; angina pectoris may occur in patients with unrecognized coronary artery disease. Obtain guidelines from prescriber for how dose should be tapered before discontinuing drug.

- Advise anesthesiologist when surgical patient is receiving a beta blocker so that isoproterenol or dobutamine can be made readily available for reversal of drug's cardiac effects.
- Beta blockers may mask tachycardia caused by hyperthyroidism. In patients with suspected thyrotoxicosis, withdraw beta blocker gradually to avoid thyroid storm.

Patient teaching

- Explain importance of taking drug as prescribed, even when feeling well. Tell patient not to discontinue drug suddenly but to call prescriber if unpleasant adverse reactions occur.
- Teach patient signs and symptoms of heart failure, including shortness of breath or difficulty breathing, unusually fast heartbeat, cough, or fatigue with exertion, and tell patient to report them immediately.
- If patient uses ophthalmic drops, tell him to shake well before instilling and to store at room temperature.

Evaluation

- Patient's blood pressure is within normal limits.
- Patient's cardiac output remains unchanged throughout therapy.
- Patient and family state understanding of drug therapy.

bethanechol chloride

(beh-THAN-eh-kol KLOR-ighd)
Duvoid

Pharmacologic class: cholinergic agonist
Therapeutic class: urinary tract stimulant
Pregnancy risk category: C

Indications and dosages

▶ **Acute postoperative and postpartum nonobstructive (functional) urinary retention, neurogenic atony of urinary bladder with urinary retention.** *Adults:* 10 to 50 mg P.O. b.i.d. to q.i.d. When used for urine retention, some patients may need 50 to 100 mg P.O. per dose. Use such doses with extreme caution. Or, 2.575 mg S.C. initially, followed by repeat dose q 15 to 30 minutes up to a maximum of 4 doses to determine minimal effective dose. Then use minimal effective dose q 6 to 8 hours. All doses must be adjusted individually.

▶ **To restore bladder function in patients with chronic neurogenic bladder.** *Adults:* 7.5 to 10 mg S.C. q 4 hours around the clock. Dosage adjustments are based on residual urine measurements.

▶ **Bladder dysfunction caused by phenothiazines‡.** *Adults:* 50 to 100 mg P.O. q.i.d.

▶ **To diagnosis flaccid or atonic neurogenic bladder‡.** *Adults:* 2.5 mg. S.C. as a single dose.

Contraindications and precautions

• Contraindicated when increased muscle activity of GI or urinary tract is harmful. Also contraindicated in patients hypersensitive to drug or its components and in those with hyperthyroidism, peptic ulceration, latent or active bronchial asthma, pronounced bradycardia or hypotension, vasomotor instability, cardiac or coronary artery disease, seizure disorder, Parkinson's disease, spastic GI disturbances, acute inflammatory lesions of GI tract, peritonitis, mechanical obstruction of GI or urinary tract, marked vagotonia, or uncertain strength or integrity of bladder wall.

Lifespan: In pregnant women, use cautiously. Breast-feeding should be discontinued. In children, safety of drug hasn't been established.

Adverse reactions

CNS: headache, malaise.
CV: ***bradycardia,*** hypotension, flushing, reflex tachycardia.
EENT: lacrimation, miosis.
GI: *abdominal cramps, diarrhea,* excessive salivation, nausea, vomiting, belching, borborygmi, esophageal spasms.
GU: urinary urgency.
Respiratory: ***bronchoconstriction,*** increased bronchial secretions.
Skin: sweating.

Interactions

Drug-drug. *Anticholinergics, atropine, procainamide, quinidine:* May reverse cholinergic effects. Watch for lack of drug effect.
Anticholinesterases, cholinergic agonists: May cause additive effects or increase toxicity. Avoid use together.
Ganglionic blockers: May cause severe abdominal pain followed by a critical drop in blood pressure. Avoid use together.

Effects on lab test results

• May increase liver enzyme, amylase, and lipase levels.

Pharmacokinetics

Absorption: Poor after P.O. administration; unknown after S.C. administration.
Distribution: Unknown.
Metabolism: Unknown.
Excretion: Unknown.

Route	Onset	Peak	Duration
P.O.	30-90 min	About 1 hr	1-6 hr
S.C.	5-15 min	5-30 min	About 2 hr

Pharmacodynamics

Chemical effect: Directly stimulates cholinergic receptors, mimicking action of acetylcholine.
Therapeutic effect: Relieves urinary retention.

Available forms

Injection: 5.15 mg/ml
Tablets: 5 mg, 10 mg, 25 mg, 50 mg

NURSING PROCESS

Assessment

• Obtain history of patient's bladder condition before therapy, and reassess regularly throughout therapy.
• Be alert for adverse reactions and drug interactions.
• Evaluate patient's and family's understanding of drug therapy.

Nursing diagnoses

• Impaired urinary elimination related to underlying bladder condition
• Ineffective breathing pattern related to drug-induced bronchoconstriction
• Deficient knowledge related to drug therapy

Planning and implementation

• **P.O. use:** Give drug on empty stomach to prevent nausea and vomiting.
• **S.C. use:** Follow normal protocol.
ALERT: Never give I.V. or I.M.

Reactions may be *common,* uncommon, ***life-threatening***, or COMMON AND LIFE-THREATENING.

• Always have atropine injection readily available and be prepared to give 0.5 mg S.C. or slow I.V. push. Provide respiratory support as needed.

Patient teaching

• Advise patient to take oral dose on an empty stomach.
• Tell patient to report breathing difficulty immediately.

☑ Evaluation

• Patient is able to void without urine retention.
• Patient's respiratory function remains normal during therapy.
• Patient and family state understanding of drug therapy.

bexarotene
(bex-AHR-oh-teen)
Targretin

Pharmacologic class: retinoid (selective retinoid X receptor activator)
Therapeutic class: tumor cell growth inhibitor
Pregnancy risk category: X

Indications and dosages

▶ **Cutaneous effects of cutaneous T-cell lymphoma in patients refractory to at least one previous systemic therapy.** *Adults:* 300 mg/m² P.O. daily as a single dose with a meal. If no response after 8 weeks, increase to 400 mg/m² daily. Adjust dose to 200 mg/m² daily, and then to 100 mg/m² daily if toxicity occurs, or drug may be temporarily suspended. When toxicity is controlled, dosage may be carefully readjusted upward. Or, for topical application, apply a sufficient amount of 1% gel and rub into the affected areas once q other day, for the first week. Allow gel to dry before applying a dressing. Then, increase at weekly intervals to b.i.d., t.i.d., and q.i.d., according to the individual skin response.
Patients with hepatic insufficiency: Lower doses may be needed. If toxicity occurs, dose may be adjusted to 200 mg/m² daily, then to 100 mg/m² daily, or drug may be temporarily suspended. When toxicity is controlled, doses may be carefully readjusted upward.

Contraindications and precautions

• Contraindicated in patients hypersensitive to drug or its components.
• Drug isn't recommended for patients taking drugs that increase triglyceride levels or cause pancreatic toxicity. Also not recommended for patients who have risk factors for pancreatitis, such as prior pancreatitis, uncontrolled hyperlipidemia, excessive alcohol consumption, uncontrolled diabetes mellitus, or biliary tract disease.
• Use cautiously in patients with hepatic insufficiency, and in patients hypersensitive to retinoids.
Lifespan: In pregnant women, drug is contraindicated. In women of childbearing potential, use cautiously.

Adverse reactions

CNS: fever, *headache,* insomnia, *asthenia,* fatigue, syncope, depression, agitation, ataxia, ***CVA,*** confusion, dizziness, hyperesthesia, hypoesthesia, neuropathy.
CV: *peripheral edema,* chest pain, ***hemorrhage,*** hypertension, angina, ***heart failure,*** tachycardia.
EENT: cataracts, pharyngitis, rhinitis, dry eyes, conjunctivitis, ear pain, blepharitis, corneal lesion, keratitis, otitis externa, visual field defect.
GI: *nausea,* diarrhea, vomiting, anorexia, ***pancreatitis,*** *abdominal pain,* constipation, dry mouth, flatulence, colitis, dyspepsia, cheilitis, gastroenteritis, gingivitis, melena.
GU: albuminuria, hematuria, incontinence, urinary tract infection, urinary urgency, dysuria, abnormal kidney function.
Hematologic: ***leukopenia,*** anemia, eosinophilia, thrombocythemia, lymphocytosis, ***thrombocytopenia.***
Hepatic: bilirubinemia, ***liver failure.***
Metabolic: *hyperlipemia, hypercholesteremia, hypothyroidism,* hyperglycemia, hypoproteinemia, hypocalcemia, hyponatremia, weight change.
Musculoskeletal: arthralgia, myalgia, back pain, bone pain, myasthenia, arthrosis.
Respiratory: pneumonia, dyspnea, hemoptysis, pleural effusion, bronchitis, cough, ***lung edema, hypoxia.***
Skin: (P.O.) *rash, dry skin, exfoliative dermatitis, alopecia, photosensitivity,* pruritus, cellulitis, acne, skin ulcer, skin nodule; **(Topical)**

contact dermatitis, pain, skin disorders, pruritus, rash.
Other: breast pain, *infection,* chills, flulike syndrome, ***sepsis.***

Interactions

Drug-drug. *Dietylotoluamide (DEET):* Increased DEET toxicity observed in animals with gel form. Avoid use together.
Erythromycin, gemfibrozil, itraconazole, ketoconazole, other inhibitors of cytochrome P-450 3A4: Increased plasma levels of bexarotene. Avoid use together.
Insulin, sulfonylureas: Enhanced hypoglycemic action of these drugs, resulting in hypoglycemia in patients with diabetes mellitus. Use together cautiously.
Phenobarbital, phenytoin, rifampin, other inducers of cytochrome P-450 3A4: Decreased plasma levels of bexarotene. Avoid use together.
Vitamin A preparations: Increased potential for vitamin A toxicity. Avoid vitamin A supplements.
Drug-food. *Any food:* Enhances drug absorption. Give with food.
Grapefruit juice: May inhibit cytochrome P-450 3A4. Don't give together.
Drug-lifestyle. *Sun exposure:* Retinoids may cause photosensitivity. Advise patient to minimize exposure to sunlight and artificial ultraviolet light.

Effects on lab test results

- May increase creatinine, LDH, AST, ALT, bilirubin, amylase, lipid, cholesterol, and glucose levels. May decrease protein, calcium, and sodium levels.
- May increase eosinophil count. May decrease hemoglobin, hematocrit, and WBC and lymphocyte counts. May alter platelet count.

Pharmacokinetics

Absorption: Increased if given with a meal that contains fat when given P.O. Unknown for topical use.
Distribution: Drug is more than 99% bound to plasma proteins. Low plasma levels with topical use.
Metabolism: Metabolized through oxidative pathways, primarily by the cytochrome P-450 3A4 system, to four metabolites. These may maintain retinoid receptor activity.
Excretion: Thought to be eliminated primarily through the hepatobiliary system. *Terminal half-life:* 7 hours.

Route	Onset	Peak	Duration
P.O., topical	Unknown	Unknown	Unknown

Pharmacodynamics

Chemical effect: Selectively binds and activates retinoid X receptor subtypes. Once activated, these receptors function as transcription factors that regulate the expression of genes that control cellular differentiation and proliferation. In vitro, bexarotene inhibits the growth of some tumor cell lines of hematopoietic and squamous cell origin; in vivo, it induces tumor cell regression in some animal models. The exact mechanism of action in the treatment of cutaneous T-cell lymphoma is unknown.
Therapeutic effect: Inhibits tumor growth in cutaneous T-cell lymphoma.

Available forms

Capsules: 75 mg
Topical gel: 1%

NURSING PROCESS

Assessment

- Assess women of childbearing potential carefully; they should use effective contraception at least 1 month before therapy starts, during therapy, and for at least 1 month after therapy stops. During therapy, patient should use two reliable forms of contraception simultaneously unless abstinence is the chosen method. A negative pregnancy test should be obtained within 1 week before therapy starts and monthly during therapy.
- Men with sexual partners who are pregnant, who could be pregnant, or who could become pregnant must use condoms during sexual intercourse during therapy and for at least 1 month after therapy ends.
- Obtain total cholesterol, high-density lipoprotein, and triglyceride levels when therapy starts, weekly until the lipid response is established (2 to 4 weeks) and at 8-week intervals thereafter. Elevated triglycerides during treatment should be treated with antilipemic therapy and the dose of bexarotene reduced or suspended as needed.

- Obtain baseline thyroid function tests, and monitor results during treatment.
- Monitor WBC with differential at baseline and periodically during treatment.
- Monitor liver function test results at baseline and after 1, 2, and 4 weeks of treatment. If patient is stable, monitor test results every 8 weeks during treatment. The prescriber may consider suspending treatment if results are three times the upper limit of normal.
- Obtain ophthalmologic evaluation for cataracts in patients who experience visual difficulties.
- Evaluate patient's and family's knowledge of drug therapy.

Nursing diagnoses

- Ineffective health maintenance related to underlying condition
- Risk for injury related to drug-induced adverse reactions
- Deficient knowledge related to drug therapy

Planning and implementation

- Lower doses may be needed for patients with hepatic insufficiency.
- Give drug with food for better absorption, although not with grapefruit or grapefruit juice.
- Start therapy on the second or third day of a normal menstrual period.
- No more than a 1-month supply of bexarotene should be given to a patient of childbearing potential so the results of pregnancy testing can be assessed regularly and the patient can be reminded to avoid pregnancy.
- Bexarotene therapy may increase CA 125 assay values in patients with ovarian cancer.

Patient teaching

- Advise patient to minimize unprotected or prolonged exposure to sunlight or artificial UV light.
- Teach patient that it may take several capsules to make the necessary dose and that these capsules should all be taken at the same time and with a meal.
- Teach women of childbearing potential the dangers of becoming pregnant while taking bexarotene and the need for monthly pregnancy tests.
- Explain the need for obtaining baseline laboratory tests and for periodic monitoring of these tests.
- Tell patient to report any visual changes.
- Advise patient to wait at least 20 minutes after bathing before applying the gel and to avoid the use of occlusive dressings.
- Tell patient to avoid gel contact with healthy skin or mucous membranes.
- Tell patient to allow the gel to dry for 5 to 10 minutes before covering area with clothing.

Evaluation

- Patient exhibits positive response to therapy.
- Patient has no injury as a result of drug-induced adverse reactions.
- Patient and family state understanding of drug therapy.

bimatoprost

(by-MAT-oh-prost)
Lumigan

Pharmacologic classification: prostaglandin analogue
Therapeutic classification: antiglaucoma agent, ocular antihypertensive
Pregnancy risk category: C

Indications and dosages

▶ **Reduction of elevated intraocular pressure (IOP) in patients with open-angle glaucoma or ocular hypertension who are intolerant of or unresponsive to other IOP-lowering drugs.** *Adults:* Instill 1 drop in the conjunctival sac of the affected eye or eyes once daily in the evening.

Contraindications and precautions

- Contraindicated in patients hypersensitive to bimatoprost, benzalkonium chloride, or other ingredients of this product. Also contraindicated in patients with angle-closure glaucoma, inflammatory glaucoma, or neovascular glaucoma.
- Use cautiously in patients with renal or hepatic impairment, active intraocular inflammation (iritis or uveitis), aphakic patients, pseudophakic patients with a torn posterior lens capsule, or patients at risk for macular edema.

Lifespan: In pregnant women, drug isn't recommended. In breast-feeding women, use cautiously because it's unknown whether drug appears in breast milk. In children, safety and efficacy haven't been established.

Adverse reactions

CNS: headache, asthenia.
EENT: *conjunctival hyperemia, growth of eyelashes, ocular pruritus,* ocular dryness, visual disturbance, ocular burning, foreign body sensation, eye pain, pigmentation of the periocular skin, blepharitis, cataract, superficial punctate keratitis, eyelid erythema, ocular irritation, eyelash darkening, eye discharge, tearing, photophobia, allergic conjunctivitis, asthenopia, increased iris pigmentation, conjunctival edema, gradual change in eye color.
Respiratory: *upper respiratory tract infection.*
Skin: hirsutism.
Other: *infection.*

Interactions

None significant.

Effects on lab test results

• May cause abnormal liver function test values.

Pharmacokinetics

Absorption: Absorbed through the cornea.
Distribution: Moderately distributed into tissues. Bimatoprost resides mainly in plasma, and about 12% remains unbound in plasma.
Metabolism: Mainly metabolized by oxidation.
Excretion: Metabolites are 67% eliminated in urine; 25% are eliminated in feces.

Route	Onset	Peak	Duration
Ophthalmic	Unknown	10 min	1½ hr

Pharmacodynamics

Chemical effect: Bimatoprost is a prostamide, which is a synthetic analog of prostaglandin. It selectively mimics the effects of naturally occurring prostaglandins. Bimatoprost is believed to lower IOP by increasing the outflow of aqueous humor through the trabecular meshwork and uveoscleral routes.
Therapeutic effect: Reduces intraocular pressure.

Available forms

Ophthalmic solution: 0.03%

NURSING PROCESS

Assessment

ALERT: Perform complete medication history. If more than one ophthalmic drug is being used, the drugs should be given at least 5 minutes apart.
• Assess patient's underlying condition and eyes before giving eyedrops.
• Monitor patient for excessive ocular irritation and evaluate the success of treatment.
• Evaluate patient's and family's knowledge of drug therapy and administration.

Nursing diagnoses

• Risk for injury to the eye related to improper administration of drug
• Impaired visual perception related to underlying condition
• Deficient knowledge related to bimatoprost therapy

Planning and implementation

ALERT: Contact lenses must be removed before using solution. Lenses may be reinserted 15 minutes after administration.
• Don't touch the tip of the dropper to the eye. Avoid contamination to the dropper.
• Apply light pressure on lacrimal sac for 1 minute after instillation to minimize systemic absorption of the drug.
• Store drug in original container at 59° to 77° F (15° to 25°C).
• Be aware that an increase in pigmentation of the iris, eyelid, and eyelashes may occur, as well as growth of the eyelashes.

Patient teaching

• Explain to patients receiving treatment in only one eye the possibility for increased brown pigmentation of iris, eyelid skin darkening, and increased length, thickness, pigmentation, or number of lashes in the treated eye.
• Teach patient to instill drops properly and advise him to wash hands before and after instilling solution. Warn him not to touch tip of dropper to eye or surrounding tissue.
• If eye trauma or infection occurs or if eye surgery is needed, tell patient to seek immediate medical advice before continuing to use multidose container.
• Urge patient to immediately report conjunctivitis or lid reactions to prescriber.

Evaluation

- Patient demonstrates proper administration of the drug, and no injury occurs.
- Patient's underlying eye condition responds positively to drug.
- Patient and family state understanding of drug therapy.

bisacodyl

(bigh-suh-KOH-dil)

Bisac-Evac†, Bisacolax♦†, Bisalax◇, Bisco-Lax**†, Bisacodyl Uniserts†, Carter's Little Pills†, Correctol†, Dacodyl†, Deficol†, Dulcolax†, Durolax◇, Feen-a-mint†, Fleet Bisacodyl†, Fleet Prep Kit†, Fleet Laxative†, Laxit♦†, Modane†, Theralax†

Pharmacologic class: diphenylmethane derivative
Therapeutic class: stimulant laxative
Pregnancy risk category: NR

Indications and dosages

▶ **Chronic constipation; preparation for childbirth, surgery, or rectal or bowel examination.** *Adults and children age 12 and older:* 10 to 15 mg P.O. in evening or before breakfast; maximum 30 mg P.O. For evacuation before examination or surgery, 10 mg P.R.
Children ages 6 to 12: 5 mg P.O. or P.R. h.s. or before breakfast.

Contraindications and precautions

- Contraindicated in patients hypersensitive to drug and in those with rectal bleeding, gastroenteritis, intestinal obstruction, or symptoms of appendicitis or acute surgical abdomen, such as abdominal pain, nausea, or vomiting.

Lifespan: In pregnant women, use cautiously.

Adverse reactions

GI: *nausea, vomiting, abdominal cramps,* diarrhea (with high doses), *burning sensation in rectum* (with suppositories), protein-losing enteropathy (with excessive use), laxative dependence (with long-term or excessive use).
Metabolic: *alkalosis,* hypokalemia, fluid and electrolyte imbalance.
Musculoskeletal: tetany, muscle weakness (with excessive use).

Interactions

Drug-drug. *Antacids:* May cause gastric irritation or dyspepsia from premature dissolution of enteric coating. Avoid use together.
Drug-food. *Milk:* May cause gastric irritation or dyspepsia from premature dissolution of enteric coating. Avoid use together.

Effects on lab test results

- May increase phosphate and sodium levels. May decrease calcium, magnesium, and potassium levels.

Pharmacokinetics

Absorption: Minimal.
Distribution: Distributed locally.
Metabolism: Up to 15% of P.O. dose may enter enterohepatic circulation.
Excretion: Excreted primarily in feces; some excreted in urine.

Route	Onset	Peak	Duration
P.O.	6-12 hr	Variable	Variable
P.R.	15-60 min	Variable	Variable

Pharmacodynamics

Chemical effect: Increases peristalsis, probably by acting directly on smooth muscle of intestine. Thought to irritate musculature or stimulate colonic intramural plexus. Also promotes fluid accumulation in colon and small intestine.
Therapeutic effect: Relieves constipation.

Available forms

Enema: 0.33 mg/dl†, 10 mg/5 ml (microenema)◇, 10 mg/30 ml
Powder for rectal solution (bisacodyl tannex): 1.5 mg bisacodyl and 2.5 g tannic acid
Suppositories: 10 mg†
Tablets (enteric-coated): 5 mg†

NURSING PROCESS

Assessment

- Obtain history of bowel disorder, GI status, fluid intake, nutritional status, exercise habits, and normal patterns of elimination.
- Monitor effectiveness by checking frequency and characteristics of stools.
- Be alert for adverse reactions and drug interactions.

• Auscultate bowel sounds at least once per shift. Check for pain and cramping.
• Evaluate patient's and family's understanding of drug therapy.

Nursing diagnoses

• Constipation related to interruption of normal pattern of elimination
• Acute pain related to drug-induced abdominal cramps
• Deficient knowledge related to drug therapy

Planning and implementation

• **P.O. use:** Don't give tablets within 60 minutes of milk or antacid.
• **P.R. use:** Insert suppository as high as possible into rectum, and try to position suppository against rectal wall. Avoid embedding within fecal material because this may delay onset of action.
• Time administration of drug so as not to interfere with scheduled activities or sleep. Soft, formed stool usually produced 15 to 60 minutes after P.R. administration.
• Tablets and suppositories are used together to clean colon before and after surgery and before barium enema.
• Store tablets and suppositories below 86° F (30° C).

Patient teaching

• Advise patient to swallow enteric-coated tablet whole to avoid GI irritation. Tell him not to take tablet within 1 hour of milk or antacid.
• Advise patient to report adverse effects to prescriber.
• Teach patient about dietary sources of fiber, including bran and other cereals, fresh fruit, and vegetables.
• Caution patient against excessive use of drug.

Evaluation

• Patient reports return of normal bowel pattern of elimination.
• Patient is free from abdominal pain and cramping.
• Patient and family state understanding of drug therapy.

bismuth subgallate

(BIS-muth sub-GAL-ayt)
Devrom

bismuth subsalicylate

Maximum Strength Pepto-Bismol†, Pepto-Bismol†

Pharmacologic class: adsorbent
Therapeutic class: antidiarrheal
Pregnancy risk category: NR

Indications and dosages

▶ **To control fecal odors in colostomy, ileostomy, or incontinence. *subgallate.***
Adults: 1 to 2 tablets P.O. t.i.d. with meals. Tablet can be chewed or swallowed whole.
▶ **Mild, nonspecific diarrhea. *subsalicylate.***
Adults and children older than age 12: 30 ml or 2 tablets P.O. q 30 to 60 minutes up to maximum of eight doses and for no longer than 2 days.
Children ages 3 to 5: 5 ml or ⅓ tablet P.O.
Children ages 6 to 8: 10 ml or ⅔ tablet P.O.
Children ages 9 to 12: 15 ml or 1 tablet P.O.

Children's doses may be given q 30 minutes to 1 hour up to a maximum of 8 doses in 24 hours and for no longer than 2 days.

Contraindications and precautions

• Contraindicated in patients hypersensitive to salicylates.
• Use cautiously in patients already taking aspirin.
Lifespan: In pregnant or breast-feeding women, use cautiously.

Adverse reactions

GI: temporary darkening of tongue and stools.
Other: salicylism (with high doses).

Interactions

Drug-drug. *Aspirin, other salicylates:* May increase risk of salicylate toxicity. Monitor patient closely.
Oral anticoagulants, oral antidiabetics: Theoretical risk of increased effects of these drugs after high doses of bismuth subsalicylate. Monitor patient closely.
Probenecid: Theoretical risk of decreased uricosuric effects after high doses of bismuth subsalicylate. Monitor patient closely.

Tetracycline: Decreases tetracycline absorption. Give drugs at least 2 hours apart.

Effects on lab test results

None reported.

Pharmacokinetics

Absorption: Poor; significant salicylate absorption may occur after using bismuth subsalicylate.
Distribution: Distributed locally in gut.
Metabolism: Metabolized minimally.
Excretion: Bismuth subsalicylate is excreted in urine.

Route	Onset	Peak	Duration
P.O.	1 hr	Unknown	Unknown

Pharmacodynamics

Chemical effect: Unknown; has mild water-binding capacity. Also may adsorb toxins and provide protective coating for mucosa.
Therapeutic effect: Relieves diarrhea.

Available forms

bismuth subgallate
Tablets (chewable): 200 mg†
bismuth subsalicylate
Oral suspension: 262.5 mg/15 ml†, 525 mg/15 ml†
Tablets (chewable): 262.5 mg†

NURSING PROCESS

Assessment

- Obtain history of patient's bowel disorder, GI status, and frequency of loose stools before therapy.
- Monitor drug's effectiveness by checking frequency and characteristics of stools.
- Be alert for adverse reactions and drug interactions.
- Check patient's hearing if he takes drug in large doses.
- Evaluate patient's and family's understanding of drug therapy.

Nursing diagnoses

- Diarrhea related to underlying GI condition
- Disturbed sensory perception (auditory) related to drug-induced salicylism
- Deficient knowledge related to drug therapy

Planning and implementation

- Avoid use before GI radiologic procedures because bismuth is radiopaque and may interfere with X-rays.
- Read label carefully because dosage varies with form of drug.
- Discontinue therapy and notify prescriber if tinnitus occurs.

Patient teaching

- Advise patient that drug contains large amount of salicylate. (Each tablet contains 102 mg; regular-strength liquid contains 130 mg/15 ml, and extra-strength liquid contains 230 mg/15 ml.)
- Instruct patient to chew tablets well or to shake liquid before measuring dose.
- Tell patient to report diarrhea that persists for more than 2 days or is accompanied by high fever.
- Tell patient to consult with prescriber before giving bismuth subsalicylate to children or teenagers who have or are recovering from flu or chickenpox.
- Inform patient that both liquid and tablet forms of Pepto-Bismol are effective against traveler's diarrhea. Tablets may be more convenient to carry.
- Tell patient that any darkening of stool or the tongue is temporary.

Evaluation

- Patient reports decrease or absence of loose stools.
- Patient remains free from signs and symptoms of salicylism.
- Patient and family state understanding of drug therapy.
- Patient reports being free from heartburn and indigestion.

bisoprolol fumarate

(bis-OP-roh-lol FYOO-muh-rayt)
Zebeta

Pharmacologic class: beta blocker
Therapeutic class: antihypertensive
Pregnancy risk category: C

Indications and dosages

▶ **Hypertension.** *Adults:* Initially, 5 mg P.O. once daily. If response is inadequate, increase to 10 mg or 20 mg P.O. daily; 20 mg is maximum recommended dosage.

Patients with renal impairment or a creatinine clearance of less than 40 ml/minute or hepatic dysfunction, cirrhosis, or hepatitis: Start with 2.5 mg P.O. daily. Subsequent dosage adjustment is done cautiously.

▶ **Heart failure‡.** *Adults:* 1.25 mg P.O. daily for 2 to 4 weeks. This low-dose strength isn't available in the U.S. If dose is tolerated, increase dose to 2.5 mg daily for 2 to 4 weeks. Subsequent doses can be doubled q 2 to 4 weeks, if tolerated.

Contraindications and precautions

- Contraindicated in patients hypersensitive to drug and in those with cardiogenic shock, overt cardiac failure, marked sinus bradycardia, or second- or third-degree AV block.
- Use cautiously in patients with bronchospastic disease. These patients should avoid beta blockers because blockade of $beta_1$-receptors isn't absolute and blockage of pulmonary $beta_2$-receptors may result in worsening of symptoms. A bronchodilator should be made available. Also use cautiously in patients with diabetes, peripheral vascular disease, or thyroid disease; and in those with history of heart failure.

Lifespan: In pregnant or breast-feeding women, use cautiously. In children, safety of drug hasn't been established.

Adverse reactions

CNS: asthenia, fatigue, dizziness, headache, hypoesthesia, vivid dreams, depression, insomnia.
CV: ***bradycardia,*** peripheral edema, chest pain, ***heart failure.***
EENT: pharyngitis, rhinitis, sinusitis.
GI: nausea, vomiting, diarrhea, dry mouth.
Musculoskeletal: arthralgia.
Respiratory: cough, dyspnea.
Skin: sweating.

Interactions

Drug-drug. *Beta blockers:* May cause extreme hypotension. Don't use together.
Calcium channel blockers: May cause myocardial depression and AV conductive inhibition. Monitor ECG closely.
Guanethidine, reserpine: Can cause hypotension. Monitor patient closely.
NSAIDs: May decrease antihypertensive effect. Monitor blood pressure and adjust dosage.
Rifampin: May increase metabolic clearance of bisoprolol. Monitor patient.

Effects on lab test results

None reported.

Pharmacokinetics

Absorption: Bioavailability after 10-mg dose is about 80%.
Distribution: About 30% of drug binds to serum proteins.
Metabolism: First-pass metabolism of drug is about 20%.
Excretion: Excreted equally by renal and nonrenal pathways, with about 50% of dose appearing unchanged in urine and remainder appearing as inactive metabolites. Less than 2% of dose is excreted in feces. *Half-life:* 9 to 12 hours.

Route	Onset	Peak	Duration
P.O.	Unknown	2-4 hr	About 24 hr

Pharmacodynamics

Chemical effect: Not completely defined. Bisoprolol is a $beta_1$-selective blocker that decreases myocardial contractility, heart rate, and cardiac output; lowers blood pressure; and reduces myocardial oxygen consumption.
Therapeutic effect: Decreases blood pressure.

Available forms

Tablets: 5 mg, 10 mg

NURSING PROCESS

Assessment

- Obtain history of patient's hypertensive status before therapy, and check blood pressure regularly throughout therapy.
- Be alert for adverse reactions and drug interactions.
- Monitor patient's hydration status if adverse GI reactions occur.
- Closely monitor glucose level in patient with diabetes. Beta blockers may mask some evidence of hypoglycemia, such as tachycardia.

• Evaluate patient's and family's understanding of drug therapy.

Nursing diagnoses

• Risk for injury related to presence of hypertension
• Risk for deficient fluid volume related to drug-induced adverse GI reactions
• Deficient knowledge related to drug therapy

Planning and implementation

• A $beta_2$-agonist (bronchodilator) should be available for patients with bronchospastic disease.

ALERT: Don't discontinue drug abruptly because angina may occur in patients with unrecognized coronary artery disease.

Patient teaching

• Tell patient to take drug as prescribed, even when he's feeling better. Warn him that abruptly discontinuing drug can worsen angina and precipitate MI. Explain that drug must be withdrawn gradually over 1 to 2 weeks.
• Instruct patient to call prescriber if adverse reactions occur.
• Tell patient with diabetes to closely monitor glucose levels.
• Tell patient to check with prescriber or pharmacist before taking OTC medications or herbal remedies.

Evaluation

• Patient's blood pressure is normal.
• Patient maintains adequate fluid balance throughout therapy.
• Patient and family state understanding of drug therapy.

bivalirudin

(bye-VAL-ih-roo-din)
Angiomax

Pharmacologic classification: direct thrombin inhibitor
Therapeutic classification: anticoagulant
Pregnancy risk category: B

Indications and dosages

▶ **Decrease risk of acute ischemic complications in patients with unstable angina who are undergoing percutaneous transluminal coronary angioplasty (PTCA), given with aspirin.** *Adults:* 1 mg/kg I.V. bolus just before PTCA; then begin 4-hour I.V. infusion at 2.5 mg/kg per hour. After the first 4-hour infusion, another I.V. infusion at 0.2 mg/kg per hour for up to 20 hours may be given as needed. Give with 300 to 325 mg of aspirin. *Patients with renal impairment:* If GFR is 30 to 59 ml/minute, reduce dosage by 20%. If GFR is 10 to 29 ml/minute, reduce dosage by 60%. *Dialysis-dependent patients (off dialysis):* Reduce dose by 90%.

Contraindications and precautions

• Contraindicated in patients hypersensitive to bivalirudin or its components and in patients with active major bleeding. Don't use drug in patients with unstable angina who aren't undergoing PTCA or in patients with other acute coronary conditions, or who aren't taking aspirin.
• Use cautiously in patients with heparin-induced thrombocytopenia or heparin-induced thrombocytopenia-thrombosis syndrome and in patients with an increased risk of bleeding.

Lifespan: In breast-feeding women, use cautiously. It isn't known whether bivalirudin appears in breast milk. In children, safety and efficacy haven't been established. Elderly patients are more likely to have puncture site hemorrhage and catheterization site hematoma.

Adverse reactions

CNS: ***cerebral ischemia,*** anxiety, *headache,* insomnia, nervousness, fever, *pain,* confusion.
CV: ***bradycardia,*** hypertension, *hypotension,* ***syncope, ventricular fibrillation,*** vascular anomaly.
GI: abdominal pain, dyspepsia, *nausea,* vomiting.
GU: urinary retention, ***kidney failure,*** oliguria.
Hematologic: ***severe, spontaneous bleeding*** (cerebral, retroperitoneal, GU, GI), ***arterial site hemorrhage.***
Musculoskeletal: *back pain,* pelvic pain, facial paralysis.
Respiratory: ***lung edema.***
Other: pain at injection site, infection, ***sepsis.***

Interactions

Drug-drug. *Glycoprotein IIb/IIIa platelet inhibitors:* Safety and effectiveness haven't been established. Avoid using together.
Heparin, warfarin, other oral anticoagulants: Increases risk of bleeding. Use together cautiously. If using low molecular weight heparin, discontinue use at least 8 hours before giving bivalirudin.
Alteplase, amiodarone HCl, amphotericin B, chlorpromazine HCl, diazepam, prochlorperazine edisylate, reteplase, streptokinase, vancomycin HCl: Incompatible with bivalirudin and causes haze formation, microparticulate formation, or gross precipitation. Avoid giving in the same I.V. line.

Effects on lab test results

- May increase ACT, APTT, thrombin time, and PT.

Pharmacokinetics

Absorption: Administered I.V.
Distribution: Binds rapidly to thrombin and has a rapid onset of action.
Metabolism: Rapidly cleared from plasma by a combination of renal mechanisms and proteolytic cleavage.
Excretion: Eliminated renally. Total body clearance is similar in patients with normal renal function and mild renal impairment. Clearance is reduced about 20% in patients with moderate and severe renal impairment and is reduced about 80% in dialysis-dependent patients. Bivalirudin is hemodialyzable. *Half-life:* 25 minutes in patients with normal renal function.

Route	Onset	Peak	Duration
I.V.	Rapid	Immediate	Duration of infusion

Pharmacodynamics

Chemical effect: Highly specific for thrombin and directly inhibits both clot-bound and circulating thrombin. By inhibiting thrombin, bivalirudin prevents generation of fibrin and further activation of the clotting cascade and inhibits thrombin-induced platelet activation, granule release, and aggregation. Bivalirudin doesn't require the presence of antithrombin to produce an anticoagulant effect.
Therapeutic effect: Prevents blood clots.

Available forms

Injection: 250-mg vial

NURSING PROCESS

Assessment

- Obtain and monitor baseline coagulation tests and hemoglobin and hematocrit before and throughout drug therapy.
- Monitor effectiveness by measuring APTT, PT, and thrombin time values regularly.
- Monitor venipuncture sites for bleeding, hematoma, or inflammation.
- Be alert for any drug-induced adverse reactions.

ALERT: If the patient has an unexplained drop in hematocrit, blood pressure, or other unexplained symptom, consider the possibility of hemorrhage.

- Assess access site for bleeding regularly.
- Evaluate patient's and family's knowledge of anticoagulant drug therapy.

Nursing diagnoses

- Risk for injury related to potential acute ischemic event caused by impaired cardiovascular status
- Ineffective protection related to increased risk of bleeding from anticoagulant therapy
- Deficient knowledge related to drug therapy

Planning and implementation

- Patients with renal failure require reduced dosage.
- Don't give by I.M. route.
- Reconstitute each 250-mg vial with 5 ml of sterile water for injection. Further dilute each reconstituted vial in 50 ml D_5W or normal saline solution to yield a final concentration of 5 mg/ml.
- To prepare low-rate infusion, further dilute each reconstituted vial in 500 ml D_5W or normal saline solution to yield a final concentration of 0.5 mg/ml.
- Don't mix other drugs with bivalirudin before or during administration.
- The prepared solution is stable and may be stored for up to 24 hours at 36° to 46° (2° to 8° C).

Patient teaching

- Advise patient that drug can cause bleeding. Urge patient to report any unusual bruising or bleeding (nosebleeds, bleeding gums, petechiae, and hematuria) or tarry or bloody stools immediately to a clinician.

- Caution patient to avoid other aspirin-containing drugs and drugs used to treat swelling or pain (such as Motrin, Naprosyn, Aleve).
- Advise patient to avoid activities that carry a risk of injury, and instruct patient to use a soft toothbrush and electric razor while taking bivalirudin.

Evaluation

- Patient doesn't suffer acute ischemic event after PTCA.
- Patient doesn't suffer drug-induced adverse reactions or bleeding.
- Patient and family state understanding of drug therapy.

bleomycin sulfate

(blee-oh-MIGH-sin SUL-fayt)
Blenoxane

Pharmacologic class: antibiotic, antineoplastic (specific to G2 and M phases of cell cycle)
Therapeutic class: antineoplastic
Pregnancy risk category: D

Indications and dosages

▶ **Hodgkin's lymphoma, squamous cell carcinoma, non-Hodgkin's lymphoma, testicular cancer.** *Adults:* 10 to 20 units/m^2 (0.25 to 0.5 units/kg) I.V., I.M., or S.C. once or twice weekly. After 50% response in patients with Hodgkin's disease, maintenance dosage is 1 unit I.V. or I.M. daily or 5 units I.V. or I.M. weekly.

▶ **Malignant pleural effusion, prevention of recurrent pleural effusions or to manage pneumothorax related to AIDS or *Pneumocystis carinii* pneumonia.** *Adults:* 60 units given as a single-dose bolus in 50 to 100 ml of normal saline solution by intrapleural injection through a thoracostomy tube. Leave in for 4 hours, then drain and resume suction. Maximum dose is 1 unit/kg.
Geriatric patients receiving intrapleural injection: Don't exceed 40 units/m^2.

▶ **AIDS-related Kaposi's sarcoma‡.** *Adults:* 20 units/m^2 daily I.V. continuously over 72 hours q 3 weeks.

Contraindications and precautions

- Contraindicated in patients hypersensitive to drug.
- Use cautiously in patients with renal or pulmonary impairment.

Lifespan: In pregnant or breast-feeding women or in children, safety of drug hasn't been established.

Adverse reactions

CNS: hyperesthesia of scalp and fingers, headache, fever.
GI: *stomatitis, prolonged anorexia, nausea, vomiting,* diarrhea.
Hematologic: leukocytosis.
Musculoskeletal: swelling of interphalangeal joints.
Respiratory: PNEUMONITIS, ***pulmonary fibrosis, fine crackles, dyspnea, nonproductive cough.***
Skin: *reversible alopecia; erythema; vesiculation; hardening and discoloration of palmar and plantar skin;* desquamation of hands, feet, and pressure areas; *hyperpigmentation; acne.*
Other: ***hypersensitivity reactions (fever up to 106° F [41.1° C] with chills up to 5 hours after injection, anaphylaxis).***

Interactions

Drug-drug. *Cardiac glycosides:* May decrease digoxin level. Monitor patient closely for loss of therapeutic effect.
Phenytoin: May decrease phenytoin level. Monitor patient closely.

Effects on lab test results

- May increase uric acid level.
- May increase WBC count.

Pharmacokinetics

Absorption: I.M. administration results in lower levels than those produced by equivalent I.V. doses.
Distribution: Distributed widely into total body water, mainly in skin, lungs, kidneys, peritoneum, and lymphatic tissue.
Metabolism: Unknown; however, extensive tissue inactivation occurs in liver and kidneys, with much less in skin and lungs.

Excretion: Drug and its metabolites excreted primarily in urine. *Half-life:* 2 hours.

Route	Onset	Peak	Duration
I.V., I.M., S.C.	Unknown	Unknown	Unknown
Intrapleural	Unknown	Unknown	Unknown

Pharmacodynamics

Chemical effect: Unknown; thought to inhibit DNA synthesis and cause scission of single- and double-stranded DNA.
Therapeutic effect: Kills selected types of cancer cells.

Available forms

Injection: 15- and 30-unit vials (1 unit = 1 mg)

NURSING PROCESS

Assessment

- Obtain history of patient's overall physical status (especially respiratory status, CBC, and pulmonary and renal function tests) before therapy and reassess regularly thereafter.
- Be alert for adverse reactions and drug interactions.
- Adverse pulmonary reactions are common in patients older than age 70. Fatal pulmonary fibrosis occurs in 1% of patients, especially when cumulative dose exceeds 400 units.
- Monitor patient for bleomycin-induced fever, which is common and usually occurs within 3 to 6 hours after giving drug.
- Watch for hypersensitivity reactions, which may be delayed for several hours, especially in patients with lymphoma.
- Assess patient for development of fine crackles and dyspnea.
- Evaluate patient's and family's understanding of drug therapy.

Nursing diagnoses

- Risk for injury related to underlying neoplastic condition
- Impaired gas exchange related to drug-induced adverse pulmonary reactions
- Deficient knowledge related to drug therapy

Planning and implementation

- Follow institutional policy for administration of drug to reduce risks. Preparation and administration of parenteral form of this drug cause carcinogenic, mutagenic, and teratogenic risks for personnel.
- **I.V. use:** Reconstitute drug with 5 ml or more of normal saline solution for injection. For I.V. infusion, dilute with 50 to 100 ml of normal saline solution for injection. Administer slowly over 10 minutes. Bleomycin may adsorb to plastic I.V. bags. For prolonged stability, use glass containers.
- **I.M. use:** Dilute drug in 1 to 5 ml of sterile water for injection, bacteriostatic water for injection, or normal saline solution for injection.
- **S.C. use:** Follow manufacturer's guidelines for administering bleomycin S.C.
- **Intrapleural use:** Dissolve drug in 50 to 100 ml normal saline solution injection. Administer through a thoracotomy tube after excess intrapleural fluid has been drained and complete lung expansion has been confirmed.
- Refrigerate unopened vials containing dry powder.
- Refrigerated, reconstituted solution is stable for 4 weeks; at room temperature, it's stable for 2 weeks.
- Drug should be stopped if pulmonary function test shows a marked decline.
- To prevent linear streaking from drug concentrating in keratin of squamous epithelium, don't use adhesive dressings on skin.
- In patients susceptible to post-treatment fever, give acetaminophen before treatment and for 24 hours after treatment.
- If ordered after treatment, give supplemental oxygen at an FIO_2 no higher than 25% to avoid potential lung damage.

Patient teaching

- Explain the risks of drug therapy, especially the danger of serious pulmonary reactions in high-risk patients.
- Explain the need for monitoring and the type of monitoring to be done.
- Tell patient that alopecia may occur, but that it's usually reversible.

Evaluation

- Patient exhibits positive response to therapy, as evidenced by follow-up diagnostic test results.
- Patient's gas exchange remains normal throughout therapy.
- Patient and family state understanding of drug therapy.

bosentan

(bow-SEN-tan)
Tracleer

Pharmacologic classification: nonselective endothelin receptor antagonist
Therapeutic classification: antihypertensive
Pregnancy risk category: X

Indications and dosages

▶ **Pulmonary arterial hypertension in patients with World Health Organization class III or IV symptoms to improve exercise ability and decrease clinical worsening.** *Adults:* 62.5 mg P.O. b.i.d. for 4 weeks. Increase to maintenance dose of 125 mg P.O. b.i.d. In patients weighing less than 40 kg, the initial and maintenance dose should be 62.5 mg b.i.d.

Contraindications and precautions

- Contraindicated in patients hypersensitive to bosentan. Don't use in patients with moderate-to-severe liver impairment or in those with elevated aminotransferase levels more than 3 times upper limit of normal.
- Use cautiously in patients with mild liver impairment.

Lifespan: In pregnant women, drug is contraindicated. In breast-feeding women, drug isn't recommended because it's unknown whether drug appears in breast milk. In children, safety and efficacy of drug haven't been established. In elderly patients, select dose cautiously because of greater likelihood of decreased organ function.

Adverse reactions

CNS: *headache,* fatigue.
CV: hypotension, palpitations, flushing, edema, lower leg edema.
EENT: *nasopharyngitis.*
GI: dyspepsia.
Hematologic: anemia.
Hepatic: ***liver failure.***
Skin: pruritus.

Interactions

Drug-drug. *Cyclosporine A:* May increase concentrations of bosentan and decrease levels of cyclosporine. Avoid use together.
Glyburide: May increase risk of elevated liver enzyme levels and decrease levels of both drugs. Avoid use together.
Hormonal contraceptives: May cause contraceptive failure. Advise use of an additional method of birth control.
Ketoconazole: May increase plasma concentration of bosentan. Monitor patient for increased effects of bosentan.
Simvastatin, other statins: May decrease plasma concentrations of these drugs. Monitor cholesterol levels to assess need for statin dose adjustment.

Effects on lab test results

- May increase liver aminotransferase levels, such as AST, ALT, and bilirubin levels.
- May decrease hemoglobin and hematocrit.

Pharmacokinetics

Absorption: 50% bioavailability after oral administration.
Distribution: More than 98% bound to plasma proteins, primarily albumin.
Metabolism: Hepatically metabolized into three metabolites. Bosentan induces three CYP2C9 and CYP3A4, and possibly CYP2C19.
Excretion: Eliminated by biliary excretion. Less than 3% of oral dose is recovered in urine.

Route	Onset	Peak	Duration
P.O.	Unknown	3-5 hr	Unknown

Pharmacodynamics

Chemical effect: Bosentan acts as a specific and competitive antagonist for endothelin-1 (ET-1). ET-1 levels are elevated in patients with pulmonary arterial hypertension, suggesting a pathogenic role for ET-1 in this disease.
Therapeutic effect: Increases exercise capacity and cardiac index. Decreases blood pressure, pulmonary arterial pressure, vascular resistance, and mean right arterial pressure.

Available forms

Tablets: 62.5 mg, 125 mg

NURSING PROCESS

Assessment

- Assess patient's underlying condition before therapy and reassess regularly thereafter.

• Make sure patient isn't pregnant. Hormonal contraceptives, including oral, implantable, and injectable, shouldn't be used as the sole means of contraception because failure may occur. Major birth defects may result with fetal exposure. Obtain monthly pregnancy tests.
• Serious liver injury may occur. Measure aminotransferase levels before treatment and monthly thereafter, and adjust dosage accordingly.
• This drug may cause hematologic changes. Monitor hemoglobin after 1 and 3 months of therapy and then every 3 months thereafter.
• Be alert for any drug-induced adverse events.
• Assess patient's and family's knowledge of drug therapy.

Nursing diagnoses

• Risk of injury related to drug-induced liver enzyme elevations
• Ineffective tissue perfusion (cardiopulmonary) related to underlying condition
• Deficient knowledge related to drug therapy

Planning and implementation

• To decrease the possibility of potential serious liver injury and to limit the chance for fetal exposure, Tracleer may be prescribed only through the Tracleer access program at 1-866-228-3546. Adverse effects also may be reported through this number.
• For patients who develop aminotransferase abnormalities, the dose may need to be decreased or stopped until aminotransferase levels return to normal. If liver function abnormalities are accompanied by symptoms of liver injury, such as nausea, vomiting, fever, abdominal pain, jaundice, or unusual lethargy or fatigue, or if bilirubin level is greater than or equal to 2 times upper limit of normal, stop treatment and don't restart.
• Overdose may cause headache, nausea, and vomiting, mildly decreased blood pressure, and increased heart rate. Massive overdose may cause severe hypotension requiring CV support. Treatment is symptomatic and supportive.
• To avoid the potential for clinical deterioration, gradual dose reduction is recommended before discontinuation of drug.

Patient teaching

• Advise patient to take drug only as prescribed.
• Warn patient to avoid becoming pregnant while taking this drug. Reliable contraception must be used and a monthly pregnancy test performed.
• Advise patient to have liver tests and blood counts performed regularly.

Evaluation

• Patient doesn't suffer from adverse reactions or liver damage from drug therapy.
• Patient's pulmonary artery pressure decreases, and patient reaches pulmonary hemodynamic stability.
• Patient and family state understanding of drug therapy.

bretylium tosylate
(breh-TIL-ee-um TOH-si-layt)
Bretylate ◇

Pharmacologic class: adrenergic blocker
Therapeutic class: ventricular antiarrhythmic
Pregnancy risk category: C

Indications and dosages

▶ **Ventricular fibrillation or hemodynamically unstable ventricular tachycardia unresponsive to other antiarrhythmics.** *Adults:* 5 mg/kg by I.V. push over 1 minute. If necessary, increase dose to 10 mg/kg and repeat q 15 to 30 minutes until 35 to 40 mg/kg have been given. For continuous suppression, give diluted solution at 1 to 2 mg/minute continuously, or give 5 to 10 mg/kg diluted solution over more than 8 minutes q 6 hours. If unable to obtain I.V. access, may give 5 to 10 mg/kg undiluted I.M. q 1 to 2 hours if the arrhythmia persists or q 6 to 8 hours for maintenance therapy.

Contraindications and precautions

• Contraindicated in patients taking a cardiac glycoside unless arrhythmia is life-threatening, not caused by digitalis, and unresponsive to other antiarrhythmics.
• Use with extreme caution in patients with fixed cardiac output (aortic stenosis and pulmonary hypertension). Drug may cause severe and sudden drop in blood pressure.
Lifespan: In pregnant or breast-feeding women, use cautiously. In children, safety and efficacy of drug haven't been established.

Adverse reactions

CNS: *vertigo, dizziness, light-headedness, syncope.*
CV: SEVERE HYPOTENSION (especially orthostatic), ***bradycardia,*** angina, ***transient arrhythmias,*** transient hypertension.
GI: severe nausea, vomiting (with rapid infusion).
Musculoskeletal: muscle atrophy, tissue necrosis (with repeated injections).

Interactions

Drug-drug. *Antihypertensives:* May potentiate hypotension. Monitor blood pressure.
Other antiarrhythmics: May have additive or antagonistic antiarrhythmic effects. Monitor patient for additive toxicity.
Sympathomimetics: Bretylium may potentiate effects of drugs given to correct hypotension. Monitor blood pressure.

Effects on lab test results

None reported.

Pharmacokinetics

Absorption: Administered I.V.
Distribution: Distributed widely throughout body. Only about 1% to 10% is bound to plasma.
Metabolism: No metabolites have been identified.
Excretion: Excreted in urine. *Half-life:* 5 to 10 hours (longer in patients with renal impairment).

Route	Onset	Peak	Duration
I.V.	3 min-2 hr	6-9 hr	6-24 hr

Pharmacodynamics

Chemical effect: Unknown; considered a class III antiarrhythmic that initially exerts transient adrenergic stimulation through release of norepinephrine. Subsequent depletion of norepinephrine causes adrenergic blocking actions to predominate, prolonging repolarization and increasing duration of action potential and effective refractory period.
Therapeutic effect: Abolishes ventricular arrhythmias.

Available forms

Injection: 50 mg/ml

NURSING PROCESS

Assessment

- Obtain history of patient's heart rate and rhythm before therapy.
- Monitor drug's effectiveness by evaluating continuous ECG recordings, blood pressure, and heart rate. Initial drug-induced release of norepinephrine may cause transient hypertension and arrhythmias.
- Be alert for adverse reactions and drug interactions.
- Evaluate patient's and family's understanding of drug therapy.

Nursing diagnoses

- Decreased cardiac output related to presence of ventricular arrhythmia
- Ineffective cerebral tissue perfusion related to drug-induced severe hypotension
- Deficient knowledge related to drug therapy

Planning and implementation

- For maintenance therapy, dilute with dextrose or saline solution for injection before administering. Follow manufacturer's guidelines for specific dilution (varies according to dosage). When giving as direct I.V. injection, use 20G to 22G needle and inject over 1 minute into vein or I.V. line containing free-flowing compatible solution.
- Drug is used with other cardiac life-support measures, such as cardiopulmonary resuscitation, defibrillation, epinephrine, sodium bicarbonate, and lidocaine.
- To prevent nausea and vomiting, follow dosage directions carefully.
- Keep patient in supine position until tolerance to hypotension develops. Have patient avoid sudden position changes.
- If supine systolic blood pressure falls below 75 mm Hg, prescriber may order norepinephrine, dopamine, or volume expanders to raise blood pressure.

Patient teaching

- Tell patient to report chest pain or dyspnea immediately.
- Tell patient to avoid sudden position changes.

Evaluation

- Patient's ECG reveals that arrhythmia has been corrected.

• Patient's blood pressure remains normal throughout therapy.
• Patient and family state understanding of drug therapy.

bromocriptine mesylate
(broh-moh-KRIP-teen MES-ih-layt)
Parlodel, Parlodel SnapTabs

Pharmacologic class: dopamine receptor agonist
Therapeutic class: semisynthetic ergot alkaloid, dopaminergic agonist, antiparkinsonian, inhibitor of prolactin and growth hormone release
Pregnancy risk category: NR

Indications and dosages

▶ **Parkinson's disease.** *Adults:* 1.25 to 2.5 mg P.O. b.i.d. with meals. Increase dosage q 14 to 28 days, up to 100 mg daily, as needed. Usual dosage is 10 to 40 mg daily.
▶ **Acromegaly.** *Adults:* 1.25 to 2.5 mg P.O. h.s. with snack for 3 days. An additional 1.25 to 2.5 mg may be added q 3 to 7 days until patient receives therapeutic benefit. Maximum dosage is 100 mg daily.
▶ **Amenorrhea and galactorrhea related to hyperprolactinemia; infertility or hypogonadism in women.** *Adults:* 1.25 to 2.5 mg P.O. daily. Increase by 2.5 mg daily at 3- to 7-day intervals until desired effect is achieved. Maintenance dosage is usually 5 to 7.5 mg daily, but may be 2.5 to 15 mg daily.
▶ **Premenstrual syndrome‡.** *Adults:* 2.5 to 7.5 mg P.O. b.i.d. from day 10 of menstrual cycle until onset of menstruation.
▶ **Cushing's syndrome‡.** *Adults:* 1.25 to 2.5 mg P.O. b.i.d. to q.i.d.
▶ **Hepatic encephalopathy‡.** *Adults:* 1.25 mg P.O. daily, increase by 1.25 mg q 3 days until 15 mg is reached.
▶ **Neuroleptic malignant syndrome related to neuroleptic drug therapy‡.** *Adults:* 2.5 to 5 mg P.O. 2 to 6 times daily.

Contraindications and precautions

• Contraindicated in patients hypersensitive to ergot derivatives and in those with uncontrolled hypertension and toxemia of pregnancy.
• Use cautiously in patients with impaired renal or hepatic function or history of MI with residual arrhythmias.
Lifespan: In women who intend to breastfeed, drug shouldn't be used because it inhibits lactation. In children younger than age 15, safety of drug hasn't been established.

Adverse reactions

CNS: confusion, hallucinations, uncontrolled body movements, *dizziness, headache,* fatigue, mania, delusions, nervousness, insomnia, depression, ***seizures, CVA,*** syncope.
CV: *hypotension,* orthostatic hypotension, hypertension, ***acute MI.***
EENT: nasal congestion, tinnitus, blurred vision.
GI: *nausea,* vomiting, *abdominal cramps,* constipation, diarrhea.
GU: urine retention, urinary frequency.
Skin: coolness and pallor of fingers and toes.

Interactions

Drug-drug. *Antihypertensives:* May increase hypotensive effects. Dosage adjustment of antihypertensive may be needed.
Ergot alkaloids, estrogens, oral contraceptives, progestins: May interfere with effects of bromocriptine. Don't use together.
Erythromycin: May increase bromocriptine levels. Adjustment of bromocriptine may be needed.
Haloperidol, loxapine, MAO inhibitors, methyldopa, metoclopramide, phenothiazines, reserpine: May interfere with effects of bromocriptine. Increase of bromocriptine dosage may be needed.
Levodopa: May have additive effects. Adjustment of levodopa dosage may be needed.
Drug-lifestyle. *Alcohol use:* May cause disulfiram-like reaction. Discourage use together.

Effects on lab test results

• May increase BUN, alkaline phosphatase, uric acid, AST, ALT, and CK levels.

Pharmacokinetics

Absorption: 28% absorbed.
Distribution: 90% to 96% bound to albumin.
Metabolism: First-pass metabolism occurs with more than 90% of absorbed dose. Drug is metabolized completely in liver.

Excretion: Major route of excretion is through bile. Only 2.5% to 5.5% of dose excreted in urine. *Half-life:* 15 hours.

Route	Onset	Peak	Duration
P.O.	0.5-2 hr	1-3 hr	12-24 hr

Pharmacodynamics

Chemical effect: Inhibits secretion of prolactin and acts as dopamine-receptor agonist by activating postsynaptic dopamine receptors.
Therapeutic effect: Reverses amenorrhea and galactorrhea caused by hyperprolactinemia, increases fertility in women, improves voluntary movement, and inhibits prolactin and growth hormone release.

Available forms

Capsules: 5 mg
Tablets: 2.5 mg

NURSING PROCESS

Assessment

- Obtain history of patient's underlying condition before therapy and reassess regularly thereafter.
- Perform baseline and periodic evaluations of cardiac, hepatic, renal, and hematopoietic functions during prolonged therapy.
- Be alert for adverse reactions and drug interactions. Risk of adverse reactions is high (about 68%), particularly at beginning of therapy; most are mild to moderate, with nausea being most common. Adverse reactions are more frequent when drug is used for Parkinson's disease.
- Evaluate patient's and family's understanding of drug therapy.

Nursing diagnoses

- Ineffective health maintenance related to underlying condition
- Risk for injury related to drug-induced adverse CNS or CV reactions
- Deficient knowledge related to drug therapy

Planning and implementation

- Patients with impaired renal function may require dosage adjustments.
- Give drug with meals.
- Gradually adjust doses to effective levels to minimize adverse reactions.
- For Parkinson's disease, bromocriptine usually is given with either levodopa or carbidopa-levodopa.

Patient teaching

- Advise patient to use contraceptive methods other than oral contraceptives or subdermal implants during treatment.
- Advise patient to rise slowly to an upright position and avoid sudden position changes to avoid dizziness and fainting.
- Advise patient that resumption of menses and suppression of galactorrhea may take 6 weeks or longer.
- Warn patient to avoid hazardous activities that require alertness until CNS and CV effects of drug are known.
- Tell patient to take drug with meals to minimize GI distress.

Evaluation

- Patient exhibits improvement in underlying condition.
- Patient doesn't experience injury as a result of drug-induced adverse reactions.
- Patient and family state understanding of drug therapy.

brompheniramine maleate

(brom-fen-IR-ah-meen MAL-ee-ayt)
Bromphen*†, Dimetane*†, Dimetapp Allergy†, Nasahist B, ND-Stat

Pharmacologic class: alkylamine antihistamine
Therapeutic class: antihistamine (H_1-receptor antagonist)
Pregnancy risk category: C

Indications and dosages

▶ **Rhinitis, allergy symptoms.** *Adults:* 4 to 8 mg P.O. t.i.d. or q.i.d. Or, 8 to 12 mg extended-release P.O. b.i.d. or t.i.d. Or, 5 to 20 mg q 6 to 12 hours I.V., I.M., or S.C. Maximum dosage is 40 mg daily.
Children age 6 and older: 2 to 4 mg P.O. t.i.d. or q.i.d. Or, 8 to 12 mg extended-release P.O. q 12 hours. Or, 0.5 mg/kg I.V., I.M., or S.C. daily in divided doses t.i.d. or q.i.d.
Children younger than age 6: 0.5 mg/kg P.O., I.V., I.M., or S.C. daily in divided doses t.i.d. or q.i.d.

Contraindications and precautions

• Contraindicated in patients hypersensitive to drug's ingredients and in those with acute asthmatic attacks, severe hypertension, coronary artery disease, angle-closure glaucoma, urine retention, or peptic ulcer. Also contraindicated within 14 days of MAO inhibitor therapy.
• Use cautiously in patients with increased intraocular pressure, diabetes, ischemic heart disease, hyperthyroidism, hypertension, bronchial asthma, or prostatic hyperplasia.
Lifespan: In pregnant women, use cautiously. In breast-feeding women, drug is contraindicated. In neonates, drug isn't recommended. Children, especially those younger than age 6, may experience paradoxical hyperexcitability. In children age 11 and younger, extended-release tablets aren't recommended. In elderly patients, use cautiously.

Adverse reactions

CNS: dizziness, tremors, irritability, insomnia, syncope, *drowsiness, stimulation* (especially in elderly patients).
CV: hypotension, palpitations.
GI: anorexia, nausea, vomiting, *dry mouth and throat.*
GU: urine retention.
Hematologic: ***thrombocytopenia, agranulocytosis.***
Skin: urticaria, rash, diaphoresis.
Other: local stinging.

Interactions

Drug-drug. *CNS depressants:* May increase sedation. Use together cautiously.
MAO inhibitors: May increase anticholinergic effects. Don't use together.

Effects on lab test results

• May decrease platelet and granulocyte counts.

Pharmacokinetics

Absorption: After oral administration, absorbed readily from GI tract; unknown for parenteral administration.
Distribution: Distributed widely throughout body.
Metabolism: About 90% to 95% metabolized by liver.
Excretion: Drug and its metabolites excreted primarily in urine; small amount excreted in feces. *Half-life:* 12 to 34½ hours.

Route	Onset	Peak	Duration
P.O., I.V., I.M., S.C.	15-60 min	2-5 hr (longer for P.O. extended-release)	4-8 hr

Pharmacodynamics

Chemical effect: Competes with histamine for H_1-receptor sites on effector cells. Prevents but doesn't reverse histamine-mediated responses.
Therapeutic effect: Relieves allergy symptoms.

Available forms

Elixir: 2 mg/5 ml*†
Injection: 10 mg/ml
Tablets: 4 mg†
Tablets (extended-release): 12 mg†

NURSING PROCESS

Assessment

• Assess patient's allergy symptoms before therapy and regularly thereafter.
• Be alert for adverse reactions and drug interactions.
• Monitor CBC during long-term therapy; watch for signs of blood dyscrasias.
• Monitor patient's hydration status if adverse GI reactions occur.
• Evaluate patient's and family's understanding of drug therapy.

Nursing diagnoses

• Ineffective health maintenance related to allergy symptoms
• Risk for deficient fluid volume related to drug-induced adverse GI reactions
• Deficient knowledge related to drug therapy

Planning and implementation

• **P.O. use:** Give drug with food or milk to reduce GI distress.
• **I.V. use:** Injectable form containing 10 mg/ml can be given diluted or undiluted very slowly I.V. Don't give 100 mg/ml injection I.V.
• **I.M. and S.C. use:** Follow normal protocol.
• Alert prescriber if patient appears to be developing tolerance to drug. A different antihistamine may need to be substituted.

Patient teaching

- Tell patient to reduce GI distress by taking drug with food or milk.
- Warn patient to avoid alcohol and activities that require alertness until CNS effects of drug are known.
- Tell patient that coffee or tea may reduce drug-induced drowsiness, although drug causes less drowsiness than some other antihistamines.
- Tell patient to relieve dry mouth with ice chips, sugarless gum, or hard candy.
- Instruct patient to notify prescriber if tolerance develops because different antihistamine may need to be ordered.
- Instruct patient to stop drug 4 days before skin tests to preserve accuracy of tests.
- If patient operates machinery or motor vehicles, explain that drug has sedative effects.

Evaluation

- Patient's allergy symptoms are relieved.
- Patient maintains adequate hydration throughout therapy.
- Patient and family state understanding of drug therapy.

budesonide

(byoo-DES-oh-nighd)

Pulmicort Respules, Pulmicort Turbuhaler, Rhinocort

Pharmacologic class: glucocorticoid
Therapeutic class: anti-inflammatory
Pregnancy risk category: B (C for Rhinocort)

Indications and dosages

▶ **Symptoms of seasonal or perennial allergic rhinitis and non-allergic perennial rhinitis.** *Adults and children age 6 and older:* 2 sprays (64 mcg) in each nostril in morning and evening or 4 sprays (128 mcg) in each nostril in morning. Maintenance dosage should be fewest number of sprays needed to control symptoms.

▶ **Chronic asthma.** *Adults:* 200 to 400 mcg oral inhalation b.i.d. when patient previously used bronchodilators alone or inhaled corticosteroids; 400 to 800 mcg oral inhalation b.i.d. when patient previously used oral corticosteroids.

Children age 6 and older: Initially, 200 mcg oral inhalation b.i.d. Maximum dose is 400 mcg b.i.d.

Children ages 1 to 8: ***Respules.*** 0.25 mg via jet nebulizer with compressor once daily. Increase to 0.5 mg once daily or 0.25 mg b.i.d. in child not receiving systemic or inhaled corticosteroids or 1 mg daily or 0.5 mg b.i.d. if child is receiving oral corticosteroids.

Contraindications and precautions

- Contraindicated in patients hypersensitive to drug or its components and in those who have had recent septal ulcers, nasal surgery, or nasal trauma, until total healing has occurred. Pulmicort Turbuhaler and Pulmicort Respules are contraindicated in the primary treatment of status asthmaticus.
- Use cautiously in patients with tuberculous infections, ocular herpes simplex, or untreated fungal, bacterial, or systemic viral infections.

Lifespan: In pregnant or breast-feeding women, use cautiously. In children younger than age 6, safety of drug hasn't been established.

Adverse reactions

CNS: nervousness, *headache.*
CV: facial edema.
EENT: nasal irritation, epistaxis, pharyngitis, sinusitis, reduced sense of smell, nasal pain, hoarseness.
GI: bad taste, dry mouth, dyspepsia, nausea, vomiting.
Metabolic: weight gain
Musculoskeletal: myalgia.
Respiratory: cough, candidiasis, wheezing, dyspnea.
Skin: rash, pruritus, contact dermatitis.
Other: ***hypersensitivity reactions.***

Interactions

Drug-drug. *Alternate-day prednisone therapy, inhaled corticosteroids:* May increase risk of hypothalamic-pituitary-adrenal suppression. Monitor patient closely.
Ketoconazole: May increase budesonide level. Use together cautiously.

Effects on lab test results

None reported.

Pharmacokinetics

Absorption: Amount of intranasal dose that reaches systemic circulation is typically low (about 20%).
Distribution: 88% protein-bound in plasma.
Metabolism: Rapidly and extensively metabolized in liver.
Excretion: Excreted in urine (about 67%) and feces (about 33%). *Half-life:* About 2 hours.

Route	Onset	Peak	Duration
Nasal inhalation	10 hr	Unknown	Unknown
Oral inhalation	24 hr	1-2 wk	Unknown

Pharmacodynamics

Chemical effect: Unknown; probably decreases nasal and pulmonary inflammation, mainly by inhibiting activities of specific cells and mediators involved in allergic response.
Therapeutic effect: Decreases nasal and pulmonary congestion.

Available forms

Inhalation suspension: 0.25 mg/2 ml, 0.5 mg/2 ml
Nasal spray: 32 mcg/metered spray (7-g canister)
Oral inhalation powder: 200 mcg/dose

NURSING PROCESS

Assessment

- Obtain history of patient's condition before therapy and reassess regularly thereafter.
- Be alert for adverse reactions.
- Evaluate patient's and family's understanding of drug therapy.

Nursing diagnoses

- Ineffective health maintenance related to allergy-induced nasal congestion
- Impaired gas exchange related to drug-induced wheezing
- Deficient knowledge related to drug therapy

Planning and implementation

- Before giving nasal inhaler, shake container and invert. Have patient clear his nasal passages and then tilt his head back. Insert nozzle into nostril (pointed away from septum), holding other nostril closed. Deliver spray while patient inhales. Repeat in other nostril.
- Notify prescriber if relief isn't obtained or signs of infection appear.
- Obtain specimen for culture if signs of nasal infection occur.

Patient teaching

- Instruct patient to shake nasal inhaler before using, blow nose to clear nasal passages, and insert nozzle into nostril, pointing away from septum. Tell him to hold other nostril closed and inhale gently while spraying; then shake container again and repeat in other nostril.
- Instruct patient to hold the inhaler upright when loading Pulmicort Turbuhaler, not to blow or exhale into the inhaler, not to shake it while loaded, and to hold the inhaler upright while orally inhaling the dose. Tell patient to place the mouthpiece between the lips and inhale forcefully and deeply.
- Pulmicort Respules can be administered only via jet nebulizer connected to an air compressor with satisfactory airflow. System should be equipped with a mouthpiece or face mask.
- Inform patient that use of an oral inhaler results in improvement in asthma control within 24 hours, with maximum benefit at 1 to 2 weeks, or possibly longer.

ALERT: Advise patient that Pulmicort Turbuhaler and Pulmicort Respules aren't indicated for relief of acute asthma attacks.

- Tell patient that product should be used by only one person to prevent spread of infection.
- Advise patient not to break, incinerate, or store canister in extreme heat; contents are under pressure.
- Warn patient not to exceed prescribed dose or use for long periods because of risk of hypothalamic-pituitary-adrenal axis suppression.
- Tell patient to report worsened condition or symptoms that don't improve in 3 weeks.
- Teach patient good nasal and oral hygiene.

Evaluation

- Patient's nasal congestion subsides.
- Patient has adequate gas exchange.
- Patient and family state understanding of drug therapy.

budesonide

(byoo-DES-oh-nighd)
Entocort EC

Pharmacologic classification: corticosteroid
Therapeutic classification: anti-inflammatory
Pregnancy risk category: C

Indications and dosages

▶ **Mild-to-moderate active Crohn's disease involving the ileum, the ascending colon, or both.** *Adults:* 9 mg P.O. once daily in the morning for up to 8 weeks. For recurrent episodes of active Crohn's disease, a repeat 8-week course may be given. Treatment can be tapered to 6 mg P.O. daily for 2 weeks before complete cessation.

Contraindications and precautions

- Contraindicated in patients hypersensitive to budesonide.
- Use cautiously in patients with tuberculosis, hypertension, diabetes mellitus, osteoporosis, peptic ulcer disease, glaucoma, or cataracts. Also use cautiously in patients with a family history of diabetes or glaucoma and those with any other condition in which glucocorticosteroids may have unwanted effects.

Lifespan: In pregnant patients, use only if potential benefit justifies risks. In breast-feeding women, glucocorticoids appear in breast milk, and infants may have adverse reactions. The decision to breast-feed should be based on importance of drug to mother. In children, safety and efficacy have not been established. In elderly patients, give drug cautiously, starting at the lower end of the dosage range.

Adverse reactions

CNS: *headache,* dizziness, asthenia, hyperkinesia, paresthesia, syncope, tremor, vertigo, fatigue, malaise, agitation, confusion, insomnia, nervousness, somnolence, migraine, fever, pain, sleep disorder.
CV: chest pain, dependent edema, facial edema, hypertension, palpitations, tachycardia, flushing.
EENT: *pharyngitis,* ear infection, eye abnormality, abnormal vision, sinusitis, voice alteration, neck pain.
GI: *nausea,* dyspepsia, abdominal pain, flatulence, vomiting, anus disorder, aggravated Crohn's disease, gastroenteritis, epigastric pain, fistula, glossitis, hemorrhoids, intestinal obstruction, tongue edema, dry mouth, tooth disorder, taste perversion, increased appetite, oral candidiasis.
GU: dysuria, micturition frequency, nocturia, intermenstrual bleeding, menstrual disorder.
Hematologic: leukocytosis, anemia.
Metabolic: *hypercorticism,* hypokalemia, weight gain, ADRENAL INSUFFICIENCY.
Musculoskeletal: back pain, aggravated arthritis, cramps, myalgia, arthralgia, hypotonia.
Respiratory: *respiratory tract infection,* bronchitis, dyspnea, cough.
Skin: acne, alopecia, dermatitis, eczema, skin disorder, increased sweating, ecchymosis.
Other: flulike syndrome, infection.

Interactions

Drug-drug. *CYP3A4 inhibitors (erythromycin, ketoconazole, indinavir, itraconazole, ritonavir, saquinavir):* May increase the effects of budesonide. If drugs must be given together, monitor patient for signs of hypercorticism and consider reducing budesonide dose.
Drug-food. *Grapefruit or grapefruit juice:* May increase drug effects. Discourage use together.

Effects on lab test results

- May increase alkaline phosphatase and C-reactive protein levels. May increase or decrease potassium level.
- May increase erythrocyte sedimentation rate and atypical neutrophil and WBC counts. May decrease hemoglobin and hematocrit.

Pharmacokinetics

Absorption: Complete.
Distribution: Drug is 85% to 90% plasma protein bound.
Metabolism: Drug has extensive first-pass metabolism and is rapidly and extensively biotransformed by CYP3A4 to two major metabolites that have very little glucocorticoid activity.
Excretion: Excreted in urine and feces as metabolites, which primarily are excreted renally.

Route	Onset	Peak	Duration
P.O.	Unknown	0.5-10 hr	Unknown

*Liquid form contains alcohol. **May contain tartrazine. ♦Canada ◇Australia †OTC ‡Off-label use

Pharmacodynamics

Chemical effect: Drug has significant glucocorticoid effects because of its high affinity for glucocorticoid receptors, which leads to improvement of Crohn's disease.
Therapeutic effect: Alleviates symptoms of Crohn's disease.

Available forms

Capsules: 3 mg

NURSING PROCESS

Assessment

- Assess patient's underlying condition before starting therapy and reassess regularly thereafter.
- Monitor patient's laboratory values regularly. Monitor patient for adverse effects.
- Be alert for signs and symptoms of hypercorticism.
- Assess patient's and family's knowledge of drug therapy.

Nursing diagnoses

- Diarrhea caused by underlying Crohn's disease
- Imbalanced nutrition: less than body requirements related to underlying Crohn's disease
- Deficient knowledge related to drug therapy

Planning and implementation

- Patients undergoing surgery or other stressful situations may need systemic glucocorticoid supplementation in addition to budesonide therapy.
- When patients are transferred from systemic glucocorticoid therapy to budesonide, monitor them carefully for signs and symptoms of steroid withdrawal. Taper glucocorticoid therapy when budesonide treatment starts.
- Watch for immunosuppression, especially in patients who haven't had diseases such as chickenpox or measles; these diseases can be fatal in patients who are immunosuppressed or receiving glucocorticoids. Monitor adrenocortical function carefully and reduce dosage cautiously.
- Prevent patient exposure to chickenpox or measles. If patient is exposed to measles, consider therapy with pooled intravenous immunoglobulin (IVIG). If patient develops chickenpox, antiviral treatment and varicella zoster immune globulin (VZIG) may be considered.
- Acute toxicity after overdose is rare.
- Prolonged use of drug may cause hypercorticism (symptoms include swelling of the face and neck, acne, bruising, hirsutism, buffalo hump, and skin striae) and adrenal suppression. Treat with immediate gastric lavage or emesis, followed by supportive and symptomatic therapy. For chronic overdose in serious disease requiring continuous steroid therapy, dosage may be reduced temporarily. Dose may need to be reduced in patients with moderate-to-severe liver disease if they have increased signs or symptoms of hypercorticism.

Patient teaching

- Tell patient to swallow capsules whole and not to chew or break them.
- Advise patient not to drink grapefruit juice while taking drug.
- Tell patient to notify prescriber immediately if exposed to chickenpox or measles.

Evaluation

- Patient's symptoms of Crohn's disease, including diarrhea and abdominal pain, are relieved.
- Patient's nutrition improves as symptoms improve.
- Patient and family state understanding of drug therapy.

bumetanide

(byoo-MEH-tuh-nighd)
Bumex, Burinex◇

Pharmacologic class: loop diuretic
Therapeutic class: diuretic
Pregnancy risk category: C

Indications and dosages

▶ **Edema in heart failure, hepatic or renal disease, postoperative edema‡, premenstrual syndrome‡, disseminated cancer‡.** *Adults:* 0.5 to 2 mg P.O. once daily. If diuretic response isn't adequate, second or third dose may be given at 4- to 5-hour intervals. Maximum dosage is 10 mg daily. May be given parenterally if P.O. not feasible. Usual initial dose is 0.5 to 1 mg given I.V. over 1 to 2 minutes or I.M. If response isn't adequate, second or third dose may be given at 2- to 3-hour intervals. Maximum dosage is 10 mg daily.

▶ **Hypertension‡.** *Adults:* 0.5 mg P.O. daily. Oral maintenance dose is 1 to 4 mg daily, not to exceed 5 mg P.O. daily.

▶ **Pediatric heart failure‡.** *Children:* 0.015 mg/kg every other day to 0.1 mg/kg daily. Use with extreme caution in neonates.

Contraindications and precautions

• Contraindicated in patients hypersensitive to drug or sulfonamides (possible cross-sensitivity), in those with anuria or hepatic coma, and in those with severe electrolyte depletion.

• Use cautiously in patients with depressed renal function or hepatic cirrhosis or ascites.

Lifespan: In pregnant women, use cautiously. In breast-feeding women, drug is contraindicated. In children, safety of drug hasn't been established.

Adverse reactions

CNS: dizziness, headache.
CV: volume depletion and dehydration, orthostatic hypotension, ECG changes.
EENT: transient deafness.
GI: nausea.
GU: ***renal failure,*** nocturia, polyuria, frequent urination, oliguria.
Hematologic: azotemia, ***thrombocytopenia.***
Metabolic: hypokalemia; hypochloremic alkalosis; asymptomatic hyperuricemia; fluid and electrolyte imbalances, including dilutional hyponatremia, hypocalcemia, and hypomagnesemia; hyperglycemia; impaired glucose tolerance.
Musculoskeletal: muscle pain and tenderness.
Skin: rash.

Interactions

Drug-drug. *Aminoglycoside antibiotics:* May potentiate ototoxicity. Use together cautiously.
Antihypertensives: May increase risk of hypotension. Use together cautiously.
Cardiac glycosides: May increase risk of digitalis toxicity from bumetanide-induced hypokalemia. Monitor potassium and digoxin levels.
Indomethacin, NSAIDs, probenecid: May inhibit diuretic response. Use together cautiously.
Lithium: May decrease lithium clearance, increasing risk of lithium toxicity. Monitor lithium level.
Metolazone: May cause profound diuresis and potential electrolyte loss. Monitor patient for fluid and electrolyte imbalances.
Other potassium-wasting drugs: May increase risk of hypokalemia. Use together cautiously.
Drug-herb. *Licorice:* May contribute to excessive potassium loss. Discourage using together.

Effects on lab test results

• May increase creatinine, urine urea, glucose, and cholesterol levels. May decrease potassium, magnesium, sodium, and calcium levels.

• May decrease platelet count.

Pharmacokinetics

Absorption: After P.O. administration, 85% to 95%; food delays absorption of P.O. dose. Complete after I.M. administration.
Distribution: About 92% to 96% protein-bound; unknown whether drug enters CSF.
Metabolism: Metabolized by liver to at least five metabolites.
Excretion: Excreted in urine (80%) and feces (10% to 20%). *Half-life:* 1 to 1½ hours.

Route	Onset	Peak	Duration
P.O.	30-60 min	1-2 hr	4-6 hr
I.V.	3 min	15-30 min	3.5-4 hr
I.M.	40 min	Unknown	Unknown

Pharmacodynamics

Chemical effect: Inhibits sodium and chloride reabsorption at ascending portion of loop of Henle.
Therapeutic effect: Promotes sodium and water excretion.

Available forms

Injection: 0.25 mg/ml
Tablets: 0.5 mg, 1 mg, 2 mg

NURSING PROCESS

Assessment

• Obtain history of patient's urine output, vital signs, electrolyte levels, breath sounds, peripheral edema, and weight before therapy and reassess regularly thereafter.

• Be alert for adverse reactions and drug interactions.

• Evaluate patient's and family's understanding of drug therapy.

Nursing diagnoses

- Excess fluid volume related to underlying condition
- Impaired urinary elimination related to therapeutic effect of drug therapy
- Deficient knowledge related to drug therapy

Planning and implementation

- **P.O. use:** Give with food to prevent GI upset.
- **I.M. use:** Follow normal protocol.
- **I.V. use:** Give I.V. doses directly using 21G or 23G needle over 1 to 2 minutes. For intermittent infusion, give diluted drug through an intermittent infusion device or piggyback into an I.V. line containing free-flowing compatible solution. Infuse at ordered rate. Continuous infusion not recommended.
- To prevent nocturia, give in morning. If second dose is needed, give in early afternoon.
- The safest and most effective dosage schedule for control of edema is intermittent dosage either given on alternate days or given for 3 to 4 days with 1- or 2-day rest periods.
- Drug can be used safely in patients allergic to furosemide; 1 mg of bumetanide equals 40 mg of furosemide. Bumetanide may be less ototoxic than furosemide, but clinical relevance hasn't been determined.
- If oliguria or azotemia develops or increases, anticipate that prescriber may stop drug.
- Notify prescriber if drug-related hearing changes occur.

Patient teaching

- Advise patient to stand up slowly to prevent dizziness; also, tell him to limit alcohol intake and strenuous exercise in hot weather to avoid exacerbating orthostatic hypotension.
- Teach patient to monitor fluid volume by measuring weight and fluid intake and output daily.
- Advise patient to take drug early in day to avoid sleep interruption caused by nocturia.
- Tell patient with diabetes receiving bumetanide to monitor glucose levels closely.

Evaluation

- Patient is free from edema.
- Patient demonstrates adjustment of lifestyle to deal with altered patterns of urinary elimination.
- Patient and family state understanding of drug therapy.

buprenorphine hydrochloride

(byoo-preh-NOR-feen high-droh-KLOR-ighd)
Buprenex

Pharmacologic class: narcotic agonist-antagonist, opioid partial agonist
Therapeutic class: analgesic
Pregnancy risk category: C
Controlled substance schedule: V

Indications and dosages

▶ **Moderate-to-severe pain.** *Adults and children age 13 and older:* 0.3 mg I.M. or slow I.V. q 6 hours, p.r.n., or around the clock. May repeat 0.3 mg or increase to 0.6 mg, if needed, 30 to 60 minutes after initial dose.
Children ages 2 to 12: 2 to 6 mcg/kg I.V. or I.M. q 4 to 6 hours.

▶ **Postoperative pain‡.** *Adults:* 25 to 250 mcg/hour via I.V. infusion over 48 hours.

▶ **Pain‡.** *Adults:* 60 to 80 mcg via epidural injection.

▶ **Circumcision‡.** *Children ages 9 months to 9 years:* 3 mg/kg I.M. with surgical anesthesia.

Contraindications and precautions

- Contraindicated in patients hypersensitive to drug.
- Use cautiously in debilitated patients and patients with head injury, intracranial lesions, increased intracranial pressure, or severe respiratory, liver, or kidney impairment. Also use cautiously in patients with CNS depression or coma, thyroid irregularities, adrenal insufficiency, prostatic hyperplasia, urethral stricture, acute alcoholism, alcohol withdrawal syndrome, or kyphoscoliosis.

Lifespan: In pregnant and breast-feeding women, use cautiously. In elderly patients, also use cautiously.

Adverse reactions

CNS: *vertigo, dizziness, sedation,* fatigue, weakness, depression, dreaming, psychosis, slurred speech, parathesia, headache, confusion, nervousness, euphoria, ***increased intracranial pressure.***
CV: *hypotension,* ***bradycardia,*** tachycardia, hypertension, cyanosis, flushing, Wenckebach block.

EENT: *miosis,* blurred vision, diplopia, visual abnormalities, tinnitus, conjunctivitis.
GI: *nausea,* vomiting, constipation, dry mouth.
GU: urine retention.
Respiratory: ***respiratory depression,*** hypoventilation, dyspnea.
Skin: pruritus, *sweating,* injection site reaction.
Other: chills, withdrawal syndrome.

Interactions

Drug-drug. *CNS depressants, MAO inhibitors:* May have additive effects. Monitor patient.
Narcotic analgesics: Possible decreased analgesic effect. Avoid using together.
Drug-lifestyle. *Alcohol use:* May have additive effects. Discourage using together.

Effects on lab test results

- May decrease alkaline phosphatase level.
- May decrease hemoglobin, hematocrit, erythrocyte count, and sedimentation rate.

Pharmacokinetics

Absorption: Rapid.
Distribution: About 96% protein-bound.
Metabolism: Metabolized in liver.
Excretion: Excreted primarily in feces. *Half-life:* 1.2 to 7.2 hours.

Route	Onset	Peak	Duration
I.V., I.M.	15 min	1 hr	About 6 hr

Pharmacodynamics

Chemical effect: Binds with opiate receptors in CNS, altering perception of and emotional response to pain.
Therapeutic effect: Relieves pain.

Available forms

Injection: 0.324 mg (0.3 mg base/ml).

NURSING PROCESS

Assessment

- Obtain history of patient's pain.
- Monitor respiratory status frequently for at least 1 hour after administration. Notify prescriber if respiratory depression occurs.
- Evaluate patient's and family's understanding of drug therapy.

Nursing diagnoses

- Acute pain related to underlying condition
- Ineffective breathing pattern related to drug-induced respiratory depression
- Deficient knowledge related to drug therapy

Planning and implementation

- **I.V. use:** Give by direct I.V. injection into vein or through tubing of free-flowing compatible I.V. solution over at least 2 minutes.
- **I.M. use:** Follow normal protocol. Data are insufficient to give single I.M. doses greater than 0.6 mg for long-term use.
- Analgesic potency of 0.3 mg buprenorphine is equal to that of 10 mg morphine and 75 mg meperidine, but buprenorphine has a longer duration of action.
- Notify prescriber if pain isn't relieved.
- If patient's respiratory rate falls below 8 breaths/minute, withhold dose, arouse patient to stimulate breathing, and notify prescriber.
- Naloxone won't completely reverse respiratory depression caused by buprenorphine overdose; mechanical ventilation may be necessary. Doxapram and larger-than-usual doses of naloxone also may be ordered.
- Drug may precipitate withdrawal syndrome in narcotic-dependent patients.
- If dependence occurs, withdrawal symptoms may appear up to 14 days after drug is stopped.

Patient teaching

- Caution ambulatory patient about getting out of bed or walking because of dizziness or hypotension.
- When drug is used postoperatively, encourage patient to turn, cough, and deep-breathe to prevent atelectasis.

Evaluation

- Patient reports pain relief.
- Patient's respiratory status is within normal limits.
- Patient and family state understanding of drug therapy.

bupropion hydrochloride

(byoo-PROH-pee-on high-droh-KLOR-ighd)
Wellbutrin, Wellbutrin SR, Zyban

Pharmacologic class: aminoketone
Therapeutic class: antidepressant, aid to smoking cessation
Pregnancy risk category: B

Indications and dosages

▶ **Depression.** ***Wellbutrin, Wellbutrin SE.*** *Adults:* Initially, 100 mg P.O. b.i.d. Or, 75 mg P.O. t.i.d. Increase dosage after 3 days to 100 mg P.O. t.i.d., if needed. If no response occurs after several weeks of therapy, increase dosage to 150 mg t.i.d. For sustained-release tablets, 150 mg P.O. q morning; increased to target dose of 150 mg P.O. b.i.d., as tolerated, as early as day 4 of dosing. Usual adult dosage is 300 mg daily; maximum dosage is 450 mg daily.

▶ **Aid to smoking cessation.** ***Zyban.*** *Adults:* 150 mg P.O. daily for 3 days; increase to 150 mg P.O. b.i.d. (at least 8 hours apart) (maximum dose). Therapy is started while patient is still smoking.

▶ **Attention deficit hyperactivity disorder‡.** ***Wellbutrin.*** *Adults:* 150 mg P.O. daily with regular release tablets. Dosage may be adjusted to the maximum daily dose of 450 mg P.O.

Contraindications and precautions

- Contraindicated in patients hypersensitive to drug, in those who have taken MAO inhibitors during previous 14 days, and in those with seizure disorders, a history of bulimia, or anorexia nervosa.
- Use cautiously in patients with renal or hepatic impairment, and in patients with recent MI or unstable heart disease.

Lifespan: In pregnant women, use cautiously. If drug must be administered to breast-feeding woman, breast-feeding should be discontinued. In children, safety of drug hasn't been established.

Adverse reactions

CNS: fever, *headache,* akathisia, ***seizures, agitation,*** anxiety, *confusion,* delusions, euphoria, hostility, impaired sleep quality, insomnia, sedation, sensory disturbance, syncope, tremor.
CV: ***arrhythmias,*** hypertension, hypotension, palpitations, tachycardia.
EENT: auditory disturbance, blurred vision.
GI: dry mouth, taste disturbance, increased appetite, constipation, dyspepsia, nausea, vomiting, anorexia.
GU: impotence, menstrual complaints, urinary frequency.
Metabolic: hyperglycemia, weight gain or loss.
Musculoskeletal: arthritis.
Skin: pruritus, rash, cutaneous temperature disturbance, diaphoresis.
Other: chills, decreased libido.

Interactions

Drug-drug. *Carbamazepine:* May decrease bupropion levels. Monitor patient for loss of therapeutic effect.
Levodopa, MAO inhibitors, phenothiazines, tricyclic antidepressants; recent and rapid withdrawal of benzodiazepines: May increase risk of adverse reactions, including seizures. Monitor patient closely.
Ritonavir: May increase bupropion levels, increasing toxicity risk. Monitor patient closely.
Drug-lifestyle. *Alcohol use:* May alter seizure threshold. Discourage use together.
Sun exposure: Photosensitivity reactions may occur. Advise patient to wear protective clothing and sunblock and avoid sun exposure.

Effects on lab test results

- May increase or decrease glucose level.
- May decrease platelet count, hemoglobin, and hematocrit. May increase or decrease WBC count.

Pharmacokinetics

Absorption: Unknown.
Distribution: At plasma levels up to 200 mcg/ml, drug appears to be about 80% bound to plasma proteins.
Metabolism: Probably metabolized in liver; several active metabolites have been identified.
Excretion: Primarily excreted in urine. *Half-life:* 8 to 24 hours.

Route	Onset	Peak	Duration
P.O.	1-3 wk	≤ 2 hr	Unknown

Pharmacodynamics

Chemical effect: Unknown. Drug isn't a tricyclic antidepressant, doesn't inhibit MAO, and is a weak inhibitor of norepinephrine, dopamine, and serotonin reuptake.
Therapeutic effect: Relieves depression, smoking deterrant.

Available forms

Tablets: 75 mg, 100 mg
Tablets (sustained-release): 100 mg, 150 mg, 200 mg

NURSING PROCESS

Assessment

- Obtain history of patient's condition before therapy and reassess regularly thereafter.
- Be alert for adverse reactions and drug interactions.
- Monitor patient with history of bipolar disorder closely. Antidepressants can cause manic episodes during depressed phase of bipolar disorder.
- Evaluate patient's and family's understanding of drug therapy.

Nursing diagnoses

- Ineffective individual coping related to underlying condition
- Risk for injury related to drug-induced adverse CNS reactions
- Deficient knowledge related to drug therapy

Planning and implementation

ALERT: Risk of seizures may be minimized by not exceeding 450 mg daily and by giving daily amount in three to four equally divided doses. Many patients who experience seizures have predisposing factors, including history of head trauma, seizures, or CNS tumors, or they may be taking a drug that lowers seizure threshold.
- Make sure patient has swallowed dose before leaving bedside.
- Patient may experience period of increased restlessness, agitation, insomnia, and anxiety, especially at beginning of therapy.
- For smoking cessation, begin therapy while patient is still smoking; about 1 week is needed to achieve steady state levels of drug. Patient should cease smoking during the second week of treatment. Course of treatment is usually 7 to 12 weeks.

Patient teaching
- Advise patient to take drug as scheduled and to take each day's amount in three divided doses to minimize risk of seizures.
- Tell patient to avoid alcohol while taking drug because alcohol may contribute to development of seizures.
- Advise patient to avoid hazardous activities that require alertness and good psychomotor coordination until CNS effects of drug are known.

ALERT: Advise patient not to take Wellbutrin with Zyban and to seek medical advice before taking other prescription drugs, OTC medications, or herbal remedies.
- Tell patient not to crush, chew, or divide sustained-release tablets.

Evaluation

- Patient's behavior and communication indicate improvement of depression.
- Patient doesn't experience injury from drug-induced adverse CNS reactions.
- Patient and family state understanding of drug therapy.

buspirone hydrochloride
(byoo-SPEER-ohn high-droh-KLOR-ighd)
BuSpar

Pharmacologic class: azaspirodecanedione derivative
Therapeutic class: anxiolytic
Pregnancy risk category: B

Indications and dosages

▶ **Anxiety disorders, short-term relief of anxiety.** *Adults:* Initially, 5 mg P.O. t.i.d. Increase dosage at 2- to 4-day intervals in 5-mg/day increments. Usual maintenance dosage is 15 to 30 mg daily in two or three divided doses. Don't exceed 60 mg daily.

When given with a CYP3A4 inhibitor, lower initial dosage to 2.5 mg P.O. b.i.d. Subsequent dosage adjustment of either drug also may be needed.

Contraindications and precautions

- Contraindicated in patients hypersensitive to drug and in those who have taken an MAO inhibitor within 14 days.

• Use cautiously in patients with hepatic or renal failure.
Lifespan: In pregnant women, use cautiously. In breast-feeding women, avoid use. In children, safety of drug hasn't been established.

Adverse reactions

CNS: *dizziness, drowsiness,* nervousness, excitement, insomnia, headache, fatigue.
GI: dry mouth, nausea, diarrhea.

Interactions

Drug-drug. *CNS depressants:* May increase CNS depression. Avoid use together.
MAO inhibitors: May elevate blood pressure. Avoid using together.
Drug-lifestyle. *Alcohol use:* May increase CNS depression. Discourage use together.

Effects on lab test results

• May increase aminotransferase level.
• May decrease WBC and platelet counts.

Pharmacokinetics

Absorption: Rapidly and completely absorbed, but extensive first-pass metabolism limits absolute bioavailability to between 1% and 13% of P.O. dose. Food slows absorption but increases amount of unchanged drug in systemic circulation.
Distribution: 95% protein-bound; doesn't displace other highly protein-bound medications.
Metabolism: Metabolized in liver, resulting in at least one active metabolite.
Excretion: 29% to 63% excreted in urine in 24 hours, primarily as metabolites; 18% to 38% excreted in feces. *Half-life:* 2 to 3 hours.

Route	Onset	Peak	Duration
P.O.	Unknown	40-90 min	Unknown

Pharmacodynamics

Chemical effect: Unknown; may inhibit neuronal firing and reduce serotonin turnover in cortical, amygdaloid, and septohippocampal tissue.
Therapeutic effect: Relieves anxiety.

Available forms

Tablets: 5 mg, 10 mg, 15 mg

NURSING PROCESS

Assessment

• Obtain history of patient's anxiety before therapy and reassess regularly thereafter.
• Signs of improvement usually appear within 7 to 10 days; optimal results occur after 3 to 4 weeks of therapy.
• Be alert for adverse reactions and drug interactions.
• Evaluate patient's and family's understanding of drug therapy.

Nursing diagnoses

• Anxiety related to underlying condition
• Fatigue related to drug-induced adverse reactions
• Deficient knowledge related to drug therapy

Planning and implementation

• Although drug has shown no potential for abuse and hasn't been classified as a controlled substance, it isn't recommended for relief of everyday stress.
• Before starting therapy in patient already being treated with a benzodiazepine, make sure he doesn't stop benzodiazepine abruptly; withdrawal reaction may occur.
• Give drug with food or milk.
• Dosage may be increased in 2- to 4-day intervals, as ordered.

Patient teaching

• Tell patient to take drug with food.
• Warn patient to avoid hazardous activities that require alertness and psychomotor coordination until CNS effects of drug are known.
• Review energy-saving measures with patient and family.
• If patient is already being treated with a benzodiazepine, warn him not to abruptly discontinue it because withdrawal reaction can occur. Teach him how and when benzodiazepine can be withdrawn safely.

Evaluation

• Patient's anxiety is reduced.
• Patient states that energy-saving measures help combat fatigue caused by therapy.
• Patient and family state understanding of drug therapy.

busulfan

(byoo-SUL-fan)
Myleran

Pharmacologic class: alkylating agent (not specific to cell cycle phase)
Therapeutic class: antineoplastic
Pregnancy risk category: D

Indications and dosages

Indications and dosages may vary.

▶ **Palliative treatment of chronic myelocytic (granulocytic) leukemia (CML).** *Adults:* For remission induction, 4 to 8 mg P.O. daily (0.06 mg/kg or 1.8 mg/m^2). For maintenance therapy, 1 to 3 mg P.O. daily.
Children: 0.06 mg/kg or 1.8 mg/m^2 P.O. daily.

▶ **For use in combination with cyclophosphamide as a conditioning regimen prior to allogeneic hematopoietic progenitor cell transplantation for CML.** *Adults:* 0.8 mg/kg of ideal body weight or actual body weight (whichever is lower) via central venous catheter q 6 hours for 4 days for a total of 16 doses. Give phenytoin for seizure prophylaxis.

▶ **Myelofibrosis‡.** *Adults:* Initially, give 2 to 4 mg P.O. daily, then followed by the same dose 2 to 3 times weekly.

Contraindications and precautions

- Contraindicated in patients with drug-resistant CML.
- Use cautiously in patients recently given other myelosuppressive drugs or radiation therapy and in those with depressed neutrophil or platelet count. Because high-dose therapy has been linked to seizures, use such therapy cautiously in patients with history of head trauma or seizures and in patients receiving other drugs that lower seizure threshold.

Lifespan: In pregnant women, use with extreme caution, if at all. In breast-feeding women, use is contraindicated.

Adverse reactions

CNS: ***seizures,*** unusual tiredness or weakness.
GI: nausea, vomiting, diarrhea, cheilosis, glossitis.
GU: amenorrhea, testicular atrophy, impotence.
Hematologic: ***leukocytopenia, thrombocytopenia, anemia, severe pancytopenia.***
Metabolic: profound hyperuricemia caused by increased cell lysis.
Respiratory: persistent cough, dyspnea, ***bronchopulmonary dysplasia with irreversible pulmonary fibrosis*** (commonly termed "busulfan lung").
Skin: transient hyperpigmentation, rash, urticaria, anhidrosis, alopecia.
Other: gynecomastia, Addison-like wasting syndrome.

Interactions

Drug-drug. *Acetaminophen:* Busulfan levels increase with simultaneous administration or if given within 72 hours. Avoid using together.
Anticoagulants, aspirin: May increase risk of bleeding. Avoid using together.
Itraconazole: Decreases busulfan clearance by 25%. Avoid using together.
Phenytoin: Increases busulfan clearance by 18%. Monitor patient for reduced effectiveness.
Thioguanine: May cause hepatotoxicity, esophageal varices, or portal hypertension. Use together cautiously.

Effects on lab test results

- May increase uric acid level.
- May decrease hemoglobin, hematocrit, and WBC, RBC, and platelet counts.

Pharmacokinetics

Absorption: Well absorbed from GI tract.
Distribution: Unknown.
Metabolism: Metabolized in liver.
Excretion: Cleared rapidly from plasma and excreted in urine. *Half-life:* About 2½ hours.

Route	Onset	Peak	Duration
P.O.	1-2 wk	Unknown	Unknown

Pharmacodynamics

Chemical effect: Unknown; thought to cross-link strands of cellular DNA and interfere with RNA transcription, causing an imbalance of growth that leads to cell death.
Therapeutic effect: Kills selected type of cancer cell.

Available forms

Tablets: 2 mg

NURSING PROCESS

Assessment
- Obtain history of patient's underlying neoplastic disease.
- Monitor effectiveness by noting results of follow-up diagnostic tests and overall physical status. Note patient's response (increased appetite and sense of well-being, decreased total WBC count, reduced size of spleen), which usually begins within 1 to 2 weeks.
- Monitor WBC and platelet counts weekly while patient is receiving drug. WBC count falls about 10 days after the start of therapy and continues to fall for 2 weeks after stopping drug.
- Monitor uric acid level.

ALERT: Be alert for adverse reactions and drug interactions. Pulmonary fibrosis may occur as late as 4 to 6 months after treatment.
- Evaluate patient's and family's understanding of drug therapy.

Nursing diagnoses
- Ineffective health maintenance related to presence of neoplastic disease
- Risk for infection related to drug-induced immunosuppression
- Deficient knowledge related to drug therapy

Planning and implementation
- **I.V. use:** Premedicate patient with dilantin to decrease risk of seizures that can occur with I.V. infusion.
- Follow facility policy regarding preparation and handling of drug. Label as hazardous drug.
- Give drug at same time each day.
- Make sure patient is adequately hydrated.
- Dosage is adjusted based on patient's weekly WBC counts, and the prescriber may temporarily stop drug therapy if severe leukocytopenia develops. Therapeutic effects are often accompanied by toxicity.
- Drug usually is given with allopurinol in addition to adequate hydration to prevent hyperuricemia with resulting uric acid nephropathy.

Patient teaching
- Warn patient to watch for signs of infection (fever, sore throat, fatigue) and bleeding (easy bruising, nosebleeds, bleeding gums, melena) and to take temperature daily.

ALERT: Instruct patient to report symptoms of toxicity so that dosage adjustments can be made. Symptoms include persistent cough and progressive dyspnea with alveolar exudate, suggestive of pneumonia.
- Instruct patient to avoid OTC products that contain aspirin.
- Advise woman of childbearing age to avoid becoming pregnant during therapy. Recommend that patient consult with prescriber before becoming pregnant.
- Advise breast-feeding woman to discontinue breast-feeding because of possible risk of toxicity in infant.

Evaluation
- Patient exhibits positive response to drug therapy.
- Patient remains free from infection.
- Patient and family state understanding of drug therapy.

butorphanol tartrate
(byoo-TOR-fah-nohl TAR-trayt)
Stadol, Stadol NS

Pharmacologic class: narcotic agonist-antagonist; opioid partial agonist
Therapeutic class: analgesic, adjunct to anesthesia
Pregnancy risk category: C

Indications and dosages
▶ **Moderate-to-severe pain.** *Adults:* 0.5 to 2 mg I.V. q 3 to 4 hours, p.r.n. or around the clock. Or, 1 to 4 mg I.M. q 3 to 4 hours, p.r.n. or around the clock. Maximum 4 mg per dose. Alternatively, 1 mg by nasal spray q 3 to 4 hours (1 spray in one nostril); repeated in 60 to 90 minutes if pain relief is inadequate.
▶ **Labor for pregnant women at full term and in early labor.** *Adults:* 1 to 2 mg I.V. or I.M., repeated after 4 hours, p.r.n.
▶ **Preoperative anesthesia or preanesthesia.** *Adults:* 2 mg I.M. 60 to 90 minutes before surgery.
▶ **Adjunct to balanced anesthesia.** *Adults:* 2 mg I.V. shortly before induction or 0.5 to 1 mg I.V. in increments during anesthesia.
Patients with hepatic or renal impairment and geriatric patients: Reduce dose to one-half of

the usual parenteral adult dose at 6-hour intervals p.r.n. For nasal spray, the initial dose (1 spray/nostril) is the same, but repeat dose is in 90 to 120 minutes, if needed. Repeat doses thereafter q 6 hours, p.r.n.

Contraindications and precautions

• Contraindicated in patients with narcotic addiction; may precipitate withdrawal syndrome. Also contraindicated in patients hypersensitive to drug or to preservative (benzethonium chloride).

• Use cautiously in patients with head injury, increased intracranial pressure, acute MI, ventricular dysfunction, coronary insufficiency, respiratory disease or depression, or renal or hepatic dysfunction. Also use cautiously in patients who have recently received repeated doses of narcotic analgesic.

Lifespan: In pregnant women, use with extreme caution, if at all. In breast-feeding women, drug is contraindicated. Use cautiously in children; drug may cause paradoxical excitement.

Adverse reactions

CNS: *sedation, headache, vertigo, floating sensation,* lethargy, *confusion,* nervousness, unusual dreams, agitation, euphoria, hallucinations, flushing, increased intracranial pressure.
CV: palpitations, fluctuation in blood pressure.
EENT: diplopia, blurred vision, *nasal congestion* (with nasal spray).
GI: nausea, vomiting, constipation, *dry mouth.*
Respiratory: ***respiratory depression.***
Skin: rash, urticaria, *clamminess, excessive sweating.*

Interactions

Drug-drug. *CNS depressants:* May have additive effects. Use together cautiously.
Narcotic analgesics: Possible decreased analgesic effect. Avoid using together.
Drug-lifestyle. *Alcohol use:* May have additive depressant effects. Discourage using together.

Effects on lab test results

None reported.

Pharmacokinetics

Absorption: Well absorbed after I.M. administration; unknown after nasal administration.
Distribution: About 80% bound to plasma proteins. After I.V. administation, mean volume of distribution is about 500 L. Drug rapidly crosses placenta, and neonatal levels are 0.4 to 1.4 times maternal levels.
Metabolism: Extensively metabolized in liver to inactive metabolites.
Excretion: Excreted in inactive form, mainly by kidneys. About 11% to 14% of parenteral dose excreted in feces.

Route	Onset	Peak	Duration
I.V.	2-3 min	0.5-1 hr	2-4 hr
I.M.	10-30 min	0.5-1 hr	3-4 hr
Intranasal	≤ 15 min	1-2 hr	4-5 hr

Pharmacodynamics

Chemical effect: Binds with opiate receptors in CNS, altering both perception of and emotional response to pain through unknown mechanism.
Therapeutic effect: Relieves pain and enhances anesthesia.

Available forms

Injection: 1 mg/ml, 2 mg/ml
Nasal spray: 10 mg/ml

NURSING PROCESS

Assessment

• Obtain history of patient's pain before and after drug administration.
• Be alert for adverse reactions and drug interactions.
• Periodically monitor postoperative vital signs and bladder function. Because drug decreases both rate and depth of respirations, monitoring arterial oxygen saturation may aid in assessing respiratory depression.
• Evaluate patient's and family's understanding of drug therapy.

Nursing diagnoses

• Acute pain related to underlying condition
• Risk for injury related to drug-induced adverse CNS reactions
• Deficient knowledge related to drug therapy

Planning and implementation

• **I.V. use:** Give drug by direct I.V. injection into vein or into I.V. line containing free-flowing compatible solution.
• **I.M. use:** Follow normal protocol.

• **Intranasal use:** Have patient clear nasal passages before administering drug. Shake container. Tilt patient's head slightly backward; insert nozzle into nostril, pointing away from septum. Have patient hold other nostril closed, and then spray while patient inhales gently.
• S.C. route isn't recommended.
• Psychological and physical addiction may occur.
• Notify prescriber and discuss increasing dose or frequency if pain persists.
• Keep narcotic antagonist (naloxone) and resuscitative equipment readily available.

Patient teaching
• Caution ambulatory patient about getting out of bed or walking. Warn outpatient to refrain from driving and performing other activities that require mental alertness until drug's CNS effects are known.
• Warn patient that drug can cause physical and psychological dependence. Tell him that he should use drug only as directed and that abrupt withdrawal after prolonged use produces intense withdrawal symptoms.

☑ Evaluation
• Patient reports relief of pain.
• Patient doesn't experience injury as a result of therapy.
• Patient and family state understanding of drug therapy.

C

calcitonin (salmon)
(kal-sih-TOH-nin)
Miacalcin, Salmonine

Pharmacologic class: thyroid hormone, calcium and bone metabolism regulator
Therapeutic class: hypocalcemic, bone resorption inhibitor
Pregnancy risk category: C

Indications and dosages
▶ **Paget's disease of bone (osteitis deformans).** *Adults:* Initially, 100 IU daily I.M. or S.C.; maintenance dosage is 50 to 100 IU daily or every other day.
▶ **Hypercalcemia.** *Adults:* 4 IU/kg q 12 hours I.M. or S.C. If response is inadequate after 1 or 2 days, dosage increased to 8 IU/kg I.M. q 12 hours. If response remains unsatisfactory after 2 more days, dosage increased to maximum of 8 units/kg q 6 hours. Or,‡ 2 to 16 IU/kg I.V. q 12 hours.
▶ **Postmenopausal osteoporosis.** *Adults:* 100 IU daily I.M. or S.C. Or, 200 IU (one activation) daily intranasally, alternating nostrils daily. Patients should receive adequate vitamin D and calcium supplements.
▶ **Osteogenesis imperfecta‡.** *Adults:* 2 IU/kg S.C. or I.M. three times weekly with daily calcium supplementation.

Contraindications and precautions
• Contraindicated in patients hypersensitive to drug.
Lifespan: With pregnant women, use cautiously. In breast-feeding women, don't use because drug may inhibit lactation. In children, safety of drug hasn't been established.

Adverse reactions
CV: *facial flushing.*
CNS: headache.
EENT: *nasal symptoms (irritation, redness, sores)* with nasal spray use, *rhinitis,* epitaxis.
GI: transient nausea, unusual taste, diarrhea, anorexia, *nausea with or without vomiting.*
GU: transient diuresis, urinary frequency, nocturia.
Metabolic: hypocalcemia, hyperglycemia, hyperthyroidism.
Musculoskeletal: back pain, arthralgia.
Skin: *inflammation at injection site;* rash.
Other: hand swelling, tingling, and tenderness; hypersensitivity reactions, ***anaphylaxis.***

Interactions
None significant.

Effects on lab test results
• May increase glucose level. May decrease calcium level.

Pharmacokinetics
Absorption: For parenteral administration, drug is absorbed directly into the circulation.

Distribution: Unknown; however, calcitonin doesn't cross the placenta.
Metabolism: Rapidly metabolized in kidneys; additional activity in blood and peripheral tissues.
Excretion: Excreted in urine as inactive metabolites. *Half-life:* Calcitonin human, 60 minutes; calcitonin salmon, 70 to 90 minutes.

Route	Onset	Peak	Duration
I.V.	Immediate	Unknown	12 hr
I.M., S.C.	≤ 15 min	≤ 4 hr	8-24 hr
Intranasal	Rapid	30 min	1 hr

Pharmacodynamics

Chemical effect: Decreases osteoclastic activity by inhibiting osteocytic osteolysis; decreases mineral release and matrix or collagen breakdown in bone.
Therapeutic effect: Prohibits bone and kidney (tubular) resorption of calcium.

Available forms

Injection: 100 IU/ml, 1-ml ampules; 200 IU/ml, 2-ml ampules
Nasal spray: 200 IU/activation in 2-ml bottle (0.09 ml/dose)

NURSING PROCESS

Assessment

- Assess patient's calcium level before therapy and regularly thereafter.
- If using nasal spray, assess nasal passages before beginning treatment and periodically thereafter.
- Monitor alkaline phosphatase and 24-hour urine hydroxyproline levels to evaluate drug effectiveness.
- Periodic examinations of urine sediment are advisable.
- Be alert for adverse reactions.
- Evaluate patient's and family's knowledge of drug therapy.

Nursing diagnoses

- Risk for trauma related to patient's underlying bone condition
- Ineffective protection related to potential for drug-induced anaphylaxis
- Deficient knowledge related to drug therapy

Planning and implementation

- Skin test usually is performed before therapy.
- Give drug at bedtime when possible to minimize nausea and vomiting.
- **I.M. use:** I.M. route is preferred if dose exceeds 2 ml. Follow normal protocol.
- **S.C. use:** S.C. route is the preferred route for outpatient self-administration. Follow normal protocol.
- **Intranasal use:** Alternate nostrils daily.
- Use freshly reconstituted solution within 2 hours.
- Keep parenteral calcium available during first doses in case hypocalcemic tetany occurs.
- Refrigerate calcitonin salmon at 36° to 46° F (2° to 8° C). Store open nasal spray at room temperature.
- In patients who relapse after a positive initial response, expect to evaluate for antibody response to hormone protein.
- Keep epinephrine handy; systemic allergic reactions are possible because hormone is protein.
- If symptoms have been relieved after 6 months, treatment may be discontinued until symptoms or radiologic signs recur.

Patient teaching

- Teach patient how to take drug.
- Teach patient to activate nasal spray before first use. He should hold bottle upright and depress side arms six times until a faint mist occurs. This signifies that pump is primed and ready for use. Patient doesn't need to reprime the pump before each use.
- Instruct patient to report signs of nasal irritation with nasal spray.
- Tell patient to handle missed doses as follows: With daily dosing, take as soon as possible, but don't double the dose. With alternate-day dosing, take missed dose as soon as possible, and then restart alternate days from this dose.
- Reassure patient that facial flushing and warmth (which occur in 20% to 30% of patients within minutes of injection) usually subside in about 1 hour.
- Remind patient with postmenopausal osteoporosis to take adequate calcium and vitamin D supplements.

Evaluation

- Patient's calcium levels are normal.
- Patient doesn't experience anaphylaxis.

• Patient and family state understanding of drug therapy.

calcitriol (1,25-dihydroxycholecalciferol)

(kal-SIH-tree-ohl)

Calcijex, Rocaltrol

Pharmacologic class: vitamin D analogue
Therapeutic class: antihypocalcemic
Pregnancy risk category: C

Indications and dosages

▶ **Hypocalcemia in patients undergoing long-term dialysis.** *Adults:* Initially, 0.25 mcg P.O. daily, increase by 0.25 mcg daily at 4- to 8-week intervals. Maintenance dosage is 0.25 mcg q other day up to 1.25 mcg daily, or 1 to 2 mcg I.V. three times weekly about q other day. Dosages from 0.5 to 4 mcg three times weekly have been used initially. If response to initial dose is inadequate, may increase by 0.5 to 1 mcg at 2- to 4-week intervals. Maintenance dosage is 0.5 to 3 mcg I.V. three times weekly.

▶ **Hypoparathyroidism and pseudohypoparathyroidism.** *Adults and children age 6 and older:* Initially, 0.25 mcg P.O. daily. Dosage may be increased at 2- to 4-week intervals. Maintenance dosage is 0.25 to 2 mcg daily.

▶ **Hypoparathyroidism.** *Children and infants ages 1 to 5 years:* 0.25 to 0.75 mcg P.O. daily.

▶ **Management of secondary hyperparathyroidism and resulting metabolic bone disease in predialysis patients (moderate-to-severe chronic renal failure with creatinine clearance of 15 to 55 ml/minute).** *Adults and children age 3 and older:* Initially, 0.25 mcg P.O. daily. Dosage may be increased to 0.5 mcg daily, if necessary.
Children younger than age 3: Initially, 10 to 15 mcg/kg P.O. daily.

▶ **Psoriasis vulgaris‡.** *Adults:* 0.5 mcg P.O. daily for 6 months and topically (0.5 mcg/g petroleum) daily for 8 weeks.

Contraindications and precautions

• Contraindicated in patients with hypercalcemia or vitamin D toxicity.
Lifespan: In pregnant or breast-feeding women, use cautiously.

Adverse reactions

CNS: headache, somnolence.
EENT: conjunctivitis, photophobia, rhinorrhea.
GI: nausea, vomiting, constipation, metallic taste, dry mouth, anorexia.
GU: polyuria.
Musculoskeletal: weakness, bone and muscle pain.

Interactions

Drug-drug. *Cardiac glycosides:* May increase risk of arrhythmias. Avoid using together.
Cholestyramine, colestipol, excessive use of mineral oil: May decrease absorption of orally administered vitamin D analogues. Avoid using together.
Corticosteroids: Counteracts vitamin D analogue effects. Don't use together.
Ketoconazole: May decrease endogenous calcitriol level. Monitor patient.
Magnesium-containing antacids: May induce hypermagnesemia, especially in patients with chronic renal failure. Avoid using together.
Phenytoin, phenobarbital: May reduce plasma calcitriol levels. Higher doses of calcitriol may be needed.
Thiazides: May induce hypercalcemia. Monitor calcium levels and patient closely.
Verapamil: May cause atrial fibrillation due to increased risk of hypercalcemia. Follow levels and monitor patient closely.

Effects on lab test results

• May increase BUN, ALT, AST, albumin, and cholesterol levels.

Pharmacokinetics

Absorption: Absorbed readily.
Distributed: Distributed widely; protein-bound.
Metabolism: Metabolized in liver and kidneys.
Excretion: Excreted primarily in feces. *Half-life:* 3 to 6 hours.

Route	Onset	Peak	Duration
P.O.	2-6 hr	3-6 hr	3-5 days
I.V.	Immediate	Unknown	3-5 days

Pharmacodynamics

Chemical effect: Stimulates calcium absorption from GI tract; promotes calcium secretion from bone to blood.
Therapeutic effect: Raises calcium levels.

Available forms

Capsules: 0.25 mcg, 0.5 mcg
Injection: 1 mcg/ml, 2 mcg/ml
Oral solution: 1 mcg/ml

NURSING PROCESS

Assessment

- Assess patient's calcium level before therapy and reassess regularly thereafter to monitor drug effectiveness; calcium level times phosphate level shouldn't exceed 70. During dosage adjustment, determine calcium level twice weekly.
- Be alert for adverse reactions and drug interactions.
- Evaluate patient's and family's knowledge of drug therapy.

Nursing diagnoses

- Risk for injury related to patient's underlying condition
- Ineffective protection related to potential for drug-induced vitamin D intoxication
- Deficient knowledge related to drug therapy

Planning and implementation

- **P.O. use:** Follow normal protocol.
- **I.V. use:** Administer I.V. dose by rapid injection via dialysis catheter at end of hemodialysis treatment.
- Keep drug away from heat and light.
- Give drug at same time daily.
- Discontinue drug and notify prescriber if hypercalcemia occurs; resume drug after calcium level returns to normal. Patient should receive 1,000 mg of calcium daily.

Patient teaching

- Tell patient to immediately report early symptoms of vitamin D intoxication, such as weakness, nausea, vomiting, dry mouth, constipation, muscle or bone pain, or metallic taste.
- Instruct patient to adhere to diet and calcium supplements and to avoid unapproved OTC drugs and magnesium-containing antacids.
- Warn patient that calcitriol is most potent form of vitamin D available; severe toxicity can occur if ingested by anyone for whom it wasn't prescribed.
- Teach patient to protect medication from light.

Evaluation

- Patient's calcium level is normal.
- Patient doesn't experience injury from drug-induced vitamin D toxicity.
- Patient and family state understanding of drug therapy.

calcium acetate

(KAL-see-um AS-ih-tayt)
Phos-Lo

calcium carbonate

Apo-Cal ♦ †, Cal-Carb-HD†, Calci-Chew†, Calciday 667†, Calci-Mix†, Calcite 500 ♦ †, Calcium 600†, Cal-Plus†, Calsan ♦ †, Caltrate†, Caltrate 600 ♦ †, Chooz†, Fem Cal†, Florical†, Gencalc 600†, Mallamint†, Nephro-Calci†, Nu-Cal ♦ †, Os-Cal ♦ †, Os-Cal 500†, Os-Cal Chewable ♦ †, Oysco†, Oysco 500 Chewable†, Oyst-Cal 500†, Oystercal 500†, Oyster Shell Calcium-500†, Rolaids Calcium Rich†, Super Calcium 1200†, Titralac†, Tums†, Tums 500†, Tums E-X†

calcium chloride†

Calciject ♦

calcium citrate†

Citrical†, Citrical Liquitabs ♦ †

calcium glubionate†

Calcium-Sandoz ♦, Neo-Calglucon

calcium gluceptate†

calcium gluconate

calcium lactate†

calcium phosphate, dibasic†

calcium phosphate, tribasic

Posture†

Pharmacologic class: calcium supplement
Therapeutic class: therapeutic agent for electrolyte balance, cardiotonic
Pregnancy risk category: C

Indications and dosages

▶ **Hypocalcemic emergency.** *Adults:* 7 to 14 mEq calcium I.V. May be given as 10% calcium gluconate solution, 2% to 10% calcium chloride solution, or 22% calcium gluceptate solution. (Calcium gluceptate sodium may be given I.M. only in emergencies.)
Children: 1 to 7 mEq calcium I.V.
Infants: Up to 1 mEq calcium I.V.
▶ **Hypocalcemic tetany.** *Adults:* 4.5 to 16 mEq calcium I.V. Repeat until tetany is controlled.
Children: 0.5 to 0.7 mEq calcium I.V. t.i.d. or q.i.d. until tetany is controlled.
Neonates: 2.4 mEq I.V. daily in divided doses.
▶ **Adjunct treatment of cardiac arrest.** *Adults:* 0.027 to 0.054 mEq calcium chloride I.V., 4.5 to 6.3 mEq calcium gluceptate I.V., or 2.3 to 3.7 mEq calcium gluconate I.V.
Children: 0.27 mEq/kg calcium chloride I.V. Repeated in 10 minutes if necessary; determine calcium levels before giving further doses.
▶ **Adjunct treatment of magnesium intoxication.** *Adults:* Initially, 7 mEq I.V. Subsequent doses based on patient's response.
▶ **During exchange transfusions.** *Adults:* 1.35 mEq with each 100 ml citrated blood.
Neonates: 0.45 mEq after each 100 ml citrated blood.
▶ **Hyperphosphatemia in end-stage renal failure.** *Adults:* 2 to 4 tablets calcium acetate P.O. with each meal.
▶ **Dietary supplement.** *Adults:* 800 mg to 1.2 g P.O. daily.

Contraindications and precautions

- Contraindicated in patients with ventricular fibrillation, hypercalcemia, hypophosphatemia, or renal calculi.
- Use all calcium products with extreme caution in digitalized patients and in patients with sarcoidosis and renal or cardiac disease.
- Use calcium chloride cautiously in patients with cor pulmonale, respiratory acidosis, and respiratory failure.

Lifespan: In children, use I.V. route cautiously.

Adverse reactions

CNS: pain, tingling sensations, sense of oppression or heat waves with I.V. use; syncope with rapid I.V. injection.
CV: mild decrease in blood pressure; vasodilation, ***bradycardia, arrhythmias,*** and ***cardiac arrest*** with rapid I.V. injection.
GI: irritation, hemorrhage, *constipation* with oral use; chalky taste with I.V. use; hemorrhage, nausea, vomiting, thirst, abdominal pain with oral calcium chloride.
GU: hypercalcemia, polyuria, renal calculi.
Skin: local reactions including burning, necrosis, tissue sloughing, cellulitis, soft-tissue calcification with I.M. use.
Other: irritation (with S.C. injection); *vein irritation* with I.V. use.

Interactions

Drug-drug. *Atenolol, fluoroquinolones, tetracyclines:* May decrease bioavailability of these drugs and calcium when oral forms are taken together. Separate administration times.
Calcium channel blockers: May decrease calcium effectiveness. Avoid using together.
Cardiac glycosides: May increase digitalis toxicity. Give calcium cautiously (if at all) to digitalized patients.
Sodium polystyrene sulfonate: May increase risk of metabolic acidosis in patients with renal disease. Avoid using together in patients with renal disease.
Thiazide diuretics: May increase risk of hypercalcemia. Avoid using together.
Drug-food. *Foods containing oxalic acid (rhubarb, spinach), phytic acid (bran, whole cereals), or phosphorus (milk, dairy products):* May interfere with calcium absorption. Tell patient to avoid these foods.

Effects on lab test results

- May increase calcium and plasma 11-hydroxycorticosteroid levels.
- May produce false-negative values for serum and urinary magnesium as measured by the Titan yellow method.

Pharmacokinetics

Absorption: Absorbed actively in duodenum and proximal jejunum and, to lesser extent, in distal part of small intestine after oral administration. Pregnancy and reduced calcium intake may enhance absorption. Vitamin D in active form is required for absorption.
Distribution: Enters extracellular fluid and is incorporated rapidly into skeletal tissue. Bone contains 99% of total calcium; 1% is distrib-

uted equally between intracellular and extracellular fluids. Levels in CSF are about half those in serum.
Metabolism: Insignificant.
Excretion: Excreted mainly in feces, minimally in urine.

Route	Onset	Peak	Duration
P.O., I.M.	Unknown	Unknown	Unknown
I.V.	Immediate	Immediate	0.5-2 hr

Pharmacodynamics

Chemical effect: Replaces and maintains calcium.
Therapeutic effect: Raises calcium level.

Available forms

calcium acetate
Contains 253 mg or 12.7 mEq of elemental calcium/g
Injection: 0.5 mEq Ca‡ per ml
Tablets: 250 mg†, 500 mg†, 667 mg, 668 mg†, 1,000 mg†
calcium carbonate
Contains 400 mg or 20 mEq of elemental calcium/g
Capsules: 364 mg†, 1.25 g†
Oral suspension: 1.25 g/5 ml†
Powder packets: 6.5 g (2,400 mg calcium) per packet†
Tablets: 650 mg†, 667 mg†, 750 mg†, 1.25 g†, 1.5 g†
Tablets (chewable): 350 mg†, 420 mg†, 500 mg†, 625 mg†, 750 mg†, 850 mg†, 1.25 g†
calcium chloride
Contains 270 mg or 13.5 mEq of elemental calcium/g
Injection: 10% solution in 10-ml ampules, vials, and syringes
calcium citrate
Contains 211 mg or 10.6 mEq of elemental calcium/g
Effervescent tablets: 2,376 mg†
Tablets: 950 mg†
calcium glubionate
Contains 64 mg or 3.2 mEq of elemental calcium/g
Syrup: 1.8 g/5 ml
calcium gluceptate
Contains 82 mg or 4.1 mEq of elemental calcium/g
Injection: 1.1 g/5 ml in 5-ml ampules or 10-ml vials
calcium gluconate
Contains 90 mg or 4.5 mEq of elemental calcium/g
Injection: 10% solution in 10-ml ampules and vials, 10-ml or 50-ml vials
Tablets: 500 mg†, 650 mg†, 975 mg†, 1 g†
calcium lactate
Contains 130 mg or 6.5 mEq of elemental calcium/g
Tablets: 325 mg, 650 mg
calcium phosphate, dibasic
Contains 230 mg or 11.5 mEq of elemental calcium/g
Tablets: 468 mg†
calcium phosphate, tribasic
Contains 400 mg or 20 mEq of elemental calcium/g
Tablets: 600 mg†

NURSING PROCESS

Assessment

• Assess patient's calcium level before therapy and reassess frequently thereafter to monitor drug effectiveness. Hypercalcemia may result after large doses in patients with chronic renal failure.
• Be alert for adverse reactions and drug interactions.
• Evaluate patient's and family's knowledge of drug therapy.

Nursing diagnoses

• Ineffective protection related to calcium deficiency
• Risk for injury related to drug-induced adverse reactions
• Deficient knowledge related to drug therapy

Planning and implementation

• **P.O. use:** If GI upset occurs, give oral calcium products 1 to 1½ hours after meals.
• **I.V. use:** Give direct injection slowly through small needle into large vein or through I.V. line containing free-flowing, compatible solution at no more than 1 ml/minute (1.5 mEq/minute) for calcium chloride, 1.5 to 5 ml/minute for calcium gluconate, and 2 ml/minute for calcium gluceptate. Don't use scalp veins in children.
– When giving intermittent infusion, infuse diluted solution through I.V. line containing compatible solution. Maximum 200 mg/minute

*Liquid form contains alcohol. **May contain tartrazine. ♦Canada ◇Australia †OTC ‡Off-label use

suggested for calcium gluceptate and calcium gluconate.

ALERT: Make sure prescriber specifies which calcium form to administer because code carts usually contain both calcium gluconate and calcium chloride.

– Give calcium chloride only by I.V. route. When adding to parenteral solutions that contain other additives (especially phosphorus or phosphate), observe solution closely for precipitate. Use in-line filter.

– Warm solutions to body temperature before administration.

– After injection, make sure patient remains recumbent for 15 minutes.

– Monitor ECG when giving calcium I.V. Stop if patient complains of discomfort, and notify prescriber.

– Stop drug immediately if extravasation occurs (severe necrosis and tissue sloughing), and change I.V. site before continuing drug.

- **I.M. use:** give injection in gluteal region in adults; lateral thigh in infants. Only calcium gluceptate can be given via the I.M. route in emergencies when no I.V. route available.
- Withhold drug and notify prescriber if hypercalcemia occurs. Be prepared to provide emergency supportive care as needed until calcium level returns to normal.

Patient teaching

- Tell patient to take oral calcium 1 to 1½ hours after meals if GI upset occurs.

ALERT: Warn patient to avoid oxalic acid (found in rhubarb and spinach), phytic acid (in bran and whole cereals), and phosphorus (in milk and dairy products) because these substances may interfere with calcium absorption.

- Teach patient to recognize and report signs and symptoms of hypercalcemia.
- Stress importance of follow-up care and regular blood samples to monitor calcium level.

Evaluation

- Patient's calcium level is normal.
- Patient doesn't experience injury from calcium-induced adverse reactions.
- Patient and family state understanding of drug therapy.

calcium carbonate

(KAL-see-um KAR-buh-nayt)
Alka-Mints†, Amitone†, Cal-Sup ◇, Chooz†, Equilet†, Mallamint†, Rolaids Calcium Rich†, Titralac†, Titralac Extra Strength†, Titralac Plus†, Tums†, Tums E-X†, Tums Extra Strength†

Pharmacologic class: calcium supplement
Therapeutic class: therapeutic agent for electrolyte balance, antacid
Pregnancy risk category: NR

Indications and dosages

▶ **Antacid, calcium supplement.** *Adults:* 350 mg to 1.5 g P.O. or two pieces of chewing gum 1 hour after meals and h.s. p.r.n.

Contraindications and precautions

- Contraindicated in patients with ventricular fibrillation or hypercalcemia.
- Use cautiously, if at all, in patients receiving cardiac glycosides and in patients with sarcoidosis or renal or cardiac disease.

Lifespan: No contraindications or precautions reported.

Adverse reactions

GI: *constipation,* gastric distention, flatulence, rebound hyperacidity, *nausea.*

Interactions

Drug-drug. *Antibiotics (including quinolones and tetracyclines), hydantoins, iron, isoniazid, salicylates:* May decrease effects of these drugs because of possible impaired absorption. Separate administration times.
Enteric-coated drugs: May release prematurely in stomach. Separate doses by at least 1 hour.
Drug-food. *Milk, other foods high in vitamin D:* Possible milk-alkali syndrome (headache, confusion, distaste for food, nausea, vomiting, hypercalcemia, hypercalciuria, calcinosis, and hypophosphatemia). Discourage intake together.

Effects on lab test results

- May increase calcium levels. May decrease phosphate levels.

Pharmacokinetics

Absorption: Absorbed actively in small intestine. Pregnancy and reduced calcium intake may enhance absorption. Vitamin D in its active form is required for absorption.
Distribution: Enters extracellular fluid and is incorporated rapidly into skeletal tissue. Bone contains 99% of total calcium; 1% is distributed equally between intracellular and extracellular fluids. Levels in CSF are about half those of serum.
Metabolism: Insignificant.
Excretion: Excreted mainly in feces, minimally in urine.

Route	Onset	Peak	Duration
P.O.	≤ 20 min	Unknown	20-60 min (fasting), 3 hr (non-fasting)

Pharmacodynamics

Chemical effect: Reduces total acid load in GI tract, elevates gastric pH to reduce pepsin activity, strengthens gastric mucosal barrier, and increases esophageal sphincter tone.
Therapeutic effect: Raises calcium level and relieves mild gastric discomfort.

Available forms

Contains 40% calcium; 20 mEq calcium/g.
Chewing gum: 500 mg/piece
Lozenges: 600 mg†
Oral suspension: 250 mg/5 ml, 1 g/5 ml†
Tablets: 500 mg†, 600 mg†, 650 mg†, 1,000 mg†, 1,250 mg†
Tablets (chewable): 350 mg†, 420 mg†, 500 mg†, 750 mg, 850 mg, 1,000 mg, 1,250 mg ◇

NURSING PROCESS

Assessment

- Assess patient's underlying condition before therapy and regularly thereafter.
- Monitor calcium level, especially in patient with mild renal impairment.
- Be alert for adverse reactions and drug interactions.
- Evaluate patient's and family's knowledge of drug therapy.

Nursing diagnoses

- Imbalanced nutrition: less than body requirements related to insufficient calcium intake
- Risk for injury related to calcium-induced hypercalcemia
- Deficient knowledge related to drug therapy

Planning and implementation

- Give 1 hour after meals, as needed.
- Make sure patient with calcium deficiency is receiving adequate calcium in diet.

Patient teaching

- Advise patient not to take calcium carbonate indiscriminately or to switch antacids without consulting prescriber.
- Tell patient to take drug 1 hour after meals and at bedtime, as needed.

Evaluation

- Patient's symptoms are alleviated.
- Patient's calcium level is normal.
- Patient and family state understanding of drug therapy.

calcium polycarbophil

(KAL-see-um pah-lee-KAR-boh-fil)
Equalactin†, Fiberall†, FiberCon†, Fiber-Lax†, FiberNorm†, Mitrolan†

Pharmacologic class: hydrophilic agent
Therapeutic class: bulk laxative, antidiarrheal
Pregnancy risk category: NR

Indications and dosages

▶ **Constipation.** *Adults and children older than age 12:* 1 g P.O. q.i.d. as required. Maximum dosage is 6 g daily.
Children ages 6 to 12: 500 mg P.O. one to three times daily. Maximum dosage is 3 g daily.
Children ages 3 to 6: 500 mg P.O. b.i.d. Maximum dosage is 1.5 g daily. Use must be directed by prescriber.
▶ **Diarrhea related to irritable bowel syndrome; acute nonspecific diarrhea.** *Adults and children age 12 and older:* 1 g P.O. q.i.d. Maximum dosage is 6 g daily.
Children age 6 to 12: 500 mg P.O. t.i.d. Maximum dosage is 3 g daily.

Children ages 2 to 6: 500 mg P.O. b.i.d. Maximum dosage is 1.5 g daily. Use must be directed by prescriber.

Contraindications and precautions

- Contraindicated in patients with signs of GI obstruction.

Lifespan: No contraindications or precautions reported.

Adverse reactions

GI: abdominal fullness, increased flatus, intestinal obstruction.
Other: laxative dependence with long-term or excessive use.

Interactions

Drug-drug. *Tetracyclines:* May impair tetracycline absorption. Avoid using together.

Effects on lab test results

None reported.

Pharmacokinetics

Absorption: None.
Distribution: None.
Metabolism: None.
Excretion: Excreted in feces.

Route	Onset	Peak	Duration
P.O.	12-24 hr	≤ 3 days	Varies

Pharmacodynamics

Chemical effect: As a laxative, absorbs water and expands to increase bulk and moisture content of stool, which encourages peristalsis and bowel movement. As an antidiarrheal, absorbs free fecal water, thereby producing formed stools.
Therapeutic effect: Relieves constipation; relieves diarrhea caused by irritable bowel syndrome.

Available forms

Tablets: 500 mg†, 625 mg†, 1,250 mg†
Tablets (chewable): 500 mg†

NURSING PROCESS

Assessment

- Assess patient's bowel condition.
- Before giving drug for constipation, determine whether patient has adequate fluid intake, exercise, and diet.
- Monitor drug effectiveness by evaluating frequency and characteristics of patient's stools.
- Be alert for adverse reactions and drug interactions.
- Evaluate patient's and family's knowledge of drug therapy.

Nursing diagnoses

- Constipation related to underlying condition
- Diarrhea related to irritable bowel syndrome
- Deficient knowledge related to drug therapy

Planning and implementation

- Give drug with full glass of water when used to treat constipation. Don't give drug with water when used for diarrhea.
- Dose may be repeated every 30 minutes for severe diarrhea, but maximum daily dosage shouldn't be exceeded.
- Don't give to patient who has signs of GI obstruction.

Patient teaching

- Advise patient to chew Equalactin or Mitrolan tablets thoroughly before swallowing and to drink a full glass of water with each dose. If drug is used as an antidiarrheal, tell patient not to drink water with dose.
- Teach patient about dietary sources of bulk, including bran and other cereals, fresh fruit, and vegetables.
- For severe diarrhea, advise patient to repeat dose every 30 minutes, but tell him not to exceed maximum daily dosage.

Evaluation

- Patient's elimination pattern returns to normal.
- Patient reports improvement of diarrhea.
- Patient and family state understanding of drug therapy.

calfactant

(kal-FAK-tant)
Infasurf

Pharmacologic class: surfactant
Therapeutic class: respiratory distress syndrome (RDS) agent
Pregnancy risk category: NR

Indications and dosages

▶ **Prevention of RDS in premature infants under 29 weeks' gestational age at high risk for RDS; treatment of infants under 72 hours of age in whom RDS develops (confirmed by clinical and radiologic findings) and who need endotracheal intubation.** *Neonates:* 3 ml/kg body weight at birth intratracheally, administered in two aliquots of 1.5 ml/kg each, q 12 hours for total of three doses.

Contraindications and precautions

• None reported.
Lifespan: Indicated for premature infants only.

Adverse reactions

CV: BRADYCARDIA.
Respiratory: AIRWAY OBSTRUCTION, APNEA, *reflux of drug into endotracheal tube,* dislodgment of endotracheal tube, *hypoventilation, cyanosis.*

Interactions

None significant.

Effects on lab test results

None reported.

Pharmacokinetics

Absorption: Unknown.
Distribution: Unknown.
Metabolism: Unknown.
Excretion: Unknown.

Route	Onset	Peak	Duration
Intratracheal	24-48 hr	Unknown	Unknown

Pharmacodynamics

Chemical effect: Nonpyrogenic lung surfactant that modifies alveolar surface tension, thereby stabilizing the alveoli.
Therapeutic effect: Prevents RDS in premature infants or infants with specific characteristics.

Available forms

Intratracheal suspension: 35 mg phospholipids and 0.65 mg proteins/ml; 6-ml vial

NURSING PROCESS

Assessment

• Obtain history of patient's underlying condition before therapy and reassess regularly thereafter.
• Monitor patient for reflux of drug into endotracheal tube, cyanosis, bradycardia, or airway obstruction during the dosing procedure. If these occur, stop drug and take appropriate measures to stabilize infant. After infant is stable, resume dosing with appropriate monitoring.
• After giving drug, carefully monitor infant so that oxygen therapy and ventilatory support can be modified in response to improvements in oxygenation and lung compliance.
• Evaluate parents' knowledge of drug therapy.

Nursing diagnoses

• Risk for injury related to potential for RDS
• Impaired gas exchange related to presence of RDS
• Deficient knowledge related to drug therapy

Planning and implementation

• Drug should be given under supervision of a prescriber experienced in the acute care of newborn infants with respiratory failure who need intubation.
• Drug is intended only for intratracheal use; give for prophylaxis of RDS as soon as possible after birth, preferably within 30 minutes.
• Suspension settles during storage. Gentle swirling or agitation of the vial is often needed for redispersion, but don't shake. Visible flecks in the suspension and foaming at the surface are normal.
• Withdraw dose into a syringe from single-use vial using a 20G or larger needle; avoid excessive foaming.
• Each single-use vial should be entered only once; discard unused material after use.
• Give through a side-port adapter into the endotracheal tube. Two medical personnel should be present during dosing. Give dose in two aliquots of 1.5 ml/kg each. Give while ventila-

tion continues over 20 to 30 breaths for each aliquot, with small bursts timed only during the inspiratory cycles. Evaluate respiratory status and reposition infant between each aliquot.
- Store drug at 36° to 46° F (2° to 8° C). It isn't necessary to warm drug before use. Unopened, unused vials that have warmed to room temperature can be returned to refrigerated storage within 24 hours for future use. Avoid repeated warming to room temperature.

Patient teaching
- Explain to parents the reason for using drug to prevent or treat RDS.
- Notify parents that, although infant may improve rapidly after treatment, he may continue to need intubation and mechanical ventilation.
- Notify parents of the potential adverse effects of drug, including bradycardia, reflux into endotracheal tube, airway obstruction, cyanosis, dislodgment of endotracheal tube, and hypoventilation.
- Reassure parents that infant will be carefully monitored.

☑ Evaluation
- Premature infant doesn't develop RDS.
- Patient's gas exchange improves because of oxygenation and increased lung compliance.
- Family states understanding of drug therapy.

candesartan cilexetil
(kan-dih-SAR-ten se-LEKS-ih-til)
Atacand

Pharmacologic class: angiotensin II receptor antagonist
Therapeutic class: antihypertensive
Pregnancy risk category: C (D in second and third trimesters)

Indications and dosages
▶ **Treatment of hypertension (alone or with other antihypertensives).** *Adults:* Initially, 16 mg P.O. once daily when used as monotherapy; usual dosage is 8 to 32 mg P.O. daily as single dose or divided b.i.d.

Contraindications and precautions
- Contraindicated in patients hypersensitive to drug or its components.
- Use cautiously in patients whose renal function depends on the renin-angiotensin-aldosterone system (such as patients with heart failure) because of risk of oliguria and progressive azotemia with acute renal failure or death.
- Use cautiously in patients who are volume- or salt-depleted because of risk of symptomatic hypotension.

Lifespan: In pregnant women, don't use because drugs that act directly on the renin-angiotension system (such as candesartan) can cause fetal and neonatal harm and death. These problems haven't been detected when exposure has been limited to first trimester. If pregnancy is suspected, notify prescriber because drug should be discontinued. Breast-feeding women should stop either breast-feeding or drug.

Adverse reactions
CNS: dizziness, fatigue, headache.
CV: chest pain, peripheral edema.
EENT: pharyngitis, rhinitis, sinusitis.
GI: abdominal pain, diarrhea, nausea, vomiting.
GU: albuminuria.
Musculoskeletal: arthralgia, back pain.
Respiratory: cough, bronchitis, upper respiratory tract infection.

Interactions
None reported.

Effects on lab test results
- May decrease hemoglobin and hematocrit.

Pharmacokinetics
Absorption: Absolute bioavailability is about 15%.
Distribution: More than 99% binds to plasma protein and doesn't penetrate RBCs.
Metabolism: Rapidly and completely bioactivated by ester hydrolysis to candesartan.
Excretion: About 33% is recovered in urine (26% unchanged) and 67% in feces. *Half-life:* 9 hours.

Route	Onset	Peak	Duration
P.O.	Unknown	3-4 hr	24 hr

Pharmacodynamics
Chemical effect: Inhibits the vasoconstrictive action of angiotensin II by blocking the angio-

tensin II receptor on the surface of vascular smooth muscle and other tissue cells.
Therapeutic effect: Dilates blood vessels and decreases blood pressure.

Available forms

Tablets: 4 mg, 8 mg, 16 mg, 32 mg

NURSING PROCESS

Assessment

- Monitor patient's electrolytes, and assess patient for volume or salt depletion (as from vigorous diuretic use) before starting drug.
- Carefully monitor therapeutic response and adverse reactions, especially in elderly patients and patients with renal impairment.
- Evaluate patient's and family's knowledge of drug therapy.

Nursing diagnoses

- Decreased cardiac output related to risk for symptomatic hypotension in volume- or salt-depleted patients
- Risk for imbalanced fluid volume in patients with impaired renal function related to drug-induced oliguria
- Deficient knowledge related to drug therapy

Planning and implementation

- Make sure patient is adequately hydrated before starting therapy.
- Observe patient for hypotension. If it occurs after a dose of candesartan, place patient in supine position and, if necessary, give an I.V. infusion of normal saline solution.
- Most of antihypertensive effect is present within 2 weeks. Maximal antihypertensive effect is obtained within 4 to 6 weeks. Diuretic may be added if blood pressure isn't controlled by drug alone.
- Drug can't be removed by hemodialysis.

Patient teaching

- Advise woman of childbearing age about risk of second- and third-trimester exposure to drug. If pregnancy is suspected, tell her to notify prescriber immediately.
- Tell patient to store drug at room temperature and to keep container tightly sealed.
- Inform patient to report adverse reactions promptly.
- Instruct patient to take drug exactly as directed.
- Tell patient that drug may be taken without regard to meals.

Evaluation

- Patient's volume or salt depletion is corrected so that symptomatic hypotension doesn't occur.
- Patient maintains fluid balance.
- Patient and family state understanding of drug therapy.

capecitabine

(ka-pe-SITE-a-been)
Xeloda

Pharmacologic class: fluoropyrimidine carbamate
Therapeutic class: antineoplastic
Pregnancy risk category: D

Indications and dosages

▶ **Metastatic breast cancer resistant to both paclitaxel and an anthracycline-containing chemotherapy regimen or resistant to paclitaxel when further anthracycline therapy isn't indicated; first-line treatment of patients with metastatic colorectal cancer when treatment with fluoropyrimidine therapy alone is preferred; metastatic breast cancer, given with docetaxel after failure of prior anthracycline-containing chemotherapy.** *Adults:* 2,500 mg/m² P.O. daily in two divided doses, taken about 12 hours apart and after a meal, for 2 weeks; followed by 1-week rest period. Repeat as an q 3-week cycle. Dosage may need to be adjusted, based on toxicity. See manufacturer's insert for details on specific dosage reduction.

Contraindications and precautions

- Contraindicated in patients hypersensitive to 5-fluorouracil (5-FU).

Lifespan: In pregnant women, use only in life-threatening situations or severe disease for which safer drugs can't be used or are ineffective. Breast-feeding should be discontinued during therapy. In children younger than age 18, safety and efficacy haven't been established. Patients older than age 80 may have a greater risk of GI adverse effects.

Adverse reactions

CNS: *fever,* dizziness, *fatigue, headache,* insomnia, *paresthesia, peripheral neuropathy.*
CV: *edema.*
EENT: *eye irritation.*
GI: *diarrhea, nausea, vomiting, stomatitis, abdominal pain, constipation, anorexia,* intestinal obstruction, *dyspepsia.*
Hematologic: NEUTROPENIA, THROMBOCYTOPENIA, LEUKOPENIA, *anemia, lymphopenia.*
Hepatic: *hyperbilirubinemia.*
Musculoskeletal: myalgia, limb pain, *back pain.*
Skin: *hand-and-foot syndrome, dermatitis,* nail disorder.
Other: dehydration.

Interactions

Drug-drug. *Leucovorin:* May increase levels of 5-FU with enhanced toxicity. Monitor patient carefully.
Warfarin: May increase risk of bleeding and death. Avoid this combination, monitor PT and INR levels frequently, and adjust warfarin dose, if necessary.

Effects on lab test results

- May increase bilirubin level.
- May decrease hemoglobin, hematocrit, and platelet, lymphocyte, and neutrophil counts.

Pharmacokinetics

Absorption: Drug is readily absorbed from the GI tract. Levels of parent drug peak in 1½ hours; levels of active metabolite peak in 2 hours. Rate and extent of absorption is decreased by food.
Distribution: About 60% is bound to plasma proteins.
Metabolism: Drug is extensively metabolized to 5-FU, an active metabolite.
Excretion: 70% excreted in urine. *Half-life:* About 45 minutes.

Route	Onset	Peak	Duration
P.O.	Unknown	1.5-2 hr	Unknown

Pharmacodynamics

Chemical effect: Drug is converted to active drug 5-FU, which is metabolized by both normal and tumor cells to metabolites that cause cellular injury via two mechanisms: interference with DNA synthesis to inhibit cell division and interference with RNA processing and protein synthesis.
Therapeutic effect: Inhibits cell growth of selected cancer.

Available forms

Tablets: 150 mg, 500 mg

NURSING PROCESS

Assessment

- Obtain history of patient's underlying condition before therapy and reassess regularly thereafter.
- Assess patient for coronary artery disease, mild-to-moderate hepatic dysfunction caused by liver metastases, hyperbilirubinemia, renal insufficiency.
- Monitor patient for severe diarrhea, and notify prescriber if it occurs.
- Monitor patient for hand-and-foot syndrome (numbness, paresthesia, tingling, painless or painful swelling, erythema, desquamation, blistering, and severe pain of hands or feet), hyperbilirubinemia, and severe nausea. Drug therapy will need to be immediately adjusted.
- Evaluate patient's and family's knowledge of drug therapy.

Nursing diagnoses

- Risk for infection related to adverse effects of drug
- Risk for impaired skin integrity related to potential for hand-and-foot syndrome
- Deficient knowledge related to drug therapy

Planning and implementation

- If diarrhea occurs and patient becomes dehydrated, give fluid and electrolyte replacement. Drug may need to be immediately interrupted until diarrhea resolves or decreases in intensity.
- Hyperbilirubinemia may require stopping drug.
- Monitor patient carefully for toxicity. Toxicity may be managed by symptomatic treatment, dose interruptions, and dosage adjustments.

Patient teaching

- Inform patient and caregiver of expected adverse effects of drug, especially nausea, vomit-

ing, diarrhea, and hand-and-foot syndrome (pain, swelling, and redness of hands or feet). Explain that patient-specific dose adaptations during therapy are expected and needed.
ALERT: Instruct patient to stop taking drug and to contact prescriber immediately if he develops diarrhea (more than four bowel movements daily or diarrhea at night), vomiting (two to five episodes in 24 hours), nausea, appetite loss or decrease in amount of food taken each day, stomatitis (pain, redness, swelling or sores in mouth), hand-and-foot syndrome, fever of 100.5° F (38° C) or more, or other evidence of infection.
- Tell patient that most adverse effects improve within 2 or 3 days after stopping drug and that if they don't, he should contact prescriber.
- Tell patient how to take drug. Dosage cycle is usually to take drug for 14 days followed by 7-day rest period. Prescriber determines number of treatment cycles.
- Instruct patient to take drug with water within 30 minutes after breakfast and after dinner.
- If a combination of tablets is prescribed, teach patient importance of correctly identifying the tablets to avoid error.
- For missed doses, instruct patient not to take the missed dose and not to double the next one. Instead, he should continue with regular dosing schedule and check with prescriber.
- Instruct patient to inform prescriber if he's taking folic acid.

Evaluation
- Patient doesn't develop infection.
- Patient doesn't develop hand-and-foot syndrome.
- Patient and family state understanding of drug therapy.

captopril
(KAP-toh-pril)
Capoten

Pharmacologic class: ACE inhibitor
Therapeutic class: antihypertensive, adjunct treatment of heart failure and diabetic nephropathy
Pregnancy risk category: C (D in second and third trimesters)

Indications and dosages
▶ **Hypertension.** *Adults:* Initially, 25 mg P.O. b.i.d. or t.i.d. If blood pressure isn't controlled in 1 to 2 weeks, dosage increased to 50 mg b.i.d. or t.i.d. If not controlled after another 1 to 2 weeks, expect a thiazide diuretic to be added to regimen. If further blood pressure reduction is necessary, dosage may be raised to as high as 150 mg t.i.d. while continuing diuretic. Maximum daily dose is 450 mg.
▶ **Heart failure; to reduce risk of death and to slow development of heart failure after MI.** *Adults:* 6.25 to 12.5 mg P.O. t.i.d. initially. Gradually increased to 50 to 100 mg t.i.d. as needed. Maximum daily dosage is 450 mg.
▶ **Prevention of diabetic nephropathy.** *Adults:* 25 mg P.O. t.i.d.
▶ **Left ventricular dysfunction after MI.** *Adults:* 6.25 mg P.O. as a single dose 3 days after an MI; then 12.5 mg t.i.d. increasing dose to 25 mg t.i.d. Target dose is 50 mg t.i.d.

Contraindications and precautions
- Contraindicated in patients hypersensitive to drug or other ACE inhibitors.
- Use cautiously in patients with impaired renal function or serious autoimmune disease (particularly systemic lupus erythematosus), and in patients exposed to other drugs known to affect WBC counts or immune response.

Lifespan: In pregnant women, use with extreme caution. If patient becomes pregnant, drug usually is discontinued. With breastfeeding women, use cautiously. In children, safety of drug hasn't been established.

Adverse reactions
CNS: fever, dizziness, fainting.
CV: *tachycardia, hypotension,* angina pectoris, ***heart failure,*** pericarditis.
GI: anorexia, *dysgeusia.*
GU: *proteinuria, nephrotic syndrome, membranous glomerulopathy,* ***renal failure*** (in patients with renal disease or those receiving high dosages), urinary frequency.
Hematologic: ***leukopenia, agranulocytosis, pancytopenia, thrombocytopenia.***
Hepatic: transient increase in hepatic enzymes.
Metabolic: ***hyperkalemia.***
Respiratory: dry, persistent, tickling, nonproductive cough.

Skin: urticarial rash, maculopapular rash, pruritus.
Other: *angioedema of face and limbs.*

Interactions

Drug-drug. *Antacids:* May decrease captopril effect. Separate administration times.
Cardiac glycosides: May increase digoxin levels by 15% to 30%. Monitor patient for digitalis toxicity.
Diuretics, other antihypertensives: May increase risk of excessive hypotension. Diuretic may need to be discontinued or captopril dosage lowered.
Insulin, oral antidiabetics: May increase risk of hypoglycemia when captopril therapy starts. Monitor patient closely.
Lithium: May increase lithium level and cause lithium toxicity. Monitor patient closely.
NSAIDs: May reduce antihypertensive effect. Monitor blood pressure.
Potassium supplements, potassium-sparing diuretics: May increase risk of hyperkalemia. Avoid these drugs unless hypokalemic levels are confirmed.
Probenecid: May increase captopril level. Avoid using together.
Drug-herb. *Black catechu:* May have additional hypotensive effects of catechu. Discourage using together.
Capsaicin: May cause or worsen coughing related to ACE inhibitors. Discourage using together.
Licorice: May cause sodium retention, which counteracts ACE effects. Monitor blood pressure.
Drug-food. *Any food:* May reduce absorption of drug. Give drug 1 hour before meals.

Effects on lab test results

- May increase alkaline phosphatase, bilirubin, and potassium levels.
- May decrease hemoglobin, hematocrit, and WBC, granulocyte, RBC, and platelet counts.

Pharmacokinetics

Absorption: Absorbed through GI tract; food may reduce absorption by up to 40%.
Distribution: Distributed into most body tissues except CNS; 25% to 30% protein-bound.
Metabolism: About 50% metabolized in liver.
Excretion: Excreted primarily in urine, minimally in feces. *Half-life:* Less than 2 hours.

Route	Onset	Peak	Duration
P.O.	15-60 min	30-90 min	6-12 hr

Pharmacodynamics

Chemical effect: Thought to inhibit ACE, preventing conversion of angiotensin I to angiotensin II. Reduced formation of angiotensin II decreases peripheral arterial resistance, thus decreasing aldosterone secretion.
Therapeutic effect: Reduces sodium and water retention, lowers blood pressure, and helps improve renal function adversely affected by diabetes.

Available forms

Tablets: 12.5 mg, 25 mg, 50 mg, 100 mg

NURSING PROCESS

Assessment

- Assess patient's underlying condition before therapy and regularly thereafter.
- Monitor blood pressure and pulse rate frequently.
- Monitor WBC and differential counts before therapy, every 2 weeks for first 3 months of therapy, and periodically thereafter.
- Monitor potassium level and renal function (BUN and creatinine clearance levels, urinalysis).
- Be alert for adverse reactions and drug interactions.
- Evaluate patient's and family's knowledge of drug therapy.

Nursing diagnoses

- Risk for injury related to patient's underlying condition
- Ineffective protection related to drug-induced blood disorder
- Deficient knowledge related to drug therapy

Planning and implementation

- Give 1 hour before meals because food may reduce absorption.
- Because antacids decrease drug's effect, separate administration times.
- Withhold dose and notify prescriber if patient develops fever, sore throat, leukopenia, hypotension, or tachycardia.

• Notify prescriber of abnormal laboratory studies.

Patient teaching

• Instruct patient to take drug 1 hour before meals.
• Inform patient that light-headedness may occur, especially during first few days of therapy. Tell patient to rise slowly to minimize this effect and to report symptoms to prescriber. Tell patient who experiences syncope to stop taking drug and call prescriber immediately.
• Tell patient to use caution in hot weather and during exercise. Inadequate fluid intake, vomiting, diarrhea, and excessive perspiration can lead to light-headedness and syncope.
• Advise patient to report signs of infection, such as fever and sore throat.
• Tell woman to notify prescriber if she becomes pregnant because drug should be discontinued.

☑ Evaluation

• Patient's underlying condition improves.
• Patient's WBC and differential counts are normal.
• Patient and family state understanding of drug therapy.

carbamazepine
(kar-buh-MEH-zuh-peen)

Apo-Carbamazepine♦, Atretol, Carbatrol, Epitol, Novo-Carbamaz♦, Tegretol, Tegretol CR♦, Tegretol-XR, Teril

Pharmacologic class: iminostilbene derivative
Therapeutic class: anticonvulsant, analgesic
Pregnancy risk category: D

Indications and dosages

▶ **Generalized tonic-clonic and complex partial seizures, mixed seizure patterns.** *Adults and children older than age 12:* Initially, 200 mg P.O. b.i.d. for tablets or 100 mg of suspension P.O. q.i.d. May be increased at weekly intervals by 200 mg P.O. daily, in divided doses at 6- to 8-hour intervals. Adjusted to minimum effective level when control is achieved. Maximum daily dosage is 1 g in children ages 12 to 15, or 1.2 g in patients older than age 15.
Children ages 6 to 12: Initially, 100 mg P.O. b.i.d., or 50 mg of suspension P.O. q.i.d. Increased at weekly intervals by 100 mg P.O. daily. Maximum daily dosage is 1 g.
▶ **Trigeminal neuralgia.** *Adults:* Initially, 100 mg P.O. b.i.d. or 50 mg of suspension P.O. q.i.d. with meals. Increase by 100 mg q 12 hours for tablets or 50 mg of suspension q.i.d. until pain is relieved. Maximum daily dosage is 1,200 mg. Maintenance dosage is 200 to 1,200 mg P.O. daily. Decrease dose to minimum effective level, or discontinue drug at least once q 3 months.
▶ **Bipolar effective disorder, intermittent explosive disorder‡.** *Adults:* Initially, 200 mg P.O. b.i.d.; increase p.r.n. q 3 to 4 days. Maintenance dose may range from 600 to 1,600 mg daily.
▶ **Restless leg syndrome‡.** *Adults:* 100 to 300 mg P.O. q h.s.
▶ **Chorea‡.** *Children:* 15 to 25 mg/kg P.O. daily.

Contraindications and precautions

• Contraindicated in patients hypersensitive to drug or tricyclic antidepressants, in patients with previous bone marrow suppression, and in patients who have taken an MAO inhibitor within 14 days of therapy.
• Use cautiously in patients with mixed seizure disorders because these patients may have increased risk of seizures, usually atypical absence or generalized.
Lifespan: In pregnant women, use cautiously. If breast-feeding women must use drug, breast-feeding should be discontinued.

Adverse reactions

CNS: fever, *dizziness, vertigo, drowsiness,* fatigue, *ataxia,* ***worsening of seizures*** (usually in patients with mixed seizure disorders, including atypical absence seizures).
CV: ***heart failure,*** hypertension, hypotension, aggravation of coronary artery disease.
EENT: conjunctivitis, dry mouth and pharynx, blurred vision, diplopia, nystagmus.
GI: *nausea, vomiting,* abdominal pain, diarrhea, anorexia, stomatitis, glossitis.
GU: urinary frequency, urine retention, impotence, albuminuria, glycosuria.
Hematologic: ***aplastic anemia, agranulocytosis,*** eosinophilia, leukocytosis, ***thrombocytopenia.***

Hepatic: ***hepatitis.***
Respiratory: pulmonary hypersensitivity.
Skin: excessive sweating, rash, urticaria, erythema multiforme, ***Stevens-Johnson syndrome.***
Other: chills, water intoxication.

Interactions

Drug-drug. *Cimetidine, danazol, diltiazem, macrolides (such as erythromycin), isoniazid, propoxyphene, valproic acid, verapamil:* May increase carbamazepine level. Use together cautiously.
Doxycycline, haloperidol, oral contraceptives, phenytoin, theophylline, warfarin: May decrease levels of these drugs. Monitor patient for decreased effect.
Lithium: May increase risk of CNS toxicity of lithium. Avoid using together.
MAO inhibitors: May increase depressant and anticholinergic effects. Don't use together.
Phenobarbital, phenytoin, primidone: May decrease carbamazepine level. Monitor patient for decreased effect.
Drug-herb. *Plantains:* Psyllium seed has been reported to inhibit GI absorption. Discourage using together.

Effects on lab test results

- May increase BUN levels.
- May increase eosinophil count and liver function test values. May decrease hemoglobin, hematocrit, thyroid function test values, and granulocyte, WBC, and platelet counts.

Pharmacokinetics

Absorption: Absorbed slowly from GI tract.
Distribution: Distributed widely throughout body; about 75% protein-bound.
Metabolism: Metabolized by liver to active metabolite; may also induce its own metabolism.
Excretion: Excreted in urine (70%) and feces (30%). *Half-life:* 25 to 65 hours with single dose; 8 to 29 hours with long-term dosing.

Route	Onset	Peak	Duration
P.O.	Hr-days	1.5 hr (suspension), 4-12 hr (tablets)	Unknown

Pharmacodynamics

Chemical effect: May stabilize neuronal membranes and limit seizure activity by increasing efflux or decreasing influx of sodium ions across cell membranes in motor cortex during generation of nerve impulses.
Therapeutic effect: Prevents seizure activity; eliminates pain caused by trigeminal neuralgia.

Available forms

Capsules (extended-release): 200 mg, 300 mg
Oral suspension: 100 mg/5 ml
Tablets: 200 mg
Tablets (chewable): 100 mg, 200 mg
Tablets (extended-release): 100 mg, 200 mg, 400 mg

NURSING PROCESS

Assessment

- Assess patient's seizure disorder or trigeminal neuralgia before therapy and regularly thereafter.
- Obtain baseline determinations of urinalysis, BUN level, liver function, CBC, platelet and reticulocyte counts, and iron level. Reassess regularly.
- Monitor drug level and effects closely. Therapeutic level is 4 to 12 mcg/ml.
- Be alert for adverse reactions and drug interactions.
- Evaluate patient's and family's knowledge of drug therapy.

Nursing diagnoses

- Risk for injury related to seizure disorder
- Acute pain related to trigeminal neuralgia
- Deficient knowledge related to drug therapy

Planning and implementation

- Give drug in divided doses, when possible, to maintain consistent blood level.
- Give drug with food to minimize GI distress.
- Shake oral suspension well before measuring dose.
- When giving by nasogastric tube, mix dose with equal volume of water, normal saline solution, or D_5W. Flush tube with 100 ml of diluent after administering dose.

ALERT: Never discontinue suddenly when treating seizures or status epilepticus. Notify prescriber immediately if adverse reactions occur. Expect prescriber to increase dosage gradually to minimize adverse reactions.

Patient teaching

- Tell patient to take drug with food to minimize GI distress.
- Tell patient to keep tablets in original container, tightly closed, and away from moisture. Some formulations may harden when exposed to excess moisture, resulting in decreased bioavailability and loss of seizure control.
- Inform patient with trigeminal neuralgia that prescriber may attempt to decrease dosage or withdraw drug every 3 months.

ALERT: Tell patient to notify prescriber immediately about fever, sore throat, mouth ulcers, or easy bruising or bleeding.

- Warn patient that drug may cause mild-to-moderate dizziness and drowsiness at first. Advise patient to avoid hazardous activities until effects disappear (usually within 3 to 4 days).
- Advise patient to have periodic ophthalmic examinations.

Evaluation

- Patient remains free from seizures.
- Patient reports pain relief.
- Patient and family state understanding of drug therapy.

carbidopa and levodopa

(kar-bih-DOH-puh LEE-vuh-doh-puh)
Sinemet, Sinemet CR

Pharmacologic class: decarboxylase inhibitor-dopamine precursor combination
Therapeutic class: antiparkinsonian
Pregnancy risk category: C

Indications and dosages

► **Idiopathic Parkinson's disease, postencephalitic parkinsonism, and symptomatic parkinsonism resulting from carbon monoxide or manganese intoxication.** *Adults:* 1 tablet of 25 mg carbidopa/100 mg levodopa or carbidopa 10 mg/levodopa 100 mg P.O. daily t.i.d. followed by increase of 1 tablet daily or every other day as necessary; maximum daily dosage 8 tablets. 25 mg carbidopa/250 mg levodopa or 10 mg carbidopa/100 mg levodopa tablets are substituted as required to obtain maximum response. Optimum daily dosage must be determined by careful adjustment for each patient. Patients treated with conventional tablets may receive extended-release tablets; dosage is calculated on current levodopa intake. Initially, extended-release tablets given equal to 10% more levodopa per day, increased as needed and tolerated to 30% more levodopa per day. Give in divided doses at intervals of 4 to 8 hours.

Contraindications and precautions

- Contraindicated in patients hypersensitive to drug; in patients with acute angle-closure glaucoma, melanoma, or undiagnosed skin lesions; and in patients who have taken an MAO inhibitor within 14 days.
- Use cautiously in patients with severe CV, renal, hepatic, endocrine, or pulmonary disorders; history of peptic ulcer; psychiatric illness; MI with residual arrhythmias; bronchial asthma; emphysema; or well-controlled, chronic, open-angle glaucoma.

Lifespan: In pregnant women, use with extreme caution. In breast-feeding women, drug is contraindicated. In children, safety of drug hasn't been established.

Adverse reactions

CNS: *choreiform, dystonic, dyskinetic movements; involuntary grimacing, head movements, myoclonic body jerks, ataxia,* tremors, muscle twitching; bradykinetic episodes; psychiatric disturbances, memory loss, nervousness, anxiety, disturbing dreams, euphoria, malaise, fatigue, severe depression, suicidal tendencies, dementia, delirium, hallucinations.
CV: *orthostatic hypotension, **cardiac irregularities,*** flushing, hypertension, phlebitis.
EENT: blepharospasm, blurred vision, diplopia, mydriasis or miosis, widening of palpebral fissures, activation of latent Horner's syndrome, oculogyric crises, nasal discharge, excessive salivation.
GI: dry mouth, bitter taste, nausea, vomiting, anorexia, and weight loss at start of therapy; constipation; flatulence; diarrhea; epigastric pain.
GU: urinary frequency, urine retention, urinary incontinence, darkened urine, excessive and inappropriate sexual behavior, priapism.
Hematologic: hemolytic anemia.
Hepatic: ***hepatotoxicity.***

Respiratory: hyperventilation, hiccups.
Skin: dark perspiration.

Interactions

Drug-drug. *Antacids:* May increase absorption of levodopa components. Monitor patient closely.
Antihypertensives: May have additive hypotensive effects. Use together cautiously.
MAO inhibitors: Increases risk of severe hypertension. Don't use together.
Papaverine, phenytoin: Antagonism of antiparkinsonian actions. Don't use together.
Phenothiazines, other antipsychotics: May antagonize antiparkinsonian actions. Use together cautiously.
Drug-herb. *Kava:* Could interfere with action of levodopa and natural dopamine, worsening Parkinson's symptoms. Discourage use together.
Octacosanol: May worsen dyskinesia. Discourage use together.
Drug-food. *Foods high in protein:* May decrease absorption of levodopa. Don't give levodopa with high-protein foods.

Effects on lab test results

- May decrease hemoglobin, hematocrit, and platelet, granulocyte, and WBC counts.
- May falsely increase levels of uric acid, urine ketones, urine catecholamines, and urine vanillylmandelic acid, depending on reagent and test method used.

Pharmacokinetics

Absorption: 40% to 70%.
Distribution: Distributed widely in body tissues except CNS.
Metabolism: Carbidopa isn't metabolized extensively. It inhibits metabolism of levodopa in GI tract, thus increasing its absorption from GI tract and its concentration in plasma.
Excretion: 30% of dose excreted unchanged in urine within 24 hours. When given with carbidopa, amount of levodopa excreted unchanged in urine is increased by about 6%. *Half-life:* 1 to 2 hours.

Route	Onset	Peak	Duration
P.O.	Unknown	40 min (regular-release), 2.5 hr (extended-release)	Unknown

Pharmacodynamics

Chemical effect: Unknown for levodopa. Thought to be decarboxylated to dopamine, countering depletion of striatal dopamine in extrapyramidal centers. Carbidopa inhibits peripheral decarboxylation of levodopa without affecting levodopa's metabolism within CNS. Therefore, more levodopa is available to be decarboxylated to dopamine in brain.
Therapeutic effect: Improves voluntary movement.

Available forms

Tablets: carbidopa 10 mg with levodopa 100 mg (Sinemet 10-100), carbidopa 25 mg with levodopa 100 mg (Sinemet 25-100), carbidopa 25 mg with levodopa 250 mg (Sinemet 25-250)
Tablets (extended-release): carbidopa 25 mg with levodopa 100 mg, carbidopa 50 mg with levodopa 200 mg (Sinemet CR)

NURSING PROCESS

Assessment

- Assess patient's underlying condition before therapy and regularly thereafter; therapeutic response usually follows each dose and disappears within 5 hours; may vary considerably.
- Be alert for adverse reactions and drug interactions.

ALERT: Immediately report muscle twitching and blepharospasm (twitching of eyelids), which may be early signs of drug overdose.

- Patients receiving long-term therapy should be tested regularly for diabetes and acromegaly and should have periodic tests of liver, renal, and hematopoietic function.
- Evaluate patient's and family's knowledge of drug therapy.

Nursing diagnoses

- Impaired physical mobility related to underlying parkinsonian syndrome
- Disturbed thought processes related to drug-induced CNS adverse reactions
- Deficient knowledge related to drug therapy

Planning and implementation

- If patient is being treated with levodopa, it should be discontinued at least 8 hours before starting carbidopa-levodopa.

• Give drug with food to minimize adverse GI reactions.
• Be aware that dosage will be adjusted according to patient's response and tolerance.
• Withhold dose and notify prescriber if vital signs or mental status change significantly. Reduced dosage or discontinuation may be necessary.
• Be aware of patients with open-angle glaucoma and treat with caution. Monitor patient closely. Watch for change in intraocular pressure and arrange for periodic eye exams.

Patient teaching
• Tell patient to take drug with food to minimize GI upset.
• Caution patient and family not to increase dosage without prescriber's orders.
• Warn patient of possible dizziness and orthostatic hypotension, especially at start of therapy. Tell patient to change positions slowly and to dangle legs before getting out of bed. Elastic stockings may control this adverse reaction in some patients.
• Instruct patient to report adverse reactions and therapeutic effects.
• Inform patient that pyridoxine (vitamin B_6) doesn't reverse beneficial effects of carbidopa-levodopa. Multivitamins can be taken without losing control of symptoms.

☑ Evaluation
• Patient exhibits improved mobility with reduction of muscular rigidity and tremor.
• Patient remains mentally alert.
• Patient and family state understanding of drug therapy.

carboplatin
(KAR-boh-plat-in)
Paraplatin, Paraplatin-AQ♦

Pharmacologic class: alkylating agent (not specific to cell cycle phase)
Therapeutic class: antineoplastic
Pregnancy risk category: D

Indications and dosages
▶ **Palliative treatment of ovarian cancer.** *Adults:* 360 mg/m² I.V. on day 1 q 4 weeks; doses shouldn't be repeated until platelet count exceeds 100,000/mm³ and neutrophil count exceeds 2,000/mm³. Subsequent doses are based on blood counts.
Patients with renal dysfunction: Starting dose is 250 mg/m² I.V. in patients with creatinine clearance of 41 to 59 ml/minute or 200 mg/m² in those with creatinine clearance of 16 to 40 ml/minute. Recommended dosage adjustments aren't available for patients with creatinine clearance of 15 ml/minute or less.
▶ **Initial treatment of advanced ovarian cancer with cyclophosphamide.** *Adults:* Initial dose is 300 mg/m² I.V. on day 1 q 4 weeks for six cycles. Don't repeat cycles until the neutrophil count is greater than or equal to 2,000/mm³ and the platelet count is greater than or equal to 100,000/mm³.

Contraindications and precautions
• Contraindicated in patients hypersensitive to cisplatin, platinum-containing compounds, or mannitol. Also contraindicated in patients with severe bone marrow suppression or bleeding.
Lifespan: Pregnant women shouldn't use drug. In breast-feeding women and children, safety of drug hasn't been established. Patients older than age 65 are at greater risk for neurotoxicity.

Adverse reactions
CNS: dizziness, confusion, *peripheral neuropathy, ototoxicity, central neurotoxicity, CVA.*
CV: ***cardiac failure, embolism.***
GI: constipation, diarrhea, *nausea, vomiting.*
Hematologic: **THROMBOCYTOPENIA,** *leukopenia,* **NEUTROPENIA,** *anemia,* **BONE MARROW SUPPRESSION.**
Hepatic: ***hepatotoxicity.***
Skin: *alopecia.*
Other: ***hypersensitivity reactions.***

Interactions
Drug-drug. *Bone marrow depressants, including radiation therapy:* May increase hematologic toxicity. Monitor patient closely.
Nephrotoxic agents: May enhance nephrotoxicity of carboplatin. Monitor patient closely.

Effects on lab test results
• May increase BUN, creatinine, bilirubin, AST, and alkaline phosphatase levels. May de-

crease magnesium, calcium, potassium, and sodium levels.
• May decrease hemoglobin, hematocrit, and neutrophil, WBC, RBC, and platelet counts.

Pharmacokinetics

Absorption: Administered I.V.
Distribution: Volume distributed is about equal to that of total body water; no significant protein binding occurs.
Metabolism: Hydrolyzed to form hydroxylated and aquated species.
Excretion: 65% excreted by kidneys within 12 hours, 71% within 24 hours. *Half-life:* 5 hours.

Route	Onset	Peak	Duration
I.V.	Unknown	Unknown	Unknown

Pharmacodynamics

Chemical effect: Probably produces cross-linking of DNA strands.
Therapeutic effect: Impairs ovarian cancer cells replication.

Available forms

Injection: 50-mg, 150-mg, 450-mg vials

NURSING PROCESS

Assessment

• Assess patient's condition before therapy and regularly thereafter.
• Determine electrolyte, creatinine, and BUN levels; creatinine clearance; CBC; and platelet count before first infusion and before each course of treatment. WBC and platelet count nadirs usually occur by day 21. Levels usually return to baseline by day 28.
• Be alert for adverse reactions and drug interactions.
• Evaluate patient's and family's knowledge of drug therapy.

Nursing diagnoses

• Ineffective health maintenance related to ovarian cancer
• Ineffective protection related to drug-induced adverse reactions
• Deficient knowledge related to drug therapy

Planning and implementation

• Follow facility policy to reduce risks because preparation and administration of parenteral form is linked to mutagenic, teratogenic, and carcinogenic risks for personnel.
• Check ordered dose against laboratory test results carefully. Only one increase in dosage is recommended. Subsequent doses shouldn't exceed 125% of starting dose.
• Reconstitute with D_5W, normal saline solution, or sterile water for injection to make 10 mg/ml. Add 5 ml of diluent to 50-mg vial, 15 ml of diluent to 150-mg vial, or 45 ml of diluent to 450-mg vial. Drug can then be further diluted for infusion with normal saline solution or D_5W. Concentration as low as 0.5 mg/ml can be prepared. Give drug by continuous or intermittent infusion over at least 15 minutes.
• Don't use needles or I.V. administration sets that contain aluminum to administer carboplatin; precipitation and loss of drug's potency may occur.
• Bone marrow suppression may be more severe in patients with creatinine clearance below 60 ml/minute; dosage adjustments are recommended for such patients.
ALERT: Dose shouldn't be repeated unless platelet count exceeds 100,000/mm^3.
• Store unopened vials at room temperature. Once reconstituted and diluted, drug is stable at room temperature for 8 hours; discard unused drug at this time.
ALERT: Have epinephrine, corticosteroids, and antihistamines available when giving carboplatin because anaphylactoid reactions may occur within minutes of administration.
• Provide antiemetic therapy. Carboplatin can produce severe vomiting.

Patient teaching

• Warn patient to watch for signs of infection (fever, sore throat, fatigue) and bleeding (easy bruising, nosebleeds, bleeding gums, melena). Take temperature daily.
• Instruct patient to avoid OTC products that contain aspirin.
• Advise woman of childbearing age to avoid pregnancy during therapy and to consult prescriber before becoming pregnant.
• Advise breast-feeding patient to discontinue breast-feeding because of risk of toxicity in infant.

Evaluation
- Patient has positive response to carboplatin as evidenced by follow-up diagnostic tests.
- Patient doesn't experience injury from drug therapy.
- Patient and family state understanding of drug therapy.

carboprost tromethamine
(KAR-boh-prost troh-METH-ah-meen)
Hemabate

Pharmacologic class: prostaglandin
Therapeutic class: oxytocic
Pregnancy risk category: C

Indications and dosages
▶ **Abortion between 13th and 20th weeks of gestation.** *Adults:* Initially, 250 mcg deep I.M. Subsequent doses of 250 mcg administered at intervals of 1½ to 3½ hours, depending on uterine response. Dosage may be increased in increments to 500 mcg if contractility is inadequate after several 250-mcg doses. Total dosage shouldn't exceed 12 mg.

▶ **Postpartum hemorrhage caused by uterine atony not managed by conventional methods.** *Adults:* 250 mcg by deep I.M. injection. Repeat doses given at 15- to 90-minute intervals, p.r.n. Maximum total dose is 2 mg.

Contraindications and precautions
- Contraindicated in patients hypersensitive to drug and in those with acute pelvic inflammatory disease or active cardiac, pulmonary, renal, or hepatic disease.
- Use cautiously in patients with history of asthma; hypotension; hypertension; CV, adrenal, renal, or hepatic disease; anemia; jaundice; diabetes; seizure disorders; or previous uterine surgery.

Lifespan: No contraindications or precautions.

Adverse reactions
CNS: *fever.*
CV: ***arrhythmias,*** flushing.
GI: *vomiting, diarrhea,* nausea.
GU: uterine rupture.
Other: chills.

Interactions
Drug-drug. *Other oxytocics:* May potentiate action. Avoid use together.

Effects on lab test results
None reported.

Pharmacokinetics
Absorption: Unknown.
Distribution: Unknown.
Metabolism: Enzymatic deactivation occurs in maternal tissues.
Excretion: Excreted primarily in urine.

Route	Onset	Peak	Duration
I.M.	Unknown	15-60 min	16-24 hr

Pharmacodynamics
Chemical effect: Produces strong, prompt contractions of uterine smooth muscle, possibly mediated by calcium and cAMP.
Therapeutic effect: Aborts fetus and stops postpartum hemorrhage.

Available forms
Injection: 250 mcg/ml

NURSING PROCESS

Assessment
- Assess patient's pregnancy status before therapy.
- Monitor drug effectiveness by evaluating uterine contractions, expulsion of products of conception, or cessation of postpartum hemorrhage.
- Be alert for adverse reactions.
- Evaluate patient's and family's knowledge of drug therapy.

Nursing diagnoses
- Impaired adjustment related to pregnancy
- Risk for altered body temperature related to drug-induced fever
- Deficient knowledge related to drug therapy

Planning and implementation
- Unlike other prostaglandin abortifacients, carboprost is administered by I.M. injection. Injectable form avoids risk of expelling vaginal suppositories, which may occur with profuse vaginal bleeding.

• Drug should be used only by trained personnel in hospital setting.
• Consult prescriber if uterine contractions are ineffective or postpartum bleeding persists.

Patient teaching
• Explain importance of follow-up care.
• Tell patient to report adverse reactions immediately.

Evaluation
• Patient aborts successfully.
• Patient's temperature remains normal.
• Patient and family state understanding of drug therapy.

carisoprodol
(kar-ih-soh-PROH-dol)
Soma

Pharmacologic class: caramate derivative
Therapeutic class: skeletal muscle relaxant
Pregnancy risk category: NR

Indications and dosages

▶ **Adjunct in acute, painful musculoskeletal conditions.** *Adults:* 350 mg P.O. t.i.d. and h.s.

Contraindications and precautions

• Contraindicated in patients hypersensitive to related compounds (such as meprobamate, tybamate) and in patients with intermittent porphyria.
• Use cautiously in patients with impaired hepatic or renal function. Prolonged use may lead to dependence; thus, use cautiously in addiction-prone patients.
Lifespan: In pregnant women, breast-feeding women, and children younger than age 12, safety of drug hasn't been established.

Adverse reactions

CNS: fever, *drowsiness, dizziness,* vertigo, ataxia, tremor, agitation, irritability, headache, depressive reactions, insomnia.
CV: orthostatic hypotension, tachycardia, facial flushing.
GI: nausea, vomiting, increased bowel activity, epigastric distress.
Hematologic: eosinophilia.
Respiratory: asthmatic episodes, hiccups.
Skin: rash, ***erythema multiforme,*** pruritus.
Other: ***angioedema, anaphylaxis.***

Interactions

Drug-drug. *CNS depressants:* May increase CNS depression. Avoid using together.
Drug-lifestyle. *Alcohol use:* May increase CNS depression. Discourage using together.

Effects on lab test results

• May increase eosinophil count.

Pharmacokinetics

Absorption: Unknown.
Distribution: Widely distributed throughout body.
Metabolism: Metabolized in liver.
Excretion: Excreted in urine mainly as metabolites; less than 1% of dose excreted unchanged. *Half-life:* 8 hours.

Route	Onset	Peak	Duration
P.O.	≤ 30 min	≤ 4 hr	4-6 hr

Pharmacodynamics

Chemical effect: Appears to modify central perception of pain without modifying pain reflexes. Blocks interneuronal activity in descending reticular activating system and in spinal cord.
Therapeutic effect: Relieves musculoskeletal pain.

Available forms

Tablets: 350 mg

NURSING PROCESS

Assessment
• Assess patient's pain before and after giving drug.
• Monitor drug effectiveness by regularly assessing severity and frequency of muscle spasms.
• Be alert for adverse reactions and drug interactions.
ALERT: Watch for idiosyncratic reactions after first to fourth doses (weakness, ataxia, visual and speech difficulties, fever, skin eruptions, and mental changes) and for severe reactions (bronchospasm, hypotension, and anaphylaxis).
• Assess patient for history of drug addiction. Prolonged use of drug may lead to dependence.

• Evaluate patient's and family's knowledge of drug therapy.

Nursing diagnoses
• Acute pain related to patient's underlying condition
• Risk for injury related to drug-induced drowsiness
• Deficient knowledge related to drug therapy

Planning and implementation
• Give drug with meals or milk to prevent GI distress.
• If adequate amount of pain relief is obtained, dosage can be reduced.
• Withhold dose and notify prescriber immediately if unusual reactions occur.
• Don't stop drug abruptly as mild withdrawal effects (such as insomnia, headache, nausea, and abdominal cramps) may result.

Patient teaching
• Warn patient to avoid activities that require alertness until drug's CNS effects are known. Drowsiness is usually temporary.
• Advise patient to avoid combining drug with alcohol or other CNS depressants.
• Advise patient to follow prescriber's orders about rest and physical therapy.
• Tell patient to take drug with meals or milk to prevent GI distress.
• Warn patient that carisoprodol may impair ability to perform hazardous activities requiring mental alertness or physical dexterity, such as operating machinery or a motor vehicle.

Evaluation
• Patient reports pain has ceased.
• Patient doesn't experience injury from drug-induced CNS adverse reactions.
• Patient and family state understanding of drug.

carmustine (BCNU)
(kar-MUHS-teen)
BiCNU, Gliadel

Pharmacologic class: alkylating agent, nitrosourea (not specific to cell cycle phase)
Therapeutic class: antineoplastic
Pregnancy risk category: D

Indications and dosages
▶ **Hodgkin's disease, non-Hodgkin's lymphoma, and multiple myeloma.** *Adults:* 150 to 200 mg/m² I.V. by slow infusion as single dose, repeat q 6 weeks or 75 to 100 mg/m² I.V. by slow infusion daily for 2 days; repeat q 6 weeks if platelet count is above 100,000/mm³ and WBC count is above 4,000/mm³. Dosage is reduced by 30% when WBC count is 2,000 to 3,000/mm³ and platelet count is 25,000 to 75,000/mm³. Dosage is reduced by 50% when WBC count is below 2,000/mm³ and platelet count is below 25,000/mm³.
▶ **Recurrent glioblastoma and metastatic brain tumors (adjunct to surgery to prolong survival).** *Adults:* 8 wafers implanted into resection cavity as size of cavity allows.
▶ **Brain‡, breast‡, GI tract‡, lung‡, and hepatic cancer‡ and malignant melanomas‡.** *Adults:* 75 to 100 mg/m² I.V. by slow infusion daily for 2 consecutive days; repeat q 6 weeks if platelet count is above 100,000/mm³ and WBC count is above 4,000/mm³.

Contraindications and precautions
• Contraindicated in patients hypersensitive to drug.
Lifespan: In pregnant or breast-feeding women, use is contraindicated. In children, safety of drug hasn't been established.

Adverse reactions
CNS: ataxia, drowsiness.
CV: facial flushing.
GI: *nausea* beginning in 2 to 6 hours (can be severe), *vomiting, anorexia, dysphagia, esophagitis, diarrhea.*
GU: ***nephrotoxicity, renal failure.***
Hematologic: ***cumulative bone marrow suppression*** (delayed 4 to 6 weeks, lasting 1 to 2 weeks), ***leukopenia, thrombocytopenia, acute leukemia or bone marrow dysplasia*** (may occur after long-term use).
Hepatic: ***hepatotoxicity.***
Metabolic: possible hyperuricemia (in lymphoma patients when rapid cell lysis occurs).
Respiratory: ***pulmonary fibrosis.***
Skin: hyperpigmentation (if drug contacts skin).
Other: *intense pain* (at infusion site from venous spasm).

Interactions

Drug-drug. *Anticoagulants, aspirin:* May increase risk of bleeding. Avoid using together.
Cimetidine: May increase carmustine's bone marrow toxicity. Avoid using together, if possible.
Digoxin, phenytoin: May reduce levels of these drugs. Use together cautiously.

Effects on lab test results

• May increase urine urea, AST, bilirubin, and alkaline phosphatase levels.
• May decrease hemoglobin, hematocrit, and WBC and platelet counts.

Pharmacokinetics

Absorption: Administered I.V.
Distribution: Distributed rapidly into CSF.
Metabolism: Metabolized extensively in liver.
Excretion: 60% to 70% excreted in urine within 96 hours, 6% to 10% excreted as carbon dioxide by lungs, and 1% excreted in feces.
Half-life: 15 to 30 minutes.

Route	Onset	Peak	Duration
I.V., wafer	Unknown	Unknown	Unknown

Pharmacodynamics

Chemical effect: Inhibits enzymatic reactions involved with DNA synthesis, cross-links strands of cellular DNA, and interferes with RNA transcription, causing growth imbalance that leads to cell death.
Therapeutic effect: Kills selected cancer cells.

Available forms

Injection: 100-mg vial (lyophilized), with 3-ml vial of absolute alcohol supplied as diluent
Wafer: 7.7 mg

NURSING PROCESS

Assessment

• Assess patient's neoplastic disorder before therapy and regularly thereafter.
• Obtain baseline pulmonary function tests before therapy because pulmonary toxicity appears to be related to dose. Be sure to evaluate results of liver, renal, and pulmonary function tests periodically thereafter.
• Monitor CBC and uric acid level.
• Be alert for adverse reactions and drug interactions.
• Evaluate patient's and family's knowledge of drug therapy.

Nursing diagnoses

• Ineffective health maintenance related to neoplastic disease
• Risk for injury related to drug-induced adverse reactions
• Deficient knowledge related to drug therapy

Planning and implementation

• Follow facility policy to reduce risks because preparation and administration of parenteral form is linked to carcinogenic, mutagenic, and teratogenic risks for personnel.
• To reduce nausea, give antiemetic before giving drug.
• **I.V. use:**To reconstitute, dissolve 100 mg of carmustine in 3 ml of absolute alcohol provided by manufacturer. Dilute solution with 27 ml of sterile water for injection. Resulting solution contains 3.3 mg of carmustine/ml in 10% alcohol. Dilute in normal saline solution or D_5W for I.V. infusion. Give at least 250 ml over 1 to 2 hours. To reduce pain on infusion, dilute further or slow infusion rate.
– Discard drug if powder liquefies or appears oily (decomposition has occurred).
– Use only in glass containers. Solution is unstable in plastic I.V. bags.
– Don't mix with other drugs during administration.
– Store reconstituted solution in refrigerator for 48 hours. May decompose at temperatures above 80° F (27° C).
– Avoid contact with skin because carmustine will cause brown stain. If drug contacts skin, wash off thoroughly.
• **Wafer use:**Unopened foil packs are stable at room temperature for 6 hours. Store below -4° F.
– Use double gloves if handling wafer in operating room.
• Allopurinol may be used with adequate hydration to prevent hyperuricemia and uric acid nephropathy.

Patient teaching

• Warn patient to watch for signs of infection (fever, sore throat, fatigue) and bleeding (easy

bruising, nosebleeds, bleeding gums, melena). Take temperature daily.
• Instruct patient to avoid OTC products containing aspirin.
• Advise breast-feeding women to discontinue breast-feeding during therapy because of possible infant toxicity.
• Advise women of childbearing age to avoid pregnancy during therapy and to consult prescriber before becoming pregnant.

☑ Evaluation
• Patient shows positive response to drug therapy as evidenced by follow-up diagnostic studies.
• Patient doesn't experience injury from drug-induced adverse reactions.
• Patient and family state understanding of drug therapy.

carvedilol
(kar-VAY-deh-lol)
Coreg

Pharmacologic class: $alpha_1$-adrenergic and beta blocker
Therapeutic class: antihypertensive, adjunct treatment for heart failure
Pregnancy risk category: C

Indications and dosages
▶ **Hypertension.** *Adults:* Dosage highly individualized. Initially, 6.25 mg P.O. b.i.d. with food. Obtain a standing blood pressure 1 hour after initial dose. If tolerated, continue dosage for 7 to 14 days. May increase to 12.5 mg P.O. b.i.d. for 7 to 14 days, following blood pressure monitoring protocol noted above. Maximum dosage is 25 mg P.O. b.i.d. as tolerated.
▶ **Mild-to-severe heart failure.** *Adults:* Dosage highly individualized and adjusted carefully. Initially, 3.125 mg P.O. b.i.d. with food for 2 weeks; if tolerated, can increase to 6.25 mg P.O. b.i.d. Dosage may be doubled q 2 weeks as tolerated. At start of new dosage, observe patient for dizziness or light-headedness for 1 hour. Maximum dosage for patients weighing less than 85 kg (187 lb) is 25 mg P.O. b.i.d.; for those weighing over 85 kg, maximum dosage is 50 mg P.O. b.i.d.

Contraindications and precautions
• Contraindicated in patients hypersensitive to drug and in those with New York Heart Association class IV decompensated cardiac failure requiring I.V. inotropic therapy, bronchial asthma or related bronchospastic conditions, second- or third-degree AV block, sick sinus syndrome (unless a permanent pacemaker is in place), cardiogenic shock, or severe bradycardia. Drug isn't recommended for patients with symptomatic hepatic impairment.
• Use cautiously in hypertensive patients with left ventricular failure, perioperative patients who receive anesthetics that depress myocardial function, patients with diabetes who receive insulin or oral antidiabetics, and patients subject to spontaneous hypoglycemia. Also use cautiously in patients with thyroid disease, pheochromocytoma, Prinzmetal's variant angina, bronchospastic disease, or peripheral vascular disease.
Lifespan: Breast-feeding should be discontinued during drug therapy. In patients younger than age 18, safety and efficacy haven't been established. In elderly patients, plasma levels are about 50% higher; monitor these patients closely.

Adverse reactions
CNS: fever, *dizziness, fatigue,* headache, hypesthesia, insomnia, pain, paresthesia, somnolence, vertigo, malaise.
CV: aggravated angina pectoris, edema, ***AV block, bradycardia,*** *chest pain,* fluid overload, hypertension, hypotension, orthostatic hypotension, syncope.
EENT: abnormal vision, rhinitis, pharyngitis, sinusitis.
GI: abdominal pain, *diarrhea,* melena, nausea, periodontitis, vomiting.
GU: abnormal renal function, albuminuria, hematuria, impotence, urinary tract infection.
Hematologic: purpura, ***thrombocytopenia.***
Metabolic: dehydration, glycosuria, gout, hypercholesterolemia, *hyperglycemia,* hypertriglyceridemia, hypervolemia, hypovolemia, hyperuricemia, hypoglycemia, hyponatremia, weight gain.
Musculoskeletal: arthralgia, myalgia, back pain.
Respiratory: bronchitis, dyspnea, *upper respiratory tract infection.*

Skin: increased sweating.

Other: allergy, peripheral edema, viral infection.

Interactions

Drug-drug. *Calcium channel blockers:* May cause isolated conduction disturbances. Monitor patient's heart rhythm and blood pressure.
Catecholamine-depleting drugs (such as MAO inhibitors, reserpine): May cause bradycardia or severe hypotension. Monitor patient closely.
Cimetidine: May increase bioavailability of carvedilol. Monitor vital signs carefully.
Clonidine: May potentiate blood pressure and heart rate–lowering effects. Monitor vital signs closely.
Digoxin: May increase digoxin level by about 15% during therapy. Monitor digoxin levels and vital signs carefully.
Insulin, oral antidiabetics: May enhance hypoglycemic properties. Monitor glucose levels.
Rifampin: May reduce levels of carvedilol by 70%. Monitor vital signs closely.

Drug-food. *Any food:* Delays carvedilol absorption but doesn't alter extent of bioavailability. Advise patient to take drug with food to minimize orthostatic effects.

Effects on lab test results

- May increase BUN, ALT, AST, alkaline phosphatase, cholesterol, and triglyceride levels. May decrease sodium level. May increase or decrease glucose level.
- May decrease platelet count, PT, and INR.

Pharmacokinetics

Absorption: Rapidly and extensively absorbed with absolute bioavailability of 25% to 35% because of significant first-pass metabolism.
Distribution: Extensively distributed into extravascular tissues; about 98% bound to plasma proteins.
Metabolism: Primarily metabolized by aromatic ring oxidation and glucuronidation.
Excretion: Metabolites are primarily excreted via bile in the feces. Less than 2% is excreted unchanged in urine. *Half-life:* 7 to 10 hours.

Route	Onset	Peak	Duration
P.O.	Unknown	1-2 hr	7-10 hr

Pharmacodynamics

Chemical effect: Nonselective beta-adrenergic blocker with $alpha_1$-blocking activity causes significant reductions in systemic blood pressure, pulmonary arterial pressure, pulmonary capillary wedge pressure, and heart rate.
Therapeutic effect: Lowers blood pressure and heart rate.

Available forms

Tablets: 3.125 mg, 6.25 mg, 12.5 mg, 25 mg

NURSING PROCESS

Assessment

- Monitor patient for decreased PT and increased alkaline phosphatase, BUN, ALT, and AST levels.
- Assess patient with heart failure for worsened condition, renal dysfunction, or fluid retention; diuretics may need to be increased.
- Monitor patient with diabetes closely; drug may mask signs of hypoglycemia, or hyperglycemia may be worsened.
- Observe patient for dizziness or lightheadedness for 1 hour after giving each dose.
- Evaluate patient's and family's knowledge of drug therapy.

Nursing diagnoses

- Ineffective health maintenance related to underlying disorder
- Ineffective cerebral tissue perfusion secondary to therapeutic action of drug
- Deficient knowledge related to drug therapy

Planning and implementation

- Before therapy begins, dosages of digoxin, diuretics, or ACE inhibitors should be stabilized.
- Give drug with food to reduce risk of orthostatic hypotension.
- Notify prescriber if pulse drops below 55 beats/minute; dosage may need to be reduced.

Patient teaching

- Tell patient not to interrupt or discontinue drug without medical approval. Drug should be withdrawn gradually over 1 to 2 weeks.
- Advise heart failure patient to call prescriber if weight gain or shortness of breath occurs.

• Inform patient that he may experience low blood pressure when standing. If he's dizzy or faints, advise him to sit or lie down.
• Caution patient against driving or performing hazardous tasks until CNS effects of drug are known.
• Tell patient to notify prescriber if dizziness or faintness occurs; dosage may need to be adjusted.
• Advise patient with diabetes to report changes in glucose level promptly.
• Inform patient who wears contact lenses that decreased lacrimation may occur.

☑ Evaluation
• Patient responds well to therapy.
• Patient doesn't experience dizziness or lightheadedness.
• Patient and family state understanding of drug therapy.

caspofungin acetate
(kas-poh-FUN-jin AS-ih-tayt)
Cancidas

Pharmacologic classification: glucan synthesis inhibitor, echinocandin
Therapeutic classification: antifungal antibiotic
Pregnancy risk category: C

Indications and dosages
▶ **Invasive aspergillosis in patients refractory to or intolerant of other drugs, such as amphotericin B, lipid formulations of amphotericin B, itraconazole.** *Adults:* A single 70-mg loading dose on day 1, followed by 50 mg daily thereafter. Give by slow I.V. infusion over about 1 hour. Duration of treatment based on severity of patient's underlying disease, recovery from immunosuppression, and clinical response.

Contraindications and precautions
• Contraindicated in patients hypersensitive to any components of caspofungin.
Lifespan: In breast-feeding women, use cautiously because it's not known whether drug appears in breast milk. In children, safety and efficacy haven't been established.

Adverse reactions
CNS: *headache,* paresthesia, *fever,* chills.
CV: *tachycardia, phlebitis, thrombophlebitis.*
GI: nausea, vomiting, diarrhea, abdominal pain, anorexia.
GU: proteinuria, hematuria.
Hematologic: eosinophilia, anemia.
Musculoskeletal: pain, myalgia.
Respiratory: *tachypnea.*
Skin: histamine-mediated symptoms including rash, facial swelling, pruritus, sensation of warmth, erythema, and sweating.

Interactions
Drug-drug. *Carbamazepine, dexamethasone, efavirenz, nelfinavir, nevirapine, phenytoin, rifampin:* May decrease caspofungin levels. Consider increasing caspofungin dosage to 70 mg daily if patient fails to respond clinically.
Cyclosporine: Significantly increases AST and ALT levels. Avoid using together unless potential benefit outweighs potential risk.
Tacrolimus: Decreased tacrolimus levels. Monitor tacrolimus levels and adjust tacrolimus dosage accordingly.

Effects on lab test results
• May increase ALT, AST, and alkaline phosphatase levels. May decrease potassium level.
• May increase eosinophil count, urine protein, and urine RBC. May decrease hemoglobin and hematocrit.

Pharmacokinetics
Absorption: Administered I.V.
Distribution: Extensively bound to albumin (about 97%).
Metabolism: Slowly metabolized in the liver.
Excretion: 35% of drug and metabolites is excreted in feces and 41% in urine. Renal clearance of parent drug is very low.

Route	Onset	Peak	Duration
I.V.	Unknown	Unknown	Unknown

Pharmacodynamics
Chemical effect: Caspofungin inhibits synthesis of beta (1,3)-D-glucan, an integral component of the cell walls of susceptible filamentous fungi that isn't found in mammal cells. Caspofungin has in vitro activity against *Aspergillus fumigatus, A. flavus,* and *A. terreus.*

Development of resistance to caspofungin by *Aspergillus sp.* in vitro hasn't been studied.
Therapeutic effect: Prevents fungi formation.

Available forms

Lyophilized powder for injection: 50-mg, 70-mg single-use vials

NURSING PROCESS

Assessment

- Assess patient's hepatic function before starting drug therapy.
- Observe patient for histamine-mediated reactions (rash, facial swelling, pruritus, sensation of warmth).
- Monitor I.V. site carefully for phlebitis.
- Monitor patient's lab test results carefully during drug therapy for any increase in liver function test values.
- Assess patient's and family's knowledge of drug therapy.

Nursing diagnoses

- Risk for infection and impaired skin integrity related to adverse effects of intravenous drug administration
- Ineffective health maintenance related to underlying disease process and immunocompromised state
- Deficient knowledge related to aspergillosis infection and caspofungin acetate drug therapy

Planning and implementation

ALERT: Never mix or dilute caspofungin acetate with any dextrose solution.

- Don't mix or infuse caspofungin acetate with any other drugs.
- Reconstituted vials should be used within 1-hour or discarded.
- Drug generally should be diluted in 250 ml of normal saline solution for all (70-mg, 50-mg, 35-mg) doses. In patients with fluid restrictions, the 50-mg and 35-mg doses may be diluted in 100 ml of normal saline solution.
- Give drug by slow I.V. infusion of about 1 hour.
- Diluted solutions may be stored at 25° C (77° F) for up to 24 hours.
- Safety and efficacy of a 70-mg dose regimen in patients who aren't clinically responding to the 50-mg daily dose hasn't been adequately studied. An increase in dosage to 70 mg daily may be well tolerated.
- Safety information on treatment durations longer than 2 weeks is limited. Drug may continue to be well tolerated during longer courses of therapy.
- Dosage adjustment is necessary for patients with moderate hepatic insufficiency.

Patient teaching

- Instruct patient to report signs and symptoms of phlebitis.
- Tell patient to report any adverse events during drug therapy.

Evaluation

- Patient does not experience any adverse reactions during drug therapy.
- Patient responds positively to antifungal drug therapy.
- Patient and family state understanding of intravenous caspofungin acetate therapy.

castor oil

(KAS-tir oyl)

Emulsoil†, Purge†, Neoloid† (sugar-free)

Pharmacologic class: glyceride, *Ricinus communis* derivative
Therapeutic class: stimulant laxative
Pregnancy risk category: NR

Indications and dosages

▶ **Preparation for rectal or bowel examination or for surgery.** For all patients, given as single dose about 16 hours before surgery or procedure.
Adults and children older than 12: 15 to 60 ml P.O.
Children ages 2 to 12: 5 to 15 ml P.O.
Infants younger than age 2: 1 to 5 ml P.O. Increased dose produces no greater effect.

Contraindications and precautions

- Contraindicated in patients with evidence of appendicitis or acute surgical abdomen (such as abdominal pain, nausea, vomiting), ulcerative bowel lesions, anal or rectal fissures, fecal impaction, or intestinal obstruction or perforation.

• Use cautiously in patients with rectal bleeding.

Lifespan: In menstruating and pregnant women, use is contraindicated. Breast-feeding women should seek medical approval before using castor oil.

Adverse reactions

GI: *nausea,* vomiting, diarrhea, and loss of normal bowel function with excessive use; *abdominal cramps,* especially in severe constipation; malabsorption of nutrients; "cathartic colon" (syndrome resembling ulcerative colitis radiologically and pathologically) with long-term misuse; laxative dependence with long-term or excessive use; protein-losing enteropathy. May cause constipation after catharsis.
GU: pelvic congestion (in menstruating women).
Metabolic: hypokalemia, other electrolyte imbalances (with excessive use).

Interactions

Drug-herb. *Male fern:* May increase absorption and increase risk of toxicity. Discourage using together.

Effects on lab test results

• May decrease potassium level
• May cause electrolyte imbalances.

Pharmacokinetics

Absorption: Unknown.
Distribution: Distributed locally, primarily in small intestine.
Metabolism: Metabolized by intestinal enzymes into its active form, ricinoleic acid.
Excretion: Excreted in feces.

Route	Onset	Peak	Duration
P.O.	2-6 hr	Varies	Varies

Pharmacodynamics

Chemical effect: Increases peristalsis, probably by direct effect on smooth muscle of intestine. Thought to irritate musculature or stimulate colonic intramural plexus. Also promotes fluid accumulation in colon and small intestine.
Therapeutic effect: Cleans bowel.

Available forms

Emulsion: 95% castor oil; 36.4% castor oil
Oral liquid: 95% castor oil

NURSING PROCESS

Assessment

• Assess patient's underlying condition.
• Monitor drug effectiveness by noting whether diagnostic testing provides accurate results.
• Failure to respond to drug may indicate acute condition requiring surgery.
• Be alert for adverse reactions and drug interactions.
• Evaluate patient's and family's knowledge of drug therapy.

Nursing diagnoses

• Health-seeking behavior (seeking diagnostic testing) related to underlying condition
• Acute pain related to drug-induced abdominal cramps
• Deficient knowledge related to drug therapy

Planning and implementation

• Have patient suck on ice before drug administration and give drug with juice or carbonated beverage to mask oily taste. Stir mixture and have patient drink it promptly.
• Shake emulsion well before measuring dose. Emulsion is better tolerated but more expensive. Store below 40° F (44° C). Don't freeze.
• Time drug administration so it doesn't interfere with scheduled activities or sleep.
• Give drug on empty stomach for best results.
• Increased intestinal motility lessens absorption of other oral drugs. Separate administration times.

Patient teaching

• Tell patient not to expect another bowel movement for 1 to 2 days after castor oil has emptied bowel.

Evaluation

• Patient obtains accurate results of diagnostic testing.
• Patient doesn't experience pain from therapy.
• Patient and family state understanding of drug therapy.

cefaclor
(SEH-fuh-klor)
Ceclor, Ceclor CD

Pharmacologic class: second-generation cephalosporin
Therapeutic class: antibiotic
Pregnancy risk category: B

Indications and dosages

▶ **Respiratory, urinary tract, skin, and soft-tissue infections and otitis media caused by *Haemophilus influenzae, Streptococcus pneumoniae, S. pyogenes, Escherichia coli, Proteus mirabilis, Klebsiella sp.,* and staphylococci.** *Adults:* 250 to 500 mg P.O. q 8 hours. Total daily dosage shouldn't exceed 4 g. For extended-release forms, 500 mg P.O. q 12 hours for 7 days for bronchitis. For pharyngitis or skin and skin-structure infections, 375 mg P.O. q 12 hours for 10 days and 7 to 10 days, respectively.
Children: 10 mg/kg P.O. b.i.d. q 8 hours. For pharyngitis or otitis media, b.i.d. q 12 hours. For more serious infections, 40 mg/kg daily are recommended, not to exceed 1 g daily. If given for otitis media, dose can be divided equally and given q 12 hours.
▶ **Acute uncomplicated urinary tract infection‡.** *Adults:* 2 g P.O. as a single dose.

Contraindications and precautions

- Contraindicated in patients hypersensitive to other cephalosporins.
- Use cautiously in patients with a history of sensitivity to penicillin because of reports of partial cross-allergenicity.
- Watch renal function; administer cautiously to patients with renal impairment.

Lifespan: In pregnant and breast-feeding women, use cautiously. Safety and efficacy of the extended-release tablets in children younger than age 16 and capsules and oral suspension in children younger than age 1 month haven't been established.

Adverse reactions

CNS: dizziness, headache, somnolence, malaise, fever.
GI: *nausea,* vomiting, *diarrhea,* anorexia, dyspepsia, abdominal cramps, ***pseudomembranous colitis,*** oral candidiasis.
GU: red and white cells in urine, vaginal candidiasis, vaginitis.
Hematologic: ***transient leukopenia,*** lymphocytosis, anemia, eosinophilia, ***thrombocytopenia.***
Skin: *maculopapular rash,* dermatitis.
Other: ***hypersensitivity reactions*** (serum sickness, ***anaphylaxis***).

Interactions

Drug-drug. *Chloramphenicol:* May have an antagonistic effect. Don't use together.
Probenecid: May inhibit excretion and increase levels of cefaclor. Monitor patient.

Effects on lab test results

- May increase ALT, AST, alkaline phosphatase, bilirubin, GGT, and LDH levels.
- May increase eosinophil count. May decrease hemoglobin, hematocrit, and WBC and platelet counts.
- May cause false-positive urine glucose determinations with copper sulfate tests (Clinitest).

Pharmacokinetics

Absorption: Well absorbed from GI tract. Food will delay but not prevent complete GI tract absorption.
Distribution: Distributed widely into most body tissues and fluids; CSF penetration is poor. Drug is 25% protein-bound.
Metabolism: None.
Excretion: Excreted primarily in urine by renal tubular secretion and glomerular filtration. *Half-life:* 0.5 to 1 hour.

Route	Onset	Peak	Duration
P.O.	Unknown	30-60 min	Unknown

Pharmacodynamics

Chemical effect: Inhibits cell-wall synthesis, promoting osmotic instability; usually bactericidal.
Therapeutic effect: Hinders or kills susceptible bacteria: many gram-positive cocci, including penicillinase-producing *Staphylococcus aureus, S. epidermidis, S. pneumoniae,* group B streptococci, and group A beta-hemolytic streptococci; gram-negative organisms, including *Klebsiella pneumoniae, Escherichia coli, Proteus mirabilis,* and *Shigella;* and other

organisms, such as *Moraxella catarrhalis, Haemophilus influenzae, Enterobacter, Citrobacter, Providencia, Acinetobacter, Serratia,* and *Neisseria.*

Available forms

Capsules: 250 mg, 500 mg
Oral suspension: 125 mg/5 ml, 250 mg/5 ml, 187 mg/5 ml, 375 mg/5 ml
Tablets: (extended-release): 375 mg, 500 mg

NURSING PROCESS

Assessment

- Assess patient's infection before therapy and regularly thereafter.
- Obtain specimen for culture and sensitivity tests before first dose. Therapy may begin pending test results.
- Ask patient about previous reactions to cephalosporins or penicillin before administering first dose.
- Be alert for adverse reactions and drug interactions.
- Monitor patient's hydration status if adverse GI reactions occur.
- Evaluate patient's and family's knowledge of drug therapy.

Nursing diagnoses

- Infection related to bacteria susceptible to drug
- Risk for deficient fluid volume related to drug-induced adverse GI reactions
- Deficient knowledge related to drug therapy

Planning and implementation

- Give drug with food to prevent or minimize GI upset.
- Store reconstituted suspension in refrigerator (stable for 14 days). Keep tightly closed and shake well before using.

ALERT: Don't confuse with other cephalosporins with similar sounding names.

Patient teaching

- Tell patient that drug may be taken with meals.
- Advise patient to take drug exactly as prescribed, even after he feels better.
- Instruct patient to call prescriber if rash develops.
- Teach patient how to store drug.

Evaluation

- Patient is free from infection.
- Patient maintains adequate hydration.
- Patient and family state understanding of drug therapy.

cefadroxil monohydrate

(seh-fuh-DROKS-il MON-oh-HIGH-drayt)
Cefadroxil, Duricef

Pharmacologic class: first-generation cephalosporin
Therapeutic class: antibiotic
Pregnancy risk category: B

Indications and dosages

▶ **Urinary tract infections caused by *Escherichia coli, Proteus mirabilis,* and *Klebsiella sp.;* skin and soft-tissue infections; and streptococcal pharyngitis.** *Adults:* 1 to 2 g P.O. daily, depending on infection treated, usually once or twice daily.
Children: 30 mg/kg P.O. daily in two divided doses. Course of treatment is usually at least 10 days.

Contraindications and precautions

- Contraindicated in patients hypersensitive to drug or other cephalosporins.
- Use cautiously in patients with impaired renal function (dosage adjustments may be necessary) or who have a history of sensitivity to penicillin.

Lifespan: In pregnant or breast-feeding women, use cautiously.

Adverse reactions

CNS: dizziness, headache, malaise, paresthesia.
GI: ***pseudomembranous colitis,*** *nausea,* anorexia, vomiting, *diarrhea,* glossitis, *dyspepsia,* abdominal cramps, anal pruritus, tenesmus, oral candidiasis.
GU: genital pruritus, candidiasis.
Hematologic: ***transient neutropenia,*** eosinophilia, ***leukopenia,*** anemia, ***agranulocytosis, thrombocytopenia.***
Respiratory: dyspnea.
Skin: *maculopapular and erythematous rashes.*

Other: ***hypersensitivity reactions*** (serum sickness, ***anaphylaxis***).

Interactions

Drug-drug. *Probenecid:* May inhibit excretion and increase levels of cefadroxil. Monitor patient.

Effects on lab test results

- May increase ALT, AST, alkaline phosphatase, bilirubin, GGT, and LDH levels.
- May increase eosinophil count. May decrease hemoglobin, hematocrit, and neutrophil, WBC, granulocyte, and platelet counts.
- May cause false-positive urine glucose determinations with copper sulfate tests (Clinitest).

Pharmacokinetics

Absorption: Rapid and complete.
Distribution: Distributed widely into most body tissues and fluids; CSF penetration is poor. Drug is 20% protein-bound.
Metabolism: None.
Excretion: Excreted primarily unchanged in urine. *Half-life:* About 1 to 2 hours.

Route	Onset	Peak	Duration
P.O.	Unknown	1-2 hr	Unknown

Pharmacodynamics

Chemical effect: Inhibits cell-wall synthesis, promoting osmotic instability; usually bactericidal.
Therapeutic effect: Hinders or kills susceptible bacteria: many gram-positive cocci, including penicillinase-producing *Staphylococcus aureus, S. epidermidis, Streptococcus pneumoniae,* group B streptococci, and group A beta-hemolytic streptococci; and gram-negative organisms, including *K. pneumoniae, E. coli, P. mirabilis, and Shigella.*

Available forms

Capsules: 500 mg
Oral suspension: 125 mg/5 ml, 250 mg/5 ml, 500 mg/5 ml
Tablets: 1 g

NURSING PROCESS

Assessment

- Assess patient's infection before therapy and regularly thereafter.
- Obtain specimen for culture and sensitivity tests before first dose. Therapy may begin pending test results.
- Be alert for adverse reactions and drug interactions.
- Monitor patient's hydration status if adverse GI reactions occur.
- Evaluate patient's and family's knowledge of drug therapy.

Nursing diagnoses

- Infection related to bacteria susceptible to drug
- Risk for deficient fluid volume related to drug-induced adverse GI reactions
- Deficient knowledge related to drug therapy

Planning and implementation

- Drug's half-life permits once- or twice-daily dosing.
- Expect prescriber to lengthen dosage interval to prevent drug accumulation if creatinine clearance is below 50 ml/minute.
- Store reconstituted suspension in refrigerator. Keep container tightly closed and shake well before using.
- About 40% to 75% of patients receiving cephalosporins show false-positive direct Coombs' test.

ALERT: Don't confuse with other cephalosporins with similar-sounding names.

Patient teaching

- Tell patient to take drug exactly as prescribed, even after he feels better.
- Advise patient to take drug with food or milk to lessen GI discomfort.
- Tell patient to call prescriber if rash develops.
- Inform patient using oral suspension to shake it well before using and to refrigerate mixture in tightly closed container.

Evaluation

- Patient is free from infection.
- Patient maintains adequate hydration.
- Patient and family state understanding of drug therapy.

cefazolin sodium
(sef-EH-zoh-lin SOH-dee-um)
Ancef, Kefzol, Zolicef

Pharmacologic class: first-generation cephalosporin
Therapeutic class: antibiotic
Pregnancy risk category: B

Indications and dosages

▶ **Serious infections of respiratory, biliary, and GU tracts; skin, soft-tissue, bone, and joint infections; septicemia; endocarditis caused by *Escherichia coli, Enterobacteriaceae,* gonococci, *Haemophilus influenzae, Klebsiella, Proteus mirabilis, Staphylococcus aureus, Streptococcus pneumoniae,* and group A beta-hemolytic streptococci; perioperative prophylaxis‡.** *Adults:* 250 mg I.V. or I.M. q 8 hours to 1 g q 6 hours. Maximum 12 g daily in life-threatening situations.
Children and infants older than 1 month: 50 to 100 mg/kg or 1.25 g/m^2 daily I.V. or I.M. in three or four divided doses.

▶ **Perioperative prophylaxis in contaminated surgery.** *Adults:* 1 g I.V. or I.M. 30 to 60 minutes before surgery; then 0.5 to 1 g I.V. or I.M. q 6 to 8 hours for 24 hours. In operations lasting over 2 hours, another 0.5- to 1-g dose may be given intraoperatively. In cases where infection would be devastating, prophylaxis may be continued for 3 to 5 days. After initial dose, dosage should be adjusted in patients with renal failure.

Contraindications and precautions

- Contraindicated in patients hypersensitive to other cephalosporins.
- Use cautiously in patients with a history of sensitivity to penicillin because of reports of cross-allergenicity, and patients with renal failure (dosage adjustments may be needed).

Lifespan: In pregnant and breast-feeding women, use cautiously.

Adverse reactions

CNS: dizziness, headache, malaise, paresthesia.
GI: ***pseudomembranous colitis,*** nausea, anorexia, vomiting, *diarrhea,* glossitis, dyspepsia, abdominal cramps, anal pruritus, tenesmus, oral candidiasis.
GU: genital pruritus and candidiasis, vaginitis.
Hematologic: *transient neutropenia, leukopenia,* eosinophilia, anemia, ***thrombocytopenia.***
Respiratory: dyspnea.
Skin: *maculopapular and erythematous rashes, urticaria,* ***Stevens-Johnson syndrome.***
Other: ***hypersensitivity reactions*** (serum sickness, ***anaphylaxis***).

Interactions

Drug-drug. *Probenecid:* May inhibit excretion and increase levels of cefazolin. Monitor patient.

Effects on lab test results

- May increase ALT, AST, alkaline phosphatase, bilirubin, GGT, and LDH levels.
- May increase eosinophil count. May decrease neutrophil, WBC, and platelet counts.
- May cause false-positive urine glucose determinations with copper sulfate tests (Clinitest).

Pharmacokinetics

Absorption: Unknown after I.M. administration.
Distribution: Distributed widely into most body tissues and fluids; CSF penetration is poor; 74% to 86% protein-bound.
Metabolism: None.
Excretion: Excreted primarily in urine. *Half-life:* About 1 to 2 hours.

Route	Onset	Peak	Duration
I.V.	Immediate	Immediate	Unknown
I.M.	Unknown	1-2 hr	Unknown

Pharmacodynamics

Chemical effect: Inhibits cell-wall synthesis, promoting osmotic instability; usually bactericidal.
Therapeutic effect: Hinders or kills susceptible bacteria: many gram-positive cocci, including penicillinase-producing *Staphylococcus aureus, S. pneumoniae,* group A beta-hemolytic streptococci, *Klebsiella, E. coli, Enterobacteriaceae,* gonococci, *P. mirabilis,* and *H. influenzae.*

Available forms

Infusion: 500 mg/50-ml or 100-ml vial, 1 g/50-ml or 100-ml vial, 500 mg or 1 g RediVials, Faspaks, or ADD-Vantage vials
Injection (parenteral): 250 mg, 500 mg, 1 g

NURSING PROCESS

Assessment
- Assess patient's infection before therapy and reassess regularly thereafter.
- Obtain specimen for culture and sensitivity tests. Therapy may begin pending test results.
- Ask patient about previous reactions to cephalosporins or penicillin before administering first dose.
- Be alert for adverse reactions and drug interactions.
- Monitor patient's hydration status if adverse GI reactions occur.
- Evaluate patient's and family's knowledge of drug therapy.

Nursing diagnoses
- Infection related to bacteria susceptible to drug
- Risk for deficient fluid volume related to drug-induced adverse GI reactions
- Deficient knowledge related to drug therapy

Planning and implementation
- **I.V. use:** Reconstitute with sterile water, bacteriostatic water, or normal saline solution as follows: 2 ml to 500-mg vial to yield 225 mg/ml or 2.5 ml to 1-g vial to yield 330 mg/ml. Shake well until dissolved.
– For direct injection, further dilute Ancef with 5 ml of sterile water (Kefzol with 10 ml). Inject into large vein or into tubing of free-flowing I.V. solution over 3 to 5 minutes. For intermittent infusion, add reconstituted drug to 50 to 100 ml of compatible solution or use premixed solution. Commercially available frozen solutions of cefazolin in D_5W should be given only by intermittent or continuous I.V. infusion.
– Alternate injection sites if I.V. therapy lasts longer than 3 days. Use of small I.V. needles in larger available veins may be preferable.
- **I.M. use:** After reconstitution, inject I.M. drug without further dilution (not as painful as other cephalosporins). Inject deep into large muscle mass, such as gluteus maximus or lateral aspect of thigh.
- Reconstituted drug is stable for 24 hours at room temperature and 96 hours if refrigerated.
- Because of long duration of effect, most infections can be treated with dose every 8 hours.
- **ALERT:** Don't confuse with other cephalosporins with similar-sounding names.

Patient teaching
- Tell patient to report adverse reactions.

Evaluation
- Patient is free from infection.
- Patient maintains adequate hydration.
- Patient and family state understanding of drug therapy.

cefdinir
(SEF-dih-neer)
Omnicef

Pharmacologic class: third-generation cephalosporin
Therapeutic class: antibiotic
Pregnancy risk category: B

Indications and dosages

▶ **Treatment of mild-to-moderate infections caused by susceptible strains of microorganisms for conditions of community-acquired pneumonia, acute exacerbations of chronic bronchitis, acute maxillary sinusitis, acute bacterial otitis media, and uncomplicated skin and skin-structure infections.** *Adults and adolescents:* 300 mg P.O. q 12 hours or 600 mg P.O. q 24 hours for 10 days. (Use 300-mg doses q 12 hour for pneumonia and skin infections.)
Children ages 6 months to 12 years: 7 mg/kg P.O. q 12 hours or 14 mg/kg P.O. q 24 hours for 10 days; maximum daily dose 600 mg. (Use q-12-hour dosages for skin infections.) Dosage is adjusted for patients with impaired renal function and is based on creatinine clearance.

▶ **Treatment of pharyngitis and tonsillitis.** *Adults and children older than age 12:* 300 mg P.O. q 12 hours for 5 to 10 days or 600 mg P.O. q 24 hours for 10 days.
Children ages 6 months to 12 years: 7 mg/kg P.O. q 12 hours for 5 to 10 days or 14 mg/kg

P.O. q 24 hours for 10 days, up to a maximum dose of 600 mg daily.

Contraindications and precautions

- Contraindicated in patients hypersensitive to cephalosporins.
- Use cautiously in patients hypersensitive to penicillin because of risk of cross-sensitivity with other beta-lactam antibiotics.
- Use cautiously in patients with history of colitis or renal insufficiency.

Lifespan: In breast-feeding women, use cautiously. In children younger than age 6 months, safety and efficacy haven't been established.

Adverse reactions

CNS: headache.
GI: abdominal pain, *diarrhea,* nausea, vomiting.
GU: vaginal candidiasis, vaginitis.
Skin: rash.

Interactions

Drug-drug. *Antacids (aluminum- and magnesium-containing), iron supplements, multivitamins containing iron:* May decrease cefdinir's absorption and bioavailability. Give such preparations 2 hours before or after cefdinir dose.
Probenecid: Inhibits the renal excretion of cefdinir. Monitor patient.

Effects on lab test results

- May increase GGT and alkaline phosphatase levels.
- May increase RBC count and urine protein.

Pharmacokinetics

Absorption: Bioavailability of drug is about 21% after 300-mg capsule dose, 16% after 600-mg capsule dose, and 25% for suspension.
Distribution: 60% to 70% bound to plasma proteins.
Metabolism: Not appreciably metabolized; activity results mainly from parent drug.
Excretion: Eliminated primarily by renal excretion. *Half-life:* 1.7 hours.

Route	Onset	Peak	Duration
P.O.	Unknown	2-4 hr	Unknown

Pharmacodynamics

Chemical effect: Kills bacteria by inhibition of cell-wall synthesis.
Therapeutic effect: Is stable in the presence of some beta-lactamase enzymes, causing some microorganisms resistant to penicillins and cephalosporins to be susceptible to cefdinir. Excluding *Pseudomonas, Enterobacter, Enterococcus,* and methicillin-resistant *Staphylococcus sp.,* cefdinir kills a broad range of gram-positive and gram-negative aerobic microorganisms.

Available forms

Capsules: 300 mg
Suspension: 125 mg/5 ml

NURSING PROCESS

Assessment

- Ask patient about previous reactions to cephalosporins or penicillin before giving first dose.
- Obtain specimen for culture and sensitivity tests before giving first dose.
- Monitor patient for symptoms of superinfection.
- Assess patient with diarrhea carefully; pseudomembranous colitis has been reported with drug.
- Evaluate patient's and family's knowledge of drug therapy.

Nursing diagnoses

- Infection related to susceptible bacteria
- Risk for deficient fluid volume related to drug-induced adverse GI reactions
- Deficient knowledge related to drug therapy

Planning and implementation

- Begin therapy pending culture and sensitivity test results.
- Patients with renal insufficiency require reduced dosage.
- Notify prescriber if allergic reaction is suspected; drug should be discontinued and emergency treatment given as needed.

ALERT: Don't confuse with other cephalosporins with similar-sounding names.

Patient teaching

- Instruct patient to take antacids and iron supplements 2 hours before or after dose of cefdinir.

• Inform patient with diabetes that each teaspoon of suspension contains 2.86 g of sucrose.
• Tell patient that drug may be taken without regard to meals.
• Advise patient to report severe diarrhea or diarrhea accompanied by abdominal pain.
• Tell patient to report adverse reactions or symptoms of superinfection promptly.

Evaluation
• Patient is free from infection.
• Patient maintains adequate hydration.
• Patient and family state understanding of drug therapy.

cefditoren pivoxil

(sef-da-TOR-en pa-VOX-ill)
Spectracef

Pharmacologic classification: semisynthetic third-generation cephalosporin
Therapeutic classification: antibiotic
Pregnancy risk category: B

Indications and dosages

▶ **Acute bacterial exacerbation of chronic bronchitis caused by *Haemophilus influenzae, H. parainfluenzae, Streptococcus pneumoniae* (penicillin-susceptible strains only), or *Moraxella catarrhalis*.** *Adults and children age 12 and older:* 400 mg P.O. b.i.d with meals for 10 days.

▶ **Pharyngitis, tonsillitis, and uncomplicated skin and skin-structure infections caused by *S. pyogenes*.** *Adults and children age 12 and older:* 200 mg P.O. b.i.d. with meals for 10 days.

Contraindications and precautions

• Contraindicated in patients hypersensitive to cefditoren, other cephalosporins, and penicillins. Also contraindicated in patients with carnitine deficiency or inborn errors of metabolism that may result in clinically significant carnitine deficiency. Because cefditoren tablets contain sodium caseinate, a milk protein, they shouldn't be given to patients hypersensitive to milk protein (distinct from those with lactose intolerance).
• Use cautiously in patients with impaired renal function. Drug is dialyzable.

Lifespan: In breast-feeding women, use cautiously because cephalosporins appear in breast milk. In patients younger than age 12, safety and efficacy haven't been established.

Adverse reactions

CNS: headache.
GI: abdominal pain, dyspepsia, *diarrhea,* nausea, vomiting, ***colitis,*** hepatic dysfunction (including cholestasis).
GU: vaginal candidiasis, hematuria, ***nephrotoxicity.***
Hematologic: anemia.
Metabolic: hyperglycemia.
Skin: ***Stevens-Johnson syndrome, toxic epidermal necrolysis.***
Other: hypersensitivity reactions (including serum sickness, rash, fever, ***anaphylaxis***).

Interactions

Drug-drug. *Aluminum antacids, H_2-receptor antagonists, magnesium:* Reduces cefditoren absorption. Avoid using together.
Oral anticoagulants: May increase bleeding time. Monitor PT levels and patient closely for unusual bleeding or bruising.
Probenecid: Increases plasma cefditoren levels. Avoid using together.
Drug-food. *Moderate or high-fat meal:* Increases cefditoren bioavailability. Advise patient to take drug with meals.

Effects on lab test results

• May increase liver enzyme levels. May decrease plasma carnitine level.
• May decrease hematocrit, hemoglobin, and PT.
• May cause a false-positive direct Coombs' test result and false-positive reaction for glucose in urine, using copper reduction tests (those involving Benedict's solution, Fehling's solution, or Clinitest tablets).

Pharmacokinetics

Absorption: Absorbed from the GI tract and hydrolyzed by esterases to cefditoren. Giving drug with a meal increases its absolute bioavailability.
Distribution: Distributed widely into most body tissues and fluids based on volume of distribution. CSF penetration is unknown. Drug is about 88% protein-bound.
Metabolism: Not appreciably metabolized.

Excretion: Excreted unchanged mainly in urine by glomerular filtration and tubular secretion. *Half-life:* 1.6 ± 0.4 hours in patients with normal renal function.

Route	Onset	Peak	Duration
P.O.	Unknown	1½-3 hr	Unknown

Pharmacodynamics

Chemical effect: Primarily bactericidal. Drug acts by adhering to bacterial penicillin-binding proteins, thereby inhibiting cell-wall synthesis. Cefditoren is active against many gram-positive and gram-negative organisms, including *Staphylococcus aureus* (methicillin-susceptible strains, including beta-lactamase–producing strains), *S. pneumoniae* (penicillin-susceptible strains only), *S. pyogenes, H. influenzae* (including beta-lactamase–producing strains), *H. parainfluenzae* (including beta-lactamase–producing strains), and *M. catarrhalis* (including beta-lactamase–producing strains).
Therapeutic effects: Kills susceptible bacteria.

Available forms

Tablets: 200 mg

NURSING PROCESS

Assessment

- Assess patient's history for hypersensitivity to cefditoren, cephalosporins, penicillins, or other contraindications for drug therapy.
- Monitor patient for overgrowth or recurrence of resistant organisms with prolonged or repeated drug therapy.
- Because cefditoren has been linked to *Clostridium difficile*-associated colitis, monitor patient for diarrhea during therapy.
- Monitor patient for hypersensitivity reactions during drug therapy as well as any unusual bleeding or bruising.
- Assess patient's and family's knowledge of drug therapy.

Nursing diagnoses

- Noncompliance related to completion of 10-day antibiotic regimen
- Risk for infection with non-susceptible bacteria or fungi related to prolonged or repeated drug therapy
- Deficient knowledge related to cephalosporin therapy

Planning and implementation

- Give drug with a meal to increase its bioavailability.
- If patient develops diarrhea after receiving cefditoren, keep in mind that this drug may cause pseudomembranous colitis. Notify prescriber immediately, as colitis may be fatal.
- Don't use this drug if patient needs prolonged treatment.
- Signs and symptoms of overdose may include nausea, vomiting, epigastric distress, diarrhea, and seizures. Treatment is symptomatic and supportive.
- If hypersensitivity or allergic reaction occurs, discontinue drug and provide emergency measures as clinically indicated.
- Dosage adjustment is necessary in patients with renal impairment.

Patient teaching

- Instruct patient to take drug with food to increase its absorption.
- Caution patient not to take drug with an H_2 antagonist or an antacid because they may reduce cefditoren absorption. If an H_2 antagonist or antacid must be used, instruct patient to take them 2 hours apart from drug, despite feeling better.
- Explain to patient the importance of taking drug for the entire treatment duration to prevent any future drug resistance.
- Instruct patient to immediately stop taking drug and call prescriber if any adverse reactions develop, such as rash, hives, difficulty breathing, unusual bleeding or bruising, or diarrhea.
- Encourage patient to contact prescriber if signs and symptoms of infection don't improve after several days of therapy.
- Urge patient not to miss any doses. However, if patient misses a dose, instruct him to take the missed dose immediately and wait 12 hours before taking the next dose. Tell him not to double the dose.

Evaluation

- Patient completes prescribed 10-day therapy.
- Patient doesn't suffer from any adverse reactions during drug therapy.

• Patient and family state understanding of drug therapy and importance of completing entire drug regimen as prescribed.

cefixime

(sef-IKS-eem)
Suprax

Pharmacologic class: third-generation cephalosporin
Therapeutic class: antibiotic
Pregnancy risk category: B

Indications and dosages

▶ **Uncomplicated urinary tract infections caused by *Escherichia coli* and *Proteus mirabilis;* otitis media caused by *Haemophilus influenzae* (beta-lactamase positive and negative strains), *Moraxella catarrhalis,* and *Streptococcus pyogenes;* pharyngitis and tonsillitis caused by *S. pyogenes;* acute bronchitis and acute exacerbations of chronic bronchitis caused by *S. pneumoniae* and *H. influenzae* (beta-lactamase positive and negative strains).** *Adults and adolescents older than age 12 and weighing more than 50 kg (110 lb):* 400 mg P.O. daily or 200 mg q 12 hours.
Children age 12 and younger or weighing 50 kg or less: 8 mg/kg P.O. daily in one or two divided doses. For otitis media, use suspension only.

▶ **Uncomplicated gonorrhea caused by *Neisseria gonorrhoeae.*** *Adults:* 400 mg P.O. as single dose.

▶ **Disseminated gonococcal infections.** *Adults:* 400 mg P.O. b.i.d. after initial treatment with I.M. or I.V. parenteral antibiotics to complete 7 days of treatment.

Contraindications and precautions

• Contraindicated in patients hypersensitive to drug or to other cephalosporins or beta-lactam antibiotics.
• Use cautiously in patients with renal dysfunction (reduced dosage necessary with creatinine clearance below 60 ml/minute) or history of sensitivity to penicillin.
Lifespan: In pregnant or breast-feeding women, use cautiously.

Adverse reactions

CNS: headache, dizziness, nervousness, malaise, fatigue, somnolence, insomnia.
GI: *diarrhea,* loose stools, abdominal pain, nausea, vomiting, dyspepsia, flatulence, ***pseudomembranous colitis.***
GU: genital pruritus, vaginitis, genital candidiasis.
Hematologic: ***thrombocytopenia, leukopenia,*** eosinophilia.
Hepatic: ***hepatitis,*** jaundice.
Skin: pruritus, rash, urticaria, ***Stevens-Johnson syndrome.***
Other: drug fever, ***hypersensitivity reactions*** (serum sickness, ***anaphylaxis***).

Interactions

Drug-drug. *Nifedipine:* May increase cefixime level. Avoid using together.
Probenecid: May inhibit excretion and increase level of cefixime. Monitor patient.
Salicylates: May displace cefixime from plasma protein–binding sites. Clinical significance is unknown.

Effects on lab test results

• May increase BUN, creatinine, ALT, AST, alkaline phosphatase, bilirubin, GGT, and LDH levels.
• May increase eosinophil count. May decrease platelet and WBC counts.
• May cause false-positive urine glucose determinations with copper sulfate tests (Clinitest).

Pharmacokinetics

Absorption: Well absorbed from GI tract.
Distribution: Widely distributed; enters CSF in patients with inflamed meninges; about 65% bound to plasma proteins.
Metabolism: About 50% of drug is metabolized.
Excretion: Excreted primarily in urine. *Half-life:* 3 to 4 hours.

Route	Onset	Peak	Duration
P.O.	Unknown	3-4½ hr	Unknown

Pharmacodynamics

Chemical effect: Inhibits cell-wall synthesis, promoting osmotic instability; usually bactericidal.

Therapeutic effect: Hinders or kills bacteria, including *H. influenzae, M. catarrhalis, S. pyogenes, S. pneumoniae, E. coli,* and *P. mirabilis.*

Available forms

Oral suspension: 100 mg/5 ml (after reconstitution)
Tablets: 200 mg, 400 mg

NURSING PROCESS

Assessment

- Assess patient's infection before therapy and reassess regularly thereafter.
- Obtain specimen for culture and sensitivity tests before first dose. Therapy may begin pending test results.
- Ask patient about previous reactions to cephalosporins or penicillin before giving first dose.
- Be alert for adverse reactions and drug interactions.
- Monitor patient's hydration status if adverse GI reactions occur.
- Evaluate patient's and family's knowledge of drug therapy.

Nursing diagnoses

- Infection related to bacteria susceptible to drug
- Risk for deficient fluid volume related to drug-induced adverse GI reactions
- Deficient knowledge related to drug therapy

Planning and implementation

- To prepare oral suspension, add required amount of water to powder in two portions. Shake well after each addition. After mixing, suspension is stable for 14 days (no need to refrigerate). Keep tightly closed. Shake well before using.

ALERT: Don't confuse with other cephalosporins with similar-sounding names.

Patient teaching

- Tell patient to take drug exactly as prescribed, even after he feels better.
- Tell patient to call prescriber if rash develops.
- Teach patient how to store drug.

Evaluation

- Patient is free from infection.
- Patient maintains adequate hydration.
- Patient and family state understanding of drug therapy.

cefmetazole sodium (cefmetazone)

(sef-MET-ah-zohl SOH-dee-um)
Zefazone

Pharmacologic class: second-generation cephalosporin
Therapeutic class: antibiotic
Pregnancy risk category: B

Indications and dosages

▶ **Lower respiratory tract infections caused by *Streptococcus pneumoniae, Staphylococcus aureus* (penicillinase- and non-penicillinase–producing strains), *Escherichia coli,* and *Haemophilus influenzae* (non-penicillinase–producing strains); intra-abdominal infections caused by *E. coli* or *Bacteroides fragilis;* skin and skin-structure infections caused by *S. aureus* (penicillinase- and non-penicillinase–producing strains), *S. epidermidis, S. pyogenes, S. agalactiae, E. coli, Proteus mirabilis, Klebsiella pneumoniae,* and *B. fragilis.*** *Adults:* 2 g I.V. q 6 to 12 hours for 5 to 14 days.

▶ **Urinary tract infections caused by *E. coli.*** *Adults:* 2 g I.V. q 12 hours.

▶ **Prophylaxis in patients undergoing vaginal hysterectomy.** *Adults:* 2 g I.V. 30 to 90 minutes before surgery as single dose. Or, 1 g I.V. 30 to 90 minutes before surgery; repeat after 8 and 16 hours.

▶ **Prophylaxis in patients undergoing abdominal hysterectomy.** *Adults:* 1 g I.V. 30 to 90 minutes before surgery; repeat after 8 and 16 hours.

▶ **Prophylaxis in patients undergoing cesarean section.** *Adults:* 2 g I.V. as single dose after clamping cord; or 1 g I.V. after clamping cord; repeat after 8 and 16 hours.

▶ **Prophylaxis in patients undergoing colorectal surgery.** *Adults:* 2 g I.V. as single dose 30 to 90 minutes before surgery. Some clinicians follow with additional 2-g doses after 8 and 16 hours.

▶ **Prophylaxis in high-risk patients undergoing cholecystectomy.** *Adults:* 1 g I.V. 30 to 90 minutes before surgery; repeat after 8 and 16 hours.

Patients with renal impairment: If creatinine clearance is 50 to 90 ml/minute, give 1 to 2 g I.V. q 12 hours; 30 to 49 ml/minute, give 1 to 2 g I.V. q 16 hours; 10 to 29 ml/minute, give 1 to 2 g I.V. q 24 hours; less than 10 ml/minute, give 1 to 2 g I.V. q 48 hours.

Contraindications and precautions

- Contraindicated in patients hypersensitive to drug or other cephalosporins.
- Use cautiously in patients with history of sensitivity to penicillin because of reported cross-reactivity.

Lifespan: In pregnant women, use cautiously. Breast-feeding should be discontinued during therapy because traces of drug have appeared in breast milk. In children, safety of drug hasn't been established.

Adverse reactions

CNS: fever, headache.
CV: ***shock,*** hypotension, phlebitis.
EENT: altered color perception, epistaxis.
GI: nausea, vomiting, *diarrhea,* epigastric pain, ***pseudomembranous colitis.***
GU: vaginitis.
Respiratory: pleural effusion, dyspnea, ***respiratory distress.***
Skin: rash, pruritus, generalized erythema.
Other: bacterial or fungal superinfection, ***hypersensitivity reactions*** (serum sickness, ***anaphylaxis***), pain at injection site.

Interactions

Drug-drug. *Aminoglycosides:* May increase risk of nephrotoxicity. Monitor patient closely. *Probenecid:* May inhibit excretion and increase levels of cefmetazole. Sometimes used for this effect.
Drug-lifestyle. *Alcohol use:* May cause disulfiram-like reaction. Discourage alcohol use for 24 hours before and after cefmetazole.

Effects on lab test results

- May increase ALT, AST, alkaline phosphatase, bilirubin, GGT, and LDH levels.
- May cause false-positive urine glucose determinations with copper sulfate tests (Clinitest).

Pharmacokinetics

Absorption: Administered I.V.
Distribution: Distributed widely into most body tissues and fluids; CSF penetration is P.O.; 65% protein-bound.
Metabolism: About 15% of dose is metabolized, probably in liver.
Excretion: Excreted primarily in urine. *Half-life:* About 1.5 hours.

Route	Onset	Peak	Duration
I.V.	Unknown	Immediate	Unknown

Pharmacodynamics

Chemical effect: Inhibits cell-wall synthesis, promoting osmotic instability; usually bactericidal.
Therapeutic effect: Hinders or kills susceptible bacteria: many gram-positive organisms and enteric gram-negative bacilli, including *S. aureus, S. epidermidis,* streptococci, *Klebsiella, E. coli* and other coliform bacteria, *H. influenzae,* and *Bacteroides sp.*

Available forms

Injection: 1 g, 2 g

NURSING PROCESS

Assessment

- Assess patient's infection before therapy and reassess regularly thereafter.
- Obtain specimen for culture and sensitivity tests before first dose. Therapy may begin pending test results.
- Ask patient about previous reactions to cephalosporins or penicillin before administering first dose.
- Be alert for adverse reactions and drug interactions. Watch for superinfection, especially in elderly patients or those with chronic conditions.
- Monitor patient's hydration status for adverse GI reactions.
- Evaluate patient's and family's knowledge of drug therapy.

Nursing diagnoses

- Infection related to bacteria susceptible to drug
- Risk for deficient fluid volume related to drug-induced adverse GI reactions
- Deficient knowledge related to drug therapy

Planning and implementation

• Reconstitute with bacteriostatic water, sterile water, or normal saline solution for injection. After reconstitution, drug may be further diluted to concentrations ranging from 1 to 20 mg/ml by adding it to normal saline solution for injection, D_5W, or lactated Ringer's injection. Reconstituted or dilute solutions are stable for 24 hours at room temperature (77° F [25° C]) or 1 week if refrigerated at 46° F (8° C).

ALERT: Don't confuse with other cephalosporins with similar-sounding names.

Patient teaching

• Instruct patient to report adverse reactions.

Evaluation

• Patient is free from infection.
• Patient maintains adequate hydration.
• Patient and family state understanding of drug therapy.

cefonicid sodium

(sef-ON-eh-sid SOH-dee-um)

Monocid

Pharmacologic class: second-generation cephalosporin
Therapeutic class: antibiotic
Pregnancy risk category: B

Indications and dosages

▶ **Perioperative prophylaxis in contaminated surgery.** *Adults:* 1 g I.M. or I.V. 60 minutes before surgery.

▶ **Serious infections of lower respiratory and urinary tracts, skin and skin-structure infections, septicemia, bone and joint infections, and perioperative prophylaxis. Susceptible microorganisms include *Streptococcus pneumoniae, S. pyogenes, Klebsiella pneumoniae, Escherichia coli, Haemophilus influenzae, Proteus mirabilis, Staphylococcus aureus,* and *S. epidermidis.*** *Adults:* Usual dosage is 1 g I.V. or I.M. q 24 hours. In life-threatening infections, 2 g q 24 hours.

Contraindications and precautions

• Contraindicated in patients hypersensitive to drug or other cephalosporins.
• Use cautiously in patients with history of sensitivity to penicillin and in patients with renal failure (may need dosage adjustment).

Lifespan: In pregnant or breast-feeding women, use cautiously. In children, safety of drug hasn't been established.

Adverse reactions

CNS: dizziness, headache, malaise, paresthesia.
GI: ***pseudomembranous colitis,*** nausea, anorexia, vomiting, diarrhea, glossitis, dyspepsia, abdominal cramps, anal pruritus, tenesmus, oral candidiasis.
GU: genital pruritus and candidiasis, vaginitis, ***acute renal failure.***
Hematologic: ***transient neutropenia, leukopenia,*** eosinophilia, anemia, ***thrombocytopenia.***
Respiratory: dyspnea.
Skin: *maculopapular and erythematous rashes, urticaria.*
Other: ***hypersensitivity reactions*** (serum sickness, ***anaphylaxis***); *pain, induration, sterile abscesses, tissue sloughing* (at injection site); *phlebitis, thrombophlebitis* (with I.V. injection).

Interactions

Drug-drug. *Aminoglycosides:* Potential increased risk of nephrotoxicity. Monitor patient's renal function closely.
Probenecid: May inhibit excretion and increase levels of cefonicid. Monitor patient.

Effects on lab test results

• May increase ALT, AST, alkaline phosphatase, bilirubin, GGT, and LDH levels.
• May increase PT and INR and eosinophil counts. May decrease hemoglobin, hematocrit, and neutrophil and WBC counts. May increase or decrease platelet count.
• May cause false-positive urine glucose determinations with copper sulfate tests (Clinitest).

Pharmacokinetics

Absorption: Unknown after I.M. administration.
Distribution: Distributed widely into most body tissues and fluids; CSF penetration is poor; 90% to 98% protein-bound.
Metabolism: None.

Excretion: Excreted primarily in urine. *Half-life:* About 3½ to 6 hours.

Route	Onset	Peak	Duration
I.V.	Immediate	Immediate	Unknown
I.M.	Unknown	1-2 hr	Unknown

Pharmacodynamics

Chemical effect: Inhibits cell-wall synthesis, promoting osmotic instability; usually bactericidal.
Therapeutic effect: Hinders or kills susceptible bacteria: many gram-positive organisms and enteric gram-negative bacilli, such as *S. aureus, S. epidermidis, S. pyogenes, S. pneumoniae, K. pneumoniae, E. coli, P. mirabilis,* and *H. influenzae.*

Available forms

Infusion: 1 g/100 ml
Injection: 1 g

NURSING PROCESS

Assessment

- Assess patient's infection before therapy and reassess regularly thereafter.
- Obtain specimen for culture and sensitivity tests before first dose. Therapy may begin pending test results.
- Ask patient about previous reactions to cephalosporins or penicillin before giving first dose.
- Be alert for adverse reactions and drug interactions. Monitor patient for superinfection.
- Monitor patient's hydration status if adverse GI reactions occur.
- Evaluate patient's and family's knowledge of drug therapy.

Nursing diagnoses

- Infection related to bacteria susceptible to drug
- Risk for deficient fluid volume related to drug-induced adverse GI reactions
- Deficient knowledge deficit related to drug therapy

Planning and implementation

- **I.V. use:** Reconstitute 500-mg vial with 2 ml sterile water for injection (yields 225 mg/ml) and 1-g vial with 2.5 ml sterile water for injection (yields 325 mg/ml). Shake well. Reconstitute piggyback vials with 50 to 100 ml D_5W or normal saline solution.
- **I.M. use:** When administering 2-g I.M. doses once daily, divide dose equally and inject deeply into two different large muscle masses, such as gluteus maximus and lateral aspect of thigh.
- Dosing interval will be adjusted for patients with renal impairment.

ALERT: Don't confuse with other cephalosporins with similar-sounding names.

Patient teaching

- Tell patient to report adverse reactions.

Evaluation

- Patient is free from infection.
- Patient maintains adequate hydration.
- Patient and family state understanding of drug therapy.

cefoperazone sodium

(sef-oh-PER-ah-zohn SOH-dee-um)
Cefobid

Pharmacologic class: third-generation cephalosporin
Therapeutic class: antibiotic
Pregnancy risk category: B

Indications and dosages

▶ **Serious infections of respiratory tract; intra-abdominal, gynecologic, and skin infections; bacteremia; and septicemia. Susceptible microorganisms include *Streptococcus pneumoniae* and *S. pyogenes; Staphylococcus aureus* (penicillinase- and non-penicillinase–producing) and *S. epidermidis;* enterococci; *Escherichia coli; Klebsiella; Haemophilus influenzae; Enterobacter; Citrobacter; Proteus;* some *Pseudomonas,* including *P. aeruginosa;* and *Bacteroides fragilis.*** *Adults:* Usual dosage is 1 to 2 g q 12 hours I.V. or I.M. In severe infections or those caused by less sensitive organisms, total daily dosage may be increased to 16 g.

Contraindications and precautions

- Contraindicated in patients hypersensitive to drug or other cephalosporins.

• Use cautiously in patients with impaired renal function and in patients with a history of sensitivity to penicillin.

Lifespan: In pregnant or breast-feeding women, use cautiously. In children younger than age 12, safety of drug hasn't been established.

Adverse reactions

CNS: headache, malaise, paresthesia, dizziness.
GI: ***pseudomembranous colitis,*** nausea, anorexia, vomiting, *diarrhea,* glossitis, dyspepsia, abdominal cramps, tenesmus, anal pruritus, oral candidiasis.
GU: genital pruritus and candidiasis.
Hematologic: ***transient neutropenia,*** eosinophilia, hemolytic anemia, hypoprothrombinemia, bleeding.
Respiratory: dyspnea.
Skin: *maculopapular and erythematous rashes, urticaria.*
Other: ***hypersensitivity reactions*** (serum sickness, ***anaphylaxis***); *pain, induration, sterile abscesses, warmth, tissue sloughing* at injection site; *phlebitis, thrombophlebitis* with I.V. injection.

Interactions

Drug-drug. *Anticoagulants:* May increase anticoagulant effects. Use with caution and monitor patient for bleeding.
Probenecid: May inhibit excretion and increase levels of cefoperazone. Monitor patient.
Drug-lifestyle. *Alcohol use:* Possible disulfiram-like reaction. Caution patient to avoid alcohol use for several days after stopping cefoperazone.

Effects on lab test results

• May increase ALT, AST, alkaline phosphatase, bilirubin, GGT, and LDH levels.
• May increase INR and eosinophil count. May decrease hemoglobin, hematocrit, and neutrophil count. May increase or decrease PT.
• May cause false-positive urine glucose determinations with copper sulfate tests (Clinitest).

Pharmacokinetics

Absorption: Unknown after I.M. administration.
Distribution: Distributed widely into most body tissues and fluids; CSF penetration in patients with inflamed meninges; 82% to 93% protein-bound.
Metabolism: Insignificant.
Excretion: Excreted primarily in urine. *Half-life:* About 1.5 to 2.5 hours.

Route	Onset	Peak	Duration
I.V.	Immediate	Immediate	Unknown
I.M.	Unknown	1-2 hr	Unknown

Pharmacodynamics

Chemical effect: Inhibits cell-wall synthesis, promoting osmotic instability; usually bactericidal.
Therapeutic effect: Hinders or kills susceptible bacteria: some gram-positive organisms and many enteric gram-negative bacilli, including *S. pneumoniae* and *S. pyogenes, S. aureus, S. epidermidis,* enterococcus, *E. coli, Klebsiella, H. influenzae, Enterobacter, Citrobacter, Proteus,* some *Pseudomonas sp.* (including *P. aeruginosa*), and *B. fragilis.*

Available forms

Infusion: 1-g, 2-g piggyback
Parenteral: 1 g, 2 g

NURSING PROCESS

Assessment

• Assess patient's infection before therapy and reassess regularly thereafter.
• Obtain specimen for culture and sensitivity tests before first dose. Therapy may begin pending test results.
• Ask patient about previous reactions to cephalosporins or penicillin before administering first dose.
• Be alert for adverse reactions and drug interactions.
• Monitor hydration status if patient develops adverse GI reactions. Cefoperazone may increase risk of diarrhea more than other cephalosporins.
• Evaluate patient's and family's knowledge of drug therapy.

Nursing diagnoses

• Infection related to bacteria susceptible to drug

• Risk for deficient fluid volume related to drug-induced adverse GI reactions
• Deficient knowledge related to drug therapy

Planning and implementation

• Give doses of 4 g daily cautiously to patients with hepatic disease or biliary obstruction. Higher dosages require monitoring of serum levels.
• **I.M. use:** To prepare drug for I.M. injection, using 1-g vial, dissolve drug with 2 ml of sterile water for injection; add 0.6 ml of 2% lidocaine hydrochloride for final concentration of 333 mg/ml. Alternatively, dissolve drug with 2.8 ml of sterile water for injection; then add 1 ml of 2% lidocaine hydrochloride for final concentration of 250 mg/ml. When using 2-g vial, dissolve drug with 3.8 ml of sterile water for injection; then add 1.2 ml of 2% lidocaine hydrochloride for final concentration of 333 mg/ml. Alternatively, dissolve drug with 5.4 ml of sterile water for injection; then add 1.8 ml of 2% lidocaine hydrochloride for final concentration of 250 mg/ml.
– Inject deeply into large muscle mass, such as gluteus maximus or lateral aspect of thigh.
• **I.V. use:** Reconstitute 1- or 2-g vial with minimum of 2.8 ml of compatible I.V. solution; manufacturer recommends using 5 ml/g.
– Give by direct injection into large vein or into tubing of free-flowing I.V. solution over 3 to 5 minutes.
– When giving by intermittent infusion, add reconstituted drug to 20 to 40 ml of compatible I.V. solution and infuse over 15 to 30 minutes.
ALERT: Don't confuse with other cephalosporins with similar-sounding names.

Patient teaching

• Tell patient to report adverse reactions.

Evaluation

• Patient is free from infection.
• Patient maintains adequate hydration.
• Patient and family state understanding of drug therapy.

cefotaxime sodium

(sef-oh-TAKS-eem SOH-dee-um)
Claforan

Pharmacologic class: third-generation cephalosporin
Therapeutic class: antibiotic
Pregnancy risk category: B

Indications and dosages

▶ **Perioperative prophylaxis in contaminated surgery.** *Adults:* 1 g I.V. or I.M. 30 to 60 minutes before surgery. Patients undergoing cesarean section should receive 1 g I.V. or I.M. as soon as umbilical cord is clamped, followed by 1 g I.V. or I.M. 6 and 12 hours later.
▶ **Serious infections of lower respiratory and urinary tracts, CNS, skin, bone, and joints; gynecologic and intra-abdominal infections; bacteremia; and septicemia. Susceptible microorganisms include streptococci, including *Streptococcus pneumoniae* and *S. pyogenes; Staphylococcus aureus* (penicillinase- and non-penicillinase–producing) and *S. epidermidis; Escherichia coli; Klebsiella; Haemophilus influenzae; Enterobacter; Proteus;* and *Peptostreptococcus;* and pelvic inflammatory disease‡.** *Adults:* Usual dosage is 1 g I.V. or I.M. q 6 to 12 hours. Up to 12 g daily can be given in life-threatening infections.
Children weighing at least 50 kg (110 lb): Usual adult dose but dosage shouldn't exceed 12 g daily.
Children ages 1 month to 12 years weighing less than 50 kg: 50 to 180 mg/kg I.V. or I.M. daily in four to six divided doses.
Neonates ages 1 to 4 weeks: 50 mg/kg I.V. q 8 hours.
Neonates up to age 1 week: 50 mg/kg I.V. q 12 hours.
▶ **Disseminated gonococcal infection‡.** *Adults:* 1 g I.V. q 8 hours.
Neonates and infants: 25 to 50 mg/kg I.V. q 8 to 12 hours for 7 days, or 50 to 100 mg/kg I.M or I.V. q 12 hours for 7 days.
▶ **Gonococcal ophthalmia‡.** *Adults:* 500 mg I.V. q.i.d.
Neonates: 100 mg I.V. or I.M. for one dose; may continue until ocular cultures are negative at 48 to 72 hours.

▶ **Gonorrheal meningitis or arthritis‡.** *Neonates and infants:* 25 to 50 mg/kg I.V. q 8 to 12 hours for 10 to 14 days. Or, 50 to 100 mg/kg I.M. or I.V. q 12 hours for 10 to 14 days.

Contraindications and precautions

• Contraindicated in patients hypersensitive to drug or other cephalosporins.
• Use cautiously in patients with history of sensitivity to penicillin, and patients with renal failure (may need dosage adjustment).
Lifespan: In pregnant and breast-feeding women, use cautiously.

Adverse reactions

CNS: headache, malaise, paresthesia, dizziness.
GI: ***pseudomembranous colitis,*** nausea, anorexia, vomiting, *diarrhea,* glossitis, dyspepsia, abdominal cramps, tenesmus, anal pruritus, oral candidiasis.
GU: genital pruritus and candidiasis.
Hematologic: ***transient neutropenia,*** eosinophilia, hemolytic anemia, ***thrombocytopenia, agranulocytosis.***
Respiratory: dyspnea.
Skin: *maculopapular and erythematous rashes, urticaria.*
Other: ***hypersensitivity reactions*** (serum sickness, ***anaphylaxis***); elevated temperature; *pain, induration, sterile abscesses, warmth, tissue sloughing* at injection site; *phlebitis, thrombophlebitis* with I.V. injection.

Interactions

Drug-drug. *Aminoglycosides:* May increase risk of nephrotoxicity. Monitor renal function closely.
Probenecid: May inhibit excretion and increase levels of cefotaxime. Use together cautiously.

Effects on lab test results

• May increase ALT, AST, alkaline phosphatase, bilirubin, GGT, and LDH levels.
• May increase eosinophil count. May decrease hemoglobin, hematocrit, and neutrophil, platelet, and granulocyte counts.
• May cause false-positive urine glucose determinations with copper sulfate tests (Clinitest).

Pharmacokinetics

Absorption: Unknown after I.M. administration.
Distribution: Distributed widely into most body tissues and fluids; adequate CSF penetration when meninges are inflamed; 13% to 38% protein-bound.
Metabolism: Partially metabolized to active metabolite, desacetylcefotaxime.
Excretion: Excreted primarily in urine. *Half-life:* 1 to 2 hours.

Route	Onset	Peak	Duration
I.V.	Immediate	Immediate	Unknown
I.M.	Unknown	30 min	Unknown

Pharmacodynamics

Chemical effect: Inhibits cell-wall synthesis, promoting osmotic instability; usually bactericidal.
Therapeutic effect: Hinders or kills susceptible bacteria: some gram-positive organisms and many enteric gram-negative bacilli, including streptococci (*S. pneumoniae* and *pyogenes*), *S. aureus, S. epidermidis, E. coli, Klebsiella sp., H. influenzae, Enterobacter sp., Proteus sp., Peptostreptococcus sp.,* and some strains of *Pseudomonas aeruginosa.*

Available forms

Infusion: 1 g, 2 g
Injection: 500 mg, 1 g, 2 g

NURSING PROCESS

Assessment

• Assess patient's infection before therapy and reassess regularly thereafter.
• Obtain specimen for culture and sensitivity tests. Therapy may begin before test results are known.
• Ask patient about previous reactions to cephalosporins or penicillin before administering first dose.
• Be alert for adverse reactions and drug interactions.
• Monitor patient's hydration status if adverse GI reactions occur.
• Evaluate patient's and family's knowledge of drug therapy.

Nursing diagnoses
- Infection related to bacteria susceptible to drug
- Risk for deficient fluid volume related to drug-induced adverse GI reactions
- Deficient knowledge related to drug therapy

Planning and implementation
- **I.M. use:** Inject deeply into large muscle mass, such as gluteus maximus or lateral aspect of thigh.
- **I.V. use:** For direct injection, reconstitute 500-mg, 1-g, or 2-g vials with 10 ml sterile water for injection. Solutions containing 1 g/14 ml are isotonic.

– Inject drug into large vein or into tubing of free-flowing I.V. solution over 3 to 5 minutes.

– For I.V. infusion, reconstitute infusion vials with 50 to 100 ml D_5W or normal saline solution. Infuse drug over 20 to 30 minutes. Interrupt flow of primary I.V. solution during infusion.

ALERT: Don't confuse with other cephalosporins with similar-sounding names.

Patient teaching
- Tell patient to report adverse reactions.
- Teach patient to report decrease in urinary output. May have to decrease total daily dosage.

Evaluation
- Patient is free from infection.
- Patient maintains adequate hydration.
- Patient and family state understanding of drug therapy.

cefotetan disodium
(SEF-oh-teh-tan die-SOH-dee-um)
Cefotan

Pharmacologic class: second-generation cephalosporin
Therapeutic class: antibiotic
Pregnancy risk category: B

Indications and dosages
▶ **Serious urinary tract infections, lower respiratory tract infections, and gynecologic, skin and skin-structure, intra-abdominal, and bone and joint infections caused by susceptible streptococci, *Staphylococcus aureus* and *S. epidermidis, Escherichia coli, Klebsiella, Enterobacter, Proteus, Haemophilus influenzae, Neisseria gonorrhoeae,* and *Bacteroides,* including *B. fragilis.*** *Adults:* 1 mg to 2 g I.V. or I.M. q 12 hours for 5 to 10 days. In life-threatening infections, up to 6 g daily. *Children‡:* 40 to 60 mg/kg daily I.V. divided in equally divided doses q 12 hours.

▶ **Perioperative prophylaxis; used in contaminated surgery‡.** *Adults:* 1 to 2 g I.V. given once 30 to 60 minutes before surgery. In cesarean section, dose should be given as soon as umbilical cord is clamped.

Contraindications and precautions
- Contraindicated in patients hypersensitive to drug or other cephalosporins.
- Use cautiously in patients with history of sensitivity to penicillin and in patients with renal failure (may need dosage adjustment).

Lifespan: In pregnant and breast-feeding women, use cautiously. In children, safety of drug hasn't been established.

Adverse reactions
CNS: headache, malaise, paresthesia, dizziness.
GI: ***pseudomembranous colitis,*** nausea, anorexia, vomiting, *diarrhea,* glossitis, dyspepsia, abdominal cramps, tenesmus, anal pruritus.
GU: genital pruritus and candidiasis, ***nephrotoxicity.***
Hematologic: ***transient neutropenia,*** eosinophilia, hemolytic anemia, hypoprothrombinemia, bleeding, ***agranulocytosis, thrombocytopenia.***
Respiratory: dyspnea.
Skin: *maculopapular and erythematous rashes, urticaria.*
Other: ***hypersensitivity reactions*** (serum sickness, ***anaphylaxis***); elevated temperature; *pain, induration, sterile abscesses, tissue sloughing* at injection site; *phlebitis, thrombophlebitis* with I.V. injection.

Interactions
Drug-drug. *Aminoglycosides:* May have synergistic effect and increase risk of nephrotoxicity. Use with caution.
Anticoagulants: May increase anticoagulants effects. Use with caution and monitor patient for bleeding.

Probenecid: May inhibit excretion and increase levels of cefotetan. Sometimes used for this effect.

Drug-lifestyle. *Alcohol use:* May cause disulfiram-like reaction. Tell patient to avoid alcohol for several days after stopping cefotetan.

Effects on lab test results

- May increase ALT, AST, alkaline phosphatase, bilirubin, and LDH levels.
- May increase PT and INR and eosinophil count. May decrease hemoglobin, hematocrit, and neutrophil and granulocyte counts. May increase or decrease platelet count.
- May cause false-positive urine glucose determinations with copper sulfate tests (Clinitest).

Pharmacokinetics

Absorption: Unknown after I.M. administration.

Distribution: Distributed widely into most body tissues and fluids; CSF penetration is poor; 75% to 90% protein-bound.

Metabolism: None.

Excretion: Excreted primarily in urine. *Half-life:* About 3 to 4.5 hours.

Route	Onset	Peak	Duration
I.V.	Immediate	Immediate	Unknown
I.M.	Unknown	1.5-2 hr	Unknown

Pharmacodynamics

Chemical effect: Inhibits cell-wall synthesis, promoting osmotic instability; usually bactericidal.

Therapeutic effect: Hinders or kills susceptible bacteria: many gram-positive organisms and enteric gram-negative bacilli, such as streptococci, *S. aureus* and *S. epidermidis, E. coli, Klebsiella sp., Enterobacter sp., Proteus sp., H. influenzae, N. gonorrhoeae,* and *Bacteroides sp.*

Available forms

Infusion: 1-g, 2-g piggyback

Injection: 1 g, 2 g

NURSING PROCESS

Assessment

- Assess patient's infection before therapy and reassess regularly thereafter.
- Obtain specimen for culture and sensitivity tests before first dose. Therapy may begin pending test results.
- Ask patient about previous reactions to cephalosporins or penicillin before giving first dose.
- Be alert for adverse reactions and drug interactions.
- Monitor patient's hydration status if adverse GI reactions occur.
- Evaluate patient's and family's knowledge of drug therapy.

Nursing diagnoses

- Infection related to bacteria susceptible to drug
- Risk for deficient fluid volume related to drug-induced adverse GI reactions
- Deficient knowledge related to drug therapy

Planning and implementation

- **I.V. use:** Reconstitute drug with sterile water for injection. Then may be mixed with 50 to 100 ml of D_5W or normal saline solution.
  - Interrupt flow of primary I.V. solution during drug infusion.
  - For direct injection, give solutions containing 1 or 2 g of solution over 3 to 5 minutes.
- **I.M. use:** Reconstitute I.M. injection with sterile water or bacteriostatic water for injection, normal saline solution for injection, or 0.5% or 1% lidocaine hydrochloride.
  - Shake to dissolve and let stand until clear.
- Reconstituted solution remains stable for 24 hours at room temperature or 96 hours if refrigerated.

ALERT: Don't confuse with other cephalosporins with similar-sounding names.

Patient teaching

- Tell patient to report adverse reactions.
- Alert patient to signs of superinfection. Careful observation by patient is essential.

Evaluation

- Patient is free from infection.
- Patient maintains adequate hydration.
- Patient and family state understanding of drug therapy.

cefoxitin sodium

(sef-OKS-ih-tin SOH-dee-um)
Mefoxin

Pharmacologic class: second-generation cephalosporin
Therapeutic class: antibiotic
Pregnancy risk category: B

Indications and dosages

▶ **Serious infections of respiratory and GU tracts; skin, soft-tissue, bone, and joint infections; bloodstream and intra-abdominal infections caused by susceptible *Escherichia coli* and other coliform bacteria, *Staphylococcus aureus* (penicillinase- and non-penicillinase–producing), *S. epidermidis*, streptococci, *Klebsiella, Haemophilus influenzae*, and *Bacteroides*, including *B. fragilis*; and perioperative prophylaxis.** *Adults:* 1 to 2 g I.V. q 6 to 8 hours for uncomplicated forms of infection. In life-threatening infections, up to 12 g daily.
Children and infants older than age 3 months: 80 to 160 mg/kg I.V. or I.M. daily given in four to six equally divided doses. Maximum daily dose is 12 g.
▶ **Prophylactic use in surgery.** *Adults:* 2 g I.V. 30 to 60 minutes before surgery; then 2 g I.M. or I.V. q 6 hours for 24 hours.
Children age 3 months and older: 30 to 40 mg/kg I.M. or I.V. 30 to 60 minutes before surgery; then 30 mg/kg q 6 hours for 24 hours.

Contraindications and precautions

• Contraindicated in patients hypersensitive to drug or other cephalosporins.
• Use cautiously in patients with history of sensitivity to penicillin and in patients with renal failure (may need dosage adjustment).
Lifespan: In pregnant or breast-feeding women, use cautiously.

Adverse reactions

CNS: headache, malaise, paresthesia, dizziness.
GI: ***pseudomembranous colitis,*** nausea, anorexia, vomiting, *diarrhea,* glossitis, dyspepsia, abdominal cramps, tenesmus, anal pruritus, oral candidiasis.
GU: genital pruritus and candidiasis, **acute renal failure.**
Hematologic: ***transient neutropenia,*** eosinophilia, hemolytic anemia, ***thrombocytopenia.***
Respiratory: dyspnea.
Skin: *maculopapular and erythematous rashes, urticaria.*
Other: ***hypersensitivity reactions*** (serum sickness, ***anaphylaxis***), elevated temperature, *phlebitis, thrombophlebitis* (with I.V. injection).

Interactions

Drug-drug. *Nephrotoxic drugs:* May increase risk of nephrotoxicity. Monitor renal function closely.
Probenecid: May inhibit excretion and increase levels of cefoxitin. Sometimes used for this effect.

Effects on lab test results

• May increase ALT, AST, alkaline phosphatase, bilirubin, and LDH levels.
• May increase eosinophil count. May decrease hemoglobin, hematocrit, and neutrophil and platelet counts.
• May cause false-positive urine glucose determinations with copper sulfate tests (Clinitest).

Pharmacokinetics

Absorption: Unknown for I.M. administration.
Distribution: Distributed widely into most body tissues and fluids; CSF penetration is poor; 50% to 80% protein-bound.
Metabolism: Insignificant (about 2%).
Excretion: Excreted primarily in urine. *Half-life:* About 0.5 to 1 hours.

Route	Onset	Peak	Duration
I.V.	Immediate	Immediate	Unknown
I.M.	Rapid	20–30 min	< 6 hr

Pharmacodynamics

Chemical effect: Inhibits cell-wall synthesis, promoting osmotic instability; usually bactericidal.
Therapeutic effect: Hinders or kills susceptible bacteria: many gram-positive organisms and enteric gram-negative bacilli, such as *E. coli* and other coliform bacteria, streptococci, *S. aureus, S. epidermidis, Klebsiella, H. influenzae,* and *Bacteroides sp.*

Available forms

Infusion: 1 g, 2 g in 50-ml or 100-ml
Injection: 1 g, 2 g

NURSING PROCESS

Assessment

- Assess patient's infection before therapy and reassess regularly thereafter.
- Obtain specimen for culture and sensitivity tests before first dose. Therapy may begin pending test results.
- Ask patient about previous reactions to cephalosporins or penicillin before giving first dose.
- Be alert for adverse reactions and drug interactions.
- Assess I.V. site frequently for thrombophlebitis.
- Monitor patient's hydration status if adverse GI reactions occur.
- Evaluate patient's and family's knowledge of drug therapy.

Nursing diagnoses

- Infection related to bacteria susceptible to drug
- Risk for deficient fluid volume related to drug-induced adverse GI reactions
- Deficient knowledge related to drug therapy

Planning and implementation

- **I.V. use:** Reconstitute 1 g with at least 10 ml of sterile water for injection and 2 g with 10 to 20 ml of sterile water for injection. Solutions of D_5W and normal saline solution for injection also can be used.
- For direct injection, inject reconstituted drug into large vein or into tubing of free-flowing I.V. solution over 3 to 5 minutes.
- For intermittent infusion, add reconstituted drug to 50 or 100 ml D_5W, $D_{10}W$, or normal saline solution for injection. Interrupt flow of primary I.V. solution during infusion.
- **I.M. use:** Reconstitute by adding 2 ml of sterile water for injection or 0.5 or 1% lidocaine hydrochloride (without epinephrine) to each g of cefoxitin.
- Inject deeply into large muscle, such as the upper quadrant of the gluteus maximus.
- Patients with renal dysfunction require dosage adjustment.
- After reconstitution, drug may be stored for 24 hours at room temperature or refrigerated for 1 week.

ALERT: Don't confuse with other cephalosporins with similar-sounding names.

Patient teaching

- Tell patient to report adverse reactions and signs and symptoms of superinfection promptly.
- Instruct patient to notify prescriber if he experiences loose stools or diarrhea.

Evaluation

- Patient is free from infection.
- Patient maintains adequate hydration.
- Patient and family state understanding of drug therapy.

cefpodoxime proxetil

(sef-poh-DOKS-eem PROKS-eh-til)
Vantin

Pharmacologic class: third-generation cephalosporin
Therapeutic class: antibiotic
Pregnancy risk category: B

Indications and dosages

▶ **Acute, community-acquired pneumonia caused by non-beta-lactamase–producing strains of *Haemophilus influenzae* or *Streptococcus pneumoniae*.** *Adults and children age 13 and older:* 200 mg P.O. q 12 hours for 14 days.

▶ **Acute bacterial exacerbation of chronic bronchitis caused by *S. pneumoniae, H. influenzae* (non-beta-lactamase–producing strains), or *Moraxella catarrhalis*.** *Adults and children age 13 and older:* 200 mg P.O. q 12 hours for 10 days.

▶ **Uncomplicated gonorrhea in men and women; rectal gonococcal infections in women.** *Adults and children age 13 and older:* 200 mg P.O. as single dose. Follow with doxycycline 100 mg P.O. b.i.d. for 7 days.

▶ **Uncomplicated skin and skin-structure infections caused by *S. aureus* or *S. pyogenes*.** *Adults and children age 13 and older:* 400 mg P.O. q 12 hours for 7 to 14 days.

▶ **Acute otitis media caused by *S. pneumoniae, H. influenzae,* or *M. catarrhalis*.** *Chil-*

dren ages 6 months to 12 years: 5 mg/kg (not to exceed 200 mg) P.O. q 12 hours or 10 mg/kg (not to exceed 400 mg) P.O. daily for 10 days.

▶ **Pharyngitis or tonsillitis caused by *S. pyogenes.*** *Adults and children age 13 and older:* 100 mg P.O. q 12 hours for 5 to 10 days.
Children ages 2 months to 12 years: 5 mg/kg (not to exceed 100 mg) P.O. q 12 hours for 10 days.

▶ **Uncomplicated urinary tract infections caused by *E. coli, Klebsiella pneumoniae, Proteus mirabilis,* or *S. saprophyticus.*** *Adults:* 100 mg P.O. q 12 hours for 7 days.

▶ **Mild-to-moderate acute maxillary sinusitis caused by *H. influenzae, S. pneumoniae,* or *M. catarrhalis.*** *Adults and children older than age 12:* 200 mg P.O. q 12 hours for 10 days.
Children ages 2 months to 12 years: 5 mg/kg P.O. q 12 hours for 10 days; maximum dose is 200 mg.
Patients with creatinine clearance below 30 ml/minute: Dosage interval should be increased to q 24 hours. Patients receiving dialysis should get drug three times weekly, after dialysis.

Contraindications and precautions

- Contraindicated in patients hypersensitive to drug or other cephalosporins.
- Use cautiously in patients with history of hypersensitivity to penicillin (risk of cross-sensitivity), and patients receiving nephrotoxic drugs (other cephalosporins have had nephrotoxic potential).

Lifespan: In pregnant or breast-feeding women, use cautiously.

Adverse reactions

CNS: headache.
GI: *diarrhea,* nausea, vomiting, abdominal pain.
GU: vaginal fungal infections.
Skin: rash.
Other: hypersensitivity reactions (***anaphylaxis***).

Interactions

Drug-drug. *Antacids, H_2-receptor antagonists:* May decrease absorption of cefpodoxime. Avoid using together.
Probenecid: May decrease excretion of cefpodoxime. Monitor patient for toxicity.
Drug-food. *Any food:* May increase drug absorption. Give drug with food.

Effects on lab test results

- May cause false-positive urine glucose determinations with copper sulfate tests (Clinitest).

Pharmacokinetics

Absorption: Absorbed from GI tract.
Distribution: Distributed widely into most body tissues and fluids except CSF; 22% to 33% protein-bound in serum and 21% to 29% protein-bound in plasma.
Metabolism: Drug is de-esterified to its active metabolite, cefpodoxime.
Excretion: Excreted primarily in urine. *Half-life:* 2.1 to 2.8 hours.

Route	Onset	Peak	Duration
P.O.	Unknown	2-3 hr	Unknown

Pharmacodynamics

Chemical effect: Inhibits cell-wall synthesis, promoting osmotic instability; usually bactericidal.
Therapeutic effect: Hinders or kills susceptible bacteria: many gram-positive aerobes, such as *S. aureus, S. saprophyticus, S. pneumoniae,* and *S. pyogenes;* and gram-negative aerobes, including *K. pneumoniae, E. coli, P. mirabilis, M. catarrhalis, H. influenzae,* and *N. gonorrhoeae.*

Available forms

Oral suspension: 50 mg/5 ml, 100 mg/5 ml in 100-ml bottles
Tablets (film-coated): 100 mg, 200 mg

NURSING PROCESS

Assessment

- Assess patient's infection before therapy and reassess regularly thereafter.
- Obtain specimen for culture and sensitivity tests before first dose. Therapy may begin pending test results.
- Ask patient about previous reactions to cephalosporins or penicillin before giving first dose.
- Be alert for adverse reactions and drug interactions.
- Monitor patient's hydration status if adverse GI reactions occur.

• Evaluate patient's and family's knowledge of drug therapy.

Nursing diagnoses

• Infection related to bacteria susceptible to drug
• Risk for deficient fluid volume related to drug-induced adverse GI reactions
• Deficient knowledge related to drug therapy

Planning and implementation

• Give drug with food to minimize adverse GI reactions. Shake well before using.
• Store suspension in refrigerator (36° to 46° F [2° to 8° C]). Discard unused portion after 14 days.
ALERT: Don't confuse with other cephalosporins with similar-sounding names.

Patient teaching

• Advise patient to take drug with meals to minimize adverse GI reactions.
• Tell patient to take drug exactly as prescribed, even after he feels better.
• Instruct patient to notify prescriber if rash develops.
• Teach patient how to store drug.
• Instruct patient to notify prescriber about a reduction in urinary output, especially if patient takes a diuretic.

Evaluation

• Patient is free from infection.
• Patient maintains adequate hydration.
• Patient and family state understanding of drug therapy.

cefprozil

(SEF-pruh-zil)
Cefzil

Pharmacologic class: second-generation cephalosporin
Therapeutic class: antibiotic
Pregnancy risk category: B

Indications and dosages

▶ **Pharyngitis or tonsillitis caused by *Streptococcus pyogenes*.** *Adults and children older than age 12:* 500 mg P.O. daily for 10 days.
Children ages 2 to 12: 7.5 mg/kg P.O. q 12 hours for 10 days.

▶ **Otitis media caused by *Streptococcus pneumoniae, Haemophilus influenzae,* or *Moraxella catarrhalis*.** *Infants and children ages 6 months to 12 years:* 15 mg/kg P.O. q 12 hours for 10 days.

▶ **Secondary bacterial infections of acute bronchitis and acute bacterial exacerbation of chronic bronchitis caused by *S. pneumoniae, H. influenzae,* and *M. catarrhalis*.** *Adults and children older than age 12:* 500 mg P.O. q 12 hours for 10 days.

▶ **Uncomplicated skin and skin-structure infections caused by *Staphylococcus aureus* or *S. pyogenes*.** *Adults and children older than age 12:* 250 mg P.O. b.i.d., or 500 mg daily to b.i.d. for 10 days.
Children ages 2 to 12: 20 mg/kg P.O. q 24 hours for 10 days. Maximum dose is 1 g P.O. daily.

▶ **Acute sinusitis caused by *Streptococcus pneumoniae, Haemophilus influenzae,* and *Moraxella (Branhamella) catarrhalis*.** *Adults and children older than age 12:* 250 mg or 500 mg P.O. q 12 hours for 10 days.
Children ages 6 months to 12 years: 7.5 mg/kg P.O. q 12 hours or 15 mg/kg P.O. daily for 10 days.
Patients with creatinine clearance less than 30 ml/minute: Give 50% of usual dose.

Contraindications and precautions

• Contraindicated in patients hypersensitive to drug or other cephalosporins.
• Use cautiously in patients with history of sensitivity to penicillin and patients with impaired hepatic or renal function.
Lifespan: In pregnant and breast-feeding women, use cautiously. Pediatric doses shouldn't exceed the recommended adult doses.

Adverse reactions

CNS: dizziness, hyperactivity, headache, nervousness, insomnia.
GI: *diarrhea, nausea,* vomiting, abdominal pain.
GU: genital pruritus, vaginitis.
Hematologic: eosinophilia.
Skin: rash, urticaria.
Other: superinfection, ***hypersensitivity reactions*** (serum sickness, ***anaphylaxis***).

Interactions

Drug-drug. *Aminoglycosides:* May increase risk of nephrotoxicity. Monitor patient closely. *Probenecid:* May inhibit excretion and increase levels of cefprozil. Monitor patient.

Effects on lab test results

• May increase BUN, creatinine, ALT, AST, alkaline phosphatase, bilirubin, and LDH levels.
• May increase eosinophil count. May decrease WBC, leukocyte, and platelet counts.
• May cause false-positive urine glucose determinations with copper sulfate tests (Clinitest).

Pharmacokinetics

Absorption: About 95% absorbed from GI tract.
Distribution: About 35% protein-bound; distributed into various body tissues and fluids.
Metabolism: Probably metabolized by the liver.
Excretion: Excreted primarily in urine. *Half-life:* 1.3 hours in patients with normal renal function; 2 hours in patients with impaired hepatic function; and 5.2 to 5.9 hours in patients with end-stage renal disease.

Route	Onset	Peak	Duration
P.O.	Unknown	Unknown	Unknown

Pharmacodynamics

Chemical effect: Inhibits cell-wall synthesis, promoting osmotic instability; usually bactericidal.
Therapeutic effect: Hinders or kills susceptible bacteria, including *S. aureus, S. pyogenes, S. pneumoniae, M. catarrhalis,* and *H. influenzae.*

Available forms

Oral suspension: 125 mg/5 ml, 250 mg/5 ml
Tablets: 250 mg, 500 mg

NURSING PROCESS

Assessment

• Assess patient's infection before therapy and reassess regularly thereafter.
• Obtain specimen for culture and sensitivity tests before first dose. Therapy may begin pending test results.
• Ask patient about previous reactions to cephalosporins or penicillin before giving first dose.
• Be alert for adverse reactions and drug interactions.
• Monitor patient's hydration status if adverse GI reactions occur.
• Monitor patient's renal function.
• Evaluate patient's and family's knowledge of drug therapy.

Nursing diagnoses

• Infection related to bacteria susceptible to drug
• Risk for deficient fluid volume related to drug-induced adverse GI reactions
• Deficient knowledge related to drug therapy

Planning and implementation

• Give drug after hemodialysis treatment is completed; drug is removed by hemodialysis.
• Refrigerate reconstituted suspension (stable for 14 days). Keep tightly closed and shake well before using.
ALERT: Don't confuse with other cephalosporins with similar-sounding names.

Patient teaching

• Tell patient to shake suspension well before measuring dose.
• Advise patient to take drug as prescribed, even after he feels better.
• Inform patient that oral suspensions contain drug in bubble-gum flavor to improve palatability and promote compliance in children. Tell him to refrigerate reconstituted suspension and to discard any unused portion after 14 days.
• Advise elderly patients also receiving diuretic therapy to notify prescriber of decreased urine output.

Evaluation

• Patient is free from infection.
• Patient maintains adequate hydration.
• Patient and family state understanding of drug therapy.

ceftazidime

(sef-TAZ-ih-deem)
Ceptaz, Fortaz, Tazicef, Tazidime

Pharmacologic class: third-generation cephalosporin
Therapeutic class: antibiotic
Pregnancy risk category: B

Indications and dosages

▶ **Serious infections of lower respiratory and urinary tracts; gynecologic, intra-abdominal, CNS, and skin infections; bacteremia; and septicemia. Among susceptible microorganisms are streptococci, including *Streptococcus pneumoniae* and *S. pyogenes, Staphylococcus aureus, Escherichia coli, Klebsiella, Proteus, Enterobacter, Haemophilus influenzae, Pseudomonas,* and some strains of *Bacteroides*.** *Adults and children older than age 12:* 1 g I.V. or I.M. q 8 to 12 hours; maximum 6 g daily for life-threatening infections.
Children ages 1 month to 12 years: 25 to 50 mg/kg I.V. q 8 hours. Maximum 6 g daily.
Neonates age 4 weeks or younger: 30 mg/kg I.V. q 12 hours.

▶ **Uncomplicated urinary tract infection.** *Adults:* 250 mg I.V. or I.M. q 12 hours.

▶ **Complicated urinary tract infection.** *Adults:* 500 mg I.V. or I.M. q 8 to 12 hours.

▶ **Uncomplicated pneumonia or mild skin and skin-structure infection.** *Adults:* 0.5 to 1 g I.V. or I.M. q 8 hours.

▶ **Bone and joint infection.** *Adults:* 2 g I.V. q 12 hours.

▶ **Empiric therapy in febrile neutropenic patients.** *Adults:* 100 mg/kg I.V. daily in three divided doses; or 2 g I.V. q 8 hours either alone or with an aminoglycoside, such as amikacin.

Contraindications and precautions

- Contraindicated in patients hypersensitive to drug or other cephalosporins.
- Use cautiously in patients with history of sensitivity to penicillin and in patients with renal failure (dosage adjustment may be needed).

Lifespan: In pregnant and breast-feeding women, use cautiously. In children age 12 and younger, safety and efficacy haven't been established.

Adverse reactions

CNS: headache, dizziness, ***seizures.***
GI: ***pseudomembranous colitis,*** nausea, vomiting, diarrhea, dysgeusia, abdominal cramps.
GU: genital pruritus, candidiasis.
Hematologic: eosinophilia, ***thrombocytosis, leukopenia, agranulocytosis.***
Respiratory: dyspnea.
Skin: *maculopapular and erythematous rashes, urticaria.*
Other: ***hypersensitivity reactions*** (serum sickness, ***anaphylaxis***); elevated temperature; *pain, induration, sterile abscesses, tissue sloughing at injection site; phlebitis, thrombophlebitis with I.V. injection.*

Interactions

Drug-drug. *Chloramphenicol:* May have an antagonistic effect. Avoid using together.

Effects on lab test results

- May increase ALT, AST, alkaline phosphatase, bilirubin, and LDH levels.
- May increase eosinophil count. May decrease hemoglobin, hematocrit, and WBC and granulocyte counts. May increase or decrease platelet count.
- May cause false-positive urine glucose determinations with copper sulfate tests (Clinitest).

Pharmacokinetics

Absorption: Unknown with I.M. administration.
Distribution: Distributed widely into most body tissues and fluids, including CSF (unlike most other cephalosporins); 5% to 24% protein-bound.
Metabolism: None.
Excretion: Excreted primarily in urine. *Half-life:* About 1.5 to 2 hours.

Route	Onset	Peak	Duration
I.V.	Immediate	Immediate	Unknown
I.M.	Unknown	≤ 1 hr	Unknown

Pharmacodynamics

Chemical effect: Inhibits cell-wall synthesis, promoting osmotic instability; usually bactericidal.
Therapeutic effect: Hinders or kills susceptible bacteria: some gram-positive organisms and many enteric gram-negative bacilli, as well

as streptococci *(S. pneumoniae* and *S. pyogenes); S. aureus; E. coli; Klebsiella sp.; Proteus sp.; Enterobacter sp.; H. influenzae; Pseudomonas sp.;* and some strains of *Bacteroides.*

Available forms

Infusion: 1 g, 2 g in 50-ml and 100-ml vials (premixed)
Injection (with arginine): 1 g, 2 g, 6 g
Injection (with sodium carbonate): 500 mg, 1 g, 2 g

NURSING PROCESS

Assessment

- Assess patient's infection before therapy and reassess regularly thereafter.
- Obtain specimen for culture and sensitivity tests before first dose. Therapy may begin pending test results.
- Ask patient about previous reactions to cephalosporins or penicillin before giving first dose.
- Be alert for adverse reactions and drug interactions.
- Monitor patient's hydration status if adverse GI reactions occur.
- Evaluate patient's and family's knowledge of drug therapy.

Nursing diagnoses

- Infection related to bacteria susceptible to drug
- Risk for deficient fluid volume related to drug-induced adverse GI reactions
- Deficient knowledge related to drug therapy

Planning and implementation

- **I.V. use:** Reconstitute sodium carbonate-containing solutions with sterile water for injection. Add 5 ml to 500-mg vial; 10 ml to 1-g or 2-g vial. Shake well to dissolve drug. Carbon dioxide is released during dissolution, and positive pressure will develop in vial. Reconstitute arginine-containing solutions with 10 ml sterile water for injection; this formulation won't release gas bubbles. Each brand of ceftazidime includes instructions for reconstitution. Read and follow these instructions carefully.
- **I.M. use:** Inject deeply into large muscle mass, such as gluteus maximus or lateral aspect of thigh.
- Ceftazidime is removed by hemodialysis; supplemental dose of drug is indicated after each dialysis period.

ALERT: Commercially available preparations contain either sodium carbonate (Fortaz, Tazicef, Tazidime) or arginine (Ceptaz) to facilitate dissolution of drug.

ALERT: Don't confuse with other cephalosporins with similar-sounding names.

Patient teaching

- Tell patient to report adverse reactions.
- Instruct patient to report any change in urinary output to prescriber immediately. Dosage may need to be reduced to compensate for decreased excretion.

Evaluation

- Patient is free from infection.
- Patient maintains adequate hydration.
- Patient and family state understanding of drug therapy.

ceftibuten

(sef-tih-BYOO-tin)
Cedax

Pharmacologic class: third-generation cephalosporin
Therapeutic class: antibiotic
Pregnancy risk category: B

Indications and dosages

▶ **Acute bacterial exacerbation of chronic bronchitis caused by *Haemophilus influenzae, Moraxella catarrhalis,* or penicillin-susceptible strains of *Streptococcus pneumoniae.*** *Adults and children age 12 and older:* 400 mg P.O. daily for 10 days.

▶ **Pharyngitis and tonsillitis caused by *Streptococcus pyogenes,* acute bacterial otitis media caused by *H. influenzae, M. catarrhalis,* or *S. pyogenes. Capsules.*** *Adults and children age 12 and older:* 400 mg P.O. daily for 10 days.

Children younger than age 12: 9 mg/kg P.O. daily for 10 days. Maximum daily dose is 400 mg.

Oral suspension. *Children weighing more than 45 kg (99 lb):* 400 mg P.O. daily for 10 days.

Children older than age 6 months and weighing 45 kg or less: 9 mg/kg P.O. daily for 10 days.
Patients with renal impairment: If creatinine clearance is 30 to 49 ml/minute, 4.5 mg/kg or 200 mg P.O. q 24 hours; if creatinine clearance is 5 to 29 ml/minute, 2.25 mg/kg or 100 mg P.O. q 24 hours.
Patients undergoing hemodialysis: Give 400 mg P.O. as a single dose at the end of each dialysis session.

Contraindications and precautions

- Contraindicated in patients hypersensitive to cephalosporins.
- Use cautiously in patients with history of hypersensitivity to penicillin and in patients with GI disease or impaired renal function.

Lifespan: In breast-feeding women and elderly patients, use cautiously. Monitor elderly patient's renal function. Dosage may need to be adjusted.

Adverse reactions

CNS: headache, dizziness, aphasia, psychosis.
GI: nausea, vomiting, diarrhea, dyspepsia, abdominal pain, loose stools, ***pseudomembranous colitis.***
GU: ***toxic nephropathy,*** renal dysfunction.
Hematologic: ***aplastic anemia,*** hemolytic anemia, ***hemorrhage, neutropenia, agranulocytosis, pancytopenia.***
Hepatic: hepatic cholestasis.
Skin: ***Stevens-Johnson syndrome.***
Other: allergic reaction, ***anaphylaxis,*** drug fever.

Interactions

Drug-food. *Any food:* Decreases bioavailability of drug. Administer drug 2 hours before or 1 hour after a meal.

Effects on lab test results

- May increase ALT, AST, alkaline phosphatase, bilirubin, and BUN and creatinine levels.
- May increase eosinophil count. May decrease hemoglobin, hematocrit, and leukocyte count. May increase or decrease platelet count.

Pharmacokinetics

Absorption: Rapidly absorbed.
Distribution: 65% bound to plasma proteins.
Metabolism: Metabolized by the kidneys.
Excretion: Excreted mainly in urine.

Route	Onset	Peak	Duration
P.O.	Unknown	2-4 hr	Unknown

Pharmacodynamics

Chemical effect: Exerts its bacterial action by binding to essential target proteins of the bacterial cell wall, thus inhibiting cell-wall synthesis.
Therapeutic effect: Hinders or kills susceptible bacteria.

Available forms

Capsules: 400 mg
Oral suspension: 90 mg/5 ml, 180 mg/5 ml

NURSING PROCESS

Assessment

- Obtain specimen for culture and sensitivity tests before starting drug.
- Monitor patient for superinfection.
- Obtain specimen for *Clostridium difficile* in patient who develops diarrhea after therapy.
- Evaluate patient's and family's knowledge of drug therapy.

Nursing diagnoses

- Infection related to bacteria susceptible to drug
- Deficient knowledge related to drug therapy

Planning and implementation

- To prepare oral suspension, tap bottle to loosen powder. Follow chart supplied by manufacturer for mixing instructions. Suspension is stable for 14 days if refrigerated.
- Shake suspension well before use.
- Stop drug and notify prescriber if allergic reaction occurs.

ALERT: Don't confuse with other cephalosporins with similar-sounding names.

Patient teaching

- Instruct patient to take drug as prescribed, even if he feels better.
- Instruct patient using oral suspension to shake bottle before use and to take it at least 2 hours before or 1 hour after a meal.

- Instruct patient to store oral suspension in the refrigerator, with lid tightly closed, and to discard unused drug after 14 days.
- Warn breast-feeding woman that it's unclear whether drug appears in breast milk.
- Tell patient with diabetes that suspension has 1 g sucrose per teaspoon.

☑ Evaluation

- Patient is free from infection.
- Patient and family state understanding of drug therapy.

ceftizoxime sodium
(sef-tih-ZOKS-eem SOH-dee-um)
Cefizox

Pharmacologic class: third-generation cephalosporin
Therapeutic class: antibiotic
Pregnancy risk category: B

Indications and dosages

▶ **Serious infections of lower respiratory and urinary tracts, gynecologic infections, bacteremia, septicemia, meningitis, intra-abdominal infections, bone and joint infections, and skin infections. Among susceptible microorganisms are *Streptococcus pneumoniae* and *S. pyogenes, Staphylococcus aureus* (penicillinase- and non-penicillinase–producing) and *S. epidermidis, Escherichia coli, Klebsiella, Haemophilus influenzae, Enterobacter, Proteus,* some *Pseudomonas,* and *Peptostreptococcus.*** *Adults:* 1 to 2 g I.V. or I.M. q 8 to 12 hours. In life-threatening infections, 3 to 4 g I.V. q 8 hours.
Children and infants older than age 6 months: 50 mg/kg I.V. q 6 to 8 hours. For serious infections, up to 200 mg/kg daily in divided doses may be used. Maximum 12 g daily.
▶ **Acute bacterial otitis media.** *Children:* 50 mg/kg (not to exceed 1 g) I.M. as a single dose.
Patients with creatinine clearance between 10 and 30 ml/minute: Give 1 g I.V. q 12 hours; with creatinine clearance of less than 10 ml/minute, give 1 g I.V. q 24 hours.

Contraindications and precautions

- Contraindicated in patients hypersensitive to drug or other cephalosporins.
- Use cautiously in patients with history of sensitivity to penicillin and in patients with renal failure.

Lifespan: In pregnant and breast-feeding women, use cautiously. In infants younger than age 6 months, safety of drug hasn't been established.

Adverse reactions

CNS: fever; *pain,* headache, malaise, paresthesia, dizziness.
GI: ***pseudomembranous colitis,*** nausea, anorexia, vomiting, *diarrhea,* glossitis, dyspepsia, abdominal cramps, tenesmus, anal pruritus.
GU: genital pruritus and candidiasis.
Hematologic: ***transient neutropenia,*** eosinophilia, hemolytic anemia, ***thrombocytopenia.***
Respiratory: dyspnea.
Skin: *maculopapular and erythematous rashes, urticaria.*
Other: ***hypersensitivity reactions*** (serum sickness, ***anaphylaxis***); *induration, sterile abscesses, tissue sloughing at injection site; phlebitis, thrombophlebitis* with I.V. injection.

Interactions

Drug-drug. *Probenecid:* May inhibit excretion and increase levels of ceftizoxime. Sometimes used for this effect.

Effects on lab test results

- May increase BUN, creatinine, ALT, AST, alkaline phosphatase, bilirubin, GGT, and LDH levels. May decrease albumin and protein levels.
- May increase eosinophil count. May decrease hemoglobin, hematocrit, PT, and RBC, WBC, platelet, granulocyte, and neutrophil counts.
- May cause false-positive urine glucose determinations with copper sulfate tests (Clinitest).

Pharmacokinetics

Absorption: Unknown with I.M. administration.
Distribution: Distributed widely into most body tissues and fluids; unlike many other cephalosporins, ceftizoxime has good CSF penetration and achieves adequate levels in in-

flamed meninges. Drug is 28% to 31% protein-bound.
Metabolism: None.
Excretion: Excreted primarily in urine. *Half-life:* About 1.5 to 2 hours.

Route	Onset	Peak	Duration
I.V.	Immediate	Immediate	Unknown
I.M.	Unknown	0.5-1.5 hr	Unknown

Pharmacodynamics

Chemical effect: Inhibits cell-wall synthesis, promoting osmotic instability; usually bactericidal.
Therapeutic effect: Hinders or kills susceptible bacteria, including some gram-positive organisms and many enteric gram-negative bacilli, as well as *S. pneumoniae, S. pyogenes, S. aureus, E. coli, Klebsiella sp., Proteus sp., Enterobacter sp., H. influenzae, Pseudomonas sp.,* and some strains of *Bacteroides*.

Available forms

Infusion: 1 g, 2 g in 100-mg vials or in 50 ml of D_5W
Injection: 500 mg, 1 g, 2 g

NURSING PROCESS

Assessment

- Assess patient's infection before therapy and reassess regularly thereafter.
- Obtain specimen for culture and sensitivity tests before giving first dose. Therapy may begin pending test results.
- Ask patient about previous reactions to cephalosporins or penicillin before giving first dose.
- Be alert for adverse reactions and drug interactions.
- Monitor patient's hydration status if adverse GI reactions occur.
- Evaluate patient's and family's knowledge of drug therapy.

Nursing diagnoses

- Infection related to bacteria susceptible to drug
- Risk for deficient fluid volume related to drug-induced adverse GI reactions
- Deficient knowledge related to drug therapy

Planning and implementation

- **I.V. use:** To reconstitute powder, add 5 ml sterile water to 500-mg vial, 10 ml to 1-g vial, or 20 ml to 2-g vial. Reconstitute piggyback vials with 50 to 100 ml of normal saline solution or D_5W. Shake vial well.
- **I.M. use:** Inject deeply into large muscle mass, such as gluteus maximus or lateral aspect of thigh. Larger doses (2 g) should be divided and given at two sites.

ALERT: Don't confuse with other cephalosporins with similar-sounding names.

Patient teaching

- Tell patient to report adverse reactions and signs and symptoms of superinfection promptly.
- Instruct patient to report discomfort at the I.V. site.
- Tell patient to notify prescriber if loose stools or diarrhea occur.

Evaluation

- Patient is free from infection.
- Patient maintains adequate hydration.
- Patient and family state understanding of drug therapy.

ceftriaxone sodium

(sef-trigh-AKS-ohn SOH-dee-um)
Rocephin

Pharmacologic class: third-generation cephalosporin
Therapeutic class: antibiotic
Pregnancy risk category: B

Indications and dosages

▶ **Uncomplicated gonococcal vulvovaginitis.** *Adults and children older than age 12 or weighing more than 45 kg (99 lb):* 125 to 250 mg I.M. as single dose, followed by 100 mg of doxycycline P.O. q 12 hours for 7 days. *Children younger than age 12 or weighing less than 45 kg:* 125 mg I.M. as a single dose.

▶ **Serious infections of lower respiratory and urinary tracts; gynecologic, bone, joint, intra-abdominal, and skin infections; Lyme disease; bacteremia; and septicemia caused by such susceptible microorganisms as *Streptococcus pneumoniae, S. pyogenes,***

Staphylococcus aureus, S. epidermidis, Escherichia coli, Klebsiella, Haemophilus influenzae, Neisseria meningitides, N. gonorrhoeae, Enterobacter, Proteus, Pseudomonas, Peptostreptococcus,* and *Serratia marcescens.
Adults and children older than age 12: 1 to 2 g I.V. or I.M. daily or in equally divided doses, maximum 4 g.
Children age 12 and younger: 50 to 75 mg/kg, maximum 2 g daily, given in divided doses q 12 hours.

▶ **Meningitis.** *Adults and children:* Initially, 100 mg/kg I.M. or I.V. (maximum 4 g); thereafter, 100 mg/kg I.M. or I.V. given once daily or in divided doses q 12 hours. Maximum 4 g, for 7 to 14 days.

▶ **Preoperative prophylaxis.** *Adults:* 1 g I.V. as single dose 30 minutes to 2 hours before surgery.

▶ **Acute bacterial otitis media.** *Children:* 50 mg/kg I.M. as a single dose; maximum I.M. dose is 1 g.

▶ **Sexually transmitted epididymitis, pelvic inflammatory disease‡.** *Adults:* 250 mg I.M. as a single dose; follow up with other antibiotics.

▶ **Anti-infectives for sexual assault victims‡.** *Adults:* 125 mg I.M. as a single dose given with other antibiotics.

▶ **Lyme disease‡.** *Adults:* 1 to 2 g I.M. or I.V. q 12 to 24 hours.

▶ **Persisting or relapsing otitis media in children‡.** *Children and infants age 3 months and older:* 50 mg/kg I.M daily for 3 days.

Contraindications and precautions

- Contraindicated in patients hypersensitive to drug or other cephalosporins.
- Use cautiously in patients with history of sensitivity to penicillin.

Lifespan: In pregnant and breast-feeding women, use cautiously.

Adverse reactions

CNS: headache, dizziness, fever.
GI: ***pseudomembranous colitis,*** nausea, vomiting, diarrhea, dysgeusia.
GU: genital pruritus and candidiasis.
Hematologic: eosinophilia, ***thrombocytosis, leukopenia.***
Skin: pain, induration, and tenderness at injection site; phlebitis; *rash.*
Other: ***hypersensitivity reactions*** (serum sickness, ***anaphylaxis***).

Interactions

Drug-drug. *Aminoglycosides:* May have additive effect. Monitor drug levels and adjust dosage as required.
Probenecid: High doses may shorten half-life of ceftriaxone. Avoid use together.
Quinolones: Has synergistic effect against *S. pneumoniae*. Using together against this organism is recommended.
Drug-lifestyle. *Alcohol use:* May cause disulfiram-like reaction. Discourage use together.

Effects on lab test results

- May increase BUN, ALT, AST, alkaline phosphatase, bilirubin, and LDH levels.
- May increase eosinophil and platelet counts. May decrease WBC count.
- May cause false-positive urine glucose determinations with copper sulfate tests (Clinitest).

Pharmacokinetics

Absorption: Unknown with I.M. administration.
Distribution: Distributed widely into most body tissues and fluids; unlike many other cephalosporins, ceftriaxone has good CSF penetration. Drug is 58% to 96% protein-bound.
Metabolism: Partially metabolized.
Excretion: Excreted primarily in urine, minimally in bile. *Half-life:* about 5.5 to 11 hours.

Route	Onset	Peak	Duration
I.V.	Immediate	Immediate	Unknown
I.M.	Unknown	1.5-4 hr	Unknown

Pharmacodynamics

Chemical effect: Inhibits cell-wall synthesis, promoting osmotic instability; usually bactericidal.
Therapeutic effect: Hinders or kills susceptible bacteria: some gram-positive organisms and many enteric gram-negative bacilli, as well as *S. epidermidis, E. coli, Klebsiella sp., Proteus sp., Enterobacter sp., H. influenzae,* some strains of *Pseudomonas sp., Peptostreptococcus sp.,* and spirochetes such as *Borrelia burgdorferi*.

Available forms

Infusion: 1 g, 2 g
Injection: 250 mg, 500 mg, 1 g, 2 g

NURSING PROCESS

Assessment

- Assess patient's infection before therapy and reassess regularly thereafter.
- Obtain specimen for culture and sensitivity tests. Therapy may begin before test results are known.
- Ask patient about previous reactions to cephalosporins or penicillin before giving first dose.
- Be alert for adverse reactions and drug interactions.
- Monitor patient's hydration status if adverse GI reactions occur.
- Evaluate patient's and family's knowledge of drug therapy.

Nursing diagnoses

- Infection related to bacteria susceptible to drug
- Risk for deficient fluid volume related to drug-induced adverse GI reactions
- Deficient knowledge related to drug therapy

Planning and implementation

- **I.V. use:** Reconstitute with sterile water for injection, normal saline solution for injection, D_5W or $D_{10}W$ injection, or combination of saline solution and dextrose injection and other compatible solutions. Reconstitute by adding 2.4 ml of diluent to 250-mg vial, 4.8 ml to 500-mg vial, 9.6 ml to 1-g vial, and 19.2 ml to 2-g vial. All reconstituted solutions yield concentration that averages 100 mg/ml. After reconstitution, dilute further for intermittent infusion to desired concentration. I.V. dilutions are stable for 24 hours at room temperature.
- **I.M. use:** Inject deeply into large muscle mass, such as gluteus maximus or lateral aspect of thigh. May use lidocaine 1% without epinephrine to dilute for I.M. use.

ALERT: Don't confuse with other cephalosporins with similar-sounding names.

Patient teaching

- Tell patient to report adverse reactions and signs and symptoms of superinfection promptly.
- Instruct patient to report pain at the I.V. site.
- Tell patient to notify prescriber if loose stools or diarrhea occur.

Evaluation

- Patient is free from infection.
- Patient maintains adequate hydration.
- Patient and family state understanding of drug therapy.

cefuroxime axetil

(sef-yoor-OKS-eem AKS-eh-til)
Ceftin

cefuroxime sodium

Kefurox, Zinacef

Pharmacologic class: second-generation cephalosporin
Therapeutic class: antibiotic
Pregnancy risk category: B

Indications and dosages

▶ **Serious infections of lower respiratory and urinary tracts, skin and skin-structure infections, bone and joint infections, septicemia, meningitis, gonorrhea, and perioperative prophylaxis.** ***cefuroxime sodium.*** *Adults and children age 13 and older:* 750 mg to 1.5 g I.V. or I.M. q 8 hours for 5 to 10 days. For life-threatening infections and infections caused by less-susceptible organisms, 1.5 g I.V. or I.M. q 6 hours; for bacterial meningitis, up to 3 g I.V. q 8 hours. *Children ages 3 months to 12 years:* 50 to 100 mg/kg daily I.V. or I.M. in equally divided doses q 6 to 8 hours. Higher doses of 100 mg/kg daily (not to exceed adult maximum dosage) should be used for more severe or serious infections. For bacterial meningitis, 200 to 240 mg/kg I.V. in divided doses q 6 to 8 hours. For other infections, 125 to 250 mg or cefuroxime axetil P.O. q 12 hours for a child who can swallow pills.

▶ **Pharyngitis, tonsillitis, infections of urinary and lower respiratory tracts, and skin and skin-structure infections. Susceptible organisms are *Streptococcus pneumoniae* and *S. pyogenes, Haemophilus influenzae, Klebsiella, Staphylococcus aureus, Escherichia coli, Enterobacter,* and *Neisseria gonorrhoeae. cefuroxime axetil.*** *Adults and children* *age 13 and older:* 250 mg P.O. q 12 hours for 10 days. For severe infections, dosage may be increased to 500 mg q 12 hours.

▶ **Uncomplicated urinary tract infections.** *Adults and children age 13 and older:* 125 to 250 mg P.O. q 12 hours for 10 days.

▶ **Otitis media.** *Children ages 3 months to 12 years:* 30 mg/kg oral suspension P.O. daily divided in two doses (maximum dose, 1 g), or 250-mg tablet P.O. b.i.d. for 10 days.

▶ **Perioperative prophylaxis.** *Adults:* 1.5 g I.V. 30 to 60 minutes before surgery; in lengthy operations, 750 mg I.V. or I.M. q 8 hours. For open-heart surgery, 1.5 g I.V. at induction of anesthesia and q 12 hours; total dosage 6 g.

▶ **Acute bacterial maxillary sinusitis caused by *S. pneumoniae* or *H. influenzae*.** *Adults and children age 13 and older:* 250 mg (tablet) P.O. b.i.d. for 10 days.

Infants and children ages 3 months to 12 years: 30 mg/kg (suspension) by mouth daily in two divided doses for 10 days. Maximum daily suspension dose is 1,000 mg. For children who can swallow tablets whole, give 250 mg (tablet) by mouth b.i.d. for 10 days.

▶ **Early Lyme disease as manifested by erythema migrans.** *Adults and children age 13 and older:* 500 mg P.O. b.i.d. for 20 days.

▶ **Gonorrhea.** *Adults and children age 13 and older:* Give a one-time dose of 1.5 g I.V. or I.M. (I.M. dose to be divided and given at two different sites) with 1 g oral probenecid. Or, 1 g P.O. as a single dose.

Patients with renal impairment with a creatinine clearance between 10 and 20 ml/minute: Give 750 mg I.V. or I.M. q 12 hours; if less than 10 ml/minute, give 750 mg I.V. or I.M q 24 hours.

Contraindications and precautions

• Contraindicated in patients hypersensitive to drug or other cephalosporins.

• Use cautiously in patients with history of sensitivity to penicillin and in patients with impaired renal function.

Lifespan: In pregnant and breast-feeding women, use cautiously. In infants younger than age 3 months, safety of drug hasn't been established.

Adverse reactions

CNS: headache, malaise, paresthesia, dizziness.

GI: ***pseudomembranous colitis,*** nausea, anorexia, vomiting, *diarrhea,* glossitis, dyspepsia, abdominal cramps, tenesmus, anal pruritus.

GU: genital pruritus and candidiasis.

Hematologic: ***transient neutropenia,*** eosinophilia, hemolytic anemia, ***thrombocytopenia.***

Respiratory: dyspnea.

Skin: *maculopapular and erythematous rashes, urticaria.*

Other: ***hypersensitivity reactions*** (serum sickness, ***anaphylaxis***); *pain, induration, sterile abscesses, warmth, tissue sloughing at injection site; phlebitis, thrombophlebitis with I.V. injection.*

Interactions

Drug-drug. *Diuretics:* May increase risk of adverse renal reactions. Monitor renal function closely.

Probenecid: May inhibit excretion and increase levels of cefuroxime. Sometimes used for this effect.

Drug-food. *Any food:* May increase drug absorption and bioavailability. Give drug with food.

Effects on lab test results

• May increase ALT, AST, alkaline phosphatase, bilirubin, and LDH levels.

• May increase PT and INR and eosinophil count. May decrease hemoglobin, hematocrit, and neutrophil and platelet counts.

• May cause urine glucose determinations to be false-positive with copper sulfate tests (Clinitest).

Pharmacokinetics

Absorption: Cefuroxime axetil is absorbed from GI tract with 37% to 52% of oral dose reaching systemic circulation. Food appears to enhance absorption. Cefuroxime sodium isn't well absorbed from GI tract; absorption from I.M. administration is unknown.

Distribution: Distributed widely into most body tissues and fluids; CSF penetration is greater than that of most first- and second-generation cephalosporins and achieves adequate therapeutic levels in inflamed meninges. It's 33% to 50% protein-bound.

Metabolism: None.

Excretion: Excreted primarily in urine. *Half-life:* 1 to 2 hours.

Route	Onset	Peak	Duration
P.O.	Unknown	2 hr	Unknown
I.V.	Unknown	Immediate	Unknown
I.M.	Unknown	15-60 min	Unknown

Pharmacodynamics

Chemical effect: Inhibits cell-wall synthesis, promoting osmotic instability; usually bactericidal.

Therapeutic effect: Hinders or kills susceptible bacteria, including many gram-positive organisms and enteric gram-negative bacilli.

Available forms

cefuroxime axetil

Suspension: 125 mg/5 ml, 250 mg/5 ml

Tablets: 125 mg, 250 mg, 500 mg

cefuroxime sodium

Infusion: 750 mg, 1.5 g premixed, frozen solution

Injection: 750 mg, 1.5 g

NURSING PROCESS

Assessment

- Assess patient's infection before therapy and reassess regularly thereafter.
- Obtain specimen for culture and sensitivity tests before first dose. Therapy may begin pending test results.
- Ask patient about previous reactions to cephalosporins or penicillin before giving first dose.
- Be alert for adverse reactions and drug interactions.
- Monitor patient's hydration status if adverse GI reactions occur.
- Evaluate patient's and family's knowledge of drug therapy.

Nursing diagnoses

- Infection related to bacteria susceptible to drug
- Risk for deficient fluid volume related to drug-induced adverse GI reactions
- Deficient knowledge related to drug therapy

Planning and implementation

- **P.O. use:** Food enhances absorption of cefuroxime axetil.

– Cefuroxime axetil is available only in tablet form, which may be crushed for patients who can't swallow tablets. Tablets may be dissolved in small amounts of apple, orange, or grape juice or chocolate milk. However, drug has bitter taste that's difficult to mask, even with food.

ALERT: Cefuroxime tablets and oral suspensions aren't bioequivalent and can't be substituted on a mg-for-mg basis.

- **I.V. use:** For each 750-mg vial of Kefurox, reconstitute with 9 ml sterile water for injection. Withdraw 8 ml from vial for proper dose. For each 1.5-g vial of Kefurox, reconstitute with 14 ml sterile water for injection; withdraw entire contents of vial for dose. For each 750-mg vial of Zinacef, reconstitute with 8 ml sterile water for injection; for each 1.5-g vial, reconstitute with 16 ml. In each case, withdraw entire contents of vial for dose.

– To give by direct injection, inject into large vein or into tubing of free-flowing I.V. solution over 3 to 5 minutes.

– For intermittent infusion, add reconstituted drug to 100 ml D_5W, normal saline solution for injection, or other compatible I.V. solution. Infuse over 15 to 60 minutes.

- **I.M. use:** Inject deeply into large muscle mass, such as gluteus maximus or lateral aspect of thigh. Prior to I.M. injection, aspirate to avoid injection into a blood vessel.

ALERT: Don't confuse with other cephalosporins with similar-sounding names.

ALERT: Patients with renal impairment may require reduced dosage.

Patient teaching

- Instruct patient to take drug exactly as prescribed, even after he feels better.
- Advise patient to take oral drug with food to enhance absorption. Explain that tablets may be crushed, but drug has bitter taste that's difficult to mask, even with food.
- Tell patient to report adverse reactions.

Evaluation

- Patient is free from infection.
- Patient maintains adequate hydration.
- Patient and family state understanding of drug therapy.

celecoxib
(sel-eh-COKS-ib)
Celebrex

Pharmacologic classification: cyclooxygenase-2 inhibitor
Therapeutic classification: anti-inflammatory
Pregnancy risk category: C

Indications and dosages

▶ **Relief of signs and symptoms of osteoarthritis.** *Adults:* 200 mg P.O. daily as a single dose or divided equally b.i.d.
▶ **Relief of signs and symptoms of rheumatoid arthritis.** *Adults:* 100 to 200 mg P.O. b.i.d.
▶ **Adjunct to treatment for familial adenomatous polyposis to reduce the number of adenomatous colorectal polyps.** *Adults:* 400 mg P.O. b.i.d. with food for up to 6 months.
▶ **Acute pain and primary dysmenorrhea.** *Adults:* Initially, give 400 mg P.O., followed by an additional 200-mg dose on the first day, if needed. On subsequent days, 200 mg P.O. b.i.d. p.r.n.
Patients with hepatic impairment: Reduce dose by 50%.
Elderly patients who weigh less than 50 kg (110 lb): Use the lowest recommended dose.

Contraindications and precautions

• Contraindicated in patients hypersensitive to celecoxib, sulfonamides, aspirin, or other NSAIDs and in patients with severe hepatic or renal impairment.
• Use cautiously in patients with known or suspected history of poor P-450 2C9 metabolism and in patients with history of ulcers, GI bleeding, dehydration, anemia, symptomatic liver disease, hypertension, edema, heart failure, or asthma.
• Use cautiously in patients who smoke or drink alcohol frequently, and in those who take oral corticosteroids or anticoagulants.
Lifespan: In women in the third trimester of pregnancy, use is contraindicated. In children younger than age 18, safety and efficacy haven't been established. In elderly and debilitated patients, use cautiously because of the increased risk of GI bleeding and acute renal failure.

Adverse reactions

CNS: dizziness, *headache,* insomnia.
CV: peripheral edema.
EENT: pharyngitis, rhinitis, sinusitis.
GI: abdominal pain, diarrhea, dyspepsia, flatulence, nausea.
Metabolic: hyperchloremia, hypophosphatemia.
Musculoskeletal: back pain.
Respiratory: upper respiratory tract infection.
Skin: rash.
Other: accidental injury.

Interactions

Drug-drug. *ACE inhibitors:* May diminish antihypertensive effects. Monitor patient's blood pressure.
Aluminum- and magnesium-containing antacids: May reduce celecoxib levels. Separate administration times.
Aspirin: Increases risk of ulcers; low aspirin dosages can be used safely to prevent CV events. Monitor patient for signs and symptoms of GI bleeding.
Fluconazole: May increase celecoxib levels. Reduce dosage of celecoxib to minimal effective level.
Furosemide: NSAIDs can reduce sodium excretion caused by diuretics, leading to sodium retention. Monitor patient for swelling and increased blood pressure.
Lithium: May increase lithium level. Monitor lithium levels closely during treatment.
Warfarin: May increase PT level and bleeding complications. Monitor PT and INR, and check for signs and symptoms of bleeding.
Drug-herb. *Dong quai, feverfew, garlic, ginger, ginkgo, horse chestnut, red clover:* May increase the risk of bleeding. Discourage using together.
Drug-lifestyle. *Chronic alcohol use, smoking:* Increases risks of GI irritation or bleeding. Check for signs and symptoms of bleeding, and discourage using together.

Effects on lab test results

• May increase BUN, ALT, AST, and chloride levels. May decrease phosphate levels.

Pharmacokinetics

Absorption: Plasma levels peak in about 3 hours. Steady state plasma levels can be expected within 5 days if celecoxib is given in

multiple doses. Elderly patients have higher levels than younger adult patients.
Distribution: Drug is highly protein-bound, primarily to albumin. It also is extensively distributed into the tissues.
Metabolism: Metabolized in the liver by cytochrome P-450 2C9. No active metabolites of celecoxib have been identified.
Excretion: Excreted primarily through hepatic metabolism, with less than 3% as unchanged drug excreted in urine and feces. *Elimination half-life:* About 11 hours.

Route	Onset	Peak	Duration
P.O.	Unknown	3 hr	Unknown

Pharmacodynamics

Chemical effect: Celecoxib is thought to selectively inhibit cyclooxygenase-2, resulting in decreased prostaglandin synthesis. Its anti-inflammatory effects along with its analgesic and antipyretic properties are thought to be related to a decrease in prostaglandin synthesis.
Therapeutic effect: Relieves osteoarthritis and rheumatoid arthritis symptoms.

Available forms

Capsules: 100 mg, 200 mg

NURSING PROCESS

Assessment

• Assess patient for appropriateness of therapy. Drug must be used cautiously in patients with history of ulcers or GI bleeding, advanced renal disease, dehydration, anemia, symptomatic liver disease, hypertension, edema, heart failure, or asthma.
• Obtain accurate list of patient's allergies. Patients may be allergic to celecoxib if they're allergic and have had anaphylactic reactions to sulfonamides, aspirin, or other NSAIDs.
• Assess patients for risk factors for GI bleeding, including treatment with corticosteroids or anticoagulants, longer duration of NSAID treatment, smoking, alcoholism, older age, and poor overall health. Patients with a history of ulcers or GI bleeding are at higher risk for GI bleeding while taking NSAIDs such as celecoxib.
• Celecoxib has been linked to a relatively high risk of heart attacks. Monitor patient closely for any signs or symptoms of a MI.
• Monitor patient for signs and symptoms of overt and occult bleeding.
• Celecoxib may be hepatotoxic; monitor patient for signs and symptoms of liver toxicity.
• Evaluate patient's and family's knowledge of drug therapy.

Nursing diagnoses

• Acute pain related to underlying condition
• Risk for injury related to drug-induced adverse reactions
• Deficient knowledge related to drug therapy

Planning and implementation

• In patients weighing less than 50 kg (110 lb), therapy should start at lowest recommended dosage.
• Although drug can be given without regard to meals, food may decrease GI upset.
• Before starting treatment, be sure to rehydrate patient.
• Although celecoxib may be used with low aspirin dosages, the combination may increase the risk of GI bleeding.
• NSAIDs such as celecoxib can cause fluid retention; closely monitor patient who has hypertension, edema, or heart failure while taking this drug.

Patient teaching

• Tell patient to report history of allergic reactions to sulfonamides, aspirin, or other NSAIDs before starting therapy.
• Instruct patient to report to prescriber immediately signs of GI bleeding (such as bloody vomitus, blood in urine or stool, and black, tarry stools).
ALERT: Advise patient to report to prescriber immediately rash, unexplained weight gain, or edema.
• Tell woman to notify prescriber if she becomes pregnant or is planning to become pregnant while taking this drug.
• Instruct patient to take drug with food if stomach upset occurs.
• Teach patient that all NSAIDs, including celecoxib, may adversely affect the liver. Signs and symptoms of liver toxicity include nausea, fatigue, lethargy, itching, jaundice, right upper quadrant tenderness, and flulike syndrome. Advise patient to stop therapy and seek immediate medical advice if he experiences any of these signs or symptoms.

• Inform patient that it may take several days before he feels consistent pain relief.

Evaluation

• Patient is free from pain.
• Patient doesn't experience injury as a result of drug-induced adverse reactions.
• Patient and family state understanding of drug therapy.

cephalexin hydrochloride
(sef-uh-LEK-sin high-droh-KLOR-ighd)
Keftab

cephalexin monohydrate
Apo-Cephalex◆, Biocef, Keflex, Novo-Lexin◆, Nu-Cephalex◇

Pharmacologic class: first-generation cephalosporin
Therapeutic class: antibiotic
Pregnancy risk category: B

Indications and dosages

▶ **Respiratory tract, GI tract, skin, soft-tissue, bone, and joint infections and otitis media caused by *Escherichia coli* and other coliform bacteria, group A beta-hemolytic streptococci, *Haemophilus influenzae, Klebsiella, Moraxella catarrhalis, Proteus mirabilis, Streptococcus pneumoniae,* and staphylococci.** *Adults:* 250 mg to 1 g P.O. q 6 hours or 500 mg q 12 hours; maximum 4 g daily.
Children: 6 to 12 mg/kg P.O. q 6 hours (monohydrate only); maximum 25 mg/kg q 6 hours or 4 g daily.

Contraindications and precautions

• Contraindicated in patients hypersensitive to cephalosporins.
• Use cautiously in patients hypersensitive to penicillin and in patients with impaired renal function.
Lifespan: In pregnant and breast-feeding women, use cautiously.

Adverse reactions

CNS: dizziness, headache, malaise, paresthesia.
GI: ***pseudomembranous colitis,*** *nausea, anorexia,* vomiting, *diarrhea,* glossitis, dyspepsia, abdominal cramps, anal pruritus, tenesmus, oral candidiasis.
GU: genital pruritus, candidiasis, vaginitis.
Hematologic: ***transient neutropenia,*** eosinophilia, anemia, ***thrombocytopenia.***
Respiratory: dyspnea.
Skin: *maculopapular and erythematous rashes, urticaria.*
Other: ***hypersensitivity reactions*** (serum sickness, ***anaphylaxis***).

Interactions

Drug-drug. *Probenecid:* May increase levels of cephalosporins. Sometimes used for this effect.

Effects on lab test results

• May increase ALT, AST, alkaline phosphatase, bilirubin, and LDH levels.
• May increase eosinophil count. May decrease hemoglobin, hematocrit, and neutrophil and platelet counts.
• May cause false-positive urine glucose determinations with copper sulfate tests (Clinitest).

Pharmacokinetics

Absorption: Rapid and complete. Food delays but doesn't prevent complete absorption.
Distribution: Distributed widely into most body tissues and fluids; CSF penetration is poor. Drug is 6% to 15% protein-bound.
Metabolism: None.
Excretion: Excreted primarily unchanged in urine. *Half-life:* About 30 minutes to 1 hour.

Route	Onset	Peak	Duration
P.O.	Unknown	≤ 1 hr	Unknown

Pharmacodynamics

Chemical effect: Inhibits cell-wall synthesis, promoting osmotic instability; usually bactericidal.
Therapeutic effect: Hinders or kills susceptible bacteria: many gram-positive cocci, including penicillinase-producing *S. aureus* and *S. epidermidis, S. pneumoniae,* group B streptococci, and group A beta-hemolytic streptococci; and gram-negative organisms, including *Klebsiella pneumoniae, E. coli, P. mirabilis,* and *Shigella.*

Available forms

cephalexin hydrochloride
Tablets: 500 mg
cephalexin monohydrate
Capsules: 250 mg, 500 mg
Oral suspension: 125 mg/5 ml, 250 mg/5 ml
Tablets: 250 mg, 500 mg, 1 g

NURSING PROCESS

Assessment

- Assess patient's infection before therapy and reassess regularly thereafter.
- Obtain specimen for culture and sensitivity tests before giving first dose. Therapy may begin pending test results.
- Ask patient about previous reactions to cephalosporins or penicillin before giving first dose.
- Be alert for adverse reactions and drug interactions.
- Monitor patient's hydration status if adverse GI reactions occur.
- Evaluate patient's and family's knowledge of drug therapy.

Nursing diagnoses

- Infection related to bacteria susceptible to drug
- Risk for deficient fluid volume related to drug-induced adverse GI reactions
- Deficient knowledge related to drug therapy

Planning and implementation

- To prepare oral suspension, first add required amount of water to powder in two portions. Shake well after each addition. After mixing, store in refrigerator (stable for 14 days without significant loss of potency). Keep tightly closed and shake well before using.
- Give drug with food or milk to minimize adverse GI reactions.
- Group A beta-hemolytic streptococcal infections should be treated for minimum of 10 days.
- If a dosage greater than 4 g daily is required, initial treatment with a parenteral cephalosporin should be considered.

ALERT: Don't confuse with other cephalosporins with similar-sounding names.

Patient teaching

- Inform patient that drug may be taken with meals.
- Instruct patient to take drug exactly as prescribed, even after he feels better.
- Tell patient to call prescriber if rash develops.
- Teach patient how to store drug.

Evaluation

- Patient is free from infection.
- Patient maintains adequate hydration.
- Patient and family state understanding of drug therapy.

cetrorelix acetate

(set-RO-rel-icks AS-ih-tayt)
Cetrotide

Pharmacologic classification: gonadotropin-releasing hormone (GnRH) analog
Therapeutic classification: infertility agent
Pregnancy risk category: X

Indications and dosages

▶ **Treatment of infertility; inhibition of premature luteinizing hormone (LH) surges in women undergoing controlled ovarian stimulation.** *Adults:* Therapy may be given once daily with the 0.25-mg dose or once during the early- to mid-follicular phase with the 3-mg dose. Dose is adjusted according to patient response. If choosing the 3-mg dose, give it S.C. once during early- to mid-follicular phase, when the estradiol level indicates an appropriate stimulation response, usually on stimulation day 7 (range, days 5 to 9). If human chorionic gonadotropin (hCG) hasn't been given within 4 days after the 3-mg injection, 0.25 mg of cetrorelix should be given S.C. once daily until the day of hCG administration. Or, if choosing the 0.25-mg dose regimen, give 0.25 mg S.C. on either stimulation day 5 (morning or evening) or day 6 (morning) and continue once daily until the day of hCG administration. hCG is given only when ultrasound shows a sufficient number of follicles of adequate size.

Contraindications and precautions

- Contraindicated in patients hypersensitive to cetrorelix acetate, extrinsic peptide hormones, mannitol, GnRH, or any other GnRH analogs.

Lifespan: In pregnant women, use is contraindicated. Rule out pregnancy before starting treatment. Avoid use in breast-feeding mothers because it's unknown whether drug appears in breast milk. In women older than age 65, drug is not to be used.

Adverse reactions

CNS: headache.
GI: nausea.
GU: ovarian hyperstimulation syndrome.
Skin: local site reactions (including erythema, bruising, itching, and swelling).
Other: ***anaphylaxis.***

Interactions

None reported.

Effects on lab test results

- May increase ALT, AST, GGT, and alkaline phosphatase levels.

Pharmacokinetics

Absorption: Rapid. Mean absolute bioavailability is 85%.
Distribution: Drug is 86% bound to plasma.
Metabolism: After giving 10 mg cetrorelix, small amounts were found in bile samples over 24 hours.
Excretion: Drug is excreted unchanged in urine and as metabolites in bile.

Route	Onset	Peak	Duration
S.C.	1-2 hr	1-2 hr	≥ 4 days

Pharmacodynamics

Chemical effect: Drug competes with natural GnRH for binding to membrane receptors on the gonadotrophic cells of the anterior pituitary and induces the production and release of LH and follicle-stimulating hormone (FSH).
Therapeutic effect: Results in the LH-surge, which induces ovulation, resumes oocyte meiosis, and causes luteinization as indicated by the rising progesterone levels.

Available forms

Powder for injection: 0.25 mg, 3 mg

NURSING PROCESS

Assessment

- Before giving drug, test patient for pregnancy; it must be ruled out before starting treatment.
- Assess patient's history for any hypersensitivity to drug therapy.
- Assess patient's and family's knowledge of infertility treatment.

Nursing diagnoses

- Ineffective coping related to underlying difficulty and frustration with conception
- Risk for impaired skin integrity related to local skin reaction from drug administration
- Noncompliance related to strict drug regimen and monitoring
- Deficient knowledge related to drug therapy and self-administration

Planning and implementation

- Drug should be prescribed by clinicians experienced in fertility treatment.
- Monitor patient carefully for anaphylaxis after initial dose. Symptoms include cough, rash, difficulty breathing, and hypotension. Provide supportive measures, such as airway management, oxygen, epinephrine, corticosteroids, intravenous fluids, antihistamines, and pressor amines, as clinically indicated.

Patient teaching

- Instruct patient to store 3-mg form at room temperature (77° F [25° C]). Instruct her to store 0.25-mg form in refrigerator at 36° to 46° F (2° to 8° C).
- Instruct patient to report any adverse effects that become bothersome.
- Educate patient on the importance of following the regimen exactly as prescribed to achieve optimal results.
- Instruct patient on the proper administration technique, as follows. Wash hands thoroughly with soap and water. Flip off the plastic cover of the vial and wipe the top with an alcohol swab. Attach the needle with the yellow mark to the prefilled syringe. Push the needle through the rubber stopper of the vial and slowly inject the liquid into the vial. Leave the syringe in place and gently swirl the vial until the solution is clear and without residue. Don't shake. Draw liquid from the vial into the syringe. If necessary, invert the vial and pull the

needle back as far as needed to withdraw the entire contents of the vial. Detach the needle with the yellow mark from the syringe and replace it with the needle with the gray mark. Invert the syringe and push the plunger until all air bubbles are gone.

• Tell patient to choose an injection site on the lower abdomen, around the navel. If she receives a multiple dose (0.25-mg) regimen, tell her to choose a different site each day to minimize local irritation. Instruct her to clean the site with an alcohol swab and gently pinch a skinfold surrounding the site of injection. Instruct her to insert the needle completely into the skin at about a 45-degree angle and, once the needle has been inserted completely, to release her grasp of the skin. Tell her to gently pull back the plunger of the syringe to check for correct positioning of the needle. If no blood appears, tell her to inject the entire solution by slowly pushing the plunger. She should then withdraw the needle and gently press an alcohol swab on the injection site.

• If blood appears when the patient pulls back on the plunger, tell her to withdraw the needle and gently press an alcohol swab on the injection site. Explain that she'll need to discard the syringe and the drug vial and to repeat the procedure using a new pack.

• Instruct patient to use a syringe and needle only once and dispose properly. Suggest that she use a medical waste container for disposal, if available.

☑ Evaluation

• Patient responds positively to drug therapy.
• Patient completes drug regimen as prescribed until administration of hCG.
• Patient doesn't suffer adverse effects from drug therapy.
• Patient and family state understanding of drug therapy and patient properly performs self-administration of subcutaneous injections.

cevimeline hydrochloride

(seh-vih-MEH-leen high-droh-KLOR-ighd)
Evoxac

Pharmacologic class: cholinergic agonist
Therapeutic class: pro-secretory agent
Pregnancy risk category: C

Indications and dosages

▶ **Dry mouth in patients with Sjögren's syndrome.** *Adults:* 30 mg P.O. t.i.d.

Contraindications and precautions

• Contraindicated in patients hypersensitive to drug. Also contraindicated in patients with uncontrolled asthma or when miosis is undesirable, as in acute iritis or angle-closure glaucoma.

• Use cautiously in patients with significant CV disease, such as angina pectoris or MI, because drug can alter cardiac conduction and heart rate. Also use cautiously in patients with controlled asthma, chronic bronchitis, or COPD, because drug can cause bronchial constriction and increase bronchial secretions.

• Use cautiously in patients with a history of nephrolithiasis because an increase in ureteral smooth muscle tone could cause renal colic or ureteral reflux. Also use cautiously in patients with cholelithiasis because contractions of the gallbladder or biliary smooth muscle could cause cholecystitis, cholangitis, and biliary obstruction.

Lifespan: In breast-feeding women, drug therapy or breast-feeding must be discontinued because it's unknown whether drug appears in breast milk. In children, safety and efficacy haven't been established. In patients age 65 and older, use with caution.

Adverse reactions

CNS: fever, anxiety, depression, dizziness, fatigue, *headache,* hypoesthesia, insomnia, migraine, pain, tremor, vertigo.
CV: chest pain, palpitations, peripheral edema, edema.
EENT: abnormal vision, conjunctivitis, earache, epistaxis, eye infection, eye pain, otitis media, pharyngitis, *rhinitis, sinusitis,* xerophthalmia, eye abnormality.
GI: abdominal pain, anorexia, constipation, *diarrhea,* dry mouth, eructation, excessive salivation, flatulence, gastroesophageal reflux, *nausea,* salivary gland enlargement and pain, sialoadenitis, ulcerative stomatitis, vomiting, dyspepsia.
GU: cystitis, candidiasis, urinary tract infection, vaginitis.
Hematologic: anemia.

Musculoskeletal: arthralgia, back pain, hypertonia, hyporeflexia, leg cramps, myalgia, rigors, skeletal pain.
Respiratory: *upper respiratory tract infection,* bronchitis, pneumonia, cough, hiccups.
Skin: rash, pruritus, skin disorder, erythematous rash, *excessive sweating.*
Other: fungal infections, flulike symptoms, injury, surgical intervention, hot flushes, postoperative pain, allergic reaction, infection, abscess, tooth disorder, toothache.

Interactions

Drug-drug. *Beta blockers:* May cause conduction disturbances. Use cautiously.
Drugs with parasympathomimetic effects: May have additive effects. Use cautiously.
Drugs that inhibit CYP2D6, CYP3A4, CYP3A3: May inhibit metabolism of cevimeline. Monitor patient closely.

Effects on lab test results

- May increase amylase level.
- May decrease hemoglobin and hematocrit.

Pharmacokinetics

Absorption: Rapid, reaching peak plasma levels at 1.5 to 2 hours. Food decreases absorption, and peak level is reduced by 17.3%.
Distribution: Less than 20% protein-bound.
Metabolism: Liver enzymes CYP2D6, CYP3A3, and CYP3A4 are involved in the metabolism of cevimeline. The drug is metabolized to a number of metabolites.
Excretion: Mostly excreted in urine. *Half-life:* About 5 hours.

Route	Onset	Peak	Duration
P.O.	Unknown	1.5 to 2 hr	Unknown

Pharmacodynamics

Chemical effect: As a cholinergic agonist, cevimeline binds to and stimulates muscarinic receptors. This results in increased secretion of exocrine glands that cause salivation, sweating, and increased tone of smooth muscles in the GI and GU tracts.
Therapeutic effect: Helps counteract the dry mouth linked to Sjögren's syndrome.

Available forms

Tablets: 30 mg

NURSING PROCESS

Assessment

- Make sure patient has a thorough physical examination before starting drug therapy.
- Assess patient's fluid balance before therapy.
- Be alert for adverse reactions and drug interactions.
- Monitor liver function test results during therapy if patient has risk of liver dysfunction.
- Evaluate patient's and family's knowledge of drug therapy.

Nursing diagnoses

- Impaired oral mucous membrane related to Sjögren's syndrome
- Risk for injury related to drug-induced adverse reactions
- Deficient knowledge related to drug therapy

Planning and implementation

- Rehydrate patient who is dehydrated, as needed.
- Monitor patient with a history of asthma, COPD, or chronic bronchitis for an increase in symptoms (such as wheezing, sputum production, or cough) during therapy.
- Monitor patient with a history of cardiac disease for increased frequency, severity, or duration of angina or changes in heart rate during therapy.

Patient teaching

- Tell patient not to interrupt or stop treatment without medical approval.
- Tell patient that sweating is a common effect of the drug. Fluid intake is important to prevent dehydration.
- Inform patient that cevimeline may cause visual disturbances, especially at night, which can impair driving ability.

Evaluation

- Increased salivation as a result of drug therapy.
- Patient doesn't experience injury as a result of drug-induced adverse reactions.
- Patient and family state understanding of drug therapy.

chloral hydrate

(KLOR-ul HIGH-drayt)

Aquachloral Supprettes, Noctec, Novo-Chlorhydrate ♦

Pharmacologic class: general CNS depressant
Therapeutic class: sedative-hypnotic
Pregnancy risk category: C
Controlled substance schedule: IV

Indications and dosages

▶ **Sedation.** *Adults:* 250 mg P.O. or P.R. t.i.d. after meals.
Children: 8.3 mg/kg P.O. or P.R. t.i.d.; maximum 500 mg per dose daily; doses may be divided.

▶ **Insomnia.** *Adults:* 500 mg to 1 g P.O. or P.R. 15 to 30 minutes before bedtime.
Children: 50 mg/kg P.O. or P.R. 15 to 30 minutes before bedtime; maximum single dose 1 g.

▶ **Preoperatively.** *Adults:* 500 mg to 1 g P.O. or P.R. 30 minutes before surgery.

▶ **Premedication for EEG.** *Children:* 20 to 25 mg/kg P.O. or P.R.

▶ **Alcohol withdrawal.** *Adults:* 500 mg to 1 g P.O. or P.R.; repeat at 6-hour intervals, p.r.n. Maximum daily dose is 2 g.

Contraindications and precautions

• Contraindicated in patients hypersensitive to chloral hydrate and in those with hepatic or renal impairment. Oral administration contraindicated in patients with gastric disorders.
• Use with extreme caution in patients with severe cardiac disease.
• Use cautiously in patients with mental depression, suicidal tendencies, or history of drug abuse.

Lifespan: In breast-feeding women, avoid use because small amounts of drug appear in breast milk and may cause drowsiness in infants.

Adverse reactions

CNS: hangover, drowsiness, nightmares, dizziness, ataxia, paradoxical excitement.
GI: *nausea, vomiting, diarrhea,* flatulence.
Hematologic: eosinophilia, ***leukopenia.***
Other: hypersensitivity reactions.

Interactions

Drug-drug. *Alkaline solutions:* Incompatible with aqueous solutions of chloral hydrate. Don't mix together.
CNS depressants, including narcotic analgesics: May cause excessive CNS depression or vasodilation reaction. Use together cautiously.
Furosemide I.V.: May cause sweating, flushes, variable blood pressure, and uneasiness. Use together cautiously or use different hypnotic drug.
Oral anticoagulants: May increase risk of bleeding. Monitor patient closely.
Phenytoin: May decrease phenytoin levels. Monitor levels closely.
Drug-lifestyle. *Alcohol use:* May cause excessive CNS depression or vasodilation reaction. Discourage using together.

Effects on lab test results

• May increase BUN level.
• May increase eosinophil count. May decrease WBC count.
• May interfere with fluorometric tests for urine catecholamines and Reddy-Jenkins-Thorn test for urine 17-hydroxycorticosteroids. May cause false-positive tests for urine glucose when using copper sulfate tests (Clinitest).

Pharmacokinetics

Absorption: Well absorbed after oral and rectal administration.
Distribution: Distributed throughout body tissue and fluids; trichloroethanol (the active metabolite) is 35% to 41% protein-bound.
Metabolism: Metabolized rapidly and nearly completely in liver and erythrocytes to trichloroethanol; further metabolized in liver and kidneys to trichloroacetic acid and other inactive metabolites.
Excretion: Inactive metabolites are excreted primarily in urine, minimally in bile. *Half-life:* 8 to 10 hours for trichloroethanol.

Route	Onset	Peak	Duration
P.O.	≤ 30 min	Unknown	4-8 hr
P.R.	Unknown	Unknown	4-8 hr

Pharmacodynamics

Chemical effect: Unknown; sedative effects may be caused by trichloroethanol.
Therapeutic effect: Promotes sleep and calmness.

Available forms

Capsules: 250 mg, 500 mg
Suppositories: 324 mg, 500 mg, 648 mg
Syrup: 250 mg/5 ml, 500 mg/5 ml

NURSING PROCESS

Assessment

- Assess patient's underlying condition.
- Evaluate drug effectiveness after administration.
- Be alert for adverse reactions and drug interactions.
- Evaluate patient's and family's knowledge of drug therapy.

Nursing diagnoses

- Disturbed sleep pattern related to patient's underlying condition
- Risk for trauma related to adverse CNS reactions
- Deficient knowledge related to drug therapy

Planning and implementation

ALERT: There are two strengths of oral liquid form; double-check dose, especially when giving to children. Fatal overdose may occur.

- To minimize unpleasant taste and stomach irritation, dilute or give drug with liquid. Drug should be taken after meals.
- **P.R. use:** Store rectal suppositories in refrigerator.
- Long-term use isn't recommended; drug loses its efficacy in promoting sleep after 14 days of continued use. Long-term use may cause drug dependence, and patient may experience withdrawal symptoms if drug is suddenly stopped.

Patient teaching

- Caution patient about performing activities that require mental alertness or physical coordination. For inpatients, supervise walking and raise bed rails, particularly for elderly patients.
- Tell patient to store capsules or syrup in dark container; store suppositories in refrigerator.
- Explain that drug may cause morning hangover. Encourage patient to report severe hangover or feelings of oversedation so prescriber can be consulted to adjust dosage or change drug.

Evaluation

- Patient states drug effectively induced sleep.
- Patient's safety is maintained.
- Patient and family state understanding of drug therapy.

chlorambucil

(klor-AM-byoo-sil)
Leukeran

Pharmacologic class: alkylating agent (not specific to cell cycle phase)
Therapeutic class: antineoplastic
Pregnancy risk category: D

Indications and dosages

▶ **Chronic lymphocytic leukemia; malignant lymphomas, including lymphosarcoma, giant follicular lymphoma, non-Hodgkin's lymphoma, Hodgkin's disease, autoimmune hemolytic anemia‡, nephrotic syndrome‡, polycythemia vera‡, and ovarian neoplasms‡.** *Adults:* 0.1 to 0.2 mg/kg P.O. daily for 3 to 6 weeks; then adjusted for maintenance (usually 4 to 10 mg daily).
Children: 0.1 to 0.2 mg/kg or 3 to 6 mg/m^2 P.O. as a single daily dose. Initial dosage should be reduced if given within 4 weeks after a full course of radiation therapy or myelosuppressive drugs or if pretreatment leukocyte or platelet counts are depressed from bone marrow disease.

▶ **Macroglobulinemia‡.** *Adults:* 2 to 10 mg P.O. daily.

▶ **Metastatic trophoblastic neoplasia‡.** *Adults:* 6 to 10 mg P.O. daily for 5 days; repeat q 1 to 2 weeks.

▶ **Idiopathic uveitis‡.** *Adults:* 6 to 12 mg P.O. daily for 1 year.

▶ **Rheumatoid arthritis‡.** *Adults:* 0.1 to 0.3 mg/kg P.O. daily.

Contraindications and precautions

- Contraindicated in patients hypersensitive or resistant to previous therapy (those hypersensitive to other alkylating agents also may be hypersensitive to chlorambucil).
- Use cautiously in patients with history of head trauma or seizures and in patients receiving other drugs that lower seizure threshold.

Lifespan: In pregnant women, use with extreme caution, if at all, because fetal harm may occur. In breast-feeding women, use is contraindicated. In children, safety of drug hasn't been established; the potential benefits versus risks must be evaluated.

Adverse reactions

CNS: ***seizures.***
GI: *nausea, vomiting, stomatitis.*
GU: *azoospermia, infertility.*
Hematologic: ***neutropenia*** (delayed up to 3 weeks, lasting up to 10 days after last dose), ***thrombocytopenia, anemia, myelosuppression*** (usually moderate, gradual, and rapidly reversible).
Hepatic: ***hepatotoxicity.***
Metabolic: hyperuricemia.
Respiratory: interstitial pneumonitis, ***pulmonary fibrosis.***
Skin: exfoliative dermatitis, rash, ***Stevens-Johnson syndrome.***
Other: ***allergic febrile reaction.***

Interactions

Drug-drug. *Anticoagulants, aspirin:* May increase risk of bleeding. Avoid using together.

Effects on lab test results

- May increase AST, ALT, and alkaline phosphatase levels. May increase blood and urine uric acid levels.
- May decrease hemoglobin, hematocrit, and neutrophil, platelet, WBC, granulocyte, and RBC counts.

Pharmacokinetics

Absorption: Well absorbed from GI tract.
Distribution: Not well understood; drug and its metabolites are highly bound to plasma and tissue proteins.
Metabolism: Metabolized in liver; primary metabolite, phenylacetic acid mustard, also possesses cytotoxic activity.
Excretion: Metabolites are excreted in urine. *Half-life:* 2 hours for parent compound; 2.5 hours for phenylacetic acid metabolite.

Route	Onset	Peak	Duration
P.O.	3-4 wk	1 hr	Unknown

Pharmacodynamics

Chemical effect: Cross-links strands of cellular DNA and interferes with RNA transcription, causing growth imbalance that leads to cell death.
Therapeutic effect: Kills selected cancer cells.

Available forms

Tablets: 2 mg

NURSING PROCESS

Assessment

- Assess patient's underlying neoplastic disorder before therapy and reassess regularly throughout therapy.
- Monitor CBC and uric acid level.
- Be alert for adverse reactions and drug interactions.
- Evaluate patient's and family's knowledge of drug therapy.

Nursing diagnoses

- Ineffective health maintenance related to presence of neoplastic disease
- Ineffective protection related to drug-induced hematologic adverse reactions
- Deficient knowledge related to drug therapy

Planning and implementation

- Dose is individualized according to patient's response.
- Give drug 1 hour before breakfast and at least 2 hours after evening meal.
- Nausea and vomiting caused by drug use can usually be controlled with antiemetics.
- Allopurinol may be used with adequate hydration to prevent hyperuricemia with resulting uric acid nephropathy.
- Follow institutional policy for infection control in immunocompromised patients if WBC count falls below 2,000/mm³ or granulocyte count falls below 1,000/mm³. Severe neutropenia is reversible up to cumulative dosage of 6.5 mg/kg in single course.

Patient teaching

- Warn patient to watch for signs of infection (fever, sore throat, fatigue) and bleeding (easy bruising, nosebleeds, bleeding gums, melena). Tell him to take temperature daily.

• Instruct patient to avoid OTC products that contain aspirin.
• Tell patient to take drug 1 hour before breakfast and 2 hours after evening meal if bothered by nausea and vomiting.
• Instruct patient to maintain fluid intake of 2,400 to 3,000 ml daily, if not contraindicated.

Evaluation

• Patient shows improvement in underlying neoplastic condition on follow-up diagnostic tests.
• Patient remains infection free and doesn't bleed abnormally.
• Patient and family state understanding of drug therapy.

chloramphenicol sodium succinate

(klor-am-FEN-eh-kol SOH-dee-um SUK-seh-nayt)

Chloromycetin, Chloromycetin Sodium Succinate, Pentamycetin ♦

Pharmacologic class: dichloroacetic acid derivative
Therapeutic class: antibiotic
Pregnancy risk category: C

Indications and dosages

▶ ***Haemophilus influenzae*** **meningitis; acute** ***Salmonella typhi*** **infection; meningitis, bacteremia, or other severe infection caused by sensitive** ***Salmonella*** **sp.,** ***Rickettsia,*** **or various sensitive gram-negative organisms; lymphogranuloma; or psittacosis.** *Adults and children:* 50 to 100 mg/kg P.O. or I.V. daily (depending on the severity of infection), divided q 6 hours. Maximum dosage is 100 mg/kg daily.
Full-term infants older than age 2 weeks with normal metabolic processes: Up to 50 mg/kg I.V. daily, divided q 6 hours.
Premature infants, neonates age 2 weeks or younger, and infants and children with immature metabolic processes: 25 mg/kg I.V. once daily. I.V. route must be used to treat meningitis.

Contraindications and precautions

• Contraindicated in patients hypersensitive to drug.
• Use cautiously in patients with impaired hepatic or renal function, acute intermittent porphyria, or G6PD deficiency, and in those taking other drugs that cause bone marrow suppression or blood disorders. Indicated for only serious infections.
Lifespan: In pregnant women, use cautiously. Breast-feeding women should temporarily stop breast-feeding during therapy because drug appears in breast milk, posing risk of bone marrow depression and slight risk of gray syndrome.

Adverse reactions

CNS: headache, mild depression, confusion, delirium; peripheral neuropathy (with prolonged therapy).
EENT: optic neuritis (in patients with cystic fibrosis), glossitis, decreased visual acuity.
GI: nausea, vomiting, stomatitis, diarrhea, enterocolitis.
Hematologic: ***aplastic anemia, hypoplastic anemia, thrombocytopenia, agranulocytosis, granulocytopenia.***
Other: infection with nonsusceptible organisms, hypersensitivity reactions (fever, rash, urticaria, ***anaphylaxis***), jaundice, ***gray syndrome in neonates.***

Interactions

Drug-drug. *Chlorpropamide, dicumarol, phenobarbital, phenytoin, tolbutamide:* May increase drug levels. Monitor patient for toxicity.
Folic acid, iron supplements, vitamin B_{12}: Possible delayed response in patients with anemia. Monitor patient closely.

Effects on lab test results

• May decrease hemoglobin, hematocrit, and RBC, granulocyte, and platelet counts.

Pharmacokinetics

Absorption: Well absorbed from GI tract after oral administration.
Distribution: Distributed widely to most body tissues and fluids. About 50% to 60% bound to plasma protein.
Metabolism: Parent drug is metabolized primarily by hepatic glucuronyl transferase to inactive metabolites.
Excretion: 8% to 12% of dose is excreted by kidneys as unchanged drug; remainder is ex-

creted as inactive metabolites. *Half-life:* about 1.5 to 4.5 hours.

Route	Onset	Peak	Duration
P.O.	Unknown	1-3 hr	Unknown
I.V.	Immediate	Immediate	Unknown

Pharmacodynamics

Chemical effect: Inhibits bacterial protein synthesis by binding to 50S subunit of ribosome; bacteriostatic.
Therapeutic effect: Inhibits growth of susceptible bacteria, including *Rickettsia, Chlamydia, Mycoplasma,* and certain *Salmonella* strains, as well as most gram-positive and gram-negative organisms.

Available forms

Capsules: 250 mg
Injection: 100 mg/ml (as sodium succinate)
Oral suspension: 150 mg/5ml (as palmitate)

NURSING PROCESS

Assessment

- Assess patient's infection before therapy and reassess regularly throughout therapy.
- Obtain specimen for culture and sensitivity tests before first dose. Therapy may begin pending results.
- Monitor drug level. Therapeutic drug level is 5 to 25 mcg/ml.
- Monitor CBC, platelets, iron, and reticulocytes before and every 2 days during therapy.
- Be alert for adverse reactions and drug interactions.

ALERT: Signs and symptoms of gray syndrome in neonates include abdominal distention, gray cyanosis, vasomotor collapse, respiratory distress, and death within few hours after onset of symptoms.
- Evaluate patient's and family's knowledge about drug therapy.

Nursing diagnoses

- Infection related to presence of bacteria susceptible to drug
- Impaired protection related to drug-induced aplastic anemia
- Deficient knowledge related to drug therapy

Planning and implementation

- **P.O. use:** Give oral drug 1 hour before or 2 hours after meals. If patient develops adverse GI effects, give with food.
- **I.V. use:** Give I.V. slowly over at least 1 minute. Check injection site daily for phlebitis and irritation.
  - Reconstitute 1-g vial of powder for injection with 10 ml sterile water for injection. Concentration will be 100 mg/ml. Stable for 30 days at room temperature, but refrigeration recommended. Don't use cloudy solutions.
- Stop drug immediately and notify prescriber if anemia, reticulocytopenia, leukopenia, or thrombocytopenia develops.
- If patient's drug level exceeds 25 mcg/ml, take bleeding precautions and infection-control measures because bone marrow suppression can occur.

Patient teaching

- Instruct patient to report adverse reactions to prescriber, especially nausea, vomiting, diarrhea, fever, confusion, sore throat, or mouth sores.
- Stress importance of having frequent blood tests to monitor therapeutic effectiveness and adverse reactions.

Evaluation

- Patient is free from infection after drug therapy.
- Patient's hematologic status remains unchanged with drug therapy.
- Patient and family state understanding of drug therapy.

chlordiazepoxide

(klor-digh-eh-zuh-POKS-ighd)
Libritabs

chlordiazepoxide hydrochloride

Apo-Chlordiazepoxide ♦, Librium, Novo-Poxide ♦

Pharmacologic class: benzodiazepine
Therapeutic class: antianxiety agent, sedative-hypnotic
Pregnancy risk category: D
Controlled substance schedule: IV

Indications and dosages

▶ **Mild-to-moderate anxiety.** *Adults:* 5 to 10 mg P.O. t.i.d. or q.i.d.
Children older than age 6: 5 mg P.O. b.i.d. to q.i.d. Maximum dosage 10 mg P.O. b.i.d. or t.i.d.

▶ **Severe anxiety.** *Adults:* 20 to 25 mg P.O. t.i.d. or q.i.d. Or, 50 to 100 mg I.V. initially, followed by 25 to 50 mg I.V. 3 or 4 times daily as needed.
Elderly patients: 5 mg P.O. b.i.d. to q.i.d.

▶ **Withdrawal symptoms of acute alcoholism.** *Adults:* 50 to 100 mg P.O., I.V., or I.M. Repeated in 2 to 4 hours, p.r.n. Maximum dosage is 300 mg daily.

▶ **Preoperative apprehension and anxiety.** *Adults:* 5 to 10 mg P.O. t.i.d. or q.i.d. on day preceding surgery. Or, 50 to 100 mg I.M. 1 hour before surgery.

Contraindications and precautions

- Contraindicated in patients hypersensitive to drug.
- Use cautiously in patients with mental depression, porphyria, or hepatic or renal disease.

Lifespan: In pregnant women, use is contraindicated. In breast-feeding women, drug shouldn't be given because of risk of adverse effects in infant. In children younger than age 6, safety of drug hasn't been established. In children younger than age 12, parenteral use isn't recommended. In elderly patients, use smallest effective dose to avoid ataxia and oversedation. In elderly or debilitated patients, dosage should be reduced.

Adverse reactions

CNS: *drowsiness, lethargy, hangover,* fainting, restlessness, psychosis, ***suicidal tendencies.***
CV: *thrombophlebitis,* transient hypotension.
EENT: visual disturbances.
GI: nausea, vomiting, abdominal discomfort.
GU: incontinence, urine retention, menstrual irregularities.
Hematologic: ***agranulocytosis.***
Skin: *swelling, pain at injection site.*

Interactions

Drug-drug. *Cimetidine:* May increase sedation. Monitor patient carefully.
CNS depressants: May increase CNS depression. Avoid use together.
Digoxin: May increase digoxin levels and risk of toxicity. Monitor patient closely.
Drug-herb. *Kava:* May lead to excessive sedation. Discourage use together.
Drug-lifestyle. *Alcohol use:* May increase CNS depression. Discourage use together.
Smoking: May increase clearance of benzodiazepines. Monitor patient for lack of effect.

Effects on lab test results

- May increase liver function test values. May decrease granulocyte count.
- May cause false-positive reaction in Gravindex pregnancy test. May interfere with certain tests for urine 17-ketosteroids.

Pharmacokinetics

Absorption: When given orally, drug is absorbed well through GI tract.
Distribution: Distributed widely throughout body. Drug is 80% to 90% protein-bound.
Metabolism: Metabolized in liver to several active metabolites.
Excretion: Most metabolites of drug are excreted in urine. *Half-life:* 5 to 30 hours.

Route	Onset	Peak	Duration
P.O., I.V., I.M.	Unknown	0.5-4 hr	Unknown

Pharmacodynamics

Chemical effect: Unknown. Thought to depress CNS at limbic and subcortical levels of brain.
Therapeutic effect: Relieves anxiety and promotes sleep and calmness.

Available forms

chlordiazepoxide
Tablets: 10 mg, 25 mg
chlordiazepoxide hydrochloride
Capsules: 5 mg, 10 mg, 25 mg
Powder for injection: 100 mg/ampule

NURSING PROCESS

Assessment

- Assess patient's underlying condition before therapy and reassess regularly thereafter.
- Monitor respirations every 5 to 15 minutes after I.V. administration and before each repeated I.V. dose.

• Monitor liver, renal, and hematopoietic function studies periodically in patients receiving repeated or prolonged therapy.
• Monitor patient for abuse and addiction.
• Be alert for adverse reactions and drug interactions.
• Evaluate patient's and family's knowledge of drug therapy.

Nursing diagnoses
• Anxiety related to patient's underlying condition
• Risk for injury related to drug-induced CNS reactions
• Deficient knowledge related to drug therapy

Planning and implementation
• Drug shouldn't be prescribed regularly for everyday stress.
• **P.O. use:** Make sure patient has swallowed tablets before you leave the bedside.
ALERT: Chlordiazepoxide 5 mg and 25 mg unit-dose capsules may appear similar in color when viewed through the package. Verify contents and read label carefully.
• **I.M. use:** Add 2 ml of diluent to powder and agitate gently until clear. Use immediately. I.M. form may be erratically absorbed.
– Recommended for I.M. use only, but may be given I.V.
– Injectable form (as hydrochloride) comes in two types of ampules: as diluent and as powdered drug. Read directions carefully.
– Don't mix injectable form with any other parenteral drug.
• **I.V. use:** Use 5 ml normal saline solution or sterile water for injection as diluent. Give over 1 minute.
ALERT: Don't give packaged diluent I.V. because air bubbles may form.
– Be sure equipment and personnel needed for emergency airway management are available.
• Refrigerate powder and keep away from light; mix just before use and discard remainder.
• Drug shouldn't be withdrawn abruptly after long-term administration; withdrawal symptoms may occur.

Patient teaching
• Warn patient to avoid hazardous activities that require alertness and good psychomotor coordination until CNS effects of drug are known.
• Tell patient to avoid alcohol while taking drug.
• Warn patient to take this drug only as directed and not to discontinue it without prescriber's approval. Inform patient of drug's potential for dependence if taken longer than directed.

Evaluation
• Patient says he's less anxious.
• Patient's safety is maintained.
• Patient and family state understanding of drug therapy.

chloroquine hydrochloride
(KLOR-uh-qwin high-droh-KLOR-ighd)
Aralen HCl

chloroquine phosphate
Aralen Phosphate, Chlorquin ◇

Pharmacologic class: 4-amino-quinoline
Therapeutic class: antimalarial, amebicide
Pregnancy risk category: C

Indications and dosages
▶ **Acute malarial attacks caused by *Plasmodium vivax, P. malariae, P. ovale,* and susceptible strains of *P. falciparum.*** *Adults:* 1 g (600-mg base) P.O. followed by 500 mg (300-mg base) P.O. after 6 to 8 hours; for next 2 days a single dose of 500 (300-mg base) P.O. or 4 to 5 ml (160- to 200-mg base) I.M., repeated in 6 hours, if needed, changing to P.O. as soon as possible.
Children: Initially, 10 mg (base)/kg P.O., then 5 mg (base)/kg at 6, 24, and 48 hours (don't exceed adult dose). Or, 5 mg (base)/kg I.M. initially; repeated in 6 hours p.r.n. Don't exceed 10 mg (base)/kg/24 hours. Patient should be switched to oral therapy as soon as possible.
▶ **Malaria prophylaxis.** *Adults:* 500 mg (300-mg base) P.O. on the same day once weekly, beginning 2 weeks before exposure. Continue for 4 weeks after leaving endemic area.
Children: 5 mg (base)/kg P.O. on the same day once weekly (not to exceed adult dosage), beginning 2 weeks before exposure.
▶ **Extraintestinal amebiasis.** *Adults:* 1 g (600-mg base) chloroquine phosphate P.O. dai-

ly for 2 days; then 500 mg (300-mg base) daily for at least 2 to 3 weeks. Treatment usually is combined with intestinal amebicide.

▶ **Rheumatoid arthritis‡.** *Adults:* 250 mg P.O. daily (chloroquine phosphate) with evening meal.

▶ **Lupus erythematosus‡.** *Adults:* 250 mg P.O. daily (chloroquine phosphate) with evening meal; reduce dosage gradually over several months when lesions regress.

Contraindications and precautions

- Contraindicated in patients hypersensitive to drug and in patients with retinal changes, visual field changes, or porphyria.
- Use with extreme caution in patients with severe GI, neurologic, or blood disorders.
- Use cautiously in patients with hepatic disease or alcoholism (drug concentrates in liver), and in those with G6PD deficiency or psoriasis (drug may exacerbate these conditions).

Lifespan: In pregnant women, drug isn't recommended except for suppression or treatment of malaria (since malaria poses greater danger to mother and fetus than prophylactic administration) or hepatic amebiasis. In breast-feeding women, use cautiously.

Adverse reactions

CNS: mild and transient headache, neuromyopathy, psychic stimulation, fatigue, irritability, nightmares, ***seizures,*** dizziness.
CV: hypotension, ECG changes.
EENT: *visual disturbances* (blurred vision; difficulty in focusing; reversible corneal changes; typically irreversible, sometimes progressive or delayed retinal changes, such as narrowing of arterioles; macular lesions; pallor of optic disk; optic atrophy; patchy retinal pigmentation, typically leading to blindness), ototoxicity (nerve deafness, vertigo, tinnitus).
GI: anorexia, abdominal cramps, diarrhea, nausea, vomiting, stomatitis.
Hematologic: ***agranulocytosis, aplastic anemia,*** hemolytic anemia, ***thrombocytopenia.***
Skin: pruritus, lichen planus eruptions, skin and mucosal pigmentary changes, pleomorphic skin eruptions.

Interactions

Drug-drug. *Aluminum salts, kaolin, magnesium:* May decrease GI absorption. Separate administration times.
Cimetidine: May decrease hepatic metabolism of chloroquine. Monitor patient for toxicity.
Drug-lifestyle. *Sun exposure:* May worsen drug-induced dermatomes. Tell patient to avoid excessive sun exposure and wear protective clothing and sunblock.

Effects on lab test results

- May decrease hemoglobin, hematocrit, and granulocyte and platelet counts.

Pharmacokinetics

Absorption: Absorbed readily and almost completely.
Distribution: Distributed in liver, spleen, kidneys, heart, and brain and is strongly bound in melanin-containing cells.
Metabolism: About 30% of dose is metabolized by liver to monodesethylchloroquine and bidesethylchloroquine.
Excretion: About 70% of dose is excreted unchanged in urine; unabsorbed drug is excreted in feces. Small amounts of drug may be present in urine for months after drug is discontinued. Renal excretion is enhanced by urine acidification. *Half-life:* 1 to 2 months.

Route	Onset	Peak	Duration
P.O.	Unknown	1-3 hr	Unknown
I.M.	Unknown	30 min	Unknown

Pharmacodynamics

Chemical effect: Unknown. As antimalarial, chloroquine is thought to bind to and alter properties of DNA in susceptible parasites.
Therapeutic effect: Prevents or eradicates malarial infections; eradicates amebiasis.

Available forms

chloroquine hydrochloride
Injection: 50 mg/ml (40-mg/ml base)
chloroquine phosphate
Tablets: 250 mg (150-mg base), 500 mg (300-mg base)

NURSING PROCESS

Assessment

- Assess patient's infection before therapy and reassess regularly throughout therapy.
- Ensure that baseline and periodic ophthalmic examinations are performed. Check periodical-

ly for ocular muscle weakness after long-term use.
- Assist patient with obtaining audiometric examinations before, during, and after therapy, especially if long-term.
- Monitor CBC and liver function studies periodically during long-term therapy.
- Be alert for adverse reactions and drug interactions.
- Assess patient for possible overdose, which can quickly lead to toxic symptoms: headache, drowsiness, visual disturbances, CV collapse, and seizures, followed by cardiopulmonary arrest. Children are extremely susceptible to toxicity.
- Evaluate patient's and family's knowledge of drug therapy.

Nursing diagnoses
- Infection related to presence of organisms susceptible to drug
- Disturbed sensory perception (visual or auditory) related to adverse reactions to drug
- Deficient knowledge related to drug therapy

Planning and implementation
- Give drug at same time of same day each week.

ALERT: Missed doses should be given as soon as possible. To avoid doubling doses in regimens requiring more than one dose per day, give missed dose within 1 hour of scheduled time or omit dose altogether.
- **I.M. use:** Replace with oral administration as soon as possible.
- **P.O. use:** Give drug with milk or meals to minimize GI distress. Tablets may be crushed and mixed with food or chocolate syrup for patients who have trouble swallowing; however, drug has bitter taste and patients may find mixture unpleasant. Crushed tablets may be placed inside empty gelatin capsules, which are easier to swallow.
- Store drug in amber-colored containers to protect from light.
- Prophylactic antimalarial therapy should begin 2 weeks before exposure and should continue for 4 weeks after patient leaves endemic area.
- Monitor patient's weight for significant changes because dosage is calculated by patient's weight.
- Notify prescriber if patient develops severe blood disorder not attributable to disease; drug may need to be discontinued.

Patient teaching
- Tell patient to take drug with food at same time on same day each week.
- Instruct patient to avoid excessive sun exposure to prevent exacerbation of drug-induced dermatoses.
- Tell patient to report blurred vision, increased sensitivity to light, and muscle weakness.
- Warn patient to avoid alcohol while taking drug.
- Teach patient how to take missed doses.

Evaluation
- Patient is free from infection.
- Patient maintains normal visual and auditory function.
- Patient and family state understanding of drug therapy.

chlorothiazide
(klor-oh-THIGH-uh-zighd)
Chlotride ◇, Diurigen, Diuril

chlorothiazide sodium

Pharmacologic class: thiazide diuretic
Therapeutic class: diuretic, antihypertensive
Pregnancy risk category: D

Indications and dosages
▶ **Edema, hypertension.** *Adults:* 500 mg to 1 g P.O. or I.V. daily or in divided doses.
▶ **Diuresis, hypertension.** *Children and infants age 6 months and older:* 10 to 20 mg/kg P.O. daily in divided doses, not to exceed 375 mg daily.
Infants younger than age 6 months: May require 30 mg/kg P.O. daily in two divided doses.

Contraindications and precautions
- Contraindicated in patients hypersensitive to other thiazides or other sulfonamide-derived drugs and in patients with anuria.
- Use cautiously in patients with severe renal disease and impaired hepatic function.

Lifespan: In pregnant or breast-feeding women, safety of drug hasn't been established.

In children, I.V. administration isn't recommended.

Adverse reactions

CV: orthostatic hypotension.
GI: anorexia, nausea, ***pancreatitis.***
GU: impotence, nocturia, polyuria, frequent urination, ***renal failure.***
Hematologic: ***aplastic anemia, agranulocytosis, leukopenia, thrombocytopenia.***
Hepatic: ***hepatic encephalopathy.***
Metabolic: asymptomatic hyperuricemia; hypokalemia; hyperglycemia and impaired glucose tolerance; fluid and electrolyte imbalances, including dilutional hyponatremia and hypochloremia, ***metabolic alkalosis,*** and hypercalcemia; gout.
Skin: dermatitis, photosensitivity, rash.
Other: hypersensitivity reactions.

Interactions

Drug-drug. *Barbiturates, opiates:* May increase orthostatic hypotension. Monitor patient closely.
Cardiac glycosides: May increase risk of digitalis toxicity from chlorothiazide-induced hypokalemia. Monitor potassium and digitalis levels.
Cholestyramine, colestipol: May decrease intestinal absorption of thiazides. Give doses separately.
Diazoxide: May increase antihypertensive, hyperglycemic, and hyperuricemic effects. Use together cautiously.
Lithium: May decrease lithium clearance, increasing risk of lithium toxicity. Monitor lithium level.
NSAIDs: May increase risk of NSAID-induced renal failure. Monitor patient for renal failure.
Drug-herb. *Licorice root:* Could worsen the potassium depletion caused by thiazides. Discourage using together.
Drug-lifestyle. *Alcohol use:* May increase orthostatic hypotension. Monitor patient closely and place patient on fall precautions.

Effects on lab test results

- May increase uric acid, glucose, and calcium levels. May decrease potassium, sodium, and chloride levels.
- May decrease hemoglobin, hematocrit, and granulocyte, WBC, and platelet counts.

Pharmacokinetics

Absorption: Absorbed incompletely and variably from GI tract.
Distribution: Unknown.
Metabolism: None.
Excretion: Excreted unchanged in urine. *Half-life:* 1 to 2 hours.

Route	Onset	Peak	Duration
P.O.	≤ 2 hr	4 hr	6-12 hr
I.V.	≤ 15 min	30 min	6-12 hr

Pharmacodynamics

Chemical effect: Increases sodium and water excretion by inhibiting sodium reabsorption in nephron's cortical diluting site.
Therapeutic effect: Promotes sodium and water excretion.

Available forms

Injection: 500-mg vial
Oral suspension: 250 mg/5 ml
Tablets: 250 mg, 500 mg

NURSING PROCESS

Assessment

- Assess patient's underlying condition.
- Monitor effectiveness by regularly checking blood pressure, fluid intake, urine output, blood pressure, and weight.
- Expect that therapeutic response may be delayed several days in patients with hypertension
- Monitor electrolyte and glucose levels.
- Monitor creatinine and BUN levels regularly. Drug not as effective if these levels are more than twice normal.
- Monitor blood uric acid level, especially in patients with history of gout.
- Be alert for adverse reactions and drug interactions.
- Evaluate patient's and family's knowledge about drug therapy.

Nursing diagnoses

- Excessive fluid volume related to patient's underlying condition
- Impaired urinary elimination related to drug therapy
- Deficient knowledge related to drug therapy

Planning and implementation

- To prevent nocturia, give drug in the morning.
- **I.V. use:** Reconstitute 500 mg with 18 ml sterile water for injection. Inject reconstituted drug directly into vein, through I.V. line containing free-flowing, compatible solution, or through intermittent infusion device. Compatible with I.V. dextrose or saline solutions.
  - Store reconstituted solutions at room temperature up to 24 hours.
  - Avoid I.V. infiltration, as it can be very painful.
  - Avoid simultaneous administration with whole blood and its derivatives.
  - Stop giving drug and notify prescriber if hypersensitivity reactions occur.
- **P.O. use:** Don't give more than 250 mg P.O. per dose. Bioavailability studies show that 250 mg P.O. every 6 hours is absorbed better than single dose of 1 g.

ALERT: Never inject I.M. or S.C.

- Drug may be used with potassium-sparing diuretic to prevent potassium loss.
- Discontinue thiazides and thiazide-like diuretics before parathyroid function tests are performed.

Patient teaching

- Teach patient and family to identify and report signs of hypersensitivity and hypokalemia.
- Teach patient to monitor fluid intake and output and daily weight.
- Instruct patient to avoid high-sodium foods and to choose high-potassium foods.
- Tell patient to take drug early in day to avoid nocturia.
- Advise patient to avoid sudden posture changes and to rise slowly to avoid orthostatic hypotension.
- Advise patient to use sunblock to prevent photosensitivity reactions.
- Teach patient the importance of periodic laboratory tests to detect possible electrolyte imbalances.

Evaluation

- Patient is free from edema.
- Patient adjusts lifestyle to cope with altered patterns of urine elimination.
- Patient and family state understanding of drug therapy.

chlorpheniramine maleate

(klor-fen-EER-uh-meen MAL-ee-ayt)

Aller-Chlor *†, Chlo-Amine†, Chlor-Trimeton Allergy 4 Hour†, Chlor-Trimeton Allergy 8 Hour†, Chlor-Trimeton Allergy 12 Hour†, Chlor-Tripolon ♦

Pharmacologic class: propylamine-derivative antihistamine
Therapeutic class: antihistamine (H_1-receptor antagonist)
Pregnancy risk category: B

Indications and dosages

▶ **Rhinitis, allergy symptoms.** *Adults and children age 12 and older:* 4 mg P.O. q 4 to 6 hours or 8 to 12 mg timed-release P.O. q 8 to 12 hours; maximum 24 mg daily.
Children ages 6 to 11: 2 mg P.O. q 4 to 6 hours; maximum 12 mg daily. Or, may give 8 mg timed-release P.O. h.s.
Children ages 2 to 5: 1 mg P.O. q 4 to 6 hours; maximum 4 mg daily.

Contraindications and precautions

- Contraindicated in patients with acute asthmatic attacks.
- Use cautiously in patients with increased intraocular pressure, hyperthyroidism, CV or renal disease, hypertension, bronchial asthma, urine retention, prostatic hyperplasia, bladder-neck obstruction, and stenosing peptic ulcerations.

Lifespan: In pregnant women, safety of drug hasn't been established. In breast-feeding women, antihistamines aren't recommended because small amounts of drug appear in breast milk. In premature or newborn infants, use is also not recommended. For children younger than age 12, extended-release tablets aren't recommended. In elderly patients, use cautiously.

Adverse reactions

CNS: *stimulation,* sedation, *drowsiness* (especially in elderly patients), excitability in children.
CV: hypotension, palpitations.
GI: epigastric distress, *dry mouth.*
GU: urine retention.
Respiratory: thick bronchial secretions.
Skin: rash, urticaria.

Interactions

Drug-drug. *CNS depressants:* May increase sedation. Use together cautiously.
MAO inhibitors: May increase anticholinergic effects. Don't use together.
Drug-lifestyle. *Alcohol use:* May increase sedation. Tell patient to use together cautiously.

Effects on lab test results

None reported.

Pharmacokinetics

Absorption: Well absorbed from GI tract after oral administration. Food delays absorption but doesn't affect bioavailability.
Distribution: Distributed extensively into body; drug is about 72% protein-bound.
Metabolism: Metabolized largely in GI mucosal cells and liver (first-pass effect).
Excretion: Drug and metabolites are excreted in urine. *Half-life:* 12 to 43 hours in adults; 10 to 13 hours in children.

Route	Onset	Peak	Duration
P.O.	15-60 min	2-6 hr	< 24 hr

Pharmacodynamics

Chemical effect: Competes with histamine for H_1-receptor sites on effector cells. Prevents, but doesn't reverse, histamine-mediated responses.
Therapeutic effect: Relieves allergy symptoms.

Available forms

Capsules (sustained-release) ♦**:** 8 mg, 12 mg
Syrup: 2 mg/5 ml*
Tablets: 4 mg
Tablets (chewable): 2 mg
Tablets (timed-release): 8 mg, 12 mg

NURSING PROCESS

Assessment

- Assess patient's underlying allergy condition and reassess regularly thereafter.
- Be alert for adverse reactions and drug interactions.
- Evaluate patient's and family's knowledge about drug therapy.

Nursing diagnoses

- Ineffective health maintenance related to underlying allergy condition
- Risk for injury related to drug-induced CNS adverse reactions
- Deficient knowledge related to drug therapy

Planning and implementation

- Give drug with food or milk to reduce GI distress.
- Notify prescriber if patient develops tolerance. Prescriber may substitute another antihistamine.

Patient teaching

- Instruct patient to take oral drug with food or milk.
- Warn patient to avoid alcohol and other CNS depressants and driving or other activities that require alertness until drug's CNS effects are known.
- Tell patient that coffee or tea may reduce drowsiness. Also, recommend sugarless gum, sugarless hard candy, or ice chips to relieve dry mouth.
- Advise patient to stop drug 4 days before allergy skin tests to preserve accuracy of tests.
- Tell patient to notify prescriber if tolerance develops because different antihistamine may need to be prescribed.
- Tell parents that drug shouldn't be used in children under age 6 unless directed by prescriber.

Evaluation

- Patient's allergic symptoms are relieved with drug therapy.
- Patient doesn't experience injury as a result of drug-induced adverse reactions.
- Patient and family state understanding of drug therapy.

chlorpromazine hydrochloride

(klor-PROH-meh-zeen high-droh-KLOR-ighd)
Chlorpromanyl-20 ♦, Chlorpromanyl-40 ♦, Largactil ♦◇, Novo-Chlorpromazine ♦, Thorazine

Pharmacologic class: aliphatic phenothiazine
Therapeutic class: antipsychotic, antiemetic
Pregnancy risk category: C

Indications and dosages

▶ **Psychosis.** *Adults:* Initially, 30 to 75 mg P.O. daily in two to four divided doses. Increase dosage by 20 to 50 mg twice weekly until symptoms are controlled. Some patients may need up to 800 mg daily. Switch to oral therapy as soon as possible.
Children age 6 months and older: 0.55 mg/kg P.O. q 4 to 6 hours or I.M. q 6 to 8 hours. Or, 1.1 mg/kg P.R. q 6 to 8 hours. Maximum I.M. dose in children younger than age 5 or weighing less than 22.7 kg (50 lb) is 40 mg. Maximum I.M. dose in children ages 5 to 12 or weighing 22.7 to 45.5 kg (100 lb) is 75 mg.
▶ **Nausea and vomiting.** *Adults:* 10 to 25 mg P.O. q 4 to 6 hours, p.r.n. Or, 50 to 100 mg P.R. q 6 to 8 hours, p.r.n. Or, 25 mg I.M. If no hypotension occurs, give 25 to 50 mg I.M. q 3 to 4 hours p.r.n. until vomiting stops.
Children and infants age 6 months and older: 0.55 mg/kg P.O. q 4 to 6 hours or I.M. q 6 to 8 hours. Or, 1.1 mg/kg P.R. q 6 to 8 hours. Maximum I.M. dose in children younger than age 5 or weighing less than 22.7 kg is 40 mg. Maximum I.M. dose in children ages 5 to 12 or weighing 22.7 to 45.5 kg is 75 mg.
▶ **Intractable hiccups, acute intermittent porphyria.** *Adults:* 25 to 50 mg P.O. t.i.d. or q.i.d. If symptoms persist for 2 to 3 days, 25 to 50 mg I.M. If symptoms still persist, 25 to 50 mg diluted in 500 to 1,000 ml normal saline solution and infused slowly.
▶ **Tetanus.** *Adults:* 25 to 50 mg I.V. or I.M. t.i.d. or q.i.d.
Children and infants age 6 months and older: 0.55 mg/kg I.M. or I.V. q 6 to 8 hours. Maximum parenteral dosage in children weighing less than 22.7 kg is 40 mg daily; in children weighing 22.7 to 45.5 kg, 75 mg daily, except in severe cases.
▶ **Relief of apprehension and nervousness before surgery.** *Adults:* Preoperatively, 25 to 50 mg P.O. 2 to 3 hours before surgery or 12.5 to 25 mg I.M. 1 to 2 hours before surgery. During surgery, 12.5 mg I.M.; repeat after 30 minutes if needed or fractional 2-mg doses I.V. at 2-minute intervals; maximum dose 25 mg. Postoperatively, 10 to 25 mg P.O. q 4 to 6 hours or 12.5 mg to 25 mg I.M.; repeat in 1 hour if needed.
Children and infants age 6 months and older: Preoperatively, 0.55 mg/kg P.O. 2 to 3 hours before surgery or I.M. 1 to 2 hours before surgery. During surgery, 0.275 mg/kg I.M. repeated after 30 minutes, if needed or fractional 1-mg doses I.V. at 2-minute intervals, maximum dose 0.275 mg/kg. May repeat fractional I.V. regimen in 30 minutes, if needed; postoperatively, 0.55 mg/kg P.O. q 4 to 6 hours or 0.55 mg/kg I.M.; repeat in 1 hour if needed and hypotension doesn't occur.

Contraindications and precautions

- Contraindicated in patients hypersensitive to drug and in patients with CNS depression, bone marrow suppression, subcortical damage, and coma.
- Use cautiously in debilitated patients and in those with hepatic or renal disease, severe CV disease (may cause sudden drop in blood pressure), exposure to extreme heat or cold (including antipyretic therapy), exposure to organophosphate insecticides, respiratory disorders, hypocalcemia, seizure disorders (may lower seizure threshold), severe reactions to insulin or electroconvulsive therapy, glaucoma, or prostatic hyperplasia.

Lifespan: In pregnant or breast-feeding women, drug isn't recommended. In acutely ill or dehydrated children, use cautiously. In elderly patients, also use cautiously.

Adverse reactions

CNS: *extrapyramidal reactions, sedation, **seizures**, tardive dyskinesia,* pseudoparkinsonism, dizziness, ***neuroleptic malignant syndrome.***
CV: *orthostatic hypotension,* tachycardia, ECG changes.
EENT: ocular changes, blurred vision.
GI: *dry mouth, constipation.*
GU: *urine retention,* menstrual irregularities, inhibited ejaculation.
Hematologic: ***transient leukopenia, agranulocytosis,*** hyperprolactinemia, ***aplastic anemia, thrombocytopenia.***
Hepatic: cholestatic jaundice.
Skin: *mild photosensitivity.*
Other: gynecomastia, allergic reactions, *I.M. injection site pain,* sterile abscess.

Interactions

Drug-drug. *Antacids:* Inhibits absorption of oral phenothiazines. Separate antacid and phenothiazine doses by at least 2 hours.
Anticholinergics, including antidepressants and antiparkinsonians: May increase anti-

cholinergic activity and aggravate parkinsonian symptoms. Use with caution.
Barbiturates, lithium: May decrease phenothiazine effect. Observe patient.
Centrally acting antihypertensives: May decrease antihypertensive effect. Monitor patient's blood pressure carefully.
CNS depressants: May increase CNS depression. Avoid using together.
Propranolol: May increase levels of both propranolol and chlorpromazine. Monitor patient.
Warfarin: May decrease effect of oral anticoagulants. Monitor PT and INR.
Drug-herb. *Kava:* Can increase the risk or severity of dystonic reactions. Discourage using together.
Dong quai, St. John's wort: Increased risk of photosensitivity. Advise patient to avoid prolonged or unprotected exposure to sunlight.
Yohimbe: May increase risk of toxicity. Discourage using together.
Drug-lifestyle. *Alcohol use:* May increase CNS depression. Discourage use together.
Sun exposure: May increase risk of photosensitivity. Discourage prolonged or unprotected exposure to sun.

Effects on lab test results

• May increase GGT and prolactin levels.
• May increase creatine phosphokinase values and eosinophil count. May decrease hemoglobin, hematocrit, and WBC, granulocyte, and platelet counts.

Pharmacokinetics

Absorption: Absorption is erratic and variable for oral administration; rapid for I.M. administration.
Distribution: Distributed widely into body; concentration is usually higher in CNS than plasma. Drug is 91% to 99% protein-bound.
Metabolism: Metabolized extensively by liver and forms 10 to 12 metabolites; some are pharmacologically active.
Excretion: Most of drug is excreted as metabolites in urine; some is excreted in feces. Chlorpromazine may undergo enterohepatic circulation.

Route	Onset	Peak	Duration
P.O., I.V., I.M, P.R	Varies	Varies	Varies

Pharmacodynamics

Chemical effect: Unknown. Probably blocks postsynaptic dopamine receptors in brain and inhibits medullary chemoreceptor trigger zone.
Therapeutic effect: Relieves nausea and vomiting; hiccups; and signs and symptoms of psychosis, acute intermittent porphyria, and tetanus. Produces calmness and sleep preoperatively.

Available forms

Capsules (controlled-release): 30 mg, 75 mg, 150 mg, 200 mg, 300 mg
Injection: 25 mg/ml
Oral concentrate: 30 mg/ml, 100 mg/ml
Suppositories: 25 mg, 100 mg
Syrup: 10 mg/5 ml
Tablets: 10 mg, 25 mg, 50 mg, 100 mg, 200 mg

NURSING PROCESS

Assessment

• Assess patient's underlying condition and reassess regularly thereafter.
• Be alert for adverse reactions and drug interactions.
• Monitor blood pressure regularly. Watch for orthostatic hypotension, especially with parenteral administration. Monitor blood pressure before and after I.M. administration.
• Monitor patient for tardive dyskinesia, which may occur after prolonged use. It may not appear until months or years later and may disappear spontaneously or persist for life despite discontinuation of drug.
• Watch for symptoms of neuroleptic malignant syndrome. It's rare, but commonly fatal. It isn't necessarily related to length of drug use or type of neuroleptic, but over 60% of affected patients are men.
• Monitor therapy with weekly bilirubin tests during first month, periodic blood tests (CBC and liver function), and ophthalmic tests (long-term use).
• Evaluate patient's and family's knowledge about drug therapy.

Nursing diagnoses

• Ineffective health maintenance related to patient's underlying condition
• Impaired physical mobility related to drug-induced extrapyramidal reactions
• Deficient knowledge related to drug therapy

Planning and implementation

- Wear gloves when preparing solutions and prevent any contact with skin and clothing. Oral liquid and parenteral forms can cause contact dermatitis.
- Slight yellowing of injection or concentrate is common; potency isn't affected. Discard markedly discolored solutions.
- **P.O. use:** Protect liquid concentrate from light.
– Dilute with fruit juice, milk, or semisolid food just before giving.
– Sustained-release preparations shouldn't be crushed but given whole.
– Shake syrup before giving.
- **I.V. use:** For direct injection, drug may be diluted with normal saline solution for injection and injected into large vein or through tubing of free-flowing I.V. solution. Don't exceed 1 mg/minute for adults or 0.5 mg/minute for children.
– Drug also may be given as I.V. infusion; dilute with 500 or 1,000 ml normal saline solution and infuse slowly.
– Chlorpromazine is compatible with most common I.V. solutions, including D_5W, Ringer's injection, lactated Ringer's injection, and normal saline solution for injection.
- **I.M. use:** Give deep I.M. only in upper outer quadrant of buttocks. Massage slowly afterward to prevent sterile abscess. Injection stings.
- **P.R. use:** Follow normal protocol for inserting suppository.
– Store suppositories in cool place.
- Keep patient supine for 1 hour after parenteral administration and advise him to get up slowly.
- Don't withdraw drug abruptly unless required by severe adverse reactions. After abrupt withdrawal from long-term therapy patient may experience gastritis, nausea, vomiting, dizziness, and tremors.
- Withhold dose and notify prescriber if patient develops jaundice, symptoms of blood dyscrasia (fever, sore throat, infection, cellulitis, weakness), persistent extrapyramidal reactions (longer than a few hours), or any such reaction in pregnancy or in children.
- Dystonic reactions may be treated with diphenhydramine.

Patient teaching

- Warn patient to avoid activities that require alertness or good psychomotor coordination until CNS effects of drug are known. Drowsiness and dizziness usually subside after first few weeks.
- Instruct patient to avoid alcohol while taking drug.
- Tell patient to notify prescriber if urine retention or constipation occurs.
- Tell patient to use sunblock and wear protective clothing to avoid photosensitivity reactions. Chlorpromazine causes higher risk of photosensitivity than other drugs in its class.
- Tell patient to use sugarless gum or hard candy to relieve dry mouth.
- Tell patient not to stop taking drug suddenly but to take it exactly as prescribed and not to double doses to compensate for missed ones.
- Instruct patient about fluids that are appropriate for diluting concentrate, and show dropper technique for measuring dose. Warn patient to avoid spilling liquid on skin because it may cause rash and irritation.
- Advise patient that injection stings.

Evaluation

- Patient has reduced signs and symptoms.
- Patient maintains physical mobility throughout drug therapy.
- Patient and family state understanding of drug therapy.

chlorpropamide

(klor-PROH-puh-mighd)

Apo-Chlorpropamide ♦, Diabinese, Novo-Propamide ♦

Pharmacologic class: sulfonylurea
Therapeutic class: antidiabetic
Pregnancy risk category: C

Indications and dosages

▶ **Adjunct to diet to lower glucose level in patients with type 2 (non–insulin-dependent) diabetes mellitus.** *Adults:* 250 mg P.O. daily with breakfast or in divided doses if GI disturbances occur. First dosage increased after 5 to 7 days because of extended duration of action; then increased q 3 to 5 days by 50 to 125 mg, if needed, to maximum of 750 mg daily. Some

patients with mild diabetes respond well to dosages of 100 mg or less daily.
Adults older than age 65: Initially, 100 to 125 mg P.O. daily.
▶ **To change from S.C. insulin to oral therapy.** *Adults:* If insulin dosage is less than 40 units daily, insulin stopped and oral therapy started as above. If insulin dosage is 40 units or more daily, oral therapy started as above with insulin reduced 50%. Insulin dosage reduced further based on patient response.

Contraindications and precautions

- Contraindicated in patients hypersensitive to drug; in patients with type 1 (insulin-dependent) diabetes mellitus or diabetes that can be adequately controlled by diet; and in patients with type 2 diabetes complicated by ketosis, acidosis, diabetic coma, major surgery, severe infections, or severe trauma.
- Use cautiously in debilitated patients, malnourished patients, and patients with porphyria or impaired hepatic or renal function.

Lifespan: In pregnant or breast-feeding women, use is contraindicated. In children, safety of drug hasn't been established. In elderly patients, use cautiously.

Adverse reactions

CV: facial flushing.
GI: nausea, heartburn, vomiting.
GU: tea-colored urine.
Hematologic: ***thrombocytopenia, aplastic anemia, agranulocytosis.***
Metabolic: ***prolonged hypoglycemia, dilutional hyponatremia.***
Skin: rash, pruritus, .
Other: allergic reactions, disulfiram-like reactions.

Interactions

Drug-drug. *Anabolic steroids, chloramphenicol, clofibrate, guanethidine, MAO inhibitors, phenylbutazone, salicylates, sulfonamides:* May increase hypoglycemic activity. Monitor glucose level.
Beta blockers, clonidine: May prolong hypoglycemic effect and mask symptoms of hypoglycemia. Use together cautiously and monitor glucose levels.
Corticosteroids, glucagon, rifampin, thiazide diuretics: May decrease hypoglycemic response. Monitor glucose level.
Hydantoins: May increase levels of hydantoins. Monitor patient closely.
Oral anticoagulants: May increase hypoglycemic activity or enhance anticoagulant effect. Monitor glucose level, PT, and INR. Monitor patient for bleeding.
Drug-herb. *Aloe, bilberry leaf, bitter melon, burdock, dandelion, fenugreek, garlic, ginseng:* May improve glucose control and allow reduced dosage of oral antidiabetic. Tell patient to discuss use of herbal remedies with prescriber before using them.
Drug-lifestyle. *Alcohol use:* May cause disulfiram-like reaction. Discourage use together.

Effects on lab test results

- May increase BUN, creatinine, alkaline phosphatase, bilirubin, AST, LDH, and cholesterol levels. May decrease glucose and sodium levels.
- May decrease hemoglobin, hematocrit, and WBC, platelet, and granulocyte counts.

Pharmacokinetics

Absorption: Absorbed readily from GI tract.
Distribution: Unknown, although it's highly protein-bound.
Metabolism: About 80% of drug is metabolized by liver.
Excretion: Excreted in urine. Rate of excretion depends on urinary pH; it increases in alkaline urine and decreases in acidic urine. *Half-life:* 36 hours.

Route	Onset	Peak	Duration
P.O.	1 hr	3-6 hr	< 60 hr

Pharmacodynamics

Chemical effect: Unknown. A sulfonylurea that may stimulate insulin release from pancreatic beta cells, reduce glucose output by liver, and increase peripheral sensitivity to insulin. Also exerts antidiuretic effect in patients with diabetes insipidus.
Therapeutic effect: Lowers glucose level; also promotes water excretion in patients with diabetes insipidus.

Available forms

Tablets: 100 mg, 250 mg

NURSING PROCESS

Assessment
- Assess patient's diabetes mellitus before therapy.
- Monitor drug's effectiveness by checking patient's glucose level regularly and monitoring patient for signs and symptoms of hyperglycemia, which may indicate drug is ineffective.
- Monitor patient's hemoglobin A1C regularly.
- Monitor alkaline phosphatase levels routinely. Progressive increases may indicate need to discontinue drug.
- Be alert for adverse reactions and drug interactions. Be aware that adverse effects of chlorpropamide, especially hypoglycemia, may be more frequent or severe than with some other sulfonylureas because of its long duration of action.
- If hypoglycemia occurs, monitor patient closely for at least 3 to 5 days.
- Evaluate patient's and family's knowledge of drug therapy.

Nursing diagnoses
- Ineffective health maintenance related to hyperglycemia
- Risk for injury related to drug-induced hypoglycemia
- Deficient knowledge related to drug therapy

Planning and implementation
- Give once-daily doses with breakfast; divided doses are usually given before morning and evening meals.
- Notify prescriber if glucose level remains elevated or frequent episodes of hypoglycemia occur.
- Treat hypoglycemic reaction with oral form of rapid-acting glucose if patient can swallow or with glucagon or I.V. glucose if patient can't swallow. Give complex carbohydrate snack when patient is awake and determine cause of reaction.

ALERT: Don't confuse chlorpropamide with chlorpromazine.

Patient teaching
- Instruct patient about nature of disease; importance of following therapeutic regimen; adhering to specific diet, weight loss, exercise, and personal hygiene program; and avoiding infection. Explain how and when to monitor glucose level, and teach recognition of and intervention for hypoglycemia and hyperglycemia.
- Make sure patient understands that therapy relieves symptoms but doesn't cure disease.
- Tell patient not to change dosage without prescriber's consent and to report abnormal blood or urine glucose test results.
- Instruct patient to carry candy or other simple sugars to treat mild hypoglycemic episodes. Severe episodes may need hospital treatment.
- Advise patient not to take other medications, including OTC drugs, without first checking with prescriber.
- Advise patient to avoid alcohol. Chlorpropamide-alcohol flush is characterized by facial flushing, light-headedness, headache, and occasional breathlessness. Even very small amounts of alcohol can produce this reaction.
- Advise patient to wear or carry medical identification indicating that he has diabetes.
- Teach patient about hypoglycemia; symptoms may be especially difficult to recognize in elderly patients and in patients taking beta blockers.

Evaluation
- Patient's glucose level is normal with drug therapy.
- Patient doesn't experience injury as a result of drug-induced hypoglycemia.
- Patient and family state understanding of drug therapy.

chlorzoxazone
(klor-ZOKS-uh-zohn)
Paraflex, Parafon Forte DSC, Remular-S

Pharmacologic class: benzoxazole derivative
Therapeutic class: skeletal muscle relaxant
Pregnancy risk category: C

Indications and dosages
▶ **Adjunct in acute, painful musculoskeletal conditions.** *Adults:* 250 to 750 mg P.O. t.i.d. or q.i.d.

Contraindications and precautions
- Contraindicated in patients hypersensitive to drug and in those with impaired hepatic function.

• Use cautiously in patients with history of drug allergies.

Lifespan: In pregnant or breast-feeding women, use cautiously.

Adverse reactions

CNS: *drowsiness, dizziness, light-headedness,* malaise, headache, overstimulation, tremor.
GI: anorexia, nausea, vomiting, heartburn, abdominal distress, constipation, diarrhea.
GU: urine discoloration (orange or purple-red).
Hematologic: anemia, ***agranulocytosis.***
Hepatic: hepatic dysfunction.
Skin: urticaria, redness, itching, petechiae, bruising.
Other: ***anaphylaxis.***

Interactions

Drug-drug. *CNS depressants:* May increase CNS depression. Avoid using together.
Drug-lifestyle. *Alcohol use:* May increase CNS depression. Discourage using together.

Effects on lab test results

• May increase AST, ALT, alkaline phosphatase, and bilirubin levels.
• May decrease granulocyte count, hemoglobin, and hematocrit.

Pharmacokinetics

Absorption: Rapid and complete.
Distribution: Widely distributed in body.
Metabolism: Metabolized in liver to inactive metabolites.
Excretion: Excreted in urine as glucuronide metabolite. *Half-life:* 1 to 2 hours.

Route	Onset	Peak	Duration
P.O.	1 hr	1-2 hr	3-4 hr

Pharmacodynamics

Chemical effect: Unknown. Appears to modify central perception of pain without modifying pain reflexes. Blocks interneuronal activity in descending reticular activating system and in spinal cord.
Therapeutic effect: Relaxes skeletal muscles.

Available forms

Caplets: 500 mg
Tablets: 250 mg, 500 mg

NURSING PROCESS

Assessment

• Assess patient's underlying condition before therapy.
• Monitor drug's effectiveness by regularly assessing severity and frequency of muscle spasms.
• Amount of relief determines if dosage (and drowsiness) can be reduced.
• Be alert for adverse reactions and drug interactions.
• Evaluate patient's and family's knowledge of drug therapy.

Nursing diagnoses

• Acute pain related to patient's underlying condition
• Risk for injury related to drug-induced adverse CNS reactions
• Deficient knowledge related to drug therapy

Planning and implementation

• Give drug with meals or milk to prevent GI distress.
• Withhold dose and notify prescriber of unusual reactions.

Patient teaching

• Tell patient to avoid activities that require mental alertness, such as driving, until full CNS effects of drug are known.
• Advise patient to avoid combining drug with alcohol or other CNS depressants.
• Instruct patient to take drug with food or milk to prevent GI distress.
• Tell patient that drug may discolor urine orange or purple-red.
• Advise patient to follow prescriber's orders regarding physical activity.

Evaluation

• Patient reports that pain has decreased or ceased as result of chlorzoxazone therapy.
• Patient doesn't experience injury as result of drug-induced adverse CNS reactions.
• Patient and family state understanding of drug therapy.

cholestyramine

(koh-leh-STIGH-ruh-meen)
LoCHOLEST, Prevalite, Questran**, Questran Light, Questran Lite ◇

Pharmacologic class: anion exchange resin
Therapeutic class: antilipemic, bile acid sequestrant
Pregnancy risk category: C

Indications and dosages

▶ **Primary hyperlipidemia or pruritus caused by partial bile obstruction; adjunct for reduction of elevated cholesterol level in patients with primary hypercholesterolemia.** *Adults:* 4 g P.O. once or twice daily. Maintenance dosage is 8 to 16 g P.O. daily. Maximum daily dosage is 24 g P.O.

Contraindications and precautions

- Contraindicated in patients hypersensitive to bile-acid sequestering resins and in patients with complete biliary obstruction.
- Use cautiously in patients at risk for constipation and those with conditions aggravated by constipation, such as severe, symptomatic coronary artery disease.

Lifespan: In pregnant and breast-feeding women, use cautiously because of possible interference with fat-soluble vitamin absorption. In children, safety of drug hasn't been established.

Adverse reactions

GI: *constipation,* fecal impaction, hemorrhoids, *abdominal discomfort,* flatulence, *nausea,* vomiting, steatorrhea.
Metabolic: *vitamin A, D, E, and K deficiency;* hyperchloremic acidosis (with long-term use or very high dosage).
Skin: *rash;* irritation of skin, tongue, and perianal area.

Interactions

Drug-drug. *Acetaminophen, beta blockers, cardiac glycosides, corticosteroids, fat-soluble vitamins (A, D, E, and K), iron preparations, thiazide diuretics, thyroid hormones, warfarin and other coumarin derivatives:* Reduces absorption of the drugs listed. Administer at least 2 hours apart.

Effects on lab test results

- May increase alkaline phosphatase and chloride levels.
- May decrease hemoglobin and hematocrit.

Pharmacokinetics

Absorption: Not absorbed.
Distribution: None.
Metabolism: None.
Excretion: Insoluble cholestyramine with bile acid complex is excreted in feces.

Route	Onset	Peak	Duration
P.O.	1-2 wk	Unknown	2-4 wk

Pharmacodynamics

Chemical effect: A bile-acid sequestrant that combines with bile acid to form insoluble compound that's excreted. The liver must synthesize new bile acid from cholesterol, which reduces low-density-lipoprotein cholesterol levels.
Therapeutic effect: Lowers cholesterol levels and relieves itching caused by partial bile obstruction.

Available forms

Powder: 78-g cans, 9-g single-dose packets. Each scoop of powder or single-dose packet contains 4 g of cholestyramine resin.

NURSING PROCESS

Assessment

- Assess patient's cholesterol level and pruritus before therapy.
- Monitor drug's effectiveness by checking cholesterol and triglyceride levels every 4 weeks or asking patient whether pruritus has diminished or abated.
- Be alert for adverse reactions and drug interactions.
- Monitor patient for fat-soluble vitamin deficiency because long-term use may be linked to deficiency of vitamins A, D, E, and K and folic acid.
- Evaluate patient's and family's knowledge of drug therapy.

Nursing diagnoses

- Risk for injury related to elevated cholesterol levels

• Constipation related to drug-induced adverse GI reactions
• Deficient knowledge related to drug therapy

Planning and implementation

• To mix powder, sprinkle on surface of preferred beverage or wet food (soup, applesauce, crushed pineapple). Let stand a few minutes, then stir to obtain uniform suspension. Mixing with carbonated beverages may result in excess foaming. Use large glass and mix slowly.
• Give drug before meals and at bedtime.
• If drug therapy is discontinued, adjust dosage of cardiac glycosides, as ordered and applicable, to avoid toxicity.
• If severe constipation develops, decrease dosage, add stool softener, or discontinue drug.
• Give all other drugs at least 1 hour before or 4 to 6 hours after cholestyramine to avoid blocking their absorption.

Patient teaching

• Instruct patient never to take drug in its dry form; esophageal irritation or severe constipation may result. Using large glass, patient should sprinkle powder on surface of preferred beverage; let mixture stand a few minutes; then stir thoroughly. The best diluents are water, milk, and juice (especially pulpy fruit juice). Mixing with carbonated beverages may result in excess foaming. After drinking this preparation, patient should swirl small additional amount of liquid in same glass and then drink it to ensure ingestion of entire dose.
• Advise patient to take all other drugs at least 1 hour before or 4 to 6 hours after cholestyramine to avoid blocking their absorption.
• Teach patient about proper dietary management of serum lipids (restricting total fat and cholesterol intake), as well as measures to control other cardiac disease risk factors.
• When appropriate, recommend weight control, exercise, and smoking cessation programs.

Evaluation

• Patient's cholesterol level is normal with drug therapy.
• Patient maintains normal bowel patterns throughout drug therapy.
• Patient and family state understanding of drug therapy.

cidofovir

(sigh-doh-FOH-veer)
Vistide

Pharmacologic class: inhibitor of viral DNA synthesis
Therapeutic class: antiviral
Pregnancy risk category: C

Indications and dosages

▶ CMV retinitis in patients with AIDS. *Adults:* 5 mg/kg I.V. infused over 1 hour once weekly for 2 consecutive weeks, followed by maintenance dosage of 5 mg/kg I.V. infused over 1 hour once q 2 weeks. Probenecid and prehydration with normal saline solution I.V. must be given at the same time and may reduce risk of nephrotoxicity. Dosage may need adjustment in patients with renal impairment.

Contraindications and precautions

• Contraindicated in patients hypersensitive to drug and in those with history of clinically severe hypersensitivity to probenecid or other sulfa-containing drugs.
• Use cautiously in patients with impaired renal function.
Lifespan: In breast-feeding women, don't give drug as intraocular injection.

Adverse reactions

CNS: *fever, asthenia, headache,* amnesia, anxiety, confusion, ***seizures,*** depression, dizziness, malaise, abnormal gait, hallucinations, insomnia, neuropathy, paresthesia, somnolence.
CV: hypotension, facial edema, orthostatic hypotension, pallor, syncope, tachycardia, vasodilation.
EENT: amblyopia, conjunctivitis, eye disorders, *ocular hypotony,* iritis, pharyngitis, retinal detachment, rhinitis, sinusitis, uveitis, abnormal vision.
GI: *nausea, vomiting, diarrhea, anorexia, abdominal pain,* dry mouth, taste perversion, colitis, constipation, tongue discoloration, dyspepsia, dysphagia, flatulence, gastritis, melena, oral candidiasis, rectal disorders, stomatitis, aphthous stomatitis, mouth ulcerations.
GU: ***nephrotoxicity,*** *proteinuria,* glycosuria, hematuria, urinary incontinence, urinary tract infection.

Hematologic: ***neutropenia, thrombocytopenia, anemia.***
Hepatic: hepatomegaly.
Metabolic: fluid imbalance, hyperglycemia, hyperlipemia, hypocalcemia, hypokalemia, weight loss, decreased bicarbonate level.
Musculoskeletal: arthralgia, myasthenia, myalgia, pain in back, chest, or neck.
Respiratory: asthma, bronchitis, cough, *dyspnea,* hiccups, increased sputum, lung disorders, pneumonia.
Skin: *rash, alopecia,* acne, skin discoloration, dry skin, herpes simplex, pruritus, sweating, urticaria.
Other: *infections, chills,* allergic reactions, ***sarcoma, sepsis.***

Interactions

Drug-drug. *Nephrotoxic drugs (such as aminoglycosides, amphotericin B, foscarnet, I.V. pentamidine):* May increase nephrotoxicity. Avoid using together.
Probenecid: Interacts with metabolism or renal tubular excretion of many drugs. Monitor patient closely.

Effects on lab test results

- May increase BUN, creatinine, urine glucose, protein levels, alkaline phosphatase, ALT, AST, and LDH levels. May decrease calcium, potassium, and bicarbonate levels.
- May decrease neutrophil and platelet counts, creatinine clearance, hemoglobin, and hematocrit.

Pharmacokinetics

Absorption: Administered I.V.
Distribution: Less than 6% plasma protein–bound.
Metabolism: Metabolized mainly by kidneys.
Excretion: Excreted by renal tubular secretion.

Route	Onset	Peak	Duration
I.V.	Unknown	Unknown	Unknown

Pharmacodynamics

Chemical effect: Selective inhibition of CMV DNA polymerase; inhibits DNA viral synthesis.
Therapeutic effect: Reduces CMV replication.

Available forms

Injection: 75 mg/ml in 5-ml ampule

NURSING PROCESS

Assessment

- Monitor WBC and neutrophil counts with differential and renal function before each dose.
- Monitor intraocular pressure, visual acuity, and ocular symptoms periodically.
- Don't use drug in patients with baseline creatinine above 1.5 mg/dl or calculated creatinine clearance of 55 ml/minute or below unless potential benefits outweigh risks. Monitor creatinine and urine protein within 48 hours before each dose and adjust dose according to renal function.
- Evaluate patient's and family's knowledge of drug therapy.

Nursing diagnoses

- Infection related to presence of virus
- Ineffective protection related to adverse renal reactions
- Deficient knowledge related to drug therapy

Planning and implementation

- Use I.V. prehydration with normal saline solution, and give probenecid with each cidofovir infusion.
- Give 1 L normal saline solution, usually over 1- to 2-hour period immediately before each cidofovir infusion.
- To prepare drug for infusion, remove appropriate amount of drug from vial using syringe, and transfer dose to an infusion bag containing 100 ml normal saline solution. Infuse entire volume I.V. at constant rate over 1 hour. Use a standard infusion pump.
- Prepare drug in a class II laminar flow biological safety cabinet.
- Cidofovir infusion admixtures should be given within 24 hours of preparation. Let drug reach room temperature before use.

Patient teaching

- Inform patient that drug doesn't cure CMV retinitis and that regular ophthalmologic follow-up examinations are needed.
- Explain that close monitoring of renal function is critical.
- Tell patient to take probenecid with food to reduce drug-related nausea and vomiting.
- Advise men to practice barrier contraception during and for 3 months after drug treatment.

Evaluation
- Patient's infection is eradicated.
- Patient doesn't experience serious renal reactions.
- Patient and family state understanding of drug therapy.

cilostazol
(sil-OS-tah-zol)
Pletal

Pharmacologic class: quinolinone phosphodiesterase inhibitor
Therapeutic class: antiplatelet drug
Pregnancy risk category: C

Indications and dosages
▶ **Reduction of symptoms of intermittent claudication.** *Adults:* 100 mg P.O. b.i.d. taken at least 30 minutes before or 2 hours after breakfast and dinner. Decrease dosage to 50 mg P.O. b.i.d during coadministration with CYP3A4- or CYP2C19-inhibiting drugs, which may interact to increase cilostazol levels.

Contraindications and precautions
- Contraindicated in patients with heart failure and in those hypersensitive to cilostazol or its components.
- Use cautiously in patients with severe underlying heart disease and with other drugs that have antiplatelet activity.

Lifespan: In breast-feeding women, avoid use. In children, safety and efficacy haven't been established.

Adverse reactions
CNS: *headache, dizziness,* vertigo.
CV: *palpitations,* tachycardia, peripheral edema.
EENT: *pharyngitis, rhinitis.*
GI: *abnormal stools, diarrhea,* dyspepsia, abdominal pain, flatulence, nausea.
Musculoskeletal: back pain, myalgia.
Respiratory: increased cough.
Other: *infection.*

Interactions
Drug-drug. *Diltiazem:* Increases cilostazol levels. Reduce cilostazol dosage to 50 mg b.i.d.
Erythromycin, other macrolides: Increases levels of cilostazol and one of the metabolites. Reduce cilostazol dosage to 50 mg b.i.d.
Omeprazole: May increase levels of active cilostazol metabolite. Reduce cilostazol dosage to 50 mg b.i.d.
Strong inhibitors of CYP3A4, such as fluconazole, fluoxetine, fluvoxamine, itraconazole, ketoconazole, miconazole, nefazodone, sertraline: Possible increased levels of cilostazol and its metabolites. Reduce cilostazol dosage to 50 mg b.i.d.
Drug-food. *Grapefruit juice:* May increase cilostazol levels. Tell patient to avoid grapefruit juice during therapy.
Drug-lifestyle. *Smoking:* May decrease cilostazol exposure by about 20%. Monitor patient closely and discourage patient from smoking.

Effects on lab test results
- May increase HDL levels. May decrease triglyceride levels.

Pharmacokinetics
Absorption: Absorption is increased by 90% when given with a high-fat meal. Absolute bioavailability is unknown.
Distribution: Drug is highly protein-bound, primarily to albumin.
Metabolism: In the liver, cytochrome P-450 enzyme system (primarily CYP3A4) extensively metabolizes the drug. There are two active metabolites, one of which accounts for at least 50% of pharmacologic activity.
Excretion: Drug is eliminated primarily through urine excretion of metabolites (74%). The remainder of the drug is eliminated in feces (20%). The half-life of cilostazol and its active metabolites is 11 to 13 hours.

Route	Onset	Peak	Duration
P.O.	Unknown	2-4 hr	Unknown

Pharmacodynamics
Chemical effect: Not fully understood. Drug is thought to inhibit the enzyme phosphodiesterase III, causing an increase of cAMP in platelets and blood vessels, thus inhibiting platelet aggregation. Cilostazol reversibly inhibits the aggregation of platelets induced by various stimuli. Drug also has a vasodilating

effect that's greatest in the femoral vascular beds.
Therapeutic effect: Reduces symptoms of intermittent claudication.

Available forms

Tablets: 50 mg, 100 mg

NURSING PROCESS

Assessment

- Obtain history of patient's underlying condition before therapy and reassess regularly thereafter.
- Cilostazol and similar drugs that inhibit the enzyme phosphodiesterase decrease the likelihood of survival in patients with class III and IV heart failure. Cilostazol is contraindicated in patients with heart failure of any severity.
- Make sure patient has a thorough physical examination before therapy starts.
- Be alert for adverse reactions and drug interactions.
- Evaluate patient's and family's knowledge of drug therapy.

Nursing diagnoses

- Acute pain related to underlying disease
- Ineffective peripheral tissue perfusion secondary to underlying disease
- Deficient knowledge related to drug therapy

Planning and implementation

- Give drug at least 30 minutes before or 2 hours after breakfast and dinner.
- Beneficial effects may not be apparent for up to 12 weeks following start of therapy.
- Dosage of cilostazol can be reduced or discontinued without such rebound effects as platelet hyperaggregability. Notify prescriber of coagulation study results.

Patient teaching

- Instruct patient to take cilostazol on an empty stomach, at least 30 minutes before or 2 hours after breakfast and dinner.
- Tell patient that the beneficial effect of cilostazol on intermittent claudication isn't likely to be noticed for 2 to 4 weeks and that it may take as long as 12 weeks.
- Instruct patient not to drink grapefruit juice while taking this drug.
- Inform patient that CV risk is unknown in patients who use the drug on a long-term basis and in patients who have severe underlying heart disease.
- Tell patient that drug may cause dizziness. Caution patient not to drive or perform other activities that require alertness until response to drug is known.

Evaluation

- Patient experiences a decrease in pain.
- Patient has adequate tissue perfusion.
- Patient and family state understanding of drug therapy.

cimetidine

(sih-MEH-tih-deen)
Tagamet, Tagamet HB†

Pharmacologic class: H_2-receptor antagonist
Therapeutic class: antiulcer agent
Pregnancy risk category: B

Indications and dosages

▶ **Duodenal ulcer (short-term treatment).** *Adults and children age 16 and older:* 800 mg P.O. h.s. Or, 400 mg P.O. b.i.d. or 300 mg q.i.d. (with meals and h.s.). Treatment continued for 4 to 6 weeks unless endoscopy shows healing. For maintenance therapy, 400 mg h.s. For parenteral therapy, 300 mg diluted to 20 ml with normal saline solution or other compatible I.V. solution by I.V. push over at least 5 minutes q 6 hours. Or, 300 mg diluted in 100 ml D_5W or other compatible I.V. solution by I.V. infusion over 15 to 20 minutes q 6 hours. Or, 300 mg I.M. q 6 hours (no dilution necessary). Parenteral dosage increased by giving 300-mg doses more frequently to maximum daily dosage of 2,400 mg as needed. Or, 900 mg/day (37.5 mg/hour) I.V. diluted in 100 to 1,000 ml of compatible solution by continuous I.V. infusion.

▶ **Active benign gastric ulceration.** *Adults:* 800 mg P.O. h.s., or 300 mg P.O. q.i.d., with meals and h.s., for up to 8 weeks.

▶ **Pathologic hypersecretory conditions (such as Zollinger-Ellison syndrome, systemic mastocytosis, and multiple endocrine adenomas).** *Adults and children age 16 and older:* 300 mg P.O. q.i.d. with meals and h.s.;

adjusted to patient needs. Maximum oral daily dosage is 2,400 mg. For parenteral therapy, 300 mg diluted to 20 ml with normal saline solution or other compatible I.V. solution by I.V. push over at least 5 minutes q 6 hours. Or, 300 mg diluted in 100 ml D_5W or other compatible I.V. solution by I.V. infusion over 15 to 20 minutes q 6 hours. Parenteral dosage increased by giving 300-mg doses more frequently to maximum daily dosage of 2,400 mg as needed.

▶ **Gastroesophageal reflux disease.** *Adults:* 800 mg P.O. b.i.d. or 400 mg q.i.d. before meals and h.s. for up to 12 weeks.

▶ **Prevention of upper GI bleeding in critically ill patients.** *Adults:* 50 mg/hour by continuous I.V. infusion for up to 7 days.

Patients with creatinine clearance below 30 ml/minute: 25 mg/hour by continuous I.V. infusion.

▶ **Heartburn.** *Adults:* 200 mg (Tagamet HB only) P.O. with water as symptoms occur, or as directed, up to b.i.d. Maximum 400 mg daily. Drug shouldn't be taken daily for more than 2 weeks.

▶ **Active upper GI bleeding, peptic esophagitis, stress ulcers‡.** *Adults:* 1 to 2 g I.V. or P.O. daily in four divided doses.

Contraindications and precautions

• Contraindicated in patients hypersensitive to drug.

• Use cautiously in debilitated patients because they may be more susceptible to drug-induced confusion.

Lifespan: In pregnant women, use cautiously. In breast-feeding women, drug is contraindicated. In patients younger than age 16, safety of drug hasn't been established. In elderly patients, use cautiously.

Adverse reactions

CNS: confusion, dizziness, headaches, peripheral neuropathy.

CV: ***bradycardia.***

GI: *mild and transient diarrhea.*

Hematologic: ***agranulocytosis, neutropenia, thrombocytopenia, aplastic anemia.***

Hepatic: jaundice.

Musculoskeletal: muscle pain.

Skin: acnelike rash, urticaria.

Other: hypersensitivity reactions, mild gynecomastia (if used longer than 1 month).

Interactions

Drug-drug. *Antacids:* May interfere with cimetidine absorption. Separate administration by at least 1 hour, if possible.

Lidocaine, phenytoin, propranolol, some benzodiazepines, warfarin: May inhibit hepatic microsomal enzyme metabolism of these drugs. Monitor levels of these drugs.

Drug-herb. *Pennyroyal:* May change the rate at which toxic metabolites of pennyroyal form. Discourage use while on drug therapy.

Yerba maté: May decrease clearance of yerba maté methylxanthines and cause toxicity. Tell patient to use together cautiously.

Effects on lab test results

• May increase creatinine, alkaline phosphatase, AST, and ALT levels.

• May decrease hemoglobin, hematocrit, and neutrophil, granulocyte, leukocyte, and platelet counts.

Pharmacokinetics

Absorption: 60% to 75% of oral dose is absorbed. Absorption rate but not extent may be affected by food. Degree of absorption unknown after I.M. administration.

Distribution: Distributed to many body tissues. About 15% to 20% of drug is protein-bound.

Metabolism: 30% to 40% of dose is metabolized in liver.

Excretion: Excreted primarily in urine (48% of oral dose, 75% of parenteral dose); 10% of oral dose excreted in feces. *Half-life:* 2 hours.

Route	Onset	Peak	Duration
P.O.	Unknown	45-90 min	4-5 hr
I.V.	Unknown	Immediate	Unknown
I.M.	Unknown	Unknown	Unknown

Pharmacodynamics

Chemical effect: Competitively inhibits action of H_2 at receptor sites of parietal cells, decreasing gastric acid secretion.

Therapeutic effect: Lessens upper GI irritation caused by increased gastric acid secretion.

Available forms

Injection: 150 mg/ml; 300 mg in 50 ml normal saline solution for injection

Oral liquid: 300 mg/5 ml

Tablets: 200 mg†, 300 mg, 400 mg, 800 mg

NURSING PROCESS

Assessment
• Assess patient's underlying upper GI condition before therapy and reassess regularly throughout therapy.
• Be alert for adverse reactions and drug interactions.
• Identify tablet strength when obtaining drug history.
• Monitor patient's CV status during I.V. administration; drug can cause profound bradycardia and other cardiotoxic effects when given too rapidly I.V.
• Evaluate patient's and family's knowledge of drug therapy.

Nursing diagnoses
• Impaired tissue integrity related to patient's underlying condition
• Diarrhea related to drug-induced adverse reaction
• Deficient knowledge related to drug therapy

Planning and implementation
• **P.O. use:** Give tablets with meals to ensure more consistent therapeutic effect.
• **I.V. use:** Dilute drug before direct injection and give over 5 minutes.
ALERT: Rapid I.V. injection may result in arrhythmias and hypotension. Infuse drug over at least 30 minutes to minimize risk of adverse cardiac effects.
– If cimetidine is given as continuous I.V. infusion, use infusion pump if giving in a total volume of 250 ml over 24 hours or less.
– Don't dilute with sterile water for injection.
• **I.M. use:** I.M. administration may be painful.
• Hemodialysis reduces levels of cimetidine. Schedule cimetidine dose at end of hemodialysis treatment. Adjust dosage in patients with renal failure.
ALERT: Don't confuse cimetidine with simethicone.

Patient teaching
• Remind patient taking drug once daily to take it at bedtime for best results.
• Warn patient to take drug as directed and to continue taking it even after pain subsides, to allow for adequate healing.
• Remind patient not to take antacid within 1 hour of taking drug.
• Urge patient to avoid cigarette smoking because it may increase gastric acid secretion and worsen disease.
• Instruct patient to immediately report black tarry stools, diarrhea, confusion, or rash.

Evaluation
• Patient experiences decrease in or relief of upper GI symptoms with drug therapy.
• Patient maintains normal bowel habits throughout drug therapy.
• Patient and family state understanding of drug therapy.

ciprofloxacin
(sih-proh-FLOKS-uh-sin)
Cipro, Cipro I.V., Ciproxin◇

Pharmacologic class: fluoroquinolone antibiotic
Therapeutic class: antibiotic
Pregnancy risk category: C

Indications and dosages
▶ **Mild-to-moderate urinary tract infections.** *Adults:* 250 mg P.O. or 200 mg I.V. q 12 hours.
▶ **Severe or complicated urinary tract infections; mild-to-moderate bone and joint infections; mild-to-moderate respiratory tract infections; mild to moderate skin and skin-structure infections; infectious diarrhea, intra-abdominal infection.** *Adults:* 500 mg P.O. or 400 mg I.V. q 12 hours.
▶ **Severe or complicated bone or joint infections; severe respiratory tract infections; severe skin and skin-structure infections.** *Adults:* 750 mg P.O. q 12 hours. Or, 400 mg I.V. q 8 hours.
▶ **Treatment of mild-to-moderate acute sinusitis caused by *Haemophilus influenzae, Streptococcus pneumoniae,* or *Moraxella catarrhalis;* mild-to moderate-chronic bacterial prostatitis caused by *Escherichia coli* or *Proteus mirabilis.*** *Adults:* 400 mg I.V. infusion given over 60 minutes q 12 hours.
▶ **Febrile neutropenia.** *Adults:* 400 mg I.V. q 8 hours (given in conjunction with piperacillin sodium [50 mg/kg I.V. q 4 hours, not to exceed 24 g daily]) for 7 to 14 days.
▶ **Inhalation anthrax (post-exposure).** *Adults:* 400 mg I.V. q 12 hours initially until

susceptibility tests are known, then switch to 500 mg P.O. b.i.d. when patient's condition improves.
Children: 10 mg/kg I.V. q 12 hours, then switch to 15 mg/kg P.O. q 12 hours when patient's clinical condition improves. Don't exceed 800 mg I.V. daily or 1,000 mg P.O. daily.
For all patients: Also use one or two additional antimicrobials. Treat for a total of 60 days (I.V. and P.O. combined).
▶ **Cutaneous anthrax‡.** *Adults:* 500 mg P.O. b.i.d. for 60 days.
Children: 10 to 15 mg/kg q 12 hours, not to exceed 1,000 mg daily, for 60 days.
▶ **Uncomplicated gonorrhea‡.** *Adults:* 250 mg P.O. as a single dose.
▶ ***Neisseria meningitidis* in nasal passages‡.** *Adults:* 500 to 750 mg P.O. as a single dose, or 250 mg P.O. b.i.d. for 2 days, or 500 mg P.O. b.i.d. for 5 days.

Contraindications and precautions

• Contraindicated in patients hypersensitive to fluoroquinolones.
• Use cautiously in patients with CNS disorders, such as severe cerebral arteriosclerosis or seizure disorders, and in those at increased risk for seizures. May cause CNS stimulation.
• Immunocompromised patients should receive the usual doses and regimens for anthrax.
Lifespan: In pregnant women, use cautiously. Pregnant women should receive the usual doses and regimens for anthrax. In breast-feeding women, use is contraindicated. In children, safety of drug for indications other than anthrax hasn't been established.

Adverse reactions

CNS: headache, restlessness, tremor, lightheadedness, confusion, hallucinations, ***seizures,*** paresthesia.
CV: thrombophlebitis.
GI: *nausea, diarrhea,* vomiting, abdominal pain or discomfort, oral candidiasis.
GU: crystalluria, interstitial nephritis.
Hematologic: eosinophilia, ***leukopenia, neutropenia, thrombocytopenia.***
Musculoskeletal: arthralgia, joint or back pain, joint inflammation, joint stiffness, achiness, neck or chest pain.
Skin: *rash,* photosensitivity, ***Stevens-Johnson syndrome.***
Other: burning, pruritus, erythema, swelling with I.V. administration.

Interactions

Drug-drug. *Antacids containing aluminum hydroxide or magnesium hydroxide, iron supplements, sucralfate:* May decrease ciprofloxacin absorption. Give ciprofloxacin 2 hours before or 6 hours after antacid.
Probenecid: May elevate level of ciprofloxacin. Monitor patient for toxicity.
Theophylline: May increase theophylline levels and prolong theophylline half-life. Monitor levels of theophylline and observe patient for adverse effects.
Drug-herb. *Yerba maté:* May decrease clearance of yerba maté methylxanthines and cause toxicity. Discourage using together.
Drug-lifestyle. *Caffeine:* May increase effect of caffeine. Monitor patient.

Effects on lab test results

• May increase BUN, creatinine, ALT, AST, alkaline phosphatase, bilirubin, LDH, and GGT levels.
• May increase eosinophil count. May decrease WBC, neutrophil, and platelet counts.

Pharmacokinetics

Absorption: About 70%. Food delays rate of absorption but not extent.
Distribution: Drug is 20% to 40% protein-bound. CSF levels are only about 10% of plasma levels.
Metabolism: Unknown but probably hepatic. Four metabolites have been identified; each has less antimicrobial activity than parent compound.
Excretion: Primarily renal. *Half-life:* About 4 hours.

Route	Onset	Peak	Duration
P.O.	Unknown	0.5-2.3 hr	Unknown
I.V.	Immediate	Immediate	Unknown

Pharmacodynamics

Chemical effect: Unknown. Bactericidal effects may result from inhibition of bacterial DNA gyrase and prevention of replication in susceptible bacteria.
Therapeutic effect: Kills susceptible bacteria, including *Campylobacter jejuni, Citrobacter diversus, Citrobacter freundii, Enterobacter*

cloacae, E. coli, H. influenzae, Klebsiella pneumoniae, Morganella morganii, P. mirabilis, P. vulgaris, Providencia stuartii, P. rettgeri, Pseudomonas aeruginosa, Serratia marcescens, Shigella flexneri, S. sonnei, Staphylococcus aureus, S. epidermidis, Streptococcus faecalis, and *S. pyogenes.*

Available forms

Infusion (premixed): 200 mg in 100 ml D_5W, 400 mg in 200 ml D_5W
Injection: 200 mg, 400 mg
Tablets: 250 mg, 500 mg, 750 mg

NURSING PROCESS

Assessment

- Assess patient's infection before therapy and reassess regularly throughout therapy.
- Obtain specimen for culture and sensitivity tests before first dose. Therapy may begin pending results.
- Be alert for adverse reactions and drug interactions.
- Monitor patient's hydration status if adverse GI reactions occur.
- Evaluate patient's and family's knowledge of drug therapy.

Nursing diagnoses

- Infection related to presence of bacteria susceptible to drug
- Risk for deficient fluid volume related to drug-induced adverse GI reactions
- Deficient knowledge related to drug therapy

Planning and implementation

- **P.O. use:** Give oral form 2 hours after meal or 2 hours before or 6 hours after taking antacids, sucralfate, or products that contain iron (such as vitamins with mineral supplements). Food doesn't affect absorption but may delay peak levels.
- **I.V. use:** Dilute drug using D_5W or normal saline solution for injection to final concentration of 1 to 2 mg/ml before use. Infuse slowly (over 1 hour) into large vein.
- Dosage adjustments are necessary in patients with renal dysfunction.
- Have patient drink plenty of fluids to reduce risk of crystalluria.
- Additional antimicrobials for anthrax multidrug regimens can include rifampin, vancomycin, penicillin, ampicillin, chloramphenicol, imipenem, clindamycin, and clarithromycin.
- Steroids may be considered as adjunctive therapy for anthrax patients with severe edema and for meningitis, based on experience with bacterial meningitis of other etiologies.
- Ciprofloxacin and doxycycline are first-line therapy for anthrax. Amoxicillin 500 mg P.O. t.i.d. for adults and 80 mg/kg daily divided q 8 hours for children is an option for completion of therapy after clinical improvement.
- Follow current CDC recommendations for anthrax.

Patient teaching

- Tell patient to take drug 2 hours after meal and to take prescribed antacids at least 2 hours after taking drug.
- Advise patient to drink plenty of fluids to reduce risk of crystalluria.
- Warn patient to avoid hazardous tasks that require alertness, such as driving, until CNS effects of drug are known.
- Advise patient to avoid caffeine while taking drug because of potential for cumulative caffeine effects.
- Advise patient that hypersensitivity reactions may occur even after first dose. If he notices rash or other allergic reactions, tell him to stop drug immediately and notify prescriber.
- Instruct patient to either discontinue breastfeeding during treatment or take a different drug. Drug appears in breast milk.

Evaluation

- Patient is free from infection after drug therapy.
- Patient maintains adequate hydration throughout drug therapy.
- Patient and family state understanding of drug therapy.

cisplatin (cis-platinum)

(sis-PLAH-tin)
Platinol-AQ

Pharmacologic class: alkylating agent (not specific to cell cycle phase)
Therapeutic class: antineoplastic
Pregnancy risk category: D

Indications and dosages

▶ **Adjunct therapy in metastatic testicular cancer.** *Adults:* 20 mg/m² I.V. daily for 5 days. Repeat q 3 weeks for three cycles or longer.
▶ **Adjunct therapy in metastatic ovarian cancer.** *Adults:* 100 mg/m² I.V.; repeat q 4 weeks. Or, 50 to 100 mg/m² I.V. once q 4 weeks with cyclophosphamide.
▶ **Advanced bladder cancer.** *Adults:* 50 to 70 mg/m² I.V. q 3 to 4 weeks. Patients who have received other antineoplastic drugs or radiation therapy should receive 50 mg/m² q 4 weeks.
▶ **Head and neck cancer‡.** *Adults:* 80 to 120 mg/m² I.V. once q 3 weeks.
▶ **Cervical cancer‡.** *Adults:* 50 mg/m² I.V. once q 3 weeks.
▶ **Non-small-cell lung cancer‡.** *Adults:* 75 to 100 mg/m² I.V. q 3 to 4 weeks with other drugs.
▶ **Brain tumor‡.** *Children:* 60 mg/m² I.V. for 2 days q 3 to 4 weeks.
▶ **Osteogenic sarcoma or neuroblastoma‡.** *Children:* 90 mg/m² I.V. q 3 weeks.
▶ **Advanced esophageal cancer‡.** *Adults:* 50 to 120 mg/m² I.V. once q 3 to 4 weeks when used alone, or 75 to 100 mg/m² I.V. once q 3 to 4 weeks when used with chemotherapy.

Contraindications and precautions

• Contraindicated in patients hypersensitive to drug or other platinum-containing compounds. Also contraindicated in patients with severe renal disease, hearing impairment, or myelosuppression.
Lifespan: In pregnant women, use with extreme caution and only when absolutely necessary because fetal harm may occur. In breast-feeding patients, use isn't recommended. In children, safety of drug hasn't been established.

Adverse reactions

CNS: *peripheral neuritis, **seizures**.*
EENT: *tinnitus, hearing loss.*
GI: *nausea and vomiting beginning 1 to 4 hours after dose and lasting 24 hours,* diarrhea, loss of taste, metallic taste.
GU: *more prolonged and* SEVERE RENAL TOXICITY *with repeated courses of therapy.*
Hematologic: MILD MYELOSUPPRESSION, ***leukopenia, thrombocytopenia, anemia,*** nadirs in circulating platelet and WBC counts on days 18 to 23 with recovery by day 39.
Metabolic: *hypomagnesemia,* hypokalemia, hypocalcemia.
Other: ***anaphylactoid reaction.***

Interactions

Drug-drug. *Aminoglycoside antibiotics:* May cause additive nephrotoxicity. Monitor renal function studies carefully.
Bumetanide, ethacrynic acid, furosemide: May cause additive ototoxicity. Avoid using together.
Phenytoin: May decrease phenytoin levels. Monitor serum levels.

Effects on lab test results

• May increase uric acid levels. May decrease magnesium, potassium, calcium, sodium, and phosphate levels.
• May decrease hemoglobin, hematocrit, and WBC, RBC, and platelet counts.

Pharmacokinetics

Absorption: Administered I.V.
Distribution: Distributed widely into tissues, with highest levels in kidneys, liver, and prostate. Drug doesn't readily cross blood-brain barrier. Drug is extensively and irreversibly bound to plasma and tissue proteins.
Metabolism: Unknown.
Excretion: Excreted primarily unchanged in urine. *Half-life:* Initial phase, 25 to 79 minutes; terminal phase, 58 to 78 hours.

Route	Onset	Peak	Duration
I.V.	Unknown	Unknown	Several days

Pharmacodynamics

Chemical effect: Probably cross-links strands of cellular DNA and interferes with RNA transcription, causing imbalance of growth that leads to cell death.
Therapeutic effect: Kills selected cancer cells.

Available forms

Injection: 0.5 mg/ml, 1 mg/ml

NURSING PROCESS

Assessment

• Assess patient's underlying neoplastic disease before therapy and reassess regularly throughout therapy.

• Monitor CBC, electrolyte levels (especially potassium and magnesium), platelet count, and renal function studies before initial and subsequent dosages.
• To detect permanent hearing loss, obtain audiometry test results before initial dose and subsequent courses.
• Be alert for adverse reactions and drug interactions.
• Evaluate patient's and family's knowledge of drug therapy.

Nursing diagnoses
• Ineffective health maintenance related to presence of neoplastic disease
• Ineffective protection related to drug-induced adverse reactions
• Deficient knowledge related to drug therapy

Planning and implementation
• Follow facility policy to reduce risks because preparation and administration of parenteral form of drug is linked to carcinogenic, mutagenic, and teratogenic risks for personnel.
• Give mannitol or furosemide boluses or infusions before and with cisplatin infusion to maintain diureses of 100 to 400 ml/hour during and for 24 hours after therapy. Prehydration and diuresis may reduce renal toxicity and ototoxicity significantly.
• Manufacturer recommends giving drug as I.V. infusion in 2 L normal saline solution with 37.5 g mannitol over 6 to 8 hours.
• Dilute with D_5W in one-third normal saline solution for injection or dextrose 5% in half-normal saline solution for injection. Solutions are stable for 20 hours at room temperature. Don't refrigerate.
• Infusions are most stable in chloride-containing solutions (such as normal, half-normal, and one-quarter saline solution).
• Don't use needles or I.V. administration sets that contain aluminum because it will displace platinum, causing loss of potency and formation of black precipitate.
• Renal toxicity is cumulative. Renal function must return to normal before next dose can be given.
• Dosage shouldn't be repeated unless platelet count is over 100,000/mm^3, WBC count is over 4,000/mm^3, creatinine level is under 1.5 mg/dl, or BUN level is under 25 mg/dl.
• Check current protocol. Some clinicians use I.V. sodium thiosulfate to minimize toxicity.
• Give antiemetics as ordered. Nausea and vomiting may be severe and protracted (up to 24 hours). Provide I.V. hydration until patient can tolerate adequate oral intake.
• Ondansetron, granisetron, and high-dose metoclopramide have been used effectively to prevent and treat nausea and vomiting. Some clinicians combine metoclopramide with dexamethasone and antihistamines, or ondansetron or granisetron with dexamethasone.
• Delayed-onset vomiting (3 to 5 days after treatment) has been reported. Patients may need prolonged antiemetic treatment.
• To prevent hypokalemia, potassium chloride (10 to 20 mEq/L) is commonly added to I.V. fluids before and after cisplatin therapy.
• Immediately give epinephrine, corticosteroids, or antihistamines for anaphylactoid reactions.
ALERT: Don't confuse cisplatin with carboplatin.

Patient teaching
• Warn patient to watch for signs of infection (fever, sore throat, fatigue) and bleeding (easy bruising, nosebleeds, bleeding gums, melena). Tell him to take his temperature daily.
• Tell patient to report tinnitus immediately.
• Instruct patient to avoid OTC products that contain aspirin.
• Teach patient to record intake and output on daily basis and to report edema or decrease in urine output.
• Encourage patient to notify prescriber if any concerns arise during drug therapy.

Evaluation
• Patient exhibits positive response to cisplatin therapy according to follow-up diagnostic studies.
• Patient doesn't experience permanent injury as a result of drug-induced adverse reactions.
• Patient and family state understanding of drug therapy.

citalopram hydrobromide
(sih-TAL-oh-pram high-droh-BROH-mighd)
Celexa

Pharmacologic class: selective serotonin reuptake inhibitor (SSRI)
Therapeutic class: antidepressant
Pregnancy risk category: C

Indications and dosages

▶ **Depression.** *Adults:* Initially, 20 mg P.O. once daily, increasing to maximum dose of 40 mg daily after no less than 1 week.
Elderly patients: 20 mg P.O. daily with adjustment to 40 mg daily only for nonresponding patients.

Contraindications and precautions

• Contraindicated in patients taking MAO inhibitors or within 14 days of stopping MAO inhibitor therapy. Also contraindicated in patients hypersensitive to drug, its ingredients, or escitalopram.
• Use cautiously in patients with history of mania, seizures, suicidal ideation, hepatic impairment, or renal impairment.
Lifespan: In nursing infants, potential for serious adverse reactions exists because drug appears in breast milk. In children, safety and effectiveness haven't been established. In elderly patients, reduced dosage is indicated.

Adverse reactions

CNS: fever, tremor, somnolence, insomnia, anxiety, agitation, dizziness, paresthesia, migraine, impaired concentration, amnesia, depression, apathy, ***suicide attempt,*** confusion, fatigue.
CV: tachycardia, orthostatic hypotension, hypotension.
EENT: rhinitis, sinusitis, abnormal accommodation.
GI: *nausea, dry mouth,* diarrhea, anorexia, dyspepsia, vomiting, abdominal pain, increased saliva, taste perversion, flatulence, weight changes, increased appetite.
GU: dysmenorrhea, amenorrhea, ejaculation disorder, impotence, polyuria.
Musculoskeletal: arthralgia, myalgia.
Respiratory: upper respiratory tract infection, cough.
Skin: rash, pruritus, *increased sweating.*
Other: yawning, decreased libido.

Interactions

Drug-drug. *Carbamazepine:* May increase citalopram clearance. Monitor patient.
CNS drugs: May increase CNS effects. Use together cautiously.
Drugs that inhibit cytochrome P-450 isoenzymes 3A4 (such as fluconazole) and 2C19 (such as omeprazole): May decrease citalopram clearance. Monitor patient for toxicity.
Imipramine, other tricyclic antidepressants: May increase level of imipramine metabolite desipramine by about 50%. Use together cautiously.
Lithium: May enhance serotonergic effect of citalopram. Use cautiously and monitor lithium levels.
MAO inhibitors: Serious, sometimes fatal, reactions may occur. Don't use drug with MAO inhibitors or within 14 days of stopping MAO inhibitor use.
Sumatriptan: May cause weakness, hyperreflexia, and incoordination. Monitor patient closely.
Warfarin: PT increased by 5%. Monitor patient carefully.
Drug-herb. *St. John's wort:* Serotonin levels may rise too high, causing serotonin syndrome. Discourage using together.

Effects on lab test results

None reported.

Pharmacokinetics

Absorption: Absolute bioavailability is 80%.
Distribution: About 80% bound to plasma proteins.
Metabolism: Metabolized primarily by the liver.
Excretion: About 10% of drug is recovered in urine. *Half-life:* 35 hours.

Route	Onset	Peak	Duration
P.O.	Unknown	4 hr	Unknown

Pharmacodynamics

Chemical effect: Probably enhances serotonergic activity in CNS resulting from its in-

hibition of CNS neuronal reuptake of serotonin.
Therapeutic effect: Relieves depression.

Available forms

Oral solution: 10 mg/5 ml
Tablets: 10 mg, 20 mg, 40 mg

NURSING PROCESS

Assessment

- Assess patient's underlying condition before therapy and reassess regularly thereafter.
- Check vital signs regularly for decreased blood pressure or tachycardia.
- Closely supervise high-risk patients at start of drug therapy.
- Evaluate patient's and family's knowledge of drug therapy.

Nursing diagnoses

- Risk for injury related to patient's underlying condition
- Ineffective coping related to patient's underlying condition
- Deficient knowledge related to drug therapy

Planning and implementation

ALERT: Don't start citaprolam therapy within 14 days of MAO inhibitor therapy.

- A reduced dosage is indicated for those with hepatic impairment.

ALERT: Don't confuse Celexa with Celebrex or Cerebyx.

Patient teaching

- Inform patient that, although improvement may occur within 1 to 4 weeks, he should continue therapy as prescribed.
- Instruct patient to exercise caution when operating hazardous machinery, including automobiles, because psychoactive drugs can impair judgment, thinking, and motor skills.
- Advise patient to consult prescriber before taking other prescription drugs, OTC medicines, or herbal remedies.

ALERT: If the patient wishes to switch from an SSRI to St. John's wort, tell him to wait a few weeks for the SSRI to leave his system before he starts the herb. Urge him to ask his prescriber for advice.

- Warn patient not to consume alcohol during therapy.
- Instruct woman of childbearing age to use birth control during drug therapy and to notify prescriber immediately if she suspects pregnancy.

Evaluation

- Patient's safety is maintained.
- Patient's condition is improved with drug.
- Patient and family state understanding of drug therapy.

clarithromycin

(klah-rith-roh-MIGH-sin)
Biaxin, Biaxin XL

Pharmacologic class: macrolide
Therapeutic class: antibiotic
Pregnancy risk category: C

Indications and dosages

▶ **Pharyngitis or tonsillitis caused by *Streptococcus pyogenes*.** *Adults:* 250 mg P.O. q 12 hours for 10 days.
Children: 7.5 mg/kg P.O. daily q 12 hours for 10 days.

▶ **Acute maxillary sinusitis caused by *Streptococcus pneumoniae, Haemophilus influenzae,* or *Moraxella catarrhalis*.** *Adults:* 500 mg P.O. q 12 hours for 14 days or two 500-mg tablets P.O. (extended-release) daily for 14 days.
Children: 7.5 mg/kg P.O. daily q 12 hours for 10 days.

▶ **Acute exacerbations of chronic bronchitis caused by *M. catarrhalis, S. pneumoniae;* community-acquired pneumonia (CAP) caused by *H. influenzae, S. pneumoniae, Mycoplasma pneumoniae,* or *C. pneumoniae*.** *Adults:* 250 mg P.O. q 12 hours for 7 days (*H. influenzae*) or 7 to 14 days (others).

▶ **Acute exacerbations of chronic bronchitis caused by *H. influenzae or H. parainfluenzae*.** *Adults:* 500 mg P.O. q 12 hours for 7 days (*H. parainfluenzae*) or 7 to 14 days (*H. influenzae*).

▶ **Acute exacerbations of chronic bronchitis caused by *M. catarrhalis, S. pneumoniae; H. parainfluenzae,* or *H. influenzae*.** *Adults:* Two 500-mg tablets P.O. (extended-release) daily for 7 days.

▶ **Mild-to-moderate community-acquired pneumonia (CAP), caused by *H. influenzae, H. parainfluenzae, Moraxella catarrhalis, S. pneumoniae, Chlamydia pneumoniae,* and *Mycoplasma pneumoniae.*** *Adults:* Two 500-mg tablets (extended-release) P.O. daily for 7 days.

▶ **Community-acquired pneumonia (CAP), caused by *S. pneumoniae, Chlamydia pneumoniae,* and *Mycoplasma pneumoniae.*** *Children:* 7.5 mg/kg P.O. q 12 hours for 10 days.

▶ **Uncomplicated skin and skin-structure infections caused by *Staphylococcus aureus* or *S. pyogenes.*** *Adults:* 250 mg P.O. q 12 hours for 7 to 14 days. *Children:* 7.5 mg/kg P.O. q 12 hours for 10 days.

▶ **Acute otitis media caused by *H. influenzae, M. catarrhalis,* or *S. pneumoniae.*** *Children:* 7.5 mg/kg P.O. q 12 hours for 10 days.

▶ **Prophylaxis and treatment of disseminated infection due to *Mycobacterium avium* complex.** *Adults:* 500 mg P.O. b.i.d.
Children: 7.5 mg/kg P.O. b.i.d. up to 500 mg b.i.d.

▶ ***H. pylori* eradication to reduce risk of duodenal ulcer recurrence.** *Adults:* 500 mg clarithromycin with 30 mg lansoprazole and 1 g amoxicillin, all given q 12 hours for 10 to 14 days. Or, 500 mg clarithromycin with 20 mg omeprazole and 1 g amoxicillin, given q 12 hours for 10 days. Alternatively, dual therapy with 500 mg clarithromycin q 8 hours and 40 mg omeprazole once daily for 14 days. Or, dual therapy with 500 mg clarithromycin q 12 hours or q 8 hours and 400 mg ranitidine bismuth citrate q 12 hours for 14 days.
Patients with renal impairment: Decrease dose by 50% in patients with a creatinine clearance of less than 30 ml/minute. Dual therapy for *H. pylori* with clarithromycin and ranitidine bismuth citrate is not recommended in patients with a creatinine clearance of less than 25 ml/minute.

Contraindications and precautions

- Contraindicated in patients hypersensitive to clarithromycin, erythromycin, or other macrolides and in those also taking pimozide or other drugs that prolong the QT interval or cause arrhythmias.
- Use cautiously in patients with hepatic or renal impairment.

Lifespan: In pregnant and breast-feeding women, use cautiously. In infants younger than age 6 months, safety of drug hasn't been established.

Adverse reactions

CNS: headache.
CV: ***arrhythmias.***
GI: ***pseudomembranous colitis,*** diarrhea, nausea, abnormal taste, dyspepsia, abdominal pain or discomfort, vomiting (in children).
Hematologic: ***leukopenia,*** coagulation abnormalities.
Skin: rash (in children).

Interactions

Drug-drug. *Carbamazepine, theophylline:* May increase levels of these drugs. Monitor blood levels.
Disopyramide, pimozide, quinidine: May cause torsades de pointes. Monitor ECG for QT prolongation.
Oral anticoagulants: Increased anticoagulant effects. Monitor PT and INR carefully.

Effects on lab test results

- May increase BUN, ALT, AST, alkaline phosphatase, bilirubin, GGT, and LDH levels.
- May increase PT and INR. May decrease WBC count.

Pharmacokinetics

Absorption: Rapid.
Distribution: Widely distributed.
Metabolism: Drug's major metabolite has significant antimicrobial activity.
Excretion: Excreted in urine. *Half-life:* 5 to 6 hours with 250 mg q 12 hours; 7 hours with 500 mg q 12 hours.

Route	Onset	Peak	Duration
P.O.	Unknown	2-3 hr	Unknown
P.O. (extended-release)	Unknown	5-6 hr	Unknown

Pharmacodynamics

Chemical effect: Binds to 50S subunit of bacterial ribosomes, blocking protein synthesis; bacteriostatic or bactericidal, depending on concentration.
Therapeutic effect: Hinders or kills susceptible bacteria.

Available forms

Suspension: 125 mg/5 ml, 250 mg/5 ml
Tablets: 250 mg, 500 mg
Tablets (extended-release): 500 mg

NURSING PROCESS

Assessment

- Assess patient's infection before therapy and reassess regularly throughout therapy.
- Obtain urine specimen for culture and sensitivity tests before first dose. Therapy may begin pending results.
- Be alert for adverse reactions and drug interactions.
- Monitor patient's hydration status if adverse GI reactions occur.
- Evaluate patient's and family's knowledge of drug therapy.

Nursing diagnoses

- Infection related to presence of bacteria susceptible to drug
- Risk for deficient fluid volume related to drug-induced adverse GI reactions
- Deficient knowledge related to drug therapy

Planning and implementation

- Give drug without regard to meals and may be taken with milk.

ALERT: Don't confuse or interchange Biaxin XL (extended-release) with Biaxin (immediate release).

Patient teaching

- Tell patient to take all of drug, as prescribed, even after he feels better.
- Tell patient to notify prescriber if adverse reactions occur.
- Tell patient not to chew or crush extended-release tablets.

Evaluation

- Patient is free from infection after drug therapy.
- Patient maintains adequate hydration throughout drug therapy.
- Patient and family state understanding of drug therapy.

clemastine fumarate

(KLEM-eh-steen FYU-muh-rayt)
Dayhist-1, Tavist

Pharmacologic class: ethanolamine-derivative antihistamine
Therapeutic class: antihistamine (H_1-receptor antagonist)
Pregnancy risk category: B

Indications and dosages

▶ **Rhinitis, allergy symptoms.** *Adults and children older than 12:* 1.34 mg (1 mg clemastine) P.O. q 12 hours, or 2.68 mg P.O. once daily to t.i.d. as needed.
Children ages 6 to 12: 0.67 to 1.34 mg P.O. b.i.d.

Contraindications and precautions

- Contraindicated in patients hypersensitive to drug or other antihistamines of similar chemical structure and in patients with acute asthma attacks.
- Use cautiously in patients with angle-closure glaucoma, increased intraocular pressure, hyperthyroidism, CV disease, hypertension, bronchial asthma, prostatic hyperplasia, bladder-neck obstruction, pyloroduodenal obstruction, and stenosing peptic ulcerations.

Lifespan: In pregnant women, use cautiously. In breast-feeding women and in neonates and premature infants, drug is contraindicated. Children younger than age 12 should use only as directed by prescriber. In elderly patients, use cautiously.

Adverse reactions

CNS: *sedation, drowsiness,* ***seizures.***
CV: hypotension, palpitations, tachycardia.
GI: epigastric distress, anorexia, nausea, vomiting, constipation, *dry mouth.*
GU: urine retention.
Hematologic: hemolytic anemia, ***thrombocytopenia, agranulocytosis.***
Respiratory: thick bronchial secretions.
Skin: rash, urticaria.
Other: ***anaphylaxis.***

Interactions

Drug-drug. *CNS depressants:* May increase sedation. Use together cautiously.

MAO inhibitors: May increase anticholinergic effects. Don't use together.
Drug-lifestyle. *Sun exposure:* Photosensitivity may occur. Urge patient to avoid sun exposure and wear protective clothing and sunblock.

Effects on lab test results

• May decrease hemoglobin, hematocrit, and platelet and granulocyte counts.

Pharmacokinetics

Absorption: Absorbed readily from GI tract.
Distribution: Unknown.
Metabolism: Metabolized extensively, probably in liver.
Excretion: Excreted in urine.

Route	Onset	Peak	Duration
P.O.	15-60 min	2-4 hr	12 hr

Pharmacodynamics

Chemical effect: Competes with histamine for H_1-receptor sites on effector cells. Prevents, but doesn't reverse, histamine-mediated responses.
Therapeutic effect: Relieves allergy symptoms.

Available forms

Syrup: 0.67 mg/5 ml
Tablets: 1.34 mg†, 2.68 mg

NURSING PROCESS

Assessment

• Assess patient's allergy condition before therapy and reassess regularly thereafter.
• Monitor blood counts during long-term therapy; watch for signs of blood dyscrasias.
• Be alert for adverse reactions and drug interactions.
• Evaluate patient's and family's knowledge of drug therapy.

Nursing diagnoses

• Ineffective health maintenance related to patient's underlying allergy condition
• Ineffective airway clearance related to drug-induced thickening of bronchial secretions
• Deficient knowledge related to drug therapy

Planning and implementation

• Give drug with food or milk to minimize GI distress.
• Notify prescriber if tolerance occurs because another antihistamine may need to be substituted for clemastine.

Patient teaching

• Warn patient to avoid driving or other activities that require alertness until drug's CNS effects are known.
• Warn patient to avoid alcohol while taking drug; it will increase drowsiness.
• Tell patient that coffee or tea may reduce drowsiness and that sugarless gum, hard candy, or ice chips may relieve dry mouth.
• Advise patient to stop drug 4 days before allergy skin tests to preserve accuracy of tests.
• Tell patient to notify prescriber if tolerance develops because different antihistamine may need to be prescribed.
• Advise patient to increase fluid intake, if not contraindicated, to help thin bronchial secretions.

Evaluation

• Patient's allergy symptoms are relieved with drug therapy.
• Patient maintains adequate air exchange throughout drug therapy.
• Patient and family state understanding of drug therapy.

clindamycin hydrochloride

(klin-duh-MIGH-sin high-droh-KLOR-ighd)
Dalacin C ◆ ◇

clindamycin palmitate hydrochloride

Cleocin Pediatric

clindamycin phosphate

Pharmacologic class: lincomycin derivative
Therapeutic class: antibiotic
Pregnancy risk category: B

Indications and dosages

▶ **Infections caused by sensitive staphylococci, streptococci, pneumococci, *Bac-***

***teroides, Fusobacterium, Clostridium perfringens,* and other sensitive aerobic and anaerobic organisms.** *Adults:* 150 to 450 mg P.O. q 6 hours. Or, 600 to 2,700 mg I.M. or I.V. q 6, 8, or 12 hours. Single I.M. doses should not exceed 600 mg. No greater than 1.2 g I.V. should be given in a 1-hour period. Maximum adult I.V. dose is 4.8 g daily.
Children ages 1 month to 16 years: 8 to 25 mg/kg P.O. daily in three or four equally divided doses. Or, 20 to 40 mg/kg I.M. or I.V. daily, in three or four equally divided doses, or 350 to 450 mg/m^2 daily.
Neonates younger than 1 month old: 15 to 20 mg /kg I.V. daily in three or four equally divided doses.

▶ **Endocarditis prophylaxis for dental procedures in patients allergic to penicillin.** *Adults:* 600 mg P.O. 1 hour before procedure or 600 mg I.V. 30 minutes before procedure.
Children ages 1 month to 16 years: 20 mg/kg P.O. 1 hour before procedure or 20 mg/kg I.V. 30 minutes before procedure (not to exceed adult dosage).

▶ **Acne vulgaris.** *Adults:* Apply a thin film of topical solution, gel, or lotion to affected areas b.i.d.

▶ ***Pneumocystis carinii* pneumonia‡.** *Adults:* 600 mg I.V. q 6 hours. Or, 300 to 450 mg P.O. q.i.d. With primaquine, give 15 to 30 mg P.O. daily.

▶ **Toxoplasmosis (cerebral or ocular) in immunocompromised patients‡.** *Adults:* 300 to 450 mg P.O. q 6 to 8 hours with pyrimethamine (25 to 75 mg once daily) and leucovorin (10 to 25 mg once daily).
Infants and children age 16 and younger: 20 to 30 mg/kg P.O. daily in four divided doses with oral pyrimethamine (1 mg/kg daily) and oral leucovorin (5 mg once q 3 days).

Contraindications and precautions

- Contraindicated in patients hypersensitive to antibiotic congener lincomycin.
- Use cautiously in patients with renal or hepatic disease, asthma, history of GI disease, or significant allergies.

Lifespan: Breast-feeding women should use a different feeding method during drug therapy. In neonates, use cautiously.

Adverse reactions

CV: thrombophlebitis.
GI: unpleasant or bitter taste, *nausea,* vomiting, abdominal pain, ***diarrhea, pseudomembranous colitis,*** esophagitis, flatulence, anorexia, *bloody or tarry stools, dysphagia.*
Hematologic: ***transient leukopenia,*** eosinophilia, ***thrombocytopenia.***
Skin: maculopapular rash, urticaria.
Other: ***anaphylaxis;*** *pain,* induration, *sterile abscess* (I.M. injection); erythema, pain (I.V. administration).

Interactions

Drug-drug. *Erythromycin:* May block clindamycin site of action. Don't use together.
Kaolin: May decrease absorption of oral clindamycin. Separate administration times.
Neuromuscular blockers: May potentiate neuromuscular blockade. Monitor patient closely.
Drug-food. *Diet foods with sodium cyclamate:* May decrease drug level. Discourage using together.

Effects on lab test results

- May increase bilirubin, AST, and alkaline phosphatase levels.
- May increase eosinophil count. May decrease WBC and platelet counts.

Pharmacokinetics

Absorption: Rapid and almost complete when administered P.O. Drug is absorbed well after I.M. administration.
Distribution: Distributed widely to most body tissues and fluids (except CSF). Drug is about 93% bound to plasma proteins.
Metabolism: Metabolized partially to inactive metabolites.
Excretion: About 10% of clindamycin dose is excreted unchanged in urine; rest is excreted as inactive metabolites. *Half-life:* 2.5 to 3 hours.

Route	Onset	Peak	Duration
P.O.	Unknown	45-60 min	Unknown
I.V.	Immediate	Immediate	Unknown
I.M.	Unknown	3 hr	Unknown

Pharmacodynamics

Chemical effect: Inhibits bacterial protein synthesis by binding to 50S subunit of ribosome.
Therapeutic effect: Hinders or kills susceptible bacteria. Spectrum of activity includes most aerobic gram-positive cocci and anaero-

bic gram-negative and gram-positive organisms. It's considered first-line drug in treating *Bacteroides fragilis* and most other gram-positive and gram-negative anaerobes. It's also effective against *Mycoplasma pneumoniae, Leptotrichia buccalis,* and some gram-positive cocci and bacilli.

Available forms

clindamycin hydrochloride
Capsules: 75 mg, 150 mg, 300 mg
clindamycin palmitate hydrochloride
Oral solution: 75 mg/5 ml
clindamycin phosphate
Injection: 150 mg/ml

NURSING PROCESS

Assessment

- Assess patient's infection before therapy and reassess regularly throughout therapy.
- Obtain urine specimen for culture and sensitivity tests before first dose. Therapy may begin pending results.
- Monitor renal, hepatic, and hematopoietic functions during prolonged therapy.
- Be alert for adverse reactions and drug interactions.
- Monitor patient's hydration status if adverse GI reactions occur.
- Evaluate patient's and family's knowledge about drug therapy.

Nursing diagnoses

- Infection related to presence of bacteria susceptible to drug
- Risk for deficient fluid volume related to drug-induced adverse GI reactions
- Deficient knowledge related to drug therapy

Planning and implementation

- **P.O. use:** Don't refrigerate reconstituted oral solution because it will thicken. Drug is stable for 2 weeks at room temperature.
– Give capsule form with full glass of water to prevent dysphagia.
- **I.V. use:** Check I.V. site daily for phlebitis and irritation. For I.V. infusion, dilute each 300 mg in 50 ml solution, and give no faster than 30 mg/minute (over 10 to 60 minutes). Never give undiluted as bolus.
- **I.M. use:** Inject drug deeply. Rotate sites. Warn patient that I.M. injection may be painful. Doses over 600 mg per injection aren't recommended.
– I.M. injection may raise CK in response to muscle irritation.

ALERT: Don't give opioid antidiarrheals to treat drug-induced diarrhea; they may prolong and worsen diarrhea.

ALERT: Because of an association with severe and even fatal colitis, reserve clindamycin for serious infections only.

Patient teaching

- Advise patient taking capsule form to take with full glass of water to prevent dysphagia.
- Teach patient how to store oral solution.
- Instruct patient to take drug for as long as prescribed, exactly as directed.
- Tell patient to take entire amount prescribed even after he feels better.
- Warn patient that I.M. injection may be painful.
- Instruct patient to report diarrhea and to avoid self-treatment because of the risk of life-threatening pseudomembranous colitis.
- Tell patient receiving drug I.V. to report discomfort at infusion site.

Evaluation

- Patient is free from infection after drug therapy.
- Patient maintains adequate hydration during drug therapy.
- Patient and family state understanding of drug therapy.

clobetasol propionate

(kloh-BAY-tah-sol PRO-pee-uh-nayt)
Cormax, Dermovate*, Embeline E, Temovate, Temovate Emollient, Olux

Pharmacologic class: topical adrenocorticoid
Therapeutic class: anti-inflammatory
Pregnancy risk category: C

Indications and dosages

▶ **Inflammation and pruritic manifestations of moderate-to-severe corticosteroid-responsive dermatoses (including dermatoses of the scalp).** *Adults:* Apply a thin layer to affected skin areas b.i.d., once in the morning and once at night. Limit treatment to

14 days, with no more than 50 g cream or ointment or 50 ml lotion (25 mg total) weekly.

Contraindications and precautions

- Contraindicated in patients hypersensitive to corticosteroids. Also contraindicated for the treatment of acne, rosacea, perioral dermatitis, or as monotherapy for the treatment of widespread plaque psoriasis.
- Use extreme caution when applying drug to face, groin, or axillae, because these areas are at an increased risk for atrophic changes.
- Use cautiously in patients with glaucoma and diabetes.

Lifespan: In pregnant women, avoid use because of possibility of teratogenic effects. In breast-feeding women, use cautiously and avoid applying to breasts because it's unknown whether drug appears in breast milk. In patients younger than age 12, drug isn't recommended. In elderly patients a beginning treatment at the low end of the dosage range and adjusting carefully is recommended.

Adverse reactions

GU: glucosuria.
Metabolic: hyperglycemia.
Skin: burning and stinging sensation, pruritus, irritation, dryness and cracking, erythema, folliculitis, perioral dermatitis, allergic contact dermatitis, hypopigmentation, hypertrichosis, acneiform eruptions, skin atrophy, telangiectasia (dilatation of capillaries), striae.
Other: ***hypothalamic-pituitary-adrenal axis suppression,*** Cushing's syndrome, numbness of fingers.

Interactions

None reported.

Effects on lab test results

- May increase glucose level.
- May cause false-positive results with the ACTH stimulation, a.m. plasma cortisol, and urinary-free cortisol tests.

Pharmacokinetics

Absorption: Dependent on the potency of the preparation, the amount applied, the nature of the skin at the application site, and the use of occlusive dressings. Absorption increases in areas of skin damage, inflammation, or occlusion. Some systemic absorption of topical steroids occurs, especially through the oral mucosa.
Distribution: After topical application, clobetasol is distributed throughout the local skin. Any drug absorbed into the circulation is rapidly removed from the blood and distributed into muscle, liver, skin, intestines, and kidneys.
Metabolism: After topical administration, drug is metabolized primarily in the skin. The small amount absorbed into systemic circulation is metabolized primarily in the liver to inactive compounds.
Excretion: Clobetasol and its metabolites are excreted in the liver and in the bile. Inactive metabolites are excreted by the kidneys, primarily as glucuronides and sulfates, but also as unconjugated products. Small amounts of the metabolites are also excreted in the urine and feces.

Route	Onset	Peak	Duration
Topical	Unknown	Unknown	Unknown

Pharmacodynamics

Chemical effect: Drug is effective because of anti-inflammatory, antipruritic, and vasoconstrictive actions; however, the exact mechanism of its actions is unknown. Clobetasol is a high-potency group I fluorinated corticosteroid that's usually reserved for the management of severe dermatoses that haven't responded satisfactorily to a less potent formulation.
Therapeutic effect: Decreases inflammation and itching.

Available forms

Cream: 0.05%
Foam: 0.05%
Gel: 0.05%
Ointment: 0.05%
Solution: 0.05%

NURSING PROCESS

Assessment

- Assess patient before and during therapy. Topical corticosteroid therapy may adversely affect and exacerbate symptoms in patients with diabetes or glaucoma.
- Monitor patient for adverse effects of corticosteroid therapy.
- Observe frequently for skin atrophy if applied to face, groin, or axillae.

- Obtain ACTH stimulation test, and a.m. plasma cortisol testing and urine free cortisol testing to monitor patient for HPA axis suppression.
- Evaluate patient's and family's knowledge of topical corticosteroid therapy.

Nursing diagnoses

- Risk of infection related to prolonged and very potent corticosteroid therapy.
- Impaired skin integrity related to underlying skin disease process
- Situational low self-esteem due to underlying skin disease process
- Deficient knowledge related to topical corticosteroid therapy.

Planning and implementation

- Not recommended for treatment over 2 weeks.
- For external use only. Avoid rubbing eyes during and after application. If drug gets into the eyes, flush affected eye with copious amounts of water.
- Don't dispense directly onto hand because cream will begin to melt immediately upon contact with warm skin.
- Apply sparingly in light film; then massage into skin gently until foam disappears.
- Don't use occlusive dressings or bandages. Don't cover or wrap treated area unless instructed by prescriber.
- If skin infection develops, institute appropriate antifungal or antibacterial treatment. If infection does not respond promptly to treatment, discontinue until infection has been controlled adequately.
- Discontinue drug and notify prescriber if irritation, skin infection, striae, or atrophy occurs.
- Drug can suppress HPA axis at doses as low as 2 g daily. If HPA axis suppression, attempt to withdraw drug, reduce dosage, or substitute a less potent steroid.
- Cushing's syndrome may have deleterious effects, especially in children because they have a larger skin surface area. Monitor carefully.
- If no improvement within 2 weeks, reassess diagnoses.
- Don't refrigerate. Store drug at room temperature, at or less than 25° C.

Patient teaching

- Advise patient that drug is for external use only and to avoid contact with eyes.
- Instruct patient to use medication only as prescribed and only for the indications specified.
- Teach patient proper application of the topical steroid to affected area(s). Explain that occlusive dressings aren't recommended and may increase absorption and skin atrophy.
- Inform patient of potential adverse reactions, signs and symptoms of infection, or failure to heal; urge patient to notify prescriber immediately.
- Warn patient not to use drug for longer than 14 days.
- Caution patient that drug is flammable and to avoid flames or smoking during and immediately after application.
- Instruct patients using Olux foam that the contents are under pressure and container shouldn't be punctured or incinerated. Also, tell patient not to expose to heat or store at temperatures above 120° F (49° C).

Evaluation

- Patient doesn't suffer from any infection caused by drug therapy.
- Patient is relieved of symptoms and remains free from any adverse effects due to drug therapy.
- Patient's self-esteem increases as patient's skin improves.
- Patient and family state understanding of topical corticosteroid therapy.

clofibrate

(kloh-FIGH-brayt)
Atromid-S

Pharmacologic class: fibric acid derivative
Therapeutic class: antilipemic
Pregnancy risk category: C

Indications and dosages

▶ **Hyperlipidemia.** *Adults:* 1 g P.O. b.i.d. Some patients may respond to lower doses as assessed by lipid monitoring.

▶ **Diabetes insipidus‡.** *Adults:* 1.5 to 2 g P.O. daily in divided doses.

Patients with renal impairment: Reduce dosage frequency to q 12 to 18 hours.

Contraindications and precautions

• Contraindicated in patients hypersensitive to drug and patients with significant hepatic or renal dysfunction or primary biliary cirrhosis.
• Use cautiously in patients with peptic ulcer.
Lifespan: In pregnant or breast-feeding women, drug is contraindicated. In children, safety of drug hasn't been established.

Adverse reactions

CNS: fatigue, weakness, fever.
CV: ***arrhythmias.***
GI: *nausea, diarrhea, vomiting,* stomatitis, *dyspepsia,* flatulence.
GU: impotence, ***acute renal failure.***
Hematologic: ***leukopenia,*** anemia.
Hepatic: gallstones.
Metabolic: *weight gain, polyphagia.*
Musculoskeletal: myalgia and arthralgia resembling flulike syndrome.
Skin: rash, urticaria, pruritus, dry skin and hair.
Other: decreased libido.

Interactions

Drug-drug. *Furosemide, sulfonylureas:* Clofibrate may potentiate effects of these drugs. Monitor patient closely.
Lovastatin, pravastatin, simvastatin: Risk of myositis, rhabdomyolysis, and renal failure. Avoid using together.
Oral anticoagulants: May potentiate anticoagulant effects of warfarin or dicumarol. Decrease anticoagulant dosage and monitor patient for bleeding.
Oral contraceptives, rifampin: May antagonize clofibrate's lipid-lowering effect. Monitor lipids.
Probenecid: May increase clofibrate effect. Monitor patient for toxicity.

Effects on lab test results

• May increase liver function test values. May decrease WBC count, hemoglobin, and hematocrit.

Pharmacokinetics

Absorption: Absorption is slow but complete from GI tract.
Distribution: Distributed into extracellular space as its active form, clofibric acid, which is up to 98% protein-bound.
Metabolism: Drug is hydrolyzed by serum enzymes to clofibric acid, which is metabolized by liver.
Excretion: 20% of clofibric acid is excreted unchanged in urine; 70% is eliminated in urine as conjugated metabolite. *Half-life:* 6 to 25 hours.

Route	Onset	Peak	Duration
P.O.	2-5 days	3 wk	≤ 3 wk

Pharmacodynamics

Chemical effect: Unknown. Appears to inhibit biosynthesis of cholesterol at early stage.
Therapeutic effect: Lowers cholesterol levels.

Available forms

Capsules: 500 mg

NURSING PROCESS

Assessment

• Assess patient's cholesterol level before therapy.
• Monitor drug's effectiveness by evaluating cholesterol and triglyceride levels regularly during therapy.
• Monitor renal and hepatic function, blood counts, and electrolyte and glucose levels.
• Be alert for adverse reactions and drug interactions.
• Evaluate patient's and family's knowledge of drug therapy.

Nursing diagnoses

• Risk for injury related to elevated cholesterol
• Impaired urinary elimination related to drug-induced acute renal failure
• Deficient knowledge related to drug therapy

Planning and implementation

• Drug may be discontinued if liver function tests show steady rise.
• Drug typically is discontinued if lipids aren't lowered significantly within 3 months.

Patient teaching

• Teach patient about proper dietary management of serum lipids (restricting total fat and cholesterol intake) as well as measures to control other cardiac disease risk factors. When

*Liquid form contains alcohol. **May contain tartrazine. ♦ Canada ◇ Australia †OTC ‡Off-label use

appropriate, recommend weight control, exercise, and smoking cessation programs.
- Advise patient to report flulike symptoms immediately because they may indicate rhabdomyolysis-induced renal failure.

Evaluation
- Patient's cholesterol level is normal with drug therapy.
- Patient maintains normal urine elimination pattern throughout drug therapy.
- Patient and family state understanding of drug therapy.

clomiphene citrate
(KLOH-meh-feen SIGH-trayt)
Clomid, Serophene

Pharmacologic class: chlorotrianisene derivative
Therapeutic class: ovulation stimulant
Pregnancy risk category: X

Indications and dosages
▶ **Induction of ovulation.** *Adults:* 50 mg P.O. daily for 5 days starting on day 5 of menstrual cycle if bleeding occurs (first day of menstrual flow is day 1), or at any time if patient hasn't had recent uterine bleeding. If ovulation doesn't occur, may increase dose to 100 mg P.O. daily for 5 days as soon as 30 days after previous course. Repeat until conception occurs or until three courses of therapy are completed.
▶ **Male infertility‡.** *Adults:* 50 to 400 mg P.O. daily for 2 to 12 months.

Contraindications and precautions
- Contraindicated in patients with undiagnosed abnormal genital bleeding, ovarian cyst not caused by polycystic ovarian syndrome, hepatic disease or dysfunction, uncontrolled thyroid or adrenal dysfunction, or organic intracranial lesion (such as pituitary tumor).

Lifespan: In pregnant women, drug is contraindicated.

Adverse reactions
CNS: headache, restlessness, insomnia, dizziness, light-headedness, depression, fatigue, tension, *vasomotor flushes.*
CV: hypertension.
EENT: blurred vision, diplopia, scotoma, photophobia.
GI: nausea, vomiting, bloating, distention.
GU: urinary frequency and polyuria; *ovarian enlargement and cyst formation,* which regress spontaneously when drug is stopped.
Metabolic: *hyperglycemia,* increased appetite, weight gain.
Skin: reversible alopecia, urticaria, rash, dermatitis.
Other: *hot flushes, breast discomfort.*

Interactions
None significant.

Effects on lab test results
- May increase glucose level.

Pharmacokinetics
Absorption: Absorbed readily from GI tract.
Distribution: May undergo enterohepatic recirculation or may be stored in body fat.
Metabolism: Metabolized by liver.
Excretion: Excreted principally in feces via biliary elimination. *Half-life:* About 5 days.

Route	Onset	Peak	Duration
P.O.	Unknown	Unknown	Unknown

Pharmacodynamics
Chemical effect: Appears to stimulate release of pituitary gonadotropins, follicle-stimulating hormone, and luteinizing hormone. This results in maturation of ovarian follicle, ovulation, and development of corpus luteum.
Therapeutic effect: Causes women to ovulate.

Available forms
Tablets: 50 mg

NURSING PROCESS

Assessment
- Assess patient's underlying condition before therapy.
- Monitor drug's effectiveness by assessing ovulation through biphasic body temperature measurement, postovulatory urinary levels of pregnanediol, estrogen excretion, and changes in endometrial tissues.
- Be alert for adverse reactions.

• Evaluate patient's and family's knowledge of drug therapy.

Nursing diagnoses

• Excess fluid volume related to drug-induced fluid retention
• Sexual dysfunction related to underlying condition
• Deficient knowledge related to drug therapy

Planning and implementation

• Prepare administration instructions for patient: Begin daily dosage on fifth day of menstrual flow for 5 consecutive days.
• No more than three courses of therapy should be given to attempt conception.

Patient teaching

• Tell patient about risk of multiple births with drug use; risk increases with higher doses.
• Teach patient how to take and chart basal body temperature and to ascertain whether ovulation has occurred.
• Reassure patient that ovulation typically occurs after first course of therapy. If pregnancy doesn't occur, course of therapy may be repeated twice.
ALERT: Advise patient to stop drug and contact prescriber immediately if pregnancy is suspected because drug may have teratogenic effect.
• Advise patient to stop drug and contact prescriber immediately if abdominal symptoms or pain occurs because these may indicate ovarian enlargement or ovarian cyst.
• Tell patient to immediately report signs of impending visual toxicity, such as blurred vision, diplopia, scotoma, or photophobia.
• Warn patient to avoid hazardous activities until CNS effects of drug are known. Drug may cause dizziness or visual disturbances.

Evaluation

• Patient is free from fluid retention at end of drug therapy.
• Patient ovulates with drug therapy.
• Patient and family state understanding of drug therapy.

clomipramine hydrochloride

(kloh-MIH-pruh-meen high-droh-KLOR-ighd)
Anafranil

Pharmacologic class: tricyclic antidepressant (TCA)
Therapeutic class: antiobsessional agent
Pregnancy risk category: C

Indications and dosages

▶ **Obsessive-compulsive disorder.** *Adults:* Initially, 25 mg P.O. daily in divided doses with meals, gradually increased to 100 mg daily during first 2 weeks. Thereafter, increased to maximum dosage of 250 mg daily in divided doses with meals as needed. After dosage adjustment, total daily dosage may be given h.s. *Adolescents and children:* Initially, 12.5 mg P.O. b.i.d. with meals, gradually increased to daily maximum of 3 mg/kg or 100 mg P.O., whichever is smaller. Maximum daily dosage is 3 mg/kg or 200 mg, whichever is smaller; may be given h.s. after adjustment. Periodic reassessment and adjustment are necessary.

Contraindications and precautions

• Contraindicated in patients hypersensitive to drug or other TCAs, in those who have taken MAO inhibitors within the previous 14 days, and in patients in acute recovery period after MI.
• Use cautiously in patients with history of seizure disorders or with brain damage of varying etiology; in those receiving other seizure threshold–lowering drugs; in patients at risk for suicide; in patients with history of urine retention or angle-closure glaucoma, increased intraocular pressure, CV disease, impaired hepatic or renal function, or hyperthyroidism; in patients with tumors of the adrenal medulla; in patients receiving thyroid drug or electroconvulsive therapy; and in those undergoing elective surgery.
Lifespan: In pregnant and breast-feeding women, use cautiously.

Adverse reactions

CNS: *somnolence, tremors, dizziness,* headache, insomnia, *nervousness, myoclonus, fatigue, EEG changes, seizures,* extrapyramidal reactions, asthenia, aggressiveness.

CV: orthostatic hypotension, palpitations, tachycardia.
EENT: otitis media in children, abnormal vision, laryngitis, pharyngitis, rhinitis.
GI: dry mouth, constipation, nausea, dyspepsia, diarrhea, anorexia, abdominal pain, eructation, *nausea.*
GU: *urinary hesitancy,* urinary tract infection, dysmenorrhea, *ejaculation failure,* impotence.
Hematologic: anemia, ***bone marrow suppression.***
Metabolic: increased appetite, weight gain.
Musculoskeletal: myalgia.
Skin: *diaphoresis,* rash, pruritus, photosensitivity, dry skin.
Other: *altered libido.*

Interactions

Drug-drug. *Barbiturates:* May decrease TCA levels. Monitor patient for decreased antidepressant effect.
Cimetidine, methylphenidate: May increase TCA levels. Monitor patient for enhanced antidepressant effect.
Clonidine, epinephrine, norepinephrine: May increase hypertensive effect. Use with caution and monitor blood pressure.
CNS depressants: Enhances CNS depression. Avoid use together.
MAO inhibitors: May cause hyperpyretic crisis, seizures, coma, or death. Don't use together.
Drug-herb. *St. John's wort:* Serotonin levels may rise too high, causing serotonin syndrome. Discourage use together.
Drug-lifestyle. *Alcohol use:* May enhance CNS depression. Discourage use together.
Sun exposure: Photosensitivity may occur. Urge patient to avoid sun exposure and wear protective clothing and sunblock.

Effects on lab test results

- May decrease hemoglobin and hematocrit.

Pharmacokinetics

Absorption: Well absorbed from the GI tract, but extensive first-pass metabolism limits bioavailability to about 50%.
Distribution: Distributed well into lipophilic tissues; about 98% bound to plasma proteins.
Metabolism: Primarily hepatic. Several metabolites have been identified; desmethylclomipramine is primary active metabolite.
Excretion: About 66% is excreted in urine; remainder in feces. *Half-life:* Parent compound, about 36 hours; desmethylclomipramine, 4 to 233 days.

Route	Onset	Peak	Duration
P.O.	≥ 2 wk	Unknown	Unknown

Pharmacodynamics

Chemical effect: Unknown but a TCA that selectively inhibits reuptake of serotonin.
Therapeutic effect: Reduces obsessive-compulsive behaviors.

Available forms

Capsules: 25 mg, 50 mg, 75 mg

NURSING PROCESS

Assessment

- Assess patient's underlying condition before therapy and reassess regularly throughout therapy.
- Evaluate patient's and family's knowledge of drug therapy.

Nursing diagnoses

- Ineffective coping related to patient's underlying condition
- Risk for injury related to drug-induced adverse reactions
- Deficient knowledge related to drug therapy

Planning and implementation

- Total daily dose may be taken at bedtime after dosage adjustment. During dosage adjustment, dosage may be divided and given with meals to minimize GI effects.
- Don't withdraw drug abruptly.
- Because hypertensive episodes have occurred during surgery in patients receiving TCAs, drug should be gradually discontinued several days before surgery.

ALERT: Don't confuse clomipramine with chlorpromazine or clomiphene; don't confuse Anafranil with enalapril, nafarelin, or alfentanil.

Patient teaching

- Warn patient to avoid hazardous activities requiring alertness and good psychomotor coordination, especially during dosage adjustment. Daytime sedation and dizziness may occur.
- Tell patient to avoid alcohol while taking drug.

• Warn patient not to withdraw drug suddenly.
• Advise patient to use sunblock, wear protective clothing, and avoid prolonged exposure to strong sunlight to prevent photosensitivity reactions.

Evaluation

• Patient's behavior and communication indicate improvement of obsessive-compulsive pattern.
• Patient doesn't experience injury from drug-induced adverse CNS reactions.
• Patient and family state understanding of drug therapy.

clonazepam
(kloh-NEH-zuh-pam)
Klonopin, Rivotril ◇ ♦

Pharmacologic class: benzodiazepine
Therapeutic class: anticonvulsant
Controlled substance schedule: IV
Pregnancy risk category: C

Indications and dosages

▶ **Lennox-Gastaut syndrome; atypical absence seizures; akinetic and myoclonic seizures.** *Adults:* Initially, not to exceed 1.5 mg P.O. t.i.d. May be increased by 0.5 to 1 mg q 3 days until seizures are controlled. If given in unequal doses, largest dose should be given h.s. Maximum daily dosage is 20 mg.
Children age 10 and younger or weighing 30 kg (66 lb) or less: Initially, 0.01 to 0.03 mg/kg P.O. daily (maximum 0.05 mg/kg daily), in two or three divided doses. Increase by 0.25 to 0.5 mg q third day to maximum maintenance dosage of 0.1 to 0.2 mg/kg daily as needed.
▶ **Status epilepticus (where parenteral form is available).** *Adults:* 1 mg by slow I.V. infusion.
Children: 0.5 mg by slow I.V. infusion.
▶ **Panic disorder.** *Adults:* Initially, 0.25 mg P.O. b.i.d.; increase to target dose of 1 mg daily after 3 days. Some patients may benefit from doses up to maximum of 4 mg daily. To achieve 4 mg daily, increase dosage in increments of 0.125 to 0.25 mg b.i.d. q 3 days as tolerated until panic disorder is controlled. Discontinue drug gradually with decrease of 0.125 mg b.i.d. q 3 days until drug is stopped.
▶ **Leg movement during sleep or as an adjunct treatment to schizophrenia‡.** *Adults:* 0.5 to 2 mg P.O. q h.s.
▶ **Parkinsonian dysarthria‡.** *Adults:* 0.25 to 0.5 mg P.O. daily.
▶ **Acute manic episodes‡.** *Adults:* 0.75 to 16 mg P.O. daily.
▶ **Multifocal tic disorders‡.** *Adults:* 1.5 to 12 mg P.O. daily.
▶ **Neuralgia ‡.** *Adults:* 2 to 4 mg P.O. daily.

Contraindications and precautions

• Contraindicated in patients hypersensitive to benzodiazepines and in those with acute angle-closure glaucoma or significant hepatic disease.
• Use cautiously in patients with mixed type of seizure because drug may precipitate generalized tonic-clonic seizures. Also, use cautiously in patients with chronic respiratory disease or open-angle glaucoma.
Lifespan: In breast-feeding women, safety of drug hasn't been established. In children, use cautiously.

Adverse reactions

CNS: *drowsiness, ataxia, behavioral disturbances* (especially in children), slurred speech, tremor, confusion, psychosis, agitation.
EENT: *increased salivation,* diplopia, nystagmus, abnormal eye movements, sore gums.
GI: constipation, gastritis, nausea, abnormal thirst.
GU: dysuria, enuresis, nocturia, urine retention.
Hematologic: ***leukopenia, thrombocytopenia,*** eosinophilia.
Metabolic: change in appetite.
Musculoskeletal: muscle weakness or pain.
Respiratory: ***respiratory depression.***
Skin: rash.

Interactions

Drug-drug. *CNS depressants:* May increase CNS depression. Monitor patient closely.
Drug-herb. *Catnip, kava, lady's slipper, lemon balm, passion flower, sassafras, skullcap, valerian:* May enhance sedative effects of clonazepam. Discourage using together.
Drug-lifestyle. *Alcohol use:* May increase CNS depression. Discourage using together.

Effects on lab test results

- May increase liver function test values and eosinophil count. May decrease WBC and platelet counts.

Pharmacokinetics

Absorption: Well absorbed from GI tract.
Distribution: Distributed widely throughout body; about 47% protein-bound.
Metabolism: Metabolized by liver to several metabolites.
Excretion: Excreted in urine. *Half-life:* 18 to 50 hours.

Route	Onset	Peak	Duration
P.O.	Unknown	1-2 hr	Unknown
I.V.	Unknown	Unknown	Unknown

Pharmacodynamics

Chemical effect: Unknown. It probably acts by facilitating effects of inhibitory neurotransmitter gamma-aminobutyric acid.
Therapeutic effect: Prevents or stops seizure activity.

Available forms

Injection: 1 mg/ml ◆
Tablets: 0.5 mg, 1 mg, 2 mg

NURSING PROCESS

Assessment

- Assess patient's seizure condition before therapy and reassess regularly thereafter.
- Monitor blood levels. Therapeutic blood level is 20 to 80 ng/ml.
- Monitor CBC and liver function tests.
- Be alert for adverse reactions and drug interactions.
- Evaluate patient's and family's knowledge of drug therapy.

Nursing diagnoses

- Risk for injury related to potential for seizure activity
- Activity intolerance related to drug-induced sedation
- Deficient knowledge related to drug therapy

Planning and implementation

- **P.O. use:** Dosage should be increased gradually.
- **I.V. use:** Give slowly by direct injection or by slow I.V. infusion. Drug may be diluted with D_5W, dextrose 2.5% in water, normal saline solution, or half-normal saline solution.
  – Mix solutions in glass bottles because drug binds to polyvinyl chloride plastics. If polyvinyl chloride infusion bags are used, give immediately and infuse at 60 ml/hour or greater.

ALERT: Never withdraw therapy suddenly because seizures may worsen. Call prescriber at once if adverse reactions develop.

- Withdrawal symptoms are similar to those of barbiturates.
- Maintain seizure precautions.

Patient teaching

- Advise patient to avoid driving or other potentially hazardous activities until CNS effects of drug are known.
- Instruct parents to monitor child's school performance because drug may interfere with attentiveness.
- Instruct patient and family never to stop drug abruptly because seizures may occur.
- Instruct patient or family to notify prescriber if oversedation or other adverse reactions develop or questions arise about drug therapy.

Evaluation

- Patient is free from seizure activity during drug therapy.
- Patient is able to meet daily activity needs.
- Patient and family state understanding of drug therapy.

clonidine hydrochloride

(KLON-uh-deen high-droh-KLOR-ighd)
Catapres, Catapres-TTS, Dixarit ◆ ◇, Duraclon

Pharmacologic class: centrally acting antiadrenergic
Therapeutic class: antihypertensive
Pregnancy risk category: C

Indications and dosages

▶ **Essential, renal, and malignant hypertension.** *Adults:* Initially, 0.1 mg P.O. b.i.d. Then, increase by 0.1 to 0.2 mg daily q week. Usual dosage range is 0.1 to 0.3 mg b.i.d.; infrequently, dosages as high as 2.4 mg daily are used. Or, transdermal patch applied to nonhairy area of intact skin on upper arm or torso q 7 days. Start with 0.1-mg system and adjust after 1 to 2 weeks with another 0.1-mg system or larger system if increases are needed to maintain normal blood pressure.

▶ **Prophylaxis for vascular headache‡.** *Adults:* 0.025 mg P.O. b.i.d. to q.i.d., up to 0.15 mg P.O. daily in divided doses.

▶ **Adjunctive therapy for nicotine withdrawal‡.** *Adults:* Initially, 0.1 mg P.O. b.i.d., then gradually increase dose by 0.1 mg daily q week, up to 0.75 mg P.O. daily, as tolerated. Alternatively, apply transdermal patch (0.1 to 0.2 mg/24 hours) and replace weekly for the first 2 or 3 weeks after smoking cessation.

▶ **Adjunctive treatment in opiate withdrawal‡.** *Adults:* 5 to 17 mcg/kg P.O. daily in divided doses for up to 10 days. Adjust dosage to avoid hypotension and excessive sedation, and slowly withdraw drug.

▶ **Adjunctive treatment of menopausal symptoms‡.** *Adults:* 0.025 to 0.2 mg P.O. b.i.d. Alternatively, apply transdermal patch (0.1 mg/24 hours) and replace weekly.

▶ **Dysmenorrhea‡.** *Adults:* 0.025 mg P.O. b.i.d. for 14 days before onset of menses and during menses.

▶ **Ulcerative colitis‡.** *Adults:* 0.3 mg P.O. t.i.d.

▶ **Diabetic diarrhea‡.** *Adults:* 0.15 to 1.2 mg P.O. daily. Or, 1 to 2 patches q week (0.3mg/24 hours).

▶ **Neuralgia‡.** *Adults:* 0.2 mg P.O. daily.

▶ **Growth delay in children‡.** *Children:* 0.0375 to 0.15 mg/m^2 P.O. daily.

▶ **Attention deficit hyperactivity disorder (ADHD)‡.** *Children:* Initially, 0.05 mg P.O. q h.s. Increase dose cautiously over 2 to 4 weeks to reach maintenance dose of 0.05 to 0.4 mg daily depending on the patient's weight and tolerance.

▶ **Severe pain.** *Adults:* Starting dose for continuous epidural infusion is 30 mcg/hour. Titrate up or down according to patient's response.

Contraindications and precautions

- Contraindicated in patients hypersensitive to drug. Transdermal form is contraindicated in patients hypersensitive to any component of adhesive layer. I.V. form is contraindicated in patients receiving anti-coagulation therapy and patients with a bleeding diathesis or injection-site infection.
- Use cautiously in patients with severe coronary insufficiency, recent MI, cerebrovascular disease, chronic renal failure, or impaired liver function.

Lifespan: In pregnant women, safety of drug hasn't been established. In breast-feeding women, use cautiously. In children, safety hasn't been established. In children with severe intractable pain from malignancy that is unresponsive to epidural or spinal opiates or other conventional analgesic techniques, I.V. form is restricted.

Adverse reactions

CNS: *anxiety, somnolence, confusion, drowsiness, dizziness, dry mouth,* fatigue, sedation, nervousness, headache, vivid dreams.
CV: orthostatic hypotension, *hypotension,* ***bradycardia, severe rebound hypertension.***
GI: *constipation, dry mouth, nausea, vomiting.*
GU: urine retention, impotence, *urinary tract infection.*
Metabolic: transient glucose intolerance.
Skin: *pruritus and dermatitis* with transdermal patch.

Interactions

Drug-drug. *CNS depressants:* May enhance CNS depression. Use together cautiously.
MAO inhibitors, tricyclic antidepressants: May decrease antihypertensive effect. Use together cautiously.
Propranolol, other beta blockers: May cause severe rebound hypertension. Monitor patient carefully.
Drug-herb. *Capsicum, yohimbe:* May reduce antihypertensive effectiveness. Discourage using together.

Effects on lab test results

- May increase glucose and CK levels.

Pharmacokinetics

Absorption: Absorbed well when given P.O. Also absorbed well percutaneously after transdermal topical administration.
Distribution: Distributed widely into body.
Metabolism: Metabolized in liver, where nearly 50% is transformed to inactive metabolites.

Excretion: About 65% of drug is excreted in urine; 20% in feces. *Half-life:* 6 to 20 hours.

Route	Onset	Peak	Duration
P.O.	15-30 min	1.5-2.5 hr	6-8 hr
I.V.	Immediate	19 min	< 4 days
Transdermal	2-3 days	2-3 days	Several days

Pharmacodynamics

Chemical effect: Thought to inhibit central vasomotor centers, thereby decreasing sympathetic outflow to heart, kidneys, and peripheral vasculature; this results in decreased peripheral vascular resistance, decreased systolic and diastolic blood pressure, and decreased heart rate.

Therapeutic effect: Lowers blood pressure.

Available forms

Injectable: 100 mg/ml
Tablets: 0.025 mg ♦, 0.1 mg, 0.2 mg, 0.3 mg
Transdermal: TTS-1 (releases 0.1 mg/24 hours), TTS-2 (releases 0.2 mg/24 hours), TTS-3 (releases 0.3 mg/24 hours)

NURSING PROCESS

Assessment

- Assess patient's blood pressure before therapy and reassess regularly thereafter.
- Antihypertensive effects of transdermal clonidine may take 2 to 3 days to become apparent. Oral antihypertensive therapy may have to be continued in interim.
- Be alert for adverse reactions and drug interactions.
- Observe patient for tolerance to drug's therapeutic effects; patient may require increased dosage.
- Periodic eye examinations are recommended.
- Monitor site of transdermal patch for dermatitis. Ask patient about pruritus.
- Evaluate patient's and family's knowledge about drug therapy.

Nursing diagnoses

- Risk for injury related to presence of hypertension
- Ineffective protection related to severe rebound hypertension caused by abrupt cessation of drug
- Deficient knowledge related to drug therapy

Planning and implementation

- Drug may be given to lower blood pressure rapidly in some hypertensive emergency situations.
- Dosage is usually adjusted to patient's blood pressure and tolerance.
- Give last dose of day at bedtime.
- **I.V. use:** Epidural clonidine is more likely to be effective in patients with neuropathic pain than somatic or visceral pain.
  – Monitor patient closely, especially during the first few days of therapy; respiratory depression or deep sedation may occur.
- **P.O. use:** Follow normal protocol.
- **Transdermal use:** To improve adherence of patch, apply adhesive overlay. Place patch at different site each week.
  – Remove transdermal patch before defibrillation to prevent arcing.
- When stopping therapy in patients receiving both clonidine and beta blocker, gradually withdraw beta blocker first to minimize adverse reactions.
- Discontinuation of clonidine for surgery isn't recommended.

Patient teaching

- Advise patient that abrupt discontinuation of drug may cause severe rebound hypertension. Reduce dosage gradually over 2 to 4 days.
- Tell patient to take last dose of day immediately before bedtime.
- Reassure patient that transdermal patch usually adheres despite showering and other routine daily activities. Instruct him on use of adhesive overlay to improve skin adherence if necessary. Also tell patient to place patch at different site each week.
- Caution patient that drug can cause drowsiness, but that tolerance to this adverse effect will develop.
- Inform patient that orthostatic hypotension can be minimized by rising slowly and avoiding sudden position changes.

Evaluation

- Patient's blood pressure is normal with drug therapy.
- Patient states understanding of need to not stop drug abruptly.
- Patient and family state understanding of drug therapy.

clopidogrel bisulfate
(kloh-PIH-doh-grel bigh-SUL-fayt)
Plavix

Pharmacologic class: inhibitor of adenosine diphosphate (ADP)-induced platelet aggregation
Therapeutic class: antiplatelet
Pregnancy risk category: B

Indications and dosages

▶ **To reduce atherosclerotic events in patients with atherosclerosis documented by recent CVA, MI, or peripheral arterial disease.** *Adults:* 75 mg P.O. daily.

▶ **To reduce atherosclerotic events in patients with acute coronary syndrome (unstable angina, non–Q-wave MI), including those managed medically and those who are to be managed with percutaneous coronary intervention (with or without stent) or coronary artery bypass graft.** *Adults:* Start therapy with a single 300-mg P.O. loading dose, then continue at 75 mg P.O. once daily. Aspirin (75 to 325 mg once daily) should be started and continued with clopidogrel.

Contraindications and precautions

- Contraindicated in patients hypersensitive to drug or its components and in those with pathologic bleeding, such as peptic ulcer or intracranial hemorrhage.
- Use cautiously in patients with hepatic impairment and in those at risk for increased bleeding from trauma, surgery, or other conditions.

Lifespan: In breast-feeding women, use is contraindicated. In children, safety and efficacy haven't been established.

Adverse reactions

CNS: headache, dizziness, fatigue, depression.
CV: chest pain, edema, hypertension.
EENT: epistaxis, rhinitis.
GI: ***hemorrhage,*** abdominal pain, dyspepsia, gastritis, constipation, diarrhea, ulcers.
GU: urinary tract infection.
Hematologic: purpura.
Musculoskeletal: arthralgia, back pain.
Respiratory: bronchitis, cough, dyspnea, upper respiratory tract infection.
Skin: *rash,* pruritus.
Other: flulike symptoms, pain.

Interactions

Drug-drug. *Aspirin, NSAIDs:* May increase risk for GI bleeding. Use together cautiously.
Heparin, warfarin: Safety hasn't been established. Use together cautiously and monitor patient for bleeding.
Drug-herb. *Dong quai, feverfew, garlic, ginger, horse chestnut, red clover:* Possible increased risk of bleeding. Monitor patient closely.

Effects on lab test results

- May decrease platelet count.

Pharmacokinetics

Absorption: Rapid.
Distribution: Highly bound to plasma protein.
Metabolism: Extensively metabolized by the liver.
Excretion: About 50% is excreted in urine and 46% in feces. *Half-life:* 8 hours.

Route	Onset	Peak	Duration
P.O.	2 hr	Unknown	5 days

Pharmacodynamics

Chemical effect: Inhibits binding of ADP to its platelet receptor, which inhibits ADP-mediated activation and subsequent platelet aggregation. Because clopidogrel acts by irreversibly modifying the platelet ADP receptor, platelets exposed to drug are affected for their lifespan.
Therapeutic effect: Prevents clot formation.

Available forms

Tablets: 75 mg

NURSING PROCESS

Assessment

- Assess current use of OTC drugs, such as aspirin or NSAIDs, and herbal remedies.
- Assess patient for increased bleeding or bruising tendencies before and during drug therapy.
- Evaluate patient's and family's knowledge of drug therapy.

Nursing diagnoses

- Risk for injury related to potential for atherosclerotic events from underlying condition
- Ineffective protection related to increased risk of bleeding
- Deficient knowledge related to drug therapy

Planning and implementation

- Platelet aggregation will return to normal 5 days after drug has been discontinued.
- Withhold drug from patients with hepatic impairment and those at increased risk for bleeding from trauma, surgery, or other pathologic conditions.

ALERT: Don't confuse Plavix (clopidogrel bisulfate) with Paxil (paroxetine).

Patient teaching

- Inform patient it may take longer than usual to stop bleeding. Tell him to refrain from activities in which trauma and bleeding may occur; encourage use of seat belt when in a car.
- Instruct patient to notify prescriber if unusual bleeding or bruising occurs.
- Tell patient to inform prescriber or dentist that he's taking drug before having surgery or starting new drug therapy.
- Inform patient that drug may be taken without regard to meals.

Evaluation

- Patient has reduced risk of CVA, MI, and vascular death.
- Patient states appropriate bleeding precautions to take.
- Patient and family state understanding of drug therapy.

clorazepate dipotassium

(klor-AYZ-eh-payt digh-po-TAH-see-um)

Apo-Clorazepate ♦, ClorazeCaps, Gen-Xene, Novoclopate ♦, Tranxene, Tranxene-SD, Tranxene T-Tab

Pharmacologic class: benzodiazepine
Therapeutic class: anxiolytic, anticonvulsant, sedative-hypnotic agent
Pregnancy risk category: D
Controlled substance schedule: IV

Indications and dosages

▶ **Acute alcohol withdrawal.** *Adults:* Day 1 dose is 30 mg P.O. initially, followed by 30 to 60 mg P.O. in divided doses; day 2 dose is 45 to 90 mg P.O. in divided doses; day 3 dose is 22.5 to 45 mg P.O. in divided doses; day 4 dose is 15 to 30 mg P.O. in divided doses; then gradually reduce dosage to 7.5 to 15 mg daily. Maximum daily dose is 90 mg.

▶ **Anxiety.** *Adults:* 15 to 60 mg P.O. daily. *Elderly patients:* Initially, 7.5 to 15 mg daily in divided doses or as a single dose.

▶ **Adjunct in partial seizure disorder.** *Adults and children older than age 12:* Maximum recommended initial dosage is 7.5 mg P.O. t.i.d. Maximum dosage increase is 7.5 mg weekly; maximum dosage is 90 mg daily.
Children ages 9 to 12: Maximum recommended initial dosage is 7.5 mg P.O. b.i.d. Maximum dosage increase is 7.5 mg weekly; maximum dosage is 60 mg daily.

Contraindications and precautions

- Contraindicated in patients hypersensitive to drug and in those with acute angle-closure glaucoma.
- Use cautiously in patients with suicidal tendencies, renal or hepatic impairment, or history of drug abuse.
- Dosage should be reduced in debilitated patients.

Lifespan: During pregnancy, especially first trimester, avoid drug. For children younger than age 9, safety of drug hasn't been established. In elderly patients, dosage should be reduced.

Adverse reactions

CNS: *drowsiness, lethargy, hangover,* fainting, restlessness, psychosis.
CV: transient hypotension.
EENT: visual disturbances.
GI: nausea, vomiting, abdominal discomfort, dry mouth.
GU: urine retention, incontinence.

Interactions

Drug-drug. *Cimetidine:* May increase sedation. Monitor patient carefully.
CNS depressants: May increase CNS depression. Avoid use together.

Digoxin: May increase levels of digoxin, increasing digoxin toxicity. Monitor patient closely.
Drug-herb. *Catnip, kava, lady's slipper, lemon balm, passion flower, sassafras, skullcap, valerian:* Sedative effects may be enhanced. Discourage use together.
Drug-lifestyle. *Alcohol use:* Increases CNS depression. Don't use together.
Smoking: May increase clearance of benzodiazepines. Monitor patient for lack of effect and discourage patient from smoking.

Effects on lab test results

- May increase liver function test values.

Pharmacokinetics

Absorption: Complete and rapid after being hydrolyzed in stomach to desmethyldiazepam.
Distribution: Distributed widely throughout body. About 80% to 95% of drug is bound to plasma protein.
Metabolism: Metabolized in liver to oxazepam.
Excretion: Inactive glucuronide metabolites are excreted in urine. *Half-life:* 30 to 200 hours.

Route	Onset	Peak	Duration
P.O.	Unknown	0.5-2 hr	Unknown

Pharmacodynamics

Chemical effect: Unknown. Drug is thought to be a benzodiazepine that facilitates action of inhibitory neurotransmitter gamma-aminobutyric acid. Depresses CNS at limbic and subcortical levels of brain and suppresses spread of seizure activity produced by epileptogenic foci in cortex, thalamus, and limbic structures.
Therapeutic effect: Relieves anxiety, prevents seizure activity, and promotes sleep and calmness.

Available forms

Capsules: 3.75 mg, 7.5 mg, 15 mg
Tablets: 3.75 mg, 7.5 mg, 11.25 mg, 15 mg, 22.5 mg

NURSING PROCESS

Assessment

- Assess patient's underlying condition before therapy and reassess regularly thereafter.
- Monitor liver, renal, and hematopoietic function studies periodically in patients receiving repeated or prolonged therapy.
- Be alert for adverse reactions and drug interactions.
- Evaluate patient's and family's knowledge of drug therapy.

Nursing diagnoses

- Anxiety related to patient's underlying condition
- Risk of injury related to drug-induced adverse CNS reactions
- Deficient knowledge related to drug therapy

Planning and implementation

- Possibility of abuse and addiction exists. Don't withdraw drug abruptly after prolonged use; withdrawal symptoms may occur.

ALERT: Don't confuse clorazepate with clofibrate.

Patient teaching

- Warn patient to avoid activities that require alertness and good psychomotor coordination until CNS effects of drug are known.
- Tell patient to avoid alcohol while taking drug.
- Suggest sugarless chewing gum or hard candy to relieve dry mouth.
- Warn patient to take drug only as directed and not to stop without prescriber's approval. Inform patient of drug's potential for dependence if taken longer than directed.

Evaluation

- Patient says he's less anxious after taking drug therapy.
- Patient doesn't experience injury as a result of drug-induced adverse CNS reactions.
- Patient and family state understanding of drug therapy.

clozapine

(KLOH-zuh-peen)
Clozaril

Pharmacologic class: tricyclic dibenzodiazepine derivative
Therapeutic class: antipsychotic
Pregnancy risk category: B

Indications and dosages

▶ **Schizophrenia in severely ill patients unresponsive to other therapies.** *Adults:* Initially, 12.5 mg P.O. once daily or b.i.d.; increase by 25 to 50 mg daily (if tolerated) to 300 to 450 mg daily by end of 2 weeks. Individual dosage based on clinical response, patient tolerance, and adverse reactions. Dosage shouldn't be increased more than once or twice weekly and shouldn't exceed 100 mg. Many patients respond to 300 to 600 mg daily, but some may need as much as 900 mg daily. Don't exceed 900 mg daily.

Use lowest recommended dose when starting therapy in geriatric patients.

Contraindications and precautions

- Contraindicated in patients with uncontrolled epilepsy, history of drug-induced agranulocytosis, myelosuppressive disorders, severe CNS depression or coma, or WBC count below 3,500/mm^3; and in those taking other drugs that suppress bone marrow function.
- Use cautiously in patients with prostatic hyperplasia or angle-closure glaucoma because clozapine has potent anticholinergic effects. Also use cautiously patients receiving general anesthesia, and patients with hepatic, renal, or cardiac disease.

Lifespan: In pregnant women, use cautiously. In breast-feeding women, use is contraindicated. In children, safety of drug hasn't been established and is not recommended in children younger than age 12. In elderly patients, use cautiously.

Adverse reactions

CNS: fever, *drowsiness, sedation, seizures,* dizziness, syncope, vertigo, headache, tremor, disturbed sleep or nightmares, restlessness, hypokinesia or akinesia, agitation, rigidity, akathisia, confusion, fatigue, insomnia, hyperkinesia, weakness, lethargy, ataxia, slurred speech, depression, myoclonus, anxiety.
CV: tachycardia, hypotension, hypertension, chest pain, ECG changes, orthostatic hypotension, ***cardiomyopathy.***
GI: dry mouth, constipation, nausea, vomiting, *excessive salivation,* heartburn, constipation.
GU: urinary frequency, urinary urgency, urine retention, incontinence, abnormal ejaculation.
Hematologic: ***leukopenia, agranulocytosis.***
Metabolic: weight gain.
Musculoskeletal: muscle pain or spasm, muscle weakness.
Skin: rash.

Interactions

Drug-drug. *Anticholinergics:* May potentiate anticholinergic effects of clozapine. Avoid use together.
Antihypertensives: May potentiate hypotensive effects. Monitor blood pressure.
Bone marrow suppressants: May increase bone marrow toxicity. Don't use together.
Digoxin, warfarin, other highly protein-bound drugs: May increase levels of these drugs. Monitor patient closely for adverse reactions.
Psychoactive drugs: May produce additive effects. Use together cautiously.
Drug-herb. *St. John's wort:* May reduce drug levels causing a loss of symptom control in patients taking an antipsychotic. Discourage use together.
Drug-food. *Caffeinated beverages:* May inhibit antipsychotic effects of clozapine. Monitor patient closely and discourage caffeine intake.
Drug-lifestyle. *Alcohol use:* May increase CNS depression. Discourage use together.

Effects on lab test results

- May decrease glucose level.
- May decrease WBC and granulocyte counts.

Pharmacokinetics

Absorption: Thought to be absorbed from GI tract.
Distribution: About 95% bound to serum proteins.
Metabolism: Nearly complete.
Excretion: About 50% of drug appears in urine and 30% in feces, mostly as metabolites. *Half-life:* Appears proportional to dose and may range from 8 to 12 hours.

Route	Onset	Peak	Duration
P.O.	Unknown	2.5 hr	4-12 hr

Pharmacodynamics

Chemical effect: Unknown. Binds to dopaminergic receptors (both D1 and D2) within limbic system of CNS and may interfere with adrenergic, cholinergic, histaminergic, and serotoninergic receptors.

Therapeutic effect: Relieves psychotic signs and symptoms.

Available forms

Tablets: 25 mg, 100 mg

NURSING PROCESS

Assessment

- Assess patient's psychotic condition before therapy and reassess regularly thereafter.
- Baseline WBC and differential counts are required before therapy and weekly thereafter.
- Be alert for adverse reactions and drug interactions.
- Monitor WBC counts weekly for at least 4 weeks after drug therapy is discontinued and monitor patient closely for recurrence of psychotic symptoms.
- Evaluate patient's and family's knowledge about drug therapy.

Nursing diagnoses

- Disturbed thought processes related to patient's underlying condition
- Risk of infection related to potential for drug-induced agranulocytosis
- Deficient knowledge related to drug therapy

Planning and implementation

- Drug carries significant risk of agranulocytosis. If possible, patients should receive at least two trials of standard antipsychotic drug therapy before clozapine therapy begins.

ALERT: Watch for signs and symptoms of cardiomyopathy, including exertional dyspnea, fatigue, orthopnea, paroxysmal nocturnal dyspnea, and peripheral edema, and report them immediately.

- WBC count is used to help determine safety of therapy. If WBC count drops below 3,500/mm^3 after therapy starts or it drops substantially from baseline, monitor patient closely for signs of infection. If WBC count is 3,000 to 3,500/mm^3 and granulocyte count is above 1,500/mm^3, obtain WBC and differential counts twice weekly as directed. If WBC count drops below 3,000/mm^3 and granulocyte count drops below 1,500/mm^3, interrupt therapy, notify prescriber, and monitor patient for signs of infection. Therapy may be restarted cautiously if WBC count returns to above 3,000/mm^3 and granulocyte count returns to above 1,500/mm^3. Continue monitoring WBC and differential counts twice weekly until WBC count exceeds 3,500/mm^3.
- If WBC count drops below 2,000/mm^3 and granulocyte count drops below 1,000/mm^3, patient may require protective isolation. If patient develops infection, prepare cultures according to institutional policy and give antibiotics. Some clinicians may perform bone marrow aspiration to assess bone marrow function. Future clozapine therapy is contraindicated in such patients.

ALERT: Clozapine is linked to an increased risk of fatal myocarditis, especially during, but not limited to the first month of therapy. In patients in whom myocarditis is suspected (unexplained fatigue, dyspnea, tachypnea, chest pain, tachycardia, fever, palpitations, and other signs or symptoms of heart failure or ECG abnormalities such as ST-T wave abnormalities or arrhythmias), clozapine therapy should be discontinued immediately. The drug shouldn't be rechallenged.

ALERT: Drug is usually withdrawn gradually (over 1- to 2-week period) if it must be discontinued. However, changes in patient's medical condition (including development of leukopenia) may require abrupt discontinuation of drug. Abrupt withdrawal of long-term therapy may cause an abrupt recurrence of psychotic symptoms.

- Follow usual guidelines for dosage increase if therapy is reinstated in patients withdrawn from drug. However, reexposure of patient to drug may increase severity and risk of adverse reactions. If therapy was withdrawn for WBC counts below 2,000/mm^3 or granulocyte counts below 1,000/mm^3, don't expect drug to be continued.

ALERT: If dose was adjusted for a patient already taking St. John's wort, stopping the herb could cause drug level to rise, potentially causing dangerous toxic symptoms.

- Severe hypoglycemia has been reported in patients without a history of hypoglycemia while receiving this therapy.
- Give no more than a 1-week supply of drug.

Patient teaching

- Warn patient about risk of agranulocytosis. Tell him drug is available only through special monitoring program that requires weekly blood tests to monitor patient for agranulocytosis.

Advise patient to report flulike symptoms, fever, sore throat, lethargy, malaise, or other signs of infection.
• Warn patient to avoid hazardous activities that require alertness and good psychomotor coordination while taking drug.
• Tell patient to rise slowly to avoid orthostatic hypotension.
• Advise patient to check with prescriber before taking OTC medicines, herbal remedies, or alcohol.
• Recommend ice chips or sugarless candy or gum to help relieve dry mouth.

Evaluation
• Patient demonstrates reduction in psychotic symptoms with drug therapy.
• Patient doesn't develop infection throughout drug therapy.
• Patient and family state understanding of drug therapy.

codeine phosphate
(KOH-deen FOS-fayt)
Paveral ◆

codeine sulfate

Pharmacologic class: opioid
Therapeutic class: analgesic, antitussive
Pregnancy risk category: C
Controlled substance schedule: II

Indications and dosages

▶ **Mild-to-moderate pain.** *Adults:* 15 to 60 mg P.O. or 15 to 60 mg (phosphate) S.C., I.M., or I.V. q 4 to 6 hours, p.r.n.
Children over age 1: 0.5 mg/kg P.O., I.M., or S.C. q 4 hours, p.r.n.
▶ **Nonproductive cough.** *Adults:* 10 to 20 mg P.O. q 4 to 6 hours. Maximum daily dosage is 120 mg.
Children ages 6 to 12: 5 to 10 mg P.O. q 4 to 6 hours. Maximum daily dosage is 60 mg.
Children ages 2 to 6: 2.5 to 5 mg P.O. q 6 hours. Maximum daily dosage is 30 mg.

Contraindications and precautions

• Contraindicated in patients hypersensitive to drug.
• Use with extreme caution in debilitated patients and in patients with head injury, increased intracranial pressure, increased CSF pressure, hepatic or renal disease, hypothyroidism, Addison's disease, acute alcoholism, seizures, severe CNS depression, bronchial asthma, COPD, respiratory depression, and shock.
Lifespan: In pregnant and breast-feeding women and in children, use cautiously. In elderly patients, use with extreme caution.

Adverse reactions

CNS: *sedation, clouded sensorium, euphoria,* dizziness, ***seizures.***
CV: hypotension, flushing, ***bradycardia.***
GI: *nausea, vomiting, constipation, dry mouth,* ileus.
GU: *urine retention.*
Respiratory: ***respiratory depression.***
Skin: pruritus.
Other: physical dependence.

Interactions

Drug-drug. *CNS depressants, general anesthetics, hypnotics, MAO inhibitors, other narcotic analgesics, sedatives, tranquilizers, tricyclic antidepressants:* May have additive effects. Use together with extreme caution. Monitor patient response.
Drug-lifestyle. *Alcohol use:* May have additive effects. Discourage using together.

Effects on lab test results

• May increase amylase and lipase levels.

Pharmacokinetics

Absorption: Well absorbed after oral or parenteral administration. About two-thirds as potent orally as parenterally.
Distribution: Distributed widely throughout body.
Metabolism: Metabolized mainly in liver.
Excretion: Excreted mainly in urine. *Half-life:* 2.5 to 4 hours.

Route	Onset	Peak	Duration
P.O.	30-45 min	1-2 hr	4-6 hr
I.V.	Immediate	Immediate	4-6 hr
I.M.	10-30 min	0.5-1 hr	4-6 hr
S.C.	10-30 min	Unknown	4-6 hr

Pharmacodynamics

Chemical effect: Binds with opiate receptors in CNS, altering both perception of and emotional response to pain through unknown mechanism. Also suppresses cough reflex by direct action on cough center in medulla.
Therapeutic effect: Relieves pain and cough.

Available forms

codeine phosphate
Injection: 15 mg/ml, 30 mg/ml, 60 mg/ml
Oral solution: 15 mg/5 ml, 10 mg/ml ♦
Soluble tablets: 30 mg, 60 mg
codeine sulfate
Tablets: 15 mg, 30 mg, 60 mg

NURSING PROCESS

Assessment

- Assess patient's pain or cough before and after drug administration.
- Be alert for adverse reactions and drug interactions.
- Evaluate patient's and family's knowledge of drug therapy.

Nursing diagnoses

- Acute pain related to patient's underlying condition
- Fatigue related to presence of cough
- Deficient knowledge related to drug therapy

Planning and implementation

- For full analgesic effect, give drug before patient has intense pain.
- Drug is an antitussive and shouldn't be used when cough is valuable diagnostic sign or is beneficial (as after thoracic surgery).
- **P.O. use:** Give drug with food or milk to minimize adverse GI reactions.
- **I.V. use:** Give drug very slowly by direct injection into large vein. Don't mix with other solutions because codeine phosphate is incompatible with many drugs.

ALERT: Don't give drug to children by I.V. route.

- **I.M. and S.C. use:** Follow normal protocol.
– Don't give discolored injection solution.
- Codeine is often prescribed with aspirin or acetaminophen to provide enhanced pain relief.
- Codeine's abuse potential is much lower than that of morphine.
- Notify prescriber if patient doesn't experience pain or cough relief after treatment.
- Keep narcotic antagonist (naloxone) and resuscitative equipment available if giving drug I.V.

Patient teaching

- Advise patient to take drug with milk or meals to minimize GI distress caused by oral administration.
- Advise patient to ask for or take drug (if at home) before pain becomes severe.
- Caution ambulatory patient about getting out of bed or walking. Warn outpatient to avoid driving and other hazardous activities until CNS effects of drug are known.
- Tell patient to report adverse drug reactions.

Evaluation

- Patient is free of pain after drug administration.
- Patient's cough is suppressed after drug administration.
- Patient and family state understanding of drug therapy.

colchicine

(KOHL-chih-seen)
Colgout ◇

Pharmacologic class: *Colchicum autumnale* alkaloid
Therapeutic class: antigout agent
Pregnancy risk category: C (P.O.), D (I.V.)

Indications and dosages

▶ **Prevention of acute gout attacks as prophylactic or maintenance therapy.** *Adults:* 0.5 or 0.6 mg P.O. daily. Patients who normally have one attack per year or fewer should receive drug only 1 to 4 days per week; patients who have more than one attack per year should receive drug daily. In severe cases, 1 to 1.8 mg daily.

▶ **Prevention of gout attacks in patients undergoing surgery.** *Adults:* 0.5 to 0.6 mg P.O. t.i.d. 3 days before and 3 days after surgery.

▶ **Acute gout, acute gouty arthritis.** *Adults:* Initially, 0.5 to 1.2 mg P.O.; then 0.5 or 0.6 mg q 1 to 2 hours until pain is relieved, nausea, vomiting, or diarrhea ensues, or a maximum dose of 8 mg is reached. Or, 2 mg I.V. followed by 0.5 mg I.V. q 6 hours if necessary. (Some clinicians prefer to give a single injection of 3 mg I.V.) Total I.V. dosage over 24 hours (one course of treatment) shouldn't exceed 4 mg. Don't give any further colchine (I.V. or P.O.) for 7 days or more.

▶ **Familial Mediterranean fever.** *Adults:* 1 to 2 mg P.O. daily in divided doses.

▶ **Dermatitis herpetiformis suppressant.** *Adults:* 0.6 mg P.O. b.i.d. or t.i.d.

▶ **Hepatic cirrhosis.** *Adults:* 1 mg P.O. 5 days weekly.

Patients with hepatic impairment or creatinine clearance of 10 to 50 ml/minute: Decrease dosage by 50%.

Contraindications and precautions

- Contraindicated in patients with serious cardiac disease, renal disease, or GI disorders.
- Use cautiously in debilitated patients and in patients with early evidence of cardiac, renal, or GI disease.

Lifespan: With pregnant women, use with extreme caution, if at all, because fetal harm may occur. In breast-feeding women and in children, safety of drug hasn't been established. In elderly patients, use cautiously.

Adverse reactions

CNS: peripheral neuritis.
GI: *nausea, vomiting, abdominal pain, diarrhea.*
Hematologic: ***aplastic anemia, thrombocytopenia, agranulocytosis*** (with prolonged use); nonthrombocytopenic purpura.
Hepatic: ***hepatic necrosis.***
Skin: alopecia, urticaria, dermatitis.
Other: severe local irritation (if extravasation occurs), ***hypersensitivity reactions, anaphylaxis.***

Interactions

Drug-drug. *Loop diuretics:* May decrease efficacy of colchicine prophylaxis. Avoid using together.
Phenylbutazone: May increase risk of leukopenia or thrombocytopenia. Don't use together.
Vitamin B_{12}: May impair absorption of vitamin B_{12}. Avoid using together.
Drug-lifestyle. *Alcohol use:* May impair efficacy of colchicine prophylaxis. Discourage using together.

Effects on lab test results

- May increase alkaline phosphatase, AST, and ALT levels. May decrease carotene and cholesterol levels.
- May decrease hemoglobin, hematocrit, and platelet and granulocyte counts.
- May cause false-positive results in urine tests for hemoglobin and erythrocytes. May interfere with urinary determinations of 17-hydroxycorticosteroids using the Reddy, Jenkins, and Thorn procedure.

Pharmacokinetics

Absorption: Rapid. Unchanged drug may be reabsorbed from intestine by biliary processes.
Distribution: Distributed rapidly into various tissues. Concentrated in leukocytes and distributed into kidneys, liver, spleen, and intestinal tract, but absent in heart, skeletal muscle, and brain.
Metabolism: Metabolized partially in liver and also slowly metabolized in other tissues.
Excretion: Drug and its metabolites are excreted primarily in feces, with lesser amounts excreted in urine. *Half-life:* 1 to 10.5 hours.

Route	Onset	Peak	Duration
P.O.	≤ 12 hr	0.5-2 hr	Unknown
I.V.	6-12 hr	0.5-2 hr	Unknown

Pharmacodynamics

Chemical effect: As antigout agent, apparently decreases WBC motility, phagocytosis, and lactic acid production, decreasing urate crystal deposits and reducing inflammation. As antiosteolytic agent, apparently inhibits mitosis of osteoprogenitor cells and decreases osteoclast activity.
Therapeutic effect: Relieves gout signs and symptoms.

Available forms

Injection: 0.5 mg/ml
Tablets: 0.5 mg (1/120 grain), 0.6 mg (1/100 grain) as sugar-coated granules

NURSING PROCESS

Assessment

- Assess patient's underlying condition before therapy and reassess regularly thereafter.

• Obtain baseline laboratory studies, including CBC and uric acid levels, before therapy and repeat regularly.
• Be alert for adverse reactions and drug interactions.
• Evaluate patient's and family's knowledge of drug therapy.

Nursing diagnoses
• Acute pain related to presence of gout
• Ineffective protection related to drug-induced hematologic adverse reactions
• Deficient knowledge related to drug therapy

Planning and implementation
• **P.O. use:** Give drug with meals to reduce GI effects as maintenance therapy. May be used with uricosuric agents.
• **I.V. use:** Give drug by slow I.V. push over 2 to 5 minutes. Avoid extravasation because colchicine is very irritating to tissues.
– Don't dilute colchicine injection with D_5W injection or other fluids that might change pH of colchicine solution. If lower concentration of colchicine injection is needed, dilute with normal saline solution or sterile water for injection and administer over 2 to 5 minutes by direct injection. Preferably, inject into tubing of free-flowing I.V. solution. However, don't inject if diluted solution becomes turbid.
ALERT: After full course of I.V. colchicine (4 mg), no more colchicine should be given by any other route for at least 7 days. Colchicine is toxic and death can result from overdose.
• Don't give I.M. or S.C.; severe local irritation occurs.
• Store drug in tightly closed, light-resistant container.
• Stop drug as soon as gout pain is relieved or at first sign of GI symptoms.
• Force fluids to maintain output at 2,000 ml daily.

Patient teaching
• Teach patient how to take drug.
• Advise patient to report rash, sore throat, fever, unusual bleeding, bruising, fatigue, weakness, numbness, or tingling.
• Instruct patient on when drug should be stopped.
• Tell patient to avoid alcohol during drug therapy because it may inhibit drug action.
• Advise patient to avoid all drugs containing aspirin because they may precipitate gout.

Evaluation
• Patient becomes pain free after drug therapy.
• Patient's CBC and platelet counts remain normal throughout drug therapy.
• Patient and family state understanding of drug therapy.

colesevelam hydrochloride
(koh-leh-SEV-eh-lam high-droh-KLOR-ighd)
Welchol

Pharmacologic classification: polymeric bile acid sequestrant
Therapeutic classification: antilipemic
Pregnancy risk category: B

Indications and dosages
▶ **Reduction of elevated LDL cholesterol in patients with primary hypercholesterolemia (Frederickson Type IIa). May be given either alone or with an HMG-CoA reductase inhibitor.** *Adults:* If given alone, give three tablets (1,875 mg) P.O. twice daily with meals and liquid or six tablets (3,750 mg) once daily with a meal and liquid. Maximum dose is seven tablets (4,375 mg). If used with an HMG-CoA reductase inhibitor, recommended dose is four to six tablets P.O. daily.

Contraindications and precautions
• Colesevelam is contraindicated in patients hypersensitive to any of its components and in patients with bowel obstruction.
• Use cautiously in patients susceptible to vitamin K deficiency or deficiencies of fat-soluble vitamins. Also use cautiously in patients with dysphagia, swallowing disorders, severe GI motility disorders, and major GI tract surgery. Due to lack of clinical studies in patients with triglyceride levels above 300 mg/dl, use cautiously in these patients.
Lifespan: In pregnant women, use only if necessary. In breast-feeding women, safety and efficacy haven't been established; use only if necessary. In children, safety and efficacy haven't been established.

Adverse reactions

CNS: headache, pain, asthenia.
EENT: pharyngitis, rhinitis, sinusitis.
GI: abdominal pain, *constipation,* diarrhea, dyspepsia, *flatulence,* nausea.
Musculoskeletal: myalgia, back pain.
Respiratory: increased cough.
Other: accidental injury, *infection,* flu-like syndrome.

Interactions

None reported.

Effects on lab test results

- May increase HDL cholesterol and triglyceride levels. May decrease total cholesterol, LDL cholesterol, and apolipoprotein B levels.

Pharmacokinetics

Absorption: Not absorbed.
Distribution: None.
Metabolism: None.
Excretion: Mainly excreted in feces as a complex bound to bile acids. Less than 0.05% of drug is excreted in urine.

Route	Onset	Peak	Duration
P.O.	Unknown	2 wk	Unknown

Pharmacodynamics

Chemical effect: Following oral intake, colesevelam binds to bile acids in the intestinal tract and forms a nonabsorbable complex that is eliminated in feces. Partial removal of bile acids from the enterohepatic circulation via this mechanism results in an increased conversion of cholesterol to bile acids in the liver in an attempt to restore the depleted bile acids. The resultant increase in cholesterol causes systemic clearance of circulating LDL levels in the blood.
Therapeutic effect: Lowers LDL and total cholesterol levels.

Available forms

Tablets: 625 mg

NURSING PROCESS

Assessment

- Rule out secondary causes of hypercholesterolemia before starting drug, such as poorly controlled diabetes, hypothyroidism, nephrotic syndrome, dysproteinemias, obstructive liver disease, other drug therapy, and alcoholism.
- Monitor total cholesterol, LDL, and triglyceride levels before and periodically during therapy.
- Monitor patient's bowel habits. If severe constipation develops, decrease dosage, add a stool softener, or discontinue drug.
- Assess patient's compliance with restricted diet and exercise program adjunctive to antilipemic therapy.
- Determine patient's and family's knowledge of antilipemic drug therapy and importance of diet and exercise regimen.

Nursing diagnoses

- Imbalanced nutrition: more than body requirements of saturated fat and cholesterol related to dietary intake and lack of exercise program
- Risk for constipation related to drug-induced adverse gastrointestinal reactions
- Risk for injury related to presence of elevated LDL cholesterol levels
- Deficient knowledge related to antilipemic drug therapy

Planning and implementation

- Give drug with a meal and a liquid.
- Discuss with prescriber adding antilipemic agent (for example, statins) for maximum additive antilipemic effect.

Patient teaching

- Instruct patient to take drug with a meal and a liquid.
- Teach patient to monitor bowel habits. Encourage a diet high in fiber and fluids. Instruct patient to notify prescriber promptly if severe constipation develops.
- Encourage patient to follow prescribed diet that is restricted in saturated fat and cholesterol and high in vegetables and fiber. Also discuss and encourage an exercise program that is appropriate for patient.
- Discuss with patient the importance of regular monitoring of lipid levels.
- Tell patient to notify prescriber if she's pregnant or breast-feeding.

Evaluation

- Patient begins a balanced diet and exercise regimen that's approved by his prescriber.

• Patient doesn't suffer adverse GI effect from drug therapy.
• Patient's LDL cholesterol and total cholesterol levels are within normal limits.
• Patient and family state understanding of drug therapy.

corticotropin (adrenocorticotropic hormone, ACTH)

(kor-teh-koh-TROH-pin)
ACTH, Acthar

repository corticotropin

Pharmacologic class: anterior pituitary hormone
Therapeutic class: diagnostic aid, replacement hormone
Pregnancy risk category: C

Indications and dosages

▶ **Diagnostic test of adrenocortical function.** *Adults:* 40 units repository form I.M. or S.C. q 12 hours for 1 to 2 days. Or, 10 to 25 units aqueous form in 500 ml D_5W I.V. over 8 hours, between blood samplings. Individual dosages generally vary with adrenal glands' sensitivity to stimulation and with specific disease. Infants and younger children require larger doses per kilogram than older children and adults.

▶ **For therapeutic use.** *Adults:* 20 units aqueous form S.C. or I.M. in four divided doses. Or, 40 to 80 units q 24 to 72 hours (repository form).

Contraindications and precautions

• Contraindicated in patients hypersensitive to pork and pork products and in patients with peptic ulcer, scleroderma, osteoporosis, systemic fungal infections, ocular herpes simplex, peptic ulceration, heart failure, hypertension, adrenocortical hyperfunction or primary insufficiency, or Cushing's syndrome. Also contraindicated in those who have had recent surgery.
• Use cautiously in patients being immunized and in those with latent tuberculosis or tuberculin reactivity, hypothyroidism, cirrhosis, acute gouty arthritis, psychotic tendencies, renal insufficiency, diverticulitis, nonspecific ulcerative colitis, thromboembolic disorders, seizures, uncontrolled hypertension, or myasthenia gravis.
Lifespan: In pregnant women and women of childbearing age, use cautiously. In breastfeeding women, safety of drug hasn't been established. In children, use cautiously because prolonged use of drug will inhibit skeletal growth; intermittent administration is recommended.

Adverse reactions

CNS: ***seizures,*** *dizziness,* ***papilledema,*** headache, *euphoria, insomnia,* mood swings, personality changes, depression, psychosis, ***increased intracranial pressure.***
CV: ***shock.***
EENT: cataracts, glaucoma.
GI: peptic ulceration (with perforation and hemorrhage), ***pancreatitis,*** abdominal distention, ulcerative esophagitis, nausea, vomiting.
GU: menstrual irregularities.
Metabolic: activation of latent diabetes mellitus, suppression of growth in children, *sodium and fluid retention,* calcium and potassium loss, hypokalemic alkalosis, negative nitrogen balance.
Musculoskeletal: muscle weakness, steroid myopathy, loss of muscle mass, osteoporosis, vertebral compression fractures.
Skin: impaired wound healing, thin and fragile skin, petechiae, ecchymoses, facial erythema, diaphoresis, acne, hyperpigmentation, allergic skin reactions, hirsutism.
Other: cushingoid symptoms, progressive increase in antibodies, loss of corticotropin stimulatory effect, ***hypersensitivity reactions*** (rash, ***bronchospasm***).

Interactions

Drug-drug. *Anticonvulsants, barbiturates, rifampin:* May increase metabolism of corticotropin and decrease effectiveness. Monitor patient for lack of effect.
Estrogens: May potentiate effects of cortisol. Dosage adjustments may be necessary.
NSAIDs, salicylates: May increase risk of GI bleeding. Avoid using together.
Oral anticoagulants: May alter PT. Monitor PT and INR. Dosage adjustments may be necessary.

Potassium-wasting diuretics: May increase risk of hypokalemia. Monitor potassium levels.

Effects on lab test results

• May increase glucose level. May decrease potassium and calcium levels.

Pharmacokinetics

Absorption: Rapid after I.M. administration; unknown for S.C. administration.
Distribution: Unknown.
Metabolism: Unknown.
Excretion: Excreted by kidneys. *Half-life:* About 15 minutes.

Route	Onset	Peak	Duration
I.V, I.M., S.C.	Rapid	Varies	2 hr (zinc form), ≤ 3 days (repository)

Pharmacodynamics

Chemical effect: By replacing body's own tropic hormone, drug stimulates secretion of adrenal cortex hormones.
Therapeutic effect: Diagnoses or treats adrenocortical hormonal deficiency.

Available forms

Aqueous injection: 25 units/vial, 40 units/vial
Repository injection: 40 units/ml, 80 units/ml

NURSING PROCESS

Assessment

• Assess patient's underlying condition before therapy and reassess regularly during therapy.
• Corticotropin treatment should be preceded by verification of adrenal responsiveness and test for hypersensitivity and allergic reactions.
• Be alert for adverse reactions and drug interactions.
• Note and record weight changes, fluid exchange, and resting blood pressures until minimal effective dosage is achieved.
• Watch neonates of corticotropin-treated mothers for signs of hypoadrenalism.
• Monitor patient for stress.
• Evaluate patient's and family's knowledge about drug test or therapy.

Nursing diagnoses

• Ineffective protection related to underlying condition
• Risk for injury related to drug-induced adverse reactions
• Deficient knowledge related to drug test or therapy

Planning and implementation

• Corticotropin should be adjunct, not sole, therapy. Oral form is preferred for long-term therapy.
• **I.V. use:** Use only aqueous form for I.V. administration. Dilute in 500 ml D_5W and infuse over 8 hours.
• **I.M. use:** If administering gel, warm it to room temperature, draw into large needle, and give slowly as deep I.M. injection with 21G or 22G needle. Warn patient that injection is painful.
• Refrigerate reconstituted solution and use within 24 hours.
• Counteract edema with low-sodium, high-potassium intake; nitrogen loss with a high-protein diet; and psychotic changes with a reduction in corticotropin dosage or use of sedatives.
• Unusual stress may require additional use of rapidly acting corticosteroids. When possible, gradually reduce corticotropin dosage to smallest effective dose to minimize induced adrenocortical insufficiency. Therapy can be reinstituted if stressful situation (trauma, surgery, severe illness) occurs shortly after stopping drug.

Patient teaching

• Stress importance of informing health care team members about corticotropin use because unusual stress may need additional use of rapidly acting corticosteroids. If corticotropin was recently stopped, therapy may have to be reinstituted.
• Tell patient to restrict sodium intake and consume high-protein, high-potassium diet.
• Advise patient to have close follow-up care.
• Warn patient that injections, especially I.M. injections, are painful.

Evaluation

• Patient's underlying condition improves with drug therapy.

• Patient doesn't experience injury as result of drug-induced adverse reactions.
• Patient and family state understanding of drug test or therapy.

cortisone acetate

(KOR-tih-sohn AS-ih-tayt)
Cortisone Acetate, Cortone Acetate

Pharmacologic class: glucocorticoid, mineralocorticoid
Therapeutic class: anti-inflammatory, replacement therapy
Pregnancy risk category: C

Indications and dosages

▶ **Adrenal insufficiency, allergy, inflammation.** *Adults:* 25 to 300 mg P.O. or 20 to 300 mg I.M. daily or on alternate days. Dosages are highly individualized, depending on severity of disease.

Contraindications and precautions

• Contraindicated in patients hypersensitive to drug or its ingredients and in those with systemic fungal infections.
• Use with extreme caution in patient with recent MI.
• Use cautiously in patients with GI ulcer, renal disease, hypertension, osteoporosis, diabetes mellitus, hypothyroidism, cirrhosis, diverticulitis, nonspecific ulcerative colitis, recent intestinal anastomoses, thromboembolic disorders, seizures, myasthenia gravis, heart failure, tuberculosis, ocular herpes simplex, emotional instability, and psychotic tendencies.
Lifespan: In pregnant and breast-feeding women, use cautiously. In children, long-term use of drug isn't recommended because growth and maturation may be delayed.

Adverse reactions

CNS: *euphoria, insomnia,* psychotic behavior, pseudotumor cerebri, ***seizures.***
CV: ***arrhythmias, heart failure, thromboembolism,*** hypertension, edema.
EENT: cataracts, glaucoma.
GI: *peptic ulceration,* GI irritation, increased appetite, ***pancreatitis.***
Metabolic: possible hypokalemia, growth suppression in children, hyperglycemia, and carbohydrate intolerance.
Musculoskeletal: muscle weakness, osteoporosis.
Skin: hirsutism, delayed wound healing, acne, various skin eruptions, atrophy at I.M. injection site.
Other: susceptibility to infections, ***acute adrenal insufficiency*** following increased stress (infection, surgery, or trauma) or abrupt withdrawal after long-term therapy.

Interactions

Drug-drug. *Aspirin, indomethacin, other NSAIDs:* May increase risk of GI distress and bleeding. Give together cautiously.
Barbiturates, phenytoin, rifampin: May decrease corticosteroid effect. Increase corticosteroid dosage.
Live-attenuated virus vaccines, other toxoids and vaccines: May decrease antibody response and increase risk of neurologic complications. Don't use together.
Oral anticoagulants: May alter dosage requirements. Monitor PT closely and monitor patient for bleeding.
Potassium-depleting drugs (such as thiazide diuretics): Enhanced potassium-wasting effects of cortisone. Monitor potassium levels.
Skin-test antigens: Decreases response. Defer skin testing until therapy is completed.
Drug-lifestyle. *Alcohol use:* May increase risk of GI irritation. Discourage using together.

Effects on lab test results

• May increase glucose and cholesterol levels. May decrease potassium, calcium, T_3, and T_4 levels.

Pharmacokinetics

Absorption: Absorbed readily after oral administration; unknown for I.M. administration.
Distribution: Distributed rapidly to muscle, liver, skin, intestines, and kidneys. Cortisone is extensively bound to plasma proteins. Only unbound portion is active.
Metabolism: Metabolized in liver to active metabolite hydrocortisone, which is metabolized to inactive glucuronide and sulfate metabolites.

Excretion: Inactive metabolites and small amounts of unmetabolized drug are excreted by kidneys. Insignificant quantities of drug also excreted in feces. *Half-life:* 8 to 12 hours.

Route	Onset	Peak	Duration
P.O.	Rapid	2 hr	30-36 hr
I.M.	Slow	20-48 hr	Varies

Pharmacodynamics

Chemical effect: Not completely defined. Decreases inflammation, mainly by stabilizing leukocyte lysosomal membranes; suppresses immune response; stimulates bone marrow; and influences protein, fat, and carbohydrate metabolism.
Therapeutic effect: Reduces inflammation; raises corticosteroid therapy.

Available forms

Injection (suspension): 50 mg/ml
Tablets: 5 mg, 10 mg, 25 mg

NURSING PROCESS

Assessment

- Assess patient's underlying condition before therapy and reassess regularly thereafter.
- Monitor electrolyte and glucose levels. Check patient's weight and vital signs regularly.
- Monitor patient's stress level.
- Be alert for adverse reactions and drug interactions; most adverse reactions are dose- or duration-dependent.
- Evaluate patient's and family's knowledge of drug therapy.

Nursing diagnoses

- Ineffective protection related to underlying condition
- Risk for injury related to drug-induced adverse reactions
- Deficient knowledge related to drug therapy

Planning and implementation

- **P.O. use:** Give drug with milk or food to reduce GI irritation.
  – Give once-daily dose in morning for best results and least toxicity.
- **I.M. use:** I.M. route causes slow onset of action. Shouldn't be used in acute conditions where rapid effect is required. May be used on twice-daily schedule matching diurnal variation. Rotate injection sites to prevent muscle atrophy.
  – Mixing or diluting parenteral suspension may alter absorption and decrease drug's effectiveness.
- Drug isn't for I.V. use.
- Drug should always be adjusted to lowest effective dose.
- Gradually reduce drug dosage after long-term therapy.
- Notify prescriber if signs of adrenal insufficiency increase. Unusual stress may require additional use of rapidly acting corticosteroids.

Patient teaching

ALERT: Tell patient not to discontinue drug abruptly or without prescriber's consent. Abrupt withdrawal may cause rebound inflammation, fatigue, weakness, arthralgia, fever, dizziness, lethargy, depression, fainting, orthostatic hypotension, dyspnea, anorexia, and hypoglycemia. After prolonged use, sudden withdrawal may be fatal.

- Advise patient receiving long-term therapy to consider exercise or physical therapy. Also tell him to ask prescriber about vitamin D or calcium supplements.
- Tell patient to restrict sodium intake and consume high-protein, high-potassium diet.
- Tell patient to report slow healing.
- Warn patient receiving long-term therapy about cushingoid symptoms and the need to report sudden weight gain or swelling to prescriber.
- Instruct patient to wear or carry medical identification indicating his need for supplemental glucocorticoids during stress.

Evaluation

- Patient shows improvement in underlying condition with drug therapy.
- Patient doesn't experience injury as result of drug-induced adverse reactions.
- Patient and family state understanding of drug therapy.

cosyntropin

(koh-sin-TROH-pin)

Cortrosyn

Pharmacologic class: anterior pituitary hormone
Therapeutic class: diagnostic agent
Pregnancy risk category: C

Indications and dosages

▶ **Diagnostic test of adrenocortical function.** *Adults and children age 2 and older:* 0.25 to 1 mg I.M. or I.V. over 2 minutes (unless label prohibits I.V. administration) between blood samplings.
Infants younger than age 2: 0.125 mg I.V. or I.M.

Contraindications and precautions

- Contraindicated in patients hypersensitive to drug.
- Use cautiously in patients hypersensitive to natural corticotropin.

Lifespan: In pregnant or breast-feeding women and in children younger than age 2, safety of drug hasn't been established.

Adverse reactions

CNS: ***seizures, increased intracranial pressure with papilledema.***
CV: flushing.
Metabolism: cushingoid state, growth suppression.
Skin: pruritus.
Other: hypersensitivity reactions.

Interactions

Drug-drug. *Blood and plasma products:* Inactivates cosyntropin. Give separately.
Cortisone, hydrocortisone: May interfere with test results of cortisol levels if given on test day. Give on separate days.
Spironolactone: May interfere with fluorometric analysis of cortisol levels. Avoid using together.

Effects on lab test results

- May increase glucose level.
- May falsely increase plasma cortisol level when fluorometric analysis is used.

Pharmacokinetics

Absorption: Rapid.
Distribution: Unknown.
Metabolism: Unknown.
Excretion: Thought to be excreted by kidneys.

Route	Onset	Peak	Duration
I.V.	≤ 5 min	1 hr	Unknown
I.M.	Unknown	1 hr	Unknown

Pharmacodynamics

Chemical effect: By replacing body's own tropic hormone, drug stimulates secretion of adrenal cortex hormones.
Therapeutic effect: Aids in diagnosing adrenocortical dysfunction.

Available forms

Injection: 0.25 mg/vial

NURSING PROCESS

Assessment

- Assess patient's reason for test before administration. Evaluate test results.
- Be alert for adverse reactions and drug interactions.
- Monitor patient for allergic reactions, rashes, dyspnea, wheezing, or evidence of anaphylaxis.
- Evaluate patient's and family's knowledge about drug test.

Nursing diagnoses

- Risk for injury related to potential for cosyntropin to cause hypersensitivity reactions
- Deficient knowledge related to drug test

Planning and implementation

- **I.V. use:** Reconstitute drug with 1 ml of supplied diluent. For direct injection, administer over at least 2 minutes. May be further diluted with D_5W or normal saline solution and infused at 0.04 mg/hr over 6 hours. Solution is stable for 12 hours at room temperature.
- **I.M. use:** Follow normal protocol.
- Notify prescriber if hypersensitivity occurs, and be prepared to provide emergency care.

Patient teaching

- Instruct patient to notify prescriber immediately if pruritus or other signs of hypersensitivity occur.
- Explain how drug test is performed.

Evaluation
• Patient doesn't have hypersensitivity reaction to drug.
• Patient and family state understanding of drug test.

co-trimoxazole (sulfamethoxazole-trimethoprim)
(koh-trigh-MOX-uh-zohl)
Apo-Sulfatrim ♦, Apo-Sulfatrim DS ♦, Bactrim*, Bactrim DS, Bactrim IV, Cotrim, Cotrim DS, Novo-Trimel ♦, Novo-Trimel D.S. ♦, Resprim ◇, Roubac ♦, Septra*, Septra DS, Septra-I.V., Septrin ◇, SMZ-TMP

Pharmacologic class: sulfonamide and folate antagonist
Therapeutic class: antibiotic
Pregnancy risk category: C (contraindicated at term)

Indications and dosages
▶ **Urinary tract infections and shigellosis.** *Adults:* 160 mg trimethoprim/800 mg sulfamethoxazole (double-strength tablet) P.O. q 12 hours for 10 to 14 days in urinary tract infections and for 5 days in shigellosis. If indicated, I.V. infusion is given at 8 to 10 mg/kg daily (based on trimethoprim component) in two to four divided doses q 6, 8, or 12 hours for up to 14 days. Maximum dose is 960 mg daily trimethoprim.
Children age 2 months and older: 8 mg/kg trimethoprim/40 mg/kg sulfamethoxazole P.O. daily, in two divided doses q 12 hours (10 days for urinary tract infections; 5 days for shigellosis). If indicated, I.V. infusion is given at 8 to 10 mg/kg daily (based on trimethoprim component) in two to four divided doses q 6, 8, or 12 hours. Don't exceed adult dose.
▶ **Otitis media in patients with penicillin allergy or penicillin-resistant infections.** *Children and infants age 2 months and older:* 8 mg/kg daily (based on trimethoprim component) P.O., in two divided doses q 12 hours for 10 days.
▶ ***Pneumocystis carinii* pneumonia.** *Adults, children, and infants age 2 months and older:* 20 mg/kg trimethoprim/100 mg/kg sulfamethoxazole P.O. daily, in equally divided doses q 6 hours for 14 days. If indicated, I.V. infusion may be given 15 to 20 mg/kg daily (based on trimethoprim component) in three or four divided doses q 6 to 8 hours for up to 14 days.
▶ **Chronic bronchitis.** *Adults:* 160 mg trimethoprim/800 mg sulfamethoxazole P.O. q 12 hours for 10 to 14 days.
▶ **Traveler's diarrhea.** *Adults:* 160 mg trimethoprim/800 mg sulfamethoxazole P.O. b.i.d. for 3 to 5 days. Some patients may require 2 days of therapy or less.
▶ **Urinary tract infections in men with prostatitis.** *Adults:* 160 mg trimethoprim/800 mg sulfamethoxazole P.O. b.i.d. for 3 to 6 months.
▶ **Chronic urinary tract infections.** *Adults:* 40 mg trimethoprim/200 mg sulfamethoxazole (½ tablet) or 80 mg trimethoprim/400 mg sulfamethoxazole P.O. daily or three times weekly for 3 to 6 months.
▶ **Septic agranulocytosis‡.** *Adults:* 2.5 mg/kg I.V. q.i.d.; for prophylaxis, 80 to 160 mg b.i.d.
▶ **Nocardia infection‡.** *Adults:* 640 mg P.O. daily for 7 months.
▶ **Pharyngeal gonococcal infections‡.** *Adults:* 720 mg P.O. daily for 5 days.
▶ **Chancroid‡.** *Adults:* 160 mg P.O. b.i.d. for 7 days.
▶ **Pertussis‡.** *Adults:* 320 mg P.O. daily in two divided doses. *Children:* 40 mg/kg P.O. daily in two divided doses.
▶ **Cholera‡.** *Adults:* 160 mg P.O. b.i.d. for 3 days.

Contraindications and precautions
• Contraindicated in patients with megaloblastic anemia caused by folate deficiency, porphyria, severe renal impairment (creatinine clearance less than 15 ml/minute), or hypersensitivity to trimethoprim or sulfonamides.
• Use cautiously and in reduced dosages in patients with impaired hepatic or renal function (creatinine clearance of 15 to 30 ml/minute), severe allergy or bronchial asthma, G6PD deficiency, and blood dyscrasia.
Lifespan: In pregnant women at term and in breast-feeding women, drug is contraindicated. In infants younger than age 2 months, safety of drug hasn't been established.

Adverse reactions
CNS: headache, mental depression, ***seizures,*** hallucinations, ataxia, nervousness, fatigue, vertigo, insomnia.

CV: thrombophlebitis.
GI: *nausea, vomiting, diarrhea,* abdominal pain, anorexia, stomatitis.
GU: ***toxic nephrosis with oliguria and anuria,*** crystalluria, hematuria.
Hematologic: ***agranulocytosis, aplastic anemia,*** megaloblastic anemia, ***thrombocytopenia, leukopenia,*** hemolytic anemia.
Hepatic: jaundice, ***hepatic necrosis.***
Musculoskeletal: muscle weakness.
Skin: ***erythema multiforme, Stevens-Johnson syndrome,*** *generalized skin eruption,* ***epidermal necrolysis,*** exfoliative dermatitis, photosensitivity, urticaria, pruritus.
Other: ***hypersensitivity reactions*** (serum sickness, drug fever, ***anaphylaxis***).

Interactions

Drug-drug. *Oral anticoagulants:* May increase anticoagulant effect. Monitor patient for bleeding.
Oral antidiabetics: May increase hypoglycemic effect. Monitor glucose level.
Oral contraceptives: Decreases contraceptive effectiveness and increases risk of breakthrough bleeding. Suggest nonhormonal form of contraception.
Phenytoin: May inhibit hepatic metabolism of phenytoin. Monitor phenytoin levels.
Drug-herb. *Dong quai, St. John's wort:* Increases risk of photosensitivity. Advise patient to avoid unprotected exposure to sunlight.
Drug-lifestyle. *Sun exposure:* Photosensitivity reactions may occur. Urge patient to avoid sun exposure and wear protective clothing and sunblock.

Effects on lab test results

- May increase BUN, creatinine, aminotransferase, and bilirubin levels.
- May decrease hemoglobin, hematocrit, and granulocyte, platelet, and WBC counts.

Pharmacokinetics

Absorption: Well absorbed from GI tract after oral administration.
Distribution: Distributed widely into body tissues and fluids, including middle ear fluid, prostatic fluid, bile, aqueous humor, and CSF. Protein binding is 44% for trimethoprim, 70% for sulfamethoxazole.
Metabolism: Both components of drug are metabolized by liver.
Excretion: Both components of drug are excreted primarily in urine. *Half-life:* Trimethoprim, 8 to 11 hours; sulfamethoxazole, 10 to 13 hours.

Route	Onset	Peak	Duration
P.O.	Unknown	1-4 hr	Unknown
I.V.	Immediate	Immediate	Unknown

Pharmacodynamics

Chemical effect: Sulfamethoxazole component inhibits formation of dihydrofolic acid from PABA; trimethoprim component inhibits dihydrofolate reductase. Both decrease bacterial folic acid synthesis.
Therapeutic effect: Inhibits susceptible bacteria, including *Escherichia coli, Klebsiella, Enterobacter, Proteus mirabilis, Haemophilus influenzae, Streptococcus pneumoniae, Staphylococcus aureus, Acinetobacter, Salmonella, Shigella,* and *P. carinii.*

Available forms

Injection: trimethoprim 16 mg and sulfamethoxazole 80 mg/ml (5 ml/ampule)
Oral suspension: trimethoprim 40 mg and sulfamethoxazole 200 mg/5 ml
Tablets: trimethoprim 80 mg and sulfamethoxazole 400 mg; trimethoprim 160 mg and sulfamethoxazole 800 mg

NURSING PROCESS

Assessment

- Assess patient's infection before therapy and reassess regularly thereafter.
- Obtain specimen for culture and sensitivity tests before first dose. Therapy may begin pending results.
- Be alert for adverse reactions and drug interactions.
- Monitor patient's hydration status if adverse GI reactions occur.
- Monitor intake and output. Urine output should be at least 1,500 ml daily to ensure proper hydration. Inadequate urine output can lead to crystalluria or tubular deposits of drug.
- Evaluate patient's and family's knowledge of drug therapy.

Nursing diagnoses

- Infection related to presence of bacteria susceptible to drug

• Risk for deficient fluid volume related to drug induced adverse GI reactions
• Deficient knowledge related to drug therapy

Planning and implementation

• **P.O. use:** Give drug with full glass of water at least 1 hour before or 2 hours after meals for maximum absorption. Shake oral suspension thoroughly before giving.
• **I.V. use:** Dilute contents of 5-ml ampule of drug in 125 ml D_5W before giving. If patient is on a fluid restriction, dilute 5 ml of drug in 75 ml D_5W. Don't mix with other drugs or solutions. Infuse slowly over 60 to 90 minutes. Don't give by rapid infusion or bolus injection. Don't refrigerate.
• Never give I.M.
• Note that DS in product name means double strength.

Patient teaching

• Tell patient to take entire amount of medication exactly as prescribed, even if he feels better.
• Tell patient to take drug with full glass of water and to drink at least 3 to 4 L of water daily.
• Advise patient to avoid exposure to direct sunlight because of risk of photosensitivity reaction.
• Tell patient to report signs of rash, sore throat, fever, or mouth sores because drug may need to be discontinued.

Evaluation

• Patient is free from infection after drug therapy.
• Patient maintains adequate hydration after drug therapy.
• Patient and family state understanding of drug therapy.

cromolyn sodium (sodium cromoglycate)

(KROH-moh-lin SOH-dee-um)
Crolom, Gastrocrom, Intal, Nasalcrom, Rynacrom ♦

Pharmacologic class: chromone derivative
Therapeutic class: mast cell stabilizer, antiasthmatic
Pregnancy risk category: B

Indications and dosages

▶ **Mild-to-moderate persistent asthma.** *Adults and children age 5 and older:* 2 metered sprays using inhaler q.i.d. at regular intervals. Or, 20 mg via nebulization q.i.d. at regular intervals.
▶ **Prevention and treatment of allergic rhinitis.** *Adults and children older than age 6:* 1 spray in each nostril t.i.d. or q.i.d. Maximum frequency is six times daily.
▶ **Prevention of exercise-induced bronchospasm.** *Adults and children age 5 and older:* 2 metered sprays inhaled no more than 1 hour before anticipated exercise.
▶ **Conjunctivitis.** *Adults and children age 4 and older:* 1 to 2 drops in each eye four to six times daily at regular intervals.
▶ **Systemic mastocytosis.** *Adults and children older than age 12:* 200 mg P.O. q.i.d. before meals and h.s.
Children ages 2 to 12: 100 mg P.O. q.i.d. 30 minutes before meals or h.s.
▶ **Food allergy, inflammatory bowel disease‡.** *Adults:* 200 mg P.O. q.i.d. 15 to 20 minutes before meals.

Contraindications and precautions

• Contraindicated in patients hypersensitive to drug and in those experiencing acute asthma attacks and status asthmaticus.
• Use inhalation form cautiously in patients with coronary artery disease or history of arrhythmias.
Lifespan: In pregnant and breast-feeding women, use cautiously. In children, use with caution. In infants younger than age 2, use of cromolyn oral inhalation solution isn't recommended. In children younger than age 5, cromolyn powder or aerosol for oral inhalation isn't recommended. In children younger than age 6, cromolyn nasal solution isn't recommended.

Adverse reactions

CNS: dizziness, headache.
EENT: *irritation of throat and trachea,* nasal congestion, pharyngeal irritation, lacrimation.
GI: nausea, esophagitis.
GU: dysuria, urinary frequency.
Respiratory: ***bronchospasm*** (after inhalation of dry powder), *cough,* wheezing, *eosinophilic pneumonia.*
Skin: rash, urticaria.

Other: joint swelling and pain, swollen parotid gland, ***angioedema.***

Interactions

None significant.

Effects on lab test results

- May decrease neutrophil count. May cause abnormal liver function test values.

Pharmacokinetics

Absorption: 0.5% to 2% of oral dose, 7% of intranasal dose, and 0.03% of ophthalmic dose.
Distribution: Drug doesn't cross most biological membranes.
Metabolism: None significant.
Excretion: Excreted unchanged in urine (50%) and bile (about 50%). Small amounts may be excreted in feces or exhaled. *Half-life:* 81 minutes.

Route	Onset	Peak	Duration
P.O., ophthalmic, inhalation, intranasal	Unknown	Unknown	Unknown

Pharmacodynamics

Chemical effect: Inhibits degranulation of sensitized mast cells that occurs after patient's exposure to specific antigens. Also inhibits release of histamine and slow-reacting substance of anaphylaxis.
Therapeutic effect: Adjunct to preventing bronchospasms and allergy symptoms.

Available forms

Aerosol: 800 mcg/metered spray
Capsules (for oral solution): 100 mg
Nasal solution: 5.2 mg/metered spray (40 mg/ml)
Ophthalmic solution: 4% (with benzalkonium chloride 0.01%, EDTA 0.01%, and phenylethyl ethanol 0.4%)
Solution (for nebulization): 20 mg/2 ml

NURSING PROCESS

Assessment

- Assess patient's underlying condition before therapy and reassess regularly thereafter.
- Monitor pulmonary function tests to demonstrate bronchodilator-reversible component of airway obstruction.
- Monitor patient for eosinophilic pneumonia.
- Watch for recurrence of asthma symptoms when dosage is decreased, especially when corticosteroids are also used.
- Be alert for adverse reactions.
- Evaluate patient's and family's knowledge of drug therapy.

Nursing diagnoses

- Impaired gas exchange related to patient's underlying condition
- Impaired tissue integrity related to drug-induced adverse EENT reactions
- Deficient knowledge related to drug therapy

Planning and implementation

- Drug should be used only when acute episode of asthma has been controlled, airway is cleared, and patient can inhale independently.
- **P.O. use:** Dissolve powder in capsules for oral dose in hot water and further dilute with cold water before ingestion. Don't mix with fruit juice, milk, or food.
  – Oral cromolyn sodium should be used in full-term neonates and infants only for severe, incapacitating disease when benefits clearly outweigh risks.
- **Inhalation use:** Insert inhalation capsule into inhalation device as described in manufacturer's directions. Have patient exhale completely. Then place mouthpiece between patient's lips; have him inhale deeply and rapidly with a steady, even breath; remove inhaler from mouth, have patient hold his breath for few seconds, and then exhale. Repeat until all powder has been inhaled.
- **Intranasal and ophthalmic use:** Follow normal protocol.
- Discontinue drug if patient develops eosinophilic pneumonia, indicated by eosinophilia and infiltrates on chest X-ray.
- Use antacids or milk to relieve esophagitis.

Patient teaching

- Instruct patient on how to give form of drug prescribed. Warn him to avoid excessive handling of capsules for inhalation.
- Tell patient that antacids or milk may relieve esophagitis.

• Instruct patient to notify prescriber if adverse reactions occur frequently or become troublesome or severe.

Evaluation

• Patient exhibits adequate gas exchange with drug therapy.
• Patient demonstrates appropriate management of adverse EENT reactions.
• Patient and family state understanding of drug therapy.

cyanocobalamin (vitamin B_{12})

(sigh-an-oh-koh-BAH-luh-meen)

Anacobin ♦, Bedoz ♦, Crystamine, Crysti 1000, Cyanocobalamin, Cyanoject, Cyomin

hydroxocobalamin (vitamin B_{12})

Hydro-Cobex, LA-12

Pharmacologic class: water-soluble vitamin
Therapeutic class: vitamin, nutrition supplement
Pregnancy risk category: A (C if used in doses above RDA)

Indications and dosages

▶ **RDA for cyanocobalamin.** *Adults and children age 11 and older:* 2 mcg.
Pregnant women: 2.2 mcg.
Breast-feeding women: 2.6 mcg.
Children ages 7 to 10: 1.4 mcg.
Children ages 4 to 6: 1 mcg.
Children ages 1 to 3: 0.7 mcg.
Infants ages 6 months to 1 year: 0.5 mcg.
Neonates and infants younger than age 6 months: 0.3 mcg.

▶ **Vitamin B_{12} deficiency caused by inadequate diet, subtotal gastrectomy, or any other condition, disorder, or disease except malabsorption related to pernicious anemia or other GI disease.** *Adults:* 30 mcg hydroxocobalamin I.M. daily for 5 to 10 days, depending on severity of deficiency. Maintenance dosage is 100 to 200 mcg I.M. once monthly. For subsequent prophylaxis, advise adequate nutrition and daily RDA vitamin B_{12} supplements.
Children: 1 to 5 mg hydroxocobalamin spread over 2 or more weeks in doses of 100 mcg I.M., depending on severity of deficiency. Maintenance dosage is 30 to 50 mcg I.M. monthly. For subsequent prophylaxis, advise adequate nutrition and daily RDA vitamin B_{12} supplements.

▶ **Pernicious anemia or vitamin B_{12} malabsorption.** *Adults:* Initially, 100 mcg cyanocobalamin I.M. or S.C. daily for 6 to 7 days; then 100 mcg I.M. or S.C. once monthly.
Children: 30 to 50 mcg I.M. or S.C. daily over 2 or more weeks; then 100 mcg I.M. or S.C. monthly for life.

▶ **Methylmalonic aciduria.** *Neonates:* 1,000 mcg cyanocobalamin I.M. daily.

▶ **Schilling test flushing dose.** *Adults and children:* 1,000 mcg hydroxocobalamin I.M. as a single dose.

Contraindications and precautions

• Contraindicated in patients with early Leber's disease or hypersensitivity to vitamin B_{12} or cobalt.
• Use cautiously in anemic patients with cardiac, pulmonary, or hypertensive disease and in those with severe vitamin B_{12}-dependent deficiencies.
Lifespan: In premature infants, use cautiously; some products contain benzyl alcohol, which may cause gasping syndrome.

Adverse reactions

CV: peripheral vascular thrombosis, ***pulmonary edema, heart failure.***
GI: transient diarrhea.
Skin: itching, transitory exanthema, urticaria.
Other: ***anaphylaxis, anaphylactoid reactions*** (with parenteral administration); pain, burning (at S.C. or I.M. injection sites).

Interactions

Drug-drug. *Aminoglycosides, chloramphenicol, colchicine, para-aminosalicylic acid and salts:* May cause malabsorption of vitamin B_{12}. Don't use together.
Drug-lifestyle. *Alcohol use:* May cause malabsorption of vitamin B_{12}. Discourage use together.

Effects on lab test results

• May decrease potassium level.
• May cause false-positive results for intrinsic factor antibody test.

Pharmacokinetics

Absorption: After oral administration, absorbed irregularly from distal small intestine. Depends on sufficient intrinsic factor and calcium. Rapid after I.M. and S.C. administration sites. Vitamin B_{12} is protein-bound.
Distribution: Distributed into liver, bone marrow, and other tissues.
Metabolism: Metabolized in liver.
Excretion: Amount of vitamin B_{12} needed by body is reabsorbed; excess is excreted in urine. *Half-life:* About 6 days.

Route	Onset	Peak	Duration
P.O.	Unknown	8-12 hr	Unknown
I.M.	Unknown	60 min	Unknown
S.C.	Unknown	Unknown	Unknown

Pharmacodynamics

Chemical effect: Acts as a coenzyme that stimulates metabolic functions. Needed for cell replication, hematopoiesis, and nucleoprotein and myelin synthesis.
Therapeutic effect: Increases vitamin B_{12} level.

Available forms

cyanocobalamin
Injection: 1,000 mcg/ml
Tablets: 25 mcg†, 50 mcg†, 100 mcg†, 250 mcg†, 500 mcg†, 1,000 mcg†
hydroxocobalamin
Injection: 1,000 mcg/ml

NURSING PROCESS

Assessment

- Assess patient's vitamin B_{12} deficiency before therapy.
- Determine reticulocyte count, hematocrit, and B_{12}, iron, and folate levels before beginning therapy.
- Monitor drug's effectiveness by assessing patient for improvement in signs and symptoms of vitamin B_{12} deficiency. Also monitor reticulocyte count, hematocrit, and B_{12}, iron, and folate levels between fifth and seventh day of therapy and periodically thereafter.
- Infection, tumors, and renal, hepatic, and other debilitating diseases may reduce therapeutic response.
- Closely monitor potassium levels for first 48 hours. Be alert for adverse reactions and drug interactions.
- Evaluate patient's and family's knowledge of drug therapy.

Nursing diagnoses

- Ineffective health maintenance related to underlying vitamin B_{12} deficiency
- Risk for injury related to parenteral administration and drug-induced hypersensitivity reactions
- Deficient knowledge related to drug therapy

Planning and implementation

- Don't mix parenteral liquids in same syringe with other medications.
- Drug is physically incompatible with dextrose solutions, alkaline or strongly acidic solutions, oxidizing or reducing agents, heavy metals, chlorpromazine, phytonadione, prochlorperazine, and many other drugs.
- **I.M. use:** Follow normal protocol. Hydroxocobalamin is approved only for I.M. use.
- **P.O. use:** Don't give large oral doses of vitamin B_{12} routinely because drug is lost through excretion.
- **S.C. use:** Follow normal protocol.
- Protect vitamin from light. Don't refrigerate or freeze.
- Give potassium supplement, if necessary.

Patient teaching

- Stress need for patient with pernicious anemia to return for monthly injections. Although total body stores may last 3 to 6 years, anemia will recur without monthly treatment.
- Emphasize importance of well-balanced diet.
- Tell patient to store oral tablets in tightly closed container at room temperature.

Evaluation

- Patient's vitamin B_{12} deficiency is resolved with drug therapy.
- Patient doesn't experience hypersensitivity reactions following parenteral administration of drug.
- Patient and family state understanding of drug therapy.

cyclobenzaprine hydrochloride

(sigh-kloh-BEN-zah-preen high-droh-KLOR-ighd)
Flexeril

Pharmacologic class: tricyclic antidepressant derivative
Therapeutic class: skeletal muscle relaxant
Pregnancy risk category: B

Indications and dosages

▶ **Short-term treatment of muscle spasm.** *Adults:* 10 mg P.O. t.i.d. for 7 days. Maximum dosage is 60 mg daily; maximum duration is 2 to 3 weeks.
▶ **Fibrositis‡.** *Adults:* 10 to 40 mg P.O. daily.

Contraindications and precautions

- Contraindicated in patients hypersensitive to drug and in patients who have received MAO inhibitors within 14 days, patients in the acute recovery phase of MI, and patients with hyperthyroidism, heart block, arrhythmias, conduction disturbances, or heart failure.
- Use cautiously in debilitated patients and in patients with history of urine retention, acute angle-closure glaucoma, or increased intraocular pressure.
- Caution use in patients taking anticholinergics.

Lifespan: In pregnant women, breast-feeding women, and in children younger than age 15, safety of drug hasn't been established. In elderly patients, use cautiously.

Adverse reactions

CNS: *drowsiness,* euphoria, weakness, headache, insomnia, nightmares, paresthesia, dizziness, depression, visual disturbances, ***seizures.***
CV: tachycardia, ***arrhythmias.***
EENT: blurred vision.
GI: dry mouth, abdominal pain, dyspepsia, abnormal taste, constipation.
GU: urine retention.
Skin: rash, urticaria, pruritus.

Interactions

Drug-drug. *Anticholinergics:* May have additive anticholinergic effects. Avoid using together.
CNS depressants: May cause additive CNS depression. Avoid using together.
MAO inhibitors: May exacerbate CNS depression or anticholinergic effects. Don't give within 14 days after discontinuing MAO inhibitors.
Drug-lifestyle. *Alcohol use:* May cause additive CNS depression. Discourage use together.

Effects on lab test results

None reported.

Pharmacokinetics

Absorption: Almost complete during first pass through GI tract.
Distribution: 93% plasma protein–bound.
Metabolism: During first pass through GI tract and liver, drug and metabolites undergo enterohepatic recycling.
Excretion: Excreted primarily in urine as conjugated metabolites; also in feces via bile as unchanged drug. *Half-life:* 1 to 3 days.

Route	Onset	Peak	Duration
P.O.	≤ 1 hr	3-8 hr	12-24 hr

Pharmacodynamics

Chemical effect: Unknown.
Therapeutic effect: Relieves muscle spasms.

Available forms

Tablets: 10 mg

NURSING PROCESS

Assessment

- Assess patient's underlying condition before therapy.
- Monitor drug's effectiveness by assessing severity and frequency of patient's muscle spasms.
- Be alert for nausea, headache, and malaise, which may occur if drug is stopped abruptly after long-term use.
- Evaluate patient's and family's knowledge about drug therapy.

Nursing diagnoses

- Acute pain related to presence of muscle spasms
- Risk for injury related to potential for drug-induced CNS adverse reactions
- Deficient knowledge related to drug therapy

Planning and implementation

ALERT: Watch for symptoms of overdose, including cardiac toxicity. Keep physostigmine available, and notify prescriber immediately if you suspect toxicity.

- Don't give drug with other CNS depressants.
- With high doses, watch for adverse reactions similar to those of other TCAs.

ALERT: Don't confuse Flexeril with Flaxedil.

Patient teaching

- Advise patient to report urinary hesitancy or urine retention. If constipation occurs, tell patient to increase fluid intake and suggest use of a stool softener.
- Warn patient to avoid activities that require alertness until drug's CNS effects are known.
- Warn patient to avoid combining drug with alcohol or other CNS depressants.
- Tell patient that dry mouth may be relieved with sugarless candy or gum.

Evaluation

- Patient is free from pain with drug therapy.
- Patient doesn't experience injury as a result of drug-induced adverse CNS reactions.
- Patient and family state understanding of drug therapy.

cyclophosphamide

(sigh-kloh-FOS-fuh-mighd)

Cycloblastin ◇, Cytoxan**, Cytoxan Lyophilized, Endoxan-Asta ◇, Neosar, Procytox ♦

Pharmacologic class: alkylating agent (not specific to cell cycle phase)
Therapeutic class: antineoplastic
Pregnancy risk category: D

Indications and dosages

▶ **Breast, head, neck, prostate, lung, and ovarian cancers; Hodgkin's disease; chronic lymphocytic leukemia; chronic myelocytic leukemia; acute lymphoblastic leukemia; acute myelocytic leukemia; neuroblastoma; retinoblastoma; non-Hodgkin's lymphoma; multiple myeloma; mycosis fungoides; sarcoma.** *Adults and children:* Initially, 40 to 50 mg/kg I.V. in divided doses over 2 to 5 days. Or, 10 to 15 mg/kg I.V. q 7 to 10 days, 3 to 5 mg/kg I.V. twice weekly, or 1 to 5 mg/kg P.O. daily, based on patient tolerance. Subsequent dosage adjusted according to evidence of antitumor activity or leukopenia.

▶ **"Minimal change" nephrotic syndrome in children.** *Children:* 2.5 to 3 mg/kg P.O. daily for 60 to 90 days.

▶ **Polymyositis ‡.** *Adults:* 1 to 2 mg/kg P.O. daily.

▶ **Rheumatoid arthritis‡.** *Adults:* 1.5 to 3 mg/kg P.O. daily.

▶ **Wegener's granulomatosis‡.** *Adults:* 1 to 2 mg/kg P.O. daily (usually given with prednisone).

Contraindications and precautions

- Contraindicated in patients with severe bone marrow depression.
- Use cautiously in patients who have recently undergone radiation therapy or chemotherapy and in patients with leukopenia, thrombocytopenia, malignant cell infiltration of bone marrow, or hepatic or renal disease.

Lifespan: In pregnant women, use with extreme caution, if at all, because fetal harm may occur. In breast-feeding women, drug is contraindicated.

Adverse reactions

CV: *cardiotoxicity* (with very high doses and with doxorubicin).
GI: anorexia, *nausea and vomiting* beginning within 6 hours, stomatitis, mucositis.
GU: gonadal suppression (may be irreversible), STERILE HEMORRHAGIC CYSTITIS, bladder fibrosis.
Hematologic: ***leukopenia,*** nadir between days 8 and 15, recovery in 17 to 28 days; ***thrombocytopenia; anemia.***
Metabolic: hyperuricemia.
Respiratory: ***pulmonary fibrosis*** (with high doses).
Skin: *reversible alopecia* in 50% of patients, especially with high doses.
Other: ***secondary malignancies, anaphylaxis,*** SIADH (with high doses), *sterility, gonadal suppression.*

Interactions

Drug-drug. *Barbiturates:* May increase pharmacologic effect and enhance cyclophosphamide toxicity caused by induction of hepatic enzymes. Avoid use together.

Cardiotoxic drugs: Additive adverse cardiac effects. Avoid use together.
Chloramphenicol, corticosteroids: Reduces activity of cyclophosphamide. Use cautiously.
Digoxin: May decrease digoxin levels. Monitor levels closely and adjust dosage as necessary.
Succinylcholine: Prolongs neuromuscular blockade. Don't use together.

Effects on lab test results

- May increase uric acid level. May decrease pseudocholinesterase level.
- May decrease hemoglobin, hematocrit, and WBC, RBC, and platelet counts.

Pharmacokinetics

Absorption: Almost complete with P.O. doses of 100 mg or less. Higher doses (300 mg) are about 75% absorbed.
Distribution: Distributed throughout body, although only minimal amounts have been found in saliva, sweat, and synovial fluid. Active metabolites are about 50% bound to plasma proteins.
Metabolism: Metabolized to its active form by hepatic microsomal enzymes. Activity of these metabolites is terminated by metabolism to inactive forms.
Excretion: Drug and its metabolites are eliminated primarily in urine, with 15% to 30% excreted as unchanged drug. *Half-life:* 4 to 6.5 hours.

Route	Onset	Peak	Duration
P.O., I.V.	Unknown	Unknown	Unknown

Pharmacodynamics

Chemical effect: Cross-links strands of cellular DNA and interferes with RNA transcription, causing imbalance of growth that leads to cell death.
Therapeutic effect: Kills specific types of cancer cells; improves renal function in mild nephrotic syndrome in children.

Available forms

Injection: 100-mg, 200-mg, 500-mg, 1-g, 2-g vials
Tablets: 25 mg, 50 mg

NURSING PROCESS

Assessment

- Assess patient's underlying condition before therapy and reassess regularly during therapy.
- Monitor CBC, uric acid levels, and renal and liver function tests.
- Monitor patient for cyclophosphamide toxicity if corticosteroid therapy is discontinued.
- Be alert for adverse reactions and drug interactions.
- Evaluate patient's and family's knowledge of drug therapy.

Nursing diagnoses

- Ineffective health maintenance related to underlying condition
- Risk for injury related to drug-induced adverse reactions
- Deficient knowledge related to drug therapy

Planning and implementation

- Follow facility policy to reduce risks. Preparation and administration of parenteral form of this drug is linked to carcinogenic, mutagenic, and teratogenic risks for personnel.
- **P.O. use:** Tablets are used for children with "minimal change" nephrotic syndrome and not to treat neoplastic disease.
- **I.V. use:** Reconstitute powder using sterile water for injection or bacteriostatic water for injection that contains only parabens. For nonlyophilized product, add 5 ml to 100-mg vial, 10 ml to 200-mg vial, 25 ml to 500-mg vial, 50 ml to 1-g vial, or 100 ml to 2-g vial to produce solution containing 20 mg/ml. Shake to dissolve; this may take up to 6 minutes and it may be difficult to completely dissolve drug. Lyophilized preparation is much easier to reconstitute; check package insert for quantity of diluent needed to reconstitute drug.
– After reconstitution, give by direct I.V. injection or infusion. For I.V. infusion, further dilute with D_5W, dextrose 5% in normal saline solution, dextrose 5% in Ringer's injection, lactated Ringer's injection, sodium lactate injection, or half-normal saline solution for injection.
– Check reconstituted solution for small particles. Filter solution if necessary.
– Reconstituted solution is stable for 6 days refrigerated or 24 hours at room temperature. However, use stored solutions cautiously because drug contains no preservatives.

• To prevent hyperuricemia with resulting uric acid nephropathy, allopurinol may be used with adequate hydration.

Patient teaching

• Warn patient that alopecia is likely to occur but that it's reversible.
• Warn patient to watch for signs of infection (fever, sore throat, fatigue) and bleeding (easy bruising, nosebleeds, bleeding gums, melena) and to take temperature daily.
• Instruct patient to avoid OTC products that contain aspirin.
• Encourage patient to void every 1 to 2 hours while awake and to drink at least 3 L of fluid daily to minimize risk of hemorrhagic cystitis. Tell patient not to take drug at bedtime; infrequent urination during night may increase possibility of cystitis. If cystitis occurs, tell patient to discontinue drug and notify prescriber. Cystitis can occur months after therapy ends. Mesna may be given to lower risk and severity of bladder toxicity.
• Advise both men and women to practice contraception while taking drug and for 4 months after; drug is potentially teratogenic.
• Advise women of childbearing age to avoid becoming pregnant during therapy. Also recommend consulting with prescriber before becoming pregnant.

Evaluation

• Patient shows positive response to drug therapy.
• Patient doesn't experience injury as a result of drug-induced adverse reactions.
• Patient and family state understanding of drug therapy.

cycloserine
(sigh-kloh-SER-een)
Seromycin

Pharmacologic class: isoxizolidone, d-alanine analogue
Therapeutic class: antituberculotic
Pregnancy risk category: C

Indications and dosages

► **Adjunct treatment in pulmonary or extrapulmonary tuberculosis.** *Adults:* Initially, 250 mg P.O. q 12 hours for 2 weeks; then, if blood levels are below 25 to 30 mcg/ml and no toxicity has developed, 250 mg q 8 hours for 2 weeks. If optimum blood levels aren't achieved and no toxicity has developed, increase to 250 mg q 6 hours. Maximum dosage is 1 g daily. If CNS toxicity occurs, drug is discontinued for 1 week and then resumed at 250 mg daily for 2 weeks. If no serious toxic effects occur, increase by 250-mg increments q 10 days until blood level is 25 to 30 mcg/ml.

Contraindications and precautions

• Contraindicated in patients hypersensitive to drug; in patients who consume excessive amounts of alcohol; and in patients with seizure disorders, depression, severe anxiety, psychosis, or severe renal insufficiency.
• Use cautiously in patients with impaired renal function; reduced dosage is required.
Lifespan: In pregnant and breast-feeding women, use cautiously. In children, safety of drug hasn't been established.

Adverse reactions

CNS: ***seizures,*** drowsiness, headache, tremor, dysarthria, vertigo, confusion, loss of memory, ***possible suicidal tendencies*** and other psychotic symptoms, ***nervousness, hallucinations, depression,*** hyperirritability, paresthesia, paresis, hyperreflexia, ***coma.***
Other: hypersensitivity reactions (allergic dermatitis).

Interactions

Drug-drug. *Ethionamide, isoniazid:* Increases risk of CNS toxicity (seizures, dizziness, or drowsiness). Monitor patient closely.
Drug-lifestyle. *Alcohol use:* Increases risk of CNS toxicity. Advise patient to refrain from alcohol consumption during therapy.

Effects on lab test results

• May increase transaminase level.

Pharmacokinetics

Absorption: About 80%.
Distribution: Distributed widely into body tissues and fluids, including CSF. It doesn't bind to plasma proteins.
Metabolism: May be metabolized partially.

Excretion: Excreted primarily in urine. *Half-life:* 10 hours.

Route	Onset	Peak	Duration
P.O.	Unknown	3-4 hr	Unknown

Pharmacodynamics

Chemical effect: Inhibits cell-wall biosynthesis by interfering with bacterial use of amino acids (bacteriostatic).
Therapeutic effect: Aids in eradicating tuberculosis.

Available forms

Capsules: 250 mg

NURSING PROCESS

Assessment

- Assess patient's underlying condition before therapy.
- Obtain specimen for culture and sensitivity tests before therapy begins and periodically thereafter to detect possible resistance.
- Monitor drug's effectiveness by evaluating culture and sensitivity results; watch for improvement in patient's underlying condition.
- Monitor cycloserine levels periodically, especially in patients receiving high doses (more than 500 mg daily) because toxic reactions may occur with blood levels above 30 mcg/ml.
- Monitor results of hematologic tests and renal and liver function studies.
- Be alert for adverse reactions and drug interactions.
- Evaluate patient's and family's knowledge of drug therapy.

Nursing diagnoses

- Ineffective health maintenance related to presence of tuberculosis
- Risk for injury related to drug-induced CNS adverse reactions
- Deficient knowledge related to drug therapy

Planning and implementation

- Cycloserine is considered second-line drug in treatment of tuberculosis and always should be given with other antituberculotics to prevent development of resistant organisms.
- Expect to adjust dosage according to blood levels, clinical toxicity, or ineffectiveness.
- Give pyridoxine, anticonvulsants, tranquilizers, or sedatives to relieve adverse reactions.

Patient teaching

- Warn patient to avoid alcohol, which may cause serious neurologic reactions.
- Instruct patient to take drug exactly as prescribed; warn against discontinuing drug without prescriber's approval.
- Stress importance of having laboratory studies done to monitor drug effectiveness and toxicity.

Evaluation

- Patient maintains health after drug therapy.
- Patient has no injury as a result of drug-induced adverse reactions.
- Patient and family state understanding of drug therapy.

cyclosporine (cyclosporin)

(sigh-kloh-SPOOR-een)
Neoral, Sandimmun◇, Sandimmune

Pharmacologic class: polypeptide antibiotic
Therapeutic class: immunosuppressant
Pregnancy risk category: C

Indications and dosages

▶ **Prophylaxis of organ rejection in kidney, liver, or heart transplantation.** *Adults and children:* 15 mg/kg P.O. 4 to 12 hours before transplantation and continued daily postoperatively for 1 to 2 weeks. Dosage is reduced by 5% each week to maintenance level of 5 to 10 mg/kg daily. Or, 5 to 6 mg/kg I.V. concentrate 4 to 12 hours before transplantation. Postoperatively, dosage repeated daily until patient can tolerate P.O. forms. For microemulsion, oral doses are the same and dosage adjustments are made according to a predefined cyclosporine level.

▶ **Severe, active rheumatoid arthritis that hasn't adequately responded to methotrexate.** *Neoral. Adults:* 1.25 mg/kg P.O. b.i.d.

▶ **Recalcitrant, plaque psoriasis that isn't adequately responsive to at least one systemic therapy or in patients for whom other systemic therapy is contraindicated or isn't tolerated.** *Neoral. Adults:* Initially, 2.5 mg/kg P.O. daily divided b.i.d. Initial dose should be maintained for 4 weeks. If dosage increase is necessary, increase by 0.5 mg/kg daily to a maximum of 4 mg/kg daily at 2-week intervals.

Contraindications and precautions

- Contraindicated in patients hypersensitive to drug or to polyoxyethylated castor oil (found in injectable form). Neoral is contraindicated in patients with psoriasis or rheumatoid arthritis who also have abnormal renal function, uncontrolled hypertension, or malignancies.

Lifespan: In pregnant women, use cautiously. In breast-feeding women, safety of drug hasn't been established.

Adverse reactions

CNS: *tremor,* headache, ***seizures.***
CV: flushing, hypertension.
EENT: sinusitis.
GI: *gum hyperplasia,* oral thrush, nausea, vomiting, diarrhea.
GU: **NEPHROTOXICITY.**
Hematologic: anemia, **LEUKOPENIA, THROMBOCYTOPENIA.**
Hepatic: ***hepatotoxicity.***
Skin: *hirsutism,* acne.
Other: ***infections, anaphylaxis.***

Interactions

Drug-drug. *Aminoglycosides, amphotericin B, co-trimoxazole, NSAIDs:* May increase risk of nephrotoxicity. Monitor patient for toxicity.
Amphotericin B, cilastatin, cimetidine, diltiazem, erythromycin, imipenem, ketoconazole, metoclopramide, prednisolone: May increase levels of cyclosporine. Monitor patient for increased toxicity.
Azathioprine, corticosteroids, cyclophosphamide, verapamil: Increase immunosuppression. Monitor patient closely for infection.
Carbamazepine, isoniazid, phenobarbital, phenytoin, rifampin: Possible decreased immunosuppressant effect. May need to increase cyclosporine dosage.
Vaccines: Decrease immune response. Postpone routine immunization.
Drug-herb. *Pill-bearing spurge:* May inhibit CYP3A enzymes affecting drug metabolism. Discourage using together.
St. John's wort: May significantly lower cyclosporine levels in the blood, contributing to organ rejection. Strongly advise against use together.
Drug-food. *Grapefruit juice:* Slows metabolism of drug. Avoid using together.

Effects on lab test results

- May increase BUN, creatinine, LDL, bilirubin, AST, ALT, and glucose levels.
- May decrease hemoglobin, hematocrit, and WBC and platelet counts.

Pharmacokinetics

Absorption: Absorption varies widely. Only 30% of Sandimmune oral dose reaches systemic circulation, while 60% of Neoral reaches systemic circulation.
Distribution: Distributed widely outside blood volume. In plasma, about 90% is bound to proteins.
Metabolism: Metabolized extensively in liver.
Excretion: Excreted primarily in feces with only 6% of drug found in urine. *Half-life:* 10 to 27 hours.

Route	Onset	Peak	Duration
P.O.			
Sandimmune	Unknown	3.5 hr	Unknown
Neoral	Unknown	1.5-2 hr	Unknown
I.V.	Unknown	Unknown	Unknown

Pharmacodynamics

Chemical effect: Inhibits proliferation of T lymphocytes.
Therapeutic effect: Prevents organ rejection.

Available forms

Capsules: 25 mg, 50 mg, 100 mg
Capsules for microemulsion: 25 mg, 100 mg
Injection: 50 mg/ml
Oral solution: 100 mg/ml

NURSING PROCESS

Assessment

- Assess patient's organ transplant before therapy.
- Monitor effectiveness by evaluating patient for signs and symptoms of organ rejection.
- Monitor cyclosporine level at regular intervals.
- Monitor BUN and creatinine levels because nephrotoxicity may develop 2 to 3 months after transplant surgery, possibly requiring dosage reduction.

• Monitor liver function tests for hepatotoxicity, which usually occurs during first month after transplant.
• Monitor CBC and platelet counts regularly.
• Be alert for adverse reactions and drug interactions.
• Evaluate patient's and family's knowledge of drug therapy.

Nursing diagnoses
• Risk for injury related to potential for organ rejection
• Ineffective protection related to drug-induced immunosuppression
• Deficient knowledge related to drug therapy

Planning and implementation
• **P.O. use:** Measure oral doses carefully in oral syringe. To increase palatability, mix with whole milk, chocolate milk, or fruit juice (except grapefruit juice). Oral cyclosporine solution for emulsion is less palatable when mixed with milk. Use glass container to minimize adherence to container walls.
– Give drug with meals to minimize GI distress.
• **I.V. use:** Give cyclosporine I.V. concentrate at one-third oral dose and dilute before use. Dilute each ml of concentrate in 20 to 100 ml of D_5W or normal saline solution for injection. Dilute immediately before infusion; infuse over 2 to 6 hours. Usually reserved for patients who cannot tolerate oral drugs.
ALERT: Sandimmune and Neoral aren't bioequivalent and can't and shouldn't be used interchangeably without prescriber supervision. Conversion from Neoral to Sandimmune should be made with increased monitoring to avoid underdosing.
• Psoriasis patients who are treated with Neoral shouldn't also receive PUVA or UVB therapy, methotrexate or other immunosuppressive agents, coal tar, or radiation therapy.
• Always give drug with adrenal corticosteroids.

Patient teaching
• Encourage patient to take drug at same times each day.
• Advise patient to take Neoral on an empty stomach and not to mix with grapefruit juice.
• Advise patient to take with meals if drug causes nausea. Anorexia, nausea, and vomiting are usually transient and most frequently occur at start of therapy.
• Stress that therapy shouldn't be stopped without prescriber's approval.
• Instruct patient to swish and swallow nystatin four times daily to prevent oral thrush.
• Instruct patient on infection control and bleeding precautions, as indicated by CBC and platelet count results.

Evaluation
• Patient doesn't experience organ rejection while taking drug.
• Patient is free from infection and serious bleeding episodes throughout drug therapy.
• Patient and family state understanding of drug therapy.

cyproheptadine hydrochloride
(sigh-proh-HEP-tah-deen high-droh-KLOR-ighd)
Periactin

Pharmacologic class: piperidine-derivative antihistamine
Therapeutic class: antihistamine (H_1-receptor antagonist), antipruritic
Pregnancy risk category: B

Indications and dosages
▶ **Allergy symptoms, pruritus.** *Adults:* 4 to 20 mg P.O. daily in divided doses. Maximum dosage is 0.5 mg/kg daily.
Children ages 7 to 14: 4 mg P.O. b.i.d. or t.i.d. Maximum dosage is 16 mg daily.
Children ages 2 to 6: 2 mg P.O. b.i.d. or t.i.d. Maximum dosage is 12 mg daily.
▶ **Cushing's syndrome‡.** *Adults:* 8 to 24 mg P.O. daily in divided doses.

Contraindications and precautions
• Contraindicated in debilitated patients; in patients hypersensitive to drug or other drugs of similar chemical structure; in those with acute asthmatic attacks, angle-closure glaucoma, stenosing peptic ulcer, symptomatic prostatic hypertrophy, bladder-neck obstruction, and pyloroduodenal obstruction; and in patients taking MAO inhibitors.
• Use cautiously in patients with increased intraocular pressure, hyperthyroidism, CV disease, hypertension, or bronchial asthma.

Lifespan: In pregnant women, use cautiously. In breast-feeding women, neonates, premature infants, and elderly patients, drug is contraindicated.

Adverse reactions

CNS: *drowsiness,* dizziness, headache, fatigue, ***seizures*** (especially in elderly patients).
GI: nausea, vomiting, epigastric distress, *dry mouth.*
GU: urine retention.
Hematologic: ***agranulocytosis, thrombocytopenia.***
Metabolic: weight gain.
Skin: rash.
Other: ***anaphylaxis.***

Interactions

Drug-drug. *CNS depressants:* May increase sedation. Use together cautiously.
MAO inhibitors: May increase anticholinergic effects. Don't use together.
Drug-lifestyle. *Sun exposure:* Photosensitivity reactions may occur. Urge patient to avoid sun exposure and wear protective clothing and sunblock.

Effects on lab test results

- May decrease hemoglobin, hematocrit, and WBC, platelet, and granulocyte counts.

Pharmacokinetics

Absorption: Well absorbed from GI tract.
Distribution: Unknown.
Metabolism: Appears to be almost completely metabolized in liver.
Excretion: Metabolites are excreted primarily in urine; unchanged drug isn't excreted in urine, but small amounts of unchanged cyproheptadine and metabolites are excreted in feces.

Route	Onset	Peak	Duration
P.O.	15-60 min	6-9 hr	8 hr

Pharmacodynamics

Chemical effect: Competes with histamine for H_1-receptor sites on effector cells. Prevents, but doesn't reverse, histamine-mediated responses.
Therapeutic effect: Relieves allergy symptoms and itching.

Available forms

Syrup: 2 mg/5 ml
Tablets: 4 mg

NURSING PROCESS

Assessment

- Assess patient's underlying condition before therapy and reassess regularly during therapy.
- Be alert for adverse reactions and drug interactions.
- Evaluate patient's and family's knowledge of drug therapy.

Nursing diagnoses

- Ineffective health maintenance related to underlying condition
- Risk for injury related to potential for drug-induced adverse CNS reactions
- Deficient knowledge related to drug therapy

Planning and implementation

- Reduce GI distress by giving drug with food or milk.
- Notify prescriber if tolerance is suspected; another antihistamine may need to be used.

Patient teaching

- Instruct patient to take drug with food or milk to reduce GI distress.
- Warn patient to avoid alcohol and hazardous activities until CNS effects of drug are known.
- Tell patient that coffee or tea may reduce drowsiness. Sugarless gum, hard candy, or ice chips may relieve dry mouth.
- Advise patient to stop drug 4 days before allergy skin tests to preserve accuracy of tests.
- Instruct patient to notify prescriber if tolerance develops; different antihistamine may be needed.

Evaluation

- Patient is free from allergy symptoms or pruritus with drug therapy.
- Patient has no injury as result of drug-induced CNS adverse reactions.
- Patient and family state understanding of drug therapy.

cytarabine (ara-C, cytosine arabinoside)

(sigh-TAR-uh-been)
Cytosar ♦, Cytosar-U

Pharmacologic class: antimetabolite (specific to S phase of cell cycle)
Therapeutic class: antineoplastic
Pregnancy risk category: D

Indications and dosages

▶ **Acute nonlymphocytic leukemia, acute lymphocytic leukemia, blast phase of chronic myelocytic leukemia.** *Adults and children:* 100 mg/m^2 daily by continuous I.V. infusion or 100 mg/m^2 I.V. q 12 hours, given for 5 days and repeated q 2 weeks. For maintenance, 1 mg/kg S.C. once or twice weekly.

▶ **Meningeal leukemia.** *Adults and children:* Highly variable from 5 to 75 mg/m^2 intrathecally. Frequency also varies from once a day for 4 days to once q 4 days. Most common dosage is 30 mg/m^2, q 4 days until CSF is normal, followed by one more dose.

Contraindications and precautions

- Contraindicated in patients hypersensitive to drug.
- Use cautiously in patients with hepatic disease.

Lifespan: In pregnant women, drug isn't recommended because fetal harm may occur. In breast-feeding women, use is contraindicated.

Adverse reactions

CNS: neurotoxicity, including ataxia and cerebellar dysfunction (with high doses).
EENT: keratitis, nystagmus.
GI: nausea, vomiting, diarrhea, dysphagia; reddened area at juncture of lips, followed by sore mouth and oral ulcers in 5 to 10 days; high dose given by rapid I.V. may cause projectile vomiting.
GU: urate nephropathy.
Hematologic: ***leukopenia,*** with initial WBC count nadir 7 to 9 days after drug is stopped and second (more severe) nadir 15 to 24 days after drug is stopped; anemia; reticulocytopenia; ***thrombocytopenia,*** with platelet count nadir occurring on day 10; *megaloblastosis.*
Hepatic: ***hepatotoxicity*** (usually mild and reversible).
Metabolic: hyperuricemia.
Skin: rash.
Other: flu syndrome, ***anaphylaxis.***

Interactions

Drug-drug. *Digoxin:* May decrease digoxin levels. Monitor digoxin levels.
Flucytosine: Decreases flucytosine activity. Monitor patient closely.
Gentamicin: May decrease activity against *Klebsiella pneumoniae*. Don't use together.

Effects on lab test results

- May increase uric acid level.
- May increase megaloblasts. May decrease hemoglobin, hematocrit, and WBC, RBC, platelet, and reticulocyte counts.

Pharmacokinetics

Absorption: Unknown.
Distribution: Rapidly distributed widely throughout body. About 13% of drug is bound to plasma proteins. Drug penetrates the blood-brain barrier only slightly after rapid I.V. dose; however, when drug is given by continuous I.V. infusion, CSF levels achieve 40% to 60% of that of plasma levels.
Metabolism: Metabolized primarily in liver but also in kidneys, GI mucosa, and granulocytes.
Excretion: Drug and its metabolites are excreted in urine. Less than 10% of dose is excreted as unchanged drug in urine. *Half-life:* Elimination of cytarabine is biphasic, with initial half-life of 8 minutes and terminal phase half-life of 1 to 3 hours.

Route	Onset	Peak	Duration
I.V., intrathecal	Unknown	Unknown	Unknown
S.C.	Unknown	20-60 min	Unknown

Pharmacodynamics

Chemical effect: Inhibits DNA synthesis.
Therapeutic effect: Kills selected cancer cells.

Available forms

Injection: 100-mg, 500-mg, 1-g, 2-g vials

NURSING PROCESS

Assessment
• Assess patient's underlying condition before therapy and reassess regularly throughout therapy.
• Monitor uric acid level, hepatic and renal function studies, and CBC.
• Be alert for adverse reactions and drug interactions.
• If patient receives high doses, watch for neurotoxicity, which may first appear as nystagmus but can progress to ataxia and cerebellar dysfunction.
• Evaluate patient's and family's knowledge of drug therapy.

Nursing diagnoses
• Ineffective health maintenance related to underlying condition
• Risk for injury related to drug-induced adverse hematologic reactions
• Deficient knowledge related to drug therapy

Planning and implementation
• Follow facility policy to reduce risks. Preparation and administration of parenteral form of this drug are linked to carcinogenic, mutagenic, and teratogenic risks for personnel.
• **I.V. use:** To reduce nausea, give antiemetic before drug. Nausea and vomiting are more frequent when large doses are given rapidly by I.V. push. These reactions are less frequent when given by infusion.
– Reconstitute drug using provided diluent, which is bacteriostatic water for injection containing benzyl alcohol. Avoid this diluent when preparing drug for neonates or for intrathecal use. Reconstitute 100-mg vial with 5 ml of diluent or 500-mg vial with 10 ml of diluent. Reconstituted solution is stable for 48 hours. Discard cloudy reconstituted solution.
– For I.V. infusion, further dilute using normal saline solution for injection, D_5W, or sterile water for injection.
• **S.C. use:** Follow manufacturer guidelines.
• **Intrathecal use:** Use preservative-free normal saline solution. Add 5 ml to 100-mg vial or 10 ml to 500-mg vial. Use immediately after reconstitution. Discard unused drug.
• Maintain high fluid intake and give allopurinol to avoid urate nephropathy in leukemia induction therapy.
• Therapy may be modified or stopped if granulocyte count is below 1,000/mm^3 or if platelet count is below 50,000/mm^3.
• Corticosteroid eye drops are prescribed to prevent drug-induced keratitis.
• Prescriber must judge possible benefit against known adverse effects.

Patient teaching
• Warn patient to watch for signs of infection (fever, sore throat, fatigue) and bleeding (easy bruising, nosebleeds, bleeding gums, melena). Tell patient to take temperature daily.
• Instruct patient on infection control and bleeding precautions.
• Advise woman of childbearing age to avoid becoming pregnant during therapy. Also recommend consulting with prescriber before becoming pregnant.
• Encourage patient to drink at least 3 L of fluids daily.
• Instruct patient about need for frequent oral hygiene.

Evaluation
• Patient demonstrates positive response to drug therapy.
• Patient doesn't experience injury as result of drug therapy.
• Patient and family state understanding of drug therapy.

cytomegalovirus immune globulin, intravenous (CMV-IGIV)
(sigh-toh-meh-GEH-loh-VIGH-rus ih-MYOON GLOH-byoo-lin)
CytoGam

Pharmacologic class: immune globulin
Therapeutic class: immune serum
Pregnancy risk category: C

Indications and dosages
▶ **To attenuate primary CMV disease in seronegative kidney transplant recipients who receive kidney from a CMV seropositive donor.** *Adults:* Give I.V. based on time after transplantation:
within 72 hours: 150 mg/kg
2 weeks after: 100 mg/kg

4 weeks after: 100 mg/kg
6 weeks after: 100 mg/kg
8 weeks after: 100 mg/kg
12 weeks after: 50 mg/kg
16 weeks after: 50 mg/kg.
Give first dose at 15 mg/kg/hour. Increase to 30 mg/kg/hour after 30 minutes if no adverse reactions occur, then increase to 60 mg/kg/hour after another 30 minutes if no adverse reactions occur. Volume shouldn't exceed 75 ml/hour. Subsequent doses may be given at 15 mg/kg/hour for 15 minutes, increasing at 15-minute intervals in stepwise fashion to 60 mg/kg/hour.

▶ **Prophylaxis of CMV disease related to lung, liver, pancreas, and heart transplants.** *Adults:* Use with ganciclovir in organ transplants from CMV seropositive donors into seronegative recipients. Maximum total dose per infusion is 150 mg/kg I.V. Given as follows based on time after transplantation:
within 72 hours: 150 mg/kg
2 weeks after: 150 mg/kg
4 weeks after: 150 mg/kg
6 weeks after: 150 mg/kg
8 weeks after: 150 mg/kg
12 weeks after: 100 mg/kg
16 weeks after: 100 mg/kg.
Give first dose at 15 mg/kg/hour. If no adverse reactions occur after 30 minutes, increase rate to 30 mg/kg/hour. If no adverse reactions occur after another 30 minutes, infusion may be increased to 60 mg/kg/hour (volume shouldn't exceed 75 ml/hour). Subsequent doses may be given at 15 mg/kg/hour for 15 minutes, increasing every 15 minutes in a stepwise fashion to a maximum of 60 mg/kg/hour (volume shouldn't exceed 75 ml/hour). Monitor patient closely during and after each rate change.

Contraindications and precautions

- Contraindicated in patients with selective IgA deficiency or history of sensitivity to other human immunoglobulin preparations.

Lifespan: In pregnant women, use cautiously. In breast-feeding women and in children, safety of drug hasn't been established.

Adverse reactions

CNS: flushing, fever.
CV: hypotension.
GI: nausea, vomiting.
Musculoskeletal: muscle cramps, back pain.
Respiratory: wheezing.
Other: *anaphylaxis,* chills.

Interactions

Drug-drug. *Live-virus vaccines:* Drug may interfere with immune response to live-virus vaccines. Defer vaccination for at least 3 months.

Effects on lab test results

None reported.

Pharmacokinetics

Absorption: Administered I.V.
Distributed: Unknown.
Metabolism: Unknown.
Excretion: Unknown.
Unknown.

Route	Onset	Peak	Duration
I.V.	Unknown	Unknown	Unknown

Pharmacodynamics

Chemical effect: Supplies relatively high concentration of immunoglobulin G (IgG) antibodies against CMV. Increasing these antibody levels in CMV-exposed patients may attenuate or reduce risk of serious CMV disease.
Therapeutic effect: Provides passive immunity to CMV.

Available forms

Solution for injection: 50 (± 10) mg (of protein) per ml.

NURSING PROCESS

Assessment

- Assess patient's kidney transplant before therapy.
- Take vital signs before starting therapy and then mid-infusion, post-infusion, and before any increase in infusion rate.
- Monitor drug's effectiveness by evaluating kidney function.
- Be alert for adverse reactions and drug interactions.
- Evaluate patient's and family's knowledge of drug therapy.

Nursing diagnoses

- Risk for injury related to potential for organ rejection

• Decreased cardiac output related to drug-induced hypotension
• Deficient knowledge related to drug therapy

Planning and implementation

• Remove tab portion of vial cap and clean rubber stopper with 70% alcohol or equivalent. Don't shake vial; avoid foaming. Infuse solution only if it is colorless, free of particulate matter, and not turbid. Pre-dilution isn't recommended.
• If possible, give through separate I.V. line using constant infusion pump. Filters are unnecessary. If unable to give through separate line, piggyback into existing line of saline solution injection or one of the following dextrose solutions with or without saline solution: dextrose 2.5% in water, D_5W, dextrose 10% in water, or dextrose 20% in water. Don't dilute more than 1:2 with any of these solutions.
• Refrigerate drug at 36° F to 46° F (2° C to 8° C).
• If patient develops anaphylaxis or if blood pressure drops, discontinue infusion, notify prescriber, and be prepared to administer CPR and drugs, such drugs as diphenhydramine and epinephrine.

Patient teaching

• Teach patient about drug therapy.
• Instruct patient to notify prescriber immediately if adverse reactions develop.

Evaluation

• Patient doesn't reject transplanted kidney during drug therapy.
• Patient maintains normal cardiac output throughout drug therapy.
• Patient and family state understanding of drug therapy.

D

dacarbazine (DTIC)

(deh-KAR-buh-zeen)
DTIC ♦, DTIC-Dome

Pharmacologic class: alkylating agent (cell cycle–phase nonspecific)
Therapeutic class: antineoplastic
Pregnancy risk category: C

Indications and dosages

▶ **Metastatic malignant melanoma.** *Adults:* 2 to 4.5 mg/kg I.V. daily for 10 days; then q 4 weeks, as tolerated. Or, 250 mg/m² I.V. daily for 5 days; repeat at 3-week intervals.
▶ **Hodgkin's disease.** *Adults:* 150 mg/m² I.V. daily (combined with other drugs) for 5 days; repeat q 4 weeks. Or, 375 mg/m² on first day of combination regimen; repeat q 15 days.
Patients with renal impairment: Use lower dose. For patients with severely impaired renal function, reduce dosage when giving repeated doses.

Contraindications and precautions

• Contraindicated in patients hypersensitive to drug.
• Use cautiously if patient's bone marrow function is impaired.
Lifespan: In pregnant women, use with extreme caution and only when absolutely necessary because fetal harm may occur. In breast-feeding women, use is contraindicated. In children, safety of drug hasn't been established.

Adverse reactions

GI: *severe nausea and vomiting, anorexia.*
Hematologic: ***leukopenia, thrombocytopenia*** (nadir at 3 to 4 weeks).
Metabolic: hyperuricemia.
Skin: alopecia, phototoxicity.
Other: *flulike syndrome* (fever, malaise, myalgia beginning 7 days after treatment and possibly lasting 7 to 21 days), ***anaphylaxis,*** severe pain with concentrated solution or extravasation, tissue damage.

Interactions

Drug-drug. *Allopurinol:* May have additive hypouricemic effects. Monitor patient closely.
Anticoagulants, aspirin: May increase risk of bleeding. Avoid using together.
Bone marrow suppressants: May increase toxicity. Monitor patient closely.
Phenobarbital, phenytoin, other drugs that induce hepatic metabolism: May enhance dacarbazine metabolism. Dosage adjustment may be needed.
Drug-lifestyle. *Sun exposure:* May cause photosensitivity reactions, especially during the

first 2 days of therapy. Advise patient to avoid prolonged sun exposure and to wear protective clothing and sunblock.

Effects on lab test results

- May increase BUN and liver enzyme levels.
- May decrease WBC, RBC, and platelet counts.

Pharmacokinetics

Absorption: Administered I.V.
Distribution: Thought to localize in body tissues, especially the liver; minimally bound to plasma proteins.
Metabolism: Rapidly metabolized in liver to several compounds, some of which may be active.
Excretion: About 30% to 45% of dose excreted in urine. *Half-life:* Initial, 19 minutes; terminal, 5 hours.

Route	Onset	Peak	Duration
I.V.	Unknown	Unknown	Unknown

Pharmacodynamics

Chemical effect: Probably cross-links strands of cellular DNA and interferes with RNA transcription, causing imbalance of growth that leads to cell death.
Therapeutic effect: Kills selected cancer cells.

Available forms

Injection: 100-mg, 200-mg vials

NURSING PROCESS

Assessment

- Obtain history of patient's underlying disease before therapy, and reassess regularly throughout therapy.
- Monitor CBC, platelet count, and liver enzyme levels.
- Be alert for adverse reactions and drug interactions.
- Evaluate patient's and family's knowledge of drug therapy.

Nursing diagnoses

- Ineffective health maintenance related to presence of neoplastic disease
- Risk for injury related to risk of drug-induced adverse reactions
- Deficient knowledge related to drug therapy

Planning and implementation

- Follow facility policy to reduce risks. Preparation and administration of parenteral form raises risk of carcinogenic, mutagenic, and teratogenic effects for personnel.
- Give antiemetics before giving dacarbazine to help decrease nausea. Nausea and vomiting may subside after several doses.
- Reconstitute drug with sterile water for injection. Add 9.9 ml to 100-mg vial or 19.7 ml to 200-mg vial. The resulting solution should be colorless to clear yellow. For infusion, further dilute, using up to 250 ml of normal saline injection or D_5W. Infuse over 30 minutes.
- During infusion, protect bag from direct sunlight to avoid drug breakdown. Solution may be diluted further or infusion slowed to decrease pain at infusion site.
- Reconstituted solutions are stable for 8 hours at room temperature and under normal lighting conditions, up to 3 days if refrigerated. Diluted solutions are stable for 8 hours at room temperature and normal light, up to 24 hours if refrigerated. If solutions turn pink, this is a sign of decomposition; discard drug.
- Take care to avoid extravasation during infusion. If I.V. site infiltrates, discontinue infusion immediately, apply ice to area for 24 to 48 hours, and notify prescriber.
- For Hodgkin's disease, drug is usually given with bleomycin, vinblastine, and doxorubicin.

Patient teaching

- Warn patient to watch for signs of infection (fever, sore throat, fatigue) and bleeding (easy bruising, nosebleeds, bleeding gums, melena). Tell patient to take temperature daily.
- Instruct patient to avoid OTC products containing aspirin.
- Advise patient to avoid sunlight and sunlamps for first 2 days after treatment.
- Reassure patient that flulike syndrome may be treated with mild antipyretics, such as acetaminophen.

Evaluation

- Patient exhibits positive response to therapy, as evidenced on follow-up diagnostic studies and overall physical status.
- Patient has no injury from drug-induced adverse reactions.
- Patient and family state understanding of drug therapy.

daclizumab

(da-KLIZ-yoo-mab)
Zenapax

Pharmacologic class: humanized immunoglobulin G_1 monoclonal antibody
Therapeutic class: immunosuppressant
Pregnancy risk category: C

Indications and dosages

▶ **Prevention of acute organ rejection in patients receiving renal transplants with an immunosuppressive regimen that includes cyclosporine and corticosteroids.** *Adults:* 1 mg/kg I.V. Standard course of therapy is five doses. Give first dose no more than 24 hours before transplantation; give remaining four doses at 14-day intervals.

Contraindications and precautions

- Contraindicated in patients hypersensitive to daclizumab and its components.

Lifespan: In pregnant or breast-feeding women, use with extreme caution. Women of childbearing age should use contraception before beginning drug therapy, during therapy, and for 4 months after ending therapy.

Adverse reactions

CNS: tremors, headache, dizziness, insomnia, generalized weakness, prickly sensation, fever, pain, fatigue, depression, anxiety.
CV: tachycardia, hypertension, hypotension, aggravated hypertension, edema, fluid overload, chest pain.
EENT: blurred vision, pharyngitis, rhinitis.
GI: constipation, nausea, diarrhea, vomiting, abdominal pain, dyspepsia, pyrosis, abdominal distention, epigastric pain, flatulence, gastritis, hemorrhoids.
GU: ***oliguria,*** dysuria, ***renal tubular necrosis,*** renal damage, urine retention, hydronephrosis, urinary tract bleeding, urinary tract disorder, renal insufficiency.
Hematologic: lymphocele, bleeding.
Metabolic: diabetes mellitus, dehydration.
Musculoskeletal: musculoskeletal or back pain, arthralgia, myalgia, leg cramps.
Respiratory: dyspnea, coughing, atelectasis, congestion, ***hypoxia,*** rales, abnormal breath sounds, pleural effusion, ***pulmonary edema.***
Skin: acne, impaired wound healing without infection, pruritus, hirsutism, rash, night sweats, increased sweating.
Other: shivering, limb edema.

Interactions

None significant.

Effects on lab test results

- May increase BUN and creatinine levels.

Pharmacokinetics

Absorption: Level increases between first and fifth doses.
Distribution: Unknown.
Metabolism: Unknown.
Excretion: Unknown. *Estimated terminal elimination half-life:* 20 days (480 hours).

Route	Onset	Peak	Duration
I.V.	Unknown	Unknown	Unknown

Pharmacodynamics

Chemical effect: Drug is an interleukin (IL)-2 receptor antagonist that inhibits IL-2 binding to prevent IL-2–mediated activation of lymphocytes, a critical pathway in the cellular immune response against allografts. Once in circulation, drug impairs response of immune system to antigenic challenges.
Therapeutic effect: Prevents organ rejection.

Available forms

Injection: 25 mg/5 ml

NURSING PROCESS

Assessment

- Obtain history of patient's underlying condition before therapy, and reassess regularly thereafter.
- Check for opportunistic infections.
- Monitor patient for anaphylactoid reactions.
- Evaluate patient's and family's knowledge of drug therapy.

Nursing diagnoses

- Risk for injury related to potential for organ rejection
- Ineffective protection related to drug-induced immunosuppression
- Deficient knowledge related to drug therapy

Planning and implementation

• Drug should be used only under supervision of a prescriber experienced in immunosuppressant therapy and management of organ transplantation.
• Drug is used as part of an immunosuppressant regimen that includes corticosteroids and cyclosporine.
• Keep drugs used to treat anaphylactic reactions immediately available.
• Don't use drug as a direct I.V. injection. Dilute in 50 ml of sterile normal saline solution before administration. To avoid foaming, don't shake. Inspect for particulates or discoloration before use; don't use if either occurs.
• Infuse over 15 minutes via a central or peripheral line. Don't add or infuse other drugs simultaneously through the same line.
• Drug may be refrigerated at 36° to 46° F (2° to 8° C) for 24 hours and is stable at room temperature for 4 hours. Discard solution if not used within 24 hours.
• Protect undiluted solution from direct light.

Patient teaching
• Tell patient to consult prescriber before taking other drugs during therapy.
• Advise patient to take precautions against infection.
• Inform patient that neither he nor any household member should receive vaccinations unless medically approved.
• Tell patient to report immediately wounds that fail to heal, unusual bruising or bleeding, or fever.
• Advise patient to drink plenty of fluids during therapy and to report painful urination, blood in the urine, or a decrease in urine amount.
• Instruct woman of childbearing age to use effective contraception before starting therapy and to continue until 4 months after completing therapy.

Evaluation

• Patient doesn't experience organ rejection while taking drug.
• Patient is free from infection and serious bleeding episodes throughout drug therapy.
• Patient and family state understanding of drug therapy

dactinomycin (actinomycin-D)

(dak-tih-noh-MIGH-sin)
Cosmegen

Pharmacologic class: antibiotic antineoplastic (cell cycle–phase nonspecific)
Therapeutic class: antineoplastic
Pregnancy risk category: D

Indications and dosages

▶ **Sarcoma, trophoblastic tumors in women, testicular cancer, Wilms' tumor, rhabdomyosarcoma, Ewing's sarcoma, Kaposi's sarcoma‡, acute organ (kidney or heart) rejection‡, malignant melanoma‡, acute lymphocytic leukemia‡, Paget's disease of bone‡.** *Adults:* 500 mcg (0.5 mg) I.V. daily for 5 days. Maximum, 15 mcg/kg/day or 400 to 600 mcg/m²/day for 5 days. Course may be repeated after 3 weeks if all signs of toxicity have disappeared.
Children: 10 to 15 mcg/kg or 450 mcg/m²/day I.V. for 5 days. Maximum, 500 mcg/day or 2.5 mg/m² I.V. in equally divided daily doses over 7-day period. Course may be repeated after 3 weeks if all signs of toxicity have disappeared.

Contraindications and precautions

• Contraindicated in patients with chickenpox or herpes zoster.
Lifespan: In pregnant women, use with extreme caution and only when absolutely necessary because fetal harm may occur. Contraindicated in breast-feeding women.

Adverse reactions

CNS: fever, malaise, fatigue, lethargy.
GI: *anorexia, nausea, vomiting,* abdominal pain, diarrhea, *stomatitis,* ulceration, proctitis.
Hematologic: ***anemia, leukopenia, thrombocytopenia, pancytopenia, aplastic anemia, agranulocytosis.***
Hepatic: ***hepatotoxicity.***
Musculoskeletal: myalgia.
Skin: reversible alopecia, *erythema,* desquamation, *hyperpigmentation of skin (especially in previously irradiated areas), acnelike eruptions (reversible).*
Other: phlebitis and severe damage to soft tissue at injection site, ***anaphylaxis.***

Interactions

Drug-drug. *Bone marrow suppressants:* May increase toxicity. Monitor patient closely. *Vitamin K derivatives:* Decreases effectiveness. Monitor patient closely.

Effects on lab test results

• May increase uric acid and liver enzyme levels. May decrease calcium level.
• May decrease hemoglobin, hematocrit, and WBC, RBC, granulocyte, and platelet counts.

Pharmacokinetics

Absorption: Administered I.V.
Distribution: Widely distributed in body tissues, with highest levels found in bone marrow and nucleated cells.
Metabolism: Minimally metabolized in liver.
Excretion: Drug and its metabolites excreted in urine and bile. *Half-life:* 36 hours.

Route	Onset	Peak	Duration
I.V.	Unknown	Unknown	Unknown

Pharmacodynamics

Chemical effect: Thought to interfere with DNA-dependent RNA synthesis by intercalation.
Therapeutic effect: Kills selected cancer cells.

Available forms

Injection: 500 mcg/vial

NURSING PROCESS

Assessment

• Obtain history of patient's underlying cancer before therapy, and reassess regularly throughout therapy.
• Monitor CBC, platelet count, and kidney and liver function tests.
• Be alert for adverse reactions and drug interactions.
• Evaluate patient's and family's knowledge of drug therapy.

Nursing diagnoses

• Ineffective health maintenance related to presence of cancer
• Risk for injury related to risk of drug-induced adverse reactions
• Deficient knowledge related to drug therapy

Planning and implementation

• Follow facility policy to reduce risks. Preparation and administration of parenteral form carry risk of carcinogenic, mutagenic, and teratogenic effects for staff.
• If accidental skin contact occurs, irrigate area with copious amounts of water for at least 15 minutes.
• To help decrease nausea, give antiemetics before giving drug.
• Use only sterile water (without preservatives) as diluent for reconstitution. Add 1.1 ml to vial to yield gold-colored solution containing 0.5 mg/ml. Give by direct injection into vein or through I.V. line of free-flowing compatible I.V. solution of normal saline injection or D_5W.
• For I.V. infusion, dilute with up to 50 ml of D_5W or normal saline solution for injection and infuse over 15 minutes.
• Dosage must be reduced if patient has recently received or will receive simultaneous radiation therapy or other chemotherapy drugs.
• If drug spills, manufacturer recommends using a solution of trisodium phosphate 5% to inactivate it.
• Discard unused portion of solution because it contains no preservative.
• Stomatitis, diarrhea, leukopenia, and thrombocytopenia may indicate that dosage and schedule should be modified.
• Dactinomycin is a vesicant. If infiltration occurs, apply cold compresses to area and notify prescriber.

Patient teaching

• Warn patient to watch for signs of infection (fever, sore throat, fatigue) and bleeding (easy bruising, nosebleeds, bleeding gums, melena). Tell patient to take temperature daily.
• Instruct patient to avoid OTC products containing aspirin.
• Tell patient that alopecia may occur but that it's usually reversible.

Evaluation

• Patient has positive response to therapy, as shown by follow-up diagnostic studies and overall physical status.
• Patient has no injury from drug-induced adverse reactions.
• Patient and family state understanding of drug therapy.

dalteparin sodium
(dal-TEH-peh-rin SOH-dee-um)
Fragmin

Pharmacologic class: low–molecular-weight heparin
Therapeutic class: anticoagulant
Pregnancy risk category: B

Indications and dosages

▶ **Prevention of deep vein thrombosis (DVT) in patients undergoing abdominal surgery or hip replacement surgery who are at risk for thromboembolic complications.** *Adults:* 2,500 IU S.C. daily, starting 1 to 2 hours before surgery and repeated once daily for 5 to 10 days postoperatively until patient is mobile. Or, 5,000 IU S.C. the evening before surgery, repeated once daily q evening for 5 to 10 days until patient is mobile.

▶ **Treatment of unstable angina, non-Q wave MI.** *Adults:* 120 IU/kg up to 10,000 IU S.C. q 12 hours with oral aspirin (75 to 165 mg/day) therapy. Continue until patient is stable.

Contraindications and precautions

- Contraindicated in patients hypersensitive to drug, heparin, or pork products and in patients with active major bleeding or thrombocytopenia with positive in vitro tests for antiplatelet antibody in presence of drug.
- Use with extreme caution in patients with a history of heparin-induced thrombocytopenia; in patients with an increased risk of hemorrhage, such as those with severe uncontrolled hypertension, bacterial endocarditis, congenital or acquired bleeding disorders, active ulceration, angiodysplastic GI disease, or hemorrhagic CVA; and in those who recently underwent brain, spinal, or ophthalmologic surgery.
- Use cautiously in patients with bleeding diathesis, thrombocytopenia, platelet defects, severe liver or kidney insufficiency, hypertensive or diabetic retinopathy, or recent GI bleeding.

Lifespan: With pregnant and breast-feeding women, use cautiously. In children, safety of drug hasn't been established.

Adverse reactions

CNS: fever.
Hematologic: ***hemorrhage,*** ecchymosis, bleeding complications, ***thrombocytopenia.***
Skin: pruritus, rash.
Other: ***anaphylaxis,*** *hematoma at injection site,* pain at injection site.

Interactions

Drug-drug. *Antiplatelet drugs, oral anticoagulants:* May increase risk of bleeding. Use together cautiously; monitor patient for bleeding.

Effects on lab test results

- May increase ALT and AST levels.
- May decrease platelet count.

Pharmacokinetics

Absorption: Absolute bioavailability of anti-factor Xa is 87%.
Distribution: Volume of distribution is 40 to 60 ml/kg.
Metabolism: Unknown.
Excretion: Excreted in urine. *Half-life:* 3 to 5 hours after S.C. administration.

Route	Onset	Peak	Duration
S.C.	Unknown	4 hr	Unknown

Pharmacodynamics

Chemical effect: Enhances inhibition of factor Xa and thrombin by antithrombin.
Therapeutic effect: Prevents DVT in selected patients.

Available forms

Multidose vial: 10,000 anti-factor Xa IU/ml
Syringe: 2,500 anti-factor Xa IU/0.2 ml; 5,000 anti-factor Xa IU/0.2 ml

NURSING PROCESS

Assessment

- Obtain history of patient's underlying condition before starting therapy.
- Monitor effectiveness by assessing patient for evidence of DVT.
- Routine CBCs (including platelet count) and fecal occult blood tests are recommended during treatment.
- Be alert for adverse reactions and drug interactions.
- Evaluate patient's and family's knowledge of drug therapy.

Nursing diagnoses

- Risk for injury related to risk of DVT as result of underlying condition
- Ineffective protection related to drug-induced adverse hematologic reactions
- Deficient knowledge related to drug therapy

Planning and implementation

- Candidates for dalteparin therapy are at risk for DVT. Risk factors include being older than age 40, being obese, and having surgery under general anesthesia lasting longer than 30 minutes. Additional risk factors include cancer and a history of DVT or pulmonary embolism.
- Place patient in sitting or supine position when giving drug. Give S.C. injection deeply. Injection sites include U-shaped area below navel, upper outer side of thigh, and upper outer quadrangle of buttock. Rotate sites daily.

ALERT: Drug should never be given I.M. or I.V.

- Don't mix with other injections or infusions unless specific compatibility data are available that support such mixing.

ALERT: Drug isn't interchangeable (unit for unit) with unfractionated heparin or other low–molecular-weight heparin derivatives.

- Stop drug and notify prescriber if a thromboembolic event occurs despite dalteparin therapy.

Patient teaching

- Instruct patient and family to watch for signs of bleeding and notify prescriber immediately.
- Tell patient to avoid OTC medications containing aspirin or other salicylates.

Evaluation

- Patient doesn't develop DVT.
- Patient maintains stable hematologic function.
- Patient and family state understanding of drug therapy.

dantrolene sodium

(DAN-troh-leen SOH-dee-um)

Dantrium, Dantrium Intravenous

Pharmacologic class: hydantoin derivative
Therapeutic class: skeletal muscle relaxant
Pregnancy risk category: C

Indications and dosages

▶ **Spasticity and sequelae from severe chronic disorders (such as multiple sclerosis, cerebral palsy, spinal cord injury, CVA).** *Adults:* 25 mg P.O. daily. Increase in 25-mg increments up to 100 mg b.i.d. to q.i.d. Maximum, 400 mg daily. Maintain each dosage level for 4 to 7 days to determine response.
Children: Initially, 0.5 mg/kg P.O. b.i.d., increase to t.i.d. and then to q.i.d. Increase dose as needed by 0.5 mg/kg daily to 3 mg/kg b.i.d. to q.i.d. Maximum, 100 mg q.i.d.

▶ **Management of malignant hyperthermic crisis.** *Adults and children:* 1 mg/kg I.V. initially, then repeat as needed up to a total dose of 10 mg/kg.

▶ **Prevention or attenuation of malignant hyperthermia in susceptible patients who need surgery.** *Adults:* 4 to 8 mg/kg P.O. daily in three or four divided doses for 1 or 2 days before procedure. Final dose 3 to 4 hours before procedure. Or, 2.5 mg/kg I.V. infused over 1 hour about 1 hour before anesthesia. Additional doses, which must be individualized, may be given intraoperatively, if necessary.

▶ **Prevention of recurrence of malignant hyperthermia.** *Adults:* 4 to 8 mg/kg/day P.O. in four divided doses for up to 3 days after hyperthermic crisis.

▶ **To reduce succinylcholine-induced muscle fasciculations and postoperative muscle pain‡.** *Adults weighing less than 45 kg (99 lb):* 100 mg P.O. 2 hours before succinylcholine.
Adults weighing more than 45 kg: 150 mg P.O. 2 hours before succinylcholine.

Contraindications and precautions

- Contraindicated in patients whose spasticity is used to maintain motor function and in patients with upper motor neuron disorders, spasms from rheumatic disorders, or active hepatic disease.
- Use cautiously in women and in patients with hepatic disease or severely impaired cardiac or pulmonary function.

Lifespan: In pregnant women and patients older than age 35, use cautiously. In breast-feeding women, use is contraindicated.

Adverse reactions

CNS: *muscle weakness, drowsiness, dizziness,* light-headedness, *malaise,* headache, confu-

sion, nervousness, insomnia, hallucinations, ***seizures,*** fever.
CV: tachycardia, blood pressure changes.
EENT: excessive tearing, auditory or visual disturbances.
GI: anorexia, constipation, cramping, dysphagia, metallic taste, severe diarrhea, drooling, ***bleeding.***
GU: urinary frequency, hematuria, incontinence, nocturia, dysuria, crystalluria, difficulty achieving erection.
Hepatic: ***hepatitis.***
Musculoskeletal: myalgia.
Respiratory: pleural effusion.
Skin: diaphoresis, abnormal hair growth, eczematous eruption, pruritus, urticaria, photosensitivity.
Other: chills.

Interactions

Drug-drug. *CNS depressants:* May increase CNS depression. Avoid using together.
Estrogens: May increase risk of hepatotoxicity. Use together cautiously.
I.V. verapamil: May cause CV collapse. Never give together. Stop verapamil before giving I.V. dantrolene.
Drug-lifestyle. *Alcohol use:* May increase CNS depression. Discourage using together.
Sunlight: Photosensitivity may occur. Urge patient to avoid prolonged and unprotected sun exposure.

Effects on lab test results

- May increase BUN, ALT, AST, and bilirubin levels.

Pharmacokinetics

Absorption: 35% of P.O. dose absorbed through GI tract.
Distribution: Substantially bound to plasma protein, mainly albumin.
Metabolism: Metabolized in liver to its less active 5-hydroxy derivatives and to its amino derivative by reductive pathways.
Excretion: Excreted in urine as metabolites. *Half-life:* P.O., 9 hours; I.V., 4 to 8 hours.

Route	Onset	Peak	Duration
P.O.	≤ 1 wk	5 hr	Unknown
I.V.	Unknown	Unknown	Unknown

Pharmacodynamics

Chemical effect: Acts directly on skeletal muscle to interfere with intracellular calcium movement.
Therapeutic effect: Relieves muscle spasms.

Available forms

Capsules: 25 mg, 50 mg, 100 mg
Injection: 20 mg/vial

NURSING PROCESS

Assessment

- Obtain history of patient's spasticity disorder before therapy.
- Obtain liver function tests at start of therapy.
- Monitor effectiveness by evaluating severity of spasticity.
- Be alert for adverse reactions and drug interactions.
- Evaluate patient's and family's knowledge of drug therapy.

Nursing diagnoses

- Acute pain related to presence of spasticity disorder
- Risk for injury related to drug-induced adverse reactions
- Deficient knowledge related to drug therapy

Planning and implementation

- For optimum drug effect, give daily amount in four divided doses.
- **P.O. use:** Give drug with meals or milk to prevent GI distress.

– Prepare oral suspension for single dose by dissolving capsule contents in juice or other suitable liquid. For multiple doses, use acid vehicle, such as citric acid in USP syrup. Refrigerate, and use within several days.

- **I.V. use:** Give as soon as malignant hyperthermia reaction is recognized. Reconstitute each vial with 60 ml of sterile water for injection, and shake vial until clear. Don't use diluent that contains bacteriostatic agent. Protect contents from light and use within 6 hours. Be careful to avoid extravasation.
- Amount of relief determines whether dosage can be reduced.
- If hepatitis, severe diarrhea, severe weakness, or sensitivity reactions occur, withhold dose and immediately notify prescriber.

Patient teaching

- Tell patient to use caution when eating to avoid choking. Some patients may have trouble swallowing during therapy.
- Warn patient to avoid hazardous activities until full CNS effects of drug are known.
- Advise patient to avoid combining dantrolene with alcohol or other CNS depressants.
- Tell patient to use sunblock and wear protective clothing, to report GI problems immediately, and to follow prescriber's orders regarding rest and physical therapy.

Evaluation

- Patient states that pain from muscle spasticity has lessened.
- Patient has no injury from drug-induced adverse reactions.
- Patient and family state understanding of drug therapy.

dapsone (DDS)

(DAP-sohn)

Avlosulfon ♦, Dapsone 100 ◇

Pharmacologic class: synthetic sulfone
Therapeutic class: antileprotic, antimalarial
Pregnancy risk category: C

Indications and dosages

▶ **Treatment of multibacillary leprosy.** *Adults:* 100 mg P.O. daily given with rifampin and clofazimine for 12 months.
Children ages 10 to 14: 50 mg P.O. daily given with rifampin and clofazimine for 12 months.

▶ **Treatment of paucibacillary leprosy.** *Adults:* 100 mg P.O. daily given with rifampin for 6 months.
Children ages 10 to 14: 50 mg P.O. daily given with rifampin for 6 months.

▶ **Dermatitis herpetiformis.** *Adults:* Initially, 50 mg P.O. daily; increase to 300 mg daily if symptoms aren't completely controlled. Dose should be reduced to lowest effective level as soon as possible.

▶ **Malaria suppression or prophylaxis‡.** *Adults:* 100 mg P.O. weekly, given with pyrimethamine 12.5 mg P.O. weekly.
Children: 2 mg/kg P.O. weekly given with pyrimethamine 0.25 mg/kg weekly. Continue prophylaxis throughout exposure and for 6 months after exposure.

▶ **Treatment of *Pneumocystis carinii* pneumonia‡.** *Adults:* 100 mg P.O. daily. Usually given with trimethoprim 20 mg/kg daily, for 21 days.

▶ **Prophylaxis of *P. carinii* pneumonia‡.** *Adults:* 50 mg P.O. b.i.d. or 100 mg P.O. daily.

▶ **Prophylaxis of toxoplasmosis in HIV-infected patients‡.** *Adults and adolescents:* 50 mg P.O. daily given with pyrimethamine 50 mg P.O. once weekly and leucovorin 25 mg P.O. once weekly.
Children and neonates older than age 1 month: 2 mg/kg or 15 mg/m^2 (maximum 25 mg) P.O. once daily given with pyrimethamine and leucovorin.

Contraindications and precautions

- Contraindicated in patients hypersensitive to drug.
- Use cautiously in patients with chronic renal, hepatic, or CV disease; refractory types of anemia; or G6PD deficiency.

Lifespan: In pregnant women, use cautiously. In breast-feeding women, use is contraindicated.

Adverse reactions

CNS: fever, insomnia, psychosis, headache, dizziness, lethargy, severe malaise, paresthesia, peripheral neuropathy, vertigo.
CV: tachycardia.
EENT: tinnitus, blurred vision, allergic rhinitis.
GI: anorexia, abdominal pain, ***pancreatitis,*** nausea, vomiting.
GU: albuminuria, nephrotic syndrome, renal papillary necrosis, male infertility.
Hematologic: ***aplastic anemia, agranulocytosis,*** hemolytic anemia, ***methemoglobinemia, leukopenia.***
Hepatic: ***hepatitis,*** cholestatic jaundice.
Respiratory: pulmonary eosinophilia.
Skin: allergic dermatitis, lupus erythematosus, phototoxicity, exfoliative dermatitis, toxic erythema, ***erythema multiforme, toxic epidermal necrolysis,*** morbilliform and scarlatiniform reactions, urticaria, erythema nodosum.
Other: infectious mononucleosis–like syndrome, ***sulfone syndrome,*** lymphadenopathy.

Interactions

Drug-drug. *Activated charcoal:* Decreases GI absorption of dapsone. Monitor patient.
Folic acid antagonists (such as methotrexate): May increase risk of adverse hematologic reactions. Monitor patient carefully.
Didanosine: May increase dapsone absorption, leading to therapeutic failure and an increase in infection. Give drug at least 2 hours before or after didanosine.
Rifampin: May increase hepatic metabolism and renal excretion of dapsone. Monitor patient closely.
PABA: May antagonize effect of dapsone by interfering with the primary mechanism of action. Monitor patient.
Probenecid: Decreases urinary excretion of dapsone metabolites, increasing plasma levels. Monitor patient.
Trimethoprim: Increases levels of both drugs, increasing pharmacologic and toxic effects. Monitor patient closely for toxicity.
Drug-lifestyle. *Sunlight:* Photosensitivity may occur. Advise patient to avoid sun exposure and wear protective clothing and sunblock.

Effects on lab test results

- May increase liver enzyme levels.
- May decrease hemoglobin, hematocrit, and WBC, RBC, and granulocyte count.

Pharmacokinetics

Absorption: Rapid and almost complete.
Distribution: Distributed widely in most body tissues and fluids; 70% to 90% is plasma protein-bound.
Metabolism: Undergoes acetylation by liver enzymes; rate varies and is genetically determined. Almost 50% of blacks and whites are slow acetylators, whereas more than 80% of Chinese, Japanese, and Eskimos are fast acetylators. Dosage adjustment may be needed.
Excretion: Dapsone and metabolites excreted primarily in urine; small amounts excreted in feces. *Half-life:* 10 to 50 hours.

Route	Onset	Peak	Duration
P.O.	Unknown	4-8 hr	Unknown

Pharmacodynamics

Chemical effect: Unknown; may inhibit folic acid biosynthesis in susceptible organisms (bacteriostatic).
Therapeutic effect: Hinders or kills selected bacteria, including *Mycobacterium leprae* and *Mycobacterium tuberculosis*. Drug also effects *Pneumocystis carinii* and *Plasmodium*.

Available forms

Tablets: 25 mg, 100 mg

NURSING PROCESS

Assessment

- Obtain history of patient's underlying infection and CBC before therapy.
- Monitor effectiveness by assessing for improvement of infection and evaluating culture and sensitivity test results.
- Monitor CBC weekly for first month, monthly for 6 months, and semiannually thereafter.
- Be alert for adverse reactions and drug interactions.
- Evaluate patient's and family's knowledge of drug therapy.

Nursing diagnoses

- Infection related to presence of susceptible bacteria
- Risk of impaired skin integrity related to drug-induced adverse dermatologic reactions
- Deficient knowledge related to drug therapy

Planning and implementation

- Be prepared to reduce dosage or temporarily discontinue drug if hemoglobin falls below 9 g/dl, if WBC count falls below 5,000/mm^3, or if RBC count falls below 2.5 million/mm^3 or remains low.
- If generalized diffuse dermatitis occurs, notify prescriber and prepare to interrupt therapy regimen.
- Give antihistamines to combat drug-induced allergic dermatitis.
- In severe erythema nodosum, therapy should be stopped and glucocorticoids given cautiously.
- Evidence of sulfone syndrome includes fever, malaise, and jaundice with hepatic necrosis. If symptoms occur, immediately stop drug therapy and notify prescriber.

Patient teaching

- Inform patient of need for periodic laboratory studies.

• Teach patient to watch for and promptly report adverse dermatologic changes because such reactions may necessitate stopping drug.
• Warn patient to avoid hazardous activities that require alertness if adverse CNS reactions occur.

Evaluation
• Patient is free from infection.
• Patient maintains normal skin integrity throughout therapy.
• Patient and family state understanding of drug therapy.

darbepoetin alfa
(dar-be-POE-e-tin AL-fa)
Aranesp

Pharmacologic class: hematopoietic
Therapeutic class: antianemic
Pregnancy risk category: C

Indications and dosages
▶ **Anemia related to chronic renal failure (CRF) for patient on or off dialysis.** *Adults:* Initially, 0.45 mcg/kg I.V. or S.C. once weekly. Doses should be titrated to achieve and maintain a target hemoglobin level not exceeding 12 g/dl. Dose shouldn't be increased more often than monthly. In patients being converted from epoetin alfa, starting dose should be based on the previous epoetin alfa dose, as follows:

Previous weekly epoetin alfa dose (units/wk)	Weekly darbepoetin alfa dose (mcg/wk)
< 2,500	6.25
2,500-4,999	12.5
5,000-10,999	25
11,000-17,999	40
18,000-33,999	60
34,000-89,999	100
> 90,000	200

ALERT: Darbepoetin alfa should be given less often than epoetin alfa because its half-life is 3 times longer. If patient was receiving epoetin alfa two to three times weekly, he should receive darbepoetin alfa once weekly. If patient was receiving epoetin alfa once weekly, he should receive darbepoetin alfa once every 2 weeks.

If hemoglobin level is increasing and approaching 12 g/dl, dose should be reduced by 25%. If it continues to increase, dose should be withheld until hemoglobin level begins to decrease, and then drug should be restarted at a dose 25% below the previous dose. If hemoglobin level increases by more than 1 g/dl over 2 weeks, decrease dose by 25%. If increase is less than 1 g/dl over 4 weeks and iron stores are adequate, increase the dose by 25% of previous dose. Further increases can be made at 4-week intervals until target hemoglobin is reached.

Patients who don't need dialysis may need lower maintenance doses because predialysis patients may be more responsive to the effects of darbepoetin alfa and need close monitoring of blood pressure, hemoglobin, renal function, and electrolyte balance.

Treatment with darbepoetin alfa decreases plasma volume, thereby reducing dialysis efficiency. Thus, patients who are on dialysis may need adjustments in their dialysis prescription.

▶ **Anemia related to chemotherapy in patients with nonmyeloid malignancies.** *Adults:* 2.25 mcg/kg S.C. once weekly. If hemoglobin increases less than 1 g/dl after 6 weeks of therapy, increase dose to 4.5 mcg/kg. If hemoglobin increases by more than 1 g/dl in a 2-week period or if it exceeds 12 g/dl, reduce dose by 25%. If hemoglobin exceeds 13 g/dl, withhold drug until hemoglobin drops to 12 g/dl and restart dose at 25% below the previous dose.

Contraindications and precautions
• Contraindicated in patients hypersensitive to drug or its components and in patients with uncontrolled hypertension.
• Use with caution in patients with underlying hematologic disease, such as hemolytic anemia, sickle cell anemia, thalassemia, or porphyria, because safety and efficacy haven't been established.
Lifespan: In pregnant women and children, safety and efficacy haven't been established. With breast-feeding women, use cautiously because it's unknown whether drug appears in breast milk. Elderly patients may have greater sensitivity to the drug.

Adverse reactions
CNS: *headache, dizziness, fatigue, fever,* asthenia, ***seizure.***

CV: *hypertension, hypotension,* **CARDIAC ARRHYTHMIA, CARDIAC ARREST,** angina, ***heart failure, thrombosis vascular access,*** *peripheral edema,* ***acute MI, TIA, CVA.***
GI: *diarrhea, vomiting, nausea, abdominal pain, constipation.*
Metabolic: dehydration.
Musculoskeletal: *myalgia, arthralgia, limb pain,* back pain.
Respiratory: *upper respiratory tract infection, dyspnea, cough,* bronchitis, ***pulmonary embolism.***
Skin: rash, pruritus.
Other: injection site pain, hemorrhage at access site, *infection (including sepsis, bacteremia, pneumonia, peritonitis, and abscess),* flulike symptoms.

Interactions

None reported.

Effects on lab test results

- May decrease ferritin level.
- May increase hemoglobin, hematocrit, and RBC count.

Pharmacokinetics

Absorption: Slow and rate-limiting. Bioavailability ranges from 30 to 50% (mean: 37%).
Distribution: Predominantly confined to the vascular space.
Metabolism: Unknown.
Excretion: Steady-state levels occur within 4 weeks. *Half-life:* 21 hours for I.V. route; 49 hours for S.C. injection.

Route	Onset	Peak	Duration
I.V.	Unknown	Unknown	21 hr
S.C.	Unknown	34 hr	49 hr

Pharmacodynamics

Chemical effect: Darbepoetin alfa stimulates erythropoiesis, which increases hemoglobin levels, by the same mechanism as endogenous erythropoietin. Endogenous erythropoietin, produced by the kidneys, is released into the bloodstream in response to hypoxia and increases RBC production. Production of endogenous erythropoietin is impaired in patients with chronic renal failure, and erythropoietin deficiency is the primary cause of anemia.
Therapeutic effect: Increases RBC production and corrects anemia in patients with CRF.

Available forms

Injection (albumin solution): 25 mcg/ml, 40 mcg/ml, 60 mcg/ml, 100 mcg/ml, 200 mcg/ml single-dose vials
Injection (polysorbate solution): 25 mcg/ml, 40 mcg/ml, 60 mcg/ml, 100 mcg/ml, 200 mcg/ml single-dose vials

NURSING PROCESS

Assessment

- Drug may increase blood pressure. Blood pressure should be adequately controlled before starting therapy. Obtain baseline blood pressure before initiating therapy. Carefully monitor and control patient's blood pressure during drug therapy.
- Monitor renal function and electrolytes in predialysis patients.

ALERT: Hemoglobin level may not increase until 2 to 6 weeks after therapy starts. Monitor hemoglobin weekly until stabilized. Don't exceed the target level of 12 g/dl in patients with CRF.

- Drug may increase risk of CV events; carefully monitor and assess patient.
- Patient may have seizures. Follow patient closely, especially during the first several months of therapy.

Nursing diagnoses

- Risk for injury related to drug-induced adverse cardiac events
- Fatigue related to underlying anemia
- Deficient knowledge related to darbepoetin alfa therapy

Planning and implementation

ALERT: Don't shake drug because doing so can denature it. Don't use if vials have particulate matter or are discolored. Don't dilute.
ALERT: Don't give with other drug solutions. Darbepoetin alfa is provided in single-dose vials without a preservative. Don't pool or retain unused portions.

- Store drug in refrigerator; don't freeze. Protect drug from light.

ALERT: Dose should be decreased if hemoglobin increases 1 g/dl in any 2-week period. Any increase greater than 1 g/dl within a 2-week period will increase the risk of CV events related to an excessive rate of increase in hemoglobin. Such CV events can be sei-

zures, CVA, exacerbation of hypertension, congestive heart failure, vascular thrombosis, infarction, or ischemia, acute MI, or fluid overload or edema. If symptoms of any of these events arise, decrease drug dose by 25%.
- Monitor iron before and during treatment. Provide supplemental iron if ferritin level is less than 100 mcg/L and transferrin saturation is less than 20%.
- Serious allergic reactions, including rash and urticaria, may occur. If an anaphylactic reaction occurs, stop drug and give appropriate therapy as clinically indicated.
- The maximum safe dosage hasn't been determined. Although doses greater than 3 mcg/kg/week for up to 28 weeks can be given, an excessive rise or rate of rise of hemoglobin leads to adverse effects. If patient has polycythemia, don't give drug.
- If patient fails to respond to drug therapy, reevaluate patient for other etiologies that may inhibit erythropoiesis, such as folic acid or vitamin B_{12} deficiencies, infections, inflammatory or malignant processes, osteofibrosis cystica, occult blood loss, hemolysis, severe aluminum toxicity, and bone marrow fibrosis.

Patient teaching
- Teach patient how to give drug properly, including how to use and dispose of needles.
- Advise patient of possible adverse effects and allergic reactions.
- Inform patient of need to frequently monitor blood pressure, hemoglobin, and hematocrit. Also, advise patient to comply with any prescribed antihypertensive drug therapy and dietary restrictions to keep blood pressure under control. Uncontrolled blood pressure is believed to cause seizures and hypertensive encephalopathy in patients with chronic renal failure who are treated with darbepoetin alfa.

☑ Evaluation
- Patient's hemoglobin level increases to no more than the target level of 12 g/dl.
- Patient's blood pressure remains adequately controlled and patient doesn't suffer any adverse events related to drug therapy.
- Patient and family state understanding of drug therapy.

daunorubicin citrate liposomal
(daw-noh-roo-BYE-sin SIH-trayt li-po-SOE-mul)
DaunoXome

Pharmacologic class: anthracycline
Therapeutic class: antineoplastic
Pregnancy risk category: D

Indications and dosages
▶ **First-line cytotoxic therapy for advanced HIV-related Kaposi's sarcoma.** *Adults:* 40 mg/m^2 I.V. over 60 minutes once q 2 weeks. Treatment should continue unless patient shows signs of progressive disease or until other complications of HIV prevent continuing.
Patients with renal or hepatic impairment: If bilirubin is 1.2 to 3 mg/dl, give ¾ of normal dose; if bilirubin or creatinine is greater than 3 mg/dl, give ½ the normal dose.

Contraindications and precautions
- Contraindicated in patients who have had a severe hypersensitivity reaction to daunorubicin citrate liposomal or its constituents.
- Use cautiously in patients with myelosuppression, cardiac disease, previous radiotherapy involving the heart, previous anthracycline use (doxorubicin > 300 mg/m^2 or equivalent), or hepatic or renal dysfunction.

Adverse reactions
CNS: *fever, headache, neuropathy,* depression, dizziness, insomnia, amnesia, anxiety, ataxia, confusion, ***seizures,*** hallucinations, tremor, hypertonia, meningitis, *fatigue,* malaise, emotional lability, abnormal gait, hyperkinesia, somnolence, abnormal thinking, syncope.
CV: ***cardiomyopathy,*** chest pain, hypertension, palpitations, ***arrhythmias, pericardial effusion, cardiac tamponade, cardiac arrest,*** angina pectoris, ***pulmonary hypertension,*** flushing, edema, tachycardia, ***MI.***
EENT: *rhinitis,* sinusitis, abnormal vision, conjunctivitis, tinnitus, eye pain, deafness, taste disturbances, earache, gingival bleeding, tooth caries, dry mouth.
GI: *nausea, diarrhea, abdominal pain, vomiting, anorexia,* constipation, ***GI hemorrhage,*** gastritis, dysphagia, stomatitis, increased appetite, melena, hemorrhoids, tenesmus.
GU: dysuria, nocturia, polyuria.

Hematologic: NEUTROPENIA.
Hepatic: hepatomegaly.
Musculoskeletal: *rigors, back pain,* arthralgia, myalgia.
Respiratory: *cough, dyspnea,* hemoptysis, hiccups, pulmonary infiltration, increased sputum.
Skin: alopecia, pruritus, *increased sweating,* dry skin, seborrhea, folliculitis.
Other: splenomegaly, lymphadenopathy, *opportunistic infections, allergic reactions,* flulike symptoms, dehydration, thirst, injection site inflammation.

Interactions

None reported.

Effects on lab test results

- May decrease neutrophil and platelet counts.

Pharmacokinetics

Absorption: Administered I.V.
Distribution: Thought to be distributed primarily in the vascular fluid volume.
Metabolism: Metabolized by the liver into active metabolites.
Excretion: Apparent elimination half-life is 4.4 hours.

Route	Onset	Peak	Duration
I.V.	Unknown	Unknown	Unknown

Pharmacodynamics

Chemical effect: Daunorubicin exerts cytotoxic effects by intercalating between DNA base pairs and uncoiling the DNA helix. This inhibits DNA synthesis and DNA-dependent RNA synthesis. Drug may also inhibit polymerase activity. The liposomal preparation maximizes the selectivity of daunorubicin for solid tumors in situ. After penetrating the tumor, daunorubicin is released over time to exert antineoplastic effects.
Therapeutic effect: Decreases tumor growth for advanced HIV-related Kaposi's sarcoma.

Available forms

Injection: 2 mg/ml (equivalent to 50 mg daunorubicin base)

NURSING PROCESS

Assessment

- Obtain history of patient's underlying condition before therapy, and reassess regularly thereafter.
- Obtain hepatic and renal studies before therapy.
- Monitor cardiac function regularly and before giving each dose because of the risk of cardiac toxicity and heart failure. Left ventricular ejection fraction should be determined at a total cumulative dose of 320 mg/m^2 and every 160 mg/m^2 thereafter.
- Monitor patient closely for signs of opportunistic infections, especially since patients with HIV infection are immunocompromised.
- Be alert for adverse reactions and drug interactions.
- Evaluate patient's and family's knowledge of drug therapy.

Nursing diagnoses

- Risk for injury related to drug-induced adverse reactions
- Risk for infection related to myelosuppression
- Deficient knowledge related to drug therapy

Planning and implementation

- Follow proper institutional procedures for handling and disposing of antineoplastics.

ALERT: Drug should be diluted with D_5W—and only D_5W—before administration. Don't mix daunorubicin citrate liposomal with other drugs, saline solution, bacteriostatic agents, or any other solution.

- Withdraw the calculated volume of drug from the vial, and transfer it into an equivalent amount of D_5W. The recommended concentration after dilution is 1 mg/ml.
- After dilution, immediately administer I.V. over 60 minutes. If unable to use drug immediately, refrigerate at 2° to 8° C (36° to 46° F) for a maximum of 6 hours.
- Because local tissue necrosis is possible, monitor I.V. site closely to avoid extravasation.
- Don't use in-line filters for I.V. infusion.
- Give only under the supervision of a prescriber specializing in cancer chemotherapy.
- Monitor patient for adverse reactions. A triad of back pain, flushing, and chest tightness may occur within the first 5 minutes of the infusion. This triad subsides after stopping the infusion

and typically doesn't recur when the infusion resumes at a slower rate.

ALERT: Monitor hematologic status closely because severe myelosuppression may occur. Blood counts should be repeated and checked before each dose. Withhold treatment if absolute granulocyte count is below 750 cells/mm³.

ALERT: Daunorubicin citrate liposomal has unique kinetic properties that are different from the conventional daunorubicin hydrochloride. Thus, don't substitute or interchange the drugs on a mg-to-mg basis.

Patient teaching

- Inform patient that alopecia may occur but usually is reversible.
- Tell patient to notify prescriber about sore throat, fever, or other signs of infection. Tell patient to avoid exposure to people with infections.
- Advise patient to report suspected or known pregnancy during therapy.
- Tell patient to report back pain, flushing, and chest tightness during the infusion.

Evaluation

- Patient has no injury as a result of drug-induced adverse reactions.
- Patient remains free of infection.
- Patient and family state understanding of drug therapy.

daunorubicin hydrochloride

(daw-noh-ROO-buh-sin high-droh-KLOR-ighd)
Cerubidine

Pharmacologic class: antibiotic antineoplastic (cell cycle–phase nonspecific)
Therapeutic class: antineoplastic
Pregnancy risk category: D

Indications and dosages

▶ **Remission induction in acute nonlymphocytic (myelogenous, monocytic, erythroid) leukemia.** *Adults:* When given with other drugs, 30 to 45 mg/m² I.V. daily on days 1, 2, and 3 of first course and on days 1 and 2 of subsequent courses with cytarabine infusions.

▶ **Remission induction in acute lymphocytic leukemia.** *Adults:* 45 mg/m² I.V. daily on days 1, 2, and 3.

Children age 2 and older: 25 mg/m² I.V. on day 1 q week for up to 6 weeks, if needed.
Children younger than age 2 or with body surface area of less than 0.5 mg/m²: Dose should be calculated based on body weight (mg/kg).

Contraindications and precautions

- No known contraindications.
- Use cautiously in patients with myelosuppression and in those with impaired cardiac, renal, or hepatic function.

Lifespan: In pregnant women, use with extreme caution, if at all. Breast-feeding isn't recommended during therapy.

Adverse reactions

CNS: fever.
CV: ***irreversible cardiomyopathy,*** ECG changes, ***arrhythmias,*** pericarditis, ***myocarditis.***
GI: *nausea, vomiting, stomatitis, esophagitis,* anorexia, diarrhea.
GU: red urine.
Hematologic: ***bone marrow suppression.***
Hepatic: ***hepatotoxicity.***
Metabolic: hyperuricemia.
Skin: rash, pigmentation of fingernails and toenails, *generalized alopecia, tissue sloughing* with extravasation.
Other: *severe cellulitis,* chills, ***anaphylaxis.***

Interactions

Drug-drug. *Bone marrow suppressants:* May increase risk of cardiotoxicity. Monitor patient closely.
Doxorubicin: May increase risk of cardiotoxicity. Monitor patient closely.
Hepatotoxic drugs: May increase risk of hepatotoxicity. Monitor patient closely.

Effects on lab test results

- May increase uric acid level.

Pharmacokinetics

Absorption: Administered I.V.
Distribution: Widely distributed in body tissues; drug doesn't cross blood-brain barrier.
Metabolism: Extensively metabolized in liver. One of metabolites has cytotoxic activity.
Excretion: Daunorubicin and its metabolites primarily excreted in bile, with small portion

excreted in urine. *Half-life:* Initial, 45 minutes; terminal, 18½ hours.

Route	Onset	Peak	Duration
I.V.	Unknown	Unknown	Unknown

Pharmacodynamics

Chemical effect: Thought to interfere with DNA-dependent RNA synthesis by intercalation.

Therapeutic effect: Kills selected cancer cells.

Available forms

Injection: 20 mg/vial

NURSING PROCESS

Assessment

- Obtain history of patient's underlying disease before therapy, and reassess regularly throughout therapy.
- Check ECG before treatment.
- Monitor CBC and liver function tests; monitor ECG every month (or more, if needed) during therapy.
- Monitor pulse rate closely.
- Be alert for adverse reactions and drug interactions.
- Monitor patient for nausea and vomiting, which may be severe and may last 24 to 48 hours. Monitor patient's hydration status during episodes of nausea and vomiting.
- Evaluate patient's and family's knowledge of drug therapy.

Nursing diagnoses

- Risk for injury related to presence of neoplastic disease
- Risk for deficient fluid volume related to drug-induced nausea and vomiting
- Deficient knowledge related to drug therapy

Planning and implementation

- Follow institutional policy to reduce risks. Preparing and giving parenteral form have carcinogenic, mutagenic, and teratogenic risks.
- Reconstitute drug using 4 ml of sterile water for injection to produce a 5-mg/ml solution.
- Withdraw desired dose into syringe containing 10 to 15 ml of normal saline solution for injection. Inject into I.V. line containing free-flowing compatible solution of D_5W or normal saline solution for injection over 2 to 3 minutes. Or, dilute in 50 ml of normal saline solution and infuse over 10 to 15 minutes. Or, dilute in 100 ml and infuse over 30 to 45 minutes.
- Avoid extravasation. If it occurs, discontinue I.V. infusion immediately, notify prescriber, and apply ice to area for 24 to 48 hours.

ALERT: Don't infuse with dexamethasone or heparin; a precipitate may form.

ALERT: Never give drug I.M. or S.C.

- Cumulative dosage is limited to 500 to 600 mg/m² (450 mg/m² if patient also receives or has received cyclophosphamide or radiation therapy to cardiac area).

ALERT: Color is similar to that of doxorubicin. Don't confuse these two drugs.

- Optimally, use within 8 hours of preparation. Reconstituted solution is stable 24 hours at room temperature, 48 hours if refrigerated.
- Notify prescriber if adverse cardiac reactions occur. Stop drug immediately and notify prescriber if signs of heart failure or cardiomyopathy develop.
- Give antiemetics to help control nausea and vomiting.

Patient teaching

- Warn patient to watch for signs of infection and bleeding.
- Advise patient that red urine for 1 to 2 days is normal and doesn't indicate blood in urine.
- Inform patient that alopecia may occur but that it's usually reversible.
- Advise women of childbearing age to avoid becoming pregnant during therapy.
- Instruct patient about need for protective measures, including conservation of energy, balanced diet, adequate rest, personal hygiene, clean environment, and avoidance of people with infections.

Evaluation

- Patient shows positive response to therapy as evidenced by reports of follow-up diagnostic tests and improved physical status.
- Patient maintains adequate hydration throughout therapy.
- Patient and family state understanding of drug therapy.

delavirdine mesylate
(deh-luh-VEER-deen MES-ih-layt)
Rescriptor

Pharmacologic class: nonnucleoside reverse transcriptase inhibitor
Therapeutic class: antiviral
Pregnancy risk category: C

Indications and dosages

▶ **Treatment of HIV-1 infection.** *Adults:* 400 mg P.O. t.i.d. with other appropriate antiretroviral agents.

Contraindications and precautions

• Contraindicated in patients hypersensitive to drug's formulation.
• Use cautiously in patients with impaired hepatic function.

Adverse reactions

CNS: *asthenia, headache, fatigue.*
GI: *nausea,* vomiting, diarrhea, abdominal pain.
Skin: *rash,* maculopapular rash.
Other: flulike symptoms.

Interactions

Drug-drug. *Amphetamines, benzodiazepines, calcium channel blockers, dapsone, ergot alkaloid preparations, indinavir, quinidine, warfarin:* May result in serious or life-threatening adverse events. Avoid using together.
Antacids: May reduce delavirdine absorption. Separate doses by at least 2 hours.
Carbamazepine, phenobarbital, phenytoin: Substantially decreases delavirdine level. Avoid using together.
Didanosine: Coadministration with delavirdine results in a 20% decrease in absorption of both drugs. Separate administration by at least 1 hour.
Fluoxetine, ketoconazole: May increase delavirdine trough levels. Monitor patient; decrease clarithromycin dose.
H_2-receptor antagonists: May reduce absorption of delavirdine. Long-term use of these drugs with delavirdine isn't recommended.
HMG-CoA reductase inhibitors: May increase levels of these drugs and risk of rhabdomyolysis and myopathy. Avoid using together.
Rifabutin, rifampin: May decrease delavirdine levels. Avoid using together.
Saquinavir: Fivefold increase in systemic levels of saquinavir. Monitor AST and ALT levels frequently when used together.
Sildenafil: May increase risk of sildenafil-associated adverse events including hypotension, visual changes, and priapism. Don't exceed 25 mg of sildenafil in a 48-hour period. Monitor patient.

Effects on lab test results

• May increase ALT, GGT, amylase, bilirubin, and AST levels. May increase or decrease glucose level.
• May increase PTT and eosinophil count. May decrease hemoglobin, hematocrit, and granulocyte, neutrophil, WBC, RBC, and platelet counts.

Pharmacokinetics

Absorption: Rapidly absorbed after oral administration.
Distribution: 98% bound to plasma protein.
Metabolism: Extensively converted to inactive metabolites. Primarily metabolized in liver by cytochrome enzyme systems.
Excretion: 51% excreted in the urine (less than 5% unchanged), 44% excreted in the feces. *Half-life:* 5.8 hours.

Route	Onset	Peak	Duration
P.O.	Unknown	1 hr	Unknown

Pharmacodynamics

Chemical effect: Drug binds directly to reverse transcriptase and blocks RNA- and DNA-dependent DNA polymerase activities.
Therapeutic effect: Inhibits HIV replication.

Available forms

Tablets: 100 mg, 200 mg.

NURSING PROCESS

Assessment

• Assess patient's underlying condition before therapy and regularly thereafter.
• Be alert for adverse reactions and drug interactions.
• Monitor patient for drug-induced rash.

• Evaluate patient's and family's knowledge of drug therapy.

Nursing diagnoses

• Risk for impaired skin integrity related to potential adverse effects of medication
• Risk for infection related to patient's underlying condition
• Deficient knowledge related to drug therapy

Planning and implementation

• If rash develops, give diphenhydramine, hydroxyzine, or topical corticosteroids to relieve symptoms.
• Resistance develops rapidly when drug is used as monotherapy. Always give with appropriate antiretroviral therapy.
• Drug may be dispersed in water before ingestion. Add tablets to at least 3 oz (90 ml) of water, let stand for a few minutes, then stir well. Have patient drink promptly, rinse glass, and swallow the rinse to make sure entire dose is consumed.

Patient teaching

• Tell patient to stop drug and call prescriber if he develops severe rash or rash accompanied by such symptoms as fever, blistering, oral lesions, conjunctivitis, swelling, or muscle or joint aches.
• Tell patient that drug doesn't cure HIV-1 infection and that he may continue to acquire illnesses related to HIV-1 infection.
• Urge patient to remain under medical supervision when taking drug because long-term effects aren't known.
• Advise patient to take drug as prescribed and not to alter doses without prescriber's approval. If a dose is missed, tell him to take the next dose as soon as possible but not to double the next dose.
• Inform patient that drug may be taken without regard to food.
• Tell patient with achlorhydria to take drug with an acidic beverage, such as orange or cranberry juice.
• Tell patient not to exceed 25 mg of sildenafil in a 48-hour period.
• Advise patient to report use of other prescription drugs, OTC medicines, or herbal remedies.

Evaluation

• Patient's skin integrity is maintained.
• Patient is free from opportunistic infections.
• Patient and family state understanding of drug therapy.

desipramine hydrochloride

(deh-SIP-rah-meen high-droh-KLOR-ighd)
Norpramin**

Pharmacologic class: dibenzazepine tricyclic antidepressant (TCA)
Therapeutic class: antidepressant
Pregnancy risk category: C

Indications and dosages

▶ **Depression.** *Adults:* Initially, 100 to 200 mg P.O. daily in divided doses; increase to maximum of 300 mg daily. Or, entire dose can be given h.s.
Elderly patients and adolescents: 25 to 100 mg P.O. daily in divided doses; increase gradually to maximum of 150 mg daily, if needed.

Contraindications and precautions

• Contraindicated in patients hypersensitive to drug, in those who have taken an MAO inhibitor within previous 14 days, and in patients in acute recovery phase of MI.
• Use with extreme caution in patients taking thyroid medication and in those with CV disease, seizure disorder, glaucoma, thyroid disorder, or history of urine retention.
Lifespan: In pregnant and breast-feeding women, use cautiously. In children younger than age 12, safety of drug hasn't been established.

Adverse reactions

CNS: *drowsiness, dizziness,* excitation, tremors, weakness, confusion, headache, nervousness, EEG changes, ***seizures,*** extrapyramidal reactions.
CV: orthostatic hypotension, *tachycardia, ECG changes,* hypertension.
EENT: *blurred vision,* tinnitus, mydriasis.
GI: *dry mouth, constipation,* nausea, vomiting, anorexia, paralytic ileus.
GU: *urine retention.*
Skin: rash, urticaria, *diaphoresis,* photosensitivity.
Other: ***sudden death,*** hypersensitivity reaction.

Interactions

Drug-drug. *Anticholinergics:* May enhance anticholinergic effects. Monitor patient closely.
Barbiturates, CNS depressants: May enhance CNS depression. Avoid using together.
Cimetidine, methylphenidate: May increase desipramine levels. Monitor patient for adverse reactions.
Clonidine, epinephrine, norepinephrine: May increase hypertensive effect. Use together cautiously.
MAO inhibitors: May cause severe excitation, hyperpyrexia, or seizures, usually with high dosage. Use together cautiously.
Selective serotonin reuptake inhibitors (SSRIs): May inhibit the metabolism of TCAs, causing toxicity. Symptoms of TCA toxicity may persist for several weeks after stopping SSRI. At least 5 weeks may be necessary when switching from fluoxetine to a TCA because of the long half-life of the active and parent metabolite.
Drug-lifestyle. *Alcohol use:* May enhance CNS depression. Discourage using together.
Smoking: May lower desipramine level. Monitor patient for lack of effect; encourage smoking cessation.
Sun exposure: Increases risk of photosensitivity. Advise against unprotected or prolonged sun exposure.

Effects on lab test results

- May increase or decrease glucose levels.
- May increase liver function test values.

Pharmacokinetics

Absorption: Rapid.
Distribution: Distributed widely throughout body, including CNS; 90% protein-bound.
Metabolism: Metabolized by liver; significant first-pass effect may explain variability of serum levels in different patients taking same dosage.
Excretion: Excreted primarily in urine.

Route	Onset	Peak	Duration
P.O.	2-4 wk	4-6 hr	Unknown

Pharmacodynamics

Chemical effect: Unknown; increases amount of norepinephrine, serotonin, or both in the CNS by blocking their reuptake by neurons.
Therapeutic effect: Relieves depression.

Available forms

Tablets: 10 mg, 25 mg, 50 mg, 75 mg, 100 mg, 150 mg

NURSING PROCESS

Assessment

- Obtain history of patient's depression before therapy, and reassess regularly thereafter.
- Be alert for adverse reactions and drug interactions.
- Evaluate patient's and family's knowledge of drug therapy.

Nursing diagnoses

- Ineffective individual coping related to depression
- Risk for injury related to drug-induced adverse reactions
- Deficient knowledge related to drug therapy

Planning and implementation

- Don't stop drug abruptly. Abrupt withdrawal of long-term therapy may cause nausea, headache, and malaise.
- Because desipramine produces fewer anticholinergic effects than other TCAs, it's prescribed often for patients with cardiac problems.
- Because hypertensive episodes have occurred during surgery in patients receiving TCAs, this drug should be discontinued gradually several days before surgery.

ALERT: Although the cause isn't clearly defined, this drug may cause sudden death in children.

- If signs of psychosis occur or increase, expect prescriber to reduce dosage.

Patient teaching

- Warn patient to avoid hazardous activities until CNS effects of drug are known. Drowsiness and dizziness usually subside after a few weeks.
- Tell patient to avoid alcohol during therapy because it may antagonize effects of desipramine.
- Warn patient not to stop drug suddenly.
- Advise patient to consult prescriber before taking other prescription drugs, OTC medications, or herbal remedies.
- Instruct patient to use sunblock, wear protective clothing, and avoid prolonged exposure to strong sunlight.

Evaluation
- Patient behavior and communication indicate improvement of depression.
- Patient has no injury as a result of drug-induced adverse reactions.
- Patient and family state understanding of drug therapy.

desloratadine
(des-lor-AT-a-deen)
Clarinex, Clarinex Reditabs

Pharmacologic class: selective H_1-receptor antagonist
Therapeutic class: antihistamine
Pregnancy risk category: C

Indications and dosages
▶ **Relief of nasal and non-nasal symptoms of allergic rhinitis (seasonal and perennial); symptomatic relief of pruritus, reduction in the number and size of hives, in patients with chronic idiopathic urticaria.** *Adults and children age 12 and older:* 5 mg P.O. daily.
Patients with hepatic or renal impairment: Start dosage at 5 mg P.O. q other day.

Contraindications and precautions
- Contraindicated in patients hypersensitive to drug, to any of its components, or to loratadine. Desloratadine and 3-hydroxydesloratadine can't be eliminated by hemodialysis.

Lifespan: Breast-feeding patients should stop nursing or stop taking the drug because drug appears in breast milk. In children younger than age 12, safety and effectiveness of drug haven't been established. In elderly patients, use cautiously because of possible decreased hepatic, renal, or cardiac function and because elderly patients may have other diseases and may be taking other drugs.

Adverse reactions
CNS: *headache,* somnolence, fatigue, dizziness.
CV: tachycardia.
EENT: pharyngitis.
GI: nausea, dry mouth, dyspepsia.
Musculoskeletal: myalgia.
Other: flulike symptoms, dysmenorrhea, ***hypersensitivity reaction*** (including rash, edema, or ***anaphylaxis***).

Interactions
None reported.

Effects on lab test results
- May increase liver enzyme and bilirubin levels.

Pharmacokinetics
Absorption: Serum level peaks in about 3 hours. Drug doesn't cross the blood-brain barrier.
Distribution: Desloratadine is 82% to 87% bound to plasma proteins. Drug's active metabolite (3-hydroxydesloratadine) is 85% to 89% protein bound.
Metabolism: Desloratadine is extensively metabolized in the liver to 3-hydroxydesloradatine.
Excretion: It's equally eliminated in the urine and feces, primarily as metabolites. *Mean half-life:* 27 hours.

Route	Onset	Peak	Duration
P.O.	Unknown	3 hr	Unknown
P.O. (orally disintegrating)	Unknown	2.5-4 hours	Unknown

Pharmacodynamics
Chemical effect: Long-acting tricyclic antihistamine with selective H_1-receptor histamine antagonist activity. It inhibits histamine release from human mast cells *in vitro*.
Therapeutic effect: Relieves allergy symptoms.

Available forms
Orally disintegrating tablets (Reditabs): 5 mg
Tablets: 5 mg

NURSING PROCESS

Assessment
- Assess patient's condition before therapy and regularly thereafter.
- Be alert for any adverse reactions.
- Evaluate patient's and family's knowledge of drug therapy.

Nursing diagnoses
- Ineffective health maintenance related to underlying allergic condition
- Fatigue related to drug-induced reaction
- Deficient knowledge related to drug therapy

Planning and implementation
- Drug may be taken with or without food.
- Overdose may cause somnolence and increased heart rate. If these symptoms occur, consider removing unabsorbed drug through standard measures and provide symptomatic and supportive treatment.

Patient teaching
- Advise patient not to exceed recommended dosage. Doses of more than 5 mg don't increase effectiveness and may cause somnolence.
- Tell patient to report adverse effects.
- Store orally disintegrating tablets at 25° C (77° F); excursions permitted between 15° to 30° C (59° to 86° F)
- Instruct patient to remove orally disintegrating tablet from blister pack and immediately place on the tongue.
- Inform patient that orally disintegrating tablet may be taken with or without water.

Evaluation
- Patient's allergic symptoms are relieved.
- Patient doesn't suffer any drug-induced adverse effects.
- Patient and family state understanding of drug therapy.

desmopressin acetate
(dez-moh-PREH-sin AS-ih-tayt)
DDAVP, Stimate

Pharmacologic class: posterior pituitary hormone
Therapeutic class: antidiuretic, hemostatic agent
Pregnancy risk category: B

Indications and dosages
▶ **Nonnephrogenic diabetes insipidus, temporary polyuria and polydipsia from pituitary trauma.** *Adults:* 10 to 40 mcg intranasally daily in one to three divided doses. Morning and evening doses adjusted separately for adequate diurnal rhythm of water turnover. Or, 0.05 mg P.O. b.i.d. Each dose should be adjusted separately for an adequate diurnal rhythm of water turnover. Total oral daily dosage should be increased or decreased as needed to achieve desired response. Doses may range from 0.1 to 1.2 mg, divided into two or three daily doses. Oral therapy should start 12 hours after last intranasal dose. Or, give 2 to 4 mcg I.V. or S.C. daily, usually in two equally divided doses.
Children ages 3 months to 12 years (nasal spray): 0.05 to 0.3 ml intranasally daily in one or two doses.
Children age 4 and older (oral form): Begin with 0.05 mg P.O. b.i.d. Each dose should be adjusted separately for an adequate diurnal rhythm of water turnover. Total oral daily dosage should be increased or decreased as necessary to achieve desired response. Doses may range from 0.1 to 1.2 mg, divided into two or three daily doses. Oral therapy should start 12 hours after the last intranasal dose.
Children younger than age 4 (oral form): Dosage must be individually adjusted to prevent an excessive decrease in plasma osmolality.
▶ **Hemophilia A and von Willebrand's disease.** *Adults and children:* 0.3 mcg/kg diluted in normal saline solution and infused I.V. over 15 to 30 minutes. May repeat dose, if necessary, based on laboratory response and patient's condition. Intranasal dose is 1 spray (of solution containing 1.5 mg/ml) into each nostril to provide total of 300 mcg.
Adults and children weighing less than 50 kg (110 lb): 1 spray into a single nostril (150 mcg).
▶ **Primary nocturnal enuresis.** *Children age 6 and older:* Initially, 20 mcg intranasally h.s. Adjust dosage according to response. Maximum recommended dosage is 40 mcg daily. Or, 0.2 mg P.O. h.s. Dose may be adjusted up to 0.6 mg P.O. to achieve desired response. Oral therapy may start 24 hours after last intranasal dose.

Contraindications and precautions
- Contraindicated in patients hypersensitive to drug and in those with type IIB von Willebrand's disease.
- Use cautiously in patients with coronary artery insufficiency or hypertensive CV disease and in those with conditions linked to fluid and electrolyte imbalance, such as cystic fibrosis, because these patients are prone to hyponatremia.

Lifespan: With pregnant and breast-feeding women, use cautiously. In infants younger than age 3 months, use of drug isn't recommended because of their increased tendency to develop fluid imbalance. In children younger than age 12, safety of parenteral form of drug hasn't been established for management of diabetes insipidus.

Adverse reactions

CNS: headache.
CV: slight rise in blood pressure.
EENT: nasal congestion, rhinitis, epistaxis, sore throat.
GI: nausea, abdominal cramps.
GU: vulvar pain.
Respiratory: cough.
Other: flushing, local erythema, swelling or burning after injection.

Interactions

Drug-drug. *Clofibrate:* May enhance and prolong effects of desmopressin. Monitor patient carefully.
Demeclocycline, epinephrine, heparin, lithium: Decreases response to desmopressin. Monitor patient closely.
Drug-lifestyle. *Alcohol use:* May increase risk of adverse effects. Discourage using together.

Effects on lab test results

None reported.

Pharmacokinetics

Absorption: After intranasal administration, 10% to 20% of dose through nasal mucosa. After S.C. administration, unknown. After P.O. administration, minimal.
Distribution: Unknown.
Metabolism: Unknown.
Excretion: Unknown. *Half-life:* Fast phase, about 8 minutes; slow phase, 75½ minutes.

Route	Onset	Peak	Duration
P.O.	1 hr	4-7 hr	8-12 hr
I.V.	15-30 min	1.5-2 hr	4-12 hr
S.C.	Unknown	Unknown	Unknown
Intranasal	≤ 1 hr	1-5 hr	8-12 hr

Pharmacodynamics

Chemical effect: Increases permeability of renal tubular epithelium to adenosine monophosphate and water; epithelium promotes reabsorption of water and produces concentrated urine (ADH effect). Desmopressin also increases factor VIII activity by releasing endogenous factor VIII from plasma storage sites.
Therapeutic effect: Decreases diuresis and promotes clotting.

Available forms

Injection: 4 mcg/ml
Nasal solution: 0.1 mg/ml, 1.5 mg/ml
Tablets: 0.1 mg, 0.2 mg

NURSING PROCESS

Assessment

- Obtain history of patient's underlying condition before therapy.
- Monitor effectiveness by checking patient's fluid intake and output, serum and urine osmolality, and urine specific gravity for treatment of diabetes insipidus or relief of symptoms of other disorders.
- Be alert for adverse reactions and drug interactions.
- Monitor patient carefully for hypertension during high-dose treatment.
- Evaluate patient's and family's knowledge of drug therapy.

Nursing diagnoses

- Deficient fluid volume related to underlying condition
- Acute pain related to drug-induced headache
- Deficient knowledge related to drug therapy

Planning and implementation

- **P.O. use:** Follow normal protocol.
- **I.V. use:** Dilute drug with normal saline solution according to prescriber's instructions when administering I.V. for treatment of hemophilia A and von Willebrand's disease.
- **S.C. use:** Follow normal protocol. Rotate injection sites.
- **Intranasal use:** Follow manufacturer's instructions exactly for administration.
  – Intranasal use can cause changes in nasal mucosa, resulting in erratic, unreliable absorption. Report worsening condition to prescriber, who may prescribe injectable DDAVP.
- Desmopressin injection shouldn't be used to treat severe cases of von Willebrand's disease or hemophilia A with factor VIII levels of 0% to 5%.
- When drug is used to treat diabetes insipidus, dosage or frequency of administration may be adjusted according to patient's fluid output. Morning and evening doses are adjusted separately for adequate diurnal rhythm of water turnover.

Patient teaching
- Instruct patient to clear nasal passages before using drug intranasally.
- Patient may have trouble measuring and inhaling drug into nostrils. Teach patient and caregiver correct method of administration.
- Advise patient to report conditions such as nasal congestion, allergic rhinitis, or upper respiratory tract infection; dosage adjustment may be required.
- Teach patient using S.C. desmopressin to rotate injection sites to avoid tissue damage.
- Warn patient to drink only enough water to satisfy thirst.
- Inform patient that when treating hemophilia A and von Willebrand's disease, giving desmopressin may avoid hazards of using blood products.
- Advise patient to wear or carry medical identification indicating use of drug.

☑ Evaluation
- Patient achieves normal fluid and electrolyte balance.
- Patient states that headache is relieved with mild analgesic.
- Patient and family state understanding of drug therapy.

dexamethasone
(deks-ah-METH-uh-sohn)
Decadron*, DexaMeth, Dexamethasone Intensol*, Dexasone♦, Dexone 0.5, Dexone 0.75, Dexone 1.5, Dexone 4, Hexadrol*, Mymethasone*, Oradexon♦

dexamethasone acetate
Cortostat LA, Dalalone D.P., Dalalone L.A., Decadron-LA, Decaject-L.A., Dexacen LA-8, Dexasone-L.A., Dexone L.A., Solurex-LA

dexamethasone sodium phosphate
AK-Dex, Cortastat, Cortastat 10, Dalalone, Decadrol, Decadron Phosphate, Decaject, Dexacen-4, Dexacorten, Dexone, Hexadrol Phosphate, Primethasone, Solurex

Pharmacologic class: glucocorticoid
Therapeutic class: anti-inflammatory, immunosuppressant
Pregnancy risk category: NR

Indications and dosages
▶ **Cerebral edema.** ***phosphate.*** *Adults:* Initially, 10 mg I.V. Then, 4 mg I.M. q 6 hours until symptoms subside (usually 2 to 4 days). Then, taper down over 5 to 7 days.
▶ **Inflammatory conditions, allergic reactions, neoplasias.** ***phosphate.*** *Adults:* 4 mg I.M. as a single dose. Continue maintenance therapy with dexamethasone tablets, 1.5 mg P.O. b.i.d. for 2 days; then, 0.75 mg P.O. b.i.d. for 1 day; then, 0.75 mg P.O. once daily for 2 days; then, discontinue drug.
acetate. *Adults:* 4 to 16 mg I.M. into joint or soft tissue q 1 to 3 weeks. Or, 0.8 to 1.6 mg into lesions q 1 to 3 weeks.
▶ **Shock.** ***phosphate.*** *Adults:* 1 to 6 mg/kg I.V. as single dose or 40 mg I.V. q 2 to 6 hours, p.r.n. Or, 20 mg I.V. as a single dose, followed by continuous infusion of 3 mg/kg q 24 hours.
▶ **Dexamethasone suppression test for Cushing's syndrome.** *Adults:* After determining baseline 24-hour urine levels of 17-hydroxycorticosteroids, 0.5 mg P.O. q 6 hours for 48 hours; 24-hour urine collection made for determination of 17-hydroxycorticosteroid excretion again during second 24 hours of dexamethasone administration. Or, 1 mg P.O. as a single dose at 11 p.m. Draw plasma cortisol level at 8 a.m. the following day.
▶ **Prevention of hyaline membrane disease in premature infants‡** ***phosphate.*** *Adults:* 5 mg I.M. t.i.d. to mother for 2 days before delivery.
▶ **Prevention of chemotherapy-induced nausea and vomiting‡.** *Adults:* 10 to 20 mg I.V. before giving chemotherapy. Additional doses (individualized for each patient and usually lower than initial dose) may be given I.V. or P.O. for 24 to 72 hours following cancer chemotherapy, if needed.

Contraindications and precautions
- Contraindicated in patients hypersensitive to drug or its components and in those with systemic fungal infections.
- Use with extreme caution in patient with recent MI.
- Use cautiously in patients with GI ulcer, renal disease, hypertension, osteoporosis, diabetes mellitus, hypothyroidism, cirrhosis, diverticulitis, nonspecific ulcerative colitis, recent intes-

tinal anastomoses, thromboembolic disorders, seizures, myasthenia gravis, heart failure, tuberculosis, ocular herpes simplex, emotional instability, or psychotic tendencies. Because some forms contain sulfite preservatives, use cautiously in patients sensitive to sulfites.

Lifespan: In pregnant women, use cautiously. In breast-feeding women, drug isn't recommended for use. In children and adolescents, long-term use of drug may delay growth and maturation.

Adverse reactions

CNS: *euphoria, insomnia,* psychotic behavior, pseudotumor cerebri, ***seizures.***
CV: ***heart failure,*** hypertension, edema, ***arrhythmias, thromboembolism.***
EENT: cataracts, glaucoma.
GI: *peptic ulceration,* GI irritation, increased appetite, ***pancreatitis.***
GU: menstrual irregularities.
Metabolic: hypokalemia, hyperglycemia, carbohydrate intolerance.
Musculoskeletal: muscle weakness, osteoporosis, growth suppression in children.
Skin: hirsutism, delayed wound healing, acne, skin eruptions, atrophy at I.M. injection sites.
Other: cushingoid state (moonface, buffalo hump, central obesity), susceptibility to infections, ***acute adrenal insufficiency may follow increased stress (infection, surgery, or trauma) or abrupt withdrawal after long-term therapy.***

Interactions

Drug-drug. *Antidiabetics, including insulin:* May decrease corticosteroid response. May need dosage adjustment.
Aspirin, indomethacin, other NSAIDs: May increase risk of GI distress and bleeding. Give together cautiously.
Barbiturates, phenytoin, rifampin: May decrease corticosteroid effect. Increase corticosteroid dosage.
Digoxin: May increase risk of arrhythmia from hypokalemia. May need dosage adjustment.
Oral anticoagulants: May alter dosage requirements. Monitor PT and INR closely.
Potassium-depleting drugs: May enhance potassium-wasting effects of dexamethasone. Monitor potassium levels.
Salicylates: May decrease salicylate levels. Monitor patient for lack of therapeutic effects.
Skin-test antigens: May decrease response of skin test antigens. Defer skin testing until therapy is completed.
Toxoids, vaccines: May decrease antibody response and increased risk of neurologic complications. Avoid using together.
Drug-lifestyle. *Alcohol use:* Increases risk of gastric irritation and GI ulceration. Discourage using together.

Effects on lab test results

- May increase glucose and cholesterol levels. May decrease potassium, calcium, T_3, and T_4 levels.

Pharmacokinetics

Absorption: Absorbed readily after P.O. administration. Absorption of suspension for injection depends on whether it's injected into an intra-articular space, a muscle, or blood supply to a muscle.
Distribution: Distributed to muscle, liver, skin, intestines, and kidneys. Drug is bound weakly to plasma proteins (transcortin and albumin). Only unbound portion is active.
Metabolism: Metabolized in liver to inactive glucuronide and sulfate metabolites.
Excretion: Inactive metabolites and small amounts of unmetabolized drug excreted by kidneys. Insignificant quantities of drug also are excreted in feces. *Half-life:* 36 to 54 hours.

Route	Onset	Peak	Duration
P.O.	1-2 hr	1-2 hr	2.5 days
I.V., I.M.	≤ 1 hr	1 hr	2 days-3 wk

Pharmacodynamics

Chemical effect: Not clearly defined; decreases inflammation, mainly by stabilizing leukocyte lysosomal membranes; suppresses immune response; stimulates bone marrow; and influences protein, fat, and carbohydrate metabolism.
Therapeutic effect: Relieves cerebral edema, reduces inflammation and immune response, and reverses shock.

Available forms

dexamethasone
Elixir: 0.5 mg/5 ml*
Oral solution: 0.5 mg/5 ml, 1 mg/ml*
Tablets: 0.25 mg, 0.5 mg, 0.75 mg, 1 mg, 1.5 mg, 2 mg, 4 mg, 6 mg

dexamethasone acetate
Injection: 8 mg/ml, 16 mg/ml suspension
dexamethasone sodium phosphate
Injection: 4 mg/ml, 10 mg/ml, 20 mg/ml, 24 mg/ml

NURSING PROCESS

Assessment

- Obtain history of patient's underlying condition before therapy.
- Monitor patient's weight, blood pressure, glucose level, and electrolyte levels.
- Be alert for adverse reactions and drug interactions. Most adverse reactions to corticosteroids are dose- or duration-dependent.
- Watch for depression or psychotic episodes, especially in high-dose therapy.
- Evaluate patient's and family's knowledge of drug therapy.

Nursing diagnoses

- Ineffective health maintenance related to underlying condition
- Risk for injury related to drug-induced adverse reactions
- Deficient knowledge related to drug therapy

Planning and implementation

- For better results and less toxicity, give once-daily dose in morning.
- **P.O. use:** Give with food when possible.
- **I.V. use:** When giving as direct injection, inject undiluted over at least 1 minute. When giving as intermittent or continuous infusion, dilute solution according to manufacturer's instructions and give over prescribed duration. If given by continuous infusion, change solution every 24 hours.
- **I.M. use:** Give I.M. injection deeply into gluteal muscle. Rotate injection sites to prevent muscle atrophy.
- Avoid S.C. injection because atrophy and sterile abscesses may occur.
- Always adjust to lowest effective dose.

ALERT: Gradually reduce dosage after long-term therapy. Abrupt withdrawal may cause rebound inflammation, fatigue, weakness, arthralgia, fever, dizziness, lethargy, depression, fainting, orthostatic hypotension, dyspnea, anorexia, and hypoglycemia. After prolonged use, abrupt withdrawal may be fatal.

ALERT: Unless contraindicated, give patient low-sodium diet high in potassium and protein. Also, give potassium supplements as directed.

- If patient's stress level (physical or psychological) increases, notify prescriber because dosage may need to be increased.
- If patient has adverse reaction, notify prescriber and be prepared to provide supportive and symptomatic treatment.

Patient teaching

- Tell patient not to stop drug abruptly or without prescriber's consent because abrupt withdrawal may be fatal.
- Teach patient signs of early adrenal insufficiency: fatigue, muscle weakness, joint pain, fever, anorexia, nausea, dyspnea, dizziness, and fainting.
- Instruct patient to wear or carry medical identification that indicates need for supplemental systemic glucocorticoids during stress, especially as dosage is decreased.
- Warn patient receiving long-term therapy about cushingoid symptoms and the need to notify prescriber about sudden weight gain or swelling.
- Warn patient about easy bruising.
- Advise patient receiving long-term therapy to consider exercise or physical therapy. Give vitamin D or calcium supplements.
- Advise patient receiving long-term therapy to have periodic ophthalmologic examinations.

Evaluation

- Patient's condition improves with drug therapy.
- Patient has no injury as a result of drug therapy.
- Patient and family state understanding of drug therapy.

dexmedetomidine hydrochloride

(DEX-meh-dih-TOE-mih-deen high-droh-KLOR-ighd)
Precedex

Pharmacologic class: selective $alpha_2$-adenoreceptor agonist with sedative properties
Therapeutic class: sedative
Pregnancy risk category: C

Indications and dosages

▶ **Sedation of initially intubated and mechanically ventilated patients in ICU setting.** *Adults:* Loading infusion of 1 mcg/kg I.V. over 10 minutes; then a maintenance infusion of 0.2 to 0.7 mcg/kg/hr for up to 24 hours, adjusted to achieve the desired level of sedation.

Contraindications and precautions

- Use cautiously in patients with advanced heart block or renal or hepatic impairment.

Lifespan: In elderly patients, use cautiously.

Adverse reactions

CNS: pain.
CV: *hypotension,* ***bradycardia, arrhythmias.***
GI: *nausea,* thirst.
GU: oliguria.
Hematologic: anemia, leukocytosis.
Respiratory: ***hypoxia,*** pleural effusion, ***pulmonary edema.***
Other: infection.

Interactions

Drug-drug. *Anesthetics, hypnotics, opioids, sedatives:* May enhance effects. May need to reduce dexmedetomidine dose.

Effects on lab test results

- May increase WBC count. May decrease hemoglobin and hematocrit.

Pharmacokinetics

Absorption: Administered I.V.
Distribution: After I.V. administration, drug is rapidly and widely distributed. Drug is 94% protein-bound.
Metabolism: Almost completely hepatically metabolized to inactive metabolites.
Excretion: Inactive metabolites are 95% renally eliminated and 4% fecally eliminated. *Elimination half-life:* About 2 hours.

Route	Onset	Peak	Duration
I.V.	Unknown	Unknown	Unknown

Pharmacodynamics

Chemical effect: Selectively stimulates alpha$_2$-adenoceptor in the CNS.
Therapeutic effect: Produces sedation of initially intubated and mechanically ventilated patients.

Available forms

Injection: 100 mcg/ml in 2-ml vials and 2-ml ampules

NURSING PROCESS

Assessment

- Assess renal and hepatic function before administration, particularly in elderly patients.
- Assess patient's response to drug. Some patients receiving dexmedetomidine have been observed to stir and be alert when stimulated. This alone shouldn't be considered evidence of lack of efficacy in the absence of other clinical signs and symptoms.
- Be alert for adverse reactions and drug interactions.
- Evaluate patient's and family's knowledge of drug therapy.

Nursing diagnoses

- Risk for injury related to drug-induced adverse reactions
- Impaired spontaneous ventilation related to underlying disease process
- Deficient knowledge related to drug therapy

Planning and implementation

- Elderly patients and those with renal or hepatic failure may need a reduced dosage.
- Dexmedetomidine must be diluted in normal saline solution before administration. To prepare the infusion, withdraw 2 ml of dexmedetomidine and add to 48 ml of normal saline injection to a total of 50 ml. Shake gently to mix well.

ALERT: Don't give through the same I.V. catheter with blood or plasma because physical compatibility hasn't been established. Dexmedetomidine infusion is compatible with lactated Ringer's solution, D_5W, normal saline solution, and 20% mannitol. It's also compatible with thiopental sodium, etomidate, vecuronium bromide, pancuronium bromide, succinylcholine, atracurium besylate, mivacurium chloride, glycopyrrolate bromide, phenylephrine hydrochloride, atropine sulfate, midazolam, morphine sulfate, fentanyl citrate, and plasma substitute. Give using a controlled infusion device at the rate calculated for body weight.

ALERT: Don't give infusion for longer than 24 hours.

- Continuously monitor cardiac status.

• Dexmedetomidine can be continuously infused in mechanically ventilated patients before, during, and after extubation. You don't need to stop dexmedetomidine before extubation.

Patient teaching
• Tell patient that he'll be sedated while the drug is given, but that he may awake when stimulated.
• Tell patient that he'll be closely monitored and attended while sedated.

Evaluation
• Patient has no injury as a result of drug-induced adverse reactions.
• Patient regains spontaneous ventilation.
• Patient and family state understanding of drug therapy.

dexmethylphenidate hydrochloride
(dex-meth-il-FEN-uh-date high-droh-KLOR-ighd)
Focalin

Pharmacologic class: CNS stimulant
Therapeutic class: CNS stimulant
Pregnancy risk category: C
Controlled substance schedule: II

Indications and dosages
▶ **Attention deficit hyperactivity disorder (ADHD).** *Children age 6 and older:* For patients who aren't taking racemic methylphenidate or are taking another stimulant, starting dosage is 2.5 mg P.O. twice daily, spaced at least 4 hours apart. For patients who are being switched from methylphenidate, starting dose is one-half of the current methylphenidate dosage. Additional adjustment should be made weekly in increments of 2.5 to 5 mg daily, up to a maximum dosage of 20 mg daily in divided doses.

Contraindications and precautions
• Contraindicated in patients hypersensitive to methylphenidate or other components. Also contraindicated in patients with severe anxiety, tension, agitation, or glaucoma, and in those who have motor tics or a family history or diagnosis of Tourette's syndrome. Also contraindicated in patients taking MAO inhibitors or within 14 days of discontinuing these drugs because hypertensive crisis may occur. Not used to treat severe depression or to prevent or treat normal fatigue states.
• Use cautiously in patients with a history of drug abuse, alcoholism, psychosis, seizures, hypertension, hyperthyroidism, heart failure, or recent MI.
Lifespan: In pregnant women, use only if benefits outweigh risks. With breast-feeding women, use cautiously because it's unknown whether drug appears in breast milk. For children younger than age 6, don't give drug.

Adverse reactions
CNS: fever, insomnia, nervousness, growth suppression, psychosis, blurred vision.
CV: tachycardia, hypertension
GI: anorexia, *abdominal pain,* nausea.
Hematologic: ***leukopenia,*** *anemia.*
Musculoskeletal: twitching (motor or vocal tics), arthralgia.
Other: weight loss.

Interactions
Drug-drug. *Anticoagulants, anticonvulsants, and selected serotonin reuptake inhibitors, tricyclics:* Inhibits metabolism of these drugs. May need to decrease dosage of these drugs; monitor drug levels.
Antihypertensives: Decreases effectiveness of these drugs. Use together cautiously; monitor blood pressure.
Clonidine, other centrally acting alpha-2 agonists: May cause serious adverse effects. Use together cautiously.
MAO inhibitors: Increases risk of hypertensive crisis. Avoid using together or within 14 days after stopping MAO inhibitor.

Effects on lab test results
• May increase liver function test results. May decrease hemoglobin, hematocrit, and WBC count.

Pharmacokinetics
Absorption: Rapid, with peak levels occurring in 1 to 1½ hours. Food delays rate of peak concentration but doesn't affect the maximum concentration absorbed.
Distribution: Distributes rapidly to the tissues.
Metabolism: Extensively metabolized via de-esterification. Doesn't inhibit the cytochrome P450 system. No active metabolites.

Excretion: Renal excretion is about 90%.
Half-life: 2.2 hours.

Route	Onset	Peak	Duration
P.O.	Unknown	1-1.5 hr	Unknown

Pharmacodynamics

Chemical effect: The exact mechanism of action is unknown. However, the dextro isomer is thought to block presynaptic reuptake of norepinephrine and dopamine and increase the release of these neurotransmitters.
Therapeutic effect: Increases attention span and decreases hyperactivity and impulsiveness related to ADHD.

Available forms

Tablets: 2.5 mg, 5 mg, 10 mg

NURSING PROCESS

Assessment
- Diagnosis of ADHD must be based on complete history and evaluation of the child with consultation of psychological, educational, and social resources.
- Monitor blood pressure and pulse routinely during drug therapy.
- Be alert for any drug-induced adverse reactions during therapy.
- Check CBC with differential and platelet counts with long-term use.

Nursing diagnoses
- Ineffective health maintenance related to underlying condition
- Ineffective coping by family of patient's underlying hyperactivity condition
- Deficient knowledge of drug therapy

Planning and implementation
- Drug is meant to be an adjunct to comprehensive treatment program that includes psychological, educational, and social support.
- Growth may be suppressed with long-term stimulant use. Monitor children for growth and weight gain. Stop treatment if growth is suppressed or if weight gain is lower than expected.
- Reduce dosage or stop treatment if symptoms are aggravated or adverse reactions occur.
- Stop treatment if seizures occur.
- Symptoms of overdose include vomiting, agitation, tremors, hyperreflexia, muscle twitching, convulsions, euphoria, confusion, hallucinations, delirium, sweating, flushing, headache, hyperpyrexia, tachycardia, palpitations, cardiac arrhythmias, hypertension, mydriasis, and dry mucous membranes. Primary treatment is supportive care and protection against self-injury and additional overstimulation.
- Stop treatment if symptoms don't improve after 1 month of treatment.

Patient teaching
- Advise parents to monitor child's height and weight and to tell prescriber if they suspect any growth suppression.
- Advise patient to take drug at the same time every day at the prescribed dose. Tell patient to report any adverse reactions to prescriber immediately.

Evaluation
- Patient responds positively with drug therapy.
- Patient and family are effectively coping with patient's underlying condition.
- Patient and family state understanding of drug therapy.

dextran, high–molecular-weight (dextran 70, dextran 75)

(DEKS-tran, high moh-LEH-kyoo-ler wayt)
Dextran 70, Dextran 75, Gentran 70, Gendex 75, Macrodex

Pharmacologic class: glucose polymer
Therapeutic class: plasma volume expander
Pregnancy risk category: C

Indications and dosages

▶ **Plasma expander.** *Adults:* 30 g (500 ml of 6% solution) I.V. In emergencies, may give 1.2 to 2.4 g (20 to 40 ml)/minute. In normovolemic or nearly normovolemic patients, rate of infusion shouldn't exceed 240 mg (4 ml)/minute. Total dosage during first 24 hours shouldn't exceed 1.2 g/kg. Actual dosage depends on amount of fluid loss and resulting hemoconcentration and must be determined for each patient.

Contraindications and precautions

• Contraindicated in patients hypersensitive to dextran and in those with marked hemostatic defects, marked cardiac decompensation, renal disease with severe oliguria or anuria, hypervolemic conditions, or severe bleeding disorders.

• Use cautiously in patients with active hemorrhage, thrombocytopenia, impaired renal clearance, chronic liver disease, or abdominal conditions and in patients undergoing bowel surgery.

Lifespan: In pregnant women, use cautiously. Breast-feeding women should stop nursing or stop the drug. In children, safety of drug hasn't been established.

Adverse reactions

CNS: fever.
CV: fluid overload, thrombophlebitis.
EENT: nasal congestion.
GI: nausea, vomiting.
GU: increased specific gravity and viscosity of urine, tubular stasis and blocking, oliguria, anuria.
Musculoskeletal: arthralgia.
Skin: urticaria.
Other: hypersensitivity reactions, ***anaphylaxis.***

Interactions

Drug-drug. *Abciximab, aspirin, heparin, thrombolytics, warfarin:* May increase bleeding. Use together cautiously; monitor patient for bleeding.

Effects on lab test results

• May increase ALT and AST levels.

• May increase bleeding time. May decrease hemoglobin and hematocrit. May significantly suppress platelet function with doses of 15 ml/kg.

Pharmacokinetics

Absorption: Administered I.V.
Distribution: Distributed throughout vascular system.
Metabolism: Dextran molecules with molecular weights above 50,000 are enzymatically degraded by dextranase to glucose at rate of about 70 to 90 mg/kg/day. This process is variable.
Excretion: Dextran molecules with molecular weights below 50,000 are eliminated by renal excretion.

Route	Onset	Peak	Duration
I.V.	Immediate	Immediate	Unknown

Pharmacodynamics

Chemical effect: Expands plasma volume by way of colloidal osmotic effect, drawing fluid from interstitial to intravascular space, providing fluid replacement.
Therapeutic effect: Expands plasma volume.

Available forms

Injection: dextran 70 in normal saline solution or D_5W; 6% dextran 75 in normal saline solution or D_5W

NURSING PROCESS

Assessment

• Obtain history of patient's underlying condition and hydration status before therapy, and reassess regularly throughout therapy. Frequently assess vital signs, fluid intake and output, and urine or serum osmolarity levels.

• Be alert for adverse reactions.

• Observe patient closely during early phase of infusion, when most anaphylactic reactions occur.

• Watch for circulatory overload and rise in central venous pressure. Plasma expansion is slightly greater than volume infused.

• Check hemoglobin and hematocrit levels.

• Evaluate patient's and family's knowledge of drug therapy.

Nursing diagnoses

• Decreased cardiac output related to underlying condition

• Risk for injury related to potential for drug-induced hypersensitivity reaction

• Deficient knowledge related to drug therapy

Planning and implementation

ALERT: Use D_5W instead of normal saline solution because drug is hazardous for patients with heart failure, especially when given in normal saline solution.

• Prescriber may order dextran 1, a dextran adjunct, to protect against drug-induced anaphylaxis. Give 20 ml of dextran 1 (containing

150 mg/ml) I.V. over 60 seconds 1 to 2 minutes before I.V. infusion of dextran.
• Store drug at constant 77° F (25° C). Dextran may precipitate in storage, but it can be heated to dissolve, if necessary.
• If oliguria or anuria occurs or isn't relieved by infusion, stop dextran and give loop diuretic.
• If hematocrit values fall below 30% by volume, notify prescriber.
• Drug may interfere with analyses of blood grouping, crossmatching, and bilirubin, glucose, and protein levels.

Patient teaching
• Inform patient, if alert, and family about dextran therapy.
• Instruct patient to notify prescriber if adverse reactions occur, such as itching.

Evaluation
• Patient's vital signs and urine output return to normal.
• Patient doesn't develop hypersensitivity reaction to drug.
• Patient and family state understanding of drug therapy.

dextran, low–molecular-weight (dextran 40)
(DEKS-tran, loh moh-LEH-kyoo-ler wayt)
Dextran 40, Gentran 40, 10% LMD, Rheomacrodex

Pharmacologic class: glucose polymer
Therapeutic class: plasma volume expander
Pregnancy risk category: C

Indications and dosages
▶ **Plasma volume expansion.** *Adults:* Dosage by I.V. infusion depends on amount of fluid loss. Initially, 10 ml/kg of dextran infused rapidly with central venous pressure monitoring; remainder of dose given slowly. Total dosage not to exceed 20 ml/kg in the first 24 hours. If therapy is continued longer than 24 hours, don't exceed 10 ml/kg daily. Continue for no longer than 5 days.
▶ **Prevention of venous thrombosis.** *Adults:* 10 ml/kg (500 to 1,000 ml) I.V. on day of procedure; 500 ml on days 2 and 3.
▶ **Hemodiluent in extracorporeal circulation.** *Adults:* 10 to 20 ml/kg added to perfusion circuit. Total dosage not to exceed 20 ml/kg.

Contraindications and precautions
• Contraindicated in patients hypersensitive to drug and in those with marked hemostatic defects, marked cardiac decompensation, and renal disease with severe oliguria or anuria.
• Use cautiously in patients with active hemorrhage, thrombocytopenia, or diabetes mellitus.
Lifespan: In pregnant women, use cautiously. Breast-feeding women should stop breast-feeding or not use drug. In children, safety of drug hasn't been established.

Adverse reactions
CV: thrombophlebitis.
GI: nausea, vomiting.
GU: tubular stasis and blocking, increased urine viscosity.
Hematologic: *anemia.*
Skin: urticaria.
Other: ***hypersensitivity reactions, anaphylaxis.***

Interactions
None significant.

Effects on lab test results
• May increase ALT and AST levels.
• May increase bleeding time. May decrease hemoglobin and hematocrit.

Pharmacokinetics
Absorption: Administered I.V.
Distribution: Distributed throughout vascular system.
Metabolism: Dextran molecules with molecular weights above 50,000 are enzymatically degraded by dextranase to glucose at about 70 to 90 mg/kg/day. This is a variable process.
Excretion: By kidneys for drug molecules with molecular weights below 50,000.

Route	Onset	Peak	Duration
I.V.	Immediate	Immediate	≤ 3 hr

Pharmacodynamics
Chemical effect: Expands plasma volume by way of colloidal osmotic effect, drawing fluid

from interstitial to intravascular space, providing fluid replacement.
Therapeutic effect: Expands plasma volume.

Available forms

Injection: 10% dextran 40 in D_5W or normal saline solution

NURSING PROCESS

Assessment

- Obtain history of patient's underlying condition and hydration status before therapy, and reassess regularly throughout therapy. Frequently assess vital signs, fluid intake and output, and urine or serum osmolarity levels.
- Be alert for adverse reactions.
- Observe patient closely during early phase of infusion, when most anaphylactic reactions occur.
- Watch for circulatory overload and rise in central venous pressure. Plasma expansion is slightly greater than volume infused.
- Check hemoglobin and hematocrit levels.
- Evaluate patient's and family's knowledge of drug therapy.

Nursing diagnoses

- Decreased cardiac output related to underlying condition
- Risk for injury related to potential for drug-induced hypersensitivity reaction
- Deficient knowledge related to drug therapy

Planning and implementation

ALERT: Use D_5W solution instead of normal saline solution because drug is hazardous for patients with heart failure, especially when given in normal saline solution.
- Prescriber may order dextran 1, a dextran adjunct, to protect against drug-induced anaphylaxis. Give 20 ml of dextran 1 (containing 150 mg/ml) I.V. over 60 seconds, 1 to 2 minutes before I.V. infusion of dextran.
- Store at constant 77° F (25° C). Dextran may precipitate in storage, but it can be heated to dissolve, if necessary.
- If oliguria or anuria occurs or isn't relieved by infusion, stop dextran and give loop diuretic.
- If hematocrit values fall below 30% by volume, notify prescriber.
- Drug may interfere with analyses of blood grouping, crossmatching, and bilirubin, glucose, and protein levels.

Patient teaching
- Inform patient, if alert, and family about dextran therapy.
- Instruct patient to notify prescriber if adverse reactions, such as itching, occur.

Evaluation

- Patient's vital signs and urine output return to normal.
- Patient has no hypersensitivity reaction to drug.
- Patient and family state understanding of drug therapy.

dextroamphetamine sulfate

(deks-troh-am-FET-uh-meen SUL-fayt)
Dexedrine* **, Dexedrine Spansule, Dextrostat**, Ferndex, Oxydess II, Spancap #1

Pharmacologic class: amphetamine
Therapeutic class: CNS stimulant
Pregnancy risk category: C
Controlled substance schedule: II

Indications and dosages

▶ **Narcolepsy.** *Adults:* 5 to 60 mg P.O. daily in divided doses.
Children age 12 and older: 10 mg P.O. daily; increase by 10-mg increments weekly until desired response occurs or adult dose is reached.
Children ages 6 to 11: 5 mg P.O. daily; increase by 5-mg increments weekly until desired response occurs. Give first dose on awakening, additional doses (one or two) at intervals of 4 to 6 hours.
▶ **Attention deficit hyperactivity disorder (ADHD).** *Children age 6 and older:* 5 mg P.O. once daily or b.i.d.; increase by 5-mg increments weekly, p.r.n.
Children ages 3 to 5: 2.5 mg P.O. daily; increase by 2.5-mg increments weekly, p.r.n. Only in rare cases is it necessary to exceed 40 mg daily.
▶ **Short-term adjunct in exogenous obesity‡.** *Adults:* 5 to 30 mg P.O. daily 30 to 60 minutes before meals in divided doses of 5 to 10 mg. Or, give one 10- or 15-mg sustained-released capsule daily as a single dose in the morning.

Contraindications and precautions

• Contraindicated in patients hypersensitive to sympathomimetic amines, patients with idiosyncratic reactions to them, patients who took an MAO inhibitor within 14 days, and patients with hyperthyroidism, moderate-to-severe hypertension, symptomatic CV disease, glaucoma, advanced arteriosclerosis, or a history of drug abuse.
• Use cautiously in patients with motor and phonic tics, Tourette syndrome, and agitated states.
Lifespan: In pregnant women, use cautiously. In breast-feeding women, safety of drug hasn't been established.

Adverse reactions

CNS: *restlessness,* tremors, *insomnia,* dizziness, headache, overstimulation, dysphoria.
CV: *tachycardia, palpitations,* hypertension, ***arrhythmias.***
GI: dry mouth, unpleasant taste, diarrhea, constipation, anorexia, weight loss, and other GI disturbances.
GU: impotence.
Skin: urticaria.
Other: altered libido, chills.

Interactions

Drug-drug. *Acetazolamide, alkalizing agents, antacids, sodium bicarbonate:* May increase renal reabsorption. Monitor patient for enhanced amphetamine effects.
Acidifying agents, ammonium chloride, ascorbic acid: May decrease level and increase renal clearance of dextroamphetamine. Monitor patient for decreased amphetamine effects.
Adrenergic blockers: Adrenergic blockers are inhibited by amphetamines. Avoid using together.
Antihistamines: Amphetamines may counteract sedative effects of antihistamines. Monitor patient for loss of therapeutic effects.
Chlorpromazine: Inhibits central stimulant effects of amphetamines; may be used to treat amphetamine poisoning. Monitor patient closely.
Haloperidol, phenothiazines, tricyclic antidepressants: Decreases amphetamine effect. Increase dose as needed.
Insulin, oral antidiabetics: May decrease antidiabetic requirement. Monitor glucose levels.
Lithium carbonate: May inhibit antiobesity and stimulating effects of amphetamines. Monitor patient closely.
MAO inhibitors: May cause severe hypertension; possibly hypertensive crisis. Don't use within 14 days of MAO inhibitor therapy.
Meperidine: Amphetamines potentiate analgesic effect. Use together cautiously.
Methenamine: Increases urinary excretion and reduced efficacy of amphetamines. Monitor effects.
Norepinephrine: Amphetamines enhance adrenergic effect of norepinephrine. Monitor patient closely.
Phenobarbital, phenytoin: Amphetamines may delay absorption. Monitor patient closely.
Propoxyphene: In cases of propoxyphene overdose, amphetamine CNS stimulation is potentiated and fatal seizures can occur. Don't use together.
Drug-food. *Caffeine:* May increase amphetamine and related amine effects. Monitor patient closely.

Effects on lab test results

• May increase corticosteroid level.

Pharmacokinetics

Absorption: Rapid; sustained-release capsules more slowly.
Distribution: Distributed widely throughout body.
Metabolism: Unknown.
Excretion: Excreted in urine. *Half-life:* 10 to 12 hours.

Route	Onset	Peak	Duration
P.O.	Unknown	Unknown	Unknown

Pharmacodynamics

Chemical effect: Unknown; probably promotes nerve impulse transmission by releasing stored norepinephrine from nerve terminals in brain. Main sites of activity appear to be the cerebral cortex and reticular activating system. In children with hyperkinesis, amphetamines have paradoxical calming effect.
Therapeutic effect: Helps prevent sleep and calms hyperactive children.

Available forms

Capsules (sustained-release): 5 mg, 10 mg, 15 mg
Tablets: 5 mg, 10 mg

NURSING PROCESS

Assessment

- Obtain history of patient's underlying condition before therapy, and reassess regularly throughout therapy.
- Be alert for adverse reactions and drug interactions.
- Monitor sleeping pattern, and observe patient for signs of excessive stimulation.
- Evaluate patient's and family's knowledge of drug therapy.

Nursing diagnoses

- Ineffective health maintenance related to underlying condition
- Disturbed sleep pattern related to drug-induced insomnia
- Deficient knowledge related to drug therapy

Planning and implementation

- Give at least 6 hours before bedtime to avoid sleep interference.
- Prolonged use may cause psychological dependence or habituation, especially in patients with history of drug addiction. After prolonged use, reduce dosage gradually to prevent acute rebound depression.

Patient teaching

- Warn patient to avoid hazardous activities until CNS effects of drug are known.
- Tell patient to avoid drinks containing caffeine, which increases effects of amphetamines and related amines.
- Inform patient that fatigue may result as drug effects wear off.
- Instruct patient to report signs of excessive stimulation.
- Inform patient that when tolerance to anorexigenic effect develops, drug should be discontinued, not increased. Tell him to report decreased effectiveness of drug. Warn patient against stopping drug abruptly.

Evaluation

- Patient shows improvement in underlying condition.
- Patient can sleep without difficulty.
- Patient and family state understanding of drug therapy.

dextromethorphan hydrobromide

(deks-troh-meth-OR-fan high-droh-BROH-mighd)

Balminil D.M. ◆, Benylin DM†, Broncho-Grippol-DM ◆, Children's Hold†, DexAlone†, Hold†, Koffex ◆, Pertussin Cough Suppressant†, Pertussin CS†, Pertussin ES*†, Robitussin Pediatric†, St. Joseph Cough Suppressant for Children†, Sucrets Cough Control Formula†, Trocal†, Vicks Formula 44 Pediatric Formula†

More commonly available in combination products such as: Anti-Tuss DM Expectorant†, Cheracol D Cough†, Extra Action Cough†, Glycotuss dm†, Guiamid D.M. Liquid†, Guiatuss-DM†, Halotussin-DM Expectorant†, Kolephrin GG/DM†, Mytussin DM†, Naldecon Senior DX†, Pertussin All-Night CS†, Rhinosyn-DMX Expectorant†, Robitussin-DM†, Silexin Cough†, Tolu-Sed DM†, Tuss-DM†, Unproco†, Vicks Children's Cough Syrup†, Vicks DayQuil Liquicaps†

Pharmacologic class: levorphanol derivative (dextrorotatory methyl ether)
Therapeutic class: antitussive (nonnarcotic)
Pregnancy risk category: C

Indications and dosages

▶ **Nonproductive cough.** *Adults and children older than age 12:* 10 to 30 mg P.O. q 4 hours, or 30 mg gelcaps q 6 to 8 hours. Or, 60 mg extended-release liquid b.i.d. Maximum, 120 mg daily.
Children ages 6 to 12: 5 to 10 mg P.O. q 4 hours, or 15 mg q 6 to 8 hours. Or, 30 mg extended-release liquid b.i.d. Maximum, 60 mg daily.
Children ages 2 to 5: 2.5 to 5 mg P.O. q 4 hours, or 7.5 mg q 6 to 8 hours. Or, 15 mg extended-release liquid b.i.d. Maximum, 30 mg daily. Dosages for children younger than age 2 must be individualized.

Contraindications and precautions

- Contraindicated in patients taking MAO inhibitors or within 2 weeks of stopping an MAO inhibitor.
- Use cautiously in sedated or debilitated patients, and patients confined to supine position. Also, use cautiously in patients with aspirin sensitivity.

Lifespan: In pregnant women, use cautiously. In breast-feeding women, safety of drug hasn't been established. In atopic children, use cautiously.

Adverse reactions

CNS: drowsiness, dizziness.
GI: nausea, vomiting, stomach pain.

Interactions

Drug-drug. *MAO inhibitors:* May increase risk of hypotension, coma, hyperpyrexia, and death. Don't use within 2 weeks of dextromethorphan hydrobromide therapy.
Selegiline: May increase risk of confusion, coma, hyperpyrexia. Avoid using together.
Drug-herb. *Parsley:* May cause serotonin syndrome. Discourage using together.

Effects on lab test results

None reported.

Pharmacokinetics

Absorption: Absorbed readily from GI tract.
Distribution: Unknown.
Metabolism: Metabolized extensively by liver.
Excretion: Small amount excreted unchanged. Metabolites excreted primarily in urine; about 7% to 10% excreted in feces. *Half-life:* About 11 hours.

Route	Onset	Peak	Duration
P.O.	≤ 30 min	Unknown	3-12 hr

Pharmacodynamics

Chemical effect: Suppresses cough reflex by direct action on cough center in medulla.
Therapeutic effect: Prevents cough.

Available forms

Gelcaps: 30 mg†
Liquid (extended-release): 30 mg/5 ml
Lozenges: 2.5 mg, 5 mg†, 7.5 mg†, 15 mg†
Solution: 3.5 mg/5 ml, 5 mg/5 ml*†, 7.5 mg/5 ml*†, 10 mg/5 ml*†, 15 mg/5 ml*†, 10 mg/15 ml* **

NURSING PROCESS

Assessment

- Obtain history of patient's cough before and after giving drug.
- Be alert for adverse reactions and drug interactions.
- Evaluate patient's and family's knowledge of drug therapy.

Nursing diagnoses

- Fatigue related to presence of nonproductive cough
- Risk for injury related to drug-induced adverse CNS reactions
- Deficient knowledge related to drug therapy

Planning and implementation

- Don't use drug when cough is valuable diagnostic sign or is beneficial (such as after thoracic surgery).
- As an antitussive, 15 to 30 mg of dextromethorphan is equivalent to 8 to 15 mg of codeine.
- Use drug with chest percussion and vibration.
- Notify prescriber if cough isn't relieved by drug.

Patient teaching

- Instruct patient to follow directions on medication bottle exactly; stress importance of not taking more drug than directed.
- Tell patient to call prescriber if cough persists more than 7 days.
- Suggest sugarless throat lozenges to decrease throat irritation and resulting cough.
- Advise patient to use humidifier to moisten air and ionizer or air filter to filter dust, smoke, and air pollutants.

Evaluation

- Patient's cough is relieved.
- Patient has no injury as a result of therapy.
- Patient and family state understanding of drug therapy.

dextrose (d-glucose)

(DEKS-trohs)

Pharmacologic class: carbohydrate
Therapeutic class: total parenteral nutrition (TPN) component, caloric agent, fluid volume replacement
Pregnancy risk category: C

Indications and dosages

▶ **Fluid replacement and calorie supplement in patients who can't maintain adequate oral intake or who are restricted from doing so.** *Adults and children:* Dosage depends on fluid and calorie requirements. Peripheral I.V. infusion of 2.5%, 5%, or 10% solution or central I.V. infusion of 20% solution is used for minimal fluid needs; 25% solution is used to treat acute hypoglycemia in neonate or older infant; 50% solution is used to treat insulin-induced hypoglycemia; 10%, 20%, 30%, 40%, 50%, 60%, and 70% solutions diluted in admixtures, normally amino acid solutions, for TPN are given through the central vein.

Contraindications and precautions

- Contraindicated in patients in diabetic coma while glucose level remains excessively high. Use of concentrated solutions is contraindicated in patients with intracranial or intraspinal hemorrhage, in dehydrated patients with delirium tremens, and in patients with severe dehydration, anuria, hepatic coma, or glucose-galactose malabsorption syndrome.
- Use cautiously in patients with cardiac or pulmonary disease, hypertension, renal insufficiency, urinary obstruction, or hypovolemia.

Lifespan: In pregnant patients, use only if necessary. With breast-feeding patients and children (especially infants of diabetic mothers), use cautiously.

Adverse reactions

CNS: confusion, ***unconsciousness in hyperosmolar hyperglycemic nonketotic syndrome.***
CV: ***pulmonary edema, worsened hypertension, heart failure*** (with fluid overload in susceptible patients), *phlebitis, venous sclerosis.*
GU: glycosuria, osmotic diuresis.
Metabolic: hyperglycemia, hypervolemia, hyperosmolarity (with rapid infusion of concentrated solution or prolonged infusion), ***hypoglycemia*** from rebound hyperinsulinemia (rapid termination of long-term infusions).
Skin: sloughing, tissue necrosis with prolonged or concentrated infusions or extravasation, especially with peripheral administration.

Interactions

None significant.

Effects on lab test results

- May increase or decrease glucose level.

Pharmacokinetics

Absorption: Administered I.V.
Distribution: Distributed throughout plasma volume.
Metabolism: Metabolized to carbon dioxide and water.
Excretion: Excess excreted in urine.

Route	Onset	Peak	Duration
I.V.	Immediate	Immediate	Unknown

Pharmacodynamics

Chemical effect: Simple water-soluble sugar that minimizes glyconeogenesis and promotes anabolism in patient who can't receive sufficient oral caloric intake.
Therapeutic effect: Provides supplemental calories and fluid.

Available forms

Injection: 3-ml ampule (10%); 5-ml ampule (10%); 10 ml (25%); 50 ml (5% and 50% available in vial, ampule, and Bristoject); 70-ml pin-top vial (70% for additive use only); 100 ml (5%); 250 ml (5%, 10%); 500 ml (5%, 10%, 20%, 30%, 40%, 50%, 60%, 70%); 1,000 ml (2.5%, 5%, 10%, 20%, 30%, 40%, 50%, 60%, 70%)

NURSING PROCESS

Assessment

- Obtain history of patient's underlying condition before therapy, and reassess regularly throughout therapy.
- Be alert for adverse reactions.
- Evaluate patient's and family's knowledge of drug therapy.

Nursing diagnoses

- Imbalanced nutrition: less than body requirements related to underlying condition
- Ineffective health maintenance related to drug-induced hyperglycemia
- Deficient knowledge related to drug therapy

Planning and implementation

ALERT: Control infusion rate carefully; maximal rate is 0.5 g/kg/hour. Use infusion pump when infusing with amino acids for TPN. Never infuse concentrated solutions rapidly; this may cause hyperglycemia and fluid shift.

ALERT: Don't give dextrose solutions without saline solution in blood transfusions; this may cause clumping of RBCs. Use central veins to infuse dextrose solutions with concentrations greater than 10%.

ALERT: Verify percentage before giving. Concentrations aren't interchangeable.

- Take care to prevent extravasation.

ALERT: Never stop hypertonic solutions abruptly. If necessary, have $D_{10}W$ available to treat hypoglycemia if rebound hyperinsulinemia occurs.

Patient teaching

- Inform patient of need for dextrose therapy, method by which it will be given, and adverse reactions that should be reported.

Evaluation

- Patient shows improvement of underlying condition.
- Patient maintains normal glucose level throughout therapy.
- Patient and family state understanding of drug therapy.

diazepam

(digh-AZ-uh-pam)

Diastat, Apo-Diazepam♦, Diazemuls♦ ◇, Diazepam Intensol, Novo-Dipam♦, PMS-Diazepam♦, Valium, Vivol♦

Pharmacologic class: benzodiazepine
Therapeutic class: anxiolytic, skeletal muscle relaxant, anticonvulsant, sedative-hypnotic
Pregnancy risk category: D
Controlled substance schedule: IV

Indications and dosages

▶ **Anxiety.** *Adults:* Depending on severity, 2 to 10 mg P.O. b.i.d. to q.i.d. Or, 2 to 10 mg I.M. or I.V. q 3 to 4 hours, if needed.
Elderly patients: 2 to 2.5 mg P.O. once or twice daily; increase gradually, as needed.
Children age 6 months and older: 1 to 2.5 mg P.O. t.i.d. or q.i.d.; increase gradually, as needed and tolerated.

▶ **Acute alcohol withdrawal.** *Adults:* 10 mg P.O. t.i.d. or q.i.d. for the first 24 hours, reduced to 5 mg P.O. t.i.d. or q.i.d., p.r.n. Or, initially, 10 mg I.M. or I.V.; then 5 to 10 mg I.M. or I.V. in 3 to 4 hours, if needed.

▶ **Before endoscopic procedures.** *Adults:* I.V. dose titrated to desired sedative response (up to 20 mg). Or, 5 to 10 mg I.M. 30 minutes before procedure.

▶ **Muscle spasm.** *Adults:* 2 to 10 mg P.O. b.i.d. to q.i.d. daily. Or, 5 to 10 mg I.M. or I.V. initially; then 5 to 10 mg I.M. or I.V. in 3 to 4 hours, p.r.n. For tetanus, larger doses may be required.
Elderly patients: 2 to 2.5 mg I.M. or I.V. once or twice daily; increase, as needed.
Children age 5 and older: 5 to 10 mg I.M. or I.V. q 3 to 4 hours, p.r.n.
Infants older than age 30 days and children younger than 5 years: 1 to 2 mg I.M. or I.V. slowly repeated q 3 to 4 hours, p.r.n.

▶ **Preoperative sedation.** *Adults:* 10 mg I.M. (preferred) or I.V. before surgery.

▶ **Cardioversion.** *Adults:* 5 to 15 mg I.V. 5 to 10 minutes before procedure.

▶ **Adjunct in seizure disorders.** *Adults:* 2 to 10 mg P.O. b.i.d. to q.i.d.
Elderly patients: 2 to 2.5 mg P.O. once or twice daily, increased as needed.
Children and infants age 6 months and older: 1 to 2.5 mg P.O. t.i.d. or q.i.d. initially; increased as tolerated and needed.

▶ **Status epilepticus.** *Adults:* 5 to 10 mg I.V. (preferred) or I.M. initially. Repeat q 10 to 15 minutes, p.r.n., up to maximum dose of 30 mg. Repeat in 2 to 4 hours, p.r.n.
Children age 5 and older: 1 mg I.V. q 2 to 5 minutes up to maximum of 10 mg. Repeat in 2 to 4 hours, p.r.n.
Infants older than age 30 days and children younger than age 5 years: 0.2 to 0.5 mg I.V. slowly q 2 to 5 minutes up to maximum of 5 mg. Repeat in 2 to 4 hours, p.r.n.

▶ **Control of acute repetitive seizure activity in patients already taking anticonvulsants.** *Adults and children age 12 and older:* 0.2 mg/kg P.R. using applicator. A second dose may be given 4 to 12 hours after the first dose, if needed.
Children ages 6 to 11: 0.3 mg/kg P.R. using applicator. A second dose may be given 4 to 12 hours after the first dose, if needed.
Children ages 2 to 5: 0.5 mg/kg P.R. using applicator. A second dose may be given 4 to 12 hours after the first dose, if needed.

Contraindications and precautions

• Contraindicated in patients hypersensitive to drug and in those with angle-closure glaucoma, shock, coma, or acute alcohol intoxication (parenteral form).
• Use cautiously in patients with hepatic or renal impairment, depression, or chronic open-angle glaucoma.
Lifespan: In pregnant women (especially during the first trimester) and in breast-feeding women, avoid use of drug. In infants younger than age 6 months, oral form of drug is contraindicated. In elderly and debilitated patients, use cautiously. Dosage should be reduced because these patients may be more susceptible to adverse CNS effects of drug.

Adverse reactions

CNS: *pain, drowsiness, lethargy, hangover, ataxia,* fainting, depression, restlessness, anterograde amnesia, psychosis, slurred speech, tremors, headache, insomnia.
CV: transient hypotension, ***bradycardia, CV collapse.***
EENT: diplopia, blurred vision, nystagmus.
GI: nausea, vomiting, abdominal discomfort, constipation.
GU: incontinence, urine retention.
Respiratory: ***respiratory depression.***
Skin: rash, urticaria, desquamation.
Other: physical or psychological dependence, ***acute withdrawal syndrome*** after sudden discontinuation in physically dependent people, *phlebitis at injection site.*

Interactions

Drug-drug. *Cimetidine:* May increase sedation. Monitor patient carefully.
CNS depressants: May increase CNS depression. Avoid using together.
Digoxin: May increase level of digoxin, increasing toxicity. Monitor patient closely.
Phenobarbital: May increase effects of both drugs. Use together cautiously.
Phenytoin: May increase level of phenytoin. Monitor patient for toxicity.
Ranitidine: May decrease absorption. Monitor patient for decreased effect.
Drug-herb. *Kava, sassafras, valerian:* Sedative effects may be enhanced. Discourage using together.
Drug-lifestyle. *Alcohol use:* May increase CNS depression. Discourage using together.
Smoking: May increase benzodiazepine clearance. Monitor patient for lack of drug effect.

Effects on lab test results

• May increase liver function test values. May decrease neutrophil count.

Pharmacokinetics

Absorption: When given P.O., absorbed through GI tract. Administration by I.M. route results in erratic absorption.
Distribution: Distributed widely throughout body; about 85% to 95% bound to plasma protein.
Metabolism: Metabolized in liver to active metabolite, desmethyldiazepam.
Excretion: Most metabolites of diazepam excreted in urine, with only small amount excreted in feces. *Half-life:* 30 to 200 hours.

Route	Onset	Peak	Duration
P.O.	30 min	0.5-2 hr	3-8 hr
I.V.	1-5 min	≤ 15 min	15-60 min
I.M.	Unknown	2 hr	Unknown
P.R.	Unknown	1-5 hr	Unknown

Pharmacodynamics

Chemical effect: Unknown; probably depresses CNS at limbic and subcortical levels of brain; suppresses spread of seizure activity produced by epileptogenic foci in cortex, thalamus, and limbic structures.
Therapeutic effect: Relieves anxiety, muscle spasms, and seizures (parenteral form); promotes calmness and sleep.

Available forms

Injection: 5 mg/ml
Oral solution: 5 mg/ml, 5 mg/5 ml
Rectal gel: 2.5 mg*, 5 mg*, 10 mg*, 15 mg*, 20 mg*
Sterile emulsion for injection: 5 mg/ml ♦
Tablets: 2 mg, 5 mg, 10 mg

NURSING PROCESS

Assessment

• Obtain history of patient's underlying condition before therapy, and reassess regularly thereafter.
• Monitor respirations every 5 to 15 minutes and before each repeated I.V. dose.

*Liquid form contains alcohol. **May contain tartrazine. ♦ Canada ◇ Australia †OTC ‡Off-label use

• Periodically monitor liver, kidney, and hematopoietic function studies in patient receiving repeated or prolonged therapy.
• Be alert for adverse reactions and drug interactions.
• Evaluate patient's and family's knowledge of drug therapy.

Nursing diagnoses

• Ineffective health maintenance related to underlying condition
• Risk for injury related to drug-induced adverse CNS reactions
• Deficient knowledge related to drug therapy

Planning and implementation

• **P.O. use:** When oral concentrate solution is used, dilute dose just before giving. Use water, juice, or carbonated beverages, or mix with semisolid food such as applesauce or pudding.
• **P.R. use:** Avoid P.R. use of Diastat for more than 5 episodes per month or one episode every 5 days.
ALERT: Diastat rectal gel should be given only by caregivers who can distinguish the distinct cluster of seizures or events from the patient's ordinary seizure activity, who have been instructed and can give the treatment competently, who understand which seizure characteristics may or may not be treated with Diastat, and who can monitor the clinical response and recognize when immediate professional medical evaluation is needed.
• **I.V. use:** Give drug at no more than 5 mg/minute. When injecting, give directly into vein. If this is impossible, inject slowly through infusion tubing as near to venous insertion site as possible. Watch daily for phlebitis at injection site.
– Avoid extravasation. Don't inject into small veins.
– Have emergency resuscitation equipment and oxygen at bedside when giving drug I.V.
• **I.M. use:** I.M. administration isn't recommended because absorption is variable and injection is painful. Used only when I.V. route and P.O. route aren't applicable.
ALERT: Don't mix injectable form with other drugs because diazepam is incompatible with most drugs.
ALERT: Don't store parenteral solution in plastic syringes.
ALERT: Parenteral emulsion—a stabilized oil-in-water emulsion—should appear milky white and uniform. Avoid mixing with any other drugs or solutions, and avoid infusion sets or containers made from polyvinyl chloride. If dilution is necessary, drug may be mixed with I.V. fat emulsion. Use admixture within 6 hours.
• Possibility of abuse and addiction exists. Don't withdraw drug abruptly after long-term use; withdrawal symptoms may occur.

Patient teaching
• Warn patient to avoid hazardous activities until CNS effects of drug are known.
• Tell patient to avoid alcohol during drug therapy.
• Warn patient to take drug only as directed and not to discontinue it without prescriber's approval.
• Warn patient about risk of physical and psychological dependence.

Evaluation

• Patient shows improvement in underlying condition.
• Patient has no injury as result of drug-induced adverse CNS reactions.
• Patient and family state understanding of drug therapy.

diazoxide

(digh-uz-OKS-ighd)
Hyperstat IV, Proglycem

Pharmacologic class: peripheral vasodilator
Therapeutic class: antihypertensive
Pregnancy risk category: C

Indications and dosages

▶ **Hypertensive crisis.** *Adults and children:* 1 to 3 mg/kg by I.V. bolus (maximum, 150 mg) q 5 to 15 minutes until adequate response occurs. Repeat at 4- to 24-hour intervals, p.r.n.
▶ **Hypoglycemia from hyperinsulinism.** *Adults and children:* Initially, 3 mg/kg P.O. daily in 3 divided doses q 8 hours. Then, 3 to 8 mg/kg daily in 2 or 3 divided doses q 12 to 8 hours, respectively.

Infants and newborns: Initially, 10 mg/kg daily in 3 divided doses q 8 hours. Then, 8 to 15 mg/kg/day in 2 or 3 divided doses q 8 to 12 hours.

Contraindications and precautions

• Contraindicated in patients hypersensitive to drug, other thiazides, or other sulfonamide-derived drugs. Also contraindicated in treatment of compensatory hypertension (as in coarctation of the aorta or arteriovenous shunt).
• Use cautiously in patients with impaired cerebral or cardiac function or uremia.
Lifespan: In pregnant women, use cautiously. In breast-feeding women, use of drug not recommended.

Adverse reactions

CNS: *headache,* dizziness, light-headedness, euphoria, ***cerebral ischemia, seizures, paralysis.***
CV: *orthostatic hypotension,* flushing, warmth, angina, ***myocardial ischemia, arrhythmias,*** ECG changes, ***shock, MI.***
GI: *nausea, vomiting,* abdominal discomfort, dry mouth, constipation, diarrhea.
Hematologic: ***thrombocytopenia.***
Metabolic: *sodium and water retention, hyperglycemia,* hyperuricemia.
Skin: diaphoresis.
Other: inflammation, pain (with extravasation).

Interactions

Drug-drug. *Antihypertensives:* May cause severe hypotension. Use together cautiously; monitor blood pressure closely.
Hydantoins: May decrease levels of hydantoins, resulting in decreased anticonvulsant action. Monitor patient closely.
Sulfonylureas: May cause hyperglycemia. Monitor glucose level.
Thiazide diuretics: May increase diazoxide effects. Use together cautiously.
Insulin and oral antidiabetics: May alter insulin and oral antidiabetic requirements in previously stable patients. Monitor glucose level.

Effects on lab test results

• May increase glucose and uric acid levels.
• May decrease platelet count.

Pharmacokinetics

Absorption: After oral administration, hyperglycemic effect begins in 1 hour. After I.V. administration, blood pressure should decrease promptly with maximum effect in 1 hour.
Distribution: Distributed throughout body; about 90% protein-bound.
Metabolism: Metabolized partially in liver.
Excretion: Diazoxide and its metabolites excreted slowly by kidneys. *Half-life:* 21 to 36 hours.

Route	Onset	Peak	Duration
P.O.	≤ 1 hr	unknown	< 8 hr
I.V.	≤ 1 min	2-5 min	2-12 hr

Pharmacodynamics

Chemical effect: Directly relaxes arteriolar smooth muscle and decreases peripheral vascular resistance. Increases glucose levels by inhibiting pancreatic release of insulin, stimulating catecholamine release or increasing hepatic release of glucose.
Therapeutic effect: Lowers blood pressure; increases blood sugar.

Available forms

Capsules: 50 mg
Injection: 15 mg/ml, 300 mg/20 ml
Oral suspension: 50 mg/ml

NURSING PROCESS

Assessment

• Obtain history of patient's blood pressure before therapy.
• Monitor effectiveness by monitoring blood pressure and ECG continuously during drug administration.
• Weigh patient daily.
• Monitor glucose levels daily; watch closely for signs of severe hyperglycemia or hyperosmolar nonketotic syndrome.
• Check patient's uric acid levels frequently.
• Be alert for adverse reactions and drug interactions.
• Evaluate patient's and family's knowledge of drug therapy.

Nursing diagnoses

• Risk for injury related to presence of hypertension

- Excess fluid volume related to drug-induced fluid retention
- Deficient knowledge related to drug therapy

Planning and implementation

- Place patient in supine or Trendelenburg position during and for 1 hour after infusion.
- Protect I.V. solutions from light. Darkened I.V. solutions of diazoxide are subpotent and shouldn't be used.
- Take care to avoid extravasation.
- Check patient's standing blood pressure before stopping drug.
- Notify prescriber immediately if severe hypotension develops, and keep norepinephrine available.
- If fluid or sodium retention develops, prescriber may order diuretics.

ALERT: Don't confuse diazoxide with Diamox.

Patient teaching

- Inform patient that orthostatic hypotension can be minimized by rising slowly and avoiding sudden position changes.
- Instruct patient to remain in supine position for 30 minutes after injection.

Evaluation

- Patient's blood pressure returns to normal.
- Patient maintains normal fluid and electrolyte balance during therapy.
- Patient and family state understanding of drug therapy.

diclofenac potassium

(digh-KLOH-fen-ek poh-TAH-see-um)
Cataflam

diclofenac sodium

Solaraze, Voltaren, Voltaren SR♦, Voltaren-XR

Pharmacologic class: NSAID
Therapeutic class: antiarthritic, anti-inflammatory
Pregnancy risk category: B

Indications and dosages

▶ **Ankylosing spondylitis.** ***delayed-release tablets.*** *Adults:* 25 mg P.O. q.i.d. (and h.s., p.r.n.).

▶ **Osteoarthritis.** ***immediate-release tablets.*** *Adults:* 50 mg P.O. b.i.d. or t.i.d. Or, 75 mg P.O. b.i.d. Or, 100 mg P.O. a day of extended release.

▶ **Rheumatoid arthritis.** ***immediate- or delayed-release.*** *Adults:* 50 mg P.O. t.i.d. or q.i.d. Or, 75 mg P.O. b.i.d. (. Or, 50 to 100 mg P.R. (where available) h.s. as substitute for last P.O. dose of day. Not to exceed 225 mg daily.

▶ **Analgesia and primary dysmenorrhea.** ***diclofenac potassium.*** *Adults:* 50 mg P.O. t.i.d. If necessary, 100 mg may be given for first dose only.

▶ **Actinic keratosis.** *Adults:* Apply gel over affected lesions b.i.d.

Contraindications and precautions

- Contraindicated in patients hypersensitive to drug and in those with hepatic porphyria or a history of asthma, urticaria, or other allergic reactions after taking aspirin or other NSAIDs.
- Use cautiously in patients with history of peptic ulcer disease, hepatic dysfunction, cardiac disease, hypertension, conditions that cause fluid retention, or impaired kidney function.

Lifespan: During late pregnancy or while breast-feeding, drug isn't recommended. In children, safety of drug hasn't been established.

Adverse reactions

CNS: anxiety, depression, dizziness, drowsiness, insomnia, irritability, myoclonus, migraine, *headache.*
CV: ***heart failure,*** hypertension, edema, fluid retention.
EENT: *tinnitus,* ***laryngeal edema,*** swelling of lips and tongue, blurred vision, eye pain, night blindness, epistaxis, reversible hearing loss.
GI: taste disorder, *abdominal pain or cramps, constipation, diarrhea, indigestion, nausea,* abdominal distention, flatulence, peptic ulceration, ***bleeding,*** melena, bloody diarrhea, appetite change, colitis.
GU: azotemia, proteinuria, ***acute renal failure,*** oliguria, interstitial nephritis, papillary necrosis, nephrotic syndrome, *fluid retention.*
Hepatic: jaundice, ***hepatitis, hepatotoxicity.***
Metabolic: ***hypoglycemia,*** hyperglycemia.
Musculoskeletal: back, leg, or joint pain.

Respiratory: asthma.
Skin: rash, pruritus, urticaria, eczema, dermatitis, alopecia, photosensitivity, bullous eruption, ***Stevens-Johnson syndrome,*** allergic purpura.
Other: ***anaphylaxis, angioedema.***

Interactions

Drug-drug. *Anticoagulants, including warfarin:* May increase risk of bleeding. Monitor patient closely for bleeding.
Aspirin: May increase risk of bleeding. Don't use together.
Beta blockers: Antihypertensive effect may be blunted. Monitor blood pressure closely.
Cyclosporine, digoxin, lithium, methotrexate: Diclofenac may reduce renal clearance of these drugs and increase risk of toxicity. Monitor patient closely.
Diuretics: May decrease effectiveness of diuretics. Monitor patient closely.
Insulin, oral antidiabetics: Diclofenac may alter antidiabetic requirement. Monitor patient closely.
Potassium-sparing diuretics: Enhances potassium retention and increased potassium levels. Monitor patient for hyperkalemia.
Drug-herb. *Dong quai, feverfew, garlic, ginger, horse chestnut, red clover:* May increase risk of bleeding. Discourage using together.
St. John's wort: May increase risk of photosensitivity. Advise patient to avoid unprotected and prolonged exposure to sunlight.
Drug-lifestyle. *Sun exposure:* May cause photosensitivity reactions. Urge patient to wear protective clothing and sunblock.

Effects on lab test results

- May increase ALT, AST, alkaline phosphatase, bilirubin, BUN, creatinine, and LDH levels. May increase or decrease glucose level.

Pharmacokinetics

Absorption: After P.O. or P.R. administration, rapidly and almost completely absorbed. Absorption is delayed by food.
Distribution: Highly (nearly 100%) protein-bound.
Metabolism: Undergoes first-pass metabolism, with 60% of unchanged drug reaching systemic circulation.
Excretion: About 40% to 60% excreted in urine; balance is excreted in bile. *Half-life:* 1.2 to 1.8 hours after P.O. dose.

Route	Onset	Peak	Duration
P.O., P.R.	30 min	Unknown	8 hr
P.O. (enteric-coated)	30 min	2-3 hr	8 hr

Pharmacodynamics

Chemical effect: Produces anti-inflammatory, analgesic, and antipyretic effects, possibly by inhibiting prostaglandin synthesis.
Therapeutic effect: Relieves inflammation, pain, and fever.

Available forms

diclofenac potassium
Tablets: 50 mg
diclofenac sodium
Suppositories: 50 mg ♦, 100 mg ♦
Tablets (delayed-release/enteric-coated): 25 mg, 50 mg, 75 mg
Tablets (extended-release): 100 mg ♦

NURSING PROCESS

Assessment

- Obtain history of patient's underlying condition before therapy.
- Monitor effectiveness by assessing patient for pain relief.
- Liver function test results may become elevated during therapy. Monitor transaminase levels, especially ALT levels, periodically in patients undergoing long-term therapy. First transaminase measurement should be no later than 8 weeks after therapy starts.
- Be alert for adverse reactions and drug interactions.
- Evaluate patient's and family's knowledge of drug therapy.

Nursing diagnoses

- Acute pain related to underlying condition
- Risk for injury related to drug-induced adverse reactions
- Deficient knowledge related to drug therapy

Planning and implementation

- **P.O. use:** Give drug with milk or food if GI distress occurs.

– Notify prescriber immediately if patient develops signs of GI bleeding, hepatotoxicity, or other adverse reactions.
• **P.R. use:** Not commercially available in the United States. May be substituted for the last oral dose of the day.

Patient teaching
• Tell patient to take drug with milk or food to minimize GI distress.
• Instruct patient not to crush, break, or chew enteric-coated tablets.
• Teach patient signs and symptoms of GI bleeding, and tell him to contact prescriber immediately if they occur.
• Teach patient signs and symptoms of hepatotoxicity, including nausea, fatigue, lethargy, pruritus, jaundice, right upper quadrant tenderness, and flulike symptoms. Tell him to contact prescriber immediately if these symptoms appear.

Evaluation
• Patient is free from pain.
• Patient has no injury as result of drug-induced adverse reactions.
• Patient and family state understanding of drug therapy.

dicloxacillin sodium
(digh-kloks-uh-SIL-in SOH-dee-um)
Dycill, Dynapen, Pathocil

Pharmacologic class: penicillinase-resistant penicillin
Therapeutic class: antibiotic
Pregnancy risk category: B

Indications and dosages
▶ **Systemic infection with penicillinase-producing staphylococci.** *Adults and children weighing more than 40 kg (88 lb):* 125 to 250 mg P.O. q 6 hours.
Children weighing 40 kg or less: 25 to 50 mg/kg P.O. daily in divided doses q 6 hours.

Contraindications and precautions
• Contraindicated in patients hypersensitive to drug or other penicillins.
• Use cautiously in patients with other drug allergies, especially to cephalosporins (possible cross-sensitivity), and in those with mononucleosis (high risk of maculopapular rash).
Lifespan: With pregnant and breast-feeding women, use cautiously.

Adverse reactions
CNS: neuromuscular irritability, ***seizures,*** lethargy, hallucinations, anxiety, confusion, agitation, depression, dizziness, fatigue.
GI: *nausea,* vomiting, *epigastric distress,* flatulence, *diarrhea,* enterocolitis, ***pseudomembranous colitis,*** black "hairy" tongue, abdominal pain.
Hematologic: eosinophilia, anemia, ***thrombocytopenia, agranulocytosis, leukopenia,*** hemolytic anemia.
Other: ***hypersensitivity reactions*** (pruritus, urticaria, rash, ***anaphylaxis***), overgrowth of nonsusceptible organisms.

Interactions
Drug-drug. *Hormonal contraceptives:* Contraceptive efficacy may be decreased. Additional form of contraception recommended during penicillin therapy.
Probenecid: Increases levels of dicloxacillin and other penicillins. Probenecid may be used for this purpose.

Effects on lab test results
• May increase ALT, AST, alkaline phosphatase, and LDH levels.
• May increase eosinophil count. May decrease hemoglobin, hematocrit, and platelet, WBC, and granulocyte counts.

Pharmacokinetics
Absorption: Absorbed rapidly but incompletely (35% to 76%) from GI tract; food may decrease rate and extent of absorption.
Distribution: Distributed widely in bone, bile, and pleural and synovial fluids. CSF penetration is poor but is enhanced by meningeal inflammation. Drug is 95% to 99% protein-bound.
Metabolism: Metabolized only partially.
Excretion: Dicloxacillin and metabolites excreted in urine. *Half-life:* 30 to 60 minutes.

Route	Onset	Peak	Duration
P.O.	Unknown	30 min-2 hr	6 hr

Pharmacodynamics

Chemical effect: Inhibits cell wall synthesis during microorganism multiplication. Bacteria resist penicillins by producing penicillinases—enzymes that convert penicillins to inactive penicilloic acid. Dicloxacillin resists these enzymes.
Therapeutic effect: Kills susceptible bacteria, including many strains of penicillinase-producing bacteria. This activity is most important against penicillinase-producing staphylococci; some strains may remain resistant. Dicloxacillin is also active against a few gram-positive aerobic and anaerobic bacilli but has no significant effect on gram-negative bacilli.

Available forms

Capsules: 125 mg, 250 mg, 500 mg
Oral suspension: 62.5 mg/5 ml (after reconstitution)

NURSING PROCESS

Assessment

- Obtain history of patient's infection before therapy, and reassess regularly thereafter.
- Before giving drug, ask patient about any allergic reaction to penicillin. Negative history of penicillin allergy is no guarantee against future allergic reactions.
- Obtain specimen for culture and sensitivity tests before first dose. Therapy may begin pending test results.
- Periodically assess renal, hepatic, and hematopoietic function in patients receiving long-term therapy.
- Be alert for adverse reactions and drug interactions.
- Monitor patient's hydration status if adverse GI reactions occur.
- Evaluate patient's and family's knowledge of drug therapy.

Nursing diagnoses

- Infection related to presence of susceptible bacteria
- Risk for deficient fluid volume related to drug-induced adverse GI reactions
- Deficient knowledge related to drug therapy

Planning and implementation

- Give drug 1 to 2 hours before or 2 to 3 hours after meals. It may cause GI disturbances. Food may interfere with absorption.
- Give drug at least 1 hour before bacteriostatic antibiotics.
- Notify prescriber if adverse reactions occur, especially rash, because dicloxacillin may need to be discontinued and another antibiotic substituted.

ALERT: Don't confuse dicloxacillin with cloxacillin.

Patient teaching

- Tell patient to complete the entire quantity of medication exactly as prescribed, even if symptoms subside.
- Tell patient to call prescriber if rash develops.
- Warn patient not to use leftover drug for new illness or share it with others.
- Teach patient that hormonal contraceptive may be ineffective.

Evaluation

- Patient is free from infection.
- Patient maintains adequate hydration throughout therapy.
- Patient and family state understanding of drug therapy.

dicyclomine hydrochloride

(digh-SIGH-kloh-meen high-droh-KLOR-ighd)
Antispas, Bemote, Bentyl, Bentylol ♦, Byclomine, Dibent, Dilomine, Di-Spaz, Formulex ♦, Lomine ♦, Merbentyl ◇, Or-Tyl, Spasmoban ♦

Pharmacologic class: anticholinergic
Therapeutic class: antimuscarinic, GI antispasmodic
Pregnancy risk category: B

Indications and dosages

▶ **Irritable bowel syndrome and other functional GI disorders.** *Adults:* Initially, 20 mg P.O. q.i.d.; increase to 40 mg q.i.d. Or, 20 mg I.M. q 4 to 6 hours.
Children age 2 and older: 10 mg P.O. t.i.d. or q.i.d.

Infants ages 6 months to 2 years: 5 to 10 mg P.O. t.i.d. or q.i.d.

▶ **Infant colic‡.** *Infants age 6 months and older:* 5 to 10 mg P.O. t.i.d. or q.i.d. Adjust dosage according to patient's needs and response.

Contraindications and precautions

• Contraindicated in patients hypersensitive to anticholinergics and in those with obstructive uropathy, obstructive disease of GI tract, reflux esophagitis, severe ulcerative colitis, myasthenia gravis, unstable CV status in acute hemorrhage, or glaucoma.

• Use cautiously in patients with autonomic neuropathy, hyperthyroidism, coronary artery disease, arrhythmias, heart failure, hypertension, hiatal hernia, hepatic or renal disease, prostatic hypertrophy, or ulcerative colitis.

Lifespan: In pregnant patients, use cautiously. In breast-feeding women and infants younger than age 6 months, drug is contraindicated.

Adverse reactions

CNS: fever, *headache, dizziness,* insomnia, drowsiness; nervousness, confusion, excitement (in elderly patients).
CV: *palpitations,* tachycardia.
EENT: blurred vision, increased intraocular pressure, mydriasis.
GI: nausea, vomiting, *constipation, dry mouth,* abdominal distention, heartburn, paralytic ileus.
GU: *urinary hesitancy, urine retention,* impotence.
Skin: urticaria, decreased sweating or possibly anhidrosis, other dermal changes.
Other: allergic reactions.

Interactions

Drug-drug. *Amantadine, antihistamines, antiparkinsonians, disopyramide, glutethimide, meperidine, phenothiazines, procainamide, quinidine, tricyclic antidepressants:* May cause additive adverse effects. Avoid using together.
Antacids: May decrease absorption of oral anticholinergics. Separate administration times by 2 to 3 hours.
Ketoconazole: Anticholinergics may interfere with ketoconazole absorption. Give at least 2 hours after ketoconazole.

Effects on lab test results

None reported.

Pharmacokinetics

Absorption: About 67% of P.O. dose absorbed from GI tract; unknown after I.M. administration.
Distribution: Unknown.
Metabolism: Unknown.
Excretion: After P.O. administration, 80% excreted in urine and 10% in feces; unknown after I.M. administration. *Half-life:* Initial, 1.8 hours; secondary, 9 to 10 hours.

Route	Onset	Peak	Duration
P.O.	Unknown	1-1.5 hr	Unknown
I.M.	Unknown	Unknown	Unknown

Pharmacodynamics

Chemical effect: Appears to exert nonspecific, indirect spasmolytic action on smooth muscle. Dicyclomine also possesses local anesthetic properties that may be partly responsible for spasmolysis.
Therapeutic effect: Relieves GI spasms.

Available forms

Capsules: 10 mg, 20 mg
Injection: 10 mg/ml
Syrup: 5 mg/5 ml ◇, 10 mg/5 ml
Tablets: 10 mg ◇, 20 mg

NURSING PROCESS

Assessment

• Obtain history of patient's underlying condition before therapy.

• Monitor effectiveness by regularly assessing patient for pain relief and improvement of underlying condition.

• Be alert for adverse reactions and drug interactions.

• Evaluate patient's and family's knowledge of drug therapy.

Nursing diagnoses

• Acute pain related to underlying condition

• Risk for injury related to drug-induced adverse CNS reactions

• Deficient knowledge related to drug therapy

Planning and implementation

ALERT: Drug is synthetic tertiary derivative that may cause atropine-like adverse reactions. Overdose may cause curare-like effects, such as respiratory paralysis.

Reactions may be *common,* uncommon, ***life-threatening***, or COMMON AND LIFE-THREATENING.

ALERT: High environmental temperatures may induce heatstroke during drug use. If symptoms occur, discontinue drug use.
- **P.O. use:** Give 30 to 60 minutes before meals and at bedtime. Bedtime dose can be larger; give at least 2 hours after last meal of day.
- **I.M. use:** Follow normal protocol.

ALERT: Don't give by S.C. or I.V. route.
- Be prepared to adjust dosage according to patient's needs and response. Doses up to 40 mg P.O. q.i.d. may be used in adults, but safety and efficacy for more than 2 weeks haven't been established.

Patient teaching
- Instruct patient to refrain from driving and performing other hazardous activities if he's drowsy or dizzy or has blurred vision.
- Tell him to drink plenty of fluids to help prevent constipation.
- Urge patient to report rash or skin eruption.
- Tell patient to use sugarless gum or hard candy to relieve dry mouth.

Evaluation
- Patient is free from pain.
- Patient doesn't experience injury as a result of drug-induced adverse CNS reactions.
- Patient and family state understanding of drug therapy.

didanosine (ddI)
(digh-DAN-uh-zeen)
Videx, Videx EC

Pharmacologic class: purine analogue
Therapeutic class: antiviral
Pregnancy risk category: B

Indications and dosages
► **Treatment of HIV infection when antiretroviral therapy is warranted.** *Adults weighing 60 kg (132 lb) and over:* 200 mg tablets P.O. q 12 hours or 400 mg tablets P.O. once daily. Or, 250 mg buffered powder q 12 hours.
Adults weighing less than 60 kg: 125 mg (one 100-mg tablet and one 25-mg tablet) P.O. q 12 hours or 250 mg P.O. once daily. Or, 167 mg buffered powder q 12 hours.
Children: 120 mg/m^2 P.O. q 12 hours.

Contraindications and precautions
- Contraindicated in patients hypersensitive to drug or its components.
- Use cautiously in patients with a history of pancreatitis and in patients with peripheral neuropathy, renal or hepatic impairment, or hyperuricemia.

Lifespan: With pregnant women, use cautiously. In breast-feeding women, drug isn't recommended.

Adverse reactions
CNS: *headache, fever,* insomnia, *dizziness, seizures,* confusion, anxiety, nervousness, hypertonia, abnormal thinking, twitching, depression, asthenia, pain, *peripheral neuropathy.*
CV: hypertension, edema, hyperlipemia, ***heart failure.***
GI: *diarrhea, nausea, vomiting, abdominal pain,* ***pancreatitis,*** dry mouth, dyspepsia, flatulence.
Hematologic: ***thrombocytopenia, leukopenia,*** granulocytosis, anemia.
Hepatic: liver abnormalities, ***hepatic failure.***
Musculoskeletal: myalgia, arthritis, myopathy.
Respiratory: cough, dyspnea, pneumonia.
Skin: rash, pruritus, alopecia.
Other: infection, sarcoma, ***anaphylactoid reaction,*** *chills.*

Interactions
Drug-drug. *Antacids containing magnesium or aluminum hydroxides:* Enhances adverse effects of antacid component (including diarrhea or constipation) when given with didanosine tablets or pediatric suspension. Avoid using together.
Dapsone, ketoconazole, drugs that require gastric acid for adequate absorption: Decreases absorption from buffering action. Give these drugs 2 hours before didanosine.
Fluoroquinolones, tetracyclines: May decrease absorption from buffering agents in didanosine tablets or antacids in pediatric suspension. Monitor patient for decreased effectiveness.
Itraconazole: May decrease levels of itraconazole. Avoid using together.
Drug-food. *Any food:* Increases rate of absorption. Give drug on an empty stomach.

Effects on lab test results
- May increase uric acid, AST, ALT, alkaline phosphatase, and bilirubin levels.

• May decrease hemoglobin, hematocrit, WBC, granulocyte, and platelet counts.

Pharmacokinetics

Absorption: Degrades rapidly in gastric acid. Commercially available preparations contain buffers to raise stomach pH. Bioavailability averages 33%; tablets may exhibit better bioavailability than buffered powder for oral solution. Food can decrease absorption by 50%.
Distribution: Widely distributed; drug penetration into CNS varies, but CSF levels average 46% of concurrent plasma levels.
Metabolism: Not fully understood; probably similar to that of endogenous purines.
Excretion: Excreted in urine. *Half-life:* 48 minutes.

Route	Onset	Peak	Duration
P.O.	Unknown	30 min-1 hr	Unknown

Pharmacodynamics

Chemical effect: Unknown; appears to inhibit replication of HIV by preventing DNA replication.
Therapeutic effect: Inhibits replication of HIV.

Available forms

Delayed-release capsules: 125 mg, 200 mg, 250 mg, 400 mg
Powder for oral solution (buffered): 100 mg/packet, 167 mg/packet, 250 mg/packet
Powder for oral solution (pediatric): 10 mg/ml in 2- and 4-g bottles
Tablets (chewable): 25 mg, 50 mg, 100 mg, 150 mg, 200 mg

NURSING PROCESS

Assessment

• Obtain history of patient's underlying condition before therapy, and reassess regularly thereafter.
• Be alert for adverse reactions and drug interactions.
• Evaluate patient's and family's knowledge of drug therapy.

Nursing diagnoses

• Infection related to presence of HIV infection
• Diarrhea related to drug-induced adverse effect on bowel
• Deficient knowledge related to drug therapy

Planning and implementation

• Give drug on empty stomach, regardless of dosage form used; giving drug with meals can decrease absorption by 50%.
• Most patients should receive two tablets per dose.
• To give single-dose packets containing buffered powder for oral solution, pour contents into 4 oz of water. Don't use fruit juice or other beverages that may be acidic. Stir for 2 to 3 minutes until powder dissolves completely. Give immediately.
• Use care when preparing powder or crushing tablets to avoid excessive dispersal of powder into air.
• Pharmacist must prepare pediatric powder for oral solution before dispensing. It must be constituted with Purified Water, USP, and then diluted with antacid (either Mylanta Double Strength Liquid or Maalox TC Suspension) to final concentration of 10 mg/ml. The admixture is stable for 30 days if refrigerated (at 36° to 46° F [2° to 8° C]). Shake solution well before measuring dose.
• If patient has diarrhea while using powdered form, consider switching to tablet form.

Patient teaching

• Instruct patient to chew tablets thoroughly before swallowing and to drink at least 1 oz of water with each dose because tablets contain buffers that raise stomach pH to levels that prevent degradation of active drug. If tablets are manually crushed, stir them thoroughly in 1 oz of water to disperse particles uniformly; then have patient drink mixture immediately.
• Inform patient on sodium-restricted diet that each two-tablet dose of didanosine contains 529 mg of sodium; each single packet of buffered powder for oral solution contains 1.38 g of sodium.
• Warn patient about adverse CNS reactions, and tell patient to take safety precautions.
• Tell patient to notify prescriber if adverse GI reactions occur.

Evaluation

• Patient improves with therapy.
• Patient regains normal bowel pattern.
• Patient and family state understanding of drug therapy.

diflunisal

(digh-FLOO-neh-sol)
Dolobid

Pharmacologic class: NSAID, salicylic acid derivative
Therapeutic class: nonnarcotic analgesic, antipyretic, anti-inflammatory
Pregnancy risk category: C

Indications and dosages

▶ **Mild-to-moderate pain, osteoarthritis, rheumatoid arthritis.** *Adults:* 500 to 1,000 mg P.O. daily in two divided doses, usually q 12 hours. Maximum, 1,500 mg daily.
Patients older than age 65: Give half the usual adult dose.

Contraindications and precautions

• Contraindicated in patients hypersensitive to drug and in those who develop acute asthmatic attacks, urticaria, or rhinitis after taking aspirin or other NSAIDs.
• Use cautiously in patients with GI bleeding, history of peptic ulcer disease, renal impairment, compromised cardiac function, hypertension, or other conditions predisposing patient to fluid retention.
Lifespan: In breast-feeding women, drug isn't recommended. In children and teenagers with chickenpox or flulike illness, salicylates aren't recommended because of epidemiologic connection to Reye's syndrome.

Adverse reactions

CNS: *dizziness,* somnolence, insomnia, *headache,* fatigue.
EENT: *tinnitus,* visual disturbances.
GI: *nausea, dyspepsia, GI pain, diarrhea,* vomiting, constipation, flatulence.
GU: renal impairment, hematuria, interstitial nephritis.
Skin: rash, pruritus, sweating, stomatitis, ***erythema multiforme, Stevens-Johnson syndrome.***
Other: dry mucous membranes.

Interactions

Drug-drug. *Acetaminophen, hydrochlorothiazide, indomethacin:* Diflunisal may substantially increase levels of these drugs, increasing risk of toxicity. Avoid using together.
Antacids: May decrease diflunisal level. Monitor patient for possible decreased therapeutic effect.
Aspirin: May increase adverse effects. Monitor patient closely.
Cyclosporine: Diflunisal may increase nephrotoxicity of cyclosporine. Avoid using together.
Methotrexate: May increase toxicity of methotrexate. Avoid using together.
Oral anticoagulants, thrombolytics: May enhance effects of these drugs. Use together cautiously.
Sulindac: Diflunisal may decrease level of sulindac's active metabolite. Monitor patient for decreased effect.
Drug-herb. *Dong quai, feverfew, garlic, ginger, horse chestnut, red clover:* May increase risk of bleeding. Discourage using together.

Effects on lab test results

None reported.

Pharmacokinetics

Absorption: Absorbed rapidly and completely by way of GI tract.
Distribution: Highly protein-bound.
Metabolism: Metabolized in liver.
Excretion: Excreted in urine. *Half-life:* 8 to 12 hours.

Route	Onset	Peak	Duration
P.O.	1 hr	2-3 hr	8-12 hr

Pharmacodynamics

Chemical effect: Probably related to inhibition of prostaglandin synthesis.
Therapeutic effect: Relieves inflammation and pain; reduces body temperature.

Available forms

Tablets: 250 mg, 500 mg

NURSING PROCESS

Assessment

• Obtain history of patient's underlying condition before therapy, and reassess regularly thereafter.
• Be alert for adverse reactions and drug interactions.
• Evaluate patient's and family's knowledge of drug therapy.

Nursing diagnoses
- Acute pain related to underlying condition
- Risk for deficient fluid volume related to drug-induced adverse reactions
- Deficient knowledge related to drug therapy

Planning and implementation
- Give drug with milk or food to minimize adverse GI reactions.

Patient teaching
- Advise patient to take with water, milk, or meals.
- Warn patient to check with prescriber or pharmacist before taking OTC medications or herbal remedies to avoid possible interactions with drugs, such as those containing aspirin or salicylates.

Evaluation
- Patient is free from pain.
- Patient maintains adequate hydration throughout therapy.
- Patient and family state understanding of drug therapy.

digoxin
(dih-JOKS-in)
Digitek, Digoxin, Lanoxicaps, Lanoxin*

Pharmacologic class: cardiac glycoside
Therapeutic class: antiarrhythmic, inotropic
Pregnancy risk category: C

Indications and dosages
▶ **Heart failure, atrial fibrillation and flutter, paroxysmal atrial tachycardia. *Tablets, elixir.*** *Adults:* For rapid digitalization, give 0.75 to 1.25 mg P.O. over 24 hours in two or more divided doses q 6 to 8 hours. For slow digitalization, give 0.125 to 0.5 mg daily for 5 to 7 days. Maintenance dose is 0.125 to 0.5 mg daily.
Children age 10 and older: 10 to 15 mcg/kg P.O. over 24 hours in two or more divided doses q 6 to 8 hours. Maintenance dose is 25% to 35% of total digitalizing dose.
Children ages 5 to 10: 20 to 35 mcg/kg P.O. over 24 hours in two or more divided doses q 6 to 8 hours. Maintenance dose is 25% to 35% of total digitalizing dose.
Children ages 2 to 5: 30 to 40 mcg/kg P.O. over 24 hours in two or more divided doses q 6 to 8 hours. Maintenance dose is 25% to 35% of total digitalizing dose.
Infants ages 1 month to 2 years: 35 to 60 mcg/kg P.O. over 24 hours in two or more divided doses q 6 to 8 hours. Maintenance dose is 25% to 35% of total digitalizing dose.
Neonates: 25 to 35 mcg/kg P.O. over 24 hours in two or more divided doses q 6 to 8 hours. Maintenance dose is 25% to 35% of total digitalizing dose.
Premature infants: 20 to 30 mcg/kg P.O. over 24 hours in two or more divided doses q 6 to 8 hours. Maintenance dose is 20% to 30% of total digitalizing dose.
Capsules. *Adults:* For rapid digitalization, give 0.4 to 0.6 mg P.O. initially, followed by 0.1 to 0.3 mg q 6 to 8 hours, as needed and tolerated, for 24 hours. For slow digitalization, give 0.05 to 0.35 mg daily in two divided doses for 7 to 22 days, as needed, until therapeutic serum levels are reached. Maintenance dose is 0.05 to 0.35 mg daily in one or two divided doses.
Children: Digitalizing dose is based on child's age and is given in three or more divided doses over the first 24 hours. Initial dose should be 50% of the total dose; subsequent doses are given q 4 to 8 hours as needed and tolerated.
Children age 10 and older: For rapid digitalization, give 8 to 12 mcg/kg P.O. over 24 hours, divided as above. Maintenance dose is 25% to 35% of total digitalizing dose, given daily as a single dose.
Children ages 5 to 10: For rapid digitalization, give 15 to 30 mcg/kg P.O. over 24 hours, divided as above. Maintenance dose is 25% to 35% of total digitalizing dose, divided and given in two or three equal portions daily.
Children ages 2 to 5: For rapid digitalization, give 25 to 35 mcg/kg P.O. over 24 hours, divided as above. Maintenance dose is 25% to 35% of total digitalizing dose, divided and given in two or three equal portions daily.
Injection. *Adults:* For rapid digitalization, give 0.4 to 0.6 mg I.V. initially, followed by 0.1 to 0.3 mg I.V. q 4 to 8 hours, as needed and tolerated, for 24 hours. For slow digitalization, give appropriate daily maintenance dose for 7 to 22 days as needed until therapeutic serum levels are reached. Maintenance dose is

0.125 to 0.5 mg I.V. daily in one or two divided doses.
Children: Digitalizing dose is based on child's age and is given in three or more divided doses over the first 24 hours. Initial dose should be 50% of total dose; subsequent doses are given q 4 to 8 hours as needed and tolerated.
Children age 10 and older: For rapid digitalization, give 8 to 12 mcg/kg I.V. over 24 hours, divided as above. Maintenance dose is 25% to 35% of total digitalizing dose, given daily as a single dose.
Children ages 5 to 10: For rapid digitalization, give 15 to 30 mcg/kg I.V. over 24 hours, divided as above. Maintenance dose is 25% to 35% of total digitalizing dose, divided and given in two or three equal portions daily.
Children ages 2 to 5: For rapid digitalization, give 25 to 35 mcg/kg I.V. over 24 hours, divided as above. Maintenance dose is 25% to 35% of total digitalizing dose, divided and given in two or three equal portions daily.
Infants age 1 month to 2 years: For rapid digitalization, give 30 to 50 mcg/kg I.V. over 24 hours, divided as above. Maintenance dose is 25% to 35% of total digitalizing dose, divided and given in two or three equal portions daily.
Neonates: For rapid digitalization, give 20 to 30 mcg/kg I.V. over 24 hours, divided as above. Maintenance dose is 25% to 35% of the total digitalizing dose, divided and given in two or three equal portions daily.
Premature infants: For rapid digitalization, give 15 to 25 mcg/kg I.V. over 24 hours, divided as above. Maintenance dose is 20% to 30% of the total digitalizing dose, divided and given in two or three equal portions daily.
Patients with renal impairment: Decrease dosage.
Patients with hyperthyroidism: May need to increase dosage.

Contraindications and precautions

- Contraindicated in patients hypersensitive to drug and in those with digitalis-induced toxicity, ventricular fibrillation, or ventricular tachycardia unless caused by heart failure.
- Use with extreme caution patients with acute MI, incomplete AV block, sinus bradycardia, PVCs, chronic constrictive pericarditis, hypertrophic cardiomyopathy, renal insufficiency, severe pulmonary disease, or hypothyroidism.

Lifespan: In pregnant and breast-feeding women, use cautiously. In elderly patients, use with extreme caution.

Adverse reactions

CNS: *fatigue, generalized muscle weakness, agitation, hallucinations,* headache, malaise, dizziness, vertigo, stupor, paresthesia.
CV: ***arrhythmias, heart failure,*** hypotension.
EENT: yellow-green halos around visual images, blurred vision, light flashes, photophobia, diplopia.
GI: *anorexia, nausea,* vomiting, diarrhea.

Interactions

Drug-drug. *Amiloride:* Inhibits digoxin effect and increases digoxin excretion. Monitor patient for altered digoxin effect.
Amiodarone, diltiazem, nifedipine, quinidine, verapamil: Increases digoxin levels. Monitor patient for digoxin toxicity.
Amphotericin B, carbenicillin, corticosteroids, diuretics (including loop diuretics, chlorthalidone, metolazone, and thiazides), ticarcillin: May decrease potassium level, predisposing patient to digitalis toxicity. Monitor potassium levels.
Antacids, kaolin-pectin: May decrease digoxin absorption. Schedule doses as far as possible from P.O. digoxin administration.
Cholestyramine, colestipol, metoclopramide: May decrease absorption of P.O. digoxin. Monitor patient for decreased effect and low blood levels. Increase dosage, if necessary, as directed.
Parenteral calcium, thiazides: May increase calcium level and decrease magnesium level, predisposing patient to digitalis toxicity. Monitor calcium and magnesium levels.
Drug-herb. *Betel palm, fumitory, goldenseal, lily of the valley, motherwort, rue, shepherd's purse:* Possible increased cardiac effect. Discourage using together.
Horsetail, licorice: May deplete potassium stores, leading to digitalis toxicity. Monitor potassium level closely.
Oleander, Siberian ginseng, squill: Possible enhanced toxicity. Discourage using together.
St. John's wort: May reduce therapeutic effect of digoxin, requiring an increased dosage. Monitor patient for loss of therapeutic effect, and advise patient to avoid this herb.

Drug-lifestyle. *Alcohol use:* May increase CNS effects. Discourage using together.

Effects on lab test results

None reported.

Pharmacokinetics

Absorption: With tablet or elixir form, 60% to 85% of dose is absorbed. With capsule form, bioavailability increases, with about 90% to 100% of dose absorbed.
Distribution: Distributed widely in body tissues; about 20% to 30% bound to plasma proteins.
Metabolism: Small amount of digoxin is thought to be metabolized in liver and gut by bacteria. This metabolism varies and may be substantial in some patients. Drug undergoes some enterohepatic recirculation (also variable). Metabolites have minimal cardiac activity.
Excretion: Most of dose excreted by kidneys as unchanged drug, although some patients excrete a substantial amount of metabolized or reduced drug. In patients with renal failure, biliary excretion is more important excretion route. *Half-life:* 30 to 40 hours.

Route	Onset	Peak	Duration
P.O.	30 min-2 hr	2-6 hr	3-4 days
I.V.	5-30 min	1-4 hr	3-4 days

Pharmacodynamics

Chemical effect: Inhibits sodium-potassium-activated adenosine triphosphatase, thereby promoting movement of calcium from extracellular to intracellular cytoplasm and strengthening myocardial contraction. Digoxin also acts on CNS to enhance vagal tone, slowing conduction through SA and AV nodes and providing antiarrhythmic effect.
Therapeutic effect: Strengthens myocardial contractions and slows conduction through SA and AV nodes.

Available forms

Capsules: 0.05 mg, 0.1 mg, 0.2 mg
Elixir: 0.05 mg/ml
Injection: 0.05 mg/ml ♦, 0.1 mg/ml (pediatric), 0.25 mg/ml
Tablets: 0.125 mg, 0.25 mg

NURSING PROCESS

Assessment

- Obtain history of patient's underlying condition before therapy.
- Monitor effectiveness by taking apical pulse for 1 full minute before each dose. Evaluate ECG when ordered, and regularly assess patient's cardiopulmonary status for signs of improvement.
- Monitor digoxin levels. Therapeutic blood levels of digoxin range from 0.5 to 2 ng/ml. Obtain blood for digoxin levels 8 hours after last P.O. dose.
- Monitor potassium level carefully.
- Be alert for adverse reactions and drug interactions.
- Evaluate patient's and family's knowledge of drug therapy.

Nursing diagnoses

- Decreased cardiac output related to underlying condition
- Ineffective protection related to digoxin toxicity caused by drug
- Deficient knowledge related to drug therapy

Planning and implementation

- Hypothyroid patients are extremely sensitive to glycosides; hyperthyroid patients may need larger doses. Reduce dosage in patients with impaired renal function.
- Before giving loading dose, obtain baseline data (heart rate and rhythm, blood pressure, and electrolyte levels) and question patient about recent use of cardiac glycosides (within previous 2 to 3 weeks).
- Loading dose is always divided over first 24 hours unless clinical situation indicates otherwise.
- Before giving drug, take apical pulse for 1 full minute. Record and report to prescriber significant changes (sudden increase or decrease in pulse rate, pulse deficit, irregular beats, and regularization of previously irregular rhythm). If these changes occur, check blood pressure and obtain 12-lead ECG.

ALERT: Withhold drug and notify prescriber if pulse rate slows to 60 beats/minute or less.

- **P.O. use:** Because absorption of digoxin from parenteral route and from liquid-filled capsules is superior to absorption from tablets or elixir, expect dosage reduction of 20% to

25% when changing from tablets or elixir to liquid-filled capsules or parenteral therapy.
• **I.V. use:** Infuse drug slowly over at least 5 minutes.
• For digoxin, give agents that bind drug in intestine (for example, colestipol or cholestyramine). Treat arrhythmias with phenytoin I.V. or lidocaine I.V. and potentially life-threatening toxicity with specific antigen-binding fragments (such as digoxin immune Fab).
• Withhold drug for 1 to 2 days before elective cardioversion. Adjust dose after cardioversion.
ALERT: Be careful when calculating doses. Tenfold errors can easily occur with children's dosages.

Patient teaching
• Instruct patient and responsible family member about drug action, dosage regimen, pulse taking, reportable signs, and follow-up plans.
• Instruct patient not to substitute one brand of digoxin for another.
• Tell patient to eat potassium-rich foods.

Evaluation
• Patient has adequate cardiac output.
• Patient has no digoxin toxicity.
• Patient and family state understanding of drug therapy.

digoxin immune Fab (ovine)
(dih-JOKS-in ih-MYOON Fab)
Digibind, DigiFab

Pharmacologic class: antibody fragment
Therapeutic class: cardiac glycoside antidote
Pregnancy risk category: C

Indications and dosages
▶ **Potentially life-threatening digoxin or digitoxin intoxication.** *Adults and children:* I.V. dosage varies according to amount of digoxin or digitoxin to be neutralized. Each vial binds about 0.5 mg of digoxin or digitoxin. Average dose is 6 vials (228 mg). If toxicity resulted from acute digoxin ingestion and neither digoxin level nor estimated ingestion amount is known, 20 vials (760 mg) may be required. See package insert for complete, specific dosage instructions.

Contraindications and precautions
• No known contraindications.
• Use cautiously in patients allergic to ovine proteins. In these high-risk patients, skin testing is recommended because drug is derived from digoxin-specific antibody fragments obtained from immunized sheep.
Lifespan: In pregnant or breast-feeding women, use cautiously.

Adverse reactions
CV: ***heart failure,*** rapid ventricular rate.
Metabolic: hypokalemia.
Other: ***hypersensitivity reactions, anaphylaxis.***

Interactions
None reported.

Effects on lab test results
• May decrease potassium levels.

Pharmacokinetics
Absorption: Administered I.V.
Distribution: Unknown.
Metabolism: Unknown.
Excretion: Excreted in urine. *Half-life:* 15 to 20 hours.

Route	Onset	Peak	Duration
I.V.	Varies	On completion of I.V. dose	2-6 hr

Pharmacodynamics
Chemical effect: Binds molecules of digoxin and digitoxin, making them unavailable for binding at site of action on cells.
Therapeutic effect: Reverses digitalis toxicity.

Available forms
Injection: 38-mg vial

NURSING PROCESS

Assessment
• Obtain history of patient's digitalis intoxication before therapy.
• Monitor effectiveness by watching for decreased signs and symptoms of digitalis toxicity; in most patients, signs of digitalis toxicity disappear within a few hours.
• Because drug interferes with digitalis immunoassay measurements, standard digoxin

levels are misleading until drug is cleared from body (about 2 days).
• Be alert for adverse reactions.
• Evaluate patient's and family's knowledge of drug therapy.

Nursing diagnoses
• Ineffective health maintenance related to digitalis intoxication
• Decreased cardiac output related to drug-induced heart failure
• Deficient knowledge related to drug therapy

Planning and implementation
• Refrigerate powder for injection. Reconstitute drug immediately before use. Reconstituted solutions may be refrigerated for 4 hours.
• Reconstitute 38-mg vial with 4 ml of sterile water for injection. Gently roll vial to dissolve powder. Reconstituted solution contains 9.5 mg/ml. Drug may be given by direct injection if cardiac arrest seems imminent. Or, dilute with normal saline solution injection to appropriate volume and give by intermittent infusion.
• Infuse drug through 0.22-micron membrane filter.
• Drug is used only for life-threatening overdose in patients with shock or cardiac arrest; ventricular arrhythmias, such as ventricular tachycardia or fibrillation; progressive bradycardia, such as severe sinus bradycardia; or second- or third-degree AV block not responsive to atropine.
• Give oxygen. Keep resuscitation equipment nearby.

Patient teaching
• Instruct patient to report respiratory difficulty, chest pain, or dizziness immediately.

Evaluation
• Patient exhibits improved health with alleviation of digitalis toxicity.
• Patient demonstrates adequate cardiac output through normal vital signs and urine output and clear mental status.
• Patient and family state understanding of drug therapy.

diltiazem hydrochloride
(dil-TIGH-uh-zem high-droh-KLOR-ighd)
Cardizem, Cardizem CD, Cardizem SR, Cartia XT, Dilacor XR, Diltia XT, Tiazac

Pharmacologic class: calcium channel blocker
Therapeutic class: antianginal
Pregnancy risk category: C

Indications and dosages
▶ **Vasospastic angina (Prinzmetal's [variant] angina), classic chronic stable angina pectoris.** *Adults:* 30 mg P.O. t.i.d. or q.i.d. before meals and h.s. Dosage increased gradually to maximum of 360 mg daily in divided doses. ***Extended-release capsules.*** 120 to 180 mg P.O. once daily. Dosage may be adjusted up to 480 mg once daily, if necessary.
▶ **Hypertension. *Sustained-release capsules.*** *Adults:* 60 to 120 mg P.O. b.i.d. Adjusted to effect. Maximum recommended dosage is 360 mg daily. ***Extended-release capsules.*** 180 to 240 mg daily initially. Dosage adjusted as necessary.
▶ **Atrial fibrillation or flutter; paroxysmal supraventricular tachycardia.** *Adults:* 0.25 mg/kg as I.V. bolus injection over 2 minutes. If response is inadequate, 0.35 mg/kg I.V. after 15 minutes, followed with continuous infusion of 10 mg/hour. May be increased in increments of 5 mg/hour. Maximum, 15 mg/hour.

Contraindications and precautions
• Contraindicated in patients hypersensitive to drug and in those with sick sinus syndrome, second- or third-degree AV block in absence of artificial pacemaker, hypotension (systolic blood pressure below 90 mm Hg), acute MI, or pulmonary congestion (documented by X-ray).
• Use cautiously in patients with heart failure and those with impaired liver or kidney function.
Lifespan: With pregnant women, use cautiously. Breast-feeding should be discontinued during drug use. In children, safety of drug hasn't been established. With elderly patients, use cautiously.

Adverse reactions

CNS: *headache,* somnolence, dizziness, insomnia, asthenia.
CV: *edema,* ***arrhythmias,*** flushing, ***bradycardia,*** hypotension, conduction abnormalities, ***heart failure, AV block,*** abnormal ECG.
GI: *nausea, constipation,* vomiting, diarrhea, abdominal discomfort.
GU: nocturia, polyuria.
Skin: rash, pruritus, photosensitivity.

Interactions

Drug-drug. *Anesthetics:* Effects may be potentiated. Monitor patient.
Cimetidine: May inhibit diltiazem metabolism. Monitor patient for toxicity.
Cyclosporine: Diltiazem may increase cyclosporine levels, possibly by decreasing its metabolism, leading to increased risk of cyclosporine toxicity. Avoid using together.
Digoxin: Diltiazem may increase levels of digoxin. Monitor patient and digoxin levels.
Propranolol, other beta-blockers: May precipitate heart failure or prolong cardiac conduction time. Use together cautiously.
Drug-lifestyle. *Sunlight:* Photosensitivity may occur. Advise patient to avoid unprotected or prolonged sun exposure.

Effects on lab test results

- May cause transient elevation of liver enzyme levels.

Pharmacokinetics

Absorption: About 80% of dose is absorbed rapidly from GI tract. Only about 40% of drug enters systemic circulation because of significant first-pass effect in liver.
Distribution: About 70% to 85% of circulating diltiazem is bound to plasma proteins.
Metabolism: Metabolized in liver.
Excretion: About 35% excreted in urine and about 65% in bile as unchanged drug and inactive and active metabolites. *Half-life:* 3 to 9 hours.

Route	Onset	Peak	Duration
P.O.	30 min-3 hr	2-14 hr	6-24 hr
I.V.	3 min	Immediate	1-3 hr (bolus); < 10 hr (infusion)

Pharmacodynamics

Chemical effect: Inhibits calcium ion influx across cardiac and smooth-muscle cells, decreasing myocardial contractility and oxygen demand; also dilates coronary arteries and arterioles.
Therapeutic effect: Relieves anginal pain, lowers blood pressure, and restores normal sinus rhythm.

Available forms

Cardizem
Injections: 5 mg/ml (25 mg and 50 mg)
Tablets: 30 mg, 60 mg, 90 mg, 120 mg
Cardizem CD
Capsules (extended-release): 120 mg, 180 mg, 240 mg, 300 mg, 360 mg
Cardizem SR
Capsules (sustained-release): 60 mg, 90 mg, 120 mg
Cartia XT
Capsules (extended-release): 120 mg, 180 mg, 240 mg, 300 mg
Dilacor XR
Capsules (extended-release) containing multiple units of 60-mg: 120 mg, 180 mg, 240 mg
Diltia XT
Capsules (extended-release) containing multiple units of 60-mg: 120 mg, 180 mg, 240 mg
Tiazac
Capsules (sustained-release): 120 mg, 180 mg, 240 mg, 300 mg, 360 mg, 420 mg

NURSING PROCESS

Assessment

- Obtain history of patient's underlying condition before therapy, and reassess regularly thereafter.
- Monitor blood pressure when therapy starts and when dosage changes.
- Monitor patient's ECG and heart rate and rhythm regularly.
- Be alert for adverse reactions and drug interactions.
- Evaluate patient's and family's knowledge of drug therapy.

Nursing diagnoses

- Ineffective health maintenance related to underlying condition

• Decreased cardiac output related to drug-induced adverse reactions
• Deficient knowledge related to drug therapy

Planning and implementation

• **P.O. use:** Give tablets before meals and at bedtime.
• **I.V. use:** Infusions lasting longer than 24 hours aren't recommended.
ALERT: Furosemide forms a precipitate when mixed with diltiazem injection. Give through separate I.V. lines.
ALERT: If systolic blood pressure is below 90 mm Hg or heart rate is below 60 beats/minute, withhold dose and notify prescriber.
• Assist patient with ambulation during start of therapy because dizziness may occur.
• Restrict patient's fluid and sodium intake to minimize edema.

Patient teaching

• If nitrate therapy is prescribed during adjustment of diltiazem dosage, urge patient compliance. Tell patient that S.L. nitroglycerin may be taken as needed and as directed when angina is acute.
• Instruct patient to call prescriber with chest pain, shortness of breath, dizziness, palpitations, or swelling of the limbs.
• Tell patient to swallow extended- and sustained-release capsules whole and not to open, crush, or chew them.
• Instruct patient to take drug exactly as prescribed, even when feeling well.
• Advise patient to minimize exposure to direct sunlight and to take precautions when in sun because of drug-induced photosensitivity.
• Instruct patient to limit fluid and sodium intake to minimize edema.

Evaluation

• Patient exhibits improvement in underlying condition.
• Patient maintains adequate cardiac output throughout therapy.
• Patient and family state understanding of drug therapy.

dimenhydrinate

(digh-men-HIGH-drih-nayt)
Apo-Dimenhydrinate ♦, Calm X†, Children's Dramamine†, Dimetabs, Dinate, Dramamine†*, Dramamine Chewable†**, Dramamine Liquid†*, Dymenate, Gravol ♦, Gravol L/A ♦, Hydrate, PMS-Dimenhydrinate ♦, Triptone Caplets†

Pharmacologic class: ethanolamine derivative antihistamine
Therapeutic class: antihistamine (H_1-receptor antagonist), antiemetic, antivertigo agent
Pregnancy risk category: B

Indications and dosages

▶ **Prevention and treatment of motion sickness.** *Adults and children age 12 and older:* 50 to 100 mg P.O. q 4 to 6 hours. Or, 50 mg I.M., p.r.n. Or, 50 mg I.V. diluted in 10 ml sodium chloride injection, injected over 2 minutes. Maximum, 400 mg daily.
Children ages 6 to 11: 25 to 50 mg P.O. q 6 to 8 hours, not to exceed 150 mg in 24 hours.
Children ages 2 to 5: 12.5 to 25 mg P.O. q 6 to 8 hours, not to exceed 75 mg in 24 hours.
▶ **Ménière's disease‡.** *Adults:* 50 mg I.M. for acute attacks. Maintenance dosage is 25 to 50 mg P.O. t.i.d.

Contraindications and precautions

• No known contraindications.
• Use cautiously in patients with seizures, acute angle-closure glaucoma, enlarged prostate gland, or in patients receiving ototoxic drugs.
Lifespan: In pregnant women, use cautiously. Drug isn't recommended for use in breast-feeding women.

Adverse reactions

CNS: *drowsiness,* headache, confusion, nervousness, insomnia, vertigo, tingling and weakness of hands, lassitude, excitation, incoordination, dizziness.
CV: palpitations, hypotension, tachycardia, tightness of chest.
EENT: blurred vision, diplopia, nasal congestion, tinnitus, dry respiratory passages.
GI: dry mouth, nausea, vomiting, diarrhea, epigastric distress, constipation, anorexia.

Respiratory: wheezing, thickened bronchial secretions.
Skin: photosensitivity, urticaria, rash.
Other: ***anaphylaxis.***

Interactions

Drug-drug. *CNS depressants:* May increase CNS depression. Avoid using together.
Drug-lifestyle. *Alcohol use:* May increase CNS depression. Discourage using together.

Effects on lab test results

None reported.

Pharmacokinetics

Absorption: Well absorbed after P.O. and I.M. administration.
Distribution: Well distributed throughout body.
Metabolism: Metabolized in liver.
Excretion: Excreted in urine. *Half-life:* 1 to 4 hours.

Route	Onset	Peak	Duration
P.O.	20-30 min	Unknown	3-6 hr
I.V.	Immediate	Unknown	3-6 hr
I.M.	15-20 min	Unknown	3-6 hr

Pharmacodynamics

Chemical effect: Unknown; may affect neural pathways originating in labyrinth.
Therapeutic effect: Prevents and relieves motion sickness.

Available forms

Capsules: 75 mg†
Elixir: 15 mg/5 ml ♦
Injection: 50 mg/ml
Syrup: 12.5 mg/4 ml*†, 15.62 mg/5 ml
Tablets: 50 mg†
Tablets (chewable): 50 mg†

NURSING PROCESS

Assessment

- Obtain history of patient's underlying condition before therapy.
- Monitor effectiveness by evaluating patient for nausea and vomiting.
- Be alert for adverse reactions and drug interactions.
- Evaluate patient's and family's knowledge of drug therapy.

Nursing diagnoses

- Risk for deficient fluid volume related to nausea and vomiting induced by motion sickness
- Risk for injury related to drug-induced adverse CNS reactions
- Deficient knowledge related to drug therapy

Planning and implementation

- **P.O. use:** To prevent motion sickness, give drug at least 30 minutes before patient travels.
- **I.V. use:** Before administration, dilute each milliliter of drug with 10 ml of sterile water for injection, D_5W, or normal saline solution injection. Give by direct injection over at least 2 minutes.

–Undiluted solution is irritating to veins and may cause sclerosis.
- **I.M. use:** Follow normal protocol.
- Because incompatibilities are common, avoid mixing parenteral form with other drugs.

Patient teaching

- Advise patient to avoid hazardous activities until CNS effects of drug are known.
- Tell patient to take drug at least 30 minutes before beginning travel.

Evaluation

- Patient maintains adequate hydration.
- Patient has no injury as result of drug-induced adverse CNS reactions.
- Patient and family state understanding of drug therapy.

dimercaprol

(digh-mer-KAP-rohl)
BAL in Oil

Pharmacologic class: chelating agent
Therapeutic class: heavy metal antagonist
Pregnancy risk category: C

Indications and dosages

▶ **Severe arsenic or gold poisoning.** *Adults and children:* 3 mg/kg deep I.M. q 4 hours for 2 days; then q.i.d. on third day; then b.i.d. for 10 days.

▶ **Mild arsenic or gold poisoning.** *Adults and children:* 2.5 mg/kg deep I.M. q.i.d. for 2 days; then b.i.d. on third day; then once daily for 10 days.

▶ **Mercury poisoning.** *Adults and children:* Initially, 5 mg/kg deep I.M.; then 2.5 mg/kg daily or b.i.d. for 10 days.

▶ **Acute lead encephalopathy or lead level exceeding 100 mcg/dl.** *Adults and children:* 4 mg/kg deep I.M.; then q 4 hours with edetate calcium disodium (250 mg/m^2 I.M.). Use separate sites. Maximum, 5 mg/kg per dose.

Contraindications and precautions

- Contraindicated in patients with hepatic dysfunction (except postarsenical jaundice).
- Use cautiously in patients with hypertension or oliguria.

Lifespan: In pregnant and breast-feeding women, safety of drug hasn't been established.

Adverse reactions

CNS: *fever,* headache, paresthesia.
CV: *transient increase in blood pressure, tachycardia.*
EENT: blepharospasm, conjunctivitis, lacrimation, rhinorrhea, excessive salivation.
GI: *halitosis; nausea; vomiting; burning sensation in lips, mouth, and throat; abdominal pain.*
GU: *dysuria,* renal damage.
Musculoskeletal: muscle pain or weakness.
Skin: diaphoresis, sterile abscess, pain at injection site.
Other: pain or tightness in throat, chest, or hands; decreased iodine uptake; pain in teeth.

Interactions

Drug-drug. *Iron:* Toxic metal complex formed; use together is contraindicated. Wait 24 hours after last dimercaprol dose.

Effects on lab test results

None reported.

Pharmacokinetics

Absorption: Unknown.
Distribution: Distributed to all tissues, mainly intracellular space.
Metabolism: Uncomplexed dimercaprol is metabolized rapidly to inactive products.
Excretion: Most dimercaprol metal complexes and inactive metabolites are excreted in urine and feces.

Route	Onset	Peak	Duration
I.M.	Unknown	30-60 min	4 hr

Pharmacodynamics

Chemical effect: Forms complexes with heavy metals.
Therapeutic effect: Treats heavy metal intoxication.

Available forms

Injection: 100 mg/ml

NURSING PROCESS

Assessment

- Obtain history of patient's toxicity before therapy.
- Assess effectiveness by monitoring serum level of substance ingested and for improvement in patient's condition.
- Be alert for adverse reactions and drug interactions.
- Monitor patient's hydration status if adverse GI reactions occur.
- Observe injection site for local reaction.
- Evaluate patient's and family's knowledge of drug therapy.

Nursing diagnoses

- Risk for poisoning related to exposure to toxic substance
- Risk for deficient fluid volume related to drug-induced nausea and vomiting
- Deficient knowledge related to drug therapy

Planning and implementation

ALERT: Don't give I.V.; give by deep I.M. route only. Massage injection site after administration.

- Be careful not to let drug come in contact with skin because it may cause skin reaction.
- Don't schedule patient for ^{131}I uptake thyroid tests during therapy because dimercaprol decreases results.
- Solution with slight sediment is usable.
- Drug is ineffective in arsine gas poisoning.

ALERT: Don't use for iron, cadmium, or selenium toxicity. Complex form is highly toxic, even fatal.

- Use ephedrine or antihistamine to prevent or relieve mild adverse reactions.
- Keep urine alkaline to prevent renal damage. Oral sodium bicarbonate may be ordered.
- Apply ice or cold compresses to injection site to alleviate local discomfort.

Patient teaching
- Warn patient that drug has unpleasant garlic-like odor.
- Advise patient that drug may cause pain at injection site.
- Instruct patient to report changes in urine output, fever, pain, nausea, or vomiting immediately.

Evaluation
- Patient's toxicity is eliminated.
- Patient maintains adequate hydration throughout therapy.
- Patient and family state understanding of drug therapy.

diphenhydramine hydrochloride
(digh-fen-HIGH-drah-meen high-droh-KLOR-ighd)
Allerdryl ♦ †, AllerMax Caplets†, Allermed†, Banophen†, Banophen Caplets†, Beldin†, Belix†, Benadryl†, Benadryl 25†, Benadryl Kapseals†, Benylin Cough†, Bydramine Cough†, Compoz†, Diphenadryl†, Diphen Cough†, Diphenhist†, Diphenhist Captabs†, Genahist†, Hyrexin-50, Nytol Maximum Strength†, Nytol with DPH†, Sleep-Eze 3†, Sominex Formula 2†, Tusstat†, Twilite Caplets†, Uni-Bent Cough†

Pharmacologic class: ethanolamine derivative antihistamine
Therapeutic class: antihistamine (H_1-receptor antagonist), antiemetic, antivertigo agent, antitussive, sedative-hypnotic, antidyskinetic (anticholinergic)
Pregnancy risk category: B

Indications and dosages
▶ **Rhinitis, allergy symptoms, motion sickness, Parkinson's disease.** *Adults and children age 12 and older:* 25 to 50 mg P.O. t.i.d. or q.i.d. Or, 10 to 50 mg deep I.M. or I.V. Maximum I.M. or I.V. dosage is 400 mg daily.
Children younger than age 12: 5 mg/kg daily P.O., deep I.M., or I.V. in divided doses q.i.d. Maximum, 300 mg daily.
▶ **Sedation.** *Adults:* 25 to 50 mg P.O. or deep I.M., p.r.n.
▶ **Nighttime sleep aid.** *Adults:* 50 mg P.O. h.s.
▶ **Nonproductive cough.** *Adults:* 25 mg P.O. q 4 to 6 hours (up to 150 mg daily).
Children ages 6 to 11: 12.5 mg P.O. q 4 to 6 hours (up to 75 mg daily).
Children ages 2 to 5: 6.25 mg P.O. q 4 to 6 hours (up to 25 mg daily).

Contraindications and precautions
- Contraindicated in patients hypersensitive to drug and patients having acute asthmatic attacks.
- Use with extreme caution in patients with angle-closure glaucoma, prostatic hyperplasia, pyloroduodenal and bladder-neck obstruction, asthma or COPD, increased intraocular pressure, hyperthyroidism, CV disease, hypertension, or stenosing peptic ulcer.

Lifespan: In pregnant women, use cautiously. In newborns, premature neonates, and breast-feeding women, use is contraindicated. Children younger than age 12 should use only as directed by prescriber.

Adverse reactions
CNS: *drowsiness,* confusion, insomnia, headache, vertigo, *sedation, sleepiness, dizziness,* incoordination, fatigue, restlessness, tremor, nervousness, ***seizures.***
CV: palpitations, hypotension, tachycardia.
EENT: diplopia, blurred vision, nasal congestion, tinnitus.
GI: *nausea,* vomiting, diarrhea, *dry mouth,* constipation, *epigastric distress,* anorexia.
GU: dysuria, urine retention, urinary frequency.
Hematologic: *hemolytic anemia,* ***thrombocytopenia, agranulocytosis.***
Respiratory: thickening of bronchial secretions.
Skin: urticaria, photosensitivity, rash.
Other: ***anaphylactic shock.***

Interactions
Drug-drug. *CNS depressants:* May increase sedation. Use together cautiously.
MAO inhibitors: May increase anticholinergic effects. Don't use together.
Other products containing diphenhydramine, including topical forms: May increase risk of adverse reactions. Avoid using together.
Drug-lifestyle. *Alcohol use:* May increase adverse CNS effects. Discourage using together.
Sun exposure: Photosensitivity reactions may occur. Urge patient to wear protective clothing and sunblock.

Effects on lab test results

- May decrease hemoglobin, hematocrit, and platelet and granulocyte counts

Pharmacokinetics

Absorption: Well absorbed from GI tract after P.O. administration; unknown after I.M. administration.
Distribution: Distributed widely throughout body, including CNS; about 82% protein-bound.
Metabolism: Metabolized in liver.
Excretion: Drug and metabolites excreted primarily in urine. *Half-life:* About 3½ hours.

Route	Onset	Peak	Duration
P.O.	≤ 15 min	1-4 hr	6-8 hr
I.V.	Immediate	1-4 hr	6-8 hr
I.M.	Unknown	1-4 hr	6-8 hr

Pharmacodynamics

Chemical effect: Competes with histamine for H_1-receptor sites on effector cells. Diphenhydramine prevents but doesn't reverse histamine-mediated responses, particularly histamine's effects on smooth muscle of bronchial tubes, GI tract, uterus, and blood vessels. Structurally related to local anesthetics, diphenhydramine provides local anesthesia by preventing initiation and transmission of nerve impulses. It also suppresses cough reflex by direct effect in medulla of brain.
Therapeutic effect: Relieves allergy symptoms, motion sickness, and cough; improves voluntary movement; and promotes sleep and calmness.

Available forms

Capsules: 25 mg†, 50 mg†
Chewable tablets: 12.5 mg†
Elixir: 12.5 mg/5 ml*†
Injection: 10 mg/ml, 50 mg/ml
Syrup: 12.5 mg/5 ml†, 6.25 mg/5 ml†
Tablets: 25 mg†, 50 mg†

NURSING PROCESS

Assessment

- Obtain history of patient's underlying condition before therapy, and reassess regularly thereafter.
- Be alert for adverse reactions and drug interactions.
- Evaluate patient's and family's knowledge of drug therapy.

Nursing diagnoses

- Ineffective health maintenance related to underlying condition
- Risk for injury related to drug-induced adverse CNS reactions
- Deficient knowledge related to drug therapy

Planning and implementation

- **P.O. use:** Reduce GI distress by giving drug with food or milk.
- **I.V. use:** Follow manufacturer's guidelines.
- **I.M. use:** Alternate injection sites to prevent irritation. Give I.M. injection deep into large muscle.
- Notify prescriber if tolerance is observed because another antihistamine may need to be substituted.

Patient teaching

- Instruct patient to take drug 30 minutes before travel to prevent motion sickness.
- Warn patient to avoid alcohol and to refrain from driving or performing other hazardous activities that require alertness.
- Tell patient that coffee or tea may reduce drowsiness.
- Inform patient that ice chips, sugarless gum, or sour hard candy may relieve dry mouth.
- Advise patient to stop drug 4 days before allergy skin tests to preserve accuracy of tests.
- Tell patient to notify prescriber if tolerance develops because different antihistamine may need to be prescribed.
- Warn patient of possible photosensitivity. Advise use of sunblock or protective clothing.
- Warn patient to avoid using other products containing diphenhydramine, including topical forms because of risk of adverse reactions.

Evaluation

- Patient shows improvement in underlying condition.
- Patient has no injury as result of therapy.
- Patient and family state understanding of drug therapy.

diphenoxylate hydrochloride and atropine sulfate

(digh-fen-OKS-ul-ayt high-droh-KLOR-ighd and AH-troh-peen SUL-fayt)
Logen, Lomanate, Lomotil*, Lonox

Pharmacologic class: opioid
Therapeutic class: antidiarrheal
Pregnancy risk category: C
Controlled substance schedule: V

Indications and dosages

▶ **Acute, nonspecific diarrhea.** *Adults:* Initially, 5 mg P.O. q.i.d.; then dosage adjusted as needed.
Children ages 2 to 12: 0.3 to 0.4 mg/kg liquid form P.O. daily in four divided doses. Maintenance dose may be ¼ of original dose.

Contraindications and precautions

• Contraindicated in patients hypersensitive to diphenoxylate or atropine and in those with acute diarrhea from poison (until toxic material is eliminated from GI tract), acute diarrhea caused by organisms that penetrate the intestinal mucosa, or diarrhea from antibiotic-induced pseudomembranous enterocolitis. Also contraindicated in jaundiced patients.
• Use cautiously in patients with hepatic disease, narcotic dependence, or acute ulcerative colitis. Stop therapy immediately if abdominal distention or other signs of toxic megacolon develop, and notify prescriber.
Lifespan: In pregnant women, use cautiously. In breast-feeding women, drug isn't recommended. In children age 2 and older, use cautiously. In children younger than age 2, use is contraindicated.

Adverse reactions

CNS: *sedation, dizziness,* headache, drowsiness, lethargy, restlessness, depression, euphoria, malaise, confusion, numbness in limbs.
CV: tachycardia.
EENT: mydriasis.
GI: *dry mouth,* nausea, vomiting, abdominal discomfort or distention, paralytic ileus, anorexia, fluid retention in bowel, possible physical dependence with long-term use, ***pancreatitis.***
GU: urine retention.
Respiratory: ***respiratory depression.***
Skin: pruritus, rash.
Other: ***angioedema, anaphylaxis.***

Interactions

Drug-drug. *Barbiturates, CNS depressants, narcotics, tranquilizers:* May enhance CNS depression. Monitor patient closely.
MAO inhibitors: May cause a hypertensive crisis. Don't use together.
Drug-lifestyle. *Alcohol use:* May enhance CNS depression. Discourage using together.

Effects on lab test results

None reported.

Pharmacokinetics

Absorption: About 90% absorbed.
Distribution: Unknown.
Metabolism: Metabolized extensively by liver.
Excretion: Metabolites excreted mainly in feces with lesser amounts excreted in urine.
Half-life: Diphenoxylate, 2½ hours; its major metabolite, diphenoxylic acid, 4½ hours; atropine, 2½ hours.

Route	Onset	Peak	Duration
P.O.	45-60 min	About 3 hr	3-4 hr

Pharmacodynamics

Chemical effect: Unknown; probably increases smooth-muscle tone in GI tract, inhibits motility and propulsion, and diminishes secretions.
Therapeutic effect: Relieves diarrhea.

Available forms

Liquid: 2.5 mg/5 ml (with atropine sulfate 0.025 mg/5 ml)*
Tablets: 2.5 mg (with atropine sulfate 0.025 mg)

NURSING PROCESS

Assessment

• Assess patient's diarrhea before and regularly during therapy.
• Be alert for adverse reactions and drug interactions.
• Evaluate patient's and family's knowledge of drug therapy.

Nursing diagnoses

• Diarrhea related to underlying condition

*Liquid form contains alcohol. **May contain tartrazine. ◆Canada ◇Australia †OTC ‡Off-label use

• Ineffective breathing pattern related to drug-induced respiratory depression
• Deficient knowledge related to drug therapy

Planning and implementation

• Fluid retention in the bowel may mask depletion of extracellular fluid and electrolytes, especially in young children treated for acute gastroenteritis. Correct fluid and electrolyte disturbances before starting drug. Dehydration may increase risk of delayed toxicity.
• Keep in mind that 2.5-mg dose is as effective as 5 ml of camphorated opium tincture.
• Drug isn't indicated for treating antibiotic-induced diarrhea.
• Drug is unlikely to be effective if no response occurs within 48 hours.
• Risk of physical dependence increases with high dosage and long-term use. Atropine sulfate helps discourage abuse.
• Use naloxone to treat respiratory depression caused by overdose.

Patient teaching

• Tell patient not to exceed recommended dosage.
• Warn patient not to use drug to treat acute diarrhea for longer than 2 days. Encourage him to seek medical attention if diarrhea persists.
• Advise patient to avoid hazardous activities, such as driving, until CNS effects of drug are known.

Evaluation

• Patient regains normal bowel pattern.
• Patient maintains normal breathing pattern throughout therapy.
• Patient and family state understanding of drug therapy.

dipyridamole

(digh-peer-IH-duh-mohl)

Apo-Dipyridamole♦, Novo-Dipiradol♦, Persantin◇, Persantin 100◇, Persantine**

Pharmacologic class: pyrimidine analogue
Therapeutic class: coronary vasodilator, platelet aggregation inhibitor
Pregnancy risk category: B

Indications and dosages

▶ **Inhibition of platelet adhesion in prosthetic heart valves.** *Adults:* 75 to 100 mg P.O. q.i.d. (with warfarin or aspirin).
▶ **Alternative to exercise in evaluation of coronary artery disease during thallium-201 myocardial perfusion scintigraphy.** *Adults:* 0.57 mg/kg as I.V. infusion at constant rate over 4 minutes (0.142 mg/kg/minute).
▶ **Chronic angina pectoris‡.** *Adults:* 50 mg P.O. t.i.d. at least 1 hour before meals; 2 to 3 months of therapy may be required to achieve clinical response.
▶ **Prevention of thromboembolic complications in patients with various thromboembolic disorders other than prosthetic heart valves‡.** *Adults:* 150 to 400 mg P.O. daily (with warfarin or aspirin).

Contraindications and precautions

• No known contraindications.
• Use cautiously in patients with hypotension.
Lifespan: In pregnant women, use cautiously. In breast-feeding women and children, safety of drug hasn't been established.

Adverse reactions

CNS: *headache, dizziness,* weakness.
CV: flushing, fainting, hypotension, chest pain, ECG abnormalities, blood pressure lability, hypertension (with I.V. infusion).
GI: *nausea,* vomiting, diarrhea, abdominal distress.
Skin: rash, irritation (with undiluted injection), pruritus.

Interactions

Drug-drug. *Heparin:* May cause increased bleeding. Monitor patient closely.
Theophylline: May prevent coronary vasodilation by I.V. dipyridamole. Avoid using together.
Drug-herb. *Dong quai, feverfew, garlic, ginger, horse chestnut, red clover:* May increase risk of bleeding. Discourage using together.

Effects on lab test results

None reported.

Pharmacokinetics

Absorption: Variable and slow; bioavailability ranges from 27% to 59%.

Distribution: Wide distribution in body tissues. Protein binding ranges from 91% to 97%.
Metabolism: Metabolized by liver.
Excretion: Elimination occurs by way of biliary excretion of glucuronide conjugates. Some dipyridamole and conjugates may undergo enterohepatic circulation and fecal excretion; small amount is excreted in urine. *Half-life:* 1 to 12 hours.

Route	Onset	Peak	Duration
P.O.	Unknown	45-150 min	Unknown
I.V.	Unknown	2 min after therapy stops	Unknown
I.M.	Unknown	Unknown	Unknown

Pharmacodynamics

Chemical effect: May involve its ability to increase adenosine, which is a coronary vasodilator and platelet aggregation inhibitor.
Therapeutic effect: Dilates coronary arteries and helps prevent clotting.

Available forms

Injection: 10 mg/2 ml
Tablets: 25 mg, 50 mg, 75 mg

NURSING PROCESS

Assessment

- Obtain history of patient's underlying condition before therapy, and reassess regularly thereafter.
- Be alert for adverse reactions and drug interactions.
- Evaluate patient's and family's knowledge of drug therapy.

Nursing diagnoses

- Ineffective cardiopulmonary tissue perfusion related to underlying condition
- Acute pain related to drug-induced headache
- Deficient knowledge related to drug therapy

Planning and implementation

- **P.O. use:** Give drug 1 hour before meals. If patient develops adverse GI reactions, give drug with meals.
- **I.V. use:** If giving drug as diagnostic agent, dilute in half-normal or normal saline solution or D_5W in at least a 1:2 ratio for total volume of 20 to 50 ml. Inject thallium-201 within 5 minutes after completing 4-minute dipyridamole infusion.
- **I.M. use:** Follow normal protocol.

Patient teaching

- Instruct patient when to take drug.
- Tell patient to have his blood pressure checked frequently.
- Advise patient to take mild analgesic if headache occurs.
- Instruct patient to notify prescriber if chest pain occurs.

Evaluation

- Patient maintains adequate tissue perfusion and cellular oxygenation.
- Patient obtains relief from drug-induced headache with use of mild analgesic.
- Patient and family state understanding of drug therapy.

disopyramide

(digh-so-PEER-uh-mighd)
Rythmodan ♦ ◇

disopyramide phosphate

Norpace, Norpace CR, Rythmodan LA♦

Pharmacologic class: pyridine derivative
Therapeutic class: antiarrhythmic
Pregnancy risk category: C

Indications and dosages

▶ **Symptomatic PVCs (unifocal, multifocal, or coupled); ventricular tachycardia not severe enough to require cardioversion.** *Adults weighing over 50 kg (110 lb):* Initial loading dose: 300 mg P.O. for rapid control of ventricular arrhythmia.
Follow with 150 mg q 6 hours, 300 mg q 12 hours with controlled-release capsules.
Adults weighing 50 kg or less: Initial loading dose is 200 mg P.O., then 100 mg P.O. q 6 hours as conventional capsules or 200 mg P.O. q 12 hours with controlled-release capsules.
Children ages 12 to 18: 6 to 15 mg/kg P.O. daily.
Children ages 4 to 12: 10 to 15 mg/kg P.O. daily.

Children ages 1 to 4: 10 to 20 mg/kg P.O. daily.
Children younger than age 1: 10 to 30 mg/kg P.O. daily.

For pediatric dosages, divide into equal amounts and give q 6 hours.

Give drug until arrhythmia is gone or patient has received 150 mg. Repeat dosage if conversion is successful but arrhythmia returns. Total I.V. dosage shouldn't exceed 300 mg in first hour. Follow with I.V. infusion of 0.4 mg/kg/ hour (usually 20 to 30 mg/hour) to maximum of 800 mg daily.
Recommended dosages in advanced renal insufficiency: If creatinine clearance is 30 to 40 ml/minute, 100 mg q 8 hours; if creatinine clearance is 15 to 30 ml/minute, 100 mg q 12 hours; if creatinine clearance is less than 15 ml/minute, 100 mg q 24 hours.

Contraindications and precautions

- Contraindicated in patients hypersensitive to drug and in those with cardiogenic shock or second- or third-degree heart block without an artificial pacemaker.
- Use with extreme caution and avoid, if possible, in patients with heart failure.
- Use cautiously in patients with underlying conduction abnormalities, urinary tract diseases (especially prostatic hypertrophy), hepatic or renal impairment, myasthenia gravis, or acute angle-closure glaucoma.

Lifespan: In pregnant women, use cautiously. In breast-feeding women, drug isn't recommended.

Adverse reactions

CNS: dizziness, agitation, depression, syncope, fatigue, headache, acute psychosis.
CV: ***hypotension, heart failure, heart block,*** edema, ***arrhythmias,*** chest pain.
EENT: blurred vision, dry eyes, dry nose.
GI: nausea, vomiting, anorexia, bloating, abdominal pain, constipation, dry mouth, diarrhea.
GU: urine retention, urinary hesitancy.
Hepatic: cholestatic jaundice.
Metabolic: weight gain.
Musculoskeletal: aches, pain, muscle weakness.
Respiratory: shortness of breath.
Skin: rash, pruritus, dermatosis.

Interactions

Drug-drug. *Antiarrhythmics:* May cause additive or antagonized antiarrhythmic effects. Monitor patient closely.
Erythromycin: May increase disopyramide levels may occur, causing arrhythmias and prolonged QTc interval. Monitor ECG closely.
Phenytoin: May increase metabolism of disopyramide. Monitor patient for decreased antiarrhythmic effect.
Rifampin: Disopyramide levels may be decreased. Monitor patient for decreased effectiveness.
Drug-herb. *Jimson weed:* May adversely affect CV function. Discourage using together.

Effects on lab test results

None reported.

Pharmacokinetics

Absorption: Rapidly and well absorbed from GI tract with P.O. administration.
Distribution: Well distributed throughout extracellular fluid but not extensively bound to tissues. Plasma–protein-binding varies but generally ranges from about 50% to 65%.
Metabolism: Metabolized in liver.
Excretion: Excreted in urine. *Half-life:* About 7 hours.

Route	Onset	Peak	Duration
P.O.	30 min-3.5 hr	2-2.5 hr	1.5-8.5 hr
I.V.	Unknown	Unknown	Unknown

Pharmacodynamics

Chemical effect: Unknown; considered class Ia antiarrhythmic that depresses phase 0 and prolongs action potential. All class I drugs have membrane-stabilizing effects.
Therapeutic effect: Restores normal sinus rhythm.

Available forms

disopyramide
Capsules: 100 mg ♦, 150 mg ♦
disopyramide phosphate
Capsules: 100 mg, 150 mg
Capsules (controlled-release): 100 mg, 150 mg
Injection: 10 mg/ml ♦ ◊
Tablets (sustained-release): 150 mg ♦

NURSING PROCESS

Assessment
- Obtain history of patient's arrhythmia before therapy.
- Monitor effectiveness by assessing patient's ECG pattern and apical pulse rate.
- Be alert for adverse reactions and drug interactions.
- Evaluate patient's and family's knowledge of drug therapy.

Nursing diagnoses
- Decreased cardiac output related to underlying arrhythmia
- Ineffective protection related to drug-induced proarrhythmias
- Deficient knowledge related to drug therapy

Planning and implementation
- Correct any underlying electrolyte abnormalities before therapy begins.
- Check apical pulse before giving drug. Notify prescriber if pulse rate is slower than 60 beats/minute or faster than 120 beats/minute.
- **P.O. use:** Sustained- and controlled-release preparations shouldn't be used for rapid control of ventricular arrhythmias, when therapeutic blood levels must be rapidly attained; in patients with cardiomyopathy or possible cardiac decompensation; or in those with severe renal impairment.

– For administration to young children, pharmacist may prepare disopyramide suspension from 100-mg capsules using cherry syrup. Suspension should be dispensed in amber glass bottles and protected from light.
- **I.V. use:** Add 200 mg to 500 ml of compatible solution, such as normal saline solution or D_5W. Use an infusion pump to give drug. Don't mix with other drugs; switch to P.O. therapy as soon as possible.
- Discontinue drug if heart block develops, if QRS complex widens by more than 25%, or if QTc interval lengthens by more than 25% above baseline; also notify prescriber.

Patient teaching
- When transferring patient from immediate- to sustained-release capsules, advise him to take sustained-release capsule 6 hours after last immediate-release capsule was taken.
- Teach patient importance of taking drug on time and exactly as prescribed. This may require use of alarm clock for night doses.
- Advise patient to chew gum or hard candy to relieve dry mouth.
- Tell patient not to crush or chew extended-release tablets.

Evaluation
- Patient's ECG reveals that arrhythmia has been corrected.
- Patient develops no new arrhythmias as result of therapy.
- Patient and family state understanding of drug therapy.

disulfiram
(digh-SUL-fih-ram)
Antabuse

Pharmacologic class: aldehyde dehydrogenase inhibitor
Therapeutic class: alcohol deterrent
Pregnancy risk category: NR

Indications and dosages
▶ **Adjunct in management of chronic alcoholism.** *Adults:* 250 to 500 mg P.O. as single dose in morning for 1 to 2 weeks. Can be taken in evening if drowsiness occurs. Maintenance dosage is 125 to 500 mg P.O. daily (average dosage 250 mg) until permanent self-control is established. Treatment may continue for months or years.

Contraindications and precautions
- Contraindicated during alcohol intoxication and within 12 hours of alcohol ingestion. Also contraindicated in patients hypersensitive to disulfiram or thiram derivatives used in pesticides and rubber vulcanization; patients with psychoses, myocardial disease, or coronary occlusion; and patients receiving metronidazole, paraldehyde, alcohol, or alcohol-containing preparations.
- Use with extreme caution in patients receiving concurrent phenytoin therapy and in patients with diabetes mellitus, hypothyroidism, seizure disorder, cerebral damage, nephritis, or hepatic cirrhosis or insufficiency.

Lifespan: Pregnant women shouldn't be given drug. With breast-feeding women, use cautiously. In children, safety of drug hasn't been established.

Adverse reactions

CNS: drowsiness, headache, fatigue, delirium, depression, neuritis, peripheral neuritis, polyneuritis, restlessness, and psychotic reactions.
EENT: optic neuritis.
GI: metallic or garlic aftertaste.
GU: impotence.
Skin: acneiform or allergic dermatitis.
Other: ***disulfiram reaction.***

Interactions

Drug-drug. *Alfentanil:* May prolong duration of effect. Monitor patient closely.
Anticoagulants: May increase anticoagulant effect. Dosage of anticoagulant may need to be adjusted accordingly; monitor patient for bleeding.
Bacampicillin: Bacampicillin metabolism produces low levels of ethanol and acetaldehyde. Monitor patient closely.
CNS depressants: Increases CNS depression. Use together cautiously.
Isoniazid: May cause ataxia or marked change in behavior. Don't use together.
Metronidazole: Will cause psychotic reaction. Don't use together; wait for 2 weeks following disulfiram.
Midazolam: May increase plasma levels of midazolam. Use together cautiously.
Paraldehyde: Will cause toxic levels of acetaldehyde. Don't use together.
Phenytoin: May increase levels of phenytoin. Monitor phenytoin blood levels, and expect prescriber to adjust phenytoin dosages.
Tricyclic antidepressants, especially amitriptyline: May cause transient delirium. Monitor patient closely.
Drug-herb. *Passion flower, pill-bearing spurge, pokeweed, squaw vine, squill, sundew, sweet flag, tormentil, valerian, yarrow:* Disulfiram reaction may occur if herb form contains alcohol. Discourage using together.
Drug-lifestyle. *Alcohol use (all sources, including cough syrups, liniments, shaving lotion, back-rub preparations):* May precipitate disulfiram reaction. Don't use together. Alcohol reaction may occur as long as 2 weeks after a single disulfiram dose; the longer patient remains on drug, the more sensitive he is to alcohol.

Effects on lab test results

- May increase cholesterol level.

Pharmacokinetics

Absorption: Absorbed completely from GI tract.
Distribution: Drug is highly lipid-soluble and initially localized in adipose tissue.
Metabolism: Mostly oxidized in liver.
Excretion: Primarily excreted in urine; 5% to 20% eliminated in feces.

Route	Onset	Peak	Duration
P.O.	1-2 hr	Unknown	< 14 days

Pharmacodynamics

Chemical effect: Blocks oxidation of ethanol at acetaldehyde stage. Excess acetaldehyde produces highly unpleasant reaction in presence of even small amounts of ethanol.
Therapeutic effect: Deters alcohol consumption.

Available forms

Tablets: 250 mg, 500 mg

NURSING PROCESS

Assessment

- Obtain history of patient's alcoholism before therapy.
- Complete physical examination and laboratory studies, including CBC, chemistry panel, and transaminase determination, should precede therapy. Repeat physical examination and laboratory studies regularly.
- Monitor effectiveness by assessing patient's abstinence from alcohol.
- Measure serum alcohol level weekly.
- Be alert for adverse reactions and drug interactions. Disulfiram reaction is precipitated by alcohol use and may include flushing, throbbing headache, dyspnea, nausea, copious vomiting, diaphoresis, thirst, chest pain, palpitations, hyperventilation, hypotension, syncope, anxiety, weakness, blurred vision, and confusion. In severe reactions patient may experience respiratory depression, CV collapse, arrhythmias, MI, acute heart failure, seizures, unconsciousness, and death.

• Mild reactions may occur in sensitive patients with blood alcohol levels of 5 to 10 mg/dl; symptoms are fully developed at 50 mg/dl; unconsciousness typically occurs at 125- to 150-mg/dl level. Reaction may last from 30 minutes to several hours or as long as alcohol remains in blood.
• Evaluate patient's and family's knowledge of drug therapy.

Nursing diagnoses
• Ineffective health maintenance related to alcoholism
• Acute pain related to drug-induced headache
• Deficient knowledge related to drug therapy

Planning and implementation
• Use only under close medical and nursing supervision. Only give drug to patient who hasn't used alcohol for at least 12 hours. Patient should clearly understand consequences of disulfiram therapy and give permission for its use. Use drug only if patient is cooperative, well-motivated, and receiving supportive psychiatric therapy.
• Administration is usually during the day, although drug may be given at night if drowsiness occurs. Establish lowered maintenance dose until permanent self-control is practiced. Keep in mind that treatment may continue for months or years.

Patient teaching
• Caution patient's family that disulfiram should never be given to the patient without his knowledge; severe reaction or death could result if the patient ingests alcohol.
• Warn patient to avoid all sources of alcohol (for example, sauces and cough syrups). Even external application of liniments, shaving lotion, and back-rub preparations may precipitate disulfiram reaction. Tell patient that alcohol reaction may occur as long as 2 weeks after single dose of disulfiram; the longer patient remains on drug, the more sensitive he becomes to alcohol.
• Tell patient to wear or carry medical identification identifying him as a disulfiram user.
• Reassure patient that drug-induced adverse reactions (unrelated to alcohol use), such as drowsiness, fatigue, impotence, headache, peripheral neuritis, and metallic or garlic taste, subside after about 2 weeks of therapy.

Evaluation
• Patient abstains from alcohol consumption.
• Patient's headache is relieved with mild analgesic therapy.
• Patient and family state understanding of drug therapy.

dobutamine hydrochloride
(doh-BYOO-tuh-meen high-droh-KLOR-ighd)
Dobutrex

Pharmacologic class: adrenergic, $beta_1$ agonist
Therapeutic class: inotropic agent
Pregnancy risk category: B

Indications and dosages
▶ **To increase cardiac output in short-term treatment of cardiac decompensation caused by depressed contractility, such as during refractory heart failure, and as adjunct in cardiac surgery.** *Adults:* 2 to 20 mcg/kg/minute I.V. infusion. Rarely, rates up to 40 mcg/kg/minute may be needed; however, such doses may worsen ischemia.

Contraindications and precautions
• Contraindicated in patients hypersensitive to drug or its components and in those with idiopathic hypertrophic subaortic stenosis.
• Use cautiously in patients with history of hypertension. Drug may cause exaggerated pressor response.
Lifespan: In pregnant and breast-feeding women and in children, safety of drug hasn't been established.

Adverse reactions
CNS: headache.
CV: *increased heart rate,* hypertension, PVCs, angina, nonspecific chest pain, phlebitis, hypotension.
GI: nausea, vomiting.
Musculoskeletal: mild leg cramps or tingling sensation.
Respiratory: shortness of breath, ***asthma attacks.***
Other: ***anaphylaxis.***

Interactions

Drug-drug. *Beta blockers:* May antagonize dobutamine effects. Don't use together.
Bretylium: May potentiate action of vasopressors on adrenergic receptors; arrhythmias may result. Monitor ECG closely.
General anesthetics: Greater risk of ventricular arrhythmias. Monitor patient closely.
Tricyclic antidepressants: May potentiate pressor response. Monitor patient closely.
Drug-herb. *Rue:* Increases inotropic potential. Monitor vital signs closely.

Effects on lab test results

- May decrease potassium level.

Pharmacokinetics

Absorption: Administered I.V.
Distribution: Widely distributed throughout body.
Metabolism: Metabolized by liver.
Excretion: Excreted mainly in urine with minor amounts in feces. *Half-life:* About 2 minutes.

Route	Onset	Peak	Duration
I.V.	1-2 min	≤ 10 min	< 5 min after therapy stops

Pharmacodynamics

Chemical effect: Directly stimulates $beta_1$ receptors to increase myocardial contractility and stroke volume. At therapeutic dosages, drug decreases peripheral vascular resistance (afterload), reduces ventricular filling pressure (preload), and may facilitate AV node conduction.
Therapeutic effect: Increases cardiac output.

Available forms

Injection: 12.5 mg/ml in 20-ml vials
Premixed: 0.5 mg/ml (125 mg or 250 mg) in D_5W, 1 mg/ml (250 mg or 500 mg) in D_5W, 2 mg/ml (500 mg) in D_5W, 4 mg/ml (1000 mg) in D_5W

NURSING PROCESS

Assessment

- Assess patient's condition before therapy and regularly thereafter.
- Continuously monitor ECG, blood pressure, pulmonary capillary wedge pressure, cardiac condition, and urine output.
- Monitor electrolyte level.
- Be alert for adverse reactions and drug interactions.
- Evaluate patient's and family's knowledge of drug therapy.

Nursing diagnoses

- Decreased cardiac output related to underlying condition
- Acute pain related to headache
- Deficient knowledge related to drug therapy

Planning and implementation

- Before starting dobutamine, correct hypovolemia with plasma volume expanders.
- Give cardiac glycoside before dobutamine. Because drug increases AV node conduction, patients with atrial fibrillation may develop rapid ventricular rate.
- Give drug using central venous catheter or large peripheral vein. Titrate infusion according to prescriber's orders and patient's condition. Use infusion pump.
- Dilute concentrate for injection before administration. Compatible solutions include D_5W, half-normal saline solution injection, normal saline solution injection, and lactated Ringer's injection. The contents of one vial (250 mg) diluted with 1,000 ml of solution yield 4 mg/ml; diluted with 500 ml, 2 mg/ml; diluted with 250 ml, 1 mg/ml. Concentration shouldn't exceed 5 mg/ml.
- Avoid extravasation; it may cause inflammatory response.

ALERT: Don't give in same I.V. line with other drugs. Drug is incompatible with heparin, hydrocortisone sodium succinate, cefazolin, cefamandole, neutral cephalothin, penicillin, and ethacrynate sodium.

- Don't mix with sodium bicarbonate injection because drug is incompatible with alkaline solutions.
- I.V. solutions remain stable for 24 hours.
- Oxidation of drug may slightly discolor admixtures containing dobutamine. This doesn't indicate significant loss of potency, provided drug is used within 24 hours of reconstitution.
- Change I.V. sites regularly to avoid phlebitis.

Patient teaching
- Tell patient to report chest pain, shortness of breath, and headache.

Evaluation
- Patient regains adequate cardiac output exhibited by stable vital signs, normal urine output, and clear mental status.
- Patient's headache is relieved with analgesic administration.
- Patient and family state understanding of drug therapy.

docetaxel
(doks-uh-TAKX-ul)
Taxotere

Pharmacologic class: taxoid antineoplastic
Therapeutic class: antineoplastic
Pregnancy risk category: D

Indications and dosages
▶ **Treatment of patients with locally advanced or metastatic breast cancer for which prior chemotherapy has failed.** *Adults:* 60 to 100 mg/m² I.V. over 1 hour q 3 weeks.

If patient initially receives 100 mg/m² and experiences febrile neutropenia, neutrophils < 500 cells/mm³ for more than 1 week, or severe or cumulative cutaneous reactions, decrease dose to 75 mg/m². If reactions continue, decrease dose to 55 mg/m² or discontinue therapy.

If patient is dosed initially at 60 mg/m² and doesn't experience febrile neutropenia, neutrophils < 500 cells/mm³, severe or cumulative cutaneous reactions, or severe peripheral neuropathy, dosage may be increased. Discontinue therapy in patient who develops grade 3 periph eral neuropathy.

▶ **Locally advanced or metastatic non–small-cell lung cancer after failure of platinum-based chemotherapy.** *Adults:* 75 mg/m² I.V. over 1 hour q 3 weeks. Premedicate with dexamethasone 16 mg daily for 3 days, starting 1 day before docetaxel therapy.

For patients with febrile neutropenia, neutrophils less than 500 cells/mm³ for more than 1 week, severe or cumulative cutaneous reactions, or other grade 3 or 4 nonhematologic toxicity, discontinue docetaxel until toxicity is resolved; then restart at 55 mg/m². For patients who develop grade 3 or higher peripheral neuropathy, discontinue docetaxel entirely.

▶ **Unresectable, locally advanced, or metastatic non–small-cell lung cancer in patient who has not previously received chemotherapy for this condition, in combination with cisplatin.** *Adults:* 75 mg/m² docetaxel I.V. over 1 hour immediately followed by cisplatin 75 mg/m² I.V. over 30 to 60 minutes every 3 weeks.

Patient whose lowest platelet count during the previous course of therapy was < 25,000 cells/m³, those with febrile neutropenia, and those with serious nonhematologic toxicities. Decrease docetaxel dosage to 65 mg/m². In patients who require a further dose reduction, a dose of 50 mg/m² is recommended. For cisplatin dosage adjustments, see manufacturers' prescribing information.

Contraindications and precautions
- Contraindicated in patients hypersensitive to drug or to other polysorbate 80–containing drugs and in those with neutrophil counts below 1,500 cells/mm³.

Lifespan: In pregnant and breast-feeding women, drug is contraindicated. In children younger than age 16, safety and efficacy haven't been established.

Adverse reactions
CNS: pain, *asthenia,* paresthesia, dysesthesia, weakness.
CV: *fluid retention,* hypotension.
GI: *stomatitis, nausea, vomiting, diarrhea.*
Hematologic: *anemia,* NEUTROPENIA, FEBRILE NEUTROPENIA, MYELOSUPPRESSION, LEUKOPENIA, THROMBOCYTOPENIA, ***septic and nonseptic death.***
Musculoskeletal: back pain, *myalgia,* arthralgia.
Respiratory: dyspnea.
Skin: *alopecia,* skin eruptions, desquamation, nail pigmentation alterations, nail pain, flushing, rash.
Other: HYPERSENSITIVITY REACTIONS, infection, chest tightness, drug fever, chills.

Interactions
Drug-drug. *Agents that are induced, inhibited, or metabolized by cytochrome P-450 3A4 (cyclosporin, ketoconazole, erythromycin, trolean-*

domycin): May modify docetaxel metabolism when given together. Use together cautiously.

Effects on lab test results

- May increase ALT, AST, bilirubin, and alkaline phosphatase levels.
- May decrease hemoglobin, hematocrit, and WBC and platelet counts.

Pharmacokinetics

Absorption: Administered I.V.
Distribution: 94% is protein-bound.
Metabolism: Partly by liver.
Excretion: Mainly in feces.

Route	Onset	Peak	Duration
I.V.	Immediate	Unknown	Unknown

Pharmacodynamics

Chemical effect: Disrupts the microtubular network essential for mitotic and interphase cellular functions.
Therapeutic effect: Inhibits mitosis, producing antineoplastic effect.

Available forms

Injection: 20 mg, 80 mg

NURSING PROCESS

Assessment

- Premedicate patient with oral corticosteroids.
- Monitor blood count frequently during therapy.
- Evaluate patient's and family's knowledge of drug therapy.

Nursing diagnoses

- Ineffective health maintenance related to neoplastic disease
- Deficient knowledge related to drug therapy

Planning and implementation

ALERT: Premedicate with oral corticosteroids for 3 days, starting 1 day before treatment to reduce fluid retention and hypersensitivty reactions.

- Dilute drug with diluent supplied before administration. Allow drug and diluent to stand at room temperature for 5 minutes before mixing. After adding diluent contents to vial, rotate vial gently for 15 seconds. Let solution stand for a few minutes for foam to dissipate.
- To prepare solution for infusion, withdraw required amount of premixed solution from vial and inject it into 250 ml normal saline solution or D_5W to yield 0.3 to 0.9 mg/ml.
- Wear gloves during drug preparation and administration.

Patient teaching

- Warn patient that alopecia occurs in almost 80% of patients.
- Tell patient to promptly report sore throat, fever, unusual bruising or bleeding, or signs of fluid retention.

Evaluation

- Patient shows positive response to drug.
- Patient and family state understanding of drug therapy.

docosanol

(doe-KOE-san-ole)
Abreva

Pharmacologic class: topical antiviral
Therapeutic class: antiviral
Pregnancy risk category: B

Indications and dosages

▶ **Recurrent oral-facial herpes simplex (cold sores).** *Adults, adolescents, and children age 12:* Apply topically 5 times daily to affected area.

Contraindications and precautions

- Contraindicated in patients hypersensitive to drug or any of its components.

Lifespan: In breast-feeding women, use cautiously because it's unknown whether drug appears in breast milk. In children younger than age 12, safety and efficacy haven't been established.

Adverse reactions

CNS: *headache.*
Skin: reaction at application site.

Interactions

None reported.

Effects on lab test results

None reported.

Pharmacokinetics

Absorption: Not absorbed.
Distribution: Not applicable.
Metabolism: Not applicable.
Excretion: Not applicable.

Route	Onset	Peak	Duration
Topical	Unknown	Unknown	Unknown

Pharmacodynamics

Chemical effect: Inhibits the fusion between the cell's plasma membrane and the herpes simplex virus lipid envelope, thereby blocking the viral entry into cells and the subsequent replication of the virus.
Therapeutic effect: Shortens healing time and relieves pain from the herpes simplex lesions.

Available forms

Cream: 10%

NURSING PROCESS

Assessment
- Assess patient before and during therapy.
- Monitor patient for any adverse drug effects.

Nursing diagnoses
- Acute pain related to underlying lesions
- Deficient knowledge related to drug therapy

Planning and implementation
- Use drug only to treat oral-facial herpes simplex. Avoid application in or near patient's eyes.
- Start treatment as early as possible after symptoms start and continue until lesions have healed.
- Enforce strict handwashing before and after application.

Patient teaching
- Advise patient to start treatment as soon as symptoms appear and continue until the lesions heal.
- Notify patient that lesions are considered contagious until completely healed.
- Urge patient to report worsening condition or any adverse reactions to drug therapy.
- Urge patient to wash hands with soap and warm water before and immediately after application.

Evaluation
- Patient's symptoms are relieved with drug therapy.
- Patient and family state understanding of drug therapy.

docusate calcium (dioctyl calcium sulfosuccinate)
(DOK-yoo-sayt KAL-see-um)
DC Softgels , Pro-Cal-Sof , Surfak

docusate potassium (dioctyl potassium sulfosuccinate)
Diocto-K†, Kasof†

docusate sodium (dioctyl sodium sulfosuccinate)
Colace†, Coloxyl ◇, Coloxyl Enema Concentrate ◇, Dialose†, Diocto†, Dioeze†, Disonate†, DOK†, DOS Softgels†, Doxinate†, D-S-S†, Modane Soft†, Pro-Sof†, Regulax SS†, Regulex ◆ †, Regutol†, Therevac Plus†, Therevac-SB†

Pharmacologic class: surfactant
Therapeutic class: emollient laxative
Pregnancy risk category: C

Indications and dosages

▶ **Stool softener.** *Adults and children age 12 and older:* 50 to 300 mg P.O. daily until bowel movements are normal. Or, give enema (where available). Dilute 1:24 with sterile water before administration, and give 100 to 150 ml (retention enema), 300 to 500 ml (evacuation enema), or 0.5 to 1.5 liters (flushing enema).
Children ages 6 to 12: 40 to 120 mg docusate sodium P.O. daily.
Children ages 3 to 6: 20 to 60 mg docusate sodium P.O. daily.
Children younger than age 3: 10 to 40 mg docusate sodium P.O. daily.

Higher dosages used for initial therapy. Dosage adjusted to individual response.
docusate calcium. *Adults and children:* Usual dosage 240 mg P.O. daily until bowel movements are normal.

Contraindications and precautions

• Contraindicated in patients hypersensitive to drug and in those with intestinal obstruction, undiagnosed abdominal pain, signs of appendicitis, fecal impaction, or acute surgical abdomen.

Lifespan: In pregnant women, use cautiously.

Adverse reactions

EENT: throat irritation.
GI: bitter taste, mild abdominal cramping, diarrhea, laxative dependence with long-term or excessive use.

Interactions

Drug-drug. *Mineral oil:* May increase mineral oil absorption and cause toxicity and lipoid pneumonia. Separate administration times.

Effects on lab test results

None reported.

Pharmacokinetics

Absorption: Absorbed minimally in duodenum and jejunum.
Distribution: Distributed primarily locally, in gut.
Metabolism: None.
Excretion: Excreted in feces.

Route	Onset	Peak	Duration
P.O.	Varies	Varies	24-72 hr
P.R.	Unknown	Unknown	Unknown

Pharmacodynamics

Chemical effect: Reduces surface tension of interfacing liquid contents of bowel. This detergent activity promotes incorporation of additional liquid into stool, thus forming softer mass.
Therapeutic effect: Softens stool.

Available forms

docusate calcium
Capsules: 50 mg†, 240 mg†
docusate potassium
Capsules: 100 mg†, 240 mg†
docusate sodium
Capsules: 50 mg†, 60 mg†, 100 mg†, 240 mg†, 250 mg†
Enema concentrate: 18 g/100 ml (must be diluted) ◇
Oral liquid: 150 mg/15 ml†
Oral solution: 50 mg/ml†
Syrup: 20 mg/5ml*†, 50 mg/15 ml†, 60 mg/15 ml†, 100 mg/30 ml†
Tablets: 100 mg†

NURSING PROCESS

Assessment

• Obtain history of patient's bowel patterns before therapy, and reassess regularly thereafter.
• Before giving drug for constipation, determine if patient has adequate fluid intake, exercise, and diet.
• Be alert for adverse reactions and drug interactions.
• Evaluate patient's and family's knowledge of drug therapy.

Nursing diagnoses

• Constipation related to underlying condition
• Diarrhea related to prolonged or excessive use of drug
• Deficient knowledge related to drug therapy

Planning and implementation

• **P.O. use:** Give liquid in milk, fruit juice, or infant formula to mask bitter taste.
• **P.R. use:** Follow manufacturer's directions.
• Drug is laxative of choice for patients who shouldn't strain during defecation, including patients recovering from MI or rectal surgery, for those with rectal or anal disease that makes passage of firm stool difficult, and for those with postpartum constipation.
• Store drug at 59° to 86° F (15° to 30° C), and protect liquid from light.
• Discontinue if abdominal cramping occurs, and notify prescriber.
• Docusate doesn't stimulate intestinal peristaltic movements.

Patient teaching

• Teach patient about dietary sources of bulk, which include bran and other cereals, fresh fruit, and vegetables.
• Instruct patient to use only occasionally and not to use for more than 1 week without prescriber's knowledge.
• Tell patient to discontinue if severe cramping occurs and notify prescriber.

☑ Evaluation

- Patient's constipation is relieved.
- Patient remains free from diarrhea during therapy.
- Patient and family state understanding of drug therapy.

dofetilide

(doh-FET-eh-lighd)
Tikosyn

Pharmacologic class: antiarrhythmic
Therapeutic class: class III antiarrhythmic
Pregnancy risk category: C

Indications and dosages

▶ **Maintenance of normal sinus rhythm in patients with symptomatic atrial fibrillation or atrial flutter of greater than one week's duration who have been converted to normal sinus rhythm; conversion of atrial fibrillation and atrial flutter to normal sinus rhythm.** *Adults:* Dosage is individualized and is based on creatinine clearance and QT interval, which must be determined before first dose (QT interval should be used if heart rate is less than 60 beats/minute). Usual recommended dosage is 500 mcg b.i.d. for patients with creatinine clearance above 60 ml/minute.
Patients with renal impairment: If creatinine clearance is 40 to 60 ml/minute, give 250 mcg P.O. b.i.d. If creatinine clearance is 20 to 39 ml/minute, give 125 mcg P.O. b.i.d.

Contraindications and precautions

- Contraindicated in patients with congenital or acquired long-QT syndromes. Drug shouldn't be used in patients with baseline QTc interval greater than 440 msec (500 msec in patients with ventricular conduction abnormalities). Also contraindicated in patients with severe renal impairment (creatinine clearance below 20 ml/min) and in patients hypersensitive to drug and in those receiving verapamil, cimetidine, trimethoprim (alone or with sulfamethoxazole), or ketoconazole.
- Use cautiously in patients with severe hepatic impairment.

Lifespan: In pregnant patients, use cautiously. Not recommended for breast-feeding women. In children, safety and efficacy haven't been established.

Adverse reactions

CNS: *headache,* dizziness, insomnia, anxiety, migraine, ***cerebral ischemia, CVA,*** asthenia, paresthesia, syncope.
CV: ***ventricular fibrillation, ventricular tachycardia, torsades de pointes, AV block,*** bundle branch block, ***heart block,*** *chest pain,* angina, atrial fibrillation, peripheral edema, hypertension, palpitations, ***bradycardia,*** edema, ***cardiac arrest, MI.***
EENT: facial paralysis.
GI: nausea, diarrhea, abdominal pain.
GU: urinary tract infection.
Hepatic: ***liver damage.***
Musculoskeletal: back pain, arthralgia.
Respiratory: respiratory tract infection, dyspnea, increased cough.
Skin: rash, sweating.
Other: flulike syndrome, ***angioedema.***

Interactions

Drug-drug. *Amiodarone, diltiazem, macrolide antibiotics, nefazodone, norfloxacin, protease inhibitors, quinine, serotonin reuptake inhibitors, zafirlukast:* May increase dofetilide plasma levels. Use with extreme caution.
Cimetidine, ketoconazole, sulfamethoxazole, trimethoprim, verapamil: Increases plasma levels of dofetilide. Don't use together.
Inhibitors of renal cationic secretion (prochlorperazine, megestrol): May increase dofetilide levels. Avoid using together.
Inhibitors of CYP3A4 (macrolide antibiotics, azole antifungals, protease inhibitors, serotonin reuptake inhibitors, amiodarone, cannabinoids, diltiazem, nefazodone, norfloxacin, quinine, zafirlukast): May decrease metabolism and increase dofetilide levels. Use together cautiously.
Triamterene, metformin, amiloride: May increase dofetilide levels. Use together cautiously.
Drug-food. *Grapefruit juice:* May decrease hepatic metabolism and increase plasma levels. Avoid using together.

Effects on lab test results

None reported.

Pharmacokinetics

Absorption: Bioavailability after oral administration is greater than 90%; plasma levels peak at 2 to 3 hours. Steady-state plasma levels are achieved in 2 to 3 days. Absorption is unaffected by food or antacid.
Distribution: Drug is widely distributed throughout the body and has a volume of distribution of 3 L/kg. Plasma protein–binding is 60% to 70%.
Metabolism: Drug is metabolized to a small extent by the CYP3A4 isoenzyme of the cytochrome P-450 system of the liver.
Excretion: About 80% is excreted in the urine, of which 80% is excreted as unchanged drug with the remaining 20% consisting of inactive or minimally active metabolites.

Route	Onset	Peak	Duration
P.O.	Unknown	2-3 hr	Unknown

Pharmacodynamics

Chemical effect: As a class III antiarrhythmic, dofetilide prolongs repolarization without affecting conduction velocity by blocking the cardiac ion channel carrying potassium current. No effect is seen on sodium channels, alpha-adrenergic receptors, or beta-adrenergic receptors.
Therapeutic effect: Maintains normal sinus rhythm in patients with symptomatic atrial fibrillation or atrial flutter who have been converted to normal sinus rhythm; converts atrial fibrillation and atrial flutter to normal sinus rhythm.

Available forms

Distributed only to hospitals and other institutions with applicable dosing and treatment initiation programs. Inpatient and subsequent outpatient discharge and refills of prescriptions are allowed only upon confirmation that prescriber has access to these programs.
Capsules: 125 mcg (0.125 mg), 250 mcg (0.25 mg), 500 mcg (0.5 mg)

NURSING PROCESS

Assessment

- Obtain accurate medication list from patient before starting dofetilide; antiarrhythmic therapy should be stopped under careful monitoring for a minimum of three plasma half-lives. Dofetilide shouldn't be given after amiodarone therapy unless amiodarone level is below 0.3 mcg/ml or unless amiodarone was stopped at least 3 months ago.
- Assess patient's QTc interval, cardiac rhythm, and vital signs before starting medication. Prolongation of the QTc interval requires subsequent dosage adjustments or discontinuation. Continuous ECG monitoring is required for a minimum of 3 days.
- Obtain potassium level before starting therapy and then regularly thereafter. Hypokalemia and hypomagnesemia may occur when giving potassium-depleting diuretics, increasing the risk of torsades de pointes. Potassium levels should be within the normal range before giving dofetilide and maintained in a normal range.
- Monitor patient for prolonged diarrhea, sweating, and vomiting; report them to prescriber because electrolyte imbalance may increase the risk of arrhythmias.
- Monitor renal function and QTc interval every 3 months.
- Evaluate patient's and family's knowledge of drug therapy.

Nursing diagnoses

- Decreased cardiac output related to underlying arrhythmia
- Risk for injury related to drug-induced adverse reactions
- Deficient knowledge related to drug therapy

Planning and implementation

- If patient doesn't convert to normal sinus rhythm within 24 hours after starting dofetilide, electrical conversion should be considered.
- Patient shouldn't be discharged within 12 hours of conversion to normal sinus rhythm.
- If dofetilide must be discontinued to allow administration of other interacting drugs, a washout period of at least 2 days should be observed before starting other drug.

Patient teaching

- Inform the patient to notify prescriber about any change in prescription drugs, OTC medications, or herbal remedies.
- Urge patient to immediately report excessive or prolonged diarrhea, sweating, vomiting, or loss of appetite or thirst to prescriber.

• Inform the patient that dofetilide can be taken without regard to meals or antacids.
• Tell patient not to take drug with grapefruit juice.
• Caution patient not to use OTC Tagamet-HB for ulcers or heartburn. Explain that antacids and OTC acid reducers such as Zantac 75 mg, Pepcid, Axid, and Prevacid are acceptable.
• Instruct woman to notify prescriber about planned, suspected, or known pregnancy.
• Advise patient not to breast-feed while taking dofetilide.
• If patient misses dose, tell him to skip it and wait for the next scheduled dose. Caution against doubling the dose.

Evaluation
• Patient maintains normal sinus rhythm.
• Patient has no injury as a result of drug-induced adverse reactions.
• Patient and family state understanding of drug therapy.

dolasetron mesylate
(doh-LEH-seh-trohn MES-ih layt)
Anzemet

Pharmacologic class: selective serotonin ($5\text{-}HT_3$) receptor antagonist
Therapeutic class: antiemetic
Pregnancy risk category: B

Indications and dosages
▶ **Prevention of nausea and vomiting from cancer chemotherapy.** *Adults:* 100 mg P.O. given as a single dose 1 hour before chemotherapy. Or, 1.8 mg/kg (or a fixed dose of 100 mg) as a single I.V. dose given 30 minutes before chemotherapy.
Children ages 2 to 16: 1.8 mg/kg P.O. 1 hour before chemotherapy. Or, 1.8 mg/kg as single I.V. dose 30 minutes before chemotherapy. Injectable form can be mixed with apple juice and given P.O. Maximum dose is 100 mg.
▶ **Prevention of postoperative nausea and vomiting.** *Adults:* 100 mg P.O. within 2 hours before surgery. Or, 12.5 mg as single I.V. dose about 15 minutes before cessation of anesthesia.
Children ages 2 to 16: 1.2 mg/kg P.O. given within 2 hours before surgery, up to maximum of 100 mg. Or, 0.35 mg/kg (up to 12.5 mg) as single I.V. dose about 15 minutes before cessation of anesthesia. Injectable form can be mixed with apple juice and given P.O.
▶ **Treatment of postoperative nausea and vomiting.** *Adults:* 12.5 mg as a single I.V. dose as soon as nausea or vomiting begins.
Children ages 2 to 16: 0.35 mg/kg, up to maximum dose of 12.5 mg, as a single I.V. dose as soon as nausea or vomiting begins.

Contraindications and precautions
• Contraindicated in patients hypersensitive to drug.
• Give cautiously in patients who have or may develop prolonged cardiac conduction intervals, such as those with electrolyte abnormalities, history of arrhythmias, and cumulative high-dose anthracycline therapy.
Lifespan: In breast-feeding women, use cautiously. In infants, drug isn't recommended.

Adverse reactions
CNS: fever, *headache,* dizziness, drowsiness, fatigue.
CV: ***arrhythmias, bradycardia,*** ECG changes, hypotension, hypertension, tachycardia.
GI: *diarrhea,* dyspepsia, abdominal pain, constipation, anorexia.
GU: oliguria, urine retention.
Skin: pruritus, rash.
Other: chills, pain at injection site.

Interactions
Drug-drug. *Drugs that prolong ECG intervals (such as antiarrhythmics):* May increase risk of arrhythmia. Monitor patient closely.
Drugs that inhibit P450 enzymes (such as cimetidine): May increase hydrodolasetron levels. Monitor patient for adverse effects.
Drugs that induce P450 enzymes (such as rifampin): May decrease hydrodolasetron levels. Monitor patient for decreased efficacy of drug.

Effects on lab test results
• May increase ALT and AST levels.

Pharmacokinetics
Absorption: Rapid for hydrodolasetron, an active metabolite that has an absolute bioavailability of 75%. Absorption of the parent compound is rarely seen.

Distribution: Widely distributed with 69% to 77% bound to plasma protein.
Metabolism: Dolasetron is metabolized to an active metabolite, hydrodolasetron, by carbonyl reductase. Rarely detected in plasma because of rapid and complete metabolism.
Excretion: About two-thirds of hydrodolasetron is recovered in urine; one-third in feces. *Half-life:* 8 hours.

Route	Onset	Peak	Duration
P.O.	Rapid	1 hr	8 hr
I.V.	Rapid	36 min	7 hr

Pharmacodynamics

Chemical effect: Dolasetron is a selective serotonin ($5\text{-}HT_3$) receptor antagonist that blocks the action of serotonin, thereby preventing serotonin from stimulating the vomiting reflex.
Therapeutic effect: Prevents nausea and vomiting.

Available forms

Injection: 20 mg/ml as 12.5 mg/0.625 ml ampule or 100 mg/5 ml vial
Tablets: 50 mg, 100 mg

NURSING PROCESS

Assessment

- Assess patient for history of nausea and vomiting related to chemotherapy or postoperative recovery.
- Be alert for potential adverse reactions and drug interactions.
- Monitor ECG carefully in patients who have or may develop prolonged cardiac conduction intervals.
- Evaluate patient's and family's knowledge of drug therapy.

Nursing diagnoses

- Imbalanced nutrition: less than body requirements, related to nausea and vomiting
- Risk for injury related to drug-induced adverse CNS reaction
- Deficient knowledge related to drug therapy

Planning and implementation

- **P.O. use:** Injection for P.O. administration is stable in apple juice for 2 hours at room temperature.
- **I.V. use:** Injection can be infused as rapidly as 100 mg/30 seconds, or diluted in 50 ml of compatible solution and infused over 15 minutes.
- Discontinue drug and notify prescriber immediately if arrhythmia develops.

ALERT: Don't confuse Avandamet with Anzemet.

Patient teaching

- Tell patient about potential adverse effects.
- Instruct patient not to mix injection in juice for P.O. use until just before dosing.
- Tell patient to report nausea or vomiting.

Evaluation

- Patient has no nausea and vomiting.
- Patient is free from injury.
- Patient and family state understanding of drug therapy

donepezil hydrochloride

(doh-NEH-peh-zil high-droh-KLOR-ighd)
Aricept

Pharmacologic class: reversible inhibitor of acetylcholinesterase
Therapeutic class: psychotherapeutic agent for Alzheimer's disease
Pregnancy risk category: C

Indications and dosages

▶ **Mild-to-moderate dementia of the Alzheimer's type.** *Adults:* Initially, 5 mg P.O. daily h.s. After 4 to 6 weeks, may increase dosage to 10 mg daily.

Contraindications and precautions

- Contraindicated in patients hypersensitive to drug or to piperidine derivatives.
- Use cautiously in patients with history of ulcer disease, CV disease, asthma or obstructive pulmonary disease, or urinary outflow impairment.
- Use cautiously in patients currently taking NSAIDs.

Lifespan: In pregnant patients, use only if benefit justifies risk to fetus. Tell breast-feeding patient to avoid breast-feeding during therapy. In children, safety and effectiveness haven't been established.

Adverse reactions

CNS: syncope, pain, *headache, insomnia,* dizziness, depression, abnormal dreams, somnolence, ***seizures,*** tremor, irritability, paresthesia, aggression, vertigo, ataxia, restlessness, abnormal crying, fatigue, nervousness, aphasia.
CV: chest pain, hypertension, vasodilation, atrial fibrillation, hot flushes, hypotension.
EENT: cataracts, *sore throat,* blurred vision, eye irritation.
GI: *nausea, diarrhea,* vomiting, anorexia, fecal incontinence, ***GI bleeding,*** bloating, epigastric pain.
GU: frequent urination.
Hematologic: ecchymosis.
Metabolic: weight decrease.
Musculoskeletal: muscle cramps, arthritis, toothache, bone fracture.
Respiratory: *dyspnea, bronchitis.*
Skin: pruritus, urticaria, diaphoresis.
Other: increased libido, accident, influenza, dehydration.

Interactions

Drug-drug. *Anticholinergics:* May interfere with anticholinergic activity. Monitor patient.
Bethanechol, succinylcholine: May have additive effects. Monitor patient closely.
Carbamazepine, dexamethasone, phenytoin, phenobarbital, rifampin: May increase rate of donepezil elimination. Monitor patient.
Cholinomimetics, cholinesterase inhibitors: Synergistic effect. Monitor patient closely.
Drug-herb. *Jaborandi tree, pill-bearing spurge:* Additive effect may occur when combined, and risk of toxicity may be increased. Discourage using together.

Effects on lab test results

None reported.

Pharmacokinetics

Absorption: Well absorbed.
Distribution: 96% plasma protein–bound, mainly to albumin.
Metabolism: Extensively metabolized.
Excretion: Excreted in urine and feces.

Route	Onset	Peak	Duration
P.O.	Unknown	3-4 hr	Unknown

Pharmacodynamics

Chemical effect: Reversibly inhibits acetylcholinesterase in the CNS, thereby increasing the acetylcholine level.
Therapeutic effect: Temporarily improves cognitive function in patients with Alzheimer's disease.

Available forms

Tablets: 5 mg, 10 mg

NURSING PROCESS

Assessment

- Monitor patient for symptoms of active or occult GI bleeding.
- Evaluate patient's and family's knowledge of drug therapy.

Nursing diagnoses

- Risk for injury related to adverse effects of drug
- Deficient knowledge related to drug therapy

Planning and implementation

Patient teaching

- Explain that drug doesn't alter underlying degenerative disease but can alleviate symptoms.
- Tell caregiver to give drug in the evening, just before bedtime.
- Advise patient and caregiver to immediately report significant adverse effects or changes in overall health status.
- Tell caregiver to inform health-care team that patient is taking drug before patient receives anesthesia.

Evaluation

- Patient remains free from injury.
- Patient and family state understanding of drug therapy.

dopamine hydrochloride

(DOH-puh-meen high-droh-KLOR-ighd)
Intropin, Revimine ♦

Pharmacologic class: adrenergic
Therapeutic class: inotropic, vasopressor
Pregnancy risk category: C

Indications and dosages

▶ **To treat shock and correct hemodynamic imbalances; to improve perfusion to vital organs; to increase cardiac output; to correct hypotension.** *Adults:* Initially, 1 to 5 mcg/kg/minute by I.V. infusion. Dosage adjusted to desired hemodynamic or renal response, increased by 1 to 4 mcg/kg/minute at 10- to 30-minute intervals.

Contraindications and precautions

- Contraindicated in patients with uncorrected tachyarrhythmias, pheochromocytoma, or ventricular fibrillation.
- Use cautiously in patients with occlusive vascular disease, cold injuries, diabetic endarteritis, and arterial embolism; and in those taking MAO inhibitors.

Lifespan: With pregnant women, use cautiously. In breast-feeding women and children, safety of drug hasn't been established.

Adverse reactions

CNS: headache.
CV: ***arrhythmias,*** ectopic beats, tachycardia, anginal pain, palpitations, ***hypotension, bradycardia, widening of QRS complex,*** conduction disturbances, vasoconstriction, hypertension.
GI: nausea, vomiting.
GU: azotemia.
Respiratory: ***asthma attacks,*** dyspnea.
Skin: necrosis, tissue sloughing with extravasation, piloerection.
Other: ***anaphylaxis.***

Interactions

Drug-drug. *Alpha-adrenergic blockers, beta blockers:* May antagonize dopamine effects. Monitor patient closely.
Ergot alkaloids: May cause extreme elevations in blood pressure. Don't use together.
Inhaled anesthetics: Increases risk of arrhythmias or hypertension. Monitor patient closely.
MAO inhibitors: May cause hypertensive crisis. Don't use together.
Oxytocic drugs: May potentiate pressor effect resulting in severe hypertension. Avoid using together, if possible.
Phenytoin: May lower blood pressure of dopamine-stabilized patients. Monitor blood pressure carefully.
Tricyclic antidepressants: May potentiate adverse sympathomimetic effects of dopamine. Monitor patient closely.

Effects on lab test results

- May increase glucose and urea levels.

Pharmacokinetics

Absorption: Administered I.V.
Distribution: Widely distributed throughout body; doesn't cross blood-brain barrier.
Metabolism: Metabolized to inactive compounds in liver, kidneys, and plasma.
Excretion: Excreted in urine, mainly as its metabolites. *Half-life:* About 9 minutes.

Route	Onset	Peak	Duration
I.V.	≤ 5 min	Unknown	≤ 10 min after therapy stops

Pharmacodynamics

Chemical effect: Stimulates dopaminergic, beta-adrenergic, and alpha-adrenergic receptors of sympathetic nervous system.
Therapeutic effect: Increases cardiac output and blood pressure.

Available forms

Injection: 40 mg/ml, 80 mg/ml, 160 mg/ml as concentrate for injection for I.V. infusion; 0.8 mg/ml (200 or 400 mg) in D_5W; 1.6 mg/ml (400 or 800 mg) in D_5W; 3.2 mg/ml (800 mg) in D_5W as parenteral injection for I.V. infusion.

NURSING PROCESS

Assessment

- Obtain history of patient's underlying condition before therapy.
- During infusion, frequently monitor ECG, blood pressure, cardiac output, central venous pressure, pulmonary capillary wedge pressure, pulse rate, urine output, and color and temperature of limbs.
- Be alert for adverse reactions and drug interactions.
- Be aware that acidosis decreases effectiveness of dopamine.
- After drug is stopped, watch closely for sudden drop in blood pressure.
- Evaluate patient's and family's knowledge of drug therapy.

Nursing diagnoses

- Ineffective tissue perfusion (cerebral, cardiopulmonary, and renal) related to underlying condition
- Risk for injury related to drug-induced adverse reactions
- Deficient knowledge related to drug therapy

Planning and implementation

- Drug isn't used to treat blood or fluid volume deficit. If deficit exists, replace fluid before giving vasopressors.
- Use central line or large vein, such as in antecubital fossa, to minimize risk of extravasation.

ALERT: Don't mix with alkaline solutions. Use D_5W, normal saline solution, or combination of D_5W and normal saline solution. Mix just before use.

- Don't mix other drugs in I.V. container with dopamine. Don't give alkaline drugs (for example, sodium bicarbonate or phenytoin sodium) through I.V. line containing dopamine.
- Use continuous infusion pump to regulate flow rate.
- Keep in mind that patient response depends on dosage and pharmacologic effect. Dosages of 0.5 to 2 mcg/kg/minute stimulate mainly dopamine receptors and dilate renal vasculature. Dosages of 2 to 10 mcg/kg/minute stimulate beta-adrenergic receptors for positive inotropic effect. Higher dosages also stimulate alpha-adrenergic receptors, causing vasoconstriction and increased blood pressure.
- Most patients are satisfactorily maintained on dosages below 20 mcg/kg/minute.
- Taper dosage slowly to evaluate stability of blood pressure.
- Discard after 24 hours or earlier if solution is discolored.
- If disproportionate rise in diastolic pressure (a marked decrease in pulse pressure) is observed in patient receiving dopamine, decrease infusion rate and watch carefully for further evidence of predominant vasoconstrictor activity, unless such effect is desired.
- If extravasation occurs, stop infusion immediately and call prescriber. Extravasation may require treatment by infiltration of area with 5 to 10 mg of phentolamine and 10 to 15 ml of normal saline solution.
- If adverse reactions develop, notify prescriber, who will adjust or discontinue dosage. Also, if urine flow decreases without hypotension, notify prescriber because dosage may need to be reduced.

Patient teaching

- Emphasize importance of reporting discomfort at I.V. site immediately.
- Explain to patient the necessity of dopamine hydrochloride therapy.

Evaluation

- Patient regains adequate cerebral, cardiopulmonary, and renal tissue perfusion.
- Patient doesn't experience injury as result of drug-induced adverse reactions.
- Patient and family state understanding of drug therapy.

dorzolamide hydrochloride

(dor-ZOLE-uh-mighd high-droh-KLOR-ighd)
Trusopt

Pharmacologic class: carbonic anhydrase inhibitor; sulfonamide
Therapeutic class: antiglaucoma agent
Pregnancy risk category: C

Indications and dosages

▶ **Treatment of increased intraocular pressure (IOP) in patients with ocular hypertension or open-angle glaucoma.** *Adults:* Instill 1 drop in the conjunctival sac of affected eye t.i.d.

Contraindications and precautions

- Contraindicated in patients hypersensitive to any component of drug or in those with impaired renal function.
- Use cautiously in patients with impaired hepatic function.

Lifespan: In breast-feeding women, drug isn't recommended because it's unknown if it appears in breast milk. In children, safety and effectiveness haven't been established. In elderly patients, use cautiously because they may have greater sensitivity to drug.

Adverse reactions

CNS: asthenia, fatigue, headache, dizziness, paresthesia.

EENT: *ocular burning, stinging, discomfort; superficial punctate keratitis; ocular allergic reactions (including conjunctivitis, itching, and lid reactions);* blurred vision; lacrimation; dryness; photophobia; iridocyclitis; redness; transient myopia; eyelid crusting; ocular pain; throat irritation.
GI: *bitter taste,* nausea.
GU: urolithiasis.
Respiratory: ***bronchospasm,*** dyspnea.
Skin: rash, pruritus, urticaria, contact dermatitis.
Other: ***angioedema.***

Interactions

Drug-drug. *Oral carbonic anhydrase inhibitors:* May cause additive effects. Don't use together.
Topical beta-adrenergic blockers: May cause additive effects. Give drugs 10 minutes apart.

Effects on lab tests results

- May decrease potassium and pH levels.

Pharmacokinetics

Absorption: Reaches the systemic circulation when applied topically.
Distribution: 33% bound to plasma proteins. Accumulates in RBCs during chronic dosing as a result of binding to carbonic anhydrase II.
Metabolism: Metabolized in the liver by cytochrome P450 isoenzymes.
Excretion: Primarily excreted unchanged in urine. *Half-life:* 120 days.

Route	Onset	Peak	Duration
Ophthalmic	1-2 hours	2-3 hours	8 hours

Pharmacodynamics

Chemical effect: Dorzolamide inhibits carbonic anhydrase in the ciliary processes of the eye. By inhibiting carbonic anhydrase, aqueous humor secretion is reduced, presumably by slowing the formation of bicarbonate ions with subsequent reduction in sodium and fluid transport.
Therapeutic effect: Reduces IOP.

Available forms

Ophthalmic solution: 2%

NURSING PROCESS

Assessment

- Assess patient before starting therapy.
- Because dorzolamide is a sulfonamide and is absorbed systemically, the adverse allergic reactions caused by sulfonamides, such as Stevens-Johnson syndrome, agranulocytosis, and aplastic anemia, may occur. Although these symptoms haven't been shown with dorzolamide hydrochloide, be alert for any signs and symptoms of them during therapy.
- Overdose may result in electrolyte imbalance, acidosis, and possible CNS effects. Monitor electrolyte levels (especially potassium) and pH levels. Treatment is supportive.
- Evaluate patient's and family's understanding of drug therapy.

Nursing diagnoses

- Risk for infection to the eyes related to inadvertent contamination of the multidose container
- Disturbed visual perception related to underlying ocular condition
- Deficient knowledge related to drug therapy

Planning and implementation

- If patient is wearing contact lenses, remove lenses before administration. Contact lenses may be reinserted 15 minutes after administration.
- Apply light finger pressure on lacrimal sac for 1 minute after instillation to minimize systemic absorption of drug.
- If more than one topical ophthalmic drug is being used, give drugs at least 10 minutes apart.

Patient teaching

- Teach patient how to instill drops properly. Advise him to wash hands before and after instilling solution, and warn him not to touch dropper or tip to eye or surrounding tissue to prevent contamination to the dropper.
- Instruct patient to remove contact lenses, if any, before administration and to reinsert 15 minutes after dosage.
- Advise patient to report ocular reactions, particularly conjunctivitis and lid reactions, immediately to prescriber and to discontinue drug.

✓ Evaluation

- Patient doesn't suffer from any infection related to drug administration.
- Patient's underlying condition is resolved with drug therapy.
- Patient and family state understanding of drug therapy.

doxacurium chloride

(doks-uh-KYOO-ree-um KLOR-ighd)
Nuromax

Pharmacologic class: nondepolarizing neuromuscular blocker
Therapeutic class: skeletal muscle relaxant
Pregnancy risk category: C

Indications and dosages

▶ **To provide skeletal muscle relaxation during surgery as adjunct to general anesthesia.** Dosage is highly individualized. All times of onset and duration of neuromuscular blockade are averages, and considerable individual variation is normal.
Adults: 0.05 mg/kg rapid I.V. produces adequate conditions for endotracheal intubation in 5 minutes in about 90% of patients when used as part of thiopental-narcotic induction technique. Lower doses may require longer delay before intubation is possible. Neuromuscular blockade at this dose lasts for average of 100 minutes.
Children older than age 2: Initial dose of 0.03 mg/kg I.V. given during halothane anesthesia produces effective blockade in 7 minutes with duration of 30 minutes. Under same conditions, 0.05 mg/kg produces blockade in 4 minutes with duration of 45 minutes.
▶ **Maintenance of neuromuscular blockade during long procedures.** *Adults and children:* After initial dose of 0.05 mg/kg I.V., maintenance doses of 0.005 to 0.01 mg/kg prolong neuromuscular blockade for an average of 30 minutes. Children usually require more frequent administration of maintenance doses.

Contraindications and precautions

- Contraindicated in patients hypersensitive to drug. Because of lack of data supporting safety, this drug isn't recommended for patients requiring prolonged mechanical ventilation in ICU, before or after administration of nondepolarizing neuromuscular blocking agents, or during cesarean delivery.
- Use cautiously, possibly at reduced dosage, in debilitated patients; patients with metastatic cancer, severe electrolyte disturbances, or neuromuscular diseases; and patients in whom neuromuscular blockade may be difficult to initiate or reverse. Patients with myasthenia gravis or myasthenic syndrome (Eaton-Lambert syndrome) are particularly sensitive to effects of nondepolarizing relaxants. Shorter-acting agents are recommended for use in such patients.

Lifespan: In breast-feeding women, use cautiously. In infants younger than age 2, safety of drug hasn't been established. In neonates, use is contraindicated because drug contains benzyl ethanol, which has been linked to fatalities in neonates.

Adverse reactions

Musculoskeletal: prolonged muscle weakness.
Respiratory: dyspnea, ***respiratory depression, respiratory insufficiency or apnea.***

Interactions

Drug-drug. *Aminoglycosides (gentamicin, kanamycin, neomycin, streptomycin), bacitracin, colistimethate, colistin, polymyxin B, tetracyclines:* May potentiate neuromuscular blockade, leading to increased skeletal muscle relaxation and prolongation of effect. Use together cautiously.
Carbamazepine, phenytoin: May prolong time to maximal block or shorten duration of block with neuromuscular blocking agents. Monitor patient closely.
Inhaled anesthetics, quinidine: May enhance activity or prolong action of nondepolarizing neuromuscular blockers. Monitor patient closely.
Magnesium salts: May enhance neuromuscular blockade. Monitor patient for excessive weakness.

Effects on lab test results

None reported.

Pharmacokinetics

Absorption: Administered I.V.
Distribution: Plasma protein–binding is about 30% in human plasma.
Metabolism: Thought not to be metabolized.

Excretion: Eliminated primarily unchanged in urine and bile. *Half-life:* 86 to 123 minutes.

Route	Onset	Peak	Duration
I.V.	≤ 5 min	3-9 min	1-4 hr

Pharmacodynamics

Chemical effect: Competes with acetylcholine for receptor sites at motor end plate. Because cholinesterase inhibitors may antagonize this action, doxacurium is considered a competitive antagonist.

Therapeutic effect: Relaxes skeletal muscles.

Available forms

Injection: 1 mg/ml

NURSING PROCESS

Assessment

- Obtain history of patient's underlying condition before therapy.
- Monitor patient continuously throughout drug administration.
- Be alert for adverse reactions and drug interactions.
- Because drug has minimal vagolytic action, watch for bradycardia, which may occur during anesthesia.
- Monitor respirations closely until patient is fully recovered from neuromuscular blockade, as evidenced by tests of muscle strength (hand grip, head lift, and ability to cough).
- Evaluate patient's and family's knowledge of drug therapy.

Nursing diagnoses

- Ineffective health maintenance related to underlying condition
- Impaired spontaneous ventilation related to drug's effects on respiratory muscles
- Deficient knowledge related to drug therapy

Planning and implementation

- To avoid distress to patient, don't give drug until patient's consciousness is obtunded by general anesthetic. Doxacurium has no effect on consciousness or pain threshold.
- Dosage should be adjusted to ideal body weight in obese patients (patients 30% or more above their ideal weight) to avoid prolonged neuromuscular blockade.
- Use drug only under direct medical supervision by personnel skilled in use of neuromuscular blocking agents and techniques for maintaining patent airway. Don't use unless facilities and equipment for intubation, mechanical ventilation, oxygen therapy, and drug antagonist are within reach.
- Patients with severe burns and some patients with severe liver disease may need higher initial doses. Higher doses (0.8 mg/kg) produce intubating conditions more rapidly (4 minutes), with neuromuscular blockade lasting 160 minutes or longer. Consequently, higher doses should be reserved for long procedures. Administration during steady-state anesthesia with enflurane, halothane, or isoflurane may allow 33% reduction of dose.
- Prepare drug for I.V. use with D_5W, normal saline solution injection, dextrose 5% in normal saline solution injection, lactated Ringer's injection, or dextrose 5% in lactated Ringer's injection.
- When diluted as directed, doxacurium is compatible with alfentanil, fentanyl, and sufentanil.
- Product should be given immediately after reconstitution. Diluted solutions are stable for 24 hours at room temperature; however, because reconstitution dilutes preservative, risk of contamination increases. Unused solutions should be discarded after 8 hours.
- Acid-base and electrolyte balance may influence actions of nondepolarizing neuromuscular blockers. Alkalosis may counteract paralysis, and acidosis may enhance it.
- Nerve stimulator and train-of-four monitoring are recommended to document antagonism of neuromuscular blockade and recovery of muscle strength. Before attempting pharmacologic reversal with neostigmine, some evidence of spontaneous recovery should be evident.
- Provide respiratory support as needed.
- Give pain medication regularly if pain is thought to be present; patient may experience pain but not be able to show it.

Patient teaching

- If patient isn't under influence of anesthesia, talk to him and keep him informed of surroundings because drug doesn't affect consciousness. Reassure him that all his vital needs are being met and that he's being monitored constantly.

Evaluation

- Patient shows improvement in underlying condition.
- Patient regains ability to maintain spontaneous ventilation after effects of drug have subsided.
- Patient and family state understanding of drug therapy.

doxapram hydrochloride

(DOKS-uh-prahm high-droh-KLOR-ighd)
Dopram

Pharmacologic class: analeptic
Therapeutic class: CNS and respiratory stimulant
Pregnancy risk category: B

Indications and dosages

▶ **Postanesthesia respiratory stimulation, drug-induced CNS depression, chronic pulmonary disease with acute hypercapnia.** *Adults:* 0.5 to 1 mg/kg of body weight (up to 2 mg/kg in CNS depression) by I.V. injection or infusion. Repeated q 5 minutes, if needed. Maximum, 4 mg/kg, up to 3 g daily.

▶ **COPD.** *Adults:* 1 to 2 mg/minute by I.V. infusion. Maximum, 3 mg/minute for maximum duration of 2 hours.

Contraindications and precautions

- Contraindicated in patients with seizure disorders; head injury; CV disorders; frank, uncompensated heart failure; severe hypertension; CVA; respiratory failure or incompetence secondary to neuromuscular disorders, muscle paresis, flail chest, obstructed airway, pulmonary embolism, pneumothorax, restrictive respiratory disease, acute bronchial asthma, or extreme dyspnea; or hypoxia not related to hypercapnia.
- Use cautiously in patients with bronchial asthma, severe tachycardia or arrhythmias, cerebral edema or increased CSF pressure, hyperthyroidism, pheochromocytoma, or metabolic disorders.

Lifespan: With pregnant women, use cautiously. In breast-feeding women and children, safety of drug hasn't been established.

Adverse reactions

CNS: ***seizures, headache,*** dizziness, apprehension, disorientation, pupillary dilation, bilateral Babinski's signs, paresthesia, fever.
CV: *chest pain and tightness, variations in heart rate, hypertension,* depressed T waves, ***arrhythmias,*** flushing.
EENT: sneezing, ***laryngospasm.***
GI: nausea, vomiting, diarrhea.
GU: urine retention, bladder stimulation with incontinence.
Musculoskeletal: muscle spasms.
Respiratory: hiccups, rebound hypoventilation, cough, ***bronchospasm,*** dyspnea.
Skin: pruritus, diaphoresis.

Interactions

Drug-drug. *MAO inhibitors, sympathomimetics:* May potentiate adverse CV effects. Use together cautiously.

Effects on lab test results

- May increase BUN levels.
- May decrease hemoglobin, hematocrit, and erythrocyte, WBC, and RBC counts.

Pharmacokinetics

Absorption: Administered I.V.
Distribution: Distributed throughout body.
Metabolism: 99% metabolized by liver.
Excretion: Metabolites excreted in urine.

Route	Onset	Peak	Duration
I.V.	20-40 sec	1-2 min	5-12 min

Pharmacodynamics

Chemical effect: Not clearly defined; acts either directly on central respiratory centers in medulla or indirectly on chemoreceptors.
Therapeutic effect: Stimulates respirations.

Available forms

Injection: 20 mg/ml (benzyl alcohol 0.9%)

NURSING PROCESS

Assessment

- Obtain history of patient's underlying condition before therapy.
- Assess blood pressure, heart rate, deep tendon reflexes, and arterial blood gases before giving drug, and closely throughout therapy.

• Monitor effectiveness by observing patient for improvement in CNS and respiratory function.
• Be alert for adverse reactions and drug interactions.
• Evaluate patient's (if appropriate) and family's knowledge of drug therapy.

Nursing diagnoses

• Ineffective breathing pattern related to underlying condition
• Risk for trauma related to potential for drug-induced seizure activity
• Deficient knowledge related to drug therapy

Planning and implementation

• Establish adequate airway before giving drug. Prevent patient from aspirating vomitus by placing him on his side. Have suction equipment nearby.
• Give drug slowly; rapid infusion may cause hemolysis. Doxapram is physically incompatible with strongly alkaline drugs such as thiopental sodium, aminophylline, and sodium bicarbonate.
• Avoid extravasation, which may lead to thrombophlebitis and local skin irritation.
• Drug is used only in surgical- or emergency-department situations.
• Discontinue drug and notify prescriber if patient shows signs of increased arterial carbon dioxide or oxygen tension, or if mechanical ventilation is started.

Patient teaching

• If patient is alert, instruct him to report chest pain or tightness immediately.

Evaluation

• Patient regains normal respiratory pattern.
• Patient has no seizures as result of therapy.
• Patient and family state understanding of drug therapy.

doxazosin mesylate

(doks-AY-zoh-sin MES-ih-layt)
Cardura

Pharmacologic class: alpha-adrenergic blocker
Therapeutic class: antihypertensive
Pregnancy risk category: C

Indications and dosages

▶ **Essential hypertension.** *Adults:* Initially, 1 mg P.O. daily. If necessary, increase to 2 mg daily. To minimize adverse reactions, adjust dosage slowly (typically increased only q 2 weeks). If necessary, increase to 4 mg daily; then to 8 mg. Maximum, 16 mg daily, but dosage above 4 mg daily increases risk of adverse reactions.

▶ **BPH.** *Adults:* Initially, 1 mg P.O. once daily morning or evening; may increase to 2 mg and, thereafter, to 4 mg and to 8 mg once daily p.r.n. Recommended adjustment interval is 1 to 2 weeks.

Contraindications and precautions

• Contraindicated in patients hypersensitive to drug and to quinazoline derivatives (including prazosin and terazosin).
• Use cautiously in patients with impaired liver function.

Lifespan: In pregnant women, use cautiously. In breast-feeding women, drug isn't recommended because it accumulates in breast milk at levels about 20 times greater than those in maternal plasma. In children, safety hasn't been established.

Adverse reactions

CNS: *dizziness,* vertigo, *asthenia, headache,* somnolence, drowsiness, pain.
CV: *orthostatic hypotension,* hypotension, edema, palpitations, ***arrhythmias,*** tachycardia.
EENT: rhinitis, pharyngitis, abnormal vision.
GI: nausea, vomiting, diarrhea, constipation.
Musculoskeletal: arthralgia, myalgia.
Respiratory: dyspnea.
Skin: rash, pruritus.

Interactions

Drug-drug. *Clonidine:* May decrease clonidine effects. Dosage adjustments may be necessary.
Drug-herb. *Butcher's broom:* May reduce effects of drug. Discourage using together.

Effects on lab test results

• May decrease WBC and neutrophil counts.

Pharmacokinetics

Absorption: Readily absorbed from GI tract.
Distribution: 98% protein-bound.
Metabolism: Extensively metabolized in liver.

Excretion: 63% excreted in bile and feces; 9% excreted in urine. *Half-life:* 19 to 22 hours.

Route	Onset	Peak	Duration
P.O.	1-2 hr	5-6 hr	24 hr

Pharmacodynamics

Chemical effect: Acts on peripheral vasculature to produce vasodilation.
Therapeutic effect: Lowers blood pressure.

Available forms

Tablets: 1 mg, 2 mg, 4 mg, 8 mg

NURSING PROCESS

Assessment
- Obtain history of patient's blood pressure before therapy, and reassess regularly thereafter.
- Determine effect on standing and supine blood pressure at 2 to 6 hours and 24 hours after administration.
- Be alert for adverse reactions.
- Monitor patient's ECG for arrhythmias.
- Evaluate patient's and family's knowledge of drug therapy.

Nursing diagnoses
- Risk for injury related to presence of hypertension
- Decreased cardiac output related to drug-induced adverse CV reactions
- Deficient knowledge related to drug therapy

Planning and implementation
- Dosage must be increased gradually, with adjustments every 2 weeks for hypertension and every 1 to 2 weeks for BPH.
- If syncope occurs, place patient in recumbent position and treat supportively. A transient hypotensive response isn't considered a contraindication to continued therapy.

Patient teaching
- Advise patient taking doxazosin that he's susceptible to a first-dose effect similar to that produced by other alpha-adrenergic blockers—marked orthostatic hypotension accompanied by dizziness or syncope. Orthostatic hypotension is most common after first dose, but it also can occur when therapy is interrupted or dosages are adjusted.
- Warn patient that dizziness or fainting may occur. Advise patient to refrain from driving and performing other hazardous activities until drug's adverse CNS effects are known.
- Stress importance of regular follow-up visits.

Evaluation
- Patient's blood pressure becomes normal.
- Patient maintains adequate cardiac output throughout therapy.
- Patient and family state understanding of drug therapy.

doxepin hydrochloride

(DOKS-eh-pin high-droh-KLOR-ighd)
Novo-Doxepin ◆, Sinequan, Triadapin ◆

Pharmacologic class: tricyclic antidepressant
Therapeutic class: antidepressant
Pregnancy risk category: C

Indications and dosages

▶ **Depression, anxiety.** *Adults:* Initially, 25 to 75 mg P.O. daily in divided doses to maximum of 300 mg daily. Or, entire maintenance dose may be given once daily with maximum dose of 150 mg P.O.

Dosage should be reduced in elderly or debilitated patients, adolescents, and those receiving other drugs (especially anticholinergics).

Contraindications and precautions

- Contraindicated in patients hypersensitive to drug and in those with glaucoma or a tendency for urine retention.

Lifespan: In pregnant women and children younger than age 12, safety of drug hasn't been established. In breast-feeding women, use isn't recommended.

Adverse reactions

CNS: *drowsiness, dizziness,* excitation, tremors, weakness, confusion, headache, nervousness, EEG changes, ***seizures,*** extrapyramidal reactions, ataxia, paresthesia, hallucinations.
CV: *orthostatic hypotension, tachycardia, ECG changes,* hypertension.
EENT: *blurred vision,* tinnitus, mydriasis.
GI: *dry mouth, glossitis, constipation,* nausea, vomiting, anorexia.

GU: *urine retention.*
Hematologic: eosinophilia, ***bone marrow depression, including leukopenia, thrombocytopenia, aplastic anemia, and agranulocytosis.***
Skin: rash, urticaria, photosensitivity.
Other: *diaphoresis,* ***hypersensitivity reaction.***

Interactions

Drug-drug. *Barbiturates, CNS depressants:* May enhance CNS depression. Avoid using together.
Cimetidine, fluoxetine, sertraline, methylphenidate: May increase doxepin levels. Monitor patient for increased adverse reactions.
Clonidine, epinephrine, norepinephrine: May increase hypertensive effect. Use cautiously; monitor blood pressure closely.
MAO inhibitors: May cause severe excitation, hyperpyrexia, or seizures, usually with high dosage. Avoid using together.
Drug-herb. *St. John's wort, SAMe, yohimbe:* May elevate serotonin levels. Discourage using together.
Drug-food. *Carbonated beverages, grape juice:* Drug is physically incompatible with these beverages. Discourage using together.
Drug-lifestyle. *Alcohol use:* May enhance CNS depression. Discourage using together.
Sun exposure: Increases risk of photosensitivity reactions. Discourage unprotected or prolonged exposure to the sun.

Effects on lab test results

- May increase or decrease glucose levels.
- May increase liver function test values and eosinophil count. May decrease hemoglobin, hematocrit, and RBC, WBC, granulocyte, and platelet counts.

Pharmacokinetics

Absorption: Absorbed rapidly from GI tract.
Distribution: Distributed widely in body, including CNS; 90% protein-bound.
Metabolism: Metabolized by liver. A significant first-pass effect may explain variability of serum levels in different patients taking same dosage.
Excretion: Most of drug excreted in urine.

Route	Onset	Peak	Duration
P.O.	Unknown	≤ 2 hr	Unknown

Pharmacodynamics

Chemical effect: Unknown; increases amount of norepinephrine, serotonin, or both in CNS by blocking their reuptake by presynaptic neurons.
Therapeutic effect: Relieves depression and anxiety.

Available forms

Capsules: 10 mg, 25 mg, 50 mg, 75 mg, 100 mg, 150 mg
Oral concentrate: 10 mg/ml

NURSING PROCESS

Assessment

- Assess patient's depression or anxiety before and during therapy.
- Be alert for adverse reactions and drug interactions.
- Evaluate patient's and family's knowledge of drug therapy.

Nursing diagnoses

- Ineffective individual coping related to underlying condition
- Risk for injury related to drug-induced adverse CNS reactions
- Deficient knowledge related to drug therapy

Planning and implementation

- Dilute oral concentrate with 120 ml of water, milk, or juice (except grape juice). Don't mix with carbonated beverages because of incompatibility.
- Don't withdraw drug abruptly. Abrupt withdrawal of long-term therapy may cause nausea, headache, and malaise, which don't indicate addiction.
- Because hypertensive episodes have occurred during surgery in patients receiving tricyclic antidepressants, drug should be discontinued gradually several days before surgery.
- If signs of psychosis occur or increase, notify prescriber and expect dosage to be reduced.

Patient teaching

- Tell patient to dilute oral concentrate with 120 ml of water, milk, or juice (orange, grapefruit, tomato, prune, or pineapple). Drug is incompatible with carbonated beverages and grape juice.

• Advise patient to take full dose at bedtime, but warn of possible morning orthostatic hypotension.
• Warn patient to avoid hazardous activities that require alertness and good psychomotor coordination until CNS effects of drug are known. Drowsiness and dizziness usually subside after a few weeks.
• Tell patient to avoid alcohol during drug therapy.
• Warn patient not to stop drug therapy suddenly.
• Advise patient to consult prescriber before taking prescription drugs, OTC medications, or herbal remedies.
• Advise patient to use sunblock, wear protective clothing, and avoid prolonged exposure to strong sunlight.

☑ Evaluation

• Patient behavior and communication indicate improvement of depression or anxiety.
• Patient has no injury as result of drug-induced adverse CNS reactions.
• Patient and family state understanding of drug therapy.

doxercalciferol

(dox-er-kal-SIF-eh-rol)
Hectorol

Pharmacologic class: synthetic vitamin D analogue
Therapeutic class: parathyroid hormone antagonist
Pregnancy risk category: B

Indications and dosages

▶ **Reduction of elevated intact parathyroid hormone (PTH) levels in the management of secondary hyperparathyroidism in patients undergoing long-term renal dialysis.** *Adults:* Initially, 10 mcg P.O. three times weekly at dialysis. Dosage adjusted as needed to lower intact PTH levels to 150 to 300 pg/ml. Dosage may be increased by 2.5 mcg at 8-week intervals if the intact PTH level isn't decreased by 50% and fails to reach target range. Maximum, 20 mcg P.O. three times weekly. If intact PTH levels fall below 100 pg/ml, drug should be suspended for 1 week and then resumed at a dose that's at least 2.5 mcg lower than the last administered dose.

Contraindications and precautions

• Contraindicated in patients with a recent history of hypercalcemia, hyperphosphatemia, or vitamin D toxicity.
• Use cautiously in patients with hepatic insufficiency, and frequently monitor calcium, phosphorus, and intact PTH levels in these patients.
Lifespan: In breast-feeding women and children younger than age 12, drug isn't recommended. In elderly patients, use cautiously because adverse CNS reactions, orthostatic hypotension, and GI and GU distresses are more likely to develop.

Adverse reactions

CNS: *dizziness, headache, malaise,* sleep disorder.
CV: ***bradycardia,*** edema.
GI: anorexia, dyspepsia, *nausea, vomiting,* constipation.
Metabolic: weight gain or loss.
Musculoskeletal: arthralgia.
Respiratory: *dyspnea.*
Skin: pruritus.
Other: abscess.

Interactions

Drug-drug. *Cholestyramine, mineral oil:* Reduces intestinal absorption of doxercalciferol. Avoid using together.
Glutethimide, phenobarbital, and other enzyme inducers; phenytoin and other enzyme inhibitors: May affect doxercalciferol metabolism. Adjust dosage as directed.
Magnesium-containing antacids: May cause hypermagnesemia. Monitor patient for toxicity.
Calcium-containing or non-aluminum-containing phosphate binders: May cause hypercalcemia or hyperphosphatemia and decrease effectiveness of doxercalciferol. Use cautiously together, and adjust dosage of phosphate binders as directed.
Vitamin D supplements: May cause additive effects and hypercalcemia. Monitor patient for toxicity.
Orlistat: May interfere with intestinal absorption of vitamin D analogues. Give drug at least 2 hours before or 2 hours after Orlistat administration.

Effects on lab test results

None reported.

Pharmacokinetics

Absorption: Absorbed from the GI tract.
Distribution: Unknown.
Metabolism: Metabolized to its active forms in the liver.
Excretion: Major metabolite of doxercalciferol attains peak blood levels at 11 to 12 hours after repeated oral doses. *Elimination half-life:* 32 to 37 hours, with a range of up to 96 hours.

Route	Onset	Peak	Duration
P.O.	Unknown	11-12 hr	Unknown

Pharmacodynamics

Chemical effect: Once activated, doxercalciferol and other biologically active vitamin D metabolites regulate calcium levels required for essential body functions. Doxercalciferol acts directly on the parathyroid glands to suppress PTH synthesis and secretion.
Therapeutic effect: Reduces elevated intact PTH levels.

Available forms

Capsules: 2.5 mcg

NURSING PROCESS

Assessment

- Assess hepatic function before starting therapy.
- Monitor calcium, phosphorus, and intact PTH levels. Monitor them more frequently in patients with hepatic insufficiency.
- Be alert for adverse reactions and drug interactions.
- Evaluate patient's and family's knowledge about drug therapy.

Nursing diagnoses

- Imbalanced nutrition: less than body requirements related to adverse GI effects
- Risk for injury related to adverse CNS effects
- Deficient knowledge related to drug therapy

Planning and implementation

- Give doxercalciferol with dialysis (about every other day). Dosing must be individualized and based on intact PTH levels, with monitoring of calcium and phosphorus levels before doxercalciferol therapy and weekly thereafter.
- If patient has hypercalcemia or hyperphosphatemia, or if the product of serum calcium 2 serum phosphorus (Ca 2 P) is greater than 70, immediately stop doxercalciferol until these values decrease.
- Progressive hypercalcemia from vitamin D overdose may require emergency attention. Acute hypercalcemia may worsen arrhythmias and seizures and affects the action of digoxin. Chronic hypercalcemia can lead to vascular and soft-tissue calcification.
- Calcium-based or non-aluminum-containing phosphate binders and a low-phosphate diet are used to control phosphorus levels in patients undergoing dialysis. Expect dosage adjustments in doxercalciferol and concurrent therapies, such as dietary phosphate binders, to sustain PTH suppression and to maintain calcium and phosphorus levels within acceptable ranges.

Patient teaching

- Inform patient that dosage must be adjusted over several months to achieve satisfactory PTH suppression.
- Tell patient to adhere to a low-phosphorus diet and to follow instructions regarding calcium supplementation.
- Tell patient to obtain prescriber's approval before using OTC drugs, including antacids and vitamin preparations containing calcium or vitamin D.
- Inform patient that early signs and symptoms of hypercalcemia include weakness, headache, somnolence, nausea, vomiting, dry mouth, constipation, muscle pain, bone pain, and metallic taste. Late signs and symptoms include polyuria, polydipsia, anorexia, weight loss, nocturia, conjunctivitis, pancreatitis, photophobia, rhinorrhea, pruritus, hyperthermia, decreased libido, hypertension, and arrhythmias.

Evaluation

- Patient has no nausea and vomiting.
- Patient remains free from injury.
- Patient and family state understanding of drug therapy.

doxorubicin hydrochloride

(doks-oh-ROO-bih-sin high-droh-KLOR-ighd)

Adriamycin ◇, Adriamycin PFS, Adriamycin RDF, Rubex

Pharmacologic class: antineoplastic antibiotic (cell cycle–phase nonspecific)
Therapeutic class: antineoplastic
Pregnancy risk category: D

Indications and dosages

▶ **Bladder, breast, lung, ovarian, stomach, testicular, and thyroid cancers; Hodgkin's disease; acute lymphoblastic and myeloblastic leukemia; Wilms' tumor; neuroblastoma; lymphoma; sarcoma.** *Adults:* 60 to 75 mg/m^2 I.V. as single dose q 3 weeks; or 30 mg/m^2 I.V. in single daily dose on days 1 through 3 of 4-week cycle. Alternatively, 20 mg/m^2 I.V. once weekly. Maximum cumulative dose is 550 mg/m^2.

Contraindications and precautions

• Contraindicated in patients with marked myelosuppression induced by previous treatment with other antitumor drugs or radiotherapy and in those who have received lifetime cumulative dose of 550 mg/m^2.

Lifespan: In pregnant and breast-feeding women, drug isn't recommended. In children, safety of drug hasn't been established.

Adverse reactions

CV: cardiac depression, seen in such ECG changes as sinus tachycardia, T-wave flattening, ST-segment depression, voltage reduction; ***arrhythmias; irreversible cardiomyopathy.***
EENT: conjunctivitis.
GI: *nausea, vomiting,* diarrhea, *stomatitis,* esophagitis, anorexia.
GU: transient red urine.
Hematologic: ***leukopenia*** during days 10 through 15, with recovery by day 21; ***thrombocytopenia;*** **MYELOSUPPRESSION.**
Skin: *complete alopecia;* urticaria; facial flushing; *hyperpigmentation of nails, dermal creases, or skin* (especially in previously irradiated areas).
Other: *severe cellulitis or tissue sloughing if drug extravasates,* hyperuricemia, ***anaphylaxis.***

Interactions

Drug-drug. *Calcium channel blockers:* May potentiate cardiotoxic effects. Monitor patient closely.
Digoxin: May decrease digoxin levels. Monitor patient closely.
Phenytoin: Decreases levels of phenytoin. Check levels.
Streptozocin: May increase and prolong blood levels. Dosage may need adjustment.
Drug-herb. *Green tea:* May enhance antitumor effects of doxorubicin. Urge patient to discuss with prescriber before using together.

Effects on lab test results

• May increase bilirubin and glucose levels. May decrease calcium levels.
• May decrease hemoglobin, hematocrit, and WBC, neutrophil, and platelet counts.

Pharmacokinetics

Absorption: Administered I.V.
Distribution: Distributed widely in body tissues; doesn't cross blood-brain barrier.
Metabolism: Extensively metabolized by hepatic microsomal enzymes to several metabolites, one of which possesses cytotoxic activity.
Excretion: Excreted primarily in bile, minimally in urine. *Half-life:* Initial, 30 minutes; terminal, 16½ hours.

Route	Onset	Peak	Duration
I.V.	Unknown	Unknown	Unknown

Pharmacodynamics

Chemical effect: Unknown; thought to interfere with DNA-dependent RNA synthesis by intercalation.
Therapeutic effect: Hinders or kills certain cancer cells.

Available forms

Injection (preservative-free): 2 mg/ml
Powder for injection: 10-mg, 20-mg, 50-mg, 100-mg, 150-mg vials

NURSING PROCESS

Assessment

• Obtain history of patient's neoplastic disorder before therapy, and reassess regularly thereafter.
• Assess ECG before treatment.

• Monitor CBC and liver function tests; monitor ECG monthly during therapy.
• Be alert for adverse reactions and drug interactions.
• Evaluate patient's and family's knowledge of drug therapy.

Nursing diagnoses

• Ineffective health maintenance related to presence of neoplastic disease
• Decreased cardiac output related to drug-induced cardiotoxicity
• Deficient knowledge related to drug therapy

Planning and implementation

• To reduce nausea, premedicate with antiemetic.
• Follow facility policy to reduce risks. Preparation and administration of parenteral form create carcinogenic, mutagenic, and teratogenic risks for staff.
• Dosage may need adjustment in elderly patients and those with myelosuppression or impaired cardiac or hepatic function.
• Never give this drug by I.M. or S.C. route.
ALERT: Red color of doxorubicin is similar to that of daunorubicin. Take care to avoid confusing these two drugs.
• Reconstitute using preservative-free normal saline solution injection. Add 5 ml to 10-mg vial, 10 ml to 20-mg vial, or 25 ml to 50-mg vial. Shake vial, and allow drug to dissolve; final concentration is 2 mg/ml. Give by direct injection into I.V. line of free-flowing compatible I.V. solution containing D_5W or normal saline solution injection.
• Avoid extravasation; don't place I.V. line over joints or in limbs with poor venous or lymphatic drainage.
• If extravasation occurs, stop I.V. infusion immediately, notify prescriber, and apply ice to area for 24 to 48 hours. Monitor area closely because extravasation reaction may be progressive. Early consultation with plastic surgeon may be advisable.
• Precipitate may form if drug is mixed with aminophylline, cephalothin, dexamethasone, fluorouracil, heparin, or hydrocortisone.
• If skin or mucosal contact occurs, immediately wash area with soap and water.
• In case of leak or spill, inactivate drug with 5% sodium hypochlorite solution (household bleach).
• Be prepared to stop drug or slow rate of infusion if tachycardia develops; notify prescriber.
• Stop drug immediately if signs of heart failure develop, and notify prescriber. Limit cumulative dosage to 550 mg/m² (400 mg/m² when patient also receives or has received cyclophosphamide or radiation therapy to cardiac area) to prevent heart failure.
• Alternative dosage schedule (once-weekly dosing) causes a lower risk of cardiomyopathy.
• If vein streaking occurs, slow administration rate. If welts occur, stop administration and notify prescriber.
• Be prepared to decrease dosage if bilirubin level is increased: 50% dosage when bilirubin level is 1.2 to 3 mg/dl; 25% dosage when bilirubin level is greater than 3 mg/dl.
• Refrigerated, reconstituted solution is stable for 48 hours; at room temperature, it's stable for 24 hours.
• Provide adequate hydration; alkalinizing urine or giving allopurinol may prevent or minimize uric acid nephropathy.
• Report adverse reactions to prescriber, and be prepared to provide supportive care to treat such reactions.
ALERT: Liposomal doxorubicin and conventional doxorubicin aren't interchangable. Plasma clearance of liposomal form is significantly reduced compared with the conventional form, requiring decreased dosing with liposomal doxorubicin.

Patient teaching

• Warn patient to watch for signs of infection (fever, sore throat, fatigue) and bleeding (easy bruising, nosebleeds, bleeding gums, melena). Have patient take temperature daily.
• Advise patient that orange to red urine for 1 to 2 days is normal and doesn't indicate presence of blood in urine.
• Tell patient that total alopecia may occur within 3 to 4 weeks. Hair may regrow 2 to 5 months after drug is stopped.
• Instruct patient to report symptoms of heart failure and other cardiac signs and symptoms promptly to prescriber.
• Tell patient to use safety precautions to prevent injury.

Evaluation

• Patient exhibits positive response to therapy, as noted on improved follow-up studies.

• Patient maintains adequate cardiac output throughout therapy.
• Patient and family state understanding of drug therapy.

doxorubicin hydrochloride liposomal

(doks-oh-ROO-bih-sin high-droh-KLOR-ighd li-po-SOE-mal)
Doxil

Pharmacologic class: anthracycline
Therapeutic class: antineoplastic
Pregnancy risk category: D

Indications and dosages

▶ **Metastatic carcinoma of the ovary in patients with disease refractory to paclitaxel- and platinum-based chemotherapy regimens.** *Adults:* 50 mg/m^2 (doxorubicin hydrochloride equivalent) I.V. at an initial infusion rate of 1 mg/minute once q 4 weeks for at least 4 courses. Continue treatment as long as patient doesn't progress, shows no evidence of cardiotoxicity, and continues to tolerate treatment. If no infusion-related adverse events are observed, increase infusion rate to complete administration over 1 hour.

▶ **AIDS-related Kaposi's sarcoma in patients with disease that has progressed with previous combination chemotherapy or in patients who are intolerant to such therapy.** *Adults:* 20 mg/m^2 (doxorubicin hydrochloride equivalent) I.V. over 30 minutes, once q 3 weeks, for as long as patient responds satisfactorily and tolerates treatment.

Contraindications and precautions

• Contraindicated in patients hypersensitive to the conventional form of doxorubicin hydrochloride or any component in the liposomal form. Also, contraindicated in patients with marked myelosuppression or those who have received a lifetime cumulative dose of 550 mg/m^2 (400 mg/m^2 if patient received radiotherapy to the mediastinal area or simultaneous therapy with other cardiotoxic drugs, such as cyclophosphamide).
• Use in patients with a history of cardiovascular disease only when benefit of drug outweighs risk to patient.
• Use cautiously in patients who have received other anthracycline. The total dose of doxorubicin hydrochloride should also take into account any previous or concomitant therapy with related compounds, such as daunorubicin. Heart failure and cardiomyopathy may occur after therapy stops.
Lifespan: In breast-feeding women, drug isn't recommended because it's unknown if it appears in breast milk. In children, safety and effectiveness haven't been established. In elderly patients, use cautiously because of a possible greater sensitivity to the drug.

Adverse reactions

CNS: fever, *asthenia,* paresthesia, headache, somnolence, dizziness, depression, insomnia, anxiety, malaise, emotional lability, fatigue.
CV: chest pain, hypotension, tachycardia, peripheral edema, ***cardiomyopathy, heart failure, arrhythmias,*** pericardial effusion.
EENT: *mucous membrane disorder,* mouth ulceration, pharyngitis, rhinitis, conjunctivitis, retinitis, optic neuritis.
GI: *nausea, vomiting, constipation, anorexia, diarrhea,* abdominal pain, taste perversion, dyspepsia, oral candidiasis, enlarged abdomen, esophagitis, dysphagia, *stomatitis,* glossitis.
GU: albuminuria.
Hematologic: ***leukopenia, neutropenia,*** **THROMBOCYTOPENIA**, anemia, ***increased PT.***
Hepatic: hyperbilirubinemia.
Metabolic: dehydration, weight loss, hypocalcemia, hyperglycemia.
Musculoskeletal: myalgia, back pain.
Respiratory: dyspnea, increased cough, pneumonia.
Skin: *rash, alopecia,* dry skin, pruritus, skin discoloration, skin disorder, exfoliative dermatitis, herpes zoster, sweating, *palmar-plantar erythrodysesthesia,* alopecia.
Other: ***allergic reaction,*** chills, infection, infusion-related reactions.

Interactions

None reported.

Effects on lab test results

• May increase bilirubin and glucose levels. May decrease calcium levels.
• May increase PT. May decrease hemoglobin, hematocrit, and WBC, neutrophil, and platelet counts.

Pharmacokinetics

Absorption: Administered I.V..
Distribution: Distributed mostly to vascular fluid. Plasma protein–binding hasn't been determined; however, plasma protein–binding of doxorubicin is about 70%.
Metabolism: Doxorubicinol, the major metabolite of doxorubicin, is detected at very low levels in plasma.
Excretion: Plasma elimination is slow and biphasic. *Half-life:* About 5 hours in the first phase, 55 hours in the second phase at doses of 10 to 20 mg/m^2.

Route	Onset	Peak	Duration
I.V.	Unknown	Unknown	Unknown

Pharmacodynamics

Chemical effect: Doxil is doxorubicin hydrochloride encapsulated in liposomes that, because of their small size and persistence in circulation, can penetrate the altered vasculature of tumors. The mechanism of action of doxorubicin hydrochloride is probably related to its ability to bind DNA and inhibit nucleic acid synthesis.
Therapeutic effect: Hinders or kills certain cancer cells in patients with ovarian cancer or AIDS-related Kaposi's sarcoma.

Available forms

Injection: 2 mg/ml

NURSING PROCESS

Assessment

- Obtain an accurate medication list from patient, including previous or current chemotherapeutic drugs.
- Evaluate patient's hepatic function before therapy, and adjust dosage accordingly.
- Monitor cardiac function closely by endomyocardial biopsy, echocardiography, or gated radionuclide scans. If results indicate possible cardiac injury, the benefit of continued therapy must be weighed against the risk of myocardial injury.
- Be alert for adverse reactions.
- Evaluate patient's and family's knowledge about drug therapy.

Nursing diagnoses

- Risk for infection related to myelosuppression
- Risk for injury related to drug-induced adverse reactions
- Deficient knowledge related to drug therapy

Planning and implementation

- Patients with impaired hepatic function need a reduced dosage.
- Dosage modifications are recommended for managing adverse reactions, including palmar-plantar erythrodysesthesia, hematologic toxicity, and stomatitis.
- Follow facility procedures for proper handling and disposal of antineoplastic drugs.

ALERT: Carefully check label on the I.V. bag before giving drug. Accidentally substituting Doxil for conventional doxorubicin hydrochloride can cause severe adverse effects. Dilute appropriate dose (maximum, 90 mg) in 250 ml of D_5W using aseptic technique. Refrigerate diluted solution at 36° to 46° F (2° to 8° C), and give within 24 hours.

- Infuse I.V. over 30 to 60 minutes, depending on the dose. Don't use with in-line filters.
- Monitor patient carefully during infusion. Acute infusion reactions (flushing, shortness of breath, facial swelling, headache, chills, back pain, tightness in the chest or throat, or hypotension) may occur. These reactions resolve over several hours to a day once the infusion is stopped. The reaction may resolve by slowing the infusion rate.
- Don't give drug by I.M. or S.C. route. Avoid extravasation. If it occurs, stop infusion immediately and restart in another vein. Applying ice over the extravasation site for about 30 minutes may help to alleviate the local reaction.

ALERT: Doxil has unique pharmacokinetic properties and shouldn't be substituted on a mg-by-mg basis for conventional doxorubicin hydrochloride.

- No drug interactions have been reported; however, Doxil may interact with drugs known to interact with the conventional form of doxorubicin hydrochloride.
- Drug may potentiate the toxicity of other antineoplastic therapies.
- The total dose of doxorubicin hydrochloride should also take into account any previous or simultaneous therapy with related compounds, such as daunorubicin. Heart failure and cardiomyopathy may occur after therapy stops.
- Monitor CBC, including platelets, before each dose and frequently throughout therapy.

Leukopenia is usually transient. Hematologic toxicity may require dosage reduction or suspension or delay of therapy. Persistent severe myelosuppression may result in superinfection or hemorrhage. Patient may need granulocyte colony-stimulating factor (or granulocyte-macrophage colony-stimulating factor) to support blood counts.

Patient teaching

- Tell patient to notify prescriber about symptoms of hand-foot syndrome, such as tingling or burning, redness, flaking, bothersome swelling, small blisters, or small sores on the palms of hands or soles of feet.
- Advise patient to report symptoms of stomatitis, such as painful redness, swelling, or sores in the mouth.
- Advise patient to avoid exposure to people with infections. Tell patient to report fever of 100.5° F (38° C) or higher.
- Urge patient to report nausea, vomiting, tiredness, weakness, rash, or mild hair loss.
- Advise woman of childbearing age to avoid pregnancy during therapy.

☑ Evaluation

- Patient has no infection.
- Patient has no injury as a result of drug-induced adverse reactions.
- Patient and family state understanding of drug therapy.

doxycycline

(doks-ee-SIGH-kleen)

Doxylin ◇, Monodox, Vibramycin, Adoxa

doxycycline calcium

Vibramycin

doxycycline hyclate

Apo-Doxy ◆, BioTab, Doryx, DoxyCaps, Doxychel Hyclate, Doxytec ◆, Novo-Doxylin ◆, Periostat, Vibramycin, Vibra-Tabs, Vibramycin IV

doxycycline hydrochloride

Doryx ◇, Vibramycin ◇, Vibra-Tabs ◇

Pharmacologic class: tetracycline

Therapeutic class: antibiotic

Pregnancy risk category: D

Indications and dosages

▶ **Infections caused by sensitive gram-negative and gram-positive organisms, *Chlamydia, Mycoplasma, Rickettsia,* and organisms that cause trachoma.** *Adults and children weighing more than 45 kg (99 lb):* 100 mg P.O. q 12 hours on first day; then 100 mg P.O. daily. Or, 200 mg I.V. on first day in one or two infusions; then 100 to 200 mg I.V. daily. For severe infections 100 mg P.O. q 12 hours may be used.

Children older than age 8 and weighing less than 45 kg: 4.4 mg/kg P.O. or I.V. daily in divided doses q 12 hours on first day, then 2.2 to 4.4 mg/kg daily.

▶ **Gonorrhea in patients allergic to penicillin.** *Adults:* 100 mg P.O. b.i.d. for 7 days. Or, 300 mg P.O. initially; repeat dose in 1 hour.

▶ **Primary or secondary syphilis in patients allergic to penicillin.** *Adults and children age 8 and older:* 100 mg P.O. b.i.d. for 2 weeks (early detection) or for 4 weeks (if more than 1 year's duration).

▶ **Uncomplicated urethral, endocervical, or rectal infection caused by *Chlamydia trachomatis* or *Ureaplasma urealyticum.*** *Adults:* 100 mg P.O. b.i.d. for at least 7 days.

▶ **Prevention of malaria.** *Adults:* 100 mg P.O. daily.

Children older than age 8: 2 mg/kg P.O. once daily. Dosage shouldn't exceed adult dose. Therapy should begin 1 to 2 days before travel to malarious area and be continued throughout travel and for 4 weeks thereafter.

▶ **Adjunct to scaling and root planing to promote attachment level gain and to reduce pocket depth in patients with adult periodontitis. *Periostat.*** *Adults:* 20 mg P.O. b.i.d. more than 1 hour before or 2 hours after the morning and evening meals and after scaling and root planing. Effective for 9 months.

▶ **Adjunct to other antibiotics for inhalation, gastrointestinal, and oropharyngeal anthrax.** *Adults:* 100 mg I.V. q 12 hours initially until susceptibility test are known. Switch to 100 mg P.O. b.i.d. when clinically appropriate. Treat for 60 days total.

Children older than age 8 and weighing more than 45 kg: 100 mg I.V. q 12 hours, then

switch to 100 mg P.O. b.i.d. when clinically appropriate. Treat for 60 days total.
Children older than age 8 and weighing 45 kg or less: 2.2 mg/kg I.V. q 12 hours, then switch to 2.2 mg/kg P.O. b.i.d. when clinically appropriate. Treat for 60 days total.
Children age 8 and younger: 2.2 mg/kg I.V. q 12 hours, then switch to 2.2 mg/kg P.O. b.i.d. when clinically appropriate. Treat for 60 days total.

▶ **Cutaneous anthrax.** *Adults:* 100 mg P.O. b.i.d. for 60 days.
Children older than age 8 and weighing more than 45 kg: 100 mg P.O. q 12 hours for 60 days.
Children older than age 8 and weighing 45 kg or less: 2.2 mg/kg P.O. q 12 hours for 60 days.
Children age 8 and younger: 2.2 mg/kg P.O. q 12 hours for 60 days.

▶ **Adjunctive treatment of severe acne.** ***Adoxa.*** *Adults:* 200 mg P.O. on day 1 (give as 100 mg q 12 hours or 50 mg q 6 hrs); follow with a maintenance dose of 100 mg P.O. daily, or 50 mg P.O. b.i.d.

▶ **Prevention of traveler's diarrhea commonly caused by enterotoxigenic *E. coli*‡.** *Adults:* 100 mg P.O. daily for up to 3 days.

▶ **Prophylaxis for rape victims‡.** *Adults and adolescents:* 100 mg P.O. b.i.d. for 7 days after a single 2-g oral dose of metronidazole is given with a single 125-mg I.M. dose of ceftriaxone.

▶ **Lyme disease‡.** *Adults and children older than age 9:* 100 mg P.O. b.i.d. or t.i.d. for 10 to 30 days.

▶ **Pleural effusions related to cancer‡.** *Adults:* 500 mg of doxycycline diluted in 250 ml of normal saline solution and instilled into pleural space via chest tube.

Contraindications and precautions

- Contraindicated in patients hypersensitive to drug or other tetracyclines.
- Use cautiously in patients with impaired kidney or liver function.

Lifespan: In breast-feeding women, avoid use of drug. Pregnant women and immunocompromised patients should receive the usual doses and regimens for anthrax. During last half of pregnancy and in children younger than age 8, use of these drugs may cause permanent discoloration of teeth, enamel defects, and bone growth retardation. These effects are dose-limited; therefore, drug may be used for a short time (7 to 14 days) before 6 months of gestation.

Adverse reactions

CNS: ***intracranial hypertension (pseudotumor cerebri).***
CV: pericarditis, thrombophlebitis.
EENT: glossitis, dysphagia.
GI: anorexia, *epigastric distress, nausea,* vomiting, *diarrhea,* oral candidiasis, enterocolitis, anogenital inflammation.
Hematologic: ***neutropenia,*** eosinophilia, ***thrombocytopenia,*** hemolytic anemia.
Musculoskeletal: bone growth retardation if used in children under age 8.
Skin: *maculopapular and erythematous rash, photosensitivity, increased pigmentation, urticaria.*
Other: hypersensitivity reactions, ***anaphylaxis,*** superinfection, permanent discoloration of teeth, enamel defects.

Interactions

Drug-drug. *Antacids (including sodium bicarbonate) and laxatives containing aluminum, magnesium, or calcium; antidiarrheals:* May decrease antibiotic absorption. Give antibiotic 1 hour before or 2 hours after these drugs.
Ferrous sulfate and other iron products, zinc: May decrease antibiotic absorption. Give drug 3 hours after or 2 hours before iron administration.
Methoxyflurane: May cause nephrotoxicity with tetracyclines. Avoid using together.
Oral anticoagulants: May increase anticoagulant effect. Monitor PT and INR, and adjust dosage.
Hormonal contraceptives: Decreases contraceptive effectiveness and increased risk of breakthrough bleeding. Recommend nonhormonal form of birth control.
Penicillins: May interfere with bactericidal action of penicillins. Avoid using together.
Carbamazepine, phenobarbital: May decrease antibiotic effect. Avoid using together, if possible.
Drug-lifestyle. *Alcohol use:* Decreases antibiotic effect. Discourage using together.
Sun exposure: Photosensitivity reactions may occur. Urge patient to avoid unprotected and prolonged sun exposure.

Effects on lab test results

- May increase BUN and liver enzyme levels.

• May increase eosinophil count. May decrease hemoglobin, hematocrit, and platelet, neutrophil, and WBC counts.

Pharmacokinetics

Absorption: 90% to 100% absorbed after P.O. administration; milk or other dairy products insignificantly alter absorption.
Distribution: Distributed widely in body tissues and fluids. Poor penetration in CSF. Drug is 25% to 93% protein-bound.
Metabolism: Insignificantly metabolized; some hepatic degradation occurs.
Excretion: Excreted primarily unchanged in urine; some drug is excreted in feces. *Half-life:* 22 to 24 hours after multiple dosing.

Route	Onset	Peak	Duration
P.O.	Unknown	1.5-4 hr	Unknown
I.V.	Immediate	Unknown	Unknown

Pharmacodynamics

Chemical effect: Thought to exert bacteriostatic effect by binding to 30S ribosomal subunit of microorganisms, thus inhibiting protein synthesis.
Therapeutic effect: Hinders bacterial growth. Spectrum of activity includes many gram-negative and gram-positive organisms, *Chlamydia, Mycoplasma, Rickettsia,* and spirochetes.

Available forms

doxycycline
Capsules: 50 mg, 100 mg
Oral suspension: 25 mg/5 ml
Tablets: 50 mg, 100 mg
doxycycline calcium
Oral suspension: 50 mg/5 ml
doxycycline hyclate
Capsules: 20 mg, 50 mg, 100 mg
Capsules (coated pellets): 100 mg
Injection: 100 mg, 200 mg
Tablets: 20 mg, 50 mg, 100 mg
doxycycline hydrochloride
Capsules: 50 mg ◇, 100 mg ◇
Tablets: 50 mg ◇, 100 mg ◇

NURSING PROCESS

Assessment

• Obtain history of patient's infection before therapy, and reassess regularly thereafter.
• Obtain specimen for culture and sensitivity tests before first dose. Therapy may begin pending test results.
• Be alert for adverse reactions and drug interactions.
• Monitor I.V. infusion site for signs of thrombophlebitis, which may occur with I.V. administration.
• Monitor patient's hydration status if adverse GI reactions occur.
• Evaluate patient's and family's knowledge of drug therapy.

Nursing diagnoses

• Infection related to presence of susceptible bacteria
• Risk for deficient fluid volume related to drug-induced adverse GI reactions
• Deficient knowledge related to drug therapy

Planning and implementation

• Check expiration date. Outdated or deteriorated tetracyclines may cause reversible nephrotoxicity (Fanconi's syndrome).
• **P.O. use:** Give drug with milk or food if adverse GI reactions develop.
• **I.V. use:** Reconstitute powder for injection with sterile water for injection. Use 10 ml in 100-mg vial and 20 ml in 200-mg vial. Dilute solution to 100 to 1,000 ml for I.V. infusion. Avoid extravasation. Don't infuse solutions that are more concentrated than 1 mg/ml. Depending on the dose, duration of infusion is typically 1 to 4 hours.
– Don't expose drug to light or heat. Protect it from sunlight during infusion.
– Reconstituted injectable solution is stable for 72 hours if refrigerated.
– Parenteral form may cause false-positive reading of copper sulfate tests (Clinitest). All forms may cause false-negative reading of glucose oxidase reagent (Diastix or Chemstrip uG).
• Follow current CDC recommendations for anthrax.
• Ciprofloxacin and doxycycline are first-line therapy for anthrax. Amoxicillin 500 mg P.O. t.i.d. for adults and 80 mg/kg/day divided every 8 hours for children is an option for completion of therapy after clinical improvement.
• Cutaneous anthrax with signs of systemic involvement, extensive edema, or lesions on the head or neck requires I.V. therapy and a multidrug approach.

• Additional antimicrobials for anthrax multidrug regimens can include rifampin, vancomycin, penicillin, ampicillin, chloramphenicol, imipenem, clindamycin, and clarithromycin.
• Steroids may be considered as adjunctive therapy for anthrax patients with severe edema and for meningitis, based on experience with bacterial meningitis of other etiologies.
• If meningitis is suspected, doxycycline would be less optimal because of poor CHS penetration.
• Notify prescriber of adverse reactions. Some adverse reactions, such as superinfection, may necessitate substitution of another antibiotic.

Patient teaching
• Tell patient to take entire amount of medication exactly as prescribed, even after he feels better.
• Instruct patient to take oral doxycycline with milk or food but not antacids if adverse GI reactions develop. Tell patient to take drug no less than 1 hour before bedtime to prevent irritation from esophageal reflux.
• Tell patient to use sunscreen and avoid strong sunlight during therapy to prevent photosensitivity reactions.
• Stress good oral hygiene.
• Tell patient to check expiration dates and to discard outdated doxycycline because it may become toxic.
• Advise patient taking oral contraceptive to use alternative means of contraception during doxycycline therapy and for 1 week after therapy is discontinued.

☑ Evaluation
• Patient is free from infection.
• Patient maintains adequate hydration throughout therapy.
• Patient and family state understanding of drug therapy.

dronabinol (delta-9-tetrahydrocannabinol)
(droh-NAB-eh-nohl)
Marinol

Pharmacologic class: cannabinoid
Therapeutic class: antiemetic, appetite stimulant
Pregnancy risk category: C
Controlled substance schedule: III

Indications and dosages
▶ **Nausea and vomiting from chemotherapy.** *Adults:* 5 mg/m^2 P.O. 1 to 3 hours before administration of chemotherapy. Then, same dose q 2 to 4 hours after chemotherapy for total of four to six doses daily. If needed, dosage increased in increments of 2.5 mg/m^2 to maximum of 15 mg/m^2 per dose.
▶ **Anorexia and weight loss in patients with AIDS.** *Adults:* 2.5 mg P.O. b.i.d. before lunch and dinner, increase p.r.n. to maximum of 20 mg daily.

Contraindications and precautions
• Contraindicated in patients hypersensitive to sesame oil or cannabinoids.
• Use cautiously in patients with heart disease, psychiatric illness, or history of drug abuse.
Lifespan: In breast-feeding women, drug isn't recommended. In children, safety of drug hasn't been established. In elderly patients, use cautiously.

Adverse reactions
CNS: *dizziness, drowsiness, euphoria, ataxia,* depersonalization, disorientation, hallucinations, somnolence, headache, muddled thinking, asthenia, amnesia, confusion, *paranoia.*
CV: tachycardia, orthostatic hypotension, palpitations, vasodilation.
EENT: visual disturbances.
GI: *dry mouth, nausea, vomiting, abdominal pain,* diarrhea.

Interactions
Drug-drug. *CNS depressants, psychotomimetic substances, sedatives:* May have additive effects. Avoid using together.
Drug-lifestyle. *Alcohol use:* May have additive effects. Discourage using together.

Effects on lab test results
None reported.

Pharmacokinetics
Absorption: Almost 95% absorbed.
Distribution: Distributed rapidly in many tissue sites; 97% to 99% protein-bound.

Metabolism: Undergoes extensive metabolism in liver. Metabolite activity is unknown.
Excretion: Excreted primarily in feces. *Half-life:* 25 to 35 hours.

Route	Onset	Peak	Duration
P.O.	Unknown	2-4 hr	4-6 hr

Pharmacodynamics

Chemical effect: Unknown.
Therapeutic effect: Relieves nausea and vomiting caused by chemotherapy and stimulates appetite.

NURSING PROCESS

Assessment

- Obtain history of patient's underlying condition before therapy.
- Monitor effectiveness by assessing for nausea, vomiting, or weight gain. Drug effects may persist for days after therapy ends.
- Be alert for adverse reactions and drug interactions.
- Monitor patient for dependence. Dronabinol is the principal active substance in *Cannabis sativa* (marijuana). It can produce physical and psychological dependence and has high potential for abuse.
- Monitor patient's hydration status, weight, and nutritional status regularly.
- Evaluate patient's and family's knowledge of drug therapy.

Nursing diagnoses

- Risk for deficient fluid volume related to nausea and vomiting from chemotherapy
- Disturbed thought processes related to drug-induced adverse CNS reactions
- Deficient knowledge related to drug therapy

Planning and implementation

- Expect drug to be prescribed only for patients who haven't responded satisfactorily to other antiemetics.
- Give drug 1 to 3 hours before chemotherapy starts and again 2 to 4 hours after chemotherapy.

Patient teaching

- Inform patient that drug may cause unusual changes in mood or other adverse behavioral effects.
- Caution patient to avoid hazardous activities until full CNS effects of drug are known.
- Warn family members to make sure patient is supervised by a responsible person during and immediately after treatment.

Evaluation

- Patient maintains adequate hydration.
- Patient regains normal thought processes after effects of drug therapy have dissipated.
- Patient and family state understanding of drug therapy.

drotrecogin alfa (activated)

(droh-truh-KO-jin al-fa)
Xigris

Pharmacologic class: recombinant protease of human activated protein C
Therapeutic class: antithrombotic
Pregnancy risk category: C

Indications and dosages

▶ **Reduction of mortality in patients with severe sepsis (sepsis from acute organ dysfunction) who are at a high risk of dying.** *Adults:* 24 mcg/kg/hr I.V. infusion for a total of 96 hours.

Contraindications and precautions

- Contraindicated in patients with active internal bleeding, recent (within 3 months) hemorrhagic CVA, recent (within 2 months) intracranial or intraspinal surgery, severe head trauma, trauma with an increased risk of life-threatening bleeding, an epidural catheter, intracranial neoplasm or mass lesion, or evidence of cerebral herniation. Drug is also contraindicated in patients hypersensitive to drotrecogin alfa (activated) or any of its components.
- Use caution in patients with an increased risk of bleeding, such as those who are taking heparin (15 units/kg/hour or more); those with a platelet count of less than 30,000 × 10^6/L (even if the platelet count is increased after transfusions), those with an INR greater than 3; those who have experienced GI bleeding within 6 weeks; those who have had thrombolytic therapy within 3 days; those who have been given oral anticoagulants, glycoprotein IIb/IIIa inhibitors, aspirin (more than 650 mg/day) or

other platelet inhibitors within 7 days; those who have had ischemic CVA within 3 months; those who have had intracranial arteriovenous malformation or aneurysm, bleeding diathesis, chronic severe hepatic disease, or any other condition in which bleeding constitutes a significant hazard or would be particularly difficult to manage because of its location.
Lifespan: In pregnant women, drug should be used only if clearly needed. Breast-feeding women should stop nursing or stop taking the drug, taking into account the importance of the drug to the mother; it's unknown whether drug appears in breast milk. In children, safety and effectiveness of drug haven't been established.

Adverse reactions

Hematologic: ***hemorrhage.***

Interactions

Drug-drug. *Drugs that affect hemostasis:* Increases risk of bleeding. Use together cautiously; monitor patient for bleeding.

Effects on lab test results

- May increase APTT and PT. May interfere with APTT and one-stage coagulation assays based on APTT (such as factors VIII, IX, and XI assays).

Pharmacokinetics

Absorption: Complete bioavailability. Administered I.V.
Distribution: Steady-state levels attained within 2 hours after starting infusion.
Metabolism: Unknown.
Excretion: Unknown.

Route	Onset	Peak	Duration
I.V.	Rapid	Unknown	Unknown

Pharmacodynamics

Chemical effect: The antisepsis action of drotrecogin alfa is unknown. The drug is thought to produce dose-dependent reductions in D-dimer and IL-6. Activated Protein C exerts an anti-thrombotic effect by inhibiting factors Va and VIIIa. Also thought to exert an anti-inflammatory effect by inhibiting human tumor necrosis factor production by monocytes, by blocking leukocyte adhesion to selectins, and by limiting the thrombin-induced inflammatory responses.
Therapeutic effect: Prevents clots and blocks cell death.

Available forms

Injection: 5 mg; 20 mg

NURSING PROCESS

Assessment

- Assess patient before starting and during drug therapy for risk of bleeding or contraindications.
- Monitor patient closely for bleeding. If clinically important bleeding occurs, immediately stop the infusion.
- Because drug may prolong APTT, it can't be used reliably to assess the status of the coagulopathy during infusion. Because drug has minimal effect on PT, PT may be used to monitor the status of the coagulopathy in these patients.

Nursing diagnoses

- Risk for injury caused by increased bleeding potential related to drug therapy.
- Deficient knowledge related to drug therapy.

Planning and implementation

- If the infusion is interrupted, restart at the 24-mcg/kg per hour infusion rate. Dose escalation, bolus doses, and dose adjustment based on clinical or laboratory parameters aren't recommended.
- Stop drug 2 hours before an invasive surgical procedure with a risk of bleeding. After hemostasis is reached, drug may be restarted 12 hours after major invasive procedures or surgery or immediately after uncomplicated, less-invasive procedures.
- Reconstitute 5-mg vials with 2.5 ml sterile water for injection, USP and 20-mg vials with 10 ml of sterile water for injection, USP. The resulting concentration is about 2 mg/ml. Gently swirl each vial until powder is completely dissolved; avoid inverting or shaking the vial.
- Further dilute the reconstituted solution with sterile normal saline injection. Withdraw appropriate amount of reconstituted drug into a prepared infusion bag of sterile normal saline solution. When adding the drug, direct the stream to the side of the bag to minimize agitation of the solution.

• Gently invert the infusion bag to obtain a homogenous solution. Don't transport the infusion bag between locations using mechanical delivery systems.
• If the reconstituted vial isn't used immediately, it may be held at controlled room temperature of 15° to 30° C (59° to 86° F) but must be used within 3 hours.
• I.V. administration must be completed within 12 hours after the I.V. solution is prepared.
• Inspect for particle matter and discoloration before administration.
• When using an I.V. pump to give the drug, the solution of reconstituted drotrecogin alfa is typically diluted into an infusion bag containing sterile normal saline solution to a final concentration between 100 mcg/ml and 200 mcg/ml.
• When using a syringe pump to give the drug, the reconstituted solution is typically diluted with sterile normal saline solution to a final concentration between 100 mcg/ml and 1,000 mcg/ml. When giving at low concentrations (less than about 200 mcg/ml) at low flow rates (less than about 5 ml/hr), the infusion set must be primed for about 15 minutes at a flow rate of about 5 ml/hour.
ALERT: Give via a dedicated I.V. line or lumen of a multilumen central venous catheter. The only other solutions that can be given through the same line are normal saline solution, lactated Ringer's injection, dextrose, or dextrose and saline mixtures.
• Store in a refrigerator at 2° to 8° C (35° to 46° F). Don't freeze. Avoid heat or direct sunlight.

Patient teaching
• Inform patient of potential adverse reactions.
• Instruct patient to promptly report signs of bleeding.
• Advise patient that bleeding may occur for up to 28 days after treatment.

Evaluation
• Patient doesn't experience any hemorrhaging during and 28 days after drug therapy.
• Patient and family state understanding of drug therapy.

E

edetate calcium disodium (calcium EDTA)
(ED-eh-tayt KAL-see-um digh-SOH-dee-um)
Calcium Disodium Versenate

Pharmacologic class: chelating agent
Therapeutic class: heavy metal antagonist
Pregnancy risk category: B

Indications and dosages
▶ **Acute lead encephalopathy or blood lead levels above 70 mcg/dl.** *Adults and children:* 1.5 g/m² I.V. or I.M. daily in divided doses at 12-hour intervals for 3 to 5 days, usually with dimercaprol. A second course may be given in 5 to 7 days.
▶ **Lead poisoning without encephalopathy, or asymptomatic patient with blood levels below 70 mcg/dl.** *Children:* 1 g/m² I.V. or I.M. daily in divided doses.

Contraindications and precautions
• Contraindicated in patients with anuria, hepatitis, or acute renal disease.
• Use with extreme caution in patients with mild renal disease. Expect dosages to be reduced.
Lifespan: In pregnant women, use cautiously.

Adverse reactions
CNS: sudden fever, headache, paresthesia, numbness, fatigue.
CV: ***arrhythmias,*** hypotension.
EENT: sneezing and nasal congestion.
GI: anorexia, nausea, vomiting, excessive thirst.
GU: proteinuria, hematuria, ***nephrotoxicity with renal tubular necrosis leading to fatal nephrosis.***
Metabolic: hypercalcemia.
Musculoskeletal: arthralgia, myalgia.
Other: chills.

Interactions

Drug-drug. *Zinc insulin:* Interferes with action of insulin by binding with zinc. Monitor patient closely.
Zinc supplements: May decrease effectiveness of edetate calcium disodium and zinc supplements because of chelation. Withhold zinc supplements until therapy is complete.

Effects on lab test results

- May increase AST, ALT, and calcium levels.
- May decrease hemoglobin and hematocrit.

Pharmacokinetics

Absorption: Well absorbed after I.M. administration.
Distribution: Distributed primarily in extra cellular fluid.
Metabolism: None.
Excretion: Excreted in urine. *Half-life:* 20 minutes to 1½ hours.

Route	Onset	Peak	Duration
I.V., I.M.	1 hr	24-48 hr	Unknown

Pharmacodynamics

Chemical effect: Forms stable, soluble complexes with metals, particularly lead.
Therapeutic effect: Abolishes effects of lead poisoning.

Available forms

Injection: 200 mg/ml

NURSING PROCESS

Assessment

- Obtain history of patient's underlying condition before therapy.
- Monitor effectiveness by checking lead level and observing for decreasing signs and symptoms of lead poisoning.
- Monitor fluid intake and output, urinalysis, BUN, and ECG daily.
- Be alert for adverse reactions.
- Observe injection site for local reaction.
- Evaluate patient's and family's knowledge of drug therapy.

Nursing diagnoses

- Risk for injury related to lead poisoning
- Ineffective renal tissue perfusion related to drug-induced fatal nephrosis
- Deficient knowledge related to drug therapy

Planning and implementation

- **I.V. use:** Dilute drug with D_5W or normal saline injection to 2 to 4 mg/ml. Infuse half of daily dose over 1 hour in asymptomatic patients or 2 hours in symptomatic patients. Give rest of infusion at least 6 hours later. Or, give by slow infusion over at least 8 hours.
- **I.M. use:** Add procaine hydrochloride to I.M. solution to minimize pain. Watch for local reactions.
- Because I.V. use may increase intracranial pressure, don't give by that route to treat lead encephalopathy. Give by I.M. route instead.
- The I.M. route is preferred, especially for children and patients with lead encephalopathy.
- Force fluids to facilitate lead excretion, except in patients with lead encephalopathy.
- To avoid toxicity, use with dimercaprol.
- Apply ice or cold compresses to injection site to ease local reaction.

ALERT: Don't confuse edetate calcium with edetate disodium, which is used to treat hypercalcemia.

Patient teaching

- Warn patient that some adverse reactions—such as fever, chills, thirst, and nasal congestion—may occur 4 to 8 hours after administration.
- Encourage patient and family to identify and remove source of lead in home.

Evaluation

- Patient sustains no injury as result of lead poisoning.
- Patient has no signs of altered renal tissue perfusion.
- Patient and family state understanding of drug therapy.

edetate disodium

(ED-eh-tayt digh-SOH-dee-um)
Disodium EDTA, Edathamil Disodium, Endrate, Sodium Edetate

Pharmacologic class: chelating agent
Therapeutic class: heavy metal antagonist
Pregnancy risk category: C

Indications and dosages

▶ **Hypercalcemic crisis.** *Adults:* 50 mg/kg by slow I.V. infusion added to 500 ml of D_5W or normal saline solution and given over 3 or more hours. Maximum dose is 3 g I.V. daily. *Children:* 40 to 70 mg/kg by slow I.V. infusion, diluted to maximum of 30 mg/ml in D_5W or normal saline solution and given over 3 or more hours. Maximum dose is 70 mg/kg I.V. daily.

▶ **Cardiac glycoside–induced arrhythmias.** *Adults and children:* 15 mg/kg/hour I.V. daily. Maximum dose is 60 mg/kg I.V. daily.

Contraindications and precautions

• Contraindicated in patients hypersensitive to drug and in those with anuria, known or suspected hypocalcemia, significant renal disease, active or healed tubercular lesions, or a history of seizures or intracranial lesions.

• Use cautiously in patients with limited cardiac reserve, heart failure, or hypokalemia.

Lifespan: In pregnant and breast-feeding women, use cautiously.

Adverse reactions

CNS: circumoral paresthesia, numbness, headache.

CV: hypertension, thrombophlebitis, orthostatic hypotension.

GI: nausea, vomiting, diarrhea, anorexia, abdominal cramps.

GU: ***nephrotoxicity*** with urinary urgency, nocturia, dysuria, polyuria, proteinuria, renal insufficiency, ***renal failure, tubular necrosis.***

Metabolic: ***severe hypocalcemia, hypomagnesia.***

Skin: dermatitis, erythema.

Other: pain at site of infusion.

Interactions

Drug-drug. *Digoxin:* Sudden drop in calcium caused by edetate disodium may reverse effects of digoxin. Monitor patient closely.

Insulin: Decreases glucose and may cause possible chelation of zinc in insulin. Dosage adjustments of insulin may be required.

Effects on lab test results

• May decrease calcium and magnesium levels.

Pharmacokinetics

Absorption: Administered I.V.

Distribution: Distributed widely throughout body but doesn't enter CSF in significant amounts.

Metabolism: None.

Excretion: Excreted in urine.

Route	Onset	Peak	Duration
I.V.	Unknown	Unknown	Unknown

Pharmacodynamics

Chemical effect: Chelates with metals, such as calcium, to form stable, soluble complex.

Therapeutic effect: Lowers calcium level.

Available forms

Injection: 150 mg/ml

NURSING PROCESS

Assessment

• Obtain history of patient's calcium level before therapy.

• Monitor effectiveness by obtaining calcium level after each dose. If used to treat cardiac glycoside–induced arrhythmias, evaluate patient's ECG frequently.

• Monitor kidney function tests frequently.

• Be alert for adverse reactions.

• Evaluate patient's and family's knowledge of drug therapy.

Nursing diagnoses

• Risk for injury related to hypercalcemia

• Ineffective protection related to drug-induced hypocalcemia

• Deficient knowledge related to drug therapy

Planning and implementation

ALERT: Read label carefully; don't confuse with edetate calcium disodium, which is used for lead toxicity.

• Dilute before use. Avoid rapid I.V. infusion; profound hypocalcemia may occur, leading to tetany, seizures, arrhythmias, and respiratory arrest. Drug isn't recommended for direct or intermittent injection. Avoid extravasation.

• Record I.V. site used, and avoid repeated use of same site, which increases likelihood of thrombophlebitis.

• Keep I.V. calcium available to treat hypocalcemia.

• Keep patient in bed for 15 minutes after infusion to avoid orthostatic hypotension.

• If generalized systemic reactions (fever, chills, back pain, emesis, muscle cramps, urinary urgency) occur 4 to 8 hours after infusion, report them to prescriber. Treatment is usually supportive. Symptoms usually subside within 12 hours.
• Don't use to treat lead toxicity; use edetate calcium disodium instead.
• Other drug treatments for hypercalcemia are safer and more effective than edetate disodium.

Patient teaching
• Instruct patient to report immediately respiratory difficulty, dizziness, and muscle cramping.
• Advise patient to move from sitting or lying position slowly to avoid dizziness.
• Reassure patient that generalized systemic reaction usually subsides within 12 hours.

Evaluation
• Patient sustains no injury as result of hypercalcemia.
• Patient's calcium level doesn't fall below normal after edetate disodium therapy.
• Patient and family state understanding of drug therapy.

edrophonium chloride
(ed-roh-FOH-nee-um KLOR-ighd)
Enlon, Reversol, Tensilon

Pharmacologic class: cholinesterase inhibitor
Therapeutic class: cholinergic agonist, diagnostic agent
Pregnancy risk category: NR

Indications and dosages
▶ **As curare antagonist (to reverse nondepolarizing neuromuscular blocking action).** *Adults:* 10 mg I.V. given over 30 to 45 seconds. Dose may be repeated as needed to maximum of 40 mg. Larger dosages may potentiate effect of curare.
▶ **Diagnostic aid in myasthenia gravis (Tensilon test).** *Adults:* 1 to 2 mg I.V. over 15 to 30 seconds; then 8 mg if no response (increase in muscle strength) occurs. Or, 10 mg I.M. If cholinergic reaction occurs, 2 mg I.M. is given 30 minutes later to rule out false-negative response.
Children weighing more than 34 kg (75 lb): 2 mg I.V. If no response within 45 seconds, 1 mg q 45 seconds to maximum of 10 mg. Or, 5 mg I.M.
Children weighing less than 34 kg: 1 mg I.V. If no response within 45 seconds, 1 mg q 45 seconds to maximum of 5 mg. Or, 2 mg I.M. (I.M. route may be used in children because of difficulty with I.V. route.) Expect same reactions as with I.V. test, but they appear after 2- to 10-minute delay.
Infants: 0.5 mg to 1 mg I.M. or S.C.
▶ **To differentiate myasthenic crisis from cholinergic crisis.** *Adults:* 1 mg I.V. If no response in 1 minute, may repeat dose once. Increased muscle strength confirms myasthenic crisis; no increase or exaggerated weakness confirms cholinergic crisis.

Contraindications and precautions
• Contraindicated in patients hypersensitive to anticholinesterases and in those with mechanical obstruction of intestine or urinary tract.
• Use cautiously in patients with bronchial asthma or arrhythmias.
Lifespan: In pregnant and breast-feeding women, safety of drug hasn't been established.

Adverse reactions
CNS: ***seizures,*** weakness, dysarthria.
CV: hypotension, ***bradycardia, AV block, cardiac arrest.***
EENT: excessive lacrimation, diplopia, ***laryngospasm,*** miosis, conjunctival hyperemia, dysphagia.
GI: nausea, vomiting, *diarrhea, abdominal cramps,* excessive salivation.
GU: urinary frequency, incontinence.
Musculoskeletal: muscle cramps, muscle fasciculation.
Respiratory: ***respiratory paralysis, bronchospasm,*** increased bronchial secretions.
Skin: diaphoresis.

Interactions
Drug-drug. *Aminoglycosides, anesthetics:* May prolong or enhance muscle weakness. Monitor patient closely.
Cardiac glycosides: May increase heart's sensitivity to edrophonium. Use together cautiously.
Cholinergics: May increase effects. Stop all other cholinergics before giving drug.
Corticosteroids, magnesium, procainamide, quinidine: May antagonize cholinergic effects. Observe patient for lack of drug effect.

Drug-herb. *Jaborandi tree, pill-bearing spurge:* Possible additive effect with risk of toxicity. Discourage using together.

Effects on lab test results

None reported.

Pharmacokinetics

Absorption: Administered I.M. or I.V.
Distribution: Unknown.
Metabolism: Unknown.
Excretion: Unknown.

Route	Onset	Peak	Duration
I.V.	30-60 sec	Unknown	5-10 min
I.M.	2-10 min	Unknown	5-30 min

Pharmacodynamics

Chemical effect: Inhibits destruction of acetylcholine released from parasympathetic and somatic efferent nerves. Acetylcholine accumulates, promoting increased stimulation of receptor.
Therapeutic effect: Reverses nondepolarizing neuromuscular blocker.

Available forms

Injection: 10 mg/ml in 1-ml ampules and in 10- or 15-ml vials

NURSING PROCESS

Assessment

- Obtain history of patient's underlying condition before therapy.
- Monitor effectiveness by evaluating reduction of symptoms of underlying condition. When giving drug to differentiate myasthenic crisis from cholinergic crisis, observe patient's muscle strength closely.
- Be alert for adverse reactions and drug interactions.
- Evaluate patient's and family's knowledge of drug therapy.

Nursing diagnoses

- Ineffective health maintenance related to underlying condition
- Impaired gas exchange related to drug-induced bronchospasm
- Deficient knowledge related to drug therapy

Planning and implementation

- Stop all other cholinergics before giving this drug.
- **I.V. use:** For easier parenteral administration, use tuberculin syringe with I.V. needle.
- **I.M. use:** Use I.M. route to give drug to children because of difficulty with I.V. insertion in children.

ALERT: Keep atropine injection readily available, and be prepared to give 0.5 to 1 mg S.C. or slow I.V. push. Provide respiratory support, as needed.

Patient teaching

- Tell patient to report adverse reactions immediately, especially difficulty breathing.

Evaluation

- Patient shows improvement in underlying condition.
- Patient maintains adequate gas exchange throughout therapy.
- Patient and family state understanding of drug therapy.

efavirenz

(eh-fah-VEER-enz)
Sustiva

Pharmacologic class: nonnucleoside, reverse transcriptase inhibitor
Therapeutic class: antiretroviral agent
Pregnancy risk category: C

Indications and dosages

▶ **Treatment of HIV-1 infection.** ***Capsules.*** *Adults:* 600 mg P.O. daily with a protease inhibitor or nucleoside analogue reverse transcriptase inhibitors. ***Tablets.*** *Adults:* 600 mg (one tablet) P.O. daily on an empty stomach, preferably at bedtime.
Children age 3 and older weighing 10 to under 15 kg (22 to under 33 lb): 200 mg P.O. daily.
Children weighing 15 to under 20 kg (33 to under 44 lb): 250 mg P.O. daily.
Children weighing 20 to under 25 kg (44 to under 55 lb): 300 mg P.O. daily.
Children weighing 25 to under 32.5 kg (55 to under 72 lb): 350 mg P.O. daily.
Children weighing 32.5 to under 40 kg (72 to under 88 lb): 400 mg P.O. daily.

Children weighing 40 kg (88 lb) or more: 600 mg P.O. once daily.

Give above doses with protease inhibitor or nucleoside analogue reverse transcriptase inhibitors.

Contraindications and precautions

- Contraindicated in patients hypersensitive to drug or its components.
- Use cautiously in patients with hepatic impairment or in those also receiving hepatotoxic drugs.

Lifespan: In pregnant and breast-feeding women, drug is contraindicated. In children and elderly patients, use cautiously.

Adverse reactions

CNS: abnormal dreams or thinking, agitation, amnesia, confusion, depersonalization, depression, *dizziness,* euphoria, fatigue, hallucinations, headache, hypesthesia, impaired concentration, insomnia, somnolence, nervousness, fever.
GI: abdominal pain, anorexia, *diarrhea,* dyspepsia, flatulence, *nausea,* vomiting.
GU: hematuria, renal calculi.
Skin: increased sweating, ***erythema multiforme, Stevens-Johnson syndrome, toxic epidermal necrolysis,*** *rash,* pruritus.

Interactions

Drug-drug. *Clarithromycin, indinavir, amprenavir, lopinavir and ritonavir:* May decrease plasma levels of these drugs. Consider alternative therapy or dosage adjustment.
Drugs that induce the cytochrome P-450 enzyme system (such as phenobarbital, rifampin): Increases clearance of efavirenz, resulting in lower plasma concentration of efavirenz. Avoid using together.
Ergot derivatives, midazolam, and triazolam: Competition for cytochrome P-450 enzyme system may result in inhibition of the metabolism of these drugs and cause serious or life-threatening adverse events (such as arrhythmias, prolonged sedation, or respiratory depression). Avoid using together.
Estrogens: Increases plasma levels. Monitor patient.
Hormonal contraceptives: Increases levels of ethinyl estradiol, no data on progesterone component. Advise use of a reliable method of barrier contraception in addition to use of hormonal contraceptives.
Psychoactive drugs: May cause additive CNS effects. Avoid using together.
Rifabutin: Decreases rifabutin concentrations. Increase the dose to 450 to 600 mg once daily or 600 mg 2 to 3 times a week.
Ritonavir: Increases levels of both drugs by 20%. Monitor patient closely.
Saquinavir: Plasma levels of saquinavir decrease significantly. Don't use with saquinavir as sole protease inhibitor. Use of saquinavir also decreases AUC of efavirenz by 12% to 13%.
Warfarin: Plasma levels and effects of warfarin are potentially increased or decreased. Monitor INR.
Drug-herb. *St. John's wort:* Decreases efavirenz levels. Discourge using together.
Drug-food. *High-fat meals:* May increase absorption of drug. Instruct patient to maintain a proper low-fat diet.
Drug-lifestyle. *Alcohol use:* Enhances CNS effects. Advise patient to avoid alcohol use.

Effects on lab test results

- May increase ALT, AST, and cholesterol levels.

Pharmacokinetics

Absorption: Oral absorption produces peak levels in 3 to 5 hours with steady-state levels in 6 to 10 days.
Distribution: Highly bound to human plasma proteins, predominantly albumin.
Metabolism: Primarily metabolized by cytochrome P-450 system to metabolites that are inactive against HIV-1.
Excretion: Excreted primarily in feces with a small number of metabolites excreted in urine.

Route	Onset	Peak	Duration
P.O.	Unknown	3-5 hr	Unknown

Pharmacodynamics

Chemical effect: A nonnucleoside, reverse transcriptase inhibitor that inhibits the transcription of HIV-1 RNA to DNA, a critical step in the viral replication process.
Therapeutic effect: Lowers amount of HIV in the blood (viral load) and increases CD4 lymphocytes.

Available forms

Capsules: 50 mg, 100 mg, 200 mg
Tablets: 600 mg

NURSING PROCESS

Assessment

• Monitor liver function test results in patients with history of hepatitis B or C and in those taking ritonavir.
• Monitor cholesterol levels.
• Children may be more prone to adverse reactions, especially diarrhea, nausea, vomiting, and rash.
• Evaluate patient's and family's knowledge of drug therapy.

Nursing diagnoses

• Risk for infection related to patient's underlying condition
• Risk for impaired skin integrity related to potential adverse effects of drug
• Deficient knowledge related to drug therapy

Planning and implementation

• Drug should be used with other antiretrovirals because resistant viruses emerge rapidly when used alone. Drug shouldn't be used as monotherapy or added on as a single agent to a failing regimen.
• Combination with ritonavir may cause a higher occurrence of adverse effects (such as dizziness, nausea, paresthesia) and laboratory abnormalities (elevated liver enzyme levels).
• Pregnancy must be ruled out before therapy is started in women of childbearing age.
• Give drug at bedtime to decrease noticeable CNS adverse effects.

Patient teaching

• Instruct patient to take drug with water, juice, milk, or soda. It may be taken without regard to meals.
• Inform patient about need for scheduled blood tests to monitor liver function and cholesterol levels.
• Tell patient to use reliable method of barrier contraception in addition to oral contraceptives and to notify prescriber immediately if pregnancy is suspected.
• Inform patient that drug doesn't cure HIV infection and that it won't affect the development of opportunistic infections and other complications of HIV disease. Explain that it doesn't reduce the risk of HIV transmission through sexual contact or blood contamination.
• Instruct patient to take drug at same time daily and always with other antiretroviral drugs.
• Tell patient to take drug exactly as prescribed and not to discontinue without medical approval.
• Inform patient that rash is most common adverse effect. If it occurs, tell patient to report it, or any other adverse effects, immediately because it may be serious in rare cases.
• Instruct patient to report use of other medications.
• Advise patient that dizziness, difficulty sleeping or concentrating, drowsiness, or unusual dreams may occur the first few days of therapy. Reassure patient that these symptoms typically resolve after 2 to 4 weeks and may be less problematic if drug is taken at bedtime.
• Tell patient to avoid alcoholic beverages, driving, or operating machinery until drug's effects are known.

Evaluation

• Patient is free from opportunistic infections.
• Patient's skin integrity is maintained.
• Patient and family state understanding of drug therapy.

eflornithine hydrochloride

(ee-FLOR-ni-theen high-droh-KLOR-ighd)
Vaniqa

Pharmacologic class: ornithine decarboxylase (ODC) inhibitor
Therapeutic class: hair growth retardant
Pregnancy risk category: C

Indications and dosages

▶ **Reduction of unwanted facial hair in women.** *Adults and children age 12 and older:* Apply a thin layer to affected areas of the face and adjacent areas under chin and rub in thoroughly twice daily, at least 8 hours apart.

Contraindications and precautions

• Contraindicated in patients with a history of sensitivity to any components of the preparation.
Lifespan: In breast-feeding women, use cautiously because it's unknown whether drug appears in breast milk. In children younger than age 12, drug is contraindicated.

Adverse reactions

CNS: headache, dizziness, asthenia, vertigo, numbness.
GI: dyspepsia, anorexia, nausea.
Skin: *acne, pseudofolliculitis barbae,* dry skin, pruritus, erythema, skin irritation, rash, alopecia, folliculitis, ingrown hair, facial edema, bleeding, cheilitis, contact dermatitis, swollen lips, herpes simplex, rosacea, stinging, tingling, or burning sensation.

Interactions

None reported.

Effects on lab test results

- May increase ALT and AST levels.

Pharmacokinetics

Absorption: Less than 1% of the radioactive dose is absorbed.
Distribution: Time to reach steady state is 4 days of twice-daily application. The steady-state plasma half-life of eflornithine is approximately 8 hours.
Metabolism: Not metabolized.
Excretion: Unchanged in urine.

Route	Onset	Peak	Duration
Topical	Unknown	8 hr	Unknown

Pharmacodynamics

Chemical effect: Thought to irreversibly inhibit skin ODC activity. ODC is an enzyme that synthesizes polyamines.
Therapeutic effect: Decreases facial hair growth rate.

Available forms

Cream: 13.9 %

NURSING PROCESS

Assessment

- Assess patient's affected areas before and during treatment.
- Be alert for any adverse skin reactions.

Nursing diagnoses

- Disturbed body image related to unwanted facial hair
- Impaired skin integrity related to drug-induced adverse skin reactions

Planning and implementation

ALERT: Drug is indicated for reducing unwanted facial hair in women only. The cream should be applied only to affected areas on the face and chin.
- If adverse effects become bothersome, instruct patient to limit use to once a day. If side effects persist, tell patient to consult prescriber.
- Drug should be stored at room temperature 15° to 30° C (59° to 86° F).

Patient teaching

- Tell patient that Vaniqa cream use should be limited to face and chin involvement.
- Instruct patient to apply Vaniqa in a thin layer to affected areas twice daily, at least 8 hours apart. Avoid washing treated area for at least 4 hours.
- If skin irritation or intolerance develops, tell patient to temporarily reduce the frequency of application to once a day. If irritation continues, patient should discontinue use of product.
- Advise patient that drug isn't a depilatory, but rather is believed to retard hair growth. Patient will likely need to continue using a hair-removal method in conjunction with Vaniqa. Cream shouldn't be applied within 5 minutes of hair removal.
- Tell patient that improvement was seen in as little as 4 to 8 weeks of initial treatment in 24-week clinical trials. The condition may return to pretreatment levels 8 weeks after discontinuing treatment.

Evaluation

- Patient's rate of facial hair growth decreases and skin improves in response to drug therapy.
- Patient doesn't suffer any adverse reactions from drug therapy.

enalaprilat

(eh-NAH-leh-prel-at)
Vasotec IV

enalapril maleate

Amprace ◇, Renitec ◇, Vasotec

Pharmacologic class: ACE inhibitor
Therapeutic class: antihypertensive
Pregnancy risk category: C (D in second and third trimesters)

Indications and dosages

▶ **Hypertension.** *Adults:* For patient not taking a diuretic, initially 5 mg P.O. once daily, adjust according to response. Usual dosage range is 10 to 40 mg daily as single dose or two divided doses. Or, 1.25 mg I.V. over 5 minutes q 6 hours. For patient taking a diuretic, initially 2.5 mg P.O. once daily. Or, 0.625 mg I.V. over 5 minutes, repeat in 1 hour if needed, followed by 1.25 mg I.V. q 6 hours.

▶ **To convert from I.V. to P.O. therapy.** *Adults:* Initially, 5 mg P.O. once daily; if patient was receiving 0.625 mg I.V., then 2.5 mg P.O. once daily. Dosage is adjusted to response.

▶ **To convert from P.O. to I.V. therapy.** *Adults:* 1.25 mg I.V. over 5 minutes q 6 hours. Higher amounts haven't shown greater efficacy.

▶ **Heart failure.** *Adults:* Initially, 2.5 mg P.O. once daily. Dosage may be increased after a few days or weeks according to clinical response. Recommended range is 2.5 to 20 mg twice daily.

▶ **Asymptomatic left ventricular dysfunction.** *Adults:* 2.5 mg P.O. b.i.d., adjust as tolerated to target of 20 mg P.O. daily in divided doses.

Contraindications and precautions

• Contraindicated in patients hypersensitive to drug and those with history of angioedema from previous treatment with ACE inhibitor.

• Use cautiously in patients with renal impairment, especially those with bilateral renal artery stenosis or unilateral renal artery stenosis in a solitary functioning kidney.

Lifespan: In pregnant women, use with extreme caution and only when absolutely necessary because fetal harm may occur. In breastfeeding women and children, safety of drug hasn't been established.

Adverse reactions

CNS: *headache, dizziness, fatigue,* vertigo, asthenia, syncope.
CV: *hypotension,* chest pain.
GI: diarrhea, nausea, abdominal pain, vomiting.
GU: decreased renal function (in patients with bilateral renal artery stenosis or heart failure).
Hematologic: ***neutropenia, thrombocytopenia, agranulocytosis.***
Metabolic: ***hyperkalemia.***
Respiratory: *dry, persistent, tickling, nonproductive cough;* dyspnea.
Skin: rash.
Other: ***angioedema.***

Interactions

Drug-drug. *Diuretics:* May cause excessive reduction of blood pressure. Monitor patient.
Insulin, oral antidiabetics: May increase risk of hypoglycemia, especially at start of enalapril therapy. Monitor patient and glucose levels closely.
Lithium: May increase risk of lithium toxicity. Monitor lithium levels.
NSAIDs: May reduce antihypertensive effect. Monitor blood pressure.
Potassium supplements, potassium-sparing diuretics: May increase risk of hyperkalemia. Avoid these drugs unless hypokalemic blood levels are confirmed.
Drug-herb. *Licorice:* May cause sodium retention and increase blood pressure, interfering with therapeutic effects of ACE inhibitors. Discourage licorice intake during drug therapy.
Drug-lifestyle. *Alcohol use:* May produce additive hypotensive effect. Discourage using together.
Sunlight: Photosensitivity reaction may occur. Urge patient to avoid unprotected or prolonged sun exposure.

Effects on lab test results

• May increase BUN, creatinine, and potassium levels. May decrease sodium and bilirubin levels.

• May decrease liver function test values, hemoglobin, hematocrit, and neutrophil, granulocyte, and platelet counts.

Pharmacokinetics

Absorption: About 60% of P.O. dose absorbed from GI tract.
Distribution: Unknown.
Metabolism: Metabolized extensively to active metabolite.
Excretion: About 94% excreted in urine and feces as enalaprilat and enalapril. *Half-life:* 12 hours.

Route	Onset	Peak	Duration
P.O.	1 hr	4-6 hr	24 hr
I.V.	15 min	1-4 hr	6 hr

Pharmacodynamics

Chemical effect: Unknown; inhibits ACE, which prevents conversion of angiotensin I to angiotensin II, a potent vasoconstrictor. Reduced formation of angiotensin II decreases peripheral arterial resistance, thus decreasing aldosterone secretion.
Therapeutic effect: Lowers blood pressure.

Available forms

Injection: 1.25 mg/ml
Tablets: 2.5 mg, 5 mg, 10 mg, 20 mg

NURSING PROCESS

Assessment

- Obtain history of patient's blood pressure before therapy, and reassess regularly thereafter.
- Monitor CBC with differential counts before therapy, every 2 weeks for first 3 months of therapy, and periodically thereafter.
- Monitor potassium intake and potassium level.
- Be alert for adverse reactions and drug interactions.
- Evaluate patient's and family's knowledge of drug therapy.

Nursing diagnoses

- Risk for injury related to presence of hypertension
- Risk for infection related to drug-induced adverse hematologic reactions
- Deficient knowledge related to drug therapy

Planning and implementation

- Patient with renal insufficiency or hyponatremia should start with 2.5 mg P.O. daily, adjusted slowly.
- **P.O. use:** Follow normal protocol.
- **I.V. use:** Inject drug slowly over at least 5 minutes, or dilute in 50 ml of compatible solution and infuse over 15 minutes. Compatible solutions include D_5W, normal saline injection, dextrose 5% in lactated Ringer's injection, and D_5W in normal saline injection.
- If patient has hypotension after first dose, adjust dose as long as patient is under medical supervision.
- If CBC becomes abnormal or if evidence of infection arises, notify prescriber immediately.
- If angioedema occurs, notify prescriber and stop treatment immediately. Institute appropriate therapy (epinephrine solution 1:1,000 [0.3 to 0.5 ml] S.C.), and take measures to ensure patent airway.

Patient teaching

- Advise patient to report evidence of angioedema, such as breathing difficulty and swelling of face, eyes, lips, or tongue. Angioedema (including laryngeal edema) may occur, especially after first dose.
- Instruct patient to report signs of infection, such as fever and sore throat.
- Advise patient that light-headedness can occur, especially during first few days of therapy. Tell patient to rise slowly to minimize this effect and to report symptoms to prescriber. If patient experiences syncope, he should stop taking drug and call prescriber immediately.
- Tell patient to use caution in hot weather and during exercise. Inadequate fluid intake, vomiting, diarrhea, and excessive perspiration can lead to light-headedness and syncope.
- Advise patient to avoid sodium substitutes; these products may contain potassium, which can cause hyperkalemia in patients taking drug.
- Tell woman to notify prescriber if pregnancy occurs. Drug will need to be discontinued.

Evaluation

- Patient's blood pressure becomes normal.
- Patient's CBC remains normal throughout therapy.
- Patient and family state understanding of drug therapy.

enoxaparin sodium

(eh-NOKS-uh-pah-rin SOH-dee-um)
Lovenox

Pharmacologic class: low–molecular-weight heparin derivative
Therapeutic class: anticoagulant
Pregnancy risk category: B

Indications and dosages

▶ **Prevention of deep vein thrombosis (DVT), which may lead to pulmonary embolism, following hip or knee replacement surgery.** *Adults:* 30 mg S.C. q 12 hours for 7 to 10 days. Initial dose given 12 to 24 hours after surgery, provided hemostasis has been established. Or, for hip replacement surgery, 40 mg S.C. once daily given initially 12 hours before surgery. May continue with 40 mg S.C. once daily or 30 mg S.C. q 12 hours for 3 weeks.

▶ **Prevention of DVT, which may lead to pulmonary embolism, following abdominal surgery.** *Adults:* 40 mg S.C. once daily for 7 to 10 days with initial dose given 2 hours before surgery.

▶ **Prevention of ischemic complications of unstable angina and non-Q-wave MI, when given with aspirin.** *Adults:* 1 mg/kg S.C. q 12 hours for 2 to 8 days together with oral aspirin therapy (100 to 325 mg/day).

▶ **Inpatient treatment of acute DVT with and without pulmonary embolism when given with warfarin sodium.** *Adults:* 1 mg/kg S.C. q 12 hours. Or, 1.5 mg/kg S.C. once daily (at same time every day) for 5 to 7 days until therapeutic oral anticoagulant effect (INR of 2 to 3) has been achieved. Warfarin sodium therapy is usually started within 72 hours of enoxaparin injection.

▶ **Outpatient treatment of acute DVT without pulmonary embolism when given in conjunction with warfarin sodium.** *Adults:* 1 mg/kg S.C. q 12 hours for 5 to 7 days until therapeutic oral anticoagulant effect (INR of 2 to 3) has been achieved. Warfarin sodium therapy is usually started within 72 hours of enoxaparin injection.

▶ **Medical patients during acute illness who are at risk of embolism due to decreased mobility.** *Adults:* 40 mg S.C. once daily for 6 to 11 days. Up to 14 days may be tolerated.

Contraindications and precautions

• Contraindicated in patients hypersensitive to drug, heparin, or pork products; in those with active major bleeding or thrombocytopenia; and in those who demonstrate antiplatelet antibodies in presence of drug.
• Not recommended for thromboprophylaxis in patients with prosthetic heart valves.
• Use with extreme caution, if at all, in patients with postoperative indwelling epidural catheters or patients who have had epidural or spinal anesthesia. Epidural and spinal hematomas have been reported, resulting in long-term or permanent paralysis.
• Use with extreme caution in patients with history of heparin-induced thrombocytopenia.
• Use cautiously in patients with conditions that put them at increased risk for hemorrhage, such as bacterial endocarditis, and in patients with congenital or acquired bleeding disorders, ulcer disease, angiodysplastic GI disease, hemorrhagic CVA, or recent spinal, eye, or brain surgery.

Lifespan: In pregnant or breast-feeding women, use cautiously; in infants born to women who receive drug during pregnancy, congenital anomalies may occur. In pregnant women with prosthetic heart valves, drug is contraindicated. In children, safety hasn't been established.

Adverse reactions

CNS: fever, pain, confusion, ***neurologic injury*** (when used with spinal or epidural puncture).
CV: edema, peripheral edema, ***CV toxicity.***
GI: nausea.
Hematologic: ecchymosis, hypochromic anemia, ***thrombocytopenia, hemorrhage, bleeding complications.***
Skin: irritation, pain, hematoma, or erythema at injection site; *rash; urticaria.*
Other: ***angioedema.***

Interactions

Drug-drug. *Anticoagulants, antiplatelet drugs, NSAIDs:* May increase risk of bleeding. Don't use together.
Plicamycin, valproic acid: May cause hypoprothrombinemia and inhibit platelet aggregation. Monitor patient closely.

Effects on lab test results

• May increase ALT and AST levels.
• May decrease hemoglobin, hematocrit, and platelet count.

Pharmacokinetics

Absorption: Unknown.
Distribution: Unknown.
Metabolism: Unknown.
Excretion: Unknown. *Half-life:* About 4½ hours after S.C. administration.

Route	Onset	Peak	Duration
S.C.	Unknown	3-5 hr	< 24 hr

Pharmacodynamics

Chemical effect: Accelerates formation of antithrombin IIIB–thrombin complex and deactivates thrombin, preventing conversion of

fibrinogen to fibrin. Enoxaparin has higher antifactor Xa–antifactor IIa activity ratio.
Therapeutic effect: Prevents pulmonary embolism and DVT.

Available forms

Injection: 30 mg/0.3 ml; 40 mg/0.4 ml; 60 mg/0.6 ml; 80 mg/0.8 ml; 90 mg/0.6 ml, 100 mg/ml, 120 mg/0.8 ml, 150 mg/ml

NURSING PROCESS

Assessment

- Obtain history of patient's coagulation parameters before therapy.
- Monitor effectiveness by evaluating patient for signs and symptoms of pulmonary embolism or DVT.
- Monitor platelet counts regularly. Patient with normal coagulation doesn't require regular monitoring of PT, INR, and PTT.
- Frequently monitor neurological status in patients who have had spinal or epidural anesthesia. Alert prescriber immediately if neurological compromise is noted.
- Pregnant women should be carefully monitored. Pregnant women and women of childbearing potential should be apprised of the potential hazard to the fetus and the mother if enoxaparin is given during pregnancy.
- Be alert for adverse reactions and drug interactions.
- Evaluate patient's and family's knowledge of drug therapy.

Nursing diagnoses

- Risk for injury related to risk for pulmonary embolism or DVT after knee or hip replacement surgery
- Ineffective protection related to drug-induced bleeding complications
- Deficient knowledge related to drug therapy

Planning and implementation

ALERT: To avoid drug loss, don't expel air bubble from 30- or 40-mg prefilled syringes.
ALERT: Never give drug I.M.
- Don't massage after S.C. injection. Rotate sites and keep accurate record.

ALERT: Enoxaparin can't be used interchangeably (unit for unit) with unfractionated heparin or other low–molecular-weight heparins.
- Don't mix enoxaparin with other injections or infusions.
- Avoid excessive I.M. injections of other drugs to prevent or minimize hematomas. If possible, don't give I.M. injections when patient is anticoagulated.
- To treat severe overdose, give protamine sulfate (a heparin antagonist) by slow I.V. infusion at concentration of 1% to equal dosage of enoxaparin injected.

ALERT: Don't confuse enoxacin with enoxaparin sodium.

Patient teaching
- Instruct patient and family to watch for signs of bleeding and notify prescriber immediately.
- Tell patient to avoid OTC drugs that contain aspirin or other salicylates.

Evaluation

- Patient doesn't develop pulmonary embolism or DVT.
- Patient has no bleeding complications during therapy.
- Patient and family state understanding of drug therapy.

entacapone

(en-TAK-uh-pohn)
Comtan

Pharmacologic class: catechol-O-methyltransferase (COMT) inhibitor
Therapeutic class: antiparkinsonian
Pregnancy risk category: C

Indications and dosages

▶ **Adjunct to levodopa-carbidopa for treatment of idiopathic Parkinson's disease in patients who experience end-of-dose wearing-off.** *Adults:* 200 mg P.O. with each dose of levodopa-carbidopa to maximum of eight times daily. Maximum recommended dosage of entacapone is 1,600 mg daily. Reducing daily levodopa dose or extending the interval between doses may be necessary to optimize patient's response.

Contraindications and precautions

- Contraindicated in patients hypersensitive to drug.

• Use cautiously in patients with hepatic impairment, biliary obstruction, or orthostatic hypotension.
Lifespan: In breast-feeding women, use cautiously.

Adverse reactions

CNS: *dyskinesia, hyperkinesia,* hypokinesia, dizziness, anxiety, somnolence, agitation, fatigue, asthenia, hallucinations.
GI: *nausea, diarrhea,* abdominal pain, constipation, vomiting, dry mouth, dyspepsia, flatulence, gastritis, taste perversion.
GU: *urine discoloration.*
Hematologic: purpura.
Musculoskeletal: back pain.
Respiratory: dyspnea.
Skin: sweating.
Other: bacterial infection.

Interactions

Drug-drug. *Ampicillin, chloramphenicol, cholestyramine, erythromycin, probenecid, rifampin:* May block biliary excretion, resulting in higher levels of entacapone. Use cautiously.
CNS depressants: May have additive effects. Use cautiously.
Drugs metabolized by COMT (bitolterol, dobutamine, dopamine, epinephrine, isoetharine, isoproterenol, norepinephrine): May cause higher levels of these drugs, resulting in increased heart rate, changes in blood pressure, or possibly arrhythmias. Use cautiously.
Nonselective MAO inhibitors (such as phenelzine, tranylcypromine): May inhibit normal catecholamine metabolism. Don't use together.
Drug-lifestyle. *Alcohol use:* May cause additive CNS effects. Discourage using together.

Effects on lab test results

None reported.

Pharmacokinetics

Absorption: Rapid, with serum levels peaking in about 1 hour. Food doesn't affect absorption.
Distribution: About 98% protein-bound, mainly to albumin, and doesn't distribute widely into tissues.
Metabolism: Almost completely metabolized by glucuronidation before elimination. No active metabolites have been identified.
Excretion: About 10% is excreted in urine; the remainder is excreted in bile and feces.
Half-life: 0.4 to 0.7 hours for first phase and 2.4 hours for second phase.

Route	Onset	Peak	Duration
P.O.	1 hr	1 hr	6 hr

Pharmacodynamics

Chemical effect: Entacapone is a reversible inhibitor of peripheral COMT, which is responsible for elimination of various catecholamines, including dopamine. Blocking this pathway when giving levodopa-carbidopa should result in higher levels of levodopa, thereby allowing greater dopaminergic stimulation in the CNS and leading to a greater clinical effect in treating parkinsonian symptoms.
Therapeutic effect: Controls idiopathic Parkinson's disease signs and symptoms.

Available forms

Tablets: 200 mg

NURSING PROCESS

Assessment

• Assess hepatic and biliary function before starting therapy.
• Monitor blood pressure closely. Watch for orthostatic hypotension.
• Monitor patient for hallucinations.
• Evaluate patient's and family's knowledge about drug therapy.

Nursing diagnoses

• Impaired physical mobility related to presence of parkinsonism
• Disturbed thought processes related to drug-induced adverse reactions
• Deficient knowledge related to drug therapy

Planning and implementation

• Drug can be given with immediate or sustained-release levodopa-carbidopa and can be taken with or without food.
• Drug should be used only with levodopa-carbidopa; no antiparkinsonian effects will occur when drug is given as monotherapy.
• Levodopa-carbidopa dosage requirements are usually lower when given with entacapone; levodopa-carbidopa dose should be lowered or dosing interval increased to avoid adverse effects.

- Drug may cause or worsen dyskinesia despite reduction of levodopa dosage.
- Watch for the onset of diarrhea. It usually begins 4 to 12 weeks after therapy starts, but may begin as early as first week or as late as many months after therapy starts.
- Rapid withdrawal or abrupt reduction in dose could lead to signs and symptoms of Parkinson's disease; it may also lead to hyperpyrexia and confusion, a symptom complex resembling neuroleptic malignant syndrome. Discontinue drug slowly and monitor patient closely. Adjust other dopaminergic treatments.
- Observe for urine discoloration.
- Rarely, rhabdomyolysis has occurred with drug use.

Patient teaching
- Instruct patient not to crush or break tablet and to take it at same time as levodopa-carbidopa.
- Warn patient to avoid hazardous activities until CNS effects of drug are known.
- Advise patient to avoid alcohol during treatment.
- Instruct patient to use caution when standing after a prolonged period of sitting or lying down because dizziness may occur. This effect is more common early in therapy.
- Warn patient that hallucinations, increased dyskinesia, nausea, and diarrhea may occur.
- Inform patient that drug may cause urine to turn brownish orange.
- Advise patient to notify prescriber if she's pregnant or breast-feeding or if she plans to become pregnant.

☑ Evaluation
- Patient exhibits improved physical mobility.
- Patient maintains normal thought process.
- Patient and family state understanding of drug therapy.

ephedrine sulfate
(eh-FED-rin SUL-fayt)
Kondon's Nasal†, Pretz-D†

Pharmacologic class: adrenergic
Therapeutic class: bronchodilator, vasopressor (parenteral form), nasal decongestant
Pregnancy risk category: C

Indications and dosages
▶ **To correct hypotension.** *Adults:* 25 to 50 mg I.M. or S.C., or 10 to 25 mg I.V., p.r.n., to maximum of 150 mg/24 hours.
Children: 3 mg/kg or 100 mg/m^2 S.C. or I.V. daily in four to six divided doses.
▶ **Bronchodilation, nasal decongestion.** *Adults and adolescents:* 25 to 50 mg P.O. q 3 to 4 hours p.r.n. For patient use as a bronchodilator, 12.5 to 25 mg P.O. q 4 hr. Maximum, 150 mg in 24 hours. As a nasal decongestant, 0.5% solution applied topically to nasal mucosa as drops or on nasal pack. Instill no more often than q 4 hours.
Children ages 2 to 12: 2 to 3 mg/kg P.O. daily in four to six divided doses.

Contraindications and precautions
- Contraindicated in patients hypersensitive to ephedrine and other sympathomimetic drugs; in those with porphyria, severe coronary artery disease, arrhythmias, angle-closure glaucoma, psychoneurosis, angina pectoris, substantial organic heart disease, or CV disease; and in those taking MAO inhibitors.
- Use with extreme caution in patients with hypertension, hyperthyroidism, nervous or excitable states, diabetes, or prostatic hyperplasia.

Lifespan: In pregnant women and children, use cautiously. Breast-feeding should be avoided during treatment with drug. In elderly men, use with extreme caution.

Adverse reactions
CNS: *insomnia, nervousness,* dizziness, headache, euphoria, confusion, delirium.
CV: *palpitations,* tachycardia, hypertension, precordial pain.
EENT: dryness of nose and throat.
GI: nausea, vomiting, anorexia.
GU: urine retention, painful urination from visceral sphincter spasm.
Musculoskeletal: muscle weakness.
Skin: diaphoresis.

Interactions
Drug-drug. *Acetazolamide:* Increases ephedrine levels. Monitor patient for toxicity.
Alpha-adrenergic blockers: Doesn't counteract beta-adrenergic effects, resulting in hypotension. Monitor blood pressure.

Antihypertensives: Decreases effects. Monitor blood pressure.
Beta blockers: Doesn't counteract alpha-adrenergic effects, resulting in hypertension. Monitor blood pressure.
Digoxin, general anesthetics (halogenated hydrocarbons): Increases risk of ventricular arrhythmias. Monitor patient closely.
Ergot alkaloids: Enhances vasoconstrictor activity. Monitor patient closely.
Guanadrel, guanethidine: Enhances pressor effects of ephedrine. Monitor patient closely.
MAO inhibitors, TCAs: When given with sympathomimetics, may cause severe hypertension (hypertensive crisis). Don't use together.
Methyldopa, reserpine: May inhibit effects of ephedrine. Use together cautiously.

Effects on lab test results

None reported.

Pharmacokinetics

Absorption: Rapid and complete after P.O., I.M., or S.C. administration; unknown after nasal administration.
Distribution: Widely distributed throughout body.
Metabolism: Slowly metabolized in liver.
Excretion: Excreted unchanged in urine. Rate of excretion depends on urine pH. *Half-life:* 3 to 6 hours.

Route	Onset	Peak	Duration
P.O.	15-60 min	Unknown	3-5 hr
I.V.	≤ 5 min	Unknown	Unknown
I.M.	10-20 min	Unknown	30 min-1 hr
S.C.	Unknown	Unknown	30 min-1 hr
Intranasal	Unknown	Unknown	Unknown

Pharmacodynamics

Chemical effect: Stimulates alpha- and beta-adrenergic receptors; direct- and indirect-acting sympathomimetic.
Therapeutic effect: Raises blood pressure, causes bronchodilation, and relieves nasal congestion.

Available forms

Capsules: 25 mg, 50 mg
Injection: 25 mg/ml, 50 mg/ml
Nasal solution: 0.25%†, 0.5%†, 1%†
Tablets: 30 mg ◊

NURSING PROCESS

Assessment

- Obtain history of patient's underlying condition before therapy, and reassess regularly thereafter.
- Be alert for adverse reactions and drug interactions.
- Evaluate patient's and family's knowledge of drug therapy.

Nursing diagnoses

- Ineffective health maintenance related to underlying condition
- Risk for deficient fluid volume related to drug-induced adverse GI reactions
- Deficient knowledge related to drug therapy

Planning and implementation

- Hypoxia, hypercapnia, and acidosis, which may reduce drug effectiveness or increase adverse reactions, must be identified and corrected before or during ephedrine administration.
- Volume deficit must be corrected before giving vasopressors. This drug isn't a substitute for blood or fluid volume replenishment.
- To prevent insomnia, avoid giving within 2 hours before bedtime.
- **P.O. use:** Follow normal protocol.
- **I.V. use:** Give 10 to 25 mg by I.V. injection slowly; repeat in 5 to 10 minutes, if necessary. Compatible with most common I.V. solutions.
- **I.M., S.C., and intranasal use:** Follow normal protocol.
- Notify prescriber if effectiveness decreases. Effectiveness decreases after 2 to 3 weeks, as tolerance develops. Prescriber may need to increase dosage. Drug isn't addictive.

Patient teaching

- Warn patient not to take OTC drugs that contain ephedrine without consulting prescriber.
- Teach patient how to instill nose drops and caution him not to exceed recommended dosage.
- Advise patient to notify prescriber if effectiveness decreases because dosage may need to be adjusted.
- Instruct patient to notify prescriber if adverse reactions occur.
- Caution patient not to perform hazardous activities if adverse CNS reactions occur.

Evaluation

- Patient exhibits improvement in underlying condition.
- Patient maintains adequate hydration throughout therapy.
- Patient and family state understanding of drug therapy.

epinephrine (adrenaline)

(eh-pih-NEF-rin)

Adrenalin†, Bronkaid Mist†, Bronkaid Mistometer ♦, Primatene Mist†

epinephrine bitartrate

AsthmaHaler Mist†, Bronitin Mist†, Bronkaid Mist Suspension†, Medihaler-Epi†, Primatene Mist Suspension†

epinephrine hydrochloride

Adrenalin Chloride†, Ana-Guard, EpiPen Auto-Injector, EpiPen Jr. Auto-Injector, Sus-Phrine

Pharmacologic class: adrenergic
Therapeutic class: bronchodilator, vasopressor, cardiac stimulant, local anesthetic, topical antihemorrhagic
Pregnancy risk category: C

Indications and dosages

▶ **Bronchospasm, hypersensitivity reactions, anaphylaxis.** *Adults:* 0.1 to 0.5 ml of 1:1,000 S.C. or I.M.; repeated q 10 to 15 minutes, p.r.n. Or, 0.1 to 0.25 ml of 1:1,000 (1 to 2.5 ml of commercially available 1:10,000 injection or of 1:10,000 dilution prepared by diluting 1 ml of commercially available 1:1,000 injection with 10 ml of water for injection or normal saline injection) I.V. slowly over 5 to 10 minutes.
Children: 0.01 ml (10 mcg) of 1:1,000/kg S.C.; repeated q 20 minutes to 4 hours, p.r.n. Or, 0.005 ml/kg of 1:200 of Sus-Phrine S.C.; repeated q 8 to 12 hours, p.r.n.

▶ **Hemostasis.** *Adults:* 1:50,000 to 1:1,000 applied topically.

▶ **Acute asthma attacks.** *Adults and children age 4 and older:* 160 to 250 mcg (metered aerosol), which is equivalent to one inhalation, repeated once if necessary after at least 1 minute; subsequent doses shouldn't be given for at least 3 hours. Or, 1% (1:100) solution of epinephrine or 2.25% solution of racepinephrine given by hand-bulb nebulizer as one to three deep inhalations, repeated q 3 hours, p.r.n.

▶ **Prolongation of local anesthetic effect.** *Adults and children:* 1:500,000 to 1:50,000 mixed with local anesthetic.

▶ **Restoration of cardiac rhythm in cardiac arrest.** *Adults:* 1 mg I.V. or 2-2.5 mg into endotracheal tube. Drug may be given intracardiac if no I.V. route or intratracheal route is available. Intracardiac dose is 0.3-0.5 mg (1:10,000 solution). Some clinicians advocate higher dose (up to 5 mg), especially in patients who don't respond to usual I.V. dose. After initial I.V. administration, drug may be infused I.V. at 1 to 4 mcg/minute.
Children: 10 mcg/kg I.V., or 5 to 10 mcg (0.05 to 0.1 ml of 1:10,000)/kg intracardiac.

Contraindications and precautions

- Contraindicated in patients with angle-closure glaucoma, shock (other than anaphylactic shock), organic brain damage, cardiac dilation, arrhythmias, coronary insufficiency, or cerebral arteriosclerosis. Also contraindicated in patients receiving general anesthesia with halogenated hydrocarbons or cyclopropane and in patients in labor (may delay second stage).
- Some commercial products contain sulfites and are contraindicated in patients with sulfite allergies except when epinephrine is being used for treatment of serious allergic reactions or in other emergency situations.
- In conjunction with local anesthetics, epinephrine is contraindicated for use in fingers, toes, ears, nose, or genitalia.
- Use with extreme caution in patients with long-standing bronchial asthma or emphysema who have developed degenerative heart disease and in those with hyperthyroidism, CV disease, hypertension, psychoneurosis, or diabetes.

Lifespan: In pregnant women not in labor and in children, use cautiously. Breast-feeding women should not nurse during drug therapy. In elderly patients, use cautiously.

Adverse reactions

CNS: *nervousness, tremors,* euphoria, anxiety, cold limbs, vertigo, *headache, drowsiness,* diaphoresis, disorientation, agitation, fear, weakness, ***cerebral hemorrhage, CVA,*** increased

rigidity and tremors (in patients with Parkinson's disease).
CV: *palpitations,* widened pulse pressure, *hypertension, tachycardia,* ***ventricular fibrillation, shock,*** anginal pain, ECG changes (including decreased T-wave amplitude).
GI: *nausea,* vomiting.
Metabolic: hyperglycemia, glycosuria.
Respiratory: dyspnea.
Skin: urticaria, pain, hemorrhage at injection site.
Other: pallor.

Interactions

Drug-drug. *Alpha-adrenergic blockers:* May cause hypotension from unopposed beta-adrenergic effects. Monitor blood pressure.
Antihistamines, thyroid hormones, tricyclic antidepressants: When given with sympathomimetics, may cause severe adverse cardiac effects. Avoid giving together.
Beta blockers (such as propranolol): May cause vasoconstriction and reflex bradycardia. Monitor patient carefully.
Cardiac glycosides, general anesthetics (halogenated hydrocarbons): May increase risk of ventricular arrhythmias. Monitor patient closely.
Doxapram, methylphenidate: May enhance CNS stimulation or pressor effects. Monitor patient closely.
Ergot alkaloids: May enhance vasoconstrictor activity. Monitor patient closely.
Guanadrel, guanethidine: Enhances pressor effects of epinephrine. Monitor patient closely.
Levodopa: Enhances risk of cardiac arrhythmias. Monitor patient closely.
MAO inhibitors: Increases risk of hypertensive crisis. Don't use together.

Effects on lab test results

- May increase BUN, glucose, and lactic acid levels.

Pharmacokinetics

Absorption: Well absorbed after S.C. or I.M. injection. Rapidly absorbed after inhalation administration.
Distribution: Distributed widely throughout body.
Metabolism: Metabolized at sympathetic nerve endings, liver, and other tissues to inactive metabolites.
Excretion: Excreted in urine, mainly as its metabolites and conjugates.

Route	Onset	Peak	Duration
I.V.	Immediate	≤ 5 min	1-4 hr
I.M.	Varies	Unknown	1-4 hr
S.C.	6-15 min	≤ 30 min	1-4 hr
Inhalation	3-5 min	Unknown	1-3 hr

Pharmacodynamics

Chemical effect: Stimulates alpha- and beta-adrenergic receptors in sympathetic nervous system.
Therapeutic effect: Relaxes bronchial smooth muscle, causes cardiac stimulation, relieves allergic signs and symptoms, stops local bleeding, and decreases pain sensation.

Available forms

Aerosol inhaler: 160 mcg†, 200 mcg†, 220 mcg†, 250 mcg/metered spray†
Nebulizer inhaler: 0.5%†, 1% (1:100) ◆ †, 2.25% (racepinephrine) ◇ †
Injection: 0.01 mg/ml (1:100,000), 0.1 mg/ml (1:10,000), 0.5 mg/ml (1:2,000), 1 mg/ml (1:1,000) parenteral; 5 mg/ml (1:200) parenteral suspension

NURSING PROCESS

Assessment

- Obtain history of patient's underlying condition before therapy, and reassess regularly thereafter.
- When administering I.V., monitor blood pressure, heart rate, and ECG when therapy starts and frequently thereafter.
- Be alert for adverse reactions and drug interactions.
- Evaluate patient's and family's knowledge of drug therapy.

Nursing diagnoses

- Ineffective health maintenance related to underlying condition
- Decreased cardiac output related to drug-induced adverse CV effects
- Deficient knowledge related to drug therapy

Planning and implementation

- Keep in mind that 1 mg of epinephrine is equal to 1 ml of 1:1,000 or 10 ml of 1:10,000.

• Epinephrine is drug of choice in emergency treatment of acute anaphylactic reactions.
• Discard epinephrine solution after 24 hours or if solution is discolored or contains precipitate. Keep solution in light-resistant container, and don't remove before use.
• **I.V. use:** Don't mix with alkaline solutions. Use D_5W, normal saline injection, lactated Ringer's injection, or combinations of dextrose in sodium chloride. Mix just before use.
• **I.M. use:** Avoid I.M. administration of parenteral suspension into buttocks. Gas gangrene may occur because epinephrine reduces oxygen tension of tissues, encouraging growth of contaminating organisms.
– Massage site after I.M. injection to counteract possible vasoconstriction. Repeated local injection can cause necrosis, resulting from vasoconstriction at injection site.
• **S.C. use:** Follow normal protocol.
• **Inhalation use:** If bronchodilator is given by inhalation and more than one inhalation is ordered, wait 2 minutes between inhalations. Always give bronchodilator first and wait 5 minutes before giving the other if more than one type of inhalant is ordered. Remember that the patient shouldn't receive more than 12 bronchodilator inhalations in 24 hours.
• Giving medication on time is extremely important.
• Notify prescriber if adverse reactions develop; he may adjust dosage or discontinue drug. Also notify prescriber if patient's pulse increases by 20% or more when epinephrine is given.
• If blood pressure rises sharply, rapid-acting vasodilators, such as nitrites or alpha-adrenergic blockers, can be given to counteract marked pressor effect of large doses of epinephrine.
• Epinephrine is destroyed rapidly by oxidizing agents, such as iodine, chromates, nitrates, nitrites, oxygen, and salts of easily reducible metals (such as iron).

Patient teaching

• Tell patient to take drug exactly as prescribed and to take it around the clock.
• Teach patient to perform oral inhalation correctly. Give following instructions for using metered-dose inhaler:
– Clear nasal passages and throat.
– Breathe out, expelling as much air from lungs as possible.
– Place mouthpiece well into mouth and inhale deeply as dose from inhaler is released.
– Hold breath for several seconds, remove mouthpiece, and exhale slowly.
• If more than one inhalation is ordered, tell patient to wait at least 2 minutes before repeating procedure.
• Tell patient who also is using corticosteroid inhaler to use bronchodilator first, then wait about 5 minutes before using corticosteroid. This allows bronchodilator to open air passages for maximum effectiveness.
• Instruct patient who has acute hypersensitivity reactions, such as to bee stings, to self-inject epinephrine at home.
• Tell patient to reduce intake of foods containing caffeine, such as coffee, colas, and chocolates, when taking bronchodilator.
• Instruct patient to contact prescriber immediately if he experiences fluttering of heart, rapid beating of heart, shortness of breath, or chest pain.
• Tell patient not to take any OTC medicines or herbal remedies without medical approval while taking this drug.
• Show patient how to check pulse. Instruct him to check pulse before and after using bronchodilator and to call prescriber if pulse rate increases by more than 20 beats/minute.

☑ Evaluation

• Patient shows improvement in underlying condition.
• Patient maintains adequate cardiac output throughout therapy.
• Patient and family state understanding of drug therapy.

epirubicin hydrochloride

(ep-uh-ROO-bih-sin high-droh-KLOR-ighd)
Ellence

Pharmacologic class: anthracycline
Therapeutic class: antineoplastic
Pregnancy risk category: D

Indications and dosages

▶ **Adjuvant therapy in patients with evidence of axillary node tumor involvement following resection of primary breast cancer.** *Adults:* 100 to120 mg/m² I.V. infusion over 3 to

5 minutes via a free-flowing I.V. solution on day 1 of each cycle q 3 to 4 weeks; or divided equally in two doses on days 1 and 8 of each cycle. Maximum cumulative (lifetime) dose is 900 mg/m^2.

Dosage modification after the first cycle is based on toxicity. For patient with platelet count below 50,000/mm^3, absolute neutrophil count (ANC) below 250/mm^3, neutropenic fever, or grade 3 or 4 nonhematologic toxicity, the day 1 dose in subsequent cycles should be reduced to 75% of the day 1 dose given in the current cycle. Day 1 therapy in subsequent cycles should be delayed until platelets are 100,000/mm^3 or above, ANC is 1,500/mm^3 or above, and nonhematologic toxicities recover to grade 1.

For patients receiving divided doses (days 1 and 8), the day 8 dose should be 75% of the day 1 dose if platelet counts are 75,000 to 100,000/mm^3 and ANC is 1,000 to 1,499/mm^3. If day 8 platelet counts are below 75,000/mm^3, ANC is below 1,000/mm^3, or grade 3 or 4 nonhematologic toxicity has occurred, the day 8 dose should be omitted.

Contraindications and precautions

- Contraindicated in patient hypersensitive to this drug, other anthracyclines, or anthracenediones. Also contraindicated in patients with baseline neutrophil counts below 1,500 cells/mm^3, in those with severe myocardial insufficiency or recent MI, in those previously treated with anthracyclines to total cumulative doses, and in those with severe hepatic dysfunction.
- Use cautiously in patients with active or dormant cardiac disease, previous or simultaneous radiotherapy to the mediastinal and pericardial area, previous therapy with other anthracyclines or anthracenediones, or simultaneous use of other cardiotoxic drugs.

Lifespan: In pregnant and breast-feeding women, drug is contraindicated. In children, safety hasn't been established. In elderly patients, especially women older than age 70, use cautiously because of greater chance of toxicity.

Adverse reactions

CNS: *lethargy,* fever.
CV: ***cardiomyopathy, heart failure,*** *hot flushes.*
EENT: *conjunctivitis, keratitis.*
GI: *nausea, vomiting, diarrhea,* anorexia, *mucositis.*
GU: *amenorrhea.*
Hematologic: **LEUKOPENIA, NEUTROPENIA,** ***febrile neutropenia,*** *anemia,* **THROMBOCYTOPENIA.**
Skin: *alopecia,* rash, itch, skin changes.
Other: *infection, local toxicity.*

Interactions

Drug-drug. *Cytotoxic drugs:* Additive toxicities (especially hematologic and GI) may occur. Monitor patient closely.
Calcium channel blockers, other cardioactive compounds: May increase risk of heart failure. Monitor cardiac function closely.
Cimetidine: Increases epirubicin level (by 50%) and decreases clearance. Avoid using together.
Radiation therapy: Effects may be enhanced. Monitor patient carefully.

Effects on lab test results

- May decrease hemoglobin, hematocrit, and WBC, neutrophil, and platelet counts.

Pharmacokinetics

Absorption: Administered I.V.
Distribution: Rapidly and widely distributed into tissues. Plasma protein–binding is about 77%, mainly to albumin, and appears to concentrate in RBCs.
Metabolism: Extensively and rapidly metabolized by the liver. Several metabolites form with little to no cytotoxic activity.
Excretion: Eliminated mostly by biliary excretion and, to a lesser extent, urinary excretion.

Route	Onset	Peak	Duration
I.V.	Unknown	Unknown	Unknown

Pharmacodynamics

Chemical effect: The precise mechanism of epirubicin's cytotoxic effects isn't completely known. It's thought to form a complex with DNA by intercalation between nucleotide base pairs, thereby inhibiting DNA, RNA, and protein synthesis. DNA cleavage occurs, resulting in cytocidal activity. Drug may also interfere with replication and transcription of DNA, and it generates cytotoxic free radicals.
Therapeutic effect: Kills certain cancer cells.

Available forms

Injection: 2 mg/ml

NURSING PROCESS

Assessment

- Obtain baseline total bilirubin, AST, creatinine, and CBC (including ANC), and evaluate cardiac function by measuring left ventricular ejection fraction (LVEF) before therapy.
- Monitor LVEF regularly during therapy, and discontinue drug at the first sign of impaired cardiac function. Monitor patient for early signs of cardiac toxicity, including sinus tachycardia, ECG abnormalities, tachyarrhythmias, bradycardia, AV block, and bundle branch block.
- Obtain total and differential WBC, RBC, and platelet counts before and during each cycle of therapy.
- Evaluate patient's and family's knowledge about drug therapy.

Nursing diagnoses

- Risk for injury related to drug-induced adverse reactions
- Risk for infection related to myelosuppression
- Deficient knowledge related to drug therapy

Planning and implementation

- Patients with bone marrow dysfunction, hepatic dysfunction, or severe renal dysfunction should receive lower dosages.
- Epirubicin should be given under the supervision of a prescriber experienced in the use of cancer chemotherapy. Pregnant women shouldn't handle this drug.
- Wear protective clothing (goggles, gown, disposable gloves) when handling this drug.

ALERT: Drug is a vesicant. Never give I.M. or S.C. Always give through free-flowing I.V. solution of normal saline solution or D_5W over 3 to 5 minutes.

- Facial flushing and local erythematous streaking along the vein may indicate too-rapid administration.
- Avoid veins over joints or in limbs with compromised venous or lymphatic drainage.
- Immediately stop infusion if burning or stinging occurs, and restart in another vein.
- Don't mix drug with heparin or fluorouracil because precipitation may result.
- Don't mix in same syringe with other drugs.
- Discard unused solution in vial 24 hours after vial penetrated.
- Patients receiving 120 mg/m^2 of epirubicin should also receive prophylactic antibiotic therapy with trimethoprim-sulfamethoxazole or a fluoroquinolone.
- Giving antiemetics before epirubicin may be necessary to reduce nausea and vomiting.
- Delayed cardiac toxicity may occur 2 to 3 months after completion of treatment. It causes reduced LVEF, evidence of heart failure (tachycardia, dyspnea, pulmonary edema, dependent edema, hepatomegaly, ascites, pleural effusion, and gallop rhythm). Delayed cardiac toxicity is dependent upon the cumulative dose of epirubicin. Don't exceed a cumulative dose of 900 mg/m^2.
- Monitor uric acid, potassium, calcium phosphate, and creatinine immediately after initial chemotherapy administration in patients susceptible to tumor lysis syndrome. Hydration, urine alkalinization, and prophylaxis with allopurinol may prevent hyperuricemia and minimize complications of tumor lysis syndrome.
- The WBC nadir usually occurs 10 to14 days after drug administration and returns to normal by day 21.
- Anthracycline-induced leukemia may occur.
- Administration of drug after previous radiation therapy may induce an inflammatory cell reaction at the site of irradiation.

Patient teaching

- Advise patient to report nausea, vomiting, stomatitis, dehydration, fever, evidence of infection, or symptoms of heart failure (tachycardia, dyspnea, edema) or injection site pain.
- Inform patient of the risk of cardiac damage and treatment-related leukemia with use of drug.
- Women of childbearing age should avoid getting pregnant, and men should use effective contraception during treatment.
- Advise women that irreversible amenorrhea or premature menopause may occur.
- Advise patient about probable hair loss. Tell patient that hair regrowth usually occurs 2 to 3 months after therapy is discontinued.
- Advise patient that urine may appear red 1 to 2 days after administration of the drug.

Evaluation

- Patient sustains no injury from drug-induced adverse reactions.

• Patient remains free of infection.
• Patient and family state understanding of drug therapy.

epoetin alfa (erythropoietin)

(ee-POH-eh-tin AL-fah)
Epogen, Eprex ♦, Procrit

Pharmacologic class: glycoprotein
Therapeutic class: hematopoietic agent
Pregnancy risk category: C

Indications and dosages

▶ **Anemia from reduced production of endogenous erythropoietin caused by end-stage renal disease.** *Adults:* Dosage is individualized. Starting dose is 50 to 100 units/kg I.V. three times weekly. (Patients with chronic renal failure who are not on dialysis or patients receiving continuous peritoneal dialysis may receive drug by S.C. injection or I.V.) Dosage reduced when target hematocrit is reached or if hematocrit rises more than 4% in any 2-week period. Dosage increased if hematocrit doesn't increase by 5 to 6 points after 8 weeks of therapy. Maintenance dosage is individualized.

▶ **Anemia in children with chronic renal failure who are undergoing dialysis.** *Infants and children ages 1 month to 16 years:* 50 units/kg I.V. or S.C. three times weekly. Reduce dosage when target hematocrit is reached or if hematocrit rises more than 4 points in a 2-week period. Increase dosage if hematocrit doesn't rise by 5 to 6 points after 8 to 12 weeks of therapy and is below target range. Maintenance dose is highly individualized to maintain hematocrit in target range.

▶ **Adjunct treatment of HIV-infected patients with anemia secondary to zidovudine therapy.** *Adults:* 100 units/kg I.V. or S.C. three times weekly for 8 to 12 weeks or until target hematocrit is reached.

▶ **Anemia secondary to chemotherapy.** *Adults:* 150 units/kg S.C. three times weekly for 8 weeks or until target hematocrit is reached. Dosage then increased up to 300 units/kg S.C. three times weekly, if needed.

▶ **Anemia related to rheumatoid arthritis and rheumatic disease‡.** *Adults:* 50 to 200 units/kg S.C. three times weekly.

▶ **Anemia related to prematurity‡.** *Neonates:* 25 to 100 units/kg S.C. three times weekly.

Contraindications and precautions

• Contraindicated in patients with uncontrolled hypertension, hypersensitivity to mammal-cell–derived products or albumin (human).
Lifespan: In pregnant and breast-feeding women, use cautiously. In children, safety of drug hasn't been established.

Adverse reactions

CNS: *headache,* ***seizures,*** *paresthesia, fatigue,* dizziness, *asthenia.*
CV: increased clotting of arteriovenous grafts, *hypertension, edema.*
GI: *nausea, vomiting, diarrhea.*
Hematologic: iron deficiency, thrombocytosis.
Musculoskeletal: *arthralgia.*
Respiratory: *cough, shortness of breath.*
Skin: *rash, injection site reactions, urticaria.*
Other: *pyrexia.*

Interactions

None significant.

Effects on lab test results

• May increase BUN, creatinine, uric acid, potassium, and phosphate levels.
• May increase platelet count.

Pharmacokinetics

Absorption: After S.C. administration, systemic absorption is delayed, incomplete, and variable compared with I.V. administration.
Distribution: Unknown.
Metabolism: Unknown.
Excretion: Unknown.

Route	Onset	Peak	Duration
I.V.	1-6 wk	Immediate	Unknown
S.C.	1-6 wk	5-24 hr	Unknown

Pharmacodynamics

Chemical effect: Mimics effects of erythropoietin, a naturally occurring hormone produced by the kidneys. Epoetin alfa is one of factors controlling rate of RBC production. It acts on erythroid tissues in bone marrow, stimulating mitotic activity of erythroid progenitor cells and early precursor cells. It functions as a

growth factor and as a differentiating factor, enhancing rate of RBC production.
Therapeutic effect: Corrects anemia.

Available forms

Injection: 2,000 units/ml, 3,000 units/ml, 4,000 units/ml, 10,000 units/ml, 20,000 units/ml, 40,000 units/ml

NURSING PROCESS

Assessment

- Assess patient's blood count and blood pressure before therapy.
- Assess effectiveness by monitoring blood count results. Hematocrit may rise and cause excessive clotting. Watch for evidence of blood clot formation such as shortness of breath and cold, swollen, or pulseless limb.
- Patient's response to epoetin alfa depends on amount of endogenous erythropoietin in plasma. Patients with 500 units/L or more usually have transfusion-dependent anemia and probably won't respond to drug. Those with levels below 500 units/L usually respond well.
- Be alert for adverse reactions.
- Monitor blood pressure closely. Up to 80% of patients with chronic renal failure have hypertension. Blood pressure may rise, especially when hematocrit is increasing in early part of therapy.
- After injection (usually within 2 hours), some patients complain of pain or discomfort in their limbs (long bones) and pelvis and of coldness and sweating. Symptoms may persist for up to 12 hours and then disappear.
- Monitor patient's hydration status if adverse GI reactions occur.
- Evaluate patient's and family's knowledge of drug therapy.

Nursing diagnoses

- Ineffective protection related to reduced production of endogenous erythropoietin
- Risk for deficient fluid volume related to drug-induced adverse GI reactions
- Deficient knowledge related to drug therapy

Planning and implementation

- **I.V. use:** Give drug by direct injection without dilution. Solution contains no preservatives. Discard unused portion. Don't mix with other drugs.
- **S.C. use:** Follow normal protocol.
- When used in HIV-infected patient, be prepared to individualize dosage based on response. Dosage recommendations are for patients with endogenous erythropoietin levels of 500 units/L or less and cumulative zidovudine doses of 4.2 g/week or less.
- Patient treated with epoetin alfa may need additional heparin to prevent clotting during dialysis.
- Institute diet restrictions or drug therapy to control blood pressure. Reduce dosage in patient who exhibits rapid rise in hematocrit (more than 4 points in a 2-week period) because of risk of hypertension.

Patient teaching

- Advise patient that blood specimens will be drawn weekly for blood counts and that dosage adjustments may be made based on results.
- Warn patient to avoid hazardous activities, such as driving or operating heavy machinery, early in therapy. Excessively rapid rise in hematocrit may increase the risk of seizures.
- Tell patient to notify prescriber if adverse reactions occur.

Evaluation

- Patient's blood count is normal.
- Patient maintains adequate hydration throughout therapy.
- Patient and family state understanding of drug therapy.

eprosartan mesylate

(eh-proh-SAR-ten MEH-sih-layt)
Teveten

Pharmacologic class: angiotensin II receptor antagonist
Therapeutic class: antihypertensive
Pregnancy risk category: C (D in second and third trimesters)

Indications and dosages

▶ **Hypertension, alone or with other antihypertensives.** *Adults:* Initially, 600 mg P.O. daily. Daily dosage ranges from 400 to 800 mg given as single daily dose or two divided doses.

Contraindications and precautions

- Contraindicated in patients hypersensitive to drug or its components.
- Use cautiously in patients with an activated renin-angiotensin system, such as volume- or salt-depleted patients, and in patients whose renal function may depend on the activity of the renin-angiotensin-aldosterone system, such as patients with severe heart failure.
- Use cautiously in patients with renal artery stenosis.

Lifespan: In pregnant and breast-feeding women, drug is contraindicated. In children, safety and efficacy haven't been established. In elderly patients, use cautiously because of decreased response to drug.

Adverse reactions

CNS: depression, fatigue, headache, dizziness.
CV: chest pain, dependent edema.
EENT: pharyngitis, rhinitis, sinusitis.
GI: abdominal pain, dyspepsia, diarrhea.
GU: urinary tract infection.
Hematologic: ***neutropenia.***
Metabolic: hypertriglyceridemia.
Musculoskeletal: arthralgia, myalgia.
Respiratory: cough, upper respiratory tract infection, bronchitis.
Other: injury, viral infection.

Interactions

None significant.

Effects on lab test results

- May increase BUN and triglyceride levels.
- May decrease neutrophil count.

Pharmacokinetics

Absorption: Absolute bioavailability of single oral dose is about 13%. Plasma levels peak in 1 to 2 hours.
Distribution: Plasma protein–binding is about 98%.
Metabolism: No active metabolites.
Excretion: Eliminated by biliary and renal excretion, primarily as unchanged drug. Following P.O. administration, about 90% is recovered in feces and about 7% in urine. *Terminal elimination half-life:* Typically 5 to 9 hours.

Route	Onset	Peak	Duration
P.O.	1-2 hr	1-3 hr	24 hr

Pharmacodynamics

Chemical effect: Drug is an angiotensin II receptor that blocks vasoconstrictor and aldosterone-secreting effects of angiotensin II by selectively blocking binding of angiotensin II to its receptor sites in many tissues, such as vascular smooth muscle and the adrenal gland.
Therapeutic effect: Lowers blood pressure.

Available forms

Tablets: 400 mg, 600 mg

NURSING PROCESS

Assessment

- Monitor blood pressure closely during start of treatment. If hypotension occurs, place patient in supine position and, if necessary, give I.V. infusion of normal saline solution.
- Determine patient's fluid balance status and sodium level before starting drug therapy.
- Elderly patients have a slightly decreased response to drug.
- Be alert for adverse reactions.
- Evaluate patient's and family's knowledge of drug therapy.

Nursing diagnoses

- Risk for injury related to presence of hypertension
- Risk for infection related to neutropenia
- Deficient knowledge related to drug therapy

Planning and implementation

- Correct hypovolemia and hyponatremia before starting therapy to reduce risk of symptomatic hypotension.
- A transient episode of hypotension doesn't contraindicate continued treatment. Drug may be restarted once patient's blood pressure has stabilized.
- Drug may be used alone or with other antihypertensives, such as diuretics and calcium channel blockers. Maximum blood pressure response may take 2 to 3 weeks.
- Monitor patient for facial or lip swelling because angioedema has occurred with other angiotensin II antagonists.

Patient teaching

- Advise woman of childbearing age to use reliable form of contraception and to notify prescriber immediately if pregnancy is suspected.

Drug may need to be discontinued under medical supervision.

- Advise patient to report facial or lip swelling and signs and symptoms of infection, such as fever or sore throat.
- Tell patient to notify prescriber before taking OTC product to treat a dry cough.
- Inform patient that drug may be taken without regard to meals.
- Tell patient to store drug at a controlled room temperature (68° to 77° F [20° to 25° C]).

Evaluation

- Patient's blood pressure is well controlled, and patient remains free of injury.
- WBCs are within normal limits.
- Patient and family state understanding of drug therapy.

eptifibatide

(ep-tih-FY-beh-tide)
Integrilin

Pharmacologic class: glycoprotein IIb/IIIa (GP IIb/IIIa) inhibitor
Therapeutic class: antiplatelet agent
Pregnancy risk category: B

Indications and dosages

▶ **Acute coronary syndrome (unstable angina or non–Q-wave MI) in patients being managed medically and in those undergoing percutaneous coronary intervention (PCI).** *Adults with creatinine less than 2 mg/dl:* 180 mcg/kg I.V. bolus as soon as possible following diagnosis, followed by a continuous I.V. infusion of 2 mcg/kg per minute until hospital discharge or initiation of coronary artery bypass graft surgery, up to 72 hours. If undergoing PCI, continue infusion until hospital discharge, or for up to 18 to 24 hours after the procedure, whichever comes first, up to 96 hours. Patients weighing more than 121 kg (266 lb) should receive a bolus maximum of 22.6 mg followed by a maximum infusion rate of 15 mg/hour.
Adults with creatinine between 2 and 4 mg/dl: 180 mcg/kg I.V. bolus as soon as possible following diagnosis, followed by an infusion rate of 1 mcg/kg per minute. For patients weighing more than 121 kg (266 lb), the maximum bolus dose is 22.6 mg and the maximum infusion rate is 7.5 mg/hour.

▶ **Treatment in patients who are undergoing percutaneous coronary intervention (PCI).** *Adults with creatinine less than 2 mg/dl initiated at the time of PCI:* 180 mcg/kg I.V. bolus given immediately before the procedure, immediately followed by an infusion of 2 mcg/kg/minute and a second IV bolus of 180 mcg/kg given 10 minutes after the first bolus. Continue infusion until hospital discharge or for up to 18 to 24 hours, whichever comes first; a minimum of 12 hours of eptifibatide infusion is recommended. Patients weighing more than 121 kg should receive a maximum bolus of 22.6 mg/bolus followed by a maximum of 15 mg/hour.
Adults with creatinine between 2 and 4 mg/dl initiated at the time of PCI: 180 mcg/kg given immediately before the procedure, immediately followed by an infusion of 1 mcg/kg per minute and a second bolus of 180 mcg/kg given 10 minutes after the first bolus. Patients weighing more than 121 kg should receive a maximum of 22.6 mg/bolus followed by a maximum rate of 7.5 mg/hour.

Contraindications

- Contraindicated in patients hypersensitive to drug or its ingredients and in those with history of bleeding diathesis, evidence of active abnormal bleeding within previous 30 days, severe hypertension (systolic blood pressure over 200 mm Hg or diastolic blood pressure over 110 mm Hg) not adequately controlled with antihypertensives, major surgery within previous 6 weeks, history of CVA within 30 days, history of hemorrhagic CVA, current or planned use of another parenteral GP IIb/IIIa inhibitor, or platelet count below 100,000/mm^3. Also, contraindicated in patients whose creatinine is 2 mg/dl or higher (for the 180-mcg/kg bolus and 2-mcg/kg/minute infusion) or 4 mg/dl or higher (for the 135-mcg/kg bolus and 0.5-mcg/kg/minute infusion) and in patients dependent on renal dialysis.

Lifespan: In breast-feeding women, use cautiously. In children, safety hasn't been established.

Adverse reactions

CV: hypotension.
GU: hematuria.

Hematologic: BLEEDING, *thrombocytopenia.*
Other: bleeding at femoral artery access site.

Interactions

Drug-drug. *Clopidogrel, dipyridamole, NSAIDs, oral anticoagulants (warfarin), thrombolytics, ticlopidine:* May increase risk of bleeding. Monitor patient closely.
Other inhibitors of platelet receptor IIb/IIIa: May have potential for serious bleeding. Don't give together.

Effects on lab test results

- May decrease platelet count.

Pharmacokinetics

Absorption: Administered I.V.
Distribution: Drug is 25% bound to plasma proteins.
Metabolism: Not reported. No major metabolites have been detected in human plasma.
Excretion: Most of drug is excreted in urine. *Elimination half-life:* 2.5 hours.

Route	Onset	Peak	Duration
I.V.	Immediate	Immediate	4-6 hr after therapy stops

Pharmacodynamics

Chemical effect: Drug reversibly binds to the glycoprotein IIb/IIIa (GP IIb/IIIa) receptor on human platelets and inhibits platelet aggregation.
Therapeutic effect: Prevents clot formation.

Available forms

Injection: 10-ml (2 mg/ml), 100-ml (0.75 mg/ml) vials

NURSING PROCESS

Assessment

- Obtain history of patient's underlying medical conditions, especially conditions that put patient at increased risk for bleeding.
- Obtain accurate patient weight. Use drug cautiously in patients weighing more than 315 lb (143 kg).
- Perform baseline laboratory tests before start of drug therapy; also determine hemoglobin, hematocrit, platelet count, and PT, INR, PTT, and creatinine levels.
- Monitor patient for bleeding.
- Evaluate patient's and family's knowledge about drug therapy.

Nursing diagnoses

- Ineffective cardiopulmonary tissue perfusion related to presence of acute coronary syndrome
- Risk for injury related to increased bleeding tendencies
- Deficient knowledge related to drug therapy

Planning and implementation

- Withdraw bolus dose from 10-ml vial into a syringe and give by I.V. push over 1 to 2 minutes. Give I.V. infusion undiluted directly from 100-ml vial using an infusion pump.
- Inspect solution for particulate matter before use. If particles are visible, the sterility is suspect; discard solution.
- Drug may be given in same I.V. line as alteplase, atropine, dobutamine, heparin, lidocaine, meperidine, metoprolol, midazolam, morphine, nitroglycerin, or verapamil.
- Don't give drug in same I.V. line as furosemide.
- Drug may be given in same I.V. line with normal saline solution or normal saline and 5% dextrose; main infusion may also contain up to 60 mEq/L of potassium chloride.
- Drug is intended for use with heparin and aspirin.
- Discontinue eptifibatide and heparin, and achieve sheath hemostasis by standard compressive techniques at least 4 hours before hospital discharge.
- If patient will undergo coronary artery bypass graft surgery, infusion should be stopped before surgery.
- Minimize use of arterial and venous punctures, I.M. injections, urinary catheters, and nasotracheal and nasogastric tubes.
- When obtaining I.V. access, avoid use of noncompressible sites (such as subclavian or jugular veins).
- If patient's platelet count is below 100,000/mm^3, notify prescriber and discontinue eptifibatide and heparin.
- Store vials in refrigerator at 36° to 46° F (2° to 8° C). Protect from light until administration.

Patient teaching

• Explain that drug is a blood thinner used to prevent chest pain and heart attack.
• Explain that the benefits of the drug far outweigh the risk of serious bleeding.
• Instruct patient to report chest discomfort or other adverse events immediately.

Evaluation

• Patient maintains adequate cardiopulmonary tissue perfusion.
• Patient has no life-threatening bleeding episode.
• Patient and family state understanding of drug therapy.

ergotamine tartrate

(er-GAH-tuh-meen TAR-trayt)
Cafergot, Ergodryl Mono ◇, Ergomar, Ergostat, Gynergen ♦, Medihaler Ergotamine ♦

Pharmacologic class: sympatholytic adrenergic blocker
Therapeutic class: vasoconstrictor
Pregnancy risk category: X

Indications and dosages

▶ **Vascular or migraine headache.** *Adults:* Initially, 2 mg P.O. or S.L.; then 1 to 2 mg P.O. or S.L. q 30 minutes to maximum of 6 mg per attack or 10 mg weekly. For aerosol inhaler, 1 spray (360 mcg) initially, repeated q 5 minutes, p.r.n., to maximum of 6 sprays (2.16 mg) per 24 hours or 15 sprays (5.4 mg) weekly. For suppositories, initially, 2 mg P.R. at onset of attack, repeated in 1 hour, p.r.n. Maximum dosage is two suppositories per attack or five suppositories weekly.

Contraindications and precautions

• Contraindicated in patients with peripheral or occlusive vascular diseases, coronary artery disease, hypertension, hepatic or renal dysfunction, severe pruritus, sepsis, or hypersensitivity to ergot alkaloids. Avoid prolonged or excessive use because of risk of ergotism and gangrene. Cafergot is contraindicated with use of a potent CYP3A4 inhibitor.
Lifespan: In pregnant women, drug is contraindicated. In breast-feeding women, use cautiously. Excessive dosage or prolonged administration of drug may inhibit lactation. In children, safety of drug hasn't been established; however, some clinicians may give 1 mg S.L. or P.O. in older children and adolescents. If no improvement, may give another 1 mg S.L. or P.O. after 30 minutes.

Adverse reactions

CV: numbness and tingling in fingers and toes, transient tachycardia or ***bradycardia,*** precordial distress and pain, increased arterial pressure, angina pectoris, peripheral vasoconstriction.
GI: *nausea, vomiting.*
GU: uterine contractions.
Musculoskeletal: weakness in legs, muscle pain in limbs.
Skin: itching, localized edema.

Interactions

Drug-drug. *Erythromycin, other macrolides:* May cause symptoms of ergot toxicity. Vasodilators (nitroprusside, nifedipine, or prazosin) may be ordered to treat such an attack. Monitor patient closely.
Potent CYP3A4 inhibitors: May cause ergot toxicity. Don't use together.
Propranolol and other beta blockers, vasoconstrictors, sympathomimetics: Blocks natural pathway for vasodilation in patients receiving ergot alkaloids; may result in excessive vasoconstriction and hypertension. Watch closely if drugs are used together.
Drug-lifestyle. *Smoking:* May cause vasoconstriction. Discourage smoking.

Effects on lab test results

None reported.

Pharmacokinetics

Absorption: Rapid after inhalation and variable after P.O. or P.R. administration.
Distribution: Widely distributed throughout body.
Metabolism: Extensively metabolized in liver.
Excretion: Thought to be primarily excreted in feces; 4% excreted in urine.

Route	Onset	Peak	Duration
P.O.	Varies	30 min-3 hr	Varies
P.R., S.L., inhalation	Varies	Unknown	Varies

Pharmacodynamics

Chemical effect: Stimulates alpha-adrenergic receptors, causing peripheral vasoconstriction. Drug also inhibits reuptake of norepinephrine, increasing vasoconstrictor activity.
Therapeutic effect: Relieves vascular or migraine headache.

Available forms

Aerosol inhaler: 360 mcg/metered spray ♦
Capsules: 1 mg ◇
Suppositories: 2 mg
Tablets: 1 mg ♦
Tablets (sublingual): 2 mg

NURSING PROCESS

Assessment

- Obtain history of patient's headache before therapy, and reassess regularly thereafter.
- Be alert for adverse reactions and drug interactions.
- Be alert for ergotamine rebound or increase in frequency and duration of headache, which may occur if drug is discontinued suddenly.
- Evaluate patient's and family's knowledge of drug therapy.

Nursing diagnoses

- Acute pain related to presence of vascular or migraine headache
- Decreased peripheral tissue perfusion related to vasoconstriction
- Deficient knowledge related to drug therapy

Planning and implementation

- Drug is most effective when used during prodromal stage of headache or as soon as possible after onset.
- Avoid prolonged administration; don't exceed recommended dosage.
- Store drug in light-resistant container.
- **P.O. and Inhalation use:** Follow normal protocol.
- **P.R. use:** If suppository softens, chill it in ice-cold water while still in wrapper.
- **S.L. use:** Don't give drug with food or drink while tablets are dissolving.
– S.L. tablets are preferred for use during early stage of attack because of their rapid absorption.

Patient teaching

- Tell patient not to eat, drink, or smoke while S.L. tablet is dissolving.
- Warn patient not to increase dosage without first consulting prescriber.
- Advise patient to avoid prolonged exposure to cold weather whenever possible. Cold may increase adverse reactions to drug.
- Instruct patient receiving long-term therapy to check for and report coldness in limbs or tingling in fingers and toes. Severe vasoconstriction may result in tissue damage.
- Instruct patient on correct use of inhaler.
- Help patient evaluate underlying causes of stress, which may precipitate attacks.

Evaluation

- Patient is free from pain.
- Patient maintains adequate tissue perfusion to limbs throughout therapy.
- Patient and family state understanding of drug therapy.

ertapenem sodium
(er-ta-PEN-uhm SOH-dee-um)
Invanz

Pharmacologic class: 1-beta methyl-carbapenem
Therapeutic class: anti-infective
Pregnancy risk category: B

Indications and dosages

▶ **Complicated intra-abdominal infections caused by *Escherichia coli, Clostridium clostridiiforme, Eubacterium lentum, Peptostreptococcus species, Bacteroides fragilis, B. distasonis, B. ovatus, B. thetaiotaomicron, B. uniformis*.** *Adults:* 1 g I.V. or I.M. once daily for 5 to 14 days.
▶ **Complicated skin and skin-structure infections caused by *Staphylococcus aureus* (methicillin-susceptible strains), *Streptococcus pyogenes, E. coli, Peptostreptococcus* species.** *Adults:* 1 g I.V. or I.M. once daily for 7 to 14 days.
▶ **Community-acquired pneumonia caused by *S. pneumoniae* (penicillin-susceptible strains), *Haemophilus influenzae* (beta-lactamase–negative strains), *Moraxella catarrhalis*.** *Adults:* 1 g I.V. or I.M. once daily for

10 to 14 days. If clinical improvement occurs after at least 3 days of treatment, appropriate oral therapy may be used to complete the full course of therapy.

▶ **Complicated UTI, including pyelonephritis caused by *E. coli, Klebsiella pneumoniae.*** *Adults:* 1 g I.V. or I.M. once daily for 10 to 14 days. After at least 3 days of treatment, if clinical improvement occurs, appropriate oral therapy may be used to complete the full course of therapy.

▶ **Acute pelvic infections including postpartum endomyometritis, septic abortion, and postsurgical gynecologic infections caused by *S. agalactiae, E. coli, B. fragilis, Porphyromonas asaccharolyticus, Peptostreptococcus species, Prevotella bivia.*** *Adults:* 1 g I.V. or I.M. once daily for 3 to 10 days.

Patients with renal impairment: If creatinine clearance is less than or equal to 30 ml/minute, give 500 mg daily. A supplemental dose of 150 mg is recommended after a hemodialysis session only in patients who are given the recommended daily ertapenem dose of 500 mg within 6 hours before hemodialysis.

Contraindications and precautions

- Contraindicated in patients hypersensitive to any component of the drug or to other drugs in the same class and in patients who have had anaphylactic reactions to beta-lactams. I.M. use is contraindicated in patients hypersensitive to local anesthetics of the amide type (because lidocaine hydrochloride is the diluent). Methicillin-resistant *Staphylococci* and *Enterococci sp.* are resistant to ertapenem.
- Use cautiously in patients with CNS disorders or compromised renal function, as seizures may occur. Ertapenem sodium may be removed by hemodialysis if necessary.

Lifespan: In pregnant women, use only if clearly needed. In breast-feeding women, use only when the expected benefit outweighs the risk because drug appears in breast milk. In children, safety and effectiveness haven't been established. In elderly patients with impaired renal function, select dose carefully and monitor renal function.

Adverse reactions

CNS: asthenia, fatigue, anxiety, altered mental status, dizziness, headache, insomnia, ***seizures,*** fever, pain.
CV: edema, swelling, chest pain, hypertension, ***hypotension,*** tachycardia.
EENT: pharyngitis.
GI: abdominal pain, acid regurgitation, oral candidiasis, constipation, *diarrhea,* dyspepsia, nausea, vomiting, abdominal distention, *C. difficile* infection, ***pseudomembranous colitis.***
GU: vaginitis, renal dysfunction, hematuria, urinary retention.
Hematologic: coagulation abnormalities, eosinophilia, anemia, ***neutropenia, leukopenia, thrombocytopenia, thrombocytosis.***
Hepatic: jaundice.
Metabolic: hyperglycemia, ***hyperkalemia,*** hypernatremia.
Musculoskeletal: leg pain.
Respiratory: cough, dyspnea, rales, rhonchi, ***respiratory distress.***
Skin: erythema, pruritus, rash, extravasation, infused vein complication, phlebitis, thrombophlebitis.
Other: ***septicemia, death,*** chills.

Interactions

Drug-drug. *Probenecid:* Reduces renal clearance and increases half-life. Avoid using together.

Effects on lab test results

- May increase albumin, ALT, AST, alkaline phosphatase, BUN, creatinine, glucose, potassium, sodium, and bilirubin levels. May decrease bicarbonate level.
- May increase PT, PTT, eosinophil count, and urinary RBC and WBC counts. May decrease hemoglobin, hematocrit, and segmented neutrophil and WBC counts. May increase or decrease platelet count.

Pharmacokinetics

Absorption: Almost completely absorbed after intramuscular administration. Mean bioavailability of 90%.
Distribution: Highly bound to plasma proteins, primarily albumin.
Metabolism: Doesn't inhibit metabolism mediated by any of the following cytochrome P450 (CYP) isoforms: 1A2, 2C9, 2C19, 2D6, 2E1, and 3A4. Ertapenem is stable against hydrolysis by a variety of beta-lactamases, including penicillinase, cephalosporinase, and extended-spectrum beta-lactamase. Ertapenem is hydrolyzed by metallo-beta-lactamases.

Excretion: Eliminated primarily by the kidneys. *Half-life:* 4 hours.

Route	Onset	Peak	Duration
I.V.	Immediate	30 min	24 hr
I.M.	Unknown	2 hr	24 hr

Pharmacodynamics

Chemical effect: The bactericidal activity of ertapenem results from the inhibition of cell wall synthesis and is mediated through ertapenem binding to penicillin-binding proteins. Ertapenem has *in vitro* activity against gram-positive bacteria, including *Staphylococcus aureus* (methicillin-susceptible strains only), *Streptococcus agalactiae, S. pneumoniae* (penicillin-susceptible strains only), *S. pyogenes;* gram-negative bacteria including *Escherichia coli, Haemophilus influenzae* (beta-lactamase–negative strains only), *Klebsiella pneumoniae, Moraxella catarrhalis;* and anaerobic bacteria including *Bacteroides fragilis, B. distasonis, B. ovatus, B. thetaiotaomicron, B. uniformis, Clostridium clostridiiforme, Eubacterium lentum, Peptostreptococcus species, Porphyromonas asaccharolyticus, Prevotella bivia.*

Therapeutic effect: Kills susceptible bacteria.

Available forms

Injection: 1 g

NURSING PROCESS

Assessment

- Check for previous penicillin, cephalosporin, or other beta-lactam hypersensitivity.
- Check for hypersensitivity to local anesthetics of the amide type if dose is given I.M.
- Obtain specimens for culture and sensitivity testing before giving first dose. Therapy may start before results are available.
- Monitor renal, hepatic, and hematopoietic function during prolonged therapy.
- Be alert for any adverse reactions, particularly diarrhea and seizures.
- Be alert for any signs or symptoms of superinfection with prolonged therapy.

Nursing diagnoses

- Diarrhea related to drug-induced adverse reaction
- Ineffective health maintenance related to underlying infectious disease process
- Deficient knowledge related to anti-infective therapy

Planning and implementation

ALERT: Don't use diluents containing dextrose (alpha-d-glucose).

ALERT: Don't mix or infuse together with other medications.

ALERT: Don't confuse Avinza (morphine sulfate) with Invanz (ertapenem)

- **I.V. use:** Reconstitute the contents of a 1-g vial of ertapenem with 10 ml of water for injection, normal saline injection, or bacteriostatic water for injection. Shake well to dissolve, and immediately transfer contents of the reconstituted vial to 50 ml of normal saline injection.
  – Infuse over 30 minutes. Complete the infusion within 6 hours of reconstitution.
- **I.M. use:** Reconstitute the contents of a 1-g vial of ertapenem with 3.2 ml of 1% lidocaine hydrochloride injection (without epinephrine). Refer to prescribing information for lidocaine hydrochloride. Shake vial thoroughly to form solution. Immediately withdraw the contents of the vial and give by deep I.M. injection into a large muscle, such as the gluteal muscles or lateral part of the thigh. The reconstituted I.M. solution should be used within 1 hour after preparation. Don't give reconstituted solution I.V.
  – Avoid inadvertent injection into a blood vessel during I.M. administration.
- Don't store lyophilized powder above 25° C (77° F). The reconstituted solution, immediately diluted in normal saline injection, may be stored at room temperature (25° C) and used within 6 hours or stored for 24 hours under refrigeration (5° C [41° F]) and used within 4 hours after removal from refrigeration. Don't freeze solutions of ertapenem.
- If diarrhea persists during therapy, stop drug and collect stool specimen for culture to rule out pseudomembranous colitis.
- If allergic reaction occurs, stop drug immediately. Serious anaphylactic reactions require immediate emergency treatment with airway management, epinephrine, oxygen, and I.V. steroids.
- Continue anticonvulsants in patients with known seizure disorders. If focal tremors, myoclonus, or seizures occur, evaluate patients neurologically and give anticonvulsants if not

done earlier. Reexamine the dosage of drug to determine whether it should be decreased or discontinued.
• Signs and symptoms of overdose may include nausea, diarrhea, and dizziness. If an overdose occurs, stop drug and treat supportively until drug has been eliminated from the body.

Patient teaching
• Inform patient of potential adverse reactions and urge him to notify prescriber immediately if they occur.
• Tell patient to alert prescriber if he develops diarrhea.

Evaluation
• Patient tolerates and responds well to drug therapy.
• Patient doesn't develop colitis or any other adverse reactions from drug therapy.
• Patient and family state understanding of drug therapy.

erythromycin base
(eh-rith-roh-MIGH-sin bays)
Apo-Erythro ♦, EMU-V ◊, E-Mycin, Erybid ♦, ERYC, ERYC-125 ♦, ERYC-250 ♦, Ery-Tab, Erythromid ♦, Erythromycin Base Filmtab, Novo-Rythro ♦, PCE Dispertab

erythromycin estolate
Ilosone, Novo-Rythro ♦

erythromycin ethylsuccinate
Apo-Erythro-ES ♦, EES, EES-400 ◊, EES granules ◊, EryPed

erythromycin gluceptate
Ilotycin Gluceptate

erythromycin lactobionate
Erythrocin

erythromycin stearate
Apo-Erythro-S ♦, Erythrocin, My-E, Novo-Rythro ♦

Pharmacologic class: erythromycin
Therapeutic class: antibiotic
Pregnancy risk category: B

Indications and dosages

▶ **Acute pelvic inflammatory disease caused by *Neisseria gonorrhoeae*.** *Adults:* 500 mg erythromycin gluceptate or lactobionate I.V. q 6 hours for 3 days; then 250 mg erythromycin base, estolate, or stearate. Or 400 mg ethylsuccinate P.O. q 6 hours for 7 days.

▶ **Endocarditis prophylaxis for dental procedures in patients allergic to penicillin.** *Adults:* Initially, 800 mg ethylsuccinate or 1 g stearate P.O. 2 hours before procedure; then 400 mg ethylsuccinate or 500 mg stearate P.O. 6 hours later.
Children: Initially, 20 mg/kg ethylsuccinate or stearate P.O. 2 hours before procedure; then one-half initial dose 6 hours later.

▶ **Intestinal amebiasis.** *Adults:* 250 mg base, estolate, or stearate, or 400 mg ethylsuccinate, P.O. q 6 hours for 10 to 14 days.
Children: 30 to 50 mg/kg base, estolate, ethylsuccinate, or stearate P.O. daily in divided doses q 6 hours for 10 to 14 days.

▶ **Mild to moderately severe respiratory tract, skin, and soft-tissue infections caused by sensitive group A beta-hemolytic streptococci, *Bordetella pertussis, Corynebacterium diphtheriae, Diplococcus pneumoniae, Listeria monocytogenes, Mycoplasma pneumoniae*.** *Adults:* 250 to 500 mg base, estolate, or stearate P.O. q 6 hours; or 400 to 800 mg erythromycin ethylsuccinate P.O. q 6 hours; or 15 to 20 mg/kg I.V. daily as continuous infusion or in divided doses q 6 hours.
Children: 30 to 50 mg/kg oral erythromycin salts P.O. daily in divided doses q 6 hours; or 15 to 20 mg/kg I.V. daily in divided doses q 4 to 6 hours.

▶ **Syphilis.** *Adults:* 500 mg base, estolate, or stearate P.O. q.i.d. for 15 days.

▶ **Legionnaires' disease.** *Adults:* 1 to 4 g P.O. or I.V. daily in divided doses for 10 to 21 days.

▶ **Uncomplicated urethral, endocervical, or rectal infections when tetracyclines are contraindicated.** *Adults:* 500 mg base, estolate, or stearate or 800 mg ethylsuccinate P.O. q.i.d. for at least 7 days.

▶ **Urogenital *Chlamydia trachomatis* infections during pregnancy.** *Adults:* 500 mg base, estolate, or stearate P.O. q.i.d. for at least 7 days, or 250 mg base, estolate, or stearate or 400 mg ethylsuccinate P.O. q.i.d. for at least 14 days.

▶ **Conjunctivitis caused by *C. trachomatis* in neonates.** *Neonates:* 50 mg/kg P.O. daily in four divided doses for 10 to 14 days.
▶ **Pneumonia of infancy caused by *C. trachomatis*.** *Infants:* 50 mg/kg P.O. daily in four divided doses for at least 3 weeks; a second course may be necessary.
▶ **Early form of Lyme disease in persons allergic to penicillins and cephalosporins and in whom tetracyclines are contraindicated‡.** *Adults:* 250 to 500 mg base P.O. t.i.d. or q.i.d. Or, 30 to 40 mg/kg P.O. daily in divided doses for 10 to 30 days.
Children younger than age 8: 30 to 40 mg/kg base P.O. daily in divided doses (not to exceed adult dose) for 10 to 30 days.
▶ **Early Lyme disease manifested as erythema migrans‡.** *Adults:* 500 mg base P.O. q.i.d. for 14 to 21 days.
Children: 12.5 mg/kg base P.O. q.i.d. (maximum dose 500 mg/dose) for 14 to 21 days.

Contraindications and precautions

- Contraindicated in patients hypersensitive to drug or other macrolides. Erythromycin estolate is contraindicated in patients with hepatic disease.
- Use other erythromycin salts cautiously in patients with impaired liver function.

Lifespan: In pregnant and breast-feeding women, use cautiously. Erythromycin lactobionate may contain benzyl alcohol, which should be avoided in neonates.

Adverse reactions

CNS: fever.
CV: ***ventricular arrhythmias,*** *venous irritation or thrombophlebitis* after I.V. injection.
EENT: hearing loss with high I.V. doses.
GI: *abdominal pain and cramping, nausea, vomiting, diarrhea.*
Hepatic: cholestatic jaundice (erythromycin estolate).
Skin: urticaria, rash, eczema.
Other: overgrowth of nonsusceptible bacteria or fungi, ***anaphylaxis.***

Interactions

Drug-drug. *Carbamazepine:* Increases carbamazepine levels and increases risk of toxicity. Monitor patient closely.
Clindamycin, lincomycin: May be antagonistic. Don't use together.
Cyclosporine: Increases cyclosporine levels. Monitor patient closely.
Digoxin: Increases digoxin levels. Monitor patient for digoxin toxicity.
Disopyramide: Increases disopyramide plasma levels, resulting, in some cases, in arrhythmias and increased QT intervals. Monitor ECG.
Midazolam, triazolam: Increases effects of these drugs. Monitor patient closely.
Oral anticoagulants: Increases anticoagulant effects. Monitor PT and INR closely; monitor patient for bleeding.
Theophylline: Decreases erythromycin level and increases risk of theophylline toxicity. Use together cautiously.
Drug-herb. *Pill-bearing spurge:* May inhibit CYP3A enzymes and alter drug metabolism. Use together cautiously.

Effects on lab test results

- May falsely elevate urinary catecholamines, 17-hydroxycorticosterone, and 17-ketosteroids. May interfere with colorimetric assays, resulting in falsely elevated AST and ALT levels.

Pharmacokinetics

Absorption: Most erythromycin salts are absorbed in duodenum. Because erythromycin base is acid-sensitive, it must be buffered or have enteric coating to prevent destruction by gastric acid. Acid salts and esters (estolate, ethylsuccinate, and stearate) aren't affected by gastric acidity and, therefore, are well absorbed; they're unaffected or possibly even enhanced by presence of food. Base and stearate preparations should be given on empty stomach.
Distribution: Widely distributed in most body tissues and fluids except CSF, where it appears at low levels. About 80% of erythromycin base and 96% of erythromycin estolate are protein-bound.
Metabolism: Partially metabolized in liver to inactive metabolites.
Excretion: Mainly excreted unchanged in bile; small amount (less than 5%) excreted in urine. *Half-life:* about 1½ hours.

Route	Onset	Peak	Duration
P.O.	Unknown	1-4 hr	Unknown
I.V.	Immediate	Immediate	Unknown

Pharmacodynamics

Chemical effect: Inhibits bacterial protein synthesis by binding to 50S subunit of ribosome.
Therapeutic effect: Inhibits bacterial growth including *B. pertussis, C. diphtheriae, Corynebacterium minutissimum, Entamoeba histolytica, Haemophilus influenzae, Legionella pneumophila,* and *M. pneumoniae.* It also may be used to treat infections caused by *C. trachomatis, L. monocytogenes, N. gonorrhoeae, Staphylococcus aureus, Streptococcus pneumoniae, Streptococcus viridans,* and *Treponema pallidum.*

Available forms

erythromycin base
Capsules (enteric-coated pellets): 250 mg, 333 mg
Tablets (enteric-coated): 250 mg, 333 mg, 500 mg
Tablets (filmtabs): 250 mg, 500 mg
erythromycin estolate
Capsules: 250 mg
Oral suspension: 125 mg/5 ml, 250 mg/5 ml
erythromycin ethylsuccinate
Drops: 100 mg/2.5 ml
Oral suspension: 200 mg/5 ml, 400 mg/5 ml
Tablets: 400 mg, 600 mg ♦
Tablets (chewable): 200 mg
erythromycin gluceptate
Injection: 1-g vial
erythromycin lactobionate
Injection: 500-mg, 1-g vials
erythromycin stearate
Tablets (film-coated): 250 mg, 500 mg

NURSING PROCESS

Assessment

- Obtain history of patient's infection before therapy, and reassess regularly thereafter.
- Obtain urine specimen for culture and sensitivity tests before first dose. Therapy may begin, pending test results.
- Be alert for adverse reactions and drug interactions.
- Monitor patient's hydration status if adverse GI reactions occur.
- Monitor liver function (increased levels of alkaline phosphatase, ALT, AST, and bilirubin may occur). Erythromycin estolate may cause serious hepatotoxicity in adults (reversible cholestatic jaundice). Other erythromycin salts cause hepatotoxicity to lesser degree. Patients who develop hepatotoxicity from estolate may react similarly to treatment with other erythromycin preparations.
- Evaluate patient's and family's knowledge of drug therapy.

Nursing diagnoses

- Infection related to presence of susceptible bacteria
- Risk for deficient fluid volume related to potential for drug-induced adverse GI reactions
- Deficient knowledge related to drug therapy

Planning and implementation

ALERT: American Heart Association recommendations no longer include using erythromycins to prevent bacterial endocarditis. However, practitioners who have successfully used the drug as prophylaxis in individual patients may continue to do so.

- **P.O. use:** When giving suspension, be sure to note concentration.
– For best absorption, give oral form of drug with full glass of water 1 hour before or 2 hours after meals. Coated tablets may be taken with meals. Tell patient not to drink fruit juice with drug. Chewable erythromycin tablets shouldn't be swallowed whole.
– Coated tablets or encapsulated pellets cause less GI upset; they may be more tolerable in patients who can't tolerate erythromycin.
- **I.V. use:** Reconstitute drug according to manufacturer's directions, and dilute each 250 mg in at least 100 ml of normal saline solution. Infuse over 1 hour.
– Don't give erythromycin lactobionate with other drugs.

Patient teaching

- Instruct patient how to take oral drug.
- Tell patient to take entire amount of drug exactly as prescribed, even after he feels better.
- Instruct patient to notify prescriber if adverse reactions occur, especially nausea, abdominal pain, and fever.

Evaluation

- Patient is free from infection.
- Patient maintains adequate hydration with therapy.
- Patient and family state understanding of drug therapy.

esmolol hydrochloride

(EZ-moh-lohl high-droh-KLOR-ighd)
Brevibloc

Pharmacologic class: beta blocker
Therapeutic class: antiarrhythmic
Pregnancy risk category: C

Indications and dosages

▶ **Supraventricular tachycardia; control of ventricular rate in patients with atrial fibrillation or flutter in perioperative, postoperative, or other emergent circumstances; noncompensatory sinus tachycardia when heart rate requires specific interventions.** *Adults:* Loading dose is 500 mcg/kg/minute by I.V. infusion over 1 minute, followed by 4-minute maintenance infusion of 50 mcg/kg/minute. If adequate response doesn't occur within 5 minutes, loading dose is repeated and followed by maintenance infusion of 100 mcg/kg/minute for 4 minutes. Loading dose is repeated and maintenance infusion increased in stepwise manner, p.r.n. Maximum maintenance infusion for tachycardia is 200 mcg/kg/minute.

▶ **Management of perioperative and postoperative tachycardia or hypertension.** *Adults:* For perioperative treatment, 80 mg (about 1 mg/kg) I.V. bolus over 30 seconds, followed by 150 mcg/kg/minute I.V., if needed. Adjust infusion rate, p.r.n., to maximum of 300 mcg/kg/minute. Postoperative treatment is same as for supraventricular tachycardia, although dosages adequate for control may be as high as 300 mcg/minute.

Contraindications and precautions

- Contraindicated in patients with sinus bradycardia, heart block greater than first-degree, cardiogenic shock, or overt heart failure.
- Use cautiously in patients with impaired kidney function, diabetes, or bronchospasm.

Lifespan: In pregnant and breast-feeding women, use cautiously. In children, safety of drug hasn't been established.

Adverse reactions

CNS: dizziness, somnolence, headache, agitation, fatigue, confusion.
CV: HYPOTENSION, peripheral ischemia.
EENT: nasal congestion.
GI: *nausea,* vomiting.
Respiratory: ***bronchospasm,*** wheezing, dyspnea.
Other: inflammation, induration at infusion site.

Interactions

Drug-drug. *Digoxin:* Esmolol may increase digoxin levels by 10% to 20%. Monitor digoxin levels.
Morphine: May increase esmolol levels. Adjust esmolol carefully.
Reserpine, other catecholamine-depleting drugs: May cause additive bradycardia and hypotension. Adjust esmolol carefully.
Succinylcholine: Esmolol may prolong neuromuscular blockade. Monitor patient.

Effects on lab test results

None reported.

Pharmacokinetics

Absorption: Administered I.V.
Distribution: Distributed rapidly throughout plasma; 55% protein-bound.
Metabolism: Hydrolyzed rapidly by plasma esterase.
Excretion: Excreted by kidneys as metabolites. *Half-life:* About 9 minutes.

Route	Onset	Peak	Duration
I.V.	Almost immediate	About 30 min	< 30 min

Pharmacodynamics

Chemical effect: A class II antiarrhythmic, esmolol is an ultrashort-acting selective $beta_1$-adrenergic blocker that decreases heart rate, myocardial contractility, and blood pressure.
Therapeutic effect: Restores normal sinus rhythm.

Available forms

Injection: 10 mg/ml, 250 mg/ml

NURSING PROCESS

Assessment

- Obtain history of patient's arrhythmias before therapy.
- Monitor ECG and blood pressure continuously during infusion. Up to 50% of patients treated with esmolol develop hypotension.

Monitor patient closely, especially if pretreatment blood pressure was low.
• Be alert for adverse reactions and drug interactions.
• Evaluate patient's and family's knowledge of drug therapy.

Nursing diagnoses
• Decreased cardiac output related to presence of arrhythmias
• Ineffective cerebral tissue perfusion related to drug-induced hypotension
• Deficient knowledge related to drug therapy

Planning and implementation
• Don't give by I.V. push; use infusion-control device. The 10-mg/ml single-dose vial may be used without diluting, but injection concentrate (250 mg/ml) must be diluted to no more than 10 mg/ml before infusion. Remove 20 ml from 500 ml of D_5W, lactated Ringer's solution, half-normal saline solution, or normal saline solution, and add two ampules of esmolol (final concentration 10 mg/ml).
• Hypotension can usually be reversed within 30 minutes by decreasing dose or, if necessary, stopping infusion. Notify prescriber if this becomes necessary.
• Esmolol solutions are incompatible with diazepam, furosemide, sodium bicarbonate, and thiopental sodium.
• When patient's heart rate becomes stable, esmolol will be replaced by a longer-acting antiarrhythmic, such as propranolol, digoxin, or verapamil. Reduce infusion rate by 50% 30 minutes after first dose of alternative drug is given. Monitor patient response, and if heart rate is controlled for 1 hour after administration of second dose of alternative drug, discontinue esmolol infusion.
• If local reaction develops at infusion site, change to another site. Avoid using butterfly needles.

Patient teaching
• Inform patient of need for continuous ECG, blood pressure, and heart rate monitoring to assess effectiveness of drug and detect adverse reactions.

Evaluation
• Patient regains normal cardiac output with correction of arrhythmias.
• Patient's blood pressure remains normal throughout therapy.
• Patient and family state understanding of drug therapy.

esomeprazole magnesium
(e-soh-MEP-rah-zohl)
Nexium

Pharmacologic class: proton pump inhibitor, s-isomer of omeprazole
Therapeutic class: gastroesophageal agent
Pregnancy risk category: B

Indications and dosages
▶ **Gastroesophageal reflux disease (GERD), healing of erosive esophagitis.** *Adults:* 20 or 40 mg P.O. daily for 4 to 8 weeks. If symptoms persist, treatment may be extended for an additional 4 to 8 weeks.
▶ **Long-term maintenance of healing in erosive esophagitis.** *Adults:* 20 mg P.O. daily for no more than 6 months.
▶ **Eradication of *Helicobacter pylori* to reduce duodenal ulcer recurrence.** *Adults:* Combination triple therapy with esomeprazole magnesium 40 mg P.O. daily plus amoxicillin 1,000 mg P.O. b.i.d. and clarithromycin 500 mg P.O. b.i.d., all for 10 days.
Patients with severe hepatic failure: The maximum dose is 20 mg P.O. daily.

Contraindications and precautions
• Contraindicated in patients hypersensitive to any component of esomeprazole or omeprazole. Combination triple therapy for the eradication of *H. pylori* is contraindicated in patients hypersensitive to clarithromycin, macrolide antibiotics, amoxicillin, or penicillin.
• Use cautiously in patients with severe hepatic insufficiency.
Lifespan: In breast-feeding women, use cautiously because it's unknown whether drug appears in breast milk. In children, safety and efficacy haven't been established.

Adverse reactions
CNS: headache.
GI: diarrhea, abdominal pain, nausea, flatulence, dry mouth, vomiting, constipation.

Interactions

Drug-drug. *Amoxicillin, clarithromycin:* Increases esomeprazole levels. Monitor patient for toxicity. Don't give clarithromycin and pimozide together.
Diazepam: Decreases diazepam clearance and increases plasma levels of diazepam. Monitor patient for diazepam toxicity.
Ketoconazole, iron salts, and digoxin: May interfere with drug absorption. Monitor patient closely.
Other drugs metabolized by cytochrome P-450-2C19: Alters esomeprazole clearance. Monitor patient closely, especially elderly patient or patient with hepatic insufficiency.
Drug-food. *Any food:* Reduces bioavailability. Advise patient to take drug 1 hour before eating.

Effects on lab test results

- May increase creatinine, uric acid, bilirubin, alkaline phosphatase, ALT, AST potassium, sodium, thyroxine, and TSH levels.
- May increase hemoglobin, hematocrit, and WBC and platelet counts.

Pharmacokinetics

Absorption: Plasma levels peak 1½ hours after oral administration. The plasma level following a 40-mg dose is three times higher than after a 20-mg dose. Repeated daily dosing of 40 mg yields systemic bioavailability of 90% compared with a single 40-mg dose, which yields 64%. Giving esomeprazole with food reduces mean plasma level by 33% to 53%.
Distribution: Esomeprazole is about 97% protein-bound.
Metabolism: Esomeprazole is extensively metabolized in the liver by cytochrome P450-2C19 to form hydroxy and desmethyl metabolites. CYP2C19 exhibits polymorphism and people who are poor metabolizers (approximately 3% of Whites and 15% to 20% of Asians who lack cytochrome P450-2C19) have decreased esomeprazole plasma levels. Cytochrome P450-3A4 metabolizes the remaining amount.
Excretion: Less than 1% of active parent drug is excreted in urine. About 80% of the drug is excreted as inactive metabolites in urine. Remaining inactive metabolites are excreted in feces. Systemic clearance of esomeprazole decreases with multiple-dose administration. *Half-life:* 1 to 1½ hours.

Route	Onset	Peak	Duration
P.O.	Unknown	1.5 hr	13-17 hr

Pharmacodynamics

Chemical effect: Suppresses gastric secretion through proton pump inhibition. Inhibits the H^+-K^+-ATPase pump in gastric parietal cells, thereby reducing gastric acidity by blocking the final step in acid production. Esomeprazole magnesium is the s-isomer of omeprazole.
Therapeutic effect: Decreases gastric acid.

Available forms

Capsules (delayed-release containing enteric-coated pellets): 20 mg, 40 mg

NURSING PROCESS

Assessment

- Assess patient's condition before and during drug therapy.
- Monitor liver function test results because drug is extensively metabolized by cytochrome P450-2C19. Patients with hepatic insufficiency have a risk of increased liver function test results.
- Long-term therapy with omeprazole has caused atrophic gastritis. Be alert for any adverse reactions.
- Evaluate patient's and family's knowledge of drug therapy.

Nursing diagnoses

- Impaired tissue integrity related to underlying gastroesophageal condition
- Imbalanced nutrition: Less than body requirements related to decreased oral intake due to underlying gastroesophageal disorder
- Deficient knowledge related to drug therapy

Planning and implementation

- Food decreases the extent of absorption; give esomeprazole at least 1 hour before meals.
- Overdosage may result in confusion, drowsiness, blurred vision, tachycardia, nausea, diaphoresis, dry mouth, and headache. Because drug isn't dialyzable, supportive care is recommended.
- Urge patient to avoid alcohol and foods that increase gastric secretions.

Patient teaching

- Tell patient to take drug exactly as prescribed and at least 1 hour before meals.
- If patient has trouble swallowing capsule, suggest that he open it, sprinkle contents into applesauce, and swallow applesauce immediately. Warn against crushing or chewing the drug pellets.
- Tell patient to report continued or worsened symptoms or any adverse reactions.

Evaluation

- Patient responds positively to drug therapy.
- Patient is able to tolerate liquids and foods orally without any nausea or vomiting.
- Patient and family state understanding of drug therapy.

estazolam

(eh-STAZ-uh-lam)

ProSom

Pharmacologic class: benzodiazepine
Therapeutic class: hypnotic
Pregnancy risk category: X
Controlled substance schedule: IV

Indications and dosages

▶ **Insomnia.** *Adults:* 1 mg P.O. h.s. Some patients may need 2 mg.
Elderly patients: 1 mg P.O. h.s. Use higher doses with extreme care. Frail elderly or debilitated patients may take 0.5 mg, but this low dose may be only marginally effective.

Contraindications and precautions

- Contraindicated in patients hypersensitive to drug.
- Use cautiously in patients with hepatic, renal, or pulmonary disease; depression; or suicidal tendencies.

Lifespan: In pregnant or breast-feeding women, drug is contraindicated. In children, safety of drug hasn't been established.

Adverse reactions

CNS: fatigue, dizziness, *daytime drowsiness, somnolence, asthenia, hypokinesia,* headache, abnormal thinking.
GI: dyspepsia, abdominal pain.
Musculoskeletal: back pain, stiffness.

Interactions

Drug-drug. *Cimetidine, disulfiram, isoniazid, oral contraceptives:* May impair metabolism and clearance of benzodiazepines and prolong their plasma half-life. Monitor patient for increased CNS depression.
CNS depressants, including antihistamines, opioid analgesics, and benzodiazepines: Increases CNS depression. Avoid using together.
Digoxin, phenytoin: Increases levels of these drugs, resulting in toxicity. Monitor levels closely.
Rifampin: May increase metabolism and clearance and decrease plasma half-life. Watch for decreased effectiveness.
Theophylline: May act as a drug antagonist. Watch for decreased effectiveness.
Drug-herb. *Catnip, kava, lady's slipper, lemon balm, passionflower, sassafras, skullcap, valerian:* Sedative effects may be enhanced. Discourage using together.
Drug-lifestyle. *Alcohol use:* Increases CNS and respiratory depression. Discourage using together.
Smoking: May increase drug metabolism and clearance and decrease plasma half-life. Monitor patient for decreased effectiveness.

Effects on lab test results

- May increase ALT and AST levels.

Pharmacokinetics

Absorption: Rapidly and completely absorbed through GI tract.
Distribution: 93% protein-bound.
Metabolism: Extensively metabolized in liver.
Excretion: Metabolites excreted primarily in urine. Less than 5% excreted in urine as unchanged drug; 4% of 2-mg dose excreted in feces. *Half-life:* 10 to 24 hours.

Route	Onset	Peak	Duration
P.O.	Unknown	1-3 hr	Unknown

Pharmacodynamics

Chemical effect: Unknown; thought to act on limbic system and thalamus of CNS by binding to specific benzodiazepine receptors.
Therapeutic effect: Promotes sleep.

Available forms

Tablets: 1 mg, 2 mg

NURSING PROCESS

Assessment
- Obtain history of patient's sleep pattern before therapy, and reassess regularly thereafter.
- Monitor liver and kidney function and CBC periodically during long-term therapy.
- Be alert for adverse reactions and drug interactions.
- Watch for possible withdrawal symptoms. Patients who receive prolonged treatment with benzodiazepines may experience withdrawal symptoms if drug is discontinued suddenly (possibly after 6 weeks of continuous therapy).
- Evaluate patient's and family's knowledge of drug therapy.

Nursing diagnoses
- Disturbed sleep pattern related to underlying condition
- Risk for trauma related to drug-induced adverse CNS reactions
- Deficient knowledge related to drug therapy

Planning and implementation
- Before leaving bedside, make sure patient has swallowed drug.
- Take precautions to prevent hoarding by depressed, suicidal, or drug-dependent patient or patient who has history of drug abuse.

Patient teaching
- Tell patient not to increase dosage of drug but to inform prescriber if he thinks that drug is no longer effective.
- Caution patient to avoid hazardous activities that require mental alertness or physical coordination. For inpatient (particularly elderly patient), supervise walking and raise side rails.
- Warn patient that additive depressant effects can occur if alcohol is consumed while taking drug or within 24 hours afterward.
- If patient uses an oral contraceptive, recommend an alternative birth-control method during therapy because drug may enhance contraceptive hormone metabolism and decrease its effect.

Evaluation
- Patient is able to sleep.
- Patient's safety is maintained.
- Patient and family state understanding of drug therapy.

estradiol (oestradiol)
(eh-struh-DIGH-ol)
Climara, Esclim, Alora, Estrace**, Estrace Vaginal Cream, Estraderm, Estring, FemPatch, Vivelle, Vivelle-Dot

estradiol cypionate
Depo-Estradiol Cypionate, Depogen

estradiol valerate (oestradiol valerate)
Delestrogen, Estradiol Valerate, Gynogen LA 20, Menaval, Valergen 20, Valergen-40, Primogyn Depot ◇

Pharmacologic class: estrogen
Therapeutic class: estrogen replacement, antineoplastic
Pregnancy risk category: X

Indications and dosages

▶ **Vasomotor symptoms, vulval and vaginal atrophy, hypoestrogenism due to hypogonadism, castration, or primary ovarian failure.** ***estradiol.*** *Adults:* 1 to 2 mg P.O. daily in cycles of 21 days on and 7 days off or cycles of 5 days on and 2 days off. *Adults:* Initially, 0.025-mg/day Esclim system applied to a clean, dry area of the trunk twice weekly. Adjust dose; if necessary, after the first 2 or 3 weeks of therapy, then 3 to 6 months p.r.n. Or, 1 Estraderm transdermal system delivering 0.05 mg/24 hours applied twice weekly. Or, as a Vivelle system delivering either 0.05 mg/24 hours or 0.0375 mg/24 hours applied twice weekly. Or, as a Climara system delivering 0.05 mg/24 hours or 0.1 mg/24 hours applied once weekly in cycles of 3 weeks on and 1 week off.

cypionate. *Adults:* 1 to 5 mg I.M. q 3 to 4 weeks.

valerate. *Adults:* 10 to 20 mg I.M. q 4 weeks, p.r.n.

▶ **Atrophic vaginitis, kraurosis vulvae.** ***estradiol.*** *Adults:* 2 to 4 g intravaginal applications of cream daily for 1 to 2 weeks. When vaginal mucosa is restored, maintenance dosage of 1 g one to three times weekly in cyclic regimen. Or, 0.05 mg/24 hours Climara applied weekly in a cyclic regimen. Or, 0.05 mg/24

hours Estraderm applied twice weekly in a cyclic regimen.
valerate. *Adults:* 10 to 20 mg I.M. q 4 weeks, p.r.n.

▶ **Palliative treatment of advanced, inoperable breast cancer.** ***estradiol.*** *Men and postmenopausal women:* 10 mg P.O. t.i.d. for 3 months.

▶ **Palliative treatment of advanced inoperable prostate cancer.** ***estradiol.*** *Men:* 1 to 2 mg P.O. t.i.d.
valerate. *Men:* 30 mg I.M. q 1 to 2 weeks.

▶ **Prevention of postmenopausal osteoporosis in high risk patients.** *Adults:* 0.025 mg/day Vivelle, Vivelle-Dot, or Alora system applied to a clean, dry area of the trunk twice weekly. Or, 0.025 mg/day Climara patch applied once weekly in a continuous regimen.

▶ **Vasomotor symptoms.** *Adults:* 0.05 mg/day Climara patch applied once weekly in a continuous regimen.

Contraindications and precautions

• Contraindicated in patients with thrombophlebitis, thromboembolic disorders, estrogen-dependent neoplasia, breast or reproductive organ cancer (except for palliative treatment), or undiagnosed abnormal genital bleeding. Also, contraindicated in patients with history of thrombophlebitis or thromboembolic disorders linked to estrogen use (except for palliative treatment of breast and prostate cancer).
• Use cautiously in patients with cerebrovascular or coronary artery disease, asthma, bone diseases, migraine, seizures, or cardiac, hepatic, or renal dysfunction and in women with strong family history of breast cancer or who have breast nodules, fibrocystic disease, or abnormal mammogram findings.
Lifespan: In pregnant and breast-feeding women, drug is contraindicated. In children, drug shouldn't be used.

Adverse reactions

CNS: headache, dizziness, chorea, depression, ***seizures.***
CV: thrombophlebitis, ***thromboembolism,*** hypertension, edema.
EENT: worsening of myopia or astigmatism, intolerance of contact lenses.
GI: *nausea,* vomiting, abdominal cramps, bloating, diarrhea, constipation, ***pancreatitis.***
GU: breakthrough bleeding, altered menstrual flow, dysmenorrhea, amenorrhea, ***increased risk of endometrial cancer,*** cervical erosion, altered cervical secretions, enlargement of uterine fibromas, vaginal candidiasis, testicular atrophy, impotence.
Hepatic: cholestatic jaundice, gallbladder disease, ***hepatic adenoma.***
Metabolic: increased appetite, weight changes, hyperglycemia, hypercalcemia.
Skin: melasma, urticaria, erythema nodosum, dermatitis, hair loss.
Other: ***possibility of increased risk of breast cancer,*** breast changes (tenderness, enlargement, secretion), gynecomastia.

Interactions

Drug-drug. *Bromocriptine:* May cause amenorrhea, interfering with bromocriptine effects. Avoid using together.
Carbamazepine, phenobarbital, rifampin: Decreases effectiveness of estrogen therapy. Monitor patient closely.
Corticosteroids: May enhance effects. Monitor patient closely.
Cyclosporine: Increases risk of toxicity. Use together with caution, and frequently monitor cyclosporine levels.
Dantrolene, other hepatotoxic drugs: Increases risk of hepatotoxicity. Monitor patient closely.
Oral anticoagulants: May decrease anticoagulant effects. Dosage adjustments may be necessary. Monitor PT and INR.
Tamoxifen: Estrogens may interfere with effectiveness of tamoxifen. Avoid using together.
Drug-food. *Caffeine:* May increase caffeine levels. Monitor effects.
Drug-lifestyle. *Smoking:* Increases risk of CV effects. If smoking continues, may need alternative therapy; urge patient to stop smoking.

Effects on lab test results

• May increase total T_4, thyroid-binding globulin, triglyceride, and clotting factor VII, VIII. IX, and X levels.
• May increase PT and norepinephrine-induced platelet aggregation.

Pharmacokinetics

Absorption: After P.O. administration, estradiol and other natural unconjugated estrogens are well absorbed but substantially inactivated by liver. After I.M. administration, absorption be-

gins rapidly and continues for days. Topically applied estradiol is absorbed readily into systemic circulation.
Distribution: Distributed throughout body with highest levels in fat. Estradiol and other natural estrogens are about 50% to 80% plasma protein–bound.
Metabolism: Metabolized primarily in liver.
Excretion: Primarily through kidneys.

Route	Onset	Peak	Duration
P.O., I.M., intravaginal	Unknown	Unknown	Unknown
Transdermal (Esclim)	Unknown	27-30 hours	Unknown

Pharmacodynamics

Chemical effect: Increases synthesis of DNA, RNA, and protein in responsive tissues; also reduces release of follicle-stimulating hormone and luteinizing hormone from pituitary gland.
Therapeutic effect: Relieves vasomotor menopausal symptoms, provides estrogen replacement, relieves vaginal dryness, and provides palliative action for advanced prostate or breast cancer.

Available forms

estradiol
Tablets (micronized): 0.5 mg, 1 mg, 1.5 mg, 2 mg
Transdermal: 0.025 mg/24 hours, 0.0375 mg/24 hours, 0.05 mg/24 hours, 0.075 mg/24 hours, 0.1 mg/24 hours
Vaginal cream (in nonliquefying base): 0.1 mg/g
Vaginal ring: 2 mg
estradiol cypionate
Injection (in oil): 5 mg/ml
estradiol valerate
Injection (in oil): 10 mg/ml, 20 mg/ml, 40 mg/ml

NURSING PROCESS

Assessment

- Obtain history of patient's underlying condition before therapy, and reassess regularly thereafter.
- Make sure patient has thorough physical examination before starting estrogen therapy.
- Ask patient about allergies, especially to foods or plants. Estradiol is available as aqueous solution or as solution in peanut oil; estradiol cypionate, as solution in cottonseed oil or vegetable oil; estradiol valerate, as solution in castor oil, sesame oil, or vegetable oil.
- Patient receiving long-term therapy should have yearly examinations. Periodically monitor lipid levels, blood pressure, body weight, and liver function.
- Evaluate patient's and family's knowledge of drug therapy.

Nursing diagnoses

- Ineffective health maintenance related to underlying condition
- Ineffective tissue perfusion (cerebral, peripheral, pulmonary, or myocardial) related to drug-induced thromboembolism
- Deficient knowledge related to drug therapy

Planning and implementation

- **P.O. use:** Give oral preparations at mealtimes or bedtime (if only one daily dose is required) to minimize nausea.
- **I.M. use:** To give as I.M. injection, make sure drug is well dispersed in solution by rolling vial between palms. Inject deep into large muscle. Rotate injection sites to prevent muscle atrophy. Never give drug I.V.
- **Intravaginal use:** Follow normal protocol.
- **Transdermal use:** Apply transdermal patch to clean, dry, hairless, intact skin on abdomen or buttocks. Don't apply to breasts, waistline, or other areas where clothing can loosen patch. When applying, ensure good contact with skin, especially around edges, and hold in place with palm for about 10 seconds. Rotate application sites.
- In women who take oral estrogen, treatment with Estraderm transdermal patch can begin 1 week after withdrawal of oral therapy, or sooner if menopausal symptoms appear before end of week.
- Because of risk of thromboembolism, therapy should be discontinued at least 1 month before procedures that increase risk of prolonged immobilization or thromboembolism, such as knee or hip surgery. Withhold drug and notify prescriber if you suspect a thromboembolic event.
- Notify pathologist if patient receives estrogen therapy.

ALERT: Estrogen preparations aren't interchangeable.

Patient teaching

- Inform patient about package insert that describes adverse effects of estrogen; also provide verbal explanation.
- Emphasize importance of regular physical examinations. Postmenopausal women who use estrogen replacement for more than 5 years to treat menopausal symptoms may be at increased risk for endometrial cancer. This risk is reduced by using cyclic rather than continuous therapy and lowest possible dosages of estrogen. Adding progestins to regimen decreases risk of endometrial hyperplasia; it's unknown if progestins affect risk of endometrial carcinoma. Most studies show no increased risk of breast cancer.
- Teach patient how to use vaginal cream. Patient should wash vaginal area with soap and water before applying. Tell her to apply drug at bedtime or to lie flat for 30 minutes after application to minimize drug loss.
- Warn patient to immediately report abdominal pain; pain, numbness, or stiffness in legs or buttocks; pressure or pain in chest; shortness of breath; severe headaches; visual disturbances, such as blind spots, flashing lights, or blurriness; vaginal bleeding or discharge; breast lumps; swelling of hands or feet; yellow skin or sclera; dark urine; and light-colored stools.
- Explain to patient receiving cyclic therapy for postmenopausal symptoms that, although withdrawal bleeding may occur during week off drug, fertility hasn't been restored. Pregnancy can't occur because patient hasn't ovulated.
- Tell diabetic patient to report elevated blood glucose test results so antidiabetic dosage can be adjusted.
- Teach woman how to perform routine breast self-examination.

☑ Evaluation

- Patient shows improvement in underlying condition.
- Patient has no thromboembolic event during therapy.
- Patient and family state understanding of drug therapy.

estrogens, conjugated (estrogenic substances, conjugated; oestrogens, conjugated)

(ES-troh-jenz, KAHN-jih-gayt-ed)

C.E.S.♦, Cenestin, Premarin, Premarin Intravenous

Pharmacologic class: estrogen
Therapeutic class: estrogen replacement, antineoplastic, antiosteoporotic
Pregnancy risk category: X

Indications and dosages

▶ **Abnormal uterine bleeding (hormonal imbalance).** *Women:* 25 mg I.V. or I.M. Repeated in 6 to 12 hours, p.r.n.

▶ **Palliative treatment of breast cancer (at least 5 years after menopause).** *Men and postmenopausal women:* 10 mg P.O. t.i.d. for 3 months or more.

▶ **Female castration, primary ovarian failure.** *Women:* 1.25 mg P.O. daily in cycles of 3 weeks on and 1 week off.

▶ **Osteoporosis.** *Postmenopausal women:* 0.625 mg P.O. daily in cyclic regimen (3 weeks on, 1 week off).

▶ **Hypogonadism.** *Women:* 2.5 to 7.5 mg P.O. daily in divided doses for 20 consecutive days each month.

▶ **Vasomotor menopausal symptoms.** *Women:* 0.3 to 1.25 mg P.O. daily in cycles of 3 weeks on and 1 week off.

▶ **Atrophic vaginitis, kraurosis vulvae.** *Women:* 2 to 4 g intravaginally once daily on cyclic basis (3 weeks on and 1 week off).

▶ **Palliative treatment of inoperable prostate cancer.** *Men:* 1.25 to 2.5 mg P.O. t.i.d.

▶ **Vulvar and vaginal arrophy.** ***Cenestin.*** *Women:* 0.3 mg P.O. daily.

Contraindications and precautions

- Contraindicated in patients with thrombophlebitis, thromboembolic disorders, estrogen-dependent neoplasia, breast or reproductive organ cancer (except for palliative treatment), or undiagnosed abnormal genital bleeding.
- Use cautiously in patients with cerebrovascular or coronary artery disease, asthma, bone disease, migraine, seizures, or cardiac, hepatic,

or renal dysfunction and in women with family history (mother, grandmother, sister) of breast or genital tract cancer or who have breast nodules, fibrocystic disease, or abnormal mammogram findings.

- These drugs shouldn't be used for the prevention of CV disease.

Lifespan: In pregnant and breast-feeding women, drug is contraindicated. In children, drug shouldn't be used.

Adverse reactions

CNS: headache, dizziness, chorea, depression, lethargy, ***seizures.***
CV: thrombophlebitis; ***thromboembolism;*** hypertension; edema; ***increased risk of CVA, pulmonary embolism, and MI.***
EENT: worsening of myopia or astigmatism, intolerance of contact lenses.
GI: *nausea,* vomiting, abdominal cramps, bloating, diarrhea, constipation, anorexia, ***pancreatitis.***
GU: breakthrough bleeding, altered menstrual flow, dysmenorrhea, amenorrhea, ***increased risk of endometrial cancer,*** cervical erosion, altered cervical secretions, enlargement of uterine fibromas, vaginal candidiasis, testicular atrophy, impotence.
Hepatic: gallbladder disease, cholestatic jaundice, ***hepatic adenoma.***
Metabolic: increased appetite, weight changes, hyperglycemia, hypercalcemia.
Skin: melasma, urticaria, erythema nodosum, dermatitis, flushing (with rapid I.V. administration), hirsutism, hair loss.
Other: breast changes (tenderness, enlargement, secretion), ***possibility of increased risk of breast cancer,*** gynecomastia.

Interactions

Drug-drug. *Bromocriptine:* May cause amenorrhea, interfering with bromocriptine effects. Avoid using together.
Carbamazepine, phenobarbital, rifampin: Decreases estrogen effectiveness. Monitor patient closely.
Corticosteroids: Possible enhanced effects. Monitor patient closely.
Cyclosporine: Increases risk of toxicity. Use together with caution, and frequently monitor cyclosporine levels.
Dantrolene, other hepatotoxic drugs: Increases risk of hepatotoxicity. Monitor patient closely.
Oral anticoagulants: May decrease anticoagulant effects. Dosage adjustments may be necessary. Monitor PT and INR.
Tamoxifen: Estrogens may interfere with effectiveness of tamoxifen. Avoid using together.
Drug-food. *Caffeine:* May increase caffeine levels. Monitor effects.
Drug-lifestyle. *Smoking:* Increases risk of CV effects. If smoking continues, patient may need alternative therapy. Urge patient to stop smoking.

Effects on lab test results

- May increase glucose, calcium, total T_4, thyroid-binding globulin, phospholipid, triglyceride, and clotting factor VII, VII, IX, and X levels.
- May increase PT and norepinephrine-induced platelet aggregation.

Pharmacokinetics

Absorption: Not well characterized after P.O. or intravaginal administration. After I.M. administration, absorption begins rapidly and continues for days.
Distribution: Distributed throughout body with highest levels in fat; about 50% to 80% plasma protein–bound.
Metabolism: Metabolized primarily in liver.
Excretion: Majority of estrogen elimination occurs through kidneys.

Route	Onset	Peak	Duration
All routes	Unknown	Unknown	Unknown

Pharmacodynamics

Chemical effect: Increases synthesis of DNA, RNA, and protein in responsive tissues; also reduces release of follicle-stimulating hormone and luteinizing hormone from pituitary gland.
Therapeutic effect: Provides estrogen replacement, relieves vasomotor menopausal symptoms and vaginal dryness, helps prevent severity of osteoporosis, and provides palliative action for prostate and breast cancer.

Available forms

Injection: 25 mg/5 ml
Tablets: 0.3 mg, 0.625 mg, 0.9 mg, 1.25 mg, 2.5 mg
Vaginal cream: 0.625 mg/g

NURSING PROCESS

Assessment
- Obtain history of patient's underlying condition before therapy, and reassess regularly thereafter.
- Make sure patient has thorough physical examination before starting estrogen therapy.
- Patient receiving long-term therapy should have yearly examinations. Periodically monitor lipid levels, blood pressure, body weight, and liver function.
- Be alert for adverse reactions and drug interactions.
- Evaluate patient's and family's knowledge of drug therapy.

Nursing diagnoses
- Ineffective health maintenance related to underlying condition
- Ineffective tissue perfusion (cerebral, peripheral, pulmonary, or myocardial) related to drug-induced thromboembolism
- Deficient knowledge related to drug therapy

Planning and implementation
- **P.O. use:** Give oral forms at mealtimes or h.s. (if only one daily dose is required) to minimize nausea.
- **Intravaginal use:** Follow normal protocol.
- **I.V. use:** When giving by direct I.V. injection, administer slowly to avoid flushing reaction. Reconstitute powder for injection with diluent provided (sterile water for injection with benzyl alcohol). To facilitate introduction of diluent, withdraw 5 ml of air from vial before adding diluent. Gently agitate to mix drug. Avoid shaking container. Avoid mixing with solutions of acidic pH to prevent incompatibility.
- **I.M. use:** When giving by I.M. injection, inject deep into large muscle. Rotate injection sites to prevent muscle atrophy.
- I.M. or I.V. use is preferred for rapid treatment of dysfunctional uterine bleeding or reduction of surgical bleeding.
- Refrigerate before reconstituting. Agitate gently after adding diluent.
- Because of risk of thromboembolism, therapy should be discontinued at least 1 month before procedures that may cause prolonged immobilization or thromboembolism, such as knee or hip surgery.
- Withhold drug and notify prescriber if thromboembolic event is suspected; be prepared to provide supportive care as indicated.
- Notify pathologist if patient receives estrogen therapy.

ALERT: Estrogens aren't interchangeable.

Patient teaching
- Inform patient about package insert that describes adverse effects of estrogen; also provide verbal explanation.
- Emphasize importance of regular physical examinations. Postmenopausal women who use estrogen replacement for more than 5 years to treat menopausal symptoms may be at increased risk for endometrial carcinoma. This risk is reduced by using cyclic rather than continuous therapy and lowest possible dosages of estrogen. Adding progestins to regimen decreases risk of endometrial hyperplasia; it's unknown if progestins decrease or increase risk of endometrial cancer. Most studies show no increased risk of breast cancer.
- Teach patient how to use vaginal cream. Patient should wash vaginal area with soap and water before applying. Tell her to apply drug at bedtime or to lie flat for 30 minutes after application to minimize drug loss.
- Explain to patient on cyclic therapy for postmenopausal symptoms that, although withdrawal bleeding may occur during week off drug, fertility hasn't been restored. Pregnancy can't occur because she hasn't ovulated.
- Warn patient to immediately report abdominal pain; pain, numbness, or stiffness in legs or buttocks; pressure or pain in chest; shortness of breath; severe headaches; visual disturbances, such as blind spots, flashing lights, or blurriness; vaginal bleeding or discharge; breast lumps; swelling of hands or feet; yellow skin or sclera; dark urine; and light-colored stools.
- Tell diabetic patient to report elevated glucose test results so antidiabetic dosage can be adjusted.
- Teach woman how to perform routine breast self-examination.

Evaluation
- Patient shows improvement in underlying condition.
- Patient has no thromboembolic event during therapy.

• Patient and family state understanding of drug therapy.

estrogens, esterified

(ES-troh-jenz, ES-ter-eh-fighd)
Estratab, Menest, Neo-Estrone ♦

Pharmacologic class: estrogen
Therapeutic class: antineoplastic
Pregnancy risk category: X

Indications and dosages

▶ **Inoperable prostate cancer.** *Men:* 1.25 to 2.5 mg P.O. t.i.d.
▶ **Breast cancer.** *Men and postmenopausal women:* 10 mg P.O. t.i.d. for 3 or more months.
▶ **Female hypogonadism.** *Women:* 2.5 to 7.5 mg P.O. daily in divided doses in cycles of 20 days on, 10 days off.
▶ **Female castration, primary ovarian failure.** *Women:* 2.5 mg P.O. daily to t.i.d. in cycles of 3 weeks on, 1 week off.
▶ **Vasomotor menopausal symptoms.** *Women:* Average dosage is 1.25 mg P.O. daily in cycles of 3 weeks on, 1 week off.
▶ **Atrophic vaginitis or urethritis.** *Women:* 0.3 to 1.25 mg P.O. daily in cycles of 3 weeks on, 1 week off.
▶ **Osteoporosis prevention.** *Adults:* Initially, 0.3 mg P.O. daily; may be increased to maximum 1.25 mg daily.

Contraindications and precautions

• Contraindicated in patients with breast cancer (except metastatic disease), estrogen-dependent neoplasia, active thrombophlebitis or thromboembolic disorders, undiagnosed abnormal genital bleeding, hypersensitivity to drug, or history of thromboembolic disease.
• Use cautiously in patients with history of hypertension, depression, cardiac or renal dysfunction, liver impairment, bone diseases, migraine, seizures, or diabetes mellitus.
Lifespan: In pregnant or breast-feeding women, drug is contraindicated. In children, drug shouldn't be used.

Adverse reactions

CNS: headache, dizziness, chorea, depression, lethargy, ***seizures.***
CV: thrombophlebitis; ***thromboembolism;*** hypertension; edema; ***increased risk of CVA, pulmonary embolism, and MI.***
EENT: worsening of myopia or astigmatism, intolerance of contact lenses.
GI: *nausea,* vomiting, abdominal cramps, bloating, diarrhea, constipation, anorexia, ***pancreatitis.***
GU: breakthrough bleeding, altered menstrual flow, dysmenorrhea, amenorrhea, ***possibility of increased risk of breast cancer,*** cervical erosion, altered cervical secretions, enlargement of uterine fibromas, vaginal candidiasis, testicular atrophy, impotence.
Hepatic: cholestatic jaundice, ***hepatic adenoma,*** gallbladder disease.
Metabolic: increased appetite, weight changes, hypercalcemia.
Skin: melasma, rash, erythema nodosum, dermatitis, hirsutism, hair loss.
Other: ***increased risk of endometrial cancer,*** gynecomastia, breast changes (tenderness, enlargement, secretion).

Interactions

Drug-drug. *Bromocriptine:* May cause amenorrhea, interfering with bromocriptine effects. Avoid using together.
Carbamazepine, phenobarbital, rifampin: Decreases effectiveness of estrogen therapy. Monitor patient closely.
Corticosteroids: Possible enhanced effects. Monitor patient closely.
Cyclosporine: Increases risk of toxicity. Use together with caution and frequently monitor cyclosporine levels.
Dantrolene, other hepatotoxic drugs: Increases risk of hepatotoxicity. Monitor patient closely.
Oral anticoagulants: May increase anticoagulant effect. Dosage adjustments may be necessary. Monitor PT and INR.
Tamoxifen: Estrogens may interfere with effectiveness of tamoxifen. Avoid using together.
Drug-food. *Caffeine:* May increase caffeine levels. Monitor effects.
Drug-lifestyle. *Smoking:* Increases risk of CV effects. Urge patient to stop smoking. If smoking continues, patient may need alternative therapy.

Effects on lab test results

• May increase calcium and clotting factor VII, VIII, IX, and X levels.

• May increase PT and norepinephrine-induced platelet aggregation.

Pharmacokinetics

Absorption: Well absorbed but substantially inactivated by liver.
Distribution: Distributed throughout body with highest levels in fat; about 50% to 80% plasma protein bound.
Metabolism: Metabolized primarily in liver.
Excretion: Excreted primarily by kidneys.

Route	Onset	Peak	Duration
P.O.	Unknown	Unknown	Unknown

Pharmacodynamics

Chemical effect: Increases synthesis of DNA, RNA, and protein in responsive tissues; also reduces release of follicle-stimulating hormone and luteinizing hormone from pituitary gland.
Therapeutic effect: Provides estrogen replacement, hinders prostate and breast cancer cell growth, and relieves vasomotor menopausal symptoms and vaginal dryness.

Available forms

Tablets: 0.3 mg, 0.625 mg, 1.25 mg, 2.5 mg
Tablets (film-coated): 0.3 mg, 0.625 mg, 1.25 mg, 2.5 mg

NURSING PROCESS

Assessment

• Obtain history of patient's underlying condition before therapy, and reassess regularly thereafter.
• Make sure patient has thorough physical examination before starting esterified estrogens therapy.
• Patient receiving long-term therapy should have yearly examinations. Periodically monitor lipid levels, blood pressure, body weight, and liver function.
• Be alert for adverse reactions and drug interactions.
• Evaluate patient's and family's knowledge of drug therapy.

Nursing diagnoses

• Ineffective health maintenance related to underlying condition
• Ineffective tissue perfusion (cerebral, peripheral, pulmonary, or myocardial) related to drug-induced thromboembolism
• Deficient knowledge related to drug therapy

Planning and implementation

• Give oral forms at mealtimes or bedtime (if only one daily dose is required) to minimize nausea.
• Because of risk of thromboembolism, therapy should be discontinued at least 1 month before procedures that may cause prolonged immobilization or thromboembolism, such as knee or hip surgery.
• Withhold drug and notify prescriber if thromboembolic event is suspected; be prepared to provide supportive care as indicated.
• Notify pathologist if patient receives estrogen therapy.
ALERT: Estrogens aren't interchangeable.

Patient teaching

• Inform patient about package insert that describes adverse effects of estrogens; also provide verbal explanation.
• Emphasize importance of regular physical examinations. Postmenopausal women who use estrogen replacement for more than 5 years to treat menopausal symptoms may be at increased risk for endometrial carcinoma. This risk is reduced by using cyclic rather than continuous therapy and lowest possible dosages of estrogen. Adding progestins to regimen decreases risk of endometrial hyperplasia; it's unknown if progestins increase or decrease risk of endometrial cancer. Most studies show no increased risk of breast cancer.
• Explain to patient on cyclic therapy for postmenopausal symptoms that although withdrawal bleeding may occur during week off drug, fertility hasn't been restored. Pregnancy can't occur because she hasn't ovulated.
• Warn patient to immediately report abdominal pain; pain, numbness, or stiffness in legs or buttocks; pressure or pain in chest; shortness of breath; severe headaches; visual disturbances, such as blind spots, flashing lights, or blurriness; vaginal bleeding or discharge; breast lumps; swelling of hands or feet; yellow skin or sclera; dark urine; and light-colored stools.
• Tell diabetic patient to report elevated glucose test results so antidiabetic dosage can be adjusted.

• Teach woman how to perform routine breast self-examination.

Evaluation

• Patient shows improvement in underlying condition.
• Patient has no thromboembolic event during therapy.
• Patient and family state understanding of drug therapy.

estropipate (piperazine estrone sulfate)

(ES-troh-pih-payt)
Ogen, Ortho-Est

Pharmacologic class: estrogen
Therapeutic class: estrogen replacement
Pregnancy risk category: X

Indications and dosages

▶ **Management of moderate-to-severe vasomotor symptoms, vulvar and vaginal atrophy.** *Women:* 0.75 to 6 mg P.O. daily 3 weeks on, 1 week off, or 2 to 4 g of vaginal cream daily. Typically, dosage given on cyclic, short-term basis.

▶ **Primary ovarian failure, female castration, female hypogonadism.** *Women:* Given on cyclic basis—1.5 to 9 mg P.O. daily for first 3 weeks, followed by rest period of 8 to 10 days. If bleeding doesn't occur by end of rest period, repeat cycle.

▶ **Prevention of osteoporosis.** *Women:* 0.625 mg P.O. daily for 25 days of 31-day cycle. Regimen may be repeated p.r.n.

Contraindications and precautions

• Contraindicated in patients with active thrombophlebitis, thromboembolic disorders, estrogen-dependent neoplasia, undiagnosed genital bleeding, or breast, reproductive organ, or genital cancer.
• Use cautiously in patients with cerebrovascular or coronary artery disease, asthma, depression, bone disease, migraine, seizures, or cardiac, hepatic, or renal dysfunction and in women with family history (mother, grandmother, sister) of breast or genital tract cancer or who have breast nodules, fibrocystic disease, or abnormal mammogram findings.

Lifespan: In pregnant and breast-feeding women, drug is contraindicated. Drug shouldn't be used in children.

Adverse reactions

CNS: depression, headache, dizziness, migraine, ***seizures.***
CV: edema; thrombophlebitis; ***increased risk of CVA, pulmonary embolism, thromboembolism, and MI.***
GI: nausea, vomiting, abdominal cramps, bloating.
GU: increased size of uterine fibromas, ***increased risk of endometrial cancer,*** vaginal candidiasis, cystitis-like syndrome, dysmenorrhea, amenorrhea, breakthrough bleeding.
Hepatic: cholestatic jaundice.
Metabolic: hypercalcemia, weight changes.
Skin: hemorrhagic eruption, erythema nodosum, ***erythema multiforme,*** hirsutism, melasma, hair loss.
Other: ***possibility of increased risk of breast cancer,*** breast engorgement or enlargement, libido changes, aggravation of porphyria.

Interactions

Drug-drug. *Bromocriptine:* May cause amenorrhea, interfering with bromocriptine effects. Avoid using together.
Carbamazepine, phenobarbital, rifampin: Decreases effectiveness of estrogen therapy. Monitor patient closely.
Corticosteroids: Possible enhanced effects. Monitor patient closely.
Cyclosporine: Increases risk of toxicity. Use together with caution and frequently monitor cyclosporine levels.
Dantrolene, other hepatotoxic drugs: Increases risk of hepatotoxicity. Monitor patient closely.
Oral anticoagulants: May decrease anticoagulant effects. Dosage adjustments may be necessary. Monitor PT and INR.
Tamoxifen: Estrogens may interfere with effectiveness of tamoxifen. Avoid using together.
Drug-food. *Caffeine:* May increase caffeine levels. Monitor effects.
Drug-lifestyle. *Smoking:* Increases risk of CV effects. Urge patient to stop smoking. If smoking continues, patient may need alternate therapy.

Effects on lab test results

• May increase calcium, total T_4, thyroid-binding globulin, phospholipid, triglyceride, and clotting factor VII, VIII, IX, and X levels.
• May increase PT and norepinephrine-induced platelet aggregation.

Pharmacokinetics

Absorption: Not well characterized after P.O. or intravaginal administration.
Distribution: Distributed throughout body with highest levels in fat; about 50% to 80% plasma protein–bound.
Metabolism: Metabolized primarily in liver.
Excretion: Eliminated primarily by kidneys.

Route	Onset	Peak	Duration
P.O., intravaginal	Unknown	Unknown	Unknown

Pharmacodynamics

Chemical effect: Increases synthesis of DNA, RNA, and protein in responsive tissues. Also reduces release of follicle-stimulating hormone and luteinizing hormone from pituitary gland.
Therapeutic effect: Provides estrogen replacement, relieves vasomotor menopausal symptoms, and helps reduce severity of osteoporosis.

Available forms

Tablets: 0.75 mg, 1.5 mg, 3 mg, 6 mg
Vaginal cream: 1.5 mg/g (0.15%)

NURSING PROCESS

Assessment

• Obtain history of patient's underlying condition before therapy, and reassess regularly thereafter.
• Make sure patient has thorough physical examination before starting estropipate therapy.
• Patient receiving long-term therapy should have yearly examinations. Periodically monitor lipid levels, blood pressure, body weight, and liver function.
• Be alert for adverse reactions and drug interactions.
• Evaluate patient's and family's knowledge of drug therapy.

Nursing diagnoses

• Ineffective health maintenance related to underlying condition
• Ineffective tissue perfusion (cerebral, peripheral, pulmonary, or myocardial) related to drug-induced thromboembolism
• Deficient knowledge related to drug therapy

Planning and implementation

• **P.O. use:** Give oral forms with meals or at bedtime (if only one daily dose is required) to minimize nausea.
• **Intravaginal use:** Follow normal protocol.
• Because of risk of thromboembolism, therapy should be discontinued at least 1 month before procedures that may cause prolonged immobilization or thromboembolism, such as knee or hip surgery.
• Withhold drug and notify prescriber if thromboembolic event is suspected; be prepared to provide supportive care as indicated.
• Notify pathologist if patient receives this drug.
ALERT: Estrogens aren't interchangeable.

Patient teaching

• Inform patient about package insert that describes adverse effects of estrogens; also provide verbal explanation.
• Emphasize importance of regular physical examinations. Postmenopausal women who use estrogen replacement for more than 5 years to treat menopausal symptoms may be at increased risk for endometrial carcinoma. This risk is reduced by using cyclic rather than continuous therapy and lowest possible dosages of estrogen. Adding progestins to regimen decreases risk of endometrial hyperplasia; it's unknown if progestins increase or decrease risk of endometrial cancer. Most studies show no increased risk of breast cancer.
• Teach patient how to use vaginal cream. Patient should wash vaginal area with soap and water before applying. Tell her to use drug at bedtime or to lie flat for 30 minutes after application to minimize drug loss.
• Explain to patient on cyclic therapy for postmenopausal symptoms that, although withdrawal bleeding may occur during week off drug, fertility hasn't been restored. Pregnancy can't occur because she hasn't ovulated.
• Explain to patient being treated for hypogonadism that duration of therapy needed to produce withdrawal bleeding depends on patient's endometrial response to drug. If satisfactory withdrawal bleeding doesn't occur, oral prog-

estin is added to regimen. Explain to patient that despite return of withdrawal bleeding, pregnancy can't occur because she isn't ovulating.
• Warn patient to immediately report abdominal pain; pain, numbness, or stiffness in legs or buttocks; pressure or pain in chest; shortness of breath; severe headaches; visual disturbances, such as blind spots, flashing lights, or blurriness; vaginal bleeding or discharge; breast lumps; swelling of hands or feet; yellow skin or sclera; dark urine; and light-colored stools.
• Tell diabetic patient to report elevated glucose test results so antidiabetic dosage can be adjusted.
• Teach woman how to perform routine breast self-examination.

Evaluation
• Patient shows improvement in underlying condition.
• Patient has no thromboembolic event during therapy.
• Patient and family state understanding of drug therapy.

etanercept
(ee-TAN-er-sept)
Enbrel

Pharmacologic class: tumor necrosis factor (TNF) blocker
Therapeutic class: antirheumatic
Pregnancy risk category: B

Indications and dosages
▶ **Reducing signs and symptoms and delaying structural damage in patients with moderately to severely active rheumatoid arthritis.** *Adults:* 25 mg S.C. twice weekly, 72 to 96 hours apart.
▶ **Reducing signs and symptoms of moderately to severely active polyarticular-course juvenile rheumatoid arthritis in patients who have had an inadequate response to one or more disease-modifying antirheumatic drugs.** *Children ages 4 to 17:* 0.4 mg/kg (maximum, 25 mg/dose) S.C. twice weekly, 72 to 96 hours apart.
▶ **Psoriatic arthritis.** *Adults:* 25 mg given twice weekly S.C. 72 to 96 hours apart. Methotrexate, glucocorticoids, salicylates, NSAIDs, or analgesics may be continued during treatment with etanercept.

Contraindications and precautions
• Contraindicated in patients hypersensitive to drug and in those with sepsis.
• Discontinue drug in patients who develop serious infections or sepsis.
• Use cautiously in patients with a history of recurring infections or conditions that may predispose them to infections.
Lifespan: In pregnant women, use cautiously. In breast-feeding women and children younger than age 4, drug isn't recommended.

Adverse reactions
CNS: asthenia, *headache,* dizziness.
EENT: *rhinitis,* pharyngitis, sinusitis.
GI: abdominal pain, dyspepsia.
Respiratory: *upper respiratory tract infections,* cough, respiratory disorder.
Skin: *injection site reaction,* rash.
Other: *infections,* ***malignancies.***

Interactions
None significant.

Effects on lab test results
None reported.

Pharmacokinetics
Absorption: Serum levels peak in 72 hours.
Distribution: Unknown.
Metabolism: Unknown.
Excretion: Unknown. *Elimination half-life:* 115 hours.

Route	Onset	Peak	Duration
S.C.	Unknown	72 hr	Unknown

Pharmacodynamics
Chemical effect: Binds specifically to TNF and blocks its action with cell surface TNF receptors, reducing inflammatory and immune responses found in rheumatoid arthritis.
Therapeutic effect: Reduces signs and symptoms of rheumatoid arthritis.

Available forms
Injection: 25 mg single-use vial

NURSING PROCESS

Assessment
• Obtain history of patient's underlying condition before therapy, and reassess regularly thereafter.
• Obtain accurate immunization history from parents or guardians of juvenile rheumatoid arthritis patients; if possible, they should be brought up to date with all immunizations in compliance with current guidelines before treatment is started.
• Monitor patient for infection.
• Evaluate patient's and family's knowledge about drug therapy.

Nursing diagnoses
• Acute pain related to underlying condition
• Risk for infection related to drug-induced adverse reactions
• Deficient knowledge related to drug therapy

Planning and implementation
• Drug is for S.C. injection only.
• Reconstitute aseptically with 1 ml of supplied sterile bacteriostatic water for injection, USP (0.9% benzyl alcohol). Don't filter reconstituted solution during preparation or administration. Inject diluent slowly into vial. Minimize foaming by gently swirling during dissolution rather than shaking. Dissolution takes less than 5 minutes.
• Inspect solution for particulates and discoloration before use. Reconstituted solution should be clear and colorless. Don't use solution if it's discolored, cloudy, or if particulates exist.
• Don't add other drugs or diluents to reconstituted solution.
• Use reconstituted solution as soon as possible; may be refrigerated in vial for up to 6 hours at 36° to 46° F (2° to 8° C).
• Injection sites should be at least 1 inch apart; don't use areas where skin is tender, bruised, red, or hard. Recommended sites include the thigh, abdomen, and upper arm. Rotate sites regularly.
• Patient may develop positive antinuclear antibody or positive anti–double-stranded DNA antibodies measured by radioimmunoassay and *Crithidia luciliae* assay.
• Don't give live vaccines during therapy.
• Anti-TNF therapies, including etanercept, may affect defenses against infection. Notify prescriber, and discontinue therapy if serious infection occurs.
• Needle cover of diluent syringe contains dry natural rubber (latex) and shouldn't be handled by persons sensitive to latex.

Patient teaching
• If patient will be administering drug, teach mixing and injection techniques, including rotation of injection sites.
• Instruct patient to use puncture-resistant container to dispose of needles and syringes.
• Tell patient that injection site reactions typically occur within first month of therapy and decrease thereafter.
• Urge patient to avoid live vaccines during therapy. Stress importance of alerting other health care providers of etanercept use.
• Instruct patient to promptly report evidence of infection to prescriber.
• Advise breast-feeding women to discontinue breast-feeding during drug therapy.

Evaluation
• Patient has decreased pain.
• Patient is free from infection.
• Patient and family state understanding of drug therapy.

ethacrynate sodium
(eth-uh-KRIH-nayt SOH-dee-um)
Sodium Edecrin

ethacrynic acid
Edecril ◇, Edecrin

Pharmacologic class: loop diuretic
Therapeutic class: diuretic
Pregnancy risk category: B

Indications and dosages
▶ **Acute pulmonary edema.** *Adults:* 50 mg or 0.5 to 1 mg/kg I.V. to maximum dose of 100 mg. Usually only one dose is needed; occasionally, second dose may be required.
▶ **Edema.** *Adults:* 50 to 200 mg P.O. daily. Refractory cases may require up to 200 mg b.i.d.
Children: Initial dose is 25 mg P.O., increase cautiously in 25-mg increments daily until desired effect is achieved.

▶ **Hypertension‡.** *Adults:* Initially, 25 mg P.O. daily. Adjust dosage p.r.n. Maximum maintenance dose is 200 mg P.O. daily in 2 divided doses.

Contraindications and precautions

• Contraindicated in patients hypersensitive to drug, and in those with anuria. Use cautiously in patients with electrolyte abnormalities or hepatic impairment.

Lifespan: In pregnant women, use cautiously. In breast-feeding women, drug isn't recommended. In infants, drug is contraindicated.

Adverse reactions

CNS: fever, malaise, confusion, fatigue, vertigo, headache, nervousness.
CV: volume depletion and dehydration, orthostatic hypotension.
EENT: transient deafness (with too-rapid I.V. injection), blurred vision, tinnitus, hearing loss.
GI: cramping, diarrhea, anorexia, nausea, vomiting, **GI BLEEDING,** ***pancreatitis.***
GU: nocturia, polyuria, frequent urination, oliguria, hematuria.
Hematologic: ***agranulocytosis, neutropenia, thrombocytopenia,*** azotemia.
Metabolic: asymptomatic hyperuricemia; hypochloremic alkalosis; fluid and electrolyte imbalances, including dilutional hyponatremia, hypokalemia, hypocalcemia, hypomagnesemia; hyperglycemia and impairment of glucose tolerance.
Skin: dermatitis, rash.
Other: chills.

Interactions

Drug-drug. *Aminoglycoside antibiotics:* Potentiated ototoxic adverse reactions of both drugs. Use together cautiously.
Antihypertensives: Increases risk of hypotension. Use together cautiously.
Cardiac glycosides: Increases risk of digoxin toxicity from ethacrynate-induced hypokalemia. Monitor potassium and digoxin levels.
Cisplatin: Increases risk of ototoxicity. Avoid using together.
Lithium: Decreases lithium clearance, increasing risk of lithium toxicity. Monitor lithium level.
Metolazone: May cause profound diuresis and enhanced electrolyte loss. Use together cautiously.
NSAIDs: May decrease diuretic effectiveness. Use together cautiously.
Warfarin: Potentiates anticoagulant effect. Use together cautiously.
Drug-herb. *Licorice root:* May contribute to potassium depletion caused by diuretics. Discourage licorice root intake.
Drug-lifestyle. *Sun exposure:* Photosensitivity may occur. Discourage prolonged or unprotected exposure to sunlight.

Effects on lab test results

• May increase glucose and uric acid levels. May decrease potassium, sodium, calcium, and magnesium levels.
• May decrease granulocyte, neutrophil, and platelet counts.

Pharmacokinetics

Absorption: Ethacrynic acid is absorbed rapidly from GI tract. Ethacrynate sodium is administered I.V.
Distribution: Unknown.
Metabolism: Unknown.
Excretion: Unknown.

Route	Onset	Peak	Duration
P.O.	30 min	2 hr	6-8 hr
I.V.	5 min	15-30 min	2 hr

Pharmacodynamics

Chemical effect: Inhibits sodium and chloride reabsorption at renal tubules and ascending loop of Henle.
Therapeutic effect: Promotes sodium and water excretion.

Available forms

Injection: 50 mg (with 62.5 mg of mannitol and 0.1 mg of thimerosal)
Tablets: 25 mg, 50 mg

NURSING PROCESS

Assessment

• Obtain history of patient's underlying condition before therapy.
• Monitor effectiveness by regularly checking urine output, weight, peripheral edema, and breath sounds.

• Monitor fluid intake, blood pressure, and electrolyte levels.
• Monitor uric acid levels, especially in patients with history of gout.
• Be alert for adverse reactions and drug interactions.
• Evaluate patient's and family's knowledge of drug therapy.

Nursing diagnoses
• Excess fluid volume related to underlying condition
• Impaired urinary elimination related to diuretic therapy
• Deficient knowledge related to drug therapy

Planning and implementation
• **P.O. use:** Give drug with food or milk. P.O. use may cause GI upset.
– To prevent nocturia, give P.O. doses in morning.
• **I.V. use:** Reconstitute vacuum vial with 50 ml of D_5W or normal saline solution. Give slowly through I.V. line of running infusion over several minutes. Discard unused solution after 24 hours. Don't use cloudy or opalescent solutions.
– If more than one I.V. dose is necessary, use new injection site to avoid thrombophlebitis.
– Don't mix with whole blood or its derivatives.
• Don't give S.C. or I.M. because of local pain and irritation.
• Potassium chloride and sodium supplements may be needed.
• Notify prescriber if diarrhea occurs because severe diarrhea may necessitate discontinuing drug.

Patient teaching
• Advise patient to avoid sudden posture changes and to rise slowly to avoid orthostatic hypotension.
• Advise diabetic patient to closely monitor glucose levels.
• Teach patient and family to identify and report signs of hypersensitivity or fluid and electrolyte disturbances.
• Teach patient to monitor fluid volume by daily weight and intake and output.
• Tell patient to take oral drug early in day to avoid interruption of sleep by nocturia.

Evaluation
• Patient is free from edema.
• Patient demonstrates adjustment of lifestyle to deal with altered patterns of urinary elimination.
• Patient and family state understanding of drug therapy.

ethambutol hydrochloride
(ee-THAM-byoo-tol high-droh-KLOR-ighd)
Etibi♦, Myambutol

Pharmacologic class: semisynthetic antituberculotic
Therapeutic class: antituberculotic
Pregnancy risk category: B

Indications and dosages
▶ **Adjunct treatment in pulmonary tuberculosis.** *Adults and children age 13 and older:* For patients who haven't received previous antitubercular therapy, 15 mg/kg P.O. daily. For patients who have received previous antitubercular therapy, 25 mg/kg P.O. daily for 60 days until cultures are negative; then, decrease to 15 mg/kg P.O. daily.
▶ **Adjunctive therapy for pulmonary *Mycobacterium avium* complex infections in patients without HIV‡.** *Adults:* 25 mg/kg P.O. daily for 2 months followed by 15 mg/kg P.O. daily until cultures are negative for 1 year.
▶ **Adjunctive therapy for disseminated *Mycobacterium avium* complex infections‡.** *Adults:* 15 mg/kg P.O. daily for patient's lifetime.

Contraindications and precautions
• Contraindicated in patients hypersensitive to drug and in patients with optic neuritis.
• Use cautiously in patients with impaired kidney function, cataracts, recurrent eye inflammations, gout, and diabetic retinopathy.
Lifespan: In pregnant and breast-feeding women, use cautiously. In children younger than age 13, drug is contraindicated.

Adverse reactions
CNS: fever, malaise, headache, dizziness, confusion, possibly hallucinations, peripheral neuritis.

EENT: dose-related optic neuritis (vision loss and loss of color discrimination, especially red and green).
GI: anorexia, nausea, vomiting, abdominal pain.
Hematologic: ***thrombocytopenia.***
Respiratory: bloody sputum.
Skin: dermatitis, pruritus, ***toxic epidermal necrolysis.***
Other: ***anaphylactoid reactions,*** precipitation of gout.

Interactions

Drug-drug. *Aluminum salts:* May delay and reduce absorption of ethambutol. Separate administrations by several hours.

Effects on lab test results

- May increase ALT, AST, bilirubin, and uric acid levels. May decrease glucose level.
- May decrease platelet count.

Pharmacokinetics

Absorption: Absorbed rapidly from GI tract.
Distribution: Distributed widely in body tissues and fluids; 8% to 22% protein-bound.
Metabolism: Undergoes partial hepatic metabolism.
Excretion: After 24 hours, about 50% of unchanged drug and 8% to 15% of its metabolites are excreted in urine; 20% to 25% is excreted in feces. *Half-life:* About 3½ hours.

Route	Onset	Peak	Duration
P.O.	Unknown	2-4 hr	Unknown

Pharmacodynamics

Chemical effect: Unknown; appears to interfere with synthesis of one or more metabolites of susceptible bacteria, altering cellular metabolism during cell division (bacteriostatic).
Therapeutic effect: Hinders bacterial growth. Spectrum of activity includes *Mycobacterium bovis, Mycobacterium marinum, Mycobacterium tuberculosis,* and some strains of *Mycobacterium avium, Mycobacterium fortuitum, Mycobacterium intracellulare,* and *Mycobacterium kansasii.*

Available forms

Tablets: 100 mg, 400 mg

NURSING PROCESS

Assessment

- Obtain history of patient's infection before therapy.
- Perform visual acuity and color discrimination tests before therapy and during treatment.
- Monitor effectiveness by regularly assessing for improvement in patient's condition and evaluating culture and sensitivity test results.
- Obtain AST and ALT levels before starting therapy. Then, monitor AST and ALT levels every 2 to 4 weeks.
- Monitor uric acid level; observe patient for symptoms of gout.
- Be alert for adverse reactions and drug interactions.
- Evaluate patient's and family's knowledge of drug therapy.

Nursing diagnoses

- Infection related to presence of susceptible bacteria
- Disturbed sensory perception (visual) related to drug-induced adverse reactions
- Deficient knowledge related to drug therapy

Planning and implementation

- Anticipate dosage reduction in patient with impaired kidney function.
- Always give ethambutol with other antituberculotics to prevent development of resistant organisms.

Patient teaching

- Reassure patient that visual disturbances will disappear several weeks to months after drug is stopped. Caution patient not to perform hazardous activities if visual disturbances or adverse CNS reactions occur.
- Emphasize need for regular follow-up care.

Evaluation

- Patient is free from infection.
- Patient regains pretreatment visual ability after therapy has stopped.
- Patient and family state understanding of drug therapy.

ethinyl estradiol (ethinyloestradiol)

(ETH-uh-nil es-truh-DIGH-ol)
Estinyl**

Pharmacologic class: estrogen
Therapeutic class: estrogen replacement, antineoplastic
Pregnancy risk category: X

Indications and dosages

▶ **Palliative treatment of metastatic breast cancer (at least 5 years after menopause).** *Women:* 1 mg P.O. t.i.d. for at least 3 months.
▶ **Female hypogonadism.** *Women:* 0.05 mg P.O. once daily to t.i.d. 2 weeks a month, followed by 2 weeks of progesterone therapy; continued for three to six monthly dosing cycles, followed by 2 months off.
▶ **Vasomotor menopausal symptoms.** *Women:* 0.02 to 0.05 mg P.O. daily for cycles of 3 weeks on and 1 week off.
▶ **Palliative treatment of metastatic inoperable prostate cancer.** *Men:* 0.15 to 2 mg P.O. daily.

Contraindications and precautions

- Contraindicated in patients with thrombophlebitis, thromboembolic disorders, estrogen-dependent neoplasia, breast or reproductive organ cancer (except for palliative treatment), or undiagnosed abnormal genital bleeding.
- Use cautiously in patients with cerebrovascular or coronary artery disease, asthma, depression, bone disease, or cardiac, hepatic, or renal dysfunction and in women with family history (mother, grandmother, sister) of breast or genital tract cancer or who have breast nodules, fibrocystic disease, or abnormal mammogram findings.

Lifespan: In pregnant and breast-feeding women, drug is contraindicated. Drug shouldn't be used in children.

Adverse reactions

CNS: headache, dizziness, chorea, depression, lethargy, ***seizures.***
CV: thrombophlebitis; ***thromboembolism;*** hypertension; edema; ***increased risk of CVA, pulmonary embolism, and MI.***
EENT: worsening of myopia or astigmatism, intolerance to contact lenses.
GI: *nausea,* vomiting, abdominal cramps, bloating, diarrhea, constipation, anorexia.
GU: breakthrough bleeding, altered menstrual flow, dysmenorrhea, amenorrhea, cervical erosion, increased risk of endometrial cancer, altered cervical secretions, enlarged uterine fibromas, vaginal candidiasis; testicular atrophy, impotence.
Hepatic: cholestatic jaundice, gallbladder disease, ***hepatic adenoma.***
Metabolic: hyperglycemia, hypercalcemia, increased appetite, weight changes.
Skin: melasma, urticaria, acne, seborrhea, oily skin, hirsutism or hair loss, erythema nodosum, dermatitis.
Other: ***increased risk of breast cancer,*** gynecomastia, breast changes (tenderness, enlargement, secretion).

Interactions

Drug-drug. *Bromocriptine:* May cause amenorrhea, interfering with bromocriptine effects. Avoid using together.
Carbamazepine, phenobarbital, rifampin: Decreases effectiveness of estrogen therapy. Monitor patient closely.
Corticosteroids: Possible enhanced effects. Monitor patient closely.
Cyclosporine: Increases risk of toxicity. Use together with caution, and frequently monitor cyclosporine levels.
Dantrolene, other hepatotoxic drugs: Increases risk of hepatotoxicity. Monitor patient closely.
Oral anticoagulants: May decrease anticoagulant effects. Dosage adjustments may be necessary. Monitor PT and INR.
Tamoxifen: Estrogens may interfere with effectiveness of tamoxifen. Avoid using together.
Drug-food. *Caffeine:* May increase caffeine levels. Monitor effects.
Drug-lifestyle. *Smoking:* Increases risk of CV effects. If smoking continues, patient may need alternate therapy. Urge patient to stop smoking.

Effects on lab test results

- May increase glucose; calcium; clotting factor VII, VIII, IX, and X; total T_4; thyroid-binding globulin; phospholipid; triglyceride; and liver enzyme levels.

• May increase PT and norepinephrine-induced platelet aggregation. May decrease antithrombin III activity.

Pharmacokinetics

Absorption: Well absorbed but substantially inactivated by liver.
Distribution: Distributed throughout body with highest levels in fat; about 50% to 80% plasma protein–bound.
Metabolism: Metabolized primarily in liver.
Excretion: Excreted primarily by kidneys.

Route	Onset	Peak	Duration
P.O.	Unknown	Unknown	Unknown

Pharmacodynamics

Chemical effect: Increases synthesis of DNA, RNA, and protein in responsive tissues; also reduces release of follicle-stimulating hormone and luteinizing hormone from pituitary gland.
Therapeutic effect: Replaces estrogen, hinders prostate and breast cancer cell growth, and relieves vasomotor menopausal symptoms.

Available forms

Tablets: 0.02 mg, 0.05 mg

NURSING PROCESS

Assessment

• Obtain history of patient's underlying condition before therapy, and reassess regularly thereafter.
• Make sure patient has thorough physical examination before starting ethinyl estradiol therapy.
• Patient receiving long-term therapy should have yearly examinations. Periodically monitor lipid levels, blood pressure, body weight, and liver function.
• Be alert for adverse reactions and drug interactions.
• Evaluate patient's and family's knowledge of drug therapy.

Nursing diagnoses

• Ineffective health maintenance related to underlying condition
• Ineffective tissue perfusion (cerebral, peripheral, pulmonary, or myocardial) related to drug-induced thromboembolism
• Deficient knowledge related to drug therapy

Planning and implementation

• Give oral forms with meals or at bedtime (if only one daily dose is required) to minimize nausea.
• Because of risk of thromboembolism, therapy should be discontinued at least 1 month before procedures that may cause prolonged immobilization or thromboembolism, such as knee or hip surgery.
• Withhold drug and notify prescriber if thromboembolic event is suspected; be prepared to provide supportive care as indicated.
• Notify pathologist if patient receives this drug.
ALERT: Estrogen preparations aren't interchangeable.

Patient teaching

• Inform patient about package insert that describes estrogen's adverse effects; also provide verbal explanation.
• Emphasize importance of regular physical examinations. Postmenopausal women who use estrogen replacement for more than 5 years to treat menopausal symptoms may be at increased risk for endometrial cancer. This risk is reduced by using cyclic rather than continuous therapy and lowest possible dosages of estrogen. Adding progestins to regimen decreases risk of endometrial hyperplasia; it's unknown if progestins decrease or increase risk of endometrial cancer. Most studies show no increased risk of breast cancer.
• Explain to patient on cyclic therapy for postmenopausal symptoms that although withdrawal bleeding may occur during week off drug, fertility hasn't been restored. Pregnancy can't occur because patient hasn't ovulated.
ALERT: Warn patient to immediately report abdominal pain; pain, numbness, or stiffness in legs or buttocks; pressure or pain in chest; shortness of breath; severe headaches; visual disturbances, such as blind spots, flashing lights, or blurriness; vaginal bleeding or discharge; breast lumps; swelling of hands or feet; yellow skin or sclera; dark urine; and light-colored stools.
• Tell diabetic patient to report elevated glucose test results so antidiabetic dosage can be adjusted.
• Teach woman how to perform routine breast self-examination.

Evaluation
- Patient shows improvement in underlying condition.
- Patient has no thromboembolic event during therapy.
- Patient and family state understanding of drug therapy.

ethinyl estradiol and desogestrel
(ETH-uh-nil es-truh-DIGH-ol and DAY-so-jest-rul)
monophasic: Apri, Desogen, Ortho-Cept
biphasic: Mircette
triphasic: Cyclessa, Kariva

ethinyl estradiol and ethynodiol diacetate
monophasic: Demulen 1/35, Demulen 1/50, Zovia 1/35E, Zovia 1/50E

ethinyl estradiol and levonorgestrel
Emergency: Preven
monophasic: Levlen, Nordette, Alesse, Aviane, Lessina, Portia
triphasic: Tri-Levlen, Triphasil, Trivora, Enpresse

ethinyl estradiol and norethindrone
monophasic: Brevicon, Genora 0.5/35, Genora 1/35, ModiCon, NEE 1/35, Nelova 0.5/35E, Nelova 1/35E, Norethin 1/35E, Norinyl 1+35, Ortho-Novum 1/35, Ovcon-35, Ovcon-50
biphasic: Necon 10/11, Nortrel, Ortho-Novum 10/11, Jenest-28
triphasic: Ortho-Novum 7/7/7, Tri-Norinyl

ethinyl estradiol and norethindrone acetate
monophasic: Loestrin 21 1/20, Loestrin 21 1.5/30
triphasic: Estrostep

ethinyl estradiol and norgestimate
monophasic: Ortho-Cyclen
triphasic: Ortho Tri-Cyclen

ethinyl estradiol and norgestrel
monophasic: Lo/Ovral, Ovral, Ogestrel

ethinyl estradiol, norethindrone acetate, and ferrous fumarate
monophasic: Loestrin Fe 1/20, Loestrin Fe 1.5/30, Microgestin Fe 1/20, Microgestin Fe 1.5/30

mestranol and norethindrone
monophasic: Necon, Norinyl 1+50, Ortho-Novum 1/50
triphasic: Estrostep Fe, Estrostep 21

Pharmacologic class: estrogen with progestin
Therapeutic class: oral contraceptive
Pregnancy risk category: X

Indications and dosages

▶ **Contraception.** ***monophasic oral contraceptives.*** *Women:* 1 tablet P.O. daily, beginning on day 5 of menstrual cycle (first day of menstrual flow is day 1). With 20- and 21-tablet packages, new dosing cycle begins 7 days after last tablet taken. With 28-tablet packages, dosage is 1 tablet daily without interruption; extra tablets are placebos or contain iron.
biphasic oral contraceptives. *Women:* First color tablet P.O. daily for 10 days; then next color tablet for 11 days.
triphasic oral contraceptives. *Women:* 1 tablet P.O. daily in sequence specified by brand.
▶ **Moderate acne vulgaris in women and girls age 15 and older who have no known contraindications to oral contraceptive therapy, desire oral contraception, have achieved menarche, and are unresponsive to topical antiacne medications.** *Women and girls age 15 and older:* 1 tablet Estrostep or Ortho Tri-Cyclen P.O. daily (21 tablets contain active ingredients and 7 are inert).

Contraindications and precautions

- Contraindicated in patients with thromboembolic disorders, cerebrovascular or coronary artery disease, diplopia or ocular lesion arising from ophthalmic vascular disease, classic migraine, MI, known or suspected breast cancer, known or suspected estrogen-dependent neoplasia, benign or malignant liver tumors, active liver disease or history of cholestatic jaundice with pregnancy or prior use of oral contraceptives, or undiagnosed abnormal vaginal bleeding.

- Use cautiously in patients with cardiac, renal, or hepatic insufficiency; hyperlipidemia; hypertension; migraine; seizure disorders; or asthma.

Lifespan: To avoid later fertility and menstrual problems, hormonal contraception isn't advised for adolescents until after at least 2 years of well-established menstrual cycles and completion of physiologic maturation. In known or suspected pregnancy and in breast-feeding women, drug is contraindicated.

Adverse reactions

CNS: *headache, dizziness,* depression, lethargy, migraine.
CV: ***thromboembolism,*** hypertension, edema, ***pulmonary embolism, CVA.***
EENT: worsening of myopia or astigmatism, intolerance of contact lenses, exophthalmos, diplopia.
GI: granulomatous colitis, *nausea,* vomiting, abdominal cramps, bloating, diarrhea, constipation, anorexia, ***pancreatitis.***
GU: *breakthrough bleeding,* dysmenorrhea, amenorrhea, cervical erosion or abnormal secretions, enlargement of uterine fibromas, vaginal candidiasis.
Hepatic: gallbladder disease, cholestatic jaundice, ***liver tumors.***
Metabolic: changes in appetite, weight gain, hyperglycemia, hypercalcemia.
Skin: rash, acne, ***erythema multiforme.***
Other: breast changes (*tenderness,* enlargement, secretion).

Interactions

Drug-drug. *Bromocriptine:* May cause amenorrhea, interfering with bromocriptine effects. Avoid using together.
Carbamazepine, phenobarbital, phenytoin, rifampin: Decreases effectiveness of estrogen therapy. Monitor patient closely.
Corticosteroids: Possibly enhanced effects. Monitor patient closely.
Dantrolene, other hepatotoxic drugs: Increases risk of hepatotoxicity. Monitor patient closely.
Griseofulvin, penicillins, sulfonamides, tetracyclines: May decrease effectiveness of oral contraceptives. Avoid using together, if possible, or use barrier contraception for the duration of therapy.
Oral anticoagulants: May decrease anticoagulant effects. Dosage adjustments may be necessary. Monitor PT and INR.
Tamoxifen: Estrogens may interfere with effectiveness of tamoxifen. Avoid using together.
Drug-food. *Caffeine:* May increase caffeine levels. Monitor effects.
Drug-lifestyle. *Smoking:* Increases risk of CV effects. Discourage patient from smoking. If smoking continues, may need an alternate therapy.

Effects on lab test results

- May increase glucose, calcium, fibrinogen, triglyceride, total T_4, thyroid-binding globulin, plasminogen, liver enzyme, and clotting factor II, VII, VIII, IX, X, and XII levels.
- May increase PT, phospholipid concentrations, and norepinephrine-induced platelet aggregation.

Pharmacokinetics

Absorption: Mostly well absorbed.
Distribution: Widely distributed and extensively bound to plasma proteins.
Metabolism: Metabolized mainly in liver.
Excretion: Excreted in urine and feces.

Route	Onset	Peak	Duration
P.O.	Unknown	Varies	Unknown

Pharmacodynamics

Chemical effect: Inhibits ovulation through negative feedback mechanism directed at hypothalamus. Estrogen suppresses secretion of follicle-stimulating hormone, blocking follicular development and ovulation. Progestin suppresses secretion of luteinizing hormone so ovulation cannot occur even if follicle develops. Progestin thickens cervical mucus, which interferes with sperm migration, and causes endometrial changes that prevent implantation of fertilized ovum.
Therapeutic effect: Prevents pregnancy and relieves signs and symptoms of endometriosis.

Available forms

Monophasic oral contraceptives
ethinyl estradiol and desogestrel
Tablets: ethinyl estradiol 30 mcg and desogestrel 0.15 mg (Apri, Desogen, Ortho-Cept), ethinyl estradiol 25 mcg and desogestrel 0.1 mg, ethinyl estradiol 20 mcg and desogestrel 0.15 mg

(Kariva, Mircette), ethinyl estradiol 25 mcg and desogestrel 0.15 mg (Cyclessa)
ethinyl estradiol and ethynodiol diacetate
Tablets: ethinyl estradiol 35 mcg and ethynodiol diacetate 1 mg (Demulen 1/35, Zovia 1/35E); ethinyl estradiol 50 mcg and ethynodiol diacetate 1 mg (Demulen 1/50, Zovia 1/50E)
ethinyl estradiol and levonorgestrel
Tablets: ethinyl estradiol 30 mcg and levonorgestrel 0.15 mg (Levlen, Levora, Nordette, Portia); ethinyl estradiol 20 mcg, levonorgestrel 0.1 mg. (Alesse, Aviane, Lessina)
ethinyl estradiol and norethindrone
Tablets: ethinyl estradiol 35 mcg and norethindrone 0.4 mg (Ovcon-35); ethinyl estradiol 35 mcg and norethindrone 0.5 mg (Brevicon, Necon, Nortel, ModiCon, Nelova 0.5/35E); ethinyl estradiol 35 mcg and norethindrone 1 mg (Necon 1/35, Nortel 1/35, Norinyl 1+35, Ortho-Novum 1/35); ethinyl estradiol 50 mcg and norethindrone 1 mg (Ovcon-50)
ethinyl estradiol and norethindrone acetate
Tablets: ethinyl estradiol 20 mcg and norethindrone acetate 1 mg (Loestrin 21 1/20); ethinyl estradiol 30 mcg and norethindrone acetate 1.5 mg (Loestrin 21 1.5/30)
ethinyl estradiol and norgestimate
Tablets: ethinyl estradiol 35 mcg and norgestimate 0.25 mg (Ortho Cyclen,)
ethinyl estradiol and norgestrel
Tablets: ethinyl estradiol 30 mcg and norgestrel 0.3 mg (Lo/Ovral, Lo/Ovral 28); ethinyl estradiol 50 mcg and norgestrel 0.5 mg (Ovral, Ovral 28, Ogestrel 0.5/50)
ethinyl estradiol, norethindrone acetate, and ferrous fumarate
Tablets: ethinyl estradiol 20 mcg, norethindrone acetate 1 mg, and ferrous fumarate 75 mg (Loestrin Fe 1/20, Microgestin Fe 1/20); ethinyl estradiol 30 mcg, norethindrone acetate 1.5 mg, and ferrous fumarate 75 mg (Loestrin Fe 1.5/30, Microgestin Fe 1.5/30)
mestranol and norethindrone
Tablets: mestranol 50 mcg and norethindrone 1 mg (Necon 1/50, Norinyl 1+50, Ortho-Novum 1/50)
Biphasic oral contraceptives
ethinyl estradiol and norethindrone
Tablets: ethinyl estradiol 35 mcg and norethindrone 0.5 mg during phase 1 [10 days]; ethinyl estradiol 35 mcg and norethindrone 1 mg during phase 2 [11 days] (Necon 10/11, Ortho-Novum 10/11)
Triphasic oral contraceptives
ethinyl estradiol and desogestrel
Tablets: desogestrel 0.1 mg and ethinyl estradiol 25 mcg (7 tablets); desogestrel 0.125 mg and ethinyl estradiol 25 mcg (7 tablets); desogestrel 0.15 mg and ethinyl estradiol 25 mcg (7 tablets) (Cyclessa); ethinyl estradiol 0.02 mg and desogestrel 0.15 mg (21 tablets), then inert tablets, (2 tablets), then ethinyl estradiol 0.01 mg (5 tablets) (Kariva, Mircette)
ethinyl estradiol and levonorgestrel
Tablets: ethinyl estradiol 30 mcg and levonorgestrel 0.05 mg during phase 1 [6 days]; ethinyl estradiol 40 mcg and levonorgestrel 0.075 mg during phase 2 [5 days]; ethinyl estradiol 30 mcg and levonorgestrel 0.125 mg during phase 3 [10 days]. (Tri-Levlen, Triphasil, Trivora-28, Enpresse)
ethinyl estradiol and norethindrone
Tablets: ethinyl estradiol 35 mcg and norethindrone 0.5 mg during phase 1 [7 days]; ethinyl estradiol 35 mcg and norethindrone 1 mg during phase 2 [9 days]; ethinyl estradiol 35 mcg and norethindrone 0.5 mg during phase 3 [5 days](Tri-Norinyl); ethinyl estradiol 35 mcg and norethindrone 0.5 mg during phase 1 [7 days]; ethinyl estradiol 35 mcg and norethindrone 0.75 mg during phase 2 [7 days]; ethinyl estradiol 35 mcg and norethindrone 1 mg during phase 3 [7 days]. (Ortho-Novum 7/7/7)
ethinyl estradiol and norethindrone acetate
Tablets: ethinyl estradiol 0.02 mg and norethindrone acetate 1 mg (5 tablets), ethinyl estradiol 0.03 mg and norethindrone acetate 1 mg (7 tablets), ethinyl estradiol 0.035 mg and norethindrone acetate 1 mg (9 tablets). (Estrostep Fe, Estrostep 21)
ethinyl estradiol and norgestimate
Tablets: ethinyl estradiol 35 mcg and norgestimate 0.18 mg during phase 1 [7days]; ethinyl estradiol 35 mcg and norgestimate 0.215 mg during phase 2 [7 days]; ethinyl estradiol 35 mcg and norgestimate 0.25 mg during phase 3 [7 days] (Ortho Tri-Cyclen)

NURSING PROCESS

Assessment

- Obtain history of patient's pregnancy status or underlying endometriosis before therapy.
- Monitor effectiveness by determining if pregnancy test is negative or if patient with endometriosis has diminished signs and symptoms.

• Periodically monitor lipid levels, blood pressure, body weight, and liver function.
• Be alert for adverse reactions and drug interactions.
• Evaluate patient's and family's knowledge of drug therapy.

Nursing diagnoses
• Health-seeking behavior (prevention of pregnancy) related to family planning
• Acute pain related to drug-induced headache
• Deficient knowledge related to drug therapy

Planning and implementation
• Make sure patient has been properly instructed about prescribed oral contraceptive before she takes first dose.
ALERT: Make sure patient has negative pregnancy test before drug therapy starts.
• Many laboratory tests are affected by oral contraceptives.
• Stop therapy if patient develops granulomatous colitis, and notify prescriber.
• Drug should be stopped at least 1 week before surgery to decrease risk of thromboembolism. Tell patient to use alternative method of birth control.

Patient teaching
• Tell patient to take tablets at same time each day; nighttime dosing may reduce nausea and headaches.
• Advise patient to use additional method of birth control, such as condoms or diaphragm with spermicide, for first week of first cycle.
• Tell patient that missed doses in midcycle greatly increase likelihood of pregnancy.
• If one tablet is missed, tell patient to take it as soon as remembered or to take two tablets the next day and continue regular schedule. If patient misses 2 consecutive days, instruct her to take two tablets daily for 2 days and then resume normal schedule. Also advise her to use additional method of birth control for 7 days after two missed doses. If she misses three or more doses, tell her to discard remaining tablets in monthly package and to substitute another contraceptive method. If next menstrual period doesn't begin on schedule, warn patient to rule out pregnancy before starting new dosing cycle. If menstrual period begins, have patient start new dosing cycle 7 days after last tablet was taken.
• Warn patient that headache, nausea, dizziness, breast tenderness, spotting, and breakthrough bleeding are common at first. These effects should diminish after three to six dosing cycles (months).
• Instruct patient to weigh herself at least twice weekly and to report sudden weight gain or edema to prescriber.
• Warn patient to avoid exposure to ultraviolet light or prolonged exposure to sunlight.
ALERT: Warn patient to immediately report abdominal pain; numbness, stiffness, or pain in legs or buttocks; pressure or pain in chest; shortness of breath; severe headache; visual disturbances, such as blind spots, blurriness, or flashing lights; undiagnosed vaginal bleeding or discharge; two consecutive missed menstrual periods; lumps in breast; swelling of hands or feet; or severe pain in abdomen.
• Advise patient of increased risks caused by simultaneous use of cigarettes and oral contraceptives.
• Teach patient how to perform routine breast self-examination.
• If one menstrual period is missed and tablets have been taken on schedule, tell patient to continue taking them. If two consecutive menstrual periods are missed, tell patient to stop drug and have pregnancy test. Progestins may cause birth defects if taken early in pregnancy.
• Advise patient not to take same drug for longer than 12 months without consulting prescriber. Stress importance of Papanicolaou test and annual gynecologic examination.
• Advise patient to check with prescriber about how soon pregnancy may be attempted after hormonal therapy is stopped. Many prescribers recommend that women not become pregnant within 2 months after stopping drug.
• Warn patient of possible delay in achieving pregnancy when drug is discontinued.
• Tell patient that many prescribers advise women on prolonged therapy (5 years or longer) to stop drug and use other birth control methods. Periodically reassess patient while off hormone therapy.

Evaluation
• Patient doesn't become pregnant.
• Patient obtains relief from drug-induced headache with administration of mild analgesic.
• Patient and family state understanding of drug therapy.

ethinyl estradiol (EE) and drospirenone (DRSP)

(ETH-in-il es-tra-DIE-ol and droh-SPEER-ih-nohn)

Yasmin

Pharmacologic class: combination, low-dose monophasic hormonal contraceptive
Therapeutic class: hormonal contraceptive
Pregnancy risk category: X

Indications and dosages

▶ **Prevention of pregnancy.** *Women and postpubertal female adolescents:* ***Day 1 start.*** 1 yellow tablet P.O. daily beginning on day 1 of menstrual cycle (first day of menstruation). Continue taking 1 yellow tablet P.O. daily for 21 consecutive days, at the same time each day, preferably after the evening meal or at bedtime; then take 1 white inert tablet P.O. daily on days 22 through 28. Begin the next and all subsequent 28-day regimens on the same day of the week that the first regimen began, following the same schedule. Restart taking yellow tablets on the next day after taking the last white tablet.

Sunday start. 1 yellow tablet P.O. daily, beginning on the first Sunday after the onset of menstruation. Continue taking 1 yellow tablet P.O. daily for 21 consecutive days, at the same time each day, preferably after the evening meal or at bedtime; then take 1 white inert tablet P.O. daily on days 22 through 28. Begin the next and all subsequent 28-day regimens on the same day of the week that the first regimen began, following the same schedule. Restart taking yellow tablets on the next day after taking the last white tablet.

Contraindications and precautions

- Contraindicated in women with hepatic dysfunction, tumor, or disease; renal or adrenal insufficiency; thrombophlebitis, thromboembolic disorders, or history of deep-vein thrombosis or thromboembolic disorders; cerebrovascular or coronary artery disease; known or suspected breast cancer, endometrial cancer, or other estrogen-dependent neoplasia; unexplained vaginal bleeding; or cholestatic jaundice of pregnancy or jaundice with other contraceptive pill use. Also contraindicated in women older than age 35 who smoke 15 or more cigarettes daily.
- Use cautiously in patients with risk factors for CV disease, such as hypertension, hyperlipidemias, obesity, and diabetes.

Lifespan: In women who are pregnant or suspect they may be pregnant, drug is contraindicated. In breast-feeding women, drug is also contraindicated because small amounts of drug appear in breast milk and jaundice and breast enlargement may occur in breast-fed infants. Drug may also decrease the quantity and quality of breast milk. Advise use of other forms of contraception until infant is completely weaned. Don't use in girls before menarche. Use in women of reproductive age only.

Adverse reactions

CNS: asthenia, ***cerebral hemorrhage, cerebral thrombosis,*** depression, dizziness, emotional lability, headache, migraine nervousness.
CV: ***arterial thromboembolism,*** hypertension, edema, ***mesenteric thrombosis, MI, thrombophlebitis.***
EENT: cataracts, change in corneal curvature (steepening), intolerance to contact lenses, pharyngitis, retinal thrombosis, sinusitis.
GI: abdominal pain, abdominal cramping, bloating, changes in appetite, colitis, diarrhea, gastroenteritis, nausea, vomiting.
GU: amenorrhea, breakthrough bleeding, change in cervical erosion and secretion, change in menstrual flow, cystitis, cystitis-like syndrome, dysmenorrhea, ***hemolytic uremic syndrome,*** impaired renal function, leukorrhea, menstrual disorder, premenstrual syndrome, spotting, temporary infertility after discontinuing treatment, urinary tract infection, vaginal candidiasis, vaginitis, breast changes, decreased lactation.
Hepatic: ***Budd-Chiari syndrome,*** cholestatic jaundice, gallbladder disease, ***hepatic adenomas,*** benign liver tumors.
Metabolic: reduced tolerance to carbohydrates, porphyria, weight gain.
Musculoskeletal: back pain.
Respiratory: bronchitis, ***pulmonary embolism,*** upper respiratory tract infection.
Skin: acne, ***erythema multiforme,*** erythema nodosum, hemorrhagic eruption, hirsutism, loss of scalp hair, melasma, pruritus, rash.
Other: changes in libido.

Interactions

Drug-drug. *ACE inhibitors, aldosterone antagonists, angiotensin-II receptor antagonists, NSAIDs, potassium-sparing diuretics, heparin:* Increases risk of hyperkalemia. Monitor potassium levels.
Acetaminophen: Decreases plasma concentrations of acetaminophen. Adjust acetaminophen dose as needed.
Ampicillin, griseofulvin, tetracycline: Decreases contraceptive effect. Encourage use of additional method of birth control while taking the antibiotic.
Ascorbic acid, atorvastatin: Increases concentrations of contraceptive. Monitor patient for adverse effects.
Carbamazepine, phenobarbital, phenytoin: Increases metabolism of EE and decreased contraceptive effectiveness. Encourage use of alternative method of birth control.
Clofibrate, morphine, salicylic acid, temazepam: Decreases plasma concentrations and increases clearance of these drugs. Monitor patient for effectiveness.
Cyclosporine, prednisolone, theophylline: Increases plasma concentrations of these drugs. Monitor patient for adverse effects and toxicity.
Phenylbutazone, rifampin: Decreases contraceptive effectiveness and increases breakthrough bleeding. Encourage use of alternative method of birth control.
Drug-herb. *St. John's wort:* Decreases contraceptive effect and increases breakthrough bleeding. Encourage use of additional method of birth control or avoid using together.
Drug-lifestyle. *Smoking:* Increases risk of CV adverse effects. Warn patient to avoid smoking and tobacco products while taking oral contraceptives.

Effects on lab test results

- May increase circulating total thyroid hormone, triglyceride, other binding protein, sex hormone-binding globulin, total circulating endogenous sex steroid, corticoid, potassium, folate, liver enzyme, and factor VII, VIII, IX, and X levels.
- May increase PT. May decrease glucose tolerance.

Pharmacokinetics

Absorption: Plasma levels of DRSP and EE peak within 1 to 3 hours. Steady state plasma levels of DRSP occur after 10 days and EE occur during the second half of the treatment cycle.
Distribution: Drug is widely distributed into the tissues and fluids. DRSP is about 97% bound to nonspecific proteins. EE is about 98.5% bound to serum albumin and other nonspecific proteins.
Metabolism: DRSP is metabolized mainly by metabolites found in plasma, and to a minor extent in the liver by CYP3A4 to inactive metabolites. EE is primarily metabolized by hydroxylation and subject to pre-systemic conjugation in the small bowel and the liver.
Excretion: Small amounts of DRSP are excreted unchanged in the urine and feces. EE is excreted as metabolites in the urine and feces. *DRSP half-life:* 30 hours. *EE half-life:* 24 hours.

Route	Onset	Peak	Duration
P.O.	Unknown	1-3 hr	Unknown

Pharmacodynamics

Chemical effect: Suppresses gonadotropins follicle-stimulating hormone (FSH) and luteinizing hormone (LH), thereby preventing ovulation, changing the cervical mucus to increase the difficulty of the sperm to penetrate, and changing the endometrium to increase the difficulty of implantation.
Therapeutic effect: Reduces the opportunity for conception.

Available forms

Tablets: 21 yellow tablets containing 3 mg DRSP and 0.03 mg EE, and 7 inert, white tablets.

NURSING PROCESS

Assessment

- Determine if patient is pregnant before starting drug.
- Obtain patient's medical history, smoking status, CV status, and potassium level before starting drug.
- Assess and be alert for any drug-induced adverse reactions. The use of contraceptives causes increased risk of MI, thromboembolism, CVA, hepatic neoplasia, gallbladder disease, and hypertension, especially in patients with hypertension, diabetes, hyperlipidemia, and obesity.

• Monitor patients laboratory results during drug therapy.
• Evaluate patient's and family's knowledge of contraception and drug therapy.

Nursing diagnoses

• Risk for injury related to drug-induced adverse reactions
• Health seeking behavior for the prevention of pregnancy related to family planning
• Deficient knowledge of contraceptive drug therapy

Planning and implementation

• Because of increased risk of thromboembolism in the postpartum period, don't start contraceptive earlier than 4 to 6 weeks after delivery.
• If patient misses two consecutive periods, she should obtain a negative pregnancy test result before continuing contraceptive. Immediately discontinue use if pregnancy is confirmed.
• In patients scheduled to have elective surgery that may increase the risk of thromboembolism, discontinue contraceptive use from at least 4 weeks before until 2 weeks after surgery. Also avoid use during and after prolonged immobilization. Advise patient to use alternative methods of birth control.
• Overdose may cause nausea and withdrawal bleeding. Monitor concentrations of potassium and sodium and watch for signs of metabolic acidosis.
• Discontinue use and evaluate patient if loss of vision, proptosis, diplopia, papilledema, or retinal vascular lesions occur. Recommend that contact lens wearers be evaluated by an ophthalmologist if they have changes in vision or lens intolerance.
• Evaluate patient who experiences unusual breakthrough bleeding for malignancy or pregnancy.
• Stop drug if patient suffers from sharp or crushing chest pains, hemoptysis, sudden shortness of breath, calf pain, breast lumps, severe stomach pains, difficulty sleeping, weakness, fatigue, or jaundice. Notify prescriber immediately, and offer supportive treatment as necessary.

Patient teaching

• Inform patient that pills are used to prevent pregnancy and don't protect against HIV and other sexually transmitted diseases.
• Advise patient of the dangers of smoking while taking oral contraceptives. Suggest that she choose a different form of birth control if she's a smoker.
• Tell patient to schedule gynecological examinations yearly and perform breast self-examination monthly.
• Inform patient that spotting, light bleeding, or stomach upset may occur during the first one to three packs of pills. Tell her to continue taking the pills and to notify prescriber if these symptoms persist.
• Tell patient to take the pill at the same time each day, preferably during the evening or at bedtime.
• Tell patient to immediately report sharp chest pain, coughing of blood, or sudden shortness of breath, pain in the calf, crushing chest pain or chest heaviness, sudden severe headache or vomiting, dizziness or fainting, visual or speech disturbances, weakness, or numbness in an arm or leg, loss of vision, breast lumps, severe stomach pain or tenderness, difficulty sleeping, lack of energy, fatigue, or change in mood, jaundice with fever, fatigue, loss of appetite, dark urine, or light-colored bowel movements.
• Tell patient to notify prescriber if she wears contact lenses and notices a change in vision or has difficulty wearing the lenses.
• Advise patient to use additional method of birth control during the first 7 days of the first cycle of oral contraceptive.
• Tell patient to continue taking drug as directed if spotting or breakthrough bleeding occurs. If bleeding is persistent or prolonged, advise patient to notify prescriber.
• Tell patient that the risk of pregnancy increases with each active yellow tablet she forgets to take.
• If patient misses one tablet, tell her to take it as soon as she remembers and to take the next pill at the regular time.
• If patient misses two tablets during week 1 or 2 of the pack, tell her to use an additional method of birth control for 7 days. Instruct her to take two pills on the day she remembers and two pills the next day, and then to resume the normal schedule.
• If patient misses two tablets during week 3, tell patient to use an additional method of birth control for 7 days. If patient uses the "day 1 start" method, tell her to throw away the rest of

the pack and start a new pack the same day. If patient uses the "Sunday start" method, tell her to keep taking one pill each day until Sunday. She should throw away the pack on Sunday and start a new pack that day. Tell patient that she may miss her period this month, but to notify prescriber if she misses it 2 months in a row because it may mean she's pregnant.

• If patient misses three or more tablets during the first 3 weeks, tell her to use an additional method of birth control for 7 days. If patient uses the "day 1 start" method, tell her to throw away the rest of the pack and start a new pack the same day. If the patient uses the "Sunday start" method, tell her to keep taking one pill each day until Sunday. She should throw away the pack on Sunday and start a new pack that day. Tell patient that she may miss her period this month, but to notify prescriber if she misses it 2 months in a row because it may mean she's pregnant.

• If patient misses any of the white tablets, tell her to throw away the missed pills and keep taking one pill each day until the pack is empty. She doesn't need to use an additional method of birth control.

• Tell patient to use an additional method of birth control and notify prescriber if she isn't sure what to do about missed pills.

☑ Evaluation

• Patient doesn't suffer from any drug-induced adverse reactions.

• Patient doesn't become pregnant.

• Patient and family state understanding of drug therapy.

ethinyl estradiol and etonogestrel vaginal ring

(ETH-ih-nil es-tra-DYE-ole and et-oh-noe-JES-trel)

NuvaRing

Pharmacologic class: progestin/estrogen intravaginal contraceptive

Therapeutic class: combination hormonal contraceptive vaginal ring

Pregnancy risk category: X

Indications and dosages

▶ **Contraception.** *Women:* Insert one ring vaginally, and leave in place for 3 weeks. Insert new ring exactly 1 week after the previous ring was removed, even if menstrual bleeding is still present.

Contraindications and precautions

• Contraindicated in patients hypersensitive to any component of drug and patients older than age 35 who smoke 15 or more cigarettes daily. Also contraindicated in patients with thrombophlebitis, thromboembolic disorder, history of deep vein thrombophlebitis, cerebral vascular or coronary artery disease (current or previous), valvular heart disease with complications, severe hypertension, diabetes with vascular complications, headache with focal neurological symptoms, major surgery with prolonged immobilization, known or suspected cancer of the endometrium or breast, estrogen-dependent neoplasia, abnormal undiagnosed vaginal bleeding, jaundice related to pregnancy or previous use of hormonal contraceptive, active liver disease, or benign or malignant hepatic tumors.

• Use cautiously in patients with hypertension, hyperlipidemias, obesity, or diabetes. Also use cautiously in patients with conditions that could be aggravated by fluid retention, a history of depression, or impaired liver function.

Lifespan: In patients who are or may be pregnant, drug is contraindicated. In breast-feeding women, drug isn't recommended. Tell patient to use alternative forms of contraception until baby is weaned. Don't start drug earlier than 4 weeks after delivery in women who choose not to breast-feed. In women who haven't reached menarche, drug is contraindicated. Don't use in postmenopausal women.

Adverse reactions

CNS: *headache,* emotional lability.
EENT: *sinusitis.*
GI: *nausea.*
GU: *vaginitis, leukorrhea,* device-related events (such as foreign body sensation, coital difficulties, device expulsion), vaginal discomfort.
Metabolic: *weight gain.*
Respiratory: *upper respiratory tract infection.*

Interactions

Drug-drug. *Acetaminophen, ascorbic acid, atorvastatin, itraconazole:* Increases ethinyl estradiol levels. Monitor patient for adverse effects.
Ampicillin, barbiturates, carbamazepine, felbamate, griseofulvin, oxcarbazepine, phenylbutazone, phenytoin, rifampin, tetracyclines, topiramate: Decreases contraceptive efficacy and increased risk of pregnancy, breakthrough bleeding, or both. Tell patient to use an additional form of contraception while taking these drugs.
Cyclosporine, prednisolone, theophylline: Increases levels of these drugs. Cyclosporine and theophylline levels should be monitored and dosages adjusted as needed, based on results.
Anti-HIV protease inhibitors: May increase or decrease the bioavailability of estrogen or progestin. Consider other methods of birth control.
Clofibric acid, morphine, salicylic acid, temazepam: Increases clearance of these drugs. Monitor patient for effectiveness.
Drug-herb. *St. John's wort:* May reduce contraceptive effectiveness, increase risk of pregnancy, and increase risk of breakthrough bleeding. Tell patient to avoid using together.
Drug-lifestyle. *Tobacco use:* Increases risk of serious CV side effects, especially in those older than age 35 who smoke 15 or more cigarettes daily. Urge patient to avoid tobacco use of any kind.

Effects on lab test results

- May increase levels of prothrombin; factor VII, VIII, IX, and X; thyroid-binding globulin (leading to increased circulating total thyroid hormone levels); other binding protein; sex hormone–binding globulin; triglyceride; lipoprotein; and other lipids. May decrease antithrombin III and folate levels.
- May increase norepinephrine-induced platelet aggregation. May decrease T_3 resin uptake and glucose tolerance.

Pharmacokinetics

Absorption: Both hormonal components are rapidly absorbed after release from the ring. Bioavailability of etonogestrel and ethinyl estradiol is 100% and 55.6%, respectively.
Distribution: Etonogestrel is 66% protein-bound and 32% bound to sex hormone–binding globulin. Ethinyl estradiol is about 98.5% nonspecific protein-bound and increases levels of sex hormone–binding globulin.
Metabolism: Both components of drug are metabolized in the liver by cytochrome P450 3A4. Many metabolites are present as free metabolites, sulfate, and glucuronide conjugates.
Excretion: Both components are eliminated mainly in urine, bile, and feces.

Route	Onset	Peak	Duration
Vaginal	Immediate	Unknown	Unknown

Pharmacodynamics

Chemical effect: Suppresses gonadotropins, which inhibits ovulation, increases the viscosity of cervical mucus (decreasing the ability of sperm to enter the uterus), and alters the endometrial lining (reducing potential for implantation).
Therapeutic effect: Decreases risk of pregnancy.

Available forms

Vaginal ring: Delivers 0.120 mg etonogestrel and 0.015 mg ethinyl estradiol daily.

NURSING PROCESS

Assessment

- Assess patient for pregnancy before starting drug.
- Obtain patient's medical history, smoking status, CV status, and risk factors before starting drug.
- Be alert for any drug-induced adverse reactions.
- The use of contraceptives causes increased risk of MI, thromboembolism, CVA, hepatic neoplasia, gallbladder disease, and hypertension, especially in patients with hypertension, diabetes, hyperlipidemia, and obesity. Monitor patient for signs and symptoms related to these occurrences.
- Monitor patients laboratory results during drug therapy.
- Evaluate patient's knowledge of contraception and drug therapy.

Nursing diagnoses

- Risk for injury related to drug-induced adverse reactions
- Health seeking behavior for the prevention of pregnancy related to family planning

• Deficient knowledge of contraceptive drug therapy

▶ Planning and implementation

• Stop drug at least 4 weeks before and for 2 weeks after procedures that may increase the risk of thromboembolism and during and after prolonged immobilization.
• Stop drug if patient develops unexplained partial or complete loss of vision, proptosis, diplopia, papilledema, or retinal vascular lesions.
• Monitor blood pressure closely if patient has hypertension or renal disease. Stop drug if blood pressure rises.
• Stop drug if migraine begins or worsens or if patient has recurrent, persistent, or severe headaches.
• Stop drug if jaundice occurs. The hormones may be poorly metabolized in patients with liver disease.
• If patient has persistent or severe abnormal menstrual bleeding, look for cause. If amenorrhea occurs, pregnancy should be ruled out.
• If depression occurs, stop drug to determine whether depression is drug-related.
• If no hormonal contraceptive is used in the preceding month, insert ring on day 5 of the menstrual cycle (counting the first day of menstruation as day 1). For the first cycle of use, an additional form of birth control should be used until 7 days after the ring was inserted.
• When switching from other combination (estrogen plus progestin) oral contraceptives, insert the ring within 7 days after the last dose of combined oral contraceptive. This should be no later than the day that a new cycle of tablets would have begun. No back-up form of contraception is needed.
• When switching from a progestin-only form of contraception, use a back-up form of contraception for the first 7 days of using the ring in any of the following situations: If switching from progestin-only tablets, insert ring on any day of the month; don't skip any days between the last oral dose and insertion of the ring. If switching from progestin-only implants (such as Norplant), insert the vaginal ring on the same day that the implants are removed. If switching from progestin-only intrauterine device (IUD), insert the vaginal ring on the same day that the IUD is removed. If switching from contraceptive injections (such as Depo-Provera), insert the vaginal ring on the same day that the next injection would be due. Begin use within the first 5 days after complete first-trimester abortion, 4 weeks postpartum in women who aren't breast-feeding, or 4 weeks after a second-trimester abortion.
• If the ring is removed or expelled (for example, while removing a tampon or moving the bowels), it should be washed with cool to lukewarm water and reinserted immediately. If the ring stays out for more than 3 hours, contraceptive efficacy may be compromised, and a back-up method of contraception is recommended until the newly reinserted ring is used continuously for 7 days.
• Rule out pregnancy if patient hasn't adhered to the prescribed regimen and a menstrual period is missed, if prescribed regimen is adhered to and two periods are missed, or if the patient has retained the ring for longer than 4 weeks.
• Overdose may cause nausea, vomiting, vaginal bleeding, or other menstrual irregularities. Offer supportive treatment.

Patient teaching

• Teach patient or provide patient with instructions for proper placement of vaginal ring. Also encourage proper handwashing before and after ring insertion to prevent vaginal infections.
• Emphasize the importance of having regular annual physical examinations to check for adverse effects or developing contraindications.
• Tell patient that drug doesn't protect against HIV and other sexually transmitted diseases.
• Advise patient not to smoke while using contraceptive.
• Tell patient not to use a diaphragm if a back-up method of birth control is needed.
• Tell patient who wears contact lenses to contact an ophthalmologist if vision or lens tolerance change.
• Advise patient that if the ring is removed or expelled (for example, while removing a tampon, straining, or moving bowels) it should be washed with cool to lukewarm (not hot) water and reinserted immediately. Stress that contraceptive efficacy may be compromised if the ring stays out for more than 3 hours, and a back-up method of contraception should be used until the newly reinserted ring is used continuously for 7 days.

Evaluation

- Patient doesn't suffer from any drug-induced adverse reactions or vaginal infections.
- Patient doesn't become pregnant.
- Patient and family state understanding of drug therapy.

ethinyl estradiol and norelgestromin transdermal system

(ETH-ih-nil es-tra-DYE-ole and nor-el-GES-tro-min)

Ortho Evra

Pharmacologic class: transdermal contraceptive patch
Therapeutic class: combination hormonal contraceptive
Pregnancy risk category: X

Indications and dosages

▶ **Contraception.** *Women:* Apply one patch weekly for 3 weeks. Week 4 is patch-free. On the day after week 4 ends, apply a new patch to start a new 4-week cycle. Apply each new patch on the same day of the week.

Contraindications and precautions

- Contraindicated in patients hypersensitive to any component of drug and in those with a history of deep vein thrombosis or related disorder, current or past history of cerebrovascular or coronary artery disease, past or current known or suspected breast cancer, endometrial cancer or other known or suspected estrogen-dependent neoplasia, hepatic adenoma or carcinoma, or known or suspected pregnancy. Also contraindicated in patients with thrombophlebitis, thromboembolic disorders, valvular heart disease with complications, severe hypertension, diabetes with vascular involvement, headaches with focal neurological symptoms, major surgery with prolonged immobilization, undiagnosed abnormal genital bleeding, cholestatic jaundice of pregnancy or jaundice with previous hormonal contraceptive use, or acute or chronic hepatocellular disease with abnormal liver function.
- Use cautiously in patients with CV disease risk factors, with conditions that might be aggravated by fluid retention, or with a history of depression.

Lifespan: In breast-feeding women, safety and efficacy haven't been established. Advise them to use alternative methods of birth control. In women who haven't reached menarche, safety and efficacy of contraceptive patch haven't been evaluated and drug shouldn't be used.

Adverse reactions

CNS: *headache,* emotional lability.
CV: ***thromboembolic events, MI,*** hypertension, edema, ***cerebral hemorrhage.***
EENT: contact lens intolerance.
GI: *nausea, abdominal pain,* vomiting.
GU: *menstrual cramps,* changes in menstrual flow, vaginal candidiasis.
Hepatic: ***hepatic adenomas, benign liver tumors,*** gallbladder disease.
Metabolic: weight changes.
Respiratory: *upper respiratory tract infection.*
Skin: *application site reaction.*
Other: *breast tenderness, enlargement, or secretion.*

Interactions

Drug-drug. *Acetaminophen, clofibric acid, morphine, salicylic acid, temazepam:* Decreases plasma concentrations or increases clearance of these drugs. Monitor patient for lack of effect.
Ampicillin, barbiturates, carbamazepine, felbamate, griseofulvin, oxcarbazepine, phenylbutazone, phenytoin, rifampin, topiramate: Contraceptive effectiveness may be reduced, resulting in unintended pregnancy or breakthrough bleeding. Encourage back-up method of contraception if used together.
Anti-HIV protease inhibitors: Efficacy and safety of contraceptives may be affected. Use together cautiously.
Ascorbic acid, atorvastatin, itraconazole, ketoconazole: Increases plasma hormone levels. Use together cautiously.
Cyclosporine, prednisolone, theophylline: Increases plasma concentrations of these drugs. Monitor patient for adverse effects.
Drug-herb. *St John's wort:* May reduce effectiveness of contraceptive and cause breakthrough bleeding. Discourage using together.
Drug-lifestyle. *Tobacco use:* Increases risk of serious CV side effects, especially in those old-

er than age 35 who smoke 15 or more cigarettes daily. Urge patient to avoid tobacco use of any kind.

Effects on lab test results

• May increase factor VII, VIII, IX, and X; circulating total thyroid hormone; triglyceride; other binding protein; sex hormone-binding globulin; total circulating endogenous sex steroid; and corticoid levels. May decrease antithrombin III and folate levels.
• May increase prothrombin. May decrease free T_3 resin uptake and glucose tolerance.

Pharmacokinetics

Absorption: After patch application, both components of drug rapidly appear in serum, peak at or about 48 hours, and are maintained at a steady state while the patch is worn.
Distribution: Norelgestromin and norgestrel (a serum metabolite of norelgestromin) are more than 97% protein bound. Norelgestromin is bound to albumin and not to SHBGs, but norgestrel is bound primarily to SHBG, which limits its biological activity. Ethinyl estradiol is extensively bound to albumin.
Metabolism: Drug and its metabolites are metabolized through the liver. Ethinyl estradiol is metabolized to various hydroxylated products.
Excretion: Upon removal of the patch, the elimination of norelgestromin and ethinyl estradiol takes 28 hours and 17 hours, respectively. The metabolites are eliminated in the urine and feces.

Route	Onset	Peak	Duration
Transdermal	Rapid	2 days	Unknown

Pharmacodynamics

Chemical effect: Combination hormonal contraceptives act by suppressing gonadotropins. The primary mechanism of action is inhibition of ovulation. However, changes in cervical mucus increase the difficulty of sperm entry into the uterus and changes in the endometrium decrease the likelihood of implantation.
Therapeutic effect: Reduces risk of pregnancy.

Available forms

Transdermal patch: norelgestromin 6 mg and ethinyl estradiol 0.75 mg (releases 150 mcg of norelgestromin and 20 mcg of ethinyl estradiol every 24 hours)

NURSING PROCESS

Assessment

• Assess patient for pregnancy before starting drug.
• Obtain patient's medical history, smoking status, and CV status before starting drug.
• Be alert for any drug-induced adverse reactions.
• The use of contraceptives causes increased risk of MI, thromboembolism, CVA, hepatic neoplasia, gallbladder disease, and hypertension, especially in patients with hypertension, diabetes, hyperlipidemia, and obesity. Monitor patient for signs and symptoms related to these occurrences.
• Monitor patient's laboratory results during drug therapy.
• Evaluate patient's knowledge of contraception and drug therapy.

Nursing diagnoses

• Risk for injury related to drug-induced adverse reactions
• Health seeking behavior for the prevention of pregnancy related to family planning
• Deficient knowledge of contraceptive drug therapy

Planning and implementation

• Encourage women with a history of hypertension or renal disease to use a different method of contraception. If Ortho Evra is used, monitor blood pressure closely and discontinue use if hypertension occurs.
• Drug may be less effective in women weighing 198 lb (90 kg) or more.
• Cigarette smoking increases the risk of serious CV adverse effects. This risk increases with women older than age 35 who smoke 15 or more cigarettes per day.
• If woman is starting the patch for the first time, she should wait until the day she begins her menstrual period. She will then choose a first-day start or a Sunday start.
• If woman chooses a first-day start, the patch should be applied during the first 24 hours of her menstrual period. If therapy starts after day 1 of the menstrual cycle, a non-hormonal back-up method of birth control should be used for the first week of the first treatment cycle.
• If the woman chooses a Sunday start, the patch should be applied on the first Sunday af-

ter her menstrual period starts. She must use back-up contraception for the first week of her cycle. If the woman's menstrual period begins on a Sunday, she should apply the first patch on that day, and no back-up contraception is needed.
• To switch from an oral contraceptive, begin treatment on the first day of withdrawal bleeding. If therapy starts later than the first day of withdrawal bleeding, back-up contraception should be used for the first week.
• Therapy should be started no sooner than 4 weeks after childbirth. If the woman hasn't had a menstrual period, pregnancy should be ruled out, and a back-up contraception should be used for the first week.
• After abortion or miscarriage in the first trimester, the patch may be started immediately. If it isn't started within 5 days of a first-trimester abortion, follow directions for a woman starting therapy for the first time.
• Therapy should be started no earlier than 4 weeks after a second-trimester abortion or miscarriage.
• The risk of thromboembolic disease increases if therapy is used postpartum or postabortion.
• If breakthrough bleeding occurs, stop treatment and have cause evaluated if bleeding lasts longer than a few cycles.
• If no withdrawal bleeding occurs on patch-free week, resume treatment on the next scheduled patch-change day. Rule out pregnancy if withdrawal bleeding fails to occur for two consecutive cycles.
• If skin becomes irritated, the patch may be removed and a new patch applied at a different site until the next patch-change day.
• Discontinue use at least 4 weeks before and for 2 weeks after elective surgery of a type associated with increased risk of thromboembolism and during and after prolonged immobilization.
• Discontinue use if patient has vision loss, proptosis, diplopia, papilledema, retinal vascular lesions, or recurrent, persistent, or severe headaches.
• Discontinue use if jaundice occurs.
• Discontinue use if patient becomes severely depressed, and evaluate whether the depression is drug-related.

Patient teaching

• Emphasize the importance of keeping regular annual physical examination appointments to monitor patient for any adverse effects or developing contraindications of the contraceptive patch.
• Tell patient that the contraceptive patch doesn't protect against HIV and other sexually transmitted diseases.
• Advise patient to immediately apply a new patch once the used patch is removed, on the same day of the week, every 7 days for 3 weeks. Week 4 is patch-free. Bleeding is expected to occur during this time.
• Advise patient to start a new cycle, applying a new patch on the usual patch-change day, regardless of when the menstrual period starts or ends.
• Teach patient how to properly apply the patch.
• Tell patient to apply each patch to a new clean, dry area of the skin on the buttocks, abdomen, upper outer arm, or upper torso, to avoid irritation. Tell patient not to apply to the breasts or to skin that's red, irritated, or cut. Instruct patient to avoid creams, oils, powder, or makeup on or near the skin where the patch will be placed because it may cause the patch to become loose.
• Tell patient what to do if a patch is partially or completely detached:
– If patch is detached for less than 24 hours, try to reapply it to the same place or replace it with a new patch immediately. No back-up contraception is needed.
– If the patch is detached for 24 hours or more, or if the woman isn't sure how long the patch has been detached, she should stop the current cycle and start a new cycle immediately by applying a new patch. Back-up contraception must be used for the first week of the new cycle because the patient may not be protected from pregnancy.
– Tell patient not to attempt to reapply patch if it's no longer sticky, if it has become stuck to itself or another surface, if it has other material stuck to it, or if it has previously become loose or fallen off. If patient can't reapply a patch, she must apply a new patch immediately. She shouldn't use adhesives or wraps to hold the patch in place.
• Tell patient what to do if she forgets to change her patch:

– *At the start of the cycle:* Tell patient to apply the first patch of the new cycle as soon as she remembers and to use back-up contraception for the first week of the new cycle.
– *In the middle of the patch cycle for 1 or 2 days:* Advise patient to apply a new patch immediately. She should apply the next patch on the usual patch-change day. No back-up contraception is needed.
– *In the middle of the patch cycle for more than 2 days:* Tell patient to stop the current contraceptive cycle and start a new 4-week cycle immediately by applying a new patch. She should use back-up contraception for 1 week.
– *At the end of a patch cycle:* If patient forgets to take off her patch, tell her to remove it as soon as she remembers. Tell patient to start next cycle on the usual patch-change day, the day after day 28. No back-up contraception is needed.
- If patient wants to change her patch-change day, tell her to complete her current cycle and apply a new patch on the desired day during the patch-free week. There shouldn't be more than 7 consecutive patch-free days.
- Tell patient what to do if she misses a menstrual period:
– If patient hasn't adhered to the prescribed schedule, pregnancy should be ruled out at the time of the first missed period.
– If patient adhered to the prescribed regimen and missed one period, she should continue using the patches. If she adhered to the prescribed regimen and missed two consecutive periods, pregnancy should be ruled out.
- Tell patient to immediately discontinue use if pregnancy is confirmed.
- Tell patient who wears contact lenses to contact an ophthalmologist if visual changes or changes in lens tolerance develop.
- Stress that if patient isn't sure what to do about mistakes with patch use, she should use a back-up method of birth control, such as a condom, spermicide, or diaphragm. She should contact her prescriber for further instructions.

☑ Evaluation
- Patient doesn't suffer from any drug-induced adverse reactions.
- Patient doesn't become pregnant.
- Patient and family state understanding of drug therapy.

etidronate disodium
(eh-tih-DROH-nayt digh-SOH-dee-um)
Didronel

Pharmacologic class: pyrophosphate analogue
Therapeutic class: antihypercalcemic
Pregnancy risk category: C

Indications and dosages
▶ **Symptomatic Paget's disease of bone (osteitis deformans).** *Adults:* 5 to 10 mg/kg P.O. daily in single dose 2 hours before meal with water or juice. Maximum dosage is 20 mg/kg P.O. daily.
▶ **Heterotopic ossification in spinal cord injuries.** *Adults:* 20 mg/kg P.O. daily for 2 weeks; then 10 mg/kg daily for 10 weeks. Total treatment period is 12 weeks.
▶ **Heterotopic ossification after total hip replacement.** *Adults:* 20 mg/kg P.O. daily for 1 month before total hip replacement and for 3 months afterward.
▶ **Malignancy-related hypercalcemia.** *Adults:* 7.5 mg/kg I.V. daily for 3 consecutive days. Maintenance dosage is 20 mg/kg P.O. daily for 30 days. May be used for maximum of 90 days.

Contraindications and precautions
- No known contraindications.
- Use cautiously in patients with impaired renal function.

Lifespan: With pregnant and breast-feeding women, use cautiously. In children, safety of drug hasn't been established.

Adverse reactions
CNS: fever, ***seizures.***
CV: fluid overload.
GI: diarrhea, increased frequency of bowel movements, nausea, constipation, stomatitis (at 20 mg/kg/day).
Musculoskeletal: *Paget's disease, increased or recurrent bone pain, pain at previously asymptomatic sites,* increased risk of fracture.
Respiratory: dyspnea.
Other: allergic skin reaction.

Interactions
Drug-drug. *Antacids containing calcium, magnesium, or aluminum; mineral supple-*

ments containing calcium, iron, magnesium, or aluminum: Can inhibit absorption. Avoid use within 2 hours of dose.
Drug-food. *Foods containing large amounts of calcium (such as milk, dairy products):* May prevent oral absorption. Avoid use within 2 hours of dose.

Effects on lab test results

- May increase BUN, creatinine, and phosphate levels. May decrease calcium level.
- May decrease granulocyte, platelet, RBC, and WBC counts.

Pharmacokinetics

Absorption: Absorption after P.O. dose is variable and decreases in presence of food. Absorption may also be dose-related.
Distribution: About half of dose is distributed to bone.
Metabolism: Not metabolized.
Excretion: About 50% excreted within 24 hours in urine. *Half-life:* 5 to 7 hours.

Route	Onset	Peak	Duration
P.O., I.V.	Variable	Variable	Variable

Pharmacodynamics

Chemical effect: Decreases osteoclastic activity by inhibiting osteocytic osteolysis and decreases mineral release and matrix or collagen breakdown in bone.
Therapeutic effect: Slows excessive remodeling of pagetic or heterotropic bone and lowers calcium level in malignant disease.

Available forms

Injection: 50 mg/ml
Tablets: 200 mg, 400 mg

NURSING PROCESS

Assessment

- Obtain history of patient's underlying condition before therapy.
- Assess kidney function before therapy and then during therapy.
- Monitor effectiveness by evaluating alkaline phosphatase level and urinary hydroxyproline excretion; both decrease if therapy is effective.
- Evaluate patient's and family's knowledge of drug therapy.

Nursing diagnoses

- Risk for injury related to underlying bone condition
- Diarrhea related to drug-induced adverse GI reactions
- Deficient knowledge related to drug therapy

Planning and implementation

- Don't give drug for longer than 3 months at doses above 10 mg/kg daily. Therapy can be resumed after 3 months, if needed, but shouldn't exceed 6 months.
- **P.O. use:** Don't give drug with food, milk, or antacids; they may reduce absorption.
- **I.V. use:** Dilute daily dose in at least 250 ml of normal saline solution or D_5W, and infuse over at least 2 hours.
  – Some patients may receive I.V. etidronate for up to 7 days. However, risk of hypokalemia increases after 3 days of treatment.
- Notify prescriber about elevated phosphate level, especially in patients receiving higher doses. However, phosphate level usually returns to normal 2 to 4 weeks after drug is discontinued.

Patient teaching

- Stress importance of diet high in calcium and vitamin D.
- Tell patient not to eat for 2 hours after daily dose.
- Tell patient that improvement may not occur for up to 3 months but may continue for months after drug is stopped.

Evaluation

- Patient shows improvement of underlying condition.
- Patient doesn't have severe diarrhea during therapy.
- Patient and family state understanding of drug therapy.

etodolac (ultradol)

(eh-toh-DOH-lak)
Lodine, Lodine XL

Pharmacologic class: NSAID
Therapeutic class: antiarthritic
Pregnancy risk category: C

Indications and dosages

▶ **Acute pain.** *Adults:* 200 to 400 mg P.O. of conventional tablets or capsules q 6 to 8 hours.
▶ **Acute or long-term management of osteoarthritis or rheumatoid arthritis.** *Adults:* 600 to 1,000 mg P.O. daily of conventional tablets or capsules in 2 divided doses. For extended-release tablets, usual dosage is 400 to 1,000 mg P.O. once daily.

Contraindications and precautions

- Contraindicated in patients hypersensitive to drug and in those with history of aspirin- or NSAID-induced asthma, rhinitis, urticaria, or other allergic reactions.
- Use cautiously in patients with history of GI bleeding, ulceration, and perforation and renal or hepatic impairment.
- Use with caution in patients with congestive heart failure, hypertension, cardiac function impairments, and those who are predisposed to fluid retention.

Lifespan: During third trimester of pregnancy, drug isn't recommended. In pregnant women during first and second trimesters and breast-feeding women, use cautiously. In children younger than age 18, safety of drug hasn't been established.

Adverse reactions

CNS: *asthenia, malaise, dizziness,* depression, drowsiness, nervousness, insomnia, headache, fever, syncope.
CV: hypertension, ***heart failure,*** flushing, palpitations, edema, fluid retention.
EENT: blurred vision, tinnitus, photophobia, dry mouth.
GI: *dyspepsia,* flatulence, abdominal pain, diarrhea, nausea, constipation, gastritis, melena, vomiting, anorexia, peptic ulceration with or without ***GI bleeding*** or ***perforation,*** ulcerative stomatitis, thirst.
GU: dysuria, urinary frequency, ***renal failure.***
Hematologic: hemolytic anemia, ***leukopenia, thrombocytopenia, agranulocytosis.***
Hepatic: ***hepatitis.***
Metabolic: weight gain.
Respiratory: ***asthma.***
Skin: pruritus, rash, photosensitivity, ***Stevens-Johnson syndrome.***
Other: chills.

Interactions

Drug-drug. *Antacids:* May decrease peak levels of drug. Monitor patient for decreased etodolac effect.
Aspirin: Reduces protein-binding of etodolac without altering its clearance. Clinical significance unknown. Recommend avoiding use together.
Beta blockers, diuretics: Effects may be blunted. Monitor patient closely.
Cyclosporine: Impairs elimination and increases risk of nephrotoxicity. Avoid using together.
Digoxin, lithium, methotrexate: Etodolac may impair elimination of these drugs, resulting in increased levels and risk of toxicity. Monitor blood levels.
Phenytoin: Increases levels of phenytoin. Monitor patient and levels for toxicity.
Warfarin: Etodolac decreases protein-binding of warfarin but doesn't change its clearance. Although no dosage adjustment is necessary, monitor PT and INR closely and watch for bleeding.
Drug-herb. *Dong quai, feverfew, garlic, ginger, horse chestnut, red clover:* May increase risk of bleeding. Discourage using together.
St. John's wort: Increases risk of photosensitivity. Advise patient to avoid unprotected or prolonged exposure to sunlight.
Drug-lifestyle. *Alcohol use:* Increases chance of adverse effects. Discourage using together.
Sun exposure: Photosensitivity reactions may occur. Urge patient to avoid unprotected or prolonged exposure to sunlight.

Effects on lab test results

- May increase BUN and creatinine levels. May decrease uric acid levels.
- May increase liver function tests. May decrease hemoglobin, hematocrit, and platelet, granulocyte, and WBC counts.
- May cause false-positive test for urinary bilirubin.

Pharmacokinetics

Absorption: Well absorbed from GI tract.
Distribution: Distributed to liver, lungs, heart, and kidneys.
Metabolism: Extensively metabolized in liver.
Excretion: Excreted in urine primarily as metabolites; 16% is excreted in feces.

Route	Onset	Peak	Duration
P.O.	≤ 30 min	1-2 hr	4-12 hr

Pharmacodynamics

Chemical effect: Unknown; may inhibit prostaglandin synthesis.
Therapeutic effect: Relieves inflammation and pain.

Available forms

Capsules: 200 mg, 300 mg
Tablets (extended-release): 400 mg, 500 mg, 600 mg
Tablets (film-coated): 400 mg, 500 mg

NURSING PROCESS

Assessment

- Obtain history of patient's underlying condition before therapy.
- Monitor effectiveness by evaluating patient for decreased inflammation and pain.
- Be alert for adverse reactions and drug interactions.
- Evaluate patient's and family's knowledge of drug therapy.

Nursing diagnoses

- Acute pain related to underlying condition
- Risk for injury related to drug-induced adverse reactions
- Deficient knowledge related to drug therapy

Planning and implementation

- Give drug with milk or meals to minimize GI discomfort.

ALERT: Don't confuse Lodine (etodolac) with iodine.

Patient teaching

- Advise patient that serious GI toxicity, including peptic ulceration and bleeding, can occur as a result of taking NSAIDs, despite absence of GI symptoms. Teach patient the signs and symptoms of GI bleeding, such as dark tarry stools, generalized weakness, coffee ground emesis, and tell him to contact prescriber immediately if they occur. Also, tell patient to take drug with milk or food.
- Instruct patient to notify prescriber if other adverse reactions occur or if drug doesn't relieve pain.
- Advise patient to use sunblock, wear protective clothing, and avoid prolonged exposure to sunlight to prevent photosensitivity reactions.
- Tell patient not to use drug during last trimester of pregnancy.

Evaluation

- Patient is free from pain.
- Patient has no injury as result of drug-induced adverse reactions.
- Patient and family state understanding of drug therapy.

etoposide (VP-16)

(eh-toh-POH-sighd)
VePesid, Toposar

Pharmacologic class: podophyllotoxin (cell cycle–phase specific, G2 and late S phases)
Therapeutic class: antineoplastic
Pregnancy risk category: D

Indications and dosages

▶ **Testicular cancer.** *Adults:* 50 to 100 mg/m^2 I.V. on 5 consecutive days q 3 to 4 weeks; or 100 mg/m^2 on days 1, 3, and 5 q 3 to 4 weeks for 3 to 4 courses of therapy.
▶ **Small-cell carcinoma of lung.** *Adults:* 35 mg/m^2/day I.V. for 4 days; or 50 mg/m^2/day I.V. for 5 days. P.O. dose is two times I.V. dose rounded to nearest 50 mg.
▶ **AIDS-related Kaposi's sarcoma‡.** *Adults:* 150 mg/m^2 I.V. for 3 consecutive days q 4 weeks. Repeat cycles p.r.n.

Contraindications and precautions

- Contraindicated in patients hypersensitive to drug.
- Use cautiously in patients who have had previous cytotoxic or radiation therapy.

Lifespan: In pregnant women, drug isn't recommended unless absolutely necessary because fetal harm may occur. In breast-feeding women, drug isn't recommended. In children, safety of drug hasn't been established.

Adverse reactions

CNS: peripheral neuropathy.
CV: hypotension.
GI: *nausea, vomiting, anorexia, diarrhea,* abdominal pain, *stomatitis.*
Hematologic: *anemia,* ***myelosuppression*** (dose-limiting), **LEUKOPENIA, THROMBOCYTOPENIA.**

Skin: reversible alopecia.
Other: ***anaphylaxis,*** rash.

Interactions

Drug-drug. *Warfarin:* May further prolong PT. Monitor patient for bleeding; monitor PT and INR levels closely.

Effects on lab test results

- May decrease hemoglobin, hematocrit, and WBC, RBC, platelet, and neutrophil counts.

Pharmacokinetics

Absorption: Only moderately absorbed across GI tract after P.O. administration. Bioavailability ranges from 25% to 75%, with average of 50% of dose being absorbed.
Distribution: Distributed widely in body tissues; crosses blood-brain barrier to limited and variable extent. Etoposide is about 94% protein-bound.
Metabolism: Only small portion of dose is metabolized in liver.
Excretion: Excreted primarily in urine as unchanged drug; smaller portion excreted in feces. *Half-life:* Initial, 30 minutes to 2 hours; terminal, 5½ to 11 hours.

Route	Onset	Peak	Duration
P.O., I.V.	Unknown	Unknown	Unknown

Pharmacodynamics

Chemical effect: Unknown.
Therapeutic effect: Inhibits selected cancer cell growth.

Available forms

Capsules: 50 mg
Injection: 20 mg/ml

NURSING PROCESS

Assessment

- Obtain history of patient's underlying condition before therapy.
- Obtain baseline blood pressure before therapy, and monitor blood pressure at 30-minute intervals during infusion.
- Monitor effectiveness by noting results of follow-up diagnostic tests and overall physical status and by regularly checking tumor size and rate of growth through appropriate studies. Etoposide has produced complete remission in small-cell lung cancer and testicular cancer.
- Monitor CBC. Observe patient for signs of bone marrow suppression.
- Be alert for adverse reactions and drug interactions.
- Evaluate patient's and family's knowledge of drug therapy.

Nursing diagnoses

- Ineffective health maintenance related to presence of neoplastic disease
- Ineffective protection related to drug induced adverse hematologic reactions
- Deficient knowledge related to drug therapy

Planning and implementation

- Follow facility policy to reduce risks. Preparation and administration of parenteral form create carcinogenic, mutagenic, and teratogenic risks for staff.
- **P.O. use:** Store capsules in refrigerator.
- **I.V. use:** Give drug by slow I.V. infusion (over at least 30 minutes) to prevent severe hypotension.

ALERT: If systolic blood pressure falls below 90 mm Hg, stop infusion and notify prescriber.
– Dilute drug for infusion in either D_5W or normal saline solution to 0.2 or 0.4 mg/ml. Higher concentrations may crystallize.
– Don't give through membrane-type in-line filter because diluent may dissolve filter.
– Solutions diluted to 0.2 mg/ml are stable 96 hours at room temperature in plastic of glass unprotected from light; solutions diluted to 0.4 mg/ml are stable 48 hours under same conditions.
- Keep diphenhydramine, hydrocortisone, epinephrine, and necessary emergency equipment available to establish airway in case of anaphylaxis.

Patient teaching
- Warn patient to watch for signs of infection and bleeding. Teach patient how to take infection-control and bleeding precautions.
- Tell patient that hair loss is possible but reversible.
- Instruct patient to report discomfort, pain, or burning at I.V. insertion site.

Evaluation

- Patient exhibits positive response to therapy.

• Patient's immune function returns to normal with cessation of therapy.
• Patient and family state understanding of drug therapy.

exemestane

(ecks-eh-MES-tayn)
Aromasin

Pharmacologic class: aromatase inhibitor
Therapeutic class: antineoplastic
Pregnancy risk category: D

Indications and dosages

▶ **Advanced breast cancer in postmenopausal women whose disease has progressed following treatment with tamoxifen.** *Adults:* 25 mg P.O. once daily after a meal.

Contraindications and precautions

• Contraindicated in patients hypersensitive to drug or its components.
Lifespan: Don't give to premenopausal women.

Adverse reactions

CNS: fever, *depression, insomnia, anxiety, fatigue, pain,* dizziness, headache, paresthesia, generalized weakness, asthenia, confusion, hypoesthesia.
CV: *hot flushes,* hypertension, edema, chest pain.
EENT: sinusitis, rhinitis, pharyngitis.
GI: *nausea,* vomiting, abdominal pain, anorexia, constipation, diarrhea, dyspepsia.
GU: urinary tract infection.
Metabolic: increased appetite.
Musculoskeletal: pathologic fractures, arthralgia, back pain, skeletal pain.
Respiratory: *dyspnea,* bronchitis, coughing, upper respiratory tract infection.
Skin: rash, increased sweating, alopecia, itching.
Other: infection, flulike syndrome, lymphedema.

Interactions

Drug-drug. *Drugs that induce CYP3A4:* May decrease exemestane plasma levels. Monitor patient closely for toxicity.
Estrogen-containing drugs: May affect drug. Don't give together.

Effects on lab test results

None reported.

Pharmacokinetics

Absorption: Rapidly absorbed, with about 42% of dose absorbed from the GI tract following P.O. administration. Plasma levels increase by 40% after a high-fat breakfast.
Distribution: Extensively distributed in tissues and 90% bound to plasma proteins.
Metabolism: Extensively metabolized by the liver. The main liver isoenzyme involved is cytochrome P-450 3A4.
Excretion: Excreted equally in urine and feces. Less than 1% is excreted unchanged in urine. *Elimination half-life:* About 24 hours.

Route	Onset	Peak	Duration
P.O.	Unknown	1-2 hr	Unknown

Pharmacodynamics

Chemical effect: Drug is an irreversible, steroidal aromatase inactivator that acts as a false substrate for the aromatase enzyme, the principal enzyme that converts androgens to estrogens in premenopausal and postmenopausal women. Exemestane is then processed to an intermediate that binds irreversibly to the enzyme's active site, causing inactivation. This effect is known as "suicide inhibition" and results in lower levels of circulating estrogens. Deprivation of estrogen is an effective and selective way to treat estrogen-dependent breast cancer in postmenopausal women.
Therapeutic effect: Hinders function of breast cancer cells.

Available forms

Tablets: 25 mg

NURSING PROCESS

Assessment

• Assess patient's breast cancer before therapy and regularly thereafter.
• Monitor patient for adverse reactions.
• Monitor patient's hydration status if adverse GI reactions occur.
• Evaluate patient's and family's knowledge about drug therapy.

Nursing diagnoses
- Ineffective health maintenance related to presence of breast cancer
- Risk for impaired physical mobility related to potential adverse musculoskeletal effects
- Deficient knowledge related to drug therapy

Planning and implementation
- Drug should be given only to postmenopausal women.
- Don't give with estrogen-containing drugs because doing so could interfere with intended action.
- Treatment should continue until tumor progression is evident.

Patient teaching
- Tell patient to take drug after a meal.
- Inform patient that she may need to take drug for a long period of time.
- Advise patient to report adverse effects to prescriber.

Evaluation
- Patient responds well to drug.
- Patient has no musculoskeletal adverse reactions.
- Patient and family state understanding of drug therapy.

F

factor IX complex
(FAK-tor nighn KOM-pleks)
Bebulin VH Immuno, Benefix, Konyne 80, Profilnine SD, Proplex T

factor IX (human)
AlphaNine SD, Mononine

Pharmacologic class: blood derivative
Therapeutic class: systemic hemostatic
Pregnancy risk category: C

Indications and dosages
▶ **Factor IX deficiency (hemophilia B or Christmas disease), anticoagulant overdosage.** *Adults and children:* To calculate approximate units of factor IX needed, use the following equations.
Human product. 1 unit/kg × body weight in kilograms × percentage of desired increase of factor IX level.
Recombinant product. 1-1.2 units/kg × body weight in kilograms × percentage of desired increase of factor IX level.
Proplex T. 0.5 units/kg × body weight in kilograms × percentage of desired increase of factor IX level.

Infusion rates vary with product and patient comfort. Dosage is highly individualized, depending on degree of deficiency, level of factor IX desired, patient weight, and severity of bleeding.

Contraindications and precautions
- Contraindicated in patients with hepatic disease in whom there's suspicion of intravascular coagulation or fibrinolysis. Mononine is contraindicated in patients hypersensitive to mouse protein. Benefix is contraindicated in patients hypersensitive to hamster protein.

Lifespan: In pregnant and breast-feeding women and in neonates and infants, use cautiously.

Adverse reactions
CNS: *transient fever,* headache.
CV: ***thromboembolic reactions, MI, disseminated intravascular coagulation, pulmonary embolism,*** *flushing,* changes in blood pressure.
GI: nausea, vomiting.
Skin: urticaria.
Other: *chills, tingling,* ***hypersensitivity reactions (anaphylaxis).***

Interactions
Drug-drug. *Aminocaproic acid:* May increase risk of thrombosis. Avoid using together.

Effects on lab test results
None reported.

Pharmacokinetics
Absorption: Administered I.V.
Distribution: Equilibration within extravascular space takes 4 to 6 hours.
Metabolism: Cleared by plasma.

Excretion: Unknown. *Half-life:* About 24 hours.

Route	Onset	Peak	Duration
I.V.	Immediate	10-30 min	Unknown

Pharmacodynamics

Chemical effect: Directly replaces deficient clotting factor.
Therapeutic effect: Causes clotting.

Available forms

Injection: Vials, with diluent. Units specified on label.

NURSING PROCESS

Assessment

- Assess patient's coagulation studies and bleeding disorder before and after therapy.
- Be alert for adverse reactions and drug interactions.
- Monitor vital signs regularly.
- Evaluate patient's and family's knowledge of drug therapy.

Nursing diagnoses

- Ineffective health maintenance related to underlying disorder
- Ineffective protection related to drug-induced intravascular hemolysis
- Deficient knowledge related to drug therapy

Planning and implementation

- Give hepatitis B vaccine before factor IX complex.
- Avoid rapid infusion. If tingling sensation, fever, chills, or headache develop, decrease flow rate and notify prescriber.
- Reconstitute with 20 ml of sterile water for injection for each vial of lyophilized drug. Keep refrigerated until ready to use; warm to room temperature before reconstituting. Use within 3 hours of reconstitution. Unstable in solution. Don't shake, refrigerate, or mix solution with other I.V. solutions. Store away from heat.
- Risk of hepatitis must be weighed against risk of not receiving drug. Because of manufacturing process, risk of HIV transmission is extremely low.

Patient teaching

- Explain drug action to patient.
- Tell patient to report adverse reactions promptly.

Evaluation

- Patient is free from bleeding.
- Patient doesn't experience injury.
- Patient and family state understanding of drug therapy.

famciclovir

(fam-SIGH-kloh-veer)
Famvir

Pharmacologic class: synthetic acyclic guanine derivative
Therapeutic class: antiviral
Pregnancy risk category: B

Indications and dosages

▶ **Acute herpes zoster.** *Adults:* 500 mg P.O. q 8 hours for 7 days.
▶ **Recurrent episodes of genital herpes.** *Adults:* 125 mg P.O. b.i.d. for 5 days. Therapy begins as soon as symptoms occur.
▶ **Treatment of recurrent herpes simplex virus infections in HIV-infected patients.** *Adults:* 500 mg P.O. b.i.d. for 7 days.
▶ **Long-term suppressive therapy of recurrent episodes of genital herpes.** *Adults:* 250 mg P.O. q 12 hours for up to 1 year.

Contraindications and precautions

- Contraindicated in patients hypersensitive to drug.
- Use cautiously in patients with renal or hepatic impairment. Dosage adjustment may be needed.

Lifespan: With pregnant women, use cautiously. In breast-feeding women, nursing isn't recommended during drug therapy. In children, safety of drug hasn't been established.

Adverse reactions

CNS: *headache,* fatigue, dizziness, paresthesia, somnolence.
EENT: pharyngitis, sinusitis.
GI: diarrhea, *nausea,* vomiting, constipation, anorexia, abdominal pain.
Musculoskeletal: back pain, arthralgia.

Skin: pruritus; zoster-related signs, symptoms, and complications.

Interactions

Drug-drug. *Probenecid:* May increase plasma levels of famciclovir. Monitor patient for increased adverse effects.

Effects on lab test results

None reported.

Pharmacokinetics

Absorption: Absolute bioavailability is 77%.
Distribution: Less than 20% is bound to plasma proteins.
Metabolism: Extensively metabolized in liver to active drug, penciclovir (98.5%), and other inactive metabolites.
Excretion: Primarily in urine.

Route	Onset	Peak	Duration
P.O.	Unknown	≤ 1 hr	Unknown

Pharmacodynamics

Chemical effect: Converted to penciclovir, which enters viral cells and inhibits DNA polymerase and viral DNA synthesis.
Therapeutic effect: Inhibits viral replication. Spectrum of activity includes herpes simplex types 1 and 2 and varicella-zoster viruses.

Available forms

Tablets: 125 mg, 250 mg, 500 mg

NURSING PROCESS

Assessment

- Assess patient's viral infection before therapy, and reassess regularly throughout therapy.
- Be alert for adverse reactions and drug interactions.
- Monitor patient's hydration status if adverse GI reactions occur.
- Evaluate patient's and family's knowledge of drug therapy.

Nursing diagnoses

- Infection related to presence of virus susceptible to famciclovir
- Risk for deficient fluid volume related to drug's adverse GI reactions
- Deficient knowledge related to drug therapy

Planning and implementation

- Patients with renal insufficiency need a reduced dosage.
- Drug may be taken without regard to meals.

Patient teaching

- Teach patient how to prevent spread of infection to others.
- Urge patient to recognize and report early symptoms of herpes infection, such as tingling, itching, or pain.

Evaluation

- Patient is free from infection.
- Patient maintains adequate hydration.
- Patient and family state understanding of drug therapy.

famotidine

(fam-OH-tih-deen)

Pepcid, Pepcid AC , Pepcid RPD, Pepcidine ◇

Pharmacologic class: H_2-receptor antagonist
Therapeutic class: antiulcer agent
Pregnancy risk category: B

Indications and dosages

▶ **Duodenal ulcer (short-term treatment).** *Adults:* For acute therapy, 40 mg P.O. once daily h.s. or 20 mg P.O. b.i.d. Maintenance, 20 mg P.O. once daily h.s.

▶ **Benign gastric ulcer (short-term treatment).** *Adults:* 40 mg P.O. daily h.s. for 8 weeks.

▶ **Pathologic hypersecretory conditions (such as Zollinger-Ellison syndrome).** *Adults:* 20 mg P.O. q 6 hours up to 160 mg q 6 hours.

▶ **Gastroesophageal reflux disease (GERD).** *Adults:* 20 mg P.O. b.i.d. for up to 6 weeks. For esophagitis caused by GERD, 20 to 40 mg b.i.d. for up to 12 weeks.

▶ **Prevention or treatment of heartburn.** *Adults:* 10 mg Pepcid AC P.O. 1 hour before meals (prevention) or 10 mg Pepcid AC P.O. with water when symptoms occur. Maximum, 20 mg daily. Drug shouldn't be taken daily for more than 2 weeks.

▶ **Hospitalized patients with intractable ulcerations or hypersecretory conditions or**

patients who can't take oral medication‡. *Adults:* 20 mg I.V. q 12 hours.

Contraindications and precautions

• Contraindicated in patients hypersensitive to drug.

Lifespan: In pregnant and breast-feeding women, use cautiously. In children, safety of drug hasn't been established.

Adverse reactions

CNS: *headache,* dizziness, vertigo, malaise, paresthesia, fever.
CV: palpitations, flushing.
EENT: tinnitus, orbital edema.
GI: diarrhea, constipation, anorexia, taste disorder, dry mouth.
Musculoskeletal: musculoskeletal pain.
Skin: acne, dry skin.
Other: transient irritation at I.V. site.

Interactions

None significant.

Effects on lab test results

• May increase BUN, creatinine, and liver enzyme levels.

Pharmacokinetics

Absorption: When given orally, about 40% to 45% is absorbed.
Distribution: Distributed widely to many body tissues.
Metabolism: About 30% to 35% of dose is metabolized by liver.
Excretion: Most of drug is excreted unchanged in urine. *Half-life:* 2½ to 3½ hours.

Route	Onset	Peak	Duration
P.O.	≤ 1 hr	1-3 hr	10-12 hr
I.V.	≤ 1 hr	20 min	10-12 hr

Pharmacodynamics

Chemical effect: Competitively inhibits action of H_2 at receptor sites of parietal cells, decreasing gastric acid secretion.
Therapeutic effect: Decreases gastric acid levels and prevents heartburn.

Available forms

Gelcaps: 10 mg
Injection: 10 mg/ml, 20 mg/50 ml (premixed)
Powder for oral suspension: 40 mg/5 ml after reconstitution
Tablets: 10 mg, 20 mg, 40 mg
Tablets, chewable: 10 mg†
Tablets, orally disintegrating: 20 mg, 40 mg

NURSING PROCESS

Assessment

• Assess patient's GI disorder before therapy, and reassess regularly throughout therapy.
• Be alert for adverse reactions.
• Evaluate patient's and family's knowledge of drug therapy.

Nursing diagnoses

• Impaired tissue integrity related to underlying GI disorder
• Constipation related to drug's adverse effect on GI tract
• Deficient knowledge related to drug therapy

Planning and implementation

• **P.O. use:** Give drug at bedtime or, if more than one daily dose is ordered, give last dose of day at bedtime.
– Store reconstituted oral suspension below 86° F (30° C). Discard after 30 days.
• **I.V. use:** To prepare I.V. injection, dilute 2 ml (20 mg) drug with compatible I.V. solution to total volume of either 5 or 10 ml, and inject over at least 2 minutes. Compatible solutions include sterile water for injection, normal saline injection, D_5W or $D_{10}W$ injection, 5% sodium bicarbonate injection, and lactated Ringer's injection.
– Or, give by intermittent I.V. infusion. Dilute 20 mg (2 ml) drug in 100 ml of compatible solution and infuse over 15 to 30 minutes. Solution is stable for 48 hours at room temperature after dilution.
– Store I.V. injection in refrigerator at 36° to 46° F (2° to 8° C).
– Change I.V. site if infiltration or signs of phlebitis occur. Apply warm compresses to site.

Patient teaching

• Tell patient to take drug with snack if desired. Remind him that drug is most effective if taken at bedtime. Tell patient taking 20 mg b.i.d. to take one dose at bedtime.

• With prescriber's knowledge, allow patient to take antacids, especially at beginning of therapy when pain is severe.
• Urge patient to avoid cigarette smoking because it may increase gastric acid secretion and worsen disease.
• Advise patient not to take drug for more than 8 weeks unless specifically ordered by prescriber. Patient shouldn't self-medicate for heartburn longer than 2 weeks without prescriber's knowledge.

☑ Evaluation
• Patient reports decrease in or relief of GI pain with drug.
• Patient regains normal bowel pattern.
• Patient and family state understanding of drug therapy.

felodipine
(feh-LOH-dih-peen)
Agon ◇, Agon SR ◇, Plendil, Plendil ER ◇, Renedil ♦

Pharmacologic class: calcium channel blocker
Therapeutic class: antihypertensive
Pregnancy risk category: C

Indications and dosages
▶ **Hypertension.** *Adults:* Initially, 5 mg P.O. daily. Dosage adjusted based on patient response, usually at no less than 2-week intervals. Usual dosage is 2.5 to 10 mg daily. Maximum recommended dosage is 20 mg daily. *Elderly patients:* 5 mg P.O. daily, adjusted as for adults. Maximum recommended dosage is 10 mg daily.

Contraindications and precautions
• Contraindicated in patients hypersensitive to drug.
• Use cautiously in patients with heart failure, particularly those receiving beta blockers, and in patients with impaired hepatic function because clearance of drug from blood is dependent on liver.
Lifespan: In pregnant women, use cautiously. Breast-feeding isn't recommended during therapy. In children, safety of drug hasn't been established.

Adverse reactions
CNS: *headache,* dizziness, paresthesia, asthenia.
CV: *flushing, peripheral edema,* chest pain, palpitations.
EENT: rhinorrhea, pharyngitis, gingival hyperplasia.
GI: abdominal pain, nausea, constipation, diarrhea.
Musculoskeletal: muscle cramps, back pain.
Respiratory: upper respiratory infection, cough.
Skin: rash.

Interactions
Drug-drug. *Anticonvulsants:* May decrease plasma felodipine level. Avoid using together.
Cimetidine: Decreases felodipine clearance. Give lower doses of felodipine.
Metoprolol: May alter pharmacokinetics of metoprolol. No dosage adjustment necessary. Monitor patient for adverse effects.
Theophylline: May slightly decrease theophylline levels. Monitor patient's response carefully.
Drug-food. *Grapefruit juice:* Increases bioavailability and effect when taken together. Caution patient not to take with grapefruit juice.

Effects on lab test results
None reported.

Pharmacokinetics
Absorption: Almost completely absorbed, but extensive first-pass metabolism reduces absolute bioavailability to about 20%.
Distribution: Over 99% bound to plasma proteins.
Metabolism: Unknown, although thought to be hepatic.
Excretion: Over 70% of dose appears in urine and 10% in feces as metabolites. *Half-life:* 11 to 16 hours.

Route	Onset	Peak	Duration
P.O.	2-5 hr	2.5-5 hr	24 hr

Pharmacodynamics
Chemical effect: Unknown; however, drug is a dihydropyridine derivative that prevents entry of calcium ions into vascular smooth muscle and cardiac cells.
Therapeutic effect: Lowers blood pressure.

Available forms

Tablets: 5 mg ◇
Tablets (extended-release): 2.5 mg, 5 mg, 10 mg

NURSING PROCESS

Assessment
• Assess patient's blood pressure before therapy, and reassess regularly thereafter.
• Be alert for adverse reactions and drug interactions.
• Evaluate patient's and family's knowledge of drug therapy.

Nursing diagnoses
• Risk for injury related to presence of hypertension
• Excessive fluid volume related to drug-induced peripheral edema
• Deficient knowledge related to drug therapy

Planning and implementation
• Drug may be given without regard to food.

Patient teaching
• Instruct patient to swallow tablets whole and not to crush or chew them.
• Tell patient to take drug even when he feels better; to watch his diet; and to check with prescriber or pharmacist before taking other medications, including OTC medicines and herbal remedies.
• Advise patient to observe good oral hygiene and to see dentist regularly.

Evaluation
• Patient's blood pressure is normal.
• Patient doesn't develop complications from peripheral edema.
• Patient and family state understanding of drug therapy.

fenofibrate
(feh-noh-FIGH-brayt)
Tricor

Pharmacologic class: fibric acid derivative
Therapeutic class: antilipemic
Pregnancy risk category: C

Indications and dosages

▶ **Adjunct to diet for treatment of hypertriglyceridemia (type IV and V hyperlipidemia).** *Adults:* 67- to 200-mg capsule or 54- to 160-mg tablet P.O. daily. Based on response, increase dose if necessary following repeat triglyceride levels at 4- to 8-week intervals to maximum dose of 200-mg capsule or 160-mg tablet daily.

▶ **Adjunct to diet for the treatment of primary hypercholesterolemia or mixed dyslipidemia (Frederickson types IIa and IIb).** *Adults:* 200-mg capsule or 160-mg tablet P.O. daily.

Minimize dose in patients with creatinine clearance less than 50 ml/minute and elderly patients. Initiate therapy at dose of 67-mg capsule or 54-mg tablet daily, and increase only after effects on renal function and triglyceride levels have been evaluated at this dose.

Contraindications and precautions

• Contraindicated in patients hypersensitive to drug and in those with gallbladder disease, hepatic dysfunction, primary biliary cirrhosis, severe renal dysfunction, or unexplained persistent liver function abnormalities.
• Use cautiously in patients with history of pancreatitis.
Lifespan: In children, safety and efficacy haven't been established.

Adverse reactions

CNS: dizziness, pain, asthenia, fatigue, paresthesia, insomnia, increased appetite, headache.
CV: ***arrhythmias.***
EENT: eye irritation, eye floaters, earache, conjunctivitis, blurred vision, rhinitis, sinusitis.
GI: dyspepsia, eructation, flatulence, nausea, vomiting, abdominal pain, constipation, diarrhea, ***pancreatitis,*** cholelithiasis.
GU: polyuria, vaginitis.
Musculoskeletal: arthralgia.
Respiratory: cough.
Skin: pruritus, rash.
Other: hypersensitivity reaction, *infection,* flu syndrome, decreased libido.

Interactions

Drug-drug. *Bile acid sequestrants:* May bind and inhibit absorption of drug. Give drug 1

hour before or 4 to 6 hours after bile acid sequestrants.
Coumarin-type anticoagulants: Potentiation of anticoagulant effect. Monitor PT and INR closely. Dosage of anticoagulant may need to be reduced.
Cyclosporine, immunosuppressants, nephrotoxic agents: May cause renal dysfunction, which may compromise the elimination of drug. Use together cautiously.
3-Hydroxy-3-methylglutaryl coenzyme A (HMG-CoA) reductase inhibitors: No data available; however, because of risk of myopathy, rhabdomyolysis, and acute renal failure reported with combined use of HMG-CoA reductase inhibitors and gemfibrozil (another fibrate derivative), these drugs shouldn't be given together.
Drug-food. *Any food:* Absorption of drug is increased. Give drug with meals.
Drug-lifestyle. *Alcohol use:* May elevate triglyceride levels. Discourage using together.

Effects on lab test results

- May increase BUN, creatinine, ALT, and AST levels. May decrease uric acid levels.
- May decrease hemoglobin, hematocrit, and WBC count.

Pharmacokinetics

Absorption: Well absorbed from GI tract.
Distribution: About 99% bound to plasma proteins.
Metabolism: Rapidly hydrolyzed by esterases to active metabolite, fenofibric acid.
Excretion: About 60% excreted in urine mainly as metabolites and 25% in feces. *Half-life:* 20 hours.

Route	Onset	Peak	Duration
P.O.	Unknown	6-8 hr	Unknown

Pharmacodynamics

Chemical effect: Exact mechanism unknown. May inhibit triglyceride synthesis, resulting in a decrease in the quantity of very-low-density lipoproteins released into circulation. Drug also may stimulate breakdown of triglyceride-rich protein.
Therapeutic effect: Decreases serum triglyceride levels.

Available forms

Micronized capsules: 67 mg, 134 mg, 200 mg (are being phased-out)
Tablets: 54 mg, 160 mg

NURSING PROCESS

Assessment

- Assess baseline lipid levels and liver function tests before starting therapy and periodically thereafter.
- Be alert for adverse reactions and drug interactions.
- Evaluate patient's and family's knowledge of drug.

Nursing diagnoses

- Imbalanced nutrition: less than body requirements related to drug-induced adverse GI reactions
- Risk for infection related to adverse drug reactions
- Deficient knowledge related to drug therapy

Planning and implementation

- Therapy should be withdrawn in patients who don't have an adequate response after 2 months of treatment with maximum dose.
- Give tablets with meals to increase bioavailability.
- Patients with severe renal impairment need evaluation of renal function and triglyceride levels before dosage increase.
- Counsel patient on importance of adhering to triglyceride-lowering diet.

Patient teaching

- Advise patient to promptly report symptoms of unexplained muscle weakness, pain, or tenderness, especially if accompanied by malaise or fever.
- Urge patient to take drug with meals to optimize drug absorption.
- Advise patient to continue weight-control measures, including diet and exercise, and to reduce alcohol intake before starting drug therapy.
- Instruct patient who also takes bile acid resin to take fenofibrate 1 hour before or 4 to 6 hours after bile acid resin.

Evaluation

- Patient maintains adequate nutritional intake.

• Patient remains free from infection.
• Patient and family state understanding of drug therapy.

fentanyl citrate
(FEN-tuh-nihl SIGH-trayt)
Sublimaze

fentanyl transdermal system
Duragesic-25, Duragesic-50, Duragesic-75, Duragesic-100

fentanyl transmucosal
Actiq, Fentanyl Oralet

Pharmacologic class: opioid analgesic
Therapeutic class: analgesic, adjunct to anesthesia, anesthetic
Pregnancy risk category: C
Controlled substance schedule: II

Indications and dosages

▶ **Adjunct to general anesthetic.** *Adults:* For low-dose therapy, 2 mcg/kg I.V. For moderate-dose therapy, 2 to 20 mcg/kg I.V.; then 25 to 100 mcg I.V. or I.M., p.r.n. For high-dose therapy, 20 to 50 mcg/kg I.V.; then 25 mcg to one-half initial loading dose I.V. p.r.n.
Children ages 2 to 12: 2 to 3 mcg/kg I.V. or I.M. during induction and maintenance phases of general anesthesia.
▶ **Adjunct to regional anesthesia.** *Adults:* 50 to 100 mcg I.M. or slow I.V. over 1 to 2 minutes.
▶ **Postoperatively.** *Adults:* 50 to 100 mcg I.M. q 1 to 2 hours, p.r.n.
▶ **Preoperatively.** *Adults:* 50 to 100 mcg I.M. 30 to 60 minutes before surgery. Or, 5 mcg/kg dispensed transmucosally.
Children age 2 and older weighing more than 15 kg (33 lb) and less than 40 kg (44 lb): 5 mcg/kg transmucosally. May need a dose 10 to 15 mcg/kg as an Oralet.
▶ **Management of chronic pain.** *Adults:* One transdermal system applied to upper torso on area of skin that isn't irritated and hasn't been irradiated. Therapy started with 25-mcg/hour system; dosage adjusted as needed and tolerated. Each system may be worn for up to 72 hours.
▶ **Breakthrough cancer pain in opioid-tolerant patients.** ***Actiq.*** *Adults:* 200 mcg P.O. initially, adjusted based on response. Each dose should be consumed over 15 minutes. An additional lozenge may be taken 30 minutes after start of the previous dose. Don't use more than 2 units per episode of breakthrough pain.

Contraindications and precautions

• Contraindicated in patients intolerant of drug.
• Use cautiously in debilitated patients and in patients with head injury, increased CSF pressure, COPD, decreased respiratory reserve, potentially compromised respirations, hepatic or renal disease, or bradyarrhythmias.
Lifespan: With pregnant and breast-feeding women, use cautiously. In infants younger than age 2, safety of drug hasn't been established. In elderly patients, use cautiously.

Adverse reactions

CNS: *sedation, somnolence, clouded sensorium, euphoria,* dizziness, headache, *confusion, asthenia,* nervousness, hallucinations, anxiety, depression.
CV: *hypotension,* hypertension, ***arrhythmias,*** chest pain, ***bradycardia.***
EENT: *dry mouth.*
GI: *nausea, vomiting, constipation,* ileus, abdominal pain.
GU: *urine retention.*
Respiratory: ***respiratory depression,*** hypoventilation, dyspnea, ***apnea.***
Skin: reaction at application site (erythema, papules, edema), *pruritus, diaphoresis.*
Other: physical dependence.

Interactions

Drug-drug. *CNS depressants, general anesthetics, hypnotics, MAO inhibitors, other narcotic analgesics, sedatives, tricyclic antidepressant:* May have additive effects. Use together with extreme caution. Fentanyl dose should be reduced by one-quarter to one-third. Also, give above drugs in reduced dosages.
Diazepam: CV depression may occur when given with high doses of fentanyl. Monitor patient closely.
Droperidol: May cause hypotension and decreased pulmonary arterial pressure. Monitor patient closely.

Drug-lifestyle. *Alcohol use:* May have additive effects. Discourage using together.

Effects on lab test results

None reported.

Pharmacokinetics

Absorption: Varies with transmucosal or transdermal use.
Distribution: Distributes and accumulates to adipose tissue and skeletal muscle.
Metabolism: Metabolized in liver.
Excretion: Excreted in urine. *Half-life:* About 3½ hours after parenteral use, 5 to 15 hours after transmucosal use, 18 hours after transdermal use.

Route	Onset	Peak	Duration
I.V.	1-2 min	3-5 min	30 min-1 hr
I.M.	7-15 min	20-30 min	1-2 hr
Transmucosal	15 min	20-30 min	Unknown
Transdermal	12-24 hr	1-3 days	Varies

Pharmacodynamics

Chemical effect: Unknown; binds with opioid receptors in CNS, altering both perception of and emotional response to pain.
Therapeutic effect: Relieves pain.

Available forms

Injection: 50 mcg/ml
Transdermal system: patches designed to release 25, 50, 75, or 100 mcg of fentanyl per hour
Transmucosal: 200 mcg, 400 mcg, 600 mcg, 800 mcg, 1,200 mcg, 1,600 mcg

NURSING PROCESS

Assessment

- Assess patient's underlying condition before therapy.
- Evaluate degree of pain relief obtained after administration.
- Periodically monitor postoperative vital signs and bladder function. Because drug decreases both rate and depth of respirations, monitoring of arterial oxygen saturation (SaO_2) may help assess respiratory depression.
- Monitor patient who develops adverse reactions to transdermal system for at least 12 hours after removal. Serum drug levels may take as long as 17 hours to decline by 50%.
- Be alert for adverse reactions and drug interactions.
- Evaluate patient's and family's knowledge of drug therapy.

Nursing diagnoses

- Acute pain related to underlying condition
- Ineffective breathing pattern related to respiratory depression
- Deficient knowledge related to drug therapy

Planning and implementation

- For better analgesic effect, give drug before patient has intense pain.
- **I.V. use:** Only staff trained in giving I.V. anesthetics and managing their adverse effects should give I.V. fentanyl.
  – Keep naloxone and resuscitation equipment available when giving drug I.V.
  – Drug is commonly used I.V. with droperidol to produce neuroleptanalgesia.
- **I.M. use:** Follow normal protocol.
- **Transmucosal use:** Remove foil overwrap of fentanyl Oralet just before administration.
  – Instruct patient to place fentanyl Oralet in mouth and suck (not chew) it.
  – Remove fentanyl Oralet unit using handle after it has been consumed, patient shows adequate effect, or patient shows signs of respiratory depression. Place any remaining portion in plastic overwrap, and dispose of accordingly for Schedule II drugs.
  ALERT: Ask patient and caregivers about the presence of children in the home. Actiq lozenges contain enough fentanyl citrate to be fatal to a child.
  – Because high doses may cause hypoventilation, transmucosal doses shouldn't exceed 15 mcg/kg (maximum, 400 mcg) in children or 5 mcg/kg (maximum, 400 mcg) in adults.
- **Transdermal use:** Transdermal fentanyl isn't recommended for postoperative pain.
  – Dosage equivalency charts are available to calculate fentanyl transdermal dose based on daily morphine intake—for example, for every 90 mg of oral morphine or 15 mg of I.M. morphine per 24 hours, 25 mcg/hour of transdermal fentanyl is needed.
  – Dosage adjustments in patient using transdermal system should be made gradually. Reaching steady-state levels of new dosage may take up to 6 days; delay dosage adjustment until after at least two applications.

– High doses can produce muscle rigidity, which can be reversed with neuromuscular blockers; however, patient must be ventilated artificially.
– Immediately report respiratory rate below 12 breaths/minute or decreased respiratory volume or SaO^2.
– When drug is used postoperatively, encourage patient to turn, cough, and breathe deeply to prevent atelectasis.
– Most patients have good control of pain for 3 days while wearing transdermal system, but a few may need new application after 48 hours. Because fentanyl level rises for first 24 hours after application, analgesic effect can't be evaluated for first day. Make sure patient has adequate supplemental analgesic to prevent breakthrough pain.
– When reducing opioid therapy or switching to different analgesic, transdermal system should be withdrawn gradually. Because fentanyl level drops gradually after removal, give half of equianalgesic dose of new analgesic 12 to 18 hours after removal.

Patient teaching

- Teach patient proper application of transdermal patch. Instruct patient to clip hair at application site, but to avoid razor, which may irritate skin. Tell him to wash area with clear water if necessary, but not with soaps, oils, lotions, alcohol, or other substances that may irritate skin or prevent adhesion. Urge him to dry area completely before application.
- Tell patient to remove transdermal system from package just before applying, to hold in place for 10 to 20 seconds, and to be sure edges of patch adhere to the skin.
- Teach patient to dispose of transdermal patch by folding so adhesive side adheres to itself and then flushing it down toilet.
- If patient needs another patch after 72 hours, tell him to apply it to new site.
- Inform patient that heat from fever or environment may increase transdermal delivery and cause toxicity, which requires dosage adjustment. Instruct patient to notify prescriber if fever occurs or if he will be spending time in hot climate.

ALERT: Strongly warn patient to keep drug safely secured, away from children.

Evaluation

- Patient is free from pain.
- Patient maintains adequate ventilation throughout drug therapy.
- Patient and family state understanding of drug therapy.

ferrous fumarate

(FEH-rus FYOO-muh-rayt)

Femiron†, Feostat†, Feostat Drops†, Fumasorb†, Fumerin†, Hemocyte†, Ircon†, Neo-Fer♦†, Nephro-Fer†, (OTC) Novofumar♦, (OTC) Palafer♦, Palafer Pediatric Drops♦, Span-FF†

ferrous gluconate

Fergon†, Fertinic♦, Novoferrogluc♦

ferrous sulfate

Apo-Ferrous Sulfate♦, Feosol*†, Feratab, Fer-Gen-Sol Drops†, Fer-In-Sol*†, Fer-Iron Drops†, Fero-Grad♦, Fero-Gradumet†, Mol-Iron

ferrous sulfate, dried

Feosol, Fer-In-Sol, Fe^{50}, Slow-Fe†

Pharmacologic class: oral iron supplement
Therapeutic class: hematinic
Pregnancy risk category: A

Indications and dosages

▶ **Iron deficiency.** ***fumarate.*** *Adults:* 50 to 100 mg elemental iron P.O. t.i.d.
Children: 4 to 6 mg/kg P.O. daily, divided into three doses.

▶ **Iron deficiency.** ***gluconate.*** *Adults:* 325 mg P.O. q.i.d., increased to 650 mg q.i.d. if needed and tolerated.
Children age 2 and older: 3 mg/kg/day P.O. in three to four divided doses.

▶ **Iron deficiency.** ***sulfate.*** *Adults:* 300 mg P.O. b.i.d. to q.i.d. Or, 1 extended-release capsule (160 to 525 mg) P.O. daily to b.i.d.
Children age 2 and older: 3 mg/kg P.O. daily in three or four divided doses.

Contraindications and precautions

- Contraindicated in patients with primary hemochromatosis, hemosiderosis, hemolytic anemia (unless iron deficiency anemia is also pres-

ent), peptic ulcer disease, regional enteritis, or ulcerative colitis, and in those receiving repeated blood transfusions.
- Use cautiously on long-term basis.

Lifespan: Iron supplements usually are recommended for breast-feeding women. In children, use cautiously. Extended-release forms aren't recommended for children. In elderly patients, may cause constipation.

Adverse reactions

GI: *nausea, epigastric pain, vomiting, constipation,* diarrhea, black stools, anorexia.
Other: suspension and drops may temporarily stain teeth.

Interactions

Drug-drug. *Antacids, cholestyramine resin, fluoroquinolones, levodopa, penicillamine, tetracycline, vitamin E:* Decreases iron absorption. Separate doses by 2 to 4 hours.
Chloramphenicol: Increases iron response. Watch patient carefully.
Fluoroquinolones, penicillamine, tetracyclines: Decreases GI absorption, possibly resulting in decreased serum levels or efficacy. Separate doses by 2 to 4 hours.
L-thyroxine: Decreases L-thyroxine absorption. Separate doses by at least 2 hours. Monitor thyroid function.
Levodopa, methyldopa: Decreases absorption and efficacy of levodopa and methyldopa. Monitor patient for decreased effects of these drugs.
Vitamin C: May increase iron absorption. Beneficial drug interaction.
Drug-food. *Yogurt, cheese, eggs, milk, whole-grain breads, cereals, tea, coffee:* May impair oral iron absorption. Advise patient not to use together.

Effects on lab test results

None reported.

Pharmacokinetics

Absorption: Absorbed from entire length of GI tract, but primary absorption sites are duodenum and proximal jejunum. Up to 10% of iron absorbed by healthy people; patients with iron-deficiency anemia may absorb up to 60%. Enteric coating and some extended-release formulas have decreased absorption because they're designed to release iron past points of highest GI absorption. Food may decrease absorption by 33% to 50%.
Distribution: Iron is transported through GI mucosal cells directly into blood, where it's bound immediately to carrier protein, transferrin, and transported to bone marrow for incorporation into hemoglobin. Iron is highly protein-bound.
Metabolism: Iron is liberated by destruction of hemoglobin, but is conserved and reused by body.
Excretion: Healthy people lose only small amounts of iron each day. Men and postmenopausal women lose about 1 mg/day, and premenopausal women about 1.5 mg/day. The loss usually occurs in nails, hair, feces, and urine; trace amounts are lost in bile and sweat.

Route	Onset	Peak	Duration
P.O.	≤ 4 days	7-10 days	2-4 mo

Pharmacodynamics

Chemical effect: Provides elemental iron, an essential component in formation of hemoglobin.
Therapeutic effect: Relieves iron deficiency.

Available forms

ferrous fumarate
(Each 100 mg provides 33 mg of elemental iron.)
Drops: 45 mg/0.6 ml†
Oral suspension: 100 mg/5 ml†
Tablets 200 mg, 324 mg, 325 mg, 350 mg
Tablets (chewable): 100 mg†
ferrous gluconate
(Each 100 mg provides 11.6 mg of elemental iron.)
Capsules: 86 mg†
Tablets: 240 mg, 300 mg†, 320 mg† (contains 37 mg elemental iron), 325 mg†
ferrous sulfate
(About 20% elemental iron; dried and powdered, it's about 32% elemental iron.)
Capsules: 150 mg†, 159 mg (dried), 190 mg (dried), 250 mg†, 390 mg†
Capsules (extended-release): 150 mg (dried), 160 mg (dried)
Drops: 75 mg/0.6 ml, 125 mg/ml
Elixir: 220 mg/5 ml*†
Solution: 75 mg/0.6 ml, 300 mg/5 ml
Syrup: 90 mg/5 ml*†

Tablets: 195 mg†, 300 mg†, 325 mg†, 187 mg (dried), 200 mg (dried)
Tablets (extended-release): 160 mg (dried)†, 525 mg

NURSING PROCESS

Assessment
• Obtain baseline assessment of patient's iron deficiency before therapy.
• Evaluate hemoglobin and hematocrit levels and reticulocyte counts during therapy.
• Be alert for adverse reactions and drug interactions.
• Evaluate patient's and family's knowledge of drug therapy.

Nursing diagnoses
• Fatigue related to iron deficiency
• Constipation related to adverse effect of drug therapy on GI tract
• Deficient knowledge related to drug therapy

Planning and implementation
• Give tablets with juice or water, but not with milk or antacids.
• Dilute liquid forms in juice or water, but not in milk or antacids.
• To avoid staining teeth, give suspension or elixir with straw and place drops at back of throat.
• Don't crush or allow patient to chew extended-release forms.
• GI upset may be related to dose. Between-meal dosing is preferable, but iron can be given with some foods, although absorption may be decreased. Enteric-coated products reduce GI upset but also reduce amount of iron absorbed.
• Oral iron may turn stools black. Although this unabsorbed iron is harmless, it could mask presence of melena.

Patient teaching
ALERT: Inform parents that as few as three or four tablets can cause poisoning in children.
• If patient misses dose, tell him to take it as soon as he remembers but not to double-dose.
• Advise patient to avoid certain foods that may impair oral iron absorption, including yogurt, cheese, eggs, milk, whole-grain breads and cereals, tea, and coffee.
• Teach dietary measures for preventing constipation.

Evaluation
• Patient reports fatigue is no longer a problem in daily life.
• Patient states appropriate measures to prevent or relieve constipation.
• Patient and family state understanding of drug therapy.

fexofenadine hydrochloride
(feks-oh-FEN-uh-deen high-droh-KLOR-ighd)
Allegra, Telfast ◇

Pharmacologic class: H_1-receptor antagonist
Therapeutic class: antihistamine
Pregnancy risk category: C

Indications and dosages
▶ **Seasonal allergic rhinitis.** *Adults and children age 12 and older:* 60 mg P.O. b.i.d. or 180 mg P.O. once daily.
Children ages 6 to 11: 30 mg P.O. b.i.d.
▶ **Chronic idiopathic urticaria.** *Children age 12 and older:* 60 mg P.O. b.i.d.
Children ages 6 to 11: 30 mg P.O. b.i.d.
Patients with creatinine clearance less than 80 ml/minute: Increase dosage interval to q 24 hours.

Contraindications and precautions
• Contraindicated in patients hypersensitive to drug or its components.
• Use cautiously in patients with impaired renal function.
Lifespan: With breast-feeding women, use cautiously because it's unknown whether drug appears in breast milk. In children younger than age 6, safety and effectiveness haven't been established.

Adverse reactions
CNS: fatigue, drowsiness.
GI: nausea, dyspepsia.
GU: dysmenorrhea.
Other: viral infection.

Interactions
Drug-drug. *Erythromycin, ketoconazole:* Increases fexofenadine levels. Prolonged QT interval has been seen with other antihistamines. Monitor patient closely.

Effects on lab test results

None reported.

Pharmacokinetics

Absorption: Drug is rapidly absorbed.
Distribution: Plasma protein–binding is 60% to 70%.
Metabolism: Not reported.
Excretion: About 80% in feces and 11% in urine. *Half-life:* 14.4 hours.

Route	Onset	Peak	Duration
P.O.	Unknown	3 hr	14 hr

Pharmacodynamics

Chemical effect: Principal effects are mediated through a selective inhibition of peripheral H_1-receptors.
Therapeutic effect: Relieves symptoms of seasonal allergies.

Available forms

Capsules: 180 mg
Tablets: 30 mg, 60 mg, 120 mg ◇, 180 mg

NURSING PROCESS

Assessment

- Assess patient's seasonal allergy symptoms before therapy and thereafter.
- Monitor patient for adverse reactions.
- Evaluate patient's and family's knowledge of drug therapy.

Nursing diagnoses

- Risk for injury related to fatigue and drowsiness caused by drug
- Ineffective health maintenance related to underlying condition
- Deficient knowledge related to drug therapy

Planning and implementation

- Patient with impaired renal function or currently on dialysis should receive a reduced daily dosage.

Patient teaching

- Caution patient not to perform hazardous activities if drowsiness occurs as a result of drug use.
- Instruct patient not to exceed prescribed dosage and to take drug only during seasonal allergy symptoms.
- Warn patient to avoid alcohol and hazardous activities that require alertness until CNS effects of drug are known.
- Tell patient that coffee or tea may reduce drowsiness. Suggest sugarless gum, sugarless sour hard candy, or ice chips to relieve dry mouth.

Evaluation

- Patient experiences limited fatigue and drowsiness caused by the drug.
- Patient responds well to the drug.
- Patient and family state understanding of drug therapy.

filgrastim (granulocyte colony-stimulating factor; G-CSF)

(fil-GRAH-stem)
Neupogen

Pharmacologic class: biologic response modifier
Therapeutic class: colony-stimulating factor, hematopoietic
Pregnancy risk category: C

Indications and dosages

▶ **To decrease risk of infection in patients with nonmyeloid cancers receiving myelosuppressive antineoplastics, to treat agranulocytosis‡, pancytopenia with colchine overdose‡, acute leukemia‡, or hematologic toxicity with zidovudine antiviral therapy‡.** *Adults and children:* 5 mcg/kg I.V. or S.C. daily as single dose. May be increased in increments of 5 mcg/kg for each chemotherapy cycle, depending on duration and severity of nadir of absolute neutrophil count (ANC).

▶ **To decrease risk of infection in patients with nonmyeloid cancers receiving myelosuppressive antineoplastics followed by bone marrow transplant.** *Adults and children:* 10 mcg/kg I.V. or S.C. daily at least 24 hours after cytotoxic chemotherapy and bone marrow infusion. Subsequent dosages adjusted according to neutrophil response.

▶ **Congenital neutropenia.** *Adults:* 6 mcg/kg S.C. b.i.d. Dosage adjusted according to patient's response.

▶ **Idiopathic or cyclic neutropenia.** *Adults:* 5 mcg/kg S.C. daily. Dosage adjusted based on response.
▶ **Peripheral blood progenitor cell collection.** *Adults:* 10 mcg/kg S.C. daily for at least 4 days before first leukapheresis and continuing until the last leukapheresis is completed.
▶ **Aplastic anemia‡.** *Adults:* 800 to 1,200 mcg/m² S.C. or I.V. daily.
▶ **Hairy cell leukemia, myelodysplasia‡.** *Adults:* 15 to 500 mcg/m² S.C. or I.V. daily. Or, for myelodysplasia, 0.3 to 10 mcg/kg S.C. daily.
▶ **AIDS‡.** *Adults:* 0.3 to 3.6 mcg/kg S.C. or I.V. daily.
▶ **Neutropenia from HIV infection‡.** *Adults and adolescents:* 5 to 10 mcg/kg S.C. or I.V. daily for 2 to 4 weeks.

Contraindications and precautions

• Contraindicated in patients hypersensitive to proteins derived from *Escherichia coli* or to drug or its components.
Lifespan: In pregnant or breast-feeding women, use cautiously.

Adverse reactions

CNS: *fever, fatigue,* headache, weakness.
CV: ***MI, arrhythmias,*** chest pain.
GI: *nausea, vomiting, diarrhea, mucositis,* stomatitis, constipation.
GU: hematuria, proteinuria.
Hematologic: ***thrombocytopenia,*** leukocytosis.
Musculoskeletal: *skeletal pain.*
Respiratory: dyspnea, cough.
Skin: *alopecia,* rash, cutaneous vasculitis.
Other: ***hypersensitivity reactions.***

Interactions

Drug-drug. *Chemotherapy drugs:* Rapidly dividing myeloid cells are sensitive to cytotoxic drugs. Don't use filgrastim within 24 hours before or after a chemotherapy dose.

Effects on lab test results

• May increase creatinine, uric acid, alkaline phosphatase, and LDH levels.
• May increase WBC count. May decrease platelet count.

Pharmacokinetics

Absorption: Rapid after S.C. administration.
Distribution: Unknown.
Metabolism: Unknown.
Excretion: Unknown. *Half-life:* About 3½ hours.

Route	Onset	Peak	Duration
I.V.	5-60 min	24 hr	1-7 days
S.C.	5-60 min	2-8 hr	1-7 days

Pharmacodynamics

Chemical effect: Glycoprotein that stimulates proliferation and differentiation of hematopoietic cells. Drug is specific for neutrophils.
Therapeutic effect: Raises WBC levels.

Available forms

Injection: 300 mcg/ml

NURSING PROCESS

Assessment

• Assess patient's underlying condition before therapy.
• Obtain baseline CBC and platelet counts before therapy.
• Evaluate CBC and platelet count during therapy.
• Be alert for adverse reactions and drug interactions.
• Ask patient about skeletal pain.
• Evaluate patient's and family's knowledge of drug therapy.

Nursing diagnoses

• Ineffective protection related to underlying condition or treatment
• Acute pain related to adverse drug effects on skeletal muscle
• Deficient knowledge related to drug therapy

Planning and implementation

• **I.V. use:** Dilute in 50 to 100 ml of D_5W, and give by intermittent infusion over 15 to 60 minutes or continuous infusion over 24 hours. If final concentration will be 2 to 15 mcg/ml, add albumin at 2 mg/ml (0.2%) to minimize binding of drug to plastic containers or tubing.
• **S.C. use:** Follow normal protocol.
• Don't give drug within 24 hours of cytotoxic chemotherapy.
• Once dose is withdrawn, don't reenter vial. Discard unused portion. Vials are for single-dose use and contain no preservatives.

• Give daily for up to 2 weeks or until ANC has returned to 10,000/mm³ after expected chemotherapy-induced neutrophil nadir.
• Refrigerate drug at 36° to 46° F (2° to 8° C). Don't freeze; avoid shaking. Store at room temperature for maximum of 6 hours; discard after 6 hours.

Patient teaching
• Teach patient how to give drug and how to dispose of used needles, syringes, drug containers, and unused drug.
• Tell patient to report bruising or spontaneous bleeding, such as frequent nosebleeds.
• Teach patient how to manage skeletal pain.

Evaluation
• Patient's WBC count is normal.
• Patient reports skeletal pain is bearable or relieved with analgesic administration and comfort measures.
• Patient and family state understanding of drug therapy.

finasteride
(fin-ES-teh-righd)
Proscar, Propecia

Pharmacologic class: steroid (synthetic 4-azasteroid) derivative
Therapeutic class: androgen synthesis inhibitor
Pregnancy risk category: X

Indications and dosages

▶ **Symptomatic BPH (*Proscar*); reduction of risk for acute urinary retention and need for surgery, including prostatectomy and transurethral resection of prostate, adjuvant therapy after radical prostatectomy‡, first-stage prostate cancer‡, acne‡, or hirsutism‡.** *Adults:* 5 mg P.O. daily
▶ **Male pattern baldness (*Propecia*).** *Adult men only:* 1 mg P.O. daily.

Contraindications and precautions

• Contraindicated in patients hypersensitive to drug or to other 5-alpha-reductase inhibitors, such as dutasteride. Use cautiously in patients with liver dysfuncion.

Lifespan: In women and children, drug is contraindicated.

Adverse reactions

GU: impotence, decreased volume of ejaculate.
Other: decreased libido.

Interactions

None significant.

Effects on lab test results

• May decrease PSA level.

Pharmacokinetics

Absorption: Not clearly defined, although average bioavailability was 63% in one study.
Distribution: About 90% bound to plasma proteins; crosses blood-brain barrier.
Metabolism: Extensively metabolized by liver.
Excretion: 39% of dose is excreted in urine as metabolites; 57% in feces.

Route	Onset	Peak	Duration
P.O.	Unknown	1-2 hr	About 2 wk

Pharmacodynamics

Chemical effect: Competitively inhibits steroid 5-reductase, an enzyme responsible for formation of potent androgen 5-dihydrotestosterone (DHT) from testosterone. Because DHT influences development of prostate gland, decreasing levels of this hormone in adult men should relieve symptoms of BPH. In men with male pattern baldness, the balding scalp contains miniaturized hair follicles and increased amounts of DHT. Finasteride decreases scalp and serum DHT concentrations in these men.
Therapeutic effect: Relieves symptoms of BPH, reduces hair loss, and promotes hair growth.

Available forms

Tablets: 1 mg, 5 mg

NURSING PROCESS

Assessment
• Before therapy, assess patient's BPH, and evaluate him for conditions that could mimic BPH, including hypotonic bladder; prostate cancer, infection, or stricture; or relevant neurologic conditions. Carefully monitor patients

with large residual urine volume or severely diminished urine flow. These patients may not be candidates for finasteride therapy.
• Evaluate patient for improvement in BPH symptoms.
• Anticipate periodic digital rectal examinations.
• Be alert for adverse reactions and drug interactions.
• Carefully evaluate sustained increases in serum prostate-specific antigen levels, which could indicate noncompliance.
• Evaluate patient's and family's knowledge of drug therapy.

Nursing diagnoses

• Impaired urinary elimination related to BPH
• Ineffective sexuality patterns related to drug-induced impotence
• Deficient knowledge related to drug therapy

Planning and implementation

• Because it's impossible to identify which patients will respond to therapy, keep in mind that a minimum of 6 months of therapy may be necessary.

Patient teaching

• Warn woman who is or may become pregnant not to handle crushed or broken tablets because of risk of adverse effects on male fetus.
• Caution man whose sexual partner is or may become pregnant to stop drug or to take precautions to avoid exposing her to his semen.
• Reassure patient that although drug may decrease volume of ejaculate, it doesn't appear to impair normal sexual function. Impotence and decreased libido have occurred in less than 4% of patients.
• Tell patient taking drug for male pattern baldness that he may not notice any effects for 3 months or more.

Evaluation

• Patient's BPH symptoms diminish.
• Patient states appropriate ways to manage sexual dysfunction.
• Patient and family state understanding of drug therapy.

flecainide acetate

(FLEH-kay-nighd AS-ih-tayt)
Tambocor

Pharmacologic class: benzamide derivative
Therapeutic class: antiarrhythmic
Pregnancy risk category: C

Indications and dosages

▶ **Paroxysmal supraventricular tachycardia; paroxysmal atrial fibrillation or flutter in patients without structural heart disease; life-threatening ventricular arrhythmias, such as sustained ventricular tachycardia.** *Adults:* For paroxysmal supraventricular tachycardia, 50 mg P.O. q 12 hours. Increase in increments of 50 mg b.i.d. q 4 days until efficacy is achieved. Maximum, 300 mg daily. For life-threatening ventricular arrhythmias, 100 mg P.O. q 12 hours. Increase in increments of 50 mg b.i.d. q 4 days until efficacy is achieved. Maximum, 400 mg daily for most patients. Initial dosage for patients with renal failure is 50 mg P.O. q 12 hours. Where available, flecainide may be given to adults by I.V. injection: 2 mg/kg I.V. push over at least 10 minutes; or dilute dose and give as infusion.
Patients with renal impairment: If creatinine clearance is 35 ml/minute or less, initial dose is 100 mg once daily or 50 mg b.i.d.

Contraindications and precautions

• Contraindicated in patients hypersensitive to drug and in those with cardiogenic shock or second- or third-degree AV block or right bundle branch block related to left hemiblock (in absence of artificial pacemaker).
• Use cautiously in patients with heart failure, cardiomyopathy, severe renal or hepatic disease, prolonged QT interval, sick sinus syndrome, or blood dyscrasia.
Lifespan: In pregnant women, use cautiously. Breast-feeding isn't recommended during drug use. In children, safety of drug hasn't been established.

Adverse reactions

CNS: *dizziness, headache,* fatigue, tremor, anxiety, insomnia, depression, malaise, paresthesia, ataxia, vertigo, *light-headedness, syncope,* asthenia, fever.

CV: edema, ***new or worsened arrhythmias,*** chest pain, ***heart failure, cardiac arrest,*** palpitations, flushing.
EENT: *blurred vision and other visual disturbances.*
GI: nausea, constipation, abdominal pain, dyspepsia, vomiting, diarrhea, anorexia.
Respiratory: *dyspnea.*
Skin: rash.

Interactions

Drug-drug. *Amiodarone, cimetidine:* May alter pharmacokinetics. Watch for toxicity.
Digoxin: May increase plasma digoxin level by 15% to 25%. Monitor digoxin level; watch for toxicity.
Disopyramide, verapamil: Negative inotropic properties may be additive with flecainide. Avoid giving together.
Propranolol, other beta blockers: Both flecainide and propranolol plasma levels increase by 20% to 30%. Monitor patient for propranolol and flecainide toxicity.
Urine acidifying and alkalinizing agents: Extremes of urine pH may substantially alter excretion of flecainide. Monitor patient for flecainide toxicity or decreased effectiveness.
Drug-lifestyle. *Smoking:* May lower drug level. Discourage smoking.

Effects on lab test results

None reported.

Pharmacokinetics

Absorption: Rapidly and almost completely absorbed from GI tract; bioavailability is 85% to 90%.
Distribution: Thought to be well distributed throughout body. Only about 40% binds to plasma proteins.
Metabolism: Metabolized in liver to inactive metabolites. About 30% of oral dose escapes metabolism.
Excretion: Excreted in urine. *Half-life:* About 20 hours.

Route	Onset	Peak	Duration
P.O.	Unknown	2-3 hr	Unknown
I.V.	Immediate	Immediate	Unknown

Pharmacodynamics

Chemical effect: Decreases excitability, conduction velocity, and automaticity as result of slowed atrial, AV node, His-Purkinje system, and intraventricular conduction and causes slight but significant prolongation of refractory periods in these tissues.
Therapeutic effect: Restores normal sinus rhythm.

Available forms

Injection: 10 mg/ml ◇
Tablets: 50 mg, 100 mg, 150 mg

NURSING PROCESS

Assessment

- Assess patient's arrhythmia before therapy.
- Monitor effectiveness by continuous ECG monitoring initially; long-term oral administration requires regular ECG readings.
- Monitor flecainide level, especially in patient with renal failure or heart failure. Therapeutic levels range from 0.2 to 1 mcg/ml. Risk of adverse effects increases when trough blood levels exceed 1 mcg/ml.
- Monitor potassium level regularly.
- Be alert for adverse reactions and drug interactions.
- Evaluate patient's and family's knowledge of drug therapy.

Nursing diagnoses

- Decreased cardiac output related to underlying arrhythmia
- Ineffective protection related to drug-induced new arrhythmias
- Deficient knowledge related to drug therapy

Planning and implementation

- When used to prevent ventricular arrhythmias, flecainide should be reserved for patient with documented life-threatening arrhythmias.
- If patient has pacemaker, check that pacing threshold was determined 1 week before and after starting therapy because flecainide can alter endocardial pacing thresholds.
- Correct hypokalemia or hyperkalemia before giving flecainide because these electrolyte disturbances may alter flecainide effect.
- **P.O. use:** Follow normal protocol.
- **I.V. use:** When giving by I.V. push, give over at least 10 minutes. For I.V. infusion, mix only with D_5W.

ALERT: Dosage adjustments should be made only once every 3 to 4 days.

• Twice-daily dosing for flecainide enhances patient compliance.
• Because of drug's long half-life, its full effect may take 3 to 5 days. Give I.V. lidocaine with drug for first several days.
• Keep emergency equipment nearby when giving drug.
• If ECG disturbances occur, withhold drug, obtain rhythm strip, and notify prescriber immediately.

Patient teaching
• Stress importance of taking oral drug exactly as prescribed.
• Warn patient to avoid hazardous activities that require alertness or good vision if adverse CNS or visual reactions occur.
• Tell patient to limit fluid and sodium intake to minimize heart failure or fluid retention and to weigh himself daily. Urge him to report promptly sudden weight gain.

✓ Evaluation
• Patient regains normal cardiac output with abolishment of underlying arrhythmia after drug therapy.
• Patient doesn't develop new arrhythmias.
• Patient and family state understanding of drug therapy.

fluconazole
(floo-KON-uh-zohl)
Diflucan

Pharmacologic class: bis-triazole derivative
Therapeutic class: antifungal
Pregnancy risk category: C

Indications and dosages

▶ **Oropharyngeal and esophageal candidiasis.** *Adults:* 200 mg P.O. or I.V. on first day, followed by 100 mg once daily. Higher doses (up to 400 mg daily) have been used for esophageal disease. Treatment should continue for 2 weeks after symptoms resolve.
Children: 6 mg/kg P.O. or I.V. on first day, followed by 3 mg/kg once daily for at least 2 weeks.
▶ **Vulvovaginal candidiasis.** *Adults:* 150 mg P.O. as a single dose.
▶ **Systemic candidiasis.** *Adults:* 400 mg P.O. or I.V. on first day, followed by 200 mg once daily. Treatment should continue at least 4 weeks or for 2 weeks after symptoms resolve.
Children: 6 to 12 mg/kg P.O. or I.V. daily.
▶ **Cryptococcal meningitis.** *Adults:* 400 mg P.O. or I.V. on first day, followed by 200 mg once daily. Higher doses (up to 400 mg daily) may be used. Treatment should continue for 10 to 12 weeks after CSF cultures are negative.
Children: 12 mg/kg P.O. or I.V. on first day, followed by 6 mg/kg P.O. or I.V. daily for 10 to 12 weeks after CSF culture becomes negative.
▶ **Prevention of candidiasis in bone marrow transplant.** *Adults:* 400 mg. P.O. or I.V. once daily. Start prophylaxis several days before anticipated granulocytopenia. Continue therapy for 7 days after neutrophil count rises above 1,000 cells/mm^3.
▶ **Suppression of relapse of cryptococcal meningitis in patients with AIDS.** *Adults:* 200 mg P.O. or I.V. daily.
Children: 3 to 6 mg/kg P.O. daily.
Patients with renal impairment: If creatinine clearance is below 50 ml/minute, reduce dose by 50% in patients not receiving dialysis. Patients receiving hemodialysis should receive 100% of usual dose after each session.
▶ **Candidal infection, long-term suppression in patients with HIV infection‡.** *Adults:* 100 to 200 mg P.O. or I.V. daily.
▶ **Prophylaxis against mucocutaneous candidiasis, cryptococcosi, coccidioidmycosis, or histoplasmosis in patients with HIV infection‡.** *Adults:* 200 to 400 mg P.O. or I.V. daily.
Children and infants: 2 to 8 mg/kg P.O. daily.
Patients with renal impairment: If creatinine clearance is 21 to 49 ml/minute, give 50% of usual adult dose. If creatinine clearance is 11 to 20 ml/minute, give 25% of usual adult dose. For patients on hemodialysis, give one full dose after each session.

Contraindications and precautions

• Contraindicated in patients hypersensitive to drug.
• Although no information exists regarding cross-sensitivity, use cautiously in patients hypersensitive to other antifungal azole compounds.
Lifespan: In pregnant women, use cautiously. In breast-feeding women, drug isn't recommended.

Adverse reactions

CNS: headache.
GI: *nausea,* vomiting, abdominal pain, diarrhea.
Hepatic: ***hepatotoxicity.***
Skin: rash, ***Stevens-Johnson syndrome.***
Other: ***anaphylaxis.***

Interactions

Drug-drug. *Cyclosporine, tacrolimus, phenytoin:* May increase plasma levels of these drugs. Monitor serum cyclosporine or phenytoin levels.
Amitriptyline: Increases amitriptyline levels. Avoid combination, if possible.
Carbamazepine: Increases carbamazepine levels. Monitor levels closely.
Isoniazid, phenytoin, rifampin, valproic acid, oral sulfonylureas: May increase risk of elevated hepatic transaminases. Monitor patient and serum levels closely.
Oral antidiabetics (tolbutamide, glyburide, glipizide): May increase plasma levels of these drugs. Monitor patient for enhanced hypoglycemic effect.
Rifampin: Enhances fluconazole metabolism. Monitor patient for lack of response.
Theophylline: Decreases theophylline clearance. Monitor serum levels.
Warfarin: May increase risk of bleeding. Monitor PT and INR.
Zidovudine: Zidovudine activity may be increased. Monitor patient closely.
Drug-lifestyle. *Alcohol use:* May increase risk of hepatotoxicity. Discourage using together.

Effects on lab test results

- May increase alkaline phosphatase, ALT, AST, bilirubin, and GGT levels.
- May decrease WBC and platelet counts.

Pharmacokinetics

Absorption: Rapid and complete after P.O. administration.
Distribution: Well distributed to various sites, including CNS, saliva, sputum, blister fluid, urine, normal skin, nails, and blister skin. Drug is 12% protein-bound.
Metabolism: Partially metabolized.
Excretion: Primarily excreted by kidneys; over 80% excreted unchanged in urine.

Route	Onset	Peak	Duration
P.O.	Unknown	1-2 hr	Unknown
I.V.	Immediate	Immediate	Unknown

Pharmacodynamics

Chemical effect: Inhibits fungal cytochrome P450, an enzyme responsible for fungal sterol synthesis, and weakens fungal cell walls.
Therapeutic effect: Hinders fungal growth, including *Cryptococcus neoformans, Candida sp.* (including systemic *C. albicans*), *Aspergillus flavus, A. fumigatus, Coccidioides immitis,* and *Histoplasma capsulatum.*

Available forms

Injection: 200 mg/100 ml, 400 mg/200 ml
Powder for oral suspension: 10 mg/ml, 40 mg/ml
Tablets: 50 mg, 100 mg, 150 mg, 200 mg

NURSING PROCESS

Assessment

- Assess patient's fungal infection before therapy, and reassess regularly throughout therapy.
- Periodically monitor liver function during prolonged therapy. Although adverse hepatic effects are rare, they can be serious.
- Be alert for adverse reactions and drug interactions.
- Monitor patient's hydration status if adverse GI reactions occur.
- Evaluate patient's and family's knowledge of drug therapy.

Nursing diagnoses

- Infection related to presence of susceptible fungi
- Risk for deficient fluid volume related to adverse GI reactions
- Deficient knowledge related to drug therapy

Planning and implementation

- **P.O. use:** Follow normal protocol.
- **I.V. use:** Don't remove protective overwrap from I.V. bags of fluconazole until just before use to ensure product sterility. Plastic container may show some opacity from moisture absorbed during sterilization. This is normal, won't affect drug, and will diminish over time.
– Give by continuous infusion at no more than 200 mg/hour. Use infusion pump. To prevent air embolism, don't connect in series with other infusions. Don't add any other drugs to solution.

• If patient develops mild rash, monitor him closely. Discontinue drug if lesions progress, and notify prescriber.

Patient teaching
• Urge patient to adhere to regimen and to return for follow-up.
• Tell patient to report adverse reactions to prescriber.

✓ Evaluation
• Patient is free from infection.
• Patient maintains adequate hydration.
• Patient and family state understanding of drug therapy.

flucytosine (5-fluorocytosine, 5-FC)
(floo-SIGH-toh-seen)
Ancobon, Ancotil ◇

Pharmacologic class: fluorinated pyrimidine
Therapeutic class: antifungal
Pregnancy risk category: C

Indications and dosages
▶ **Severe fungal infections caused by susceptible strains of *Candida* (including septicemia, endocarditis, urinary tract and pulmonary infections) and *Cryptococcus* (meningitis, pulmonary infection, and possible urinary tract infections).** *Adults:* 50 to 150 mg/kg P.O. daily in divided doses given q 6 hours.

▶ **Chromomycosis‡.** *Adults:* 150 mg/kg P.O. daily.

Contraindications and precautions
• Contraindicated in patients hypersensitive to drug.
• Use with extreme caution in those with impaired hepatic or renal function or bone marrow suppression.
Lifespan: In pregnant women, use cautiously. In breast-feeding women, a decision should be made to discontinue breast-feeding or the drug. In children, safety hasn't been established.

Adverse reactions
CNS: dizziness, confusion, headache, vertigo, sedation, fatigue, weakness, hallucinations, psychosis, ataxia, paresthesia, parkinsonism, peripheral neuropathy.
CV: chest pain, ***cardiac arrest.***
EENT: hearing loss.
GI: nausea, vomiting, diarrhea, abdominal pain, dry mouth, duodenal ulcer, ***hemorrhage,*** ulcerative colitis.
GU: azotemia, crystalluria, ***renal failure.***
Hematologic: anemia, eosinophilia, ***leukopenia, bone marrow suppression, thrombocytopenia, agranulocytosis, aplastic anemia.***
Hepatic: jaundice.
Metabolic: ***hypoglycemia,*** hypokalemia.
Respiratory: ***respiratory arrest,*** dyspnea.
Skin: occasional rash, pruritus, urticaria, photosensitivity.

Interactions
Drug-drug. *Amphotericin B:* May have synergistic effects and enhance toxicity when used together. Monitor patient.

Effects on lab test results
• May increase urine urea, alkaline phosphatase, ALT, AST, bilirubin, creatinine, and BUN levels. May decrease glucose and potassium levels.
• May increase eosinophil count. May decrease hemoglobin, hematocrit, and WBC, platelet, and granulocyte counts.

Pharmacokinetics
Absorption: From 75% to 90% of dose is absorbed; food decreases absorption rate.
Distribution: Distributed widely into liver, kidneys, spleen, heart, bronchial secretions, joints, peritoneal fluid, and aqueous humor. CSF levels vary from 60% to 100% of serum levels. Drug is 2% to 4% bound to plasma proteins.
Metabolism: Only small amounts of drug are metabolized.
Excretion: About 75% to 95% excreted unchanged in urine; less than 10% excreted unchanged in feces. *Half-life:* 2½ to 6 hours.

Route	Onset	Peak	Duration
P.O.	Unknown	1-2 hr	Unknown

Pharmacodynamics

Chemical effect: Unknown; appears to penetrate fungal cells, where it's converted to fluorouracil—a known metabolic antagonist—and causes defective protein synthesis.
Therapeutic effect: Hinders fungal growth, including some strains of *Cryptococcus* and *Candida.*

Available forms

Capsules: 250 mg, 500 mg

NURSING PROCESS

Assessment
- Assess patient's fungal infection before therapy, and reassess regularly throughout therapy.
- Before therapy, obtain hematologic tests and renal and liver function studies. Make sure susceptibility tests showing that organism is flucytosine-sensitive are on chart.
- Monitor blood, liver, and renal function studies frequently; obtain susceptibility tests weekly to monitor drug resistance.
- If possible, regularly perform blood level assays of drug to maintain flucytosine at therapeutic level (25 to 120 mcg/ml). Higher blood levels may be toxic.
- Be alert for adverse reactions and drug interactions.
- Monitor patient's hydration status if adverse GI reactions occur.
- Evaluate patient's and family's knowledge of drug therapy.

Nursing diagnoses
- Infection related to presence of susceptible fungi
- Risk for deficient fluid volume related to adverse GI reactions
- Deficient knowledge related to drug therapy

Planning and implementation
- Give capsules over 15 minutes to reduce adverse GI reactions.

Patient teaching
- Inform patient that therapeutic response may take weeks or months.
- Tell patient how to take capsules.
- Warn patient to avoid hazardous activities requiring mental alertness if adverse CNS reactions occur.

Evaluation
- Patient is free from infection.
- Patient maintains adequate hydration throughout drug therapy.
- Patient and family state understanding of drug therapy.

fludarabine phosphate
(floo-DAR-uh-been FOS-fayt)
Fludara

Pharmacologic class: antimetabolite, purine antagonist
Therapeutic class: antineoplastic
Pregnancy risk category: D

Indications and dosages

▶ **B-cell chronic lymphocytic leukemia in patients who either haven't responded or have responded inadequately to at least one standard alkylating agent regimen, mycosis fungoides‡, hairy cell leukemia‡, and Hodgkin's and malignant lymphoma‡.** *Adults:* 25 mg/m² I.V. over 30 minutes for 5 consecutive days. Cycle repeated q 28 days.
Patients with renal impairment: If creatinine clearance is 30 to 70 ml/minute, decrease dose by 20%. Drug isn't recommended for patients with creatinine clearance of less than 30 ml/minute.
▶ **Chronic lymphocytic leukemia‡.** *Adults:* Usually, 18 to 30 mg/m² I.V. over 30 minutes for 5 consecutive days q 28 days. Therapy is based upon patient's response and tolerance.

Contraindications and precautions

- Contraindicated in patients hypersensitive to drug or its components.
- Use cautiously in patients with renal insufficiency.

Lifespan: In pregnant women, use with extreme caution and only when necessary. In breast-feeding women and children, safety of drug hasn't been established.

Adverse reactions

CNS: *fever,* diaphoresis, *fatigue, malaise, weakness, paresthesia,* headache, peripheral neuropathy, sleep disorder, depression, pain, cerebellar syndrome, ***CVA,*** transient ischemic attack, agitation, *confusion,* ***coma.***

CV: *edema,* angina, phlebitis, ***arrhythmias, heart failure, MI,*** supraventricular tachycardia, deep venous thrombosis, ***aneurysm, hemorrhage.***
EENT: *visual disturbances,* hearing loss, delayed blindness (with high doses), sinusitis, pharyngitis, epistaxis.
GI: *nausea, vomiting, diarrhea,* constipation, *anorexia,* stomatitis, **GI BLEEDING,** esophagitis, mucositis.
GU: dysuria, *urinary infection,* urinary hesitancy, proteinuria, hematuria, ***renal failure.***
Hematologic: *anemia,* **MYELOSUPPRESSION, NEUTROPENIA, THROMBOCYTOPENIA.**
Hepatic: ***liver failure,*** cholelithiasis.
Metabolic: hyperglycemia, dehydration, hyperuricemia, hyperphosphatemia.
Musculoskeletal: myalgia.
Respiratory: *cough, pneumonia, dyspnea, upper respiratory infection,* allergic pneumonitis, hemoptysis, hypoxia, bronchitis.
Skin: alopecia, *rash,* pruritus, seborrhea.
Other: *chills,* **INFECTION,** ***tumor lysis syndrome, anaphylaxis.***

Interactions

Drug-drug. *Other myelosuppressants:* May increase toxicity. Avoid using together.
Pentostatin: Increases risk of pulmonary toxicity. Avoid using together.

Effects on lab test results

- May increase glucose, phosphate, potassium, and uric acid levels.
- May decrease hemoglobin, hematocrit, and platelet and neutrophil counts.

Pharmacokinetics

Absorption: Administered I.V.
Distribution: Unknown.
Metabolism: Rapidly dephosphorylated and then phosphorylated intracellularly to its active metabolite.
Excretion: 23% is excreted in urine as unchanged active metabolite. *Half-life:* About 10 hours.

Route	Onset	Peak	Duration
I.V.	7-21 hr	Unknown	Unknown

Pharmacodynamics

Chemical effect: Unknown; actions may be multifaceted. After conversion to its active metabolite, fludarabine interferes with DNA synthesis by inhibiting DNA polymerase alpha, ribonucleotide reductase, and DNA primase.
Therapeutic effect: Kills susceptible cancer cells.

Available forms

Powder for injection: 50 mg

NURSING PROCESS

Assessment

- Assess patient's underlying condition before therapy, and reassess regularly thereafter.
- Careful hematologic monitoring is needed, especially of neutrophil and platelet counts. Bone marrow suppression can be severe.
- Be alert for adverse reactions and drug interactions.
- Evaluate patient's and family's knowledge of drug therapy.

Nursing diagnoses

- Ineffective health maintenance related to presence of leukemia
- Ineffective protection related to drug-induced immunosuppression
- Deficient knowledge related to drug therapy

Planning and implementation

- Follow facility policy to reduce risks. Preparation and administration of parenteral form create mutagenic, teratogenic, and carcinogenic risks for staff.
- To prepare solution, add 2 ml of sterile water for injection to solid cake of drug. Dissolution should occur within 15 seconds; each ml will contain 25 mg of drug. Dilute further in 100 or 125 ml of D_5W or normal saline injection. Use within 8 hours of reconstitution.
- Optimal duration of therapy isn't known. Current recommendations suggest three additional cycles after achieving maximal response.
- Store drug in refrigerator at 36° to 46° F (2° to 8° C).

Patient teaching

- Warn patient to watch for evidence of infection and bleeding.
- Tell patient to notify prescriber if adverse reactions occur.

Evaluation
- Patient shows positive response to fludarabine therapy.
- Patient develops no serious infections or bleeding complications.
- Patient and family state understanding of drug therapy.

fludrocortisone acetate
(floo-droh-KOR-tuh-sohn AS-ih-tayt)
Florinef

Pharmacologic class: mineralocorticoid, glucocorticoid
Therapeutic class: mineralocorticoid replacement therapy
Pregnancy risk category: C

Indications and dosages
▶ **Adrenal insufficiency (partial replacement), adrenogenital syndrome.** *Adults:* 0.1 to 0.2 mg P.O. daily.
▶ **Orthostatic hypotension‡.** *Adults:* 0.1 to 0.4 mg P.O. daily.

Contraindications and precautions
- Contraindicated in patients hypersensitive to drug and in those with systemic fungal infections.
- Use cautiously in patients with hypothyroidism, cirrhosis, ocular herpes simplex, emotional instability and psychotic tendencies, nonspecific ulcerative colitis, diverticulitis, fresh intestinal anastomoses, active or latent peptic ulcer, renal insufficiency, hypertension, osteoporosis, and myasthenia gravis.

Lifespan: In children, long-term use may delay growth and maturation.

Adverse reactions
CV: *sodium and water retention,* hypertension, cardiac hypertrophy, edema, ***heart failure.***
Metabolic: hypokalemia.
Skin: bruising, diaphoresis, urticaria, allergic rash.

Interactions
Drug-drug. *Barbiturates, phenytoin, rifampin:* Increases clearance of fludrocortisone acetate. Monitor patient for effect.
Potassium-depleting drugs (such as thiazide diuretics): Enhances potassium-wasting effects of fludrocortisone. Monitor serum potassium levels.
Drug-food. *Sodium-containing drugs or foods:* May increase blood pressure. Sodium intake may need to be adjusted.

Effects on lab test results
- May decrease potassium level.

Pharmacokinetics
Absorption: Absorbed readily from GI tract.
Distribution: Distributed to muscle, liver, skin, intestines, and kidneys. It's extensively bound to plasma proteins. Only unbound portion is active.
Metabolism: Metabolized in liver to inactive metabolites.
Excretion: Excreted in urine; insignificant quantities are excreted in feces. *Half-life:* 18 to 36 hours.

Route	Onset	Peak	Duration
P.O.	Varies	Varies	1-2 days

Pharmacodynamics
Chemical effect: Increases sodium reabsorption and potassium and hydrogen secretion at distal convoluted tubule of nephron.
Therapeutic effect: Increases sodium levels and decreases potassium and hydrogen levels.

Available forms
Tablets: 0.1 mg

NURSING PROCESS

Assessment
- Assess patient's underlying condition before therapy, and reassess regularly thereafter.
- Monitor patient's blood pressure, weight, and electrolyte levels.
- Be alert for adverse reactions and drug interactions.
- Evaluate patient's and family's knowledge of drug therapy.

Nursing diagnoses
- Ineffective health maintenance related to underlying adrenal condition
- Excessive fluid volume related to drug-induced adverse reactions
- Deficient knowledge related to drug therapy

Planning and implementation
- Drug is used with cortisone or hydrocortisone in patients with adrenal insufficiency.
- If hypertension occurs, notify prescriber, who may lower dosage by 50%.
- Potassium supplements may be needed.

Patient teaching
- Tell patient to notify prescriber about worsened symptoms, such as hypotension, weakness, cramping, and palpitations.
- Warn patient that mild peripheral edema is common.

Evaluation
- Patient's health is improved.
- Patient develops no sodium and water retention.
- Patient and family state understanding of drug therapy.

flumazenil
(floo-MAZ-ih-nil)
Romazicon

Pharmacologic class: benzodiazepine antagonist
Therapeutic class: antidote
Pregnancy risk category: C

Indications and dosages
▶ **Complete or partial reversal of sedative effects of benzodiazepines after anesthesia or short diagnostic procedures (conscious sedation).** *Adults:* Initially, 0.2 mg I.V. over 15 seconds. If patient doesn't reach desired level of consciousness after 45 seconds, dose is repeated. Repeat at 1-minute intervals until cumulative dose of 1 mg has been given (initial dose plus four more doses), if needed. Most patients respond after 0.6 to 1 mg of drug. In case of resedation, dose may be repeated after 20 minutes; however, no more than 1 mg should be given at any one time and no more than 3 mg/hour.

▶ **Suspected benzodiazepine overdose.** *Adults:* Initially, 0.2 mg I.V. over 15 seconds. If patient doesn't reach desired level of consciousness after 30 seconds, 0.3 mg is given over 30 seconds. If patient still doesn't respond adequately, 0.5 mg is given over 30 seconds; 0.5-mg doses are repeated as needed at 1-minute intervals until cumulative dose of 3 mg has been given. Most patients with benzodiazepine overdose respond to cumulative doses between 1 and 3 mg; rarely, patients who respond partially after 3 mg may need additional doses. No more than 5 mg over 5 minutes should be given initially. Sedation that persists after this dosage is unlikely to be caused by benzodiazepines. In case of resedation, dose may be repeated after 20 minutes; however, no more than 1 mg should be given at any one time and no more than 3 mg/hour.

Contraindications and precautions
- Contraindicated in patients hypersensitive to drug or benzodiazepines; in patients who show evidence of serious cyclic antidepressant overdose; and in those who received benzodiazepine to treat potentially life-threatening condition (such as status epilepticus).
- Use cautiously in patients at high risk for developing seizures; in patients who recently have received multiple doses of parenteral benzodiazepine; in patients displaying signs of seizure activity; in patients who may be at risk for unrecognized benzodiazepine dependence, such as ICU patients; and in patients with head injury, psychiatric, or alcohol-dependent problems.

Lifespan: In pregnant or breast-feeding women, use cautiously. In children, safety of drug hasn't been established.

Adverse reactions
CNS: *dizziness, headache,* ***seizures,*** agitation, emotional lability, tremor, insomnia.
CV: ***arrhythmias,*** cutaneous vasodilation, palpitations.
EENT: *abnormal or blurred vision.*
GI: *nausea, vomiting.*
Respiratory: dyspnea, hyperventilation.
Skin: *diaphoresis.*
Other: *pain at injection site.*

Interactions
Drug-drug. *Antidepressants, drugs that can cause seizures or arrhythmias:* Seizures or arrhythmias can develop after effect of benzodiazepine overdose is removed. Use with caution, if at all, in cases of mixed overdose.

Effects on lab test results

None reported.

Pharmacokinetics

Absorption: Administered I.V.
Distribution: Redistributes rapidly; 50% bound to plasma proteins.
Metabolism: Metabolized by liver. Ingestion of food during I.V. infusion enhances extraction of drug from plasma, probably by increasing hepatic blood flow.
Excretion: About 90% to 95% appears in urine as metabolites; remainder excreted in feces. *Half-life:* About 54 minutes.

Route	Onset	Peak	Duration
I.V.	Unknown	Unknown	Unknown

Pharmacodynamics

Chemical effect: Competitively inhibits actions of benzodiazepines on GABA–benzodiazepine receptor complex.
Therapeutic effect: Awakens patient from sedative effects of benzodiazepines.

Available forms

Injection: 0.1 mg/ml in 5- and 10-ml multiple-dose vials

NURSING PROCESS

Assessment

- Assess patient's sedation before therapy.
- Assess patient's level of consciousness frequently.
- Be alert for adverse reactions and drug interactions.

ALERT: Monitor patient closely for resedation that may occur after reversal of benzodiazepine effects; flumazenil's duration of action is shorter than that of all benzodiazepines. Monitor patient closely after long-acting benzodiazepines, such as diazepam, or high doses of short-acting benzodiazepines, such as 10 mg of midazolam. In most cases, severe resedation is unlikely in patient who fails to show signs of resedation 2 hours after 1-mg dose of flumazenil.

- Monitor patient's ECG for evidence of arrhythmias.
- Evaluate patient's and family's knowledge of drug therapy.

Nursing diagnoses

- Ineffective protection related to sedated state
- Decreased cardiac output related to drug-induced seizures
- Deficient knowledge related to drug therapy

Planning and implementation

- Give drug by direct injection, or dilute with compatible solution. Discard within 24 hours any unused drug that has been drawn into syringe or diluted.
- Give drug into I.V. line in large vein with free-flowing I.V. solution to minimize pain at injection site. Compatible solutions include D_5W, lactated Ringer's injection, and normal saline solution.
- Notify prescriber if arrhythmias or other adverse reactions occur, and be prepared to treat accordingly.

Patient teaching

- Warn patient to avoid hazardous activities within 24 hours of procedure.
- Tell patient to avoid alcohol, CNS depressants, and OTC drugs for 24 hours.
- Give family members important instructions, or provide patient with written instructions.

Evaluation

- Patient is awake and alert.
- Patient maintains adequate cardiac output.
- Patient and family state understanding of drug therapy.

flunisolide

(floo-NIH-soh-lighd)

AeroBid, AeroBid-M, Bronalide ◆ (oral inhalant), Nasalide, Nasarel, Rhinalar Nasal Mist ◇ (nasal inhalant)

Pharmacologic class: glucocorticoid
Therapeutic class: anti-inflammatory, antiasthmatic
Pregnancy risk category: C

Indications and dosages

▶ **Steroid-dependent asthma.** ***Oral inhalant.*** *Adults and children age 6 and older:* 2 inhalations (500 mcg) b.i.d. Maximum, 4 inhalations b.i.d. (for adults) and 4 inhalations daily (for children).

▶ **Symptoms of seasonal or perennial rhinitis.** ***Nasal inhalant.*** *Adults:* Starting dose is 2 sprays (50 mcg) in each nostril b.i.d. Total, 200 mcg daily. If necessary, dosage may be increased to 2 sprays in each nostril t.i.d. Maximum, 8 sprays in each nostril (400 mcg) daily. *Children ages 6 to 14:* Starting dose is 1 spray (25 mcg) in each nostril t.i.d. or 2 sprays (50 mcg) in each nostril b.i.d. Total, 150 to 200 mcg daily. Maximum, 4 sprays in each nostril (200 mcg) daily.

Contraindications and precautions

- Contraindicated in patients hypersensitive to drug and in those with status asthmaticus or respiratory infection.
- Nasal inhalant shouldn't be used in presence of untreated localized infection involving nasal mucosa.
- Use nasal inhalant cautiously, if at all, in patients with active or quiescent respiratory tract tubercular infections or with untreated fungal, bacterial, or systemic viral or ocular herpes simplex infections. Also use cautiously in patients who recently have had nasal septal ulcers, nasal surgery, or nasal trauma.

Lifespan: In pregnant or breast-feeding women, use cautiously. In children younger than age 6, safety of drug hasn't been established.

Adverse reactions

CNS: headache, dizziness, irritability, nervousness, fever.
CV: chest pain, edema, palpitations.
EENT: dry mouth, watery eyes, throat irritation, hoarseness, nasopharyngeal fungal infections, *sore throat, nasal congestion, mild and transient nasal burning and stinging,* dryness, sneezing, epistaxis.
GI: *unpleasant taste, nausea, vomiting, upset stomach,* abdominal pain, decreased appetite, *diarrhea.*
Respiratory: *upper respiratory tract infection.*
Skin: pruritus, rash.
Other: *cold symptoms, flu.*

Interactions

None significant.

Effects on lab test results

None reported.

Pharmacokinetics

Absorption: About 50% of nasally inhaled dose is absorbed systemically. After oral inhalation, about 70% of dose is absorbed from lungs and GI tract. Only about 20% of orally inhaled dose reaches systemic circulation unmetabolized because of extensive metabolism in liver.
Distribution: Unknown after intranasal use. After oral inhalation, 10% to 25% of drug is distributed to lungs; remainder is deposited in mouth and swallowed. No evidence exists of tissue storage of drug or its metabolites. When absorbed, it's 50% bound to plasma proteins.
Metabolism: Drug that's swallowed undergoes rapid metabolism in liver or GI tract to variety of metabolites, one of which has glucocorticoid activity. Flunisolide and its active metabolite are eventually conjugated in liver to inactive metabolites.
Excretion: Unknown for inhalation routes.

Route	Onset	Peak	Duration
Nasal or oral inhalation	1-4 wk	Unknown	Unknown

Pharmacodynamics

Chemical effect: Unknown; may stabilize leukocyte lysosomal membranes.
Therapeutic effect: Relieves inflammation.

Available forms

Nasal inhalant: 25 mcg/metered spray, 200 doses/bottle ◇
Nasal solution: 0.25 mg/ml in pump spray bottle
Oral inhalant: 250 mcg/metered spray (at least 100 metered inhalations/container)

NURSING PROCESS

Assessment

- Assess patient's underlying condition before therapy, and reassess regularly thereafter.
- Be alert for adverse reactions and drug interactions.
- Evaluate patient's and family's knowledge of drug therapy.

Nursing diagnoses

- Ineffective health maintenance related to underlying condition

• Impaired tissue integrity related to adverse EENT reactions
• Deficient knowledge related to drug therapy

Planning and implementation
• **Nasal inhalation:** Drug isn't effective for acute exacerbations of rhinitis. Decongestants or antihistamines may be needed.
– To instill, shake container before using; have patient blow nose to clear nasal passages; have patient tilt head slightly forward. Insert nozzle into nostril, pointing away from septum. Hold other nostril closed, and then have patient inhale gently and spray. Next, shake container and repeat in other nostril. Clean nosepiece with warm water if it becomes clogged.
• **Oral inhalation:** Not recommended in patients with asthma controlled by bronchodilators or other noncorticosteroids alone, or in those with nonasthmatic bronchial diseases.
– Spacer device may help to ensure proper dosage administration.
• Store drug between 36° and 86° F (2° and 30° C).
• Withdraw drug slowly in patient who has received long-term oral corticosteroid therapy.
• After withdrawal of systemic corticosteroids, patient may need supplemental systemic steroids if he shows evidence of adrenal insufficiency when exposed to trauma, surgery, or infections.

Patient teaching
Nasal inhalation
• Explain that therapeutic effects of drug, unlike those of decongestants, aren't immediate. Most patients achieve benefit within a few days, but some need 2 to 3 weeks.
• Advise patient to use drug regularly, as prescribed, because its effectiveness depends on regular use.
• Teach patient how to instill drug.
• Warn patient not to exceed recommended dosage to avoid suppression of hypothalamic-pituitary-adrenal function.
Oral inhalation
• Warn patient that drug doesn't relieve acute asthma attacks.
• Advise patient to ensure delivery of proper dose by gently warming canister to room temperature before using. Some patients carry canister in pocket to keep it warm.
• Tell patient who also is using bronchodilator to use it several minutes before flunisolide.
• Instruct patient to allow 1 minute to elapse before repeating inhalations and to hold breath for few seconds to enhance drug action.
• Teach patient to keep inhaler clean and unobstructed by washing with warm water and drying thoroughly after use.
• Teach patient to check mucous membranes frequently for signs of fungal infection.
• Advise patient to prevent oral fungal infections by gargling or rinsing mouth with water after each inhaler use. Caution patient not to swallow the water.
• Tell patient to stop drug and notify prescriber if symptoms persist after 3 weeks.

Evaluation
• Patient's health improves.
• Patient maintains upper airway and buccal tissue integrity.
• Patient and family state understanding of drug therapy.

fluorouracil (5-fluorouracil, 5-FU)
(floo-roh-YOOR-uh-sil)
Adrucil, Efudex, Fluoroplex, Carac

Pharmacologic class: antimetabolite (cell cycle–phase specific, S phase)
Therapeutic class: antineoplastic
Pregnancy risk category: D

Indications and dosages
▶ **Colon, rectal, breast, stomach, and pancreatic cancers.** *Adults:* 12 mg/kg I.V. daily for 4 days; if no toxicity, give 6 mg/kg on 6th, 8th, 10th, and 12th day; then single weekly maintenance dose of 10 to 15 mg/kg I.V. begun after toxicity (if any) from initial course has subsided. Dosages recommended based on lean body weight. Maximum single recommended dose is 800 mg.
▶ **Palliative treatment of advanced colorectal cancer.** *Adults:* 425 mg/m^2 I.V. daily for 5 consecutive days. Give with 20 mg/m^2 of leucovorin I.V. Repeat at 4-week intervals for two additional courses; then repeat at intervals of 4 to 5 weeks, if tolerated.

▶ **Multiple actinic (solar) keratoses; superficial basal cell carcinoma.** *Adults:* Apply cream or topical solution b.i.d.

▶ **Topical treatment of multiple actinic or solar keratosis of the face and anterior scalp.** *Adults:* Apply a thin layer to the washed and dried affected area daily for up to 4 weeks.

Contraindications and precautions

- Contraindicated in patients hypersensitive to drug and in those with poor nutrition, bone marrow suppression (WBC counts of 5,000/mm^3 or less or platelet counts of 100,000/mm^3 or less), or potentially serious infections, and in those who have had major surgery within previous month.
- Use cautiously after high-dose pelvic radiation therapy and in patients who received alkylating agents, or have impaired hepatic or renal function or widespread neoplastic infiltration of bone marrow.

Lifespan: In pregnant and breast-feeding women, drug isn't recommended. In children, safety of drug hasn't been established.

Adverse reactions

CNS: acute cerebellar syndrome, ataxia, confusion, disorientation, euphoria, headache, nystagmus, *weakness, malaise.*
CV: thrombophlebitis, ***myocardial ischemia,*** angina.
EENT: epistaxis, photophobia, lacrimation, lacrimal duct stenosis, visual changes.
GI: *stomatitis, GI ulcer* (may precede leukopenia), *nausea and vomiting, diarrhea, anorexia,* GI bleeding.
Hematologic: ***leukopenia, thrombocytopenia, agranulocytosis,*** anemia; WBC count nadir 9 to 14 days after first dose; platelet count nadir in 7 to 14 days.
Skin: *reversible alopecia; dermatitis; erythema; scaling; pruritus;* contact dermatitis; nail changes; pigmented palmar creases; erythematous, desquamative rash of hands and feet with long-term use ("hand-foot syndrome"); photosensitivity; *pain, burning,* soreness, suppuration, and swelling with topical use.
Other: ***anaphylaxis.***

Interactions

Drug-drug. *Leucovorin calcium, previous treatment with alkylating agents:* Increases fluorouracil toxicity. Use with extreme caution.

Drug-lifestyle. *Sun exposure:* Photosensitivity reactions may occur. Urge patient to avoid unprotected or prolonged sun exposure.

Effects on lab test results

- May increase alkaline phosphatase, AST, ALT, bilirubin, and LDH levels. May increase 5-hydroxyindoleacetic acid level in urine.
- May decrease hemoglobin, hematocrit, and WBC, RBC, platelet, and granulocyte counts.

Pharmacokinetics

Absorption: Unknown for topical forms.
Distribution: Distributes widely into all areas of body water and tissues; crosses blood-brain barrier.
Metabolism: Small amount converted in tissues to active metabolite with majority of drug degraded in liver.
Excretion: Metabolites primarily excreted through lungs as carbon dioxide; small portion excreted in urine as unchanged drug.

Route	Onset	Peak	Duration
I.V., topical	Unknown	Unknown	Unknown

Pharmacodynamics

Chemical effect: Inhibits DNA synthesis.
Therapeutic effect: Inhibits cell growth of selected cancers.

Available forms

Cream: 1%, 5%
Injection: 50 mg/ml
Topical solution: 1%, 2%, 5%

NURSING PROCESS

Assessment

- Assess patient's condition before therapy, and reassess regularly thereafter.
- Monitor fluid intake and output, CBC, platelet count, and renal and hepatic function tests.
- Be alert for adverse reactions and drug interactions.
- Fluorouracil toxicity may be delayed for 1 to 3 weeks.
- Monitor patient receiving topical form for serious adverse reactions. Ingestion and systemic absorption may cause leukopenia, thrombocytopenia, stomatitis, diarrhea, or GI ulceration, bleeding, and hemorrhage. Application to large ulcerated areas may cause systemic toxicity.

• Watch for stomatitis or diarrhea (signs of toxicity).
• Evaluate patient's and family's knowledge of drug therapy.

Nursing diagnoses

• Ineffective health maintenance related to underlying neoplastic condition
• Ineffective protection related to adverse hematologic reactions
• Deficient knowledge related to drug therapy

Planning and implementation

• Follow facility policy to reduce risks. Preparation and administration of parenteral form create carcinogenic, mutagenic, and teratogenic risks for staff.
ALERT: Drug sometimes is ordered as 5-fluorouracil or 5-FU. The numeral 5 is part of drug name and shouldn't be confused with dosage units.
• Give antiemetic to reduce nausea before giving parenteral form of drug.
• **I.V. use:** Drug may be given by direct injection without dilution. For I.V. infusion, drug may be diluted with D_5W, sterile water for injection, or normal saline injection. Infuse slowly over 2 to 8 hours.
– Don't use cloudy solution. If crystals form, redissolve by warming.
– Use plastic I.V. containers for giving continuous infusions. Solution is more stable in plastic I.V. bags than in glass bottles.
• **Topical use:** Apply with caution near eyes, nose, and mouth.
– Avoid occlusive dressings because they increase risk of inflammatory reactions in adjacent normal skin.
– Wash hands immediately after handling topical form.
– Wash and dry affected area; wait 10 minutes. Apply thin layer of medication to affected area.
– Expect to use 1% topical concentration on face. Higher concentrations are used for thicker-skinned areas or resistant lesions.
– Expect to use 5% topical strength for superficial basal cell carcinoma confirmed by biopsy.
• Don't refrigerate fluorouracil.
• Use sodium hypochlorite 5% (household bleach) to inactivate drug in event of spill.
• Discontinue drug if diarrhea occurs, and notify prescriber.
• Consider protective isolation if WBC count is less than 2,000/mm^3.

Patient teaching

• Warn patient that alopecia may occur but is reversible.
• Caution patient to avoid prolonged exposure to sunlight or ultraviolet light when topical form is used.
• Tell patient to use sunblock to avoid inflammatory erythematous dermatitis. Long-term use of drug may cause erythematous, desquamative rash of hands and feet. May be treated with pyridoxine (50 to 150 mg P.O. daily) for 5 to 7 days.
• Warn patient that topically treated area may be unsightly during therapy and for several weeks after. Full healing may take 1 or 2 months. Local irritation generally resolves after 2 weeks of cessation of drug treatment.
• Inform patient that sunscreen and a moisturizer may be applied 2 hours after drug application.

Evaluation

• Patient shows positive response to fluorouracil therapy.
• Patient develops no serious adverse hematologic reactions.
• Patient and family state understanding of drug therapy.

fluoxetine hydrochloride

(floo-OKS-eh-teen high-droh-KLOR-ighd)
Prozac, Prozac-20 ◇, Prozac Weekly, Sarafem

Pharmacologic class: selective serotonin reuptake inhibitor (SSRI)
Therapeutic class: antidepressant
Pregnancy risk category: B

Indications and dosages

▶ **Depression, obsessive-compulsive disorder.** *Adults:* Initially, 20 mg P.O. in morning; dosage increased according to patient response. May be given b.i.d. in morning and at noon. Maximum, 80 mg daily.
Children ages 7 to 17: For obsessive-compulsive disorder, 10 mg P.O. daily. After 2 weeks,

increase dose to 20 mg/day to maximum of 60 mg/day.
Children ages 8 to 18: For depression, 10 to 20 mg P.O. daily. After 1 week, increase to 20 mg daily .

▶ **Maintenance therapy for depression in stabilized patients (not for newly diagnosed depression).** *Adults:* 90 mg Prozac Weekly P.O. once weekly. Start 7 days after the last daily dose of Prozac 20 mg.

▶ **Treatment of depression in elderly patients.** *Adults age 65 and older:* Initially, 20 mg P.O. daily in the morning. Increase dosage based on clinical response. Doses may be given twice daily, in the morning and at noon. Maximum, 80 mg daily. A lower dosage or less frequent dosing should be considered in these patients, especially those with systemic illness and those who take multiple drugs for other illnesses.

▶ **Treatment of binge eating and vomiting behaviors in patients with moderate-to-severe bulimia nervosa.** *Adults:* 60 mg daily P.O. in the morning.

▶ **Premenstrual dysphoric disorder (PMDD).** *Adults:* 20 mg Sarafem P.O. daily continuously (every day of the menstrual cycle) or intermittently (daily dose starting 14 days prior to the anticipated onset of menstruation through the first full day of menses and repeating with each new cycle). Maximum dose is 80 mg P.O. daily.

▶ **Anorexia nervosa‡.** *Adults:* 40 mg P.O. daily in weight-restored patients.

▶ **Depression linked to bipolar disorder‡.** *Adults:* 20 to 60 mg P.O. daily.

▶ **Panic disorder with or without agoraphobia.** *Adults:* 10 mg P.O. daily. May increase in 10-mg increments at intervals of no less than 1 week to maximum dose of 60 mg.

▶ **Cataplexy‡.** *Adults:* 20 mg P.O. daily or b.i.d. in conjunction with CNS stimulant therapy.

▶ **Alcohol dependence‡.** *Adults:* 60 mg P.O. daily.

Contraindications and precautions

- Contraindicated in patients hypersensitive to drug and in those taking MAO inhibitors within 14 days of starting therapy.
- Use cautiously in patients at high risk for suicide; in those with history of mania, seizures, diabetes mellitus, or hepatic, renal, or CV disease.

Lifespan: In pregnant women, use cautiously. In breast-feeding women, drug isn't recommended. In children, safety of drug hasn't been established.

Adverse reactions

CNS: fever, *nervousness, anxiety, insomnia, somnolence, headache, drowsiness,* fatigue, tremor, dizziness, asthenia.
CV: palpitations, hot flushes.
EENT: nasal congestion, pharyngitis, sinusitis.
GI: *nausea, diarrhea, dry mouth, anorexia,* dyspepsia, constipation, abdominal pain, vomiting, flatulence, increased appetite.
GU: sexual dysfunction.
Metabolic: weight loss.
Musculoskeletal: muscle pain.
Respiratory: cough, upper respiratory infection, ***respiratory distress.***
Skin: rash, pruritus, urticaria.
Other: flulike syndrome.

Interactions

Drug-drug. *Amphetamines, SSRIs, trazadone, dextromethorphan, meperidine, tramadol, sumatriptan, dihydroergotamine:* May increase risk of serotonin syndrome. Avoid use together.
Benzodiazines: Increases CNS effects. Monitor patient closely.
Cyproheptadine: May reverse or decrease pharmacologic effect. Monitor patient closely.
Flecainide, carbamazepine, vinblastine: Increases serum levels of these drugs. Monitor serum levels and patient for adverse effects.
Insulin, oral antidiabetics: Alters glucose levels and alters need for antidiabetic. Adjust dosage.
Lithium, tricyclic antidepressants: May increase serum levels. Monitor levels, and adjust doses, as needed.
MAO inhibitors, thioridazine: Fatal reactions may occur. Avoid giving drug within 14 days after MAO inhibitor has been given. Don't give these drugs 5 weeks or shorter after fluoxetine has been discontinued
Phenytoin: May increase plasma phenytoin levels and risk of toxicity. Monitor serum phenytoin levels; adjust dosage.
Tryptophan: May increase toxic reaction with agitation, GI distress, and restlessness. Don't use together.

Warfarin, other highly protein-bound drugs: May increase plasma levels of fluoxetine or other highly protein-bound drugs. Monitor serum levels closely.
Drug-herb. *St. John's wort:* Increases risk of serotonin syndrome. Discourage use together.
Drug-lifestyle. *Alcohol use:* Increases CNS depression. Discourage use together.

Effects on lab test results

None reported.

Pharmacokinetics

Absorption: Well absorbed after P.O. administration.
Distribution: Apparently highly protein-bound (about 95%).
Metabolism: Metabolized primarily in liver to active metabolites.
Excretion: Excreted by kidneys. *Half-life:* 2 to 3 days.

Route	Onset	Peak	Duration
P.O.	1-4 wk	6-8 hr	Unknown

Pharmacodynamics

Chemical effect: Unknown; presumed to be linked to inhibition of CNS neuronal uptake of serotonin.
Therapeutic effect: Relieves depression and obsessive-compulsive behaviors.

Available forms

Capsules: 90 mg ***(Prozac Weekly)***
Oral solution: 20 mg/5 ml
Pulvules: 10 mg, 20 mg, 40 mg
Tablets: 10 mg

NURSING PROCESS

Assessment

- Assess patient's condition before therapy, and reassess regularly throughout therapy.
- Be alert for adverse reactions and drug interactions.
- Evaluate patient's and family's knowledge of drug therapy.

Nursing diagnoses

- Ineffective individual coping related to patient's underlying condition
- Disturbed sleep pattern related to drug-induced insomnia
- Deficient knowledge related to drug therapy

Planning and implementation

- Elderly or debilitated patients and patients with renal or hepatic dysfunction may need lower dosages or less frequent dosing.
- Give drug in morning to prevent insomnia.
- Give antihistamines or topical corticosteroids to treat rashes or pruritus.
- Lower-weight children may need several weeks between dosage increases.

Patient teaching

- Tell patient not to take drug in afternoon because fluoxetine commonly causes nervousness and insomnia.
- Tell patient to take drug without regard to meals or food.
- Warn patient to avoid hazardous activities that require alertness and psychomotor coordination until CNS effects of drug are known.
- Advise patient to consult prescriber before taking any other prescription or OTC medications.

Evaluation

- Patient behavior and communication indicate improvement of depression with drug therapy.
- Patient has no insomnia with drug use.
- Patient and family state understanding of drug therapy.

fluphenazine decanoate

(floo-FEN-uh-zeen deh-kuh-NOH-ayt)
Modecate ♦ ◇, Modecate Concentrate ♦, Prolixin Decanoate

fluphenazine enanthate

Moditen Enanthate ♦, Prolixin Enanthate

fluphenazine hydrochloride

Anatensol ◇ *, Apo-Fluphenazine ♦, Modecate Concentrate ♦, Moditen HCl ♦, Permitil* **, Permitil Concentrate, Prolixin* **, Prolixin Concentrate* ♦

Pharmacologic class: phenothiazine (piperazine derivative)
Therapeutic class: antipsychotic
Pregnancy risk category: C

*Liquid form contains alcohol. **May contain tartrazine. ♦ Canada ◇ Australia †OTC ‡Off-label use

Indications and dosages

▶ **Psychotic disorders.** *Adults:* Initially, 0.5 to 10 mg hydrochloride P.O. daily in divided doses q 6 to 8 hours; may increase cautiously to 20 mg. Higher doses (50 to 100 mg) have been given. Maintenance, 1 to 5 mg P.O. daily. I.M. doses are one-third to one-half of oral doses. Use lower dosages for elderly patients (1 to 2.5 mg daily). Or, 12.5 to 25 mg of long-acting esters (decanoate or enanthate) I.M. or S.C. q 1 to 6 weeks. Maintenance, 25 to 100 mg, p.r.n.

Contraindications and precautions

• Contraindicated in patients hypersensitive to drug and in those with CNS depression, bone marrow suppression, other blood dyscrasia, subcortical damage, liver damage, or coma.
• Use cautiously in debilitated patients, and those with pheochromocytoma, severe CV disease (may cause sudden drop in blood pressure), peptic ulcer, exposure to extreme heat or cold (including antipyretic therapy) or phosphorous insecticides, respiratory disorder, hypocalcemia, seizure disorder (may lower seizure threshold), severe reactions to insulin or electroconvulsive therapy, mitral insufficiency, glaucoma, or prostatic hyperplasia. Use parenteral form cautiously in patients with asthma and patients allergic to sulfites.
Lifespan: In pregnant or breast-feeding women and elderly patients, use cautiously.

Adverse reactions

CNS: *extrapyramidal reactions, tardive dyskinesia,* sedation, pseudoparkinsonism, EEG changes, drowsiness, ***seizures,*** dizziness, ***neuroleptic malignant syndrome.***
CV: orthostatic hypotension, tachycardia, ECG changes.
EENT: *dry mouth,* ocular changes, *blurred vision,* nasal congestion.
GI: *constipation.*
GU: *urine retention,* dark urine, menstrual irregularities, gynecomastia, inhibited ejaculation.
Hematologic: ***leukopenia, agranulocytosis, aplastic anemia,*** eosinophilia, hemolytic anemia.
Hepatic: cholestatic jaundice.
Metabolic: weight gain, increased appetite.
Skin: *mild photosensitivity,* allergic reactions.

Interactions

Drug-drug. *Antacids:* Inhibits absorption of oral phenothiazines. Separate doses by at least 2 hours.
Anticholinergics: Increases anticholinergic effects. Avoid using together.
Barbiturates, lithium: May decrease phenothiazine effect. Observe patient.
Centrally acting antihypertensives: Decreases antihypertensive effect. Monitor blood pressure.
CNS depressants: Increases CNS depression. Avoid using together.
Drug-lifestyle. *Alcohol use:* Increases CNS depression. Discourage using together.
Sun exposure: Increases risk of photosensitivity. Discourage prolonged or unprotected exposure to sun.

Effects on lab test results

• May increase eosinophil count and liver function test values. May decrease hemoglobin, hematocrit, and WBC, granulocyte, and platelet counts.

Pharmacokinetics

Absorption: Rate and extent of absorption vary with route of administration; oral tablet absorption is erratic and variable.
Distribution: Distributed widely into body. CNS levels are usually higher than those in plasma. Drug is 91% to 99% protein-bound.
Metabolism: Metabolized extensively by liver, but no active metabolites are formed.
Excretion: Most of drug excreted in urine; some excreted in feces by way of biliary tract.

Route	Onset	Peak	Duration
P.O.	≤ 1 hr	0.5 hr	6-8 hr
I.M., S.C.	1-3 days	Unknown	1-6 wk

Pharmacodynamics

Chemical effect: Unknown; may block dopamine receptors in brain.
Therapeutic effect: Relieves psychotic signs and symptoms.

Available forms

fluphenazine decanoate
Depot injection: 25 mg/ml, 100 mg/ml ◆
fluphenazine enanthate
Depot injection: 25 mg/ml
fluphenazine hydrochloride
Elixir: 2.5 mg/5 ml*

I.M. injection: 2.5 mg/ml
Oral concentrate: 5 mg/ml*
Tablets: 1 mg, 2.5 mg, 5 mg, 10 mg

NURSING PROCESS

Assessment
- Assess patient's condition before therapy and regularly thereafter.
- Monitor therapy with weekly bilirubin tests during first month, periodic blood tests (CBC and liver function), and periodic renal function and ophthalmic tests (long-term use).
- Be alert for adverse reactions and drug interactions.
- Monitor patient for tardive dyskinesia, which may occur after prolonged use. It may not appear until months or years later and may disappear spontaneously or persist for life despite discontinuation of drug.
- Evaluate patient's and family's knowledge of drug therapy.

Nursing diagnoses
- Impaired thought processes related to psychosis
- Impaired physical mobility related to extrapyramidal reactions
- Deficient knowledge related to drug therapy

Planning and implementation
ALERT: Prolixin concentrate and Permitil concentrate are 10 times more concentrated than Prolixin elixir (5 mg/ml vs. 0.5 mg/ml). Check dosage order carefully.
- **P.O. use:** Dilute liquid concentrate with water, fruit juice (except apple), milk, or semisolid food just before administration.
- **I.M. and S.C. use:** For long-acting forms (decanoate and enanthate), which are oil preparations, use dry needle of at least 21G. Allow 24 to 96 hours for onset of action. Note and report adverse reactions in patient taking these drug forms.
- Oral liquid and parenteral forms can cause contact dermatitis. Wear gloves when preparing solutions, and avoid contact with skin and clothing.
- Protect drug from light. Slight yellowing of injection or concentrate is common and doesn't affect potency. Discard markedly discolored solutions.
- Withhold dose and notify prescriber if patient develops symptoms of blood dyscrasia (fever, sore throat, infection, cellulitis, weakness) or persistent extrapyramidal reactions (longer than a few hours), especially in a pregnant woman or a child.
- Acute dystonic reactions may be treated with diphenhydramine.
- Don't withdraw drug abruptly unless severe adverse reactions occur. After abrupt withdrawal of long-term therapy, patient may experience gastritis, nausea, vomiting, dizziness, tremor, feeling of warmth or cold, diaphoresis, tachycardia, headache, and insomnia.

Patient teaching
- Warn patient to avoid activities that require alertness and psychomotor coordination until CNS effects of drug are known.
- Tell patient not to mix concentrate with beverages containing caffeine, tannics (such as tea) or pectinates (such as apple juice).
- Tell patient to avoid alcohol during therapy.
- Advise patient to relieve dry mouth with sugarless gum or hard candy.
- Have patient report urine retention or constipation.
- Tell patient to use sunblock and to wear protective clothing.
- Inform patient that drug may discolor urine.
- Stress importance of not stopping drug suddenly.

Evaluation
- Patient demonstrates decrease in psychotic behavior.
- Patient maintains pretreatment physical mobility.
- Patient and family state understanding of drug therapy.

flurazepam hydrochloride
(floo-RAH-zuh-pam high-droh-KLOR-ighd)
Apo-Flurazepam ♦, Dalmane, Novo-Flupam ♦

Pharmacologic class: benzodiazepine
Therapeutic class: sedative-hypnotic
Pregnancy risk category: X
Controlled substance schedule: IV

Indications and dosages

▶ **Insomnia.** *Adults:* 15 to 30 mg P.O. h.s. Dose repeated once, p.r.n.

Contraindications and precautions

- Contraindicated in patients hypersensitive to drug.
- Use cautiously in patients with impaired hepatic or renal function, chronic pulmonary insufficiency, mental depression, suicidal tendencies, or history of drug abuse.

Lifespan: In pregnant women, drug is contraindicated. In breast-feeding women, drug isn't recommended. In children younger than age 15, safety of drug hasn't been established. In elderly patients, use cautiously and at a lower dose because they're more susceptible to CNS effects from drug.

Adverse reactions

CNS: *daytime sedation, dizziness, drowsiness, disturbed coordination,* lethargy, confusion, *headache,* light-headedness, nervousness, hallucinations, staggering, ataxia, disorientation, ***coma.***

GI: nausea, vomiting, heartburn, diarrhea, abdominal pain.

Other: physical or psychological dependence.

Interactions

Drug-drug. *Cimetidine:* May increase sedation. Monitor patient carefully.

CNS depressants, including narcotic analgesics: May cause excessive CNS depression. Use together cautiously.

Digoxin: Digoxin serum levels may increase, resulting in toxicity. Monitor patient and digoxin levels closely.

Disulfiram, isoniazid, oral contraceptives: May decrease metabolism of benzodiazepines, leading to toxicity. Monitor patient closely.

Phenytoin: May increase phenytoin levels. Monitor patient for toxicity.

Rifampin: Enhances metabolism of benzodiazepines. Monitor patient for decreased effectiveness.

Theophylline: May antagonize with flurazepam. Monitor patient for decreased effectiveness.

Drug-herb. *Catnip, kava, lady's slipper, lemon balm, passionflower, sassafras, skullcap, valerian:* Sedative effects may be enhanced. Discourage using together.

Drug-lifestyle. *Alcohol use:* May cause excessive CNS and respiratory depression. Discourage using together.

Smoking: Enhances metabolism of benzodiazepines. Discourage using together.

Effects on lab test results

- May increase AST, ALT, total and direct bilirubin, and alkaline phosphatase levels.

Pharmacokinetics

Absorption: Absorbed rapidly through GI tract.

Distribution: Distributed widely throughout body; about 97% bound to plasma protein.

Metabolism: Metabolized in liver to active metabolite desalkylflurazepam.

Excretion: Excreted in urine. *Half-life:* 50 to 100 hours.

Route	Onset	Peak	Duration
P.O.	Unknown	0.5-1 hr	Unknown

Pharmacodynamics

Chemical effect: Unknown; may act on limbic system, thalamus, and hypothalamus of CNS to produce hypnotic effects.

Therapeutic effect: Promotes sleep and calmness.

Available forms

Capsules: 15 mg, 30 mg

NURSING PROCESS

Assessment

- Assess patient's sleep patterns and CNS status before therapy.
- Evaluate patient's ability to sleep. Drug is more effective on second, third, and fourth nights of use.
- Be alert for adverse reactions and drug interactions.
- Evaluate patient's and family's knowledge of drug therapy.

Nursing diagnoses

- Disturbed sleep pattern related to underlying patient problem
- Risk for trauma related to drug-induced adverse CNS reactions
- Deficient knowledge related to drug therapy

Planning and implementation

- Before leaving bedside, make sure patient has swallowed capsule.

Patient teaching

- Encourage patient to continue drug, even if it doesn't relieve insomnia on first night.
- Warn patient to avoid activities that require alertness or physical coordination. For inpatient, supervise walking and raise bed rails, particularly for elderly patient.
- Advise patient that physical and psychological dependence is possible with long-term use.

Evaluation

- Patient notes drug-induced sleep.
- Patient's safety is maintained.
- Patient and family state understanding of drug therapy.

flutamide

(FLOO-tuh-mighd)

Euflex♦, Eulexin

Pharmacologic class: nonsteroidal antiandrogen
Therapeutic class: antineoplastic
Pregnancy risk category: D

Indications and dosages

▶ **Metastatic prostatic carcinoma (stage D2).** *Adults:* 250 mg P.O. q 8 hours. Used with luteinizing hormone–releasing hormone analogues such as leuprolide acetate.

Contraindications and precautions

- Contraindicated in patients hypersensitive to drug and in those with severe hepatic impairment.
- Drug isn't indicated for female patients.

Lifespan: In male children, safety of drug hasn't been established.

Adverse reactions

CNS: drowsiness, confusion, depression, anxiety, nervousness, paresthesia.
CV: *hot flushes,* peripheral edema, hypertension.
GI: *diarrhea, nausea, vomiting,* anorexia.
GU: *impotence.*
Hematologic: ***thrombocytopenia, leukopenia,*** anemia, hemolytic anemia.
Hepatic: ***hepatitis,*** hepatic encephalopathy.
Skin: rash, photosensitivity.
Other: *loss of libido,* gynecomastia.

Interactions

Drug-drug. *Warfarin:* May increase PT. Monitor patient's PT and INR.
Drug-lifestyle. *Sun exposure:* May cause sensitivity reactions. Warn patient to avoid unprotected or prolonged sun exposure.

Effects on lab test results

- May increase BUN, creatinine, and liver enzyme levels.
- May decrease hemoglobin, hematocrit, and WBC and platelet counts.

Pharmacokinetics

Absorption: Absorbed rapidly and completely.
Distribution: Animal studies show drug concentrates in prostate. Drug and its active metabolite are about 95% protein-bound.
Metabolism: Over 97% of drug is metabolized rapidly, with at least six metabolites identified.
Excretion: Over 95% excreted in urine. *Half-life:* 6 hours.

Route	Onset	Peak	Duration
P.O.	Unknown	2 hr	Unknown

Pharmacodynamics

Chemical effect: Inhibits androgen uptake or prevents androgen binding in cell nuclei in target tissues.
Therapeutic effect: Hinders prostatic cancer cell activity.

Available forms

Capsules: 125 mg
Tablets: 250 mg♦

NURSING PROCESS

Assessment

- Assess patient's prostatic cancer before therapy.
- Monitor liver function tests periodically.
- Be alert for adverse reactions.
- Monitor hydration status if adverse GI reactions occur.

• Evaluate patient's and family's knowledge of drug therapy.

Nursing diagnoses

• Ineffective health maintenance related to presence of prostatic cancer
• Risk for deficient fluid volume related to adverse GI reactions
• Deficient knowledge related to drug therapy

Planning and implementation

• Drug may be given without regard to meals.
• Give with luteinizing hormone–releasing antagonist (such as leuprolide acetate).

Patient teaching

• Make sure patient knows that flutamide must be taken continuously with drug used for medical castration (such as leuprolide acetate) to allow full benefit of therapy. Leuprolide suppresses testosterone production while flutamide inhibits testosterone action at cellular level. Together they can impair growth of androgen-responsive tumors. Advise patient not to discontinue either drug.
• Tell patient to notify prescriber if adverse reactions occur.

Evaluation

• Patient responds well to drug.
• Patient maintains adequate hydration throughout drug therapy.
• Patient and family state understanding of drug therapy.

fluticasone propionate

(FLU-tih-ka-sohn proh-PIGH-oh-nayt)
Flovent Inhalation Aerosol, Flovent Rotadisk, Flonase

Pharmacologic class: corticosteroid
Therapeutic class: topical and inhalation anti-inflammatory
Pregnancy risk category: C

Indications and dosages

▶ **Maintenance treatment of asthma as prevention and for patients who need oral corticosteroid for chronic asthma.** ***Flovent Inhalation Aerosol.*** *Adults and children age 12 and older:* In those previously taking bronchodilators alone, initially, inhale dose of 88 mcg b.i.d. to maximum of 440 mcg b.i.d.
Patients previously taking inhaled corticosteroids: Initially, inhale dose of 88 to 220 mcg b.i.d. to maximum of 440 mcg b.i.d.
Patients previously taking oral corticosteroids: Inhaled dose of 880 mcg b.i.d.
Flovent Rotadisk. *Adults and adolescents:* In patients previously taking bronchodilators alone, initially, inhale dose of 100 mcg b.i.d. to maximum of 500 mcg b.i.d.
Patients previously taking inhaled corticosteroids: Initially, inhale dose of 100 to 250 mcg b.i.d. to maximum of 500 mcg b.i.d.
Patients previously taking oral corticosteroids: Inhale dose of 1,000 mcg b.i.d.
Children ages 4 to 11: For patients previously on bronchodilators alone or on inhaled corticosteroids, initially, inhale dose of 50 mcg b.i.d. to maximum of 100 mcg b.i.d.
Patients starting therapy who are currently receiving oral corticosteroid therapy: Reduce prednisone dose to no more than 2.5 mg/day on a weekly basis, beginning after at least 1 week of therapy with fluticasone.

▶ **Management of nasal symptoms of seasonal and perennial allergic and nonallergic rhinitis.** ***Flonase.*** *Adults:* 2 sprays (100 mcg) in each nostril once daily or 1 spray (50 mcg) b.i.d. Reduce dosage to 1 spray in each nostril daily for maintenance therapy.
Alternatively for seasonal allergic rhinitis, 2 sprays (100 mcg) in each nostril once daily as needed for symptom control, although greater symptom control maybe achieved with regular use.
Children age 4 and older: Initially, 1 spray (50 mcg) in each nostril once daily. If patient doesn't respond, increase to 2 sprays (100 mcg) in each nostril daily. Once adequate control is achieved, decrease dose to 1 spray in each nostril daily. Maximum dose is 2 sprays in each nostril daily.

Contraindications and precautions

• Contraindicated in patients hypersensitive to ingredients of these preparations.
• Also contraindicated as primary treatment of patients with status asthmaticus or other acute episodes of asthma in whom intensive measures are needed.

Lifespan: With breast-feeding women, use cautiously. In children younger than age 4, use is not recommended.

Adverse reactions

CNS: fever, *headache,* dizziness, migraine, nervousness.
EENT: mouth irritation, *oral candidiasis, pharyngitis,* acute nasopharyngitis, nasal congestion, sinusitis, dysphonia, rhinitis, otitis media, tonsillitis, nasal discharge, earache, laryngitis, epistaxis, sneezing, hoarseness, conjunctivitis, eye irritation.
GI: diarrhea, abdominal pain, viral gastroenteritis, colitis, abdominal discomfort, nausea, vomiting.
GU: dysmenorrhea, candidiasis of vagina, pelvic inflammatory disease, vaginitis, vulvovaginitis, irregular menstrual cycle.
Metabolic: cushingoid features, weight gain.
Musculoskeletal: growth retardation in children, pain in joints, aches and pains, disorder or symptoms of neck sprain or strain, sore muscles.
Respiratory: *upper respiratory tract infection,* bronchitis, chest congestion, dyspnea, irritation from inhalant.
Skin: dermatitis, urticaria.
Other: dental problems, influenza.

Interactions

Drug-drug. *Ketoconazole:* May increase mean fluticasone levels. Use care when giving fluticasone with long-term ketoconazole and other known cytochrome P-450 3A4 inhibitors.

Effects on lab test results

- May increase glucose level.

Pharmacokinetics

Absorption: Rapidly and completely absorbed after P.O. administration.
Distribution: Animal studies show drug concentrates in prostate. Drug and its active metabolite are about 95% protein-bound.
Metabolism: Rapid, with at least 6 metabolites identified. More than 97% of drug is metabolized within 1 hour of administration.
Excretion: More than 95% of drug is excreted in urine.

Route	Onset	Peak	Duration
Inhalation	24 hr	1-2 wk	Several days

Pharmacodynamics

Chemical effect: Synthetic glucocorticoid with potent anti-inflammatory activity inhibits many cell types and mediator production or secretion involved in asthma. These anti-inflammatory actions may contribute to drug's efficacy in asthma.
Therapeutic effect: Improves breathing ability.

Available forms

Nasal suspension: 50 mcg metered inhaler
Oral inhalation aerosol: 44 mcg, 110 mcg, 220 mcg
Oral inhalation powder: 50 mcg, 100 mcg, 250 mcg

NURSING PROCESS

Assessment

- Obtain history of patient's underlying condition before therapy, and reassess regularly thereafter.
- Because of risk of systemic absorption of inhaled corticosteroids, observe patient carefully for evidence of systemic corticosteroid effects.
- Monitor patient, especially postoperatively or during periods of stress, for evidence of inadequate adrenal response.
- Evaluate patient's and family's knowledge of drug therapy.

Nursing diagnoses

- Ineffective breathing pattern related to respiratory condition
- Impaired oral mucous membrane related to potential adverse effect of oral candidiasis
- Deficient knowledge related to drug therapy

Planning and implementation

- During withdrawal from oral corticosteroids, some patients may have symptoms of systemically active corticosteroid withdrawal, such as joint or muscle pain, lassitude, and depression, despite maintenance or even improvement of respiratory function.
- As with other inhaled asthma drugs, bronchospasm may occur with an immediate increase in wheezing after dosing. If bronchospasm occurs following fluticasone inhalation aerosol, it should be treated immediately with a fast-acting inhaled bronchodilator.

• Some patients on high doses of fluticasone may have an abnormal response to the 6-hour cosyntropin stimulation test.

Patient teaching

• Tell patient that drug isn't intended to relieve acute bronchospasm.
• For proper use of drug and to attain maximum improvement, tell patient to follow carefully the accompanying patient instructions.
• Advise patient to use drug at regular intervals as directed.
• Instruct patient not to increase dosage but to contact prescriber if symptoms don't improve or if condition worsens.
• Instruct patient to contact prescriber immediately when episodes of asthma that aren't responsive to bronchodilators occur during course of treatment with fluticasone. During such episodes, patients may need therapy with oral corticosteroids.
• Warn patient to avoid exposure to chickenpox or measles and, if exposed, to consult prescriber immediately.
• Tell patient to carry or wear medical identification indicating that he may need supplementary corticosteroids during stress or a severe asthma attack.
• During periods of stress or a severe asthma attack, instruct patient who has been withdrawn from systemic corticosteroids to resume oral corticosteroids (in large doses) immediately and to contact prescriber for further instruction. Instruct him to rinse his mouth after inhalation.
• Advise patient to avoid spraying inhalation aerosol into eyes.
• Instruct patient to shake canister well before using inhalation aerosol.
• Advise patient to store fluticasone powder in a dry place.

☑ Evaluation

• Patient has normal breathing pattern.
• Patient doesn't develop oral candidiasis.
• Patient and family state understanding of drug therapy.

fluticasone propionate and salmeterol inhalation powder

(FLU-tih-ka-sohn proh-PIGH-oh-nayt and sal MEH teh rohl)

Advair Diskus 100/50, Advair Diskus 250/50, Advair Diskus 500/50

Pharmacologic class: corticosteroid, long-acting beta$_2$-adrenergic agonist
Therapeutic class: anti-inflammatory, bronchodilator
Pregnancy risk category: C

Indications and dosages

▶ **Chronic asthma.** *Adults and adolescents:* 1 oral inhalation twice daily, morning and evening, at least 12 hours apart. Maximum oral inhalation of Advair Diskus is 500/50 twice daily.
Adults and adolescents older than age 12 not currently taking an inhaled corticosteroid: 1 oral inhalation of Advair Diskus 100/50 twice daily.
Adults and adolescents currently taking beclomethasone dipropionate: If daily dose of beclomethasone dipropionate is 420 mcg or less, start with 1 oral inhalation of Advair Diskus 100/50 twice daily. If beclomethasone dipropionate daily dose is 462 to 840 mcg, start with one oral inhalation of Advair Diskus 250/50 twice daily.
Adults and adolescents currently taking budesonide: If daily dose of budesonide is 400 mcg or less, start with 1 oral inhalation of Advair Diskus 100/50 twice daily. If budesonide daily dose is 800 to 1,200 mcg, start with 1 oral inhalation of Advair Diskus 250/50 twice daily. If budesonide daily dose is 1,600 mcg, start with 1 oral inhalation of Advair Diskus 500/50 twice daily.
Adults and adolescents currently taking flunisolide: If daily dose of flunisolide is 1,000 mcg or less, start with 1 oral inhalation of Advair Diskus 100/50 twice daily. If flunisolide daily dose is 1,250 to 2,000 mcg, start with 1 oral inhalation of Advair Diskus 250/50 twice daily.
Adults and adolescents currently taking fluticasone propionate inhalation aerosol: If daily dose of fluticasone propionate inhalation aerosol is 176 mcg or less, start with 1 oral inhalation of Advair Diskus 100/50 twice daily.

If fluticasone propionate inhalation aerosol daily dose is 440 mcg, start with 1 oral inhalation of Advair Diskus 250/50 twice daily. If fluticasone propionate inhalation aerosol daily dose is 660 to 880 mcg, start with 1 oral inhalation of Advair Diskus 500/50 twice daily.
Adults and adolescents currently taking fluticasone propionate inhalation powder: If fluticasone propionate inhalation powder daily dose is 200 mcg or less, start with 1 oral inhalation of Advair Diskus 100/50 twice daily. If fluticasone propionate inhalation powder daily dose is 500 mcg, start with 1 oral inhalation of Advair Diskus 250/50 twice daily. If fluticasone propionate inhalation powder daily dose is 1,000 mcg, start with 1 oral inhalation of Advair Diskus 500/50 twice daily.
Adults and adolescents currently taking triamcinolone acetonide: If triamcinolone acetonide daily dose is 1,000 mcg or less, start with 1 oral inhalation of Advair Diskus 100/50 twice daily. If triamcinolone acetonide daily dose is 1,100 to 1,600 mcg, start with 1 oral inhalation of Advair Diskus 250/50 twice daily.

Contraindications and precautions

• Contraindicated in patients hypersensitive to any component of the drug. Also, contraindicated as primary treatment of status asthmaticus or other acute asthmatic episodes.
• Use extreme caution in patients with active or quiescent respiratory tuberculosis infection; untreated systemic fungal, bacterial, viral, or parasitic infection; or ocular herpes simplex.
• Use cautiously in patients with CV disorders, especially coronary insufficiency, cardiac arrhythmias, and hypertension; in patients with seizure disorders or thyrotoxicosis; in patients unusually responsive to sympathomimetic amines; and in patients with hepatic impairment (because salmeterol is metabolized mainly in the liver).
Lifespan: In children, safety and efficacy haven't been established. Closely monitor growth in children because growth suppression may occur. Maintain child on lowest effective dose to minimize potential for growth suppression.

Adverse reactions

CNS: pain, sleep disorder, tremor, hypnagogic effects, fever, compressed nerve syndromes, *headache.*
CV: palpitations, chest pains, fluid retention, rapid heart rate, ***arrhythmias.***
EENT: *pharyngitis,* sinusitis, hoarseness/dysphonia, oral candidiasis, rhinorrhea, rhinitis, sneezing, nasal irritation, blood in nasal mucosa, keratitis, conjunctivitis, eye redness, viral eye infections, congestion.
GI: nausea, vomiting, abdominal pain and discomfort, diarrhea, gastroenteritis, oral discomfort and pain, constipation, oral ulcerations, oral erythema and rashes, appendicitis, dental discomfort and pain, unusual taste.
Musculoskeletal: muscle pain, arthralgia, articular rheumatism, muscle stiffness, tightness, rigidity, bone and cartilage disorders, back pain.
Respiratory: *upper respiratory tract infection,* lower viral respiratory infections, bronchitis, cough, pneumonia, ***paradoxical bronchospasms.***
Skin: viral skin infections, urticaria, skin flakiness, disorders of sweat and sebum, sweating.
Other: bacterial infections, allergies, allergic reactions, influenza, agitation, nervousness.

Interactions

Drug-drug. *Beta blockers:* Blocked pulmonary effect of salmeterol may produce severe bronchospasm in patients with asthma. Avoid using together. If necessary, use a cardioselective beta blocker with extreme caution.
Ketoconazole, other inhibitors of cytochrome P-450: May increase fluticasone levels and adverse effects. Use together cautiously.
Loop diuretics, thiazide diuretics: ECG changes or hypokalemia may result from or be worsened by potassium-wasting diuretics. Use together cautiously.
MAO inhibitors, tricyclic antidepressants: May potentiate the action of salmeterol on the vascular system. Avoid use within 2 weeks of taking these drugs.

Effects on lab test results

None reported.

Pharmacokinetics

Absorption: Most of the fluticasone propionate delivered to the lung is systemically absorbed. Salmeterol acts locally in the lung; therefore, plasma levels don't predict therapeutic effect. Because of the small therapeutic dose, systemic levels of salmeterol are low and

undetectable after inhalation of recommended doses. Following long-term administration of an inhaled dose of 50 mcg of salmeterol inhalation twice daily, salmeterol was detected in plasma within 5 to 45 minutes and peaked at 20 minutes.
Distribution: Fluticasone is 91% bound to plasma proteins, is weakly and reversibly bound to erythrocytes, and isn't bound significantly to human transcortin. Salmeterol is 96% bound to human plasma proteins.
Metabolism: Metabolized mainly in the liver by cytochrome P-450 (CYP) 3A4 isoenzyme, with renal clearance accounting for less than 0.02% of the total. The only circulating metabolite is the 17 beta-carboxylic acid derivative, which is formed via the cytochrome P-450 3A4 pathway. Salmeterol base is extensively metabolized by hydroxylation.
Excretion: Fluticasone has less than 5% of a dose excreted in urine as metabolites, with the remainder excreted in feces as an unchanged drug and metabolite. *Half-life:* 7.8 hours. Salmeterol xinafoate is about 25% to 60% eliminated in urine and feces, respectively, over a period of 7 days. No significant amount of unchanged salmeterol base was detected in either urine or feces. *Half-life:* 5.5 hours.

Route	Onset	Peak	Duration
Inhalation	Unknown	5 min (salmeterol); 1 to 2 hr (fluticasone)	Unknown

Pharmacodynamics

Chemical effect: Fluticasone is a synthetic corticosteroid with potent anti-inflammatory activity, although precise mechanisms of action in asthma are unknown. Corticosteroids inhibit mast cells, eosinophils, basophils, lymphocytes, macrophages, and neutrophils, and they inhibit production or secretion of histamine, eicosanoids, leukotrienes, and cytokines, which are involved in the asthmatic response.

Salmeterol xinafoate is a long-acting beta-adrenergic agonist selective for $beta_2$-adrenoceptors. Pharmacologic effects are at least in part attributable to stimulation of intracellular adenyl cyclase, the enzyme that catalyzes conversion of adenosine triphosphate (ATP) to cyclic AMP. Increased cyclic AMP levels relax bronchial smooth muscle and inhibit release of mediators of immediate hypersensitivity from cells, especially mast cells. In vitro tests show that salmeterol is a potent and long-lasting inhibitor of the release of mast cell mediators, such as histamine, leukotrienes, and prostaglandin D_2, from human lung.
Therapeutic effect: Reduces inflammation in the lungs and opens airways to improve pulmonary function.

Available forms

Inhalation powder: 100 mcg fluticasone/50 mcg salmeterol, 250 mcg fluticasone/50 mcg salmeterol, 500 mcg fluticasone/50 mcg salmeterol

NURSING PROCESS

Assessment

- Obtain patient's medical history, and assess patient before initiating therapy.

ALERT: Chronic overdose of fluticasone may cause signs and symptoms of hypercorticism. Salmeterol overdose may cause seizures, angina, hypertension, hypotension, tachycardia, arrhythmias, nervousness, headache, tremor, muscle cramps, dry mouth, palpitations, nausea, prolonged QTc interval, ventricular arrhythmia, hypokalemia, hyperglycemia, cardiac arrest, and death. Treatment consists of discontinuing drug and possibly using a cardioselective beta blocker. Cardiac monitoring is necessary.

- Monitor patient for urticaria, angioedema, rash, bronchospasm, or other signs of hypersensitivity, which may occur immediately after a dose of Advair Diskus.
- Monitor patient for increased use of inhaled short-acting $beta_2$-agonist. The dose of Advair Diskus may need to be increased.
- Monitor patient for hypercorticism and adrenal suppression. If these occur, reduce dosage slowly.
- Monitor patient for eosinophilia, vasculitic rash, worsening pulmonary symptoms, cardiac complications, or neuropathy, which may be signs of a serious eosinophilic condition.
- Monitor patient for signs or symptoms of thrush.
- Evaluate patient's and family's knowledge of drug therapy.

Nursing diagnoses
- Ineffective airway clearance related to underlying asthmatic condition
- Risk of impaired gas exchange related to poor pulmonary function
- Activity intolerance related to underlying asthmatic condition
- Deficient knowledge related to proper inhalation with the Diskus device and drug therapy

Planning and implementation
ALERT: Don't switch patient from systemic corticosteroids to Advair Diskus because of HPA axis suppression. Death can occur from adrenal insufficiency.
ALERT: Don't start Advair Diskus therapy during rapidly deteriorating or potentially life-threatening episodes of asthma. Serious acute respiratory events, including death, can occur.
ALERT: Don't use Advair Diskus to treat status asthmaticus. When a patient uses Advair Diskus, make sure the patient has an inhaled, short-acting beta$_2$-agonist (such as albuterol) for acute symptoms.
ALERT: Advair Diskus can produce paradoxical bronchospasm. If it does, treat immediately with a short-acting, inhaled bronchodilator (such as albuterol) and discontinue Advair Diskus therapy.
- If patient is exposed to chickenpox, consider prophylaxis with varicella zoster immune globulin. If chickenpox develops, consider antiviral treatment.
- If patient is exposed to measles, consider prophylaxis with pooled I.M. immunoglobulin.
- Store at controlled room temperature (20° to 25° C [68° F to 77° F]) in a dry place away from direct heat or sunlight. Discard the device 1 month after removal from the moisture-protective over-wrap pouch or after every foil-wrapped blister has been used, whichever comes first. Don't attempt to take the device apart.

Patient teaching
- Instruct patient on proper use of Diskus device to provide the most effective treatment.
- Tell patient to avoid exhaling into the Diskus and to activate and use the Diskus in a level, horizontal position.
- Instruct patient to keep the Diskus in a dry place, to avoid washing the mouthpiece or other parts of the device, and to avoid taking the Diskus apart.
- Tell patient to stop taking an oral or inhaled long-acting beta$_2$-agonist simultaneously when beginning treatment with Advair Diskus.
- Explain to patient that Advair Diskus is used only for long-term maintenance and not for acute symptoms of asthma or for prevention of exercise-induced bronchospasm. Urge patient to use a short-acting beta$_2$-agonist (e.g., albuterol) for relief of acute symptoms.
- Instruct patient to rinse mouth after each inhalation to prevent oral candidiasis.
- Inform patient that improvement may be seen within 30 minutes after an Advair dose; however, the full benefit may not occur for 1 week or more.
- Instruct patient not to exceed recommended prescribing dose under any circumstances.
- Instruct patient to report decreasing effects or increasing use of the short-acting beta$_2$-agonist inhaler immediately to his prescriber.
- Instruct patient not to use Advair Diskus with a spacer device.
- Tell patient to report palpitations, chest pain, rapid heart rate, tremor, or nervousness immediately to the prescriber. Also instruct patient to avoid stimulants, such as caffeine, while on Advair Diskus therapy because they may increase these adverse reactions.
- Instruct patient to contact prescriber immediately if exposed to chickenpox or measles.

Evaluation
- Patient's activity tolerance increases.
- Patient doesn't suffer from any adverse effects related to fluticasone propionate and salmeterol inhalation powder.
- Patient has a normal breathing pattern and optimal air exchange.
- Patient and family state understanding of drug therapy.

fluvastatin sodium
(floo-vuh-STAH-tin SOH-dee-um)
Lescol, Lescol XL

Pharmacologic class: hydroxymethylglutaryl-coenzyme A (HMG-CoA) reductase inhibitor
Therapeutic class: cholesterol inhibitor
Pregnancy risk category: X

Indications and dosages

▶ **Reduction of LDL and total cholesterol levels in patients with primary hypercholesterolemia (types IIa and IIb) or to slow progression of coronary atherosclerosis in patients with coronary artery disease; treatment of elevated triglyceride and apolipoprotein B levels in patients with primary hypercholesterolemia and mixed dyslipidemia whose response to dietary restriction and other nonpharmacologic measures has been inadequate.** *Adults:* Initially, 20 to 40 mg P.O. h.s. Increase dosage as needed to maximum of 80 mg daily (given in divided doses).
Elderly patients or patients with increased sensitivity to the CNS effects: Initial dose may be 25 mg, with subsequent adjustments as necessary.

Contraindications and precautions

- Contraindicated in patients hypersensitive to drug and in those with active liver disease or conditions that cause unexplained persistent elevations of serum transaminase levels.
- Use cautiously in patients with severe renal impairment or with history of liver disease or heavy alcohol use.

Lifespan: In pregnant and breast-feeding women and women of childbearing age who have the potential to become pregnant, drug is contraindicated. In children younger than age 18, safety of drug hasn't been established.

Adverse reactions

CNS: headache, fatigue, dizziness, insomnia.
EENT: sinusitis, rhinitis, pharyngitis.
GI: dyspepsia, diarrhea, nausea, vomiting, abdominal pain, constipation, flatulence.
Hematologic: ***thrombocytopenia, leukopenia,*** hemolytic anemia.
Musculoskeletal: arthropathy, muscle pain.
Respiratory: *upper respiratory infection,* cough, bronchitis.
Skin: hypersensitivity reactions (rash, pruritus).
Other: tooth disorder.

Interactions

Drug-drug. *Cholestyramine, colestipol:* May bind with fluvastatin in GI tract and decrease absorption. Separate administration times by at least 4 hours.
Cimetidine, omeprazole, ranitidine: May decrease fluvastatin metabolism. Monitor patient for enhanced effects.
Cyclosporine and other immunosuppressants, erythromycin, gemfibrozil, niacin: Possible increased risk of polymyositis and rhabdomyolysis. Avoid using together.
Digoxin: May alter digoxin pharmacokinetics. Monitor serum digoxin levels carefully.
Rifampin: Enhances fluvastatin metabolism and decreases plasma level. Monitor patient for lack of effect.
Warfarin: Increases anticoagulant effect with bleeding. Monitor patient.
Drug-herb. *Red yeast rice:* Contains components similar to those of statin drugs, increasing the risk of adverse events or toxicity. Discourage using together.
Drug-lifestyle. *Alcohol use:* May increase risk of hepatotoxicity. Discourage using together.

Effects on lab test results

- May increase ALT, AST, and CK levels.
- May decrease hemoglobin, hematocrit, and platelet and WBC counts.

Pharmacokinetics

Absorption: Rapid and almost complete after P.O. administration on empty stomach.
Distribution: More than 98% bound to plasma proteins.
Metabolism: Completely metabolized in liver.
Excretion: About 5% excreted in urine, 90% in feces.

Route	Onset	Peak	Duration
P.O.	Unknown	Unknown	Unknown

Pharmacodynamics

Chemical effect: Inhibits 3-hydroxy-3-methylglutaryl coenzyme A reductase. This enzyme is early (and rate-limiting) step in synthetic pathway of cholesterol.
Therapeutic effect: Lowers blood LDL and cholesterol levels.

Available forms

Capsules: 20 mg, 40 mg
Tablets (extended release): 80 mg

NURSING PROCESS

Assessment
- Assess patient's blood LDL and cholesterol levels before therapy, and evaluate regularly thereafter.
- Liver function tests should be performed periodically.
- Be alert for adverse reactions and drug interactions.
- Evaluate patient's and family's knowledge of drug therapy.

Nursing diagnoses
- Risk for injury related to elevated LDL and cholesterol blood levels
- Diarrhea related to adverse effect of drug on GI tract
- Deficient knowledge related to drug therapy

Planning and implementation
- Drug should be started only after diet and other nondrug therapies have proven ineffective.
- Give drug at bedtime to enhance effectiveness.
- Maintain standard low-cholesterol diet during therapy.

Patient teaching
- Tell patient that drug may be taken without regard to meals; efficacy is enhanced if taken in evening.
- Teach patient about proper dietary management, weight control, and exercise. Explain their importance in controlling serum lipid levels.
- Warn patient to restrict alcohol consumption.
- Tell patient to inform prescriber of any adverse reactions, particularly muscle aches and pains.
- Tell patient to stop drug and notify prescriber about planned, suspected, or known pregnancy.

Evaluation
- Patient's blood LDL and cholesterol levels are within normal limits.
- Patient maintains normal bowel pattern.
- Patient and family state understanding of drug therapy.

fluvoxamine maleate
(floo-VOKS-uh-meen MAL-ee-ayt)
Luvox

Pharmacologic class: serotonin reuptake inhibitor
Therapeutic class: antidepressant
Pregnancy risk category: C

Indications and dosages
▶ **Obsessive-compulsive disorder.** *Adults:* Initially, 50 mg P.O. daily h.s. Increase in 50-mg increments q 4 to 7 days until maximum benefit occurs. Maximum, 300 mg daily. Total daily doses of more than 100 mg should be given in two divided doses.
Children ages 8 to 17: 25 mg P.O. daily h.s. Dose may be increased in 25-mg increments q 4 to 7 days as tolerated until maximum benefit achieved. Maximum, 200 mg daily for children ages 8 to 11 and 300 mg for children ages 12 to 17. Total daily doses exceeding 50 mg should be given in two divided doses.
Elderly patients: Initially, 25 mg P.O. daily, then adjust upward gradually.

Contraindications and precautions
- Contraindicated in patients hypersensitive to drug or to other phenylpiperazine antidepressants and within 14 days of MAO inhibitor therapy.
- Coadministration with thioridazine or pimozide is contraindicated because ventricular arrhythmias and death may occur.
- Use cautiously in patients with hepatic dysfunction, conditions that may affect hemodynamic responses or metabolism, or history of mania or seizures.

Lifespan: With pregnant women, use cautiously. In breast-feeding women, drug isn't recommended. In children and adolescents younger than age 18, safety of drug hasn't been established. In elderly patients, use cautiously and start at a lower dose.

Adverse reactions
CNS: *headache, asthenia, somnolence, insomnia, nervousness, dizziness,* tremor, anxiety, hypertonia, *agitation,* depression, CNS stimulation.
CV: palpitations, vasodilation.

EENT: amblyopia.
GI: *nausea, diarrhea, constipation, dyspepsia,* anorexia, *vomiting,* flatulence, dysphagia, taste perversion, *dry mouth.*
GU: abnormal ejaculation, urinary frequency, impotence, anorgasmia, urine retention.
Respiratory: upper respiratory tract infection, dyspnea, yawning.
Skin: sweating.
Other: decreased libido, flulike syndrome, chills, tooth disorder.

Interactions

Drug-drug. *Benzodiazepines, theophylline, warfarin:* Reduces clearance of these drugs by fluvoxamine. Use together cautiously (except for diazepam, which shouldn't be given with fluvoxamine). Dosage adjustments may be necessary.
Carbamazepine, clozapine, methadone, metoprolol, propranolol, tricyclic antidepressants: Elevates serum levels of these drugs. Use together cautiously. Monitor patient closely for adverse reactions. Dosage adjustments may be necessary.
Diltiazem: Bradycardia may occur. Monitor heart rate.
Lithium, tryptophan: May enhance fluvoxamine effects. Use together cautiously.
MAO inhibitors: May cause severe excitation, hyperpyrexia, myoclonus, delirium, and coma. Don't use together.
Pimozide, thiorazidine: May prolong QT interval. Avoid using together.
Sumatriptan: May cause weakness, hyperreflexia, and incoordination. Monitor patient closely.
Drug-herb. *St. John's wort:* May cause serotonin syndrome. Discourage using together.
Drug-food. *Caffeine:* Decreases caffeine elimination and increases caffeine effects. Discourage using together.
Drug-lifestyle. *Alcohol use:* May increase CNS effects. Discourage using together.
Smoking: Decreases effectiveness of drug. Discourage patient from smoking.

Effects on lab test results

None reported.

Pharmacokinetics

Absorption: Unknown.
Distribution: 77% protein-bound.
Metabolism: Metabolized in liver.
Excretion: Excreted in urine. *Half-life:* 17 hours.

Route	Onset	Peak	Duration
P.O.	Unknown	3-8 hr	Unknown

Pharmacodynamics

Chemical effect: Unknown; selectively inhibits neuronal uptake of serotonin, which is thought to reduce obsessive-compulsive disorders.
Therapeutic effect: Decreases obsessive-compulsive behavior.

Available forms

Tablets: 25 mg, 50 mg, 100 mg

NURSING PROCESS

Assessment

- Assess patient's condition before therapy, and reassess regularly thereafter. Several weeks of therapy may be needed before positive response occurs.
- Be alert for adverse reactions and drug interactions.
- Evaluate patient's and family's knowledge of drug therapy.

Nursing diagnoses

- Ineffective individual coping related to underlying condition
- Diarrhea related to adverse effect of drug on GI tract
- Deficient knowledge related to drug therapy

Planning and implementation

- At least 14 days should elapse after stopping fluvoxamine before patient starts an MAO inhibitor, and at least 14 days should elapse before patient starts fluvoxamine after MAO inhibitor therapy has stopped.
- Give drug at bedtime and without regard to meals.

Patient teaching

- Warn patient to avoid hazardous activities until CNS effects of drug are known.
- Advise patient to avoid alcoholic beverages during drug therapy.
- Alert patient that smoking may decrease effectiveness of drug.
- Instruct woman to notify prescriber about planned, suspected, or known pregnancy.

• Tell patient who develops rash, hives, or related allergic reaction to notify prescriber.
• Inform patient that several weeks of therapy may be needed to obtain full antidepressant effect. Once improvement occurs, advise patient not to stop drug unless directed by prescriber.
• Advise patient to check with prescriber before taking OTC medications or herbal remedies; interactions can occur.

☑ Evaluation

• Patient's obsessive-compulsive behaviors are diminished.
• Patient maintains normal bowel patterns.
• Patient and family state understanding of drug therapy.

folic acid (vitamin B)

(FOH-lek AS-id)
Apo-Folic ♦, Folvite, Novo-Folacid ♦

Pharmacologic class: folic acid derivative
Therapeutic class: vitamin supplement
Pregnancy risk category: A

Indications and dosages

▶ **To maintain health.** *Infants:* Up to 0.1 mg P.O. daily.
Children younger than age 4: Up to 0.3 mg P.O. daily.
Adults and children age 4 and older: 0.4 mg P.O. daily.
Pregnant or lactating women: 0.8 mg P.O. daily.

▶ **Megaloblastic or macrocytic anemia caused by folic acid or other nutritional deficiency, hepatic disease, alcoholism, intestinal obstruction, excessive hemolysis.** *Adults and children age 4 and older:* 0.4 mg to 1 mg P.O., S.C., or I.M. daily. After anemia caused by folic acid deficiency is corrected, proper diet and supplements are needed to prevent recurrence.
Children younger than age 4: Up to 0.3 mg P.O., S.C., or I.M. daily.
Pregnant and breast-feeding women: 0.8 mg P.O., S.C., or I.M. daily.

▶ **Prevention of megaloblastic anemia in pregnancy and fetal damage.** *Adults:* Up to 1 mg P.O., S.C., or I.M. daily throughout pregnancy.

▶ **Nutritional supplement.** *Adults:* 0.1 mg P.O., S.C., or I.M. daily.
Children: 0.05 mg P.O. daily.

▶ **To test folic acid deficiency in patients with megaloblastic anemia without masking pernicious anemia.** *Adults and children:* 0.1 to 0.2 mg P.O. or I.M. for 10 days, with diet low in folate and vitamin B_{12}.

▶ **Tropical sprue.** *Adults:* 3 to 15 mg P.O. daily.

Contraindications and precautions

• Contraindicated in patients with B_{12} deficiency or undiagnosed anemia.
Lifespan: In pregnant women, folic acid therapy is recommended to prevent neural tube defects.

Adverse reactions

CNS: general malaise.
GI: bitter taste, anorexia, nausea, flatulence.
Respiratory: ***bronchospasm.***
Skin: allergic reactions (rash, pruritus, erythema).

Interactions

Drug-drug. *Aminosalicylic acid, chloramphenicol, methotrexate, sulfasalazine, trimethoprim:* Antagonism of folic acid. Monitor patient for decreased folic acid effect. Use together cautiously.
Anticonvulsants (such as phenobarbital, phenytoin): May increase anticonvulsant metabolism and decrease anticonvulsant blood levels. Monitor patient closely.

Effects on lab test results

• May decrease folate level.
• May decrease RBC count.

Pharmacokinetics

Absorption: Absorbed rapidly from GI tract, mainly from proximal part of small intestine, when given orally. Absorption unknown after S.C. or I.M. administration.
Distribution: Distributed into all body tissues; liver contains about half of total body folate stores. Folate is concentrated actively in CSF.
Metabolism: Metabolized in liver.
Excretion: Excess folate is excreted unchanged in urine; small amounts of folic acid have been recovered in feces. About 0.05 mg/day of normal body folate stores is lost by

combination of urinary and fecal excretion and oxidative cleavage of molecule.

Route	Onset	Peak	Duration
P.O., I.M., S.C.	Unknown	30-60 min	Unknown

Pharmacodynamics

Chemical effect: Stimulates normal erythropoiesis and nucleoprotein synthesis.
Therapeutic effect: Nutritional supplement.

Available forms

Injection: 5 mg/ml with 1.5% benzyl alcohol or 10 mg/ml with 1.5% benzyl alcohol and 0.2% EDTA
Tablets: 0.1 mg†, 0.4 mg†, 0.8 mg†, 1 mg

NURSING PROCESS

Assessment

- Assess patient's folic acid deficiency before therapy.
- Evaluate CBC, and assess patient's physical status throughout therapy.
- Be alert for adverse reactions and drug interactions.
- Evaluate patient's and family's knowledge of drug therapy.

Nursing diagnoses

- Imbalanced nutrition: less than body requirements related to presence of folic acid deficiency
- Deficient knowledge related to drug therapy

Planning and implementation

- Patient with small-bowel resection and intestinal malabsorption may need parenteral administration.
- **P.O. and S.C. use:** Follow normal protocol.
- **I.M. use:** Don't mix with other drugs in same syringe for I.M. injections. Follow normal protocol.
- Protect from light and heat; store at room temperature.
- Concurrent folic acid and vitamin B_{12} therapy may be used if supported by diagnosis.
- Make sure patient is getting properly balanced diet.

Patient teaching

- Teach patient proper nutrition to prevent recurrence of anemia.
- Tell patient to report hypersensitivity reactions or breathing difficulty.
- Urge patient to avoid alcohol because it increases folic acid requirements.

Evaluation

- Patient's CBC is normal.
- Patient and family state understanding of drug therapy.

fondaparinux sodium

(fon-duh-PAIR-in-ux)
Arixtra

Pharmacologic class: inhibitor of activated factor X (Xa)
Therapeutic class: anticoagulant
Pregnancy risk category: B

Indications and dosages

▶ **Prevention of deep vein thrombosis, which may lead to pulmonary embolism, in patients undergoing surgery for hip fracture, hip replacement, or knee replacement.** *Adults:* 2.5 mg S.C. once daily for 5 to 9 days; maximum 11 days. Give initial dose after hemostasis is established, approximately 6 to 8 hours after surgery. Giving the dose earlier than 6 hours after surgery increases the risk for major bleeding.

Contraindications and precautions

- Contraindicated in patients with creatinine clearance less than 30 ml/minute; in those who are hypersensitive to the drug or weigh less than 50 kg (110 lbs); and in those with active major bleeding, bacterial endocarditis, or thrombocytopenia with a positive test result for antiplatelet antibody while taking drug.
- Use with extreme caution in patients also being treated with platelet inhibitors and in those at increased risk for bleeding, such as patients with congenital or acquired bleeding disorders, with active ulcerative and angiodysplastic GI disease, with hemorrhagic CVA, or shortly after brain, spinal, or ophthalmologic surgery.
- Use cautiously in patients who have had epidural or spinal anesthesia or spinal puncture; they have an increased risk for developing

an epidural or spinal hematoma (which may cause permanent paralysis).

• Use caution in patients undergoing elective hip surgery with mild or moderate renal impairment.

• Also use cautiously in patients with creatinine clearance 30 to 50 ml/minute, with a history of heparin-induced thrombocytopenia, or with a bleeding diathesis, uncontrolled arterial hypertension, or a history of recent GI ulceration, diabetic retinopathy, and hemorrhage. Patients with mild renal impairment had approximately 25% lower total clearance. Patients with moderate renal impairment had a 40% lower total clearance. Hemodialysis may increase clearance by 20%.

Lifespan: In pregnant women, avoid using drug unless clearly needed because no adequate studies have been done in pregnant women. In breast-feeding women, use cautiously because it's unknown whether drug appears in breast milk. In children, safety and effectiveness of drug haven't been established. In elderly patients, use cautiously because the risk of major bleeding increases with age. In patients older than age 75, total clearance of drug was approximately 25% lower than in patients younger than age 65.

Adverse reactions

CNS: insomnia, dizziness, confusion, pain, headache, *fever, **spinal and epidural hematomas.***
CV: hypotension, edema.
GI: *nausea,* constipation, vomiting, diarrhea, dyspepsia.
GU: urinary tract infection, urinary retention.
Hematologic: ***hemorrhage,*** *anemia,* hematoma, ***postoperative hemorrhage, thrombocytopenia.***
Metabolic: hypokalemia.
Skin: mild local irritation (injection site bleeding, rash, pruritus), bullous eruption, purpura increased wound drainage, rash.

Interactions

Drug-drug. *Drugs that increase risk of bleeding (NSAIDs, platelet inhibitors, anticoagulants):* Increases risk of hemorrhage. Stop use before starting fondaparinux. If must be used together, monitor patient closely for bleeding.

Effects on lab results

• May increase creatinine, AST, ALT, and bilirubin levels. May decrease potassium level.

• May decrease hemoglobin, hematocrit, and platelet count.

Pharmacokinetics

Absorption: Rapid and complete when given by S.C. injection; 100% bioavailability.
Distribution: Mainly in blood. Fondaparinux is at least 94% bound to AT-III.
Metabolism: In vivo metabolism of fondaparinux hasn't been investigated since most of the drug is eliminated unchanged in urine in people with normal kidney function.
Excretion: Up to 77% of a single I.V. or S.C. dose is eliminated in urine unchanged in 72 hours. Elimination is prolonged in patients over age 75; in patients who weigh less than 50 kg (110 lbs); and in patients with renal impairment. (See Contraindications and precautions). *Half-life:* 17 to 21 hours.

Route	Onset	Peak	Duration
S.C.	Unknown	2-3 hr	Unknown

Pharmacodynamics

Chemical effect: Binds to antithrombin III (AT-III) and potentiates by about 300 times the natural neutralization of factor Xa by AT-III. Neutralization of factor Xa interrupts the coagulation cascade, thereby inhibiting formation of thrombin and thrombus development.
Therapeutic effect: Prevents the formation of blood clots.

Available forms

Injection: 2.5 mg/0.5 ml prefilled syringe

NURSING PROCESS

Assessment

• Assess patient's underlying condition before initiating therapy.

• Be alert for any adverse reactions or drug interactions.

• Patients who have received epidural or spinal anesthesia are at increased risk for developing an epidural or spinal hematoma, which may result in long-term or permanent paralysis. Monitor these patients closely for neurological impairment.

• Monitor renal function periodically and discontinue drug in patients who develop unstable renal function or severe renal impairment while on therapy.

• Routinely assess patient for signs and symptoms of bleeding, and regularly monitor CBC, platelet count, creatinine level, and stool occult blood test results. Stop use if platelet count is less than 100,000/mm³.
• Anticoagulant effects may last for 2 to 4 days after stopping drug in patients with normal renal function.
• PT and aPTT are unsuitable tests to measure fondaparinux activity.
• Evaluate patient's and family's knowledge of drug therapy.

Nursing diagnoses
• Risk for injury related to potential for thrombosis or pulmonary emboli development from underlying condition
• Increased risk for trauma related to increased risk of bleeding and hemorrhaging due to drug therapy
• Deficient knowledge related to anticoagulant therapy

Planning and implementation
• Give by S.C. injection only. Give the drug S.C. in fatty tissue only, rotating administration injection sites.
• Visually inspect the single-dose, prefilled syringe for particulate matter and discoloration before administration.
• Don't mix with other injections or infusions.
ALERT: Don't use interchangeably with heparin, low–molecular-weight heparins, or heparinoids.
• To avoid loss of drug, don't expel air bubble from the syringe.
• Should patient begin to overtly bleed during therapy, apply strong pressure to area and notify prescriber immediately.
• Overdosage may lead to hemorrhagic complications. Stop drug and treat bleeding appropriately.
ALERT: Don't confuse fondaparinux (Arixtra) with the lab test anti-factor Xa, sometimes written anti-Xa.
ALERT: Don't confuse Arixtra with Bextra.

Patient teaching
• Teach patient signs and symptoms of bleeding. If any occur, patient should contact a clinician immediately.
• Instruct patient to avoid OTC products that contain aspirin, other salicylates, or NSAIDs and other prescribed anticoagulants.
• Teach patient the correct technique of S.C. drug administration if patient is to self-administer.
• Show patient the different sites for injection and explain to patient that he must alternate injection sites to prevent hardening of fatty tissues.
• Teach patient the proper disposal of the syringe.

Evaluation
• Patient doesn't suffer from any pulmonary embolus or thrombus during drug therapy.
• Patient is free from any injury or bleeding.
• Patient and family state understanding of drug therapy.

formoterol fumarate inhalation powder
(for-MOE-tur-all FOO-muh-rayt)
Foradil Aerolizer

Pharmacologic class: long-acting selective $beta_2$-adrenergic agonist
Therapeutic class: bronchodilator
Pregnancy risk category: C

Indications and dosages
▶ **Prevention and maintenance treatment of bronchospasm in patients with reversible obstructive airway disease or nocturnal asthma who usually need treatment with short-acting inhaled $beta_2$-adrenergic agonists.** *Adults and children age 5 and older:* One 12-mcg capsule by inhalation via Aerolizer inhaler q 12 hours. Total amount shouldn't exceed one capsule twice daily (24 mcg daily). If symptoms are present between doses, use a short-acting $beta_2$-adrenergic agonist for immediate relief.
▶ **Prevention of exercise-induced bronchospasm.** *Adults, adolescents, and children age 12:* One 12-mcg capsule by inhalation via Aerolizer inhaler at least 15 minutes before exercise, given occasionally, p.r.n. Avoid giving additional doses within 12 hours of first dose.

▶ **Maintenance treatment of COPD.** *Adults:* One 12-mcg capsule q 12 hours using the Aerolizer inhaler. Total daily dose of greater than 24 mcg isn't recommended.

Contraindications and precautions

• Contraindicated in patients hypersensitive to drug or its components.
• Use cautiously in patients with CV disease, particularly coronary insufficiency, cardiac arrhythmias, and hypertension; in those who are unusually responsive to sympathomimetic amines; and in those with diabetes mellitus because hyperglycemia and ketoacidosis have occurred rarely with use of beta agonists.
• Use cautiously in patients with seizure disorders or thyrotoxicosis.
Lifespan: In breast-feeding women, use cautiously because it isn't known whether drug appears in breast milk. In children younger than age 5, safety and efficacy haven't been established. In elderly patients, no overall differences in safety or efficacy have been observed. However, increased sensitivity of some elderly patients is possible.

Adverse reactions

CNS: tremor, dizziness, insomnia, nervousness, headache, fatigue, malaise.
CV: chest pain, angina, hypertension, hypotension, tachycardia, ***arrhythmias,*** palpitations.
EENT: dry mouth, tonsillitis, dysphonia.
GI: nausea.
Metabolic: hypokalemia, hyperglycemia, ***metabolic acidosis.***
Musculoskeletal: muscle cramps.
Respiratory: bronchitis, chest infection, dyspnea.
Skin: rash.
Other: viral infection.

Interactions

Drug-drug. *Adrenergics:* May potentiate sympathetic effects of formoterol. Use together cautiously.
Beta blockers: May antagonize effects of beta agonists, causing bronchospasm in asthmatic patients. Avoid use except when benefits outweigh risks. Use cardioselective beta blockers cautiously to minimize risk of bronchospasm.
Corticosteroids, diuretics, xanthine derivatives: May potentiate hypokalemic effect of formoterol. Use together cautiously.
MAO inhibitors, tricyclic antidepressants, and other drugs that prolong the QT interval: May increase risk of ventricular arrhythmias. Use together cautiously.
Non–potassium-sparing diuretics (such as loop or thiazide diuretics): May worsen ECG changes or hypokalemia with beta agonists. Use together cautiously, and monitor patient closely.

Effects on lab test results

• May decrease potassium level. May increase glucose and blood pH levels.

Pharmacokinetics

Absorption: Rapidly absorbed into plasma. Drug levels peak within 5 minutes after a 120-mcg dose. Similar to other products for oral inhalation, most of inhaled dose is probably swallowed and absorbed from the GI tract.
Distribution: 61% to 64% bound to human plasma proteins.
Metabolism: Occurs primarily via direct glucuronidation and O-demethylation (involving cytochrome P450 isoenzymes 2D6, 2C19, 2C9, and 2A6). Doesn't appear to inhibit CYP450 enzymes at therapeutic levels.
Excretion: 59% to 62% eliminated in urine and 32% to 34% eliminated in feces over 104 hours. When 12 to 24 mcg formoterol is given to asthma patients, about 10% of total dose is excreted in urine as unchanged drug and 15% to 18% is eliminated in urine as direct glucuronide conjugates of formoterol.

Route	Onset	Peak	Duration
Oral inhalation	≤ 15 min	1-3 hr	12 hr

Pharmacodynamics

Chemical effect: Relaxes bronchial and cardiac smooth muscle by acting on $beta_2$ adrenergic receptors; stimulates intracellular adenyl cyclase, the enzyme responsible for catalyzing the conversion of adenosine triphosphate (ATP) to cAMP. This increase in cAMP leads to relaxation of bronchial smooth muscle and inhibition of mediator release from mast cells.
Therapeutic effect: Prevents and controls bronchospasm.

Available forms

Capsules for inhalation: 12 mcg

NURSING PROCESS

Assessment
• Assess patient's underlying condition before therapy, and reassess regularly throughout therapy.
• Evaluate patient's use of short acting $beta_2$ agonists for immediate relief of bronchospasm. Drug may be used with short-acting $beta_2$ agonists, inhaled corticosteroids, and theophylline therapy to manage asthma.
• Evaluate patient's and family's knowledge of drug therapy.

Nursing diagnoses
• Impaired gas exchange related to underlying pulmonary condition
• Risk for activity intolerance related to underlying pulmonary condition
• Knowledge deficit related to formoterol fumarate therapy

Planning and implementation
• Patients using drug twice daily shouldn't take additional doses to prevent exercise-induced bronchospasm.
• Don't use as a substitute for short-acting $beta_2$ agonists for immediate relief of bronchospasm or as a substitute for inhaled or oral corticosteroids.
• Don't begin use in patients with rapidly deteriorating or significantly worsening asthma.
• If usual dose doesn't control symptoms of bronchoconstriction, and the patient's short-acting $beta_2$ agonist becomes less effective, reevaluate patient and treatment regimen.
• For patients who formerly used regularly scheduled short-acting $beta_2$ agonists, use of the short-acting drug should be decreased to an as-needed basis when long-acting formoterol therapy starts.
• Before dispensing, store drug in refrigerator. Once dispensed to patient, drug may be stored at room temperature. Capsules should remain in the unopened blister until immediately before administration. Capsules should be given only by oral inhalation and used only with the Aerolizer inhaler. They aren't for oral ingestion. Don't let the patient exhale into the device. Don't use Foradil Aerolizer with a spacer device. Pierce capsules only once. In rare instances, the gelatin capsule may break into small pieces and enter the patient's mouth or throat with inhalation. However, the Aerolizer contains a screen that should catch any broken pieces before they leave the device. To minimize the possibility of shattering the capsule, strictly follow storage and use instructions.
• As with all $beta_2$ agonists, drug may produce life-threatening paradoxical bronchospasm. If this occurs, discontinue formoterol immediately and use an alternative drug.
• Monitor patient for tachycardia, hypertension, and other adverse CV effects. If they occur, drug may need to be discontinued.
• Watch for immediate hypersensitivity reactions, such as anaphylaxis, urticaria, angioedema, rash, and bronchospasm.
• Signs and symptoms of overdose include excessive beta-adrenergic stimulation and exaggeration of adverse effects. Cardiac arrest and death may result. Treatment of overdose should include discontinuation of drug, cardiac monitoring, appropriate symptomatic relief or supportive therapy, and possibly judicious use of cardioselective beta blockers. It's unknown whether dialysis is beneficial.

ALERT: Don't confuse Foradil (formoterol fumarate) with Toradol (ketorolac).

Patient teaching
• Tell patient not to increase the dose or frequency of use without medical advice.
• Warn patient not to stop or reduce other medication taken for asthma.
• Advise patient that drug isn't for acute asthmatic episodes. A short-acting $beta_2$ agonist should be prescribed for this use.
• Advise patient to report worsening symptoms, less-effective treatment, or increasing use of short-acting $beta_2$ agonist.
• Tell patient to report nausea, vomiting, shakiness, headache, fast or irregular heartbeat, chest pain, or sleeplessness.
• Tell patient being treated for exercise-induced bronchospasm to take drug at least 15 minutes before exercise. Additional doses can't be taken for 12 hours.
• Tell patient not to use the Foradil Aerolizer with a spacer device or to exhale or blow into the inhaler.
• Advise patient to avoid washing the Aerolizer and to always keep it dry. Advise patient to use the new device that comes with each refill.

• Tell patient to avoid exposing capsules to moisture and to handle them only with dry hands.

Evaluation

• Patient's pulmonary symptoms improve.
• Patient's activity intolerance improves.
• Patient and family state understanding of drug therapy.

foscarnet sodium (phosphonoformic acid)

(fos-KAR-net SOH-dee-um)
Foscavir

Pharmacologic class: pyrophosphate analogue
Therapeutic class: antiviral
Pregnancy risk category: C

Indications and dosages

▶ **CMV retinitis in patients with AIDS.** *Adults:* Initially, in patients with normal renal function, 60 mg/kg I.V. over 1 hour q 8 hours for 2 to 3 weeks, depending on clinical response. Or, 90 mg/kg I.V. q 12 hours over 1.5 to 2 hours for 2 to 3 weeks, depending on clinical response. Follow with maintenance infusion of 90 mg/kg I.V. daily over 2 hours; dose may be increased as needed and tolerated to 120 mg/kg daily if disease progresses.

▶ **Mucocutaneous acyclovir-resistant herpes simplex virus (HSV) infections.** *Adults:* 40 mg/kg I.V. infused over at least 1 hour, either q 8 or 12 hours for 2 to 3 weeks or until healed.

▶ **Varicella zoster infection‡.** *Adults:* 40 mg/kg I.V. q 8 hours for 10 to 21 days.

Contraindications and precautions

• Contraindicated in patients hypersensitive to drug.
• Use cautiously and in reduced amounts in patients with abnormal renal function because drug will accumulate and toxicity will increase. Because foscarnet is nephrotoxic, it may worsen renal impairment. Some nephrotoxicity occurs in most patients treated with drug.

Lifespan: In pregnant or breast-feeding women, use cautiously. In children, safety of drug hasn't been established.

Adverse reactions

CNS: *fever,* pain, *headache,* ***seizures,*** *fatigue, malaise, asthenia, paresthesia, dizziness, hypesthesia, neuropathy,* tremor, ataxia, generalized spasms, dementia, stupor, sensory disturbances, meningitis, aphasia, abnormal coordination, EEG abnormalities, depression, confusion, anxiety, insomnia, somnolence, nervousness, amnesia, agitation, aggressive reaction.
CV: *hypertension, palpitations, ECG abnormalities, sinus tachycardia,* cerebrovascular disorder, *first-degree AV block, hypotension, flushing,* edema.
EENT: visual disturbances, eye pain, conjunctivitis, sinusitis, pharyngitis, rhinitis.
GI: taste perversion, dry mouth, *nausea, diarrhea, vomiting, abdominal pain, anorexia,* constipation, dysphagia, ***rectal hemorrhage,*** melena, flatulence, ulcerative stomatitis, ***pancreatitis.***
GU: *abnormal renal function, albuminuria, dysuria, polyuria, urethral disorder, urine retention, urinary tract infection,* ***acute renal failure, nephrotoxicity,*** candidiasis.
Hematologic: anemia, granulocytopenia, ***leukopenia, bone marrow suppression, thrombocytopenia,*** platelet abnormalities, thrombocytosis, WBC count abnormalities, lymphadenopathy.
Hepatic: abnormal hepatic function.
Metabolic: hypokalemia, hypomagnesemia, hypophosphatemia or hyperphosphatemia, hypocalcemia, hyponatremia.
Musculoskeletal: leg cramps, arthralgia, myalgia.
Respiratory: *cough, dyspnea,* pneumonitis, respiratory insufficiency, pulmonary infiltration, stridor, pneumothorax, ***bronchospasm,*** hemoptysis.
Skin: *rash, increased sweating,* pruritus, skin ulceration, erythematous rash, seborrhea, skin discoloration, facial edema.
Other: ***sepsis,*** rigors, inflammation, pain at infusion site, lymphoma-like disorder, sarcoma, back or chest pain, bacterial or fungal infections, abscess, flulike symptoms.

Interactions

Drug-drug. *Nephrotoxic drugs (such as amphotericin B, aminoglycosides):* May increase risk of nephrotoxicity. Avoid using together.
Pentamidine: May increase risk of nephrotoxicity and severe hypocalcemia. Don't use together.

Zidovudine: Possible increased risk or severity of anemia. Monitor blood counts.

Effects on lab test results

• May increase BUN, creatinine, phosphate, ALT, AST, alkaline phosphatase, and bilirubin levels. May decrease calcium, magnesium, phosphate, potassium, and sodium levels.

• May decrease hemoglobin, hematocrit, and granulocyte and WBC counts. May increase or decrease platelet count.

Pharmacokinetics

Absorption: Administered I.V.
Distribution: Unknown.
Metabolism: Unknown.
Excretion: 80% to 90% appears unchanged in urine. *Half-life:* About 3 hours.

Route	Onset	Peak	Duration
I.V.	Immediate	Immediate	Unknown

Pharmacodynamics

Chemical effect: Inhibits all known herpes viruses in vitro by blocking pyrophosphate binding site on DNA polymerases and reverse transcriptases.
Therapeutic effect: Inhibits herpes virus activity.

Available forms

Injection: 24 mg/ml in 250- and 500-ml bottles

NURSING PROCESS

Assessment

• Assess patient's infection before therapy and regularly thereafter.

• Obtain serum electrolyte levels and creatinine clearance before beginning therapy.

• Monitor creatinine clearance two to three times weekly during induction and at least once every 1 to 2 weeks during maintenance.

• Because drug can adversely affect potassium, calcium, magnesium, and phosphorus, monitor levels using schedule similar to that established for creatinine clearance.

• Drug may cause dose-related transient decrease in ionized serum calcium, which may not be reflected in laboratory values. Assess for tetany and seizures with abnormal electrolyte levels.

• Monitor patient's hemoglobin and hematocrit levels. Anemia is common (in up to 33% of patients treated with drug). It may be severe enough that patient needs transfusions.

• Be alert for adverse reactions and drug interactions.

• Evaluate patient's and family's knowledge of drug therapy.

Nursing diagnoses

• Infection related to presence of herpes virus susceptible to drug

• Disturbed sensory perception (tactile) related to drug's adverse effect

• Deficient knowledge related to drug therapy

Planning and implementation

• Use infusion pump to give drug over at least 1 hour. To minimize renal toxicity, ensure adequate hydration before and during infusion.

• Don't exceed recommended dosage, infusion rate, or frequency of administration. All doses must be individualized based on patient's renal function.

• Because drug is highly toxic and toxicity is probably dose-related, use lowest effective maintenance dose.

ALERT: Dosage must be adjusted when creatinine clearance is below 1.5 ml/minute/kg. If creatinine clearance falls below 0.4 ml/minute/kg, drug should be discontinued.

Patient teaching

• Advise patient to report circumoral tingling, numbness in limbs, and paresthesia.

Evaluation

• Patient is free from infection.

• Patient has no adverse neurologic reactions.

• Patient and family state understanding of drug therapy.

fosinopril sodium

(foh-SIN-oh-pril SOH-dee-um)
Monopril

Pharmacologic class: ACE inhibitor
Therapeutic class: antihypertensive
Pregnancy risk category: C (D in second and third trimesters)

Indications and dosages

▶ **Hypertension.** *Adults:* Initially, 10 mg P.O. daily. Dosage is adjusted based on blood pressure response at peak and trough levels. Usual dosage is 20 to 40 mg, up to 80 mg daily. Dosage is divided, if needed.

▶ **Adjunctive therapy for heart failure.** *Adults:* Initially, 10 mg P.O. once daily. Dosage should be increased over several weeks to maximum tolerable, but no more than 40 mg P.O. daily. If possible, discontinue diuretic therapy.

Patients who have heart failure with moderate-to-severe renal impairment or who are being vigorously diuresed: Give initial dose of 5 mg P.O. daily.

Contraindications and precautions

- Contraindicated in patients hypersensitive to drug or other ACE inhibitors.
- Use cautiously in patients with impaired renal or hepatic function. Avoid use in patients with renal artery stenosis.

Lifespan: In pregnant women, use with extreme caution and only when necessary to prevent fetal harm. In breast-feeding women, drug is contraindicated. In children, safety of drug hasn't been established.

Adverse reactions

CNS: headache, dizziness, fatigue, syncope, paresthesia, sleep disturbance, ***CVA.***
CV: chest pain, angina, ***MI,*** rhythm disturbances, palpitations, hypotension, orthostatic hypotension.
EENT: tinnitus, sinusitis.
GI: dry mouth, nausea, vomiting, diarrhea, ***pancreatitis,*** abdominal distention, abdominal pain, constipation.
GU: sexual dysfunction, renal insufficiency.
Hepatic: ***hepatitis.***
Metabolic: ***hyperkalemia.***
Musculoskeletal: arthralgia, musculoskeletal pain, myalgia.
Respiratory: *dry, persistent, tickling, nonproductive cough;* ***bronchospasm.***
Skin: urticaria, rash, photosensitivity, pruritus.
Other: decreased libido, gout, ***angioedema.***

Interactions

Drug-drug. *Antacids:* May impair absorption. Separate administration times by at least 2 hours.
Diuretics, other antihypertensives: May increase risk of excessive hypotension. Diuretic may need to be discontinued or fosinopril dosage lowered.
Lithium: May increase serum lithium levels and lithium toxicity. Avoid using together.
Potassium-sparing diuretics, potassium supplements, sodium substitutes containing potassium: May increase risk of hyperkalemia. Monitor serum potassium levels.
Drug-herb. *Licorice:* May cause sodium retention and increase blood pressure, interfering with therapeutic effect of ACE inhibitor. Discourage ingestion of licorice during drug therapy.
Drug-food. *Salt substitutes containing potassium:* May increase risk of hyperkalemia. Monitor serum potassium closely.
Drug-lifestyle. *Alcohol use:* May have additive hypotensive effects. Discourage using together.

Effects on lab test results

- May increase BUN, creatinine, and potassium levels.
- May increase liver function test values. May decrease hemoglobin and hematocrit.

Pharmacokinetics

Absorption: Absorbed slowly through GI tract, primarily in proximal small intestine.
Distribution: More than 95% protein-bound.
Metabolism: Hydrolyzed mainly in liver and gut.
Excretion: 50% excreted in urine; remainder in feces. *Half-life:* 11½ hours.

Route	Onset	Peak	Duration
P.O.	≤ 1 hr	2-6 hr	24 hr

Pharmacodynamics

Chemical effect: Antihypertensive action not clearly defined. Inhibits ACE, preventing conversion of angiotensin I to angiotensin II, a potent vasoconstrictor. Reduced formation of angiotensin II decreases peripheral arterial resistance, thus decreasing aldosterone secretion.
Therapeutic effect: Lowers blood pressure.

Available forms

Tablets: 10 mg, 20 mg, 40 mg

NURSING PROCESS

Assessment
- Assess blood pressure before therapy and regularly thereafter.
- Assess renal and hepatic function before and during therapy.
- Monitor potassium intake and potassium level. Diabetic patients, those with impaired renal function, and those receiving drugs that can increase serum potassium may develop hyperkalemia.
- Other ACE inhibitors have been linked to agranulocytosis and neutropenia. Monitor CBC with differential counts before therapy, every 2 weeks for first 3 months of therapy, and periodically thereafter.
- Monitor patient's hydration status if adverse GI reactions occur.
- Evaluate patient's and family's knowledge of drug therapy.

Nursing diagnoses
- Risk for injury related to presence of hypertension
- Risk for deficient fluid volume related to adverse GI reactions
- Deficient knowledge related to drug therapy

Planning and implementation
- Drug may be taken without regard to meals. However, taking drug with food slows absorption of drug.

Patient teaching
- Tell patient to avoid sodium substitutes; they may contain potassium, which increases the risk of hyperkalemia.
- Urge patient to report signs of infection (such as fever and sore throat); easy bruising or bleeding; swelling of tongue, lips, face, eyes, mucous membranes, or limbs; difficulty swallowing or breathing; and hoarseness.
- Tell patient to use caution in hot weather and during exercise. Inadequate fluid intake, vomiting, diarrhea, and excessive perspiration can lead to light-headedness and syncope.
- Tell woman to notify prescriber about planned, suspected, or known pregnancy. Drug will probably need to be discontinued.

Evaluation
- Patient's blood pressure is normal.
- Patient maintains adequate hydration throughout drug therapy.
- Patient and family state understanding of drug therapy.

fosphenytoin sodium
(fahs-FEN-eh-toyn SOH-dee-um)
Cerebyx

Pharmacologic class: prodrug of phenytoin; hydantoin
Therapeutic class: anticonvulsant
Pregnancy risk category: D

Indications and dosages
▶ **Status epilepticus.** *Adults:* 15 to 20 mg phenytoin sodium equivalent (PE)/kg I.V. at 100 to 150 mg PE/minute as loading dose; then 4 to 6 mg PE/kg I.V. daily as maintenance dose. (Phenytoin may be used instead of fosphenytoin as maintenance, using the appropriate dose.)
▶ **Prevention and treatment of seizures during neurosurgery (nonemergent loading or maintenance dosing).** *Adults:* Loading dose of 10 to 20 mg PE/kg I.M. or I.V. at infusion rate not exceeding 150 mg PE/minute. Maintenance dose is 4 to 6 mg PE/kg I.V. or I.M. daily.
▶ **Short-term substitution for oral phenytoin therapy.** *Adults:* Same total daily dosage equivalent as oral phenytoin sodium therapy given as a single daily dose I.M. or I.V. at infusion rate not exceeding 150 mg PE/minute. Some patients may need more frequent dosing.

Contraindications and precautions
- Contraindicated in patients hypersensitive to drug, its components, phenytoin, or other hydantoins. Also, contraindicated in patients with sinus bradycardia, SA block, second- or third-degree AV block, or Adams-Stokes syndrome.

Lifespan: In breast-feeding women, drug isn't recommended.

Adverse reactions
CNS: increased or decreased reflexes, speech disorders, dysarthria, asthenia, ***intracranial hypertension,*** thinking abnormalities, nervousness, hypesthesia, extrapyramidal syndrome, ***cerebral edema,*** headache, *nystagmus, dizziness, somnolence, ataxia,* stupor, incoordination, paresthesia, tremor, agitation, vertigo.

CV: hypertension, vasodilation, tachycardia, hypotension.
GI: taste perversion, constipation, dry mouth. nausea, vomiting, tongue disorder.
Hematologic: ***thrombocytopenia, leukopenia, agranulocytosis, granulocytopenia, pancytopenia.***
Metabolic: hypokalemia, hyperglycemia.
Musculoskeletal: back pain, myasthenia, pelvic pain.
Respiratory: pneumonia.
Skin: ecchymosis, injection-site reaction and pain, rash, *pruritus.*
Other: lymphadenopathy, accidental injury, infection, chills.

Interactions

Drug-drug. *Amiodarone, chloramphenicol, chlordiazepoxide, cimetidine, diazepam, dicumarol, disulfiram, estrogens, ethosuximide, fluoxetine, H_2-receptor antagonists, halothane, isoniazid, methylphenidate, phenothiazines, phenylbutazone, salicylates, succinimides, sulfonamides, tolbutamide, trazodone:* May increase plasma phenytoin levels and thus its therapeutic effects. Use together cautiously.
Carbamazepine, reserpine: May decrease plasma phenytoin levels. Monitor patient.
Coumarin, digitoxin, doxycycline, estrogens, furosemide, oral contraceptives, rifampin, quinidine, theophylline, vitamin D: Efficacy may be decreased by phenytoin because of increased hepatic metabolism. Monitor patient closely.
Phenobarbital, valproic acid, sodium valproate: May increase or decrease plasma phenytoin levels. Monitor patient.
Tricyclic antidepressants: May lower seizure threshold and require adjustments in phenytoin dosage. Use cautiously.
Drug-lifestyle. *Acute alcohol use:* May increase plasma phenytoin levels and thus its therapeutic effects. Discourage alcohol intake.
Chronic alcohol use: May decrease plasma phenytoin levels. Monitor patient; discourage alcohol intake.

Effects on lab test results

- May increase alkaline phosphatase, GGT, and glucose levels. May decrease potassium and T_4 levels.
- May decrease platelet, WBC, granulocyte, leukocyte, and RBC counts.

Pharmacokinetics

Absorption: Completely absorbed following I.M. and I.V. use.
Distribution: Widely throughout body; 95% plasma protein–bound.
Metabolism: Metabolized in the liver.
Excretion: Excreted in the urine.

Route	Onset	Peak	Duration
I.V.	Unknown	Immediate	Unknown
I.M.	Unknown	30 min	Unknown

Pharmacodynamics

Chemical effect: Because fosphenytoin is a prodrug of phenytoin, its anticonvulsant action is the same. Phenytoin is thought to stabilize neuronal membranes and limit seizure activity.
Therapeutic effect: Prevents and controls seizures.

Available forms

Injection: 2 ml (150 mg fosphenytoin sodium equivalent to 100 mg phenytoin sodium), 10 ml (750 mg fosphenytoin sodium equivalent to 500 mg phenytoin sodium)

NURSING PROCESS

Assessment

- Don't give drug I.M. for status epilepticus because therapeutic phenytoin levels may not occur as rapidly as with I.V. administration.
- After drug administration, phenytoin levels shouldn't be monitored until about 2 hours after the end of I.V. infusion or 4 hours after I.M. administration.
- Evaluate patient's and family's knowledge of drug therapy.

Nursing diagnoses

- Risk for trauma related to seizures
- Deficient knowledge related to drug therapy

Planning and implementation

- Drug should always be prescribed and dispensed in PE units. Don't make any adjustments in recommended doses when substituting fosphenytoin for phenytoin, and vice versa.
- **I.V. use:** Before I.V. infusion, dilute drug in D_5W or normal saline solution for injection to a level ranging from 1.5 to 25 mg PE/ml. Don't exceed 150 mg PE/minute.

– Monitor patient's ECG, blood pressure, and respiration throughout period of maximal serum phenytoin levels—about 10 to 20 minutes after end of fosphenytoin infusion.
• **I.M. use:** I.M. use generates systemic phenytoin levels similar to oral phenytoin sodium, allowing essentially interchangeable use.
• Abrupt withdrawal of drug may cause status epilepticus.
ALERT: Don't confuse Cerebyx with Celexa or Celebrex.

Patient teaching
• Warn patient that sensory disturbances may occur with I.V. use.
• Instruct patient to immediately report adverse reactions, especially rash.
• Warn patient not to stop drug abruptly or to adjust dosage without consulting prescriber.

Evaluation
• Patient is free from seizures.
• Patient and family state understanding of drug therapy.

frovatriptan succinate
(froh-vah-TRIP-tan SUK-seh-nayt)
Frova

Pharmacologic class: serotonin 5HT1 receptor agonist with high affinity for 5HT1B/1D receptors
Therapeutic class: antimigraine drug
Pregnancy risk category: C

Indications and dosages

▶ **Acute treatment of migraine attacks with or without aura.** *Adults:* 2.5 mg P.O. taken at the first sign of migraine attack. If the headache recurs after initial relief, a second tablet may be taken providing there's an interval of at least 2 hours between doses. The total daily dose shouldn't exceed three tablets.

Contraindications and precautions

• Contraindicated in patients who are hypersensitive to drug or any of the inactive ingredients in the tablets. Also contraindicated in patients with ischemic heart disease (such as angina pectoris, history of myocardial infarction, or documented silent ischemia) and in patients who have symptoms or findings consistent with ischemic heart disease, coronary artery vasospasm (including Prinzmetal's variant angina), or other significant underlying cardiovascular conditions. Don't use in patients with cerebrovascular syndromes such as CVAs of any types or transient ischemic attacks or in patients with peripheral vascular disease, including, but not limited to, ischemic bowel disease. Contraindicated in patients with uncontrolled hypertension and in patients with hemiplegic or basilar migraine.
Lifespan: In pregnant women, use drug only if potential benefit justifies risk to the fetus. In breast-feeding women, use cautiously because it's unknown whether drug appears in breast milk. In children, safety and effectiveness of drug haven't been established. In elderly patients, mean blood concentrations are 1.5 to 2 times higher. No special dosing is suggested. Because migraine is uncommon in the elderly, clinical experience with drug in older patients is limited.

Adverse reactions

CNS: dizziness, headache, fatigue, pain, paresthesia, insomnia, anxiety, somnolence, dysesthesia, hypoesthesia.
CV: flushing, palpitations, chest pain.
EENT: abnormal vision, tinnitus, sinusitis, rhinitis.
GI: dry mouth, dyspepsia, vomiting, abdominal pain, diarrhea, nausea.
Musculoskeletal: skeletal pain.
Skin: increased sweating.
Other: hot or cold sensation.

Interactions

Drug-drug. *Ergotamine-containing or ergot-type medications (such as dihydroergotamine or methysergide):* May cause prolonged vasospastic reactions. Use of ergot-containing medications and frovatriptan within 24 hours of each other should be avoided.
5HT 1B/1D Agonists: May have additive effects. Use of other 5HT1 agonists within 24 hours of frovatriptan isn't recommended.
Selective serotonin reuptake inhibitors (SSRIs, such as citalopram, fluoxetine, fluvoxamine, paroxetine, sertraline): May cause weakness, hyperreflexia, and incoordination when coadministered with 5HT1 agonists. Monitor patient closely.

Hormonal contraceptives, propranolol: Increases bioavailablity of frovatriptan. Monitor patient for adverse effects.

Effects on lab test results

None reported.

Pharmacokinetics

Absorption: Oral bioavailability of 20% in males and 30% in females. Peak concentrations are achieved in 2 to 4 hours. Food delays the time to peak, but not the bioavailabilty of the drug.
Distribution: Distributed to blood cells and plasma. Protein binding is low (about 15%).
Metabolism: Metabolized in the liver by cytochrome P450 1A2. Among the minor metabolites, desmethyl frovatriptan has low affinity for 5HT1B/1D receptors compared with the active compound. Frovatriptan doesn't appear to be an inducer or inhibitor of cytochrome P450.
Excretion: The drug is excreted in the urine and feces as unchanged frovatriptan and various metabolites (hydroxylated frovatriptan, N-acetyl desmethyl frovatriptan, hydroxylated N-acetyl desmethyl frovatriptan and desmethyl frovatriptan). *Half-life:* 26 hours.

Route	Onset	Peak	Duration
P.O.	Unknown	2-4 hr	Unknown

Pharmacodynamics

Chemical effect: Believed to inhibit excessive dilation of extracerebral, intracranial arteries in migraine headaches.
Therapeutic effect: Relieves pain caused by migraines.

Available forms

Tablets: 2.5 mg

NURSING PROCESS

Assessment

- Assess underlying condition before therapy and reassess regularly throughout therapy.
- Obtain complete medical history, paying particular attention to history of cardiovascular and cerebrovascular disease.
- Evaluate patient's and family's knowledge of drug therapy.

Nursing diagnoses

- Acute pain related to migraine headache
- Activity intolerance related to migraine headache
- Knowledge deficit related to frovatriptan succinate therapy

Planning and implementation

ALERT: Don't give within 24 hours of treatment with another 5HT1 agonist, an ergotamine-containing, or ergot-like medication.
ALERT: Serious cardiac events, including acute myocardial infarction, life-threatening cardiac rhythm disturbances, and death have been reported within a few hours of administration of 5HT1 agonists.

- Prescribers should be aware of the possibility of ophthalmic effects due to the possibility that drug may bind to the melanin of the eye. No specific ophthalmic monitoring is recommended.
- The safety of treating an average of more than four migraine attacks in a 30-day period hasn't been established.
- If frovatriptan is used in patients with risk factors for unrecognized coronary artery disease (such as hypertension, hypercholesterolemia, smoking, obesity, strong family history of coronary artery disease, female with surgical or physiological menopause, male over 40 years of age), it's strongly recommended that the first dose be given in prescriber's office or other medically staffed and equipped facility. Consider obtaining an ECG following the first dose. It's further suggested that intermittent, long-term users of 5HT1 agonists or those who have or acquire risk factors undergo periodic cardiac evaluation while using frovatriptan.

Patient teaching

- Instruct patient to take the dose at the first sign of a migraine headache. If the headache comes back after the first dose, a second dose may be taken after 2 hours. Don't take more than three tablets in a 24-hour period.
- Inform patient that in rare cases patients have experienced serious heart problems, CVA, or increased blood pressure after taking the drug.
- Caution the patient to take extra care or avoid driving and operating machinery if dizziness or fatigue develops after taking the drug.

• Emphasize importance of immediately reporting pain, tightness, heaviness, or pressure in the chest, throat, neck, or jaw, or rash or itching after taking the drug.
• Instruct patient not to take drug within 24 hours of taking another serotonin receptor agonist or ergotamine-type medication.

☑ Evaluation

• Patient is relieved of pain.
• Patient's activity tolerance returns to baseline.
• Patient and family state understanding of drug therapy.

furosemide (frusemide◆)

(fyoo-ROH-seh-mighd)

Apo-Furosemide◆, Furoside◆, Lasix*, Lasix Special◆, Myrosemide*, Novosemide◆, Uritol◆

Pharmacologic class: loop diuretic
Therapeutic class: diuretic, antihypertensive
Pregnancy risk category: C

Indications and dosages

▶ **Acute pulmonary edema.** *Adults:* 40 mg I.V. injected slowly over 1 to 2 minutes; then 80 mg I.V. in 1 to 1½ hours, if needed.
Infants and children: 1 mg/kg I.M. or I.V. If desired results don't occur after 2 hours, may increase initial dose by 1 mg/kg. Dosing interval should be at least 2 hours.
▶ **Edema.** *Adults:* 20 to 80 mg P.O. daily in morning, second dose in 6 to 8 hours; carefully adjusted up to 600 mg daily if needed. Or, 20 to 40 mg I.M. or I.V., increased by 20 mg q 2 hours until desired response occurs. Give I.V. dose slowly over 1 to 2 minutes.
Infants and children: 2 mg/kg P.O. daily, increase by 1 to 2 mg/kg in 6 to 8 hours if needed; carefully adjust up to 6 mg/kg daily, if needed.
▶ **Hypertension.** *Adults:* 40 mg P.O. b.i.d. Dosage adjusted according to response.
▶ **Hypercalcemia‡.** *Adults:* 80 to 100 mg I.V. q 1 to 2 hours; or 120 mg P.O. daily.

Contraindications and precautions

• Contraindicated in patients with anuria or history of hypersensitivity to drug.
• Use cautiously in patients with hepatic cirrhosis.
Lifespan: In pregnant women, use only if benefits outweigh risks. In breast-feeding women, drug isn't recommended.

Adverse reactions

CNS: fever, vertigo, headache, dizziness, paresthesia, restlessness, weakness.
CV: volume depletion and dehydration, orthostatic hypotension, thrombophlebitis (with I.V. use).
EENT: transient deafness (with too-rapid I.V. injection), blurred or yellow vision.
GI: abdominal discomfort and pain, diarrhea, anorexia, nausea, vomiting, constipation, ***pancreatitis.***
GU: azotemia, nocturia, polyuria, frequent urination, oliguria.
Hematologic: ***agranulocytosis, leukopenia, thrombocytopenia,*** anemia, ***aplastic anemia.***
Hepatic: ***hepatic dysfunction.***
Metabolic: hypokalemia, hypochloremic alkalosis, asymptomatic hyperuricemia, hyperglycemia and glucose intolerance, fluid and electrolyte imbalances, including dilutional hyponatremia, hypocalcemia, and hypomagnesemia.
Musculoskeletal: muscle spasm.
Skin: dermatitis, purpura, photosensitivity.
Other: gout, transient pain at I.M. injection site.

Interactions

Drug-drug. *Aminoglycoside antibiotics, cisplatin:* Potentiates ototoxicity. Use together cautiously.
Amphotericin B, corticosteroids, corticotropin, metolazone: May increase risk of hypokalemia. Monitor potassium levels closely.
Antidiabetics: Decreases hypoglycemic effects. Monitor glucose levels.
Antihypertensives: May increase risk of hypotension. Use together cautiously.
Cardiac glycosides, neuromuscular blockers: May increase toxicity from furosemide-induced hypokalemia. Monitor potassium levels closely.
Ethacrynic acid: May increase risk of ototoxicity. Don't use together.
Lithium: Decreases lithium excretion, resulting in lithium toxicity. Monitor lithium level.
NSAIDs: Inhibits diuretic response. Use together cautiously.

Salicylates: May cause salicylate toxicity. Use together cautiously.
Drug-herb. *Aloe.* Possible increased drug effects. Monitor patient for dehydration.
Licorice: May cause rapid potassium loss. Monitor patient for hypokalemia; discourage licorice intake.
Drug-lifestyle. *Alcohol use:* Additive hypotensive and diuretic effect. Discourage using together.
Sun exposure: Photosensitivity reactions may occur. Urge patient to avoid unprotected or prolonged sun exposure.

Effects on lab test results

- May increase glucose, cholesterol, and uric acid levels. May decrease potassium, sodium, calcium, and magnesium levels.
- May decrease hemoglobin, hematocrit, and granulocyte, WBC, and platelet counts.

Pharmacokinetics

Absorption: About 60% absorbed from GI tract after P.O. administration; unknown after I.M. use.
Distribution: About 95% plasma protein-bound.
Metabolism: Metabolized minimally by liver.
Excretion: About 50% to 80% excreted in urine. *Half-life:* About 30 minutes.

Route	Onset	Peak	Duration
P.O.	20-60 min	1-2 hr	6-8 hr
I.V.	5 min	30 min	2 hr
I.M.	Unknown	Unknown	Unknown

Pharmacodynamics

Chemical effect: Inhibits sodium and chloride reabsorption at proximal and distal tubules and ascending loop of Henle.
Therapeutic effect: Promotes water and sodium excretion.

Available forms

Injection: 10 mg/ml
Oral solution: 40 mg/5 ml, 10 mg/ml*
Tablets: 20 mg, 40 mg, 80 mg, 500 mg ♦

NURSING PROCESS

Assessment

- Assess patient's underlying condition before therapy.
- Monitor weight, peripheral edema, breath sounds, blood pressure, fluid intake and output, and serum electrolyte, blood glucose, BUN, and carbon dioxide levels.
- Monitor blood uric acid, especially if patient has a history of gout.
- Be alert for adverse reactions and drug interactions.
- Evaluate patient's and family's knowledge of drug therapy.

Nursing diagnoses

- Excessive fluid volume related to presence of edema
- Impaired urinary elimination related to diuretic therapy
- Deficient knowledge related to drug therapy

Planning and implementation

- **P.O. and I.M. use:** Give P.O. and I.M. doses in morning to prevent nocturia. Give second doses in early afternoon.
- **I.V. use:** Give drug by direct injection over 1 to 2 minutes. Or, dilute with D_5W, normal saline solution, or lactated Ringer's solution, and infuse no faster than 4 mg/minute to avoid ototoxicity. Use prepared infusion solution within 24 hours.
- Store tablets in light-resistant container to prevent discoloration. Don't use yellowed injectable preparation.
- Refrigerate oral furosemide solution to ensure drug stability.
- Notify prescriber if oliguria or azotemia develops or increases.

Patient teaching

- Advise patient to stand slowly to prevent dizziness, to avoid alcohol, and to minimize strenuous exercise in hot weather.
- Instruct patient to report ringing in ears, severe abdominal pain, or sore throat and fever because they may indicate furosemide toxicity.

ALERT: Discourage patient from storing different drugs in same container, because this increases risk of errors. The most popular strengths of furosemide and digoxin are white tablets of similar size.
- Tell patient to check with prescriber before taking OTC medications or herbal remedies.

Evaluation

- Patient is free from edema.

• Patient demonstrates adjustment of lifestyle to cope with altered patterns of urinary elimination.
• Patient and family state understanding of drug therapy.

G

gabapentin
(geh-buh-PEN-tin)
Neurontin

Pharmacologic class: 1-aminomethyl cyclohexoneacetic acid
Therapeutic class: anticonvulsant
Pregnancy risk category: C

Indications and dosages

▶ **Adjunct treatment of partial seizures with and without secondary generalization in adults with epilepsy.** *Adults:* Initially, 300 mg P.O. h.s. on day 1, then 300 mg P.O. b.i.d. on day 2, then 300 mg P.O. t.i.d. on day 3. Dosage increased as needed and tolerated to 1,800 mg daily in divided doses. Dosages up to 3,600 mg daily have been well tolerated.
Starting dosage, children ages 3 to 12: 10 to 15 mg/kg P.O. daily in three divided doses, adjusting over 3 days to reach effective dosage.
Effective dosage, children ages 5 to 12: 25 to 35 mg/kg P.O. daily in three divided doses.
Effective dosage, children ages 3 to 4: 40 mg/kg P.O. daily in three divided doses.
Adults and children age 12 or older with compromised renal function or undergoing hemodialysis: If creatinine clearance is 30 to 59 ml/minute, give 400 to 1,400 mg daily, divided b.i.d. If creatinine clearance is 15 to 29 ml/minute, give 200 to 700 mg P.O. daily. If creatinine clearance is less than 15 ml/minute, 100 to 300 mg daily; reduce dose in proportion to creatinine clearance (for example, patients with a creatinine clearance of 7.5 ml/minute should receive ½ the dose that a patient with 15 ml/minute would receive. Patients on dialysis should receive maintenance dosages based on estimated creatinine clearance. Supplemental postdialysis dose of 125 to 350 mg should be given after each 4 hours of dialysis

▶ **Postherpetic neuralgia.** *Adults:* 300 mg P.O. once daily on day 1, then 300 mg b.i.d. on day 2, and 300 mg t.i.d. on day 3. Adjust as needed for pain relief to a maximum daily dose of 1,800 mg, divided t.i.d.

Contraindications and precautions

• Contraindicated in patients hypersensitive to drug.
Lifespan: With pregnant women, use cautiously. In breast-feeding women and children younger than age 12, safety of drug hasn't been established.

Adverse reactions

CNS: *somnolence, dizziness, ataxia, fatigue, nystagmus, tremor,* nervousness, dysarthria, amnesia, depression, abnormal thinking, twitching, abnormal coordination.
CV: peripheral edema, vasodilation.
EENT: *diplopia, rhinitis,* pharyngitis, dry throat, *amblyopia.*
GI: nausea, vomiting, dyspepsia, dry mouth, constipation.
GU: impotence.
Hematologic: ***leukopenia.***
Metabolic: increased appetite, weight gain.
Musculoskeletal: back pain, myalgia, fractures.
Respiratory: cough.
Skin: pruritus, abrasion.
Other: dental abnormalities.

Interactions

Drug-drug. *Antacids:* Decreases gabapentin absorption. Separate administration times by at least 2 hours.
Drug-lifestyle. *Alcohol use:* Increases CNS depression. Discourage use.

Effects on lab test results

• May decrease WBC count.
• May cause false-positive tests for urine protein when Ames-N-Multistix SG dipstick test is used.

Pharmacokinetics

Absorption: Bioavailability isn't dose-proportional but averages 60%.
Distribution: Drug circulates largely unbound to plasma protein.
Metabolism: Not appreciably metabolized.

Excretion: Excreted by kidneys as unchanged drug. *Half-life:* 5 to 7 hours.

Route	Onset	Peak	Duration
P.O.	Unknown	Unknown	Unknown

Pharmacodynamics

Chemical effect: Unknown; although structurally related to GABA, drug doesn't interact with GABA receptors and isn't converted metabolically into GABA or a GABA agonist.
Therapeutic effect: Prevents and treats partial seizures.

Available forms

Capsules: 100 mg, 300 mg, 400 mg
Solution: 250 mg/5 ml
Tablets (film-coated): 600 mg, 800 mg

NURSING PROCESS

Assessment

- Assess patient's disorder before therapy and regularly thereafter.
- Routine monitoring of plasma drug levels isn't necessary. Drug doesn't appear to alter plasma levels of other anticonvulsants.
- Be alert for adverse reactions and drug interactions.
- Evaluate patient's and family's knowledge of drug therapy.

Nursing diagnoses

- Risk for trauma related to seizures
- Risk for injury related to drug-induced adverse CNS reactions
- Deficient knowledge related to drug therapy

Planning and implementation

- Give first dose at bedtime to minimize drowsiness, dizziness, fatigue, and ataxia.

ALERT: If gabapentin is discontinued or alternative drug is substituted, do so gradually over at least 1 week to minimize risk of seizures. Don't suddenly withdraw other anticonvulsants in patient starting gabapentin therapy.

- Take seizure precautions.

ALERT: Don't confuse Neurontin (gabapentin) for Noroxin (norfloxacin).

Patient teaching

- Tell patient to take drug without regard to meals.
- Warn patient to avoid hazardous activities until CNS effects of drug are known.

Evaluation

- Patient is free from seizures.
- Patient has no injury from adverse CNS reactions.
- Patient and family state understanding of drug therapy.

galantamine hydrobromide

(gah-LAN-tah-meen high-droh-BROH-mide)
Reminyl

Pharmacologic class: reversible, competitive acetylcholinesterase inhibitor
Therapeutic class: cholinomimetic
Pregnancy risk category: B

Indications and dosages

▶ **Mild-to-moderate dementia of Alzheimer's type.** *Adults:* Initially, 4 mg b.i.d., preferably with morning and evening meals. If dose is well tolerated after minimum of 4 weeks of therapy, increase to 8 mg b.i.d. A further increase to 12 mg b.i.d. may be attempted only after at least 4 weeks of the previous dose. Recommended dosage range is 16 to 24 mg daily in two divided doses.
Patients with hepatic or renal impairment: Don't exceed 16 mg daily for patients with a Child-Pugh score of 7 to 9 or with moderate renal impairment. Not recommended for patients with a Child-Pugh score of 10 to 15 or with a creatinine clearance less than 9 ml/minute.

Contraindications and precautions

- Contraindicated in patients hypersensitive to drug or its components.
- Use cautiously in patients with supraventricular cardiac conduction disorders and in those taking other drugs that significantly slow the heart rate.
- Use cautiously before or during procedures involving anesthesia with succinylcholine-type or other similar neuromuscular blockers.
- Use cautiously in patients with history of peptic ulcer disease and in those taking NSAIDs.
- Because of the potential for cholinomimetic effects, use cautiously in patients with bladder outflow obstruction, seizures, asthma, or COPD.

Lifespan: In breast-feeding women, drug is contraindicated because it's unknown whether drug appears in breast milk. In children, safety and efficacy haven't been established.

Adverse reactions

CNS: dizziness, headache, tremor, depression, insomnia, somnolence, fatigue, syncope.
CV: ***bradycardia.***
EENT: rhinitis.
GI: *nausea, vomiting,* anorexia, *diarrhea,* abdominal pain, dyspepsia, anorexia.
GU: urinary tract infection, hematuria.
Hematologic: anemia.
Metabolic: weight loss.

Interactions

Drug-drug. *Amitriptyline, fluoxetine, fluvoxamine, quinidine:* Decreases galantamine clearance. Monitor patient closely.
Anticholinergics: May antagonize activity of anticholinergics. Monitor patient.
Cholinergics (such as bethanechol, succinylcholine): May have a synergistic effect. Monitor patient closely. May need to avoid use before procedures using general anesthesia with succinylcholine-type neuromuscular blockers.
Cimetidine, erythromycin, ketoconazole, paroxetine: Increases bioavailability of galantamine. Monitor patient closely.

Effects on lab test results

- May decrease hemoglobin and hematocrit.

Pharmacokinetics

Absorption: Rapidly and well absorbed, with an oral bioavailability of about 90%. Levels peak in about 1 hour. In elderly patients, drug levels are 30% to 40% higher than in young, healthy people.
Distribution: Primarily distributed to blood cells. Protein binding isn't significant.
Metabolism: Metabolized in the liver by cytochrome P450 enzymes (CYP2D6 and CYP3A4) and glucuronidated. Using together with inhibitors of these enzyme systems may result in modest increases in galantamine bioavailability.
Excretion: Excreted in the urine unchanged, as the glucuronide, and as metabolites. *Terminal half-life:* About 7 hours.

Route	Onset	Peak	Duration
P.O.	Unknown	1 hr	Unknown

Pharmacodynamics

Chemical effect: Unknown; drug is a competitive and reversible inhibitor of acetylcholinesterase, which is believed to enhance cholinergic function by increasing the level of acetylcholine in the brain.
Therapeutic effect: Improves cognition in patients with Alzheimer's disease.

Available forms

Oral solution: 4 mg/ml
Tablets: 4 mg, 8 mg, 12 mg
Oral solution and tablets are bioequivalent.

NURSING PROCESS

Assessment

- Assess underlying condition before therapy, and reassess regularly throughout therapy.
- Bradycardia and heart block have been reported in patients with and without underlying cardiac conduction abnormalities. Consider all patients at risk for adverse effects on cardiac conduction.
- Patients taking drug are at an increased risk of developing gastric ulcers because of the potential for increased gastric acid secretion. Monitor patient closely for symptoms of active or occult GI bleeding.
- Evaluate patient's and family's knowledge of drug therapy.

Nursing diagnoses

- Risk for injury due to wandering related to Alzheimer's disease
- Risk for imbalanced fluid volume related to drug-induced adverse GI reactions
- Deficient knowledge related to galantamine hydrobromide therapy

Planning and implementation

- Give drug with food and antiemetics and ensure adequate fluid intake to decrease the risk of nausea and vomiting.
- If drug is stopped for several days, dose should be restarted at the lowest dose and increased, at a minimum of 4-week intervals, to the previous dosage level.
- Use proper technique when dispensing the oral solution with the pipette. Dispense measured amount in a liquid and give right away.

• Dosage shouldn't exceed 16 mg daily in patients with moderately impaired hepatic or renal function.
• In case of overdose, contact a poison control center for the latest management recommendations. Treatment is supportive and symptomatic. Atropine I.V. may be used as an antidote. An initial dose of 0.5 to 1 mg is recommended, with subsequent doses based on clinical response. It's unknown if drug is removed by dialysis.

Patient teaching
• Advise patient or caretaker to take drug with morning and evening meals.
• Inform patient or caretaker that dosage increases should occur at no more than 4-week intervals.
• Explain that nausea and vomiting are common adverse effects.
• Advise patient or caretaker that following the recommended dosing and administration schedule can minimize common adverse effects.
• Tell patient or caretaker that, if therapy is interrupted for several days or longer, the drug should be restarted at the lowest dose and increased based on the prescriber's dosing schedule.
• Advise patient or caretaker to report signs and symptoms of bradycardia immediately to the prescriber.
• Advise patient or caretaker that drug is believed to enhance cognitive function, but there's no evidence that it alters the underlying disease process.

☑ Evaluation
• Patient's cognition improves and tendency to wander decreases.
• Patient and family state that drug-induced adverse GI reactions haven't occurred.
• Patient and family state understanding of drug therapy.

ganciclovir (DHPG)
(jan-SIGH-kloh-veer)
Cytovene

Pharmacologic class: synthetic nucleoside
Therapeutic class: antiviral
Pregnancy risk category: C

Indications and dosages
▶ **Treatment of CMV retinitis in immunocompromised patients, including those with AIDS.** *Adults:* Induction treatment is 5 mg/kg I.V. over 1 hour q 12 hours for 14 to 21 days (normal renal function); maintenance treatment is 5 mg/kg I.V. daily for 7 days weekly, or 6 mg/kg I.V. daily for 5 days weekly. Or, following induction treatment, give 1,000 mg P.O. t.i.d. with food.
▶ **Prevention of CMV disease in transplant recipients at risk for CMV disease.** *Adults:* 5 mg/kg I.V. over 1 hour q 12 hours for 7 to 14 days, followed by 5 mg/kg once daily, or 6 mg/kg once daily 5 days weekly. Alternatively, 1,000 mg P.O. t.i.d. with food. Duration of treatment with I.V. ganciclovir in transplant recipients depends on duration and degree of immunosuppression.
▶ **Prevention of CMV disease in patients with advanced HIV infection at risk for development of CMV disease.** *Adults:* 1,000 mg P.O. t.i.d. with food.
▶ **Other CMV infections‡.** *Adults:* 5 mg/kg I.V. over 1 hour q 12 hours for 14 to 21 days. Or, 2.5 mg/kg I.V. over 1 hour q 8 hours for 14 to 21 days.
Patients with impaired renal function: Dosage should be adjusted according to the table on page 636.

Contraindications and precautions
• Contraindicated in patients hypersensitive to drug and in those with absolute neutrophil count below 500/mm^3 or platelet count below 25,000/mm^3.
• Use cautiously and at reduced dosage in patients with renal impairment.
Lifespan: In pregnant women, use cautiously and at reduced dosage. In breastfeeding women, drug isn't recommended. In children, safety of drug hasn't been established.

Adverse reactions
CNS: pain, altered dreams, confusion, ataxia, dizziness, headache, ***seizures, coma,*** behavioral changes.
CV: ***arrhythmias,*** hypotension, hypertension.
EENT: retinal detachment in CMV retinitis patients.
GI: nausea, vomiting, diarrhea, anorexia.
GU: hematuria.

	Initial I.V. dose		Maintenance I.V. therapy		P.O. therapy	
Creatinine clearance (ml/min)	Dose (mg/kg)	Interval	Dose (mg/kg)	Interval	Dose (mg)	Interval
50-69	2.5	12 hours	2.5	24 hours	1,500	24 hours
					500	8 hours
25-49	2.5	24 hours	1.25	24 hours	1,000	24 hours
					500	12 hours
10-24	1.25	24 hours	0.625	24 hours	500	24 hours
< 10 or on hemodialysis	1.25	3 times weekly	0.625	3 times weekly	500	3 times weekly

Hematologic: ***thrombocytopenia, agranulocytosis, leukopenia, granulocytopenia,*** anemia.
Other: inflammation, phlebitis at injection site.

Interactions

Drug-drug. *Cytotoxic drugs:* Increases toxic effects, especially hematologic effects and stomatitis. Monitor patient closely.
Imipenem and cilastatin: Heightens seizure activity. Monitor patient closely.
Immunosuppressants (such as azathioprine, corticosteroids, cyclosporine): Enhances immune and bone marrow suppression. Use together cautiously.
Probenecid: Increases ganciclovir blood levels. Monitor patient closely.
Zidovudine: Increases risk of granulocytopenia. Monitor patient closely.

Effects on lab test results

- May increase creatinine, ALT, AST, GGT, and alkaline phosphatase levels.
- May decrease hemoglobin, hematocrit, and granulocyte, platelet, neutrophil, and WBC counts.

Pharmacokinetics

Absorption: Poorly absorbed after P.O. administration. Bioavailability is about 5% under fasting conditions.
Distribution: Preferentially concentrates in CMV-infected cells; only 2% to 3% protein-bound.
Metabolism: Over 90% of drug isn't metabolized.
Excretion: Mostly excreted unchanged. *Half-life:* About 3 hours.

Route	Onset	Peak	Duration
P.O.	Unknown	Unknown	Unknown
I.V.	Immediate	Immediate	Unknown

Pharmacodynamics

Chemical effect: Unknown; may inhibit viral DNA synthesis of CMV.
Therapeutic effect: Inhibits CMV.

Available forms

Capsules: 250 mg, 500 mg
Injection: 500 mg/vial

NURSING PROCESS

Assessment

- Assess patient's condition before therapy and regularly thereafter.
- Obtain CBC, neutrophil, and platelet counts every 2 days during twice-daily ganciclovir dosing and at least weekly thereafter.
- Monitor hydration if adverse GI reactions occur with oral drug.
- Be alert for adverse reactions and drug interactions.
- Evaluate patient's and family's knowledge of drug therapy.

Nursing diagnoses

- Infection related to CMV retinitis
- Ineffective protection related to adverse hematologic reactions
- Deficient knowledge related to drug therapy

Planning and implementation

- **P.O. use:** Give drug with food.
- **I.V. use:** Reconstitute with 10 ml sterile water for injection. Shake vial to dissolve drug. Further dilute appropriate dose in normal saline solution, D_5W, Ringer's lactate, or Ringer's solutions (typically 100 ml), and infuse over 1 hour. Faster infusions will cause increased toxicity. Use infusion pump. Don't give as I.V. bolus. Infusion concentrations greater than 10 mg/ml aren't recommended.

ALERT: Use caution when preparing solution, which is alkaline.
ALERT: Don't give drug S.C. or I.M. because severe tissue irritation could result.
ALERT: Encourage fluid intake; ganciclovir infusion therapy should be accompanied by adequate hydration.
- Alert prescriber to signs of renal failure because the dosage will need adjustment.
- Oral capsules are linked to a risk of rapid rate of CMV retinitis progression and should only be used as maintenance therapy in patients who benefit from avoiding I.V. infusions.

Patient teaching
- Tell patient to take oral form of drug with food.
- Stress importance of drinking adequate fluid throughout therapy.
- Advise patient to report pain or discomfort at I.V. site.
- Instruct patient about infection-control and bleeding precautions.

Evaluation
- Patient is free from infection.
- Patient has no serious adverse hematologic reactions.
- Patient and family state understanding of drug therapy.

ganirelix acetate
(gan-eh-REL-iks AS-ih-tayt)
Antagon

Pharmacologic class: gonadotropin-releasing hormone (Gn-RH) antagonist
Therapeutic class: fertility agent
Pregnancy risk category: X

Indications and dosages
▶ **Inhibition of premature luteinizing hormone (LH) surges in women undergoing medically supervised, controlled ovarian hyperstimulation.** *Adults:* 250 mcg S.C. once daily during early to midfollicular phase of menstrual cycle. Continue daily until enough follicles of sufficient size are confirmed by ultrasound; human chorionic gonadotropin will then be given to induce final maturation of follicles.

Contraindications and precautions
- Contraindicated in patients hypersensitive to ganirelix or its components or to Gn-RH or Gn-RH analogue.
- Use with caution in patients with potential hypersensitivity to Gn-RH and in those with latex allergies because the product packaging contains natural rubber latex.

Lifespan: In pregnant women, drug is contraindicated.

Adverse reactions
CNS: headache.
GI: abdominal pain, nausea.
GU: vaginal bleeding, gynecologic abdominal pain, ovarian hyperstimulation syndrome, miscarriage.
Skin: injection site reaction.

Interactions
None reported.

Effects on lab test results
- May decrease bilirubin levels.
- May increase WBC count. May decrease hemoglobin and hematocrit.

Pharmacokinetics
Absorption: Rapid after S.C. injection with an average of 91.1% absorbed.
Distribution: 81.9% bound to plasma proteins.
Metabolism: Unmetabolized drug is found in urine up to 24 hours after dose. Two metabolites have been detected in feces.
Excretion: Primary excretion route is fecal; metabolites can be detected nearly 8 days after a dose.

Route	Onset	Peak	Duration
S.C.	Unknown	1 hr	Unknown

Pharmacodynamics
Chemical effect: Gn-RH, secreted by the pituitary gland, stimulates the synthesis and secretion of gonadotropins LH and follicle-stimulating hormone (FSH). In midcycle, a large increase in Gn-RH leads to a large surge in LH secretion, causing ovulation, a rise in progesterone levels, and a decrease in estradiol levels. Ganirelix blocks pituitary Gn-RH receptors and suppresses LH and, to a smaller degree, FSH secretion. By suppressing LH and FSH secretion in the early-to-mid

menstrual cycle, ganirelix stops premature gonadotropin surges that could interfere with medically supervised, controlled ovarian hyperstimulation.
Therapeutic effect: Increases fertility.

Available forms

Injection: 250 mcg/0.5 ml in prefilled syringes

NURSING PROCESS

Assessment

- Before starting treatment, make sure patient isn't pregnant.
- Monitor patient who reports previous potential hypersensitivity to Gn-RH carefully; monitor patient closely after first injection.
- Evaluate patient's and family's knowledge about drug therapy.

Nursing diagnoses

- Disturbed self-esteem related to infertility
- Acute pain secondary to drug-induced adverse reactions
- Deficient knowledge related to drug therapy

Planning and implementation

- Only prescribers experienced in infertility treatments should prescribe this drug.
- Natural rubber latex packaging of this product may cause allergic reactions in a hypersensitive patient.

Patient teaching

- Tell patient that the correct use of ganirelix injection is extremely important to the success of the fertility treatments. Patient should be able to follow strict administration schedule.
- Teach patient proper technique for S.C. administration of drug.
- Advise patient to use the abdomen or upper thigh for injection and to alternate injection sites with each dose.
- Advise patient to store drug at room temperature, away from heat and light, and out of children's reach.

Evaluation

- Patient becomes pregnant.
- Patient has no adverse reactions.
- Patient and family state understanding of drug therapy.

gatifloxacin
(ga-tih-FLOCKS-ah-sin)
Tequin

Pharmacologic class: fluoroquinolone antibiotic
Therapeutic class: antibiotic
Pregnancy risk category: C

Indications and dosages

▶ **Acute bacterial exacerbation of chronic bronchitis caused by *Streptococcus pneumoniae, Haemophilus influenzae, Haemophilus parainfluenzae, Moraxella catarrhalis,* or *Staphylococcus aureus;* complicated urinary tract infection caused by *Escherichia coli, Klebsiella pneumoniae,* or *Proteus mirabilis;* acute pyelonephritis caused by *E. coli.*** *Adults:* 400 mg I.V. or P.O. daily for 5 days.

▶ **Acute sinusitis caused by *S. pneumoniae* or *H. influenzae*.** *Adults:* 400 mg I.V. or P.O. daily for 10 days.

▶ **Community-acquired pneumonia caused by *S. pneumoniae, H. influenzae, H. parainfluenzae, M. catarrhalis, S. aureus, Mycoplasma pneumoniae, Chlamydia pneumoniae,* or *Legionella pneumophila.*** *Adults:* 400 mg I.V. or P.O. daily for 7 to 14 days.

▶ **Uncomplicated urethral gonorrhea in men and cervical gonorrhea or acute uncomplicated rectal infections in women caused by *Neisseria gonorrhoeae*.** *Adults:* 400 mg P.O. as single dose.

▶ **Uncomplicated urinary tract infection caused by *E. coli, K. pneumoniae,* or *P. mirabilis*.** *Adults:* 400 mg I.V. or P.O. as single dose, or 200 mg I.V. or P.O. daily for 3 days.

▶ **Uncomplicated skin and skin-structure infections caused by *S. aureus* (methicillin-susceptible strains only) *or Streptococcus pyogenes*.** *Adults:* 400 mg I.V. or P.O. daily for 7 to 10 days.

Patients with renal impairment: If creatinine clearance is less than 40 ml/minute, or if the patient is on hemodialysis or continuous peritoneal dialysis, give initial dose of 400 mg P.O., followed by 200 mg P.O. daily.

Contraindications and precautions

- Contraindicated in patients hypersensitive to fluoroquinolones or in patients with pro-

longed QTc interval or uncorrected hypokalemia.
• Use cautiously in patients with clinically significant bradycardia, acute myocardial ischemia, known or suspected CNS disorders, or renal insufficiency.
Lifespan: Breast-feeding patients should either stop nursing or not take the drug, taking into account the importance of the drug to the mother. In children, safety and efficacy haven't been established.

Adverse reactions

CNS: headache, dizziness, abnormal dreams, insomnia, paresthesia, tremor, fever, vertigo.
CV: palpitations, chest pain, peripheral edema.
EENT: tinnitus, abnormal vision, pharyngitis.
GI: nausea, diarrhea, abdominal pain, constipation, dyspepsia, oral candidiasis, ***pseudomembranous colitis,*** glossitis, stomatitis, mouth ulcer, vomiting, disturbed taste.
GU: dysuria, hematuria, vaginitis.
Musculoskeletal: arthralgia, myalgia, back pain.
Respiratory: dyspnea.
Skin: rash, redness at injection site, sweating.
Other: ***anaphylaxis,*** chills.

Interactions

Drug-drug. *Antacids:* Decreases absorption of antibiotic. Give gatifloxacin 4 hours before antacids.
Antidiabetics (glyburide, insulin): Possible symptomatic hypoglycemia or hyperglycemia. Monitor glucose level.
Antipsychotics, cisapride, erythromycin, tricyclic antidepressants: May prolong QT interval. Use cautiously.
Class IA antiarrhythmics (quinidine, procainamide), class III antiarrhythmics (amiodarone, sotalol): May prolong QT interval. Avoid using together.
Digoxin: May increase digoxin levels. Watch for signs of digoxin toxicity.
NSAIDs: May increase risk of CNS stimulation and seizures. Use together cautiously.
Probenecid: Increases gatifloxacin levels and prolongs its half-life. Monitor patient closely.
Warfarin: May enhance effects of warfarin. Monitor PT and INR.
Drug-lifestyle. *Sun exposure:* Photosensitivity reactions may occur. Urge patient to avoid unprotected or prolonged sun exposure.

Effects on lab test results

None reported.

Pharmacokinetics

Absorption: 96% of gatifloxacin is absorbed after P.O. administration; levels peak in 1 to 2 hours.
Distribution: Drug is 20% protein-bound. It's widely distributed into many tissues and fluids.
Metabolism: Limited biotransformation.
Excretion: More than 70% excreted unchanged by the kidneys. *Half-life:* 7-14 hours.

Route	Onset	Peak	Duration
P.O.	Unknown	1-2 hr	Unknown
I.V.	Unknown	Unknown	Unknown

Pharmacodynamics

Chemical effect: Inhibits DNA gyrase and topoisomerase, preventing cell replication and division. It's active against gram-positive and gram-negative organisms, including *S. aureus, S. pneumoniae, E. coli, H. influenzae, H. parainfluenzae, K. pneumoniae, M. catarrhalis, N. gonorrhoeae, P. mirabilis, C. pneumoniae, L. pneumophila,* and *M. pneumoniae.*
Therapeutic effect: Kills susceptible bacteria.

Available forms

Injection: 200 mg/20-ml vial, 400 mg/40-ml vial; 200 mg in 100 ml D_5W, 400 mg in 200 ml D_5W
Tablets: 200 mg, 400 mg

NURSING PROCESS

Assessment

• In patient being treated for gonorrhea, test for syphilis at time of diagnosis.
• In patient with renal insufficiency, monitor kidney function.
• In patient with diabetes, monitor glucose level.
• Monitor patient on digoxin for digoxin toxicity.
• Be alert for adverse reactions and drug interactions.
• Evaluate patient's and family's knowledge about drug therapy.

Nursing diagnoses

- Infection related to presence of bacteria susceptible to drug
- Risk for injury related to drug-induced adverse reactions
- Deficient knowledge related to drug therapy

Planning and implementation

- **P.O. use:** Give gatifloxacin 4 hours before antacids containing aluminum or magnesium, didanosine buffered solution tablets or buffered powder, or products containing zinc, magnesium, or iron.
- **I.V. use:** Dilute drug in single-use vials with D_5W or normal saline solution to 2 mg/ml before administration. Diluted solutions are stable 14 days at room temperature or refrigerated. Frozen solutions are stable up to 6 months, except for 5% sodium bicarbonate solutions. Thaw at room temperature. After being thawed, solutions are stable 14 days when stored at room temperature or refrigerated. Don't mix with other drugs. Infuse over 60 minutes.
  – Discard any unused portion of single-dose vials.
- Discontinue drug and notify prescriber if patient experiences seizures, increased intracranial pressure, psychosis, or CNS stimulation leading to tremors, restlessness, lightheadedness, confusion, hallucinations, paranoia, depression, nightmares, and insomnia.
- Discontinue drug and notify prescriber about skin rash or other sign of hypersensitivity.
- Discontinue drug and notify prescriber if patient experiences pain, inflammation, or rupture of a tendon.
- Monitor patient for diarrhea because pseudomembranous colitis may occur in patients taking antibiotics.

Patient teaching

- Tell patient to take drug as prescribed and to finish all of the medication even if symptoms disappear.
- Advise patient to take drug 4 hours before products containing aluminum, magnesium, zinc, or iron.
- Advise patient to use sunblock and protective clothing when exposed to excessive sunlight.
- Warn patient to avoid hazardous tasks until adverse CNS effects of drugs are known.
- Advise diabetic patient to monitor glucose levels and notify prescriber if hypoglycemia occurs.
- Advise patient to report immediately palpitations, fainting spells, skin rash, hives, difficulty swallowing or breathing, swelling of the lips, tongue, face, tightness in throat, hoarseness, or other symptoms of allergic reaction.
- Advise patient to stop drug, refrain from exercise, and notify prescriber if pain, inflammation, or rupture of a tendon occur.

Evaluation

- Patient is free from infection after drug therapy.
- Patient has no injury as a result of drug-induced adverse reactions.
- Patient and family state understanding of drug therapy.

gemfibrozil

(jem-FIGH-broh-zil)
Lopid

Pharmacologic class: fibric acid derivative
Therapeutic class: antilipemic
Pregnancy risk category: C

Indications and dosages

▶ **Type IV and V hyperlipidemia unresponsive to diet and other drugs; reduction of risk of coronary heart disease in patients with type IIb hyperlipidemia who can't tolerate or who are refractory to treatment with bile acid sequestrants or niacin.** *Adults:* 1,200 mg P.O. daily in two divided doses, 30 minutes before morning and evening meals. If no benefit occurs after 3 months, drug should be discontinued.

Contraindications and precautions

- Contraindicated in patients hypersensitive to drug and in those with hepatic or severe renal dysfunction (including primary biliary cirrhosis) or gallbladder disease.

Lifespan: With pregnant women, use cautiously. In breast-feeding women and in children, safety of drug hasn't been established.

Adverse reactions

CNS: blurred vision, headache, dizziness.
GI: *abdominal and epigastric pain,* diarrhea, nausea, vomiting, flatulence, *dyspepsia.*
Hematologic: ***severe anemia, leukopenia, thrombocytopenia, bone marrow hypoplasia.***
Hepatic: bile duct obstruction.
Musculoskeletal: painful limbs.
Skin: rash, dermatitis, pruritus.

Interactions

Drug-drug. *HMG-CoA reductase inhibitors:* Myopathy with rhabdomyolysis may occur. Don't use together.
Oral anticoagulants: Gemfibrozil may enhance clinical effects of oral anticoagulants. Monitor patient.

Effects on lab test results

- May increase ALT, AST, and CK levels. May decrease potassium level.
- May decrease hemoglobin, hematocrit, and eosinophil, WBC, and platelet counts.

Pharmacokinetics

Absorption: Well absorbed from GI tract.
Distribution: 95% protein-bound.
Metabolism: Metabolized by liver.
Excretion: Excreted primarily in urine, with some excretion in feces. *Half-life:* About 1.25 hours. Biological half-life is considerably longer, as a result of enterohepatic circulation and reabsorption in the GI tract.

Route	Onset	Peak	Duration
P.O.	2-5 days	> 4 wk	Unknown

Pharmacodynamics

Chemical effect: Inhibits peripheral lipolysis and also reduces triglyceride synthesis in liver.
Therapeutic effect: Lowers triglyceride levels and raises HDL levels.

Available forms

Capsules: 300 mg ♦
Tablets: 600 mg

NURSING PROCESS

Assessment

- Obtain patient's triglyceride and HDL levels before therapy and regularly thereafter.
- Periodic CBCs and liver function tests should be performed during first 12 months of therapy.
- Be alert for adverse reactions and drug interactions.
- Evaluate patient's and family's knowledge of drug therapy.

Nursing diagnoses

- Risk for injury related to elevated blood lipids and cholesterol levels
- Diarrhea related to drug's adverse effect on GI tract
- Deficient knowledge related to drug therapy

Planning and implementation

- Give drug 30 minutes before breakfast and dinner.
- Make sure patient is following standard low-cholesterol diet.

Patient teaching

- Instruct patient to take drug 30 minutes before breakfast and dinner.
- Teach patient dietary management of lipids (restricting total fat and cholesterol intake) and measures to control other cardiac disease risk factors. If appropriate, suggest weight control, exercise, and smoking cessation programs.
- Advise patient to avoid driving or other potentially hazardous activities until drug's CNS effects are known.
- Tell patient to observe bowel movements and to report signs of steatorrhea or bile duct obstruction.

Evaluation

- Patient's triglyceride and cholesterol levels are normal.
- Patient regains normal bowel patterns.
- Patient and family state understanding of drug therapy.

gentamicin sulfate

(jen-tuh-MIGH-sin SUL-fayt)
Cidomycin ♦, Garamycin, Gentamicin Sulfate ADD-Vantage, Jenamicin

Pharmacologic class: aminoglycoside
Therapeutic class: antibiotic
Pregnancy risk category: D

Indications and dosages

▶ **Serious infections caused by sensitive strains of *Pseudomonas aeruginosa, Escherichia coli, Proteus, Klebsiella, Serratia, Enterobacter, Citrobacter, Staphylococcus.*** *Adults:* 3 mg/kg daily in divided doses I.M. or I.V. infusion q 8 hours (in 50 to 200 ml of normal saline solution or D_5W infused over 30 minutes to 2 hours). For life-threatening infections, patient may receive up to 5 mg/kg daily in three to four divided doses. Reduce dosage to 3 mg/kg daily as soon as clinically indicated.
Children: 2 to 2.5 mg/kg q 8 hours I.M. or by I.V. infusion.
Neonates older than age 1 week and infants: 2.5 mg/kg daily I.M. or I.V. q 8 hours.
Preterm infants and neonates age 1 week and younger: 2.5 mg/kg I.V. q 12 hours.

▶ **Meningitis.** *Adults:* Systemic therapy as above; 4 to 8 mg intrathecally daily also may be used.
Children and infants older than age 3 months: Systemic therapy as above; 1 to 2 mg intrathecally daily may also be used.

▶ **Endocarditis prophylaxis for GI or GU procedure or surgery.** *Adults:* 1.5 mg/kg I.M., or I.V. 30 to 60 minutes before procedure or surgery and q 8 hours after, for two doses. Give separately with aqueous penicillin or ampicillin.
Children: 2 mg/kg I.M. or I.V. 30 to 60 minutes before procedure or surgery and q 8 hours after, for two doses. Given separately with aqueous penicillin G or ampicillin G.

▶ **Posthemodialysis to maintain therapeutic blood levels.** *Adults:* 1 to 1.7 mg/kg I.M. or by I.V. infusion after each dialysis.
Children: 2 to 2.5 mg/kg I.M. or by I.V. infusion after each dialysis.

Contraindications and precautions

• Contraindicated in patients hypersensitive to drug or other aminoglycosides.
• Use cautiously in patients with impaired renal function or neuromuscular disorders.
Lifespan: In pregnant women, don't use because drug is teratogenic. In neonates, infants, and the elderly, use cautiously.

Adverse reactions

CNS: headache, lethargy, numbness, paresthesias, twitching, peripheral neuropathy, ***seizures, neurotoxicity.***
EENT: *ototoxicity.*
GU: NEPHROTOXICITY.
Hematologic: *thrombocytopenia, leukopenia, agranulocytosis.*
Other: hypersensitivity reactions.

Interactions

Drug-drug. *Acyclovir, amphotericin B, cisplatin, methoxyflurane, other aminoglycosides, vancomycin:* Increases ototoxicity and nephrotoxicity. Use together cautiously.
Cephalothin: Increases nephrotoxicity. Use together cautiously; monitor renal function.
Dimenhydrinate: May mask symptoms of ototoxicity. Use with caution.
Diuretics: May increase ototoxicity. Avoid using together.
General anesthetics, neuromuscular blockers: May potentiate neuromuscular blockade. Monitor patient closely.
Indomethacin: May increase peak and trough levels of gentamicin. Monitor gentamicin levels.
I.V. loop diuretics (such as furosemide): Increases ototoxicity. Use cautiously.
Neurotoxic agents: Increases neurotoxicity. Avoid using together.
Parenteral penicillins (such as ampicillin, ticarcillin): Gentamicin inactivation in vitro. Don't mix together.

Effects on lab test results

• May increase BUN, creatinine, nonprotein nitrogen, ALT, AST, bilirubin, and LDH levels.
• May increase eosinophil count. May decrease hemoglobin, hematocrit, and WBC, platelet, and granulocyte counts.

Pharmacokinetics

Absorption: Unknown after I.M. administration.
Distribution: Distributed widely. CSF penetration is low even in patients with inflamed meninges. Protein binding is minimal.
Metabolism: Not metabolized.
Excretion: Excreted primarily in urine; small amounts may be excreted in bile. *Half-life:* 2 to 3 hours.

Route	Onset	Peak	Duration
I.V.	Immediate	30-90 min	Unknown
I.M.	Unknown	30-90 min	Unknown
Intrathecal	Unknown	Unknown	Unknown

Pharmacodynamics

Chemical effect: Inhibits protein synthesis by binding to ribosomes.
Therapeutic effect: Kills susceptible bacteria (many aerobic gram-negative organisms and some aerobic gram-positive organisms). Drug may act against some aminoglycoside-resistant bacteria.

Available forms

Injection: 40 mg/ml (adult), 10 mg/ml (pediatric), 2 mg/ml (intrathecal)
I.V. infusion (premixed): 40 mg, 60 mg, 70 mg, 80 mg, 90 mg, 100 mg, 120 mg, available in normal saline solution

NURSING PROCESS

Assessment

- Assess patient's infection before therapy and regularly thereafter.
- Obtain specimen for culture and sensitivity tests before first dose.
- Evaluate patient's hearing before therapy and regularly thereafter.
- Weigh patient and review baseline renal function studies before therapy and then regularly during therapy. Notify prescriber of any changes, so that dosage may be adjusted.
- Obtain blood for peak drug level 1 hour after I.M. injection and 30 minutes to 1 hour after I.V. infusion; for trough levels, draw blood just before next dose. Don't collect blood in heparinized tube because heparin is incompatible with aminoglycosides.
- Peak blood levels above 12 mcg/ml and trough levels above 2 mcg/ml may increase risk of toxicity.
- Be alert for adverse reactions and drug interactions.
- Evaluate patient's and family's knowledge of drug therapy.

Nursing diagnoses

- Infection related to presence of susceptible bacteria
- Impaired urinary elimination related to nephrotoxicity
- Deficient knowledge related to drug therapy

Planning and implementation

- **I.V. use:** When giving drug by intermittent I.V. infusion, dilute with 50 to 200 ml of D_5W or normal saline injection and infuse over 30 minutes to 2 hours. After infusion, flush line with normal saline solution or D_5W.
- **I.M. use:** Give drug deep into large muscle mass (gluteal or midlateral thigh); rotate injection sites. Don't inject more than 2 g of drug per site.
- **Intrathecal use:** Use preservative-free forms of gentamicin for intrathecal route.
- Hemodialysis (8 hours) removes up to 50% of drug from blood.
- Notify prescriber about signs of decreasing renal function or changes in hearing.
- Therapy usually continues for 7 to 10 days. If no response occurs in 3 to 5 days, therapy may be stopped and new specimens obtained for culture and sensitivity testing.
- Encourage adequate fluid intake; patient should be well hydrated while taking drug to minimize chemical irritation of renal tubules.

Patient teaching

- Instruct patient to notify prescriber about adverse reactions, such as changes in hearing.
- Emphasize importance of drinking at least 2,000 ml of fluids daily, if not contraindicated.

Evaluation

- Patient is free from infection.
- Patient maintains normal renal function throughout drug therapy.
- Patient and family state understanding of drug therapy.

glimepiride
(gligh-MEH-peh-righd)
Amaryl

Pharmacologic class: sulfonylurea
Therapeutic class: antidiabetic
Pregnancy risk category: C

Indications and dosages

▶ **Adjunct to diet and exercise to lower blood glucose in patients with type 2 (non-insulin-dependent) diabetes mellitus whose hyperglycemia can't be managed by diet and exercise alone.** *Adults:* Initially, 1 to 2 mg P.O. once daily with first main meal of day. Usual maintenance dosage is 1 to 4 mg P.O. once daily. After reaching 2 mg, dosage increased in increments not exceeding 2 mg q 1 to 2 weeks, based on patient's blood glucose response. Maximum, 8 mg daily.

▶ **Adjunct to insulin therapy in patients with type 2 (non-insulin-dependent) diabetes mellitus whose hyperglycemia can't be managed by diet and exercise in conjunction with oral hypoglycemic agents.** *Adults:* 8 mg P.O. once daily with first main meal of day with low-dose insulin. Adjust insulin upward weekly as needed, based on patient's blood glucose response.

Patients with renal impairment: Initial dose of 1 mg P.O. daily, then adjust based on the patient's fasting glucose levels.

Contraindications and precautions

- Contraindicated in patients hypersensitive to drug and in those with diabetic ketoacidosis.
- Use cautiously in debilitated or malnourished patients and in those with adrenal, pituitary, hepatic, or renal insufficiency.

Lifespan: In breast-feeding women, drug is contraindicated. In children, safety and efficacy haven't been established. In elderly patients, use cautiously because they might be more sensitive to the drug.

Adverse reactions

CNS: dizziness, asthenia, headache.
EENT: changes in accommodation.
GI: nausea.
Hematologic: ***leukopenia,*** hemolytic anemia, ***agranulocytosis, thrombocytopenia, aplastic anemia, pancytopenia.***
Hepatic: cholestatic jaundice.
Metabolic: ***hypoglycemia.***
Skin: allergic skin reactions (pruritus, erythema, urticaria, and morbilliform or maculopapular eruptions).

Interactions

Drug-drug. *Beta-blockers:* May mask symptoms of hypoglycemia. Monitor glucose levels carefully.
Drugs that produce hyperglycemia, other diuretics: May lead to loss of glucose control. May require dosage adjustment.
Insulin: May increase potential for hypoglycemia. Monitor glucose levels closely.
NSAIDs, other highly protein-bound drugs: May potentiate hypoglycemic action of sulfonylureas, such as glimepiride. Monitor patient carefully.
Drug-herb. *Aloe, bitter melon, bilberry leaf, burdock, dandelion, fenugreek, garlic, ginseng:* May improve glucose control, which may allow reduction of oral hypoglycemic. Tell patient to discuss herbs with prescriber before use.
Drug-lifestyle. *Alcohol use:* Alters glycemic control, most commonly hypoglycemia. May cause disulfiram-like reaction. Discourage using together.

Effects on lab test results

- May increase BUN, creatinine, alkaline phosphatase, ALT, and AST levels. May decrease glucose and sodium levels.
- May decrease hemoglobin, hematocrit, and WBC, RBC, platelet, and granulocyte counts.

Pharmacokinetics

Absorption: Completely absorbed.
Distribution: 99.5% protein-bound.
Metabolism: Completely metabolized.
Excretion: Excreted in urine and feces.

Route	Onset	Peak	Duration
P.O.	≤ 1 hr	2-3 hr	Unknown

Pharmacodynamics

Chemical effect: Stimulates release of insulin from pancreatic beta cells; increases sensitivity of peripheral tissues to insulin.
Therapeutic effect: Lowers glucose levels.

Available forms

Tablets: 1 mg, 2 mg, 4 mg

NURSING PROCESS

Assessment

- Monitor fasting glucose periodically to determine therapeutic response. Also monitor glycosylated hemoglobin, usually every 3 to 6 months, to more precisely assess long-term glycemic control.
- Evaluate patient's and family's knowledge of drug therapy.

Nursing diagnoses

- Ineffective health maintenance related to hyperglycemia
- Risk for injury related to drug-induced hypoglycemia
- Deficient knowledge related to drug therapy

Planning and implementation

- Oral hypoglycemic drugs have been linked with an increased risk of CV mortality compared with diet alone or with diet and insulin therapy.
- Give drug with the first meal of the day.

Patient teaching

- Tell patient to take drug with first meal of day.
- Stress importance of adhering to diet, weight-reduction, exercise, and personal hygiene programs. Explain to patient and family how to monitor glucose levels, and teach them signs, symptoms, and treatment of hyperglycemia and hypoglycemia.
- Advise patient to wear or carry medical identification that describes his condition.
- Instruct patient to avoid alcohol consumption during therapy.

Evaluation

- Patient's glucose level is normal.
- Patient recognizes hypoglycemia early and treats it before injury occurs.
- Patient and family state understanding of drug therapy.

glipizide

(GLIGH-peh-zighd)

Glucotrol, Glucotrol XL, Minidiab ◇

Pharmacologic class: sulfonylurea
Therapeutic class: antidiabetic
Pregnancy risk category: C

Indications and dosages

▶ **Adjunct to diet to lower glucose level in patients with type 2 (non–insulin-dependent) diabetes mellitus.** *Adults:* Initially, 5 mg P.O. daily before breakfast. Elderly patients or those with liver disease may be started on 2.5 mg. Maximum once-daily dose is 15 mg. Maximum recommended total daily dose is 40 mg.
Extended-release tablets. *Adults:* 5 mg P.O. daily. Adjust in 5-mg increments q 3 months depending on level of glycemic control. Maximum daily dosage for these tablets is 20 mg.
▶ **To replace insulin therapy.** *Adults:* If insulin dosage is more than 20 units daily, patient is started at usual dosage in addition to 50% of insulin. If insulin dosage is less than 20 units, insulin may be discontinued.

Contraindications and precautions

- Contraindicated in patients hypersensitive to drug, and in patients with diabetic ketoacidosis.
- Use cautiously in patients with renal and hepatic disease and in debilitated or malnourished patients.

Lifespan: In pregnant and breast-feeding women, drug is contraindicated. In children, safety of drug hasn't been established because of the rarity of type 2 diabetes mellitus in this population. In elderly patients, use cautiously.

Adverse reactions

CNS: dizziness.
CV: facial flushing.
GI: nausea, vomiting, constipation.
Hematologic: ***agranulocytosis, thrombocytopenia, aplastic anemia.***
Hepatic: cholestatic jaundice.
Metabolic: ***hypoglycemia.***
Skin: rash, pruritus.

Interactions

Drug-drug. *Anabolic steroids, chloramphenicol, clofibrate, guanethidine, MAO inhibitors, phenylbutazone, probenecid, salicylates, sulfonamides:* Increases hypoglycemic activity. Monitor glucose level.
Beta blockers, clonidine: Prolongs hypoglycemic effect and masked symptoms of hypoglycemia. Use together cautiously.
Corticosteroids, glucagon, rifampin, thiazide diuretics: Decreases hypoglycemic response. Monitor glucose level.
Hydantoins: Increases levels of hydantoins. Monitor levels.
Oral anticoagulants: Increases hypoglycemic activity or enhanced anticoagulant effect. Monitor glucose level, PT, and INR.
Drug-herb. *Aloe, bitter melon, bilberry leaf, burdock, dandelion, fenugreek, garlic, ginseng:* Improves glucose control, which may allow reduction of oral hypoglycemic. Tell patient to discuss herbs with prescriber before use.
Drug-lifestyle. *Alcohol use:* Alters glycemic control, most commonly hypoglycemia. May also cause disulfiram-like reaction. Discourage using together.

Effects on lab test results

- May increase BUN, creatinine, alkaline phosphatase, AST, and cholesterol levels. May decrease glucose levels.
- May decrease hemoglobin, hematorcrit, and granulocyte and platelet counts.

Pharmacokinetics

Absorption: Rapid and complete from GI tract.
Distribution: Distributed within extracellular fluid; about 92% to 99% protein-bound.
Metabolism: Metabolized by liver to inactive metabolites.
Excretion: Primarily in urine; small amounts in feces. *Half-life:* 2 to 4 hours.

Route	Onset	Peak	Duration
P.O.	15-30 min	1-3 hr	10-16 hr

Pharmacodynamics

Chemical effect: May stimulate insulin release from pancreas, reduce glucose output by liver, and increase peripheral sensitivity to insulin.
Therapeutic effect: Lowers glucose levels.

Available forms

Tablets: 5 mg, 10 mg
Tablets (extended-release): 2.5 mg, 5 mg, 10 mg

NURSING PROCESS

Assessment

- Assess glucose level before therapy and regularly thereafter.
- Patient transferring from insulin therapy to oral antidiabetic needs glucose monitoring at least three times daily before meals.
- During periods of increased stress, such as from infection, fever, surgery, or trauma, patient may need insulin therapy. Monitor patient closely for hyperglycemia in these situations.
- Be alert for adverse reactions and drug interactions.
- Evaluate patient's and family's knowledge of drug therapy.

Nursing diagnoses

- Ineffective health maintenance related to hyperglycemia
- Risk for injury related to drug-induced hypoglycemia
- Deficient knowledge related to drug therapy

Planning and implementation

- Give drug about 30 minutes before meals.
- Some patients taking drug may attain effective control on once-daily regimen; others show better response with divided dosing.
- Treat hypoglycemic reaction with oral form of rapid-acting carbohydrates if patient can swallow or with glucagon or I.V. glucose if patient can't swallow or is comatose. Follow up treatment with complex carbohydrate snack when patient is awake, and determine cause of reaction.
- Make sure adjunct therapies, such as diet and exercise, are being used appropriately.

Patient teaching

- Instruct patient about nature of disease; importance of following therapeutic regimen; adhering to specific diet, weight reduction, exercise, and personal hygiene programs; and avoiding infection. Explain how and when to monitor glucose level, and teach recognition and treatment of hypoglycemia and hyperglycemia.
- Tell patient not to change dosage without prescriber's consent and to report any adverse reactions.
- Advise patient not to take other medications, including OTC drugs or herbal remedies, without first checking with prescriber.
- Instruct patient to avoid alcohol consumption during drug therapy.
- Advise patient to carry medical identification at all times.

Evaluation

- Patient's glucose level is normal with drug therapy.
- Patient doesn't experience hypoglycemia or hyperglycemia.
- Patient and family state understanding of drug therapy.

glucagon
(GLOO-kuh-gon)

Pharmacologic class: pancreatic hormone
Therapeutic class: antihypoglycemic
Pregnancy risk category: B

Indications and dosages

▶ **Hypoglycemia.** *Adults and children weighing more than 20 kg (44 lb):* 1 mg I.V., I.M., or S.C.
Children weighing 20 kg or less: 0.5 mg I.V., I.M., or S.C.
▶ **Diagnostic aid for radiologic examination.** *Adults:* 0.25 to 2 mg I.V. or I.M. before start of radiologic procedure.

Contraindications and precautions

- Contraindicated in patients hypersensitive to drug and in those with pheochromocytoma.
- Use cautiously in patients with history of insulinoma or pheochromocytoma.

Lifespan: In pregnant women, use only if absolutely necessary. In breast-feeding women, use cautiously. In children, safety and efficacy as a diagnostic aid haven't been established.

Adverse reactions

GI: nausea, vomiting.
Other: allergic reactions (including urticaria, ***respiratory distress,*** and hypotension).

Interactions

Drug-drug. *Oral anticoagulants:* Anticoagulant effect may be increased. Monitor PT and INR closely; monitor patient for bleeding.

Effects on lab test results

- May decrease potassium level.

Pharmacokinetics

Absorption: Unknown.
Distribution: Unknown.
Metabolism: Drug is degraded extensively by liver, in kidneys and plasma, and at its tissue receptor sites in plasma membranes.
Excretion: Excreted by kidneys. *Half-life:* 3 to 10 minutes.

Route	Onset	Peak	Duration
I.V., I.M., S.C.	Almost immediate	≤ 30 min	1-2 hr

Pharmacodynamics

Chemical effect: Promotes catalytic depolymerization of hepatic glycogen to glucose.
Therapeutic effect: Raises glucose level.

Available forms

Powder for injection: 1 mg (1 unit)/vial

NURSING PROCESS

Assessment

- Assess patient's glucose level before therapy and after drug administration.
- Be alert for adverse reactions and drug interactions.
- Monitor patient's hydration if vomiting occurs.
- Evaluate patient's and family's knowledge of drug therapy.

Nursing diagnoses

- Risk for injury related to patient's hypoglycemia
- Risk for deficient fluid volume related to drug-induced vomiting
- Deficient knowledge related to drug therapy

Planning and implementation

- **I.M. and S.C. use:** Follow normal protocol.
- Reconstitute drug in 1-unit vial with 1 ml of diluent; reconstitute drug in 10-unit vial with 10 ml of diluent. Use only diluent supplied by manufacturer when preparing doses of 2 mg or less. For larger doses, dilute with sterile water for injection.
- **I.V. use:** For I.V. drip infusion, use dextrose solution, which is compatible with glucagon; drug forms precipitate in chloride solutions. Inject directly into vein or into I.V. tubing of free-flowing compatible solution over 2 to 5 minutes. Interrupt primary infusion during glucagon injection if using same I.V. line. May repeat in 15 minutes if necessary. I.V. glucose must be given if patient fails to respond. When patient responds, supplemental carbohydrate needs to be given promptly.
- Arouse lethargic patient as quickly as possible and give additional carbohydrates orally to prevent secondary hypoglycemic reactions. Notify prescriber that patient's hypoglycemic episode required glucagon use. Be prepared to provide emergency intervention if patient doesn't respond to glucagon administration. Unstable hypoglycemic diabetic patient may not respond to glucagon; give dextrose I.V. instead.
- Notify prescriber if patient can't retain some form of sugar for 1 hour because of nausea or vomiting.

Patient teaching

• Instruct patient and family in proper drug administration.

• Teach them to recognize signs and symptoms of hypoglycemia, and tell them to notify prescriber immediately in emergencies.

Evaluation

• Patient's glucose level returns to normal.

• Patient remains well hydrated.

• Patient and family state understanding of drug therapy.

glyburide (glibenclamide)

(GLIGH-byoo-righd)

Albert Glyburide ♦, Apo-Glyburide ♦, DiaBeta**, Euglucon ♦, Gen-Glybe ♦, Glynase PresTab, Micronase, Novo-Glyburide ♦, Nu-Glyburide ♦

Pharmacologic class: sulfonylurea
Therapeutic class: antidiabetic
Pregnancy risk category: B

Indications and dosages

▶ **Adjunct to diet to lower glucose level in patients with type 2 (non–insulin-dependent) diabetes mellitus.** *Adults:* Initially, 1.25 to 5 mg regular tablets P.O. once daily with breakfast. For maintenance, 1.25 to 20 mg daily as single dose or in divided doses. Or initially, 0.75 to 3 mg micronized formulation P.O. daily. For maintenance, 0.75 to 12 mg P.O. daily in single or divided doses.

▶ **To replace insulin therapy.** *Adults:* Initially, if insulin dosage is more than 40 units daily, 5 mg regular tablets or 3 mg micronized formulation P.O. once daily in addition to 50% of insulin dosage. If insulin dosage is 20 to 40 units daily, 5 mg regular tablets or 3 mg micronized formulation P.O. once daily with abrupt insulin discontinuation. If insulin dosage is less than 20 units daily, 2.5 to 5 mg regular tablets or 1.5 to 3 mg micronized formulation P.O. once daily with abrupt insulin discontinuation.

Contraindications and precautions

• Contraindicated in patients hypersensitive to drug and in patients with diabetic ketoacidosis.

• Use cautiously in patients with hepatic or renal impairment and in debilitated or malnourished patients.

Lifespan: In pregnant and breast-feeding women and in children, drug is contraindicated. In elderly patients, use cautiously.

Adverse reactions

CV: facial flushing.
GI: nausea, epigastric fullness, heartburn.
Hematologic: ***agranulocytosis, thrombocytopenia, aplastic anemia.***
Hepatic: cholestatic jaundice.
Metabolic: ***hypoglycemia.***
Skin: rash, pruritus.

Interactions

Drug-drug. *Anabolic steroids, chloramphenicol, clofibrate, guanethidine, MAO inhibitors, phenylbutazone, salicylates, sulfonamides:* Increases hypoglycemic activity. Monitor glucose level.
Beta blockers, clonidine: Prolongs hypoglycemic effect and masks symptoms of hypoglycemia. Use together cautiously.
Corticosteroids, glucagon, rifampin, thiazide diuretics: Decreases hypoglycemic response. Monitor glucose level.
Hydantoins: Increases levels of hydantoins. Monitor blood levels.
Oral anticoagulants: Increases hypoglycemic activity or enhanced anticoagulant effect. Monitor glucose level, PT, and INR.
Drug-herb. *Aloe, bitter melon, bilberry leaf, burdock, dandelion, fenugreek, garlic, ginseng:* Improvement in glucose control may allow reduction of oral hypoglycemic. Tell patient to discuss herbs with prescriber before use.
Drug-lifestyle. *Alcohol use:* Alters glycemic control, most commonly hypoglycemia. May also cause disulfiram-like reaction. Discourage using together.

Effects on lab test results

• May increase BUN, alkaline phosphatase, bilirubin, AST, ALT, and cholesterol levels. May decrease glucose levels.

• May decrease hemoglobin, hematocrit, and WBC, platelet, and granulocyte counts.

Pharmacokinetics

Absorption: Absorbed almost completely from GI tract.

Distribution: Unknown, although it's 99% protein-bound.
Metabolism: Metabolized completely by liver to inactive metabolites.
Excretion: Excreted as metabolites in urine and feces in equal proportions. *Half-life:* 10 hours.

Route	Onset	Peak	Duration
P.O.	1-4 hr	2-4 hr	24 hr

Pharmacodynamics

Chemical effect: Unknown; may stimulate insulin release from pancreas, reduce glucose output by liver, increase peripheral sensitivity to insulin, and cause mild diuresis.
Therapeutic effect: Lowers glucose levels.

Available forms

Tablets: 1.25 mg, 2.5 mg, 5 mg
Tablets (micronized): 1.5 mg, 3 mg, 4.5 mg, 6 mg

NURSING PROCESS

Assessment

- Assess glucose level before therapy and regularly thereafter.
- Patient transferring from insulin therapy to oral antidiabetic needs glucose monitoring at least three times daily before meals.
- During periods of increased stress, such as from infection, fever, surgery, or trauma, patient may need insulin therapy. Monitor patient closely for hyperglycemia in these situations.
- Be alert for adverse reactions and drug interactions.
- Evaluate patient's and family's knowledge of drug therapy.

Nursing diagnoses

- Ineffective health maintenance related to hyperglycemia
- Risk for injury related to drug-induced hypoglycemia
- Deficient knowledge related to drug therapy

Planning and implementation

- Micronized glyburide (Glynase PresTab) contains drug in smaller particle size and isn't bioequivalent to regular tablets. Dosage for patient who has been taking Micronase or DiaBeta needs adjustment.
- Although most patients take glyburide once daily, patient taking more than 10 mg daily may achieve better results with twice-daily dosage.
- Treat hypoglycemic reaction with oral form of rapid-acting carbohydrates if patient can swallow or with glucagon or I.V. glucose if patient can't swallow or is comatose. Follow up treatment with complex carbohydrate snack when patient is awake, and determine cause of reaction.
- Make sure that adjunct therapy, such as diet and exercise, is being used appropriately.

Patient teaching

- Instruct patient about nature of disease; importance of following therapeutic regimen; adhering to specific diet, weight reduction, exercise, and personal hygiene programs; and avoiding infection. Explain how and when to monitor glucose levels, and teach recognition and treatment of hypoglycemia and hyperglycemia.
- Tell patient not to change dosage without prescriber's consent and to report any adverse reactions.
- Advise patient not to take other medications, including OTC drugs and herbal remedies, without first checking with prescriber.
- Instruct patient to avoid alcohol consumption during drug therapy.
- Advise patient to wear or carry medical identification at all times.

Evaluation

- Patient's glucose level is normal with drug therapy.
- Patient doesn't experience hypoglycemia.
- Patient and family state understanding of drug therapy.

glyburide and metformin hydrochloride

(GLIGH-byoo-righd and met-FOR-min high-droh-KLOR-ighd)
Glucovance

Pharmacologic class: combination sulfonylurea and biguanide
Therapeutic class: antidiabetic
Pregnancy risk category: B

Indications and dosages

▶ **Adjunct to diet and exercise to improve glycemic control in patients with type 2 diabetes whose hyperglycemia cannot be controlled with diet and exercise alone.** *Adults:* Initially, 1.25 mg/250 mg P.O. once daily or b.i.d. with meals. In patients whose hyperglycemia cannot be managed with diet and exercise alone, start with 1.25 mg/250 mg once daily with meals. In patients with glycosylated hemoglobin above 9% or a fasting glucose level above 200 mg/dl, start with 1.25 mg/250 mg twice daily with morning and evening meals. Daily dose may be increased in increments of 1.25 mg/250 mg per day q 2 weeks up to the minimum dose needed to adequately control glucose. Maximum, 20 mg glyburide and 2,000 mg metformin daily.

▶ **Second-line therapy in patients with type 2 diabetes when diet, exercise, and initial treatment with a sulfonylurea or metformin don't provide adequate glycemic control.** *Adults:* Initially 2.5 mg/500 mg or 5 mg/500 mg twice daily with meals. Increase in increments of no more than 5 mg/500 mg up to the minimum effective dose needed to adequately control glucose. Maximum, 20 mg glyburide and 2,000 mg metformin daily.

Contraindications and precautions

- Contraindicated in patients hypersensitive to glyburide or metform, and in patients with renal disease, renal dysfunction, or metabolic acidosis (including diabetic ketoacidosis). Contraindicated in heart failure that needs pharmacologic treatment.
- Use cautiously in hepatically impaired, debilitated, or malnourished patients and those with adrenal or pituitary insufficiency because of increased risk of hypoglycemia.

Lifespan: In breast-feeding women, drug isn't recommended. In children, safety and efficacy haven't been established. In elderly patients, use cautiously. Monitor their renal function, and don't give the maximum dose of Glucovance. In patients age 80 and older, treatment shouldn't begin unless creatinine clearance measurement shows that renal function isn't reduced.

Adverse reactions

CNS: headache, dizziness.
GI: *diarrhea,* nausea, vomiting, abdominal pain.
Metabolic: HYPOGLYCEMIA.
Respiratory: *upper respiratory infection.*

Interactions

Drug-drug. *Beta blockers, chloramphenicol, ciprofloxacin, coumarins, highly protein-bound drugs, MAO inhibitors, miconazole, NSAIDs, probenecid, salicylates, sulfonamides:* Increases hypoglycemic activity of glyburide. Monitor glucose level.
Calcium channel blockers, corticosteroids, estrogens, isoniazid, nicotinic acid, oral contraceptives, phenothiazines, phenytoin, sympathomimetics, thiazides and other diuretics, thyroid agents: Increases risk of hyperglycemia. Monitor patient's glucose level.
Cationic drugs (such as amiloride, cimetidine, digoxin, morphine, procainamide, quinidine, quinine, ranitidine, triamterene, trimethoprim, vancomycin): May increase metformin level. Monitor patient.
Furosemide: Increases metformin level and decreases furosemide level. Monitor patient closely.
Nifedipine: Increases metformin level. Metformin dosage may need to be decreased.
Drug-lifestyle. *Alcohol use:* Alters glycemic control, most commonly hypoglycemia. May also cause disulfiram-like reaction with glyburide component. Avoid using together.

Effects on lab test results

- May increase lactate levels. May decrease glucose level.

Pharmacokinetics

glyburide
Absorption: Absorbed almost completely from the GI tract.
Distribution: Extensively protein-bound.
Metabolism: Metabolized completely by the liver to weakly active metabolites.
Excretion: Excreted as metabolites in urine and bile in equal proportions. *Half-life:* 10 hours.
metformin
Absorption: Absorbed from GI tract, with food decreasing extent and slightly delaying rate of absorption.
Distribution: Negligibly bound to plasma proteins.
Metabolism: Not metabolized.

Excretion: Excreted unchanged in urine. *Half-life:* 6.2 hours.

Route	Onset	Peak	Duration
P.O.			
glyburide	1 hr	4 hr	24 hr
metformin	Unknown	Unknown	Unknown

Pharmacodynamics

Chemical effect: Glyburide stimulates the release of insulin from the pancreas. Metformin decreases hepatic glucose production and intestinal absorption of glucose and improves insulin sensitivity.
Therapeutic effect: Lowers glucose level.

Available forms

Tablets: 1.25 mg glyburide and 250 mg metformin, 2.5 mg glyburide and 500 mg metformin, 5 mg glyburide and 500 mg metformin.

NURSING PROCESS

Assessment

• Assess underlying condition before therapy, and reassess regularly throughout therapy.
• Obtain list of current and past medications taken by the patient. For patients previously treated with glyburide or metformin, the starting dose of Glucovance shouldn't exceed the daily dose of the glyburide (or equivalent dose of another sulfonylurea) and metformin already being taken.
• Assess glucose level before therapy and regularly thereafter. Monitor glycosylated hemoglobin to assess long-term therapy.
• Obtain baseline renal function studies and don't start drug if creatinine levels are 1.5 mg/dl or more for men or 1.4 mg/dl or more for women. Monitor renal function at least once yearly while the patient takes drug and more often in those with increased risk of renal dysfunction. If renal impairment is detected, drug should be discontinued.
• Monitor patient closely during times of increased stress, such as infection, fever, surgery, or trauma; insulin therapy may be needed.
• Monitor patient's hematologic status for megaloblastic anemia. Patients with inadequate vitamin B_{12} or calcium intake or absorption seem predisposed to developing subnormal vitamin B_{12} levels when taking metformin. They should have vitamin B_{12} level determinations every 2 to 3 years.
• Evaluate patient's and family's knowledge of drug therapy.

Nursing diagnoses

• Ineffective tissue perfusion, peripheral, related to presence of hyperglycemia
• Risk for injury related to drug-induced hypoglycemia
• Deficient knowledge related to glyburide and metformin hydrochloride therapy

Planning and implementation

• Make sure that adjunct therapy, such as diet and exercise, is being used appropriately.
• Drug should be temporarily discontinued in patients undergoing radiologic studies involving intravascular administration of iodinated contrast materials, because use of such products may result in acute alteration of renal function.
• Drug therapy should be temporarily suspended for any surgical procedure that requires restricted intake of food and fluids and shouldn't be restarted until oral intake has resumed.
• Mild hypoglycemic symptoms, without loss of consciousness or neurologic findings, should be treated aggressively with oral glucose and adjustments in drug, dosage, or meal patterns. Severe hypoglycemic reactions with coma, seizure, or other neurologic impairment occur infrequently but demand immediate hospitalization. If hypoglycemic coma is diagnosed or suspected, the patient should be given a rapid I.V. injection of concentrated (50%) glucose solution followed by continuous infusion of a more dilute (10%) glucose solution at a rate that will maintain glucose at a level above 100 mg/dl. Any patient with hypoglycemia should be monitored closely until out of danger and, if the reaction is severe, for a minimum of 24 to 48 hours, because hypoglycemia may recur after apparent clinical recovery.
• For patients requiring additional glycemic control, a thiazolidenedione may be added.
• Lactic acidosis is a rare, but serious (50% fatal), metabolic complication that can result from metformin accumulation. The risk of lactic acidosis increases with the degree of renal impairment and patient's age. Early symptoms of lactic acidosis may include malaise, myalgias, respiratory distress, increasing somno-

lence, and nonspecific abdominal distress. GI symptoms that occur after a patient is stabilized with Glucovance are unlikely to be drug-related and could be from lactic acidosis or other serious disease. Lactic acidosis should be suspected in any diabetic patient with metabolic acidosis lacking evidence of ketoacidosis.
• Discontinue drug if CV collapse, acute heart failure, acute MI, or other conditions characterized by hypoxemia occur because these conditions may be related to lactic acidosis and may cause prerenal azotemia.
• Evaluate patient for evidence of ketoacidosis or lactic acidosis, including electrolytes, ketones, glucose, blood pH, lactate, pyruvate, and metformin levels. Discontinue drug if evidence of acidosis occurs.

Patient teaching
• Tell patient to take once-daily dose with breakfast and, if prescribed, twice-daily doses with breakfast and dinner.
• Teach patient about diabetes and the importance of following therapeutic regimen; adhering to diet, weight reduction, regular exercise, and hygiene programs; and avoiding infection.
• Explain how and when to monitor glucose level and how to differentiate between hypoglycemia and hyperglycemia.
• Instruct patient to stop drug and report unexplained hyperventilation, myalgia, malaise, unusual somnolence, or other symptoms of early lactic acidosis.
• Tell patient that GI symptoms are common early in drug therapy. GI symptoms that occur after prolonged therapy may be related to lactic acidosis or other serious disease and should be reported promptly.
• Counsel patient against excessive alcohol intake, either acute or chronic.
• Advise patient not to take any other medications, including OTC drugs, without checking with prescriber.
• Instruct patient to wear or carry medical identification.

☑ Evaluation
• Patient's glucose level is normal with drug therapy.
• Patient doesn't experience hypoglycemia.
• Patient and family state understanding of drug therapy.

glycerin
(GLIH-seh-rin)
Fleet Babylax†, Fleet†, Sani-Supp†

Pharmacologic class: trihydric alcohol
Therapeutic class: laxative (osmotic)
Pregnancy risk category: NR

Indications and dosages
▶ **Constipation.** *Adults and children age 6 and older:* 2 to 3 g as rectal suppository or 5 to 15 ml as enema.
Children younger than age 6: 1 to 1.7 g as rectal suppository, or 2 to 5 ml as enema.

Contraindications and precautions
• Contraindicated in patients hypersensitive to drug and in those with intestinal obstruction, undiagnosed abdominal pain, vomiting or other signs of appendicitis, fecal impaction, or acute surgical abdomen.
Lifespan: In pregnant women, use drug only when potential benefits outweigh potential risks to fetus.

Adverse reactions
GI: *cramping pain,* rectal discomfort, hyperemia of rectal mucosa.

Interactions
None significant.

Effects on lab test results
None reported.

Pharmacokinetics
Absorption: Suppositories are absorbed poorly.
Distribution: Distributed locally.
Metabolism: Unknown.
Excretion: Excreted in feces.

Route	Onset	Peak	Duration
P.R.	15-60 min	15-60 min	15-60 min

Pharmacodynamics
Chemical effect: Hyperosmolar laxative that draws water from tissues into feces to stimulate evacuation.
Therapeutic effect: Promotes stool evacuation.

Available forms

Enema (pediatric): 4 ml/applicator†
Suppositories: adult, children, and infant sizes†

NURSING PROCESS

Assessment

- Obtain assessment of patient's constipation before therapy.
- Monitor effectiveness by noting patient's response after administration.
- Be alert for adverse GI reactions.
- Evaluate patient's and family's knowledge of drug therapy.

Nursing diagnoses

- Constipation related to interruption of normal pattern of elimination
- Acute pain related to abdominal cramping
- Deficient knowledge related to drug therapy

Planning and implementation

- Drug is used mainly to reestablish proper toilet habits in laxative-dependent patient.
- Drug must be retained for at least 15 minutes; usually acts within 1 hour. Entire suppository need not melt to be effective.
- Make sure that patient has easy and immediate access to a bathroom, bedside commode, or bedpan after giving drug.
- Notify prescriber if drug isn't effective.

Patient teaching

- Warn patient that abdominal cramping may occur but will subside when bowel is emptied.
- Teach patient a proper diet high in fiber and water.

Evaluation

- Patient reports return of normal bowel pattern of elimination.
- Patient states that abdominal cramping is transient.
- Patient and family state understanding of drug therapy.

goserelin acetate

(GOH-seh-reh-lin AS-ih-tayt)
Zoladex, Zoladex 3-Month

Pharmacologic class: synthetic decapeptide
Therapeutic class: luteinizing hormone-releasing hormone (LH-RH; Gn-RH) analogue
Pregnancy risk category: X

Indications and dosages

▶ **Endometriosis, advanced breast carcinoma.** *Adults:* One 3.6-mg implant S.C. q 28 days into upper abdominal wall for 6 months. For endometriosis, maximum duration of therapy is 6 months.

▶ **Palliative treatment of advanced carcinoma of the prostate.** *Adult men:* One 10.8-mg implant S.C. q 12 weeks into upper abdominal wall.

▶ **Endometrial thinning before endometrial ablation for dysfunctional uterine bleeding.** *Adults:* One or two 3.6-mg implants S.C. into upper abdominal wall. Each implant should be given 4 weeks apart.

Contraindications and precautions

- Contraindicated in patients hypersensitive to LH-RH, LH-RH agonist analogues, or goserelin acetate.
- The 10.8-mg implant is contraindicated for use in women.
- Use cautiously in patients with risk factors for osteoporosis, such as family history of osteoporosis, chronic alcohol or tobacco abuse, or use of drugs that affect bone density.

Lifespan: In pregnant and breast-feeding women, drug is contraindicated. In children, drug shouldn't be used.

Adverse reactions

CNS: ***CVA,*** lethargy, pain (worsened in first 30 days), dizziness, insomnia, anxiety, depression, headache, emotional lability, fever.
CV: edema, ***heart failure, arrhythmias,*** hypertension, ***MI,*** peripheral vascular disorder, chest pain.
GI: nausea, vomiting, diarrhea, constipation, ulcer.
GU: *impotence, sexual dysfunction, lower urinary tract symptoms,* renal insufficiency, uri-

nary obstruction, urinary tract infection, amenorrhea, vaginal dryness.
Hematologic: anemia.
Metabolic: gout, hyperglycemia, weight increase.
Musculoskeletal: loss of bone mineral density (in women).
Respiratory: COPD, upper respiratory tract infection.
Skin: rash, diaphoresis.
Other: chills, *hot flushes,* breast swelling and tenderness, changes in breast size.

Interactions

None reported.

Effects on lab test results

- May increase calcium and glucose levels.
- May decrease hemoglobin and hematocrit.

Pharmacokinetics

Absorption: Slowly absorbed from implant site.
Distribution: Unknown.
Metabolism: Unknown.
Excretion: Route unknown. *Half-life:* About 4.2 hours.

Route	Onset	Peak	Duration
S.C.	2-4 wk	12-15 days	Throughout therapy

Pharmacodynamics

Chemical effect: LH-RH analogue that acts on pituitary to decrease release of follicle-stimulating hormone and LH, resulting in dramatically lowered levels of sex hormones.
Therapeutic effect: Decreases effects of sex hormones on tumor growth in prostate gland and tissue growth in uterus.

Available forms

Implants: 3.6 mg, 10.8 mg

NURSING PROCESS

Assessment

- Assess patient's condition before therapy and regularly thereafter.
- When used for prostate cancer, LH-RH analogues such as goserelin may initially worsen symptoms because drug initially increases testosterone levels. Some patients may have increased bone pain. Rarely, disease (spinal cord compression or ureteral obstruction) may worsen.
- Be alert for adverse reactions.
- Evaluate patient's and family's knowledge of drug therapy.

Nursing diagnoses

- Ineffective health maintenance related to underlying condition
- Acute pain related to drug's adverse effect
- Deficient knowledge related to drug therapy

Planning and implementation

- Drug should be given under supervision of prescriber.
- Administer drug into upper abdominal wall using aseptic technique. After cleaning area with alcohol swab (and injecting local anesthetic), stretch patient's skin with one hand while grasping barrel of syringe with the other. Insert needle into S.C. fat; then change direction of needle so that it parallels abdominal wall. Needle should then be pushed in until hub touches patient's skin and then withdrawn about 1 cm (this creates gap for drug to be injected) before depressing plunger completely.
- To avoid need for new syringe and injection site, don't aspirate after inserting needle.
- Implant comes in preloaded syringe. If package is damaged, don't use syringe. Make sure drug is visible in translucent chamber.
- After implantation, area requires bandage after needle is withdrawn.
- Be prepared to schedule patient for ultrasound to locate goserelin implants if they require removal.
- Notify prescriber of adverse reactions and provide supportive care as indicated and ordered.

Patient teaching

- Advise patient to report every 28 days for new implant. A delay of a couple of days is permissible.
- Tell patient to call prescriber if menstruation persists or breakthrough bleeding occurs. Menstruation should stop during treatment.
- After therapy ends, inform patient that she may experience delayed return of menses. Persistent amenorrhea is rare.
- Warn patient that pain may occur.

Evaluation

- Patient responds well to drug.

• Patient has no pain.
• Patient and family state understanding of drug therapy.

granisetron hydrochloride
(grah-NEEZ-eh-trohn high-droh-KLOR-ighd)
Kytril

Pharmacologic class: selective 5-hydroxy tryptamine (5-HT_3) receptor antagonist
Therapeutic class: antiemetic, antinauseant
Pregnancy risk category: B

Indications and dosages

▶ **Prevention of nausea and vomiting caused by emetogenic cancer chemotherapy.** *Adults and children age 2 and older:* 10 mcg/kg undiluted by direct injection over 30 seconds, or diluted and infused over 5 minutes. Begin infusion within 30 minutes before chemotherapy starts. Or, for adults, 1 mg P.O. up to 1 hour before chemotherapy and repeated 12 hours later. Or, for adults, 2 mg P.O. daily within 1 hour before chemotherapy.

▶ **Prevention of nausea and vomiting from radiation, including total body irradiation and fractionated abdominal radiation.** *Adults:* 2 mg P.O. once daily within 1 hour of radiation.

▶ **Postoperative nausea and vomiting.** *Adults:* 1 mg I.V. undiluted and given over 30 seconds. For prevention, give before anesthesia induction or immediately before reversal.

Contraindications and precautions

• Contraindicated in patients hypersensitive to drug.

Lifespan: In pregnant and breast-feeding women, use cautiously. In children younger than age 2, safety hasn't been established. Safety of oral granisetron hasn't been established in children of any age. In children, safety hasn't been established for the prevention or treatment of postoperative nausea and vomiting.

Adverse reactions

CNS: *fever, headache, asthenia, pain,* somnolence.
CV: hypertension.
GI: taste disorder, diarrhea, *constipation, nausea, vomiting.*
GU: UTI, oliguria.
Hematologic: ***thrombocytopenia, leukopenia,*** *anemia,* leukocytosis.
Respiratory: cough, increased sputum.
Skin: rash, dermatitis, alopecia.
Other: ***hypersensitivity reactions*** **(*anaphylaxis,*** urticaria, dyspnea, hypotension), infection.

Interactions

Drug-herb. *Horehound:* May enhance serotonergic effects. Discourage using together.

Effects on lab test results

• May increase ALT and AST levels. May alter fluid and electrolyte levels with prolonged use.
• May decrease hemoglobin, hematocrit, and WBC and platelet counts.

Pharmacokinetics

Absorption: Unknown after P.O. administration.
Distribution: Distributed freely between plasma and RBCs; plasma protein binding about 65%.
Metabolism: Metabolized by liver.
Excretion: Excreted in urine and feces.

Route	Onset	Peak	Duration
P.O., I.V.	Unknown	Unknown	Unknown

Pharmacodynamics

Chemical effect: Located in CNS at area postrema (chemoreceptor trigger zone) and in peripheral nervous system on nerve terminals of vagus nerve. Drug's blocking action may occur at both sites.
Therapeutic effect: Prevents nausea and vomiting from chemotherapy.

Available forms

Injection: 1 mg/ml
Oral solution: 1 mg/5 ml
Tablets: 1 mg

NURSING PROCESS

Assessment

• Assess patient's chemotherapy and GI reactions before therapy.
• Monitor patient for nausea and vomiting.
• Be alert for adverse reactions.
• Monitor hydration if drug is ineffective or diarrhea occurs.

• Evaluate patient's and family's knowledge of drug therapy.

Nursing diagnoses
• Risk for deficient fluid volume related to nausea and vomiting
• Acute pain related to drug-induced headache
• Deficient knowledge related to drug therapy

Planning and implementation
• **P.O. use:** Give drug 1 hour before chemotherapy; repeat in 12 hours.
• **I.V. use:** Dilute drug with normal saline injection or D_5W to make 20 to 50 ml. Infuse over 5 minutes beginning within 30 minutes before chemotherapy starts, and only on day(s) chemotherapy is given. Diluted solutions are stable for 24 hours at room temperature.
ALERT: Don't mix with other drugs; compatibility data are limited.
• Alert prescriber if patient experiences nausea or vomiting.

Patient teaching
• Tell patient to notify prescriber if adverse drug reactions occur.

Evaluation
• Patient has no nausea or vomiting with chemotherapy.
• Patient's headache is relieved with mild analgesic.
• Patient and family state understanding of drug therapy.

griseofulvin microsize
(gris-ee-oh-FUHL-vin MIGH-kroh-sighz)
Fulcin ◇, Fulvicin U/F, Grifulvin V*, Grisactin, Grisovin ◇

griseofulvin ultramicrosize
Fulvicin P/G, Grisactin Ultra, Gris-PEG

Pharmacologic class: *Penicillium* antibiotic
Therapeutic class: antifungal
Pregnancy risk category: C

Indications and dosages
▶ **Ringworm infection of skin, hair, nails (tinea corporis, tinea capitis) when caused by *Trichophyton, Microsporum,* or *Epidermophyton.*** *Adults:* 500 mg microsize P.O. daily in single or divided doses. Severe infections may require up to 1 g daily. Or, 330 to 375 mg ultramicrosize daily in single or divided doses.
▶ **Tinea pedis and tinea unguium.** *Adults:* 0.75 to 1 g microsize P.O. daily. Or, 660 to 750 mg ultramicrosize P.O. daily in divided doses.
Children: 11 mg/kg microsize daily P.O. Or, 7.3 mg/kg ultramicrosize daily.

Contraindications and precautions
• Contraindicated in patients hypersensitive to drug and in those with porphyria or hepatocellular failure.
• Use cautiously in penicillin-sensitive patients because drug is penicillin derivative.
Lifespan: In pregnant women and women who intend to become pregnant, drug is contraindicated. In breast-feeding women, safety of drug hasn't been established.

Adverse reactions
CNS: headache, transient decrease in hearing, fatigue with large doses, occasional mental confusion, impaired performance of routine activities, psychotic symptoms, dizziness, insomnia.
GI: oral thrush, nausea, vomiting, excessive thirst, flatulence, diarrhea, ***bleeding.***
Hematologic: ***leukopenia, agranulocytosis,*** porphyria.
Hepatic: ***hepatic toxicity.***
Skin: rash, urticaria, photosensitivity, ***toxic epidermal necrolysis.***
Other: estrogen-like effects in children, hypersensitivity reactions (rash, ***angioedema,*** serum sickness-like reactions), lupus-like syndrome or worsening of existing lupus erythematosus.

Interactions
Drug-drug. *Coumarin anticoagulants:* Decreases effectiveness. Monitor PT and INR.
Cyclosporine: Cyclosporine levels may be reduced, resulting in decreased pharmacologic effects. Avoid using together.
Hormonal contraceptives: Decreases effectiveness. Suggest alternate methods of contraception.
Phenobarbital: Decreases griseofulvin level as a result of decreased absorption or increased metabolism. Avoid using together, or give griseofulvin t.i.d.

Drug-food. *High-fat meals:* Increases absorption. Give together.
Drug-lifestyle. *Alcohol use:* May cause tachycardia, diaphoresis, and flushing. Discourage using together.
Sunlight: Photosensitivity may occur. Urge patient to avoid unprotected or prolonged sun exposure.

Effects on lab test results

- May decrease WBC and granulocyte counts.

Pharmacokinetics

Absorption: Absorbed primarily in duodenum; varies among patients. Ultramicrosize preparations are absorbed almost completely; microsize absorption ranges from 25% to 70% and may be increased by giving with high-fat meal.
Distribution: Concentrates in skin, hair, nails, fat, liver, and skeletal muscle; tightly bound to new keratin.
Metabolism: Metabolized in liver.
Excretion: About 50% excreted in urine, 33% in feces, less than 1% unchanged in urine; also excreted in perspiration. *Half-life:* 9 to 24 hours.

Route	Onset	Peak	Duration
P.O.	Unknown	4-8 hr	Unknown

Pharmacodynamics

Chemical effect: Disrupts mitotic spindle structure of fungal cells.
Therapeutic effect: Inhibits fungal cell growth, including *Trichophyton, Microsporum,* and *Epidermophyton.*

Available forms

griseofulvin microsize
Capsules: 250 mg
Oral suspension: 125 mg/5 ml*
Tablets: 250 mg, 500 mg
griseofulvin ultramicrosize
Tablets: 125 mg, 165 mg, 250 mg, 330 mg
Tablets (film-coated): 125 mg, 250 mg

NURSING PROCESS

Assessment

- Assess patient's fungal infection before therapy.
- Monitor patient for improvement of signs and symptoms and for laboratory confirmation of complete eradication of organism.
- Assess hematologic, renal, and hepatic function periodically during prolonged therapy.
- Be alert for adverse reactions and drug interactions.
- Evaluate patient's and family's knowledge of drug therapy.

Nursing diagnoses

- Infection related to presence of susceptible fungi
- Ineffective protection related to drug-induced granulocytopenia
- Deficient knowledge related to drug therapy

Planning and implementation

- Because of potential toxicity, drug is used only when topical treatment fails to arrest mycotic disease.
- Obtain laboratory test results to confirm diagnosis of infecting organism. Continue drug until clinical and laboratory examinations confirm complete eradication.
- Because griseofulvin ultramicrosize is dispersed in polyethylene glycol, it's absorbed more rapidly and completely than microsize preparations and is effective at one-half to two-thirds the usual griseofulvin dose.
- Give after high-fat meal to enhance absorption and minimize GI distress.
- Keep in mind that effective treatment of tinea pedis may require use of topical agent.
- Notify prescriber immediately of granulocytopenia or agranulocytosis, which requires discontinuation of drug.

Patient teaching

- Advise patient that prolonged treatment may be needed to control infection and prevent relapse, even if symptoms abate in first few days. Tell him to keep skin clean and dry and to maintain good hygiene.
- Instruct woman not to become pregnant while on drug therapy.
- Caution patient to avoid intense sunlight.
- Instruct patient to avoid alcohol consumption during therapy.
- Instruct patient to take drug after high-fat meal.

• Warn patient to avoid hazardous activities that require alertness if adverse CNS reactions occur.

Evaluation
• Patient's infection is alleviated.
• Patient's CBC remains within normal limits.
• Patient and family state understanding of drug therapy.

guaifenesin (glyceryl guaiacolate)
(gwah-FEH-nih-sin)

Anti-Tuss*†, Balminil Expectorant♦, Breonesin†, Diabetic Choice Phanasin, Diabetic Tussin EX, Duratuss G, Fenesin, Ganidin NR, Gee-Gee†, Genatuss, GG-Cen*†, Glyate*†, Glytuss, Guaifenex G, Guaifenex LA, Guiatuss*†, Halotussin*, Humavent LA, Humibid LA, Humibid pediatric, Hytuss†, Hytuss-2X†, Mucinex†, Muco-Fen LA, Mytussin AF, Naldecon Senior EX†, Organidin NR, Respa-GF, Resyl♦†, Robitussin*†, Touro EX

Pharmacologic class: propanediol derivative
Therapeutic class: expectorant
Pregnancy risk category: C

Indications and dosages
▶ **Expectorant.** *Adults and children 12 years and older:* 200 to 400 mg P.O. q 4 hours, or 600 to 1,200 mg extended-release capsules q 12 hours. Maximum, 2,400 mg daily.
Children ages 6 to 11: 100 to 200 mg P.O. q 4 hours. Maximum, 1,200 mg daily.
Children ages 2 to 5: 50 to 100 mg P.O. q 4 hours. Maximum, 600 mg daily.

Contraindications and precautions
• Contraindicated in patients hypersensitive to drug.
Lifespan: In pregnant women, use cautiously. In breast-feeding women, safety of drug hasn't been established.

Adverse reactions
CNS: drowsiness.
GI: stomach pain, diarrhea, vomiting, nausea (with large doses).
Skin: rash.

Interactions
None significant.

Effects on lab test results
None reported.

Pharmacokinetics
Absorption: Unknown.
Distribution: Unknown.
Metabolism: Unknown.
Excretion: Unknown.

Route	Onset	Peak	Duration
P.O.	Unknown	Unknown	Unknown

Pharmacodynamics
Chemical effect: Increases production of respiratory tract fluids to help liquefy and reduce viscosity of tenacious secretions.
Therapeutic effect: Thins respiratory secretions for easier removal.

Available forms
Capsules: 200 mg†
Capsules (extended-release): 300 mg
Liquid: 100 mg/5 ml
Solution: 50 mg/ml, 100 mg/5 ml*†, 200 mg/5 ml*†
Syrup: 100 mg/5 ml
Tablets: 100 mg†, 200 mg†
Tablets (extended-release): 575 mg, 600 mg, 800 mg, 1,200 mg
Tablets (extended-release, film-coated): 600 mg, 1,200 mg

NURSING PROCESS

Assessment
• Assess patient's sputum production before and after giving drug.
• Be alert for adverse reactions and drug interactions.
• Monitor patient's hydration if adverse GI reactions occur.
• Evaluate patient's and family's knowledge of drug therapy.

Nursing diagnoses
• Ineffective airway clearance related to underlying condition
• Risk for deficient fluid volume related to adverse GI reactions
• Deficient knowledge related to drug therapy

Planning and implementation
- Give drug with a full glass of water.
- Drug may interfere with laboratory tests for 5-hydroxyindoleacetic acid and vanillylmandelic acid.

Patient teaching
- Inform patient that persistent cough may indicate a serious condition. Tell him to contact prescriber if cough lasts longer than 1 week, recurs frequently, or accompanies a high fever, rash, or severe headache.
- Advise patient to take each dose with a full glass of water before and after dose; increasing fluid intake may prove beneficial.
- Encourage patient to perform deep-breathing exercises.

Evaluation
- Patient's lungs are clear, and respiratory secretions are normal.
- Patient maintains adequate hydration.
- Patient and family state understanding of drug therapy.

guanfacine hydrochloride
(GWAHN-fuh-seen high-droh-KLOR-ighd)
Tenex

Pharmacologic class: centrally acting antiadrenergic
Therapeutic class: antihypertensive
Pregnancy risk category: B

Indications and dosages
▶ **Hypertension.** *Adults:* Initially, 1 mg P.O. daily h.s. May be increased to 2 mg P.O. h.s. after 3 to 4 weeks, p.r.n. May be further increased to 3 mg P.O. h.s. after another 3 to 4 weeks, p.r.n. Average is 1 to 3 mg daily.

Contraindications and precautions
- Contraindicated in patients hypersensitive to drug.
- Use cautiously in patients with severe coronary insufficiency, cerebrovascular disease, recent MI, or chronic renal or hepatic insufficiency.

Lifespan: In pregnant women, use cautiously. In children and breast-feeding women, safety of drug hasn't been established.

Adverse reactions
CNS: *drowsiness, dizziness,* fatigue, headache, insomnia.
CV: ***bradycardia,*** orthostatic hypotension, rebound hypertension.
GI: *constipation,* diarrhea, nausea, *dry mouth.*
Skin: dermatitis, pruritus.

Interactions
Drug-drug. *CNS depressants:* Potential for increased sedation. Avoid using together.
Drug-lifestyle. *Alcohol use:* May enhance CNS effect. Discourage use.

Effects on lab test results
None reported.

Pharmacokinetics
Absorption: Absorbed well and completely; about 80% bioavailable.
Distribution: Thought to be highly distributed; about 70% protein-bound.
Metabolism: Metabolized in liver.
Excretion: Excreted in urine. *Half-life:* About 17 hours.

Route	Onset	Peak	Duration
P.O.	Unknown	1-4 hr	24 hr

Pharmacodynamics
Chemical effect: Unknown; may inhibit central vasomotor center, decreasing sympathetic outflow to heart, kidneys, and peripheral vasculature.
Therapeutic effect: Lowers blood pressure.

Available forms
Tablets: 1 mg, 2 mg

NURSING PROCESS

Assessment
- Assess blood pressure before therapy and regularly thereafter.
- Be alert for adverse reactions. Risk and severity increase with higher dosages.
- Evaluate patient's and family's knowledge of drug therapy.

Nursing diagnoses
- Risk for injury related to presence of hypertension

• Constipation related to adverse effects on GI tract
• Deficient knowledge related to drug therapy

Planning and implementation
• Give daily dose at bedtime to minimize daytime drowsiness.
• Drug may be used alone or with diuretic.

Patient teaching
• Tell patient not to stop therapy abruptly. Rebound hypertension is less common than with similar drugs but may occur.
• Advise patient to avoid activities that require alertness until CNS response to drug is known.
• Instruct patient to check with prescriber before taking other OTC medications.

Evaluation
• Patient's blood pressure is normal.
• Patient's bowel pattern is normal.
• Patient and family state understanding of drug therapy.

H

haloperidol
(hal-oh-PER-uh-dol)
Apo-Haloperidol ♦, Haldol**, Novo-Peridol ♦, Peridol ♦, PMS Haloperidol, Serenace ◇

haloperidol decanoate
Haldol Decanoate, Haldol LA ♦

haloperidol lactate
Haldol

Pharmacologic class: phenylbutylpiperdine derivative
Therapeutic class: antipsychotic
Pregnancy risk category: C

Indications and dosages
▶ **Psychotic disorders.** *Adults and children age 12 and older:* Dosage varies for each patient. Initial range, 0.5 to 5 mg P.O. b.i.d. or t.i.d. Or, 2 to 5 mg I.M. q 4 to 8 hours, although hourly administration may be needed until control is obtained. Maximum, 100 mg P.O. daily.
Children ages 3 to 11: 0.05 to 0.15 mg/kg P.O. given b.i.d. or t.i.d. Severely disturbed children may need higher doses.
▶ **Chronically psychotic patients who need prolonged therapy.** *Adults:* 50 to 100 mg I.M. decanoate q 4 weeks.
▶ **Nonpsychotic behavior disorders.** *Children ages 3 to 12:* 0.05 to 0.075 mg/kg P.O. b.i.d. or t.i.d. Maximum, 6 mg P.O. daily.
▶ **Tourette syndrome.** *Adults:* 0.5 to 5 mg P.O. b.i.d., t.i.d., or p.r.n.
Children ages 3 to 12: 0.05 to 0.075 mg/kg P.O. b.i.d. or t.i.d.
▶ **Delirium‡.** *Adults:* 1 to 2 mg I.V. q 2 to 4 hours.

Contraindications and precautions
• Contraindicated in patients hypersensitive to drug or in those with parkinsonism, coma, or CNS depression.
• Use cautiously in debilitated patients; in patients who take anticonvulsants, anticoagulants, antiparkinsonians, or lithium; and in patients with history of seizures or EEG abnormalities, severe CV disorders, allergies, glaucoma, or urine retention.
Lifespan: In pregnant women, safety of drug hasn't been established. In breast-feeding women, drug isn't recommended. In elderly patients, use cautiously; they need a lower initial dose and a more gradual dose adjustment.

Adverse reactions
CNS: *severe extrapyramidal reactions, tardive dyskinesia,* sedation, ***seizures, neuroleptic malignant syndrome.***
CV: tachycardia, ECG changes (including prolonged QT interval and ***torsades de pointes***), hypotension, hypertension, ***bradycardia.***
EENT: *blurred vision.*
GU: urine retention, menstrual irregularities.
Hematologic: transient ***leukopenia*** and leukocytosis.
Hepatic: jaundice.
Skin: rash.
Other: gynecomastia.

Interactions
Drug-drug. *Carbamazepine:* May decrease haloperidol level. Monitor patient.

CNS depressants: Increases CNS depression. Avoid using together.
Fluoxetine: Possibility of severe extrapyramidal reaction. Don't use together.
Lithium: May cause lethargy and confusion with high doses. Monitor patient.
Methyldopa: May cause symptoms of dementia or psychosis to appear. Monitor patient.
Phenytoin: May decrease haloperidol level. Monitor patient.
Drug-herb. *Nutmeg:* Possible loss of symptom control or interference with therapy for psychiatric illness. Discourage using together.
Drug-lifestyle. *Alcohol use:* Increases CNS depression. Discourage using together.

Effects on lab test results

- May increase liver function test values. May increase or decrease WBC count.

Pharmacokinetics

Absorption: About 60% of P.O. dose absorbed; about 70% of I.M. dose absorbed within 30 minutes.
Distribution: Distributed widely, with high levels in adipose tissue; 91% to 99% protein-bound.
Metabolism: Metabolized extensively by liver.
Excretion: About 40% excreted in urine within 5 days; about 15% excreted in feces by way of biliary tract. *Half-life:* P.O., 24 hours; I.M., 21 hours.

Route	Onset	Peak	Duration
P.O.	Unknown	3-6 hr	Unknown
I.M.	Unknown	10-20 min	Unknown (lactate); 3-9 days (decanoate)

Pharmacodynamics

Chemical effect: May block postsynaptic dopamine receptors in brain.
Therapeutic effect: Decreases psychotic behaviors.

Available forms

haloperidol
Tablets: 0.5 mg, 1 mg, 2 mg, 5 mg, 10 mg, 20 mg
haloperidol decanoate
Injection: 50 mg/ml, 100 mg/ml
haloperidol lactate
Injection: 5 mg/ml
Oral concentrate: 2 mg/ml

NURSING PROCESS

Assessment

- Assess patient's disorder before therapy and regularly thereafter.
- Be alert for adverse reactions and drug interactions.
- Monitor patient for tardive dyskinesia. It may occur after prolonged use. It may not appear until months or years later and may disappear spontaneously or persist for life despite discontinuation of drug.
- Evaluate patient's and family's knowledge of drug therapy.

Nursing diagnoses

- Disturbed thought processes related to underlying condition
- Impaired physical mobility related to extrapyramidal effects
- Deficient knowledge related to drug therapy

Planning and implementation

- **P.O. use:** Follow normal protocol.
- **I.M. use:** Give drug by deep I.M. injection in gluteal region, using a 21G needle. Maximum volume of injection shouldn't exceed 3 ml.

ALERT: Don't give I.V.

- When changing from oral to injection form, patient should be given 10 to 15 times oral dose once monthly (maximum, 100 mg).
- Protect drug from light. Slight yellowing of injection or concentrate is common and doesn't affect potency. Discard markedly discolored solutions.
- Don't stop drug abruptly unless severe adverse reactions occur.
- Acute dystonic reactions may be treated with diphenhydramine.

Patient teaching

- Warn patient to avoid activities that require alertness and psychomotor coordination until CNS effects of drug are known.
- Tell patient to avoid alcohol while taking drug.
- Tell patient to relieve dry mouth with sugarless gum or hard candy.

• Instruct patient to take drug exactly as prescribed and not to double doses to compensate for missed ones.

Evaluation
• Patient demonstrates decreased psychotic behavior and agitation.
• Patient maintains physical mobility.
• Patient and family state understanding of drug therapy.

heparin sodium
(HEH-puh-rin SOH-dee-um)
Hepalean ♦, Heparin Leo ♦, Heparin Lock Flush Solution (with Tubex), Hep-Lock, Liquaemin Sodium, Uniparin ◇

Pharmacologic class: anticoagulant
Therapeutic class: anticoagulant
Pregnancy risk category: C

Indications and dosages
Heparin dosing is highly individualized, depending upon patient's disease state, age, and renal and hepatic status.

▶ **Deep vein thrombosis, pulmonary embolism.** *Adults:* Initially, 10,000 units I.V. bolus; then adjust according to PTT and give I.V. q 4 to 6 hours (5,000 to 10,000 units). Or, 5,000 units I.V. bolus; then 20,000 to 40,000 units in 24 hours by I.V. infusion pump. Adjust hourly rate 4 to 6 hours after bolus dose according to PTT.
Children: Initially, 50 units/kg I.V. drip. Maintenance dosage is 100 units/kg I.V. drip q 4 hours. Constant infusion: 20,000 units/m^2 daily. Adjust dosages according to PTT.

▶ **Embolism prevention.** *Adults:* 5,000 units S.C. q 8 to 12 hours. In surgical patients, first dose given 2 hours before procedure; follow with 5,000 units S.C. q 8 to 12 hours for 5 to 7 days or until patient is fully ambulatory.

▶ **Open-heart surgery.** *Adults:* (total body perfusion) 150 to 400 units/kg continuous I.V. infusion.

▶ **Disseminated intravascular coagulation.** *Adults:* 50 to 100 units/kg I.V. q 4 hours as a single injection or constant infusion. Discontinue if no improvement in 4 to 8 hours.
Children: 25 to 50 units/kg I.V. q 4 hours, as a single injection or constant infusion. Discontinue if no improvement in 4 to 8 hours.

▶ **Maintaining patency of I.V. indwelling catheters.** *Adults:* 10 to 100 units I.V. flush. Use sufficient volume to fill device. Not intended for therapeutic use.

▶ **Unstable angina‡.** *Adults:* 70 to 80 mg/kg I.V. loading dose; follow by infusion maintaining PTT at 1.5 to 2 times control level during first week of anginal pain.

▶ **Post MI, cerebral thrombosis in evolving CVA, left ventricular thrombi, heart failure, history of embolism, and atrial fibrillation‡.** *Adults:* 5,000 units S.C. q 12 hours empirically. Or, 75 units/kg continuous infusion to maintain PTT at 1.5 to 2 times control value; follow by warfarin sodium.

Contraindications and precautions
• Contraindicated in patients hypersensitive to drug.
• Conditionally contraindicated in patients with active bleeding; blood dyscrasia; bleeding tendencies, such as hemophilia, thrombocytopenia, or hepatic disease with hypoprothrombinemia; suspected intracranial hemorrhage; suppurative thrombophlebitis; inaccessible ulcerative lesions (especially of GI tract) and open ulcerative wounds; extensive denudation of skin; ascorbic acid deficiency and other conditions causing increased capillary permeability; subacute bacterial endocarditis; shock; advanced renal disease; threatened abortion; severe hypertension; during or after brain, eye, or spinal cord surgery; during spinal tap or spinal anesthesia; and during continuous tube drainage of stomach or small intestine. Although heparin is clearly hazardous in these conditions, risk versus benefits must be evaluated.
• Use cautiously in patients with mild hepatic or renal disease, alcoholism, or occupations with risk of physical injury; and in patients with history of allergies, asthma, or GI ulcerations.
Lifespan: In pregnant women who need anticoagulation, most clinicians use heparin. During menses and immediately postpartum, use cautiously. Elderly patients require lower dosages.

Adverse reactions
CNS: fever.

EENT: rhinitis, conjunctivitis, lacrimation.
Hematologic: ***hemorrhage*** (with excessive dosage), *overly prolonged clotting time,* ***thrombocytopenia.***
Musculoskeletal: arthralgia.
Skin: irritation, mild pain, hematoma, ulceration, pruritus, urticaria, cutaneous or subcutaneous necrosis.
Other: ***white clot syndrome; hypersensitivity reactions,*** chills, burning of feet, ***anaphylaxis.***

Interactions

Drug-drug. *Oral anticoagulants:* May cause additive anticoagulation. Monitor PT, INR, and PTT; monitor patient for bleeding.
Salicylates, other antiplatelet drugs: Increases anticoagulant effect. Don't use together.
Thrombolytics: Increases risk of hemorrhage. Monitor patient closely for bleeding.
Drug-herb. *Dong quai, feverfew, garlic, ginger, horse chestnut, motherwort, red clover:* Possible increased risk of bleeding. Monitor patient closely for bleeding if he has been using these herbal products.

Effects on lab test results

- May increase ALT and AST levels.
- May increase INR, PT, and PTT. May decrease platelet count.

Pharmacokinetics

Absorption: Immediately absorbed after I.V. infusion. Peak plasma levels can vary with S.C. administration.
Distribution: Distributed in plasma and extensively bound to lipoprotein, globulins, and fibrinogen.
Metabolism: Thought to be removed by reticuloendothelial system, with some metabolism occurring in liver.
Excretion: Small amount excreted in urine as unchanged drug. *Half-life:* 1 to 2 hours. Half-life is dose-dependent and nonlinear and may be disproportionately prolonged at higher doses.

Route	Onset	Peak	Duration
I.V.	Immediate	Unknown	Unknown
S.C.	20-60 min	2-4 hr	Unknown

Pharmacodynamics

Chemical effect: Accelerates formation of antithrombin III–thrombin complex and deactivates thrombin, preventing conversion of fibrinogen to fibrin.
Therapeutic effect: Decreases ability of blood to clot.

Available forms

Products are derived from beef lung or porcine intestinal mucosa.
heparin sodium
Carpuject: 5,000 units/ml
Disposable syringes: 1,000 units/ml, 2,500 units/ml, 5,000 units/ml, 7,500 units/ml, 10,000 units/ml, 15,000 units/ml, 20,000 units/ml, 40,000 units/ml
Premixed I.V. solutions: 1,000 units in 500 ml of normal saline solution; 2,000 units in 1,000 ml of normal saline solution; 12,500 units in 250 ml of half-normal saline solution; 25,000 units in 250 ml of half-normal saline solution; 25,000 units in 500 ml of half-normal saline solution; 10,000 units in 100 ml of D_5W; 12,500 units in 250 ml of D_5W; 25,000 units in 250 ml of D_5W; 25,000 units in 500 ml of D_5W; 20,000 units in 500 ml of D_5W
Unit-dose ampules: 1,000 units/ml, 5,000 units/ml, 10,000 units/ml
Vials: 1,000 units/ml, 2,500 units/ml, 5,000 units/ml, 7,500 units/ml, 10,000 units/ml, 15,000 units/ml, 20,000 units/ml, 40,000 units/ml
heparin sodium flush
Disposable syringes: 10 units/ml, 100 units/ml
Vials: 10 units/ml, 100 units/ml

NURSING PROCESS

Assessment

- Assess patient's underlying condition before therapy.
- Draw blood to establish baseline coagulation values before therapy.
- Monitor effectiveness by measuring PTT carefully and regularly. Anticoagulation present when PTT values are 1½ to 2 times control values.
- During intermittent I.V. therapy, always draw blood 30 minutes before next dose to avoid falsely elevated PTT. Blood for PTT may be drawn 8 hours after start of continuous I.V. heparin therapy. Blood for PTT should never be drawn from I.V. tubing of heparin infusion or from infused vein; falsely elevated

PTT will result. Always draw blood from opposite arm.
- Be alert for adverse reactions and drug interactions.
- Monitor platelet counts regularly. Thrombocytopenia caused by heparin may be linked to a type of arterial thrombosis known as white clot syndrome.
- Concentrated heparin solutions (greater than 100 units/ml) can irritate blood vessels.
- Evaluate patient's and family's knowledge of drug therapy.

Nursing diagnoses
- Risk for injury related to potential for thrombosis or emboli development from underlying condition
- Ineffective protection related to increased bleeding risks
- Deficient knowledge related to drug therapy

Planning and implementation
- Check order and vial carefully. Heparin comes in various concentrations.
- **I.V. use:** Give drug I.V. using infusion pump to provide maximum safety because of long-term effect and irregular absorption when given S.C. Check constant I.V. infusions regularly, even when pumps are in good working order, to prevent giving too much or too little.

ALERT: Never piggyback other drugs into infusion line while heparin infusion is running. Many antibiotics and other drugs deactivate heparin. Never mix any drug with heparin in syringe when bolus therapy is used.

ALERT: Don't skip dose or "catch up" with I.V. containing heparin. If I.V. is out, restart it as soon as possible, and reschedule bolus dose immediately.
- **S.C. use:** Give low-dose injections sequentially between iliac crests in lower abdomen deep into S.C. fat. Inject drug slowly. Leave needle in place for 10 seconds after injection; then withdraw. Don't massage after S.C. injection, and watch for bleeding at injection site. Alternate sites every 12 hours.
- Drug requirements are higher in early phases of thrombogenic diseases and febrile states; lower when patient's condition stabilizes.
- Place notice above patient's bed to inform I.V. team or laboratory staff to apply pressure dressings after taking blood.
- Take bleeding precautions.
- To minimize the risk of hematoma, avoid excessive I.M. injection of other drugs. If possible, don't give I.M. injections at all.
- To treat severe heparin calcium or heparin sodium overdose, use protamine sulfate, a heparin antagonist. Dosage is based on dose of heparin, its route of administration, and time elapsed since it was given. As a general rule, 1 to 1.5 units of protamine/100 units of heparin are given if only a few minutes have elapsed; 0.5 to 0.75 mg protamine/100 units heparin if 30 to 60 minutes have elapsed; and 0.25 to 0.375 mg protamine/100 units heparin if 2 hours or more have elapsed.
- Abrupt withdrawal may cause increased coagulability, and heparin therapy is usually followed by oral anticoagulants for prophylaxis.

Patient teaching
- Instruct patient and family to watch for signs of bleeding and to notify prescriber immediately if they occur.
- Tell patient to avoid OTC medications containing aspirin, other salicylates, some herbal remedies, and other drugs that may interact with heparin.

Evaluation
- Patient's PTT is reflective of goal of heparin therapy.
- Patient has no injury from bleeding.
- Patient and family state understanding of drug therapy.

hepatitis B immune globulin, human
(hep-uh-TIGH-tus bee ih-MYOON GLOH-byoo-lin, HYOO-mun)

HBIG, BayHep B, Nabi-HB

Pharmacologic class: immune serum
Therapeutic class: hepatitis B prophylaxis
Pregnancy risk category: C

Indications and dosages
▶ **Hepatitis B exposure in high-risk patients.** *Adults and children:* 0.06 ml/kg I.M. within 7 days after exposure (preferably within first 24 hours). Dosage repeated 28 days after exposure if patient refuses hepatitis B vaccine.

Neonates born to patients who test positive for hepatitis B surface antigen (HBsAg): 0.5 ml I.M. within 12 hours of birth.

Contraindications and precautions

- Contraindicated in patients with history of anaphylactic reactions to immune serum.

Lifespan: In pregnant and breast-feeding women, use cautiously. It's unknown whether drug appears in breast milk.

Adverse reactions

Skin: urticaria; *pain, tenderness* at injection site.
Other: ***anaphylaxis, angioedema.***

Interactions

Drug-drug. *Live-virus vaccines:* May interfere with response to live-virus vaccines. Defer routine immunization for 3 months.

Effects on lab test results

None reported.

Pharmacokinetics

Absorption: Absorbed slowly after I.M. injection.
Distribution: Unknown.
Metabolism: Unknown.
Excretion: Unknown. *Half-life:* Antibodies to HBsAg, 21 days.

Route	Onset	Peak	Duration
I.M.	1-6 days	3-11 days	≥ 2 mo

Pharmacodynamics

Chemical effect: Provides passive immunity to hepatitis B.
Therapeutic effect: Prevents hepatitis B.

Available forms

Injection: 1-ml, 4-ml, 5-ml vials

NURSING PROCESS

Assessment

- Assess patient's allergies and reaction to immunizations before therapy.
- Monitor effectiveness by checking patient's antibody titers.
- Be alert for anaphylaxis.
- Evaluate patient's and family's knowledge of drug therapy.

Nursing diagnoses

- Ineffective protection related to lack of immunity to hepatitis B
- Deficient knowledge related to drug therapy

Planning and implementation

- Inject drug into anterolateral aspect of thigh or deltoid muscle in older children and adults; inject into anterolateral aspect of thigh for neonates and children under age 3.
- Make sure epinephrine 1:1,000 is available in case anaphylaxis occurs.
- For postexposure prophylaxis (for example, needle stick, direct contact), drug is usually given with hepatitis B vaccine.

Patient teaching

- Instruct patient to report respiratory difficulty immediately.

Evaluation

- Patient exhibits passive immunity to hepatitis B.
- Patient and family state understanding of drug therapy.

hetastarch

(HET-uh-starch)
Hespan

Pharmacologic class: amylopectin derivative
Therapeutic class: plasma volume expander
Pregnancy risk category: C

Indications and dosages

▶ **Plasma expander.** *Adults:* 500 to 1,000 ml I.V., depending on amount of blood lost and resulting hemoconcentration. Total dosage usually not to exceed 1,500 ml daily. Up to 20 ml/kg hourly may be used in hemorrhagic shock.

Contraindications and precautions

- Contraindicated in patients with severe bleeding disorders, severe heart failure, and renal failure with oliguria and anuria.

Lifespan: In pregnant women, use cautiously. Breast-feeding women should temporarily stop nursing. In children, safety of drug hasn't been established.

Adverse reactions

CNS: mild fever, headaches.
CV: peripheral edema of legs.
EENT: periorbital edema.
GI: nausea, vomiting.
Respiratory: wheezing.
Skin: urticaria.
Other: ***hypersensitivity reactions.***

Interactions

None significant.

Effects on lab test results

None reported.

Pharmacokinetics

Absorption: Administered I.V.
Distribution: Distributed in blood plasma.
Metabolism: Hetastarch molecules larger than 50,000 molecular weight are slowly enzymatically degraded to molecules that can be excreted.
Excretion: 40% of hetastarch molecules smaller than 50,000 molecular weight are excreted in urine within 24 hours. Hetastarch molecules that aren't hydroxyethylated are slowly degraded to glucose. *Half-life:* 17 to 48 days.

Route	Onset	Peak	Duration
I.V.	Immediate	Immediate	Unknown

Pharmacodynamics

Chemical effect: Expands plasma volume.
Therapeutic effect: Reverses fluid volume deficit.

Available forms

Injection: 500 ml (6 g/100 ml in normal saline solution)

NURSING PROCESS

Assessment

- Assess patient's underlying condition before therapy.
- Check for improvement in underlying condition. Assess vital signs and cardiopulmonary status.
- To avoid circulatory overload, monitor patient with impaired renal function carefully.
- Monitor CBC, total leukocyte and platelet counts, leukocyte differential count, hemoglobin, hematocrit, PT, INR, PTT, and electrolyte, BUN, and creatinine levels.
- Be alert for adverse reactions.
- Evaluate patient's and family's knowledge of drug therapy.

Nursing diagnoses

- Deficient fluid volume related to underlying condition
- Ineffective health maintenance related to hypersensitivity reaction
- Deficient knowledge related to drug therapy

Planning and implementation

- Hetastarch isn't a substitute for blood or plasma.
- During continuous-flow centrifugation, leukapheresis ratio is usually 1 part hetastarch to 8 parts venous whole blood.
- Discard partially used bottles.
- Discontinue drug if allergic or sensitivity reaction occurs and notify prescriber. If necessary, give antihistamine.

Patient teaching

- Inform patient about need for drug.
- Tell patient to report difficulty breathing.

Evaluation

- Patient regains normal fluid volume after drug therapy.
- Patient doesn't develop hypersensitivity reaction to drug.
- Patient and family state understanding of drug therapy.

hydralazine hydrochloride

(high-DRAL-uh-zeen high-droh-KLOR-ighd)
Alphapress◇, Apresoline**, Novo-Hylazin◆

Pharmacologic class: peripheral vasodilator
Therapeutic class: antihypertensive
Pregnancy risk category: C

Indications and dosages

▶ **Essential hypertension (orally, alone or with other antihypertensives); severe essential hypertension (parenterally, to lower blood pressure quickly).** *Adults:* Initially, 10 mg P.O. q.i.d.; gradually increase to 50 mg q.i.d., p.r.n. Maximum recommended dosage is

200 mg daily, but some patients may need 300 to 400 mg daily. Or, 10 to 20 mg I.V. given slowly and repeated, as necessary. Switch to P.O. antihypertensives as soon as possible. Or, 10 to 50 mg I.M., repeated as necessary. Switch to P.O. form as soon as possible.

▶ **Management of severe heart failure‡.** *Adults:* Initially 50 to 75 mg P.O., then adjust according to patient's response. Most patients respond to 200 to 600 mg daily, divided q 6 to 12 hours, but doses as high as 3 g daily have been given.

Contraindications and precautions

- Contraindicated in patients hypersensitive to drug and in those with coronary artery disease or mitral valvular rheumatic heart disease.
- Use cautiously in patients with suspected cardiac disease, CVA, or severe renal impairment, and in those taking other antihypertensives.

Lifespan: In pregnant women, use cautiously. In breast-feeding women and in children, safety of drug hasn't been established.

Adverse reactions

CNS: peripheral neuritis, *headache,* dizziness.
CV: orthostatic hypotension, tachycardia, ***arrhythmias,*** angina, palpitations, sodium retention.
GI: nausea, vomiting, diarrhea, anorexia.
Hematologic: *neutropenia, leukopenia, agranulocytopenia.*
Metabolic: *weight gain.*
Skin: rash.
Other: *lupus-like syndrome* (especially with high doses).

Interactions

Drug-drug. *Diazoxide, MAO inhibitors:* May cause severe hypotension. Use together cautiously.
Indomethacin: May decrease hydralazine effects. Monitor patient.
Metoprolol, propranolol (beta blockers): Serum levels of either drug may be increased. Avoid using together.

Effects on lab test results

- May decrease hemoglobin, hematocrit, and neutrophil, WBC, RBC, granulocyte, and platelet counts.

Pharmacokinetics

Absorption: Absorbed rapidly from GI tract. Food enhances absorption. Degree of absorption is unknown after I.M. administration.
Distribution: Distributed widely throughout body; about 88% to 90% protein-bound.
Metabolism: Metabolized extensively in GI mucosa and liver.
Excretion: Excreted primarily in urine; about 10% of P.O. dose is excreted in feces. *Half-life:* 3 to 7 hours.

Route	Onset	Peak	Duration
P.O.	20-30 min	1-2 hr	3-8 hr
I.V.	≤ 5 min	15-30 min	3-8 hr
I.M.	Unknown	Unknown	3-8 hr

Pharmacodynamics

Chemical effect: Unknown. As a direct-acting vasodilator, its predominant effect relaxes arteriolar smooth muscle.
Therapeutic effect: Lowers blood pressure.

Available forms

Injection: 20 mg/ml
Tablets: 10 mg, 25 mg, 50 mg, 100 mg

NURSING PROCESS

Assessment

- Assess blood pressure before therapy and regularly thereafter.
- Monitor CBC, lupus erythematosus cell preparation, and antinuclear antibody titer determination during long-term therapy.
- Be alert for adverse reactions and drug interactions.
- Evaluate patient's and family's knowledge of drug therapy.

Nursing diagnoses

- Risk for injury related to presence of hypertension
- Excessive fluid volume related to sodium retention
- Deficient knowledge related to drug therapy

Planning and implementation

- **P.O. use:** Give drug with meals to increase absorption.
- **I.V. use:** Give drug slowly, and repeat as necessary, usually every 4 to 6 hours.

– Hydralazine changes color in most infusion solutions, but the change doesn't indicate loss of potency.
– Drug is compatible with normal saline solution, Ringer's and lactated Ringer's solutions, and several other common I.V. solutions. Drug may react with dextrose. Manufacturer doesn't recommend mixing drug in infusion solutions. Check with pharmacist for additional compatibility information.
- **I.M. use:** Follow normal protocol.
- Some clinicians combine hydralazine therapy with diuretics and beta blockers to decrease sodium retention and tachycardia and to prevent angina.
- Compliance may be improved by giving drug twice daily. Check with prescriber.

Patient teaching
- Instruct patient to take oral form with meals to increase absorption.
- Inform patient that orthostatic hypotension can be minimized by rising slowly and avoiding sudden position changes.
- Tell patient not to stop drug suddenly but to call prescriber if unpleasant adverse reactions occur.
- Tell patient to limit sodium intake.

☑ Evaluation
- Patient's blood pressure is normal.
- Fluid retention doesn't develop.
- Patient and family state understanding of drug therapy.

hydrochlorothiazide

(high-droh-klor-oh-THIGH-uh-zighd)
Apo-Hydro ♦, Dichlotride ◇, Diuchlor H ♦, Esidrix, Ezide, HydroDIURIL, Hydro-Par, Microzide, Neo-Codema ♦, Novo-Hydrazide ♦, Oretic, Urozide ♦, Aquazide-25, Aquazide-H

Pharmacologic class: thiazide diuretic
Therapeutic class: diuretic, antihypertensive
Pregnancy risk category: D

Indications and dosages

▶ **Edema.** *Adults:* 25 to 100 mg P.O. daily or intermittently.

▶ **Hypertension.** *Adults:* 12.5 to 50 mg P.O. once daily. May increase or decrease daily dose based on blood pressure.
Children ages 2 to 12: 2.2 mg/kg or 60 mg/m² P.O. daily in 2 divided doses. Usual dosage range is 37.5 to 100 mg P.O. daily.
Infants and children ages 6 months to younger than 2 years: 2.2 mg/kg or 60 mg/m² P.O. daily in 2 divided doses. Usual dosage range is 12.5 to 37.5 mg P.O. daily.
Infants younger than age 6 months: Up to 3.3 mg/kg daily in 2 divided doses.

Contraindications and precautions

- Contraindicated in patients with anuria and in patients hypersensitive to other thiazides or sulfonamide derivatives.
- Use cautiously in patients with severe renal disease, impaired hepatic function, and progressive hepatic disease.

Lifespan: In pregnant women, drug isn't recommended because fetal harm may occur. In breast-feeding women, safety of drug hasn't been established.

Adverse reactions

CV: volume depletion and dehydration, orthostatic hypotension.
GI: anorexia, nausea, ***pancreatitis.***
GU: nocturia, polyuria, frequent urination, ***renal failure.***
Hematologic: ***aplastic anemia, agranulocytosis, leukopenia, thrombocytopenia.***
Hepatic: hepatic encephalopathy.
Metabolic: gout, hypokalemia, asymptomatic hyperuricemia, hyperglycemia and impairment of glucose tolerance, fluid and electrolyte imbalances, including dilutional hyponatremia and hypochloremia, ***metabolic alkalosis,*** and hypercalcemia.
Skin: dermatitis, photosensitivity, rash.
Other: ***anaphylactic reactions,*** hypersensitivity reactions, such as pneumonitis and vasculitis.

Interactions

Drug-drug. *Antidiabetics:* Decreases effectiveness of hypoglycemics. Adjust dosage as needed; monitor glucose level.
Antihypertensives: May have additive antihypertensive effect. Use together cautiously; monitor blood pressure closely.

Barbiturates, opiates: Increases orthostatic hypotensive effect. Monitor patient closely.
Cholestyramine, colestipol: Decreases intestinal absorption of thiazides. Give drugs separately.
Diazoxide: Increases antihypertensive, hyperglycemic, and hyperuricemic effects. Use together cautiously.
Digoxin: Increases risk of digoxin toxicity from hydrochlorothiazide-induced hypokalemia. Monitor potassium and digoxin levels.
Lithium: Decreases lithium excretion, increasing risk of lithium toxicity. Monitor lithium level.
NSAIDs: Increases risk of NSAID-induced renal failure. Monitor patient closely.
Drug-herb. *Dandelion:* May interfere with diuretic activity. Discourage using together.
Licorice root: May contribute to the potassium depletion caused by thiazides. Discourage using together.
Drug-lifestyle. *Alcohol use:* Increases orthostatic hypotensive effect. Discourage using together.
Sun exposure: Increases photosensitivity. Urge patient to avoid unprotected or prolonged sun exposure.

Effects on lab test results

• May increase glucose, cholesterol, triglyceride, calcium, and uric acid levels. May decrease potassium, sodium, and chloride levels.
• May decrease hemoglobin, hematocrit, and granulocyte, WBC, and platelet counts.

Pharmacokinetics

Absorption: Rate and extent vary with different forms of drug.
Distribution: Unknown.
Metabolism: None.
Excretion: Excreted unchanged in urine.

Route	Onset	Peak	Duration
P.O.	2 hr	4-6 hr	6-12 hr

Pharmacodynamics

Chemical effect: Increases sodium and water excretion by inhibiting sodium and chloride reabsorption in nephron's distal segment.
Therapeutic effect: Promotes sodium and water excretion and lowers blood pressure.

Available forms

Capsules: 12.5 mg
Oral solution: 50 mg/5 ml
Tablets: 25 mg, 50 mg, 100 mg

NURSING PROCESS

Assessment

• Assess patient's edema or blood pressure before starting therapy.
• Monitor effectiveness by regularly checking blood pressure, urine output, and weight. In patient with hypertension, therapeutic response may be delayed several days.
• Monitor electrolyte levels.
• Monitor creatinine and BUN levels regularly. Drug isn't as effective if these levels are more than twice normal.
• Monitor uric acid levels, especially in patient with history of gout.
• Be alert for adverse reactions and drug interactions.
• Evaluate patient's and family's knowledge of drug therapy.

Nursing diagnoses

• Ineffective health maintenance related to presence of edema or hypertension
• Impaired urinary elimination related to diuretic effect of drug
• Deficient knowledge related to drug therapy

Planning and implementation

• Give drug in morning to prevent nocturia.
• Give with food if nausea occurs.
• Drug may be used with potassium-sparing diuretic to prevent potassium loss.

Patient teaching

• Advise patient to take drug with food to minimize GI upset.
• Caution patient to avoid sudden posture changes and to rise slowly to avoid orthostatic hypotension.
• Instruct patient to avoid alcohol consumption during drug therapy.
• Advise patient to use sunblock to prevent photosensitivity reactions.
• Tell patient to check with prescriber before taking OTC medications or herbal remedies.

☑ Evaluation

- Patient's blood pressure is normal, and no edema is present.
- Patient demonstrates adjustment of lifestyle to deal with altered patterns of urinary elimination.
- Patient and family state understanding of drug therapy.

hydrocortisone
(high-droh-KOR-tuh-sohn)
Cortef, Cortenema, Hydrocortone

hydrocortisone acetate
Cortifoam, Hydrocortone Acetate

hydrocortisone cypionate
Cortef

hydrocortisone sodium phosphate
Hydrocortone Phosphate

hydrocortisone sodium succinate
A-hydroCort, Solu-Cortef

Pharmacologic class: glucocorticoid, mineralocorticoid
Therapeutic class: adrenocorticoid replacement
Pregnancy risk category: NR

Indications and dosages

▶ **Severe inflammation, adrenal insufficiency.** *Adults:* 20 to 240 mg hydrocortisone or cipionate P.O. daily. Or, 5 to 75 mg acetate injected into joints or soft tissue. Dosage varies with degree of inflammation and size and location of the joint or soft tissues. Or, 15 to 240 mg phosphate I.V., I.M., or S.C. daily, divided into 12-hour intervals. Or, initially, 100 to 500 mg succinate I.V. or I.M.; may repeat q 2 to 10 hours p.r.n.

▶ **Adjunct for ulcerative colitis and proctitis.** *Adults:* 1 enema (100 mg) hydrocortisone or acetate P.R. nightly for 21 days.

Contraindications and precautions

- Contraindicated in patients allergic to drug or its components, in those with systemic fungal infections, and in premature infants ***(succinate)***.
- Use with extreme caution in patients with recent MI.
- Use cautiously in patients with GI ulcer, renal disease, hypertension, osteoporosis, diabetes mellitus, hypothyroidism, cirrhosis, diverticulitis, nonspecific ulcerative colitis, recent intestinal anastomoses, thromboembolic disorders, seizures, myasthenia gravis, heart failure, tuberculosis, ocular herpes simplex, emotional instability, and psychotic tendencies.

Lifespan: In pregnant women, use cautiously. In breast-feeding women, drug isn't recommended in high doses. In children, long-term use may delay growth and maturation.

Adverse reactions

Most adverse reactions are dose- or duration-dependent.
CNS: *euphoria, insomnia,* psychotic behavior, pseudotumor cerebri, ***seizures.***
CV: ***heart failure,*** hypertension, edema, ***arrhythmias, thromboembolism.***
EENT: cataracts, glaucoma.
GI: *peptic ulceration,* GI irritation, increased appetite, ***pancreatitis.***
Metabolic: possible hypokalemia, hyperglycemia, and carbohydrate intolerance.
Musculoskeletal: muscle weakness, growth suppression in children, osteoporosis.
Skin: hirsutism, delayed wound healing, acne, various skin eruptions, easy bruising.
Other: susceptibility to infections, ***acute adrenal insufficiency with increased stress (infection, surgery, or trauma) or abrupt withdrawal after long-term therapy.***

Interactions

Drug-drug. *Aspirin, indomethacin, other NSAIDs:* Increases risk of GI distress and bleeding. Give together cautiously.
Barbiturates, phenytoin, rifampin: Decreases corticosteroid effect. May require increased corticosteroid dosage.
Live-attenuated virus vaccines, other toxoids and vaccines: Decreases antibody response and increases risk of neurologic complications. Avoid using together.
Oral anticoagulants: Alters dosage requirements. Monitor PT and INR closely.
Potassium-depleting drugs (such as thiazide diuretics): Enhances potassium-wasting effects of hydrocortisone. Monitor potassium level.

Skin-test antigens: Decreases skin response. Defer skin testing until therapy is completed.
Drug-lifestyle. *Alcohol use:* Increases risk of GI effects. Discourage using together.

Effects on lab test results

• May increase glucose and cholesterol levels. May decrease potassium and calcium levels.

Pharmacokinetics

Absorption: Rapid after P.O. use. Variable after I.M. or intra-articular injection. Unknown after rectal use.
Distribution: Distributed to muscle, liver, skin, intestines, and kidneys. Drug is bound extensively to plasma proteins. Only unbound portion is active.
Metabolism: Metabolized in liver.
Excretion: Inactive metabolites and small amounts of unmetabolized drug excreted in urine; insignificant quantities excreted in feces. *Half-life:* 8 to 12 hours.

Route	Onset	Peak	Duration
P.O., I.V., I.M., P.R.	Varies	Varies	Varies

Pharmacodynamics

Chemical effect: Not clearly defined; decreases inflammation, mainly by stabilizing leukocyte lysosomal membranes; suppresses immune response; stimulates bone marrow; and influences nutrient metabolism.
Therapeutic effect: Reduces inflammation, suppresses immune function and raises adrenocorticoid hormonal levels.

Available forms

hydrocortisone
Enema: 100 mg/60 ml
Tablets: 5 mg, 10 mg, 20 mg
hydrocortisone acetate
Enema: 10% aerosol foam (provides 90 mg/application)
Injection: 25 mg/ml*, 50 mg/ml* suspension
Suppositories: 25 mg
hydrocortisone cypionate
Oral suspension: 10 mg/5 ml
hydrocortisone sodium phosphate
Injection: 50 mg/ml solution
hydrocortisone sodium succinate
Injection: 100 mg/vial*, 250 mg/vial*, 500 mg/vial*, 1,000 mg/vial*

NURSING PROCESS

Assessment

• Assess patient's condition before therapy and regularly thereafter.
• Monitor patient's weight, blood pressure, and electrolyte levels.
• Monitor patient for stress. Fever, trauma, surgery, and emotional problems may increase adrenal insufficiency.
• Periodic measurement of growth and development may be needed during high-dose or prolonged therapy in child.
• Be alert for adverse reactions and drug interactions.
• Evaluate patient's and family's knowledge of drug therapy.

Nursing diagnoses

• Ineffective health maintenance related to underlying condition
• Ineffective protection related to immunosuppression
• Deficient knowledge related to drug therapy

Planning and implementation

• For better results and less toxicity, give once-daily dose in morning.
• **P.O. use:** Give P.O. dose with food.
• **I.V. use:** Don't use acetate or suspension form for I.V. use. When giving as direct injection, inject directly into vein or I.V. line containing free-flowing compatible solution over 30 seconds to several minutes. When giving as intermittent or continuous infusion, dilute solution according to manufacturer's instructions and give over prescribed duration. If used for continuous infusion, change solution every 24 hours.
– Hydrocortisone sodium phosphate may be added directly to D_5W or normal saline solution for I.V. administration.
– Reconstitute hydrocortisone sodium succinate with bacteriostatic water or bacteriostatic sodium chloride solution before adding to I.V. solutions. When giving by direct I.V. injection, inject over at least 30 seconds. For infusion, dilute with D_5W, normal saline solution, or D_5W in normal saline solution to 1 mg/ml or less.
• **I.M. use:** Give I.M. injection deep into gluteal muscle. Rotate injection sites to prevent muscle atrophy.
• **P.R. use:** Enema may produce the same systemic effects as other forms of hydrocortisone.

If therapy must exceed 21 days, discontinue gradually by reducing administration to every other night for 2 or 3 weeks.

ALERT: Avoid S.C. injection because atrophy and sterile abscesses may occur.

ALERT: Don't confuse Solu-Cortef with Solu-Medrol (methylprednisolone sodium succinate).

- Injectable forms aren't used for alternate-day therapy.
- High-dose therapy usually doesn't continue beyond 48 hours.
- Always adjust to lowest effective dose, and gradually reduce dosage after long-term therapy.
- Give potassium supplements.
- Notify prescriber if evidence of adrenal insufficiency appears. Dosage may need to be increased.
- Notify prescriber about adverse reactions. Provide supportive care.

Patient teaching

- Teach patient signs of early adrenal insufficiency: fatigue, muscle weakness, joint pain, fever, anorexia, nausea, dyspnea, dizziness, and fainting.
- Instruct patient to carry or wear medical identification that identifies need for supplemental systemic glucocorticoids during stress.

ALERT: Tell patient not to discontinue drug abruptly or without prescriber's consent. Abrupt withdrawal may lead to rebound inflammation, fatigue, weakness, arthralgia, fever, dizziness, lethargy, depression, fainting, orthostatic hypotension, dyspnea, anorexia, and hypoglycemia. After prolonged use, sudden withdrawal may be fatal.

- Warn patient receiving long-term therapy about cushingoid symptoms and tell him to report sudden weight gain or swelling to prescriber. Also, advise him to consider exercise or physical therapy, to ask his prescriber about vitamin D or calcium supplements, and to have periodic ophthalmic examinations.
- Caution patient about easy bruising.

☑ Evaluation

- Patient's condition improves.
- Serious complications related to drug-induced immunosuppression don't develop.
- Patient and family state understanding of drug therapy.

hydromorphone hydrochloride (dihydromorphinone hydrochloride)

(high-droh-MOR-fohn high-droh-KLOR-ighd)
Dilaudid, Dilaudid-HP

Pharmacologic class: opioid
Therapeutic class: analgesic, antitussive
Pregnancy risk category: C
Controlled substance schedule: II

Indications and dosages

▶ **Moderate-to-severe pain.** *Adults:* 2 to 4 mg P.O. q 4 to 6 hours, p.r.n. Or, 1 to 2 mg I.M., S.C., or I.V. (slowly over at least 2 to 3 minutes) q 4 to 6 hours p.r.n. Or, 3-mg rectal suppository q 6 to 8 hours p.r.n.

▶ **Cough.** *Adults:* 1 mg P.O. q 3 to 4 hours p.r.n.
Children ages 6 to 12: 0.5 mg P.O. q 3 to 4 hours p.r.n.

Contraindications and precautions

- Contraindicated in patients hypersensitive to drug, in patients with intracranial lesions from increased intracranial pressure, and whenever ventilator function is depressed, as in status asthmaticus, COPD, cor pulmonale, emphysema, or kyphoscoliosis.
- Use with extreme caution in patients with hepatic or renal disease, hypothyroidism, Addison's disease, prostatic hypertrophy, or urethral stricture.

Lifespan: In pregnant and breast-feeding women and in elderly and debilitated patients, use cautiously.

Adverse reactions

CNS: *sedation, somnolence, clouded sensorium,* dizziness, *euphoria,* ***seizures.***
CV: hypotension, ***bradycardia.***
EENT: blurred vision, diplopia, nystagmus.
GI: nausea, vomiting, constipation, ileus.
GU: urine retention.
Respiratory: ***respiratory depression, bronchospasm.***
Other: induration with repeated S.C. injections, physical dependence.

Interactions

Drug-drug. *CNS depressants, general anesthetics, hypnotics, MAO inhibitors, other narcotic analgesics, sedatives, tranquilizers, tricyclic antidepressants:* May have additive effects. Use together with extreme caution. Reduce hydromorphone dose, and monitor patient response.
Drug-lifestyle. *Alcohol use:* May have additive effects. Discourage using together.

Effects on lab test results

- May increase amylase and lipase levels.

Pharmacokinetics

Absorption: Well absorbed after oral, rectal, or parenteral administration.
Distribution: Unknown.
Metabolism: Metabolized primarily in liver.
Excretion: Excreted primarily in urine. *Half-life:* 2.6 to 4 hours.

Route	Onset	Peak	Duration
P.O.	30 min	30 min-2 hr	4-5 hr
I.V.	10-15 min	15-30 min	2-3 hr
I.M.	15 min	30-60 min	4-5 hr
S.C.	15 min	30-90 min	4 hr
P.R.	Unknown	Unknown	4 hr

Pharmacodynamics

Chemical effect: Binds with opioid receptors in CNS, altering perception of and emotional response to pain. Suppresses cough reflex by direct action on cough center in medulla.
Therapeutic effect: Relieves pain and cough.

Available forms

Injection: 1 mg/ml, 2 mg/ml, 4 mg/ml, 10 mg/ml
Injection (lyophilized powder): 250 mg/vial
Liquid: 5 mg/5 ml
Suppositories: 3 mg
Tablets: 2 mg, 4 mg, 8 mg

NURSING PROCESS

Assessment

- Assess patient's pain or cough before and after drug administration.
- Respiratory depression and hypotension can occur with I.V. administration. Monitor respiratory and circulatory status frequently.
- Drug may worsen or mask gallbladder pain.
- Drug is a commonly abused narcotic. Be alert for addictive behavior or drug abuse.
- Be alert for adverse reactions and drug interactions.
- Evaluate patient's and family's knowledge of drug therapy.

Nursing diagnoses

- Acute pain related to underlying condition
- Ineffective breathing pattern related to respiratory depression
- Deficient knowledge related to drug therapy

Planning and implementation

- For better analgesic effect, give drug before patient has intense pain.
- Dilaudid-HP, a highly concentrated form (10 mg/ml), may be given in smaller volumes to prevent discomfort caused by large-volume I.M. or S.C. injections. Check dosage carefully.
- **P.O., I.M., and P.R. use:** Follow normal protocol.
- **I.V. use:** Give drug by direct injection over at least 2 minutes. For infusion, drug may be mixed in D_5W, normal saline solution, D_5W in normal saline solution, D_5W in half-normal saline solution, or Ringer's or lactated Ringer's solutions.
- **S.C. use:** Rotate injection sites to avoid induration with S.C. injection.
- Keep resuscitation equipment and narcotic antagonist (naloxone) available.
- Postoperatively, encourage patient to turn, cough, and deep-breathe to avoid atelectasis.

Patient teaching

- Caution ambulatory patient about getting out of bed or walking. Warn patient to avoid activities that require mental alertness until CNS effects of drug are known.
- Suggest measures to prevent constipation during maintenance therapy.
- Encourage patient to ask for drug before pain becomes severe.
- Tell patient or family caregiver to notify health care professional if patient's respiratory rate decreases.
- Instruct patient to avoid alcohol consumption during drug therapy.

Evaluation

- Patient is free from pain.
- Patient maintains adequate breathing patterns.

• Patient and family state understanding of drug therapy.

hydroxychloroquine sulfate

(high-droks-ee-KLOR-oh-kwin SUL-fayt)
Plaquenil

Pharmacologic class: 4-aminoquinoline
Therapeutic class: antimalarial, anti-inflammatory
Pregnancy risk category: NR

Indications and dosages

▶ **Suppressive prophylaxis of malaria attacks caused by *Plasmodium vivax, P. malariae, P. ovale,* and susceptible strains of *P. falciparum.*** *Adults:* 310 mg base P.O. weekly on same day of week. Begin 1 to 2 weeks before exposure and continue for 4 weeks after leaving endemic areas.
Children: 5 mg base/kg P.O. weekly, not to exceed 310 mg.
Patients who have not started treatment before exposure: Initial loading dose is doubled (620 mg for adults, 10 mg/kg for children) P.O. in two divided doses 6 hours apart.

▶ **Acute malarial attacks.** *Adults:* Initially, 620 mg base P.O.; then 310 mg base after 6 hours; then 310 mg base daily for 2 days.
Children: Initial dose, 10 mg base/kg (up to 620 mg base); second dose, 5 mg base/kg (up to 310 mg base) 6 hours after first dose; third dose, 5 mg base/kg 18 hours after second dose; fourth dose, 5 mg base/kg 24 hours after third dose.

▶ **Lupus erythematosus (chronic discoid and systemic).** *Adults:* 400 mg (sulfate) P.O. daily or b.i.d., continued for several weeks or months, depending on response. Prolonged maintenance dosage: 200 to 400 mg (sulfate) daily.

▶ **Rheumatoid arthritis.** *Adults:* Initially, 400 to 600 mg (sulfate) P.O. daily. When good response occurs (usually in 4 to 12 weeks), reduce doage by 50% and continue at a level of 200 to 400 mg daily.

Contraindications and precautions

• Contraindicated in patients hypersensitive to drug, and in patients with retinal or visual field changes or porphyria.
• Use with extreme caution in patients with severe GI, neurologic, or blood disorders.
• Use cautiously in patients with hepatic disease or alcoholism because drug concentrates in liver. Also, use cautiously in those with G6PD deficiency or psoriasis because drug may worsen these conditions.
Lifespan: With pregnant women, use cautiously. In breast-feeding women, safety of drug hasn't been established. In children who need long-term therapy, drug is contraindicated.

Adverse reactions

CNS: irritability, nightmares, ataxia, ***seizures,*** psychic stimulation, toxic psychosis, vertigo, nystagmus, lassitude, fatigue, dizziness, hypoactive deep tendon reflexes.
EENT: visual disturbances (blurred vision; difficulty in focusing; reversible corneal changes; typically irreversible, sometimes progressive or delayed retinal changes, such as narrowing of arterioles; macular lesions; pallor of optic disk; optic atrophy; visual field defects; patchy retinal pigmentation, commonly leading to blindness), ototoxicity (irreversible nerve deafness, tinnitus, labyrinthitis).
GI: anorexia, abdominal cramps, diarrhea, nausea, vomiting.
Hematologic: ***agranulocytosis, leukopenia, thrombocytopenia, aplastic anemia; hemolysis*** (in patients with G6PD deficiency).
Metabolic: weight loss.
Musculoskeletal: skeletal muscle weakness.
Skin: pruritus, lichen planus eruptions, skin and mucosal pigmentary changes, pleomorphic skin eruptions, alopecia, bleaching of hair.

Interactions

Drug-drug. *Aluminum and magnesium salts, kaolin:* Decreases GI absorption. Separate administration times.
Cimetidine: Decreases hepatic metabolism of hydroxychloroquine. Monitor patient for toxicity.

Effects on lab test results

• May decrease hemoglobin, hematocrit, and granulocyte, WBC, and platelet counts.

Pharmacokinetics

Absorption: Absorbed readily and almost completely.

Distribution: Concentrates in liver, spleen, kidneys, heart, and brain and is strongly bound in melanin-containing cells. Drug is bound to plasma proteins.
Metabolism: Metabolized by liver.
Excretion: Most excreted unchanged in urine. *Half-life:* 32 to 50 days.

Route	Onset	Peak	Duration
P.O.	Unknown	2-4.5 hr	Unknown

Pharmacodynamics

Chemical effect: Unknown; may bind to and alter properties of DNA in susceptible organisms.
Therapeutic effect: Prevents or hinders growth of *P. malariae, P. ovale, P. vivax,* and *P. falciparum*. Relieves inflammation.

Available forms

Tablets: 200 mg (equivalent to 155 mg base)

NURSING PROCESS

Assessment

- Assess patient's condition before therapy and regularly thereafter.
- Make sure baseline and periodic ophthalmic examinations are performed. Check periodically for ocular muscle weakness after long-term use.
- Obtain audiometric examinations before, during, and after therapy, especially during long-term therapy.
- Monitor CBCs and liver function studies periodically during long-term therapy.
- Assess patient for overdose, which can quickly lead to toxic symptoms: headache, drowsiness, visual disturbances, CV collapse, and seizures, followed by cardiopulmonary arrest. Children are extremely susceptible to toxicity; long-term treatment should be avoided.
- Be alert for adverse reactions and drug interactions.
- Evaluate patient's and family's knowledge of drug therapy.

Nursing diagnoses

- Infection related to susceptible organisms
- Disturbed sensory perception (visual and auditory) related to adverse reactions to drug
- Deficient knowledge related to drug therapy

Planning and implementation

- Give drug right before or after meals on same day of each week.
- Notify prescriber immediately about severe blood disorder that can't be attributed to disease under treatment. Blood reaction may require discontinuation.

Patient teaching

- Advise patient to take drug immediately before or after meals on same day each week to enhance compliance for prophylaxis.
- Warn patient to avoid hazardous activities if adverse CNS or visual disturbances occur.
- Tell patient to promptly report visual or auditory changes.

Evaluation

- Patient is free from infection.
- Patient maintains normal visual and auditory function.
- Patient and family state understanding of drug therapy.

hydroxyurea

(high-droks-ee-yoo-REE-uh)
Droxia, Hydrea**

Pharmacologic class: antimetabolite (cell cycle–phase specific, S phase)
Therapeutic class: antineoplastic; antisickling agent
Pregnancy risk category: D

Indications and dosages

▶ **Melanoma; resistant chronic myelocytic leukemia; recurrent, metastatic, or inoperable ovarian cancer; head and neck cancers.** *Adults:* 80 mg/kg P.O. as single dose q 3rd day; or, 20 to 30 mg/kg P.O. as single daily dose.

▶ **Reduction of frequency of painful crises and need for transfusions in adult sickle-cell anemia patients with recurrent moderate-to-severe painful crises.** *Adults:* Initially, 15 mg/kg P.O. once daily. If blood counts are in acceptable range, dosage may be increased by 5 mg/kg daily q 12 weeks until maximum tolerated dosage or 35 mg/kg daily has been reached. If blood counts are considered toxic, withhold drug until hematologic recovery occurs. Resume treatment after reducing dose by

2.5 mg/kg daily. Every 12 weeks, drug may then be adjusted up or down in 2.5-mg/kg daily increments until patient is at a stable, nontoxic dose for 24 weeks.

Contraindications and precautions

• Contraindicated in patients hypersensitive to drug and in those with marked bone marrow depression.
• Use cautiously in patients with renal dysfunction.
Lifespan: In pregnant and breast-feeding women, drug isn't recommended. In children, safety of drug hasn't been established.

Adverse reactions

CNS: drowsiness, hallucinations, ***seizures.***
GI: anorexia, nausea, vomiting, diarrhea, stomatitis.
Hematologic: ***leukopenia, thrombocytopenia,*** anemia, *megaloblastosis,* **bone marrow suppression** (dose-limiting and dose-related, with rapid recovery).
Metabolic: hyperuricemia.
Skin: rash, pruritus.

Interactions

Drug-drug. *Cytotoxic drugs, radiation therapy:* Enhances toxicity of hydroxyurea. Use together cautiously.

Effects on lab test results

• May increase BUN, creatinine, and uric acid levels.
• May decrease hemoglobin, hematocrit, and WBC, RBC, and platelet counts.

Pharmacokinetics

Absorption: Well absorbed. Serum levels are higher with a large, single dose than with divided doses.
Distribution: Crosses blood-brain barrier.
Metabolism: About 50% of dose is degraded in liver.
Excretion: 50% of drug excreted in urine as unchanged drug; metabolites excreted through lungs as carbon dioxide and in urine as urea. *Half-life:* 3 to 4 hours.

Route	Onset	Peak	Duration
P.O.	Unknown	2 hr	Unknown

Pharmacodynamics

Chemical effect: Unknown; thought to inhibit DNA synthesis.
Therapeutic effect: Hinders growth of certain cancer cells.

Available forms

Capsules: 200 mg, 300 mg, 400 mg, 500 mg
Tablets: 1,000 mg

NURSING PROCESS

Assessment

• Assess patient's condition before therapy and regularly thereafter.
• Measure CBC, BUN, uric acid, and creatinine levels.
• Auditory and visual hallucinations and hematologic toxicity increase with decreased renal function.
• Radiation therapy may increase risk or severity of GI distress or stomatitis.
• Be alert for adverse reactions and drug interactions.
• Evaluate patient's and family's knowledge of drug therapy.

Nursing diagnoses

• Ineffective health maintenance related to presence of neoplastic disease
• Ineffective protection related to adverse hematologic reactions
• Deficient knowledge related to drug therapy

Planning and implementation

• Keep patient hydrated.
• Dosage modification may be needed after chemotherapy or radiation therapy.
• Bone marrow suppression is dose-limited and dose-related with rapid recovery.

Patient teaching

• If patient can't swallow capsules, tell him to empty contents of capsules into water and drink immediately.
• Warn patient to watch for signs of infection (fever, sore throat, fatigue) and bleeding (easy bruising, nosebleeds, bleeding gums, melena). Instruct patient to take infection-control and bleeding precautions. Tell patient to take temperature daily.

• Advise woman of childbearing age to avoid becoming pregnant during therapy and to consult with prescriber before becoming pregnant.

☑ Evaluation

• Patient responds well to drug therapy.
• Serious infections or bleeding complications don't develop.
• Patient and family state understanding of drug therapy.

hydroxyzine embonate ◇

(high-DROKS-ih-zeen EM-boh-nayt)
Atarax

hydroxyzine hydrochloride

Anx, Apo-Hydroxyzine ♦, Atarax*, Hydroxacen, Hyzine-50, Multipax ♦, Neucalm, Novo-Hydroxyzin ♦, QYS, Vistacon-50, Vistaject-50, Vistaril

hydroxyzine pamoate

Vistaril

Pharmacologic class: antihistamine (piperazine derivative)
Therapeutic class: antianxiety, sedative, antipruritic, antiemetic, antispasmodic
Pregnancy risk category: NR

Indications and dosages

▶ **Anxiety.** *Adults:* 50 to 100 mg P.O. q.i.d.
Children age 6 and older: 50 to 100 mg P.O. daily in divided doses.
Children younger than age 6: 50 mg P.O. daily in divided doses.
▶ **Preoperative and postoperative adjunct therapy.** *Adults:* 25 to 100 mg I.M. q 4 to 6 hours.
Children: 1.1 mg/kg I.M. q 4 to 6 hours.
▶ **Pruritus from allergies.** *Adults:* 25 mg P.O. t.i.d. or q.i.d.
Children age 6 and older: 50 to 100 mg P.O. daily in divided doses.
Children younger than age 6: 50 mg P.O. daily in divided doses.
▶ **Psychiatric and emotional emergencies, including acute alcoholism.** *Adults:* 50 to 100 mg I.M. q 4 to 6 hours, p.r.n.
▶ **Nausea and vomiting (excluding nausea and vomiting of pregnancy).** *Adults:* 25 to 100 mg I.M.
Children: 1.1 mg/kg I.M.
▶ **Prepartum and postpartum adjunct therapy.** *Adults:* 25 to 100 mg I.M.

Contraindications and precautions

• Contraindicated in patients hypersensitive to drug.
Lifespan: In early pregnancy, drug is contraindicated. In breast-feeding women, safety of drug hasn't been established.

Adverse reactions

CNS: *drowsiness,* involuntary motor activity.
GI: *dry mouth.*
Other: marked discomfort at I.M. injection site, hypersensitivity reactions (wheezing, dyspnea, chest tightness).

Interactions

Drug-drug. *MAO inhibitors:* Enhances anticholinergic effects. Use cautiously together.
CNS depressants: Increases CNS depression. Avoid using together.
Drug-lifestyle. *Alcohol use:* Increases CNS depression. Discourage using together.
Sunlight: Photosensitivity may occur. Urge patient to avoid unprotected or prolonged sun exposure.

Effects on lab test results

• Drug may cause false elevations of urine 17-hydroxycorticosteroids, depending on test method used.

Pharmacokinetics

Absorption: Rapid and complete after P.O. administration. Unknown for I.M. administration.
Distribution: Unknown.
Metabolism: Metabolized almost completely in liver.
Excretion: Metabolites excreted primarily in urine; small amounts of drug and metabolites excreted in feces. *Half-life:* 3 hours.

Route	Onset	Peak	Duration
P.O.	15-30 min	About 2 hr	4-6 hr
I.M.	Unknown	Unknown	4-6 hr

Pharmacodynamics

Chemical effect: Unknown; may suppress activity in key regions of subcortical area of CNS.
Therapeutic effect: Relieves anxiety and itching, promotes calmness, and alleviates nausea and vomiting.

Available forms

hydroxyzine embonate ◇
Capsules: 25 mg, 50 mg
hydroxyzine hydrochloride
Capsules: 10 mg ◆ ◇, 25 mg ◆ ◇, 50 mg ◆ ◇
Injection: 25 mg/ml, 50 mg/ml
Syrup: 10 mg/5 ml
Tablets: 10 mg, 25 mg, 50 mg, 100 mg
Tablets (film-coated): 10 mg, 25 mg, 50 mg
hydroxyzine pamoate
Capsules: 25 mg, 50 mg, 100 mg
Oral suspension: 25 mg/5 ml

NURSING PROCESS

Assessment

- Assess patient's condition before therapy and regularly thereafter.
- Be alert for adverse reactions and drug interactions.
- Evaluate patient's and family's knowledge of drug therapy.

Nursing diagnoses

- Ineffective health maintenance related to underlying condition
- Risk for injury related to adverse CNS reactions
- Deficient knowledge related to drug therapy

Planning and implementation

- Dosage should be reduced in elderly or debilitated patients.
- **P.O. use:** Follow normal protocol.
- **I.M. use:** Parenteral form (hydroxyzine hydrochloride) for I.M. use only; Z-track injection method is preferred. Aspirate I.M. injection carefully to prevent inadvertent intravascular injection. Inject deep into large muscle mass.

ALERT: Never give I.V.

Patient teaching

- Warn patient to avoid hazardous activities until CNS effects of drug are known.
- Tell patient to avoid alcohol during drug therapy.
- Suggest sugarless hard candy or gum to relieve dry mouth.

Evaluation

- Patient exhibits improved health.
- Patient doesn't experience injury.
- Patient and family state understanding of drug therapy.

I-J

ibuprofen

(igh-byoo-PROH-fen)

ACT-3 ◇, Advil†, Advil Children's, Advil Infants' Drops†, Advil Liqui-Gels†, Advil Migraine†, Apo-Ibuprofen ◆, Brufen ◇, Genpril Caplets†, Genpril Tablets†, Haltran†, IBU†, Ibu-Tab†, Menadol, Midol Cramp†, Midol IB, Motrin, Motrin Children's†, Motrin Drops†, Motrin IB Caplets†, Motrin IB Gelcaps†, Motrin IB Tablets†, Motrin Infants' Drops†, Motrin Migraine Pain Caplets†, Novo-Profen ◆, Nurofen ◇, Rafen ◇, Saleto-200

Pharmacologic class: NSAID
Therapeutic class: nonnarcotic analgesic, antipyretic, anti-inflammatory
Pregnancy risk category: NR

Indications and dosages

▶ **Rheumatoid arthritis, osteoarthritis.** *Adults:* 300 to 800 mg P.O. t.i.d. or q.i.d. not to exceed 3.2 g P.O. daily.
Children: 20 to 40 mg/kg P.O. daily, divided into 3 to 4 doses.

▶ **Mild-to-moderate pain, dysmenorrhea.** *Adults:* 400 mg P.O. q 4 to 6 hours, p.r.n.

▶ **Fever.** *Adults and adolescents:* 200 to 400 mg P.O. q 4 to 6 hours, p.r.n. Don't exceed 1.2 g P.O. daily or give for longer than 3 days.
Children ages 6 months to 12 years: If temperature is below 102.5° F (39.2° C), recommended dosage is 5 mg/kg P.O. q 6 to 8 hours, p.r.n. Treat higher temperatures with 10 mg/kg P.O. q 6 to 8 hours, p.r.n., to maximum dosage of 40 mg/kg daily.

Contraindications and precautions

- Contraindicated in patients hypersensitive to drug and in those with syndrome of nasal polyps, angioedema, and bronchospastic reactivity to aspirin or other NSAIDs.
- Use cautiously in patients with GI disorders, history of peptic ulcer disease, hepatic or renal disease, cardiac decompensation, hypertension, or intrinsic coagulation defects.

Lifespan: For pregnant or breast-feeding women, drug isn't recommended. In infants younger than age 6 months, safety and efficacy haven't been established.

Adverse reactions

CNS: *headache, drowsiness, dizziness,* cognitive dysfunction, aseptic meningitis.
CV: *peripheral edema,* edema, hypertension, ***heart failure.***
EENT: visual disturbances, *tinnitus.*
GI: *epigastric distress, nausea, occult blood loss, peptic ulceration.*
GU: ***reversible renal failure.***
Hematologic: prolonged bleeding time, anemia, ***neutropenia, pancytopenia, thrombocytopenia, aplastic anemia, leukopenia, agranulocytosis.***
Respiratory: ***bronchospasm.***
Skin: pruritus, rash, urticaria, photosensitivity reactions, ***Stevens-Johnson syndrome.***

Interactions

Drug-drug. *Antihypertensives, furosemide, thiazide diuretics:* May decrease effectiveness of diuretics or antihypertensives. Monitor patient.
Aspirin: May decrease drug level and increase risk of adverse GI reactions. Avoid using together.
Corticosteroids: May increase risk of adverse GI reactions. Avoid using together.
Cyclosporine: May increase nephrotoxicity of both drugs. Avoid using together.
Digoxin, hydantoins: May increase levels of these drugs. Monitor levels closely.
Lithium, oral anticoagulants: May increase levels or effects of these drugs. Monitor patient for toxicity.
Methotrexate: May increase risk of methotrexate toxicity. Monitor patient closely.
Probenecid: Probenecid may increase level and toxicity of NSAIDs. Monitor patient for signs of toxicity.
Drug-herb. *Dong quai, feverfew, garlic, ginger, horse chestnut, red clover:* May increase risk of bleeding. Monitor patient closely for bleeding.
St. John's wort: May increase risk of photosensitivity reactions. Advise patient to avoid unprotected or prolonged exposure to sunlight.
Drug-lifestyle. *Alcohol use:* May increase risk of adverse GI reactions. Discourage using together.
Sun exposure: May cause photosensitivity reactions. Advise patient to avoid unprotected or prolonged exposure to sunlight.

Effects on lab test results

- May increase BUN, creatinine, ALT, AST, and potassium levels. May decrease glucose level.
- May decrease hemoglobin, hematocrit, and neutrophil, WBC, RBC, platelet, and granulocyte counts.

Pharmacokinetics

Absorption: Rapid and complete from GI tract.
Distribution: Highly protein-bound.
Metabolism: Undergoes biotransformation in liver.
Excretion: Excreted mainly in urine, with some biliary excretion. *Half-life:* 2 to 4 hours.

Route	Onset	Peak	Duration
P.O.	≤ 30 min	2-4 hr	≥4 hr

Pharmacodynamics

Chemical effect: Unknown; produces anti-inflammatory, analgesic, and antipyretic effects, possibly by inhibiting prostaglandin synthesis.
Therapeutic effect: Relieves pain, fever, and inflammation.

Available forms

Caplets: 200 mg†
Capsules (liquid-filled): 200 mg†
Oral drops: 40 mg/ml†
Oral suspension: 100 mg/5 ml†
Tablets: 100 mg†, 200 mg†, 400 mg, 600 mg, 800 mg
Tablets (chewable): 50 mg†, 100 mg†
Tablets (film-coated): 100 mg†, 200 mg†, 400 mg, 600 mg, 800 mg

NURSING PROCESS

Assessment
- Obtain assessment of patient's underlying condition before starting drug therapy.
- Assess patient for relief from pain, fever, or inflammation. Full effects on arthritis may take 2 to 4 weeks.
- Check renal and hepatic function periodically in long-term therapy.
- Be alert for adverse reactions and drug interactions.
- Evaluate patient's and family's knowledge of drug therapy.

Nursing diagnoses
- Chronic pain related to underlying condition
- Risk for injury related to drug-induced adverse reactions
- Deficient knowledge related to drug therapy

Planning and implementation
- Give with meals or milk to reduce adverse GI reactions.
- Notify prescriber if drug is ineffective.
- If renal or hepatic abnormalities occur, stop drug and notify prescriber.

Patient teaching
- Tell patient to take drug with meals or milk to reduce adverse GI reactions.

ALERT: Tell patient not to exceed 1.2 g daily, not to give drug to children younger than age 12, and not to take drug for extended periods without consulting prescriber.
- Caution patient that using drug with aspirin, alcohol, or corticosteroids may increase risk of adverse GI reactions.
- Serious GI toxicity, including peptic ulceration and bleeding, can occur in patients taking NSAIDs despite absence of GI symptoms.
- Teach patient to recognize and report signs and symptoms of GI bleeding.
- Instruct patient to avoid alcohol during drug therapy.
- Instruct patient to use sunblock, wear protective clothing, and avoid prolonged exposure to sunlight.

Evaluation
- Patient is free from pain.
- Patient doesn't experience injury from adverse reactions.
- Patient and family state understanding of drug therapy.

ibutilide fumarate
(igh-BYOO-tih-lighd FYOO-muh-rayt)
Corvert

Pharmacologic class: ibutilide derivative
Therapeutic class: supraventricular antiarrhythmic
Pregnancy risk category: C

Indications and dosages
▶ **Rapid conversion of recent atrial fibrillation or atrial flutter to sinus rhythm.** *Adults weighing 60 kg (132 lb) or more:* 1 mg I.V. infused over 10 minutes.
Adults weighing less than 60 kg: 0.01 mg/kg I.V. infused over 10 minutes.

Stop infusion if arrhythmia stops or if patient develops sustained or nonsustained ventricular tachycardia or marked prolongation of QT interval. If arrhythmia doesn't stop within 10 minutes after infusion ends, a second 10-minute infusion of equal strength may be given.

Contraindications and precautions
- Contraindicated in patients hypersensitive to drug or its components.
- Drug isn't recommended for use in patients with history of polymorphic ventricular tachycardia, such as torsades de pointes.
- Use cautiously in patients with hepatic or renal dysfunction (usually, no dosage adjustments are needed).

Lifespan: In pregnant women, use cautiously. In breast-feeding women and in children, safety of drug hasn't been established.

Adverse reactions
CNS: headache.
CV: ventricular extrasystoles, ***nonsustained ventricular tachycardia,*** hypotension, bundle branch block, ***sustained polymorphic ventricular tachycardia, AV block,*** hypertension, QT interval prolongation, ***bradycardia,*** palpitations, tachycardia.
GI: nausea.

Interactions

Drug-drug. *Class Ia antiarrhythmics (such as disopyramide, procainamide, quinidine), other class III drugs (such as amiodarone, sotalol):* May increase risk of prolonged refractory state. Avoid using together.
Digoxin: Supraventricular arrhythmias may mask cardiotoxicity from excessive digoxin levels. Use cautiously.
H_1-receptor antagonist antihistamines, phenothiazines, tetracyclic antidepressants, tricyclic antidepressants, other drugs that prolong QT interval: May increase risk of proarrhythmias. Monitor patient closely.

Effects on lab test results

None reported.

Pharmacokinetics

Absorption: Administered I.V.
Distribution: Highly distributed; about 40% protein-bound.
Metabolism: Not clearly defined.
Excretion: Excreted in urine and feces. *Half-life:* Averages about 6 hours.

Route	Onset	Peak	Duration
I.V.	Unknown	Unknown	Unknown

Pharmacodynamics

Chemical effect: Prolongs action potential in isolated cardiac myocyte and increases atrial and ventricular refractoriness; has predominantly class III properties.
Therapeutic effect: Restores normal sinus rhythm.

Available forms

Injection: 0.1 mg/ml

NURSING PROCESS

Assessment

- Assess patient's arrhythmia before therapy.

ALERT: Monitor ECG continuously during therapy and for at least 4 hours afterward (or until QT interval returns to baseline) because drug can induce or worsen ventricular arrhythmias. Monitor longer if ECG shows arrhythmic activity.

- Be alert for adverse reactions and drug interactions.
- Evaluate patient's and family's knowledge of drug therapy.

Nursing diagnoses

- Decreased cardiac output related to arrhythmias
- Risk for injury related to life-threatening arrhythmias
- Deficient knowledge related to drug therapy

Planning and implementation

- Drug should only be given by skilled personnel. During and after administration, proper equipment and facilities, such as cardiac monitoring, intracardiac pacing, cardioverter/defibrillator, and medication for treatment of sustained ventricular tachycardia, should be available.
- Hypokalemia and hypomagnesemia should be corrected before therapy to reduce risk of proarrhythmia.
- Drug may be given undiluted or diluted in 50 ml of diluent. It may be added to normal saline solution for injection or D_5W injection before infusion. Contents of one 10-ml vial (0.1 mg/ml) may be added to a 50-ml infusion bag to form admixture of about 0.017 mg/ml ibutilide fumarate. Use strict aseptic technique. Drug is compatible with polyvinyl chloride plastic bags and polyolefin bags.
- Admixtures with approved diluents are chemically and physically stable for 24 hours at room temperature or 48 hours if refrigerated.
- Inspect parenteral drugs for particles and discoloration before administration.

Patient teaching

- Tell patient to promptly report adverse reactions, especially headaches, dizziness, weakness, palpitations, or chest pains.
- Instruct patient to report any discomfort at injection site.

Evaluation

- Patient regains normal sinus rhythm.
- Life-threatening arrhythmia doesn't develop.
- Patient and family state understanding of drug therapy.

idarubicin hydrochloride

(igh-duh-ROO-bih-sin high-droh-KLOR-ighd)
Idamycin, Idamycin PFS

Pharmacologic class: anthracycline antibiotic
Therapeutic class: antineoplastic
Pregnancy risk category: D

Indications and dosages

▶ **Acute myeloid leukemia, including French-American-British classifications M1 through M7, with other approved anti-leukemic drugs.** *Adults:* 12 mg/m² by slow I.V. injection (over 10 to 15 minutes) daily for 3 days with 100 mg/m² of cytarabine by continuous I.V. infusion daily for 7 days or cytarabine as 25-mg/m² bolus followed by 200 mg/m² by continuous infusion daily for 5 days. A second course may be given, if needed. If patient develops severe mucositis, administration should be delayed until recovery is complete, and dosage may be reduced by 25%. Dosage also should be reduced in patients with hepatic or renal impairment. Idarubicin shouldn't be given if bilirubin level is above 5 mg/dl.

Contraindications and precautions

- No known contraindications.
- Use with extreme caution in patients with bone marrow suppression induced by previous drug therapy or radiotherapy and in patients with impaired hepatic or renal function.

Lifespan: For pregnant or breast-feeding women, drug isn't recommended. In children, safety of drug hasn't been established.

Adverse reactions

CNS: *fever,* headache, changed mental status, peripheral neuropathy, ***seizures.***
CV: ***heart failure,*** atrial fibrillation, chest pain, ***MI, myocardial insufficiency, arrhythmias,*** **HEMORRHAGE,** ***myocardial toxicity.***
GI: *nausea, vomiting,* cramps, diarrhea, *mucositis,* ***severe enterocolitis with perforation.***
Hematologic: MYELOSUPPRESSION.
Skin: alopecia, rash, urticaria, bullous erythrodermatous rash on palms and soles, urticaria at injection site, erythema at previously irradiated sites, tissue necrosis at injection site if extravasation occurs.
Other: INFECTION.

Interactions

Drug-drug. *Alkaline solutions, heparin:* Incompatible. Idarubicin shouldn't be mixed with other drugs unless specific compatibility data are available.

Effects on lab test results

- May increase BUN and creatinine levels.
- May incease liver function test results. May decrease hemoglobin, hematocrit, and RBC, WBC, and platelet counts.

Pharmacokinetics

Absorption: Administered I.V.
Distribution: Drug is highly lipophilic and tissue-bound (97%), with highest levels in nucleated blood and bone marrow cells.
Metabolism: Extensive extrahepatic metabolism is indicated. Metabolite has cytotoxic activity.
Excretion: Primarily biliary excretion, minimally by renal excretion. *Half-life:* 20 to 22 hours.

Route	Onset	Peak	Duration
I.V.	Unknown	≤ 3 min	Unknown

Pharmacodynamics

Chemical effect: May inhibit nucleic acid synthesis by intercalation; interacts with enzyme topoisomerase II.
Therapeutic effect: Hinders growth of susceptible cancer cells.

Available forms

Powder for injection: 1 mg/ml available in 5-, 10-, and 20-mg vials

NURSING PROCESS

Assessment

- Assess patient's condition before therapy and regularly thereafter.
- Assess patient for systemic infection, which should be controlled before therapy begins.
- Monitor CBC and hepatic and renal function test results frequently.
- Be alert for adverse reactions and drug interactions, especially signs of heart failure.
- Evaluate patient's and family's knowledge of drug therapy.

Nursing diagnoses

- Ineffective health maintenance related to presence of underlying condition
- Ineffective protection related to adverse hematologic reactions
- Deficient knowledge related to drug therapy

Planning and implementation

- Follow facility policy to reduce risks. Preparation and administration of parenteral form are linked to carcinogenic, mutagenic, and teratogenic risks for personnel.
- Take appropriate preventive measures (including adequate hydration) before starting treatment.

ALERT: Don't confuse idarubicin with daunorubicin.

- Reconstitute to final concentration of 1 mg/ml using normal saline solution for injection. Add 5 ml to 5-mg vial or 10 ml to 10-mg vial. Don't use bacteriostatic saline solution. Vial is under negative pressure.
- Give over 10 to 15 minutes into free-flowing I.V. infusion of normal saline solution or D_5W that is running into large vein.

ALERT: Never give drug by I.M. or S.C. route.

- Reconstituted solutions are stable for 72 hours at 59° to 86°F (15° to 30°C), 7 days if refrigerated. Label unused solutions with chemotherapy hazard label.
- Hyperuricemia may result from rapid destruction of leukemic cells. Allopurinol may be ordered.
- If extravasation occurs, discontinue infusion immediately, elevate limb, and notify prescriber. Treat with intermittent ice packs—30 minutes immediately and then 30 minutes q.i.d. for 4 days.

Patient teaching

- Teach patient to recognize and report signs of extravasation, infection, bleeding, and heart failure, such as shortness of breath and leg swelling.
- Advise patient that red urine for several days is normal and doesn't indicate blood in urine.
- Advise women of childbearing age to use a reliable contraceptive during therapy and to consult with prescriber before becoming pregnant.

Evaluation

- Patient responds well to drug.
- Serious adverse hematologic reactions don't develop.
- Patient and family state understanding of drug therapy.

ifosfamide

(igh-FOHS-fuh-mighd)
IFEX

Pharmacologic class: alkylating agent (cell cycle–phase nonspecific)
Therapeutic class: antineoplastic
Pregnancy risk category: D

Indications and dosages

▶ **Testicular cancer.** *Adults:* 1.2 g/m^2 I.V. daily for 5 consecutive days. Repeat q 3 weeks or after patient recovers from hematologic toxicity.
▶ **Lung cancer, Hodgkin's and malignant lymphoma, breast cancer, acute lymphocytic leukemia, ovarian cancer, gastric cancer, pancreatic cancer, sarcomas, cervical cancer, and uterine cancer‡.** *Adults:* 1.2 to 2.5 g/m^2 I.V. daily for 3 to 5 days, with cycles of therapy repeated p.r.n.

Contraindications and precautions

- Contraindicated in patients hypersensitive to drug and in those with severely depressed bone marrow function.
- Use cautiously in patients with renal impairment or compromised bone marrow from leukopenia, granulocytopenia, extensive bone marrow metastases, previous radiation therapy, or previous therapy with cytotoxic drugs.

Lifespan: In children, safety of drug hasn't been established.

Adverse reactions

CNS: *lethargy, somnolence, confusion, depressive psychosis,* ***coma, seizures,*** ataxia.
GI: *nausea, vomiting.*
GU: *hemorrhagic cystitis* (dose-limiting, occurring in up to 50% of patients), *hematuria,* ***nephrotoxicity.***
Hematologic: ***leukopenia, thrombocytopenia, myelosuppression.***
Skin: *alopecia.*

Interactions

Drug-drug. *Allopurinol:* May produce excessive ifosfamide effect by prolonging half-life. Monitor patient for enhanced toxicity.

Anticoagulants, aspirin: May increase risk of bleeding. Avoid using together.
Barbiturates, chloral hydrate, phenytoin: May increase ifosfamide toxicity by inducing hepatic enzymes that hasten formation of toxic metabolites. Monitor patient closely.
Corticosteroids: May inhibit hepatic enzymes and reduce the effect of ifosfamide. Monitor patient for enhanced ifosfamide toxicity if corticosteroid dosage is abruptly reduced or discontinued.
Myelosuppressants: May enhance hematologic toxicity. Dosage adjustment may be needed.

Effects on lab test results

- May increase BUN, creatinine, bilirubin, and liver enzyme levels.
- May decrease hemoglobin, hematocrit, and WBC, RBC, and platelet counts.

Pharmacokinetics

Absorption: Administered I.V.
Distribution: Drug crosses blood-brain barrier but its metabolites don't; therefore, alkylating activity doesn't occur in CSF.
Metabolism: About 50% of dose is metabolized in liver.
Excretion: Excreted primarily in urine. *Half-life:* About 14 hours.

Route	Onset	Peak	Duration
I.V.	Unknown	Unknown	Unknown

Pharmacodynamics

Chemical effect: Cross-links strands of cellular DNA and interferes with RNA transcription, which causes growth imbalance that leads to cell death.
Therapeutic effect: Kills testicular cancer cells.

Available forms

Injection: 1 g (supplied with 200-mg ampule of mesna), 2 g, 3 g (supplied with 400-mg ampule of mesna)

NURSING PROCESS

Assessment

- Assess patient's condition before therapy and regularly thereafter.
- Obtain urinalysis before each dose. If microscopic hematuria is present, patient should be evaluated for hemorrhagic cystitis. Dosage adjustments of mesna—a protecting agent given with ifosfamide—may be needed.
- Monitor CBC and renal and liver function tests.
- Be alert for adverse reactions and drug interactions.
- Assess patient for mental status changes; dosage may need to be decreased.
- Evaluate patient's and family's knowledge of drug therapy.

Nursing diagnoses

- Ineffective health maintenance related to presence of cancer
- Ineffective protection related to adverse CNS and hematologic reactions
- Deficient knowledge related to drug therapy

Planning and implementation

- Give antiemetics before giving drug to decrease nausea.
- Give drug with protecting agent (mesna) to prevent hemorrhagic cystitis. Mesna must be given with or before drug to prevent cystitis. Adequate fluid intake (2 L/day, either P.O. or I.V.) is essential.
- Follow facility policy to reduce risks. Preparation and administration of parenteral form are linked to carcinogenic, mutagenic, and teratogenic risks for personnel.

ALERT: Don't confuse ifosfamide with cyclophosphamide.

- Reconstitute each gram of drug with 20 ml of diluent to yield 50 mg/ml. Use sterile water for injection or bacteriostatic water for injection. Solutions may be further diluted with sterile water, dextrose 2.5% or 5% in water, half-normal or normal saline solution for injection, D_5W and normal saline solution for injection, or lactated Ringer's injection.
- Infuse each dose over at least 30 minutes.
- Ifosfamide and mesna are physically compatible and may be mixed in same I.V. solution.
- Reconstituted solution is stable for 1 week at room temperature or 6 weeks if refrigerated. However, use solution within 6 hours if drug was reconstituted with sterile water.
- Don't give drug at bedtime; infrequent voiding during night may increase risk of cystitis. If cystitis develops, discontinue drug and notify prescriber.

• Bladder irrigation with normal saline solution may decrease possibility of cystitis.
• Institute infection-control and bleeding precautions.

Patient teaching
• Tell patient to void frequently to minimize contact of drug and its metabolites with bladder mucosa.
• Warn patient to watch for evidence of infection (fever, sore throat, fatigue), CNS effects (somnolence and dizziness), and bleeding (easy bruising, nosebleeds, bleeding gums, melena). Teach patient about infection-control and bleeding precautions, and tell him to report adverse effects. Tell him to take his temperature daily.
• Instruct patient to avoid OTC drugs that contain aspirin.
• Stress importance of adequate fluid intake during therapy. Explain that it may help prevent hemorrhagic cystitis.
• Warn patient that hyperpigmentation may occur.

Evaluation
• Patient responds well to drug.
• Serious infections and CNS and bleeding complications don't develop.
• Patient and family state understanding of drug therapy.

imatinib mesylate
(i-MAH-tin-nib MES-uh-late)
Gleevec

Pharmacologic classification: protein-tyrosine kinase inhibitor
Therapeutic classification: antineoplastic
Pregnancy risk category: D

Indications and dosages

▶ **Newly diagnosed Philadelphia chronic myeloid leukemia (CML) and Philadelphia chromosome positive CML in blast crisis, in accelerated phase, or in chronic phase after failure of interferon-alpha therapy.**
Adults: ***Chronic-phase CML.*** 400 mg P.O. daily as single dose with a meal and large glass of water. ***Accelerated-phase CML or blast crisis.*** 600 mg P.O. daily as single dose with a meal and large glass of water. Continue treatment as long as patient continues to benefit. May increase daily dose to 600 mg P.O. in chronic phase or to 800 mg P.O. (400 mg P.O. b.i.d.) in accelerated phase or blast crisis.
Patients with neutropenia or thrombocytopenia: See table on page 686.
▶ **Kit (CD117) positive unresectable or metastatic malignant GI stromal tumors (GIST).** *Adults:* 400 or 600 mg P.O. daily.

Contraindications and precautions

• Contraindicated in patients hypersensitive to drug or its components.
• Use cautiously in patients with hepatic impairment.
Lifespan: Breast-feeding women shouldn't take this drug. It's unknown if drug appears in breast milk. In children, safety and efficacy haven't been established. In elderly patients, use cautiously because they may have an increased risk of edema when taking this drug.

Adverse reactions

CNS: *headache,* **CEREBRAL HEMORRHAGE,** *fatigue, weakness, fever.*
CV: *edema.*
EENT: nasopharyngitis, *epistaxis.*
GI: *anorexia, nausea, diarrhea, abdominal pain, constipation, vomiting, dyspepsia,* **GI HEMORRHAGE.**
Hematologic: **HEMORRHAGE, NEUTROPENIA, THROMBOCYTOPENIA,** *anemia.*
Metabolic: *hypokalemia,* weight increase.
Musculoskeletal: *myalgia, muscle cramps, musculoskeletal pain, arthralgia.*
Respiratory: *cough, dyspnea, pneumonia.*
Skin: *rash,* pruritus, *petechiae.*
Other: *night sweats.*

Interactions

Drug-drug. *CYP3A4 inhibitors (clarithromycin, erythromycin, itraconazole, ketoconazole):* May decrease metabolism and increase imatinib level. Monitor patient for toxicity.
CYP3A4 inducers (carbamazepine, dexamethasone, phenobarbital, phenytoin, rifampin): May increase metabolism and decrease imatinib level. Use cautiously.
Dihydropyridine calcium channel blockers, certain HMG-CoA reductase inhibitors, cyclosporine, pimozide, triazolo-benzodiazepines:

DOSAGE ADJUSTMENTS FOR NEUTROPENIA AND THROMBOCYTOPENIA

Indication	Laboratory values	Treatment guidelines
Chronic phase CML (starting dose 400 mg) GIST (starting dose 400 mg or 600 mg)	Absolute neutrophil count (ANC) is less than 1×10^9/L or platelets are less than 50×10^9/L	1. Stop drug until ANC is greater than or equal to 1.5×10^9/L and platelets are greater than or equal to 75×10^9/L. 2. Resume treatment at original dose of 400 mg or 600 mg. 3. If recurrence of ANC is less than 1×10^9/L or platelets are less than 50×10^9/L, repeat step 1 and resume at 300 mg if starting dose was 400 mg or at 400 mg if starting dose was 600 mg.
Accelerated phase CML and blast crisis (starting dose 600 mg)	ANC is less than 0.5×10^9/L after at least 1 month of treatment or platelets are less than 10×10^9/L	1. Check if cytopenia is related to leukemia using marrow aspirate or biopsy. 2. If cytopenia is unrelated to leukemia, reduce dose to 400 mg. 3. If cytopenia persists 2 weeks, reduce dose further to 300 mg. 4. If cytopenia persists 4 weeks and is still unrelated to leukemia, stop drug until ANC is greater than or equal to 1×10^9/L and platelets are greater than or equal to 20×10^9/L and then resume treatment at 300 mg.

May increase levels of these drugs. Monitor patient for toxicity and obtain drug levels, if appropriate.
Warfarin: May alter metabolism of warfarin. Avoid use together; instead, use standard heparin or a low-molecular-weight heparin.
Drug-herb. *St. John's wort:* May decrease drug effects. Warn patient not to use together.

Effects on lab test results

- May increase creatinine, bilirubin, alkaline phosphatase, AST, and ALT levels. May decrease potassium level.
- May decrease hemoglobin, hematocrit, and neutrophil and platelet counts.

Pharmacokinetics

Absorption: Well absorbed.
Distribution: 98% protein-bound.
Metabolism: Metabolized via cytochrome P-450 system, primarily CYP3A4.
Excretion: Excreted primarily in feces as metabolites.

Route	Onset	Peak	Duration
P.O.	Unknown	2-4 hr	Unknown

Pharmacodynamics

Chemical effect: Inhibits Bcr-Abl tyrosine kinase, which is the abnormal tyrosine kinase created by the Philadelphia chromosome abnormality in CML; in vivo, it inhibits tumor growth of Bcr-Abl transfected murine myeloid cells as well as Bcr-Abl positive leukemia lines derived from CML patients in blast crisis.
Therapeutic effect: Stops tumor growth.

Available forms

Capsules: 100 mg

NURSING PROCESS

Assessment

- Assess neoplastic disease before therapy and reassess regularly during therapy.
- Obtain baseline weight before beginning therapy and weigh patient daily throughout therapy. Evaluate and treat unexpected and rapid weight gain.
- Evaluate patient's and family's knowledge of drug therapy.

Nursing diagnoses

- Ineffective health maintenance related to neoplastic disease
- Risk for falls related to drug-induced adverse reactions
- Deficient knowledge related to drug therapy

Planning and implementation

- For the treatment of CML, consider dosage increases only if there is an absence of severe adverse reactions and absence of severe non–leukemia-related neutropenia or thrombocy-

topenia in these circumstances: disease progression (at any time), failure to achieve a satisfactory hematologic response after at least 3 months of treatment, or loss of a previously achieved hematologic response.
- Dosage adjustments are needed for hepatic impairment and nonhematologic and hematologic adverse reactions.
- Monitor patients closely for fluid retention, which can be severe.
- Monitor CBC weekly for first month, then monitor biweekly for second month, and periodically thereafter.
- Because GI irritation is common, give this drug with food.
- Monitor liver function tests carefully because hepatotoxicity (occasionally severe) may occur; decrease dosage as needed.
- Because the long-term safety of this drug isn't known, monitor renal and liver toxicity and immunosuppression carefully.

Patient teaching
- Instruct patient to take drug with food and a large glass of water.
- Urge patient to report any adverse effects, such as fluid retention, to prescriber.
- Advise patient to have periodic liver and kidney function tests and blood work to determine blood counts.

Evaluation
- Patient shows positive response to drug therapy on follow-up studies.
- Patient does not experience falls.
- Patient and family state understanding of imatinib mesylate therapy.

imipenem and cilastatin sodium
(im-ih-PEN-em and sigh-luh-STAT-in SO-dee-um)
Primaxin IM, Primaxin IV

Pharmacologic class: carbapenem (thienamycin class); beta-lactam antibiotic
Therapeutic class: antibiotic
Pregnancy risk category: C

Indications and dosages
▶ **Mild-to-moderate lower respiratory tract, skin, skin-structure, and gynecologic infections.** *Adults weighing at least 70 kg (154 lb):* 500 to 750 mg I.M. q 12 hours. Or, 250 to 500 mg I.V. q 6 hours. Maximum I.V. dosage is 50 mg/kg or 4 g daily, whichever is less.
Children age 3 months and older: 15 to 25 mg/kg I.V. q 6 hours. Maximum dosage for fully susceptible organisms is 2 g daily and for moderately susceptible organisms, 4 g daily (based on adult studies).
Infants ages 4 weeks to 3 months and weighing at least 1.5 kg (3.3 lb): 25 mg/kg I.V. q 6 hours.
Neonates ages 1 to 4 weeks and weighing at least 1.5 kg: 25 mg/kg I.V. q 8 hours.
Neonates younger than 1 week old and weighing at least 1.5 kg: 25 mg/kg I.V. q 12 hours.
▶ **Mild-to-moderate intra-abdominal infections.** *Adults:* 750 mg I.M. q 12 hours.
Children age 3 months and older: 15 to 25 mg/kg I.V. q 6 hours. Maximum dosage for fully susceptible organisms is 2 g daily and for moderately susceptible organisms, 4 g daily (based on adult studies).
Infants ages 4 weeks to 3 months and weighing at least 1.5 kg (3.3 lb): 25 mg/kg I.V. q 6 hours.
Neonates ages 1 to 4 weeks and weighing at least 1.5 kg: 25 mg/kg I.V. q 8 hours.
Neonates younger than 1 week old and weighing at least 1.5 kg: 25 mg/kg I.V. q 12 hours.
▶ **Serious infections of lower respiratory and urinary tracts, intra-abdominal and gynecologic infections, bacterial septicemia, bone and joint infections, skin and soft-tissue infections, and endocarditis.** *Adults weighing at least 70 kg (154 lb):* 500 mg I.V. q 6 hours or 1 g q 6 to 8 hours by I.V. infusion. Maximum dosage is 50 mg/kg or 4 g daily, whichever is less.
Patients with renal impairment or who weigh less than 70 kg (154 lb): Lower dose or longer intervals between doses may be needed.
▶ **Infections (other than CNS infections) in children.** *Children age 3 months and older:* 15 to 25 mg/kg I.V. q 6 hours. Maximum dosage for fully susceptible organisms is 2 g daily and for moderately susceptible organisms, 4 g daily (based on adult studies).
Infants ages 4 weeks to 3 months and weighing at least 1.5 kg (3.3 lb): 25 mg/kg I.V. q 6 hours.
Neonates ages 1 to 4 weeks and weighing at least 1.5 kg: 25 mg/kg I.V. q 8 hours.
Neonates younger than 1 week old and weighing at least 1.5 kg: 25 mg/kg I.V. q 12 hours.
Patients with renal impairment: If creatinine clearance is 6 to 20 ml/minute, give 125 to

250 mg I.V. q 12 hours. If creatinine clearance is less then 5 ml/minute, drug should not be given unless hemodialysis is instituted within 48 hours.

Contraindications and precautions

- Contraindicated in patients hypersensitive to drug.
- Use cautiously in patients allergic to penicillins or cephalosporins, and in those with history of seizure disorders, especially if they also have compromised renal function.

Lifespan: In pregnant or breast-feeding women, use cautiously. In children younger than age 12, I.M. safety and efficacy haven't been established. In children with CNS infections, I.V. use isn't recommended because of risk of seizures; in children weighing less than 30 kg (66 lb) with impaired renal function, use is also not recommended because no data are available.

Adverse reactions

CNS: ***seizures,*** dizziness, somnolence, fever.
CV: hypotension, thrombophlebitis.
GI: nausea, vomiting, diarrhea, ***pseudomembranous colitis.***
Skin: rash, urticaria, pruritus.
Other: ***hypersensitivity reactions (anaphylaxis),*** pain at injection site.

Interactions

Drug-drug. *Beta-lactam antibiotics:* May cause in vitro antagonism. Avoid use together.
Cyclosporine: May increase adverse CNS effects of both drugs, possibly because of additive or synergistic toxicity. Avoid use together.
Ganciclovir: May cause seizures. Avoid use together.
Probenecid: May increase cilastatin levels. Avoid use together.

Effects on lab test results

- May increase BUN, creatinine, ALT, AST, alkaline phosphatase, bilirubin, and LDH levels.
- May increase eosinophil count. May decrease WBC and platelet counts.

Pharmacokinetics

Absorption: Imipenem is about 75% bioavailable; cilastatin is about 95% bioavailable after I.M. use.
Distribution: Distributed rapidly and widely. About 20% of imipenem is protein-bound; 40% of cilastatin is protein-bound.
Metabolism: Imipenem is metabolized by kidney dehydropeptidase I, resulting in low urine levels. Cilastatin inhibits this enzyme, thereby reducing imipenem metabolism.
Excretion: About 70% excreted unchanged by kidneys. *Half-life:* 1 hour after I.V. dose; 2 to 3 hours after I.M. dose.

Route	Onset	Peak	Duration
I.V.	Unknown	Immediate	Unknown
I.M.	Unknown	1-2 hr	Unknown

Pharmacodynamics

Chemical effect: Imipenem is bactericidal and inhibits bacterial cell wall synthesis. Cilastatin inhibits enzymatic breakdown of imipenem in kidneys, making it effective in urinary tract.
Therapeutic effect: Kills susceptible organisms, including many gram-positive, gram-negative, and anaerobic bacteria, including *Staphylococcus* and *Streptococcus sp., Escherichia coli, Klebsiella, Proteus, Enterobacter sp., Pseudomonas aeruginosa,* and *Bacteroides sp., including B. fragilis.*

Available forms

Powder for I.M. injection: 500- and 750-mg vials
Powder for I.V. injection: 250- and 500-mg vials

NURSING PROCESS

Assessment

- Assess patient's infection before therapy and regularly thereafter.
- Obtain urine specimen for culture and sensitivity tests before first dose. Therapy may begin pending results.
- Be alert for adverse reactions and drug interactions.
- Monitor patient's hydration status if adverse GI reactions occur.
- Evaluate patient's and family's knowledge of drug therapy.

Nursing diagnoses

- Infection related to presence of susceptible organisms

- Risk for deficient fluid volume related to adverse GI reactions
- Deficient knowledge related to drug therapy

Planning and implementation

- **I.V. use:** Don't give drug by direct I.V. bolus injection. Give 250- or 500-mg dose by I.V. infusion over 20 to 30 minutes. Infuse each 1-g dose over 40 to 60 minutes. If nausea occurs, slow infusion.

– When reconstituting powder, shake until solution is clear. Solutions may range from colorless to yellow, and variations of color within this range don't affect drug's potency. After reconstitution, solution is stable for 10 hours at room temperature and for 48 hours when refrigerated.

- **I.M. use:** Follow normal protocol. Reconstitute drug for I.M. injection with 1% lidocaine hydrochloride (without epinephrine) as directed.

ALERT: If seizures develop and persist despite anticonvulsants, notify prescriber, who may discontinue the drug and institute seizure precautions and protocols.

Patient teaching

- Instruct patient to report adverse reactions because supportive therapy may be needed.
- Warn patient about pain at injection site.

Evaluation

- Patient is free from infection.
- Patient maintains adequate hydration throughout therapy.
- Patient and family state understanding of drug therapy.

imipramine hydrochloride

(ih-MIP-ruh-meen high-droh-KLOR-ighd)

Apo-Imipramine ♦, Impril ♦, Melipramine ◇, Norfranil, Novopramine ♦, Tipramine, Tofranil**

imipramine pamoate

Tofranil-PM**

Pharmacologic class: dibenzazepine tricyclic antidepressant
Therapeutic class: antidepressant
Pregnancy risk category: D

Indications and dosages

▶ **Depression.** *Adults:* 75 to 100 mg P.O. daily in divided doses, increased in 25- to 50-mg increments to maximum dosage. Or, 25 mg P.O. daily, increased in 25-mg increments every other day. Or, entire dosage may be given h.s. Maximum dosage is 200 mg P.O. daily for outpatients, 300 mg P.O. daily for inpatients, and 100 mg P.O. daily for elderly patients.

▶ **Childhood enuresis‡.** *Children age 6 and older:* 25 mg P.O. 1 hour before bedtime. If no response within 1 week, dosage may be increased to 50 mg nightly for children younger than age 12 or 75 mg nightly for children age 12 and older. Maximum dosage shouldn't exceed 2.5 mg/kg P.O. daily.

Contraindications and precautions

- Contraindicated in patients hypersensitive to drug, patients receiving MAO inhibitors, and patients in acute recovery phase of MI.
- Use with extreme caution in patients at risk for suicide; patients receiving thyroid drugs; patients with history of urine retention or angle-closure glaucoma, increased intraocular pressure, CV disease, impaired hepatic function, hyperthyroidism, seizure disorder, or renal impairment.

Lifespan: In pregnant or breast-feeding women, drug isn't recommended. In children, safety of drug hasn't been established for treating depression.

Adverse reactions

CNS: *drowsiness, dizziness,* excitation, tremor, weakness, confusion, headache, nervousness, EEG changes, ***seizures,*** extrapyramidal reactions.
CV: *orthostatic hypotension, tachycardia, ECG changes,* hypertension, ***MI, CVA, arrhythmias, heart block.***
EENT: *blurred vision,* tinnitus, mydriasis.
GI: *dry mouth, constipation,* nausea, vomiting, anorexia, paralytic ileus.
GU: *urine retention,* impotence, testicular swelling.
Metabolic: ***hypoglycemia,*** hyperglycemia.
Skin: rash, urticaria, *diaphoresis,* photosensitivity reactions.
Other: hypersensitivity reactions, gynecomastia, galactorrhea and breast enlargement, altered libido, SIADH.

Interactions

Drug-drug. *Barbiturates, CNS depressants:* May enhance CNS depression. Avoid using together.
Cimetidine, methylphenidate: May increase imipramine level. Monitor patient for adverse reactions.
Clonidine, epinephrine, norepinephrine: May increase hypertensive effect. Use cautiously; monitor patient's blood pressure.
Fluoxetine: May increase the pharmacologic and toxic effects of tricyclic antidepressants; symptoms may persist several weeks after fluoxetine therapy stops. Monitor symptoms closely.
MAO inhibitors: May cause hyperpyretic crisis, severe seizures, and death. Don't use together.
Drug-herb. *SAMe, St. John's wort, yohimbe:* May elevate serotonin level. Discourage using together.
Drug-lifestyle. *Alcohol use:* May enhance CNS depression. Discourage using together.
Smoking: May decrease imipramine level. Monitor patient for lack of effect; discourage patient from smoking.
Sun exposure: May increase risk of photosensitivity reactions. Advise patient to avoid unprotected or prolonged exposure to sunlight.

Effects on lab test results

- May increase or decrease glucose level.
- May increase liver function test values.

Pharmacokinetics

Absorption: Rapid and complete from GI tract after P.O. use; rapid after IM use.
Distribution: Distributed widely into body, including CNS. Drug is 90% protein-bound.
Metabolism: Metabolized by liver. A significant first-pass effect may explain variable level in different patients taking same dose.
Excretion: Most of drug is excreted in urine.

Route	Onset	Peak	Duration
P.O.	Unknown	1-2 hr	Unknown

Pharmacodynamics

Chemical effect: Increases amount of norepinephrine, serotonin, or both in CNS by blocking their reuptake by presynaptic neurons.
Therapeutic effect: Relieves depression and childhood enuresis (hydrochloride form).

Available forms

imipramine hydrochloride
Tablets: 10 mg, 25 mg, 50 mg
imipramine pamoate
Capsules: 75 mg, 100 mg, 125 mg, 150 mg

NURSING PROCESS

Assessment

- Assess patient's condition before therapy and regularly thereafter.
- Be alert for adverse reactions and drug interactions.
- Evaluate patient's and family's knowledge of drug therapy.

Nursing diagnoses

- Ineffective individual coping related to depression
- Deficient knowledge related to drug therapy

Planning and implementation

- Dosage should be reduced in elderly or debilitated patients, adolescents, and patients with aggravated psychotic symptoms.

ALERT: Don't confuse imipramine with desipramine.

- Although doses can be given up to four times daily, patients also may receive entire daily dose at one time because of drug's long action.
- Don't withdraw drug abruptly.
- Drug causes high risk of orthostatic hypotension. Check sitting and standing blood pressures after initial dose.
- Because of hypertensive episodes during surgery in patients receiving tricyclic antidepressants, drug should be gradually discontinued several days before surgery. After abrupt withdrawal of long-term therapy, patient may experience nausea, headache, and malaise. Treat patient symptomatically. These symptoms don't indicate addiction.
- If signs of psychosis occur or increase, notify prescriber, expect to reduce dosage, and institute safety precautions.

Patient teaching

- Advise patient to take full dose at bedtime but warn about possible morning orthostatic hypotension.
- Suggest taking drug with food or milk if it causes stomach upset.

• Suggest relieving dry mouth with sugarless chewing gum or hard candy. Encourage good dental prophylaxis because persistent dry mouth may increase the risk of dental caries.
• Tell patient to avoid alcohol and smoking during drug therapy.
• Warn patient to avoid hazardous activities until CNS effects of drug are known.
• Warn patient not to discontinue drug suddenly.
• Advise patient to consult prescriber before taking other prescription drugs, OTC drugs, or herbal remedies.
• Advise patient to use sunblock, wear protective clothing, and avoid prolonged exposure to sunlight to prevent photosensitivity reactions.

☑ Evaluation

• Patient behavior and communication show diminished depression.
• Patient and family state understanding of drug therapy.

immune globulin intramuscular (gamma globulin, IG, IGIM)

(ih-MYOON GLOB-yoo-lin in-truh-MUS-kyoo-ler)
BayGam

immune globulin intravenous (IGIV)

Gamimune N, Gammagard S/D, Gammar-P IV, Iveegam EN, Panglobulin, Polygam S/D, Sandoglobulin, Venoglobulin-S

Pharmacologic class: immune serum
Therapeutic class: immune serum
Pregnancy risk category: C

Indications and dosages

▶ **Primary humoral immunodeficiency (IGIV); treatment of primary defective antibody synthesis such as agammaglobulinemia or hypogammaglobulinemia in patients who are at increased risk of infection.**
I.V.
Gamimune N. *Adults and children:* 100 to 200 mg/kg I.V. monthly, at 0.01 to 0.02 ml/kg/minute for 30 minutes. If no discomfort, rate can slowly be increased to a maximum of 0.08 ml/kg/minute.
Gammagard S/D. *Adults and children:* 200 to 400 mg/kg I.V.; then monthly doses of 100 mg/kg. Start infusion at 0.5 ml/kg/hour and increase to maximum of 4 ml/kg/hour. Dose is related to patient response.
Gammar-P IV. *Adults and children:* 200 to 400 mg/kg I.V. q 3 to 4 weeks. Infuse at 0.01 ml/kg/minute and increase to 0.02 ml/kg/minute after 15 to 30 minutes if no problems occur. Maximum infusion rate is 0.06 ml/kg/minute.
Iveegam EN. *Adults and children:* 200 ml/kg I.V. monthly. May increase dose to maximum of 800 mg/kg or give more frequently to produce desired effect. Infusion rate is 1 to 2 ml/minute for 5% solution.
Panglobulin or Sandoglobulin. *Adults and children:* 200 mg/kg I.V. monthly. Start with 0.5 to 1 ml/minute of 3% solution; gradually increase dose to 2.5 ml/minute after 15 to 30 minutes.
Polygam S/D. *Adults and children:* 200 to 400 mg/kg I.V. at 0.5 ml/kg/hour, increasing to a maximum of 4 ml/kg/hour. Subsequent dose is 100 mg/kg I.V. monthly.
Venoglobulin-S. *Adults and children:* 200 mg/kg I.V. monthly. Dose may be increased to 300 to 400 mg/kg and given more often than once monthly if IgG levels aren't adequate. Infuse at 0.01 to 0.02 ml/kg/minute for 30 minutes; if tolerated, increase 5% solutions to 0.04 ml/kg/minute and 10% solutions to 0.05 ml/kg/minute.
I.M.
Adults and children: Initially, 1.3 ml/kg I.M. Maintenance dose of 0.66 ml/kg (at least 100 mg/kg) q 3 to 4 weeks. Maximum single dose of IGIM is 30 to 50 ml in adults and 20 to 30 ml in infants and small children.

▶ **Idiopathic thrombocytopenic purpura (IGIV).** ***Gamimune N.*** *Adults and children:* 400 mg/kg 5% solution I.V. for 5 days; or 1,000 mg/kg 10% solution I.V. for 1 to 2 days with maintenance dose of 10% solution at 400 to 1,000 mg/kg I.V. single infusion to maintain 30,000/mm³ platelet count.
Gammagard S/D or Polygam S/D. *Adults and children:* 1,000 mg/kg I.V. as a single dose. Give up to three doses on alternate days, if needed.

Panglobulin or *Sandoglobulin.* *Adults and children:* 400 mg/kg I.V. for 2 to 5 consecutive days, depending on platelet count and immune response.
Venoglobulin-S. *Adults and children:* Maximum of 2,000 mg/kg I.V. over 5 days or less. Maintenance dose is 1,000 mg/kg given as needed.
▶ **Bone marrow transplant (IGIV).** *Gamimune N. Adults older than age 20:* 500 mg/kg 5% or 10% solution I.V. on days 7 and 2 pretransplantation; then weekly until 90 days posttransplantation.
▶ **B-cell chronic lymphocytic leukemia (IGIV).** ***Gammagard S/D or Polygam S/D.*** *Adults:* 400 mg/kg I.V. q 3 to 4 weeks.
▶ **Pediatric HIV infection (IGIV).** *Gamimune N. Children:* 400 mg/kg I.V. q 28 days, at 0.01 to 0.02 ml/kg/minute for 30 minutes; increase to maximum of 0.08 ml/kg/minute.
▶ **Kawasaki Syndrome (IGIV).** *Iveegam EN. Adults:* 400 mg/kg I.V. daily over 2 hours for 4 consecutive days, or a single dose of 2,000 mg/kg I.V. over 10 to 12 hours. Start within 10 days of disease onset. Treat concurrently with aspirin (80 to 100 mg/kg P.O. daily through day 14; then 3 to 10 mg/kg P.O. daily for 5 weeks).
▶ **Hepatitis A exposure (IGIM).** *Adults and children:* 0.02 ml/kg I.M. as soon as possible after exposure. Up to 0.01 ml/kg may be given for prolonged or intense exposure.
▶ **Measles exposure (IGIM).** *Adults and children:* 0.025 ml/kg I.M. within 6 days after exposure.
▶ **Measles postexposure prophylaxis (IGIM).** *Children:* 0.5 ml/kg I.M. (maximum, 15 ml) within 6 days after exposure.
▶ **Chickenpox exposure (IGIM).** *Adults and children:* 0.6 to 1.2 ml/kg I.M. as soon as possible after exposure.
▶ **Rubella exposure in first trimester of pregnancy (IGIM).** *Women:* 0.55 ml/kg I.M. as soon as possible after exposure (within 72 hours).

Contraindications and precautions

- Contraindicated in patients hypersensitive to drug and in patients with selective IgA deficiencies.
- I.M. administration contraindicated in patients with severe thrombocytopenia or other coagulation-bleeding disorders.
- Use Gammagard S/D cautiously in patients with a history of cardiovascular disease or thrombotic episodes. Use cautiously in patients with renal impairment.

Lifespan: In pregnant or breast-feeding women, use cautiously.

Adverse reactions

CNS: pain, fever, severe headache, malaise.
CV: chest pain, ***MI, heart failure*** (Gammagard S/D).
GI: nausea, vomiting.
GU: nephrotic syndrome, acute tubular necrosis, osmotic nephrosis, ***acute renal failure.***
Musculoskeletal: muscle stiffness at injection site.
Respiratory: ***pulmonary embolism.***
Skin: urticaria, erythema.
Other: ***anaphylaxis.***

Interactions

Drug-drug. *Live-virus vaccines:* Antibodies in the vaccine may interfere with drug therapy. Don't give within 3 months after giving immune globulin.

Effects on lab test results

None reported.

Pharmacokinetics

Absorption: Absorbed slowly.
Distribution: Distributed evenly between intravascular and extravascular spaces.
Metabolism: Unknown.
Excretion: Unknown. *Half-life:* 21 to 24 days in immunocompromised patients.

Route	Onset	Peak	Duration
I.V.	Immediate	Immediate	Unknown
I.M.	Unknown	2-5 days	Unknown

Pharmacodynamics

Chemical effect: Provides passive immunity by increasing antibody titer. The primary component is IgG.
Therapeutic effect: Helps prevent infections.

Available forms

IGIM
Injection: 2- and 10-ml vials
IGIV
Injection: 5% and 10% in 10-, 50-, 100-, 200-, and 250-ml vials (Gamimune N); 5%

and 10% in 50-, 100-, and 200-ml vials (Venoglobulin-S)
Powder for injection: 50 mg protein/ml in 2.5-, 5-, and 10-g vials (Gammagard S/D); 1-, 2.5-, and 5-g vials (Gammar-P IV); 500-mg and 1-, 2.5-, and 5-g vials (Iveegam); 2.5-, 5-, and 10-g vials (Polygam S/D); 3-, 6-, and 12-g vials (Panglobulin, Sandoglobulin)

NURSING PROCESS

Assessment
- Obtain history of allergies and reactions to immunizations.
- Observe patient for signs of anaphylaxis or other adverse reactions immediately after injection.
- Inspect injection site for local reactions.
- Monitor effectiveness by checking antibody titers after administration.
- Evaluate patient's and family's knowledge of drug therapy.

Nursing diagnoses
- Ineffective protection related to lack of or decreased immunity
- Ineffective breathing pattern related to anaphylaxis
- Deficient knowledge related to drug therapy

Planning and implementation
- **I.V. use:** I.V. products aren't interchangeable. Gammagard requires a filter, which is supplied by manufacturer.
- **I.M. use:** Give in gluteal region. Doses over 10 ml should be divided and injected into several muscle sites to reduce local pain and discomfort.
- Most adverse effects are related to rapid infusion rate. Infuse slowly.

ALERT: Don't confuse Sandoglobulin with Sandimmune or Sandostatin.
- Immune globulin shouldn't be given for prophylaxis against hepatitis A if 6 weeks or more have passed since exposure or since clinical symptoms have begun.
- If there is a possible risk of a thrombotic event, the recommended infusion concentration is no more than 5%, and the infusion rate should be initiated no faster than 0.5 ml/kg per hour and advanced slowly only if well tolerated to a maximum rate of 4 ml/kg per hour.
- Make sure epinephrine 1:1,000 is available in case of anaphylaxis.

ALERT: I.V. and I.M. products aren't interchangeable.

Patient teaching
- Instruct patient to report respiratory difficulty immediately.
- Tell patient that local reactions may occur at injection site.
- Instruct patient to notify prescriber promptly if adverse reaction persists or becomes severe.

Evaluation
- Patient exhibits increased passive immunity.
- Patient shows no signs of anaphylaxis.
- Patient and family state understanding of drug therapy.

indapamide
(in-DAP-uh-mighd)
Lozide ♦, Lozol, Natrilix ◇

Pharmacologic class: thiazide-like diuretic
Therapeutic class: diuretic, antihypertensive
Pregnancy risk category: B

Indications and dosages
▶ **Edema.** *Adults:* Initially, 2.5 mg P.O. daily in morning. Increase to 5 mg daily after 1 week, if needed.
▶ **Hypertension.** *Adults:* Initially, 1.25 mg P.O. daily in morning. Increased to 2.5 mg daily after 4 weeks, if needed. Increase to 5 mg daily after 4 more weeks, if needed.

Contraindications and precautions
- Contraindicated in patients hypersensitive to other sulfonamide-derived drugs and in those with anuria.
- Use cautiously in patients with severe renal disease, impaired hepatic function, and progressive hepatic disease.

Lifespan: In pregnant women, use cautiously. In breast-feeding women and in children, safety of drug hasn't been established.

Adverse reactions
CNS: headache, irritability, nervousness, dizziness, light-headedness, weakness.

CV: volume depletion and dehydration, orthostatic hypotension.
GI: nausea, ***pancreatitis.***
GU: nocturia, polyuria, frequent urination.
Metabolic: anorexia, hypokalemia, asymptomatic hyperuricemia, ***metabolic alkalosis,*** dilutional hyponatremia, hypochloremia, gout.
Musculoskeletal: muscle cramps and spasms.
Skin: dermatitis, photosensitivity reactions, rash.

Interactions

Drug-drug. *Cardiac glycosides:* Increases risk of digoxin toxicity from indapamide-induced hypokalemia. Monitor potassium and digoxin levels.
Diazoxide: Increases antihypertensive, hyperglycemic, and hyperuricemic effects. Use together cautiously.
NSAIDs: Increases risk of NSAID-induced renal failure. Monitor patient for signs of renal failure.

Effects on lab test results

- May increase glucose, cholesterol, triglyceride, and uric acid levels. May decrease potassium, sodium, and chloride levels.

Pharmacokinetics

Absorption: Complete from GI tract.
Distribution: Distributed widely into body tissues because of its lipophilicity; 71% to 79% plasma protein–bound.
Metabolism: Undergoes significant hepatic metabolism.
Excretion: Primarily excreted in urine; smaller amounts excreted in feces. *Half-life:* About 14 hours.

Route	Onset	Peak	Duration
P.O.	1-2 hr	≤ 2 hr	≤ 36 hr

Pharmacodynamics

Chemical effect: Unknown; probably inhibits sodium reabsorption in distal segment of nephron. Also has direct vasodilating effect, possibly from calcium channel–blocking action.
Therapeutic effect: Promotes water and sodium excretion and lowers blood pressure.

Available forms

Tablets: 1.25 mg, 2.5 mg

NURSING PROCESS

Assessment

- Assess patient's underlying condition before therapy.
- Monitor effectiveness by assessing fluid intake and output, weight, and blood pressure. In hypertensive patient, therapeutic response may be delayed several days.
- Monitor electrolytes and glucose levels.
- Monitor creatinine and BUN levels regularly. Drug isn't as effective if these levels are more than twice normal.
- Monitor uric acid level, especially if patient has history of gout.
- Be alert for adverse reactions and drug interactions.
- Evaluate patient's and family's knowledge of drug therapy.

Nursing diagnoses

- Risk for injury related to presence of hypertension
- Excessive fluid volume related to presence of edema
- Deficient knowledge related to drug therapy

Planning and implementation

- To prevent nocturia, give drug in morning.
- Drug may be used with potassium-sparing diuretic to prevent potassium loss.

Patient teaching

- Advise patient to avoid sudden postural changes and to rise slowly to avoid orthostatic hypotension.
- Advise patient to use sunblock and avoid prolonged exposure to sunlight to prevent photosensitivity reactions.
- Teach patient to monitor fluid volume by recording daily weight and intake and output.
- Tell patient to avoid high-sodium foods and to choose high-potassium foods.
- Advise patient to take drug early in day to avoid nocturia.

Evaluation

- Patient's blood pressure is normal.
- Patient is free from edema.
- Patient and family state understanding of drug therapy.

indinavir sulfate

(in-DIH-nuh-veer SUL-fayt)
Crixivan

Pharmacologic class: protease inhibitor
Therapeutic class: antiviral
Pregnancy risk category: C

Indications and dosages

▶ **Treatment of patients with HIV infection when antiretroviral therapy is warranted.** *Adults:* 800 mg P.O. q 8 hours.
Patients with mild-to-moderate hepatic insufficiency resulting in cirrhosis: Reduce dosage to 600 mg P.O. q 8 hours.

Contraindications and precautions

- Contraindicated in patients hypersensitive to drug.

Lifespan: In breast-feeding patients, use is not recommended. In children, safety and efficacy haven't been established.

Adverse reactions

CNS: headache, insomnia, dizziness, malaise, somnolence, asthenia, fatigue.
GI: abdominal pain, *nausea,* diarrhea, vomiting, acid regurgitation, anorexia, dry mouth, taste perversion.
GU: nephrolithiasis.
Hematologic: anemia, ***neutropenia.***
Hepatic: *hyperbilirubinemia.*
Musculoskeletal: flank pain, back pain.

Interactions

Drug-drug. *Amprenavir, saquinavir:* May increase plasma levels of these drugs. Dosage adjustments probably are probably not needed.
Carbamazepine: Decreases indinavir concentration. Avoid using together; consider an alternative agent.
Clarithromycin: Alters plasma level of clarithromycin. Monitor patient.
Didanosine: May need normal gastric pH for optimal absorption of indinavir. Give these drugs and indinavir at least 1 hour apart on an empty stomach.
Efavirenz, nevirapine: May decrease level of indinavir. Increase indinavir to 1,000 mg q 8 hours.
HMG-CoA reductase inhibitors: May increase levels of these drugs and increase risk of myopathy and rhabdomyolysis. Avoid using together.
Ketoconazole, itraconazole, delavirdine: May increase level of indinavir. Consider a dosage reduction of indinavir to 600 mg q 8 hours.
Lopinavir/ritonavir fixed combination: May increase level of indinavir. Adjust indinavir dosage to 600 mg b.i.d.
Midazolam, triazolam: Competition for CYP3A4 by indinavir may result in inhibition of the metabolism of these drugs and create the potential for serious or life-threatening events, such as arrhythmias or prolonged sedation. Don't give together.
Nelfinavir: May increase levels of indinavir by 50% and nelfinavir by 80%. There is limited data on adjusting the dosage to indinavir 1,200 mg b.i.d. and nelfinavir 1,250 mg b.i.d. Monitor patient closely.
Rifabutin: May increase level of rifabutin and decrease level of indinavir. Give indinavir 1,000 mg q 8 hours and decrease the rifabutin dose to either 150 mg daily or 300 mg two to three times a week.
Rifampin: May significantly diminish level of indinavir because rifampin is a potent inducer of CYP3A4. Use together isn't recommended.
Ritonavir: May increase level of indinavir by 2 to 5 times. Adjust dosage to indinavir 400 mg b.i.d. and ritonavir 400 mg b.i.d., or indinavir 800 mg b.i.d. and ritonavir 100 to 200 mg b.i.d.
Sildenafil: May increase sildenafil level, and increase risk of adverse effects (hypotension, visual changes, and priapism). Do not exceed 25 mg of sildenafil in a 48-hour period.
Drug-herb. *St. John's wort:* May reduce plasma levels of indinavir by over 50%. Discourage use together.
Drug-food. *Any food:* Substantially decreases absorption of oral indinavir. Give drug on an empty stomach.
Grapefruit juice: May decrease level and therapeutic effect of indinavir. Take with liquid other than grapefruit juice.

Effects on lab test results

- May increase ALT, AST, bilirubin, amylase, and glucose levels.
- May decrease hemoglobin, hematocrit, and neutrophil and platelet counts.

Pharmacokinetics

Absorption: Rapid.
Distribution: 60% bound to plasma proteins.
Metabolism: Metabolized by liver and kidneys.
Excretion: Excreted in urine.

Route	Onset	Peak	Duration
P.O.	Unknown	< 1 hr	1-8 hr

Pharmacodynamics

Chemical effect: Binds to protease active sites and inhibits their activity.
Therapeutic effect: Prevents cleavage of viral polyproteins, resulting in formation of immature, noninfectious viral particles.

Available forms

Capsules: 100 mg, 200 mg, 333 mg, and 400 mg

NURSING PROCESS

Assessment

- Monitor adverse reactions and drug interactions.
- Evaluate patient's and family's knowledge of drug therapy.

Nursing diagnoses

- Infection related to presence of virus
- Risk for deficient fluid volume related to effect on kidneys
- Deficient knowledge related to drug therapy

Planning and implementation

- Patient should maintain adequate hydration (at least 48 oz [1.5 L] of fluids every 24 hours while taking indinavir).
- Give drug on an empty stomach, 1 hour before or 2 hours after a meal.

Patient teaching

- Instruct patient to use barrier protection during sexual intercourse.
- Advise patient that if a dose is missed, he should take the next dose at regularly scheduled time and not double the dose.
- Instruct patient to take drug on an empty stomach with water 1 hour before or 2 hours after a meal.
- Instruct patient to store capsules in the original container and to keep the desiccant in the bottle.
- Instruct patient to drink at least 48 oz (1.5 L) of fluid daily.
- Advise HIV-positive women to avoid breast-feeding to prevent transmitting virus to infant.
- Instruct patient to report evidence of nephrolithiasis (flank pain, hematuria) or diabetes (increased thirst, polyuria) promptly.
- Advise patient receiving sildenafil that he may be at an increased risk of sildenafil-associated adverse events including hypotension, visual changes, and priapism, and should promptly report any symptoms to the prescriber. Patient should not take more than 25 mg of sildenafil in a 48-hour period.

Evaluation

- Patient's health improves and signs and symptoms of underlying condition diminish with use of drug.
- Patient maintains adequate hydration.
- Patient and family state understanding of drug therapy.

indomethacin

(in-doh-METH-uh-sin)

Apo-Indomethacin ◆, Arthrexin ◇, Indocid ◆ ◇, Indocid SR ◆, Indocin, Indocin SR, Novo-Methacin ◆

indomethacin sodium trihydrate

Apo-Indomethacin ◆, Indocid PDA ◆, Indocin I.V., Novo-Methacin ◆

Pharmacologic class: NSAID
Therapeutic class: nonnarcotic analgesic, antipyretic, anti-inflammatory
Pregnancy risk category: NR

Indications and dosages

▶ **Moderate-to-severe rheumatoid arthritis or osteoarthritis, ankylosing spondylitis.** *Adults:* 25 mg P.O. b.i.d. or t.i.d. with food or antacids. Increase by 25 mg or 50 mg daily q 7 days up to 200 mg daily. Or, 50 mg P.R. q.i.d. Or, 75 mg sustained-release capsules P.O. to start, in morning or h.s., followed, if needed, by another 75 mg b.i.d.

▶ **Acute gouty arthritis.** *Adults:* 50 mg P.O. t.i.d. Reduce dose soon as possible, then discontinue. Don't use sustained-release capsules for this condition.

▶ **Acute painful shoulders (bursitis or tendinitis).** *Adults:* 75 to 150 mg P.O. daily b.i.d. or t.i.d. with food or antacids for 7 to 14 days.
▶ **To close hemodynamically significant patent ductus arteriosus in premature infants.** *Neonates less than 48 hours old:* 0.2 mg/kg I.V. followed by two doses of 0.1 mg/kg at 12- to 24-hour intervals.
Neonates ages 2 to 7 days: 0.2 mg/kg I.V. followed by two doses of 0.2 mg/kg at 12- to 24-hour intervals.
Neonates more than 7 days old: 0.2 mg/kg I.V. followed by two doses of 0.25 mg/kg at 12- to 24-hour intervals.
▶ **Pericarditis‡.** *Adults:* 75 to 200 mg P.O. daily in 3 to 4 divided doses.
▶ **Dysmenorrhea‡.** *Adults:* 25 mg P.O. t.i.d. with food or antacids.
▶ **Bartter's syndrome‡.** *Adults:* 150 mg P.O. daily with food or antacids.
Children: 0.5 to 2 mg/kg P.O. in divided doses.

Contraindications and precautions

• Contraindicated in patients hypersensitive to drug and with history of aspirin- or NSAID-induced asthma, rhinitis, or urticaria. Suppositories contraindicated in patients with history of proctitis or recent rectal bleeding.
• Because of its high risk of adverse effects during prolonged use, indomethacin shouldn't be used routinely as analgesic or antipyretic.
• Use cautiously in patients with epilepsy, parkinsonism, hepatic or renal disease, CV disease, infection, mental illness or depression, or history of GI disease.
Lifespan: In pregnant or breast-feeding women, use is contraindicated. In infants with untreated infection, active bleeding, coagulation defects, thrombocytopenia, congenital heart disease (in whom patency of ductus arteriosus is needed for satisfactory pulmonary or systemic blood flow), necrotizing enterocolitis, or impaired renal function, use also is contraindicated. In elderly patients, use cautiously.

Adverse reactions

P.O. and P.R.
CNS: *headache, dizziness,* depression, drowsiness, confusion, peripheral neuropathy, ***seizures,*** psychic disturbances, syncope, *vertigo.*
CV: hypertension, *edema,* ***heart failure.***
EENT: blurred vision, corneal and retinal damage, hearing loss, tinnitus.
GI: *nausea, vomiting,* anorexia, *diarrhea, peptic ulceration,* ***GI bleeding, pancreatitis.***
GU: hematuria, ***acute renal failure.***
Hematologic: hemolytic anemia, ***aplastic anemia, agranulocytosis, leukopenia, thrombocytopenic purpura,*** iron-deficiency anemia.
Metabolic: ***hyperkalemia.***
Skin: pruritus, urticaria, ***Stevens-Johnson syndrome.***
Other: ***hypersensitivity reactions*** (rash, ***respiratory distress, anaphylaxis, angioedema***).
I.V.
GI: ***bleeding,*** vomiting.
GU: ***renal dysfunction,*** azotemia.
Metabolic: hyponatremia, ***hyperkalemia, hypoglycemia.***
Other: ***hypersensitivity reactions*** (rash, ***respiratory distress, anaphylaxis, angioedema***).

Interactions

Drug-drug. *Aminoglycosides, cyclosporine, methotrexate:* Indomethacin may enhance toxicity of these drugs. Avoid using together.
Antihypertensives: May reduce antihypertensive effect. Monitor blood pressure closely.
Aspirin: May decrease indomethacin level. Avoid using together.
Corticosteroids: May increase risk of GI toxicity. Don't use together.
Diflunisal, probenecid: May decrease indomethacin excretion. Monitor patient for increased adverse reactions to indomethacin.
Digoxin: Indomethacin may prolong half-life of digoxin. Use together cautiously; monitor digoxin level.
Dipyridamole: May enhance fluid retention. Avoid using together.
Furosemide, thiazide diuretics: May impair response to both drugs. Avoid using together, if possible.
Lithium: May increase lithium levels. Monitor patient for lithium toxicity.
Triamterene: May cause nephrotoxicity. Monitor patient closely.
Drug-herb. *Dong quai, feverfew, garlic, ginger, horse chestnut, red clover:* May increase risk of bleeding. Monitor patient closely for bleeding.
St. John's wort: May increase risk of photosensitivity. Advise patient to avoid unprotected or prolonged exposure to sunlight.

Senna: May block laxative effects. Discourage using together.

Drug-lifestyle. *Alcohol use:* May increase risk of GI toxicity. Discourage using together.

Effects on lab test results

- May increase AST, ALT, BUN, creatinine, and potassium levels. May decrease glucose and sodium levels.
- May decrease hemoglobin, hematocrit, and WBC, granulocyte, and platelet counts.

Pharmacokinetics

Absorption: Rapidly and completely from GI tract after P.O. and P.R. administration.

Distribution: Highly protein-bound.

Metabolism: Metabolized in liver.

Excretion: Excreted mainly in urine, with some biliary excretion.

Route	Onset	Peak	Duration
P.O.	30 min	1-4 hr	4-6 hr
I.V.	Immediate	Immediate	Unknown
P.R.	2-4 hr	Unknown	4-6 hr

Pharmacodynamics

Chemical effect: Unknown; produces anti-inflammatory, analgesic, and antipyretic effects, possibly by inhibiting prostaglandin synthesis.

Therapeutic effect: Relieves pain, fever, and inflammation.

Available forms

indomethacin

Capsules: 25 mg, 50 mg

Capsules (sustained-release): 75 mg

Oral suspension: 25 mg/5 ml

Suppositories: 50 mg

indomethacin sodium trihydrate

Injection: 1-mg vials

NURSING PROCESS

Assessment

- Assess patient's condition before therapy and regularly thereafter.
- Monitor patient carefully for bleeding and for reduced urine output during I.V. use.
- Be alert for adverse reactions and drug interactions.
- Evaluate patient's and family's knowledge of drug therapy.

Nursing diagnoses

- Chronic pain related to underlying condition
- Risk for injury related to adverse reactions
- Deficient knowledge related to drug therapy

Planning and implementation

- **P.O. use:** Give drug with food, milk, or antacid if GI upset occurs.
- **I.V. use:** Reconstitute powder for injection with sterile water for injection or normal saline solution. For each 1-mg vial, add 1 ml of diluent to yield 1 mg/ml; add 2 ml of diluent to yield 0.5 mg/ml. Give by direct injection over 5 to 10 seconds.

ALERT: Use only preservative-free diluents to prepare I.V. injection. Never use diluents containing benzyl alcohol because it has been linked to fatal gasping syndrome in neonates. Because injection contains no preservatives, reconstitute immediately before administration and discard unused solution.

- Don't give second or third scheduled I.V. dose if patient has anuria or marked oliguria; instead, notify prescriber.
- **P.R. use:** Follow normal protocol.
- If ductus arteriosus reopens, second course of one to three doses may be given. If ineffective, surgery may be needed.
- Discontinue drug and notify prescriber if patient has bleeding or reduced urine output.
- Drug may enhance hypothalamic-pituitary-adrenal axis response to dexamethasone suppression test.
- Notify prescriber if drug is ineffective.

Patient teaching

- Tell patient to take oral form of drug with food, milk, or antacid if GI upset occurs.
- Alert patient that use of oral form with aspirin, alcohol, or corticosteroids may increase risk of adverse GI reactions.
- Teach patient to recognize and urge him to report signs and symptoms of GI bleeding. Serious GI toxicity, including peptic ulceration and bleeding, can occur in patients taking oral NSAIDs despite absence of GI symptoms.
- Instruct patient to avoid alcohol consumption during drug therapy.
- Tell patient to notify prescriber immediately about visual or hearing changes. Patient receiving long-term oral therapy should have regular eye examinations, hearing tests, CBC, and renal function tests to detect toxicity.

• Advise patient to avoid hazardous activities if adverse CNS reactions occur.

Evaluation

• Patient is free from pain.
• Patient doesn't experience injury from adverse reactions.
• Patient and family state understanding of drug therapy.

infliximab

(in-FLIX-i-mab)
Remicade

Pharmacologic class: monoclonal antibody
Therapeutic class: anti-inflammatory
Pregnancy risk category: B

Indications and dosages

▶ **Reduction of signs and symptoms, and inducing and maintaining clinical remission in patients with moderate to severe Crohn's disease who have had an inadequate response to conventional therapy.** *Adults:* 5 mg/kg I.V. infusion (over a period of no less than 2 hours), given as an induction regimen at 0, 2, and 6 weeks followed by a maintenance regimen of 5 mg/kg q 8 weeks thereafter. For patients who respond and then lose their response, consider treating with 10 mg/kg. Patients who do not respond by week 14 are unlikely to respond with continued dosing; consider discontinuing infliximab.

▶ **Reduction in the number of draining enterocutaneous fistulas in patients with fistulizing Crohn's disease.** *Adults:* 5 mg/kg I.V. infused over a period of not less than 2 hours. Give additional doses of 5 mg/kg at 2 and 6 weeks after initial infusion. The safety and efficacy of treatment for fistulizing Crohn's disease beyond 3 doses have not been established.

▶ **Reducing signs and symptoms, inhibiting the progression of structural damage and improving physical function in patients with moderate to severe rheumatoid arthritis who have had an inadequate response to methotrexate.** *Adults:* 3 mg/kg I.V. infusion over a period of not less than 2 hours. Give additional doses of 3 mg/kg at 2 and 6 weeks after initial infusion and q 8 weeks thereafter. Dose may be increased up to 10 mg/kg or doses may be given q 4 weeks if response is inadequate.

Contraindications and precautions

• Contraindicated in patients hypersensitive to murine proteins or other components of drug.
• In patients with mild heart failure (NYHA Class I or II), use cautiously. Patients with moderate to severe heart failure (NYHA Class III or IV) should not use this drug.
Lifespan: In pregnant women, give only if clearly needed. It is unknown whether drug is excreted in breast milk. In children, safety hasn't been established. In elderly patients, use drug cautiously.

Adverse reactions

CNS: pain, *headache, fatigue, fever,* dizziness, malaise, insomnia.
CV: hypertension, peripheral edema, hypotension, tachycardia, chest pain, flushing.
EENT: pharyngitis, rhinitis, sinusitis, conjunctivitis.
GI: *nausea, abdominal pain,* vomiting, constipation, dyspepsia, flatulence, intestinal obstruction, mouth pain, ulcerative stomatitis.
GU: dysuria, increased micturition frequency.
Hematologic: anemia, ecchymosis, hematoma.
Musculoskeletal: myalgia, arthralgia, arthritis, back pain.
Respiratory: *upper respiratory tract infections,* bronchitis, coughing, dyspnea.
Skin: rash, pruritus, candidiasis, acne, alopecia, eczema, erythema, erythematous rash, maculopapular rash, papular rash, dry skin, increased sweating, urticaria.
Other: chills, flulike syndrome, hot flushes, abscess, toothache, hypersensitivity reaction, allergic reaction.

Interactions

None significant.

Effects on lab test results

• May increase liver enzyme levels.
• May decrease hemoglobin and hematocrit.

Pharmacokinetics

Absorption: Administered I.V.
Distribution: Unknown.
Metabolism: Unknown.

Excretion: Unknown. *Terminal half-life:* 9½ days.

Route	Onset	Peak	Duration
I.V.	Unknown	Unknown	Unknown

Pharmacodynamics

Chemical effect: A monoclonal antibody that binds to human tumor necrosis factor (TNF)-alpha to neutralize its activity and inhibit its binding with receptors, thereby reducing the infiltration of inflammatory cells and production of TNF-alpha in inflamed areas of the intestine.

Therapeutic effect: Relieves inflammation in the GI tract.

Available forms

Injection: 100-mg vials

NURSING PROCESS

Assessment

- Obtain history of patient's underlying condition before therapy, and reassess regularly thereafter.
- Observe patient for infusion-related reactions, including fever, chills, pruritus, urticaria, dyspnea, hypotension, hypertension, and chest pain, during and for 2 hours after administration.
- Monitor liver function test values.
- Observe patient for development of lymphomas and infection. Patients with chronic Crohn's disease and long-term exposure to immunosuppressants are more likely to develop lymphomas and infections.
- Drug may affect normal immune responses. Monitor patient for development of autoimmune antibodies and lupus-like syndrome; drug should be discontinued. Expect symptoms to resolve.
- Monitor patient's cardiac status if drug is used in patients with heart failure.
- Evaluate patient's and family's knowledge of drug therapy.

Nursing diagnoses

- Chronic pain related to inflammation of the GI tract
- Imbalanced nutrition: Less than body requirements related to underlying medical condition
- Deficient knowledge related to drug therapy

Planning and implementation

- Drug is incompatible with plasticized polyvinyl chloride equipment or devices; prepare only in glass infusion bottles or polypropylene or polyolefin infusion bags. Give through polyethylene-lined administration sets with an in-line, sterile, nonpyrogenic, low–protein-binding filter (pore size of 1.2 mm or less).
- Vials don't contain antibacterial preservatives; use reconstituted drug immediately. Reconstitute with 10 ml sterile solution for injection using syringe with 21G or smaller needle. Don't shake; gently swirl to dissolve powder. Solution should be colorless to light yellow and opalescent; it may contain a few translucent particles. Don't use if you see other particles or discoloration.
- Dilute total volume of reconstituted drug to 250 ml with normal saline solution for injection. Infusion concentration range is 0.4 to 4 mg/ml. Infusion should begin within 3 hours of preparation and must last at least 2 hours.
- Don't infuse drug in same I.V. line with other drugs.
- If an infusion reaction occurs, discontinue drug, notify prescriber, and be prepared to give acetaminophen, antihistamines, corticosteroids, and epinephrine.
- Stop treatment if patient develops new or worsening symptoms of heart failure.
- Patients receiving infliximab may develop tuberculosis (frequently disseminated or extrapulmonary at clinical presentation), invasive fungal infections, and other, sometimes fatal, opportunistic infections. Patients should be evaluated for latent tuberculosis infection with a tuberculin skin test. Treatment of latent tuberculosis infection should be initiated before therapy with infliximab.
- Patient receiving infliximab may develop histoplasmosis, listeriosis, and pneumocystosis. For patients who have resided in regions where histoplasmosis is endemic, the benefits and risks of infliximab therapy should be carefully considered before initiation of the therapy.

Patient teaching

- Tell patient about infusion reaction symptoms, and instruct him to report them.

• Inform patient of postinfusion adverse effects, and tell him to report them promptly.
• Tell breast-feeding woman to stop breast-feeding if drug is to be given.

☑ Evaluation
• Patient is free from pain.
• Patient maintains adequate nutrition.
• Patient and family state understanding of drug therapy.

insulin aspart (rDNA origin) injection

(IN-suh-lin AS-part)
NovoLog

Pharmacologic classification: human insulin analogue
Therapeutic classification: antidiabetic
Pregnancy risk category: C

Indications and dosages

▶ **Control of hyperglycemia in diabetes mellitus.** *Adults:* Dosage is based on the needs of the patient. Typical daily insulin requirements are 0.5 to 1 unit/kg S.C. daily divided in a meal-related treatment regimen. About 50% to 70% of this dose may be provided with NovoLog and the remainder by intermediate-acting or long-acting insulin. Give within 5 to 10 minutes of start of meal.
External insulin infusion pumps: Initially, based on the total daily insulin dose of the previous regimen. Usually 50% of the total dose is given as meal-related boluses, and the remainder as basal infusion. Adjust dose as needed.

Contraindications and precautions

• Contraindicated during episodes of hypoglycemia and in patients hypersensitive to NovoLog or one of its excipients.
• Use cautiously in patients prone to hypoglycemia and hypokalemia, such as patients who are fasting, have autonomic neuropathy, or who are using potassium-lowering drugs or drugs sensitive to potassium levels.
Lifespan: In breast-feeding women, use caution; may appear in breast milk. In children under age 12, safety and efficacy haven't been established.

Adverse reactions

Metabolic: ***hypoglycemia.***
Skin: injection site reactions, lipodystrophy, pruritus, rash.
Other: allergic reactions.

Interactions

Drug-drug. *ACE inhibitors, disopyramide, fibrates, fluoxetine, MAO inhibitors, oral antidiabetics, propoxyphene, salicylates, somatostatin analogue (octreotide), and sulfonamide antibiotics:* May enhance the glucose-lowering effects of insulin and may potentiate hypoglycemia. Monitor glucose level and signs of hypoglycemia. May require insulin dose adjustment.
Beta blockers, clonidine: May potentiate or weaken glucose-lowering effect of insulin, causing hypoglycemia or hyperglycemia. May mask signs and symptoms of hypoglycemia (may be reduced or absent). Monitor glucose level.
Corticosteroids, danazol, diuretics, estrogens, progestogens such as in oral contraceptives, isoniazid, niacin, phenothiazine derivatives, somatropin, sympathomimetics such as epinephrine, salbutamol, and terbutaline, and thyroid hormones: May reduce the glucose-lowering effect of insulin and may cause hyperglycemia. Monitor glucose level. May require insulin dosage adjustment.
Guanethidine, reserpine: May mask signs and symptoms of hypoglycemia (may be reduced or absent). Monitor glucose level.
Lithium salts, pentamidine: May potentiate or weaken glucose-lowering effect of insulin, causing hypoglycemia or hyperglycemia. Pentamidine may cause hypoglycemia, which may sometimes be followed by hyperglycemia. Monitor glucose level.
Drug-lifestyle. *Alcohol:* May potentiate or weaken glucose-lowering effect of insulin, resulting in hypoglycemia or hyperglycemia. Monitor glucose level.

Effects on lab test results

• May decrease glucose and potassium levels.

Pharmacokinetics

Absorption: Bioavailable as regular human insulin. Faster absorption and onset and shorter duration of action compared to regular human insulin.

Distribution: Low plasma protein binding (0% to 9%), similar to regular insulin.
Metabolism: Unknown.
Excretion: *Half life:* Shorter than that of regular human insulin (81 minutes compared with 141 minutes).

Route	Onset	Peak	Duration
S.C.	Rapid	1-3 hr	3-5 hr

Pharmacodynamics

Chemical effect: Binds to insulin receptors on muscle and fat cells, lowering glucose level, facilitating the cellular uptake of glucose, and inhibiting the output of glucose from the liver.
Therapeutic effect: Lowers glucose level.

Available forms

10-ml vial for injection: 100 units of insulin aspart per ml (U-100)
3-ml PenFill cartridges: 100 units/ml

NURSING PROCESS

Assessment

- Assess underlying condition before therapy and reassess regularly throughout therapy.
- Monitor glucose levels before therapy and regularly throughout therapy.
- Monitor patient's glycosylated hemoglobin level regularly.
- Monitor urine ketones when glucose level is elevated.
- Monitor patient for injection site reactions.
- Monitor patient with an external insulin pump for erythematous, pruritic, or thickened skin at injection site.
- Determine patient's and family's knowledge of drug therapy.

Nursing diagnoses

- Risk for impaired skin integrity related to adverse drug effects
- Risk for injury related to drug-induced hypoglycemia
- Deficient knowledge related to insulin aspart therapy

Planning and implementation

- Monitor patient for hypoglycemia, which may occur as a result of an excess of insulin relative to food intake, energy expenditure, or both. The warning signs and symptoms of hypoglycemia include shaking, sweating, dizziness, fatigue, hunger, irritability, confusion, blurred vision, headaches, or nausea and vomiting. Mild episodes of hypoglycemia can be treated with oral glucose. Adjustments in drug dosage, meal patterns, or exercise may be needed. More severe episodes involving coma, seizure, or neurologic impairment may be treated with I.M. or S.C. glucagon or concentrated I.V. glucose. Sustained carbohydrate intake and observation may be needed because hypoglycemia may recur after apparent clinical recovery.
- Give 5 to 10 minutes before the start of a meal. Because of drug's rapid onset and short duration of action, patients may require the addition of longer-acting insulins to prevent premeal hyperglycemia.
- Give by S.C. injection into the abdominal wall, thigh, or upper arm. It's important to rotate sites to minimize lipodystrophies.
- Vials should be inspected visually before use. Drug should appear as a clear, colorless solution and should never contain particulate matter, appear cloudy or viscous, or have discoloration. Don't use after the expiration date.
- Store drug between 2° and 8° C (36° and 46° F). Don't freeze. Don't expose vials to excessive heat or sunlight. Open vials are stable at room temperature for 28 days.

ALERT: Pump or infusion-set malfunctions or insulin degradation can lead to hyperglycemia and ketosis in a short time because there is an S.C. depot of fast-acting insulin.

- Don't dilute or mix insulin aspart with any other insulin when using an external insulin pump.
- Insulin aspart is recommended for use with Disetronic H-TRON plus V100 with Disetronic 3.15 plastic cartridges and Classic or Tender infusion sets, and MiniMed Models 505, 506, and 507 with MiniMed 3-ml syringes and Polyfin or Sof-set infusion sets. The use of insulin aspart in quick-release infusion sets and cartridge adapters has not been assessed.
- Replace infusion sets and insulin aspart in the reservoir and choose a new infusion site every 48 hours or less to avoid insulin degradation and infusion set malfunction.
- Drug exposed to temperatures higher than 37°C (98.6°F) should be discarded. The temperature may exceed ambient temperature

when the pump housing, cover, tubing, or sport case is exposed to sunlight or radiant heat.

Patient teaching
- Inform patient of the possible risks and benefits of drug.
- Teach patient to recognize symptoms of hypoglycemia and hyperglycemia and how to treat them.
- Instruct patient on injection techniques, timing of dose to meals, adherence to meal planning, importance of regular glucose monitoring and periodic glycosylated hemoglobin testing, and proper storage of insulin.
- Tell woman to notify prescriber if she plans to become or becomes pregnant; information on drug in pregnancy or lactation isn't available.
- Instruct patient to report changes at injection site, including redness, itchiness, or thickened skin.
- Tell patient not to dilute or mix insulin aspart with any other insulin when using an external insulin pump.
- Teach patient how to properly use the external insulin pump.

☑ Evaluation
- Patient does not experience adverse reactions caused by drug.
- Patient's glucose level is within the normal range.
- Patient and family state understanding of insulin aspart therapy.

insulin glargine (rDNA) injection
IN-suh-lin GLAR-gene (rDNA) in-JEK-shun
Lantus

Pharmacologic class: pancreatic hormone
Therapeutic class: antidiabetic
Pregnancy risk category: C

Indications and dosages
▶ **Management of type 1 diabetes mellitus in patients who need basal (long-acting) insulin for the control of hyperglycemia.** *Adults and children:* For patients taking once-daily NPH or ultralente human insulin, start drug at the same dose as the current insulin dose. For patients taking twice-daily NPH human insulin, start drug at a dose that is 20% less than the current daily dose of insulin. Adjust dose based on patient response.
▶ **Management of type 2 diabetes mellitus in patients previously treated with oral antidiabetics.** *Adults:* 10 units S.C. once daily h.s. Adjust as needed to total daily dosage of 2 units to 100 units S.C. h.s.

Contraindications and precautions
- Contraindicated in patients hypersensitive to insulin glargine or its excipients. Don't use drug during episodes of hypoglycemia.
- Use cautiously in patients with renal or hepatic impairment, and adjust dosage as directed.

Lifespan: In breast-feeding women, use cautiously. In children younger than age 6 months, safety and efficacy haven't been established. In elderly patients, use conservatively to avoid hypoglycemia.

Adverse reactions
Metabolic: ***hypoglycemia.***
Skin: lipodystrophy, pruritus, rash.
Other: allergic reactions, pain at injection site.

Interactions
Drug-drug. *ACE inhibitors, disopyramide, fibrates, fluoxetine, MAO inhibitors, octreotide, oral antidiabetics, propoxyphene, salicylates, sulfonamide antibiotics:* May cause hypoglycemia and increased insulin effect. Monitor glucose level. Insulin glargine dosage may need adjustment.
Beta blockers, clonidine: May mask signs of hypoglycemia and may either potentiate or weaken glucose-lowering effect of insulin. Monitor glucose level carefully. Insulin glargine dosage may need adjustment.
Corticosteroids, danazol, diuretics, estrogens, isoniazid, phenothiazines (prochlorperazine, promethazine), progestins (oral contraceptives), sympathomimetics (albuterol, epinephrine, terbutaline), thyroid hormones: May reduce the glucose-lowering effect of insulin. Monitor glucose level. Insulin glargine dosage may need adjustment.
Guanethidine, reserpine: May mask signs of hypoglycemia. Avoid using together, if possible. Monitor glucose level carefully.
Lithium: May either potentiate or weaken the glucose-lowering effect of insulin. Monitor

glucose level. Insulin glargine dosage may need adjustment.
Pentamidine: May cause hypoglycemia, which may be followed by hyperglycemia. Avoid using together, if possible.
Drug-herb. *Aloe, bitter melon, bilberry leaf, burdock, dandelion, fenugreek, garlic, ginseng:* May improve glucose control and allow a reduced antidiabetic dosage. Tell patient to discuss the use of herbal remedies with prescriber before use.
Licorice root: May increase dosage requirements of insulin. Discourage using together.
Drug-lifestyle. *Alcohol use, emotional stress, exercise:* May potentiate or weaken the glucose-lowering effect of insulin. Monitor glucose level. Insulin glargine dosage may need adjustment.

Effects on lab test results

- May decrease glucose level.

Pharmacokinetics

Absorption: Slower, more prolonged absorption than NPH insulin and a relatively constant level over 24 hours with no pronounced peak when compared with NPH insulin. After injection into S.C. tissue, the acidic solution is neutralized, leading to formation of microprecipitates. From these microprecipitates, small amounts of insulin glargine are slowly released.
Distribution: Unknown.
Metabolism: Partly metabolized to form two active metabolites with in vitro activity similar to that of insulin.
Excretion: Unknown.

Route	Onset	Peak	Duration
S.C.	Slow	None	10.8-24 hr

Pharmacodynamics

Chemical effect: Increases glucose transport across muscle and fat cell membranes to reduce glucose level. Promotes conversion of glucose to its storage form, glycogen. Triggers amino acid uptake and conversion to protein in muscle cells and inhibits protein degradation. Stimulates triglyceride formation and inhibits release of free fatty acids from adipose tissue. Stimulates lipoprotein lipase activity, which converts circulating lipoproteins to fatty acids.
Therapeutic effect: Lowers glucose level.

Available forms

Injection: 100 units/ml

NURSING PROCESS

Assessment

- Obtain history of patient's underlying condition before therapy, and reassess regularly thereafter. As with any insulin, the desired glucose level and the doses and timing of antidiabetic drug must be determined individually.
- Monitor glucose level closely.
- Monitor patient for hypoglycemia. Early symptoms may be different or less pronounced in patients with longstanding diabetes, diabetic nerve disease, or intensified diabetes control.
- Evaluate patient's and family's knowledge of drug therapy.

Nursing diagnoses

- Ineffective health maintenance related to hyperglycemia
- Risk for injury related to drug-induced hypoglycemia
- Deficient knowledge related to drug therapy

Planning and implementation

- Drug isn't intended for I.V. use. Its prolonged duration of activity depends on injection into the S.C. space.
- Because of its prolonged duration, insulin glargine isn't the insulin of choice for diabetic ketoacidosis.
- The rate of absorption and onset and the duration of action may be affected by exercise and other circumstances such as illness and emotional stress.
- Don't dilute drug or mix it with any other insulin or solution.
- As with any insulin therapy, lipodystrophy may occur at injection site and delay insulin absorption. Rotate injection sites to reduce lipodystrophy.

ALERT: Don't confuse Lantus with Lente.

Patient teaching

- Teach patient proper glucose-monitoring techniques and proper diabetes management.
- Teach diabetic patient signs and symptoms of hypoglycemia, such as fatigue, weakness, confusion, headache, and pale skin.
- Advise patient to treat mild episodes of hypoglycemia with oral glucose tablets. Encour-

age patient to always carry glucose tablets in case of a hypoglycemic episode.
- Teach patient the importance of maintaining a diabetic diet. Explain that adjustments in drug dosage, meal patterns, and exercise may be needed to regulate blood glucose.
- Any change of insulin should be made cautiously and only under medical supervision. Changes in insulin strength, manufacturer, type (regular, NPH, insulin analogs), species (animal, human), or method of manufacture (rDNA versus animal source), may necessitate a dosage change. Oral antidiabetic treatment may need to be adjusted.
- Tell patient to consult prescriber before using OTC drugs.
- Advise patient not to dilute or mix any other insulin or solution with insulin glargine. Tell patient to discard the vial if the solution is cloudy.
- Instruct patient to store insulin glargine vials and cartridges in the refrigerator.

☑ Evaluation
- Patient's blood glucose level is normal.
- Patient doesn't experience hypoglycemic reactions.
- Patient and family state understanding of drug therapy.

insulins
(IN-suh-linz)

insulin analog injection (lispro)
Humalog, Humalog mix 75/25, Humalog mix 50/50

insulin injection (regular insulin, crystalline zinc insulin)
Actrapid HM ◇, Actrapid HM Penfill ◇, Actrapid MC ◇, Actrapid MC Penfill ◇, Humulin R†, Hypurin Neutral ◇, Insulin 2 Neutral ◇, Novolin R†, Novolin R PenFill†, Pork Regular Iletin II†, Regular (Concentrated) Iletin II, Regular Purified Pork Insulin†, Velosulin Human ◇, Velosulin Insuject ◇

insulin zinc suspension (lente)
Humulin L†, Lente Iletin II†, Lente Insulin†, Lente MC ◇, Lente Purified Pork Insulin†, Monotard HM ◇, Monotard MC ◇, Novolin L†

insulin zinc suspension, extended (ultralente)
Humulin U†, Ultralente Insulin†, Ultratard HM ◇, Ultratard MC ◇

insulin zinc suspension, prompt (semilente)
Semilente MC ◇

isophane insulin suspension (neutral protamine Hagedorn insulin, NPH)
Humulin N†, Hypurin Isophane ◇, Insulatard ◇, Insulatard Human ◆, Isotard MC ◇, Novolin N†, Novolin N PenFill†, NPH Insulin†, Pork NPH Iletin II†, Protaphane HM ◇, Protaphane HM Penfill ◇, Protaphane MC ◇

isophane insulin suspension with insulin injection
Actraphane HM ◇, Actraphane HM Penfill ◇, Actraphane MC ◇, Humulin 50/50†, Humulin 70/30†, Novolin 70/30, Novolin 70/30 PenFill†

protamine zinc suspension (PZI)
Protamine Zinc Insulin MC ◇

Pharmacologic class: pancreatic hormone
Therapeutic class: antidiabetic
Pregnancy risk category: NR

Indications and dosages
▶ **Diabetic ketoacidosis. *Regular insulin.*** *Adults:* 0.15 units/kg as I.V. bolus, followed by 0.1 units/kg/hour by continuous infusion. Continue infusion until glucose level drops to 250 mg/dl; then start S.C. insulin with dose and interval adjusted according to patient's glucose level. Or, 50 to 100 units I.V. and 50 to 100 units S.C. immediately; then additional doses q 1 to 2 hours based on glucose level.

Children: 0.1 unit/kg as I.V. bolus; then 0.1 unit/kg hourly by continuous infusion until glucose level drops to 250 mg/dl; then start S.C. insulin. Or, 0.5 to 1 unit/kg in two divided doses, one I.V. and the other S.C., followed by 0.5 to 1 unit/kg I.V. q 1 to 2 hours based on glucose levels.

▶ **Type 1 diabetes mellitus (insulin-dependent), adjunct to type 2 diabetes mellitus (non–insulin-dependent) inadequately controlled by diet and oral antidiabetics.** *Adults and children:* Therapeutic regimen is adjusted based on patient's glucose level.

▶ **Control of hyperglycemia with longer-acting insulin in patients with type 1 diabetes mellitus and with sulfonylureas in patients with type 2 diabetes mellitus. *Insulin lispro rDNA origin, Humalog.*** *Adults and children older than age 3:* Dosage varies and must be determined by a prescriber familiar with patient's metabolic needs, eating habits, and other lifestyle variables. Inject S.C. up to 15 minutes before or immediately after a meal.

▶ **Control of hyperglycemia with Humalog and longer-acting insulin in patients with type 1 diabetes mellitus.** *Adults:* Dosage varies among patients and must be determined by prescriber familiar with patient's metabolic needs, eating habits, and other lifestyle variables. Inject S.C. within 15 minutes before or immediately after a meal.

▶ **Control of hyperglycemia with Humalog and sulfonylureas in patients with type 2 diabetes mellitus.** *Adults and children older than age 3:* Dosage varies among patients and must be determined by prescriber familiar with patient's metabolic needs, eating habits, and other lifestyle variables. Inject S.C. within 15 minutes before or immediately after a meal.

Contraindications and precautions

- No known contraindications.

Lifespan: In pregnant and breast-feeding women, insulin is drug of choice to treat diabetes.

Adverse reactions

Metabolic: ***hypoglycemia,*** hyperglycemia (rebound, or Somogyi, effect).
Skin: urticaria, itching, swelling, redness, stinging, warmth at injection site, rash.
Other: *lipoatrophy, lipohypertrophy,* hypersensitivity reactions, ***anaphylaxis,*** rash.

Interactions

Drug-drug. *AIDS antivirals, corticosteroids, dextrothyroxine, epinephrine, thiazide diuretics:* Diminishes insulin response. Monitor patient for hyperglycemia.
Anabolic steroids, beta blockers, clofibrate, fenfluramine, guanethidine, MAO inhibitors, salicylates, tetracyclines: Prolonged hypoglycemic effect. Monitor glucose level carefully.
Diazoxide, phenytoin (high doses): May inhibit endogenous insulin secretion and may cause hypoglycemia in patients with diabetes. Carefully adjust insulin dosage.
Oral contraceptives: May decrease glucose tolerance in diabetic patients. Monitor glucose levels and adjust insulin dosage carefully.
Drug-herb. *Basil, bay, bee pollen, burdock, ginseng, glucomannan, horehound, marshmallow, myrrh, sage:* May affect glycemic control. Monitor glucose level carefully.
Drug-lifestyle. *Alcohol use:* May cause hypoglycemic effect. Discourage using together.
Marijuana use: May increase glucose level. Tell patient about this interaction.
Smoking: May increase glucose level and decrease response to insulin. Discourage patient from smoking; have patient monitor glucose level closely.

Effects on lab test results

- May decrease glucose, magnesium, and potassium levels.

Pharmacokinetics

Absorption: Highly variable after S.C. administration depending on insulin type and injection site.
Distribution: Distributed widely throughout body.
Metabolism: Some is bound and inactivated by peripheral tissues, but most appears to be degraded in liver and kidneys.
Excretion: Filtered by renal glomeruli; undergoes some tubular reabsorption. *Half-life:* About 9 minutes after I.V. administration.

Route	Onset	Peak	Duration
I.V.	≤ 30 min	15-30 min	30 min-1 hr
S.C.	15 min-8 hr	2-30 hr	5-36 hr

Pharmacodynamics

Chemical effect: Increases glucose transport across muscle and fat cell membranes to re-

duce blood glucose level. Promotes conversion of glucose to its storage form, glycogen; triggers amino acid uptake and conversion to protein in muscle cells and inhibits protein degradation; stimulates triglyceride formation and inhibits release of free fatty acids from adipose tissue; stimulates lipoprotein lipase activity, which converts circulating lipoproteins to fatty acids.
Therapeutic effect: Lowers glucose level.

Available forms

insulin injection
Injection (human): 100 units/ml (Actrapid HM ◇, Humulin R†, Novolin R†, Humalog [lispro], Velosulin Human ◇); 100 units/ml in 1.5-ml cartridge system† (Actrapid HM Penfill ◇, Novolin R PenFill†)
Injection (from pork): 100 units/ml†
Injection (purified beef): 100 units/ml (Hypurin Neutral ◇, Insulin 2 ◇)
Injection (purified pork): 100 units/ml (Actrapid MC ◇, Pork Regular Iletin II†, Regular Purified Pork Insulin†); 100 units/ml in 1.5-ml cartridge system ◇ (Actrapid MC Penfill ◇); 100 units/ml in 2-ml cartridge system ◇; 500 units/ml (Regular [Concentrated] Iletin II)
insulin zinc suspension, prompt
Injection (purified pork): 100 units/ml† (Semilente MC ◇)
isophane insulin suspension
Injection (from beef): 100 units/ml† (NPH Insulin†)
Injection (human, recombinant): 100 units/ml (Humulin N†, Humulin NPH ◇, Insulatard Human ♦, Novolin N†, Protaphane HM ◇); 100 units/ml in 1.5-ml cartridge system (Protaphane HM PenFill ◇, Novolin N PenFill†)
Injection (purified beef): 100 units/ml (Hypurin Isophane ◇, Isotard MC ◇)
Injection (purified pork): 100 units/ml (Insulatard ◇, NPH Purified Pork†, Pork NPH Iletin II, Protaphane MC ◇)
isophane insulin suspension 50% with insulin injection 50%
Injection (human): 100 units/ml (Humulin 50/50†)
isophane insulin suspension 70% with insulin injection 30%
Injection (human): 100 units/ml (Actraphane HM ◇, Humulin 70/30†, Novolin 70/30†); 100 units/ml in 1.5-ml cartridge system (Actraphane HM Penfill ◇, Novolin 70/30 PenFill†)
Injection (purified pork): 100 units/ml (Actraphane MC ◇)
insulin zinc suspension
Injection (from beef): 100 units/ml (Lente Insulin†, Lente MC ◇)
Injection (purified beef): 100 units/ml (Lente MC ◇)
Injection (purified pork): 100 units/ml (Lente Iletin II†, Monotard MC ◇, Lente Purified Pork Insulin†)
Injection (human): 100 units/ml† (Humulin L†, Monotard HM ◇, Novolin L†)
protamine zinc suspension
Injection (purified pork): Protamine Zinc Insulin MC ◇
insulin zinc suspension, extended
Injection (from beef): 100 units/ml† (Ultralente Insulin†)
Injection (human): 100 units/ml (Ultratard HM ◇, Humulin U†)
Injection (purified pork): 100 units/ml ◇ (Ultratard MC ◇)

NURSING PROCESS

Assessment

- Assess patient's glucose level before therapy and regularly thereafter. Monitor level more frequently if patient is under stress, unstable, pregnant, recently diagnosed, or taking drugs that can interact with insulin.
- Monitor patient's glycosylated hemoglobin level regularly.
- Monitor urine ketone level when glucose level is elevated.
- Be alert for adverse reactions and drug interactions.
- Monitor injection sites for local reactions.
- Evaluate patient's and family's knowledge of drug therapy.

Nursing diagnoses

- Ineffective health maintenance related to hyperglycemia
- Risk for injury related to drug-induced hypoglycemia
- Deficient knowledge related to drug therapy

Planning and implementation

ALERT: Regular insulin is used in patients with circulatory collapse, diabetic ketoacidosis, or hyperkalemia. Don't use regular insulin concentrated (500 units/ml) I.V. Don't use intermediate- or long-acting insulins for coma or other emergency that needs rapid drug action.

ALERT: Dosage is always expressed in USP units. Use only syringes calibrated for particular concentration of insulin given. U-500 insulin must be given with U-100 syringe because no syringes are made for this strength.

- Insulin resistance may develop and large insulin doses are needed to control symptoms of diabetes in these patients. U-500 insulin is available as Regular (Concentrated) Iletin II for such patients. Although not normally stocked in every pharmacy, it's readily available. Give hospital pharmacy sufficient notice before needing to refill in-house prescription. Never store U-500 insulin in same area with other insulin preparations because of danger of severe overdose if given accidentally to other patients.
- To mix insulin suspension, swirl vial gently or rotate between palms or between palm and thigh. Don't shake vigorously because doing so causes bubbling and air in syringe.
- Humalog insulin has a rapid onset of action and should be given within 15 minutes before meals.
- Lente, semilente, and ultralente insulins may be mixed in any proportion.
- Regular insulin may be mixed with NPH or lente insulins in any proportion.
- Switching from separate injections to prepared mixture may alter patient response. Whenever NPH or lente is mixed with regular insulin in same syringe, give immediately to avoid loss of potency.
- Don't use insulin that has changed color or become clumped or granular.
- Check expiration date on vial before using.
- **I.V. use:** Use only regular insulin. Inject directly at ordered rate into vein, through intermittent infusion device, or into port close to I.V. access site. Intermittent infusion isn't recommended. If given by continuous infusion, infuse drug diluted in normal saline solution at prescribed rate.
- **S.C. use:** Usual route is S.C. Pinch fold of skin with fingers starting at least 3 inches apart, and insert needle at 45- to 90-degree angle.

– Press but don't rub site after injection. Rotate and chart injection sites to avoid overuse of one area. Diabetic patients may achieve better control if injection sites are rotated within same anatomic region.

- Ketosis-prone type 1, severely ill, and newly diagnosed diabetic patients with very high glucose levels may require hospitalization and I.V. treatment with regular fast-acting insulin.
- Store drug in cool area. Refrigeration is desirable but not essential except for concentrated regular insulin.
- Notify prescriber of sudden changes in glucose levels, dangerously high or low levels, or ketosis.
- Be prepared to provide supportive measures if patient develops diabetic ketoacidosis or hyperglycemic hyperosmolar nonketotic coma.
- Treat hypoglycemic reaction with oral form of rapid-acting glucose if patient can swallow or with glucagon or I.V. glucose if patient can't be roused. Follow with complex carbohydrate snack when patient is awake, and determine cause of reaction.
- Make sure patient is following appropriate diet and exercise programs. Expect to adjust insulin dosage when other aspects of regimen are altered.
- Discuss with prescriber how to deal with noncompliance.
- Treat lipoatrophy or lipohypertrophy according to prescribed protocol.

Patient teaching

- Tell patient that insulin relieves symptoms but doesn't cure disease.
- Inform patient about nature of disease; importance of following therapeutic regimen; adherence to specific diet, weight reduction, exercise, and personal hygiene programs; and ways of avoiding infection. Review timing of injections and eating, and explain that meals must not be skipped.
- Stress that accuracy of measurement is very important, especially with concentrated regular insulin. Aids, such as magnifying sleeve or dose magnifier, may improve accuracy. Instruct patient and family how to measure and give insulin.
- Advise patient not to alter order of mixing insulins or change model or brand of syringe or needle.

• Tell patient that glucose monitoring and urine ketone tests are essential guides to dosage and success of therapy. Stress the importance of recognizing hypoglycemic symptoms because insulin-induced hypoglycemia is hazardous and may cause brain damage if prolonged; most adverse effects are self-limiting and temporary.
• Teach patient about proper use of equipment for monitoring glucose level.
• Instruct patient to avoid alcohol consumption during drug therapy.
• Advise patient not to smoke within 30 minutes after insulin injection. Smoking decreases absorption.
• Tell patient that marijuana use may increase insulin requirements.
• Advise patient to wear or carry medical identification at all times, to carry ample insulin supply and syringes on trips, to have carbohydrates (lump of sugar or candy) on hand for emergencies, and to note time-zone changes for dose scheduling when traveling.

☑ Evaluation
• Patient's glucose level is normal.
• Patient sustains no injury from drug-induced hypoglycemia.
• Patient and family state understanding of drug therapy.

interferon alfa-2a, recombinant (rIFN-A)

(in-ter-FEER-on AL-fuh too-ay ree-COM-bih-nent)
Roferon-A

interferon alfa-2b, recombinant (IFN-alpha 2)

Intron-A

Pharmacologic class: antiviral
Therapeutic class: antineoplastic
Pregnancy risk category: C

Indications and dosages

▶ **Hairy cell leukemia.** ***alfa-2a.*** *Adults:* For induction, 3 million IU S.C. or I.M. daily for 16 to 24 weeks. For maintenance, 3 million IU S.C. or I.M. three times weekly.
alfa-2b. *Adults:* For induction and maintenance, 2 million IU/m² I.M. or S.C. three times weekly.
▶ **Condylomata acuminata.** ***alfa-2b.*** *Adults:* 1 million IU per lesion, intralesionally, three times weekly for 3 weeks.
▶ **Kaposi's sarcoma.** ***alfa-2a.*** *Adults:* For induction, 36 million IU S.C. or I.M. daily for 10 to 12 weeks; for maintenance, 36 million IU three times weekly. Doses may begin at 3 million IU and escalate every 3 days until patient is given 36 million IU daily, in order to decrease toxicity.
alfa-2b. *Adults:* 30 million IU/m² S.C. or I.M. three times weekly. Maintain dose unless disease progresses rapidly or intolerance occurs.
▶ **Chronic hepatitis C.** ***alfa-2a.*** *Adults:* 3 million IU three times weekly S.C. or I.M. for 12 months (48 to 52 weeks). Alternatively, induction dose of 6 million IU three times weekly for the first 3 months (12 weeks) followed by 3 million IU three times weekly for 9 months (36 weeks). If no response after 3 months, discontinue therapy. Re-treatment with either 3 or 6 million IU three times weekly for 6 to 12 months may be considered.
alfa-2b. *Adults:* 3 million IU S.C. or I.M. three times weekly. In patients tolerating therapy with normalization of ALT at 16 weeks of treatment, extend therapy to 18 to 24 months. If no normalization of ALT at 16 weeks of treatment, consider discontinuing therapy.
▶ **Chronic hepatitis B.** ***alfa-2b.*** *Adults:* 30 to 35 million IU S.C. or I.M. weekly either as 5 million IU daily or 10 million IU three times weekly for 16 weeks.
Children ages 1 to 17: 3 million IU/m² S.C. three times weekly for 1 week, then escalate dose to 6 million IU/m² S.C. three times weekly (up to 10 million IU/m² S.C. three times weekly) for 16 to 24 weeks.
▶ **Chronic myelogenous leukemia.** ***alfa-2a.*** *Adults:* 9 million IU daily I.M or S.C. An escalating dosing regimen in which daily doses of 3 million and 6 million IU are given over 3 days, followed by 9 million IU daily for remainder of therapy, may produce increased short-term tolerance.
Children: 2.5 to 5 million IU/m² I.M. daily.
▶ **Malignant melanoma.** ***alfa-2b.*** *Adults:* 20 million IU/m² daily given as I.V. infusion 5 days in a row for 4 weeks. For maintenance

therapy, 10 million IU/m² S.C. three times weekly for 48 weeks. If adverse effects occur, discontinue therapy until they abate and then resume therapy at 50% of the previous dose. If intolerance persists, discontinue therapy.

▶ **Initial treatment of clinically aggressive follicular non-Hodgkin's lymphoma in conjunction with anthracycline-containing combination chemotherapy.** ***alfa-2b.*** *Adults:* 5 million IU S.C. three times weekly for up to 18 months.

▶ **Renal cell carcinoma‡.** *Adults:* 5 to 20 million IU daily or three times weekly.

Contraindications and precautions

• Contraindicated in patients hypersensitive to drug or to mouse immunoglobulin.
• Use cautiously in patients with severe hepatic or renal function impairment, seizure disorders, compromised CNS function, cardiac disease, or myelosuppression.
Lifespan: In pregnant women, use cautiously. In breast-feeding women, drug isn't recommended. In children, safety of drug hasn't been established.

Adverse reactions

CNS: *dizziness,* confusion, paresthesia, numbness, lethargy, depression, nervousness, difficulty in thinking or concentrating, insomnia, sedation, apathy, anxiety, irritability, syncope, fatigue, vertigo, gait disturbances, poor coordination.
CV: hypotension, chest pain, ***arrhythmias,*** palpitations, ***heart failure,*** hypertension, edema, flushing, ***MI.***
EENT: excessive salivation, visual disturbances, dry or inflamed oropharynx, rhinorrhea, sinusitis, conjunctivitis, earache, eye irritation, rhinitis.
GI: *anorexia, nausea, diarrhea,* vomiting, abdominal fullness, abdominal pain, flatulence, constipation, hypermotility, gastric distress, dysgeusia.
GU: transient impotence.
Hematologic: *anemia,* ***leukopenia, neutropenia, mild thrombocytopenia.***
Hepatic: ***hepatitis.***
Respiratory: coughing, dyspnea, tachypnea, ***cyanosis.***
Skin: *rash,* dryness, *pruritus,* partial alopecia, diaphoresis, urticaria.
Other: flulike syndrome (fever, fatigue, myalgia, headache, chills, arthralgia), hot flushes.

Interactions

Drug-drug. *Aminophylline, theophylline:* May reduce theophylline clearance. Monitor serum levels.
Cardiotoxic, hematotoxic, or neurotoxic drugs: Effects of previously or concurrently administered drugs may be increased by interferons. Monitor patient closely.
CNS depressants: May enhance CNS effects. Avoid using together.
Interleukin-2: Increases risk of renal failure from interleukin-2. Monitor patient closely.
Live-virus vaccines: Increases risk of adverse reactions and decreased antibody response. Don't use together.
Zidovudine: Possible synergistic adverse effects between alfa-2b and zidovudine. Carefully monitor WBC count.
Drug-lifestyle. *Alcohol use:* Increases risk of GI bleeding. Discourage using together.

Effects on lab test results

• May increase calcium, phosphate, AST, ALT, alkaline phosphatase, LDH, and fasting glucose levels.
• May increase PT, INR, and PTT. May decrease hemoglobin, hematocrit, and WBC, neutrophil, and platelet counts.

Pharmacokinetics

Absorption: More than 80% absorbed after I.M. or S.C. injection.
Distribution: Not applicable.
Metabolism: Drug appears to be metabolized in liver and kidney.
Excretion: Reabsorbed from glomerular filtrate with minor biliary elimination.

Route	Onset	Peak	Duration
I.M.	Unknown	3.8 hr	Unknown
S.C.	Unknown	7.3 hr	Unknown
Intralesional	Unknown	Unknown	Unknown

Pharmacodynamics

Chemical effect: Unknown; appears to involve direct antiproliferative action against tumor cells or viral cells to inhibit replication and modulation of host immune response by enhancing phagocytic activity of macrophages

and by augmenting specific cytotoxicity of lymphocytes for target cells.
Therapeutic effect: Inhibits growth of certain tumor cells and viral cells.

Available forms

alfa-2a
Powder for injection with diluent: 18 million IU/multidose vial
Prefilled syringes: 6 million IU/0.5 ml, 9 million IU/0.5 ml
alfa-2b
Powder for injection with diluent: 3 million IU/vial; 5 million IU/vial; 10 million IU/vial; 18 million IU/multidose vial; 25 million IU/vial; 50 million IU/vial
Solution for injection: 3 million IU/vial or syringe, 5 million IU/vial or syringe, 10 million IU/vial, 18 million IU/multidose vial, 25 million IU/vial
Solution for injection: 3 million IU/vial, 6 million IU/vial, 9 million IU/vial, 9 million IU/multidose vial, 18 million IU/multidose vial, 36 million IU/multidose vial

NURSING PROCESS

Assessment

- Assess patient's condition before therapy and regularly thereafter.
- Obtain allergy history. Drug contains phenol as preservative and serum albumin as stabilizer.
- At beginning of therapy, assess for flulike symptoms, which tend to diminish with continued therapy.
- Alpha interferons may cause or aggravate fatal or life-threatening neuropsychiatric, autoimmune, ischemic, and infectious disorders. Monitor patients closely with periodic clinical and laboratory evaluations. Patients with persistently severe or worsening signs or symptoms of these conditions should be withdrawn from therapy. In many but not all cases these disorders resolve after stopping therapy.
- Monitor blood studies. Any effects are dose-related and reversible. Recovery occurs within several days or weeks after withdrawal.
- Be alert for adverse reactions and drug interactions.
- Evaluate patient's and family's knowledge of drug therapy.

Nursing diagnoses

- Ineffective health maintenance related to underlying condition
- Risk for injury related to drug-induced adverse CNS reactions
- Deficient knowledge related to drug therapy

Planning and implementation

- Premedicate patient with acetaminophen to minimize flulike symptoms.
- Give drug at bedtime to minimize daytime drowsiness.
- Make sure patient is well hydrated, especially during initial stages of treatment.

ALERT: Different brands of interferon may not be equivalent and may require different dosages.

- **I.M. use:** Follow normal protocol.
- **S.C. use:** Use S.C. administration route in patients whose platelet count is below 50,000/mm^3.
- **Intralesional use:** When giving interferon alfa-2b for condylomata acuminata, use only 10 million-IU vial because dilution of other strengths is needed for intralesional use results in hypertonic solution. Don't reconstitute 10-million-IU vial with more than 1 ml of diluent. Use tuberculin or similar syringe and 25G to 30G needle. Don't inject too deeply beneath lesion or too superficially. As many as five lesions can be treated at one time. To ease discomfort, give drug in evening with acetaminophen.
- Refrigerate drug.
- Notify prescriber of severe adverse reactions, which may require dosage reduction or discontinuation.
- Using drug with blood dyscrasia-causing drugs, bone marrow suppressants, or radiation therapy may increase bone marrow suppression. Dosage reduction may be needed.

Patient teaching

- Advise patient that laboratory tests will be performed before and periodically during therapy. Tests include CBC with differential, platelet count, blood chemistry and electrolyte studies, liver function tests, and, if patient has cardiac disorder or advanced stages of cancer, ECGs.
- Instruct patient in proper oral hygiene during treatment because bone-marrow–suppressant

effects of interferon may lead to microbial infection, delayed healing, and gingival bleeding. This drug also may decrease salivary flow.
• Emphasize need to follow prescriber's instructions about taking and recording temperature. Explain how and when to take acetaminophen.
• Advise patient to check with prescriber for instructions after missing dose.
• Tell patient that drug may cause temporary hair loss; explain that it should grow back when therapy ends.
• Teach patient how to prepare and give drug and how to dispose of used needles, syringes, containers, and unused drug. Give him a copy of information for patients included with product, and make sure he understands it. Also provide information on drug stability.
• Warn patient not to receive any immunization without prescriber's approval and to avoid contact with people who have taken oral polio vaccine. Use with live-virus vaccine may potentiate replication of vaccine virus, increase adverse reactions, and decrease patient's antibody response. Patient is at increased risk for infection during therapy.
• Instruct patient to avoid alcohol during drug therapy.
• Advise patient to report signs of depression.

Evaluation
• Patient shows improved health.
• Patient sustains no injury from adverse CNS reactions.
• Patient and family state understanding of drug therapy.

interferon beta-1b, recombinant
(in-ter-FEER-on BAY-tuh wun bee ree-COM-bih-nent)
Betaseron

Pharmacologic class: biological response modifier
Therapeutic class: antiviral, immunoregulator
Pregnancy risk category: C

Indications and dosages
▶ **To reduce frequency of exacerbations in patients with relapsing-remitting multiple sclerosis.** *Adults:* 0.25 mg S.C. every other day.

Contraindications and precautions
• Contraindicated in patients hypersensitive to interferon beta or human albumin.
Lifespan: In pregnant or breast-feeding women, drug isn't recommended. It is unknown whether drug appears in breast milk. In women of childbearing age, use cautiously. In children, safety of drug hasn't been established.

Adverse reactions
CNS: depression, anxiety, emotional lability, depersonalization, *malaise,* ***suicidal tendencies,*** confusion, somnolence, ***seizures,*** headache, dizziness.
CV: ***hemorrhage.***
EENT: laryngitis.
GI: *nausea, diarrhea, constipation.*
GU: *menstrual disorders (bleeding or spotting, early or delayed menses, decreased days of menstrual flow, menorrhagia).*
Hematologic: ***leukopenia, neutropenia.***
Respiratory: dyspnea.
Other: *flulike symptoms (fever, chills, myalgia, diaphoresis);* breast pain; *pelvic pain; lymphadenopathy;* hypersensitivity reaction, *inflammation, pain, and necrosis* at injection site.

Interactions
None significant.

Effects on lab test results
• May increase ALT and bilirubin levels.
• May decrease WBC and neutrophil counts.

Pharmacokinetics
Absorption: Unknown.
Distribution: Unknown.
Metabolism: Unknown.
Excretion: Unknown.

Route	Onset	Peak	Duration
S.C.	Unknown	1-8 hr	Unknown

Pharmacodynamics
Chemical effect: Attaches to membrane receptors and causes cellular changes, including increased protein synthesis.

Therapeutic effect: Decreases exacerbations in multiple sclerosis.

Available forms

Powder for injection: 0.3 mg

NURSING PROCESS

Assessment

- Obtain assessment of patient's underlying condition before therapy.
- Monitor frequency of exacerbations after drug therapy begins.
- Monitor WBC counts, platelet counts, and blood chemistries, including liver function tests.
- Be alert for adverse reactions.
- Monitor patient for depression and suicidal ideation.
- Evaluate patient's and family's knowledge of drug therapy.

Nursing diagnoses

- Ineffective health maintenance related to exacerbations of multiple sclerosis
- Risk for injury related to drug-induced adverse CNS reactions
- Deficient knowledge related to drug therapy

Planning and implementation

- Premedicate patient with acetaminophen to minimize flulike symptoms.
- To reconstitute, inject 1.2 ml of supplied diluent (0.54% saline solution for injection) into vial and gently swirl to dissolve drug. Don't shake. Reconstituted solution will contain 8 million units (0.25 mg)/ml. Discard vials that contain particles or discolored solution.
- Inject immediately after preparation.
- Store at room temperature. Once reconstituted, may refrigerate for up to 3 hours before use.
- Rotate injection sites to minimize local reactions.

Patient teaching

- Warn woman of childbearing age about dangers to fetus. Tell her to notify prescriber promptly if she becomes pregnant during therapy.
- Teach patient how to give S.C. injections, including solution preparation, use of aseptic technique, rotation of injection sites, and equipment disposal. Periodically reevaluate patient's technique.
- Advise patient to take drug at bedtime to minimize mild flulike symptoms.
- Advise patient to report thoughts of depression or suicidal ideation.

Evaluation

- Patient exhibits decreased frequency of exacerbations.
- Patient sustains no injury from adverse CNS reactions.
- Patient and family state understanding of drug therapy.

interferon gamma-1b

(in-ter-FEER-on GAH-muh wun bee)
Actimmune

Pharmacologic class: biological response modifier
Therapeutic class: antineoplastic
Pregnancy risk category: C

Indications and dosages

▶ **To delay disease progression in patients with severe, malignant osteopetrosis; chronic granulomatous disease.**
Patients with body surface area greater than 0.5 m²: 50 mcg/m² (1 million IU/m²) S.C. three times weekly in the deltoid or anterior thigh.
Patients with body surface area 0.5 m² or less: 1.5 mcg/kg/dose S.C. 3 times weekly in the deltoid or anterior thigh.

Contraindications and precautions

- Contraindicated in patients hypersensitive to drug or to genetically engineered products derived from *Escherichia coli.*
- Use cautiously in patients with cardiac disease, compromised CNS function, or seizure disorders.

Lifespan: In pregnant women, use cautiously. In breast-feeding women, use isn't recommended. In children younger than age 18, safety of drug hasn't been established.

Adverse reactions

CNS: *fatigue, decreased mental status, gait disturbance.*
GI: *nausea, vomiting, diarrhea.*
Hematologic: ***neutropenia, thrombocytopenia.***
Skin: erythema and tenderness at injection site, rash.
Other: flulike syndrome.

Interactions

Drug-drug. *Myelosuppressive drugs:* Possible additive myelosuppression. Monitor patient closely.
Zidovudine: Increases plasma zidovudine levels. Adjust dosages as directed.

Effects on lab test results

- May increase liver enzyme levels.
- May decrease neutrophil and platelet counts.

Pharmacokinetics

Absorption: About 90% absorbed after S.C. administration.
Distribution: Unknown.
Metabolism: Unknown.
Excretion: Unknown. *Half-life:* 6 hours.

Route	Onset	Peak	Duration
S.C.	Unknown	≤ 7 hr	Unknown

Pharmacodynamics

Chemical effect: Acts as interleukin-type lymphokine. Drug has potent phagocyte-activating properties and enhances oxidative metabolism of tissue macrophages.
Therapeutic effect: Promotes phagocyte activity.

Available forms

Injection: 100 mcg (2 million IU)/0.5-ml vial

NURSING PROCESS

Assessment

- Assess patient's condition before therapy and regularly thereafter.
- Be alert for adverse reactions and drug interactions. Symptoms of flulike syndrome include headache, fever, chills, myalgia, and arthralgia.
- Monitor patient's hydration status if adverse GI reactions occur.
- Evaluate patient's and family's knowledge of drug therapy.

Nursing diagnoses

- Ineffective health maintenance related to underlying condition
- Risk for fluid volume deficit related to adverse GI reactions
- Deficient knowledge related to drug therapy

Planning and implementation

- Premedicate with acetaminophen to minimize symptoms at beginning of therapy. Flulike symptoms tend to diminish with continued therapy.
- Discard unused portion. Each vial is for single-dose use and doesn't contain preservative.
- Give drug at bedtime to reduce discomfort from flulike symptoms.
- Refrigerate drug immediately. Vials must be stored at 36° to 46° F (2° to 8° C); don't freeze. Don't shake vial; avoid excessive agitation. Discard vials that have been left at room temperature for more than 12 hours.

Patient teaching

- Teach patient how to give drug and how to dispose of used needles, syringes, containers, and unused drug. Give him a copy of patient information included with product, and make sure he understands it.
- Instruct patient to notify prescriber if adverse reactions occur.

Evaluation

- Patient responds well to drug.
- Patient maintains adequate hydration.
- Patient and family state understanding of drug therapy.

ipecac syrup
(IH-pih-kak SIH-rup)

Pharmacologic class: alkaloid emetic
Therapeutic class: emetic
Pregnancy risk category: C

Indications and dosages

▶ **To induce vomiting in poisoning.** *Adults and children age 12 and older:* 30 ml P.O., followed by 200 to 300 ml of water.
Children ages 1 to 11: 15 ml P.O., followed by about 200 ml of water or milk.
Children younger than age 1 year: 5 ml P.O., followed by 100 to 200 ml of water or milk. If needed, repeat dose once after 20 minutes.

Contraindications and precautions

- Contraindicated in semicomatose or unconscious patients and in those with severe inebriation, seizures, shock, or loss of gag reflex.
- Don't use if patient has ingested strychnine, corrosives (such as alkalies and strong acids), or petroleum distillates.

Lifespan: In pregnant patients, use only if clearly needed. In breast-feeding women, use cautiously.

Adverse reactions

CNS: depression.
CV: ***arrhythmias, bradycardia,*** hypotension, atrial fibrillation, ***fatal myocarditis*** (after excessive dose).
GI: diarrhea.

Interactions

Drug-drug. *Activated charcoal:* Neutralizes emetic effect. Don't give together; may give activated charcoal after patient vomits.

Effects on lab test results

None reported.

Pharmacokinetics

Absorption: Absorbed in significant amounts mainly when it doesn't produce emesis.
Distribution: Unknown.
Metabolism: Unknown.
Excretion: Slowly excreted in urine.

Route	Onset	Peak	Duration
P.O.	20-30 min	Unknown	20-25 min

Pharmacodynamics

Chemical effect: Acts locally on gastric mucosa and centrally on the chemoreceptor trigger zone.
Therapeutic effect: Induces vomiting.

Available forms

Syrup: 70 mg powdered ipecac/ml (contains glycerin 10% and alcohol 1% to 2.5%)†*

NURSING PROCESS

Assessment

- Assess patient to determine substance ingested before starting therapy.
- Monitor effectiveness by observing patient for vomiting. Ipecac syrup usually induces vomiting in 20 to 30 minutes. In antiemetic toxicity, ipecac syrup is usually effective if less than 1 hour has passed since ingestion of antiemetic.
- No systemic toxicity occurs with doses of 30 ml or less.
- Monitor blood pressure, ECG, and fluid and electrolyte balance.
- Be alert for adverse reactions and drug interactions.
- Evaluate patient's and family's knowledge of drug therapy.

Nursing diagnoses

- Ineffective health maintenance related to ingestion of poisonous substance
- Decreased cardiac output related to adverse cardiac reactions
- Deficient knowledge related to drug therapy

Planning and implementation

ALERT: Unless advised otherwise by poison control center, don't give ipecac syrup after patient ingests petroleum distillates (for example, kerosene, gasoline) or volatile oils; retching and vomiting may cause aspiration and lead to bronchospasm, pulmonary edema, or aspiration pneumonitis. Vegetable oil will delay absorption of these substances. Don't give ipecac syrup after patient ingests caustic substances, such as lye; additional injury to esophagus and mediastinum can occur.

ALERT: Clearly indicate ipecac *syrup,* not single word "ipecac," to avoid confusion with fluid extract, which is 14 times more concentrated and, if inadvertently used instead of syrup, may cause death.

- Give 200 to 300 ml of water after dose.
- If two doses don't induce vomiting, be prepared to perform gastric lavage.

• Position patient on side to prevent aspiration of vomitus. Have airway and suction equipment nearby.

Patient teaching

• Recommend that parents keep 1 oz (30 ml) of syrup available in home for use in emergency when child reaches age 1.
• Advise parent or guardian to consult prescriber or poison control center before giving to child.

Evaluation

• Patient regains health after elimination of poisonous substance.
• Patient's cardiac output remains adequate.
• Patient and family state understanding of drug therapy.

ipratropium bromide

(ip-ruh-TROH-pee-um BROH-mighd)

Atrovent

Pharmacologic class: anticholinergic
Therapeutic class: bronchodilator
Pregnancy risk category: B

Indications and dosages

▶ **Bronchospasm caused by COPD.** *Adults and children older than age 12:* 1 to 2 inhalations q.i.d. Additional inhalations may be needed. However, total inhalations shouldn't exceed 12 in 24 hours. Or, use inhalation solution, giving up to 500 mcg q 6 to 8 hours via oral nebulizer.

▶ **Rhinorrhea linked to allergic and nonallergic perennial rhinitis (0.03% nasal spray).** *Adults and children age 6 and older:* 2 sprays (42 mcg) in each nostril b.i.d. or t.i.d.

▶ **Rhinorrhea caused by the common cold (0.06% nasal spray).** *Adults and children age 12 and over:* 2 sprays (84 mcg) per nostril t.i.d. or q.i.d.
Children ages 5 to 11: 2 sprays (84 mcg) per nostril t.i.d.

▶ **Rhinorrhea associated with seasonal allergic rhinitis (0.06% nasal spray).** *Adults and children age 5 and older:* 2 sprays (84 mcg) per nostril q.i.d.

Contraindications and precautions

ALERT: Contraindicated in patients hypersensitive to drug or to atropine or its derivatives and in those hypersensitive to soya lecithin or related food products such as soybeans and peanuts.
• Use cautiously in patients with angle-closure glaucoma, prostatic hyperplasia, or bladder-neck obstruction.
• Safety and efficacy of use beyond 4 days for rhinorrhea from the common cold haven't been established.
Lifespan: In pregnant or breast-feeding patients, use cautiously. In children younger than age 12, safety of inhaler or nebulizer hasn't been established.

Adverse reactions

CNS: nervousness, dizziness, headache.
CV: palpitations.
EENT: blurred vision, epistaxis.
GI: nausea, GI distress, dry mouth.
Respiratory: cough, *upper respiratory tract infection, bronchitis,* ***bronchospasm.***
Skin: rash.

Interactions

Drug-drug. *Anticholinergics:* Increases anticholinergic effects. Avoid using together.
Cromolyn sodium: Will form precipitate if mixed in same nebulizer. Don't use together.
Drug-herb. *Jaborandi tree, pill-bearing spurge:* Decreases drug effects. Use cautiously.

Effects on lab test results

None reported.

Pharmacokinetics

Absorption: Not readily absorbed into systemic circulation.
Distribution: Not applicable.
Metabolism: Small amount that is absorbed is metabolized in liver.
Excretion: Absorbed drug excreted in urine and bile; remainder excreted unchanged in feces. *Half-life:* About 2 hours.

Route	Onset	Peak	Duration
Inhalation	5-15 min	1-2 hr	3-6 hr

Pharmacodynamics

Chemical effect: Inhibits vagally mediated reflexes by antagonizing acetylcholine.

Therapeutic effect: Relieves bronchospasms and symptoms of seasonal allergic rhinitis.

Available forms

Inhaler: each metered dose supplies 18 mcg
Nasal spray: 0.03% (21 mcg), 0.06% (42 mcg)
Solution for inhalation: 0.02% (500 mcg vial)
Solution for nebulizer: 0.025% (250 mcg/ml) ◇ 0.02% (200 mcg/ml)

NURSING PROCESS

Assessment
- Assess patient's condition before and after drug administration; monitor peak expiratory flow.
- Be alert for adverse reactions and drug interactions.
- Evaluate patient's and family's knowledge of drug therapy.

Nursing diagnoses
- Ineffective breathing pattern related to patient's underlying condition
- Acute pain related to drug-induced headache
- Deficient knowledge related to drug therapy

Planning and implementation
ALERT: Don't confuse Atrovent with Alupent.
- Drug isn't effective for treating acute episodes of bronchospasm when rapid response is needed.
- Total inhalations shouldn't exceed 12 in 24 hours, and total nasal sprays shouldn't exceed eight in each nostril in 24 hours.
- If more than one inhalation is ordered, 2 minutes should elapse between inhalations. If more than one type of inhalant is ordered, always give bronchodilator first and wait 5 minutes before giving the other.
- Give drug on time to ensure maximal effect.
- Notify prescriber if drug fails to relieve bronchospasms.

Patient teaching
- Warn patient that drug isn't effective for treating acute episodes of bronchospasm where rapid response is needed.
- Give patient these instructions for using metered-dose inhaler: Clear nasal passages and throat. Breathe out, expelling as much air from lungs as possible. Place mouthpiece well into mouth and inhale deeply as you release dose from inhaler. Hold breath for several seconds, remove mouthpiece, and exhale slowly.
- Tell patient to avoid accidentally spraying into eyes. Temporary blurring of vision may result.
- If more than one inhalation is ordered, tell patient to wait at least 2 minutes before repeating procedure.
- If patient also uses a corticosteroid inhaler, tell him to use ipratropium first, and then wait about 5 minutes before using the corticosteroid. This process allows bronchodilator to open air passages for maximum effectiveness of the corticosteroid.
- Tell patient to take a missed dose as soon as remembered, unless it's almost time for next dose. In that case, tell him to skip the missed dose. Advise against doubling the dose.

Evaluation
- Patient's bronchospasms are relieved.
- Patient does not suffer from any drug-induced headaches.
- Patient and family state understanding of drug therapy.

irbesartan
(ir-buh-SAR-tun)
Avapro

Pharmacologic class: angiotensin II receptor antagonist
Therapeutic class: antihypertensive
Pregnancy risk category: C (D in second and third trimesters)

Indications and dosages

▶ **Hypertension.** *Adults and children age 13 and older:* Initially, 150 mg P.O. daily, increased to a maximum of 300 mg daily, if needed.
Children ages 6 to 12 years: Initially, 75 mg P.O. daily, increased to a maximum of 150 mg daily, if necessary.

▶ **Nephropathy in type 2 diabetic patients.** *Adults:* 300 mg P.O. daily.

*Liquid form contains alcohol. **May contain tartrazine. ◆ Canada ◇ Australia †OTC ‡Off-label use

Contraindications and precautions

- Contraindicated in patients hypersensitive to drug or its components.
- Use cautiously in volume- or salt-depleted patients and in patients with impaired renal function or renal artery stenosis.

Lifespan: In pregnant women, drug is contraindicated. In children younger than age 6, safety hasn't been established.

Adverse reactions

CNS: fatigue, anxiety, dizziness, headache.
CV: chest pain, edema, tachycardia.
EENT: pharyngitis, rhinitis, sinus abnormality.
GI: diarrhea, dyspepsia, abdominal pain, nausea, vomiting.
GU: urinary tract infection.
Musculoskeletal: musculoskeletal trauma or pain.
Respiratory: upper respiratory tract infection.
Skin: rash.

Interactions

None reported.

Effects on lab test results

None reported.

Pharmacokinetics

Absorption: Rapid and complete with an average absolute bioavailability of 60% to 80%.
Distribution: Widely distributed into body tissues; 90% bound to plasma proteins.
Metabolism: Metabolized primarily by conjugation and oxidation.
Excretion: Excreted by biliary and renal routes. About 20% is recovered in urine and the rest in feces. *Half-life:* 11 to 15 hours.

Route	Onset	Peak	Duration
P.O.	Unknown	1.5-2 hr	24 hr

Pharmacodynamics

Chemical effect: Inhibits the vasoconstricting and aldosterone-secreting effects of angiotensin II by selectively blocking binding of angiotensin II to receptor sites in many tissues.
Therapeutic effect: Lowers blood pressure.

Available forms

Tablets: 75 mg, 150 mg, 300 mg

NURSING PROCESS

Assessment

- Monitor patient's blood pressure regularly. Dizziness and orthstatic hypotension may occur more frequently in patients with type 2 diabetes mellitus and renal disease
- Monitor patient's electrolytes, and assess patient for volume or salt depletion before starting drug therapy.
- Make sure woman of childbearing age is using effective birth control before starting this drug because of danger to fetus.
- Evaluate patient's and family's knowledge of drug therapy.

Nursing diagnoses

- Risk for hypotension in volume- or salt-depleted patients
- Risk of injury related to the presence of hypertension
- Deficient knowledge related to drug therapy

Planning and implementation

- Drug may be given with a diuretic or other antihypertensive if needed to control blood pressure.
- If patient becomes hypotensive, place in a supine position and give an I.V. infusion of normal saline solution.

Patient teaching

- Warn woman of childbearing age about consequences of exposing fetus to drug. Tell her to call prescriber immediately if pregnancy is suspected.
- Tell patient that drug may be taken once daily with or without food.
- Instruct patient to avoid driving and hazardous activities until CNS effects of drug are known.

Evaluation

- Patient doesn't experience hypotension as a result of volume or salt depletion.
- Patient's blood pressure remains within normal limits and drug therapy doesn't cause injury.
- Patient and family state understanding of drug therapy.

iron dextran

(IGH-ern DEKS-tran)

DexFerrum, Dexiron ♦, InFeD

Pharmacologic class: parenteral iron supplement
Therapeutic class: hematinic
Pregnancy risk category: C

Indications and dosages

▶ **Iron-deficiency anemia.** Dosage (in ml) is based on patient's weight and hemoglobin level using the following formula:

$0.0476 \times$ weight (kg) $\times$ [Hemoglobin$_N$ − Hemoglobin$_O$] + 1 ml/5 kg of weight (max. 14 ml)

One ml iron dextran provides 50 mg elemental iron.

Adults and children: For I.M. use, 0.5-ml test dose injected by Z-track method. If no reactions occur, maximum daily doses are 0.5 ml (25 mg) for infants weighing less than 5 kg (11 lb), 1 ml (50 mg) for children weighing less than 10 kg (22 lb), and 2 ml (100 mg) for heavier children and adults. For I.V. use, 0.5-ml test dose injected over 30 seconds. If no reactions occur in 1 hour, remainder of therapeutic dose is given I.V. Therapeutic dose repeated I.V. daily. Maximum single dose is 100 mg. Give slowly (1 ml/minute).

Contraindications and precautions

- Contraindicated in patients hypersensitive to drug and in those with acute infectious renal disease or anemia disorders (except iron-deficiency anemia).
- Use with extreme caution in patients who have serious hepatic impairment, rheumatoid arthritis, and other inflammatory diseases.
- Use cautiously in patients with history of significant allergies or asthma.

Lifespan: In pregnant women, use only when the potential benefits to the mother outweigh the potential risks to the fetus. In breast-feeding women, use cautiously. In children younger than age 4 months, use is contraindicated.

Adverse reactions

CNS: headache, transitory paresthesia, arthralgia, myalgia, dizziness, malaise, syncope.
CV: chest pain, chest tightness, ***shock,*** hypertension, ***arrhythmias,*** *hypotensive reaction, peripheral vascular flushing with overly rapid I.V. administration, tachycardia.*
GI: nausea, vomiting, metallic taste, transient loss of taste, abdominal pain, diarrhea.
Respiratory: ***bronchospasm.***
Skin: rash, urticaria, *brown discoloration* at I.M. injection site.
Other: *soreness, inflammation, and local phlebitis* at I.V. injection site; sterile abscess; necrosis; atrophy; fibrosis; ***anaphylaxis;*** delayed sensitivity reactions.

Interactions

None significant.

Effects on lab test results

None reported.

Pharmacokinetics

Absorption: In two stages: 60% after 3 days and up to 90% by 3 weeks. Remainder is absorbed over several months or longer.
Distribution: During first 3 days, local inflammation facilitates passage of drug into lymphatic system; drug is then ingested by macrophages, which enter lymph and blood.
Metabolism: Drug is cleared from plasma by reticuloendothelial cells of liver, spleen, and bone marrow.
Excretion: Trace amounts excreted in urine, bile, and feces. *Half-life:* 6 hours.

Route	Onset	Peak	Duration
I.V., I.M.	72 hr	Unknown	3-4 wk

Pharmacodynamics

Chemical effect: Provides elemental iron, a component of hemoglobin.
Therapeutic effect: Increases level of plasma iron, an essential component of hemoglobin.

Available forms

Injection: 50 mg elemental iron/ml

NURSING PROCESS

Assessment

- Assess patient's iron deficiency before therapy.

• Monitor effectiveness by evaluating hemoglobin, hematocrit, and reticulocyte count, and monitor patient's health status.
• Be alert for adverse reactions and drug interactions.
• Observe patient for delayed reactions (1 to 2 days), which may include arthralgia, backache, chills, dizziness, headache, malaise, fever, myalgia, nausea, and vomiting.
• Evaluate patient's and family's knowledge of drug therapy.

Nursing diagnoses
• Ineffective health maintenance related to iron deficiency
• Risk for injury related to potential drug-induced anaphylaxis
• Deficient knowledge related to drug therapy

Planning and implementation
• Don't give iron dextran with oral iron preparations.
• I.M. or I.V. injections of iron are recommended only for patients for whom oral administration is impossible or ineffective.
ALERT: I.M. or I.V. test dose is required.
• **I.V. use:** Check facility policy before giving I.V.
– Use I.V. when patient has insufficient muscle mass for deep I.M. injection, impaired absorption from muscle as a result of stasis or edema, possibility of uncontrolled I.M. bleeding from trauma (as may occur in hemophilia), or massive and prolonged parenteral therapy (as may be needed in chronic substantial blood loss).
– When I.V. dose is complete, flush vein with 10 ml of normal saline solution. The patient should rest 15 to 30 minutes after I.V. administration.
• **I.M. use:** Use a 19G or 20G needle that is 2 to 3 inches long. Inject drug deep into upper outer quadrant of buttock—never into arm or other exposed area. Use Z-track method to avoid leakage into S.C. tissue and staining of skin.
• Minimize skin staining by using separate needle to withdraw drug from its container.
• Keep epinephrine and resuscitation equipment readily available to treat anaphylaxis.

Patient teaching
• Warn patient to avoid OTC vitamins that contain iron.
• Teach patient to recognize and report symptoms of reaction or toxicity.

Evaluation
• Patient's hemoglobin, hematocrit, and reticulocyte counts are normal.
• Patient doesn't experience anaphylaxis.
• Patient and family state understanding of drug therapy.

iron sucrose injection
(IGH-ern SOO-krohs)
Venofer

Pharmacologic classification: polynuclear iron (III)-hydroxide in sucrose
Therapeutic classification: hematinic
Pregnancy risk category: B

Indications and dosages
▶ **Iron deficiency anemia in patients undergoing long-term hemodialysis who are receiving supplemental erythropoietin therapy.** *Adults:* 100 mg (5 ml) of elemental iron I.V. directly in the dialysis line either by slow injection (1 ml per minute) or by infusion over 15 minutes during the dialysis session, one to three times weekly for a total of 1,000 mg in 10 doses. Repeat, if needed.

Contraindications and precautions
• Contraindicated in patients with evidence of iron overload, patients hypersensitive to drug or any of its inactive components, and patients with anemia not caused by iron deficiency.
Lifespan: In breast-feeding women, use cautiously; it's not known whether drug appears in breast milk. In children, safety and efficacy haven't been established. In elderly patients, dose selection should be conservative; these patients may have decreased hepatic, renal, and cardiac function and other diseases and drug therapies.

Adverse reactions
CNS: fever, headache, asthenia, malaise, dizziness, pain.
CV: *hypotension,* chest pain, hypertension, fluid retention.
GI: nausea, vomiting, diarrhea, abdominal pain.

Musculoskeletal: *leg cramps,* bone and muscle pain.
Respiratory: dyspnea, pneumonia, cough.
Skin: pruritus, application site reaction.
Other: accidental injury.

Interactions

Drug-drug. *Oral iron preparations:* Reduces absorption of these compounds. Avoid using together.

Effects on lab test results

- May increase liver enzyme levels.

Pharmacokinetics

Absorption: Administered I.V.
Distribution: Distributed mainly in blood and somewhat in extravascular fluid. A significant amount of iron is also distributed in the liver, spleen, and bone marrow.
Metabolism: Dissociated by the reticuloendothelial system into iron and sucrose.
Excretion: About 75% of sucrose and 5% of the iron component are eliminated by urinary excretion in 24 hours. *Elimination half-life:* 6 hours.

Route	Onset	Peak	Duration
I.V.	Unknown	Unknown	Variable

Pharmacodynamics

Chemical effect: Dissociated by the reticuloendothelial system into iron and sucrose. The released iron component eventually replenishes depleted body iron stores, resulting in significant increases in iron and ferritin levels and significant decreases in total iron binding capacity.
Therapeutic effect: Increases plasma iron level.

Available forms

Injection: 20 mg/ml of elemental iron

NURSING PROCESS

Assessment

- Assess underlying condition before therapy and reassess regularly throughout therapy.
- Monitor hemoglobin, hematocrit, ferritin level, and transferrin saturation.
- Evaluate patient's and family's knowledge of iron sucrose therapy.

Nursing diagnoses

- Acute pain related to adverse drug effects
- Ineffective health maintenance related to iron deficiency
- Deficient knowledge related to iron sucrose therapy

Planning and implementation

- Monitor patient for symptoms of overdose or too-rapid infusion, which include hypotension, headache, nausea, dizziness, joint aches, paresthesia, abdominal and muscle pain, edema, and CV collapse.
- Observe patient for rare but fatal hypersensitivity reactions characterized by anaphylaxis, loss of consciousness, collapse, hypotension, dyspnea, or seizures.
- For administration by slow injection, administer at 1 ml (20 mg elemental iron) undiluted solution per minute, not exceeding one vial (100 mg elemental iron) per injection.
- For administration by infusion, dilute to a maximum of 100 ml in normal saline solution immediately before infusion, and infuse 100 mg elemental iron over at least 15 minutes. Administering by infusion may reduce the risk of hypotension.
- Transferrin saturation values increase rapidly after I.V. administration of iron sucrose. Obtain iron level values 48 hours after I.V. dosing.
- Withhold dose in patients with evidence of iron overload.
- Don't mix with other drugs or add to parenteral nutrition solutions of I.V. infusion.
- Inspect for particulate matter and discoloration before administration.

Patient teaching

- Instruct patient to notify prescriber if symptoms of overdose occur, such as headache, nausea, dizziness, joint aches, paresthesia, or abdominal and muscle pain.
- Warn patient not to take OTC vitamins containing iron.

Evaluation

- Patient does not experience pain.
- Patient's hemoglobin and hematocrit are normal.
- Patient and family state understanding of iron sucrose therapy.

isoniazid (isonicotinic acid hydride INH)

(igh-soh-NIGH-uh-sid)

Isotamine ♦, Laniazid, Nydrazid**, PMS Isoniazid ♦

Pharmacologic class: isonicotinic acid hydrazine
Therapeutic class: antituberculotic
Pregnancy risk category: C

Indications and dosages

▶ **Actively growing tubercle bacilli.** *Adults:* 5 mg/kg P.O. or I.M. daily in single dose, maximum 300 mg P.O. or I.M. daily, continued for 6 months to 2 years.
Infants and children: 10 mg/kg P.O. or I.M. daily in single dose, maximum 300 mg P.O. or I.M. daily, continued for 18 months to 2 years. Administration with at least one other antituberculotic is recommended.

▶ **Prevention of tubercle bacilli in those closely exposed to tuberculosis or those with positive skin tests whose chest X-rays and bacteriologic studies are consistent with nonprogressive tuberculosis.** *Adults:* 300 mg P.O. daily in single dose, for 6 months to 1 year.
Infants and children: 10 mg/kg P.O. daily in single dose. Maximum 300 mg P.O. daily for 1 year.

Contraindications and precautions

- Contraindicated in patients with acute hepatic disease or isoniazid-related liver damage.
- Use cautiously in patients with chronic non–isoniazid-related liver disease, seizure disorders (especially in those taking phenytoin), severe renal impairment, or chronic alcoholism.

Lifespan: In pregnant or breast-feeding women and in elderly patients, use cautiously.

Adverse reactions

CNS: *peripheral neuropathy* (especially in patients who are malnourished, alcoholic, diabetic, or slow acetylators), usually preceded by paresthesia of hands and feet; psychosis; ***seizures.***
GI: nausea, vomiting, epigastric distress, constipation, dry mouth.
Hematologic: ***agranulocytosis,*** hemolytic anemia, ***aplastic anemia,*** eosinophilia, ***leukopenia, neutropenia, thrombocytopenia, methemoglobinemia,*** pyridoxine-responsive hypochromic anemia.
Hepatic: ***hepatitis*** (occasionally severe and sometimes fatal, especially in elderly patients).
Metabolic: hyperglycemia, metabolic acidosis.
Other: rheumatic syndrome and lupus-like syndrome, hypersensitivity reactions (fever, rash, lymphadenopathy, vasculitis), irritation at I.M. injection site.

Interactions

Drug-drug. *Acetaminophen:* Increases hepatotoxic effects of acetaminophen. Don't give together.
Antacids and laxatives containing aluminum: May decrease rate and amount of isoniazid absorbed. Give isoniazid at least 1 hour before antacid or laxative.
Carbamazepine: Increases risk of isoniazid hepatotoxicity. Use together cautiously.
Carbamazepine, phenytoin: Increases plasma levels of these anticonvulsants. Monitor patient closely.
Corticosteroids: May decrease therapeutic effect of isoniazid. Monitor patient's need for larger isoniazid dose.
Cyclosporine: Possible increased adverse CNS effects of cyclosporine. Monitor patient closely.
Disulfiram: May cause neurologic symptoms, including changes in behavior and coordination. Avoid using together.
Ketoconazole: Decreases ketoconazole levels. Monitor patient closely.
Oral anticoagulants: Possible increased anticoagulant activity. Monitor patient for signs of bleeding.
Rifampin: Increases risk of hepatotoxicity. Monitor patient closely.
Theophylline: Increases theophylline levels. Monitor serum levels closely, and adjust theophylline dosage as directed.
Drug-food. *Foods containing tyramine:* May cause hypertensive crisis. Tell patients to avoid such foods altogether.
Drug-lifestyle. *Alcohol use:* May increase risk of isoniazid-related hepatitis. Discourage using together.

Effects on lab test results

- May increase transaminase, glucose, and bilirubin levels. May decrease calcium and phosphate levels.
- May increase eosinophil count. May decrease hemoglobin, hematocrit, and WBC, granulocyte, neutrophil, and platelet counts.

Pharmacokinetics

Absorption: Complete and rapid after P.O. administration. Also absorbed readily after I.M. injection.
Distribution: Distributed widely into body tissues and fluids.
Metabolism: Metabolized primarily in liver. Rate of metabolism varies individually; fast acetylators metabolize drug five times as rapidly as others. About 50% of blacks and whites are slow acetylators, whereas more than 80% of Chinese, Japanese, and Eskimos are fast acetylators.
Excretion: Excreted primarily in urine; some drug excreted in saliva, sputum, feces, and breast milk. *Half-life:* 1 to 4 hours.

Route	Onset	Peak	Duration
P.O., I.M.	Unknown	1-2 hr	Unknown

Pharmacodynamics

Chemical effect: Appears to inhibit cell wall biosynthesis by interfering with lipid and DNA synthesis.
Therapeutic effect: Kills susceptible bacteria, such as *Mycobacterium tuberculosis, M. bovis,* and some strains of *M. kansasii.*

Available forms

Injection: 100 mg/ml
Oral solution: 50 mg/5 ml
Tablets: 100 mg, 300 mg

NURSING PROCESS

Assessment

- Assess patient's infection before therapy.
- Monitor patient for improvement, and evaluate culture and sensitivity tests.
- Be alert for adverse reactions and drug interactions.
- Monitor hepatic function closely for changes.
- Monitor patient for paresthesia of hands and feet, which usually precedes peripheral neuropathy, especially in patients who are malnourished, alcoholic, diabetic, or slow acetylators.
- Evaluate patient's and family's knowledge of drug therapy.

Nursing diagnoses

- Infection related to presence of susceptible bacteria
- Disturbed sensory perception (tactile) related to drug-induced peripheral neuropathy
- Deficient knowledge related to drug therapy

Planning and implementation

- **P.O. use:** Give drug 1 hour before or 2 hours after meals to avoid decreased absorption.
- **I.M. use:** Follow normal protocol. Switch to P.O. form as soon as possible.
- Always give isoniazid with other antituberculotics to prevent development of resistant organisms.
- Give pyridoxine to prevent peripheral neuropathy, especially in malnourished patients.

Patient teaching

- Tell patient to take drug as prescribed; warn against stopping drug without prescriber's consent.
- Advise patient to take with food if GI irritation occurs.
- Instruct patient to avoid alcohol during drug therapy.
- Instruct patient to avoid certain foods (fish, such as skipjack and tuna, and tyramine-containing products, such as aged cheese, beer, and chocolate) because drug has some MAO inhibitor activity.
- Tell patient to notify prescriber immediately if symptoms of liver impairment occur (loss of appetite, fatigue, malaise, jaundice, dark urine).
- Urge patient to comply with treatment, which may last for months or years.

Evaluation

- Patient is free from infection.
- Patient maintains normal peripheral nervous system function.
- Patient and family state understanding of drug therapy.

isoproterenol (isoprenaline)
(igh-soh-proh-TEER-uh-nol)
Isuprel

isoproterenol hydrochloride

isoproterenol sulfate
Medihaler-Iso

Pharmacologic class: adrenergic
Therapeutic class: bronchodilator, cardiac stimulant
Pregnancy risk category: C

Indications and dosages

▶ **Bronchospasm.** *Adults and children:* For acute dyspneic episodes, one inhalation of sulfate form initially. Repeat, if needed, after 2 to 5 minutes. Maintenance dosage is one to two inhalations four to six times daily. Repeat once more 10 minutes after second dose. No more than three doses should be given for each attack.

▶ **Bronchospasm in COPD.** Give by IPPB or for nebulization by compressed air or oxygen. *Adults:* 2 ml of 0.125% or 2.5 ml of 0.1% solution (prepared by diluting 0.5 ml of 0.5% solution to 2 or 2.5 ml or by diluting 0.25 ml of 1% solution to 2 or 2.5 ml with water or half-normal or normal saline solution) up to five times daily.
Children: 2 ml of 0.125% solution or 2.5 ml of 0.1% solution up to five times daily.

▶ **Heart block and ventricular arrhythmias.** *Adults: **hydrochloride.*** Initially, 0.02 to 0.06 mg I.V. Subsequent doses 0.01 to 0.2 mg I.V. or 5 mcg/minute I.V. Or, 0.2 mg I.M. initially; then 0.02 to 1 mg, p.r.n.
*Children: **hydrochloride.*** Give half of initial adult dose.

▶ **Shock.** *Adults and children: **hydrochloride.*** 0.5 to 5 mcg/minute by continuous I.V. infusion. Usual concentration is 1 mg (5 ml) in 500 ml D_5W. Infusion rate adjusted according to heart rate, CVP, blood pressure, and urine flow.

▶ **Postoperative cardiac patients with bradycardia‡.** *Children:* I.V. infusion of 0.029 mcg/kg/minute.

▶ **As an aid in diagnosing the cause of mitral regurgitation‡.** *Adults:* 4 mcg/minute I.V. infusion.

▶ **As an aid in diagnosing coronary artery disease or lesions‡ .** *Adults:* 1 to 3 mcg/minute I.V. infusion.

Contraindications and precautions

- Contraindicated in patients with tachycardia caused by digitalis intoxication, in those with arrhythmias (other than those that may respond to treatment with isoproterenol), and in those with angina pectoris.
- Use cautiously in patients with renal or CV disease, coronary insufficiency, diabetes, hyperthyroidism, or history of sensitivity to sympathomimetic amines.

Lifespan: In pregnant or breast-feeding women, children, and elderly patients, use cautiously.

Adverse reactions

CNS: *headache,* mild tremor, weakness, dizziness, nervousness, insomnia, ***Stokes-Adams seizures.***
CV: *palpitations, tachycardia, angina,* flushing of face, ***cardiac arrest,*** *blood pressure that rises and then falls,* ***arrhythmias.***
GI: nausea, vomiting.
Metabolic: hyperglycemia.
Respiratory: ***bronchospasm.***
Skin: diaphoresis.

Interactions

Drug-drug. *Epinephrine, other sympathomimetics:* Increases risk of arrhythmias. Avoid using together.
Propranolol, other beta blockers: Blocks bronchodilating effect of isoproterenol. Monitor patient carefully if used together.

Effects on lab test results

- May increase glucose level.

Pharmacokinetics

Absorption: Rapid after P.O. inhalation.
Distribution: Distributed widely throughout body.
Metabolism: Metabolized by conjugation in GI tract and by enzymatic reduction in liver, lungs, and other tissues.
Excretion: Excreted primarily in urine.

Route	Onset	Peak	Duration
I.V.	Immediate	Unknown	< 1 hr
Inhalation	2-5 min	Unknown	0.5-2 hr

Pharmacodynamics

Chemical effect: Relaxes bronchial smooth muscle by acting on $beta_2$-adrenergic receptors. As cardiac stimulant, acts on $beta_1$-adrenergic receptors in heart.
Therapeutic effect: Relieves bronchospasms and heart block and restores normal sinus rhythm after ventricular arrhythmia.

Available forms

isoproterenol
Nebulizer inhaler: 0.25%, 0.5%, 1%
isoproterenol hydrochloride
Aerosol inhaler: 131 mcg/metered spray
Injection: 20 mcg/ml, 200 mcg/ml
Solution for inhalation: 0.5%, 1%
isoproterenol sulfate
Aerosol inhaler: 80 mcg/metered spray

NURSING PROCESS

Assessment

- Assess patient's underlying condition before therapy.
- Monitor cardiopulmonary status frequently.
- Be alert for adverse reactions and drug interactions.
- This drug may aggravate ventilation and perfusion abnormalities. Even when ease of breathing is improved, arterial oxygen tension may fall paradoxically.
- Evaluate patient's and family's knowledge of drug therapy.

Nursing diagnoses

- Ineffective health maintenance related to underlying condition
- Risk for injury related to drug-induced adverse reactions
- Deficient knowledge related to drug therapy

Planning and implementation

- Drug doesn't treat blood or fluid volume deficit. Volume deficit should be corrected before giving vasopressors.
- Don't use injection or inhalation solution if it's discolored or contains precipitate.
- **I.V. use:** Give drug by direct injection or I.V. infusion. For infusion, drug may be diluted with most common I.V. solutions. However, don't use with sodium bicarbonate injection; drug decomposes rapidly in alkaline solutions.

ALERT: If heart rate exceeds 110 beats/min with I.V. infusion, notify prescriber. Doses sufficient to increase heart rate to more than 130 beats/min may induce ventricular arrhythmias.
– When giving I.V. isoproterenol to treat shock, closely monitor blood pressure, CVP, ECG, arterial blood gas measurements, and urine output. Carefully adjust infusion rate according to these measurements. Use continuous infusion pump to regulate flow rate.
ALERT: Don't confuse Isuprel with Ismelin or Isordil.

- **Inhalation use:** If drug is given by inhalation with oxygen, make sure oxygen concentration won't suppress respiratory drive.
- Follow same instructions for metered powder nebulizer, although deep inhalation isn't necessary.
- Notify prescriber if adverse reactions occur. Dosage adjustment or discontinuation of drug may be needed.
- Stop drug immediately if precordial distress or angina occurs.

Patient teaching

- Give patient the following instructions for using metered-dose inhaler: Clear nasal passages and throat. Breathe out, expelling as much air from lungs as possible. Place mouthpiece well into mouth and inhale deeply as you release dose from inhaler. Hold breath for several seconds, remove mouthpiece, and exhale slowly.
- If more than one inhalation is ordered, tell patient to wait at least 2 minutes before repeating procedure.
- If patient also uses a corticosteroid inhaler, tell him to use bronchodilator first, and then wait about 5 minutes before using corticosteroid. This process allows bronchodilator to open air passages for maximum effectiveness of the corticosteroid.
- Warn patient using oral inhalant that this drug may turn sputum and saliva pink.
- Tell patient to stop drug and notify prescriber about chest tightness or dyspnea.
- Warn patient against overuse of drug. Tell him that tolerance can develop.
- Tell patient to reduce caffeine intake during drug therapy.

Evaluation
• Patient exhibits improved health.
• Patient doesn't experience injury from adverse reactions.
• Patient and family state understanding of drug therapy.

isosorbide dinitrate
(igh-soh-SOR-bighd digh-NIGH-trayt)
Apo-ISDN ♦, Cedocard SR ♦, Coronex ♦, Dilatrate-SR, Isordil, Isordil Titradose, Isotrate, Sorbitrate

isosorbide mononitrate
IMDUR, ISMO, Isotrate ER, Monoket

Pharmacologic class: nitrate
Therapeutic class: antianginal, vasodilator
Pregnancy risk category: C

Indications and dosages
▶ **Acute angina, prophylaxis in situations likely to cause angina.** ***isosorbide dinitrate.*** *Adults:* 2.5 to 10 mg S.L. for prompt relief of angina pain, repeated q 2 to 3 hours during acute phase, or q 4 to 6 hours for prophylaxis. Or, 2.5 to 10 mg chewable tablets, p.r.n., for acute attack or q 2 to 3 hours for prophylaxis but only after initial test dose of 5 mg to determine risk of severe hypotension. Or, initially, 5 to 20 mg P.O., then maintain on 10 to 40 mg P.O. q 6 hr. Or. initially, 40 mg extended-release tablets P.O., then maintain on 40 to 80 mg P.O. q 8 to 12 hours.
isosorbide mononitrate. *Adults:* For prophylaxis only, 20 mg P.O. b.i.d. with doses 7 hours apart and first dose upon awakening. For sustained-release form, 30 to 60 mg P.O. once daily on arising; after several days, dosage may be increased to 120 mg once daily; rarely, 240 mg may be needed.
▶ **Adjunctive treatment of heart failure‡.** ***isosorbide dinitrate.*** *Adults:* 80 mg P.O. daily with hydralazine. Maximum dose is 160 mg isosorbide dinitrate and 300 mg hydralazine.
▶ **Diffuse esophageal spasm without gastroesophageal reflux‡.** ***isosorbide dinitrate.*** *Adults:* 10 to 30 mg P.O. q.i.d.

Contraindications and precautions
• Contraindicated in patients hypersensitive to nitrates, in those with idiosyncratic reactions to nitrates, and in those with severe hypotension, shock, or acute MI with low left ventricular filling pressure.
• Use cautiously in patients with blood volume depletion (such as that resulting from diuretic therapy) or mild hypotension.
Lifespan: In pregnant or breast-feeding women, use cautiously. In children, safety of drug hasn't been established.

Adverse reactions
CNS: *headache, sometimes with throbbing; dizziness;* weakness.
CV: orthostatic hypotension, tachycardia, palpitations, ankle edema, fainting, *flushing.*
GI: nausea, vomiting.
Skin: cutaneous vasodilation.
Other: hypersensitivity reactions, S.L. burning.

Interactions
Drug-drug. *Antihypertensives:* Possibly increased hypotensive effects. Monitor patient closely during initial therapy.
Sildenafil: May increase hypotensive effects. Avoid using together.
Drug-lifestyle. *Alcohol use:* May increase hypotension. Discourage using together.

Effects on lab test results
None reported.

Pharmacokinetics
Absorption: Dinitrate is well absorbed from GI tract but undergoes first-pass metabolism, resulting in bioavailability of about 50% (depending on dosage form used). Mononitrate is also absorbed well, with almost 100% bioavailability.
Distribution: Distributed widely throughout body.
Metabolism: Metabolized in liver to active metabolites.
Excretion: Excreted in urine. *Half-life:* Dinitrate P.O., 5 to 6 hours; S.L., 2 hours; mononitrate, about 5 hours.

Route	Onset	Peak	Duration
P.O.	2-60 min	2-60 min	1-12 hr
S.L.	2-5 min	2-5 min	1-2 hr

Pharmacodynamics

Chemical effect: May reduce cardiac oxygen demand by decreasing left-ventricular-end diastolic pressure (preload) and, to a lesser extent, systemic vascular resistance (afterload). Drug also may increase blood flow through collateral coronary vessels. Most isosorbide dinitrate activity is attributed to its active metabolite, isosorbide mononitrate.
Therapeutic effect: Relieves angina.

Available forms

isosorbide dinitrate
Tablets: 5 mg, 10 mg, 20 mg, 30 mg, 40 mg
Tablets (chewable): 5 mg, 10 mg
Tablets (S.L.): 2.5 mg, 5 mg, 10 mg
Tablets (sustained-release): 40 mg
isosorbide mononitrate
Tablets: 10 mg, 20 mg
Tablets (extended-release): 30 mg, 60 mg, 120 mg

NURSING PROCESS

Assessment

- Assess patient's angina before therapy and regularly thereafter.
- Monitor blood pressure, heart rate and rhythm, and intensity and duration of drug response.
- Be alert for adverse reactions and drug interactions.
- Evaluate patient's and family's knowledge of drug therapy.

Nursing diagnoses

- Acute pain related to angina
- Risk for injury related to drug-induced adverse reactions
- Deficient knowledge related to drug therapy

Planning and implementation

ALERT: Don't confuse Isordil with Isuprel or Inderal.
Don't confuse Coronex isosorbide dinitrate with Coronex the herbal supplement.

- To prevent development of tolerance, don't give drug during an 8- to 12-hour period daily. The dosage regimen for isosorbide mononitrate (one tablet upon awakening with second dose in 7 hours, or one extended-release tablet daily) is intended to offer nitrate-free period during the day to minimize nitrate tolerance.
- **P.O. use:** Give drug on empty stomach, either 30 minutes before or 1 to 2 hours after meals, and have patient swallow tablets whole. Have patient chew chewable tablets thoroughly before swallowing.
- **S.L. use:** Give drug at first sign of angina. Have patient wet tablet with saliva, place it under his tongue until completely absorbed, and sit down and rest. Dose may be repeated every 10 to 15 minutes for maximum of three doses.
- Don't discontinue drug abruptly because coronary vasospasm may occur.
- Notify prescriber immediately if patient's pain doesn't subside.

Patient teaching

- Caution patient to take drug regularly, as prescribed, and to keep it accessible at all times.

ALERT: Advise patient that abrupt discontinuation causes coronary vasospasm.

- Tell patient to take S.L. tablet at first sign of attack. Explain that tablet should be wet with saliva and placed under tongue until completely absorbed, and that patient should sit down and rest until pain subsides. Tell patient that dose may be repeated every 10 to 15 minutes for maximum of three doses. If drug doesn't provide relief, medical help should be obtained promptly.
- Tell patient who complains of tingling sensation with drug placed S.L. to try holding tablet in buccal pouch.

ALERT: Warn patient not to confuse S.L. form with P.O. form.

- Teach patient taking P.O. form to take tablet on empty stomach, either 30 minutes before or 1 to 2 hours after meals, and to swallow tablet whole or chew chewable tablet thoroughly before swallowing.
- Tell patient to minimize orthostatic hypotension by changing to upright position slowly. Tell him to go up and down stairs carefully and to lie down at first sign of dizziness.
- Instruct patient to avoid alcohol consumption during drug therapy.
- Tell patient to store drug in cool place, in tightly closed container, away from light.

Evaluation

- Patient is free from pain.
- Patient doesn't experience injury from adverse reactions.

• Patient and family state understanding of drug therapy.

isotretinoin

(igh-soh-TREH-tih-noyn)
Accutane, Accutane Roche ♦, Roaccutane ◇, Amnesteem, Sotret

Pharmacologic class: retinoic acid derivative
Therapeutic class: antiacne
Pregnancy risk category: X

Indications and dosages

▶ **Severe recalcitrant nodular acne unresponsive to conventional therapy.** *Adults and children ages 12 to 17:* 0.5 to 2 mg/kg P.O. daily in two divided doses for 15 to 20 weeks.
▶ **Keratinization disorders resistant to conventional therapy, prevention of skin cancer‡.** *Adults:* Dosage varies with specific disease and severity of the disorder. Dosages up to 2 to 4 mg/kg P.O. daily have been used. Consult literature for specific recommendations.
▶ **Squamous cell cancer of the head and neck‡.** *Adults:* 50 to 100 mg/m² P.O.

Contraindications and precautions

• Contraindicated in patients hypersensitive to parabens, which are used as preservatives.
• Use cautiously in patients with genetic predisposition or history of osteoporosis, osteomalacia or other disorders of bone metabolism.
Lifespan: In women of childbearing age, use is contraindicated unless patient has had negative serum pregnancy test within 2 weeks of beginning therapy, will begin drug therapy on second or third day of next menstrual period, and will comply with stringent contraceptive measures for 1 month before therapy, during therapy, and at least 1 month after therapy. In breast-feeding women, drug isn't recommended. In children younger than age 12, safety of drug hasn't been established.
• Use cautiously in children ages 12 to 17.
ALERT: Severe fetal abnormalities may occur if drug is used during pregnancy.

Adverse reactions

CNS: headache, fatigue, depression, psychosis, ***suicide,*** emotional instability, *pseudotumor cerebri* (benign intracranial hypertension).
EENT: *conjunctivitis,* corneal deposits, dry eyes, visual disturbances, hearing impairment.
GI: nonspecific GI symptoms, gum bleeding and inflammation, nausea, vomiting, ***acute pancreatitis,*** inflammatory bowel disease.
Hepatic: ***hepatitis.***
Hematologic: anemia.
Metabolic: *hypertriglyceridemia,* hyperglycemia.
Musculoskeletal: skeletal hyperostosis, calcification of tendons and ligaments, premature epiphyseal closure, decreases in bone mineral density, musculoskeletal symptoms (sometimes severe) including back pain and arthralgia, arthritis, tendonitis, other types of bone abnormalities, ***rhabdomyolysis.***
Skin: *cheilosis, rash, dry skin,* peeling of palms and toes, skin infection, thinning of hair, photosensitivity.

Interactions

Drug-drug. *Corticosteroids:* May increase risk of osteoporosis. Use cautiously together.
Medicated soaps and cleansers, medicated cover-ups, topical resorcinol peeling agents (benzoyl peroxide), and alcohol-containing preparations: Cumulative drying effect. Use cautiously.
Micro-dosed progesterone birth control pills "minipills" that don't contain estrogen: Decreases effectiveness of birth control. Advise women to use two alternative contraceptive methods.
Phenytoin: May increase risk of osteomalacia. Use cautiously together.
Tetracyclines: Increases risk of pseudotumor cerebri. Avoid using together.
Vitamin A, products that contain vitamin A: Increases toxic effects of isotretinoin. Don't use together without prescriber's permission.
Drug-food. *Any food:* Enhances absorption of drug. Take drug with food.
Drug-lifestyle. *Alcohol use:* Increases risk of hypertriglyceridemia. Discourage using together.
Sun exposure: Increases photosensitivity reactions. Advise patient to use sunscreen and wear protective clothing.

Effects on lab test results

• May increase CPK, ALT, AST, alkaline phosphatase, glucose, and triglyceride levels.

• May increase platelet count. May decrease hemoglobin and hematocrit.

Pharmacokinetics

Absorption: Rapid from GI tract.
Distribution: Distributed widely in body; 99.9% protein-bound, primarily to albumin.
Metabolism: Metabolized in liver and possibly in gut wall.
Excretion: Unknown.

Route	Onset	Peak	Duration
P.O.	Unknown	3 hr	Unknown

Pharmacodynamics

Chemical effect: Unknown; thought to normalize keratinization, reversibly decrease size of sebaceous glands, and alter composition of sebum to less viscous form that is less likely to cause follicular plugging.
Therapeutic effect: Improves skin integrity.

Available forms

Capsules: 10 mg, 20 mg, 40 mg

NURSING PROCESS

Assessment

• Assess patient's skin before therapy and regularly thereafter.
• Obtain baseline serum lipid studies and liver function tests before therapy. Monitor these values at regular intervals until response to drug is established (usually about 4 weeks).
• Monitor glucose and CK levels in patients who engage in vigorous physical activity.
• Be alert for adverse reactions and drug interactions.
• Osteoporosis, osteopenia, bone fractures, and delayed healing of bone fractures have been seen in patients taking isotretinoin. While causality to drug hasn't been established, an effect can't be ruled out. Long-term effects haven't been studied. It is important to not exceed the recommended dose duration.
• Most adverse reactions appear to be dose-related, occurring at dosages greater than 1 mg/kg daily. They're usually reversible when therapy is discontinued or dosage reduced.
• Evaluate patient's and family's knowledge of drug therapy.

Nursing diagnoses

• Impaired skin integrity related to underlying skin condition
• Impaired tissue integrity related to adverse reactions
• Deficient knowledge related to drug therapy

Planning and implementation

• Anticipate second course of therapy, if needed, to start at least 8 weeks after completion of first course because improvement may continue after withdrawal of drug.
• Give drug with meals or shortly thereafter to enhance absorption.
ALERT: Patient who experiences headache, nausea, vomiting, or visual disturbances should be screened for papilledema. Signs and symptoms of pseudotumor cerebri require immediate discontinuation of therapy and prompt neurologic intervention.

Patient teaching

• Advise patient to take drug with milk, meals, or shortly after meals to ensure adequate absorption.
• Tell patient to immediately report visual disturbances and bone, muscle, or joint pain.
• Warn patient that contact lenses may feel uncomfortable during drug therapy.
• Warn patient against using abrasives, medicated soaps and cleansers, acne preparations containing peeling agents, and topical alcohol preparations (including cosmetics, after-shave, cologne) because these agents cause cumulative irritation or excessive drying of skin.
• Instruct patient to avoid alcohol during drug therapy.
• Tell patient to avoid prolonged exposure to sunlight, to use sunblock, and to wear protective clothing.
ALERT: Advise patient not to donate blood during or for 30 days after therapy; severe fetal abnormalities may occur if a pregnant woman receives blood containing isotretinoin.
• Advise women of childbearing age to use two reliable forms of contraception simultaneously for 1 month before, during, and 1 month after treatment.

Evaluation

• Patient has improved skin condition.
• Patient is free from conjunctivitis, corneal deposits, and dry eyes.

• Patient and family state understanding of drug therapy.

isradipine

(is-RAH-deh-peen)

DynaCirc

Pharmacologic class: calcium channel blocker
Therapeutic class: antihypertensive
Pregnancy risk category: C

Indications and dosages

▶ **Essential hypertension.** *Adults:* Initially, 2.5 mg P.O. b.i.d., alone or with thiazide diuretic. Dosage increased gradually. If response is inadequate after first 2 to 4 weeks, increase dose by 5 mg daily at 2- to 4-week intervals to maximum of 20 mg daily.

Contraindications and precautions

• Contraindicated in patients hypersensitive to drug.

• Use cautiously in patients with heart failure, especially those who take beta blockers.

Lifespan: In pregnant or breast-feeding women, use cautiously. In children, safety of drug hasn't been established.

Adverse reactions

CNS: dizziness.
CV: edema, flushing, palpitations, tachycardia, orthostatic hypotension.
GI: nausea, diarrhea.
GU: frequent urination.
Respiratory: dyspnea.
Skin: rash.

Interactions

Drug-drug. *Cimetidine:* Increases isradipine levels. Monitor patient for increased effects.
Fentanyl anesthesia: Severe hypotension has been reported with concomitant use of beta blocker and calcium channel blocker. Avoid using together.
Rifampin: Reduces isradipine effects. Monitor patient closely.

Effects on lab test results

None reported.

Pharmacokinetics

Absorption: 90% to 95% absorbed after P.O. administration.
Distribution: 95% is bound to plasma protein.
Metabolism: Completely metabolized before elimination with extensive first-pass metabolism.
Excretion: 60% to 65% of drug excreted in urine; 25% to 30% in feces. *Half-life:* About 8 hours.

Route	Onset	Peak	Duration
P.O.	≤ 20 min	≤ 1.5 hr	12 hr

Pharmacodynamics

Chemical effect: Inhibits calcium ion influx across cardiac and smooth-muscle cells and may decrease arteriolar resistance and blood pressure.
Therapeutic effect: Lowers blood pressure.

Available forms

Capsules: 2.5 mg, 5 mg

NURSING PROCESS

Assessment

• Assess blood pressure before therapy and regularly thereafter.

• Be alert for adverse reactions and drug interactions.

• Monitor patient's hydration status if adverse GI reactions occur.

• Evaluate patient's and family's knowledge of drug therapy.

Nursing diagnoses

• Risk for injury related to presence of hypertension

• Risk for deficient fluid volume related to adverse GI reactions

• Deficient knowledge related to drug therapy

Planning and implementation

• Drug may be given without regard to meals. However, giving drug with food slows its absorption.

• Before surgery, inform anesthesiologist that patient is taking calcium channel blocker.

ALERT: Don't confuse DynaCirc with Dynacin.

Patient teaching
- Explain that patient may note increased need to void because drug has some diuretic activity.
- Instruct patient to notify prescriber of adverse reactions or significant changes in blood pressure.

Evaluation
- Patient's blood pressure is normal.
- Patient maintains normal hydration.
- Patient and family state understanding of drug therapy.

itraconazole
(ih-truh-KAHN-uh-zohl)
Sporanox

Pharmacologic class: synthetic triazole
Therapeutic class: antifungal
Pregnancy risk category: C

Indications and dosages

▶ **Pulmonary and extrapulmonary blastomycosis, histoplasmosis.** ***Capsules.*** *Adults:* 200 mg P.O. daily. Dosage may be increased as needed and tolerated in 100-mg increments to maximum of 400 mg daily. Amounts that exceed 200 mg daily should be divided into two doses. Treatment should continue for at least 3 months. In life-threatening illness, loading dose of 200 mg t.i.d. is given for 3 days. Or, give 200 mg by I.V. infusion over 1 hour twice daily for four doses; then 200 mg I.V. once daily.

▶ **Aspergillosis.** ***Capsules.*** *Adults:* 200 to 400 mg P.O. daily. Or, give 200 mg by I.V. infusion over 1 hour twice daily for four doses; then decrease to 200 mg I.V. once daily for up to 14 days.

▶ **Onychomycosis for toenails with or without fingernail involvement.** ***Capsules.*** *Adults:* 200 mg P.O. once daily for 12 weeks.

▶ **Onychomycosis for fingernails.** ***Capsules.*** *Adults:* Two treatment phases each consisting of 200 mg P.O. b.i.d. for 1 week. Phases are separated by a 3-week period without drug.

▶ **Esophageal candidiasis.** ***Oral solution.*** *Adults:* 100 mg to 200 mg swished in mouth vigorously and swallowed daily for a minimum of 3 weeks.

▶ **Oropharyngeal candidiasis.** ***Oral solution.*** *Adults:* 200 mg swished in mouth vigorously and swallowed daily for 1 to 2 weeks. For patients unresponsive to fluconazole tablets, give 100 mg swished in mouth vigorously and swallowed twice daily for 2 to 4 weeks.

Contraindications and precautions
- Contraindicated in patients hypersensitive to drug and in those receiving oral triazolam or oral midazolam. Also contraindicated in patients with ventricular dysfunction, heart failure, or a history of heart failure. Don't use injection in patients with a creatinine clearance less than 30 ml/minute.
- Use cautiously in patients with hypochlorhydria (they may not absorb drug as readily as patients with normal gastric acidity), in HIV-infected patients (hypochlorhydria can accompany HIV infection), and in those with liver disease.

Lifespan: In pregnant women, use cautiously. In breast-feeding women, use is contraindicated because drug appears in breast milk. In children, safety of drug hasn't been established.

Adverse reactions
CNS: malaise, fatigue, *headache*, dizziness, somnolence, fever, asthenia, pain, tremor, abnormal dreaming, anxiety, depression.
CV: edema, hypertension, orthostatic hypotension, ***heart failure.***
EENT: rhinitis, sinusitis, pharyngitis.
GI: *nausea,* vomiting, diarrhea, abdominal pain, anorexia, dyspepsia, flatulence, incrfeased appetite, constipation, gastritis, gastroenteritis, ulcerative stomatitis, gingivitis.
GU: albuminuria, impotence, cystitis, UTI.
Hematologic: ***neutropenia.***
Hepatic: impaired hepatic function, ***hepatotoxicity, liver failure.***
Metabolic: hypokalemia, hypertriglyceridemia.
Musculoskeletal: myalgia
Respiratory: upper respiratory tract infection, ***pulmonary edema.***
Skin: rash, pruritus.
Other: decreased libido, injury, herpes zoster, ***hypersensitivity reactions (urticaria, angioedema, Steven-Johnson syndrome).***

Interactions

Drug-drug. *Antacids, H_2-receptor antagonists, phenytoin, rifampin:* Possible decreased plasma itraconazole levels. Avoid using together.
Cyclosporine, digoxin: Possible increased plasma levels of these drugs. Monitor plasma levels closely.
Dofetilide, pimozide, quinidine: May increase the plasma levels of these drugs by CYP-3A4 metabolism, causing serious CV events, including torsades de pointes, QT prolongation, ventricular tachycardia, cardiac arrest, or sudden death. Avoid using together.
Isoniazid: May decrease plasma itraconazole levels. Monitor patient closely.
Oral anticoagulants: Possible enhanced anticoagulant effects. Monitor PT and INR closely.
Oral antidiabetics: Similar antifungals have caused hypoglycemia. Monitor glucose level.

Effects on lab test results

• May increase alkaline phosphatase, ALT, AST, bilirubin, and GGT levels. May decrease potassium level.

Pharmacokinetics

Absorption: Bioavailability is maximal when taken without food. Absolute bioavailability is 55%.
Distribution: Plasma protein binding of itraconazole is 99.8%; that of its metabolite, hydroxyitraconazole, is 99.5%. Extensively distributed in tissues susceptible to infection.
Metabolism: Extensively metabolized by liver into large number of metabolites, including hydroxyitraconazole, the major metabolite.
Excretion: Excreted in feces and urine.

Route	Onset	Peak	Duration
P.O.	Unknown	2 hr (fasting); 5 hr (not fasting)	Unknown
I.V.	Unknown	Unknown	Unknown

Pharmacodynamics

Chemical effect: Interferes with fungal cell wall synthesis by inhibiting formation of ergosterol and increasing cell wall permeability.
Therapeutic effect: Hinders fungi, including *Aspergillus sp.* and *Blastomyces dermatitidis.*

Available forms

Capsules: 100 mg
Injection: 10 mg/ml
Oral solution: 10 mg/ml

NURSING PROCESS

Assessment

• Assess patient's infection before therapy and regularly thereafter.
• Before initiating treatment, appropriate nail specimens for laboratory testing (KOH preparation, fungal culture, or nail biopsy) should be obtained to confirm the diagnosis of onychomycosis.
• Monitor liver and renal function test results.
• Be alert for adverse reactions and drug interactions.
• Evaluate patient's and family's knowledge of drug therapy.

Nursing diagnoses

• Infection related to presence of susceptible fungi
• Risk for deficient fluid volume related to adverse reactions
• Deficient knowledge related to drug therapy

Planning and implementation

• Therapy is discouraged in patients with baseline liver impairment, unless there is a life-threatening situation where benefit exceeds risk. Monitor liver function closely and stop therapy if signs of liver dysfunction occur. Restarting of therapy is strongly discouraged, unless the benefit exceeds risk.
• Give capsules with food. Don't give oral solution with food.
ALERT: Oral solution and capsules aren't interchangeable.
• If signs and symptoms of heart failure occur, discontinue itraconazole.
• Report signs and symptoms of liver disease and abnormal liver test results.
• **P.O. use:** Instruct patient to swish solution vigorously in the mouth (10 ml at a time) for several seconds and then swallow.
• **I.V. use:** Dilute in normal saline solution for injection. Add dose to 50-ml I.V. bag of normal saline solution. Infuse over 60 minutes, using an infusion set with a filter. Flush I.V. line with 15 to 20 ml of normal saline solution after each infusion. Compatibility with other drugs is unknown.

Patient teaching
- Teach patient to recognize and report signs and symptoms of liver disease (anorexia, dark urine, pale feces, unusual fatigue, or jaundice).
- Tell patient to take capsules with food to ensure maximal absorption.

Evaluation
- Patient is free from infection.
- Patient maintains adequate fluid balance.
- Patient and family state understanding of drug therapy.

K

kaolin and pectin mixtures
(KAY-oh-lin and PEK-tin MIX-cherz)
K-Pek, Kaodene Non-Narcotic†, Kaolin w/Pectin†, Kao-Spen, Kapectolin†

Pharmacologic class: absorbent
Therapeutic class: antidiarrheal
Pregnancy risk category: NR

Indications and dosages
▶ **Mild, nonspecific diarrhea.** ***Regular-strength suspension.*** *Adults:* 60 to 120 ml P.O. after each bowel movement.
Adolescents: 60 ml P.O. after each bowel movement.
Children ages 6 to 12: 30 to 60 ml P.O. after each bowel movement.
Children ages 3 to 6: 15 to 30 ml P.O. after each bowel movement.
Liquid. *Adults:* 45 ml P.O. one to three times daily or after each loose bowel movement.
Children ages 6 to 12: 22.5 ml P.O. one to three times daily or after each loose bowel movement.
Children ages 3 to 6: 15 ml P.O. one to three times daily or after each loose bowel movement.

Contraindications and precautions
- Do not use in patients with diarrhea associated with pseudomembranous colitis or caused by toxigenic bacteria. Use cautiously in patients with bleeding disorders or salicylate sensitivity.

Lifespan: In pregnant women and in children, use cautiously.

Adverse reactions
GI: constipation; fecal impaction or ulceration (in infants and elderly or debilitated patients after long-term use).

Interactions
Drug-drug. *Oral drugs:* Decreases drug absorption. Separate administration times by at least 2 to 3 hours.

Effects on lab test results
None reported.

Pharmacokinetics
Absorption: None.
Distribution: None.
Metabolism: None.
Excretion: Excreted in stool.

Route	Onset	Peak	Duration
P.O.	Unknown	Unknown	Unknown

Pharmacodynamics
Chemical effect: Decreases fluid content of feces, although total water loss seems to remain the same.
Therapeutic effect: Alleviates diarrhea.

Available forms
Liquid: 3.9 g kaolin and 194.4 mg pectin per 30 ml with bismuth subsalicylate (Kaodene)
Oral suspension: 5.2 g kaolin and 260 mg pectin per 30 ml† (Kao-Spen), 90 g kaolin and 2 g pectin per 30 ml† (Kapectolin†, Kaolin w/Pectin†)

NURSING PROCESS

Assessment
- Assess patient's bowel patterns before and after therapy.
- Be alert for adverse GI reactions and drug interactions.
- Evaluate patient's and family's knowledge of drug therapy.

Nursing diagnoses
- Diarrhea related to underlying condition
- Constipation related to long-term use of drug
- Deficient knowledge related to drug therapy

Planning and implementation
- Read label carefully. Check dosage and strength.
- Give dose after each loose bowel movement.
- Don't use in place of specific therapy for underlying cause of diarrhea.

Patient teaching
- Warn patient not to use drug to replace therapy for underlying cause.
- Advise patient not to use drug for more than 2 days.

Evaluation
- Patient reports decrease in or absence of loose stools.
- Patient doesn't have constipation.
- Patient and family state understanding of drug therapy.

ketoconazole
(kee-toh-KAHN-uh-zohl)
Nizoral, Nizoral A-D

Pharmacologic class: imidazole derivative
Therapeutic class: antifungal
Pregnancy risk category: C

Indications and dosages

▶ **Systemic candidiasis, chronic mucocandidiasis, oral thrush, candiduria, coccidioidomycosis, histoplasmosis, chromomycosis, paracoccidioidomycosis, severe cutaneous dermatophyte infection resistant to therapy with topical or oral griseofulvin.** *Adults and children weighing more than 40 kg (88 lb):* Initially, 200 mg P.O. daily in single dose. Dosage may be increased to 400 mg once daily in patients who don't respond to lower dosage.
Children age 2 and older: 3.3 to 6.6 mg/kg P.O. daily as single dose.

Contraindications and precautions
- Contraindicated in patients hypersensitive to drug and in those taking oral midazolam or triazolam. Use cautiously in patients with hepatic disease, and in those taking other hepatotoxic drugs.

Lifespan: In pregnant women, use cautiously. Breast-feeding women should use other feeding methods during therapy.

Adverse reactions
CNS: headache, nervousness, dizziness, ***suicidal tendencies.***
GI: *nausea, vomiting,* abdominal pain, diarrhea, constipation.
Hematologic: ***thrombocytopenia.***
Hepatic: ***hepatotoxicity.***
Skin: itching.
Other: gynecomastia with tenderness.

Interactions
Drug-drug. *Antacids, anticholinergics, H_2-receptor antagonists, proton pump inhibitors, sucralfate:* Decreases ketoconazole absorption. Wait at least 2 hours after ketoconazole dose before giving these drugs.
Corticosteroids: Corticosteroid bioavailability may be increased and clearance may be decreased, possibly resulting in toxicity. Monitor patient closely.
Cyclosporine, methylprednisolone, tacrolimus: Increases serum levels of these drugs. Adjust their dosages as directed, and monitor their levels closely.
Isoniazid, rifampin: Increases ketoconazole metabolism. Monitor patient for decreased antifungal effect.
Oral anticoagulants: Anticoagulant response may be enhanced. Monitor PT and INR.
Oral midazolam, triazolam: Elevates plasma levels of these drugs, which may potentiate or prolong sedative or hypnotic effects. Avoid using together.

Effects on lab test results
- May increase lipid, alkaline phosphatase, ALT, and AST levels.
- May decrease hemoglobin, hematocrit, and platelet and WBC counts.

Pharmacokinetics
Absorption: Decreased by raised gastric pH and may be increased in extent and consistency by food.
Distribution: Distributed into bile, saliva, cerumen, synovial fluid, and sebum. Penetra-

tion into CSF is erratic and probably minimal. Drug is 84% to 99% bound to plasma proteins.
Metabolism: Metabolized in liver.
Excretion: Primarily in feces, with smaller amount excreted in urine. *Half-life:* 8 hours.

Route	Onset	Peak	Duration
P.O.	Unknown	1-2 hr	Unknown

Pharmacodynamics

Chemical effect: Inhibits purine transport and DNA, RNA, and protein synthesis; increases cell wall permeability, making fungus more susceptible to osmotic pressure.
Therapeutic effect: Kills or hinders growth of susceptible fungi, including most pathogenic fungi.

Available forms

Tablets: 200 mg
Shampoo: 1%†

NURSING PROCESS

Assessment

- Assess patient's infection before therapy and regularly thereafter.
- Evaluate laboratory studies for eradication of fungi.
- Be alert for adverse reactions and drug interactions.
- Monitor patient's hydration status if adverse GI reactions occur.
- Evaluate patient's and family's knowledge of drug therapy.

Nursing diagnoses

- Infection related to presence of susceptible fungi
- Risk for deficient fluid volume related to adverse GI reactions
- Deficient knowledge related to drug therapy

Planning and implementation

- Because of risk of serious hepatotoxicity, drug shouldn't be used for less serious conditions, such as fungus infections of skin or nails.
- To minimize nausea, divide daily amount into two doses. Also, giving drug with meals helps to decrease nausea.
- Have patient dissolve each tablet in 4 ml aqueous solution of 0.2*N* hydrochloric acid and sip mixture through straw to avoid contact with teeth. Have patient drink full glass (8 oz) of water afterward.

Patient teaching

- Instruct patient with achlorhydria to dissolve each tablet in 4 ml aqueous solution of 0.2*N* hydrochloric acid, sip mixture through a straw (to avoid contact with teeth), and drink a glass of water after the dose because ketoconazole requires gastric acidity for dissolution and absorption.
- Make sure patient understands that treatment should continue until all clinical and laboratory tests indicate that active fungal infection has subsided. If drug is discontinued too soon, infection will recur. Minimum treatment for candidiasis is 7 to 14 days; for other systemic fungal infections, 6 months; for resistant dermatophyte infections, at least 4 weeks.
- Reassure patient that nausea will subside.

Evaluation

- Patient is free from infection.
- Patient maintains adequate hydration.
- Patient and family state understanding of drug therapy.

ketoprofen

(kee-toh-PROH-fen)

Actron caplets†, Apo-Keto ♦, Apo-Keto-E ♦, Novo-Keto-EC ♦, Orudis, Orudis-E ♦, Orudis KT†, Orudis SR ♦ ◇, Oruvail, Rhodis ♦, Rhodis-EC ♦

Pharmacologic class: NSAID
Therapeutic class: nonnarcotic analgesic, antipyretic, anti-inflammatory
Pregnancy risk category: B

Indications and dosages

▶ **Rheumatoid arthritis and osteoarthritis.** *Adults:* 75 mg t.i.d., 50 mg q.i.d., or 200 mg as sustained-release tablet once daily. Maximum, 300 mg daily. Or, where suppository is available, 100 mg P.R. b.i.d. or one suppository h.s. (with ketoprofen P.O. during day).
▶ **Mild-to-moderate pain; dysmenorrhea.** *Adults:* 25 to 50 mg P.O. q 6 to 8 hours, p.r.n.
▶ **Minor aches and pain or fever.** *Adults:* 12.5 mg with full glass of water q 4 to 6 hours.

Don't exceed 25 mg in 4 hours or 75 mg in 24 hours.

Contraindications and precautions

- Contraindicated in patients hypersensitive to drug and in those with a history of aspirin- or NSAID-induced asthma, urticaria, or other allergic reactions.
- Use cautiously in patients with history of peptic ulcer disease, renal dysfunction, hypertension, heart failure, or fluid retention.

Lifespan: In pregnant women, avoid use of drug during third trimester of pregnancy. For breast-feeding women, drug isn't recommended. In children, safety of drug hasn't been established. Children younger than age 16 shouldn't be given drug unless directed by prescriber.

Adverse reactions

CNS: *headache,* dizziness, *CNS excitation* or depression.
EENT: tinnitus, visual disturbances, ***laryngeal edema.***
GI: *nausea, abdominal pain, diarrhea, constipation, flatulence,* peptic ulceration, anorexia, vomiting, stomatitis.
GU: ***nephrotoxicity.***
Hematologic: prolonged bleeding time, ***thrombocytopenia, agranulocytosis.***
Respiratory: dyspnea, ***bronchospasm.***
Skin: rash, photosensitivity, exfoliative dermatitis.

Interactions

Drug-drug. *Anticoagulants:* May increase anticoagulant effect. Monitor PT and INR.
Aspirin: Increases risk of adverse GI reactions and increased ketoprofen levels. Avoid using together.
Corticosteroids: Increases risk of adverse GI reactions. Avoid using together.
Hydrochlorothiazide, other diuretics: Decreases diuretic effectiveness. Monitor patient for lack of effect.
Lithium, methotrexate: Increases levels of these drugs, leading to toxicity. Monitor levels closely.
Oral anticoagulants: Increases risk of bleeding. Monitor patient for bleeding.
Probenecid: Increases plasma ketoprofen levels. Avoid using together.
Drug-herb. *Dong quai, feverfew, garlic, ginger, horse chestnut, red clover:* Possible increased risk of bleeding. Monitor patient closely.
St. John's wort: Increases risk of photosensitivity reactions. Advise patient to avoid unprotected or prolonged exposure to sunlight.
Drug-lifestyle. *Alcohol use:* Increases risk of GI toxicity. Discourage using together.
Sun exposure: May cause photosensitivity reactions. Advise patient to avoid unprotected or prolonged exposure to sunlight.

Effects on lab test results

- May increase BUN level.
- May increase bleeding time. May decrease WBC and platelet counts.

Pharmacokinetics

Absorption: Absorbed rapidly and completely from GI tract.
Distribution: Highly protein-bound.
Metabolism: Metabolized extensively in liver.
Excretion: Excreted in urine.

Route	Onset	Peak	Duration
P.O., P.R.	1-2 hr	30 min-2 hr	3-4 hr

Pharmacodynamics

Chemical effect: May inhibit prostaglandin synthesis.
Therapeutic effect: Relieves pain, fever, and inflammation.

Available forms

Capsules: 25 mg, 50 mg, 75 mg
Capsules (extended-release): 100 mg, 150 mg, 200 mg
Suppositories: 100 mg ♦
Tablets: 12.5 mg†**
Tablets (enteric-coated): 50 mg ♦, 100 mg ♦
Tablets (sustained-release): 200 mg ♦

NURSING PROCESS

Assessment

- Assess patient's pain before and after drug administration. Full effect may not occur for 2 to 4 weeks.
- Check renal and hepatic function every 6 months or as directed during long-term therapy.

• Be alert for adverse reactions and drug interactions.
• Monitor patient's hydration status if adverse GI reactions occur.
• Evaluate patient's and family's knowledge of drug therapy.

Nursing diagnoses
• Chronic pain related to underlying condition
• Risk for deficient fluid volume related to adverse GI reactions
• Deficient knowledge related to drug therapy

Planning and implementation
• **P.O. use:** Sustained-release form isn't recommended for patients in acute pain.
• May give drug with antacids, food, or milk to minimize adverse GI effects.
• **P.R. use:** Follow normal protocol.
• Inform laboratory personnel that patient is taking ketoprofen. Drug may interfere with some laboratory determinations of glucose and iron levels, depending on testing method used.

Patient teaching
• Patient may take drug with milk or meals if he experiences adverse GI effects.
• Tell patient that full therapeutic effect may be delayed for 2 to 4 weeks.
• Instruct patient to report adverse visual or auditory reactions immediately.
• Teach patient to recognize and immediately report evidence of GI bleeding. Also, explain that serious GI toxicity, including peptic ulceration and bleeding, can occur in patients taking NSAIDs despite an absence of GI symptoms.
• Alert patient that use with aspirin, alcohol, or corticosteroids may increase risk of adverse GI reactions.
• Advise patient to use sunblock, wear protective clothing, and avoid prolonged exposure to sunlight. Explain that drug may cause photosensitivity reactions.

Evaluation
• Patient is free from pain.
• Patient maintains normal hydration status.
• Patient and family state understanding of drug therapy.

ketorolac tromethamine
(KEE-toh-roh-lak troh-METH-uh-meen)
Toradol

Pharmacologic class: NSAID
Therapeutic class: analgesic
Pregnancy risk category: C

Indications and dosages
▶ **Short-term management of pain.** *Adults younger than age 65:* Dosage based on patient response. Initially, 60 mg I.M. or 30 mg I.V. as single dose or doses of 30 mg I.M. or I.V. q 6 hours. Maximum, 120 mg daily. To switch to P.O. dosing, initially give 20 mg P.O., and then 10 mg P.O. q 4 to 6 hours, p.r.n., up to 40 mg daily.
Adults age 65 or older, renally impaired patients, and those weighing less than 50 kg (110 lb): Initially, 30 mg I.M. or 15 mg I.V. as single dose or doses of 15 mg I.M. or I.V. q 6 hours. Maximum, 60 mg daily. To switch to P.O. dosing, 10 mg P.O. q 4 to 6 hours, p.r.n., up to 40 mg daily. Maximum combined use of drug not to exceed 5 days.

Contraindications and precautions
• Contraindicated in patients hypersensitive to drug and in those with a history of syndrome of nasal polyps, angioedema, bronchospastic reactivity, or allergic reactions to aspirin or other NSAIDs; in patients currently receiving aspirin or other NSAIDs; in those with advanced renal impairment; and in those at risk for renal failure as a result of volume depletion. Also contraindicated in patients with a high risk of bleeding and in those with suspected or confirmed cerebrovascular bleeding, hemorrhage diathesis, and incomplete hemostasis.
• Not recommended for intrathecal or epidural administration because of its alcohol content.
• Use cautiously in women, patients in the perioperative period; and patients with hepatic or renal impairment, history of serious GI events or peptic ulcer disease, cardiac decompensation, hypertension, or coagulation disorders.
Lifespan: In women giving birth and in breast-feeding patients, use cautiously; trace amounts have been detected in breast milk. In children, safety of drug hasn't been established

Adverse reactions

CNS: drowsiness, insomnia, syncope, dizziness, *headache.*
CV: edema, hypertension, palpitations.
GI: *nausea, dyspepsia, GI pain,* diarrhea.
GU: hematuria, polyuria.
Hematologic: purpura, eosinophilia, anemia.
Skin: pain at injection site, sweating.

Interactions

Drug-drug. *Antihypertensives, diuretics:* Decreases effectiveness of these drugs. Monitor reactions closely.
Lithium: Increases lithium levels. Monitor levels closely.
Methotrexate: Decreases methotrexate clearance and increased toxicity. Don't use together.
Salicylates, warfarin: Ketorolac may increase levels of free (unbound) salicylates or warfarin in blood. Clinical significance is unknown.
Drug-herb. *Dong quai, feverfew, garlic, ginger, horse chestnut, red clover:* Possible increased risk of bleeding. Monitor patient closely.
St. John's wort: Increases risk of photosensitivity reactions. Advise patient to avoid unprotected or prolonged exposure to sunlight.

Effects on lab test results

- May increase eosinophil count. May decrease hemoglobin and hematocrit.

Pharmacokinetics

Absorption: Completely absorbed after I.M. use. After P.O. use, food delays absorption but doesn't decrease total amount absorbed.
Distribution: More than 99.9% protein-bound.
Metabolism: Metabolized mainly in liver.
Excretion: More than 90% excreted in urine, with the remainder excreted in feces. *Half-life:* 3.8 to 6.3 hours.

Route	Onset	Peak	Duration
P.O.	30-60 min	30-60 min	6-8 hr
I.V.	Immediate	Immediate	8 hr
I.M.	≤ 10 min	30-60 min	6-8 hr

Pharmacodynamics

Chemical effect: Unknown; may inhibit prostaglandin synthesis.
Therapeutic effect: Relieves pain.

Available forms

Injection: 15 mg/ml, 30 mg/ml
Tablets: 10 mg

NURSING PROCESS

Assessment

- Assess patient's pain before and after drug administration.
- Be alert for adverse reactions and drug interactions.
- Evaluate patient's and family's knowledge of drug therapy.

Nursing diagnoses

- Acute pain related to underlying condition
- Risk for injury related to drug-induced adverse CNS reactions
- Deficient knowledge related to drug therapy

Planning and implementation

- **P.O. use:** When switching from injectable to P.O. form, don't exceed 120 mg of drug (including maximum of 40 mg P.O.) on day of transition.
- **I.V. use:** Give I.V. bolus over at least 15 seconds.
- **I.M. use:** Administration by I.M. route may cause pain at injection site. Apply pressure to site for 15 to 30 seconds after injection to minimize local effects.
- Notify prescriber if pain persists or worsens.

ALERT: Don't confuse Toradol with Foradil.

Patient teaching

- Teach patient to recognize and immediately report signs and symptoms of GI bleeding. Also explain that serious GI toxicity, including peptic ulceration and bleeding, can occur in patient taking oral NSAIDs despite an absence of GI symptoms.
- Advise patient to report persistent or worsening pain.
- Explain that drug is intended only for short-term use.

Evaluation

- Patient is free from pain.
- Patient sustains no injury from adverse reactions.
- Patient and family state understanding of drug therapy.

ketotifen fumarate

(kee-toe-TYE-fen FOO-muh-rayt)
Zaditor

Pharmacologic classification: histamine (H_1-receptor) antagonist and mast cell stabilizer
Therapeutic classification: ophthalmic antihistamine
Pregnancy risk category: C

Indications and dosages

▶ **Temporary prevention of itching of eye caused by allergic conjunctivitis.** *Adults and children age 3 and older:* Instill 1 drop in affected eye q 8 to 12 hours.

Contraindications and precautions

• Contraindicated in patients hypersensitive to drug or its component.
Lifespan: In breast-feeding women, use cautiously; it's unknown if topical ocular product appears in breast milk. In children younger than age 3, safety and effectiveness haven't been established.

Adverse reactions

CNS: *headaches.*
EENT: *conjunctival infection, rhinitis,* ocular allergic reactions, burning or stinging of eyes, conjunctivitis, eye discharge, dry eyes, eye pain, eyelid disorder, itching of eyes, keratitis, lacrimation disorder, mydriasis, photophobia, ocular rash, pharyngitis.
Other: flulike syndrome.

Interactions

None reported.

Effects on lab test results

None reported.

Pharmacokinetics

Absorption: Effect is seen within minutes after administration.
Distribution: Unknown.
Metabolism: Unknown.
Excretion: Unknown.

Route	Onset	Peak	Duration
Ophthalmic	Within minutes	Unknown	Unknown

Pharmacodynamics

Chemical effect: Inhibits release of mediators from cells involved in hypersensitivity reactions.
Therapeutic effect: Temporary prevention of eye itching.

Available forms

Ophthalmic solution: 0.025%; supplied as 5-ml solution in 7.5-ml bottles

NURSING PROCESS

Assessment

• Assess underlying condition before therapy and reassess regularly throughout therapy.
• Monitor patient for sensitivity reactions.
• Monitor patient for signs of infection.
• Evaluate patient's and family's knowledge of ketotifen fumarate therapy.

Nursing diagnoses

• Risk for injury related to ocular infection and possible altered vision
• Impaired tissue integrity related to drug-induced adverse EENT reactions
• Deficient knowledge related to ketotifen fumarate therapy

Planning and implementation

• Drug is for ophthalmic use only; not for injection or oral use.
• Drug isn't indicated for use with irritation related to contact lenses.
• Preservative in drug may be absorbed by soft contact lenses. Contact lenses should be removed before giving drops and shouldn't be inserted until at least 10 minutes after drug is instilled.

Patient teaching

• Teach patient proper instillation technique. Tell him to avoid contaminating dropper tip and solution and not to touch eyelids or surrounding areas with dropper tip of bottle.
• Tell patient not to wear contact lenses if eyes are red. Warn patient not to use drug to treat irritation related to contact lenses.
• Instruct patient who wears soft contact lenses and whose eyes aren't red to wait at least 10 minutes after instilling drug before inserting contact lenses.

• Advise patient to report adverse reactions to drug.
• Advise patient to keep bottle tightly closed when not in use.

Evaluation

• Patient does not sustain any injury.
• Patient demonstrates appropriate management of any adverse EENT reactions.
• Patient and family state understanding of therapy.

L

labetalol hydrochloride

(lah-BAY-tuh-lol high-droh-KLOR-ighd)
Normodyne, Presolol ◇, Trandate

Pharmacologic class: alpha-adrenergic and beta blocker
Therapeutic class: antihypertensive
Pregnancy risk category: C

Indications and dosages

▶ **Hypertension.** *Adults:* 100 mg P.O. b.i.d. with or without diuretic. If needed, increase dosage to 200 mg b.i.d. after 2 days as directed. Increases further q 2 to 3 days until ideal response is reached. Usual maintenance dosage is 200 to 400 mg b.i.d.
▶ **Severe hypertension, hypertensive emergencies.** *Adults:* 200 mg diluted in 160 ml of D_5W, infused at 2 mg/minute until satisfactory response is obtained; then stop infusion. Dose may be repeated q 6 to 12 hours. Or, give by repeated I.V. injection; initially, 20 mg I.V. slowly over 2 minutes. Then repeat injections of 40 to 80 mg q 10 minutes until maximum dosage of 300 mg is reached, p.r.n.

Contraindications and precautions

• Contraindicated in patients hypersensitive to drug and in those with bronchial asthma, overt cardiac failure, greater than first-degree heart block, cardiogenic shock, severe bradycardia, and other conditions linked to severe and prolonged hypotension.
• Use cautiously in patients with heart failure, hepatic failure, chronic bronchitis, emphysema, peripheral vascular disease, or pheochromocytoma.
Lifespan: In pregnant or breast-feeding women, use cautiously. In children, safety of drug hasn't been established.

Adverse reactions

CNS: vivid dreams, *dizziness,* fatigue, headache, transient scalp tingling.
CV: *orthostatic hypotension,* peripheral vascular disease, ***bradycardia, ventricular arrhythmias.***
EENT: nasal stuffiness.
GI: nausea, vomiting, diarrhea.
GU: sexual dysfunction, urine retention.
Respiratory: increased airway resistance.
Skin: rash.

Interactions

Drug-drug. *Beta-adrenergic agonists:* May blunt the bronchodilator effect of these drugs in patients with bronchospasm. Increase dosages of these bronchodilators may be needed.
Cimetidine: May enhance labetalol's effect. Give together cautiously.
Diuretics and other hypotensives: May increase hypotensive effects. Monitor patient; adjust dosages as necessary.
Halothane: May have additive hypotensive effect. Monitor blood pressure.
Insulin, oral antidiabetics: May need altered dosages in previously stabilized diabetic patients. Observe patient carefully.

Effects on lab test results

• May increase transaminase and blood urea levels.

Pharmacokinetics

Absorption: 90% to 100%; however, drug undergoes extensive first-pass metabolism in liver and only about 25% reaches systemic circulation unchanged.
Distribution: Distributed widely throughout body; about 50% protein-bound.
Metabolism: Metabolized extensively in liver and, possibly, GI mucosa.
Excretion: About 5% excreted unchanged in urine; remainder excreted as metabolites in

urine and feces. *Half-life:* About 5½ hours after I.V. dose; 6 to 8 hours after P.O. dose.

Route	Onset	Peak	Duration
P.O.	≤ 20 min	2-4 hr	8-12 hr
I.V.	≤ 2-5 min	5 min	2-4 hr

Pharmacodynamics

Chemical effect: Unknown; may be related to reduced peripheral vascular resistance as result of alpha-adrenergic blockade.
Therapeutic effect: Lowers blood pressure.

Available forms

Injection: 5 mg/ml
Tablets: 100 mg, 200 mg, 300 mg

NURSING PROCESS

Assessment

- Obtain history of patient's hypertension before therapy.
- Monitor blood pressure frequently. Drug masks common signs of shock.
- When given I.V. for hypertensive emergencies, labetalol produces rapid, predictable fall in blood pressure within 5 to 10 minutes.
- Be alert for adverse reactions and drug interactions.
- Evaluate patient's and family's knowledge of drug therapy.

Nursing diagnoses

- Ineffective health maintenance related to presence of hypertension
- Risk for trauma related to drug-induced hypotension
- Deficient knowledge related to drug therapy

Planning and implementation

- **P.O. use:** If dizziness occurs, ask prescriber if patient may take dose at bedtime or take smaller doses t.i.d. to help minimize this reaction.
- **I.V. use:** Give diluted infusion with infusion-control device. Monitor blood pressure q 5 minutes for 30 minutes, then q 30 minutes for 2 hours, then hourly for 6 hours. Patient should remain lying down for 3 hours after infusion. For I.V. injection, blood pressure should be monitored immediately before and 5 to 10 minutes after injection.

ALERT: Don't confuse Trandate with Tridrate.

ALERT: Sodium bicarbonate injection and furosemide are incompatible with I.V. labetalol.

Patient teaching

- Tell patient that abrupt discontinuation of therapy can worsen angina and cause MI.
- Inform patient that dizziness can be minimized by rising slowly and avoiding sudden position changes.

Evaluation

- Patient's blood pressure is normal.
- Patient doesn't experience trauma caused by drug-induced hypotension.
- Patient and family state understanding of drug therapy.

lactulose

(LAK-tyoo-lohs)
Cephulac, Cholac, Chronulac, Constilac, Constulose, Duphalac, Enulose, Generlac, Kristalose, Lac-Dol ◇

Pharmacologic class: disaccharide
Therapeutic class: laxative
Pregnancy risk category: B

Indications and dosages

▶ **Constipation.** *Adults:* 10 to 20 g (15 to 30 ml) P.O. daily, increase to 60 ml/day, if needed.

▶ **Prevention and treatment of hepatic encephalopathy, including hepatic precoma and coma in patients with severe hepatic disease.** *Adults:* Initially, 20 to 30 g (30 to 45 ml) P.O. t.i.d. or q.i.d. until two to three soft stools are produced daily. Usual dosage is 30 to 50 g daily t.i.d. Or, 200 g (300 ml) diluted with 700 ml of water or normal saline solution and given as retention enema q 4 to 6 hours, p.r.n.

▶ **To induce bowel evacuation in geriatric patients with colonic retention of barium and severe constipation after a barium meal examination‡.** *Adults:* 3.3 to 6.7 g P.O. b.i.d. for 1 to 4 weeks.

▶ **To restore bowel movements after hemorrhoidectomy‡.** *Adults:* 10 g P.O. twice during day before surgery and for 5 days postoperatively.

Contraindications and precautions

- Contraindicated in patients on low-galactose diet.
- Use cautiously in patients with diabetes mellitus.

Lifespan: In breast-feeding women, use cautiously. In elderly patients, use cautiously because they may be more susceptible to hyponatremia.

Adverse reactions

GI: *abdominal cramps, belching, diarrhea, distention, flatulence.*

Interactions

Drug-drug. *Antacids, antibiotics, orally administered neomycin:* May decrease effectiveness of lactulose. Avoid using together.

Effects on lab test results

None reported.

Pharmacokinetics

Absorption: Minimal.
Distribution: Distributed locally, primarily in colon.
Metabolism: Metabolized by colonic bacteria (absorbed portion isn't metabolized).
Excretion: Most excreted in feces; absorbed portion excreted in urine.

Route	Onset	Peak	Duration
P.O.	24-48 hr	Varies	Varies
P.R.	Unknown	Unknown	Unknown

Pharmacodynamics

Chemical effect: Produces osmotic effect in colon. Resulting distention promotes peristalsis. Lactulose also decreases blood ammonia, probably as result of bacterial degradation, which lowers pH of colon contents.
Therapeutic effect: Relieves constipation.

Available forms

Crystals for reconstitution: 10 g/packet, 20 g/packet
Solution: 10 g/15 ml, 3.33 g/5 ml

NURSING PROCESS

Assessment

- Assess patient's condition before therapy and regularly thereafter, including mental status if patient has hepatic encephalopathy.
- Monitor sodium level.
- Be alert for adverse reactions and drug interactions.
- Evaluate patient's and family's knowledge of drug therapy.

Nursing diagnoses

- Constipation related to underlying condition
- Deficient knowledge related to drug therapy

Planning and implementation

ALERT: Don't confuse lactulose with lactose.

- Be prepared to replace fluid loss.
- Store drug at room temperature, preferably below 86° F (30° C). Don't freeze.
- To minimize sweet taste, dilute with water or fruit juice or give with food.
- If enema isn't retained for at least 30 minutes, be prepared to repeat dose.

Patient teaching

- Advise patient to dilute drug with juice or water or to take with food to improve taste.
- Inform patient of adverse reactions and tell him to notify prescriber if reactions become bothersome or if diarrhea occurs.

Evaluation

- Patient's constipation is relieved.
- Patient and family state understanding of drug therapy.

lamivudine

(la-MI-vyoo-deen)
Epivir, Epivir-HBV

Pharmacologic class: synthetic nucleoside analogue
Therapeutic class: antiviral
Pregnancy risk category: C

Indications and dosages

▶ **Treatment of HIV infection in patients taking zidovudine.** *Epivir. Adults and adoles-*

cents age 16 and older weighing 50 kg (110 lb) or more: 150 mg P.O. b.i.d.
Adults and adolescents age 16 and older weighing less than 50 kg (110 lb): 2 mg/kg P.O. b.i.d.
Children ages 3 months to 16 years: 4 mg/kg P.O. b.i.d. Maximum dose is 150 mg b.i.d.
Neonates 30 days and younger‡ : 2 mg/kg P.O. b.i.d.
Patients with renal impairment: If creatinine clearance is 30 to 49 ml/minute, give 150 mg P.O. daily; if clearance is 15 to 29 ml/minute, give 150 mg P.O. on day 1, then 100 mg daily; if 5 to 14 ml/minute, give 150 mg on day 1, then 50 mg daily; if less than 5 ml/minute, give 50 mg on day 1, then 25 mg daily.
▶ **Treatment of chronic hepatitis B with evidence of hepatitis B viral replication and active liver inflammation.** ***Epivir-HBV.*** *Adults:* 100 mg P.O. once daily.
Children ages 2 to 17: 3 mg/kg once daily, up to a maximum dose of 100 mg. Safety and efficacy of treatment beyond 1 year haven't been established; optimum duration of treatment isn't known.
Adult patients with renal impairment: If creatinine clearance is 30 to 49 ml/minute, give 100 mg as first dose, then 50 mg P.O. daily; if clearance is 15 to 29 ml/minute, give 100 mg first dose, then 25 mg P.O. daily; if 5 to 14 ml/minute, give 35 mg first dose, then 15 mg P.O. daily; if less than 5 ml/minute, give 35 mg first dose, then 10 mg P.O. daily.

Contraindications and precautions

- Contraindicated in patients hypersensitive to drug.

Lifespan: Women infected with HIV and those taking lamivudine shouldn't breast-feed. In children with history of pancreatitis or other significant risk factors for development of pancreatitis, drug should be used with extreme caution, if at all.

Adverse reactions

Adverse reactions pertain to the combination therapy of lamivudine and zidovudine.
CNS: *fever, headache, fatigue, neuropathy, malaise, dizziness, insomnia, sleep disorders,* depressive disorders.
EENT: *nasal symptoms.*
GI: *nausea, diarrhea, vomiting, anorexia,* abdominal pain, abdominal cramps, dyspepsia, ***pancreatitis.***
Hematologic: ***neutropenia,*** anemia, ***thrombocytopenia.***
Musculoskeletal: *musculoskeletal pain,* myalgia, arthralgia.
Respiratory: *cough.*
Skin: rash.
Other: *chills.*

Interactions

Drug-drug. *Trimethoprim–sulfamethoxazole:* May decrease lamivudine clearance and increase blood levels. Monitor patient closely.
Zalcitabine: May inhibit one another. Avoid using together.
Zidovudine: May increase zidovudine level. Monitor patient closely.

Effects on lab test results

- May increase ALT and bilirubin levels.
- May decrease hemoglobin, hematocrit, and neutrophil and platelet counts.

Pharmacokinetics

Absorption: Rapid in HIV-infected patients.
Distribution: Believed to distribute into extravascular spaces. Volume of distribution is independent of dose and doesn't correlate with body weight. Less than 36% is bound to plasma proteins.
Metabolism: Drug has a minor route of elimination. The only known metabolite is the trans-sulfoxide metabolite.
Excretion: Drug is primarily eliminated unchanged in urine. *Mean elimination half-life:* 5 to 7 hours.

Route	Onset	Peak	Duration
P.O.	Unknown	1-3 hr	Unknown

Pharmacodynamics

Chemical effect: A synthetic nucleoside analogue that inhibits HIV reverse transcription via viral DNA chain termination. RNA- and DNA-dependent DNA polymerase activities are also inhibited.
Therapeutic effect: Reduces the symptoms linked to HIV infection.

Available forms

Oral solution: 5 mg/ml, 10 mg/ml
Tablets: 100 mg, 150 mg, 300 mg

NURSING PROCESS

Assessment

- Obtain history of patient's underlying condition before therapy, and reassess regularly thereafter.
- Patients should be tested for HIV before and during treatment because formulation and dosage of lamivudine in Epivir-HBV aren't appropriate for those dually infected with hepatitis B virus and HIV.
- Monitor renal function before and during therapy.
- Monitor patient's CBC, platelet count, and renal and liver function studies. Report any abnormalities to prescriber.
- Evaluate patient's and family's knowledge of drug therapy.

Nursing diagnoses

- Risk for infection related to the presence of HIV
- Risk for injury related to drug-induced CNS adverse reactions
- Deficient knowledge related to drug therapy

Planning and implementation

- If lamivudine is given to patients with hepatitis B virus and HIV, the higher dosage indicated for HIV therapy should be used as part of an appropriate combination regimen.
- Give drug with zidovudine. Drug is not currently indicated for use alone unless for chronic hepatitis B virus infection.
- Safety and effectiveness of treatment with Epivir-HBV beyond 1 year haven't been established; optimum duration of treatment isn't known.
- Stop lamivudine treatment immediately and notify prescriber if clinical signs, symptoms, or laboratory abnormalities suggest pancreatitis.
- An Antiretroviral Pregnancy Registry has been established to monitor maternal-fetal outcomes of pregnant women exposed to lamivudine. To register a pregnant patient, the prescriber can call 1-800-258-4263.

Patient teaching

- Inform patient that long-term effects of lamivudine are unknown.
- Stress importance of taking lamivudine exactly as prescribed.
- Teach parents the signs and symptoms of pancreatitis. Advise them to report signs and symptoms immediately.

Evaluation

- Patient responds well to drug therapy.
- Patient sustains no injury as a result of drug-induced CNS adverse reactions.
- Patient and family state understanding of drug therapy.

lamivudine and zidovudine

(la-MI-vyoo-deen and zye-DOE-vyoo-deen)
Combivir

Pharmacologic class: reverse transcriptase inhibitor
Therapeutic class: antiretroviral
Pregnancy risk category: C

Indications and dosages

▶ **Treatment of HIV infection.** *Adults and children age 12 and older weighing more than 50 kg (110 lb):* One tablet P.O. b.i.d.

Contraindications and precautions

- Contraindicated in patients hypersensitive to drug or its components, in those who need dosage adjustments (such as those weighing less than 50 kg), and in those with creatinine clearance below 50 ml/minute. Also contraindicated in patients experiencing dose-limiting adverse effects.

Lifespan: Women infected with HIV and those taking Combivir shouldn't breast-feed. In children younger than age 12, drug is contraindicated.

Adverse reactions

CNS: *fever, headache, malaise, fatigue, insomnia, dizziness, neuropathy,* depression.
EENT: *nasal signs and symptoms.*
GI: *nausea, diarrhea, vomiting, anorexia,* abdominal pain, abdominal cramps, dyspepsia.
Hematologic: ***neutropenia,*** anemia.
Musculoskeletal: *musculoskeletal pain,* myalgia, arthralgia.
Respiratory: *cough.*
Skin: rash.
Other: *chills.*

Interactions

Drug-drug. *Atovaquone, fluconazole, methadone, probenecid, and valproic acid coadministered with zidovudine:* Increased bioavailability of zidovudine. Dosage modification isn't needed.
Co-trimoxazole or nelfinavir coadministered with lamivudine: Increased bioavailability of lamivudine. Dosage modification isn't needed.
Ganciclovir, inteferon-alpha, and other bone marrow suppressive or cytotoxic agents: May increase hematologic toxicity of zidovudine. Use cautiously as with other reverse transcriptase inhibitors.
Nelfinavir, ritonavir: Decreased bioavailability of zidovudine may occur with administration together. Dosage modification isn't needed.
Zalcitabine: Zalcitabine and lamivudine may inhibit intracellular phosphorylation of one another. Use of drugs together isn't recommended.

Effects on lab test results

- May increase ALT, AST, and amylase levels.
- May decrease hemoglobin, hematocrit, and neutrophil count.

Pharmacokinetics

Absorption: Rapid for both drugs, with bioavailability of 86% and 64%, respectively.
Distribution: Both drugs are extensively distributed with low protein binding.
Metabolism: Only about 5% of lamivudine is metabolized; zidovudine is primarily metabolized (74%) in the liver.
Excretion: Lamivudine is primarily eliminated unchanged in the urine. Zidovudine and its major metabolite are primarily eliminated in the urine. Elimination half-lives of lamivudine and zidovudine are 5 to 7 hours and ½ to 3 hours, respectively. Renal excretion is a principal route of elimination, and dosage adjustments are necessary in patients with compromised renal function making this fixed ratio combination unsuitable. Hemodialysis and peritoneal dialysis have negligible effect on the removal of zidovudine, but removal of its metabolite, GZDV, is enhanced. The effect of dialysis on lamivudine is unknown.

Route	Onset	Peak	Duration
P.O.	Unknown	Unknown	Unknown

Pharmacodynamics

Chemical effect: Inhibits reverse transcriptase via DNA chain termination. Both drugs are also weak inhibitors of DNA polymerase. Together, they have synergistic antiretroviral activity. Combination therapy with lamivudine and zidovudine is targeted at suppressing or delaying the emergence of resistant strains that can occur with retroviral monotherapy, because dual resistance requires multiple mutations.
Therapeutic effect: Reduces the symptoms of HIV infection.

Available forms

Tablets: 150 mg lamivudine and 300 mg zidovudine

NURSING PROCESS

Assessment

- Obtain history of patient's underlying condition before therapy, and reassess regularly thereafter.
- Watch for bone marrow toxicity with frequent blood counts, particularly in patients with advanced HIV infection.
- Monitor patient for signs of lactic acidosis or hepatotoxicity (abdominal pain, jaundice) and notify the prescriber.
- Assess patient's fine motor skills and peripheral sensation for evidence of peripheral neuropathies.
- Evaluate patient's and family's knowledge of drug therapy.

Nursing diagnoses

- Risk for infection related to the presence of HIV
- Disturbed sensory perception (tactile) related to drug-induced peripheral neuropathy
- Deficient knowledge related to drug therapy

Planning and implementation

- This drug combination may be inappropriate for patients with compromised renal function.
- Use drug cautiously in patients with bone marrow suppression (granulocyte count below 1,000 cells/mm³ or hemoglobin level below 9.5 g/dl).
- An Antiretroviral Pregnancy Registry has been established to monitor maternal-fetal outcomes of pregnant women exposed to Com-

bivir. To register a pregnant patient, prescriber can call 1-800-258-4263.
• Patients with chronic hepatitis B virus (HBV) may experience recurrence of hepatitis upon discontinuation of lamivudine. Patients with liver disease may have more severe consequences. Periodically monitor liver function tests and markers of HBV replication in patients with liver disease and HBV.
• Safety and efficacy of lamivudine haven't been established for treatment of chronic hepatitis B in patients infected with both HIV and HBV. Lamivudine-resistant hepatitis B virus variants may emerge in patients with HBV and HIV who have received lamivudine-containing antiretroviral regimens.

Patient teaching
• Advise patient that therapy with lamivudine and zidovudine won't cure HIV infection and that he may continue to experience illness, including opportunistic infections.
• Warn patient that HIV transmission can still occur with drug therapy.
• Educate patient about using barrier contraception when engaging in sexual activities to prevent disease transmission.
• Teach patient signs and symptoms of neutropenia and anemia (fever, chills, infection, fatigue) and instruct him to report such occurrences immediately to prescriber.
• Tell patient to have blood counts followed closely while on drug, especially if he has advanced disease.
• Advise patient to consult prescriber or pharmacist before taking other drugs.
• Warn patient to report abdominal pain immediately.
• Instruct patient to report signs and symptoms of myopathy or myositis (muscle inflammation, pain, weakness, decrease in muscle size).
• Stress importance of taking combination drug therapy exactly as prescribed to reduce the development of resistance.
• Tell patient he may take combination with or without food.
• Inform women that breast-feeding is contraindicated in HIV infection and during drug therapy.

☑ Evaluation
• Patient responds well to drug.
• Patient doesn't develop peripheral neuropathy.
• Patient and family state understanding of drug therapy.

lamotrigine
(lah-MOH-trigh-jeen)
Lamictal

Pharmacologic class: phenyltriazine
Therapeutic class: anticonvulsant
Pregnancy risk category: C

Indications and dosages
▶ **Adjunct therapy in treatment of partial seizures caused by epilepsy or generalized seizures of Lennox-Gastout syndrome.** *Adults and adolescents older than age 12:* For patients taking valproic acid with other enzyme-inducing antiepileptics, 25 mg P.O. every other day for 2 weeks; then 25 mg P.O. daily for 2 weeks. Continue to increase, p.r.n., by 25 to 50 mg/day q 1 to 2 weeks until an effective maintenance dosage of 100 to 400 mg daily given in one or two divided doses is reached. When added to valproic acid alone, the usual maintenance dose is 100 to 200 mg/day. For patients receiving enzyme-inducing antiepileptics but not valproic acid, 50 mg P.O. daily for 2 weeks; then 100 mg P.O. daily in two divided doses for 2 weeks. Increase, p.r.n., by 100 mg daily q 1 to 2 weeks. Usual maintenance dosage is 300 to 500 mg P.O. daily in two divided doses.
Children ages 2 to 12 years weighing 6.7 to 40 kg (15 to 88 lb): For patients taking valproic acid with other enzyme-inducing antiepileptics, 0.15 mg/kg P.O. daily in 1 or 2 divided doses (rounded down to nearest whole tablet) for 2 weeks, followed by 0.3 mg/kg daily in 1 or 2 divided doses for another 2 weeks. Thereafter, usual maintenance dosage is 1 to 5 mg/kg daily (maximum, 200 mg daily in one to two divided doses). For patients receiving enzyme-inducing antiepileptics but not valproic acid, 0.6 mg/kg P.O. daily in 2 divided doses (rounded down to nearest whole tablet) for 2 weeks, followed by 1.2 mg/kg daily in 2 divided doses for another 2 weeks. Thereafter, usual maintenance dosage is 5 to 15 mg/kg daily (maximum 400 mg/day in 2 divided doses).

▶ **To convert patients from monotherapy with a hepatic enzyme-inducing anticonvulsant drug to lamotrigine therapy.** *Adults and children age 16 and older:* Add lamotrigine 50 mg P.O. once daily to current drug regimen for 2 weeks, followed by 100 mg P.O. daily in two divided doses for 2 weeks. Then increase daily dosage by 100 mg q 1 to 2 weeks until maintenance dose of 500 mg daily in two divided doses is reached. Then the hepatic enzyme-inducing anticonvulsant can be gradually withdrawn by 20% weekly for 4 weeks.
Patients with severe renal impairment: Use lower maintenance dosage.

Contraindications and precautions

- Contraindicated in patients hypersensitive to drug.
- Use cautiously in patients with renal, hepatic, or cardiac impairment.

Lifespan: In pregnant women, use cautiously. In breast-feeding women, drug isn't recommended. In children younger than age 16, use is contraindicated.

Adverse reactions

CNS: fever, *dizziness, headache, ataxia, somnolence,* incoordination, insomnia, tremor, depression, anxiety, ***seizures,*** irritability, speech disorder, decreased memory, aggravated reaction, concentration disturbance, sleep disorder, emotional lability, vertigo, malaise, mind racing, ***suicide attempts.***
CV: palpitations.
EENT: *diplopia, blurred vision,* vision abnormality, nystagmus, rhinitis, pharyngitis.
GI: *nausea, vomiting,* diarrhea, dyspepsia, abdominal pain, constipation, anorexia, dry mouth.
GU: dysmenorrhea, vaginitis, amenorrhea.
Musculoskeletal: dysarthria, muscle spasm, neck pain.
Respiratory: cough, dyspnea.
Skin: ***Stevens-Johnson syndrome, toxic epidermal necrolysis,*** *rash,* pruritus, hot flushes, alopecia, acne.
Other: flulike syndrome, infection, chills, tooth disorder.

Interactions

Drug-drug. *Acetaminophen:* May reduce lamotrigine level, decreasing therapeutic effects. Monitor patient.
Carbamazepine, phenobarbital, phenytoin, primidone: Decreases steady-state level of lamotrigine. Monitor patient closely.
Folate inhibitors (such as co-trimoxazole, methotrexate): May have additive effect because lamotrigine inhibits dihydrofolate reductase, an enzyme involved in folic acid synthesis. Monitor patient closely.
Valproic acid: Decreases lamotrigine clearance, which increases steady-state levels. Monitor patient closely for toxicity.
Drug-lifestyle. *Sun exposure:* Photosensitivity reactions may occur. Urge patient to avoid unprotected or prolonged exposure to sunlight.

Effects on lab test results

None reported.

Pharmacokinetics

Absorption: Rapid and complete with negligible first-pass metabolism.
Distribution: 55% protein-bound.
Metabolism: Predominantly by glucuronic acid conjugation.
Excretion: Excreted primarily in urine. *Half-life:* 14.4 to 70.3 hours, depending on dosage schedule and use of other anticonvulsants.

Route	Onset	Peak	Duration
P.O.	Unknown	1.4-4.8 hr	Unknown

Pharmacodynamics

Chemical effect: Unknown; may inhibit release of glutamate and aspartate, excitatory neurotransmitters in the brain, through action at sodium channels.
Therapeutic effect: Prevents partial seizure activity.

Available forms

Tablets: 25 mg, 100 mg, 150 mg, 200 mg
Tablets (chewable dispersible): 2 mg, 5 mg, 25 mg

NURSING PROCESS

Assessment

- Obtain history of patient's seizure disorder before therapy.
- Evaluate patient for reduction in frequency and duration of seizures after therapy begins. Check adjunct anticonvulsant's level periodically.

• Evaluate patient's and family's knowledge of drug therapy.

Nursing diagnoses
• Risk for trauma related to seizures
• Risk for impaired skin integrity related to dermatologic reactions
• Deficient knowledge related to drug therapy

Planning and implementation
• Dosage should be lowered if drug is added to multidrug regimen that includes valproic acid.
• Lowered maintenance dosage should be used in patients with severe renal impairment.
• Don't stop drug abruptly because doing so increases the risk of seizures. Instead, drug should be tapered over at least 2 weeks.
ALERT: Rash may be life-threatening. Stop drug and notify prescriber at first sign of rash.
ALERT: Don't confuse Lamictal with Lamisil.

Patient teaching
• Inform patient that lamotrigine may cause rash. Combination therapy with valproic acid and lamotrigine is more likely to cause a serious rash. Tell patient to report rash or signs or symptoms of hypersensitivity immediately because they could be life-threatening.
• Instruct patient to avoid prolonged exposure to sunlight, use sunblock, and wear protective clothing.
• Warn patient not to engage in hazardous activity until CNS effects of drug are known.

Evaluation
• Patient is seizure-free.
• Patient doesn't develop drug-induced skin reactions.
• Patient and family state understanding of drug therapy.

lansoprazole
(lan-soh-PRAY-zohl)
Prevacid, Prevacid SoluTab

Pharmacologic class: substituted benzimidazole
Therapeutic class: antiulcer agent
Pregnancy risk category: B

Indications and dosages
▶ **Short-term treatment of active duodenal ulcer.** *Adults:* 15 mg P.O. daily before meals for 4 weeks.
▶ **Maintenance of healed duodenal ulcers.** *Adults:* 15 mg P.O. once daily.
▶ **Short-term treatment of erosive esophagitis.** *Adults:* 30 mg P.O. daily before meals for up to 8 weeks. If healing doesn't occur, additional 8 weeks of therapy may be given. Maintenance dosage for healing is 15 mg P.O. daily.
▶ **Short-term treatment of active benign gastric ulcer.** *Adults:* 30 mg P.O. once daily for up to 8 weeks.
▶ ***Helicobacter pylori* eradication to reduce risk of duodenal ulcer recurrence.** ***Triple therapy.*** *Adults:* 30 mg P.O. lansoprazole with 500 mg P.O. clarithromycin and 1 g P.O. amoxicillin, each given q 12 hours for 14 days. ***Dual therapy.*** *Adults:* 30 mg P.O. lansoprazole with 1 g P.O. amoxicillin, each given q 8 hours for 14 days.
▶ **Long-term treatment of pathologic hypersecretory conditions, including Zollinger-Ellison syndrome.** *Adults:* Initially, 60 mg P.O. once daily. Dosage increased as needed. If more than 120 mg daily, give in divided doses.
▶ **Short-term treatment of symptomatic gastroesophageal reflux disease (GERD).** *Adults:* 15 mg P.O. daily for up to 8 weeks. *Children ages 1 to 11 years old, weighing 30 kg or less:* 15 mg P.O. daily for up to 12 weeks.
Children ages 1 to 11 years old, weighing more than 30 kg (66 lb): 30 mg P.O. daily for up to 12 weeks.
▶ **Treatment of NSAID-related ulcer in patients who continue to take NSAIDs.** *Adults:* 30 mg P.O. daily for 8 weeks.
▶ **Reduction in risk of NSAID-related ulcer in patients who have a history of gastric ulcer but who need NSAIDs.** *Adults:* 15 mg P.O. daily for up to 12 weeks.

Contraindications and precautions
• Contraindicated in patients hypersensitive to drug.
• Drug isn't recommended as maintenance therapy for patients with active duodenal ulcers or erosive esophagitis.
Lifespan: In pregnant women, use cautiously. For breast-feeding women, drug isn't recommended. In children less than age 1 or

ages 12 to 17, safety of drug hasn't been established.

Adverse reactions

GI: diarrhea, nausea, abdominal pain.

Interactions

Drug-drug. *Ampicillin esters, digoxin, iron salts, ketoconazole:* Lansoprazole may interfere with absorption. Monitor patient closely.
Sucralfate: Delays lansoprazole absorption. Give lansoprazole at least 30 minutes before sucralfate.
Theophylline: Theophylline clearance may increase slightly. Use together cautiously. Dosage adjustment of theophylline may be necessary when lansoprazole is started or stopped.
Drug-food. *Food:* Decreases absorption of drug when taken with meals. Take drug on an empty stomach, before meals.
Drug-herb. *Male fern:* Inactivated in alkaline environments. Discourage using together.
St. John's wort: Increases risk of photosensitivity reactions. Advise patient to avoid unprotected or prolonged exposure to sunlight.

Effects on lab test results

None reported.

Pharmacokinetics

Absorption: Rapid.
Distribution: 97% bound to plasma proteins.
Metabolism: Metabolized extensively in liver.
Excretion: Excreted mainly in feces, minimally in urine. *Half-life:* Less than 2 hours.

Route	Onset	Peak	Duration
P.O.	Unknown	2 hr	> 24 hr

Pharmacodynamics

Chemical effect: Inhibits activity of proton pump and binds to hydrogen or potassium adenosine triphosphatase, located at secretory surface of gastric parietal cells.
Therapeutic effect: Decreases gastric acid formation.

Available forms

Capsules (delayed-release): 15 mg, 30 mg
Oral suspension (delayed-release): 15 mg/packet, 30 mg/packet
Tablets (orally disintegrating, delayed-release): 15 mg, 30 mg

NURSING PROCESS

Assessment

- Assess patient's condition before therapy and regularly thereafter.
- Be alert for adverse reactions and drug interactions.
- Evaluate patient's and family's knowledge of drug therapy.

Nursing diagnoses

- Impaired tissue integrity related to underlying condition
- Ineffective health maintenance related to drug-induced adverse reactions
- Deficient knowledge related to drug therapy

Planning and implementation

- Give drug on empty stomach.
- Contents of capsule can be mixed with 40 ml of apple juice in a syringe and given within 3 to 5 minutes via a nasogastric tube. Flush with additional apple juice to ensure entire dose is given and to maintain patency of the tube.
- Contents of capsule may be emptied into a small volume of apple, cranberry, grape, orange, pineapple, prune, tomato, or vegetable juice (60 ml is about 2 ounces), mixed briefly and used within 30 minutes. To ensure complete delivery of the dose, the glass should be rinsed with two or more volumes of juice and the contents swallowed immediately.
- Contents of capsule also can be mixed with 1 tablespoon of applesauce, pudding, cottage cheese, yogurt, or strained pears and swallowed immediately. The granules should not be chewed or crushed.
- For the oral suspension, empty packet contents into 30 ml of water. Stir well and have patient drink immediately. Tell patient not to chew or crush the contents of the capsules or the suspension. Don't use with other liquids or food. If any material remains after drinking, add more water, stir, and have patient drink immediately.
- Dosage adjustment may be needed for patients with severe liver disease.
- Orally disintegrating tablets should be placed on the tongue and allowed to dissolve until the particles can be swallowed. Water isn't necessary.

• Notify prescriber if adverse reactions occur, and be prepared to provide supportive care.

Patient teaching
• Instruct patient to take drug before eating. Tell the patient who has trouble swallowing capsules to open and sprinkle contents over applesauce, and to swallow immediately. The contents shouldn't be chewed or crushed.
• Instruct patient to notify prescriber if any adverse reactions occur.

Evaluation
• Patient regains normal GI tissue integrity.
• Patient doesn't experience serious adverse reactions.
• Patient and family state understanding of drug therapy.

leflunomide
(leh-FLOO-noh-mighd)
Arava

Pharmacologic class: pyrimidine synthesis inhibitor
Therapeutic class: immunomodulatory agent
Pregnancy risk category: X

Indications and dosages

▶ **Treatment of active rheumatoid arthritis to reduce signs and symptoms and to retard structural damage as evidenced by X-ray erosions and joint space narrowing.** *Adults:* 100 mg P.O. q 24 hours for 3 days followed by 20 mg (maximum daily dose) P.O. q 24 hours. Dosage may be decreased to 10 mg daily if higher dosage isn't tolerated well.

Contraindications and precautions

• Contraindicated in patients hypersensitive to drug or its components.
• Drug isn't recommended for patients with hepatic insufficiency, hepatitis B or C, severe immunodeficiency, bone marrow dysplasia, or severe uncontrolled infections.
• Vaccination with live vaccines isn't recommended. Long half-life of drug should be considered when contemplating administration of a live vaccine after stopping drug treatment.
• Use cautiously in patients with renal insufficiency.
• Some immunosuppression drugs, including leflunomide, cause an increased risk of malignancy, particularly lymphoproliferative disorders.
• Drug isn't recommended for men attempting to father children.
Lifespan: In pregnant or breast-feeding women, drug is contraindicated. For children younger than age 18, drug isn't recommended.

Adverse reactions

CNS: asthenia, dizziness, fever, headache, paresthesia, malaise, migraine, sleep disorder, vertigo, neuritis, anxiety, depression, insomnia, neuralgia.
CV: angina pectoris, *hypertension,* chest pain, peripheral edema, palpitations, tachycardia, vasculitis, vasodilation, varicose veins.
EENT: pharyngitis, rhinitis, sinusitis, epistaxis, enlarged salivary gland, blurred vision, cataracts, conjunctivitis, eye disorders.
GI: mouth ulcer, oral candidiasis, stomatitis, dry mouth, anorexia, *diarrhea,* dyspepsia, gastroenteritis, nausea, abdominal pain, vomiting, cholelithiasis, colitis, constipation, esophagitis, flatulence, gastritis, melena, gingivitis, taste perversion.
GU: urinary tract infection, albuminuria, cystitis, dysuria, hematuria, menstrual disorder, pelvic pain, vaginal candidiasis, prostate disorder, urinary frequency.
Hematologic: anemia, hyperlipidemia.
Metabolic: weight loss, diabetes mellitus, hyperglycemia, hyperthyroidism, hypokalemia.
Musculoskeletal: arthrosis, back pain, bursitis, muscle cramps, myalgia, bone necrosis, bone pain, arthralgia, leg cramps, joint disorder, neck pain, synovitis, tendon rupture, tenosynovitis.
Respiratory: bronchitis, increased cough, pneumonia, *respiratory infection,* asthma, dyspnea, lung disorders.
Skin: *alopecia,* eczema, pruritus, *rash,* dry skin, acne, contact dermatitis, fungal dermatitis, hair discoloration, hematoma, nail disorder, skin nodule, subcutaneous nodule, maculopapular rash, skin disorder, skin discoloration, skin ulcer, increased sweating, ecchymosis.
Other: allergic reaction, flulike syndrome, injury or accident, pain, abscess, cyst, hernia, tooth disorder, herpes simplex, herpes zoster.

Interactions

Drug-drug. *Cholestyramine, charcoal:* Decreases plasma leflunomide levels. Sometimes used for this effect in overdose.
Methotrexate, other hepatotoxic drugs: Increases risk of hepatotoxicity. Monitor liver enzyme levels.
NSAIDs (diclofenac, ibuprofen): Increases NSAID levels. Clinical significance is unknown; monitor patient.
Rifampin: Increases active leflunomide metabolite level. Use together cautiously.
Tolbutamide: Increases tolbutamide levels. Clinical significance is unknown; monitor patient.

Effects on lab test results

- May increase AST, ALT, glucose, lipid, T_4, and CK levels. May decrease potassium and TSH levels.
- May decrease hemoglobin and hematocrit.

Pharmacokinetics

Absorption: 80% of dose is absorbed after P.O. administration.
Distribution: Extensively bound to albumin; has low volume of distribution.
Metabolism: Primary route of metabolism hasn't been identified.
Excretion: Excreted renally as well as by direct biliary elimination; 43% excreted in urine, 48% eliminated in feces.

Route	Onset	Peak	Duration
P.O.	Unknown	6-12 hr	Unknown

Pharmacodynamics

Chemical effect: Inhibits dihydroorotate dehydrogenase, an enzyme involved in pyrimidine synthesis, and has antiproliferative activity and anti-inflammatory effects.
Therapeutic effect: Reduces pain and inflammation related to rheumatoid arthritis.

Available forms

Tablets: 10 mg, 20 mg, 100 mg

NURSING PROCESS

Assessment

- Assess patient's condition before therapy and regularly thereafter.
- Be alert for adverse reactions and drug interactions.
- Monitor liver enzymes (ALT and AST) before starting therapy and monthly thereafter until stable. Frequency of monitoring can then be decreased based on clinical situation.
- Evaluate patient's and family's knowledge of drug therapy.

Nursing diagnoses

- Ineffective health maintenance related to underlying disease
- Deficient knowledge related to drug therapy

Planning and implementation

ALERT: Drug can cause fetal harm when given to pregnant women. Discontinue drug in women planning to become pregnant, and notify prescriber.
- Drug should be discontinued in man who plans to father a child. Tell patient to follow recommended leflunomide removal protocol (cholestyramine 8 g P.O. t.i.d. for 11 days).

Patient teaching

- Explain need for and frequency of required blood test monitoring.
- Instruct patient to use contraceptive measures during drug therapy and until drug is no longer active.
- Advise patient to notify prescriber immediately if pregnancy is suspected.
- Advise breast-feeding patient to discontinue breast-feeding during drug therapy.
- Inform patient that aspirin, other NSAIDs, and low-dose corticosteroids may be continued during treatment; however, combined use of drug with antimalarials, I.M. or P.O. gold, penicillamine, azathioprine, or methotrexate hasn't been adequately studied.

Evaluation

- Patient's symptoms of rheumatoid arthritis improve.
- Patient and family state understanding of drug therapy.

leucovorin calcium (citrovorum factor, folinic acid)

(loo-koh-VOR-in KAL-see-um)

Pharmacologic class: formyl derivative (active reduced form of folic acid)
Therapeutic class: vitamin, antidote
Pregnancy risk category: C

Indications and dosages

▶ **Overdose of folic acid antagonist.** *Adults and children:* P.O., I.M., or I.V. dose equivalent to weight of antagonist given.

▶ **Rescue after high methotrexate dose in treatment of cancer.** *Adults and children:* 10 mg/m² P.O., I.M., or I.V. q 6 hours until methotrexate level falls below 5×10^{-8} M.

▶ **Megaloblastic anemia caused by congenital enzyme deficiency.** *Adults and children:* 3 to 6 mg I.M. daily; then 1 mg P.O. or I.M. daily for life.

▶ **Folate-deficient megaloblastic anemia.** *Adults and children:* Up to 1 mg P.O. or I.M daily. Duration of treatment depends on hematologic response.

▶ **Treatment of hematologic toxicity caused by pyrimethamine or trimethoprim therapy.** *Adults and children:* 5 to 15 mg P.O. or I.M. daily.

▶ **Palliative treatment of advanced colorectal carcinoma.** *Adults:* 20 mg/m² I.V., followed by fluorouracil, for 5 consecutive days. Repeated q 4 weeks for two additional courses; then q 4 to 5 weeks, if tolerated.

Contraindications and precautions

• Contraindicated in patients with pernicious anemia and other megaloblastic anemias caused by lack of vitamin B_{12}.

Lifespan: In breast-feeding women, use cautiously. In children, use cautiously; may increase risk of seizures. In neonates, injection form is contraindicated because it contains benzyl alcohol.

Adverse reactions

Respiratory: ***bronchospasm.***
Skin: hypersensitivity reactions (rash, pruritus, erythema).

Interactions

Drug-drug. *Anticonvulsants:* May decrease anticonvulsant effectiveness. Monitor patient closely.
Fluorouracil: May enhance fluorouracil toxicity. Avoid using together.
Methotrexate: May decrease efficacy of intrathecal methotrexate. Avoid using together.

Effects on lab test results

None reported.

Pharmacokinetics

Absorption: Absorbed rapidly after P.O. administration.
Distribution: Distributed throughout body; liver contains about one-half of total body folate stores.
Metabolism: Metabolized in liver.
Excretion: Excreted by kidneys. *Half-life:* 6.2 hours.

Route	Onset	Peak	Duration
P.O.	20-30 min	2-3 hr	3-6 hr
I.V.	5 min	10 min	3-6 hr
I.M.	10-20 min	< hr	3-6 hr

Pharmacodynamics

Chemical effect: Readily converts to other folic acid derivatives.
Therapeutic effect: Raises folic acid level in body.

Available forms

Injection: 1-ml ampule (3 mg/ml with 0.9% benzyl alcohol)
Powder for injection: 50-, 100-, and 350-mg vials
Tablets: 5 mg, 15 mg, 25 mg

NURSING PROCESS

Assessment

• Assess patient's condition before therapy and regularly thereafter.
• Monitor creatinine level daily to detect renal dysfunction.
• Be alert for adverse reactions and drug interactions.
• Monitor patient for rash, wheezing, pruritus, and urticaria, which can be signs of drug allergy.

• Evaluate patient's and family's knowledge of drug therapy.

Nursing diagnoses

• Ineffective health maintenance related to underlying condition
• Deficient knowledge related to drug therapy

Planning and implementation

• **P.O. and I.M. use:** Follow normal protocol.
• **I.V. use:** When using powder for injection, reconstitute drug in 50-mg vial with 5 ml, 100-mg vial with 10 ml, or 350-mg vial with 17 ml of sterile water or bacteriostatic water for injection. When doses are greater than 10 mg/m^2, don't use diluents containing benzyl alcohol, especially in neonates.
ALERT: Don't exceed 160 mg/minute when giving by direct injection.
• To avoid confusion, don't refer to leucovorin as folinic acid.
• Follow leucovorin rescue schedule and protocol closely to maximize therapeutic response.
• Don't give simultaneously with systemic methotrexate.
• Protect drug from light and heat, especially reconstituted parenteral forms.
ALERT: Don't confuse leucovorin (folinic acid) with folic acid.

Patient teaching

• Explain to patient reasons for drug therapy.

Evaluation

• Patient's condition improves.
• Patient and family state understanding of drug therapy.

leuprolide acetate

(loo-PROH-lighd AS-ih-tayt)

Eligard, Lupron for Pediatric use, Lucrin ◇, Lupron, Lupron Depot, Lupron Depot-Ped, Lupron Depot-3 Month, Lupron Depot-4 Month

Pharmacologic class: gonadotropin-releasing hormone
Therapeutic class: antineoplastic, luteinizing hormone-releasing hormone analogue
Pregnancy risk category: X

Indications and dosages

▶ **Advanced prostate cancer.** *Adults:* 1 mg S.C. daily. Or, 7.5 mg I.M. (depot injection) monthly. Or, 22.5 mg I.M. q 3 months (84 days). Or, 30 mg I.M. (depot injection) q 4 months (16 weeks).
▶ **Endometriosis.** *Adults:* 3.75 mg I.M. as single injection once monthly. Or, 11.25 mg I.M. q 3 months (depot injection only) for up to 6 months.
▶ **Central precocious puberty.** *Children:* Initially, 0.3 mg/kg (minimum 7.5 mg) I.M. (depot injection only) as single injection q 4 weeks. Dosage may be increased in increments of 3.75 mg q 4 weeks, if needed. Or, (injection form) 50 mcg/kg S.C. daily. If total downregulation isn't achieved, adjust dosage upward by 10 mcg/kg daily. This becomes the maintenance dosage. Therapy should be discontinued before girl reaches age 11 and before boy reaches age 12.

Contraindications and precautions

• Contraindicated in patients hypersensitive to drug or other gonadotropin-releasing hormone analogues, and in women with undiagnosed vaginal bleeding.
• Use cautiously in patients hypersensitive to benzyl alcohol.
Lifespan: In pregnant or breast-feeding women, use is contraindicated. In neonates, benzyl alcohol is contraindicated. In women, the 30-mg depot formulation is contraindicated.

Adverse reactions

CNS: dizziness, depression, headache.
CV: ***arrhythmias,*** angina, ***MI,*** peripheral edema.
GI: nausea, vomiting.
GU: impotence.
Musculoskeletal: transient bone pain (during first week of treatment).
Respiratory: ***pulmonary embolism.***
Skin: skin reactions at injection site.
Other: *hot flushes,* decreased libido, gynecomastia.

Interactions

None significant.

Effects on lab test results

- May increase BUN, creatinine, bilirubin, alkaline phosphatase, LDH, glucose, uric acid, albumin, calcium, and phosphorus levels.
- May decrease hemoglobin and hematocrit.
- May give inaccurate reading of pituitary gonadotropic and gonadal functions during treatment and for up to 12 weeks afterwards.

Pharmacokinetics

Absorption: After S.C. administration, drug is rapidly and completely absorbed; unknown for I.M. use.
Distribution: Unknown; about 7% to 15% bound to plasma proteins.
Metabolism: Unknown.
Excretion: Unknown. *Half-life:* 3 hours.

Route	Onset	Peak	Duration
I.M., S.C.	Unknown	1-2 mo	1-3 mo

Pharmacodynamics

Chemical effect: Initially stimulates but then inhibits release of follicle-stimulating hormone and luteinizing hormone, resulting in testosterone suppression.
Therapeutic effect: Hinders prostatic cancer cell growth and eases signs and symptoms of endometriosis.

Available forms

Depot injection: *Lupron Depot*—3.75 mg, 7.5 mg. *Lupron Depot-Ped*—7.5 mg, 11.25 mg, 15 mg. *Lupron Depot-3 month*—11.25 mg, 22.5 mg. *Lupron Depot-4 month*—30 mg
Injection: 5 mg/ml in 2.8-ml multiple-dose vial

NURSING PROCESS

Assessment

- Assess patient's condition before therapy and regularly thereafter.
- Be alert for adverse reactions.
- Evaluate patient's and family's knowledge of drug therapy.

Nursing diagnoses

- Ineffective health maintenance related to underlying condition
- Disturbed thought processes related to drug-induced depression
- Deficient knowledge related to drug therapy

Planning and implementation

- Never give drug by I.V. injection.
- **I.M. use:** Once-monthly depot injection should be given under medical supervision. Use supplied diluent to reconstitute drug (extra diluent is provided and should be discarded).
  – Draw 1 ml into syringe with 22G needle. (When preparing Lupron Depot-3 Month 22.5 mg, use a 23G or larger needle.) Withdraw 1.5 ml from ampule for the 3-month formulation.
  – Inject into vial, then shake well. Suspension will appear milky.
  – Although suspension is stable for 24 hours after reconstitution, it contains no bacteriostatic agent. Use immediately.
- When using prefilled dual-chamber syringes, prepare for injection by screwing white plunger into end stopper until stopper begins to turn. Remove and discard tab around base of needle. Hold syringe upright and release diluent by slowly pushing plunger until first stopper is at blue line in middle of barrel. Gently shake syringe to form a uniform milky suspension. If particles adhere to stopper, tap syringe against finger. Remove needle guard and advance plunger to expel air from syringe. Inject entire contents I.M. as for a normal injection.
- **S.C. use:** Follow normal protocol.
- Leuprolide is nonsurgical alternative to orchiectomy for prostate cancer.
- A fractional dose of drug formulated to give every 3 months isn't equivalent to same dose of once-monthly formulation.

Patient teaching

- Before starting therapy in child for central precocious puberty, make sure parents understand importance of continuous therapy.
- Carefully instruct patient who will give S.C. injection about proper administration techniques, and advise him to use only syringes provided by manufacturer.
- Advise patient that if another syringe must be substituted, a low-dose insulin syringe (U-100, 0.5 ml) is acceptable.
- Advise patient to store drug at room temperature, protected from light and heat.
- Reassure patient with history of undesirable effects from other endocrine therapies that leuprolide is much easier to tolerate. Tell patient

that adverse effects are transient and will disappear after about 1 week.
• Warn patient that worsening of prostate cancer symptoms may occur when therapy starts.

Evaluation
• Patient exhibits improvement in underlying condition.
• Patient demonstrates pretreatment thought processes.
• Patient and family state understanding of drug therapy.

levalbuterol hydrochloride
(leev-al-BYOO-teh-rohl high-droh-KLOR-ighd)
Xopenex

Pharmacologic class: $beta_2$ agonist
Therapeutic class: bronchodilator
Pregnancy risk category: C

Indications and dosages
▶ **To prevent or treat bronchospasm in patients with reversible obstructive airway disease.** *Adults and adolescents age 12 and older:* 0.63 mg given t.i.d. every 6 to 8 hours by P.O. inhalation via a nebulizer. Patients with more severe asthma who don't respond adequately to 0.63-mg doses may benefit from 1.25 mg t.i.d. *Children ages 6 to 11:* 0.31 mg given t.i.d. by nebulization. Routine dosing should not exceed 0.63 mg t.i.d.

Contraindications and precautions
• Contraindicated in patients hypersensitive to levalbuterol or racemic albuterol, or any of its components.
• Use cautiously in patients with CV disorders, especially coronary insufficiency, hypertension, and arrhythmias. Also use cautiously in patients with seizure disorders, hyperthyroidism, or diabetes mellitus and in patients who are unusually responsive to sympathomimetic amines.
Lifespan: In pregnant women, use only if the potential benefits outweigh the potential harm to the fetus. In breast-feeding women, use cautiously. In children younger than age 6 or in patients age 65 and older, safety has not been established.

Adverse reactions
CNS: dizziness, migraine, nervousness, tremor, anxiety, pain.
CV: tachycardia.
EENT: *rhinitis,* sinusitis, turbinate edema.
GI: dyspepsia.
Musculoskeletal: leg cramps.
Respiratory: increased cough.
Other: flulike syndrome, accidental injury, *viral infection.*

Interactions
Drug-drug. *Beta blockers:* Blocks pulmonary effect of the drug and, possibly, severe bronchospasm. Don't use together, if possible. If drug is necessary, a cardioselective beta blocker could be considered but should be given with caution.
Digoxin: Decreases digoxin levels (up to 22%). Monitor digoxin level and for loss of therapeutic effect.
Epinephrine, short-acting sympathomimetic aerosol bronchodilators: Increases adverse adrenergic effects. To avoid serious CV effects, additional adrenergics should be used with caution.
Loop or thiazide diuretics: Increases risk of ECG changes and hypokalemia. Use together cautiously; monitor cardiac status.
MAO inhibitors, tricyclic antidepressants: May potentiate action of levalbuterol on the vascular system. Use extreme caution when giving these drugs within 2 weeks of each other.

Effects on lab test results
None reported.

Pharmacokinetics
Absorption: Some is absorbed.
Distribution: Unknown.
Metabolism: Unknown.
Excretion: Unknown.

Route	Onset	Peak	Duration
Inhalation	10-17 min	90 min	5-8 hr

Pharmacodynamics
Chemical effect: Levalbuterol activates $beta_2$ receptors on airway smooth muscle, which causes smooth muscle from trachea to terminal bronchioles to relax, thereby relieving bronchospasm and reducing airway resistance.

Drug also inhibits the release of mediators from mast cells in the airway.
Therapeutic effect: Improves ventilation.

Available forms

Solution for inhalation: 0.31 mg, 0.63 mg or 1.25 mg in 3-ml vials

NURSING PROCESS

Assessment

- Obtain history of patient's underlying condition before therapy, and reassess regularly thereafter.
- Make sure that patient has a thorough physical examination before starting drug therapy.
- Be alert for adverse reactions and drug interactions.
- Evaluate patient's and family's knowledge of drug therapy.

Nursing diagnoses

- Impaired gas exchange related to underlying respiratory condition
- Risk for injury related to drug-induced adverse reactions
- Deficient knowledge related to drug therapy

Planning and implementation

- Like other inhaled beta agonists, levalbuterol can produce paradoxical bronchospasm, which may be life-threatening. If this occurs, discontinue levalbuterol immediately and start alternative therapy.
- Like other beta agonists, levalbuterol can produce significant CV effects in some patients. Although such effects are uncommon at recommended doses, drug may be discontinued if they occur.
- Compatibility, efficacy, and safety of levalbuterol when mixed with other drugs in a nebulizer haven't been established.

Patient teaching

- Warn patient to stop drug and notify prescriber if drug causes breathing to worsen.
- Urge patient not to increase the dosage or frequency without consulting prescriber.
- Tell patient to seek medical attention immediately if levalbuterol becomes less effective, if signs and symptoms worsen, or if drug is needed more often than usual.
- Tell patient that the effects of levalbuterol may last up to 8 hours.
- Urge patient to use other inhalations and antiasthma drugs only as directed while taking levalbuterol.
- Inform patient that common adverse reactions include palpitations, rapid heart rate, headache, dizziness, tremor, and nervousness.
- Caution woman to notify prescriber if she becomes pregnant or intends to breast-feed.
- Tell patient to keep unopened vials in foil pouch. Once the foil pouch is opened, the vials should be used within 2 weeks. Inform patient that vials removed from the pouch, if not used immediately, should be protected from light and heat and used within 1 week.
- Teach patient to correctly use nebulizer.
- Tell patient to breathe as calmly, deeply, and evenly as possible until no more mist is formed in the nebulizer reservoir (5 to 15 minutes). At this point, the treatment is finished.

Evaluation

- Patient's respiratory status improves.
- Patient doesn't experience injury from adverse reactions caused by drug.
- Patient and family state understanding of drug therapy.

levetiracetam

(leev-ah-tah-RACE-ah-tam)
Keppra

Pharmacologic class: anticonvulsant
Therapeutic class: anticonvulsant
Pregnancy risk category: C

Indications and dosages

▶ **Adjunctive therapy for partial seizures.** *Adults:* Initially, 500 mg b.i.d. Dosage can be increased by 500 mg b.i.d., as needed, for seizure control at 2-week intervals to maximum dose of 1,500 mg b.i.d.
Patients with renal impairment: If creatinine clearance is more than 80 ml/minute, give 500 to 1,500 mg q 12 hours; if clearance is 50 to 80 ml/minute, give 500 to 1,000 mg q 12 hours; if 30 to 50 ml/minute, 250 to 750 mg q 12 hours; if less than 30 ml/minute, 250 to 500 mg q 12 hours. For dialysis patients, give

500 to 1,000 mg q 24 hours. A 250- to 500-mg dose should be given after dialysis.

Contraindications and precautions

- Contraindicated in patients hypersensitive to drug.
- Use cautiously in immunocompromised patients and in those with poor renal function.

Lifespan: In breast-feeding women, use cautiously because it's not known if drug appears in breast milk. In children younger than16, use is contraindicated. In elderly patients, use cautiously because they are at an increased risk for falls.

Adverse reactions

CNS: *asthenia, headache, somnolence,* dizziness, depression, vertigo, paresthesia, nervousness, hostility, emotional lability, ataxia, amnesia, anxiety.
EENT: diplopia, pharyngitis, rhinitis, sinusitis.
GI: anorexia.
Hematologic: *leukopenia, neutropenia.*
Musculoskeletal: pain.
Respiratory: cough.
Other: infection.

Interactions

Drug-drug. *Antihistamines, benzodiazepines, narcotics, tricyclic antidepressants, other drugs that cause drowsiness:* May lead to severe sedation. Avoid using together.
Carbamazepine, clozapine, and other drugs known to cause leukopenia or neutropenia: May increase the risk of infection. Monitor patient closely.
Drug-lifestyle. *Alcohol:* Increases risk of severe sedation. Discourage using together.

Effects on lab test results

- May decrease WBC and neutrophil counts.

Pharmacokinetics

Absorption: Rapid. Serum levels peak in about 1 hour. Although drug can be taken with food, time to reach peak levels is delayed by about 1.5 hours and serum levels are slightly lower. Serum levels reach steady-state in about 2 days.
Distribution: Protein binding is minimal.
Metabolism: No active metabolites. Drug isn't metabolized through the cytochrome P450 system.
Excretion: About 66% of drug is eliminated unchanged by glomerular filtration and tubular reabsorption. *Elimination half-life:* About 7 hours in patients with normal renal function.

Route	Onset	Peak	Duration
P.O.	1 hr	1 hr	12 hr

Pharmacodynamics

Chemical effect: Unknown. Thought to inhibit kindling activity in hippocampus, thus preventing simultaneous neuronal firing that leads to seizure activity.
Therapeutic effect: Prevents seizure activity.

Available forms

Tablets: 250 mg, 500 mg, 750 mg

NURSING PROCESS

Assessment

- Obtain history of patient's underlying condition before therapy, and reassess regularly thereafter.
- Assess renal function before therapy starts.
- Monitor patient closely for such adverse reactions as dizziness, which may lead to falls.
- Evaluate patient's and family's knowledge of drug therapy.

Nursing diagnoses

- Risk for trauma related to seizures
- Risk for infection related to drug-induced leukopenia and neutropenia
- Deficient knowledge related to drug therapy

Planning and implementation

- Drug can be taken with or without food.
- Use drug only with other anticonvulsants; not recommended for monotherapy.
- Seizures can occur if drug is stopped abruptly. Tapering is recommended.

ALERT: Don't confuse Keppra with Kaletra.

Patient teaching

- Warn patient to use extra care when rising to a sitting or standing position to avoid dizziness and falling.
- Advise patient to call prescriber and not to stop drug suddenly if adverse reactions occur.
- Tell patient to take with other prescribed seizure drugs.

• Inform patient that drug can be taken with or without food.

Evaluation
• Patient is free from seizure activity.
• Patient doesn't develop infection.
• Patient and family state understanding of drug therapy.

levocarnitine (L-carnitine)
(lee-voh-KAR-nuh-teen)
Carnitor, L-Carnitine

Pharmacologic class: amino acid derivative
Therapeutic class: nutritional supplement
Pregnancy risk category: B

Indications and dosages
▶ **Primary and secondary systemic carnitine deficiency.** All dosages based on clinical response. Higher dosages may be given.
Adults: 990 mg P.O. b.i.d. or t.i.d. Or, 10 to 30 ml (1 to 3 g) of oral liquid daily.
Children: 50 to 100 mg/kg P.O. daily in divided doses. Maximum, 3 g P.O. daily.
▶ **Acute and long-term treatment of secondary carnitine deficiency.** *Adults:* 50 mg/kg daily divided and given I.V. slowly over 2 to 3 minutes q 3 to 4 hours.

Contraindications and precautions
• Use of oral formulations isn't approved in patients with end stage renal disease, those on dialysis, and those with severely compromised renal function. Only the I.V. formulation is approved for these patients. The major metabolites formed during oral administration of high doses over long periods can't be efficiently removed by the kidneys and will accumulate.
Lifespan: In pregnant women, use cautiously. In breast-feeding women, drug isn't recommended.

Adverse reactions
GI: *nausea, vomiting, cramps, diarrhea.*
Other: body odor.

Interactions
Drug-drug. *Valproic acid:* Increases levocarnitine requirement. Adjust dosage as ordered.
Drug-lifestyle. *Any food:* Decreases GI upset. Give drug with food.

Effects on lab test results
None reported.

Pharmacokinetics
Absorption: Unknown after P.O. administration.
Distribution: Not bound to plasma proteins or albumin.
Metabolism: Major metabolites are trimethylamine *N*-oxide and gamma butyrobetaine.
Excretion: Excreted mainly in urine; small amount excreted in feces.

Route	Onset	Peak	Duration
P.O., I.V.	Unknown	Unknown	Unknown

Pharmacodynamics
Chemical effect: Facilitates transport of fatty acids (used to produce energy) into cellular mitochondria.
Therapeutic effect: Relieves signs and symptoms of carnitine deficiency.

Available forms
Capsules: 250 mg
Injection: 1 g/5 ml
Oral liquid: 100 mg/ml
Tablets: 330 mg, 500 mg

NURSING PROCESS

Assessment
• Assess patient's underlying condition before therapy and regularly thereafter.
• Monitor blood chemistry and drug level periodically.
• Monitor patient's tolerance during first week of therapy and after increasing dosage.
• Be alert for adverse reactions and drug interactions.
• Monitor patient's hydration status if adverse GI reactions occur.
• Evaluate patient's and family's knowledge of drug therapy.

Nursing diagnoses
• Fatigue related to levocarnitine deficiency
• Risk for deficient fluid volume related to drug-induced adverse GI reactions
• Deficient knowledge related to drug therapy

Planning and implementation

- **P.O. use:** Give enteral liquid alone or dissolve in drinks or liquid food.
- **I.V. use:** Give drug slowly over 2 to 3 minutes.
- Space doses evenly every 3 to 4 hours, and give drug with or after meals, if possible.
- Don't refrigerate solution.

Patient teaching

- Tell patient to consume oral liquid slowly to minimize GI distress. If GI intolerance persists, dosage may have to be reduced.
- Instruct patient to dissolve drug in drink or liquid food or take with meals to reduce GI upset.
- Warn patient to avoid vitamin$_{B-T}$ in health-food stores because it contains both dextrocarnitine and levocarnitine, which renders levocarnitine ineffective.
- Caution patient not to share drug with others. Some people have used it to improve athletic performance.

Evaluation

- Patient's energy level is increased.
- Patient maintains adequate hydration throughout therapy.
- Patient and family state understanding of drug therapy.

levodopa

(lee-voh-DOH-puh)
Dopar, Larodopa

Pharmacologic class: precursor of dopamine
Therapeutic class: antiparkinsonian
Pregnancy risk category: C

Indications and dosages

▶ **Idiopathic parkinsonism, postencephalitic parkinsonism, and symptomatic parkinsonism after carbon monoxide or manganese intoxication or with cerebral arteriosclerosis.** *Adults and children older than age 12:* Initially, 0.5 to 1 g P.O. daily divided into two or more doses with food; increased by no more than 0.75 g daily q 3 to 7 days until usual optimal daily dose of 3 to 6 g is reached. Maximum, 8 g daily. Dosage carefully adjusted to patient requirements, tolerance, and response. Higher dosage needs closer supervision.

Contraindications and precautions

- Contraindicated in patients hypersensitive to drug, in those who have taken an MAO inhibitor within 14 days, and in those with acute angle-closure glaucoma, melanoma, or undiagnosed skin lesions.
- Use cautiously in patients with severe CV, renal, hepatic, or pulmonary disorders; peptic ulcer; psychiatric illness; MI with residual arrhythmias; bronchial asthma; emphysema; or endocrine disease.

Lifespan: In pregnant women, use cautiously. Breast-feeding women shouldn't use drug. In children age 12 and younger, safety of drug hasn't been established.

Adverse reactions

CNS: *aggressive behavior, abnormal movements (choreiform, dystonic, dyskinetic), involuntary grimacing and head movements, myoclonic body jerks,* ***seizures,*** *ataxia, tremor, muscle twitching, bradykinetic episodes, psychiatric disturbance, memory loss, mood changes, nervousness, anxiety, disturbing dreams, euphoria, malaise, fatigue, severe depression,* ***suicidal tendencies,*** *dementia, delirium, hallucinations* (may necessitate reduction or withdrawal of drug).
CV: *orthostatic hypotension,* cardiac irregularities, flushing, hypertension, phlebitis.
EENT: blepharospasm, blurred vision, diplopia, mydriasis or miosis, widening of palpebral fissures, activation of latent Horner's syndrome, oculogyric crises, nasal discharge.
GI: dry mouth, excessive salivation, bitter taste, *nausea, vomiting, anorexia,* constipation, flatulence, diarrhea, epigastric pain.
GU: urinary frequency, urine retention, incontinence, darkened urine, priapism.
Hematologic: hemolytic anemia, ***leukopenia, agranulocytosis.***
Hepatic: ***hepatotoxicity.***
Metabolic: weight loss.
Respiratory: hyperventilation, hiccups.
Other: dark perspiration, excessive and inappropriate sexual behavior.

Interactions

Drug-drug. *Antacids:* Increases levodopa absorption. Administer antacids 1 hour after levodopa.
Anticholinergics: Increases gastric deactivation and decreases intestinal absorption of levodopa. Avoid using together.
Benzodiazepine: Levodopa's therapeutic value may be attenuated. Monitor patient closely.
Furazolidone, MAO inhibitors, procarbazine: May increase risk of severe hypertension. Avoid using together.
Inhaled halogen anesthetics, sympathomimetics: May increase risk of arrhythmias. Monitor patient closely.
Metoclopramide: May accelerate gastric emptying of levodopa. Give metoclopramide 1 hour after levodopa.
Papaverine, phenothiazines and other antipsychotics, phenytoin, rauwolfia alkaloids: May decrease levodopa effect. Use together cautiously.
Pyridoxine: May reverse antiparkinsonian effects. Check vitamin preparations and nutritional supplements for pyridoxine (vitamin B_6) content. Don't give together.
Tricyclic antidepressants: Delays absorption and decreases bioavailability of levodopa. Hypertensive episodes have occurred. Monitor patient closely.
Drug-herb. *Kava:* May interfere with drug and with natural dopamine, worsening symptoms of Parkinson's disease. Discourage using together.
Rauwolfia: May decrease effectiveness of levodopa. Discourage using together.
Drug-food. *Foods high in protein:* May decrease levodopa absorption. Don't give with high-protein foods.
Drug-lifestyle. *Cocaine:* Increases risk of arrhythmias. Inform patient of this interaction.

Effects on lab test results

- May increase BUN, ALT, AST, alkaline phosphatase, LDH, and bilirubin levels.
- May decrease hemoglobin, hematocrit, and WBC and granulocyte counts.
- Coombs' test results may be positive. Uric acid levels may be elevated with colorimetric method. Reagents that use copper sulfate may cause false-positive tests for urine glucose. Tests that use glucose enzymatic methods may cause false-negative results. May interfere with tests for urine ketones and urine phenylketonuria. May falsely elevate urine catecholamine levels. May falsely decrease urine vanillylmandelic acid levels.

Pharmacokinetics

Absorption: Absorbed rapidly from small intestine by active amino acid transport system, with 30% to 50% reaching general circulation.
Distribution: Distributed widely to most body tissues but not to CNS, which receives less than 1% of dose because of extensive metabolism in periphery.
Metabolism: 95% of levodopa is converted to dopamine in lumen of stomach and intestines and on first pass through liver.
Excretion: Excreted primarily in urine. *Half-life:* 1 to 3 hours.

Route	Onset	Peak	Duration
P.O.	Unknown	1-3 hr	About 5 hr but varies greatly

Pharmacodynamics

Chemical effect: Unknown; may be decarboxylated to dopamine, countering dopamine depletion in extrapyramidal centers.
Therapeutic effect: Relieves signs and symptoms of parkinsonism.

Available forms

Capsules: 100 mg, 250 mg, 500 mg
Tablets: 100 mg, 250 mg, 500 mg

NURSING PROCESS

Assessment

- Assess patient's condition before therapy and regularly thereafter.
- Observe and monitor vital signs, especially during dosage adjustments.
- Patient receiving long-term therapy should be tested regularly for diabetes and acromegaly; periodically monitor kidney, liver, and hematopoietic function.
- Be alert for adverse reactions and drug interactions.
- Evaluate patient's and family's knowledge of drug therapy.

Nursing diagnoses
- Impaired physical mobility related to presence of parkinsonism
- Disturbed thought processes related to drug-induced adverse reactions
- Deficient knowledge related to drug therapy

Planning and implementation
- To minimize GI upset, give drug with food. However, keep in mind that high-protein meals can impair absorption and reduce effectiveness.
- Patient who must undergo surgery should continue levodopa as long as oral intake is permitted, usually until 6 to 24 hours before surgery. Drug should be resumed as soon as patient can take oral medication.
- Protect drug from heat, light, and moisture. If preparation darkens, it has lost potency and should be discarded.
- Report significant changes in vital signs.

ALERT: Muscle twitching and eyelid twitching may be early signs of drug overdose; report immediately.
- Prescriber-supervised period of drug discontinuance (called a drug holiday) may reestablish effectiveness of lower dosage regimen.

Patient teaching
- Advise patient to take drug with food but not with high-protein meals. If patient has trouble swallowing pills, tell him or family member to crush tablets and mix with applesauce or baby food.
- Warn patient and family not to increase dosage without prescriber's orders.
- Warn patient about possible dizziness and light-headedness, especially at start of therapy. Tell patient to change positions slowly and dangle legs before getting out of bed. Elastic stockings may help control this reaction.
- Advise patient and family that multivitamin preparations, fortified cereals, and certain OTC drugs may contain pyridoxine (vitamin B_6), which can block effects of levodopa.
- Warn patient about risk of arrhythmias if he uses cocaine, especially when used with drug.

Evaluation
- Patient has improved physical mobility.
- Patient maintains normal thought process.
- Patient and family state understanding of drug therapy.

levofloxacin
(lee-voe-FLOX-a-sin)
Levaquin

Pharmacologic class: fluorinated carboxyquinolone
Therapeutic class: broad-spectrum antibacterial
Pregnancy risk category: C

Indications and dosages
▶ **Acute maxillary sinusitis caused by susceptible strains of *Streptococcus pneumoniae, Moraxella catarrhalis,* or *Haemophilus influenzae*.** *Adults:* 500 mg P.O. or I.V. daily for 10 to 14 days.

▶ **Acute bacterial exacerbation of chronic bronchitis caused by *Staphylococcus aureus, S. pneumoniae, M. catarrhalis,* or *H. influenzae* or *parainfluenzae*.** *Adults:* 500 mg P.O. or I.V. daily for 7 days.

▶ **Community-acquired pneumonia caused by *S. aureus, S. pneumoniae, M. catarrhalis, H. influenzae, H. parainfluenzae, Klebsiella pneumoniae, Chlamydia pneumoniae, Legionella pneumophila,* or *Mycoplasma pneumoniae*.** *Adults:* 500 mg P.O. or I.V. daily for 7 to 14 days.

▶ **Mild-to-moderate skin and skin-structure infections caused by *S. aureus* or *Streptococcus pyogenes*.** *Adults:* 500 mg P.O. or I.V. daily for 7 to 10 days.

▶ **Mild-to-moderate uncomplicated urinary tract infection caused by *Escherichia coli, K. pneumoniae,* or *Staphylococcus saprophyticus*.** *Adults:* 250 mg P.O. daily for 3 days.

▶ **Mild-to-moderate urinary tract infections caused by *Enterococcus faecalis, Enterobacter cloacae, E. coli, K. pneumoniae, Proteus mirabilis,* or *Pseudomonas aeruginosa*.** *Adults:* 250 mg P.O. or I.V. daily for 10 days.

▶ **Mild-to-moderate acute pyelonephritis caused by *E. coli*.** *Adults:* 250 mg P.O. or I.V. daily for 10 days.

▶ **Community-acquired pneumonia caused by penicillin-resistant *S. pneumoniae*.** *Adults:* 500 mg P.O. or I.V. infusion over 60 minutes once daily for 7 to 14 days.

Patients with renal impairment: If creatinine clearance is 20 to 49 ml/minute, give initial dose of 500 mg, then 250 mg once daily; if clearance is 10 to 19 ml/minute, initial dose is 500 mg, then 250 mg q 48 hours. For patients on hemodialysis or chronic ambulatory peritoneal dialysis, give initial dose of 500 mg, then 250 mg q 48 hours.

▶ **Complicated skin and skin structure infections caused by methicillin-sensitive *S. aureus, E. faecalis, S. pyogenes, P. mirabilis;* nosocomial pneumonia caused by methicillin-susceptible *S. aureus, P. aeruginosa, Serratia marcescens, E. coli, K. pneumoniae, H. influenzae, or S. pneumoniae.*** *Adults:* 750 mg P.O or I.V. infusion over 90 minutes q 24 hours for 7 to 14 days.

Patients with renal impairment: If creatinine clearance is 20 to 49 ml/min, give 750 mg initially, then 750 mg q 48 hours; if clearance is 10 to 19 ml/minute or patient is on hemodialysis or chronic ambulatory peritoneal dialysis, give 750 mg initially, then 500 mg q 48 hours.

▶ **Traveler's diarrhea‡.** *Adults:* 500 mg P.O. as a single dose with loperamide hydrochloride.

▶ **Prevention of traveler's diarrhea‡.** *Adults:* 500 mg P.O. daily during period of risk, for up to 3 weeks.

Contraindications and precautions

• Contraindicated in patients hypersensitive to drug, its components, or other fluoroquinolones.

Lifespan: Breast-feeding women should either stop taking drug or stop breast-feeding. In children younger than age 18, safety hasn't been established. In elderly patients, adjust dose if they have renal impairment.

Adverse reactions

CNS: headache, insomnia, dizziness, encephalopathy, paresthesia, pain, ***seizures.***

CV: chest pain, palpitations, vasodilation, abnormal ECG.

GI: nausea, diarrhea, constipation, vomiting, abdominal pain, dyspepsia, flatulence, ***pseudomembranous colitis.***

GU: vaginitis.

Hematologic: eosinophilia, hemolytic anemia, lymphocytopenia.

Metabolic: ***hypoglycemia.***

Musculoskeletal: back pain, tendon rupture.

Respiratory: allergic pneumonitis.

Skin: rash, photosensitivity reactions, pruritus, ***erythema multiforme, Stevens-Johnson syndrome.***

Other: hypersensitivity reactions, ***anaphylaxis, multisystem organ failure.***

Interactions

Drug-drug. *Antacids:* Decreases absorption of antibiotic. Do not take levofloxacin 2 hours before or 6 hours after antacids.

Antidiabetics: May alter glucose levels. Monitor them closely.

Iron salts, products containing zinc, sucralfate: May interfere with GI absorption of levofloxacin. Administer at least 2 hours apart.

NSAIDs: May increase CNS stimulation. Monitor patient for seizure activity.

Theophylline: Decreases theophylline clearance with some fluoroquinolones. Monitor theophylline levels.

Warfarin and derivatives: May increase effect of oral anticoagulant with some fluoroquinolones. Monitor PT and INR.

Drug-lifestyle. *Sun exposure:* Possible photosensitivity reactions. Urge patient to avoid unprotected or prolonged exposure to sunlight.

Effects on lab test results

• May decrease glucose level.

• May increase eosinophil count. May decrease hemoglobin, hematocrit, and WBC and lymphocyte counts.

• May cause false-positive opiate assay results.

Pharmacokinetics

Absorption: Plasma level after I.V. administration is comparable to that observed for equivalent P.O. doses (on a mg-per-mg basis). Therefore, P.O. and I.V. routes can be considered interchangeable. Plasma levels peak within 1 to 2 hours after P.O. dosing. Steady state occurs within 48 hours on a 500 mg/day regimen.

Distribution: Mean volume of distribution ranges from 89 to 112 L after single and multiple 500-mg doses, indicating widespread distribution into body tissues. Drug also penetrates well into lung tissues; levels are generally two to five times higher than plasma levels.

Metabolism: Drug undergoes limited metabolism. The only identified metabolites are the desmethyl and *N*-oxide metabolites, which have little relevant pharmacologic activity.
Excretion: Primarily excreted unchanged in the urine. *Mean terminal half-life:* About 6 to 8 hours.

Route	Onset	Peak	Duration
P.O., I.V.	Unknown	1-2 hr	Unknown

Pharmacodynamics

Chemical effect: Inhibits bacterial DNA gyrase and prevents DNA replication, transcription, repair, and recombination in susceptible bacteria.
Therapeutic effect: Kills susceptible bacteria. Spectrum of activity includes *S. pneumoniae, M. catarrhalis, H. influenzae, H. parainfluenzae, S. aureus, S. pyogenes, K. pneumoniae, C. pneumoniae, L. pneumophila, M. pneumoniae, E. coli, K. pneumoniae, S. saprophyticus, E. faecalis, E. cloacae,* and *P. aeruginosa.*

Available forms

Infusion (premixed): 250 mg in 50 ml D_5W, 500 mg in 100 ml D_5W, 750 mg in 150 ml D_5W (5 mg/ml)
Single-use vials: 500 mg, 750 mg (25 mg/ml)
Tablets: 250 mg, 500 mg, 750 mg

NURSING PROCESS

Assessment

- Obtain specimen for culture and sensitivity tests before starting therapy and as needed to detect bacterial resistance.
- Obtain history of seizure disorders or other CNS diseases, such as cerebral arteriosclerosis, before therapy starts.
- Monitor glucose level and renal, hepatic, and hematopoietic blood studies.
- Evaluate patient's and family's knowledge of drug therapy.

Nursing diagnoses

- Risk for infection related to presence of bacteria susceptible to drug
- Risk for deficient fluid volume related to drug-induced adverse GI reactions
- Deficient knowledge related to drug therapy

Planning and implementation

- **P.O. use:** Give dose with plenty of fluids. Antacids, sucralfate, and products containing iron or zinc should be avoided for at least 2 hours before and after each dose.
- **I.V. use:** Levofloxacin injection should be given only by I.V. infusion.
  – Dilute drug in single-use vials, according to manufacturer's instructions, with D_5W or normal saline solution for injection to a final concentration of 5 mg/ml.
  – Reconstituted solution should be clear, slightly yellow, and free of particulates. It's stable 72 hours at room temperature, 14 days when refrigerated in plastic containers, and 6 months when frozen. Thaw at room temperature or in refrigerator.
  – Don't mix with other drugs. Infuse over 60 minutes.
- Acute hypersensitivity reactions may need treatment with epinephrine, oxygen, I.V. fluids, antihistamines, corticosteroids, pressor amines, and airway management.
- If patient has symptoms of excessive CNS stimulation (restlessness, tremor, confusion, hallucinations), stop drug and notify prescriber. Take seizure precautions.
- Most antibacterial drugs can cause pseudomembranous colitis. Notify prescriber if diarrhea occurs. Drug may be discontinued.

Patient teaching

- Tell patient to take drug as prescribed, even if symptoms resolve.
- Advise patient to take drug with plenty of fluids and to avoid antacids, sucralfate, and products containing iron or zinc for at least 2 hours before and after each dose.
- Warn patient to avoid hazardous tasks until adverse CNS effects of drug are known.
- Advise patient to avoid excessive sunlight, use sunblock, and wear protective clothing when outdoors.
- Instruct patient to stop drug and notify prescriber if rash or other signs or symptoms of hypersensitivity develop.
- Tell patient to notify prescriber if he experiences pain or inflammation; tendon rupture can occur with drug.
- Instruct diabetic patient to monitor glucose level and notify prescriber if a hypoglycemic reaction occurs.

• Instruct patient to notify prescriber about loose stools or diarrhea.

Evaluation
• Patient is free from infection after drug therapy.
• Patient maintains adequate hydration throughout drug therapy.
• Patient and family state understanding of drug therapy.

levonorgestrel
(lee-voh-nor-JES-trel)
Norplant System

Pharmacologic class: progestin
Therapeutic class: contraceptive
Pregnancy risk category: X

Indications and dosages
▶ **Prevention of pregnancy.** *Women:* Six capsules implanted subdermally in midportion of upper arm, about 8 cm above elbow crease, during first 7 days after menses starts. Capsules are placed fanlike, 15 degrees apart (total of 75 degrees). Contraceptive effect lasts for 5 years.

Contraindications and precautions
• Contraindicated in patients with active thrombophlebitis or thromboembolic disorders, undiagnosed abnormal genital bleeding, acute liver disease, malignant or benign liver tumors, or known or suspected breast cancer.
• Use cautiously in patients with hyperlipidemia or history of depression and in diabetic or prediabetic patients.
Lifespan: In known or suspected pregnancy, drug is contraindicated. In breast-feeding women, little is known about effects of drug.

Adverse reactions
CNS: headache, nervousness, dizziness.
GI: nausea, *abdominal discomfort,* appetite change.
GU: *amenorrhea, prolonged bleeding, spotting, irregular onset of bleeding, frequent onset of bleeding, scanty bleeding, cervicitis, vaginitis, leukorrhea.*
Metabolic: weight gain.
Musculoskeletal: *musculoskeletal pain.*
Skin: dermatitis; acne; hirsutism; hypertrichosis; scalp hair loss; infection, transient pain, or itching at implant site.
Other: adnexal enlargement, mastalgia, *removal difficulty, breast discharge.*

Interactions
Drug-drug. *Carbamazepine, phenytoin, rifampin:* May reduce contraceptive efficacy of levonorgestrel implants. Avoid using together.
Drug-food. *Caffeine:* May increase caffeine levels. Monitor effects.
Drug-lifestyle. *Smoking:* May increase risk of adverse CV effects. Advise patient to stop smoking.

Effects on lab test results
• May decrease sex hormone-binding globulin (SHBG) and T_4 levels.
• May increase T_3 uptake.

Pharmacokinetics
Absorption: 100% bioavailable.
Distribution: Bound by circulating protein SHBG.
Metabolism: Metabolized by liver.
Excretion: Metabolites excreted in urine.

Route	Onset	Peak	Duration
Subdermal	≤ 24 hr	≤ 24 hr	5 yr

Pharmacodynamics
Chemical effect: Slowly releases synthetic progestin levonorgestrel into bloodstream. How progestins provide contraception isn't understood, but they alter mucus covering the cervix, prevent implantation of ovum and, in some patients, prevent ovulation.
Therapeutic effect: Prevents pregnancy.

Available forms
Implants: 36 mg/capsule; each kit contains six capsules

NURSING PROCESS

Assessment
• Obtain pregnancy test before therapy, and retest if pregnancy is suspected.

• Closely monitor patient with condition that may be aggravated by fluid retention because steroid hormones may cause fluid retention.
• Be alert for adverse reactions and drug interactions.
• Evaluate patient's and family's knowledge of drug therapy.

Nursing diagnoses
• Health-seeking behavior related to desire to prevent pregnancy
• Chronic pain related to drug-induced adverse reactions
• Deficient knowledge related to drug therapy

Planning and implementation
ALERT: Drug has been discontinued and product is being phased out. Counsel patients on alternative contraceptive options.
• Expect implants to be removed if active thrombophlebitis or thromboembolic disease develops or if patient will be immobilized for a long time.
• If jaundice develops, expect implants to be removed because steroid hormone metabolism is impaired in patients with liver failure.
• Although retinal thrombosis after use of oral contraceptives has been reported, no similar incidents have been documented after use of implant system. However, patients with sudden, unexplained vision problems, including contact lens wearers in whom vision or lens tolerance changes, should be immediately evaluated by an ophthalmologist.

Patient teaching
ALERT: Tell patient to report to prescriber immediately if implant capsule falls out. Efficacy may be impaired.
• After drug is removed from the body, advise woman of contraceptive alternatives.
• Warn patient that missed menstrual periods aren't accurate indicators of early pregnancy because drug may induce amenorrhea. Advise patient that 6 weeks or more of amenorrhea (after pattern of regular menstrual periods) could indicate pregnancy. If pregnancy is confirmed, implants must be removed.
• Encourage regular (at least annual) physical examinations.
• Inform patient that most patients develop variations in menstrual bleeding patterns, including irregular bleeding, prolonged bleeding, spotting, and amenorrhea. These irregularities usually diminish over time.
• Instruct patient to avoid caffeine consumption and smoking while on drug therapy.

Evaluation
• Patient doesn't become pregnant.
• Patient is free from pain.
• Patient and family state understanding of drug therapy.

levothyroxine sodium (T_4, L-thyroxine sodium)
(lee-voh-thigh-ROKS-een SOH-dee-um)
Eltroxin, Levo-T, Levothroid, Levoxine, Levoxyl, Novothyrox, Oroxine ◇, Synthroid**, Unithroid

Pharmacologic class: thyroid hormone
Therapeutic class: thyroid hormone replacement
Pregnancy risk category: A

Indications and dosages
▶ **Congenital hypothyroidism.** *Neonates:* 0.0375 mg (0.025 to 0.05 mg) P.O. daily.
Infants younger than age 1: Initially, 0.025 to 0.05 mg P.O. daily; increase to 0.05 mg P.O. in 4 to 6 weeks, as needed.
Children ages 1 year and older: 0.03 to 0.05 mg/kg P.O. daily until adult dose (0.15 mg) is reached in early or mid-adolescence.
▶ **Myxedema coma.** *Adults:* 300 to 500 mcg I.V., followed by parenteral maintenance dosage of 75 to 100 mcg I.V. daily. Patient should be switched to P.O. maintenance as soon as possible.
▶ **Hypothyroidism and thyroid hormone replacement.** *Adults age 65 and younger:* Initially, 0.025 to 0.05 mg P.O. daily, increased by 0.025 mg P.O. q 2 to 4 weeks until desired response occurs. Maintenance dosage is 0.1 to 0.2 mg P.O. daily. May give I.V. or I.M. when P.O. ingestion is precluded for long periods. Dosage adjustment may be necessary.
Adults older than age 65: 0.0125 to 0.025 mg P.O. daily. Increase by 0.0125 to 0.025 mg at 3- to 8-week intervals, depending on response.

Children: Initially, 0.025 to 0.075 mg (children younger than age 1) or 3 to 5 mcg/kg (children age 1 and older) P.O. daily, gradually increased by 0.025 to 0.05 mg q 2 to 4 weeks until desired response occurs.

Contraindications and precautions

- Contraindicated in patients hypersensitive to drug and in patients with acute MI uncomplicated by hypothyroidism, untreated thyrotoxicosis, or uncorrected adrenal insufficiency.
- Use with extreme caution in patients with angina pectoris, hypertension, other CV disorders, renal insufficiency, or ischemia.
- Rapid replacement in patients with arteriosclerosis may precipitate angina, coronary occlusion, or CVA. Use cautiously in these patients.
- Use cautiously in patients with diabetes mellitus, diabetes insipidus, or myxedema.

Lifespan: In breast-feeding women, use cautiously. In elderly patients, use with extreme caution.

Adverse reactions

Adverse reactions to thyroid hormones are extensions of their pharmacologic properties and reflect patient sensitivity to them.
CNS: fever, headache, *nervousness, insomnia, tremor.*
CV: *tachycardia, palpitations,* ***arrhythmias,*** angina pectoris, hypertension, ***cardiac arrest.***
GI: appetite change, nausea, diarrhea.
GU: menstrual irregularities.
Metabolic: weight loss.
Musculoskeletal: leg cramps.
Skin: diaphoresis.
Other: heat intolerance.

Interactions

Drug-drug. *Cholestyramine, colestipol:* Impairs levothyroxine absorption. Separate doses by 4 to 5 hours.
Insulin, oral antidiabetics: Alters glucose level. Monitor glucose level. Dosage adjustments may be necessary.
I.V. phenytoin: Free thyroid released. Monitor patient for tachycardia.
Oral anticoagulants: Alters PT. Monitor PT and INR; monitor patient for bleeding. Dosage adjustments may be necessary.
Sympathomimetics (such as epinephrine): Increases risk of coronary insufficiency. Monitor patient closely.

Effects on lab test results

None reported.

Pharmacokinetics

Absorption: Well absorbed from GI tract after P.O. administration.
Distribution: Distributed widely; 99% protein-bound.
Metabolism: Metabolized in peripheral tissues, primarily in liver, kidneys, and intestines.
Excretion: 20% to 40% excreted in feces.
Half-life: 6 to 7 days.

Route	Onset	Peak	Duration
P.O., I.V., I.M.	24 hr	Unknown	Unknown

Pharmacodynamics

Chemical effect: Not fully defined; stimulates metabolism by accelerating cellular oxidation.
Therapeutic effect: Raises thyroid hormone levels in body.

Available forms

Injection: 200 mcg/vial, 500 mcg/vial
Tablets: 0.025 mg, 0.05 mg, 0.075 mg, 0.088 mg, 0.1 mg, 0.112 mg, 0.125 mg, 0.137 mg, 0.15 mg, 0.175 mg, 0.2 mg, 0.3 mg

NURSING PROCESS

Assessment

- Assess patient's condition before therapy and regularly thereafter. Normal levels of T_4 should occur within 24 hours, followed by threefold increase in T_3 level in 3 days.
- Be alert for adverse reactions and drug interactions.
- In patients with coronary artery disease who must receive thyroid hormone, watch carefully for possible coronary insufficiency.
- Evaluate patient's and family's knowledge of drug therapy.

Nursing diagnoses

- Ineffective health maintenance related to presence of hypothyroidism

• Risk for injury related to drug-induced adverse reactions
• Deficient knowledge related to drug therapy

Planning and implementation

ALERT: Don't confuse mg with mcg dosage (1 mg = 1,000 mcg).
• Thyroid hormone replacement requirements are about 25% lower in patients older than age 60 than in young adults.
• Patients with adult hypothyroidism are unusually sensitive to thyroid hormone. Patient should be started at lowest dosage and adjusted to higher dosage until reaching a euthyroid state based on symptoms and laboratory data.
• **P.O. use:** When changing from levothyroxine to liothyronine, levothyroxine should be stopped and liothyronine begun. Dosage is increased in small increments after residual effects of levothyroxine disappear. When changing from liothyronine to levothyroxine, levothyroxine is started several days before withdrawing liothyronine to avoid relapse.
• **I.V. use:** Prepare I.V. dose immediately before injection. Don't mix with other solutions. Inject into vein over 1 to 2 minutes.
• **I.M. use:** Follow normal protocol.
• Thyroid hormones alter thyroid function test results. Patients taking levothyroxine who need radioactive iodine uptake studies must discontinue drug 4 weeks before test.
• Patients taking a prescribed anticoagulant with thyroid hormones usually need a reduced anticoagulant dosage.
ALERT: Don't confuse levothyroxine sodium with liothyronine sodium.

Patient teaching
• Stress importance of compliance. Tell patient to take thyroid hormones at same time each day, preferably before breakfast, to maintain constant hormone levels. Suggest morning dosage to prevent insomnia.
• Warn patient (especially elderly patient) to notify prescriber at once of chest pain, palpitations, sweating, nervousness, shortness of breath, or other signs of overdose or aggravated CV disease.
• Advise patient who has achieved stable response not to change brands.
• Tell patient to report unusual bleeding and bruising.

Evaluation

• Patient's thyroid hormone levels are normal.
• Patient doesn't experience any adverse reactions.
• Patient and family state understanding of drug therapy.

lidocaine hydrochloride (lignocaine hydrochloride)

(LIGH-doh-kayn high-droh-KLOR-ighd)
LidoPen Auto-Injector, Xylocaine, Xylocard ◆ ◇

Pharmacologic class: amide derivative
Therapeutic class: ventricular antiarrhythmic
Pregnancy risk category: B

Indications and dosages

▶ **Ventricular arrhythmias resulting from MI, cardiac manipulation, or cardiac glycosides.** *Adults:* 50 to 100 mg (1 to 1.5 mg/kg) by I.V. bolus at 25 to 50 mg/minute. Bolus dose is repeated q 3 to 5 minutes until arrhythmias subside or adverse reactions develop. Don't exceed 300-mg total bolus during 1-hour period. Simultaneously, constant infusion of 20 to 50 mcg/kg/minute (1 to 4 mg/minute) is begun. If single bolus has been given, smaller bolus dose may be repeated 5 to 10 minutes after start of infusion to maintain therapeutic serum level. After 24 hours of continuous infusion, rate is decreased by one-half. Or, 200 to 300 mg I.M., followed by second I.M. dose 60 to 90 minutes later, if needed.
Children: 1 mg/kg by I.V. bolus, followed by infusion of 20 to 50 mcg/kg/minute.
Elderly patients or patients weighing less than 50 kg (110 lb) and those with heart failure or hepatic disease: Give half the normal adult dose.
▶ **Status epilepticus‡.** *Adults:* 1 mg/kg I.V. bolus; then, if seizures continue, give 0.5 mg/kg 2 minutes after first dose. May use an infusion of 30 mcg/kg/minute.

Contraindications and precautions

• Contraindicated in patients hypersensitive to amide-type local anesthetics and in those with Adams-Stokes syndrome, Wolff-Parkinson-White syndrome, or severe degrees of SA, AV,

or intraventricular block in absence of artificial pacemaker.
• Use cautiously in patients with complete or second-degree heart block or sinus bradycardia, in those with heart failure or renal or hepatic disease, and in those weighing less than 50 kg. These patients need reduced dosage.
Lifespan: In breast-feeding women and in children, safety of drug hasn't been established. In elderly patients, use cautiously.

Adverse reactions

CNS: *confusion, tremor,* lethargy, somnolence, *stupor, restlessness,* slurred speech, euphoria, depression, *light-headedness,* paresthesia, muscle twitching, ***seizures.***
CV: *hypotension,* ***bradycardia, new or worsened arrhythmias, cardiac arrest.***
EENT: *tinnitus, blurred or double vision.*
Respiratory: ***respiratory arrest, status asthmaticus.***
Skin: diaphoresis.
Other: ***anaphylaxis,*** soreness at injection site, cold sensation.

Interactions

Drug-drug. *Beta blockers, cimetidine:* Decreases lidocaine metabolism. Monitor patient for toxicity.
Phenytoin, procainamide, propranolol, quinidine: May have additive cardiac depressant effects. Monitor patient.
Succinylcholine: Possible prolonged neuromuscular blockage. Monitor patient for increased effects.
Tocainide: May increase risk of adverse reactions. Avoid using together.
Drug-herb. *Pareira:* May add to or potentiate neuromuscular blockade. Avoid using together.
Drug-lifestyle. *Smoking:* May increase lidocaine metabolism. Monitor patient closely; discourage patient from smoking.

Effects on lab test results

• May increase creatine phosphokinase.

Pharmacokinetics

Absorption: Nearly complete after I.M. administration.
Distribution: Distributed widely, especially to adipose tissue.
Metabolism: Most of drug metabolized in liver to two active metabolites.
Excretion: 90% excreted as metabolites; less than 10% excreted in urine unchanged. *Half-life:* 1.5 to 2 hours (may be prolonged in patients with heart failure or hepatic disease).

Route	Onset	Peak	Duration
I.V. (no bolus)	Immediate	30-60 min	10-20 min
I.M.	5-15 min	10 min	2 hr

Pharmacodynamics

Chemical effect: Decreases depolarization, automaticity, and excitability in ventricles during diastolic phase by direct action on tissues.
Therapeutic effect: Abolishes ventricular arrhythmias.

Available forms

Infusion (premixed): 0.2% (2 mg/ml), 0.4% (4 mg/ml), 0.8% (8 mg/ml)
Injection for direct I.V. use: 1% (10 mg/ml), 2% (20 mg/ml)
Injection for I.M. use: 300 mg/3 ml automatic injection device
Injection for I.V. admixtures: 4% (40 mg/ml), 10% (100 mg/ml), 20% (200 mg/ml)

NURSING PROCESS

Assessment

• Assess patient's condition before therapy and regularly thereafter.
• Patient receiving infusion must be on cardiac monitor and be attended to at all times.
• Monitor patient's response, especially ECG, blood pressure, and selectrolyte, BUN, and creatinine levels.
• Check for therapeutic level (2 to 5 mcg/ml).
• Be alert for adverse reactions and drug interactions.
ALERT: Monitor patient for toxicity. Seizures may be first clinical sign. Severe reactions usually are preceded by somnolence, confusion, and paresthesia.
• Evaluate patient's and family's knowledge of drug therapy.

Nursing diagnoses

• Decreased cardiac output related to presence of ventricular arrhythmia
• Disturbed thought processes related to adverse CNS reactions
• Deficient knowledge related to drug therapy

Planning and implementation

- Remind prescriber to test isoenzymes if I.M. route is prescribed in patients with suspected MI. This is necessary because patients who received I.M. lidocaine show sevenfold increase in CK level. Such an increase originates in skeletal muscle, not cardiac muscle.
- **I.V. use:** Use infusion-control device to administer infusion precisely. Don't exceed 4 mg/minute; faster rate greatly increases risk of toxicity.

ALERT: Don't give concentrated lidocaine solutions (4%, 10%, 20%) by direct I.V. injection. Lidocaine injections containing 40, 100, or 200 mg/ml are for the preparation of I.V. infusion solutions and must be diluted before use.

- **I.M. use:** Give I.M. injections only in deltoid muscle.
- If signs of toxicity (such as dizziness) occur, stop drug at once and notify prescriber. Continued infusion could lead to seizures and coma. Give oxygen by way of nasal cannula, if not contraindicated. Keep oxygen and cardiopulmonary resuscitation equipment available.
- Discontinue drug and notify prescriber if arrhythmias worsen or if ECG changes, such as widening QRS complex or substantially prolonged PR interval, are evident.

Patient teaching

- Explain purpose of drug to patient.
- Tell patient or caregiver to report any adverse reactions.
- Instruct patient to avoid smoking during drug therapy.

Evaluation

- Patient's cardiac output returns to normal with abolishment of ventricular arrhythmia.
- Patient maintains normal thought processes throughout therapy.
- Patient and family state understanding of drug therapy.

linezolid

(linn-AYE-zoe-lid)

Zyvox

Pharmacologic class: oxazolidinone
Therapeutic class: antibiotic
Pregnancy risk category: C

Indications and dosages

▶ **Vancomycin-resistant *Enterococcus faecium* infections, including cases with bacteremia.** *Adults:* 600 mg I.V. or P.O. (tablets or suspension) q 12 hours for 14 to 28 days.

▶ **Nosocomial pneumonia caused by *Staphylococcus aureus* (methicillin-susceptible [MSSA] and methicillin-resistant [MRSA] strains) or penicillin-susceptible strains of *Streptococcus pneumonia.*** *Adults:* 600 mg I.V. or P.O. (tablets or suspension) q 12 hours for 10 to 14 days.

▶ **Complicated skin and skin-structure infections caused by *S. aureus* (MSSA and MSRA), *Streptococcus pyogenes,* or *Streptococcus agalactiae.*** *Adults:* 600 mg I.V. or P.O. (tablets or suspension) q 12 hours for 10 to 14 days.

▶ **Uncomplicated skin and skin-structure infections caused by *S. aureus* (MSSA) or *S. pyogenes.*** *Adults:* 400 mg P.O. (tablets or suspension) q 12 hours for 10 to 14 days.

▶ **Community-acquired pneumonia caused by *S. pneumoniae* (penicillin-susceptible strains), including case with or *S. aureus* (MSSA).** *Adults:* 600 mg I.V. or P.O. (tablets or suspension) q 12 hours for 10 to 14 days.

Contraindications and precautions

- Contraindicated in patients hypersensitive to linezolid or any inactive components of the formulation.

Lifespan: In children, safety and efficacy haven't been established.

Adverse reactions

CNS: *headache*, insomnia, fever, dizziness.
GI: *diarrhea, nausea,* vomiting, constipation, altered taste, tongue discoloration, oral candidiasis.
GU: vaginal candidiasis.
Hematologic: anemia, ***leukopenia, neutropenia, thrombocytopenia.***
Skin: rash.
Other: fungal infection.

Interactions

Drug-drug. *Adrenergics such as dopamine, epinephrine, and pseudoephedrine:* Increases risk of hypertension. Monitor blood pressure and heart rate. Start continuous infusions of dopamine and epinephrine at lower doses, and adjust to response.

Serotoninergic drugs: Increases risk of serotonin syndrome (confusion, delirium, restlessness, tremor, blushing, diaphoresis, hyperpyrexia). If these symptoms occur, consider stopping serotoninergic drug as directed.
Drug-food. *Foods and beverages high in tyramine, such as aged cheese, tap beer, red wine, air-dried meat, soy sauce, sauerkraut:* Increases blood pressure. Advise patient to avoid these foods, if possible. Tyramine content of meals shouldn't exceed 100 mg.

Effects on lab test results

- May increase amylase, lipase, ALT, AST, alkaline phosphatase, LDH, total bilirubin, and BUN levels.
- May decrease hemoglobin, hematocrit, and WBC, neutrophil, and platelet counts.

Pharmacokinetics

Absorption: Rapid and complete. Levels peak in 1 to 2 hours. Bioavailability is about 100%.
Distribution: Distributed readily into well-perfused tissues. Protein-binding is about 31%.
Metabolism: Undergoes oxidative metabolism to two inactive metabolites. Linezolid doesn't appear to be metabolized by the cytochrome P450 oxidative system.
Excretion: At steady-state, about 30% of a dose appears in urine as linezolid and about 50% as metabolites. Linezolid undergoes significant renal tubular reabsorption, such that renal clearance is low. Non-renal clearance accounts for about 65% of the total clearance.

Route	Onset	Peak	Duration
P.O. (tablet)	Unknown	1 hr	4.7-5.4 hr
P.O. (suspension)	Unknown	1 hr	4.6 hr
I.V.	Unknown	0.5 hr	4.8 hr

Pharmacodynamics

Chemical effect: Bacteriostatic against enterococci and staphylococci. Bactericidal against most strains of streptococci. Linezolid is active against methicillin-susceptible and resistant strains of *S. aureus* and penicillin-susceptible strains of *S. pneumoniae.* It's also active against *S. pyogenes* and *S. agalactiae.* Linezolid exerts antimicrobial effects by interfering with bacterial protein synthesis. It binds to the 23S ribosomal DNA on the bacterial 50S ribosomal subunit. This action prevents formation of a functional 70S ribosomal subunit, thereby blocking the translation step of bacterial protein synthesis.
Therapeutic effect: Hinders or kills susceptible bacteria.

Available forms

Injection: 2 mg/ml
Powder for oral suspension: 100 mg/5 ml when constituted
Tablets: 400 mg, 600 mg

NURSING PROCESS

Assessment

- Obtain history of patient's underlying condition before therapy, and reassess regularly thereafter.
- Obtain specimen for culture and sensitivity tests before starting linezolid therapy. Sensitivity results should be used to guide subsequent therapy.
- Monitor platelet count in patients with increased risk of bleeding, patients with thrombocytopenia, patients receiving drugs that may cause thrombocytopenia, and patients receiving linezolid for more than 14 days.
- Monitor patient for persistent diarrhea; consider pseudomembranous colitis.
- Evaluate patient's and family's knowledge of drug therapy.

Nursing diagnoses

- Infection related to susceptible bacteria
- Risk for injury related to drug-induced adverse reactions
- Deficient knowledge related to drug therapy

Planning and implementation

- Because inappropriate use of antibiotics may lead to resistant organisms, careful consideration should be given to alternative drugs before starting linezolid therapy, especially in the outpatient setting.
- **P.O. use:** Reconstitute suspension according to manufacturer's instructions. Store at room temperature and use within 21 days.
- **I.V. use:** Inspect for particulate matter and leaks.

– Infuse over 30 to 120 minutes. Don't infuse linezolid in a series connection.
– Don't inject additives into the infusion bag. Give other I.V. drugs separately or in a separate I.V. line to avoid physical incompatibilities. If a single I.V. line is used, flush the line with a compatible solution before and after linezolid infusion.
– Linezolid is compatible with the following I.V. solutions: D_5W, USP; normal saline solution for injection, USP; and lactated Ringer's injection, USP.
– Drugs known to be incompatible with linezolid include amphotericin B, ceftriaxone sodium, chlorpromazine hydrochloride, diazepam, erythromycin lactobionate, pentamidine isethionate, phenytoin sodium, and trimethoprim-sulfamethoxazole.

- Store drug at room temperature in its protective overwrap. The solution may turn yellow over time, but this doesn't indicate a change in potency.
- No dosage adjustment is needed when switching from I.V. to P.O. dosage forms.
- Safety and efficacy of linezolid therapy for longer than 28 days haven't been studied.

ALERT: Don't confuse Zyvox with Zovirax.

Patient teaching

- Inform patient that tablets and oral suspension may be taken with or without meals.
- Stress the importance of completing the entire course of therapy, even if the patient feels better.
- Tell patient to alert prescriber if he has hypertension, is taking cough or cold preparations, or is being treated with selective serotonin-reuptake inhibitors or other antidepressants.
- Inform patient with phenylketonuria that each 5 ml of linezolid oral suspension contains 20 mg of phenylalanine. Linezolid tablets and injection don't contain phenylalanine.

Evaluation

- Patient is free from infection.
- Patient doesn't experience injury as a result of drug-induced adverse reactions.
- Patient and family state understanding of drug therapy.

liothyronine sodium (T_3)

(lee-oh-THIGH-roh-neen SOH-dee-um)
Cytomel, Tertroxin ◇, Triostat

Pharmacologic class: thyroid hormone
Therapeutic class: thyroid hormone replacement
Pregnancy risk category: A

Indications and dosages

▶ **Congenital hypothyroidism.** *Children:* 5 mcg P.O. daily with a 5-mcg increase q 3 to 4 days until desired response is achieved.

▶ **Myxedema.** *Adults:* Initially, 5 mcg P.O. daily, increased by 5 to 10 mcg q 1 to 2 weeks until daily dose reaches 25 mcg. Then, increase by 12.5 to 25 mcg daily q 1 to 2 weeks. Maintenance dose is 50 to 100 mcg daily.

▶ **Myxedema coma, precoma.** *Adults:* Initially, 10 to 20 mcg I.V. for patients with known or suspected CV disease; 25 to 50 mcg I.V. for those not known to have CV disease. Subsequent dosages are based on patient's condition and response.

▶ **Nontoxic goiter.** *Adults:* Initially, 5 mcg P.O. daily; may increase by 5 to 10 mcg daily q 1 to 2 weeks until daily dose reaches 25 mcg. Then, increase by 12.5 to 25 mcg daily q 1 to 2 weeks. Usual maintenance dose is 75 mcg daily.

▶ **Thyroid hormone replacement.** *Adults:* Initially, 25 mcg P.O. daily, increased by 12.5 to 25 mcg q 1 to 2 weeks until satisfactory response is achieved. Usual maintenance dose is 25 to 75 mcg daily.

▶ **T_3 suppression test to differentiate hyperthyroidism from euthyroidism.** *Adults:* 75 to 100 mcg P.O. daily for 7 days.

Contraindications and precautions

- Contraindicated in patients hypersensitive to drug and in those with untreated thyrotoxicosis, uncorrected adrenal insufficiency, and acute MI uncomplicated by hypothyroidism.
- Use with extreme caution in patients with angina pectoris, hypertension, other CV disorders, renal insufficiency, or ischemia.
- Rapid replacement in patients with arteriosclerosis may precipitate angina, coronary occlusion, or CVA. Use cautiously in these patients.

• Use cautiously in patients with diabetes mellitus, diabetes insipidus, or myxedema.

Lifespan: In breast-feeding women, use cautiously. In elderly patients, use with extreme caution.

Adverse reactions

Adverse reactions to thyroid hormones are extensions of their pharmacologic properties and reflect patient sensitivity to them.

CNS: irritability, *nervousness, insomnia, tremor,* headache.

CV: *tachycardia,* ***arrhythmias,*** angina pectoris, hypertension, ***cardiac arrest.***

GI: diarrhea, abdominal cramps, vomiting.

GU: menstrual irregularities.

Metabolic: weight loss.

Musculoskeletal: accelerated bone maturation in infants and children.

Skin: diaphoresis.

Other: heat intolerance.

Interactions

Drug-drug. *Cholestyramine, colestipol:* Impairs liothyronine absorption. Separate doses by 4 to 5 hours.

Insulin, oral antidiabetics: Initial thyroid replacement therapy may increase insulin or oral hypoglycemic requirements. Monitor blood glucose levels. Dosage adjustments may be necessary.

I.V. phenytoin: Free thyroid released. Monitor patient for tachycardia.

Oral anticoagulants: Alters PT. Monitor PT and INR; monitor patient for bleeding. Dosage adjustments may be necessary.

Sympathomimetics (such as epinephrine): Increases risk of coronary insufficiency. Monitor patient closely.

Effects on lab test results

None reported.

Pharmacokinetics

Absorption: 95%.

Distribution: Highly protein-bound.

Metabolism: Unknown.

Excretion: Unknown. *Half-life:* 1 to 2 days.

Route	Onset	Peak	Duration
P.O.	Unknown	2-3 days	About 3 days
I.V.	Unknown	Unknown	Unknown

Pharmacodynamics

Chemical effect: Not clearly defined; enhances oxygen consumption by most body tissues and increases basal metabolic rate and metabolism of carbohydrates, lipids, and proteins.

Therapeutic effect: Raises thyroid hormone levels in body.

Available forms

Injection: 10 mcg/ml

Tablets: 5 mcg, 25 mcg, 50 mcg

NURSING PROCESS

Assessment

• Assess patient's condition before therapy and regularly thereafter.

• Monitor pulse rate and blood pressure.

• Observe patient with coronary artery disease for coronary insufficiency.

• Be alert for adverse reactions and drug interactions.

• Evaluate patient's and family's knowledge of drug therapy.

Nursing diagnoses

• Ineffective health maintenance related to underlying thyroid condition

• Disturbed sleep pattern related to drug-induced insomnia

• Deficient knowledge related to drug therapy

Planning and implementation

• **P.O. use:** Give drug at same time every day, preferably in the morning to prevent insomnia.

• **I.V. use:** Repeat doses should be given more than 4 hours but less than 12 hours apart.

ALERT: Don't give I.M. or S.C.

• Levothyroxine is usually preferred for thyroid hormone replacement therapy. Liothyronine may be used when rapid onset or rapidly reversible agent is desirable or in patients with impaired peripheral conversion of levothyroxine to liothyronine.

• In most patients, regulation of liothyronine dosage is difficult.

• Thyroid hormone replacement requirements are about 25% lower in patients older than age 60 than in young adults.

• When changing from levothyroxine to liothyronine, levothyroxine should be stopped and liothyronine begun at low dosage and increased in small increments after residual ef-

fects of levothyroxine have disappeared. When changing from liothyronine to levothyroxine, levothyroxine is started several days before withdrawing liothyronine to avoid relapse.
• Thyroid hormones alter thyroid function tests. Patient taking liothyronine who needs radioactive iodine uptake studies must discontinue drug 7 to 10 days before test.
• Patient who takes thyroid hormone and anticoagulant usually needs decreased anticoagulant dosage.
ALERT: Don't confuse liothyronine with levothyroxine.

Patient teaching
• Stress importance of compliance. Tell patient to take thyroid hormones at same time each day, preferably before breakfast, to maintain constant hormone levels and prevent insomnia.
• Advise patient who has achieved stable response not to change brands to avoid problems with bioequivalence.
• Warn patient (especially elderly patient) to notify prescriber at once if chest pain, palpitations, sweating, nervousness, or other signs of overdose occur or if signs of aggravated CV disease (chest pain, dyspnea, and tachycardia) develop.
• Tell patient to report unusual bleeding and bruising.

Evaluation
• Patient's thyroid hormone levels are normal.
• Patient doesn't have insomnia.
• Patient and family state understanding of drug therapy.

lisinopril
(ligh-SIN-uh-pril)
Prinivil, Zestril

Pharmacologic class: ACE inhibitor
Therapeutic class: antihypertensive
Pregnancy risk category: C (D in second and third trimesters)

Indications and dosages
▶ **Hypertension.** *Adults:* Initially, 10 mg P.O. daily. If patient also takes a diuretic, reduce initial dosage to 5 mg P.O. daily. Most patients are well controlled on 20 to 40 mg daily.
▶ **Treatment adjunct in heart failure (with diuretics and cardiac glycosides).** *Adults:* Initially, 5 mg P.O. daily. Usual effective dosage range is 5 to 20 mg daily. In patients with hyponatremia (sodium level below 130 mEq/L) or serum creatinine above 3 mg/dl, start with 2.5 mg P.O. once daily.
▶ **Treatment of hemodynamically stable patients within 24 hours of acute MI to improve survival.** *Adults:* Initially, 5 mg P.O. Then 5 mg P.O. after 24 hours, 10 mg P.O. after 48 hours, and 10 mg P.O. once daily for 6 weeks. Patients with systolic blood pressure of 120 mm Hg or less at start of therapy or during first 3 days after an infarct should receive reduced dosage of 2.5 mg P.O.

Contraindications and precautions
• Contraindicated in patients hypersensitive to ACE inhibitors and in those with a history of angioedema from previous treatment with an ACE inhibitor.
• Use cautiously in patients with impaired kidney function; adjust dosage as directed. Also use cautiously in patients at risk for hyperkalemia (those with renal insufficiency or diabetes or who use drugs that raise potassium level).
Lifespan: In pregnant women, use is contraindicated. In breast-feeding women, use cautiously. In children, safety of drug hasn't been established.

Adverse reactions
CNS: *dizziness, headache, fatigue,* depression, somnolence, paresthesia.
CV: hypotension, *orthostatic hypotension,* chest pain.
EENT: *nasal congestion.*
GI: *diarrhea,* nausea, dyspepsia, dysgeusia.
GU: impotence.
Metabolic: ***hyperkalemia.***
Musculoskeletal: *muscle cramps.*
Respiratory: *dry, persistent, tickling, nonproductive cough.*
Skin: rash.
Other: ***angioedema, anaphylaxis,*** decreased libido.

Interactions
Drug-drug. *Capsaicin:* May cause or worsen coughing caused by ACE inhibitors. Monitor patient closely.

Diuretics: May cause excessive hypotension. Monitor blood pressure.
Indomethacin: Attenuated hypotensive effect. Monitor blood pressure.
Insulin, oral antidiabetics: May increase risk of hypoglycemia, especially when starting lisinopril. Monitor blood glucose closely.
Lithium: May increase lithium level. Monitor patient for toxicity.
Potassium-sparing diuretics, potassium supplements: May increase risk of hyperkalemia. Monitor potassium level.
Thiazide diuretics: Attenuation of potassium loss caused by thiazide diuretics. Discontinue diuretics 2 to 3 days before lisinopril therapy or reduce lisinopril dosage to 5 mg P.O. once daily.
Drug-herb. *Licorice:* May cause sodium retention and increase blood pressure, thereby interfering with the therapeutic effects of ACE inhibitors. Discourage using together.
Drug-food. *Potassium-containing salt substitutes:* May increase risk of hyperkalemia. Monitor patient closely; discourage patient from using.

Effects on lab test results

- May increase BUN, creatinine, potassium, and bilirubin levels.
- May elevate liver function test values.

Pharmacokinetics

Absorption: Variable.
Distribution: Distributed widely in tissues, although only minimal amount enters brain. Plasma protein–binding appears insignificant.
Metabolism: Not metabolized.
Excretion: Excreted unchanged in urine. *Half-life:* 12 hours.

Route	Onset	Peak	Duration
P.O.	1 hr	7 hr	24 hr

Pharmacodynamics

Chemical effect: Unknown; may result primarily from suppression of renin-angiotensin-aldosterone system.
Therapeutic effect: Lowers blood pressure.

Available forms

Tablets: 2.5 mg, 5 mg, 10 mg, 20 mg, 40 mg

NURSING PROCESS

Assessment

- Assess patient's condition before therapy and regularly thereafter. Beneficial effects of drug may require several weeks of therapy.
- Monitor WBC with differential counts before therapy, every 2 weeks for first 3 months of therapy, and periodically thereafter.
- Be alert for adverse reactions and drug interactions.
- Evaluate patient's and family's knowledge of drug therapy.

Nursing diagnoses

- Risk for injury related to presence of hypertension
- Decreased cardiac output related to drug-induced hypotension
- Deficient knowledge related to drug therapy

Planning and implementation

- If drug doesn't control blood pressure, diuretics may be added.

ALERT: Don't confuse lisinopril with fosinopril or Lioresal.
ALERT: Don't confuse Prinivil with Proventil or Prilosec.
ALERT: Don't confuse Zestril with Zostrix.

Patient teaching

- Advise patient to report signs or symptoms of angioedema (including laryngeal edema), such as breathing difficulty or swelling of face, eyes, lips, or tongue.
- Tell patient that light-headedness may occur, especially during first few days of therapy. Tell him to rise slowly to avoid this effect and to report symptoms to prescriber. If syncope occurs, tell patient to stop taking drug and call prescriber immediately.
- Tell patient not to discontinue drug suddenly but to call prescriber if adverse reactions occur.
- Advise patient to report signs of infection, such as fever and sore throat.
- Tell patient to notify prescriber if she becomes pregnant. Drug will need to be discontinued.

Evaluation

- Patient's blood pressure is within normal limits.

• Patient maintains adequate cardiac output throughout therapy.
• Patient and family state understanding of drug therapy.

lithium carbonate

(LITH-ee-um KAR-buh-nayt)

Carbolith ♦, Duralith ♦, Eskalith, Eskalith CR, Lithane**, Lithicarb ◇, Lithizine ♦, Lithobid, Lithonate, Lithotabs

lithium citrate

Lithium Citrate Syrup*

Pharmacologic class: alkali metal
Therapeutic class: antimanic agent
Pregnancy risk category: D

Indications and dosages

▶ **Prevention or control of mania.** *Adults:* 300 to 600 mg P.O. up to q.i.d., increasing on basis of blood levels to achieve optimal dosage, usually 1,800 mg P.O. daily. Recommended therapeutic lithium blood levels: 1 to 1.5 mEq/L for acute mania; 0.6 to 1.2 mEq/L for maintenance therapy; and 2 mEq/L as maximum dosage.

▶ **Major depression, schizoaffective disorder, schizophrenic disorder, alcohol dependence‡.** *Adults:* 300 mg lithium carbonate P.O. t.i.d. or q.i.d.

▶ **Apparent mixed bipolar disorder in children‡.** *Children:* Initially, 15 to 60 mg/kg or 0.5 to 1.5 g/m² lithium carbonate P.O. daily in three divided doses. Don't exceed usual adult dosage. Adjust dosage based upon patient's response and serum lithium levels. Usual dosage range is 150 to 300 mg daily in divided doses to maintain lithium levels of 0.5 to 1.2 mEq/L.

▶ **Chemotherapy-induced neutropenia in children and patients with AIDS receiving zidovudine‡.** *Adults and children:* 300 to 1,000 mg P.O. daily.

Contraindications and precautions

• Contraindicated if therapy can't be closely monitored.
• Use with extreme caution in patients receiving neuroleptics, neuromuscular blockers, or diuretics; in debilitated patients; and in patients with thyroid disease, seizure disorder, renal or CV disease, severe debilitation or dehydration, or sodium depletion.

Lifespan: In pregnant or breast-feeding women, drug shouldn't be used. In children younger than age 12, drug isn't recommended. In elderly patients, use with extreme caution.

Adverse reactions

CNS: tremor, drowsiness, headache, confusion, restlessness, dizziness, psychomotor retardation, stupor, lethargy, ***coma,*** syncope, ***epileptiform seizures,*** EEG changes, worsened organic mental syndrome, impaired speech, ataxia, weakness, incoordination.
CV: *reversible ECG changes,* ***arrhythmias,*** hypotension, ankle and wrist edema.
EENT: tinnitus, blurred vision.
GI: dry mouth, metallic taste, nausea, vomiting, anorexia, diarrhea, thirst, abdominal pain, flatulence, indigestion.
GU: polyuria, glycosuria, ***renal toxicity*** with long-term use, albuminuria.
Hematologic: *leukocytosis with leukocyte count of 14,000 to 18,000/mm³* (reversible).
Metabolic: transient hyperglycemia, goiter, hypothyroidism, hyponatremia.
Skin: pruritus, rash, diminished or absent sensation, drying and thinning of hair, psoriasis, acne, alopecia.

Interactions

Drug-drug. *Aminophylline, sodium bicarbonate, urine alkalinizers:* Increases lithium excretion. Avoid salt loads and monitor lithium levels.
Carbamazepine, indomethacin, methyldopa, piroxicam, probenecid: Increases effect of lithium. Monitor patient for lithium toxicity.
Diuretics: Increases reabsorption of lithium by kidneys with possible toxic effect. Use with extreme caution, and monitor lithium and electrolyte levels (especially sodium).
Fluoxetine: Increases lithium levels. Monitor patient for toxicity.
Neuroleptics: May cause encephalopathy. Watch for signs and symptoms (lethargy, tremor, extrapyramidal symptoms), and stop drug if they occur.
Neuromuscular blockers: May cause prolonged paralysis or weakness. Monitor patient closely.

Thyroid hormones: May induce hypothyroidism. Monitor thyroid function.

Drug-herb. *Parsley:* May promote or produce serotonin syndrome. Discourage using together.

Effects on lab test results

- May increase glucose level. May decrease sodium, T_3, T_4, and protein-bound iodine levels.
- May increase ^{131}I uptake and WBC and neutrophil counts.

Pharmacokinetics

Absorption: Rate and extent vary with dosage form; absorption is complete within 8 hours of P.O. use.

Distribution: Distributed widely; levels in thyroid gland, bone, and brain exceed serum levels.

Metabolism: Not metabolized.

Excretion: 95% excreted unchanged in urine. *Half-life:* 18 hours (adolescents) to 36 hours (elderly).

Route	Onset	Peak	Duration
P.O.	1-3 wk	30 min-3 hr	Unknown

Pharmacodynamics

Chemical effect: Unknown; probably alters chemical transmitters in CNS, possibly by interfering with ionic pump mechanisms in brain cells, and may compete with sodium ions.

Therapeutic effect: Prevents or controls mania.

Available forms

lithium carbonate

Capsules: 150 mg, 300 mg, 600 mg

Tablets: 300 mg (300 mg = 8.12 mEq lithium)

Tablets (controlled-release): 300 mg, 450 mg

lithium citrate

Syrup (sugarless): 8 mEq (of lithium) per 5 ml (8 mEq lithium = 300 mg of lithium carbonate)

NURSING PROCESS

Assessment

- Assess patient's condition before therapy and regularly thereafter. Expect delay of 1 to 3 weeks before drug's beneficial effects are noticed.
- Monitor baseline ECG, thyroid and kidney studies, and electrolyte levels. Monitor lithium blood levels 8 to 12 hours after first dose, usually before morning dose, two or three times weekly in first month, then weekly to monthly during maintenance therapy.
- With blood levels of lithium below 1.5 mEq/L, adverse reactions usually remain mild.
- Check urine-specific gravity and report level below 1.005, which may indicate diabetes insipidus.
- Lithium may alter glucose tolerance in diabetic patient. Monitor glucose level closely.
- Perform outpatient follow-up of thyroid and kidney function every 6 to 12 months. Palpate thyroid to check for enlargement.
- Be alert for adverse reactions and drug interactions.
- Evaluate patient's and family's knowledge of drug therapy.

Nursing diagnoses

- Disturbed thought processes related to presence of manic disorder
- Ineffective health maintenance related to drug-induced endocrine dysfunction
- Deficient knowledge related to drug therapy

Planning and implementation

ALERT: Don't confuse Lithobid with Levbid, Lithonate with Lithostat, or Lithotabs with Lithobid or Lithostat.

- Determination of lithium blood levels is crucial to safe use of drug. Drug shouldn't be used in patients who can't have blood level checked regularly.
- Give with plenty of water and after meals to minimize GI reactions.
- Before leaving bedside, make sure patient has swallowed drug.
- Notify prescriber if patient's behavior hasn't improved in 3 weeks or if it worsens.

Patient teaching

- Tell patient to take drug with plenty of water and after meals to minimize GI upset.
- Explain that lithium has narrow therapeutic margin of safety. A blood level that is even slightly high can be dangerous.
- Warn patient and family to watch for signs of toxicity (diarrhea, vomiting, tremor, drowsiness, muscle weakness, ataxia) and to expect

transient nausea, polyuria, thirst, and discomfort during first few days. Tell patient to withhold one dose and call prescriber if toxic symptoms appear but not to stop drug abruptly.
• Warn patient to avoid activities that require alertness and good psychomotor coordination until CNS effects of drug are known.
• Tell patient not to switch brands or take other prescription or OTC drugs without prescriber's approval.
• Advise patient to wear or carry medical identification.

Evaluation
• Patient exhibits improved behavior and thought processes.
• Patient maintains normal endocrine function throughout therapy.
• Patient and family state understanding of drug therapy.

lomustine (CCNU)
(loh-MUH-steen)
CeeNU

Pharmacologic class: alkylating agent, nitrosourea (cell cycle–phase nonspecific)
Therapeutic class: antineoplastic
Pregnancy risk category: D

Indications and dosages
▶ **Brain tumor, Hodgkin's disease, lymphomas.** *Adults and children:* 100 to 130 mg/m² P.O. as single dose q 6 weeks. Dosage reduced according to degree of bone marrow suppression. Repeat doses shouldn't be given until WBC count is more than 4,000/mm³ and platelet count is more than 100,000/mm³.

Contraindications and precautions
• Contraindicated in patients hypersensitive to drug.
• Use cautiously in patients with decreased platelet, WBC, or RBC count and in those receiving other myelosuppressant drugs.
Lifespan: In pregnant or breast-feeding women, drug isn't recommended.

Adverse reactions
GI: *nausea, vomiting* (beginning within 4 to 5 hours), stomatitis.
GU: ***nephrotoxicity,*** progressive azotemia, ***renal failure.***
Hematologic: anemia, ***leukopenia*** (delayed up to 6 weeks, lasting 1 to 2 weeks), ***thrombocytopenia*** (delayed up to 4 weeks, lasting 1 to 2 weeks), ***bone marrow suppression*** (delayed up to 6 weeks).
Hepatic: ***hepatotoxicity.***
Respiratory: ***pulmonary fibrosis.***
Other: ***secondary malignant disease.***

Interactions
Drug-drug. *Anticoagulants, aspirin:* Increases bleeding risk. Avoid using together.

Effects on lab test results
• May increase urine urea, liver enzyme, BUN, and creatinine levels.
• May decrease hemoglobin, hematocrit, and WBC, RBC, and platelet counts.

Pharmacokinetics
Absorption: Absorbed rapidly and well.
Distribution: Distributed widely in body tissues and crosses blood-brain barrier to significant extent.
Metabolism: Rapidly and extensive in liver.
Excretion: Metabolites excreted primarily in urine with smaller amounts excreted in feces and through lungs. *Half-life:* 1 to 2 days.

Route	Onset	Peak	Duration
P.O.	Unknown	Unknown	Unknown

Pharmacodynamics
Chemical effect: Cross-links strands of cellular DNA and interferes with RNA transcription.
Therapeutic effect: Kills selected cancer cells.

Available forms
Capsules: 10 mg, 40 mg, 100 mg, dose pack (two 10-mg, two 40-mg, two 100-mg capsules)

NURSING PROCESS
Assessment
• Assess patient's condition before therapy and regularly thereafter.
• Monitor CBC weekly; bone marrow toxicity is delayed.
• Periodically monitor liver function tests.

• Be alert for adverse reactions and drug interactions.
• Evaluate patient's and family's knowledge of drug therapy.

Nursing diagnoses
• Ineffective health maintenance related to presence of neoplastic disease
• Ineffective protection related to adverse hematologic reactions
• Deficient knowledge related to drug therapy

Planning and implementation
• To avoid nausea, give antiemetic before giving drug.
• Give 2 to 4 hours after meals; drug is better absorbed if taken on empty stomach.
• Drug administration is repeated only when CBC results reveal safe hematologic parameters.
• Institute infection control and bleeding precautions.

Patient teaching
• Warn patient to watch for signs of infection (fever, sore throat, fatigue) and bleeding (easy bruising, nosebleeds, bleeding gums, melena) and to take temperature daily.
• Instruct patient to avoid OTC products containing aspirin.
• Advise woman of childbearing age to avoid becoming pregnant during therapy and to consult with prescriber before becoming pregnant.

Evaluation
• Patient responds well to therapy.
• Patient regains normal hematologic function.
• Patient and family state understanding of drug therapy.

loperamide

(loh-PEH-ruh-mighd)
Imodium, Imodium A-D†, Kaopectate II Caplets†, Maalox Anti-Diarrheal Caplets†, Neo-Diaral†, Pepto Diarrhea Control†

Pharmacologic class: piperidine derivative
Therapeutic class: antidiarrheal
Pregnancy risk category: B

Indications and dosages

▶ **Acute diarrhea.** *Adults and children age 12 and older:* Initially, 4 mg P.O.; then 2 mg after each unformed stool. Maximum dosage is 16 mg daily.
Children ages 9 to 11: 10 ml (2 mg) t.i.d. P.O. on first day. Subsequent doses of 5 ml (1 mg)/ 10 kg (22 lb) of body weight may be given after each unformed stool. Maximum dosage is 6 mg daily.
Children ages 6 to 8: 10 ml (2 mg) P.O. b.i.d. on first day. Report persistent diarrhea.
Children ages 2 to 5: 5 ml (1 mg) P.O. t.i.d. on first day. Report persistent diarrhea.
▶ **Chronic diarrhea.** *Adults:* Initially, 4 mg P.O.; then 2 mg after each unformed stool until diarrhea subsides. Dosage adjusted to individual response.
Children‡ : 0.08 to 0.24 mg/kg P.O. daily in two to three divided doses.
▶ **Acute diarrhea including traveler's diarrhea†.** *Adults:* 4 mg after first loose bowel movement followed by 2 mg after each subsequent loose bowel movement; maximum, 8 mg P.O. daily for 2 days.

Contraindications and precautions

• Contraindicated in patients hypersensitive to drug, and in patients in whom constipation must be avoided. OTC form is contraindicated in patients with bloody diarrhea and those with temperature over 101° F (38° C).
• Use cautiously in patients with hepatic disease.
Lifespan: In pregnant or breast-feeding women, use cautiously. In children younger than age 2, drug is contraindicated.

Adverse reactions

CNS: drowsiness, fatigue, dizziness.
GI: dry mouth; abdominal pain, distention, or discomfort; *constipation;* nausea; vomiting.
Skin: rash.
Other: hypersensitivity reactions.

Interactions

None significant.

Effects on lab test results

None reported.

Pharmacokinetics

Absorption: Poor.

Distribution: Unknown.
Metabolism: Metabolized in liver.
Excretion: Excreted primarily in feces; less than 2% excreted in urine. *Half-life:* 9.1 to 14.4 hours.

Route	Onset	Peak	Duration
P.O.	Unknown	2.5-5 hr	24 hr

Pharmacodynamics

Chemical effect: Inhibits peristaltic activity, prolonging transit of intestinal contents.
Therapeutic effect: Relieves diarrhea.

Available forms

Capsules: 2 mg
Oral liquid*: 1 mg/5 ml†, 1 mg/ml†
Tablets: 2 mg†

NURSING PROCESS

Assessment

- Assess patient's diarrhea before therapy and regularly thereafter.
- Be alert for adverse reactions.

ALERT: Monitor children closely for CNS effects because they may be more sensitive than adults to such effects.

- Monitor patient's hydration status if adverse GI reactions occur.
- Evaluate patient's and family's knowledge of drug therapy.

Nursing diagnoses

- Diarrhea related to underlying condition
- Risk for deficient fluid volume related to drug-induced adverse GI reactions
- Deficient knowledge related to drug therapy

Planning and implementation

- Notify prescriber if acute abdominal signs occur or drug is ineffective.
- If drug is given by nasogastric tube, flush tube to clear it and ensure drug's passage to stomach.

ALERT: Oral liquids are available in different concentrations. Check dosage carefully. For children, consider an oral liquid product that doesn't contain alcohol.

ALERT: Don't confuse Imodium with Ionamin.

Patient teaching

- Advise patient not to exceed recommended dosage.
- Tell patient with acute diarrhea to discontinue drug and seek medical attention if no improvement occurs within 48 hours; for chronic diarrhea, tell him to notify prescriber and discontinue drug if no improvement occurs after giving 16 mg daily for at least 10 days.
- Advise patient to stop taking drug and to notify prescriber immediately if abdominal distention or other symptoms develop in acute colitis.

Evaluation

- Patient's diarrhea is relieved.
- Patient maintains adequate hydration throughout therapy.
- Patient and family state understanding of drug therapy.

lopinavir and ritonavir

(loe-PIN-a-veer and rih-TOH-nuh-veer)
Kaletra

Pharmacologic class: protease inhibitor
Therapeutic class: antiviral
Pregnancy risk category: C

Indications and dosages

▶ **Treatment of HIV infection in combination therapy with other antiretroviral agents.** *Adults and adolescents older than age 12:* 400 mg lopinavir/100 mg ritonavir (3 capsules or 5 ml) P.O. b.i.d. with food. In treatment-experienced patient also taking efavirenz or nevirapine in whom reduced susceptibility to lopinavir might be suspected, consider a dose of 533/33 mg (4 capsules or 6.5 ml) P.O. b.i.d. with food.

Children ages 6 months to 12 years weighing 15 to 40 kg (33 to 88 lb): 10 mg/kg (lopinavir content) P.O. b.i.d. with food, up to a maximum of 400/100 mg in children weighing more than 40 kg. In treatment-experienced patient also taking efavirenz or nevirapine who weighs 15 to 50 kg (33 to 110 lb) and in whom reduced susceptibility to lopinavir is suspected, consider a dose of 11 mg/kg (lopinavir content) P.O. b.i.d. Children who weigh more than 50 kg can receive the adult dose.

Children ages 6 months to 12 years weighing 7 to 14 kg (15 to 31 lb): 12 mg/kg (lopinavir content) P.O. b.i.d. with food. In treatment-experienced patient also taking efavirenz or nevirapine in whom reduced susceptibility to lopinavir is suspected, consider a dose of 13 mg/kg (lopinavir content) P.O. b.i.d. with food.

Contraindications and precautions

• Contraindicated in patients hypersensitive to any of drug's ingredients.
• Use cautiously in patients with a history of pancreatitis or with hepatic impairment, hepatitis B or C, marked elevations in liver enzyme levels, or hemophilia.
Lifespan: HIV-infected mothers shouldn't breast-feed to avoid HIV transmission. In infants younger than age 6 months, safety and effectiveness haven't been established. In elderly patients, use cautiously.

Adverse reactions

CNS: pain, asthenia, headache, fever, insomnia, malaise, abnormal dreams, agitation, amnesia, anxiety, ataxia, confusion, depression, dizziness, dyskinesia, emotional lability, ***encephalopathy,*** hypertonia, nervousness, neuropathy, paresthesia, peripheral neuritis, somnolence, abnormal thinking, tremor.
CV: chest pain, ***deep vein thrombosis,*** hypertension, palpitations, peripheral edema, thrombophlebitis, vasculitis, facial edema, edema.
EENT: sinusitis, abnormal vision, eye disorder, otitis media, tinnitus.
GI: abdominal pain, abnormal stools, *diarrhea, nausea,* vomiting, anorexia, cholecystitis, constipation, dry mouth, dyspepsia, dysphagia, enterocolitis, eructation, esophagitis, fecal incontinence, flatulence, gastritis, gastroenteritis, GI disorder, ***hemorrhagic colitis,*** increased appetite, ***pancreatitis,*** sialadenitis, stomatitis, ulcerative stomatitis.
GU: abnormal ejaculation, taste perversion, hypogonadism, renal calculus, urine abnormality.
Hematologic: anemia, ***leukopenia, neutropenia; thrombocytopenia*** in children.
Hepatic: hyperbilirubinemia in children.
Metabolic: Cushing's syndrome, hypothyroidism, dehydration, decreased glucose tolerance, lactic acidosis, weight loss, hyperglycemia, hyperuricemia, *hypercholesterolemia,* hyponatremia in children.
Musculoskeletal: back pain, arthralgia, arthrosis, myalgia.
Respiratory: bronchitis, dyspnea, lung edema.
Skin: rash, acne, alopecia, dry skin, exfoliative dermatitis, furunculosis, nail disorder, pruritus, benign skin neoplasm, skin discoloration, sweating.
Other: chills, flulike syndrome, viral infection, lymphadenopathy, gynecomastia, decreased libido.

Interactions

Drug-drug. *Amiodarone, bepridil, lidocaine, quinidine:* Increases levels of antiarrhythmics. Use cautiously. Monitor levels of these drugs, if possible.
Amprenavir, indinavir, saquinavir: Increases levels of these drugs. Avoid using together.
Antiarrhythmics (flecainide, propafenone), pimozide: Increases risk of cardiac arrhythmias. Don't use together.
Atovaquone, methadone: Decreases levels of these drugs. Consider increasing doses of these drugs.
Carbamazepine, dexamethasone, phenobarbital, phenytoin: Decreases lopinavir levels. Use cautiously.
Clarithromycin: Increases clarithromycin levels in patients with renal impairment. Adjust clarithromycin dose.
Cyclosporine, rapamycin, tacrolimus: Increases levels of these drugs. Monitor therapeutic levels.
Delavirdine, ritonavir: Increases levels of lopinavir. Avoid using together.
Didanosine: Decreases absorption of didanosine because lopinavir and ritonavir is taken with food. Give didanosine 1 hour before or 2 hours after lopinavir and ritonavir.
Dihydroergotamine, ergonovine, ergotamine, methylergonovine: Increases risk of ergot toxicity characterized by peripheral vasospasm and ischemia. Don't use together.
Disulfiram, metronidazole: May increase risk of disulfiram-like reaction. Avoid using together.
Efavirenz, nevirapine: Decreases lopinavir levels. Consider increasing lopinavir and ritonavir dose.
Felodipine, nicardipine, nifedipine: Increases levels of these drugs. Use cautiously. Monitor patient.

Itraconazole, ketoconazole: Increases levels of these drugs. Don't give more than 200 mg/day of these drugs.
HMG-CoA reductase inhibitors: Increases risk of adverse reactions, such as myopathy, rhabdomyolysis. Avoid using together.
Methadone: Methadone AUC decreased. May need to increase dose. Monitor patient closely.
Midazolam, triazolam: Increases risk of prolonged or increased sedation or respiratory depression. Don't use together.
Oral contraceptives (ethinyl estradiol): Decreases effectiveness of contraceptives. Recommend alternative contraception measures.
Rifabutin: Increases rifabutin levels. Decrease rifabutin dose by 75%; monitor patient for adverse effects.
Rifampin: Decreases effectiveness of lopinavir and ritonavir. Avoid using together.
Sildenafil: Increases sildenafil levels. Don't exceed 25 mg of sildenafil in a 48-hour period. Use cautiously, and monitor patient for adverse reactions.
Warfarin: May affect warfarin level. Monitor PT and INR.
Drug-herb. *St. John's wort:* Loss of virologic response and possible resistance to Kaletra. Discourage using together.
Drug-food. *Any food:* Increases absorption of drug. Give drug with food.

Effects on lab test results

- May increase amylase, liver enzyme, glucose, uric acid, cholesterol, and triglyceride levels. In children, may increase bilirubin level and decrease sodium level.
- May decrease hemoglobin, hematocrit, and WBC, neutrophil, and platelet counts.

Pharmacokinetics

Absorption: Peak levels are achieved in 4 hours. Lopinavir and ritonavir is better absorbed when taken with food.
Distribution: Lopinavir is highly bound to plasma proteins (98-99%).
Metabolism: Lopinavir is extensively metabolized by the CYP3A isoenzyme, which is part of the P450 pathway. Ritonavir is a potent inhibitor of the CYP3A, which inhibits the metabolism of lopinavir, and therefore increases plasma levels of lopinavir.
Excretion: The drug is excreted in the urine and feces. Less than 3% of the drug is excreted unchanged. *Half-life:* about 5-6 hours.

Route	Onset	Peak	Duration
P.O.	Unknown	4 hr	5-6 hr

Pharmacodynamics

Chemical effects: Inhibits the HIV protease. Ritonavir inhibits the metabolism of lopinavir, thereby increasing plasma levels of lopinavir.
Therapeutic effect: Prevents the cleavage of the Gag-Pol polyprotein, resulting in the production of immature, noninfectious viral particles.

Available forms

Capsules: lopinavir 133.3 mg/ritonavir 33.3 mg.
Solution: lopinavir 400 mg/ritonavir 100 mg per 5 ml (80 mg/20 mg per ml)

NURSING PROCESS

Assessment

- Assess underlying condition before therapy and reassess regularly throughout therapy.
- Monitor total cholesterol and triglycerides before starting therapy and periodically thereafter.
- To monitor maternal-fetal outcomes of pregnant women exposed to lopinavir/ritonavir, an antiretroviral registry has been established. Health care providers are encouraged to enroll patients by calling 1-800-258-4263.

ALERT: Be aware that many drug interactions are possible. Review current drugs that patient is taking.

- Evaluate patient's and family's knowledge of drug therapy.

Nursing diagnoses

- Risk for falls related to drug-induced adverse CNS effects
- Risk for powerlessness related to chronic disease and need for aggressive medical management
- Deficient knowledge related to drug therapy

Planning and implementation

- Give drug with food.
- Refrigerated drug remains stable until expiration date on package. If stored at room temperature, drug should be used within 2 months.

• Monitor patient for signs of fat redistribution, including central obesity, buffalo hump, peripheral wasting, breast enlargement, and cushingoid appearance.
• Monitor patient for signs of pancreatitis: nausea, vomiting, abdominal pain, increased lipase and amylase values.
• Monitor patient for signs of bleeding.
• For an overdose, induce emesis or perform gastric lavage. Activated charcoal may be used to aid in the removal of unabsorbed drug. Dialysis is unlikely to help remove drug.
ALERT: Don't confuse Kaletra with Keppra.

Patient teaching
• Tell patient to take drug with food.
• Tell patient also taking didanosine to take it 1 hour before or 2 hours after lopinavir and ritonavir.
• Advise patient to report side effects to prescriber.
• Tell patient to immediately report severe nausea, vomiting, or abdominal pain.
• Warn patient to tell prescriber about any other prescription or nonprescription medicine that he is taking, including herbal supplements.
• Tell patient that drug is not a cure for HIV.
• Advise patient receiving sildenafil that there is an increased risk of sildenafil-associated adverse events including hypotension, visual changes, and priapism, and he should promptly report any symptoms. Tell him not to exceed 25 mg of sildenafil in a 48-hour period.

Evaluation
• Patient doesn't experience falls.
• Patient has adequate support, personal and professional, to deal with emotional aspects of having HIV disease.
• Patient and family state understanding of drug therapy.

loracarbef
(loh-ruh-KAR-bef)
Lorabid

Pharmacologic class: synthetic beta-lactam antibiotic of carbacephem class
Therapeutic class: antibiotic
Pregnancy risk category: B

Indications and dosages
▶ **Secondary bacterial infections of acute bronchitis.** *Adults:* 200 to 400 g P.O. q 12 hours for 7 days.
▶ **Acute bacterial exacerbations of chronic bronchitis.** *Adults:* 400 mg P.O. q 12 hours for 7 days.
▶ **Pneumonia.** *Adults:* 400 mg P.O. q 12 hours for 14 days.
▶ **Pharyngitis, sinusitis, tonsillitis.** *Adults:* 200 to 400 mg P.O. q 12 hours for 10 days. *Children:* 15 mg/kg P.O. daily in divided doses q 12 hours for 10 days.
▶ **Acute otitis media.** *Children:* 30 mg/kg (oral suspension) P.O. daily in divided doses q 12 hours for 10 days.
▶ **Uncomplicated skin and skin-structure infections.** *Adults:* 200 mg P.O. q 12 hours for 7 days.
▶ **Impetigo.** *Children:* 15 mg/kg P.O. daily in divided doses q 12 hours for 7 days.
▶ **Uncomplicated cystitis.** *Adults:* 200 mg P.O. daily for 7 days.
▶ **Uncomplicated pyelonephritis.** *Adults:* 400 mg P.O. q 12 hours for 14 days.
Patients with renal impairment: If creatinine clearance is 10 to 49 ml/minute, patient should receive half of usual dose at same interval. If clearance is below 10 ml/minute, patient should receive usual dose q 3 to 5 days. Hemodialysis patients need another dose after dialysis.

Contraindications and precautions
• Contraindicated in patients hypersensitive to drug or other cephalosporins and in patients with diarrhea caused by pseudomembranous colitis.
Lifespan: In pregnant or breast-feeding women, use cautiously. In infants younger than age 6 months, safety and efficacy haven't been established.

Adverse reactions
CNS: headache, somnolence, nervousness, insomnia, dizziness.
CV: vasodilation.
GI: diarrhea, nausea, vomiting, abdominal pain, anorexia, ***pseudomembranous colitis.***
GU: vaginal candidiasis.
Hematologic: ***transient thrombocytopenia, leukopenia,*** eosinophilia.

Skin: rash, urticaria, pruritus, ***erythema multiforme.***
Other: hypersensitivity reactions, ***anaphylaxis.***

Interactions

Drug-drug. *Probenecid:* Decreases loracarbef excretion, causing increased plasma levels. Monitor patient for toxicity.
Drug-food. *Any food:* Decreases absorption. Give drug 1 hour before or 2 hours after meals.

Effects on lab test results

- May increase BUN, creatinine, ALT, AST, and alkaline phosphatase levels.
- May increase PT, INR, and eosinophil count. May decrease platelet, WBC, RBC, and neutrophil counts.

Pharmacokinetics

Absorption: About 90%. Absorption of suspension is greater than that of capsule.
Distribution: About 25% of circulating drug is bound to plasma proteins.
Metabolism: Doesn't appear to be metabolized.
Excretion: Excreted primarily in urine. *Half-life:* About 1 hour.

Route	Onset	Peak	Duration
P.O.	Unknown	30-60 min	Unknown

Pharmacodynamics

Chemical effect: Inhibits cell-wall synthesis, promoting osmotic instability; usually bactericidal.
Therapeutic effect: Kills susceptible bacteria, including gram-positive aerobes, such as *Staphylococcus aureus* and *saprophyticus, Streptococcus pneumoniae* and *pyogenes;* and gram-negative aerobes, such as *Escherichia coli, Haemophilus influenzae,* and *Moraxella catarrhalis.*

Available forms

Powder for oral suspension: 100 mg/5 ml, 200 mg/5 ml in 50-, 75-, and 100-ml bottles
Pulvules: 200 mg, 400 mg

NURSING PROCESS

Assessment

- Assess patient's infection before therapy and regularly thereafter.
- Obtain specimen for culture and sensitivity tests before giving first dose. Therapy may begin pending test results.
- Be alert for adverse reactions and drug interactions.

ALERT: Watch for seizures. Beta-lactam antibiotics may trigger seizures in susceptible patients, especially when given without dosage modification to those with renal impairment.

- Monitor patient's hydration status if adverse GI reactions occur.
- Evaluate patient's and family's knowledge of drug therapy.

Nursing diagnoses

- Infection related to presence of susceptible bacteria
- Risk for deficient fluid volume related to drug-induced adverse GI reactions
- Deficient knowledge related to drug therapy

Planning and implementation

- To reconstitute powder for oral suspension, add 30 ml of water in two portions to 50-ml bottle or 60 ml of water in two portions to 100-ml bottle. Shake after each addition.
- After reconstitution, store oral suspension for 14 days at constant room temperature (59° to 86° F [15° to 30° C]).
- If seizures occur, stop drug and tell prescriber. Give anticonvulsants.
- Between 40% and 75% of patients receiving cephalosporins show false-positive direct Coombs' test; only some indicate hemolytic anemia.

ALERT: Don't confuse Lorabid with Lortab.

Patient teaching

- Tell patient to take drug on an empty stomach, at least 1 hour before or 2 hours after meals.
- Tell patient to shake suspension well before measuring dose.
- Tell patient to take drug exactly as prescribed.
- Instruct patient to discard unused portion after 14 days.

Evaluation

- Patient is free from infection.
- Patient maintains adequate hydration throughout therapy.
- Patient and family state understanding of drug therapy.

loratadine

(loo-RAH-tuh-deen)
Alavert†, Claratyne ◇, Claritin†, Claritin Reditabs†, Claritin Syrup†, Claritin-D 12-hour†, Claritin-D 24 hour†

Pharmacologic class: tricyclic antihistamine
Therapeutic class: antihistamine
Pregnancy risk category: B

Indications and dosages

▶ **Symptomatic treatment of seasonal or perennial allergic rhinitis, chronic idiopathic urticaria.** *Adults and children age 6 and older:* 10 mg P.O. daily.
Children ages 2 to 5: 5 mg syrup P.O. daily.
Patients older than 5 years with renal impairment or hepatic failure: If creatinine clearance is 30 ml/minute or less, initial dose is 10 mg P.O. every other day.
Children ages 2 to 5 with renal insufficiency or hepatic failure: Initial dose is 5 mg P.O. every other day.

Contraindications and precautions

- Contraindicated in patients hypersensitive to drug.
- Use cautiously in patients with hepatic impairment.

Lifespan: In pregnant women, use only when absolutely necessary. In breast-feeding women, use isn't recommended. In children younger than age 2, safety of drug hasn't been established.

Adverse reactions

CNS: headache, somnolence, fatigue.
GI: dry mouth.

Interactions

Drug-drug. *Erythromycin, ketoconazole:* Increases plasma loratadine levels. Monitor patient closely.
Drug-lifestyle. *Alcohol use:* Increases CNS depression. Discourage using together.
Sun exposure: Photosensitivity reactions may occur. Tell patient to avoid unprotected or prolonged exposure to sunlight.

Effects on lab test results

None reported.

Pharmacokinetics

Absorption: Readily absorbed. Food may delay peak plasma levels by 1 hour.
Distribution: Doesn't readily cross blood-brain barrier; about 97% bound to plasma protein.
Metabolism: Extensively metabolized, although specific enzyme systems responsible for metabolism haven't been identified.
Excretion: About 80% distributed equally between urine and feces. *Half-life:* 8.4 hours.

Route	Onset	Peak	Duration
P.O.	1 hr	4-6 hr	24 hr

Pharmacodynamics

Chemical effect: Blocks effects of histamine at H_1-receptor sites. Loratadine is a nonsedating antihistamine; its chemical structure prevents entry into CNS.
Therapeutic effect: Relieves allergy symptoms.

Available forms

Syrup: 1 mg/ml
Tablets: 10 mg
Tablets (rapidly disintegrating): 10 mg

NURSING PROCESS

Assessment

- Assess patient's condition before therapy and regularly thereafter.
- Be alert for adverse reactions and drug interactions.
- Evaluate patient's and family's knowledge of drug therapy.

Nursing diagnoses

- Ineffective health maintenance related to underlying allergy condition
- Fatigue related to drug's adverse effect
- Deficient knowledge related to drug therapy

Planning and implementation

- Dosage for patients with hepatic failure or renal insufficiency should be reduced.
- Give drug on empty stomach.
- Notify prescriber if drug is ineffective.

Patient teaching

• Tell patient to take drug at least 2 hours after meal, to avoid eating for at least 1 hour after taking drug, and to take drug only once daily.
• Advise patient taking Claritin Reditabs to place tablet on the tongue, where it disintegrates within a few seconds. It can be swallowed with or without water.
• Tell patient to contact prescriber if symptoms persist or worsen.
• Advise patient to stop taking drug 4 days before allergy skin tests to preserve accuracy of tests.
• Instruct patient to avoid prolonged exposure to the sun and to wear sunblock and protective clothing during drug therapy.
• Tell patient to avoid alcohol and driving or other activities that require alertness until CNS effects of drug are known.

☑ Evaluation

• Patient states that allergy symptoms are relieved.
• Patient describes coping strategies for fatigue.
• Patient and family state understanding of drug therapy.

lorazepam

(loo-RAZ-eh-pam)

Apo-Lorazepam ♦, Ativan, Lorazepam Intensol, Novo-Lorazem ♦, Nu-Loraz ♦

Pharmacologic class: benzodiazepine
Therapeutic class: antianxiety agent, sedative-hypnotic
Pregnancy risk category: D
Controlled substance schedule: IV

Indications and dosages

▶ **Anxiety.** *Adults:* 2 to 6 mg P.O. daily in divided doses. Maximum, 10 mg daily.
▶ **Insomnia caused by anxiety.** *Adults:* 2 to 4 mg P.O. h.s.
▶ **Premedication before operative procedure.** *Adults:* 0.05 mg/kg I.M. 2 hours before procedure. Total dosage shouldn't exceed 4 mg. Or, 2 mg total or 0.044 mg/kg I.V., whichever is smaller. Larger doses up to 0.05 mg/kg I.V. (to total of 4 mg) may be needed.
▶ **Management of nausea and vomiting caused by emetogenic cancer chemotherapy‡.** *Adults:* 2.5 mg P.O. the evening before chemotherapy; repeat just after the initiation of chemotherapy. Alternatively, 1.5 mg/m^2 (maximum, 3 mg) I.V. over 5 minutes, 45 minutes before chemotherapy.
Elderly: Initially, 1 to 2 mg P.O. daily in divided doses. Then dosage is divided, p.r.n.
▶ **Status epilepticus‡.** *Adults and children:* 0.05 to 0.1 mg/kg I.V. Doses may be repeated at 10- to 15-minute intervals p.r.n. for seizure control. Alternatively, adults may be given 4 to 8 mg I.V.

Contraindications and precautions

• Contraindicated in patients hypersensitive to drug, other benzodiazepines, or vehicle used in parenteral dosage form; also contraindicated in patients with acute angle-closure glaucoma.
• Use cautiously in patients with pulmonary, renal, or hepatic impairment. Also use cautiously in acutely ill or debilitated patients.
Lifespan: In pregnant women, avoid use, especially during first trimester. In breast-feeding women, avoid use. In children, safety of drug hasn't been established. In elderly patients, use cautiously.

Adverse reactions

CNS: *drowsiness, lethargy, hangover,* fainting, anterograde amnesia, restlessness, psychosis.
CV: transient hypotension.
EENT: visual disturbances.
GI: dry mouth, abdominal discomfort.
GU: incontinence, urine retention.
Other: ***acute withdrawal syndrome*** (after sudden discontinuation in physically dependent patients).

Interactions

Drug-drug. *CNS depressants:* May increase CNS depression. Avoid using together.
Digoxin: May increase serum digoxin levels, increasing toxicity. Monitor patient closely.
Drug-herb. *Catnip, kava, lady's slipper, lemon balm, passion flower, sassafras, skullcap, valerian:* Sedative effects may be enhanced. Discourage using together.
Drug-lifestyle. *Alcohol use:* Increases CNS depression. Discourage using together.

Smoking: Decreases benzodiazepine effectiveness. Monitor patient closely; discourage patient from smoking.

Effects on lab test results

• May increase liver function test values.

Pharmacokinetics

Absorption: Well absorbed after P.O. administration; unknown after I.M. administration.
Distribution: Distributed widely throughout body; about 85% protein-bound.
Metabolism: Metabolized in liver.
Excretion: Excreted in urine. *Half-life:* 10 to 20 hours.

Route	Onset	Peak	Duration
P.O.	1 hr	2 hr	12-24 hr
I.V.	1-5 min	1-1.5 hr	6-8 hr
I.M.	15-30 min	1-1.5 hr	6-8 hr

Pharmacodynamics

Chemical effect: Unknown; probably stimulates gamma-aminobutyric receptors in ascending reticular activating system.
Therapeutic effect: Relieves anxiety and promotes calmness and sleep.

Available forms

Injection: 2 mg/ml, 4 mg/ml
Oral solution (concentrated): 2 mg/ml
Tablets: 0.5 mg, 1 mg, 2 mg
Tablets (S.L.): 0.5 mg♦, 1 mg♦, 2 mg♦

NURSING PROCESS

Assessment

• Assess patient's condition before therapy and regularly thereafter.
ALERT: Check respirations before each I.V. dose and every 5 to 15 minutes thereafter until respiratory status is stable.
• Monitor liver, kidney, and hematopoietic function studies periodically in patient receiving repeated or prolonged therapy.
• Be alert for adverse reactions and drug interactions.
• Evaluate patient's and family's knowledge of drug therapy.

Nursing diagnoses

• Anxiety related to underlying condition
• Risk for injury related to drug-induced adverse CNS effects
• Deficient knowledge related to drug therapy

Planning and implementation

• **P.O. use:** Follow normal protocol.
• **I.V. use:** Give drug slowly, at no more than 2 mg/minute. Dilute with equal volume of sterile water for injection, normal saline solution for injection, or D_5W injection.
• **I.M. use:** Inject drug deep into muscle mass. Don't dilute.
• Reduce dosage in elderly or debilitated patient. Preoperative I.V. dose shouldn't exceed 2 mg in patients older than age 50.
• Have emergency resuscitation equipment and oxygen available.
• Refrigerate parenteral form to prolong shelf life.
• Possibility of abuse and addiction exists. Don't withdraw drug abruptly after long-term use; withdrawal symptoms may occur.
ALERT: Don't confuse lorazepam with alprazolam.

Patient teaching

• Warn patient to avoid hazardous activities until CNS effects of drug are known.
• Tell patient to avoid alcohol and smoking during drug therapy.
• As premedication before surgery, lorazepam provides substantial preoperative amnesia. Patient teaching requires extra care to ensure adequate recall. Provide written materials or inform family member, if possible.

Evaluation

• Patient is less anxious.
• Patient doesn't experience injury as result of adverse CNS reactions.
• Patient and family state understanding of drug therapy.

losartan potassium

(loh-SAR-tan poh-TAH-see-um)
Cozaar

Pharmacologic class: angiotensin II receptor antagonist
Therapeutic class: antihypertensive

Pregnancy risk category: C (D in second and third trimesters)

Indications and dosages

▶ **Nephropathy in type 2 diabetes mellitus.** *Adults:* 50 mg P.O. daily. Increase dose to 100 mg daily based on blood pressure response.
▶ **Hypertension.** *Adults:* Initially, 25 to 50 mg P.O. daily. Maximum daily dose is 100 mg in one or two divided doses.

Contraindications and precautions

- Contraindicated in patients hypersensitive to drug.
- Use cautiously in patients with impaired kidney or liver function.

Lifespan: In pregnant women, drug should be used only when absolutely necessary. Breast-feeding isn't recommended during drug therapy. In children, safety of drug hasn't been established.

Adverse reactions

Hypertension
CNS: dizziness, asthenia, fatigue, headache, insomnia.
CV: edema, chest pain.
EENT: nasal congestion, sinusitis, pharyngitis, sinus disorder.
GI: abdominal pain, nausea, diarrhea, dyspepsia.
Musculoskeletal: muscle cramps, myalgia, back or leg pain.
Respiratory: cough, upper respiratory tract infection.
Other: *angioedema.*
Nephropathy
CNS: *asthenia, fatigue*, fever, hypesthesia.
CV: *chest pain,* hypotension, orthostatic hypotension.
EENT: sinusitis, cataract.
GI: *diarrhea,* dyspepsia, gastritis.
GU: *urinary tract infection.*
Hematologic: *anemia.*
Metabolic: hyperkalemia, *hypoglycemia,* weight gain.
Musculoskeletal: *back pain,* leg or knee pain, muscle weakness.
Respiratory: *cough, bronchitis.*
Skin: cellulitis.
Other: infection, *flulike syndrome,* trauma, diabetic neuropathy, *diabetic vascular disease, angioedema.*

Interactions

Drug-drug. *Potassium-sparing diuretics, potassium supplements:* May cause possible hyperkalemia. Monitor patient closely.
Drug-herb. *Red yeast rice:* Contains components similar to those of statin drugs, increasing the risk of adverse events or toxicity. Discourage using together.
Drug-food: *Salt substitutes containing potassium:* May increase risk of hyperkalemia. Monitor patient closely.

Effects on lab test results

None reported.

Pharmacokinetics

Absorption: Absorbed well and undergoes extensive first-pass metabolism; systemic bioavailability of drug is about 33%.
Distribution: Highly bound to plasma proteins.
Metabolism: Cytochrome P450 2C9 and 3A4 are involved in biotransformation of losartan to its metabolites.
Excretion: Excreted primarily in feces with smaller amount excreted in urine. *Half-life:* About 2 hours.

Route	Onset	Peak	Duration
P.O.	Unknown	1-4 hr	Unknown

Pharmacodynamics

Chemical effect: Inhibits vasoconstricting and aldosterone-secreting effects of angiotensin II by selectively blocking binding of angiotensin II to receptor sites in many tissues, including vascular smooth muscle and adrenal glands.
Therapeutic effect: Lowers blood pressure.

Available forms

Tablets: 25 mg, 50 mg, 100 mg

NURSING PROCESS

Assessment

- Assess patient's blood pressure before therapy and regularly thereafter. When drug is used alone, its effect on blood pressure is notably less in black patients than in those of other races.
- Regularly assess patient's kidney function (by way of creatinine and BUN levels). Pa-

tients with severe heart failure whose kidney function depends on angiotensin-aldosterone system have experienced acute renal failure during ACE inhibitor therapy. Manufacturer states that losartan would be expected to do the same. Closely monitor patient, especially during first few weeks of therapy.
• Be alert for adverse reactions.
• Monitor patient for symptomatic hypotension if he is taking a diuretic.
• Evaluate patient's and family's knowledge of drug therapy.

Nursing diagnoses
• Risk for injury related to presence of hypertension
• Disturbed sleep pattern related to drug-induced insomnia
• Deficient knowledge related to drug therapy

Planning and implementation
• Lowest dosage (25 mg) should be used initially in patients with impaired liver function and in those with volume depletion (such as those receiving diuretics).
• Drug can be used alone or with other antihypertensives.
• If antihypertensive effect measured by serum trough level of drug using once-daily dosing is inadequate, a twice-daily regimen using same total daily dose or an increase in dosage may give better response.
• Give once-daily dosing in morning to prevent insomnia.
• If pregnancy is suspected, notify prescriber because drug should probably be discontinued.
ALERT: Don't confuse Cozaar with Zocor.

Patient teaching
• Tell patient to avoid sodium substitutes; these products may contain potassium, which can cause hyperkalemia in patients taking losartan.
• Inform woman of childbearing age about consequences of second- and third-trimester exposure to losartan, and instruct her to notify prescriber immediately if pregnancy occurs or is suspected.

Evaluation
• Patient's blood pressure is normal.
• Patient states that insomnia hasn't occurred.
• Patient and family state understanding of drug therapy.

lovastatin (mevinolin)
(loh-vuh-STAH-tin)
Altocor, Mevacor

Pharmacologic class: HMG-CoA reductase inhibitor
Therapeutic class: cholesterol-lowering agent
Pregnancy risk category: X

Indications and dosages
▶ **Primary prevention of primary hypercholesterolemia (types IIa and IIb), atherosclerosis.** *Adults:* Initially, 20 mg P.O. once daily with evening meal. Patients requiring reductions in LDL cholesterol of 20% or more to achieve their goal should be started on 20 mg P.O. daily. Recommended range is 10 to 80 mg in single or divided doses; the maximum recommended dose is 80 mg P.O. daily.
▶ **Adolescents with heterozygous familial hypercholesterolemia.** *Adolescents and children ages 10 to 17 (girls should be 1 year postmenarche):* 10 to 40 mg P.O. daily with evening meal. Patients requiring reductions in LDL cholesterol of 20% or more should be started on 20 mg daily.
Patients also taking immunosuppressive drugs: 10 mg P.O. daily, not to exceed 20 mg daily.
Patients also taking lipid-lowering therapy: Use of lovastatin with fibrates or niacin should generally be avoided; if used with either, the dose of lovastatin should not exceed 20 mg P.O. daily.
▶ **Primary prevention of coronary artery disease in patients without symptomatic CV disease, average to moderately elevated total cholesterol and LDL cholesterol levels, and below average HDL cholesterol levels; reduction of LDL and total cholesterol levels in patients with primary hypercholesterolemia (types IIa and IIb), to slow the progression of coronary atherosclerosis with coronary artery disease.** *Adults:* Initially, 20 mg P.O. once daily with evening meal. Recommended dosage range is 10 to 80 mg daily in one or two divided doses.

Patients receiving immunosuppressants: Initial dosage is 10 mg P.O. daily; maximum, 20 mg daily.

▶ **Adjunct to diet to slow the progression of coronary atherosclerosis in patients with coronary heart disease as part of a treatment strategy to lower total cholesterol levels and LDL cholesterol levels to target levels; adjunct to diet for the reduction of elevated total cholesterol levels, LDL cholesterol levels, Apo B, and TG, and to increase HDL cholesterol levels in patients with primary hypercholesterolemia (heterozygous familial and non-familial) and mixed dyslipidemia (Fredrickson types IIa and IIb).**

Altocor ER. *Adults:* 20 to 60 mg P.O. h.s. Starting dose of 10 mg can be used for patients requiring smaller reductions. Usual dosage range is 10 to 60 mg P.O. daily.

Patients also taking immunosuppressive drugs: Dosage is 10 mg P.O. daily, not to exceed 20 mg P.O. daily.

Patients also taking lipid-lowering therapy: Use of lovastatin with fibrates or niacin should generally be avoided; if used with either, the dose of lovastatin should not exceed 20 mg P.O. daily.

Patients with severe renal insufficiency (creatinine clearance less than 30 ml/min): A dosage increase above 20 mg P.O. daily should be carefully considered and, if necessary, implemented cautiously.

Contraindications and precautions

- Contraindicated in patients hypersensitive to drug, and in those with active liver disease or conditions linked to unexplained persistent elevations of serum transaminase levels.
- Use cautiously in patients who consume substantial quantities of alcohol or have history of liver disease.

Lifespan: In pregnant or breast-feeding women, use is contraindicated. In women of childbearing age, use is contraindicated unless they have no risk of pregnancy. In children younger than 10, safety of drug hasn't been established.

Adverse reactions

CNS: headache, dizziness, peripheral neuropathy.
EENT: blurred vision.
GI: constipation, diarrhea, dyspepsia, flatulence, abdominal pain or cramps, heartburn, dysgeusia, nausea.
Musculoskeletal: muscle cramps, myalgia, myositis, ***rhabdomyolysis.***
Skin: rash, pruritus.

Interactions

Drug-drug. *Bile acid sequestrants:* Decreases lovastatin bioavailability. Administer separately.
Cyclosporine or other immunosuppressants, erythromycin, gemfibrozil, niacin: Increases risk of polymyositis and rhabdomyolysis. Monitor patient closely.
Digoxin: Slight elevation in digoxin levels is possible. Monitor patient.
Isradipine: Increases clearance of lovastatin and its metabolites via increased hepatic blood flow. Monitor patient for loss of therapeutic effect.
Itraconazole: May increase HMG-CoA reductase inhibitor levels about twentyfold. Temporarily interrupt HMG-CoA reductase inhibitor if patient needs systemic azole antifungal.
Oral anticoagulants: Lovastatin may enhance oral anticoagulant effects. Monitor patient closely.
Drug-herb. *Red yeast rice:* Contains components similar to those of statin drugs, increasing the risk of adverse events or toxicity. Discourage using together.
Drug-lifestyle. *Alcohol use:* Increases risk of hepatotoxicity. Discourage using together.
Sun exposure: Photosensitivity reactions may occur. Tell patient to avoid unprotected or prolonged exposure to sunlight.

Effects on lab test results

- May increase ALT, AST, and CK levels.

Pharmacokinetics

Absorption: About 30%. Administration with food improves plasma levels of total inhibitors by about 30%. Extended-release tablets have greater bioavailability than immediate-release tablets.
Distribution: Less than 5% of dose reaches systemic circulation because of extensive first-pass hepatic extraction; liver is principal site of action. Drug and its principal metabolite are more than 95% bound to plasma proteins.

Metabolism: Metabolized in liver. Studies with extended-release tablets have not been conducted.
Excretion: About 80% excreted in feces, about 10% in urine. *Half-life:* 3 hours. Extended-release tablets incur negligible excretion through the kidneys.

Route	Onset	Peak	Duration
P.O.	Unknown	2-6 hr	4-6 wk
P.O. (extended-release)	Unknown	14 hours	Unknown

Pharmacodynamics

Chemical effect: Inhibits 3-hydroxy-3-methylglutaryl coenzyme A reductase. This enzyme is an early (and rate-limiting) step in synthetic pathway of cholesterol.
Therapeutic effect: Lowers LDL and total cholesterol levels.

Available forms

Tablets: 10 mg, 20 mg, 40 mg
Tablets (extended-release): 10 mg, 20 mg, 40 mg, 60 mg

NURSING PROCESS

Assessment
- Obtain history of patient's lipoprotein and cholesterol levels before therapy, and reassess regularly thereafter.
- Criteria for heterozygous familial hypercholesterolemia include adolescent girls who are at least 1 year post-menarche and boys, ages 10 to 17, who have these findings after an adequate trial of diet therapy:
  – LDL cholesterol levels remains >189 mg/dl, or
  – LDL cholesterol levels remains >160 mg/dl, and
  – Family history of premature CV disease or two or more other CV disease risk factors.
- Liver function tests should be performed at start of therapy and periodically thereafter.
- Be alert for adverse reactions and drug interactions.
- Evaluate patient's and family's knowledge of drug therapy.

Nursing diagnoses
- Risk for injury related to underlying condition
- Pain related to drug-induced adverse musculoskeletal reactions
- Deficient knowledge related to drug therapy

Planning and implementation
- Drug therapy should begin only after diet and other nonpharmacologic therapies have proven ineffective. Patient should follow a standard low-cholesterol diet during therapy.
- Give drug with evening meal; absorption is enhanced and cholesterol biosynthesis is greater in evening.

ALERT: Don't confuse lovastatin with Lotensin, Leustatin, or Livostin. Don't confuse Mevacor with Mivacron.

ALERT: Don't confuse Altocor (lovastatin, extended-release) with Advicor (niacin/lovastatin, extended-release).

Patient teaching
- Instruct patient to take drug with evening meal.
- Advise patient not to crush or chew extended-release tablets.
- Teach patient dietary management of serum lipids (restricting total fat and cholesterol intake) and measures to control other cardiac disease risk factors. If appropriate, recommend weight control, exercise, and smoking cessation programs.
- Advise patient to have periodic eye examinations.
- Tell patient to store drug at room temperature in light-resistant container.
- Instruct patient to avoid alcohol consumption during drug therapy.

ALERT: Inform woman that drug is contraindicated during pregnancy. Tell her to notify prescriber immediately if she becomes pregnant.

Evaluation
- Patient's LDL and cholesterol levels are within normal limits.
- Patient doesn't experience musculoskeletal pain.
- Patient and family state understanding of drug therapy.

loxapine hydrochloride

(LOKS-uh-peen high-droh-KLOR-ighd)
Loxapac ♦, Loxitane C, Loxitane IM

loxapine succinate

Loxapac ♦, Loxitane

Pharmacologic class: dibenzoxazepine
Therapeutic class: antipsychotic
Pregnancy risk category: NR

Indications and dosages

▶ **Psychotic disorders.** *Adults:* 10 mg P.O. b.i.d. to q.i.d., rapidly increasing to 60 to 100 mg P.O. daily for most patients (dosage varies from patient to patient); or 12.5 to 50 mg I.M. q 4 to 6 hours or longer, both dose and interval depending on patient response. Maximum dose is 250 mg daily.

Contraindications and precautions

• Contraindicated in patients hypersensitive to dibenzoxazepines and in patients experiencing coma, severe CNS depression, or drug-induced depression.
• Use with extreme caution in those with seizure disorder, CV disorder, glaucoma, or history of urine retention.
Lifespan: In pregnant women, safety of drug hasn't been established. In breast-feeding women, drug isn't recommended. In children, safety of drug hasn't been established.

Adverse reactions

CNS: *extrapyramidal reactions, sedation, tardive dyskinesia,* ***seizures,*** pseudoparkinsonism, EEG changes, dizziness, ***neuroleptic malignant syndrome.***
CV: *orthostatic hypotension,* tachycardia, ECG changes.
EENT: *blurred vision.*
GI: *dry mouth, constipation.*
GU: *urine retention,* dark urine, menstrual irregularities.
Hematologic: ***leukopenia, agranulocytosis, thrombocytopenia.***
Metabolic: weight gain, increased appetite.
Skin: *mild photosensitivity reactions,* allergic reactions.
Other: gynecomastia.

Interactions

Drug-drug. *CNS depressants:* May increase CNS depression. Avoid using together.
Drug-lifestyle. *Alcohol use:* May increase CNS depression. Discourage using together.

Effects on lab test results

• May increase liver function test values. May decrease WBC, granulocyte, and platelet counts.

Pharmacokinetics

Absorption: Rapid and complete.
Distribution: Distributed widely in body; 91% to 99% protein-bound.
Metabolism: Metabolized extensively by liver.
Excretion: Most of drug excreted as metabolites in urine; some excreted in feces. *Half-life:* P.O. form, 3 to 4 hours; I.M. form, 12 hours.

Route	Onset	Peak	Duration
P.O.	30 min	1.5-3 hr	≤ 2 hr
I.M.	30 min	1.5-3 hr	≤ 12 hr

Pharmacodynamics

Chemical effect: Unknown; probably blocks postsynaptic dopamine receptors in brain.
Therapeutic effect: Relieves psychotic symptoms.

Available forms

loxapine hydrochloride
Injection: 50 mg/ml
Oral concentrate: 25 mg/ml
loxapine succinate
Capsules: 5 mg, 10 mg, 25 mg, 50 mg
Tablets: 5 mg ♦, 10 mg ♦, 25 mg ♦, 50 mg ♦

NURSING PROCESS

Assessment

• Assess patient's condition before therapy and regularly thereafter.
• Assess blood pressure before therapy and monitor regularly.
• Be alert for adverse reactions and drug interactions.
• Monitor patient for tardive dyskinesia. It may occur after prolonged use. It may not appear until months or years later and may disappear spontaneously or persist for life despite discontinuation of drug.

• Evaluate patient's and family's knowledge of drug therapy.

Nursing diagnoses

• Disturbed thought processes related to underlying psychotic condition
• Impaired physical mobility related to drug-induced extrapyramidal symptoms
• Deficient knowledge related to drug therapy

Planning and implementation

• **P.O. use:** Dilute liquid concentrate with orange or grapefruit juice just before giving.
• **I.M. use:** Follow normal protocol.
• Acute dystonic reactions may be treated with diphenhydramine.

Patient teaching
• Warn patient to avoid activities that require alertness and psychomotor coordination until CNS effects of drug are known.
• Urge patient to avoid alcohol consumption during drug therapy.
• Advise patient to get up slowly to avoid orthostatic hypotension.
• Tell patient to relieve dry mouth with sugarless gum or hard candy.
• Urge patient to get periodic eye examinations.

Evaluation

• Patient's psychotic behavior declines.
• Patient maintains physical mobility throughout therapy.
• Patient and family state understanding of drug therapy.

lymphocyte immune globulin (antithymocyte globulin [equine], ATG), (LIG)

(LIM-foh-sight ih-MYOON GLOH-byoo-lin)
Atgam

Pharmacologic class: immunoglobulin
Therapeutic class: immunosuppressant
Pregnancy risk category: C

Indications and dosages

▶ **Prevention of acute renal allograft rejection.** *Adults and children:* 15 mg/kg I.V. daily for 14 days, followed by alternate-day dosing for 14 days. First dose should be given within 24 hours of transplantation.
▶ **Treatment of acute renal allograft rejection.** *Adults and children:* 10 to 15 mg/kg I.V. daily for 14 days, followed by alternate-day dosing for 14 days. Therapy should start when rejection is diagnosed.
▶ **Aplastic anemia.** *Adults:* 10 to 20 mg/kg I.V. daily for 8 to 14 days. Additional alternate-day therapy up to total of 21 doses can be given.
▶ **Skin allotransplantation‡.** *Adults:* 10 mg/kg I.V. 24 hours before allograft; then 10 to 15 mg/kg every other day. Maintenance dose ranges from 5 to 40 mg/kg daily based on response. Therapy usually continues until allograft covers less than 20% of total body surface area, usually 40 to 60 days.

Contraindications and precautions

• Contraindicated in patients hypersensitive to drug. An intradermal skin test is recommended at least 1 hour before first dose. Marked local swelling or erythema larger than 10 mm indicates increased risk of severe systemic reaction, such as anaphylaxis. Severe reactions to skin test, such as hypotension, tachycardia, dyspnea, generalized rash, or anaphylaxis, usually preclude further administration.
• Use cautiously in patients receiving additional immunosuppressive therapy (such as corticosteroids and azathioprine) because of increased potential for infection.
Lifespan: In pregnant women, use cautiously. In breast-feeding women, drug isn't recommended.

Adverse reactions

CNS: malaise, ***seizures,*** headache.
CV: *hypotension, chest pain,* thrombophlebitis, tachycardia, edema, iliac vein obstruction, renal artery stenosis.
EENT: ***laryngospasm.***
GI: *nausea, vomiting,* diarrhea, epigastric pain, abdominal distention, stomatitis.
Hematologic: ***leukopenia, thrombocytopenia,*** hemolysis, ***aplastic anemia.***
Metabolic: hyperglycemia.
Musculoskeletal: arthralgia.
Respiratory: *dyspnea,* hiccups, pulmonary edema.
Skin: rash.

Other: febrile reactions, serum sickness, ***anaphylaxis,*** infection, night sweats, lymphadenopathy.

Interactions

Drug-drug. *Muromonab-CD3:* May increase risk of infection. Monitor patient closely.

Effects on lab test results

- May increase liver enzyme and glucose levels.
- May decrease hemoglobin, hematocrit, and WBC and platelet counts.

Pharmacokinetics

Absorption: Administered I.V.
Distribution: Unknown.
Metabolism: Unknown.
Excretion: About 1% excreted in urine, principally as unchanged drug. *Half-life:* About 6 days.

Route	Onset	Peak	Duration
I.V.	Unknown	5 days	Unknown

Pharmacodynamics

Chemical effect: Unknown; inhibits cell-mediated immune responses by either altering T-cell function or eliminating antigen-reactive T cells.
Therapeutic effect: Prevents or relieves signs and symptoms of renal allograft rejection; also relieves signs and symptoms of aplastic anemia.

Available forms

Injection: 50 mg of equine IgG/ml in 5-ml ampules

NURSING PROCESS

Assessment

- Assess patient's condition before therapy and regularly thereafter.
- Be alert for adverse reactions and drug interactions.
- Evaluate patient's and family's knowledge of drug therapy.

Nursing diagnoses

- Ineffective health maintenance related to underlying condition
- Ineffective immune protection related to adverse hematologic reactions
- Deficient knowledge related to drug therapy

Planning and implementation

- Dilute concentrated drug before administration. Dilute dose in 250 to 1,000 ml of half-normal or normal saline solution for injection. Final concentration of drug shouldn't exceed 1 mg/ml.
  – When adding ATG to infusion solution, make sure container is inverted so drug doesn't contact air inside container. Gently rotate or swirl container to mix contents; don't shake because this may cause excessive foaming or denature drug protein.
  – Infuse with in-line filter with pore size of 0.2 to 1 micron over no less than 4 hours (most facilities specify 4 to 8 hours). ATG solutions must be filtered during administration; filters with pore sizes of 0.2 to 5 microns have been used.
  – Don't use solutions that are more than 12 hours old, including actual infusion time.
- Don't dilute ATG concentrate with dextrose solutions or solutions with low salt concentration because precipitate may form. The proteins in ATG can be denatured by air. ATG is unstable in acidic solutions.
- Refrigerate drug at 35° to 47° F (2° to 8° C). Don't freeze. ATG concentrate is heat-sensitive.

Patient teaching

- Warn patient that fever is likely. Instruct him to report adverse drug effects.
- Instruct patient to take infection-control and bleeding precautions.

Evaluation

- Patient responds well to therapy.
- Patient doesn't experience serious adverse hematologic reactions.
- Patient and family state understanding of drug therapy.

M

magaldrate (aluminum-magnesium complex)

(muh-GAL-drayt)
Iosopan†, Riopan†

Pharmacologic class: aluminum-magnesium salt
Therapeutic class: antacid
Pregnancy risk category: A

Indications and dosages

▶**Antacid.** *Adults:* 540 to 1,080 mg (5 to 10 ml) P.O. of suspension or liquid with water between meals and h.s.

Contraindications and precautions

• Contraindicated in patients with severe renal disease. Drug isn't typically used in patients with renal failure to help control hypophosphatemia because it contains magnesium, which may accumulate.
• Use cautiously in patients with mild renal impairment.
Lifespan: In pregnant or breast-feeding women, use cautiously.

Adverse reactions

GI: mild constipation, diarrhea.

Interactions

Drug-drug. *Allopurinol, antibiotics (including fluoroquinolones and tetracyclines), diflunisal, digoxin, iron, isoniazid, penicillamine, phenothiazines, quinidine:* May decrease pharmacologic effects of these drugs because of impaired absorption. Separate administration times.
Enteric-coated drugs: May release prematurely in stomach. Separate doses by at least 1 hour.

Effects on lab test results

• May increase gastrin levels. May decrease potassium levels.

Pharmacokinetics

Absorption: May be absorbed systemically, posing risk to patient with renal failure. Absorption is unrelated to mechanism of action.
Distribution: Primarily local.
Metabolism: None.
Excretion: Excreted in feces.

Route	Onset	Peak	Duration
P.O.	≤ 20 min	Unknown (fasting); 3 hr (non-fasting)	20-60 min

Pharmacodynamics

Chemical effect: Reduces total acid load in GI tract, elevates gastric pH to reduce pepsin activity, strengthens gastric mucosal barrier, and increases esophageal sphincter tone.
Therapeutic effect: Soothes stomach upset.

Available forms

Liquid, oral suspension: 540 mg/5 ml†

NURSING PROCESS

Assessment

• Assess patient's condition before therapy and regularly thereafter.
• Record amount and consistency of stools.
• Monitor magnesium level in patient with mild renal impairment. Symptomatic hypermagnesemia usually occurs only in severe renal failure.
• Be alert for adverse reactions and drug interactions.
• Evaluate patient's and family's knowledge of drug therapy.

Nursing diagnoses

• Chronic pain related to gastric hyperacidity
• Diarrhea related to drug-induced adverse GI reactions
• Deficient knowledge related to drug therapy

Planning and implementation

• Shake suspension well. Give with water to facilitate passage.
• When giving through NG tube, make sure tube is placed properly and is patent. After instilling drug, flush tube with water to ensure passage to stomach and to clear tube.

• Drug has very low sodium content and is acceptable for patient on restricted sodium intake.

Patient teaching
• Advise patient not to take drug indiscriminately or to switch antacids without prescriber's advice.

✔ Evaluation
• Patient states that pain is relieved.
• Patient maintains normal bowel patterns throughout therapy.
• Patient and family state understanding of drug therapy.

magnesium chloride
(mag-NEE-see-um KLOR-ighd)
Slow-Mag

magnesium sulfate

Pharmacologic class: magnesium salt
Therapeutic class: anticonvulsant, electrolyte supplement, antiarrhythmic
Pregnancy risk category: A

Indications and dosages

▶ **Mild hypomagnesemia.** *Adults:* 1 g I.M. q 6 hours for four doses, depending on magnesium level.
▶ **Severe hypomagnesemia (magnesium level 0.8 mEq/L or less with symptoms).** *Adults:* 5 g I.V. in 1 L of solution over 3 hours. Subsequent doses depend on serum magnesium level.
▶ **Magnesium supplementation.** *Adults:* 54 to 483 mg P.O. daily in divided doses.
▶ **Magnesium supplementation in total parenteral nutrition (TPN).** *Adults:* 4 to 24 mEq I.V. daily added to TPN solution.
Infants: 2 to 10 mEq I.V. daily added to TPN solution. Each 2 ml of 50% solution contains 1 g, or 8.12 mEq, magnesium sulfate.
▶ **Hypomagnesemic seizures.** *Adults:* 1 to 2 g of 10% solution I.V. over 15 minutes; then 1 g I.M. q 4 to 6 hours, based on patient's response and magnesium level.
▶ **Seizures caused by hypomagnesemia in acute nephritis.** *Children:* 0.2 ml/kg of 50% solution I.M. q 4 to 6 hours, p.r.n., or 100 mg/kg of 10% solution I.V. very slowly. Adjust dosage according to magnesium level and seizure response.
▶ **Paroxysmal atrial tachycardia unresponsive to other treatments.** *Adults:* 3 to 4 g I.V. of 10% solution over 30 seconds with close monitoring of ECG.
▶ **Reduction of CV morbidity and mortality caused by acute MI.** *Adults:* 2 g I.V. over 5 to 15 minutes, followed by infusion of 18 g over 24 hours (12.5 mg/min). Initiate therapy as soon as possible, but no longer than 6 hours after MI.

Contraindications and precautions

• Contraindicated in patients with myocardial damage or heart block.
• Use parenteral magnesium with extreme caution in patients with impaired kidney function.
Lifespan: In women who are actively progressing in labor, drug is contraindicated.

Adverse reactions

CNS: *weak or absent deep tendon reflexes,* flaccid paralysis, hypothermia, drowsiness, perioral paresthesia, twitching carpopedal spasm, tetany, ***seizures.***
CV: flushing; slow, weak pulse; ***arrhythmias;*** *hypotension;* ***circulatory collapse.***
Metabolic: hypocalcemia.
Respiratory: ***respiratory paralysis.***
Skin: diaphoresis,.

Interactions

Drug-drug. *Cardiac glycosides:* May cause serious cardiac conduction changes. Give with extreme caution.
Neuromuscular blockers: May increase neuromuscular blockage. Use cautiously.
Nitrofurantoin, penicillamine, tetracyclines: Decreases bioavailability with oral magnesium supplements. Separate administration times by 2 to 3 hours.

Effects on lab test results

• May decrease calcium level.

Pharmacokinetics

Absorption: 35% to 40% of P.O. dose is absorbed through GI tract. High-fat diets may interfere with absorption.

Distribution: About 30% of magnesium is bound intracellularly to proteins and energy-rich phosphates.
Metabolism: Unknown.
Excretion: Parenteral dose excreted primarily in urine; P.O. dose excreted in urine and feces.

Route	Onset	Peak	Duration
P.O.	Unknown	4 hr	4-6 hr
I.V., I.M.	Unknown	Unknown	4-6 hr

Pharmacodynamics

Chemical effect: Replaces and maintains magnesium levels; as anticonvulsant, reduces muscle contractions by interfering with release of acetylcholine at myoneural junction.
Therapeutic effect: Raises magnesium levels, alleviates seizure activity, and restores normal sinus rhythm.

Available forms

magnesium chloride
Injectable solutions: 20% in 50-ml vials
Tablets (delayed-release): 64 mg
magnesium sulfate
Injectable solutions: 10%, 12.5%, 50% in 2-ml, 5-ml, 10-ml, 20-ml, and 30-ml ampules, vials, and prefilled syringes

NURSING PROCESS

Assessment

- Assess patient's condition before therapy and regularly thereafter.
- When giving I.V. for severe hypomagnesemia, watch for respiratory depression and signs of heart block. Respirations should be more than 16 breaths/minute before dose is given.
- Check magnesium level after repeated doses.
- Monitor patient's fluid intake and output. Output should be 100 ml or more during 4-hour period before dose.
- Be alert for adverse reactions and drug interactions.
- Evaluate patient's and family's knowledge of drug therapy.

Nursing diagnoses

- Ineffective health maintenance related to underlying condition
- Risk for injury related to drug-induced adverse reactions
- Deficient knowledge related to drug therapy

Planning and implementation

- **P.O. use:** Follow normal protocol.
- **I.V. use:** Inject I.V. bolus dose slowly, using infusion pump for continuous infusion if available, to avoid respiratory or cardiac arrest. Infusion shouldn't exceed 150 mg/minute. Rapid drip causes feeling of heat.

ALERT: When giving I.V. for severe hypomagnesemia, watch for respiratory depression and signs and symptoms of heart block. Respirations should be more than 16 breaths/minute before dose is given.

- Magnesium sulfate may form precipitate when mixed with solutions containing arsenates, barium, calcium, clindamycin, ethanol, heavy metals, hydrocortisone sodium succinate, phosphates, polymyxin B sulfate, procaine, salicylates, or tartrates. Drug is also incompatible with alkalis, including carbonates and bicarbonates.
- Keep I.V. calcium available to reverse magnesium intoxication.
- **I.M. use:** Undiluted 50% solutions may be given to adults by deep I.M. injection. When giving to children, dilute solutions to 20% or less.

ALERT: Test knee-jerk and patellar reflexes before each additional dose. If no reflex, notify prescriber and don't give magnesium until reflexes return; otherwise, patient may develop temporary respiratory failure and need cardiopulmonary resuscitation or I.V. administration of calcium.

Patient teaching

- Instruct patient receiving parenteral drug to report adverse reactions immediately.
- Review oral administration schedule with patient. Tell him not to take more than prescribed.

Evaluation

- Patient has positive response to drug administration.
- Patient sustains no injury from adverse reactions.
- Patient and family state understanding of drug therapy.

magnesium citrate (citrate of magnesia)

(mag-NEE-see-um SIH-trayt)
Citro-Mag♦, Evac-Q-Mag

magnesium hydroxide (milk of magnesia)

Milk of Magnesia†, Milk of Magnesia Concentrate†, Phillips' Milk of Magnesia†, Phillips' Milk of Magnesia Concentrated †

magnesium sulfate (epsom salts)

Pharmacologic class: magnesium salt
Therapeutic class: saline laxative
Pregnancy risk category: NR

Indications and dosages

▶ **Constipation; to evacuate bowel before surgery.** ***magnesium citrate.*** *Adults and children age 12 and older:* 11 to 25 g P.O. daily as single dose or divided.
Children ages 6 to 11: 5.5 to 12.5 g P.O. daily as single dose or divided.
Children ages 2 to 5: 2.7 to 6.25 g P.O. daily as single dose or divided.
▶ **Laxative use.** ***magnesium hydroxide.*** *Adults and children 12 years and older:* 2 to 4 tablespoons at bedtime or upon rising, followed by a full glass (8 ounces) of liquid.
Children ages 6 to 11 years: Don't use dosage cup. 1 to 2 tablespoons followed by a full glass (8 ounces) of liquid.
Children ages 2 to 5 years: Don't use dosage cup. 1 to 3 teaspoons followed by a full glass (8 ounces) of liquid.
magnesium sulfate. *Adults and children age 12 and older:* 10 to 30 g P.O. daily as single dose or divided.
Children ages 6 to 11: 5 to 10 g P.O. daily as single dose or divided.
Children ages 2 to 5: 2.5 to 5 g P.O. daily as single dose or divided.
▶ **Antacid use.** ***magnesium hydoxide.*** *Adults and children 12 years and older:* Don't use dosage cup. 1 to 3 teaspoons with a little water, up to four times a day.
magnesium citrate. *Adults:* 5 to 15 ml P.O. t.i.d. or q.i.d.

Contraindications and precautions

- Contraindicated in patients with abdominal pain, nausea, vomiting, other symptoms of appendicitis or acute surgical abdomen, myocardial damage, heart block, fecal impaction, rectal fissures, intestinal obstruction or perforation, or renal disease.
- Use cautiously in patients with rectal bleeding.

Lifespan: In women, during labor and delivery, use is contraindicated. In pregnant or breast-feeding women, use cautiously.

Adverse reactions

GI: *abdominal cramping, nausea, diarrhea,* laxative dependence with long-term or excessive use.
Metabolic: fluid and electrolyte disturbances.

Interactions

Drug-drug. *Oral drugs:* Impairs absorption. Separate administration times.

Effects on lab test results

- May alter fluid and electrolyte levels with prolonged use.

Pharmacokinetics

Absorption: About 15% to 30% may be absorbed systemically (posing risk to patients with renal failure).
Distribution: Unknown.
Metabolism: Unknown.
Excretion: Unabsorbed drug excreted in feces; absorbed drug excreted rapidly in urine.

Route	Onset	Peak	Duration
P.O.	30 min-3 hr	Varies	Varies

Pharmacodynamics

Chemical effect: Reduces total acid load in GI tract, elevates gastric pH to reduce pepsin activity, strengthens gastric mucosal barrier, and increases esophageal sphincter tone.
Therapeutic effect: Soothes stomach upset, relieves constipation, and raises magnesium level.

Available forms

magnesium citrate
Oral solution: about 168 mEq magnesium/240 ml†
magnesium hydroxide
Oral suspension: 7% to 8.5% (about 80 mEq magnesium/30 ml)†
magnesium sulfate
Granules: about 40 mEq magnesium/5 g†

NURSING PROCESS

Assessment
- Assess patient's condition before therapy and regularly thereafter.
- Before giving for constipation, determine whether patient has adequate fluid intake, exercise, and diet.

ALERT: Monitor electrolyte levels during prolonged use. Magnesium may accumulate in patient with renal insufficiency.
- Be alert for adverse reactions and drug interactions.
- Evaluate patient's and family's knowledge of drug therapy.

Nursing diagnoses
- Constipation related to underlying condition
- Diarrhea related to therapy
- Deficient knowledge related to drug therapy

Planning and implementation
- Time drug administration so that it doesn't interfere with scheduled activities or sleep.
- Chill magnesium citrate before use to improve its palatability.
- Shake suspension well. Give with large amount of water when used as laxative. When giving through NG tube, make sure tube is placed properly and is patent. After instilling drug, flush tube with water to ensure passage to stomach and to maintain tube patency.
- Drug is for short-term therapy.
- Magnesium sulfate is more potent than other saline laxatives.

Patient teaching
- Teach patient about dietary sources of bulk, such as bran and other cereals, fresh fruit, and vegetables.
- Warn patient that frequent or prolonged use may cause dependence.

Evaluation
- Patient's constipation is relieved.
- Diarrhea doesn't develop.
- Patient and family state understanding of drug therapy.

magnesium oxide

(mag-NEE-see-um OKS-ighd)
Mag-Ox 400 , Maox , Uro-Mag

Pharmacologic class: magnesium salt
Therapeutic class: antacid, laxative
Pregnancy risk category: NR

Indications and dosages

▶ **Antacid.** *Adults:* 140 mg P.O. with water or milk after meals and h.s.
▶ **Laxative.** *Adults:* 4 g P.O. with water or milk, usually h.s.
▶ **Oral replacement therapy in mild hypomagnesemia.** *Adults:* 400 to 840 mg P.O. daily. Monitor serum magnesium response.

Contraindications and precautions

- Contraindicated in patients with severe renal disease.
- Use cautiously in patients with mild renal impairment.

Lifespan: In pregnant or breast-feeding women, use cautiously.

Adverse reactions

GI: *diarrhea,* nausea, abdominal pain.
Metabolic: hypermagnesemia.

Interactions

Drug-drug. *Allopurinol, antibiotics (including fluoroquinolones and tetracyclines), diflunisal, digoxin, iron, isoniazid, penicillamine, phenothiazines, quinidine:* Decreases pharmacologic effect, possibly because of impaired absorption. Separate administration times.
Enteric-coated drugs: May release prematurely in stomach. Separate doses by at least 1 hour.

Effects on lab test results

- May increase magnesium level.

Pharmacokinetics

Absorption: Small amount absorbed from GI tract.

Distribution: Unknown.
Metabolism: None.
Excretion: Unabsorbed drug excreted in feces; absorbed drug excreted in urine.

Route	Onset	Peak	Duration
P.O.	20 min	Unknown (fasting); 3 hr (non-fasting)	20-60 min

Pharmacodynamics

Chemical effect: Reduces total acid load in GI tract, elevates gastric pH to reduce pepsin activity, strengthens gastric mucosal barrier, and increases esophageal sphincter tone.
Therapeutic effect: Soothes stomach upset, relieves constipation, and raises magnesium level.

Available forms

Capsules: 140 mg†
Tablets: 400 mg†, 420 mg†, 500 mg†

NURSING PROCESS

Assessment

- Assess patient's condition before therapy and regularly thereafter.

ALERT: Monitor magnesium level. With prolonged use and renal impairment, watch for symptoms of hypermagnesemia (signs and symptoms include hypotension, nausea, vomiting, depressed reflexes, respiratory depression, and coma).

- Be alert for adverse reactions and drug interactions.
- Evaluate patient's and family's knowledge of drug therapy.

Nursing diagnoses

- Ineffective health maintenance related to underlying condition
- Risk for injury related to potential for hypermagnesemia
- Deficient knowledge related to drug therapy

Planning and implementation

- When using as laxative, don't give other oral drugs 1 to 2 hours before or after treatment.
- If diarrhea occurs, be prepared to suggest alternative preparation.

Patient teaching

- Advise patient not to take drug indiscriminately or to switch antacids without prescriber's advice.

Evaluation

- Patient responds well to therapy.
- Patient maintains normal magnesium level throughout therapy.
- Patient and family state understanding of drug therapy.

magnesium sulfate

(mag-NEE-see-um SUL-fayt)

Pharmacologic class: mineral, electrolyte
Therapeutic class: anticonvulsant
Pregnancy risk category: A

Indications and dosages

▶ **Prevention or control of seizures in preeclampsia or eclampsia.** *Women:* Initially, 4 g I.V. in 250 ml of D_5W and 4 to 5 g deep I.M. each buttock; then 4 g deep I.M. into alternate buttock q 4 hours, p.r.n. Or, 4 g I.V. loading dose, followed by 1 to 2 g hourly as I.V. infusion.

▶ **Hypomagnesemia.** *Adults:* 1 g I.M. q 6 hours for four doses for mild deficiency; up to 250 mg/kg I.M. over 4 hours for severe deficiency.

▶ **Seizures, hypertension, and encephalopathy linked to acute nephritis in children.** *Children:* 0.2 ml/kg of 50% solution I.M. q 4 to 6 hours, p.r.n. For severe symptoms, 100 to 200 mg/kg I.V. very slowly over 1 hour with one-half of dose given in first 15 to 20 minutes. Dosage adjusted according to serum magnesium level and seizure response.

▶ **Management of paroxysmal atrial tachycardia.** *Adults:* 3 to 4 g I.V. over 30 seconds.

▶ **Management of life-threatening ventricular arrhythmias, such as sustained ventricular tachycardia or torsades de pointes.** *Adults:* 2 to 6 g I.V. over several minutes, followed by continuous infusion of 3 to 20 mg/minute for 5 to 48 hours. Dosage and duration of therapy based on patient response and serum magnesium level.

▶ **Management of preterm labor‡.** *Adults:* 4 to 6 g I.V. over 20 minutes as a loading dose, followed by maintenance infusions of 2 to 4 g/hour for 12 to 24 hours, as tolerated, after contractions subside.

▶ **Asthma‡.** *Adults:* 1 to 2 g I.V.

Contraindications and precautions

- Parenteral administration contraindicated in patients with heart block or myocardial damage.
- Use cautiously in patients with impaired kidney function.

Lifespan: In women who are in labor, use cautiously. In breast-feeding women, drug isn't recommended.

Adverse reactions

CNS: drowsiness, *depressed reflexes,* flaccid paralysis, hypothermia.
CV: *hypotension, flushing,* ***circulatory collapse,*** depressed cardiac function, ***heart block.***
Metabolic: hypocalcemia.
Respiratory: ***respiratory paralysis.***
Skin: diaphoresis.

Interactions

Drug-drug. *Anesthetics, CNS depressants:* May cause additive CNS depression. Use together cautiously.
Cardiac glycosides: May exacerbate arrhythmias. Use together cautiously.
Neuromuscular blockers: May increase neuromuscular blockade. Use together cautiously.

Effects on lab test results

- May increase magnesium level. May decrease calcium level.

Pharmacokinetics

Absorption: Unknown.
Distribution: Throughout body.
Metabolism: None.
Excretion: Unchanged in urine.

Route	Onset	Peak	Duration
I.V.	1-2 min	Almost immediate	About 30 min
I.M.	1 hr	Unknown	3-4 hr

Pharmacodynamics

Chemical effect: May decrease acetylcholine released by nerve impulses, but anticonvulsant mechanism is unknown.

Therapeutic effect: Prevents or controls seizures, raises magnesium level, stops paroxysmal atrial tachycardia, and alleviates selected symptoms of acute nephritis in children.

Available forms

Injection: 10%, 12.5%, 50%

NURSING PROCESS

Assessment

- Assess patient's condition before therapy and regularly thereafter.
- Monitor vital signs every 15 minutes when giving drug I.V.

ALERT: Watch for respiratory depression and signs of heart block. Respirations should be about 16 breaths/minute before each dose.

- Monitor fluid intake and output. Output should be 100 ml or more in 4-hour period before each dose.
- Be alert for adverse reactions and drug interactions.
- Check magnesium level after repeated doses. Disappearance of knee-jerk and patellar reflexes is sign of early stages of magnesium toxicity. Signs of hypermagnesemia begin to appear at a level of 4 mEq/L.
- Observe neonate for signs of magnesium toxicity, including neuromuscular or respiratory depression, when giving I.V. form to toxemic mother within 24 hours before delivery.
- Evaluate patient's and family's knowledge of drug therapy.

Nursing diagnoses

- Ineffective health maintenance related to underlying condition
- Risk for injury related to drug-induced adverse reactions
- Deficient knowledge related to drug therapy

Planning and implementation

- **I.V. use:** Dilute to maximum concentration of 200 mg/ml (20%). Drug is compatible with D_5W.
  – Infuse no faster than 150 mg/minute (1.5 ml/minute of 10% solution or 0.75 ml/minute of 20% solution). Rapid drip induces uncomfortable feeling of heat.
- Keep I.V. calcium gluconate available to reverse magnesium intoxication; use cautiously

in patients undergoing digitalization because of danger of arrhythmias.
• If used to treat seizures, institute appropriate seizure precautions.
• **I.M. use:** Follow normal protocol.
ALERT: Don't confuse magnesium sulfate with manganese sulfate.

Patient teaching
• Stress importance of reporting adverse reactions immediately.

Evaluation
• Patient responds well to therapy.
• Patient doesn't experience injury.
• Patient and family state understanding of drug therapy.

mannitol
(MAN-ih-tol)
Osmitrol

Pharmacologic class: osmotic diuretic
Therapeutic class: diuretic, diagnostic and nephrotic treatment agent, treatment of drug intoxication, reduction of intracranial or intraocular pressure
Pregnancy risk category: C

Indications and dosages
▶ **Test dose for marked oliguria or suspected inadequate kidney function.** *Adults and adolescents older than age 12:* 200 mg/kg or 12.5 g as 15% or 20% I.V. solution over 3 to 5 minutes. Response is adequate if 30 to 50 ml of urine/hour is excreted over 2 to 3 hours. If response is inadequate, second test dose is given. If still no response after second dose, drug should be discontinued.
Children younger than age 12‡: 0.2 g/kg or 6 g/m^2 I.V. over 3 to 5 minutes.
▶ **Oliguria.** *Adults and adolescents older than age 12:* 100 g I.V. as 15% to 20% solution over 90 minutes to several hours.
Children younger than age 12‡: 2 g/kg or 60 g/m^2 I.V.
▶ **Prevention of oliguria or acute renal failure.** *Adults and adolescents older than age 12:* 50 to 100 g I.V. of concentrated solution, followed by 5% to 10% solution. Exact concentration determined by fluid requirements.
▶ **Edema; ascites caused by renal, hepatic, or cardiac failure.** *Adults and adolescents older than age 12:* 100 g I.V. as 10% to 20% solution over 2 to 6 hours.
Children younger than age 12‡: 2 g/kg or 60 g/m^2 I.V. as a 15% to 20% solution over 2 to 6 hours.
▶ **Reduction of intraocular or intracranial pressure.** *Adults and adolescents older than age 12:* 1.5 to 2 g/kg as 15% to 25% I.V. solution over 30 to 60 minutes.
Children younger than age 12‡: 2 g/kg or 60 g/m^2 I.V. as a 15% to 20% solution over 30 to 60 minutes.
▶ **Diuresis in drug intoxication.** *Adults and adolescents older than age 12:* 25-g loading dose followed by an infusion maintaining 100- to 500-ml urine output/hour and positive fluid balance.
Children younger than age 12‡: 2 g/kg or 60 g/m^2 I.V. of a 5% to 10% solution, p.r.n.
▶ **Irrigating solution during transurethral resection of prostate.** *Adults:* 2.5% solution, p.r.n.

Contraindications and precautions
• Contraindicated in patients hypersensitive to drug and in those with anuria, severe pulmonary congestion, frank pulmonary edema, severe heart failure, severe dehydration, metabolic edema, progressive renal disease or dysfunction, or active intracranial bleeding except during craniotomy.
Lifespan: In pregnant women, use cautiously. In breast-feeding women, drug isn't recommended.

Adverse reactions
CNS: headache, confusion, ***seizures.***
CV: transient expansion of plasma volume during infusion, causing ***circulatory overload*** and ***heart failure;*** tachycardia; chest pains.
EENT: blurred vision, rhinitis.
GI: thirst, nausea, vomiting, *diarrhea.*
GU: urine retention.
Metabolic: water intoxication, cellular dehydration.

Interactions
Drug-drug. *Lithium:* Increases urinary excretion of lithium. Monitor patient closely.

Effects on lab test results

• May cause electrolyte imbalance.

Pharmacokinetics

Absorption: Given I.V.
Distribution: Remains in extracellular compartment; doesn't cross blood-brain barrier.
Metabolism: Metabolized minimally to glycogen in liver.
Excretion: Excreted in urine. *Half-life:* About 100 minutes.

Route	Onset	Peak	Duration
I.V.	30-60 min	≤ 1 hr	6-8 hr

Pharmacodynamics

Chemical effect: Increases osmotic pressure of glomerular filtrate, inhibiting tubular reabsorption of water and electrolytes. This elevates blood plasma osmolality, enhancing water flow into extracellular fluid.
Therapeutic effect: Increases water excretion, decreases intracranial or intraocular pressure, prevents or treats kidney dysfunction, and alleviates drug intoxication.

Available forms

Injection: 5%, 10%, 15%, 20%, 25%

NURSING PROCESS

Assessment

• Assess patient's condition before therapy and regularly thereafter.
• Monitor vital signs, central venous pressure, and fluid intake and output hourly. Insert urethral catheter in comatose or incontinent patient because therapy is based on strict evaluation of fluid intake and output. In patient with urethral catheter, use hourly urometer collection bag to facilitate accurate evaluation.
• Monitor weight, kidney function, and serum and urine sodium and potassium levels daily.
• Be alert for adverse reactions and drug interactions.
• Evaluate patient's and family's knowledge of drug therapy.

Nursing diagnoses

• Ineffective health maintenance related to underlying condition
• Risk for deficient fluid volume related to drug-induced adverse GI reactions
• Deficient knowledge related to drug therapy

Planning and implementation

• To dissolve crystallized solution (occurs at low temperatures or in concentrations greater than 15%), warm bottle in hot water bath and shake vigorously. Cool to body temperature before giving. Don't use solution with undissolved crystals.
• Give as intermittent or continuous infusion at prescribed rate, using in-line filter and infusion pump. Direct injection isn't recommended. Check I.V. line patency at infusion site before and during administration.
• Avoid infiltration; if it occurs, observe for inflammation, edema, and necrosis.
• For maximum intraocular pressure reduction before surgery, give 1 to 1½ hours preoperatively.
• When used as irrigating solution for prostate surgery, a concentration of 3.5% or greater is needed to avoid hemolysis.
• Notify prescriber immediately if oliguria increases or adverse reactions occur.

Patient teaching

• Tell patient he may feel thirsty or have a dry mouth, and emphasize the importance of drinking only amount of fluid provided.
• Instruct patient to immediately report pain in chest, back, or legs, or shortness of breath.

Evaluation

• Patient responds well to mannitol.
• Patient maintains adequate hydration throughout therapy.
• Patient and family state understanding of drug therapy.

mebendazole

(meh-BEN-duh-zohl)
Vermox

Pharmacologic class: benzimidazole
Therapeutic class: anthelmintic
Pregnancy risk category: C

Indications and dosages

▶ **Pinworm.** *Adults and children older than age 2:* 100 mg P.O. as single dose. If infection persists 3 weeks later, treatment is repeated.
▶ **Roundworm, whipworm, hookworm.** *Adults and children older than age 2:* 100 mg P.O. b.i.d. for 3 days. If infection persists 3 weeks later, treatment is repeated.
▶ **Trichinosis‡.** *Adults and children older than age 2:* 200 to 400 mg P.O. t.i.d. for 3 days, then 400 to 500 mg t.i.d. for 10 days.
▶ **Capillariasis‡.** *Adults and children older than age 2:* 200 mg P.O. b.i.d. for 20 days.
▶ **Toxocariasis‡.** *Adults and children:* 100 to 200 mg P.O. b.i.d. for 5 days.
▶ **Dracunculiasis‡.** *Adults and children older than age 2:* 400 to 800 mg P.O. daily for 6 days.

Contraindications and precautions

- Contraindicated in patients hypersensitive to drug.

Lifespan: In pregnant women, use cautiously. In breast-feeding women, safety of drug hasn't been established.

Adverse reactions

GI: transient abdominal pain, diarrhea.

Interactions

Drug-drug. *Carbamazepine, hydantoins:* May reduce plasma levels of mebendazole, possibly decreasing its therapeutic effect. Monitor patient.
Cimetidine: Increases mebendazole levels. Monitor patient closely.

Effects on lab test results

None reported.

Pharmacokinetics

Absorption: About 5% to 10% of dose is absorbed; varies widely among patients.
Distribution: Highly bound to plasma proteins.
Metabolism: Metabolized to inactive metabolites.
Excretion: Mostly excreted in feces; 2% to 10% excreted in urine. *Half-life:* 3 to 9 hours.

Route	Onset	Peak	Duration
P.O.	Unknown	2-5 hr	Varies

Pharmacodynamics

Chemical effect: Selectively and irreversibly inhibits uptake of glucose and other nutrients in susceptible helminths.
Therapeutic effect: Kills helminth infestation.

Available forms

Oral suspension: 100 mg/5 ml ◇
Tablets (chewable): 100 mg

NURSING PROCESS

Assessment

- Assess patient's condition before therapy and regularly thereafter.
- Be alert for adverse reactions and drug interactions.
- Evaluate patient's and family's knowledge of drug therapy.

Nursing diagnoses

- Infection related to presence of helminths
- Diarrhea related to drug-induced adverse GI reactions
- Deficient knowledge related to drug therapy

Planning and implementation

- Tablets may be chewed, swallowed whole, or crushed and mixed with food.
- Give drug to all family members to decrease risk of spreading infection.
- No dietary restrictions, laxatives, or enemas are needed.

Patient teaching

- Teach patient about personal hygiene, especially good hand-washing technique. To avoid reinfection, teach patient to wash perianal area daily, to change undergarments and bedclothes daily, and to wash hands and clean fingernails before meals and after bowel movements.
- Advise patient not to prepare food for others.

Evaluation

- Patient is free from infestation.
- Patient's bowel pattern returns to normal after therapy is stopped.
- Patient and family state understanding of drug therapy.

mechlorethamine hydrochloride (nitrogen mustard)

(meh-klor-ETH-uh-meen high-droh-KLOR-ighd)
Mustargen

Pharmacologic class: alkylating agent (cell cycle–phase nonspecific)
Therapeutic class: antineoplastic
Pregnancy risk category: D

Indications and dosages

▶ **Polycythemia vera, chronic lymphocytic leukemia, chronic myelocytic leukemia, malignant effusions (pericardial, peritoneal, pleural), mycosis fungoides, Hodgkin's disease, lymphosarcoma, bronchogenic cancer.** *Adults:* 0.4 mg/kg or 10 mg/m^2 I.V. as single dose or in divided doses of 0.1 to 0.2 mg/kg I.V. daily for 2 to 4 successive days q 3 to 6 weeks. Given through running I.V. infusion. Subsequent courses given when patient has recovered hematologically from previous course (usually 3 to 6 weeks).

▶ **Malignant effusions.** *Adults:* 0.2 to 0.4 mg/kg intracavitarily.

▶ **Treatment of malignant Hodgkin's disease as part of MOPP (mechlorethamine, vincristine, procarbazine, prednisone) regimen.** *Adults:* 6 mg/m^2 given I.V. on days 1 and 8 of 28-day cycle. In subsequent cycles, dose is based on leukocyte count.

Adverse reactions

CNS: headache, weakness, drowsiness, vertigo.
CV: *thrombophlebitis.*
EENT: tinnitus, hearing loss with high doses.
GI: *metallic taste, nausea, vomiting, anorexia.*
Hematologic: ***thrombocytopenia, agranulocytosis, lymphocytopenia, myelosuppression*** that peaks in 4 to 10 days and lasts 10 to 21 days, mild anemia that begins in 2 to 3 weeks.
Skin: *alopecia,* rash, sloughing, severe irritation if drug extravasates or touches skin.
Other: precipitation of herpes zoster, ***anaphylaxis, secondary malignant disease.***

Interactions

Drug-drug. *Anticoagulants, aspirin:* Increases risk of bleeding. Avoid using together.

Effects on lab test results

- May increase urine urea level.
- May decrease hemoglobin, hematocrit, and platelet, granulocyte, lymphocyte, WBC, and RBC counts.

Pharmacokinetics

Absorption: Incomplete, probably from deactivation by body fluids in cavity.
Distribution: Doesn't cross blood-brain barrier.
Metabolism: Converted rapidly to its active form, which reacts quickly with various cellular components before being deactivated.
Excretion: Metabolites excreted in urine.

Route	Onset	Peak	Duration
I.V., intracavitary	Rapid	Unknown	Unknown

Pharmacodynamics

Chemical effect: Cross-links strands of cellular DNA and interferes with RNA transcription, causing imbalance of growth that leads to cell death.
Therapeutic effect: Kills certain cancer cells.

Available forms

Injection: 10-mg vials

NURSING PROCESS

Assessment

- Assess patient's condition before therapy and regularly thereafter.
- Monitor CBC and platelet counts regularly.
- Monitor uric acid level.
- Be alert for adverse reactions and drug interactions.
- Neurotoxicity increases with dose and patient age.
- Evaluate patient's and family's knowledge of drug therapy.

Nursing diagnoses

- Ineffective health maintenance related to presence of neoplastic disease
- Ineffective immune protection related to adverse hematologic reactions
- Deficient knowledge related to drug therapy

Planning and implementation

- Follow facility policy to reduce risks. Preparation and administration of parenteral form are linked to carcinogenic, mutagenic, and teratogenic risks for personnel.

- **I.V. use:** Reconstitute drug using 10 ml of sterile water for injection or normal saline solution injection. Resulting solution contains 1 mg/ml of mechlorethamine.
– Give by direct injection into vein or into I.V. line containing free-flowing solution.

ALERT: Make sure I.V. solution doesn't extravasate because mechlorethamine is a potent vesicant. If it does, apply cold compresses and infiltrate area with isotonic sodium thiosulfate.

- **Intracavitary use:** When giving for sclerosing effect, dilute with up to 100 ml of normal saline solution for injection. Turn patient from side to side every 15 minutes to 1 hour to distribute drug.
- Prepare immediately before infusion. Solution is very unstable. Use within 15 minutes, and discard unused solution.
- Don't use solutions that are discolored or contain particulates. Don't use vials that appear to contain droplets of water.
- Dispose of equipment used in drug preparation and administration properly and according to facility policy. Neutralize unused solution with equal volume of 5% sodium bicarbonate and 5% sodium thiosulfate.
- To prevent hyperuricemia with resulting uric acid nephropathy, make sure patient is adequately hydrated.

Patient teaching

- Warn patient to watch for signs of infection (fever, sore throat, fatigue) and bleeding (easy bruising, nosebleeds, bleeding gums, melena). Have patient take temperature daily.
- Instruct patient to avoid OTC products that contain aspirin.
- Advise woman of childbearing age to avoid becoming pregnant during therapy and to consult with prescriber before becoming pregnant.

☑ Evaluation

- Patient responds positively to drug.
- Patient regains normal hematologic parameters.
- Patient and family state understanding of drug therapy.

meclizine hydrochloride (meclozine hydrochloride)

(MEK-lih-zeen high-droh-KLOR-ighd)

Ancolan ◇, Antivert†, Antivert/25, Antivert/50, Antrizine, Bonamine ♦, Bonine†, Dramamine Less Drowsy Formula†, Meni-D, Vergon†

Pharmacologic class: piperazine-derivative antihistamine
Therapeutic class: antiemetic, antivertigo agent
Pregnancy risk category: B

Indications and dosages

▶ **Vertigo, dizziness.** *Adults:* 25 to 100 mg P.O. daily in divided doses. Dosage varies with patient response.

▶ **Motion sickness.** *Adults:* 25 to 50 mg P.O. 1 hour before travel, repeated daily for duration of journey.

Contraindications and precautions

- Contraindicated in patients hypersensitive to drug.
- Use cautiously in patients with asthma, glaucoma, or prostatic hyperplasia.

Lifespan: In pregnant women, safety of drug hasn't been established. In breast-feeding women, use cautiously. In children, safety of drug hasn't been established.

Adverse reactions

CNS: *drowsiness,* fatigue.
EENT: blurred vision.
GI: dry mouth.

Interactions

Drug-drug. *CNS depressants:* May increase drowsiness. Use together cautiously.

Effects on lab test results

None reported.

Pharmacokinetics

Absorption: Unknown.
Distribution: Well distributed throughout body.
Metabolism: Unknown. Thought to be metabolized in liver.

Excretion: Excreted unchanged in feces; metabolites found in urine. *Half-life:* About 6 hours.

Route	Onset	Peak	Duration
P.O.	About 1 hr	Unknown	8-24 hr

Pharmacodynamics

Chemical effect: Unknown; may affect neural pathways originating in labyrinth to inhibit nausea and vomiting.
Therapeutic effect: Relieves vertigo and nausea.

Available forms

Capsules: 25 mg, 30 mg†
Tablets: 12.5 mg, 25 mg†, 50 mg
Tablets (chewable): 25 mg†

NURSING PROCESS

Assessment

- Assess patient's condition before therapy and regularly thereafter.
- Be alert for adverse reactions and drug interactions.
- Evaluate patient's and family's knowledge of drug therapy.

Nursing diagnoses

- Risk for injury related to vertigo
- Risk for deficient fluid volume related to motion sickness
- Deficient knowledge related to drug therapy

Planning and implementation

- Don't discontinue abruptly after long-term therapy because paradoxical reactions or sudden reversal of improved state may occur.

ALERT: Don't confuse Antivert with Axert.

Patient teaching

- Advise patient to refrain from driving and performing other hazardous activities that require alertness until CNS effects of drug are known.
- If drug is to be used long-term, stress importance of not stopping abruptly.
- Advise patient not to use alcohol while taking this drug and to consult a prescriber before taking drug if already taking sedatives or tranquilizers.

Evaluation

- Patient states that vertigo is relieved.
- Patient states that motion sickness doesn't occur.
- Patient and family state understanding of drug therapy.

medroxyprogesterone acetate

(med-roks-ee-proh-JES-ter-ohn AS-ih-tayt)
Amen, Cycrin, Depo-Provera, Provera

Pharmacologic class: progestin
Therapeutic class: progestin antineoplastic
Pregnancy risk category: X

Indications and dosages

▶ **Abnormal uterine bleeding caused by hormonal imbalance.** *Women:* 5 to 10 mg P.O. daily for 5 to 10 days beginning on day 16 of menstrual cycle. If patient also has received estrogen, 10 mg P.O. daily for 10 days beginning on day 16 of cycle.
▶ **Secondary amenorrhea.** *Women:* 5 to 10 mg P.O. daily for 5 to 10 days.
▶ **Endometrial or renal carcinoma.** *Women:* 400 to 1,000 mg I.M. weekly.
▶ **Contraception.** *Women:* 150 mg I.M. once q 3 months.
▶ **Paraphilia.** *Men:* Initially, 200 mg I.M. b.i.d. or t.i.d. or 500 mg I.M. weekly. Adjust dosage based on response.

Contraindications and precautions

- Contraindicated in patients hypersensitive to drug, in pregnant women, and in those with active thromboembolic disorders, breast cancer, undiagnosed abnormal vaginal bleeding, missed abortion, hepatic dysfunction, or a history of thromboembolic disorders, cerebrovascular disease, or apoplexy. Tablets are also contraindicated in patients with liver dysfunction or known or suspected cancer of genital organs.
- Use cautiously in patients with diabetes mellitus, seizure disorder, migraine, cardiac or renal disease, asthma, or depression.

Lifespan: In breast-feeding women, use isn't recommended.

Adverse reactions

CNS: dizziness, migraine, lethargy, depression, nervousness, asthenia.

CV: hypertension, thrombophlebitis, ***pulmonary embolism,*** edema, ***thromboembolism, CVA.***
EENT: intolerance to contact lenses.
GI: nausea, vomiting, abdominal cramps.
GU: breakthrough bleeding, dysmenorrhea, amenorrhea, cervical erosion, abnormal secretions, uterine fibromas, vaginal candidiasis.
Hepatic: cholestatic jaundice, ***tumors,*** gallbladder disease.
Metabolic: hyperglycemia, weight gain.
Skin: melasma, rash, pain, induration, sterile abscesses, acne, alopecia.
Other: breast tenderness, enlargement, or secretion; decreased libido, hypersensitivity reactions.

Interactions

Drug-drug. *Aminoglutethimide, rifampin:* May decrease progestin effects. Monitor patient for diminished therapeutic response. Tell patient to use nonhormonal contraceptive during therapy with these drugs.
Bromocriptine: May cause amenorrhea, interfering with bromocriptine's effects. Avoid using together.
Drug-food. *Caffeine:* May increase caffeine levels. Monitor patient for effect.
Drug-lifestyle. *Smoking:* Increases risk of adverse CV effects. If smoking continues, may need alternative therapy. Discourage patient from smoking.

Effects on lab test results

- May increase thyroxin-binding globulin and T_4 levels.
- May increase liver function test values.

Pharmacokinetics

Absorption: Slow after I.M. use; unknown for P.O. use.
Distribution: Unknown.
Metabolism: Primarily in liver.
Excretion: Primarily in urine.

Route	Onset	Peak	Duration
P.O.	Unknown	Unknown	Unknown
I.M.	Unknown	Unknown	Unknown

Pharmacodynamics

Chemical effect: Suppresses ovulation, possibly by inhibiting pituitary gonadotropin secretion, and forms thick cervical mucus.
Therapeutic effect: Stops abnormal uterine bleeding, reverses secondary amenorrhea, prevents pregnancy, and hinders cancer cell growth.

Available forms

Injection (suspension): 150 mg/ml, 400 mg/ml
Tablets: 2.5 mg, 5 mg, 10 mg

NURSING PROCESS

Assessment

- Assess patient's condition before therapy and regularly thereafter.
- Be alert for adverse reactions and drug interactions.
- Monitor injection sites for evidence of sterile abscess.
- Evaluate patient's and family's knowledge of drug therapy.

Nursing diagnoses

- Ineffective health maintenance related to underlying condition
- Excessive fluid volume related to drug-induced edema
- Deficient knowledge related to drug therapy

Planning and implementation

- **P.O. use:** Follow normal protocol.
- **I.M. use:** Rotate injection sites to prevent muscle atrophy.

Patient teaching

- Have patient read package insert explaining possible adverse effects of progestins before first dose; then provide verbal explanation.
- Instruct patient to avoid caffeine and smoking during drug therapy.

ALERT: Tell patient to report unusual symptoms immediately and to stop drug and notify prescriber if visual disturbance or migraine occurs.

- Teach woman how to perform routine monthly breast self-examination.
- Warn patient that I.M. injection may be painful.

Evaluation

- Patient responds well to drug therapy.
- Patient doesn't develop fluid excess throughout drug therapy.
- Patient and family state understanding of drug therapy.

mefloquine hydrochloride

(MEF-loh-kwin high-droh-KLOR-ighd)

Lariam

Pharmacologic class: quinine derivative
Therapeutic class: antimalarial
Pregnancy risk category: C

Indications and dosages

▶ **Acute malaria infections caused by mefloquine-sensitive strains of *Plasmodium falciparum* and *P. vivax*.** *Adults:* 1,250 mg P.O. as single dose. Patients with *P. vivax* infections should receive primaquine or other 8-aminoquinolones to avoid relapse after treatment of initial infection.

▶ **Malaria prophylaxis.** *Adults:* 250 mg P.O. once weekly. Prophylaxis should start 1 week before entering endemic area and continue for 4 weeks after return.

Contraindications and precautions

- Contraindicated in patients hypersensitive to mefloquine or related compounds and in patients with active depression, generalized anxiety disorder, psychosis, schizophrenia, or other major psychiatric disorder, or a history of seizures.
- Use cautiously in patients with cardiac disease or seizure disorders.

Lifespan: In pregnant or breast-feeding women, use cautiously. In children, safety of drug hasn't been established.

Adverse reactions

CNS: dizziness, fever, fatigue, syncope, headache, ***seizures,*** tremor, ataxia, mood changes, panic attacks, ***suicide.***
CV: extrasystoles, chest pain, edema.
EENT: tinnitus.
GI: loss of appetite, vomiting, *nausea,* loose stools, diarrhea, GI discomfort, dyspepsia.
Skin: rash.
Other: chills.

Interactions

Drug-drug. *Beta blockers, quinidine, quinine:* ECG abnormalities and cardiac arrest may occur. Avoid using together.
Chloroquine, quinine: May increase risk of seizures. Monitor patient.
Halofantrine: May increase risk of fatal prolongation of QTc interval. Don't use together.
Valproic acid: Decreases valproic acid level and may cause loss of seizure control at start of mefloquine therapy. Check anticonvulsant level.

Effects on lab test results

- May increase transaminase levels.
- May decrease hematocrit, hemoglobin, and WBC and platelet counts.

Pharmacokinetics

Absorption: Well absorbed.
Distribution: Concentrated in RBCs; about 98% protein-bound.
Metabolism: Metabolized by liver.
Excretion: Excreted primarily by liver; small amounts found in urine. *Half-life:* About 21 days.

Route	Onset	Peak	Duration
P.O.	Unknown	7-24 hr	Unknown

Pharmacodynamics

Chemical effect: Unknown; may be related to its ability to form complexes with hemin.
Therapeutic effect: Kills malaria-causing organisms. Spectrum of activity includes all human types of malaria, including chloroquine-resistant malaria and strains of *P. falciparum* and *P. vivax.*

Available forms

Tablets: 250 mg

NURSING PROCESS

Assessment

- Assess patient's condition before therapy and regularly thereafter.
- Monitor liver function tests periodically.
- Be alert for adverse reactions and drug interactions.
- Monitor patient's hydration status if adverse GI reactions occur.
- Evaluate patient's and family's knowledge of drug therapy.

Nursing diagnoses

- Infection related to presence of malaria organisms

• Risk of deficient fluid volume related to drug-induced adverse reactions
• Deficient knowledge related to drug therapy

Planning and implementation

ALERT: If psychiatric symptoms such as anxiety, depression, restlessness, or confusion occur, discontinue drug.
• Because health risks from simultaneous administration of quinine and mefloquine are great, drug therapy shouldn't begin less than 12 hours after last dose of quinine or quinidine.
• Patients with infections caused by *P. vivax* are at high risk for relapse because drug doesn't eliminate hepatic phase (exoerythrocytic parasites). Follow-up therapy with primaquine is advisable.
• Give drug with food and full glass of water to minimize adverse GI reactions.

Patient teaching
• Advise patient to take drug on same day of week when using it for prophylaxis.
• Advise patient to use caution when performing hazardous activities that require alertness and coordination because dizziness, disturbed sense of balance, and neuropsychiatric reactions may occur.
• Instruct patient taking mefloquine prophylaxis to discontinue drug and notify prescriber if he notices signs or symptoms of impending toxicity, such as unexplained anxiety, depression, confusion, or restlessness.
• For patient undergoing long-term therapy, recommend that he have periodic ophthalmologic examinations.

Evaluation
• Patient is free from infection.
• Patient maintains adequate hydration throughout therapy.
• Patient and family state understanding of drug therapy.

megestrol acetate
(meh-JES-trol AS-ih-tayt)
Megace, Megostat ◇

Pharmacologic class: progestin
Therapeutic class: antineoplastic
Pregnancy risk category: D

Indications and dosages
▶ **Breast cancer.** *Adults:* 40 mg P.O. q.i.d.
▶ **Endometrial cancer.** *Adults:* 40 to 320 mg P.O. daily in divided doses.
▶ **Treatment of anorexia, cachexia, or unexplained significant weight loss in patients with AIDS.** *Adults:* 800 mg P.O. (oral suspension) daily in divided doses; 100 to 400 mg for AIDS-related cachexia.
▶ **Anorexia or cachexia in patients with neoplastic disease.** *Adults:* 480 to 600 mg P.O. daily.

Contraindications and precautions
• Contraindicated in patients hypersensitive to drug.
• Use cautiously in patients with history of thrombophlebitis.
Lifespan: In pregnant women, use is contraindicated. In breast-feeding women, drug isn't recommended. In children, safety of drug hasn't been established.

Adverse reactions
CV: hypertension, thrombophlebitis, ***heart failure.***
GI: nausea, vomiting.
GU: breakthrough menstrual bleeding.
Metabolic: weight gain, increased appetite.
Musculoskeletal: carpal tunnel syndrome.
Respiratory: ***pulmonary embolism.***
Skin: alopecia, hirsutism.
Other: breast tenderness.

Interactions
None significant.

Effects on lab test results
• May increase glucose level.

Pharmacokinetics
Absorption: Well absorbed across GI tract.
Distribution: Appears to be stored in fatty tissue; highly bound to plasma proteins.
Metabolism: Completely metabolized in liver.
Excretion: Excreted in urine.

Route	Onset	Peak	Duration
P.O.	Unknown	Unknown	Unknown

Pharmacodynamics
Chemical effect: Changes tumor's hormonal environment and alters neoplastic process.

Mechanism of appetite stimulation is unknown.
Therapeutic effect: Hinders cancer cell growth and increases appetite.

Available forms

Oral suspension: 40 mg/ml
Tablets: 20 mg, 40 mg

NURSING PROCESS

Assessment

- Assess patient's condition before therapy and regularly thereafter.
- Be alert for adverse reactions.
- Monitor patient's hydration status if adverse GI reactions occur.
- Evaluate patient's and family's knowledge of drug therapy.

Nursing diagnoses

- Ineffective health maintenance related to underlying condition
- Risk for deficient fluid volume related to drug-induced adverse GI reactions
- Deficient knowledge related to drug therapy

Planning and implementation

- Two months is adequate trial when treating cancer.

Patient teaching

- Inform patient that therapeutic response isn't immediate.
- Advise breast-feeding woman to stop during therapy because of possible infant toxicity.

Evaluation

- Patient responds well to therapy.
- Patient maintains adequate hydration throughout therapy.
- Patient and family state understanding of drug therapy.

meloxicam

(mell-OX-ih-kam)
Mobic

Pharmacologic class: enolic acid NSAID
Therapeutic class: anti-inflammatory, analgesic
Pregnancy risk category: C

Indications and dosages

▶ **Relief of signs and symptoms of osteoarthritis.** *Adults:* 7.5 mg P.O. once daily. May increase to maximum of 15 mg daily, p.r.n.

Contraindications and precautions

- Contraindicated in patients hypersensitive to meloxicam and in those who have experienced asthma, urticaria, or allergic-type reactions after taking aspirin or other NSAIDs.
- Use with extreme caution in patients with a history of ulcers or GI bleeding. Use cautiously in patients with dehydration, anemia, hepatic disease, renal disease, hypertension, fluid retention, heart failure, and asthma.

Lifespan: During late pregnancy, avoid using. In elderly and debilitated patients, use cautiously because of increased risk of fatal GI bleeding.

Adverse reactions

CNS: dizziness, headache, insomnia, fatigue, ***seizures,*** paresthesia, fever, tremor, vertigo, anxiety, confusion, depression, nervousness, somnolence, malaise, syncope.
CV: ***arrhythmias,*** palpitations, tachycardia, angina, ***heart failure,*** hypertension, hypotension, ***MI,*** edema.
EENT: pharyngitis, abnormal vision, conjunctivitis, tinnitus.
GI: abdominal pain, diarrhea, dyspepsia, flatulence, nausea, constipation, colitis, dry mouth, duodenal ulcer, esophagitis, gastric ulcer, gastritis, GI reflux, ***hemorrhage, pancreatitis,*** vomiting, increased appetite, taste perversion.
GU: albuminuria, hematuria, urinary frequency, ***renal failure,*** urinary tract infection.
Hematologic: anemia, ***leukopenia,*** purpura, ***thrombocytopenia.***
Hepatic: bilirubinemia, ***hepatitis.***
Metabolic: dehydration, weight changes.
Musculoskeletal: arthralgia, back pain.
Respiratory: upper respiratory tract infection, asthma, ***bronchospasm,*** dyspnea, cough.
Skin: rash, pruritus, alopecia, bullous eruption, photosensitivity reactions, sweating, urticaria.
Other: accidental injury, allergic reaction, ***angioedema,*** flulike symptoms.

Interactions

Drug-drug. *ACE inhibitors:* Diminishes antihypertensive effects. Monitor patient's blood pressure.

Aspirin: Increases risk of adverse effects. Avoid using together.
Furosemide, thiazide diuretics: NSAIDs may reduce sodium excretion linked to diuretics, leading to sodium retention. Monitor patient for edema and increased blood pressure.
Lithium: Increases lithium levels. Monitor plasma lithium levels closely for toxicity during treatment.
Warfarin: Increases PT or INR and risk of bleeding complications. Monitor PT and INR, and check for signs and symptoms of bleeding.
Drug-herb. *Dong quai, feverfew, garlic, ginger, horse chestnut, red clover:* Possible increased risk of bleeding. Monitor patient closely.
St. John's wort: Increases risk of photosensitivity reactions. Advise patient to avoid unprotected or prolonged exposure to sunlight.
Drug-lifestyle. *Smoking:* Increases risk of GI irritation and bleeding. Monitor patient for bleeding; discourage patient from smoking.
Alcohol: Increases risk of GI irritation and bleeding. Monitor patient for bleeding; discourage using together.

Effects on lab test results

- May increase BUN, creatinine, ALT, AST, and bilirubin levels.
- May decrease hemoglobin, hematocrit, and WBC and platelet counts.

Pharmacokinetics

Absorption: Bioavailability is 89% and doesn't appear to be affected by food or antacids. Steady-state conditions are reached after 5 days of daily administration.
Distribution: 99.4% bound to human plasma proteins.
Metabolism: Almost completely metabolized to pharmacologically inactive metabolites.
Excretion: Excreted in both urine and feces, primarily as metabolites. *Half-life:* 15 to 20 hours.

Route	Onset	Peak	Duration
P.O.	Unknown	Unknown	Unknown

Pharmacodynamics

Chemical effect: Mechanism of action may be related to prostaglandin (cyclooxygenase) synthetase inhibition.
Therapeutic effect: Relief of signs and symptoms of osteoarthritis.

Available forms

Tablets: 7.5 mg

NURSING PROCESS

Assessment

- Obtain accurate history of drug allergies; drug can produce allergic-like reactions in patients hypersensitive to aspirin and other NSAIDs.
- Assess patient for increased risk of GI bleeding. Risk factors include history of ulcers or GI bleeding, treatment with corticosteroids or anticoagulants, longer duration of NSAID treatment, smoking, alcoholism, older age, and poor overall health.
- Monitor patient for signs and symptoms of overt and occult bleeding.
- Monitor patient for fluid retention; closely monitor patients who have hypertension, edema, or heart failure.
- Monitor liver function.
- Evaluate patient's and family's knowledge of drug therapy.

Nursing diagnoses

- Chronic pain related to underlying condition
- Risk for injury related to drug-induced adverse reactions
- Deficient knowledge related to drug therapy

Planning and implementation

- Drug may be taken with food to prevent GI upset.
- Rehydrate patients who are dehydrated before starting treatment.
- If patient develops evidence of liver disease (eosinophilia, rash), drug should be discontinued.

Patient teaching

- Tell patient to notify prescriber about history of allergic reactions to aspirin or other NSAIDs before starting therapy.
- Teach patient to report signs and symptoms of GI ulcerations and bleeding, such as vomiting blood, blood in stool, and black, tarry stools.
- Instruct patient to report skin rash, weight gain, or edema.
- Advise patient to report warning signs of hepatotoxicity (nausea, fatigue, lethargy, pruritus, jaundice, right upper quadrant tenderness, and flulike symptoms).

• Warn patient with a history of asthma that it may recur during therapy and that he should stop taking the drug and notify prescriber if it does.
• Tell woman to notify prescriber if she becomes pregnant or is planning to become pregnant during therapy.
• Inform patient that it may take several days before consistent pain relief is achieved.

✓ Evaluation

• Patient is free from pain.
• Patient sustains no injury as a result of drug-induced adverse reactions.
• Patient and family state understanding of drug therapy.

melphalan (L-phenylalanine mustard)

(MEL-feh-len)
Alkeran

Pharmacologic class: alkylating agent (cell cycle–phase nonspecific)
Therapeutic class: antineoplastic
Pregnancy risk category: D

Indications and dosages

▶ **Multiple myeloma.** *Adults:* 6 mg P.O. daily for 2 to 3 weeks; then stop drug for up to 4 weeks or until WBC and platelet counts begin to rise again; then give maintenance dosage of 2 mg daily.
Alternative therapy: 0.15 mg/kg P.O. daily for 7 days at 2- to 6-week intervals. Or, 0.25 mg/kg P.O. daily for 4 days, repeat q 4 to 6 weeks. Or, give I.V. to patients who can't tolerate oral therapy: 16 mg/m^2 given by infusion over 15 to 20 minutes q 2 weeks for four doses. After patient has recovered from toxicity, drug given q 4 weeks.
Patients with renal impairment: Reduce I.V. dosage by 50% to reduce risk of severe leukopenia and drug-related death.
▶ **Nonresectable advanced ovarian cancer.** *Adults:* 0.2 mg/kg P.O. daily for 5 days. Repeat q 4 to 6 weeks, depending on bone marrow recovery.

Contraindications and precautions

• Contraindicated in patients hypersensitive to drug and in those whose disease is resistant to drug. Patients hypersensitive to chlorambucil may have cross-sensitivity to melphalan.
• Drug isn't recommended for patients with severe leukopenia, thrombocytopenia, anemia, or chronic lymphocytic leukemia.
Lifespan: For pregnant or breast-feeding women, drug isn't recommended. In children, safety of drug hasn't been established.

Adverse reactions

Hematologic: ***thrombocytopenia, leukopenia, bone marrow suppression.***
Hepatic: ***hepatotoxicity.***
Respiratory: pneumonitis, ***pulmonary fibrosis.***
Skin: dermatitis, pruritus, rash, alopecia.
Other: ***anaphylaxis,*** hypersensitivity reactions.

Interactions

Drug-drug. *Anticoagulants, aspirin:* Increases risk of bleeding. Avoid using together.
Antigout agents: Decreases effectiveness. Dosage adjustments may be needed.
Bone marrow suppressants: May have additive toxicity. Monitor patient closely.
Carmustine: Carmustine lung toxicity threshold may be reduced. Monitor patient closely.
Cisplatin: Cisplatin may affect melphalan kinetics by inducing renal dysfunction and subsequently altering melphalan clearance. Monitor patient closely.
Cyclosporine: Increases toxicity of cyclosporine, particularly nephrotoxicity. Use cautiously together.
Interferon alpha: May decrease melphalan level. Monitor level closely.
Nalidixic acid: May increase risk of severe hemorrhagic necrotic enterocolitis in children. Monitor patient closely.
Vaccines: Decreases effectiveness of killed-virus vaccines and increases risk of toxicity from live-virus vaccines. Postpone routine immunization for at least 3 months after last dose of melphalan.
Drug-food. *Any food:* Decreases absorption of oral drug. Separate administration times; give drug on an empty stomach.

Effects on lab test results

• May increase urine urea level.

• May decrease hemoglobin, hematocrit, and RBC, WBC, and platelet counts.

Pharmacokinetics

Absorption: Incomplete and variable.
Distribution: Distributed rapidly and widely in total body water; initially 50% to 60% bound to plasma proteins and increases to 80% to 90% over time.
Metabolism: Extensively deactivated by hydrolysis.
Excretion: Excreted primarily in urine. *Half-life:* 2 hours.

Route	Onset	Peak	Duration
P.O., I.V.	Unknown	Unknown	Unknown

Pharmacodynamics

Chemical effect: Cross-links strands of cellular DNA and interferes with RNA transcription.
Therapeutic effect: Kills certain cancer cells.

Available forms

Injection: 50 mg
Tablets (scored): 2 mg

NURSING PROCESS

Assessment

• Assess patient's condition before therapy and regularly thereafter.
• Monitor uric acid level and CBC.
• Be alert for adverse reactions and drug interactions.
• Evaluate patient's and family's knowledge of drug therapy.

Nursing diagnoses

• Ineffective health maintenance related to presence of neoplastic disease
• Ineffective immune protection related to adverse hematologic reactions
• Deficient knowledge related to drug therapy

Planning and implementation

• Follow facility policy to reduce risks. Preparation and administration of parenteral form are linked to carcinogenic, mutagenic, and teratogenic risks for personnel.
• Dosage may need to be reduced in patient with renal impairment.
• Melphalan is drug of choice in combination with prednisone in patients with multiple myeloma.
• **P.O. use:** Give drug on empty stomach.
• **I.V. use:** Because drug isn't stable in solution, reconstitute immediately before giving with 10 ml of sterile diluent supplied by manufacturer. Shake vigorously until solution is clear. Resulting solution contains 5 mg of melphalan per ml.
– Immediately dilute required dose in normal saline solution for injection. Final concentration shouldn't exceed 0.45 mg/ml.
– Give by I.V. infusion over 15 to 20 minutes.
– Give promptly after diluting; reconstituted product begins to degrade within 30 minutes. After final dilution, nearly 1% of drug degrades every 10 minutes.
– Don't refrigerate reconstituted product because precipitate will form.
ALERT: Don't confuse melphalan with Mephyton.

Patient teaching

• Tell patient to take oral drug on empty stomach.
• Warn patient to watch for signs of infection (fever, sore throat, fatigue) and bleeding (easy bruising, nosebleeds, bleeding gums, melena). Have patient take temperature daily.
• Instruct patient to avoid OTC products that contain aspirin.
• Advise woman of childbearing age to avoid becoming pregnant during therapy and to consult with prescriber before becoming pregnant.

Evaluation

• Patient responds well to therapy.
• Patient regains normal hematologic function when therapy is completed.
• Patient and family state understanding of drug therapy.

menotropins

(meh-noh-TROH-pins)
Humegon, Pergonal, Repronex

Pharmacologic class: gonadotropin
Therapeutic class: ovulation stimulant, spermatogenesis stimulant
Pregnancy risk category: X

Indications and dosages

▶ **Anovulation.** *Women:* 75 IU each of follicle-stimulating hormone (FSH) and luteinizing hormone (LH) I.M. daily for 7 to 12 days; follow by 5,000 to 10,000 USP units of human chorionic gonadotropin (HCG) I.M. 1 day after last dose of menotropins. Repeat for 1 to 3 to three menstrual cycles until ovulation occurs.

▶ **Infertility with ovulation.** *Women:* 75 IU each of FSH and LH I.M. daily for 7 to 12 days; follow by 5,000 to 10,000 USP units of HCG I.M. 1 day after last dose of menotropins. Repeat for 2 menstrual cycles and then increase to 150 IU each of FSH and LH daily for 7 to 12 days; follow by 5,000 to 10,000 USP units of HCG I.M. 1 day after last dose of menotropins. Repeat for 2 menstrual cycles.

▶ **Infertility.** *Men:* Treat with HCG of 5,000 USP units 3 times a week for 4 to 6 months; then 75 IU each of FSH and LH I.M. 3 times weekly (given with 2,000 USP units of HCG twice weekly) for at least 4 months. If spermatogenesis doesn't increase, dosage increased to 150 IU each of FSH and LH 3 times weekly (dosage of HCG remains unchanged).

Contraindications and precautions

- Contraindicated in patients hypersensitive to drug; in women with primary ovarian failure, uncontrolled thyroid or adrenal dysfunction, pituitary tumor, abnormal uterine bleeding, uterine fibromas, or ovarian cysts or enlargement; and in men with normal pituitary function, primary testicular failure, or infertility disorders other than hypogonadotropic hypogonadism.

Lifespan: In pregnant women, drug is contraindicated. In breast-feeding women or children, drug shouldn't be used.

Adverse reactions

CV: *CVA,* fever, tachycardia.
GI: nausea, vomiting, diarrhea.
GU: *ovarian enlargement with pain and abdominal distention,* multiple births, ovarian hyperstimulation syndrome (sudden ovarian enlargement, ascites, or pleural effusion).
Hematologic: hemoconcentration with fluid loss into abdomen.
Respiratory: atelectasis, ***acute respiratory distress syndrome, pulmonary embolism, pulmonary infarction, arterial occlusion.***
Other: *gynecomastia,* hypersensitivity reactions, ***anaphylaxis.***

Interactions

None significant.

Effects on lab test results

None reported.

Pharmacokinetics

Absorption: Unknown.
Distribution: Unknown.
Metabolism: Unknown.
Excretion: Excreted in urine.

Route	Onset	Peak	Duration
I.M.	9-12 days	Unknown	Unknown

Pharmacodynamics

Chemical effect: When given to women who haven't had primary ovarian failure, mimics FSH in inducing follicular growth and LH in aiding follicular maturation.
Therapeutic effect: Stimulates ovulation and fertility.

Available forms

Injection: 75 IU of LH and 75 IU of FSH activity/ampule; 150 IU of LH and 150 IU of FSH activity/ampule

NURSING PROCESS

Assessment

- Assess patient's condition before therapy and regularly thereafter.
- Be alert for adverse reactions.
- Evaluate patient's and family's knowledge of drug therapy.

Nursing diagnoses

- Sexual dysfunction related to underlying disorder
- Risk for deficient fluid volume related to drug-induced adverse reactions
- Deficient knowledge related to drug therapy

Planning and implementation

- Monitor patient closely to ensure adequate ovarian stimulation.
- Reconstitute with 1 to 2 ml of sterile normal saline solution. Use immediately.
- Rotate injection sites.

Patient teaching
- Discuss risk of multiple births.
- In infertility, encourage daily intercourse from day before HCG is given until ovulation occurs.
- Tell patient that pregnancy usually occurs 4 to 6 weeks after therapy.
- Instruct patient to immediately report severe abdominal pain, bloating, swelling of hands or feet, nausea, vomiting, diarrhea, substantial weight gain, or shortness of breath.

Evaluation
- Patient or partner becomes pregnant.
- Patient maintains adequate hydration throughout therapy.
- Patient and family state understanding of drug therapy.

meperidine hydrochloride (pethidine hydrochloride)

(meh-PER-uh-deen high-droh-KLOR-ighd)
Demerol

Pharmacologic class: opioid
Therapeutic class: analgesic, adjunct to anesthesia
Pregnancy risk category: C
Controlled substance schedule: II

Indications and dosages

▶ **Moderate-to-severe pain.** *Adults:* 50 to 150 P.O., I.M., or S.C. q 3 to 4 hours, p.r.n. Or, 15 to 35 mg/hour by continuous I.V. infusion. *Children:* 1.1 to 1.76 mg/kg P.O., I.M., or S.C. q 3 to 4 hours. Maximum dosage is 100 mg q 4 hours, p.r.n.

▶ **Preoperatively.** *Adults:* 50 to 100 mg I.M., I.V., or S.C. 30 to 90 minutes before surgery. *Children:* 1 to 2.2 mg/kg I.M., I.V., or S.C. up to adult dose 30 to 90 minutes before surgery.

▶ **Adjunct to anesthesia.** *Adults:* Repeat slow I.V. injections of fractional doses (i.e., 10 mg/ml). Or, continuous I.V. infusion of more dilute solution (1 mg/ml) adjusted to needs of patient.

▶ **Obstetric analgesia.** *Adults:* 50 to 100 mg I.M. or S.C. when pain becomes regular, repeat at 1- to 3-hour intervals.

Contraindications and precautions

- Contraindicated in patients hypersensitive to drug and in those who have received MAO inhibitors within 14 days.
- Use with extreme caution in debilitated patients and patients with increased intracranial pressure, head injury, asthma, other respiratory conditions, supraventricular tachycardias, seizures, acute abdominal conditions, hepatic or renal disease, hypothyroidism, Addison's disease, urethral stricture, or prostatic hyperplasia.

Lifespan: In pregnant or breast-feeding women, use cautiously. In elderly patients, use with extreme caution.

Adverse reactions

CNS: *sedation, somnolence, clouded sensorium, euphoria,* paradoxical excitement, tremors, dizziness, ***seizures.***
CV: *hypotension,* ***bradycardia,*** tachycardia, ***cardiac arrest, shock.***
GI: *nausea, vomiting, constipation,* ileus.
GU: *urine retention.*
Musculoskeletal: muscle twitching.
Respiratory: ***respiratory depression, respiratory arrest.***
Skin: pain at injection site, local tissue irritation and induration (after S.C. injection), phlebitis (after I.V. use).
Other: physical dependence.

Interactions

Drug-drug. *CNS depressants, general anesthetics, hypnotics, other narcotic analgesics, phenothiazines, sedatives, tricyclic antidepressants:* Possible respiratory depression, hypotension, profound sedation, or coma. Use together with extreme caution. Reduce meperidine dosage as directed.
MAO inhibitors: Increases CNS excitation or depression that can be severe or fatal. Don't use together.
Phenytoin: Decreases serum levels of meperidine. Monitor patient for decreased analgesia.
Drug-herb. *Parsley:* May promote or produce serotonin syndrome. Discourage using together.
Drug-lifestyle. *Alcohol use:* May have additive CNS effects. Discourage using together.

Effects on lab test results

- May increase amylase and lipase levels.

Pharmacokinetics

Absorption: Unknown.
Distribution: Distributed widely throughout body.
Metabolism: Metabolized primarily by hydrolysis in liver.
Excretion: Excreted primarily in urine. Excretion enhanced by acidifying urine. *Half-life:* 2.4 to 4 hours.

Route	Onset	Peak	Duration
P.O.	15 min	60-90 min	2-4 hr
I.V.	1 min	5-7 min	2-4 hr
I.M., S.C.	10-15 min	30-50 min	2-4 hr

Pharmacodynamics

Chemical effect: binds with opioid receptors in CNS, altering both perception of and emotional response to pain through unknown mechanism.
Therapeutic effect: relieves pain.

Available forms

Injection: 25 mg/ml, 50 mg/ml, 75 mg/ml, 100 mg/ml
Injection (for infusion only): 10 mg/ml
Syrup: 50 mg/5 ml
Tablets: 50 mg, 100 mg

NURSING PROCESS

Assessment

- Assess patient's pain before therapy and regularly thereafter.
- Be alert for adverse reactions and drug interactions.
- Meperidine and its active metabolite normeperidine accumulate in body. Monitor patient for increased toxic effect, especially in patient with impaired renal function.
- Monitor respirations of neonate exposed to drug during labor.
- Monitor patient for withdrawal symptoms if drug is discontinued abruptly after long-term use.
- Evaluate patient's and family's knowledge of drug therapy.

Nursing diagnoses

- Acute pain related to underlying condition
- Risk for injury related to drug-induced adverse reactions
- Deficient knowledge related to drug therapy

Planning and implementation

- Drug may be used in some patients who are allergic to morphine.
- Because meperidine toxicity often appears after several days of treatment, it isn't recommended for treatment of chronic pain.
- Keep resuscitation equipment and naloxone available.
- Don't give drug if respirations are below 12 breaths/minute, if respiratory rate or depth is decreased, or if change in pupils is noted.
- **P.O. use:** P.O. dose is less than half as effective as parenteral dose. Give I.M., if possible. When changing from parenteral to P.O. route, dosage should be increased.
– Syrup has local anesthetic effect. Give with full glass of water.
- **I.V. use:** Give slowly by direct I.V. injection or slow continuous I.V. infusion. Drug is compatible with most I.V. solutions, including D_5W, normal saline solution, and Ringer's or lactated Ringer's solutions.
- **I.M. use:** Follow normal protocol.

ALERT: Drug is incompatible with aminophylline, barbiturates, heparin, morphine sulfate, phenytoin, sodium bicarbonate, or sulfonamides.

- **S.C. use:** Not recommended because it's painful.

ALERT: Don't confuse Demerol with Demulen, Dymelor, or Temaril.

Patient teaching

- Warn outpatient to avoid hazardous activities until CNS effects of drug are known.
- Instruct patient to avoid alcohol consumption during drug therapy.
- Teach patient to manage adverse reactions, such as constipation.
- Tell family members to withhold drug and notify prescriber if patient's respiratory rate decreases.

Evaluation

- Patient is free from pain.
- Patient doesn't experience injury.
- Patient and family state understanding of drug therapy.

Photoguide to tablets and capsules

This photoguide provides full-color photographs of some of the most commonly prescribed tablets and capsules. These drugs, organized by generic name, are shown in actual size and color with cross-references to drug information. Each product is labeled with its trade name and its strength.

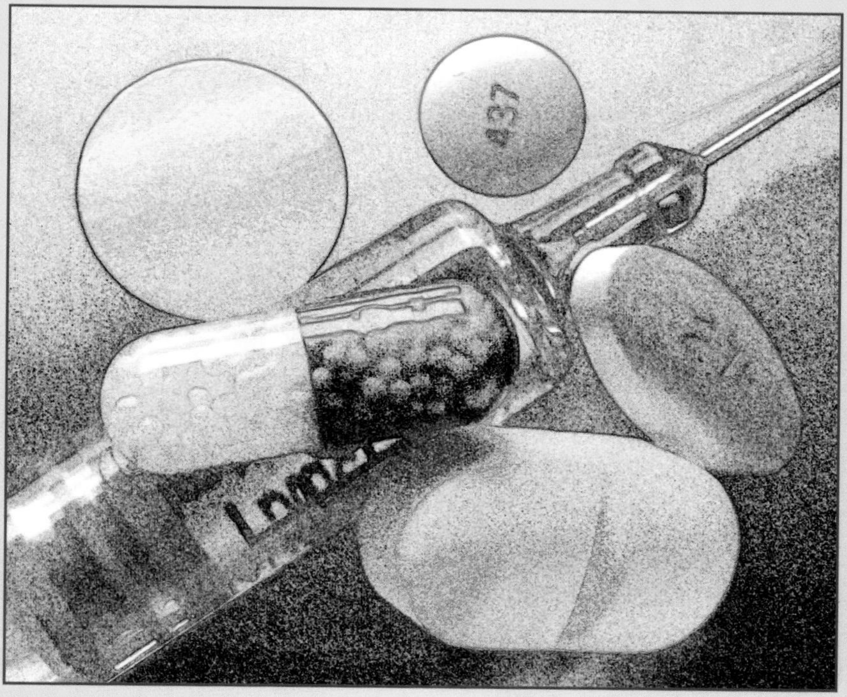

ADAPTED FROM FACTS AND COMPARISONS, ST. LOUIS, MISSOURI

ALENDRONATE SODIUM

Fosamax
(page 113)

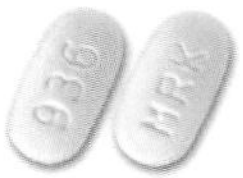

10 mg

40 mg

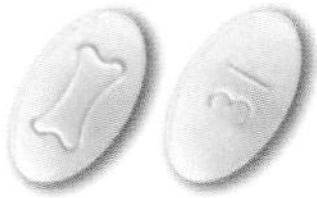

70 mg

ALPRAZOLAM

Xanax
(page 120)

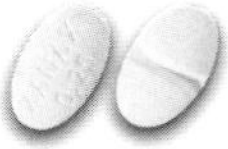
0.25 mg

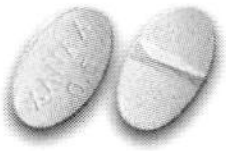
0.5 mg

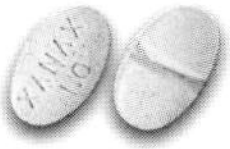
1 mg

AMLODIPINE BESYLATE

Norvasc
(page 146)

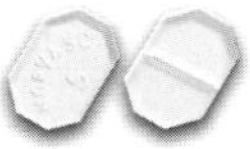
5 mg

10 mg

AMOXICILLIN AND POTASSIUM CLAVULANATE

Augmentin
(page 147)

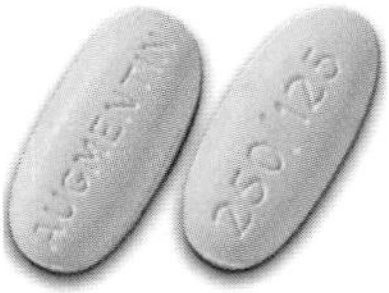

250 mg

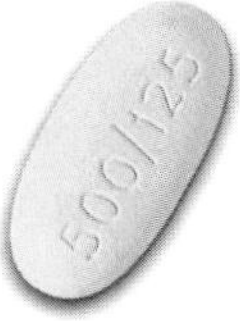

500 mg

AMOXICILLIN TRIHYDRATE

Amoxil
(page 149)

250 mg

500 mg

ATENOLOL

Tenormin
(page 182)

25 mg

50 mg

100 mg

ATORVASTATIN CALCIUM

Lipitor
(page 183)

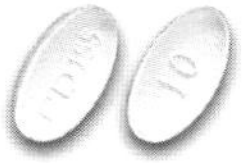

10 mg

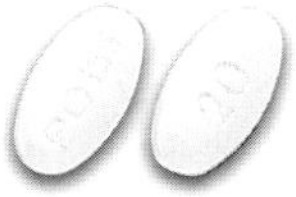

20 mg

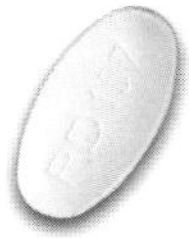

40 mg

AZITHROMYCIN

Zithromax
(page 198)

250 mg

BUPROPION HYDROCHLORIDE

Wellbutrin SR
(page 252)

150 mg

CAPTOPRIL

Capoten
(page 271)

12.5 mg

25 mg

CARVEDILOL

Coreg
(page 283)

3.125 mg

6.25 mg

12.5 mg

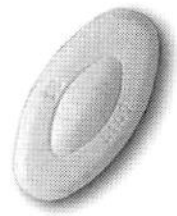

25 mg

CEFADROXIL

Duricef
(page 289)

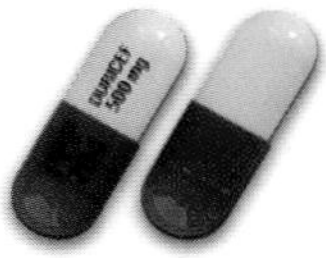

500 mg

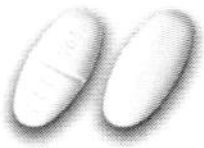

1000 mg

CEFUROXIME

Ceftin
(page 317)

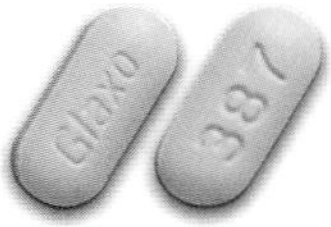

250 mg

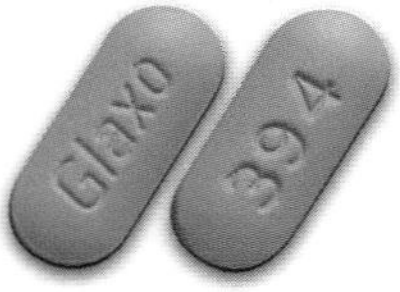

500 mg

CELECOXIB

Celebrex
(page 320)

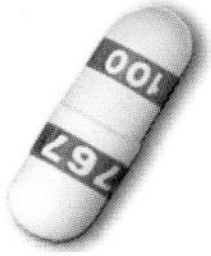

100 mg

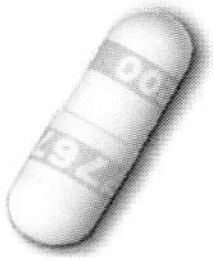

200 mg

CIPROFLOXACIN

Cipro
(page 351)

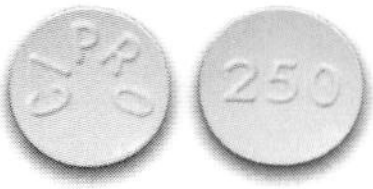

250 mg

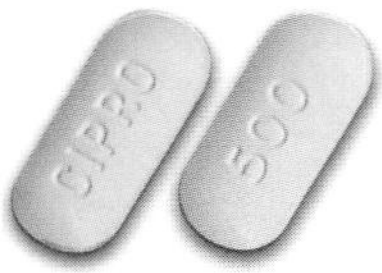

500 mg

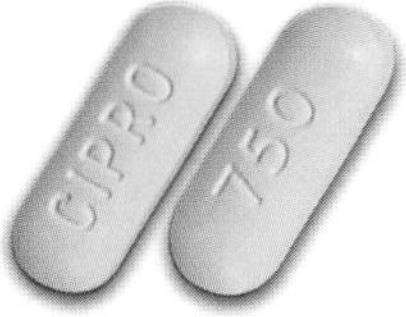

750 mg

CITALOPRAM HYDROBROMIDE

Celexa
(page 356)

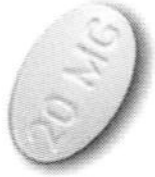

20 mg

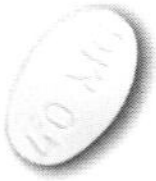

40 mg

DESLORATADINE

Clarinex
(page 424)

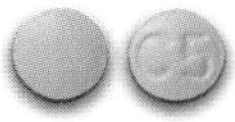

5 mg

DIAZEPAM

Valium
(page 440)

2 mg

5 mg

10 mg

DIGOXIN

Lanoxin
(page 452)

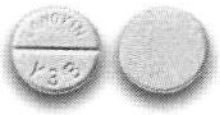

0.125 mg

0.25 mg

DILTIAZEM HYDROCHLORIDE

Cardizem
(page 456)

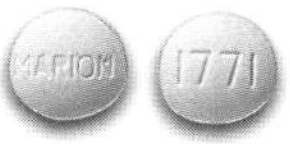

30 mg

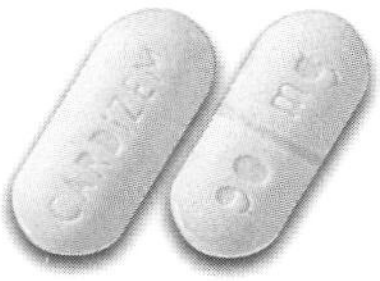

90 mg

ENALAPRIL MALEATE

Vasotec
(page 508)

2.5 mg

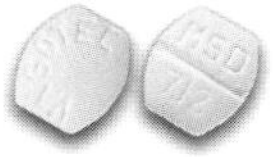

5 mg

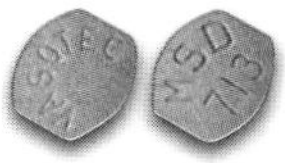

10 mg

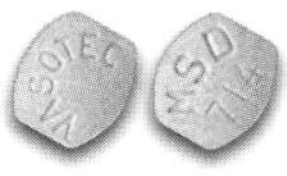

20 mg

ERYTHROMYCIN BASE

Eryc
(page 530)

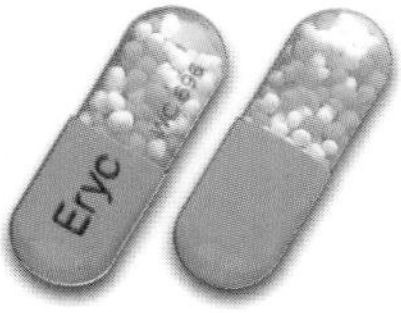

250 mg

ESTRADIOL

Estrace
(page 537)

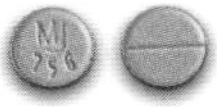

2 mg

ESTROGENS, CONJUGATED

Premarin
(page 540)

0.3 mg

0.625 mg

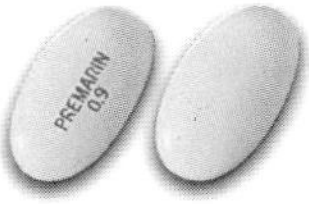

0.9 mg

1.25 mg

2.5 mg

ETHINYL ESTRADIOL AND NORETHINDRONE

Ovcon-35
(page 554)

0.4/35-28

FAMOTIDINE

Pepcid
(page 575)

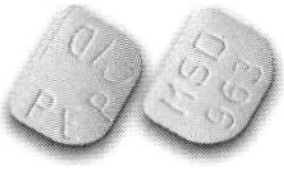

20 mg

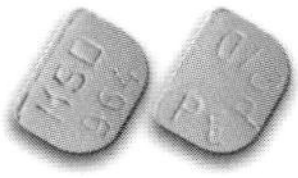

40 mg

FLUCONAZOLE

Diflucan
(page 590)

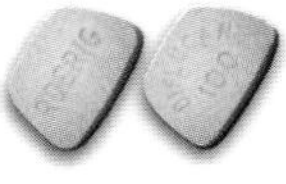

100 mg

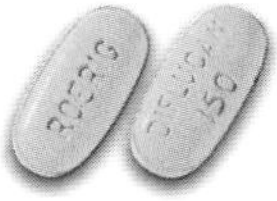

150 mg

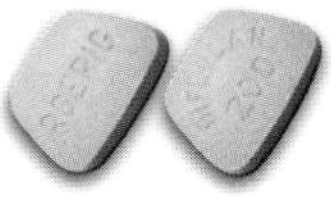

200 mg

FLUOXETINE HYDROCHLORIDE

Prozac
(page 601)

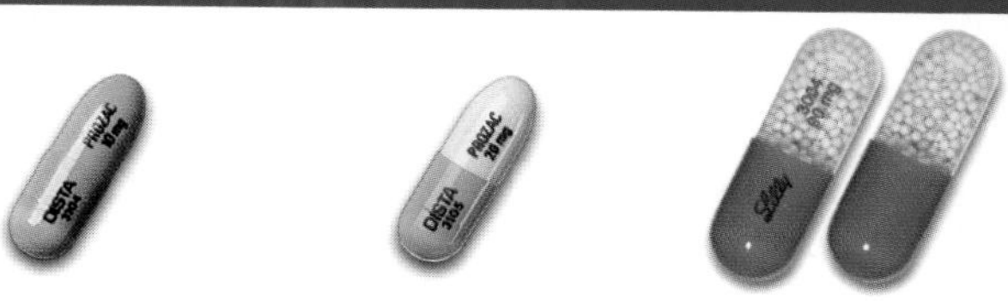

10 mg | 20 mg | 90 mg

FOSINOPRIL SODIUM

Monopril
(page 625)

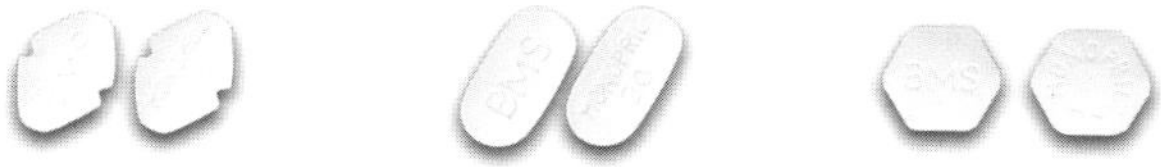

10 mg | 20 mg | 40 mg

FROVATRIPTAN SUCCINATE

Frova
(page 628)

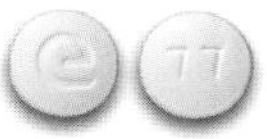

2.5 mg

FUROSEMIDE

Lasix
(page 630)

20 mg | 40 mg

GABAPENTIN

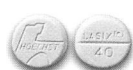

Neurontin
(page 632)

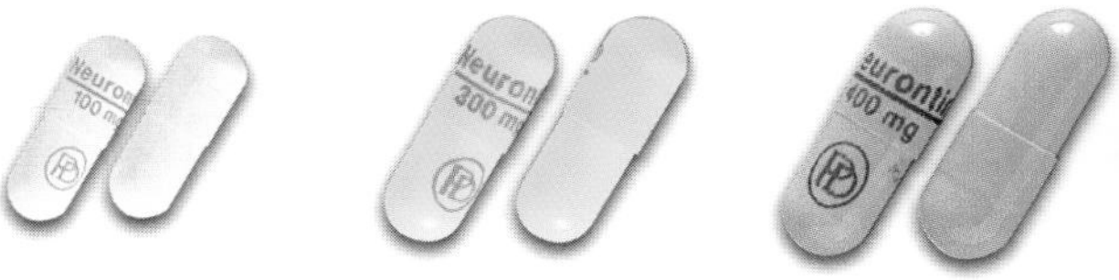

100 mg | 300 mg | 400 mg

GLIPIZIDE

Glucotrol
(page 645)

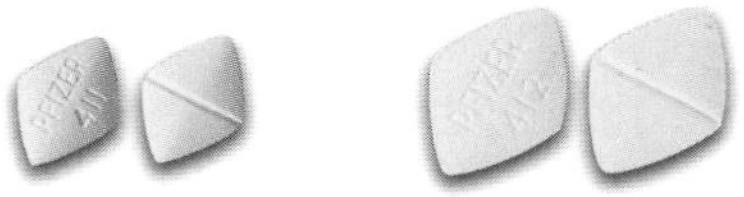

5 mg | 10 mg

Glucotrol XL
(page 645)

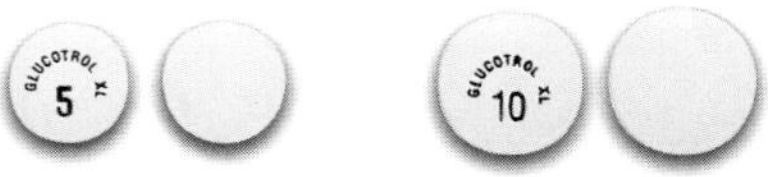

5 mg | 10 mg

GLYBURIDE

DiaBeta
(page 648)

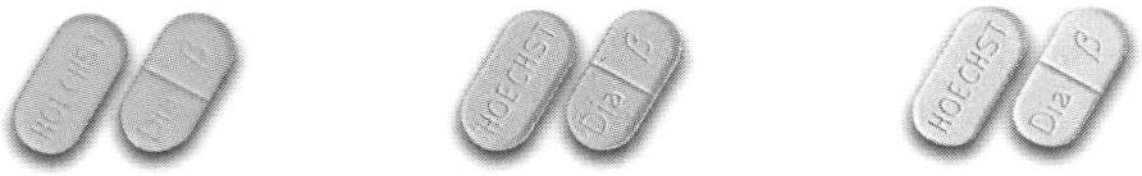

1.25 mg | 2.5 mg | 5 mg

Micronase
(page 648)

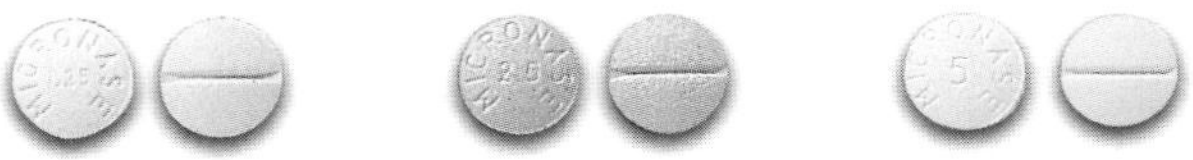

1.25 mg | 2.5 mg | 5 mg

LANSOPRAZOLE

Prevacid
(page 748)

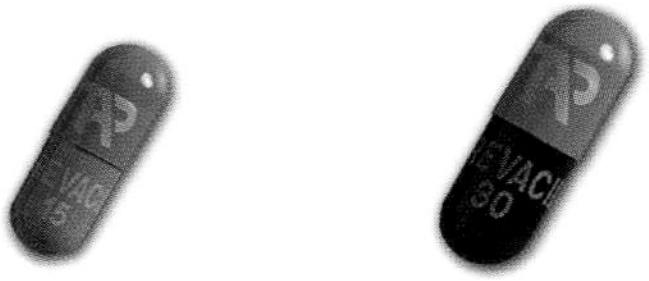

15 mg | 30 mg

LEVOFLOXACIN

Levaquin
(page 761)

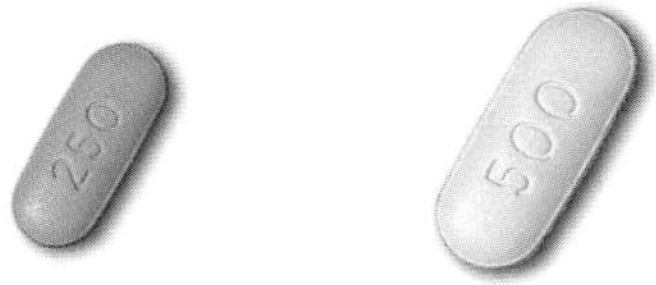

250 mg | 500 mg

LEVOTHYROXINE SODIUM

Levoxyl
(page 765)

25 mcg

50 mcg

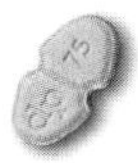
75 mcg

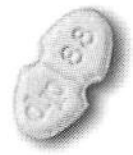
88 mcg

100 mcg

112 mcg

125 mcg

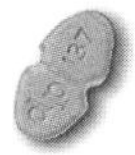
137 mcg

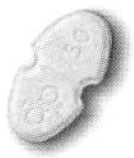
150 mcg

175 mcg

200 mcg

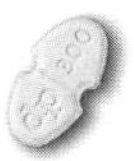
300 mcg

LISINOPRIL

Prinivil
(page 773)

2.5 mg

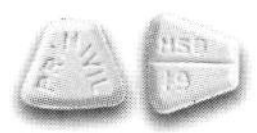
5 mg

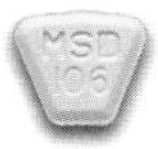

10 mg

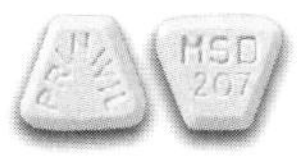

20 mg

40 mg

LORATADINE

Claritin
(page 784)

10 mg

LOSARTAN POTASSIUM

Cozaar
(page 786)

25 mg

50 mg

LOVASTATIN

Mevacor
(page 788)

10 mg

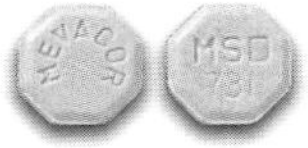
20 mg

40 mg

MEDROXYPROGESTERONE ACETATE

Provera
(page 806)

2.5 mg

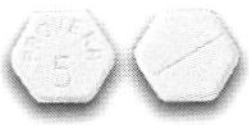
5 mg

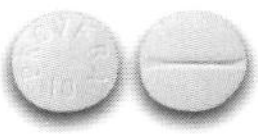
10 mg

METFORMIN HYDROCHLORIDE

Glucophage
(page 826)

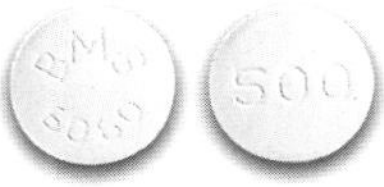
500 mg

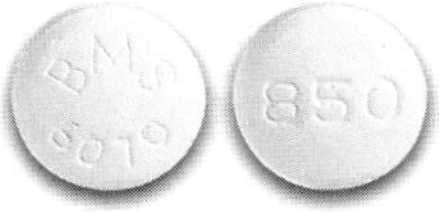
850 mg

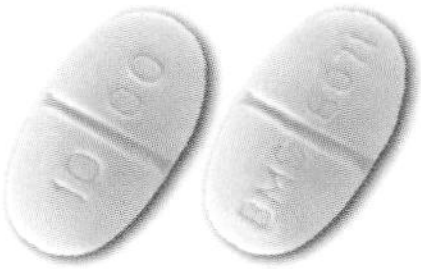
1000 mg

Glucophage XR
(page 826)

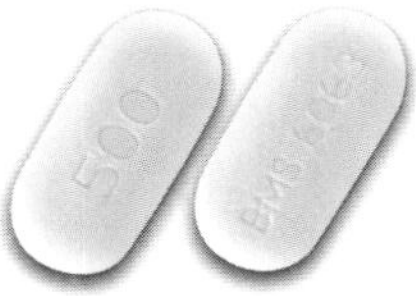
500 mg

METHYLPHENIDATE HYDROCHLORIDE

Ritalin
(page 839)

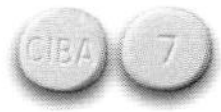
5 mg

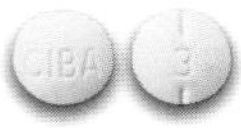
10 mg

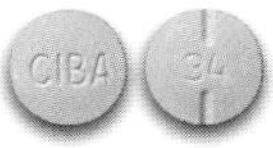
20 mg

Ritalin SR
(page 839)

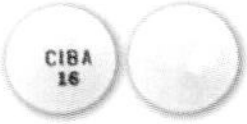
20 mg

METOPROLOL SUCCINATE

Toprol-XL
(page 847)

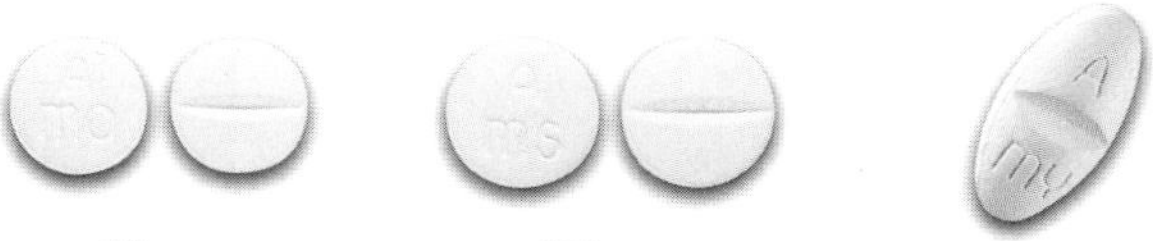

50 mg | 100 mg | 200 mg

MONTELUKAST SODIUM

Singulair
(page 875)

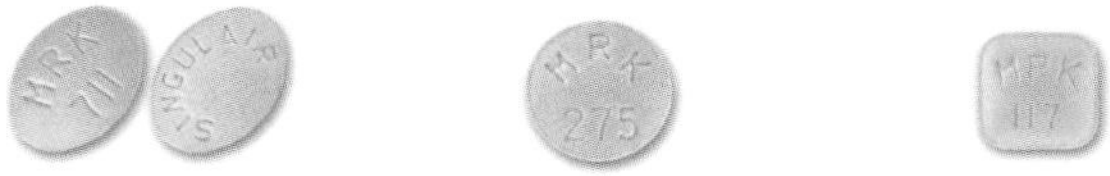

4 mg | 5 mg | 10 mg

NABUMETONE

Relafen
(page 885)

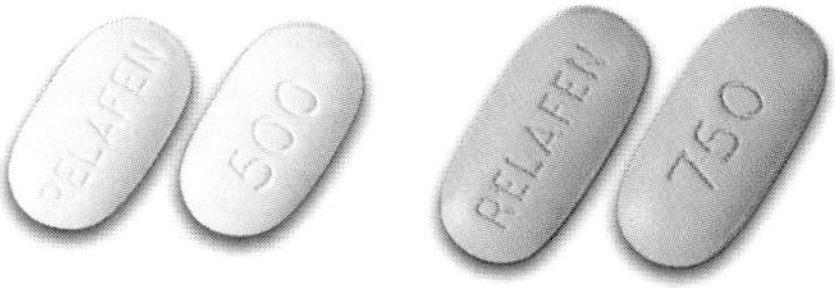

500 mg | 750 mg

NEFAZODONE HYDROCHLORIDE

Serzone
(page 901)

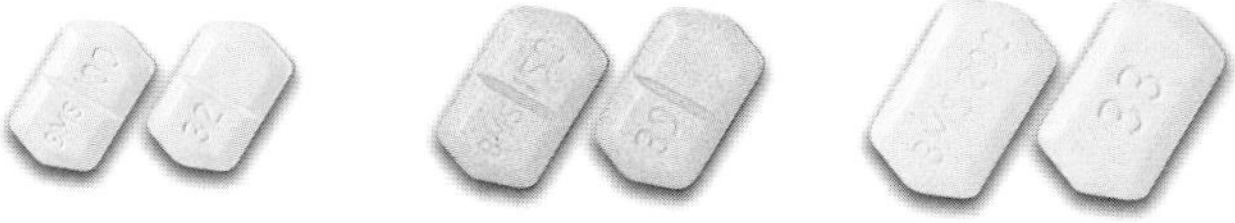

100 mg | 150 mg | 200 mg

NIFEDIPINE

Procardia XL
(page 918)

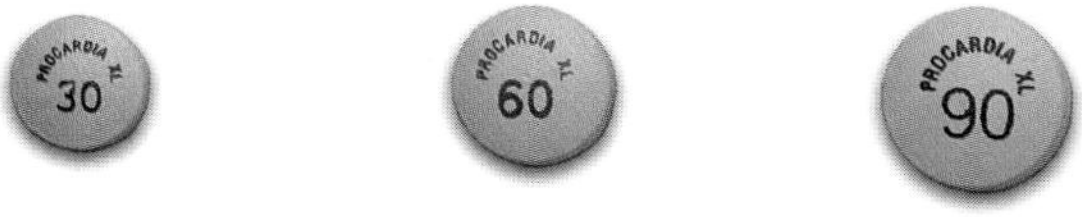

30 mg | 60 mg | 90 mg

NORTRIPTYLINE HYDROCHLORIDE

Pamelor
(page 932)

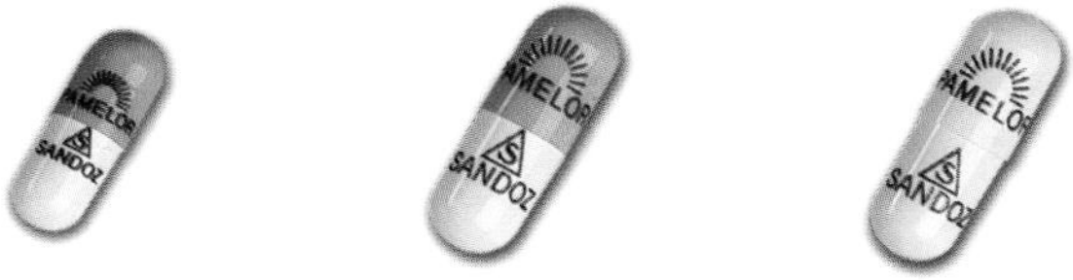

10 mg | 25 mg | 50 mg

OMEPRAZOLE

Prilosec
(page 941)

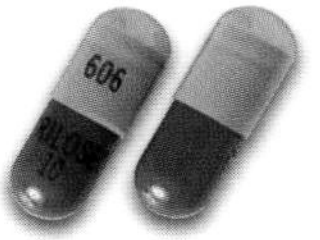

10 mg

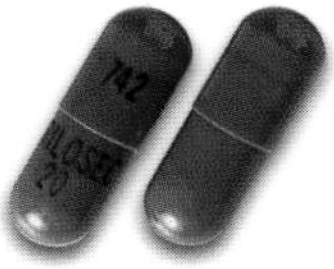

20 mg

OXYCODONE HYDROCHLORIDE

OxyContin
(page 955)

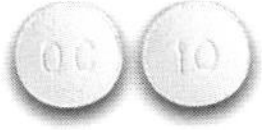

10 mg

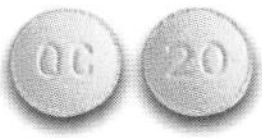

20 mg

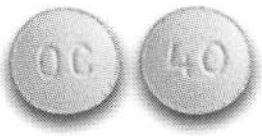

40 mg

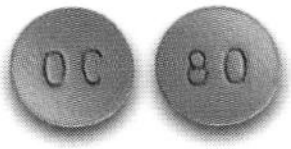

80 mg

PAROXETINE HYDROCHLORIDE

Paxil
(page 974)

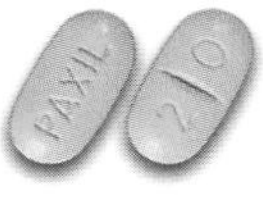

20 mg

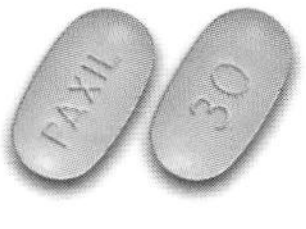

30 mg

PHENYTOIN SODIUM

Dilantin Kapseals
(page 1014)

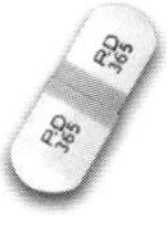

30 mg

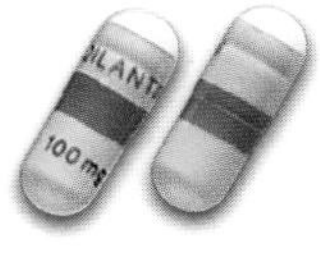
100 mg

POTASSIUM CHLORIDE

K-Dur 20
(page 1040)

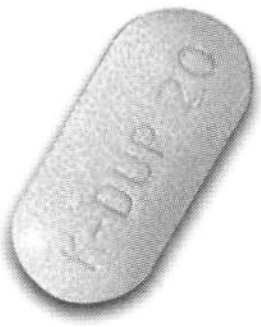

20 mEq

PRAVASTATIN SODIUM

Pravachol
(page 1048)

10 mg

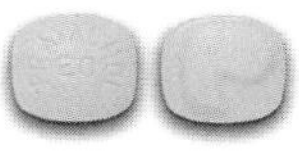

20 mg

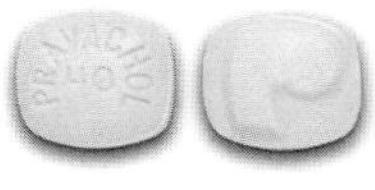

40 mg

PROCHLORPERAZINE

Compazine
(page 1063)

5 mg

10 mg

PROMETHAZINE HYDROCHLORIDE

Phenergan
(page 1067)

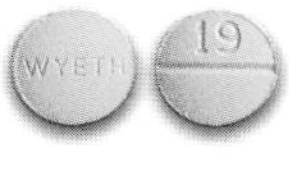

12.5 mg

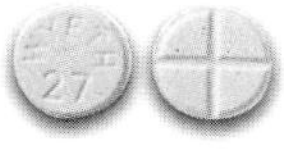

25 mg

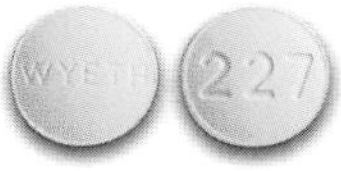

50 mg

QUINAPRIL HYDROCHLORIDE

Accupril
(page 1088)

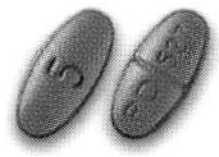

5 mg

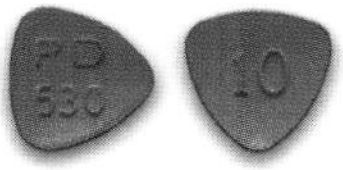

10 mg

20 mg

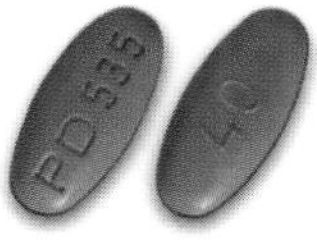

40 mg

RANITIDINE HYDROCHLORIDE

Zantac
(page 1102)

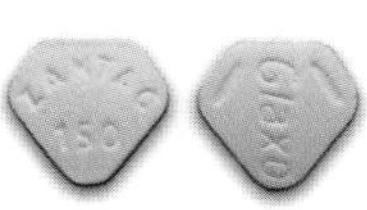

150 mg

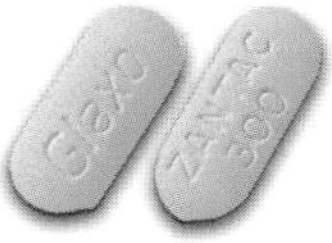

300 mg

RISEDRONATE SODIUM

Actonel
(page 1120)

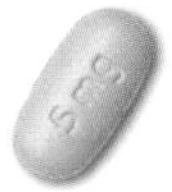

5 mg

RISPERIDONE

Risperdal
(page 1122)

0.25 mg

0.5 mg

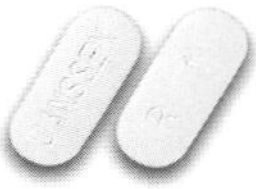
1 mg

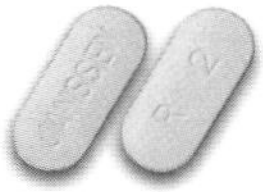

2 mg

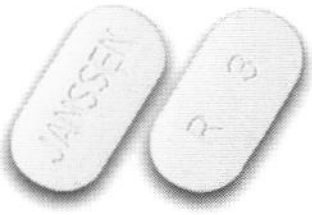

3 mg

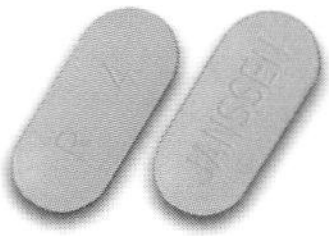

4 mg

ROFECOXIB

Vioxx
(page 1130)

12.5 mg

25 mg

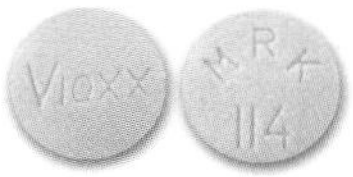

50 mg

ROSIGLITAZONE MALEATE

Avandia
(page 1134)

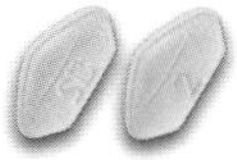
2 mg

4 mg

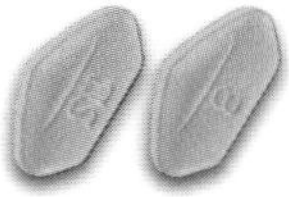
8 mg

SERTRALINE HYDROCHLORIDE

Zoloft
(page 1148)

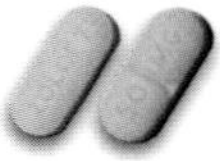
50 mg

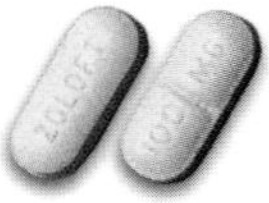

100 mg

SILDENAFIL CITRATE

Viagra
(page 1152)

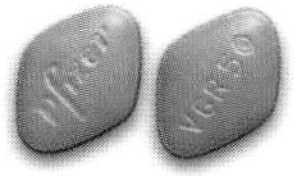

50 mg

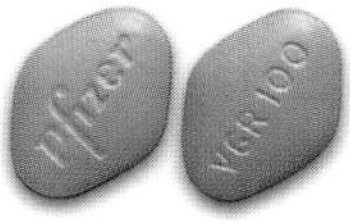

100 mg

SIMVASTATIN

Zocor
(page 1155)

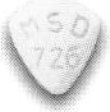

5 mg

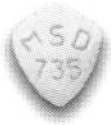

10 mg

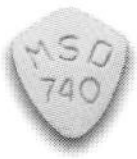

20 mg

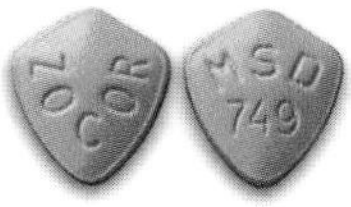

40 mg

TERAZOSIN HYDROCHLORIDE

Hytrin
(page 1213)

1 mg

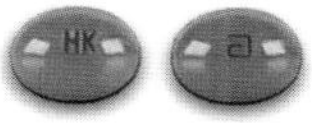

5 mg

10 mg

TICLOPIDINE HYDROCHLORIDE

Ticlid
(page 1241)

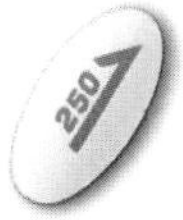

250 mg

VALDECOXIB

Bextra
(page 1297)

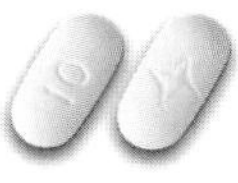

10 mg

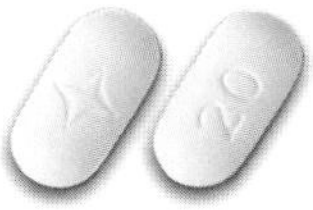

20 mg

VALPROIC ACID

Depakote

(page 1301)

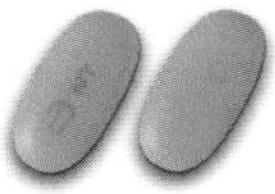

125 mg

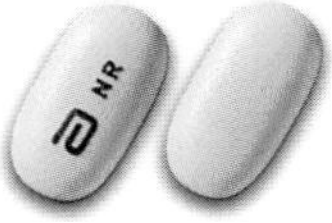

250 mg

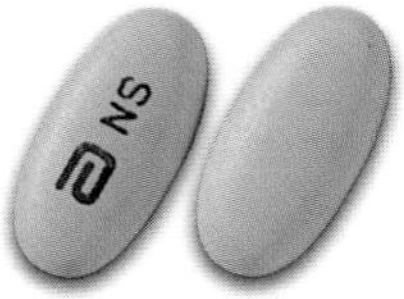

500 mg

VENLAFAXINE HYDROCHLORIDE

Effexor XR

(page 1311)

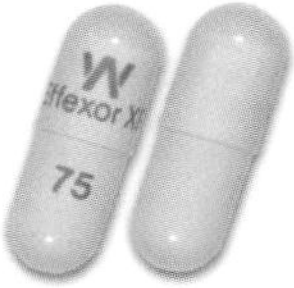

75 mg

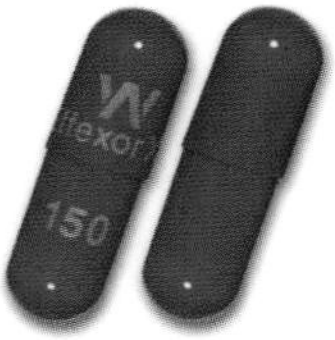

150 mg

WARFARIN SODIUM

Coumadin

(page 1326)

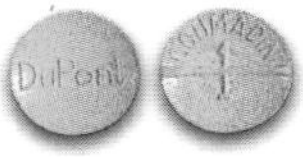

1 mg

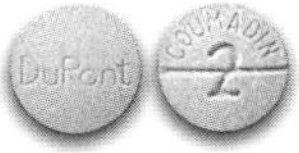

2 mg

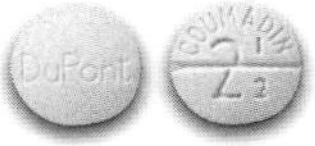

2.5 mg

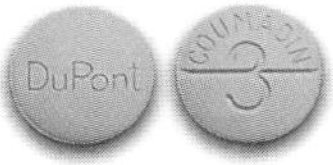

3 mg

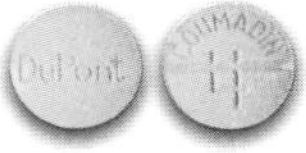

4 mg

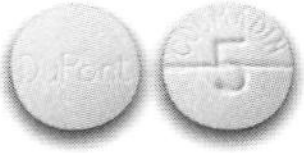

5 mg

6 mg

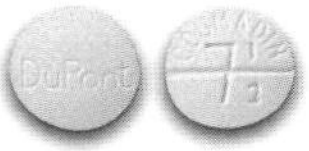

7.5 mg

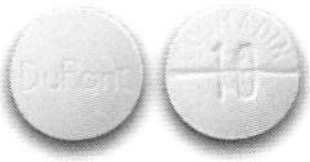

10 mg

ZOLPIDEM TARTRATE

Ambien

(page 1343)

5 mg

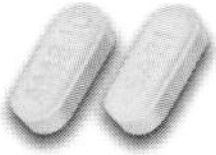

10 mg

mercaptopurine (6-mercaptopurine, 6-MP)

(mer-cap-toh-PYOO-reen)
Purinethol

Pharmacologic class: antimetabolite (cell cycle–phase specific, S phase)
Therapeutic class: antineoplastic
Pregnancy risk category: D

Indications and dosages

▶ **Acute lymphoblastic leukemia in children, chronic myelocytic leukemia.** *Adults:* 2.5 mg/kg P.O. daily as single dose, up to 5 mg/kg P.O. daily. Maintenance dosage is 1.5 to 2.5 mg/kg P.O. daily.
Children age 5 and older: 2.5 mg/kg P.O. daily. Maintenance dosage is 1.5 to 2.5 mg/kg P.O. daily.

▶ **Acute myeloblastic leukemia‡.** *Adults:* 500 mg/m^2 P.O. daily with other therapies.

Contraindications and precautions

• Contraindicated in patients whose disease has resisted drug.
Lifespan: In pregnant or breast-feeding women, drug isn't recommended.

Adverse reactions

GI: *nausea, vomiting, anorexia,* painful oral ulcers.
Hematologic: ***leukopenia, thrombocytopenia,*** *anemia* (may persist several days after drug is stopped).
Hepatic: biliary stasis, *jaundice,* ***hepatotoxicity.***
Metabolic: hyperuricemia.
Skin: rash, hyperpigmentation.

Interactions

Drug-drug. *Allopurinol:* Slows inactivation of mercaptopurine. Decrease mercaptopurine to one-fourth or one-third normal dose, as directed.
Hepatotoxic drugs: May enhance hepatotoxicity of mercaptopurine. Monitor patient closely.
Nondepolarizing neuromuscular blockers: Antagonized muscle relaxant effect. Notify anesthesiologist that patient is receiving drug.
Warfarin: Antagonizes anticoagulant effect. Monitor PT and INR.

Effects on lab test results

• May increase uric acid level.
• May decrease hemoglobin, hematocrit, and WBC, RBC, and platelet counts.

Pharmacokinetics

Absorption: Incomplete and variable; about 50% of dose is absorbed.
Distribution: Distributed widely in total body water.
Metabolism: Extensively metabolized in liver.
Excretion: Excreted in urine.

Route	Onset	Peak	Duration
P.O.	Unknown	Unknown	Unknown

Pharmacodynamics

Chemical effect: Inhibits RNA and DNA synthesis.
Therapeutic effect: Inhibits growth of certain cancer cells.

Available forms

Tablets (scored): 50 mg

NURSING PROCESS

Assessment

• Assess patient's condition before therapy and regularly thereafter.
• Monitor blood count and transaminase, alkaline phosphatase, and bilirubin levels weekly during induction and monthly during maintenance.
• Observe for signs of bleeding and infection.
• Monitor fluid intake and output and uric acid level.
• Be alert for adverse reactions and drug interactions. Adverse GI reactions are less common in children.
ALERT: Watch for jaundice, clay-colored stools, and frothy, dark urine. Hepatic dysfunction is reversible when drug is stopped. If hepatic tenderness occurs, stop drug and notify prescriber.
• Evaluate patient's and family's knowledge of drug therapy.

Nursing diagnoses

• Ineffective health maintenance related to presence of leukemia

• Ineffective immune protection related to drug-induced adverse hematologic reactions
• Deficient knowledge related to drug therapy

Planning and implementation

• Dosage modifications may be needed after chemotherapy or radiation therapy and in patient with depressed neutrophil or platelet count or impaired liver or kidney function.
ALERT: Sometimes drug is ordered as 6-mercaptopurine or 6-MP. The numeral 6 is part of drug name and doesn't signify number of dosage units. To prevent confusion, avoid these designations.
• Drug regimen must continue despite nausea and vomiting. Notify prescriber if adverse GI reactions occur, and obtain order for antiemetic.
• Encourage adequate fluid intake (3 L daily).
• If allopurinol is ordered, use cautiously.
• Discontinue drug if hepatic tenderness occurs and notify prescriber.

Patient teaching
• Tell patient to notify prescriber if vomiting occurs shortly after taking dose because antiemetic will be needed so drug therapy can continue.
• Warn patient to watch for signs of infection (fever, sore throat, fatigue) and bleeding (easy bruising, nosebleeds, bleeding gums, melena). Have patient take his temperature daily.
• Advise woman of childbearing age to avoid becoming pregnant during therapy and to consult with prescriber before becoming pregnant.

Evaluation

• Patient responds well to therapy.
• Patient doesn't develop serious ill effects when hematologic studies are abnormal.
• Patient and family state understanding of drug therapy.

meropenem

(mer-oh-PEN-em)
Merrem I.V.

Pharmacologic class: synthetic broad-spectrum carbapenem antibiotic
Therapeutic class: antibiotic
Pregnancy risk category: B

Indications and dosages

▶ **Complicated appendicitis and peritonitis caused by viridans group streptococci, *Escherichia coli, Klebsiella pneumoniae, Pseudomonas aeruginosa, Bacteroides fragilis, Bacteroides thetaiotaomicron,* and *Peptostreptococcus* species; bacterial meningitis (children only) caused by *Streptococcus pneumoniae, Haemophilus influenzae,* and *Neisseria meningitidis.*** *Adults:* 1 g I.V. q 8 hours over 15 to 30 minutes as I.V. infusion or over 3 to 5 minutes as I.V. bolus injection (5 to 20 ml).
Adults with renal impairment: If creatinine clearance is 26 to 50 ml/minute, give usual dose q 12 hours; if 10 to 25 ml/minute, give ½ usual dose q 12 hours; if less than 10 ml/minute, give ½ dose q 24 hours.
Children weighing more than 50 kg (110 lb): 1 g I.V. q 8 hours for intra-abdominal infections and 2 g I.V. q 8 hours for meningitis.
Children age 3 months and older: 20 mg/kg (intra-abdominal infection) or 40 mg/kg (bacterial meningitis) q 8 hours over 15 to 30 minutes as I.V. infusion or over 3 to 5 minutes as I.V. bolus injection (5 to 20 ml). Maximum dosage is 2 g I.V. q 8 hours.

Contraindications and precautions

• Contraindicated in patients hypersensitive to drug, its components, or other drugs in same class. Also contraindicated in those who have had anaphylactic reactions to beta-lactams.
Lifespan: In pregnant patients, use only if clearly needed. In breast-feeding women, use cautiously; it is unknown whether drug appears in breast milk. In infants younger than age 3 months, safety and efficacy haven't been established.

Adverse reactions

CNS: ***seizures,*** headache.
CV: phlebitis, thrombophlebitis at injection site.
GI: diarrhea, nausea, vomiting, constipation, oral candidiasis, ***pseudomembranous colitis,*** glossitis.
Hematologic: anemia, eosinophilia.
Respiratory: ***apnea.***
Skin: rash, pruritus.
Other: hypersensitivity reactions, ***anaphylaxis,*** inflammation.

Interactions

Drug-drug. *Probenecid:* Inhibits renal excretion of meropenem. Don't give together.

Effects on lab test results

- May increase ALT, AST, bilirubin, alkaline phosphatase, LDH, creatinine, and BUN levels.
- May increase eosinophil count. May decrease hemoglobin, hematocrit, and WBC count. May increase or decrease platelet count and PT.

Pharmacokinetics

Absorption: Given I.V.
Distribution: Plasma protein–binding is 2%. Penetrates into most body fluids and tissues including CSF.
Metabolism: Metabolized in kidneys.
Excretion: Excreted in urine. *Half-life:* 1 hour.

Route	Onset	Peak	Duration
I.V.	Unknown	Within 1 hr	Unknown

Pharmacodynamics

Chemical effect: Readily penetrates the cell wall of most gram-positive and gram-negative bacteria to reach penicillin binding protein targets, where it inhibits cell wall synthesis.
Therapeutic effect: Bactericidal.

Available forms

Powder for injection: 500 mg/15 ml, 500 mg/20 ml, 500 mg/100 ml, 1 g/15 ml, 1 g/30 ml, 1 g/100 ml

NURSING PROCESS

Assessment

- Obtain specimen for culture and sensitivity tests before giving first dose.

ALERT: Serious and occasionally fatal hypersensitivity reactions have been reported in patients receiving therapy with beta-lactams. Before starting therapy, determine whether previous hypersensitivity reactions have occurred to penicillins, cephalosporins, other beta-lactams, or other allergens.

- Monitor patient for signs and symptoms of superinfection.
- Periodically assess organ system functions during prolonged therapy.
- Evaluate patient's and family's knowledge of drug therapy.

Nursing diagnoses

- Infection related to bacteria
- Risk for deficient fluid volume related to effect on kidneys
- Deficient knowledge related to drug therapy

Planning and implementation

- For I.V. bolus administration, add 10 ml of sterile water for injection to 500-mg/20-ml vial or add 20 ml to 1-g/30-ml vial.
- For I.V. infusion, reconstitute drug in infusion vials (500 mg/100 ml and 1 g/100 ml) with compatible infusion fluid. Or, reconstitute drug in injection vial, add resulting solution to an I.V. container, and further dilute with appropriate infusion fluid.
- Dosages need to be adjusted for patients with renal insufficiency or renal failure or with creatinine clearance below 51 ml/minute.
- Follow manufacturer's guidelines closely when using ADD-Vantage vials.

Patient teaching

- Advise breast-feeding patient of risk of drug transmission to infant.
- Instruct patient to report adverse reactions.

Evaluation

- Patient is free from infection.
- Patient maintains adequate hydration.
- Patient and family state understanding of drug therapy.

mesalamine

(mez-AL-uh-meen)
Asacol, Canasa, Pentasa, Rowasa

Pharmacologic class: salicylate
Therapeutic class: anti-inflammatory
Pregnancy risk category: B

Indications and dosages

▶ **Active mild-to-moderate distal ulcerative colitis, proctitis, proctosigmoiditis.** *Adults: P.O.* 800 mg P.O. (tablets) t.i.d. for total dose of 2.4 g daily for 6 weeks, or 1 g P.O. (capsules) q.i.d. for total dose of 4 g up to 8 weeks. *P.R.* 500 mg P.R. (suppository) b.i.d., increased to t.i.d. after 2 wk; retain for 1 to 3 hours or longer, or 4 g as retention enema once daily (preferably h.s.) retained overnight (for about

8 hours). Usual course of therapy for P.R. form is 3 to 6 weeks.

▶ **Maintenance of remission of ulcerative colitis.** *Adults:* 1.6 g P.O. daily in divided doses for 6 months. Or, 60 ml (4 g) rectal suspension q 2 to 3 nights or 1 to 3 g rectal suspension daily.

Contraindications and precautions

• Contraindicated in patients hypersensitive to drug, its components, or salicylates.
• Use cautiously in patients with renal impairment. Nephrotoxic potential from absorbed mesalamine exists.
Lifespan: In pregnant women, use cautiously. In breast-feeding women, drug isn't recommended for use. In children, drug is contraindicated. In the elderly, use cautiously.

Adverse reactions

CNS: headache, dizziness, fatigue, fever, malaise.
GI: abdominal pain, cramps, or discomfort; flatulence; diarrhea; rectal pain; bloating; *nausea;* vomiting; *belching;* ***pancreatitis.***
Respiratory: wheezing.
Skin: pruritus, rash, urticaria, hair loss, acne.
Other: ***anaphylaxis***.

Interactions

None significant.

Effects on lab test results

• May increase BUN, creatinine, AST, ALT, alkaline phosphatase, LDH, amylase, and lipase levels.

Pharmacokinetics

Absorption: Poorly absorbed with P.R. administration; P.O. tablets and capsules are made to have delayed absorption from GI tract.
Distribution: Not clearly defined.
Metabolism: Undergoes acetylation, but whether this takes place at colonic or systemic sites is unknown.
Excretion: P.O. form primarily excreted in urine; most of P.R. form excreted in feces. *Half-life:* Mesalamine, 30 to 75 minutes; acetylated metabolite, about 5 to 10 hours.

Route	Onset	Peak	Duration
P.O., P.R.	Unknown	3-12 hr	Unknown

Pharmacodynamics

Chemical effect: Unknown; probably acts topically by inhibiting prostaglandin production in colon.
Therapeutic effect: Relieves inflammation in lower GI tract.

Available forms

Capsules (controlled-release): 250 mg
Rectal suspension: 4 g/60 ml
Suppositories: 500 mg
Tablets (delayed-release): 400 mg

NURSING PROCESS

Assessment

• Assess patient's condition before therapy and regularly thereafter.
• Monitor periodic kidney function studies in patient on long-term therapy.
• Because it contains potassium metabisulfite, drug may cause hypersensitivity reactions in patient sensitive to sulfites.
• Be alert for adverse reactions.
• Evaluate patient's and family's knowledge of drug therapy.

Nursing diagnoses

• Impaired tissue integrity related to underlying condition
• Acute pain related to drug-induced adverse GI reactions
• Deficient knowledge related to drug therapy

Planning and implementation

• **P.O. use:** Patient should swallow tablets and capsules whole and not crush or chew them.
• **P.R. use:** For maximum effectiveness, have patient retain suppository as long as possible (1 to 3 hours). When giving suspension, shake bottle before application.
ALERT: Don't confuse Asacol with Os-Cal.

Patient teaching

• Teach patient how to take oral and rectal form, and instruct him to carefully follow instructions supplied with drug.
• Instruct patient to discontinue drug if he experiences fever or rash. Patient intolerant of sulfasalazine may also be hypersensitive to mesalamine.

Evaluation

- Patient reports relief from GI symptoms.
- Patient states that no new pain is experienced during therapy.
- Patient and family state understanding of drug therapy.

mesna

(MEZ-nah)
MESNEX

Pharmacologic class: thiol derivative
Therapeutic class: uroprotectant
Pregnancy risk category: B

Indications and dosages

▶ **Prophylaxis of hemorrhagic cystitis in patients receiving ifosfamide.** *Adults:* Dosage varies with amount of ifosfamide given. Usual dosage is 240 mg/m^2 as I.V. bolus with ifosfamide. Dosage repeated at 4 hours and 8 hours after ifosfamide is given.

▶ **Prophylaxis of hemorrhagic cystitis in bone marrow recipients receiving cyclophosphamide‡.** *Adults:* 60% to 160% of the cyclophosphamide daily dose given I.V. in three to five divided doses or by continuous infusion. Or, in patients receiving cyclophosphamide (50 to 60 mg/kg I.V. daily for 2 to 4 days), give 10 mg/kg I.V. loading dose of mesna followed by 60 mg/kg mesna by continuous infusion over 24 hours. Give mesna regimen with each cyclophosphamide dose and continue for an additional 24 hours once cyclophosphamide is discontinued.

Contraindications and precautions

- Contraindicated in patients hypersensitive to mesna or thiol-containing compounds.

Lifespan: In pregnant women, use cautiously. In breast-feeding women and in children, safety of drug hasn't been established.

Adverse reactions

CNS: *fatigue, fever, asthenia,* dizziness, headache, somnolence, anxiety, confusion, insomnia, pain.
CV: chest pain, edema, hypotension, tachycardia, flushing.
GI: *nausea, vomiting,* diarrhea, *constipation, anorexia, abdominal pain,* dyspepsia.
GU: hematuria.
Hematologic: ***leukopenia, thrombocytopenia, anemia, granulocytopenia.***
Metabolic: hypokalemia, dehydration.
Musculoskeletal: back pain.
Respiratory: dyspnea, coughing, pneumonia.
Skin: alopecia, increased sweating, injection site reaction, pallor
Other: ***allergy.***

Interactions

None significant.

Effects on lab test results

None reported.

Pharmacokinetics

Absorption: Given I.V.
Distribution: Remains in vascular compartment; isn't distributed through tissues.
Metabolism: Rapidly metabolized to mesna disulfide, its only metabolite.
Excretion: Excreted in urine. *Half-life:* Mesna, 1¼ hour; mesna disulfide, 1 hour.

Route	Onset	Peak	Duration
I.V.	Unknown	Unknown	Unknown

Pharmacodynamics

Chemical effect: Prevents ifosfamide-induced hemorrhagic cystitis by reacting with urotoxic ifosfamide metabolites.
Therapeutic effect: Prevents ifosfamide from adversely affecting bladder tissue.

Available forms

Injection: 100 mg/ml in 2- and 10-ml vials.

NURSING PROCESS

Assessment

- Assess patient's condition before therapy and regularly thereafter.
- Up to 6% of patients may not respond to drug's protective effects.
- Monitor urine samples daily in patient receiving mesna for hematuria.
- Be alert for adverse reactions.
- Monitor patient's hydration status if adverse GI reactions occur.
- Evaluate patient's and family's knowledge of drug therapy.

Nursing diagnoses

- Risk for deficient fluid volume related to drug-induced adverse GI reactions
- Deficient knowledge related to drug therapy

Planning and implementation

- Because mesna is used with ifosfamide and other chemotherapeutic drugs, it's difficult to determine adverse reactions attributable solely to mesna.
- Mesna isn't effective in preventing hematuria from other causes (such as thrombocytopenia).
- Although formulated to prevent hemorrhagic cystitis from ifosfamide, drug won't protect against other toxicities linked to ifosfamide.
- Mesna may interfere with diagnostic tests for urine ketones.
- Prepare I.V. solution by diluting drug in commercially available ampules of D_5W, D_5W and normal saline solution for injection, normal saline solution for injection, or lactated Ringer's solution to obtain final solution of 20 mg/ml of mesna.
- Refrigerate diluted solutions after preparation, and use within 6 hours. Diluted solutions are stable for 24 hours at room temperature.
- After opening ampule, discard any unused drug because it decomposes quickly into inactive compound.

ALERT: Don't mix mesna with cisplatin because they're incompatible.

Patient teaching

- Instruct patient to report hematuria immediately and to notify prescriber about adverse GI reactions.

Evaluation

- Patient maintains adequate hydration throughout therapy.
- Patient and family state understanding of drug therapy.

mesoridazine besylate

(mes-oh-RID-eh-zeen BES-eh-layt)
Serentil*, Serentil Concentrate

Pharmacologic class: phenothiazine (piperidine derivative)
Therapeutic class: antipsychotic
Pregnancy risk category: C

Indications and dosages

▶ **Management of psychotic disorders and for schizophrenic patients who don't show an acceptable response to adequate treatment with other antipsychotic drugs.** *Adults and adolescents older than age 12:* Initially, 50 mg P.O. t.i.d., up to 400 mg P.O. daily. Or, 25 mg I.M. repeated in 30 to 60 minutes, if needed, up to 200 mg I.M. daily.

Contraindications and precautions

- Contraindicated in patients hypersensitive to drug and in those experiencing severe CNS depression or coma.

Lifespan: In pregnant women, use cautiously. For breast-feeding women, drug isn't recommended. In children younger than age 12, safety of drug hasn't been established.

Adverse reactions

CNS: extrapyramidal reactions, drowsiness, *tardive dyskinesia, sedation,* EEG changes, dizziness, ***neuroleptic malignant syndrome.***
CV: *orthostatic hypotension,* tachycardia, ECG changes, ***prolonged QTc interval, torsades de pointes, sudden death.***
EENT: *ocular changes, blurred vision,* retinitis pigmentosa.
GI: *dry mouth, constipation,* increased appetite.
GU: *urine retention,* dark urine, menstrual irregularities, inhibited ejaculation.
Hematologic: ***leukopenia, agranulocytosis,*** hyperprolactinemia, ***aplastic anemia, thrombocytopenia.***
Hepatic: cholestatic jaundice.
Metabolic: weight gain.
Skin: *mild photosensitivity reactions,* pain at I.M. injection site, sterile abscess.
Other: allergic reactions, gynecomastia.

Interactions

Drug-drug. *Antacids:* Inhibits absorption of oral phenothiazines. Separate doses by at least 2 hours.
Anticholinergics: May increase anticholinergic effects. Use together cautiously.
Barbiturates: May decrease phenothiazine effect. Observe patient.
CNS depressants: Increases CNS depression. Use together cautiously.

Lithium, phenothiazine: May cause possible disorientation, unconsciousness, and extrapyramidal symptoms. Use cautiously.
Metrizamide: Increases risk of seizures. Monitor patient closely.
Drug-herb. *Dong quai, St. John's wort:* Increases risk of photosensitivity reactions. Advise patient to avoid unprotected or prolonged exposure to sunlight.
Kava: Increases risk or severity of dystonic reactions. Discourage using together.
Yohimbe: Phenothiazines may increase the risk of toxicity. Discourage using together.
Drug-lifestyle. *Alcohol use:* Increases CNS depression. Discourage using together.
Sun exposure: Increases photosensitivity reactions. Urge patient to avoid unprotected or prolonged exposure to sunlight.

Effects on lab test results

- May increase liver function test values and eosinophil count. May decrease hemoglobin, hematocrit, and WBC, granulocyte, and platelet counts.

Pharmacokinetics

Absorption: Erratic and variable with P.O. use; unknown with I.M. use.
Distribution: Distributed widely in body; 91% to 99% protein-bound.
Metabolism: Metabolized extensively by liver.
Excretion: Excreted primarily in urine with some excretion in feces by way of biliary tract.

Route	Onset	Peak	Duration
P.O., I.M.	Up to several wks	Unknown	Unknown

Pharmacodynamics

Chemical effect: Unknown. A piperidine phenothiazine and major sulfoxide metabolite of thioridazine, mesoridazine may block postsynaptic dopamine receptors in brain.
Therapeutic effect: Relieves psychotic and alcoholic signs and symptoms.

Available forms

Injection: 25 mg/ml
Oral concentrate: 25 mg/ml*
Tablets: 10 mg, 25 mg, 50 mg, 100 mg

NURSING PROCESS

Assessment

- Assess patient's condition before therapy and regularly thereafter.
- Obtain baseline measures of blood pressure before starting therapy and monitor regularly. Watch for orthostatic hypotension, especially with parenteral administration.
- Monitor therapy with weekly bilirubin tests during first month, periodic blood tests (CBC and liver function), and ophthalmologic tests (long-term use).

ALERT: Because mesoridazine is linked to a dose-related prolongation of the QTc interval, which is potentially life threatening, its use should be reserved for schizophrenic patients who fail to respond to other antipsychotic drugs.

ALERT: Before treatment, obtain baseline ECG and measure potassium level. Potassium level should be normalized before starting therapy. Patient with a baseline QTc interval longer than 450 msec shouldn't receive drug. Patients with a QTc interval above 500 msec should discontinue use.

- Monitor patient for tardive dyskinesia. It may occur after prolonged use, although it may not appear until months or years later and may disappear spontaneously or persist for life, despite discontinuation of drug.

ALERT: Watch for symptoms of neuroleptic malignant syndrome (extrapyramidal effects, hyperthermia, autonomic disturbance), which is rare but can be fatal.

- Evaluate patient's and family's knowledge of drug therapy.

Nursing diagnoses

- Disturbed thought processes related to underlying condition
- Constipation related to drug-induced adverse GI reactions
- Deficient knowledge related to drug therapy

Planning and implementation

- Oral liquid and parenteral forms may cause contact dermatitis. Wear gloves when preparing solutions, and avoid contact with skin and clothing.
- **P.O. use:** P.O. therapy should replace parenteral therapy as soon as possible. When P.O. concentrate solution is used, dilute dose with

water, orange juice, or grape juice just before administration.
- **I.M. use:** Give drug deep in upper outer quadrant of buttocks. Massage slowly afterward to prevent sterile abscess. Injection may sting.
- Protect drug from light. Slight yellowing of injection or concentrate is common; this doesn't affect potency. Discard markedly discolored solutions.

ALERT: Withhold dose and notify prescriber if jaundice, symptoms of blood dyscrasia (fever, sore throat, infection, cellulitis, weakness), or persistent extrapyramidal reactions (longer than a few hours) develop, especially in pregnant woman or in children.
- Acute dystonic reactions may be treated with diphenhydramine.
- Don't discontinue drug abruptly unless severe adverse reactions occur. After abrupt withdrawal of long-term therapy, patient may experience gastritis, nausea, vomiting, dizziness, tremors, feeling of warmth or cold, diaphoresis, tachycardia, headache, and insomnia.

ALERT: Don't confuse Serentil with Serevent or Aventyl.

Patient teaching
- Warn patient to avoid activities that require alertness and psychomotor coordination until CNS effects of drug are known.
- Advise patient to change positions slowly.
- Tell patient to avoid alcohol during drug therapy.
- Have patient report urine retention or constipation.
- Tell patient that drug may discolor urine.
- Advise patient to relieve dry mouth with sugarless gum or hard candy.
- Tell patient to avoid prolonged exposure to sunlight, use sunblock, and wear protective clothing to avoid photosensitivity reactions.

Evaluation
- Patient exhibits improved behavior.
- Patient maintains normal bowel pattern.
- Patient and family state understanding of drug therapy.

metaproterenol sulfate
(met-uh-proh-TER-eh-nul SUL-fayt)
Alupent

Pharmacologic class: adrenergic agonist
Therapeutic class: bronchodilator
Pregnancy risk category: C

Indications and dosages
▶ **Acute episodes of bronchial asthma.** *Adults and children:* 2 to 3 inhalations. Don't repeat inhalations more often than q 3 to 4 hours. Maximum 12 inhalations daily.
▶ **Bronchial asthma and reversible bronchospasm.** *Adults:* 20 mg P.O. q 6 to 8 hours. *Children older than age 9 or weighing more than 27 kg (60 lb):* 20 mg P.O. q 6 to 8 hours. *Children ages 6 to 9 or weighing less than 27 kg:* 10 mg P.O. q 6 to 8 hours.

Or, by way of IPPB or nebulizer. *Adults and children age 12 and older:* by IPPB, 0.2 to 0.3 ml of 5% solution diluted in 2.5 ml of normal saline solution or 2.5 ml of commercially available 0.4% or 0.6% solution q 4 hours, p.r.n. By hand-bulb nebulizer, 10 inhalations of an undiluted 5% solution.
Children ages 6 to 12: 0.1 to 0.2 ml of 5% solution diluted in normal saline solution to final volume of 3 ml q 4 hours, p.r.n.

Contraindications and precautions
- Contraindicated in patients hypersensitive to drug or its ingredients, in those receiving cyclopropane or halogenated hydrocarbon general anesthetics, and in those with tachycardia or arrhythmias caused by tachycardia, peripheral or mesenteric vascular thrombosis, or profound hypoxia or hypercapnia.
- Use cautiously in patients with hypertension, hyperthyroidism, heart disease, diabetes, or cirrhosis; in those who are receiving cardiac glycosides.

Lifespan: In pregnant or breast-feeding women, use cautiously.

Adverse reactions
CNS: nervousness, weakness, drowsiness, tremors.
CV: tachycardia, hypertension, palpitations, ***cardiac arrest.***
GI: vomiting, nausea, bad taste.

Respiratory: ***paradoxical bronchiolar constriction.***

Interactions

Drug-drug. *Levodopa:* Increases risk of arrhythmias. Avoid using together.
Propranolol, other beta blockers: Blocks bronchodilating effect of metaproterenol. Monitor patient.

Effects on lab test results

None reported.

Pharmacokinetics

Absorption: Well absorbed.
Distribution: Widely distributed.
Metabolism: Extensively metabolized on first pass through liver.
Excretion: Excreted in urine.

Route	Onset	Peak	Duration
P.O.	1 min	≤ 1 hr	1-4 hr
Inhalation	15 min	≤ 1 hr	2-6 hr
Nebulization	5-30 min	≤ 1 hr	2-6 hr

Pharmacodynamics

Chemical effect: Relaxes bronchial smooth muscle by acting on $beta_2$-adrenergic receptors.
Therapeutic effect: Improves breathing.

Available forms

Aerosol inhaler: 0.65 mg/metered spray
Solution for nebulizer inhalation: 0.4%, 0.6%, 5% solution
Syrup: 10 mg/5 ml
Tablets: 10 mg, 20 mg

NURSING PROCESS

Assessment

- Assess patient's condition before therapy and regularly thereafter.
- Be alert for adverse reactions and drug interactions.
- Monitor patient's hydration status if adverse GI reactions occur.
- Evaluate patient's and family's knowledge of drug therapy.

Nursing diagnoses

- Impaired gas exchange related to underlying respiratory condition
- Risk for deficient fluid volume related to drug-induced adverse GI reactions
- Deficient knowledge related to drug therapy

Planning and implementation

- Patient may use tablets and aerosol together. Watch for toxicity.
- **P.O. and oral inhalation use:** Follow normal protocol.
- **Aerosol nebulization use:** Solution can be given by IPPB with drug diluted in normal saline solution or by hand-bulb nebulizer at full strength.

ALERT: Don't confuse metaproterenol with metoprolol or metipranolol.
ALERT: Don't confuse Alupent with Atrovent.

Patient teaching

- Give patient the following instructions for using metered-dose inhaler: Clear nasal passages and throat. Breathe out, expelling as much air from lungs as possible. Place mouthpiece well into mouth and inhale deeply as you release a dose from inhaler. Hold breath for several seconds, remove mouthpiece, and exhale slowly. Allow 2 minutes between inhalations.
- Instruct patient to store drug in light-resistant container.
- Advise patient that metaproterenol inhalations should precede corticosteroid inhalations (when prescribed) by 10 to 15 minutes to maximize effectiveness of corticosteroid therapy.
- Tell patient using corticosteroid inhaler to use bronchodilator first, and then wait 5 minutes before using corticosteroid. This allows bronchodilator to open air passages for maximum effectiveness of corticosteroid.
- If more than one inhalation of metaproterenol is ordered, tell patient to wait at least 2 minutes before repeating procedure.
- Warn patient to discontinue immediately and notify prescriber if paradoxical bronchospasm occurs.
- If no response is derived from dosage, tell patient to notify prescriber or request dosage adjustments.

Evaluation

- Patient's status improves.
- Patient maintains adequate hydration.
- Patient and family state understanding of drug therapy.

metformin hydrochloride

(met-FOR-min high-droh-KLOR-ighd)
Glucophage, Glucophage XR

Pharmacologic class: biguanide
Therapeutic class: antidiabetic
Pregnancy risk category: B

Indications and dosages

▶ **Adjunct to diet to lower blood glucose level in patients with type 2 (non-insulin-dependent) diabetes mellitus.** *Adults:* Initially, 500 mg P.O. b.i.d. with morning and evening meals, or 850 mg P.O. once daily with morning meal. When 500-mg dose form is used, increase dosage to 500 mg weekly, maximum 2,500 mg P.O. daily, as needed. When 850-mg dose form is used, increase dosage to 850 mg q other week, maximum 2,550 mg P.O. daily, as needed. If using extended-release formulation, initiate therapy at 500 mg P.O. daily with the evening meal. May increase dose weekly in increments of 500 mg P.O. daily, up to a maximum dose of 2,000 mg P.O. once daily. If higher doses are needed, consider using the regular release formulation up to its maximum dose.

Contraindications and precautions

- Contraindicated in patients hypersensitive to drug and in those with renal disease or metabolic acidosis. Drug should be temporarily withheld in patients undergoing radiologic studies involving parenteral administration of iodinated contrast materials; using such products may result in acute renal dysfunction. Drug also should be stopped if patient enters hypoxic state. Metformin should be avoided in patients with hepatic disease.
- Use cautiously in debilitated or malnourished patients and those with adrenal or pituitary insufficiency because of increased risk of hypoglycemia.

Lifespan: In pregnant women, safety hasn't been established. In breast-feeding women, drug isn't recommended. In children, safety hasn't been established. In elderly patients, use cautiously.

Adverse reactions

GI: diarrhea, nausea, vomiting, abdominal bloating, flatulence, anorexia, unpleasant or metallic taste.
Hematologic: megaloblastic anemia.
Metabolic: ***lactic acidosis.***
Skin: rash, dermatitis.

Interactions

Drug-drug. *Calcium channel blockers, corticosteroids, estrogens, isoniazid, nicotinic acid, oral contraceptives, phenothiazines, phenytoin, sympathomimetics, thiazide and other diuretics, thyroid agents:* May produce hyperglycemia. Monitor patient's glycemic control. Metformin dosage may need to be increased.
Cationic drugs (such as amiloride, cimetidine, digoxin, morphine, procainamide, quinidine, quinine, ranitidine, triamterene, trimethoprim, vancomycin): May compete for common renal tubular transport systems, which may increase plasma metformin levels. Monitor patient's glucose level.
Furosemide, nifedipine: Increases metformin levels. Monitor patient. Metformin dosage may need to be decreased.
Iodinated contrast material: Parenteral contrast studies with iodinated materials have been linked to lactic acidosis leading to acute renal failure. Withhold metformin on or before the day of the study, and resume after 48 hours, provided renal function is within normal limits.
Drug-herb. *Aloe, bilberry leaf, bitter melon, burdock, dandelion, fenugreek, garlic, ginseng:* Improved glucose control may allow reduction of antidiabetic. Tell patient to discuss use of herbal remedies with prescriber before therapy.
Drug-lifestyle. *Alcohol use:* May potentiate drug effects. Discourage using together.

Effects on lab test results

- May decrease pH and bicarbonate levels.
- May decrease hemoglobin, hematocrit, and RBC count.

Pharmacokinetics

Absorption: Absorbed from GI tract, with food decreasing extent of absorption as well as slightly delaying absorption.
Distribution: Only negligibly bound to plasma proteins in contrast to sulfonylureas, which are more than 90% protein-bound.
Metabolism: Not metabolized.

Excretion: Excreted unchanged in urine. *Plasma half-life:* About 6.2 hours.

Route	Onset	Peak	Duration
P.O.	Unknown	Unknown	Unknown
P.O. (extended release)	Unknown	4-8 hrs	Unknown

Pharmacodynamics

Chemical effect: Decreases hepatic glucose production and intestinal absorption of glucose and improves insulin sensitivity (increases peripheral glucose uptake and utilization).
Therapeutic effect: Lowers glucose level.

Available forms

Tablets: 500 mg, 850 mg, 1,000 mg
Tablets (extended-release): 500 mg

NURSING PROCESS

Assessment

- Assess patient's glucose level before therapy and regularly thereafter.
- Before beginning therapy, assess patient's kidney function, and then reassess at least annually. If renal impairment is detected, expect prescriber to switch to different antidiabetic agent.
- Monitor patient's hematologic status for megaloblastic anemia. Patients with inadequate vitamin B_{12} or calcium intake or absorption seem predisposed to developing subnormal vitamin B_{12} levels when taking metformin. They should have serum vitamin B_{12} level determinations every 2 to 3 years.
- Be alert for adverse reactions and drug interactions.
- Monitor patient closely during times of increased stress, such as infection, fever, surgery, or trauma; insulin therapy may be needed.
- Risk of metformin-induced lactic acidosis is very low. Cases have been reported primarily in diabetic patients with significant renal insufficiency; with other medical or surgical problems; and with multiple, concomitant drug regimens. The risk of lactic acidosis increases with the degree of renal impairment and patient's age.
- Evaluate patient's and family's knowledge of drug therapy.

Nursing diagnoses

- Ineffective health maintenance related to presence of hyperglycemia
- Risk for deficient fluid volume related to drug-induced adverse GI reactions
- Deficient knowledge related to drug therapy

Planning and implementation

- When switching from standard oral antidiabetic (except chlorpropamide) to metformin, no transition period usually is needed. When switching patient from chlorpropamide to metformin, use care during first 2 weeks of metformin therapy because prolonged retention of chlorpropamide increases risk of hypoglycemia during this time.
- Notify prescriber if glucose level rises despite therapy.
- If patient hasn't responded to 4 weeks of therapy using maximum dosage, prescriber may add oral sulfonylurea while continuing metformin at maximum dosage. If patient still doesn't respond after several months, prescriber may stop both drugs and start insulin therapy.

ALERT: If patient develops conditions linked to hypoxemia or dehydration, stop drug immediately and notify prescriber because of risk of lactic acidosis.

- Metformin therapy may be temporarily suspended for surgical procedure (except minor procedures not related to restricted intake of food and fluids) and not restarted until patient's oral intake has resumed and kidney function is normal.

Patient teaching

- Tell patient to take once-daily dose with breakfast and twice-daily dose with breakfast and dinner.
- Instruct patient to stop drug and tell prescriber about unexplained hyperventilation, myalgia, malaise, unusual somnolence, or other symptoms of early lactic acidosis.
- Warn patient to minimize alcohol consumption while taking drug.

ALERT: Teach patient about diabetes and the importance of following therapeutic regimen; adhering to diet, weight reduction, exercise, and hygiene programs; and avoiding infection. Explain how and when to monitor glucose level and how to differentiate between hypoglycemia and hyperglycemia.

• Tell patient not to change dosage without prescriber's consent. Encourage patient to report abnormal glucose test results.
• Advise patient not to take other drugs, including OTC drugs, without checking with prescriber.
• Instruct patient to wear or carry medical identification.

☑ Evaluation

• Patient's glucose level is normal.
• Patient maintains adequate hydration throughout therapy.
• Patient and family state understanding of drug therapy.

methadone hydrochloride

(METH-eh-dohn high-droh-KLOR-ighd)
Dolophine, Methadose, Physeptone ◇

Pharmacologic class: opioid
Therapeutic class: analgesic, narcotic detoxification adjunct
Pregnancy risk category: C
Controlled substance schedule: II

Indications and dosages

▶ **Severe pain.** *Adults:* 2.5 to 10 mg P.O., I.M., or S.C. q 3 to 4 hours, p.r.n.
Children‡: 0.7 mg/kg P.O. q 4 to 6 hours.
▶ **Narcotic withdrawal syndrome.** *Adults:* 15 to 20 mg P.O. daily (highly individualized). Maintenance dosage is 20 to 120 mg P.O. daily. Dosage adjusted as needed. Daily doses greater than 120 mg require state and federal approval.

Contraindications and precautions

• Contraindicated in patients hypersensitive to drug.
• Use with extreme caution in patients with acute abdominal conditions, severe hepatic or renal impairment, hypothyroidism, Addison's disease, prostatic hyperplasia, urethral stricture, head injury, increased intracranial pressure, asthma, or other respiratory conditions.
• Use cautiously in debilitated patients.
Lifespan: In pregnant or breast-feeding women, use cautiously. In children, safety of drug hasn't been established. In elderly patients, use cautiously.

Adverse reactions

CNS: *sedation, somnolence, clouded sensorium, euphoria,* dizziness, chorea, ***seizures.***
CV: *hypotension,* ***bradycardia, shock, cardiac arrest, arrhythmias.***
EENT: visual disturbances.
GI: *nausea, vomiting, constipation,* ileus.
GU: *urine retention.*
Respiratory: ***respiratory depression, respiratory arrest.***
Skin: pain at injection site, tissue irritation, induration after S.C. injection, diaphoresis.
Other: decreased libido, physical dependence.

Interactions

Drug-drug. *Ammonium chloride and other urine acidifiers, phenytoin:* May reduce methadone effect. Monitor patient for decreased pain control.
CNS depressants, general anesthetics, hypnotics, MAO inhibitors, sedatives, tranquilizers, tricyclic antidepressants: Possible respiratory depression, hypotension, profound sedation, or coma. Use together cautiously. Monitor patient.
Rifampin: May cause withdrawal symptoms; reduces blood levels of methadone. Use together cautiously.
Drug-lifestyle. *Alcohol use:* May have additive effects. Discourage patient from using together.

Effects on lab test results

• May increase amylase level.

Pharmacokinetics

Absorption: Well absorbed from GI tract; unknown for I.M. route.
Distribution: Highly bound to tissue protein.
Metabolism: Metabolized primarily in liver.
Excretion: Excreted primarily in urine; metabolites excreted in feces. *Half-life:* 15 to 25 hours.

Route	Onset	Peak	Duration
P.O.	30-60 min	1.5-2 hr	4-6 hr
I.M.	10-20 min	1-2 hr	4-5 hr
S.C.	Unknown	Unknown	Unknown

Pharmacodynamics

Chemical effect: Binds with opioid receptors at many sites in CNS, altering both perception of and emotional response to pain through unknown mechanism.
Therapeutic effect: Relieves pain and symptoms of opioid withdrawal.

Available forms

Dispersible tablets (for methadone maintenance therapy): 40 mg
Injection: 10 mg/ml
Oral solution: 5 mg/5 ml, 10 mg/5 ml, 10 mg/ml (concentrate)
Tablets: 5 mg, 10 mg

NURSING PROCESS

Assessment

- Assess patient's pain or opioid dependence before and during therapy.
- Monitor patient closely because drug has cumulative effect; marked sedation can occur after repeated doses.
- Be alert for adverse reactions and drug interactions.
- Evaluate patient's and family's knowledge of drug therapy.

Nursing diagnoses

- Chronic pain related to underlying condition
- Ineffective individual coping related to opioid dependence
- Deficient knowledge related to drug therapy

Planning and implementation

- **P.O. use:** Liquid form is legally required in maintenance programs. Dissolve tablets in 120 ml of orange juice or powdered citrus drink.
  – P.O. dose is one-half as potent as injected dose.
- **I.M. and S.C. use:** For parenteral use, I.M. injection is preferred. Rotate injection sites.
- Around-the-clock regimen is needed to manage severe, chronic pain.

ALERT: Very high doses of methadone may cause QT interval prolongation and torsades de pointe.

Patient teaching

- Caution patient about getting out of bed or walking. Warn outpatient to avoid hazardous activities until drug's CNS effects are known.
- Instruct patient to avoid alcohol consumption during drug therapy.

Evaluation

- Patient is free from pain.
- Patient doesn't exhibit opioid withdrawal symptoms.
- Patient and family state understanding of drug therapy.

methamphetamine hydrochloride

(meth-am-FET-uh-meen high-droh-KLOR-ighd)
Desoxyn

Pharmacologic class: amphetamine
Therapeutic class: CNS stimulant, short-term adjunct anorexigenic, sympathomimetic amine
Pregnancy risk category: C
Controlled substance schedule: II

Indications and dosages

▶ **Attention deficit hyperactivity disorder.** *Children age 6 and older:* Initially, 5 mg P.O. once daily or b.i.d., with 5-mg increments weekly, p.r.n. Usual effective dosage is 20 to 25 mg daily.

▶ **Short-term adjunct in exogenous obesity.** *Adults:* 2.5 to 5 mg P.O. b.i.d. to t.i.d. 30 minutes before meals. Or, 10 to 15 mg of long-acting tablet P.O. once daily in the morning.

Contraindications and precautions

- Contraindicated in patients hypersensitive to sympathomimetic amines; patients with idiosyncratic reactions to sympathomimetic amines; patients with moderate to severe hypertension, hyperthyroidism, symptomatic CV disease, advanced arteriosclerosis, glaucoma, or history of drug abuse; patients who have taken an MAO inhibitor within 14 days; and agitated patients.
- Use cautiously in patients who are debilitated, asthenic, or psychopathic or who have history of suicidal or homicidal tendencies.

Lifespan: In pregnant women, don't use. In breast-feeding women, safety of drug hasn't been established. In elderly patients, use cautiously.

Adverse reactions

CNS: *nervousness, insomnia,* irritability, *talkativeness,* dizziness, headache, hyperexcitability, tremors.
CV: hypertension, hypotension, *tachycardia, palpitations,* ***arrhythmias.***
EENT: blurred vision, mydriasis.
GI: metallic taste, dry mouth, nausea, vomiting, abdominal cramps, diarrhea, constipation, anorexia.

GU: impotence.
Skin: urticaria.
Other: altered libido.

Interactions

Drug-drug. *Acetazolamide, antacids, sodium bicarbonate:* Increases renal reabsorption. Monitor patient for enhanced effects.
Ammonium chloride, ascorbic acid: Decreases level and increases renal excretion of methamphetamine. Monitor patient for decreased methamphetamine effects.
Guanethidine: Amphetamines may decrease the antihypertensive effectiveness of guanethidine. Monitor blood pressure.
Haloperidol, phenothiazines, tricyclic antidepressants: Increases CNS effects. Avoid using together.
Insulin, oral antidiabetics: May decrease antidiabetic requirement. Monitor glucose level.
MAO inhibitors: May cause severe hypertension; possible hypertensive crisis. Don't use within 14 days of MAO inhibitor therapy.
Drug-herb. *Melatonin:* Enhances monoaminergic effects of methamphetamine; may worsen insomnia. Discourage using together.
Drug-food. *Caffeine-containing beverages:* May increase amphetamine and related amine effects. Discourage using together.

Effects on lab test results

- May increase corticosteroid level.

Pharmacokinetics

Absorption: Rapid.
Distribution: Widely distributed.
Metabolism: Metabolized in liver to at least seven metabolites.
Excretion: Excreted in urine. *Half-life:* 4 to 5 hours.

Route	Onset	Peak	Duration
P.O.	Unknown	Unknown	≤ 24 hr

Pharmacodynamics

Chemical effect: Unknown; probably promotes nerve impulse transmission by releasing stored norepinephrine from nerve terminals in brain. Main sites of activity appear to be cerebral cortex and reticular activating system. In hyperkinetic children, drug has paradoxical calming effect.
Therapeutic effect: Promotes calmness in children with attention deficit disorder and causes weight loss.

Available forms

Tablets: 5 mg

NURSING PROCESS

Assessment

- Assess patient's condition before therapy and regularly thereafter.
- Be alert for adverse reactions and drug interactions.
- Evaluate patient's and family's knowledge of drug therapy.

Nursing diagnoses

- Ineffective health maintenance related to underlying condition
- Disturbed sleep pattern related to drug-induced insomnia
- Deficient knowledge related to drug therapy

Planning and implementation

ALERT: Don't confuse Desoxyn with digitoxin or digoxin.

- Drug isn't the first-line treatment for obesity. Use as anorexigenic is prohibited in some states.
- When used for obesity, make sure patient is on weight-reduction program.
- If tolerance to anorexigenic effect develops, notify prescriber because drug will need to be discontinued.

Patient teaching

- Warn patient of high potential for abuse. Advise him that drug shouldn't be used to prevent fatigue.
- Advise patient to take last dose of drug at least 6 hours before bedtime.
- Warn patient to avoid activities that require alertness or good coordination until CNS effects are known.
- Tell patient to avoid caffeine during drug therapy.
- Instruct patient to report signs of excessive stimulation.
- Instruct patient not to crush long-acting tablets.

Evaluation
• Patient exhibits positive response to methamphetamine therapy.
• Patient doesn't experience insomnia.
• Patient and family state understanding of drug therapy.

methimazole
(meth-IH-muh-zohl)
Tapazole

Pharmacologic class: thyroid hormone antagonist
Therapeutic class: antihyperthyroid agent
Pregnancy risk category: D

Indications and dosages
▶ **Hyperthyroidism.** *Adults:* If mild, 15 mg P.O. daily. If moderately severe, 30 to 40 mg daily. If severe, 60 mg daily. Daily dose divided into three doses at 8-hour intervals. Maintenance dosage is 5 to 15 mg daily.
Children: 0.4 mg/kg P.O. daily in divided doses q 8 hours. Maintenance dosage is 0.2 mg/kg P.O. daily in divided doses q 8 hours.

Contraindications and precautions
• Contraindicated in patients hypersensitive to drug.
Lifespan: In pregnant women, use with extreme caution. For breast-feeding women, drug isn't recommended.

Adverse reactions
CNS: headache, drowsiness, vertigo.
GI: diarrhea, nausea, vomiting, salivary gland enlargement, loss of taste.
Hematologic: ***agranulocytosis, leukopenia, thrombocytopenia, aplastic anemia.***
Hepatic: jaundice.
Metabolic: hypothyroidism.
Musculoskeletal: arthralgia, myalgia.
Skin: rash, urticaria, skin discoloration.
Other: drug-induced fever, lymphadenopathy.

Interactions
Drug-drug. *Anticoagulants:* Enhances effects from anti-vitamin K activity attributed to drug. Monitor PT and INR as indicated.

Effects on lab test results
• May decrease hemoglobin, hematocrit, and granulocyte, WBC, RBC, and platelet counts.

Pharmacokinetics
Absorption: Rapid.
Distribution: Concentrated in thyroid and isn't protein-bound.
Metabolism: Hepatic.
Excretion: Primarily in urine. *Half-life:* 5 to 13 hours.

Route	Onset	Peak	Duration
P.O.	≤ 5 days	30 min-1 hr	Unknown

Pharmacodynamics
Chemical effect: Inhibits oxidation of iodine in thyroid gland, blocking iodine's ability to combine with tyrosine to form T_4. Also may prevent coupling of monoiodotyrosine and diiodotyrosine to form T_4 and T_3.
Therapeutic effect: Reduces thyroid hormone level.

Available forms
Tablets: 5 mg, 10 mg

NURSING PROCESS

Assessment
• Assess patient's thyroid condition before therapy and regularly thereafter.
• Monitor thyroid function studies.
• Monitor CBC and liver function periodically.
ALERT: Dosages higher than 30 mg daily increase risk of agranulocytosis, especially in patients older than age 40.
• Be alert for adverse reactions.
• Evaluate patient's and family's knowledge of drug therapy.

Nursing diagnoses
• Ineffective health maintenance related to presence of hyperthyroidism
• Ineffective immune protection related to drug-induced adverse hematologic reactions
• Deficient knowledge related to drug therapy

Planning and implementation
• Pregnant women may need reduced dose as pregnancy progresses. Thyroid hormone may be added. Drug may be stopped during last weeks of pregnancy.

• Notify prescriber about signs and symptoms of hypothyroidism because dosage may need to be adjusted.

ALERT: Stop drug and notify prescriber if severe rash occurs or cervical lymph nodes become enlarged.

ALERT: Don't confuse methimazole with mebendazole or methazolamide.

Patient teaching

• Tell patient to take drug with meals.
• Warn patient to immediately report fever, sore throat, or mouth sores (signs of agranulocytosis); skin eruptions (sign of hypersensitivity); and anorexia, pruritus, right upper quadrant pain, and yellow skin or sclera (signs of hepatic dysfunction).
• Tell patient to ask prescriber about using iodized salt and eating shellfish.
• Warn patient against taking OTC cough medications; many contain iodine.
• Instruct patient to store drug in light-resistant container.

Evaluation

• Patient has normal thyroid hormone level.
• Patient maintains normal hematologic parameters throughout therapy.
• Patient and family state understanding of drug therapy.

methocarbamol

(meth-oh-KAR-buh-mol)
Robaxin, Robaxin-750

Pharmacologic class: carbamate derivative of guaifenesin
Therapeutic class: skeletal muscle relaxant
Pregnancy risk category: NR

Indications and dosages

▶ **As adjunct in acute, painful musculoskeletal conditions.** *Adults:* 1.5 g P.O. q.i.d. for 2 to 3 days; then 1 g P.O. q.i.d., or not more than 500 mg (5 ml) I.M. into each buttock. Repeat q 8 hours, p.r.n. Or, 1 to 3 g daily (10 to 30 ml) I.V. directly into vein at 3 ml/minute, or 10 ml may be added to no more than 250 ml of D_5W or normal saline solution. Maximum dosage is 3 g daily I.M. or I.V. for 3 consecutive days.

▶ **Supportive therapy in tetanus management.** *Adults:* 1 to 2 g by direct I.V., or 1 to 3 g as infusion q 6 hours.
Children: 15 mg/kg or 500 mg/m^2 I.V. q 6 hours.

Contraindications and precautions

• Contraindicated in patients hypersensitive to drug and in those with impaired kidney function or seizure disorder (injectable form).

Lifespan: In pregnant women, use cautiously. In breast-feeding women, drug isn't recommended.

Adverse reactions

CNS: drowsiness, dizziness, light-headedness, headache, syncope, fever, mild muscle incoordination with I.M. or I.V. use, ***seizures*** with I.V. use.
CV: hypotension, ***bradycardia*** with I.M. or I.V. use, thrombophlebitis, flushing.
GI: nausea, anorexia, GI upset, metallic taste.
GU: hematuria with I.V. use, discoloration of urine.
Hematologic: hemolysis.
Skin: urticaria, pruritus, rash.
Other: extravasation with I.V. use, ***anaphylaxis*** with I.M. or I.V. use.

Interactions

Drug-drug. *CNS depressants:* Increases CNS depression. Avoid using together.
Drug-lifestyle. *Alcohol use:* Increases CNS depression. Discourage using together.

Effects on lab test results

• May decrease hemoglobin and hematocrit (with I.V. use).

Pharmacokinetics

Absorption: Rapid and complete after P.O. administration; unknown after I.M. administration.
Distribution: Widely distributed throughout body.
Metabolism: Extensively metabolized in liver.
Excretion: Excreted primarily in urine. *Half-life:* 0.9 to 2.2 hours.

Route	Onset	Peak	Duration
P.O.	≤ 30 min	≤ 2 hr	Unknown
I.V.	Immediate	Immediate	Unknown
I.M.	Unknown	Unknown	Unknown

Pharmacodynamics

Chemical effect: Unknown; probably modifies central perception of pain without modifying pain reflexes.
Therapeutic effect: Relieves skeletal muscle pain.

Available forms

Injection: 100 mg/ml
Tablets: 500 mg, 750 mg

NURSING PROCESS

Assessment

• Assess patient's condition before therapy and regularly thereafter.
• Watch for orthostatic hypotension, especially with parenteral route.
• Monitor CBC periodically during prolonged therapy.
• Be alert for adverse reactions and drug interactions.
• Monitor patient's hydration status if adverse GI reactions occur.
• Evaluate patient's and family's knowledge of drug therapy.

Nursing diagnoses

• Acute pain related to underlying musculoskeletal condition
• Risk for deficient fluid volume related to drug-induced adverse GI reactions
• Deficient knowledge related to drug therapy

Planning and implementation

• **P.O. use:** Give tablets with meals or milk.
– Prepare liquid by crushing tablets into water or saline solution. Give through NG tube.
• **I.V. use:** Dilute 10 ml of drug in no more than 250 ml of D_5W or normal saline solution injection. Infuse slowly; maximum rate is 300 mg (3 ml)/minute.
– Drug irritates veins; may cause phlebitis and fainting and aggravate seizures if injected rapidly. Keep patient supine during infusion and for 15 minutes afterward. Drug is an irritant. Watch for irritation and infiltration; extravasation can cause tissue damage and necrosis.
• **I.M. use:** Give drug I.M. deep into upper outer quadrant of buttocks, with maximum of 5 ml in each buttock.
ALERT: Don't give drug S.C.
• For tetanus, methocarbamol is used with tetanus antitoxin, penicillin, tracheotomy, and aggressive supportive care. Long course of I.V. methocarbamol therapy is needed.
• Have epinephrine, antihistamines, and corticosteroids available.
• Drug may interfere with urine tests to determine 5-hydroxyindoleacetic acid and vanillylmandelic acid levels.
ALERT: Don't confuse methocarbamol with mephobarbital.

Patient teaching

• Advise patient to get up slowly after parenteral administration.
• Tell patient that urine may turn green, black, or brown.
• Advise patient to follow prescriber's orders regarding physical activity.
• Warn patient to avoid activities that require alertness until drug's CNS effects are known.
• Tell patient not to combine drug with alcohol or other CNS depressants. Instruct patient to avoid alcohol consumption during drug therapy.

Evaluation

• Patient is free from pain.
• Patient maintains adequate hydration throughout therapy.
• Patient and family state understanding of drug therapy.

methotrexate (amethopterin, MTX)

(meth-oh-TREKS-ayt)
Trexall

methotrexate sodium

Methotrexate LPF, Rheumatrex Dose Pack

Pharmacologic class: antimetabolite (cell cycle–phase specific, S phase)
Therapeutic class: antineoplastic
Pregnancy risk category: X

Indications and dosages

▶ **Trophoblastic tumors (choriocarcinoma, hydatidiform mole).** *Adults:* 15 to 30 mg P.O. or I.M. daily for 5 days. Repeat course after

1 or more weeks, based on response or toxicity. 3 to 5 courses usually are used.

▶ **Acute lymphoblastic and lymphatic leukemia.** *Adults and children:* 3.3 mg/m^2 P.O. or I.M. daily for 4 to 6 weeks or until remission occurs; then 20 to 30 mg/m^2 P.O. or I.M. twice weekly. Or, 2.5 mg/kg I.V. q 14 days.

▶ **Meningeal leukemia.** *Adults and adolescents older than age 12:* 12 mg/m^2 intrathecally, or an empirical dose of 15 mg q 2 to 5 days and repeat until cell count of CSF returns to normal, then give one additional dose. Or, 12 mg/m^2 once weekly for 2 weeks, then once monthly thereafter.

▶ **Burkitt's lymphoma (stage I or stage II).** *Adults:* 10 to 25 mg P.O. daily for 4 to 8 days with 1-week rest intervals.

▶ **Lymphosarcoma (stage III).** *Adults:* 0.625 to 2.5 mg/kg P.O., I.M., or I.V. daily.

▶ **Osteosarcoma.** *Adults:* Initially, 12 g/m^2 I.V. as 4-hour infusion. Subsequent doses 12 to 15 g/m^2 I.V. as 4-hour infusion given weeks 4, 5, 6, 7, 11, 12, 15, 16, 29, 30, 44, and 45 after surgery. Give with leucovorin, 15 mg P.O. q 6 hours for 10 doses after start of methotrexate infusion.

▶ **Mycosis fungoides.** *Adults:* 2.5 to 10 mg P.O. daily, or 50 mg I.M. weekly, or 25 mg I.M. twice weekly.

▶ **Psoriasis.** *Adults:* 10 to 25 mg P.O., I.M., or I.V. as single weekly dose.

▶ **Rheumatoid arthritis.** *Adults:* Initially, 7.5 mg P.O. once weekly, or divided as 2.5 mg P.O. q 12 hours for three doses once a week. Dosage may be gradually increased to maximum of 20 mg weekly.

Adults‡: 7.5 to 15 mg I.M. once weekly.

▶ **Head and neck carcinoma‡.** *Adults:* 40 to 60 mg/m^2 I.V. once weekly. Response to therapy is limited to 4 months.

Contraindications and precautions

• Contraindicated in patients hypersensitive to drug; and in those with psoriasis or rheumatoid arthritis who also have alcoholism, alcoholic liver, chronic liver disease, immunodeficiency syndromes, or blood dyscrasias.

• Use cautiously and at modified dosage in patients with impaired liver or kidney function, bone marrow suppression, aplasia, leukopenia, thrombocytopenia, or anemia. Also use cautiously in patients with infection, peptic ulceration, or ulcerative colitis and in debilitated patients.

Lifespan: In pregnant or breast-feeding women, use is contraindicated. In very young and in very elderly patients, use cautiously.

Adverse reactions

CNS: ***arachnoiditis*** (within hours of intrathecal use), subacute neurotoxicity (may begin few weeks later), demyelination, ***leukoencephalopathy.***

EENT: pharyngitis.

GI: *stomatitis, diarrhea,* enteritis, ***intestinal perforation,*** *nausea, vomiting.*

GU: nephropathy, *tubular necrosis,* ***renal failure.***

Hematologic: WBC and platelet count nadirs on day 7, ***anemia, leukopenia, thrombocytopenia.***

Hepatic: ***acute toxicity, chronic toxicity, cirrhosis, hepatic fibrosis.***

Metabolic: hyperuricemia.

Musculoskeletal: osteoporosis in children with long-term use.

Respiratory: ***pulmonary fibrosis, pulmonary interstitial infiltrates,*** pneumonitis.

Skin: *urticaria,* pruritus, alopecia, hyperpigmentation, psoriatic lesions, rash, photosensitivity reactions.

Other: ***sudden death.***

Interactions

Drug-drug. *Digoxin:* May decrease digoxin level. Monitor patient closely.

Folic acid derivatives: Antagonizes methotrexate effect. Monitor patient.

NSAIDs, phenylbutazone, probenecid, salicylates, sulfonamides: Increases methotrexate toxicity. Don't use together.

Phenytoin: May decrease phenytoin level. Monitor patient.

Procarbazine: May increase hepatotoxicity of methotrexate. Monitor liver function closely.

Vaccines: Immunizations may be ineffective; may increase risk of disseminated infection with live-virus vaccines. Consult with prescriber about safe time to give vaccine.

Drug-lifestyle. *Alcohol use:* May increase hepatotoxicity. Discourage using together.

Sun exposure: Photosensitivity reactions may occur. Urge patient to avoid unprotected or prolonged exposure to sunlight.

Drug-food. *Food:* Delays drug absorption and reduces peak levels of methotrexate. Take on empty stomach.

Effects on lab test results

- May increase uric acid, BUN, creatinine, and liver enzyme levels.
- May decrease hemoglobin, hematocrit, and WBC, RBC, and platelet counts.

Pharmacokinetics

Absorption: Smaller P.O. doses are almost completely absorbed, but absorption of larger doses is incomplete and variable. I.M. doses are absorbed completely.
Distribution: Distributed widely throughout body with highest levels in kidneys, gallbladder, spleen, liver, and skin; about 50% bound to plasma protein.
Metabolism: Metabolized only slightly in liver.
Excretion: Excreted primarily in urine. *Half-life:* 4 hours. *Terminal half-life:* About 3 to 10 hours for patients receiving low-dose antineoplastic therapy (below 30 mg/m^2). For patients receiving high doses, the terminal half-life is 8 to 15 hours.

Route	Onset	Peak	Duration
P.O.	Unknown	1-2 hr	Unknown
I.V., intrathecal	Unknown	Immediate	Unknown
I.M.	Unknown	30 min-1 hr	Unknown

Pharmacodynamics

Chemical effect: Prevents reduction of folic acid to tetrahydrofolate by binding to dihydrofolate reductase.
Therapeutic effect: Kills certain cancer cells and reduces inflammation.

Available forms

Injection: 20-mg, 25-mg, 50-mg, and 1-g vials, lyophilized powder, preservative-free; 25-mg/ml vials, preservative-free solution; 2.5-mg/ml and 25-mg/ml vials, lyophilized powder, preserved
Tablets (scored): 2.5 mg

NURSING PROCESS

Assessment

- Assess patient's condition before therapy and regularly thereafter.
- Perform baseline pulmonary function tests and repeat periodically.
- Monitor fluid intake and output daily.
- Monitor uric acid level.
- Watch for increases in AST, ALT, and alkaline phosphatase levels—signs of hepatic dysfunction.
- Monitor CBC regularly.
- Be alert for adverse reactions and drug interactions.
- Evaluate patient's and family's knowledge of drug therapy.

Nursing diagnoses

- Ineffective health maintenance related to underlying condition
- Ineffective immune protection related to drug-induced adverse hematologic reactions
- Deficient knowledge related to drug therapy

Planning and implementation

- **P.O. use:** Follow normal protocol.
- **I.V. use:** Give undiluted by direct injection. Or, dilute with D_5W or normal saline solution. Dilute 20 and 50 ml vials to a maximum of 25 mg/ml and for 1 g vials, maximum of 50 mg/ml.
- Drug may be given daily or weekly, depending on the disease. Be aware of disease process and protocol to avoid medication errors.
- **I.M. use:** Follow normal protocol.
- **Intrathecal use:** Use only 20-, 50-, or 100-mg vials of powder with no preservatives. Reconstitute immediately before using with preservative-free normal saline solution injection. Dilute to maximum of 1 mg/ml. Use only new vials of drug and diluent.
- Follow facility policy to reduce risks. Preparation and administration of parenteral forms are linked to carcinogenic, mutagenic, and teratogenic risks.
- Reconstitute solutions without preservatives immediately before use, and discard unused drug.
- CSF volume depends on age, not body surface area (BSA). Using BSA for dosing when treating meningeal leukemia has resulted in low CSF methotrexate level in children and high level and neurotoxicity in adults. Or, a dosing regimen based on age may be used. Elderly patients may require a reduced dosage because CSF volume and turnover may decrease with age.

• Have patient drink 2 to 3 L of fluids daily.
ALERT: Alkalinize urine by giving sodium bicarbonate tablets to prevent precipitation of drug, especially with high doses. Maintain urine pH at more than 6.5. Reduce dosage if BUN level reaches 20 to 30 mg/dl or creatinine level reaches 1.2 to 2 mg/dl. Report BUN level over 30 mg/dl or creatinine level over 2 mg/dl, and stop drug.
• Rash, redness, or ulcerations in mouth or adverse pulmonary reactions may signal serious complications. Therapy may be discontinued if ulcerative stomatitis or other severe adverse GI reaction occurs or if pulmonary toxicity is detected.
• Leucovorin rescue is used with high-dose (greater than 100 mg) protocols. This technique works against systemic toxicity but doesn't interfere with tumor cells' absorption of methotrexate.

Patient teaching
• Teach and encourage diligent mouth care to reduce risk of superinfection in mouth.
• Tell patient to take P.O. form on empty stomach.
• Warn patient to avoid prolonged exposure to sunlight, wear protective clothing, and use highly protective sunblock.
• Tell patient to continue leucovorin rescue despite severe nausea and vomiting and to tell prescriber. Parenteral leucovorin therapy may be needed.
• Warn patient to avoid becoming pregnant during and immediately after therapy because of risk of abortion or congenital anomalies.
• Instruct patient to avoid alcohol consumption during drug therapy.

Evaluation
• Patient exhibits positive response to drug therapy.
• Patient doesn't experience serious complications when hematologic parameters are depressed during therapy.
• Patient and family state understanding of drug therapy.

methylcellulose
(meth-il-SEL-yoo-lohs)
Citrucel†, Citrucel Sugar Free†

Pharmacologic class: adsorbent
Therapeutic class: bulk-forming laxative
Pregnancy risk category: NR

Indications and dosages
▶ **Chronic constipation.** *Adults:* 1 to 3 heaping tablespoons in 8 oz (240 ml) cold water daily to t.i.d. Usual dosage up to 6 g daily (3 tablespoons).
Children ages 6 to 12: 1 to 1½ level tablespoons in 4 oz (120 ml) cold water daily to t.i.d. Usual dosage up to 3 g daily (1½ tablespoons).

Contraindications and precautions
• Contraindicated in patients with abdominal pain, nausea, vomiting, or other symptoms of appendicitis or acute surgical abdomen and in those with intestinal obstruction or ulceration, disabling adhesions, or difficulty swallowing.
Lifespan: In pregnant or breast-feeding women, use cautiously.

Adverse reactions
GI: *nausea,* vomiting, and diarrhea with excessive use; esophageal, gastric, small intestinal, or colonic strictures when drug is chewed or taken in dry form; *abdominal cramps,* especially in severe constipation; laxative dependence with long-term or excessive use.

Interactions
None significant.

Effects on lab test results
None reported.

Pharmacokinetics
Absorption: Not absorbed.
Distribution: Distributed in intestine.
Metabolism: None.
Excretion: Excreted in feces.

Route	Onset	Peak	Duration
P.O.	12-24 hr	≤ 3 days	Varies

Pharmacodynamics

Chemical effect: Absorbs water and expands to increase bulk and moisture content of stool, which encourages peristalsis and bowel movement.

Therapeutic effect: Relieves constipation.

Available forms

Powder: 2 g/heaping tablespoon†

NURSING PROCESS

Assessment

- Assess patient's constipation before therapy and regularly thereafter.
- Before giving drug for constipation, determine whether patient has adequate fluid intake, exercise, and diet.
- Be alert for adverse reactions.
- Monitor patient's hydration status if adverse GI reactions occur.
- Evaluate patient's and family's knowledge of drug therapy.

Nursing diagnoses

- Constipation related to underlying condition
- Risk for deficient fluid volume related to drug-induced adverse GI reactions
- Deficient knowledge related to drug therapy

Planning and implementation

- Drug is especially useful in debilitated patients and in those with postpartum constipation, irritable bowel syndrome, diverticulitis, or colostomies. Drug is also used to treat laxative abuse and to empty colon before barium enema.

ALERT: Don't confuse Citrucel with Citracal.

Patient teaching

- Tell patient to take drug with at least 8 ounces of pleasant-tasting liquid.
- Teach patient about dietary sources of bulk, such as bran and other cereals, fresh fruit, and vegetables.

Evaluation

- Patient's constipation is relieved.
- Patient maintains adequate hydration throughout therapy.
- Patient and family state understanding of drug therapy.

methyldopa

(meth-il-DOH-puh)

Aldomet, Apo-Methyldopa ♦, Dopamet ♦, Hydopa ◇, Novomedopa ♦, Nu-Medopa ♦

methyldopate hydrochloride

Aldomet

Pharmacologic class: centrally acting antiadrenergic agent

Therapeutic class: antihypertensive

Pregnancy risk category: B (P.O.), C (I.V.)

Indications and dosages

▶ **Hypertension, hypertensive crisis.** *Adults:* Initially, 250 mg P.O. b.i.d. to t.i.d. in first 48 hours. Then increased as needed q 2 days. Entire daily dose may be given in evening or h.s. Adjust dosages, as needed, if other antihypertensives are added to or deleted from therapy. Maintenance dosage is 500 mg to 2 g daily in two to four divided doses. Maximum recommended daily dose is 3 g.

Adults: 250 to 500 mg I.V. q 6 hours, diluted in D_5W and given over 30 to 60 minutes. Maximum dosage is 1 g q 6 hours. Switch to P.O. antihypertensives as soon as possible.

Children: Initially, 10 mg/kg P.O. daily in two to four divided doses. Or, 20 to 40 mg/kg I.V. daily in four divided doses. Increase dosage at least q 2 days until desired response occurs. Maximum 65 mg/kg, 2 g/m^2, or 3 g daily, whichever is least.

Contraindications and precautions

- Contraindicated in patients hypersensitive to drug and in those with active hepatic disease (such as acute hepatitis) or active cirrhosis. Also contraindicated if previous methyldopa therapy has been linked to liver disorders.
- Use cautiously in patients with history of impaired liver function.

Lifespan: In breast-feeding women, use cautiously.

Adverse reactions

CNS: *sedation,* headache, asthenia, weakness, dizziness, *decreased mental acuity,* involuntary choreoathetoid movements, psychic disturbances, depression, nightmares.

CV: ***bradycardia,*** *orthostatic hypotension,* aggravated angina, ***myocarditis,*** *edema.*
EENT: *nasal congestion.*
GI: nausea, vomiting, diarrhea, ***pancreatitis,*** *dry mouth.*
GU: impotence.
Hematologic: hemolytic anemia, reversible agranulocytosis, ***thrombocytopenia.***
Hepatic: ***hepatic necrosis.***
Metabolic: *weight gain.*
Skin: rash.
Other: gynecomastia, galactorrhea, *drug-induced fever.*

Interactions

Drug-drug. *Amphetamines, norepinephrine, phenothiazines, tricyclic antidepressants:* Possible hypertensive effects. Monitor patient carefully.
Antihypertensives, diuretics: Increases hypotensive effects. Decreased methyldopa dosage may be needed.
Barbiturates: May reduce the action of methyldopa. Monitor patient.
Haloperidol: May produce dementia and sedation. Use together cautiously.
Levodopa: May have additive hypotensive effects and may increase adverse CNS reactions. Monitor patient closely.
Lithium: May increase lithium levels. Monitor patient for increased lithium levels and lithium toxicity.
Oral iron therapy: May increase hypotensive effects. Use together cautiously; monitor blood pressure.
Drug-herb. *Capsicum:* May reduce antihypertensive effectiveness. Discourage using together.
Yohimbe: May interfere with blood pressure. Discourage using together.

Effects on lab test results

- May increase creatinine level.
- May decrease hemoglobin, hematocrit, liver function test values, and granulocyte, platelet, RBC, and WBC counts.

Pharmacokinetics

Absorption: Partial.
Distribution: Distributed throughout body; bound weakly to plasma proteins.
Metabolism: Metabolized extensively in liver and intestinal cells.
Excretion: Absorbed drug excreted in urine; unabsorbed drug excreted in feces. *Half-life:* About 2 hours.

Route	Onset	Peak	Duration
P.O.	Unknown	4-6 hr	12-48 hr
I.V.	Unknown	4-6 hr	10-16 hr

Pharmacodynamics

Chemical effect: Unknown; thought to involve inhibition of central vasomotor centers, thereby decreasing sympathetic outflow to heart, kidneys, and peripheral vasculature.
Therapeutic effect: Lowers blood pressure.

Available forms

methyldopa
Oral suspension: 250 mg/5 ml
Tablets: 125 mg, 250 mg, 500 mg
methyldopate hydrochloride
Injection: 50 mg/ml in 5- and 10-mg vials

NURSING PROCESS

Assessment

- Assess patient's blood pressure before therapy and regularly thereafter.
- Monitor CBC with differential counts before therapy, every 2 weeks for first 3 months of therapy, and periodically thereafter.
- Monitor patient's Coombs' test results. In patient who has received this drug for several months, positive reaction to direct Coombs' test indicates hemolytic anemia.
- Be alert for adverse reactions and drug interactions.
- Evaluate patient's and family's knowledge of drug therapy.

Nursing diagnoses

- Ineffective health maintenance related to presence of hypertension
- Risk for injury related to drug-induced adverse CNS reactions
- Deficient knowledge related to drug therapy

Planning and implementation

- **I.V. use:** Report involuntary choreoathetoid movements; drug may be stopped.
- **P.O. use:** Follow normal protocol.
- After dialysis, notify prescriber if hypertension occurs; patient may need extra dose of methyldopa.

• Patient who needs blood transfusions should have direct and indirect Coombs' tests to prevent crossmatching problems.
ALERT: Don't confuse Aldomet with Aldoril or Anzemet.

Patient teaching
• Advise patient to report signs of infection, such as fever and sore throat.
• Tell patient to report adverse reactions but not to stop taking drug.
• Tell patient to check his weight daily and to report weight gain over 5 lb (2.27 kg). Diuretics can relieve sodium and water retention.
• Warn patient that drug may impair mental alertness, particularly at start of therapy. Once-daily dose at bedtime minimizes daytime drowsiness.
• Tell patient to rise slowly and avoid sudden position changes.
• Tell patient that dry mouth can be relieved with ice chips, sugarless gum, or hard candy.
• Advise patient that urine may turn dark in bleached toilet bowls.

☑ Evaluation
• Patient's blood pressure is normal.
• Patient doesn't experience injury as result of drug-induced adverse CNS reactions.
• Patient and family state understanding of drug therapy.

methylphenidate hydrochloride
(meth-il-FEN-ih-dayt high-droh-KLOR-ighd)
Concerta, Metadate CD, Metadate ER, Methylin, Methylin ER, Ritalin, Ritalin LA, Ritalin SR

Pharmacologic classification: piperidine CNS stimulant
Therapeutic classification: CNS stimulant (analeptic)
Pregnancy risk category: NR (Metadate ER, Methylin, Methylin ER, Ritalin, Ritalin SR); C (Concerta, Metadate CD, Ritalin LA)
Controlled substance schedule: II

Indications and dosages
▶ **Attention deficit hyperactivity disorder (ADHD).** ***Metadate ER, Methylin, Methylin ER, Ritalin, Ritalin SR.*** *Children age 6 and older:* Initially 5 mg P.O. daily before breakfast and lunch, increased in 5- to 10-mg increments weekly, p.r.n., until an optimum daily dose of 2 mg/kg is reached, not to exceed 60 mg/day. Ritalin SR, Metadate ER, and Methylin ER tablets may be used in place of methylphenidate tablets by calculating the dose of methylphenidate in intervals of 8 hours.
Concerta. *Children age 6 and older not currently on methylphenidate or for patients on stimulants other than methylphenidate:* 18 mg P.O. (extended-release) once daily in the morning. Adjust dosage by 18 mg at weekly intervals to a maximum of 54 mg P.O. once daily in the morning.
Children age 6 and older currently on methylphenidate: If the previous methylphenidate daily dose is 5 mg b.i.d. or t.i.d. or 20 mg sustained-release, the recommended dose of Concerta is 18 mg P.O. q morning. If the previous methylphenidate daily dose is 10 mg b.i.d. or t.i.d. or 40 mg sustained-release, the recommended dose of Concerta is 36 mg P.O. q morning. If the previous methylphenidate daily dose is 15 mg b.i.d. or t.i.d. or 60 mg sustained release, the recommended dose of Concerta is 54 mg P.O. q morning. Maximum daily dose is 54 mg.
Metadate CD. *Children age 6 and older:* Initially 20 mg P.O. daily before breakfast, increased in 20 mg increments weekly to a maximum of 60 mg daily.
Ritalin LA. *Children ages 6 and older:* 20 mg P.O. once daily. Adjust dosage in weekly 10-mg increments to a maximum of 60 mg daily. If the previous methylphenidate daily dose is 10 mg b.i.d. or 20 mg sustained-release, the recommended dose of Ritalin LA is 20 mg P.O. once daily. If the previous methylphenidate daily dose is 15 mg b.i.d., the recommended dose of Ritalin LA is 30 mg P.O. once daily. If the previous methylphenidate daily dose is 20 mg b.i.d. or 40 mg sustained-release, the recommended dose of Ritalin LA is 40 mg P.O. once daily. If the previous methylphenidate daily dose is 30 mg b.i.d. or 60 mg sustained-release, the recommended dose of Ritalin LA is 60 mg P.O. once daily.
▶ **Narcolepsy.** ***Metadate ER, Methylin, Methylin ER, Ritalin, Ritalin SR.*** *Adults:* 10 mg P.O. b.i.d. or t.i.d. 30 to 45 minutes before meals. Dosage varies with patient needs; average dose is 40 to 60 mg P.O. daily.

Ritalin SR, Metadate ER, and Methylin ER tablets may be used in place of methylphenidate tablets by calculating the dose of methylphenidate in intervals of 8 hours.

Contraindications and precautions

• Contraindicated in patients hypersensitive to drug and in those with glaucoma, motor tics, family history or diagnosis of Tourette syndrome, or history of marked anxiety, tension, or agitation. Ritalin, Ritalin SR, and Ritalin LA are contraindicated during treatment with monoamine oxidase (MAO) inhibitors, and also within a minimum of 14 days after discontinuation of a MAO inhibitor.
• Use cautiously in patients with hypertension, history of drug abuse, seizures, or EEG abnormalities.
Lifespan: In pregnant or breast-feeding women, use cautiously. In children younger than age 6, drug isn't recommended.

Adverse reactions

CNS: *nervousness, insomnia,* Tourette syndrome, dizziness, headache, akathisia, dyskinesia, ***seizures.***
CV: *palpitations,* angina, *tachycardia,* changes in blood pressure and pulse rate.
EENT: dry throat, pharyngitis and sinusitis (Concerta).
GI: vomiting; nausea, abdominal pain, and anorexia (Concerta).
Hematologic: ***thrombocytopenia,*** thrombocytopenic purpura, ***leukopenia.***
Metabolic: weight loss, delayed growth.
Respiratory: upper respiratory tract infection (Concerta), cough.
Skin: rash, urticaria, exfoliative dermatitis, ***erythema multiforme.***

Interactions

Drug-drug. *Anticonvulsants (phenytoin, phenobarbital, primidone):* Increases level of anticonvulsants. Patient may need dosage adjustment.
Centrally acting antihypertensives: Decreases antihypertensive effect. Monitor blood pressure.
Clonidine: Serious adverse events have been reported, although no causality for the combination has been established. The safety of using methylphenidate with clonidine or other centrally acting alpha-2 agonists has not been systemically evaluated.
MAO inhibitors: May cause severe hypertension; possible hypertensive crisis. Don't use together or within 14 days of MAO inhibitor therapy.
Tricyclic antidepressants: Increases levels of these drugs. Avoid using together.
Drug-food. *Caffeine:* May increase amphetamine and related amine effects. Discourage using together.

Effects on lab test results

• May decrease hemoglobin, hematocrit, and WBC and platelet counts.

Pharmacokinetics

Absorption: Absorbed rapidly and completely after oral administration. Ritalin LA has bimodal absorption (two distinct peaks).
Distribution: Unknown. Ritalin LA is 10% to 33% plasma protein bound.
Metabolism: Metabolized by the liver.
Excretion: Excreted in urine.

Route	Onset	Peak	Duration
P.O.			
Concerta	Unknown	6-8 hr	Unknown
Metadate CD	Unknown	1st peak 1.5 hr; 2nd peak 4.5 hr	Unknown
Methylin, Ritalin	Unknown	1.9 hr	Unknown
Methylin ER, Ritalin-SR	Unknown	4.7 hr	8 hr
Ritalin LA	Unknown	1st peak 1 to 3 hr; 2nd peak 4 to 7 hr	Unknown

Pharmacodynamics

Chemical effect: Unknown; probably promotes nerve impulse transmission by releasing stored norepinephrine from nerve terminals in brain. Main site of activity appears to be cerebral cortex and reticular activating system. In hyperkinetic children, drug has paradoxical calming effect.
Therapeutic effect: Promotes calmness and prevents sleep.

Available forms

Capsules: 20 mg
Capsules (extended-release): 20 mg, 30 mg, 40 mg
Tablets: 5 mg, 10 mg, 20 mg

Tablets (extended release): 10 mg, 18 mg, 20 mg, 27 mg, 36 mg, 54 mg
Tablets (sustained-release): 20 mg

NURSING PROCESS

Assessment
- Assess patient's condition before therapy and regularly thereafter.
- Drug may precipitate Tourette syndrome in children. Monitor effects, especially at start of therapy.
- Observe patient for signs of excessive stimulation. Monitor blood pressure.
- Monitor results of periodic CBC, differential, and platelet counts with long-term use.
- Monitor height and weight in child receiving prolonged therapy. Drug may delay growth, but child will attain normal height when drug is stopped.

ALERT: Chronic abuse can lead to marked tolerance and psychic dependence. Careful supervision is needed. Monitor patient for tolerance or psychological dependence.
- Be alert for adverse reactions and drug interactions.
- Evaluate patient's and family's knowledge of drug therapy.

Nursing diagnoses
- Ineffective health maintenance related to underlying condition
- Disturbed sleep pattern related to drug-induced insomnia
- Deficient knowledge related to drug therapy

Planning and implementation
- This is drug of choice for ADHD. It's usually discontinued after puberty.
- Drug shouldn't be used to prevent fatigue.
- Metadate CD may be swallowed whole, or the contents of the capsule may be sprinkled onto a small amount of applesauce and given immediately.
- Give at least 6 hours before bedtime to prevent insomnia. Give after meals to reduce appetite suppression.
- Ritalin SR tablets have a duration of about 8 hours and may be used in place of regular tablets when 8-hour dosage of SR tablets corresponds to the adjusted dosage of the regular tablets.

ALERT: Don't confuse Ritalin with Rifadin.

Patient teaching
- Tell patient to swallow Ritalin SR and Concerta tablets whole and not to chew or crush them. Metadate CD may be swallowed whole, or the contents of the capsule may be sprinkled onto a small amount of applesauce and given immediately.
- Caution patient to avoid activities that require alertness until CNS effects of drug are known.
- Tell patient to avoid caffeine.
- Advise patient with seizure disorder to notify prescriber if seizure occurs.
- Inform patient that he will need more rest as drug effects wear off.
- Warn patient that the shell of the Concerta tablet may appear in the stool.

Evaluation
- Patient responds positively to drug therapy.
- Patient doesn't experience insomnia during therapy.
- Patient and family state understanding of drug therapy.

methylprednisolone
(meth-il-pred-NIS-uh-lohn)
Medrol**, Meprolone

methylprednisolone acetate
depMedalone 40, depMedalone 80, Depoject-40, Depoject-80, Depo-Medrol, Depopred-40, Depopred-80, Depo-Predate 40, Duralone-40, Duralone-80, M-Prednisol-40, M-Prednisol-80, Medralone 40, Medralone 80

methylprednisolone sodium succinate
A-MethaPred, Solu-Medrol

Pharmacologic class: glucocorticoid
Therapeutic class: anti-inflammatory, immunosuppressant
Pregnancy risk category: NR

Indications and dosages

▶ **Severe inflammation or immunosuppression.** ***methylprednisolone.*** *Adults:* 2 to 60 mg P.O. daily in four divided doses.

methylprednisolone acetate. *Adults:* 10 to 80 mg I.M. daily, or 4 to 80 mg into joint or soft tissue, p.r.n.
methylprednisolone succinate. *Adults:* 10 to 250 mg I.M. or I.V. q 4 hours.
Children: 0.03 to 0.2 mg/kg or 1 to 6.25 mg/m^2 I.M. or I.V. daily in divided doses.
▶ **Shock. *methylprednisolone succinate.*** *Adults:* 100 to 250 mg I.V. at 2- to 6-hour intervals. Or, 30 mg/kg I.V. initially, repeat q 4 to 6 hours, p.r.n. Continue therapy for 2 to 3 days or until patient is stable.
▶ **Treatment of acute exacerbations of multiple sclerosis.** *Adults:* Give 200 mg I.M. daily for 2 weeks, followed by 800 mg every other day for 1 month.
▶ **Severe lupus nephritis‡.** *Adults:* 1 g I.V. over 1 hour for 3 days. Continue orally at 0.5 mg/kg daily.
Children: 30 mg/kg I.V. every other day for 6 doses.
▶ **Treatment or minimization of motor and sensory defects caused by acute spinal cord injury‡.** *Adults:* Initially, 30 mg/kg I.V. over 15 minutes followed in 45 minutes by 5.4 mg/kg/hour I.V. infusion for 23 hours.
▶ **Adjunct to moderate-to-severe *Pneumocystis carinii* pneumonia‡.** *Adults and adolescents older than age 13:* 30 mg I.V. b.i.d. for 5 days; 30 mg I.V. daily for 5 days; 15 mg I.V. daily for 11 days (or until completion of anti-infective regimen).

Contraindications and precautions

- Contraindicated in patients allergic to drug or its components and in those with systemic fungal infections.
- Use cautiously in patients with GI ulceration or renal disease, hypertension, osteoporosis, diabetes mellitus, hypothyroidism, cirrhosis, diverticulitis, nonspecific ulcerative colitis, recent intestinal anastomoses, thromboembolic disorders, seizures, myasthenia gravis, heart failure, tuberculosis, ocular herpes simplex, emotional instability, or psychotic tendencies.

Lifespan: In pregnant women, use cautiously. For breast-feeding women, drug isn't recommended. In premature infants, methylprednisolone acetate and methylprednisolone succinate are contraindicated.

Adverse reactions

CNS: *euphoria, insomnia,* psychotic behavior, pseudotumor cerebri.
CV: ***heart failure,*** hypertension, edema, ***thromboembolism, fatal arrest or circulatory collapse*** after rapid administration of large I.V. doses.
EENT: cataracts, glaucoma.
GI: peptic ulceration, GI irritation, increased appetite, ***pancreatitis.***
Metabolic: hypokalemia, hyperglycemia, carbohydrate intolerance, growth suppression in children.
Musculoskeletal: muscle weakness, osteoporosis.
Skin: hirsutism, delayed wound healing, acne, various skin eruptions.
Other: susceptibility to infections, ***acute adrenal insufficiency*** with increased stress (infection, surgery, or trauma) or abrupt withdrawal after long-term therapy.

Interactions

Drug-drug. *Anticholinesterases:* May cause profound weakness. Use together cautiously.
Aspirin, indomethacin, other NSAIDs: Increases risk of GI distress and bleeding. Give together cautiously.
Barbiturates, phenytoin, rifampin: Decreases corticosteroid effect. Increase corticosteroid dosage.
Cholestyramine: Decreases corticosteroid effect. Separate administration times.
Cyclosporins: May increase risk of adverse events and convulsions. May need to increase methylprednisolone dose.
Macrolide antibiotics: Significant decrease in methylprednisolone clearance. May need reduced dosage.
Oral anticoagulants: Alters dosage requirements. Monitor PT closely.
Oral contraceptives: Reduces metabolism of corticosteroids. Monitor patient.
Potassium-depleting drugs (such as thiazide diuretics): Enhances potassium-wasting effects. Monitor potassium level.
Skin-test antigens: Decreases response. Defer skin testing until therapy is completed.
Toxoids, vaccines: Decreases antibody response and increases risk of neurologic complications. Avoid using together.

Effects on lab test results

• May increase glucose and cholesterol levels. May decrease potassium and calcium levels.

Pharmacokinetics

Absorption: Absorbed readily after P.O. administration; unknown after I.M. administration.
Distribution: Distributed rapidly to muscle, liver, skin, intestines, and kidneys.
Metabolism: Metabolized in liver.
Excretion: Excreted primarily in urine; insignificant amount excreted in feces. *Half-life:* 18 to 36 hours.

Route	Onset	Peak	Duration
P.O.	Rapid	1-2 hr	30-36 hr
I.V.	Immediate	Immediate	Unknown
I.M.	6-48 hr	4-8 days	1-4 wk

Pharmacodynamics

Chemical effect: Not clear; decreases inflammation, mainly by stabilizing leukocyte lysosomal membranes. Drug also suppresses immune response, stimulates bone marrow, and influences protein, fat, and carbohydrate metabolism.
Therapeutic effect: Relieves inflammation and suppresses immune system function.

Available forms

methylprednisolone
Tablets: 2 mg, 4 mg, 8 mg, 16 mg, 24 mg, 32 mg
methylprednisolone acetate
Injection (suspension): 20 mg/ml, 40 mg/ml, 80 mg/ml
methylprednisolone sodium succinate
Injection: 40-, 125-, 500-, 1,000-, and 2,000-mg vials

NURSING PROCESS

Assessment

• Assess patient's condition before therapy and regularly thereafter.
• Watch for enhanced response in patient with hypothyroidism or cirrhosis.
• Monitor patient's weight, blood pressure, electrolyte levels (especially glucose), and sleep patterns. Euphoria may initially interfere with sleep, but patient typically adjusts to drug after 1 to 3 weeks.
• Be alert for adverse reactions and drug interactions.
• Evaluate patient's and family's knowledge of drug therapy.

Nursing diagnoses

• Ineffective health maintenance related to underlying condition
• Risk for injury related to drug-induced adverse reactions
• Deficient knowledge related to drug therapy

Planning and implementation

• Drug may be used for alternate-day therapy.
• For better results and less risk of toxicity, give once-daily dose in morning.
• Avoid S.C. injection because atrophy and sterile abscesses may occur.
• **P.O. use:** Give with food when possible. Critically ill patients may also need antacid or H_2-receptor antagonist therapy.
• **I.V. use:** Give only methylprednisolone sodium succinate this way, never the acetate form. Reconstitute according to manufacturer's directions using supplied diluent or bacteriostatic water for injection with benzyl alcohol.
– For direct injection, inject diluted drug into vein or I.V. line containing free-flowing compatible solution over at least 1 minute. For treatment of shock, give massive doses over at least 10 minutes to prevent arrhythmias and circulatory collapse.
– When giving as intermittent or continuous infusion, dilute solution according to manufacturer's instructions and give over prescribed duration.
– If used for continuous infusion, change solution every 24 hours.
– Compatible solutions include D_5W, normal saline solution, and D_5W in normal saline solution.
• **I.M. use:** Give deep into gluteal muscle.
– Dermal atrophy may occur with large doses of acetate salt. Use multiple small injections rather than single large dose and rotate injection sites.
ALERT: Manufacturers of Solu-Medrol state that drug should not be given intrathecally because severe adverse reactions have been reported.
• Don't use acetate salt when immediate onset of action is needed.
• Discard reconstituted solutions after 48 hours.

• Always adjust to lowest effective dose.
• Give potassium supplements, as needed.
• Gradually reduce drug dosage after long-term therapy. Abrupt withdrawal may cause inflammation, fatigue, weakness, arthralgia, fever, dizziness, lethargy, depression, fainting, orthostatic hypotension, dyspnea, anorexia, and hypoglycemia. After prolonged use, sudden withdrawal may be fatal.
ALERT: Don't confuse Solu-Medrol with Solu-Cortef (hydrocortisone sodium succinate).
ALERT: Don't confuse methylprednisolone with medroxyprogesterone.

Patient teaching

• Tell patient most adverse reactions are dose- or duration-dependent.
• Tell patient not to discontinue drug abruptly or without prescriber's consent.
• Teach patient signs of early adrenal insufficiency: fatigue, muscle weakness, joint pain, fever, anorexia, nausea, dyspnea, dizziness, and fainting.
• Instruct patient to wear or carry medical identification.
• Warn patient receiving long-term therapy about cushingoid symptoms, and tell him to report sudden weight gain or swelling. Suggest exercise or physical therapy, and advise him to ask prescriber about vitamin D or calcium supplements.

Evaluation

• Patient responds positively to drug therapy.
• Patient sustains no injury from adverse reactions.
• Patient and family state understanding of drug therapy.

metoclopramide hydrochloride

(met-oh-KLOH-preh-mighd high-droh-KLOR-ighd)

Apo-Metoclop ♦, Clopra, Maxeran ♦, Maxolon, Octamide, Octamide PFS, Pramin ◇, Reclomide, Reglan

Pharmacologic class: para-aminobenzoic acid derivative
Therapeutic class: antiemetic, GI stimulant
Pregnancy risk category: B

Indications and dosages

▶ **Prevention or reduction of nausea and vomiting induced by cisplatin and other chemotherapeutic agents.** *Adults:* 1 to 2 mg/kg I.V. 30 minutes before chemotherapy; then repeat q 2 hours for two doses; then q 3 hours for three doses.
▶ **Prevention or reduction of postoperative nausea and vomiting.** *Adults:* 10 to 20 mg I.M. near end of surgical procedure, repeat q 4 to 6 hours, p.r.n.
▶ **To facilitate small-bowel intubation and aid in radiologic examinations.** *Adults and adolescents older than age 14:* 10 mg (2 ml) I.V. as single dose over 1 to 2 minutes.
Children ages 6 to 14: 2.5 to 5 mg I.V. (0.5 to 1 ml).
Children younger than age 6: 0.1 mg/kg I.V.
▶ **Delayed gastric emptying caused by diabetic gastroparesis.** *Adults:* 10 mg P.O. for mild symptoms; slow I.V. infusion for severe symptoms 30 minutes before meals and h.s. for 2 to 8 weeks, depending on response.
▶ **Gastroesophageal reflux disease.** *Adults:* 10 to 15 mg P.O. q.i.d., p.r.n., 30 minutes before meals and h.s.
Patients with renal impairment: If creatinine clearance is less than 40 ml/minute, reduce initial dose by 50% and adjust dose, as tolerated.

Contraindications and precautions

• Contraindicated in patients hypersensitive to drug, in those for whom stimulation of GI motility might be dangerous (such as those with hemorrhage), and in those with pheochromocytoma or seizure disorder.
• Use cautiously in patients with a history of depression, Parkinson's disease, or hypertension.
• Safety and effectiveness haven't been established for therapy that lasts longer than 12 weeks.
Lifespan: In pregnant and breast-feeding women, use cautiously.

Adverse reactions

CNS: *restlessness, anxiety, drowsiness,* fatigue, fever, *lassitude,* insomnia, ***suicide ideation, seizures,*** headache, dizziness, extrapyramidal symptoms, tardive dyskinesia, dystonic reactions, sedation.
CV: transient hypertension.
GI: nausea, bowel disturbances.
Hematologic: ***agranulocytosis, neutropenia.***

Skin: rash.
Other: prolactin secretion, loss of libido.

Interactions

Drug-drug. *Acetaminophen, aspirin, cyclosporine, diazepam, levodopa, lithium, tetracycline:* Increases absorption of these drugs. Monitor patient.
Anticholinergics, opioid analgesics: Antagonizes GI motility effects of metoclopramide. Use together cautiously.
Butyrophenones, phenothiazines: Increases risk of extrapyramidal effects. Monitor patient closely.
CNS depressants: May cause additive CNS depression. Avoid using together.
Digoxin: Decreases absorption of digoxin. Monitor digoxin levels.
Insulin: Metoclopramide influences the rate of absorption of food. Adjustments of insulin dosage or timing may be needed.
Drug-lifestyle. *Alcohol use:* May cause additive CNS depression. Discourage using together.

Effects on lab test results

- May increase aldosterone and prolactin levels.
- May decrease neutrophil and granulocyte counts.

Pharmacokinetics

Absorption: After P.O. dose, rapid and complete. After I.M. dose, about 74% to 96% bioavailable.
Distribution: Distributed to most body tissues and fluids, including brain.
Metabolism: Not metabolized extensively; small amount metabolized in liver.
Excretion: Excreted in urine and feces. *Half-life:* 4 to 6 hours.

Route	Onset	Peak	Duration
P.O.	30-60 min	1-2 hr	1-2 hr
I.V.	1-3 min	Unknown	1-2 hr
I.M.	10-15 min	Unknown	1-2 hr

Pharmacodynamics

Chemical effect: Stimulates motility of upper GI tract by increasing lower esophageal sphincter tone and blocks dopamine receptors at chemoreceptor trigger zone.
Therapeutic effect: Prevents or minimizes nausea and vomiting from chemotherapy or surgery. Also reduces gag reflex in small-bowel intubation and radiologic examinations, improves gastric emptying when diabetic gastroparesis is present, and reduces gastric reflux.

Available forms

Injection: 5 mg/ml
Syrup: 5 mg/5 ml, 10 mg/ml
Tablets: 5 mg, 10 mg

NURSING PROCESS

Assessment

- Assess patient's condition before therapy and regularly thereafter.
- Monitor blood pressure frequently in patient receiving I.V. form of drug.
- Be alert for adverse reactions and drug interactions.
- Evaluate patient's and family's knowledge of drug therapy.

Nursing diagnoses

- Risk for deficient fluid volume related to nausea and vomiting
- Risk for injury related to drug-induced adverse CNS reactions
- Deficient knowledge related to drug therapy

Planning and implementation

- **P.O. use:** Follow normal protocol. Dilute concentrate just before administration in water, juice, or carbonated beverage. Semisolid food such as applesauce or pudding also may be used.
- **I.V. use:** Give doses of 10 mg or less by direct injection over 1 to 2 minutes.
  – Dilute doses larger than 10 mg in 50 ml of compatible diluent and infuse over at least 15 minutes.
  – Protection from light is unnecessary if infusion mixture is given within 24 hours.
  – Drug is compatible with D_5W, normal saline solution injection, and D_5W in half-normal saline solution.
- **I.M. use:** Commercially available preparation may be used without further dilution.

ALERT: Diphenhydramine 25 mg I.V. counteracts extrapyramidal effects caused by high drug doses.

Patient teaching

- Instruct patient to avoid alcohol consumption during drug therapy.

• Advise patient to avoid activities requiring alertness for 2 hours after taking each dose.

Evaluation

• Patient responds positively to drug and doesn't develop fluid volume deficit.
• Patient doesn't experience injury from adverse reactions.
• Patient and family state understanding of drug therapy.

metolazone

(meh-TOH-luh-zohn)
Mykrox, Zaroxolyn**

Pharmacologic class: quinazoline derivative (thiazide-like) diuretic
Therapeutic class: diuretic, antihypertensive
Pregnancy risk category: B

Indications and dosages

▶ **Edema in heart failure or renal disease.** *Adults:* 5 to 20 mg (extended) P.O. daily.
▶ **Hypertension.** *Adults:* 2.5 to 5 mg (extended) P.O. daily. Maintenance dosage determined by patient's blood pressure. Or, 0.5 mg (prompt) P.O. once daily in morning, increased to 1 mg P.O. daily, p.r.n. If response is inadequate, another antihypertensive is added.

Contraindications and precautions

• Contraindicated in patients hypersensitive to thiazides or other sulfonamide-derived drugs and in patients with anuria, hepatic coma, or precoma.
• Use cautiously in patients with impaired kidney or liver function.
Lifespan: In pregnant women, drug isn't recommended. In breast-feeding women and in children, safety of drug hasn't been established.

Adverse reactions

CNS: dizziness, headache, fatigue.
CV: volume depletion and dehydration, orthostatic hypotension.
GI: anorexia, nausea, ***pancreatitis.***
GU: nocturia, polyuria, frequent urination.
Hematologic: ***aplastic anemia, agranulocytosis, leukopenia, thrombocytopenia.***
Hepatic: ***hepatic encephalopathy.***
Metabolic: hyperglycemia and glucose tolerance impairment; fluid and electrolyte imbalances, including hypokalemia, ***metabolic alkalosis,*** hypercalcemia, and dilutional hyponatremia and hypochloremia.
Musculoskeletal: gout, muscle cramps, swelling.
Skin: dermatitis, photosensitivity reactions, rash.
Other: hypersensitivity reactions.

Interactions

Drug-drug. *Amphotericin B, corticosteroids:* May potentiate hypokalemia. Monitor serum potassium levels.
Barbiturates, opioids: Increases orthostatic hypotensive effect. Monitor patient closely.
Cardiac glycosides: Increases risk of digitalis toxicity from metolazone-induced hypokalemia. Monitor potassium and digitalis levels.
Cholestyramine, colestipol: Decreases intestinal absorption of thiazides. Separate doses by 1 hour.
Diazoxide: Increases antihypertensive, hyperglycemic, and hyperuricemic effects. Use together cautiously.
Insulin, sulfonylureas: Increases requirements in diabetic patients. Dosages may need to be adjusted.
Lithium: Decreases lithium clearance, increasing risk of lithium toxicity. Monitor lithium level.
NSAIDs: Increases risk of NSAID-induced renal failure. Monitor patient for signs of renal failure.
Drug-lifestyle. *Alcohol use:* Increases orthostatic hypotensive effect. Discourage using together.
Sun exposure: Photosensitivity reactions may occur. Urge patient to avoid unprotected or prolonged exposure to sunlight.

Effects on lab test results

• May increase glucose, calcium, cholesterol, pH, bicarbonate, and triglyceride levels. May decrease potassium, sodium, magnesium, and chloride levels.
• May decrease hemoglobin, hematocrit, and granulocyte, platelet, and WBC counts.

Pharmacokinetics

Absorption: About 65% in healthy people; in cardiac patients, falls to 40%. Rate and extent vary among preparations.

Distribution: 50% to 70% erythrocyte-bound; 33% protein-bound.
Metabolism: Insignificant.
Excretion: 70% to 95% excreted unchanged in urine. *Half-life:* About 14 hours.

Route	Onset	Peak	Duration
P.O.	1 hr	2-8 hr	12-24 hr

Pharmacodynamics

Chemical effect: Increases sodium and water excretion by inhibiting sodium reabsorption in cortical diluting site of ascending loop of Henle.
Therapeutic effect: Promotes water and sodium elimination and lowers blood pressure.

Available forms

Tablets (extended): 2.5 mg, 5 mg, 10 mg
Tablets (prompt): 0.5 mg

NURSING PROCESS

Assessment

- Assess patient's condition before therapy and regularly thereafter. In hypertensive patients, therapeutic response may be delayed several days.
- Unlike thiazide diuretics, drug is effective in patient with decreased kidney function.
- Monitor fluid intake and output, weight, blood pressure, and electrolyte level.
- Monitor uric acid level, especially in patient with history of gout.
- Be alert for adverse reactions and drug interactions.
- Evaluate patient's and family's knowledge of drug therapy.

Nursing diagnoses

- Excessive fluid volume related to presence of edema
- Risk for injury related to presence of hypertension
- Deficient knowledge related to drug therapy

Planning and implementation

- Drug may be used with potassium-sparing diuretic to prevent potassium loss.
- Give drug in morning to prevent nocturia.
- Drug is used as adjunct in furosemide-resistant edema.

ALERT: Don't confuse Zaroxolyn with Zarontin or Metolazone with Metoprolol.

ALERT: Mykrox (prompt) tablets are more rapidly and completely absorbed than other brands, mimicking oral solution. Don't interchange Mykrox with Zaroxolyn (extended) tablets.

Patient teaching

- Advise patient to avoid sudden posture changes and to rise slowly to avoid orthostatic hypotension.
- Advise patient to wear protective clothing, avoid prolonged exposure to sunlight, and use sunblock to prevent photosensitivity reactions.
- Instruct patient to avoid alcohol consumption during drug therapy.

Evaluation

- Patient doesn't have edema.
- Patient's blood pressure is normal.
- Patient and family state understanding of drug therapy.

metoprolol succinate
(meh-TOH-pruh-lol SUHK-seh-nayt)
Toprol-XL

metoprolol tartrate
(meh-TOH-pruh-lol TAR-trayt)
Apo-Metoprolol ♦, Apo-Metoprolol (Type L) ♦, Betaloc ♦ ◇, Betaloc Durules ♦, Lopresor ♦, Lopressor, Minax ◇, Novometoprol ♦, Nu-Metop ♦

Pharmacologic class: beta blocker
Therapeutic class: antihypertensive, adjunct treatment of acute MI
Pregnancy risk category: C

Indications and dosages

▶ **Hypertension.** ***metoprolol succinate.*** *Adults:* Initially, 100 to 150 mg (extended-release tablets) P.O. once daily. Dosage is adjusted as needed and tolerated at intervals of not less than 1 week to maximum of 400 mg daily.
metoprolol tartrate. *Adults:* 100 mg P.O. daily in single or divided doses; usual maintenance dosage is 100 to 450 mg daily.
▶ **Early intervention in acute MI.** ***metoprolol tartrate.*** *Adults:* 2.5 to 5 mg I.V. push q 2 to 5 minutes to a total of 15 mg within 15 min-

utes. Then, 15 minutes after last dose, 25 to 50 mg P.O. q 6 hours for 48 hours. Maintenance dosage is 100 mg P.O. b.i.d.

▶ **Angina pectoris. *metoprolol succinate.*** *Adults:* Initially, 100 mg (extended-release tablets) P.O. daily as single dose. Dosage increased at weekly intervals until adequate response or pronounced decrease in heart rate is seen. Daily dose beyond 400 mg hasn't been studied.

metoprolol tartrate. *Adults:* 100 mg P.O. in two divided doses. Dosage increased at weekly intervals until adequate response or pronounced decrease in heart rate is seen. Maintenance dosage is 100 to 400 mg/day.

▶ **Treatment of stable, symptomatic heart failure (New York Heart Association class II) resulting from ischemia, hypertension, or cardiomyopathy. *metoprolol succinate.*** *Adults:* 25 mg P.O. once daily for 2 weeks. Double the dose every 2 weeks as tolerated to a maximum of 200 mg daily. In patients with more severe heart failure, start with 12.5 mg P.O. once daily for 2 weeks.

▶ **Atrial tachyarrhythmias after acute MI‡.** *Adults:* 2.5 to 5 mg I.V. q 2 to 5 minutes to control rate up to 15 mg over a 10- to 15-minute period. Once heart rate is controlled or normal sinus rhythm is restored, therapy may continue with 50 mg P.O. b.i.d. for 24 hours starting 15 minutes after the last I.V. dose. Increase dosage to 100 mg P.O. b.i.d. as tolerated. Discontinue when therapeutic efficacy is achieved or if systolic blood pressure is less than 100 mm Hg or heart rate is less than 50 beats/minute.

Contraindications and precautions

- Contraindicated in patients hypersensitive to drug or other beta blockers and in those with sinus bradycardia, heart block greater than first-degree, cardiogenic shock, or overt cardiac failure when used to treat hypertension or angina. When used to treat MI, drug is also contraindicated in patients with heart rate below 45 beats/minute, second- or third-degree heart block, PR interval of 0.24 second or more with first-degree heart block, systolic blood pressure under 100 mm Hg, or moderate-to-severe cardiac failure.
- Use cautiously in patients with heart failure, diabetes, or respiratory or hepatic disease.

Lifespan: In pregnant women, use cautiously. For breast-feeding women, drug isn't recommended. In children, safety of drug hasn't been established.

Adverse reactions

CNS: fatigue, lethargy, dizziness, fever.
CV: ***bradycardia,*** *hypotension,* ***heart failure, AV block,*** peripheral vascular disease.
GI: nausea, vomiting, diarrhea.
Musculoskeletal: arthralgia.
Respiratory: dyspnea, ***bronchospasm.***
Skin: rash.

Interactions

Drug-drug. *Barbiturates, cholestyramine, colestipol, rifampin:* Increases metabolism of metoprolol. Monitor patient for decreased effect.
Cardiac glycosides, diltiazem, verapamil: May cause excessive bradycardia and increase depressant effect on myocardium. Use together cautiously.
Chlorpromazine, cimetidine, verapamil: Decreases hepatic clearance. Monitor patient for increased beta-blocking effect.
Hydralazine: Serum levels and, hence, pharmacologic effects of beta blockers and hydralazine may be enhanced. Monitor patient closely.
Indomethacin: Decreases antihypertensive effect. Monitor blood pressure and adjust dosage.
Insulin, oral antidiabetics: Alters dosage requirements in previously stabilized diabetic patient. Observe patient carefully.
MAO inhibitors: Bradycardia may develop during use with MAO inhibitors. Monitor ECG and patient closely.
Thioamines: Pharmacokinetics of metoprolol may be altered, increasing the effects of metoprolol. Monitor patient.
Thyroid hormones: Actions of metoprolol may be impaired when patient is converted to euthyroid state. Monitor patient.
Drug-food. *Any food:* May increase absorption. Give together.

Effects on lab test results

- May increase transaminase, alkaline phosphatase, LDH, and uric acid levels.

Pharmacokinetics

Absorption: Rapidly and almost complete; food enhances absorption.

Distribution: Distributed widely throughout body; about 12% protein-bound.
Metabolism: Metabolized in liver.
Excretion: About 95% excreted in urine. *Half-life:* 3 to 7 hours.

Route	Onset	Peak	Duration
P.O.	≤ 15 min	1-12 hr	6-24 hr
I.V.	≤ 5 min	20 min	5-8 hr

Pharmacodynamics

Chemical effect: Unknown for antihypertensive action. Drug decreases myocardial contractility, heart rate, and cardiac output; lowers blood pressure; reduces myocardial oxygen consumption; and depresses renin secretion.
Therapeutic effect: Reduces blood pressure and angina and helps to prevent myocardial tissue damage.

Available forms

metoprolol succinate
Tablets (extended-release): 25 mg, 50 mg, 100 mg, 200 mg
metoprolol tartrate
Injection: 1 mg/ml in 5-ml ampules
Tablets: 50 mg, 100 mg
Tablets (extended-release): 100 mg ♦, 200 mg ♦

NURSING PROCESS

Assessment

- Assess patient's condition before therapy and regularly thereafter.
- Monitor blood pressure frequently. Drug masks common signs of shock.
- Be alert for adverse reactions and drug interactions.
- Evaluate patient's and family's knowledge of drug therapy.

Nursing diagnoses

- Ineffective health maintenance related to underlying disorder
- Risk for injury related to drug-induced adverse CNS reactions
- Deficient knowledge related to drug therapy

Planning and implementation

ALERT: Always check patient's apical pulse rate before giving drug. If it's slower than 60 beats/minute, withhold drug and call prescriber immediately.
- **P.O. use:** Give drug with meals because food may increase absorption.
- **I.V. use:** Give drug undiluted and by direct injection.
  – Although mixing with other drugs should be avoided, studies have shown that metoprolol is compatible with meperidine hydrochloride or morphine sulfate, or with alteplase infusions at Y-site connection.
  – Store drug at room temperature and protect from light. Discard solution if discolored or contains particulates.

ALERT: Don't confuse metoprolol with metaproterenol or metolazone or Toprol XL with Topamax.

Patient teaching
- Tell patient that abrupt discontinuation of therapy can worsen angina and precipitate MI. Withdraw drug gradually over 1 to 2 weeks.
- Instruct patient to take oral form of drug with meals to enhance absorption.
- Advise patient to report adverse reactions to prescriber.
- Warn patient to avoid performing hazardous activities until CNS effects of drug are known.

Evaluation

- Patient responds well to therapy.
- Patient doesn't experience injury from adverse CNS reactions.
- Patient and family state understanding of drug therapy.

metronidazole

(met-roh-NIGH-duh-zohl)
Apo-Metronidazole ♦, Flagyl, Flagyl ER, Flagyl 375, Metric 21, Metrogyl ◇, Metrozine ◇, Novonidazol ♦, Protostat, Trikacide ♦

metronidazole hydrochloride

Flagyl I.V. RTU, Metro I.V., Novonidazol ♦

Pharmacologic class: nitroimidazole
Therapeutic class: antibacterial, antiprotozoal, amebicide
Pregnancy risk category: B

Indications and dosages

▶ **Amebic hepatic abscess.** *Adults:* 500 to 750 mg P.O. t.i.d. for 5 to 10 days.
Children: 35 to 50 mg/kg daily (in three doses) for 10 days.

▶ **Intestinal amebiasis.** *Adults:* 750 mg P.O. t.i.d. for 5 to 10 days.
Children: 35 to 50 mg/kg daily (in three doses) for 10 days. Therapy is followed by P.O. iodoquinol.

▶ **Trichomoniasis.** *Adults:* 375 mg P.O. b.i.d. for 7 days or 2 g P.O. in single dose (may give 2-g dose in two 1-g doses on same day); 4 to 6 weeks should elapse between courses of therapy.
Children: 5 mg/kg dose P.O. t.i.d. for 7 days.

▶ **Refractory trichomoniasis.** *Adults:* 500 mg P.O. b.i.d. for 10 days.

▶ **Bacterial infections caused by anaerobic microorganisms.** *Adults:* Loading dose is 15 mg/kg I.V. infused over 1 hour (about 1 g for 70-kg [154-lb] adult). Maintenance dosage is 7.5 mg/kg I.V. or P.O. q 6 hours (about 500 mg for 70-kg adult). First maintenance dose should be given 6 hours after loading dose. Maximum, 4 g daily.

▶ **Prevention of postoperative infection in contaminated or potentially contaminated colorectal surgery.** *Adults:* 15 mg/kg I.V. infused over 30 to 60 minutes and completed about 1 hour before surgery. Then, 7.5 mg/kg I.V. infused over 30 to 60 minutes at 6 and 12 hours after initial dose.

▶ **Pelvic inflammatory disease‡.** *Adults:* 500 mg I.V. q 12 hours with other drugs. Or, 500 mg P.O. b.i.d. for 14 days given with ofloxacin, 400 mg P.O. b.i.d.

▶ **Bacterial vaginosis‡.** *Adults:* 500 mg P.O. b.i.d. for 7 days. Or, 2 g P.O. as a single dose. Or, 250 mg P.O. t.i.d. for 7 days.

▶ **Active Crohn's disease‡.** *Adults:* 400 mg P.O. b.i.d. For refractory perineal disease, 20 mg/kg (1 to 1.5 g) P.O. daily in 3 to 5 divided doses.

▶ **Prophylaxis in sexual assault victims‡.** *Adults:* 2 g P.O. given with other drugs.

▶ ***Helicobacter pylori* with peptic ulcer disease‡.** *Adults:* 250 to 500 mg P.O. t.i.d. to q.i.d. given with other drugs. Continue for 7 to 14 days depending on the regimen used. *Children:* 15 to 20 mg/kg P.O. daily, divided in 2 doses for 4 weeks given with other drugs.

Contraindications and precautions

- Contraindicated in patients hypersensitive to drug or other nitroimidazole derivatives.
- Use cautiously in patients receiving hepatotoxic drugs and in patients with history of blood dyscrasia or CNS disorder, retinal or visual field changes, hepatic disease, or alcoholism.

Lifespan: For breast-feeding women, drug isn't recommended.

Adverse reactions

CNS: vertigo, headache, ataxia, fever, incoordination, confusion, irritability, depression, restlessness, weakness, fatigue, drowsiness, insomnia, sensory neuropathy, paresthesia of limbs, psychic stimulation, ***seizures,*** neuropathy.
CV: flattened T wave, edema, flushing.
GI: abdominal cramping, stomatitis, *nausea, vomiting, anorexia,* diarrhea, constipation, proctitis, dry mouth, metallic taste.
GU: darkened urine, polyuria, dysuria, pyuria, incontinence, cystitis, dyspareunia, dry vagina and vulva, sense of pelvic pressure.
Hematologic: ***transient leukopenia, neutropenia.***
Skin: pruritus, rash.
Other: decreased libido, gynecomastia, overgrowth of nonsusceptible organisms, especially *Candida* (glossitis, furry tongue), thrombophlebitis after I.V. infusion.

Interactions

Drug-drug. *Barbiturates, phenobarbital, phenytoin:* Decreases metronidazole effectiveness because of increased hepatic clearance. Monitor patient closely.
Cimetidine: Increases risk of metronidazole toxicity because of inhibited hepatic metabolism. Monitor patient.
Disulfiram: May cause acute psychoses and confusional states. Don't use together.
Fluoracil, azathioprine: May increase risk of transient neutropenia. Use cautiously.
Lithium: Increases lithium level, possibly resulting in toxicity. Monitor lithium level closely.
Oral anticoagulants: Increases anticoagulant effects. Monitor patient for bleeding.
Drug-lifestyle. *Alcohol use:* May cause disulfiram-like reaction (nausea, vomiting,

headache, cramps, flushing). Discourage using together.

Effects on lab test results

- May decrease WBC and neutrophil counts.

Pharmacokinetics

Absorption: About 80%; food delays peak levels to about 2 hours.
Distribution: Distributed in most body tissues and fluids; less than 20% bound to plasma proteins.
Metabolism: Metabolized to active metabolite and to other metabolites.
Excretion: Excreted primarily in urine; 6% to 15% in feces. *Half-life:* 6 to 8 hours (may be longer in patients with impaired liver function).

Route	Onset	Peak	Duration
P.O.	Unknown	1-2 hr	Unknown
I.V.	Immediate	Immediate	Unknown

Pharmacodynamics

Chemical effect: Direct-acting trichomonacide and amebicide that works at both intestinal and extraintestinal sites.
Therapeutic effect: Hinders growth of selected organisms, including most anaerobic bacteria and protozoa, including *Bacteroides fragilis, Bacteroides melaninogenicus, Balantidium coli, Clostridium, Entamoeba histolytica, Fusobacterium, Giardia lamblia, Peptococcus, Peptostreptococcus, Trichomonas vaginalis,* and *Veillonella.*

Available forms

Capsules: 375 mg
Injection: 500 mg/100 ml
Oral suspension (benzoyl metronidazole): 200 mg/5 ml ◇
Powder for injection: 500-mg single-dose vials
Tablets: 200 mg ◇, 250 mg, 400 mg ◇, 500 mg
Tablets (extended release): 750 mg

NURSING PROCESS

Assessment

- Assess patient's infection before therapy and regularly thereafter.
- Watch carefully for edema, especially in patients also receiving corticosteroids, because Flagyl I.V. RTU may cause sodium retention.
- Record number and character of stools when used in amebiasis.
- Be alert for adverse reactions and drug interactions.
- Evaluate patient's and family's understanding of drug therapy.

Nursing diagnoses

- Infection related to presence of susceptible organisms
- Risk for deficient fluid volume related to drug-induced adverse GI reactions
- Deficient knowledge related to drug therapy

Planning and implementation

- **P.O. use:** Give drug with meals to minimize GI distress.
- **I.V. use:** No preparation is needed for RTU form.
  - To prepare lyophilized vials of metronidazole, add 4.4 ml of sterile water for injection, bacteriostatic water for injection, sterile normal saline solution injection, or bacteriostatic normal saline solution injection. Reconstituted drug contains 100 mg/ml.
  - Add contents of vial to 100 ml of D_5W, lactated Ringer's injection, or normal saline solution for final concentration of 5 mg/ml.
  - Resulting highly acidic solution must be neutralized before giving. Carefully add 5 mEq of sodium bicarbonate for each 500 mg of metronidazole. Carbon dioxide will form and may need to be vented.
  - Don't refrigerate neutralized diluted solution. Precipitation may occur. If Flagyl I.V. RTU is refrigerated, crystals may form. These will disappear after solution is gently warmed to room temperature.

ALERT: Infuse drug over at least 1 hour. Don't give I.V. push.

- Metronidazole should be used only after *T. vaginalis* has been confirmed by wet smear or culture or *E. histolytica* has been identified. Asymptomatic sexual partners of patients being treated for *T. vaginalis* infection should be treated simultaneously to avoid reinfection.
- During pregnancy, 7-day regimen is preferred over 2-g single-dose regimen for trichomoniasis.

Patient teaching
- Tell patient to avoid alcohol or alcohol-containing drugs during therapy and for at least 48 hours after therapy is completed.
- Tell patient that metallic taste and dark or red-brown urine may occur.
- Instruct patient to take oral form with meals to minimize reactions.
- Instruct patient in proper hygiene.

Evaluation
- Patient is free from infection.
- Patient maintains adequate hydration throughout therapy.
- Patient and family state understanding of drug therapy.

mexiletine hydrochloride
(MEKS-il-eh-teen high-droh-KLOR-ighd)
Mexitil

Pharmacologic class: lidocaine analogue, sodium channel antagonist
Therapeutic class: ventricular antiarrhythmic
Pregnancy risk category: C

Indications and dosages

▶ **Refractory life-threatening ventricular arrhythmias, including ventricular tachycardia and PVCs.** *Adults:* 200 to 400 mg P.O., followed by 200 mg q 8 hours. Dose increased q 2 to 3 days to 400 mg q 8 hours if satisfactory control isn't obtained. Patients who respond well to q-12-hour schedule may be given up to 450 mg q 12 hours. Maximum daily dose is 1,200 mg.

▶ **Diabetic neuropathy‡.** *Adults:* 150 mg P.O. daily for 3 days; then give 300 mg P.O. daily for 3 days followed by 10 mg/kg P.O. daily.

Contraindications and precautions

- Contraindicated in patients with cardiogenic shock or second- or third-degree AV block in absence of artificial pacemaker.
- Use cautiously in patients with first-degree heart block, ventricular pacemaker, sinus node dysfunction, intraventricular conduction disturbances, hypotension, severe heart failure, or seizure disorder.

Lifespan: In pregnant patients, use cautiously. For breast-feeding women, drug isn't recommended. In children, safety of drug hasn't been established.

Adverse reactions

CNS: *tremor, dizziness,* blurred vision, ataxia, diplopia, confusion, nystagmus, nervousness, headache.
CV: hypotension, ***bradycardia,*** widened QRS complex, ***arrhythmias,*** palpitations, chest pain.
GI: nausea, vomiting.
Skin: rash.

Interactions

Drug-drug. *Antacids, atropine, narcotics:* Slows mexiletine absorption. Monitor patient.
Cimetidine: Increases or decreases mexiletine level. Monitor patient carefully.
Methylxanthines (such as theophylline): Reduces clearance of methylxanthines, possibly resulting in toxicity. Monitor patient.
Metoclopramide: Mexiletine absorption may be accelerated. Monitor patient for toxicity.
Phenobarbital, phenytoin, rifampin, urine acidifiers: Decreases mexiletine blood levels. Monitor patient.
Urine alkalinizers: Increases mexiletine blood levels. Monitor patient.
Drug-food. *Caffeine:* Reduces clearance of methylxanthines, possibly resulting in toxicity. Monitor patient.

Effects on lab test results

- May increase AST level.

Pharmacokinetics

Absorption: About 90%.
Distribution: Distributed widely throughout body. Distribution volume declines in patients with liver disease, resulting in toxic serum drug levels with usual doses. About 50% to 60% of circulating drug is bound to plasma proteins.
Metabolism: Most of drug metabolized in liver.
Excretion: Excreted in urine. *Half-life:* 10 to 12 hours.

Route	Onset	Peak	Duration
P.O.	0.5-2 hr	2-3 hr	Unknown

Pharmacodynamics

Chemical effect: Class Ib antiarrhythmic that blocks fast sodium channel in cardiac tissues, especially Purkinje network, without involvement of autonomic nervous system. Drug reduces rate of rise and amplitude of action potential and decreases automaticity in Purkinje fibers. It also shortens action potential and, to a lesser extent, decreases effective refractory period in Purkinje fibers.
Therapeutic effect: Abolishes ventricular arrhythmias.

Available forms

Capsules: 100 mg ♦, 150 mg, 200 mg, 250 mg

NURSING PROCESS

Assessment

- Assess patient's condition until arrhythmia is abolished.
- Monitor drug levels. Therapeutic levels range from 0.75 to 2 mcg/ml.
- Be alert for adverse reactions and drug interactions.
- Monitor patient for toxicity. An early sign is tremors, usually fine tremor of hands. This progresses to dizziness and later to ataxia and nystagmus as drug's blood level increases. Ask patient about these symptoms.
- Monitor patient's hydration status if adverse GI reactions occur.
- Evaluate patient's and family's knowledge of drug therapy.

Nursing diagnoses

- Decreased cardiac output related to presence of ventricular arrhythmia
- Risk for deficient fluid volume related to drug-induced adverse GI reactions
- Deficient knowledge related to drug therapy

Planning and implementation

- **P.O. use:** Give with meals or antacids to lessen GI distress.
- If patient appears to be good candidate for q 12-hour therapy, notify prescriber. Twice-daily dose enhances compliance.
- Notify prescriber of any significant changes in blood pressure, heart rate, and heart rhythm.

Patient teaching

- Instruct patient taking oral form of drug to take it with food.
- Instruct patient to report adverse reactions.

Evaluation

- Patient regains normal cardiac output.
- Patient maintains adequate hydration throughout therapy.
- Patient and family state understanding of drug therapy.

midazolam hydrochloride

(MID-ayz-oh-lam high-droh-KLOR-ighd)
Hypnovel◇, Versed, Versed Syrup

Pharmacologic class: benzodiazepine
Therapeutic class: preoperative sedative, agent for conscious sedation, adjunct for induction of general anesthesia
Controlled substance schedule: IV
Pregnancy risk category: D

Indications and dosages

▶ **Preoperative sedation (to induce sleepiness or drowsiness and relieve apprehension).** *Adults younger than age 60:* 0.07 mg to 0.08 mg/kg I.M. about 1 hour before surgery.

▶ **Conscious sedation before short diagnostic or endoscopic procedures.** *Adults younger than age 60:* Initially, small dose not to exceed 2.5 mg I.V. given slowly; repeated in 2 minutes if needed in small increments of initial dose over at least 2 minutes to achieve desired effect. Total dose of up to 5 mg may be given.

Adults age 60 and older: 1.5 mg or less over at least 2 minutes. If additional adjustment is needed, give at no more than 1 mg over 2 minutes. Total doses exceeding 3.5 mg aren't usually needed.

▶ **Induction of general anesthesia.** *Adults younger than age 55:* 0.3 to 0.35 mg/kg I.V. over 20 to 30 seconds if patient hasn't received preanesthesia drug, or 0.15 to 0.35 mg/kg I.V. over 20 to 30 seconds if patient has received preanesthesia drug. Additional increments of 25% of initial dose may be needed to complete induction.

Adults age 55 and older: 0.3 mg/kg I.V. over 20 to 30 seconds if patient hasn't received premedication, or 0.2 mg/kg I.V. over 20 to 30 seconds if patient has received sedation or narcotic premedication. Additional increments of 25% of initial dose may be needed to complete induction.

▶ **To induce sleepiness and amnesia and to relieve apprehension before anesthesia or before or during procedures in children.**
Children: 0.1 to 0.15 mg/kg I.M. Doses up to 0.5 mg/kg can be used for more anxious patients.
Children ages 6 months to 5 years: 0.05 to 0.1 mg/kg I.V. over 2 to 3 minutes. Additional doses may be given in small increments after 2 to 3 minutes. Total dose of up to 0.6 mg/kg (not to exceed 6 mg) may be given.
Children ages 6 to 12: 0.025 to 0.05 mg/kg I.V. over 2 to 3 minutes. Additional doses may be given in small increments after 2 to 3 minutes. Total dose of up to 0.4 mg/kg (not to exceed 10 mg) may be given.

▶ **Continuous infusion for sedation of intubated patients in the critical care setting.**
Adults: Initially 0.01 to 0.05 mg/kg may be given I.V. over several minutes, repeated at 10- to 15-minute intervals, until adequate sedation is achieved. For maintenance of sedation, usual initial infusion rate is 0.02 to 0.1 mg/kg/hour. Higher loading dose or infusion rates may be needed in some patients. Use the lowest effective rate.
Children: Initially, 0.05 to 0.2 mg/kg may be given I.V. over at least 2 to 3 minutes; then continuous infusion at 0.06 to 0.12 mg/kg/hour. Increase or decrease infusion to maintain desired effect.
Neonates born at 32 weeks gestation or later: Initially 0.06 mg/kg/hr. Adjust rate, p.r.n., using lowest possible rate.
Neonates born earlier than 32 weeks gestation: Initially 0.03 mg/kg/hr. Adjust rate, p.r.n., using lowest possible rate.

Contraindications and precautions

- Contraindicated in patients hypersensitive to drug and in those with acute angle-closure glaucoma, shock, coma, or acute alcohol intoxication.
- Use cautiously in patients with uncompensated acute illness and in debilitated patients.

Lifespan: In pregnant women, drug isn't recommended. In breast-feeding women and in elderly patients, use cautiously.

Adverse reactions

CNS: headache, oversedation, involuntary movements, combativeness, amnesia.
CV: variations in blood pressure ***(hypotension)*** and pulse rate, ***cardiac arrest.***
GI: *nausea,* vomiting, *hiccups.*
Respiratory: *decreased respiratory rate,* **APNEA.**
Skin: pain, tenderness at injection site.

Interactions

Drug-drug. *Cimetidine, verapamil:* Effects of benzodiazepine may be increased. Monitor patient closely.
CNS depressants: May increase risk of apnea. Avoid using together.
Indinavir, ritonavir: Possible prolonged or severe sedation and respiratory depression. Monitor patient closely.
Narcotic analgesics: May increase midazolam's hypnotic effect and increase risk of hypotension. Monitor patient closely; adjust dosage.
Oral contraceptives: May prolong benzodiazepine half-life. Monitor patient closely.
Rifamycin: May decrease midazolam levels. Monitor patient for effect.
Drug-lifestyle. *Alcohol use:* May increase risk of apnea. Discourage using together.

Effects on lab test results

None reported.

Pharmacokinetics

Absorption: 80% to 100%.
Distribution: Drug has large volume of distribution; about 97% protein-bound.
Metabolism: Metabolized in liver.
Excretion: Excreted in urine. *Half-life:* 2 to 6 hours.

Route	Onset	Peak	Duration
I.V.	1.5-5 min	Rapid	2-6 hr
I.M.	≤ 15 min	15-60 min	2-6 hr

Pharmacodynamics

Chemical effect: Unknown; thought to depress CNS at limbic and subcortical levels of brain by potentiating effects of GABA.
Therapeutic effect: Promotes calmness and sleep.

Available forms

Injection: 1 mg/ml, 5 mg/ml
Syrup: 2 mg/ml

NURSING PROCESS

Assessment

- Assess patient's condition before therapy and regularly thereafter.
- Monitor blood pressure, heart rate and rhythm, respirations, airway integrity, and arterial oxygen saturation during procedure, especially in patients premedicated with narcotics.
- Be alert for adverse reactions and drug interactions.
- Evaluate patient's and family's knowledge of drug therapy.

Nursing diagnoses

- Anxiety related to surgery
- Ineffective breathing pattern related to drug's effect on respiratory system
- Deficient knowledge related to drug therapy

Planning and implementation

- Before giving drug, have oxygen and resuscitation equipment available in case of severe respiratory depression. Excessive dosage or rapid infusion has been linked to respiratory arrest, particularly in elderly or debilitated patients.
- Midazolam may be mixed in same syringe with morphine sulfate, meperidine, atropine sulfate, or scopolamine.
- **I.V. use:** Give slowly over at least 2 minutes, and wait at least 2 minutes when adjusting doses to effect.
– Watch for irritation and infiltration; extravasation can cause tissue damage and necrosis.
- **I.M. use:** Give deep into large muscle mass.

ALERT: Don't confuse Versed with VePesid.

Patient teaching

- Drug's beneficial amnesic effect diminishes recall of perioperative events. This effect requires extra caution when teaching patients. Written information, family member instruction, and follow-up contact may be needed to ensure that patient has adequate information.
- Instruct patient to avoid alcohol consumption during drug therapy.

Evaluation

- Patient exhibits calmness.
- Patient maintains adequate breathing pattern throughout therapy.
- Patient and family state understanding of drug therapy.

miglitol

(MIG-lih-tall)
Glyset

Pharmacologic class: alpha-glucosidase inhibitor
Therapeutic class: antidiabetic
Pregnancy risk category: B

Indications and dosages

▶ **Monotherapy as an adjunct to diet to improve glycemic control in patients with type 2 diabetes mellitus whose hyperglycemia can't be managed with diet alone, or with a sulfonylurea when diet plus either miglitol or sulfonylurea alone yield inadequate glycemic control.** *Adults:* 25 mg P.O. t.i.d. at the start (with the first bite) of each main meal; may be increased after 4 to 8 weeks to a maintenance dosage of 50 mg P.O. t.i.d. The dosage may then be further increased after 3 months, based on glycosylated hemoglobin level, to maximum of 100 mg P.O. t.i.d.

Contraindications and precautions

- Contraindicated in patients hypersensitive to drug or its components. Also contraindicated in patients with diabetic ketoacidosis, inflammatory bowel disease, colonic ulceration, or partial intestinal obstruction; patients predisposed to intestinal obstruction or those with chronic intestinal diseases related to disorders of digestion or absorption; and patients with conditions that may deteriorate as a result of increased gas formation in the intestine.
- Drug isn't recommended for patients with significant renal dysfunction (serum creatinine more than 2 mg/dl).

• Use cautiously in patients also receiving insulin or oral sulfonylureas.

Lifespan: In pregnant patients, use only if clearly needed. In breast-feeding women, don't use. In children, safety and efficacy haven't been established.

Adverse reactions

GI: abdominal pain, diarrhea, flatulence.
Skin: rash.

Interactions

Drug-drug. *Digoxin, propranolol, ranitidine:* May decrease the bioavailability of these drugs. Monitor patient for loss of efficacy and adjust dosages.
Intestinal absorbents (such as charcoal) and digestive enzyme preparations (such as amylase, pancreatin): May reduce the effectiveness of miglitol. Avoid using together.
Drug-herb. *Aloe, bilberry leaf, bitter melon, burdock, dandelion, fenugreek, garlic, ginseng, stinging nettle:* May improve glucose level control, allowing for a reduced antidiabetic dosage. Advise patient to discuss the use of herbal remedies with prescriber before therapy.

Effects on lab test results

• May decrease iron level.

Pharmacokinetics

Absorption: Saturable absorption at high doses. A 25-mg dose of miglitol is completely absorbed, whereas a dose of 100 mg is only 50% to 70% absorbed; levels peak 2 to 3 hours after P.O. dose.
Distribution: Distributed primarily into the extracellular fluid. Protein-binding is negligible (less than 4%).
Metabolism: None.
Excretion: Primarily renal. More than 95% of a dose appears in urine as unchanged drug. *Half-life:* About 2 hours.

Route	Onset	Peak	Duration
P.O.	Unknown	2-3 hr	Unknown

Pharmacodynamics

Chemical effect: Lowers glucose level through reversible inhibition of alpha-glucosidases in the brush border of the small intestine. Alpha-glucosidases are responsible for the conversion of oligosaccharides and disaccharides to glucose. Inhibition of these enzymes results in delayed glucose absorption and a lowering of postprandial hyperglycemia. In contrast to sulfonylureas, miglitol has no effect on insulin secretion.
Therapeutic effect: Lowers glucose level.

Available forms

Tablets: 25 mg, 50 mg, 100 mg

NURSING PROCESS

Assessment

• Obtain history of patient's underlying condition before therapy, and reassess regularly thereafter.
• Monitor glucose level regularly, especially during situations of increased stress, such as infection, fever, surgery, and trauma.
• Check glycosylated hemoglobin every three months to monitor long-term glycemic control.
• Evaluate patient's and family's knowledge about drug therapy.

Nursing diagnoses

• Ineffective health maintenance related to hyperglycemia
• Risk for injury related to drug-induced hypoglycemia
• Deficient knowledge related to drug therapy

Planning and implementation

• Miglitol should be given with the first bite of each main meal.
• In patients also receiving insulin or oral sulfonylureas, miglitol may increase the hypoglycemic potential of insulin or sulfonylureas. Dosage adjustments of these drugs may be needed, as ordered. Monitor these patients for an increased frequency of hypoglycemia.
• Management of type 2 diabetes should include diet control, exercise program, and regular testing of urine and blood glucose.
• Treat mild-to-moderate hypoglycemia with a form of dextrose such as glucose tablets or gel. Severe hypoglycemia may require I.V. glucose or glucagon.

Patient teaching

• Instruct patient about the importance of adhering to prescriber's diet, weight reduction, and exercise instructions and to have glucose

level and glycosylated hemoglobin tested regularly.
- Inform patient that treatment with miglitol relieves symptoms but doesn't cure diabetes.
- Teach patient to recognize the signs and symptoms of hyperglycemia and hypoglycemia.
- Instruct patient to treat hypoglycemia with glucose tablets and to have a source of glucose readily available when miglitol is taken with a sulfonylurea or insulin.
- Advise patient to seek medical advice promptly during periods of stress such as fever, trauma, infection, or surgery because drug requirements may change.
- Instruct patient to take miglitol t.i.d. with the first bite of each main meal.
- Show patient how and when to monitor glucose level.
- Advise patient that adverse GI effects are most common during the first few weeks of therapy and should improve over time.
- Urge patient to wear or carry medical identification at all times.

✓ Evaluation
- Patient's glucose level is normal.
- Patient sustains no injury from drug-induced hypoglycemia.
- Patient and family state understanding of drug therapy.

milrinone lactate
(MIL-rih-nohn LAK-tayt)
Primacor

Pharmacologic class: bipyridine phosphodiesterase inhibitor
Therapeutic class: inotropic vasodilator
Pregnancy risk category: C

Indications and dosages
▶ **Short-term treatment of heart failure.** *Adults:* Loading dose is 50 mcg/kg I.V., given slowly over 10 minutes, followed by continuous I.V. infusion of 0.375 to 0.75 mcg/kg/minute. Adjust infusion dose based on clinical and hemodynamic responses, as ordered.
Patients with creatinine clearance of 50 ml/minute or less: Adjust dosage to maximum clinical effect, not to exceed 1.13 mg/kg I.V. daily.

Contraindications and precautions
- Contraindicated in patients hypersensitive to drug.
- Drug isn't recommended for patients with severe aortic or pulmonic valvular disease in place of surgical correction of obstruction, or for patients in acute phase of MI.
- Use cautiously in patients with atrial flutter or fibrillation because drug slightly shortens AV node conduction time and may increase ventricular response rate.

Lifespan: In pregnant or breast-feeding women, use cautiously. In children, safety of drug hasn't been established.

Adverse reactions
CNS: headache.
CV: VENTRICULAR ARRHYTHMIAS, *ventricular ectopic activity,* nonsustained ventricular tachycardia, ***sustained ventricular tachycardia, ventricular fibrillation.***

Interactions
Drug-drug. *Natrecor:* May increase hypotensive effect. Avoid using together.

Effects on lab test results
None reported.

Pharmacokinetics
Absorption: Given I.V.
Distribution: About 70% bound to plasma protein.
Metabolism: About 12% metabolized to glucuronide metabolite.
Excretion: About 83% excreted unchanged in urine. *Half-life:* 2.3 to 2.7 hours.

Route	Onset	Peak	Duration
I.V.	5-15 min	1-2 hr	3-6 hr

Pharmacodynamics
Chemical effect: Produces inotropic action by increasing cellular levels of cAMP; produces vasodilation by relaxing vascular smooth muscle.
Therapeutic effect: Relieves acute signs and symptoms of heart failure.

Available forms

Injection: 1 mg/ml
Premixed injection: 200 mcg/ml in 100 ml D_5W injection; 200 mcg/ml in 200 ml D_5W injection.

NURSING PROCESS

Assessment

- Assess patient's heart failure before therapy and regularly thereafter.
- Monitor fluid and electrolyte status, blood pressure, heart rate, and kidney function during therapy.
- Monitor patient's ECG continuously during therapy.
- Be alert for adverse reactions.
- Evaluate patient's and family's knowledge of drug therapy.

Nursing diagnoses

- Impaired gas exchange related to presence of heart failure
- Decreased cardiac output related to drug-induced cardiac arrhythmias
- Deficient knowledge related to drug therapy

Planning and implementation

- Milrinone typically is given with digoxin and diuretics.
- Inotropics may aggravate outflow tract obstruction in hypertrophic subaortic stenosis.
- Prepare I.V. infusion solution using half-normal or normal saline solution or D_5W. Prepare 100-mcg/ml solution by adding 180 ml of diluent per 20-mg (20-ml) vial, 150-mcg/ml solution by adding 113 ml of diluent per 20-mg (20-ml) vial, and 200-mcg/ml solution by adding 80 ml of diluent per 20-mg (20-ml) vial.

ALERT: Improvement of cardiac output may result in enhanced urine output. Expect dosage reduction in diuretic therapy as heart failure improves. Potassium loss may predispose patient to digitalis toxicity.

- Excessive decrease in blood pressure requires discontinuation or slower infusion.

ALERT: Giving furosemide into an I.V. line containing milrinone causes precipitate to form. Don't give in the same line.

ALERT: Don't confuse milrinone with inamrinone.

Patient teaching

- Tell patient to report headache; mild analgesic can be given for relief.

Evaluation

- Patient exhibits adequate gas exchange as heart failure is resolved.
- Drug-induced arrhythmias don't develop during therapy.
- Patient and family state understanding of drug therapy.

mineral oil (liquid petrolatum)

(MIN-er-ul OYL)

Fleet Enema Mineral Oil†, Fleet Mineral Oil, Kondremul†, Kondremul Plain†, Lansoyl ♦, Milkinol†, Petrogalar Plain†

Pharmacologic class: lubricant oil
Therapeutic class: laxative
Pregnancy risk category: C

Indications and dosages

▶ **Constipation, preparation for bowel studies or surgery.** *Adults and children age 12 and older:* 15 to 45 ml P.O. h.s. Or, 120 ml P.R. (as enema).
Children ages 6 to 11: 5 to 15 ml P.O. h.s. Or, 30 to 60 ml P.R. (as enema).
Children ages 2 to 5: 30 to 60 ml P.R. (as enema).

Contraindications and precautions

- Contraindicated in patients with abdominal pain, nausea, vomiting, or other symptoms of appendicitis or acute surgical abdomen and in those with fecal impaction or intestinal obstruction or perforation.
- Use cautiously in debilitated patients because of susceptibility to lipid pneumonia through aspiration, absorption, and transport from intestinal mucosa; and in patients with rectal bleeding.

Lifespan: In pregnant or breast-feeding women, in young children, and in elderly patients, use cautiously because of susceptibility to lipid pneumonia through aspiration, absorption, and transport from intestinal mucosa.

Adverse reactions

GI: *nausea,* vomiting, decreased absorption of nutrients and fat-soluble vitamins, anal pruritus, diarrhea with excessive use, *abdominal cramps* (especially in severe constipation), slowed healing after hemorrhoidectomy.
Respiratory: ***lipid pneumonia.***
Other: laxative dependence with long-term or excessive use.

Interactions

Drug-drug. *Anticoagulants, fat-soluble vitamins (A, D, E, and K), oral contraceptives, sulfonamides:* May decrease absorption after prolonged administration. Monitor patient for deficiencies.
Docusate salts: May increase mineral oil absorption and cause lipid pneumonia. Separate administration times.

Effects on lab test results

• May alter fluid and electrolyte balances.

Pharmacokinetics

Absorption: Minimal except for emulsified form, which has significant absorption.
Distribution: Distributed locally, primarily in colon.
Metabolism: None.
Excretion: Excreted in feces.

Route	Onset	Peak	Duration
P.O., P.R.	6-8 hr	Varies	Varies

Pharmacodynamics

Chemical effect: Increases water retention in stool by creating barrier between colon wall and feces that prevents colonic reabsorption of fecal water.
Therapeutic effect: Relieves constipation.

Available forms

Emulsion: 50%†
Oral liquid: in pints, quarts, gallons†
Rectal oil enema: 120 ml†, 133 ml†
Suspension: 2.75 mg/ml, 4.75 mg/ml

NURSING PROCESS

Assessment

• Assess patient's condition before therapy and regularly thereafter.
• Before giving drug for constipation, determine whether patient has adequate fluid intake, exercise, and diet.
• Be alert for adverse reactions and drug interactions.
• Evaluate patient's and family's knowledge of drug therapy.

Nursing diagnoses

• Constipation related to underlying condition
• Risk for deficient fluid volume related to drug-induced adverse GI reactions
• Deficient knowledge related to drug therapy

Planning and implementation

• **P.O. use:** Give drug on empty stomach.
– Give drug with fruit juice or carbonated drink to disguise taste.
• **P.R. use:** Follow normal protocol.

Patient teaching

• Advise patient to take drug only at bedtime and not for more than 1 week.
• Warn patient of possible rectal leakage from excessive dosages.
• Teach patient about dietary sources of bulk, such as bran and cereals, fresh fruit, and vegetables.

Evaluation

• Patient regains normal bowel pattern.
• Patient maintains adequate hydration throughout therapy.
• Patient and family state understanding of drug therapy.

minocycline hydrochloride

(migh-noh-SIGH-kleen high-droh-KLOR-ighd)
Apo-Minocycline ◇, Dynacin ♦, Minocin*, Minocin IV, Minomycin ◇, Minomycin IV ◇, Vectrin

Pharmacologic class: tetracycline
Therapeutic class: antibiotic
Pregnancy risk category: D

Indications and dosages

▶ **Infections caused by sensitive gram-negative and gram-positive organisms, trachoma, amebiasis.** *Adults:* 200 mg I.V.; then 100 mg I.V. q 12 hours. Maximum 400 mg I.V.

daily. Or, 200 mg P.O. initially; then 100 mg P.O. q 12 hours. Some clinicians use 100 or 200 mg P.O. initially, followed by 50 mg q.i.d. *Children older than age 8:* Initially, 4 mg/kg P.O. or I.V., followed by 2 mg/kg P.O. q 12 hours. Give I.V. in 500- to 1,000-ml solution without calcium over 6 hours.

▶ **Gonorrhea in patients sensitive to penicillin.** *Adults:* Initially, 200 mg P.O.; then 100 mg q 12 hours for at least 4 days.

▶ **Syphilis in patients sensitive to penicillin.** *Adults:* Initially, 200 mg P.O.; then 100 mg q 12 hours for 10 to 15 days.

▶ **Meningococcal carrier state.** *Adults:* 100 mg P.O. q 12 hours for 5 days.

▶ **Uncomplicated urethral, endocervical, or rectal infection caused by *Chlamydia trachomatis* or *Ureaplasma urealyticum*.** *Adults:* 100 mg P.O. b.i.d. for at least 7 days.

▶ **Uncomplicated gonococcal urethritis in men.** *Adults:* 100 mg P.O. b.i.d. for 5 days.

▶ **Treatment of multibacillary leprosy‡.** *Adults:* 100 mg P.O. daily with clofazimine and ofloxacin for 6 months, followed by 100 mg P.O. daily for an additional 18 months in conjunction with clofazimine.

▶ **Nocardiosis‡.** *Adults:* Usual dose for 12 to 18 months.

▶ **Nongonococcal urethritis caused by *C. trachomatis* or *mycoplasma*‡.** *Adults:* 100 mg P.O. daily in 1 or 2 divided doses for 1 to 3 weeks.

Contraindications and precautions

- Contraindicated in patients hypersensitive to drug or other tetracyclines.
- Use cautiously in patients with impaired kidney or liver function.

Lifespan: During last half of pregnancy and in children younger than age 8, drug may cause permanent discoloration of teeth, enamel defects, and bone growth retardation. For breast-feeding women, drug isn't recommended.

Adverse reactions

CNS: *light-headedness or dizziness from vestibular toxicity,* ***intracranial hypertension (pseudotumor cerebri).***
CV: pericarditis, *thrombophlebitis.*
EENT: dysphagia, glossitis.
GI: *anorexia,* epigastric distress, oral candidiasis, *nausea,* vomiting, *diarrhea,* enterocolitis, inflammatory lesions in anogenital region.
Hematologic: ***neutropenia,*** eosinophilia, ***thrombocytopenia.***
Musculoskeletal: bone growth retardation if used in children younger than age 8; superinfection.
Skin: *maculopapular and erythematous rashes, photosensitivity reactions, increased pigmentation, urticaria.*
Other: permanent discoloration of teeth, enamel defects, hypersensitivity reactions ***(anaphylaxis).***

Interactions

Drug-drug. *Antacids (including sodium bicarbonate) and laxatives containing aluminum, magnesium, or calcium; antidiarrheals:* May decrease antibiotic absorption. Give antibiotic 1 hour before or 2 hours after these drugs.
Cimetidine: May decrease absorption of minocycline. Monitor patient.
Digoxin: Increases serum digoxin levels. Decreased digoxin dose may be needed.
Ferrous sulfate, other iron products, zinc: Decreases antibiotic absorption. Give drug 3 hours after or 2 hours before iron.
Methoxyflurane: May cause nephrotoxicity with tetracyclines. Avoid using together; monitor patient carefully.
Oral anticoagulants: May increase anticoagulant effect. Monitor PT and INR and adjust dosage, as ordered.
Oral contraceptives: Decreases contraceptive effectiveness and increased risk of breakthrough bleeding. Recommend nonhormonal form of birth control.
Penicillins: May interfere with bactericidal action of penicillins. Avoid using together.
Drug-lifestyle. *Sun exposure:* Photosensitivity reactions may occur. Urge patient to avoid unprotected or prolonged exposure to sunlight.
Drug-herb. *St. John's wort:* May increase photosensitivity reactions. Urge patient to avoid unprotected or prolonged exposure to sunlight.

Effects on lab test results

- May increase BUN and liver enzyme levels.
- May increase eosinophil count. May decrease hemoglobin and hematocrit and platelet and neutrophil counts.

Pharmacokinetics

Absorption: 90% to 100%.
Distribution: Distributed widely in body tissues and fluids, including synovial, pleural, prostatic, and seminal fluids; bronchial secretions; saliva; and aqueous humor. CSF penetration is poor. Drug is 70% to 80% protein-bound.
Metabolism: Partial.
Excretion: Excreted primarily unchanged in liver. *Half-life:* 11 to 26 hours.

Route	Onset	Peak	Duration
P.O.	Unknown	1-4 hr	Unknown
I.V.	Immediate	Immediate	Unknown

Pharmacodynamics

Chemical effect: Unknown; may exert bacteriostatic effect by binding to ribosomal subunit of microorganisms, inhibiting protein synthesis.
Therapeutic effect: Hinders bacterial cell growth, including many gram-negative and gram-positive organisms, *Chlamydia, Mycoplasma, Rickettsia,* and spirochetes.

Available forms

Capsules: 50 mg, 100 mg
Capsules (pellet-filled): 50 mg, 100 mg
Injection: 100 mg
Oral suspension: 50 mg/5 ml
Tablets (film-coated): 50 mg, 100 mg

NURSING PROCESS

Assessment

- Assess patient's infection before therapy and regularly thereafter.
- Obtain specimen for culture and sensitivity tests before giving first dose. Therapy may begin pending results.
- Be alert for adverse reactions and drug interactions.
- Monitor patient's hydration status if adverse GI reactions occur.
- Evaluate patient's and family's knowledge of drug therapy.

Nursing diagnoses

- Infection related to presence of susceptible bacteria
- Risk for deficient fluid volume related to drug-induced adverse reactions
- Deficient knowledge related to drug therapy

Planning and implementation

ALERT: Check expiration date. Outdated or deteriorated tetracyclines have been linked to reversible nephrotoxicity (Fanconi's syndrome).

- Don't expose these drugs to light or heat. Keep cap tightly closed.
- **P.O. use:** Follow normal protocol.
- **I.V. use:** Reconstitute 100 mg of powder with 5 ml of sterile water for injection, with further dilution of 500 to 1,000 ml for I.V. infusion. Solution is stable for 24 hours at room temperature.
  – Thrombophlebitis may develop with I.V. administration of drug. Watch for irritation and infiltration; extravasation can cause tissue damage and necrosis. Switch to P.O. form as soon as possible.
  – Parenteral form may cause false-positive reading of copper sulfate tests (Clinitest). All forms may cause false-negative reading of glucose enzymatic tests (Diastix).
- Drug may cause tooth discoloration in children and young adults. Inform prescriber if brown pigmentation occurs.

ALERT: Don't confuse Minocin with niacin and Mithracin.
ALERT: Don't confuse Dynacin with DynaCirc.

Patient teaching

- Inform patient that drug may be taken with food, and instruct him to take drug exactly as prescribed.
- Instruct patient to take oral form of drug with full glass of water, and to avoid taking it within 1 hour of bedtime to avoid esophagitis.
- Warn patient to avoid hazardous tasks until adverse CNS effects of drug are known.
- Warn patient to avoid direct sunlight and ultraviolet light, to use a sunblock, and wear protective clothing.
- Advise patient using oral contraceptives that another form of birth control should be used. Also inform her that she may experience breakthrough bleeding.

Evaluation

- Patient is free from infection.
- Patient maintains adequate hydration throughout therapy.
- Patient and family state understanding of drug therapy.

minoxidil

(migh-NOKS-uh-dil)
Loniten

Pharmacologic class: peripheral vasodilator
Therapeutic class: antihypertensive
Pregnancy risk category: C

Indications and dosages

▶ **Severe hypertension.** *Adults:* Initially, 5 mg P.O. as single dose. Effective dosage range is usually 10 to 40 mg daily. Maximum dosage is 100 mg P.O. daily.
Children younger than age 12: 0.2 mg/kg P.O. (maximum 5 mg) as single daily dose. Effective dosage range usually is 0.25 to 1 mg/kg daily. Maximum dosage is 50 mg P.O. daily.

Contraindications and precautions

- Contraindicated in patients hypersensitive to drug and in those with pheochromocytoma.
- Use cautiously in patients with impaired kidney function or recent acute MI.

Lifespan: In pregnant women, use cautiously. For breast-feeding women, drug isn't recommended.

Adverse reactions

CV: *edema, tachycardia, pericardial effusion and tamponade,* ***heart failure,*** ECG changes.
Metabolic: weight gain.
Skin: *hypertrichosis* (elongation, thickening, and enhanced pigmentation of fine body hair), rash, ***Stevens-Johnson syndrome.***
Other: breast tenderness.

Interactions

Drug-drug. *Guanethidine:* May cause severe orthostatic hypotension. Advise patient to stand up slowly.
Drug-herb. *Yohimbe:* May interfere with blood pressure control. Monitor blood pressure closely.

Effects on lab test results

- May increase BUN, creatinine, and alkaline phosphatase levels.
- May decrease hemoglobin and hematocrit.

Pharmacokinetics

Absorption: Rapid.
Distribution: Distributed widely in body tissues; not bound to plasma proteins.
Metabolism: About 90%.
Excretion: Excreted primarily in urine. *Half-life:* 4.2 hours.

Route	Onset	Peak	Duration
P.O.	About 30 min	≤ 1 hr	2-5 days

Pharmacodynamics

Chemical effect: Unknown; produces direct arteriolar vasodilation.
Therapeutic effect: Lowers blood pressure.

Available forms

Tablets: 2.5 mg, 10 mg, 25 mg ◇

NURSING PROCESS

Assessment

- Obtain history of patient's blood pressure and pulse rate before therapy and reassess regularly thereafter.
- Be alert for adverse reactions and drug interactions.
- Monitor fluid intake and output and check for weight gain and edema.
- Evaluate patient's and family's knowledge of drug therapy.

Nursing diagnoses

- Risk for injury related to presence of hypertension
- Excessive fluid volume related to drug-induced edema
- Deficient knowledge related to drug therapy

Planning and implementation

- Drug is removed by hemodialysis. Give dose after dialysis.
- Drug usually is prescribed with a beta blocker to control tachycardia and a diuretic to counteract fluid retention.
- Notify prescriber if blood pressure changes significantly or pulse rate rises more than 20 beats/minute from baseline.

ALERT: Don't confuse Loniten with Lotensin.

Patient teaching

- Make sure patient reads package insert describing drug's adverse reactions. Provide verbal explanation.

• Teach patient how to take his own pulse and instruct him to report increases over 20 beats/minute to prescriber.
• Tell patient not to suddenly stop taking drug but to call prescriber if unpleasant adverse effects occur.
• Tell patient to weigh himself at least weekly and to report weight gain of more than 5 lb (2.27 kg).
• Inform patient that excessive hair growth commonly occurs within 3 to 6 weeks of beginning treatment. Unwanted hair can be removed by depilatory cream or by shaving. Assure patient that extra hair will disappear within 1 to 6 months of stopping minoxidil. Advise him not to discontinue drug without prescriber's approval.

Evaluation

• Patient's blood pressure is normal.
• Patient exhibits no evidence of edema throughout therapy.
• Patient and family state understanding of drug therapy.

mirtazapine

(mir-TAH-zuh-peen)
Remeron, Remeron SolTab

Pharmacologic class: piperazinoazepine group of compounds
Therapeutic class: antidepressant
Pregnancy risk category: C

Indications and dosages

▶ **Depression.** *Adults:* Initially, 15 mg P.O. h.s. Maintenance dosage is 15 to 45 mg daily. Adjust dosage at intervals of at least 1 to 2 weeks.

Contraindications and precautions

• Contraindicated in patients hypersensitive to drug. Giving with MAO inhibitors is contraindicated.
• Use cautiously in patients with CV or cerebrovascular disease, seizure disorders, suicidal ideations, impaired hepatic or renal function, or history of mania or hypomania.
Lifespan: In breast-feeding women, use cautiously.

Adverse reactions

CNS: somnolence, dizziness, asthenia, abnormal dreams, abnormal thinking, tremor, confusion.
CV: edema, peripheral edema.
GI: nausea, increased appetite, dry mouth, constipation.
GU: urinary frequency.
Metabolic: weight gain.
Musculoskeletal: back pain, myalgia.
Respiratory: dyspnea.
Other: flulike syndrome.

Interactions

Drug-drug. *Diazepam, other CNS depressants:* Possible additive CNS effects. Avoid using together.
MAO inhibitors: May cause potentially serious, sometimes fatal reactions. Don't use drug within 14 days of an MAO inhibitor.
Drug-lifestyle. *Alcohol use:* May have possible additive CNS effects. Discourage using together.

Effects on lab test results

• May increase ALT levels.

Pharmacokinetics

Absorption: Rapid.
Distribution: 85% bound to plasma proteins.
Metabolism: Extensively metabolized in liver.
Excretion: Mainly excreted in urine; some in feces. *Mean elimination half-life:* About 20 to 40 hours.

Route	Onset	Peak	Duration
P.O.	Unknown	Within 2 hr	Unknown

Pharmacodynamics

Chemical effect: Enhances central noradrenergic and serotonergic activity; potent antagonist of histamine receptors.
Therapeutic effect: Relieves depression.

Available forms

Orally disintegrating tablets: 15 mg, 30 mg, 45 mg
Tablets: 15 mg, 30 mg, 45 mg

NURSING PROCESS

Assessment

• Stop drug and monitor patient closely if he develops a sore throat, fever, stomatitis, or oth-

er signs of infection together with a low WBC count.
- Evaluate patient's and family's knowledge of drug therapy.

Nursing diagnoses
- Disturbed thought processes related to adverse effects
- Risk for injury related to sedation and orthostatic hypotension
- Deficient knowledge related to drug therapy

Planning and implementation
- Use cautiously when giving drug to breast-feeding women.

Patient teaching
- Instruct patient to remove orally disintegrating tablet from blister pack and immediately place on the tongue. Patient does not need water to swallow the tablet because drug rapidly dissolves.
- Caution patient not to break or split tablet.
- Warn patient to avoid hazardous activities if somnolence occurs.
- Tell patient to report signs and symptoms of infection or flulike symptoms.
- Advise patient to avoid alcohol or other CNS depressants.
- Stress importance of compliance with therapy.
- Instruct patient not to take other drugs without prescriber's approval.
- Tell woman to notify prescriber if she suspects pregnancy or if she is breast-feeding.

Evaluation
- Patient regains normal thought processes.
- Patient sustains no injury from adverse reactions.
- Patient and family state understanding of drug therapy.

misoprostol
(mee-SOH-pruh-stol)
Cytotec

Pharmacologic class: prostaglandin E_1 analogue
Therapeutic class: gastric mucosal protectant
Pregnancy risk category: X

Indications and dosages
▶ **Prevention of NSAID-induced gastric ulcer in elderly or debilitated patients at high risk for complications from gastric ulcer and in patients with history of NSAID-induced ulcer.** *Adults:* 200 mcg P.O. q.i.d. with food. If dosage isn't tolerated, decrease to 100 mcg P.O. q.i.d.
▶ **Duodenal or gastric ulcer‡.** *Adults:* 100 to 200 mcg P.O. q.i.d. with meals and h.s. for 4 to 8 weeks.

Contraindications and precautions
- Contraindicated in those with a known allergy to prostaglandins.

Lifespan: Pregnant women shouldn't take drug for reducing the risk of NSAID-induced ulcers.

Adverse reactions
CNS: headache.
GI: *diarrhea, abdominal pain,* nausea, flatulence, dyspepsia, vomiting, constipation.
GU: hypermenorrhea, dysmenorrhea, spotting, cramps, menstrual disorders.

Interactions
Drug-drug. *Antacids:* Reduces misoprostol level insignificantly. Monitor patient.

Effects on lab test results
None reported.

Pharmacokinetics
Absorption: Rapid.
Distribution: Highly bound to plasma proteins.
Metabolism: Rapidly de-esterified to misoprostol acid, the biologically active metabolite.
Excretion: About 15% excreted in feces; balance excreted in urine. *Half-life:* 20 to 40 minutes.

Route	Onset	Peak	Duration
P.O.	30 min	10-15 min	3 hr

Pharmacodynamics
Chemical effect: Replaces gastric prostaglandins depleted by NSAID therapy. Decreases basal and stimulated gastric acid secretion and may increase gastric mucus and bicarbonate production.

Therapeutic effect: Protects gastric mucosa from ulcerating.

Available forms

Tablets: 100 mcg, 200 mcg

NURSING PROCESS

Assessment

- Obtain history of patient's GI condition before therapy.
- In woman of childbearing age, make sure that negative pregnancy test is obtained within 2 weeks before therapy begins.
- Be alert for adverse reactions and drug interactions.
- Evaluate patient's and family's knowledge of drug therapy.

Nursing diagnoses

- Risk for injury related to potential for gastric ulceration
- Acute pain related to headache
- Deficient knowledge related to drug therapy

Planning and implementation

ALERT: Take special precautions to prevent use of drug during pregnancy. Make sure patient is fully aware of dangers of misoprostol to fetus and that she receives both verbal and written warnings regarding these dangers. Also make sure patient can comply with effective contraceptive means.

- Uterine rupture is linked to certain risk factors, including later trimester pregnancies, higher doses of the drug, prior cesarean delivery or uterine surgery, or five or more previous pregnancies.

ALERT: Don't confuse misoprostol with mifepristone.

Patient teaching

- Instruct patient not to share drug. Remind her that drug may cause miscarriage, usually with life-threatening bleeding.
- Advise her not to begin therapy until second or third day of next normal menstrual period.

Evaluation

- Patient remains free from signs and symptoms of gastric ulceration.
- Patient states that drug-induced headache doesn't occur.
- Patient and family state understanding of drug therapy.

mitomycin (mitomycin-C)

(might-oh-MIGH-sin)
Mutamycin, Mitozytrex

Pharmacologic class: antineoplastic antibiotic (cell cycle–phase nonspecific)
Therapeutic class: antineoplastic
Pregnancy risk category: NR

Indications and dosages

▶ **Pancreatic and stomach cancers.** *Adults:* 15 mg/m² (Mitozytrex) or 20 mg/m² (Mutamycin) I.V. as single dose. Cycle repeated after 6 to 8 weeks, with dosage adjusted if needed based on nadir WBC and platelet counts.

▶ **Bladder cancer‡.** ***Mutamycin.*** *Adults:* 20 to 60 mg intravesically once per week for 8 weeks.

Contraindications and precautions

- Contraindicated in patients hypersensitive to drug and in those with thrombocytopenia, coagulation disorder, or increased bleeding tendency from other causes.

Lifespan: For pregnant or breast-feeding women, drug isn't recommended. In children, safety of drug hasn't been established.

Adverse reactions

GI: *nausea, vomiting,* anorexia, stomatitis.
Hematologic: THROMBOCYTOPENIA, LEUKOPENIA (may be delayed up to 8 weeks and be cumulative with successive doses), ***microangiopathic hemolytic anemia.***
Respiratory: ***interstitial pneumonitis.***
Skin: desquamation, induration, pruritus, and *pain* at injection site; ***septicemia,*** cellulitis, ulceration, and sloughing with extravasation; *reversible alopecia;* purple coloration of nail beds.

Interactions

Drug-drug. *Vinca alkaloids:* May cause acute respiratory distress. Avoid using together.

Effects on lab test results

- May decrease hemoglobin, hematocrit, and platelet and WBC counts.

Pharmacokinetics

Absorption: Given I.V.
Distribution: Distributed widely in body tissues; doesn't cross blood-brain barrier.
Metabolism: Metabolized by hepatic microsomal enzymes and deactivated in kidneys, spleen, brain, and heart.
Excretion: Excreted primarily in urine; small portion excreted in bile and feces. *Half-life:* About 50 minutes.

Route	Onset	Peak	Duration
I.V.	Unknown	Unknown	Unknown

Pharmacodynamics

Chemical effect: Acts like alkylating agent, cross-linking strands of DNA. This causes imbalance of cell growth, leading to cell death.
Therapeutic effect: Kills certain cancer cells.

Available forms

Injection: 5-, 20-, and 40-mg vials

NURSING PROCESS

Assessment

- Assess patient's condition before therapy and regularly thereafter.
- Obtain CBC and blood studies.
- Monitor kidney function tests.
- Be alert for adverse reactions and drug interactions.
- Evaluate patient's and family's knowledge of drug therapy.

Nursing diagnoses

- Ineffective health maintenance related to presence of neoplastic disease
- Ineffective protection related to adverse hematologic reactions
- Deficient knowledge related to drug therapy

Planning and implementation

- Follow facility policy to reduce risks. Preparation and administration of parenteral form are related to mutagenic, teratogenic, and carcinogenic risks to personnel.
- To reconstitute 5-mg vial Mitozytrex, use 8.5 ml sterile water for injection; for 5-mg vial Mutamycin, use 10 ml of sterile water for injection; to reconstitute 20-mg vial, use 40 ml of sterile water for injection; to reconstitute a 40-mg vial, use 80 ml sterile water for injection, to give a concentration of 0.5 mg/ml. Allow to stand at room temperature until complete dissolution occurs.
- Mitozytrex: When reconstituted with sterile water for injection to a concentration of 0.5 mg/ml, is stable for 24 hours. When diluted, stable in D_5W for 4 hours, 0.9% NaCl for 48 hours, sodium lactate for 24 hours.
- Mutamycin: When reconstituted with sterile water for injection to a concentration of 0.5 mg/ml, is stable for 14 days refrigerated or 7 days at room temperature. When diluted, stable in D_5W for 3 hours, 0.9% NaCl for 12 hours, sodium lactate for 24 hours.
- The combination of mitomycin (5 mg to 15 mg) and heparin (1,000 units to 10,000 units) in 30 ml of 0.9% Sodium Chloride Injection is stable for 48 hours (Mutamycin), 72 hours (Mitozytrex) at room temperature.
- Watch for irritation and infiltration; extravasation can cause tissue damage and necrosis. If extravasation occurs, stop infusion immediately and notify prescriber because of potential for severe ulceration and necrosis.
- Never give drug I.M. or S.C.
- Discontinue drug if WBC count is less than 4,000/mm^3 and platelet count is less than 150,000/mm^3. Restart drug when counts rise above those levels.

ALERT: Don't confuse mitomycin with mithramycin.

Patient teaching

- Instruct patient to watch for signs of infection and bleeding and to take temperature daily.
- Warn patient that alopecia may occur but assure him that it's reversible.
- Tell patient to report adverse reactions to prescriber promptly.

Evaluation

- Patient responds well to therapy.
- Patient doesn't develop serious complications.
- Patient and family state understanding of drug therapy.

mitotane (o,p′-DDD)

(MIGH-toh-tayn)
Lysodren

Pharmacologic class: chlorophenothane (DDT) analogue
Therapeutic class: antineoplastic
Pregnancy risk category: C

Indications and dosages

▶ **Inoperable adrenocortical cancer.** *Adults:* Initially, 2 to 6 g P.O. daily in divided doses t.i.d. or q.i.d.; increased to 9 to 10 g P.O. daily in divided doses t.i.d. or q.i.d. Dosage is adjusted until maximum tolerated dosage is achieved (varies from 2 to 19 g P.O. daily but is usually 8 to 10 g P.O. daily).

Contraindications and precautions

- Contraindicated in patients hypersensitive to drug and in those who are in shock or have suffered trauma.
- Use cautiously in patients with hepatic disease.

Lifespan: In pregnant women, use cautiously. For breast-feeding women, drug isn't recommended. In children, safety of drug hasn't been established.

Adverse reactions

CNS: *depression, somnolence, lethargy, vertigo,* brain damage and dysfunction in long-term high-dose therapy.
CV: hypertension.
EENT: visual disturbances.
GI: *severe nausea, vomiting,* diarrhea, anorexia.
GU: hemorrhagic cystitis.
Metabolic: hypercholesteremia, adrenal insufficiency.
Skin: dermatitis, maculopapular rash.

Interactions

Drug-drug. *Corticosteroids:* Corticosteroid metabolism may be altered; higher corticosteroid doses may be needed.
Warfarin: May increase metabolism, which may require higher warfarin doses. Monitor PT and INR closely.

Effects on lab test results

- May increase plasma cortisol, protein-bound iodine, cholesterol, and uric acid levels.

Pharmacokinetics

Absorption: 35% to 40%.
Distribution: Widely distributed in body tissue; fatty tissue is primary storage site. Slow release of drug from fatty tissue into plasma occurs after drug is discontinued.
Metabolism: Metabolized in liver and other tissue.
Excretion: Excreted in urine and bile. *Half-life:* 18 to 159 days.

Route	Onset	Peak	Duration
P.O.	2-3 days (steroid); ≤ 6 mo (tumor)	3-5 hr	Unknown

Pharmacodynamics

Chemical effect: Unknown; thought to selectively destroy adrenocortical tissue and hinder extra-adrenal metabolism of cortisol.
Therapeutic effect: Hinders adrenocortical cancer cell growth.

Available forms

Tablets (scored): 500 mg

NURSING PROCESS

Assessment

- Obtain history of patient's adrenocortical cancer before therapy.
- Monitor effectiveness according to reduction in pain, weakness, and anorexia.
- Assess and record behavioral and neurologic signs daily throughout therapy. Prolonged therapy has been linked to significant neurologic impairment.
- Be alert for adverse reactions.
- Monitor patient's hydration status if adverse GI reactions occur.
- Evaluate patient's and family's knowledge of drug therapy.

Nursing diagnoses

- Ineffective health maintenance related to presence of neoplastic disease

• Risk for deficient fluid volume related to drug-induced adverse GI reactions
• Deficient knowledge related to drug therapy

Planning and implementation

• Give antiemetic before mitotane.
• Be prepared to reduce dosage if adverse GI or skin reactions are severe.
• Use of corticosteroids may avoid acute adrenocorticoid insufficiency and is usually needed. Glucocorticoid dosage should be increased in periods of stress, such as infection or trauma.
• Drug is distributed mostly to body fat. Obese patients may need higher dosage and have longer-lasting adverse reactions.
• Adequate therapeutic trial is at least 3 months, but treatment can continue if clinical benefits are observed.
• Monitor PT and INR in patient receiving mitotane with warfarin.

Patient teaching

• Warn patient to avoid activities that require alertness and good motor coordination until CNS effects of drug are known.
• Tell patient to report adverse reactions promptly.
• For patient also receiving warfarin, instruct him to watch for and report signs of bleeding.

Evaluation

• Patient responds well to therapy.
• Patient maintains adequate hydration throughout therapy.
• Patient and family state understanding of drug therapy.

mitoxantrone hydrochloride

(migh-toh-ZAN-trohn high-droh-KLOR-ighd)
Novantrone

Pharmacologic class: antibiotic antineoplastic
Therapeutic class: antineoplastic
Pregnancy risk category: D

Indications and dosages

▶ **Combination initial therapy for acute nonlymphocytic leukemia.** *Adults:* Induction begins with 12 mg/m^2 I.V. daily on days 1 through 3, given with 100 mg/m^2 daily of cytarabine on days 1 through 7. A second induction may be given if response isn't adequate. Maintenance therapy: 12 mg/m^2 on days 1 and 2, given with cytarabine on days 1 through 5.

▶ **To reduce neurologic disability and frequency of relapse in chronic progressive, progressive relapsing, or worsening relapsing-remitting multiple sclerosis.** *Adults:* 12 mg/m^2 I.V. over 5 to 15 minutes q 3 months.

▶ **Combination initial therapy for pain from advanced hormone-refractory prostate cancer.** *Adults:* 12 to 14 mg/m2 I.V. infusion over 15 to 30 minutes q 21 days.

Contraindications and precautions

• Contraindicated in patients hypersensitive to drug.
• Use cautiously in patients previously exposed to anthracyclines or other cardiotoxic drugs.
Lifespan: For pregnant or breast-feeding women, drug isn't recommended. In children, safety of drug hasn't been established.

Adverse reactions

CNS: *seizures,* headache.
CV: ***heart failure, arrhythmias,*** tachycardia.
EENT: conjunctivitis.
GI: *bleeding, abdominal pain, diarrhea, nausea, mucositis, vomiting, stomatitis.*
GU: uric acid nephropathy, ***renal failure.***
Hematologic: ***myelosuppression.***
Hepatic: jaundice.
Metabolic: hyperuricemia.
Respiratory: dyspnea, cough.
Skin: petechiae, ecchymoses, alopecia.

Interactions

None significant.

Effects on lab test results

• May increase ALT, AST, bilirubin, BUN, creatinine, and uric acid levels.
• May decrease hemoglobin, hematocrit, and WBC, RBC, and platelet counts.

Pharmacokinetics

Absorption: Given I.V.
Distribution: 78% plasma protein–bound.
Metabolism: Metabolized by liver.

Excretion: Excreted by way of renal and hepatobiliary systems. *Half-life:* 5.8 days.

Route	Onset	Peak	Duration
I.V.	Unknown	Unknown	Unknown

Pharmacodynamics

Chemical effect: Not fully understood; probably cell cycle–nonspecific. Drug reacts with DNA, producing cytotoxic effect.
Therapeutic effect: Hinders susceptible cancer cell growth.

Available forms

Injection: 2 mg/ml in 10-, 12.5-, and 15-ml vials

NURSING PROCESS

Assessment
- Assess patient's condition before therapy and regularly thereafter.
- Monitor hematologic and laboratory chemistry parameters.
- Left ventricular ejection fraction should be monitored.
- Be alert for adverse reactions and drug interactions.
- Evaluate patient's and family's knowledge of drug therapy.

Nursing diagnoses
- Ineffective health maintenance related to presence of leukemia
- Ineffective immune protection related to drug-induced myelosuppression
- Deficient knowledge related to drug therapy

Planning and implementation
- Patients with significant myelosuppression (neutrophil count below 1,500 cells/mm^3) shouldn't receive drug unless benefits outweigh risks.
- Follow facility policy to minimize risks. Preparation and administration of parenteral form are linked to mutagenic, teratogenic, and carcinogenic risks to personnel.
- Dilute dose (available as aqueous solution of 2 mg/ml in volumes of 10, 12.5, and 15 ml) in at least 50 ml of normal saline solution injection or D_5W injection. Give drug by direct injection into free-flowing I.V. line of normal saline solution or D_5W injection over at least 3 minutes.

ALERT: Don't mix with other drugs, especially heparin because it's physically incompatible.
- Although drug isn't a vesicant, discontinue infusion immediately and notify prescriber if it extravasates.
- Be prepared to give allopurinol. Uric acid nephropathy can be avoided by adequately hydrating patient before and during therapy.
- If severe nonhematologic toxicity occurs during first course of therapy, second course should be delayed until patient recovers.
- Store undiluted solution at room temperature. Once diluted, mixture is stable for 7 days at room temperature.

Patient teaching
- Inform patient that urine may appear blue-green within 24 hours after administration and that some bluish discoloration of sclera may occur. These effects aren't harmful.
- Teach patient infection control and bleeding precautions. Tell him to watch for and report signs of bleeding and infection.
- Advise woman of childbearing age to avoid pregnancy during therapy and to consult prescriber before becoming pregnant.

Evaluation
- Patient responds well to therapy.
- Patient develops no serious complications from drug-induced myelosuppression.
- Patient and family state understanding of drug therapy.

mivacurium chloride
(migh-vuh-KYOO-ree-um KLOR-ighd)
Mivacron

Pharmacologic class: nondepolarizing neuromuscular blocker
Therapeutic class: skeletal muscle relaxant
Pregnancy risk category: C

Indications and dosages

▶**Adjunct to general anesthesia, to facilitate endotracheal intubation, and to relax skeletal muscles during surgery or mechanical ventilation.** *Adults:* Dosage is highly individualized. Usually, 0.15 mg/kg I.V. push over 5 to 15 seconds provides adequate muscle relaxation within 135 seconds for endotracheal

intubation. Supplemental doses of 0.1 mg/kg I.V. q 15 minutes is usually sufficient to maintain muscle relaxation. Or, maintain neuromuscular blockade with continuous infusion of 4 mcg/kg/minute begun simultaneously with initial dose, or 9 to 10 mcg/kg/minute started after evidence of spontaneous recovery caused by initial dose. When used with isoflurane or enflurane anesthesia, dosage usually is reduced about 35% to 40%.
Children ages 2 to 12: 0.2 mg/kg I.V. push given over 5 to 15 seconds. Neuromuscular blockade is usually evident in less than 2 minutes. Maintenance doses are generally needed more frequently in children. Or, neuromuscular blockade maintained with continuous I.V. infusion adjusted to effect. Most children respond to 5 to 31 mcg/kg/minute (average 14 mcg/kg/minute).
Patients with end-stage renal or hepatic disease: decrease infusion rates by as much as 50%.

Contraindications and precautions

- Contraindicated in patients hypersensitive to drug.
- Use cautiously, if at all, in patients who are homozygous for atypical plasma pseudocholinesterase gene. Drug is metabolized to inactive compounds by plasma pseudocholinesterase.
- Use cautiously in patients with significant CV disease and in those who may be adversely affected by release of histamine (such as asthmatic patients).
- Also use cautiously, possibly at reduced dosage, in debilitated patients; in patients with metastatic cancer, severe electrolyte disturbances, or neuromuscular diseases; and in those in whom potentiation or difficulty in reversal of neuromuscular blockade is anticipated. Patients with myasthenia gravis or myasthenic syndrome (Eaton-Lambert syndrome) are particularly sensitive to effects of nondepolarizing relaxants.

Lifespan: In pregnant or breast-feeding women, use cautiously.

Adverse reactions

CNS: dizziness.
CV: *flushing,* hypotension, tachycardia, ***bradycardia, arrhythmias,*** phlebitis.
Musculoskeletal: prolonged muscle weakness, muscle spasms.
Respiratory: ***bronchospasm,*** wheezing, ***respiratory insufficiency, apnea.***
Skin: rash, urticaria, erythema.

Interactions

Drug-drug. *Alkaline solutions (such as barbiturate solutions):* Physically incompatible; precipitate may form. Don't give through same I.V. line.
Aminoglycosides (gentamicin, kanamycin, neomycin, streptomycin), bacitracin, clindamycin, colistimethate, colistin, ketamine, parenteral verapamil, polymyxin B sulfate, tetracycline: May potentiate neuromuscular blockade, leading to increased skeletal muscle relaxation and prolonged effect. Use together cautiously.
Carbamazepine, phenytoin: May prolong time to maximal blockade or shorten duration of neuromuscular blockers. Monitor patient.
Inhaled anesthetics (especially enflurane, isoflurane), magnesium salts, quinidine: May enhance activity or prolong action of nondepolarizing neuromuscular blockers. Monitor patient for excessive weakness.

Effects on lab test results

None reported.

Pharmacokinetics

Absorption: Given I.V.
Distribution: Not extensively distributed to tissues.
Metabolism: Rapidly hydrolyzed by plasma pseudocholinesterase to inactive components.
Excretion: Metabolites excreted in urine and bile. *Half-life: cis-trans* and *trans-trans* isomers, less than 2.3 minutes; *cis-cis* isomer, 55 minutes.

Route	Onset	Peak	Duration
I.V.	1-2 min	2-5 min	20-35 min

Pharmacodynamics

Chemical effect: Competes with acetylcholine for receptor sites at motor end plate. Because cholinesterase inhibitors may antagonize this action, drug is considered a competitive antagonist. Drug is mixture of three stereoisomers, each with neuromuscular blocking activity.
Therapeutic effect: Relaxes skeletal muscles.

Available forms

Infusion: 0.5 mg/ml in 50 ml of D_5W
Injection: 2 mg/ml in 5- and 10-ml vials

NURSING PROCESS

Assessment

- Assess patient's need for drug before therapy and regularly thereafter.
- Monitor respiratory rate closely until patient is fully recovered from neuromuscular blockade, as evidenced by tests of muscle strength (hand grip, head lift, and ability to cough).
- Be alert for adverse reactions and drug interactions.
- Evaluate patient's and family's knowledge of drug therapy.

Nursing diagnoses

- Ineffective breathing pattern related to drug's effect on respiratory muscle
- Deficient knowledge related to drug therapy

Planning and implementation

ALERT: Give only under direct medical supervision of clinician skilled in use of neuromuscular blockers and techniques for maintaining airway. Don't use unless emergency equipment for respiratory support and antagonist are within reach.

- To avoid patient distress, don't give until patient is unconscious by general anesthetic because drug has no effect on consciousness or pain threshold.
- Give test dose to assess patient's sensitivity to drug. Patients with severe burns develop resistance to nondepolarizing neuromuscular blockers; however, they also may have reduced plasma pseudocholinesterase activity.
- Drug may be given by direct injection over 5 to 15 seconds.
- Prepare drug for I.V. use with D_5W, normal saline solution injection, D_5W in normal saline solution injection, lactated Ringer's injection, or D_5W in lactated Ringer's injection. Diluted solutions are stable for 24 hours at room temperature.
- When diluted as directed, drug is compatible with alfentanil, fentanyl, sufentanil, droperidol, and midazolam.
- For drug available as premixed infusion in D_5W, remove protective outer wrap and check container for minor leaks by squeezing bag before giving. Don't add other drugs to container, and don't use container in series connections.
- Nerve stimulator and train-of-four monitoring are recommended to document antagonism of neuromuscular blockade and recovery of muscle strength. Before attempting reversal with neostigmine or edrophonium, some signs of spontaneous recovery should be evident.
- Experimental evidence suggests that acid-base and electrolyte balances may influence actions of nondepolarizing neuromuscular blockers. Alkalosis may counteract paralysis; acidosis may enhance it.
- Dosage should be adjusted to ideal body weight in obese patients (patients 30% or more above their ideal weight) to avoid prolonged neuromuscular blockade.
- Duration of effect is increased about 150% in patients with end-stage renal disease and 300% in patients with hepatic dysfunction.
- Like other neuromuscular blockers, dosage requirements for children are higher on mg/kg basis than those for adults. Onset and recovery of neuromuscular blockade occur more rapidly in children.

ALERT: Don't confuse Mivacron with Mazicon or Mevacor.

Patient teaching

- Describe use of drug to patient and family, and answer their questions.

Evaluation

- Patient maintains adequate ventilation with or without assistance.
- Patient and family state understanding of drug therapy.

modafinil

(moh-DAF-ih-nil)

Provigil

Pharmacologic class: nonamphetamine CNS stimulant
Therapeutic class: analeptic
Pregnancy risk category: C
Controlled substance schedule: IV

Indications and dosages

▶ **Improvement of wakefulness in patients with excessive daytime sleepiness caused by narcolepsy.** *Adults:* 200 mg P.O. daily, given as a single dose in the morning.
Patients with severe hepatic impairment: Reduce dosage by 50%.

Contraindications and precautions

• Contraindicated in patients hypersensitive to modafinil. Don't use in patients with a history of left ventricular hypertrophy or ischemic ECG changes, chest pain, arrhythmias, or other signs or symptoms of mitral valve prolapse caused by CNS stimulant use.
• Use cautiously in patients with recent MI or unstable angina and in those with history of psychosis.
• Use cautiously and at reduced dosage in patients with severe hepatic impairment, with or without cirrhosis.
• Also use cautiously in patients receiving treatment with MAO inhibitors.
Lifespan: In pregnant patients, use only when the potential benefits outweigh the potential harm to the fetus. In breast-feeding women, use cautiously. In patients younger than age 16 or older than age 65, safety and efficacy haven't been established. In elderly patients with renal or hepatic impairment, use cautiously and at a reduced rate.

Adverse reactions

CNS: *headache,* nervousness, dizziness, depression, anxiety, fever, cataplexy, insomnia, paresthesia, dyskinesia, hypertonia, confusion, amnesia, emotional lability, ataxia, syncope, tremor.
CV: hypotension, hypertension, vasodilation, ***arrhythmias,*** chest pain.
EENT: *rhinitis,* pharyngitis, epistaxis, amblyopia, abnormal vision.
GI: *nausea,* diarrhea, dry mouth, mouth ulcer, gingivitis, thirst, anorexia, vomiting.
GU: abnormal urine, urine retention, abnormal ejaculation.
Hematologic: eosinophilia.
Metabolic: hyperglycemia.
Musculoskeletal: neck pain, rigid neck, joint disorder.
Respiratory: lung disorders, dyspnea, asthma.
Skin: herpes simplex, dry skin.
Other: chills.

Interactions

Drug-drug. *Carbamazepine, phenobarbital, rifampin, other inducers of CYP3A4; itraconazole, ketoconazole, other inhibitors of CYP3A4:* Alters modafinil levels. Monitor patient closely.
Cyclosporine, theophylline: Reduces levels of these drugs. Use together cautiously.
Diazepam, phenytoin, propranolol, other drugs metabolized by CYP2C19: Modafinil is a reversible inhibitor of cytochrome P-450 isoenzyme CYP2C19, and thus may increase levels of drugs that this enzyme metabolizes. Use together cautiously. Adjust dosage as needed.
Hormonal contraceptives: Reduces levels of these drugs, resulting in reduced contraceptive effectiveness. Recommend additional or alternative contraceptive method during modafinil therapy and for 1 month afterward.
Methylphenidate: Delays modafinil absorption. Separate administration times.
Phenytoin, warfarin: May cause concentration-dependent inhibition of CYP2C9 activity and increase levels of phenytoin and warfarin. Monitor patient closely for signs of toxicity.
Tricyclic antidepressants (such as clomipramine, desipramine): May increase tricyclic antidepressant levels. Reduce dosage of these drugs.

Effects on lab test results

• May increase glucose, GGT, and AST levels.
• May increase eosinophil count.

Pharmacokinetics

Absorption: Rapid, with plasma levels peaking in 2 to 4 hours.
Distribution: Well distributed in body tissue. About 60% binds to plasma protein, primarily albumin.
Metabolism: About 90% of drug is metabolized in the liver, with subsequent renal elimination of the metabolites.
Excretion: Less than 10% is excreted from the kidneys as unchanged drug.

Route	Onset	Peak	Duration
P.O.	Unknown	2-4 hr	Unknown

Pharmacodynamics

Chemical effect: Unknown. It has wake-promoting actions similar to those of sympathomimetics, including amphetamines, but it's structurally distinct from amphetamines and doesn't appear to alter the release of either dopamine or norepinephrine to produce CNS stimulation.
Therapeutic effect: Improves daytime wakefulness.

Available forms

Tablets: 100 mg, 200 mg

NURSING PROCESS

Assessment

- Obtain history of patient's underlying condition before therapy, and reassess regularly thereafter.
- Assess patient's renal function before starting drug therapy.
- Monitor hypertensive patients on modafinil therapy closely.
- Evaluate patient's and family's knowledge about drug therapy.

Nursing diagnoses

- Disturbed sleep pattern related to drug-induced insomnia
- Risk for injury related to drug-induced CNS adverse effects
- Deficient knowledge related to drug therapy

Planning and implementation

- Food has no effect on overall bioavailability, but it may delay modafinil absorption by 1 hour.
- Although single, daily, 400-mg doses have been well tolerated, no consistent evidence exists that this dosage provides additional benefit beyond the 200-mg dose.

Patient teaching

- Modafinil may impair judgment. Advise patient to be careful while driving or performing other activities that require alertness until full effects of drug are known.
- Instruct patient not to take other prescription or OTC drugs without consulting prescriber because of possible drug interactions.
- Advise patient to avoid alcohol while taking modafinil.
- Tell patient to notify prescriber if he develops a rash, hives, or a related allergic reaction.
- Caution woman that use of hormonal contraceptives (including depot or implantable contraceptives) with modafinil tablets may increase the risk of pregnancy. Recommend an alternative or additional method of contraception during modafinil therapy and for 1 month afterward.
- Advise woman to notify prescriber if she becomes pregnant or intends to become pregnant during therapy.
- Tell woman to notify prescriber if she's breast-feeding.

Evaluation

- Patient develops and maintains normal sleep-wake patterns.
- Patient has no adverse CNS effects.
- Patient and family state understanding of drug therapy.

moexipril hydrochloride

(moh-EKS-eh-pril high-droh-KLOR-ighd)

Univasc

Pharmacologic class: ACE inhibitor
Therapeutic class: antihypertensive
Pregnancy risk category: C (D in second and third trimesters)

Indications and dosages

▶ **Hypertension.** *Adults:* 7.5 mg P.O. once daily before meals (3.75 mg for patients receiving diuretics). Inadequate response may lead to increased dose or divided dosing. Recommended dosage is 7.5 to 30 mg daily, in one or two divided doses 1 hour before meals. Subsequent adjustments made based on patient response.

Patients with renal impairment: If creatinine clearance is 40 ml/minute or less, initiate dose at 3.75 mg P.O. daily. Maximum dose is 15 mg P.O. daily.

Contraindications and precautions

- Contraindicated in patients hypersensitive to drug and in those with history of angioedema with previous treatment with ACE inhibitor.
- Use cautiously in patients with impaired kidney function, heart failure, or renal artery stenosis.

Lifespan: For pregnant women, drug isn't recommended. In breast-feeding women, use cautiously. In children, safety of drug hasn't been established.

Adverse reactions

CNS: *dizziness,* headache, fatigue.
CV: peripheral edema, hypotension, orthostatic hypotension, chest pain, flushing.
EENT: pharyngitis, rhinitis, sinusitis.
GI: diarrhea, dyspepsia, nausea.

GU: urinary frequency.
Hematologic: ***neutropenia.***
Metabolic: ***hyperkalemia.***
Musculoskeletal: myalgia.
Respiratory: *persistent, nonproductive cough,* upper respiratory tract infection.
Skin: rash.
Other: ***anaphylaxis, angioedema,*** flulike syndrome, pain.

Interactions

Drug-drug. *Antacids:* Bioavailability of ACE inhibitors may be decreased. Give drug on an empty stomach.
Digoxin: Increases digoxin level. Monitor digoxin level and patient closely.
Diuretics: May increase risk of excessive hypotension. Monitor blood pressure closely.
Indomethacin: May reduce hypotensive effects of ACE inhibitors. Avoid using together; monitor blood pressure.
Lithium: Increases lithium level and lithium toxicity. Use together cautiously. Monitor lithium level frequently.
Potassium-sparing diuretics, potassium supplements: Increases risk of hyperkalemia. Monitor potassium level closely.
Drug-herb. *Capsaicin:* May cause or worsen coughing linked to ACE inhibitor treatment. Discourage using together.
Drug-food. *Salt substitutes that contain potassium:* May increase risk of hyperkalemia. Monitor potassium level closely; urge patient to avoid salt substitutes containing potassium.

Effects on lab test results

- May increase potassium level.
- May decrease neutrophil count.

Pharmacokinetics

Absorption: Incomplete, with bioavailability of about 13%. Food significantly decreases bioavailability.
Distribution: About 50% protein-bound.
Metabolism: Metabolized extensively to the active metabolite moexiprilat.
Excretion: Excreted primarily in feces, with small amount in urine. *Half-life:* 2 to 9 hours.

Route	Onset	Peak	Duration
P.O.	1 hr	3-6 hr	24 hr

Pharmacodynamics

Chemical effect: Unknown; thought to result mainly from suppression of renin-angiotensin-aldosterone system. Inhibits ACE, thereby inhibiting production of angiotensin II (a potent vasoconstrictor and stimulator of aldosterone secretion). Other mechanisms also may be involved.
Therapeutic effect: Lowers blood pressure.

Available forms

Tablets: 7.5 mg, 15 mg

NURSING PROCESS

Assessment

- Assess patient's blood pressure before therapy.
- Measure blood pressure at trough (just before dose) to verify adequate control. Drug is less effective in reducing trough blood pressure in blacks than in nonblacks.
- Monitor patient for hypotension.
- Assess kidney function before therapy and periodically thereafter. Monitor potassium level.
- Other ACE inhibitors have been linked to agranulocytosis and neutropenia. Monitor CBC with differential counts before therapy, especially in patient who has collagen-vascular disease with impaired kidney function.
- Be alert for adverse reactions and interactions.
- Evaluate patient's and family's knowledge of drug therapy.

Nursing diagnoses

- Risk for injury related to presence of hypertension
- Disturbed sleep pattern related to cough
- Deficient knowledge related to drug therapy

Planning and implementation

- Excessive hypotension can occur when drug is given with diuretics. If possible, diuretic therapy should be discontinued 2 to 3 days before starting moexipril to decrease potential for excessive hypotensive response. If moexipril doesn't adequately control blood pressure, prescriber may reinstitute diuretic with care.
- Angioedema involving tongue, glottis, or larynx may be fatal because of airway obstruction. Be prepared with appropriate therapy,

such as epinephrine and equipment to ensure a patent airway.
- Notify prescriber if drug-induced cough interferes with patient's ability to sleep.

Patient teaching
- Instruct patient to take drug on an empty stomach; high-fat meals can impair absorption.
- Tell patient to avoid salt substitutes; these products may contain potassium, which can cause hyperkalemia.
- Advise patient to rise slowly to minimize light-headedness. If syncope occurs, tell him to stop drug and call prescriber immediately.
- Urge patient to use caution in hot weather and during exercise. Inadequate fluid intake, vomiting, diarrhea, and excessive perspiration can lead to light-headedness and syncope.
- Advise patient to report signs of infection, such as fever and sore throat; easy bruising or bleeding; swelling of tongue, lips, face, eyes, mucous membranes, or limbs; difficulty swallowing or breathing; and hoarseness.
- Tell woman to notify prescriber if pregnancy occurs.

☑ Evaluation
- Patient's blood pressure is normal.
- Patient states that sleep disturbance doesn't occur.
- Patient and family state understanding of drug therapy.

montelukast sodium
(mon-tih-LOO-kist SOH-dee-um)
Singulair

Pharmacologic class: leukotriene receptor antagonist
Therapeutic class: antiasthmatic
Pregnancy risk category: B

Indications and dosages
▶ **Prevention and long-term treatment of asthma, seasonal allergic rhinitis.** *Adults and adolescents age 15 and older:* 10 mg P.O. once daily in evening.
Children ages 6 to 14: 5-mg chewable tablet P.O. once daily in evening.
Children ages 2 to 5: 4-mg chewable tablet P.O. once daily in evening.
▶ **Prevention of exercise-induced bronchoconstriction.** *Adults and adolescents ages 15 and older:* 10 mg P.O. daily.
Children ages 6 to 14‡: 5 mg P.O. daily.
▶ **Asthma.** *Children under age 2:* One packet of 4-mg granules P.O. daily in evening.

Contraindications and precautions
- Contraindicated in patients hypersensitive to drug or its components and in patients with acute asthmatic attacks or status asthmaticus.
- Use cautiously and with appropriate monitoring when systemic corticosteroid dosages are reduced.

Lifespan: For children younger than age 2, safety and efficacy haven't been established.

Adverse reactions
CNS: *headache,* dizziness, fatigue, fever, asthenia.
EENT: nasal congestion.
GI: dyspepsia, infectious gastroenteritis, abdominal pain.
GU: pyuria.
Respiratory: cough.
Skin: rash.
Other: trauma, influenza, dental pain.

Interactions
Drug-drug. *Phenobarbital, rifampin:* May decrease bioavailability of montelukast via induction of hepatic metabolism. Monitor patient closely.

Effects on lab test results
- May increase ALT and AST levels.

Pharmacokinetics
Absorption: Rapid with an oral bioavailability of 64%.
Distribution: Over 99% bound to plasma proteins.
Metabolism: Extensively metabolized by cytochrome P450 isoenzymes.
Excretion: About 86% is recovered in the feces, indicating montelukast and its metabolites are excreted almost exclusively via the bile.
Half-life: 2.7 to 5.5 hours.

Route	Onset	Peak	Duration
P.O.			
(coated)	Unknown	3-4 hr	Unknown
(chewable)	Unknown	2-2.5 hr	Unknown

Pharmacodynamics

Chemical effect: Inhibits airway cysteinyl leukotriene ($CysLT_1$) receptors. Binds with high affinity and selectivity to the $CysLT_1$ receptor, and inhibits physiologic action of the cysteinyl leukotriene LTD_4. This receptor inhibition reduces early- and late-phase bronchoconstriction caused by antigen challenge.

Therapeutic effect: Improves breathing.

Available forms

Granules: 4 mg packets
Tablets (chewable): 4 mg, 5 mg
Tablets (film-coated): 10 mg

NURSING PROCESS

Assessment

- Assess patient's underlying condition and monitor drug's effectiveness.
- Monitor patient for adverse reactions and drug interactions.
- Evaluate patient's and family's knowledge of drug therapy.

Nursing diagnoses

- Impaired gas exchange related to asthma
- Activity intolerance related to asthma
- Deficient knowledge related to drug therapy

Planning and implementation

- Don't abruptly substitute drug for inhaled or oral corticosteroids.
- Drug isn't indicated for patients with acute asthmatic attacks or status asthmaticus. Also not indicated as monotherapy for managing exercise-induced bronchospasm. Appropriate rescue drug should be continued for acute exacerbations.
- Oral granules can be given either directly in the mouth, or mixed with a teaspoonful of cold or room temperature applesauce, carrots, rice, or ice cream. The packet should not be opened until ready to use. After opening packet, administer within 15 minutes. If mixed with food, don't store excess for future use; discard any unused portion.
- Oral granules shouldn't be dissolved in liquid for administration. However, liquids may be taken after administration.
- Oral granules can be given without regard to meals.
- Give drug daily; not intended for use on an as-needed basis.

Patient teaching

- Advise patient to take drug daily, even if asymptomatic, and to contact prescriber if asthma isn't well controlled.
- Warn patient not to reduce or stop taking other prescribed antiasthma drugs without prescriber's approval.
- Give patient directions for administration of oral granules mixed in with applesauce, carrots, rice, or ice cream. Tell him to discard any unused portion.
- Warn patient that drug isn't beneficial in acute asthma attacks or in exercise-induced bronchospasm, and advise him to keep appropriate rescue drugs available.
- Advise patient with known aspirin sensitivity to continue to avoid using aspirin and NSAIDs.
- Advise patient with phenylketonuria that chewable tablet contains phenylalanine.

Evaluation

- Patient's respiratory signs and symptoms improve.
- Patient can perform normal activities of daily living.
- Patient and family state understanding of drug therapy.

moricizine hydrochloride

(MOR-ih-sigh-zeen high-droh-KLOR-ighd)
Ethmozine

Pharmacologic class: sodium channel blocker
Therapeutic class: antiarrhythmic
Pregnancy risk category: B

Indications and dosages

▶ **Life-threatening ventricular arrhythmias.** *Adults:* Individualized dosage is based on clinical response and patient tolerance. Therapy should begin in hospital. Most patients respond to 600 to 900 mg P.O. daily in divided doses q 8 hours. Daily dose is increased within this range q 3 days by 150 mg until desired clinical effect is achieved.
Patients with hepatic or renal impairment: Give 600 mg or less P.O. daily. Advise clinician to monitor ECG before increasing dosage.

Contraindications and precautions

- Contraindicated in patients hypersensitive to drug, in patients with second- or third-degree AV block or right bundle-branch heart block when linked to left hemiblock (bifascicular block) unless artificial pacemaker is present, and in patients with cardiogenic shock.
- Use with extreme caution in patients with sick-sinus syndrome because drug may cause sinus bradycardia or sinus arrest.
- Use with extreme caution in patients with coronary artery disease and left ventricular dysfunction because these patients may be at risk for sudden death when treated with drug.
- Give cautiously to patients with hepatic or renal impairment.

Lifespan: In pregnant women, give cautiously. For breast-feeding women, drug isn't recommended. In children, safety of drug hasn't been established.

Adverse reactions

CNS: *dizziness, headache, fatigue,* anxiety, hypoesthesia, asthenia, nervousness, paresthesia, sleep disorders.
CV: ***proarrhythmic events (ventricular tachycardia, PVCs, supraventricular arrhythmias),*** *ECG abnormalities (including conduction defects, sinus pause, junctional rhythm, or AV block),* ***heart failure,*** *palpitations,* ***cardiac death,*** *chest pain.*
EENT: blurred vision.
GI: *nausea, vomiting, abdominal pain, dyspepsia, diarrhea, dry mouth.*
GU: urine retention, urinary frequency, dysuria.
Musculoskeletal: muscle pain.
Respiratory: dyspnea.
Skin: diaphoresis, rash.
Other: drug-induced fever.

Interactions

Drug-drug. *Cimetidine:* Increases plasma levels and decreases clearance of moricizine. Begin moricizine therapy at low dosage (not more than 600 mg daily) and monitor plasma levels and therapeutic effect closely.
Digoxin, propranolol: May cause additive prolongation of PR interval. Monitor patient closely.
Theophylline: Increases clearance and reduces plasma levels of theophylline. Monitor plasma levels and therapeutic response; adjust theophylline dosage.

Effects on lab test results

- May increase liver function test results.

Pharmacokinetics

Absorption: Administration within 30 minutes of mealtime delays absorption and lowers peak plasma levels but has no effect on extent of absorption.
Distribution: 95% protein-bound.
Metabolism: Undergoes significant first-pass metabolism. At least 26 metabolites have been found; none represent more than 1% of a dose. Drug induces its own metabolism.
Excretion: 50% excreted in feces; 39% excreted in urine; some recycled through enterohepatic circulation. *Half-life:* 1½ to 3½ hours.

Route	Onset	Peak	Duration
P.O.	≤ 2 hr	30 min-2 hr	10-24 hr

Pharmacodynamics

Chemical effect: Reduces fast inward current carried by sodium ions across myocardial cell membranes. Moricizine has potent local anesthetic activity and membrane-stabilizing effect.
Therapeutic effect: Alleviates ventricular arrhythmias.

Available forms

Tablets: 200 mg, 250 mg, 300 mg

NURSING PROCESS

Assessment

- Assess patient's condition before therapy and regularly thereafter.
- Be alert for adverse reactions and drug interactions.
- Evaluate patient's and family's knowledge of drug therapy.

Nursing diagnoses

- Decreased cardiac output related to presence of ventricular arrhythmia
- Risk for injury related to drug-induced adverse reactions
- Deficient knowledge related to drug therapy

Planning and implementation

• When substituting moricizine for another antiarrhythmic, previous drug should be withdrawn for one or two of drug's half-lives before moricizine is started. Patients with tendency to develop life-threatening arrhythmias after drug withdrawal should be hospitalized during withdrawal of therapy and adjustment to moricizine. Guidelines that prescribers use for starting moricizine therapy are as follows:
– disopyramide, 6 to 12 hours after last dose.
– mexiletine, 8 to 12 hours after last dose.
– procainamide, 3 to 6 hours after last dose.
– propafenone, 8 to 12 hours after last dose.
– quinidine, 6 to 12 hours after last dose.
– tocainide, 8 to 12 hours after last dose.
• Determine electrolyte status and correct imbalances before therapy. Hypokalemia, hyperkalemia, and hypomagnesemia may alter effects of drug.
ALERT: Don't confuse Ethmozine with Erythrocin.

Patient teaching

• Tell patient to report adverse reactions promptly.

Evaluation

• Patient regains normal cardiac output with alleviation of ventricular arrhythmia.
• Patient sustains no injury from adverse reactions.
• Patient and family state understanding of drug therapy.

morphine hydrochloride

(MOR-feen high-droh-KLOR-ighd)
M.O.S.♦, M.O.S.-SR♦

morphine sulfate

Astramorph PF, Avinza, DMS Concentrate, Duramorph PF, Infumorph 200, Infumorph 500, Kadian, Morphine H.P.♦, MS Contin, MSIR, MS/L, MS/L concentrate, OMS concentrate, Oramorph SR, RMS Uniserts, Roxanol, Roxanol 100, Roxanol T, Statex♦

morphine tartrate◇

Pharmacologic class: opioid
Therapeutic class: narcotic analgesic
Pregnancy risk category: C
Controlled substance schedule: II

Indications and dosages

▶ **Severe pain.** *Adults:* 10 mg S.C. or I.M. Or, 2.5 to 15 mg I.V. q 4 hours, p.r.n. Or, 10 to 30 mg P.O. Or, 10 to 20 mg P.R. q 4 hours, p.r.n. When given by continuous I.V. infusion, loading dose of 15 mg I.V. may be followed by continuous infusion of 0.8 to 10 mg/hour. Or, 30 mg controlled-release tablets P.O. q 8 to 12 hours may be given. As epidural injection, 5 mg by epidural catheter. If adequate pain relief not obtained within 1 hour, additional doses of 1 to 2 mg are given at intervals sufficient to assess efficacy. Maximum total epidural dosage shouldn't exceed 10 mg.
Children: 0.1 to 0.2 mg/kg S.C. q 4 hours. Maximum single dose is 15 mg.

Contraindications and precautions

• Contraindicated in patients hypersensitive to drug and in those with conditions that preclude I.V. administration of opioids (acute bronchial asthma or upper airway obstruction).
• Use with extreme caution in debilitated patients and in patients with head injury, increased intracranial pressure, seizures, chronic pulmonary disease, prostatic hyperplasia, severe hepatic or renal disease, acute abdominal conditions, hypothyroidism, Addison's disease, or urethral stricture.
Lifespan: In pregnant women, use cautiously. Breast-feeding women should wait 2 to 3 hours after last dose before breast-feeding to avoid sedation in infant. In elderly patients, use with extreme caution.

Adverse reactions

CNS: *sedation, somnolence, clouded sensorium, euphoria,* ***seizures*** (with large doses), dizziness, *nightmares* (with long-acting oral forms).
CV: *hypotension,* flushing, ***bradycardia, shock, cardiac arrest.***
GI: *nausea, vomiting, constipation,* ileus.
GU: *urine retention.*
Hematologic: ***thrombocytopenia.***
Respiratory: ***respiratory depression, respiratory arrest.***
Skin: pruritus and flushing with epidural administration.
Other: *physical dependence.*

Interactions

Drug-drug. *Antihistamines, chloral hydrate, CNS depressants, general anesthetics, glutethimide, hypnotics, MAO inhibitors, methocarbamol, other narcotic analgesics, sedatives, tranquilizers, tricyclic antidepressants:* May cause possible respiratory depression, hypotension, profound sedation, or coma. Use together with extreme caution. Reduce morphine dosage and monitor patient response.
Drug-lifestyle. *Alcohol use:* May have additive CNS effects. Urge patient to avoid using alcohol during drug therapy.

Effects on lab test results

- May increase amylase level.
- May decrease platelet count.

Pharmacokinetics

Absorption: Variable when given P.O.; unknown for other routes.
Distribution: Distributed widely throughout body.
Metabolism: Metabolized primarily in liver.
Excretion: Excreted in urine and bile. *Half-life:* 2 to 3 hours.

Route	Onset	Peak	Duration
P.O.	1 hr	1-2 hr	4-12 hr
I.V.	< 5 min	20 min	4-5 hr
I.M.	10-30 min	30-60 min	4-5 hr
S.C.	10-30 min	50-90 min	4-5 hr
P.R.	20-60 min	20-60 min	4-5 hr
Epidural	15-60 min	15-60 min	24 hr
Intrathecal	15-60 min	Unknown	24 hr

Pharmacodynamics

Chemical effect: Binds with opioid receptors in CNS, altering both perception of and emotional response to pain through unknown mechanism.
Therapeutic effect: Relieves pain.

Available forms

morphine hydrochloride
Oral solution ♦: 1 mg/ml, 5 mg/ml, 10 mg/ml, 20 mg/ml, 50 mg/ml
Suppositories: 10 mg ♦, 20 mg ♦, 30 mg ♦
Syrup: 1 mg/ml ♦, 5 mg/ml ♦, 10 mg/ml ♦, 20 mg/ml ♦, 50 mg/ml ♦
Tablets: 10 mg ♦, 20 mg ♦, 40 mg ♦, 60 mg ♦
Tablets (extended-release): 30 mg ♦, 60 mg ♦

morphine sulfate
Capsules: 15 mg, 30 mg
Capsules (extended-release) (Avinza): 30 mg, 60 mg, 90 mg, 120 mg
Capsules (sustained-release): 20 mg, 50 mg, 100 mg
Injection (with preservative): 500 mcg/ml, 1 mg/ml, 2 mg/ml, 3 mg/ml, 4 mg/ml, 5 mg/ml, 8 mg/ml, 10 mg/ml, 15 mg/ml, 25 mg/ml, 50 mg/ml
Injection (without preservative): 500 mcg/ml, 1 mg/ml, 10 mg/ml, 15 mg/ml, 25 mg/ml
Oral solution: 10 mg/5 ml, 20 mg/5 ml, 20 mg/ml
Oral solution (concentrated): 20 mg/ml, 30 mg/1.5 ml, 100 mg/5 ml
Soluble tablets: 10 mg, 15 mg, 30 mg
Suppositories: 5 mg, 10 mg, 20 mg, 30 mg
Syrup: 1 mg/ml, 5 mg/ml
Tablets: 15 mg, 30 mg
Tablets (controlled-release): 15 mg, 30 mg, 60 mg, 100 mg, 200 mg
Tablets (extended-release): 15 mg, 30 mg, 60 mg, 100 mg, 200 mg
morphine tartrate
Injection: 80 mg/ml ◇

NURSING PROCESS

Assessment

- Assess patient's pain before therapy and regularly thereafter.
- Morphine may worsen or mask gallbladder pain.
- Monitor patient for respiratory depression after administration. When given epidurally, monitor patient for up to 24 hours after injection. Check respiratory rate and depth every 30 to 60 minutes for 24 hours.
- Be alert for adverse reactions and drug interactions.
- Evaluate patient's and family's knowledge of drug therapy.

Nursing diagnoses

- Acute pain related to underlying condition
- Ineffective breathing pattern related to drug's depressive effect on respiratory system
- Deficient knowledge related to drug therapy

Planning and implementation

• **Epidural and intrathecal use:** Preservative-free preparations are available for epidural or intrathecal administration.
• **P.O. use:** Solutions of various concentrations are available as well as intensified P.O. solution (20 mg/ml). Carefully note the strength you are giving.
• **I.V. use:** When given by direct injection, 2.5 to 15 mg may be diluted in 4 or 5 ml of sterile water for injection and given over 4 to 5 minutes.
– Or, drug may be mixed with D_5W to yield 0.1 to 1 mg/ml and given by continuous infusion device.
– Morphine sulfate is compatible with most common I.V. solutions.
• **I.M. and S.C. use:** Follow normal protocol.
– Don't crush or break extended-release tablets.
– If S.L. administration is ordered, measure solution with tuberculin syringe. Give dose a few drops at a time to allow maximal S.L. absorption and minimize swallowing.
• **P.R. use:** Refrigeration of rectal suppository isn't needed.
– In some patients, P.R. and P.O. absorption may not be equivalent.
• Morphine is drug of choice in relieving pain of MI. It may cause transient decrease in blood pressure.
• Keep narcotic antagonist and resuscitation equipment available.
• An around-the-clock regimen best manages severe, chronic pain.
ALERT: Withhold dose and notify prescriber if respiratory rate is below 12 breaths/minute.
• Because constipation is often severe with maintenance dosage, make sure prescriber has ordered stool softener or other laxative.
ALERT: Don't confuse morphine with hydromorphone.
ALERT: Don't confuse Avinza (morphine sulfate) with Invanz (ertapenem).

Patient teaching

• Caution patient about getting out of bed or walking. Warn outpatient not to drive or perform other potentially hazardous activities until full CNS effects of drug are known.
• Tell patient to report continued pain.
• Instruct patient to avoid alcohol consumption during drug therapy.

Evaluation

• Patient states that pain is relieved.
• Patient maintains adequate breathing patterns throughout therapy.
• Patient and family state understanding of drug therapy.

moxifloxacin hydrochloride

(mox-ih-FLOX-uh-sin high-droh-CLOR-ighd)
Avelox, Avelox I.V.

Pharmacologic class: fluoroquinolone
Therapeutic class: antibiotic
Pregnancy risk category: C

Indications and dosages

▶ **Acute bacterial sinusitis caused by *Streptococcus pneumoniae, Haemophilus influenzae,* or *Moraxella catarrhalis.*** *Adults:* 400 mg P.O. or I.V. once daily for 10 days.
▶ **Acute bacterial exacerbation of chronic bronchitis caused by *S. pneumoniae, H. influenzae, H. parainfluenzae, Klebsiella pneumoniae, Staphylococcus aureus,* or *M. catarrhalis.*** *Adults:* 400 mg P.O. or I.V. once daily for 5 days.
▶ **Mild-to-moderate community-acquired pneumonia caused by *S. pneumoniae, H. influenzae, Mycoplasma pneumoniae, Chlamydia pneumoniae,* or *M. catarrhalis.*** *Adults:* 400 mg P.O. or I.V. once daily for 10 days.
▶ **Uncomplicated skin and skin-structure infections caused by *Staphylococcus aureus* and *Streptococcus pyogenes.*** *Adults:* 400 mg P.O daily for 7 days.

Contraindications and precautions

• Contraindicated in patients hypersensitive to drug, its components, or other fluoroquinolones.
• Use cautiously in patients with known or suspected CNS disorders and in patients with risk factors that may predispose them to seizures or lower the seizure threshold. Use cautiously in patients with prolonged QT interval or uncorrected hypokalemia.
Lifespan: In pregnant or breast-feeding women or children younger than age 18, safety and efficacy haven't been established. In elderly patients, monitor cardiac function carefully, especially with I.V. form of drug.

Adverse reactions

CNS: dizziness, headache, asthenia, pain, malaise, insomnia, nervousness, anxiety, confusion, somnolence, tremor, vertigo, paresthesia.
CV: ***prolonged QT interval,*** chest pain, palpitations, tachycardia, hypertension, peripheral edema.
GI: ***pseudomembranous colitis,*** nausea, diarrhea, abdominal pain, vomiting, dyspepsia, dry mouth, constipation, oral candidiasis, anorexia, stomatitis, glossitis, flatulence, gastrointestinal disorder, taste perversion.
GU: vaginitis, vaginal candidiasis.
Hematologic: ***thrombocytosis, thrombocytopenia, leukopenia,*** eosinophilia.
Hepatic: liver dysfunction, cholestatic jaundice.
Musculoskeletal: leg pain, back pain, arthralgia, myalgia, tendon rupture.
Respiratory: dyspnea.
Skin: injection site reaction, rash (maculopapular, purpuric, pustular), pruritus, sweating.
Other: candidiasis, ***allergic reaction.***

Interactions

Drug-drug. *Antacids; didanosine; metal cations, such as aluminum, magnesium, iron, zinc; multivitamins; sucralfate:* Metal cations chelate with moxifloxacin, resulting in decreased absorption and lower drug level. Give drug at least 4 hours before or 8 hours after drugs containing metal cations.
Class IA (quinidine, procainamide) or Class III (amiodarone, sotalol) antiarrhythmics: May have possible enhanced adverse CV effects. Avoid using together.
Drugs known to prolong the QT interval, such as erythromycin, antipsychotics, and tricyclic antidepressants: May have an additive effect when combined with these drugs. Avoid using together.
NSAIDs: May increase risk of CNS stimulation and seizures. Don't use together.
Drug-lifestyle. *Sun exposure:* Although photosensitivity reactions haven't occurred with moxifloxacin, it has been reported with other fluoroquinolones. Discourage prolonged or unprotected exposure to sunlight.

Effects on lab test results

- May increase ALT, AST, alkaline phosphatase, and bilirubin levels.
- May increase eosinophil counts. May decrease WBC count. May increase or decrease platelet counts, and PT.

Pharmacokinetics

Absorption: Well absorbed, with an absolute bioavailability of about 90%. Plasma levels peak in 1 to 3 hours. Steady-state is reached after 3 days on a 400 mg once-daily dose.
Distribution: Widely distributed with a distribution volume of 1.7 to 2.7 L/kg. Plasma protein-binding is about 50%. Penetrates well into nasal and bronchial secretions, sinus mucosa, and saliva.
Metabolism: Drug is metabolized to inactive glucuronide and sulfate conjugates. About 14% of dose is converted to the glucuronide metabolite. Sulfate metabolite accounts for about 38% of the dose.
Excretion: About 45% of dose is excreted unchanged, about 20% in urine and 25% in feces. Sulfate metabolite is eliminated mainly in feces; glucuronide metabolite undergoes renal Excretion. *Half-life:* About 12 hours.

Route	Onset	Peak	Duration
P.O., I.V.	Unknown	1-3 hr	Unknown

Pharmacodynamics

Chemical effect: Inhibits the activity of topoisomerase I (DNA gyrase) and topoisomerase IV in susceptible bacteria. These enzymes are needed for bacterial DNA replication, transcription, repair, and recombination.
Therapeutic effect: Kills susceptible bacteria, including *S. pneumoniae, H. influenzae, H. parainfluenzae, K. pneumoniae, S. aureus, M. pneumoniae, C. pneumoniae,* and *M. catarrhalis.*

Available forms

Injection (premixed solution): 400 mg
Tablets (film-coated): 400 mg

NURSING PROCESS

Assessment

- Obtain history of patient's underlying condition before therapy, and reassess regularly thereafter.

• Obtain specimen for culture and sensitivity tests before first dose. Therapy may begin pending culture results.
• Monitor patient for hypersensitivity reactions, CNS toxicities including seizures, QT interval prolongation, pseudomembranous colitis, phototoxicity, and tendon rupture.
• Evaluate patient's and family's knowledge about drug therapy.

Nursing diagnoses

• Infection related to presence of bacteria susceptible to drug
• Risk for injury related to drug-induced adverse reactions
• Deficient knowledge related to drug therapy

Planning and implementation

• **IV use:** Infuse I.V. over 60 minutes by direct infusion or through a Y-type IV infusion set. Avoid rapid or bolus infusion.
ALERT: Do not mix or infuse drug simultaneously with other substances as compatibility data are limited.
– Switch from I.V. to P.O. form when warranted.
• Correct hypokalemia before starting therapy.
• Drug may be given without regard to meals. Give at same time to provide consistent absorption.
• Provide liberal fluid intake.
• Give moxifloxacin 4 hours before or 8 hours after antacids, sucralfate, and products containing iron or zinc.
• The most common adverse reactions are nausea, vomiting, stomach pain, diarrhea, dizziness, and headache.
• Monitor patient for seizures and other adverse CNS reactions linked to fluoroquinolones including dizziness, confusion, tremors, hallucinations, depression, and, rarely, suicidal thoughts or acts. These may occur after the initial dose. Notify prescriber and discontinue moxifloxacin; institute appropriate therapy if any of these reactions occur.
• Store drug at controlled room temperature.

Patient teaching

• Instruct patient to take drug once daily, at the same time each day.
• Tell patient to finish the entire course of therapy, even if symptoms resolve.
• Advise the patient to drink plenty of fluids and to take moxifloxacin 4 hours before or 8 hours after antacids, sucralfate, and products containing iron and zinc.
• Most common adverse reactions are nausea, vomiting, stomach pain, diarrhea, dizziness, and headache.
• Tell patient to avoid hazardous activities, such as driving or operating machinery, until effects of drug are known.
• Instruct patient to contact prescriber if he experiences allergic reaction, palpitations, fainting, persistent diarrhea, severe sunburn, injury to a muscle tendon, or seizures.

Evaluation

• Patient is free from infection after drug therapy.
• Patient sustains no injury as a result of drug-induced adverse reactions.
• Patient and family state understanding of drug therapy.

muromonab-CD3

(myoo-roh-MOH-nab see dee three)
Orthoclone OKT3

Pharmacologic class: monoclonal antibody
Therapeutic class: immunosuppressive
Pregnancy risk category: C

Indications and dosages

▶ **Acute allograft rejection in kidney transplant patients; steroid-resistant hepatic or cardiac allograft rejection.** *Adults:* 5 mg I.V. bolus over less than 1 minute once daily for 10 to 14 days.

Contraindications and precautions

• Contraindicated in patients hypersensitive to drug or to other products of murine origin. Also contraindicated in patients who have antimouse antibody titers of 1:1,000 or more, who have fluid overload, as evidenced by chest X-ray or weight gain greater than 3% within week before treatment, and who have history of or predisposition to seizures.

Lifespan: In pregnant or breast-feeding women, use is contraindicated. In children, safety of drug hasn't been established.

Adverse reactions

CNS: *fever, tremor,* headache, ***seizures, encephalopathy, aseptic meningitis, cerebral edema.***
CV: *chest pain,* tachycardia, ***cardiac arrest, shock, heart failure.***
GI: *nausea, vomiting,* diarrhea.
Respiratory: ***severe pulmonary edema, adult respiratory distress syndrome,*** *dyspnea.*
Other: *chills,* INFECTION, ***anaphylaxis, cytokine release syndrome, risk of neoplasia.***

Interactions

Drug-drug. *Immunosuppressants:* Increases risk of infection. Monitor patient closely.
Indomethacin: Increases muromonab-CD3 levels with CNS effects. Encephalopathy may occur. Monitor patient closely.
Live-virus vaccines: May increase replication and effects of vaccine. Postpone vaccination when possible and consult prescriber.

Effects on lab test results

- May increase BUN and creatinine levels.

Pharmacokinetics

Absorption: Given I.V.
Distribution: Unknown.
Metabolism: Unknown.
Excretion: Unknown.

Route	Onset	Peak	Duration
I.V.	Almost immediately	Unknown	1 wk after drug stopped

Pharmacodynamics

Chemical effect: IgG antibody that reacts in T-lymphocyte membrane with a molecule (CD3) needed for antigen recognition. This drug depletes blood of CD3-positive T cells, which leads to restoration of allograft function and reversal of rejection.
Therapeutic effect: Halts acute allograft rejection in kidney transplantation.

Available forms

Injection: 1 mg/ml in 5-ml ampules

NURSING PROCESS

Assessment

- Assess patient's condition before therapy and regularly thereafter.
- Obtain chest X-ray within 24 hours before drug treatment.
- Assess patient for signs of fluid overload before treatment.
- Be alert for adverse reactions and drug interactions.
- Monitor patient's hydration status if adverse GI reactions occur.
- Evaluate patient's and family's knowledge of drug therapy.

Nursing diagnoses

- Risk for injury related to presence of acute allograft rejection
- Risk for deficient fluid volume related to drug-induced adverse GI reactions
- Deficient knowledge related to drug therapy

Planning and implementation

- Treatment should begin in facility equipped and staffed for cardiopulmonary resuscitation where patient can be monitored closely.
- Most adverse reactions develop within 30 minutes to 6 hours after first dose.
- Give antipyretic before giving drug to help lower risk of expected pyrexia and chills. Corticosteroids also may be given before first injection to help decrease risk of adverse reactions. Methylprednisolone sodium succinate (1 mg/kg) preinjection followed by hydrocortisone sodium succinate (100 mg) 30 minutes postinjection may alleviate severity of first-dose reaction.
- Muromonab-CD3 is a monoclonal antibody. Patients develop antibodies to it that can lead to loss of effectiveness and more severe adverse reactions if second course of therapy is attempted; this drug should only be used for one course of treatment.

ALERT: Do not give by I.V. infusion or with other drug solutions.

Patient teaching

- Inform patient of expected adverse reactions, and reassure him that they will lessen as treatment progresses.

☑ Evaluation

- Patient shows no signs of organ rejection.
- Patient maintains adequate hydration.
- Patient and family state understanding of drug therapy.

mycophenolate mofetil

(migh-koh-FEN-oh-layt MOH-feh-til)
CellCept

mycophenolate mofetil hydrochloride

CellCept Intravenous

Pharmacologic class: mycophenolic acid derivative
Therapeutic class: immunosuppressant
Pregnancy risk category: C

Indications and dosages

▶ **Prevention of organ rejection in patients receiving allogeneic renal transplant.** *Adults:* 1 g P.O. or I.V. infused over 2 hours b.i.d. with corticosteroids and cyclosporine (begun within 72 hours after transplantation).

▶ **Prevention of organ rejection in patients receiving allogeneic cardiac transplant.** *Adults:* 1.5 g P.O. or I.V. b.i.d. with cyclosporine and corticosteroids.

▶ **Prophylaxis of organ rejection, with cyclosporine and corticosteroids, in patients receiving allogenic hepatic transplants.** *Adults:* 1 gram I.V. b.i.d. over no less than 2 hours or 1.5 grams P.O. b.i.d.

Patients with severe chronic renal impairment (GFR less than 25 ml/minute) outside the immediate posttransplant period: Avoid doses above 1 g b.i.d.

Contraindications and precautions

- Contraindicated in patients hypersensitive to drug, mycophenolic acid, or other components of product.
- Use cautiously in patients with GI disorders.

Lifespan: In pregnant or breast-feeding women, use is contraindicated unless benefits outweigh risks. In children, safety of drug hasn't been established.

Adverse reactions

CNS: *tremor,* insomnia, dizziness, *headache, pain, fever, asthenia.*
CV: *chest pain, hypertension, edema,* peripheral edema.
EENT: pharyngitis.
GI: *diarrhea, constipation, nausea, dyspepsia, vomiting, oral candidiasis, abdominal pain,* HEMORRHAGE.
GU: urinary tract infection, hematuria, kidney tubular necrosis.
Hematologic: anemia, ***leukopenia,*** THROMBOCYTOPENIA, hypochromic anemia, leukocytosis.
Metabolic: *hypercholesteremia, hypophosphatemia, hypokalemia,* ***hyperkalemia,*** hyperglycemia.
Musculoskeletal: *back pain.*
Respiratory: *dyspnea, cough,* infection, bronchitis, pneumonia.
Skin: *acne,* rash.
Other: *infection,* ***sepsis.***

Interactions

Drug-drug. *Acyclovir, ganciclovir, other drugs known to undergo tubular secretion:* Increases risk of toxicity for both drugs. Monitor patient closely.
Antacids with magnesium and aluminum hydroxides: Decreases absorption of mycophenolate mofetil. Separate administration times.
Azathioprine: Hasn't been clinically studied. Avoid using together.
Cholestyramine: May interfere with enterohepatic recirculation, reducing mycophenolate bioavailability. Don't give together.
Oral contraceptives: May affect efficacy of oral contraceptives. Advise patient to use barrier birth control methods.

Effects on lab test results

- May increase cholesterol and glucose levels. May decrease phosphorous level. May increase or decrease potassium level.
- May decrease hemoglobin, hematocrit, and platelet counts. May increase or decrease WBC count.

Pharmacokinetics

Absorption: Absorbed from GI tract.
Distribution: 97% bound to plasma proteins.

Metabolism: Undergoes complete presystemic metabolism to mycophenolic acid.
Excretion: Excreted primarily in urine, with small amount in feces. *Half-life:* About 18 hours.

Route	Onset	Peak	Duration
P.O.	Unknown	Unknown	Unknown
I.V.	Unknown	Unknown	10-17 hr

Pharmacodynamics

Chemical effect: Inhibits proliferative responses of T- and B-lymphocytes, suppresses antibody formation by B-lymphocytes, and may inhibit recruitment of leukocytes into sites of inflammation and graft rejection.
Therapeutic effect: Prevents organ rejection.

Available forms

mycophenolate mofetil
Capsules: 250 mg
Powder for oral suspension: 200 mg/ml
Tablets: 500 mg
mycophenolate mofetil hydrochloride
Injection: 500 mg/vial

NURSING PROCESS

Assessment

- Obtain history of patient's kidney transplant.
- Monitor CBC regularly.
- Be alert for adverse reactions and drug interactions.
- Evaluate patient's and family's knowledge of drug therapy.

Nursing diagnoses

- Ineffective health maintenance related to need for kidney transplant
- Ineffective immune protection related to drug-induced immunosupression
- Deficient knowledge related to drug therapy

Planning and implementation

- **I.V. use:** CellCept Intravenous must be reconstituted and diluted to 6 mg/ml using D_5W injection.

ALERT: Never give drug by rapid or bolus I.V. injection. Give infusion over at least 2 hours.

- **P.O. use:** Give drug on an empty stomach.

ALERT: Because of potential teratogenic effects, don't open or crush capsules. Avoid inhaling powder in capsules or letting it contact skin or mucous membranes. If contact occurs, wash skin thoroughly with soap and water and rinse eyes with plain water.

- Notify prescriber if neutropenia occurs.

Patient teaching

- Warn patient not to open or crush capsule but to swallow it whole on an empty stomach.
- Stress importance of not interrupting therapy without consulting prescriber.
- Inform woman that a pregnancy test should be done 1 week before therapy. Advise her to use effective contraception until at least 6 weeks after therapy stops, even if she has a history of infertility (unless she has had a hysterectomy). Tell her to use two forms of contraception simultaneously unless abstinence is the chosen method. If pregnancy occurs despite these measures, have patient contact prescriber immediately.

Evaluation

- Patient shows no signs and symptoms of organ rejection.
- Neutropenia doesn't develop.
- Patient and family state understanding of drug therapy.

N

nabumetone

(nuh-BYOO-meh-tohn)
Apo-Nabumetone ◆, Relafen

Pharmacologic class: NSAID
Therapeutic class: antiarthritic
Pregnancy risk category: C

Indications and dosages

▶ **Rheumatoid arthritis, osteoarthritis.** *Adults:* Initially, 1,000 mg P.O. daily as single dose or in divided doses b.i.d. Maximum dose, 2,000 mg daily.

Contraindications and precautions

• Contraindicated in patients hypersensitive to drug and patients with history of aspirin- or NSAID-induced asthma, urticaria, or other allergic reactions.
• Use cautiously in patients with renal or hepatic impairment, peptic ulcer disease, heart failure, hypertension, or other conditions that may predispose patient to fluid retention.
Lifespan: For women in the third trimester of pregnancy and breast-feeding women, drug is not recommended. In children, safety of drug hasn't been established. In geriatric patients, use cautiously.

Adverse reactions

CNS: *dizziness, headache,* fatigue, increased sweating, insomnia, nervousness, somnolence.
CV: vasculitis, *edema.*
EENT: *tinnitus.*
GI: *diarrhea, dyspepsia, abdominal pain, constipation, flatulence, nausea,* dry mouth, gastritis, stomatitis, vomiting, ***bleeding,*** ulceration.
Respiratory: dyspnea, pneumonitis.
Skin: *pruritus, rash.*

Interactions

Drug-drug. *Diuretics:* NSAIDs may decrease diuretic effectiveness. Monitor patient closely.
Drugs highly bound to plasma proteins (such as warfarin): Increased risk of adverse effects from displacement of drug by nabumetone. Use together cautiously.
Drug-herb. *Dong quai, feverfew, garlic, ginger, horse chestnut, red clover:* Increased risk of bleeding. Discourage using together.
St. John's wort: Increases risk of photosensitivity. Advise patient to avoid unprotected or prolonged exposure to sunlight.
Drug-food. *Any food:* Increases the rate of absorption. Give together.
Drug-lifestyle. *Alcohol use:* Increases risk of additive GI toxicity. Discourage using together.

Effects on lab test results

None reported.

Pharmacokinetics

Absorption: Well absorbed from GI tract. Administration with food increases absorption rate and peak levels of principal metabolite but doesn't change total drug absorbed.
Distribution: Over 99% of metabolite is bound to plasma proteins.
Metabolism: Metabolized to inactive metabolites in liver.
Excretion: Metabolites excreted primarily in urine; about 9% appears in feces. *Half-life:* About 24 hours.

Route	Onset	Peak	Duration
P.O.	Unknown	2-4 hr	Unknown

Pharmacodynamics

Chemical effect: Unknown; may inhibit prostaglandin synthesis.
Therapeutic effect: Relieves pain.

Available forms

Tablets: 500 mg, 750 mg

NURSING PROCESS

Assessment

• Assess patient's arthritis before therapy and regularly thereafter.
• During long-term therapy, periodically monitor renal and liver function, CBC, and hematocrit; assess these patients for evidence of GI bleeding.
• Watch for fluid retention, especially among patients with heart failure and hypertension.
• Be alert for adverse reactions and drug interactions.
• Evaluate patient's and family's knowledge of drug therapy.

Nursing diagnoses

• Chronic pain related to arthritic condition
• Impaired tissue integrity related to adverse drug effect on GI mucosa
• Deficient knowledge related to drug therapy

Planning and implementation

• Give drug with food to increase absorption rate.
• Notify prescriber about adverse reactions.
ALERT: Do not confuse Relafen with Rifadin.

Patient teaching

• Instruct patient to take drug with food, milk, or antacids for best absorption.
• Advise patient to limit alcohol intake because of additive GI toxicity.

• Teach patient to recognize and report signs and symptoms of GI bleeding.

Evaluation

• Patient is free from pain.
• Patient's GI tissue integrity is maintained throughout drug therapy.
• Patient and family state understanding of drug therapy.

nadolol
(nay-DOH-lol)
Apo-Nadol ♦, Corgard

Pharmacologic class: beta blocker
Therapeutic class: antihypertensive, antianginal
Pregnancy risk category: C

Indications and dosages

▶ **Angina pectoris.** *Adults:* Initially, 40 mg P.O. once daily. Increase by 40- to 80-mg increments q 3 to 7 days until optimum response occurs. Usual maintenance dosage is 40 to 240 mg daily.
▶ **Hypertension.** *Adults:* Initially, 20 to 40 mg P.O. once daily. Increase by 40- to 80-mg increments q 2 to 14 days until optimum response occurs. Usual maintenance dosage is 40 to 320 mg daily (in rare cases, 640 mg).
Patients with renal impairment: If creatinine clearance is > 50 ml/minute, dosing interval is q 24 hours; if 31 to 50 ml/minute, give q 24 to 36 hours; if 10 to 30 ml/minute, give q 24 to 48 hours; if < 10 ml/minute, give q 40 to 60 hours.
▶ **Arrhythmias‡.** *Adults:* 60 to 160 mg P.O. daily.
▶ **Prevention of vascular headaches‡.** *Adults:* 20 to 40 mg P.O. daily; may gradually increase to 120 mg daily, if necessary.

Contraindications and precautions

• Contraindicated in patients with bronchial asthma, sinus bradycardia, greater than first-degree heart block, and cardiogenic shock.
• Use cautiously in patients undergoing major surgery involving general anesthesia and in those with heart failure, chronic bronchitis, emphysema, renal or hepatic impairment, or diabetes.

Lifespan: In breast-feeding women, drug isn't recommended. In children, safety of drug hasn't been established.

Adverse reactions

CNS: fatigue, lethargy, dizziness, fever.
CV: ***bradycardia***, *hypotension*, ***heart failure***, peripheral vascular disease.
GI: nausea, vomiting, diarrhea, constipation.
Respiratory: *increased airway resistance.*
Skin: rash.

Interactions

Drug-drug. *Antihypertensives:* Enhances antihypertensive effect. Monitor patient's blood pressure closely.
Cardiac glycosides: May cause excessive bradycardia and affect AV conduction. Use together cautiously.
Epinephrine: Severe vasoconstriction and reflex bradycardia. Monitor patient closely.
Insulin, oral antidiabetics: Can alter dosage requirements in diabetic patients. Monitor patient.
NSAIDs: Decreases antihypertensive effect. Monitor blood pressure and adjust dosage.

Effects on lab test results

None reported.

Pharmacokinetics

Absorption: 30% to 40%.
Distribution: Distributed throughout body; about 30% protein-bound.
Metabolism: None.
Excretion: Most excreted unchanged in urine; remainder in feces. *Half-life:* About 20 hours.

Route	Onset	Peak	Duration
P.O.	Unknown	2-4 hr	Unknown

Pharmacodynamics

Chemical effect: Reduces cardiac oxygen demand by blocking catecholamine-induced increases in heart rate, blood pressure, and myocardial contraction. Depresses renin secretion.
Therapeutic effect: Lowers blood pressure and relieves angina.

Available forms

Tablets: 20 mg, 40 mg, 80 mg, 120 mg, 160 mg

NURSING PROCESS

Assessment

- Assess patient's condition before therapy and regularly thereafter.
- Drug masks common signs of shock and hyperthyroidism.
- Be alert for adverse reactions and drug interactions.
- Evaluate patient's and family's knowledge of drug therapy.

Nursing diagnoses

- Risk for injury related to presence of hypertension
- Acute pain related to angina
- Deficient knowledge related to drug therapy

Planning and implementation

- Always check apical pulse before giving drug. If slower than 60 beats/minute, withhold drug and notify prescriber.
- If patient develops severe hypotension, give vasopressor, as prescribed.

ALERT: Reduce dosage gradually over 1 to 2 weeks. Abrupt discontinuation can worsen angina and MI.

ALERT: Do not confuse Corgard with Coreg.

Patient teaching

- Explain importance of taking drug as prescribed, even when feeling well. Caution patient not to stop drug suddenly.

Evaluation

- Patient's blood pressure is normal.
- Patient reports reduced angina.
- Patient and family state understanding of drug therapy.

nafcillin sodium
(naf-SIL-in SOH-dee-um)

Pharmacologic class: penicillinase-resistant penicillin
Therapeutic class: antibiotic
Pregnancy risk category: B

Indications and dosages

▶ **Systemic infections caused by susceptible organisms (methicillin-sensitive *Staphylococcus aureus*).** *Adults:* 500 mg to 1 g I.V. q 4 hours depending on severity of the infection.
Infants and children older than age 1 month: 50 to 200 mg/kg/day I.V. in divided doses q 4 to 6 hours depending on the severity of the infection.
Neonates age 7 days or younger weighing less than 2 kg: 25 mg/kg I.V. q 12 hours.
Neonates age 7 days or younger weighing more than 2 kg: 25 mg/kg I.V. q 8 hours.
Neonates older than 7 days weighing less than 2 kg: 25 mg/kg I.V. q 8 hours.
Neonates older than 7 days weighing more than 2 kg: 25 mg/kg I.V. q 6 hours.

▶ **Meningitis.** *Adults:* 100 to 200 mg/kg/day I.V. in divided doses q 4 to 6 hours.
Neonates age 7 days or younger weighing less than 2 kg: 50 mg/kg I.V. q 12 hours.
Neonates age 7 days or younger weighing more than 2 kg: 50 mg/kg I.V. q 8 hours.
Neonates older than 7 days weighing less than 2 kg: 50 mg/kg I.V. q 8 hours.
Neonates older than 7 days weighing more than 2 kg: 50 mg/kg I.V. q 6 hours.

▶ **Native valve endocarditis.** *Adults:* 2 g I.V. q 4 hours for 4 to 6 weeks in combination with gentamicin.

▶ **Osteomyelitis.** *Adults:* 1 to 2 g I.V. q 4 hours for 4 to 8 weeks.

Contraindications and precautions

- Contraindicated in patients hypersensitive to drug or other penicillins.
- Use cautiously in patients with GI distress and those with other drug allergies, especially to cephalosporins.

Lifespan: In pregnant and breast-feeding women, use cautiously.

Adverse reactions

GI: *nausea,* vomiting, diarrhea.
Hematologic: ***transient leukopenia, neutropenia, granulocytopenia, thrombocytopenia*** (with high doses).
Other: hypersensitivity reactions (chills, fever, rash, pruritus, urticaria, ***anaphylaxis***), vein irritation, thrombophlebitis.

Interactions

Drug-drug. *Aminoglycosides:* May have synergistic effect. Monitor patient closely.
Cyclosporine: May cause subtherapeutic cyclosporine level. Monitor level.

Probenecid: Increases level of nafcillin. Probenecid may be used for this purpose.
Rifampin: Dose-dependent antagonism. Monitor patient closely.
Warfarin: Increases risk of bleeding when used with I.V. nafcillin. Monitor patient for bleeding.

Effects on lab test results

- May decrease neutrophil, granulocyte, WBC, and platelet counts.
- Drug may falsely elevate urine or serum proteins or cause false-positive results in certain tests for them.

Pharmacokinetics

Absorption: Given I.V.
Distribution: Distributed widely. CSF penetration is poor but enhanced by meningeal inflammation. Drug is 70% to 90% protein-bound.
Metabolism: Metabolized primarily in liver; undergoes enterohepatic circulation.
Excretion: Excreted primarily in bile; 25% to 30% is excreted in urine unchanged. *Half-life:* 30 to 90 minutes.

Route	Onset	Peak	Duration
I.V.	Immediate	Immediate	Unknown

Pharmacodynamics

Chemical effect: Inhibits cell wall synthesis during microorganism multiplication; bacteria resist penicillins by producing penicillinases—enzymes that hydrolyze penicillins. Drug resists these enzymes.
Therapeutic effect: Kills susceptible bacteria, such as penicillinase-producing staphylococci, and some gram-positive aerobic and anaerobic bacilli.

Available forms

Injection (for I.V. infusion): 1 g, 2 g

NURSING PROCESS

Assessment

- Assess patient's infection before therapy and regularly thereafter.
- Before giving drug, ask patient about allergic reactions to penicillin. Remember that allergic reactions may occur even in patients with no history of penicillin allergy.
- Obtain specimen for culture and sensitivity tests before giving first dose. Therapy may begin pending results.
- Be alert for adverse reactions and drug interactions.
- Monitor patient's hydration status if adverse GI reactions occur.
- Evaluate patient's and family's knowledge of drug therapy.

Nursing diagnoses

- Infection related to susceptible bacteria
- Risk for deficient fluid volume related to drug-induced adverse GI reactions
- Deficient knowledge related to drug therapy

Planning and implementation

- Give drug at least 1 hour before bacteriostatic antibiotics.
- **I.V. use:** Check container for leaks, cloudiness or precipitate prior to use. Discard if present. Give by intermittent I.V. infusion over 30 to 60 minutes.
  – Avoid continuous I.V. infusions to prevent vein irritation. Change site every 48 hours.

ALERT: Aminoglycosides are chemically and physically incompatible with drug; don't mix together in same I.V. solution.

Patient teaching

- Tell patient to call prescriber if rash, fever, or chills develop.

Evaluation

- Patient is free from infection.
- Patient maintains adequate hydration throughout drug therapy.
- Patient and family state understanding of drug therapy.

nalbuphine hydrochloride

(NAL-byoo-feen high-droh-KLOR-ighd)
Nubain

Pharmacologic class: narcotic agonist-antagonist, opioid partial agonist
Therapeutic class: analgesic, adjunct to anesthesia
Pregnancy risk category: B

Indications and dosages

▶ **Moderate-to-severe pain.** *Adults:* For average (70 kg [154 lb]) person, give 10 to 20 mg I.V., I.M., or S.C., q 3 to 6 hours, p.r.n. Maximum daily dosage is 160 mg.

▶ **Adjunct to balanced anesthesia.** *Adults:* 0.3 mg/kg to 3 mg/kg I.V. over 10 to 15 minutes, followed by maintenance doses of 0.25 to 0.5 mg/kg in single I.V. doses p.r.n.

Contraindications and precautions

- Contraindicated in patients hypersensitive to drug.
- Use cautiously in substance abusers and in those with emotional instability, head injury, increased intracranial pressure, impaired ventilation, MI accompanied by nausea and vomiting, upcoming biliary surgery, and hepatic or renal disease.

Lifespan: With pregnant and breast-feeding women, use cautiously. In children younger than age 18, safety hasn't been established.

Adverse reactions

CNS: *headache, sedation, dizziness, vertigo,* nervousness, depression, restlessness, crying, euphoria, hostility, unusual dreams, confusion, hallucinations, speech difficulty, delusions.
CV: hypertension, hypotension, tachycardia, ***bradycardia.***
EENT: blurred vision.
GI: cramps, dyspepsia, bitter taste, *dry mouth, nausea, vomiting,* constipation.
GU: urinary urgency.
Respiratory: ***respiratory depression, pulmonary edema.***
Skin: itching; burning; urticaria; *sweaty, clammy feeling.*

Interactions

Drug-drug. *CNS depressants, general anesthetics, hypnotics, MAO inhibitors, sedatives, tranquilizers, tricyclic antidepressants:* May cause respiratory depression, hypertension, profound sedation, or coma. Don't use together.
Narcotic analgesics: May cause decrease in analgesic effect and increase withdrawal symptoms. Avoid using together.

Drug-lifestyle. *Alcohol use:* May cause respiratory depression, hypertension, profound sedation, or coma. Discourage using together.

Effects on lab test results

None reported.

Pharmacokinetics

Absorption: Unknown.
Distribution: Not measurably bound to plasma proteins.
Metabolism: Metabolized in liver.
Excretion: Excreted in urine and bile. *Half-life:* 5 hours.

Route	Onset	Peak	Duration
I.V.	2-3 min	≤ 30 min	3-4 hr
I.M.	≤ 15 min	≤ 60 min	3-6 hr
S.C.	≤ 15 min	Unknown	3-6 hr

Pharmacodynamics

Chemical effect: Binds with opioid receptors in CNS, altering pain perception and response to pain by unknown mechanism.
Therapeutic effect: Relieves pain and enhances anesthesia.

Available forms

Injection: 10 mg/ml, 20 mg/ml
I.V. PCA infusion: 1.5 mg/ml

NURSING PROCESS

Assessment

- Assess patient's pain or anesthetic requirement before therapy and regularly thereafter.
- Observe for signs of withdrawal in patient receiving long-term opioid therapy.
- Monitor patient closely for respiratory depression.
- Monitor patient for signs and symptoms of constipation.
- Be alert for adverse reactions and drug interactions.
- Evaluate patient's and family's knowledge of drug therapy.

Nursing diagnoses

- Acute pain related to condition
- Disturbed thought processes related to drug's effect on CNS
- Deficient knowledge related to drug therapy

Planning and implementation
- Psychological and physical dependence may occur with prolonged use.
- Drug acts as a narcotic antagonist and may precipitate withdrawal syndrome. For patients receiving long-term opioid therapy, start with 25% of usual dose.
- Suggest that a stool softener or other laxative be ordered to prevent constipation. Encourage patient to drink fluids and eat fiber.
- Withhold dose and notify prescriber if patient's respirations are shallow or rate is below 12 breaths/minute.
- Respiratory depression can be reversed with naloxone. Keep resuscitation equipment available, particularly when administering I.V.
- **I.V. use:** Inject slowly over at least 2 minutes into vein or into I.V. line containing compatible, free-flowing I.V. solution, such as D_5W, normal saline solution, or lactated Ringer's solution.
- **I.M. and S.C. use:** Follow normal protocol.

ALERT: Don't confuse Nubain with Navane.

Patient teaching
- Caution ambulatory patient about getting out of bed or walking.
- Warn outpatient to avoid hazardous activities until CNS effects of drug are known.

Evaluation
- Patient is free from pain.
- Patient maintains normal thought processes throughout therapy.
- Patient and family state understanding of drug therapy.

naloxone hydrochloride
(nal-OKS-ohn high-droh-KLOR-ighd)
Narcan

Pharmacologic class: narcotic (opioid) antagonist
Therapeutic class: narcotic antagonist
Pregnancy risk category: B

Indications and dosages
▶ **Known or suspected narcotic-induced respiratory depression, including that caused by pentazocine and propoxyphene.** *Adults:* 0.4 to 2 mg I.V., I.M., or S.C. Repeated q 2 to 3 minutes, p.r.n. If no response is observed after 10 mg has been given, diagnosis of narcotic-induced toxicity should be questioned.

▶ **Postoperative narcotic depression.** *Adults:* 0.1 to 0.2 mg I.V. q 2 to 3 minutes, p.r.n.
Children: 0.005 to 0.01 mg/kg dose I.V. Repeated q 2 to 3 minutes, p.r.n.
Neonates (asphyxia neonatorum): 0.01 mg/kg I.V. into umbilical vein. May be repeated q 2 to 3 minutes for three doses.

▶ **Naloxone challenge for diagnosing opiate dependence‡.** *Adults:* 0.16 mg I.M. naloxone; if no signs of withdrawal after 20 to 30 minutes, give second dose of 0.24 mg I.V.

Contraindications and precautions
- Contraindicated in patients hypersensitive to drug.
- Use cautiously in patients with cardiac irritability and opioid addiction. Abrupt reversal of opioid-induced CNS depression may cause nausea, vomiting, diaphoresis, tachycardia, CNS excitement, and increased blood pressure.

Lifespan: In pregnant women, use cautiously. In breast-feeding women, safety of drug hasn't been established.

Adverse reactions
CNS: tremors, ***seizures.***
CV: tachycardia and hypertension with high doses, ***ventricular fibrillation.***
GI: nausea and vomiting with high doses.
Respiratory: ***pulmonary edema.***
Other: withdrawal symptoms in narcotic-dependent patients with higher-than-recommended doses.

Interactions
None significant.

Effects on lab test results
None reported.

Pharmacokinetics
Absorption: Unknown.
Distribution: Rapidly distributed into body tissues and fluids.
Metabolism: Rapidly metabolized in liver.

Excretion: Excreted in urine. *Half-life:* 60 to 90 minutes in adults, 3 hours in neonates.

Route	Onset	Peak	Duration
I.V.	1-2 min	Unknown	Varies
I.M., S.C.	2-5 min	Unknown	Varies

Pharmacodynamics

Chemical effect: Unknown; may displace narcotic analgesics from their receptors (competitive antagonism). Has no pharmacologic activity of its own.
Therapeutic effect: Reverses opioid effects.

Available forms

Injection: 0.02 mg/ml, 0.4 mg/ml, 1 mg/ml

NURSING PROCESS

Assessment

- Assess patient's opioid use before therapy.
- Assess effectiveness of drug regularly throughout therapy.
- Duration of narcotic may exceed that of naloxone, causing relapse into respiratory depression. Monitor patient's respiratory depth and rate.
- Patients who receive naloxone to reverse opioid-induced respiratory depression may develop tachypnea.
- Monitor patient's hydration status if adverse GI reactions occur.
- Evaluate patient's and family's knowledge of drug therapy.

Nursing diagnoses

- Ineffective health maintenance related to opioid use
- Risk for deficient fluid volume related to drug-induced adverse GI reactions
- Deficient knowledge related to drug therapy

Planning and implementation

ALERT: Drug is effective only in reversing respiratory depression caused by opioids. Flumazenil should be used to treat respiratory depression caused by diazepam or other benzodiazepines.
ALERT: Provide oxygen, ventilation, and other resuscitation measures when drug is used in the management of acute opiate overdosage and patient has severe respiratory depression.
- **I.V. use:** Be prepared to give continuous I.V. infusion to control adverse effects of epidural morphine.
– To make neonatal concentration (0.02 mg/ml), adult concentration (0.4 mg) may be diluted by mixing 0.5 ml with 9.5 ml of sterile water or saline solution for injection.
- **I.M. and S.C. use:** Follow normal protocol.

ALERT: Don't confuse naloxone with naltrexone.

Patient teaching

- Instruct patient and family to report adverse reactions.

Evaluation

- Patient responds well to drug.
- Patient maintains adequate hydration.
- Patient and family state understanding of drug therapy.

naltrexone hydrochloride

(nal-TREKS-ohn high-droh-KLOR-ighd)
ReVia, Depade

Pharmacologic class: narcotic (opioid) antagonist
Therapeutic class: narcotic detoxification adjunct
Pregnancy risk category: C

Indications and dosages

▶ **Adjunct for maintenance of opioid-free state in detoxified patients.** *Adults:* Initially, 25 mg P.O. If no withdrawal signs occur within 1 hour, additional 25 mg is given. Once patient receives 50 mg q 24 hours, flexible maintenance schedule may be used.
▶ **Treatment of alcohol dependence.** *Adults:* 50 mg P.O. once daily for up to 12 weeks.

Contraindications and precautions

- Contraindicated in patients hypersensitive to drug; in those who are receiving opioid analgesics, have a positive urine screen for opioids, or are opioid dependent; in those who have acute opioid withdrawal; and in those with acute hepatitis or liver failure.

- Use cautiously in patients with mild hepatic disease or history of recent hepatic disease.

Lifespan: In pregnant women, use cautiously. In breast-feeding women and children younger than age 18, safety of drug hasn't been established.

Adverse reactions

CNS: *insomnia, anxiety, nervousness, headache,* depression, ***suicidal ideation.***
GI: *nausea, vomiting,* anorexia, *abdominal pain.*
Hematologic: lymphocytosis.
Hepatic: ***hepatotoxicity.***
Musculoskeletal: *muscle and joint pain.*

Interactions

Drug-drug. *Products containing opioids (such as cough and cold and antidiarrheal products):* Decreases response to these products. Recommend using other non-opioid agents.
Thioridazine: Increases somnolence and lethargy. Monitor patient closely.

Effects on lab test results

- May increase AST, ALT, and LDH levels.
- May increase lymphocyte count.

Pharmacokinetics

Absorption: Well absorbed from GI tract.
Distribution: Widely distributed throughout body but varies considerably. Drug is about 21% to 28% protein-bound.
Metabolism: Undergoes extensive first-pass hepatic metabolism. Its major metabolite may be pure antagonist and contribute to its efficacy. Drug and metabolites may undergo enterohepatic recirculation.
Excretion: Excreted mainly by kidneys. *Half-life:* About 4 hours.

Route	Onset	Peak	Duration
P.O.	15-30 min	> 12 hr	24 hr

Pharmacodynamics

Chemical effect: Unknown; may reversibly block subjective effects of I.V. opioids by occupying opioid receptors in brain.
Therapeutic effect: Helps prevent opioid dependence and treats alcohol dependence.

Available forms

Tablets: 50 mg

NURSING PROCESS

Assessment

- Assess patient's opioid or alcohol dependence before therapy.
- Monitor effectiveness of drug.
- Evaluate patient's and family's knowledge of drug therapy.

Nursing diagnoses

- Health-seeking behavior related to desire to remain free from opioid dependence
- Disturbed sleep pattern related to drug-induced insomnia
- Deficient knowledge related to drug therapy

Planning and implementation

ALERT: Treatment for opioid dependency should begin after patient receives naloxone challenge, a provocative test of opioid dependency. If signs of opioid withdrawal persist after challenge, don't give naltrexone.

- Patient must be completely free from opioids before taking naltrexone or severe withdrawal symptoms may occur. Patient who has been addicted to short-acting opioids, such as heroin and meperidine, must wait at least 7 days after last opioid dose before starting naltrexone. Patient who has been addicted to longer-acting opioids, such as methadone, should wait at least 10 days.
- In emergency, expect patient receiving naltrexone to be given an opioid analgesic, but in a higher dose than usual to surmount naltrexone's effect. Respiratory depression caused by opioid analgesic may be longer and deeper.
- For patient with opioid dependence who isn't expected to comply, use flexible maintenance regimen: 100 mg on Monday and Wednesday, 150 mg on Friday.
- Use naltrexone only as part of comprehensive rehabilitation program.

ALERT: Don't confuse naloxone and naltrexone.

Patient teaching

- Advise patient to wear or carry medical identification. Warn him to tell medical personnel that he takes naltrexone.

• Give patient names of nonopioid drugs he can continue to take for pain, diarrhea, or cough.

Evaluation

• Patient maintains opioid-free state.
• Patient reports no insomnia.
• Patient and family state understanding of drug therapy.

nandrolone decanoate

(NAN-druh-lohn deh-kuh-NOH-ayt)
Androlone-D, Deca-Durabolin, Hybolin Decanoate, Kabolin, Neo-Durabolic

nandrolone phenpropionate

Durabolin, Hybolin Improved

Pharmacologic class: anabolic steroid
Therapeutic class: erythropoietic and anabolic (nandrolone decanoate), antineoplastic (nandrolone phenpropionate)
Pregnancy risk category: X
Controlled substance schedule: III

Indications and dosages

▶ **Severe debility or disease states, refractory anemias.** ***nandrolone decanoate.*** *Adults:* 50 to 100 mg I.M. weekly for women; 100 to 200 mg I.M. weekly for men. Therapy should be intermittent.
Children ages 2 to 13: 25 to 50 mg I.M. q 3 to 4 weeks.
▶ **Control of metastatic breast cancer.** ***nandrolone phenpropionate.*** *Adults:* 50 to 100 mg I.M. weekly.

Contraindications and precautions

• Contraindicated in patients hypersensitive to anabolic steroids, in men with breast or prostate cancer, in patients with nephrosis, in patients experiencing the nephrotic phase of nephritis, in women with breast cancer and hypercalcemia.
• Use cautiously in patients with diabetes; cardiac, renal, or hepatic disease; epilepsy; or migraine or other conditions that may be aggravated by fluid retention.
Lifespan: In pregnant and breast-feeding women, drug is contraindicated. In children, use cautiously.

Adverse reactions

CV: edema.
GI: gastroenteritis, nausea, vomiting, diarrhea, change in appetite.
GU: bladder irritability.
Hematologic: ***thrombocytopenia.***
Hepatic: reversible jaundice, ***peliosis hepatis, liver cell tumors.***
Metabolic: hypercalcemia.
Musculoskeletal: muscle cramps or spasms.
Skin: pain, induration at injection site.
Other: androgenic effects in women (acne, edema, *weight gain, hirsutism,* hoarseness, clitoral enlargement, *decreased breast size,* altered libido, male-pattern baldness, *oily skin or hair*), hypoestrogenic effects in women (flushing, diaphoresis, vaginitis, vaginal bleeding, nervousness, emotional lability, menstrual irregularities), excessive hormonal effects in prepubertal men (premature epiphyseal closure, *acne,* priapism, *growth of body and facial hair,* phallic enlargement), excessive hormonal effects in postpubertal men (testicular atrophy, oligospermia, decreased ejaculatory volume, impotence, gynecomastia, epididymitis).

Interactions

Drug-drug. *Hepatotoxic drugs:* Increases risk of hepatotoxicity. Monitor patient closely.
Insulin, oral antidiabetics: Alters antidiabetic dosage requirements. Monitor glucose levels in diabetic patients.
Oral anticoagulants: Alters anticoagulant dosage requirements. Monitor PT and INR.

Effects on lab test results

• May increase creatinine, lipid, sodium, potassium, calcium, phosphate, cholesterol, and liver enzyme levels.
• May decrease platelet count and thyroid function test values.

Pharmacokinetics

Absorption: Nandrolone decanoate is slowly released from I.M. depot. Nandrolone phenpropionate's absorption is unknown.
Distribution: Unknown.
Metabolism: Nandrolone decanoate is hydrolyzed to free nandrolone by plasma esterase and metabolized in liver. Nandrolone phenpropionate is metabolized in liver.

Excretion: Excreted in urine. *Half-life:* 6 to 8 days for nandrolone decanoate; unknown for nandrolone phenpropionate.

Route	Onset	Peak	Duration
I.M.	Unknown	3-6 days (decanoate); 1-2 days (phenpropionate)	Unknown

Pharmacodynamics

Chemical effect: Promotes tissue building, reverses catabolism, and stimulates erythropoiesis.
Therapeutic effect: Promotes tissue building and RBC growth (decanoate); hinders growth of breast cancer cells (phenpropionate).

Available forms

nandrolone decanoate
Injection (in oil): 50 mg/ml, 100 mg/ml, 200 mg/ml
nandrolone phenpropionate
Injection (in oil): 25 mg/ml, 50 mg/ml

NURSING PROCESS

Assessment

- Assess patient's condition before therapy and regularly thereafter.
- Make sure that pregnancy test is negative for woman of childbearing age before therapy starts.
- In child, X-rays of wrist bones should be taken before treatment to assess bone maturation. During treatment, bone maturation may proceed rapidly; periodically review X-ray results to monitor it.
- Closely observe boy younger than age 7 for precocious development of male sexual characteristics.
- Semen evaluation is routinely performed every 3 to 4 months, especially in adolescent male.
- Evaluate hepatic function.
- Watch for symptoms of hypoglycemia in diabetic patient. Check glucose level regularly because antidiabetic dosage may need to be adjusted.
- Check quantitative urine and serum calcium levels.
- Be alert for adverse reactions and drug interactions.
- Evaluate patient's and family's knowledge of drug therapy.
- Check weight regularly and assess for fluid retention.

Nursing diagnoses

- Ineffective health maintenance related to underlying condition
- Disturbed body image related to adverse androgenic reactions
- Deficient knowledge related to drug therapy

Planning and implementation

- Inject I.M. drug deeply, preferably into upper outer quadrant of gluteal muscle in adults. Rotate injection sites to prevent muscle atrophy.
- Notify prescriber immediately about signs of virilization; they may be irreversible despite stopping therapy promptly.
- Dosage adjustment may reverse jaundice. If liver function test results are abnormal, therapy should be stopped.
- Drug-induced edema usually can be controlled with sodium restrictions or diuretics.
- When used to promote erythropoiesis, make sure patient has adequate daily iron intake.
- Anabolic steroids may alter results of laboratory studies performed during therapy and for 2 to 3 weeks after therapy ends.

Patient teaching

- Make sure patient understands importance of using effective nonhormonal contraceptive during therapy.
- Advise washing after intercourse to decrease risk of vaginitis. Instruct patient to wear only cotton underwear.
- Tell woman to report menstrual irregularities and to stop therapy until the cause of irregularity has been determined.
- Instruct patient to report sudden weight gain.

Evaluation

- Patient responds well to therapy.
- Patient states acceptance of body image changes.
- Patient and family state understanding of drug therapy.

naproxen
(nuh-PROK-sin)
Apo-Naproxen ♦, EC-Naprosyn, Naprosyn, Naprosyn SR ♦ ◇, Naxen ♦ ◇, Novo-Naprox ♦, Nu-Naprox ♦

naproxen sodium
Aleve†, Anaprox, Anaprox DS, Apo-Napro-Na ♦, Apo-Napro-Na DS ♦, Naprelan, Novo-Naprox Sodium ♦, Synflex ♦, Synflex DS ♦

Pharmacologic class: NSAID
Therapeutic class: nonnarcotic analgesic, antipyretic, anti-inflammatory
Pregnancy risk category: B

Indications and dosages

▶ **Rheumatoid arthritis, osteoarthritis, ankylosing spondylitis.** *Adults:* 250 to 500 mg naproxen P.O. b.i.d. Or, 375 mg to 500 mg EC-Naprosyn P.O. b.i.d. Or, 275 to 550 mg naproxen sodium P.O. b.i.d. Or, 750 mg or 1,000 mg Naprelan P.O. daily. Or, where suppository is available, 500 mg P.R. h.s. with naproxen P.O. during day.
▶ **Juvenile arthritis.** *Children:* 10 mg/kg naproxen P.O. in two divided doses.
▶ **Acute gout.** *Adults:* 750 mg naproxen P.O., followed by 250 mg q 8 hours until attack subsides. Or, 825 mg naproxen sodium initially; then 275 mg q 8 hours until attack subsides. Or, 1,000 mg to 1,500 mg Naprelan P.O. on the first day, then 1,000 mg daily until attack subsides.
▶ **Mild-to-moderate pain, primary dysmenorrhea, acute tendinitis and bursitis.** *Adults:* 500 mg naproxen P.O., followed by 250 mg q 6 to 8 hours p.r.n. Or, 550 mg naproxen sodium P.O. initially; then 275 mg P.O. q 6 to 8 hours p.r.n. Or, 1,000 mg Naprelan P.O. daily; may use 1,500 mg P.O. daily for limited period, if needed.

Contraindications and precautions

- Contraindicated in patients hypersensitive to drug and patients with asthma, rhinitis, or nasal polyps.
- Use cautiously in those with renal disease, CV disease, GI disorders, hepatic disease, or peptic ulcer disease.

Lifespan: In women in the last trimester of pregnancy and in breast-feeding women, drug is contraindicated. In geriatric patients, use cautiously.

Adverse reactions

CNS: *headache, drowsiness, dizziness,* tinnitus, cognitive dysfunction, aseptic meningitis.
CV: *peripheral edema,* palpitations, digital vasculitis.
EENT: visual disturbances, *tinnitus.*
GI: *epigastric distress, occult blood loss, nausea,* peptic ulceration.
GU: ***nephrotoxicity.***
Hematologic: ***agranulocytosis, thrombocytopenia, neutropenia.***
Metabolic: ***hyperkalemia.***
Respiratory: dyspnea.
Skin: *pruritus, rash,* urticaria.

Interactions

Drug-drug. *Antihypertensives, diuretics:* Decreases effect of these drugs. Monitor patient.
Aspirin, corticosteroids: Increases risk of adverse GI reactions. Use cautiously.
Cyclosporine: Increases nephrotoxicity of both agents. Monitor renal function tests.
Methotrexate: Increases risk of toxicity. Monitor patient closely.
Oral anticoagulants, sulfonylureas, drugs that are highly protein-bound: Increases risk of toxicity. Monitor patient closely.
Probenecid: Decreases elimination of naproxen. Monitor patient for toxicity.
Drug-herb. *Dong quai, feverfew, garlic, ginger, horse chestnut, red clover:* Increases risk of bleeding. Discourage using together.
St. John's wort: Increases risk of photosensitivity. Advise patient to avoid unprotected or prolonged exposure to sunlight.
Drug-lifestyle. *Alcohol use:* Increases risk of adverse GI reactions. Discourage using together.

Effects on lab test results

- May increase BUN, creatinine, ALT, AST, and potassium levels.
- May increase bleeding time. May decrease granulocyte, platelet, and neutrophil counts.
- May interfere with urinary assays of 5-hydroxyindoleacetic acid and may falsely elevate urine 17-ketosteroid concentrations.

Pharmacokinetics

Absorption: Rapid and complete.
Distribution: Highly protein-bound.
Metabolism: Metabolized in liver.
Excretion: Excreted in urine. *Half-life:* 1.3 hours.

Route	Onset	Peak	Duration
P.O.	≤ 1 hr	1-6 hr	7-12 hr
P.R.	Unknown	Unknown	Unknown

Pharmacodynamics

Chemical effect: Unknown; produces anti-inflammatory, analgesic, and antipyretic effects, possibly by inhibiting prostaglandin synthesis.
Therapeutic effect: Relieves pain, fever, and inflammation.

Available forms

naproxen
Oral suspension: 125 mg/5 ml
Suppositories: 500 mg ◊
Tablets: 250 mg, 375 mg, 500 mg
Tablets (delayed-release, enteric coated): 375 mg, 500 mg
Tablets (extended-release) ♦: 750 mg, 1,000 mg
naproxen sodium
275 mg naproxen sodium = 250 mg naproxen
Tablets (controlled-release): 375 mg, 500 mg (equivalent to 412.5 mg or 550 mg naproxen sodium, respectively)
Tablets (film-coated): 220 mg, 275 mg, 550 mg

NURSING PROCESS

Assessment

- Assess patient's condition before therapy and regularly thereafter.
- Monitor CBC and renal and hepatic function every 4 to 6 months during long-term therapy.
- NSAIDs may mask signs and symptoms of infection.
- Monitor patient's hydration status if adverse GI reactions occur.
- Evaluate patient's and family's knowledge of drug therapy.

Nursing diagnoses

- Acute pain related to condition
- Risk for deficient fluid volume related to drug-induced adverse GI reactions
- Deficient knowledge related to drug therapy

Planning and implementation

ALERT: Do not exceed 1.25 g of naproxen or 1.375 of naproxen sodium daily.
- **P.O. use:** Give drug with food or milk to minimize GI upset.
– Tell patient to take a full glass of water or other liquid with each dose.
– Do not break, crush or chew delayed-release tablets.
- **P.R. use:** Not commercially available in the United States.
– Don't use in patients with inflammatory lesion of the rectum or anus.

Patient teaching
- Tell patient taking prescription doses of naproxen for arthritis that full therapeutic effect may take 2 to 4 weeks.

ALERT: Warn patient against taking naproxen and naproxen sodium at the same time.
- Teach patient to recognize and report evidence of GI bleeding. Serious GI toxicity, including peptic ulceration and bleeding, can occur in patients taking NSAIDs, despite absence of GI symptoms.
- Caution patient that use with aspirin, alcohol, or corticosteroids may increase risk of adverse GI reactions.
- Advise patient to have periodic eye examinations.

Evaluation

- Patient is free from pain.
- Patient maintains adequate hydration.
- Patient and family state understanding of drug therapy.

naratriptan hydrochloride
(nah-rah-TRIP-tin high-droh-KLOR-ighd)
Amerge

Pharmacologic class: selective 5-hydroxytryptamine 1 (5-HT1) receptor subtype agonist
Therapeutic class: antimigraine agent
Pregnancy risk category: C

Indications and dosages

▶ **Treatment of acute migraine headaches with or without aura.** *Adults:* 1 or 2.5 mg P.O. as a single dose. If headache returns or responds only partially, dose may be repeated after 4 hours, for maximum dose of 5 mg in 24 hours.
Patients with mild renal or hepatic impairment: Do not use more than 2.5 mg P.O. in 24 hours. If creatinine clearance is < 15 ml/minute or patient has severe hepatic impairment, do not use drug.

Contraindications and precautions

• Contraindicated in patients who are hypersensitive to drug or its components; who have received ergot-containing, ergot-type, or other 5-HT1 agonists in the previous 24 hours; or who have a history, symptoms, or signs of cardiac ischemia, cerebrovascular disease, peripheral vascular disease, significant underlying CV disease, a history of uncontrolled hypertension, severe renal impairment (creatinine clearance below 15 ml/minute), or severe hepatic impairment (Child-Pugh grade C).
• Unless a CV evaluation has determined that patient is free from cardiac disease, use cautiously in patients with risk factors for coronary artery disease, such as hypertension, hypercholesterolemia, obesity, diabetes, a strong family history of coronary artery disease, surgical or physiologic menopause (women), age older than 40 (men), and smoking. For patients with cardiac risk factors but a satisfactory CV evaluation, give first dose in a medical facility and consider ECG monitoring.
Lifespan: In pregnant women and geriatric patients, drug is contraindicated.

Adverse reactions

CNS: paresthesias, dizziness, drowsiness, malaise, fatigue, vertigo, syncope.
CV: palpitations, increased blood pressure, ***tachyarrhythmias, abnormal ECG changes (PR and QTc interval prolongation, ST/T wave abnormalities, PVCs, atrial flutter or fibrillation), coronary vasospasm.***
EENT: ear, nose, and throat infections; photophobia.
GI: nausea, hyposalivation, vomiting.
Other: warm or cold temperature sensations; pressure, tightness, and heaviness sensations.

Interactions

Drug-drug. *Ergot-containing or ergot-type drugs (methysergide, dihydroergotamine), other 5-HT1 agonists:* Prolong vasospastic reactions. Don't give within 24 hours of naratriptan.
Oral contraceptives: Slightly higher naratriptan levels. Monitor patient.
Selective serotonin reuptake inhibitors (fluoxetine, fluvoxamine, paroxetine, sertraline): May cause weakness, hyperreflexia, and incoordination. Monitor patient.
Sibutramine: Signs of serotonin syndrome including CNS irritability, motor weakness, shivering, myoclonus may occur. Use together cautiously.
Drug-lifestyle. *Smoking:* Increases naratriptan clearance. Discourage using together; urge patient to stop smoking.

Effects on lab test results

None reported.

Pharmacokinetics

Absorption: Well absorbed with a bioavailability of 70%.
Distribution: About 28% to 31% plasma protein–bound.
Metabolism: Metabolized to a number of inactive metabolites by wide range of cytochrome P-450 isoenzymes.
Excretion: Primarily excreted in urine with 50% of dose recovered unchanged and 30% as metabolites. *Half-life:* 6 hours.

Route	Onset	Peak	Duration
P.O.	Unknown	2-3 hr	Unknown

Pharmacodynamics

Chemical effect: Thought to activate receptors in intracranial blood vessels leading to vasoconstriction and relief of migraine headache; activation of receptors on sensory nerve endings in trigeminal system may inhibit proinflammatory neuropeptide release.
Therapeutic effect: Relieves migraine pain.

Available forms

Tablets: 1 mg, 2.5 mg

NURSING PROCESS

Assessment
• Assess baseline cardiac function before starting therapy. Perform periodic cardiac reevaluation in patients who develop risk factors for coronary artery disease.
• Monitor renal and liver function test results before starting drug therapy, and report abnormalities.
• Evaluate patient's and family's knowledge of drug therapy.

Nursing diagnoses
• Acute pain related to presence of migraine headache
• Risk for injury related to drug-induced adverse CV reactions
• Deficient knowledge related to drug therapy

Planning and implementation
• Give drug only if a definite diagnosis of migraine has been established. Drug isn't intended for preventing migraine headaches or treating hemiplegic headaches, basilar migraines, or cluster headaches.
• Withhold drug and notify prescriber if patient has pain or tightness in chest or throat, arrhythmias, or increased blood pressure.
• Don't give drug to patients with history of coronary artery disease, hypertension, arrhythmias, or risk factors for coronary artery disease because drug may cause coronary vasospasm and hypertension.
• For patients with cardiac risk factors who have had a satisfactory cardiac evaluation, give first dose while monitoring ECG. Keep emergency equipment readily available.
• Safety and effectiveness haven't been established for cluster headaches or for treating more than four migraine headaches in a 30-day period.

Patient teaching
• Instruct patient to take drug only as prescribed.
• Tell patient that drug is intended to relieve migraine headaches, not prevent them.
• Instruct patient to take dose soon after headache starts. If no response occurs to first tablet, tell patient to seek medical approval before taking second tablet. If prescriber approves a second dose, patient may take a second tablet, but no sooner than 4 hours after first tablet. Warn patient not to exceed two tablets in 24 hours.
• Teach patient to alert prescriber about bothersome adverse effects or risk factors for coronary artery disease.

Evaluation
• Patient has relief of migraine headache.
• Patient has no pain or tightness in chest or throat, arrhythmias, or increase in blood pressure.
• Patient and family state understanding of drug therapy.

nateglinide
(na-TEG-li-nide)
Starlix

Pharmacologic class: amino acid derivative
Therapeutic class: antidiabetic
Pregnancy risk category: C

Indications and dosages
▶ **Alone or with metformin to lower glucose levels in patients with type 2 diabetes whose hyperglycemia isn't adequately controlled by diet and exercise and who haven't received long-term treatment with other antidiabetics.** *Adults:* 120 mg P.O. t.i.d., taken 1 to 30 minutes before meals. If patient's glycosylated hemoglobin (HbA1c) is near goal when treatment starts, he may receive 60 mg P.O. t.i.d.

Contraindications and precautions
• Contraindicated in patients hypersensitive to the drug and in patients with type 1 diabetes or diabetic ketoacidosis.
• Use cautiously in malnourished patients and patients with moderate-to-severe liver dysfunction or adrenal or pituitary insufficiency.
Lifespan: In breast-feeding women, drug should be avoided because it isn't known whether drug appears in breast milk. In children, safety and efficacy haven't been determined. In geriatric patients, use cautiously; some geriatric patients may have greater sensitivity to the glucose-lowering effects than others.

Adverse reactions

CNS: dizziness.
GI: diarrhea.
Metabolic: ***hypoglycemia.***
Musculoskeletal: back pain, arthropathy.
Respiratory: *upper respiratory tract infection,* bronchitis, coughing.
Other: flulike symptoms, accidental trauma.

Interactions

Drug-drug. *MAO inhibitors, nonselective beta blockers, NSAIDs, salicylates:* May increase the hypoglycemic action of nateglinide. Monitor patient for hypoglycemia and monitor glucose levels closely.
Corticosteroids, sympathomimetics, thiazides, thyroid products: May reduce the hypoglycemic action of nateglinide. Monitor patient for hyperglycemia and monitor glucose levels closely.

Effects on lab test results

- May decrease glucose level.

Pharmacokinetics

Absorption: Rapidly absorbed when taken immediately before a meal. Levels peak within 1 hour. The rate of absorption is slower when nateglinide is taken with or after a meal, but the extent of absorption is unaffected.
Distribution: Extensively bound (98%) to plasma proteins, primarily albumin.
Metabolism: Metabolized in the liver by hydroxylation followed by glucuronide conjugation. It's mainly metabolized by the cytochrome P450 isoenzymes CYP2C9 (70%) and CYP3A4 (30%).
Excretion: Nateglinide and its metabolites are rapidly and completely eliminated in urine and feces after oral use. Average elimination half-life in healthy people and those with type 2 diabetes is about 1.5 hours.

Route	Onset	Peak	Duration
P.O.	20 min	1 hr	4 hr

Pharmacodynamics

Chemical effect: Stimulates insulin secretion from the pancreas. This action is dependent on the presence of functioning beta cells in the pancreas.
Therapeutic effect: Lowers glucose level.

Available forms

Tablets: 60 mg, 120 mg

NURSING PROCESS

Assessment

- Assess underlying condition before therapy and reassess regularly throughout therapy.
- Monitor glucose level regularly to evaluate drug effectiveness.
- When other drugs are started or stopped, monitor glucose level closely to detect possible drug interactions.
- Periodically monitor HbA1c levels.
- Evaluate patient's and family's knowledge of drug therapy.

Nursing diagnoses

- Ineffective health maintenance related to hyperglycemia
- Risk for injury related to adverse drug effect of hypoglycemia
- Deficient knowledge related to nateglinide therapy

Planning and implementation

- Don't use with or instead of glyburide or other oral antidiabetics. Drug may be used with metformin.
- Give drug 1 to 30 minutes before a meal. If patient misses a meal, skip the scheduled dose.
- Risk of hypoglycemia rises with strenuous exercise, alcohol ingestion, insufficient caloric intake, and use with other oral antidiabetics.
- Symptoms of hypoglycemia may be masked in patients with autonomic neuropathy and in those who use beta blockers.
- Insulin may be needed for glycemic control in patients with fever, infection, trauma, or impending surgery.
- Effectiveness may decline over time.
- Observe patient for evidence of hypoglycemia, including sweating, rapid pulse, trembling, confusion, headache, irritability, and nausea. To minimize the risk of hypoglycemia, the dose of nateglinide should be followed immediately by a meal. If hypoglycemia occurs and the patient remains conscious, give an oral form of glucose. If unconscious, give I.V. glucose.

Patient teaching

- Tell patient to take nateglinide 1 to 30 minutes before a meal.

• To reduce the risk of hypoglycemia, advise patient to skip the scheduled dose if he misses a meal.
• Educate patient about the risk of hypoglycemia and its signs and symptoms (sweating, rapid pulse, trembling, confusion, headache, irritability, and nausea). Advise patient to treat these symptoms by eating or drinking something containing sugar.
• Teach patient how to monitor and log glucose levels to evaluate diabetes control.
• Instruct patient to adhere to the prescribed diet and exercise regimen.
• Explain the possible long-term complications of diabetes and the importance of regular preventive therapy.
• Encourage patient to wear or carry medical identification that shows he has diabetes.

☑ Evaluation

• Patient's glucose level is normal.
• Patient does not become hypoglycemic and therefore sustains no injury.
• Patient and family state understanding of drug therapy.

nefazodone hydrochloride

(nef-AZ-oh-dohn high-droh-KLOR-ighd)
Serzone

Pharmacologic class: synthetically derived phenylpiperazine
Therapeutic class: antidepressant
Pregnancy risk category: C

Indications and dosages

▶ **Depression.** *Adults:* Initially, 200 mg P.O. daily in two divided doses. Dosage increased in increments of 100 to 200 mg daily at intervals of no less than 1 week, as indicated. Usual daily dosage range is 300 to 600 mg.

Contraindications and precautions

• Contraindicated in patients hypersensitive to drug or other phenylpiperazine antidepressants and within 14 days of MAO inhibitor therapy. Also contraindicated in patients who were withdrawn from nefazodone due to liver injury.
• Use cautiously in patients with CV or cerebrovascular disease that could be worsened by hypotension (such as history of MI, angina, or CVA) and conditions that predispose to hypotension (such as dehydration, hypovolemia, and treatment with antihypertensives).
• Also use cautiously in patients with history of mania.
Lifespan: In pregnant and breast-feeding women, use cautiously. In children, safety of drug hasn't been established.

Adverse reactions

CNS: headache, fever, *somnolence, dizziness, asthenia,* insomnia, *light-headedness, confusion,* memory impairment, paresthesia, abnormal dreams, decreased concentration, ataxia, incoordination, psychomotor retardation, tremor, hypertonia.
CV: vasodilation, orthostatic hypotension, hypotension, peripheral edema.
EENT: *blurred vision, abnormal vision,* pharyngitis, tinnitus, visual field defect.
GI: *dry mouth, nausea, constipation,* dyspepsia, diarrhea, increased appetite, vomiting, taste perversion.
GU: urinary frequency, urinary tract infection, urine retention, vaginitis.
Metabolic: hyponatremia.
Musculoskeletal: neck rigidity, arthralgia.
Respiratory: cough.
Skin: pruritus, rash.
Other: infection, flulike syndrome, chills, thirst, breast pain.

Interactions

Drug-drug. *Alprazolam, triazolam:* Increases effects of these drugs. Either avoid using together or give greatly reduced dosage of alprazolam and triazolam.
Calcium channel blockers and HMG-CoA reductase inhibitors: May increase levels of these drugs. Dosage adjustment may be needed.
CNS-active drugs: May alter CNS activity. Use together cautiously.
Digoxin: May increase digoxin level. Use together cautiously, and monitor digoxin levels.
MAO inhibitors, sibutramine, sumatriptan: May cause severe excitation, hyperpyrexia, seizures, delirium, coma, or a fatal reaction. Avoid using together.
Other drugs highly bound to plasma proteins: May increase adverse reactions. Monitor patient closely.

Drug-herb. *St. John's wort:* May increase sedative-hypnotic effects. Discourage using together.
Drug-lifestyle. *Alcohol use:* Enhances CNS depression. Discourage using together.

Effects on lab test results

• May decrease sodium level.

Pharmacokinetics

Absorption: Rapid and complete with low, variable absolute bioavailability (about 20%).
Distribution: Widely distributed in body tissues, including CNS. Drug is extensively bound to plasma proteins.
Metabolism: Extensively metabolized.
Excretion: Excreted in urine. *Half-life:* 2 to 4 hours.

Route	Onset	Peak	Duration
P.O.	Unknown	1 hr	Unknown

Pharmacodynamics

Chemical effect: Not precisely defined. Drug inhibits neuronal uptake of serotonin (5-HT2) and norepinephrine; it also occupies serotonin and $alpha_1$-adrenergic receptors in CNS.
Therapeutic effect: Relieves depression.

Available forms

Tablets: 50 mg, 100 mg, 150 mg, 200 mg, 250 mg

NURSING PROCESS

Assessment

• Assess patient's depression before therapy and regularly thereafter.
• Record mood changes. Monitor patient for suicidal tendencies.
• Be alert for adverse reactions and drug interactions.
• Evaluate patient's and family's knowledge of drug therapy.

Nursing diagnoses

• Disturbed thought processes related to depression
• Risk for injury related to drug-induced adverse CNS reactions
• Deficient knowledge related to drug therapy

Planning and implementation

ALERT: Allow at least 1 week after stopping drug before patient starts an MAO inhibitor. Allow at least 14 days after stopping an MAO inhibitor before patient starts drug.
ALERT: Do not initiate therapy in patients with active liver disease or with elevated baseline serum transaminases. There is no evidence that preexisting liver disease increases the likelihood of developing liver failure; however, baseline abnormalities can complicate patient monitoring.
ALERT: Discontinue the drug if clinical signs and symptoms of liver dysfunction occur, such as increased AST or ALT levels greater than or equal to 3 times upper limit of normal. Do not restart therapy.
ALERT: Don't confuse Serzone with Seroquel.

Patient teaching
• Warn patient not to engage in hazardous activity until CNS effects of drug are known.
ALERT: Instruct man with prolonged or inappropriate erections to stop drug at once and call prescriber.
• Instruct woman to call prescriber if she becomes pregnant or intends to become pregnant during therapy.
• Teach the patient the signs and symptoms of liver dysfunction, including jaundice, anorexia, gastrointestinal complaints, and malaise. Tell the patient to report these adverse events to the prescriber immediately.
• Instruct patient not to drink alcoholic beverages during drug therapy.
• Tell patient who develops rash, hives, or related allergic reaction to notify prescriber.
• Inform patient that several weeks of therapy may be needed to obtain full antidepressant effect. Once improvement occurs, tell patient not to stop drug until directed by prescriber.
• Urge patient to notify prescriber before taking any OTC medications.

Evaluation

• Patient exhibits improved behavior.
• Patient sustains no injuries from drug-induced adverse CNS reactions.
• Patient and family state understanding of drug therapy.

nelfinavir mesylate

(nel-FIN-uh-veer MES-ih-layt)
Viracept

Pharmacologic class: HIV protease inhibitor
Therapeutic class: antiviral
Pregnancy risk category: B

Indications and dosages

▶ **Treatment of HIV infection when antiretroviral therapy is warranted.** *Adults:* 750 mg P.O. t.i.d. with meals or light snacks. *Children ages 2 to 13:* 20 to 30 mg/kg P.O. t.i.d. with meals or light snacks; not to exceed 750 mg t.i.d. Recommended children's dose given t.i.d. is shown below.

Body weight (kg)	Level 1-g scoops	Level teaspoons	Tablets
7 to < 8.5	4	1	-
8.5 to < 10.5	5	1.25	-
10.5 to < 12	6	1.5	-
12 to < 14	7	1.75	-
14 to < 16	8	2	-
16 to < 18	9	2.25	-
18 to < 23	10	2.5	2
> 23	15	3.75	3

▶ **Post-exposure prophylaxis following occupational exposure to HIV‡.** *Adults:* 750 mg P.O. t.i.d. with oral zidovudine and lamivudine for 4 weeks.

Contraindications and precautions

• Contraindicated in patients hypersensitive to drug or its components.
• Use cautiously in patients with hepatic dysfunction or hemophilia type A and B.
Lifespan: In breast-feeding women, stop breast-feeding to avoid transmitting HIV virus to infant.

Adverse reactions

CNS: asthenia, anxiety, depression, dizziness, emotional lability, hyperkinesia, insomnia, migraine, malaise, headache, paresthesia, ***seizures,*** sleep disorders, somnolence, ***suicidal ideation,*** fever.
EENT: iritis, eye disorder, pharyngitis, rhinitis, sinusitis.
GI: abdominal pain, nausea, *diarrhea,* flatulence, anorexia, dyspepsia, epigastric pain, GI bleeding, ***pancreatitis,*** mouth ulceration, vomiting.
GU: sexual dysfunction, renal calculus, urine abnormality.
Hematologic: anemia, ***leukopenia, thrombocytopenia.***
Hepatic: ***hepatitis.***
Metabolic: dehydration, hyperglycemia, hyperlipidemia, hyperuricemia, ***hypoglycemia.***
Musculoskeletal: back pain, arthralgia, arthritis, cramps, myalgia, myasthenia, myopathy.
Respiratory: dyspnea.
Skin: rash, dermatitis, folliculitis, fungal dermatitis, pruritus, diaphoresis, urticaria.
Other: ***allergic reactions.***

Interactions

Drug-drug. *Amiodarone, ergot derivatives, midazolam, quinidine, or triazolam:* Increases plasma levels of these drugs, causing increased risk of serious or life-threatening adverse events. Avoid using together.
Carbamazepine, phenobarbital, and phenytoin: May reduce the effectiveness of nelfinavir by decreasing nelfinavir plasma levels. Use together cautiously.
Delavirdine, efavirenz, HIV protease inhibitors (such as indinavir or saquinavir), nevirapine: May increase plasma levels of protease inhibitors. Use together cautiously.
Drugs primarily metabolized by cytochrome P450 (CYP3A), such as dihydropyridine or calcium channel blockers: May increase levels of these drugs and decrease plasma levels of nelfinavir. Use together cautiously.
HMG-CoA inhibitors such as lovastatin, simvastatin: May increase plasma levels of antilipemic agents. Avoid using together.
Hormonal contraceptives: Decreased plasma levels of contraceptives. Advise patient to use alternative contraceptive measures during therapy.
Methadone: May decrease methadone level. Adjust dose accordingly.
Rifabutin: Increased rifabutin plasma levels, and decreased levels of nelfinavir. Reduce dose of rifabutin to one-half the usual dose, and increase nelfinavir to 1,000 mg t.i.d.
Rifampin: Decreased nelfinavir plasma level. Don't use together.

Ritonavir: May increase concentration of nelfinavir. Use together cautiously.
Sildenafil: May increase adverse effects of sildenafil. Use together cautiously. Don't exceed 25 mg of sildenafil in a 48-hour period.
Drug-herb. *St. John's wort:* Decreases nelfinavir level. Discourage using together.

Effects on lab test results

- May increase ALT, AST, alkaline phosphatase, bilirubin, GGT, amylase, CPK, and uric acid levels. May increase or decrease glucose level.
- May decrease hemoglobin, hematocrit, and WBC and platelet counts.

Pharmacokinetics

Absorption: Not reported; plasma levels peak higher when drug is taken with food.
Distribution: More than 98% bound to plasma protein.
Metabolism: Metabolized primarily by CYP3A.
Excretion: Excreted mainly in feces. *Half-life:* 3½ to 5 hours.

Route	Onset	Peak	Duration
P.O.	Unknown	2-4 hr	Unknown

Pharmacodynamics

Chemical effect: Inhibits protease enzyme and prevents splitting of the viral polyprotein.
Therapeutic effect: Produces immature, noninfectious virus.

Available forms

Powder: 50 mg/g powder
Tablets: 250 mg

NURSING PROCESS

Assessment

- Obtain baseline assessment of patient's condition, and reassess regularly thereafter to monitor drug effectiveness.
- Monitor liver function test results.
- Assess patient for increased bleeding tendencies, especially if he has hemophilia type A or B.
- Monitor patient for excessive diarrhea, and treat as directed.
- Evaluate patient's and family's knowledge of drug therapy.

Nursing diagnoses

- Risk for injury related to adverse GI effects of drug
- Risk for impaired skin integrity secondary to drug adverse effects
- Deficient knowledge related to drug therapy

Planning and implementation

- Give oral powder to children unable to take tablets. May mix oral powder with small amount of water, milk, formula, soy formula, soy milk, or dietary supplements. Tell patient to consume entire contents.
- Don't reconstitute drug with water in its original container.
- Use reconstituted powder within 6 hours.
- Mixing with acidic foods or juice isn't recommended because of the bitter taste.

ALERT: Don't confuse nelfinavir with nevirapine.

Patient teaching

- Advise patient to take drug with food.
- Inform patient that drug doesn't cure HIV infection.
- Tell patient that long-term effects of drug are unknown and that there are no data to support assumption that drug reduces risk of HIV transmission to others.
- Advise patient to take drug daily as prescribed and not to alter dose or stop drug without medical approval.
- Tell patient that diarrhea is most common adverse effect and it can be controlled with loperamide.
- If patient misses a dose, tell him to take it as soon as possible and then return to his normal schedule. If a dose is skipped, advise patient not to double the dose.
- Instruct patient taking hormonal contraceptives to use alternate or additional contraceptive measures while taking nelfinavir.
- Warn patient with phenylketonuria that powder contains 11.2 mg phenylalanine per gram.
- Advise patient to report use of other prescribed or OTC drugs because of possible drug interactions.
- Advise patient taking sildenafil about increased risk of sildenafil-associated adverse events including hypotension, visual changes, and priapism. These events should be reported promptly.

• Tell patient not to exceed 25 mg of sildenafil in a 48-hour period.

Evaluation
• Patient has no adverse GI reactions.
• Skin integrity remains intact.
• Patient and family state understanding of drug therapy.

neomycin sulfate
(nee-oh-MIGH-sin SUL-fayt)
Mycifradin, Neo-fradin, Neo-Tabs

Pharmacologic class: aminoglycoside
Therapeutic class: antibiotic
Pregnancy risk category: D

Indications and dosages
▶ **Infectious diarrhea caused by enteropathogenic *Escherichia coli*.** *Adults:* 50 mg/kg daily P.O. in four divided doses for 2 to 3 days. *Children:* 50 to 100 mg/kg daily P.O. divided q 4 to 6 hours for 2 to 3 days.
▶ **Preoperative suppression of intestinal bacteria.** *Adults:* 1 g P.O. q hour for four doses; then 1 g q 4 hours for balance of 24 hours. A saline cathartic should precede therapy. *Children:* 40 to 100 mg/kg daily P.O. divided q 4 to 6 hours. First dose should follow saline cathartic.
▶ **Adjunct treatment in hepatic coma.** *Adults:* 1 to 3 g P.O. q.i.d. for 5 to 6 days. Or, 200 ml of 1% solution or 100 ml of 2% solution as enema retained for 20 to 60 minutes q 6 hours.

Contraindications and precautions
• Contraindicated in patients hypersensitive to other aminoglycosides and in those with intestinal obstruction.
• Use cautiously in those with impaired renal function, neuromuscular disorders, or ulcerative bowel lesions.
Lifespan: In breast-feeding women, safety of drug hasn't been established. In geriatric patients, use cautiously.

Adverse reactions
CNS: headache, lethargy.
EENT: *ototoxicity.*
GI: nausea, vomiting.
GU: *nephrotoxicity* (cells or casts in urine, oliguria, proteinuria).
Skin: rash, urticaria.
Other: ***hypersensitivity reactions.***

Interactions
Drug-drug. *Acyclovir, amphotericin B, cisplatin, methoxyflurane, other aminoglycosides, vancomycin:* Increases risk of nephrotoxicity. Use together cautiously.
Cephalothin: Increases risk of nephrotoxicity. Use together cautiously.
Digoxin: Decreases digoxin absorption. Monitor patient for loss of therapeutic effect.
Dimenhydrinate: May mask symptoms of ototoxicity. Use cautiously.
I.V. loop diuretics (such as furosemide): Increases risk of ototoxicity. Use cautiously.
Methotrexate: Decreases effects of methotrexate. Monitor patient for decreased effect.
Oral anticoagulants: Inhibits vitamin-K–producing bacteria; may increase anticoagulant effect. Monitor patient for bleeding.

Effects on lab test results
• May increase BUN, creatinine, and nonprotein nitrogen levels.

Pharmacokinetics
Absorption: About 3%. Enhanced in patients with impaired GI motility or mucosal intestinal ulcerations.
Distribution: Distributed locally in GI tract.
Metabolism: Not metabolized.
Excretion: Excreted primarily unchanged in feces. *Half-life:* 2 to 3 hours.

Route	Onset	Peak	Duration
P.O.	Unknown	1-4 hr	8 hr

Pharmacodynamics
Chemical effect: Inhibits protein synthesis by binding directly to 30S ribosomal subunit.
Therapeutic effect: Kills susceptible bacteria, such as many aerobic gram-negative organisms and some aerobic gram-positive organisms. Inhibits ammonia-forming bacteria in GI tract, reducing ammonia and improving neurologic status of patients with hepatic encephalopathy.

Available forms
Oral solution: 125 mg/5 ml
Tablets: 500 mg

NURSING PROCESS

Assessment
- Assess patient's condition before therapy and regularly thereafter.
- Evaluate patient's hearing before therapy and regularly thereafter.
- Monitor renal function (output, specific gravity, urinalysis, BUN and creatinine levels, and creatinine clearance).
- Be alert for adverse reactions and drug interactions.
- Monitor patient's hydration status if adverse GI reactions occur.
- Evaluate patient's and family's knowledge of drug therapy.

Nursing diagnoses
- Infection related to organisms
- Risk for deficient fluid volume related to drug-induced adverse GI reactions
- Deficient knowledge related to drug therapy

Planning and implementation
ALERT: Never give drug parenterally.
- Drug is nonabsorbable at recommended dosage. More than 4 g daily may be systemically absorbed and lead to nephrotoxicity.
- Make sure patient is well hydrated while taking drug to minimize chemical irritation of renal tubules.
- For preoperative disinfection, provide low-residue diet and cathartic immediately before oral administration of drug.
- In adjunct treatment of hepatic coma, decrease patient's dietary protein and assess neurologic status frequently during therapy.
- The ototoxic and nephrotoxic properties of neomycin limit its usefulness.
- Drug is available with polymyxin B as urinary bladder irrigant.
- Notify prescriber about signs of decreasing renal function or complaints of tinnitus, vertigo, or hearing loss. Deafness may begin several weeks after drug is stopped.

Patient teaching
- Instruct patient to report adverse reactions, especially hearing loss or change in urinary elimination.
- Emphasize the need to drink 2 L of fluid each day.
- Tell patient to alert prescriber if infection worsens or doesn't improve.

Evaluation
- Patient is free from infection.
- Patient maintains adequate hydration throughout drug therapy.
- Patient and family state understanding of drug therapy.

neostigmine bromide
(nee-oh-STIG-meen BROH-mighd)
Prostigmin

neostigmine methylsulfate
Prostigmin

Pharmacologic class: cholinesterase inhibitor
Therapeutic class: muscle stimulant
Pregnancy risk category: C

Indications and dosages
▶ **Treatment of myasthenia gravis.** *Adults:* 15 to 30 mg P.O. t.i.d. (range, 15 to 375 mg daily). Or, 0.5 mg S.C. or I.M.
Children: 7.5 to 15 mg P.O. t.i.d. or q.i.d. Subsequent dosages must be highly individualized, depending on response and tolerance of adverse effects. Therapy may be required day and night.
▶ **Diagnosis of myasthenia gravis.** *Adults:* 0.022 mg/kg I.M. 30 minutes after 0.011 mg/kg I.M. of atropine sulfate.
Children: 0.025 to 0.04 mg/kg. I.M. after 0.011 mg/kg atropine sulfate S.C.
▶ **Postoperative abdominal distention and bladder atony.** *Adults:* 0.25 to 0.5 mg I.M. or S.C. q 4 to 6 hours for 2 to 3 days.
▶ **Antidote for nondepolarizing neuromuscular blockers.** *Adults:* 0.5 to 2 mg I.V. slowly. Repeat p.r.n. to total of 5 mg. Before antidote dose, 0.6 to 1.2 mg atropine sulfate is given I.V.
▶ **Supraventricular tachycardia from tricyclic antidepressant overdose‡.** *Children:* 0.5 to 1 mg I.V., followed by 0.25 to 0.5 mg I.V. q 1 to 3 hours, p.r.n.
▶ **Decrease small bowel transit time during radiography‡.** *Adults:* 0.5 to 0.75 mg S.C.

Note: 1:1,000 solution of injectable solution contains 1 mg/ml; 1:2,000 solution contains 0.5 mg/ml.

Contraindications and precautions

- Contraindicated in patients hypersensitive to cholinergics or bromide and in those with peritonitis or mechanical obstruction of intestine or urinary tract.
- Use cautiously in patients with bronchial asthma, bradycardia, seizure disorders, recent coronary occlusion, vagotonia, hyperthyroidism, arrhythmias, or peptic ulcer.

Lifespan: In pregnant women, safety has not been established.

Adverse reactions

CNS: dizziness, headache, mental confusion, jitters.
CV: ***bradycardia,*** hypotension, ***cardiac arrest.***
EENT: blurred vision, lacrimation, miosis.
GI: *nausea, vomiting, diarrhea, abdominal cramps,* excessive salivation.
GU: urinary frequency.
Musculoskeletal: *muscle cramps,* muscle weakness, muscle fasciculations.
Respiratory: ***depressed respiratory drive, bronchospasm, bronchoconstriction, respiratory arrest.***
Skin: rash (with bromide), diaphoresis.
Other: ***hypersensitivity reactions (anaphylaxis).***

Interactions

Drug-drug. *Aminoglycosides, anticholinergics, atropine, corticosteroids, magnesium sulfate, procainamide, quinidine:* May reverse cholinergic effects. Observe patient for lack of drug effect.

Effects on lab test results

None reported.

Pharmacokinetics

Absorption: 1% to 2% after P.O. administration. Unknown after S.C. or I.M. administration.
Distribution: About 15% to 25% of dose binds to plasma proteins.
Metabolism: Hydrolyzed by cholinesterases and metabolized by microsomal liver enzymes.
Excretion: About 80% of drug excreted in urine.

Route	Onset	Peak	Duration
P.O.	45-75 min	1-2 hr	2-4 hr
I.V.	4-8 min	1-2 hr	2-4 hr
I.M.	20-30 min	1-2 hr	2-4 hr
S.C.	Unknown	1-2 hr	2-4 hr

Pharmacodynamics

Chemical effect: Inhibits destruction of acetylcholine released from parasympathetic and somatic efferent nerves. Acetylcholine accumulates, promoting increased stimulation of receptor.
Therapeutic effect: Stimulates muscle contraction.

Available forms

neostigmine bromide
Tablets: 15 mg
neostigmine methylsulfate
Injection: 0.25 mg/ml, 0.5 mg/ml, 1 mg/ml

NURSING PROCESS

Assessment

- Assess patient's condition before therapy.
- Monitor patient's response after each dose. Watch closely for improvement in strength, vision, and ptosis 45 to 60 minutes after each dose. Show patient how to record variations in muscle strength.
- Monitor vital signs frequently.
- Evaluate patient's and family's knowledge of drug therapy.

Nursing diagnoses

- Impaired physical mobility related to condition
- Diarrhea related to drug's adverse effect on GI tract
- Deficient knowledge related to drug therapy

Planning and implementation

- Stop all other cholinergics before giving drug.
- In myasthenia gravis, schedule doses before fatigue. For example, if patient has dysphagia, schedule dose 30 minutes before each meal.
- Be prepared to give atropine injection; provide respiratory support as needed.

• When drug is used to prevent abdominal distention and GI distress, prescriber may order a rectal tube to help passage of gas.
ALERT: Although drug is commonly used to reverse effects of nondepolarizing neuromuscular blockers in patients who have undergone surgery, be aware that it may worsen blockade produced by succinylcholine.
• Patient may develop resistance to drug.
• **P.O. use:** Give drug with food or milk.
– If appropriate, obtain order for hospitalized patient to have bedside supply of tablets. A patient with long-standing disease may insist on self-administration.
• **I.V. use:** Give drug at slow, controlled rate of no more than 1 mg/minute in adults and 0.5 mg/minute in children.
• **I.M. and S.C. use:** Follow normal protocol.
• I.M. neostigmine may be used instead of edrophonium to diagnose myasthenia gravis. May be preferable to edrophonium when limb weakness is only symptom.
ALERT: Don't confuse neostigmine with etomidate (Amidate) vials which may look alike.

Patient teaching
• Tell patient to take drug with food or milk to reduce GI distress.
• When using for myasthenia gravis, explain that drug will relieve ptosis, double vision, difficulty chewing and swallowing, and trunk and limb weakness. Stress need to take drug exactly as ordered. Explain that it may have to be taken for life.
• Advise patient to wear or carry medical identification indicating that he has myasthenia gravis.

Evaluation
• Patient performs activities of daily living without assistance.
• Patient has normal bowel patterns.
• Patient and family state understanding of drug therapy.

nesiritide
(ne-SIR-I-tide)
Natrecor

Pharmacologic class: human B-type natriuretic peptide
Therapeutic class: inotropic vasodilator
Pregnancy risk category: C

Indications and dosages
▶ **Acutely decompensated heart failure in patients with dyspnea at rest or with minimal activity.** *Adults:* 2 mcg/kg by I.V. bolus over 60 seconds followed by continuous infusion of 0.01 mcg/kg/minute.

Contraindications and precautions
• Contraindicated in patients hypersensitive to drug or its components.
• Avoid using drug as primary therapy in patients with cardiogenic shock or patients with systolic blood pressure below 90 mm Hg, low cardiac filling pressures, conditions in which cardiac output is dependent on venous return, or conditions that make vasodilators inappropriate, such as valvular stenosis, restrictive or obstructive cardiomyopathy, constrictive pericarditis, or pericardial tamponade.
Lifespan: In breast-feeding women, use cautiously because it isn't known whether drug appears in breast milk. In children, safety and efficacy haven't been established. Some older patients may be more sensitive to drug effects than younger patients, but no overall difference in effectiveness has been noted.

Adverse reactions
CNS: headache, confusion, somnolence, insomnia, dizziness, anxiety, paresthesia, tremor, fever.
CV: ***hypotension, ventricular tachycardia,*** ventricular extrasystoles, angina, ***bradycardia,*** atrial fibrillation, AV node conduction abnormalities.
GI: nausea, vomiting, abdominal pain.
Hematologic: anemia.
Musculoskeletal: back pain, leg cramps.
Respiratory: ***apnea,*** cough.
Skin: injection site reactions, pain at the site, rash, sweating, pruritus.

Interactions
Drug-drug. *ACE inhibitors:* Increases hypotension symptoms. Monitor blood pressure closely.

Effects on lab test results
• May increase creatinine level more than 0.5 mg/dl above baseline.

• May decrease hemoglobin and hematocrit.

Pharmacokinetics

Absorption: Administered I.V.
Distribution: Unknown.
Metabolism: Unknown.
Excretion: Three independent paths clear drug: lysosomal proteolysis after drug binds to cell surface receptors, proteolytic cleavage by endopeptidases in the vascular lumen, and renal filtration.

Route	Onset	Peak	Duration
I.V.	15 min	1 hr	3 hr

Pharmacodynamics

Chemical effect: Binds to receptors on vascular smooth muscle and endothelial cells, which leads to an increase in cGMP level, relaxation of smooth muscles, and dilation of veins and arteries.
Therapeutic effect: Produces a dose-dependent reduction in pulmonary capillary wedge pressure and systemic arterial pressure in patients with heart failure.

Available forms

Injection: Single-dose vials of 1.5 mg sterile, lyophilized powder

NURSING PROCESS

Assessment

• Assess underlying condition before therapy and reassess regularly throughout therapy.
ALERT: Nesiritide may cause hypotension. Monitor patient's blood pressure closely, particularly if patient also takes an ACE inhibitor.
• Evaluate patient's renal function. Nesiritide may affect renal function in some people. In patients with severe heart failure whose renal function depends on the renin-angiotensin-aldosterone system, treatment may lead to azotemia.
• Monitor patient's cardiac status before, during, and after drug administration.
• Evaluate patient's and family's knowledge of drug therapy.

Nursing diagnoses

• Ineffective tissue perfusion (cardiopulmonary) related to drug-induced hypotension
• Excess fluid volume related to heart failure
• Deficient knowledge related to nesiritide therapy

Planning and implementation

• Store drug at a controlled room temperature.
• There's limited experience giving this drug for longer than 48 hours.
• Because of possible hypotension, don't start drug at dosage higher than recommended. If hypotension develops during administration, reduce dosage or discontinue drug. Drug may be restarted at a dosage reduced by 30% with no bolus doses.
• Reconstitute one 1.5-mg vial with 5 ml of diluent (such as D_5W, normal saline solution, 5% dextrose and 0.2% saline solution injection, or 5% dextrose and half-normal saline solution) from a pre-filled 250-ml I.V. bag.
• Don't shake vial. Gently rock vial until a clear, colorless solution results.
• Withdraw contents of vial and add back to the 250-ml I.V. bag to yield 6 mcg/ml. Invert the bag several times to ensure complete mixing, and use the solution within 24 hours.
• Use these formulas to calculate bolus volume (2 mcg/kg) and infusion flow rate (0.01 mcg/kg/min:

$$\underset{\text{(ml)}}{\text{Bolus volume}} = 0.33 \times \underset{\text{(kg)}}{\text{patient weight}}$$

$$\underset{\text{(ml/hr)}}{\text{Infusion flow rate}} = 0.1 \times \underset{\text{(kg)}}{\text{patient weight}}$$

• Before starting bolus dose, prime the I.V. tubing. Withdraw the bolus and administer over 60 seconds through an I.V. port in the tubing.
• Immediately after giving bolus, infuse drug at 0.1 ml/kg/hr to deliver 0.01 mcg/kg/minute.
ALERT: Drug is incompatible with injectable forms of bumetanide, enalaprilat, ethacrynate sodium, furosemide, heparin, hydralazine, and insulin. These drugs shouldn't be given through the same line with nesiritide.
ALERT: Nesiritide binds heparin and could bind the heparin lining of a heparin-coated catheter, decreasing the amount of nesiritide delivered. Don't give nesiritide through a central heparin-coated catheter.
ALERT: The preservative sodium metabisulfite is incompatible with nesiritide. Don't give injectable drugs with this preservative in the same line as nesiritide.

Patient teaching
- Tell patient to report discomfort at I.V. site.
- Urge patient to report symptoms of hypotension, such as dizziness, light-headedness, blurred vision, or sweating.
- Tell patient to report other adverse effects promptly.

Evaluation
- Patient's blood pressure remains normal during therapy.
- Patient's volume status improves.
- Patient and family state understanding of drug therapy.

nevirapine
(neh-VEER-uh-peen)
Viramune

Pharmacologic class: nonnucleoside reverse transcriptase inhibitor
Therapeutic class: antiviral
Pregnancy risk category: C

Indications and dosages
▶ **Adjunct treatment in patients with HIV-1 infection who have experienced clinical or immunologic deterioration.** *Adults:* 200 mg P.O. daily for first 14 days, followed by 200 mg P.O. b.i.d. with nucleoside analogue antiretroviral drugs.
▶ **Adjunct treatment in children infected with HIV-1.** *Children age 8 and older:* 4 mg/kg P.O. once daily for first 14 days, followed by 4 mg/kg P.O. b.i.d. thereafter. Maximum 400 mg daily.
Children ages 2 months to 8 years: 4 mg/kg P.O. once daily for first 14 days, followed by 7 mg/kg P.O. b.i.d. thereafter. Maximum dose is 400 mg daily.
▶ **Prevention of maternal-fetal transmission of HIV‡.** *Mother:* Give 200 mg P.O. as a single dose at the onset of labor.
Neonate: Give 2 mg/kg P.O. as a single dose 48 to 72 hours after birth. Usually given with a three-part zidovudine regimen.

Contraindications and precautions
- Contraindicated in patients hypersensitive to drug.
- Use cautiously in patients with impaired renal and hepatic function.

Lifespan: Women of childbearing age should avoid using hormonal contraceptive methods during therapy. Breast-feeding women should stop nursing during therapy to reduce risk of postnatal HIV transmission. Drug appears in breast milk.

Adverse reactions
CNS: *headache,* paresthesia, *fever.*
GI: *nausea,* diarrhea, abdominal pain, ulcerative stomatitis.
Hepatic: ***hepatitis.***
Musculoskeletal: myalgia.
Skin: rash, blistering, ***Stevens-Johnson syndrome.***

Interactions
Drug-drug. *Drugs extensively metabolized by cytochrome P4503A (CYP3A):* Nevirapine may lower the plasma levels of these drugs. Dosage adjustment of these drugs may be required.
Ketoconazole: Decreases ketoconazole levels. Avoid using together.
Protease inhibitors, hormonal contraceptives: Decreases plasma levels of these drugs. Use cautiously.
Rifabutin, rifampin: More data needed to assess whether dosage adjustment is necessary. Monitor patient closely.
Drug-herb. *St. John's wort:* Decreases nevirapine levels. Discourage using together.

Effects on lab test results
- May increase ALT, AST, GGT, and bilirubin levels.
- May decrease hemoglobin, hematocrit, and neutrophil count.

Pharmacokinetics
Absorption: Readily absorbed.
Distribution: Widely distributed.
Metabolism: Metabolized by liver.
Excretion: Excreted in urine and feces.

Route	Onset	Peak	Duration
P.O.	Unknown	4 hr	Unknown

Pharmacodynamics

Chemical effect: Binds to reverse transcriptase and blocks RNA-dependent and DNA-dependent DNA polymerase activities.
Therapeutic effect: May inhibit replication of HIV-1.

Available forms

Oral suspension: 50 mg/5 ml
Tablets: 200 mg

NURSING PROCESS

Assessment

- Obtain clinical chemistry tests, including liver and renal function tests, before and during therapy.
- Monitor patient for blistering, oral lesions, conjunctivitis, muscle or joint aches, or general malaise. Be especially alert for severe rash or rash accompanied by fever. Report such signs and symptoms immediately to prescriber.

Nursing diagnoses

- Infection related to presence of virus
- Deficient knowledge related to drug therapy

Planning and implementation

- Drug should be used with at least one other antiretroviral.

ALERT: Don't confuse nelfinavir with nevirapine.

Patient teaching

- Inform patient that drug doesn't cure HIV infection and that he can still develop illnesses linked to advanced HIV infection. Explain that drug doesn't reduce the risk of HIV transmission.
- Instruct patient to report rash at once and to stop drug if rash develops.
- Tell patient not to use other drugs unless approved by prescriber.
- If therapy is interrupted for more than 7 days, instruct patient to resume it as if for the first time.

Evaluation

- Patient shows no signs of worsening condition.
- Patient and family state understanding of drug therapy.

niacin (vitamin B_3, nicotinic acid)

(NIGH-uh-sin)
Niacin TR Tablets, Niacor, Niaspan, Nico-400, Nicobid , Nicolar**, Nicotinex*, Slo-Niacin

niacinamide (nicotinamide)†

Pharmacologic class: B-complex vitamin
Therapeutic class: vitamin B_3, antilipemic, peripheral vasodilator
Pregnancy risk category: A (C in dosages that exceed the RDA)

Indications and dosages

▶ **RDA.** *Neonates and infants younger than 6 months:* 5 mg.
Infants ages 6 months to 1 year: 6 mg.
Children ages 1 to 3: 9 mg.
Children ages 4 to 6: 12 mg.
Children ages 7 to 10: 13 mg.
Men ages 11 to 14: 17 mg.
Men ages 15 to 18: 20 mg.
Men ages 19 to 50: 19 mg.
Men age 51 and older: 15 mg.
Women ages 11 to 50: 15 mg.
Women age 51 and older: 13 mg.
Pregnant women: 17 mg.
Breast-feeding women: 20 mg.
▶ **Pellagra.** *Adults:* 300 to 500 mg P.O., S.C., I.M., or I.V. infusion daily in divided doses, depending on severity of niacin deficiency.
Children: Up to 300 mg P.O. or 100 mg I.V. daily, depending on severity of niacin deficiency. After symptoms subside, advise adequate nutrition and RDA supplements to prevent recurrence.
▶ **Hartnup disease.** *Adults:* 50 to 200 mg P.O. daily.
▶ **Niacin deficiency.** *Adults:* up to 100 mg P.O. daily.
▶ **Hyperlipidemias, especially with hypercholesterolemia.** *Adults:* 1 to 2 g P.O. t.i.d. with meals, increased at intervals to 6 g daily. Or, for extended-release tablets, 500 mg to 2,000 mg P.O. daily h.s.

Contraindications and precautions

- Contraindicated in patients hypersensitive to drug and in those with hepatic dysfunction, active peptic ulcers, severe hypotension, or arterial hemorrhage.

• Use cautiously in patients with gallbladder disease, diabetes mellitus, or coronary artery disease and in patients with history of liver disease, peptic ulcer, allergy, or gout.

Lifespan: In pregnant women, the benefits and risks should be assessed. Drug appears in breast milk. In children, safety of doses that exceed the RDA has not been established.

Adverse reactions

CNS: dizziness, transient headache.
CV: *flushing, excessive peripheral vasodilation,* ***arrhythmias.***
GI: *nausea, vomiting, diarrhea,* possible activation of peptic ulceration, epigastric or substernal pain.
Hepatic: ***hepatic dysfunction.***
Metabolic: hyperglycemia, hyperuricemia.
Skin: pruritus, dryness, tingling.

Interactions

Drug-drug. *Antihypertensives:* May increase risk of orthostatic hypotension. Use together cautiously; also warn patient about orthostatic hypotension.
HMG-CoA reductase inhibitors (e.g., lovastatin): Coadministration may result in myopathy and rhabdomyolysis. Avoid using together. Monitor patient for muscle pain and weakness.

Effects on lab test results

• May increase glucose, AST, ALT, and uric acid levels.

Pharmacokinetics

Absorption: Rapid after P.O. administration. Unknown after S.C. or I.M. administration.
Distribution: Coenzymes are distributed widely in body tissues.
Metabolism: Metabolized by liver to active metabolites.
Excretion: Excreted in urine. *Half-life:* About 45 minutes.

Route	Onset	Peak	Duration
P.O.	Unknown	45 min	Unknown
I.V., I.M., S.C.	Unknown	Unknown	Unknown

Pharmacodynamics

Chemical effect: Niacin and niacinamide stimulate lipid metabolism, tissue respiration, and glycogenolysis; niacin decreases synthesis of low-density lipoproteins and inhibits lipolysis in adipose tissue.
Therapeutic effect: Restores normal level of vitamin B_3, lowers triglyceride and cholesterol levels, and dilates peripheral blood vessels.

Available forms

niacin
Capsules (timed-release): 125 mg†, 250 mg†, 300 mg†, 400 mg†, 500 mg
Elixir: 50 mg/5 ml†
Injection: 100 mg/ml in 30-ml vials
Tablets: 50 mg†, 100 mg†, 250 mg†, 500 mg
Tablets (extended-release): 500 mg, 750 mg, 1 g
Tablets (timed-release): 250 mg†, 500 mg†, 750 mg†
niacinamide
Tablets: 50 mg†, 100 mg†, 500 mg†

NURSING PROCESS

Assessment

• Assess patient's condition before therapy and regularly thereafter.
• Monitor hepatic function and glucose levels.
• Be alert for adverse reactions and drug interactions.
• Monitor patient's hydration status if adverse GI reactions occur.
• Evaluate patient's and family's knowledge of drug therapy.

Nursing diagnoses

• Imbalanced nutrition: less than body requirements related to decreased intake of vitamin B3
• Risk for deficient fluid volume related to drug-induced adverse GI reactions
• Deficient knowledge related to drug therapy

Planning and implementation

• Administer aspirin (325 mg P.O. 30 minutes before niacin dose) to help reduce flushing.
• Timed-release niacin or niacinamide may prevent excessive flushing that occurs with large doses. However, timed-release niacin has been linked to hepatic dysfunction, even at doses as low as 1 g daily.
• **P.O. use:** Give drug with meals to minimize GI adverse effects.
• **I.V. use:** Give drug by slow I.V. (no more than 2 mg/minute).
• **I.M. and S.C. use:** Follow normal protocol.

Patient teaching

- Explain that flushing sensation is harmless.
- To decrease flushing, advise patient to take drug with a low-fat snack and to avoid taking it after alcohol, hot beverages, hot or spicy foods, a hot shower, or exercise.
- Stress that drug is a potent medication that may cause serious adverse effects. Explain importance of adhering to therapeutic regimen.
- Advise patient against self-medicating for hyperlipidemia.

Evaluation

- Patient's vitamin B_3 levels are normal.
- Patient maintains adequate hydration throughout drug therapy.
- Patient and family state understanding of drug therapy.

nicardipine hydrochloride

(nigh-KAR-dih-peen high-droh-KLOR-ighd)
Cardene, Cardene I.V., Cardene SR

Pharmacologic class: calcium channel blocker
Therapeutic class: antianginal, antihypertensive
Pregnancy risk category: C

Indications and dosages

▶ **Chronic stable angina (alone or with other antianginals).** *Adults:* Initially, 20 mg P.O. t.i.d. (immediate-release only). Dosage titrated based on response q 3 days. Usual dosage range is 20 to 40 mg t.i.d.

▶ **Hypertension.** *Adults:* Initially, 20 to 40 mg P.O. t.i.d. (immediate-release) or 30 to 60 mg b.i.d. (sustained-release). Dosage increase based on response. Or, for patients unable to take oral nicardipine, initially, 50 ml/hour (5 mg/hour) I.V. infusion, increased by 25 ml/hour (2.5 mg/hour) q 15 minutes up to 150 ml/hour (15 mg/hour).

Contraindications and precautions

- Contraindicated in patients hypersensitive to drug and in those with advanced aortic stenosis.
- Use cautiously in patients with cardiac conduction disturbances, hypotension, heart failure, and impaired hepatic or renal function.

Lifespan: In pregnant women, use cautiously. In breast-feeding women, drug isn't recommended. In children, safety of drug hasn't been established.

Adverse reactions

CNS: *dizziness, light-headedness, headache, paresthesia, drowsiness, asthenia.*
CV: *peripheral edema, palpitations,* angina, tachycardia, *flushing.*
GI: nausea, abdominal discomfort, dry mouth.
Skin: rash.

Interactions

Drug-drug. *Antihypertensives:* Enhances antihypertensive effect. Monitor patient's blood pressure closely.
Beta blockers: May increase cardiac depressant effects. Monitor patient.
Cimetidine: May decrease metabolism of calcium channel blockers. Monitor patient for toxicity.
Cyclosporine: Nicardipine may increase plasma cyclosporine levels. Monitor levels closely.
Theophylline: Pharmacologic effects of theophylline may be enhanced. Monitor patient.
Drug-food. *Grapefruit juice:* May increase bioavailability of drug. Give drug with another liquid.
High-fat meal: Decreases bioavailability of drug by 20% to 30%. Don't give drug with a high fat meal.

Effects on lab test results

None reported.

Pharmacokinetics

Absorption: Complete; may be decreased if drug is taken with food.
Distribution: Extensively (over 95%) bound to plasma proteins.
Metabolism: Absolute bioavailability of about 35%; extensively metabolized in liver.
Excretion: About 60% excreted in urine, 35% in bile. *Half-life:* 2 to 4 hours.

Route	Onset	Peak	Duration
P.O.	< 20 min	30 min-4 hr	6-12 hr
I.V.	Immediate	Within min	Rapid decline after therapy stops

Pharmacodynamics

Chemical effect: Inhibits calcium ion influx across cardiac and smooth-muscle cells, decreasing myocardial contractility and oxygen demand. Also dilates coronary arteries and arterioles.
Therapeutic effect: Lowers blood pressure and relieves angina.

Available forms

Capsules (immediate-release): 20 mg, 30 mg
Capsules (sustained-release): 30 mg, 45 mg, 60 mg
Injection: 2.5 mg/ml

NURSING PROCESS

Assessment

- Assess patient's condition before therapy and regularly thereafter.
- Measure blood pressure frequently during initial therapy. Maximum blood pressure response occurs about 1 hour after immediate-release form and 2 to 4 hours after sustained-release form. Check for orthostatic hypotension. Because blood pressure may vary widely based on blood level of drug, assess adequacy of antihypertensive effect 8 hours after dosing.
- Be alert for adverse reactions and drug interactions.
- Evaluate patient's and family's knowledge of drug therapy.

Nursing diagnoses

- Risk for injury related to hypertension
- Acute pain related to angina
- Deficient knowledge related to drug therapy

Planning and implementation

- **P.O. use:** When switching to oral nicardipine, give first dose of t.i.d. regimen 1 hour before stopping infusion. If using an oral drug other than nicardipine, start therapy after stopping infusion.
- **I.V. use:** Dilute with compatible solution before administration.
- – Administer by slow I.V. infusion at 0.1 mg/ml.
- – Closely monitor blood pressure during infusion.
- – Titrate rate if hypotension or tachycardia occurs.
- – Change peripheral infusion site every 12 hours to minimize risk of venous irritation.
- – Adjust infusion rate if hypotension or tachycardia occurs.

ALERT: Don't confuse nicardipine with nifedipine or nimodipine.

Patient teaching

- Advise patient to report chest pain immediately. Some patients may experience increased frequency, severity, or duration of chest pain at start of therapy or during dosage adjustments.
- Stress need to take drug exactly as prescribed even when feeling well.
- Instruct patient how to minimize orthostatic hypotension.

Evaluation

- Patient's blood pressure is normal.
- Patient's anginal attacks are less frequent and less severe.
- Patient and family state understanding of drug therapy.

nicotine polacrilex

(NIH-koh-teen poh-luh-KRIGH-leks)
Nicorette†, Nicorette DS

Pharmacologic class: nicotinic agonist
Therapeutic class: smoking cessation aid
Pregnancy risk category: C

Indications and dosages

▶ **Relief of nicotine withdrawal symptoms in patients undergoing smoking cessation.** *Adults:* Initially, one 2-mg square (4-mg square if highly dependent). Patient chews one piece of gum slowly and intermittently for 30 minutes whenever the urge to smoke occurs. Most patients need 9 to 12 pieces of gum daily during first month. With 4-mg squares, maximum dosage is 20 pieces daily. With 2-mg squares, maximum dosage is 30 pieces daily.

Contraindications and precautions

- Contraindicated in nonsmokers and patients with recent MI, life-threatening arrhythmias, severe or worsening angina pectoris, or active temporomandibular joint disease.
- Use cautiously in patients with hyperthyroidism, pheochromocytoma, insulin-dependent diabetes, peptic ulcer disease, history of esophagitis, oral or pharyngeal inflammation,

or dental conditions that could be worsened by chewing gum.

Lifespan: In pregnant women, drug is contraindicated. In breast-feeding women and children, drug isn't recommended.

Adverse reactions

CNS: dizziness, light-headedness.
CV: ***atrial fibrillation.***
EENT: sore throat, jaw muscle ache (from chewing).
GI: nausea, vomiting, indigestion.
Other: hiccups.

Interactions

Drug-drug. *Beta blockers, methylxanthines, propoxyphene, propranolol:* Decreases metabolism of these drugs, increasing therapeutic effects. Dosages may need to be adjusted.
Insulin: Smoking cessation may increase insulin absorption. Insulin dose may need to be adjusted.
Theophylline: Smoking cessation may increase theophylline levels. Monitor theophylline levels; theophylline dose may need to be adjusted.
Drug-herb. *Blue cohosh:* May increase effects of nicotine. Discourage using together.
Drug-food. *Caffeine:* May increase caffeine metabolism. Monitor patient for effects.
Food and acidic beverages (coffee, juice, carbonated beverages): Inhibits absorption. Avoid eating and drinking 15 minutes before and during chewing.
Drug-lifestyle. *Smoking:* Reduces effectiveness of drug. Warn patient to avoid smoking while taking drug.

Effects on lab test results

None reported.

Pharmacokinetics

Absorption: Nicotine is bound to ion-exchange resin and is released only during chewing. Blood level depends on vigor of gum chewing.
Distribution: Not clearly defined.
Metabolism: Metabolized by liver and somewhat by kidney and lung.
Excretion: Excreted in urine. Excretion increased with acidic urine and high urine output. *Half-life:* 1 to 2 hours.

Route	Onset	Peak	Duration
P.O.	Unknown	15-30 min	Unknown

Pharmacodynamics

Chemical effect: Provides nicotine, which stimulates nicotinic acetylcholine receptors in CNS, neuromuscular junction, autonomic ganglia, and adrenal medulla.
Therapeutic effect: Blocks nicotine withdrawal symptoms.

Available forms

Chewing gum†: 2 mg/square, 4 mg/square

NURSING PROCESS

Assessment

- Assess patient's smoking history before therapy.
- Evaluate effectiveness of drug by assessing patient for nicotine withdrawal signs and symptoms.
- Be alert for adverse reactions and drug interactions.
- Evaluate patient's and family's knowledge of drug therapy.

Nursing diagnoses

- Ineffective health maintenance related to smoking
- Risk for injury related to drug-induced adverse CNS reactions
- Deficient knowledge related to drug therapy

Planning and implementation

- Smokers most likely to benefit from nicotine gum are those with high physical nicotine dependence—those who smoke more than 15 cigarettes daily, prefer high-nicotine brands, usually inhale the smoke, smoke their first cigarette within 30 minutes of arising, find the first morning cigarette the hardest to give up, smoke most frequently in the morning, find it difficult to refrain from smoking in places where it's forbidden, or smoke even when ill and confined to bed.

Patient teaching

ALERT: Instruct patient to chew gum slowly and intermittently (chew several times, and then place between cheek and gum) for about 30 minutes to promote slow, even absorption. Fast chewing tends to produce more adverse reactions.

- Make sure patient reads and understands instruction sheet included in package.

• Emphasize importance of withdrawing gum gradually.
• Tell patient that successful abstainers will begin to gradually withdraw gum usage after 3 months. Use of gum for longer than 6 months isn't recommended. For gradual withdrawal, tell patient to cut gum in halves or quarters and mix with other sugarless gum.

☑ Evaluation
• Patient has no nicotine withdrawal symptoms.
• Patient sustains no injuries from drug-induced CNS reactions.
• Patient and family state understanding of drug therapy.

nicotine transdermal system

(NIH-koh-teen trans-DER-mul SIS-tum)
Habitrol†, NicoDerm CQ†, Nicotrol†, Nicotrol TD†, ProStep

Pharmacologic class: nicotinic cholinergic agonist
Therapeutic class: smoking cessation aid
Pregnancy risk category: D

Indications and dosages

▶ **Relief of nicotine withdrawal symptoms in patients trying to stop smoking.** ***Habitrol, NicoDerm CQ.*** *Adults:* One transdermal system applied to a nonhairy part of the upper trunk or upper outer arm. Dosage varies slightly with product selected.

Initially, one 21-mg daily system applied daily for 4 to 6 weeks. After 24 hours, system removed and a new system applied to a different site. Then, taper to 14 mg daily for 2 to 4 weeks. Finally, taper to 7 mg daily, if necessary. Nicotine substitution and gradual withdrawal should take 8 to 12 weeks. If patient experiences vivid dreams or sleep disturbances, remove patch h.s. and apply a new patch in morning.

In patients who weigh less than 45 kg (100 lb), have CV disease, or smoke less than half a pack of cigarettes daily, start therapy with the 14-mg daily system.

Nicotrol. *Adults:* One 15-mg system applied daily for 6 weeks. System applied upon waking and removed h.s. because patch provides systemic delivery over 16 hours.

Contraindications and precautions

• Contraindicated in patients hypersensitive to nicotine or components of transdermal system, in nonsmokers, and in patients with recent MI, life-threatening arrhythmias, or severe or worsening angina pectoris.
• Use cautiously in patients with hyperthyroidism, pheochromocytoma, hypertension, insulin-dependent diabetes, or peptic ulcer disease.
Lifespan: In pregnant women, breast-feeding women, and children, drug isn't recommended.

Adverse reactions

CNS: somnolence, dizziness, *headache, insomnia.*
EENT: pharyngitis, sinusitis.
GI: abdominal pain, constipation, dyspepsia, nausea.
GU: dysmenorrhea.
Musculoskeletal: back pain, myalgia.
Skin: *local or systemic erythema, pruritus or burning* at application site, cutaneous hypersensitivity, rash, diaphoresis.

Interactions

Drug-drug. *Acetaminophen, imipramine, oxazepam, pentazocine, propranolol, theophylline:* May decrease induction of hepatic enzymes that help metabolize certain drugs. Dosage may be reduced.
Adrenergic agonists (such as isoproterenol, phenylephrine), adrenergic antagonists (such as labetalol, prazosin): May alter circulating catecholamines. Dosage may need adjustment according to smoking status.
Insulin: May increase amount of S.C. insulin absorbed. Insulin dosage may be reduced.
Drug-herb. *Blue cohosh:* Increases effects of nicotine. Discourage using together.
Drug-lifestyle. *Caffeine:* May decrease induction of hepatic enzymes that help metabolize certain drugs. Dosage may be reduced.

Effects on lab test results

None reported.

Pharmacokinetics

Absorption: Rapid.
Distribution: Plasma protein–binding of drug is below 5%.

Metabolism: Metabolized by liver, kidney, and lung.
Excretion: Excreted primarily in urine as metabolites; about 10% excreted unchanged. With high urine flow rates or acidified urine, up to 30% can be excreted unchanged. *Half-life:* 1 to 2 hours.

Route	Onset	Peak	Duration
Transdermal	Unknown	3-9 hr	Varies

Pharmacodynamics

Chemical effect: Provides nicotine, which stimulates nicotinic acetylcholine receptors in CNS, neuromuscular junction, autonomic ganglia, and adrenal medulla.
Therapeutic effect: Blocks nicotine withdrawal symptoms.

Available forms

Habitrol
Transdermal system: 21 mg daily, 14 mg daily, and 7 mg daily
NicoDerm CQ
Transdermal system: 21 mg daily, 14 mg daily, 7 mg daily
Nicotrol
Transdermal system: 15 mg daily

NURSING PROCESS

Assessment
• Assess patient's smoking history before therapy.
• Evaluate effectiveness of drug by assessing patient for nicotine withdrawal signs and symptoms.
• Be alert for adverse reactions and drug interactions.
• Evaluate patient's and family's knowledge of drug therapy.

Nursing diagnoses
• Ineffective health maintenance related to smoking
• Risk for injury related to drug-induced adverse CNS reactions
• Deficient knowledge related to drug therapy

Planning and implementation
• Exposure of health care workers to nicotine in transdermal systems probably is minimal; however, avoid unnecessary contact. Wash hands with water alone because soap can enhance absorption.
ALERT: Don't confuse NicoDerm with Nitro-Derm.

Patient teaching
• Discourage use of transdermal system for more than 3 months. Prolonged nicotine consumption by any route can be habit forming.
• Warn patient not to smoke. If he smokes while using system, serious adverse effects may occur because peak nicotine level will be much higher than that achieved by smoking alone.
• Make sure patient reads and understands information dispensed with drug.
• Advise patient to apply patch promptly because nicotine can evaporate from transdermal system once it's removed from protective packaging. Patch shouldn't be altered in any way (folded or cut) before application.
• Urge patient not to store at temperatures above 86° F (30° C).
• Teach patient to fold patch in half after removal, bringing adhesive sides together. If system comes in protective pouch, tell patient to place used patch in it. Explain that careful disposal prevents accidental poisoning of children or pets.
• Tell patient with persistent or severe local skin reactions or generalized rash to immediately stop use of patch and contact prescriber.
• Instruct patient to remove patch and contact prescriber immediately if he experiences signs and symptoms of nicotine overdose, such as nausea and vomiting, dizziness, weakness, or rapid heart rate.
• Explain that patient who can't stop cigarette smoking during first 4 weeks of therapy probably won't benefit from continued use of drug. Unsuccessful patient may benefit from counseling to identify factors that led to treatment failure. Encourage patient to minimize or eliminate factors contributing to treatment failure and to try again after a while.

Evaluation
• Patient has no nicotine withdrawal symptoms.
• Patient sustains no injuries from drug-induced adverse CNS reactions.
• Patient and family state understanding of drug therapy.

nifedipine

(nigh-FEH-duh-peen)
Adalat, Adalat CC, Adalat P.A.♦, Adalat XL♦, Nifedical XL, Nu-Nifed♦, Procardia, Procardia XL

Pharmacologic class: calcium channel blocker
Therapeutic class: antianginal
Pregnancy risk category: C

Indications and dosages

▶ **Vasospastic angina (also called Prinzmetal's [variant] angina) and classic chronic stable angina pectoris.** *Capsules. Adults:* Starting dose is 10 mg P.O. t.i.d. Usual effective dosage range is 10 to 20 mg t.i.d. Some patients may need up to 30 mg q.i.d. Maximum daily dose is 180 mg.

▶ **Hypertension.** ***Extended-release form.*** *Adults:* 30 or 60 mg P.O. once daily. Adjusted over 7- to 14-day period. Maximum 120 mg daily.

Contraindications and precautions

- Contraindicated in patients hypersensitive to drug.
- Use cautiously in those with heart failure or hypotension.
- Use extended-release tablets cautiously in patients with severe GI narrowing because obstructive symptoms may occur.

Lifespan: In pregnant and breast-feeding women, drug is contraindicated. In children, safety of drug hasn't been established. In geriatric patients, use cautiously.

Adverse reactions

CNS: *dizziness, light-headedness, headache,* weakness, syncope.
CV: *flushing,* peripheral edema, hypotension, palpitations, ***heart failure, MI.***
EENT: nasal congestion.
GI: nausea, heartburn, diarrhea.
Metabolic: ***hypokalemia.***
Musculoskeletal: muscle cramps.
Respiratory: dyspnea, pulmonary edema.
Skin: rash, pruritus.

Interactions

Drug-drug. *Cimetidine, ranitidine:* Decreases nifedipine metabolism. Monitor patient closely.
Magnesium sulfate (I.V.): May cause neuromuscular blockade and hypotension. Don't use together. Monitor patient.
Propranolol, other beta blockers: May cause hypotension and heart failure. Use together cautiously.
Quinidine: May cause hypotension, bradycardia, ventricular tachycardia, AV block, and pulmonary edema. Quinidine level may be reduced. Monitor quinidine. Monitor ECG and vital signs if used together.
Drug-food. *Grapefruit juice:* Increases drug bioavailability. Discourage using together because effects vary.

Effects on lab test results

- May increase ALT, AST, alkaline phosphatase, and LDH levels. May decrease potassium level.

Pharmacokinetics

Absorption: About 90% of drug is absorbed rapidly from GI tract; however, only about 65% to 70% of drug reaches systemic circulation because of significant first-pass effect in liver.
Distribution: About 92% to 98% of circulating drug is bound to plasma proteins.
Metabolism: Metabolized in liver.
Excretion: Excreted in urine and feces as inactive metabolites. *Half-life:* 2 to 5 hours.

Route	Onset	Peak	Duration
P.O.	20 min	30 min-2 hr	4-24 hr

Pharmacodynamics

Chemical effect: Unknown; may inhibit calcium ion influx across cardiac and smooth-muscle cells, decreasing myocardial contractility and oxygen demand. Also may dilate coronary arteries and arterioles.
Therapeutic effect: Reduces blood pressure and prevents angina.

Available forms

Capsules: 10 mg, 20 mg
Tablets (extended-release): 30 mg, 60 mg, 90 mg

NURSING PROCESS

Assessment
- Assess patient's condition before therapy and regularly thereafter.
- Monitor blood pressure regularly, especially if patient also takes a beta blocker or an antihypertensive.
- Monitor potassium level regularly.
- Be alert for adverse reactions and drug interactions.
- Evaluate patient's and family's knowledge of drug therapy.

Nursing diagnoses
- Risk for injury related to presence of hypertension
- Pain related to angina
- Deficient knowledge related to drug therapy

Planning and implementation
- When rapid response to drug is desired, instruct patient to bite and swallow capsule. If he can't chew capsules, liquid can be withdrawn by puncturing capsule with needle and squeezing contents into mouth. When using these methods, continuous blood pressure and ECG monitoring is recommended.
- Despite widespread S.L. use of nifedipine capsules, avoid this route of administration. Peak level will be lower and it will take longer for level to peak than when capsule is bitten and swallowed.
- S.L. nitroglycerin may be taken as needed for acute angina.
- Although rebound effect hasn't been observed when drug is stopped, dosage should still be reduced slowly under prescriber's supervision.

ALERT: Don't confuse nifedipine with nicardipine or nisoldipine.

Patient teaching
- If patient is kept on nitrate therapy while nifedipine dosage is being adjusted, urge continued compliance.
- Warn patient that angina may worsen when therapy starts or dosage increases. Reassure him that this is temporary.
- Instruct patient to swallow extended-release tablets without breaking, crushing, or chewing them.
- Advise patient who takes extended-release form of drug that the wax-matrix "ghost" of tablet may be passed in stool.

ALERT: Warn patient not to switch brands. Procardia XL and Adalat CC aren't equivalent because of their differing pharmacokinetics.
- Tell patient to protect capsules from direct light and moisture and to store them at room temperature.

Evaluation
- Patient's blood pressure is normal.
- Patient's angina is less frequent and severe.
- Patient and family state understanding of drug therapy.

nisoldipine
(nigh-SOHL-dih-peen)
Sular

Pharmacologic class: calcium channel blocker
Therapeutic class: antihypertensive
Pregnancy risk category: C

Indications and dosages

▶ **Hypertension.** *Adults:* Initially, 20 mg (10 mg if patient is over age 65 or has liver dysfunction) P.O. once daily; then increase by 10 mg/week or at longer intervals, as indicated. Usual maintenance dosage is 20 to 40 mg once daily. Dosages above 60 mg daily aren't recommended.

Contraindications and precautions
- Contraindicated in patients hypersensitive to dihydropyridine calcium channel blockers.
- Use cautiously in patients with severe hepatic impairment, heart failure, or compromised ventricular function, and particularly in those taking beta blockers.

Lifespan: In pregnant women, use cautiously. In breast-feeding women, drug shouldn't be used.

Adverse reactions
CNS: *headache,* dizziness.
CV: vasodilation, palpitations, chest pain, *peripheral edema.*
EENT: sinusitis, pharyngitis.
GI: nausea.
Skin: rash.

Interactions

Drug-drug. *Cimetidine:* Increases bioavailability and peak levels of nisoldipine. Monitor patient.
Quinidine: Decreases bioavailability, but not peak levels, of nisoldipine. Monitor patient.
Drug-food. *Grapefruit juice:* Increases bioavailability and peak levels of drug. Discourage using together.
High-fat meal: Increases peak drug levels. Discourage high-fat meals with drug intake.

Effects on lab test results

None reported.

Pharmacokinetics

Absorption: Well absorbed from GI tract; high-fat foods significantly affect release of drug from coat-core form.
Distribution: About 99% protein-bound.
Metabolism: Extensively metabolized, with five major metabolites identified.
Excretion: Excreted in urine. *Half-life:* 7 to 12 hours.

Route	Onset	Peak	Duration
P.O.	Unknown	6-12 hr	Unknown

Pharmacodynamics

Chemical effect: Prevents entry of calcium ions into vascular smooth-muscle cells, causing dilation of arterioles, which decreases peripheral vascular resistance.
Therapeutic effect: Lowers blood pressure.

Available forms

Extended-release tablets: 10 mg, 20 mg, 30 mg, 40 mg

NURSING PROCESS

Assessment

- Assess patient's blood pressure before therapy and monitor regularly thereafter, especially during dosage adjustment.
- Monitor patient carefully. Some patients, especially those with severe obstructive coronary artery disease, have developed increased frequency, duration, or severity of angina or acute MI when starting calcium channel blocker therapy or increasing dosage.
- Be alert for adverse reactions and interactions.
- Evaluate patient's and family's knowledge of drug therapy.

Nursing diagnoses

- Risk for injury related to hypertension
- Excessive fluid volume related to edema
- Deficient knowledge related to drug therapy

Planning and implementation

- Don't give drug with a high-fat meal or grapefruit products.

ALERT: Do not confuse nisoldipine with nifedipine or nicardipine.

Patient teaching

- Tell patient to take drug as prescribed.
- Instruct patient to swallow tablet whole and not to chew, divide, or crush.

Evaluation

- Patient's blood pressure is normal.
- Patient doesn't exhibit signs of edema.
- Patient and family state understanding of drug therapy.

nitrofurantoin macrocrystals

(nigh-troh-fyoo-RAN-toyn MAH-kroh-kris-tuls)
Macrobid, Macrodantin

nitrofurantoin microcrystals

Apo-Nitrofurantoin ♦, Furadantin, Furalan, Macrodantin

Pharmacologic class: nitrofuran
Therapeutic class: urinary tract anti-infective
Pregnancy risk category: B

Indications and dosages

▶ **Urinary tract infection caused by susceptible *Escherichia coli, Staphylococcus aureus,* enterococci, and certain strains of *Klebsiella, Proteus,* and *Enterobacter.*** *Adults and children older than age 12:* 50 to 100 mg P.O. q.i.d. with milk or meals.
Children ages 1 month to 12 years: 5 to 7 mg/kg P.O. daily, divided q.i.d.

▶ **Long-term suppression therapy.** *Adults:* 50 to 100 mg P.O. daily h.s.
Children: 1 to 2 mg/kg P.O. daily h.s.

Contraindications and precautions

- Contraindicated in patients with moderate-to-severe renal impairment (creatinine clearance less than 60 ml/minute), anuria, or oliguria.
- Use cautiously in patients with renal impairment, anemia, diabetes mellitus, electrolyte abnormalities, vitamin B deficiency, debilitating disease, or G6PD deficiency.

Lifespan: In pregnant and breast-feeding women, use cautiously. In infants age 1 month and younger, drug is contraindicated.

Adverse reactions

CNS: ***peripheral neuropathy,*** headache, dizziness, drowsiness, *ascending polyneuropathy with high doses or renal impairment.*
GI: *anorexia, nausea, vomiting,* abdominal pain, *diarrhea.*
Hematologic: ***hemolysis in patients with G6PD deficiency*** (reversed after stopping drug), ***agranulocytosis, thrombocytopenia.***
Hepatic: ***hepatitis, hepatic necrosis.***
Respiratory: ***asthmatic attacks in patients with history of asthma,*** pulmonary sensitivity (cough, chest pains, fever, chills, dyspnea).
Skin: maculopapular, erythematous, or eczematous eruption; pruritus; urticaria; exfoliative dermatitis; ***Stevens-Johnson syndrome.***
Other: hypersensitivity reactions, ***anaphylaxis,*** transient alopecia, drug fever, overgrowth of nonsusceptible organisms in urinary tract.

Interactions

Drug-drug. *Magnesium-containing antacids:* Decreases nitrofurantoin absorption. Separate ingestion by 1 hour.
Quinolones (like nalidixic acid, norfloxacin): Possible decreased effectiveness of quinolone derivatives. Avoid using together.
Probenecid, sulfinpyrazone: Increases blood level and decreases urine level. May result in increased toxicity and lack of therapeutic effect. Don't use together.
Drug-food. *Any food:* Increases drug absorption. Give drug with food.

Effects on lab test results

- May increase bilirubin and alkaline phosphatase levels. May decrease glucose level.
- May decrease granulocyte and platelet counts.
- May cause false-positive results with urine glucose test using copper sulfate reduction method (Clinitest).

Pharmacokinetics

Absorption: Well absorbed from GI tract. Food aids drug's dissolution and speeds absorption. Macrocrystal form has slower dissolution and absorption.
Distribution: Drug crosses into bile; 60% binds to plasma proteins.
Metabolism: Metabolized partially in liver.
Excretion: About 30% to 50% of dose is eliminated in urine. *Half-life:* 15 minutes to 1 hour.

Route	Onset	Peak	Duration
P.O.	Unknown	Unknown	Unknown

Pharmacodynamics

Chemical effect: Unknown; may interfere with bacterial enzyme systems and cell wall formation.
Therapeutic effect: Hinders growth of many common gram-positive and gram-negative urinary pathogens including *E. coli, S. aureus,* enterococci, and certain strains of *Klebsiella* and *Enterobacter*.

Available forms

nitrofurantoin macrocrystals
Capsules: 25 mg, 50 mg, 100 mg
Capsules (dual-release): 100 mg
nitrofurantoin microcrystals
Capsules: 50 mg, 100 mg
Oral suspension: 25 mg/5 ml
Tablets: 50 mg, 100 mg

NURSING PROCESS

Assessment

- Assess patient's infection before therapy and regularly thereafter.
- Obtain urine specimen for culture and sensitivity tests before starting therapy, and repeat p.r.n. Therapy may begin pending results.
- Monitor fluid intake and output. May turn urine brown or darker.
- Monitor CBC and pulmonary status regularly.
- Be alert for adverse reactions and drug interactions.
- Monitor patient's hydration status if adverse GI reactions occur.
- Evaluate patient's and family's knowledge of drug therapy.

Nursing diagnoses

- Infection related to susceptible bacteria

*Liquid form contains alcohol. **May contain tartrazine. ♦ Canada ◇ Australia †OTC ‡Off-label use

• Risk for deficient fluid volume related to drug-induced adverse GI reactions
• Deficient knowledge related to drug therapy

Planning and implementation
• Drug has no effect on blood or tissue outside urinary tract.
ALERT: Hypersensitivity may develop during long-term therapy.
• Dual-release capsules (25 mg nitrofurantoin macrocrystals combined with 75 mg nitrofurantoin monohydrate) enable twice-daily dosing.
• Continue treatment for 3 days after urine specimens become sterile.
• Some patients may experience fewer adverse GI effects with nitrofurantoin macrocrystals.
• Store drug in amber container. Avoid metals other than stainless steel or aluminum to avoid precipitate formation.

Patient teaching
• Tell patient to take drug with food or milk to minimize GI distress.
• Teach patient how to measure intake and output. Warn him that drug will turn urine brown or darker.
• Instruct patient how to store drug.

Evaluation
• Patient is free from infection.
• Patient maintains adequate hydration throughout drug therapy.
• Patient and family state understanding of drug therapy.

nitroglycerin (glyceryl trinitrate)
(nigh-troh-GLIH-suh-rin)
Anginine ◇, Deponit, GTN-Pohl ◇, Minitran, Nitradisc ◇, Nitro-Bid, Nitro-Bid IV, Nitrodisc, Nitro-Dur, Nitrogard, Nitroglyn, Nitroject, Nitrol, Nitrolingual, Nitrong, NitroQuick, Nitrostat, Nitro-Time, Transderm-Nitro, Transiderm-Nitro ◇, Tridil

Pharmacologic class: nitrate
Therapeutic class: antianginal, vasodilator
Pregnancy risk category: C

Indications and dosages
▶ **Prophylaxis against chronic anginal attacks.** *Adults:* 2.5 mg or 2.6 mg sustained-release capsule q 8 to 12 hours. Or, 2% ointment: Start with ½ inch of ointment and increase by ½-inch increments until headache occurs; then decrease to previous dose. Range of dosage with ointment is ½ to 5 inches. Usual dose is 1 to 2 inches. Or, Nitrodisc, Nitro-Dur, or Transderm-Nitro transdermal disk or pad, 0.2 to 0.4 mg/hour once daily.
▶ **Acute angina pectoris; to prevent or minimize anginal attacks when taken immediately before stressful events.** *Adults:* 1 S.L. tablet (grain [gr] 1/400, 1/200, 1/150, 1/100) dissolved under tongue or in buccal pouch as soon as angina begins. Repeat q 5 minutes, if needed, for 15 minutes. Or, using Nitrolingual spray, 1 or 2 sprays into mouth, preferably onto or under tongue. Repeat q 3 to 5 minutes, if needed, to maximum of three doses in 15-minute period. Or, 1 to 3 mg transmucosally q 3 to 5 hours during waking hours.
▶ **Hypertension related to surgery; heart failure linked to MI; angina pectoris in acute situations; to produce controlled hypotension during surgery (by I.V. infusion).** *Adults:* Initial infusion rate is 5 mcg/minute. Increase p.r.n. by 5 mcg/minute q 3 to 5 minutes until response occurs. If 20-mcg/minute rate doesn't produce response, dosage is increased by as much as 20 mcg/minute q 3 to 5 minutes. Up to 100 mcg/minute may be needed.
▶ **Hypertensive crisis‡.** *Adults:* Infuse at 5 to 100 mcg/minute I.V.

Contraindications and precautions
• Contraindicated in patients hypersensitive to nitrates and in those with early MI (S.L. nitroglycerin), severe anemia, increased intracranial pressure, angle-closure glaucoma, orthostatic hypotension, and allergy to adhesives (transdermal form). I.V. nitroglycerin is contraindicated in patients with cardiac tamponade, restrictive cardiomyopathy, constrictive pericarditis, or hypersensitivity to I.V. form.
• Use cautiously in patients with hypotension or volume depletion.
Lifespan: In pregnant and breast-feeding women, use cautiously. In children, safety of drug hasn't been established.

Adverse reactions

CNS: *headache, sometimes with throbbing; dizziness;* weakness.
CV: *orthostatic hypotension, tachycardia, flushing, palpitations,* fainting.
EENT: sublingual burning.
GI: nausea, vomiting.
Skin: cutaneous vasodilation, contact dermatitis (patch), rash.
Other: hypersensitivity reactions.

Interactions

Drug-drug. *Antihypertensives:* May enhance hypotensive effect. Monitor patient closely.
Dihydroergotamine: May decrease antianginal effect. Avoid use together.
Sildenafil: Increases hypotensive effect. Do not use together.
Drug-lifestyle. *Alcohol use:* May increase hypotension. Urge patient to avoid alcohol during therapy.

Effects on lab test results

None reported.

Pharmacokinetics

Absorption: Well absorbed from GI tract. However, because it undergoes first-pass metabolism in liver, drug is incompletely absorbed into systemic circulation. For S.L. form, absorption from oral mucosa is relatively complete. For topical or transdermal form, well absorbed. Data not reported for other forms.
Distribution: Distributed widely; about 60% of circulating drug is bound to plasma proteins.
Metabolism: Metabolized in liver.
Excretion: Metabolites excreted in urine.
Half-life: About 1 to 4 minutes.

Route	Onset	Peak	Duration
P.O.	20-45 min	Unknown	8-12 hr
I.V.	Immediate	Immediate	3-5 min
S.L.	1-3 min	Unknown	30-60 min
Buccal	3 min	Unknown	5 hr
Translingual	2-4 min	Unknown	30-60 min
Topical	30 min	Unknown	4-8 hr
Transdermal	30 min	Unknown	≤ 24 hr

Pharmacodynamics

Chemical effect: Reduces cardiac oxygen demand by decreasing left ventricular end-diastolic pressure (preload) and, to a lesser extent, systemic vascular resistance (afterload). Also increases blood flow through collateral coronary vessels.
Therapeutic effect: Prevents or relieves acute angina, lowers blood pressure, and helps minimize heart failure caused by MI.

Available forms

Aerosol (translingual): 0.4 mg metered spray
Capsules (sustained-release): 2.5 mg, 6.5 mg, 9 mg, 13 mg
I.V.: 0.5 mg/ml, 0.8 mg/ml, 5 mg/ml
I.V. premixed solutions in dextrose: 100 mcg/ml, 200 mcg/ml, 400 mcg/ml
Tablets (buccal): 1 mg, 2 mg, 3 mg
Tablets (S.L.): 0.3 mg (gr 1/200), 0.4 mg (gr 1/150), 0.6 mg (gr 1/100)
Tablets (sustained-release): 2.6 mg, 6.5 mg, 9 mg
Topical: 2% ointment
Transdermal: 2.5 mg/24 hours, 5 mg/24 hours, 7.5 mg/24 hours, 10 mg/24 hours, 15 mg/24 hours

NURSING PROCESS

Assessment

- Assess patient's condition before therapy and regularly thereafter.
- Monitor vital signs and drug response. Be particularly aware of blood pressure. Excessive hypotension may worsen MI.
- Be alert for adverse reactions and drug interactions.
- Evaluate patient's and family's knowledge of drug therapy.

Nursing diagnoses

- Pain related to angina
- Risk for injury related to drug-induced adverse reactions
- Deficient knowledge related to drug therapy

Planning and implementation

- **P.O. use:** Give tablets on empty stomach, either 30 minutes before or 1 to 2 hours after meals.

– Tell patient to swallow tablets whole and not to chew them.

- **I.V. use:** Dilute drug with D_5W or normal saline solution for injection. Concentration shouldn't exceed 400 mcg/ml.

– Administer with infusion control device and titrate to desired response.
– Mix in glass bottles and avoid I.V. filters because drug binds to plastic. Regular polyvinyl chloride tubing can bind up to 80% of drug, making it necessary to infuse higher dosages. A special nonabsorbent (non-polyvinyl chloride) tubing is available from manufacturer.
– Always use same type of infusion set when changing I.V. lines.
– When changing concentration of nitroglycerin infusion, flush I.V. administration set with 15 to 20 ml of new concentration before use. This will clear line of old drug solution.
• **S.L. use:** Administer tablet at first sign of attack. The tablet should be wet with patient's saliva and placed under tongue until completely absorbed. Patient should sit down and rest until pain subsides.
– Dose may be repeated every 10 to 15 minutes for up to three doses. If drug doesn't provide relief, medical help should be obtained promptly.
– Patient who complains of tingling sensation with S.L. form may try holding tablet in buccal pouch.
• **Buccal use:** Tell patient to place transmucosal tablet between lip and gum above incisors, or between cheek and gum.
– Tablets shouldn't be swallowed or chewed.
• **Translingual use:** When administering translingual aerosol form, make sure patient doesn't inhale spray. Release it onto or under tongue, and have patient wait about 10 seconds or so before swallowing.
• **Topical use:** To apply ointment, measure prescribed amount on application paper; then place paper on any nonhairy area. Don't rub in. Cover with plastic film to aid absorption and protect clothing.
– If using Tape-Surrounded Appli-Ruler (TSAR) system, keep TSAR on skin to protect patient's clothing and to make sure that ointment remains in place.
– Remove excess ointment from previous site before applying next dose. Avoid getting ointment on your fingers.
• **Transdermal use:** Apply transdermal dosage forms to any nonhairy area except distal parts of arms or legs. Absorption won't be maximal from distal sites.
ALERT: Remove transdermal patch before defibrillation. Because of aluminum backing on patch, electric current may cause patch to explode.
– When stopping transdermal treatment of angina, gradually reduce dose and frequency of application over 4 to 6 weeks.
• Notify prescriber immediately if nitroglycerin is ineffective; keep patient at rest.
• Drug may cause headache, especially at start of therapy. Dosage may need to be reduced temporarily, but tolerance usually develops. Treat headache with aspirin or acetaminophen.
• Minimize drug tolerance with 10- to 12-hour daily nitrate-free interval. For example, remove transdermal system in early evening and apply a new system the next morning. Or omit last daily dose of buccal, sustained-release, or ointment form. Check with prescriber for alterations in dosage regimen if tolerance is suspected.
ALERT: Don't confuse Nitro-Bid with Nicobid.
ALERT: Don''t confuse nitroglycerin with nitroprusside.

Patient teaching
• Teach patient how to use form of drug prescribed.
• Caution patient to take drug regularly, as prescribed, and to have it accessible at all times.
• Tell patient that stopping drug abruptly causes coronary vasospasm.
• Inform patient that an additional dose may be taken before anticipated stress or at bedtime if angina is nocturnal.
• Instruct patient to use caution when wearing transdermal patch near microwave oven. Leaking radiation may heat metallic backing of patch and cause burns.
• Advise patient to avoid alcohol during drug therapy.
• Tell patient to change to upright position slowly. Advise him to go up and down stairs carefully and to lie down at first sign of dizziness.
• Urge patient to store drug in cool, dark place in tightly closed container. To ensure freshness, tell him to replace S.L. tablets every 3 months and to remove cotton because it absorbs drug.
• Tell patient to store S.L. tablets in original container or other container specifically approved for this use and to carry container in jacket pocket or purse, not in a pocket close to body.

Evaluation
- Patient reports pain relief.
- Patient doesn't experience injury from adverse reactions.
- Patient and family state understanding of drug therapy.

nitroprusside sodium
(nigh-troh-PRUS-ighd SOH-dee-um)
Nitropress, Nipride ◆

Pharmacologic class: vasodilator
Therapeutic class: antihypertensive
Pregnancy risk category: C

Indications and dosages
▶ **To lower blood pressure quickly in hypertensive emergencies; to produce controlled hypotension during anesthesia; to reduce preload and afterload in cardiac pump failure or cardiogenic shock (may be used with or without dopamine).** *Adults:* 50-mg vial diluted with 2 to 3 ml of D_5W and then added to 250, 500, or 1,000 ml of D_5W. Infused at 0.3 to 10 mcg/kg/minute. Average dose is 3 mcg/kg/minute. Maximum infusion rate is 10 mcg/kg/minute. Patients taking other antihypertensives are extremely sensitive to nitroprusside. Dosage is adjusted accordingly.

Contraindications and precautions
- Contraindicated in patients hypersensitive to drug and in those with compensatory hypertension (as in arteriovenous shunt or coarctation of aorta), inadequate cerebral circulation, congenital optic atrophy, or tobacco-induced amblyopia.
- Use with extreme caution in patients with increased intracranial pressure.
- Use cautiously in patients with hypothyroidism, hepatic or renal disease, hyponatremia, or low vitamin B_{12} level.

Lifespan: With pregnant women, use cautiously. In children and breast-feeding women, safety of drug hasn't been established.

Adverse reactions
CNS: *headache, dizziness,* ataxia, loss of consciousness, ***coma, increased intracranial pressure,*** weak pulse, absent reflexes, dilated pupils, *restlessness, muscle twitching.*
CV: distant heart sounds, palpitations, ***bradycardia,*** tachycardia, hypotension.
GI: vomiting, nausea, abdominal pain.
Hematologic: ***methemoglobinemia.***
Metabolic: ***acidosis.***
Respiratory: dyspnea, shallow breathing.
Skin: pink color, *diaphoresis.*
Other: ***thiocyanate toxicity, cyanide toxicity.***

Interactions
Drug-drug. *Antihypertensives:* May cause sensitivity to nitroprusside. Adjust dosage.
Ganglionic blockers, general anesthetics, negative inotropics, other antihypertensives: May have additive effects. Monitor blood pressure closely.
Sildenafil: Increases hypotensive effects. Don't use together.

Effects on lab test results
- May increase creatinine and methemoglobin levels.

Pharmacokinetics
Absorption: Administered I.V.
Distribution: Unknown.
Metabolism: Metabolized rapidly in erythrocytes and tissues to cyanide radical and then converted to thiocyanate in liver.
Excretion: Excreted primarily as metabolites in urine. *Half-life:* 2 minutes.

Route	Onset	Peak	Duration
I.V.	Almost immediate	1-2 min	10 min

Pharmacodynamics
Chemical effect: Relaxes arteriolar and venous smooth muscle.
Therapeutic effect: Lowers blood pressure and reduces preload and afterload.

Available forms
Injection: 50 mg/vial in 2-ml, 5-ml vials

NURSING PROCESS

Assessment
- Assess patient's condition before therapy.
- Obtain baseline vital signs before giving drug, and find out what parameters prescriber wants to achieve.

ALERT: Excessive doses or rapid infusion (more than 15 mcg/kg/minute) can cause cyanide toxicity; therefore, check thiocyanate levels every 72 hours. Levels above 100 mcg/ml may cause toxicity. Watch for profound hypotension, metabolic acidosis, dyspnea, headache, loss of consciousness, ataxia, and vomiting.
- Be alert for adverse reactions and drug interactions.
- Evaluate patient's (if appropriate) and family's knowledge of drug therapy.

Nursing diagnoses
- Risk for injury related to hypertension
- Decreased cardiac output related to heart failure
- Deficient knowledge related to drug therapy

Planning and implementation
- Keep patient in supine position when starting therapy or adjusting dosage.
- Don't use bacteriostatic water for injection or sterile saline solution for reconstitution.
- Because drug is sensitive to light, wrap I.V. solution in foil; it isn't necessary to wrap tubing. Fresh solution should have faint brownish tint. Discard drug after 24 hours.
- Infuse with infusion pump. Drug is best given by piggyback through peripheral line with no other medication. Don't adjust rate of main I.V. line while drug is being infused. Even small bolus of nitroprusside can cause severe hypotension.
- Check blood pressure every 5 minutes at start of infusion and every 15 minutes thereafter. If severe hypotension occurs, stop infusion. Effects of drug quickly reverse. Notify prescriber. If possible, start arterial pressure line. Adjust flow to specified level.
- If cyanide toxicity occurs, stop drug immediately and notify prescriber.

ALERT: Don't confuse nitroprusside with nitroglycerin.

Patient teaching
- Advise patient, if alert, to report adverse reactions or discomfort at the I.V. site immediately.

Evaluation
- Patient's blood pressure is normal.
- Patient has normal cardiac output.
- Patient and family state understanding of drug therapy.

nizatidine
(nigh-ZAT-ih-deen)
Axid, Axid AR†, Tazac ◇

Pharmacologic class: histamine$_2$ (H_2)-receptor antagonist
Therapeutic class: antiulcer drug
Pregnancy risk category: B

Indications and dosages
▶ **Active duodenal ulcer.** *Adults:* 300 mg P.O. daily h.s. Or, 150 mg P.O. b.i.d.
▶ **Maintenance therapy for duodenal ulcer.** *Adults:* 150 mg P.O. daily h.s.
▶ **Benign gastric ulcer.** *Adults:* 150 mg P.O. b.i.d. or 300 mg h.s. for 8 weeks.
▶ **Gastroesophageal reflux disease.** *Adults:* 150 mg P.O. b.i.d.
Patients with impaired renal function: If creatinine clearance is 20 to 50 ml/minute, give 150 mg P.O. daily for treatment of active duodenal ulcer or 150 mg every other day for maintenance therapy. If creatinine clearance is below 20 ml/minute, give 150 mg P.O. every other day for treatment or 150 mg q third day for maintenance.

Contraindications and precautions
- Contraindicated in patients hypersensitive to H_2-receptor antagonists.
- Use cautiously in patients with impaired renal function.

Lifespan: In pregnant and breast-feeding women, use cautiously. In children, safety of drug hasn't been established.

Adverse reactions
CNS: *somnolence,* fever.
CV: ***arrhythmias.***
Hematologic: ***thrombocytopenia.***
Hepatic: ***liver damage.***
Metabolic: hyperuricemia.
Skin: *diaphoresis,* rash, urticaria, exfoliative dermatitis.

Interactions
Drug-drug. *Aspirin:* May elevate salicylate levels (with high doses). Monitor patient for salicylate toxicity.

Drug-food. *Tomato-based, mixed-vegetable juices:* May decrease drug potency. Monitor diet.

Drug-lifestyle. *Alcohol:* May increase alcohol level. Discourage using together.

Effects on lab test results

- May increase liver enzyme and uric acid levels.
- May decrease platelet count.
- May cause false-positive test results for urobilinogen.

Pharmacokinetics

Absorption: Greater than 90%. May be slightly enhanced by food and slightly impaired by antacids.

Distribution: About 35% of drug is bound to plasma proteins.

Metabolism: Unknown, but may undergo hepatic metabolism.

Excretion: More than 90% excreted in urine; less than 6% in feces. *Half-life:* 1 to 2 hours.

Route	Onset	Peak	Duration
P.O.	≤ 30 min	30 min-3 hr	≤ 12 hr

Pharmacodynamics

Chemical effect: Competitively inhibits action of H_2 at receptor sites of parietal cells.

Therapeutic effect: Decreases gastric acid secretion.

Available forms

Capsules: 75 mg†, 150 mg, 300 mg

NURSING PROCESS

Assessment

- Assess patient's condition before therapy and regularly thereafter.
- Be alert for adverse reactions and drug interactions.
- Assess patient for abdominal pain. Note presence of blood in emesis, stool, or gastric aspirate.
- Evaluate patient's and family's knowledge of drug therapy.

Nursing diagnoses

- Impaired tissue integrity related to ulceration of GI mucosa
- Decreased cardiac output related to drug-induced arrhythmias
- Deficient knowledge related to drug therapy

Planning and implementation

- If necessary, open capsules and mix contents with apple juice. However, drug loses some potency when combined with tomato-based, mixed-vegetable juices.

Patient teaching

- Urge patient to avoid cigarette smoking because it may increase gastric acid secretion and worsen disease.
- Have patient report blood in stool or emesis.
- Warn patient to take drug as directed, even after pain subsides, to allow for adequate healing.

Evaluation

- Patient reports pain relief.
- Patient maintains normal cardiac output throughout drug therapy.
- Patient and family state understanding of drug therapy.

norepinephrine bitartrate (levarterenol bitartrate, noradrenaline acid tartrate)

(nor-ep-ih-NEF-rin bigh-TAR-trayt)

Levophed

Pharmacologic class: adrenergic (direct acting)

Therapeutic class: vasopressor

Pregnancy risk category: C

Indications and dosages

▶ **To restore blood pressure in acute hypotensive states.** *Adults:* Initially, 8 to 12 mcg/minute by I.V. infusion, adjusted to maintain normal blood pressure. Average maintenance dosage is 2 to 4 mcg/minute.

Children: 2 mcg/m²/minute by I.V. infusion; dosage adjusted based on patient response.

▶ **Severe hypotension during cardiac arrest.** *Children:* Initial I.V. infusion rate is 0.1 mcg/kg/minute. Rate adjusted based on response.

▶ **GI bleeding‡.** *Adults:* Give 8 mg in 250 ml normal saline solution intraperitoneally. Or give 8 mg in 100 ml of normal saline solution via NG tube q 1 hour for 6 to 8 hours and then q 2 hours for 4 to 6 hours.

Contraindications and precautions

• Contraindicated in patients receiving cyclopropane or halothane anesthesia, and patients with mesenteric or peripheral vascular thrombosis, profound hypoxia, hypercapnia, or hypotension caused by blood volume deficits.
• Use with extreme caution in patients receiving MAO inhibitors, tricyclic antidepressants, and certain antihistamines.
• Use cautiously in patients with sulfite sensitivity.
Lifespan: In pregnant and breast-feeding women, drug is contraindicated.

Adverse reactions

CNS: *headache,* anxiety, fever, weakness, dizziness, tremor, restlessness, insomnia.
CV: ***bradycardia, severe hypertension,*** marked increase in peripheral resistance, decreased cardiac output, ***arrhythmias.***
GU: decreased urine output.
Metabolic: ***metabolic acidosis,*** hyperglycemia, increased glycogenolysis.
Respiratory: ***respiratory difficulties, asthmatic episodes.***
Other: irritation with extravasation, swelling and enlargement of thyroid, ***anaphylaxis.***

Interactions

Drug-drug. *Alpha-adrenergic blockers:* May antagonize drug effects. Monitor patient.
Antihistamines, ergot alkaloids, guanethidine, methyldopa: Use with sympathomimetics may cause severe hypertension. Don't give together.
Bretylium: May cause arrhythmias. Monitor ECG closely.
Inhaled anesthetics: Increases risk of arrhythmias. Monitor ECG closely.
MAO inhibitors: Increases risk of hypertensive crisis. Monitor patient closely.
Tricyclic antidepressants: Increases vasopressor effect. Don't give together.

Effects on lab test results

• May increase glucose level.

Pharmacokinetics

Absorption: Administered I.V.
Distribution: Drug localizes in sympathetic nerve tissues.
Metabolism: Metabolized in liver and other tissues to inactive compounds.
Excretion: Excreted in urine. *Half-life:* About 1 minute.

Route	Onset	Peak	Duration
I.V.	Immediate	Immediate	1-2 min

Pharmacodynamics

Chemical effect: Stimulates alpha- and $beta_1$-adrenergic receptors in sympathetic nervous system.
Therapeutic effect: Raises blood pressure.

Available forms

Injection: 1 mg/ml

NURSING PROCESS

Assessment

• Assess patient's condition before therapy.
• During infusion, frequently monitor ECG, cardiac output, central venous pressure, pulmonary capillary wedge pressure, pulse rate, urine output, and color and temperature of limbs. Also, check blood pressure every 2 minutes until stabilized; then check every 5 minutes.
• Be alert for adverse reactions and drug interactions.
• Monitor vital signs closely when therapy ends. Watch for sudden drop in blood pressure.
• Evaluate patient's and family's knowledge of drug therapy.

Nursing diagnoses

• Decreased cardiac output related to hypotension
• Risk for injury related to drug-induced adverse reactions
• Deficient knowledge related to drug therapy

Planning and implementation

• Drug isn't a substitute for blood or fluid volume deficit. If deficit exists, replace fluid before giving vasopressors.
• Use central venous catheter or large vein, such as in antecubital fossa, to minimize risk of extravasation. Administer in dextrose 5% in normal saline solution for injection; normal saline solution for injection alone isn't recommended. Use continuous infusion pump to reg-

ulate flow rate and piggyback setup so I.V. line remains open if norepinephrine is stopped.
• Titrate infusion rate according to assessment findings and prescriber's guidelines. In previously hypertensive patients, blood pressure should be raised no higher than 40 mm Hg below previous systolic pressure.
ALERT: Never leave patient unattended during infusion.
• Check site frequently for extravasation. If it occurs, stop infusion immediately and call prescriber. Counteract effect by infiltrating area with 5 to 10 mg phentolamine and 10 to 15 ml of normal saline solution. Also check for blanching along course of infused vein; may progress to superficial sloughing.
• If prolonged I.V. therapy is needed, change injection site frequently.
• Keep emergency drugs on hand to reverse effects of norepinephrine: atropine for reflex bradycardia, phentolamine for vasopressor effects, and propranolol for arrhythmias.
• Report decreased urine output to prescriber immediately.
• When stopping drug, gradually slow infusion rate and report sudden drop in blood pressure.
• Drug solutions deteriorate after 24 hours.
• Protect drug from light. Discard discolored solutions or solutions that contain precipitate.

Patient teaching
• Tell patient to immediately report discomfort at infusion site or difficulty breathing.

Evaluation
• Patient has normal cardiac output.
• Patient sustains no injuries from drug-induced adverse reactions.
• Patient and family state understanding of drug therapy.

norethindrone
(nor-ETH-in-drohn)
Micronor, Nor-Q.D., Camila, Errin

norethindrone acetate
Aygestin, Norlutate ♦

Pharmacologic class: progestin
Therapeutic class: contraceptive
Pregnancy risk category: X

Indications and dosages
▶ **Amenorrhea, abnormal uterine bleeding.** ***norethindrone acetate.*** *Adults:* 2.5 to 10 mg P.O. daily on days 5 to 25 of menstrual cycle.
▶ **Endometriosis. *norethindrone acetate.*** *Adults:* 5 mg P.O. daily for 14 days; then increase by 2.5 mg daily q 2 weeks up to 15 mg daily.
▶ **Contraception in women. *norethindrone.*** *Adults:* Initially, 0.35 mg P.O. on first day of menstruation; then 0.35 mg daily.

Contraindications and precautions
• Contraindicated in patients hypersensitive to drug; patients with thromboembolic disorders, cerebral apoplexy, or a history of these conditions; and patients with breast cancer, undiagnosed abnormal vaginal bleeding, severe hepatic disease, or missed abortion.
• Use cautiously in patients with diabetes mellitus, seizure disorder, migraine, cardiac or renal disease, asthma, and depression.
Lifespan: In pregnant women, drug is contraindicated. In breast-feeding women, drug isn't recommended. In children, safety of drug hasn't been established.

Adverse reactions
CNS: dizziness, migraine, lethargy, depression.
CV: hypertension, thrombophlebitis, ***pulmonary embolism, thromboembolism, CVA,*** edema.
GI: nausea, vomiting, abdominal cramps.
GU: breakthrough bleeding, dysmenorrhea, amenorrhea, cervical erosion, abnormal secretions, uterine fibromas, vaginal candidiasis.
Hepatic: cholestatic jaundice.
Metabolic: hyperglycemia.
Skin: melasma, rash.
Other: decreased libido; breast tenderness, enlargement, or secretion.

Interactions
Drug-drug. *Barbiturates, carbamazepine, rifampin:* Decreases progestin effects. Monitor patient for lack of effect.
Bromocriptine: May cause amenorrhea, thus interfering with bromocriptine effects. Avoid using together.
Drug-food. *Caffeine:* May increase caffeine level. Monitor patient for caffeine effects.

Drug-lifestyle. *Smoking:* Increases risk of CV effects. If smoking continues, may need alternative therapy.

Effects on lab test results

- May increase glucose level.
- May increase liver function test values.

Pharmacokinetics

Absorption: Well absorbed from GI tract.
Distribution: Distributed widely; about 80% protein-bound.
Metabolism: Metabolized primarily in liver; it undergoes extensive first-pass metabolism.
Excretion: Excreted primarily in feces. *Half-life:* 5 to 14 hours.

Route	Onset	Peak	Duration
P.O.	Unknown	Unknown	Unknown

Pharmacodynamics

Chemical effect: Suppresses ovulation, possibly by inhibiting pituitary gonadotropin secretion, and forms thick cervical mucus.
Therapeutic effect: Prevents pregnancy and relieves symptoms of endometriosis, amenorrhea, and abnormal uterine bleeding.

Available forms

norethindrone
Tablets: 0.35 mg, 0.5 mg
norethindrone acetate
Tablets: 5 mg

NURSING PROCESS

Assessment

- Assess patient's condition before therapy and regularly thereafter.
- Be alert for adverse reactions and drug interactions.
- Evaluate patient's and family's knowledge of drug therapy.
- Monitor blood pressure and edema.

Nursing diagnoses

- Ineffective health maintenance related to underlying condition
- Excessive fluid volume related to drug-induced edema
- Deficient knowledge related to drug therapy

Planning and implementation

ALERT: Norethindrone acetate is twice as potent as norethindrone. It shouldn't be used for contraception.
- Don't use drug as test for pregnancy; norethindrone may cause birth defects and masculinization of female fetus.
- Preliminary estrogen treatment is usually needed by patients with menstrual disorders.

ALERT: If visual disturbance, migraine, or headache occurs or if pulmonary emboli are suspected, withhold drug, notify prescriber, and provide supportive care.

ALERT: Don't confuse Micronor with Micro-K or Micronase.

Patient teaching
- Make sure patient reads package insert explaining adverse effects of progestin before taking first dose. Also, provide verbal explanation.
- Instruct patient to report unusual symptoms immediately. Tell her to stop drug and call prescriber if visual disturbance or migraine occurs.
- Teach patient how to perform routine monthly breast self-examination.
- Warn patient that edema and weight gain are likely. Advise her to restrict sodium intake.

Evaluation

- Patient responds well to therapy.
- Patient's drug-induced edema is minimized with sodium restriction.
- Patient and family state understanding of drug therapy.

norfloxacin

(nor-FLOKS-uh-sin)
Noroxin

Pharmacologic class: fluoroquinolone
Therapeutic class: broad-spectrum antibiotic
Pregnancy risk category: C

Indications and dosages

▶ **Complicated or uncomplicated urinary tract infections caused by susceptible strains of *Escherichia coli, Klebsiella, Enterobacter, Proteus, Pseudomonas aeruginosa, Citrobacter, Staphylococcus aureus, Staphylococcus epidermidis,* and group D streptococci.**

Adults: For uncomplicated infections, 400 mg P.O. b.i.d. for 7 to 10 days. For complicated infections, 400 mg b.i.d. for 10 to 21 days.

▶ **Cystitis caused by *E. coli, K. pneumoniae,* or *Proteus mirabilis.*** *Adults:* 400 mg P.O. b.i.d. for 3 days.

▶ **Acute, uncomplicated gonorrhea.** *Adults:* 800 mg P.O. as single dose, followed by doxycycline therapy to treat coexisting chlamydial infection.

▶ **Gastroenteritis‡.** *Adults:* 400 mg P.O. b.i.d. for 5 days.

▶ **Traveler's diarrhea‡.** *Adults:* 400 mg P.O. b.i.d. for 3 days.

Patients with renal impairment: If creatinine clearance is < 30 ml/minute, patient should receive 400 mg once daily.

Contraindications and precautions

- Contraindicated in patients hypersensitive to fluoroquinolones.
- Use cautiously in patients with conditions that may predispose them to seizure disorders, such as cerebral arteriosclerosis.

Lifespan: In pregnant women, use cautiously. In children younger than age 18 and breast-feeding women, safety of drug hasn't been established.

Adverse reactions

CNS: fatigue, somnolence, headache, fever, dizziness, ***seizures.***
GI: nausea, constipation, flatulence, heartburn, dry mouth.
GU: crystalluria.
Hematologic: eosinophilia.
Musculoskeletal: arthralgia, arthritis, myalgia, joint swelling.
Skin: rash, photosensitivity reaction.
Other: hypersensitivity reactions (rash, ***anaphylactoid reactions***).

Interactions

Drug-drug. *Antacids, iron products, sucralfate:* May hinder absorption of antibiotic. Separate administration times by 2 hours before or 6 hours after antacid.
Cyclosporine: Increases cyclosporine level. Monitor level.
Nitrofurantoin: Decreases norfloxacin's effectiveness. Don't use together.
Oral anticoagulants: Increases anticoagulant effect. Monitor patient closely for bleeding.
Probenecid: May increase levels of norfloxacin by decreasing its excretion. Monitor patient for toxicity.
Theophylline: Possible impaired theophylline metabolism, resulting in increased plasma levels and risk of toxicity. Monitor patient closely.
Drug-food. *Any food:* Decreases absorption of norfloxacin. Give drug 1 hour before or 2 hours after meals.
Drug-lifestyle. *Sunlight:* May cause photosensitivity reaction. Urge patient to avoid unprotected or prolonged sun exposure.

Effects on lab test results

- May increase BUN, creatinine, ALT, AST, and alkaline phosphatase levels.
- May increase eosinophil count. May decrease hemoglobin, hematocrit, and neutrophil count.

Pharmacokinetics

Absorption: About 30% to 40%. As dose increases, percentage of absorbed drug decreases. Food may reduce absorption.
Distribution: Distributed into renal tissue, liver, gallbladder, prostatic fluid, testicles, seminal fluid, bile, and sputum. From 10% to 15% binds to plasma proteins.
Metabolism: Unknown.
Excretion: Most systemically absorbed drug is excreted by kidneys, with about 30% appearing in bile. *Half-life:* 3 to 4 hours.

Route	Onset	Peak	Duration
P.O.	Unknown	1-2 hr	Unknown

Pharmacodynamics

Chemical effect: Inhibits bacterial DNA synthesis, mainly by blocking DNA gyrase.
Therapeutic effect: Kills certain bacteria, such as most aerobic gram-positive and gram-negative urinary pathogens, including *P. aeruginosa.*

Available forms

Tablets: 400 mg

NURSING PROCESS

Assessment

- Assess patient's infection before therapy and regularly thereafter.

• Obtain culture and sensitivity tests before starting therapy, and repeat as needed throughout therapy.
• Be alert for adverse reactions and drug interactions.
• Evaluate patient's and family's knowledge of drug therapy.

Nursing diagnoses
• Infection related to bacteria
• Risk for injury related to drug-induced adverse CNS reactions
• Deficient knowledge related to drug therapy

Planning and implementation
• Give drug on empty stomach.
• Make sure patient is well hydrated before and during therapy to avoid crystalluria.
ALERT: Do not confuse Noroxin (norfloxacin) for Neurontin (gabapentin) or Floxin (ofloxacin).

Patient teaching
• Urge patient to take drug 1 hour before or 2 hours after meals to promote absorption.
• Warn patient not to exceed recommended dosage and to drink several glasses of water throughout day to maintain hydration and adequate urine output.
• Caution patient to avoid hazardous activities until CNS effects of drug are known.

Evaluation
• Patient is free from infection.
• Patient has no injuries from drug-induced adverse CNS reactions.
• Patient and family state understanding of drug therapy.

nortriptyline hydrochloride
(nor-TRIP-teh-leen high-droh-KLOR-ighd)
Allegron ◇, Aventyl*, Pamelor*

Pharmacologic class: tricyclic antidepressant
Therapeutic class: antidepressant
Pregnancy risk category: NR

Indications and dosages
▶ **Depression, panic disorder‡.** *Adults:* 25 mg P.O. t.i.d. or q.i.d., gradually increased to maximum of 150 mg daily. Or, entire dosage may be given h.s.
Geriatric and adolescent patients: Give 30 mg to 50 mg P.O. once daily or in divided doses.

Contraindications and precautions
• Contraindicated in patients hypersensitive to drug, patients in acute recovery phase after MI, and patients who have taken an MAO inhibitor within 14 days.
• Use with extreme caution in patients taking thyroid drugs and in patients with glaucoma, suicidal tendency, history of urine retention or seizures, CV disease, or hyperthyroidism.
Lifespan: In pregnant women, breast-feeding women, and children, drug isn't recommended.

Adverse reactions
CNS: *drowsiness, dizziness,* excitation, ***seizures,*** tremor, weakness, confusion, headache, nervousness, EEG changes, extrapyramidal reactions.
CV: *tachycardia,* ECG changes, hypertension, ***heart block, CVA, MI.***
EENT: *blurred vision,* tinnitus, mydriasis.
GI: dry mouth, *constipation,* nausea, vomiting, anorexia, paralytic ileus.
GU: urine retention.
Hematologic: ***bone marrow depression,*** eosinophilia, ***agranulocytosis, thrombocytopenia.***
Skin: diaphoresis, rash, urticaria, photosensitivity.
Other: hypersensitivity reaction.

Interactions
Drug-drug. *Anticholinergics:* Increases anticholinergic effect. Paralytic ileus may occur. Monitor patient.
Barbiturates, CNS depressants: Enhances CNS depression. Avoid using together.
Bupropion, cimetidine, methylphenidate, SSRIs, valproic acid: May increase nortriptyline levels. Monitor patient for adverse reactions.
Clonidine, epinephrine, norepinephrine: Increases hypertensive effect. Use together cautiously.
Quinolones: Increases risk of life-threatening arrhythmias, including torsade de pointes. Don't use together.
Rifamycins: Decreases nortriptylline levels. Monitor levels for decreased effect.

MAO inhibitors: May cause severe excitation, hyperpyrexia, or seizures. Use together cautiously.
Drug-herb. *SAMe, St. John's wort, yohimbe:* Use with some tricyclic antidepressants may increase serotonin levels. Discourage using together.
Drug-lifestyle. *Alcohol use:* Enhances CNS depression. Discourage using together.
Smoking: May lower nortriptyline level. Monitor patient for lack of drug effect.
Sun exposure: Increases risk of photosensitivity reaction. Urge patient to avoid unprotected or prolonged exposure to sunlight.

Effects on lab test results

- May increase or decrease glucose level.
- May increase liver function test values and eosinophil count. May decrease RBC, WBC, granulocyte, and platelet counts.

Pharmacokinetics

Absorption: Rapid.
Distribution: Distributed widely into body, including CNS. Drug is 95% protein-bound.
Metabolism: Metabolized by liver; significant first-pass effect may account for variability of serum levels in different patients taking same dosage.
Excretion: Most excreted in urine; some in feces. *Half-life:* 18 to 24 hours.

Route	Onset	Peak	Duration
P.O.	Unknown	7-8.5 hr	Unknown

Pharmacodynamics

Chemical effect: Unknown; increases amount of norepinephrine, serotonin, or both in CNS by blocking their reuptake by presynaptic neurons.
Therapeutic effect: Relieves depression.

Available forms

Capsules: 10 mg, 25 mg, 50 mg, 75 mg
Oral solution: 10 mg/5 ml*
Tablets: 10 mg ◇, 25 mg ◇

NURSING PROCESS

Assessment

- Assess patient's depression before therapy and regularly thereafter.
- Be alert for adverse reactions and drug interactions.
- Evaluate patient's and family's knowledge of drug therapy.

Nursing diagnoses

- Disturbed thought processes related to depression
- Risk for injury related to drug-induced adverse CNS reactions
- Deficient knowledge related to drug therapy

Planning and implementation

- Dosage should be reduced in geriatric or debilitated patient.
- Don't withdraw drug abruptly. After abrupt withdrawal of long-term therapy, patient may experience nausea, headache, and malaise.
- Because hypertensive episodes have occurred during surgery in patients receiving tricyclic antidepressants, drug should be gradually stopped several days before surgery.
- If signs of psychosis occur or increase, expect to reduce dosage.

ALERT: Don't confuse nortriptyline with amitriptyline.

Patient teaching

- Whenever possible, advise patient to take full dose at bedtime to reduce risk of orthostatic hypotension.
- Warn patient to avoid hazardous activities until CNS effects of drug are known. Drowsiness and dizziness usually subside after a few weeks.
- Tell patient to avoid alcohol during drug therapy.
- Warn patient not to stop drug suddenly.
- Advise patient to consult prescriber before taking other prescription or OTC drugs.
- Advise patient to use sunblock, wear protective clothing, and avoid prolonged exposure to sunlight.

Evaluation

- Patient's depression improves.
- Patient experiences no injuries due to drug-induced adverse CNS reactions.
- Patient and family state understanding of drug therapy.

nystatin

(nigh-STAT-in)

Mycostatin*, Nilstat, Nystex*

Pharmacologic class: polyene macrolide
Therapeutic class: antifungal
Pregnancy risk category: C

Indications and dosages

▶ **GI tract infections.** *Adults:* 500,000 to 1 million units as oral tablets P.O. t.i.d.

▶ **Oral, vaginal, and intestinal infections caused by *Candida albicans* and other *Candida* sp.** *Adults:* 500,000 to 1 million units suspension P.O. t.i.d. for oral candidiasis.
Children and infants older than age 3 months: 250,000 to 500,000 units suspension P.O. q.i.d.
Neonates and premature infants: 100,000 units suspension P.O. q.i.d.

▶ **Vaginal infections.** *Adults:* 100,000 units, as vaginal tablets, inserted high into vagina, daily or b.i.d. for 14 days.

Contraindications and precautions

• Contraindicated in patients hypersensitive to drug.
Lifespan: In breast-feeding women, safety of drug hasn't been established.

Adverse reactions

GI: transient nausea, vomiting, diarrhea (with large oral dosage).

Interactions

None significant.

Effects on lab test results

None reported.

Pharmacokinetics

Absorption: Not absorbed from GI tract, intact skin, or mucous membranes.
Distribution: None.
Metabolism: None.
Excretion: Oral form excreted almost entirely unchanged in feces.

Route	Onset	Peak	Duration
P.O., topical, vaginal	Unknown	Unknown	Unknown

Pharmacodynamics

Chemical effect: Unknown; probably acts by binding to sterols in fungal cell membrane, altering cell permeability and allowing leakage of intracellular components.
Therapeutic effect: Kills susceptible yeasts and fungi.

Available forms

Oral suspension: 100,000 units/ml
Tablets: 500,000 units
Vaginal suppositories: 100,000 units

NURSING PROCESS

Assessment

• Assess patient's infection before therapy and regularly thereafter.
• Be alert for adverse reactions.
• Monitor patient's hydration status if adverse GI reactions occur.
• Evaluate patient's and family's knowledge of drug therapy.

Nursing diagnoses

• Infection related to organisms
• Risk for deficient fluid volume related to drug-induced adverse GI reactions
• Deficient knowledge related to drug therapy

Planning and implementation

• Drug isn't effective against systemic infections.
• **P.O. use:** When treating oral candidiasis (thrush), clean food debris from patient's mouth and have patient hold suspension in mouth for several minutes before swallowing.
– When treating an infant, swab medication on oral mucosa.
– Immunosuppressed patients with oral candidiasis are sometimes instructed by prescriber to suck on vaginal tablets (100,000 units) because doing so provides prolonged contact with oral mucosa.
• **Vaginal use:** Pregnant patients can use vaginal tablets up to 6 weeks before term to treat infection that may cause thrush in neonates.

Patient teaching

• Advise patient to take drug for at least 2 days after symptoms disappear to prevent reinfection. Consult prescriber for duration of therapy.

• Instruct patient to continue therapy during menstruation.
• Instruct patient in oral hygiene techniques. Poorly fitting dentures and overuse of mouthwash may alter oral flora and promote infection.
• Explain that predisposing factors for vaginal infection include use of antibiotics, oral contraceptives, and corticosteroids; diabetes; reinfection by sexual partner; and tight-fitting panty hose. Encourage patient to wear cotton (not synthetic) underpants.
• Teach patient about hygiene for affected areas, including wiping perineal area from front to back.
• Advise patient to report redness, swelling, or irritation.

Evaluation
• Patient is free from infection.
• Patient maintains adequate hydration throughout drug therapy.
• Patient and family state understanding of drug therapy.

O

octreotide acetate
(ok-TREE-oh-tighd AS-ih-tayt)
Sandostatin, Sandostatin LAR Depot

Pharmacologic class: synthetic octapeptide
Therapeutic class: somatotropic hormone
Pregnancy risk category: B

Indications and dosages
▶ **Flushing and diarrhea caused by carcinoid tumors.** *Adults:* 0.1 to 0.6 mg daily S.C. in two to four divided doses for first 2 weeks (usual daily dosage is 0.3 mg). Subsequent dosage based on patient's response. Patients currently on Sandostatin can switch to Sandostatin LAR Depot 20 mg I.M. to gluteal area q 4 weeks for 2 months.
▶ **Watery diarrhea caused by vasoactive intestinal polypeptide secreting tumors (VIPomas).** *Adults:* 0.2 to 0.3 mg daily S.C. in two to four divided doses for first 2 weeks of therapy. Subsequent dosage based on individual response; typically doesn't exceed 0.45 mg daily. Patients currently on Sandostatin can switch to Sandostatin LAR Depot 20 mg I.M. to gluteal area q 4 weeks for 2 months.
▶ **Acromegaly.** *Adults:* Initially, 50 mcg S.C. t.i.d.; then adjusted according to somatomedin C levels q 2 weeks. Patients on Sandostatin can switch to Sandostatin LAR Depot 20 mg I.M. to gluteal area q 4 weeks for 3 months.

Contraindications and precautions
• Contraindicated in patients hypersensitive to drug or its components.
Lifespan: In pregnant women, use cautiously. In children and breast-feeding women, safety of drug hasn't been established.

Adverse reactions
CNS: dizziness, headache, light-headedness, fatigue.
CV: flushing, ***arrhythmias, bradycardia.***
GI: *nausea, diarrhea, abdominal pain or discomfort,* loose stools, vomiting, fat malabsorption, gallbladder abnormalities.
Metabolic: hyperglycemia, ***hypoglycemia,*** hypothyroidism.
Skin: edema, wheal, erythema and pain at injection site.
Other: pain, burning at S.C. injection site.

Interactions
Drug-drug. *Cyclosporine:* May decrease cyclosporine level. Monitor patient.
Drug-food. *Dietary fats:* Drug may alter the absorption of dietary fats. Also may decrease Vitamin B_{12} level; monitor level.

Effects on lab test results
• May decrease T_4 and thyroid-stimulating hormone levels. May increase or decrease glucose level.

Pharmacokinetics
Absorption: Rapid and complete after S.C. injection.
Distribution: Distributed to plasma, where it binds to serum lipoprotein and albumin.
Metabolism: Not clearly defined.
Excretion: About 35% of drug appears unchanged in urine. *Half-life:* About 1½ hours.

Route	Onset	Peak	Duration
I.M., S.C.	≤ 30 min	30-60 min	12 hr-6 wk

Pharmacodynamics

Chemical effect: Mimics action of naturally occurring somatostatin.
Therapeutic effect: Relieves flushing and diarrhea caused by certain tumors, and treats acromegaly.

Available forms

Depot: 10 mg/5 ml, 20 mg/5 ml, 30 mg/5 ml
Injection: 0.05-mg, 0.1-mg, 0.5-mg ampules; 0.2-mg/ml, 1-mg/ml multidose vials

NURSING PROCESS

Assessment

- Assess patient's condition before therapy and regularly thereafter.
- Monitor baseline thyroid function tests.
- Monitor somatomedin C levels every 2 weeks. Dosage is adjusted based on this level.
- Monitor laboratory tests periodically, such as thyroid function tests, urine 5-hydroxyindoleacetic acid, plasma serotonin, plasma substance P (for carcinoid tumors), and plasma vasoactive intestinal peptide (for VIPomas).
- Monitor fluid and electrolyte status.
- Be alert for adverse reactions and drug interactions.
- Evaluate patient's and family's knowledge of drug therapy.

Nursing diagnoses

- Diarrhea related to condition
- Fatigue related to drug-induced adverse CNS reaction
- Deficient knowledge related to drug therapy

Planning and implementation

- Give drug in divided doses for first 2 weeks of therapy; subsequent daily dosage depends on patient's response.
- Read drug labels carefully, and check dosage and strength.

ALERT: For LAR Depot injection, administer only by I.M. route. Don't give I.V. or S.C. Avoid deltoid muscle because of possible discomfort at site.

- Drug therapy may alter fluid and electrolyte balance and may require adjustment of other drugs.

Patient teaching

- Tell patient to report signs of gallbladder disease such as abdominal discomfort. Drug may be linked to development of cholelithiasis.
- Instruct patient that laboratory tests are needed during therapy.
- Advise diabetic patient to monitor glucose level closely. Antidiabetics may need dosage adjustment.

Evaluation

- Patient's bowel pattern is normal.
- Patient uses energy-saving measures to combat fatigue.
- Patient and family state understanding of drug therapy.

ofloxacin

(oh-FLOKS-eh-sin)
Apo-Oflox ♦, Floxin

Pharmacologic class: fluoroquinolone
Therapeutic class: antibiotic
Pregnancy risk category: C

Indications and dosages

▶ **Lower respiratory tract infections caused by susceptible strains of *Haemophilus influenzae* or *Streptococcus pneumoniae*.** *Adults:* 400 mg I.V. or P.O. q 12 hours for 10 days.
▶ **Cervicitis or urethritis caused by *Chlamydia trachomatis* or *Neisseria gonorrhoeae*.** *Adults:* 300 mg I.V. or P.O. q 12 hours for 7 days.
▶ **Acute, uncomplicated gonorrhea.** *Adults:* 400 mg I.V. or P.O. as single dose.
▶ **Mild to moderate skin and skin-structure infections caused by susceptible strains of *Staphylococcus aureus*, *Staphylococcus epidermidis*, *Streptococcus pyogenes*, or *Proteus mirabilis*.** *Adults:* 400 mg I.V. or P.O. q 12 hours for 10 days.
▶ **Cystitis caused by *Escherichia coli* or *Klebsiella pneumoniae*.** *Adults:* 200 mg I.V. or P.O. q 12 hours for 3 days.
▶ **Urinary tract infections caused by susceptible strains of *Citrobacter diversus*, *Enterobacter aerogenes*, *E. coli*, *P. mirabilis*, or *Pseudomonas aeruginosa*.** *Adults:* 200 mg I.V.

or P.O. q 12 hours for 7 days. Complicated infections may need 10 days of therapy.

▶ **Prostatitis caused by *E. coli*.** *Adults:* 300 mg I.V. or P.O. q 12 hours for 6 weeks.

Patients with renal impairment: After giving normal initial dose, adjust dose as follows: if creatinine clearance is 20 to 50 ml/minute, give usual recommended dose q 24 hours; if creatinine clearance is less than 20 ml/minute, give one-half of recommended dose q 24 hours.

▶ **Adjunct to *Brucella* infections‡.** *Adults:* 400 mg P.O. daily for 6 weeks.

▶ **Typhoid fever‡.** *Adults:* 200 to 400 mg P.O. q 12 hours for 7 to 14 days.

▶ **Antituberculosis drug (adjunct)‡.** *Adults:* 300 mg P.O. daily.

▶ **Treatment of postoperative sternotomy or soft tissue wounds caused by *Mycobacterium fortuitum*‡.** *Adults:* 300 to 600 mg P.O. daily for 3 to 6 months.

▶ **Acute Q fever pneumonia‡.** *Adults:* 600 mg P.O. daily for up to 16 days.

▶ **Mediterranean spotted fever‡.** *Adults:* 200 mg P.O. q 12 hours for 7 days.

▶ **Traveler's diarrhea‡.** *Adults:* 300 mg P.O. b.i.d. for 3 days.

Patients with renal impairment: If creatinine clearance is 10 to 50 ml/minute, no dosage adjustments necessary at 24-hour intervals; if less than 10 ml/minute, give one-half of recommended dose q 24 hours.

Patients with hepatic impairment: Maximum daily dose is 400 mg.

Contraindications and precautions

- Contraindicated in patients hypersensitive to drug or other fluoroquinolones.
- Use cautiously in patients with renal impairment, history of seizures, or other CNS diseases such as cerebral arteriosclerosis.

Lifespan: In pregnant women, use cautiously. In children and breast-feeding women, safety of drug hasn't been established.

Adverse reactions

CNS: headache, dizziness, fever, fatigue, lethargy, malaise, drowsiness, sleep disorders, nervousness, light-headedness, insomnia, ***seizures.***
CV: chest pain.
EENT: visual disturbances.
GI: nausea, anorexia, abdominal pain or discomfort, diarrhea, vomiting, dry mouth, flatulence, dysgeusia.
GU: vaginitis, vaginal discharge, genital pruritus.
Hematologic: eosinophilia, anemia, leukocytosis, ***neutropenia,*** lymphocytopenia, ***leukopenia.***
Metabolic: ***hypoglycemia,*** hyperglycemia.
Musculoskeletal: trunk pain, transient arthralgia, myalgia.
Skin: rash, pruritus, photosensitivity reaction.
Other: hypersensitivity reactions, ***anaphylaxis.***

Interactions

Drug-drug. *Antacids (containing calcium, magnesium, or aluminum), sucralfate, divalent or trivalent cations (such as iron or zinc), or didanosine (chewable/buffered tablets or pediatric powder for oral solution):* Interferes with GI absorption of ofloxacin. Take these drugs 2 hours before or 2 hours after taking ofloxacin.
Antineoplastics: May lower fluoroquinolone levels. Monitor patient for lack of effect.
Cimetidine: May intefere with the elimination of ofloxacin. Monitor patient for toxicity.
NSAIDs: Increases risk of CNS stimulation and convulsive seizures. Avoid using together; however, monitor patient for tremors and seizures if used together.
Oral anticoagulants: Increases anticoagulant effect. Monitor patient for bleeding and altered PT and INR.
Procainamide: May increase procainamide concentration. Monitor procainamide concentration; adjust dose accordingly.
Theophylline: Decreases theophylline clearance with some fluoroquinolones. Monitor theophylline level.
Drug-food. *Any food:* Decreased drug absorption. Give drug on an empty stomach.
Drug-lifestyle. *Sun exposure:* Photosensitivity reactions may occur. Urge patient to avoid unprotected or prolonged sun exposure.

Effects on lab test results

- May increase ALT, AST, and alkaline phosphatase level. May increase or decrease glucose level.
- May increase eosinophil count. May decrease hemoglobin, hematocrit, and neutrophil and lymphocyte counts. May increase or decrease WBC count.

- May produce false-positive opiate assay results.

Pharmacokinetics

Absorption: Well absorbed after P.O. administration.
Distribution: Widely distributed to body tissues and fluids.
Metabolism: Pyridobenzoxazine ring decreases extent of metabolism in liver.
Excretion: 70% to 80% of drug is excreted unchanged in urine; less than 5% in feces.

Route	Onset	Peak	Duration
P.O.	Unknown	1-2 hr	Unknown
I.V.	Almost immediate	Immediate	Unknown

Pharmacodynamics

Chemical effect: Unknown; may inhibit bacterial DNA gyrase and prevent DNA replication in susceptible bacteria.
Therapeutic effect: Kills susceptible aerobic gram-positive and gram-negative organisms.

Available forms

Injection: 20 mg/ml, 40 mg/ml; 4 mg/ml premixed in D_5W
Tablets: 200 mg, 300 mg, 400 mg

NURSING PROCESS

Assessment

- Assess patient's infection before therapy and regularly thereafter.
- Monitor regular blood studies and hepatic and renal function tests during prolonged therapy.
- Patient treated for gonorrhea should have serologic test for syphilis. Drug isn't effective against syphilis, and treatment of gonorrhea may mask or delay symptoms of syphilis.
- Be alert for adverse reactions and drug interactions.
- Monitor patient's hydration status if adverse GI reactions occur.
- Evaluate patient's and family's knowledge of drug therapy.

Nursing diagnoses

- Infection related to presence of bacteria
- Risk for deficient fluid volume related to drug-induced adverse GI reactions
- Deficient knowledge related to drug therapy

Planning and implementation

- **P.O. use:** Administer drug on empty stomach.
- **I.V. use:** Dilute concentrate for injection before use. Single-use vials containing 20 or 40 mg/ml must be diluted to maximum of 4 mg/ml using compatible I.V. solution, such as D_5W, normal saline solution for injection, D_5W in normal saline solution for injection, or sterile water for injection. Infuse over at least 1 hour.

ALERT: Because compatibility with other drugs isn't known, don't mix ofloxacin with other drugs. If giving infusion at Y-site, discontinue other solution during infusion.

ALERT: If patient experiences restlessness, tremor, confusion, or hallucinations, stop medication and notify prescriber. Take seizure precautions.

Patient teaching

- Advise patient to take drug with plenty of fluids but not with meals. Also, tell patient to avoid antacids, sucralfate, and products containing iron or zinc for at least 2 hours before and after each dose.
- Advise patient to complete full course of antibiotics, as directed.
- Warn patient to avoid hazardous tasks until CNS effects of drug are known.
- Advise patient to use sunblock and protective clothing to avoid photosensitivity reactions.
- Tell patient to stop drug and notify prescriber if rash or other signs of hypersensitivity reactions develop.

Evaluation

- Patient is free from infection.
- Patient maintains adequate hydration throughout drug therapy.
- Patient and family state understanding of drug therapy.

olanzapine

(oh-LAN-za-peen)
Zyprexa, Zyprexa Zydis

Pharmacologic class: thienobenzodiazepine derivative
Therapeutic class: antipsychotic
Pregnancy risk category: C

Indications and dosages

▶ **Short-term treatment of acute manic episodes related to bipolar I disorder.** *Adults:* Initially, 10 to 15 mg P.O. daily. Adjust dosage as needed by increments of 5 mg daily at intervals of 24 hours or more. Maximum dose is 20 mg P.O. daily. Duration of treatment is 3 to 4 weeks.

▶ **Long-term treatment of schizophrenia.** *Adults:* Initially, 5 to 10 mg P.O. daily. Goal is 10 mg P.O. daily within several days of starting therapy. Dosage may be increased weekly in increments of 5 mg daily to a maximum of 20 mg daily. Clinical assessment is recommended for dosages that exceed 10 mg daily.

The recommended starting dose is 5 mg P.O. in patients who are debilitated, have a predisposition to hypotensive reactions, have risk factors of slower metabolism of olanzapine (nonsmoking women older than age 65), or may be more pharmacodynamically sensitive to olanzapine. In these patients, increase dose with caution.

Contraindications and precautions

- Contraindicated in patients hypersensitive to drug.
- Use cautiously in patients with heart disease, cerebrovascular disease, conditions that predispose patient to hypotension, history of seizures or conditions that might lower the seizure threshold, or hepatic impairment.
- Also use cautiously in those with a history of paralytic ileus, and those at risk for aspiration pneumonia, prostatic hyperplasia, or angle-closure glaucoma.

Lifespan: In pregnant women, drug should be given only if potential benefits justify risks to fetus. Women taking drug shouldn't breast-feed. In geriatric patients, use cautiously.

Adverse reactions

CNS: *drowsiness, somnolence, asthenia, insomnia,* personality disorder, akathisia, tremor, fever, abnormal gait, articulation impairment, tardive dyskinesia, *parkinsonism,* ***neuroleptic malignant syndrome, suicide attempt.***
CV: orthostatic hypotension, chest pain, tachycardia, hypertension, ecchymosis, peripheral edema.
EENT: rhinitis, pharyngitis, amblyopia, conjunctivitis.
GI: *constipation, dry mouth, dyspepsia,* increased appetite, vomiting, increased salivation and thirst.
GU: urinary incontinence, urinary tract infection, amenorrhea, hematuria, metrorrhagia, vaginitis.
Hematologic: ***leukopenia.***
Metabolic: weight gain.
Musculoskeletal: joint pain, joint stiffness and twitching, extremity pain, back pain, hypertonia.
Respiratory: increased cough, dyspnea.
Skin: sweating.
Other: dental pain, flu syndrome, injury.

Interactions

Drug-drug. *Antihypertensives:* May increase hypotensive effects. Monitor blood pressure closely.
Carbamazepine, omeprazole, rifampin: Increases olanzapine clearance. Monitor patient.
Diazepam: Increases CNS effects. Monitor patient closely.
Dopamine agonists, levodopa: Antagonizes activity of these drugs. Monitor patient.
Fluvoxamine: Decreases the clearance of olanzapine. Consider lower doses of olanzapine.
Drug-herb. *Nutmeg:* May reduce effectiveness of or interfere with drug therapy. Discourage using together.
Drug-lifestyle. *Alcohol use:* Increases CNS effects. Discourage using together.

Effects on lab test results

- May increase AST, ALT, GGT, CK, and prolactin levels.

Pharmacokinetics

Absorption: Levels peak about 6 hours after P.O. dose. Food doesn't affect rate or extent of absorption. About 40% of dose is limited by first-pass metabolism.
Distribution: Distributes extensively throughout the body, with a volume of distribution of about 1,000 L. Drug is about 93% protein-bound, primarily to albumin and alpha$_1$-acid glycoprotein.
Metabolism: Metabolized by direct glucuronidation and cytochrome P450-mediated oxidation.
Excretion: About 57% of drug appears in urine and 30% in feces as metabolites. Only

7% of dose is recovered in urine unchanged.
Elimination half-life: 21 to 54 hours.

Route	Onset	Peak	Duration
P.O.	Unknown	6 hr	Unknown

Pharmacodynamics

Chemical effect: Unknown. Binds to dopamine and serotonin receptors; may antagonize adrenergic, cholinergic, and histaminergic receptors.
Therapeutic effect: Relieves signs and symptoms of psychosis.

Available forms

Zyprexa
Tablets: 2.5 mg, 5 mg, 7.5 mg, 10 mg, 15 mg, 20 mg
Zyprexa Zydis
Tablets (orally disintegrating): 5 mg, 10mg, 15mg, 20 mg

NURSING PROCESS

Assessment

- Obtain history of patient's underlying condition before therapy, and reassess regularly thereafter.
- Obtain baseline and periodic liver function tests.
- Monitor patient for signs of neuroleptic malignant syndrome (hyperpyrexia, muscle rigidity, altered mental status, autonomic instability), which is rare but commonly fatal. Drug should be stopped immediately and patient monitored and treated as needed.
- Monitor patient for tardive dyskinesia, which may occur after prolonged use. It may not appear until months or years later, and it may disappear spontaneously or persist for life despite discontinuation of drug.
- Monitor patient for abnormal body temperature regulation, especially if patient is exercising strenuously, exposed to extreme heat, receiving anticholinergics, or at risk for dehydration.
- Evaluate patient's and family's knowledge about drug therapy.

Nursing diagnoses

- Disturbed thought processes related to underlying condition
- Risk for injury related to drug-induced adverse CNS reactions
- Deficient knowledge related to drug therapy

Planning and implementation

- Therapy starts at 5-mg dose in patients who are debilitated, predisposed to hypotension, pharmacologically sensitive to drug, or affected by altered metabolism caused by smoking status, sex, or age.
- Orally disintegrating tablets contain phenylalanine.

ALERT: Don't confuse olanzapine with olsalazine.
ALERT: Don't confuse Zyprexa with Zyrtec.

Patient teaching

- Drug can be taken without regard to food.
- Tell patient to avoid hazardous tasks until adverse CNS effects of drug are known.
- Warn patient against exposure to extreme heat; drug may impair body's ability to reduce core temperature.
- Tell patient to avoid alcohol during therapy.
- Tell patient to rise slowly to avoid effects of orthostatic hypotension.
- Instruct patient to relieve dry mouth with ice chips or sugarless candy or gum.
- Advise woman to notify prescriber if she becomes pregnant or intends to become pregnant during drug therapy. Advise her not to breastfeed during therapy.

Evaluation

- Patient's behavior and communication show improved thought processes.
- Patient sustains no injury from adverse CNS reactions.
- Patient and family state understanding of drug therapy.

olsalazine sodium

(olh-SAL-uh-zeen SOH-dee-um)
Dipentum

Pharmacologic class: salicylate
Therapeutic class: anti-inflammatory
Pregnancy risk category: C

Indications and dosages

▶ **Maintenance of remission of ulcerative colitis in patients intolerant of sulfasalazine.** *Adults:* 500 mg P.O. b.i.d. with meals.

Contraindications and precautions

- Contraindicated in patients hypersensitive to salicylates.
- Use cautiously in patients with renal disease. Renal tubular damage may result from absorbed mesalamine or its metabolites.

Lifespan: In pregnant and breast-feeding women, use cautiously. In children, safety of drug hasn't been established.

Adverse reactions

CNS: headache, depression, vertigo, dizziness.
GI: *diarrhea,* nausea, abdominal pain, heartburn.
Musculoskeletal: arthralgia.
Skin: rash, itching.

Interactions

Drug-drug. *Anticoagulants, coumarin derivatives:* Prolongs PT and INR. Monitor patient closely for bleeding.
Drug-food. *Any food:* Decreases GI irritation. Give drug with food.

Effects on lab test results

None reported.

Pharmacokinetics

Absorption: About 2.4% of single dose is absorbed.
Distribution: Liberated mesalamine is absorbed slowly from colon, resulting in very high local levels.
Metabolism: 0.1% is metabolized in liver; remainder reaches colon, where it's rapidly converted to mesalamine by colonic bacteria.
Excretion: About 80% excreted in feces; less than 1% in urine. *Half-life:* Of two metabolites, 0.9 hours to 7 days.

Route	Onset	Peak	Duration
P.O.	Unknown	1 hr	Unknown

Pharmacodynamics

Chemical effect: Unknown; converts to 5-aminosalicylic acid (5-ASA or mesalamine) in colon, where it has local anti-inflammatory effect.
Therapeutic effect: Prevents flare-up of ulcerative colitis.

Available forms

Capsules: 250 mg

NURSING PROCESS

Assessment

- Assess patient's condition before therapy and regularly thereafter.
- Monitor BUN and creatinine levels and urinalysis in patient with renal disease.
- Be alert for adverse reactions.
- Evaluate patient's and family's knowledge of drug therapy.

Nursing diagnoses

- Impaired tissue integrity related to ulcerative colitis
- Diarrhea related to drug's adverse effect on GI tract
- Deficient knowledge related to drug therapy

Planning and implementation

- Give drug with food in evenly divided doses.
- Report diarrhea to prescriber. Although diarrhea appears dose-related, it's difficult to distinguish from worsening of disease symptoms. Worsening of disease has been noted with similar drugs.

ALERT: Don't confuse olsalazine with olanzapine.

Patient teaching

- Teach patient to take drug in evenly divided doses and with food to minimize adverse GI reactions.
- Urge patient to notify prescriber about adverse reactions, especially diarrhea or increased pain.

Evaluation

- Patient has no evidence of ulcerative colitis.
- Patient is free from diarrhea.
- Patient and family state understanding of drug therapy.

omeprazole

(oh-MEH-pruh-zohl)
Losec ♦ ◇, Prilosec

Pharmacologic class: substituted benzimidazole
Therapeutic class: gastric acid suppressant.
Pregnancy risk category: C

Indications and dosages

▶ **Erosive esophagitis; symptomatic, poorly responsive gastroesophageal reflux disease (GERD).** *Adults:* 20 mg P.O. daily for 4 to 8 weeks. (Patients with GERD should have failed therapy with H_2-receptor antagonist.)

▶ **Pathologic hypersecretory conditions (such as Zollinger-Ellison syndrome).** *Adults:* Initially, 60 mg P.O. daily, adjusted according to patient response. If daily amount exceeds 80 mg, give in divided doses. Dosages up to 120 mg t.i.d. have been given. Continue therapy as long as clinically indicated.

▶ **Duodenal ulcer (short-term treatment).** *Adults:* 20 mg P.O. daily for 4 to 8 weeks.

▶ **Gastric ulcer.** *Adults:* 40 mg P.O. daily for 4 to 8 weeks.

▶ ***Helicobacter pylori* eradication to reduce risk of duodenal ulcer recurrence; triple therapy with omeprazole, clarithromycin, amoxicillin.** *Adults:* 20 mg P.O. with clarithromycin 500 mg P.O. and amoxicillin 1,000 mg P.O., each given b.i.d. for 10 days. For patients with an ulcer present when therapy starts, another 18 days of omeprazole 20 mg P.O. once daily is recommended.

▶ **Posterior laryngitis‡.** *Adults:* 40 mg q h.s. for 6 to 24 weeks.

▶ **Increase efficacy of pancreatin (for the treatment of cystic fibrosis)‡.** *Adults:* 40 mg q h.s. for 6 to 4 weeks.

Contraindications and precautions

- Contraindicated in patients hypersensitive to drug or its components.

Lifespan: In pregnant and breast-feeding women, use cautiously. In children, safety of drug hasn't been established.

Adverse reactions

CNS: headache, dizziness.
GI: diarrhea, abdominal pain, nausea, vomiting, constipation, flatulence.
Musculoskeletal: back pain.
Respiratory: cough.
Skin: rash.

Interactions

Drug-drug. *Ampicillin esters, iron derivatives, ketoconazole:* These drugs may have poor bioavailability because optimal absorption requires low gastric pH. Administer separately.
Clarithromycin: Increases plasma levels of either drug. Monitor patient for drug toxicity.
Diazepam, phenytoin, warfarin: Decreases hepatic clearance, possibly leading to increased serum levels. Monitor patient closely.
Sucralfate: Delays absorption and reduces omeprazole bioavailability. Separate administration times by 30 minutes or more.
Drug-herb. *Male fern:* Herb is inactivated in alkaline environments. Discourage using together.
Pennyroyal: May change the rate at which toxic metabolites of pennyroyal form. Discourage using together.

Effects on lab test results

None reported.

Pharmacokinetics

Absorption: Absorbed rapidly after drug leaves stomach. However, bioavailability is about 40% because of instability in gastric acid as well as substantial first-pass effect. Bioavailability increases slightly with repeated dosing.
Distribution: Protein-binding is about 95%.
Metabolism: Metabolized primarily in liver.
Excretion: Excreted primarily in urine. *Half-life:* 30 to 60 minutes.

Route	Onset	Peak	Duration
P.O.	≤ 1 hr	2 hr	≥ 3 days

Pharmacodynamics

Chemical effect: Inhibits activity of acid (proton) pump and binds to hydrogen-potassium adenosine triphosphatase on secretory surface of gastric parietal cells to block formation of gastric acid.
Therapeutic effect: Relieves symptoms caused by excessive gastric acid.

Available forms

Capsules (delayed-release): 10 mg, 20 mg, 40 mg

NURSING PROCESS

Assessment

- Assess patient's condition before therapy and regularly thereafter.
- Be alert for adverse reactions and drug interactions.

• Monitor patient's hydration status if adverse GI reactions occur.
• Evaluate patient's and family's knowledge of drug therapy.

Nursing diagnoses
• Impaired tissue integrity related to upper gastric disorder
• Risk for deficient fluid volume related to drug-induced adverse GI reactions
• Deficient knowledge related to drug therapy

Planning and implementation
• Give drug 30 minutes before meals.
• Dosage adjustments aren't needed for patients with renal or hepatic impairment.
ALERT: Don't confuse Prilosec with Prozac, prilocaine, or Prinivil.

Patient teaching
• Explain importance of taking drug exactly as prescribed.
• Tell patient to swallow capsules whole and not to open or crush.

Evaluation
• Patient responds well to therapy.
• Patient maintains adequate hydration throughout drug therapy.
• Patient and family state understanding of drug therapy.

ondansetron hydrochloride
(on-DAN-seh-tron high-droh-KLOR-ighd)
Zofran, Zofran ODT

Pharmacologic class: serotonin (5-HT3) receptor antagonist
Therapeutic class: antiemetic
Pregnancy risk category: B

Indications and dosages
▶ **Prevention of nausea and vomiting caused by emetogenic chemotherapy.** *Adults and children age 12 and older:* 8 mg P.O. 30 minutes before start of chemotherapy. Follow with 8 mg P.O. 4 and 8 hours after first dose. Then follow with 8 mg q 8 hours for 1 to 2 days. Or, give single dose of 32 mg by I.V. infusion over 15 minutes beginning 30 minutes before chemotherapy; or three divided doses of 0.15 mg/kg I.V. (first dose given 30 minutes before chemotherapy; subsequent doses given 4 and 8 hours after first dose). Infuse drug over 15 minutes.
Children ages 4 to 11: 4 mg P.O. 30 minutes before start of chemotherapy. Follow with 4 mg P.O. 4 and 8 hours after first dose. Then follow with 4 mg q 8 hours for 1 to 2 days. Or, three doses of 0.15 mg/kg I.V. Give first dose 30 minutes before chemotherapy; give subsequent doses 4 and 8 hours after first dose. Infuse drug over 15 minutes.
▶ **Prevention of postoperative nausea and vomiting.** *Adults:* 4 mg I.V. (undiluted) over 2 to 5 minutes. Or, 4 mg I.M. as a single injection.
Children ages 2 to 12: If patient weighs ≤ 40 kg (88 lb), give 0.1 mg/kg I.V; if patient weighs > 40 kg, give 4 mg I.V. over 2 to 5 minutes as a single dose.
▶ **Prevention of nausea and vomiting related to radiotherapy, either total body irradiation or single high-dose fraction or daily fractions to the abdomen.** *Adults:* 8 mg P.O. t.i.d.
Patients with severe liver impairment: Total daily dose should not exceed 8 mg P.O. daily or a single maximum dose of 8 mg I.V. over 15 minutes.

Contraindications and precautions
• Contraindicated in patients hypersensitive to drug.
• Use cautiously in patients with liver failure.
Lifespan: In pregnant and breast-feeding women, use cautiously.

Adverse reactions
CNS: headache.
GI: diarrhea, constipation.
Skin: rash.

Interactions
Drug-drug. *Drugs that alter hepatic drug-metabolizing enzymes (such as cimetidine, phenobarbital):* May alter pharmacokinetics of ondansetron. No dosage adjustment appears necessary.
Rifampin: Ondansetron levels may be reduced, thereby decreasing antiemetic effect. Monitor patient for adequate antiemetic effect; adjust dosage as necessary.

Drug-herb. *Horehound:* May enhance serotonergic effects. Discourage using together.

Effects on lab test results

- May increase ALT and AST levels.

Pharmacokinetics

Absorption: Variable; bioavailability is 50% to 60%.
Distribution: 70% to 76% is plasma protein–bound.
Metabolism: Extensively metabolized.
Excretion: Primarily excreted in urine. *Half-life:* 4 hours.

Route	Onset	Peak	Duration
P.O., I.V.	Unknown	Unknown	Unknown

Pharmacodynamics

Chemical effect: Blocking action may take place in CNS at area postrema (chemoreceptor trigger zone) and in peripheral nervous system on terminals of vagus nerve.
Therapeutic effect: Prevents nausea and vomiting from emetogenic chemotherapy or surgery.

Available forms

Injection: 2 mg/ml, 4 mg/ml
Oral solution: 4 mg/5 ml
Tablets: 4 mg, 8 mg, 24 mg
Tablets (orally disintegrating): 4 mg, 8 mg

NURSING PROCESS

Assessment

- Assess patient's condition before therapy and regularly thereafter.
- Be alert for adverse reactions and drug interactions.
- Evaluate patient's and family's knowledge of drug therapy.

Nursing diagnoses

- Risk for deficient fluid volume related to nausea and vomiting
- Pain related to drug-induced headache
- Deficient knowledge related to drug therapy

Planning and implementation

- **P.O. use:** Follow normal protocol.
- **I.V. use:** Dilute drug in 50 ml of D_5W injection or normal saline solution for injection before administration.
– Infuse drug over 15 minutes.
– Drug is stable for up to 48 hours after dilution in 5% dextrose in normal saline solution for injection, 5% dextrose in half-normal saline solution for injection, and 3% saline solution for injection.

ALERT: Don't confuse Zofran with Zantac or Zosyn.

Patient teaching
- Instruct patient when to take drug.
- Tell patient to report adverse reactions.
- Advise patient to report any discomfort at I.V. site.

Evaluation

- Patient maintains adequate hydration.
- Patient does not experience any drug-induced headaches.
- Patient and family state understanding of drug therapy.

opium tincture*
(OH-pee-um TINK-shur)

opium tincture, camphorated* (paregoric)

Pharmacologic class: opium
Therapeutic class: antidiarrheal
Pregnancy risk category: C
Controlled substance schedule: II (III for opium tincture, camphorated)

Indications and dosages

▶ **Acute, nonspecific diarrhea.** ***Opium tincture.*** *Adults:* 0.6 ml (range 0.3 to 1 ml) P.O. q.i.d. Maximum dosage is 6 ml daily.
Camphorated opium tincture. *Adults:* 5 to 10 ml once daily, b.i.d., t.i.d., or q.i.d. until diarrhea subsides.
Children: 0.25 to 0.5 ml/kg P.O. once daily, b.i.d., t.i.d., or q.i.d. until diarrhea subsides.
▶ **Severe opiate withdrawal symptoms in neonates born to women addicted to opiates.** *Neonates:* Camphorated opium tincture (pare-

goric) or a 1:25 dilution of opium tincture in water given as 0.3 ml q 3 hours. Adjust dose to control symptoms. May be increased by 0.05 ml q 3 hours until symptoms are controlled. Maximum dose is 0.7 ml daily. Once symptoms are stabilized for 3 to 5 days, gradually decrease dose over a 2- to 4-week period.

Contraindications and precautions

- Contraindicated in patients with acute diarrhea resulting from poisoning, until toxic material is removed from GI tract. Also contraindicated in patients with diarrhea caused by organisms that penetrate intestinal mucosa.
- Use cautiously in patients with asthma, prostatic hyperplasia, hepatic disease, or opioid dependence.

Lifespan: In pregnant women and breast-feeding women, safety of drug hasn't been established.

Adverse reactions

CNS: dizziness, light-headedness.
GI: nausea, vomiting.
Other: physical dependence after long-term use.

Interactions

None significant.

Effects on lab test results

- May increase amylase and lipase levels.

Pharmacokinetics

Absorption: Variable.
Distribution: Distributed widely in body.
Metabolism: Metabolized in liver.
Excretion: Excreted in urine.

Route	Onset	Peak	Duration
P.O.	Unknown	Unknown	Unknown

Pharmacodynamics

Chemical effect: Increases smooth-muscle tone in GI tract, inhibits motility and propulsion, and diminishes secretions.
Therapeutic effect: Relieves diarrhea.

Available forms

opium tincture
Oral solution: equivalent to morphine 10 mg/ml*

opium tincture, camphorated
Oral solution: each 5 ml contains morphine, 2 mg; anise oil, 0.2 ml; benzoic acid, 20 mg; camphor, 20 mg; glycerin, 0.2 ml; and ethanol to make 5 ml*

NURSING PROCESS

Assessment

- Assess patient's condition before therapy and regularly thereafter.
- Be alert for adverse reactions.
- Monitor patient's hydration status throughout drug therapy.
- Evaluate patient's and family's knowledge of drug therapy.

Nursing diagnoses

- Diarrhea related to GI disorder
- Risk for deficient fluid volume related to diarrhea and drug-induced adverse GI reactions
- Deficient knowledge related to drug therapy

Planning and implementation

ALERT: Read label carefully. Opium content of opium tincture is 25 times greater than that of camphorated opium tincture (paregoric). Don't confuse the two. Also, camphorated opium tincture (paregoric) is more dilute, and teaspoonful doses are easier to measure than dropper quantities of opium tincture.

- Mix drug with water to form a milky fluid.
- Store drug in tightly capped, light-resistant container.
- For overdose, use narcotic antagonist naloxone to reverse respiratory depression.

Patient teaching

- Advise patient against using drug for more than 2 days; risk of dependence increases with long-term use.
- Encourage proper storage to keep drug out of children's hands.

Evaluation

- Patient's diarrhea ceases.
- Patient maintains adequate hydration.
- Patient and family state understanding of drug.

orlistat
(OR-lih-stat)
Xenical

Pharmacologic class: lipase inhibitor
Therapeutic class: antiobesity drug
Pregnancy risk category: B

Indications and dosages

▶ **Management of obesity, including weight loss and weight maintenance in conjunction with a reduced-calorie diet; reduction of risk of weight regain after weight loss.**
Adults: 120 mg P.O. t.i.d. with each main meal containing fat (during or up to 1 hour after the meal).

Contraindications and precautions

• Contraindicated in patients hypersensitive to orlistat or any component of the drug and in patients with chronic malabsorption syndrome or cholestasis.
• Use cautiously in patients with a history of hyperoxaluria or calcium oxalate nephrolithiasis, who are at risk for anorexia nervosa or bulimia, or who are receiving cyclosporine therapy because of possible changes in cyclosporine absorption related to variations in diet.
Lifespan: In pregnant or breast-feeding women, use isn't recommended. In children, safety hasn't been established.

Adverse reactions

CNS: *headache,* dizziness, fatigue, sleep disorder, anxiety, depression.
CV: pedal edema.
EENT: otitis.
GI: *oily spotting, flatus with discharge, fecal urgency, fatty or oily stool, oily evacuation, increased defecation, abdominal pain,* fecal incontinence, nausea, infectious diarrhea, rectal pain, vomiting.
GU: menstrual irregularity, vaginitis, urinary tract infection.
Musculoskeletal: *back pain,* leg pain, arthritis, myalgia, joint disorder, tendinitis.
Respiratory: *influenza, upper respiratory tract infection,* lower respiratory tract infection.
Skin: rash, dry skin.
Other: tooth and gingival disorders.

Interactions

Drug-drug. *Fat-soluble vitamins such as vitamin E, beta-carotene:* Decreases vitamin absorption. Separate administration times by 2 hours.
Pravastatin: Slightly increases pravastatin levels and increases lipid-lowering effects of drug. Monitor patient.
Warfarin: Possible change in coagulation parameters. Monitor INR.

Effects on lab test results

• May decrease vitamin D, beta-carotene, LDL, and total cholesterol levels.

Pharmacokinetics

Absorption: Systemic exposure is minimal because only a small amount of drug is absorbed.
Distribution: More than 99% of drug binds to plasma proteins. Lipoproteins and albumin are major binding proteins.
Metabolism: Drug is primarily metabolized in GI wall.
Excretion: Most unabsorbed drug is excreted in feces.

Route	Onset	Peak	Duration
P.O.	Unknown	Unknown	Unknown

Pharmacodynamics

Chemical effect: A reversible inhibitor of lipases, orlistat bonds with the active site of gastric and pancreatic lipases. These inactivated enzymes are thus unavailable to hydrolyze dietary fat, in the form of triglycerides, into absorbable free fatty acids and monoglycerides. Because the undigested triglycerides aren't absorbed, the resulting caloric deficit may help with weight control. The recommended dosage of 120 mg t.i.d. inhibits dietary fat absorption by about 30%.
Therapeutic effect: Weight loss and weight maintenance.

Available forms

Capsules: 120 mg

NURSING PROCESS

Assessment

• Obtain history of patient's underlying condition before therapy, and reassess regularly thereafter.

• Screen patient for anorexia nervosa or bulimia; as with any weight-loss drug, orlistat carries a risk of misuse in certain patient populations.
• Organic causes of obesity, such as hypothyroidism, must be ruled out before patient starts orlistat therapy.
• In diabetic patients, monitor glucose frequently during weight loss. Dosage of oral antidiabetic or insulin may need to be reduced.
• Evaluate patient's and family's knowledge about drug therapy.

Nursing diagnoses

• Imbalanced nutrition: More than body requirements related to obesity
• Disturbed body image related to obesity
• Deficient knowledge related to drug therapy

Planning and implementation

• Drug is recommended for patients with an initial body mass index of 30 kg/m^2 or more (27 kg/m^2 or more if patient has other risk factors, such as hypertension, diabetes, or dyslipidemia).
• It's unknown whether orlistat is safe and effective to use longer than 2 years.
• Tell patient to follow dietary guidelines. GI effects may increase when patient takes orlistat with high-fat foods—specifically, when more than 30% of total daily calories come from fat.
• Orlistat reduces absorption of some fat-soluble vitamins and beta-carotene.

Patient teaching

• Advise patient to follow a nutritionally balanced, reduced-calorie diet that derives only 30% of its calories from fat. Daily intake of fat, carbohydrate, and protein should be distributed over three main meals. If a meal is occasionally missed or contains no fat, tell patient that the orlistat dose can be omitted.
• To ensure adequate nutrition, advise patient to take a daily multivitamin supplement that contains fat-soluble vitamins at least 2 hours before or after taking orlistat, such as at bedtime.
• Tell patient with diabetes that weight loss may improve glycemic control, so the dosage of his oral antidiabetic or insulin may need to be reduced.
• Tell woman to inform prescriber if she is pregnant, plans to become pregnant, or is breast-feeding.

Evaluation

• Patient's nutritional intake is adequate according to proper dietary guidelines.
• Patient reaches and maintains a stable weight.
• Patient and family state understanding of drug therapy.

oseltamivir phosphate

(ah-sul-TAM-ih-veer FOS-fayt)
Tamiflu

Pharmacologic class: neuraminidase inhibitor
Therapeutic class: antiviral
Pregnancy risk category: C

Indications and dosages

▶ **Uncomplicated, acute illness from influenza in patients who have been symptomatic for 2 days or less.** *Children who weigh 15 kg (33 lb) or less:* 30 mg oral suspension P.O. b.i.d.
Children who weigh more than 15 to 23 kg (33 to 51 lb): 45 mg oral suspension P.O. b.i.d.
Children who weigh more than 23 to 40 kg (51 to 88 lb): 60 mg oral suspension P.O. b.i.d.
Children who weigh more than 40 kg (88 lb): 75 mg oral suspension P.O. b.i.d.
Adults and children age 13 and older: 75 mg P.O. b.i.d. for 5 days.
Patients with renal impairment: If creatinine clearance is 10 to 30 ml/minute, give 75 mg once daily for 5 days.
▶ **Prevention of influenza after close contact with infected person.** *Adults and children age 13 and older:* 75 mg P.O. once daily beginning within 2 days of exposure and lasting at least 7 days.
▶ **Prevention of influenza during a community outbreak.** *Adults and children age 13 and older:* 75 mg P.O. once daily for up to 6 weeks.
Patients with renal impairment: If creatinine clearance is 10 to 30 ml/minute, give 75 mg once every other day, or 30 mg of oral suspension every day.

Contraindications

• Contraindicated in patients hypersensitive to drug or its components.
Lifespan: In breast-feeding women, use drug only if potential benefits outweigh risks to the infant.

Adverse reactions

CNS: dizziness, insomnia, headache, vertigo, fatigue.
GI: abdominal pain, diarrhea, nausea, vomiting.
Respiratory: bronchitis, cough.

Interactions

None significant.

Effects on lab test results

None reported.

Pharmacokinetics

Absorption: Well absorbed after P.O. administration. More than 75% of administered dose reaches systemic circulation as oseltamivir carboxylate.
Distribution: Serum protein–binding for oseltamivir is 42%; 3% for oseltamivir carboxylate.
Metabolism: Extensively metabolized by hepatic esterases to its active component, oseltamivir carboxylate.
Excretion: Oseltamivir carboxylate is almost entirely eliminated in urine via glomerular filtration and tubular secretion. Less than 20% of orally administered dose is eliminated in feces.

Route	Onset	Peak	Duration
P.O.	Unknown	Unknown	Unknown

Pharmacodynamics

Chemical effect: Oseltamivir carboxylate, the active form of oseltamivir, inhibits the enzyme neuraminidase in influenza virus particles. This action is thought to inhibit viral replication, possibly by interfering with viral particle aggregation and release from the host cell.
Therapeutic effect: Lessens the symptoms of influenza.

Available forms

Capsules: 75 mg
Oral suspension: 12 mg/ml after reconstitution

NURSING PROCESS

Assessment

- Obtain complete medical history before treatment.
- Evaluate renal function before giving drug, as directed.
- Evaluate patient's and family's knowledge of drug therapy.

Nursing diagnoses

- Infection related to influenza virus
- Imbalanced nutrition: Less than body requirements related to drug's adverse GI effects
- Deficient knowledge related to drug therapy

Planning and implementation

- Drug is used to treat symptoms, not to prevent influenza. Drug isn't a replacement for the annual influenza vaccination.
- There's no evidence to support use of drug in treating viral infections other than influenza virus types A and B.
- Drug may be given with meals to decrease adverse GI effects.
- Safety and efficacy of repeated treatment courses haven't been established.
- Store at controlled room temperature (59° to 86° F [15° to 30° C]).

Patient teaching

- Tell patient to take drug within 2 days of start of symptoms.
- Inform patient that drug is used to treat symptoms, not to prevent influenza. Urge patient to continue receiving an annual influenza vaccination.

Evaluation

- Patient recovers from influenza.
- Patient has no adverse GI effects and maintains adequate hydration.
- Patient and family state understanding of drug therapy.

oxaprozin potassium

(oks-uh-PROH-zin)
Daypro Alta

Pharmacologic class: NSAID
Therapeutic class: nonnarcotic analgesic, antipyretic, anti-inflammatory
Pregnancy risk category: C

Indications and dosages

▶ **Osteoarthritis, rheumatoid arthritis.** *Adults:* 1,200 mg P.O. once daily. Divided doses may be used in patients unable to tolerate

single doses. For osteoarthritis patients with low body weight and milder disease, an initial dose of 600 mg once daily may be appropriate. The maximum daily dose is 1,200 mg.
Patients with renal impairment or those undergoing hemodialysis: Initial dose is 600 mg P.O. daily.

Contraindications and precautions

• Contraindicated in patients hypersensitive to drug and in those with syndrome of nasal polyps, angioedema, and bronchospastic reactivity to aspirin or other NSAIDs.
• Use cautiously in those with history of peptic ulcer disease, hepatic or renal dysfunction, hypertension, CV disease, or conditions that predispose to fluid retention.
Lifespan: In pregnant and breast-feeding women, use cautiously. In children, safety of drug has not been established.

Adverse reactions

CNS: depression, sedation, somnolence, confusion, sleep disturbances.
EENT: tinnitus, visual disturbances.
GI: *nausea, dyspepsia, diarrhea, constipation,* abdominal pain or distress, anorexia, flatulence, vomiting, ***hemorrhage.***
GU: dysuria, renal insufficiency, urinary frequency.
Skin: *rash,* photosensitivity.

Interactions

Drug-drug. *Antihypertensives, diuretics:* Decreases effect. Monitor patient closely and adjust dosage.
Aspirin: Oxaprozin displaces salicylates from plasma protein–binding sites, increasing risk of salicylate toxicity. Avoid using together.
Aspirin, corticosteroids: Increases risk of adverse GI reactions. Avoid using together.
Cyclosporine: Risk of nephrotoxicity by both agents may increase. Monitor renal function tests if used together.
Methotrexate: Increases risk of methotrexate toxicity. Avoid using together.
Oral anticoagulants: Increases risk of bleeding. Use together cautiously; monitor patient for bleeding.
Drug-herb. *Dong quai, feverfew, garlic, ginger, horse chestnut, red clover:* Possible increased risk of bleeding. Discourage using together.
St. John's wort: Increases risk of photosensitivity. Advise patient to avoid unprotected or prolonged exposure to sunlight.
Drug-lifestyle. *Alcohol use:* Increases risk of adverse GI reactions. Discourage using together.
Sun exposure: Photosensitivity reactions may occur. Urge patient to avoid unprotected or prolonged exposure to sunlight.

Effects on lab test results

• May increase ALT, AST, BUN, and creatinine levels.
• May increase bleeding time. May decrease hemoglobin and hematocrit.

Pharmacokinetics

Absorption: Oral bioavailability is 95%; food may reduce rate but not extent of absorption.
Distribution: About 99.9% protein-bound.
Metabolism: Metabolized in liver.
Excretion: Metabolites are excreted in urine (65%) and feces (35%). *Half-life:* 5 hours.

Route	Onset	Peak	Duration
P.O.	Unknown	2 hr	Unknown

Pharmacodynamics

Chemical effect: Unknown; may inhibit prostaglandin synthesis.
Therapeutic effect: Relieves pain, fever, and inflammation.

Available forms

Tablets: 600 mg

NURSING PROCESS

Assessment

• Assess patient's condition before therapy and regularly thereafter.
• Monitor liver function test results periodically during long-term therapy, and closely monitor patient with abnormal test results. Liver function values may be elevated. These abnormal findings may persist, worsen, or resolve with continued therapy. Rarely, patient may progress to severe hepatic dysfunction.
• Be alert for adverse reactions and drug interactions.
• Evaluate patient's and family's knowledge of drug therapy.

Nursing diagnoses

- Chronic pain related to condition
- Impaired tissue integrity related to adverse GI effects of drug
- Deficient knowledge related to drug therapy

Planning and implementation

- Give drug on empty stomach unless adverse GI reactions occur.
- Notify prescriber immediately about adverse reactions, especially GI symptoms.

ALERT: Don't confuse oxaprozin with oxazepam.

Patient teaching

- To minimize adverse GI effects, tell patient to take drug with milk or meals.
- Explain that full therapeutic effects may be delayed for 2 to 4 weeks.
- Tell patient to report adverse visual or auditory reactions immediately.
- Teach patient to recognize and promptly report signs and symptoms of GI bleeding.
- Advise patient to use sunscreen, wear protective clothing, and avoid prolonged exposure to sunlight.
- Warn patient to avoid hazardous activities until CNS effects of drug are known.

Evaluation

- Patient is free from pain.
- Patient maintains GI tissue integrity.
- Patient and family state understanding of drug therapy.

oxazepam

(oks-AZ-ih-pam)

Alepam◇, Apo-Oxazepam◆, Murelax◇, Serax**, Serepax◇

Pharmacologic class: benzodiazepine
Therapeutic class: antianxiety, sedative-hypnotic
Pregnancy risk category: D
Controlled substance schedule: IV

Indications and dosages

▶ **Alcohol withdrawal.** *Adults:* 15 to 30 mg P.O. t.i.d. or q.i.d.

▶ **Severe anxiety.** *Adults:* 15 to 30 mg P.O. t.i.d. or q.i.d.

▶ **Mild-to-moderate anxiety.** *Adults:* 10 to 15 mg P.O. t.i.d. or q.i.d.

▶ **Older patients with anxiety, tension, irritability, and agitation.** *Adults:* 10 mg P.O. t.i.d. May increase cautiously to 15 mg P.O. t.i.d. to q.i.d.

Contraindications and precautions

- Contraindicated in patients hypersensitive to drug.
- Use cautiously in those with history of drug abuse and in those for whom a drop in blood pressure could lead to cardiac problems.

Lifespan: In pregnant and breast-feeding women, avoid using drug. In children, safety of drug hasn't been established. In geriatric patients, use cautiously.

Adverse reactions

CNS: drowsiness, lethargy, hangover, fainting, *mental status changes.*
CV: transient hypotension.
GI: nausea, vomiting, abdominal discomfort.
Hepatic: ***hepatic dysfunction.***
Other: increased risk for falls.

Interactions

Drug-drug. *Cimetidine, CNS depressants:* Increases CNS depression. Avoid using together.
Digoxin: May increase digoxin levels, increasing toxicity. Monitor levels closely.
Oral contraceptives: Increases clearance of oxazepam. Monitor patient for decreased effect.
Phenytoin: May increase oxazepam clearance and increase phenytoin concentration. Monitor patient closely for phenytoin toxicity.
Drug-herb. *Catnip, kava, lady's slipper, lemon balm, passion flower, sassafras, skullcap, valerian:* Sedative effects may be enhanced. Discourage using together.
Drug-lifestyle. *Alcohol use:* Increases CNS depression. Discourage using together.
Smoking: Increases benzodiazepine clearance. Monitor patient for lack of drug effect.

Effects on lab test results

- May increase liver enzyme function values.

Pharmacokinetics

Absorption: Well absorbed.
Distribution: Distributed widely throughout body. Drug is 85% to 95% protein-bound.
Metabolism: Metabolized in liver.

Excretion: Metabolites are excreted in urine. *Half-life:* 5 to 13 hours.

Route	Onset	Peak	Duration
P.O.	Unknown	About 3 hr	Unknown

Pharmacodynamics

Chemical effect: Unknown; believed to stimulate gamma-aminobutyric receptors in ascending reticular activating system.
Therapeutic effect: Relieves anxiety and promotes calmness.

Available forms

Capsules: 10 mg, 15 mg, 30 mg
Tablets: 10 mg, 15 mg, 30 mg

NURSING PROCESS

Assessment

- Assess patient's condition before therapy and regularly thereafter.
- Monitor liver, renal, and hematopoietic function studies periodically in patient receiving repeated or prolonged therapy.
- Be alert for adverse reactions and drug interactions.
- Evaluate patient's and family's knowledge of drug therapy.

Nursing diagnoses

- Disturbed thought processes related to condition
- Risk for injury related to drug-induced adverse CNS reactions
- Deficient knowledge related to drug therapy

Planning and implementation

- Expect to reduce dosage in geriatric or debilitated patient.
- Possibility of abuse and addiction exists. Don't stop drug abruptly; withdrawal symptoms may occur.

ALERT: Don't confuse oxazepam with oxaprozin.

Patient teaching

- Warn patient to avoid hazardous activities until CNS effects of drug are known.
- Tell patient to avoid alcohol during drug therapy.
- Warn patient not to stop drug abruptly; withdrawal signs may occur.

Evaluation

- Patient has less anxiety.
- Patient sustains no injury as result of drug therapy.
- Patient and family state understanding of drug therapy.

oxcarbazepine

(ox-car-BAY-zah-peen)
Trileptal

Pharmacologic class: carboxamide derivative
Therapeutic class: antiepileptic
Pregnancy risk category: C

Indications and dosages

▶ **Adjunctive therapy for partial seizures in patients with epilepsy.** *Adults:* Initially, 300 mg P.O. b.i.d. Increase by maximum of 600 mg daily (300 mg P.O. b.i.d.) at weekly intervals. Recommended daily dose is 600 mg P.O. b.i.d.
Children ages 4 to 16: Initially, 4 to 5 mg/kg P.O. b.i.d., not to exceed 600 mg P.O. daily. Target maintenance dosage depends on patient weight. If patient weighs 20 to 29 kg (44 to 64 lb), target maintenance dosage is 900 mg daily. If 29.1 to 39 kg (64 to 86 lb), target maintenance dosage is 1,200 mg/day. If more than 39 kg (86 lb), target maintenance dosage is 1,800 mg daily. Target dosage should be achieved over 2 weeks.

▶ **Conversion to monotherapy for treatment of partial seizures in patients with epilepsy.** *Adults:* Initially, 300 mg P.O. b.i.d. with simultaneous reduction in dosage of concomitant antiepileptic. Increased by a maximum of 600 mg daily at weekly intervals over 2 to 4 weeks. Recommended daily dose is 2,400 mg P.O., divided b.i.d. Other antiepileptics should be completely withdrawn over 3 to 6 weeks.

▶ **Start of monotherapy for treatment of partial seizures in patients with epilepsy.** *Adults:* Initially, 300 mg P.O. b.i.d. Increase by 300 mg daily every third day to a daily dose of 600 mg b.i.d.
Patients with renal impairment: If creatinine clearance is less than 30 ml/minute, therapy starts at 150 mg P.O. b.i.d. (one-half the usual starting dose) and increases slowly to achieve desired clinical response.

Contraindications and precautions

- Contraindicated in patients hypersensitive to oxcarbazepine or its components.
- Use cautiously in patients who have had hypersensitivity reactions to carbamazepine.

Lifespan: In breast-feeding women, either discontinue breast-feeding or discontinue drug because drug appears in breast milk. Importance of drug to mother should be taken into account.

Adverse reactions

CNS: *fatigue,* fever, asthenia, feeling abnormal, *headache, dizziness, somnolence, ataxia, abnormal gait,* insomnia, *tremor,* nervousness, agitation, abnormal coordination, speech disorder, confusion, anxiety, amnesia, ***aggravated seizures,*** hypoesthesia, emotional lability, impaired concentration, *vertigo.*
CV: hypotension, edema, chest pain.
EENT: *nystagmus, diplopia, abnormal vision,* abnormal accommodation, rhinitis, sinusitis, pharyngitis, epistaxis.
GI: *nausea, vomiting, abdominal pain,* diarrhea, dyspepsia, constipation, gastritis, anorexia, dry mouth, rectal hemorrhage, taste perversion, thirst.
GU: urinary tract infection, urinary frequency, vaginitis.
Metabolic: hyponatremia, weight gain.
Musculoskeletal: muscle weakness, back pain.
Respiratory: *upper respiratory tract infection,* coughing, bronchitis, chest infection.
Skin: acne, purpura, rash, bruising, increased sweating.
Other: allergic reaction, hot flushes, toothache.

Interactions

Drug-drug. *Carbamazepine, valproic acid, verapamil:* Decreases levels of the active metabolite of oxcarbazepine. Monitor patient and levels closely.
Felodipine: Decreases felodipine level. Monitor patient closely.
Hormonal contraceptives: Decreases plasma levels of ethinyl estradiol and levonorgestrel, which reduces contraceptive effect. Women of childbearing age should use other forms of contraception.
Phenobarbital: Decreases levels of the active metabolite of oxcarbazepine and increases phenobarbital level. Monitor patient closely.
Phenytoin: Decreases levels of the active metabolite of oxcarbazepine. May increase phenytoin level in adults receiving high doses of oxcarbazepine. Monitor phenytoin levels closely when starting therapy in these patients.
Drug-lifestyle. *Alcohol use:* Increases CNS depression. Discourage using together.

Effects on lab test results

- May decrease sodium and T_4 levels.

Pharmacokinetics

Absorption: Complete.
Distribution: About 40% of 10-monohydroxy metabolite (MHD) is bound to serum proteins, mostly to albumin.
Metabolism: Rapidly metabolized in the liver to MHD, which is primarily responsible for pharmacologic effects. Minor amounts (4% of dose) are oxidized to pharmacologically inactive 10,11-dihydroxy metabolite (DHD).
Excretion: Drug and its metabolites are mainly excreted by the kidneys. More than 95% of dose appears in urine, with less than 1% as unchanged oxcarbazepine. Fecal excretion accounts for less than 4% of dose. *Half-life:* About 2 hours for parent compound, about 9 hours for MHD. Children under age 8 have about 30% to 40% increased clearance of drug.

Route	Onset	Peak	Duration
P.O.	Unknown	Variable	Unknown

Pharmacodynamics

Chemical effect: Activity is primarily in response to MHD. Antiseizure activity of oxcarbazepine and MHD is thought to result from blockade of voltage-sensitive sodium channels, which causes stabilization of hyperexcited neural membranes, inhibition of repetitive neuronal firing, and reduction of propagation of synaptic impulses. This activity is thought to prevent seizure spread in the brain. Anticonvulsant effects also may stem from increased potassium conductance and modulation of high-voltage activated calcium channels.
Therapeutic effect: Controls partial seizures.

Available forms

Oral suspension: 60 mg/ml, 300 mg/5ml*
Tablets (film-coated): 150 mg, 300 mg, 600 mg

NURSING PROCESS

Assessment

ALERT: Question patient about history of hypersensitivity reaction to carbamazepine because 25% to 30% of affected patients may develop hypersensitivity to oxcarbazepine. Discontinue drug immediately if signs or symptoms of hypersensitivity occur.

- Obtain history of patient's underlying condition before therapy, and reassess regularly thereafter.

ALERT: Oxcarbazepine has been linked to several adverse neurologic events, including psychomotor slowing, difficulty with concentration, speech or language problems, somnolence, fatigue, and abnormal coordination (including ataxia and gait disturbances). Monitor patient closely.

- Monitor patient for evidence of hyponatremia, including nausea, malaise, headache, lethargy, confusion, and decreased sensation.
- Evaluate patient's and family's knowledge of drug therapy.

Nursing diagnoses

- Risk for trauma related to seizures
- Risk for injury related to drug-induced adverse reactions
- Deficient knowledge related to drug therapy

Planning and implementation

ALERT: Withdraw drug gradually to minimize risk of increased seizure frequency.

- Correct hyponatremia as needed.
- For oral suspension, shake well before administration. Suspension can be mixed with water or may be swallowed directly from the syringe. Oral suspension and tablets may be interchanged at equal doses. Suspension can be taken without regard to food.

Patient teaching

- Advise patient to tell prescriber if he has ever had a hypersensitivity reaction to carbamazepine.
- Tell patient that drug may be taken with or without food.
- Caution patient to avoid hazardous activities until effects of drug are known.
- Caution patient to avoid alcohol while taking drug.
- Advise patient not to interrupt therapy without consulting prescriber.
- Advise patient to report signs and symptoms of hyponatremia, such as nausea, malaise, headache, lethargy, or confusion.
- Advise women using oral contraceptives for birth control to use another form of birth control while taking drug.

Evaluation

- Patient experiences no or fewer seizures during drug therapy.
- Patient sustains no injury from drug-induced adverse reactions.
- Patient and family state understanding of drug therapy.

oxybutynin chloride

(oks-ee-BYOO-tih-nin KLOR-ighd)

Apo-Oxybutynin ◆, Ditropan, Ditropan XL

Pharmacologic class: synthetic tertiary amine
Therapeutic class: antispasmodic
Pregnancy risk category: B

Indications and dosages

▶ **Antispasmodic for uninhibited or reflex neurogenic bladder.** *Adults:* 5 mg P.O. b.i.d. to t.i.d., up to 5 mg q.i.d.
Children older than age 5: 5 mg P.O. b.i.d., up to 5 mg t.i.d.

▶ **Treatment of overactive bladder.** *Adults:* Initially, 5 mg Ditropan XL P.O. once daily. Dosage adjustments may be made weekly in 5-mg increments, as needed, to a maximum of 30 mg P.O. daily.

Contraindications and precautions

- Contraindicated in patients hypersensitive to drug or debilitated patients with intestinal atony, hemorrhaging patients with unstable CV status, and patients with myasthenia gravis, GI obstruction, glaucoma, adynamic ileus, megacolon, severe colitis, ulcerative colitis with megacolon, or obstructive uropathy.
- Use cautiously in patients with autonomic neuropathy, reflux esophagitis, or hepatic or renal disease.

Lifespan: In pregnant and breast-feeding women and in geriatric patients, use cautiously.

In geriatric patients with intestinal atony, drug is contraindicated.

Adverse reactions

CNS: *drowsiness,* fever, dizziness, insomnia, restlessness, impaired alertness.
CV: flushing, palpitations, tachycardia.
EENT: *transient blurred vision,* mydriasis, cycloplegia.
GI: nausea, vomiting, *constipation,* bloated feeling, *dry mouth.*
GU: impotence, urinary hesitancy, urine retention.
Skin: decreased diaphoresis, rash, urticaria.
Other: suppressed lactation, flushing, allergic reactions.

Interactions

Drug-drug. *Anticholinergics:* Increases anticholinergic effects. Use together cautiously.
Atenolol, digoxin: Increases levels of these drugs. Monitor patient closely.
CNS depressants: Increases CNS effects. Use cautiously.
Haloperidol, levodopa: Decreases levels of these drugs. Monitor patient closely.
Drug-lifestyle. *Alcohol use:* Increases CNS effects. Discourage using together.
Exercise, hot weather: May precipitate heatstroke. Urge patient to avoid exercise or any increased activity during hot and humid weather and maintain adequate hydration.

Effects on lab test results

None reported.

Pharmacokinetics

Absorption: Rapid.
Distribution: Unknown.
Metabolism: Metabolized by liver.
Excretion: Excreted primarily in urine.

Route	Onset	Peak	Duration
P.O.	30-60 min	3-4 hr	6-10 hr

Pharmacodynamics

Chemical effect: Produces direct spasmolytic effect and antimuscarinic (atropine-like) effect on smooth muscles of urinary tract, increasing bladder capacity and providing some local anesthesia and mild analgesia.
Therapeutic effect: Relieves bladder spasms.

Available forms

Syrup: 5 mg/5 ml
Tablets: 5 mg
Tablets (extended-release): 5 mg, 10 mg, 15 mg

NURSING PROCESS

Assessment

- Assess patient's bladder condition before therapy.
- Before giving drug, prescriber will most likely confirm neurogenic bladder by cystometry and rule out partial intestinal obstruction in patients with diarrhea, especially those with colostomy or ileostomy.
- Prepare patient for periodic cystometry to evaluate response to therapy.
- Watch geriatric patients for confusion and mental status changes.
- Be alert for adverse reactions.
- Drug may aggravate symptoms of hyperthyroidism, coronary artery disease, heart failure, arrhythmias, tachycardia, hypertension, or prostatic hyperplasia.
- Evaluate patient's and family's knowledge of drug therapy.

Nursing diagnoses

- Acute pain related to bladder spasms
- Risk for injury related to drug-induced adverse CNS reactions
- Deficient knowledge related to drug therapy

Planning and implementation

- If patient has a urinary tract infection, give antibiotics.
- To minimize tendency toward tolerance, be prepared to stop therapy periodically to determine whether patient can be weaned off medication.

ALERT: Don't confuse Ditropan with diazepam or Dithranol.

Patient teaching

- Warn patient to avoid hazardous activities until CNS effects of drug are known.
- Tell patient to avoid alcohol during drug therapy.
- Caution patient that taking drug in hot weather raises the risk of fever or heatstroke and urge patient to take precautions to avoid excessive heat and maintain adequate hydration.

• Advise patient to store drug in tightly closed containers at 59° to 86° F (15° to 30° C).

Evaluation

• Patient is free from bladder pain.
• Patient sustains no injuries from drug-induced adverse CNS reactions.
• Patient and family state understanding of drug therapy.

oxycodone hydrochloride

(oks-ee-KOH-dohn high-droh-KLOR-ighd)
Endocodone, Endone ◇, M-Oxy, OxyContin, Oxydose, OxyFAST, OxyIR, OxyNorm ◇, Percolone, Roxicodone, Roxicodone Intensol, Supeudol ♦

oxycodone pectinate

Proladone ◇

Pharmacologic class: opioid
Therapeutic class: analgesic
Pregnancy risk category: B
Controlled substance schedule: II

Indications and dosages

▶ **Moderate-to-severe pain.** *Adults:* 5 mg P.O. q 6 hours, p.r.n. Or, 1 to 3 suppositories P.R. daily, p.r.n.
Patients not currently receiving opiates, who need a continuous aroung-the-clock analgesic for an extended period of time: Give 10 mg extended-release tablets P.O. q 12 hours. May increase dose q 1 to 2 days, as needed. The 80-mg formulation is for opioid-tolerant patients only.
Patients with impaired hepatic function: Extended-release tablets should be initiated at 33% to 50% of the usual dosage and titrated carefully. In patients with impaired renal function (creatinine clearance < 60 ml/minute), reduce initial extended-release dose and titrate carefully according to the clinical situation.

Contraindications and precautions

• Contraindicated in patients hypersensitive to drug.
• Use with extreme caution in debilitated patients and those with head injury, increased intracranial pressure, seizures, asthma, COPD, prostatic hyperplasia, severe hepatic or renal disease, acute abdominal conditions, urethral stricture, hypothyroidism, Addison's disease, or arrhythmias.
Lifespan: In pregnant and breast-feeding women, use cautiously. In children, drug is not recommended. In geriatric patients, use with extreme caution.

Adverse reactions

CNS: *sedation, somnolence, clouded sensorium, euphoria,* dizziness.
CV: *hypotension,* ***bradycardia.***
GI: nausea, vomiting, constipation, ileus.
GU: urine retention.
Respiratory: ***respiratory depression.***
Other: physical dependence.

Interactions

Drug-drug. *Anticoagulants:* Oxycodone products containing aspirin may increase anticoagulant effect. Monitor PT and INR. Use together cautiously; monitor patient for bleeding.
CNS depressants, general anesthetics, hypnotics, MAO inhibitors, other narcotic analgesics, protease inhibitors, sedatives, tranquilizers, tricyclic antidepressants: May have additive effects. Use together with extreme caution. Reduce oxycodone dose as directed, and monitor patient response.
Drug-lifestyle. *Alcohol use:* Increases CNS depression. Discourage using together.

Effects on lab test results

• May increase amylase and lipase levels.

Pharmacokinetics

Absorption: Unknown.
Distribution: Unknown.
Metabolism: Metabolized in liver.
Excretion: Excreted primarily in urine. *Half-life:* 2 to 3 hours.

Route	Onset	Peak	Duration
P.O.	10-15 min	≤ 1 hr	3-6 hr
P.R.	Unknown	Unknown	Unknown

Pharmacodynamics

Chemical effect: Binds with opioid receptors in CNS, altering response to pain via unknown mechanism.
Therapeutic effect: Relieves pain.

*Liquid form contains alcohol. **May contain tartrazine. ♦ Canada ◇ Australia †OTC ‡Off-label use

Available forms

oxycodone hydrochloride
Capsules: 5 mg
Oral solution: 5 mg/ml, 20 mg/ml
Tablets: 5 mg, 15 mg, 30 mg
Tablets (controlled-release): 10 mg, 20 mg, 40 mg, 80 mg
oxycodone pectinate
Suppositories: 10 mg ♦, 30 mg ◇

NURSING PROCESS

Assessment

- Assess patient's pain before and after drug administration.
- Monitor circulatory and respiratory status.
- Be alert for adverse reactions and drug interactions.
- Evaluate patient's and family's knowledge of drug therapy.

Nursing diagnoses

- Acute pain related to condition
- Ineffective breathing pattern related to drug-induced respiratory depression
- Deficient knowledge related to drug therapy

Planning and implementation

- **P.O. use:** Give drug with food or milk to avoid GI upset.

ALERT: OxyContin is not intended for p.r.n. use or for immediate postoperative pain. Drug is only indicated for postoperative use if patient was receiving it prior to surgery or if pain is expected to persist for an extended period of time.

- **P.R. use:** Not commercially available in the United States.
- For best results, give drug before patient has intense pain.
- Single-agent oxycodone solution and tablets are especially good for patient who shouldn't take aspirin or acetaminophen.

ALERT: Withhold dose and notify prescriber if respirations are shallow or rate falls below 12 breaths/minute.

ALERT: Do not confuse oxycodone immediate-release tablets with OxyContin extended-release tablets.

ALERT: OxyContin is potentially addictive and abused as much as morphine. Chewing, crushing, snorting, or injecting it can lead to overdose and death.

Patient teaching

- Instruct patient to take drug with food or milk to minimize GI upset.
- Tell patient to ask for drug before pain becomes intense.
- Tell patient not to chew or crush OxyIR or extended-release forms.
- Caution ambulatory patient about getting out of bed or walking. Warn outpatient to avoid hazardous activities until CNS effects of drug are known.

Evaluation

- Patient is free from pain.
- Patient's respiratory rate and pattern remain within normal limits.
- Patient and family state understanding of drug therapy.

oxymetazoline hydrochloride

(oks-ee-met-AHZ-oh-leen high-droh-KLOR-ighd)
Afrin, Afrin 12-Hour†, Afrin Children's Strength Nose Drops†, Allerest 12 Hour Nasal†, Benzedrex 12 Hour Nasal Spray†, Cheracol Nasal Spray†, Dristan Long Lasting†, Drixine Nasal ◇, Duramist Plus†, Duration†, 4-Way Long-Acting Nasal, Genasal Spray†, Nasal Relief†, Neo-Synephrine 12 Hour†, Nostrilla†, NTZ Long Acting Nasal†, Oxymeta-12 Spray†, Sinarest 12 Hour†, Twice-A-Day 12-Hour Nasal†, Vicks Sinex 12-Hour†

Pharmacologic class: sympathomimetic
Therapeutic class: decongestant, vasoconstrictor
Pregnancy risk category: NR

Indications and dosages

▶ **Nasal congestion.** *Adults and children ages 6 and older:* 2 to 3 gtt or sprays of 0.05% solution in each nostril b.i.d.
Children ages 2 to 5: 2 to 3 gtt or sprays of 0.025% solution in each nostril b.i.d. Don't use for more than 5 days.

Contraindications and precautions

- Contraindicated in patients hypersensitive to drug.

• Use cautiously in patients with hyperthyroidism, cardiac disease, hypertension, or diabetes mellitus.
Lifespan: In pregnant and breast-feeding women and in geriatric patients, use cautiously.

Adverse reactions

CNS: headache, *restlessness, anxiety,* dizziness, insomnia, possible sedation.
CV: palpitations, ***CV collapse,*** hypertension.
EENT: rebound nasal congestion or irritation with excessive or long-term use, dry nose and throat, increased nasal discharge, stinging, sneezing.
Other: systemic effects in children with excessive or long-term use.

Interactions

Drug-drug. *Methyldopa, tricyclic antidepressants:* May increase pressor response. Monitor blood pressure.
MAO inhibitors: May produce severe headache, hypertension, hyperpyrexia, possibly resulting in hypertensive crisis. Don't use together.

Effects on lab test results

None reported.

Pharmacokinetics

Absorption: Absorbed rapidly through the mucous membranes. Occasional systemic absorption may occur.
Distribution: Unknown.
Metabolism: Unknown.
Excretion: Unknown.

Route	Onset	Peak	Duration
Intranasal	5-10 min	≤ 6 hr	< 12 hr

Pharmacodynamics

Chemical effect: May cause local vasoconstriction of dilated arterioles, reducing blood flow and nasal congestion.
Therapeutic effect: Relieves nasal congestion.

Available forms

Nasal solution: 0.025%, 0.05%

NURSING PROCESS

Assessment

• Assess patient's congestion before therapy and regularly thereafter.
• Be alert for adverse reactions.
• Evaluate patient's and family's knowledge of drug therapy.

Nursing diagnoses

• Ineffective health maintenance related to nasal congestion
• Risk for injury related to drug-induced adverse CNS reactions
• Deficient knowledge related to drug therapy

Planning and implementation

• Have patient hold head upright, insert nozzle and then have patient sniff spray quickly.

Patient teaching

• Teach patient how to use drug.
• Tell patient not to share product to prevent spread of infection.
• Tell patient not to exceed recommended dosage and to use only when needed.
• Warn patient that excessive use may cause bradycardia, hypotension, dizziness, and weakness.

Evaluation

• Patient's nasal congestion is relieved.
• Patient sustains no injuries from drug-induced adverse CNS reactions.
• Patient and family state understanding of drug therapy.

oxymorphone hydrochloride

(oks-ee-MOR-fohn high-droh-KLOR-ighd)
Numorphan, Numorphan HP

Pharmacologic class: opioid
Therapeutic class: analgesic
Pregnancy risk category: C
Controlled substance schedule: II

Indications and dosages

▶ **Moderate-to-severe pain.** *Adults:* 1 to 1.5 mg I.M. or S.C. q 4 to 6 hours, p.r.n. Or, 0.5 mg I.V. q 4 to 6 hours, p.r.n. Or, 5 mg P.R. q 4 to 6 hours, p.r.n.

Contraindications and precautions

• Contraindicated in patients hypersensitive to drug.

• Use with extreme caution in debilitated patients and in those with head injury, increased intracranial pressure, seizures, asthma, COPD, acute abdominal conditions, prostatic hyperplasia, severe hepatic or renal disease, urethral stricture, respiratory depression, hypothyroidism, Addison's disease, or arrhythmias.

Lifespan: In pregnant and breast-feeding women, use cautiously. In children younger than age 18, drug is contraindicated. In geriatric patients, use with extreme caution.

Adverse reactions

CNS: *sedation, somnolence, clouded sensorium, euphoria,* dizziness, ***seizures*** with large doses.
CV: *hypotension,* ***bradycardia.***
GI: *nausea, vomiting, constipation,* ileus.
GU: urine retention.
Respiratory: ***respiratory depression.***
Other: physical dependence.

Interactions

Drug-drug. *CNS depressants, general anesthetics, MAO inhibitors, tricyclic antidepressants:* May have additive effects. Use together with extreme caution.
Drug-lifestyle. *Alcohol use:* May have additive effects. Discourage using together.

Effects on lab test results

• May increase amylase level.

Pharmacokinetics

Absorption: Well absorbed.
Distribution: Widely distributed.
Metabolism: Metabolized primarily in liver.
Excretion: Excreted primarily in urine.

Route	Onset	Peak	Duration
I.V.	5-10 min	15-30 min	3-4 hr
I.M.	10-15 min	30-90 min	3-6 hr
S.C.	10-20 min	60-90 min	3-6 hr
P.R.	15-30 min	About 2 hr	3-6 hr

Pharmacodynamics

Chemical effect: Binds with opioid receptors in CNS, altering response to pain via unknown mechanism.
Therapeutic effect: Relieves pain.

Available forms

Injection: 1 mg/ml, 1.5 mg/ml
Suppositories: 5 mg

NURSING PROCESS

Assessment

• Assess patient's pain before and after drug administration.
• Be alert for adverse reactions and drug interactions.
• Evaluate patient's and family's knowledge of drug therapy.

Nursing diagnoses

• Acute pain related to condition
• Ineffective breathing pattern related to drug-induced respiratory depression
• Deficient knowledge related to drug therapy

Planning and implementation

• Keep narcotic antagonist (naloxone) and resuscitation equipment available.
• Don't give drug for mild-to-moderate pain.
• Drug may worsen gallbladder pain.
• Give drug before patient's pain becomes too intense.
• Withhold dose and notify prescriber if respirations decrease or rate is below 12 breaths/minute.
• Dependence can develop with long-term use.
• Giving laxatives or stool softeners may help prevent or relieve constipation.
• **I.V. use:** Give drug by direct I.V. injection. If needed, dilute in normal saline solution.
– Keep patient supine during administration to minimize hypotension.
• **I.M., S.C., and P.R. use:** Follow normal protocol.

ALERT: Don't confuse oxymorphone with oxymetholone.

Patient teaching

• Instruct patient to take drug before pain becomes intense.
• Caution ambulatory patient about getting out of bed or walking. Warn outpatient to avoid hazardous activities until CNS effects of drug are known.
• Tell patient to refrigerate suppositories.
• Caution patient or family to report a decreased respiratory rate.

☑ Evaluation

- Patient is free from pain.
- Patient's respiratory status is within normal limits.
- Patient and family state understanding of drug therapy.

oxytocin, synthetic injection
(oks-ih-TOH-sin, sin-THET-ik in-JEK-shun)
Oxytocin, Pitocin, Syntocinon

Pharmacologic class: exogenous hormone
Therapeutic class: oxytocic, lactation stimulant
Pregnancy risk category: C

Indications and dosages

▶ **Induction or stimulation of labor.** *Adults:* Initially, 1 ml (10 units) ampule in 1,000 ml of dextrose 5% injection or normal saline solution I.V. infused at 1 to 2 milliunits/minute. Rate increased in increments of no more than 1 to 2 milliunits/minute at 15- to 30-minute intervals until normal contraction pattern is established. Rate decreased when labor is firmly established. Maximum dose is 20 milliunits/minute.

▶ **Reduction of postpartum bleeding after expulsion of placenta.** *Adults:* 10 to 40 units added to 1,000 ml of D_5W or normal saline solution infused at rate necessary to control bleeding, usually 20 to 40 milliunits/minute. Also, 1 ml (10 units) can be given I.M. after delivery of placenta.

▶ **Incomplete or inevitable abortion.** *Adults:* 10 units of oxytocin I.V. in 500 ml of normal saline solution or dextrose 5% in normal saline solution. Infuse at 20 to 40 gtt/minute.

▶ **Oxytocin challenge test to assess fetal distress in high-risk pregnancies greater than 31 weeks' gestation‡.** *Adults:* Prepare solution by adding 5 to 10 units of oxytocin to 1 L of D_5W injection, yielding a solution of 5 to 10 milliunits per ml. Infuse 0.5 milliunits/minute, gradually increasing at 15-minute intervals to a maximum infusion of 20 milliunits/minute. Discontinue infusion when three moderate uterine contractions occur within a 10-minute period. Response of fetal heart rate may be used to evaluate prognosis.

Contraindications and precautions

- Contraindicated in patients hypersensitive to drug.
- Use with extreme caution, if at all, in patients with invasive cervical carcinoma and patients with history of cervical or uterine surgery.

Lifespan: Contraindicated in cephalopelvic disproportion or delivery that requires conversion, as in transverse lie; in fetal distress when delivery isn't imminent; in prematurity; in other obstetric emergencies; and in severe toxemia, hypertonic uterine patterns, total placenta previa, or vasoprevia. Use with extreme caution during first and second stages of labor because cervical laceration, uterine rupture, and maternal and fetal death may occur. Use with extreme caution, if at all, in patients with grand multiparity, uterine sepsis, traumatic delivery, or overdistended uterus.

Adverse reactions

Maternal
CNS: ***subarachnoid hemorrhage*** from hypertension, ***seizures, coma*** from water intoxication.
CV: ***hypertension;*** increased heart rate, systemic venous return, and cardiac output; ***arrhythmias.***
GI: nausea, vomiting.
GU: tetanic uterine contractions, ***abruptio placentae, impaired uterine blood flow,*** pelvic hematoma, ***increased uterine motility.***
Hematologic: afibrinogenemia (may be related to postpartum bleeding).
Other: hypersensitivity reactions, ***anaphylaxis.***
Fetal
CV: ***bradycardia,*** tachycardia, ***PVCs.***
Hematologic: hyperbilirubinemia.
Respiratory: ***anoxia, asphyxia.***

Interactions

Drug-drug. *Cyclopropane anesthetics:* May cause less pronounced bradycardia and hypotension. Use together cautiously.
Thiopental anesthetics: Possible delayed induction. Use together cautiously.
Vasoconstrictors: May cause severe hypertension if oxytocin given within 3 or 4 hours of vasoconstrictor in patients receiving caudal block anesthetic. Avoid using together.

Effects on lab test results

None reported.

Pharmacokinetics

Absorption: Unknown.
Distribution: Distributed through extracellular fluid.
Metabolism: Metabolized rapidly in kidneys and liver. In early pregnancy, a circulating enzyme, oxytocinase, can inactivate drug.
Excretion: Small amounts excreted in urine. *Half-life:* 3 to 5 minutes.

Route	Onset	Peak	Duration
I.V.	Immediate	Unknown	1 hr
I.M.	3-5 min	Unknown	2-3 hr

Pharmacodynamics

Chemical effect: Causes potent and selective stimulation of uterine and mammary gland smooth muscle.
Therapeutic effect: Induces labor and milk ejection and reduces postpartum bleeding.

Available forms

Injection: 10 units/ml in ampule or vial

NURSING PROCESS

Assessment

- Assess patient's condition before therapy and regularly thereafter.
- Monitor and record uterine contractions, heart rate, blood pressure, intrauterine pressure, fetal heart rate, and blood loss every 15 minutes.
- Be alert for adverse reactions and drug interactions.
- Monitor fluid intake and output. Antidiuretic effect may lead to fluid overload, seizures, and coma.
- Evaluate patient's and family's knowledge of drug therapy.

Nursing diagnoses

- Risk for deficient fluid volume related to postpartum bleeding
- Excessive fluid volume related to drug-induced antidiuretic effect
- Deficient knowledge related to drug therapy

Planning and implementation

- Drug is used to induce or reinforce labor only when pelvis is known to be adequate, vaginal delivery is indicated, fetal maturity is ensured, and fetal position is favorable. Should be used only in hospital where critical care facilities and experienced clinician are immediately available.
- **I.V. use:** Don't give drug by I.V. bolus injection. Administer only by infusion.
- Give by piggyback infusion so drug can be stopped without interrupting I.V. line.
- Use an infusion pump.
- **I.M. use:** Drug isn't recommended for routine I.M. use. However, 10 units may be given I.M. after delivery of placenta to control postpartum uterine bleeding.
- Never give oxytocin simultaneously by more than one route.
- Have magnesium sulfate (20% solution) available for relaxation of myometrium.

ALERT: If contractions are less than 2 minutes apart, if they're above 50 mm Hg, or if they last 90 seconds or longer, stop infusion, turn patient on her side, and notify prescriber.
ALERT: Don't confuse Pitocin with Pitressin.

Patient teaching

- Instruct patient to report unusual feelings or adverse effects at once.
- Instruct patient to remain lying down during administration.

Evaluation

- Patient maintains adequate fluid balance with drug therapy.
- Patient does not develop edema.
- Patient and family state understanding of drug therapy.

P

paclitaxel
(pak-lih-TAK-sil)
Onxol, Taxol

Pharmacologic class: novel antimicrotubule
Therapeutic class: antineoplastic
Pregnancy risk category: D

Indications and dosages

▶ **First-line and subsequent treatment of advanced ovarian cancer.** *Adults (previously untreated):* 175 mg/m^2 I.V. over 3 hours q

3 weeks followed by cisplatin 75 mg/m²; or, 135 mg/m² I.V. over 24 hours with cisplatin 75 mg/m² q 3 weeks.
Adults (previously treated): 135 or 175 mg/m² I.V. over 3 hours q 3 weeks.

▶ **Breast cancer after failure of combination chemotherapy for metastatic disease or after relapse within 6 months of adjuvant chemotherapy (prior therapy should have included an anthracycline unless clinically contraindicated); adjuvant treatment of node-positive breast cancer administered sequentially to standard doxorubicin-containing combination chemotherapy.** *Adults:* 175 mg/m² I.V. over 3 hours q 3 weeks.

▶ **AIDS-related Kaposi's sarcoma.** *Adults:* 135 mg/m² I.V. over 3 hours q 3 weeks, or 100 mg/m² I.V. over 3 hours q 2 weeks.

▶ **Initial treatment of advanced non–small-cell lung cancer for patients who are not candidates for curative surgery or radiation.** *Adults:* 135 mg/m² I.V. infusion over 24 hours, follow with cisplatin 75 mg/m². Repeat cycle q 3 weeks.

For all indications, subsequent courses shouldn't be repeated until neutrophil count is at least 1,500 cells/mm³ and platelet count is at least 100,000 cells/mm³.

Contraindications and precautions

- Contraindicated in patients hypersensitive to drug or polyoxyethylated castor oil, a vehicle used in drug solution, and in patients with baseline neutrophil counts below 1,500/mm³.
- Use cautiously in patients who have received radiation therapy; they may have more frequent or severe myelosuppression.

Lifespan: In pregnant and breast-feeding women, drug isn't recommended. In children, safety of drug hasn't been established.

Adverse reactions

CNS: peripheral neuropathy.
CV: ***bradycardia,*** *hypotension, abnormal ECG.*
GI: *nausea, vomiting, diarrhea, mucositis.*
Hematologic: **NEUTROPENIA, LEUKOPENIA, THROMBOCYTOPENIA,** *anemia, bleeding.*
Musculoskeletal: *myalgia, arthralgia.*
Skin: alopecia, phlebitis, cellulitis at injection site.
Other: ***hypersensitivity reactions (anaphylaxis).***

Interactions

Drug-drug. *Cisplatin:* May have possible additive myelosuppressive effects. Use together cautiously.
Cyclosporine, dexamethasone, diazepam, estradiol, etoposide, ketoconazole, quinidine, retinoic acid, teniposide, testosterone, verapamil, vincristine: Inhibits paclitaxel metabolism. Use together cautiously.
Doxorubicin: May increase levels of doxorubicin and its metabolites. Dose adjustments may be needed.

Effects on lab test results

- May increase alkaline phosphatase, AST, and triglyceride levels.
- May decrease hemoglobin, hematocrit, and neutrophil, WBC, and platelet counts.

Pharmacokinetics

Absorption: Administered I.V.
Distribution: About 89% to 98% of drug is bound to serum proteins.
Metabolism: May be metabolized in liver.
Excretion: Unknown.

Route	Onset	Peak	Duration
I.V.	Unknown	Unknown	Unknown

Pharmacodynamics

Chemical effect: Prevents depolymerization of cellular microtubules, thus inhibiting normal reorganization of microtubule network necessary for mitosis and other vital cellular functions.
Therapeutic effect: Stops ovarian and breast cancer cell activity.

Available forms

Injection: 6 mg/ml

NURSING PROCESS

Assessment

- Assess patient's condition before therapy and regularly thereafter.
- Continuously monitor patient for first 30 minutes of infusion. Monitor patient closely throughout infusion.
- Monitor blood counts and liver function test results frequently during therapy.
- Be alert for adverse reactions and drug interactions.

• Evaluate patient's and family's knowledge of drug therapy.

Nursing diagnoses

• Ineffective health maintenance related to cancer
• Ineffective protection related to drug-induced adverse hematologic reactions
• Deficient knowledge related to drug therapy

Planning and implementation

• To reduce severe hypersensitivity, expect to pretreat patient with corticosteroids, such as dexamethasone, and antihistamines. H_1-receptor antagonists, such as diphenhydramine, and H_2-receptor antagonists, such as cimetidine or ranitidine, may be used.
• Follow facility protocol for safe handling, preparation, and use of chemotherapy drugs. Preparation and administration of parenteral form are linked to carcinogenic, mutagenic, and teratogenic risks for personnel. Mark all waste materials with chemotherapy hazard labels.
• Dilute concentrate to 0.3 to 1.2 mg/ml before infusion. Compatible solutions include normal saline solution for injection, D_5W, dextrose 5% in normal saline solution for injection, and dextrose 5% in lactated Ringer's injection. Diluted solutions are stable for 27 hours at room temperature.
• Prepare and store infusion solutions in glass containers. Undiluted concentrate shouldn't come in contact with polyvinyl chloride I.V. bags or tubing. Store diluted solution in glass or polypropylene bottles, or use polypropylene or polyolefin bags. Administer through polyethylene-lined administration sets, and use in-line 0.22-micron filter.
• Take care to avoid extravasation.
ALERT: Don't confuse paclitaxel with paroxetine.
ALERT: Don't confuse Taxol with Paxil.

Patient teaching

• Warn patient to watch for signs of bleeding and infection.
• Teach patient symptoms of peripheral neuropathy, such as tingling, burning, or numbness in limbs, and urge her to report them immediately to the prescriber. Although mild symptoms are common, severe symptoms occur infrequently. Dosage reduction may be necessary.
• Warn patient that alopecia occurs in up to 82% of patients.
• Advise woman of childbearing age to avoid pregnancy during therapy. Also recommend consulting with prescriber before becoming pregnant.

Evaluation

• Patient responds well to therapy.
• Patient develops no serious complications from drug-induced adverse hematologic reactions.
• Patient and family state understanding of drug therapy.

palivizumab

(pal-i-VI-zu-mab)
Synagis

Pharmacologic class: recombinant monoclonal antibody $IgG1_k$
Therapeutic class: RSV prophylactic
Pregnancy risk category: C

Indications and dosages

▶ **Prevention of serious lower respiratory tract disease caused by RSV in children at high risk.** *Children:* 15 mg/kg I.M. monthly throughout RSV season, with first administration before RSV season.

Contraindications and precautions

• Use cautiously in patients with thrombocytopenia or other coagulation disorders.
Lifespan: In children hypersensitive to drug or its components, drug is contraindicated.

Adverse reactions

CNS: nervousness, pain.
EENT: *otitis media, rhinitis,* pharyngitis, sinusitis, conjunctivitis.
GI: diarrhea, vomiting, gastroenteritis, oral candidiasis.
Hematologic: anemia.
Respiratory: *upper respiratory tract infection,* cough, wheeze, bronchiolitis, ***apnea,*** pneumonia, bronchitis, ***asthma,*** croup, dyspnea.
Skin: *rash,* fungal dermatitis, eczema, seborrhea.
Other: hernia, failure to thrive, injection site reaction, viral infection, flu-like syndrome.

Interactions

None significant.

Effects on lab test results

- May increase ALT and AST levels.
- May decrease hemoglobin and hematocrit.

Pharmacokinetics

Absorption: Unknown.
Distribution: Unknown.
Metabolism: Unknown.
Excretion: Unknown. *Half-life:* About 18 days.

Route	Onset	Peak	Duration
I.M.	Unknown	Unknown	Unknown

Pharmacodynamics

Chemical effect: Has neutralizing and fusion-inhibitory activity against RSV, which inhibits RSV replication.
Therapeutic effect: Prevents RSV infection in high-risk children.

Available forms

Injection (single use vial): 50 mg, 100 mg

NURSING PROCESS

Assessment

- Obtain accurate medical history before giving drug; ask if child has any coagulation disorders or liver dysfunction.
- Be alert for adverse reactions.
- Evaluate patient's and family's knowledge about drug therapy.

Nursing diagnoses

- Risk for infection related to RSV infection
- Risk for injury related to drug-induced adverse reactions
- Deficient knowledge related to drug therapy

Planning and implementation

- To reconstitute, slowly add 1 ml of sterile water for injection into a 100-mg vial. Gently swirl vial for 30 seconds to avoid foaming; don't shake. Let reconstituted solution stand at room temperature for 20 minutes. Give within 6 hours of reconstitution.
- Give drug in anterolateral aspect of thigh. Don't use gluteal muscle routinely as an injection site because of risk of damage to sciatic nerve. Injection volumes over 1 ml should be divided.
- Patients should receive monthly doses throughout RSV season, even if RSV infection develops. In the northern hemisphere, RSV season typically lasts from November to April.

Patient teaching

- Explain to parent or caregiver that drug is used to prevent RSV and not to treat it.
- Advise parent that monthly injections are recommended throughout RSV season.
- Advise parent to report adverse reactions immediately or any unusual bruising, bleeding, or weakness.

Evaluation

- Patient doesn't develop RSV infection.
- Patient sustains no injury from drug-induced adverse reactions.
- Patient and family state understanding of drug therapy.

pamidronate disodium

(pam-ih-DROH-nayt digh-SOH-dee-um)
Aredia

Pharmacologic class: bisphosphonate, pyrophosphate analogue
Therapeutic class: antihypercalcemic
Pregnancy risk category: D

Indications and dosages

▶ **Moderate-to-severe hypercalcemia related to malignancy (with or without metastases).** *Adults:* Dosage depends on severity of hypercalcemia. Calcium levels are corrected for serum albumin as follows:

$$\underset{\text{(in mg/dl)}}{\text{Corrected serum calcium (CCa)}} = \underset{\text{(in mg/dl)}}{\text{serum calcium}} + 0.8\,(4 - \underset{\text{(in g/dl)}}{\text{serum albumin}})$$

Patients with moderate hypercalcemia (CCa levels of 12 to 13.5 mg/dl) may receive 60 to 90 mg I.V. infusion as a single dose over 2 to 24 hours.

Patients with severe hypercalcemia (CCa levels over 13.5 mg/dl) may receive 90 mg over 2 to 24 hours. Repeat doses shouldn't be given sooner than 7 days to allow for full response to initial dose.

▶ **Osteolytic bone lesions of multiple myeloma.** *Adults:* 90 mg I.V. daily over 4 hours once monthly.

▶ **Osteolytic bone lesions of breast cancer.** *Adults:* 90 mg I.V. daily over 2 hours q 3 to 4 weeks.

▶ **Moderate-to-severe Paget's disease.** *Adults:* 30 mg I.V. as 4-hour infusion on 3 consecutive days for total dose of 90 mg. Cycle repeated, p.r.n.

Contraindications and precautions

- Contraindicated in patients hypersensitive to drug or to other bisphosphonates, such as etidronate.
- Use with extreme caution in patients with renal impairment.

Lifespan: In pregnant women, drug may cause fetal harm. In breast-feeding women, use cautiously. In children, safety of drug hasn't been established.

Adverse reactions

CNS: pain, fever, ***seizures.***
CV: *fluid overload, hypertension,* atrial fibrillation.
GI: *abdominal pain, anorexia, constipation, nausea, vomiting,* ***GI hemorrhage.***
GU: *urinary tract infection,* ***renal failure.***
Hematologic: ***leukopenia, thrombocytopenia,*** *anemia.*
Metabolism: hypophosphatemia, hypokalemia, hypomagnesemia, hypocalcemia.
Musculoskeletal: bone pain.

Interactions

None significant.

Effects on lab test results

- May increase serum creatinine levels. May decrease phosphate, potassium, magnesium, and calcium levels.
- May decrease hemoglobin, hematocrit, and WBC and platelet counts.

Pharmacokinetics

Absorption: Administered I.V.
Distribution: About 50% to 60% of dose is rapidly taken up by bone; drug is also taken up by kidneys, liver, spleen, teeth, and tracheal cartilage.
Metabolism: None.
Excretion: Excreted by kidneys. *Half-life:* Alpha, 1½ hours; beta, 27¼ hours.

Route	Onset	Peak	Duration
I.V.	Unknown	Unknown	Unknown

Pharmacodynamics

Chemical effect: Inhibits bone resorption. Adsorbs to hydroxyapatite crystals in bone and may directly block calcium phosphate dissolution.
Therapeutic effect: Lowers calcium levels.

Available forms

Injection: 30 mg/vial, 90 mg/vial

NURSING PROCESS

Assessment

- Assess patient's condition before therapy and regularly thereafter.
- Assess hydration before treatment.
- Closely monitor electrolytes, and creatinine levels, CBC counts and differential, hematocrit, and hemoglobin.
- Carefully monitor patient with anemia, leukopenia, or thrombocytopenia during first 2 weeks of therapy.
- Monitor patient's temperature. Fever is most likely 24 to 48 hours after therapy.
- Be alert for adverse reactions and drug interactions.
- Evaluate patient's and family's knowledge of drug therapy.

Nursing diagnoses

- Ineffective health maintenance related to hypercalcemia
- Risk for injury related to drug-induced hypocalcemia
- Deficient knowledge related to drug therapy

Planning and implementation

- Use drug only after patient has been vigorously hydrated with saline solution. In patients with mild-to-moderate hypercalcemia, hydration alone may be sufficient.
- Reconstitute vial with 10 ml sterile water for injection. Once drug is completely dissolved, add to 250 ml (2-hour infusion), 500 ml (4-hour infusion), or 1,000 ml (up to 24-hour infusion) bag of half-normal or normal saline solution injection or D_5W.

• Don't mix with infusion solutions that contain calcium, such as Ringer's injection or lactated Ringer's injection. Inspect for precipitate before administering.
• Give drug only by I.V. infusion. Animals have developed nephropathy when drug is given as bolus.
• Longer infusions (more than 2 hours) may reduce the risk for renal toxicity, particularly in patients with preexisting renal insufficiency.
• Short-term administration of calcium may be needed if patient has severe hypocalcemia.
• Solution is stable for 24 hours at room temperature.
• For patients with multiple myeloma, there is limited information on use in patients with serum creatinine > 3 mg/dl. Also, patients with marked Bence-Jones proteinuria and dehydration should receive adequate hydration prior to Aredia infusion. Optimal duration of therapy is unknown; in studies, 21 months demonstrated overall benefits.
ALERT: Because of the risk of renal dysfunction leading to renal failure, single doses of pamidronate shouldn't exceed 90 mg.
• Patients treated for bone metastases who have renal dysfunction should have the dose withheld until renal function returns to baseline. Treatment of bone metastases in patients with severe renal impairment is not recommended.
• For breast cancer patients, optimal duration of therapy is unknown; in studies, 24 months demonstrated overall benefits.

Patient teaching
• Instruct patient to report unusual signs or symptoms at once.
• Inform patient of need for frequent tests to monitor effectiveness of drug and detect adverse reactions.

Evaluation
• Patient's calcium level returns to normal.
• Patient doesn't develop hypocalcemia during drug therapy.
• Patient and family state understanding of drug therapy.

pancreatin
(pan-kree-AH-tin)
Creon, Digepepsin, 8X Pancreatin 900 mg†, 4X Pancreatin 600 mg†, Hi-Vegi-Lip†, Pancrezyme 4X†

Pharmacologic class: pancreatic enzyme
Therapeutic class: digestant
Pregnancy risk category: C

Indications and dosages
▶ **Exocrine pancreatic secretion insufficiency; digestive aid in diseases related to deficiency of pancreatic enzymes, such as cystic fibrosis.** *Adults and children:* Dosage varies with condition being treated. Usual initial dosage is 8,000 to 24,000 units of lipase activity before or with each meal or snack. Total daily dose also may be given in divided doses at 1- to 2-hour intervals throughout day.

Contraindications and precautions
• Contraindicated in patients hypersensitive to drug or to pork protein or enzymes and in those with acute pancreatitis or acute exacerbation of chronic pancreatitis.
Lifespan: In pregnant and breast-feeding women, use cautiously.

Adverse reactions
GI: nausea, diarrhea with high doses.
Metabolic: hyperuricuria with high doses.

Interactions
Drug-drug. *Antacids:* May negate effects of pancreatin. Avoid using together.
Iron: May decrease serum iron response. Monitor levels.

Effects on lab test results
• May increase uric acid levels.

Pharmacokinetics
Absorption: Not absorbed; it acts locally in GI tract.
Distribution: None.
Metabolism: None.
Excretion: Excreted in feces.

Route	Onset	Peak	Duration
P.O.	Unknown	1-2 hr	Unknown

Pharmacodynamics

Chemical effect: Replaces endogenous exocrine pancreatic enzymes.
Therapeutic effect: Aids digestion of starches, fats, and proteins.

Available forms

Creon
Capsules (enteric-coated microspheres): 300 mg pancreatin, 8,000 units lipase, 13,000 units protease, and 30,000 units amylase
Creon 10
Capsules: 10,000 units lipase, 37,500 units protease, and 33,200 units amylase
Creon 20
Capsules: 20,000 units lipase, 75,000 units protease, and 66,400 units amylase
Digepepsin
Tablets (enteric-coated): 300 mg pancreatin
8X Pancreatin 900 mg†
Tablets (enteric-coated): 7,200 mg pancreatin, 22,500 units lipase, 180,000 units protease, and 180,000 units amylase
4X Pancreatin 600 mg†, Pancrezyme 4X†
Tablets (enteric-coated): 2,400 mg pancreatin, 12,000 units lipase, 60,000 units protease, and 60,000 units amylase
Hi-Vegi-Lip†
Tablets (enteric-coated): 2,400 mg pancreatin, 4,800 units lipase, 60,000 units protease, and 60,000 units amylase

NURSING PROCESS

Assessment

- Assess patient's condition before therapy and regularly thereafter. Decreased number of bowel movements and improved stool consistency indicate effective therapy.
- Monitor patient's diet to ensure proper balance of fat, protein, and starch intake to avoid indigestion. Dosage varies according to degree of maldigestion and malabsorption, amount of fat in diet, and enzyme activity of drug.
- Evaluate patient's and family's knowledge of drug therapy.

Nursing diagnoses

- Imbalanced nutrition: less than body requirements related to condition
- Noncompliance related to long-term therapy
- Deficient knowledge related to drug therapy

Planning and implementation

- Give drug before or with each meal.
- USP standards dictate that each milligram of bovine or porcine pancreatin contain lipase 2 units, protease 25 units, and amylase 25 units.

ALERT: Drug isn't effective in GI disorders unrelated to pancreatic enzyme deficiency.
ALERT: Don't change brands without consulting a physician or a pharmacist.

- Enteric coating on some products may reduce availability of enzyme in upper portion of jejunum.

Patient teaching

- Tell patient not to crush or chew enteric-coated dosage forms. Capsules containing enteric-coated microspheres may be opened and contents sprinkled on small quantity of soft food, such as applesauce. Follow with a glass of water or juice.
- Tell patient to store in airtight containers at room temperature.

Evaluation

- Patient maintains normal digestion of fats, carbohydrates, and proteins.
- Patient complies with prescribed drug regimen.
- Patient and family state understanding of drug therapy.

pancrelipase

(pan-krih-LIGH-pays)
Creon 5, Creon 10, Creon 20, Kutrase, Ku-Zyme, Ku-Zyme HP, Lipram 4500, Lipram CR 5, Lipram CR 10, Lipram CR 20, Lipram PN 10, Lipram PN 16, Lipram PN 20, Lipram UL 12, Lipram UL 18, Lipram UL 20, Pancrease, Pancrease MT 4, Pancrease MT 10, Pancrease MT 16, Pancrease MT 20, Pancrecarb MS-4, Pancrecarb MS-8, Panokase, Plaretase 8000, Ultrase, Ultrase MT 12, Ultrase MT 18, Ultrase MT 20, Viokase, Viokase 8, Viokase 16

Pharmacologic class: pancreatic enzyme
Therapeutic class: digestant
Pregnancy risk category: C

Indications and dosages

▶ **Exocrine pancreatic secretion insufficiency, cystic fibrosis in adults and children, steatorrhea and other disorders of fat metabolism secondary to insufficient pancreatic enzymes.** *Adults and children:* Dosage adjusted to patient's response. Usual initial dosage is 4,000 to 33,000 units of lipase activity with each meal or snack.

Contraindications and precautions

• Contraindicated in patients hypersensitive to drug or pork protein or enzymes and in those with acute pancreatitis or acute exacerbation of chronic pancreatitis.

Lifespan: In pregnant and breast-feeding women, use cautiously.

Adverse reactions

GI: *nausea,* cramping, diarrhea with large doses.

Interactions

Drug-drug. *Antacids:* May destroy enteric coating and enhance degradation of pancrelipase. Avoid using together.
Iron: Decreases serum iron response. Monitor iron levels.

Effects on lab test results

• May increase uric acid level.

Pharmacokinetics

Absorption: None; it acts locally in GI tract.
Distribution: None.
Metabolism: None.
Excretion: Excreted in feces.

Route	Onset	Peak	Duration
P.O.	Varies	Varies	Varies

Pharmacodynamics

Chemical effect: Replaces endogenous exocrine pancreatic enzymes.
Therapeutic effect: Aids digestion of starches, fats, and proteins.

Available forms

Creon 5, Lipram CR 5
Capsules (enteric-coated microspheres): 5,000 units lipase, 18,750 units protease, 16,600 units amylase
Creon 10, Lipram CR 10
Capsules (enteric-coated microspheres): 10,000 units lipase, 37,500 units protease, 33,200 units amylase
Creon 20, Lipram CR 20
Capsules (enteric-coated microspheres): 20,000 units lipase, 75,000 units protease, 66,400 units amylase
Kutrase
Capsules: 2,400 units lipase, 30,000 units protease, 15,000 units amylase
Ku-Zyme
Capsules: 1,200 units lipase; 15,000 units protease; 15,000 units amylase
Ku-Zyme HP, Panokase, Plaretase 8000, Viokase 8
Capsules or tablets: 8,000 units lipase, 30,000 units protease, 30,000 units amylase
Lipram 4500, Pancrease, Ultrase
Capsules (enteric-coated microspheres): 4,500 units lipase, 25,000 units protease, 20,000 units amylase
Lipram PN 10, Pancrease MT 10
Capsules (enteric-coated contents): 10,000 units lipase, 30,000 units protease, 30,000 units amylase
Lipram PN 16, Pancrease MT 16
Capsules (enteric-coated contents): 16,000 units lipase, 48,000 units protease, and 48,000 units amylase
Lipram PN 20, Pancrease MT 20
Capsules (enteric-coated contents): 20,000 units lipase, 44,000 units protease, 56,000 units amylase.
Lipram UL 12, Ultrase MT 12
Capsules (enteric-coated contents): 12,000 units lipase, 39,000 units protease, and 39,000 units amylase
Lipram UL 18, Ultrase MT 18
Capsules (enteric-coated contents): 18,000 units lipase, 58,500 units protease, and 58,500 units amylase
Lipram UL 20, Ultrase MT 20
Capsules (enteric-coated contents): 20,000 units lipase, 65,000 units protease, and 65,000 units amylase
Pancrease MT 4
Capsules (enteric-coated microtablets): 4,000 units lipase, 12,000 units protease, and 12,000 units amylase

Pancrecarb MS-4
Capsules (enteric-coated microspheres): 4,000 units lipase, 25,000 units protease, and 25,000 units amylase
Pancrecarb MS-8
Capsules (enteric-coated microspheres): 8,000 units lipase; 45,000 units protease; 40,000 units amylase
Pancrelipase
Capsules (enteric-coated pellets): 4,000 units lipase, 25,000 units protease, and 20,000 units amylase
Viokase
Powder: 16,800 units lipase, 70,000 units protease, and 70,000 units amylase per 0.7 g powder
Viokase 16
Tablets: 8,000 units lipase, 30,000 units protease, 30,000 units amylase

NURSING PROCESS

Assessment
- Assess patient's condition before therapy and regularly thereafter. Decreased number of bowel movements and improved stool consistency indicate effective therapy.
- Monitor patient's diet to ensure proper balance of fat, protein, and starch intake to avoid indigestion. Dosage varies according to degree of maldigestion and malabsorption, amount of fat in diet, and enzyme activity of drug.
- Be alert for adverse reactions and drug interactions.
- Evaluate patient's and family's knowledge of drug therapy.

Nursing diagnoses
- Imbalanced nutrition: less than body requirements related to condition
- Noncompliance related to long-term therapy
- Deficient knowledge related to drug therapy

Planning and implementation
- For infant, mix powder with applesauce and give before or with meals. Avoid contact with or inhalation of powder; it may be irritating. Older child may take capsules with food.
- Enteric coating on some products may reduce availability of enzyme in upper portion of jejunum.

ALERT: Drug isn't effective in GI disorders unrelated to pancreatic enzyme deficiency.

Patient teaching
- Advise patient not to crush or chew enteric-coated dosage forms.
- Tell patient to store in airtight containers at room temperature.

Evaluation
- Patient maintains normal digestion of fats, carbohydrates, and proteins.
- Patient complies with prescribed drug regimen.
- Patient and family state understanding of drug therapy.

pancuronium bromide
(pan-kyoo-ROH-nee-um BROH-mighd)

Pharmacologic class: nondepolarizing neuromuscular blocker
Therapeutic class: skeletal muscle relaxant
Pregnancy risk category: C

Indications and dosages
▶ **Adjunct to anesthesia to induce skeletal muscle relaxation; to facilitate intubation; to lessen muscle contractions in pharmacologically or electrically induced seizures; to assist with mechanical ventilation.** Dosage depends on anesthetic used, individual needs, and response. Dosages are representative and must be adjusted.
Adults and children age 1 month and older: Initially, 0.04 to 0.1 mg/kg I.V.; then 0.01 mg/kg q 25 to 60 minutes.
Neonates younger than age 1 month: Dosages are individualized.

Contraindications and precautions
- Contraindicated in patients hypersensitive to bromides, in those with tachycardia, and in those for whom even a minor increase in heart rate is undesirable.
- Use cautiously in debilitated patients and in those with respiratory depression, myasthenia gravis, myasthenic syndrome of lung cancer, bronchogenic carcinoma, dehydration, thyroid disorders, collagen diseases, porphyria, electrolyte disturbances, hyperthermia, toxemic states, or renal, hepatic, or pulmonary impairment.

Lifespan: In pregnant women undergoing cesarean section and in breast-feeding women, use large doses cautiously. In geriatric patients, use cautiously.

Adverse reactions

CV: tachycardia, increased blood pressure.
EENT: excessive salivation.
Musculoskeletal: residual muscle weakness.
Respiratory: ***prolonged, dose-related respiratory insufficiency or apnea;*** wheezing.
Skin: transient rashes, excessive diaphoresis.
Other: burning sensation, ***allergic or idiosyncratic hypersensitivity reactions.***

Interactions

Drug-drug. *Aminoglycoside antibiotics, including amikacin, gentamicin, kanamycin, neomycin, streptomycin; clindamycin; general anesthetics; polymyxin antibiotics, such as polymyxin B sulfate and colistin; quinidine:* Potentiates neuromuscular blockade, leading to increased skeletal muscle relaxation and prolonged effect. Use cautiously during surgical and postoperative periods.
Lithium, opioid analgesics: Potentiates neuromuscular blockade, leading to increased skeletal muscle relaxation and possible respiratory paralysis. Use with extreme caution and reduce pancuronium dosage, as directed.
Succinylcholine: Increases intensity and duration of blockade. Allow succinylcholine effects to subside before giving pancuronium.

Effects on lab test results

None reported.

Pharmacokinetics

Absorption: Administered I.V.
Distribution: Little protein-binding regardless of dose.
Metabolism: Unknown.
Excretion: Excreted mainly in urine; some biliary excretion. *Half-life:* About 2 hours.

Route	Onset	Peak	Duration
I.V.	30-45 sec	3-4.5 min	35-45 min

Pharmacodynamics

Chemical effect: Prevents acetylcholine from binding to receptors on muscle end plate, thus blocking depolarization.
Therapeutic effect: Relaxes skeletal muscles.

Available forms

Injection: 1 mg/ml, 2 mg/ml

NURSING PROCESS

Assessment

- Assess patient's condition before therapy and regularly thereafter.
- Monitor baseline electrolyte determinations (electrolyte imbalance can increase neuromuscular effects) and vital signs.
- Measure fluid intake and output; renal dysfunction may prolong duration of action because 25% of drug is unchanged before excretion.
- Nerve stimulator and train-of-four monitoring are recommended to confirm antagonism of neuromuscular blockade and recovery of muscle strength. Before attempting pharmacologic reversal with neostigmine, you should see some evidence of spontaneous recovery.
- Monitor respirations closely until patient fully recovers from neuromuscular blockade, as evidenced by tests of muscle strength (hand grip, head lift, and ability to cough).
- Be alert for adverse reactions and drug interactions.
- Evaluate patient's and family's knowledge of drug therapy.

Nursing diagnoses

- Ineffective health maintenance related to condition
- Ineffective breathing pattern related to drug's effect on respiratory muscles
- Deficient knowledge related to drug therapy

Planning and implementation

- Administer sedatives or general anesthetics before neuromuscular blockers. Neuromuscular blockers don't reduce consciousness or alter pain threshold. Give analgesics for pain.
- Pancuronium should be used only by personnel skilled in airway management.
- Mix drug only with fresh solutions; precipitates will form if alkaline solutions such as barbiturate solutions are used.
- Allow succinylcholine effects to subside before giving pancuronium.
- Store drug in refrigerator. Don't store in plastic containers or syringes, although plastic syringes may be used for administration.

• Have emergency respiratory support equipment (endotracheal equipment, ventilator, oxygen, atropine, edrophonium, epinephrine, and neostigmine) immediately available.
• Once spontaneous recovery starts, drug-induced neuromuscular blockade may be reversed with anticholinesterase drug (such as neostigmine or edrophonium). Usually given with an anticholinergic such as atropine.
ALERT: Don't confuse pancuronium with pipecuronium.

Patient teaching
• Explain all events to patient because he can still hear.
• Reassure patient that he'll be monitored at all times and that pain medication will be provided, if appropriate.
• Tell patient that he may feel burning sensation at injection site.

Evaluation
• Patient's condition improves.
• Patient maintains adequate ventilation with mechanical assistance.
• Patient and family state understanding of drug therapy.

pantoprazole
(pan-TOE-pra-zole)
Protonix

pantoprazole sodium
(pan-TOE-pra-zole SOH-dee-um)
Protonix I.V.

Pharmacologic class: substituted benzimidazole
Therapeutic class: proton pump inhibitor
Pregnancy risk category: B

Indications and dosages
▶ **Short-term treatment of erosive esophagitis related to gastroesophageal reflux disease (GERD).** *Adults:* 40 mg P.O. once daily for up to 8 weeks. For those patients who haven't healed after 8 weeks of treatment, an additional 8-week course may be considered.
▶ **Short-term treatment of GERD related to history of erosive esophagitis.** *Adults:* 40 mg I.V. daily for 7 to 10 days. Switch to oral form as soon as patient is able to take oral medications.
▶ **Long-term maintenance of healing erosive esophagitis and reduction in relapse rates of daytime and nighttime heartburn symptoms in patients with GERD.** *Adults:* 40 mg P.O. once daily.
▶ **Short-term treatment of pathological hypersecretion conditions related to Zollinger-Ellison syndrome or other neoplastic conditions.** *Adults:* Individualize dosage. Usual dose is 80 mg I.V. q 12 hours for no more than 6 days. For those needing a higher dose, 80 mg q 8 hours is expected to maintain acid output below 10 mEq/h. Maximum daily dose is 240 mg.
▶ **Long-term treatment of pathological hypersecretory conditions, including with Zollinger-Ellison syndrome.** *Adults:* Individualize dosage. Usual starting dose is 40 mg P.O. b.i.d. Adjust dose to a maximum of 240 mg daily.

Contraindications and precautions
• Contraindicated in patients with a known hypersensitivity to any component of the drug.
Lifespan: In breast-feeding women, use cautiously. In children, safety and effectiveness haven't been established.

Adverse reactions
CNS: headache, insomnia, asthenia, migraine, anxiety, dizziness.
CV: chest pain.
EENT: pharyngitis, rhinitis, sinusitis.
GI: diarrhea, flatulence, abdominal pain, eructation, constipation, dyspepsia, gastroenteritis, gastrointestinal disorder, nausea, vomiting.
GU: rectal disorder, urinary frequency, urinary tract infection.
Metabolic: hyperglycemia, hyperlipidemia.
Musculoskeletal: back pain, neck pain, arthralgia, hypertonia.
Respiratory: bronchitis, increased cough, dyspnea, upper respiratory tract infection.
Skin: rash.
Other: flulike syndrome, infection, pain.

Interactions
Drug-drug. *Ampicillin esters, iron salts, ketoconazole:* May decrease absorption of these drugs. Monitor patient closely and try to space out the time intervals of administration.

Drug-herb. *St. John's wort:* Increases risk of sunburn. Advise patient to avoid unprotected or prolonged sun exposure.
Drug-food. *Food:* Delays absorption of pantoprazole for up to 2 hours, however the extent of absorption is not affected. Can be given without regard to meals.

Effects on lab test results

• May increase glucose and lipid levels. May increase or decrease liver function levels.

Pharmacokinetics

Absorption: Well absorbed with an absolute bioavailability of 77%. Peak level occurs at 2.5 hours. Food may delay its absorption up to 2 hours; however, the extent of absorption is not affected.
Distribution: Distributes mainly in the extracellular fluid. Protein binding is approximately 98%, mainly to albumin.
Metabolism: Extensively metabolized in the liver through the cytochrome P450 (CYP) system.
Excretion: About 71% of a dose is excreted in the urine with 18% excreted in the feces by biliary excretion.

Route	Onset	Peak	Duration
P.O.	Unknown	2.5 hr	Unknown
I.V.	15-30 min	Unknown	24 hr

Pharmacodynamics

Chemical effect: Inhibits the activity of the proton pump by binding to hydrogen-potassium adenosine triphosphatase, located at secretory surface of the gastric parietal cells.
Therapeutic effect: Suppresses gastric acid secretion.

Available forms

Injection: 40 mg vial.
Tablet (delayed-release): 20 mg, 40 mg

NURSING PROCESS

Assessment

• Evaluate patient's and family's knowledge of pantoprazole therapy.
• Assess underlying condition before therapy and reassess regularly throughout therapy.
• Assess patient for complaints of epigastric or abdominal pain and for bleeding (such as blood in stool or emesis).
• Be alert for adverse reactions and interactions.

Nursing diagnoses

• Risk for imbalanced fluid volume related to drug-induced adverse reactions
• Risk for aspiration related to underlying gastrointestinal disorder
• Deficient knowledge deficit related to pantoprazole therapy

Planning and implementation

• Pantoprazole can be given without regard to meals.
• Symptomatic response to therapy doesn't mean there isn't gastric malignancy.
• I.V. pantoprazole should be stopped when P.O. use is warranted.
• **I.V. use:** Reconstitute each vial with 10 ml of normal saline solution. Compatible diluents for infusion include 5% dextrose, normal saline solution, or lactated Ringer's injection.
– For GERD, further dilute with 100 ml of diluent to a final concentration of 0.4 mg/ml.
– For hypersecretion conditions, combine 2 reconstituted vials and further dilute with 80 ml of diluent to a total volume of 100 ml, with a final concentration of 0.8 mg/ml.
– Infuse diluted solutions I.V. over 15 minutes at a rate not greater than 3 mg/min (7 ml/min) for GERD and 6 mg/min (7 ml/min) for pathological hypersecretory conditions.
– Don't give another infusion simultaneously through the same line.
– The reconstituted solution may be stored for up to 2 hours at room temperature, and the diluted solutions may be stored for up to 12 hours at room temperature.
ALERT: Don't confuse Protonix with Prilosec, Prozac, or Prevacid.

Patient teaching
• Instruct patient to take exactly as prescribed and at approximately the same time every day.
• Advise patient that the medication can be taken without regard to meals.
• Advise patient that tablet is to be swallowed whole and not crushed, split, or chewed.
• Tell patient that antacids do not affect the absorption of pantoprazole.

• Instruct patient to report abdominal pain or signs of bleeding, such as tarry stool.
• Advise patient to avoid alcohol, food, or other medications (aspirin, NSAIDs) that could cause gastric irritation.

Evaluation

• Patient maintains adequate hydration throughout therapy.
• Patient responds well to therapy and doesn't aspirate.
• Patient and family state understanding of pantoprazole therapy.

papaverine hydrochloride

(puh-PAV-eh-reen high-droh-KLOR-ighd)
Pavabid Plateau Caps, Pavagen TD

Pharmacologic class: benzylisoquinoline derivative, opioid alkaloid
Therapeutic class: peripheral vasodilator
Pregnancy risk category: C

Indications and dosages

▶ **Relief of cerebral and peripheral ischemia from arterial spasm and myocardial ischemia; treatment of coronary occlusion and certain cerebral angiospastic states.** *Adults:* 150 to 300 mg sustained-release form q 8 to 12 hours. Or, 30 to 120 mg I.M. or I.V. q 3 hours, as indicated. In treatment of extrasystoles, give two doses 10 minutes apart.
Children: 6 mg/kg I.M. or I.V. divided q.i.d.
▶ **Impotence‡.** *Adults:* 2.5 to 37.5 mg by intracavernous injection.

Contraindications and precautions

• I.V. use is contraindicated in patients with Parkinson's disease or complete AV block.
• Use cautiously in patients with glaucoma, in large doses, and in patients with acute coronary thrombosis.
Lifespan: In pregnant women, use cautiously. In breast-feeding women and children, safety of drug hasn't been established.

Adverse reactions

CNS: *headache,* depression, malaise.
CV: *flushing, increased heart rate, increased blood pressure* (parenteral use), depressed AV and intraventricular conduction, hypotension, ***arrhythmias.***
GI: constipation, dry mouth, *nausea.*
Hepatic: ***hepatitis, cirrhosis.***
Respiratory: increased depth of respiration, ***apnea.***
Skin: *diaphoresis.*

Interactions

Drug-drug. *Levodopa:* Papaverine may interfere with therapeutic effects of levodopa in patients with Parkinson's disease. Monitor patient closely.
Drug-herb. *Hawthorne:* May have additive vasodilatory effects. Discourage using together.

Effects on lab test results

• May increase liver function test values.

Pharmacokinetics

Absorption: 54% of P.O. drug is bioavailable; sustained-release forms are sometimes absorbed poorly and erratically. Unknown after I.M. administration.
Distribution: Drug tends to localize in adipose tissue and in liver; remainder is distributed throughout body. About 90% of drug is protein-bound.
Metabolism: Metabolized by the liver.
Excretion: Excreted in urine as metabolites.

Route	Onset	Peak	Duration
P.O.	Rapid	1-2 hr	12 hr
I.V., I.M.	Unknown	Unknown	Unknown

Pharmacodynamics

Chemical effect: Has direct, nonspecific relaxant effect on vascular, cardiac, and other smooth muscle.
Therapeutic effect: Relieves vascular spasms.

Available forms

Capsules (sustained-release): 150 mg
Injection: 30 mg/ml in 2- and 10-ml ampules

NURSING PROCESS

Assessment

• Assess patient's condition before therapy and regularly thereafter.

• Monitor blood pressure and heart rate and rhythm, especially in patient with cardiac disease.
• Be alert for adverse reactions and drug interactions.
• Monitor patient for adverse hepatic reactions during long-term therapy.
• Evaluate patient's and family's knowledge of drug therapy.

Nursing diagnoses
• Ineffective tissue perfusion (cerebral, cardiopulmonary, peripheral, GI) related to vascular spasms
• Constipation related to drug's effect on GI tract
• Deficient knowledge related to drug therapy

Planning and implementation
• **P.O. and I.M. use:** Follow normal protocol.
• **I.V. use:** Give drug by direct injection over 1 to 2 minutes to minimize risk of serious adverse reactions. Don't add to lactated Ringer's injection because precipitate forms.
• Drug is most effective when given early in course of disorder.
• Hold dose and notify prescriber at once if vital signs change.

Patient teaching
• Tell patient to take drug regularly; long-term therapy is required.
• Advise patient to avoid hazardous activities until CNS effects of drug are known.
• Instruct patient to avoid sudden position changes.

Evaluation
• Patient maintains adequate tissue perfusion.
• Patient states measures used to prevent constipation.
• Patient and family state understanding of drug therapy.

paricalcitol
(pair-ee-KAL-sih-tohl)
Zemplar

Pharmacologic class: vitamin D analog
Therapeutic class: hyperparathyroidism agent
Pregnancy risk category: C

Indications and dosages
▶ **Prevention and treatment of secondary hyperparathyroidism caused by chronic renal failure.** *Adults:* 0.04 to 0.1 mcg/kg (2.8 to 7 mcg) I.V. no more often than every other day during dialysis. Doses as high as 0.24 mcg/kg (16.8 mcg) have been safely administered. If satisfactory response isn't observed, dosage may be increased by 2 to 4 mcg at 2- to 4-week intervals.

Contraindications and precautions
• Contraindicated in patients hypersensitive to drug or its ingredients and in those with evidence of vitamin D toxicity or hypercalcemia.
• Use cautiously in patients taking digitalis compounds. Patients taking digoxin are at greater risk for digitalis toxicity during therapy because of risk of hypercalcemia.
Lifespan: In pregnant women, the benefits should outweigh the risks to the fetus and mother. In breast-feeding women, giving large doses of drug is not recommended. In children, safety hasn't been established.

Adverse reactions
CNS: light-headedness, fever, malaise.
CV: edema, palpitations.
GI: dry mouth, ***GI bleeding,*** *nausea,* vomiting.
Respiratory: pneumonia.
Other: chills, flu syndrome, ***sepsis.***

Interactions
None significant.

Effects on lab test results
• May decrease total alkaline phosphatase level.

Pharmacokinetics
Absorption: Administered I.V.
Distribution: Unknown.
Metabolism: Unknown.
Excretion: Eliminated primarily by hepatobiliary excretion, 74% in feces and 16% in urine. *Half-life:* About 15 hours.

Route	Onset	Peak	Duration
I.V.	Immediate	Unknown	15 hr

Pharmacodynamics
Chemical effect: Synthetic vitamin D analogue that reduces parathyroid hormone (PTH) levels.

Therapeutic effect: Reduces PTH levels in patients with chronic renal failure.

Available forms

Injection: 5 mcg/ml

NURSING PROCESS

Assessment

- Obtain history of patient's underlying condition before therapy, and reassess regularly thereafter.
- Watch for ECG abnormalities.
- Monitor patient for symptoms of hypercalcemia, such as fatigue, muscle weakness, anorexia, depression, nausea, and constipation. Immediately notify prescriber if you suspect hypercalcemia.
- Monitor calcium and phosphorus levels twice weekly when dosage is being adjusted, and then monitor monthly. Measure PTH level every 3 months during therapy, as directed.
- Evaluate patient's and family's knowledge about drug therapy.

Nursing diagnoses

- Risk for injury related to drug-induced hypercalcemia
- Imbalanced nutrition: less than body requirements related to drug-induced GI adverse effects
- Deficient knowledge related to drug therapy

Planning and implementation

- Drug is only administered as an I.V. bolus. Discard unused portion.
- Inspect drug for particulates and discoloration before use.

ALERT: As PTH level decreases, paricalcitol dose may need to be decreased. Acute paricalcitol overdose may cause hypercalcemia, which may require emergency attention.

- In patients with chronic renal failure, appropriate types of phosphate-binding compounds may be needed to control phosphorus levels, but excessive use of aluminum-containing compounds should be avoided.
- Store drug at controlled room temperature (59° to 86° F [15° to 30° C]).

Patient teaching

- Stress importance of adhering to a dietary regimen of calcium supplementation and phosphorus restriction during drug therapy.
- Caution against use of phosphate or vitamin-D–related compounds during drug therapy.
- Explain need for frequent laboratory tests.
- Instruct patient with chronic renal failure to take phosphate-binding compounds as prescribed but to avoid excessive use of aluminum-containing compounds. Alert patient to early symptoms of hypercalcemia and vitamin D intoxication, such as weakness, headache, somnolence, nausea, vomiting, dry mouth, constipation, muscle pain, bone pain, and metallic taste.
- Instruct patient to promptly report adverse reactions.
- Remind patient taking digoxin to watch for signs and symptoms of digitalis toxicity.

Evaluation

- Patient doesn't experience hypercalcemia.
- Patient doesn't experience adverse GI effects.
- Patient and family state understanding of drug therapy.

paroxetine hydrochloride

(par-OKS-eh-teen high-droh-KLOR-ighd)
Paxil, Paxil CR

Pharmacologic class: selective serotonin reuptake inhibitor (SSRI)
Therapeutic class: antidepressant
Pregnancy risk category: B

Indications and dosages

▶ **Major depressive disorder.** *Adults:* Initially, 20 mg P.O. daily, preferably in morning, as directed. Increase by 10 mg daily at weekly intervals, to maximum of 50 mg daily, if necessary. Or, initially, 25 mg Paxil CR P.O. as a single daily dose, usually in the morning, with or without food. May increase dose at intervals of at least 1 week by 12.5 mg daily increments, up to a maximum of 62.5 mg daily.

▶ **Obsessive-compulsive disorder.** *Adults:* Initially, 20 mg P.O. daily, preferably in morning, as directed. Increase by 10 mg daily at weekly intervals to target of 40 mg daily. Maximum daily dose, 60 mg.

▶ **Panic disorder.** *Adults:* Initially, 10 mg P.O. daily. Increase by 10-mg increments at no less than weekly intervals to maximum daily dose of 60 mg. Or, initially, 12.5 mg Paxil CR P.O. as a single daily dose, usually in the morning, with or without food. May increase dose at intervals of at least 1 week by 12.5 mg daily increments, up to a maximum daily dose of 75 mg.

▶ **Social anxiety disorder.** *Adults:* Initially, 20 mg P.O. daily, usually in the morning. Maintain lowest effective dosage, and periodically assess patient to determine need for continued treatment. Maximum, 60 mg/day.

▶ **Generalized anxiety disorder.** *Adults:* Initially, 20 mg P.O. daily. Increase dose by 10 mg daily at increments of at least 1 week. Maximum dose is 50 mg P.O. daily.

▶ **Posttraumatic stress disorder.** *Adults:* Initially, 20 mg P.O. daily. Increase dose by 10 mg daily at increments of at least 1 week. Maximum dose is 50 mg P.O. daily.

Geriatric or debilitated patients and patients with severe hepatic or renal disease: Initially, 10 mg (immediate-release formulation) P.O. daily, preferably in morning, as directed. If patient doesn't respond, increase by 10-mg/day increments at weekly intervals to maximum daily dose of 40 mg. The recommended initial dose of Paxil CR is 12.5 mg daily. Dosage should not exceed 50 mg daily.

▶ **Diabetic neuropathy‡.** *Adults:* 10 to 60 mg P.O. daily.

▶ **Headaches‡.** *Adults:* 10 to 50 mg P.O daily.

▶ **Premature ejaculation‡.** *Adults:* 20 mg P.O. daily.

Contraindications and precautions

• Contraindicated in patients taking MAO inhibitors or thioridazine.

• Use cautiously in patients with a history of seizures or mania; patients with severe, concomitant systemic illness; and patients at risk for volume depletion.

Lifespan: In pregnant and breast-feeding women, use cautiously. In children, safety of drug hasn't been established.

Adverse reactions

CNS: asthenia, blurred vision, somnolence, dizziness, insomnia, tremor, nervousness, anxiety, paresthesia, confusion.
CV: palpitations, vasodilation, orthostatic hypotension.
EENT: lump or tightness in throat, dysgeusia.
GI: *dry mouth, nausea, constipation, diarrhea,* taste perversion, increased or *decreased* appetite, flatulence, vomiting, dyspepsia, increased appetite.
GU: *ejaculatory disturbances, male genital disorders (including anorgasmy, erectile difficulties, delayed ejaculation or orgasm, impotence, and sexual dysfunction),* urinary frequency, other urinary disorder, *female genital disorder (including anorgasmy, difficulty with orgasm).*
Metabolic: hyponatremia.
Musculoskeletal: myopathy, myalgia, myasthenia.
Skin: *diaphoresis,* rash.
Other: decreased libido, yawning.

Interactions

Drug-drug. *Cimetidine:* Decreases hepatic metabolism of paroxetine, leading to risk of toxicity. Dosage adjustments may be necessary.
Digoxin: May decrease digoxin level. Monitor level closely.
MAO inhibitors: May increase risk of serious, sometimes fatal, adverse reactions. Don't use together.
Phenobarbital, phenytoin: May alter pharmacokinetics of both drugs. Dosage adjustments may be needed.
Procyclidine: May increase procyclidine levels. Monitor patient for excessive anticholinergic effects.
Sumatriptan: Weakness, hyperreflexia, and incoordination may occur. Monitor patient closely if used together.
Theophylline: Theophylline clearance may decrease threefold. Dosage reduction may be necessary.
Thioridazine: Prolongation of QT interval and increased risk of serious ventricular arrhythmias, such as torsades de pointes and sudden death. Avoid use together.
Tricyclic antidepressants: May inhibit TCA metabolism. Dose of TCA may need to be reduced. Monitor patient closely.
Tryptophan: May increase risk of adverse reactions, such as nausea and dizziness. Avoid using together.
Warfarin: Increases risk of bleeding. Use with caution; monitor patient closely for bleeding.
Drug-herb. *St. John's wort:* May result in sedative-hypnotic intoxication with concurrent ingestion of the herb. Discourage using together.
Drug-lifestyle. *Alcohol use:* May alter psychomotor function. Discourage using together.

Effects on lab test results

- May decrease sodium level.

Pharmacokinetics

Absorption: Completely absorbed.
Distribution: Distributed throughout body, including CNS; only 1% remains in plasma. About 93% to 95% bound to plasma protein.
Metabolism: About 36% metabolized in liver.
Excretion: About 64% excreted in urine. *Half-life:* About 24 hours.

Route	Onset	Peak	Duration
P.O. (immediate-release)	1-4 wk	2-8 hr	Unknown
P.O. (controlled-release)	Unknown	6-10 hr	Unknown

Pharmacodynamics

Chemical effect: Unknown; presumed to be linked to inhibition of CNS neuronal uptake of serotonin.
Therapeutic effect: Relieves depression.

Available forms

Tablets: 10 mg, 20 mg, 30 mg, 40 mg
Tablets (controlled-release): 12.5 mg, 25 mg, 37.5 mg

NURSING PROCESS

Assessment

- Assess patient's depression before therapy and regularly thereafter.
- Be alert for adverse reactions and drug interactions.
- Evaluate patient's and family's knowledge of drug therapy.

Nursing diagnoses

- Disturbed thought processes related to depression
- Risk for injury related to drug-induced adverse CNS reactions
- Deficient knowledge related to drug therapy

Planning and implementation

- Don't give drug with, or within 14 days of discontinuing, MAO inhibitor therapy. Allow at least 2 weeks after stopping paroxetine before starting an MAO inhibitor.
- Don't crush CR tablet. If patient cannot swallow a CR tablet whole, consider giving regular-release paroxetine hydrochloride.
- If signs of psychosis occur or increase, expect to reduce dosage.

ALERT: Don't confuse paroxetine with paclitaxel.

ALERT: Don't confuse Paxil with Taxol or Plavix.

Patient teaching

- Warn patient to avoid hazardous activities until CNS effects of drug are known.
- Warn patient that the Paxil CR tablet should not be chewed or crushed, and should be swallowed whole.
- Tell patient that he may notice improvement in 1 to 4 weeks but that he must continue with prescribed regimen to obtain continued benefits.
- Tell patient to abstain from alcohol during drug therapy.

ALERT: If patient wishes to switch from an SSRI to St. John's wort, tell him to wait a few weeks for the SSRI to fully leave his system before starting the herb. The exact time required will depend on which SSRI he takes.

Evaluation

- Patient's depression improves.
- Patient sustains no injuries because of drug-induced adverse CNS reactions.
- Patient and family state understanding of drug therapy.

pegaspargase (PEG-L-asparaginase)

(peg-AHS-per-jays)
Oncaspar

Pharmacologic class: modified version of enzyme L-asparaginase
Therapeutic class: antineoplastic
Pregnancy risk category: C

Indications and dosages

▶ **Acute lymphoblastic leukemia (ALL) in patients who need L-asparaginase but have developed hypersensitivity to native forms of L-asparaginase.** *Adults and children with body*

surface area of at least 0.6 m^2: 2,500 IU/m^2 I.M. or I.V. q 14 days.
Children with body surface area less than 0.6 m^2: 82.5 IU/kg I.M. or I.V. q 14 days.

Contraindications and precautions

- Contraindicated in patients with pancreatitis or history of pancreatitis; in those who have had significant hemorrhagic events with previous L-asparaginase therapy; and in those with previous serious allergic reactions, such as generalized urticaria, bronchospasm, laryngeal edema, hypotension, or other unacceptable adverse reactions to pegaspargase.
- Use cautiously in patients with liver dysfunction.

Lifespan: In pregnant and breast-feeding women, drug isn't recommended.

Adverse reactions

CNS: ***seizures,*** headache, paresthesia, ***status epilepticus,*** somnolence, ***coma,*** mental status changes, dizziness, emotional lability, mood changes, parkinsonism, confusion, disorientation, fatigue, malaise.
CV: hypotension, tachycardia, chest pain, subacute bacterial endocarditis, hypertension, edema.
EENT: epistaxis.
GI: nausea, vomiting, abdominal pain, anorexia, diarrhea, constipation, indigestion, flatulence, GI pain, mucositis, ***pancreatitis (sometimes fulminant and fatal),*** colitis, mouth tenderness.
GU: increased urinary frequency, hematuria, severe hemorrhagic cystitis, renal dysfunction, ***renal failure.***
Hematologic: ***thrombosis, leukopenia, pancytopenia, agranulocytosis, thrombocytopenia, disseminated intravascular coagulation,*** hemolytic anemia, easy bruising, ecchymosis, ***hemorrhage.***
Hepatic: jaundice, bilirubinemia, ascites, hypoalbuminemia, fatty changes in liver, ***liver failure.***
Metabolic: hyperuricemia, hyponatremia, uric acid nephropathy, hypoproteinemia, proteinuria, weight loss, ***metabolic acidosis,*** hyperglycemia, ***hypoglycemia.***
Musculoskeletal: arthralgia, myalgia, musculoskeletal pain, joint stiffness, cramps.
Respiratory: cough, ***severe bronchospasm,*** upper respiratory tract infection.
Skin: itching, alopecia, fever blister, purpura, white hands, urticaria, fungal changes, nail whiteness and ridging, erythema simplex, petechial rash, nighttime sweating.
Other: ***hypersensitivity reactions (including anaphylaxis,*** pain, fever, chills, peripheral edema; infection); ***sepsis; septic shock;*** injection pain or reaction; localized edema.

Interactions

Drug-drug. *Aspirin, dipyridamole, heparin, NSAIDs, warfarin:* Imbalances in coagulation factors may occur, predisposing patient to bleeding or thrombosis. Use together cautiously.
Methotrexate: May interfere with action of methotrexate, which requires cell replication for its lethal effect. Monitor patient for decreased effectiveness.
Protein-bound drugs: Protein depletion may increase toxicity of other drugs that bind to proteins. Monitor patient for toxicity. May interfere with enzymatic detoxification of other drugs, particularly in liver. Administer together with caution.

Effects on lab test results

- May increase BUN, creatinine, amylase, lipase, bilirubin, ALT, AST, uric acid, and ammonia levels. May decrease sodium and protein levels. May increase or decrease glucose level.
- May increase PT, INR, PTT, and thromboplastin. May decrease antithrombin III, fibrinogen, hemoglobin, hematocrit, and WBC, RBC, platelet, and granulocyte counts.

Pharmacokinetics

Absorption: Unknown.
Distribution: Unknown.
Metabolism: Unknown.
Excretion: Unknown.

Route	Onset	Peak	Duration
I.V., I.M.	Unknown	Unknown	Unknown

Pharmacodynamics

Chemical effect: Exerts cytotoxic effect by inactivating amino acid asparagine. Asparagine is required by tumor cells to synthesize proteins. Because tumor cells can't synthesize their own asparagine, protein synthesis and, eventually, synthesis of DNA and RNA are inhibited.

Therapeutic effect: Kills selected leukemic cells.

Available forms

Injection: 750 IU/ml

NURSING PROCESS

Assessment

- Assess patient's condition before therapy and regularly thereafter.
- Monitor patient closely for hypersensitivity reactions, including life-threatening anaphylaxis, which may occur during therapy, especially in patient hypersensitive to other forms of L-asparaginase.
- Monitor patient's peripheral blood count and bone marrow. A drop in circulating lymphoblasts is often noted after therapy begins. This may be accompanied by marked rise in uric acid levels.
- Monitor amylase levels to detect early evidence of pancreatitis. Monitor patient's glucose levels during therapy because hyperglycemia may occur.
- Monitor patient for liver dysfunction when pegaspargase is used with hepatotoxic chemotherapeutic agents.
- Drug may affect a number of plasma proteins; therefore, monitor fibrinogen, PT, and PTT. Question prescriber if not ordered.
- Be alert for adverse reactions and drug interactions.
- Evaluate patient's and family's knowledge of drug therapy.

Nursing diagnoses

- Ineffective health maintenance related to leukemia
- Ineffective protection related to drug-induced adverse hematologic reactions
- Deficient knowledge related to drug therapy

Planning and implementation

- Drug should be used as sole induction agent only in unusual situation when combined regimen that uses other chemotherapeutic drugs is inappropriate because of toxicity, because patient is refractory to other therapy, or because of other specific patient-related factors.
- Don't use drug that has been frozen. Although drug may not look different, freezing destroys its activity. Obtain new dose from pharmacist.
- Avoid excessive agitation; don't shake. Keep refrigerated at 36° to 46° F (2° to 8° C). Don't use if cloudy, precipitated, or stored at room temperature for more than 48 hours. Discard unused portions. Use only one dose per vial; don't reenter vial. Don't save unused drug for later use.
- Hydrate patient before treatment. Hyperuricemia may result from rapid lysis of leukemic cells. Allopurinol may be ordered.
- **I.V. use:** Give drug over 1 to 2 hours in 100 ml of normal saline solution or D_5W through infusion that is already running.
- **I.M. use:** I.M. route is preferred over I.V. route because of its lower risk of hepatotoxicity, coagulopathy, and GI and renal disorders.
- Limit volume administered at single injection site to 2 ml. If volume is larger than 2 ml, use multiple injection sites.
- Keep patient under observation for 1 hour and keep resuscitation equipment (such as epinephrine, oxygen, and I.V. steroids) within reach to treat anaphylaxis. Moderate to life-threatening hypersensitivity reactions require discontinuation of drug.
- Handle and administer solution with care. Gloves are recommended. Avoid inhalation of vapors and contact with skin or mucous membranes, especially in eyes. If contact occurs, wash with copious amounts of water for at least 15 minutes.

Patient teaching

- Inform patient about hypersensitivity reactions and importance of alerting staff at once if they occur.
- Instruct patient not to take other drugs, including OTC preparations, until approved by prescriber. Using together may increase risk of bleeding or may increase toxicity of other drugs.
- Instruct patient to report signs and symptoms of infection (fever, chills, and malaise) to prescriber because drug may suppress immune system.

Evaluation

- Patient responds well to therapy.
- Patient develops no serious complications caused by drug-induced adverse hematologic reactions.

• Patient and family state understanding of drug therapy.

pegfilgrastim
(peg-fil-gras-tim)
Neulasta

Pharmacologic class: colony-stimulating factor
Therapeutic class: neutrophil-growth stimulator
Pregnancy risk category: C

Indications and dosages

▶ **To reduce frequency of infection in patients with nonmyeloid malignancies receiving myelosuppressive anticancer drugs that may cause febrile neutropenia.** *Adults:* 6 mg S.C. once per chemotherapy cycle. Don't give in the period between 14 days before and 24 hours after administration of cytotoxic chemotherapy.

Contraindications and precautions

• Contraindicated in patients hypersensitive to *Escherichia coli*–derived proteins, filgrastim, or any component of the drug.
• Don't give from 14 days before to 24 hours after cytotoxic chemotherapy.
• Don't use for peripheral blood progenitor cell (PBPC) mobilization.
• Use cautiously in patients with sickle cell disease, those receiving chemotherapy causing delayed myelosuppression, or those receiving radiation therapy.
Lifespan: In pregnant women, use drug only if potential benefit to mother justifies potential risk to fetus. In breast-feeding women, use cautiously. Infants, children, and adolescents weighing less than 45 kg (99 lb) shouldn't use the 6-mg single-use syringe dose. In children, efficacy and safety haven't been established.

Adverse reactions

CNS: *dizziness, headache, fatigue, insomnia, fever.*
CV: *peripheral edema.*
GI: *nausea, diarrhea, vomiting, constipation, anorexia, taste perversion, dyspepsia, abdominal pain, stomatitis, mucositis.*
Hematologic: **GRANULOCYTOPENIA, NEUTROPENIC FEVER.**
Musculoskeletal: *skeletal pain, generalized weakness, arthralgia, myalgia, bone pain.*
Respiratory: ***adult respiratory distress syndrome (ARDS).***
Skin: *alopecia.*

Interactions

Drug-drug. *Lithium:* May increase the release of neutrophils. Monitor neutrophil counts closely.

Effects on lab test results

• May increase LDH, alkaline phosphatase, and uric acid levels.
• May increase WBC, granulocyte, and neutrophil counts.

Pharmacokinetics

Absorption: Unknown.
Distribution: Unknown.
Metabolism: Unknown.
Excretion: *Half-life:* 15 to 80 hours after S.C. injection.

Route	Onset	Peak	Duration
S.C.	Unknown	Unknown	Unknown

Pharmacodynamics

Chemical effect: Binds cell receptors to stimulate proliferation, differentiation, commitment, and end-cell function of neutrophils. Pegfilgrastim and filgrastim have the same mechanism of action. Pegfilgrastim has a reduced renal clearance and therefore a longer half-life than filgrastim.
Therapeutic effect: Increases WBC count.

Available forms

Injection: 6 mg/0.6 ml single-use, preservative-free, prefilled syringes.

NURSING PROCESS

Assessment

• Assess underlying condition before therapy and reassess regularly throughout therapy.
• Obtain CBC and platelet count before therapy.
• Monitor patient's hemoglobin, hematocrit, and CBC and platelet counts; and LDH, alka-

line phosphatase, and uric acid levels during therapy.
- Evaluate patient's and family's knowledge of pegfilgrastim therapy.

Nursing diagnoses
- Acute pain related to adverse musculoskeletal effects of drug
- Risk for infection related to underlying condition and treatment
- Deficient knowledge related to pegfilgrastim therapy

Planning and implementation
- The maximum amount of filgrastim that can be given is unknown. Treat patients having symptomatic leukocytosis with leukapheresis.

ALERT: Splenic rupture has occurred rarely with filgrastim use. Patient who experiences signs or symptoms of left upper abdominal or shoulder pain should be evaluated for an enlarged spleen or splenic rupture.
- Monitor patient for allergic-type reactions, including anaphylaxis, skin rash, and urticaria, which can occur with initial or subsequent treatment.
- Patient who develops fever, lung infiltrates, or respiratory distress should be evaluated for the development of ARDS. If ARDS occurs, discontinue drug.
- Keep patient with sickle cell disease well hydrated, and monitor patient for symptoms of sickle cell crisis.
- Pegfilgrastim may act as a growth factor for tumors.

Patient teaching
- Inform patient of the potential side effects of the drug.
- Tell patient to report signs and symptoms of allergic reactions, left upper abdominal or shoulder pain, fever, or breathing problems.
- Tell patient with sickle cell disease to maintain hydration and report signs or symptoms of sickle cell crisis.
- Instruct patient or caregiver how to give drug if it is to be given at home.
- Instruct patient or caregiver that the drug shouldn't be frozen. If accidentally frozen, thaw in refrigerator before administration. Drug should be discarded if frozen twice.

Evaluation
- Patient states that pain management is adequate.
- Patient's WBC count is normal.
- Patient and family state understanding of pegfilgrastim therapy.

peginterferon alfa-2b
(pehg-in-ter-FEAR-ahn)
PEG-Intron

Pharmacologic class: biological response modifier
Therapeutic class: antiviral
Pregnancy risk category: C

Indications and dosages
▶ **Chronic hepatitis C.** *Adults:* Give the following doses S.C. once weekly for 48 weeks on the same day each week based on weight:
37 to 45 kg (81 to 99 lb): 40 mcg (0.4 ml) of 100-mcg/ml strength
46 to 56 kg (100 to 123 lb): 50 mcg (0.5 ml) of 100-mcg/ml strength
57 to 72 kg (124 to 158 lb): 64 mcg (0.4 ml) of 160-mcg/ml strength
73 to 88 kg (159 to 194 lb): 80 mcg (0.5 ml) of 160-mcg/ml strength
89 to 106 kg (195 to 233 lb): 96 mcg (0.4 ml) of 240-mcg/ml strength
107 to 136 kg (234 to 299 lb): 120 mcg (0.5 ml) of 240-mcg/ml strength
137 to 160 kg (300 to 352 lb): 150 mcg (0.5 ml) of 300-mcg/ml strength
▶ **Chronic hepatitis C in patients not previously treated with interferon alpha, in combination with ribaviron.** *Adults:* Give S.C. once weekly for 48 weeks on same day each week, initial dose based on weight. Recommended regimen is 1.5 mcg/kg/week, based on weight as follows:
Less than 40 kg (<88 lb): 50 mcg (0.5ml) of 100-mcg/ml strength
40 to 50 kg (88 to 110 lb): 64 mcg (0.4 ml) of 160-mcg/ml strength
51 to 60 kg (111 to 132 lb): 80 mcg (0.5ml) of 160-mcg/ml strength
61 to 75 kg (133 to 165 lb): 96 mcg (0.4ml) of 240 mcg-mcg/ml strength
76 to 85 kg (166 to 187 lb): 120 mcg (0.5ml) of 240 mcg-mcg/ml strength

More than 85 kg (187 lb): 150 mcg (0.5 ml) of 300-mcg/ml strength

Decrease dose by 50% in patients who have WBC counts < 1,500/mm³, neutrophil counts < 750/mm³, or platelet counts < 80,000/mm³. Oral ribavirin dose can be continued. If hemoglobin < 10 g/dl, reduce oral ribavirin dose by 200 mg. Discontinue both drugs if hemoglobin < 8.5 g/dl, WBC counts < 1000/mm³, neutrophil counts < 500/mm³, or platelet counts < 50,000/mm³. If patient develops mild depression, peginterferon alfa-2b can be continued, but patient should be evaluated once weekly. If moderate depression, reduce peginterferon alfa-2b by 50% for 4 to 8 weeks and evaluate patient every week. If symptoms improve and remain stable for 4 weeks, continue at present dose or resume previous dose. If severe depression, discontinue peginterferon alfa-2b. For patients with preexisting stable cardiovascular disease, decrease peginterferon alfa-2b by 50% and ribavirin dosage by 200 mg daily if hemoglobin concentrations decrease > 2g/dl in any 4-week period. Discontinue both drugs if hemoglobin < 12 g/dl after 4 weeks of reduced dosages.

Contraindications and precautions

• Contraindicated in patients hypersensitive to peginterferon alfa-2b or its components. Also contraindicated in patients with autoimmune hepatitis or decompensated liver disease.
• Use cautiously in patients with psychiatric disorders; diabetes mellitus; cardiovascular disease; renal impairment (creatinine clearance below 50 ml/minute); pulmonary infiltrates; pulmonary function impairment; or autoimmune, ischemic, and infectious disorders.
• Don't use drug in patients who have failed other alpha interferon treatment, patients who have received liver or other organ transplants, or patients with HIV or hepatitis B virus.

Lifespan: Breast-feeding women must decide to discontinue breast-feeding or discontinue drug because of risk of adverse reactions to the infant. It isn't known whether drug appears in breast milk. In children younger than age 18, safety and effectiveness haven't been established.

Adverse reactions

CNS: dizziness, hypertonia, fever, depression, insomnia, anxiety, emotional lability, irritability, headache, fatigue, malaise, ***suicidal behavior.***
CV: flushing.
EENT: pharyngitis, sinusitis.
GI: nausea, anorexia, diarrhea, abdominal pain, vomiting, dyspepsia, right upper quadrant pain.
Hematologic: ***neutropenia, thrombocytopenia.***
Hepatic: hepatomegaly.
Metabolic: hypothyroidism, hyperthyroidism, weight decrease.
Musculoskeletal: musculoskeletal pain.
Respiratory: cough.
Skin: alopecia, pruritus, dry skin, rash, injection site reaction (inflammation), increased sweating, injection site pain.
Other: viral infection, flulike symptoms, rigors.

Interactions

None reported.

Effects on lab test results

• May increase ALT levels. May increase or decrease TSH levels.
• May decrease neutrophil and platelet counts.

Pharmacokinetics

Absorption: Levels peak 15 to 44 hours after a dose and persist for 48 to 72 hours.
Distribution: Unknown.
Metabolism: Mean elimination half-life is about 40 hours.
Excretion: About 30% is excreted by the kidneys.

Route	Onset	Peak	Duration
S.C.	Unknown	15-44 hr	Unknown

Pharmacodynamics

Chemical effect: Binds to specific membrane receptors on the cell surface, thereby inducing certain enzymes, suppressing cell proliferation, starting immunomodulation, and inhibiting virus replication in infected cells.
Therapeutic effect: Increases effector proteins and body temperature, and it decreases leukocyte and platelet counts.

Available forms

Injection: 100 mcg/ml, 160 mcg/ml, 240 mcg/ml, 300 mcg/ml

NURSING PROCESS

Assessment
- Assess underlying condition before therapy and reassess regularly throughout therapy.
- Assess patients for preexisting uncontrolled diabetes or thyroid disorders. Peginterferon alfa-2b may cause or aggravate hypothyroidism, hyperthyroidism, or diabetes.
- Obtain ECG before starting drug if patient has cardiac history.
- Evaluate patient's volume status and make sure patient is well hydrated before starting drug.
- Obtain eye examination in patients with diabetes or hypertension before starting drug. Retinal hemorrhages, cotton wool spots, and retinal artery or vein obstruction may occur.
- Monitor CBC, platelet count, and AST, ALT, bilirubin, and TSH levels before starting drug and periodically during treatment.
- Evaluate patient's and family's knowledge of peginterferon alfa-2b therapy.

Nursing diagnoses
- Ineffective health maintenance related to underlying condition
- Risk for suicide related to adverse CNS effects of drug
- Deficient knowledge related to peginterferon alfa-2b therapy

Planning and implementation
- If patient has history of MI or arrhythmias, watch closely for hypotension, arrhythmias, tachycardia, cardiomyopathy, and MI.
- Monitor patient for depression and other psychiatric illness. If symptoms are severe, discontinue drug and refer patient for psychiatric care.
- Monitor patient for signs and symptoms of colitis, such as abdominal pain, bloody diarrhea, and fever. Discontinue drug if colitis occurs. Symptoms should resolve 1 to 3 weeks after stopping drug.
- Monitor patient for signs and symptoms of pancreatitis or hypersensitivity reactions, and discontinue drug if these occur.
- Monitor patient with pulmonary disease for dyspnea, pulmonary infiltrates, pneumonitis, and pneumonia.
- If patient has renal disease, watch for signs and symptoms of toxicity.
- Stop drug if patient has severe neutropenia or thrombocytopenia.

Patient teaching
- Explain appropriate use of the drug and the benefits and risks of treatment. Tell patient that adverse reactions may continue for several months after treatment stops.
- Advise patient that laboratory tests are required before therapy starts and periodically thereafter.
- Tell patient to take drug at bedtime and to use antipyretics to decrease the effect of flulike symptoms.
- Emphasize the importance of properly disposing of needles and syringes, and caution against reusing old needles and syringes.
- Tell patient that drug isn't known to prevent transmission of hepatitis C. It also isn't known whether drug cures hepatitis C or prevents cirrhosis, liver failure, or liver cancer that may result from hepatitis C.
- Advise patient to immediately report symptoms of depression or thoughts of suicide.

Evaluation
- Patient has improved health.
- Patient denies suicidal ideation.
- Patient and family state understanding of peginterferon alfa-2b therapy.

pemoline
(PEH-moh-leen)
Cylert, Cylert Chewable, PemADD, PemADD CT

Pharmacologic class: oxazolidinedione derivative
Therapeutic class: analeptic
Pregnancy risk category: B
Controlled substance schedule: IV

Indications and dosages
▶ **Attention deficit hyperactivity disorder (ADHD).** *Children age 6 and older:* initially, 37.5 mg P.O. in morning. Increased by 18.75 mg/day q week, as necessary. Effective dosage range is 56.25 to 75 mg daily. Maximum dosage is 112.5 mg daily.

▶ **Narcolepsy‡.** *Adults:* 50 to 200 mg P.O. daily in divided doses after breakfast and after lunch.

Contraindications and precautions

- Contraindicated in patients hypersensitive to drug, in those who have idiosyncratic reactions to drug, and in those with hepatic dysfunction.
- Because of risk of hepatic failure, drug shouldn't be considered as first-line therapy.
- Use cautiously in patients with impaired renal function.

Lifespan: In children, drug may precipitate Tourette syndrome.

Adverse reactions

CNS: *insomnia,* malaise, dyskinetic movements, irritability, fatigue, mild depression, dizziness, headache, drowsiness, hallucinations, nervousness, ***seizures,*** *Tourette syndrome,* psychosis.
CV: *tachycardia.*
GI: anorexia, abdominal pain, nausea, diarrhea.
Hematologic: ***aplastic anemia.***
Hepatic: ***hepatitis,*** jaundice, ***hepatic failure.***
Skin: rash.

Interactions

Drug-drug. *Insulin, oral antidiabetics:* May decrease antidiabetic requirement. Monitor glucose levels.

Effects on lab test results

- May increase liver enzyme and prostate-specific antigen levels.
- May decrease hemoglobin and hematocrit.

Pharmacokinetics

Absorption: Well absorbed.
Distribution: Distribution is unknown. Drug is 50% protein-bound.
Metabolism: Metabolized in liver.
Excretion: Excreted in urine. *Half-life:* 12 hours.

Route	Onset	Peak	Duration
P.O.	Unknown	2-4 hr	Unknown

Pharmacodynamics

Chemical effect: May promote nerve impulse transmission by releasing stored norepinephrine from nerve terminals in brain, mainly in cerebral cortex and reticular activating system.
Therapeutic effect: Promotes calmness in children with ADHD.

Available forms

Tablets: 18.75 mg, 37.5 mg, 75 mg
Tablets (chewable and containing povidone): 37.5 mg

NURSING PROCESS

Assessment

- Assess patient's condition, including liver function test results, before and during therapy.
- May precipitate Tourette syndrome in child. Monitor patient closely, especially at start of therapy.
- Monitor patient for blood or hepatic function changes and growth suppression.
- Drug should be stopped if significant hepatic dysfunction occurs.
- Drug may produce adverse reactions similar to those from amphetamines or methylphenidate, including lowered seizure threshold. Has potential for abuse and dependence.
- Evaluate patient's and family's knowledge of drug therapy.

Nursing diagnoses

- Risk for injury related to ADHD
- Disturbed sleep pattern related to drug-induced insomnia
- Deficient knowledge related to drug therapy

Planning and implementation

- Give drug at least 6 hours before bedtime.

ALERT: Don't confuse pemoline with pelamine.

Patient teaching

- Warn patient and parent to avoid hazardous activities until effects of drug are known.
- Tell patient to report insomnia and other adverse effects.

Evaluation

- Patient shows less hyperactivity.
- Patient can sleep without difficulty throughout drug therapy.
- Patient and family state understanding of drug therapy.

penicillamine

(pen-ih-SIL-uh-meen)
Cuprimine, Depen

Pharmacologic class: chelating agent
Therapeutic class: heavy metal antagonist, antirheumatic
Pregnancy risk category: NR

Indications and dosages

▶ **Wilson's disease.** *Adults and children:* 250 mg P.O. q.i.d. 30 to 60 minutes before meals. Dosage adjusted to achieve urinary copper excretion of 0.5 to 1 mg daily.

▶ **Cystinuria.** *Adults:* 250 mg to 1 g P.O. q.i.d. before meals. Dosage adjusted to achieve urinary cystine excretion of less than 100 mg daily when renal calculi are present or 100 to 200 mg daily when no calculi are present. Maximum daily dosage is 4 g.
Children: 30 mg/kg P.O. daily divided q.i.d. before meals. Dosage adjusted to achieve urinary cystine excretion of less than 100 mg daily when renal calculi are present or 100 to 200 mg daily when no calculi are present.

▶ **Rheumatoid arthritis.** *Adults:* Initially, 125 to 250 mg P.O. daily, with increases of 125 to 250 mg q 1 to 3 months, if necessary. Maximum daily dosage is 1.5 g.

▶ **Adjunctive treatment of heavy metal poisoning‡.** *Adults:* 500 to 1,500 mg P.O. daily for 1 to 2 months.

▶ **Primary biliary cirrhosis‡.** *Adults:* Initially, 250 mg P.O. daily with increases of 250 mg P.O. q 2 weeks. Maximum daily dose is 1 g in divided doses.

Contraindications and precautions

• Contraindicated in patients with previous penicillamine-related aplastic anemia or granulocytosis, patients with rheumatoid arthritis and renal insufficiency.

• Use with extreme caution, if at all, in patients hypersensitive to penicillin.

Lifespan: In pregnant women, except those with Wilson's disease, drug is contraindicated. In breast-feeding women, safety of drug hasn't been established.

Adverse reactions

EENT: tinnitus, *optic neuritis.*
GI: *anorexia, epigastric pain, nausea, vomiting, diarrhea, loss of taste or altered taste perception, stomatitis.*
GU: nephrotic syndrome, glomerulonephritis, proteinuria, hematuria.
Hematologic: ***leukopenia,*** *eosinophilia,* ***thrombocytopenia,*** *monocytosis,* ***agranulocytopenia, aplastic anemia,*** lupus-like syndrome.
Hepatic: ***hepatotoxicity.***
Musculoskeletal: *arthralgia.*
Respiratory: *pneumonitis.*
Skin: alopecia; friability, especially at pressure spots; wrinkling; erythema; urticaria; ecchymoses.
Other: myasthenia gravis syndrome with long-term use, allergic reactions, *lymphadenopathy.*

Interactions

Drug-drug. *Antacids, oral iron:* Decreases effectiveness of D-penicillamine. Give at least 2 hours apart.
Antimalaria drugs, cytotoxic drugs, gold therapy, oxyphenbutazone, phenylbutazone: Increases risk of toxicity. Avoid giving together.
Digoxin: May decrease digoxin effect. Dosage adjustment may be required.
Drug-food. *Any food:* Delays absorption of drug. Give drug 1 hour before or 3 hours after meals.

Effects on lab test results

• May increase liver enzyme levels.
• May increase eosinophil count and sedimentation rate. May decrease hemoglobin, hematocrit, and platelet, WBC, and granulocyte counts.

Pharmacokinetics

Absorption: Well absorbed from GI tract.
Distribution: Limited data available.
Metabolism: Uncomplexed penicillamine is metabolized in liver to inactive disulfides.
Excretion: Only small amount of penicillamine excreted unchanged; after 24 hours, 50% of drug excreted in urine, 20% in feces, and 30% is unaccounted for.

Route	Onset	Peak	Duration
P.O.	Unknown	1 hr	Unknown

Pharmacodynamics

Chemical effect: Chelates heavy metals and may inhibit collagen formation; unknown for rheumatoid arthritis.

Therapeutic effect: Chelates copper in Wilson's disease, combines with cystine to form complex more soluble than cystine alone, and relieves symptoms of rheumatoid arthritis.

Available forms

Capsules: 125 mg, 250 mg
Tablets (scored): 250 mg

NURSING PROCESS

Assessment

- Obtain history of patient's underlying condition before therapy.
- Monitor effectiveness by evaluating patient's urinary copper or cysteine excretion or improvement in rheumatoid arthritis.
- Monitor CBC and kidney and liver function every 2 weeks for first 6 months, and then monthly.
- Monitor urinalysis regularly for protein loss.
- Check patient's range of motion and joint mobility.
- Be alert for adverse reactions and drug interactions.
- Evaluate patient's and family's knowledge of drug therapy.

Nursing diagnoses

- Impaired physical mobility related to Wilson's disease
- Impaired urinary elimination related to drug-induced renal dysfunction
- Deficient knowledge related to drug therapy

Planning and implementation

- Give dose on empty stomach to facilitate absorption, preferably 1 hour before or 3 hours after meals.
- Patient should receive supplemental pyridoxine daily.
- If patient has a skin reaction, give antihistamines. Handle patient carefully to avoid skin damage.

ALERT: Report rash and fever (important signs of toxicity) to prescriber immediately.

- Withhold drug and notify prescriber if WBC count falls below 3,500/mm^3 or platelet count falls below 100,000/mm^3. A progressive decline in platelet or WBC count in three successive blood tests may necessitate temporary cessation of therapy, even if such counts are within normal limits.

ALERT: Do not confuse penicillamine with penicillin.

Patient teaching

- Tell patient that therapeutic effect may be delayed up to 3 months in treatment of rheumatoid arthritis.
- Tell patient to maintain adequate fluid intake, especially at night.
- Advise patient to report early signs of granulocytopenia: fever, sore throat, chills, bruising, and prolonged bleeding time.
- Reassure patient that taste impairment usually resolves in 6 weeks without change in dosage.

Evaluation

- Patient reports increase in physical mobility.
- Patient maintains normal urinary elimination pattern.
- Patient and family state understanding of drug therapy.

penicillin G benzathine (benzylpenicillin benzathine)

(pen-ih-SIL-in gee BENZ-uh-theen)
Bicillin L-A, Permapen

Pharmacologic class: natural penicillin
Therapeutic class: antibiotic
Pregnancy risk category: B

Indications and dosages

▶ **Congenital syphilis.** *Children under age 2:* 50,000 units/kg I.M. as single dose.

▶ **Group A streptococcal upper respiratory tract infections.** *Adults:* 1.2 million units I.M. as single injection.
Children weighing more than 27 kg (59 lb): 900,000 units I.M. as single injection.
Children weighing less than 27 kg (59 lb): 300,000 to 600,000 units I.M. as single injection.

▶ **Prophylaxis of poststreptococcal rheumatic fever.** *Adults and children:* 1.2 million units I.M. once monthly or 600,000 units twice monthly.

*Liquid form contains alcohol. **May contain tartrazine. ◆Canada ◇Australia †OTC ‡Off-label use

▶ **Syphilis of less than 1 year's duration.**
Adults: 2.4 million units I.M. as single dose.
▶ **Syphilis of more than 1 year's duration.**
Adults: 2.4 million units I.M. weekly for 3 successive weeks.

Contraindications and precautions

• Contraindicated in patients hypersensitive to drug or other penicillins.
• Use cautiously in patients with other drug allergies, especially to cephalosporins.
Lifespan: In pregnant women, use cautiously. Drug appears in breast milk. In breast-feeding women, use of drug may sensitize infant to penicillin and cause some adverse effects.

Adverse reactions

CNS: pain, neuropathy, ***seizures.***
Hematologic: eosinophilia, hemolytic anemia, ***thrombocytopenia, leukopenia.***
Other: hypersensitivity reactions (maculopapular and exfoliative dermatitis, chills, fever, edema, ***anaphylaxis***), sterile abscess at injection site.

Interactions

Drug-drug. *Colestipol:* Decreases levels of penicillin G benzathine. Give penicillin 1 hour before or 4 hours after colestipol.
Heparin, oral anticoagulants: Increases risk of bleeding. Monitor PT, PTT, and INR and patient for bleeding.
Oral contraceptives: Decreases effectiveness of oral contraceptives, and increased breakthrough bleeding may occur. Advise patient to use alternate method during therapy.
Probenecid: Increases levels of penicillin. Probenecid may be used for this purpose.

Effects on lab test results

• May increase eosinophil count. May decrease hemoglobin, hematocrit, and platelet, WBC, and granulocyte counts.

Pharmacokinetics

Absorption: Absorbed slowly from I.M. injection site.
Distribution: Distributed widely into synovial, pleural, pericardial, and ascitic fluids; bile; and liver, skin, lungs, kidneys, muscle, intestines, tonsils, maxillary sinuses, saliva, and erythrocytes. CSF penetration is poor but enhanced in patients with inflamed meninges. Drug is 45% to 68% protein-bound.
Metabolism: Between 16% and 30% of drug is metabolized to inactive compounds.
Excretion: Excreted primarily in urine. *Half-life:* 30 to 60 minutes.

Route	Onset	Peak	Duration
I.M.	Unknown	13-24 hr	1-4 wk

Pharmacodynamics

Chemical effect: Inhibits cell wall synthesis during microorganism multiplication; bacteria resist penicillins by producing penicillinases, enzymes that convert penicillins to inactive penicilloic acid. Penicillin G benzathine resists these enzymes.
Therapeutic effect: Kills susceptible bacteria, such as most non–penicillinase-producing strains of gram-positive and gram-negative aerobic cocci; spirochetes; and some gram-positive aerobic and anaerobic bacilli.

Available forms

Injection: 600,000 units/ml, 1,200,000 units/dose, 2,400,000 units/dose

NURSING PROCESS

Assessment

• Assess patient's infection before therapy and regularly thereafter.
• Before giving drug, ask patient about allergic reactions to penicillin. However, negative history of penicillin allergy is no guarantee against future allergic reaction.
• Obtain specimen for culture and sensitivity tests before giving first dose. Therapy may begin pending results.
• Be alert for adverse reactions and drug interactions.
• Observe patient closely. Large doses and prolonged therapy raise the risk of bacterial or fungal superinfection, especially in geriatric, debilitated, or immunosuppressed patients.
• Evaluate patient's and family's knowledge of drug therapy.

Nursing diagnoses

• Infection related to presence of bacteria
• Ineffective protection related to risk of hypersensitivity reactions to drug
• Deficient knowledge related to drug therapy

Planning and implementation
- Shake drug well before injection.

ALERT: Never give drug I.V.; doing so has caused cardiac arrest and death.
- Inject deep into upper outer quadrant of buttocks in adult; in midlateral thigh in infant and young child. Avoid injection into or near major nerves or blood vessels to prevent neurovascular damage.
- Give drug at least 1 hour before bacteriostatic antibiotics.
- Drug's extremely slow absorption makes allergic reactions difficult to treat. Stop drug immediately if patient develops signs of anaphylactic shock (rapidly developing dyspnea and hypotension). Notify prescriber and prepare for immediate treatment with epinephrine, corticosteroids, antihistamines, and other resuscitative measures as indicated.

ALERT: Be aware of the various preparations of penicillin. They aren't interchangable.

ALERT: Don't confuse penicillin with penicillamine.

Patient teaching
- Tell patient to call prescriber if rash, fever, or chills develop.
- Warn patient that injection may be painful but that ice applied to site may ease discomfort.

Evaluation
- Patient is free from infection.
- Patient shows no signs of allergy.
- Patient and family state understanding of drug therapy.

penicillin G potassium (benzylpenicillin potassium)
(pen-ih-SIL-in gee poh-TAH-see-um)
Pfizerpen

Pharmacologic class: natural penicillin
Therapeutic class: antibiotic
Pregnancy risk category: B

Indications and dosages
▶ **Moderate-to-severe systemic infections.** *Adults:* 12 to 24 million units I.M. or I.V. daily in divided doses q 4 hours.
Children: 25,000 to 300,000 units/kg I.M. or I.V. daily in divided doses q 4 hours.

▶ **Anthrax.** *Adults:* 5 to 20 million units I.V. daily given in divided doses q 4 to 6 hours for at least 14 days after symptoms abate. Alternatively, may give 80,000 units/kg body weight in the first hour followed by a maintenance dose of 320,000 units/kg body weight daily. The average adult dose is 4 million units q 4 hours; can also be given as 2 million units q 2 hours.
Children: 100,000 to 150,000 units/kg I.V. daily in divided doses q 4 to 6 hours for at least 14 days after symptoms abate.
Patients with renal impairment: Refer to the table for dosage adjustments. If patient is uremic and creatinine clearance is > 10 ml/min, give full loading dose, then give ½ dose q 4 to 5 hr for additional doses.

Creatinine clearance (ml/min)	Dosage (after full loading dose)
10-50	Usual dose q 8-12 hr
< 10	50% of usual dose q 8-10 hr; or, give usual dose q 12-18 hr

Contraindications and precautions
- Contraindicated in patients hypersensitive to drug or other penicillins.
- Use cautiously in patients with other drug allergies, especially to cephalosporins.

Lifespan: In pregnant women, use cautiously. Drug appears in breast milk. In breast-feeding women, use of drug may sensitize infant to penicillin and cause some adverse effects.

Adverse reactions
CNS: neuropathy, ***seizures.***
Hematologic: hemolytic anemia, ***thrombocytopenia, leukopenia.***
Metabolic: ***severe potassium poisoning with high doses (hyperreflexia, seizures, coma).***
Other: hypersensitivity reactions (rash, urticaria, maculopapular eruptions, exfoliative dermatitis, chills, fever, edema, ***anaphylaxis***), overgrowth of nonsusceptible organisms, thrombophlebitis, pain at injection site.

Interactions
Drug-drug. *Heparin, oral anticoagulants:* Increases risk of bleeding. Monitor PT, PTT, and INR and patient for bleeding.

Oral contraceptives: Decreases effectiveness of oral contraceptives, and increased breakthrough bleeding may occur. Advise patient to use alternate method during therapy.
Potassium-sparing diuretics: May increase risk of hyperkalemia. Don't use together.
Probenecid: Increases levels of penicillin. Probenecid may be used for this purpose.

Effects on lab test results

- May increase potassium level.
- May increase eosinophil count. May decrease hemoglobin and hematocrit and platelet, WBC, and granulocyte counts.

Pharmacokinetics

Absorption: Absorbed rapidly from I.M. injection site.
Distribution: Distributed widely into synovial, pleural, pericardial, and ascitic fluids; bile; and liver, skin, lungs, kidneys, muscle, intestines, tonsils, maxillary sinuses, saliva, and erythrocytes. CSF penetration is poor but is enhanced in patients with inflamed meninges. Drug is 45% to 68% protein-bound.
Metabolism: Hepatic metabolism accounts for less than 30% of biotransformation of penicillin.
Excretion: Excreted primarily in urine. *Half-life:* 30 to 60 minutes.

Route	Onset	Peak	Duration
I.V.	Immediate	Immediate	Unknown
I.M.	Unknown	15-30 min	Unknown

Pharmacodynamics

Chemical effect: Inhibits cell wall synthesis during microorganism multiplication; bacteria resist penicillins by producing penicillinases, enzymes that convert penicillins to inactive penicilloic acid. Penicillin G potassium resists these enzymes.
Therapeutic effect: Kills susceptible bacteria, such as most non–penicillinase-producing strains of gram-positive and gram-negative aerobic cocci; spirochetes; and certain gram-positive aerobic and anaerobic bacilli.

Available forms

Injection (powder): 1 million units, 5 million units, 10 million units, 20 million units
Injection (premixed in dextrose): 20,000 units, 40,000 units, 60,000 units

NURSING PROCESS

Assessment

- Assess patient's infection before therapy and regularly thereafter.
- Before giving, ask patient about any allergic reactions to penicillin. However, negative history of penicillin allergy is no guarantee against future allergic reaction.
- Obtain specimen for culture and sensitivity tests before first dose. Therapy may begin pending results.
- Be alert for adverse reactions and drug interactions.
- Observe patient closely. Large doses and prolonged therapy raise the risk of bacterial or fungal superinfection, especially in geriatric, debilitated, or immunosuppressed patients.
- Evaluate patient's and family's knowledge of drug therapy.

Nursing diagnoses

- Infection related to presence of bacteria
- Ineffective protection related to risk of hypersensitivity reactions to drug
- Deficient knowledge related to drug therapy

Planning and implementation

- Reconstitute vials with sterile water for injection, D_5W, or normal saline solution for injection. Volume of diluent varies with manufacturer.
- Give drug at least 1 hour before bacteriostatic antibiotics.

ALERT: Be aware of the various preparations of penicillin. They aren't interchangable.

- Monitor level in patients taking large doses. A high level may lead to seizures. Take precautions.
- **I.V. use:** Use continuous I.V. infusion when large doses are required (10 million units or more). Otherwise, give via intermittent I.V. infusion over 1 to 2 hours.

– Aminoglycosides are physically and chemically incompatible with drug. Administer separately.

- **I.M. use:** Give drug deep into large muscle; may be painful.

ALERT: Don't confuse penicillamine with penicillin.

Patient teaching

- Tell patient to take drug exactly as prescribed, even after he feels better.
- Warn patient never to use leftover penicillin for a new illness or to share penicillin with family and friends.
- Tell patient to call prescriber if rash, fever, or chills develop.
- Warn patient that I.M. injection may be painful but that ice applied to site may ease discomfort.

Evaluation

- Patient is free from infection.
- Patient shows no signs of allergy.
- Patient and family state understanding of drug therapy.

penicillin G procaine (benzylpenicillin procaine)

(pen-ih-SIL-in gee PROH-kayn)
Wycillin

Pharmacologic class: natural penicillin
Therapeutic class: antibiotic
Pregnancy risk category: B

Indications and dosages

▶ **Moderate-to-severe systemic infections.** *Adults:* 600,000 to 1.2 million units I.M. daily in single dose.
Children older than age 1 month: 25,000 to 50,000 units/kg I.M. daily in single dose.
▶ **Uncomplicated gonorrhea.** *Adults and adolescents older than age 12:* 1 g probenecid; after 30 minutes, 4.8 million units of penicillin G procaine I.M., divided between two injection sites.
▶ **Pneumococcal pneumonia.** *Adults and adolescents older than age 12:* 600,000 units to 1.2 million units I.M. daily for 7 to 10 days.
▶ **Anthrax due to *Bacillus anthracis,* including inhalational anthrax (postexposure).** *Adults:* 1,200,000 units I.M. q 12 hours.
Children: 25,000 units/kg I.M. (maximum 1,200,000 units) q 12 hours.
▶ **Cutaneous anthrax.** *Adults:* 600,000 to 1 million units I.M. daily.

Contraindications and precautions

- Contraindicated in patients hypersensitive to drug or other penicillins.
- Use cautiously in patients with other drug allergies, especially to cephalosporins.

Lifespan: In pregnant women, use cautiously. Drug appears in breast milk. In breastfeeding women, use of drug may sensitize infant to penicillin and cause some adverse effects.

Adverse reactions

CNS: ***seizures.***
Hematologic: ***thrombocytopenia,*** hemolytic anemia, ***leukopenia.***
Musculoskeletal: arthralgia.
Other: hypersensitivity reactions (rash, urticaria, chills, fever, edema, prostration, ***anaphylaxis***), overgrowth of nonsusceptible organisms.

Interactions

Drug-drug. *Colestipol:* Decreases levels of penicillin G procaine. Give penicillin 1 hour before or 4 hours after colestipol.
Heparin, oral anticoagulants: Increases risk of bleeding. Monitor PT, PTT, and INR and patient for bleeding.
Oral contraceptives: Decreases effectiveness of oral contraceptives, and increased breakthrough bleeding may occur. Advise patient to use alternate method during therapy.
Probenecid: Increases blood levels of penicillin. Probenecid may be used for this purpose.

Effects on lab test results

- May increase eosinophil count. May decrease hemoglobin, hematocrit, and platelet, WBC, and granulocyte counts.

Pharmacokinetics

Absorption: Slow.
Distribution: Distributed widely into synovial, pleural, pericardial, and ascitic fluids; bile; and liver, skin, lungs, kidneys, muscle, intestines, tonsils, maxillary sinuses, saliva, and erythrocytes. CSF penetration usually poor, but enhanced in patients with inflamed meninges. Drug is 45% to 68% protein-bound.

Metabolism: From 16% to 30% metabolized to inactive compounds.
Excretion: Excreted primarily in urine. *Half-life:* 30 to 60 minutes.

Route	Onset	Peak	Duration
I.M.	Unknown	1-4 hr	1-2 days

Pharmacodynamics

Chemical effect: Inhibits cell wall synthesis during microorganism multiplication; bacteria resist penicillins by producing penicillinases, enzymes that convert penicillins to inactive penicilloic acid. Penicillin G procaine resists these enzymes.
Therapeutic effect: Kills susceptible bacteria, such as most non–penicillinase-producing strains of gram-positive and gram-negative aerobic cocci, spirochetes, and some gram-positive aerobic and anaerobic bacilli.

Available forms

Injection: 600,000 units/ml, 1,200,000 units/ml, 2,400,000 units/ml

NURSING PROCESS

Assessment

- Assess patient's infection before therapy and regularly thereafter.
- Before giving, ask patient about allergic reactions to penicillin. However, negative history of penicillin allergy is no guarantee against future allergic reaction.
- Obtain specimen for culture and sensitivity tests before giving first dose. Therapy may begin pending results.
- Be alert for adverse reactions and drug interactions.
- Observe patient closely. Large doses and prolonged therapy raise the risk of bacterial or fungal superinfection, especially in geriatric, debilitated, or immunosuppressed patients.
- Evaluate patient's and family's knowledge of drug therapy.

Nursing diagnoses

- Infection related to presence of bacteria
- Ineffective protection related to risk of hypersensitivity reactions to drug
- Deficient knowledge related to drug therapy

Planning and implementation

- Shake drug well before injection.
- Never give I.V.; doing so has caused cardiac arrest and death.
- Inject deep into upper outer quadrant of buttocks in adults; in midlateral thigh in infants and small children. Avoid injection into or near major nerves or blood vessels to prevent neurovascular damage.
- Give penicillin G procaine at least 1 hour before bacteriostatic antibiotics.
- Drug's extremely slow absorption makes allergic reactions difficult to treat. Stop drug immediately if patient develops signs of anaphylactic shock (rapidly developing dyspnea and hypotension). Notify prescriber and prepare for immediate treatment with epinephrine, corticosteroids, antihistamines, and other resuscitative measures as indicated.

ALERT: Be aware of the various preparations of penicillin. They aren't interchangable.

Patient teaching

- Tell patient to call prescriber if rash, fever, or chills develop.
- Warn patient that injection may be painful but that ice applied to site may ease discomfort.

Evaluation

- Patient is free from infection.
- Patient shows no signs of allergy.
- Patient and family state understanding of drug therapy.

penicillin G sodium (benzylpenicillin sodium)

(pen-ih-SIL-in gee SOH-dee-um)
Crystapen ♦

Pharmacologic class: natural penicillin
Therapeutic class: antibiotic
Pregnancy risk category: B

Indications and dosages

▶ **Moderate-to-severe systemic infections.** *Adults:* 12 to 24 million units daily I.M. or I.V. in divided doses q 4 to 6 hours.
Children: 25,000 to 300,000 units/kg daily I.M. or I.V. in divided doses q 4 to 6 hours.

▶ **Endocarditis prophylaxis for dental surgery.** *Adults and children weighing more than 27 kg (59 lb):* 2 million units I.V. or I.M. 30 to 60 minutes before procedure; then 1 million units 6 hours later.
Patients with renal impairment: Refer to the table for dosage adjustments. If patient is uremic and creatinine clearance is >10 ml/min, give full loading dose, then give one-half dose q 4 to 5 hr.

Creatinine clearance (ml/min)	Dosage (after full loading dose)
10-50	Usual dose q 8-12 hr
< 10	50% of usual dose q 8-10 hr; or, give usual dose q 12 to 18 hr

Contraindications and precautions

- Contraindicated in patients hypersensitive to drug or other penicillins.
- Use cautiously in patients with other drug allergies, especially to cephalosporins.

Lifespan: In pregnant women, use cautiously. Drug appears in breast milk. In breast-feeding women, use of drug may sensitize infant to penicillin and cause some adverse effects.

Adverse reactions

CNS: neuropathy, ***seizures.***
Hematologic: hemolytic anemia, ***leukopenia, thrombocytopenia.***
Musculoskeletal: arthralgia.
Other: hypersensitivity reactions (exfoliative dermatitis, urticaria, ***anaphylaxis***), overgrowth of nonsusceptible organisms, vein irritation, thrombophlebitis, pain at injection site.

Interactions

Drug-drug. *Colestipol:* Decreases levels of penicillin G sodium. Give penicillin 1 hour before or 4 hours after colestipol.
Heparin, oral anticoagulants: Increases risk of bleeding. Monitor PT, PTT, and INR and patient for bleeding.
Oral contraceptives: Decreases effectiveness of oral contraceptives and increased breakthrough bleeding may occur. Advise patient to use alternate method during therapy.
Probenecid: Increases blood levels of penicillin. Probenecid may be used for this purpose.

Effects on lab test results

- May increase eosinophil count. May decrease hemoglobin, hematocrit, and platelet, WBC, and granulocyte counts.

Pharmacokinetics

Absorption: Rapid.
Distribution: Distributed widely into synovial, pleural, pericardial, and ascitic fluids; bile; and liver, skin, lungs, kidneys, muscle, intestines, tonsils, maxillary sinuses, saliva, and erythrocytes. CSF penetration is poor but is enhanced in patients with inflamed meninges. Drug is 45% to 68% protein-bound.
Metabolism: 16% to 30% of drug is metabolized to inactive compounds.
Excretion: Excreted primarily in urine. *Half-life:* 30 to 60 minutes.

Route	Onset	Peak	Duration
I.V.	Immediate	Immediate	Unknown
I.M.	Unknown	15-30 min	Unknown

Pharmacodynamics

Chemical effect: Inhibits cell wall synthesis during microorganism multiplication; bacteria resist penicillins by producing penicillinases, enzymes that convert penicillins to inactive penicilloic acid. Penicillin G sodium resists these enzymes.
Therapeutic effect: Kills susceptible bacteria, such as most non–penicillinase-producing strains of gram-positive and gram-negative aerobic cocci, spirochetes, and some gram-positive aerobic and anaerobic bacilli.

Available forms

Injection: 5-million-unit vial

NURSING PROCESS

Assessment

- Assess patient's infection before therapy and regularly thereafter.
- Before giving, ask patient about allergic reactions to penicillin. However, negative history of penicillin allergy is no guarantee against future allergic reaction.
- Obtain specimen for culture and sensitivity tests before first dose. Therapy may begin pending results.
- Be alert for adverse reactions and drug interactions.

• Observe patient closely. Large doses and prolonged therapy raise the risk of bacterial or fungal superinfection, especially in geriatric, debilitated, or immunosuppressed patients.
• Evaluate patient's and family's knowledge of drug therapy.

Nursing diagnoses
• Infection related to presence of bacteria
• Ineffective protection related to risk of hypersensitivity reactions to drug
• Deficient knowledge related to drug therapy

Planning and implementation
• **I.V. use:** Reconstitute vials with sterile water for injection, normal saline solution for injection, or D_5W. Volume of diluent varies with manufacturer and concentration needed.
– For patient receiving 10 million units of drug or more daily, dilute in 1 to 2 liters of compatible solution and administer over 24 hours. Otherwise, give by intermittent I.V. infusion: Dilute drug in 50 to 100 ml and give over 1 to 2 hours q 4 to 6 hours.
– In neonate or child, give divided doses usually over 15 to 30 minutes.
– Aminoglycosides are physically and chemically incompatible with drug. Administer separately.
• **I.M. use:** Give drug deep in upper outer quadrant of buttocks in adult; in midlateral thigh in young child. Don't massage injection site. Avoid injection near major nerves or blood vessels to prevent neurovascular damage.
ALERT: Don't give by S.C. route.
• Give penicillin G sodium at least 1 hour before bacteriostatic antibiotics.
ALERT: Be aware of the various preparations of penicillin. They aren't interchangable.
• Monitor level in patient taking large doses. A high level may lead to seizures. Take precautions.
ALERT: Do not confuse penicillamine with penicillin.

Patient teaching
• Tell patient to report discomfort at I.V. site
• Warn patient that I.M. injection may be painful but that ice applied to site may ease discomfort.

Evaluation
• Patient is free from infection.
• Patient shows no signs of allergy.
• Patient and family state understanding of drug therapy.

penicillin V (phenoxymethylpenicillin)
(pen-ih-SIL-in VEE)

penicillin V potassium (phenoxymethylpenicillin potassium)
Abbocillin VK◇, Apo-Pen-VK◇, Beepen-VK, Cilicaine VK◇, Nadopen-V-200◆, Nadopen-V 400◆, Nadopen-V◆, Novo-Pen-VK◆, Nu-Pen-VK◆, Pen-Vee K, PVF K◆, PVK◇, V-Cillin K, Veetids**

Pharmacologic class: natural penicillin
Therapeutic class: antibiotic
Pregnancy risk category: B

Indications and dosages
▶ **Mild to moderate systemic infections.** *Adults:* 125 to 500 mg (200,000 to 800,000 units) P.O. q 6 hours.
Children: 15 to 50 mg/kg (25,000 to 90,000 units/kg) P.O. daily, in divided doses q 6 to 8 hours.
▶ **Endocarditis prophylaxis for dental surgery.** *Adults:* 2 g P.O. 30 to 60 minutes before procedure; then 500 mg P.O. q 6 hours for eight doses.
Children weighing less than 30 kg (66 lb): Give half of adult dose.
▶ **Necrotizing ulcerative gingivitis.** *Adults and children older than age 12:* 250 mg to 500 mg P.O. q 6 to 8 hours.
▶ **Prophylaxis for rheumatic fever.** *Adults and children:* 250 mg P.O. b.i.d.
▶ **Prophylaxis for pneumococcal infections‡.** *Children age 5 and older:* 250 mg P.O. b.i.d.
Children younger than age 5: 125 mg P.O. b.i.d.
▶ **Lyme disease‡.** *Adults:* 250 to 500 mg P.O. q.i.d. for 10 to 20 days.

Contraindications and precautions
• Contraindicated in patients hypersensitive to drug or other penicillins.

• Use cautiously in patients with other drug allergies, especially to cephalosporins.
Lifespan: In pregnant women, use cautiously. Drug appears in breast milk. In breast-feeding women, use of drug may sensitize infant to penicillin and cause some adverse effects.

Adverse reactions

CNS: neuropathy.
GI: *epigastric distress,* vomiting, diarrhea, *nausea.*
Hematologic: eosinophilia, hemolytic anemia, ***leukopenia, thrombocytopenia.***
Other: hypersensitivity reactions (rash, urticaria, chills, fever, edema, ***anaphylaxis***), overgrowth of nonsusceptible organisms.

Interactions

Drug-drug. *Oral contraceptives containing estrogen:* Decreases effectiveness of oral contraceptive. Monitor patient for breakthrough bleeding. Advise patient to use alternative forms of birth control.
Heparin, oral anticoagulants: Increases risk of bleeding. Monitor PT, PTT, and INR and patient for bleeding.
Probenecid: Increases level of penicillin. Probenecid may be used for this purpose.

Effects on lab test results

• May increase eosinophil count. May decrease hemoglobin, hematocrit, and platelet, WBC, and granulocyte counts.

Pharmacokinetics

Absorption: About 60% to 75%.
Distribution: Distributed widely into synovial, pleural, pericardial, and ascitic fluids; bile; and liver, skin, lungs, kidneys, muscle, intestines, tonsils, maxillary sinuses, saliva, and erythrocytes. CSF penetration is poor but is enhanced in patients with inflamed meninges. Drug is 75% to 89% protein-bound.
Metabolism: Between 35% and 70% metabolized to inactive compounds.
Excretion: Excreted primarily in urine. *Half-life:* 30 minutes.

Route	Onset	Peak	Duration
P.O.	Unknown	30-60 min	Unknown

Pharmacodynamics

Chemical effect: Inhibits cell wall synthesis during microorganism multiplication; bacteria resist penicillins by producing penicillinases. Penicillin V resists those enzymes.
Therapeutic effect: Kills susceptible bacteria, such as most non–penicillinase-producing strains of gram-positive and gram-negative aerobic cocci, spirochetes, and some gram-positive aerobic and anaerobic bacilli.

Available forms

penicillin V
Oral suspension: 125 mg/5 ml, 250 mg/5 ml (after reconstitution)
Tablets: 250 mg, 500 mg
penicillin V potassium
Capsules: 250 mg ◇
Oral suspension: 125 mg/5 ml, 250 mg/5 ml (after reconstitution)
Tablets: 125 mg, 250 mg, 500 mg
Tablets (film-coated): 250 mg, 500 mg

NURSING PROCESS

Assessment

• Assess patient's infection before therapy and regularly thereafter.
• Before giving drug, ask patient about any allergic reactions to penicillin. However, negative history of penicillin allergy is no guarantee against future allergic reaction.
• Obtain specimen for culture and sensitivity tests before giving first dose. Therapy may begin pending results.
• Periodically assess renal and hematopoietic function in patient receiving long-term therapy.
• Be alert for adverse reactions and drug interactions.
• Observe patient closely. Large doses and prolonged therapy raise the risk of bacterial or fungal superinfection, especially in geriatric, debilitated, or immunosuppressed patients.
• Evaluate patient's and family's knowledge of drug therapy.

Nursing diagnoses

• Infection related to presence of bacteria
• Ineffective protection related to risk of hypersensitivity reactions to drug
• Deficient knowledge related to drug therapy

Planning and implementation

- Give drug at least 1 hour before bacteriostatic antibiotics.
- American Heart Association considers amoxicillin the preferred drug for endocarditis prophylaxis because GI absorption is better and serum levels are sustained longer. Penicillin V is considered an alternative choice.

ALERT: Be aware of the various preparations of penicillin. They aren't interchangable.

ALERT: Don't confuse penicillamine with penicillin.

Patient teaching

- Tell patient to take drug exactly as prescribed, even after he feels better.
- Tell patient that drug may be taken without regard to meals. However, if GI disturbances occur, drug may be taken with meals.
- Warn patient never to use leftover penicillin V for new illness or to share penicillin with family and friends.
- Tell patient to call prescriber if rash, fever, or chills develop.

Evaluation

- Patient is free from infection.
- Patient shows no signs of allergy.
- Patient and family state understanding of drug therapy.

pentamidine isethionate

(pen-TAM-eh-deen ighs-eh-THIGH-oh-nayt)

NebuPent, Pentacarinat, Pentam 300

Pharmacologic class: diamidine derivative
Therapeutic class: antiprotozoal
Pregnancy risk category: C

Indications and dosages

▶ ***Pneumocystis carinii* pneumonia.** *Adults and children:* 4 mg/kg I.V. or I.M. once daily for 14 to 21 days.

▶ **Prevention of *P. carinii* pneumonia in high-risk patients.** *Adults:* 300 mg by inhalation (using Respirgard II nebulizer) once q 4 weeks.

Contraindications and precautions

- Contraindicated in patients with history of anaphylactic reaction to drug.
- Use cautiously in patients with hypertension, hypotension, hypoglycemia, hypocalcemia, leukopenia, thrombocytopenia, anemia, or hepatic or renal dysfunction.

Lifespan: In pregnant women, use cautiously. In breast-feeding women, drug isn't recommended.

Adverse reactions

CNS: confusion, fever, hallucinations.
CV: ***hypotension,*** tachycardia.
GI: nausea, anorexia, metallic taste.
GU: ***renal toxicity, acute renal failure.***
Hematologic: ***leukopenia, thrombocytopenia, anemia.***
Metabolic: ***hypoglycemia,*** hyperglycemia, hypocalcemia.
Respiratory: cough, ***bronchospasm.***
Skin: rash, facial flushing, pruritus, ***Stevens-Johnson syndrome.***
Other: *sterile abscess, pain and induration* at injection site.

Interactions

Drug-drug. *Aminoglycosides, amphotericin B, capreomycin, cisplatin, colistin, methoxyflurane, polymyxin B, vancomycin:* Increases risk of nephrotoxicity. Monitor patient closely.

Effects on lab test results

- May increase BUN, creatinine, potassium, and liver enzyme levels. May decrease calcium level. May increase or decrease glucose levels.
- May decrease hemoglobin, hematocrit, and WBC and platelet counts.

Pharmacokinetics

Absorption: Limited after aerosol administration. Unknown after I.M. administration.
Distribution: Drug appears to be extensively tissue-bound. CNS penetration is poor. Extent of plasma protein–binding is unknown.
Metabolism: Unknown.
Excretion: Excreted unchanged in urine. *Half-life:* Varies according to route of administration: 9 to 13¼ hours for I.M., about 6½ hours for I.V., and unknown for aerosol.

Route	Onset	Peak	Duration
I.V.	Unknown	Immediate	Unknown
I.M.	Unknown	30 min-1 hr	Unknown
Aerosol	Unknown	Unknown	Unknown

Pharmacodynamics

Chemical effect: Interferes with organism's biosynthesis of DNA, RNA, phospholipids, and proteins.
Therapeutic effect: Hinders growth of susceptible organisms, such as *P. carinii* and *Trypanosoma.*

Available forms

Aerosol: 300-mg vial
Injection: 300-mg vial

NURSING PROCESS

Assessment

- Assess patient's infection before therapy and regularly thereafter.
- Monitor glucose, calcium, creatinine, and BUN levels daily. After parenteral administration, glucose level may decrease initially; hypoglycemia may be severe in 5% to 10% of patients. This may be followed by hyperglycemia and insulin-dependent diabetes mellitus, which may be permanent.
- Closely monitor blood pressure during I.V. administration.
- Be alert for adverse reactions and drug interactions.
- Evaluate patient's and family's knowledge of drug therapy.

Nursing diagnoses

- Infection related to presence of organisms
- Risk for injury related to drug-induced adverse CNS reactions
- Deficient knowledge related to drug therapy

Planning and implementation

- **I.V. use:** Reconstitute drug with 3 ml of sterile water for injection; then dilute in 50 to 250 ml of D_5W. Inject over at least 1 hour.
  – To minimize hypotension, infuse drug slowly with patient lying down.
- **I.M. use:** Reconstitute drug with 3 ml of sterile water for solution containing 100 mg/ml; administer deeply. Expect pain and induration.
- In patient with AIDS, pentamidine may produce less severe adverse reactions than co-trimoxazole, the alternative treatment, and may be treatment of choice.
- **Aerosol use:** Administer aerosol form only by Respirgard II nebulizer manufactured by Marquest. Dosage recommendations are based on particle size and delivery rate of this device.
  – To use aerosol, mix contents of one vial in 6 ml of sterile water for injection. Don't use normal saline solution; it will cause precipitation.
  – Don't mix with other drugs.
  – Don't use low-pressure (below 20 pounds per square inch [psi]) compressors. The flow rate should be 5 to 7 liters/minute from 40- to 50-psi air or oxygen source.

Patient teaching

- Instruct patient to use aerosol device until chamber is empty, which may take up to 45 minutes.
- Warn patient that I.M. injection is painful. However, application of warm soaks is helpful.
- Stress need to report light-headedness or signs and symptoms of hypoglycemia immediately.

Evaluation

- Patient is free from infection.
- Patient sustains no injuries because of drug-induced adverse CNS reactions.
- Patient and family state understanding of drug therapy.

pentazocine hydrochloride

(pen-TAZ-oh-seen high-droh-KLOR-ighd)
Fortral ◇

pentazocine hydrochloride and acetaminophen

Talacen

pentazocine hydrochloride and aspirin

Talwin Compound

pentazocine hydrochloride and naloxone hydrochloride

Talwin NX

pentazocine lactate

Fortral ◇, Talwin

Pharmacologic class: narcotic agonist-antagonist, opioid partial agonist

Therapeutic class: analgesic, adjunct to anesthesia
Pregnancy risk category: C
Controlled substance schedule: IV

Indications and dosages

▶ **Moderate-to-severe pain.** *Adults:* 50 to 100 mg Talwin NX P.O. q 3 to 4 hours, p.r.n. Maximum oral dosage is 600 mg daily. Or, 2 tablets Talwin Compound P.O. t.i.d. or q.i.d. Or, 1 tablet Talacen P.O. q 4 hours, up to 6 tablets daily. Or, 30 mg I.M., I.V., or S.C. q 3 to 4 hours, p.r.n. Maximum total parenteral dosage is 360 mg in 24 hours. Single doses above 30 mg I.V. or 60 mg I.M. or S.C. aren't recommended.
▶ **Labor.** *Adults:* 30 mg I.M. or 20 mg I.V. q 2 to 3 hours when contractions become regular.

Contraindications and precautions

• Contraindicated in patients hypersensitive to drug or its components.
• Use cautiously in patients with hepatic or renal disease, acute MI, head injury, increased intracranial pressure, or respiratory depression.
Lifespan: In pregnant and breast-feeding women, use cautiously. In children younger than age 12, drug isn't recommended. Geriatric patients may be more sensitive to adverse CNS effects of drug.

Adverse reactions

CNS: *sedation,* visual disturbances, hallucinations, drowsiness, *dizziness, light-headedness,* confusion, *euphoria,* headache, psychotomimetic effects.
CV: hypotension, ***shock.***
EENT: dry mouth, dysgeusia.
GI: *nausea, vomiting,* constipation.
GU: urine retention.
Respiratory: ***respiratory depression.***
Skin: induration, nodules, sloughing, and sclerosis of injection site.
Other: ***hypersensitivity reactions (anaphylaxis),*** physical and psychological dependence.

Interactions

Drug-drug. *CNS depressants:* May have additive effects. Use together cautiously.
Fluoxetine: May cause diaphoresis, ataxia, flushing, and tremor. Use together cautiously.
Narcotic analgesics: May decrease analgesic effect. Avoid using together.
Drug-lifestyle. *Alcohol use:* May have additive effects. Discourage using together.
Smoking: May increase requirements for pentazocine. Monitor drug's effectiveness; urge patient to stop smoking.

Effects on lab test results

• May interfere with laboratory tests for urinary 17-hydroxycorticosteroids.

Pharmacokinetics

Absorption: Well absorbed after P.O. or parenteral administration, although P.O. form undergoes first-pass metabolism in liver and less than 20% of dose reaches systemic circulation unchanged. Bioavailability is increased in patients with hepatic dysfunction; patients with cirrhosis absorb 60% to 70% of drug.
Distribution: Appears to be widely distributed throughout body.
Metabolism: Metabolized in liver. Metabolism may be prolonged in patients with impaired hepatic function.
Excretion: Excreted primarily in urine, with very small amounts excreted in feces. *Half-life:* 2 to 3 hours.

Route	Onset	Peak	Duration
P.O.	15-30 min	60-90 min	2-3 hr
I.V.	2-3 min	15-30 min	2-3 hr
I.M., S.C.	15-20 min	30-60 min	2-3 hr

Pharmacodynamics

Chemical effect: Binds with opioid receptors at many sites in CNS, altering pain response by unknown mechanism.
Therapeutic effect: Relieves pain.

Available forms

pentazocine hydrochloride
Tablets: 25 mg◇, 50 mg◇
pentazocine hydrochloride and acetaminophen
Tablets: 25 mg pentazocine hydrochloride and 650 mg acetaminophen
pentazocine hydrochloride and aspirin
Tablets: 12.5 mg pentazocine hydrochloride and 325 mg aspirin
pentazocine hydrochloride and naloxone hydrochloride
Tablets: 50 mg pentazocine hydrochloride and 500 mcg naloxone hydrochloride
pentazocine lactate
Injection: 30 mg/ml

NURSING PROCESS

Assessment
- Assess patient's pain before and after drug administration.
- Monitor vital signs closely, especially respirations.
- Be alert for adverse reactions and drug interactions.
- Evaluate patient's and family's knowledge of drug therapy.

Nursing diagnoses
- Acute pain related to condition
- Ineffective breathing pattern related to drug-induced respiratory depression
- Deficient knowledge related to drug therapy

Planning and implementation
- **P.O. use:** Talwin NX, the oral pentazocine available in the U.S., contains the narcotic antagonist naloxone, which prevents illicit I.V. use.
- **I.V. use:** Give drug by direct I.V. injection. Administer slowly. Don't mix in same syringe with aminophylline, barbiturates, or other alkaline substances.
- **I.M. and S.C. use:** Rotate injection sites to minimize tissue irritation. If possible, avoid giving by S.C. route.
- Drug has narcotic antagonist properties. May precipitate withdrawal syndrome in narcotic-dependent patient.
- Dependence may occur with prolonged use.

ALERT: Hold drug and notify prescriber if respiratory rate drops significantly. Have naloxone readily available to reverse respiratory depression.

Patient teaching
- Caution ambulatory patient about getting out of bed or walking. Warn outpatient to avoid hazardous activities until CNS effects of drug are known.
- Warn patient about the risk of dependence.

Evaluation
- Patient is free from pain.
- Patient maintains respiratory rate and pattern within normal limits.
- Patient and family state understanding of drug therapy.

pentobarbital (pentobarbitone)
(pen-toh-BAR-beh-tol)
Nembutal* **

pentobarbital sodium
Carbrital ◇, Nembutal Sodium*

Pharmacologic class: barbiturate
Therapeutic class: anticonvulsant, sedative-hypnotic
Pregnancy risk category: D
Controlled substance schedule: II

Indications and dosages
▶ **Sedation.** *Adults:* 20 to 40 mg P.O. b.i.d., t.i.d., or q.i.d.
Children: 2 to 6 mg/kg daily P.O. or P.R. in three divided doses. Maximum daily dosage is 100 mg.
▶ **Hypnotic.** *Adults:* 100 to 200 mg P.O. h.s. or 150 to 200 mg I.M. Or, initially, 100 mg I.V. with additional small doses, to a total of 500 mg. Or, 120 or 200 mg P.R.
Children: 2 to 6 mg/kg I.M. Maximum dosage is 100 mg. P.R. doses are 30 mg for patients ages 2 months to 1 year, 30 or 60 mg for patients ages 1 to 4, 60 mg for patients ages 5 to 12, and 60 or 120 mg for patients ages 12 to 14.
▶ **Preoperative sedation.** *Adults:* 150 to 200 mg I.M.
Children age 10 or older: 5 mg/kg P.O. or I.M.
Children younger than age 10: 5 mg/kg P.R.

Contraindications and precautions
- Contraindicated in patients with porphyria or hypersensitivity to barbiturates.
- Use cautiously in debilitated patients and in those with acute or chronic pain, depression, suicidal tendencies, history of drug abuse, or hepatic impairment.

Lifespan: In pregnant and breast-feeding women, drug isn't recommended. In geriatric patients, use cautiously.

Adverse reactions
CNS: *drowsiness, lethargy, hangover,* paradoxical excitement in geriatric patients.
GI: nausea, vomiting.
Hematologic: worsening of porphyria.
Respiratory: ***respiratory depression.***

Skin: rash, urticaria, ***Stevens-Johnson syndrome.***
Other: ***angioedema.***

Interactions

Drug-drug. *Corticosteroids, doxycycline, estrogens and oral contraceptives, oral anticoagulants:* Pentobarbital may enhance metabolism of these drugs. Monitor patient for decreased effect.
CNS depressants, including narcotic analgesics: Excessive CNS and respiratory depression may occur. Use together cautiously.
Griseofulvin: Decreases absorption of griseofulvin. Separate administration times.
MAO inhibitors: Inhibits barbiturate metabolism and prolongs CNS depression. Reduce barbiturate dosage.
Rifampin: May decrease barbiturate levels. Monitor patient for decreased effect.
Drug-lifestyle. *Alcohol use:* May cause excessive CNS and respiratory depression. Discourage using together.

Effects on lab test results

None reported.

Pharmacokinetics

Absorption: Rapid after P.O. or P.R. administration. Unknown after I.M. administration.
Distribution: Distributed widely throughout body. About 35% to 45% of drug is protein-bound.
Metabolism: Metabolized in liver.
Excretion: 99% of drug is excreted in urine. *Half-life:* 35 to 50 hours.

Route	Onset	Peak	Duration
P.O.	≤ 15 min	30-60 min	1-4 hr
I.V.	Immediate	Immediate	15 min
I.M.	10-25 min	Unknown	Unknown
P.R.	≤ 15 min	Unknown	1-4 hr

Pharmacodynamics

Chemical effect: Unknown; may interfere with transmission of impulses from thalamus to cortex of brain.
Therapeutic effect: Promotes sleep and calmness.

Available forms

pentobarbital
Elixir: 20 mg/5 ml
pentobarbital sodium
Capsules: 50 mg, 100 mg
Injection: 50 mg/ml
Suppositories: 30 mg, 60 mg, 120 mg, 200 mg

NURSING PROCESS

Assessment

- Assess patient's condition before therapy and regularly thereafter.
- Geriatric patients are more sensitive to adverse CNS effects of drug.
- Inspect patient's skin. Skin eruptions may precede life-threatening reactions to barbiturate therapy.
- Be alert for adverse reactions and drug interactions.
- Evaluate patient's and family's knowledge of drug therapy.

Nursing diagnoses

- Disturbed sleep pattern related to condition
- Risk for injury related to drug-induced adverse CNS reactions
- Deficient knowledge related to drug therapy

Planning and implementation

- **P.O. use:** Follow normal protocol.
- **I.V. use:** I.V. use of barbiturates may cause severe respiratory depression, laryngospasm, or hypotension. Have emergency resuscitation equipment available.

– To minimize deterioration, use I.V injection solution within 30 minutes after opening container. Don't use cloudy solution.
– Reserve I.V. injection for emergency treatment, which should be given under close supervision. Give slowly (50 mg/minute or less).
– Parenteral solution is alkaline. Local tissue reactions and injection site pain have followed I.V. use. Avoid extravasation. Assess patency of I.V. site before and during administration.
– Don't mix with other drugs in syringe or in I.V. solutions or lines.

- **I.M. use:** Give I.M. injection deeply. Superficial injection may cause pain, sterile abscess, and sloughing.
- **P.R. use:** To ensure accurate dosage, don't divide suppositories.

ALERT: Stop drug and notify prescriber if skin reactions occur. In some patients, high fever, stomatitis, headache, or rhinitis may precede skin reactions.

• Pentobarbital has no analgesic effect and may cause restlessness or delirium in patient with pain.
• Long-term use isn't recommended; drug loses its efficacy in promoting sleep after 14 days of continued use. Long-term high doses may cause dependence and may lead to withdrawal symptoms if drug is suddenly discontinued. Withdraw barbiturates gradually.
ALERT: Don't confuse pentobarbital with phenobarbital.

Patient teaching
• Warn patient about performing activities that require alertness or physical coordination. For inpatient, particularly geriatric patient, supervise walking and raise bed rails.
• Inform patient that morning hangover is common after hypnotic dose, which suppresses REM sleep. Patient may experience increased dreaming after therapy stops.
• Tell patient who uses oral contraceptives that she should consider a different birth control method because drug may decrease contraceptive effect.

☑ Evaluation
• Patient reports satisfactory sleep.
• Patient sustains no injuries from drug-induced adverse CNS reactions.
• Patient and family state understanding of drug therapy.

pentostatin (2′-deoxycoformycin)
(pen-toh-STAH-tin)
Nipent

Pharmacologic class: antimetabolite (adenosine deaminase [ADA] inhibitor)
Therapeutic class: antineoplastic
Pregnancy risk category: D

Indications and dosages
▶ **Alpha-interferon–refractory hairy-cell leukemia.** *Adults:* 4 mg/m² I.V. every other week.

Contraindications and precautions
• Contraindicated in patients hypersensitive to drug and in patients with renal damage (creatinine clearance of 60 ml/minute or less).

Lifespan: In pregnant and breast-feeding women, drug isn't recommended. In children, safety of drug hasn't been established.

Adverse reactions
CNS: pain, asthenia, malaise, fever, *headache, neurologic symptoms, anxiety, confusion, depression, dizziness, insomnia, nervousness, paresthesia, somnolence, abnormal thinking, fatigue.*
CV: chest pain, ***arrhythmias,*** abnormal ECG, thrombophlebitis, peripheral edema, ***hemorrhage.***
EENT: abnormal vision, conjunctivitis, ear pain, eye pain, epistaxis, pharyngitis, rhinitis, sinusitis.
GI: abdominal pain, nausea, vomiting, anorexia, diarrhea, constipation, flatulence, stomatitis.
GU: *hematuria, dysuria.*
Hematologic: ***myelosuppression,*** **LEUKOPENIA,** anemia, **THROMBOCYTOPENIA,** ***lymphocytopenia,*** lymphadenopathy.
Metabolic: weight loss.
Musculoskeletal: back pain, myalgia, arthralgia.
Respiratory: *cough, bronchitis, dyspnea,* ***pulmonary edema,*** *pneumonia.*
Skin: diaphoresis, photosensitivity reaction, contact dermatitis, ecchymosis, petechiae, rash, eczema, dry skin, herpes simplex or zoster, maculopapular rash, vesiculobullous rash, pruritus, seborrhea, discoloration.
Other: **INFECTION, HYPERSENSITIVITY REACTIONS,** ***neoplasm,*** chills, sepsis, flulike syndrome.

Interactions
Drug-drug. *Cytarabine, vidarabine:* Increases adverse reactions to either drug. Avoid using together.
Fludarabine: Increases risk of fatal pulmonary toxicity. Don't use together.

Effects on lab test results
• May increase BUN, creatinine, liver enzyme, and uric acid levels.
• May decrease hemoglobin, hematocrit, and platelet, WBC, lymphocyte, and granulocyte counts.

Pharmacokinetics
Absorption: Administered I.V.

Distribution: Plasma protein–binding is low (about 4%).
Metabolism: Unknown.
Excretion: Over 90% excreted in urine. *Half-life:* About 6 hours.

Route	Onset	Peak	Duration
I.V.	Unknown	Unknown	Unknown

Pharmacodynamics

Chemical effect: Inhibits ADA, causing increase in intracellular levels of deoxyadenosine triphosphate. This leads to cell damage and death. Greatest activity of ADA is in cells of lymphoid system (especially malignant T cells).
Therapeutic effect: Kills certain leukemic cells.

Available forms

Powder for injection: 10 mg/vial

NURSING PROCESS

Assessment

- Assess patient's condition before therapy and regularly thereafter.
- Be alert for adverse reactions and drug interactions.
- Evaluate patient's and family's knowledge of drug therapy.

Nursing diagnoses

- Ineffective health maintenance related to leukemia
- Ineffective protection related to drug-induced adverse hematologic reactions
- Deficient knowledge related to drug therapy

Planning and implementation

- Use drug only in patients with hairy-cell leukemia refractory to alpha-interferon (disease that progresses after minimum of 3 months of treatment with alpha-interferon or disease that doesn't respond after 6 months of therapy).
- Use drug only under supervision of prescriber qualified and experienced in use of chemotherapy drugs. Adverse reactions after therapy are common.
- Make sure patient is well hydrated before therapy. For hydration, administer 500 to 1,000 ml of dextrose 5% in half-normal saline solution for injection.
- Follow facility policy to reduce risks. Preparation and administration of parenteral form are linked to mutagenic, teratogenic, and carcinogenic risks for staff.
- Add 5 ml of sterile water for injection to vial containing pentostatin powder for injection. Mix thoroughly to make solution of 5 mg/ml. Drug may be administered by I.V. bolus injection or diluted further in 25 or 50 ml of D_5W or normal saline solution for injection and infused over 20 to 30 minutes.
- Use reconstituted solution within 8 hours; it contains no preservatives.
- Treat all spills and waste products with 5% sodium hypochlorite (household bleach).
- Give additional 500 ml of D_5W for hydration after drug is administered.
- Optimal duration of therapy is unknown. Current recommendations suggest two additional courses of therapy after complete response. If partial response isn't evident after 6 months, drug will be discontinued. If partial response is evident, drug will be continued for another 6 months or for two courses of therapy after complete response.
- Withhold drug in patients with CNS toxicity, severe rash, or active infection and notify prescriber. Drug may be resumed when infection clears.
- Temporarily withhold drug and notify prescriber if absolute neutrophil count falls below $200/mm^3$ and pretreatment level was over $500/mm^3$. No recommendations exist for dosage adjustments in patients with anemia, neutropenia, or thrombocytopenia.

ALERT: Don't confuse pentostatin with pentosan.

Patient teaching

- Teach patient how to take infection-control and bleeding precautions.
- Tell patient to notify prescriber of adverse reactions.

Evaluation

- Patient responds well to therapy.
- Patient doesn't develop serious complications from adverse reactions.
- Patient and family state understanding of drug therapy.

pentoxifylline

(pen-tok-SIH-fi-lin)
Trental

Pharmacologic class: xanthine derivative
Therapeutic class: hemorrheologic
Pregnancy risk category: C

Indications and dosages

▶ **Intermittent claudication caused by chronic occlusive vascular disease.** *Adults:* 400 mg P.O. t.i.d. with meals.

Contraindications and precautions

- Contraindicated in patients who are intolerant of methylxanthines, such as caffeine and theophylline, and in those with recent cerebral or retinal hemorrhage.

Lifespan: In pregnant women, use cautiously. In breast-feeding women, drug isn't recommended. In children, safety of drug hasn't been established.

Adverse reactions

CNS: headache, dizziness.
GI: dyspepsia, nausea, vomiting.

Interactions

Drug-drug. *Anticoagulants:* Increases anticoagulant effect. Adjust anticoagulant dosage; monitor patient for bleeding.
Antihypertensives: Increases hypotensive effect. Dosage adjustments may be necessary; monitor patient's blood pressure closely.
Theophylline: Increases theophylline level. Monitor level; adjust theophylline dosage.
Drug-lifestyle. *Smoking:* Vasoconstriction may result. Advise patient to avoid smoking because it may worsen his condition.

Effects on lab test results

None reported.

Pharmacokinetics

Absorption: Almost complete but slowed by food. Undergoes first-pass hepatic metabolism.
Distribution: Bound by erythrocyte membrane.
Metabolism: Metabolized extensively by erythrocytes and liver.
Excretion: Excreted primarily in urine; less than 4% of drug is excreted in feces. *Half-life:* About 30 to 45 minutes.

Route	Onset	Peak	Duration
P.O.	Unknown	2-4 hr	Unknown

Pharmacodynamics

Chemical effect: Unknown; thought to increase RBC flexibility and lower blood viscosity.
Therapeutic effect: Improves capillary blood flow.

Available forms

Tablets (extended-release): 400 mg
Tablets (controlled-release): 400 mg

NURSING PROCESS

Assessment

- Assess patient's condition before therapy and regularly thereafter.
- Be alert for adverse reactions and drug interactions.
- Be aware that geriatric patients may be more sensitive to drug's effects.
- Monitor patient's hydration status if adverse GI reactions occur.
- Evaluate patient's and family's knowledge of drug therapy.

Nursing diagnoses

- Ineffective peripheral tissue perfusion related to condition
- Risk for deficient fluid volume related to drug-induced adverse GI reactions
- Deficient knowledge related to drug therapy

Planning and implementation

- Drug is useful in patients who aren't good surgical candidates.
- Report adverse reactions to prescriber; dosage may need to be reduced.

ALERT: Don't confuse Trental with Trendar or Trandate.

Patient teaching

- Advise patient to take drug with meals to minimize GI upset.
- Instruct patient to swallow drug whole, without breaking, crushing, or chewing.
- Tell patient to report adverse GI or CNS reactions.

• Advise patient to avoid smoking because nicotine causes vasoconstriction that can worsen his condition.
• Tell patient not to stop drug during first 8 weeks of therapy unless directed by prescriber.

Evaluation

• Patient has adequate peripheral tissue perfusion.
• Patient maintains adequate hydration throughout therapy.
• Patient and family state understanding of drug therapy.

pergolide mesylate

(PER-goh-lighd MES-ih-layt)
Permax

Pharmacologic class: dopaminergic agonist
Therapeutic class: antiparkinsonian
Pregnancy risk category: B

Indications and dosages

▶ **Adjunct treatment with levodopa-carbidopa in management of symptoms caused by Parkinson's disease.** *Adults:* Initially, 0.05 mg P.O. daily for first 2 days followed by increased dosage of 0.1 to 0.15 mg q third day over 12 days. Subsequent dosage increased by 0.25 mg q third day until optimum response is seen, if needed. Drug usually is given in divided doses t.i.d. Gradual reductions in levodopa-carbidopa dosage may be made during dosage adjustment.

Contraindications and precautions

• Contraindicated in patients hypersensitive to drug or ergot alkaloids.
• Use cautiously in patients prone to arrhythmias, and in patients with a history of pleuritis, pleural effusion, pleural fibrosis, pericarditis, pericardial effusion, cardiac valvulopathy or retroperitoneal fibrosis.
Lifespan: In pregnant women, use cautiously. In children and breast-feeding women, safety of drug hasn't been established.

Adverse reactions

CNS: headache, asthenia, *dyskinesia, dizziness, hallucinations,* dystonia, confusion, *somnolence,* syncope, insomnia, anxiety, depression, tremor, abnormal dreams, personality disorder, psychosis, abnormal gait, akathisia, extrapyramidal syndrome, incoordination, akinesia, hypertonia, neuralgia, speech disorder, twitching paresthesia.
CV: chest pain; *orthostatic hypotension;* vasodilation; palpitations; hypotension; hypertension; ***arrhythmias; MI;*** facial, peripheral, or generalized edema.
EENT: *rhinitis,* epistaxis, abnormal vision, diplopia, eye disorder.
GI: dry mouth, dysgeusia, abdominal pain, *nausea, constipation,* diarrhea, dyspepsia, anorexia, vomiting.
GU: urinary frequency, urinary tract infection, hematuria.
Metabolic: weight gain.
Musculoskeletal: neck and back pain, arthralgia, bursitis, myalgia.
Skin: diaphoresis, rash.
Other: flulike syndrome, chills, infection.

Interactions

Drug-drug. *Butyrophenones, metoclopramide, other dopamine antagonists, phenothiazines, thioxanthenes:* May antagonize effects of pergolide. Avoid using together.

Effects on lab test results

None reported.

Pharmacokinetics

Absorption: Well absorbed.
Distribution: Drug is about 90% protein-bound.
Metabolism: Metabolized to at least 10 different compounds, some of which retain pharmacologic activity.
Excretion: Excreted mainly by kidneys.

Route	Onset	Peak	Duration
P.O.	Unknown	Unknown	Unknown

Pharmacodynamics

Chemical effect: Directly stimulates dopamine receptors in nigrostriatal system.
Therapeutic effect: Helps to relieve signs and symptoms of Parkinson's disease.

Available forms

Tablets: 0.05 mg, 0.25 mg, 1 mg

NURSING PROCESS

Assessment
- Assess patient's condition before therapy. Monitor drug effectiveness by regularly checking patient's body movements for improvement.
- Monitor blood pressure and heart rate and rhythm. Symptomatic orthostatic or sustained hypotension may occur in some patients, especially at start of therapy. Drug also may induce arrhythmias.
- Be alert for adverse reactions and drug interactions.
- Evaluate patient's and family's knowledge of drug therapy.

Nursing diagnoses
- Impaired physical mobility related to Parkinson's disease
- Decreased cardiac output related to drug-induced adverse CV reactions
- Deficient knowledge related to drug therapy

Planning and implementation
- Dosage is gradually increased according to patient's response and tolerance.
- Notify prescriber if patient has significant changes in vital signs or mental status.

Patient teaching
- Inform patient of potential adverse reactions, especially hallucinations and confusion.
- Warn patient to avoid activities that could result in injury from orthostatic hypotension and syncope.

Evaluation
- Patient has improved mobility.
- Patient maintains cardiac output.
- Patient and family state understanding of drug therapy.

perindopril erbumine
(PER-in-doh-pril ER-buh-mighn)
Aceon

Pharmacologic class: ACE inhibitor
Therapeutic class: antihypertensive
Pregnancy risk category: C (first trimester), D (second and third trimesters)

Indications and dosages
▶ **Treatment of essential hypertension.** *Adults:* Initially, 4 mg P.O. once daily. Increase until blood pressure is controlled or a maximum of 16 mg daily is reached. Usual maintenance dosage 4 to 8 mg daily; may be divided into two doses.
Adults older than age 65: Initially, 4 mg P.O. daily as one dose or two divided doses. Daily dosage increases exceeding 8 mg should occur only under close medical supervision.
Patients with renal impairment (creatinine clearance above 30 ml/minute): Initially, 2 mg P.O. daily with a maximum maintenance dosage of 8 mg daily.
Patients taking diuretics: Initially, 2 to 4 mg P.O. daily as one dose or divided into two doses with close medical supervision for several hours and until blood pressure has stabilized. Adjust dosage based on patient's blood pressure response.

Contraindications and precautions
- Contraindicated in patients hypersensitive to perindopril or any other ACE inhibitor. Also contraindicated in patients with a history of angioedema secondary to ACE inhibitors.
- Use cautiously in patients with a history of angioedema unrelated to ACE inhibitor therapy. Also use cautiously in patients with impaired renal function, heart failure, ischemic heart disease, cerebrovascular disease, renal artery stenosis, or collagen vascular disease, such as systemic lupus erythematosus or scleroderma.

Lifespan: In pregnant women, drug is contraindicated.

Adverse reactions
CNS: dizziness, asthenia, fever, sleep disorder, paresthesia, depression, somnolence, nervousness, *headache.*
CV: palpitations, edema, chest pain, abnormal ECG.
EENT: rhinitis, sinusitis, ear infection, pharyngitis, tinnitus.
GI: dyspepsia, diarrhea, abdominal pain, nausea, vomiting, flatulence.
GU: proteinuria, urinary tract infection, sexual dysfunction in men, menstrual disorder.
Metabolic: ***hyperkalemia.***
Musculoskeletal: back pain, hypertonia, neck pain, joint pain, myalgia, arthritis, leg or arm pain.

Respiratory: *cough,* upper respiratory tract infection.
Skin: rash.
Other: viral infection, injury, seasonal allergy.

Interactions

Drug-drug. *Antacids:* Decreases drug bioavailability. Separate administration times by at least 2 hours.
Diuretics: May have additive hypotensive effect. Monitor patient closely.
Lithium: Increases lithium levels and possible lithium toxicity. Use together cautiously, and monitor lithium levels. Use of a diuretic may further increase the risk of lithium toxicity.
Potassium supplements, potassium-sparing diuretics (spironolactone, amiloride, triamterene), other drugs capable of increasing serum potassium (indomethacin, heparin, cyclosporine): May have additive hyperkalemic effect. Use together cautiously, and monitor potassium levels frequently.
Drug-herb. *Capsaicin:* Increases risk of cough. Discourage using together.
Licorice: May cause sodium retention and increase blood pressure, interfering with therapeutic effects of ACE inhibitors. Discourage using together.
Drug-food. *Salt substitutes containing potassium:* May increase risk of hyperkalemia. Use together cautiously.

Effects on lab test results

• May increase ALT, triglyceride, and potassium levels.

Pharmacokinetics

Absorption: Rapid; level peaks at about 1 hour. Absolute P.O. bioavailability of perindopril is around 75%. Plasma perindopril and perindoprilat levels are about doubled in geriatric patients.
Distribution: Perindopril and perindoprilat are about 60% and 10% to 20% bound to plasma proteins, respectively. Drug interaction resulting from effects on protein-binding isn't anticipated.
Metabolism: Extensively metabolized by the liver to the active ACE inhibitor, perindoprilat.
Excretion: About 4% to 12% of drug is excreted in the urine as unchanged drug. Clearance is reduced in geriatric patients and patients with heart failure or renal insufficiency.

Route	Onset	Peak	Duration
P.O.	Unknown	1 hour	Unknown

Pharmacodynamics

Chemical effect: This is a prodrug converted by the liver to the active metabolite perindoprilat. Perindoprilat probably inhibits ACE activity, thereby preventing conversion of angiotensin I to angiotensin II, a potent vasoconstrictor. ACE inhibition results in decreased vasoconstriction and decreased aldosterone, thus reducing sodium and water retention.
Therapeutic effect: Lowers blood pressure.

Available forms

Tablets: 2 mg, 4 mg, 8 mg

NURSING PROCESS

Assessment

• Obtain complete medical history before therapy.
• Monitor CBC with differential before therapy, especially in renally impaired patients with systemic lupus erythematosus or scleroderma. Other ACE inhibitors have been linked to agranulocytosis and neutropenia.
• Monitor renal function before and periodically throughout therapy. Drug shouldn't be used in patients with a creatinine clearance less than 30 ml/minute.
• Assess patient for volume or sodium depletion as a result of prolonged diuretic therapy, dietary salt restriction, dialysis, diarrhea, or vomiting.
• Monitor potassium level closely.
• If patient is at risk for hypotension, watch closely during first dose, for the first 2 weeks of treatment, and whenever the dose of perindopril or a diuretic, if prescribed, is increased. If severe hypotension occurs, place patient in supine position and treat symptomatically.
• Evaluate patient's and family's knowledge of drug therapy.

Nursing diagnoses

• Risk for injury related to presence of hypertension
• Risk for activity intolerance related to drug-induced adverse effects

• Deficient knowledge related to drug therapy

Planning and implementation

• Correct volume and salt depletion before starting drug.

ALERT: Angioedema of the face, limbs, lips, tongue, glottis, and larynx has been reported in patients treated with perindopril. Angioedema involving the tongue, glottis, or larynx may cause fatal airway obstruction. Appropriate therapy, such as S.C. epinephrine solution, should be promptly given. Discontinue drug, notify prescriber, and observe patient until the swelling resolves.

• Swelling confined to the face and lips will probably resolve without treatment, but antihistamines may help relieve symptoms.

• Patients with a history of angioedema unrelated to ACE inhibitor therapy may be at increased risk of angioedema while receiving an ACE inhibitor.

• Excessive hypotension can occur when drug is given with diuretics. If possible, diuretic therapy should be stopped 2 to 3 days before starting perindopril. If diuretic can't be stopped, prescriber may consider starting perindopril at a reduced dosage, decreasing the diuretic dosage, or both.

• ACE inhibitors rarely are linked to a fatal syndrome of cholestatic jaundice and fulminant hepatic necrosis. Notify prescriber and stop drug if patient develops jaundice or marked elevation of hepatic enzyme levels during therapy.

Patient teaching

• Inform patient that angioedema, including laryngeal edema, can occur during therapy, especially with the first dose. Advise patient to stop taking the drug and immediately report any signs or symptoms that suggest angioedema (swelling of face, limbs, eyes, lips, tongue; hoarseness or difficulty in swallowing or breathing).

• Advise patient to report promptly any sign of infection (sore throat, fever) or jaundice (yellowing of eyes or skin).

• Advise patient to avoid salt substitutes containing potassium unless instructed otherwise by prescriber.

• Caution patient that light-headedness may occur, especially during the first few days of therapy. Advise patient to report light-headedness and, if fainting occurs, to discontinue the drug and consult prescriber promptly.

• Caution patient that inadequate fluid intake or excessive perspiration, diarrhea, or vomiting can lead to an excessive drop in blood pressure.

• Advise patient to notify prescriber immediately if she suspects pregnancy.

Evaluation

• Patient's blood pressure is controlled and he remains free of injury.

• Patient has no adverse effects that limit mobility.

• Patient and family state understanding of drug therapy.

perphenazine

(per-FEN-uh-zeen)

Apo-Perphenazine ♦, Trilafon, Trilafon Concentrate

Pharmacologic class: phenothiazine (piperazine derivative)
Therapeutic class: antipsychotic, antiemetic
Pregnancy risk category: NR

Indications and dosages

▶ **Psychosis in nonhospitalized patients.** *Adults:* Initially, 4 to 8 mg P.O. t.i.d., reduced as soon as possible to minimum effective dosage.
Children older than age 12: Lowest adult dose.

▶ **Psychosis in hospitalized patients.** *Adults:* Initially, 8 to 16 mg P.O. b.i.d., t.i.d., or q.i.d., increase to 64 mg daily, p.r.n. Or, 5 to 10 mg I.M. q 6 hours, p.r.n. Maximum daily I.M. dose shouldn't exceed 30 mg.
Children older than age 12: Lowest limit of adult dosage.

▶ **Severe nausea and vomiting.** *Adults:* 5 to 10 mg I.M., p.r.n.

Contraindications and precautions

• Contraindicated in patients hypersensitive to drug; patients experiencing coma; those with CNS depression, blood dyscrasia, bone marrow depression, liver damage, or subcortical damage; and those receiving large doses of CNS depressants.

• Use cautiously with other CNS depressants or anticholinergics. Also use cautiously in debilitated patients and patients with alcohol withdrawal, psychic depression, suicidal tendency, severe adverse reactions to other phenothiazines, impaired renal function, or respiratory disorders.

Lifespan: In pregnant and breast-feeding women and in geriatric patients, use cautiously. In children age 12 and younger, safety of drug hasn't been established.

Adverse reactions

CNS: *extrapyramidal reaction, tardive dyskinesia,* sedation, pseudoparkinsonism, EEG changes, dizziness, ***seizures, neuroleptic malignant syndrome.***
CV: *orthostatic hypotension,* tachycardia, ECG changes, ***cardiac arrest.***
EENT: ocular changes, blurred vision.
GI: dry mouth, constipation.
GU: *urine retention,* dark urine, menstrual irregularities, inhibited ejaculation.
Hematologic: transient ***leukopenia,*** hyperprolactinemia, ***agranulocytosis, hemolytic anemia, thrombocytopenia.***
Hepatic: cholestatic jaundice.
Metabolic: weight gain, increased appetite.
Skin: *mild photosensitivity reaction,* allergic reactions, pain at I.M. injection site, sterile abscess.
Other: gynecomastia.

Interactions

Drug-drug. *Antacids:* Inhibits oral phenothiazine absorption. Administer drugs separately.
Anticonvulsants: Phenothiazines may lower the seizure threshold. Monitor patient.
Barbiturates: May decrease phenothiazine effect. Observe patient closely.
Bromocriptine: Decreases bromocriptine effectiveness. Monitor patient for clinical effect.
Lithium: Causes severe neurological toxicity with encephalitis-like syndrome; decreased therapeutic response to perphenazine. Don't use together.
Other CNS depressants: Increases CNS depression. Avoid using together.
Drug-herb. *Dong quai, St. John's wort:* Increases photosensitivity reactions. Discourage using together.
Evening primrose oil: May increase risk of seizures. Discourage using together.
Kava: Increases risk of dystonic reactions. Discourage using together.
Milk thistle: Decreases liver toxicity caused by phenothiazines. Monitor liver enzyme levels.
Yohimbe: Increases risk of yohimbe toxicity. Discourage using together.
Drug-lifestyle. *Alcohol use:* Increases CNS depression. Discourage using together.
Sun exposure: Increases photosensitivity reaction. Urge patient to avoid unprotected or prolonged exposure to sunlight.

Effects on lab test results

• May increase prolactin levels.
• May increase liver function test values and eosinophil count. May decrease hemoglobin, hematocrit, and WBC, granulocyte, and platelet counts.

Pharmacokinetics

Absorption: Rate and extent vary. Erratic and variable for P.O. tablet; much more predictable for P.O. concentrate. Rapid from I.M. injection.
Distribution: Distributed widely; 91% to 99% of drug is protein-bound.
Metabolism: Metabolized extensively by liver.
Excretion: Most of drug excreted in urine; some in feces.

Route	Onset	Peak	Duration
P.O., I.M.	Varies	Unknown	Unknown

Pharmacodynamics

Chemical effect: Unknown; probably blocks postsynaptic dopamine receptors in brain and inhibits medullary chemoreceptor trigger zone.
Therapeutic effect: Relieves signs and symptoms of psychosis; also relieves nausea and vomiting.

Available forms

Injection: 5 mg/ml
Oral concentrate: 16 mg/5 ml*
Syrup: 2 mg/5 ml ♦
Tablets: 2 mg, 4 mg, 8 mg, 16 mg

NURSING PROCESS

Assessment

• Assess patient's condition before therapy and regularly thereafter.
• Obtain baseline blood pressure before therapy, and monitor regularly. Watch for orthosta-

tic hypotension, especially with I.M. administration.
- Monitor weekly bilirubin tests during first month; periodic blood tests (CBC and liver function); and ophthalmic tests (long-term use).
- Be alert for adverse reactions and drug interactions.
- Monitor patient for tardive dyskinesia, which may occur after prolonged use. It may not appear until months or years later and may disappear spontaneously or persist for life despite discontinuation of drug.
- Monitor patient's hydration status if drug is used for nausea and vomiting.
- Evaluate patient's and family's knowledge of drug therapy.

Nursing diagnoses
- Disturbed thought processes related to psychosis
- Risk for deficient fluid volume related to nausea or vomiting
- Deficient knowledge related to drug therapy

Planning and implementation
- **P.O. use:** Dilute liquid concentrate with fruit juice, milk, carbonated beverage, or semisolid food just before giving.
  – Concentrate causes turbidity or precipitation in colas, black coffee, grape or apple juice, or tea. Don't mix with them.
- **I.M. use:** Inject drug deep in upper outer quadrant of buttocks. Injection may sting.
  – Massage slowly afterward to prevent sterile abscess.
  – Keep patient supine for 1 hour after injection because of risk of hypotension.
- Prevent contact dermatitis by keeping drug away from skin and clothes. Wear gloves when preparing liquid forms.
- Protect drug from light. Slight yellowing of injection or concentrate doesn't affect potency. Discard markedly discolored solutions.
- Don't stop drug abruptly unless severe adverse reactions demand it. After abrupt withdrawal of long-term therapy, patient may experience gastritis, nausea, vomiting, dizziness, tremors, feeling of warmth or cold, diaphoresis, tachycardia, headache, or insomnia.
- Withhold dose and notify prescriber if patient develops jaundice, symptoms of blood dyscrasia (fever, sore throat, infection, cellulitis, weakness), or persistent extrapyramidal reactions (longer than a few hours).
- Acute dystonic reactions may be treated with diphenhydramine.

ALERT: Don't confuse perphenazine with prochlorperazine.

Patient teaching
- Advise patient to change positions slowly to minimize effects of orthostatic hypotension.
- Teach patient which fluids are appropriate for dilution of concentrate (see "P.O. use").
- Warn patient to avoid hazardous activities until CNS effects of drug are known. Drowsiness and dizziness usually subside after a few weeks.
- Tell patient to avoid alcohol during drug therapy.
- Advise patient to report urine retention or constipation.
- Tell patient to use sunblock and to wear protective clothing to avoid photosensitivity reactions.
- Tell patient to relieve dry mouth with sugarless gum or hard candy.

Evaluation
- Patient's thought processes are normal.
- Patient maintains adequate hydration throughout drug therapy.
- Patient and family state understanding of drug therapy.

phenazopyridine hydrochloride (phenylazo diamino pyridine hydrochloride)

(fen-eh-soh-PEER-eh-deen high-droh-KLOR-ighd)

Azo-Dine, Azo-Gesic, Azo-Standard†, Baridium†, Geridium, Phenazo♦, Prodium†, Pyridiate, Pyridium, Pyridium Plus, Re-Azo, Urodine†, Urogesic, UTI Relief

Pharmacologic class: azo dye
Therapeutic class: urinary analgesic
Pregnancy risk category: B

Indications and dosages

▶ **Urinary tract irritation or infection.**
Adults: 200 mg P.O. t.i.d.

Children: 12 mg/kg P.O. daily divided into three equal doses.

Contraindications and precautions

• Contraindicated in patients with glomerulonephritis, severe hepatitis, uremia, or renal insufficiency.

Lifespan: In pyelonephritis during pregnancy, drug is contraindicated. In breast-feeding women, safety of drug hasn't been established. In children, use cautiously.

Adverse reactions

CNS: headache, vertigo.
GI: nausea.
Skin: rash.

Interactions

None significant.

Effects on lab test results

• May decrease hemoglobin and hematocrit.
• May alter urine glucose results when Diastix is used.

Pharmacokinetics

Absorption: Unknown.
Distribution: Unknown.
Metabolism: Metabolized in liver.
Excretion: Excreted in urine.

Route	Onset	Peak	Duration
P.O.	Unknown	Unknown	Unknown

Pharmacodynamics

Chemical effect: Unknown; has local anesthetic effect on urinary mucosa.
Therapeutic effect: Relieves urinary tract pain.

Available forms

Tablets: 95 mg†, 97 mg, 97.2 mg, 100 mg†, 150 mg, 200 mg

NURSING PROCESS

Assessment

• Assess patient's pain before and after drug administration.
• Be alert for adverse reactions.
• Monitor patient's hydration status if nausea occurs.
• Evaluate patient's and family's knowledge of drug therapy.

Nursing diagnoses

• Acute pain related to underlying urinary tract condition
• Risk for deficient fluid volume related to drug-induced nausea
• Deficient knowledge related to drug therapy

Planning and implementation

• Administer drug with food to minimize nausea.

ALERT: Don't confuse Pyridium with pyridoxine or pyridine.

Patient teaching

• Advise patient that taking drug with meals may minimize nausea.
• Caution patient to stop taking drug and to notify prescriber if skin or sclera becomes yellow-tinged.
• Alert patient that drug colors urine red or orange. It may stain fabrics and contact lenses.
• Tell patient to notify prescriber if urinary tract pain persists. Drug isn't for long-term therapy.

Evaluation

• Patient is free from pain.
• Patient maintains adequate hydration.
• Patient and family state understanding of drug therapy.

phenobarbital (phenobarbitone)

(feen-oh-BAR-bih-tol)
Solfoton

phenobarbital sodium (phenobarbitone sodium)

Luminal Sodium

Pharmacologic class: barbiturate
Therapeutic class: anticonvulsant, sedative-hypnotic
Pregnancy risk category: D
Controlled substance schedule: IV

Indications and dosages

▶ **All forms of epilepsy except absence seizures; febrile seizures in children.** *Adults:* 60 to 250 mg P.O. daily, in divided doses t.i.d. or as single dose h.s.

Children: 1 to 6 mg/kg P.O. daily, divided q 12 hours for total of 100 mg; can be given once daily, usually h.s.

▶ **Status epilepticus.** *Adults:* 10 to 20 mg/kg I.V.; may repeat, if necessary.
Children: 15 to 20 mg/kg I.V. Don't exceed 50 mg/minute.

▶ **Sedation.** *Adults:* 30 to 120 mg P.O. daily in two or three divided doses.
Children: 3 to 5 mg/kg P.O. daily in divided doses t.i.d.

▶ **Insomnia.** *Adults:* 100 to 200 mg P.O. or I.M. h.s.

▶ **Preoperative sedation.** *Adults:* 100 to 200 mg I.M. 60 to 90 minutes before surgery.
Children: 1 to 3 mg/kg I.V. or I.M. 60 to 90 minutes before surgery.

Contraindications and precautions

- Contraindicated in patients with barbiturate hypersensitivity, history of manifest or latent porphyria, hepatic dysfunction, respiratory disease with dyspnea or obstruction, and nephritis.
- Use cautiously in debilitated patients, and patients with acute or chronic pain, depression, suicidal tendencies, history of drug abuse, altered blood pressure, CV disease, shock, or uremia.

Lifespan: In pregnant and breast-feeding women, drug isn't recommended. In geriatric patients, use cautiously; drug causes paradoxical excitement in geriatric patients.

Adverse reactions

CNS: drowsiness, lethargy, hangover.
CV: ***bradycardia,*** hypotension.
GI: nausea, vomiting.
Hematologic: exacerbation of porphyria.
Respiratory: ***respiratory depression, apnea.***
Skin: rash; ***erythema multiforme; Stevens-Johnson syndrome;*** urticaria; pain, swelling, thrombophlebitis, necrosis, nerve injury at injection site.
Other: ***angioedema.***

Interactions

Drug-drug. *Chloramphenicol, MAO inhibitors, valproic acid:* Increases barbiturate effect. Monitor patient for increased CNS and respiratory depression.
CNS depressants, including narcotic analgesics: Excessive CNS depression. Use together cautiously.
Corticosteroids, digitoxin, doxycycline, estrogens and oral contraceptives, oral anticoagulants, tricyclic antidepressants: Phenobarbital may enhance metabolism of these drugs. Monitor patient for decreased effect.
Diazepam: Increases effects of both drugs. Use together cautiously.
Griseofulvin: Decreases griseofulvin absorption. Administer drug separately.
Mephobarbital, primidone: Excessive phenobarbital levels. Monitor patient closely.
Rifampin: May decrease barbiturate levels. Monitor patient for decreased effect.
Valproic acid: Increases phenobarbital levels. Monitor patient for toxicity.
Drug-lifestyle. *Alcohol use:* Excessive CNS depression. Discourage using together.

Effects on lab test results

- May decrease bilirubin level.

Pharmacokinetics

Absorption: Absorbed well after P.O. administration. 100% from I.M. injection.
Distribution: Distributed widely throughout body. Drug is about 25% to 30% protein-bound.
Metabolism: Metabolized in liver.
Excretion: Excreted in urine. *Half-life:* 5 to 7 days.

Route	Onset	Peak	Duration
P.O.	20-60 min	Unknown	10-12 hr
I.V.	5 min	≥ 15 min	10-12 hr
I.M.	> 60 min	Unknown	10-12 hr

Pharmacodynamics

Chemical effect: Unknown; may depress CNS synaptic transmission and increase seizure activity threshold in motor cortex. As sedative, may interfere with transmission of impulses from thalamus to brain cortex.
Therapeutic effect: Prevents and stops seizure activity; promotes calmness and sleep.

Available forms

Capsules: 16 mg
Elixir*: 15 mg/5 ml, 20 mg/5 ml
Injection: 30 mg/ml, 60 mg/ml, 65 mg/ml, 130 mg/ml
Tablets: 15 mg, 16 mg, 30 mg, 32 mg, 60 mg, 65 mg, 100 mg

NURSING PROCESS

Assessment
- Assess patient's condition before therapy and regularly thereafter.
- Monitor blood level closely. Therapeutic level is 15 to 40 mcg/ml.
- Be alert for adverse reactions and drug interactions.
- Evaluate patient's and family's knowledge of drug therapy.

Nursing diagnoses
- Risk for trauma related to seizures
- Risk for injury related to drug-induced adverse CNS reactions
- Deficient knowledge related to drug therapy

Planning and implementation
- **P.O. use:** Follow normal protocol.
- **I.V. use:** I.V. injection is reserved for emergency treatment. Monitor respirations closely.
  – Don't give more than 60 mg/minute. Have resuscitation equipment available.
  – Don't mix parenteral form with acidic solutions.
  – Don't use injectable solution if it contains precipitate.
- Don't stop drug abruptly; seizures may worsen. Call prescriber immediately if adverse reactions occur.
- **I.M. use:** Give drug by deep I.M. injection. Superficial injection may cause pain, sterile abscess, and tissue sloughing.

ALERT: Don't confuse pentobarbital with phenobarbital.

Patient teaching
- Make sure patient knows that phenobarbital is available in different strengths and sizes. Advise him to check prescription and refills closely.
- Inform him that full effects don't occur for 2 to 3 weeks except when loading dose is used.
- Advise him to avoid hazardous activities until CNS effects of drug are known.
- Warn patient and parents not to stop drug abruptly.
- Advise patient using oral contraceptives to consider other birth control methods.

Evaluation
- Patient is free from seizure activity.
- Patient has no injury from drug-induced adverse CNS reactions.
- Patient and family state understanding of drug therapy.

phentermine hydrochloride
(FEN-ter-meen high-droh-KLOR-ighd)
Adipex-P, Duromine ◇ , Ionamin, Pro-Fast HS, Pro-Fast SA, Pro-Fast SR

Pharmacologic class: indirect-acting sympathomimetic amine
Therapeutic class: short-term adjunct anorexigenic
Pregnancy risk category: C
Controlled substance schedule: IV

Indications and dosages

▶ **Short-term adjunct in exogenous obesity.** *Adults:* 8 mg P.O. t.i.d. 30 minutes before meals. Or, 15 to 37.5 mg daily before breakfast. Give Pro-fast HS or Pro-fast SR capsules 2 hours after breakfast. Give Adipex-P before breakfast or 1 to 2 hours after breakfast.

Contraindications and precautions
- Contraindicated in agitated patients, patients hypersensitive to sympathomimetic amines, patients who have idiosyncratic reactions to them, patients who have taken an MAO inhibitor within 14 days, and patients with hyperthyroidism, moderate-to-severe hypertension, advanced arteriosclerosis, symptomatic CV disease, or glaucoma.
- Use cautiously in patients with mild hypertension.

Lifespan: In pregnant and breast-feeding women, drug isn't recommended. In children, safety of drug hasn't been established.

Adverse reactions
CNS: overstimulation, headache, euphoria, dysphoria, dizziness, *insomnia.*
CV: palpitations, tachycardia, increased blood pressure.
EENT: mydriasis, eye irritation, blurred vision.
GI: dry mouth, dysgeusia, constipation, diarrhea, other GI disturbances.
GU: impotence.
Skin: urticaria.
Other: altered libido.

Interactions

Drug-drug. *Acetazolamide, antacids, sodium bicarbonate:* Increases renal reabsorption. Monitor patient.
Ammonium chloride, ascorbic acid: Decreases plasma levels and increased renal excretion of phentermine. Monitor patient for decreased effects.
Guanethidine: May decrease hypotensive effect. Monitor patient closely.
Haloperidol, phenothiazines, tricyclic antidepressants: Increases CNS effects. Avoid using together.
Insulin, oral antidiabetics: May alter antidiabetic requirements. Monitor glucose levels.
MAO inhibitors: May cause severe hypertension and possible hypertensive crisis. Don't use together or within 14 days of MAO inhibitor.
Drug-food. *Caffeine:* May increase CNS stimulation. Discourage using together.

Effects on lab test results

None reported.

Pharmacokinetics

Absorption: Absorbed readily from GI tract.
Distribution: Distributed throughout body.
Metabolism: Unknown.
Excretion: Excreted in urine. *Half-life:* 19 to 24 hours.

Route	Onset	Peak	Duration
P.O.	Unknown	Unknown	12-14 hr

Pharmacodynamics

Chemical effect: Unknown; probably promotes nerve impulse transmission by releasing stored norepinephrine from nerve terminals in brain. Main sites appear to be cerebral cortex and reticular activating system.
Therapeutic effect: Depresses appetite.

Available forms

Capsules: 15 mg, 18.75 mg (15 mg base), 30 mg (24 mg base), 37.5 mg (30 mg base)
Capsules (resin complex): 15 mg, 30 mg
Tablets: 8 mg, 37.5 mg

NURSING PROCESS

Assessment

- Weigh patient before therapy and regularly thereafter.
- Be alert for adverse reactions and drug interactions.
- Monitor patient for habituation and tolerance.
- Evaluate patient's and family's knowledge of drug therapy.

Nursing diagnoses

- Imbalanced nutrition: more than body requirements related to food intake
- Disturbed sleep pattern related to drug-induced insomnia
- Deficient knowledge related to drug therapy

Planning and implementation

- Give drug at least 6 hours before bedtime to avoid insomnia.
- Make sure patient is following a weight-reduction program.

ALERT: Don't confuse phentermine with phentolamine.

Patient teaching

- Instruct patient to take drug at least 6 hours before bedtime to avoid sleep interference.
- Warn patient to avoid hazardous activities until CNS effects of drug are known.
- Tell patient to avoid caffeine because it increases the effects of amphetamines and related amines.
- Tell patient to report signs of excessive stimulation.
- Inform patient that fatigue may result as drug effects wear off.

Evaluation

- Patient loses weight.
- Patient doesn't have insomnia.
- Patient and family state understanding of drug therapy.

phenylephrine hydrochloride

(fen-il-EF-rin high-droh-KLOR-ighd)
Neo-Synephrine

Pharmacologic class: adrenergic
Therapeutic class: vasoconstrictor
Pregnancy risk category: C

Indications and dosages

▶ **Hypotensive emergencies during spinal anesthesia.** *Adults:* Initially, 0.1 to 0.2 mg I.V., followed by 0.1 to 0.2 mg, p.r.n.

▶ **Maintenance of blood pressure during spinal or inhalation anesthesia.** *Adults:* 2 to 3 mg S.C. or I.M. 3 or 4 minutes before anesthesia.

Children: 0.044 to 0.088 mg/kg S.C. or I.M.

▶ **Prolongation of spinal anesthesia.** *Adults:* 2 to 5 mg added to anesthetic solution.

▶ **Vasoconstrictor for regional anesthesia.** *Adults:* 1 mg phenylephrine added to 20 ml local anesthetic.

▶ **Mild-to-moderate hypotension.** *Adults:* 2 to 5 mg S.C. or I.M.; repeated in 1 to 2 hours as needed and tolerated. Initial dose shouldn't exceed 5 mg. Or, 0.1 to 0.5 mg slow I.V., no more than q 10 to 15 minutes.

Children: 0.1 mg/kg I.M. or S.C.; repeated in 1 to 2 hours as needed and tolerated.

▶ **Severe hypotension and shock (including drug-induced).** *Adults:* 0.1 to 0.18 mg/minute I.V. infusion. After blood pressure stabilizes, maintain at 0.04 to 0.06 mg/minute, adjusted to patient response.

▶ **Paroxysmal supraventricular tachycardia.** *Adults:* Initially, 0.5 mg rapid I.V. Subsequent doses may be increased by 0.1 to 0.2 mg. Maximum dose shouldn't exceed 1 mg.

Contraindications and precautions

- Contraindicated in patients hypersensitive to drug and patients with severe hypertension or ventricular tachycardia.
- Use with extreme caution in patients with heart disease, hyperthyroidism, severe atherosclerosis, bradycardia, partial heart block, myocardial disease, or sulfite sensitivity.

Lifespan: In pregnant and breast-feeding women, use cautiously. In geriatric patients, use with extreme caution.

Adverse reactions

CNS: *headache, restlessness, light-headedness, weakness.*

CV: palpitations, ***bradycardia, arrhythmias,*** hypertension, angina, decreased cardiac output.

EENT: blurred vision.

GI: vomiting.

Respiratory: ***asthma attacks.***

Skin: pilomotor response, feeling of coolness.

Other: tachyphylaxis, decreased organ perfusion with prolonged use, tissue sloughing with extravasation, ***anaphylaxis.***

Interactions

Drug-drug. *Alpha-adrenergic blockers, phenothiazines:* Decreases vasopressor response. Monitor patient closely.

Beta blockers: Blocks cardiostimulatory effects. Monitor patient closely.

Bretylium: Increases risk of arrhythmias. Monitor ECG.

MAO inhibitors: May cause severe hypertension (hypertensive crisis). Don't use together. Monitor patient and blood pressure closely.

Oxytocics, tricyclic antidepressants, guanethidine: Increases pressor response and causes severe, persistent hypertension. Monitor patient and blood pressure closely.

Effects on lab test results

None reported.

Pharmacokinetics

Absorption: Unknown after I.M. and S.C. administration.

Distribution: Unknown.

Metabolism: Metabolized in liver and intestine.

Excretion: Unknown.

Route	Onset	Peak	Duration
I.V.	Immediate	Unknown	15-20 min
I.M.	10-15 min	Unknown	0.5-2 hr
S.C.	10-15 min	Unknown	50-60 min

Pharmacodynamics

Chemical effect: Mainly stimulates alpha-adrenergic receptors in sympathetic nervous system.

Therapeutic effect: Raises blood pressure and stops paroxysmal supraventricular tachycardia.

Available forms

Injection: 10 mg/ml

NURSING PROCESS

Assessment

- Assess patient's condition before therapy and regularly thereafter.
- Monitor blood pressure frequently; avoid severe increase. Maintain blood pressure slightly

below patient's normal level. In previously normotensive patient, maintain systolic pressure at 80 to 100 mm Hg; in previously hypertensive patient, maintain systolic pressure at 30 to 40 mm Hg below usual level.
• Monitor ECG throughout therapy.
• Be alert for adverse reactions and drug interactions.
• Evaluate patient's and family's knowledge of drug therapy.

Nursing diagnoses
• Ineffective tissue perfusion (cerebral, cardiopulmonary, peripheral, GI, renal) related to underlying condition
• Decreased cardiac output related to drug-induced adverse reaction
• Deficient knowledge related to drug therapy

Planning and implementation
• **I.V. use:** For direct injection, dilute 10 mg (1 ml) with 9 ml sterile water for injection to provide solution containing 1 mg/ml. Prepare I.V. infusions by adding 10 mg of drug to 500 ml of D_5W or normal saline solution for injection.
– Initial infusion rate is usually 100 to 180 mcg/minute; maintenance rate is usually 40 to 60 mcg/minute.
– Use continuous infusion pump to regulate flow rate.
– During infusion, frequently monitor ECG, blood pressure, cardiac output, central venous pressure, pulmonary capillary wedge pressure, pulse rate, urine output, and color and temperature of limbs. Titrate infusion rate according to findings and prescriber's guidelines.
– Use central venous catheter or large vein, as in antecubital fossa, to minimize risk of extravasation.
– After prolonged I.V. infusion, avoid abrupt withdrawal.
– To treat extravasation, infiltrate site promptly with 10 to 15 ml of normal saline solution for injection that contains 5 to 10 mg phentolamine. Use a fine needle.
– Drug is incompatible with butacaine sulfate, alkalis, ferric salts, and oxidizing agents.
• **I.M. and S.C. use:** Follow normal protocol.

Patient teaching
• Tell patient to report discomfort at infusion site immediately.

Evaluation
• Patient maintains tissue perfusion and cellular oxygenation.
• Patient maintains adequate cardiac output.
• Patient and family state understanding of drug therapy.

phenylephrine hydrochloride
(fen-il-EF-rin high-droh-KLOR-ighd)
Afrin Children's Pump Mist†, Alconefrin 12†, Alconefrin 25†, Alconefrin 50†, Duration†, Little Colds for Infants and Children†, Little Noses Gentle Formula†, Neo-Synephrine 4 Hour†, Nostril†, Rhinall†, Vicks Sinex†

Pharmacologic class: adrenergic
Therapeutic class: vasoconstrictor
Pregnancy risk category: C

Indications and dosages
▶ **Nasal congestion.** *Adults and children age 12 and older:* 2 to 3 drops (gtt) or 1 to 2 sprays in each nostril, p.r.n.
Children ages 6 to 11: 2 to 3 gtt or 1 to 2 sprays of 0.25% solution in each nostril q 3 to 4 hours, p.r.n.
Children younger than age 6: 2 to 3 gtt of 0.125% solution q 4 hours, p.r.n.

Contraindications and precautions
• Contraindicated in patients hypersensitive to drug.
• Use cautiously in patients with hyperthyroidism, marked hypertension, type 1 diabetes mellitus, cardiac disease, or advanced arteriosclerotic changes.
Lifespan: In pregnant and breast-feeding women, children with low body weight, and geriatric patients, use cautiously.

Adverse reactions
CNS: headache, tremor, dizziness, nervousness.
CV: *palpitations, tachycardia, **PVCs**,* hypertension, pallor.
EENT: transient burning or stinging, dry nasal mucosa, rebound nasal congestion with continued use.
GI: nausea.

Interactions

Drug-drug. *Guanethidine:* May potentiate phenylephrine hydrochloride and decrease pressor response (hypotension). Monitor patient's blood pressure closely.
Methyldopa, MAO inhibitors, tricyclic antidepressants: Increases pressor response and increases risk of arrhythmias. Don't use together.

Effects on lab test results

None reported.

Pharmacokinetics

Absorption: Small amounts may be absorbed.
Distribution: Distributed locally to nasal tissue.
Metabolism: Metabolized in liver.
Excretion: Excreted in urine.

Route	Onset	Peak	Duration
Intranasal	Rapid	Unknown	0.5-4 hr

Pharmacodynamics

Chemical effect: Causes local vasoconstriction of dilated arterioles, reducing blood flow.
Therapeutic effect: Relieves nasal congestion.

Available forms

Nasal solution: 0.125%, 0.16%, 0.25%, 0.5%, 1%

NURSING PROCESS

Assessment

- Assess patient's condition before therapy and regularly thereafter.
- Be alert for adverse reactions.
- Evaluate patient's and family's knowledge of drug therapy.

Nursing diagnoses

- Ineffective health maintenance related to nasal congestion
- Impaired tissue integrity related to adverse effect on nasal tissue
- Deficient knowledge related to drug therapy

Planning and implementation

- Have patient hold head upright while you insert nozzle; have patient sniff spray briskly.

Patient teaching

- Teach patient how to give drug.
- Tell patient not to share drug to prevent spread of infection.
- Warn patient not to exceed recommended dosage.
- Advise patient to contact prescriber if symptoms persist beyond 3 days.

Evaluation

- Patient's nasal congestion is relieved with phenylephrine therapy.
- Patient maintains normal nasal tissue integrity.
- Patient and family state understanding of drug therapy.

phenytoin (diphenylhydantoin)

(FEN-uh-toyn)
Dilantin-125, Dilantin Infatabs

phenytoin sodium (prompt)

Dilantin

phenytoin sodium (extended)

Dilantin Kapseals, Phenytek

Pharmacologic class: hydantoin derivative
Therapeutic class: anticonvulsant
Pregnancy risk category: D

Indications and dosages

▶ **Control of tonic-clonic (grand mal) and complex partial (temporal lobe) seizures.**
*Adults: **extended release.*** Highly individualized. Initially, 100 mg P.O. t.i.d., increased in increments of 100 mg P.O. q 2 to 4 weeks until desired response is obtained. Usual range is 300 to 600 mg daily. If patient is stabilized with extended-release capsules, once-daily dosing with 300-mg extended-release capsules is possible as an alternative.
Children: 5 mg/kg or 250 mg/m² P.O. divided b.i.d. or t.i.d. Maximum daily dose is 300 mg.
▶ **For patient requiring a loading dose.**
Adults: Initially, 1 g P.O. daily divided into three doses and administered at 2-hour intervals. Or, 10 to 15 mg/kg I.V. at a rate not exceeding 50 mg/minute. Normal maintenance dose is started 24 hours later with frequent serum level determinations.
Children: Initially, 5 mg/kg P.O. daily in two or three equally divided doses with subsequent dose individualized to maximum of 300 mg

daily. Usual dose is 4 to 8 mg/kg P.O. daily. Children older than 6 years old may require the minimum adult dosage (300 mg daily).

▶ **Prevention and treatment of seizures occurring during neurosurgery.** *Adults:* 100 to 200 mg I.M or I.V. q 4 hours during surgery and continued in the immediate postoperative period.

▶ **Status epilepticus.** *Adults:* Loading dose of 10 to 15 mg/kg I.V. (1 to 1.5 g may be needed) at a rate not exceeding 50 mg/minute; then maintenance doses of 100 mg P.O. or I.V. q 6 to 8 hours.

Children: Loading dose of 15 to 20 mg/kg I.V., at a rate not exceeding 1 to 3 mg/kg/minute; then highly individualized maintenance doses.

Geriatric patients: May need lower dosages.

Contraindications and precautions

- Contraindicated in patients hypersensitive to hydantoin and patients with sinus bradycardia, SA block, second- or third-degree AV block, or Adams-Stokes syndrome.
- Use cautiously in debilitated patients, patients receiving other hydantoin derivatives, and patients with hepatic dysfunction, hypotension, myocardial insufficiency, diabetes, or respiratory depression.

Lifespan: In pregnant and breast-feeding women, drug isn't recommended. In geriatric patients, use cautiously; geriatric patients tend to metabolize phenytoin slowly and may need lower dosages.

Adverse reactions

CNS: *ataxia, slurred speech, confusion,* dizziness, insomnia, nervousness, twitching, headache.
CV: hypotension.
EENT: nystagmus, diplopia, blurred vision, gingival hyperplasia.
GI: nausea, vomiting.
Hematologic: ***thrombocytopenia, leukopenia, agranulocytosis, pancytopenia,*** macrocythemia, megaloblastic anemia.
Hepatic: ***toxic hepatitis.***
Metabolic: hyperglycemia.
Musculoskeletal: osteomalacia.
Skin: scarlatiniform or morbilliform rash; bullous, exfoliative, or purpuric dermatitis; ***Stevens-Johnson syndrome;*** lupus erythematosus; *hirsutism;* ***toxic epidermal necrolysis;*** photosensitivity reaction; pain, necrosis, or inflammation at injection site; discoloration (purple glove syndrome) if given by I.V. push in back of hand; hypertrichosis.
Other: periarteritis nodosa, lymphadenopathy.

Interactions

Drug-drug. *Amiodarone, antihistamines, chloramphenicol, cimetidine, clonazepam, cycloserine, diazepam, disulfiram, influenza vaccine, isoniazid, phenylbutazone, salicylates, sulfamethizole, valproate:* Increases therapeutic effects of phenytoin. Monitor patient for toxicity.
Dexamethasone, diazoxide, folic acid: Decreases phenytoin activity. Monitor patient closely.
Lithium: Increases toxicity. Monitor lithium levels.
Meperidine: Toxic effects of meperidine may be increased while decreasing analgesic effects. Monitor patient for decreased effects and toxicity.
Warfarin: Displacement of warfarin can occur. Monitor patient for bleeding complications.
Drug-herb. *Milk thistle:* May decrease risk of liver toxicity. Monitor patient.
Drug-food. *Enteral nutrition therapy:* May reduce orally administered phenytoin concentrations. Consider giving phenytoin 2 hours before starting enteral feeding, or wait 2 hours after stopping enteral feeding to administer phenytoin.
Drug-lifestyle. *Alcohol use:* Decreases phenytoin activity. Discourage using together.

Effects on lab test results

- May increase alkaline phosphatase, GGT, and glucose levels. May reduce serum protein–bound iodine, free thyroxine, urinary 17-hydroxysteroid, and 17-ketosteroid levels.
- May increase urine 6-hydroxycortisol excretion. May decrease hemoglobin, hematocrit, and platelet, WBC, RBC, and granulocyte counts.
- May decrease dexamethasone suppression and metyrapone test values.

Pharmacokinetics

Absorption: Slow after P.O. administration. Formulation-dependent; bioavailability may differ among products. Erratic from I.M. site.
Distribution: Distributed widely throughout body. Drug is about 90% protein-bound.

Metabolism: Metabolized by liver.
Excretion: Excreted in urine; exhibits dose-dependent (zero-order) elimination kinetics. Above certain dosage level, small increases in dosage disproportionately increase serum levels. *Half-life:* Varies with dose and serum concentration changes.

Route	Onset	Peak	Duration
P.O.	Unknown	1.5-2 hr	Unknown
P.O. (extended)	Unknown	4-12 hr	Unknown
I.V.	Immediate	1-2 hr	Unknown
I.M.	Unknown	Unknown	Unknown

Pharmacodynamics

Chemical effect: Unknown; probably stabilizes neuronal membranes and limits seizure activity by either increasing efflux or decreasing influx of sodium ions across cell membranes in motor cortex during generation of nerve impulses.
Therapeutic effect: Prevents and stops seizure activity.

Available forms

phenytoin
Oral suspension: 125 mg/5 ml
Tablets (chewable): 50 mg
phenytoin sodium (prompt)
Capsules: 100 mg (92-mg base)
Injection: 50 mg/ml (46-mg base)
phenytoin sodium (extended)
Capsules: 30 mg (27.6-mg base), 100 mg (92-mg base), 200 mg (184-mg base), 300 mg (276-mg base)

NURSING PROCESS

Assessment

- Assess patient's condition before therapy and regularly thereafter.
- Monitor blood levels; therapeutic level is 10 to 20 mcg/ml.
- Monitor CBC and calcium level every 6 months, and periodically monitor hepatic function.
- Check vital signs, blood pressure, and ECG during I.V. administration.
- Be alert for adverse reactions and drug interactions.
- Mononucleosis may decrease phenytoin level. Monitor patient for increased seizure activity.
- Evaluate patient's and family's knowledge of drug therapy.

Nursing diagnoses

- Risk for trauma related to seizures
- Impaired oral mucous membrane related to gingival hyperplasia
- Deficient knowledge related to drug therapy

Planning and implementation

- Use only clear or slightly yellow solution for injection. Don't refrigerate.
- **P.O. use:** Divided doses given with or after meals may decrease adverse GI reactions.
  – Dilantin capsule is only P.O. form that can be given once daily. Toxic levels may result if any other brand or form is given once daily. Dilantin tablets and P.O. suspension shouldn't be taken once daily.
- **I.V. use:** If giving as infusion, don't mix drug with D_5W because it will precipitate. Clear I.V. tubing first with normal saline solution. May mix with normal saline solution if necessary and infuse over 30 to 60 minutes when possible.
  – Infusion must begin within 1 hour after preparation and should run through in-line filter.
  – Administer drug slowly (50 mg/minute) as I.V. bolus.
  – Check patency of I.V. catheter before administering. Extravasation has caused severe local tissue damage.
  – Never use cloudy solution.
  – Discard 4 hours after preparation.
  – Avoid giving phenytoin by I.V. push into veins on back of hand to avoid discoloration known as purple glove syndrome. Inject into larger veins or central venous catheter if available.
- **I.M. use:** Don't give drug I.M. unless dosage adjustments are made. Drug may precipitate at site, cause pain, and be erratically absorbed.
- Discontinue drug if rash appears. If rash is scarlatiniform or morbilliform, drug may be resumed after rash clears. If rash reappears, therapy should be discontinued. If rash is exfoliative, purpuric, or bullous, drug shouldn't be resumed.
- Don't withdraw drug suddenly; seizures may worsen. Call prescriber at once if adverse reactions develop.

• If patient has megaloblastic anemia, prescriber may order folic acid and vitamin B_{12}.
ALERT: Don't confuse phenytoin with Mephyton or fosphenytoin.
ALERT: Don't confuse Dilantin with Dilaudid.

Patient teaching
• Advise patient to avoid hazardous activities until CNS effects of drug are known.
• Advise patient not to change brands or dosage forms.
• Warn patient and parents not to stop drug abruptly.
• Promote oral hygiene and regular dental examinations. Gingivectomy may be necessary periodically if dental hygiene is poor.
• Caution patient that drug may color urine pink, red, or red-brown.
• Inform patient that heavy alcohol use may diminish drug's benefits.

Evaluation
• Patient is free from seizure activity.
• Patient expresses importance of good oral hygiene and regular dental examinations.
• Patient and family state understanding of drug therapy.

physostigmine salicylate (eserine salicylate)
(fiz-oh-STIG-meen sa-LIS-il-ayt)
Antilirium

Pharmacologic class: cholinesterase inhibitor
Therapeutic class: antimuscarinic antidote
Pregnancy risk category: C

Indications and dosages
▶ **To reverse CNS toxicity caused by clinical or toxic dosages of drugs capable of producing anticholinergic syndrome.** *Adults:* 0.5 to 2 mg I.M. or I.V. (1 mg/minute I.V.) repeated q 10 minutes as necessary if life-threatening signs recur (coma, seizures, arrhythmias).
Children: 0.02 mg/kg I.M. or slow I.V. repeated q 5 to 10 minutes until response is obtained. Maximum dosage is 2 mg. Drug is reserved for life-threatening situations.

Contraindications and precautions
• Contraindicated in patients receiving choline esters or depolarizing neuromuscular blockers and in patients with mechanical obstruction of intestine or urogenital tract, asthma, gangrene, diabetes, CV disease, or vagotonia.
• Use cautiously in patients with sensitivity or allergy to sulfites.
Lifespan: In pregnant women, use cautiously. In breast-feeding women, safety of drug hasn't been established.

Adverse reactions
CNS: ***seizures,*** hallucinations, muscle twitching, muscle weakness, ataxia, *restlessness, excitability, sweating.*
CV: irregular pulse, palpitations, ***bradycardia,*** hypotension.
EENT: miosis.
GI: nausea, vomiting, epigastric pain, *diarrhea, excessive salivation.*
GU: urinary urgency.
Respiratory: ***bronchospasm,*** bronchial constriction, dyspnea.

Interactions
Drug-drug. *Anticholinergics, atropine, procainamide, quinidine:* May reverse cholinergic effects. Observe patient for lack of drug effect.
Ganglionic blockers: May decrease blood pressure. Avoid using together.
Drug-herb. *Jaborandi tree, pill-bearing spurge:* May have additive effects and increase risk of toxicity. Discourage using together.

Effects on lab test results
None reported.

Pharmacokinetics
Absorption: Absorbed well from injection site.
Distribution: Distributed widely and crosses blood-brain barrier.
Metabolism: Cholinesterase hydrolyzes physostigmine relatively quickly.
Excretion: Primary mode of excretion unknown; small amount excreted in urine.

Route	Onset	Peak	Duration
I.V.	3-5 min	≤ 5 min	30-60 min
I.M.	3-5 min	20-30 min	30-60 min

Pharmacodynamics

Chemical effect: Inhibits destruction of acetylcholine released from parasympathetic and somatic efferent nerves. Acetylcholine accumulates, promoting increased stimulation of receptor.
Therapeutic effect: Reverses anticholinergic signs and symptoms.

Available forms

Injection: 1 mg/ml

NURSING PROCESS

Assessment

- Assess patient's condition before therapy and regularly thereafter. Effectiveness is often immediate and dramatic, but may be transient and require repeated doses.
- Monitor vital signs frequently, especially respirations.
- Be alert for adverse reactions and drug interactions.
- Evaluate patient's and family's knowledge of drug therapy.

Nursing diagnoses

- Ineffective health maintenance related to underlying condition
- Risk for injury related to drug-induced adverse CNS reactions
- Deficient knowledge related to drug therapy

Planning and implementation

- **I.V. use:** Give drug I.V. at controlled rate; use direct injection at no more than 1 mg/minute.
- **I.M. use:** Follow normal protocol.
- Use only clear solution. Darkening of solution may indicate loss of potency.
- Position patient to ease breathing. Have atropine injection available and be prepared to give 0.5 mg S.C. or slow I.V. push. Provide respiratory support as needed. Best administered in presence of prescriber.
- Raise side rails of bed if patient becomes restless or hallucinates. Adverse reactions may indicate drug toxicity. Notify prescriber.

Patient teaching

- Tell patient to report adverse reactions, especially pain at the I.V. site.

Evaluation

- Patient responds well to therapy.
- Patient doesn't experience injury from adverse CNS reactions.
- Patient and family state understanding of drug therapy.

phytonadione (vitamin K_1)

(figh-toh-neh-DIGH-ohn)
AquaMEPHYTON, Mephyton

Pharmacologic class: vitamin K
Therapeutic class: blood coagulation modifier
Pregnancy risk category: C

Indications and dosages

▶ **RDA.** *Infants age 6 months and younger:* 5 mcg.
Infants ages 6 months to 1 year: 10 mcg.
Children ages 1 to 3: 15 mcg.
Children ages 4 to 6: 20 mcg.
Children ages 7 to 10: 30 mcg.
Children ages 11 to 14: 45 mcg.
Men ages 15 to 18: 65 mcg.
Men ages 19 to 24: 70 mcg.
Men age 25 and over: 80 mcg.
Women ages 15 to 18: 55 mcg.
Women ages 19 to 24: 60 mcg.
Women age 25 and over, pregnant or breast-feeding women: 65 mcg.

▶ **Hypoprothrombinemia secondary to vitamin K malabsorption, drug therapy, or excessive vitamin A.** *Adults:* Depending on severity, 2 to 25 mg P.O., S.C., or I.M.; repeat and increase up to 50 mg, if necessary.
Children: 5 to 10 mg P.O. or parenterally. I.V. injection rate for infants and children shouldn't exceed 3 mg/m^2/minute or total of 5 mg.
Infants: 2 mg P.O. or parenterally.

▶ **Hypoprothrombinemia secondary to effect of oral anticoagulants.** *Adults:* 2.5 to 10 mg P.O., S.C., or I.M. based on PT; repeat if necessary within 12 to 48 hours after P.O. dose or within 6 to 8 hours after parenteral dose. In emergency, 10 to 50 mg slow I.V., maximum rate 1 mg/minute; repeat q 4 hours, p.r.n.

▶ **Prevention of hemorrhagic disease of newborn.** *Neonates:* 0.5 to 1 mg I.M. or S.C. within 1 hour after birth.

▶ **Treatment of hemorrhagic disease of newborn.** *Neonates:* 1 mg S.C. or I.M. based on laboratory tests. Higher doses may be necessary if mother has been receiving anticoagulants P.O.

▶ **To differentiate between hepatocellular disease or biliary obstruction as source of hypoprothrombinemia.** *Adults and children:* 10 mg I.M. or S.C.

▶ **Prevention of hypoprothrombinemia related to vitamin K deficiency in long-term parenteral nutrition.** *Adults:* 5 to 10 mg I.M. weekly.
Children: 2 to 5 mg I.M. weekly.

▶ **Prevention of hypoprothrombinemia in infants receiving less than 0.1 mg/L vitamin K in breast milk or milk substitutes.** *Infants:* 1 mg I.M. monthly.

Contraindications and precautions

• Contraindicated in patients hypersensitive to drug.
Lifespan: In pregnant and breast-feeding women, use cautiously.

Adverse reactions

CNS: dizziness, seizurelike movements.
CV: flushing, transient hypotension after I.V. administration, rapid and weak pulse, cardiac irregularities.
Skin: diaphoresis, erythema.
Other: cramplike pain; ***anaphylaxis and anaphylactoid reactions*** (usually after rapid I.V. administration); pain, swelling, and hematoma at injection site.

Interactions

Drug-drug. *Anticoagulants:* Temporary resistance to prothrombin-depressing anticoagulants may result, especially when larger doses of phytonadione are used. Monitor patient closely. *Cholestyramine resin, mineral oil:* Inhibits GI absorption of oral vitamin K. Administer separately.

Effects on lab test results

None reported.

Pharmacokinetics

Absorption: Drug requires presence of bile salts for GI tract absorption after P.O. administration. Unknown after I.M. or S.C. administration.
Distribution: Concentrates in liver for short time.
Metabolism: Metabolized rapidly by liver.
Excretion: Not clearly defined.

Route	Onset	Peak	Duration
P.O.	6-12 hr	Unknown	12-14 hr
I.V., I.M., S.C.	1-2 hr	Unknown	12-14 hr

Pharmacodynamics

Chemical effect: An antihemorrhagic factor that promotes hepatic formation of active prothrombin.
Therapeutic effect: Controls abnormal bleeding.

Available forms

Injection (aqueous colloidal solution): 2 mg/ml, 10 mg/ml
Injection (aqueous dispersion): 2 mg/ml, 10 mg/ml
Tablets: 5 mg

NURSING PROCESS

Assessment

• Assess patient's condition before therapy and regularly thereafter.
• Monitor PT to determine dosage effectiveness
• Failure to respond to vitamin K may indicate coagulation defects.
• Be alert for adverse reactions and drug interactions.
• Monitor patient's hydration status if adverse GI reactions occur.
• Evaluate patient's and family's knowledge of drug therapy.

Nursing diagnoses

• Ineffective protection related to underlying vitamin K deficiency
• Risk for deficient fluid volume related to adverse GI reactions
• Deficient knowledge related to drug therapy

Planning and implementation

• Check brand name labels for administration route restrictions.
• **P.O. and S.C. use:** Follow normal protocol. S.C. is the preferred route of administration.
• **I.V. use:** Dilute drug with normal saline solution for injection, D_5W, or dextrose 5% in normal saline solution for injection.

– Give I.V. by slow infusion over 2 to 3 hours. Maximum infusion rate 1 mg/minute in adult or 3 mg/m^2/minute in child.
– Protect parenteral products from light. Wrap infusion container with aluminum foil.
– Anticipate order for weekly addition of 5 to 10 mg of phytonadione to total parenteral nutrition solutions.
• **I.M. use:** Give drug in upper outer quadrant of buttocks in adult or older child; inject in anterolateral aspect of thigh or deltoid region in infant.
• If severe bleeding occurs, don't delay other treatments, such as fresh frozen plasma or whole blood.

Patient teaching
• Explain drug's purpose.
• Instruct patient to report adverse reactions.

Evaluation
• Patient achieves normal PT levels with drug therapy.
• Patient maintains adequate hydration throughout drug therapy.
• Patient and family state understanding of drug therapy.

pimecrolimus
(pee-mu-croo-lime-us)
Elidel

Pharmacologic class: topical immunomodulator
Therapeutic class: topical skin product
Pregnancy risk category: C

Indications and dosages
▶ **Short-term and intermittent long-term therapy in the treatment of mild-to-moderate atopic dermatitis in non-immunocompromised patients, in whom the use of alternative, conventional therapies is deemed inadvisable or in the treatment of patients who are not adequately responding to or are intolerant of conventional therapies.** *Adults and children age 2 and older:* Apply a thin layer to the affected skin twice daily and rub in gently and completely.

Contraindications and precautions
• Contraindicated in patients hypersensitive to pimecrolimus or the components of the cream.
• Don't use on areas of active cutaneous viral infections or clinically infected atopic dermatitis.
• Not recommended for use in patients with Netherton's syndrome or in immunocompromised patients.
• Use cautiously in patients with varicella zoster virus infection, herpes simplex virus infection, or eczema herpeticum.
Lifespan: In pregnant women, safety of drug hasn't been established. In breast-feeding women, a decision should be made to discontinue nursing or discontinue the drug. In children younger than age 2, drug is not recommended. In patients age 65 and older, safety of drug hasn't been established.

Adverse reactions
CNS: *headache.*
EENT: *nasopharyngitis,* otitis media, sinusitis, pharyngitis, eye infection, nasal congestion, rhinorrhea, sinus congestion, rhinitis, epistaxis, conjunctivitis, earache.
GI: gastroenteritis, abdominal pain, sore throat, tonsillitis, vomiting, diarrhea, nausea, toothache, constipation, loose stools.
GU: dysmenorrhea.
Musculoskeletal: back pain, arthralgias.
Respiratory: *upper respiratory tract infections,* pneumonia, *bronchitis, cough,* asthma, wheezing, dyspnea.
Skin: skin infections, impetigo, folliculitis, molluscum contagiosum, herpes simplex, varicella, skin papilloma, *application site reaction* (burning, irritation, erythema, pruritus), urticaria, acne.
Other: *influenza, pyrexia,* influenzalike illness, hypersensitivity reaction, bacterial infection, staphylococcal infection, viral infection.

Interactions
Drug-drug. *CYP3A family of inhibitors (erythromycin, itraconazole, ketoconazole, fluconazole, calcium channel blockers):* May have an effect on metabolism of pimecrolimus. Use together cautiously.
Drug-lifestyle. *Natural or artificial sunlight:* Pimecrolimus may shorten the time to skin tumor formation. Avoid or minimize exposure to sunlight.

Effects on lab test results

None reported.

Pharmacokinetics

Absorption: Low systemic absorption.
Distribution: 74% to 87% bound to plasma proteins.
Metabolism: No evidence of skin mediated drug metabolism exists.
Excretion: Following the administration of a single oral radiolabeled dose of pimecrolimus, about 81% of the administered radioactivity was recovered, primarily in the feces (78.4%) as metabolites. Less than 1% of the radioactivity found in the feces was due to unchanged drug.

Route	Onset	Peak	Duration
Topical	Unknown	Unknown	Unknown

Pharmacodynamics

Chemical effect: Unknown. Pimecrolimus has been shown to inhibit T cell activation by blocking the transcription of early cytokines. Specifically, it inhibits Interleukin-2, interferon gamma, Interleukin-4, and Interleukin-10 cytokine synthesis in human T cells. It has also been shown to prevent the release of inflammatory cytokines and mediators from mast cells in vitro after stimulation by antigen/IgE.
Therapeutic effect: Improves skin integrity.

Available forms

Cream: 1% in tubes of 15 grams, 30 grams, and 100 grams. Base contains the following alcohols: benzyl alcohol, cetyl alcohol, oleyl alcohol, and stearyl alcohol.

NURSING PROCESS

Assessment

- Assess underlying skin condition before therapy and reassess regularly throughout therapy. Clinical infections at treatment sites should be cleared before using pimecrolimus.
- Evaluate patient's and family's knowledge of drug therapy.

Nursing diagnoses

- Risk for situational low self-esteem related to skin disorder
- Impaired skin integrity related to underlying skin condition
- Deficient knowledge related to pimecrolimus therapy

Planning and implementation

- May be used on all skin surfaces, including the head, neck, and intertriginous areas.
- Discontinue if resolution of disease occurs.
- If symptoms persist beyond 6 weeks, patient should be reevaluated.

ALERT: Do not use with occlusive dressing; this may promote systemic exposure.

- May cause local symptoms such as skin burning. Most local reactions started within 1 to 5 days of treatment, were mild to moderate in severity, and lasted no more than 5 days.
- Monitor patient for lymphadenopathy. In the absence of a clear etiology for the lymphadenopathy, or in the presence of acute infectious mononucleosis, consider discontinuing drug.
- Papillomas or warts may occur with use. Consider discontinuation of drug if skin papillomas worsen or do not respond to conventional treatment.

Patient teaching

- Instruct patient to use as directed; this medication is for external use on the skin only. Tell patient to report any signs or symptoms of adverse reactions.
- Tell patient not to use medication with an occlusive dressing.
- Instruct patient to wash hands after application if hands are not an area of treatment.
- Inform patient that therapy should be discontinued after signs and symptoms of atopic dermatitis have resolved. If symptoms persist beyond 6 weeks, patient should contact prescriber.
- Inform patient to resume treatment at the first signs or symptoms of recurrence.
- Emphasize that patient should minimize or avoid exposure to natural or artificial sunlight (including tanning beds and UVA/B treatment) while using this medication.
- Tell patient that application site reactions are expected, but to notify prescriber if reaction is severe or persists for more than 1 week.

Evaluation

- Patient has improved self-esteem as skin condition clears.
- Patient has improved skin condition.
- Patient and family state understanding of drug therapy.

pimozide

(PIH-mih-zighd)
Orap

Pharmacologic class: diphenylbutylpiperidine
Therapeutic class: antipsychotic
Pregnancy risk category: C

Indications and dosages

▶ **Suppression of motor and phonic tics in patients with Tourette syndrome refractory to first-line therapy.** *Adults and children older than age 12:* Initially, 1 to 2 mg P.O. daily in divided doses. Increase every other day, as needed. Maximum dosage is 20 mg daily.

Contraindications and precautions

- Contraindicated in patients hypersensitive to drug, patients with simple tics or tics other than those caused by Tourette syndrome, patients receiving concurrent therapy with drugs known to cause motor and phonic tics, and patients with congenital long-QT syndrome, history of arrhythmias, severe toxic CNS depression, or coma.
- Use cautiously in patients with hepatic or renal dysfunction, glaucoma, prostatic hyperplasia, seizure disorder, or EEG abnormalities.

Lifespan: In breast-feeding women, safety of drug hasn't been established.

Adverse reactions

CNS: *parkinsonian-like symptoms,* other extrapyramidal symptoms (dystonia, akathisia, hyperreflexia, opisthotonos, oculogyric crisis), *tardive dyskinesia, sedation.*
CV: ***ECG changes (prolonged QT interval),*** hypotension.
EENT: visual disturbances.
GI: dry mouth, constipation.
GU: impotence.
Musculoskeletal: muscle rigidity, ***neuroleptic malignant syndrome.***

Interactions

Drug-drug. *Antiarrhythmics, phenothiazines, tricyclic antidepressants:* Increases risk of ECG abnormalities. Monitor patient closely.
CNS depressants: Increases CNS depression. Avoid using together.

Drug-lifestyle. *Alcohol use:* Increases CNS depression. Discourage using together.

Effects on lab test results

None reported.

Pharmacokinetics

Absorption: Slow and incomplete.
Distribution: Distributed widely into body.
Metabolism: Metabolized by liver; significant first-pass effect.
Excretion: About 40% of drug is excreted in urine as parent drug and metabolites; about 15% is excreted in feces. *Half-life:* About 29 hours.

Route	Onset	Peak	Duration
P.O.	Unknown	4-12 hr	Unknown

Pharmacodynamics

Chemical effect: May block dopamine nonselectively at presynaptic and postsynaptic receptors on neurons in CNS.
Therapeutic effect: Stops tics linked to Tourette syndrome.

Available forms

Tablets: 1 mg, 2 mg, 4 mg♦, 10 mg♦

NURSING PROCESS

Assessment

- Assess patient's tics before therapy and regularly thereafter.
- Perform ECG before therapy and periodically thereafter. Check for prolonged QT interval.
- Monitor patient for tardive dyskinesia. It may occur after prolonged use. It may not appear until months or years later and may disappear spontaneously or persist for life despite discontinuing drug.
- Monitor patient who also is taking anticonvulsants for increased seizure activity. Pimozide may lower seizure threshold.
- Be alert for adverse reactions and drug interactions.
- Evaluate patient's and family's knowledge of drug therapy.

Nursing diagnoses

- Disturbed body image related to presence of tics

- Impaired physical mobility related to adverse reactions
- Deficient knowledge related to drug therapy

Planning and implementation

- Acute dystonic reactions may be treated with diphenhydramine.

ALERT: Avoid giving other drugs that prolong QT interval, such as antiarrhythmics.

Patient teaching

- Warn patient not to stop taking drug abruptly and not to exceed prescribed dosage.
- Tell patient to avoid alcohol during drug therapy.
- Tell patient to use sugarless hard candy, gum, and liquids to relieve dry mouth.

Evaluation

- Patient states positive feelings about self with absence of tics.
- Patient is able to perform activities of daily living.
- Patient and family state understanding of drug therapy.

pindolol

(PIN-duh-lol)

Novo-Pindol◆, Visken

Pharmacologic class: beta blocker
Therapeutic class: antihypertensive
Pregnancy risk category: B

Indications and dosages

▶ **Hypertension.** *Adults:* Initially, 5 mg P.O. b.i.d. Increase as needed and tolerated to maximum of 60 mg daily.

▶ **Angina‡.** *Adults:* 15 to 40 mg P.O. daily in four divided doses.

Contraindications and precautions

- Contraindicated in patients hypersensitive to drug and in those with bronchial asthma, severe bradycardia, heart block greater than first degree, cardiogenic shock, or cardiac failure. Contraindicated for use with thioridazine.
- Use cautiously in patients with heart failure, nonallergic bronchospastic disease, diabetes, hyperthyroidism, or impaired renal or hepatic function.

Lifespan: In pregnant women, use cautiously. In breast-feeding women, drug isn't recommended. In children, safe use of drug hasn't been established.

Adverse reactions

CNS: insomnia, fatigue, dizziness, nervousness, vivid dreams, hallucinations, lethargy.
CV: *edema,* ***bradycardia, heart failure,*** peripheral vascular disease, hypotension.
EENT: visual disturbances.
GI: *nausea,* vomiting, diarrhea.
Metabolic: ***hypoglycemia without tachycardia.***
Musculoskeletal: *muscle pain, joint pain.*
Respiratory: increased airway resistance.
Skin: rash.

Interactions

Drug-drug. *Digoxin, diltiazem, verapamil:* May cause excessive bradycardia and additive depression of AV node. Use together cautiously.
Epinephrine: May cause severe vasoconstriction. Monitor blood pressure and observe patient carefully.
Indomethacin: Decreases antihypertensive effect. Monitor blood pressure and adjust dosage, as directed.
Insulin, oral antidiabetics: May alter requirements for these drugs in previously stabilized diabetic patients. Monitor patient for hypoglycemia.
Thioridazine: May prolong QTc interval and increase the risk of potentially fatal cardiac arrhythmias. Pindolol serum concentrations may increase. Avoid using together.

Effects on lab test results

- May increase transaminase, alkaline phosphatase, LDH, and uric acid levels. May decrease glucose level.

Pharmacokinetics

Absorption: Rapid. Food doesn't reduce bioavailability but may increase rate of GI absorption.
Distribution: Distributed widely throughout body and is 40% to 60% protein-bound.
Metabolism: About 60% to 65% of drug is metabolized in liver.

Excretion: 35% to 50% of dose excreted unchanged in urine. *Half-life:* About 3 to 4 hours.

Route	Onset	Peak	Duration
P.O.	Unknown	1-2 hr	24 hr

Pharmacodynamics

Chemical effect: Unknown; possible mechanisms include reduced cardiac output, decreased sympathetic outflow to peripheral vasculature, and inhibition of renin release by kidneys.
Therapeutic effect: Lowers blood pressure.

Available forms

Tablets: 5 mg, 10 mg, 15 mg ♦

NURSING PROCESS

Assessment

- Assess patient's blood pressure before therapy and regularly thereafter.
- Always check patient's apical pulse rate before giving drug.
- Be alert for adverse reactions and drug interactions.
- Evaluate patient's and family's knowledge of drug therapy.

Nursing diagnoses

- Risk for injury related to presence of hypertension
- Fatigue related to drug's adverse effect
- Deficient knowledge related to drug therapy

Planning and implementation

- If you detect extreme pulse rates, withhold medication and call prescriber immediately.
- Notify prescriber if severe hypotension occurs.
- Abrupt discontinuation can worsen angina and precipitate MI. Withdraw over 1 to 2 weeks after long-term administration.

ALERT: Don't confuse pindolol with Parlodel, perindopril, Panadol, or Plendil.

Patient teaching

- Teach patient how to take his pulse, and tell him to do so before taking each pindolol dose. Tell him to notify prescriber before taking any more doses if his pulse rate varies significantly from its usual level.
- Tell patient not to stop drug suddenly even if he has unpleasant adverse reactions; urge him to discuss them with prescriber. Explain that stopping drug abruptly can worsen angina and increase the risk of MI.
- Instruct patient to check with prescriber before taking OTC medications.
- Teach patient and family caregiver to take blood pressure measurements. Tell them to notify prescriber of any significant change.
- Advise patient to monitor glucose levels closely. Drug may mask signs of hypoglycemia.

Evaluation

- Patient's blood pressure is normal.
- Patient states energy-conserving measures to combat fatigue.
- Patient and family state understanding of drug therapy.

pioglitazone hydrochloride

(pigh-oh-GLIH-tah-zohn high-droh-KLOR-ighd)
Actos

Pharmacologic class: thiazolidinedione
Therapeutic class: antidiabetic
Pregnancy risk category: C

Indications and dosages

▶ **Monotherapy adjunct to diet and exercise to improve glycemic control in patients with type 2 diabetes mellitus, or combination therapy with a sulfonylurea, metformin, or insulin when diet and exercise plus the single drug doesn't yield adequate glycemic control.** *Adults:* Initially, 15 or 30 mg P.O. once daily. For patients who respond inadequately to initial dose, it may be increased in increments; maximum daily dose is 45 mg. If used in combination therapy, daily dosage shouldn't exceed 30 mg.

Contraindications and precautions

- Contraindicated in patients hypersensitive to pioglitazone or its components. This drug is not recommended for New York Heart Association Class III and IV cardiac status patients.
- Drug shouldn't be used in patients with type 1 diabetes mellitus or diabetic ketoacidosis, patients with clinical evidence of active liver dis-

ease, patients with serum ALT levels more than two and one-half times the upper limit of normal, and patients who experienced jaundice while taking troglitazone.
Lifespan: With pregnant women, drug should be used only if benefit justifies risk to fetus. Insulin is the preferred antidiabetic for use during pregnancy.

Adverse reactions

CNS: headache.
CV: *edema,* ***heart failure.***
EENT: sinusitis, pharyngitis.
Hematologic: anemia.
Metabolic: ***hypoglycemia with combination therapy,*** aggravated diabetes mellitus, weight gain.
Musculoskeletal: myalgia.
Respiratory: upper respiratory tract infection.
Other: tooth disorder.

Interactions

Drug-drug. *Ketoconazole:* May inhibit pioglitazone metabolism. Monitor patient's glucose levels more frequently.
Oral contraceptives: May reduce plasma levels of oral contraceptives, resulting in less effective contraception. Advise patients taking pioglitazone and oral contraceptives to consider additional birth control measures.
Drug-herb. *Aloe, bitter melon, bilberry leaf, burdock, dandelion, fenugreek, garlic, ginseng:* May improve blood glucose control and allow reduction of antidiabetic dosage. Advise patient to discuss herbal remedies with prescriber before using them.

Effects on lab test results

- May increase high-density lipoprotein levels. May decrease glucose and triglyceride levels.
- May decrease hemoglobin and hematocrit.

Pharmacokinetics

Absorption: When taken on an empty stomach, rapidly absorbed and measurable in serum within 30 minutes; level peaks within 2 hours. Food slightly delays time to peak serum levels (to 3 to 4 hours), but doesn't affect the overall extent of absorption.
Distribution: Drug and its metabolites are extensively protein-bound (more than 98%), primarily to serum albumin.
Metabolism: Extensively metabolized by the liver. Three metabolites, M-II, M-III, and M-IV, are pharmacologically active.
Excretion: About 15% to 30% of dose is recovered in urine, primarily as metabolites and their conjugates. Most of P.O. dose is excreted in bile and eliminated in feces. *Half-life:* 3 to 7 hours.

Route	Onset	Peak	Duration
P.O.	Unknown	Within 2 hr	Unknown

Pharmacodynamics

Chemical effect: Lowers glucose levels by decreasing insulin resistance in the periphery and in the liver, resulting in increased insulin-dependent glucose disposal and decreased glucose output by the liver. A potent and highly selective agonist for receptors found in insulin-sensitive tissues, such as adipose tissue, skeletal muscle, and liver. Activation of these receptors modulates the transcription of a number of insulin-responsive genes involved in the control of glucose and lipid metabolism.
Therapeutic effect: Lowers glucose level.

Available forms

Tablets: 15 mg, 30 mg, 45 mg

NURSING PROCESS

Assessment

- Obtain history of patient's underlying condition before therapy, and reassess regularly thereafter.
- Assess patients for excessive fluid volume. Patients with heart failure should be monitored for increased edema during pioglitazone therapy.
- Measure liver enzymes at start of therapy, every 2 months for the first year of therapy, and periodically thereafter. Obtain liver function tests in patients who develop evidence of liver dysfunction, such as nausea, vomiting, abdominal pain, fatigue, anorexia, or dark urine.
- Monitor hemoglobin and hematocrit, especially during the first 4 to 12 weeks of therapy.
- Monitor glucose level regularly, especially during situations of increased stress, such as infection, fever, surgery, and trauma.
- Check glycosylated hemoglobin periodically to evaluate therapeutic response to drug.

• Evaluate patient's and family's knowledge about drug therapy.

Nursing diagnoses

• Ineffective health maintenance related to hyperglycemia
• Risk for injury related to drug-induced hyperglycemia
• Deficient knowledge related to drug therapy

Planning and implementation

• Notify prescriber and discontinue drug if patient develops jaundice or if results of liver function tests show ALT elevations greater than three times the upper limit of normal.
• Pioglitazone alone or with insulin can cause fluid retention that may lead to or exacerbate heart failure. Observe patients for these signs or symptoms of heart failure. Discontinue drug if any deterioration in cardiac status occurs.
• Management of type 2 diabetes should include diet control. Because calorie restrictions, weight loss, and exercise help improve insulin sensitivity and help make drug therapy more effective, these measures are essential for proper diabetes management.
• Watch for hypoglycemia in patients receiving pioglitazone with insulin or a sulfonylurea. Dosage adjustments of these drugs may be needed.
• Because ovulation may resume in premenopausal, anovulatory women with insulin resistance, contraceptive measures may need to be considered.

Patient teaching

• Instruct patient to adhere to dietary instructions and to have glucose level and glycosylated hemoglobin tested regularly.
• Inform patient taking pioglitazone with insulin or an oral antidiabetic about the signs and symptoms of hypoglycemia.
• Advise patient to notify prescriber about periods of stress, such as fever, trauma, infection, or surgery, because medication requirements may change.
• Notify patient that blood tests for liver function will be performed before the start of therapy, every 2 months for the first year, and periodically thereafter.
• Tell patient to report unexplained nausea, vomiting, abdominal pain, fatigue, anorexia, or dark urine immediately because these signs and symptoms may indicate liver problems.
• Warn patient to contact the prescriber if he has signs or symptoms of heart failure (unusually rapid increase in weight or edema, shortness of breath).
• Inform patient that pioglitazone can be taken with or without meals.
• If patient misses a dose, caution against doubling the dose the following day.
• Advise premenopausal, anovulatory woman with insulin resistance that pioglitazone may restore ovulation; recommend that she consider contraception as needed.

Evaluation

• Patient's glucose level is normal with drug therapy.
• Patient doesn't experience hypoglycemia.
• Patient and family state understanding of drug therapy.

piperacillin sodium

(pigh-PER-uh-sil-in SOH-dee-um)
Pipracil, Pipril ♦

Pharmacologic class: extended-spectrum penicillin, acylaminopenicillin
Therapeutic class: antibiotic
Pregnancy risk category: B

Indications and dosages

▶ **Systemic infections caused by susceptible strains of gram-positive and especially gram-negative organisms (including *Proteus* and *Pseudomonas aeruginosa*).** *Adults and children older than age 12:* 12 to 18 g I.V. daily in divided doses q 4 to 6 hours.
Patients with renal impairment: If creatinine clearance is 20 to 40 ml/minute, give 4 g I.V. q 8 ; if < 20 ml/minute, 4 g q 12 hours.
▶ **Prophylaxis of surgical infections.** *Adults:* 2 g I.V. 30 to 60 minutes before surgery. Dose may be repeated during surgery and once or twice after surgery.
▶ **Complicated UTI.** *Adults and children older than age 12:* 8 to 16 g I.V. daily in divided doses q 6 to 8 hours.
Patients with renal impairment: If creatinine clearance is 20 to 40 ml/minute, give 3 g I.V. q 8 hours; if < 20 ml/minute, 3 g q 12 hours.

▶ **Uncomplicated UTI; community-acquired pneumonia.** *Adults and children older than age 12:* 6 to 8 g I.M. or I.V. daily in divided doses q 6 to 12 hours.
Patients with renal impairment: If creatinine clearance is < 20 ml/minute, give 3 g q 12 hours.

Contraindications and precautions

• Contraindicated in patients hypersensitive to drug or other penicillins.
• Use cautiously in patients with other drug allergies, especially to cephalosporins (possible cross-sensitivity); in those with bleeding tendencies, uremia, or hypokalemia.
Lifespan: In pregnant and breast-feeding women, use cautiously. In children younger than age 12, safety of drug hasn't been established.

Adverse reactions

CNS: neuromuscular irritability, ***seizures,*** headache, dizziness.
GI: nausea, diarrhea.
Hematologic: bleeding with large doses, ***neutropenia,*** eosinophilia, ***leukopenia, thrombocytopenia.***
Metabolic: *hypokalemia.*
Other: hypersensitivity reactions (edema, fever, chills, rash, pruritus, urticaria, ***anaphylaxis***), overgrowth of nonsusceptible organisms, pain at injection site, vein irritation, phlebitis.

Interactions

Drug-drug. *Anticoagulants:* Increases risk of bleeding. Monitor PT, PTT and INR; monitor patient for bleeding.
Oral contraceptives: May decrease efficacy of oral contraceptives. Advise alternative barrier method while on drug therapy.
Probenecid: Increases blood levels of piperacillin. Probenecid may be used for this purpose.

Effects on lab test results

• May increase ALT, AST, alkaline phosphatase, LDH, and sodium levels. May decrease potassium level.
• May increase eosinophil count. May decrease hemoglobin, hematocrit, and platelet, WBC, and granulocyte counts.

Pharmacokinetics

Absorption: Unknown after I.M. administration.
Distribution: Distributed widely in body. It penetrates minimally into uninflamed meninges and slightly into bone and sputum. Drug is 16% to 22% protein-bound.
Metabolism: Unknown.
Excretion: Excreted mainly in urine (42% to 90%); some excreted in bile. *Half-life:* 30 to 90 minutes.

Route	Onset	Peak	Duration
I.V.	Immediate	Immediate	Unknown
I.M.	Unknown	30-50 min	Unknown

Pharmacodynamics

Chemical effect: Inhibits cell wall synthesis during microorganism multiplication; bacteria resist penicillins by producing penicillinases, enzymes that convert penicillins to inactive penicilloic acid. Piperacillin sodium resists these enzymes.
Therapeutic effect: Kills susceptible bacteria, including many gram-negative aerobic and anaerobic bacilli, many gram-positive and gram-negative cocci, and some gram-positive aerobic and anaerobic bacilli.

Available forms

Injection: 2 g, 3 g, 4 g

NURSING PROCESS

Assessment

• Assess patient's infection before therapy and regularly thereafter.
• Before giving drug, ask patient about allergic reactions to penicillin. However, negative history is no guarantee against future reaction.
• Obtain specimen for culture and sensitivity tests before first dose. Therapy may begin pending results.
• Check CBC and platelet counts frequently. Drug may cause thrombocytopenia.
• Monitor potassium level.
• Be alert for adverse reactions and drug interactions.
• Cystic fibrosis patients tend to be most susceptible to fever or rash.
• Monitor patient's hydration status if adverse GI reactions occur.
• Evaluate patient's and family's knowledge of drug therapy.

Nursing diagnoses
- Infection related to presence of susceptible bacteria
- Risk for deficient fluid volume related to adverse GI reactions
- Deficient knowledge related to drug therapy

Planning and implementation
- Dosage should be altered in patient with impaired renal function.
- Drug is typically used with another antibiotic, such as gentamicin.
- **I.V. use:** Reconstitute each gram of drug with 5 ml of diluent, such as sterile or bacteriostatic water for injection, normal saline solution for injection (with or without preservative), D_5W, or dextrose 5% in normal saline solution for injection. Shake until dissolved.
– Inject reconstituted solution directly into vein or into I.V. line of free-flowing solution over 3 to 5 minutes. Or, dilute with at least 50 ml of compatible I.V. solution and give by intermittent infusion over 30 minutes.
– Avoid continuous infusions to prevent vein irritation. Change site every 48 hours.
– Aminoglycoside antibiotics (such as gentamicin and tobramycin) are chemically incompatible with drug. Don't mix in same I.V. container.
- **I.M. use:** Reconstitute drug with sterile or bacteriostatic water for injection, normal saline solution for injection (with or without preservative), or 0.5% to 1% lidocaine hydrochloride. Add 2 ml of diluent for each gram of drug. Final solution will contain 1 g/2.5 ml.
- Give drug at least 1 hour before bacteriostatic antibiotics.
- Institute seizure precautions. Patients with high serum levels of this drug may have seizures.

Patient teaching
- Tell patient to report pain or discomfort at I.V. site.
- Instruct patient to limit salt intake while taking piperacillin because drug contains 1.98 mEq sodium per gram.
- Tell patient to report adverse reactions.

Evaluation
- Patient is free from infection.
- Patient maintains adequate hydration throughout drug therapy.
- Patient and family state understanding of drug therapy.

piperacillin sodium and tazobactam sodium
(pigh-PER-uh-sil-in SOH-dee-um and taz-oh-BAK-tem SOH-dee-um)
Zosyn

Pharmacologic class: extended-spectrum penicillin/beta-lactamase inhibitor
Therapeutic class: antibiotic
Pregnancy risk category: B

Indications and dosages
▶ **Appendicitis (complicated by rupture or abscess); peritonitis caused by *Escherichia coli, Bacteroides fragilis, B. ovatus, B. thetaiotaomicron,* or *B. vulgatus;* skin and skin-structure infections caused by *Staphylococcus aureus;* postpartum endometritis or pelvic inflammatory disease caused by *E. coli;* moderately severe community-acquired pneumonia caused by *Haemophilus influenzae.*** *Adults:* 3 g piperacillin and 0.375 g tazobactam I.V. q 6 hours.
Patients with renal impairment: If creatinine clearance is 20 to 40 ml/minute, 2 g piperacillin and 0.25 g tazobactam I.V. q 6 hours; if below 20 ml/minute, 2 g piperacillin and 0.25 g tazobactam I.V. q 8 hours.

Contraindications and precautions
- Contraindicated in patients hypersensitive to drug or other penicillins.
- Use cautiously in patients with other drug allergies, especially to cephalosporins (possible cross-sensitivity), and in those with bleeding tendencies, uremia, or hypokalemia.

Lifespan: In pregnant and breast-feeding women, use cautiously. In children younger than age 12, safety of drug hasn't been established.

Adverse reactions
CNS: *headache, insomnia,* agitation, fever, dizziness, anxiety.
CV: hypertension, tachycardia, chest pain, edema.
EENT: rhinitis.

GI: *diarrhea, nausea, constipation,* vomiting, dyspepsia, stool changes, abdominal pain.
Hematologic: ***thrombocytopenia.***
Respiratory: dyspnea.
Skin: rash (including maculopapular, bullous, urticarial, and eczematoid), pruritus.
Other: pain, ***anaphylaxis,*** candidiasis, inflammation and phlebitis at I.V. site.

Interactions

Drug-drug. *Anticoagulants:* Increases risk of bleeding. Monitor PT, PTT, and INR, and monitor patient for bleeding.
Oral contraceptives: Potential for decreased efficacy of oral contraceptives. Advise alternative barrier method while on drug therapy.
Probenecid: Increases blood levels of piperacillin. Probenecid may be used for this purpose.
Vecuronium: Prolongs neuromuscular blockage. Monitor patient closely.

Effects on lab test results

- May increase eosinophil count. May decrease hemoglobin, hematocrit, and WBC and platelet counts.

Pharmacokinetics

Absorption: Administered I.V.
Distribution: Both drugs are about 30% protein-bound.
Metabolism: Piperacillin is metabolized to a minor, microbiologically active desethyl metabolite. Tazobactam is metabolized to a single metabolite that lacks pharmacologic and antibacterial activities.
Excretion: Excreted in urine and bile. *Half-life:* piperacillin, 40 minutes; tazobactam, 70 minutes.

Route	Onset	Peak	Duration
I.V.	Immediate	Immediate	Unknown

Pharmacodynamics

Chemical effect: Piperacillin inhibits cell wall synthesis during microorganism multiplication; tazobactam increases piperacillin effectiveness by inactivating beta-lactamases, which destroy penicillins.
Therapeutic effect: Kills susceptible bacteria, including *E. coli, B. fragilis, B. ovatus, B. thetaiotaomicron, B. vulgatus, Staphylococcus aureus,* and *Haemophilus influenzae.*

Available forms

Powder for injection: 2 g piperacillin and 0.25 g tazobactam per vial, 3 g piperacillin and 0.375 g tazobactam per vial, 4 g piperacillin and 0.5 g tazobactam per vial

NURSING PROCESS

Assessment

- Before giving drug, ask patient about previous allergic reactions to this drug or other penicillins. However, negative history of penicillin allergy doesn't guarantee future safety.
- Assess patient's infection before therapy and regularly thereafter.
- Obtain specimen for culture and sensitivity tests before first dose. Therapy may begin pending results.
- Be alert for adverse reactions and drug interactions.
- Monitor patient's hydration status if adverse GI reactions occur.
- Evaluate patient's and family's knowledge of drug therapy.

Nursing diagnoses

- Infection related to presence of bacteria
- Risk of deficient fluid volume related to adverse GI reactions
- Deficient knowledge related to drug therapy

Planning and implementation

- Reconstitute each gram of piperacillin with 5 ml of diluent, such as sterile or bacteriostatic water for injection, normal saline solution for injection, bacteriostatic normal saline solution for injection, D_5W, dextrose 5% in normal saline solution for injection, or dextran 6% in normal saline solution for injection. Don't use lactated Ringer's injection. Shake until dissolved. Further dilute to final volume of 50 ml before infusion.

ALERT: Infuse drug over at least 30 minutes. Stop other primary infusions during administration if possible. Aminoglycoside antibiotics (such as gentamicin and tobramycin) are chemically incompatible with drug. Don't mix in same I.V. container.

- Don't mix with other drugs.
- Use drug immediately after reconstitution. Discard unused drug in single-dose vials after 24 hours if held at room temperature; after 48 hours if refrigerated. Diluted drug is stable in

I.V. bags for 24 hours at room temperature or 1 week if refrigerated.
- Change I.V. site every 48 hours.
- Because hemodialysis removes 6% of piperacillin dose and 21% of tazobactam dose, supplemental doses may be needed after hemodialysis.

Patient teaching
- Tell patient to report pain or discomfort at I.V. site.
- Advise patient to limit salt intake while taking drug because piperacillin contains 1.98 mEq of sodium per gram.
- Tell patient to report adverse reactions.

Evaluation
- Patient is free from infection.
- Patient maintains adequate hydration.
- Patient and family state understanding of drug therapy.

pirbuterol acetate
(pir-BYOO-teh-rol AS-ih-tayt)
Maxair

Pharmacologic class: beta-adrenergic agonist
Therapeutic class: bronchodilator
Pregnancy risk category: C

Indications and dosages
▶ **Prevention and reversal of bronchospasm, asthma.** *Adults and children age 12 and older:* 1 or 2 inhalations (0.2 to 0.4 mg) repeated q 4 to 6 hours. Maximum, 12 inhalations daily.

Contraindications and precautions
- Contraindicated in patients hypersensitive to drug.
- Use cautiously in patients who are unusually responsive to sympathomimetic amines, and in patients with CV disorders, hyperthyroidism, diabetes, or seizure disorders.

Lifespan: In pregnant and breast-feeding women, use cautiously. In children younger than age 12, safety of drug hasn't been established.

Adverse reactions
CNS: tremor, nervousness, dizziness, insomnia, headache.
CV: tachycardia, palpitations, increased blood pressure.
EENT: dry or irritated throat.

Interactions
Drug-drug. *MAO inhibitors, tricyclic antidepressants:* May potentiate action of beta-adrenergic agonist on vascular system. Use together cautiously.
Propranolol, other beta blockers: Decreases bronchodilating effects. Avoid using together.

Effects on lab test results
None reported.

Pharmacokinetics
Absorption: Negligible serum level after inhalation.
Distribution: Distributed locally.
Metabolism: Metabolized in liver.
Excretion: About 50% of inhaled dose is excreted in urine as parent drug and metabolites.

Route	Onset	Peak	Duration
Inhalation	≤ 5 min	30-60 min	5 hr

Pharmacodynamics
Chemical effect: Relaxes bronchial smooth muscle by acting on $beta_2$-adrenergic receptors.
Therapeutic effect: Improves breathing ability.

Available forms
Inhaler: 0.2 mg/metered dose

NURSING PROCESS

Assessment
- Assess patient's condition before therapy.
- Monitor effectiveness by checking respiratory rate, auscultating lung fields frequently, and following laboratory studies (such as arterial blood gases).
- Be alert for adverse reactions and drug interactions.
- Evaluate patient's and family's knowledge of drug therapy.

Nursing diagnoses
- Impaired gas exchange related to presence of bronchospasms
- Disturbed sleep pattern related to drug-induced insomnia
- Deficient knowledge related to drug therapy

Planning and implementation
- Shake canister well before each use.
- Store drug away from heat and direct sunlight.
- If patient also uses a corticosteroid inhaler, always give pirbuterol first, and then wait about 5 minutes before giving the corticosteroid inhaler.
- Notify prescriber if patient's condition doesn't improve or worsens.

Patient teaching
- Give these instructions for using metered-dose inhaler: Clear nasal passages and throat. Breathe out, expelling as much air from lungs as possible. Place mouthpiece well into mouth and inhale deeply as you release a dose from inhaler. Hold breath for several seconds, remove mouthpiece, and exhale slowly.
- If more than one inhalation is ordered, tell patient to wait at least 2 minutes before repeating procedure.
- If patient also uses a corticosteroid inhaler, tell him to use the bronchodilator first and then wait about 5 minutes before using the corticosteroid. This allows the bronchodilator to open air passages for maximum effectiveness.
- Tell patient to notify prescriber if bronchospasm increases after drug use.
- Advise patient to seek medical attention if previously effective dosage no longer controls symptoms; this change may signify worsening of disease.

Evaluation
- Patient has improved gas exchange, as demonstrated by improved lung sounds and arterial blood gas measurements.
- Patient doesn't have insomnia.
- Patient and family state understanding of drug therapy.

piroxicam
(peer-OK-sih-cam)
Apo-Piroxicam ◆, Feldene, Novo-Pirocam ◆

Pharmacologic class: NSAID
Therapeutic class: nonnarcotic analgesic, antipyretic, anti-inflammatory
Pregnancy risk category: C

Indications and dosages
▶ **Osteoarthritis, rheumatoid arthritis.** *Adults:* 20 mg P.O. daily. If desired, dosage may be divided b.i.d.
▶ **Juvenile rheumatoid arthritis‡.** *Children weighing 15 to 30 kg (33 to 67 lb):* 5 mg P.O. daily.
Children weighing 31 to 45 kg (68 to 100 lb): 10 mg P.O. daily.
Children weighing 46 to 55 kg (101 to 121 lb): 15 mg P.O. daily.

Contraindications and precautions
- Contraindicated in patients hypersensitive to drug, and patients with bronchospasm or angioedema caused by aspirin or NSAIDs.
- Use cautiously in those with GI disorders, history of renal or peptic ulcer disease, cardiac disease, hypertension, or conditions predisposing to fluid retention.

Lifespan: In pregnant or breast-feeding women, drug is contraindicated. In children, long-term use of drug hasn't been established. In geriatric patients, use cautiously.

Adverse reactions
CNS: headache, drowsiness, dizziness, paresthesia, somnolence.
CV: peripheral edema.
EENT: auditory disturbances.
GI: *epigastric distress, nausea, occult blood loss,* peptic ulceration, ***severe GI bleeding.***
GU: ***nephrotoxicity.***
Hematologic: anemia, ***leukopenia, aplastic anemia, agranulocytosis, thrombocytopenia.***
Metabolism: ***hyperkalemia, acidosis,*** dilutional hypernatremia.
Respiratory: ***bronchospasm.***
Skin: pruritus, rash, urticaria, *photosensitivity reaction.*

Interactions
Drug-drug. *Aspirin, corticosteroids:* Increases risk of GI toxicity. Decreases plasma piroxicam levels. Monitor patient closely.
Lithium: Increased plasma lithium levels. Monitor patient for toxicity.
Oral anticoagulants: Increases risk of bleeding. Monitor patient closely for bleeding.
Oral antidiabetics: Increases antidiabetic effects. Monitor patient and glucose levels closely.

Probenecid, ritonavir: Increases toxicity of piroxicam. Don't use together.
Drug-herb. *Dong quai, feverfew, garlic, ginger, horse chestnut, red clover:* May increase risk of bleeding. Monitor patient closely.
St. John's wort: May increase risk of photosensitivity. Advise patient to avoid unprotected or prolonged exposure to sunlight.
Drug-lifestyle. *Alcohol use:* Increases risk of GI toxicity. Decreases plasma piroxicam levels. Discourage using together.
Sun exposure: Increases risk of photosensitivity reaction. Advise patient to avoid unprotected or prolonged exposure to sunlight.

Effects on lab test results

- May increase BUN, creatinine, liver enzyme, sodium, and potassium levels. May decrease glucose level.
- May decrease hemoglobin, hematocrit, and WBC, granulocyte, platelet, and eosinophil counts. May prolong bleeding time.

Pharmacokinetics

Absorption: Rapid. Food delays absorption.
Distribution: Drug is highly protein-bound.
Metabolism: Metabolized in liver.
Excretion: Excreted in urine. *Half-life:* About 50 hours.

Route	Onset	Peak	Duration
P.O.	15-30 min	3-5 hr	About 24 hr

Pharmacodynamics

Chemical effect: Unknown; produces anti-inflammatory, analgesic, and antipyretic effects, possibly by inhibiting prostaglandin synthesis.
Therapeutic effect: Relieves pain, fever, and inflammation.

Available forms

Capsules: 10 mg, 20 mg

NURSING PROCESS

Assessment

- Assess patient's condition before therapy and regularly thereafter. Effects don't occur for at least 2 weeks after therapy begins. Evaluate response to drug by assessing for reduced symptoms.
- Check CBC and renal, hepatic, and auditory function periodically during prolonged therapy.
- Be alert for adverse reactions and drug interactions.
- Evaluate patient's and family's knowledge of drug therapy.

Nursing diagnoses

- Chronic pain related to arthritis
- Impaired tissue integrity related to adverse effect on GI mucosa
- Deficient knowledge related to drug therapy

Planning and implementation

- Give drug with milk, antacids, or food if adverse GI reactions occur.
- Stop drug and notify prescriber if laboratory abnormalities occur.

Patient teaching

- Tell patient that full therapeutic effects may be delayed for 2 to 4 weeks.
- Teach patient to recognize and report signs and symptoms of GI bleeding.
- Advise patient to use sunblock, wear protective clothing, and avoid prolonged exposure to sunlight.
- Warn patient to not take any NSAIDs during therapy.

Evaluation

- Patient is free from pain.
- Patient maintains normal GI tissue integrity.
- Patient and family state understanding of drug therapy.

plasma protein fraction

(PLAZ-muh PROH-teen FRAK-shun)
Plasmanate, Plasma-Plex, Plasmatein, Protenate

Pharmacologic class: blood derivative
Therapeutic class: plasma volume expander
Pregnancy risk category: C

Indications and dosages

▶ **Shock.** *Adults:* Varies with patient's condition and response, but usual dose is 250 to 500 ml I.V. (12.5 to 25 g protein), usually no faster than 10 ml/minute.

Infants and young children: 6.6 to 33 ml/kg (0.33 to 1.65 g/kg of protein) I.V., 5 to 10 ml/minute.

▶ **Hypoproteinemia.** *Adults:* 1,000 to 1,500 ml I.V. daily. Maximum infusion rate is 8 ml/minute.

Contraindications and precautions

- Contraindicated in patients with severe anemia or heart failure and in those having undergone cardiac bypass surgery.
- Use cautiously in patients with hepatic or renal failure, low cardiac reserve, or restricted sodium intake. Rapid infusion may cause severe, persistent hypotension.

Lifespan: In pregnant and breast-feeding women, use cautiously.

Adverse reactions

CNS: headache, fever.
CV: various effects on blood pressure after rapid infusion or intra-arterial administration, ***vascular overload*** after rapid infusion, flushing.
GI: nausea, vomiting, hypersalivation.
Musculoskeletal: back pain.
Respiratory: dyspnea, pulmonary edema.
Skin: erythema, urticaria.
Other: chills.

Interactions

None significant.

Effects on lab test results

None reported.

Pharmacokinetics

Absorption: Administered I.V.
Distribution: Distributed into intravascular space and extravascular sites, including skin, muscle, and lungs.
Metabolism: Unknown.
Excretion: Unknown.

Route	Onset	Peak	Duration
I.V.	Immediate	Immediate	Unknown

Pharmacodynamics

Chemical effect: Supplies colloid to blood and expands plasma volume.
Therapeutic effect: Raises serum protein levels and expands plasma volume.

Available forms

Injection: 5% solution in 50-ml, 250-ml, 500-ml vials

NURSING PROCESS

Assessment

- Assess patient's condition before therapy and regularly thereafter.
- Monitor vital signs at least hourly.
- Be alert for adverse reactions.
- Drug contains 130 to 160 mEq sodium/L. Monitor patients who are on sodium restriction or who have heart failure carefully for signs and symptoms of hypervolemia.
- Evaluate patient's and family's knowledge of drug therapy.

Nursing diagnoses

- Decreased cardiac output related to underlying condition
- Acute pain related to headache
- Deficient knowledge related to drug therapy

Planning and implementation

- Check expiration date before using. Don't use solutions that are cloudy, contain sediment, or have been frozen. Discard container that has been open for more than 4 hours because solution contains no preservatives.
- If patient is dehydrated, give additional fluids P.O. or I.V.

ALERT: Avoid rapid I.V. infusion. Rate is individualized according to patient's age, condition, and diagnosis. Maximum rate is 10 ml/minute. Stop or slow infusion if sudden hypotension occurs.

- Be prepared to slow or stop infusion if hypotension occurs. Vital signs should return to normal gradually.

ALERT: Don't administer drug near area of trauma, injury, or infection.

- Administer mild analgesic for drug-induced headache.

Patient teaching

- Tell patient and family the purpose of plasma protein fraction, and keep them informed of drug effectiveness.
- Instruct patient to report adverse reactions.

Evaluation

- Patient regains normal cardiac output.
- Patient is free from pain.
- Patient and family state understanding of drug therapy.

plicamycin (mithramycin)

(pligh-keh-MIGH-sin)
Mithracin

Pharmacologic class: antibiotic antineoplastic (not specific to cell cycle)
Therapeutic class: antineoplastic, hypocalcemic agent
Pregnancy risk category: X

Indications and dosages

▶ **Hypercalcemia linked to advanced malignancy.** *Adults:* 15 to 25 mcg/kg/day I.V. for 3 to 4 days. Dosage repeated at weekly intervals until desired response is obtained.
▶ **Testicular cancer.** *Adults:* 25 to 30 mcg/kg I.V. daily for 8 to 10 days or until toxicity occurs.
▶ **Paget's disease‡.** *Adults:* 15 mcg/kg I.V. daily over 4 to 6 hours for up to 10 days.

Contraindications and precautions

- Contraindicated in patients with thrombocytopenia, bone marrow suppression, or bleeding disorder.
- Use with extreme caution in patients who have significant renal or hepatic impairment.

Lifespan: In women who are or may become pregnant and in breast-feeding patients, drug is contraindicated. In children, safety of drug hasn't been established.

Adverse reactions

CNS: drowsiness, weakness, lethargy, headache, dizziness, nervousness, depression.
GI: *nausea, vomiting,* anorexia, diarrhea, stomatitis, metallic taste.
GU: proteinuria.
Hematologic: ***leukopenia, thrombocytopenia, bleeding syndrome from epistaxis to generalized hemorrhage.***
Hepatic: ***hepatotoxicity.***
Skin: *facial flushing.*
Other: vein irritation, cellulitis with extravasation.

Interactions

None significant.

Effects on lab test results

- May increase BUN, creatinine, and liver enzyme levels. May decrease calcium, potassium, and phosphate levels.
- May decrease WBC and platelet counts.

Pharmacokinetics

Absorption: Administered I.V.
Distribution: Distributes mainly into Kupffer cells of liver, into renal tubular cells, and along formed bone surfaces. Also crosses blood-brain barrier and reaches appreciable levels in CSF.
Metabolism: Unknown.
Excretion: Excreted mainly in urine.

Route	Onset	Peak	Duration
I.V.	1-2 days	3 days	7-10 days

Pharmacodynamics

Chemical effect: Unknown; may form a complex with DNA, thus inhibiting RNA synthesis. Also inhibits osteocytic activity, blocking calcium and phosphorus resorption from bone.
Therapeutic effect: Hinders growth of testicular cancer cells and lowers calcium level.

Available forms

Injection: 2.5-mg vials

NURSING PROCESS

Assessment

- Assess patient's condition before therapy and regularly thereafter.
- Obtain baseline platelet count and PT before therapy, and monitor them during therapy.
- Facial flushing is an early indicator of bleeding.
- Monitor LD, AST, ALT, alkaline phosphatase, BUN, creatinine, potassium, calcium, and phosphorus levels.
- Monitor patient for tetany, carpopedal spasm, Chvostek's sign, and muscle cramps; check calcium level. Precipitous drop is possible.
- Be alert for adverse reactions.
- Evaluate patient's and family's knowledge of drug therapy.

Nursing diagnoses

- Ineffective health maintenance related to underlying condition
- Ineffective protection related to adverse hematologic reactions
- Deficient knowledge related to drug therapy

Planning and implementation

- Give antiemetic before giving drug.
- Follow facility policy to reduce risks. Preparation and administration of parenteral form are related to carcinogenic, mutagenic, and teratogenic risks for personnel.
- To prepare solution, add 4.9 ml of sterile water for injection to vial and shake to dissolve. Then dilute for I.V. infusion in 1,000 ml of D_5W or normal saline solution. Infuse over 4 to 6 hours. Discard unused drug.
- Slow infusion reduces nausea that develops with I.V. push.
- Avoid extravasation. Drug is a vesicant. If I.V. solution infiltrates, stop immediately, notify prescriber, and use ice packs. Restart I.V. line.
- Avoid contact with skin or mucous membranes.
- Discontinue drug and notify prescriber if WBC count is less than 4,000/mm^3, platelet count falls to less than 150,000/mm^3, or PT is prolonged to more than 4 seconds longer than control.
- Store lyophilized powder in refrigerator and protect from light.

Patient teaching

- Warn patient to watch for signs of infection (fever, sore throat, fatigue) and bleeding (easy bruising, nosebleeds, bleeding gums, melena). Have patient take temperature daily. Instruct patient and family on infection-control and bleeding precautions.
- Tell patient to use salicylate-free medication for pain or fever.
- Warn patient to protect against pregnancy during therapy. If she thinks she has become pregnant, tell her to contact her prescriber immediately.

Evaluation

- Patient responds well to therapy.
- Patient doesn't develop serious complications from adverse hematologic reactions.
- Patient and family state understanding of drug therapy.

polyethylene glycol and electrolyte solution

(pol-ee-ETH-ih-leen GLIGH-kohl and ee-LEK-troh-light soh-LOO-shun)

Colovage, CoLyte, GoLYTELY, NuLYTELY, OCL

Pharmacologic class: polyethylene glycol (PEG) 3350 nonabsorbable solution

Therapeutic class: laxative and bowel evacuant

Pregnancy risk category: C

Indications and dosages

▶ **Bowel preparation before GI examination.** *Adults:* 240 ml P.O. q 10 minutes until 4 L are consumed. Typically, give 4 hours before examination, allowing 3 hours for drinking and 1 hour for bowel evacuation.

▶ **Management of acute iron overdose‡.** *Children older than age 3:* 2,953 ml/kg over 5 days.

Contraindications and precautions

- Contraindicated in patients with GI obstruction or perforation, gastric retention, toxic colitis, or megacolon.

Lifespan: In pregnant and breast-feeding women, use cautiously.

Adverse reactions

GI: nausea, bloating, cramps, vomiting.

Interactions

Drug-drug. *Oral drugs:* Decreases absorption if given within 1 hour of starting therapy. Don't give with other oral drugs.

Effects on lab test results

None reported.

Pharmacokinetics

Absorption: Not absorbed.

Distribution: Not applicable because drug isn't absorbed.

Metabolism: Not applicable because drug isn't absorbed.

Excretion: Excreted via GI tract.

Route	Onset	Peak	Duration
P.O.	≤ 1 hr	Varies	Varies

Pharmacodynamics

Chemical effect: PEG 3350, a nonabsorbable solution, acts as osmotic agent. Sodium sulfate greatly reduces sodium absorption. The electrolyte concentration causes virtually no net absorption or secretion of ions.
Therapeutic effect: Cleanses bowel.

Available forms

Oral solution: PEG 3350 (6 g), sodium sulfate decahydrate (1.29 g), sodium chloride (146 mg), potassium chloride (75 mg) sodium bicarbonate (168 mg), polysorbate-80 (30 mg) per 100 ml (OCL)
Powder for oral solution: PEG 3350 (240 g), sodium sulfate (22.72 g), sodium chloride (5.84 g), potassium chloride (2.98 g), sodium bicarbonate (6.72 g) per 4 L (CoLyte); PEG 3350 (236 g), sodium sulfate (22.74 g), sodium bicarbonate (6.74 g), sodium chloride (5.86 g), potassium chloride (2.97 g) per 4 L (GoLYTELY); PEG 3350 (420 g), sodium bicarbonate (5.72 g), sodium chloride (11.2 g), potassium chloride (1.48 g) per 4 L (NuLYTELY)

NURSING PROCESS

Assessment

- Assess patient's condition before therapy and regularly thereafter.
- Be alert for adverse reactions and drug interactions.
- Evaluate patient's and family's knowledge of drug therapy.

Nursing diagnoses

- Health-seeking behavior (testing) related to need to determine cause of underlying GI problem
- Risk for deficient fluid volume related to adverse GI reactions
- Deficient knowledge related to drug therapy

Planning and implementation

- Use tap water to reconstitute powder. Shake vigorously to make sure all powder is dissolved. Refrigerate solution but use within 48 hours.

ALERT: Don't add flavoring or additional ingredients to solution or administer chilled solution. Hypothermia has developed after ingestion of large amounts of chilled solution.

- Give solution early in morning if patient is scheduled for midmorning examination. Orally administered solution induces diarrhea (onset 30 to 60 minutes) that rapidly cleans bowel, usually within 4 hours.
- When used as preparation for barium enema, give solution the evening before examination, to avoid interfering with barium coating of colonic mucosa.
- If given to semiconscious patient or to patient with impaired gag reflex, take care to prevent aspiration.
- No major shifts in fluid or electrolyte balance have been reported.

Patient teaching

- Tell patient to fast for 4 hours before taking solution and to ingest only clear fluids until examination is complete.
- Warn patient about adverse GI reactions to drug.

Evaluation

- Patient is able to have examination.
- Patient maintains adequate fluid volume.
- Patient and family state understanding of drug therapy.

polysaccharide iron complex

(pol-ee-SAK-uh-righd IGH-ern KOM-pleks)
Hytinic, Ferrex 150, Niferex, Niferex-150, Nu-Iron, Nu-Iron 150

Pharmacologic class: oral iron supplement
Therapeutic class: hematinic
Pregnancy risk category: NR

Indications and dosages

▶ **Treatment of uncomplicated iron deficiency anemia.** *Adults and children age 12 and older:* 100 to 300 mg P.O. daily. *Children ages 6 to 12:* 50 to 100 mg P.O. daily as tablets or 1 tsp of elixir P.O. daily.

Children younger than age 6: 3 to 6 mg/kg P.O. daily in three divided doses, as directed by prescriber.
Infants: 10 to 25 mg P.O. daily in three divided doses, as directed by prescriber.

Contraindications and precautions

• Contraindicated in patients hypersensitive to drug or its components and in those with hemochromatosis or hemosiderosis.
Lifespan: In children, iron overdose may be fatal; treat patient immediately. In children younger than age 6, doses should be administered only as directed by prescriber.

Adverse reactions

GI: nausea, constipation, black stools, epigastric pain.

Interactions

Drug-drug. *Antacids, cholestyramine resin, cimetidine, tetracycline, vitamin E:* Decreases iron absorption. Separate doses by 2 to 4 hours.
Chloramphenicol: Delays response to iron therapy. Monitor patient.
Fluoroquinolones, levodopa, methyldopa, penicillamine, tetracycline: Decreases GI absorption of these drugs, possibly resulting in decreased serum level or efficacy. Administer separately; monitor patient.
Levothyroxine sodium: Decreases levothyroxine efficacy, leading to hypothyroidism. Avoid using together, or separate administration times by 2 to 4 hours.
Vitamin C: May increase iron absorption. Can be used for this effect.
Drug-food. *Cereals, coffee, dairy products, eggs, teas, whole-grain breads:* Decreases iron absorption. Separate use by 2 to 4 hours.

Effects on lab test results

• May increase hemoglobin, hematocrit, and reticulocyte count.

Pharmacokinetics

Absorption: Iron is absorbed from entire length of GI tract, but primary absorption sites are duodenum and proximal jejunum. Up to 10% of iron is absorbed by healthy people; people with iron-deficiency anemia may absorb up to 60%.
Distribution: Iron is transported through GI mucosal cells directly into blood, where it's immediately bound to carrier protein, transferrin, and transported to bone marrow for incorporation into hemoglobin. Iron is highly protein-bound.
Metabolism: Iron is liberated by destruction of hemoglobin, but is conserved and reused by body.
Excretion: Men and postmenopausal women lose about 1 mg/day; premenopausal women, about 1.5 mg/day. Loss usually occurs in nails, hair, feces, and urine; trace amounts lost in bile and sweat.

Route	Onset	Peak	Duration
P.O.	≤ 3 days	5-30 days	2 mo

Pharmacodynamics

Chemical effect: Provides elemental iron, an essential component in formation of hemoglobin.
Therapeutic effect: Restores normal iron levels in body.

Available forms

Capsules†: 150 mg
Solution†: 100 mg/5 ml
Tablets†: 50 mg

NURSING PROCESS

Assessment

• Assess patient's condition before therapy and regularly thereafter.
• Be alert for adverse reactions and drug interactions.
• Evaluate patient's and family's knowledge of drug therapy.

Nursing diagnoses

• Fatigue related to anemia
• Deficient knowledge related to drug therapy

Planning and implementation

• Give drug with juice (preferably orange juice) or water but not with milk or antacids.

Patient teaching

• Inform patient that drug may turn stools black.
• Advise patient to avoid foods that may impair absorption, including yogurt, cheese, eggs, milk, whole-grain breads and cereals, tea, and

coffee. Tell him to take drug with juice or water.
• Inform parents that as few as three tablets can cause iron poisoning, which may be fatal in children. Warn them to store drug out of reach of children.
• If patient misses a dose, tell him to take it as soon as he remembers but not to double the dose.

✓ Evaluation
• Patient states that fatigue is relieved as hemoglobin and reticulocyte count return to normal.
• Patient and family state understanding of drug therapy.

potassium acetate
(puh-TAS-ee-um AS-ih-tayt)

Pharmacologic class: potassium supplement
Therapeutic class: therapeutic agent for electrolyte balance
Pregnancy risk category: C

Indications and dosages
▶ **Hypokalemia.** *Adults:* No more than 20 mEq I.V. hourly at concentration of 40 mEq/L or less. Total 24-hour dose should not exceed 150 mEq. Potassium replacement should be done with ECG monitoring and frequent potassium tests. Use I.V. route only for life-threatening hypokalemia or when oral replacement isn't feasible.
▶ **Prevention of hypokalemia.** *Adults:* Dosage is individualized to patient's needs, not to exceed 150 mEq daily. Administer as an additive to I.V infusions. Usual dosage is 20 mEq/L infused at no more than 20 mEq/hour.
Children: Individualized dosage not to exceed 3 mEq/kg daily. Administer as an additive to I.V infusions.

Contraindications and precautions
• Contraindicated in patients with severe renal impairment with oliguria, anuria, or azotemia; those with untreated Addison's disease or adrenocortical insufficiency; and those with acute dehydration, heat cramps, hyperkalemia, hyperkalemic form of familial periodic paralysis, and conditions related to extensive tissue breakdown.
• Use cautiously in patients with cardiac disease or renal impairment.
Lifespan: In pregnant and breast-feeding women, use cautiously.

Adverse reactions
CNS: paresthesia of limbs, listlessness, mental confusion, weakness or heaviness of legs, flaccid paralysis.
CV: ***arrhythmias, possible cardiac arrest, heart block,*** ECG changes.
GI: nausea, vomiting, abdominal pain, diarrhea, bowel ulceration.
GU: oliguria.
Respiratory: ***respiratory paralysis.***
Skin: cold skin, gray pallor.
Other: pain, redness at infusion site.

Interactions
Drug-drug. *ACE inhibitors, potassium-sparing diuretics:* Increases risk of hyperkalemia. Use with extreme caution.
Drug-herb. *Cascara, licorice:* May antagonize effects of potassium supplements. Discourage using together.
Drug-food. *Salt substitutes:* Increases risk of hyperkalemia. Don't use together.

Effects on lab test results
• May increase potassium level.

Pharmacokinetics
Absorption: Administered I.V.
Distribution: Distributed throughout body.
Metabolism: None significant.
Excretion: Excreted largely by kidneys; small amounts may be excreted via skin and intestinal tract, but intestinal potassium is usually reabsorbed.

Route	Onset	Peak	Duration
I.V.	Immediate	Immediate	Unknown

Pharmacodynamics
Chemical effect: Aids in transmitting nerve impulses, contracting cardiac and skeletal muscle, and maintaining intracellular tonicity, cellular metabolism, acid-base balance, and normal renal function.
Therapeutic effect: Replaces and maintains potassium level.

Available forms

Injection: 2 mEq/ml in 20-ml, 50-ml, 100-ml vials; 4 mEq/ml in 50-ml vial

NURSING PROCESS

Assessment

- Assess patient's condition before therapy and regularly thereafter.
- During therapy, monitor ECG, renal function, fluid intake and output, and serum potassium, serum creatinine, and BUN levels.
- Be alert for adverse reactions and drug interactions.
- Evaluate patient's and family's knowledge of drug therapy.

Nursing diagnoses

- Ineffective health maintenance related to presence of hypokalemia
- Risk for injury related to drug-induced hyperkalemia
- Deficient knowledge related to drug therapy

Planning and implementation

- Give drug only by I.V. infusion, never by I.V. push or I.M. route.
- Watch for pain and redness at infusion site. Large-bore needle reduces local irritation.
- Administer drug slowly as diluted solution; life-threatening hyperkalemia may result from too-rapid infusion.
- Don't give potassium postoperatively until urine flow is established.

ALERT: Potassium preparations aren't interchangeable. Verify preparation before administration.

Patient teaching

- Inform patient of need for potassium supplementation.
- Tell patient that drug will be given through an I.V. line.
- Instruct patient to report adverse reactions.

Evaluation

- Patient's potassium level returns to normal with drug therapy.
- Patient doesn't develop hyperkalemia as result of drug therapy.
- Patient and family state understanding of drug therapy.

potassium bicarbonate

(puh-TAS-ee-um bigh-KAR-buh-nayt)
K+ Care ET

Pharmacologic class: potassium supplement
Therapeutic class: therapeutic agent for electrolyte balance
Pregnancy risk category: C

Indications and dosages

▶ **Hypokalemia.** *Adults:* 25 to 50 mEq dissolved in 4 to 8 oz (120 to 240 ml) of water and given once daily to b.i.d.

Contraindications and precautions

- Contraindicated in patients with untreated Addison's disease, acute dehydration, heat cramps, hyperkalemia, hyperkalemic form of familial periodic paralysis, other conditions linked to extensive tissue breakdown, and severe renal impairment with oliguria, anuria, or azotemia.
- Use cautiously in patients with cardiac disease or renal impairment.

Lifespan: In pregnant and breast-feeding women, use cautiously. In children, safety of drug hasn't been established.

Adverse reactions

CNS: paresthesia of limbs, listlessness, mental confusion, weakness or heaviness of legs, flaccid paralysis.
CV: ***arrhythmias, cardiac arrest, heart block,*** ECG changes (prolonged PR interval, widened QRS complex, ST-segment depression, and tall, tented T waves).
GI: *nausea, vomiting, abdominal pain,* diarrhea, ulcerations, hemorrhage, obstruction, perforation.

Interactions

Drug-drug. *ACE inhibitors, potassium-sparing diuretics:* Increases risk of hyperkalemia. Use with extreme caution.
Drug-food. *Salt substitutes:* Increases risk of hyperkalemia. Don't use together.

Effects on lab test results

- May increase potassium level.

Pharmacokinetics

Absorption: Well absorbed from GI tract.
Distribution: Distributed throughout body.
Metabolism: None significant.
Excretion: Excreted largely by kidneys; small amounts may be excreted via skin and intestinal tract, but intestinal potassium is usually reabsorbed.

Route	Onset	Peak	Duration
P.O.	Unknown	≤ 4 hr	Unknown

Pharmacodynamics

Chemical effect: Aids in transmitting nerve impulses, contracting cardiac and skeletal muscle, and maintaining intracellular tonicity, cellular metabolism, acid-base balance, and normal renal function.
Therapeutic effect: Replaces and maintains potassium level.

Available forms

Effervescent tablets: 25 mEq

NURSING PROCESS

Assessment

- Assess patient's condition before therapy and regularly thereafter.
- During therapy, monitor ECG, renal function, fluid intake and output, and serum potassium, serum creatinine, and BUN levels.
- Be alert for adverse reactions and drug interactions.
- Evaluate patient's and family's knowledge of drug therapy.

Nursing diagnoses

- Ineffective health maintenance related to presence of hypokalemia
- Risk for injury related to potassium-induced hyperkalemia
- Deficient knowledge related to drug therapy

Planning and implementation

- Dissolve potassium bicarbonate tablets completely in 6 to 8 ounces of cold water to minimize GI irritation.
- Ask patient's flavor preference. Available in lime, fruit punch, and orange flavors.
- Have patient take with meals and sip slowly over 5 to 10 minutes.
- Don't give potassium supplements postoperatively until urine flow has been established.

ALERT: Potassium preparations aren't interchangeable. Verify preparation before administration.

Patient teaching

- Inform patient about need for potassium supplementation.
- Teach patient how to prepare and take drug.
- Instruct patient to report adverse reactions.

Evaluation

- Patient's potassium level returns to normal.
- Patient doesn't develop hyperkalemia as result of drug therapy.
- Patient and family state understanding of drug therapy.

potassium chloride

(puh-TAS-ee-um KLOR-ighd)

Apo-K*, Cena-K, Gen-K, K-8, K-10*, K+ 10, Kaochlor, Kaochlor S-F*, Kaon-Cl, Kaon-Cl-10, Kaon-Cl 20%*, Kay Ciel*, K+ Care, K-Dur 10, K-Dur 20, K-Lease, K-Lor, Klor-Con, Klor-Con 8, Klor-Con 10, Klor-Con/25, Klorvess, Klotrix, K-Lyte/Cl, K-Norm, K-Tab, K-vescent Potassium Chloride, Micro-K Extencaps, Micro-K 10 Extencaps, Micro-K LS, Potasalan, Rum-K, Slow-K, Ten-K

Pharmacologic class: potassium supplement
Therapeutic class: therapeutic agent for electrolyte balance
Pregnancy risk category: C

Indications and dosages

▶ **Prevention of hypokalemia.** *Adults and children:* Initially, 20 mEq of potassium supplement P.O. daily, in divided doses. Adjust dosage, p.r.n., based on potassium level.

▶ **Hypokalemia.** *Adults and children:* 40 to 100 mEq P.O. divided into two to four doses daily. Use I.V. potassium chloride when oral replacement isn't feasible. Maximum dose of diluted I.V. potassium chloride is 20 mEq/hour at 40 mEq/L. Further dose based on potassium level. Don't exceed 150 mEq P.O. daily in adults and 3 mEq/kg daily P.O. in children. Further doses are based on serum potassium levels and blood pH. I.V. potassium replacement should be carried out only with ECG monitoring and frequent potassium level.

▶ **Severe hypokalemia.** *Adults and children:* Potassium chloride should be diluted in a suitable I.V. solution of less than 80 mEq/L and administered at no more than 40 mEq/hour. Further dose based on potassium level. Don't exceed 150 mEq I.V. daily in adults, and 3 mEq/kg I.V. daily or 40 mEq/m^2 daily for children. I.V. potassium replacement should be carried out only with ECG monitoring and frequent potassium level.

▶ **Acute MI‡.** *Adults:* High dose—80 mEq/L at 1.5 ml/kg/hour for 24 hours with an I.V. infusion of 25% dextrose and 50 units/L regular insulin. Low dose—40 mEq/L at 1 ml/kg/hour for 24 hours, with an I.V. infusion of 10% dextrose and 20 units/L regular insulin.

Contraindications and precautions

• Contraindicated in patients with untreated Addison's disease, adrenocortical insufficiency, acute dehydration, heat cramps, hyperkalemia, hyperkalemic form of familial periodic paralysis, other conditions linked to extensive tissue breakdown, and severe renal impairment with oliguria, anuria, or azotemia.

• Use cautiously in patients with cardiac disease or renal impairment.

Lifespan: In pregnant and breast-feeding women, use cautiously.

Adverse reactions

CNS: paresthesia of limbs, listlessness, mental confusion, weakness or heaviness of limbs, flaccid paralysis.

CV: ***arrhythmias, heart block, possible cardiac arrest,*** ECG changes (prolonged PR interval, widened QRS complex, ST-segment depression, and tall, tented T waves).

GI: *nausea, vomiting, abdominal pain,* diarrhea, ***GI ulcerations*** (possible stenosis, hemorrhage, obstruction, perforation).

GU: oliguria.

Respiratory: ***respiratory paralysis.***

Skin: cold skin, gray pallor.

Other: postinfusion phlebitis.

Interactions

Drug-drug. *ACE inhibitors, potassium-sparing diuretics:* Increases risk of hyperkalemia. Use with extreme caution.

Drug-herb. *Cascara, licorice:* May antagonize effects of potassium supplements. Discourage using together.

Drug-food. *Salt substitutes:* Increases risk of hyperkalemia. Don't use together.

Effects on lab test results

• May increase potassium level.

Pharmacokinetics

Absorption: Well absorbed.

Distribution: Distributed throughout body.

Metabolism: None significant.

Excretion: Excreted largely by kidneys; small amounts may be excreted via skin and intestinal tract, but intestinal potassium is usually reabsorbed.

Route	Onset	Peak	Duration
P.O.	Unknown	≤ 4 hr	Unknown
I.V.	Immediate	Immediate	Unknown

Pharmacodynamics

Chemical effect: Aids in transmitting nerve impulses, contracting cardiac and skeletal muscle, and maintaining intracellular tonicity, cellular metabolism, acid-base balance, and normal renal function.

Therapeutic effect: Replaces and maintains potassium level.

Available forms

Capsules (controlled-release): 8 mEq, 10 mEq

Injection concentrate: 1.5 mEq/ml, 2 mEq/ml

Injection for I.V. infusion: 0.1mEq/ml, 0.2 mEq/ml, 0.3 mEq/ml, 0.4 mEq/ml

Oral liquid: 20 mEq/15 ml, 30 mEq/15 ml, 40 mEq/15 ml

Powder for oral administration: 15 mEq/packet, 20 mEq/packet, 25 mEq/packet

Tablets (controlled-release): 6.7 mEq, 8 mEq, 10 mEq, 20 mEq

Tablets (extended-release): 8 mEq, 10 mEq

NURSING PROCESS

Assessment

• Assess patient's condition before therapy and regularly thereafter.

• During therapy, monitor ECG, renal function, fluid intake and output, and potassium, creatinine, and BUN levels.

• Be alert for adverse reactions and drug interactions.
• Evaluate patient's and family's knowledge of drug therapy.

Nursing diagnoses
• Ineffective health maintenance related to presence of hypokalemia
• Risk for injury related to drug-induced hyperkalemia
• Deficient knowledge related to drug therapy

Planning and implementation
• **P.O. use:** Give with extreme caution because different potassium supplements deliver varying amounts of potassium. Never switch products without prescriber's order.
– Make sure powders are completely dissolved before administering.
– Don't crush sustained-release potassium products.
– Give potassium with or after meals with full glass of water or fruit juice to lessen GI distress.
– Use sugar-free liquid (Kaochlor S-F 10%) if tablet or capsule passage is likely to be delayed, as in GI obstruction. Have patient sip slowly to minimize GI irritation.
– Enteric-coated tablets aren't recommended because of increased risk of GI bleeding and small-bowel ulcerations.
– Tablets in wax matrix sometimes lodge in esophagus and cause ulceration in cardiac patients who have esophageal compression from enlarged left atrium. Use liquid form in such patients and in those with esophageal stasis or obstruction.
– Drug is commonly given with potassium-wasting diuretics to maintain potassium levels.
• **I.V. use:** Give drug only by infusion; never by I.V. push or I.M. route.
– Give slowly as dilute solution; life-threatening hyperkalemia may result from too-rapid infusion.
ALERT: Potassium preparations aren't interchangeable. Verify preparation before administration.
ALERT: Don't give potassium postoperatively until urine flow is established.

Patient teaching
• Tell patient that controlled-release tablets may appear in stool but that the drug has already been absorbed.
• Instruct patient to report adverse reactions and pain at the I.V. site.

Evaluation
• Patient's potassium level returns to normal.
• Patient doesn't develop hyperkalemia.
• Patient and family state understanding of drug therapy.

potassium gluconate
(puh-TAS-ee-um GLOO-kuh-nayt)
Kaon, Kaylixir*, K-G Elixir*

Pharmacologic class: potassium supplement
Therapeutic class: therapeutic agent for electrolyte balance
Pregnancy risk category: C

Indications and dosages
▶ **Hypokalemia.** *Adults:* 40 to 100 mEq P.O. daily in three or four divided doses for treatment; 20 mEq P.O. daily for prevention. Further dosage based on potassium level determinations.

Contraindications and precautions
• Contraindicated in patients with untreated Addison's disease, acute dehydration, heat cramps, hyperkalemia, hyperkalemic form of familial periodic paralysis, other conditions related to extensive tissue breakdown, and severe renal impairment with oliguria, anuria, or azotemia.
• Use cautiously in patients with cardiac disease or renal impairment.
Lifespan: In pregnant and breast-feeding women, use cautiously. In children, safety of drug hasn't been established.

Adverse reactions
CNS: paresthesia of limbs, listlessness, mental confusion, weakness or heaviness of legs, flaccid paralysis.
CV: ***arrhythmias,*** ECG changes (prolonged PR interval, widened QRS complex, ST-segment depression, and tall, tented T waves).
GI: *nausea and vomiting; abdominal pain;* diarrhea; GI ulcerations that may be accompanied by stenosis, ***hemorrhage, obstruction or perforation*** (with oral products, especially enteric-coated tablets).

Interactions

Drug-drug. *ACE inhibitors, potassium-sparing diuretics:* Increases risk of hyperkalemia. Use with extreme caution.
Drug-food. *Salt substitutes:* Increases risk of hyperkalemia. Don't use together.

Effects on lab test results

- May increase potassium level.

Pharmacokinetics

Absorption: Well absorbed from GI tract.
Distribution: Distributed throughout body.
Metabolism: None significant.
Excretion: Excreted largely by kidneys; small amounts may be excreted via skin and intestinal tract, but intestinal potassium is usually reabsorbed.

Route	Onset	Peak	Duration
P.O.	Unknown	≤ 4 hr	Unknown

Pharmacodynamics

Chemical effect: Aids in transmitting nerve impulses, contracting cardiac and skeletal muscle, and maintaining intracellular tonicity, cellular metabolism, acid-base balance, and normal renal function.
Therapeutic effect: Replaces and maintains potassium level.

Available forms

Liquid: 20 mEq/15 ml *
Tablets: 500mg†, 595 mg†(83.45 mg and 99 mg potassium, respectively)

NURSING PROCESS

Assessment

- Assess patient's condition before therapy and regularly thereafter.
- During therapy, monitor ECG, renal function, fluid intake and output, and potassium, creatinine, and BUN levels.
- Be alert for adverse reactions and drug interactions.
- Evaluate patient's and family's knowledge of drug therapy.

Nursing diagnoses

- Ineffective health maintenance related to presence of hypokalemia
- Risk for injury related to potassium-induced hyperkalemia
- Deficient knowledge related to drug therapy

Planning and implementation

- Give oral potassium supplements with extreme caution because different forms deliver varying amounts of potassium. Never switch products without prescriber's order.
- Give drug with or after meals with glass of water or fruit juice.
- Have patient sip liquid potassium slowly to minimize GI irritation.
- Enteric-coated tablets aren't recommended because of increased risk of GI bleeding and small-bowel ulcerations.

ALERT: Potassium preparations aren't interchangeable. Verify preparation before administration.
ALERT: Don't give potassium supplements postoperatively until urine flow is established.

Patient teaching

- Inform patient of need for potassium supplementation.
- Teach patient how to take drug.
- Instruct patient to report adverse reactions.

Evaluation

- Patient's potassium level returns to normal.
- Patient doesn't develop hyperkalemia as result of drug therapy.
- Patient and family state understanding of drug therapy.

potassium iodide

(puh-TAS-ee-um IGH-uh-dighd)
Iosat, Pima, Thyro-Block

potassium iodide, saturated solution (SSKI)

strong iodine solution (Lugol's Solution)

Pharmacologic class: electrolyte
Therapeutic class: antihyperthyroid agent, expectorant
Pregnancy risk category: D

Indications and dosages

▶ **Preparation for thyroidectomy.** ***strong iodine solution.*** *Adults and children:* 0.1 to 0.3 ml P.O. t.i.d.
SSKI. *Adults and children:* 0.3 ml to 0.6 ml in water P.O. t.i.d., after meals for 10 to 14 days before surgery.
▶ **Thyrotoxic crisis.** *Adults and children:* 500 mg P.O. q 4 hours (about 10 gtt of SSKI).
▶ **Radiation protectant for thyroid gland.** *Adults:* 130 mg P.O. daily for 10 days after radiation exposure. Start no later than 3 to 4 hours after acute exposure.
Children older than age 3 to 18 years: 65 mg P.O. daily for 10 days after exposure. Initiate no later than 3 to 4 hours after acute exposure.
Pima. *Adults:* 3 ml P.O. daily 24 hours before and for 10 days postexposure.
Children age 1 to 18: 2 ml P.O. once daily 24 hours before and for 10 days postexposure.
Infants and children younger than age 1: 1 ml P.O. daily 24 hours before and for 10 days postexposure.

Contraindications and precautions

- Contraindicated in patients with tuberculosis, acute bronchitis, iodide hypersensitivity, impaired renal function, or hyperkalemia. Some forms contain sulfites, which may precipitate allergic reactions in hypersensitive people.
- Use cautiously in patients with hypocomplementemic vasculitis, goiter, or autoimmune thyroid disease.

Lifespan: In pregnant and breast-feeding women, drug isn't recommended.

Adverse reactions

CNS: fever, frontal headache.
EENT: acute rhinitis, inflammation of salivary glands, periorbital edema, conjunctivitis, hyperemia.
GI: burning, irritation, *nausea,* vomiting, diarrhea (sometimes bloody), *metallic taste.*
Metabolic: ***potassium toxicity*** (confusion, irregular heart beat, numbness, tingling, pain or weakness in hands and feet, tiredness).
Skin: acneform rash, mucous membrane ulceration.
Other: hypersensitivity reactions, tooth discoloration.

Interactions

Drug-drug. *ACE inhibitors, potassium-sparing diuretics:* Increases risk of hyperkalemia. Avoid using together.
Antithyroid medications: Potassium iodide may potentiate hypothyroid or goitrogenic effects. Monitor effects closely.
Lithium carbonate: Possible hypothyroidism. Use together cautiously.
Drug-food. *Salt substitutes:* Increases risk of hyperkalemia. Don't use together.

Effects on lab test results

- May increase potassium level.
- May increase or decrease thyroid function test results.

Pharmacokinetics

Absorption: Unknown.
Distribution: Unknown.
Metabolism: Unknown.
Excretion: Unknown.

Route	Onset	Peak	Duration
P.O.	≤ 24 hr	10-15 days	Unknown

Pharmacodynamics

Chemical effect: Inhibits thyroid hormone formation by blocking iodotyrosine and iodothyronine synthesis, limits iodide transport into thyroid gland, and blocks thyroid hormone release.
Therapeutic effect: Lowers thyroid hormone levels.

Available forms

potassium iodide
Oral solution: 500 mg/15 ml
Syrup: 325 mg/5 ml
Tablets: 130 mg
potassium iodide, saturated solution
Oral solution: 1 g/ml
strong iodine solution
Oral solution: iodine 50 mg/ml and potassium iodide 100 mg/ml

NURSING PROCESS

Assessment

- Assess patient's condition before therapy and regularly thereafter.

• Be alert for adverse reactions and drug interactions.
• Earliest signs of delayed hypersensitivity reactions caused by iodides are irritation and swelling of eyelids.
• Evaluate patient's and family's knowledge of drug therapy.

Nursing diagnoses

• Ineffective health maintenance related to underlying thyroid condition
• Ineffective protection related to hypersensitivity reactions
• Deficient knowledge related to drug therapy

Planning and implementation

• Potassium iodide is usually given with other antithyroid drugs.
• Prescriber may avoid prescribing enteric-coated tablets, which have been linked to small bowel lesions and can lead to serious complications, including perforation, hemorrhage, or obstruction.
• Dilute oral doses in water, milk, or fruit juice to hydrate patient and mask salty taste; give drug after meals to prevent gastric irritation.
• Give iodide through straw to prevent tooth discoloration.
• Store drug in light-resistant container.

Patient teaching

• Teach patient how to give drug.
• Warn patient that sudden withdrawal may cause thyroid crisis.
• Tell patient to ask prescriber about using iodized salt and eating shellfish.
• Tell him to report adverse reactions.

Evaluation

• Patient's thyroid hormone level is lower with potassium iodide therapy.
• Patient doesn't experience hypersensitivity reactions.
• Patient and family state understanding of drug therapy.

pralidoxime chloride (pyridine-2-aldoxime methochloride; 2-PAM chloride)

(pral-ih-DOKS-eem KLOR-ighd)
Protopam Chloride

Pharmacologic class: quaternary ammonium oxime
Therapeutic class: antidote
Pregnancy risk category: C

Indications and dosages

▶ **Antidote for organophosphate poisoning.** *Adults:* 1 to 2 g in 100 ml of saline solution by I.V. infusion over 15 to 30 minutes. If patient has pulmonary edema, give by slow I.V. push over at least 5 minutes. Repeat in 1 hour if muscle weakness persists; may give further doses cautiously. I.M. or S.C. injection may be used if I.V. route isn't feasible.
Children: 20 to 40 mg/kg I.V. administered as for adults.
▶ **Anticholinesterase overdose.** *Adults:* 1 to 2 g I.V., followed by 250 mg I.V. q 5 minutes, p.r.n.

Contraindications and precautions

• Use with extreme caution in patients with myasthenia gravis (overdose may cause myasthenic crisis).
Lifespan: In pregnant women, use cautiously. In breast-feeding women, safety of drug hasn't been established.

Adverse reactions

CNS: dizziness, headache, drowsiness, excitement, manic behavior after recovery of consciousness.
CV: tachycardia.
EENT: blurred vision, diplopia, impaired accommodation, ***laryngospasm.***
GI: nausea.
Musculoskeletal: muscle weakness, muscle rigidity.
Respiratory: hyperventilation.

Interactions

Drug-drug. *Atropine:* Atropinization may occur earlier when used together. Monitor patient.

Barbiturates: Potentiates effects of barbiturates. Use together cautiously.

Effects on lab test results

• May increase AST, ALT, and CPK levels.

Pharmacokinetics

Absorption: Unknown after I.M. or S.C. administration.
Distribution: Distributed throughout extracellular fluid; it isn't appreciably bound to plasma protein. It doesn't readily pass into CNS.
Metabolism: Unknown but hepatic metabolism is considered likely.
Excretion: Excreted rapidly in urine.

Route	Onset	Peak	Duration
I.V.	Unknown	5-15 min	Unknown
I.M.	Unknown	10-20 min	Unknown
S.C.	Unknown	Unknown	Unknown

Pharmacodynamics

Chemical effect: Reactivates cholinesterase that has been inactivated by organophosphorous pesticides and related compounds, permitting degradation of accumulated acetylcholine and facilitating normal functioning of neuromuscular junctions.
Therapeutic effect: Alleviates signs and symptoms of organophosphate poisoning and cholinergic crisis in myasthenia gravis.

Available forms

Injection: 1 g/20 ml in 20-ml vial without diluent or syringe; 1 g/20 ml in 20-ml vial with diluent, syringe, needle, and alcohol swab (emergency kit); 600 mg/2 ml auto-injector (may contain benzyl alcohol), parenteral

NURSING PROCESS

Assessment

• Assess patient's condition before therapy and regularly thereafter. Drug relieves paralysis of respiratory muscles but is less effective in relieving depression of respiratory center.
• Drug isn't effective against poisoning caused by phosphorus, inorganic phosphates, or organophosphates that have no anticholinesterase activity.
• Observe patient for 48 to 72 hours if poison was ingested. Delayed absorption may occur from lower bowel. It's difficult to distinguish between toxic effects produced by atropine or organophosphate compounds and those resulting from pralidoxime.
• Watch for signs of rapid weakening in patient with myasthenia gravis who was treated for overdose of cholinergic drugs. Patient can pass quickly from cholinergic crisis to myasthenic crisis and may need more cholinergic drugs to treat myasthenia. Keep edrophonium (Tensilon) available in such situations for establishing differential diagnosis.
• Be alert for adverse reactions.
• Evaluate patient's and family's knowledge of drug therapy.

Nursing diagnoses

• Ineffective health maintenance related to underlying condition
• Risk for injury related to adverse CNS reactions
• Deficient knowledge related to drug therapy

Planning and implementation

• Remove secretions, maintain patent airway, and start artificial ventilation if needed. After dermal exposure to organophosphate, remove patient's clothing and wash his skin and hair with sodium bicarbonate, soap, water, and alcohol as soon as possible. A second washing may be necessary. When washing patient, wear protective gloves and clothes to avoid exposure.
• Draw blood for cholinesterase levels before giving drug.
• Use drug only in hospitalized patients; have respiratory and other supportive measures available. If possible, obtain accurate medical history and chronology of poisoning. Give drug as soon as possible after poisoning; treatment is most effective if started within 24 hours after exposure.
• **I.V. use:** Give I.V. preparation slowly as diluted solution. Dilute with unpreserved sterile water.
– To lessen muscarinic effects and block accumulation of acetylcholine related to organophosphate poisoning, give atropine 2 to 6 mg I.V. along with pralidoxime if cyanosis isn't present. (If cyanosis is present, atropine should be given I.M.) Give atropine every 5 to 60 minutes in adults until muscarinic signs and symptoms disappear; if they reappear, repeat the

dose. Maintain atropinization for at least 48 hours.

ALERT: Administer slowly by I.V. infusion since tachycardia, laryngospasm, and muscle rigidity have occurred with rapid administration.

- **I.M. and S.C. use:** Follow normal protocol.

ALERT: Don't confuse pralidoxime with pramoxine or pyridoxine.

Patient teaching

- Tell patient to report adverse reactions immediately.
- Caution patient treated for organophosphate poisoning to avoid contact with insecticides for several weeks.

Evaluation

- Patient responds well to therapy.
- Patient sustains no injury from adverse CNS reactions.
- Patient and family state understanding of drug therapy.

pramipexole dihydrochloride

(pram-ih-PEKS-ohl digh-high-droh-KLOR-ighd)

Mirapex

Pharmacologic class: dopamine agonist
Therapeutic class: antiparkinsonian
Pregnancy risk category: C

Indications and dosages

▶ **Treatment of signs and symptoms of idiopathic Parkinson's disease.** *Adults:* Initially, 0.375 mg P.O. daily in three divided doses; don't increase more often than q 5 to 7 days. Maintenance daily dosage range is 1.5 to 4.5 mg in three divided doses.

Patients with renal impairment: If creatinine clearance is over 60 ml/minute, initial dose is 0.125 mg P.O. t.i.d., up to 1.5 mg t.i.d. If creatinine clearance is 35 to 59 ml/minute, initial dose is 0.125 mg P.O. b.i.d. up to 1.5 mg b.i.d. If creatinine clearance is 15 to 34 ml/minute, initial dose is 0.125 mg P.O. daily, up to 1.5 mg daily.

Contraindications and precautions

- Contraindicated in patients hypersensitive to drug or its components.
- Use cautiously in patients with renal impairment; dosage may need adjustment.

Lifespan: In breast-feeding women and geriatric patients, use cautiously.

Adverse reactions

CNS: malaise, akathisia, amnesia, *asthenia, confusion,* delusions, *dizziness, dream abnormalities, dyskinesia,* dystonia, *extrapyramidal syndrome,* gait abnormalities, *hallucinations,* hypoesthesia, hypertonia, *insomnia,* myoclonus, paranoid reaction, *somnolence,* sleep disorders, thought abnormalities, fever.
CV: chest pain, peripheral edema, general edema, *orthostatic hypotension.*
EENT: accommodation abnormalities, diplopia, rhinitis, vision abnormalities.
GI: dry mouth, anorexia, *constipation,* dysphagia, *nausea.*
GU: urinary frequency, urinary tract infection, urinary incontinence.
Metabolic: weight loss.
Musculoskeletal: arthritis, bursitis, twitching, myasthenia.
Respiratory: dyspnea, pneumonia.
Skin: skin disorders.
Other: impotence, decreased libido, *accidental injury.*

Interactions

Drug-drug. *Butyrophenones, metoclopramide, phenothiazines, thiothixenes:* May diminish pramipexole effectiveness. Monitor patient closely.
Cimetidine, diltiazem, quinidine, quinine, ranitidine, triamterene, verapamil: Decreases pramipexole clearance. Adjust dosage, as directed.
Levodopa: Increases adverse effects of levodopa. Adjust levodopa dosage, as directed.
Drug-herb. *Black horehound:* May have additive dopaminergic effects. Discourage using together.

Effects on lab test results

None reported.

Pharmacokinetics

Absorption: Rapid. Absolute bioavailability exceeds 90%.
Distribution: Extensively distributed throughout body.

Metabolism: 90% of dose is excreted unchanged in urine.
Excretion: Primary route of elimination is urinary. *Half-life:* 8 to 12 hours.

Route	Onset	Peak	Duration
P.O.	Rapid	2 hr	8-12 hr

Pharmacodynamics

Chemical effect: Precise mechanism is unknown, but drug probably stimulates dopamine receptors in striatum.
Therapeutic effect: Relieves symptoms of idiopathic Parkinson's disease.

Available forms

Tablets: 0.125 mg, 0.25 mg, 1 mg, 1.5 mg

NURSING PROCESS

Assessment

- Monitor vital signs carefully because drug may cause orthostatic hypotension, especially during dose escalation.
- Assess patient's risk for physical injury from adverse CNS effects of drug (dyskinesia, dizziness, hallucinations, and somnolence).
- Assess patient's response to drug therapy and adjust dose.
- Evaluate patient's and family's knowledge of drug therapy.

Nursing diagnoses

- Impaired physical mobility related to underlying Parkinson's disease
- Disturbed thought processes related to drug-induced CNS adverse reactions
- Deficient knowledge related to drug therapy

Planning and implementation

- Institute safety precautions.

ALERT: Don't withdraw drug abruptly. Adjust dosage gradually according to patient's response and tolerance.

- Provide ice chips, drinks, or hard, sugarless candy to relieve dry mouth. Increase fluid and fiber intake to prevent constipation as appropriate.

Patient teaching

- Instruct patient not to rise rapidly after sitting or lying down because of risk of orthostatic hypotension.
- Caution patient to avoid hazardous activities until CNS effects of drug are known.
- Tell patient to use caution before taking drug with other CNS depressants.
- Tell patient—especially geriatric patient—that hallucinations may occur.
- Advise patient to take drug with food if nausea develops.
- Tell woman to notify prescriber if she is breast-feeding or intends to do so.

Evaluation

- Patient has improved mobility and reduced muscle rigidity and tremor.
- Patient remains mentally alert.
- Patient and family state understanding of drug therapy.

pravastatin sodium (eptastatin)

(PRAH-vuh-stat-in SOH-dee-um)
Pravachol

Pharmacologic class: HMG-CoA reductase inhibitor
Therapeutic class: antilipemic
Pregnancy risk category: X

Indications and dosages

▶ **Primary hypercholesterolemia and mixed dyslipidemia; primary and secondary prevention of coronary events; hyperlipidemia; homozygous familial hypercholesterolemia.** *Adults:* Initially, 40 mg P.O. once daily at the same time each day, with or without food. Adjust dosage q 4 weeks based on patient tolerance and response; maximum daily dose is 80 mg.
Patients with renal or hepatic dysfunction: Start with 10 mg P.O. daily.

▶ **Heterozygous familial hypercholesterolemia.** *Children 14 to 18 years:* 40 mg P.O. once daily.
Children 8 to 13 years: 20 mg P.O. once daily.
Patients also taking immunosuppressive drugs: Pravastatin therapy should begin with 10 mg P.O. at bedtime and titration to higher doses should be done with caution. Most patients treated with this combination received a maximum daily dose of 20 mg.

Contraindications and precautions

• Contraindicated in patients hypersensitive to drug, and in patients with active liver disease or unexplained persistent elevations of transaminase levels.
• Use cautiously in patients who consume large quantities of alcohol or have history of liver disease.
Lifespan: In pregnant and breast-feeding women and in women of childbearing age (unless they have no risk of pregnancy), drug is contraindicated. In children under age 8, safety of drug hasn't been established.

Adverse reactions

CNS: headache, fatigue, dizziness.
CV: chest pain.
EENT: rhinitis.
GI: vomiting, diarrhea, heartburn, nausea.
GU: ***renal failure*** secondary to myoglobinuria.
Musculoskeletal: myositis, myopathy, localized muscle pain, myalgia, ***rhabdomyolysis.***
Respiratory: cough.
Skin: rash.
Other: flulike symptoms.

Interactions

Drug-drug. *Cholestyramine, colestipol:* Decreases plasma pravastatin levels. Give pravastatin 1 hour before or 4 hours after these drugs.
Drugs that decrease levels or activity of endogenous steroids (such as cimetidine, ketoconazole, spironolactone): May increase risk of endocrine dysfunction. No intervention appears necessary. Take complete drug history in patients who develop endocrine dysfunction.
Erythromycin, fibric acid derivatives (such as clofibrate, gemfibrozil), high doses of niacin, immunosuppressants: May increase risk of rhabdomyolysis. Don't use together.
Gemfibrozil: Decreases protein-binding and urinary clearance of pravastatin. Avoid using together.
Hepatotoxic drugs: Increases risk of hepatotoxicity. Avoid using together.
Drug-herb. *Kava:* Increases risk of hepatotoxicity. Discourage using together.
Red yeast rice: Contains components similar to those of statin drugs, increasing the risk of adverse events or toxicity. Discourage using together.
Drug-lifestyle. *Alcohol use:* Increases risk of hepatotoxicity. Discourage using together.

Effects on lab test results

• May increase ALT, AST, CK, alkaline phosphatase, and bilirubin levels.
• May alter thyroid function test values.

Pharmacokinetics

Absorption: Rapidly absorbed. Although food reduces bioavailability, drug effects are same if drug is taken with or 1 hour before meals.
Distribution: About 50% bound to plasma proteins. Drug undergoes extensive first-pass extraction, possibly because of active transport system into hepatocytes.
Metabolism: Metabolized in liver; at least six metabolites have been identified. Some are active.
Excretion: Excreted by liver and kidneys. *Half-life:* 1¼ to 2½ hours

Route	Onset	Peak	Duration
P.O.	Unknown	1 hr	Unknown

Pharmacodynamics

Chemical effect: Inhibits 3-hydroxy-3-methylglutaryl coenzyme A reductase. This enzyme is an early (and a rate-limiting) step in synthetic pathway of cholesterol.
Therapeutic effect: Lowers low-density lipoprotein (LDL) and total cholesterol levels in some patients.

Available forms

Tablets: 10 mg, 20 mg, 40 mg, 80 mg

NURSING PROCESS

Assessment

• Assess patient's condition before therapy and regularly thereafter.
• Obtain liver function tests at start of therapy and periodically thereafter, as directed. A liver biopsy may be performed if elevations persist.
• Be alert for adverse reactions and drug interactions.
• Monitor patient's hydration status if adverse GI reactions occur.
• Evaluate patient's and family's knowledge of drug therapy.

Nursing diagnoses

• Risk for injury related to elevated cholesterol levels

• Risk for deficient fluid volume related to adverse GI reactions
• Deficient knowledge related to drug therapy

Planning and implementation

• Drug therapy should begin only after diet and other nondrug therapies have proved ineffective. Patient should follow a standard low-cholesterol diet during therapy.

Patient teaching

• Instruct patient to take recommended dosage in evening, preferably at bedtime.
• Teach patient about proper dietary management of serum lipids (restricting total fat and cholesterol intake), as well as measures to control other cardiac disease risk factors. When appropriate, recommend weight control, exercise, and smoking cessation programs.
• Inform woman that drug is contraindicated during pregnancy. Advise her to notify prescriber immediately if she becomes pregnant.

Evaluation

• Patient's LDL and total cholesterol levels are within normal range.
• Patient maintains adequate hydration.
• Patient and family state understanding of drug therapy.

prazosin hydrochloride

(PRAH-zoh-sin high-droh-KLOR-ighd)
Minipress

Pharmacologic class: alpha-adrenergic blocker
Therapeutic class: antihypertensive
Pregnancy risk category: C

Indications and dosages

▶ **Mild-to-moderate hypertension, alone or with diuretic or other antihypertensive.** *Adults:* Initial dosage is 1 mg P.O. b.i.d. to t.i.d. Increased slowly; maximum daily dosage is 20 mg. Maintenance dosage is 6 to 15 mg daily in three divided doses. Some patients need larger dosages (up to 40 mg daily).
Children: 0.5 to 7 mg P.O. t.i.d.
Dosage adjustment: If other antihypertensives or diuretics are added to this drug, prazosin is decreased to 1 to 2 mg t.i.d. and readjusted.

▶ **BPH‡.** *Adults:* Initially, 2 mg P.O. b.i.d. Dose may range from 1 to 9 mg P.O. daily.

Contraindications and precautions

• Use cautiously in patients taking other antihypertensives.
Lifespan: With pregnant women, use cautiously. In breast-feeding women, drug isn't recommended. In children, safety of drug hasn't been established.

Adverse reactions

CNS: *dizziness,* headache, drowsiness, weakness, ***first-dose syncope,*** depression.
CV: orthostatic hypotension, *palpitations.*
EENT: blurred vision.
GI: vomiting, diarrhea, abdominal cramps, constipation, *nausea,* dry mouth.
GU: priapism, impotence.

Interactions

Drug-drug. *Diuretics, propranolol and other beta blockers:* Increases frequency of syncope with loss of consciousness. Advise patient to sit or lie down if dizziness occurs.
Drug-herb. *Yohimbine:* Antagonizes antihypertensive effects. Discourage using together.

Effects on lab test results

• May increase BUN and uric acid levels.
• May increase liver function test values.

Pharmacokinetics

Absorption: Variable.
Distribution: Distributed throughout body; highly protein-bound (about 97%).
Metabolism: Extensive in liver.
Excretion: Over 90% excreted in feces via bile; remainder excreted in urine. *Half-life:* 2 to 4 hours.

Route	Onset	Peak	Duration
P.O.	30-90 min	2-4 hr	7-10 hr

Pharmacodynamics

Chemical effect: Unknown; effects probably stem from alpha-adrenergic blocking activity.
Therapeutic effect: Lowers blood pressure.

Available forms

Capsules: 1 mg, 2 mg, 5 mg

NURSING PROCESS

Assessment
- Assess patient's condition before therapy and regularly thereafter.
- Monitor patient's blood pressure and pulse rate frequently.
- Geriatric patients may be more sensitive to hypotensive effects of drug.
- Be alert for adverse reactions and drug interactions.
- Evaluate patient's and family's knowledge of drug therapy.

Nursing diagnoses
- Risk for injury related to presence of hypertension
- Sexual dysfunction related to drug-induced impotence
- Deficient knowledge related to drug therapy

Planning and implementation
- If first dose is larger than 1 mg, severe syncope with loss of consciousness may occur (first-dose syncope).

ALERT: Don't stop therapy abruptly.
- Twice-daily dosing may improve compliance. Discuss this dosing change with prescriber if you suspect compliance problems.

Patient teaching
- Tell patient not to stop taking drug abruptly, but to call prescriber if unpleasant adverse reactions occur.
- Advise patient to minimize effects of orthostatic hypotension by rising slowly and avoiding sudden position changes. Dry mouth can be relieved with sugarless chewing gum, sour hard candy, or ice chips.

Evaluation
- Patient's blood pressure is normal.
- Patient seeks counseling for alternative methods of sexual gratification because of drug-induced impotence.
- Patient and family state understanding of drug therapy.

prednisolone (systemic)
(pred-NIS-uh-lohn)
Delta-Cortef, Prelone

prednisolone acetate
Cotolone, Key-Pred-25, Predalone 50, Predcor-50

prednisolone sodium phosphate
Hydeltrasol, Key-Pred SP, Orapred, Pediapred

prednisolone tebutate
Nor-Pred TBA, Predate TBA, Predcor-TBA, Prednisol TBA

Pharmacologic class: glucocorticoid, mineralocorticoid
Therapeutic class: anti-inflammatory, immunosuppressant
Pregnancy risk category: C

Indications and dosages
▶ **Severe inflammation, modification of body's immune response to disease.** ***prednisolone.*** *Adults:* 2.5 to 15 mg P.O. b.i.d., t.i.d., or q.i.d.
Children: Initially, 0.14 to 2 mg/kg P.O. or 4 to 60 mg/m^2 P.O. daily in 4 divided doses.
prednisolone acetate. *Adults:* 2 to 30 mg I.M. q 12 hours.
Children: 0.04 to 0.25 mg/kg or 1.5 to 7.5 mg/m^2 I.M. once or twice daily.
prednisolone sodium phosphate. *Adults:* 5 to 60 mg I.M., I.V., or P.O. daily.
Children: Initially, 0.14 to 2 mg/kg or 4 to 60 mg/m^2 I.M., I.V. or P.O. daily in three or four divided doses.
prednisolone tebutate. *Adults:* 4 to 40 mg injected into joints and lesions, p.r.n.
▶ **Acute exacerbations of multiple sclerosis.** ***prednisolone sodium phosphate.*** *Children:* 200 mg P.O. daily for a week, followed by 80 mg q other day.
▶ **Nephrotic syndrome.** ***prednisolone sodium phosphate.*** *Children:* 60 mg/m^2 P.O. daily in 3 divided doses for 4 weeks, followed by 4 weeks of single dose alternate-day therapy at 40 mg/m^2.

▶ **Uncontrolled asthma in those taking by inhaled corticosteroids and long-acting bronchodilators.** ***prednisolone sodium phosphate.*** *Children:* 1 to 2 mg/kg P.O. daily in single or divided doses. It is further recommended that short course, or "burst" therapy, be continued until a child achieves a peak expiratory flow rate of 80% of his or her personal best or symptoms resolve. This usually requires 3 to 10 days of treatment, although it can take longer. There is no evidence that tapering the dose after improvement will prevent a relapse.

Contraindications and precautions

- Contraindicated in patients hypersensitive to drug or its ingredients and in those with fungal infections.
- Use with extreme caution in patients with recent MI.
- Use cautiously in patients with GI ulcer, renal disease, hypertension, osteoporosis, diabetes mellitus, hypothyroidism, cirrhosis, diverticulitis, nonspecific ulcerative colitis, recent intestinal anastomoses, thromboembolic disorders, seizures, myasthenia gravis, heart failure, tuberculosis, ocular herpes simplex, emotional instability, and psychotic tendencies.

Lifespan: In pregnant women, use with extreme caution. In breast-feeding women, high doses aren't recommended.

Adverse reactions

Most reactions to corticosteroids are dose- or duration-dependent.

CNS: *euphoria, insomnia,* psychotic behavior, pseudotumor cerebri, ***seizures.***

CV: ***heart failure, thromboembolism,*** hypertension, edema.

EENT: cataracts, glaucoma.

GI: *peptic ulceration,* GI irritation, increased appetite, pancreatitis.

Metabolic: hypokalemia, hyperglycemia, carbohydrate intolerance.

Musculoskeletal: muscle weakness, osteoporosis, growth suppression in children.

Skin: hirsutism, delayed wound healing, acne, various skin eruptions.

Other: susceptibility to infections, ***acute adrenal insufficiency with increased stress (infection, surgery, or trauma) or abrupt withdrawal after long-term therapy.***

Interactions

Drug-drug. *Aspirin, indomethacin, other NSAIDs:* Increases risk of GI distress and bleeding. Avoid using together.

Barbiturates, phenytoin, rifampin: Decreases corticosteroid effect. Increase corticosteroid dosage.

Oral anticoagulants: Alters dosage requirements. Monitor PT and INR closely.

Potassium-depleting drugs (such as thiazide diuretics): Enhances potassium-wasting effects of prednisolone. Monitor potassium levels.

Skin-test antigens: Decreases skin test response. Defer skin testing until therapy is completed.

Toxoids, vaccines: Decreases antibody response and increases risk of neurologic complications. Check with prescriber about when to reschedule vaccine, if possible.

Effects on lab test results

- May increase glucose and cholesterol levels. May decrease potassium and calcium levels.

Pharmacokinetics

Absorption: Absorbed readily after P.O. administration; variable with other routes.

Distribution: Distributed to muscle, liver, skin, intestine, and kidneys. Drug is extensively bound to plasma proteins. Only unbound portion is active.

Metabolism: Metabolized in liver.

Excretion: Inactive metabolites and small amounts of unmetabolized drug are excreted in urine; insignificant amount excreted in feces. *Half-life:* 18 to 36 hours.

Route	Onset	Peak	Duration
P.O.	Rapid	1-2 hr	30-36 hr
I.V.	Rapid	< 1 hr	Unknown
I.M.	Rapid	< 1 hr	< 4 wk
P.R.	Unknown	Unknown	Unknown
Intralesional, intra-articular	1-2 days	Unknown	3 days-4 wk

Pharmacodynamics

Chemical effect: Not clearly defined; decreases inflammation, mainly by stabilizing leukocyte lysosomal membranes; suppresses immune response; stimulates bone marrow; and influences protein, fat, and carbohydrate metabolism.

Therapeutic effect: Relieves inflammation and induces immunosuppression.

Available forms

prednisolone
Syrup: 5 mg/ml, 15 mg/5 ml
Tablets: 5 mg
prednisolone acetate
Injection: 25 mg/ml, 50 mg/ml suspension
prednisolone sodium phosphate
Injection: 20 mg/ml solution
Oral liquid: 5 mg/5 ml, 15 mg/5ml
prednisolone tebutate
Injection: 20 mg/ml suspension

NURSING PROCESS

Assessment
- Assess patient's condition before therapy and regularly thereafter.
- Monitor patient's weight, blood pressure, and electrolyte levels.
- Watch for depression or psychotic episodes, especially at high doses.
- Diabetic patient may need increased insulin; monitor glucose levels.
- Monitor patient's stress level; dosage adjustment may be needed.
- Be alert for adverse reactions and drug interactions.
- Evaluate patient's and family's knowledge of drug therapy.

Nursing diagnoses
- Ineffective health maintenance related to underlying condition
- Ineffective protection related to drug-induced adverse reactions
- Deficient knowledge related to drug therapy

Planning and implementation
- Always adjust to lowest effective dosage. However, expect to increase dosage as specified during times of physiologic stress (such as surgery, trauma, or infection).
- Prednisolone salts (acetate, sodium phosphate, and tebutate) are used parenterally less often than other corticosteroids that have more potent anti-inflammatory action.
- Drug may be used for alternate-day therapy.
- **P.O. use:** Give dose with food when possible to reduce GI irritation.

Orapred should be stored refrigerated at 2-8° C (36-46° F).
- **I.V. use:** Use only prednisolone sodium phosphate.

ALERT: Never give acetate or tebutate form by I.V. route.

– When giving drug as direct injection, inject undiluted over at least 1 minute.
– When giving drug as intermittent or continuous infusion, dilute solution according to manufacturer's instructions and give over prescribed duration.
– D_5W and normal saline solution are recommended as diluents for I.V. infusions.
- **I.M. use:** Inject drug deep into gluteal muscle.

– Alternate injection sites to prevent muscle atrophy.
- **P.R. use:** Follow normal protocol.
- **Intralesional and intra-articular use:** Assist prescriber with administration as directed.
- Avoid S.C. injection because atrophy and sterile abscesses may occur.
- Unless contraindicated, give low-sodium diet high in potassium and protein. Administer potassium supplements as needed.
- Notify prescriber immediately if serious adverse reactions occur, and be prepared to give supportive care.
- After long-term therapy, reduce dosage gradually. Abrupt withdrawal may cause rebound inflammation, fatigue, weakness, arthralgia, fever, dizziness, lethargy, depression, fainting, orthostatic hypotension, dyspnea, anorexia, or hypoglycemia. Sudden withdrawal after prolonged use may be fatal.

ALERT: Don't confuse prednisolone with prednisone.

Patient teaching
- Tell patient not to stop drug without prescriber's knowledge.
- Tell patient to take drug as ordered. Tell patient what to do if he misses a dose.
- Advise patient to take oral form with meals to minimize GI reactions.
- Warn patient receiving long-term therapy about cushingoid symptoms.
- Teach signs of early adrenal insufficiency: fatigue, muscle weakness, joint pain, fever, anorexia, nausea, dyspnea, dizziness, and fainting.

• Instruct patient to wear or carry medical identification that indicates his need for systemic glucocorticoids during stress.
• Tell patient to report sudden weight gain, swelling, or slow healing.
• Advise patient receiving long-term therapy to consider exercise or physical therapy and to ask prescriber about vitamin D or calcium supplements.

Evaluation
• Patient responds well to therapy.
• Patient has no serious adverse reactions.
• Patient and family state understanding of drug therapy.

prednisone
(PRED-nih-sohn)
Apo-Prednisone ◆, Deltasone, Liquid Pred*, Meticorten, Novo-Prednisone ◆, Orasone, Panafcort ◆, Panasol-S, Prednicen-M, Prednisone Intensol*, Sone ◆, Sterapred, Winpred ◆

Pharmacologic class: adrenocorticoid
Therapeutic class: anti-inflammatory, immunosuppressant
Pregnancy risk category: NR

Indications and dosages

▶ **Severe inflammation or immunosuppression.** *Adults:* 5 to 60 mg P.O. daily in single or divided doses. Maximum, 250 mg daily. Maintenance dosage given once daily or q other day. Dosage must be individualized.
▶ **Acute exacerbations of multiple sclerosis.** *Adults:* 200 mg P.O. daily for 1 week; then 80 mg P.O. q other day for 1 month.

Contraindications and precautions

• Contraindicated in patients hypersensitive to drug and in those with systemic fungal infections.
• Use cautiously in patients with GI ulcer, renal disease, hypertension, osteoporosis, diabetes mellitus, hypothyroidism, cirrhosis, diverticulitis, nonspecific ulcerative colitis, recent intestinal anastomoses, thromboembolic disorders, seizures, myasthenia gravis, heart failure, tuberculosis, ocular herpes simplex, emotional instability, and psychotic tendencies.

Lifespan: In pregnant women, use with extreme caution. In breast-feeding women, high doses aren't recommended.

Adverse reactions

Most reactions are dose- or duration-dependent.
CNS: *euphoria, insomnia,* psychotic behavior, pseudotumor cerebri, ***seizures.***
CV: ***heart failure, thromboembolism,*** hypertension, edema.
EENT: cataracts, glaucoma.
GI: *peptic ulceration,* GI irritation, increased appetite, ***pancreatitis.***
Metabolic: hypokalemia, hyperglycemia, carbohydrate intolerance.
Musculoskeletal: muscle weakness, osteoporosis, growth suppression in children.
Skin: hirsutism, delayed wound healing, acne, various skin eruptions.
Other: susceptibility to infections.

Interactions

Drug-drug. *Aspirin, indomethacin, other NSAIDs:* Increases risk of GI distress and bleeding. Give together cautiously.
Barbiturates, phenytoin, rifampin: Decreases corticosteroid effect. Increase corticosteroid dosage.
Oral anticoagulants: Alters dosage requirements. Monitor PT and INR closely.
Potassium-depleting drugs (such as thiazide diuretics): Enhances potassium-wasting effects of prednisone. Monitor potassium levels.
Skin-test antigens: Decreases skin test response. Defer skin testing until therapy is completed.
Toxoids, vaccines: Decreases antibody response and increases risk of neurologic complications. Don't give together.

Effects on lab test results

• May increase glucose and cholesterol levels. May decrease potassium and calcium levels.

Pharmacokinetics

Absorption: Absorbed readily after P.O. administration.
Distribution: Distributed to muscle, liver, skin, intestine, and kidneys. Drug is extensively bound to plasma proteins. Only unbound portion is active.
Metabolism: Metabolized in liver.

Excretion: Inactive metabolites and small amounts of unmetabolized drug are excreted in urine; insignificant amounts excreted in feces. *Half-life:* 18 to 36 hours.

Route	Onset	Peak	Duration
P.O.	Varies	Varies	Varies

Pharmacodynamics

Chemical effect: Not clearly defined; decreases inflammation; suppresses immune response; stimulates bone marrow; and influences protein, fat, and carbohydrate metabolism.
Therapeutic effect: Relieves inflammation and induces immunosuppression.

Available forms

Oral solution: 5 mg/5 ml*, 5 mg/ml (concentrate)*
Syrup: 5 mg/5 ml*
Tablets: 1 mg, 2.5 mg, 5 mg, 10 mg, 20 mg, 25 mg, 50 mg

NURSING PROCESS

Assessment

- Assess patient's condition before therapy and regularly thereafter.
- Monitor patient's weight, blood pressure, and electrolyte levels.
- Watch for depression or psychotic episodes, especially at high doses.
- Diabetic patient may need increased insulin; monitor glucose level.
- Monitor patient's stress level; dosage adjustment may be needed.
- Be alert for adverse reactions and drug interactions.
- Evaluate patient's and family's knowledge of drug therapy.

Nursing diagnoses

- Ineffective health maintenance related to underlying condition
- Ineffective protection related to drug-induced adverse reactions
- Deficient knowledge related to drug therapy

Planning and implementation

- Always adjust to lowest effective dosage. Expect to increase dosage during times of physiologic stress (such as surgery, trauma, or infection).
- Drug may be used for alternate-day therapy.
- For better results and less toxicity, give once-daily dose in morning.
- Give oral dose with food when possible to reduce GI irritation.
- After long-term therapy, reduce dosage gradually. Abrupt withdrawal may cause rebound inflammation, fatigue, weakness, arthralgia, fever, dizziness, lethargy, depression, fainting, orthostatic hypotension, dyspnea, anorexia, or hypoglycemia. After long-term therapy, increased stress or abrupt withdrawal may cause acute adrenal insufficiency. Sudden withdrawal after prolonged use may be fatal.
- Unless contraindicated, give low-sodium diet high in potassium and protein. Administer potassium supplements as needed.
- Notify prescriber immediately if serious adverse reactions occur; be prepared to give supportive care.

ALERT: Don't confuse prednisone with prednisolone.

Patient teaching

- Tell patient not to stop drug without prescriber's knowledge.
- Tell patient to take drug. Tell patient what to do if he misses a dose.
- Advise patient to take oral form with meals to minimize GI reactions.
- Tell patient to report sudden weight gain, swelling, or slow healing.
- Advise patient receiving long-term therapy to consider exercise or physical therapy, to ask prescriber about vitamin D or calcium supplements, and to have periodic eye examinations.
- Instruct patient to wear or carry medical identification that indicates his need for systemic glucocorticoids during stress.
- Warn patient receiving long-term therapy about cushingoid symptoms.
- Teach signs of early adrenal insufficiency: fatigue, muscular weakness, joint pain, fever, anorexia, nausea, dyspnea, dizziness, and fainting.

Evaluation

- Patient responds well to therapy.
- Patient doesn't experience serious adverse reactions.
- Patient and family state understanding of drug therapy.

primaquine phosphate
(PRIH-muh-kwin FOS-fayt)

Pharmacologic class: 8-aminoquinoline
Therapeutic class: antimalarial
Pregnancy risk category: C

Indications and dosages

▶ **Radical cure of relapsing *Plasmodium vivax* malaria, eliminating symptoms and infection completely; prevention of relapse.** *Adults:* 15 mg (base) P.O. daily for 14 days. (26.3-mg tablet = 15 mg of base.)
Children: 0.5 mg/kg (base = 0.3 mg/kg daily) P.O. daily for 14 days.
▶ ***Pneumocystis carinii* pneumonia‡.** *Adults:* 15 to 30 mg (base) P.O. daily.

Contraindications and precautions

- Contraindicated in patients with systemic diseases in which granulocytopenia may develop (such as lupus erythematosus or rheumatoid arthritis) and in those taking bone marrow suppressants and potentially hemolytic drugs.
- Use cautiously in patients with previous idiosyncratic reaction (hemolytic anemia, methemoglobinemia, or leukopenia), in those with family or personal history of favism, and in those with erythrocytic G6PD deficiency or NADH methemoglobin reductase deficiency.

Lifespan: In pregnant women, use cautiously. In children and breast-feeding women, safety of drug hasn't been established.

Adverse reactions

GI: nausea, vomiting, epigastric distress, abdominal cramps.
Hematologic: ***leukopenia, hemolytic anemia in G6PD deficiency,*** methemoglobinemia in NADH methemoglobin reductase deficiency.

Interactions

Drug-drug. *Magnesium and aluminum salts:* Decreases GI absorption. Separate administration times.
Quinacrine: Enhances primaquine toxicity. Don't use together.

Effects on lab test results

- May increase or decrease WBC count.
- May decrease RBC count, hemoglobin, and hematocrit.

Pharmacokinetics

Absorption: Well absorbed.
Distribution: Distributed widely into liver, lungs, heart, brain, skeletal muscle, and other tissues.
Metabolism: Metabolized in liver.
Excretion: Small amount excreted unchanged in urine. *Half-life:* 4 to 10 hours.

Route	Onset	Peak	Duration
P.O.	Unknown	2-3 hr	Unknown

Pharmacodynamics

Chemical effect: Unknown; it may be effective because it can bind to and alter properties of DNA.
Therapeutic effect: Prevents or treats relapsing *P. vivax* malaria.

Available forms

Tablets: 15 mg (base)

NURSING PROCESS

Assessment

- Assess patient's condition before therapy and regularly thereafter.
- Obtain frequent blood studies and urine examinations in light-skinned patients taking more than 30 mg (base) daily, dark-skinned patients taking more than 15 mg (base) daily, and patients with severe anemia or suspected sensitivity.
- Monitor patient for sudden drop in hemoglobin level, decreased erythrocyte or leukocyte count, or marked darkening of urine, each of which suggests impending hemolytic reactions.
- Be alert for adverse reactions and drug interactions.
- Evaluate patient's and family's knowledge of drug therapy.

Nursing diagnoses

- Infection related to malaria
- Ineffective protection related to adverse hematologic reactions
- Deficient knowledge related to drug therapy

Planning and implementation
- Give drug with meals.
- A fast-acting antimalarial (such as chloroquine) is usually given with primaquine to reduce possibility of drug-resistant strains.
- Stop drug immediately and notify prescriber about abnormal CBC results or pronounced darkening of urine.

Patient teaching
- Instruct patient to take drug with meals.
- Tell patient to notify prescriber if adverse reactions occur, especially a marked darkening of urine.
- Tell patient to avoid hazardous activities if visual disturbances occur.

Evaluation
- Patient is free from malaria.
- Patient doesn't develop serious adverse hematologic reactions.
- Patient and family state understanding of drug therapy.

primidone
(PRIH-mih-dohn)

Apo-Primidone ◆, Mysoline, PMS Primidone ◆, Sertan ◆

Pharmacologic class: barbiturate analogue
Therapeutic class: anticonvulsant
Pregnancy risk category: NR

Indications and dosages
▶ **Generalized tonic-clonic, focal, and complex-partial (psychomotor) seizures.** *Adults and children age 8 and older:* Initially, 100 to 125 mg P.O. h.s. on days 1 to 3; then 100 to 125 mg P.O. b.i.d. on days 4 to 6; then 100 to 125 mg P.O. t.i.d. on days 7 to 9; followed by maintenance dosage of 250 mg P.O. t.i.d.; maintenance dosage increased to 250 mg q.i.d., if needed.
Children younger than age 8: Initially, 50 mg P.O. h.s. for 3 days; then 50 mg P.O. b.i.d. for 4 to 6 days; then 100 mg P.O. b.i.d. for 7 to 9 days followed by maintenance dosage of 125 to 250 mg P.O. t.i.d.
▶ **Benign familial tremor (essential tremor).** *Adults:* 750 mg P.O. daily.

Contraindications and precautions
- Contraindicated in patients with phenobarbital hypersensitivity or porphyria.

Lifespan: In pregnant and breast-feeding women, drug is contraindicated.

Adverse reactions
CNS: *drowsiness, ataxia,* emotional disturbances, vertigo, hyperirritability, fatigue.
CV: edema.
EENT: *diplopia,* nystagmus, edema of eyelids.
GI: anorexia, nausea, vomiting, thirst.
GU: impotence, polyuria.
Hematologic: ***leukopenia,*** eosinophilia, ***thrombocytopenia.***
Skin: morbilliform rash, alopecia.

Interactions
Drug-drug. *Acetazolamide:* May decrease primidone levels. Monitor patient for clinical effect.
Carbamazepine: Increases primidone levels. Observe patient for toxicity.
Phenytoin: Increases conversion of primidone to phenobarbital. Observe patient for increased phenobarbital effect.
Drug-herb. *Glutamate:* Antagonizes anticonvulsant effects of drug. Discourage using together.

Effects on lab test results
- May increase eosinophil count. May decrease hemoglobin, hematocrit, and WBC and platelet counts.

Pharmacokinetics
Absorption: Absorbed readily.
Distribution: Distributed widely throughout body.
Metabolism: Metabolized slowly by liver to phenylethylmalonamide (PEMA) and phenobarbital; PEMA is the major metabolite.
Excretion: Excreted in urine.

Route	Onset	Peak	Duration
P.O.	Unknown	3-4 hr	Unknown

Pharmacodynamics
Chemical effect: Unknown; some activity may be caused by PEMA and phenobarbital.
Therapeutic effect: Prevents seizures.

Available forms

Oral suspension: 250 mg/5 ml
Tablets: 50 mg, 250 mg

NURSING PROCESS

Assessment

- Assess patient's condition before therapy and regularly thereafter.
- Monitor blood levels. Therapeutic primidone level is 5 to 12 mcg/ml. Therapeutic phenobarbital level is 15 to 40 mcg/ml.
- Monitor CBC and routine blood chemistry every 6 months.
- Monitor patient's hydration status throughout drug therapy.
- Evaluate patient's and family's knowledge of drug therapy.

Nursing diagnoses

- Risk for trauma related to seizures
- Risk for deficient fluid volume related to adverse reactions
- Deficient knowledge related to drug therapy

Planning and implementation

- Shake liquid suspension well.
- Don't withdraw drug suddenly because seizures may worsen.
- Call prescriber immediately if adverse reactions develop.

ALERT: Don't confuse primidone with prednisone.

Patient teaching

- Advise patient to avoid hazardous activities until CNS effects of drug are known.
- Warn patient and parents not to stop drug suddenly.
- Tell patient that full therapeutic response may take 2 weeks or more.

Evaluation

- Patient is free from seizure activity.
- Patient maintains adequate hydration throughout drug therapy.
- Patient and family state understanding of drug therapy.

probenecid

(proh-BEN-uh-sid)
Benemid, Benuryl♦, Probalan

Pharmacologic class: sulfonamide derivative
Therapeutic class: uricosuric agent
Pregnancy risk category: B

Indications and dosages

▶ **Adjunct to penicillin therapy.** *Adults and children older than age 14 or weighing more than 50 kg (110 lb):* 500 mg P.O. q.i.d. *Children ages 2 to 14 weighing 50 kg or less:* Initially, 25 mg/kg P.O.; then 40 mg/kg in divided doses q.i.d.

▶ **Gonorrhea.** *Adults:* 3.5 g ampicillin P.O. with 1 g probenecid P.O. given together. Or, 1 g probenecid P.O. 30 minutes before 4.8 million units of aqueous penicillin G procaine I.M., injected at two different sites.

▶ **Hyperuricemia of gout, gouty arthritis.** *Adults:* 250 mg P.O. b.i.d. for first week; then 500 mg b.i.d., to maximum of 3 g daily. Maintenance dosage should be reviewed q 6 months and reduced by increments of 500 mg, if indicated.

▶ **To diagnose parkinsonian syndrome or mental depression‡.** *Adults:* 500 mg P.O. q 12 hours for 5 doses.

Contraindications and precautions

- Contraindicated in patients hypersensitive to drug and patients with uric acid kidney stones, blood dyscrasias, or acute gout attack.
- Use cautiously in patients with peptic ulcer or renal impairment.

Lifespan: In pregnant and breast-feeding women, use cautiously. In children younger than age 2, drug is contraindicated.

Adverse reactions

CNS: *headache,* fever, dizziness.
CV: flushing, hypotension.
GI: anorexia, nausea, vomiting, sore gums, *gastric distress.*
GU: urinary frequency, renal colic.
Hematologic: hemolytic anemia, ***aplastic anemia.***
Hepatic: ***hepatic necrosis.***
Skin: alopecia, dermatitis, pruritus.
Other: hypersensitivity reaction, ***anaphylaxis.***

Interactions

Drug-drug. *NSAIDs:* May increase NSAID plasma levels and increase risk of NSAID toxicity. Adjust dosage, as needed.
Methotrexate: Decreases methotrexate excretion. Lower methotrexate dosage may be needed. Serum levels should be determined.
Oral antidiabetics: Enhances hypoglycemic effect. Monitor glucose levels closely. Dosage adjustment may be needed.
Salicylates: Inhibits uricosuric effect of probenecid, causing urate retention. Don't use together.
Sulfonamides: May decrease sulfonamide excretion. Monitor patient for signs of toxicity.
Zidovudine: May increase absorption of zidovudine. Monitor patient for cutaneous drug eruption, malaise, myalgia, and fever.
Drug-lifestyle. *Alcohol use:* Increases urate levels. Discourage using together.

Effects on lab test results

- May decrease hemoglobin and hematocrit.
- May cause false-positive glucose test results with Benedict's solution or Clinitest.

Pharmacokinetics

Absorption: Complete.
Distribution: Distributed throughout body; about 75% protein-bound.
Metabolism: Metabolized in liver to active metabolites, with some uricosuric effect.
Excretion: Drug and metabolites excreted in urine; probenecid is actively reabsorbed but metabolites aren't. *Half-life:* 3 to 8 hours after 500-mg dose, 6 to 12 hours after larger doses.

Route	Onset	Peak	Duration
P.O.	Unknown	2-4 hr	About 8 hr

Pharmacodynamics

Chemical effect: Blocks renal tubular reabsorption of uric acid, increasing excretion, and inhibits active renal tubular secretion of many weak organic acids, such as penicillins and cephalosporins.
Therapeutic effect: Lowers uric acid and prolongs penicillin action.

Available forms

Tablets: 500 mg

NURSING PROCESS

Assessment

- Assess patient's condition before therapy and regularly thereafter.
- Monitor periodic BUN and renal function tests in long-term therapy.
- Drug is ineffective in patients with chronic renal insufficiency (GFR less than 30 ml/minute).
- Be alert for adverse reactions and drug interactions.
- Monitor patient's hydration status if adverse GI reactions occur.
- Evaluate patient's and family's knowledge of drug therapy.

Nursing diagnoses

- Ineffective health maintenance related to underlying condition
- Risk for deficient fluid volume related to adverse GI reactions
- Deficient knowledge related to drug therapy

Planning and implementation

- Give drug with milk, food, or antacids to minimize GI distress. Continued disturbances may indicate need to lower dosage.
- Encourage patient to drink to maintain minimum daily output of 2 L of water a day. Alkalinize urine with sodium bicarbonate or potassium citrate. These measures will prevent hematuria, renal colic, urate stone development, and costovertebral pain.
- Keep in mind that therapy doesn't start until acute attack subsides. Drug contains no analgesic or anti-inflammatory agent and isn't useful during acute gout attacks.
- Drug may increase frequency, severity, and duration of acute gout attacks during first 6 to 12 months of therapy. Prophylactic colchicine or another anti-inflammatory is given during first 3 to 6 months.

ALERT: Don't confuse probenecid with Procanbid or Benemid with Beminal.

Patient teaching

- Instruct patient to take drug with food or milk to minimize GI distress.
- Advise patient with gout to avoid all drugs that contain aspirin, which may precipitate gout. Acetaminophen may be used for pain.

• Tell patient with gout to avoid alcohol during drug therapy; it increases urate level.
• Tell patient with gout to limit intake of foods high in purine, such as anchovies, liver, sardines, kidneys, sweetbreads, peas, and lentils.
• Instruct patient and family that drug must be taken regularly as ordered or gout attacks may result. Tell him to visit prescriber regularly so uric acid can be monitored and dosage adjusted, if necessary. Lifelong therapy may be required in patients with hyperuricemia.

Evaluation

• Patient responds positively to therapy.
• Patient maintains adequate hydration.
• Patient and family state understanding of drug therapy.

procainamide hydrochloride

(proh-KAYN-uh-mighd high-droh-KLOR-ighd)

Procainamide Durules♦, Procan SR, Procanbid, Promine, Pronestyl**, Pronestyl-SR

Pharmacologic class: procaine derivative
Therapeutic class: ventricular antiarrhythmic, supraventricular antiarrhythmic
Pregnancy risk category: C

Indications and dosages

▶ **Symptomatic PVCs; life-threatening ventricular tachycardia.** *Adults:* 100 mg q 5 minutes by slow I.V. push, no faster than 25 to 50 mg/minute, until arrhythmias disappear, adverse effects develop, or 500 mg has been given. When arrhythmias disappear, give continuous infusion of 2 to 6 mg/minute. Usual effective loading dose is 500 to 600 mg. If arrhythmias recur, repeat bolus as above and increase infusion rate. For I.M. administration, give 50 mg/kg divided q 3 to 6 hours; arrhythmias during surgery, 100 to 500 mg I.M. For oral therapy, initiate dosage at 50 mg/kg P.O. in divided doses q 3 hours until therapeutic levels are reached. For the maintenance dose, substitute sustained-release form q 6 hours or extended-release form (Procanbid) at dose of 50 mg/kg in two divided doses q 12 hours.
Patients with renal or hepatic dysfunction: Decreased dosages or longer dosing intervals may be needed.

▶ **Malignant hyperthermia‡.** *Adults:* 200 to 900 mg I.V.; then a maintenance infusion.

Contraindications and precautions

• Contraindicated in patients hypersensitive to procaine and related drugs; in those with complete, second-, or third-degree heart block in absence of artificial pacemaker; and in those with myasthenia gravis or systemic lupus erythematosus. Also contraindicated in patients with atypical ventricular tachycardia (torsades de pointes) because procainamide may aggravate this condition.
• Use extreme caution when giving drug to treat ventricular tachycardia during coronary occlusion.
• Use cautiously in patients with hepatic or renal insufficiency, blood dyscrasias, bone marrow suppression, heart failure, or other conduction disturbances, such as bundle-branch heart block, sinus bradycardia, or cardiac glycoside intoxication.

Lifespan: In pregnant women, use cautiously. In breast-feeding women, drug isn't recommended. In children, safety of drug hasn't been established.

Adverse reactions

CNS: hallucinations, *fever,* confusion, depression, dizziness.
CV: hypotension, ***ventricular asystole, bradycardia,*** AV block, ***ventricular fibrillation*** after parenteral use, ***heart failure.***
GI: nausea, vomiting, anorexia, diarrhea, bitter taste with large doses.
Hematologic: ***thrombocytopenia, neutropenia*** (especially with sustained-release forms), ***agranulocytosis,*** hemolytic anemia.
Musculoskeletal: *myalgia.*
Skin: maculopapular rash.
Other: *lupuslike syndrome* (especially after prolonged administration).

Interactions

Drug-drug. *Amiodarone:* Increases procainamide levels and toxicity; additive effects on QT interval and QRS complex. Avoid using together.
Anticholinergics: May have additive anticholinergic effects. Monitor patient closely.
Anticholinesterases: Decreases anticholinesterase effect. Anticholinesterase dosage may need to be increased.

Cimetidine, ranitidine: May increase procainamide level. Monitor level closely.
Neuromuscular blockers: Increases skeletal muscle relaxant effects. Monitor patient.
Propranolol: May increase procainamide level. Monitor patient for toxicity.
Trimethoprim: May elevate procainamide and *N*-acetylprocainamide (NAPA) levels. Monitor patient for toxicity.
Drug-herb. *Jimson weed:* May adversely affect CV function. Discourage using together.
Licorice: May prolong QT interval and be additive. Discourage using together.

Effects on lab test results

- May increase ALT, AST, alkaline phosphatase, LDH, and bilirubin levels.
- May increase antinuclear antibody titer. May decrease hemoglobin, hematocrit, and neutrophil, granulocyte, and platelet counts.

Pharmacokinetics

Absorption: Usually 75% to 95% of P.O. dose. Unknown after I.M. administration.
Distribution: Distributed widely in most body tissues, including CSF, liver, spleen, kidneys, lungs, muscles, brain, and heart. About 15% binds to plasma proteins.
Metabolism: Metabolized in liver.
Excretion: Excreted in urine. *Half-life:* About 2½ to 4¾ hours.

Route	Onset	Peak	Duration
P.O.	2 hr	1-1.5 hr	Unknown
I.V.	Immediate	Immediate	Unknown
I.M.	10-30 min	15-60 min	Unknown

Pharmacodynamics

Chemical effect: Class Ia antiarrhythmic that decreases excitability, conduction velocity, automaticity, and membrane responsiveness with prolonged refractory period. Larger doses may induce AV block.
Therapeutic effect: Restores normal sinus rhythm.

Available forms

Capsules: 250 mg, 375 mg, 500 mg
Injection: 100 mg/ml, 500 mg/ml
Tablets: 250 mg, 375 mg, 500 mg
Tablets (extended-release): 500 mg, 1000 mg
Tablets (sustained-release): 250 mg, 500 mg, 750 mg

NURSING PROCESS

Assessment

- Assess patient's condition before therapy and regularly thereafter.
- Monitor plasma levels of procainamide and its active metabolite, NAPA. To suppress ventricular arrhythmias, therapeutic serum level of procainamide is 4 to 8 mcg/ml; therapeutic level of NAPA is 10 to 30 mcg/ml.
- Monitor QT interval closely in patient with renal failure.
- Hypokalemia predisposes patient to arrhythmias; monitor electrolytes, especially potassium level.
- Monitor blood pressure and ECG continuously during I.V. administration. Watch for prolonged QT intervals and QRS complexes, heart block, or increased arrhythmias.
- Monitor CBC frequently during first 3 months, particularly in patient taking sustained-release form.
- Be alert for adverse reactions and drug interactions.
- Evaluate patient's and family's knowledge of drug therapy.

Nursing diagnoses

- Decreased cardiac output related to presence of arrhythmia
- Ineffective protection related to adverse hematologic reactions
- Deficient knowledge related to drug therapy

Planning and implementation

ALERT: Some procainamide products contain tartrazine and sulfites. Ask if patient is allergic to any of these agents.
- **P.O. and I.M. use:** Follow normal protocol.
- **I.V. use:** Patient receiving infusions must be attended at all times.
  - Use infusion control device to administer infusion precisely.
  - Vials for I.V. injection contain 1 g of drug: 100 mg/ml (10 ml) or 500 mg/ml (2 ml).
  - Keep patient in supine position during I.V. administration. If drug is given too rapidly, hypotension can occur. Watch closely for adverse reactions during infusion, and notify prescriber if they occur.
  - If procainamide solution becomes discolored, check with pharmacy and expect to discard.

ALERT: If blood pressure changes significantly or ECG changes occur, withhold drug, obtain rhythm strip, and notify prescriber immediately.

• Positive antinuclear antibody titer occurs in about 60% of patients without lupuslike symptoms. This response seems to be related to prolonged use, not to dosage. May progress to systemic lupus erythematosus if drug isn't discontinued.

Patient teaching

• Instruct patient to report fever, rash, muscle pain, diarrhea, bleeding, bruises, or pleuritic chest pain.

• Stress importance of taking drug exactly as prescribed. This may require use of alarm clock for nighttime doses.

• Inform patient taking extended-release form that wax-matrix "ghost" from tablet may be passed in stool. Assure patient that drug is completely absorbed before this occurs.

• Tell patient not to crush or break sustained-release or extended-release tablets.

Evaluation

• Patient regains normal cardiac output after drug stops abnormal heart rhythm.

• Patient maintains normal CBC.

• Patient and family state understanding of drug therapy.

procarbazine hydrochloride

(proh-KAR-buh-zeen high-droh-KLOR-ighd)

Matulane, Natulan

Pharmacologic class: antibiotic antineoplastic (specific to S phase of cell cycle)
Therapeutic class: antineoplastic
Pregnancy risk category: D

Indications and dosages

▶ **Hodgkin's disease, lymphoma, brain and lung cancer.** *Adults:* 2 to 4 mg/kg P.O. daily in single dose or divided doses for first week. Then, 4 to 6 mg/kg/day until WBC count decreases to below 4,000/mm^3 or platelet count decreases to below 100,000/mm^3. After bone marrow recovers, maintenance dosage of 1 to 2 mg/kg/day resumed.

Children: 50 mg/m^2 P.O. daily for first week; then 100 mg/m^2 until response or toxicity occurs. Maintenance dosage is 50 mg/m^2 P.O. daily after bone marrow recovery.

Contraindications and precautions

• Contraindicated in patients hypersensitive to drug and those with inadequate bone marrow reserve as shown by bone marrow aspiration.

• Use cautiously in patients with impaired hepatic or renal function.

Lifespan: In pregnant and breast-feeding women, drug isn't recommended.

Adverse reactions

CNS: nervousness, depression, insomnia, nightmares, paresthesia, neuropathy, *hallucinations,* confusion, ***seizures, coma.***
EENT: retinal hemorrhage, nystagmus, photophobia.
GI: *nausea, vomiting,* anorexia, stomatitis, dry mouth, dysphagia, diarrhea, constipation.
Hematologic: ***bleeding tendency, thrombocytopenia, leukopenia,*** anemia.
Hepatic: ***hepatotoxicity.***
Respiratory: *pleural effusion,* pneumonitis.
Skin: dermatitis, reversible alopecia.

Interactions

Drug-drug. *CNS depressants:* May have additive depressant effects. Avoid using together.
Digoxin: May decrease digoxin level. Monitor level closely.
Levodopa: May cause flushing and a significant rise in blood pressure within 1 hour of levodopa administration. Separate administration times; monitor patient's blood pressure closely.
Local anesthetics, sympathomimetics, tricyclic antidepressants: May cause possible tremors, palpitations, increased blood pressure. Monitor patient closely.
Meperidine: May cause severe hypotension and possible death. Don't give together.
Drug-food. *Caffeine:* May result in arrhythmias, severe hypertension. Discourage caffeine intake.
Foods high in tyramine (cheese, Chianti wine): May cause possible tremors, palpitations, and increased blood pressure. Monitor patient closely.
Drug-lifestyle. *Alcohol use:* May cause mild disulfiram-like reaction. Warn patient to avoid alcohol.

Effects on lab test results

- May increase liver enzyme levels.
- May increase eosinophil count. May decrease hemoglobin, hematocrit, and platelet, WBC, and RBC counts.

Pharmacokinetics

Absorption: Rapid and complete.
Distribution: Distributes widely into body tissues, with highest levels in liver, kidneys, intestinal wall, and skin. Drug crosses blood-brain barrier.
Metabolism: Extensively metabolized in liver; some metabolites have cytotoxic activity.
Excretion: Drug and metabolites excreted primarily in urine. *Half-life:* About 10 minutes.

Route	Onset	Peak	Duration
P.O.	Unknown	Unknown	Unknown

Pharmacodynamics

Chemical effect: Unknown; thought to inhibit DNA, RNA, and protein synthesis.
Therapeutic effect: Kills selected cancer cells.

Available forms

Capsules: 50 mg

NURSING PROCESS

Assessment

- Assess patient's condition before therapy and regularly thereafter.
- Monitor CBC and platelet counts.
- Be alert for adverse reactions and drug interactions.
- Evaluate patient's and family's knowledge of drug therapy.

Nursing diagnoses

- Ineffective health maintenance related to presence of neoplastic disease
- Ineffective protection related to adverse hematologic reactions
- Deficient knowledge related to drug therapy

Planning and implementation

- Give drug at bedtime to lessen nausea.

ALERT: Be prepared to stop drug and notify prescriber if patient becomes confused or if paresthesia or other neuropathies develop.

Patient teaching

- Advise patient to take drug at bedtime and in divided doses.
- Warn patient to watch for signs of infection (fever, sore throat, fatigue) and bleeding (easy bruising, nosebleeds, bleeding gums, melena). Tell him to take his temperature daily.
- Warn patient to avoid alcohol during drug therapy.
- Tell patient to stop drug and check with prescriber immediately if disulfiram-like reaction occurs (chest pains, rapid or irregular heartbeat, severe headache, stiff neck).
- Warn patient to avoid hazardous activities until CNS effects of drug are known.
- Advise woman of childbearing age not to become pregnant during therapy and to consult with prescriber before becoming pregnant.

Evaluation

- Patient responds well to therapy.
- Patient develops no serious adverse hematologic reactions.
- Patient and family state understanding of drug therapy.

prochlorperazine
(proh-klor-PER-ah-zeen)
Compazine, PMS Prochlorperazine ◆, Prorazin ◆, Stemetil

prochlorperazine edisylate
Compa-Z, Compazine Syrup, Cotranzine, Ultrazine-10

prochlorperazine maleate
Anti-Naus ◆, Compazine Spansule, PMS Prochlorperazine ◆, Prorazin ◆, Stemetil

Pharmacologic class: phenothiazine (piperazine derivative)
Therapeutic class: antipsychotic, antiemetic, antianxiety agent
Pregnancy risk category: NR

Indications and dosages

▶ **Preoperative nausea control.** *Adults:* 5 to 10 mg I.M. 1 to 2 hours before induction of anesthesia; repeat once in 30 minutes, if necessary. Or, 5 to 10 mg I.V. 15 to 30 minutes before induction of anesthesia; repeat once if necessary. Or, 20 mg/L D_5W or normal saline solution by I.V. infusion. Begin infusion 15 to 30 minutes before induction of anesthesia.

▶ **Severe nausea and vomiting.** *Adults:* 5 to 10 mg P.O., t.i.d. or q.i.d. Or, 15 mg sustained-release form P.O. on arising. Or, 10-mg sustained-release form P.O. q 12 hours. Or, 25 mg P.R., b.i.d. Or, 5 to 10 mg I.M. repeated q 3 to 4 hours, p.r.n. Or, 5 to 10 mg may be given I.V. Maximum I.M. dosage is 40 mg daily.
Children weighing 18 to 39 kg (39 to 86 lb): 2.5 mg P.O. or P.R., t.i.d. Or, 5 mg P.O. or P.R., b.i.d. Maximum dosage is 15 mg daily. Or, give 0.132 mg/kg by deep I.M. injection. Control usually is obtained with one dose.
Children weighing 14 to 17 kg (31 to 38 lb): 2.5 mg P.O. or P.R., b.i.d. or t.i.d. Maximum dosage is 10 mg daily. Or give 0.132 mg/kg by deep I.M. injection. Control usually is obtained with one dose.
Children weighing 9 to 14 kg (20 to 30 lb): 2.5 mg P.O. or P.R. once daily or b.i.d. Maximum dosage is 7.5 mg daily. Or give 0.132 mg/kg by deep I.M. injection. Control usually is obtained with one dose.

▶ **To manage symptoms of psychotic disorders.** *Adults:* 5 to 10 mg P.O., t.i.d. or q.i.d.
Children ages 2 to 12: 2.5 mg P.O. or P.R., b.i.d. or t.i.d. Don't exceed 10 mg on day 1. Increase dosage gradually to recommended maximum, if necessary. In children ages 2 to 5, maximum daily dosage is 20 mg. In children ages 6 to 12, maximum daily dosage is 25 mg.

▶ **To manage symptoms of severe psychoses.** *Adults:* 10 to 20 mg I.M. repeated in 1 to 4 hours, if needed. Rarely, patients may receive 10 to 20 mg q 4 to 6 hours. Institute P.O. therapy after symptoms are controlled.
Children younger than age 12: 0.06 mg/lb. I.M., then switch to P.O. form.

▶ **Nonpsychotic anxiety.** *Adults:* 5 to 10 mg by deep I.M. injection q 3 to 4 hours, not to exceed 40 mg daily; or 5 to 10 mg P.O., t.i.d. or q.i.d. Or, give 15-mg extended-release capsule once daily or 10-mg extended-release capsule q 12 hours.

Contraindications and precautions

• Contraindicated in patients hypersensitive to phenothiazines, patients with CNS depression (including coma), patients undergoing pediatric surgery, patients taking adrenergic blockers, or patients under the influence of alcohol.
• Use cautiously in patients who have been exposed to extreme heat and patients with impaired CV function, glaucoma, or seizure disorders.

Lifespan: In pregnant women, safety of drug hasn't been established. In breast-feeding women and acutely ill children, use cautiously. In children younger than age 2 and weighing less than 20 lb (9 kg), drug is contraindicated. In geriatric patients, use cautiously with gradual increases in dosage.

Adverse reactions

CNS: *extrapyramidal reactions,* sedation, pseudoparkinsonism, EEG changes, dizziness.
CV: *orthostatic hypotension,* tachycardia, ECG changes.
EENT: *ocular changes, blurred vision.*
GI: *dry mouth, constipation.*
GU: *urine retention,* dark urine, menstrual irregularities, inhibited ejaculation.
Hematologic: ***transient leukopenia, agranulocytosis.***
Hepatic: cholestatic jaundice.
Metabolic: weight gain, increased appetite.
Skin: *mild photosensitivity,* allergic reactions, exfoliative dermatitis.
Other: hyperprolactinemia, gynecomastia.

Interactions

Drug-drug. *Antacids:* Inhibits absorption of oral phenothiazines. Separate antacid doses by at least 2 hours.
Anticholinergics, including antidepressants and antiparkinsonian agents: Increases anticholinergic activity and aggravated parkinsonian symptoms. Use together cautiously.
Barbiturates: May decrease phenothiazine effect. Monitor patient for decreased effect.
Lithium: May cause disorientation, unconsciousness, and extrapyramidal symptoms. Monitor patient closely if used together.
Drug-herb. *Dong quai, St. John's wort:* Increases photosensitivity reactions. Discourage using together.
Ginkgo: May decrease effects of phenothiazines. Monitor patient.
Kava: Increases risk of dystonic reactions. Discourage using together.

Milk thistle: Decreases liver toxicity caused by phenothiazines. Monitor liver enzyme levels if used together.
Yohimbe: Increases risk for yohimbe toxicity when used together. Discourage using together.
Drug-lifestyle. *Sun exposure:* Potential photosensitivity reaction. Urge patient to avoid unprotected or prolonged sun exposure.

Effects on lab test results

• May decrease WBC and granulocyte counts. May alter liver function test values.

Pharmacokinetics

Absorption: Erratic and variable with P.O. tablet; more predictable with P.O. concentrate. Unknown for P.R. administration. Rapid for I.M. administration.
Distribution: Distributed widely into body; 91% to 99% protein-bound.
Metabolism: Metabolized extensively by liver, but no active metabolites are formed.
Excretion: Excreted primarily in urine; some excreted in feces.

Route	Onset	Peak	Duration
P.O.	30-40 min	Unknown	3-12 hr
I.V.	Immediate	Immediate	Unknown
I.M.	10-20 min	Unknown	3-4 hr
P.R.	60 min	Unknown	3-4 hr

Pharmacodynamics

Chemical effect: Acts on chemoreceptor trigger zone to inhibit nausea and vomiting; in larger doses, partially depresses vomiting center.
Therapeutic effect: Relieves nausea and vomiting, signs and symptoms of psychosis, and anxiety.

Available forms

prochlorperazine
Injection: 5 mg/ml
Suppositories: 2.5 mg, 5 mg, 25 mg
Tablets: 5 mg, 10 mg
prochlorperazine edisylate
Syrup: 1 mg/ml
prochlorperazine maleate
Capsules (sustained-release): 10 mg, 15 mg, 30 mg
Tablets: 5 mg, 10 mg, 25 mg

NURSING PROCESS

Assessment

• Assess patient's condition before therapy and regularly thereafter.
• Watch for orthostatic hypotension, especially when giving drug I.V.
• Monitor CBC and liver function studies during prolonged therapy.
• Be alert for adverse reactions and drug interactions.
• Evaluate patient's and family's knowledge of drug therapy.

Nursing diagnoses

• Risk for deficient fluid volume related to nausea and vomiting
• Disturbed thought processes related to presence of psychosis
• Deficient knowledge related to drug therapy

Planning and implementation

• **P.O. use:** Dilute solution with tomato or fruit juice, milk, coffee, carbonated beverage, tea, water or soup; or mix with pudding.
• **I.V. use:** Drug may be given undiluted or diluted in an isotonic solution. Administration rate shouldn't exceed 5 mg/minute. Don't give by bolus injection.
• **I.M. use:** Inject deep into upper outer quadrant of gluteal region.
• **P.R. use:** Follow normal protocol.
• Don't give S.C. or mix in syringe with another drug.
• Avoid getting concentrate or injection solution on hands or clothing.
• Drug is used only if vomiting can't be otherwise controlled or if only a few doses are needed. If more than four doses are needed in 24 hours, notify prescriber.
• Store drug in light-resistant container. Slight yellowing doesn't affect potency; discard extremely discolored solutions.

Patient teaching

• Tell patient to mix oral solution with flavored liquid to mask taste.
• Advise patient to wear protective clothing when exposed to sunlight.
• Tell patient to notify prescriber about adverse reactions.

Evaluation
- Patient's nausea and vomiting are relieved.
- Patient behavior and communication show better thought processes.
- Patient and family state understanding of drug therapy.

progesterone
(proh-JES-teh-rohn)
Crinone 4%, Crinone 8%, Gesterol 50, PMS-Progesterone ♦, Progestasert, Prometrium

Pharmacologic class: progestin
Therapeutic class: hormonal agent
Pregnancy risk category: X

Indications and dosages

▶ **Amenorrhea.** *Adults:* 5 to 10 mg I.M. daily for 6 to 8 days usually beginning 8 to 10 days before anticipated start of menstruation.

▶ **Secondary amenorrhea.** *Adults:* 400 mg P.O. in the evening for 10 days. Or, Crinone 4% gel given intravaginally every other day up to 6 doses. Those who fail may try Crinone 8% gel given intravaginally every other day up to 6 doses.

▶ **Prevention of endometrial hyperplasia.** *Adult women with intact uterus:* 200 mg P.O. in the evening for 12 contiguous days per 28-day cycle, given with conjugated estrogen tablets.

▶ **Dysfunctional uterine bleeding.** *Adults:* 5 to 10 mg I.M. daily for six doses.

▶ **Contraception (with an intrauterine device [IUD]).** *Adults:* Progestasert system inserted into uterine cavity; replaced annually.

▶ **Infertility.** *Adults:* 90 mg gel administered intravaginally daily to b.i.d. May use up to 10 to 12 weeks after pregnancy to maintain placental autonomy.

Contraindications and precautions

- Contraindicated in patients hypersensitive to drug; patients with thromboembolic disorders, cerebral apoplexy, or a history of these conditions; and patients with breast cancer, undiagnosed abnormal vaginal bleeding, severe hepatic disease, or missed abortion.
- Use cautiously in patients with diabetes mellitus, seizure disorder, migraine, cardiac or renal disease, asthma, and depression.

Lifespan: In pregnant and breast-feeding women, drug is contraindicated. In children, safety of drug hasn't been established.

Adverse reactions

CNS: dizziness, migraine, lethargy, depression.
CV: hypertension, thrombophlebitis, ***thromboembolism, pulmonary embolism, CVA,*** edema.
GI: nausea, vomiting, abdominal cramps.
GU: breakthrough bleeding, dysmenorrhea, amenorrhea, cervical erosion, abnormal secretions, uterine fibromas, vaginal candidiasis.
Hepatic: cholestatic jaundice.
Metabolic: hyperglycemia.
Skin: melasma, rash.
Other: breast tenderness, enlargement, or secretion; decreased libido; pain at injection site.

Interactions

Drug-drug. *Barbiturates, carbamazepine, rifampin:* Decreases progestin effects. Avoid using together.
Bromocriptine: May cause amenorrhea. Monitor patient.

Effects on lab test results

- May increase glucose level.
- May increase liver function test values. May decrease pregnanediol excretion. May alter thyroid function test results.

Pharmacokinetics

Absorption: Unknown.
Distribution: Unknown.
Metabolism: Metabolized in liver.
Excretion: Excreted in urine. *Half-life:* Several minutes.

Route	Onset	Peak	Duration
P.O., I.M., Intravaginal	Unknown	Unknown	Unknown

Pharmacodynamics

Chemical effect: Suppresses ovulation and forms thick cervical mucus.
Therapeutic effect: Alleviates amenorrhea and dysfunctional uterine bleeding.

Available forms

Capsules: 100 mg
Gel: 4%, 8%

Injection (in oil): 50 mg/ml
IUD: 38 mg (with barium sulfate, dispersed in silicone fluid)

NURSING PROCESS

Assessment
- Assess patient's condition before therapy and regularly thereafter.
- Be alert for adverse reactions and drug interactions.
- Evaluate patient's and family's knowledge of drug therapy.

Nursing diagnoses
- Risk for deficient fluid volume related to excessive uterine bleeding
- Risk for injury related to dizziness
- Deficient knowledge related to drug therapy

Planning and implementation
- Preliminary estrogen treatment is usually needed in menstrual disorders.
- Give peanut or sesame oil solutions by deep I.M. injection. Check sites frequently for irritation. Rotate injection sites.

Patient teaching
- Make sure patient reads package insert explaining possible adverse effects of progestins before taking first dose. Also, provide verbal explanation.
- Tell patient not to perform hazardous activities if dizziness occurs.
- Tell patient to report any unusual symptoms immediately and to stop drug and call prescriber if visual disturbances or migraine occurs.
- Teach patient how to perform routine breast self-examination.

Evaluation
- Patient's uterine bleeding ceases.
- Patient doesn't experience injury from drug-induced dizziness.
- Patient and family state understanding of drug therapy.

promethazine hydrochloride
(proh-METH-uh-zeen high-droh-KLOR-ighd)
Anergan 50, Phenergan*

promethazine theoclate
Avomine ♦

Pharmacologic class: phenothiazine derivative
Therapeutic class: antiemetic, antivertigo agent, antihistamine (H_1-receptor antagonist), sedative
Pregnancy risk category: C

Indications and dosages

▶ **Motion sickness.** *Adults:* 25 mg P.O. b.i.d.
Children older than age 2: 12.5 to 25 mg P.O. or P.R. b.i.d.

▶ **Nausea.** *Adults:* 12.5 to 25 mg P.O., I.M., or P.R. q 4 to 6 hours, p.r.n.
Children older than age 2: 25 mg or 0.5 mg/lb P.O. or P.R.; doses of 12.5 mg to 25 mg may be repeated q 4 to 6 hours p.r.n. Do not exceed half of the adult dose for parenteral administration.

▶ **Rhinitis, allergy symptoms.** *Adults:* 12.5 to 25 mg P.O. q.i.d. Or, 25 mg P.O. h.s.
Children older than age 2: 6.25 to 12.5 mg P.O. t.i.d. or 25 mg P.O. or P.R. h.s.

▶ **Sedation.** *Adults:* 25 to 50 mg P.O. or I.M. h.s. or p.r.n.
Children older than age 2: 12.5 to 25 mg P.O., I.M., or P.R. h.s.

▶ **Routine preoperative or postoperative sedation or adjunct to analgesics.** *Adults:* 25 to 50 mg I.M., I.V., or P.O.
Children older than age 2: 12.5 to 25 mg I.M., I.V., or P.O.

Contraindications and precautions

- Contraindicated in patients hypersensitive to drug and in those with intestinal obstruction, prostatic hyperplasia, bladder-neck obstruction, seizure disorders, coma, CNS depression, or stenosing peptic ulcerations.
- Use cautiously in patients with pulmonary, hepatic, or CV disease or asthma.

Lifespan: In pregnant women, safety of drug hasn't been established. In breast-feeding women, newborns, premature neonates, and acutely ill or dehydrated children, drug is contraindicated. Do not use in children for nausea and vomiting when the etiology of the vomiting is unknown.

Adverse reactions

CNS: *sedation,* confusion, restlessness, tremors, *drowsiness* (especially geriatric patients).
CV: hypotension, EKG changes.
EENT: transient myopia, nasal congestion.
GI: anorexia, nausea, vomiting, constipation, *dry mouth.*
GU: urine retention.
Hematologic: ***leukopenia, agranulocytosis, thrombocytopenia.***
Skin: photosensitivity, venous thrombosis at injection site.

Interactions

Drug-drug. *CNS depressants:* Increases sedation. Use together cautiously.
Epinephrine: Promethazine may block or reverse effects of epinephrine. Other vasopressors should be used.
Levodopa: Promethazine may decrease antiparkinsonian action of levodopa. Avoid using together.
Lithium: Promethazine may reduce GI absorption or enhance renal elimination of lithium. Avoid using together.
MAO inhibitors: Increases extrapyramidal effects. Don't use together.
Protease inhibitors, selective serotonin reuptake inhibitors: Increases serum levels of these drugs and causes serious adverse cardiac effects. Don't use together.
Drug-herb. *Dong quai, St. John's wort:* Increases photosensitivity reactions. Discourage using together.
Kava: Increases risk of dystonic reactions. Discourage using together.
Yohimbe: Increases risk for yohimbe toxicity when used together. Discourage using together.
Drug-lifestyle. *Alcohol use:* Increases sedation. Discourage using together.
Sun exposure: Possible photosensitivity reaction. Urge patient to avoid unprotected or prolonged sun exposure.

Effects on lab test results

• May increase hemoglobin and hematocrit. May decrease WBC, platelet, and granulocyte counts.
• May cause false-positive immunologic urine pregnancy test using Gravindex and false-negative results using Prepurex or Dap tests. May interfere with blood typing of ABO group.

Pharmacokinetics

Absorption: Well absorbed after P.O. use; fairly rapid after P.R. or I.M. use.
Distribution: Distributed widely throughout body.
Metabolism: Metabolized in liver.
Excretion: Excreted in urine and feces.

Route	Onset	Peak	Duration
P.O.	15-60 min	Unknown	≤ 12 hr
I.V.	3-5 min	Unknown	≤ 12 hr
I.M., P.R.	20 min	Unknown	≤ 12 hr

Pharmacodynamics

Chemical effect: Competes with histamine for H_1-receptor sites on effector cells. Prevents, but doesn't reverse, histamine-mediated responses.
Therapeutic effect: Prevents motion sickness and relieves nausea, nasal congestion, and allergy symptoms. Also promotes calmness.

Available forms

promethazine hydrochloride
Injection: 25 mg/ml, 50 mg/ml (I.M. use only)
Suppositories: 12.5 mg, 25 mg, 50 mg
Syrup: 6.25 mg/5 ml*
Tablets: 12.5 mg, 25 mg, 50 mg
promethazine theoclate
Tablets: 25 mg†

NURSING PROCESS

Assessment

• Assess patient's condition before therapy and regularly thereafter.
• Be alert for adverse reactions and drug interactions.
• Evaluate patient's and family's knowledge of drug therapy.

Nursing diagnoses

• Ineffective health maintenance related to underlying condition
• Risk for injury related to drug's sedating effects
• Deficient knowledge related to drug therapy

Planning and implementation

• Pronounced sedative effect limits use in many ambulatory patients.

• Drug is used as adjunct to analgesics (usually to increase sedation); it has no analgesic activity.
• **P.O. use:** Give drug with food or milk to reduce GI distress.
• **I.V. use:** Don't give in concentration greater than 25 mg/ml or at rate exceeding 25 mg/minute. Shield I.V. infusion from direct light.
ALERT: Phenergan ampules contain sulfite.
• **I.M. use:** Inject deep into large muscle mass. Rotate injection sites.
• **P.R. use:** Follow normal protocol.
• Don't give S.C.
• Drug may be safely mixed with meperidine (Demerol) in same syringe.
• In patient scheduled for myelogram, discontinue drug 48 hours before procedure and don't resume drug until 24 hours after procedure because of risk of seizures.

Patient teaching
• When treating for motion sickness, tell patient to take first dose 30 to 60 minutes before travel. On succeeding days of travel, he should take dose after rising and with evening meal.
• Warn patient to avoid alcohol and hazardous activities until drug's CNS effects are known.
• Tell patient that coffee or tea may reduce drowsiness. Sugarless gum, sugarless sour hard candy, or ice chips may relieve dry mouth.
• Warn patient about possible photosensitivity and precautions to avoid it.
• Advise patient to stop drug 4 days before allergy skin tests.

☑ Evaluation
• Patient responds well to therapy.
• Patient doesn't experience injury from adverse reactions.
• Patient and family state understanding of drug therapy.

propafenone hydrochloride
(proh-puh-FEE-nohn high-droh-KLOR-ighd)
Rythmol

Pharmacologic class: sodium channel antagonist
Therapeutic class: antiarrhythmic (class IC)
Pregnancy risk category: C

Indications and dosages
▶ **Suppression of life-threatening ventricular arrhythmias, such as sustained ventricular tachycardia.** *Adults:* Initially, 150 mg P.O. q 8 hours. Dosage may be increased at 3- to 4-day intervals to 225 mg q 8 hours. If necessary, increase dosage to 300 mg q 8 hours. Maximum daily dosage is 900 mg.
Patients with hepatic failure: Manufacturer recommends dosage reduction of 20% to 30%.

Contraindications and precautions
• Contraindicated in patients hypersensitive to drug and in those with severe or uncontrolled heart failure, cardiogenic shock, bradycardia, marked hypotension, bronchospastic disorders, electrolyte imbalance, or SA, AV, or intraventricular disorders of impulse conduction in absence of pacemaker.
• Use cautiously in patients with heart failure because propafenone can have negative inotropic effect. Also use cautiously in patients taking other cardiac depressant drugs and in those with hepatic or renal failure.
Lifespan: In pregnant women, safety of drug hasn't been established. In breast-feeding women, drug isn't recommended. In children, safety of drug hasn't been established.

Adverse reactions
CNS: anxiety, ataxia, dizziness, drowsiness, fatigue, headache, insomnia, syncope, tremor, weakness.
CV: atrial fibrillation, ***bradycardia,*** bundle branch block, ***heart failure,*** chest pain, edema, first-degree AV block, hypotension, increased QRS duration, intraventricular conduction delay, palpitations, ***proarrhythmic events (ventricular tachycardia, PVCs).***
EENT: blurred vision.
GI: abdominal pain or cramps, constipation, diarrhea, dyspepsia, flatulence, nausea, vomiting, dry mouth, unusual taste, anorexia.
Musculoskeletal: joint pain.
Respiratory: dyspnea.
Skin: rash, diaphoresis.

Interactions
Drug-drug. *Antiarrhythmics:* Increases risk of heart failure. Monitor patient closely.
Cardiac glycosides, oral anticoagulants: Propafenone may increase levels of these drugs

by about 35% to 85%, resulting in toxicity. Monitor patient closely.
Cimetidine: Decreases metabolism of propafenone. Monitor patient closely.
Local anesthetics: Increases risk of CNS toxicity. Monitor patient closely.
Metoprolol, propranolol: Propafenone slows metabolism of these drugs. Monitor patient for toxicity.
Quinidine: Slows propafenone metabolism. Avoid using together.
Rifampin: Increases propafenone clearance. Monitor patient closely.

Effects on lab test results

None reported.

Pharmacokinetics

Absorption: Well absorbed from GI tract. Because of significant first-pass effect, bioavailability is limited; however, it increases with dosage.
Distribution: 97% protein-bound.
Metabolism: Metabolized in liver.
Excretion: Excreted mainly in feces; some in urine. *Half-life:* 2 to 32 hours.

Route	Onset	Peak	Duration
P.O.	Unknown	≤ 3.5 hr	Unknown

Pharmacodynamics

Chemical effect: Reduces inward sodium current in Purkinje and myocardial cells. Decreases excitability, conduction velocity, and automaticity in AV nodal, His-Purkinje, and intraventricular tissue; causes slight but significant prolongation of refractory period in AV nodal tissue.
Therapeutic effect: Restores normal sinus rhythm.

Available forms

Tablets: 150 mg, 225 mg, 300 mg

NURSING PROCESS

Assessment

- Assess patient's condition before therapy and regularly thereafter.
- Continuous cardiac monitoring is recommended at start of therapy and during dosage adjustments.
- Be alert for adverse reactions and drug interactions.
- Evaluate patient's and family's knowledge of drug therapy.

Nursing diagnoses

- Decreased cardiac output related to presence of arrhythmia
- Ineffective protection related to drug-induced proarrhythmias
- Deficient knowledge related to drug therapy

Planning and implementation

- Administer drug with food to minimize adverse GI reactions.

ALERT: If PR interval or QRS complex increases by more than 25%, notify prescriber because reduction in dosage may be necessary.

- During use with digoxin, monitor ECG and digoxin level frequently.

Patient teaching

- Tell patient to take drug with food.
- Stress importance of taking drug exactly as ordered.
- Warn patient to avoid hazardous activities if adverse CNS disturbances occur.

Evaluation

- Patient regains adequate cardiac output when arrhythmia is corrected.
- Patient doesn't develop any proarrhythmic events.
- Patient and family state understanding of drug therapy.

propoxyphene hydrochloride (dextropropoxyphene hydrochloride)

(proh-POK-sih-feen high-droh-KLOR-ighd)
Darvon, 642 ♦

propoxyphene napsylate (dextropropoxyphene napsylate)

Darvon-N

Pharmacologic class: opioid
Therapeutic class: analgesic
Pregnancy risk category: C
Controlled substance schedule: IV

Indications and dosages

▶ **Mild-to-moderate pain.** ***propoxyphene hydrochloride.*** *Adults:* 65 mg P.O. q 4 hours p.r.n. Maximum, 390 mg P.O. daily.
propoxyphene napsylate. *Adults:* 100 mg P.O. q 4 hours p.r.n. Maximum, 600 mg P.O. daily.

Contraindications and precautions

- Contraindicated in patients hypersensitive to drug or in patients who are suicidal or addiction-prone.
- Use cautiously in patients with hepatic or renal disease, emotional instability, or history of drug or alcohol abuse.

Lifespan: In pregnant and breast-feeding women, use cautiously. In children, safety of drug hasn't been established.

Adverse reactions

CNS: *dizziness,* headache, *sedation,* euphoria, paradoxical excitement, insomnia.
GI: nausea, vomiting, constipation.
Respiratory: ***respiratory depression.***
Other: psychological and physical dependence.

Interactions

Drug-drug. *Barbiturate anesthetics:* May increase respiratory and CNS depression. Use together cautiously.
Carbamazepine: May increase carbamazepine levels. Monitor levels closely.
CNS depressants: May have additive effects. Use together cautiously.
Protease inhibitors: May increase CNS and respiratory depression. Monitor patient.
Warfarin: Increases anticoagulant effect. Monitor PT and INR and patient for bleeding.
Drug-lifestyle. *Alcohol use:* May have additive effects. Discourage using together.

Effects on lab test results

- May increase or decrease liver function test values.

Pharmacokinetics

Absorption: Absorbed primarily in upper small intestine.
Distribution: Drug enters CSF.
Metabolism: Metabolized in liver; about one-quarter of dose is metabolized to norpropoxyphene, an active metabolite.
Excretion: Excreted in urine. *Half-life:* 6 to 12 hours.

Route	Onset	Peak	Duration
P.O.	15-60 min	2-2.5 hr	4-6 hr

Pharmacodynamics

Chemical effect: Binds with opioid receptors in CNS, altering both perception of and emotional response to pain through unknown mechanism.
Therapeutic effect: Relieves pain.

Available forms

propoxyphene hydrochloride
Capsules: 65 mg
propoxyphene napsylate
Oral suspension: 50 mg/5 ml
Tablets: 100 mg

NURSING PROCESS

Assessment

- Assess patient's pain before and after drug administration.
- Be alert for adverse reactions and drug interactions.
- Monitor patient's hydration status if adverse GI reactions occur.
- Evaluate patient's and family's knowledge of drug therapy.

Nursing diagnoses

- Acute pain related to underlying condition
- Risk for deficient fluid volume related to GI reactions
- Deficient knowledge related to drug therapy

Planning and implementation

- Give with food to minimize adverse GI reactions.
- Drug can be considered a mild narcotic analgesic, but pain relief is equivalent to that provided by aspirin. Tolerance and physical dependence have been observed. Typically used with aspirin or acetaminophen to maximize analgesia.

ALERT: A dose of 65 mg of propoxyphene hydrochloride equals 100 mg of propoxyphene napsylate.

- Drug may cause false decreases in urinary steroid excretion tests.

Patient teaching

- Advise patient to take drug with food or milk to minimize GI upset.
- Warn patient not to exceed recommended dosage. Respiratory depression, hypotension, profound sedation, and coma may result if used in excessive amounts or with other CNS depressants. Propoxyphene-containing products alone or with other drugs are major cause of drug-related overdose and death.
- Advise patient to avoid alcohol during drug therapy.
- Caution ambulatory patient about getting out of bed or walking. Warn outpatient to avoid driving and other hazardous activities until drug's CNS effects are known.

☑ Evaluation

- Patient is free from pain.
- Patient maintains adequate hydration.
- Patient and family state understanding of drug therapy.

propranolol hydrochloride

(proh-PRAH-nuh-lohl high-droh-KLOR-ighd)

Apo-Propranolol ♦, Detensol ♦, Inderal, Inderal LA, Novopranol ♦, PMS Propranolol ♦

Pharmacologic class: beta blocker
Therapeutic class: antihypertensive, antianginal, antiarrhythmic, adjunct therapy for migraine, adjunct therapy for MI
Pregnancy risk category: C

Indications and dosages

▶ **Angina pectoris.** *Adults:* Total daily doses of 80 to 320 mg P.O. when given b.i.d., t.i.d., or q.i.d. Or one 80-mg extended-release capsule daily. Dosage increased at 7- to 10-day intervals.

▶ **Mortality reduction after MI.** *Adults:* 180 to 240 mg P.O. daily in divided doses beginning 5 to 21 days after MI. Usually given t.i.d. or q.i.d.

▶ **Supraventricular, ventricular, and atrial arrhythmias; tachyarrhythmias caused by excessive catecholamine action during anesthesia, hyperthyroidism, or pheochromocytoma.** *Adults:* 0.5 to 3 mg by slow I.V. push, not to exceed 1 mg/minute. After 3 mg have been given, another dose may be given in 2 minutes; subsequent doses, no sooner than q 4 hours. May be diluted and infused slowly. Usual maintenance dosage is 10 to 30 mg P.O. t.i.d. or q.i.d.

▶ **Hypertension.** *Adults:* Initially, 80 mg P.O. daily in two to four divided doses or extended-release form once daily. Increased at 3- to 7-day intervals to maximum daily dosage of 640 mg. Usual maintenance dosage is 120 mg to 240 mg daily in two or three divided doses or 120 to 160 mg sustained-release once daily. *Children‡:* 1 mg/kg P.O. daily, up to a maximum daily dose of 16 mg/kg.

▶ **Prevention of frequent, severe, uncontrollable, or disabling migraine or vascular headache.** *Adults:* Initially, 80 mg P.O. daily in divided doses or one extended-release capsule daily. Usual maintenance dosage is 160 to 240 mg daily, t.i.d. or q.i.d.

▶ **Essential tremor.** *Adults:* 40 mg (tablets, solution) P.O. b.i.d. Usual maintenance dosage is 120 to 320 mg daily in three divided doses.

▶ **Hypertrophic subaortic stenosis.** *Adults:* 10 to 20 mg P.O. t.i.d. or q.i.d. before meals and h.s.

▶ **Adjunct therapy in pheochromocytoma.** *Adults:* 60 mg P.O. daily in divided doses with alpha-adrenergic blocker 3 days before surgery.

▶ **Adjunctive treatment to anxiety‡.** *Adults:* 10 to 80 mg P.O. 1 hour before anxiety-provoking activity.

Contraindications and precautions

- Contraindicated in patients with bronchial asthma, sinus bradycardia, heart block greater than first-degree, cardiogenic shock, and overt cardiac failure (unless failure is secondary to tachyarrhythmia that can be treated with propranolol).
- Use cautiously in patients taking other antihypertensives; in those with renal impairment, nonallergic bronchospastic diseases, Wolff-Parkinson-White syndrome, hepatic disease, diabetes mellitus (drug blocks some symptoms of hypoglycemia), or thyrotoxicosis (drug may mask some signs of that disorder).

Lifespan: In pregnant women, use cautiously. In breast-feeding women, drug isn't recommended. In children, safety of drug hasn't been established.

Adverse reactions

CNS: *fatigue, lethargy,* vivid dreams, fever, hallucinations, mental depression.

CV: ***bradycardia,*** *hypotension,* ***heart failure,*** intermittent claudication.
GI: nausea, vomiting, diarrhea.
Hematologic: ***agranulocytosis.***
Musculoskeletal: arthralgia.
Respiratory: increased airway resistance.
Skin: rash.

Interactions

Drug-drug. *Aminophylline:* Antagonizes beta-blocking effects of propranolol. Use together cautiously.
Cardiac glycosides, diltiazem, verapamil: May cause hypotension, bradycardia, and increased depressant effect on myocardium. Use together cautiously.
Cimetidine: Inhibits propranolol's metabolism. Monitor patient for increased beta-blocking effect.
Epinephrine: Causes severe vasoconstriction. Monitor blood pressure and observe patient carefully.
Glucagon, isoproterenol: Antagonizes propranolol effect. May be used therapeutically and in emergencies.
Insulin, oral antidiabetics: Can alter requirements for these drugs in previously stabilized diabetic patients. Monitor patient for hypoglycemia.
Drug-herb. *Gingko:* May alter propranolol serum concentrations. Discourage use.
Melatonin: Can reverse the negative effects of drug on nocturnal sleep. Advise patient to discuss use with prescriber.
Drug-lifestyle. *Cocaine use:* Increases angina-inducing potential of cocaine. Inform patient of this potentially dangerous combination.

Effects on lab test results

- May increase BUN, transaminase, alkaline phosphatase, and LDH levels.
- May decrease granulocyte count.

Pharmacokinetics

Absorption: Almost complete. Absorption is enhanced when given with food.
Distribution: Distributed widely throughout body. Drug is more than 90% protein-bound.
Metabolism: Metabolized almost totally in liver. P.O. form undergoes extensive first-pass metabolism.
Excretion: About 96% to 99% excreted in urine as metabolites; remainder excreted in feces as unchanged drug and metabolites. *Half-life:* about 4 hours.

Route	Onset	Peak	Duration
P.O.	30 min	60-90 min	About 12 hr
I.V.	≤ 1 min	≤ 1 min	< 5 min

Pharmacodynamics

Chemical effect: Reduces cardiac oxygen demand by blocking catecholamine-induced increases in heart rate, blood pressure, and force of myocardial contraction. Depresses renin secretion and prevents vasodilation of cerebral arteries.
Therapeutic effect: Relieves anginal and migraine pain, lowers blood pressure, restores normal sinus rhythm, and helps limit MI damage.

Available forms

Capsules (extended-release): 60 mg, 80 mg, 120 mg, 160 mg
Injection: 1 mg/ml
Oral solution: 4 mg/ml, 8 mg/ml, 80 mg/ml (concentrate)
Tablets: 10 mg, 20 mg, 40 mg, 60 mg, 80 mg, 90 mg

NURSING PROCESS

Assessment

- Assess patient's condition before therapy and regularly thereafter.
- Monitor blood pressure, ECG, and heart rate and rhythm frequently, especially during I.V. administration.
- Be alert for adverse reactions and drug interactions.
- Evaluate patient's and family's knowledge of drug therapy.

Nursing diagnoses

- Ineffective health maintenance related to underlying condition
- Impaired gas exchange related to airway resistance
- Deficient knowledge related to drug therapy

Planning and implementation

- Check patient's apical pulse before giving drug. If you detect extremes in pulse rate, withhold drug and call prescriber immediately.

ALERT: Don't confuse Inderal with Inderide or Isordil.

• Double-check dose and route. I.V. doses are much smaller than oral doses.
• **P.O. use:** Give drug with meals. Food may increase absorption of propranolol.
• **I.V. use:** Give drug by direct injection into large vessel or I.V. line containing free-flowing, compatible solution; continuous I.V. infusion generally isn't recommended.
– Or, dilute drug with normal saline solution and give by intermittent infusion over 10 to 15 minutes in 0.1- to 0.2-mg increments.
– Drug is compatible with D_5W, half-normal and normal saline solutions, and lactated Ringer's solution.
• Don't stop drug before surgery for pheochromocytoma. Before any surgical procedure, notify anesthesiologist that patient is receiving propranolol.
• Notify prescriber if patient develops severe hypotension; vasopressor may be prescribed.
• Geriatric patient may have increased adverse reactions and may need dosage adjustment.
• Don't discontinue drug abruptly.
• For overdose, give I.V. isoproterenol, I.V. atropine, or glucagon; refractory cases may require pacemaker.

Patient teaching
• Teach patient how to check pulse rate, and tell him to do so before each dose. Tell him to notify prescriber if rate changes significantly.
• Tell patient that taking drug twice daily or as extended-release capsule may improve compliance. Advise him to check with prescriber.
• Advise patient to continue taking drug as prescribed, even when he's feeling well. Tell him not to stop drug suddenly because doing so can worsen angina and MI.

Evaluation
• Patient responds well to therapy.
• Patient maintains adequate gas exchange.
• Patient and family state understanding of drug therapy.

propylthiouracil (PTU)
(proh-pil-thigh-oh-YOOR-uh-sil)
Propyl-Thyracil ♦

Pharmacologic class: thyroid hormone antagonist
Therapeutic class: antihyperthyroid agent
Pregnancy risk category: D

Indications and dosages
▶ **Hyperthyroidism.** *Adults:* 300 to 450 mg P.O. daily in divided doses. Continue until patient is euthyroid, then start maintenance dose of 100 mg P.O. daily to t.i.d.
Children age 10 and older: Initially, 100 mg P.O. t.i.d. Continue until patient is euthyroid. Individualize maintenance dose.
Children ages 6 to 10: 50 to 150 mg P.O. daily in divided doses q 8 hours. Continue until patient is euthyroid. Individualize maintenance dose.
Neonates and children: 5 to 7 mg/kg P.O. daily in divided doses q 8 hours, or give according to age.
▶ **Thyrotoxic crisis.** *Adults and children:* 200 to 400 mg P.O. q 4 to 6 hours on first day; after symptoms are under control, gradually reduce dosage to usual maintenance levels.

Contraindications and precautions
• Contraindicated in patients hypersensitive to drug.
Lifespan: In pregnant women, use cautiously. Pregnant woman may need less drug as pregnancy progresses. Monitor thyroid function studies closely. In breast-feeding women, drug is contraindicated.

Adverse reactions
CNS: headache, drowsiness, vertigo.
CV: vasculitis.
EENT: visual disturbances.
GI: diarrhea, *nausea, vomiting* (may be dose-related), salivary gland enlargement, loss of taste.
Hematologic: ***agranulocytosis, thrombocytopenia, aplastic anemia, leukopenia.***
Hepatic: jaundice, ***hepatotoxicity.***
Metabolic: dose-related hypothyroidism (mental depression; cold intolerance; hard, nonpitting edema).
Musculoskeletal: arthralgia, myalgia.
Skin: rash, urticaria, skin discoloration, pruritus.
Other: drug-induced fever, lymphadenopathy.

Interactions
Drug-drug. *Aminophylline, oxtriphylline, theophylline:* Decreases drug clearance. Dosage may need adjustment.

Anticoagulants: Anticoagulant effects may be increased. Monitor PT, PTT, or INR and patient for bleeding.
Cardiac glycosides: Increases glycoside levels. May need to decrease dose.
Potassium iodide: May decrease response to drug. May need to increase dose of antithyroid drug.

Effects on lab test results

- May increase liver enzyme levels.
- May decrease hemoglobin, hematocrit, and granulocyte, WBC, and platelet counts.

Pharmacokinetics

Absorption: About 80% of drug is absorbed rapidly and readily from GI tract.
Distribution: Drug appears to be concentrated in thyroid gland. About 75% to 80% of drug is protein-bound.
Metabolism: Metabolized rapidly in the liver.
Excretion: About 35% excreted in urine. *Half-life:* 1 to 2 hours.

Route	Onset	Peak	Duration
P.O.	Unknown	1-1.5 hr	Unknown

Pharmacodynamics

Chemical effect: Inhibits oxidation of iodine in thyroid gland, blocking iodine's ability to combine with tyrosine to form T_4, and may prevent coupling of monoiodotyrosine and diiodotyrosine to form T_4 and T_3.
Therapeutic effect: Lowers thyroid hormone level.

Available forms

Tablets: 50 mg, 100 mg ♦

NURSING PROCESS

Assessment

- Assess patient's condition before therapy and regularly thereafter.
- Watch for signs of hypothyroidism (depression; cold intolerance; hard, nonpitting edema); adjust dosage as directed.
- Monitor CBC as directed to detect impending leukopenia, thrombocytopenia, and agranulocytosis.
- Be alert for adverse reactions.
- Monitor patient's hydration status if adverse GI reactions occur.
- Evaluate patient's and family's knowledge of drug therapy.

Nursing diagnoses

- Ineffective health maintenance related to thyroid condition
- Risk for deficient fluid volume related to adverse GI reactions
- Deficient knowledge related to drug therapy

Planning and implementation

- Give drug with meals to reduce adverse GI reactions.
- Discontinue drug and notify prescriber if patient develops severe rash or enlarged cervical lymph nodes.
- Store drug in light-resistant container.

Patient teaching

- Warn patient to report skin eruptions (sign of hypersensitivity), fever, sore throat, or mouth sores (early signs of agranulocytosis).
- Tell patient to ask prescriber about using iodized salt and eating shellfish.
- Warn patient against OTC cough medicines because many contain iodine.

Evaluation

- Patient's thyroid hormone level is normal.
- Patient maintains adequate hydration.
- Patient and family state understanding of drug therapy.

protamine sulfate

(PROH-tuh-meen SUL-fayt)

Pharmacologic class: antidote
Therapeutic class: heparin antagonist
Pregnancy risk category: C

Indications and dosages

▶ **Heparin overdose.** *Adults:* Dosage based on venous blood coagulation studies, usually 1 mg for each 90 to 115 units of heparin. Give by slow I.V. injection over 10 minutes, not to exceed 50 mg.

Contraindications and precautions

- Contraindicated in patients hypersensitive to drug.
- Use cautiously after cardiac surgery.

Lifespan: In pregnant and breast-feeding women, use cautiously. In children, safety of drug hasn't been established.

Adverse reactions

CV: transitory flushing, drop in blood pressure, ***bradycardia, circulatory collapse.***
Respiratory: dyspnea, ***pulmonary edema, acute pulmonary hypertension.***
Other: feeling of warmth, ***anaphylaxis, anaphylactoid reactions.***

Interactions

None significant.

Effects on lab test results

None reported.

Pharmacokinetics

Absorption: Administered I.V.
Distribution: Unknown.
Metabolism: Unknown, although it appears to be partially degraded, with release of some heparin.
Excretion: Unknown.

Route	Onset	Peak	Duration
I.V.	30-60 sec	Unknown	2 hr

Pharmacodynamics

Chemical effect: Forms inert complex with heparin sodium.
Therapeutic effect: Blocks heparin's effects.

Available forms

Injection: 10 mg/ml

NURSING PROCESS

Assessment

- Assess patient's heparin overdose before therapy.
- Monitor patient continually. Check vital signs frequently.
- Watch for spontaneous bleeding (heparin rebound), especially in patients undergoing dialysis and in those who have undergone cardiac surgery. Protamine sulfate may act as anticoagulant in very high doses.
- Evaluate patient's and family's knowledge of drug therapy.

Nursing diagnoses

- Ineffective protection related to heparin overdose
- Risk for injury related to anaphylaxis
- Deficient knowledge related to drug therapy

Planning and implementation

- Calculate dosage carefully. One mg of protamine neutralizes 90 to 115 units of heparin depending on salt (heparin calcium or heparin sodium) and source of heparin (beef or pork).
- Give drug slowly by direct injection. Be prepared to treat shock.

ALERT: Don't confuse protamine with Protopam.

Patient teaching

- Instruct patient to report adverse reactions immediately.

Evaluation

- Patient doesn't experience injury.
- Patient and family state understanding of drug therapy.

pseudoephedrine hydrochloride

(soo-doh-eh-FED-rin high-droh-KLOR-ighd)
Cenafed, Children's Sudafed Liquid†, Decofed†, DeFed-60†, Dimetapp†, Dorcol Children's Decongestant†, Drixoral Non-Drowsy Formula†, Efidac/24†, Eltor 120♦†, Genaphed†, Halofed†, Halofed Adult Strength†, Maxenal♦†, Myfedrine†, Novafed†, PediaCare Infants' Oral Decongestant Drops†, Pseudo†, Pseudofrin♦, Pseudogest†, Robidrine♦†, Sudafed†, Sudafed 12 Hour†, Sudafed 60†, Sufedrin†, Triaminic†

pseudoephedrine sulfate

Afrin†, Drixoral♦, Drixoral 12 Hour Non-Drowsy Formula

Pharmacologic class: adrenergic
Therapeutic class: decongestant
Pregnancy risk category: C

Indications and dosages

▶ **Nasal and eustachian tube decongestion.** *Adults and adolescents age 12 and older:*

60 mg P.O. q 4 to 6 hours; or 120 mg P.O. extended-release tablet q 12 hours; or 240 mg P.O. controlled-release tablet daily. Maximum dosage is 240 mg daily.
Children ages 6 to 11: 30 mg P.O. q 4 to 6 hours. Maximum dosage is 120 mg daily.
Children ages 2 to 5: 15 mg P.O. q 4 to 6 hours. Maximum dosage is 60 mg daily, or 4 mg/kg or 125 mg/m^2 P.O. divided q.i.d.
Children younger than age 2: Consult a physician.

Contraindications and precautions

- Contraindicated in patients taking MAO inhibitors and patients with severe hypertension or severe coronary artery disease.
- Use cautiously in patients with hypertension, cardiac disease, diabetes, glaucoma, hyperthyroidism, and prostatic hyperplasia.

Lifespan: In breast-feeding women, drug is contraindicated. In children younger than age 12, extended-release forms are contraindicated.

Adverse reactions

CNS: *anxiety,* transient stimulation, tremor, dizziness, headache, insomnia, *nervousness.*
CV: ***arrhythmias,*** *palpitations,* tachycardia.
GI: anorexia, nausea, vomiting, dry mouth.
GU: difficulty urinating.
Respiratory: ***respiratory difficulty.***
Skin: pallor.

Interactions

Drug-drug. *Antihypertensives:* May attenuate hypotensive effect. Monitor patient closely.
MAO inhibitors: May cause severe hypertension (hypertensive crisis). Don't use together.
Drug-herb. *Bitter orange:* May increase risk of hypertension and increased adverse CV effects. Discourage using together.

Effects on lab test results

None reported.

Pharmacokinetics

Absorption: Unknown.
Distribution: Widely distributed throughout body.
Metabolism: Incompletely metabolized in liver to inactive compounds.
Excretion: Excreted in urine; rate is accelerated with acidic urine.

Route	Onset	Peak	Duration
P.O.	15-30 min	30-60 min	3-12 hr

Pharmacodynamics

Chemical effect: Stimulates alpha-adrenergic receptors in respiratory tract, resulting in vasoconstriction.
Therapeutic effect: Acts to relieve congestion of nasal and eustachian tube.

Available forms

pseudoephedrine hydrochloride
Capsules†: 60 mg
Capsules (Liquid gel): 30 mg
Liquid: 7.5 mg/0.8 ml, 15 mg/5 ml, 30 mg/5 ml
Tablets: 30 mg, 60 mg
Tablets (chewable): 15 mg
Tablets (controlled-release): 240 mg
Tablets (extended-release): 120 mg
pseudoephedrine sulfate
Tablets (extended-release): 120 mg (60 mg immediate-release, 60 mg delayed-release)

NURSING PROCESS

Assessment

- Assess patient's condition before therapy and regularly thereafter.
- Be alert for adverse reactions and drug interactions.
- Geriatric patients are more sensitive to drug's effects.
- Evaluate patient's and family's knowledge of drug therapy.

Nursing diagnoses

- Ineffective health maintenance related to congestion
- Disturbed sleep pattern related to drug-induced insomnia
- Deficient knowledge related to drug therapy

Planning and implementation

- Don't crush or break extended-release forms.
- Give last dose at least 2 hours before bedtime to minimize insomnia.

Patient teaching

- Warn patient against using OTC products containing other sympathomimetics.
- Caution patient not to take drug within 2 hours of bedtime because it can cause insomnia.
- Tell patient to relieve dry mouth with sugarless gum or hard candy.
- Urge patient to stop drug if he becomes unusually restless and to notify prescriber promptly.

Evaluation

- Patient's congestion is relieved.
- Patient and family state understanding of drug therapy.

psyllium

(SIL-ee-um)

Fiberall†, Genfiber†, Hydrocil Instant†, Konsyl†, Konsyl-D†, Metamucil†, Modane Bulk†, Perdiem Fiber Therapy†, Reguloid†, Serutan†, Syllact†

Pharmacologic class: adsorbent
Therapeutic class: bulk laxative
Pregnancy risk category: NR

Indications and dosages

▶ **Constipation, bowel management, irritable bowel syndrome.** *Adults:* 1 to 2 rounded tsp P.O. in full glass of liquid once daily, b.i.d., or t.i.d., followed by second glass of liquid. Or, 1 packet dissolved in water once daily, b.i.d., or t.i.d. Or, 2 wafers b.i.d. or t.i.d.
Children older than age 6: ½ to 1 level teaspoonful P.O. in a half-glass of liquid daily, b.i.d., or t.i.d.

Contraindications and precautions

- Contraindicated in patients hypersensitive to drug and those with intestinal obstruction or ulceration, disabling adhesions, difficulty swallowing, or symptoms of appendicitis, such as abdominal pain, nausea, and vomiting.

Lifespan: In pregnant or breast-feeding women, use cautiously.

Adverse reactions

GI: nausea, vomiting, and diarrhea with excessive use; esophageal, gastric, small intestinal, or colonic strictures with dry form; abdominal cramps in severe constipation.

Interactions

None significant.

Effects on lab test results

None reported.

Pharmacokinetics

Absorption: None.
Distribution: Distributed locally in GI tract.
Metabolism: None.
Excretion: Excreted in feces.

Route	Onset	Peak	Duration
P.O.	12-24 hr	≤ 3 days	Varies

Pharmacodynamics

Chemical effect: Absorbs water and expands to increase bulk and moisture content of stool, thus encouraging peristalsis and bowel movement.
Therapeutic effect: Relieves constipation.

Available forms

Granules: 2.5 g/tsp, 4 g/tsp
Powder: 3.3 g/tsp, 3.4 g/packet, 3.4 g/tsp, 3.4 g/tbs, 3.5 g/tsp, 3.5 g/scoopful, 6 g/packet, 6 g/tsp
Wafers: 3.4 g/wafer

NURSING PROCESS

Assessment

- Assess patient's condition before therapy and regularly thereafter.
- Before giving drug for constipation, determine if patient has adequate fluid intake, exercise, and diet.
- Be alert for adverse reactions.
- Evaluate patient's and family's knowledge of drug therapy.

Nursing diagnoses

- Constipation related to underlying condition
- Acute pain related to abdominal cramps
- Deficient knowledge related to drug therapy

Planning and implementation

- Mix drug with at least 8 oz (240 ml) of cold, pleasant-tasting liquid such as orange juice to mask grittiness. Stir only a few seconds. Have

patient drink mixture immediately, before it congeals. Follow with another glass of liquid.
• For dosages in children younger than age 6, consult prescriber.
• Drug may reduce appetite if taken before meals.
• Drug isn't absorbed systemically and is nontoxic. It's especially useful in debilitated patients and those with postpartum constipation, irritable bowel syndrome, and diverticular disease. Also useful to treat chronic laxative abuse and with other laxatives to empty colon before barium enema examinations.

Patient teaching
• Teach patient how to properly mix drug. To enhance effect and prevent intestinal obstruction, tell him to take drug with plenty of water. Advise him that inhaling powder may cause allergic reactions.
• Tell patient that laxative effect usually occurs in 12 to 24 hours but may be delayed up to 3 days.
• Advise diabetic patient to check label and use brand of drug that doesn't contain sugar.
• Teach patient about dietary sources of bulk, including bran and other cereals, fresh fruit, and vegetables.

Evaluation
• Patient's constipation is relieved.
• Patient's abdominal cramping is minimal and tolerable.
• Patient and family state understanding of drug therapy.

pyrantel embonate
(peer-AN-tul EM-boh-nayt)
Anthel ♦, Combantrin ♦, Early Bird ♦

pyrantel pamoate
Antiminth, Combantrin ♦, Pin-Rid†, Pin-X, Reese's Pinworm Medicine

Pharmacologic class: pyrimidine derivative
Therapeutic class: anthelmintic
Pregnancy risk category: C

Indications and dosages
▶ **Roundworm and pinworm.** *Adults and children older than age 2:* 11 mg/kg P.O. given as single dose. Maximum total dose is 1 g. For pinworm, dosage should be repeated in 2 weeks.

Contraindications and precautions
• Contraindicated in patients hypersensitive to drug.
• Use cautiously in patients with hepatic dysfunction or severe malnutrition or anemia.
Lifespan: In pregnant women, use cautiously. In children younger than age 2 and breast-feeding women, safety of drug hasn't been established.

Adverse reactions
CNS: headache, dizziness, fever, drowsiness, insomnia, weakness.
GI: anorexia, nausea, vomiting, gastralgia, cramps, diarrhea, tenesmus.
Skin: rash.

Interactions
Drug-drug. *Piperazine salts:* Possible antagonism. Don't give together.
Theophylline: Increases theophylline levels. Monitor serum level.

Effects on lab test results
• May increase AST level.

Available forms
pyrantel embonate
Granules: 100 mg/g ♦
Oral suspension: 50 mg/ml ♦
Squares (chocolate-flavored): 100 mg ♦
Tablets: 125 mg ♦, 250 mg ♦
pyrantel pamoate
Capsules: 180 mg†
Liquid: 50 mg/ml
Oral suspension: 50 mg/ml
Tablets: 125 mg ♦

Pharmacokinetics
Absorption: Poor.
Distribution: Unknown.
Metabolism: Small amount partially metabolized in liver.
Excretion: Over 50% excreted in feces; about 7% excreted in urine.

Route	Onset	Peak	Duration
P.O.	Varies	1-3 hr	Varies

Pharmacodynamics

Chemical effect: Blocks neuromuscular action, paralyzing worm and causing its expulsion by normal peristalsis.
Therapeutic effect: Relieves roundworm and pinworm infestation, including *Ancylostoma duodenale, Ascaris lumbricoides, Enterobius vermicularis, Necator americanus,* and *Trichostrongylus orientalis.*

NURSING PROCESS

Assessment

- Assess patient's condition before therapy and regularly thereafter.
- Be alert for adverse reactions and drug interactions.
- Monitor patient's hydration status if adverse GI reactions occur.
- Evaluate patient's and family's knowledge of drug therapy.

Nursing diagnoses

- Infection related to worm infestation
- Risk for deficient fluid volume related to adverse GI reactions
- Deficient knowledge related to drug therapy

Planning and implementation

- No dietary restrictions, laxatives, or enemas are needed.
- Drug should be given to all family members, as prescribed, to prevent risk of spreading infection.
- Drug may be taken with food, milk, or fruit juices. Shake suspension well.

Patient teaching

- Tell patient to shake suspension well before taking it. Inform patient that drug may be taken with food or beverages.
- Teach patient about personal hygiene, especially good hand-washing technique. To avoid reinfection, teach him to wash perianal area daily, to change undergarments and bedclothes daily, and to wash hands and clean fingernails before meals and after bowel movements. Advise patient to refrain from preparing food for others during infestation.

Evaluation

- Patient is free from infestation.
- Patient maintains adequate hydration.
- Patient and family state understanding of drug therapy.

pyrazinamide

(peer-uh-ZIN-uh-mighd)
PMS-Pyrazinamide ♦, Tebrazid ♦, Zinamide ♦

Pharmacologic class: synthetic pyrazine analogue of nicotinamide
Therapeutic class: antituberculotic
Pregnancy risk category: C

Indications and dosages

▶ **Adjunct treatment of tuberculosis when primary and secondary antituberculotics can't be used or have failed.** *Adults:* 15 to 30 mg/kg P.O. once daily, not to exceed 2 g daily. Or, twice-weekly dose of 50 to 70 mg/kg (based on lean body weight) to promote compliance.
Patients with renal impairment and geriatric patients: Use the lower dose range.

Contraindications and precautions

- Contraindicated in patients hypersensitive to drug and patients with severe hepatic disease.
- Use cautiously in patients with diabetes mellitus, renal failure, or acute gout.

Lifespan: In pregnant women, use cautiously. In children and breast-feeding women, safety of drug hasn't been established.

Adverse reactions

CNS: malaise, fever.
GI: anorexia, nausea, vomiting, diarrhea.
GU: dysuria.
Hematologic: sideroblastic anemia, ***thrombocytopenia.***
Hepatic: ***hepatitis.***
Metabolic: *hyperuricemia.*
Musculoskeletal: arthralgia.

Interactions

Drug-herb. *Kava:* May increase risk of liver damage. Discourage using together.

Effects on lab test results

- May increase uric acid level.
- May decrease platelet count, hemoglobin, and hematocrit.

Pharmacokinetics

Absorption: Well absorbed.
Distributed: Distributed widely into body tissues and fluids, including lungs, liver, and CSF. Drug is 50% protein-bound.
Metabolism: Hydrolyzed in liver and in stomach.
Excretion: Excreted almost completely in urine. *Half-life:* 9 to 10 hours.

Route	Onset	Peak	Duration
P.O.	Unknown	1-2 hr	Unknown

Pharmacodynamics

Chemical effect: Unknown.
Therapeutic effect: Helps eradicate tuberculosis. Only active against *Mycobacterium tuberculosis.*

Available forms

Tablets: 500 mg

NURSING PROCESS

Assessment

- Assess patient's condition before therapy and regularly thereafter.
- Monitor hematopoietic studies and uric acid level.
- Monitor liver function studies; examine patient for jaundice and liver tenderness or enlargement before and frequently during therapy.
- Watch closely for signs of gout and liver impairment.
- Monitor patient's hydration status if adverse GI reactions occur.
- Evaluate patient's and family's knowledge of drug therapy.

Nursing diagnoses

- Infection related to tuberculosis
- Risk for deficient fluid volume related to adverse GI reactions
- Deficient knowledge related to drug therapy

Planning and implementation

- Drug should always be given with other antituberculotics to prevent development of resistant organisms.
- Reduced dosage is needed in patients with renal impairment because nearly all of drug is excreted in urine.
- Question doses that exceed 35 mg/kg; they may cause liver damage.
- Notify prescriber at once if you suspect liver dysfunction.
- When drug is used with surgical management of tuberculosis, it's started 1 to 2 weeks before surgery and continued for 4 to 6 weeks after.
- Patients with concomitant HIV infection may need longer course.
- Pyrazinamide may interfere with Acetest and Ketostix urine tests to produce pink-brown color.

Patient teaching

- Stress importance of taking drug exactly as prescribed; warn patient against discontinuing drug without prescriber's approval.
- Teach patient to watch for and immediately report signs of gout and hepatic impairment.

Evaluation

- Patient is free from infection.
- Patient maintains adequate hydration.
- Patient and family state understanding of drug therapy.

pyridostigmine bromide

(peer-ih-doh-STIG-meen BROH-mighd)
Mestinon*, Mestinon SR♦, Mestinon Timespans, Regonol

Pharmacologic class: cholinesterase inhibitor
Therapeutic class: muscle stimulant
Pregnancy risk category: NR

Indications and dosages

▶ **Antidote for nondepolarizing neuromuscular blocking agents.** *Adults:* 10 to 20 mg I.V. preceded by atropine sulfate 0.6 to 1.2 mg I.V.

▶ **Myasthenia gravis.** *Adults:* 60 to 120 mg P.O. t.i.d. Usual dosage is 600 mg daily but higher dosage may be needed (up to 1,500 mg daily). For I.M. or I.V. use, 1/30 of oral dosage is given. Dosage must be adjusted for each patient, depending on response and tolerance. Or, 180 to 540 mg sustained-release tablets (1 to 3 tablets) P.O. daily to b.i.d., with at least 6 hours between doses.

Children: 7 mg/kg or 200 mg/m^2 P.O. daily in five or six divided doses. Or, 0.05 to 0.15 mg/kg/dose I.V. or I.M.

▶ **Supportive treatment of neonates born to myasthenic mothers.** *Neonates:* 0.05 to 0.15 mg/kg I.M. q 4 to 6 hours. Dosage decreased daily until drug can be withdrawn.

▶ **To increase survival after exposure to the nerve agent Soman.** *Adults in the military:* 30 mg P.O. q 8 hours starting at least several hours (about 8 hours) prior to Soman exposure.

Contraindications and precautions

- Contraindicated in patients hypersensitive to anticholinesterase agents, in those with mechanical obstruction of intestine or urinary tract, and in those with history of a reaction to bromides.
- Use cautiously in patients with bronchial asthma, bradycardia, or arrhythmias.

Lifespan: In pregnant and breast-feeding women, safety of drug hasn't been established.

Adverse reactions

CNS: headache with large doses, weakness, sweating, ***seizures.***
CV: ***bradycardia,*** hypotension, thrombophlebitis.
EENT: miosis.
GI: abdominal cramps, nausea, vomiting, diarrhea, excessive salivation.
Musculoskeletal: muscle cramps, muscle fasciculations.
Respiratory: ***bronchospasm, bronchoconstriction,*** increased bronchial secretions.
Skin: rash.

Interactions

Drug-drug. *Aminoglycosides, anesthetics:* May decrease response to drug. Use together cautiously.
Anticholinergics, atropine, corticosteroids, magnesium, procainamide, quinidine: May antagonize cholinergic effects. Observe patient for lack of drug effect.
Ganglionic blockers: Increases risk of hypotension. Monitor patient closely.

Effects on lab test results

None reported.

Pharmacokinetics

Absorption: Poor.
Distribution: Unknown.
Metabolism: Unknown.
Excretion: Excreted in urine.

Route	Onset	Peak	Duration
P.O.	20-60 min	1-2 hr	3-12 hr
I.V.	2-5 min	Unknown	2-3 hr
I.M.	15 min	Unknown	2-3 hr

Pharmacodynamics

Chemical effect: Inhibits destruction of acetylcholine released from parasympathetic and somatic efferent nerves. Acetylcholine accumulates, promoting increased stimulation of receptor.
Therapeutic effect: Reverses effect of nondepolarizing neuromuscular blockers and myasthenia gravis.

Available forms

Injection: 5 mg/ml in 2-ml ampules or 5-ml vials
Syrup: 60 mg/5 ml
Tablets: 60 mg
Tablets (military use only): 30 mg
Tablets (sustained-release): 180 mg

NURSING PROCESS

Assessment

- Assess patient's condition before therapy and regularly thereafter.
- Monitor and document patient's response after each dose; optimum dosage is difficult to judge.
- Monitor patient's vital signs, especially respirations.
- Be alert for adverse reactions and drug interactions.
- Evaluate patient's and family's knowledge of drug therapy.

Nursing diagnoses

- Impaired physical mobility related to underlying condition
- Ineffective breathing pattern related to adverse respiratory reactions
- Deficient knowledge related to drug therapy

Planning and implementation

- Stop all other cholinergics before giving drug.
- **P.O. use:** Don't crush extended-release tablets.

– When using sweet syrup for patient who has difficulty swallowing, pour over ice chips if he can't tolerate flavor.
• **I.V. use:** Administer I.V. injection no faster than 1 mg/minute. If I.V. administration is too rapid, bradycardia and seizures may result.
• **I.M. use:** Follow normal protocol.
• Position patient to ease breathing. Have atropine injection readily available, and provide respiratory support as needed.
• If patient's muscle weakness is severe, prescriber will determine if it's caused by drug-induced toxicity or worsening of myasthenia gravis. Test dose of edrophonium I.V. will aggravate drug-induced weakness but will temporarily relieve weakness caused by disease.
• The U.S. formulation of Regonol contains benzyl alcohol preservative that may cause toxicity in neonates if given in large doses. The Canadian formulation of this drug doesn't contain benzyl ethanol.
• If appropriate, obtain prescriber's order for hospitalized patient to have bedside supply of tablets. Patients with long-standing disease often insist on self-administration.
ALERT: If drug is taken immediately before or during Soman exposure, drug may be ineffective against Soman, and may worsen the effects of Soman.
ALERT: Don't confuse Mestinon with Mesantoin or Metatensin.

Patient teaching

• When giving drug for myasthenia gravis, stress the importance of taking it exactly as ordered, on time, in evenly spaced doses. If prescriber has ordered extended-release tablets, tell patient to take tablets at same time each day, at least 6 hours apart. Tell him that he may have to take drug for life.
• Advise patient to wear or carry medical identification at all times.

Evaluation

• Patient has improved physical mobility.
• Patient maintains adequate respiratory pattern.
• Patient and family state understanding of drug therapy.

pyridoxine hydrochloride (vitamin B_6)

(peer-ih-DOKS-een high-droh-KLOR-ighd)
Aminoxin, Beesix, Nestrex†, Rodex

Pharmacologic class: water-soluble vitamin
Therapeutic class: nutritional supplement
Pregnancy risk category: A

Indications and dosages

▶ **RDA.** *Men age 15 and older:* 2 mg.
Men ages 11 to 14: 1.7 mg.
Women age 19 and older: 1.6 mg.
Women ages 15 to 18: 1.5 mg.
Women ages 11 to 14: 1.4 mg.
Pregnant women: 2.2 mg.
Breast-feeding women: 2.1 mg.
Children ages 7 to 10: 1.4 mg.
Children ages 4 to 6: 1.1 mg.
Children ages 1 to 3: 1 mg.
Infants ages 6 months to 1 year: 0.6 mg.
Neonates and infants up to age 6 months: 0.3 mg.
▶ **Dietary vitamin B_6 deficiency.** *Adults:* 2.5 to 10 mg P.O., I.M., or I.V. daily for 3 weeks; then 2 to 5 mg daily as supplement to proper diet.
▶ **Seizures related to vitamin B_6 deficiency or dependency.** *Adults and children:* 10 to 100 mg I.M. or I.V. in single dose.
▶ **Vitamin B_6-responsive anemias or dependency syndrome (inborn errors of metabolism).** *Adults:* up to 600 mg I.M., P.O., or I.V. daily until symptoms subside; then 30 mg daily for life.
▶ **Prevention of vitamin B_6 deficiency during drug therapy.** *Adults:* 6 to 100 mg P.O. daily for isoniazid therapy.
▶ **Drug-induced vitamin B_6 deficiency.** *Adults:* 100 to 200 mg P.O. daily for 3 weeks, followed by 25 to 100 mg P.O. daily to prevent relapse.
▶ **Antidote for isoniazid poisoning.** *Adults:* 4 g I.V., followed by 1 g I.M. q 30 minutes until amount of pyridoxine administered equals amount of isoniazid ingested.
▶ **Premenstrual syndrome‡.** *Adults:* 40 to 500 mg P.O., I.M., or I.V. daily.

Contraindications and precautions

- Contraindicated in patients hypersensitive to pyridoxine.

Lifespan: No contraindications or precautions reported.

Adverse reactions

CNS: drowsiness, paresthesia, unstable gait.

Interactions

Drug-drug. *Levodopa:* Decreases levodopa effect. Avoid using together.

Phenobarbital, phenytoin: Decreases anticonvulsant level, increasing risk of seizures. Monitor serum level closely; institute seizure precautions.

Drug-lifestyle. *Alcohol use:* Increases risk of possible delirium and lactic acidosis. Discourage using together.

Effects on lab test results

- May increase AST level. May decrease folic acid level.

Pharmacokinetics

Absorption: Drug and its substituents are absorbed readily from GI tract. May be diminished in patients with malabsorption syndromes or following gastric resection.

Distribution: Drug is stored mainly in liver.

Metabolism: Metabolized in liver.

Excretion: In erythrocytes, pyridoxine is converted to pyridoxal phosphate and pyridoxamine is converted to pyridoxamine phosphate. The phosphorylated form of pyridoxine is transaminated to pyridoxal and pyridoxamine, which is phosphorylated rapidly. Conversion of pyridoxine phosphate to pyridoxal phosphate requires riboflavin. *Half-life:* 15 to 20 days.

Route	Onset	Peak	Duration
P.O, I.V., I.M.	Unknown	Unknown	Unknown

Pharmacodynamics

Chemical effect: Acts as coenzyme that stimulates various metabolic functions, including amino acid metabolism.

Therapeutic effect: Raises pyridoxine levels, prevents and relieves seizure activity related to pyridoxine deficiency or dependency, and blocks effects of isoniazid poisoning.

Available forms

Capsules: 500 mg
Capsules (timed-release): 100 mg
Injection: 100 mg/ml
Tablets: 10 mg†, 25 mg†, 50 mg†, 100 mg†, 200 mg†, 250 mg†, 500 mg†
Tablets (enteric-coated): 20 mg†
Tablets (timed-release): 100 mg

NURSING PROCESS

Assessment

- Assess patient before therapy and regularly thereafter.
- Be alert for adverse CNS reactions and drug interactions. Patient taking high doses (2 to 6 g/day) may have difficulty walking because of reduced proprioceptive and sensory function.
- Monitor patient's diet and snack habits. Excessive protein intake increases daily drug requirements.
- Evaluate patient's and family's knowledge of drug therapy.

Nursing diagnoses

- Ineffective health maintenance related to underlying condition
- Risk for injury related to drug-induced adverse CNS reactions
- Deficient knowledge related to drug therapy

Planning and implementation

- **P.O. and I.M. use:** Follow normal protocol.
- **I.V. use:** Inject undiluted drug into I.V. line containing free-flowing compatible solution. Or, infuse diluted drug over prescribed duration for intermittent infusions. Don't use for continuous infusion.
- Protect drug from light. Don't use solution if it contains precipitate, although slight darkening is acceptable.
- When using drug to treat isoniazid toxicity, expect to give anticonvulsants.
- If sodium bicarbonate is required to control acidosis in isoniazid toxicity, don't mix in same syringe with pyridoxine.

ALERT: Don't confuse pyridoxine with pralidoxime, pyrimethamine, or Pyridium.

Patient teaching

- Advise patient taking levodopa alone to avoid multivitamins containing pyridoxine because of decreased levodopa effect.

• If prescribed for maintenance therapy to prevent recurrence of deficiency, stress importance of compliance and good nutrition. Explain that pyridoxine in combination therapy with isoniazid has specific therapeutic purpose and isn't just a vitamin.

Evaluation
• Patient responds well to therapy.
• Patient doesn't experience injury from adverse CNS reactions.
• Patient and family state understanding of drug therapy.

pyrimethamine
(peer-ih-METH-uh-meen)
Daraprim

pyrimethamine with sulfadoxine
Fansidar

Pharmacologic class: aminopyrimidine derivative (folic acid antagonist)
Therapeutic class: antimalarial
Pregnancy risk category: C

Indications and dosages
▶ **Malaria prophylaxis and transmission control.** ***pyrimethamine.*** *Adults and children older than age 10:* 25 mg P.O. weekly.
Children ages 4 to 10: 12.5 mg P.O. weekly.
Children younger than age 4: 6.25 mg P.O. weekly.
Continued in all age groups at least 10 weeks after leaving endemic area.
▶ **Acute attacks of malaria.** ***pyrimethamine with sulfadoxine.*** *Adults:* 2 to 3 tablets as single dose, either alone or in sequence with quinine.
Children ages 9 to 14: 2 tablets.
Children ages 4 to 8: 1 tablet.
Children younger than age 4: ½ tablet.
▶ **Malaria prophylaxis.** ***pyrimethamine with sulfadoxine.*** *Adults:* 1 tablet weekly, or 2 tablets q 2 weeks.
Children ages 9 to 14: ¾ tablet weekly, or 1½ tablets q 2 weeks.
Children ages 4 to 8: ½ tablet weekly, or 1 tablet q 2 weeks.
Children younger than age 4: ¼ tablet weekly, or ½ tablet q 2 weeks.
▶ **Acute attacks of malaria.** ***pyrimethamine.*** *Adults and children older than age 10:* 25 mg P.O. daily for 2 days when used with faster-acting antimalarials; when used alone, 50 mg P.O. daily for 2 days.
Children ages 4 to 10: 25 mg P.O. daily for 2 days.
▶ **Toxoplasmosis.** ***pyrimethamine.*** *Adults:* Initially, 50 to 75 mg P.O. daily for 1 to 3 weeks; then 25 mg P.O. daily for 4 to 5 weeks along with 1 g sulfadiazine P.O. q 6 hours.
Children: Initially, 1 mg/kg P.O. (not to exceed 100 mg) in two equally divided doses for 2 to 4 days; then 0.5 mg/kg daily for 4 weeks along with 100 mg sulfadiazine/kg P.O. daily, divided q 6 hours.
▶ **Isosporiasis‡.** *Adults:* 50 to 75 mg P.O.daily.

Contraindications and precautions
• Contraindicated in patients hypersensitive to drug and in those with megaloblastic anemia caused by folic acid deficiency. Pyrimethamine with sulfadoxine is contraindicated in patients with porphyria because it contains sulfadoxine, a sulfonamide.
• Repeated use of pyrimethamine with sulfadoxine is contraindicated in patients hypersensitive to pyrimethamine or sulfonamides, and in patients with severe renal insufficiency, marked liver parenchymal damage or blood dyscrasias, or megaloblastic anemia caused by folate deficiency.
• Use cautiously in patients with impaired hepatic or renal function, severe allergy or bronchial asthma, or G6PD deficiency; in those with seizure disorders (smaller doses may be needed); and in those treated with chloroquine.
Lifespan: In infants younger than age 2 months, breast-feeding women, and pregnant women at term, repeated use of pyrimethamine with sulfadoxine is contraindicated.

Adverse reactions
CNS: stimulation, ***seizures.***
GI: anorexia, vomiting, diarrhea, atrophic glossitis.
Hematologic: ***agranulocytosis, aplastic anemia,*** megaloblastic anemia***, bone marrow suppression, leukopenia, thrombocytopenia, pancytopenia.***
Skin: rash, ***erythema multiforme, Stevens-Johnson syndrome, toxic epidermal necrolysis.***

Interactions

Drug-drug. *Co-trimoxazole, methotrexate, sulfonamides:* Increases risk of bone marrow suppression. Don't use together.
Folic acid, PABA: Decreases antitoxoplasmic effects. May require dosage adjustment.
Lorazepam: May cause mild hepatotoxicity. Monitor liver enzymes.

Effects on lab test results

- May decrease hemoglobin, hematocrit, and granulocyte, WBC, platelet, and RBC counts.

Pharmacokinetics

Absorption: Well absorbed from intestinal tract.
Distribution: Distributed to kidneys, liver, spleen, and lungs. About 80% bound to plasma proteins.
Metabolism: Metabolized to several unidentified compounds.
Excretion: Excreted in urine. *Half-life:* 2 to 6 hours.

Route	Onset	Peak	Duration
P.O.	Unknown	1.5-8 hr	Unknown

Pharmacodynamics

Chemical effect: Inhibits enzyme dihydrofolate reductase, thereby impeding reduction of dihydrofolic acid to tetrahydrofolic acid. Sulfadoxine competitively inhibits use of PABA.
Therapeutic effect: Prevents malaria and treats malaria and toxoplasmosis infections. Spectrum of activity includes asexual erythrocytic forms of susceptible plasmodia and *Toxoplasma gondii.*

Available forms

pyrimethamine
Tablets: 25 mg
pyrimethamine with sulfadoxine
Tablets: pyrimethamine 25 mg, sulfadoxine 500 mg

NURSING PROCESS

Assessment

- Assess patient's condition before therapy and regularly thereafter.
- Obtain twice-weekly blood counts, including platelets, for patients with toxoplasmosis because dosages used approach toxic levels.
- Be alert for adverse reactions and drug interactions.
- Evaluate patient's and family's knowledge of drug therapy.

Nursing diagnoses

- Infection related to presence of susceptible organism
- Ineffective protection related to adverse hematologic reactions
- Deficient knowledge related to drug therapy

Planning and implementation

- Give drug with meals to minimize GI distress.
- If signs of folic acid or folinic acid deficiency develop, dosage should be reduced or discontinued while patient receives parenteral folinic acid (leucovorin) until blood counts become normal.
- When used to treat toxoplasmosis in patients with AIDS, therapy may be lifelong. Long-term suppressive therapy for patient's lifetime may also be necessary.

ALERT: Because of possibly severe skin reactions, pyrimethamine with sulfadoxine should be used only in regions where chloroquine-resistant malaria is prevalent and only when traveler plans to stay in region longer than 3 weeks.

Patient teaching

- Advise patient to take drug with food.
- Teach patient to watch for and immediately report signs of folic or folinic acid deficiency and acute toxicity.
- Warn patient taking pyrimethamine with sulfadoxine to stop drug and notify prescriber at first sign of rash.
- Instruct patient to take first prophylactic dose of pyrimethamine with sulfadoxine 1 to 2 days before traveling to endemic area.

Evaluation

- Patient is free from infection.
- Patient maintains normal hematologic parameters.
- Patient and family state understanding of drug therapy.

Q

quetiapine fumarate
(KWET-ee-uh-peen FYOO-muh-rayt)
Seroquel

Pharmacologic class: dibenzothiazepine derivative
Therapeutic class: antipsychotic
Pregnancy risk category: C

Indications and dosages

▶ **Management of the symptoms of psychotic disorders.** *Adults:* Initially, 25 mg b.i.d.; increased in increments of 25 to 50 mg b.i.d. or t.i.d. on days 2 and 3, as tolerated. Target dosage range is 300 to 400 mg daily, divided into two or three daily doses by day 4. Further dosage adjustments, if indicated, usually occur at intervals of not less than 2 days. Dosages can be increased or decreased by 25 to 50 mg b.i.d. Antipsychotic efficacy typically occurs at 150 to 750 mg daily. Safety of doses above 800 daily hasn't been evaluated. Dosage adjustment may be required in patients with hepatic impairment.

Contraindications and precautions

- Contraindicated in patients hypersensitive to drug or its ingredients.
- Use cautiously in patients with CV or cerebrovascular disease with or conditions that predispose them to hypotension; in those with history of seizures or conditions that lower seizure threshold; in those at risk for aspiration pneumonia; and in those who could experience conditions in which core body temperature may be elevated.

Lifespan: In breast-feeding women, safety of drug hasn't been established. In children younger than age 12, drug is not recommended. In geriatric patients, use cautiously; they may be more sensitive to adverse effects.

Adverse reactions

CNS: fever, asthenia, *dizziness, headache, seizures, somnolence,* hypertonia, dysarthria.
CV: orthostatic hypotension, tachycardia, palpitations, peripheral edema.
EENT: pharyngitis, rhinitis, ear pain, cataracts, sinusitis, nasal congestion.
GI: dry mouth, dyspepsia, abdominal pain, constipation, anorexia.
GU: urine retention.
Hematologic: *leukopenia.*
Metabolic: *weight gain,* hypothyroidism.
Musculoskeletal: back pain.
Respiratory: increased cough, dyspnea.
Skin: rash, sweating.
Other: flulike syndrome.

Interactions

Drug-drug. *Antihypertensives:* May increase drug effects. Monitor blood pressure.
Carbamazepine, glucocorticoids, phenobarbital, phenytoin, rifampin, thioridazine: Increases quetiapine clearance. Increase quetiapine dose, as directed.
CNS depressants: Increases CNS effects. Use together cautiously.
Erythromycin, fluconazole, itraconazole, ketoconazole: Decreases quetiapine clearance. Use cautiously.
Dopamine agonists, Levodopa: Effects of these agents may be antagonized. Monitor patient for clinical effects.
Lorazepam: Reduces lorazepam clearance. Monitor patient.
Drug-lifestyle. *Alcohol use:* Increases CNS effects. Discourage using together.

Effects on lab test results

- May increase liver enzyme, cholesterol, and triglyceride levels. May decrease T_4 and thyroid-stimulating hormone levels.
- May decrease WBC count.

Pharmacokinetics

Absorption: Rapid following P.O. administration; 100% bioavailability.
Distribution: Widely distributed throughout body; 83% bound to plasma protein.
Metabolism: Extensively metabolized by liver to inactive metabolites.
Excretion: About 73% excreted in urine, 20% in feces. *Half-life:* 6 hours.

Route	Onset	Peak	Duration
P.O.	Unknown	1.5 hr	Unknown

Pharmacodynamics

Chemical effect: Unknown, but drug is thought to exert antipsychotic activity by blocking dopamine D-2 receptors and serotonin 5-HT2 receptors in the brain. It also may act at histamine H_1 receptors and alpha$_1$-adrenergic receptors.
Therapeutic effect: Reduces symptoms of psychotic disorders.

Available forms

Tablets: 25 mg, 100 mg, 200 mg, 300 mg

NURSING PROCESS

Assessment

- Monitor patient for tardive dyskinesia. Condition may not appear until months or years after starting drug and may disappear spontaneously or persist for life, despite discontinuation of drug.
- Monitor patient's vital signs carefully, especially during the 3- to 5-day period of initial dosage adjustment and when restarting treatment or increasing dosage.
- Assess patient's risk of physical injury from adverse CNS effects.
- Be alert for adverse reactions and drug interactions.
- Evaluate patient's and family's knowledge of drug therapy.

Nursing diagnoses

- Risk for imbalanced body temperature related to drug-induced hyperpyrexia
- Impaired physical mobility related to drug-induced adverse CNS effects
- Deficient knowledge related to drug therapy

Planning and implementation

- Geriatric or debilitated patients or patients with hepatic impairment or predisposition to hypotensive reactions usually require lower initial doses and more gradual dosage adjustment.

ALERT: Withhold drug and notify prescriber if symptoms of neuroleptic malignant syndrome (hyperpyrexia, muscle rigidity, altered mental status, and autonomic instability) occur.
- Provide ice chips, drinks, or sugarless hard candy to help relieve dry mouth.

ALERT: Don't confuse Serzone (nefazodone) with Seroquel (quetiapine).

Patient teaching
- Caution patient about risk of orthostatic hypotension. Risk is greatest during 3- to 5-day period of initial dosage adjustment and when restarting treatment or increasing dosage.
- Tell patient to avoid becoming overheated or dehydrated during therapy.
- Warn patient to avoid activities that require mental alertness until CNS effects of drug are known.
- Remind patient to have eye examination before starting drug therapy and every 6 months during therapy to check for cataract formation.
- Tell patient to notify prescriber of other medications (prescription or OTC) he is taking or plans to take.
- Tell woman to notify prescriber if she becomes pregnant or intends to become pregnant during drug therapy. Advise her not to breast-feed during therapy.
- Advise patient to avoid alcohol during therapy.

Evaluation

- Patient maintains normal body temperature.
- Patient maintains physical mobility and doesn't experience extrapyramidal effects of drug.
- Patient and family state understanding of drug therapy.

quinapril hydrochloride

(KWIN-eh-pril high-droh-KLOR-ighd)
Accupril, Asig ◇

Pharmacologic class: ACE inhibitor
Therapeutic class: antihypertensive
Pregnancy risk category: C (D in second and third trimesters)

Indications and dosages

▶ **Hypertension.** *Adults:* Initially, 10 mg to 20 mg P.O. daily. Dosage adjusted based on patient response at intervals of about 2 weeks. Most patients are controlled at 20, 40, or 80 mg daily as a single dose or in two divided doses.

Maximum initial dose is 10 mg P.O. if creatinine clearance exceeds 60 ml/minute; 5 mg if clearance is 30 to 60 ml/minute; and 2.5 mg if clearance is 10 to 30 ml/minute. No dose recommendations are available for creatinine clearance less than 10 ml/minute.

▶ **Heart failure.** *Adults:* Initially, 5 mg P.O. b.i.d. if patient is taking a diuretic and 10 mg P.O. b.i.d. if patient isn't taking a diuretic. Dosage increased at weekly intervals. Usual effective dosage is 20 to 40 mg b.i.d. in equally divided doses.

Patients with renal impairment: The recommended initial dose is 5 mg P.O. if creatinine clearance exceeds 30 ml/minute; 2.5 mg if clearance is 10 to 30 ml/min. No dose recommendations are available for creatinine clearance less than 10 ml/minute.

Contraindications and precautions

- Contraindicated in patients hypersensitive to ACE inhibitors, in those with a history of angioedema during previous ACE inhibitor treatment, and in those with renal artery stenosis.
- Use cautiously in patients with impaired kidney function and increased serum potassium.

Lifespan: In pregnant women in the second or third trimester, drug isn't recommended. In breast-feeding women, use cautiously. In children, safety of drug hasn't been established.

Adverse reactions

CNS: somnolence, vertigo, light-headedness, syncope, malaise, nervousness, depression.
CV: palpitations, vasodilation, tachycardia, ***hypertensive crisis,*** angina, orthostatic hypotension, ***arrhythmias.***
EENT: dry throat.
GI: dry mouth, abdominal pain, constipation, ***hemorrhage.***
Metabolic: ***hyperkalemia.***
Musculoskeletal: back pain.
Respiratory: dry, persistent, tickling, nonproductive cough.
Skin: pruritus, exfoliative dermatitis, *photosensitivity reaction,* diaphoresis.
Other: ***angioedema.***

Interactions

Drug-drug. *Diuretics, other antihypertensives:* May increase the risk of excessive hypotension. Expect to stop diuretic or lower dosage.
Lithium: May increase lithium levels and lithium toxicity. Avoid using together.
Potassium-sparing diuretics: May increase risk of hyperkalemia. Monitor patient, ECG, and potassium levels closely.
Drug-herb. *Licorice:* May cause sodium retention and increase blood pressure, interfering with the therapeutic effects of ACE inhibitors. Discourage using together.
Drug-food. *High-fat foods:* May impair absorption. Discourage using together.
Sodium substitutes containing potassium: May increase risk of hyperkalemia. Discourage using together; monitor patient closely.

Effects on lab test results

- May increase potassium level.
- May decrease liver function test values.

Pharmacokinetics

Absorption: At least 60% absorbed; rate and extent drop by 25% to 30% when taken with high-fat meals.
Distribution: About 97% of drug and active metabolite are bound to plasma proteins.
Metabolism: 38% of dose de-esterified in liver to active metabolite.
Excretion: Excreted primarily in urine. *Half-life:* About 25 hours.

Route	Onset	Peak	Duration
P.O.	≤ 1 hr	1-2 hr	About 24 hr

Pharmacodynamics

Chemical effect: Unknown; may inhibit transition of angiotensin I to angiotensin II, which lowers peripheral arterial resistance and decreases aldosterone secretion.
Therapeutic effect: Lowers blood pressure.

Available forms

Tablets: 5 mg, 10 mg, 20 mg, 40 mg

NURSING PROCESS

Assessment

- Assess patient's blood pressure before therapy and regularly thereafter. Take blood pressure when drug levels are at their peak (2 to 6 hours after dose) and at their trough (just be-

fore dose) to verify adequate blood pressure control.
- Assess kidney and liver function before and throughout therapy.
- Monitor potassium levels.
- Other ACE inhibitors have been linked to agranulocytosis and neutropenia. Monitor CBC with differential before therapy, every 2 weeks for first 3 months of therapy, and periodically thereafter.
- Be alert for adverse reactions and drug interactions.
- Evaluate patient's and family's knowledge of drug therapy.

Nursing diagnoses
- Risk for injury related to presence of hypertension
- Disturbed sleep pattern related to drug-induced cough
- Deficient knowledge related to drug therapy

Planning and implementation
- Dosage adjustment is necessary if patient has renal impairment.
- Give drug on empty stomach; high-fat meals can impair absorption.

Patient teaching
- Advise patient to report signs of infection, such as fever and sore throat.
- Tell patient to report signs of angioedema, such as breathing difficulty and swelling of face, eyes, lips, or tongue, especially after first dose.
- Warn patient that light-headedness can occur, especially at start of drug therapy. Tell him to rise slowly and to stop drug and notify prescriber if he experiences blackouts.
- Inadequate fluid intake, vomiting, diarrhea, and excessive perspiration can lead to light-headedness and syncope. Tell patient to maintain adequate hydration/fluid intake and to use caution in hot weather and during exercise.
- Warn patient to avoid potassium supplements and sodium substitutes that contain potassium during therapy.
- Tell women to notify prescriber about suspected or confirmed pregnancy. Drug will need to be stopped.

Evaluation
- Patient's blood pressure is normal.
- Patient's sleep patterns are undisturbed throughout therapy.
- Patient and family state understanding of drug therapy.

quinidine bisulfate
(KWIN-eh-deen bigh-SUL-fayt)
(66.4% quinidine base)
Biquin Durules ◆, Kinidin Durules ◇

quinidine gluconate
(62% quinidine base)
Quinaglute Dura-Tabs, Quinalan, Quinate ◆

quinidine sulfate
(83% quinidine base)
Apo-Quinidine ◆, Cin-Quin, Novoquinidin ◆, Quinidex Extentabs, Quinora

Pharmacologic class: cinchona alkaloid
Therapeutic class: antiarrhythmic
Pregnancy risk category: C

Indications and dosages
▶ **Atrial flutter or fibrillation.** *Adults:* 200 mg of quinidine sulfate or equivalent base P.O. q 2 to 3 hours for five to eight doses, with subsequent daily increases until sinus rhythm is restored or toxic effects develop. Quinidine is given only after digitalization to avoid increasing AV conduction. Maximum dosage is 3 to 4 g daily.

▶ **Paroxysmal supraventricular tachycardia.** *Adults:* 400 to 600 mg of quinidine sulfate P.O. q 2 to 3 hours until toxic adverse reactions develop or arrhythmia subsides.

▶ **Premature atrial and ventricular contractions; paroxysmal AV junctional rhythm; paroxysmal atrial tachycardia; paroxysmal ventricular tachycardia; maintenance after cardioversion of atrial fibrillation or flutter.** *Adults:* Quinidine sulfate or equivalent base 200 to 400 mg P.O. q 4 to 6 hours. Or, quinidine gluconate 400 mg I.M. q 2 hours, adjusting each dose by the effect of the previous. Or, quinidine sulfate or gluconate sustained-release tablets 300 mg to 600 mg P.O. q 8 or 12 hours. Or, quinidine gluconate infused I.V. at up to 0.25 mg/kg/minute (1 ml/kg/hour).

Children: Test dose is 2 mg/kg; then 30 mg/kg P.O. daily or 900 mg/m^2 P.O. daily in five divided doses.

▶ **Severe *Plasmodium falciparum* malaria.** *Adults:* 10 mg/kg quinidine gluconate I.V. diluted in 250 ml of normal saline solution and infused over 1 to 2 hours; then continuous maintenance infusion of 0.02 mg/kg/minute for 72 hours or until parasitemia is reduced to less than 1%. Or, 15 mg/kg quinidine gluconate I.V. diluted in 250 ml of normal saline solution infused over 4 hours; begin maintenance therapy 24 hours after the start of the loading dose, 7.5 mg/kg infused over 4 hours, q 8 hours for 7 days, or until oral therapy can be instituted.

Patients with heart failure or impaired liver function: Reduced dosage.

Contraindications and precautions

- Contraindicated in patients hypersensitive to quinidine or related cinchona derivatives, in patients with idiosyncratic reactions to them, and in patients with intraventricular conduction defects, complete heart block, left bundle branch block, history of drug-induced torsade de pointes or prolonged QT interval, digitalis toxicity with grossly impaired AV conduction, or abnormal rhythms caused by escape mechanisms.
- Use cautiously in patients with asthma, muscle weakness, or infection with fever (hypersensitivity reactions to drug may be masked); patients with hepatic, renal, or other cardiac impairment.

Lifespan: In pregnant women, use cautiously. In breast-feeding women, drug isn't recommended. In children, safety of drug hasn't been established.

Adverse reactions

CNS: *vertigo, headache, light-headedness,* confusion, restlessness, cold sweats, pallor, fainting, fever, dementia.

CV: ***PVCs, ventricular tachycardia, atypical ventricular tachycardia (torsades de pointes), severe hypotension, SA and AV block, ventricular fibrillation, cardiotoxicity,*** tachycardia, ***aggravated heart failure,*** ECG changes (widening of QRS complex, notched P waves, widened QT interval, ST-segment depression).

EENT: *tinnitus,* blurred vision.

GI: *diarrhea, nausea, vomiting,* excessive salivation, anorexia, petechial hemorrhage of buccal mucosa, abdominal pain.

Hematologic: hemolytic anemia, ***thrombocytopenia, agranulocytosis.***

Hepatic: ***hepatotoxicity.***

Respiratory: ***acute asthma attack, respiratory arrest.***

Skin: rash, pruritus.

Other: ***angioedema,*** cinchonism, hypersensitivity reaction.

Interactions

Drug-drug. *Acetazolamide, antacids, sodium bicarbonate, thiazide diuretics:* May increase quinidine levels because of alkaline urine. Monitor patient for increased effect.

Amiodarone, cimetidine: Increases quinidine levels. Monitor patient for increased effect.

Barbiturates, phenytoin, rifampin: May decrease level of quinidine. Monitor patient for decreased quinidine effect.

Digoxin: Increases digoxin level after quinidine therapy starts. Monitor patient closely for digitalis toxicity.

Nifedipine: May decrease quinidine level. Monitor patient carefully.

Other antiarrhythmics (such as lidocaine, phenytoin, procainamide, propranolol): Increases risk of toxicity. Use together cautiously.

Verapamil: May result in hypotension, bradycardia, or AV block. Monitor blood pressure and heart rate.

Warfarin: Increases anticoagulant effect. Monitor patient closely for bleeding.

Drug-herb. *Jimson weed:* May adversely effect CV function. Discourage using together.

Licorice: May prolong the QT interval. Discourage using together.

Drug-food. *Grapefruit juice:* May decrease level. Discourage using together.

Effects on lab test results

- May increase liver enzyme levels.
- May decrease hemoglobin, hematocrit, and platelet and granulocyte counts.

Pharmacokinetics

Absorption: Although all quinidine salts are well absorbed from GI tract after P.O. administration, serum drug levels vary greatly among individuals.

Distribution: Well distributed in all tissues except brain; about 80% bound to plasma proteins.

Metabolism: About 60% to 80% metabolized in liver to two metabolites that may have some pharmacologic activity.
Excretion: 10% to 30% excreted in urine. Urine acidification increases excretion; alkalinization decreases it. *Half-life:* 5 to 12 hours.

Route	Onset	Peak	Duration
P.O.	1-3 hr	1-2 hr	6-8 hr
I.V.	Immediate	Immediate	Unknown
I.M.	Unknown	Unknown	Unknown

Pharmacodynamics

Chemical effect: Class Ia antiarrhythmic that has direct and indirect (anticholinergic) effects on cardiac tissue. Automaticity, conduction velocity, and membrane responsiveness are decreased. The effective refractory period is prolonged. Anticholinergic action reduces vagal tone.
Therapeutic effect: Restores normal sinus rhythm and relieves signs and symptoms of malaria infection.

Available forms

quinidine bisulfate
Tablets (sustained-release): 250 mg ◆ ◇
quinidine gluconate
Injection: 80 mg/ml
Tablets (sustained-release): 324 mg, 325 mg ◆, 330 mg
quinidine sulfate
Capsules: 200 mg, 300 mg
Injection: 200 mg/ml
Tablets: 200 mg, 300 mg
Tablets (sustained-release): 300 mg

NURSING PROCESS

Assessment

- Assess patient's arrhythmia before therapy and regularly thereafter.
- Monitor quinidine level. Therapeutic level for antiarrhythmic effects is 2 to 5 mcg/ml.
- Check apical pulse rate and blood pressure before starting therapy.
- Monitor liver function test results during first 4 to 8 weeks of therapy.
- Be alert for adverse reactions and drug interactions.
- Evaluate patient's and family's knowledge of drug therapy.

Nursing diagnoses

- Decreased cardiac output related to presence of arrhythmia
- Risk for deficient fluid volume related to drug-induced adverse GI reactions
- Deficient knowledge related to drug therapy

Planning and implementation

- Anticoagulant therapy is commonly advised before quinidine therapy in long-standing atrial fibrillation because restoration of normal sinus rhythm may dislodge thrombi from atrial wall, causing thromboembolism.
- **P.O. use:** Don't crush sustained-release tablets.

ALERT: Sustained-release preparations are not interchangeable.

- **I.V. use:** I.V. route should only be used for treating acute arrhythmias.

– Mix 10 ml of quinidine gluconate with 40 ml of D_5W and infuse at an initial rate of up to 0.25 mg/minute (1 ml/kg/hr).
– Never use discolored (brownish) quinidine solution.

- **I.M. use:** Follow normal protocol.

ALERT: Don't confuse quinidine with clonidine.

Patient teaching

- Tell patient to take drug with meals.
- Tell patient to report signs of toxicity, including ringing in ears, visual disturbances, dizziness, headache, nausea, rash, or shortness of breath.
- Stress importance of follow-up care.

Evaluation

- Patient regains normal cardiac output with resolution of arrhythmia.
- Patient maintains adequate hydration throughout therapy.
- Patient and family state understanding of drug therapy.

quinupristin and dalfopristin

(QUIN-uh-pris-tin and DALF-oh-pris-tin)
Synercid

Pharmacologic class: streptogramin
Therapeutic class: antibiotic
Pregnancy risk category: B

Indications and dosages

▶ **Serious or life-threatening infections linked to vancomycin-resistant *Enterococcus faecium* (VREF) bacteremia.** *Adults and children age 16 and older:* 7.5 mg/kg I.V. infusion over 1 hour q 8 hours. Length of treatment determined by site and severity of infection.

▶ **Complicated skin and skin-structure infections caused by *Staphylococcus aureus* (methicillin susceptible) or *Streptococcus pyogenes*.** *Adults and children age 16 and older:* 7.5 mg/kg by I.V. infusion over 1 hour q 12 hours for at least 7 days.

Contraindications and precautions

- Contraindicated in patients hypersensitive to drug or other streptogramin antibiotics.

Lifespan: In pregnant women, use only if clearly needed. In breast-feeding women, use cautiously. In children younger than age 16, safety and efficacy haven't been established.

Adverse reactions

CNS: headache, pain.
CV: thrombophlebitis.
GI: nausea, diarrhea, vomiting.
Musculoskeletal: arthralgia, myalgia.
Skin: *inflammation, pain, and edema at infusion site;* rash; pruritus.

Interactions

Drug-drug. *Cyclosporine:* Metabolism of cyclosporine is reduced and levels may be increased. Monitor cyclosporine levels.
Drugs metabolized by cytochrome P-450 3A4 (carbamazepine, delavirdine, diazepam, diltiazem, disopyramide, docetaxel, indinavir, lidocaine, lovastatin, methylprednisolone, midazolam, nevirapine, nifedipine, paclitaxel, ritonavir, tacrolimus, verapamil, vinblastine, and others): Increases plasma levels and increases therapeutic effects and adverse reactions of these drugs. Use together cautiously.
Drugs metabolized by cytochrome P-450 3A4 that may prolong the QTc interval (such as quinidine): Decreases metabolism of these drugs, resulting in prolongation of QTc interval. Avoid using together.

Effects on lab test results

- May increase AST, ALT, and bilirubin levels.

Pharmacokinetics

Absorption: Administered I.V.
Distribution: Protein-binding is moderate.
Metabolism: Quinupristin and dalfopristin are converted to several active major metabolites by nonenzymatic reactions.
Excretion: About 75% of both drugs and their metabolites excreted in feces. About 15% of quinupristin and 19% of dalfopristin excreted in urine. *Half-life:* About 0.85 hours for quinupristin and 0.7 hours for dalfopristin.

Route	Onset	Peak	Duration
I.V.	Unknown	Unknown	Unknown

Pharmacodynamics

Chemical effect: The two antibiotics inhibit or destroy susceptible bacteria through combined inhibition of protein synthesis in bacterial cells. Dalfopristin inhibits the early phase of protein synthesis in the bacterial ribosome, and quinupristin inhibits the late phase of protein synthesis. Without the ability to manufacture new proteins, bacterial cells become inactive or die.
Therapeutic effect: Inactivation or death of bacterial cells.

Available forms

Injection: 500 mg/10 ml (150 mg quinupristin and 350 mg dalfopristin)

NURSING PROCESS

Assessment

- Obtain history of patient's underlying condition before therapy, and reassess regularly thereafter.
- Overgrowth of nonsusceptible organisms may occur; monitor patient closely for signs and symptoms of superinfection.
- Monitor liver function during therapy.
- Evaluate patient's and family's knowledge of drug therapy.

Nursing diagnoses

- Risk for infection related to presence of bacteria
- Diarrhea related to drug-induced adverse effect
- Deficient knowledge related to drug therapy

Planning and implementation

- Reconstitute powder for injection by adding 5 ml of sterile water for injection or D_5W. Gently swirl vial to dissolve powder completely; avoid shaking to limit foaming. Reconstituted solutions must be further diluted within 30 minutes.
- The dose of reconstituted solution should be added to 250 ml of D_5W; maximum concentration 2 mg/ml. This diluted solution is stable for 5 hours at room temperature or 54 hours refrigerated.

ALERT: Quinupristin and dalfopristin is incompatible with saline and heparin solutions. Don't dilute drug with saline-containing solutions or infuse into lines that contain saline or heparin. Flush line with D_5W before and after each dose.

- Fluid-restricted patient with a central venous catheter may receive dose in 100 ml of D_5W. This concentration isn't recommended for peripheral venous administration.
- Administer all doses by I.V. infusion over 1 hour. Use an infusion pump or device to control rate of infusion.
- If moderate-to-severe peripheral venous irritation occurs, consider increasing infusion volume to 500 or 750 ml, changing injection site, or infusing by central venous catheter.

ALERT: Quinupristin and dalfopristin isn't active against *Enterococcus faecalis*. Appropriate blood cultures are needed to avoid misidentifying *E. faecalis* as *E. faecium*.

- Adverse reactions, such as arthralgia and myalgia, may be reduced by decreasing dosage interval to every 12 hours.
- Notify prescriber if patient develops diarrhea during or following therapy because mild-to-life-threatening pseudomembranous colitis has been reported with use of quinupristin/dalfopristin.

Patient teaching

- Advise patient to immediately report irritation at I.V. site, pain in joints or muscles, and diarrhea.
- Tell patient about importance of reporting persistent or worsening signs and symptoms of infection, such as pain and erythema.

Evaluation

- Patient is free from infection.
- Patient doesn't experience diarrhea.
- Patient and family state understanding of drug therapy.

R

rabeprazole sodium

(rah-BEH-pruh-zohl SOH-dee-um)

Aciphex

Pharmacologic class: proton pump inhibitor
Therapeutic class: antiulcerative
Pregnancy risk category: B

Indications and dosages

▶ **Healing of erosive or ulcerative gastroesophageal reflux disease (GERD).** *Adults:* 20 mg P.O. daily for 4 to 8 weeks. Additional 8-week course may be considered, if necessary.

▶ **Maintenance of healing of erosive or ulcerative GERD.** *Adults:* 20 mg P.O. daily.

▶ **Healing of duodenal ulcers.** *Adults:* 20 mg P.O. daily after morning meal for up to 4 weeks.

▶ **Treatment of pathological hypersecretory conditions including Zollinger-Ellison syndrome.** *Adults:* 60 mg P.O. daily; increase p.r.n. to 100 mg P.O. daily or 60 mg P.O. twice daily.

▶ **Symptomatic GERD, including daytime and nighttime heartburn.** *Adults:* 20 mg P.O. daily for 4 weeks. Additional 4-week course may be considered, if necessary.

▶ ***Helicobacter pylori* eradication to reduce the risk of duodenal ulcer recurrence.** *Adults:* Three drug regimen: rabeprazole 20 mg P.O. b.i.d. in combination with amoxicillin 1,000 mg P.O. b.i.d. and clarithromycin 500 mg P.O. b.i.d. for a total of 7 days.

Contraindications and precautions

- Contraindicated in patients hypersensitive to rabeprazole, other benzimidazoles (such as lansoprazole, omeprazole), or components in these formulations. For H. pylori eradication, clarithromycin is contraindicated in patients with known hypersensitivity to any macrolide antibiotic, and in patients taking pimozide. Amoxicillin is contraindicated in patients with a known hypersensitivity to any penicillin. Use cautiously in patients with severe hepatic impairment.

Lifespan: In pregnant women, clarithromycin is contraindicated for *H. pylori* eradication. In children, safety of drug hasn't been established.

Adverse reactions

CNS: headache.

Interactions

Drug-drug. *Clarithromycin:* Increased plasma levels of rabeprazole. Monitor patient closely.
Cyclosporine: May inhibit cyclosporine metabolism. Use together cautiously.
Digoxin, ketoconazole, other gastric pH-dependent drugs: Decreases or increases drug absorption at increased pH values. Monitor patient closely.
Drug-herb. *St. John's wort:* May increase risk of sunburn. Discourage using together; urge patient to avoid unprotected or prolonged sun exposure.

Effects on lab test results

None reported.

Pharmacokinetics

Absorption: Acid labile; enteric coating allows drug to pass through the stomach relatively intact. Plasma levels peak over a period of 2 to 5 hours.
Distribution: 96.3% plasma protein-bound.
Metabolism: Extensively metabolized by the liver to inactive compounds.
Excretion: 90% eliminated in urine as metabolites. Remaining 10% of metabolites eliminated in feces. *Half-life:* 1 to 2 hours.

Route	Onset	Peak	Duration
P.O.	Within 1 hr	2-5 hr	> 24 hr

Pharmacodynamics

Chemical effect: Blocks activity of the acid (proton) pump by inhibiting gastric hydrogen-potassium adenosine triphosphatase at the secretory surface of gastric parietal cells, thereby blocking gastric acid secretion.
Therapeutic effect: Promotes healing of gastric erosion or ulceration by stopping gastric acid secretion.

Available forms

Tablets (delayed-release): 20 mg

NURSING PROCESS

Assessment

- Obtain history of patient's underlying condition before therapy, and reassess regularly thereafter.
- Be alert for adverse reactions and drug interactions.
- Evaluate patient's and family's knowledge of drug therapy.

Nursing diagnoses

- Acute pain related to underlying condition
- Risk for injury related to drug-induced adverse reactions
- Deficient knowledge related to drug therapy

Planning and implementation

- Don't crush, split, or allow patient to chew tablets.
- Prescriber may consider additional courses of therapy when duodenal ulcer or GERD isn't healed after first course of therapy.

ALERT: Symptomatic response to therapy doesn't rule out presence of gastric malignancy.

- In patients who fail therapy for *H. pylori,* susceptibility testing should be done. If resistance to clarithromycin is demonstrated or susceptibility testing is not possible, alternative antimicrobial therapy should be instituted.

ALERT: For *H. pylori* eradication, pseudomembranous colitis may occur with nearly all antibacterial agents, including clarithromycin and amoxicillin. Monitor patient closely.

Patient teaching

- Explain importance of taking drug exactly as prescribed.
- Advise patient that delayed-release tablets should be swallowed whole and not crushed, chewed, or split.
- Advise patient that drug may be taken without regard to meals.

Evaluation

- Patient experiences decreased pain with drug therapy.

• Patient sustains no injury as a result of drug-induced adverse reactions.
• Patient and family state understanding of drug therapy.

rabies immune globulin, human
(RAY-bees ih-MYOON GLOH-byoo-lin, HYOO-mun)
BayRab, Imogam Rabies-HT

Pharmacologic class: immune serum
Therapeutic class: rabies prophylaxis agent
Pregnancy risk category: C

Indications and dosages
▶ **Rabies exposure.** *Adults and children:* 20 IU/kg I.M. at time of first dose of rabies vaccine. Use half of dose to infiltrate wound area. Give remainder I.M.

Contraindications and precautions
• Rabies immune globulin should not be given in repeated doses once vaccine treatment has been initiated. Repeating the dose may interfere with maximum active immunity expected from the vaccine.
• Use cautiously in patients hypersensitive to thimerosal, in patients with a history of systemic allergic reactions after administration of human immunoglobulin preparations, and in patients with immunoglobulin A deficiency.
Lifespan: In pregnant women, use cautiously. In breast-feeding women, safety of drug hasn't been established.

Adverse reactions
CV: slight fever, slight headache, malaise.
GU: nephrotic syndrome.
Skin: *rash,* pain, redness, induration at injection site.
Other: ***anaphylaxis, angioedema.***

Interactions
Drug-drug. *Corticosteroids, immunosuppressive drugs:* May interfere with the active antibody response, predisposing patient to rabies. Avoid these drugs during postexposure immunization period.
Live-virus vaccines (measles, mumps, polio, rubella): May interfere with response to vaccine. Delay immunization, if possible.

Effects on lab test results
None reported.

Pharmacokinetics
Absorption: Slow.
Distribution: Unknown.
Metabolism: Unknown.
Excretion: Unknown. *Half-life:* About 24 days.

Route	Onset	Peak	Duration
I.M.	Unknown	24 hr	Unknown

Pharmacodynamics
Chemical effect: Provides passive immunity to rabies.
Therapeutic effect: Prevents rabies.

Available forms
Injection: 150 IU/ml in 2-ml, 10-ml vials

NURSING PROCESS

Assessment
• Obtain history of animal bites, allergies, and immunization reactions.
• Ask patient when he last received a tetanus immunization; prescriber may order booster.
• Be alert for adverse reactions and drug interactions.
• Evaluate patient's and family's knowledge of drug therapy.

Nursing diagnoses
• Risk for injury related to rabies exposure
• Ineffective protection related to drug-induced hypersensitivity reaction
• Deficient knowledge related to drug therapy

Planning and implementation
• Use only with rabies vaccine and immediate local treatment of wound. Don't give in same syringe or at same site as rabies vaccine. Give drug regardless of interval between exposure and start of therapy.
• Don't administer live-virus vaccines within 3 months of rabies immune globulin.
ALERT: Drug provides passive immunity. Don't confuse with rabies vaccine, which is suspension of attenuated or killed microorganisms used to confer active immunity. The two drugs usually are given together for prophylaxis after exposure to known or suspected rabid animals.

ALERT: Have epinephrine 1:1,000 immediately available to treat any acute anaphylactic reactions.
- Don't give more than 5 ml at one I.M. injection site; divide I.M. doses larger than 5 ml, and give at different sites. Use a large muscle, such as the gluteus.

Patient teaching
- Explain that patient may develop a slight fever and pain and redness at injection site.
- Advise patient that tetanus booster may be necessary.
- Instruct patient to report signs of hypersensitivity immediately.

Evaluation
- Patient has passive immunity to rabies.
- Patient shows no signs of hypersensitivity after receiving drug.
- Patient and family state understanding of drug therapy.

radioactive iodine (sodium iodide)
(ray-dee-oh-AK-tiv IGH-oh-dighn)
Iodotope, Sodium Iodide ^{131}I Therapeutic

Pharmacologic class: thyroid hormone antagonist
Therapeutic class: antihyperthyroid agent
Pregnancy risk category: X

Indications and dosages
▶ **Hyperthyroidism.** *Adults:* Usual dosage is 4 to 10 millicuries (mCi) P.O. Dosage based on estimated weight of thyroid gland and thyroid uptake. Treatment repeated after 6 weeks, according to serum T_4 level.
▶ **Thyroid cancer.** *Adults:* 50 to 150 mCi P.O. Dosage based on estimated malignant thyroid tissue and metastatic tissue as determined by total body scan. Treatment repeated according to clinical status.

Contraindications and precautions
- Contraindicated in patients experiencing vomiting or diarrhea.
- Drug isn't recommended for use in patients under age 30, unless other treatments are precluded.

Lifespan: In pregnant women, drug is contraindicated except to treat thyroid cancer. In breast-feeding women, drug is contraindicated.

Adverse reactions
CV: chest pain, tachycardia.
EENT: *fullness in neck,* pain with swallowing, sore throat.
Hematologic: anemia, blood dyscrasia, ***leukopenia, thrombocytopenia.***
Metabolic: hypothyroidism.
Respiratory: cough.
Skin: temporary thinning of hair.
Other: radiation-induced thyroiditis, radiation sickness (nausea, vomiting), allergic-type reactions, increased risk of leukemia later in life or birth defects in offspring after ^{131}I dosage sufficient for thyroid ablation after cancer surgery.

Interactions
Drug-drug. *Lithium carbonate:* Hypothyroidism may occur. Use cautiously.
Stable iodine (any form), thyroid, antithyroid agents: The uptake of ^{131}I will be affected by these agents. Ask patient about medication use or radiographic procedures using contrast media.

Effects on lab test results
- May decrease hemoglobin, hematocrit, and WBC and platelet counts.

Pharmacokinetics
Absorption: Readily absorbed from GI tract.
Distribution: Distributed in extracellular fluid. Selectively concentrated and bound to tyrosyl residues of thyroglobulin in thyroid gland. Also concentrated in stomach, choroid plexus, and salivary glands.
Metabolism: Converted readily to protein-bound iodine by thyroid.
Excretion: Excreted by kidneys. *Half-life:* 138 days; effective radioactive half-life is 7.6 days.

Route	Onset	Peak	Duration
P.O.	2-4 wk	2-4 mo	Unknown

Pharmacodynamics

Chemical effect: Limits thyroid hormone secretion by destroying thyroid tissue. The affinity of radioactive iodine for thyroid tissue facilitates uptake of drug by cancerous thyroid tissue that has metastasized to other sites in body.
Therapeutic effect: Decreases thyroid function.

Available forms

Iodotope
Capsules: radioactivity range is 8 to 100 mCi/capsule
Oral solution: radioactivity concentration is 7.05 mCi/ml; in vials containing about 7, 14, 28, 70, or 106 mCi
Sodium Iodide ^{131}I Therapeutic
Capsules: radioactivity range is 0.75 to 100 mCi/capsule
Oral solution: radioactivity range is 3.5 to 150 mCi/vial

NURSING PROCESS

Assessment

- Assess patient's thyroid condition before therapy and regularly thereafter.
- Monitor thyroid function via serum T_4 levels.
- Be alert for adverse reactions and drug interactions.
- Evaluate patient's and family's knowledge of drug therapy.

Nursing diagnoses

- Ineffective health maintenance related to presence of thyroid dysfunction
- Risk for injury related to drug's possible long-term effects
- Deficient knowledge related to drug therapy

Planning and implementation

- All antithyroid drugs and thyroid preparations should be stopped 1 week before ^{131}I dose. If not, patient may receive thyroid-stimulating hormone for 3 days before ^{131}I dose. When treating woman of childbearing age, give dose during or within 7 days after menstruation.
- Institute full radiation precautions. Have patient use appropriate disposal methods when coughing and expectorating. After dose for hyperthyroidism, urine and saliva are slightly radioactive for 24 hours; vomitus is highly radioactive for 6 to 8 hours.
- After dose for thyroid cancer, urine, saliva, and perspiration are radioactive for 3 days. Isolate patient. Don't allow pregnant personnel to care for patient. Instruct patient to use disposable eating utensils and linens and to save all urine in lead containers for 24 to 48 hours so amount of radioactive material excreted can be determined. Tell patient to drink as much fluid as possible for 48 hours after dose to facilitate excretion. Limit patient contact to 30 minutes per shift per person on first day and increase time, as needed, to 1 hour on second day and longer on third day.
- The following drugs can interfere with action of ^{131}I and should be withheld for the specified time before administering ^{131}I dose:

Adrenocorticoids: 1 week.
Benzodiazepines: 1 month.
Cholecystographic drugs: 6 to 9 months.
Iodine-containing contrast media: 1 to 2 months.
Iodine-containing products, including antitussives, expectorants, topical agents, and vitamins: 2 weeks.
Salicylates: 1 to 2 weeks.

Patient teaching

- Tell patient to fast overnight before dose; food may delay absorption.
- Inform patient that after therapy for hyperthyroidism, he shouldn't resume antithyroid drugs but should continue propranolol or other drugs used to treat symptoms of hyperthyroidism until onset of full ^{131}I effect (usually 6 weeks).
- Review safety precautions to take after radioactive iodine dose. If patient is discharged less than 7 days after ^{131}I dose for thyroid cancer, warn him to avoid close, prolonged contact with young children and to avoid sleeping in the same room with another person for 7 days after treatment. Tell patient he can use same bathroom as the rest of the family.
- Review symptoms of hypothyroidism and hyperthyroidism. Have patient contact his prescriber if these occur.

Evaluation

- Patient's thyroid function returns to normal.
- Patient doesn't develop complications as result of therapy.

• Patient and family state understanding of drug therapy.

raloxifene hydrochloride

(rah-LOKS-ih-feen high-droh-KLOR-ighd)
Evista

Pharmacologic class: selective estrogen receptor modulator of the benzothiophene class
Therapeutic class: antiosteoporotic
Pregnancy risk category: X

Indications and dosages

▶ **Prevention and treatment of osteoporosis in postmenopausal women.** *Adults:* 60 mg P.O. daily.

Contraindications and precautions

• Contraindicated in women hypersensitive to drug or its constituents and who have current or past venous thromboembolic events, including deep vein thrombosis (DVT), pulmonary embolism, and retinal vein thrombosis.
• Use cautiously in patients with severe hepatic impairment.
• Effect on bone mineral density with more than 2 years of drug treatment isn't known.
• Safety and efficacy haven't been evaluated in men.
Lifespan: In women who are pregnant or planning to become pregnant, in breast-feeding women, and in children, drug is contraindicated. Using this drug with hormone replacement therapy or systemic estrogen isn't recommended.

Adverse reactions

CNS: depression, insomnia, migraine, fever.
CV: *hot flushes,* chest pain, peripheral edema.
EENT: *sinusitis,* pharyngitis, laryngitis.
GI: nausea, dyspepsia, vomiting, flatulence, GI disorder, gastroenteritis, abdominal pain.
GU: vaginitis, urinary tract infection, cystitis, leukorrhea, endometrial disorder, vaginal bleeding.
Metabolic: weight gain.
Musculoskeletal: *arthralgia,* myalgia, arthritis, leg cramps.
Respiratory: increased cough, pneumonia.
Skin: rash, sweating.
Other: *infection, flulike syndrome,* breast pain.

Interactions

Drug-drug. *Cholestyramine:* Significantly reduces raloxifene absorption. Don't give these drugs together.
Highly protein-bound drugs (such as clofibrate, diazepam, diazoxide, ibuprofen, indomethacin, naproxen): May interfere with binding sites. Use together cautiously.
Warfarin: May cause a decrease in PT. Monitor PT and INR closely.

Effects on lab test results

• May increase calcium, inorganic phosphate, total protein, albumin, hormone-binding globulin, and apolipoprotein A levels. May decrease total and low-density lipoprotein cholesterol levels and apolipoprotein B levels.

Pharmacokinetics

Absorption: Rapid, with about 60% of dose absorbed after P.O. administration.
Distribution: Widely distributed and highly bound to plasma proteins.
Metabolism: Extensive first-pass metabolism to glucuronide conjugates.
Excretion: Primarily excreted in feces, with less than 0.2% excreted unchanged in urine. *Half-life:* 27½ hours.

Route	Onset	Peak	Duration
P.O.	Unknown	Unknown	24 hr

Pharmacodynamics

Chemical effect: Reduces resorption of bone and decreases overall bone turnover. These effects on bone are revealed as reduced serum and urine levels of bone turnover markers and increased bone mineral density.
Therapeutic effect: Prevents bone breakdown in postmenopausal women.

Available forms

Tablets: 60 mg

NURSING PROCESS

Assessment

• Obtain history of patient's condition, and reassess during therapy.
• Monitor patient for signs of blood clots. The greatest risk of thromboembolic events occurs during first 4 months of treatment.

• Monitor patient for breast abnormalities that occur during treatment.
• Monitor lipid levels, blood pressure, body weight, and liver function.
• Evaluate patient's and family's knowledge of drug therapy.

Nursing diagnoses
• Ineffective peripheral tissue perfusion related to potential DVT formation
• Imbalanced nutrition: less than body requirements related to drug-induced adverse GI reactions
• Deficient knowledge related to drug therapy

Planning and implementation
ALERT: Discontinue drug at least 72 hours before prolonged immobilization, and resume only after patient is fully mobile.
• Withhold drug and notify prescriber if you suspect thromboembolic event.
• Unexplained uterine bleeding should be reported immediately to prescriber.

Patient teaching
• Advise patient to avoid long periods of restricted movement (such as during traveling) because it increases the risk of venous thromboembolic events.
• Inform patient that hot flashes or flushing may occur and that drug doesn't aid in reducing them.
• Instruct patient to take other bone-loss prevention measures, including taking supplemental calcium and vitamin D if dietary intake is inadequate, performing weight-bearing exercises, and stopping alcohol consumption and smoking.
• Tell patient that drug may be taken without regard to food.
• Advise patient to report any unexplained uterine bleeding or breast abnormalities that occur during treatment.
• Explain adverse effects of drug. Instruct patient to read package insert before starting therapy and to read it again each time prescription is renewed.

Evaluation
• Patient doesn't develop pain, redness, or swelling in legs.
• Patient maintains normal dietary intake.
• Patient and family state understanding of drug therapy.

ramipril
(reh-MIH-pril)
Altace, Ramace ◇, Tritace ◇

Pharmacologic class: ACE inhibitor
Therapeutic class: antihypertensive
Pregnancy risk category: C (D in second and third trimesters)

Indications and dosages
▶ **Treatment of hypertension either alone or with thiazide diuretics.** *Adults:* Initially, 2.5 mg P.O. daily in patients not receiving diuretic therapy. Adjust dose based on blood pressure response. Usual maintenance dosage is 2.5 to 20 mg daily as a single dose or in two equal doses.
Patients with renal impairment: If creatinine clearance is below 40 ml/minute (serum creatinine above 2.5 mg/dl), recommended initial dose is 1.25 mg daily, adjusted upward to maximum dose of 5 mg based on blood pressure response.
Patients receiving diuretic therapy: Symptomatic hypotension may occur. To minimize this, discontinue diuretic, if possible, 2 to 3 days before starting ramipril. When this isn't possible, initial dose of ramipril should be 1.25 mg.
▶ **Heart failure post-MI.** *Adults:* Initially, 2.5 mg P.O. b.i.d. Adjust to target dose of 5 mg P.O. b.i.d.
Patients with renal impairment: Start therapy with 1.25 mg P.O. once daily, and increase to 1.25 mg b.i.d. Maximum dosage is 2.5 mg b.i.d.
▶ **Reduction in risk of MI, CVA, and death from cardiovascular causes.** *Adults age 55 and older:* 2.5 mg P.O. once daily for 1 week, then 5 mg P.O. once daily for 3 weeks. Increase as tolerated to a maintenance dose of 10 mg P.O. once daily.

Contraindications and precautions
• Contraindicated in patients hypersensitive to ACE inhibitors, those with history of angioedema during previous treatment with ACE inhibitor, and those with renal artery stenosis.
• Use cautiously in patients with renal impairment.
Lifespan: In pregnant and breast-feeding women, drug isn't recommended. In children, safety of drug hasn't been established.

Adverse reactions

CNS: headache, dizziness, fatigue, syncope, asthenia, malaise, light-headedness, anxiety, amnesia, ***seizures,*** depression, insomnia, nervousness, neuralgia, neuropathy, paresthesia, somnolence, tremors, vertigo.
CV: orthostatic hypotension, angina, ***arrhythmias,*** chest pain, palpitations, ***MI,*** edema.
EENT: epistaxis, tinnitus.
GI: nausea, vomiting, abdominal pain, anorexia, constipation, diarrhea, dyspepsia, dry mouth, gastroenteritis.
GU: impotence.
Metabolic: ***hyperkalemia,*** weight gain.
Musculoskeletal: arthralgia, arthritis, myalgia.
Respiratory: *dry, persistent, tickling, nonproductive cough;* dyspnea.
Skin: rash, dermatitis, pruritus, photosensitivity reaction, increased diaphoresis.
Other: hypersensitivity reactions, ***angioedema.***

Interactions

Drug-drug. *Diuretics:* Excessive hypotension, especially at start of therapy. Discontinue diuretic at least 3 days before starting ramipril, increase sodium intake, or reduce starting dose of ramipril.
Insulin, oral antidiabetics: May increase risk of hypoglycemia, especially at start of ramipril therapy. Monitor patient closely.
Lithium: May increase lithium levels. Use together cautiously, and monitor lithium levels for toxicity.
Potassium-sparing diuretics, potassium supplements: Increases risk of hyperkalemia because ramipril attenuates potassium loss. Monitor plasma potassium levels closely.
Drug-herb. *Capsaicin:* Increases risk of cough. Discourage using together.
Licorice: May cause sodium retention and increase blood pressure, interfering with therapeutic effects of ACE inhibitors. Discourage using together.
Drug-food. *Salt substitutes containing potassium:* Increases risk of hyperkalemia because ramipril attenuates potassium loss. Monitor plasma potassium levels closely.

Effects on lab test results

- May increase BUN, creatinine, bilirubin, liver enzyme, glucose, and potassium levels.
- May decrease hemoglobin and hematocrit.

Pharmacokinetics

Absorption: 50% to 60%.
Distribution: 73% serum protein-bound; ramiprilat (metabolite), 58%.
Metabolism: Almost completely converted to ramiprilat, which is six times more potent than parent drug.
Excretion: 60% in urine; 40% in feces. *Half-life:* Ramipril, 5 hours; ramiprilat, 13 to 17 hours.

Route	Onset	Peak	Duration
P.O.	1-2 hr	< 1 hr	About 24 hr (ramipril); 3 hr (ramiprilat)

Pharmacodynamics

Chemical effect: Unknown; may inhibit change from angiotensin I to angiotensin II, a potent vasoconstrictor. This decreases peripheral arterial resistance, thus decreasing aldosterone secretion.
Therapeutic effect: Lowers blood pressure.

Available forms

Capsules: 1.25 mg, 2.5 mg, 5 mg, 10 mg

NURSING PROCESS

Assessment

- Assess patient's blood pressure before therapy and regularly thereafter.
- Closely assess kidney function during first few weeks of therapy. Regular assessment (serum creatinine and BUN levels) is recommended. Patient with severe heart failure whose kidney function depends on angiotensin-aldosterone system may experience acute renal failure during ACE inhibitor therapy. Hypertensive patient with renal artery stenosis also may show signs of worsening kidney function at start of therapy.
- Monitor CBC with differential before therapy, every 2 weeks for first 3 months of therapy, and periodically thereafter.
- Monitor potassium level. Risk factors for development of hyperkalemia include renal insufficiency, diabetes, and use of drugs that raise potassium levels.
- Be alert for adverse reactions and drug interactions.
- Evaluate patient's and family's knowledge of drug therapy.

Nursing diagnoses

- Risk for injury related to presence of hypertension
- Disturbed sleep pattern related to drug-induced cough
- Deficient knowledge related to drug therapy

Planning and implementation

- Diuretic therapy should be stopped 2 to 3 days before start of ramipril therapy, if possible.
- If patient has trouble swallowing pills whole, capsule may be opened and the contents sprinkled onto 4 ounces of applesauce or mixed in 4 ounces (118 ml) of water or apple juice. These mixtures may be stored at room temperature for up to 24 hours, or refrigerated for up to 48 hours.

Patient teaching

- Warn patient to avoid sodium substitutes during therapy.
- If patient has trouble swallowing, tell him to open capsules and sprinkle contents on food.
- Tell patient to rise slowly to avoid initial light-headedness. If syncope occurs, he should stop drug and call prescriber.
- Tell patient not to stop therapy abruptly.
- Advise patient to report signs of angioedema and laryngeal edema, which may occur after first dose.
- Tell patient to report signs of infection.
- Tell woman to report pregnancy. Drug will need to be stopped.

Evaluation

- Patient's blood pressure is normal.
- Patient's sleep patterns are undisturbed throughout therapy.
- Patient and family state understanding of drug therapy.

ranitidine hydrochloride

(ruh-NIH-tuh-deen high-droh-KLOR-ighd)
Zantac*, Zantac-C ♦, Zantac EFFERdose, Zantac GELdose, Zantac 75†

Pharmacologic class: H_2-receptor antagonist
Therapeutic class: antiulcer agent
Pregnancy risk category: B

Indications and dosages

▶ **Duodenal and gastric ulcer (short-term treatment); pathologic hypersecretory conditions, such as Zollinger-Ellison syndrome.** *Adults:* 150 mg P.O. b.i.d. or 300 mg daily h.s. Or, 50 mg I.V. or I.M. q 6 to 8 hours. Patients with Zollinger-Ellison syndrome may need up to 6 g P.O. daily.
▶ **Maintenance therapy for duodenal ulcer.** *Adults:* 150 mg P.O. h.s.
▶ **Gastroesophageal reflux disease.** *Adults:* 150 mg P.O. b.i.d.
▶ **Erosive esophagitis.** *Adults:* 150 mg P.O. q.i.d.; maintenance is 150 mg P.O. b.i.d.
▶ **Relief of occasional heartburn, acid indigestion, and sour stomach.** *Adults and children age 12 and older:* 75 mg once or twice daily; maximum daily dosage is 150 mg.

Contraindications and precautions

- Contraindicated in patients hypersensitive to drug.
- Use cautiously in patients with hepatic dysfunction. Adjust dosage in patients with impaired kidney function.

Lifespan: In pregnant and breast-feeding women, use cautiously.

Adverse reactions

CNS: vertigo, malaise.
EENT: blurred vision.
Hematologic: ***reversible leukopenia, pancytopenia, thrombocytopenia.***
Hepatic: jaundice.
Other: burning and itching at injection site, ***anaphylaxis, angioedema.***

Interactions

Drug-drug. *Antacids:* May interfere with ranitidine absorption. Stagger doses, if possible.
Diazepam: Decreases diazepam absorption. Monitor patient for decreased effectiveness; adjust dose.
Glipizide: Possible increased hypoglycemic effect. Adjust glipizide dosage, as directed.
Procainamide: Possible decreased renal clearance of procainamide. Monitor patient for procainamide toxicity.
Warfarin: Possible interference with warfarin clearance. Monitor patient closely for bleeding.
Drug-lifestyle. *Smoking:* May increase gastric acid secretion and worsen disease. Discourage using together.

Effects on lab test results

- May increase creatinine and ALT levels.
- May decrease RBC, WBC, and platelet counts.

Pharmacokinetics

Absorption: About 50% to 60% of P.O. dose; rapid from parenteral sites after I.M. dose.
Distribution: Distributed to many body tissues and appears in CSF; about 10% to 19% protein-bound.
Metabolism: Metabolized in liver.
Excretion: Excreted in urine and feces. *Half-life:* 2 to 3 hours.

Route	Onset	Peak	Duration
P.O.	≤ 1 hr	1-3 hr	≤ 13 hr
I.V., I.M.	Unknown	Unknown	≤ 13 hr

Pharmacodynamics

Chemical effect: Competitively inhibits action of H_2 at receptor sites of parietal cells, decreasing gastric acid secretion.
Therapeutic effect: Relieves GI discomfort.

Available forms

Capsules: 150 mg, 300 mg
Granules (effervescent): 150 mg
Infusion: 0.5 mg/ml in 100-ml containers
Injection: 25 mg/ml
Syrup: 15 mg/ml*
Tablets: 75 mg†, 150 mg, 300 mg
Tablets (dispersible): 150 mg†
Tablets (effervescent): 150 mg

NURSING PROCESS

Assessment

- Assess patient's GI condition before therapy and regularly thereafter.
- Be alert for adverse reactions and drug interactions.
- Evaluate patient's and family's knowledge of drug therapy.

Nursing diagnoses

- Impaired tissue integrity related to underlying GI condition
- Risk for injury related to drug-induced adverse CNS reactions
- Deficient knowledge related to drug therapy

Planning and implementation

- Don't use aluminum-based needles or equipment when mixing or giving drug parenterally because drug is incompatible with aluminum.
- **P.O. use:** Follow normal protocol.
- **I.V. use:** To prepare I.V. injection, dilute 2 ml (50 mg) ranitidine with compatible I.V. solution to a total volume of 20 ml, and inject over at least 5 minutes. Compatible solutions include sterile water for injection, normal saline solution for injection, D_5W, and lactated Ringer's injection.
  - To give drug by intermittent I.V. infusion, dilute 50 mg (2 ml) ranitidine in 100 ml compatible solution and infuse at a rate of 5 to 7 ml/minute. The premixed solution is 50 ml and doesn't need further dilution. Infuse over 15 to 20 minutes. After dilution, solution is stable for 48 hours at room temperature.
  - Store I.V. injection in refrigerator at 36° to 46° F (2° to 8° C).
  - For premixed I.V. infusion, give by slow I.V. drip (over 15 to 20 minutes). Don't add other drugs to solution. If used with primary I.V. fluid system, stop primary solution during infusion.
- **I.M. use:** Follow normal protocol. No dilution is needed when giving drug I.M.

ALERT: Don't confuse ranitidine with rimantadine.

ALERT: Don't confuse Zantac with Xanax or Zyrtec.

Patient teaching

- Remind patient taking drug once daily to take it at bedtime.
- Instruct patient to take drug without regard to meals.
- Urge patient to avoid cigarette smoking because it may increase gastric acid secretion and worsen disease.

Evaluation

- Patient states that GI discomfort is relieved.
- Patient sustains no injury as result of drug-induced adverse CNS reactions.
- Patient and family state understanding of drug therapy.

repaglinide
(reh-PAG-lih-nighd)
Prandin

Pharmacologic class: meglitinide
Therapeutic class: antidiabetic
Pregnancy risk category: C

Indications and dosages

▶ **Adjunct to diet and exercise to lower glucose levels in patients with type 2 diabetes mellitus (non-insulin-dependent diabetes mellitus) whose hyperglycemia cannot be controlled satisfactorily by diet and exercise alone; adjunct to diet, exercise, and metformin, rosiglitazone, or pioglitazone.**
Adults: For patients not previously treated or whose HbA_{1c} is below 8%, starting dose is 0.5 mg P.O. given 15 minutes before meal; however, time may vary from immediately before to as long as 30 minutes before meal. For patients previously treated with glucose-lowering drugs and whose HbA_{1c} is 8% or more, initial dose is 1 to 2 mg P.O. with each meal. Recommended dosage range is 0.5 to 4 mg with meals b.i.d., t.i.d., or q.i.d. Maximum daily dose is 16 mg.

Dosage should be determined by glucose level response. May double dosage up to 4 mg with each meal until satisfactory glucose response is achieved. At least 1 week should elapse between dosage adjustments to assess response to each dose.
Patients with severe renal impairment: Starting dose is 0.5 mg P.O. with meals.

Contraindications and precautions

- Contraindicated in patients hypersensitive to drug or its inactive ingredients and in those with insulin-dependent diabetes mellitus or diabetic ketoacidosis with or without coma.
- Use cautiously in patients with hepatic insufficiency in whom reduced metabolism could increase repaglinide levels and cause hypoglycemia.
- Use cautiously in debilitated and malnourished patients and in those with adrenal or pituitary insufficiency because they're more susceptible to the hypoglycemic effect of glucose-lowering drugs.

Lifespan: In geriatric patients, use cautiously.

Adverse reactions

CNS: *headache,* paresthesia.
CV: angina, chest pain.
EENT: rhinitis, sinusitis.
GI: constipation, diarrhea, dyspepsia, nausea, vomiting.
GU: urinary tract infection.
Metabolic: HYPOGLYCEMIA, hyperglycemia.
Musculoskeletal: arthralgia, back pain.
Respiratory: bronchitis, *upper respiratory infection.*
Other: tooth disorder.

Interactions

Drug-drug. *Barbiturates, carbamazepine, rifampin:* May increase repaglinide metabolism. Monitor glucose level.
Beta blockers, chloramphenicol, coumarins, MAO inhibitors, NSAIDs, other drugs that are highly protein-bound, probenecid, salicylates, sulfonamides: May potentiate hypoglycemic action of repaglinide. Monitor glucose level.
Calcium channel blockers, corticosteroids, estrogens, isoniazid, nicotinic acid, oral contraceptives, phenothiazines, phenytoin, sympathomimetics, thiazides and other diuretics, thyroid products: May produce hyperglycemia and loss of glycemic control. Monitor glucose level.
Erythromycin, inhibitors of P450 cytochrome system 3A4, ketoconazole, miconazole: May inhibit repaglinide metabolism. Monitor glucose levels.
Drug-herb. *Aloe, bitter melon, bilberry leaf, burdock, dandelion, fenugreek, garlic, ginseng:* May improve glucose control and create a need to reduce antidiabetic dosage. Advise patient to discuss the use of herbal remedies before taking repaglinide.

Effects on lab test results

- May increase or decrease glucose level.

Pharmacokinetics

Absorption: Rapid and complete. Absolute bioavailability is 56%.
Distribution: More than 98% bound to plasma proteins.

Metabolism: Completely metabolized by oxidative biotransformation and direct conjugation with glucuronic acid.
Excretion: About 90% is recovered in feces and 8% in urine. *Half-life:* 1 hour.

Route	Onset	Peak	Duration
P.O.	Unknown	1 hr	Unknown

Pharmacodynamics

Chemical effect: Stimulates the release of insulin from beta cells in the pancreas.
Therapeutic effect: Lowers glucose level.

Available forms

Tablets: 0.5 mg, 1 mg, 2 mg

NURSING PROCESS

Assessment

- Monitor glucose level before therapy and regularly thereafter.
- Be alert for adverse reactions and drug interactions.
- Monitor geriatric patients and patients taking beta blockers carefully because hypoglycemia may be difficult to recognize in these patients.
- Evaluate patient's and family's knowledge of drug therapy.

Nursing diagnoses

- Imbalanced nutrition: more than body requirements related to patient's underlying condition
- Risk for injury related to drug-induced hypoglycemic episode
- Deficient knowledge related to drug therapy

Planning and implementation

- Increase dosage carefully in patients with impaired renal function or renal failure who need dialysis.
- Metformin may be added if repaglinide alone is inadequate.
- Loss of glycemic control can occur during stress, such as fever, trauma, infection, or surgery. Discontinue drug; administer insulin.
- Administration of oral antidiabetics has been linked to increased CV mortality compared with diet treatment alone.
- Give drug immediately or up to 30 minutes before meals.

Patient teaching

- Teach patient about importance of diet and exercise along with drug therapy.
- Discuss symptoms of hypoglycemia with patient and family.
- Advise patient to monitor glucose level periodically to determine minimum effective dose.
- Encourage patient to keep regular medical appointments and have glucose level checked to monitor long-term glucose control.
- Tell patient to take drug before meals, usually 15 minutes before start of meal; however, time can vary from immediately to up to 30 minutes before meal.
- Tell patient to skip dose if he skips a meal and to add dose if he adds a meal.
- Teach patient how to monitor glucose levels carefully and what to do when he is ill, undergoing surgery, or under added stress.

Evaluation

- Patient's glucose level is controlled and an adequate nutritional balance is maintained.
- Patient doesn't experience severe decreases in glucose level.
- Patient and family state understanding of drug therapy.

reteplase, recombinant

(REE-teh-plays, ree-KUHM-buh-nent)
Retavase

Pharmacologic class: recombinant plasminogen activator, enzyme
Therapeutic class: thrombolytic enzyme
Pregnancy risk category: C

Indications and dosages

▶ **Management of acute MI.** *Adults:* Double-bolus injection of 10 + 10 units. Give each bolus I.V. over 2 minutes. If complications don't occur after first bolus, give second bolus 30 minutes after start of first.

Contraindications and precautions

- Contraindicated in patients with active internal bleeding, bleeding diathesis, history of CVA, recent intracranial or intraspinal surgery or trauma, severe uncontrolled hypertension,

intracranial neoplasm, arteriovenous malformation, or aneurysm.
• Use cautiously in patients with recent (within 10 days) major surgery, obstetric delivery, organ biopsy, or trauma; previous puncture of noncompressible vessel; cerebrovascular disease; recent GI or GU bleeding; or heart disease.
Lifespan: In breast-feeding women, use extreme caution. In children, safety of drug hasn't been established.

Adverse reactions

CNS: ***intracranial hemorrhage.***
CV: ***arrhythmias, cholesterol embolization, hemorrhage.***
GI: ***hemorrhage.***
GU: hematuria.
Hematologic: anemia, ***bleeding tendency.***
Other: bleeding at puncture sites.

Interactions

Drug-drug. *Heparin, oral anticoagulants, platelet inhibitors (abciximab, aspirin, dipyridamole):* May increase risk of bleeding. Use together cautiously.

Effects on lab test results

• May decrease plasminogen and fibrinogen levels.
• May decrease hemoglobin and hematocrit.
• May cause unreliable results of coagulation tests or measurements of fibrinolytic activity.

Pharmacokinetics

Absorption: Administered I.V.
Distribution: Rapid distribution.
Metabolism: Unknown.
Excretion: Excreted in urine and feces.

Route	Onset	Peak	Duration
I.V.	Unknown	Unknown	Unknown

Pharmacodynamics

Chemical effect: Enhances cleavage of plasminogen to generate plasmin.
Therapeutic effect: Dissolves and breaks up clots.

Available forms

Injection: 10.8 IU (18.8 mg)/vial. Supplied in kit with components for reconstitution for 2 single-use vials.

NURSING PROCESS

Assessment

• Monitor ECG during treatment.
• Monitor patient for bleeding. Avoid I.M. injections, invasive procedures, and unnecessary handling of patient.
• Evaluate patient's and family's knowledge of drug therapy.

Nursing diagnoses

• Ineffective cardiopulmonary tissue perfusion related to underlying condition
• Risk for injury related to adverse effects of drug
• Deficient knowledge related to drug therapy

Planning and implementation

• Reteplase is administered I.V. as double-bolus injection. If bleeding or anaphylactoid reaction occurs after first bolus, notify prescriber.
• Reconstitute drug according to manufacturer's instructions.
ALERT: Don't administer drug with other I.V. drugs through the same line. Heparin and reteplase are incompatible in solution.
• Avoid noncompressible pressure sites during therapy. If an arterial puncture is needed, use an arm vessel that can be compressed manually. Apply pressure for at least 30 minutes; then apply a pressure dressing. Check site often for bleeding.

Patient teaching

• Tell patient and family about drug.
• Tell patient to report adverse reactions immediately.

Evaluation

• Patient's cardiopulmonary assessment findings show improved perfusion.
• Patient is free from serious adverse reactions caused by therapy.
• Patient and family state understanding of drug therapy.

Rh_o(D) immune globulin, human
(R H O D ih-MYOON GLOH-byoo-lin, HYOO-mun)

Rh_o(D) immune globulin, human (Rh_o[D] IGIM)
BayRho-D Full Dose, RhoGAM

Rh_o(D) immune globulin, human, microdose (Rh_o[D] IG Microdose)
BayRho-D Mini-Dose, MICRhoGAM

Rh_o(D) immune globulin, human (Rh_o[D] IGIV)
WinRho SDF

Pharmacologic class: immune serum
Therapeutic class: anti-Rh_o(D)-positive prophylaxis agent
Pregnancy risk category: C

Indications and dosages

▶ **Rh exposure (postabortion, postmiscarriage, ectopic pregnancy, postpartum, or threatened abortion 13 weeks or later).** *Women:* Transfusion unit or blood bank determines fetal packed RBC volume entering patient's blood; then give one vial I.M. if fetal packed RBC volume is below 15 ml. More than one vial I.M. may be required if large fetomaternal hemorrhage occurs. Must be given within 72 hours after delivery or miscarriage.

▶ **Transfusion accident.** *Adults and children:* Usually, 600 mcg I.V. q 8 hours or 1,200 mcg I.M. q 12 hours until total dose given. Total dose depends on volume of packed RBCs or whole blood infused. Consult blood bank or transfusion unit at once. Must be given within 72 hours.

▶ **Postabortion or postmiscarriage to prevent Rh antibody formation up to and including 12 weeks' gestation.** *Women:* Consult transfusion unit or blood bank. One microdose vial suppresses immune reaction to 2.5 ml Rh_o(D)-positive RBCs. Should be given within 3 hours but may be given up to 72 hours after abortion or miscarriage.

▶ **Amniocentesis or abdominal trauma during pregnancy.** *Women:* Dose based on extent of fetomaternal hemorrhage.

Contraindications and precautions

- Contraindicated in Rh_o(D)-positive or Du-positive patients, those previously immunized to Rh_o(D) blood factor, those with anaphylactic or severe systemic reaction to human globulin, and those with immunoglobulin A deficiency.
- Use cautiously in patients with thrombocytopenia or bleeding disorders.

Lifespan: In pregnant and breast-feeding women, use cautiously. Microdose must not be used for any indication with continuation of pregnancy.

Adverse reactions

CNS: slight fever.
Skin: discomfort at injection site.
Other: ***anaphylaxis.***

Interactions

Drug-drug. *Live-virus vaccines:* May interfere with response to Rh_o(D) immune globulin. Delay immunization for 3 months, if possible.

Effects on lab test results

None reported.

Pharmacokinetics

Absorption: Unknown.
Distribution: Unknown.
Metabolism: Unknown.
Excretion: Unknown.

Route	Onset	Peak	Duration
I.V., I.M.	Unknown	Unknown	Unknown

Pharmacodynamics

Chemical effect: Suppresses active antibody response and formation of anti-Rh_o(D) in Rh_o(D)-negative, Du-negative people exposed to Rh-positive blood.
Therapeutic effect: Blocks adverse effects of Rh-positive exposure.

Available forms

I.M. injection: 300 mcg of Rh_o(D) immune globulin/vial (standard dose); 50 mcg of Rh_o(D) immune globulin/vial (microdose)
I.V. infusion: 120 mcg, 300 mcg, 1,000 mcg

NURSING PROCESS

Assessment

- Obtain history of Rh-negative patient's Rh-positive exposure, allergies, and reactions to immunizations.
- Evaluate patient's and family's knowledge of drug therapy.

Nursing diagnoses

- Risk for injury related to Rh-positive exposure
- Ineffective protection related to drug-induced anaphylaxis
- Deficient knowledge related to drug therapy

Planning and implementation

- **I.V. use:** Reconstitute only with normal saline solution; 2.5 ml for the 120 mcg and 300 mcg vials and 8.5 ml for the 1,000 mcg vial. Slowly inject diluent into vial and gently swirl vial until dissolved. Don't shake vial. Give injection over 3 to 5 minutes.
  – Don't give in the same line as other medications.
- **I.M. use:** Inject into the anterolateral aspect of the upper thigh or deltoid muscle.
  – If administering 1,000 mcg, don't give entire dose in one muscle; divide dose to give in several different sites.
- Make sure epinephrine 1:1,000 is available in case of anaphylaxis.
- After delivery, have neonate's cord blood typed and crossmatched; confirm if mother is Rh_o(D)-negative and Du-negative. Administer to mother only if infant is Rh_o(D)-positive or Du-positive.
- Drug gives passive immunity to patient exposed to Rh_o(D)-positive fetal blood during pregnancy; it prevents formation of maternal antibodies, which would endanger future Rh_o(D)-positive pregnancies.
- Defer vaccination with live-virus vaccines for 3 months after administration of drug.
- MICRhoGAM is recommended for every patient undergoing abortion or miscarriage up to 12 weeks' gestation unless she is Rh_o(D)-positive or Du-positive, she has Rh antibodies, or father or fetus is Rh-negative.
- Refrigerate drug at 36° to 46° F (2° to 8° C).

Patient teaching

- Explain how drug protects future Rh_o(D)-positive fetuses.

Evaluation

- Patient shows evidence of passive immunity to exposure to Rh_o(D)-positive blood.
- Patient doesn't develop anaphylaxis after drug administration.
- Patient and family state understanding of drug therapy.

ribavirin

(righ-beh-VIGH-rin)

Virazole

Pharmacologic class: synthetic nucleoside
Therapeutic class: antiviral
Pregnancy risk category: X

Indications and dosages

▶ **Hospitalized infants and young children infected by RSV.** *Infants and young children:* 20-mg/ml solution delivered by small particle aerosol generator (SPAG-2) and mechanical ventilator or oxygen hood, face mask, or oxygen tent at about 12.5 L of mist per minute. Treatment lasts 12 to 18 hours daily for 3 to 7 days.

Contraindications and precautions

- Contraindicated in patients hypersensitive to drug. Use cautiously in patients with renal impairment.

Lifespan: In women who are or may become pregnant, drug is contraindicated. In breast-feeding women, drug is not indicated.

Adverse reactions

CNS: *headache,* dizziness, seizures, asthenia.
CV: ***cardiac arrest,*** hypotension, chest pains.
EENT: *conjunctivitis, rhinitis, pharyngitis, lacrimation,* rash or erythema of eyelids.
GI: *nausea.*
Hematologic: reticulocytosis, anemia.
Respiratory: ***worsening of respiratory state, bronchospasms, apnea,*** bacterial pneumonia, ***pneumothorax.***
Skin: *rash.*

Interactions

Drug-drug. *Acetaminophen, aspirin, cimetidine:* May affect drug level. Monitor patient.

Effects on lab test results

- May increase bilirubin, AST, and ALT levels.
- May increase reticulocytes. May decrease hemoglobin and hematocrit.

Pharmacokinetics

Absorption: Some ribavirin is absorbed systemically.
Distribution: Concentrates in bronchial secretions.
Metabolism: Metabolized to 1,2,4-triazole-3-carboxamide (deribosylated ribavirin).
Excretion: Most of drug excreted in urine. *Half-life:* First phase, 9½ hours; second phase, 40 hours.

Route	Onset	Peak	Duration
Inhalation	Immediate	Immediate	Unknown

Pharmacodynamics

Chemical effect: Inhibits viral activity by unknown mechanism, possibly by inhibiting RNA and DNA synthesis by depleting intracellular nucleotide pools.
Therapeutic effect: Inhibits RSV activity.

Available forms

Powder to be reconstituted for inhalation: 6 g in 100-ml glass vial

NURSING PROCESS

Assessment

- Assess patient's respiratory infection before therapy and regularly thereafter.
- Monitor ventilator function. Drug may precipitate in ventilator apparatus, causing equipment malfunction with serious consequences.
- Watch for anemia in patient receiving drug longer than 1 to 2 weeks.
- Be alert for adverse reactions.
- Evaluate patient's and family's knowledge of drug therapy.

Nursing diagnoses

- Infection related to presence of RSV
- Risk for injury related to drug-induced adverse CV reactions
- Deficient knowledge related to drug therapy

Planning and implementation

- Ribavirin aerosol is indicated only for severe lower respiratory tract infection caused by RSV. Treatment may start pending test results, but existence of RSV infection must be documented.
- Most infants and children with RSV infection don't need treatment. Infants with underlying conditions, such as prematurity or cardiopulmonary disease, benefit most from treatment with ribavirin aerosol.
- Give drug by SPAG-2 only. Don't use any other aerosol generator.
- Use sterile USP water for injection, not bacteriostatic water, for reconstitution. Water used to reconstitute this drug must not contain an antimicrobial agent.
- Discard solutions placed in SPAG-2 unit at least every 24 hours before adding newly reconstituted solution.
- Avoid unnecessary occupational exposure to drug. Adverse effects reported in health care personnel exposed to aerosolized ribavirin include eye irritation and headache.
- Store reconstituted solutions at room temperature for 24 hours.
- Continue providing supportive respiratory and fluid management.

ALERT: Don't confuse ribavirin with riboflavin.

Patient teaching

- Inform parents of need for drug therapy, and answer their questions.
- Advise patient to use correct device.

Evaluation

- Patient is free from infection.
- Patient doesn't develop adverse CV reactions after drug administration.
- Parents state understanding of drug therapy.

riboflavin (vitamin B_2)†

(righ-boh-FLAY-vin)

Pharmacologic class: water-soluble vitamin
Therapeutic class: vitamin B complex vitamin
Pregnancy risk category: A (C in doses that exceed RDA)

Indications and dosages

▶ **RDA.** *Men age 51 and older:* 1.4 mg.
Men ages 19 to 50: 1.7 mg.
Men ages 15 to 18: 1.8 mg.
Men ages 11 to 14: 1.5 mg.
Women age 51 and older: 1.2 mg.
Women ages 11 to 50: 1.3 mg.
Pregnant women: 1.6 mg.
Breast-feeding women (first 6 months): 1.8 mg.
Breast-feeding women (second 6 months): 1.7 mg.
Children ages 7 to 10: 1.2 mg.
Children ages 4 to 6: 1.1 mg.
Children ages 1 to 3: 0.8 mg.
Infants ages 6 months to 1 year: 0.5 mg.
Neonates and infants to age 6 months: 0.4 mg.

▶ **Riboflavin deficiency or adjunct to thiamine treatment for polyneuritis or cheilosis caused by pellagra.** *Adults and children age 12 and older:* 5 to 30 mg P.O. daily, depending on severity.
Children younger than age 12: 3 to 10 mg P.O. daily, depending on severity. For maintenance, increase nutritional intake and supplement with vitamin B complex.

▶ **Microcytic anemia linked to splenomegaly and glutathione reductase deficiency.** *Adults:* 10 mg P.O. daily for 10 days.

Contraindications and precautions

- No known contraindications.

Adverse reactions

GU: bright yellow urine.

Interactions

Drug-drug. *Probenecid:* Reduces urinary excretion of riboflavin. Use together cautiously.
Propantheline, other anticholinergics: Decreases rate and extent of absorption. Avoid using together.

Effects on lab test results

None reported.

Pharmacokinetics

Absorption: Absorbed readily from GI tract, although extent is limited. Occurs at specialized segment of mucosa and is limited by duration of drug's contact with this area. Before being absorbed, riboflavin 5-phosphate is rapidly dephosphorylated in GI lumen. GI absorption increases when drug is given with food and decreases when hepatitis, cirrhosis, biliary obstruction, or probenecid administration is present.
Distribution: Riboflavin, a coenzyme, functions in forms of flavin adenine dinucleotide (FAD) and flavin mononucleotide (FMN). FAD and FMN are distributed widely to body tissues. Riboflavin is stored in limited amounts in liver, spleen, kidneys, and heart, mainly in the form of FAD. FAD and FMN are about 60% protein-bound in blood.
Metabolism: Riboflavin is metabolized to FMN in erythrocytes, GI mucosal cells, and liver. FMN is converted to FAD in liver.
Excretion: Excreted in urine. *Half-life:* 66 to 84 minutes.

Route	Onset	Peak	Duration
P.O.	Unknown	Unknown	Unknown

Pharmacodynamics

Chemical effect: Converts to two other coenzymes needed for normal tissue respiration.
Therapeutic effect: Relieves riboflavin deficiency.

Available forms

Tablets: 10 mg†, 25 mg†, 50 mg†, 100 mg†
Tablets (sugar-free): 50 mg†, 100 mg†

NURSING PROCESS

Assessment

- Assess patient's riboflavin deficiency before and during therapy.
- Be alert for change in urine color.
- Evaluate patient's and family's knowledge of drug therapy.

Nursing diagnoses

- Imbalanced nutrition: less than body's needs, related to drug deficiency
- Deficient knowledge related to drug therapy

Planning and implementation

- Drug may be given I.M. or I.V. as component of multiple vitamins.
- Riboflavin deficiency usually accompanies other vitamin B–complex deficiencies and may require multivitamin therapy.
- Protect drug from air and light.

ALERT: Don't confuse riboflavin (vitamin B_2) with ribavirin (Virazole).

Patient teaching

- Encourage patient to take with meals to increase absorption.
- Stress proper nutritional habits to prevent return of deficiency.
- Inform patient that urine will likely turn to bright yellow or orange.

Evaluation

- Patient's drug deficiency is resolved.
- Patient and family state understanding of drug therapy.

rifabutin

(rif-uh-BYOO-tin)
Mycobutin

Pharmacologic class: semisynthetic ansamycin
Therapeutic class: antibiotic
Pregnancy risk category: B

Indications and dosages

▶ **Prevention of disseminated *Mycobacterium avium* complex (MAC) in patients with advanced HIV infection.** *Adults:* 300 mg P.O. daily as single dose or divided b.i.d. and taken with food.

Contraindications and precautions

- Contraindicated in patients hypersensitive to drug or other rifamycin derivatives (such as rifampin) and in those with active tuberculosis because single-agent therapy with rifabutin increases risk of bacterial resistance to both rifabutin and rifampin.
- Use cautiously in patients with neutropenia and thrombocytopenia.

Lifespan: In breast-feeding women, drug isn't recommended. In children, safety of drug hasn't been established.

Adverse reactions

CNS: fever, headache.
CV: ECG changes.
GI: dyspepsia, eructation, flatulence, diarrhea, nausea, vomiting, abdominal pain.
GU: *discolored urine.*
Hematologic: anemia, eosinophilia, LEUKOPENIA, NEUTROPENIA, ***thrombocytopenia.***
Musculoskeletal: myalgia.
Skin: *rash.*

Interactions

Drug-drug. *Corticosteroids:* Rifabutin decreases effect of drug. Double dose of corticosteroids, if needed.
Cyclosporine: Reduces immunosuppressive effects. Don't use together.
Drugs metabolized by the liver, zidovudine: Decreases zidovudine level. Because rifabutin, like rifampin, induces liver enzymes, it may lower levels of many other drugs as well. Although dosage adjustments may be necessary, further study is needed.
Oral contraceptives: Decreases effectiveness. Instruct patient to use nonhormonal forms of birth control.
Warfarin: Decreases anticoagulation effect. Increase dose of anticoagulant.
Drug-food. *High-fat foods:* Slows absorption of drug. Avoid taking drug with high-fat meals.

Effects on lab test results

- May increase alkaline phosphatase, AST, and ALT levels.
- May increase eosinophil count. May decrease hemoglobin, hematocrit, and neutrophil, WBC, and platelet counts.

Pharmacokinetics

Absorption: Readily absorbed from GI tract.
Distribution: Because of its high lipophilicity, rifabutin demonstrates high propensity for distribution and intracellular tissue uptake. About 85% of drug is bound to plasma proteins independent of concentration.
Metabolism: Metabolized in liver.
Excretion: Excreted primarily in urine; about 30% excreted in feces. *Half-life:* 45 hours.

Route	Onset	Peak	Duration
P.O.	Unknown	1.5-4 hr	Unknown

Pharmacodynamics

Chemical effect: Inhibits DNA-dependent RNA polymerase in susceptible bacteria, blocking bacterial protein synthesis.
Therapeutic effect: Prevents disseminated MAC in patients with advanced HIV infection.

Available forms

Capsules: 150 mg

NURSING PROCESS

Assessment

- Assess patient's condition before therapy and regularly thereafter.
- Perform baseline hematologic studies and repeat periodically.
- Be alert for adverse reactions and drug interactions.
- Evaluate patient's and family's knowledge of drug therapy.

Nursing diagnoses

- Infection related to advanced HIV infection and decreased immune system
- Ineffective protection related to drug-induced adverse hematologic reactions
- Deficient knowledge related to drug therapy

Planning and implementation

- High-fat meals slow rate but not extent of absorption.
- Mix with soft foods for patient who has difficulty swallowing.
- No evidence exists that drug will provide effective prophylaxis against *Mycobacterium tuberculosis*. Patients requiring prophylaxis against both *M. tuberculosis* and MAC may require rifampin and rifabutin.

ALERT: Don't confuse rifampin, rifapentine, and rifabutin.

Patient teaching

- Tell patient that drug may turn urine, feces, sputum, saliva, tears, and skin brownish-orange. Tell him not to wear soft contacts because they may be permanently stained.
- Instruct patient to report photophobia, excessive lacrimation, or eye pain. Drug may rarely cause uveitis.

Evaluation

- Patient doesn't develop disseminated MAC.
- Patient maintains normal hematologic values throughout therapy.
- Patient and family state understanding of drug therapy.

rifampin (rifampicin)

(rih-FAM-pin)

Rifadin, Rifadin IV, Rimactane, Rimycin ◇, Rofact ♦

Pharmacologic class: semisynthetic rifamycin B derivative (macrocytic antibiotic)
Therapeutic class: antituberculotic
Pregnancy risk category: C

Indications and dosages

▶ **Pulmonary tuberculosis.** *Adults:* 10 mg/kg P.O. or I.V. daily in single dose, not to exceed maximum daily dose of 600 mg.
Children older than age 5: 10 to 20 mg/kg P.O. or I.V. daily in single dose. Maximum, 600 mg daily. Use with other antituberculotics is recommended.

▶ **Meningococcal carriers.** *Adults:* 600 mg P.O. or I.V. b.i.d. for 2 days.
Children ages 1 month to 12 years: 10 mg/kg P.O. or I.V. b.i.d. for 2 days; maximum daily dose is 600 mg.
Neonates: 5 mg/kg P.O. or I.V. b.i.d. for 2 days.
Patients with liver dysfunction: Reduce dosage.

▶ **Prophylaxis of *Haemophilus influenzae* type b.** *Adults and children:* 20 mg/kg P.O. daily for 4 days; maximum daily dose is 600 mg.

▶ **Leprosy ‡.** *Adults:* 600 mg P.O. once monthly, usually with other drugs.

Contraindications and precautions

- Contraindicated in patients hypersensitive to drug.
- Use cautiously in patients with liver disease.

Lifespan: In breast-feeding women, use cautiously. In neonates of rifampin-treated mothers, drug may cause hemorrhage.

Adverse reactions

CNS: ataxia, behavioral changes, confusion, dizziness, fatigue, headache, drowsiness, generalized numbness.
EENT: visual disturbances, exudative conjunctivitis.
GI: epigastric distress, anorexia, nausea, vomiting, abdominal pain, diarrhea, flatulence, sore mouth and tongue, ***pseudomembranous colitis, pancreatitis.***
GU: hemoglobinuria, hematuria, ***acute renal failure,*** menstrual disturbances.

Hematologic: eosinophilia, ***transient leukopenia, thrombocytopenia,*** hemolytic anemia.
Hepatic: ***hepatotoxicity,*** worsening of porphyria.
Metabolic: hyperuricemia.
Musculoskeletal: osteomalacia.
Respiratory: shortness of breath, wheezing.
Skin: pruritus, urticaria, rash.
Other: flulike syndrome, discoloration of body fluids, ***shock.***

Interactions

Drug-drug. *Analgesics, anticoagulants, anticonvulsants, barbiturates, beta blockers, cardiac glycosides, chloramphenicol, clofibrate, corticosteroids, cyclosporine, dapsone, diazepam, disopyramide, methadone, mexiletine, narcotics, oral contraceptives, progestins, quinidine, sulfonylureas, theophylline, verapamil:* Reduces effectiveness of these drugs. Avoid using together.
Halothane: May increase risk of hepatotoxicity in both drugs. Monitor liver function closely.
Ketoconazole, para-aminosalicylate sodium: May interfere with absorption of rifampin. Give these drugs 8 to 12 hours apart.
Probenecid: May increase rifampin levels. Use cautiously.
Drug-herb. *Kava:* May increase the risk of hepatotoxicity. Discourage use.
Drug-lifestyle. *Alcohol use:* May increase risk of hepatotoxicity. Discourage using together.

Effects on lab test results

- May increase ALT, AST, alkaline phosphatase, bilirubin, BUN, creatinine, and uric acid levels.
- May increase eosinophil count. May decrease hemoglobin, hematocrit, and platelet and WBC counts.

Pharmacokinetics

Absorption: Complete. Food delays absorption.
Distribution: Distributed widely in body tissues and fluids, including CSF; ascitic, pleural, and seminal fluids; tears; saliva; and liver, prostate, lungs, and bone. It's 84% to 91% protein-bound.
Metabolism: Metabolized extensively in liver. Drug undergoes enterohepatic circulation.
Excretion: Drug and metabolite excreted primarily in bile; drug, but not metabolite, is reabsorbed. Some of drug and its metabolite are excreted in urine. *Half-life:* 1½ to 5 hours.

Route	Onset	Peak	Duration
P.O.	Unknown	2-4 hr	Unknown
I.V.	Unknown	Unknown	Unknown

Pharmacodynamics

Chemical effect: Inhibits DNA-dependent RNA polymerase, thus impairing RNA synthesis (bactericidal).
Therapeutic effect: Kills susceptible bacteria. Spectrum of activity includes *Mycobacterium bovis, M. kansasii, M. marinum, M. tuberculosis* and some strains of *M. avium-intracellulare* and *M. fortuitum* as well as many gram-positive and some gram-negative bacteria.

Available forms

Capsules: 150 mg, 300 mg
Injection: 600 mg

NURSING PROCESS

Assessment

- Assess patient's infection before therapy and regularly thereafter.
- Monitor liver function, hematopoiesis, and uric acid levels.
- Be alert for adverse reactions and drug interactions.
- Watch closely for signs of hepatic impairment.
- Monitor patient's hydration status if adverse GI reactions occur.
- Evaluate patient's and family's knowledge of drug therapy.

Nursing diagnoses

- Infection related to presence of susceptible bacteria
- Risk for deficient fluid volume related to drug-induced adverse reactions
- Deficient knowledge related to drug therapy

Planning and implementation

- **P.O. use:** Give drug 1 hour before or 2 hours after meals for optimal absorption; if GI irritation occurs, patient may take rifampin with meals. Rifampin has been shown to inhibit standard assays for serum folate and vitamin B_{12}. Consider alternative assay method.

• **I.V. use:** Reconstitute vial with 10 ml of sterile water for injection to make solution containing 60 mg/ml.
– Add to 100 ml of D_5W and infuse over 30 minutes, or add to 500 ml of D_5W and infuse over 3 hours.
– When dextrose is contraindicated, drug may be diluted with normal saline solution for injection. Don't use other I.V. solutions.
• Treatment with at least one additional antituberculotic is recommended.
• Report hepatic impairment.
ALERT: Don't confuse rifampin, rifapentine, and rifabutin.

Patient teaching
• Warn patient about drowsiness and possible red-orange discoloration of urine, feces, saliva, sweat, sputum, and tears. Soft contact lenses may be permanently stained.
• Advise patient to avoid alcoholic beverages while taking this drug.

Evaluation
• Patient is free from infection.
• Patient maintains adequate hydration throughout therapy.
• Patient and family state understanding of drug therapy.

rifapentine
(rif-ah-PEN-tin)
Priftin

Pharmacologic class: rifamycin-derivative antibiotic
Therapeutic class: antituberculotic
Pregnancy risk category: C

Indications and dosages

▶ **Pulmonary tuberculosis, with at least one other antituberculotic to which the isolate is susceptible.** *Adults:* During intensive phase of short-course therapy, 600 mg P.O. twice weekly for 2 months, with an interval between doses of not less than 3 days (72 hours). During the continuation phase of short-course therapy, 600 mg P.O. once weekly for 4 months with isoniazid or another drug to which the isolate is susceptible.

Contraindications and precautions

• Contraindicated in patients hypersensitive to rifamycin (rifapentine, rifampin, or rifabutin).
• Use drug cautiously and with frequent monitoring in patients with liver disease.
Lifespan: During last 2 weeks of pregnancy, drug may lead to postnatal hemorrhage in mother or infant. Monitor clotting parameters closely.

Adverse reactions

CNS: pain, headache, dizziness.
CV: hypertension.
GI: anorexia, nausea, vomiting, dyspepsia, diarrhea, ***pseudomembranous colitis.***
GU: pyuria, proteinuria, hematuria, urinary casts.
Hematologic: ***neutropenia,*** lymphopenia, anemia, ***leukopenia,*** thrombocytosis.
Metabolic: *hyperuricemia.*
Musculoskeletal: arthralgia.
Respiratory: hemoptysis.
Skin: rash, pruritus, acne, maculopapular rash.

Interactions

Drug-drug. *Antiarrhythmics (disopyramide, mexiletine, quinidine, tocainide), antibiotics (chloramphenicol, clarithromycin, dapsone, doxycycline, fluoroquinolones), anticonvulsants (phenytoin), antifungals (fluconazole, itraconazole, ketoconazole), barbiturates, benzodiazepines (diazepam), beta blockers, calcium channel blockers (diltiazem, nifedipine, verapamil), cardiac glycosides, clofibrate, corticosteroids, haloperidol, HIV protease inhibitors (indinavir, nelfinavir, ritonavir, saquinavir), immunosuppressants (cyclosporine, tacrolimus), levothyroxine, narcotic analgesics (methadone), oral anticoagulants (warfarin), oral hypoglycemics (sulfonylureas), oral or other systemic hormonal contraceptives, progestins, quinine, reverse transcriptase inhibitors (delavirdine, zidovudine), sildenafil, theophylline, tricyclic antidepressants (amitriptyline, nortriptyline):* Induces metabolism of hepatic cytochrome P-450 enzyme system, decreasing the activity of these drugs. Dosage adjustments may be needed.

Effects on lab test results

• May increase uric acid, ALT, and AST levels.

• May increase platelet count. May decrease hemoglobin, hematocrit, and neutrophil and WBC counts.

Pharmacokinetics

Absorption: Relative bioavailability is 70%.
Distribution: About 98% bound to plasma proteins.
Metabolism: Hydrolyzed by an esterase enzyme to the microbiologically active 25-desacetyl rifapentine. Rifapentine contributes 62% to drug's activity and 25-desacetyl contributes 38%.
Excretion: About 17% is excreted in urine and 70% in feces. *Half-life:* 13 hours.

Route	Onset	Peak	Duration
P.O.	Unknown	5-6 hr	Unknown

Pharmacodynamics

Chemical effect: Inhibits DNA-dependent RNA polymerase in susceptible strains of *Mycobacterium tuberculosis.* It has intracellular and extracellular bactericidal activity. Rifapentine and rifampin share similar antimicrobial action.
Therapeutic effect: Kills susceptible bacteria.

Available forms

Tablets (film-coated): 150 mg

NURSING PROCESS

Assessment

• Assess patient's condition before therapy and regularly thereafter.
• Assess patient's understanding of disease and stress importance of strict compliance with drug and daily companion medications, as well as necessary follow-up visits and laboratory tests.
• Monitor liver function, CBC, and uric acid levels.
• Monitor patient for persistent or severe diarrhea and notify prescriber if it occurs.
• Evaluate patient's and family's knowledge of drug therapy.

Nursing diagnoses

• Infection related to patient's underlying condition
• Noncompliance related to long-term therapeutic regimen
• Deficient knowledge related to drug therapy

Planning and implementation

• Administration of pyridoxine (vitamin B_6) during rifapentine therapy is recommended in malnourished patients, those predisposed to neuropathy (alcoholics, diabetics), and adolescents.
• Drug must be given with appropriate daily companion drugs. Compliance with all drugs, especially with daily companion drugs on the days when rifapentine isn't given, is crucial for early sputum conversion and protection from tuberculosis relapse.
ALERT: Don't confuse rifampin, rifapentine, and rifabutin.

Patient teaching

• Stress importance of strict compliance with drug and daily companion drugs, as well as necessary follow-up visits and laboratory tests.
• Advise patient to use nonhormonal methods of birth control.
• Tell patient to take drug with food if nausea, vomiting, or GI upset occurs.
• Instruct patient to notify prescriber if any of the following occur: fever, loss of appetite, malaise, nausea, vomiting, darkened urine, yellowish discoloration of skin and eyes, pain or swelling of joints, and excessive loose stools or diarrhea.
• Instruct patient to protect pills from excessive heat.
• Tell patient that drug can turn body fluids red-orange. Contact lenses can become permanently stained.

Evaluation

• Patient experiences sputum conversion and recovers from tuberculosis.
• Patient is compliant with therapeutic regimen.
• Patient and family state understanding of drug therapy.

riluzole

(RIGH-loo-zohl)
Rilutek

Pharmacologic class: benzothiazole
Therapeutic class: neuroprotector
Pregnancy risk category: C

Indications and dosages

▶ **Amyotrophic lateral sclerosis (ALS).** *Adults:* 50 mg P.O. q 12 hours on empty stomach.

Contraindications and precautions

- Contraindicated in patients severely hypersensitive to drug or components of the tablets.
- Use cautiously in patients with hepatic or renal dysfunction, and women and Japanese patients (who may have a lower metabolic capacity to eliminate riluzole compared with men and white patients, respectively).

Lifespan: In breast-feeding women, drug isn't recommended. In children, safety of drug hasn't been established. In geriatric patients, use cautiously.

Adverse reactions

CNS: headache, aggravation reaction, *asthenia,* hypertonia, depression, dizziness, insomnia, malaise, somnolence, vertigo, circumoral paresthesia.
CV: hypertension, tachycardia, palpitations, orthostatic hypotension, peripheral edema.
EENT: *rhinitis, sinusitis.*
GI: abdominal pain, *nausea,* vomiting, dyspepsia, anorexia, diarrhea, flatulence, stomatitis, dry mouth, oral candidiasis.
GU: urinary tract infection, dysuria.
Hematologic: *neutropenia.*
Metabolic: weight loss.
Musculoskeletal: back pain, arthralgia.
Respiratory: *decreased lung function,* increased cough.
Skin: pruritus, eczema, alopecia, exfoliative dermatitis.
Other: tooth disorder, phlebitis.

Interactions

Drug-drug. *Allopurinol, methyldopa, sulfasalazine:* Increases risk of hepatotoxicity. Monitor patient closely.
Inducers of CYP 1A2 (omeprazole, rifampicin): May increase riluzole elimination. Monitor patient for loss of therapeutic effect.
Potential inhibitors of CYP 1A2 (amitriptyline, phenacetin, quinolones, theophylline): May decrease riluzole elimination. Monitor patient closely for toxicity.
Drug-food. *Any food:* Decreases drug bioavailability. Administer 1 hour before or 2 hours after meals.
Caffeine: May decrease riluzole elimination. Monitor patient for adverse reactions.
Charbroiled foods: May increase riluzole elimination. Discourage patient from eating while on drug therapy.
Drug-lifestyle. *Alcohol use:* May increase risk of hepatotoxicity. Discourage using together.
Smoking: May increase riluzole elimination. Urge patient to stop smoking.

Effects on lab test results

- May increase AST, ALT, bilirubin, and GGT levels.
- May decrease neutrophil count.

Pharmacokinetics

Absorption: Well absorbed from GI tract, with average absolute oral bioavailability of about 60%. High-fat meal decreases absorption.
Distribution: 96% protein-bound.
Metabolism: Extensively metabolized in liver.
Excretion: Excreted primarily in urine, with small amount in feces. *Half-life:* 12 hours with repeated doses.

Route	Onset	Peak	Duration
P.O.	Unknown	Unknown	Unknown

Pharmacodynamics

Chemical effect: Unknown.
Therapeutic effect: Improves signs and symptoms of ALS.

Available forms

Tablets: 50 mg

NURSING PROCESS

Assessment

- Obtain history of patient's ALS.
- Obtain liver and renal function studies and CBC before and during therapy.
- Evaluate patient's and family's knowledge of drug therapy.

Nursing diagnoses

- Impaired physical mobility related to ALS
- Risk for deficient fluid volume related to adverse GI reactions
- Deficient knowledge related to drug therapy

Planning and implementation

- Baseline elevations in liver function studies (especially elevated bilirubin level) should preclude use of riluzole. In many patients, drug may increase aminotransferase level. If level exceeds 10 times upper limit of normal range, or if jaundice develops, notify prescriber.
- Give drug at least 1 hour before or 2 hours after a meal.

Patient teaching

- Tell patient to take drug at same time each day. If he misses a dose, discourage taking a double dose and tell him to take the next tablet as scheduled.
- Instruct patient to report febrile illness; his WBC count should be checked.
- Warn patient to avoid hazardous activities until drug's CNS effects are known.
- Advise patient to limit alcohol intake during therapy.
- Tell patient to store drug at room temperature, protected from bright light and out of children's reach.

Evaluation

- Patient responds well to therapy.
- Patient maintains adequate hydration.
- Patient and family state understanding of drug therapy.

rimantadine hydrochloride

(righ-MAN-tuh-deen high-droh-KLOR-ighd)
Flumadine

Pharmacologic class: adamantine
Therapeutic class: antiviral
Pregnancy risk category: C

Indications and dosages

▶ **Prevention of influenza A virus.** *Children younger than age 10:* 5 mg/kg (not to exceed 150 mg daily) P.O. once daily.
Adults and children age 10 and older: 100 mg P.O. b.i.d.
Geriatric patients, patients with severe hepatic or renal dysfunction: 100 mg P.O. daily.
▶ **Treatment of influenza A virus infection.** *Adults:* 100 mg P.O. b.i.d. for 7 days from onset of symptoms.
Geriatric patients, patients with severe hepatic or renal dysfunction: 100 mg P.O. daily.

Contraindications and precautions

- Contraindicated in patients hypersensitive to drug or amantadine.
- Use cautiously in patients with renal or hepatic impairment and in patients with a history of seizures.

Lifespan: In pregnant women, use cautiously. In breast-feeding women, drug is contraindicated.

Adverse reactions

CNS: insomnia, headache, dizziness, nervousness, fatigue, asthenia.
GI: nausea, vomiting, anorexia, dry mouth, abdominal pain.

Interactions

Drug-drug. *Acetaminophen, aspirin:* Reduces rimantadine level. Monitor patient for decreased rimantadine effectiveness.
Cimetidine: May decrease rimantadine clearance. Monitor patient for adverse reactions.

Effects on lab test results

None reported.

Pharmacokinetics

Absorption: Well absorbed from GI tract.
Distribution: Plasma protein–binding is about 40%.
Metabolism: Metabolized extensively in liver.
Excretion: Excreted in urine. *Half-life:* 25½ to 32 hours.

Route	Onset	Peak	Duration
P.O.	Unknown	1-4 hr	Unknown

Pharmacodynamics

Chemical effect: Unknown; appears to prevent viral uncoating, an early step in viral reproductive cycle.
Therapeutic effect: Inhibits viral reproduction of influenza A virus.

Available forms

Syrup: 50 mg/5 ml
Tablets: 100 mg

NURSING PROCESS

Assessment
• Obtain history of patient's exposure to influenza A virus before therapy, and reassess regularly thereafter.
• Monitor patient's hydration status throughout rimantadine therapy.
• Evaluate patient's and family's knowledge of drug therapy.

Nursing diagnoses
• Infection related to exposure to influenza A virus
• Risk for deficient fluid volume related to drug-induced adverse GI reactions
• Deficient knowledge related to drug therapy

Planning and implementation
• Give within 48 hours of onset of influenza symptoms and continue for 7 days after signs and symptoms appeared.
• Consider risk to contacts of treated patients, who may be subject to morbidity from influenza A. Influenza A–resistant strains can emerge during therapy. Patients taking drug may still be able to spread disease.
ALERT: Don't confuse rimantadine with amantadine.

Patient teaching
• Instruct patient to take drug several hours before bedtime to prevent insomnia.

Evaluation
• Patient is free from infection.
• Patient maintains adequate hydration throughout therapy.
• Patient and family state understanding of drug therapy.

Ringer's injection
(RING-erz in-JEK-shun)

Pharmacologic class: electrolyte solution
Therapeutic class: electrolyte and fluid replenishment
Pregnancy risk category: NR

Indications and dosages
▶ **Fluid and electrolyte replacement.** *Adults and children:* Dosage highly individualized; usually 1.5 to 3 L (2% to 6% body weight) infused I.V. over 18 to 24 hours.

Contraindications and precautions
• Contraindicated in patients with renal failure, except as emergency volume expander.
• Use cautiously in patients with heart failure, circulatory insufficiency, renal dysfunction, hypoproteinemia, or pulmonary edema.
Lifespan: In pregnant women, use cautiously.

Adverse reactions
CV: fluid overload.
Metabolic: electrolyte imbalance.

Interactions
None significant.

Effects on lab test results
• May cause electrolyte imbalances.

Pharmacokinetics
Absorption: Administered I.V.
Distribution: Widely distributed.
Metabolism: Not significant.
Excretion: Excreted primarily in urine and minimally in feces.

Route	Onset	Peak	Duration
I.V.	Immediate	Immediate	Unknown

Pharmacodynamics
Chemical effect: Replaces fluids and electrolytes.
Therapeutic effect: Restores normal fluid and electrolyte balance.

Available forms
Injection: 250 ml, 500 ml, 1,000 ml

NURSING PROCESS

Assessment
• Obtain history of patient's fluid and electrolyte status before therapy, and reassess regularly thereafter.
• Be alert for fluid overload.
• Evaluate patient's and family's knowledge of drug therapy.

Nursing diagnoses
- Deficient fluid volume related to underlying condition
- Deficient knowledge related to drug therapy

Planning and implementation
- Drug contains sodium, 147 mEq/L; potassium, 4 mEq/L; calcium, 4.5 mEq/L; and chloride, 155.5 mEq/L.
- Electrolyte content isn't enough to treat severe electrolyte deficiencies, but it provides electrolytes in levels approximating those of blood.

ALERT: Don't confuse Ringer's injection with lactated Ringer's solutions.

Patient teaching
- Inform patient of need for drug, and instruct him to report signs of fluid overload, such as difficulty breathing.

Evaluation
- Patient regains normal fluid and electrolyte balance.
- Patient and family state understanding of drug therapy.

Ringer's injection, lactated (Hartmann's solution, lactated Ringer's solution)

(RING-erz in-JEK-shun, LAK-tayt-ed)

Pharmacologic class: electrolyte and carbohydrate solution
Therapeutic class: electrolyte and fluid replenishment
Pregnancy risk category: NR

Indications and dosages

▶ **Fluid and electrolyte replacement.** *Adults and children:* Dosage highly individualized according to patient's size and clinical condition.

Contraindications and precautions

- Contraindicated in patients with renal failure, except as emergency volume expander.
- Use cautiously in patients with heart failure, circulatory insufficiency, renal dysfunction, hypoproteinemia, or pulmonary edema.

Lifespan: In pregnant women, use cautiously.

Adverse reactions

CV: fluid overload.
Metabolic: electrolyte imbalance.

Interactions

None significant.

Effects on lab test results

- May cause electrolyte imbalance.

Pharmacokinetics

Absorption: Administered I.V.
Distribution: Widely distributed.
Metabolism: Not significant for electrolytes. Lactate is oxidized to bicarbonate.
Excretion: Excreted primarily in urine and minimally in feces.

Route	Onset	Peak	Duration
I.V.	Immediate	Immediate	Unknown

Pharmacodynamics

Chemical effect: Replaces fluids and electrolytes.
Therapeutic effect: Restores normal fluid and electrolyte balance.

Available forms

Injection: 150 ml, 250 ml, 500 ml, 1,000 ml

NURSING CONSIDERATIONS

Assessment
- Obtain history of patient's fluid and electrolyte status before therapy, and reassess regularly thereafter.
- Be alert for fluid overload.
- Evaluate patient's knowledge of drug therapy.

Nursing diagnoses
- Deficient fluid volume related to underlying condition
- Deficient knowledge related to drug therapy

Planning and implementation
- Drug contains sodium, 130 mEq/L; potassium, 4 mEq/L; calcium, 3 mEq/L; chloride, 109.7 mEq/L; and lactate, 28 mEq/L.
- Lactated Ringer's injection approximates electrolyte concentration in blood plasma.

⚠ **ALERT:** Don't confuse lactated Ringer's solutions with Ringer's injection.

Patient teaching

- Inform patient of need for drug. Instruct him to report signs of fluid overload, such as difficulty breathing.

☑ Evaluation

- Patient regains normal fluid and electrolyte balance.
- Patient and family state understanding of drug therapy.

risedronate sodium

(ri-SEH-droe-nate SOE-dee-um)

Actonel

Pharmacologic class: bisphosphonate
Therapeutic class: antiresorptive agent
Pregnancy risk category: C

Indications and dosages

▶ **Prevention and treatment of postmenopausal osteoporosis.** *Adults:* 5-mg tablet P.O. once daily, or 35-mg tablet once weekly. Give at least 30 minutes before first food or drink (except water) of the day.

▶ **Glucocorticoid-induced osteoporosis in patients who are either starting or continuing glucocorticoid therapy at 7.5 mg or more of prednisone or equivalent daily.** *Adults:* 5 mg P.O. daily.

▶ **Paget's disease.** *Adults:* 30 mg P.O. daily for 2 months. If relapse occurs or alkaline phosphatase level doesn't normalize, may give same dose for 2 months or more after completing first treatment.

Contraindications and precautions

- Contraindicated in patients hypersensitive to any component of the product and in patients who are hypocalcemic or unable to stand or sit upright for 30 minutes after administration.
- Drug isn't recommended for patients with severe renal impairment (creatinine clearance below 30 ml/minute).
- Use cautiously in patients with upper GI disorders such as dysphagia, esophagitis, and esophageal or gastric ulcers.

Lifespan: In breast-feeding women, consider stopping either drug or breast-feeding, taking into account importance of drug to the mother. It isn't known whether drug appears in breast milk. In children, safety and efficacy of drug haven't been established.

Adverse reactions

CNS: asthenia, *headache,* depression, dizziness, insomnia, anxiety, neuralgia, vertigo, hypertonia, paresthesia, *pain.*
CV: *hypertension,* CV disorder, angina pectoris, chest pain, peripheral edema.
EENT: pharyngitis, rhinitis, sinusitis, cataract, conjunctivitis, otitis media, amblyopia, tinnitus.
GI: *nausea, diarrhea, abdominal pain,* flatulence, gastritis, rectal disorder, constipation.
GU: *urinary tract infection,* cystitis.
Hematologic: ecchymosis, anemia.
Musculoskeletal: *arthralgia,* neck pain, *back pain,* myalgia, bone pain, leg cramps, bursitis, tendon disorder.
Respiratory: dyspnea, pneumonia, bronchitis.
Skin: *rash,* pruritus, ***skin carcinoma.***
Other: tooth disorder, *infection.*

Interactions

Drug-drug. *Calcium supplements, antacids that contain calcium, magnesium, or aluminum:* May interfere with risedronate absorption. Advise patient to separate administration times.
Drug-food. *Any food:* May interfere with risedronate absorption. Advise patient to take drug at least 30 minutes before first food or drink of the day (other than water).

Effects on lab test results

- May decrease calcium and phosphorus levels.
- May decrease hemoglobin and hematocrit.

Pharmacokinetics

Absorption: Absorbed via the GI tract. Steady state occurs in 57 days. Mean absolute oral bioavailability of the 30-mg tablet is 0.63%. Food alters absorption; drug should be taken at least 30 minutes before breakfast.
Distribution: The mean steady-state volume of distribution is 6.3 L/kg. Plasma protein binding is about 24%.
Metabolism: No evidence of systemic metabolism.

Excretion: About 50% of a dose is excreted in urine within 24 hours. Mean renal clearance is 105 ml/minute and mean total clearance is 122 ml/minute. Unabsorbed drug is eliminated unchanged in feces. Once absorbed, risedronate has an initial half-life of 1.5 hours and a terminal exponential half-life of about 480 hours.

Route	Onset	Peak	Duration
P.O.	1 hr	Unknown	Unknown

Pharmacodynamics

Chemical effect: Reverses the loss of bone mineral density in postmenopausal women, a central factor in the progression of osteoporosis. It does so by reducing bone turnover and bone resorption at remodeling sites by inhibiting osteoclasts. In patients with Paget's disease, drug causes bone turnover to return to normal, as evidenced by reduced levels of serum alkaline phosphatase (a marker of bone formation) and urinary hydroxyproline/creatinine and deoxypyridinoline/creatinine (markers of bone resorption).
Therapeutic effect: Reverses the loss of bone mineral density.

Available forms

Tablets: 5 mg, 30 mg, 35 mg

NURSING PROCESS

Assessment

- Assess underlying condition before therapy and reassess regularly throughout therapy.
- Evaluate renal function before beginning therapy. Drug isn't recommended for patients with creatinine clearance below 30 ml/minute.
- Assess for the following risk factors for the development of osteoporosis: family history, previous fracture, smoking, a decrease in bone mineral density below the premenopausal mean, a thin body frame, white or Asian race, and early menopause.
- Evaluate patient's and family's knowledge of drug therapy.

Nursing diagnoses

- Risk for injury related to decreased bone mass
- Ineffective health maintenance related to underlying disease
- Deficient knowledge related to risedronate sodium therapy

Planning and implementation

ALERT: Follow dosing instructions carefully because benefits of the drug may be compromised by failure to take it according to instructions. Give drug at least 30 minutes before patient's first food or drink (other than water) of the day.

- Give drug with sufficient (6 to 8 ounces) plain water to facilitate delivery to the stomach. Don't allow patient to lie down for 30 minutes after taking drug.
- Weight-bearing exercise should be considered along with cessation of smoking and alcohol consumption, as appropriate.

ALERT: Bisphosphonates have been linked to such GI disorders as dysphagia, esophagitis, and esophageal or gastric ulcers. Monitor patient for symptoms of esophageal disease (such as dysphagia, retrosternal pain, or severe persistent or worsening heartburn).

- Patients should receive supplemental calcium and vitamin D if dietary intake is inadequate. However, because calcium supplements and calcium-, aluminum-, and magnesium-containing medications may interfere with risedronate absorption, the dosing times should be separated.
- Store drug at 68° to 77° F (20° to 25° C).
- Bisphosphonates can interfere with bone-imaging agents.

Patient teaching

- Explain that risedronate is used to replace bone lost as a result of certain disease processes.
- Caution patient about the importance of adhering to special dosing instructions.
- Tell patient to take drug at least 30 minutes before the first food or drink (other than water) of the day. Urge patient to take the drug with a full glass of water (6 to 8 ounces) while sitting or standing. Warn against lying down for 30 minutes after taking risedronate.
- Advise patient not to chew or suck the tablet because doing so could cause mouth irritation.
- Advise patient to contact prescriber immediately if he develops symptoms of esophageal disease (such as difficulty or pain when swallowing, retrosternal pain, or severe heartburn).

• Advise patient to take calcium and vitamin D if dietary intake is inadequate, but to take them at a different time than risedronate.
• Advise patient to stop smoking and drinking alcohol, as appropriate. Also, advise patient to perform weight-bearing exercise.
• Tell patient to store drug in a cool (room temperature), dry place and away from children.
• Urge patient to read the Patient Information Guide before starting therapy.
• Tell patient if he misses a dose of the 35-mg tablet, he should take 1 tablet on the morning after he remembers and return to taking 1 tablet once a week, as originally scheduled on his chosen day. Patients should not take 2 tablets on the same day.

Evaluation
• Patient does not suffer any injury related to decreased bone mass.
• Patient shows improvement in underlying condition.
• Patient and family state understanding of drug therapy.

risperidone
(ris-PER-ih-dohn)
Risperdal

Pharmacologic class: benzisoxazole derivative
Therapeutic class: antipsychotic
Pregnancy risk category: C

Indications and dosages
▶ **Short-term (6 to 8 weeks) treatment of schizophrenia.** *Adults:* Initially, 1 mg P.O. b.i.d. Increase in increments of 1 mg b.i.d. on days 2 and 3 of treatment to a target dose of 3 mg b.i.d. Alternatively, 1 mg P.O. on day 1, increase to 2 mg once daily on day 2, and 4 mg once daily on day 3. Wait at least 1 week before adjusting dosage further. Adjust doses by 1 to 2 mg. Doses above 6 mg daily weren't more effective than lower doses and were linked to more extrapyramidal reactions. Doses up to 8 mg daily were safe and effective. Safety of doses above 16 mg daily has not been evaluated.
▶ **Delaying relapse in the long-term (1 to 2 years) treatment of schizophrenia.** *Adults:* Initially, 1 mg P.O. on day 1, increase to 2 mg once daily on day 2, and 4 mg once daily on day 3. Dosage range is 2 to 8 mg daily. *Geriatric or debilitated patients, hypotensive patients, or patients with severe renal or hepatic impairment:* Initially, give 0.5 mg P.O. b.i.d. Increase dosage in increments of 0.5 mg b.i.d. Increases in dosages above 1.5 mg b.i.d. should occur at intervals of at least 1 week. Subsequent switches to once-daily dosing may be made after patient has received a twice-daily regimen for 2 to 3 days at the target dose.

Contraindications and precautions
• Contraindicated in patients hypersensitive to the drug or any of its components.
• Use cautiously in patients with prolonged QT interval, CV disease, cerebrovascular disease, dehydration, hypovolemia, history of seizures, exposure to extreme heat, or conditions that could affect metabolism or hemodynamic responses. Also use cautiously in patients at risk for aspiration pneumonia.
Lifespan: In pregnant women, use with extreme caution. In breast-feeding women, drug is contraindicated. In children, safety of drug hasn't been established.

Adverse reactions
CNS: *somnolence, extrapyramidal symptoms, headache,* ***suicide attempt,*** *insomnia, agitation, anxiety,* tardive dyskinesia, aggressiveness, fever, sedation, ***neuroleptic malignant syndrome.***
CV: tachycardia, chest pain, orthostatic hypotension, ***prolonged QTc interval.***
EENT: *rhinitis,* sinusitis, pharyngitis, abnormal vision.
GI: *constipation, nausea, vomiting, dyspepsia.*
Metabolic: weight gain.
Musculoskeletal: arthralgia, back pain.
Respiratory: coughing, upper respiratory tract infection.
Skin: rash, dry skin, photosensitivity reaction.
Other: priapism.

Interactions
Drug-drug. *Antihypertensives:* May enhance hypotensive effects. Monitor blood pressure.

Carbamazepine: Increases risperidone clearance, leading to decreased effectiveness. Monitor patient closely.
Clozapine: Decreases risperidone clearance, increasing toxicity. Monitor patient closely.
CNS depressants: Additive CNS depression. Avoid using together.
Dopamine agonists, levodopa: May antagonize the effects of these drugs. Monitor patient closely.
Drug-lifestyle. *Alcohol use:* Additive CNS depression. Discourage using together.
Sun exposure: Increases photosensitivity reactions. Discourage prolonged or unprotected sun exposure.

Effects on lab test results

- May increase prolactin levels.

Pharmacokinetics

Absorption: Well absorbed; absolute oral bioavailability is 70%.
Distribution: Plasma protein–binding is about 90% for risperidone and 77% for its major active metabolite.
Metabolism: Extensively metabolized in liver.
Excretion: Metabolite excreted in urine.

Route	Onset	Peak	Duration
P.O.	Unknown	About 1 hr	Unknown

Pharmacodynamics

Chemical effect: Blocks dopamine and serotonin receptors as well as $alpha_1$, $alpha_2$, and H_1 receptors in the CNS.
Therapeutic effect: Relieves signs and symptoms of psychosis.

Available forms

Oral solution: 1 mg/ml
Tablets: 0.25 mg, 0.5 mg, 1 mg, 2 mg, 3 mg, 4 mg

NURSING PROCESS

Assessment

- Assess patient's psychosis before therapy and regularly thereafter.
- Assess blood pressure before therapy, and monitor regularly. Watch for orthostatic hypotension, especially during dosage adjustment.
- Be alert for adverse reactions and drug interactions.

ALERT: Watch for tardive dyskinesia. It may occur after prolonged use; it may not appear until months or years later and may disappear spontaneously or persist for life despite stopping drug.
- Evaluate patient's and family's knowledge of drug therapy.

Nursing diagnoses

- Disturbed thought processes related to presence of psychosis
- Risk for injury related to drug-induced adverse CNS reactions
- Deficient knowledge related to drug therapy

Planning and implementation

- When restarting therapy for patient who has been off drug, follow 3-day dose initiation schedule.
- When switching patient to drug from another antipsychotic, stop other drug immediately when risperidone therapy starts.

Patient teaching

- Warn patient to rise slowly, avoid hot showers, and use extra caution during first few days of therapy to avoid fainting.
- Warn patient to avoid activities that require alertness until CNS effects of drug are known. Drowsiness and dizziness usually subside after a few days.
- Tell patient to avoid alcohol and prolonged sunlight during therapy.
- Advise patient to use caution in hot weather to prevent heatstroke; drug may affect thermoregulation.
- Tell patient to use sunblock and to wear protective clothing.
- Tell woman to notify prescriber if she is or plans to become pregnant.
- Inform patient that drug may be taken without regard to food.

Evaluation

- Patient behavior and communication indicate improved thought processes.
- Patient doesn't experience injury as result of drug-induced adverse CNS reactions.
- Patient and family state understanding of drug therapy.

ritonavir

(rih-TOH-nuh-veer)
Norvir

Pharmacologic class: protease inhibitor
Therapeutic class: antiviral
Pregnancy risk category: B

Indications and dosages

▶ **Treatment of HIV infection with nucleoside analogues or as monotherapy when antiretroviral therapy is warranted.** *Adults:* 600 mg P.O. b.i.d. with meals. If nausea occurs, dosage escalation may provide relief: 300 mg b.i.d. for 1 day, 400 mg b.i.d. for 2 days, 500 mg b.i.d. for 1 day, and 600 mg b.i.d. thereafter.

Contraindications and precautions

• Contraindicated in patients hypersensitive to drug or who are taking dihydroergotamine, ergotamine agents, or cisapride.
Lifespan: HIV-positive women should not breast-feed to prevent transmission of HIV. It isn't known whether drug appears in breast milk.

Adverse reactions

CNS: *asthenia,* headache, malaise, fever, circumoral paresthesia, dizziness, insomnia, paresthesia, peripheral paresthesia, somnolence, thinking abnormality, migraine headache.
CV: vasodilation.
EENT: local throat irritation, diplopia, blepharitis, pharyngitis, photophobia.
GI: abdominal pain, anorexia, constipation, *diarrhea, nausea, vomiting, taste perversion,* dyspepsia, flatulence.
Hematologic: ***leukopenia, thrombocytopenia.***
Metabolic: hyperlipidemia.
Musculoskeletal: myalgia.
Skin: rash, sweating.

Interactions

Drug-drug. *Agents that increase CYP3A activity, such as carbamazepine, dexamethasone, phenobarbital, phenytoin, rifabutin, and rifampin:* Increases ritonavir clearance, resulting in decreased ritonavir plasma levels. Monitor patient closely. Monitor anticonvulsant drug levels. May reduce rifabutin dose, if necessary.
Alprazolam, clorazepate, diazepam, estazolam, flurazepam, midazolam, triazolam, and zolpidem: Potential for extreme sedation and respiratory depression from these agents. Don't give together.
Methadone: Decreases level of drug. May cause opiate withdrawal symptoms. Increase methadone dose, if necessary.
Amiodarone, bepridil, bupropion, clozapine, encainide, flecainide, meperidine, piroxicam, propafenone, propoxyphene, quinidine, rifabutin: Significant increases in the plasma levels of these drugs, thus increasing the patient's risk of arrhythmias, hematologic abnormalities, seizures, or other potentially serious adverse effects. Don't give together.
Amprenavir: Increases concentration of amprenavir. There is limited data in adjusting the dose to amprenavir 600 to 1,200 mg b.i.d. and ritonavir 100 to 200 mg b.i.d.
Clarithromycin: Increases clarithromycin concentration. Patients with impaired renal function receiving drug with ritonavir require a 50% reduction in their clarithromycin if creatinine clearance is 30 to 60 ml/minute and a 75% reduction if it's below 30 ml/minute.
Delavirdine, nevirapine: Alters plasma concentrations of ritonavir. No dosage adjustment is necessary.
Desipramine: Increases overall serum concentrations of desipramine. May require dosage adjustment.
Disopyramide: Cardiac and neurologic events may occur. Use together with caution.
Disulfiram or other drugs that produce disulfiram-like reactions, such as metronidazole: Increases risk of disulfiram-like reactions. Ritonavir formulations contain alcohol that can produce reactions when given at the same time. Monitor patient.
Efavirenz: Increases plasma levels of both drugs. Leave the dose at 600 mg b.i.d., or may reduce dose of ritonavir to 500 mg b.i.d. if intolerance.
Ethinyl estradiol: Decreases ethinyl estradiol plasma concentrations. Use an alternative or additional method of birth control.
Glucuronosyltransferases, including oral anticoagulants or immunosuppressants: Loss of therapeutic effects from directly glucuronidated agents. May need dosage alteration of these

agents; monitor drug levels and drug effects. A dosage reduction greater than 50% may be required for those agents extensively metabolized by CYP3A.
HMG CoA reductase inhibitors: May cause a large increase in statin levels, causing myopathy. Avoid using together.
Ketoconazole: Increases level of ritonavir. Use together cautiously and monitor patient carefully.
Sildenafil: Increases level of drugs. Use together cautiously. Don't exceed 25 mg of sildenafil in a 48-hour period.
Nelfinavir: Increases nelfinavir plasma levels. Adjust dose by taking ritonavir 400 mg b.i.d. and nelfinavir 500 to 750 mg b.i.d.
Oral contraceptives: Decreases overall serum levels of the contraceptive. May require a dosage increase in the oral contraceptive or alternate contraceptive measures.
Saquinavir: Increases saquinavir plasma levels. Adjust dose by taking saquinavir 400 mg b.i.d. and ritonavir 400 mg b.i.d.
Theophylline: Decreases overall levels of theophylline. Increased dosage may be required.
Drug-herb. *St. John's wort:* Substantially reduces levels of the drug, which could cause loss of therapeutic effects. Discourage using together.
Drug-food. *Any food:* Increases drug absorption. Drug should be taken with food.
Drug-lifestyle. *Smoking:* Decreases levels of ritonavir. Discourage smoking.

Effects on lab test results

- May increase ALT, AST, alkaline phosphatase, GGT, bilirubin, glucose, triglyceride, lipid, potassium, CK, and uric acid levels.
- May increase PT and INR and eosinophil count. May decrease hemoglobin, hematocrit, and WBC, platelet, and neutrophil counts.

Pharmacokinetics

Absorption: Enhanced by food.
Distribution: Absolute bioavailability unknown; 98% to 100% bound to serum albumin.
Metabolism: Metabolized in the liver and kidneys.
Excretion: Excreted in the urine and feces.

Route	Onset	Peak	Duration
P.O.	Unknown	2-4 hr	Unknown

Pharmacodynamics

Chemical effect: HIV protease inhibitor with activity against HIV-1 and HIV-2 proteases; binds to protease-active site and inhibits enzyme activity.
Therapeutic effect: Prevents cleavage of viral polyproteins, resulting in formation of immature noninfectious viral particles.

Available forms

Capsules: 100 mg
Oral solution: 80 mg/ml

NURSING PROCESS

Assessment

- Use cautiously in patients with hepatic insufficiency.
- Evaluate patient's and family's understanding of drug therapy.

Nursing diagnoses

- Infection related to presence of virus
- Deficient knowledge related to drug therapy

Planning and implementation

ALERT: Do not confuse Norvir with Norvasc.

Patient teaching

- Inform patient that drug isn't a cure for HIV infection and that illnesses caused by HIV infection may occur. Drug doesn't reduce risk of HIV transmission.
- Tell patient that the taste of oral solution may be improved by mixing with flavored milk within 1 hour of dose.
- Tell patient to take drug with meal.
- If a dose is missed, instruct patient to take next dose at once; he shouldn't take double doses.
- Advise patient to report use of other drugs, including OTC drugs.
- Advise patient receiving sildenafil that there is an increased risk of sildenafil-associated adverse events, including hypotension, visual changes, and priapism. He should promptly report any symptoms to his prescriber. Tell patient not to exceed 25 mg of sildenafil in a 48-hour period.

Evaluation

- Patient's infection is eradicated.
- Patient and family state understanding of drug therapy.

rivastigmine tartrate

(ri-va-STIG-meen TAR-trayt)
Exelon

Pharmacologic class: cholinesterase inhibitor
Therapeutic class: Alzheimer's agent
Pregnancy risk category: B

Indications and dosages

▶ **Symptomatic treatment of patients with mild-to-moderate Alzheimer's disease.**
Adults: Initially, 1.5 mg P.O. b.i.d. with food. If tolerated, may be increased to 3 mg b.i.d. after 2 weeks. Further increases to 4.5 mg b.i.d. and 6 mg b.i.d. may be given as tolerated after 2 weeks on the previous dose. Effective dosage range is 6 to 12 mg daily, with maximum recommended dosage of 12 mg daily.

Contraindications and precautions

- Contraindicated in patients hypersensitive to drug, its components, or other carbamate derivatives.
- Use cautiously in patients who take NSAIDs and who have a history of ulcers or GI bleeding, sick sinus syndrome or other supraventricular cardiac conditions, asthma or obstructive pulmonary disease, or seizures.

Lifespan: In breast-feeding women, drug is not indicated; it isn't known whether drug appears in breast milk.

Adverse reactions

CNS: syncope, fatigue, asthenia, malaise, *dizziness, headache,* somnolence, tremor, insomnia, confusion, depression, anxiety, hallucination, aggressive reaction, vertigo, agitation, nervousness, delusion, paranoid reaction.
CV: hypertension, chest pain, peripheral edema.
EENT: rhinitis, pharyngitis.
GI: *nausea, vomiting, diarrhea, anorexia, abdominal pain,* dyspepsia, constipation, flatulence, eructation.
GU: urinary tract infection, urinary incontinence.
Metabolic: weight loss.
Musculoskeletal: back pain, arthralgia, bone fracture.
Respiratory: upper respiratory tract infection, cough, bronchitis.
Skin: increased sweating, rash.
Other: *accidental trauma,* flulike symptoms, pain.

Interactions

Drug-drug. *Anticholinergics:* Possible interference with anticholinergic activity. Monitor patient closely.
Bethanechol, succinylcholine, and other neuromuscular blocking agents or cholinergic antagonists: Possible synergistic effect on rivastigmine. Monitor patient closely.
Drug-lifestyle. *Nicotine:* Increases rivastigmine clearance. Monitor patient closely.

Effects on lab test results

None reported.

Pharmacokinetics

Absorption: Drug is rapidly absorbed, and serum levels peak in about 1 hour. Although drug should be taken with food, the time to reach peak levels is delayed by about 1.5 hours. Absolute bioavailability is 36%.
Distribution: Widely distributed throughout body; drug crosses the blood-brain barrier. Protein-binding is about 40%.
Metabolism: Rapidly and extensively metabolized.
Excretion: Elimination is primarily through the kidneys. *Half-life:* About 1½ hours in patients with normal renal function.

Route	Onset	Peak	Duration
P.O.	Unknown	1 hr	12 hr

Pharmacodynamics

Chemical effect: Thought to increase acetylcholine levels by reversibly inhibiting its hydrolysis by cholinesterase. Acetylcholine is probably the primary neurotransmitter that is depleted in Alzheimer's disease.
Therapeutic effect: Improves cognitive function.

Available forms

Capsules: 1.5 mg, 3 mg, 4.5 mg, 6 mg

NURSING PROCESS

Assessment

- Assess underlying condition before therapy and regularly thereafter.

• Perform complete health history, and carefully monitor patient with a history of GI bleeding, NSAID use, arrhythmias, seizures, or pulmonary conditions for adverse effects.
• Evaluate patient's and family's knowledge of drug therapy.

Nursing diagnoses
• Acute or chronic confusion related to underlying disease
• Risk for imbalanced fluid volume related to drug-induced GI effects
• Deficient knowledge related to rivastigmine tartrate therapy

Planning and implementation
• Expect significant GI adverse effects, such as nausea, vomiting, anorexia, and weight loss. They're less common during maintenance doses.
ALERT: The manufacturer has issued a warning that severe vomiting has occurred among patients who resumed rivastigmine therapy after an interruption. Revised package labeling states that therapy should resume at the recommended starting dosage (1.5 mg b.i.d.) if therapy is interrupted for more than several days. The dosage should then be adjusted upward to maintenance levels.
• Dramatic memory improvement is unlikely. As disease progresses, the benefits of rivastigmine may decline.
• Monitor patient for symptoms of active or occult GI bleeding.
• Monitor patient for severe nausea, vomiting, and diarrhea, which may lead to dehydration and weight loss.

Patient teaching
• Advise patient to report any episodes of nausea, vomiting, or diarrhea.
• Inform patient and caregiver that memory improvement may be subtle and that a more likely result of therapy is a slower decline in memory loss.
• Tell patient to take rivastigmine with food in the morning and evening.
• Urge patient to consult prescriber before taking OTC medications.

Evaluation
• Patient's cognition improves and he experiences less confusion.
• Patient and family state that adverse GI effects have not occurred or have been managed effectively.
• Patient and family state understanding of drug therapy.

rizatriptan benzoate
(rih-zah-TRIP-tin BEN-zoh-ayt)
Maxalt, Maxalt-MLT

Pharmacologic class: selective 5-hydroxytryptamine (5-HT_1) receptor agonist
Therapeutic class: antimigraine agent
Pregnancy risk category: C

Indications and dosages
▶ **Treatment of acute migraine headaches with or without aura.** *Adults:* Initially, 5 to 10 mg P.O. If first dose is ineffective, another dose can be given at least 2 hours after first dose. Maximum, 30 mg daily. For patients taking propranolol, 5 mg P.O., up to maximum of three doses (15 mg total) in 24 hours.

Contraindications and precautions
• Contraindicated in patients with ischemic heart disease (angina pectoris, history of MI, or documented silent ischemia) or those with evidence of ischemic heart disease, coronary artery vasospasm (Prinzmetal's variant angina), or other significant underlying CV disease. Also contraindicated in patients with uncontrolled hypertension and within 24 hours of treatment with another 5-HT_1 agonist or with ergotamine-containing or ergot-type drugs such as dihydroergotamine or methysergide.
• Don't use within 2 weeks of an MAO inhibitor.
• Also contraindicated in patients hypersensitive to drug or its inactive ingredients.
• Use cautiously in patients with hepatic or renal impairment.
• Use cautiously in patients with risk factors for coronary artery disease (hypertension, hypercholesterolemia, smoking, obesity, diabetes, strong family history of coronary artery disease, women with surgical or physiologic menopause, or men older than age 40), unless a cardiac evaluation provides evidence that patient is free from cardiac disease.

Lifespan: In breast-feeding women, do not use drug because the effects on infants are unknown. In children, safety and effectiveness haven't been established.

Adverse reactions

CNS: dizziness, headache, somnolence, paresthesia, asthenia, fatigue, hypesthesia, decreased mental acuity, euphoria, tremor.
CV: flushing, chest pain, pressure or heaviness, palpitations, ***coronary artery vasospasm.***
EENT: neck, throat, and jaw pain, pressure, or heaviness.
GI: dry mouth, nausea, diarrhea, vomiting.
Respiratory: dyspnea.
Other: pain, warm or cold sensations, hot flushes.

Interactions

Drug-drug. *Ergot-containing or ergot-type drugs (dihydroergotamine, methysergide), other 5-HT$_1$ agonists:* Prolongs vasospastic reactions. Don't use within 24 hours of rizatriptan.
MAO inhibitors: Increases plasma rizatriptan levels. Don't use together. Allow at least 14 days between stopping an MAO inhibitor and taking rizatriptan.
Propranolol: Increases rizatriptan levels. Reduce rizatriptan dose to 5 mg.
Selective serotonin reuptake inhibitors (fluoxetine, fluvoxamine, paroxetine, sertraline): Weakness, hyperreflexia, incoordination may occur. Monitor patient.

Effects on lab test results

None reported.

Pharmacokinetics

Absorption: Complete with an absolute bioavailability of 45%.
Distribution: Widely distributed, 14% bound to plasma proteins.
Metabolism: Metabolized primarily by oxidative deamination by MAO-A.
Excretion: Excreted primarily in the urine (82%). *Half-life:* 2 to 3 hours.

Route	Onset	Peak	Duration
P.O.	Unknown	1-1.5 hr	Unknown

Pharmacodynamics

Chemical effect: Believed to exert its effect by acting as an agonist at serotonin receptors on extracerebral intracranial blood vessels, which results in vasoconstriction of the affected vessels, inhibition of neuropeptide release, and reduction of pain transmission in the trigeminal pathways.
Therapeutic effect: Relieves migraine pain.

Available forms

Tablets: 5 mg, 10 mg
Tablets (disintegrating): 5 mg, 10 mg

NURSING PROCESS

Assessment

- Use drug only after a definite diagnosis of migraine is established.
- Assess patient for history of coronary artery disease, hypertension, arrhythmias, or presence of risk factors for coronary artery disease.
- Perform baseline and periodic CV evaluation in patients who develop risk factors for coronary artery disease during treatment.
- Monitor renal and liver function tests before starting drug therapy, and report abnormalities.
- Evaluate patient's and family's knowledge of drug therapy.

Nursing diagnoses

- Acute pain related to presence of migraine headache
- Risk for activity intolerance related to adverse drug reactions
- Deficient knowledge related to drug therapy

Planning and implementation

- Don't give to patients with hemiplegic migraine, basilar migraine, or cluster headaches.

ALERT: Don't give drug within 24 hours of an ergot-containing drug or 5-HT$_1$ agonist or within 2 weeks of an MAO inhibitor.

- For patients with cardiac risk factors who have had a satisfactory cardiac evaluation, give first dose while monitoring ECG and have emergency equipment readily available.
- Withhold drug and notify prescriber if patient develops palpitations or neck, throat, or jaw pain, pressure, or heaviness.

• Safety of treating, on average, more than four headaches in a 30-day period hasn't been established.
• Drug contains phenylalanine.

Patient teaching
• Inform patient that drug doesn't prevent headache.
• For Maxalt-MLT, tell patient to remove blister pack from sachet and to remove drug from blister pack immediately before use. Tell him not to pop tablet out of blister pack but to carefully peel pack away with dry hands, place tablet on tongue, and let it dissolve. Tablet is then swallowed with saliva. No water is needed or recommended. Tell patient that dissolving tablet doesn't provide more rapid headache relief.
• Advise patient that if headache returns after first dose, a second dose may be taken with medical approval at least 2 hours after the first dose. Don't take more than 30 mg in a 24-hour period.
• Tell patient that food may delay onset of drug action.
• Advise patient to notify prescriber if pregnancy occurs or is suspected.

☑ Evaluation
• Patient has relief from migraine headache.
• Patient maintains baseline activity level.
• Patient and family state understanding of drug therapy.

rocuronium bromide
(roh-kyoo-ROH-nee-um BROH-mighd)
Zemuron

Pharmacologic class: nondepolarizing neuromuscular blocker
Therapeutic class: skeletal muscle relaxant
Pregnancy risk category: C

Indications and dosages
▶ **Adjunct to general anesthesia, to facilitate endotracheal intubation, and to provide skeletal muscle relaxation during surgery or mechanical ventilation.** Dosage depends on anesthetic used, individual needs, and response. Dosages are representative and must be adjusted.
Adults and children age 3 months or older: Initially, 0.6 mg/kg (adults, up to 1.2 mg/kg) I.V. bolus. In most patients, perform tracheal intubation within 2 minutes; muscle paralysis should last about 31 minutes. A maintenance dosage of 0.1 mg/kg should provide additional 12 minutes of muscle relaxation, 0.15 mg/kg will add 17 minutes, and 0.2 mg/kg will add 24 minutes to duration of effect.

Contraindications and precautions
• Contraindicated in patients hypersensitive to bromides.
• Use cautiously in patients with hepatic disease, severe obesity, bronchogenic carcinoma, electrolyte disturbances, neuromuscular disease, and altered circulation time caused by CV disease or edema.
Lifespan: In pregnant women, use cautiously. In breast-feeding women, safety of drug hasn't been established. In geriatric patients, use cautiously due to altered circulation time caused by advanced age.

Adverse reactions
CV: tachycardia, abnormal ECG, ***arrhythmias,*** transient hypotension, hypertension.
GI: nausea, vomiting.
Respiratory: hiccups, asthma, ***respiratory insufficiency, apnea.***
Skin: rash, edema, pruritus.

Interactions
Drug-drug. *Aminoglycoside antibiotics (including amikacin, gentamicin, kanamycin, neomycin, streptomycin), anticonvulsants, clindamycin, general anesthetics (such as enflurane, halothane, isoflurane), opioid analgesics, polymyxin antibiotics (colistin, polymyxin B sulfate), quinidine, succinylcholine, tetracyclines:* Potentiates neuromuscular blockade, leading to increased skeletal muscle relaxation and potentiation of effect. Use cautiously during surgical and postoperative periods.

Effects on lab test results
None reported.

Pharmacokinetics
Absorption: Administered I.V.
Distribution: About 30% bound to human plasma proteins.

Metabolism: Unknown, although hepatic clearance may be significant.
Excretion: About 33% excreted in urine.

Route	Onset	Peak	Duration
I.V.	≤ 1 min	≤ 2 min	Dose-dependent

Pharmacodynamics

Chemical effect: Prevents acetylcholine from binding to receptors on motor end plate, thus blocking depolarization.
Therapeutic effect: Relaxes skeletal muscles.

Available forms

Injection: 10 mg/ml

NURSING PROCESS

Assessment

- Assess patient's condition before therapy and regularly thereafter.
- Be alert for adverse reactions and drug interactions.
- Monitor patients with liver disease; they may need higher doses to achieve adequate muscle relaxation and may exhibit prolonged effects from drug.
- Monitor respirations closely until patient is fully recovered from neuromuscular blockade, as evidenced by tests of muscle strength (hand grip, head lift, and ability to cough).
- Evaluate patient's and family's knowledge of drug therapy.

Nursing diagnoses

- Ineffective health maintenance related to underlying condition
- Ineffective breathing pattern related to drug's effect on respiratory muscles
- Deficient knowledge related to drug therapy

Planning and implementation

- Drug should be used only by personnel skilled in airway management.
- Administer sedatives or general anesthetics before neuromuscular blockers because neuromuscular blockers don't obtund consciousness or alter pain perception.
- Give analgesics for pain.
- Keep airway clear. Have emergency respiratory support equipment (endotracheal equipment, ventilator, oxygen, atropine, edrophonium, epinephrine, and neostigmine) on hand.
- Give drug by rapid I.V. injection or continuous I.V. infusion. Infusion rates are highly individualized but range from 0.004 to 0.16 mg/kg/minute. Compatible solutions include D_5W, normal saline solution for injection, dextrose 5% in normal saline solution for injection, sterile water for injection, and lactated Ringer's injection.
- Store reconstituted solution in refrigerator. Discard after 24 hours.
- Nerve stimulator and train-of-four monitoring are recommended to confirm antagonism of neuromuscular blockade and recovery of muscle strength. Before attempting pharmacologic reversal with neostigmine, some evidence of spontaneous recovery should be evident.
- Prior administration of succinylcholine may enhance neuromuscular blocking effect and duration of action.

Patient teaching

- Explain all events and happenings to patient because he can still hear.
- Reassure patient that he is being monitored and that muscle use will return when drug has worn off.

Evaluation

- Patient has positive response to drug therapy.
- Patient maintains adequate breathing pattern with mechanical assistance throughout therapy.
- Patient and family state understanding of drug therapy.

rofecoxib
(roh-feh-COKS-ib)
Vioxx

Pharmacologic class: cyclooxygenase-2 (COX-2) inhibitor
Therapeutic class: nonnarcotic analgesic, anti-inflammatory
Pregnancy risk category: C

Indications and dosages

▶ **Relief of signs and symptoms of osteoarthritis.** *Adults:* Initially, 12.5 mg P.O. once daily, increase as needed to maximum of 25 mg P.O. once daily.

▶ **Rheumatoid arthritis.** *Adults:* 25 mg P.O. once daily. The maximum recommended daily dose is 25 mg.
▶ **Management of acute pain and treatment of primary dysmenorrhea.** *Adults:* 50 mg P.O. once daily as needed for up to 5 days. Chronic use of 50 mg daily is not recommended.

Contraindications and precautions

- Contraindicated in patients hypersensitive to rofecoxib or any of its components and in patients who have experienced asthma, urticaria, or allergic-type reactions after taking aspirin or other NSAIDs.
- Drug should be avoided in patients with advanced kidney disease or moderate or severe hepatic insufficiency.
- Use cautiously in patients with asthma, renal disease, liver dysfunction, or abnormal liver function tests. Also use cautiously in patients with a history of ulcer disease or GI bleeding. Use cautiously when rofecoxib is used in patients with a medical history of ischemic heart disease. Because of its lack of platelet effects, rofecoxib is not a substitute for aspirin for cardiovascular prophylaxis. Therefore, in patients taking rofecoxib, antiplatelet therapies should not be discontinued. A recent study concluded that patients taking Vioxx had more than twice as many MIs, CVAs, and other cardiac events as patients taking naproxen.
- Use cautiously in patients being treated with oral corticosteroids or anticoagulants, patients with a history of smoking or alcoholism, and debilitated patients because of the increased risk of GI bleeding.
- Use cautiously in patients with considerable dehydration. Rehydration is recommended before therapy begins.
- Use cautiously and start therapy at the lowest recommended dosage in patients with fluid retention, hypertension, or heart failure.

Lifespan: In pregnant women, drug should be avoided because it may cause the ductus arteriosus to close prematurely. Report prenatal exposure to the Pregnancy Registry at 1-800-986-8999. In geriatric patients, use cautiously because of the increased risk of GI bleeding

Adverse reactions

CNS: headache, asthenia, fatigue, dizziness, ***aseptic meningitis.***
CV: hypertension, leg edema, ***thromboembolic events,*** fluid retention.
EENT: sinusitis.
GI: diarrhea, dyspepsia, epigastric discomfort, heartburn, nausea, abdominal pain.
GU: urinary tract infection.
Metabolic: hyponatremia.
Musculoskeletal: back pain.
Respiratory: bronchitis, upper respiratory tract infection, ***pulmonary edema.***
Other: flu-like syndrome.

Interactions

Drug-drug. *ACE inhibitors:* Decreases antihypertensive effects of ACE inhibitors. Monitor patient's blood pressure closely.
Aspirin: Increases rate of GI ulceration and other complications. Don't use together, if possible. If used together, monitor patient closely for GI bleeding.
Furosemide, thiazide diuretics: May reduce efficacy of these drugs. Monitor patient closely.
Lithium: Increases plasma lithium levels and decreases lithium clearance. Monitor patient closely for lithium toxicity.
Methotrexate: Increases plasma methotrexate levels. Monitor patient closely for toxic reaction to methotrexate.
Rifampin: Decreases rofecoxib levels by about 50%. Start therapy with a higher dosage of rofecoxib.
Theophylline: Increases theophylline concentrations. Monitor levels closely.
Warfarin: Increases effects of warfarin. Monitor INR frequently for a few days after therapy starts or dosage changes.
Drug-lifestyle. *Chronic alcohol use, smoking:* Increases risk of GI bleeding. Discourage drinking and smoking, especially during drug therapy; assess patient for bleeding.

Effects on lab test results

- May decrease sodium level.

Pharmacokinetics

Absorption: Well absorbed, with a mean bioavailability of 93%. Serum levels peak in 2 to 3 hours (median); range is 2 to 9 hours.
Distribution: About 87% of drug binds to proteins.
Metabolism: Metabolized in liver to inactive metabolites.

Excretion: Eliminated mainly through hepatic metabolism. Less than 1% of drug is eliminated via the kidneys as unchanged drug. *Half-life:* About 17 hours.

Route	Onset	Peak	Duration
P.O.	Unknown	2-3 hr	Unknown

Pharmacodynamics

Chemical effect: Unknown; anti-inflammatory, analgesic, and antipyretic effects may stem from inhibited prostaglandin synthesis caused by inhibited COX-2 isoenzyme. At therapeutic serum levels, rofecoxib doesn't inhibit cyclooxygenase-1 (COX-1) isoenzyme.
Therapeutic effect: Relieves inflammation and pain.

Available forms

Oral suspension: 12.5 mg/5 ml, 25 mg/5 ml
Tablets: 12.5 mg, 25 mg

NURSING PROCESS

Assessment

- Obtain history of patient's underlying condition before therapy, and reassess regularly thereafter.

ALERT: Ask patient if he has allergies to aspirin or other NSAIDs. Ask patient if he has asthma. Don't give drug if patient has had severe, potentially fatal bronchospasm after taking aspirin or other NSAIDs.

- Assess patient for dehydration.
- Monitor kidney function closely in patients with renal disease. Drug isn't recommended for patients with advanced kidney disease.
- Monitor patient closely for GI bleeding, which can occur any time, with or without warning.
- Monitor patient for signs and symptoms of liver toxicity. Discontinue drug if signs and symptoms consistent with liver disease develop.
- Check hemoglobin level and hematocrit in patient undergoing long-term treatment if he experiences signs or symptoms of anemia or blood loss.
- Evaluate patient's and family's knowledge about drug therapy.

Nursing diagnoses

- Acute pain related to underlying condition
- Risk for injury related to drug-induced adverse reactions
- Deficient knowledge related to drug therapy

Planning and implementation

- Shake oral suspension well before giving it. Patient may take drug with food to decrease GI upset.

ALERT: If patient has fluid retention, hypertension, or heart failure, use cautiously and start therapy at lowest recommended dosage. Monitor blood pressure and check patient for fluid retention or worsening heart failure.

- In patients older than age 65, drug therapy should start at lowest recommended dosage.
- NSAIDs may cause serious GI toxicity. To minimize the risk of an adverse GI event, use lowest effective rofecoxib dosage for shortest possible duration. The risk of GI toxicity with rofecoxib 50 mg once daily is significantly less than with naproxen 500 mg twice daily.
- If patient is dehydrated, rehydrate him before therapy begins.

Patient teaching

- Tell patient that drug may be taken without regard to food, although taking it with food may decrease GI upset.
- Tell patient that the most common adverse effects are dyspepsia, epigastric discomfort, heartburn, and nausea. Taking drug with food may help minimize these effects.
- Tell patient to avoid aspirin, products that contain aspirin, and OTC anti-inflammatories such as ibuprofen (Advil) unless his prescriber has instructed him otherwise.
- Warn patient that he may experience GI bleeding. Signs and symptoms include bloody vomitus, blood in urine and stool, and black, tarry stools. Advise patient to seek medical advice if he experiences any of these signs or symptoms.
- Advise patient to report to prescriber rash, unexplained weight gain, or edema.
- Tell patient that all NSAIDs, including rofecoxib, may adversely affect the liver. Explain that signs and symptoms of liver toxicity include nausea, fatigue, lethargy, itching, jaundice, right upper quadrant tenderness, and flu-like symptoms. Advise patient to stop therapy and seek immediate medical advice if he experiences any of these signs or symptoms.

• Instruct patient to inform her prescriber if she becomes pregnant or plans to become pregnant while taking drug.

Evaluation

• Patient is free from pain.
• Patient sustains no injury from drug-induced adverse reactions.
• Patient and family state understanding of drug therapy.

ropinirole hydrochloride

(roh-PIN-er-ohl high-droh-KLOR-ighd)
Requip

Pharmacologic class: nonergoline dopamine agonist
Therapeutic class: antiparkinsonian
Pregnancy risk category: C

Indications and dosages

▶**Idiopathic Parkinson's disease.** *Adults:* Initially, 0.25 mg P.O. t.i.d. Dosages can be adjusted weekly. After week 4, dosage may be increased by 1.5 mg daily on a weekly basis up to dosage of 9 mg daily, and then increase weekly by up to 3 mg daily to maximum daily dose of 24 mg.

Contraindications and precautions

• Contraindicated in patients hypersensitive to drug.
• Use cautiously in patients with severe hepatic or renal impairment.
Lifespan: In patients older than age 65, clearance is reduced; dosage is individually adjusted to response.

Adverse reactions

Early Parkinson's disease (without levodopa)
CNS: asthenia, *fatigue,* malaise, hallucinations, *dizziness,* aggravated Parkinson's disease, *syncope, somnolence,* headache, confusion, hyperkinesia, hypesthesia, vertigo, amnesia, impaired concentration.
CV: hypotension, orthostatic symptoms, flushing, hypertension, edema, chest pain, extrasystoles, atrial fibrillation, palpitations, tachycardia, peripheral ischemia.
EENT: pharyngitis, abnormal vision, eye abnormality, xerophthalmia, rhinitis, sinusitis.
GI: dry mouth, *nausea, vomiting, dyspepsia,* flatulence, abdominal pain, anorexia, constipation, abdominal pain.
GU: urinary tract infection, impotence (male).
Respiratory: bronchitis, dyspnea.
Skin: increased sweating.
Other: *viral infection,* pain, yawning.
Advanced Parkinson's disease (with levodopa)
CNS: *dizziness,* aggravated parkinsonism, *somnolence, headache,* insomnia, *hallucinations,* abnormal dreaming, confusion, tremor, anxiety, nervousness, amnesia, paresthesia, syncope.
CV: hypotension.
EENT: diplopia, increased saliva.
GI: *nausea,* abdominal pain, dry mouth, vomiting, constipation, diarrhea, dysphagia, flatulence.
GU: urinary tract infection, pyuria, urinary incontinence.
Hematologic: anemia.
Metabolic: weight loss.
Musculoskeletal: *dyskinesia,* hypokinesia, paresis, arthralgia, arthritis.
Respiratory: upper respiratory infection, dyspnea.
Skin: increased sweating.
Other: injury, *falls,* viral infection, pain.

Interactions

Drug-drug. *CNS depressants:* Increases CNS effects. Use together cautiously.
Dopamine antagonists (butyrophenones, metoclopramide, phenothiazines, thioxanthenes): May decrease ropinirole effectiveness. Monitor patient closely.
Estrogens: Reduces ropinirole clearance. Adjust ropinirole dosage as directed if estrogens are started or stopped during ropinirole therapy.
Inhibitors or substrates of cytochrome P-450 1A2 (cimetidine, ciprofloxacin, erythromycin, fluvoxamine, diltiazem, tacrine): Alters ropinirole clearance. Adjust ropinirole dosage if drugs are started or stopped during ropinirole therapy.
Drug-lifestyle. *Alcohol use:* Increases sedative effects. Discourage using together.
Smoking: May increase drug clearance. Urge patient to stop smoking, especially during drug therapy.

Effects on lab test results

- May increase BUN and alkaline phosphatase levels.
- May decrease hemoglobin and hematocrit.

Pharmacokinetics

Absorption: Rapid, with an absolute bioavailability of 55%.
Distribution: Widely distributed, with about 40% bound to plasma protein.
Metabolism: Extensively metabolized by the liver to inactive metabolites.
Excretion: Less than 10% excreted unchanged in urine. *Half-life:* 6 hours.

Route	Onset	Peak	Duration
P.O.	Unknown	1-2 hr	6 hr

Pharmacodynamics

Chemical effect: Unknown. A nonergoline dopamine agonist thought to stimulate postsynaptic dopamine D_2 receptors in the caudate-putamen in the brain.
Therapeutic effect: Improves physical mobility in patients with parkinsonism.

Available forms

Tablets: 0.25 mg, 0.5 mg, 1 mg, 2 mg, 5 mg

NURSING PROCESS

Assessment

- Assess patient before and during therapy to evaluate effectiveness.
- Monitor patient carefully for orthostatic hypotension, especially during dose escalation.
- Assess patient for adequate nutritional intake.
- Evaluate patient's and family's knowledge of drug therapy.

Nursing diagnoses

- Impaired physical mobility related to underlying Parkinson's disease
- Disturbed thought processes related to drug-induced CNS adverse reactions
- Deficient knowledge related to drug therapy

Planing and implementation

- Give drug with food to decrease nausea.
- Drug can potentiate dopaminergic adverse effects of levodopa and may cause or worsen dyskinesia. Levodopa dosage may need to be decreased.
- Don't abruptly stop drug. Withdraw gradually over 7 days to avoid hyperpyrexia and confusion.

Patient teaching

- Tell patient to take drug with food if nausea occurs.
- Explain that hallucinations may occur, particularly in geriatric patients.
- To minimize effects of orthostatic hypotension, instruct patient not to rise rapidly after sitting or lying down, especially when therapy starts or dosage changes.
- Advise patient to avoid hazardous activities until CNS effects of drug are known.
- Tell patient to avoid alcohol during drug therapy.
- Tell woman to notify prescriber if pregnancy is suspected or is planned; also tell her to inform prescriber if she is breast-feeding.

Evaluation

- Patient has improved mobility and reduced muscle rigidity and tremor.
- Patient remains mentally alert.
- Patient and family state understanding of drug therapy.

rosiglitazone maleate

(roh-sih-GLIH-tah-zohn MAL-ee-ayt)
Avandia

Pharmacologic class: thiazolidinedione
Therapeutic class: antidiabetic
Pregnancy risk category: C

Indications and dosages

▶ **Adjunct to diet and exercise (as monotherapy) to improve glycemic control in patients with type 2 diabetes mellitus, or (as combination therapy) with sulfonylurea or metformin when diet, exercise, and a single agent do not result in adequate glycemic control.** *Adults:* Initially, 4 mg P.O. daily in the morning or in divided doses b.i.d. in the morning and evening. Dosage may be increased to 8 mg P.O. daily or in divided doses b.i.d. if fasting plasma glucose level doesn't improve after 12 weeks of treatment.

Contraindications and precautions

- Contraindicated in patients hypersensitive to rosiglitazone or any of its components and in patients with New York Heart Association Class III and IV cardiac status unless expected benefits outweigh risks. Also contraindicated in patients who developed jaundice while taking troglitazone and in patients with active liver disease, increased baseline liver enzyme levels (ALT level is greater than 2½ times the upper limit of normal), type 1 diabetes, or diabetic ketoacidosis.
- Combination therapy with metformin and rosiglitazone is contraindicated in patients with renal impairment. Rosiglitazone can be used as monotherapy in patients with renal impairment.
- Use cautiously in patients with edema or heart failure.

Lifespan: No contraindications or precautions reported.

Adverse reactions

CNS: headache, fatigue.
CV: edema, ***heart failure,*** peripheral edema.
EENT: sinusitis.
GI: diarrhea.
Hematologic: anemia.
Metabolic: hyperglycemia.
Musculoskeletal: back pain.
Respiratory: upper respiratory tract infection.
Other: injury.

Interactions

Drug-herb. *Aloe, bitter melon, bilberry leaf, burdock, dandelion, fenugreek, garlic, ginseng:* May improve glucose control. Patient may need reduced antidiabetic dosage. Discourage using together.

Effects on lab test results

- May increase liver enzyme and glucose levels.
- May decrease hemoglobin and hematocrit.

Pharmacokinetics

Absorption: Plasma levels peak about 1 hour after a dose. Absolute bioavailability is 99%.
Distribution: About 99.8% of rosiglitazone binds to plasma proteins, primarily albumin.
Metabolism: Extensively metabolized, with no unchanged drug excreted in the urine. Primarily metabolized through N-demethylation and hydroxylation.
Excretion: After oral administration, about 64% and 23% of the dose is eliminated in urine and feces, respectively. *Half-life:* 3 to 4 hours.

Route	Onset	Peak	Duration
P.O.	Unknown	1 hr	Unknown

Pharmacodynamics

Chemical effect: Lowers glucose level by improving insulin sensitivity. Highly selective and potent agonist for receptors in key target areas for insulin action, such as adipose tissue, skeletal muscle, and liver.
Therapeutic effect: Lowers glucose level.

Available forms

Tablets: 2 mg, 4 mg, 8 mg

NURSING PROCESS

Assessment

- Obtain history of patient's underlying condition before therapy, and reassess regularly thereafter.
- Check liver enzyme levels before therapy starts. Don't use drug in patients with increased baseline liver enzyme levels. In patients with normal baseline liver enzyme levels, these levels should be monitored every 2 months for the first 12 months of treatment and periodically afterward. If ALT level is elevated during treatment, recheck levels as soon as possible. Notify prescriber because drug should be stopped if levels remain elevated.
- Monitor glucose level regularly and glycosylated hemoglobin level periodically to determine therapeutic response to drug.
- If patient has heart failure, watch for increased edema during rosiglitazone therapy.
- Evaluate patient's and family's knowledge about drug therapy.

Nursing diagnoses

- Ineffective health maintenance related to hyperglycemia
- Risk for injury related to drug-induced hypoglycemia
- Deficient knowledge related to drug therapy

Planning and implementation

- Before starting rosiglitazone, patient should be treated for other causes of poor glycemic control, such as infection.
- Management of type 2 diabetes should include diet control. Because calorie restriction, weight loss, and exercise help improve insulin sensitivity and help make drug therapy effective, these measures are essential to proper diabetes treatment.
- For patients inadequately controlled with a maximum dose of a sulfonylurea or metformin, rosiglitazone should be added to, rather than substituted for, a sulfonylurea or metformin.
- Rosiglitazone alone or with insulin can cause fluid retention that may lead to or exacerbate heart failure. Observe patients for these signs or symptoms of heart failure. Discontinue drug if any deterioration in cardiac status occurs.
- Hemoglobin level and hematocrit may decrease while patient is receiving this drug, usually during the first 4 to 8 weeks of therapy. Total cholesterol, low-density lipoprotein, and high-density lipoprotein levels may increase, and free fatty acid levels may decrease.
- Because ovulation may resume in premenopausal, anovulatory woman with insulin resistance, contraceptive measures may need to be considered.

Patient teaching

- Advise patient that rosiglitazone can be taken with or without food.
- Notify patient that blood will be tested to check liver function before therapy starts, every 2 months for the first 12 months, and periodically thereafter.
- Tell patient to immediately report unexplained signs and symptoms—such as nausea, vomiting, abdominal pain, fatigue, anorexia, or dark urine—because they may indicate liver problems.
- Warn patient to contact his prescriber if he has signs or symptoms of heart failure, such as unusually rapid increase in weight or edema or shortness of breath.
- Inform premenopausal, anovulatory woman with insulin resistance that ovulation may resume and that she may want to consider contraceptive measures.
- Advise patient that diabetes management should include diet control. Because calorie restriction, weight loss, and exercise help improve insulin sensitivity and help make drug therapy effective, these measures are essential to proper diabetes treatment.

Evaluation

- Patient's glucose level is normal with drug therapy.
- Patient doesn't experience hypoglycemia.
- Patient and family state understanding of drug therapy.

S

salmeterol xinafoate

(sal-MEE-ter-ohl zee-neh-FOH-ayt)
Serevent, Serevent Diskus

Pharmacologic class: selective $beta_2$-adrenergic agonist
Therapeutic class: bronchodilator
Pregnancy risk category: C

Indications and dosages

▶ Long-term maintenance treatment of asthma; prevention of bronchospasm in patients with nocturnal asthma or reversible obstructive airway disease who need regular treatment with short-acting beta agonists. ***Inhalation aerosol.*** *Adults and children older than age 12:* 2 inhalations b.i.d., in the morning and in the evening. Drug shouldn't be used to treat acute symptoms.
Inhalation powder. *Adults and children older than age 4:* 1 inhalation q 12 hours, in the morning and in the evening.

▶ Prevention of exercise-induced bronchospasm. ***Inhalation aerosol.*** *Adults and children age 12 and older:* 2 inhalations at least 30 to 60 minutes before exercise.
Inhalation powder. *Adults and children age 4 and older:* 1 inhalation at least 30 minutes before exercise.

▶ Maintenance treatment of bronchospasm with COPD (including emphysema and chronic bronchitis). *Adults:* ***Inhalation aerosol.*** 2 inhalations (42 mcg) q 12 hours, in the morning and in the evening. ***Inhalation***

powder. 1 inhalation (50 mcg) q 12 hours, in the morning and in the evening.

Contraindications and precautions

- Contraindicated in patients hypersensitive to drug or its components.
- Use cautiously in patients who are unusually responsive to sympathomimetics and patients with coronary insufficiency, arrhythmias, hypertension or other CV disorders, thyrotoxicosis, or seizure disorders.

Lifespan: In pregnant women, use cautiously. In breast-feeding women and in children age 12 and younger, safety of inhalation aerosol hasn't been established. In children younger than age 4, safety of inhalation powder hasn't been established.

Adverse reactions

CNS: *headache,* sinus headache, tremor, nervousness, dizziness.
CV: tachycardia, palpitations, ***ventricular arrhythmias.***
EENT: *upper respiratory tract infection, nasopharyngitis,* nasal cavity or sinus disorder.
GI: nausea, vomiting, diarrhea, heartburn.
Musculoskeletal: joint and back pain, myalgia.
Respiratory: cough, lower respiratory tract infection, ***bronchospasm.***
Other: ***hypersensitivity reactions, anaphylaxis.***

Interactions

Drug-drug. *Beta agonists, methyl-xanthines, theophylline:* Possible adverse cardiac effects with excessive use. Monitor patient closely.
MAO inhibitors: Risk of severe adverse CV effects. Avoid use within 14 days of MAO therapy.
Tricyclic antidepressants: Risk of moderate to severe adverse CV effects. Use with extreme caution.

Effects on lab test results

None reported.

Pharmacokinetics

Absorption: Low or undetectable because of low therapeutic dose.
Distribution: Local to lungs; 94% to 99% bound to plasma proteins.
Metabolism: Extensively metabolized by hydroxylation.
Excretion: Excreted primarily in feces.

Route	Onset	Peak	Duration
Inhalation	10-20 min	3 hr	12 hr

Pharmacodynamics

Chemical effect: Not clearly defined; selectively activates $beta_2$-adrenergic receptors, which results in bronchodilation. Drug also blocks release of allergic mediators from mast cells lining the respiratory tract.
Therapeutic effect: Improves breathing ability.

Available forms

Inhalation aerosol: 21 mcg per metered spray
Inhalation powder: 50 mcg/blister

NURSING PROCESS

Assessment

- Assess patient's respiratory condition before therapy and regularly thereafter.
- Assess peak flow readings before starting treatment and periodically thereafter.
- Be alert for adverse reactions and drug interactions.
- Evaluate patient's and family's knowledge of drug therapy.

Nursing diagnoses

- Ineffective breathing pattern related to respiratory condition
- Acute pain related to drug-induced headache
- Deficient knowledge related to drug therapy

Planning and implementation

- Don't give drug for acute bronchospasm.
- Report insufficient relief or worsening condition.
- Obtain order for mild analgesic if drug-induced headache occurs.

ALERT: Don't confuse Serevent with Serentil.

Patient teaching

- Tell patient to take drug at about 12-hour intervals and to take even if he is feeling better.
- Tell patient to prevent exercise-induced bronchospasm by taking drug 30 to 60 minutes before exercise.

ALERT: Instruct patient not to take drug to treat acute bronchospasm. Patient must be provided with short-acting beta agonist (such as albuterol) to treat such exacerbations.

- Tell patient to contact prescriber if short-acting agonist no longer provides sufficient relief or if he needs more than 4 inhalations daily. This may be a sign that asthma symptoms are worsening. Tell patient not to increase dosage of drug.
- If patient is taking inhaled corticosteroid, he should continue to use it. Warn him not to take other drugs without prescriber's consent.

Evaluation

- Patient exhibits normal breathing pattern.
- Patient states that drug-induced headache is relieved after analgesic administration.
- Patient and family state understanding of drug therapy.

saquinavir
(sah-KWIN-ah-veer)
Fortovase

saquinavir mesylate
Invirase

Pharmacologic class: HIV-1 and HIV-2 protease inhibitor
Therapeutic class: antiviral
Pregnancy risk category: B

Indications and dosages

▶ **Adjunct treatment of advanced HIV infection in selected patients.** *Adults:* 600-mg capsule (Invirase) or 1,200 mg (Fortovase) P.O. t.i.d. within 2 hours after full meal and with a nucleoside analogue, such as zalcitabine (0.75 mg P.O. t.i.d.) or zidovudine (200 mg P.O. t.i.d.).

Contraindications and precautions

- Contraindicated in patients hypersensitive to drug or components of capsule. Also contraindicated in patients taking triazolam, midazolam, ergot derivatives, or cisapride.

Lifespan: In pregnant or breast-feeding women and in children younger than age 16, safety of drug hasn't been established.

Adverse reactions

CNS: asthenia, paresthesia, headache, dizziness.
CV: chest pain.
GI: diarrhea, ulcerated buccal mucosa, abdominal pain, nausea, ***pancreatitis.***
Hematologic: ***pancytopenia, thrombocytopenia.***
Musculoskeletal: musculoskeletal pain.
Respiratory: bronchitis, cough.
Skin: rash.

Interactions

Drug-drug. *Amprenavir:* Decreases level of amprenavir. Use together cautiously.
Carbamazepine, phenobarbital, phenytoin: May decrease saquinavir level. Avoid using together.
Delavirdine: Increases saquinavir level. Use cautiously; monitor hepatic enzymes. Decrease dose when used together.
Dexamethasone: Decreases saquinavir level. Avoid using together.
Efavirenz: Decreases levels of both drugs. Use together isn't recommended.
HMG-CoA reductase inhibitors: Increases levels of these drugs, thus increasing risk for myopathy, including rhabdomyolysis. Avoid using together.
Indinavir, lopinavir/ritonavir combination, nelfinavir, ritonavir: Increases level of saquinavir. Use together cautiously.
Ketoconazole: Use together may increase saquinavir level. No dosage adjustment needed.
Macrolide antibiotics such as clarithromycin: Increases levels of both drugs. Use together cautiously.
Nevirapine: Decreases saquinavir level. Monitor patient.
Rifabutin, rifampin: Reduces the steady-state level of saquinavir. Use rifabutin and saquinavir together cautiously. Don't use with rifampin.
Sildenafil: Increases peak level and AUC of sildenafil. Reduce initial dose of sildenafil to 25 mg when given with saquinavir.
Triazolam, midazolam, ergot derivatives, cisapride: Potential for serious, life threatening effects caused by increased levels of these drugs. Don't use together.
Drug-herb. *Garlic:* Decreases level of saquinavir. Discourage use of garlic supplements.

St. John's wort: May substantially reduce level of the drug and cause loss of therapeutic effects. Discourage use together.
Drug-food. *Any food:* Increases drug absorption. Advise patient to take drug with food.
Grapefruit juice: Increases drug level. Take with liquid other than grapefruit juice.

Effects on lab test results

- May increase liver enzyme levels.
- May decrease WBC, RBC, and platelet counts.

Pharmacokinetics

Absorption: Poor.
Distribution: More than 98% bound to plasma proteins.
Metabolism: Rapid.
Excretion: Excreted mainly in feces. *Half-life:* 1 to 2 hours.

Route	Onset	Peak	Duration
P.O.	Unknown	Unknown	Unknown

Pharmacodynamics

Chemical effect: Inhibits activity of HIV protease and prevents cleavage of HIV polyproteins, which are essential for HIV maturation.
Therapeutic effect: Hinders HIV activity.

Available forms

saquinavir
Capsules (soft gelatin): 200 mg
saquinavir mesylate
Capsules (hard gelatin): 200 mg

NURSING PROCESS

Assessment

- Obtain history of patient's HIV infection.
- Monitor CBC and platelet counts and electrolyte, uric acid, liver enzyme, and bilirubin levels before therapy and at appropriate intervals during therapy.
- Be alert for adverse reactions and interactions, including those caused by adjunct therapy (zidovudine or zalcitabine).
- Monitor patient's hydration status if adverse GI reactions occur.
- Evaluate patient's and family's knowledge of drug therapy.

Nursing diagnoses

- Infection related to presence of HIV
- Risk for deficient fluid volume related to adverse GI reactions
- Deficient knowledge related to drug therapy

Planning and implementation

ALERT: Don't confuse the two forms of this drug because dosages are different.

- If severe toxicity occurs during treatment, drug should be discontinued until cause is identified or toxicity resolves. Therapy may resume with no dosage modifications.
- Notify prescriber of adverse reactions, and obtain an order for a mild analgesic, antiemetic, or antidiarrheal, if needed.

Patient teaching

- Tell patient to take drug within 2 hours after a full meal.
- Urge patient to notify prescriber of adverse reactions.
- Inform patient that drug is usually given with other AIDS-related antiviral drugs.
- Tell patient that a change from Invirase to Fortovase capsules should be made only under a prescriber's supervision.

ALERT: Advise patient receiving sildenafil that there is an increased risk of sildenafil-associated adverse events including hypotension, visual changes, and priapism; any symptoms should be promptly reported. Tell patient not to exceed 25 mg of sildenafil in a 48-hour period.

Evaluation

- Patient responds well to therapy.
- Patient maintains adequate hydration.
- Patient and family state understanding of drug therapy.

sargramostim (granulocyte macrophage colony-stimulating factor, GM-CSF)

(sar-GRAH-moh-stim)
Leukine

Pharmacologic class: biological response modifier

Therapeutic class: colony-stimulating factor
Pregnancy risk category: C

Indications and dosages

▶ **Acceleration of hematopoietic reconstitution after autologous bone marrow transplantation in patients with malignant lymphoma or acute lymphoblastic leukemia, or during autologous bone marrow transplantation in patients with Hodgkin's disease.** *Adults:* 250 mcg/m^2 daily for 21 consecutive days given as 2-hour I.V. infusion beginning 2 to 4 hours after bone marrow transplantation.

▶ **Bone marrow transplantation failure or engraftment delay.** *Adults:* 250 mcg/m^2 as 2-hour I.V. infusion daily for 14 days. Dose may be repeated after 7 days off therapy. If engraftment still hasn't occurred, a third course of 500 mcg/m^2 I.V. daily for 14 days may be tried after another 7 days off therapy.

▶ **Acute myelogenous leukemia.** *Adults:* 250 mcg/m^2 I.V. infusion over 4 hours daily. Start therapy about day 11 or 4 days after end of induction therapy.

Contraindications and precautions

• Contraindicated in patients hypersensitive to drug or its components or to yeast-derived products. Also contraindicated in patients with excessive leukemic myeloid blasts in bone marrow or peripheral blood.

• Use cautiously in patients with cardiac disease, hypoxia, fluid retention, pulmonary infiltrates, heart failure, or impaired kidney or liver function.

Lifespan: In pregnant or breast-feeding women, use cautiously. In children, safety of drug hasn't been established.

Adverse reactions

CNS: *malaise, CNS disorders, asthenia, fever.*
CV: *edema,* ***supraventricular arrhythmia,*** pericardial effusion.
EENT: *mucous membrane disorder.*
GI: *nausea, vomiting, diarrhea, anorexia,* ***hemorrhage,*** *GI disorder, stomatitis.*
GU: *urinary tract disorder,* abnormal kidney function.
Hematologic: *blood dyscrasias,* ***hemorrhage.***
Hepatic: ***liver damage.***
Respiratory: *dyspnea, lung disorders,* pleural effusion.
Skin: *alopecia, rash.*
Other: SEPSIS.

Interactions

Drug-drug. *Corticosteroids, lithium:* May potentiate myeloproliferative effects of sargramostim. Use together cautiously.

Effects on lab test results

• May increase BUN, creatinine, AST, ALT, and bilirubin levels.

Pharmacokinetics

Absorption: Administered I.V.
Distribution: Bound to specific receptors on target cells.
Metabolism: Unknown.
Excretion: Unknown. *Half-life:* About 2 hours.

Route	Onset	Peak	Duration
I.V.	≤ 30 min	2 hr	Unknown

Pharmacodynamics

Chemical effect: Glycoprotein manufactured by recombinant DNA technology in yeast expression system; differs from natural human GM-CSF. Drug induces cellular responses by binding to specific receptors on surfaces of target cells.
Therapeutic effect: Stimulates formation of granulocytes (neutrophils, eosinophils) and macrophages.

Available forms

Liquid: 500 mcg*
Powder for injection: 250 mcg

NURSING PROCESS

Assessment

• Assess patient's condition before therapy and regularly thereafter.

• Drug effect may be limited in patient who has received extensive radiotherapy to hematopoietic sites for treatment of primary disease in abdomen or chest or who has been exposed to multiple drugs (alkylating, anthracycline antibiotics, antimetabolites) before autologous bone marrow transplantation.

• Drug is effective in accelerating myeloid recovery in patients receiving bone marrow purged from monoclonal antibodies.

• Drug can act as growth factor for tumors, particularly myeloid cancers.
• Blood counts return to normal or baseline levels within 3 to 7 days after stopping treatment.
• Monitor CBC with differential, including examination for presence of blast cells, biweekly.
• Be alert for adverse reactions and drug interactions.
• Monitor patient's hydration status throughout drug therapy.
• Evaluate patient's and family's knowledge of drug therapy.

Nursing diagnoses

• Ineffective health maintenance related to underlying condition
• Risk for deficient fluid volume related to drug-induced adverse effects
• Deficient knowledge related to drug therapy

Planning and implementation

• Reconstitute drug with 1 ml of sterile water for injection. Direct stream of sterile water against side of vial and gently swirl contents to minimize foaming. Avoid excessive or vigorous agitation or shaking. Dilute in normal saline solution. If final level is below 10 mcg/ml, add human albumin at final level of 0.1% to saline solution before adding sargramostim to prevent adsorption to components of delivery system. For final level of 0.1% human albumin, add 1 mg human albumin per 1 ml saline solution. Give as soon as possible after mixing and no later than 6 hours after reconstituting.
• Discard unused portion. Vials are for single-dose use and contain no preservatives. Don't reenter vial.
ALERT: Don't add other drugs to infusion solution because no data exist on solution compatibility and stability.
• Notify prescriber and anticipate reducing dose by half or discontinuing drug temporarily if severe adverse reactions occur. Therapy may be resumed when reactions decrease. Transient rashes and local reactions at injection site may occur; serious allergic or anaphylactic reactions aren't common.
ALERT: Don't give drug within 24 hours of last dose of chemotherapy or within 12 hours of last dose of radiotherapy; rapidly dividing progenitor cells may be sensitive to these cytotoxic therapies and drug would be ineffective.
• Stimulation of marrow precursors may result in rapid rise of WBC count. If blast cells appear or increase to 10% or more of WBC count or if underlying disease progresses, therapy should be discontinued. If absolute neutrophil count is more than 20,000/mm^3 or if platelet count is more than 50,000/mm^3, drug is temporarily discontinued or dose is reduced by half.
• Refrigerate sterile powder, reconstituted solution, and diluted solution for injection. Don't freeze or shake.

Patient teaching

• Inform patient and family about need for therapy.
• Advise patient to report adverse reactions immediately.

Evaluation

• Patient exhibits positive response to sargramostim therapy.
• Patient maintains adequate hydration throughout therapy.
• Patient and family state understanding of drug therapy.

scopolamine (hyoscine)

(skoh-POL-uh-meen)
Scop ◇, Transderm Scōp, Transderm-V ♦

scopolamine butylbromide (hyoscine butylbromide)

Buscopan ♦ ◇

scopolamine hydrobromide (hyoscine hydrobromide)

Pharmacologic class: anticholinergic
Therapeutic class: antimuscarinic, antiemetic, antivertigo agent, antiparkinsonian
Pregnancy risk category: C

Indications and dosages

▶ **Spastic states.** *Adults:* 10 to 20 mg P.O. t.i.d. or q.i.d. Dosage adjusted, p.r.n. ***butylbromide.*** Or, 10 to 20 mg S.C., I.M., or I.V. t.i.d. or q.i.d.

▶ **Preoperatively to reduce secretions.** ***hydrobromide.*** *Adults:* 0.2 to 0.6 mg I.M. 30 to 60 minutes before induction of anesthesia.
Children ages 8 to 12: 300 mcg I.M. 45 minutes before induction of anesthesia.
Children ages 3 to 8: 200 mcg I.M. 45 minutes before induction of anesthesia.
Children ages 7 months to 3 years: 150 mcg I.M. 45 minutes before induction of anesthesia.
Infants ages 4 to 7 months: 100 mcg I.M. 45 minutes before induction of anesthesia.
▶ **Prevention of nausea and vomiting from motion sickness.** ***scopolamine.*** *Adults:* 1 Transderm Scōp patch (a circular flat unit) formulated to deliver 1 mg over 3 days (72 hours), applied to skin behind ear several hours before antiemetic is needed.
hydrobromide. *Adults:* 300 to 600 mcg S.C., I.M., or I.V. Or, 400 to 800 mcg P.O.
Children: 6 mcg/kg or 200 mcg/m² S.C., I.M., or I.V.

Contraindications and precautions

- Contraindicated in patients with angle-closure glaucoma, obstructive uropathy, obstructive disease of GI tract, asthma, chronic pulmonary disease, myasthenia gravis, paralytic ileus, intestinal atony, unstable CV status in acute hemorrhage, or toxic megacolon.
- Use cautiously in patients with autonomic neuropathy, hyperthyroidism, coronary artery disease, arrhythmias, heart failure, hypertension, hiatal hernia with reflux esophagitis, hepatic or renal disease, or ulcerative colitis; and in patients in hot or humid environments (drug-induced heatstroke is possible).

Lifespan: In pregnant women and children younger than age 6, use cautiously. Breast-feeding women should not use drug.

Adverse reactions

CNS: disorientation, restlessness, irritability, dizziness, drowsiness, headache, confusion, hallucinations, delirium, fever.
CV: palpitations, tachycardia, flushing, ***paradoxical bradycardia.***
EENT: dilated pupils, blurred vision, photophobia, increased intraocular pressure, difficulty swallowing.
GI: *constipation, dry mouth, nausea, vomiting, epigastric distress.*
GU: urinary hesitancy, urine retention.
Respiratory: bronchial plugging, ***depressed respirations.***
Skin: rash, dryness, contact dermatitis with transdermal patch.

Interactions

Drug-drug. *Centrally acting anticholinergics (antihistamines, phenothiazines, tricyclic antidepressants):* Increases risk of adverse CNS reactions. Monitor patient closely.
CNS depressants: Increases risk of CNS depression. Monitor patient closely.
Digoxin: Increases digoxin levels. Monitor patient for cardiac toxicity.
Drug-herb. *Jaborandi tree:* Effects of these drugs may be decreased. Discourage using together.
Pill-bearing spurge: Choline may decrease effect of scopolamine. Discourage using together.
Squaw vine: Tannic acid may decrease metabolic breakdown. Discourage using together.
Drug-lifestyle. *Alcohol use:* Increases risk of CNS depression. Discourage using together.

Effects on lab test results

None reported.

Pharmacokinetics

Absorption: Well absorbed percutaneously from behind ear with transdermal patch application. Well absorbed from GI tract when given P.O. or P.R. Absorbed rapidly when given I.M. or S.C.
Distribution: Distributed widely throughout body tissues; probably crosses blood-brain barrier.
Metabolism: Thought to be metabolized completely in liver.
Excretion: May be excreted in urine as metabolites. *Half-life:* 8 hours.

Route	Onset	Peak	Duration
P.O.	30-60 min	Unknown	4-6 hr
I.V., I.M., S.C.	30 min	Unknown	4 hr
P.R.	Unknown	Unknown	Unknown
Transdermal	Unknown	Unknown	≤ 72 hr

Pharmacodynamics

Chemical effect: Inhibits muscarinic actions of acetylcholine on autonomic effectors innervated by postganglionic cholinergic neurons.

Scopolamine also may affect neural pathways originating in labyrinth (inner ear) to inhibit nausea and vomiting.
Therapeutic effect: Relieves spasticity, nausea, and vomiting; reduces secretions; and blocks cardiac vagal reflexes.

Available forms

scopolamine
Transdermal patch: 1.5 mg
scopolamine butylbromide
Capsules: 0.25 mg
Suppositories: 10 mg ♦
Tablets: 10 mg ♦
scopolamine hydrobromide
Injection: 0.3, 0.4, 0.5, 0.6, and 1 mg/ml in 1-ml vials and ampules; 0.86 mg/ml in 0.5-ml ampules

NURSING PROCESS

Assessment

- Assess patient's condition before therapy and regularly thereafter.
- Be alert for adverse reactions and drug interactions.
- Evaluate patient's and family's knowledge of drug therapy.

Nursing diagnoses

- Risk for deficient fluid volume related to nausea and vomiting
- Risk for injury related to drug-induced adverse CNS reactions
- Deficient knowledge related to drug therapy

Planning and implementation

- **P.O., I.M., S.C., and P.R. use:** Follow normal protocol.
- **I.V. use:** Intermittent and continuous infusions aren't recommended.
  - For direct injection, dilute with sterile water and inject diluted drug at ordered rate through patent I.V. line.
  - Protect I.V. solutions from freezing and light, and store at room temperature.
- **Transdermal use:** Apply patch the night before patient's expected travel.
- Raise bed's side rails as precaution because some patients become temporarily excited or disoriented. Symptoms disappear when sedative effect is complete.
- In therapeutic doses, scopolamine may produce amnesia, drowsiness, and euphoria; patient may need to be reoriented.
- Tolerance may develop when scopolamine is given over a long time.

ALERT: Overdose may cause curare-like effects such as respiratory paralysis.

Patient teaching

- Advise patient to apply patch the night before planned trip. Transdermal method releases controlled therapeutic amount of drug. Transderm Scōp is effective if applied 2 to 3 hours before experiencing motion but is more effective if applied 12 hours before.
- Advise patient to wash and dry hands thoroughly before and after applying transdermal patch on dry skin behind ear and before touching eye because pupil may dilate. After removing system, he should discard it and wash hands and application site thoroughly.
- Tell patient that if patch becomes displaced, he should remove it and replace it with another patch on fresh skin site behind ear.
- Alert patient to risk of withdrawal symptoms (nausea, vomiting, headache, dizziness) if transdermal system is used longer than 72 hours.
- Tell patient to ask pharmacist for brochure that comes with transdermal product.
- Instruct patient about P.O. or P.R. administration, if applicable.
- Advise patient to refrain from activities that require alertness until drug's CNS effects are known.
- Instruct patient to report signs of urinary hesitancy or urine retention.
- Recommend use of sugarless gum or hard candy to help minimize dry mouth.

Evaluation

- Patient responds well to therapy.
- Patient doesn't experience injury from adverse CNS reactions.
- Patient and family state understanding of drug therapy.

secobarbital sodium

(sek-oh-BAR-bih-tohl SOH-dee-um)
Novosecobarb ♦, Seconal Sodium

Pharmacologic class: barbiturate
Therapeutic class: sedative-hypnotic, anticonvulsant
Pregnancy risk category: D
Controlled substance schedule: II

Indications and dosages

▶ **Preoperative sedation.** *Adults:* 200 to 300 mg P.O. 1 to 2 hours before surgery. *Children:* 2 to 6 mg/kg P.O. 1 to 2 hours before surgery. Maximum single dose is 100 mg.

▶ **Insomnia.** *Adults:* 100 mg P.O. h.s.

Contraindications and precautions

- Contraindicated in patients hypersensitive to barbiturates and patients with marked liver impairment, respiratory disease in which dyspnea or obstruction is evident, or porphyria.
- Use cautiously in patients with acute or chronic pain, depression, suicidal tendencies, history of drug abuse, or hepatic impairment.

Lifespan: In pregnant or breast-feeding women, drug isn't recommended.

Adverse reactions

CNS: *drowsiness, lethargy, hangover,* paradoxical excitement in geriatric patients, somnolence.
GI: nausea, vomiting.
Hematologic: exacerbation of porphyria.
Respiratory: ***respiratory depression.***
Skin: rash, urticaria, ***Stevens-Johnson syndrome.***
Other: ***angioedema,*** physical or psychological dependence.

Interactions

Drug-drug. *Chloramphenicol, MAO inhibitors, valproic acid:* Inhibits metabolism of barbiturates; may cause prolonged CNS depression. Reduce barbiturate dosage.
CNS depressants, including narcotic analgesics: May cause excessive CNS and respiratory depression. Use together cautiously.
Corticosteroids, digitoxin, doxycycline, estrogens and oral contraceptives, oral anticoagulants, theophylline, tricyclic antidepressants, verapamil: Secobarbital may enhance metabolism of these drugs. Monitor patient for decreased effect.
Griseofulvin: Decreases absorption of griseofulvin. Monitor patient for decreased griseofulvin effectiveness.
Rifampin: May decrease barbiturate levels. Monitor patient for decreased effect.
Drug-lifestyle. *Alcohol use:* May cause excessive CNS and respiratory depression. Discourage using together.

Effects on lab test results

None reported.

Pharmacokinetics

Absorption: Rapid with 90% of drug absorbed.
Distribution: Rapid; about 30% to 45% protein-bound.
Metabolism: Oxidized in liver to inactive metabolites.
Excretion: Excreted in urine. *Half-life:* About 30 hours.

Route	Onset	Peak	Duration
P.O.	≤ 15 min	5-30 min	1-4 hr

Pharmacodynamics

Chemical effect: Unknown; probably interferes with transmission of impulses from thalamus to cortex of brain.
Therapeutic effect: Promotes pain relief and calmness and relieves acute seizures.

Available forms

Capsules: 50 mg, 100 mg

NURSING PROCESS

Assessment

- Assess patient's condition before therapy and regularly thereafter.
- Assess mental status before therapy. Geriatric patients are more sensitive to adverse CNS effects of drug.
- Be alert for adverse reactions and drug interactions.
- Evaluate patient's and family's knowledge of drug therapy.

Nursing diagnoses

- Disturbed sleep pattern related to underlying condition

- Risk for injury related to drug-induced adverse CNS reactions
- Deficient knowledge related to drug therapy

Planning and implementation

- **P.O. use:** Prevent hoarding or intentional overdosing by patient who is depressed, suicidal, or drug-dependent or who has history of drug abuse.
- Skin eruptions may precede potentially fatal reactions to barbiturate therapy. Discontinue drug if skin reactions occur, and notify prescriber. In some patients, high fever, stomatitis, headache, or rhinitis may precede skin reactions.
- Long-term use isn't recommended; drug loses its efficacy in promoting sleep after 14 days of continued use.

Patient teaching

- Caution patient to avoid activities that require mental alertness or physical coordination. For inpatient, supervise walking and raise bed rails, particularly for the geriatric patient.
- Inform patient that morning hangover is common after hypnotic dose, which suppresses REM sleep. Patient may experience increased dreaming after drug is discontinued.
- Advise patient who uses oral contraceptives to consider a different birth control method, such as a barrier method; drug may enhance contraceptive hormone metabolism and decrease its effect.

Evaluation

- Patient states that drug effectively induces sleep.
- Patient doesn't experience injury from adverse CNS reactions.
- Patient and family state understanding of drug therapy.

selegiline hydrochloride (L-deprenyl hydrochloride)

(see-LEJ-eh-leen high-droh-KLOR-ighd)

Atapryl, Carbex, Eldepryl, Selpak

Pharmacologic class: MAO inhibitor
Therapeutic class: antiparkinsonian
Pregnancy risk category: C

Indications and dosages

▶ **Adjunct treatment with levodopa-carbidopa in managing symptoms of Parkinson's disease.** *Adults:* 10 mg P.O. daily, taken as 5 mg at breakfast and 5 mg at lunch. After 2 or 3 days of therapy, gradual decrease of levodopa-carbidopa dosage is attempted.

Contraindications and precautions

- Contraindicated in patients hypersensitive to drug and in those receiving meperidine.

Lifespan: In pregnant women, use cautiously. For breast-feeding women and children, safety of drug hasn't been established.

Adverse reactions

CNS: *dizziness,* increased tremors, chorea, loss of balance, restlessness, increased bradykinesia, facial grimacing, stiff neck, dyskinesia, involuntary movements, twitching, increased apraxia, behavioral changes, fatigue, headache, confusion, hallucinations, vivid dreams, malaise, syncope.
CV: orthostatic hypotension, hypertension, hypotension, ***arrhythmias,*** palpitations, angina, tachycardia, peripheral edema.
EENT: blepharospasm.
GI: dry mouth, *nausea,* vomiting, constipation, abdominal pain, anorexia or poor appetite, dysphagia, diarrhea, heartburn.
GU: slow urination, transient nocturia, prostatic hyperplasia, urinary hesitancy, urinary frequency, urine retention, sexual dysfunction.
Skin: rash, hair loss, diaphoresis.
Metabolic: weight loss.

Interactions

Drug-drug. *Adrenergics:* Possible increased pressor response, particularly in patients who have taken overdose of selegiline. Use together cautiously.
Meperidine: May cause stupor, muscle rigidity, severe agitation, and elevated temperature. Avoid using together.
Drug-herb. *Cacao tree:* Potential vasopressor effects. Discourage using together.
Ginseng: May increase risk of adverse reactions, including headache, tremor, and mania. Discourage using together.
Drug-food. *Foods high in tyramine:* Possible hypertensive crisis. Monitor patient's blood pressure; urge patient to avoid these foods.

Effects on lab test results

None reported.

Pharmacokinetics

Absorption: Unknown.
Distribution: Unknown.
Metabolism: Three metabolites have been detected in serum and urine: *N*-desmethyldeprenyl, L-amphetamine, and L-methamphetamine.
Excretion: 45% excreted in urine as metabolite. *Half-life:* Selegiline, 2 to 10 hours; *N*-desmethyldeprenyl, 2 hours; L-amphetamine, 17.7 hours; L-methamphetamine, 20.5 hours.

Route	Onset	Peak	Duration
P.O.	Unknown	30 min-2 hr	Unknown

Pharmacodynamics

Chemical effect: Unknown; probably acts by selectively inhibiting MAO type B (found mostly in brain). At higher-than-recommended doses, it is nonselective inhibitor of MAO, including MAO type A (found in GI tract). It also may directly increase dopaminergic activity by decreasing reuptake of dopamine into nerve cells. Its active metabolites, amphetamine and methamphetamine, may contribute to this effect.
Therapeutic effect: Improves physical mobility.

Available forms

Tablets: 5 mg

NURSING PROCESS

Assessment

- Assess patient's condition before therapy and regularly thereafter.
- Be alert for adverse reactions and drug interactions.
- Evaluate patient's and family's knowledge of drug therapy.

Nursing diagnoses

- Impaired physical mobility related to underlying condition
- Risk for injury related to drug-induced adverse CNS reactions
- Deficient knowledge related to drug therapy

Planning and implementation

- Some patients experience increased adverse reactions related to levodopa and need a 10% to 30% reduction of levodopa-carbidopa dosage.

ALERT: Don't confuse selegiline with Stelazine or Eldepryl with enalapril.

Patient teaching

- Warn patient to move cautiously at start of therapy because he may experience dizziness.
- Advise patient not to take more than 10 mg daily because greater amount of drug won't improve efficacy and may increase adverse reactions.

Evaluation

- Patient exhibits improved physical mobility.
- Patient doesn't experience injury from adverse CNS reactions.
- Patient and family state understanding of drug therapy.

senna
(SEN-uh)
Black-Draught†, Fletcher's Castoria†, Senexon†, Senokot†, Senolax†, X-Prep*†

Pharmacologic class: anthraquinone derivative
Therapeutic class: stimulant laxative
Pregnancy risk category: C

Indications and dosages

▶ **Acute constipation; preparation for bowel examination.** ***Black-Draught.*** *Adults:* 2 tablets or ¼ to ½ teaspoons of granules mixed with water.
Other preparations. *Adults and children age 12 and older:* Usual dose is 2 tablets, 1 teaspoon of granules dissolved in water, 1 suppository, or 10 to 15 ml syrup h.s. Maximum dosage varies with preparation used.
Children ages 6 to 11: 1 tablet, ½ teaspoon of granules dissolved in water, ½ suppository h.s., or 5 to 10 ml syrup. Maximum dosage is 2 tablets b.i.d. or 1 teaspoon of granules b.i.d.
Children ages 2 to 5: ½ tablet or ¼ teaspoon of granules dissolved in water. Maximum, 1 tablet b.i.d. or ½ teaspoon of granules b.i.d.
Children ages 1 to 5: 2.5 to 5 ml syrup h.s.

Children ages 1 month to 12 months: Consult prescriber.

Contraindications and precautions

- Contraindicated in patients with ulcerative bowel lesions; nausea, vomiting, abdominal pain, or other symptoms of appendicitis or acute surgical abdomen; fecal impaction; or intestinal obstruction or perforation.

Lifespan: In pregnant or breast-feeding women, use cautiously.

Adverse reactions

GI: *nausea;* vomiting; diarrhea; malabsorption of nutrients; yellow or yellow-green cast to feces; *abdominal cramps,* especially in severe constipation; "cathartic colon" (syndrome resembling ulcerative colitis radiologically) with long-term misuse; possible constipation after catharsis; diarrhea in breast-feeding infants of mothers receiving senna; darkened pigmentation of rectal mucosa with long-term use (usually reversible within 4 to 12 months after stopping drug); laxative dependence; loss of normal bowel function with excessive use.
GU: red-pink discoloration in alkaline urine; yellow-brown color to acidic urine.
Metabolic: protein-losing enteropathy, electrolyte imbalance.

Interactions

None significant.

Effects on lab test results

- May alter fluid and electrolyte levels with prolonged use.

Pharmacokinetics

Absorption: Minimal.
Distribution: In bile, saliva, colonic mucosa.
Metabolism: Absorbed portion metabolized in liver.
Excretion: Unabsorbed senna excreted mainly in feces; absorbed drug excreted in urine and feces.

Route	Onset	Peak	Duration
P.O.	6-10 hr	Varies	Varies
P.R.	30 min-2 hr	Varies	Varies

Pharmacodynamics

Chemical effect: Unknown; increases peristalsis, probably by direct effect on smooth muscle of intestine. Senna may either irritate musculature or stimulate colonic intramural plexus. It also promotes fluid accumulation in colon and small intestine.
Therapeutic effect: Relieves constipation and cleanses bowel.

Available forms

Dosages expressed as sennosides (active principle)
Granules†: 15 mg/teaspoon, 20 mg/teaspoon
Liquid†: 3 mg/ml
Suppositories†: 30 mg
Syrup†: 8.8 mg/5 ml
Tablets†: 6 mg, 8.6 mg, 17 mg

NURSING PROCESS

Assessment

- Assess patient's condition before therapy and regularly thereafter.
- Before giving drug for constipation, determine if patient has adequate fluid intake, exercise, and diet.
- Be alert for adverse reactions.
- Evaluate patient's and family's knowledge of drug therapy.

Nursing diagnoses

- Constipation related to underlying condition
- Diarrhea related to drug-induced adverse GI reactions
- Deficient knowledge related to drug therapy

Planning and implementation

- **P.O. use:** Limit diet to clear liquids after patient takes X-Prep Liquid.
- **P.R. use:** Follow normal protocol.
- Avoid exposing drug to excessive heat or light.
- Drug is used for short-term treatment.
- Senna is one of the most effective laxatives for counteracting constipation caused by narcotic analgesics.

Patient teaching

- Teach patient about dietary sources of bulk, which include bran and other cereals, fresh fruit, and vegetables.
- Tell patient to maintain adequate fluid intake of at least 6 to 8 glasses of water or juices daily unless contraindicated.

Evaluation

• Patient's constipation is relieved.
• Patient states that diarrhea doesn't occur.
• Patient and family state understanding of drug therapy.

sertraline hydrochloride

(SER-truh-leen high-droh-KLOR-ighd)
Zoloft

Pharmacologic class: serotonin uptake inhibitor
Therapeutic class: antidepressant
Pregnancy risk category: B

Indications and dosages

▶ **Depression.** *Adults:* 50 mg P.O. daily. Dosage adjusted as tolerated and needed. Dosage adjustments should be made at intervals of no less than 1 week.

▶ **Posttraumatic stress disorder, social anxiety disorder.** *Adults:* Initially, 25 mg P.O. once daily. Increase dosage to 50 mg P.O. once daily after 1 week of therapy. Dosage may be increased at weekly intervals to a maximum of 200 mg daily. Maintain patient on lowest effective dosage.

▶ **Premenstrual dysphoric disorder.** *Adults:* Initially, 50 mg daily P.O. continuously, or limited to the luteal phase of the menstrual cycle. Patients not responding may benefit from dose increases at 50-mg increments per menstrual cycle up to 150 mg daily when dosing daily throughout the menstrual cycle, or 100 mg daily when dosing during the luteal phase of the menstrual cycle. If a 100-mg daily dose has been established with luteal phase dosing, a 50-mg daily adjustment step for 3 days should be used at the beginning of each luteal phase dosing period.

▶ **Premature ejaculation‡.** *Adults:* 25 to 50 mg P.O. daily or p.r.n.

Contraindications and precautions

• Contraindicated in patients with a hypersensitivity to sertraline or any of the inactive ingredients. Contraindicated in patients receiving pimozide.
• Use cautiously in patients at risk for suicide and in those with seizure disorder, major affective disorder, or diseases or conditions that affect metabolism or hemodynamic responses.

Lifespan: In pregnant or breast-feeding women, use cautiously. In children, safety of drug hasn't been established.

Adverse reactions

CNS: *headache, tremor, dizziness, insomnia, somnolence,* paresthesia, hypesthesia, hyperesthesia, *fatigue,* twitching, hypertonia, nervousness, anxiety, confusion.
CV: palpitations, chest pain, hot flushes, flushing.
GI: *dry mouth, nausea, diarrhea, loose stools, dyspepsia,* vomiting, constipation, thirst, flatulence, anorexia, abdominal pain, increased appetite.
GU: *male sexual dysfunction.*
Musculoskeletal: myalgia.
Skin: *diaphoresis,* rash, pruritus.
Other: decreased libido.

Interactions

Drug-drug. *Benzodiazepines (except lorazepam and oxazepam), tolbutamide:* Decreases clearance of these drugs. Significance is unknown; monitor patient for increased drug effects.
Cimetidine: Decreases sertraline clearance. Monitor patient for toxicity.
Disulfiram: Oral concentrate contains alcohol that could cause a reaction. Avoid using together.
MAO inhibitors: May cause serious mental status changes, hyperthermia, autonomic instability, rapid fluctuations of vital signs, delirium, coma, and death. Drug must not be given within 14 days of an MAO inhibitor.
Pimozide: Increased pimozide level. Avoid using together.
Sumatriptan: May cause weakness, hyperreflexia, and incoordination. Monitor patient closely.
Tricyclic antidepressants (TCA): May inhibit TCA metabolism. Dose of TCA may need to be reduced. Monitor patient closely.
Warfarin, other highly protein-bound drugs: May increase levels of sertraline or other highly bound drug. Increases of 8% in PT and INR have been noted with use of warfarin. Monitor patient closely.
Drug-herb. *Ginkgo:* Herb may decrease adverse sexual effects of drug. Advise patient to

speak to prescriber before taking any herbal remedy.
St. John's wort: Increases serotonin levels and may cause serotonin syndrome. Discourage using together.
Drug-lifestyle: *Alcohol use:* May enhance CNS effects. Advise patient to avoid alcohol use.

Effects on lab test results

• May increase ALT, AST, cholesterol, and triglyceride levels. May decrease uric acid level.

Pharmacokinetics

Absorption: Well absorbed from GI tract. Rate and extent enhanced when taken with food.
Distribution: Highly protein-bound (greater than 98%).
Metabolism: Metabolism is probably hepatic.
Excretion: Excreted mostly as metabolites in urine and feces. *Half-life:* 26 hours.

Route	Onset	Peak	Duration
P.O.	2-4 wk	4.5-8.5 hr	Unknown

Pharmacodynamics

Chemical effect: Unknown; may be linked to inhibited neuronal uptake of serotonin in CNS.
Therapeutic effect: Relieves depression.

Available forms

Oral concentrate: 20 mg/ml.
Tablets: 25 mg, 50 mg, 100 mg

NURSING PROCESS

Assessment

• Assess patient's condition before therapy, and reassess regularly thereafter.
• Assess patient for risk factors for suicide.
• Be alert for adverse reactions and drug interactions.
• Evaluate patient's and family's knowledge of drug therapy.

Nursing diagnoses

• Disturbed thought processes related to presence of depression
• Risk for injury related to drug-induced adverse CNS reactions
• Deficient knowledge related to drug therapy

Planning and implementation

• Give drug once daily, either in morning or evening. Drug may be given with or without food.
• Drug shouldn't be given within 14 days of MAO inhibitor therapy. Allow 14 days after stopping drug before starting an MAO inhibitor.
• Avoid using the oral concentrate dropper, which is made of rubber, in a patient with a latex allergy.

Patient teaching

• Advise patient to use caution when performing hazardous tasks that require alertness and to avoid alcohol while taking this drug. Drugs that influence CNS may impair judgment.
• Caution patient to check with prescriber or pharmacist before taking OTC drugs.
• Advise patient to mix the oral concentrate with 4 oz of water, ginger ale, or lemon-lime soda only, and to take the dose right away.

Evaluation

• Patient behavior and communication indicate improved thought processes.
• Patient doesn't experience injury from adverse CNS reactions.
• Patient and family state understanding of drug therapy.

sevelamer hydrochloride

(seh-VEL-ah-mer high-droh-KLOR-ighd)
Renagel

Pharmacologic class: polymeric phosphate binder
Therapeutic class: hyperphosphatemia agent
Pregnancy risk category: C

Indications and dosages

▶ **Reduction of serum phosphorus in patients with end-stage renal disease.** *Adults:* Depends on severity of hyperphosphatemia. Gradually adjust dosage based on phosphorus level with goal of lowering phosphorus to 6 mg/dl or less. If phosphorus level is 9 mg/dl or more, start with 1.6 g P.O. t.i.d. with meals; if phosphorus level is between 7.5 and 9 mg/dl, 1.2 g P.O. t.i.d. with meals; if phosphorus level is between 6 and 7.5 mg/dl, 800 mg P.O. t.i.d. with meals.

Contraindications and precautions

- Contraindicated in patients hypersensitive to drug or its components and in those with hypophosphatemia or bowel obstruction.
- Use cautiously in patients with dysphagia, swallowing disorders, severe GI motility disorders, or major GI tract surgery.

Lifespan: In breast-feeding women, use cautiously. In children, safety and effectiveness haven't been established.

Adverse reactions

CNS: *headache, pain.*
CV: hypertension, *hypotension, **thrombosis.***
GI: *vomiting,* nausea, constipation, *diarrhea,* flatulence, *dyspepsia.*
Respiratory: cough.
Other: *infection.*

Interactions

Drug-drug. *Antiarrhythmics, anticonvulsants:* May have potential pharmacokinetic interaction. Give drug at least 1 hour before or 3 hours after giving these drugs and monitor blood levels of these drugs.

Effects on lab test results

- May increase alkaline phosphatase level.

Pharmacokinetics

Absorption: None.
Distribution: Unknown.
Metabolism: Unknown.
Excretion: Unknown.

Route	Onset	Peak	Duration
P.O.	Unknown	Unknown	Unknown

Pharmacodynamics

Chemical effect: Inhibits intestinal phosphate absorption.
Therapeutic effect: Decreases phosphorus level.

Available forms

Capsules: 403 mg
Tablets: 400 mg, 800 mg

NURSING PROCESS

Assessment

- Obtain history of patient's underlying condition before therapy, and reassess regularly thereafter.
- Monitor calcium, bicarbonate, and chloride levels.
- Watch for symptoms of thrombosis (numbness or tingling of limbs, chest pain, shortness of breath), and notify prescriber if they occur.
- Evaluate patient's and family's knowledge of drug therapy.

Nursing diagnoses

- Ineffective tissue perfusion (cardiopulmonary or peripheral) related to potential drug-induced thrombosis
- Imbalanced nutrition: less than body requirements related to drug-induced adverse GI effects
- Deficient knowledge related to drug therapy

Planning and implementation

- Don't crush or break capsules or tablets, and give only with meals.
- Although no known drug interactions have been studied, drug may bind to other drugs given at the same time and decrease their bioavailability. Give other drugs 1 hour before or 3 hours after sevelamer.

ALERT: Drug may reduce vitamins D, E, and K and folic acid; patient should take a multivitamin supplement.

Patient teaching

- Instruct patient to take with meals and adhere to prescribed diet.
- Inform patient that drug must be taken whole because contents expand in water; caution him not to open or chew capsules.
- Tell patient to take other drugs as directed, but they must be taken either 1 hour before or 3 hours after sevelamer.
- Inform patient about common adverse reactions and instruct him to report them immediately. Teach patient signs and symptoms of thrombosis (numbness, tingling limbs, chest pain, changes in level of consciousness).

Evaluation

- Patient doesn't develop a thrombus.
- Patient maintains adequate nutrition.

• Patient and family state understanding of drug therapy.

sibutramine hydrochloride monohydrate

(sigh-BYOO-truh-meen high-droh-KLOR-ighd muh-noh-HIGH-drayt)
Meridia

Pharmacologic class: serotonin, norepinephrine, and dopamine reuptake inhibitor
Therapeutic class: antiobesity agent
Pregnancy risk category: C
Controlled substance schedule: IV

Indications and dosages

▶ **Management of obesity.** *Adults:* 10 mg P.O. once daily with or without food. May increase dosage to 15 mg P.O. daily after 4 weeks if weight loss is inadequate. Patients who don't tolerate the 10-mg dose may receive 5 mg P.O. daily. Doses above 15 mg daily aren't recommended.

Contraindications and precautions

• Contraindicated in patients hypersensitive to drug or its active ingredients, those taking MAO inhibitors or other centrally acting appetite suppressants, and those with anorexia nervosa.
• Don't use drug in patients with severe renal or hepatic dysfunction, history of hypertension, seizures, coronary artery disease, heart failure, arrhythmias, or CVA.
• Use cautiously in patients with angle-closure glaucoma.
Lifespan: In children younger than age 16, safety and effectiveness haven't been established.

Adverse reactions

CNS: asthenia, *headache, insomnia,* dizziness, nervousness, anxiety, depression, paresthesia, somnolence, CNS stimulation, emotional lability, migraine.
CV: tachycardia, vasodilation, hypertension, palpitations, chest pain, generalized edema.
EENT: thirst, *rhinitis, pharyngitis,* sinusitis, ear disorder, ear pain, laryngitis.
GI: *dry mouth,* taste perversion, *anorexia, constipation,* increased appetite, nausea, dyspepsia, gastritis, vomiting, abdominal pain, rectal disorder.
GU: dysmenorrhea, urinary tract infection, vaginal candidiasis, metrorrhagia.
Musculoskeletal: arthralgia, myalgia, tenosynovitis, joint disorder, neck or back pain.
Respiratory: cough.
Skin: rash, sweating, herpes simplex, acne.
Other: flulike syndrome, injury, accident, allergic reaction.

Interactions

Drug-drug. *CNS depressants:* May enhance CNS depression. Use cautiously.
Dextromethorphan, dihydroergotamine, fentanyl, fluoxetine, fluvoxamine, lithium, MAO inhibitors, meperidine, paroxetine, pentazocine, sertraline, sumatriptan, tryptophan, venlafaxine: May cause hyperthermia, tachycardia, and loss of consciousness. Don't use together.
Ephedrine, pseudoephedrine: May increase blood pressure or heart rate. Use cautiously.
Drug-lifestyle. *Alcohol use:* Enhances CNS depression. Discourage using together.

Effects on lab test results

• May increase ALT, AST, GGT, LDH, alkaline phosphatase, and bilirubin levels.

Pharmacokinetics

Absorption: Rapid; about 77% of dose is absorbed.
Distribution: Rapid and extensive. Active metabolites are extensively bound to plasma proteins.
Metabolism: Extensive first-pass metabolism by the liver to two active metabolites, M_1 and M_2.
Excretion: About 77% is excreted in urine. *Half-life:* M_1 is 14 hours and M_2 is 16 hours.

Route	Onset	Peak	Duration
P.O.	Unknown	3-4 hr	Unknown

Pharmacodynamics

Chemical effect: Inhibits reuptake of norepinephrine, serotonin, and dopamine.
Therapeutic effect: Facilitates weight loss.

Available forms

Capsules: 5 mg, 10 mg, 15 mg

NURSING PROCESS

Assessment

- Monitor patient for adverse reactions and drug interactions.
- Assess patient for organic causes of obesity before starting therapy.
- Assess patient's dietary intake.
- Measure blood pressure and pulse before starting therapy, with dosage changes, and at regular intervals during therapy.
- Evaluate patient's and family's knowledge of drug therapy.

Nursing diagnoses

- Imbalanced nutrition: more than body requirements related to increased caloric intake
- Disturbed sleep pattern related to drug-induced insomnia
- Deficient knowledge related to drug therapy

Planning and implementation

- At least 2 weeks should elapse between stopping an MAO inhibitor and starting drug therapy, and vice versa.
- Give patient ice chips or sugarless hard candy to relieve dry mouth.
- Make sure patient follows appropriate diet regimen.

Patient teaching

- Advise patient to report rash, hives, or other allergic reactions immediately.
- Instruct patient to inform prescriber if he is taking or plans to take other prescription or OTC drugs.
- Advise patient to have blood pressure and pulse monitored at regular intervals. Stress importance of regular follow-up visits with prescriber.
- Advise patient to use drug with reduced calorie diet.
- Tell patient that weight loss can precipitate gallstone formation. Teach patient about signs and symptoms and the need to report them to prescriber promptly.

Evaluation

- Patient achieves nutritional balance with the use of drugs and a reduced-calorie diet.
- Patient experiences normal sleep patterns.
- Patient and family state understanding of drug therapy.

sildenafil citrate

(sil-DEN-ah-fil SIGH-trayt)
Viagra

Pharmacologic class: selective inhibitor of cyclic guanosine monophosphate-specific phosphodiesterase type 5
Therapeutic class: therapy for erectile dysfunction
Pregnancy risk category: B

Indications and dosages

▶ **Treatment of erectile dysfunction.** *Men younger than age 65:* 50 mg P.O., p.r.n., about 1 hour before sexual activity. Dosage range is 25 to 100 mg based on effectiveness and tolerance. Maximum of 1 dose daily.
Men age 65 and older: 25 mg P.O., p.r.n. about 1 hour before sexual activity. Dose may be adjusted based on patient response. Maximum of 1 dose daily.
Patients with hepatic or severe renal impairment: 25 mg P.O. about 1 hour before sexual activity. Dose may be adjusted based on patient response. Maximum of 1 dose daily.

Contraindications and precautions

- Contraindicated in patients hypersensitive to drug or its components, those with underlying CV disease, and those using organic nitrates at any frequency and in any form.
- Use cautiously in those with hepatic or severe renal impairment; those with anatomic deformation of the penis; those with conditions that may predispose them to priapism (such as sickle-cell anemia, multiple myeloma, leukemia), retinitis pigmentosa, bleeding disorders, or active peptic ulcer disease; those who have had an MI, CVA, or life-threatening arrhythmia during previous 6 months; and those with history of cardiac failure, coronary artery disease, or uncontrolled high or low blood pressure.

Lifespan: In patients age 65 and older, use cautiously.

Adverse reactions

CNS: anxiety, *headache,* dizziness, ***seizures,*** somnolence, vertigo.
CV: ***MI, sudden cardiac death, ventricular arrhythmia, cerebrovascular hemorrhage, transient ischemic attack,*** hypertension, *flushing.*
EENT: diplopia, temporary vision loss, decreased vision, ocular redness or bloodshot appearance, increased intraocular pressure, retinal vascular disease, retinal bleeding, vitreous detachment or traction, perimacular edema, abnormal vision (photophobia, color tinged vision, blurred vision), ocular burning, ocular swelling or pressure.
GI: dyspepsia, diarrhea.
GU: hematuria, prolonged erection, priapism, urinary tract infection.
Musculoskeletal: arthralgia, back pain.
Respiratory: respiratory tract infection.
Skin: rash.
Other: flulike syndrome.

Interactions

Drug-drug. *Beta blockers, loop and potassium-sparing diuretics:* Increases level of major metabolite of sildenafil. Significance of this interaction isn't known.
CYP3A4 inducers, rifampin: Reduces sildenafil level. Monitor drug effect.
Hepatic isoenzyme inhibitors (such as cimetidine, erythromycin, itraconazole, ketoconazole): May reduce clearance of sildenafil. Avoid using together.
Nitrates: Sildenafil enhances hypotensive effects. Don't use together.
Protease inhibitors, delavirdine: Increases sildenafil level and may result in an increase in sildenafil-associated adverse events, including hypotension, visual changes, and priapism. Don't exceed 25 mg in a 48-hour period.
Drug-food. *High-fat meals:* Reduces rate of absorption and decreases peak serum levels. Separate administration time from meals.

Effects on lab test results

None reported.

Pharmacokinetics

Absorption: Rapid. Absolute bioavailability is 40%.
Distribution: Extensively into body tissues. About 96% bound to plasma proteins.
Metabolism: Primarily metabolized in the liver to an active metabolite with properties similar to those of parent drug.
Excretion: About 80% is excreted in feces and 13% in urine. *Half-life:* 4 hours.

Route	Onset	Peak	Duration
P.O.	Unknown	30 min-2 hr	4 hr

Pharmacodynamics

Chemical effect: Drug has no direct relaxant effect on isolated human corpus cavernosum, but enhances the effect of nitric oxide (NO) by inhibiting phosphodiesterase type 5 (PDE5), which is responsible for degradation of cyclic guanosine monophosphate (cGMP) in the corpus cavernosum. When sexual stimulation causes local release of NO, inhibition of PDE5 by sildenafil causes increased levels of cGMP in the corpus cavernosum, resulting in smooth muscle relaxation and inflow of blood to the corpus cavernosum.
Therapeutic effect: Patient achieves an erection.

Available forms

Tablets: 25 mg, 50 mg, 100 mg

NURSING PROCESS

Assessment

- Discuss patient's history of erectile dysfunction to establish need for drug versus other therapies.
- Discuss with patient his response to drug and if he is experiencing adverse effects.
- Assess patient for CV risk factors because serious events have been reported with drug use, and report risk factors to prescriber.
- Evaluate patient's and family's knowledge of drug therapy.

Nursing diagnoses

- Sexual dysfunction related to patient's underlying condition
- Ineffective tissue perfusion (cardiopulmonary) related to drug-induced effects on blood pressure and cardiac output
- Deficient knowledge related to drug therapy

Planning and implementation

ALERT: Drug's systemic vasodilatory properties cause transient decreases in supine blood pressure and cardiac output (about 2 hours after ingestion). Together with the potential cardiac risk of sexual activity, the risk for patients with underlying CV disease is increased.

ALERT: Serious CV events, including MI, sudden cardiac death, ventricular arrhythmia, cerebrovascular hemorrhage, transient ischemic attack, and hypertension, have occurred in patients during or shortly after sexual activity.

Patient teaching

- Advise patient that drug is contraindicated with regular or intermittent use of nitrates.
- Caution patient about cardiac risk with sexual activity, especially if patient has CV risk factors. If patient has symptoms such as angina pectoris, dizziness, or nausea at the start of sexual activity, instruct him to notify prescriber and refrain from further sexual activity.
- Warn patient that erections lasting more than 4 hours and priapism (painful erections more than 6 hours) can occur and should be reported immediately. Penile tissue damage and permanent loss of potency may result if priapism isn't treated immediately.
- Inform patient that drug doesn't offer protection against sexually transmitted diseases and that protective measures, such as condoms, should be used.
- Instruct patient to take drug 30 minutes to 4 hours before sexual activity; maximum benefit can be expected less than 2 hours after ingesting drug.
- Advise patient that drug is most rapidly absorbed if taken on an empty stomach.
- Inform patient to avoid potentially hazardous activities that rely on color discrimination because blue/green discrimination may be impaired.
- Instruct patient to notify prescriber if visual changes occur.
- Advise patient that drug is effective only in the presence of sexual stimulation.
- Caution patient to take drug only as prescribed.
- Advise patient receiving HIV drugs that there is an increased risk of sildenafil-associated adverse events including hypotension, visual changes, and priapism, and he should promptly report any symptoms to his prescriber. Tell him not to exceed 25 mg of sildenafil in a 48-hour period.

Evaluation

- Sexual activity improves with drug therapy.
- Patient doesn't experience adverse CV events.
- Patient and family state understanding of drug therapy.

simethicone

(sigh-METH-ih-kohn)

Extra Strength Gas-X†, Gas Relief†, Gas-X†, Maximum Strength Gas Relief†, Maximum Strength Phazyme†, Mylanta Gas†, Mylanta Gas Maximum Strength†, Mylanta Gas Regular Strength†, Mylicon-80†, Mylicon-125†, Ovol♦, Ovol-40♦, Ovol-80♦, Phazyme†, Phazyme 95†, Phazyme 125†

Pharmacologic class: dispersant
Therapeutic class: antiflatulent
Pregnancy risk category: NR

Indications and dosages

▶ **Flatulence, functional gastric bloating.** ***Tablets.*** *Adults and children older than age 12:* 40 to 125 mg P.O. q.i.d. after each meal and h.s.

Capsules. *Adults and children older than age 12:* 125 mg P.O. q.i.d. after each meal and h.s.

Drops. *Adults and children older than age 12:* 40 to 80 mg q.i.d. after each meal and h.s., up to maximum of 500 mg daily.

Children ages 2 to 12: 40 mg P.O. q.i.d. after each meal and h.s., up to maximum of 240 mg daily.

Children younger than age 2: 20 mg P.O. q.i.d. after each meal and h.s.

Contraindications and precautions

- Contraindicated in patients hypersensitive to drug.

Lifespan: In pregnant or breast-feeding women, use cautiously.

Adverse reactions

GI: excessive belching or flatus.

Interactions

None significant.

Effects on lab test results

None reported.

Pharmacokinetics

Absorption: None.
Distribution: None.
Metabolism: None.
Excretion: Excreted in feces.

Route	Onset	Peak	Duration
P.O.	Immediate	Immediate	Unknown

Pharmacodynamics

Chemical effect: By its defoaming action, disperses or prevents formation of mucus-surrounded gas pockets in GI tract.
Therapeutic effect: Relieves gas.

Available forms

Capsules: 125 mg
Drops: 40 mg/0.6 ml†
Tablets: 40 mg†, 50 mg†, 60 mg†, 80 mg†, 95 mg†, 125 mg†

NURSING PROCESS

Assessment

- Assess patient's condition before therapy and regularly thereafter.
- Be alert for adverse GI reactions.
- Evaluate patient's and family's knowledge of drug therapy.

Nursing diagnoses

- Acute pain related to gas in GI tract
- Deficient knowledge related to drug therapy

Planning and implementation

- Make sure patient chews tablet before swallowing.

ALERT: Don't confuse simethicone with cimetidine.

Patient teaching

- Advise patient that drug doesn't prevent formation of gas.
- Encourage patient to change position frequently and ambulate to aid in passing flatus.

Evaluation

- Patient's gas pain is relieved.
- Patient and family state understanding of drug therapy.

simvastatin (synvinolin)

(sim-vuh-STAT-in)
Lipex◊, Zocor

Pharmacologic class: HMG-CoA reductase inhibitor
Therapeutic class: antilipemic, cholesterol-lowering agent
Pregnancy risk category: X

Indications and dosages

▶ **Primary and secondary prevention of coronary heart disease; hyperlipidemia.** *Adults:* Initially, 20 mg P.O. daily in the evening. Patients who require a greater than 45% reduction in LDL level can be started on 40 mg daily. Dosage adjusted q 4 weeks based on patient tolerance and response. Dosage range is 5 to 80 mg daily.

▶ **Homozygous familial hypercholesterolemia.** *Adults:* 40 mg P.O. daily in the evening or 80 mg daily given in three divided doses of 20 mg, 20 mg, and 40 mg in the evening.

Patients taking cyclosporine: Begin with 5 mg P.O. daily; don't exceed 10 mg daily.

Patients taking fibrates or niacin: Maximum is 10 mg P.O. daily. For patients with severe renal insufficiency, start with 5 mg P.O. daily.

Patients taking amiodarone or verapamil: Dose should not exceed 20 mg P.O. daily.

Contraindications and precautions

- Contraindicated in patients hypersensitive to drug and those with active liver disease or conditions that have unexplained persistent elevations of transaminase levels.
- Use cautiously in patients who consume substantial quantities of alcohol or have history of liver disease.

Lifespan: In pregnant or breast-feeding women and in women of childbearing age unless they have no risk of pregnancy, drug is contraindicated. In children, safety of drug hasn't been established.

Adverse reactions

CNS: headache, asthenia.
GI: abdominal pain, constipation, diarrhea, dyspepsia, flatulence, nausea.
Respiratory: upper respiratory tract infection.

Interactions

Drug-drug. *Amiodarone, verapamil:* Increases risk of myopathy and rhabdomyolysis. Don't exceed 20 mg simvastatin daily.
Clarithromycin, erythromycin, HIV protease inhibitors, itraconazole, ketoconazole, nefazodone: Increases risk of myopathy and rhabdomyolysis. Avoid using together or suspend therapy during treatment with clarithromycin, erythromycin, itraconazole, and ketoconazole.
Cyclosporine, fibrates, niacin: Increases risk of myopathy and rhabdomyolysis. Monitor patient closely if use together can't be avoided. Don't exceed 10 mg simvastatin daily.
Digoxin: Digoxin level may elevate slightly. Closely monitor digoxin level at the start of simvastatin therapy.
Hepatotoxic drugs: Increases risk for hepatotoxicity. Avoid using together.
Warfarin: Enhanced anticoagulant effect. Monitor PT and INR at the start of therapy and during dose adjustment.
Drug-herb. *Red yeast rice:* Contains similar components to those of statin drugs, increasing the risk of adverse events or toxicity. Discourage using together.
Drug-food. *Grapefruit juice:* Increases drug level, increasing risk of adverse effects, including myopathy and rhabdomyolysis. Give with liquids other than grapefruit juice.
Drug-lifestyle. *Alcohol use:* May increase the risk of hepatotoxicity. Discourage using together.

Effects on lab test results

• May increase liver enzyme and CK levels.

Pharmacokinetics

Absorption: Readily absorbed; however, extensive hepatic extraction limits plasma availability of active inhibitors to 5% of dose or less. Individual absorption varies considerably.
Distribution: Parent drug and active metabolites are more than 95% bound to plasma proteins.
Metabolism: Hydrolysis occurs in plasma; at least three major metabolites have been identified.
Excretion: Excreted primarily in bile. *Half-life:* 3 hours.

Route	Onset	Peak	Duration
P.O.	Unknown	1.3-2.4 hr	Unknown

Pharmacodynamics

Chemical effect: Inhibits HMG-CoA reductase. This enzyme is early (and rate-limiting) step in synthetic pathway of cholesterol.
Therapeutic effect: Lowers LDL and total cholesterol levels.

Available forms

Tablets: 5 mg, 10 mg, 20 mg, 40 mg, 80 mg

NURSING PROCESS

Assessment

• Obtain history of patient's LDL and total cholesterol levels before therapy, and reassess regularly thereafter.
• Liver function tests should be performed at start of therapy and periodically thereafter. A liver biopsy may be performed if enzyme level elevations persist.
• Be alert for adverse reactions and drug interactions.
• Assess patient's dietary fat intake.
• Evaluate patient's and family's knowledge of drug therapy.

Nursing diagnoses

• Risk for injury related to presence of elevated cholesterol levels
• Constipation related to drug-induced adverse GI reactions
• Deficient knowledge related to drug therapy

Planning and implementation

• Drug therapy starts only after diet and other nondrug therapies have proven ineffective. Patient should follow a standard low-cholesterol diet during therapy.
• Give drug with evening meal for enhanced effectiveness.
• If cholesterol level falls below target range, dosage may be reduced.
• Make sure patient follows an appropriate diet.
ALERT: Don't confuse Zocor with Cozaar.

Patient teaching

• Tell patient to take drug with evening meal because absorption and cholesterol biosynthesis are enhanced.
• Teach patient dietary management of serum lipids (restricting total fat and cholesterol intake) and measures to control other cardiac dis-

ease risk factors. If appropriate, suggest weight control, exercise, and smoking cessation programs.

- Tell patient to inform prescriber about adverse reactions, particularly muscle aches and pains.

ALERT: Inform woman that drug is contraindicated during pregnancy. Advise her to notify prescriber immediately if pregnancy occurs.

Evaluation

- Patient's LDL and total cholesterol levels are within normal limits.
- Patient regains and maintains normal bowel pattern throughout therapy.
- Patient and family state understanding of drug therapy.

sirolimus

(sir-AH-lih-mus)

Rapamune

Pharmacologic class: macrocyclic lactone
Therapeutic class: immunosuppressant
Pregnancy risk category: C

Indications and dosages

▶ **Prophylaxis, with cyclosporine and corticosteroids, of organ rejection in patients receiving renal transplants.** *Adults and adolescents ages 13 and older who weigh 40 kg (88 lb) or more:* Initially, 6 mg P.O. as a one-time loading dose as soon as possible after transplantation; then maintenance dose of 2 mg P.O. once daily.

Adolescents ages 13 and older who weigh less than 40 kg: Initially, 3 mg/m² P.O. as a one-time loading dose after transplantation; then maintenance dose of 1 mg/m² P.O. once daily.

Contraindications and precautions

- Contraindicated in patients hypersensitive to active drug or its derivatives or components. Use cautiously in patients with hyperlipidemia or impaired liver or renal function.
- The safety and efficacy of sirolimus haven't been established in liver transplant patients, and therefore, such use isn't recommended.

Lifespan: In breast-feeding women, drug is contraindicated because of potential for severe adverse effects in infants.

Adverse reactions

CNS: *headache, insomnia, tremor, anxiety, depression, asthenia,* malaise, syncope, confusion, dizziness, emotional lability, hypertonia, hypesthesia, hypotonia, neuropathy, paresthesia, somnolence, *fever, pain.*
CV: *hypertension,* ***heart failure,*** atrial fibrillation, tachycardia, hypotension, *peripheral edema, chest pain, edema,* ***hemorrhage,*** palpitations, peripheral vascular disorder, thrombophlebitis, thrombosis, vasodilation.
EENT: facial edema, *pharyngitis,* epistaxis, rhinitis, sinusitis, abnormal vision, cataracts, conjunctivitis, deafness, ear pain, otitis media, tinnitus.
GI: *diarrhea, nausea, vomiting, constipation, abdominal pain, dyspepsia,* enlarged abdomen, hernia, ascites, peritonitis, anorexia, dysphagia, eructation, esophagitis, flatulence, gastritis, gastroenteritis, gingivitis, gum hyperplasia, ileus, mouth ulcerations, oral candidiasis, stomatitis.
GU: dysuria, hematuria, albuminuria, ***kidney tubular necrosis,*** *urinary tract infection,* pelvic pain, glycosuria, bladder pain, hydronephrosis, impotence, kidney pain, nocturia, oliguria, pyuria, scrotal edema, testis disorder, ***toxic nephropathy,*** urinary frequency, urinary incontinence, urine retention.
Hematologic: *anemia,* **THROMBOCYTOPENIA,** ***leukopenia,*** thrombotic thrombocytopenic purpura, leukocytosis, polycythemia, lymphadenopathy.
Hepatic: ***hepatic artery thrombosis.***
Metabolic: *hypercholesteremia, hyperlipidemia, hypokalemia, weight gain, hypophosphatemia,* **HYPERKALEMIA,** hypervolemia, Cushing's syndrome, diabetes mellitus, ***acidosis,*** dehydration, hypercalcemia, hyperglycemia, hyperphosphatemia, hypocalcemia, ***hypoglycemia,*** hypomagnesemia, hyponatremia, weight loss.
Musculoskeletal: *back pain, arthralgia,* myalgia, arthrosis, bone necrosis, leg cramps, osteoporosis, tetany.
Respiratory: *dyspnea, cough, atelectasis, upper respiratory tract infection,* asthma, bronchitis, hypoxia, lung edema, pleural effusion, pneumonia.

Skin: *rash, acne,* hirsutism, fungal dermatitis, pruritus, skin hypertrophy, skin ulcer, ecchymoses, sweating.
Other: abscess, cellulitis, chills, flulike syndrome, infection, ***sepsis,*** lymphadenopathy, abnormal healing, including fascial dehiscence and anastomotic disruption (e.g., wound, vascular, airway, ureteral, biliary).

Interactions

Drug-drug. *Aminoglycosides, amphotericin, other nephrotoxic drugs:* Increases risk of nephrotoxicity. Use cautiously.
Bromocriptine, cimetidine, clarithromycin, clotrimazole, danazol, erythromycin, fluconazole, indinavir, itraconazole, metoclopramide, nicardipine, ritonavir, verapamil, other drugs that inhibit CYP3A4: May decrease sirolimus metabolism, thereby increasing sirolimus level. Monitor patient for loss of therapeutic effect.
Carbamazepine, phenobarbital, phenytoin, rifabutin, rifapentine, other drugs that induce CYP3A4: May increase sirolimus metabolism, thereby decreasing sirolimus level. Monitor patient closely.
Cyclosporine (oral solution and capsules): Increases sirolimus level. Give sirolimus 4 hours after cyclosporine. After long-term use, sirolimus may reduce cyclosporine clearance, leading to need for reduction in cyclosporine dosage.
Diltiazem: Increases sirolimus level. Monitor and reduce dosage of sirolimus as needed.
HMG-CoA reductase inhibitors or fibrates: Increases risk of rhabdomyolysis with the combination of sirolimus and cyclosporine. Monitor patient closely.
Ketoconazole: Increases rate and extent of sirolimus absorption. Avoid using together.
Live virus vaccines (BCG, measles, mumps, oral polio, rubella, TY21a typhoid, varicella, yellow fever): Reduces effectiveness of vaccines. Avoid using together.
Rifampin: Decreases sirolimus level. Consider alternatives to rifampin.
Drug-food. *Grapefruit juice:* Decreases metabolism of sirolimus. Avoid using together.
Drug-lifestyle. *Sun exposure:* Increases risk of skin cancer. Take precautions.

Effects on lab test results

• May increase BUN, creatinine, liver enzyme, cholesterol, and lipid levels. May decrease sodium and magnesium levels. May increase or decrease phosphate, potassium, glucose, and calcium levels.
• May increase RBC count. May decrease platelet count, hemoglobin, and hematocrit. May increase or decrease WBC count.

Pharmacokinetics

Absorption: Rapid, with mean peak levels occurring in about 1 to 3 hours. Oral bioavailability is about 14%. Food decreases peak plasma levels and increases time to peak level.
Distribution: Extensively partitioned into formed blood elements. Drug is extensively bound to plasma proteins (about 92%).
Metabolism: Extensively metabolized by the mixed function oxidase system, primarily cytochrome P-450 3A4. Seven major metabolites have been identified in whole blood.
Excretion: 91% in feces and in 2.2% urine. *Half-life:* About 62 hours.

Route	Onset	Peak	Duration
P.O.	Unknown	1-3 hr	Unknown

Pharmacodynamics

Chemical effect: An immunosuppressant that inhibits T-lymphocyte activation and proliferation that occur in response to antigenic and cytokine stimulation. Also inhibits antibody formation.
Therapeutic effect: Immunosuppression in patients receiving renal transplants.

Available forms

Oral solution: 1 mg/ml
Tablets: 1 mg

NURSING PROCESS

Assessment

• Obtain history of patient's organ transplantation before therapy.
• Monitor patient's liver and renal function and serum triglycerides before therapy.
• Monitor sirolimus levels in children, patients 13 and older who weigh less than 40 kg (88 lb); patients with hepatic impairment; patients receiving administration of drugs that induce or inhibit CYP3A4; and patients whose cyclosporine dosage is markedly reduced or discontinued.

• Monitor patient for infection and development of lymphoma, which may result from immunosuppression.
• Watch for development of rhabdomyolysis if patient is receiving sirolimus and cyclosporine is started as an HMG-CoA reductase inhibitor.
• Evaluate patient's and family's knowledge about drug therapy.

Nursing diagnoses

• Risk for injury related to potential for organ rejection
• Ineffective protection related to drug-induced immunosuppression
• Deficient knowledge related to drug therapy

Planning and implementation

• Drug should be taken consistently with or without food.
ALERT: In patients with mild-to-moderate hepatic impairment, reduce maintenance dose by about one-third. It isn't needed to reduce loading dose.
• Oral solution must be diluted before administration. After dilution, it should be used immediately.
• When diluting drug, empty correct amount into glass or plastic container filled with at least 2 ounces (60 ml) of water or orange juice. Don't use grapefruit juice or any other liquid. Stir vigorously and have patient drink immediately. Refill container with at least 4 ounces (120 ml) of water or orange juice, stir again, and have patient drink all contents.
• After opening bottle, use contents within 1 month. If needed, bottles and pouches may be stored at room temperature (up to 77° F [25° C]) for several days. Drug can be kept in oral dosing syringe for 24 hours at room temperature or refrigerated at 36° to 46° F.
• A slight haze may develop during refrigeration, but this won't affect quality of drug. If haze develops, bring drug to room temperature and shake gently until haze disappears.
• Drug should be used in a regimen with cyclosporine and corticosteroids. Sirolimus should be taken 4 hours after cyclosporine dose.
• After transplantation, give antimicrobials for 1 year as directed to prevent *Pneumocystis carinii* pneumonia and for 3 months as directed to prevent cytomegalovirus infection.
• If patient has hyperlipidemia, additional interventions, such as diet, exercise, and lipid-lowering drugs, should start. Treatment with lipid-lowering drugs during therapy is common.

Patient teaching

• Show patient how to properly store, dilute, and administer drug.
• Tell patient to take drug consistently with or without food to minimize absorption variability.
• Advise patient to take drug 4 hours after taking cyclosporine.
• Tell patient to wash area with soap and water if solution touches skin or mucous membranes; tell him to rinse eyes with plain water if solution gets in eyes.
• Inform woman of childbearing age of risks during pregnancy. Tell her to use effective contraception before, during, and for 12 weeks after stopping drug.
• Advise patient to take precautions against sun exposure.

Evaluation

• Patient doesn't experience organ rejection.
• Patient is free from infection and serious bleeding episodes throughout drug therapy.
• Patient and family state understanding of drug therapy.

sodium bicarbonate

(SOH-dee-um bigh-KAR-buh-nayt)
Arm and Hammer Pure Baking Soda, Bell/ans, Citrocarbonate, Soda Mint

Pharmacologic class: alkalinizing agent
Therapeutic class: systemic and urine alkalinizer, systemic hydrogen ion buffer, oral antacid
Pregnancy risk category: C

Indications and dosages

▶ **Adjunct to advanced cardiovascular life support during CPR.** *Adults:* Although no longer routinely recommended, inject either 300 to 500 ml of a 5% solution or 200 to 300 mEq of a 7.5% or 8.4% solution as rapidly as possible. Base further doses on subsequent blood gas values. Alternatively, 1 mEq/kg dose, then repeat 0.5 mEq/kg q 10 minutes.

Children age 2 and younger: 1 mEq/kg I.V. or intraosseous injection of a 4.2 % to 8.4% solution. Give slowly. Don't exceed daily dose of 8 mEq/kg.

▶ **Severe metabolic acidosis.** *Adults:* Dose depends on blood carbon dioxide content, pH, and patient's clinical condition. Generally, give 90 to 180 mEq/L I.V. during first hour, then adjust, p.r.n.

▶ **Less urgent metabolic acidosis.** *Adults and adolescents:* 2 to 5 mEq/kg as a 4- to 8-hour I.V. infusion.

▶ **Urine alkalization.** *Adults:* 48 mEq (4 g) P.O. initially, then 12 to 24 mEq (1 to 2 g) q 4 hours. May need doses of 30 to 48 mEq (2.5 to 4 g) q 4 hours, up to 192 mEq (16g) daily.
Children: 1 to 10 mEq (84 to 840 mg)/kg P.O. daily.

▶ **Antacid.** *Adults:* 300 mg to 2 g P.O. one to four times daily.

Contraindications and precautions

• Contraindicated in patients with metabolic or respiratory alkalosis, patients who are losing chlorides from vomiting or continuous GI suction, patients receiving diuretics known to produce hypochloremic alkalosis, and patients with hypocalcemia in which alkalosis may produce tetany, hypertension, seizures, or heart failure. Oral sodium bicarbonate is contraindicated in patients with acute ingestion of strong mineral acids.

• Use with extreme caution in patients with heart failure or other edematous or sodium-retaining conditions or renal insufficiency.

Lifespan: In pregnant or breast-feeding women, use cautiously.

Adverse reactions

GI: gastric distention, belching, flatulence.
Metabolic: ***metabolic alkalosis,*** hypernatremia, hypokalemia, hyperosmolarity (with overdose).
Skin: pain and irritation at injection site.

Interactions

Drug-drug. *Anorexigenics, flecainide, mecamylamine, quinidine, sympathomimetics:* Increased urine alkalinization causes increased renal clearance and reduces effectiveness of these drugs. Monitor patient closely.
Chlorpropamide, lithium, methotrexate, salicylates, tetracycline: Urine alkalinization causes decreased renal clearance of these drugs and increases risk of toxicity. Monitor patient closely.
Enteric-coated drugs: May be released prematurely in stomach. Avoid using together.
Ketoconazole: May decrease absorption. Use with caution.

Effects on lab test results

• May increase sodium and lactate levels. May decrease potassium level.

Pharmacokinetics

Absorption: Well absorbed after P.O. administration.
Distribution: Bicarbonate is confined to systemic circulation.
Metabolism: None.
Excretion: Bicarbonate is filtered and reabsorbed by kidneys; less than 1% of filtered bicarbonate is excreted.

Route	Onset	Peak	Duration
P.O.	Unknown	Unknown	Unknown
I.V.	Immediate	Immediate	Unknown

Pharmacodynamics

Chemical effect: Restores body's buffering capacity and neutralizes excess acid.
Therapeutic effect: Restores normal acid-base balance and relieves acid indigestion.

Available forms

Injection: 4% (2.4 mEq/5 ml), 4.2% (5 mEq/10 ml), 5% (297.5 mEq/500 ml), 7.5% (8.92 mEq/10 ml and 44.6 mEq/50 ml), 8.4% (10 mEq/10 ml and 50 mEq/50 ml)
Tablets†: 300 mg, 325 mg, 520 mg, 600 mg, 650 mg

NURSING PROCESS

Assessment

• Assess patient's condition before therapy and regularly thereafter.
• To avoid risk of alkalosis, obtain blood pH, Pao_2, $Paco_2$, and serum electrolyte levels.
• If sodium bicarbonate is being used to produce alkaline urine, monitor urine pH (should be greater than 7) every 4 to 6 hours.

• Be alert for adverse reactions and drug interactions.
• Evaluate patient's and family's knowledge of drug therapy.

Nursing diagnoses

• Ineffective health maintenance related to underlying condition
• Risk for injury related to drug-induced adverse reactions
• Deficient knowledge related to drug therapy

Planning and implementation

• Drug isn't routinely recommended for use in cardiac arrest because it may produce paradoxical acidosis from CO_2 production. It shouldn't be routinely given during early stages of resuscitation unless acidosis is clearly present. Drug may be used at team leader's discretion after such interventions as defibrillation, cardiac compression, and administration of first-line drugs.
• **P.O. use:** Give drug with water, not milk.
• **I.V. use:** Drug is usually given by I.V. infusion. When immediate treatment is needed, drug may be given by direct, rapid I.V. injection. However, in neonates and children younger than age 2, slow I.V. administration is preferred to avoid hypernatremia, decreased CSF pressure, and possible intracranial hemorrhage.
ALERT: Sodium bicarbonate inactivates such catecholamines as norepinephrine and dopamine and forms precipitate with calcium. Don't mix sodium bicarbonate with I.V. solutions of these drugs, and flush I.V. line adequately.
• Keep prescriber informed of laboratory results.

Patient teaching

• Tell patient not to take with milk. Drug may cause hypercalcemia, alkalosis, or possibly renal calculi.
• Discourage use as antacid. Offer nonabsorbable alternate antacid if it is to be used repeatedly.

Evaluation

• Patient regains normal acid-base balance.
• Patient doesn't experience injury from drug-induced adverse reactions.
• Patient and family state understanding of drug therapy.

sodium chloride
(SOH-dee-um KLOR-ighd)

Pharmacologic class: electrolyte
Therapeutic class: sodium and chloride replacement
Pregnancy risk category: C

Indications and dosages

▶ **Fluid and electrolyte replacement in hyponatremia caused by electrolyte loss, severe salt depletion.** *Adults:* Dosage is highly individualized. The 3% and 5% solutions are used only with frequent electrolyte determination and given only by slow I.V. With half-normal saline solution: 3% to 8% of body weight, according to deficiencies, over 18 to 24 hours. With normal saline solution: 2% to 6% of body weight, according to deficiencies, over 18 to 24 hours.
▶ **Management of heat cramp caused by excessive perspiration.** *Adults:* 1 g P.O. with every glass of water.

Contraindications and precautions

• Contraindicated in patients with conditions in which sodium and chloride administration is detrimental. The 3% and 5% saline solution injections are contraindicated in patients with increased, normal, or only slightly decreased electrolyte levels.
• Use cautiously in postoperative patients and patients with heart failure, circulatory insufficiency, renal dysfunction, or hypoproteinemia.
Lifespan: In pregnant and breast-feeding women and in geriatric patients, use cautiously.

Adverse reactions

CV: ***aggravation of heart failure,*** edema if given too rapidly or in excess, thrombophlebitis.
Metabolic: hypernatremia, ***aggravation of existing metabolic acidosis*** with excessive infusion, electrolyte disturbances, hypokalemia.
Respiratory: ***pulmonary edema*** if given too rapidly or in excess.

Skin: local tenderness, abscess, tissue necrosis at injection site.

Interactions

None significant.

Effects on lab test results

- May increase sodium level. May decrease potassium level.

Pharmacokinetics

Absorption: Absorbed readily from GI tract after P.O. administration.
Distribution: Distributed widely in body.
Metabolism: None significant.
Excretion: Excreted primarily in urine; some excreted in sweat, tears, and saliva.

Route	Onset	Peak	Duration
P.O.	Unknown	Unknown	Unknown
I.V.	Immediate	Immediate	Unknown

Pharmacodynamics

Chemical effect: Replaces and maintains sodium and chloride levels.
Therapeutic effect: Restores normal sodium and chloride levels.

Available forms

Injection: *Half-normal saline solution:* 500 ml, 1,000 ml
Normal saline solution: 50 ml, 100 ml, 150 ml, 250 ml, 500 ml, 1,000 ml
3% saline solution: 500 ml
5% saline solution: 500 ml
14.6% saline solution: 20 ml, 40 ml, 200 ml
23.4% saline solution: 30 ml, 50 ml, 200 ml
Tablets (enteric-coated): 650 mg, 1 g, 2.25 g
Tablets (slow-release): 600 mg

NURSING PROCESS

Assessment

- Obtain history of patient's sodium and chloride levels before therapy, and reassess regularly thereafter.
- Monitor other electrolyte levels.
- Assess patient's fluid status.
- Be alert for adverse reactions.
- Evaluate patient's and family's knowledge of drug therapy.

Nursing diagnoses

- Imbalanced nutrition: less than body requirements related to subnormal levels of sodium and chloride
- Excess fluid volume related to saline solution's water-drawing power
- Deficient knowledge related to drug therapy

Planning and implementation

- **P.O. use:** Give tablet with glass of water.
- **I.V. use:** Infuse 3% and 5% solutions very slowly and cautiously to avoid pulmonary edema. Use only for critical situations, and observe patient continually.

ALERT: Don't confuse concentrates (14.6% and 23.4%) available to add to parenteral nutrient solutions with normal saline solution injection, and never give without diluting. Read label carefully.

Patient teaching

- Tell patient to report adverse reactions promptly.

Evaluation

- Patient's sodium and chloride levels are normal.
- Patient doesn't exhibit signs and symptoms of fluid retention.
- Patient and family state understanding of drug therapy.

sodium ferric gluconate complex

(SOH-dee-um FEH-rik GLOO-kuh-nayt KOM-pleks)
Ferrlecit

Pharmacologic class: macromolecular iron complex
Therapeutic class: hematinic
Pregnancy risk category: B

Indications and dosages

▶ **Treatment of iron deficiency anemia in patients undergoing long-term hemodialysis who are receiving supplemental erythropoietin therapy.** *Adults:* Before starting therapeutic doses, give a test dose of 2 ml sodium ferric gluconate complex (25 mg elemental iron) diluted in 50 ml normal saline solution I.V. over 1 hour. If test dose is tolerated, give therapeutic dose of 10 ml (125 mg elemental iron) diluted in 100 ml normal saline solution I.V. over 1 hour. Most patients need a minimum cumulative dose of 1 g elemental iron given at more than eight sequential dialysis treatments to achieve a favorable hemoglobin or hematocrit response.

Contraindications and precautions

• Contraindicated in patients hypersensitive to sodium ferric gluconate complex or its components (such as benzyl alcohol). Also contraindicated in patients with anemias not linked to iron deficiency. Don't give to patients with iron overload.

Lifespan: In breast-feeding women and geriatric patients, use cautiously. In children, safety hasn't been established.

Adverse reactions

CNS: asthenia, headache, fatigue, malaise, dizziness, paresthesia, agitation, insomnia, somnolence, syncope, pain, fever.
CV: hypotension, hypertension, tachycardia, ***bradycardia,*** angina, chest pain, ***MI,*** edema, flushing.
EENT: conjunctivitis, abnormal vision, rhinitis.
GI: nausea, vomiting, diarrhea, rectal disorder, dyspepsia, eructation, flatulence, melena, abdominal pain.
GU: urinary tract infection.
Hematologic: abnormal erythrocytes, anemia.
Metabolic: ***hyperkalemia, hypoglycemia,*** hypokalemia, hypervolemia.
Musculoskeletal: myalgia, arthralgia, back pain, arm pain, cramps.
Respiratory: dyspnea, coughing, upper respiratory tract infections, pneumonia, pulmonary edema.
Skin: pruritus, increased sweating, rash, injection site reaction.
Other: infection, rigors, chills, flulike syndrome, ***sepsis, carcinoma, hypersensitivity reactions,*** lymphadenopathy.

Interactions

None reported.

Effects on lab test results

• May decrease glucose level. May increase or decrease potassium level.
• May decrease hemoglobin and hematocrit.

Pharmacokinetics

Absorption: Administered I.V.
Distribution: Unknown.
Metabolism: Unknown.
Excretion: Unknown.

Route	Onset	Peak	Duration
I.V.	Unknown	Unknown	Unknown

Pharmacodynamics

Chemical effect: Drug restores total body iron content, which is critical for normal hemoglobin synthesis and oxygen transport. Iron deficiency in hemodialysis patients can result from increased iron utilization (such as from erythropoietin therapy), blood loss (such as from fistula, retention in dialyzer, hematologic testing, menses), decreased dietary intake or absorption, surgery, iron sequestration because of inflammatory process, and malignancy.
Therapeutic effect: Restores total body iron content.

Available forms

Injection: 62.5 mg elemental iron (12.5 mg/ml) in 5-ml ampules

NURSING PROCESS

Assessment

• Obtain history of patient's underlying condition before therapy, and reassess regularly thereafter.
• Check with patient about other possible sources of iron, such as nonprescription iron preparations and iron-containing multiple vitamins with minerals.
• Monitor hematocrit and hemoglobin, serum ferritin, and iron saturation levels during therapy.
• Evaluate patient's and family's knowledge of drug therapy.

Nursing diagnoses

• Risk for injury related to drug-induced adverse reactions
• Activity intolerance related to underlying condition
• Deficient knowledge related to drug therapy

Planning and implementation

• Dilute test dose of sodium ferric gluconate complex in 50 ml normal saline solution and give over 1 hour. Dilute therapeutic doses of drug in 100 ml normal saline solution and give over 1 hour.

- Don't mix sodium ferric gluconate complex with other drugs or add to parenteral nutrition solutions for I.V. infusion. Use immediately after dilution in normal saline solution.

ALERT: Patient may develop profound hypotension with flushing, light-headedness, malaise, fatigue, weakness, or severe chest, back, flank, or groin pain after rapid I.V. administration of iron. These reactions don't indicate hypersensitivity and may result from too-rapid administration of drug. Don't exceed recommended rate of administration (2.1 mg/minute). Monitor patient closely during infusion.

- Dose is expressed in mg of elemental iron.
- Don't give drug to patients with iron overload, which commonly occurs in hemoglobinopathies and other refractory anemias.

ALERT: Potentially life-threatening hypersensitivity reactions may occur during infusion (characterized by CV collapse, cardiac arrest, bronchospasm, oral or pharyngeal edema, dyspnea, angioedema, urticaria, or pruritus sometimes linked with pain and muscle spasm of chest or back). Have adequate supportive measures readily available. Monitor patient closely during infusion.

- Some adverse reactions in hemodialysis patients may be related to dialysis itself or to chronic renal failure.

Patient teaching

- Abdominal pain, diarrhea, vomiting, drowsiness, or hyperventilation may indicate iron poisoning. Advise patient to report any of these symptoms immediately.

Evaluation

- Patient doesn't experience injury as a result of drug-induced adverse reactions.
- Patient experiences improved activity tolerance.
- Patient and family state understanding of drug therapy.

sodium fluoride

(SOH-dee-um FLOR-ighd)

Fluor-A-Day ♦, Fluoritab, Fluorodex, Fluotic ♦, Flura, Flura-Drops, Flura-Loz, Flura-Tab, Karidium, Luride, Luride Lozi-Tabs, Luride-SF, Luride-SF Lozi-Tabs, Pediaflor, Pedi-Dent ♦, Pharmaflur, Pharmaflur df, Pharmaflur 1.1, Phos-Flur, Solu-Flur ♦

sodium fluoride, topical

ACT†, Control RX, Fluorigard†, Fluorinse, Gel-Kam, Gel-Tin†, Karigel, Karigel-N, Listermint with Fluoride, Minute-Gel, Neutra-Foam, Point-Two, Prevident, Prevident 5000 Plus, SF 5000 Plus, Thera-Flur, Thera-Flur-N

Pharmacologic class: trace mineral
Therapeutic class: dental caries prophylactic
Pregnancy risk category: NR

Indications and dosages

▶ **Prevention of dental caries.** *Adults and children older than age 6:* 10 ml of rinse or thin ribbon of gel or cream applied to teeth with toothbrush or mouth trays for at least 1 minute h.s. When using cream, patient should brush teeth for 2 minutes and then expectorate; children ages 6 to 16 years should rinse mouth after expectorating.

Alternatively, P.O. dosing for children is as follows:

If fluoride level less than 0.3 ppm (mg/L):
Children ages 6 months to 2 years: 0.25 mg P.O. daily.
Children ages 3 to 5 years: 0.5 mg P.O. daily.
Children ages 6 to 16 years: 1 mg P.O. daily.
If fluoride level 0.3 to 0.6 ppm (mg/L):
Children ages 3 to 5 years: 0.25 mg P.O. daily.
Children ages 6 to 16 years: 0.5 mg P.O. daily.

Contraindications and precautions

- Contraindicated in patients hypersensitive to fluoride and in those whose drinking water exceeds 0.7 ppm of fluoride.

Lifespan: In pregnant or breast-feeding women, use cautiously.

Adverse reactions

CNS: headache, weakness.
GI: gastric distress.

Other: hypersensitivity reactions, staining of teeth.

Interactions

Drug-drug. *Aluminum hydroxide, calcium, iron, magnesium:* May decrease absorption. Give separately.
Drug-food. *Dairy products:* Incompatibility may occur because of formation of calcium fluoride, which is poorly absorbed. Avoid ingestion during sodium fluoride therapy.

Effects on lab test results

None reported.

Pharmacokinetics

Absorption: Absorbed readily and almost completely from GI tract. A large amount may be absorbed in stomach, and rate may depend on gastric pH. Oral fluoride absorption may be decreased by simultaneous ingestion of aluminum or magnesium hydroxide. Simultaneous ingestion of calcium also may decrease absorption of large doses.
Distribution: Stored in bones and developing teeth after absorption. Skeletal tissue also has high storage capacity for fluoride ions. Because of storage-mobilization mechanism in skeletal tissue, constant fluoride supply may be provided. Although teeth have small mass, they also serve as storage sites. Fluoride deposited in teeth isn't released readily. Fluoride has been found in all organs and tissues with low accumulation in noncalcified tissues. Fluoride is distributed into sweat, tears, hair, and saliva.
Metabolism: None.
Excretion: Excreted rapidly, mainly in urine.

Route	Onset	Peak	Duration
P.O.	Unknown	30-60 min	Unknown

Pharmacodynamics

Chemical effect: Stabilizes apatite crystal of bone and teeth.
Therapeutic effect: Prevents dental caries.

Available forms

sodium fluoride
Tablets: 1 mg
Tablets (chewable): 0.25 mg, 0.5 mg, 1 mg
Oral solution: 0.5 mg/ml, 2.21 mg/ml, 5 mg/ml

sodium fluoride, topical
Cream: 1.1%
Foam: 2%
Gel: 0.5%
Gel drops: 0.5%
Rinse: 0.01%†, 0.02%†, 0.09%

NURSING PROCESS

Assessment

• Obtain history of patient's dental history and fluoride intake before therapy, and reassess regularly thereafter.
• Be alert for adverse reactions and drug interactions.
• Chronic toxicity (fluorosis) may result from prolonged use of higher-than-recommended doses.
• Evaluate patient's and family's knowledge of drug therapy.

Nursing diagnoses

• Health-seeking behavior related to desire for good dental care
• Risk for deficient fluid volume related to drug-induced adverse GI reactions
• Deficient knowledge related to drug therapy

Planning and implementation

• Give oral drops undiluted or mixed with fluids or food.
• Fluoride in prenatal vitamins may produce healthier teeth in infants.
ALERT: Chronic toxicity (fluorosis) may result from prolonged use of higher-than-recommended doses.

Patient teaching

• Tell patient that tablets may be dissolved in mouth, chewed, or swallowed whole.
• Advise parents that topical rinses and gels shouldn't be swallowed by children younger than age 3 or used if water supply is fluorinated.
• Tell patient that sodium fluoride is most effective when used immediately after brushing teeth. Tell patient to rinse around and between teeth for 1 minute, and then spit fluid out.
• Tell patient to dilute drops or rinses in plastic rather than glass containers.
• Advise patient to notify dentist of tooth mottling.

Evaluation
- Patient is free from dental caries.
- Patient maintains adequate hydration throughout therapy.
- Patient and family state understanding of drug therapy.

sodium lactate
(SOH-dee-um LAK-tayt)

Pharmacologic class: alkalinizer
Therapeutic class: systemic alkalizer
Pregnancy risk category: NR

Indications and dosages
▶ **Urine alkalinization.** *Adults:* 30 ml of 1⁄6 molar solution per kg of body weight P.O. given in divided doses over 24 hours.
▶ **Metabolic acidosis.** *Adults:* 1⁄6 molar injection (167 mEq lactate/L) I.V.; dose depends on degree of bicarbonate deficit.

Contraindications and precautions
- Contraindicated in patients with hypernatremia, lactic acidosis, or conditions in which sodium administration is detrimental.
- Use with extreme caution in patients with metabolic or respiratory alkalosis, severe hepatic or renal disease, shock, hypoxia, or beriberi.

Lifespan: In pregnant or breast-feeding women, use cautiously.

Adverse reactions
CNS: fever.
CV: thrombophlebitis at injection site.
Metabolic: ***metabolic alkalosis,*** hypernatremia, hyperosmolarity with overdose.
Other: infection.

Interactions
None significant.

Effects on lab test results
- May increase sodium level.

Pharmacokinetics
Absorption: Administered I.V.
Distribution: Lactate ion occurs naturally throughout body.
Metabolism: Metabolized in liver.
Excretion: None.

Route	Onset	Peak	Duration
I.V.	Immediate	Immediate	Unknown

Pharmacodynamics
Chemical effect: Metabolized to sodium bicarbonate, producing buffering effect.
Therapeutic effect: Restores normal acid-base balance.

Available forms
Injection: 1/6 molar solution (167 mEq/L), 5 mEq/ml

NURSING PROCESS

Assessment
- Obtain history of patient's underlying acid-base imbalance before therapy, and reassess regularly thereafter.
- Monitor electrolyte levels.
- Evaluate patient's and family's knowledge of drug therapy.

Nursing diagnoses
- Ineffective health maintenance related to underlying condition
- Ineffective protection related to drug-induced adverse reactions
- Deficient knowledge related to drug therapy

Planning and implementation
- Add drug to other I.V. solutions or give as isotonic 1/6 molar solution. Drug is compatible with most common I.V. solutions.
- Don't mix with sodium bicarbonate because drugs are physically incompatible.

Patient teaching
- Instruct patient to report discomfort at I.V. site immediately.

Evaluation
- Patient regains normal acid-base balance.
- Patient doesn't experience serious adverse reactions.
- Patient and family state understanding of drug therapy.

sodium phosphates
(SOH-dee-um FOS-fayts)
Fleet Phospho-soda†, Fleet Enema, Fleet Pediatric Enema

Pharmacologic class: acid salt
Therapeutic class: saline laxative
Pregnancy risk category: NR

Indications and dosages

▶ **Constipation.** *Adults and children age 12 and older:* 20 to 45 ml of solution mixed with 120 ml of cold water P.O. Or, 120 ml P.R. (as enema).
Children 10 to 11 years: 10 to 20 ml of solution mixed with 120 ml of cold water P.O.
Children 5 to 9 years: 5 to 10 ml of solution mixed with 120 ml of cold water P.O.
Children older than age 2: 60 ml P.R.

Contraindications and precautions

• Contraindicated in patients on sodium-restricted diets and patients with intestinal obstruction or perforation, edema, heart failure, megacolon, impaired renal function, or symptoms of appendicitis or acute surgical abdomen, such as abdominal pain, nausea, and vomiting.
• Use cautiously in patients with large hemorrhoids or anal excoriations.
Lifespan: In pregnant or breast-feeding women, use cautiously. In children younger than age 4, use only as directed by prescriber.

Adverse reactions

GI: *abdominal cramps.*
Metabolic: fluid and electrolyte disturbances (such as hypernatremia or hyperphosphatemia) with daily use.
Other: laxative dependence with long-term or excessive use.

Interactions

None significant.

Effects on lab test results

• May increase sodium and phosphate levels. May decrease electrolyte levels with prolonged use.

Pharmacokinetics

Absorption: About 1% to 20% of P.O. dose absorbed; unknown after P.R. administration.
Distribution: Unknown.
Metabolism: Unknown.
Excretion: Unknown.

Route	Onset	Peak	Duration
P.O.	30 min-3 hr	Varies	Varies
P.R.	5-10 min	Varies	Ends with evacuation

Pharmacodynamics

Chemical effect: Produces osmotic effect in small intestine by drawing water into intestinal lumen.
Therapeutic effect: Relieves constipation.

Available forms

Enema: 160 mg/ml sodium phosphate and 60 mg/ml sodium biphosphate
Liquid: 2.4 g/5 ml sodium phosphate and 900 mg/5 ml sodium biphosphate

NURSING PROCESS

Assessment

• Assess patient's condition before therapy and regularly thereafter.
• Before giving drug for constipation, determine whether patient has adequate fluid intake, exercise, and diet.
• Be alert for adverse reactions.
ALERT: Up to 10% of sodium content of drug may be absorbed.
• Evaluate patient's and family's knowledge of drug therapy.

Nursing diagnoses

• Constipation related to underlying condition
• Acute pain related to drug-induced abdominal cramping
• Deficient knowledge related to drug therapy

Planning and implementation

• **P.O. use:** Dilute drug with water before giving. Follow administration with full glass of water.
• **P.R. use:** Follow normal protocol.
• Make sure that patient has easy access to bathroom facilities, commode, or bedpan.
ALERT: Severe electrolyte imbalances may occur if recommended dosage is exceeded.

Patient teaching

- Teach patient about dietary sources of bulk, which include bran and other cereals, fresh fruit, and vegetables.
- Tell patient to maintain adequate fluid intake of at least 6 to 8 glasses of water or juices daily unless contraindicated.

Evaluation

- Patient's constipation is relieved.
- Patient's abdominal cramping ceases.
- Patient and family state understanding of drug therapy.

sodium phosphate monohydrate

(SOE-dee-um FOS-fate maw-no-HIGH-drate)

sodium phosphate dibasic anhydrous

(SOE-dee-um FOS-fate die-BAY-sick an-HIGH-drus)

Visicol

Pharmacologic class: osmotic laxative
Therapeutic class: bowel evacuant
Pregnancy risk category: C

Indications and dosages

▶ **Cleansing of the bowel before colonoscopy.** *Adults:* 40 tablets taken in the following manner: The evening before the procedure, 3 tablets P.O. with at least 8 oz of clear liquid q 15 minutes for a total of 20 tablets. The last dose will be only 2 tablets. The day of the procedure, 3 tablets P.O. with at least 8 oz of clear liquid q 15 minutes for a total of 20 tablets, starting 3 to 5 hours before the procedure. The last dose will be only 2 tablets.

Contraindications and precautions

- Contraindicated in patients hypersensitive to sodium phosphate or any of its ingredients. Avoid giving drug to patients with heart failure, ascites, unstable angina, gastric retention, ileus, acute intestinal obstruction, pseudo-obstruction, severe chronic constipation, bowel perforation, acute colitis, toxic megacolon, or hypomotility syndrome (hypothyroidism, scleroderma).
- Use cautiously in patients with a history of electrolyte abnormalities, current electrolyte abnormalities, or impaired renal function.
- Use cautiously in patients who take drugs that can induce electrolyte abnormalities or prolong the QT interval.

Lifespan: In patients younger than age 18, safety and efficacy haven't been established. In geriatric patients, use cautiously. No dosage adjustment is needed, but greater sensitivity in some older patients cannot be ruled out.

Adverse reactions

CNS: headache, dizziness.
GI: nausea, vomiting, abdominal bloating, abdominal pain.

Interactions

Drug-drug. *Oral drugs:* Reduces absorption of these drugs because of rapid peristalsis and diarrhea induced by sodium phosphate monohydrate and sodium phosphate dibasic anhydrous. Separate administration times.

Effects on lab test results

- May increase phosphorus level. May decrease potassium and calcium levels.

Pharmacokinetics

Absorption: Quick. Duration of action is 1 to 3 hours after administration.
Distribution: Unknown.
Metabolism: Not expected to be metabolized by the liver.
Excretion: Eliminated almost entirely via the kidneys.

Route	Onset	Peak	Duration
P.O.	Unknown	3 hr	1-3 hr

Pharmacodynamics

Chemical effect: The primary mechanism is thought to be the osmotic action of sodium, which causes large amounts of water to be drawn into the colon.
Therapeutic effect: Cleanses the colon.

Available forms

Tablets: 1.5 g sodium phosphate (1.102 g sodium phosphate monohydrate and 0.398 g sodium phosphate dibasic anhydrous)

NURSING PROCESS

Assessment
- Assess underlying condition before therapy and reassess regularly throughout therapy.
- Obtain laboratory studies before beginning therapy and correct electrolyte imbalances before giving drug.
- Evaluate patient's and family's knowledge of drug therapy.

Nursing diagnoses
- Acute pain related to abdominal discomfort
- Risk for deficient fluid volume related to adverse GI effects
- Deficient knowledge related to drug therapy

Planning and implementation
- Undigested or partially digested tablets and other drugs may be seen in the stool or during colonoscopy.
- As with other sodium phosphate cathartic preparations, this drug may induce colonic mucosal ulceration.
- Monitor patient for signs of dehydration.
- Don't repeat administration within 7 days.
- No enema or laxative is needed with drug. Patients shouldn't take any additional purgatives, particularly those that contain sodium phosphate.

ALERT: Administration of other sodium phosphate products may result in death from significant fluid shifts, electrolyte abnormalities, and cardiac arrhythmias. Patients with electrolyte disturbances have an increased risk of prolonged QT interval. Use drug cautiously in patients who are taking other drugs known to prolong the QT interval.

Patient teaching
- Urge patient to drink at least 8 ounces of clear liquid with each dose. Inadequate fluid intake may lead to excessive fluid loss and hypovolemia.
- Tell patient to drink only clear liquids for at least 12 hours before starting the purgative regimen.
- Caution patient against taking an additional purgative agent (enema or laxative), particularly one that contains sodium phosphate.
- Tell patient that undigested or partially digested tablets and other drugs may appear in the stool.

Evaluation
- Patient states that pain management methods are effective.
- Patient maintains adequate hydration.
- Patient and family state understanding of therapy.

sodium polystyrene sulfonate
(SOH-dee-um pol-ee-STIGH-reen SUL-fuh-nayt)
Kayexalate, SPS

Pharmacologic class: cation-exchange resin
Therapeutic class: potassium-removing resin
Pregnancy risk category: C

Indications and dosages
▶ **Hyperkalemia.** *Adults:* 15 g P.O. daily to q.i.d. in water or sorbitol (3 to 4 ml/g of resin). Or, mix powder with appropriate medium—aqueous suspension or diet appropriate for renal failure—and instill into NG tube. Or, 30 to 50 g q 6 hours as warm emulsion deep into sigmoid colon (20 cm). In persistent vomiting or paralytic ileus, high-retention enema of sodium polystyrene sulfonate (30 g) suspended in 200 ml of 10% methylcellulose, 10% dextrose, or 25% sorbitol solution may be given.
Children: 1 g of resin P.O. or P.R. for each mEq of potassium to be removed. P.O. route preferred because drug should stay in intestine for at least 6 hours.

Contraindications and precautions
- Contraindicated in patients hypersensitive to drug and in those with hypokalemia.
- Use cautiously in patients with severe heart failure, severe hypertension, or marked edema.

Lifespan: In pregnant or breast-feeding women, use cautiously.

Adverse reactions
GI: *constipation,* fecal impaction in geriatric patients, anorexia, gastric irritation, nausea, vomiting, *diarrhea* with sorbitol emulsions.
Metabolic: hypokalemia, hypocalcemia, sodium retention.

Interactions
Drug-drug. *Antacids and laxatives (nonabsorbable cation-donating types, including magnesium hydroxide):* May cause systemic

alkalosis and reduced potassium exchange capability. Don't use together.

Effects on lab test results

- May increase sodium level. May decrease potassium, calcium, and magnesium levels.

Pharmacokinetics

Absorption: None.
Distribution: None.
Metabolism: None.
Excretion: Excreted unchanged in feces.

Route	Onset	Peak	Duration
P.O., P.R.	Unknown	Unknown	Unknown

Pharmacodynamics

Chemical effect: Exchanges sodium ions for potassium ions in intestine: 1 g of sodium polystyrene sulfonate is exchanged for 0.5 to 1.0 mEq of potassium. The resin is then eliminated. Much of exchange capacity is used for cations other than potassium (calcium and magnesium) and, possibly, fats and proteins.
Therapeutic effect: Lowers potassium level.

Available forms

Powder: 1-lb jar (3.5 g/teaspoon)
Suspension: 60 ml*, 120 ml*, 200 ml*, 480 ml*, 500 ml*

NURSING PROCESS

Assessment

- Obtain history of patient's potassium level before therapy.
- Monitor potassium level at least once daily. Treatment may result in potassium deficiency. Treatment usually stops when potassium level declines to 4 or 5 mEq/L.

ALERT: Watch for other signs of hypokalemia, such as irritability, confusion, arrhythmias, ECG changes, severe muscle weakness and paralysis, and cardiac toxicity in digitalized patients.

- Monitor patient for symptoms of other electrolyte deficiencies (magnesium, calcium) because drug is nonselective. Monitor calcium level in patient receiving sodium polystyrene therapy for more than 3 days. Supplementary calcium may be needed.
- Watch for sodium overload. Drug contains about 100 mg of sodium/g. About one-third of sodium in resin is retained.
- Be alert for adverse reactions and drug interactions.
- Watch for constipation with P.O. or NG administration.
- Evaluate patient's and family's knowledge of drug therapy.

Nursing diagnoses

- Ineffective health maintenance related to presence of hyperkalemia
- Constipation related to drug-induced adverse GI reactions
- Deficient knowledge related to drug therapy

Planning and implementation

- Don't heat resin; doing so will impair drug's effectiveness.
- **P.O. use:** Mix resin only with water or sorbitol for P.O. administration. Never mix with orange juice (high potassium content) to disguise taste.

– Chill oral suspension for greater palatability.
– If sorbitol is given, mix with resin suspension.
– Consider solid form. Resin cookie and candy recipes are available; ask pharmacist or dietitian to supply.
– To prevent constipation, use sorbitol (10 to 20 ml of 70% syrup every 2 hours, as needed) to produce one or two watery stools daily.

- **P.R. use:** Premixed forms are available (SPS and others).

– If preparing manually, mix polystyrene resin only with water and sorbitol for P.R. use. Don't use mineral oil for P.R. administration to prevent impaction; ion exchange requires aqueous medium. Sorbitol content prevents impaction.
– Prepare P.R. dose at room temperature. Stir emulsion gently during administration.
– Use #28 French rubber tube. Insert tube 20 cm into sigmoid colon and tape in place. Or, consider indwelling urinary catheter with 30-ml balloon inflated distal to anal sphincter to aid in retention. This is especially helpful for patients with poor sphincter control (for example, after CVA). Use gravity flow. Drain returns constantly through Y-tube connection. Place patient in knee-chest position or with hips on pillow for a while if back leakage occurs.

– After P.R. administration, flush tubing with 50 to 100 ml of nonsodium fluid to ensure delivery of all drug. Flush rectum to remove resin.
– Prevent fecal impaction in geriatric patient by giving resin P.R. Give cleansing enema before P.R. administration. Explain to patient the need to retain enema; 6 to 10 hours is ideal, but 30 to 60 minutes is acceptable.
- If hyperkalemia is severe, prescriber won't depend solely on polystyrene resin to lower serum potassium level. Dextrose 50% with regular insulin may be given by I.V. push.

Patient teaching
- Explain importance of following prescribed low-potassium diet.
- Explain necessity of retaining enema; 6 to 10 hours is ideal, but 30 to 60 minutes is acceptable.
- Tell patient to report adverse reactions.

☑ Evaluation
- Patient's serum potassium level is normal.
- Patient doesn't develop constipation.
- Patient and family state understanding of drug therapy.

somatrem
(SOH-muh-trem)
Protropin

Pharmacologic class: anterior pituitary hormone
Therapeutic class: human growth hormone (GH)
Pregnancy risk category: C

Indications and dosages
▶ **Long-term treatment of children who have growth failure because of lack of adequate endogenous GH secretion.** *Children (prepuberty):* Highly individualized; up to 0.1 mg/kg I.M. or S.C. three times weekly.

Contraindications and precautions
- Contraindicated in patients hypersensitive to benzyl alcohol and in those with epiphyseal closure or active neoplasia.
- Use cautiously in patients with hypothyroidism and in those whose GH deficiency results from an intracranial lesion.

Lifespan: Drug is suitable for prepubescent children only.

Adverse reactions
Metabolic: hypothyroidism, hyperglycemia.
Other: antibodies to GH.

Interactions
Drug-drug. *Glucocorticoids:* May inhibit growth-promoting action of somatrem. Adjust glucocorticoid dosage, as needed.

Effects on lab test results
- May increase glucose level. May decrease T_4 level.

Pharmacokinetics
Absorption: Unknown.
Distribution: Unknown.
Metabolism: About 90% metabolized in liver.
Excretion: About 0.1% excreted unchanged in urine. *Half-life:* 20 to 30 minutes.

Route	Onset	Peak	Duration
I.M., S.C.	Unknown	Unknown	12-48 hr

Pharmacodynamics
Chemical effect: Purified GH of recombinant DNA origin that stimulates linear, skeletal muscle, and organ growth.
Therapeutic effect: Stimulates growth in children.

Available forms
Injectable lyophilized powder: 5 mg (10 international units)/vial

NURSING PROCESS

Assessment
- Assess child's growth before therapy and regularly thereafter.
- Be alert for adverse reactions and drug interactions.

ALERT: Toxicity in neonates may occur from exposure to benzyl alcohol used in drug as preservative.
- Monitor patient's height and blood with regular checkups; radiologic studies are also needed.

• Observe patient for signs of glucose intolerance and hyperglycemia.
• Monitor patient's periodic thyroid function tests for hypothyroidism, which may require treatment with thyroid hormone.
• Evaluate patient's and family's knowledge of drug therapy.

Nursing diagnoses
• Delayed growth and development related to lack of adequate endogenous GH
• Ineffective health maintenance related to adverse metabolic reactions
• Deficient knowledge related to drug therapy

Planning and implementation
• Check drug's expiration date.
• To prepare solution, inject supplied bacteriostatic water for injection into vial containing drug. Then swirl vial with gentle rotary motion until contents are dissolved. Don't shake vial.
• After reconstitution, vial solution should be clear. Don't inject if solution is cloudy or contains particles.
• If drug is given to neonate, reconstitute immediately before use with sterile water for injection (without bacteriostat). Use vial once, then discard.
• Store reconstituted drug in refrigerator; use within 7 days.
ALERT: Don't confuse somatrem with somatropin.

Patient teaching
• Reassure patient and family members that somatrem is pure and safe. Drug replaces pituitary-derived human GH, which was removed from market in 1985 because of an association with rare but fatal viral infection (Creutzfeldt-Jakob disease).

Evaluation
• Patient exhibits growth.
• Patient's thyroid function studies and glucose level are normal.
• Patient and family state understanding of drug therapy.

somatropin
(soh-muh-TROH-pin)
Genotropin, Humatrope, Norditropin, Nutropin, Nutropin AQ, Nutropin Depot, Saizen, Serostim

Pharmacologic class: anterior pituitary hormone
Therapeutic class: human growth hormone (GH)
Pregnancy risk category: C

Indications and dosages
▶ **Long-term treatment of growth failure in children with inadequate secretion of endogenous GH.** ***Humatrope.*** *Children:* 0.18 mg/kg of body weight S.C. weekly, divided equally and given on 3 alternate days, six times weekly or daily.
Nutropin, Nutropin AQ. *Children:* 0.3 mg/kg S.C. weekly in daily divided doses.
Saizen. *Children:* 0.06 mg/kg S.C. or I.M. three times weekly.
Norditropin. *Children:* 0.024 to 0.034 mg/kg S.C. six or seven times weekly.
Genotropin. *Children:* 0.16 to 0.24 mg/kg/week divided into six or seven S.C. injections.
Serostim. *Children:* About 0.1 mg/kg S.C. daily h.s. See manufacturer's dosing chart.
▶ **Growth failure in children related to chronic renal insufficiency up to time of renal transplantation.** ***Nutropin.*** *Children:* 0.35 mg/kg of body weight S.C. weekly in daily divided doses.
▶ **Replacement of endogenous growth hormone in adult patients with growth hormone deficiency.** *Adults:* Initially, no more than 0.006 mg/kg S.C. daily. May be increased to maximum of 0.025 mg/kg daily in patients younger than age 35 or 0.0125 mg/kg daily in patients older than age 35.
Genotropin. *Adults:* Starting dose is not more than 0.04 mg/kg weekly, divided into 6 to 7 doses S.C. Dose may be increased at 4- to 8-week intervals to a maximum dose 0.08 mg/kg weekly, divided into 6 to 7 doses S.C.
▶ **Long-term treatment of growth failure in children with Prader-Willi Syndrome (PWS) diagnosed by genetic testing.** ***Genotropin.*** *Children:* 0.24 mg/kg/week, divided into 6 to 7 doses S.C.

▶ **Long-term treatment of growth failure in children born small for gestational age (SGA) and who do not achieve catch-up growth by 2 years of age.** ***Genotropin.*** *Children:* 0.48 mg/kg/week, divided into 6 to 7 doses S.C.

Contraindications and precautions

• Contraindicated in patients with closed epiphyses or an active underlying intracranial lesion. Humatrope shouldn't be reconstituted with supplied diluent for patients with known sensitivity to either m-cresol or glycerin.

Lifespan: In pregnant or breast-feeding women, drug isn't indicated. In children with hypothyroidism and those whose GH deficiency is caused by an intracranial lesion, use cautiously. These children should be examined frequently for progression or recurrence of underlying disease.

Adverse reactions

CNS: headache, weakness.
CV: mild, transient edema.
Hematologic: *leukemia.*
Metabolic: mild hyperglycemia, hypothyroidism.
Musculoskeletal: localized muscle pain.
Other: injection site pain, antibodies to GH.

Interactions

Drug-drug. *Corticosteroids, corticotropin:* Long-term use inhibits growth response to GH. Monitor patient.

Effects on lab test results

• May increase glucose, inorganic phosphorus, alkaline phosphatase, and parathyroid hormone levels.

Pharmacokinetics

Absorption: Unknown.
Distribution: Unknown.
Metabolism: About 90% metabolized in liver.
Excretion: About 0.1% excreted unchanged in urine. *Half-life:* 20 to 30 minutes.

Route	Onset	Peak	Duration
I.M, S.C.	Unknown	7.5 hr	12-48 hr

Pharmacodynamics

Chemical effect: Purified GH of recombinant DNA origin that stimulates linear, skeletal muscle, and organ growth.
Therapeutic effect: Stimulates growth.

Available forms

Depot injection: 13.5 mg, 18 mg, 22.5 mg
Injection: 1.5 mg/ml; 5 mg/5 ml; 4-mg, 5-mg, 5.8 mg, 6-mg, 8-mg, 10-mg, 12-mg, 13.8-mg, and 24-mg vials
Norditropin injection: 5 mg/1.5 ml, 10 mg/1.5 ml, 15 mg/1.5 ml

NURSING PROCESS

Assessment

• Assess child's growth before therapy and regularly thereafter.
• Be alert for adverse reactions.
• Toxicity in neonates may occur from exposure to benzyl alcohol used in drug as preservative.
• Regular checkups with monitoring of height and of blood and radiologic studies are needed.
• Observe patient for signs of glucose intolerance and hyperglycemia.
• Monitor patient's periodic thyroid function tests for hypothyroidism, which may require treatment with thyroid hormone.
• Evaluate patient's and family's knowledge of drug therapy.

Nursing diagnoses

• Delayed growth and development related to lack of adequate endogenous GH
• Ineffective health maintenance related to adverse metabolic reactions
• Deficient knowledge related to drug therapy

Planning and implementation

• To prepare solution, inject supplied diluent into vial containing drug by aiming stream of liquid against glass wall of vial. Then swirl vial with gentle rotary motion until contents are completely dissolved. Don't shake vial.
• After reconstitution, solution should be clear. Don't inject solution if it's cloudy or contains particles.
• Store reconstituted drug in refrigerator; use within 14 days.
• If sensitivity to diluent should occur, drugs may be reconstituted with sterile water for injection. When drug is reconstituted in this

manner, use only one reconstituted dose per vial, refrigerate solution if it isn't used immediately after reconstitution, use reconstituted dose within 24 hours, and discard unused portion.
• Excessive glucocorticoid therapy inhibits growth-promoting effect of somatropin. Patient with coexisting corticotropin deficiency should have glucocorticoid-replacement dosage carefully adjusted to avoid growth inhibition.
ALERT: Don't confuse somatropin with somatrem or sumatriptan.

Patient teaching
• Inform parents that child with endocrine disorders (including GH deficiency) may develop slipped capital epiphyses more frequently. Tell them that if they notice their child limping, they should notify prescriber.

Evaluation
• Patient exhibits growth.
• Patient's thyroid function studies and glucose level are normal.
• Patient and family state understanding of drug therapy.

sotalol hydrochloride
(SOH-tuh-lol high-droh-KLOR-ighd)
Betapace, Betapace AF, Sotacor♦ ◇

Pharmacologic class: beta blocker
Therapeutic class: antiarrhythmic, antihypertensive, antianginal
Pregnancy risk category: B

Indications and dosages
▶ **Documented, life-threatening ventricular arrhythmias.** *Adults:* Initially, 80 mg P.O. b.i.d. Dosage is increased q 2 to 3 days as needed and tolerated; most patients respond to 160 to 320 mg daily. A few patients with refractory arrhythmias have received as much as 640 mg daily.
Patients with renal failure: If creatinine clearance is over 60 ml/minute, dosage adjustment isn't needed. If creatinine clearance is 30 to 60 ml/minute, interval is increased to q 24 hours; if 10 to 30 ml/minute, q 36 to 48 hours; if less than 10 ml/minute, individualized dosage.
▶ **Maintenance of normal sinus rhythm (delay in time to recurrence of atrial fibrillation/atrial flutter) in patients with symptomatic atrial fibrillation/atrial flutter who are currently in sinus rhythm.** ***Betapace AF.*** *Adults:* Initially, 80 mg P.O. twice daily. If initial dose does not reduce the frequency of relapses of atrial fibrillation/atrial flutter and is tolerated without excessive QTc interval prolongation (≥ 520 msec), the dose level may be increased after 3 days to 120 mg P.O. bid. Maximum dose is 160 mg P.O. bid.
Patients with renal failure: If creatinine clearance is 40 to 60 ml/min, give once daily.

Contraindications and precautions
• Contraindicated in patients hypersensitive to drug and patients with severe sinus node dysfunction, sinus bradycardia, second- or third-degree AV block in absence of an artificial pacemaker, congenital or acquired long-QT interval syndrome, cardiogenic shock, uncontrolled heart failure, or bronchial asthma. Don't give to patients with a creatinine clearance < 40 ml/min.
• Use cautiously in patients with renal impairment or diabetes mellitus.
Lifespan: In pregnant women, use cautiously. In breast-feeding women and children, safety of drug hasn't been established.

Adverse reactions
CNS: *asthenia, headache, dizziness, weakness, fatigue,* sleep problems, *light-headedness.*
CV: ***bradycardia, arrhythmias, heart failure, AV block, proarrhythmic events (ventricular tachycardia, PVCs, ventricular fibrillation),*** edema, *palpitations, chest pain,* ECG abnormalities, hypotension.
GI: *nausea,* vomiting, diarrhea, dyspepsia.
Respiratory: *dyspnea,* ***bronchospasm.***

Interactions
Drug-drug. *Antiarrhythmics:* May have additive effects. Avoid using together.
Antihypertensives, catecholamine-depleting drugs (such as guanethidine, haloperidol, and reserpine): Enhances hypotensive effects. Monitor patient closely.
Calcium channel blockers: Enhances myocardial depression. Monitor patient carefully.
Clonidine: Beta blockers may enhance rebound effect seen after withdrawal of cloni-

dine. Discontinue sotalol several days before withdrawing clonidine.
General anesthetics: May cause additional myocardial depression. Monitor patient closely.
Insulin, oral antidiabetics: May cause hyperglycemia and may mask symptoms of hyperglycemia. Adjust dosage as directed.
Drug-food. *Any food:* Increases drug absorption. Give drug on an empty stomach.

Effects on lab test results

- May increase glucose level.

Pharmacokinetics

Absorption: Well absorbed with bioavailability of 90% to 100%. Food may interfere with absorption.
Distribution: Unknown; doesn't bind to plasma proteins and crosses blood-brain barrier poorly.
Metabolism: Not metabolized.
Excretion: Excreted primarily in urine in unchanged form. *Half-life:* 12 hours.

Route	Onset	Peak	Duration
P.O.	Unknown	2.5-4 hr	Unknown

Pharmacodynamics

Chemical effect: Depresses sinus heart rate, slows AV conduction, decreases cardiac output, and lowers systolic and diastolic blood pressure.
Therapeutic effect: Restores normal sinus rhythm, lowers blood pressure, and relieves angina.

Available forms

Tablets: 80 mg, 120 mg, 160 mg, 240 mg

NURSING PROCESS

Assessment

- Assess patient's condition before therapy and regularly thereafter.
- Monitor patient's electrolyte levels and ECG regularly, especially if patient is receiving diuretics. Electrolyte imbalances, such as hypokalemia and hypomagnesemia, may enhance QT-interval prolongation and increase risk of serious arrhythmias such as torsades de pointes.
- Be alert for adverse reactions and drug interactions.
- Evaluate patient's and family's knowledge of drug therapy.

Nursing diagnoses

- Ineffective health maintenance related to underlying condition
- Fatigue related to adverse reactions
- Deficient knowledge related to drug therapy

Planning and implementation

- Because proarrhythmic events may occur at start of therapy and during dosage adjustments, patient should be hospitalized. Facilities and personnel should be available to monitor cardiac rhythm and interpret ECG.
- Although patients receiving I.V. lidocaine have started sotalol therapy without ill effect, other antiarrhythmic drugs should be withdrawn before therapy with sotalol. Sotalol therapy typically is delayed until two or three half-lives of withdrawn drug have elapsed. After withdrawal of amiodarone, sotalol shouldn't be given until QTc interval normalizes.

ALERT: In patients with creatinine clearance of 40 to 60 ml/minute, increase dosage interval to every 24 hours.

- Dosage should be adjusted slowly, allowing 2 to 3 days between dosage increments for adequate monitoring of QTc intervals and for plasma drug levels to reach steady-state level.

ALERT: The baseline QTc interval must be ≤ 450 msec in order to start a patient on Betapace AF. During initiation and adjustment, monitor QTc interval 2 to 4 hours after each dose. If the QTc interval is 500 msec or longer, the dose must be reduced or the drug discontinued.

ALERT: Don't confuse sotalol with Statrol or Stadol. Don't substitute Betapace AF for Betapace.

Patient teaching

- Explain importance of taking drug as prescribed, even when feeling well. Caution patient not to stop drug suddenly.
- Tell patient to take drug 1 hour before or 2 hours after meals.
- Teach patient how to check his pulse rate.

Evaluation

- Patient responds well to therapy.
- Patient states energy-conserving measures to combat fatigue.

• Patient and family state understanding of drug therapy.

spironolactone

(spih-ron-uh-LAK-tohn)

Aldactone, Novospiroton ♦, Spiractin ◊

Pharmacologic class: potassium-sparing diuretic

Therapeutic class: management of edema, antihypertensive, diagnosis of primary hyperaldosteronism, treatment of diuretic-induced hypokalemia

Pregnancy risk category: NR

Indications and dosages

▶ **Edema.** *Adults:* 25 to 200 mg P.O. daily or in divided doses.

Children: 3.3 mg/kg P.O. daily or in divided doses.

▶ **Hypertension.** *Adults:* 50 to 100 mg P.O. daily or in divided doses.

▶ **Diuretic-induced hypokalemia.** *Adults:* 25 to 100 mg P.O. daily when P.O. potassium supplements are contraindicated.

▶ **Detection of primary hyperaldosteronism.** *Adults:* 400 mg P.O. daily for 4 days (short test) or 3 to 4 weeks (long test). If hypokalemia and hypertension are corrected, presumptive diagnosis of primary hyperaldosteronism is made.

▶ **Management of primary hyperaldosteronism.** *Adults:* 100 to 400 mg P.O. daily.

▶ **Hirsutism‡.** *Adults:* 50 to 200 mg P.O. daily.

▶ **Premenstrual syndrome‡.** *Adults:* 25 mg P.O. q.i.d. on day 14 of menstrual cycle.

▶ **Heart failure in patients receiving an ACE inhibitor and a loop diuretic with or without a cardiac glycoside‡.** *Adults:* Initially, 12.5 to 25 mg P.O. daily.

▶ **Decrease risk of metrorrhagia‡.** *Adults:* 50 mg P.O. b.i.d. on days 4 through 21 of menstrual cycle.

▶ **Acne vulgaris‡.** *Adults:* 100 mg P.O. daily.

Contraindications and precautions

• Contraindicated in patients with anuria, acute or progressive renal insufficiency, or hyperkalemia.

• Use cautiously in patients with fluid or electrolyte imbalances, impaired kidney function, or hepatic disease.

Lifespan: In pregnant women, use cautiously. In breast-feeding women, safety of drug hasn't been established.

Adverse reactions

CNS: headache, drowsiness, lethargy, confusion, ataxia.

GI: diarrhea, gastric bleeding, ulceration, cramping, gastritis, vomiting.

GU: inability to maintain an erection, menstrual disturbances.

Hematologic: ***agranulocytosis.***

Metabolic: ***hyperkalemia,*** hyponatremia, mild acidosis, dehydration.

Skin: urticaria, hirsutism, maculopapular eruptions.

Other: drug fever, gynecomastia, breast soreness, ***anaphylaxis.***

Interactions

Drug-drug. *ACE inhibitors, indomethacin, other potassium-sparing diuretics, potassium supplements:* Increases risk of hyperkalemia. Don't use together, especially in patients with renal impairment.

Aspirin: Possible blocked diuretic effect of spironolactone. Watch for diminished spironolactone response.

Digoxin: May alter digoxin clearance, increasing risk of digoxin toxicity. Monitor digoxin level.

Warfarin: Decreases anticoagulant effect. Monitor PT and INR.

Drug-food. *Potassium-containing salt substitutes, potassium-rich foods (such as citrus fruits, tomatoes):* Increases risk of hyperkalemia. Tell patient to use low-potassium salt substitutes and to eat high-potassium foods cautiously.

Effects on lab test results

• May increase BUN, creatinine, and potassium levels. May decrease sodium level.

• May decrease granulocyte count.

Pharmacokinetics

Absorption: About 90%.

Distribution: More than 90% plasma protein–bound.

Metabolism: Metabolized rapidly and extensively to canrenone, its major active metabolite.

Excretion: Canrenone and other metabolites excreted primarily in urine, minimally in feces. *Half-life:* 13 to 24 hours.

Route	Onset	Peak	Duration
P.O.	1-2 days	2-3 days	2-3 days

Pharmacodynamics

Chemical effect: Antagonizes aldosterone in distal tubule.
Therapeutic effect: Promotes water and sodium excretion and hinders potassium excretion, lowers blood pressure, and helps to diagnose primary hyperaldosteronism.

Available forms

Tablets: 25 mg, 50 mg, 100 mg

NURSING PROCESS

Assessment

- Assess patient's condition before therapy and regularly thereafter. Maximum antihypertensive response may be delayed up to 2 weeks.
- Monitor electrolyte levels, fluid intake and output, weight, and blood pressure.
- Be alert for adverse reactions and drug interactions.
- Evaluate patient's and family's knowledge of drug therapy.

Nursing diagnoses

- Excess fluid volume related to presence of edema
- Impaired urinary elimination related to diuretic therapy
- Deficient knowledge related to drug therapy

Planning and implementation

- Give drug with meals to enhance absorption.
- Protect drug from light.
- Inform laboratory that patient is taking spironolactone because it may interfere with some laboratory tests that measure digoxin levels.

ALERT: Don't confuse Aldactone with Aldactazide.

Patient teaching

ALERT: Warn patient to avoid excessive ingestion of potassium-rich foods, potassium-containing salt substitutes, and potassium supplements to prevent serious hyperkalemia.

- Tell patient to take drug with meals and, if possible, early in day to avoid interruption of sleep by nocturia.

Evaluation

- Patient shows no signs of edema.
- Patient demonstrates adjustment of lifestyle to deal with altered patterns of urinary elimination.
- Patient and family state understanding of drug therapy.

stavudine (2,3-didehydro-3-deoxythymidine, d4T)

(stay-VYOO-deen)
Zerit, Zerit XR

Pharmacologic class: synthetic thymidine nucleoside analogue
Therapeutic class: antiviral
Pregnancy risk category: C

Indications and dosages

▶ **Patients with advanced HIV infection who are intolerant of or unresponsive to other antivirals.** *Adults and children who weigh 60 kg (132 lb) or more:* 40 mg P.O. q 12 hours, or 100 mg P.O. extended-release daily.
Adults and children who weigh more than 30 kg (66 lb) but less than 60 kg: 30 mg P.O. q 12 hours, or 75 mg P.O. extended-release daily.
Children who weigh less than 30 kg: 1 mg/kg q 12 hours.

Contraindications and precautions

- Contraindicated in patients hypersensitive to drug.
- Don't use Zerit XR in patients with creatinine clearance of 50 ml/minute or less.
- Use cautiously in patients with renal impairment or a history of peripheral neuropathy.

Lifespan: In pregnant women, use cautiously. In breast-feeding women, safety of drug hasn't been established.

Adverse reactions

CNS: *asthenia, peripheral neuropathy, headache, malaise, insomnia, anxiety, depression, nervousness,* dizziness, *fever.*
CV: chest pain.

EENT: conjunctivitis.
GI: *abdominal pain, diarrhea, nausea, vomiting, anorexia,* dyspepsia, constipation, weight loss, ***pancreatitis.***
Hematologic: ***neutropenia, thrombocytopenia,*** anemia.
Hepatic: ***hepatotoxicity, severe hepatomegaly with steatosis.***
Metabolic: ***lactic acidosis.***
Musculoskeletal: myalgia, *back pain, arthralgia.*
Respiratory: *dyspnea.*
Skin: *rash, diaphoresis, pruritus,* maculopapular rash.
Other: *chills.*

Interactions

Drug-drug. *Ketoconazole, ritonavir:* Increases stavudine level. Monitor patient closely.
Myelosuppressants: Additive myelosuppression. Avoid using together.

Effects on lab test results

- May increase liver enzyme levels.
- May decrease hemoglobin, hematocrit, and neutrophil and platelet counts.

Pharmacokinetics

Absorption: Rapid with mean absolute bioavailability of 86.4%.
Distribution: Distributed equally between RBCs and plasma; binds poorly to plasma proteins.
Metabolism: Not extensive.
Excretion: Renal elimination accounts for about 40% of overall clearance. *Half-life:* 1 to 2 hours.

Route	Onset	Peak	Duration
P.O.	Unknown	≤ 1 hr	Unknown

Pharmacodynamics

Chemical effect: Prevents replication of HIV by inhibiting enzyme reverse transcriptase.
Therapeutic effect: Inhibits HIV growth.

Available forms

Capsules: 15 mg, 20 mg, 30 mg, 40 mg
Capsules (extended-release): 37.5 mg, 50 mg, 75 mg, 100 mg.
Powder for oral solution: 1 mg/ml

NURSING PROCESS

Assessment

- Assess patient's condition before therapy and regularly thereafter.
- Periodically monitor CBC and levels of creatinine, AST, ALT, and alkaline phosphatase.
- Be alert for adverse reactions and drug interactions.
- Evaluate patient's and family's knowledge of drug therapy.

Nursing diagnoses

- Infection related to presence of HIV
- Disturbed sensory perception (peripheral) related to drug-induced peripheral neuropathy
- Deficient knowledge related to drug therapy

Planning and implementation

ALERT: Peripheral neuropathy appears to be major dose-limiting adverse effect; withdraw drug temporarily and resume at 50% of recommeneded dose.
- Dosage is calculated based on patient's weight.

ALERT: Don't confuse drug with other antivirals that may use initials for identification.
- Monitor liver function tests.
- Motor weakness, mimicking the clinical presentation of Guillain-Barré syndrome (including respiratory failure) may occur in HIV patients taking stavudine along with other antiretrovirals. Most of the cases were reported in the setting of lactic acidosis. Monitor patient for factors of lactic acidosis, including generalized fatigue, GI problems, tachypnea, or dyspnea. Symptoms may continue or worsen upon discontinuation of drug. Patients with these symptoms should promptly interrupt antiretroviral therapy, and a full medical workup should be performed immediately. Permanent discontinuation of stavudine should be considered.
- Monitor patient for pancreatitis, especially when stavudine is used with didanosine or hydroxyurea. Use caution when restarting drug after confirmed diagnosis of pancreatitis.

Patient teaching

- Tell patient that drug may be taken without regard to meals.
- Advise patient that he can't take drug if he experienced peripheral neuropathy while tak-

ing other nucleoside analogues or if his treatment plan includes cytotoxic antineoplastics.
- Warn patient not to take any other drugs for HIV or AIDS (especially street drugs) unless prescriber has approved them.
- Teach patient signs and symptoms of peripheral neuropathy—pain, burning, aching, weakness, or pins and needles in limbs—and tell him to report these immediately.
- Tell patient to report symptoms of lactic acidosis, including fatigue, GI problems, dyspnea or tachypnea.
- Tell patient to report symptoms of pancreatitis, including abdominal pain, nausea, vomiting, weight loss or fatty stools.

✓ Evaluation

- Patient's infection is controlled.
- Patient maintains normal peripheral neurologic function.
- Patient and family state understanding of drug therapy.

streptokinase

(strep-toh-KIGH-nayz)
Kabikinase, Streptase

Pharmacologic class: plasminogen activator
Therapeutic class: thrombolytic enzyme
Pregnancy risk category: C

Indications and dosages

▶ **Arteriovenous cannula occlusion.** *Adults:* 250,000 IU in 2 ml I.V. solution by I.V. pump infusion into each occluded limb of cannula over 25 to 35 minutes. Clamp cannula for 2 hours. Then aspirate contents of cannula; flush with saline solution and reconnect.

▶ **Venous thrombosis, pulmonary embolism, arterial thrombosis and embolism.** *Adults:* Loading dose is 250,000 IU by I.V. infusion over 30 minutes. Sustaining dose is 100,000 IU/hour by I.V. infusion for 72 hours for deep vein thrombosis and 100,000 IU/hour over 24 hours by I.V. infusion pump for pulmonary embolism.

▶ **Lysis of coronary artery thrombi after acute MI.** *Adults:* The total dose for intracoronary infusion is 140,000 IU. Loading dose is 20,000 IU by coronary catheter, followed by infusion of maintenance dose of 2,000 IU/minute for 60 minutes. Or, may be given as an I.V. infusion. Usual adult dose is 1,500,000 IU infused over 60 minutes.

Contraindications and precautions

- Contraindicated in patients with ulcerative wounds, active internal bleeding, uncontrolled hypocoagulation, chronic pulmonary disease with cavitation, subacute bacterial endocarditis or rheumatic valvular disease, visceral or intracranial malignant neoplasms, ulcerative colitis, diverticulitis, severe hypertension, acute or chronic hepatic or renal insufficiency, recent CVA, recent trauma with possible internal injuries, or recent cerebral embolism, thrombosis, or hemorrhage.
- Also contraindicated within 10 days after intra-arterial diagnostic procedure or any surgery, including liver or kidney biopsy, lumbar puncture, thoracentesis, paracentesis, or extensive or multiple cutdowns.
- I.M. injections and other invasive procedures are contraindicated during streptokinase therapy.
- Use cautiously when treating arterial embolism that originates from left side of heart because of danger of cerebral infarction.

Lifespan: In pregnant women, use cautiously. In breast-feeding women and children, safety of drug hasn't been established.

Adverse reactions

CNS: polyradiculoneuropathy, headache, fever.
CV: *hypotension,* vasculitis, ***reperfusion arrhythmias.***
EENT: periorbital edema.
GI: nausea.
Hematologic: ***bleeding.***
Musculoskeletal: musculoskeletal pain.
Respiratory: minor breathing difficulty, ***bronchospasm, pulmonary edema.***
Skin: urticaria, pruritus, flushing.
Other: phlebitis at injection site, ***hypersensitivity reactions (anaphylaxis), delayed hypersensitivity reactions*** (interstitial nephritis, vasculitis, serum-sickness–like reactions), ***angioedema.***

Interactions

Drug-drug. *Anticoagulants:* Increases risk of bleeding. Monitor patient closely.

Antifibrinolytic drugs: Streptokinase activity is inhibited and reversed by antifibrinolytic drugs such as aminocaproic acid. Use only when indicated during streptokinase therapy.
Aspirin, dipyridamole, drugs that affect platelet activity, indomethacin, phenylbutazone: Increases risk of bleeding. Monitor patient closely. Combined therapy with low-dose aspirin (162.5 mg) or dipyridamole has improved acute and long-term results.

Effects on lab test results

• May increase PT, PTT, and INR. May decrease hemoglobin and hematocrit.

Pharmacokinetics

Absorption: Administered I.V.
Distribution: Unknown.
Metabolism: Insignificant.
Excretion: Removed from circulation by antibodies and reticuloendothelial system. *Half-life:* First phase, 18 minutes; second phase, 83 minutes.

Route	Onset	Peak	Duration
I.V.	Immediate	20 min-2 hr	4 hr

Pharmacodynamics

Chemical effect: Activates plasminogen in two steps. Plasminogen and streptokinase form a complex that exposes plasminogen-activating site. Plasminogen is then converted to plasmin by cleavage of peptide bond.
Therapeutic effect: Dissolves blood clots.

Available forms

Injection: 100,000 IU, 250,000 IU, 600,000 IU, 750,000 IU, and 1.5 million IU in vials for reconstitution

NURSING PROCESS

Assessment

• Assess patient's condition before therapy and regularly thereafter.
• Assess patient for increased risk of bleeding (such as from recent surgery, CVA, trauma, or hypertension) before starting therapy.
• Before starting therapy, draw blood to determine aPTT and PT. Rate of I.V. infusion depends on thrombin time and streptokinase resistance. Then repeat studies often and keep laboratory flow sheet on patient's chart to monitor aPTT, PT, hemoglobin, and hematocrit.
• Monitor patient for excessive bleeding every 15 minutes for first hour, every 30 minutes for second through eighth hours, then once every shift.
• Monitor pulse rates, color, and sensation of limbs every hour.
• Be alert for adverse reactions and drug interactions.
• Evaluate patient's and family's knowledge of drug therapy.

Nursing diagnoses

• Ineffective cardiopulmonary tissue perfusion related to condition
• Risk for deficient fluid volume related to potential for bleeding
• Deficient knowledge related to drug therapy

Planning and implementation

• Drug should be used only by prescriber with wide experience in thrombotic disease management and in a setting where clinical and laboratory monitoring can be performed.
• Before using streptokinase to clear an occluded arteriovenous cannula, try flushing with heparinized saline solution.
ALERT: To check for hypersensitivity reactions, give 100 IU I.D.; wheal and flare response within 20 minutes means patient is probably allergic. Monitor vital signs frequently.
• If patient has had either recent streptococcal infection or recent treatment with streptokinase, higher loading dose may be needed.
• Reconstitute each drug vial with 5 ml of normal saline solution for injection. Further dilute to 45 ml. Don't shake; roll gently to mix. Some flocculation may be present; discard if large amounts appear. Filter solution with 0.8-micron or larger filter. Use within 24 hours. Store powder at room temperature and refrigerate after reconstitution.
• If bleeding occurs, stop therapy and notify prescriber. Pretreatment with heparin or drugs affecting platelets causes high risk of bleeding but may improve long-term results.
• Have aminocaproic acid available to treat bleeding, and corticosteroids to treat allergic reactions.
• Have typed and crossmatched packed RBCs and whole blood ready to treat possible hemorrhage.

• Keep involved limb in straight alignment to prevent bleeding from infusion site.
• Avoid unnecessary handling of patient, and pad side rails. Bruising is more likely during therapy.
• Keep venipuncture sites to minimum; use pressure dressing on puncture sites for at least 15 minutes.
ALERT: Notify prescriber immediately if hypersensitivity occurs. Antihistamines or corticosteroids may be used to treat mild reactions. If severe reaction occurs, infusion should be stopped and prescriber notified immediately.
• Heparin by continuous infusion is usually started within 1 hour after stopping streptokinase. Use infusion pump to give heparin.
• In patient with acute MI, thrombolytic therapy may decrease infarct size, improve ventricular function, and decrease risk of heart failure. Drug must be given within 6 hours of onset of symptoms for optimal effect.

Patient teaching
• Tell patient to report oozing, bleeding, or signs of hypersensitivity immediately.

Evaluation
• Patient responds well to therapy.
• Patient maintains adequate fluid balance.
• Patient and family state understanding of drug therapy.

streptomycin sulfate
(strep-toh-MIGH-sin SUL-fayt)

Pharmacologic class: aminoglycoside
Therapeutic class: antibiotic
Pregnancy risk category: D

Indications and dosages
▶ **Streptococcal endocarditis.** *Adults:* 1 g I.M. q 12 hours for 1 week, and then 500 mg q 12 hours for 1 week, given with penicillin.
Adults older than age 60: 500 mg I.M. q 12 hours for 14 days.
▶ **Primary and adjunct treatment in tuberculosis.** *Adults:* 1 g or 15 mg/kg I.M. daily for 2 to 3 months, and then 1 g two or three times weekly.
Children: 20 to 40 mg/kg I.M. daily in divided doses injected deep into large muscle mass. Given with other antituberculars but not with capreomycin. Continue until sputum specimen becomes negative.
▶ **Enterococcal endocarditis.** *Adults:* 1 g I.M. q 12 hours for 2 weeks, and then 500 mg q 12 hours for 4 weeks, given with penicillin.
▶ **Tularemia.** *Adults:* 1 to 2 g I.M. daily in divided doses injected deep into upper outer quadrant of buttocks. Continue for 5 to 7 days until patient is afebrile.
▶ **Dosage in renal failure.** *Adults and children:* Initial dose same for normal renal function. Subsequent doses and frequency determined by renal function study results and blood levels.

Contraindications and precautions
• Contraindicated in patients hypersensitive to drug or other aminoglycosides and patients with labyrinthine disease. Never give I.V.
• Use cautiously in patients with impaired kidney function or neuromuscular disorders.
Lifespan: In pregnant women, drug is contraindicated. In breast-feeding women and geriatric patients, use cautiously.

Adverse reactions
CNS: ***neuromuscular blockade.***
EENT: *ototoxicity (tinnitus, vertigo, hearing loss).*
GI: vomiting, nausea.
GU: some ***nephrotoxicity*** (not as much as other aminoglycosides).
Hematologic: eosinophilia, ***leukopenia, thrombocytopenia.***
Respiratory: ***apnea.***
Skin: exfoliative dermatitis.
Other: hypersensitivity reactions, ***angioedema, anaphylaxis.***

Interactions
Drug-drug. *Cephalosporins:* Increases risk of nephrotoxicity. Use together cautiously.
Dimenhydrinate: May mask symptoms of streptomycin-induced ototoxicity. Use together cautiously.
General anesthetics, neuromuscular blockers: May potentiate neuromuscular blockade. Monitor patient closely.
I.V. loop diuretics (such as furosemide): Increases ototoxicity. Use together cautiously.

Other aminoglycosides, acyclovir, amphotericin B, cisplatin, methoxyflurane, vancomycin: Increases risk of nephrotoxicity. Monitor patient.

Effects on lab test results

- May increase BUN, creatinine, and nonprotein nitrogen levels.
- May increase eosinophil count. May decrease hemoglobin, hematocrit, and WBC and platelet counts.

Pharmacokinetics

Absorption: Unknown after I.M. administration.
Distribution: Wide distribution although CSF penetration is low; 36% protein-bound.
Metabolism: None.
Excretion: Mainly in urine; less so in bile. *Half-life:* 2 to 3 hours.

Route	Onset	Peak	Duration
I.M.	Unknown	1-2 hr	Unknown

Pharmacodynamics

Chemical effect: Inhibits protein synthesis by binding directly to 30S ribosomal subunit. Drug is generally bactericidal.
Therapeutic effect: Kills bacteria, including many aerobic gram-negative organisms and some aerobic gram-positive organisms. Drug is also active against *Brucella* and *Mycobacterium.*

Available forms

Injection: 400 mg/ml, 1 g/2.5 ml ampules

NURSING PROCESS

Assessment

- Assess patient's infection before therapy and regularly thereafter.
- Obtain specimen for culture and sensitivity tests before first dose except when treating tuberculosis. Therapy may begin pending results.

ALERT: Obtain blood for peak streptomycin level 1 to 2 hours after I.M. injection; for trough levels, draw blood just before next dose. Don't use heparinized tube because heparin is incompatible with aminoglycosides.

- Evaluate patient's hearing before beginning therapy, during therapy, and 6 months after therapy.
- Be alert for adverse reactions and drug interactions.
- Evaluate patient's and family's knowledge of drug therapy.

Nursing diagnoses

- Infection related to presence of susceptible bacteria
- Disturbed sensory perception (auditory) related to drug-induced adverse reactions
- Deficient knowledge related to drug therapy

Planning and implementation

- Protect hands when preparing because drug is irritating.
- Inject drug deep into upper outer quadrant of buttocks. Rotate injection sites.

ALERT: Never give streptomycin I.V.

- Encourage adequate fluid intake; patient should be well hydrated while taking drug to minimize chemical irritation of renal tubules.
- In primary treatment of tuberculosis, drug is discontinued when sputum becomes negative.

Patient teaching

- Warn patient that injection may be painful.
- Emphasize the need to drink at least 2,000 ml daily (if not contraindicated) during therapy.
- Instruct patient to report hearing loss, roaring noises, or fullness in ears immediately.

Evaluation

- Patient is free from infection.
- Patient's auditory function remains normal.
- Patient and family state understanding of drug therapy.

succimer
(SUK-sih-mer)
Chemet

Pharmacologic class: heavy metal
Therapeutic class: chelating agent
Pregnancy risk category: C

Indications and dosages

▶ **Lead poisoning in children with blood lead levels above 45 mcg/dl.** *Children:* 10 mg/

kg or 350 mg/m^2 q 8 hours for 5 days. Dose rounded to nearest 100 mg (see table). Then, frequency is decreased to q 12 hours for an additional 2 weeks.

Weight (kg)	Dose (mg)
8-15	100
16-23	200
24-34	300
35-44	400
≥ 45	500

Contraindications and precautions

• Contraindicated in patients hypersensitive to drug.
• Use cautiously in patients with compromised kidney function.
Lifespan: In pregnant or breast-feeding women, drug isn't indicated.

Adverse reactions

CNS: *drowsiness, dizziness, sensory motor neuropathy, sleepiness, paresthesia, headache.*
CV: *arrhythmias.*
EENT: plugged ears, cloudy film in eyes, otitis media, watery eyes, sore throat, rhinorrhea, nasal congestion.
GI: *nausea, vomiting, diarrhea, loss of appetite, abdominal cramps, hemorrhoidal symptoms, metallic taste, loose stools.*
GU: decreased urination, difficult urination, proteinuria.
Hematologic: intermittent eosinophilia.
Musculoskeletal: *leg, kneecap, back, stomach, rib, or flank pain.*
Respiratory: cough, head cold.
Skin: papular rash, herpetic rash, mucocutaneous eruptions, pruritus.
Other: *flulike syndrome,* candidiasis.

Interactions

None reported.

Effects on lab test results

• May increase AST, ALT, alkaline phosphatase, and cholesterol levels.
• May increase eosinophil and platelet counts.

Pharmacokinetics

Absorption: Rapid but variable.
Distribution: Unknown.
Metabolism: Rapid and extensive.
Excretion: 39% excreted in feces as nonabsorbed drug; remainder excreted mainly in urine. *Half-life:* 48 hours.

Route	Onset	Peak	Duration
P.O.	Unknown	1-2 hr	Unknown

Pharmacodynamics

Chemical effect: Forms water-soluble complexes with lead and increases its excretion in urine.
Therapeutic effect: Relieves signs and symptoms of lead poisoning.

Available forms

Capsules: 100 mg

NURSING PROCESS

Assessment

• Assess child's condition before therapy and regularly thereafter.
• Measure severity by initial blood lead level and by rate and degree of rebound of blood lead level. Severity should be used as guide for more frequent blood lead monitoring.
• Monitor transaminase level before and at least weekly during therapy. Transient, mild elevations of transaminase level may occur. Patient with history of hepatic disease should be monitored more closely.
• Monitor patient at least once weekly for rebound blood lead levels. Elevated blood lead levels and associated symptoms may return rapidly after drug is discontinued because of redistribution of lead from bone to soft tissues and blood.
• Be alert for adverse reactions.
• Monitor patient's hydration status if adverse GI reactions occur.
• Evaluate parents' knowledge of drug therapy.

Nursing diagnoses

• Ineffective health maintenance related to presence of lead poisoning
• Risk for deficient fluid volume related to drug-induced adverse GI reactions
• Deficient knowledge related to drug therapy

Planning and implementation

• Course of treatment lasts 19 days. Repeated courses may be needed if indicated by weekly monitoring of blood lead levels.

• A minimum of 2 weeks between courses is recommended unless high blood lead level indicates need for immediate therapy.
• False-positive results for ketones in urine using nitroprusside reagents (Ketostix) and falsely decreased levels of uric acid and CK have been reported.
ALERT: Administration of succimer with other chelates isn't recommended. Patient who has received edetate calcium disodium with or without dimercaprol may use succimer as subsequent therapy after 4-week interval.

Patient teaching
• Tell parents of child who can't swallow capsule to open it and sprinkle contents on small amount of soft food. Or, medicated beads from capsule may be poured on spoon and followed with flavored beverage such as a fruit drink.
• Help parents identify and remove sources of lead in child's environment. Chelation therapy isn't a substitute for preventing further exposure.
• Tell parents to consult prescriber if rash occurs. Consider possibility of allergic or other mucocutaneous reactions each time drug is used.

Evaluation
• Patient responds well to therapy.
• Patient maintains adequate hydration.
• Parents state understanding of drug therapy.

succinylcholine chloride (suxamethonium chloride)
(SUK-seh-nil-KOH-leen KLOR-ighd)
Anectine, Anectine Flo-Pack, Quelicin, Scoline ◇, Sucostrin

Pharmacologic class: depolarizing neuromuscular blocker
Therapeutic class: skeletal muscle relaxant
Pregnancy risk category: C

Indications and dosages
▶ **Adjunct to anesthesia to induce skeletal muscle relaxation; to facilitate intubation and assist with mechanical ventilation or orthopedic manipulations (drug of choice); to lessen muscle contractions in pharmacologically or electrically induced seizures.** Dosage depends on anesthetic used, individual needs, and response.
Adults: 0.6 mg/kg I.V.; then 2.5 mg/minute, p.r.n. Or, 2.5 mg/kg I.M. up to maximum of 150 mg I.M. in deltoid muscle.
Children: 1 to 2 mg/kg I.M. or I.V. Maximum I.M. dosage is 150 mg.

Contraindications and precautions
• Contraindicated in patients hypersensitive to drug and patients with abnormally low pseudocholinesterase level, angle-closure glaucoma, malignant hyperthermia, or penetrating eye injury.
• Use cautiously in debilitated patients, those receiving quinidine or cardiac glycoside therapy, and those with severe burns or trauma, electrolyte imbalances, hyperkalemia, paraplegia, spinal neuraxis injury, CVA, degenerative or dystrophic neuromuscular disease, myasthenia gravis, myasthenic syndrome of lung cancer, bronchogenic carcinoma, dehydration, thyroid disorders, collagen diseases, porphyria, fractures, muscle spasms, eye surgery, pheochromocytoma, respiratory depression, or hepatic, renal, or pulmonary impairment.
Lifespan: In women undergoing cesarean section and in breast-feeding women, use large doses cautiously. In geriatric patients, use cautiously.

Adverse reactions
CV: ***bradycardia,*** tachycardia, hypertension, hypotension, ***arrhythmias,*** flushing, ***cardiac arrest.***
EENT: increased intraocular pressure.
Musculoskeletal: muscle fasciculation, *postoperative muscle pain,* myoglobinemia.
Respiratory: ***prolonged respiratory depression, apnea, bronchoconstriction.***
Other: ***malignant hyperthermia,*** excessive salivation, allergic or idiosyncratic hypersensitivity reactions ***(anaphylaxis).***

Interactions
Drug-drug. *Aminoglycoside antibiotics, including amikacin, gentamicin, kanamycin, neomycin, streptomycin; anticholinesterase, such as echothiophate, edrophonium, neostigmine, physostigmine, or pyridostigmine; general anesthetics, such as enflurane, halothane, isoflurane; polymyxin antibiotics, such as col-*

istin and polymyxin B sulfate: Potentiates neuromuscular blockade, leading to increased skeletal muscle relaxation and potentiation of effect. Use cautiously during surgical and postoperative periods.
Cardiac glycosides: May cause arrhythmias. Use together cautiously.
Cyclophosphamide, lithium, MAO inhibitors: May cause prolonged apnea. Avoid using together; monitor patient closely.
Methotrimeprazine, opioid analgesics: Potentiates neuromuscular blockade, leading to increased skeletal muscle relaxation and, possibly, respiratory paralysis. Use with extreme caution.
Parenteral magnesium sulfate: Potentiates neuromuscular blockade, leading to increased skeletal muscle relaxation and, possibly, respiratory paralysis. Use cautiously, preferably with reduced doses.
Drug-herb. *Melatonin:* Potentiates blocking properties of succinylcholine. Avoid using together.

Effects on lab test results

- May increase myoglobin and potassium levels.

Pharmacokinetics

Absorption: Unknown after I.M. administration.
Distribution: Distributed in extracellular fluid and rapidly reaches its site of action.
Metabolism: Occurs rapidly by plasma pseudocholinesterase.
Excretion: About 10% excreted unchanged in urine.

Route	Onset	Peak	Duration
I.V.	30 sec-1 min	1-2 min	4-10 min
I.M.	2-3 min	Unknown	10-30 min

Pharmacodynamics

Chemical effect: Prolongs depolarization of muscle end plate.
Therapeutic effect: Relaxes skeletal muscles.

Available forms

Injection: 20 mg/ml, 50 mg/ml, 100 mg/ml; 100-mg, 500-mg, and 1-g vials

NURSING PROCESS

Assessment

- Assess patient's condition before therapy and regularly thereafter.
- Monitor baseline electrolyte determinations and vital signs (check respiratory rate every 5 to 10 minutes during infusion).
- Monitor respiratory rate and pulse oximetry closely until patient is fully recovered from neuromuscular blockade, as evidenced by tests of muscle strength (hand grip, head lift, and ability to cough).
- Be alert for adverse reactions and drug interactions.
- Evaluate patient's and family's knowledge of drug therapy.

Nursing diagnoses

- Ineffective health maintenance related to underlying condition
- Ineffective breathing pattern related to drug's effect on respiratory muscles
- Deficient knowledge related to drug therapy

Planning and implementation

ALERT: Only personnel skilled in airway management should give drug.
- Succinylcholine is drug of choice for short procedures (less than 3 minutes) and for orthopedic manipulations; use caution in fractures or dislocations.
- Give sedatives or general anesthetics before neuromuscular blockers. Neuromuscular blockers don't obtund consciousness or alter pain threshold.
- Keep airway clear. Have emergency respiratory support equipment immediately available.

ALERT: Careful drug calculation is essential. Always verify with another professional.
- **I.V. use:** To evaluate patient's ability to metabolize succinylcholine, give test dose (10 mg I.M. or I.V.) after patient has been anesthetized. Normal response (no respiratory depression or transient depression for up to 5 minutes) indicates drug may be given. Don't give subsequent doses if patient develops respiratory paralysis sufficient to permit endotracheal intubation. (Recovery within 30 to 60 minutes.)
- **I.M. use:** Give deep I.M., preferably high into deltoid muscle.

• Store injectable form in refrigerator. Store powder form at room temperature in tightly closed container. Use immediately after reconstitution. Don't mix with alkaline solutions (thiopental sodium, sodium bicarbonate, or barbiturates).
• Give analgesics.
ALERT: Reversing drugs shouldn't be used. Unlike what happens with nondepolarizing drugs, giving neostigmine or edrophonium with this depolarizing drug may worsen neuromuscular blockade.
• Repeated or continuous infusions of succinylcholine are not advised; this may reduce response or prolong muscle relaxation and apnea.

Patient teaching

• Explain all events and happenings to patient because he can still hear.
• Reassure patient that he is being monitored at all times.
• Inform him that postoperative stiffness is normal and will soon subside.

Evaluation

• Patient responds well to therapy.
• Patient maintains adequate respiratory patterns with mechanical assistance.
• Patient and family state understanding of drug therapy.

sucralfate

(SOO-krahl-fayt)
Carafate, SCF◇

Pharmacologic class: pepsin inhibitor
Therapeutic class: antiulcerative
Pregnancy risk category: B

Indications and dosages

▶ **Short-term (up to 8 weeks) treatment of duodenal ulcer.** *Adults:* 1 g P.O. q.i.d. 1 hour before meals and h.s.
▶ **Maintenance therapy for duodenal ulcer.** *Adults:* 1 g P.O. b.i.d.

Contraindications and precautions

• No known contraindications.
• Use cautiously in patients with chronic renal failure.

Lifespan: In pregnant or breast-feeding women, use cautiously. In children, safety of drug hasn't been established.

Adverse reactions

CNS: dizziness, sleepiness, headache, vertigo.
GI: constipation, nausea, gastric discomfort, diarrhea, bezoar formation, vomiting, flatulence, dry mouth, indigestion.
Musculoskeletal: back pain.
Skin: rash, pruritus.

Interactions

Drug-drug. *Antacids:* May decrease binding of drug to gastroduodenal mucosa, impairing effectiveness. Don't give within 30 minutes of each other.
Cimetidine, digoxin, norfloxacin, phenytoin, fluoroquinolones, ranitidine, tetracycline, theophylline: Decreases absorption. Separate administration times by at least 2 hours.

Effects on lab test results

None reported.

Pharmacokinetics

Absorption: Only about 3% to 5%. Drug acts locally at ulcer site.
Distribution: Absorbed drug is distributed to many body tissues.
Metabolism: None.
Excretion: About 90% excreted in feces; absorbed drug excreted unchanged in urine.

Route	Onset	Peak	Duration
P.O.	Unknown	≤ 6 hr	Unknown

Pharmacodynamics

Chemical effect: Unknown; probably adheres to and protects ulcer's surface by forming barrier.
Therapeutic effect: Aids in duodenal ulcer healing.

Available forms

Suspension: 500 mg/5 ml
Tablets: 1 g

NURSING PROCESS

Assessment

• Assess patient's GI symptoms before therapy and regularly thereafter.

- Be alert for adverse reactions and drug interactions.
- Monitor patient for severe, persistent constipation.
- Evaluate patient's and family's knowledge of drug therapy.

Nursing diagnoses
- Impaired tissue integrity related to presence of duodenal ulcer
- Constipation related to drug-induced adverse GI reactions
- Deficient knowledge related to drug therapy

Planning and implementation
- Give drug on an empty stomach for best results.

Patient teaching
- Instruct patient to take drug 1 hour before each meal and at bedtime.
- Tell patient to continue on prescribed regimen to ensure complete healing. Pain and ulcerative symptoms may subside within first few weeks of therapy.
- Urge patient to avoid cigarette smoking because it may increase gastric acid secretion and worsen disease. Also tell patient to avoid alcohol, chocolate, and spicy foods.
- Tell patient to elevate the head of the bed to sleep.
- Tell patient to avoid large meals within 2 hours before bedtime.

Evaluation
- Patient's ulcer pain is gone.
- Patient maintains normal bowel elimination patterns.
- Patient and family state understanding of drug therapy.

sufentanil citrate
(soo-FEN-tih-nil SIGH-trayt)
Sufenta

Pharmacologic class: opioid
Therapeutic class: analgesic, adjunct to anesthesia, anesthetic
Pregnancy risk category: C
Controlled substance schedule: II

Indications and dosages
▶ **Adjunct to general anesthetic.** *Adults:* 1 to 8 mcg/kg I.V. with nitrous oxide and oxygen.
▶ **As primary anesthetic.** *Adults:* 8 to 30 mcg/kg I.V. with 100% oxygen and muscle relaxant.

Contraindications and precautions
- Contraindicated in patients hypersensitive to drug.
- Drug isn't recommended for prolonged use.
- Use with extreme caution in debilitated patients and in patients with head injury, decreased respiratory reserve, or pulmonary, hepatic, or renal disease.

Lifespan: In pregnant women, drug isn't recommended in high doses at term. In breast-feeding women and in children, safety of drug hasn't been established. In geriatric patients, use with extreme caution.

Adverse reactions
CNS: chills, somnolence.
CV: *hypotension,* hypertension, ***bradycardia,*** tachycardia, ***arrhythmias.***
GI: nausea, vomiting.
Musculoskeletal: intraoperative muscle movement.
Respiratory: ***chest wall rigidity, apnea, bronchospasm.***
Skin: *pruritus,* erythema.

Interactions
Drug-drug. *CNS depressants:* May have additive effects. Use together cautiously.
Drug-lifestyle. *Alcohol use:* May have additive effects. Discourage using together.

Effects on lab test results
None reported.

Pharmacokinetics
Absorption: Administered I.V.
Distribution: Highly protein-bound and redistributed rapidly.
Metabolism: Unknown, although appears to be metabolized mainly in liver and small intestine.
Excretion: Drug and its metabolites excreted primarily in urine. *Half-life:* About 2½ hours.

Route	Onset	Peak	Duration
I.V.	1-2 min	1-2 min	0.7-5 min

Pharmacodynamics

Chemical effect: Binds with opioid receptors in CNS, altering perception of and emotional response to pain through unknown mechanism.
Therapeutic effect: Relieves pain and promotes loss of consciousness.

Available forms

Injection: 50 mcg/ml in 1-ml, 2-ml, and 5-ml ampules

NURSING PROCESS

Assessment

- Assess patient's condition before therapy and regularly thereafter.
- Because drug decreases rate and depth of respirations, monitoring patient's arterial oxygen saturation may aid in assessing respiratory depression.
- Monitor respiratory rate of neonates exposed to drug during labor.
- Monitor postoperative vital signs.
- Be alert for adverse reactions and drug interactions.
- Evaluate patient's and family's knowledge of drug therapy.

Nursing diagnoses

- Ineffective health maintenance related to underlying condition
- Ineffective breathing pattern related to respiratory depression
- Deficient knowledge related to drug therapy

Planning and implementation

- Only personnel specifically trained in use of I.V. anesthetics should give drug.
- Geriatric and debilitated patients need a reduced dosage.
- For obese patient who exceeds 20% of ideal body weight, dosage calculations should be based on an estimate of ideal weight.
- Give drug by direct I.V. injection. Although drug has been given by intermittent I.V. infusion, its compatibility and stability in I.V. solutions haven't been fully investigated.
- When used at doses over 8 mcg/kg, postoperative mechanical ventilation and observation are essential because of prolonged respiratory depression.
- Keep narcotic antagonist (naloxone) and resuscitation equipment available.
- Notify prescriber if respiratory rate falls below 12 breaths/minute.

ALERT: High doses can produce muscle rigidity reversible by neuromuscular blockers; however, patient must be artificially ventilated.
ALERT: Don't confuse sufentanil with alfentanil or fentanyl, or Sufenta with Survanta.

Patient teaching

- Inform patient and family that sufentanil will be used as part of patient's anesthesia. Answer questions patient or family may have.

Evaluation

- Patient responds well to therapy.
- Patient maintains adequate ventilation with mechanical support, if needed.
- Patient and family state understanding of drug therapy.

sulfadiazine

(sul-fuh-DIGH-uh-zeen)

Pharmacologic class: sulfonamide
Therapeutic class: antibiotic
Pregnancy risk category: C (contraindicated at term)

Indications and dosages

▶ **UTI.** *Adults:* Initially, 2 to 4 g P.O.; then, 2 to 4 g daily in three to six divided doses.
Children age 2 months and older: Initially, 75 mg/kg or 2 g/m^2 P.O.; then 150 mg/kg or 4 g/m^2 P.O. in four to six divided doses daily. Maximum daily dosage is 6 g.
▶ **Rheumatic fever prophylaxis, as an alternative to penicillin.** *Children who weigh 30 kg (66 lb) or more:* 1 g P.O. daily.
Children who weigh less than 30 kg: 500 mg P.O. daily.
▶ **Adjunct treatment in toxoplasmosis.** *Adults:* 2 to 8 g P.O. daily in divided doses q 6 hours. Usually given with pyrimethamine.
Children: 100 to 200 mg/kg P.O. daily. Usually given with pyrimethamine.

Contraindications and precautions

- Contraindicated in patients hypersensitive to sulfonamides and in patients with porphyria.
- Use cautiously and in reduced doses in patients with impaired liver or kidney function,

bronchial asthma, history of multiple allergies, G6PD deficiency, or blood dyscrasia.

Lifespan: In breast-feeding women, pregnant women at term, and infants younger than age 2 months (except in congenital toxoplasmosis), drug is contraindicated.

Adverse reactions

CNS: headache, mental depression, ***seizures,*** hallucinations.
GI: *nausea, vomiting, diarrhea,* abdominal pain, anorexia, stomatitis.
GU: ***toxic nephrosis with oliguria and anuria,*** crystalluria, hematuria.
Hematologic: ***agranulocytosis, aplastic anemia,*** megaloblastic anemia, ***leukopenia,*** hemolytic anemia, ***thrombocytopenia.***
Hepatic: jaundice.
Skin: ***erythema multiforme, Stevens-Johnson syndrome,*** *generalized skin eruption,* ***epidermal necrolysis,*** exfoliative dermatitis, photosensitivity reactions, urticaria, pruritus.
Other: hypersensitivity reactions (**SERUM SICKNESS,** *drug fever,* ***anaphylaxis***), local irritation, extravasation.

Interactions

Drug-drug. *Methotrexate:* May increase methotrexate level. Use together cautiously.
Oral anticoagulants: Increases anticoagulant effect. Monitor patient for bleeding.
Oral antidiabetics: Increases hypoglycemic effect. Monitor glucose level.
Oral contraceptives: Decreases contraceptive effectiveness and increases risk of breakthrough bleeding. Suggest nonhormonal contraceptive.
Drug-herb. *Dong quai, St. John's wort:* Increases risk of photosensitivity. Discourage using together.
Drug-lifestyle. *Sun exposure:* Photosensitivity reactions may occur. Urge patient to avoid unprotected or prolonged exposure to sunlight.

Effects on lab test results

- May increase BUN, creatinine, fibrinogen, transaminase, and bilirubin levels.
- May increase eosinophil count and PT. May decrease hemoglobin, hematocrit, and granulocyte, platelet, and WBC counts.

Pharmacokinetics

Absorption: Some.
Distribution: Distributed widely in most body tissues and fluids; 32% to 56% protein-bound.
Metabolism: Metabolized partially in liver.
Excretion: Excreted unchanged mainly in urine. Urine solubility of unchanged drug increases as urine pH increases. *Half-life:* About 10 hours.

Route	Onset	Peak	Duration
P.O.	Unknown	≤ 6 hr	Unknown

Pharmacodynamics

Chemical effect: Inhibits formation of dihydrofolic acid from PABA, decreasing bacterial folic acid synthesis.
Therapeutic effect: Hinders bacterial activity, including many gram-positive bacteria, *Chlamydia trachomatis,* many enterobacteriaceae, and some strains of *Plasmodium falciparum* and *Toxoplasma gondii.*

Available forms

Tablets: 500 mg

NURSING PROCESS

Assessment

- Assess patient's condition before therapy and regularly thereafter.
- Obtain specimen for culture and sensitivity tests before first dose. Therapy may begin pending results.
- Monitor urine cultures, CBCs, and urinalyses before and during therapy.
- Monitor urine pH daily.
- Be alert for adverse reactions and drug interactions.
- Monitor patient's hydration if adverse GI reactions occur.
- Evaluate patient's and family's knowledge of drug therapy.

Nursing diagnoses

- Infection related to presence of susceptible bacteria
- Risk for deficient fluid volume related to drug-induced adverse GI reactions
- Deficient knowledge related to drug therapy

Planning and implementation

- Give drug on schedule to maintain constant blood level.

• Folic or folinic acid may be used during rest periods in toxoplasmosis therapy to reverse hematopoietic depression or anemia related to pyrimethamine and sulfadiazine.
• Have adult patient drink between 3 and 4 L daily to prevent crystalluria. Sodium bicarbonate may be given to alkalinize urine.
ALERT: Don't confuse sulfadiazine with sulfasalazine. Don't confuse sulfonamide drugs.

Patient teaching
• Tell patient to drink full glass of water with each dose and plenty of water throughout day.
• Tell patient to take entire amount of drug exactly as prescribed, even if he feels better.
• Warn patient to avoid direct sunlight and ultraviolet light to prevent photosensitivity reaction.

Evaluation
• Patient is free from infection.
• Patient maintains adequate hydration.
• Patient and family state understanding of drug therapy.

sulfasalazine (salazosulfapyridine, sulphasalazine)
(sul-fuh-SAL-uh-zeen)
Azulfidine, Azulfidine EN-tabs, PMS Sulfasalazine E.C.♦, Salazopyrin♦◇, Salazopyrin EN-Tabs♦◇, S.A.S.-500♦, S.A.S. Enteric-500♦

Pharmacologic class: sulfonamide
Therapeutic class: anti-inflammatory
Pregnancy risk category: B

Indications and dosages
▶ **Mild-to-moderate ulcerative colitis, adjunct therapy in severe ulcerative colitis, Crohn's disease.** *Adults:* Initially, 3 to 4 g P.O. daily in evenly divided doses; usual maintenance dosage is 2 g P.O. daily in divided doses q 6 hours. Dosage may be started with 1 to 2 g, with gradual increase to minimize adverse effects.
Children older than age 2: Initially, 40 to 60 mg/kg P.O. daily, divided into three to six doses; then 30 mg/kg daily in four doses. Dosage may be reduced if GI intolerance occurs.
▶ **Rheumatoid arthritis in patients who have responded inadequately to salicylates or NSAIDs.** *Adults:* 2 g P.O. daily b.i.d. in evenly divided doses. Dosage may be started at 0.5 to 1 g daily and be gradually increased over 3 weeks to reduce possible GI intolerance.
▶ **Patients with polyarticular-course juvenile rheumatoid arthritis who have responded inadequately to salicylates or other NSAIDs.** *Children age 6 and older:* 30 to 50 mg/kg P.O. daily in two divided doses (as delayed release tablet). Maximum dose is 2 g daily. To reduce possible GI intolerance, start with one-fourth to one-third of planned maintenance dose and increase weekly until reaching maintenance dose at 1 month.

Contraindications and precautions
• Contraindicated in patients hypersensitive to drug or its metabolites, and patients with porphyria or intestinal or urinary obstruction.
• Use cautiously and in reduced dosages in patients with impaired liver or kidney function, severe allergy, bronchial asthma, or G6PD deficiency.
Lifespan: In pregnant or breast-feeding women, use cautiously. In infants younger than age 2, drug is contraindicated.

Adverse reactions
CNS: headache, depression, ***seizures,*** hallucinations.
GI: *nausea, vomiting, diarrhea,* abdominal pain, anorexia, stomatitis.
GU: ***toxic nephrosis with oliguria and anuria,*** crystalluria, hematuria, oligospermia, infertility.
Hematologic: ***agranulocytosis, aplastic anemia,*** megaloblastic anemia, ***thrombocytopenia, leukopenia,*** hemolytic anemia.
Hepatic: jaundice, ***hepatotoxicity.***
Skin: ***erythema multiforme, Stevens-Johnson syndrome,*** *generalized skin eruption,* ***epidermal necrolysis,*** exfoliative dermatitis, photosensitivity reactions, urticaria, pruritus.
Other: ***hypersensitivity reactions*** *(serum sickness, drug fever,* ***anaphylaxis****).*

Interactions
Drug-drug. *Antibiotics:* May alter action of sulfasalazine by altering internal flora. Monitor patient closely.

Digoxin: May reduce digoxin absorption. Monitor patient closely.
Folic acid: Absorption may be decreased. No intervention needed.
Iron: Lowers sulfasalazine level caused by iron chelation. Monitor patient closely.
Oral anticoagulants: Increases anticoagulant effect. Monitor patient for bleeding.
Oral antidiabetics: Increases hypoglycemic effect. Monitor glucose level.
Oral contraceptives: Decreases contraceptive effectiveness and increased risk of breakthrough bleeding. Suggest nonhormonal contraceptive.
Drug-herb. *Dong quai, St. John's wort:* Increases risk of photosensitivity. Discourage using together.

Effects on lab test results

- May increase AST and ALT levels.
- May decrease hemoglobin, hematocrit, and granulocyte, platelet, RBC, and WBC counts.

Pharmacokinetics

Absorption: Poor; 70% to 90% transported to colon, where intestinal flora metabolize drug to its active ingredients, which exert their effects locally. One metabolite, sulfapyridine, is absorbed from colon, but only small portion of metabolite 5-aminosalicylic acid is absorbed.
Distribution: Distributed locally in colon. Distribution of absorbed metabolites is unknown.
Metabolism: Divided by intestinal flora in colon.
Excretion: Systemically absorbed sulfasalazine is excreted chiefly in urine. *Half-life:* 6 to 8 hours.

Route	Onset	Peak	Duration
P.O.	Unknown (parent drug); 12-24 hr (metabolites)	1.5-6 hr	Unknown

Pharmacodynamics

Chemical effect: Unknown.
Therapeutic effect: Relieves inflammation in GI tract.

Available forms

Oral suspension: 250 mg/5 ml
Tablets (with or without enteric coating): 500 mg

NURSING PROCESS

Assessment

- Assess patient's condition before therapy and regularly thereafter.
- Be alert for adverse reactions and drug interactions.
- Monitor patient's hydration status throughout drug therapy.
- Evaluate patient's and family's knowledge of drug therapy.

Nursing diagnoses

- Acute pain related to inflammation of GI tract
- Risk for deficient fluid volume related to drug-induced adverse GI reactions
- Deficient knowledge related to drug therapy

Planning and implementation

- Minimize adverse GI symptoms by spacing doses evenly and giving after food intake.
- Drug colors alkaline urine orange-yellow.

ALERT: Discontinue immediately and notify prescriber if patient shows evidence of hypersensitivity.

ALERT: Don't confuse sulfasalazine with sulfisoxazole, salsalate, or sulfadiazine.

Patient teaching

- Instruct patient to take drug after meals and to space doses evenly.
- Warn patient that drug may cause skin and urine to turn orange-yellow and may permanently stain soft contact lenses yellow.
- Warn patient to avoid direct sunlight and ultraviolet light to prevent photosensitivity reaction.

Evaluation

- Patient is free from pain.
- Patient maintains adequate hydration.
- Patient and family state understanding of drug therapy.

sulfinpyrazone

(sul-fin-PEER-uh-zohn)
Anturan ♦, Anturane

Pharmacologic class: uricosuric
Therapeutic class: renal tubular-blocking agent, platelet aggregation inhibitor
Pregnancy risk category: NR

Indications and dosages

▶ **Intermittent or chronic gouty arthritis.** *Adults:* Initially, 100 mg to 200 mg P.O. b.i.d. during the first week; then 200 mg to 400 mg P.O. b.i.d. Maximum dosage is 800 mg daily. After serum urate level is controlled, dosage can sometimes be reduced to 200 mg daily in divided doses.

▶ **Prophylaxis of thromboembolic disorders, including angina, MI, transient (cerebral) ischemic attacks, and presence of prosthetic heart valves‡.** *Adults:* 600 to 800 mg P.O. daily in divided doses to decrease platelet aggregation.

Contraindications and precautions

- Contraindicated in patients hypersensitive to pyrazole derivatives (including oxyphenbutazone and phenylbutazone) and patients with active peptic ulcer, symptoms of GI inflammation or ulceration, or blood dyscrasias.
- Use cautiously in patients with healed peptic ulcer.

Lifespan: In pregnant women, use cautiously. In breast-feeding women or children, safety of drug hasn't been established.

Adverse reactions

GI: *nausea, dyspepsia,* epigastric pain, reactivation of peptic ulcerations.
Hematologic: ***blood dyscrasias*** (such as anemia, ***leukopenia, agranulocytosis, thrombocytopenia, aplastic anemia***).
Respiratory: ***bronchoconstriction*** in patients with aspirin-induced asthma.
Skin: rash.

Interactions

Drug-drug. *Aspirin, niacin, salicylates:* Inhibits uricosuric effect of sulfinpyrazone. Don't use together.
Oral anticoagulants: Increases anticoagulant effect and risk of bleeding. Use together cautiously.
Oral antidiabetics: Increases effects. Monitor patient closely.
Probenecid: Inhibits renal excretion of sulfinpyrazone. Use together cautiously.
Drug-lifestyle: *Alcohol use:* Decreases drug effectiveness. Avoid using together.

Effects on lab test results

- May increase BUN and creatinine levels.
- May decrease hemoglobin, hematocrit, and RBC, WBC, granulocyte, and platelet counts.

Pharmacokinetics

Absorption: Complete.
Distribution: 98% to 99% protein-bound.
Metabolism: Rapid.
Excretion: Excreted in urine; about 50% excreted unchanged. *Half-life:* 4 to 6 hours.

Route	Onset	Peak	Duration
P.O.	Unknown	1-2 hr	4-6 hr

Pharmacodynamics

Chemical effect: Blocks renal tubular reabsorption of uric acid, increasing excretion, and inhibits platelet aggregation.
Therapeutic effect: Relieves signs and symptoms of gouty arthritis.

Available forms

Capsules: 200 mg
Tablets: 100 mg

NURSING PROCESS

Assessment

- Assess patient's condition before therapy and regularly thereafter.
- Monitor BUN level, CBC, and kidney function studies periodically during long-term use.
- Monitor fluid intake and output. Therapy may lead to renal colic and formation of uric acid stones until acid levels are normal (about 6 mg/dl).
- Be alert for adverse reactions and drug interactions.
- Evaluate patient's and family's knowledge of drug therapy.

Nursing diagnoses

- Ineffective health maintenance related to presence of gouty arthritis
- Risk for injury related to drug-induced adverse CNS reactions
- Deficient knowledge related to drug therapy

Planning and implementation

- Give drug with milk, food, or antacids to minimize GI disturbances.
- Encourage patient to drink fluids to maintain minimum daily output of 2 to 3 L. Alkalinize urine with sodium bicarbonate or other agent.

Keep in mind that alkalinizing agents are used therapeutically to increase drug activity, preventing urolithiasis.
• Drug is recommended for patients unresponsive to probenecid. Suitable for long-term use; neither cumulative effects nor tolerance develops.
• Drug contains no analgesic or anti-inflammatory and is of no value during acute gout attacks.
• Drug may increase frequency, severity, and length of acute gout attacks during first 6 to 12 months of therapy. Prophylactic colchicine or another anti-inflammatory is given during first 3 to 6 months.
• Lifelong therapy may be needed in patient with hyperuricemia.
• Drug decreases urinary excretion of aminohippuric acid, interfering with laboratory test results.
ALERT: Don't confuse Anturane with Artane or Antabuse.

Patient teaching
• Warn patient with gout not to take aspirin-containing drugs because they may precipitate gout. Acetaminophen may be used for pain.
• Tell patient to take drug with food, milk, or antacid. Also instruct him to drink plenty of water.
• Instruct patient with gout to avoid foods high in purine, such as anchovies, liver, sardines, kidneys, sweetbreads, peas, and lentils.
• Inform patient and family that drug must be taken regularly or gout attacks may result. Tell patient to visit prescriber regularly so blood levels can be monitored and dosage adjusted if needed.

Evaluation
• Patient regains and maintains normal uric acid level.
• Patient doesn't experience injury from adverse CNS reactions.
• Patient and family state understanding of drug therapy.

sulindac
(SUL-in-dak)
Aclin ◇, Apo-Sulin ♦, Clinoril, Novo-Sundac ♦

Pharmacologic class: NSAID
Therapeutic class: nonnarcotic analgesic, antipyretic, anti-inflammatory
Pregnancy risk category: NR

Indications and dosages
▶ **Osteoarthritis, rheumatoid arthritis, ankylosing spondylitis.** *Adults:* Initially, 150 mg P.O. b.i.d.; increased to 200 mg b.i.d., as needed.
▶ **Acute subacromial bursitis or supraspinatus tendinitis, acute gouty arthritis.** *Adults:* 200 mg P.O. b.i.d. for 7 to 14 days. Reduce dose as symptoms subside.

Contraindications and precautions
• Contraindicated in patients hypersensitive to drug and in patients for whom aspirin or NSAIDs precipitate.
• Use cautiously in patients with history of ulcers and GI bleeding, renal dysfunction, compromised cardiac function or hypertension, or conditions predisposing to fluid retention.
Lifespan: In pregnant women, drug isn't recommended. In breast-feeding women and in children, safety of drug hasn't been established.

Adverse reactions
CNS: dizziness, headache, nervousness, psychosis.
CV: hypertension, ***heart failure,*** palpitations, edema.
EENT: tinnitus, transient visual disturbances.
GI: *epigastric distress,* peptic ulceration, ***pancreatitis, GI bleeding,*** occult blood loss, nausea, constipation, dyspepsia, flatulence, anorexia.
GU: interstitial nephritis, ***nephrotic syndrome, renal failure.***
Hematologic: ***aplastic anemia, thrombocytopenia, neutropenia, agranulocytosis,*** hemolytic anemia.
Skin: *rash,* pruritus.
Other: drug fever, ***anaphylaxis,*** hypersensitivity syndrome, ***angioedema.***

Interactions

Drug-drug. *Anticoagulants:* Increases risk of bleeding. Monitor PT closely.
Aspirin: Decreases sulindac level and increases risk of adverse GI reactions. Avoid using together.
Cyclosporine: Increases nephrotoxicity of cyclosporine. Monitor patient.
Diflunisal, dimethyl sulfoxide: Decreases metabolism of sulindac to its active metabolite, reducing its effectiveness. Don't use together.
Methotrexate: Increases methotrexate toxicity. Avoid using together.
Probenecid: Increases plasma levels of sulindac and its active metabolite. Monitor patient for toxicity.
Sulfonamides, sulfonylureas, other highly protein-bound drugs: Possible displacement of these drugs from protein–binding sites, leading to increased toxicity. Monitor patient closely.

Effects on lab test results

- May increase BUN, creatinine, liver enzyme, and potassium levels.
- May increase bleeding time. May decrease hemoglobin, hematocrit, and platelet, neutrophil, and granulocyte counts.

Pharmacokinetics

Absorption: Rapid and complete.
Distribution: Highly protein-bound.
Metabolism: Drug is inactive and metabolized in liver to an active sulfide metabolite.
Excretion: Excreted in urine. *Half-life:* Parent drug, 8 hours; active metabolite, about 16 hours.

Route	Onset	Peak	Duration
P.O.	Unknown	2-4 hr	Unknown

Pharmacodynamics

Chemical effect: Unknown; produces anti-inflammatory, analgesic, and antipyretic effects, possibly by inhibiting prostaglandin synthesis.
Therapeutic effect: Relieves pain, fever, and inflammation.

Available forms

Tablets: 100 mg ◇, 150 mg, 200 mg

NURSING PROCESS

Assessment

- Assess patient's condition before therapy and regularly thereafter.
- Periodically monitor liver and kidney function and CBC in patient receiving long-term therapy.
- Be alert for adverse reactions and drug interactions.
- Evaluate patient's and family's knowledge of drug therapy.

Nursing diagnoses

- Acute pain related to presence of arthritis
- Impaired tissue integrity related to drug's adverse effect on GI mucosa
- Deficient knowledge related to drug therapy

Planning and implementation

- Notify prescriber of adverse reactions.

Patient teaching

- Tell patient to take drug with food, milk, or antacids to reduce adverse GI reactions.
- Advise patient to refrain from driving or performing other hazardous activities that require mental alertness until CNS effects are known.
- Teach patient signs and symptoms of GI bleeding, and tell him to contact prescriber immediately if they occur. Serious GI toxicity, including peptic ulceration and bleeding, can occur in patient taking NSAIDs despite absence of GI symptoms.

ALERT: Tell patient to notify prescriber immediately if easy bruising or prolonged bleeding occurs.

- Instruct patient to report edema and have blood pressure checked monthly. Drug causes sodium retention but may not effect kidneys as much as other NSAIDs.
- Instruct patient not to take aspirin or aspirin-containing products with sulindac.
- Tell patient to notify prescriber and undergo complete eye examination if visual disturbances occur.

Evaluation

- Patient is free from pain.
- Patient doesn't experience adverse GI reactions.
- Patient and family state understanding of drug therapy.

sumatriptan succinate
(soo-muh-TRIP-ten SEK-seh-nayt)
Imitrex

Pharmacologic class: selective 5-hydroxytryptamine (5-HT_1) receptor agonist
Therapeutic class: antimigraine agent
Pregnancy risk category: C

Indications and dosages

▶ **Acute migraine attacks (with or without aura).** *Adults:* 6 mg S.C. Maximum recommended dose is two 6-mg injections in 24 hours, separated by at least 1 hour. Or, 25 to 100 mg P.O. If headache returns or responds only partially, dose may be repeated after 2 hours. Maximum daily dose is 300 mg P.O. Intranasally, 5 mg, 10 mg, or 20 mg in one nostril (for 10-mg dose, one spray of 5-mg concentration into each nostril); if headache returns, may repeat once after 2 hours. Maximum daily dose is 40 mg.

Contraindications and precautions

- Contraindicated in patients hypersensitive to drug, patients taking ergotamine, patients who have taken an MAO inhibitor within 14 days, and patients with uncontrolled hypertension, ischemic heart disease (such as angina pectoris, Prinzmetal's angina, history of MI, or documented silent ischemia), or hemiplegic or basilar migraine.
- Use cautiously in patients who may have unrecognized coronary artery disease (CAD), such as postmenopausal women, men older than age 40, and patients with risk factors for CAD, such as hypertension, hypercholesterolemia, obesity, diabetes, smoking, or family history of CAD.

Lifespan: In women who are pregnant or intend to become pregnant, use cautiously. In breast-feeding women and in children, safety of drug hasn't been established.

Adverse reactions

CNS: *dizziness, vertigo,* drowsiness, headache, anxiety, malaise, fatigue.
CV: ***atrial fibrillation, ventricular fibrillation, ventricular tachycardia, MI,*** pressure or tightness in chest, flushing.
EENT: discomfort of throat, nasal cavity or sinus, mouth, jaw, or tongue; altered vision.
GI: abdominal discomfort, dysphagia.
Musculoskeletal: neck pain, myalgia, muscle cramps.
Skin: diaphoresis, *injection site reaction.*
Other: *tingling; warm or hot sensation; burning sensation; heaviness, pressure, or tightness;* feeling of strangeness; tight feeling in head; cold sensation.

Interactions

Drug-drug. *Ergot, ergot derivatives:* Prolongs vasospastic effects. Don't use these drugs within 24 hours of sumatriptan.
MAO inhibitors: Increases sumatriptan effects. Don't use within 2 weeks of an MAO inhibitor.
Drug-herb. *Horehound:* May enhance serotonergic effects. Discourage using together.

Effects on lab test results

None reported.

Pharmacokinetics

Absorption: Rapid after P.O. administration but with low absolute bioavailability (about 15%); absorbed well from injection site after S.C. administration.
Distribution: Drug has low protein-binding of about 14% to 21%.
Metabolism: About 80%, in liver.
Excretion: Excreted primarily in urine. *Half-life:* About 2 hours.

Route	Onset	Peak	Duration
P.O.	30 min	2-4 hr	Unknown
S.C.	10-20 min	1-2 hr	Unknown
Intranasal	Rapid	1-2 hr	Unknown

Pharmacodynamics

Chemical effect: Unknown; thought to selectively activate vascular serotonin (5-HT) receptors. Stimulation of specific receptor subtype 5-HT_1, present on cranial arteries and the dura mater, causes vasoconstriction of cerebral vessels but has minimal effects on systemic vessels, tissue perfusion, and blood pressure.
Therapeutic effect: Relieves acute migraine pain.

Available forms

Injection: 6 mg/0.5 ml (12 mg/ml) in 0.5-ml prefilled syringes and vials

Nasal spray: 5 mg/spray; 20 mg/spray
Tablets: 25 mg, 50 mg, 100 mg (base) ♦

NURSING PROCESS

Assessment
- Assess patient's condition before therapy and regularly thereafter.
- Be alert for adverse reactions and drug interactions.
- Evaluate patient's and family's knowledge of drug therapy.

Nursing diagnoses
- Acute pain related to presence of acute migraine attack
- Risk for injury related to drug-induced adverse reactions
- Deficient knowledge related to drug therapy

Planning and implementation
- Consider giving first dose in prescriber's office if patient has risk of unrecognized CAD.
- **P.O. use:** Give single tablet whole with fluids as soon as patient complains of migraine symptoms. Give second tablet if symptoms come back, but no sooner than 2 hours after first tablet.
- **S.C. use:** Maximum recommended dosage in 24-hour period is two 6-mg injections separated by at least 1 hour. Notify prescriber if patient doesn't obtain relief.

– Patient will most likely experience relief within 1 to 2 hours.
– Redness or pain at injection site should subside within 1 hour after injection.

ALERT: Serious adverse cardiac effects can follow S.C. administration of this drug, but such events are rare.

- **Intranasal use:** Follow normal protocol.

– Notify prescriber if patient doesn't feel relief.

ALERT: Don't confuse sumatriptan with somatropin.

Patient teaching
- Make sure patient understands that drug is intended only to treat migraine attack, not to prevent or reduce number of attacks.
- Tell patient that drug may be given at any time during migraine attack but should be given as soon as symptoms appear.
- Drug is available in spring-loaded injector system that makes it easy for the patient to give injection to himself. Review detailed information with patient. Make sure patient understands how to load injector, give injection, and dispose of used syringes.
- Instruct patient taking P.O. form when and how often to take drug. Warn patient not to take more than 300 mg within 24 hours.
- Instruct patient to use intranasal spray in one nostril (if 10 mg dose is ordered, 1 spray into each nostril). A second spray may be used if headache returns, but not before 2 hours has elapsed from the first use.
- Tell patient who experiences persistent or severe chest pain to call prescriber immediately. Patient who experiences pain or tightness in throat, wheezing, heart throbbing, rash, lumps, hives, or swollen eyelids, face, or lips should stop using drug and call prescriber.
- Tell woman who is pregnant or intends to become pregnant not to take this drug. Advise her to discuss with prescriber the risks and benefits of using drug during pregnancy.

Evaluation
- Patient is free from pain.
- Patient doesn't experience injury from adverse CV reactions.
- Patient and family state understanding of drug therapy.

T

tacrine hydrochloride
(TAK-reen high-droh-KLOR-ighd)
Cognex

Pharmacologic class: centrally acting reversible anticholinesterase
Therapeutic class: psychotherapeutic for Alzheimer's disease
Pregnancy risk category: C

Indications and dosages

▶ **Mild-to-moderate dementia of Alzheimer's type.** *Adults:* Initially, 10 mg P.O. q.i.d. After 6 weeks and if patient tolerates treatment and transaminase levels aren't elevated, dosage increased to 20 mg q.i.d. After another 6 weeks, dosage adjusted upward to 30 mg q.i.d. If still tolerated, increased to 40 mg q.i.d. after another 6 weeks.

Contraindications and precautions

• Contraindicated in patients hypersensitive to drug or acridine derivatives and in those who have previously developed tacrine-related jaundice and been confirmed with elevated total bilirubin level of more than 3 mg/dl.
• Use cautiously in patients with sick sinus syndrome or bradycardia; those at risk for peptic ulceration (including patients taking NSAIDs or those with history of peptic ulcer); those with history of hepatic disease; and those with renal disease, asthma, prostatic hyperplasia, or other urinary outflow impairment.
Lifespan: In pregnant or breast-feeding women, drug isn't recommended. In children, drug isn't indicated.

Adverse reactions

CNS: agitation, ataxia, insomnia, abnormal thinking, somnolence, depression, anxiety, *headache,* fatigue, *dizziness,* confusion.
CV: chest pain, facial flushing.
EENT: rhinitis.
GI: *nausea, vomiting,* anorexia, *diarrhea,* dyspepsia, loose stools, changes in stool color, constipation.
Hepatic: jaundice.
Metabolic: weight loss.
Musculoskeletal: myalgia.
Respiratory: upper respiratory tract infection, cough.
Skin: rash.

Interactions

Drug-drug. *Anticholinergics:* Drug may decrease effectiveness of anticholinergics. Monitor patient closely.
Cholinergics (such as bethanechol), anticholinesterases: May have additive effects. Monitor patient for toxicity.
Succinylcholine: Enhances neuromuscular blockade and prolongs duration of action. Monitor patient.
Theophylline: Increases theophylline serum levels and prolonged theophylline half-life. Carefully monitor plasma theophylline levels and adjust dosage as directed.
Drug-food. *Any food:* Decreases tacrine absorption. Tell patient to take drug on empty stomach.
Drug-lifestyle. *Smoking:* Decreases plasma levels of drug. Monitor response.

Effects on lab test results

• May increase ALT and AST levels.

Pharmacokinetics

Absorption: Rapidly absorbed with absolute bioavailability of about 17%. Food reduces tacrine bioavailability by 30% to 40%.
Distribution: About 55% bound to plasma proteins.
Metabolism: Undergoes first-pass metabolism, which is dose-dependent; extensively metabolized.
Excretion: Excreted in urine. *Half-life:* 2 to 4 hours.

Route	Onset	Peak	Duration
P.O.	Unknown	30 min-3 hr	Unknown

Pharmacodynamics

Chemical effect: Reversibly inhibits enzyme cholinesterase in CNS, allowing buildup of acetylcholine.
Therapeutic effect: Improves thinking ability in patients with Alzheimer's disease.

Available forms

Capsules: 10 mg, 20 mg, 30 mg, 40 mg

NURSING PROCESS

Assessment

• Assess patient's cognitive ability before therapy and regularly thereafter.
• Monitor serum ALT levels weekly during first 18 weeks of therapy. If ALT is modestly elevated after first 18 weeks (twice upper limit of normal range), continue weekly monitoring. If no problems occur, determinations decreased to every 3 months. Whenever dosage is increased, resume weekly monitoring for at least 6 weeks.
• Be alert for adverse reactions and drug interactions.
• Evaluate patient's and family's knowledge of drug therapy.

Nursing diagnoses

- Disturbed thought processes related to Alzheimer's disease
- Diarrhea related to drug-induced adverse GI reactions
- Deficient knowledge related to drug therapy

Planning and implementation

- Give drug between meals. If GI upset becomes a problem, give drug with meals, although plasma levels may drop by 30% to 40%.
- If drug is discontinued for 4 weeks or more, full dosage adjustment and monitoring schedule must be restarted.
- Obtain order for antidiarrheal, if indicated.

Patient teaching

- Help patient and family members understand that drug only alleviates symptoms. Effect of therapy depends on drug administration at regular intervals.

ALERT: Instruct caregivers when to give drug. Explain that dosage adjustment is integral to safe use. Abrupt discontinuation or large reduction in daily dose (80 mg or more per day) may trigger behavioral disturbances and cognitive decline.

- Advise patient and caregivers to report immediately any significant adverse effects or changes in status.

Evaluation

- Patient exhibits improved cognitive ability.
- Patient or caregiver states that drug-induced diarrhea hasn't occurred.
- Patient and family state understanding of drug therapy.

tacrolimus

(tek-roh-LYE-mus)

Prograf

Pharmacologic class: bacteria-derived macrolide
Therapeutic class: immunosuppressant
Pregnancy risk category: C

Indications and dosages

▶ **Prophylaxis of organ rejection in allogenic liver transplantation.** *Adults:* 0.05 to 0.1 mg/kg I.V. daily as continuous infusion given no sooner than 6 hours after transplantation. P.O. therapy should be substituted as soon as possible, with first dose given 8 to 12 hours after discontinuing I.V. infusion. Recommended initial P.O. dosage is 0.15 to 0.3 mg/kg daily in two divided doses q 12 hours. Dosage should be adjusted according to clinical response.
Children: Initially, 0.1 mg/kg I.V. daily, followed by 0.3 mg/kg P.O. daily on schedule similar to that for adults; adjust dosage, as needed.

Contraindications and precautions

- Contraindicated in patients hypersensitive to drug. The I.V. form is contraindicated in patients hypersensitive to castor oil derivatives.

Lifespan: In pregnant or breast-feeding women, drug isn't recommended.

Adverse reactions

CNS: *asthenia, headache, tremor, insomnia, paresthesia, delirium,* ***coma,*** *pain, fever.*
CV: *hypertension, peripheral edema.*
GI: *diarrhea, nausea, constipation, anorexia, vomiting, abdominal pain.*
GU: *abnormal kidney function,* urinary tract infection, oliguria.
Hematologic: *anemia,* leukocytosis, **THROMBOCYTOPENIA.**
Metabolic: ***hyperkalemia,*** hypokalemia, *hyperglycemia, hypomagnesemia.*
Musculoskeletal: *back pain.*
Respiratory: *pleural effusion, atelectasis, dyspnea.*
Skin: *photosensitivity reactions.*
Other: *ascites,* ***anaphylaxis.***

Interactions

Drug-drug. *Bromocriptine, cimetidine, clarithromycin, clotrimazole, cyclosporine, danazol, diltiazem, erythromycin, fluconazole, itraconazole, ketoconazole, methylprednisolone, metoclopramide, nicardipine, verapamil:* May increase tacrolimus level. Monitor patient for adverse effects.
Carbamazepine, phenobarbital, phenytoin, rifabutin, rifampin: May decrease tacrolimus level. Monitor effectiveness of tacrolimus.
Cyclosporine: increased risk of excess nephrotoxicity. Don't give together.

Immunosuppressants (except adrenocorticosteroids): May over-suppress immune system. Monitor patient closely, especially during times of stress.
Inducers of cytochrome P-450 enzyme system: May increase tacrolimus metabolism and decrease plasma level. Dosage adjustment may be needed.
Inhibitors of cytochrome P-450 enzyme system: May decrease tacrolimus metabolism and increase plasma level. Dosage adjustment may be needed.
Nephrotoxic drugs (such as aminoglycosides, amphotericin B, cisplatin, cyclosporine): May cause additive or synergistic effects. Monitor patient closely.
Viral vaccines: Tacrolimus may interfere with immune response to live virus vaccines.
Drug-food. *Any food:* Inhibits drug absorption. Tell patient to take drug on an empty stomach.
Grapefruit juice: Increases drug blood levels in liver transplant patients. Discourage using together.

Effects on lab test results

- May increase glucose, creatinine, and BUN levels. May decrease magnesium level. May increase or decrease potassium level.
- May increase WBC count and liver function test values. May decrease hemoglobin, hematocrit, and platelet count.

Pharmacokinetics

Absorption: Variable. Food reduces absorption and bioavailability of drug.
Distribution: Distribution between whole blood and plasma depends on several factors, such as hematocrit, temperature of separation of plasma, drug level, and protein level. Drug is 75% to 99% protein-bound.
Metabolism: Extensively metabolized.
Excretion: Excreted primarily in bile; less than 1% excreted unchanged in urine.

Route	Onset	Peak	Duration
P.O., I.V.	Unknown	1.5-3.5 hr	Unknown

Pharmacodynamics

Chemical effect: Precise mechanism unknown; inhibits T-lymphocyte activation, which results in immunosuppression.
Therapeutic effect: Prevents organ rejection.

Available forms

Capsules: 1 mg, 5 mg
Injection: 5 mg/ml

NURSING PROCESS

Assessment

- Obtain history of patient's organ transplant before therapy and reassess regularly thereafter.
- Monitor patient continuously during first 30 minutes of infusion; then monitor frequently for anaphylaxis.
- Monitor patient for signs of neurotoxicity and nephrotoxicity, especially in those receiving high dosage or those with renal dysfunction.
- Obtain potassium and glucose levels regularly. Monitor patient for hyperglycemia.
- Drug increases risk of infections, lymphomas, and other cancers.
- Be alert for adverse reactions and drug interactions.
- Evaluate patient's and family's knowledge of drug therapy.

Nursing diagnoses

- Risk for injury related to potential organ transplant rejection
- Ineffective protection related to drug-induced immunosuppression
- Deficient knowledge related to drug therapy

Planning and implementation

- Child with normal kidney and liver function may need higher dosage than adult.
- Patient with hepatic or renal dysfunction needs lowest possible dosage.
- Expect to give adrenocorticosteroids with this drug.
- **P.O. use:** Give drug on empty stomach.
- **I.V. use:** Dilute drug with normal saline solution injection or D_5W injection to 0.004 to 0.02 mg/ml before use.

– Store diluted solution for no more than 24 hours in glass or polyethylene containers. Don't store drug in polyvinyl chloride container.
– Each required daily dose of diluted drug is infused continuously over 24 hours.

ALERT: Because of risk of anaphylaxis, use injection only in patient who cannot take oral form.

– Keep epinephrine 1:1,000 readily available to treat anaphylaxis.
• Other immunosuppressants (except for adrenocorticosteroids) shouldn't be used during therapy.
• Avoid potassium-sparing diuretics during therapy.

Patient teaching
• Instruct patient to take drug on empty stomach and not to take it with grapefruit juice.
• Explain need for repeated tests during therapy to monitor adverse reactions and drug effectiveness.
• Advise woman of childbearing age to notify prescriber if she becomes pregnant or plans to do so.
• Instruct patient to check with prescriber before taking other drugs.

☑ Evaluation
• Patient doesn't exhibit signs and symptoms of organ rejection.
• Patient doesn't develop serious complications as result of drug-induced adverse reactions.
• Patient and family state understanding of drug therapy.

tacrolimus (topical)
(tack-row-LYE-mus)
Protopic

Pharmacologic class: macrolide
Therapeutic class: immunosuppressant
Pregnancy risk category: C

Indication and dosages
▶ **Moderate-to-severe atopic dermatitis in patients unresponsive to other therapies or unable to use other therapies because of potential risks.** *Adults:* Thin layer of 0.03% or 0.1% strength applied to affected areas twice daily and rubbed in completely. Continued for 1 week after affected area clears.
Children age 2 and older: Thin layer of 0.03% strength applied to affected areas twice daily and rubbed in completely. Continued for 1 week after affected area clears.

Contraindications and precautions
• Contraindicated in patients hypersensitive to tacrolimus.
• Don't use in patients with Netherton's syndrome or generalized erythroderma.
Lifespan: In breast-feeding women, tacrolimus appears in breast milk; weigh risk and benefit before giving it. In children ages 2 to 15, use only 0.03% ointment.

Adverse reactions
CNS: *headache, fever,* hyperesthesia, asthenia, insomnia.
CV: face edema, peripheral edema.
EENT: *otitis media, pharyngitis,* rhinitis, sinusitis, conjunctivitis.
GI: diarrhea, vomiting, nausea, abdominal pain, gastroenteritis, dyspepsia.
GU: dysmenorrhea.
Musculoskeletal: back pain, myalgia.
Respiratory: *increased cough, asthma,* pneumonia, bronchitis.
Skin: *skin burning, pruritus, skin erythema, skin infection, herpes simplex,* eczema herpeticum, pustular rash, *folliculitis,* urticaria, maculopapular rash, rash, fungal dermatitis, acne, sunburn, tingling, benign skin neoplasm, skin disorder, vesiculobullous rash, dry skin, varicella zoster, herpes zoster, eczema, exfoliative dermatitis, contact dermatitis.
Other: *flulike symptoms, accidental injury, infection, lack of drug effect,* alcohol intolerance, periodontal abscess, cyst, *allergic reaction,* pain, lymphadenopathy.

Interactions
Drug-drug. *Calcium channel blockers, cimetidine, CYP3A4 inhibitors (erythromycin, itraconazole, ketoconazole, fluconazole):* May interfere with effects of tacrolimus. Use together cautiously.
Drug-lifestyle. *Sun exposure:* Risk of phototoxicity. Tell patient to avoid or minimize exposure to artificial or natural sunlight.

Effects on lab test results
None reported.

Pharmacokinetics
Absorption: Immediate, with no systemic accumulation.
Distribution: Unknown.

Metabolism: Unknown.
Excretion: Unknown.

Route	Onset	Peak	Duration
Topical	Unknown	Unknown	Unknown

Pharmacodynamics

Chemical effect: Unknown. Believed to act as an immune system modulator in the skin by inhibiting T-lymphocyte activation, which causes immunosuppression. Drug also inhibits the release of mediators from mast cells and basophils in skin.
Therapeutic effect: Improves skin condition.

Available forms

Ointment: 0.03%, 0.1%

NURSING PROCESS

Assessment
- Assess patient's underlying condition before therapy and reassess regularly throughout therapy.
- Evaluate patient with clinically infected atopic dermatitis; clear infections at treatment site before using drug.
- Evaluate patient's and family's knowledge of tacrolimus therapy.

Nursing diagnoses
- Impaired skin integrity related to underlying skin condition
- Acute pain related to drug-induced adverse effects
- Deficient knowledge related to tacrolimus therapy

Planning and implementation
- Drug is used only for short-term or intermittent long-term therapy.

ALERT: Don't use occlusive dressings over drug application. This may promote systemic absorption.
- This drug may increase the risk of varicella zoster, herpes simplex virus, and eczema herpeticum.
- Evaluate all cases of lymphadenopathy to determine etiology. If a clear etiology is unknown or acute mononucleosis is diagnosed, consider stopping drug.
- Monitor all cases of lymphadenopathy until resolution.
- Local adverse effects are most common during the first few days of treatment.

Patient teaching
- Tell patient to wash hands before and after applying drug and to avoid applying drug to wet skin. Skin should be completely dry before applying drug.
- Urge patient not to use bandages or other occlusive dressings.
- Tell patient not to bathe, shower, or swim immediately after application because doing so could wash the ointment off.
- Advise patient to avoid or minimize exposure to natural or artificial sunlight.
- Tell patient that if he needs to be outdoors after applying drug, to wear loose-fitting clothing that covers the treated area. Check with prescriber regarding sunscreen use.
- Caution patient not to use drug for any disorder other than that for which it was prescribed.
- Encourage patient to report adverse reactions.
- Tell patient to store the ointment at room temperature.

Evaluation
- Patient has improved skin condition.
- Patient states that pain management techniques are effective.
- Patient and family state understanding of tacrolimus therapy.

tamoxifen citrate
(teh-MOKS-uh-fen SIGH-trayt)
Apo-Tamox♦, Nolvadex, Nolvadex-D♦◇, Novo-Tamoxifen♦, Tamofen♦, Tamone♦

Pharmacologic class: nonsteroidal antiestrogen
Therapeutic class: antineoplastic
Pregnancy risk category: D

Indications and dosages

▶ **Advanced postmenopausal breast cancer.** *Adults:* 10 to 20 mg P.O. b.i.d.
▶ **Adjunct treatment for breast cancer.** *Adults:* 10 mg P.O. b.i.d. to t.i.d. for no more than 2 years.
▶ **Reduction of breast cancer risk in high-risk women.** *Adults:* 20 mg P.O. daily for 5 years.

▶ **Ductal carcinoma in situ (DCIS).** *Adults:* 20 mg P.O. daily for 5 years.
▶ **Stimulation of ovulation‡.** *Adults:* 5 to 40 mg P.O. b.i.d. for 4 days.
▶ **McCune–Albright syndrome and precocious puberty‡.** *Children ages 2 to 10 years:* 20 mg P.O. daily. Treat for up to 12 months.
▶ **Mastalgia‡.** *Adults:* 10 mg P.O. daily for 10 months.

Contraindications and precautions

- Contraindicated in patients hypersensitive to drug.
- Contraindicated in women receiving coumarin-type anticoagulants and those with history of deep vein thrombosis or pulmonary emboli.
- Use cautiously in patients with leukopenia or thrombocytopenia.

Lifespan: In pregnant or breast-feeding women, drug isn't recommended. In children, safety of drug hasn't been established.

Adverse reactions

CNS: confusion, weakness, headache, sleepinessm, ***CVA.***
CV: *hot flushes.*
EENT: corneal changes, cataracts, retinopathy.
GI: *nausea, vomiting, diarrhea.*
GU: *vaginal discharge* and bleeding, *irregular menses, amenorrhea,* ***endometrial cancer, uterine sarcoma.***
Hematologic: ***leukopenia, thrombocytopenia.***
Hepatic: fatty liver, cholestasis, ***hepatic necrosis.***
Metabolic: *hypercalcemia, weight changes, fluid retention.*
Musculoskeletal: brief exacerbation of pain from osseous metastases.
Respiratory: ***pulmonary embolism.***
Skin: *skin changes,* rash.
Other: temporary bone or tumor pain.

Interactions

Drug-drug. *Antacids:* May affect absorption of enteric-coated tablet. Don't use within 2 hours of tamoxifen dose.
Bromocriptine: May elevate tamoxifen level. Monitor patient for toxicity.
Coumadin-type anticoagulants: May cause significant increase in anticoagulant effect. Monitor patient, PT, and INR closely.

Effects on lab test results

- May increase BUN, creatinine, calcium, and liver enzyme levels.
- May decrease WBC and platelet counts.

Pharmacokinetics

Absorption: Appears to be well absorbed across GI tract.
Distribution: Distributed widely in total body water.
Metabolism: Metabolized extensively in liver to several metabolites.
Excretion: Drug and metabolites excreted mainly in feces, mostly as metabolites. *Half-life:* Over 7 days.

Route	Onset	Peak	Duration
P.O.	4-10 wk	Unknown	Several wk

Pharmacodynamics

Chemical effect: Exact antineoplastic action is unknown; acts as estrogen antagonist.
Therapeutic effect: Hinders function of breast cancer cells.

Available forms

Tablets: 10 mg, 20 mg
Tablets (enteric-coated)♦: 10 mg, 20 mg

NURSING PROCESS

Assessment

- Assess patient's breast cancer before therapy and regularly thereafter.
- Monitor CBC closely in patient with leukopenia or thrombocytopenia.
- Monitor lipid levels during long-term therapy in patients with hyperlipidemia.
- Monitor calcium level. Drug may compound hypercalcemia related to bone metastases during initiation of therapy.
- Be alert for adverse reactions.
- Monitor patient's hydration status if adverse GI reactions occur.
- Evaluate patient's and family's knowledge of drug therapy.

Nursing diagnoses

- Ineffective health maintenance related to presence of breast cancer
- Risk for deficient fluid volume related to drug-induced adverse GI reactions
- Deficient knowledge related to drug therapy

Planning and implementation

• Drug acts as an antiestrogen. Best results have been reported in patients with positive estrogen receptors.
• Make sure patient swallows enteric-coated tablets whole.
ALERT: Serious, life-threatening, or fatal events linked to tamoxifen in women at high risk for cancer and women with DCIS include endometrial cancer, uterine sarcoma, CVA, and pulmonary embolism. Prescribers should discuss the potential benefits versus the potential risks of these serious events with women considering Nolvadex to reduce their risk of developing breast cancer. The benefits of tamoxifen outweigh its risks in women already diagnosed with breast cancer.

Patient teaching

• Tell patient to report symptoms of pulmonary embolism (chest pain, difficulty breathing, rapid breathing, sweating or fainting).
• Tell patient to report symptoms of CVA (headache, vision changes, confusion, difficulty speaking or walking, and weakness of face, arm or leg, especially on one side of the body).
• Reassure patient that acute bone pain during drug therapy usually means that drug will produce good response. Tell her to take an analgesic for pain.
• Encourage patient who is taking or has taken drug to have regular gynecologic examinations because of increased risk of uterine cancer.
• If patient is taking drug to reduce risk of breast cancer, teach proper technique for self breast examination.
• Tell patient that annual mammograms and gynecologic examinations are important.
• Advise patient to use barrier form of contraception because short-term therapy induces ovulation in premenopausal women.
• Advise woman of childbearing age to avoid becoming pregnant during therapy and to consult with prescriber before becoming pregnant.

Evaluation

• Patient responds well to drug.
• Patient maintains adequate hydration.
• Patient and family state understanding of drug therapy.

tamsulosin hydrochloride

(tam-soo-LOH-sin high-droh-KLOR-ighd)
Flomax

Pharmacologic class: alpha-1_a antagonist
Therapeutic class: BPH agent
Pregnancy risk category: B

Indications and dosages

▶ **Treatment of BPH.** *Men:* 0.4 mg P.O. once daily, given 30 minutes after same meal each day. If no response after 2 to 4 weeks, dose may be increased to 0.8 mg P.O. once daily.

Contraindications and precautions

• Contraindicated in patients hypersensitive to drug or its components.
Lifespan: Drug is indicated for men only.

Adverse reactions

CNS: asthenia, *dizziness, headache,* insomnia, somnolence, syncope, vertigo.
CV: chest pain, orthostatic hypotension.
EENT: amblyopia, pharyngitis, *rhinitis,* sinusitis.
GI: diarrhea, nausea.
GU: abnormal ejaculation.
Musculoskeletal: back pain.
Respiratory: cough.
Other: decreased libido, *infection,* tooth disorder.

Interactions

Drug-drug. *Alpha-adrenergic blockers:* May interact with tamsulosin. Avoid using together.
Cimetidine: Decreases tamsulosin clearance. Use cautiously.

Effects on lab test results

None reported.

Pharmacokinetics

Absorption: More than 90%. Food increases bioavailability by 30%.
Distribution: Distributed into extracellular fluids. Extensively bound to protein (94% to 99%).
Metabolism: Primarily metabolized by cytochrome P450 enzymes in the liver.

Excretion: 76% of drug eliminated in urine; 21% in feces. *Half-life:* 9 to 13 hours.

Route	Onset	Peak	Duration
P.O.	Unknown	4-5 hr	9-15 hr

Pharmacodynamics

Chemical effect: Selectively blocks alpha receptors in the prostate, leading to relaxation of smooth muscles in the bladder neck and prostate, which improves urine flow and reduces symptoms of BPH.
Therapeutic effect: Improves urine flow.

Available forms

Capsules: 0.4 mg

NURSING PROCESS

Assessment

- Assess patient for signs of prostatic hyperplasia, including frequency of urination, nocturnal urination, and urinary hesitancy.
- Monitor patient for decreases in blood pressure and notify prescriber.
- Evaluate patient's and family's knowledge of drug therapy.

Nursing diagnoses

- Risk for injury related to decreased blood pressure and resulting syncope
- Impaired urinary elimination related to underlying prostatic hyperplasia
- Deficient knowledge related to drug therapy

Planning and implementation

- Symptoms of BPH and cancer of the prostate are similar; cancer should be ruled out before therapy starts.
- If treatment is interrupted for several days or more, restart therapy at one capsule daily.
- Drug may cause a sudden drop in blood pressure, especially after the first dose or when changing doses.

ALERT: Don't confuse Flomax with Fosamax.

Patient teaching

- Instruct patient not to crush, chew, or open capsules.
- Tell patient to get up slowly from chair or bed during initiation of therapy and to avoid situations where injury could occur because of syncope. Advise him that drug may cause a sudden drop in blood pressure, especially after the first dose or when changing doses.
- Instruct patient not to drive or perform hazardous tasks for 12 hours after the initial dose or changes in dose until response can be monitored.
- Tell patient to take drug about 30 minutes after same meal each day.

Evaluation

- Patient doesn't experience sudden decreases in blood pressure.
- Patient experiences normal urinary elimination patterns.
- Patient and family state understanding of drug therapy.

telmisartan

(tel-mih-SAR-tan)
Micardis

Pharmacologic class: angiotensin II receptor antagonist
Therapeutic class: antihypertensive
Pregnancy risk category: C (D in second and third trimesters)

Indications and dosages

▶ **Treatment of hypertension (used alone or with other antihypertensives).** *Adults:* 40 mg P.O. daily. Blood pressure response is dose-related between 20 and 80 mg daily.

Contraindications and precautions

- Contraindicated in patients hypersensitive to drug or its components.
- Use cautiously in patients with renal and hepatic insufficiency and in those with an activated renin-angiotensin system, such as volume- or salt-depleted patients (such as those being treated with high doses of diuretics).

Lifespan: If pregnancy is suspected, notify prescriber because drug should be discontinued. In breast-feeding women, drug isn't recommended. In patients age 18 or younger, safety and effectiveness haven't been studied.

Adverse reactions

CNS: dizziness, pain, fatigue, headache.
CV: chest pain, hypertension, peripheral edema.
EENT: pharyngitis, sinusitis.

GI: abdominal pain, diarrhea, dyspepsia, nausea.
GU: urinary tract infection.
Musculoskeletal: back pain, myalgia.
Respiratory: cough, upper respiratory tract infection.
Other: flulike symptoms.

Interactions

Drug-drug. *Digoxin:* Increases digoxin level. Monitor digoxin level closely.
Warfarin: Slightly decreases warfarin level. Monitor INR.

Effects on lab test results

- May increase liver enzyme levels.

Pharmacokinetics

Absorption: Readily absorbed after P.O. administration.
Distribution: Highly protein-bound; volume of distribution is about 500 L.
Metabolism: Metabolized by conjugation to an inactive metabolite.
Excretion: Mainly excreted unchanged in feces.

Route	Onset	Peak	Duration
P.O.	Unknown	30 min-1 hr	24 hr

Pharmacodynamics

Chemical effect: Blocks the vasoconstrictive and aldosterone-secreting effects of angiotensin II by selectively blocking the binding of angiotensin II to the AT_1 receptor in many tissues, such as vascular smooth muscle and the adrenal gland.
Therapeutic effect: Lowers blood pressure.

Available forms

Tablets: 40 mg, 80 mg

NURSING PROCESS

Assessment

- Monitor patient for hypotension after therapy starts. Place patient in supine position if hypotension occurs and give normal saline solution I.V. if needed.
- In patients whose renal function may depend on the activity of the renin-angiotensin-aldosterone system, such as those with severe heart failure, treatment with ACE inhibitors and angiotensin-receptor antagonists has been related to oliguria or progressive azotemia and (rarely) to acute renal failure or death.
- In patients with biliary obstruction, drug level may elevate because of inability to excrete drug.
- Drug isn't removed by hemodialysis. Patients undergoing dialysis may develop orthostatic hypotension. Closely monitor blood pressure.
- Evaluate patient's and family's knowledge of drug therapy.

Nursing diagnoses

- Risk for injury related to presence of hypertension
- Ineffective cerebral and cardiopulmonary tissue perfusion related to drug-induced hypotension
- Deficient knowledge related to drug therapy

Planning and implementation

- Most of the antihypertensive effect is present within 2 weeks. Maximal blood pressure reduction is generally attained after 4 weeks. Diuretic may be added if blood pressure isn't controlled by drug alone.

Patient teaching

- Inform woman of childbearing age of consequences of second- and third-trimester exposure to drug. Instruct patient to report suspected pregnancy to prescriber immediately.
- Advise breast-feeding woman about the risk of adverse effects on her infant and the need to stop breast-feeding or discontinue drug, taking into account importance of drug to patient.
- Tell patient that transient hypotension may occur. Instruct him to lie down if feeling dizzy and to climb stairs slowly and rise slowly to standing position.
- Instruct patient with heart failure to notify prescriber about decreased urine output.
- Tell patient that drug may be taken without regard to meals.
- Teach patient other means to reduce blood pressure, such as diet control, exercise, smoking cessation, and stress reduction.
- Inform patient that drug shouldn't be removed from blister-sealed packet until immediately before use.

Evaluation

- Patient doesn't experience injury from underlying disease.

• Patient doesn't experience hypotension and maintains adequate tissue perfusion.
• Patient and family state understanding of drug therapy.

temazepam

(teh-MAZ-ih-pam)
Euhypnos ◇, Normison ◇, Restoril, Temaze ◇

Pharmacologic class: benzodiazepine
Therapeutic class: sedative-hypnotic
Pregnancy risk category: X
Controlled substance schedule: IV

Indications and dosages

▶ **Insomnia.** *Adults age 65 and younger:* 7.5 to 30 mg P.O. 30 minutes before bedtime. *Adults older than age 65:* 7.5 mg P.O. h.s.

Contraindications and precautions

• Contraindicated in patients hypersensitive to benzodiazepines.
• Use cautiously in patients with chronic pulmonary insufficiency, impaired liver or kidney function, severe or latent depression, suicidal tendencies, or history of drug abuse.
Lifespan: In pregnant women, drug is contraindicated. In breast-feeding women, drug isn't recommended. In children, safety of drug hasn't been established.

Adverse reactions

CNS: *drowsiness, dizziness, lethargy,* disturbed coordination, daytime sedation, confusion, nightmares, vertigo, euphoria, weakness, headache, fatigue, nervousness, anxiety, depression.
EENT: blurred vision.
GI: diarrhea, nausea, dry mouth.
Other: physical or psychological dependence.

Interactions

Drug-drug. *CNS depressants, including narcotic analgesics:* Increases CNS depression. Use together cautiously.
Drug-herb. *Ashwagandha, calendula, catnip, hops, lady's slipper, lemon balm, passion flower, sassafras, skullcap, valerian, yerba maté:* May increase sedative effects. Monitor patient closely; discourage using together.
Kava: May cause excessive sedation. Discourage using together.
Drug-lifestyle. *Alcohol use:* Increases CNS depression. Discourage using together.

Effects on lab test results

• May increase liver enzyme level.

Pharmacokinetics

Absorption: Well absorbed through GI tract.
Distribution: Distributed widely throughout body; 98% protein-bound.
Metabolism: Metabolized in liver to primarily inactive metabolites.
Excretion: Metabolites excreted in urine.
Half-life: 10 to 17 hours.

Route	Onset	Peak	Duration
P.O.	Unknown	1-2 hr	Unknown

Pharmacodynamics

Chemical effect: Unknown; probably acts on limbic system, thalamus, and hypothalamus of CNS to produce hypnotic effects.
Therapeutic effect: Promotes sleep.

Available forms

Capsules: 7.5 mg, 15 mg, 20 mg ◇, 30 mg

NURSING PROCESS

Assessment

• Assess patient's sleeping disorder before therapy and regularly thereafter.
• Assess mental status before therapy. Geriatric patients are more sensitive to drug's adverse CNS effects.
• Be alert for adverse reactions and drug interactions.
• Evaluate patient's and family's knowledge of drug therapy.

Nursing diagnoses

• Disturbed sleep pattern related to presence of insomnia
• Risk for injury related to drug-induced adverse CNS reactions
• Deficient knowledge related to drug therapy

Planning and implementation

• Prevent hoarding or intentional overdosing by patient who is depressed, suicidal, or drug-dependent or who has history of drug abuse.
• Make sure patient has swallowed capsule before leaving bedside.

• Supervise walking and raise bed rails, particularly for geriatric patients.
ALERT: Don't confuse Restoril with Vistaril.

Patient teaching
• Warn patient to avoid activities that require mental alertness or physical coordination.

Evaluation
• Patient states that drug induces sleep.
• Patient doesn't experience injury from adverse CNS reactions.
• Patient and family state understanding of drug therapy.

temozolomide
(teh-moh-ZOHL-uh-mighd)
Temodar

Pharmacologic class: alkylating agent
Therapeutic class: antineoplastic
Pregnancy risk category: D

Indications and dosages
▶ **Refractory anaplastic astrocytoma that has relapsed after chemotherapy regimen containing a nitrosourea and procarbazine.** *Initial cycle. Adults:* 150 mg/m² P.O. once daily for first 5 days of 28-day chemotherapy treatment cycle.
Subsequent cycles. Adults: 100 to 200 mg/m² P.O. once daily for first 5 days of subsequent 28-day chemotherapy treatment cycles. Timing and dosage of subsequent cycles must be adjusted according to the absolute neutrophil count (ANC) and platelet count measured on cycle day 22 (expected nadir) and cycle day 29 (initiation of next cycle).

Dosage adjustments are based on the lowest of these ANC and platelet results.
Patients with ANC less than 1,000/mm³ or platelets less than 50,000/mm³: Hold therapy until ANC is above 1,500/mm³ and platelets are above 100,000/mm³. Reduce dose by 50 mg/m² for subsequent cycle. Minimum dose is 100 mg/m².
Patients with ANC 1,000 to 1,500/mm³ or platelets 50,000 to 100,000/mm³: Hold therapy until ANC is above 1,500/mm³ and platelets are above 100,000/mm³. Maintain prior dose for subsequent cycle.
Patients with ANC greater than 1,500/mm³ and platelets greater than 100,000/mm³: Increase dose to, or maintain at, 200 mg/m² for first 5 days of subsequent cycle.

Contraindications and precautions
• Contraindicated in patients hypersensitive to temozolomide or its components. Also contraindicated in patients allergic to dacarbazine, which is structurally similar to temozolomide.
• Use with caution in those with severe hepatic or renal impairment.
Lifespan: In geriatric patients, use with caution.

Adverse reactions
CNS: *fever, amnesia,* anxiety, *asthenia,* ataxia, confusion, SEIZURES, *coordination abnormality,* depression, *dizziness,* dysphasia, *fatigue,* gait abnormality, *headache, hemiparesis,* insomnia, local seizures, paresis, *paresthesia,* somnolence.
CV: peripheral edema.
EENT: abnormal vision, diplopia, pharyngitis, sinusitis.
GI: abdominal pain, anorexia, *constipation, diarrhea, nausea, vomiting.*
GU: increased urinary frequency, urinary incontinence, urinary tract infection.
Hematologic: anemia, LEUKOPENIA, NEUTROPENIA, THROMBOCYTOPENIA.
Metabolic: weight gain.
Musculoskeletal: back pain, myalgia.
Respiratory: cough, upper respiratory tract infection.
Skin: pruritus, rash.
Other: hyperadrenocorticism, breast pain (women), *viral infection.*

Interactions
Drug-drug. *Valproic acid:* Decreases oral clearance of temozolomide by about 5%. Use cautiously.
Drug-food. *Any food:* Reduces rate and extent of drug absorption; however, there are no dietary restrictions with drug administration. Give drug on an empty stomach to reduce nausea and vomiting.

Effects on lab test results
• May decrease hemoglobin, hematocrit, and WBC, platelet, and neutrophil counts.

Pharmacokinetics

Absorption: Rapid and complete, with plasma levels peaking in 1 hour.
Distribution: 15% bound to plasma proteins.
Metabolism: Undergoes spontaneous hydrolysis to its active form and other metabolites. After 7 days, 38% of given dose is recovered in urine and 0.8% in feces.
Excretion: Rapidly eliminated. *Half-life:* 1¾ hours.

Route	Onset	Peak	Duration
P.O.	Unknown	1 hr	Unknown

Pharmacodynamics

Chemical effect: Temozolomide is a prodrug that is rapidly hydrolyzed to the active agent. It's thought to interfere with DNA replication in rapidly dividing tissues, primarily through alkylation (methylation) of guanine nucleotides in the DNA structure.
Therapeutic effect: Hinders or kills certain cancer cells.

Available forms

Capsules: 5 mg, 20 mg, 100 mg, 250 mg

NURSING PROCESS

Assessment

- Obtain history of patient's underlying condition before therapy and reassess regularly thereafter.
- Blood count should be drawn on days 22 and 29 of each treatment cycle. If the ANC falls below 1,500/mm^3 or the platelet count falls below 100,000/mm^3, obtain a weekly CBC until the counts have recovered.
- Be alert for adverse reactions and drug interactions.
- Evaluate patient's and family's knowledge of drug therapy.

Nursing diagnoses

- Ineffective health maintenance related to presence of neoplastic disease
- Risk for injury related to drug-induced adverse reactions
- Deficient knowledge related to drug therapy

Planning and implementation

- Nausea and vomiting, which may be self-limiting, are the most common adverse effects. Giving drug on an empty stomach or at bedtime may lessen these effects. Usual antiemetics effectively control nausea and vomiting.
- Women and geriatric patients are at higher risk for developing myelosuppression.

ALERT: Avoid skin contact with or inhalation of capsule contents if capsule is accidentally opened or damaged. Follow procedures for safe handling and disposal of antineoplastics.

- Store capsules at a controlled room temperature (59° to 86° F [15° to 30° C]).

Patient teaching

- Emphasize importance of taking dose exactly as prescribed, usually on an empty stomach or at bedtime.
- Stress importance of continuing drug despite nausea and vomiting.
- Tell patient to call immediately if vomiting occurs shortly after a dose is taken.
- Tell patient to promptly report sore throat, fever, unusual bruising or bleeding, rash, or seizures.
- Advise patient to avoid exposure to people with infections.
- Advise sexually active patient to use effective birth control measures during treatment because temozolomide may cause birth defects.
- Tell patient to swallow capsules whole and to not break open the capsules.

Evaluation

- Patient exhibits positive response to therapy, as noted on improvement of follow-up studies.
- Patient doesn't experience injury as a result of drug-induced adverse reactions.
- Patient and family state understanding of drug therapy.

tenecteplase
(te-NEK-te-plase)
TNKase

Pharmacologic class: recombinant tissue plasminogen activator
Therapeutic class: thrombolytic
Pregnancy risk category: C

Indications and dosages

▶ **Reduction of mortality from acute MI.** *Adults who weigh less than 60 kg (132 lb):* 30 mg (6 ml) by I.V. bolus over 5 seconds. *Adults who weigh 60 to 69 kg (132 to 152 lb):* 35 mg (7 ml) by I.V. bolus over 5 seconds. *Adults who weigh 70 to 79 kg (154 to 174 lb):* 40 mg (8 ml) by I.V. bolus over 5 seconds. *Adults who weigh 80 to 89 kg (176 to 196 lb):* 45 mg (9 ml) by I.V. bolus over 5 seconds. *Adults who weigh 90 kg (198 lb) or more:* 50 mg (10 ml) by I.V. bolus over 5 seconds. Maximum dose is 50 mg.

Contraindications and precautions

- Contraindicated in patients with active internal bleeding; history of CVA; intracranial or intraspinal surgery or trauma within the previous 2 months; intracranial neoplasm, aneurysm, or arteriovenous malformation; severe uncontrolled hypertension; or known bleeding diathesis.
- Use cautiously in patients who have had recent major surgery (such as coronary artery bypass graft), organ biopsy, obstetrical delivery, or previous puncture of noncompressible vessels.
- Use cautiously in patients with recent trauma, recent GI or GU bleeding, high risk of left ventricular thrombus, acute pericarditis, hypertension (systolic 180 mm Hg or above, diastolic 110 mm Hg or above), severe hepatic dysfunction, hemostatic defects, subacute bacterial endocarditis, septic thrombophlebitis, diabetic hemorrhagic retinopathy, or cerebrovascular disease.

Lifespan: In pregnant or breast-feeding women, use cautiously. In children, safety and efficacy haven't been established. In patients age 75 and older, give cautiously; the drug benefit should be weighed against the risk of increased adverse effects.

Adverse reactions

CNS: ***intracranial hemorrhage.***
CV: ***CVA,*** *hematoma.*
EENT: pharyngeal bleeding, epistaxis.
GI: ***GI bleeding.***
GU: hematuria.
Hematologic: bleeding at puncture sites.

Interactions

Drug-drug. *Anticoagulants (heparin, vitamin K antagonists), drugs that alter platelet function (acetylsalicylic acid, dipyridamole, glycoprotein IIb/IIIa inhibitors):* Increases risk of bleeding when used before, during, or after therapy with tenecteplase. Use cautiously.

Effects on lab test results

- May increase PT, PTT, and INR.

Pharmacokinetics

Absorption: Administered I.V.
Distribution: Related to weight and is an approximation of plasma volume.
Metabolism: Primarily hepatic.
Excretion: Initial half-life is 20 to 24 minutes and terminal half-life is 90 to 130 minutes.

Route	Onset	Peak	Duration
I.V.	Immediate	Immediate	20-24 min

Pharmacodynamics

Chemical effect: Binds to fibrin and converts plasminogen to plasmin. The specificity to fibrin decreases systemic activation of plasminogen and the resulting breakdown of circulating fibrinogen.
Therapeutic effect: Dissolves blood clots.

Available forms

Injection: 50 mg

NURSING PROCESS

Assessment

- Assess underlying condition before therapy and reassess regularly throughout therapy.
- Monitor ECG for reperfusion arrhythmias.
- Evaluate pain before therapy and reassess regularly.
- Assess patient for contraindications to therapy.
- Monitor vital signs.
- Evaluate patient's and family's knowledge of drug therapy.

Nursing diagnoses

- Ineffective tissue perfusion, coronary, related to presence of blood clots
- Acute pain related to MI
- Deficient knowledge related to tenecteplase therapy

Planning and implementation

• Avoid arterial and venous punctures during treatment.
• Avoid noncompressible arterial punctures and internal jugular and subclavian venous punctures.
• Use syringe prefilled with sterile water for injection and inject entire contents into drug vial.
ALERT: Do not use bacteriostatic water for injection.
ALERT: Gently swirl solution once mixed. Don't shake. Make sure contents are completely dissolved.
• Draw up the appropriate dose needed from the reconstituted vial with the syringe and discard any unused portion.
• Give drug rapidly over 5 seconds.
• Give drug immediately once reconstituted, or refrigerate and use within 8 hours.
ALERT: Don't give drug in same I.V. line as dextrose. Flush dextrose-containing lines with normal saline solution before administration.
• Give tenecteplase in a designated line.
• Give heparin with tenecteplase, but not in the same I.V. line.
• Monitor patient for bleeding. If serious bleeding occurs, discontinue heparin and antiplatelet drugs immediately.
• Cholesterol embolism is rarely related to thrombolytic use, but may be lethal. Signs and symptoms may include livedo reticularis "purple toe" syndrome, acute renal failure, gangrenous digits, hypertension, pancreatitis, MI, cerebral infarction, spinal cord infarction, retinal artery occlusion, bowel infarction, and rhabdomyolysis.

Patient teaching

• Advise patient about proper dental care to avoid excessive gum bleeding.
• Advise patient to report any adverse effects or excess bleeding immediately.
• Explain use of drug to patient and family.

Evaluation

• Patient and family state understanding of tenecteplase therapy.
• Patient regains tissue perfusion with dissolution on blood clots.
• Patient is relieved of pain.

teniposide (VM-26)
(teh-NIP-uh-sighd)
Vumon

Pharmacologic class: podophyllotoxin (specific to phase of cell cycle G_2 and late S phase)
Therapeutic class: antineoplastic
Pregnancy risk category: D

Indications and dosages

▶ **Refractory childhood acute lymphoblastic leukemia.** *Children:* Optimum dosage hasn't been established. One protocol reported by manufacturer is 165 mg/m² I.V. twice weekly for 8 or 9 doses. Usually used with other drugs.

Contraindications and precautions

• Drug is contraindicated in patients who are hypersensitive to drug or to polyoxyethylated castor oil (an injection vehicle).
Lifespan: In pregnant or breast-feeding women, drug isn't recommended.

Adverse reactions

CV: hypotension from rapid infusion.
GI: *nausea, vomiting, mucositis, diarrhea.*
Hematologic: MYELOSUPPRESSION (dose-limiting), LEUKOPENIA, NEUTROPENIA, THROMBOCYTOPENIA, *anemia.*
Skin: alopecia.
Other: ***hypersensitivity reactions*** (chills, fever, urticaria, tachycardia, ***bronchospasm,*** dyspnea, hypotension, flushing), *phlebitis at injection site with extravasation.*

Interactions

Drug-drug. *Methotrexate:* May increase clearance and intracellular levels of methotrexate. Monitor patient closely.
Sodium salicylate, sulfamethizole, tolbutamide: May displace teniposide from protein-binding sites and increase toxicity. Monitor patient closely.

Effects on lab test results

• May increase uric acid level.
• May decrease hemoglobin, hematocrit, and RBC, WBC, platelet, and neutrophil counts.

Pharmacokinetics

Absorption: Administered I.V.
Distribution: Distributed mainly in liver, kidneys, small intestine, and adrenals. Drug crosses blood-brain barrier to limited extent; highly bound to plasma proteins.
Metabolism: Metabolized extensively in liver.
Excretion: About 40% eliminated through kidneys as unchanged drug or metabolites.
Half-life: 5 hours.

Route	Onset	Peak	Duration
I.V.	Unknown	Unknown	Unknown

Pharmacodynamics

Chemical effect: Acts in late S or early G_2 phase of cell cycle, thus preventing cells from entering mitosis.
Therapeutic effect: Prevents reproduction of leukemic cells.

Available forms

Injection: 50 mg/5 ml

NURSING PROCESS

Assessment

- Assess patient's condition before therapy and regularly thereafter.
- Obtain baseline blood counts and kidney and liver function tests, then monitor periodically.
- Monitor blood pressure before therapy and at 30-minute intervals during infusion.
- Be alert for adverse reactions and drug interactions.
- Evaluate patient's and family's knowledge of drug therapy.

Nursing diagnoses

- Ineffective health maintenance related to presence of leukemia
- Ineffective protection related to drug-induced immunosuppression
- Deficient knowledge related to drug therapy

Planning and implementation

- Some prescribers may decide to use drug despite patient's history of hypersensitivity because therapeutic benefits may outweigh risks. Such patients should be treated with antihistamines and corticosteroids before infusion begins and be closely watched during drug administration.

ALERT: Have diphenhydramine, hydrocortisone, epinephrine, and appropriate emergency equipment available to establish airway in case of anaphylaxis.

- Follow institutional policy to reduce risks. Preparation and administration of parenteral form are linked to carcinogenic, mutagenic, and teratogenic risks for personnel.
- Dilute drug in D_5W or normal saline solution injection to level of 0.1, 0.2, 0.4, or 1 mg/ml. Don't agitate vigorously; precipitation may form. Discard cloudy solutions. Prepare and store in glass containers. Infuse over 45 to 90 minutes to prevent hypotension.
- Don't mix with other drugs or solutions.
- Heparin is physically incompatible with drug. Don't mix.
- Ensure careful placement of I.V. catheter. Extravasation can cause local tissue necrosis or sloughing.
- Don't give drug through membrane-type inline filter because diluent may dissolve filter.
- Solutions containing 0.5 to 1 mg/ml teniposide are stable for 4 hours; those containing 0.1 to 0.2 mg/ml are stable for 6 hours at room temperature.
- Report systolic blood pressure below 90 mm Hg and stop infusion.

Patient teaching

- Tell patient to report discomfort at I.V. site immediately.
- Encourage adequate fluid intake to increase urine output and facilitate excretion of uric acid.
- Review infection-control and bleeding precautions to take during therapy.
- Reassure patient that hair should grow back after treatment stops.
- Instruct patient and parents to notify prescriber if adverse reactions occur.

Evaluation

- Patient responds well to drug.
- Patient doesn't develop serious complications from immunosuppression.
- Patient and family state understanding of drug therapy.

tenofovir disoproxil fumarate

(teh-NAH-fuh-veer diso-PRAHK-sul FOO-mah-rate)
Viread

Pharmacologic class: nucleotide reverse transcriptase inhibitor
Therapeutic class: antiviral, antiretroviral
Pregnancy risk category: B

Indications and dosages

▶ **HIV-1 infection, with other antiretroviral drugs.** *Adults:* 300 mg P.O. once daily with a meal. When given with didanosine, give 2 hours before or 1 hour after didanosine.

Contraindications and precautions

- Contraindicated in patients hypersensitive to any component of the drug.
- Don't use in patients with creatinine clearance less than 60 ml/minute.
- Use very cautiously in patients with risk factors for liver disease or with hepatic impairment.

Lifespan: In pregnant women, give this drug only if its benefits clearly outweigh the risks. Mothers receiving tenofovir for HIV infection shouldn't breast-feed. In children, safety and efficacy haven't been studied. In geriatric patients, use cautiously because these patients are more likely to have renal impairment and to be receiving other drug therapy.

Adverse reactions

CNS: asthenia, headache.
GI: abdominal pain, anorexia, diarrhea, flatulence, *nausea,* vomiting.
GU: glycosuria.
Hematologic: ***neutropenia.***
Metabolic: hyperglycemia.

Interactions

Drug-drug. *Acyclovir, cidofovir, ganciclovir, valacyclovir, valganciclovir (drugs that reduce renal function or compete for renal tubular secretion):* Increases level of tenofovir or other renally eliminated drugs. Monitor patient for adverse effects.
Didanosine (buffered formulation): Increases didanosine bioavailability. Monitor patient for didanosine-related adverse effects, such as bone marrow suppression, GI distress, and peripheral neuropathy. Give tenofovir 2 hours before or 1 hour after didanosine.

Effects on lab test results

- May increase amylase, AST, ALT, creatinine kinase, serum and urine glucose, and triglyceride levels. May decrease HIV-1 RNA levels.
- May decrease neutrophil and CD4 cell counts.

Pharmacokinetics

Absorption: In fasting patients, tenofovir is poorly absorbed (bioavailability 25%) with peak level occurring in about 1 hour. A high-fat meal delays the peak by 1 hour but increases bioavailability to 40%.
Distribution: Tenofovir has low binding to plasma (0.7%) and serum proteins (7.2%).
Metabolism: Neither tenofovir nor tenofovir disoproxil fumarate is metabolized by liver enzymes, including the CYP450 enzymes.
Excretion: Renal, through glomerular filtration and active tubular secretion.

Route	Onset	Peak	Duration
P.O.	Unknown	1-2 hr	Unknown

Pharmacodynamics

Chemical effect: Tenofovir disoproxil fumarate is a prodrug that is hydrolyzed to produce tenofovir. Tenofovir, a nucleoside analog of adenosine monophosphate, undergoes sequential phosphorylations to yield tenofovir diphosphate. Tenofovir diphosphate is a competitive antagonist of HIV reverse transcriptase, via competition with the natural substrate and through DNA chain termination.
Therapeutic effect: Inhibits HIV replication.

Available forms

Tablets: 300 mg as the fumarate salt (equivalent to 245 mg of tenofovir disoproxil)

NURSING PROCESS

Assessment

- Obtain baseline assessment of patient's viral infection and reassess regularly.
- Evaluate patient for risk factors of severe adverse reactions. Antiretrovirals, alone or com-

bined, have been linked to lactic acidosis and severe (including fatal) hepatomegaly with steatosis. These effects may occur without elevated transaminase levels. Risk factors may include prolonged exposure to antiretrovirals, being obese, and being female. Monitor all patients for hepatotoxicity, including lactic acidosis and hepatomegaly with steatosis.
• Evaluate patient's and family's knowledge of tenofovir disoproxil fumarate therapy.

Nursing diagnoses
• Noncompliance related to long-term therapy
• Risk for infection related to presence of HIV
• Deficient knowledge related to drug therapy

Planning and implementation
• Monitor patient for adverse events and begin standard supportive therapies if they occur.
• Antiretrovirals have been linked to the accumulation and redistribution of body fat, resulting in central obesity, peripheral wasting, and development of a buffalo hump. The long-term effects of these changes are unknown. Monitor patients for changes in body fat.
• Tenofovir may be linked to bone abnormalities (osteomalacia and decreased bone mineral density) and renal toxicity (increased creatinine and phosphaturia levels). Monitor patient carefully during long-term treatment.
• Drug may lead to decreased HIV-1 RNA levels and CD4 cell counts.
• The effects of tenofovir on the progression of HIV infection are unknown.

Patient teaching
• Instruct patient to take tenofovir with a meal to enhance bioavailability.
• Tell patient to report adverse effects, including nausea, vomiting, diarrhea, flatulence, and headache.

Evaluation
• Patient complies with treatment regimen.
• Patient has reduced signs and symptoms of infection.
• Patient and family state understanding of drug therapy.

terazosin hydrochloride
(ter-uh-ZOH-sin high-droh-KLOR-ighd)
Hytrin

Pharmacologic class: selective alpha$_1$-adrenergic blocker
Therapeutic class: antihypertensive
Pregnancy risk category: C

Indications and dosages
▶ **Hypertension.** *Adults:* Initially, 1 mg P.O. h.s., increased gradually based on response. Usual dosage range is 1 to 5 mg daily. Maximum daily dose is 20 mg.
▶ **Symptomatic BPH.** *Adults:* Initially, 1 mg P.O. h.s. Dosage increased in stepwise manner to 2 mg, 5 mg, and 10 mg once daily to achieve optimal response. Most patients require 10 mg daily for optimal response.

Contraindications and precautions
• Contraindicated in patients hypersensitive to drug.
Lifespan: In pregnant or breast-feeding women, use cautiously. In children, safety of drug hasn't been established.

Adverse reactions
CNS: *asthenia, dizziness, headache,* nervousness, paresthesia, somnolence.
CV: palpitations, orthostatic hypotension, tachycardia, *peripheral edema,* atrial fibrillation.
EENT: nasal congestion, sinusitis, blurred vision.
GI: nausea.
GU: impotence, priapism.
Hematologic: ***thrombocytopenia.***
Musculoskeletal: back pain, muscle pain.
Respiratory: dyspnea.
Other: decreased libido.

Interactions
Drug-drug. *Antihypertensives:* May cause excessive hypotension. Use together cautiously.
Clonidine: May decrease antihypertensive effect of clonidine. Monitor patient.
Drug-herb. *Butcher's broom:* Possible diminished effect. Discourage using together.

Effects on lab test results

- May decrease total protein and albumin levels.
- May decrease hematocrit, hemoglobin, and platelet and WBC counts.

Pharmacokinetics

Absorption: Rapid with about 90% of dose being bioavailable.
Distribution: About 90% to 94% plasma protein-bound.
Metabolism: Metabolized in liver.
Excretion: About 40% excreted in urine, 60% in feces, mostly as metabolites. Up to 30% may be excreted unchanged. *Half-life:* About 12 hours.

Route	Onset	Peak	Duration
P.O.	≤ 15 min	2-3 hr	24 hr

Pharmacodynamics

Chemical effect: Decreases blood pressure by vasodilation produced in response to blockade of alpha$_1$-adrenergic receptors. Improves urine flow in patients with BPH by blocking alpha$_1$-adrenergic receptors in smooth muscle of bladder neck and prostate, thus relieving urethral pressure and reestablishing urine flow.
Therapeutic effect: Lowers blood pressure and relieves symptoms of BPH.

Available forms

Capsules: 1 mg, 2 mg, 5 mg, 10 mg

NURSING PROCESS

Assessment

- Assess patient's condition before therapy and regularly thereafter.
- Monitor blood pressure frequently.
- Be alert for adverse reactions and drug interactions.
- Evaluate patient's and family's knowledge of drug therapy.

Nursing diagnoses

- Risk for injury related to presence of hypertension
- Sexual dysfunction related to drug-induced impotence
- Deficient knowledge related to drug therapy

Planning and implementation

ALERT: If drug is stopped for several days, dosage will need to be readjusted to initial dosing regimen.

Patient teaching

- Tell patient not to stop drug but to call prescriber if adverse reactions occur.
- Tell patient to take the first dose at bedtime. If he must get up, he should do so slowly to prevent syncope.
- Warn patient to avoid activities that require mental alertness for 12 hours after first dose.
- Teach patient other means to reduce blood pressure, such as diet control, exercise, smoking cessation, and stress reduction.

Evaluation

- Patient's blood pressure is normal.
- Patient develops and maintains positive attitude toward his sexuality despite impotence.
- Patient and family state understanding of drug therapy.

terbutaline sulfate

(ter-BYOO-tuh-leen SUL-fayt)
Brethine, Bricanyl

Pharmacologic class: beta$_2$-adrenergic agonist
Therapeutic class: bronchodilator
Pregnancy risk category: B

Indications and dosages

▶ **Bronchospasm in patients with reversible obstructive airway disease.** *Adults and children age 15 and older:* 5 mg P.O. t.i.d. at 6-hour intervals. Or, 0.25 mg S.C. may be repeated in 15 to 30 minutes; maximum 0.5 mg q 4 hours.
Children ages 12 to 15: 2.5 mg P.O. t.i.d.

▶ **Premature labor‡.** *Adults:* Initially, 2.5 to 10 mcg/minute I.V.; increase dose gradually as tolerated in 10- to 20-minute intervals until desired effects are achieved. Maximum dosages range from 17.5 to 30 mcg/minute, although dosages of up to 80 mcg/minute have been used cautiously. Continue infusion for at least 12 hours after uterine contractions stop. Maintenance therapy is 2.5 to 10 mg P.O. q 4 to 6 hours.

Contraindications and precautions

- Contraindicated in patients hypersensitive to drug or sympathomimetic amines.
- Use cautiously in patient with CV disorders, hyperthyroidism, diabetes, or seizure disorders.

Lifespan: In pregnant and breast-feeding women, use cautiously. In children age 11 and younger, safety of drug hasn't been established.

Adverse reactions

CNS: *nervousness, tremor, headache, drowsiness, dizziness,* weakness.
CV: *palpitations,* tachycardia, ***arrhythmias,*** flushing.
GI: *vomiting, nausea,* heartburn.
Metabolic: hypokalemia.
Respiratory: ***paradoxical bronchospasm,*** dyspnea.
Skin: diaphoresis.

Interactions

Drug-drug. *Cardiac glycosides, cyclopropane, halogenated inhaled anesthetics, levodopa:* Increases risk of arrhythmias. Monitor patient closely.
CNS stimulants: Increases CNS stimulation. Avoid using together.
MAO inhibitors: When given with sympathomimetics, may cause severe hypertension (hypertensive crisis). Don't use together.
Propranolol, other beta blockers: Blocks bronchodilating effects of terbutaline. Avoid using together.

Effects on lab test results

- May decrease potassium level.

Pharmacokinetics

Absorption: 33% to 50% of P.O. dose; unknown for S.C.
Distribution: Widely distributed throughout body.
Metabolism: Partially metabolized in liver to inactive compounds.
Excretion: Excreted primarily in urine.

Route	Onset	Peak	Duration
P.O.	30 min	2-3 hr	4-8 hr
S.C.	≤ 15 min	30-60 min	1.5-4 hr

Pharmacodynamics

Chemical effect: Relaxes bronchial smooth muscle by acting on beta$_2$-adrenergic receptors.
Therapeutic effect: Improves breathing ability.

Available forms

Injection: 1 mg/ml
Tablets: 2.5 mg, 5 mg

NURSING PROCESS

Assessment

- Assess patient's respiratory condition before therapy and regularly thereafter.
- Monitor patient closely for toxicity.
- Evaluate patient's and family's knowledge of drug therapy.

Nursing diagnoses

- Ineffective breathing pattern related to underlying respiratory condition
- Pain related to drug-induced headache
- Deficient knowledge related to drug therapy

Planning and implementation

- **P.O. use:** Follow normal protocol.
- **S.C. use:** Inject in lateral deltoid area.
  – Protect injection from light. Don't use if discolored.
- Notify prescriber immediately if bronchospasms develop during therapy.
- Mild analgesic may be used to treat drug-induced headache.

ALERT: Don't confuse terbutaline with tolbutamide or terbinafine.

Patient teaching

- Make sure patient and family understand why drug is needed.
- Warn patient to report paradoxical bronchospasm and stop drug.
- Warn patient that tolerance may develop with prolonged use.

Evaluation

- Patient's breathing is improved.
- Patient's headache is relieved with mild analgesic.
- Patient and family state understanding of drug therapy.

terconazole
(ter-KON-uh-zohl)
Terazol 3, Terazol 7

Pharmacologic class: triazole derivative
Therapeutic class: antifungal
Pregnancy risk category: C

Indications and dosages

▶ **Vulvovaginal candidiasis.** *Women:* 1 applicator of cream or 1 suppository inserted into vagina h.s.; 0.4% cream used for 7 consecutive days; 0.8% cream or 80-mg suppository used for 3 consecutive days. Repeat course, if needed, after reconfirmation by smear or culture.

Contraindications and precautions

• Contraindicated in patients hypersensitive to drug or inactive ingredients in formulation.
Lifespan: In pregnant women, use cautiously. In breast-feeding women, drug isn't recommended.

Adverse reactions

CNS: *headache,* fever.
GI: abdominal pain.
GU: dysmenorrhea, vulvovaginal pain or burning.
Skin: irritation, photosensitivity reactions, *pruritus.*
Other: chills, body aches.

Interactions

None significant.

Effects on lab test results

None reported.

Pharmacokinetics

Absorption: 5% to 16%.
Distribution: Mainly local.
Metabolism: Unknown.
Excretion: Unknown.

Route	Onset	Peak	Duration
Intravaginal	Unknown	Unknown	Unknown

Pharmacodynamics

Chemical effect: Unknown; may increase fungal cell membrane permeability (*Candida* species only).
Therapeutic effect: Impairs function of *Candida* sp.

Available forms

Vaginal cream: 0.4%, 0.8%
Vaginal suppositories: 80 mg

NURSING PROCESS

Assessment

• Assess patient's infection before therapy and regularly thereafter.
• Be alert for adverse reactions.
• Evaluate patient's and family's knowledge of drug therapy.

Nursing diagnoses

• Risk for infection related to presence of susceptible fungi
• Acute pain related to drug-induced burning
• Deficient knowledge related to drug therapy

Planning and implementation

• Insert cream using applicator supplied.
• If vaginal suppository is used, have patient remain supine for about 30 minutes after insertion.
• Report fever, chills, other flulike symptoms, or sensitivity, and stop drug.
ALERT: Don't confuse terconazole with tioconazole.

Patient teaching

• Instruct patient how to insert cream or suppository.
• Advise patient to continue treatment during menstrual period. Tell her not to use tampons.
• Tell patient to use for full treatment period prescribed. Explain how to prevent reinfection.

Evaluation

• Patient is free from infection.
• Patient states that drug-induced burning is tolerable.
• Patient and family state understanding of drug therapy.

testolactone
(tes-tuh-LAK-tohn)
Teslac

Pharmacologic class: androgen
Therapeutic class: antineoplastic
Pregnancy risk category: C
Controlled substance schedule: III

Indications and dosages

▶ **Advanced postmenopausal breast cancer.** *Women:* 250 mg P.O. q.i.d.

Contraindications and precautions

- Contraindicated in patients hypersensitive to drug and in men with breast cancer.

Lifespan: In pregnant women, use cautiously. In breast-feeding women, drug isn't recommended. In children, drug isn't indicated.

Adverse reactions

CNS: paresthesia, peripheral neuropathy.
CV: increased blood pressure, edema.
GI: nausea, vomiting, diarrhea, anorexia, glossitis.
Skin: erythema, nail changes, alopecia.

Interactions

Drug-drug. *Oral anticoagulants:* Increases pharmacologic effects. Monitor patient carefully.

Effects on lab test results

None reported.

Pharmacokinetics

Absorption: Absorbed well across GI tract.
Distribution: Widely distributed in total body water.
Metabolism: Extensively metabolized in liver.
Excretion: Testolactone and its metabolites excreted primarily in urine.

Route	Onset	Peak	Duration
P.O.	6-12 wk	Unknown	Unknown

Pharmacodynamics

Chemical effect: Exact antineoplastic action unknown; probably changes tumor's hormonal environment and alters neoplastic process.

Therapeutic effect: Hinders breast cancer cell activity.

Available forms

Tablets: 50 mg

NURSING PROCESS

Assessment

- Assess patient's breast cancer before therapy and regularly thereafter.
- Monitor fluid and electrolyte levels, especially calcium level.
- Be alert for adverse reactions and drug interactions.
- Evaluate patient's and family's knowledge of drug therapy.

Nursing diagnoses

- Ineffective health maintenance related to presence of breast cancer
- Disturbed sensory perception (tactile) related to drug-induced paresthesia and peripheral neuropathy
- Deficient knowledge related to drug therapy

Planning and implementation

- Encourage patient to drink to aid calcium excretion, and encourage exercise to prevent hypercalcemia. Immobilized patients are prone to hypercalcemia.
- Higher-than-recommended doses don't promote remission.

Patient teaching

- Inform patient that therapeutic response isn't immediate; it may take up to 3 months for benefit to be noted.
- Encourage patient to exercise and drink plenty of fluids to help prevent hypercalcemia.
- Tell patient to report adverse effects.

Evaluation

- Patient responds well to drug.
- Patient lists ways to protect against risk of injury caused by diminished tactile sensation.
- Patient and family state understanding of drug therapy.

testosterone

(tes-TOS-teh-rohn)

Andronaq-50, Histerone-50, Histerone 100, Testamone 100, Testaqua, Testoject-50

testosterone cypionate

Andronate 100, Andronate 200, depAndro 100, depAndro 200, Depotest, Depo-Testosterone, Duratest-100, Duratest-200, T-Cypionate, Testred Cypionate 200, Virilon IM

testosterone enanthate

Andro L.A. 200, Andropository 200, Andryl 200, Delatest, Delatestryl, Durathate-200, Everone 200, Testrin-P.A.

testosterone propionate

Malogen in Oil♦, Testex

Pharmacologic class: androgen
Therapeutic class: androgen replacement, antineoplastic
Pregnancy risk category: X
Controlled substance schedule: III

Indications and dosages

▶ **Male hypogonadism.** ***testosterone.*** *Adults:* 10 to 25 mg I.M. two to three times weekly.
testosterone cypionate, testosterone enanthate. *Adults:* 50 to 400 mg I.M. q 2 to 4 weeks.
testosterone propionate. *Adults:* 10 to 25 mg I.M. two to three times weekly.

▶ **Delayed puberty in boys.** ***testosterone, testosterone propionate.*** *Children:* 25 to 50 mg I.M. two or three times weekly for up to 6 months.

▶ **Metastatic breast cancer in women 1 to 5 years postmenopausal.** ***testosterone.*** *Adults:* 100 mg I.M. three times weekly.
testosterone propionate. *Adults:* 50 to 100 mg I.M. three times weekly.
testosterone cypionate, testosterone enanthate. *Adults:* 200 to 400 mg I.M. q 2 to 4 weeks.

▶ **Postpartum breast pain and engorgement.** ***testosterone, testosterone propionate.*** *Adults:* 25 to 50 mg I.M. daily for 3 to 4 days.

Contraindications and precautions

• Contraindicated in men with breast or prostate cancer; patients with hypercalcemia; and those with cardiac, hepatic, or renal decompensation.

Lifespan: In pregnant or breast-feeding women, use is contraindicated. In geriatric patients, use cautiously.

Adverse reactions

CNS: headache, anxiety, depression, paresthesia, sleep apnea syndrome.
CV: edema.
GI: nausea.
GU: hypoestrogenic effects in women (*acne; edema; oily skin; hirsutism; hoarseness; weight gain;* clitoral enlargement; decreased or increased libido; flushing; diaphoresis; vaginitis, including itching, drying, and burning; vaginal bleeding; menstrual irregularities), excessive hormonal effects in men (prepubertal—premature epiphyseal closure, *acne,* priapism, *growth of body and facial hair,* phallic enlargement; postpubertal—testicular atrophy, oligospermia, decreased ejaculatory volume, impotence, gynecomastia, epididymitis), bladder irritability.
Hematologic: ***polycythemia,*** suppression of clotting factors.
Hepatic: reversible jaundice, ***cholestatic hepatitis.***
Metabolic: hypercalcemia.
Skin: pain and induration at injection site, local edema, hypersensitivity skin signs and symptoms.
Other: androgenic effects in women.

Interactions

Drug-drug. *Hepatotoxic drugs:* Increases risk of hepatotoxicity. Monitor patient closely.
Insulin, oral antidiabetics: Alters dosage requirements. Monitor glucose level in diabetic patients.
Oral anticoagulants: Alters dosage requirements. Monitor PT and INR.

Effects on lab test results

• May increase sodium, potassium, phosphate, cholesterol, liver enzyme, calcium, and creatinine levels. May decrease thyroxine-binding globulin and total T_4 levels.
• May increase RBC count and resin uptake of T_3 and T_4 levels.

Pharmacokinetics

Absorption: Unknown.

Distribution: 98% to 99% plasma protein–bound, primarily to testosterone-estradiol–binding globulin.
Metabolism: Metabolized in liver.
Excretion: Excreted in urine. *Half-life:* 10 to 100 minutes.

Route	Onset	Peak	Duration
I.M.	Unknown	Unknown	Unknown

Pharmacodynamics

Chemical effect: Stimulates target tissues to develop normally in androgen-deficient men. Drug may have some antiestrogen properties, making it useful to treat certain estrogen-dependent breast cancers. Its action in postpartum breast engorgement isn't known because drug doesn't suppress lactation.
Therapeutic effect: Increases testosterone level, inhibits some estrogen activity, and relieves postpartum breast pain and engorgement.

Available forms

testosterone
Injection (aqueous suspension): 25 mg/ml, 50 mg/ml, 100 mg/ml
testosterone cypionate
Injection (in oil): 100 mg/ml, 200 mg/ml
testosterone enanthate
Injection (in oil): 100 mg/ml, 200 mg/ml
testosterone propionate
Injection (in oil): 100 mg/ml

NURSING PROCESS

Assessment

- Assess patient's condition before therapy and regularly thereafter.
- Periodically monitor calcium level and liver function test results.
- Monitor lab studies for polycythemia.
- Monitor prepubertal boys by X-ray for rate of bone maturation.
- Be alert for adverse reactions and drug interactions.
- Evaluate patient's and family's knowledge of drug therapy.

Nursing diagnoses

- Ineffective health maintenance related to underlying condition
- Disturbed body image related to drug-induced adverse androgenic reactions
- Deficient knowledge related to drug therapy

Planning and implementation

- Avoid use in women of childbearing age until pregnancy is ruled out.
- Give daily dose requirement in divided doses for best results.
- Store preparations at room temperature. If crystals appear, warm and shake bottle to disperse them.
- Inject deep into upper outer quadrant of gluteal muscle. Rotate sites to prevent muscle atrophy. Report soreness at site because of possibility of postinfection furunculosis.
- Unless contraindicated, use with diet high in calories and protein in small, frequent meals.
- Report signs of virilization in woman.
- Edema generally can be controlled with sodium restriction or diuretics.

ALERT: Therapeutic response in breast cancer usually appears within 3 months. Therapy should be stopped if signs of disease progression appear. In metastatic breast cancer, hypercalcemia usually signals progression of bone metastases. Report signs of hypercalcemia.

- Androgens may alter results of laboratory studies during therapy and for 2 to 3 weeks after therapy ends.

ALERT: Testosterone and methyltestosterone aren't interchangeable. Don't confuse testosterone with testolactone.

Patient teaching

- Make sure patient understands importance of using effective nonhormonal contraceptive during therapy.
- Instruct man to report priapism, reduced ejaculatory volume, and gynecomastia. Drug may need to be discontinued.
- Inform woman that virilization may occur. Tell her to report androgenic effects immediately. Stopping drug will prevent further androgenic changes but probably won't reverse those already present.
- Teach patient to recognize and report signs of hypoglycemia.
- Instruct patient to follow dietary measures to combat drug-induced adverse reactions.

Evaluation

- Patient responds well to drug.
- Patient states acceptance of altered body image.

• Patient and family state understanding of drug therapy.

testosterone transdermal system

(tes-TOS-teh-rohn tranz-DER-mal SIHS-tum)
Androderm, Testoderm, Testoderm TTS

Pharmacologic class: androgen
Therapeutic class: androgen replacement
Pregnancy risk category: X
Controlled substance schedule: III

Indications and dosages

▶ **Primary or hypogonadotropic hypogonadism in men age 18 and older.** *Adults: Testoderm.* One 6-mg patch applied to scrotal area daily. If scrotal area is too small for 6-mg patch, start with 4-mg patch. Patch worn for 22 to 24 hours daily.
Androderm. 5 mg daily either as two 2.5-mg systems or one 5-mg system applied h.s. to clean, dry skin on back, abdomen, upper arms, or thighs.
Testoderm TTS. one 5-mg patch applied to arm, back, or upper buttock daily.

Contraindications and precautions

• Contraindicated in patients hypersensitive to drug, women, and men with known or suspected breast or prostate cancer.
• Use cautiously in patients with renal, hepatic, or cardiac disease.
Lifespan: In children, drug isn't indicated. In geriatric men, use cautiously because they may be at greater risk for prostatic hyperplasia or prostate cancer.

Adverse reactions

CV: ***CVA,*** headache, depression.
GI: GI bleeding.
GU: prostatitis, prostate abnormalities, urinary tract infection.
Skin: acne, *pruritus,* irritation, *blister under system,* allergic contact dermatitis; burning, induration (at application site).
Other: gynecomastia, breast tenderness.

Interactions

Drug-drug. *Antidiabetics:* Alters antidiabetic dosage requirements. Monitor glucose level.
Oral anticoagulants: Alters anticoagulant dosage requirements. Monitor PT and INR.
Oxyphenbutazone: May elevate oxyphenbutazone levels. Monitor patient for adverse reactions.

Effects on lab test results

• May increase sodium, potassium, phosphate, cholesterol, liver enzyme, calcium, and creatinine levels.
• May increase RBC count.

Pharmacokinetics

Absorption: Absorbed from scrotal skin after application.
Distribution: Chiefly bound to sex-hormone–binding globulin.
Metabolism: Metabolized in liver.
Excretion: Excreted in urine. *Half-life:* 10 to 100 minutes.

Route	Onset	Peak	Duration
Transdermal	Unknown	2-4 hr	2 hr after removal

Pharmacodynamics

Chemical effect: Stimulates target tissues to develop normally in androgen-deficient men.
Therapeutic effect: Increases testosterone in androgen-deficient men.

Available forms

Transdermal system: 2.5 mg/day, 4 mg/day, 5 mg/day, 6 mg/day

NURSING PROCESS

Assessment

• Assess patient's condition before therapy and regularly thereafter.
• Because long-term use of systemic androgens is linked to polycythemia, monitor hematocrit and hemoglobin values periodically in patient on long-term therapy.
• Periodically assess liver function tests, serum lipid profiles, and prostatic acid phosphatase and prostate-specific antigen levels.
• Be alert for adverse reactions and drug interactions.
• Evaluate patient's and family's knowledge of drug therapy.

Nursing diagnoses

- Sexual dysfunction related to androgen deficiency
- Risk for impaired skin integrity related to drug-induced irritation at application site
- Deficient knowledge related to drug therapy

Planning and implementation

- Apply Testoderm system on clean, dry scrotal skin. Dry shave scrotal hair (don't use chemical depilatories).
- Apply Androderm to clean, dry skin on back, abdomen, upper arms, or thighs.
- Apply Testoderm TTS to clean, dry skin on arm, back, or upper buttock.

ALERT: Don't confuse Testoderm with Estraderm.

Patient teaching

- Teach patient how to apply transdermal system.
- Tell patient that topical testosterone preparations can cause virilization in female partners. These women should report acne or changes in body hair.
- Advise patient to report to prescriber persistent erections, nausea, vomiting, changes in skin color, or ankle edema.

Evaluation

- Patient states that he can resume normal sexual activity.
- Patient maintains normal skin integrity.
- Patient and family state understanding of drug therapy.

tetanus immune globulin, human

(TET-uh-nus ih-MYOON GLOH-byoo-lin)
Hyper-Tet

Pharmacologic class: immune serum
Therapeutic class: tetanus prophylaxis
Pregnancy risk category: C

Indications and dosages

▶ **Tetanus exposure.** *Adults and children age 7 and older:* 250 units I.M.
Children younger than age 7: 4 units/kg I.M.

▶ **Tetanus treatment.** *Adults and children:* Single doses of 3,000 to 6,000 units I.M. Optimal dosage hasn't been established.

Contraindications and precautions

- Contraindicated in patients with thrombocytopenia or coagulation disorders that would contraindicate I.M. injection unless potential benefits outweigh risks.

Lifespan: In pregnant or breast-feeding women, use cautiously.

Adverse reactions

GU: slight fever, nephrotic syndrome.
Skin: pain, stiffness, erythema at injection site.
Other: hypersensitivity reactions, ***anaphylaxis, angioedema.***

Interactions

Drug-drug. *Live-virus vaccines:* May interfere with response. Defer administration of live-virus vaccines for 3 months after administration of tetanus immune globulin.

Effects on lab test results

None reported.

Pharmacokinetics

Absorption: Slow.
Distribution: Unknown.
Metabolism: Unknown.
Excretion: Unknown. *Half-life:* About 28 days.

Route	Onset	Peak	Duration
I.M.	Unknown	2-3 days	4 wk

Pharmacodynamics

Chemical effect: Provides passive immunity to tetanus.
Therapeutic effect: Prevents tetanus.

Available forms

Injection: 250 units per vial or syringe

NURSING PROCESS

Assessment

- Obtain history of injury, tetanus immunizations, last tetanus toxoid injection, allergies, and reaction to immunizations.
- Antibodies remain at effective level for about 4 weeks (several times the duration of antitoxin-induced antibodies), which protects patient for incubation period of most tetanus cases.
- Be alert for adverse reactions and drug interactions.

• Evaluate patient's and family's knowledge of drug therapy.

Nursing diagnoses

• Risk for injury related to potential for tetanus to occur
• Deficient knowledge related to drug therapy

Planning and implementation

ALERT: Have epinephrine 1:1,000 available to treat hypersensitivity reactions.
• Drug is used only if wound is more than 24 hours old or if patient has had fewer than two tetanus toxoid injections.
• Thoroughly clean wound and remove all foreign matter.
• Inject drug into deltoid muscle for adult and child age 3 and older and into anterolateral aspect of thigh in neonate and child younger than age 3.

ALERT: Don't confuse drug with tetanus toxoid. Tetanus immune globulin isn't a substitute for tetanus toxoid, which should be given at same time to produce active immunization. Don't give at same site as toxoid.

Patient teaching
• Warn patient that pain and tenderness at injection site may occur. Suggest mild analgesic for pain relief.
• Tell patient to document date of tetanus immunization and encourage him to keep immunization current.

Evaluation

• Patient doesn't develop tetanus.
• Patient and family state understanding of drug therapy.

tetracycline hydrochloride

(tet-ruh-SIGH-kleen high-droh-KLOR-ighd)
Achromycin V, Apo-Tetra ♦, Mysteclin 250 ◇, Nor-Tet, Novo-Tetra ♦, Panmycin**, Panmycin P ◇, Robitet, Sumycin, Tetracap, Tetralan, Tetrex ◇

Pharmacologic class: tetracycline
Therapeutic class: antibiotic
Pregnancy risk category: NR

Indications and dosages

▶ **Infections caused by sensitive gram-negative and gram-positive organisms, including *Chlamydia, Mycoplasma, Rickettsia,* and organisms that cause trachoma.** *Adults:* 1 to 2 g P.O. divided into 2 to 4 doses. *Children older than age 8:* 25 to 50 mg/kg P.O. daily divided into 4 doses.

▶ **Uncomplicated urethral, endocervical, or rectal infection caused by *Chlamydia trachomatis.*** *Adults:* 500 mg P.O. q.i.d. for at least 7 days.

▶ **Brucellosis.** *Adults:* 500 mg P.O. q 6 hours for 3 weeks combined with 1 g of streptomycin I.M. q 12 hours first week and daily the second week.

▶ **Gonorrhea in patients sensitive to penicillin.** *Adults:* Initially, 1.5 g P.O.; then 500 mg q 6 hours for 4 days.

▶ **Syphilis in nonpregnant patients sensitive to penicillin.** *Adults:* 500 mg P.O. q.i.d. for 15 days.

▶ **Acne.** *Adults and adolescents:* Initially, 125 to 250 mg P.O. q 6 hours; then 125 to 500 mg daily or every other day.

▶ **Lyme disease‡.** *Adults:* 250 to 500 mg P.O. q.i.d. for 10 to 30 days.

▶ **Adjunct therapy for acute transmitted epididymitis (children older than age 8); pelvic inflammatory disease; and infection with *Helicobacter pylori*‡.** *Adults:* 500 mg P.O. q.i.d. for 10 to 14 days.

Contraindications and precautions

• Contraindicated in patients hypersensitive to tetracyclines.
• Use with extreme caution in patients with impaired kidney or liver function.

Lifespan: In women in their last half of pregnancy and in children younger than age 8, use with extreme caution (if at all) because drug may cause permanent discoloration of teeth, enamel defects, and bone growth retardation. In breast-feeding women, drug isn't recommended.

Adverse reactions

CNS: dizziness, headache, ***intracranial hypertension (pseudotumor cerebri).***
CV: ***pericarditis.***
EENT: sore throat, glossitis, dysphagia.
GI: anorexia, *epigastric distress, nausea,* vomiting, *diarrhea,* esophagitis, oral candidiasis,

stomatitis, enterocolitis, inflammatory lesions in anogenital region.
Hematologic: ***neutropenia, thrombocytopenia,*** eosinophilia.
Musculoskeletal: *retardation of bone growth if used in children younger than age 9.*
Skin: candidal superinfection, maculopapular and erythematous rashes, urticaria, photosensitivity reactions, increased pigmentation.
Other: *permanent discoloration of teeth, enamel defects,* ***hypersensitivity reactions.***

Interactions

Drug-drug. *Antacids (including sodium bicarbonate); antidiarrheals containing bismuth subsalicylate, kaolin, or pectin; laxatives containing aluminum, calcium, or magnesium:* Decreases antibiotic absorption. Give tetracyclines 1 hour before or 2 hours after these drugs.
Ferrous sulfate, other iron products, zinc: Decreases antibiotic absorption. Give tetracyclines 3 hours after or 2 hours before iron.
Lithium carbonate: May alter serum lithium level. Monitor patient.
Methoxyflurane: May cause severe nephrotoxicity with tetracyclines. Monitor patient carefully.
Oral anticoagulants: Potentiates anticoagulant effects. Monitor PT and adjust anticoagulant dosage.
Oral contraceptives: Decreases contraceptive effectiveness and increased risk of breakthrough bleeding. Recommend nonhormonal form of birth control.
Penicillins: May interfere with bactericidal action of penicillins. Avoid using together.
Drug-food. *Milk, dairy products, other foods:* Decreases antibiotic absorption. Give tetracycline 1 hour before or 2 hours after these products.
Drug-lifestyle. *Sun exposure:* Photosensitivity reactions may occur. Urge patient to avoid prolonged or unprotected exposure to sunlight.

Effects on lab test results

- May increase BUN and liver enzyme levels.
- May increase eosinophil counts. May decrease platelet and neutrophil counts.
- May cause false-negative reading with glucose enzymatic tests (Diastix).

Pharmacokinetics

Absorption: 75% to 80%. Food or milk products significantly reduces.
Distribution: Distributed widely in body tissues and fluids. CSF penetration is poor. Drug is 20% to 67% protein-bound.
Metabolism: None.
Excretion: Excreted primarily unchanged in urine. *Half-life:* 6 to 11 hours.

Route	Onset	Peak	Duration
P.O.	Unknown	2-4 hr	Unknown

Pharmacodynamics

Chemical effect: Unknown; thought to exert bacteriostatic effect by binding to 30S ribosomal subunit of microorganisms, thus inhibiting protein synthesis.
Therapeutic effect: Hinders bacterial activity. Spectrum of activity includes such gram-negative and gram-positive organisms as *Chlamydia, Mycoplasma, Rickettsia,* and spirochetes.

Available forms

Capsules: 100 mg, 250 mg, 500 mg
Oral suspension: 125 mg/5 ml
Tablets: 250 mg, 500 mg

NURSING PROCESS

Assessment

- Assess patient's infection before therapy and regularly thereafter.
- Obtain specimen for culture and sensitivity tests before first dose. Therapy may begin pending results.
- Monitor patient's hydration status if adverse GI reactions occur.
- Be alert for adverse reactions and drug interactions.
- Evaluate patient's and family's knowledge of drug therapy.

Nursing diagnoses

- Risk for infection related to presence of susceptible bacteria
- Risk for deficient fluid volume related to drug-induced adverse GI reactions
- Deficient knowledge related to drug therapy

Planning and implementation

ALERT: Check expiration date. Outdated or deteriorated tetracyclines have been linked to reversible nephrotoxicity (Fanconi's syndrome).

• Give drug on empty stomach.
• Don't expose drug to light or heat.

Patient teaching
• Explain that effectiveness of drug is reduced when taken with milk or other dairy products, food, antacids, or iron products. Tell patient to take drug with full glass of water on empty stomach, at least 1 hour before or 2 hours after meals. Also, tell him to take drug at least 1 hour before bedtime to prevent esophagitis.
• Tell patient to take drug exactly as prescribed, even after he feels better, and to take entire amount prescribed.
• Warn patient to avoid direct sunlight and ultraviolet light. Recommend sunscreen to help prevent photosensitivity reactions. Tell him that photosensitivity persists after drug is stopped.

Evaluation
• Patient is free from infection.
• Patient maintains adequate hydration.
• Patient and family state understanding of drug therapy.

theophylline
(thee-OF-ih-lin)
Immediate-release liquids
Accurbron*, Aquaphyllin, Asmalix*, Bronkodyl*, Elixomin*, Elixophyllin*, Lanophyllin*, Slo-Phyllin, Theolair
Immediate-release tablets and capsules
Bronkodyl, Elixophyllin, Nuelin ◇, Slo-Phyllin
Timed-release capsules
Elixophyllin SR, Nuelin-SR ◇, Slo-bid Gyrocaps, Slo-Phyllin, Theo-24, Theobid Duracaps, Theochron, Theospan-SR, Theovent Long-Acting
Timed-release tablets
Quibron-T/SR Dividose, Respbid, Sustaire, T-Phyl, Theocron, Theolair-SR, Theo-Sav, Theo-Time, Theo-X, Uniphyl

theophylline sodium glycinate

Pharmacologic class: xanthine derivative
Therapeutic class: bronchodilator
Pregnancy risk category: C

Indications and dosages
▶ **Oral theophylline for acute bronchospasm in patients not already receiving theophylline.** *Adults (nonsmokers):* Loading dose of 6 mg/kg P.O.; then 3 mg/kg q 6 hours for 2 doses. Maintenance dosage is 3 mg/kg q 8 hours.
Children ages 9 to 16 and young adult smokers: Loading dose of 6 mg/kg P.O.; then 3 mg/kg q 4 hours for 3 doses; then 3 mg/kg q 6 hours.
Children ages 6 months to 9 years: Loading dose of 6 mg/kg P.O.; then 4 mg/kg q 4 hours for 3 doses; then 4 mg/kg q 6 hours.
Older adults or those with cor pulmonale: Loading dose of 6 mg/kg P.O.; then 2 mg/kg q 6 hours for 2 doses; then 2 mg/kg q 8 hours.
Adults with heart failure or liver disease: Loading dose of 6 mg/kg P.O.; then 2 mg/kg q 8 hours for 2 doses; then 1 to 2 mg/kg q 12 hours.

Extended-release preparations shouldn't be used for treatment of acute bronchospasm.

▶ **Parenteral theophylline for patients not receiving theophylline.** *Adults (nonsmokers):* Loading dose of 4.7 mg/kg given slow I.V.; then maintenance infusion of 0.55 mg/kg/hour I.V. for 12 hours; then 0.39 mg/kg/hour.
Adults (otherwise healthy smokers): Loading dose of 4.7 mg/kg given slow I.V.; then maintenance infusion of 0.79 mg/kg/hr I.V. for 12 hours; then 0.63 mg/kg/hr.
Older adults or those with cor pulmonale: Loading dose of 4.7 mg/kg given slow I.V.; then maintenance infusion of 0.47 mg/kg/hour I.V. for 12 hours; then 0.24 mg/kg/hour.
Adults with heart failure or liver disease: Loading dose of 4.7 mg/kg given slow I.V.; then maintenance infusion of 0.39 mg/kg/hour I.V. for 12 hours; then 0.08 to 0.16 mg/kg/hour.
Children ages 9 to 16: Loading dose of 4.7 mg/kg given slow I.V.; then maintenance infusion of 0.79 mg/kg/hour I.V. for 12 hours; then 0.63 mg/kg/hour.
Children ages 6 months to 9 years: Loading dose of 4.7 mg/kg given slow I.V.; then maintenance infusion of 0.95 mg/kg/hour I.V. for 12 hours; then 0.79 mg/kg/hour.

▶ **Oral and parenteral theophylline for acute bronchospasm in patients receiving theophylline.** *Adults and children:* Each 0.5 mg/kg I.V. or P.O. (loading dose) increases plasma level by 1 mcg/ml. Ideally, dose is based on current theophylline level. In emergencies, some clinicians recommend 2.5 mg/kg P.O. dose of rapidly absorbed form if no obvious signs of theophylline toxicity are present.

▶ **Chronic bronchospasm.** *Adults and children:* 16 mg/kg or 400 mg P.O. daily (whichever is less) given in 3 or 4 divided doses at 6- to 8-hour intervals. Or, 12 mg/kg or 400 mg P.O. daily (whichever is less) using extended-release preparation given in 2 or 3 divided doses at 8- or 12-hour intervals. Dosage increased as tolerated at 2- to 3-day intervals to maximum dosage as follows:

Adults and children age 16 and older: 13 mg/kg or 900 mg P.O. daily (whichever is less) in divided doses.

Children ages 12 to 16: 18 mg/kg P.O. daily in divided doses.

Children ages 9 to 12: 20 mg/kg P.O. daily in divided doses.

Children younger than age 9: 24 mg/kg P.O. daily in divided doses.

▶ **Cystic fibrosis‡.** *Infants:* 10 to 20 mg/kg I.V. daily.

▶ **Promotion of diuresis; treatment of Cheyne-Stokes respirations; paroxysmal nocturnal dyspnea‡.** *Adults:* 200 to 400 mg I.V. bolus as a single dose.

Contraindications and precautions

- Contraindicated in patients with active peptic ulcer or seizure disorders, or in those who are hypersensitive to xanthine compounds (caffeine, theobromine).
- Use cautiously in those with COPD, cardiac failure, cor pulmonale, renal or hepatic disease, peptic ulceration, hyperthyroidism, diabetes mellitus, glaucoma, severe hypoxemia, hypertension, compromised cardiac or circulatory function, angina, acute MI, or sulfite sensitivity.

Lifespan: In pregnant women, use cautiously. In breast-fed infants, drug may cause irritability, insomnia, or fretting. In young children, infants, neonates, and geriatric patients, use cautiously.

Adverse reactions

CNS: *restlessness, dizziness,* headache, *insomnia,* irritability, ***seizures,*** muscle twitching.
CV: *palpitations, sinus tachycardia,* extrasystoles, flushing, marked hypotension, ***arrhythmias.***
GI: *nausea, vomiting,* diarrhea, epigastric pain.
Respiratory: increased respiratory rate, ***respiratory arrest.***

Interactions

Drug-drug. *Adenosine:* Decreases antiarrhythmic effectiveness. Higher doses of adenosine may be needed.

Barbiturates, carbamazepine, phenytoin, rifampin: Enhances metabolism and decreases theophylline blood level. Monitor patient for decreased effect.

Beta blockers: Antagonizes drug. Propranolol and nadolol, especially, may cause bronchospasm in sensitive patients. Use together cautiously.

Cimetidine, fluoroquinolone (such as ciprofloxacin), influenza virus vaccine, macrolide antibiotics (such as erythromycin), oral contraceptives: Decreases hepatic clearance of theophylline; elevates theophylline level. Monitor patient for toxicity.

Drug-food. *Any food:* Accelerates absorption. Give drug on an empty stomach.

Caffeine: Decreases hepatic clearance of theophylline and elevates theophylline level. Monitor patient for toxicity.

Drug-lifestyle. *Smoking:* Increases elimination of theophylline, increasing dosage requirements. Monitor theophylline response and level.

Drug-herb. *Cacao tree:* Possible inhibition of theophylline metabolism. Advise against using together.

Cayenne: Oral cayenne may increase the absorption of theophylline. Discourage using together.

St. John's wort: Potential for decreased effectiveness of theophylline. Discourage using together.

Effects on lab test results

- May increase plasma free–fatty-acid level.

Pharmacokinetics

Absorption: Well absorbed after P.O. administration. Food may further alter rate of absorption, especially of some extended-release preparations.
Distribution: Distributed throughout extracellular fluids; equilibrium between fluid and tissues occurs within 1 hour of I.V. loading dose.
Metabolism: Metabolized in liver to inactive compounds.

Excretion: About 10% excreted unchanged in urine. *Half-life:* Adults, 7 to 9 hours; smokers, 4 to 5 hours; children, 3 to 5 hours; premature infants, 20 to 30 hours.

Route	Onset	Peak	Duration
P.O.			
(regular)	15-60 min	1-2 hr	Unknown
(enteric-coated)	15-60 min	1-2 hr	5 hr
(extended-release)	15-60 min	1-2 hr	4-7 hr
I.V.	15 min	15-30 min	Unknown

Pharmacodynamics

Chemical effect: Inhibits phosphodiesterase, the enzyme that degrades cAMP, and relaxes smooth muscle of bronchial airways and pulmonary blood vessels.
Therapeutic effect: Improves breathing ability.

Available forms

theophylline
Capsules: 100 mg, 200 mg
Capsules (extended-release): 50 mg, 60 mg, 65 mg, 75 mg, 100 mg, 125 mg, 130 mg, 200 mg, 250 mg, 260 mg, 300 mg
D_5W injection: 200 mg in 50 ml or 100 ml; 400 mg in 100 ml, 250 ml, 500 ml, or 1,000 ml; 800 mg in 500 ml or 1,000 ml
Elixir: 27 mg/5 ml, 50 mg/5 ml*
Oral solution: 27 mg/5 ml, 50 mg/5 ml
Syrup: 27 mg/5 ml, 50 mg/5 ml
Tablets: 100 mg, 125 mg, 200 mg, 250 mg, 300 mg
Tablets (chewable): 100 mg
Tablets (extended-release): 100 mg, 200 mg, 250 mg, 300 mg, 400 mg, 500 mg, 600 mg
theophylline sodium glycinate
Elixir: 110 mg/5 ml (equivalent to 55 mg of anhydrous theophylline/5 ml)

NURSING PROCESS

Assessment

- Assess patient's condition before therapy and regularly thereafter.
- Monitor vital signs; measure fluid intake and output. Expected clinical effects include improvement in quality of pulse and respirations.
- Xanthine metabolism rate varies among individuals; dosage is determined by monitoring response, tolerance, pulmonary function, and serum theophylline level. Theophylline level should range from 10 to 20 mcg/ml in adults and 5 to 15 mcg/ml in children.
- Be alert for adverse reactions and drug interactions.

ALERT: Monitor patient for signs and symptoms of toxicity including tachycardia, anorexia, nausea, vomiting, diarrhea, restlessness, irritability, and headache. The presence of any of these signs in patients taking theophylline warrants checking theophylline level and adjusting dose as indicated.

- Monitor patient's hydration status if adverse GI reactions occur.
- Evaluate patient's and family's knowledge of drug therapy.

Nursing diagnoses

- Impaired gas exchange related to presence of bronchospasm
- Risk for deficient fluid volume related to drug-induced adverse GI reactions
- Deficient knowledge related to drug therapy

Planning and implementation

- **P.O. use:** Give drug around-the-clock, using sustained-release product at bedtime.

ALERT: Don't confuse sustained-release forms with standard-release forms.

- **I.V. use:** Use commercially available infusion solution, or mix drug in D_5W. Use infusion pump for continuous infusion.
- Dosage may need to be increased in cigarette smokers and in habitual marijuana smokers; smoking causes drug to be metabolized faster.
- Daily dose may need to be decreased in patients with heart failure or hepatic disease and in geriatric patients because metabolism and excretion may be decreased.

ALERT: Don't confuse Theolair with Thyrolar.

Patient teaching

- Warn patient not to dissolve, crush, or chew sustained-release products. For child unable to swallow capsules, sprinkle contents of capsules over soft food and tell patient to swallow without chewing.
- Supply instructions for home care and dosage schedule.

• Tell patient to relieve GI symptoms by taking oral drug with full glass of water after meals, although food in stomach delays absorption.
• Warn patient to take drug regularly, as directed. Patients tend to want to take extra "breathing pills."
• Warn geriatric patient that dizziness may occur at start of therapy.
• Have patient change position slowly and avoid hazardous activities.
• Caution patient to check with prescriber about other drugs used. OTC drugs may contain ephedrine with theophylline salts; excessive CNS stimulation may result.
• If patient's dosage is stabilized while he is smoking and then he quits smoking, tell him to notify his prescriber; the dosage may need to be reduced.

☑ Evaluation
• Patient demonstrates improved gas exchange, exhibited in arterial blood gas values and respiratory status.
• Patient maintains adequate hydration.
• Patient and family state understanding of drug therapy.

thiamine hydrochloride (vitamin B_1)
(THIGH-eh-min high-droh-KLOR-ighd)
Betamin ◇, Beta-Sol ◇, Biamine, Thiamilate†

Pharmacologic class: water-soluble vitamin
Therapeutic class: nutritional supplement
Pregnancy risk category: A

Indications and dosages
▶ **RDA.** *Men age 51 and older:* 1.2 mg P.O. daily.
Men ages 15 to 50: 1.5 mg P.O. daily.
Boys ages 11 to 14: 1.3 mg P.O. daily.
Women age 51 and over: 1 mg P.O. daily.
Women ages 11 to 50: 1.1 mg P.O. daily.
Pregnant women: 1.5 mg P.O. daily.
Breast-feeding women: 1.6 mg P.O. daily.
Children ages 7 to 10: 1 mg P.O. daily.
Children ages 4 to 6: 0.9 mg P.O. daily.
Children ages 1 to 3: 0.7 mg P.O. daily.
Infants age 6 months to 1 year: 0.4 mg P.O. daily.
Neonates and infants younger than age 6 months: 0.3 mg P.O. daily.
▶ **Beriberi.** *Adults:* Depending on severity, 10 to 20 mg I.M. t.i.d. for 2 weeks, followed by dietary correction and multivitamin supplement containing 5 to 10 mg of thiamine daily for 1 month.
Children: Depending on severity, 10 to 50 mg I.M. daily for several weeks with adequate diet.
▶ **Wet beriberi with myocardial failure.** *Adults and children:* 10 to 30 mg I.V. for emergency treatment.
▶ **Wernicke's encephalopathy.** *Adults:* Initially, 100 mg I.V.; then 50 to 100 mg I.V. or I.M. daily until patient is consuming regular balanced diet.

Contraindications and precautions
• Contraindicated in patients hypersensitive to thiamine products.
Lifespan: In pregnant women, use cautiously if dose exceeds RDA.

Adverse reactions
CNS: restlessness, weakness.
CV: ***CV collapse,*** cyanosis.
EENT: tightness of throat.
GI: nausea, ***hemorrhage.***
Respiratory: ***pulmonary edema.***
Skin: feeling of warmth, pruritus, urticaria, diaphoresis.
Other: tenderness and induration after I.M. administration, ***angioedema.***

Interactions
None significant.

Effects on lab test results
None reported.

Pharmacokinetics
Absorption: Absorbed readily after small P.O. doses; after large P.O. dose, total amount absorbed is limited. In alcoholics and in patients with cirrhosis or malabsorption, GI absorption of thiamine is decreased. When given with meals, drug's GI rate of absorption decreases, but total absorption remains same. After I.M. dose, drug is absorbed rapidly and completely.
Distribution: Distributed widely in body tissues. When intake exceeds minimal requirements, tissue stores become saturated.

Metabolism: Metabolized in liver.
Excretion: Excess thiamine excreted in urine.

Route	Onset	Peak	Duration
P.O., I.V., I.M.	Unknown	Unknown	Unknown

Pharmacodynamics

Chemical effect: Combines with adenosine triphosphate to form coenzyme needed for carbohydrate metabolism.
Therapeutic effect: Restores normal thiamine level.

Available forms

Elixir: 250 mcg/5 ml
Injection: 100 mg/ml, 200 mg/ml
Tablets: 5 mg†, 10 mg†, 25 mg†, 50 mg†, 100 mg†, 250 mg†, 500 mg†
Tablets (enteric-coated): 20 mg

NURSING PROCESS

Assessment

- Assess patient's condition before therapy and regularly thereafter.
- Be alert for adverse reactions.
- Evaluate patient's and family's knowledge of drug therapy.

Nursing diagnoses

- Imbalanced nutrition: less than body requirements related to presence of thiamine deficiency
- Diarrhea related to drug-induced adverse GI reactions
- Deficient knowledge related to drug therapy

Planning and implementation

- Use parenteral route only when P.O. route isn't feasible.
- **P.O. and I.M. use:** Follow normal protocol.
- **I.V. use:** Dilute drug before administration.

ALERT: Give large I.V. doses cautiously; apply skin test before starting therapy if patient has history of hypersensitivity reactions. Have epinephrine on hand to treat anaphylaxis if it occurs.

- For treating alcoholic patient, give thiamine before dextrose infusions to prevent encephalopathy.
- Don't use with materials that yield alkaline solutions. Unstable in alkaline solutions.
- Drug malabsorption is most likely in patients with alcoholism, cirrhosis, and GI disease.
- Clinically significant deficiency can occur in about 3 weeks of thiamine-free diet. Thiamine deficiency usually requires concurrent treatment for multiple deficiencies.
- Doses larger than 30 mg t.i.d. may not be fully utilized. Tissues may become saturated with thiamine and drug is excreted in urine as pyrimidine.
- If breast-fed infant develops beriberi, both mother and child should be treated with thiamine.

ALERT: Don't confuse thiamine with Thorazine.

Patient teaching

- Stress proper nutritional habits to prevent recurrence of deficiency.

Evaluation

- Patient regains normal thiamine level.
- Patient maintains normal bowel pattern.
- Patient and family state understanding of drug therapy.

thioguanine (6-thioguanine, 6-TG)

(thigh-oh-GWAH-neen)
Lanvis ♦

Pharmacologic class: antimetabolite (specific to S phase of cell cycle)
Therapeutic class: antineoplastic
Pregnancy risk category: D

Indications and dosages

▶ **Acute nonlymphocytic leukemia, chronic myelogenous leukemia.** *Adults and children:* Initially, 2 mg/kg P.O. daily (usually calculated to nearest 20 mg). If needed, dose is then increased gradually to 3 mg/kg daily, as tolerated.

Contraindications and precautions

- Contraindicated in patients whose disease has shown resistance to drug.
- Use cautiously in patients with renal or hepatic dysfunction.

Lifespan: For pregnant or breast-feeding women, drug isn't recommended.

Adverse reactions

GI: nausea, vomiting, stomatitis, diarrhea, anorexia.
Hematologic: ***leukopenia, anemia, thrombocytopenia*** (occurs slowly over 2 to 4 weeks).
Hepatic: ***hepatotoxicity,*** jaundice, hepatic fibrosis, ***toxic hepatitis.***
Metabolic: hyperuricemia.

Interactions

Drug-drug. *Myelosuppressant drugs:* Increases risk of toxicity, especially myelosuppression, hepatotoxicity, and bleeding. Use together cautiously.

Effects on lab test results

- May increase uric acid level.
- May decrease hemoglobin, hematocrit, and WBC, RBC, and platelet counts.

Pharmacokinetics

Absorption: Incomplete and variable; average bioavailability is 30%.
Distribution: Distributed well in bone marrow cells.
Metabolism: Extensively metabolized to less active form in liver and other tissues.
Excretion: Excreted in urine, mainly as metabolites. *Half-life:* Initial phase, 15 minutes; terminal phase, 11 hours.

Route	Onset	Peak	Duration
P.O.	Unknown	Unknown	Unknown

Pharmacodynamics

Chemical effect: Inhibits purine synthesis.
Therapeutic effect: Inhibits selected leukemic cell reproduction.

Available forms

Tablets (scored): 40 mg

NURSING PROCESS

Assessment

- Assess patient's condition before therapy and regularly thereafter.
- Monitor CBC daily during induction and then weekly during maintenance therapy.
- Monitor uric acid level.
- Watch for jaundice.
- Be alert for adverse reactions and drug interactions.
- Evaluate patient's and family's knowledge of drug therapy.

Nursing diagnoses

- Ineffective health maintenance related to presence of leukemia
- Ineffective protection related to drug-induced immunosuppression
- Deficient knowledge related to drug therapy

Planning and implementation

- Dosage modification may be required in renal or hepatic dysfunction.
- Drug may be ordered as 6-thioguanine. The numeral 6 is part of drug name and doesn't signify dosage units.
- Report jaundice; it may be reversible if drug is stopped promptly. Also, drug must be stopped if hepatotoxicity or hepatic tenderness occurs.
- Encourage patient to drink to prevent hyperuricemia.

Patient teaching

- Warn patient to watch for signs of infection and bleeding, and teach him infection-control and bleeding precautions to use in daily living.
- Tell patient to increase fluid intake.
- Advise woman of childbearing age to avoid becoming pregnant during therapy. Also recommend that she consult with prescriber before becoming pregnant.

Evaluation

- Patient responds well to drug.
- Patient doesn't develop serious complications from drug-induced immunosuppression.
- Patient and family state understanding of drug therapy.

thioridazine hydrochloride

(thigh-oh-RIGH-duh-zeen high-droh-KLOR-ighd)
Aldazine ◇, Apo-Thioridazine ♦, Mellaril*, Mellaril Concentrate, Novo-Ridazine ♦, PMS Thioridazine ♦

Pharmacologic class: phenothiazine (piperidine derivative)
Therapeutic class: antipsychotic
Pregnancy risk category: NR

Indications and dosages

▶ **Psychosis.** *Adults:* Initially, 50 to 100 mg P.O. t.i.d., with gradual, incremental increases up to 800 mg daily in divided doses, if needed. Dosage varies.

▶ **Short-term treatment of moderate-to-marked depression with variable degrees of anxiety; dementia in geriatric patients; behavioral problems in children.** *Adults:* Initially, 25 mg P.O. t.i.d. Maximum daily dose is 200 mg.

Children ages 2 to 12: 0.5 to 3 mg/kg P.O. daily in divided doses. Give 10 mg b.i.d. to t.i.d. to children with moderate disorders and 25 mg b.i.d. to t.i.d. to hospitalized, severely disturbed, or psychotic children.

Contraindications and precautions

- Contraindicated in patients hypersensitive to drug and in those with CNS depression, severe hypertensive or hypotensive cardiac disease, or coma. Also, contraindicated in patients with reduced levels of cytochrome P-450 2D6 isoenzyme, patients with congenital long QT syndrome or patients with a history of cardiac arrhythmias
- Don't give to patients taking fluvoxamine, propranolol, pindolol, fluoxetine, or drugs that inhibit the cytochrome P450 2D6 enzyme or that prolong the QTc interval.
- Use cautiously in debilitated patients and in patients with hepatic disease, CV disease, respiratory disorder, hypocalcemia, seizure disorder, severe reactions to insulin or electroconvulsive therapy, or exposure to extreme heat or cold (including antipyretic therapy), or organophosphate insecticides.

Lifespan: In pregnant or breast-feeding women and in geriatric patients, use cautiously.

Adverse reactions

CNS: extrapyramidal reactions, *tardive dyskinesia, sedation,* EEG changes, dizziness, ***neuroleptic malignant syndrome.***
CV: *orthostatic hypotension,* tachycardia, ECG changes.
EENT: *ocular changes, blurred vision,* retinitis pigmentosa.
GI: *dry mouth, constipation.*
GU: *urine retention,* dark urine, menstrual irregularities, inhibited ejaculation.
Hematologic: ***transient leukopenia, agranulocytosis,*** hyperprolactinemia.
Hepatic: cholestatic jaundice.
Metabolic: weight gain, increased appetite.
Skin: *mild photosensitivity reactions.*
Other: gynecomastia, allergic reaction.

Interactions

Drug-drug. *Antacids:* Inhibits absorption of oral phenothiazines. Separate doses by at least 2 hours.
Barbiturates, lithium: May decrease phenothiazine effect. Monitor patient.
Centrally acting antihypertensives: Decreases antihypertensive effect. Monitor blood pressure.
Fluvoxamine, propranolol, pindolol, fluoxetine, and any drug that inhibits the cytochrome P-450 2D6 enzyme and drugs known to prolong the QTc interval: Potential for serious, fatal cardiac arrhythmias. Don't use together.
Other CNS depressants: Increases CNS depression. Use together cautiously.
Drug-herb. *Dong quai, St. John's wort:* Increases photosensitivity reactions. Discourage using together.
Kava: Increases risk of dystonic reactions. Discourage using together.
Milk thistle: Decreases liver toxicity caused by phenothiazines. Monitor liver enzymes if used together.
Yohimbe: Increases risk for yohimbe toxicity when used together. Discourage using together.
Drug-lifestyle. *Alcohol use:* Increases CNS depression. Discourage using together.
Sun exposure: Increases photosensitivity reactions. Advise patient to avoid prolonged or unprotected exposure to sunlight.

Effects on lab test results

- May increase liver enzyme and prolactin levels.
- May decrease granulocyte and WBC counts.

Pharmacokinetics

Absorption: Erratic and variable, although P.O. concentrates and syrups are more predictable than tablets.
Distribution: Distributed widely in body; 91% to 99% protein-bound.
Metabolism: Metabolized extensively by liver.
Excretion: Excreted mostly as metabolites in urine, some in feces.

Route	Onset	Peak	Duration
P.O.	Varies	Unknown	Unknown

Pharmacodynamics

Chemical effect: Unknown; probably blocks postsynaptic dopamine receptors in brain.
Therapeutic effect: Relieves signs of psychosis, depression, anxiety, stress, fears, and sleep disturbances.

Available forms

Oral suspension: 25 mg/5 ml, 100 mg/5 ml
Oral concentrate: 30 mg/ml, 100 mg/ml* (3% to 4.2% alcohol)
Tablets: 10 mg, 15 mg, 25 mg, 50 mg, 100 mg, 150 mg, 200 mg

NURSING PROCESS

Assessment

- Assess patient's condition before therapy and regularly thereafter.
- Monitor patient for tardive dyskinesia. It may occur after prolonged use, or may not appear until months or years later. It may disappear spontaneously or persist for life, despite discontinuation of drug.
- Monitor therapy with weekly bilirubin tests during first month, periodic blood tests (CBC and liver function), and ophthalmologic tests (long-term therapy).

ALERT: Monitor patient for symptoms of neuroleptic malignant syndrome (extrapyramidal effects, hyperthermia, autonomic disturbance), which is rare but can be fatal. It isn't necessarily related to length of drug use or type of neuroleptic; however, more than 60% of patients are men.

- Before starting treatment, perform baseline ECG and measure potassium level. Patients with a QTc interval longer than 450 msec should not receive Mellaril. Patients with a QTc longer than 500 msec should discontinue use.
- Be alert for adverse reactions and drug interactions.
- Evaluate patient's and family's knowledge of drug therapy.

Nursing diagnoses

- Disturbed thought processes related to underlying condition
- Risk for injury related to drug-induced adverse CNS reactions
- Deficient knowledge related to drug therapy

Planning and implementation

ALERT: Different liquid formulations have different concentrations. Check dosage.
ALERT: Mellaril prolongs the QTc interval in a dose-related manner.

- Prevent contact dermatitis by keeping drug away from skin and clothes. Wear gloves when preparing liquid forms.
- Dilute liquid concentrate with water or fruit juice just before giving.
- Shake suspension well before using.
- Don't withdraw drug abruptly unless patient experiences severe adverse reactions. Abrupt withdrawal of long-term therapy may cause gastritis, nausea, vomiting, dizziness, tremors, feeling of warmth or cold, diaphoresis, tachycardia, headache, or insomnia.
- Report jaundice, symptoms of blood dyscrasia (fever, sore throat, infection, cellulitis, weakness), or persistent extrapyramidal reactions (longer than a few hours), especially in pregnant woman or in child, and withhold drug.
- Acute dystonic reactions may be treated with diphenhydramine.

ALERT: Don't confuse thioridazine with Thorazine; don't confuse Mellaril with Elavil.

Patient teaching

- Warn patient to avoid activities that require alertness until CNS effects of drug are known. Drowsiness and dizziness usually subside after a few weeks.
- Tell patient to watch for orthostatic hypotension, especially with parenteral administration. Advise patient to change position slowly.
- Tell patient to avoid alcohol while taking drug.
- Instruct patient to report urine retention or constipation.
- Inform patient that drug may discolor urine.
- Tell patient to watch for and notify prescriber of blurred vision.
- Advise patient to relieve dry mouth with sugarless gum or hard candy.
- Tell patient to use sun block and to wear protective clothing to avoid photosensitivity reactions.

Evaluation

- Patient's behavior and communication exhibit improved thought processes.

• Patient doesn't experience injury from adverse CNS reactions.
• Patient and family state understanding of drug therapy.

thiotepa
(thigh-oh-TEE-puh)
Thioplex

Pharmacologic class: alkylating agent (not specific to phase of cell cycle)
Therapeutic class: antineoplastic
Pregnancy risk category: D

Indications and dosages

▶ **Breast and ovarian cancers, lymphoma, Hodgkin's disease.** *Adults and children older than age 12:* 0.3 to 0.4 mg/kg I.V. q 1 to 4 weeks or 0.2 mg/kg for 4 to 5 days at intervals of 2 to 4 weeks.
▶ **Bladder tumor.** *Adults and children older than age 12:* 60 mg in 30 to 60 ml of normal saline solution instilled in bladder for 2 hours once weekly for 4 weeks.
▶ **Neoplastic effusions.** *Adults and children older than age 12:* 0.6 to 0.8 mg/kg intracavitarily or intratumor q 1 to 4 weeks.
▶ **Malignant meningeal neoplasm‡.** *Adults:* 1 to 10 mg/m^2 intrathecally, once to twice weekly.

Contraindications and precautions

• Contraindicated in patients hypersensitive to drug and in those with severe bone marrow, hepatic, or renal dysfunction.
• Use cautiously in patients with mild bone marrow suppression or renal or hepatic dysfunction.
Lifespan: For pregnant or breast-feeding women, drug isn't recommended. In children age 12 and younger, safety of drug hasn't been established.

Adverse reactions

CNS: headache, dizziness, fatigue, weakness, fever.
EENT: blurred vision, ***laryngeal edema,*** conjunctivitis.
GI: *nausea, vomiting,* abdominal pain, anorexia, stomatitis.
GU: amenorrhea, decreased spermatogenesis, dysuria, urine retention, hemorrhagic cystitis.
Hematologic: *leukopenia* (begins within 5 to 10 days), ***thrombocytopenia, neutropenia,*** anemia.
Respiratory: asthma.
Skin: urticaria, rash, dermatitis, alopecia, pain at injection site.
Other: hypersensitivity reactions, ***anaphylaxis.***

Interactions

Drug-drug. *Anticoagulants, aspirin:* Increases bleeding risk. Avoid using together.
Neuromuscular blockers: May prolong muscular paralysis. Monitor patient closely.
Other alkylating agents, irradiation therapy: May intensify toxicity rather than enhance therapeutic response. Avoid using together.
Succinylcholine: Increases apnea with use together. Monitor patient closely.

Effects on lab test results

• May increase uric acid level. May decrease pseudocholinesterase level.
• May decrease hemoglobin, hematocrit, and lymphocyte, platelet, WBC, RBC, and neutrophil counts.

Pharmacokinetics

Absorption: Absorption from bladder after instillation ranges from 10% to 100% of instilled dose; also variable after intracavitary administration. Increased by certain pathologic conditions.
Distribution: Crosses blood-brain barrier.
Metabolism: Metabolized extensively in liver.
Excretion: Thiotepa and its metabolites excreted in urine.

Route	Onset	Peak	Duration
I.V., bladder instillation, intracavitary	Unknown	Unknown	Unknown

Pharmacodynamics

Chemical effect: Cross-links strands of cellular DNA and interferes with RNA transcription, causing growth imbalance that leads to cell death.
Therapeutic effect: Kills certain cancer cells.

Available forms

Injection: 15-mg vials

NURSING PROCESS

Assessment
- Assess patient's condition before therapy and regularly thereafter.
- Adverse GU reactions are reversible in 6 to 8 months.
- Monitor CBC weekly for at least 3 weeks after last dose.
- Monitor uric acid level.
- Be alert for adverse reactions and drug interactions.
- Evaluate patient's and family's knowledge of drug therapy.

Nursing diagnoses
- Ineffective health maintenance related to presence of neoplastic disease
- Ineffective protection related to drug-induced immunosuppression
- Deficient knowledge related to drug therapy

Planning and implementation
- Follow facility policy to minimize risks. Preparation and administration of parenteral form are linked to mutagenic, teratogenic, and carcinogenic risks to personnel.
- **I.V. use:** Reconstitute drug with 1.5 ml of sterile water for injection. Don't reconstitute with other solutions. Further dilute solution with normal saline solution injection, D_5W, dextrose 5% in normal saline solution for injection, Ringer's injection, or lactated Ringer's injection.

– Drug may be given by rapid I.V. administration in doses of 0.3 to 0.4 mg/kg at intervals of 1 to 4 weeks. Solutions are stable for up to 5 days if refrigerated.

– If intense pain occurs, use local anesthetic at injection site.

– If pain occurs at insertion site, dilute further or use local anesthetic. Make sure drug doesn't infiltrate.

– Discard if solution appears grossly opaque or contains precipitate. Solutions should be clear to slightly opaque.
- **Bladder instillation use:** Dehydrate patient 8 to 10 hours before therapy. Instill drug into bladder by catheter; ask patient to retain solution for 2 hours. Volume may be reduced to 30 ml if discomfort is too great with 60 ml. Reposition patient every 15 minutes for maximum area contact.
- **Intracavitary use:** For neoplastic effusions, mix drug with 2% procaine hydrochloride or epinephrine hydrochloride 1:1,000.
- Drug can be given by all parenteral routes, including direct injection into tumor.
- Refrigerate and protect dry powder from direct sunlight.
- Report WBC count below 3,000/mm^3 or platelet count below 150,000/mm^3 and stop drug.
- To prevent hyperuricemia with resulting uric acid nephropathy, allopurinol may be used with adequate hydration.

Patient teaching
- Warn patient to watch for signs of infection (fever, sore throat, fatigue) and bleeding (easy bruising, nosebleeds, bleeding gums, melena). Tell patient to take temperature daily and to report even mild infections.
- Instruct patient to avoid OTC products containing aspirin.
- Advise woman to stop breast-feeding during therapy because of risk of toxicity to infant.
- Advise woman of childbearing age to avoid becoming pregnant during therapy and to consult with prescriber before becoming pregnant.

Evaluation
- Patient responds well to drug.
- Patient doesn't develop serious complications from drug-induced immunosuppression.
- Patient and family state understanding of drug therapy.

thiothixene
(thigh-oh-THIKS-een)
Navane

thiothixene hydrochloride
Navane*

Pharmacologic class: thioxanthene
Therapeutic class: antipsychotic
Pregnancy risk category: C

Indications and dosages
▶ **Mild-to-moderate psychosis.** *Adults:* Initially, 2 mg P.O. t.i.d. Increase gradually to 15 mg daily.

▶ **Severe psychosis.** *Adults:* Initially, 5 mg P.O. b.i.d. Increase gradually to 20 to 30 mg daily. Maximum recommended dosage is 60 mg daily. Or, 4 mg I.M. b.i.d. or q.i.d. Maximum dosage is 30 mg I.M. daily. Switch to P.O. form as soon as possible.

Contraindications and precautions

- Contraindicated in patients hypersensitive to drug and in those with circulatory collapse, coma, CNS depression, or blood dyscrasia.
- Use with extreme caution in patients with history of seizure disorder or during alcohol withdrawal.
- Use cautiously in debilitated patients, and patients with CV disease (may cause sudden drop in blood pressure), glaucoma, prostatic hyperplasia, or exposure to extreme heat.

Lifespan: In pregnant or breast-feeding women and in geriatric patients, use cautiously.

Adverse reactions

CNS: *extrapyramidal reactions, tardive dyskinesia,* sedation, pseudoparkinsonism, EEG changes, dizziness, restlessness, agitation, insomnia, ***neuroleptic malignant syndrome.***
CV: *orthostatic hypotension,* tachycardia, ECG changes.
EENT: ocular changes, *blurred vision,* nasal congestion.
GI: *dry mouth, constipation.*
GU: *urine retention,* menstrual irregularities, inhibited ejaculation.
Hematologic: ***transient leukopenia,*** leukocytosis, ***agranulocytosis.***
Hepatic: jaundice.
Metabolic: weight gain.
Skin: *mild photosensitivity reactions,* pain and sterile abscesses at I.M. injection site.
Other: gynecomastia, allergic reaction.

Interactions

Drug-drug. *Other CNS depressants:* Increases CNS depression. Avoid using together.
Drug-herb. *Nutmeg:* Herb may cause a loss of symptom control or interfere with therapy for psychiatric illnesses. Discourage using together.
Drug-lifestyle. *Alcohol use:* Increases CNS depression. Discourage using together.
Sun exposure: Increases photosensitivity reactions. Advise patient to avoid prolonged or unprotected exposure to sunlight.

Effects on lab test results

- May increase liver enzyme levels.
- May decrease granulocyte count. May increase or decrease WBC count.

Pharmacokinetics

Absorption: Rapid.
Distribution: Distributed widely in body; 91% to 99% protein-bound.
Metabolism: Minimal.
Excretion: Most of drug excreted as parent drug in feces.

Route	Onset	Peak	Duration
P.O., I.M.	Several wk	Unknown	Unknown

Pharmacodynamics

Chemical effect: Unknown; probably blocks postsynaptic dopamine receptors in brain.
Therapeutic effect: Relieves signs and symptoms of psychosis.

Available forms

thiothixene
Capsules: 1 mg, 2 mg, 5 mg, 10 mg, 20 mg
thiothixene hydrochloride
Injection: 2 mg/ml, 5 mg/ml
Oral concentrate: 5 mg/ml*

NURSING PROCESS

Assessment

- Assess patient's psychosis before therapy and regularly thereafter.
- Watch for orthostatic hypotension, especially with parenteral route.
- Monitor patient for tardive dyskinesia. It may occur after prolonged use or may not appear until months or years later. It may disappear spontaneously or persist for life, despite stopping drug.
- Monitor therapy with weekly bilirubin tests during first month, periodic blood tests (CBC and liver function), and ophthalmologic tests (long-term therapy).

ALERT: Monitor patient for symptoms of neuroleptic malignant syndrome (extrapyramidal effects, hyperthermia, autonomic disturbance), which is rare but can be fatal. It isn't necessarily related to length of drug use or type of neuroleptic; however, more than 60% of patients are men.

• Be alert for adverse reactions and drug interactions.
• Evaluate patient's and family's knowledge of drug therapy.

Nursing diagnoses
• Disturbed thought processes related to presence of psychosis
• Risk for injury related to drug-induced adverse CNS reactions
• Deficient knowledge related to drug therapy

Planning and implementation
• **P.O. use:** Prevent contact dermatitis by keeping drug away from skin and clothes. Wear gloves when preparing liquid forms.
– Dilute liquid concentrate with water or fruit juice just before giving.
• **I.M. use:** Give I.M. only in upper outer quadrant of buttocks or midlateral thigh. Massage slowly afterward to prevent sterile abscess. Injection may sting.
– Keep patient in supine position for 1 hour after drug administration.
• Slight yellowing of injection or concentrate is common and doesn't affect potency. Discard markedly discolored solutions.
• Don't withdraw drug abruptly unless required by severe adverse reactions. Abrupt withdrawal of long-term therapy may cause gastritis, nausea, vomiting, dizziness, tremors, feeling of warmth or cold, diaphoresis, tachycardia, headache, or insomnia.
• Report jaundice, symptoms of blood dyscrasia (fever, sore throat, infection, cellulitis, weakness), or persistent extrapyramidal reactions (longer than a few hours), especially in pregnant woman or in child, and withhold dose.
• Acute dystonic reactions may be treated with diphenhydramine.
ALERT: Don't confuse Navane with Nubain or Norvasc.

Patient teaching
• Warn patient to avoid activities that require alertness until CNS effects of drug are known. Drowsiness and dizziness usually subside after a few weeks.
• Tell patient to avoid alcohol while taking drug.
• Instruct patient to notify prescriber if urine retention or constipation occurs.
• Tell patient to relieve dry mouth with sugarless gum or hard candy.
• Tell patient to use sun block and to wear protective clothing to avoid photosensitivity reactions.
• Tell patient to watch for orthostatic hypotension, especially with parenteral administration. Advise patient to change position slowly.

Evaluation
• Patient's behavior and communication exhibit improved thought processes.
• Patient doesn't experience injury from adverse CNS reactions.
• Patient and family state understanding of drug therapy.

thyroid
(THIGH-royd)
Armour Thyroid, Thyroid USP

Pharmacologic class: thyroid hormone
Therapeutic class: thyroid agent
Pregnancy risk category: A

Indications and dosages
▶ **Hypothyroidism.** *Adults:* Initially, 30 mg P.O. daily; increased by 15 mg q 14 to 30 days, depending on disease severity, until desired response is achieved. Usual maintenance dosage is 60 to 180 mg P.O. daily as a single dose.
▶ **Congenital hypothyroidism.** *Children older than age 12:* May approach adult dosage (60 to 180 mg daily), depending on response. *Children ages 6 to 12:* 60 to 90 mg P.O. daily. *Children ages 1 to 5:* 45 to 60 mg P.O. daily. *Children ages 6 to 12 months:* 30 to 45 mg P.O. daily.
Children up to age 6 months: 15 to 30 mg P.O. daily.

Contraindications and precautions
• Contraindicated in patients hypersensitive to drug and those with acute MI uncomplicated by hypothyroidism, untreated thyrotoxicosis, or uncorrected adrenal insufficiency.
• Use with extreme caution in those with renal insufficiency, an ischemic state, or angina pectoris, hypertension, or other CV disorder.

• Use cautiously in patients with myxedema, diabetes mellitus, or diabetes insipidus.
Lifespan: In breast-feeding women, use cautiously. In geriatric patients, use with extreme caution.

Adverse reactions

CNS: *nervousness, insomnia,* tremor, headache.
CV: *tachycardia,* ***arrhythmias,*** angina pectoris, increased blood pressure, ***cardiac decompensation and collapse.***
GI: diarrhea, vomiting.
GU: menstrual irregularities.
Metabolic: weight loss, heat intolerance.
Musculoskeletal: accelerated rate of bone maturation in infants and children.
Skin: diaphoresis.
Other: allergic reactions.

Interactions

Drug-drug. *Cholestyramine:* Impairs thyroid absorption. Separate doses by 4 to 5 hours.
Insulin, oral antidiabetics: Alters glucose level. Monitor level and adjust dosage, as needed.
I.V. phenytoin: Free thyroid released. Monitor patient for tachycardia.
Oral anticoagulants: Alters PT. Monitor PT and INR; adjust dosage, as needed.
Sympathomimetics (such as epinephrine): Increases risk of coronary insufficiency. Monitor patient closely.

Effects on lab test results

None reported.

Pharmacokinetics

Absorption: Absorbed from GI tract.
Distribution: Highly protein-bound.
Metabolism: Not fully understood.
Excretion: Not fully understood. *Half-life:* T_4, 7 days; T_3, 2 days.

Route	Onset	Peak	Duration
P.O.	Unknown	Unknown	Unknown

Pharmacodynamics

Chemical effect: Not clearly defined; stimulates metabolism of body tissues by accelerating cellular oxidation.
Therapeutic effect: Raises thyroid hormone level in body.

Available forms

Tablets: 15 mg, 30 mg, 60 mg, 90 mg, 120 mg, 180 mg, 240 mg, 300 mg
Tablets (enteric-coated): 60 mg, 120 mg

NURSING PROCESS

Assessment

• Assess patient's thyroid condition before therapy and regularly thereafter.
• Monitor pulse rate and blood pressure.
• In children, sleeping pulse rate and basal morning temperature guide treatment.
• In patient with coronary artery disease who must receive drug, watch for possible coronary insufficiency.
• Be alert for adverse reactions and drug interactions.
• Evaluate patient's and family's knowledge of drug therapy.

Nursing diagnoses

• Ineffective health maintenance related to presence of hypothyroidism
• Disturbed sleep pattern related to drug-induced insomnia
• Deficient knowledge related to drug therapy

Planning and implementation

• Drug requirements are about 25% lower in patients older than age 60 than in young adults.
• Thyroid hormones alter thyroid function test results.
• Patient taking drug usually requires decreased anticoagulant dosage.
ALERT: Don't confuse Thyrolar with thyroid.

Patient teaching

• Tell patient to take drug at same time each day, preferably before breakfast, to maintain constant levels.
• Suggest that patient take drug in the morning to prevent insomnia.
• Advise patient who has achieved stable response not to change brands.
• Warn patient (especially geriatric patient) to notify prescriber promptly if chest pain, palpitations, sweating, nervousness, or other signs of overdose occur or if chest pain, dyspnea, and tachycardia develop.
• Tell patient to report unusual bleeding and bruising.

Evaluation
- Patient regains normal thyroid function.
- Patient expresses importance of taking thyroid in morning if insomnia occurs.
- Patient and family state understanding of drug therapy.

tiagabine hydrochloride
(tigh-AG-ah-been high-droh-KLOR-ighd)
Gabitril

Pharmacologic class: GABA uptake inhibitor
Therapeutic class: anticonvulsant
Pregnancy risk category: C

Indications and dosages
▶ **Adjunctive therapy in the treatment of partial seizures.** *Adults:* Initially, 4 mg P.O. once daily. Total daily dose may be increased by 4 to 8 mg at weekly intervals until clinical response or up to 56 mg/day. Dose should be divided b.i.d. to q.i.d.
Adolescents ages 12 to 18: Initially, 4 mg P.O. once daily. Total daily dosage may be increased by 4 mg at the beginning of week 2 and by 4 to 8 mg/week until clinical response or up to 32 mg daily. Daily dosage should be given in divided doses b.i.d. to q.i.d.

Contraindications and precautions
- Contraindicated in patients hypersensitive to drug or its ingredients.

Lifespan: In breast-feeding women, use cautiously.

Adverse reactions
CNS: generalized weakness, *dizziness, asthenia, somnolence, nervousness,* tremor, difficulty with concentration and attention, insomnia, ataxia, confusion, speech disorder, difficulty with memory, paresthesia, depression, emotional lability, abnormal gait, hostility, language problems, agitation, pain.
CV: vasodilation.
EENT: nystagmus, pharyngitis.
GI: abdominal pain, *nausea,* diarrhea, vomiting, increased appetite, mouth ulcerations.
Musculoskeletal: myasthenia.
Respiratory: increased cough.
Skin: rash, pruritus.

Interactions
Drug-drug. *Carbamazepine, phenobarbital, phenytoin:* Increases tiagabine clearance. Monitor patient for loss of therapeutic effect.
CNS depressants: Enhances CNS effects. Use cautiously.
Drug-lifestyle. *Alcohol use:* Enhances CNS effects. Discourage using together.

Effects on lab test results
None reported.

Pharmacokinetics
Absorption: Rapid and more than 95%. Absolute bioavailability is 90%.
Distribution: About 96% bound to plasma protein.
Metabolism: Likely to be metabolized by cytochrome P-450 3A isoenzymes.
Excretion: About 25% is excreted in urine (2% unchanged); 63% in feces. *Half-life:* 7 to 9 hours.

Route	Onset	Peak	Duration
P.O.	Rapid	45 min	7-9 hr

Pharmacodynamics
Chemical effect: Unknown, but tiagabine may act by enhancing the activity of GABA, the major inhibitory neurotransmitter in the CNS. It binds to recognition sites related to the GABA uptake carrier and may thus permit more GABA to be available for binding to receptors on postsynaptic cells.
Therapeutic effect: Prevents partial seizures.

Available forms
Tablets: 4 mg, 12 mg, 16 mg, 20 mg

NURSING PROCESS

Assessment
- Assess patient's seizure disorder before therapy and regularly thereafter.
- Assess patient's compliance with therapy at each follow-up visit.

ALERT: Monitor patient carefully for status epilepticus because sudden unexpected death has occurred in patients receiving antiepileptic drugs, including tiagabine.
- Assess patient for adverse reactions and drug interactions.

• Evaluate patient's and family's knowledge of drug therapy.

Nursing diagnoses

• Risk for injury related to seizure disorder
• Impaired physical mobility related to drug-induced generalized weakness
• Deficient knowledge related to drug therapy

Planning and implementation

• In patients with impaired liver function, reduced initial and maintenance doses or longer dosing intervals may be needed.
ALERT: Never withdraw drug suddenly because seizure frequency may increase. Withdraw gradually unless safety concerns require a more rapid withdrawal.
• Patients who aren't receiving at least one enzyme-inducing antiepilepsy drug at the time of tiagabine initiation may require lower doses or slower dosage adjustments.
• Report breakthrough seizure activity to prescriber.
ALERT: Don't confuse tiagabine with tizanidine which both have 4-mg starting doses.

Patient teaching

• Advise patient to take drug only as prescribed.
• Advise patient to take tiagabine with food.
• Warn patient that drug may cause dizziness, somnolence, and other symptoms and signs of CNS depression. Advise patient to avoid driving and other potentially hazardous activities that require mental alertness until drug's CNS effects are known.
• Tell woman to call prescriber if she becomes pregnant or plans to become pregnant during therapy.
• Tell woman to notify prescriber if planning to breast-feed because drug may appear in breast milk.

Evaluation

• Patient is free from seizure activity.
• Patient receives therapeutic dose and doesn't experience muscle weakness.
• Patient and family state understanding of drug therapy.

ticarcillin disodium

(tigh-kar-SIL-in digh-SOH-dee-um)
Ticar, Ticillin ◊

Pharmacologic class: extended-spectrum penicillin, alpha-carboxypenicillin
Therapeutic class: antibiotic
Pregnancy risk category: B

Indications and dosages

▶ **Severe systemic infections caused by susceptible strains of gram-positive and especially gram-negative organisms (including *Pseudomonas* and *Proteus*).** *Adults and children older than age 1 month:* 200 to 300 mg/kg I.V. daily in divided doses q 4 to 6 hours.
▶ **Uncomplicated UTI.** *Adults and children weighing 40 kg (88 lb) or more:* 1 g I.V. or I.M. q 6 hours.
Infants and children older than age 1 month and weighing less than 40 kg: 50 to 100 mg/kg I.V. or I.M. daily in divided doses q 6 to 8 hours.

Contraindications and precautions

• Contraindicated in patients hypersensitive to penicillins.
• Use cautiously in patients with other drug allergies, especially to cephalosporins (possible cross-sensitivity); and those with impaired kidney function, hemorrhagic conditions, hypokalemia, or sodium restrictions (contains 5.2 to 6.5 mEq sodium/g).
Lifespan: In pregnant or breast-feeding women, use cautiously.

Adverse reactions

CNS: ***seizures,*** neuromuscular excitability.
CV: vein irritation, phlebitis.
GI: nausea, diarrhea, vomiting.
Hematologic: ***leukopenia, neutropenia,*** eosinophilia, ***thrombocytopenia,*** hemolytic anemia.
Metabolic: hypokalemia.
Other: ***hypersensitivity reactions*** (rash, pruritus, urticaria, chills, fever, edema, ***anaphylaxis***), overgrowth of nonsusceptible organisms, pain at injection site.

Interactions

Drug-drug. *Lithium:* Alters renal elimination of lithium. Monitor lithium level closely.

Oral contraceptives: Efficacy of oral contraceptives may be decreased. Recommend an additional form of contraception during penicillin therapy.
Probenecid: Increases level of ticarcillin and other penicillins. Probenecid may be used for this purpose.

Effects on lab test results

• May increase ALT, AST, alkaline phosphatase, LDH, and sodium levels. May decrease potassium level.
• May increase eosinophil count. May decrease hemoglobin, hematocrit, and platelet, WBC, neutrophil, and granulocyte counts.

Pharmacokinetics

Absorption: Unknown after I.M. administration.
Distribution: Distributed widely. Penetrates minimally into CSF with non-inflamed meninges; 45% to 65% protein-bound.
Metabolism: About 13% metabolized by hydrolysis to inactive compounds.
Excretion: Excreted mostly in urine; also in bile. *Half-life:* About 1 hour.

Route	Onset	Peak	Duration
I.V.	Immediate	Immediate	Unknown
I.M.	Unknown	30-75 min	Unknown

Pharmacodynamics

Chemical effect: Inhibits cell wall synthesis during microorganism multiplication; bacteria resist penicillins by producing penicillinase enzymes that convert penicillins to inactive penicilloic acid. Ticarcillin resists these enzymes.
Therapeutic effect: Kills bacteria, including many gram-negative aerobic and anaerobic bacilli, many gram-positive and gram-negative aerobic cocci, and some gram-positive aerobic and anaerobic bacilli. May be effective against some carbenicillin-resistant gram-negative bacilli.

Available forms

Injection: 1 g, 3 g, 6 g
I.V. infusion: 3 g

NURSING PROCESS

Assessment

• Assess patient's infection before therapy and regularly thereafter.
• Before giving, ask patient if he is allergic to penicillin. Negative history of penicillin allergy is no guarantee against future allergic reaction.
• Obtain specimen for culture and sensitivity tests before giving first dose. Therapy may begin pending results.
• Monitor potassium level.
• Monitor CBC and platelet count.
• Monitor INR in patients receiving warfarin therapy because drug may prolong PT.
• Be alert for adverse reactions and drug interactions.
• Monitor patient's hydration status if adverse GI reactions occur.
• Evaluate patient's and family's knowledge of drug therapy.

Nursing diagnoses

• Risk for infection related to presence of susceptible bacteria
• Risk for deficient fluid volume related to drug-induced adverse GI reactions
• Deficient knowledge related to drug therapy

Planning and implementation

• Dosage should be decreased in patient with impaired kidney function.
• **I.V. use:** Reconstitute drug in vials using D_5W, normal saline solution injection, sterile water for injection, or other compatible solution. Add 4 ml of diluent for each gram of drug. Further dilute to maximum of 50 mg/ml, and inject slowly directly into vein or I.V. line containing free-flowing solution. Or, dilute to 10 to 100 mg/ml and infuse intermittently over 30 minutes to 2 hours in adults or 10 to 20 minutes in neonates.
– Aminoglycoside antibiotics (such as gentamicin and tobramycin) are chemically incompatible. Don't mix in same I.V. container.
– Continuous infusion may cause vein irritation. Change site every 48 hours.
• **I.M. use:** Reconstitute drug in vials with sterile water for injection, normal saline solution injection, or lidocaine 1% (without epinephrine). Use 2 ml of diluent per gram of drug.

– Inject deep into large muscle. Don't exceed 2 g per injection.
• Give drug at least 1 hour before bacteriostatic antibiotics.
• Drug is typically used with another antibiotic, such as gentamicin.
ALERT: Institute seizure precautions. Patient with high blood level of ticarcillin may develop seizures.

Patient teaching
• Instruct patient to report adverse reactions.

Evaluation
• Patient is free from infection.
• Patient maintains adequate hydration.
• Patient and family state understanding of drug therapy.

ticarcillin disodium and clavulanate potassium
(tigh-kar-SIL-in digh-SOH-dee-um and KLAV-yoo-lan-nayt poh-TAH-see-um)
Timentin

Pharmacologic class: extended-spectrum penicillin, beta-lactamase inhibitor
Therapeutic class: antibiotic
Pregnancy risk category: B

Indications and dosages
▶ **Lower respiratory tract, urinary tract, bone and joint, skin, and skin-structure infections and septicemia caused by beta-lactamase–producing strains of bacteria or by ticarcillin-susceptible organisms.** *Adults:* 3.1 g (3 g ticarcillin and 100 mg clavulanate acid) given by I.V. infusion q 4 to 6 hours.

Contraindications and precautions
• Contraindicated in patients hypersensitive to penicillins.
• Use cautiously in patients with other drug allergies, especially to cephalosporins (possible cross-sensitivity), and those with impaired kidney function, hemorrhagic condition, hypokalemia, or sodium restrictions (contains 4.5 mEq sodium/g).
Lifespan: In pregnant or breast-feeding women, use cautiously.

Adverse reactions
CNS: ***seizures,*** neuromuscular excitability, headache, giddiness.
CV: vein irritation, phlebitis.
GI: nausea, diarrhea, stomatitis, vomiting, epigastric pain, flatulence, ***pseudomembranous colitis,*** taste and smell disturbances.
Hematologic: ***leukopenia, neutropenia,*** eosinophilia, ***thrombocytopenia,*** hemolytic anemia, anemia.
Metabolic: hypokalemia.
Other: ***hypersensitivity reactions*** (rash, pruritus, urticaria, chills, fever, edema, ***anaphylaxis***), overgrowth of nonsusceptible organisms, pain at injection site.

Interactions
Drug-drug. *Oral contraceptives:* Efficacy of oral contraceptives may be decreased. Recommend an additional form of contraception during ticarcillin therapy.
Probenecid: Increases blood levels of ticarcillin. Probenecid may be used for this purpose.

Effects on lab test results
• May increase ALT, AST, alkaline phosphatase, LDH, and sodium levels. May decrease potassium level.
• May increase eosinophil count. May decrease hemoglobin, hematocrit, and platelet, WBC, neutrophil, and granulocyte counts.

Pharmacokinetics
Absorption: Administered I.V.
Distribution: Ticarcillin disodium distributed widely; penetrates minimally into CSF with noninflamed meninges. Clavulanic acid penetrates pleural fluid, lungs, and peritoneal fluid.
Metabolism: About 13% of ticarcillin dose metabolized by hydrolysis to inactive compounds; clavulanic acid is thought to undergo extensive metabolism but its fate is unknown.
Excretion: Ticarcillin excreted primarily in urine; also excreted in bile. Clavulanate's metabolites are excreted in urine. *Half-life:* About 1 hour.

Route	Onset	Peak	Duration
I.V.	Immediate	Immediate	Unknown

Pharmacodynamics

Chemical effect: Ticarcillin is an extended-spectrum penicillin that inhibits cell wall synthesis during microorganism replication; clavulanic acid increases ticarcillin's effectiveness by inactivating beta lactamases, which destroy ticarcillin.
Therapeutic effect: Kills susceptible bacteria, including many gram-negative aerobic and anaerobic bacilli, many gram-positive and gram-negative aerobic cocci, and some gram-positive aerobic and anaerobic bacilli. The combination of ticarcillin and clavulanate potassium is also effective against many beta-lactamase–producing strains, including *Bacteroides fragilis, Escherichia coli, Haemophilus influenzae, Klebsiella, Neisseria gonorrhoeae, Providencia,* and *Staphylococcus aureus.*

Available forms

Injection: 3 g ticarcillin and 100 mg clavulanic acid

NURSING PROCESS

Assessment
- Assess patient's infection before therapy and regularly thereafter.
- Before giving drug, ask patient if he's allergic to penicillin. Negative history of penicillin allergy is no guarantee against future allergic reaction.
- Obtain specimen for culture and sensitivity tests before giving first dose. Therapy may begin pending results.
- Monitor CBC and platelet count.
- Be alert for adverse reactions and drug interactions.
- Monitor patient's hydration status if adverse GI reactions occur.
- Evaluate patient's and family's knowledge of drug therapy.

Nursing diagnoses
- Risk for infection related to presence of susceptible bacteria
- Risk for deficient fluid volume related to drug-induced adverse GI reactions
- Deficient knowledge related to drug therapy

Planning and implementation
- Dosage should be decreased in patient with impaired kidney function.
- Reconstitute drug with 13 ml of sterile water for injection or normal saline solution injection. Further dilute to maximum of 10 to 100 mg/ml (based on ticarcillin component) and infuse over 30 minutes. In fluid-restricted patient, dilute to maximum of 48 mg/ml if using D_5W, 43 mg/ml if using normal saline solution injection, or 86 mg/ml if using sterile water for injection.
- Aminoglycoside antibiotics (such as gentamicin and tobramycin) are chemically incompatible. Don't mix in same I.V. container.
- Give drug at least 1 hour before bacteriostatic antibiotics.

Patient teaching
- Instruct patient to report adverse reactions immediately.

Evaluation
- Patient is free from infection.
- Patient maintains adequate hydration.
- Patient and family state understanding of drug therapy.

ticlopidine hydrochloride
(tigh-KLOH-peh-deen high-droh-KLOR-ighd)
Ticlid

Pharmacologic class: platelet aggregation inhibitor
Therapeutic class: antithrombotic
Pregnancy risk category: C

Indications and dosages

▶ **To reduce risk of thrombotic CVA in patients with history of CVA or who have experienced CVA precursors.** *Adults:* 250 mg P.O. b.i.d. with meals.

Contraindications and precautions
- Contraindicated in patients hypersensitive to drug and those with hematopoietic disorders (such as neutropenia, thrombocytopenia, or disorders of hemostasis), active pathologic bleeding (such as peptic ulceration or active intracranial bleeding), or severe hepatic impairment.
- Drug is reserved for patients intolerant to aspirin.

Lifespan: In pregnant women, use cautiously. In breast-feeding women, drug isn't recommended. In children, safety of drug hasn't been established.

Adverse reactions

CNS: dizziness, ***intracerebral bleeding.***
CV: vasculitis.
EENT: epistaxis, conjunctival hemorrhage.
GI: *diarrhea,* nausea, dyspepsia, vomiting, flatulence, anorexia, *abdominal pain,* ***bleeding.***
GU: hematuria, nephrotic syndrome, dark-colored urine.
Hematologic: ***neutropenia, agranulocytosis, pancytopenia, immune thrombocytopenia.***
Hepatic: ***hepatitis,*** cholestatic jaundice.
Metabolic: ***hyponatremia.***
Musculoskeletal: arthropathy, myositis.
Respiratory: ***allergic pneumonitis.***
Skin: *rash,* purpura, pruritus, urticaria, ***thrombocytopenic purpura,*** ecchymoses.
Other: ***hypersensitivity reactions, postoperative bleeding,*** systemic lupus erythematosus, ***serum sickness.***

Interactions

Drug-drug. *Antacids:* Decreases ticlopidine level. Separate administration times by at least 2 hours.
Aspirin: Potentiates aspirin effects on platelets. Don't use together.
Cimetidine: Decreases clearance of ticlopidine and increases risk of toxicity. Avoid using together.
Digoxin: Slightly decreases digoxin level. Monitor level.
Theophylline: Decreases theophylline clearance and risk of toxicity. Monitor patient closely and adjust theophylline dosage.
Drug-herb. *Red clover:* May increase risk of bleeding. Caution against using together.

Effects on lab test results

- May increase ALT, AST, and alkaline phosphatase levels. May decrease sodium level.
- May decrease neutrophil, WBC, RBC, platelet, and granulocyte counts.

Pharmacokinetics

Absorption: Rapid and extensive; enhanced by food.
Distribution: 98% bound to serum proteins and lipoproteins.
Metabolism: Extensively metabolized by liver. More than 20 metabolites have been identified; unknown if parent drug or active metabolites are responsible for pharmacologic activity.
Excretion: 60% excreted in urine and 23% in feces.

Route	Onset	Peak	Duration
P.O.	Unknown	2 hr	Unknown

Pharmacodynamics

Chemical effect: Unknown; probably blocks adenosine diphosphate–induced platelet-fibrinogen and platelet-platelet binding.
Therapeutic effect: Prevents blood clots from forming.

Available forms

Tablets: 250 mg

NURSING PROCESS

Assessment

- Assess patient's condition before therapy and regularly thereafter.
- Obtain baseline liver function tests before therapy. Monitor test results closely, especially during first 4 months of treatment, and repeat when liver dysfunction is suspected.
- Determine baseline CBC and WBC differentials and then repeat at second week of therapy and every 2 weeks until end of third month. Test more frequently if patient shows signs of declining neutrophil count or if count falls 30% below baseline. After first 3 months, CBC and WBC differential determinations should be performed only in patient showing signs of infection.
- Be alert for adverse reactions and drug interactions.
- Evaluate patient's and family's knowledge of drug therapy.

Nursing diagnoses

- Impaired cerebral tissue perfusion related to CVA potential or history
- Ineffective protection related to drug-induced adverse hematologic reactions
- Deficient knowledge related to drug therapy

Planning and implementation

- Thrombocytopenia has occurred rarely. Report platelet count of 80,000/mm³ or less, and stop drug. Give 20 mg of methylprednisolone

I.V. to normalize bleeding time within 2 hours. Platelet transfusions also may be used.
- When used preoperatively, drug may decrease risk of graft occlusion in patient receiving coronary artery bypass grafts and reduce severity of drop in platelet count in patient receiving extracorporeal hemoperfusion during open heart surgery.

Patient teaching
- Tell patient to take drug with meals; this substantially increases bioavailability and improves GI tolerance.
- Tell patient to avoid aspirin-containing products and to check with prescriber before taking OTC drugs.
- Explain that drug prolongs bleeding time but that patient should report unusual or prolonged bleeding. Advise him to tell dentist and other prescribers that he is taking this drug.
- Stress importance of regular blood tests. Because neutropenia can increase risk of infection, tell patient to promptly report such signs as fever, chills, and sore throat.
- If drug is substituted for fibrinolytic or anticoagulant, tell patient to discontinue those drugs before starting ticlopidine therapy.
- Advise patient to stop drug 10 to 14 days before elective surgery.
- Tell patient to report yellow skin or sclera, severe or persistent diarrhea, rashes, S.C. bleeding, light-colored stools, and dark urine.

☑ Evaluation
- Patient maintains adequate cerebral perfusion.
- Patient doesn't develop serious complications.
- Patient and family state understanding of drug therapy.

timolol maleate
(TIH-moh-lol MAL-ee-ayt)
Apo-Timol ♦, Blocadren

Pharmacologic class: beta blocker
Therapeutic class: antihypertensive, adjunct in MI, antimigraine agent
Pregnancy risk category: C

Indications and dosages
▶ **Hypertension.** *Adults:* Initially, 10 mg P.O. b.i.d. Usual daily maintenance dose is 20 to 40 mg. Maximum daily dose is 60 mg. Allow at least 7 days to elapse between increases in dosage.
▶ **MI (long-term prophylaxis in patients who have survived acute phase).** *Adults:* 10 mg P.O. b.i.d.
▶ **Prevention of migraine headache.** *Adults:* Usual dosage is 10 mg P.O. b.i.d. During maintenance therapy, 20-mg daily dose may be given once daily. Maximum daily dose is 30 mg in divided doses (10 mg in morning and 20 mg in evening). If maximum dose for 6 to 8 weeks doesn't achieve an adequate response, another form of therapy should be instituted.
▶ **Angina‡.** *Adults:* 15 to 45 mg P.O. daily given in three divided doses.

Contraindications and precautions
- Contraindicated in patients hypersensitive to drug and in those with bronchial asthma, severe COPD, sinus bradycardia and heart block greater than first-degree, cardiogenic shock, or overt heart failure.
- Use cautiously in patients with compensated heart failure; hepatic, renal, or respiratory disease; diabetes; or hyperthyroidism.

Lifespan: In pregnant women, use cautiously. In breast-feeding women, drug isn't recommended. In children, safety of drug hasn't been established.

Adverse reactions
CNS: fatigue, lethargy, dizziness.
CV: ***bradycardia,*** hypotension, peripheral vascular disease, ***arrhythmias, heart failure.***
GI: nausea, vomiting, diarrhea.
Respiratory: dyspnea, ***bronchospasm,*** *increased airway resistance.*
Skin: pruritus.

Interactions
Drug-drug. *Cardiac glycosides, diltiazem, verapamil:* Excessive bradycardia and increased depressant effect on myocardium. Use together cautiously.
Catecholamine-depleting drugs (such as reserpine): May have additive effects when given with beta blockers. Monitor patient for hypotension and bradycardia.

Insulin, oral antidiabetics: May alter requirements for these drugs in previously stabilized diabetic patients. Monitor patient for hypoglycemia.
NSAIDs (ibuprofen, indomethacin): Decreases antihypertensive effect. Monitor blood pressure and adjust dosage.
Quinidine: May increase beta-adrenergic blockade. Monitor heart rate.

Effects on lab test results

- May increase BUN, potassium, uric acid, and glucose levels.

Pharmacokinetics

Absorption: About 90%.
Distribution: Distributed throughout body; depending on assay method, drug is 10% to 60% protein-bound.
Metabolism: About 80% metabolized in liver to inactive metabolites.
Excretion: Drug and its metabolites excreted primarily in urine. *Half-life:* About 4 hours.

Route	Onset	Peak	Duration
P.O.	15-30 min	1-2 hr	6-12 hr

Pharmacodynamics

Chemical effect: Mechanism of antihypertensive action unknown. In MI, drug may decrease myocardial oxygen requirements. It also prevents arterial dilation through beta blockade for migraine headache prophylaxis.
Therapeutic effect: Lowers blood pressure and helps to prevent MI and migraine headaches.

Available forms

Tablets: 5 mg, 10 mg, 20 mg

NURSING PROCESS

Assessment

- Assess patient's condition before therapy and regularly thereafter.
- Monitor blood pressure frequently.
- Be alert for adverse reactions and drug interactions.
- Evaluate patient's and family's knowledge of drug therapy.

Nursing diagnoses

- Risk for injury related to history of hypertension or MI
- Acute pain related to migraine headache
- Deficient knowledge related to drug therapy

Planning and implementation

- Check patient's apical pulse rate before giving drug. Report extreme pulse rate, and withhold drug.
- Don't stop drug abruptly; this can exacerbate angina and precipitate MI. Dosage should be reduced gradually over 1 to 2 weeks.
- Teach patient other means to reduce blood pressure such as diet control, weight reduction, exercise, smoking cessation, and stress reduction.

ALERT: Don't confuse timolol with atenolol.

Patient teaching

- Explain importance of taking drug exactly as prescribed.
- Tell patient not to discontinue drug abruptly because serious complications can occur. Instead, tell him to report adverse reactions.

Evaluation

- Patient doesn't experience injury from underlying disease.
- Patient doesn't develop migraine headaches.
- Patient and family state understanding of drug therapy.

tinzaparin sodium

(TIN-zuh-pear-in SOE-dee-um)
Innohep

Pharmacologic class: low–molecular-weight heparin
Therapeutic class: anticoagulant
Pregnancy risk category: B

Indications and dosages

▶ **Adjunct treatment (with warfarin sodium) of symptomatic deep vein thrombosis with or without pulmonary embolism.** *Adults:* 175 anti-Xa IU per kg of body weight S.C. once daily for at least 6 days and until the patient is adequately anticoagulated with warfarin (INR at least 2) for 2 consecutive days. Warfarin therapy should begin when appropriate, usually within 1 to 3 days after tinzaparin starts. The volume to be given may be calculated as follows:

Patient weight in kg × 0.00875 ml/kg = volume to be given (in ml).

Contraindications and precautions

- Contraindicated in patients hypersensitive to tinzaparin, heparin, sulfites, benzyl alcohol, or pork products.
- Contraindicated in patients with active major bleeding and patients with heparin-induced thrombocytopenia or a history of it.
- Use cautiously in patients with increased risk of hemorrhage, such as those with bacterial endocarditis, uncontrolled hypertension, diabetic retinopathy, or congenital or acquired bleeding disorders such as hepatic failure, amyloidosis, GI ulceration, or hemorrhagic CVA.
- Use cautiously in patients being treated with platelet inhibitors and patients who have recently undergone brain, spinal, or ophthalmologic surgery.
- Use cautiously in patients with renal insufficiency.

Lifespan: In breast-feeding mothers, it isn't known whether tinzaparin sodium appears in breast milk, so give drug cautiously. In children, safety and efficacy haven't been established. Geriatric patients may show reduced elimination of tinzaparin sodium; use drug cautiously.

Adverse reactions

CNS: headache, fever, dizziness, insomnia, confusion, ***cerebral or intracranial bleeding.***
CV: ***arrhythmias,*** chest pain, hypotension, hypertension, ***MI, thromboembolism,*** tachycardia, dependent edema, angina pectoris.
EENT: epistaxis, ocular hemorrhage.
GI: anorectal bleeding, constipation, flatulence, hematemesis, hemarthrosis, ***GI hemorrhage,*** nausea, vomiting, dyspepsia, retroperitoneal or intra-abdominal bleeding.
GU: dysuria, hematuria, urinary tract infection, urine retention, ***vaginal hemorrhage.***
Hematologic: granulocytopenia, ***thrombocytopenia,*** anemia, ***agranulocytosis, pancytopenia, hemorrhage.***
Musculoskeletal: back pain.
Respiratory: pneumonia, respiratory disorder, ***pulmonary embolism,*** dyspnea.
Skin: bullous eruption, cellulitis, *injection site hematoma,* pruritus, purpura, rash, melena, skin necrosis, wound hematoma.
Other: ***hypersensitivity reactions, spinal or epidural hematoma,*** pain, infection, impaired healing, allergic reaction, congenital anomaly, ***fetal death, fetal distress.***

Interactions

Drug-drug. *Oral anticoagulants, platelet inhibitors (such as dextran, dipyridamole, NSAIDs, salicylates, sulfinpyrazone), thrombolytics:* May increase the risk of bleeding. Use together cautiously and monitor patient.

Effects on lab test results

- May increase AST and ALT levels.
- May increase granular leukocyte count. May decrease hemoglobin, hematocrit, and granulocyte, platelet, RBC, and WBC counts.

Pharmacokinetics

Absorption: Plasma levels peak in 4 to 5 hours.
Distribution: The volume of distribution is similar in magnitude to that of blood volume, which suggests that distribution is limited to the central compartment.
Metabolism: Drug is partially metabolized by desulfation and depolymerization, similar to that seen by other low–molecular-weight heparins.
Excretion: The primary route of elimination is renal. *Half-life:* 3 to 4 hours.

Route	Onset	Peak	Duration
S.C.	2-3 hr	4-5 hr	Unknown

Pharmacodynamics

Chemical effect: Inhibits reactions that lead to blood clotting, including the formation of fibrin clots. It also acts as a potent co-inhibitor of several activated coagulation factors, especially factors Xa and IIa (thrombin). The main inhibitory action is activated by binding with the plasma protease inhibitor antithrombin. Binding with antithrombin increases the ability to inactivate coagulation enzymes, factor Xa, and thrombin. Tinzaparin sodium also induces release of tissue factor pathway inhibitor, which may contribute to the antithrombotic effect.
Therapeutic effect: Reduces the ability of the blood to clot.

Available forms

Injection: 20,000 anti-Xa IU per ml in 2-ml vials

NURSING PROCESS

Assessment

- Assess underlying condition before therapy, and reassess regularly throughout therapy.
- Monitor platelet count during therapy. If platelet count falls below 100,000/mm^3, discontinue drug.
- Monitor CBC and stool tests for occult blood periodically during treatment.
- Drug may affect PT and INR levels. Patients who also receive warfarin should have blood drawn for PT and INR tests just before the next scheduled tinzaparin dose.
- Drug contains sodium metabisulfite, which may cause allergic reactions in susceptible people.
- Assess weight before therapy to calculate accurate dose.
- Evaluate patient's and family's knowledge of tinzaparin sodium therapy.

Nursing diagnoses

- Ineffective protection related to increased risk of bleeding
- Ineffective tissue perfusion, peripheral, related to deep vein thrombosis
- Deficient knowledge related to tinzaparin sodium therapy

Planning and implementation

- If patient develops serious bleeding or receives a large overdose, replace volume and hemostatic blood elements (such as RBCs, fresh frozen plasma, and platelets) as needed. If this is ineffective, consider giving protamine sulfate.
- Tinzaparin isn't intended for I.M. or I.V. use and it shouldn't be mixed with other injections or infusions.
- Tinzaparin can't be interchanged (unit for unit) with heparin or other low–molecular-weight heparins.
- During administration, the patient should be lying or sitting down. Give drug by deep S.C. injection into the abdominal wall. Insert the whole length of the needle into a skin fold held between thumb and forefinger. Hold skin fold throughout injection. To minimize bruising, don't rub the injection site after administration.
- Rotate injection sites between the right and left anterolateral and posterolateral abdominal wall.
- Use an appropriate calibrated syringe to ensure withdrawal of the correct volume of drug from vial.

ALERT: When neuraxial anesthesia (epidural or spinal anesthesia) or spinal puncture is used, the patient is at risk for spinal hematoma, which can result in long-term or permanent paralysis. Watch for evidence of neurologic impairment. Consider the risks and benefits of neuraxial intervention in patients being anticoagulated with low–molecular-weight heparins or heparinoids.

- Store tinzaparin sodium at room temperature.

Patient teaching

- Inform patient that co-administration of warfarin will begin within 1 to 3 days of tinzaparin administration. Explain the importance of warfarin therapy.
- Stress the importance of laboratory monitoring to ensure effectiveness and safety of therapy.
- Caution patient to take safety measures to prevent cuts and bruises (such as using a soft toothbrush and an electric razor).
- Review the warning signs of bleeding, and instruct the patient to report evidence of bleeding immediately.
- Warn patient about the risks of becoming pregnant while taking tinzaparin sodium. Cases of gasping syndrome have occurred in premature infants who received large amounts of benzyl alcohol.

Evaluation

- Patient states appropriate bleeding precautions to take.
- Patient's peripheral neurovascular status returns to baseline.
- Patient and family state understanding of tinzaparin sodium therapy.

tirofiban hydrochloride

(ty-roh-FYE-ban high-droh-KLOR-ighd)
Aggrastat

Pharmacologic class: GP IIb/IIIa receptor antagonist
Therapeutic class: platelet aggregation inhibitor
Pregnancy risk category: B

Indications and dosages

▶ **Acute coronary syndrome, with heparin, aspirin, or both, including patients who are to be managed medically and those undergoing percutaneous transluminal coronary angioplasty (PTCA) or atherectomy.** *Adults:* I.V. loading dose of 0.4 mcg/kg/minute for 30 minutes; then continuous I.V. infusion of 0.1 mcg/kg/minute. Continue through angiography and for 12 to 24 hours after angioplasty or atherectomy.

Contraindications and precautions

- Contraindicated in patients hypersensitive to drug or its ingredients, those with active internal bleeding or history of bleeding diathesis within the previous 30 days, and those with history of intracranial hemorrhage, intracranial neoplasm, arteriovenous malformation, aneurysm, thrombocytopenia after prior exposure to tirofiban, CVA within 30 days, or hemorrhagic CVA.
- Contraindicated in those with history, symptoms, or findings suggestive of aortic dissection; severe hypertension (systolic blood pressure over 180 mm Hg or diastolic blood pressure over 110 mm Hg); acute pericarditis; those who have had major surgical procedure or severe physical trauma within previous 30 days; or patients receiving another parenteral GP IIb/IIIa inhibitor.
- Use cautiously in patients with increased risk of bleeding, including those with hemorrhagic retinopathy or platelet count below 150,000/mm^3.

Lifespan: In breast-feeding women, discontinue drug use or breast-feeding because of potential adverse effects in infants. In patients younger than 18, safety and effectiveness have not been determined.

Adverse reactions

CNS: fever, dizziness, headache.
CV: ***bradycardia, coronary artery dissection,*** edema, vasovagal reaction.
GI: nausea, *occult bleeding.*
Hematologic: *bleeding,* ***thrombocytopenia.***
Musculoskeletal: pelvic pain, leg pain.
Skin: sweating.
Other: bleeding at arterial access site.

Interactions

Drug-drug. *Clopidogrel, dipyridamole, heparin, NSAIDs, oral anticoagulants such as warfarin, thrombolytics, ticlopidine:* Increases risk of bleeding. Monitor patient closely.
Levothyroxine, omeprazole: Increases renal clearance of tirofiban. Monitor patient.
Drug-herb. *Dong quai, feverfew, garlic, ginger:* May increase the risk of bleeding. Tell patient to discontinue use before planned invasive procedures.

Effects on lab test results

- May decrease hemoglobin, hematocrit, and platelet count.

Pharmacokinetics

Absorption: Administered I.V.
Distribution: 65% protein-bound. Volume ranges from 22 to 42 liters.
Metabolism: Limited. *Half-life:* 2 hours.
Excretion: Renal clearance accounts for 39 to 69% of elimination; feces accounts for 25%.

Route	Onset	Peak	Duration
I.V.	Immediate	Immediate	4-8 hr after end of infusion

Pharmacodynamics

Chemical effect: Reversibly binds to the glycoprotein IIb/IIIa (GP IIb/IIIa) receptor on human platelets and inhibits platelet aggregation.
Therapeutic effect: Prevents clot formation.

Available forms

Injection: 25- and 50-ml vials (250 mcg/ml), 250- and 500-ml premixed vials (50 mcg/ml)

NURSING PROCESS

Assessment

- Obtain history of patient's underlying condition before therapy, and reassess regularly thereafter.
- Monitor hemoglobin level and hematocrit and platelet counts before starting therapy, 6 hours after loading dose, and at least daily during therapy.
- Monitor patient for bleeding.
- Notify prescriber if thrombocytopenia occurs.

• Evaluate patient's and family's knowledge of drug therapy.

Nursing diagnoses

• Ineffective cardiopulmonary tissue perfusion related to presence of acute coronary syndrome
• Risk for injury related to increased bleeding tendencies
• Deficient knowledge related to drug therapy

Planning and implementation

• **I.V. use:** Dilute 50-ml injection vials (250 mcg/ml) to same strength as 500-ml premixed vials (50 mcg/ml) as follows: Withdraw and discard 100 ml from a 500-ml bag of sterile saline solution or D_5W and replace this volume with 100 ml of tirofiban injection (from two 50-ml vials or four 25-ml vials) or withdraw 50 ml from a 250-ml bag of sterile saline solution or D_5W and replace this volume with 50 ml of tirofiban injection, to achieve 50 mcg/ml.
• Inspect solution for particulate matter before administration, and check for leaks by squeezing the inner bag firmly. If particles are visible or if leaks occur, discard solution.
• Discard unused solution 24 hours after the start of infusion.
• Heparin and tirofiban can be given through same I.V. catheter.
• Minimize injection and avoid noncompressible I.V. sites.
• The most common adverse effect is bleeding at the arterial access site for cardiac catheterization.

ALERT: In patients with renal insufficiency (creatinine clearance below 30 ml/minute), give a loading dose of 0.2 mcg/kg/minute for 30 minutes; then continuous infusion of 0.05 mcg/kg/minute. Continue infusion through angiography and for 12 to 24 hours after angioplasty or atherectomy.

• Store drug at room temperature, and protect from light.

ALERT: Do not confuse Aggrastat (tirofiban) with Argatroban (argatroban).

Patient teaching

• Explain that drug is a blood thinner used to prevent chest pain and heart attack.
• Explain that risk of serious bleeding is far outweighed by the benefits of drug.
• Instruct patient to report chest discomfort or other adverse events immediately.
• Inform patient that frequent blood sampling may be needed to evaluate therapy.

Evaluation

• Patient maintains adequate cardiopulmonary tissue perfusion.
• Patient doesn't experience life-threatening bleeding episode.
• Patient and family state understanding of drug therapy.

tobramycin sulfate

(toh-breh-MIGH-sin SUL-fayt)
Nebcin

Pharmacologic class: aminoglycoside
Therapeutic class: antibiotic
Pregnancy risk category: D

Indications and dosages

▶ **Serious infections caused by sensitive strains of *Citrobacter, Enterobacter, Escherichia coli, Klebsiella, Proteus, Providencia, Pseudomonas, Serratia,* and *Staphylococcus aureus.*** *Adults and children with normal renal function:* 3 mg/kg I.M. or I.V. daily divided q 8 hours. Up to 5 mg/kg daily divided q 6 to 8 hours for life-threatening infections.
Neonates younger than age 1 week or premature infants: Up to 4 mg/kg I.V. or I.M. daily in two equal doses q 12 hours.

Contraindications and precautions

• Contraindicated in patients hypersensitive to aminoglycosides.
• Use cautiously in patients with impaired kidney function or neuromuscular disorders.

Lifespan: For pregnant or breast-feeding women, drug isn't recommended. In geriatric patients, use cautiously.

Adverse reactions

CNS: headache, lethargy, confusion, disorientation.
EENT: *ototoxicity.*
GI: nausea, vomiting, diarrhea.
GU: ***nephrotoxicity.***
Hematologic: anemia, eosinophilia, ***leukopenia, thrombocytopenia, agranulocytosis.***

Other: hypersensitivity reactions *(anaphylaxis).*

Interactions

Drug-drug. *Acyclovir, amphotericin B, cisplatin, methoxyflurane, other aminoglycosides, vancomycin:* Increases nephrotoxicity. Use together cautiously.
Cephalothin: Increases nephrotoxicity. Use together cautiously.
Dimenhydrinate: May mask symptoms of ototoxicity. Use cautiously.
General anesthetics, neuromuscular blockers: May potentiate neuromuscular blockade. Monitor patient closely.
I.V. loop diuretics (such as furosemide): Increases ototoxicity. Use together cautiously.
Parenteral penicillins (such as ticarcillin): Tobramycin inactivation in vitro. Don't mix.

Effects on lab test results

- May increase BUN, creatinine, and nonprotein nitrogen and nitrogenous compound levels. May decrease calcium, magnesium, and potassium levels.
- May increase eosinophil count. May decrease hemoglobin, hematocrit, and WBC, platelet, and granulocyte counts.

Pharmacokinetics

Absorption: Unknown.
Distribution: Wide, although CSF penetration is low, even in patients with inflamed meninges. Protein-binding is minimal.
Metabolism: Not metabolized.
Excretion: Excreted primarily in urine; small amount may be excreted in bile. *Half-life:* 2 to 3 hours.

Route	Onset	Peak	Duration
I.V.	Immediate	Immediate	8 hr
I.M.	Unknown	30-90 min	8 hr

Pharmacodynamics

Chemical effect: Inhibits protein synthesis by binding directly to 30S ribosomal subunit. Drug is generally bactericidal.
Therapeutic effect: Kills susceptible bacteria, including many aerobic gram-negative organisms (such as most strains of *Pseudomonas aeruginosa)* and some aerobic gram-positive organisms.

Available forms

Injection: 40 mg/ml, 10 mg/ml (pediatric)
Powder for injection: 30 mg/ml after reconstitution
Premixed parenteral injection for I.V. infusion: 60 mg or 80 mg in normal saline solution

NURSING PROCESS

Assessment

- Assess patient's infection before therapy and regularly thereafter.
- Obtain specimen for culture and sensitivity tests before giving first dose. Therapy may begin pending results.
- Draw blood for peak tobramycin level 1 hour after I.M. injection and 30 minutes to 1 hour after infusion ends; draw blood for trough level just before next dose. Don't collect blood in heparinized tube because heparin is incompatible with drug.
- Weigh patient and review baseline kidney function studies before therapy.
- Evaluate patient's hearing before and during therapy. Report tinnitus, vertigo, or hearing loss.

ALERT: Peak levels higher than 12 mcg/ml and trough levels higher than 2 mcg/ml may be linked to increased risk of toxicity.

- Monitor kidney function (output, specific gravity, urinalysis, BUN and creatinine levels, and creatinine clearance).
- Be alert for adverse reactions and drug interactions.
- Evaluate patient's and family's knowledge of drug therapy.

Nursing diagnoses

- Risk for infection related to susceptible bacteria
- Risk for injury related to potential for drug-induced nephrotoxicity
- Deficient knowledge related to drug therapy

Planning and implementation

- **I.V. use:** Dilute in 50 to 100 ml of normal saline solution or D_5W for adults and in less volume for children. Infuse over 20 to 60 minutes. After I.V. infusion, flush line with normal saline solution or D_5W.
- **I.M. use:** Follow normal protocol.
- Notify prescriber of signs of decreasing kidney function.

• Patient should be well hydrated while taking drug to minimize chemical irritation of renal tubules.
• If no response occurs in 3 to 5 days, therapy may be stopped and new specimens obtained for culture and sensitivity testing.
ALERT: Don't confuse tobramycin with Trobicin.

Patient teaching
• Emphasize need to drink 2,000 ml of fluid each day.
• Instruct patient to report adverse reactions.

Evaluation
• Patient is free from infection.
• Patient maintains normal kidney function.
• Patient and family state understanding of drug therapy.

tocainide hydrochloride
(TOH-kay-nighd high-droh-KLOR-ighd)
Tonocard

Pharmacologic class: local anesthetic
Therapeutic class: ventricular antiarrhythmic
Pregnancy risk category: C

Indications and dosages
▶ **Suppression of symptomatic life-threatening ventricular arrhythmias, such as sustained ventricular tachycardia.** *Adults:* Initially, 400 mg P.O. q 8 hours. Usual dosage is between 1,200 and 1,800 mg daily in three divided doses.
▶ **Myotonic dystrophy‡.** *Adults:* 800 to 1,200 mg P.O. daily.

Contraindications and precautions
• Contraindicated in patients hypersensitive to lidocaine or other amide-type local anesthetics and those with second- or third-degree AV block in absence of artificial pacemaker.
• Use cautiously in patients with heart failure or diminished cardiac reserve and those with hepatic or renal impairment. These patients often may be treated effectively with lower dose.
Lifespan: In breast-feeding women and in children, safety of drug hasn't been established. In geriatric patients, dizziness and falling are more likely to occur.

Adverse reactions
CNS: *light-headedness, tremor,* restlessness, paresthesia, confusion, *dizziness, vertigo,* drowsiness, fatigue, confusion, headache.
CV: hypotension, ***new or worsened arrhythmias, heart failure, bradycardia,*** palpitations.
EENT: blurred vision, tinnitus.
GI: *nausea,* vomiting, diarrhea, anorexia.
Hematologic: ***blood dyscrasia.***
Hepatic: ***hepatitis.***
Respiratory: ***respiratory arrest, pulmonary fibrosis,*** pneumonitis, ***pulmonary edema.***
Skin: rash, diaphoresis.

Interactions
Drug-drug. *Beta blockers:* Decreases myocardial contractility; increases CNS toxicity. Avoid using together.
Cimetidine: May decrease peak tocainide level. Monitor cardiac rhythm closely.
Disopyramide, lidocaine, mexiletine, phenytoin, procainamide, quinidine: May have additive pharmacologic effect and CNS toxicity. Monitor patient closely.
Rifampin: Increases clearance of tocainide. Monitor efficacy of tocainide.

Effects on lab test results
• May increase liver function test values. May decrease hemoglobin, hematocrit, and platelet and granulocyte counts.

Pharmacokinetics
Absorption: Rapid and complete.
Distribution: Not clearly defined, although drug appears to be widely distributed and apparently crosses blood-brain barrier. Only about 10% to 20% bound to plasma protein.
Metabolism: Metabolized, apparently in liver, to inactive metabolites.
Excretion: Excreted in urine. *Half-life:* About 11 to 23 hours.

Route	Onset	Peak	Duration
P.O.	Unknown	30 min-2 hr	8 hr

Pharmacodynamics
Chemical effect: Class Ib antiarrhythmic that blocks fast sodium channel in cardiac tissues, especially Purkinje network, without involvement of autonomic nervous system. It reduces rate of rise and amplitude of action potential and decreases automaticity in Purkinje fibers.

It shortens duration of action potential and, to lesser extent, decreases effective refractory period in Purkinje fibers.
Therapeutic effect: Restores normal sinus rhythm.

Available forms

Tablets: 400 mg, 600 mg

NURSING PROCESS

Assessment

- Assess patient's condition before therapy and regularly thereafter.
- Monitor therapeutic blood level. Therapeutic level ranges from 4 to 10 mcg/ml. Report any abnormalities.

ALERT: Monitor patient for tremors, which may indicate that maximum dosage has been reached.

- Monitor patient during transition from lidocaine to tocainide.
- Be alert for adverse reactions and drug interactions.
- Evaluate patient's and family's knowledge of drug therapy.

Nursing diagnoses

- Decreased cardiac output related to presence of cardiac arrhythmia
- Risk for injury related to drug-induced adverse reactions
- Deficient knowledge related to drug therapy

Planning and implementation

- Cardiologists commonly call drug "oral lidocaine." It may ease transition from I.V. lidocaine to oral antiarrhythmic therapy.

Patient teaching

- Instruct patient to take drug with food.
- Tell patient to report unusual bruising or bleeding or signs of infection. Agranulocytosis and bone marrow suppression have been reported in patients taking usual doses of drug. Most cases have been reported within first 12 weeks of therapy.
- Tell patient to report sudden onset of pulmonary symptoms, such as coughing, wheezing, and exertional dyspnea. Drug has been linked to serious pulmonary toxicity.

Evaluation

- Patient exhibits normal cardiac output with abolishment of arrhythmia.
- Patient doesn't experience injury from adverse reactions.
- Patient and family state understanding of drug therapy.

tolcapone

(TOHL-cah-pohn)
Tasmar

Pharmacologic class: catechol-O-methyltransferase (COMT) inhibitor
Therapeutic class: antiparkinsonian
Pregnancy risk category: C

Indications and dosages

▶ **Adjunct to levodopa and carbidopa for treatment of signs and symptoms of idiopathic Parkinson's disease.** *Adults:* Initially, 100 mg P.O. t.i.d. (with levodopa-carbidopa). Recommended daily dose is 100 mg P.O. t.i.d. although 200 mg P.O. t.i.d. may be given if the anticipated clinical benefit is justified. If starting treatment with 200 mg t.i.d. and dyskinesia occurs, reduce dosage of levodopa. Maximum daily dose is 600 mg.

Contraindications and precautions

- Contraindicated in patients hypersensitive to drug or its components and patients with liver disease or elevated ALT or AST values. Also contraindicated in patients withdrawn from tolcapone because of evidence of drug-induced hepatocellular injury and patients with history of nontraumatic rhabdomyolysis, hyperpyrexia, and confusion possibly related to drug.
- Use cautiously in patients with severe renal impairment.

Lifespan: In pregnant patients, use only if potential benefits outweigh risks. In breast-feeding women, use cautiously.

Adverse reactions

CNS: *dyskinesia, sleep disorder, dystonia, excessive dreaming, somnolence,* dizziness, *confusion, headache, hallucinations,* hyperkinesia, hypertonia, fatigue, falling, syncope, balance loss, depression, tremor, speech disorder,

paresthesia, agitation, irritability, mental deficiency, hyperactivity, hypokinesia, fever.
CV: *orthostatic complaints,* chest pain, chest discomfort, palpitations, hypotension.
EENT: pharyngitis, tinnitus, sinus congestion.
GI: *nausea, anorexia, diarrhea,* flatulence, *vomiting,* constipation, abdominal pain, dyspepsia, dry mouth.
GU: urinary tract infection, urine discoloration, hematuria, micturition disorder, urinary incontinence, impotence.
Hematologic: ***bleeding.***
Musculoskeletal: *muscle cramps,* stiffness, arthritis, neck pain.
Respiratory: bronchitis, dyspnea, upper respiratory tract infection.
Skin: increased sweating, rash.
Other: burning, influenza.

Interactions

Drug-drug. *CNS depressants:* Enhances sedative effects. Use cautiously.
Desipramine: Increases risk of adverse effects. Use cautiously.
Nonselective MAO inhibitors (phenelzine, tranylcypromine): Possible hypertensive crisis. Don't use together.

Effects on lab test results

- May increase liver function test values.

Pharmacokinetics

Absorption: Rapid. Absolute bioavailability is 65%.
Distribution: Not widely distributed into tissues; over 99.9% is bound to plasma proteins.
Metabolism: Almost complete, mainly by glucuronidation.
Excretion: 60% excreted in urine and 40% in feces. *Half-life:* 2 to 3 hours.

Route	Onset	Peak	Duration
P.O.	Unknown	2 hr	Unknown

Pharmacodynamics

Chemical effect: Exact mechanism unknown. Thought to reversibly inhibit human erythrocyte catechol-O-methyltransferase when given with levodopa-carbidopa, resulting in a decrease in levodopa clearance and a twofold increase in levodopa bioavailability. Decreased clearance of levodopa prolongs elimination half-life of levodopa from 2 to 3.5 hours.

Therapeutic effect: Improves physical mobility in patients with parkinsonism.

Available forms

Tablets: 100 mg, 200 mg

NURSING PROCESS

Assessment

- Assess patient's history of Parkinson's disease, and reassess during therapy.
- Monitor liver enzyme levels before therapy, then every 2 weeks during first 3½ years of therapy, then every 8 weeks thereafter because of risk of liver toxicity. Stop drug if results are elevated or if patient appears jaundiced. Assess patient's risk for physical injury because of drug's CNS adverse effects.
- Monitor patient for orthostatic hypotension and syncope.
- Evaluate patient's and family's knowledge of drug therapy.

Nursing diagnoses

- Impaired physical mobility related to underlying Parkinson's disease
- Disturbed thought processes related to drug-induced CNS adverse reactions
- Deficient knowledge related to drug therapy

Planning and implementation

ALERT: Patient should provide written informed consent before drug is used. Give drug only to patients receiving levodopa and carbidopa who don't respond to or who aren't appropriate candidates for other adjunctive therapies because of risk of liver toxicity.
- Give first dose of day with first daily dose of levodopa-carbidopa.
- Patients with severe renal dysfunction may need a reduced dose.
- Withhold drug and notify prescriber if hepatic transaminases are elevated or if patient appears jaundiced.
- Because of risk of liver toxicity, stop treatment if patient shows no benefit within 3 weeks.
- Because of highly protein-bound nature of tolcapone, dialysis does not significantly remove drug.
- Notify prescriber if severe diarrhea occurs that is linked to drug therapy.

Patient teaching

- Advise patient to take drug exactly as prescribed.
- Teach patient signs of liver injury (jaundice, fatigue, loss of appetite, persistent nausea, pruritus, dark urine or right upper quadrant tenderness) and instruct him to report them immediately.
- Warn patient about risk of orthostatic hypotension; tell him to use caution when rising from a seated or recumbent position.
- Caution patient to avoid hazardous activities until CNS effects of drug are known.
- Tell patient that nausea may occur at the start of therapy.
- Inform patient about risk of increased dyskinesia or dystonia.
- Tell patient to report planned, suspected, or known pregnancy during therapy.
- Instruct patient to report to prescriber adverse effects, including diarrhea and hallucinations.
- Inform patient that drug may be taken without regard to meals.

✓ Evaluation

- Patient exhibits improved mobility with reduction of muscular rigidity and tremor.
- Patient remains mentally alert.
- Patient and family state understanding of drug therapy.

tolterodine tartrate

(tohl-TER-oh-deen TAR-trate)

Detrol, Detrol LA

Pharmacologic class: muscarinic receptor antagonist
Therapeutic class: anticholinergic
Pregnancy risk category: C

Indications and dosages

▶ **Overactive bladder in patients with symptoms of urinary frequency, urgency, or urge incontinence.** *Adults:* 2 mg P.O. b.i.d. Dose may be lowered to 1 mg P.O. b.i.d. based on patient response and tolerance. Or, 4 mg of extended-release capsule P.O. daily; may be decreased to 2 mg P.O. daily.

Adults with significantly reduced hepatic function , adults taking drug that inhibits cytochrome P450 3A4 isoenzyme system: 1 mg P.O. b.i.d. or 2 mg P.O. daily of extended-release capsules.

Contraindications and precautions

- Contraindicated in patients hypersensitive to drug or its components and those with uncontrolled angle-closure glaucoma or urine or gastric retention.
- Use with caution in patients with significant bladder outflow obstruction, GI obstructive disorders (such as pyloric stenosis), controlled angle-closure glaucoma, and hepatic or renal impairment.

Lifespan: In nursing mothers, discontinue drug or breast-feeding. In children, safety and effectiveness have not been established.

Adverse reactions

CNS: fatigue, paresthesia, vertigo, dizziness, *headache,* nervousness, somnolence.
CV: hypertension, chest pain.
EENT: abnormal vision, xerophthalmia, pharyngitis, rhinitis, sinusitis.
GI: *dry mouth,* abdominal pain, constipation, diarrhea, dyspepsia, flatulence, nausea, vomiting.
GU: dysuria, micturition frequency, urine retention, urinary tract infection.
Metabolic: weight gain.
Musculoskeletal: arthralgia, back pain.
Respiratory: bronchitis, cough, upper respiratory tract infection.
Skin: pruritus, rash, erythema, dry skin.
Other: flulike syndrome, falls, fungal infection, infection.

Interactions

Drug-drug. *Antifungals (itraconazole, ketoconazole, miconazole), cytochrome P-450 3A4 inhibitors (such as macrolide antibiotics clarithromycin and erythromycin), cyclosporin, vincristine:* Effects haven't been studied. However, tolterodine doses above 1 mg b.i.d. (2 mg daily of extended-release capsules) shouldn't be given together with these drugs.
Fluoxetine: Increases tolterodine levels. Avoid using together.

Effects on lab test results

None reported.

Pharmacokinetics

Absorption: Well absorbed with about 77% bioavailability. Peak level occurs within 1 to 2 hours after administration. Food increases bioavailability by 53%.
Distribution: Volume of distribution is about 113 L, 96% protein-bound.
Metabolism: Metabolized by the liver primarily by oxidation by the cytochrome P-450 2D6 pathway and leads to the formation of a pharmacologically active 5-hydroxymethyl metabolite.
Excretion: Mostly recovered in urine; the rest in feces. Less than 1% of dose is recovered as unchanged drug, and 5% to 14% is recovered as the active metabolite. *Half-life:* 1¾ to 3½ hours.

Route	Onset	Peak	Duration
P.O.	Unknown	1-2 hr	Unknown

Pharmacodynamics

Chemical effect: A competitive muscarinic receptor antagonist. Both urinary bladder contraction and salivation are mediated via cholinergic muscarinic receptors.
Therapeutic effect: Relieves symptoms of overactive bladder.

Available forms

Tablets: 1 mg, 2 mg
Capsules (extended-release): 2 mg, 4 mg

NURSING PROCESS

Assessment

- Assess baseline bladder function and monitor therapeutic effects.
- Be alert for adverse reactions and drug interactions.
- Evaluate patient's and family's knowledge about drug therapy.

Nursing diagnoses

- Impaired urinary elimination related to underlying medical condition
- Urine retention related to drug-induced adverse effects
- Deficient knowledge related to drug therapy

Planning and implementation

- Food increases the absorption of tolterodine, but no dosage adjustment is needed.
- In the case of urine retention, notify prescriber and prepare for urinary catheterization.
- Dry mouth is the most frequently reported adverse reaction.

Patient teaching

- Tell patient that sugarless gum, hard candy, or saliva substitute may help relieve dry mouth.
- Advise patient to avoid driving or other potentially hazardous activities until visual effects of drug are known.
- Instruct patient to immediately report signs of infection, urine retention, or GI problems.

Evaluation

- Patient experiences improved bladder function with drug therapy.
- Patient doesn't experience urine retention.
- Patient and family state understanding of drug therapy.

topiramate

(toh-PEER-uh-mayt)
Topamax

Pharmacologic class: sulfamate-substituted monosaccharide
Therapeutic class: antiepileptic
Pregnancy risk category: C

Indications and dosages

▶ **Partial onset seizures, primary generalized tonic-clonic seizures.** *Adults:* 400 mg P.O. daily in two divided doses. Initiate therapy at 25 to 50 mg daily followed by adjustment to an effective dose in increments of 25 to 50 mg/week.

▶ **Adjunctive therapy for partial seizures, primary generalized tonic-clonic seizures, or Lennox-Gastaut syndrome.** *Children ages 2 to 16:* 5 to 9 mg/kg P.O. daily in two divided doses. Dosage adjustment should begin at 1 to 3 mg/kg nightly for 1 week. Then increase at 1- to 2-week intervals by 1 to 3 mg/kg daily to achieve optimal clinical response. Dosage adjustment should be guided by clinical outcome.

Contraindications and precautions

- Contraindicated in patients hypersensitive to drug or its components.

• Use cautiously in patients with hepatic impairment.
Lifespan: In pregnant or breast-feeding women, use cautiously.

Adverse reactions

CNS: fever, *fatigue,* abnormal coordination, aggression, agitation, apathy, asthenia, *ataxia, confusion,* depression, depersonalization, *dizziness,* emotional lability, euphoria, ***generalized tonic-clonic seizures,*** hallucinations, hyperkinesia, hypertonia, hypesthesia, hypokinesia, insomnia, *nervousness, nystagmus, paresthesia,* personality disorder, *psychomotor slowing,* psychosis, *somnolence, speech disorders,* stupor, ***suicide attempts,*** *tremor,* vertigo, malaise, mood problems, difficulty with concentration, attention, language, or *memory.*
CV: chest pain, palpitations, edema, hot flushes.
EENT: *abnormal vision,* conjunctivitis, *diplopia,* eye pain, hearing problems, pharyngitis, sinusitis, tinnitus.
GI: taste perversion, abdominal pain, anorexia, constipation, diarrhea, dry mouth, dyspepsia, flatulence, gastroenteritis, gingivitis, *nausea,* vomiting.
GU: amenorrhea, dysuria, dysmenorrhea, hematuria, impotence, intermenstrual bleeding, menstrual disorder, menorrhagia, micturition frequency, renal calculi, urinary incontinence, urinary tract infection, vaginitis, leukorrhea.
Hematologic: anemia, epistaxis, ***leukopenia.***
Metabolic: weight changes.
Musculoskeletal: arthralgia, back or leg pain, muscular weakness, myalgia, rigors.
Respiratory: bronchitis, cough, dyspnea, *upper respiratory tract infection.*
Skin: acne, alopecia, increased sweating, pruritus, rash.
Other: body odor, flulike syndrome, breast pain, decreased libido.

Interactions

Drug-drug. *Carbamazepine:* Decreases topiramate levels. Monitor patient.
Carbonic anhydrase inhibitors (acetazolamide, dichlorphenamide): Increases risk of renal calculus formation. Avoid using together.
CNS depressants: Possible topiramate-induced CNS depression, as well as other adverse cognitive and neuropsychiatric events. Use cautiously.
Oral contraceptives: Decreases efficacy. Report changes in bleeding patterns; urge patient to use other nonhormonal but effective contraceptives.
Phenytoin: Decreases topiramate levels and increases phenytoin levels. Monitor levels.
Valproic acid: Decreases valproic acid and topiramate levels. Monitor patient.
Drug-lifestyle. *Alcohol use:* Possible topiramate-induced CNS depression, as well as other adverse cognitive and neuropsychiatric events. Discourage using together.

Effects on lab test results

• May increase liver enzyme levels.
• May decrease hemoglobin, hematocrit, and WBC count.

Pharmacokinetics

Absorption: Rapid.
Distribution: Up to 17% bound to plasma proteins.
Metabolism: Not extensively metabolized.
Excretion: Primarily eliminated unchanged in urine. *Half-life:* 21 hours.

Route	Onset	Peak	Duration
P.O.	Unknown	2 hr	Unknown

Pharmacodynamics

Chemical effect: Precise mechanism of action unknown. Thought to block action potential, suggestive of a sodium channel blocking action. Drug may also potentiate activity of GABA and antagonize ability of kainate to activate the kainate/alpha-amino-3-hydroxy-5-methylisoxazole-4-proprionic acid subtype of excitatory amino acid (glutamate) receptor. Drug also has weak carbonic anhydrase inhibitor activity, which is unrelated to its antiepileptic properties.
Therapeutic effect: Prevents partial-onset seizures.

Available forms

Capsules: 15 mg, 25 mg
Tablets: 25 mg, 100 mg, 200 mg

NURSING PROCESS

Assessment

• Assess patient's seizure disorder before therapy and regularly thereafter.

• Carefully monitor patient taking topiramate in conjunction with other antiepileptic drugs; dosage adjustments may be needed to achieve optimal response.
• Assess patient's compliance with therapy at each follow-up visit.
• Evaluate patient's and family's knowledge of drug therapy.

Nursing diagnoses
• Risk for injury related to seizure disorder
• Acute pain related to increased risk of renal calculi formation
• Deficient knowledge related to drug therapy

Planning and implementation
• Renal insufficiency requires a reduced dose. For hemodialysis patients, supplemental doses may be needed to avoid rapid drops in drug levels during prolonged dialysis treatment.
• Dosage must be adjusted according to patient's response.
• Initiate safety precautions as indicated.
ALERT: Discontinue the drug if an ocular adverse event occurs, characterized by acute myopia and secondary angle-closure glaucoma.
ALERT: Don't confuse Topamax with Toprol XL.

Patient teaching
• Tell patient to maintain adequate fluid intake during therapy to minimize risk of forming renal calculi.
• Advise patient not to drive or operate hazardous machinery until CNS effects of drug are known.
• Tell patient that drug may decrease effectiveness of oral contraceptives and to use a barrier form of birth control.
• Tell patient to avoid crushing or breaking tablets because of bitter taste.
• Tell patient that drug can be taken without regard to food.
• Tell patient to notify prescriber immediately if he experiences changes in vision.

Evaluation
• Patient is free from seizure activity.
• Patient maintains adequate hydration to prevent renal calculus formation.
• Patient and family state understanding of drug therapy.

topotecan hydrochloride
(toh-poh-TEE-ken high-droh-KLOR-ighd)
Hycamtin

Pharmacologic class: antitumor agent
Therapeutic class: antineoplastic
Pregnancy risk category: D

Indications and dosages
▶ **Metastatic carcinoma of ovary after failure of initial or subsequent chemotherapy; treatment of small cell lung cancer sensitive disease after failure of first-line chemotherapy.** *Adults:* 1.5 mg/m^2 by I.V. infusion over 30 minutes, daily for 5 consecutive days, starting on day 1 of a 21-day cycle, for minimum of four cycles.
Patients with renal impairment: If creatinine clearance is 20 to 39 ml/minute, decrease dosage to 0.75 mg/m^2.

If severe neutropenia occurs, reduce dose by 0.25 mg/m^2 for subsequent courses. Or, in severe neutropenia, give granulocyte-colony stimulating factor (GSF) after subsequent course (before resorting to dose reduction) starting from day 6 of the course (24 hours after topotecan administration).

Contraindications and precautions
• Contraindicated in patients hypersensitive to drug or its components and in patients with severe bone marrow depression.
Lifespan: In pregnant or breast-feeding women, drug is contraindicated.

Adverse reactions
CNS: *fever, fatigue, asthenia, headache,* paresthesia.
GI: *nausea, vomiting, diarrhea, constipation, abdominal pain, stomatitis, anorexia.*
Hematologic: NEUTROPENIA, LEUKOPENIA, THROMBOCYTOPENIA, *anemia.*
Respiratory: *dyspnea.*
Skin: *alopecia.*
Other: ***sepsis.***

Interactions
Drug-drug. *Cisplatin:* Increases severity of myelosuppression. Use both drugs very cautiously.

GSF: Prolongs duration of neutropenia. Don't give GSF until day 6 of regimen, 24 hours after completion of topotecan treatment.

Effects on lab test results

- May increase ALT, AST, and bilirubin levels.
- May decrease hemoglobin, hematocrit, and WBC, platelet, and neutrophil counts.

Pharmacokinetics

Absorption: Administered I.V.
Distribution: About 35% bound to plasma proteins.
Metabolism: Metabolized by liver.
Excretion: 30% excreted in urine.

Route	Onset	Peak	Duration
I.V.	Unknown	Unknown	Unknown

Pharmacodynamics

Chemical effect: Relieves torsional strain in DNA and prevents relegation of single-strand breaks.
Therapeutic effect: Cytotoxicity is thought to result from double-strand DNA damage produced during DNA synthesis when replication enzymes interact with the complex formed.

Available forms

Injection: 4-mg single-dose vial

NURSING PROCESS

Assessment

ALERT: Patient must have a baseline neutrophil count greater than 1,500 cells/mm³ and platelet count greater than 100,000 cells/mm³ before therapy can start.

- Frequent monitoring of peripheral blood cell count is critical. Don't give repeated doses until neutrophil count is greater than 1,000 cells/mm³, platelet count is greater than 100,000 cells/mm³, and hemoglobin is greater than 9 mg/dl.
- Evaluate patient's and family's understanding of drug therapy.

Nursing diagnoses

- Ineffective health maintenance related to neoplastic disease
- Deficient knowledge related to drug therapy

Planning and implementation

- Prepare drug under a vertical laminar flow hood while wearing gloves and protective clothing. If drug contacts skin, wash immediately and thoroughly with soap and water. If mucous membranes are affected, flush with water.
- Reconstitute drug in each 4-mg vial with 4 ml sterile water for injection. Dilute appropriate volume of reconstituted solution in normal saline solution or D_5W before use. Infuse over 30 minutes.
- Protect unopened vials of drug from light. Reconstituted vials stored at 68° to 77° F (20° to 25° C) and exposed to ambient lighting are stable for 24 hours.

Patient teaching

- Instruct patient to report promptly sore throat, fever, chills, or unusual bleeding or bruising.
- Advise woman of childbearing age to avoid pregnancy and breast-feeding during treatment.
- Tell patient and family about need for close monitoring of blood counts.

Evaluation

- Patient shows positive response to drug.
- Patient and family state understanding of drug therapy.

torsemide

(TOR-seh-mighd)
Demadex

Pharmacologic class: loop diuretic
Therapeutic class: diuretic, antihypertensive
Pregnancy risk category: B

Indications and dosages

▶ **Diuresis in patients with heart failure.** *Adults:* Initially, 10 to 20 mg P.O. or I.V. once daily. If response is inadequate, dose is doubled until response is obtained. Maximum dose is 200 mg daily.

▶ **Diuresis in patients with chronic renal impairment.** *Adults:* Initially, 20 mg P.O. or I.V. once daily. If response is inadequate, dose is doubled until response is obtained. Maximum dose is 200 mg daily.

▶ **Diuresis in patients with hepatic cirrhosis.** *Adults:* Initially, 5 to 10 mg P.O. or I.V. once daily with aldosterone antagonist or potassium-sparing diuretic. If response is inadequate, dose is doubled until response is obtained. Maximum dose is 40 mg daily.
▶ **Hypertension.** *Adults:* Initially, 5 mg P.O. daily. Increase to 10 mg in 4 to 6 weeks if needed and tolerated. If response is still inadequate, another antihypertensive drug should be added.

Contraindications and precautions

- Contraindicated in patients hypersensitive to drug or other sulfonylurea derivatives and in those with anuria.
- Use cautiously in patients with hepatic disease, cirrhosis, and ascites; sudden changes in fluid and electrolyte balance may precipitate hepatic coma in these patients.

Lifespan: In pregnant or breast-feeding women, use cautiously. In children, safety of drug hasn't been established. In geriatric patients, use cautiously.

Adverse reactions

CNS: asthenia, dizziness, headache, nervousness, insomnia, syncope.
CV: ECG abnormalities, chest pain, edema, ***dehydration,*** orthostatic hypertension.
EENT: rhinitis, sore throat.
GI: *excessive thirst,* diarrhea, constipation, nausea, dyspepsia, **HEMORRHAGE.**
GU: *excessive urination,* impotence.
Metabolic: electrolyte imbalances, including *hypokalemia, hypomagnesemia,* hypocalcemia, hyperuricemia, gout, hyperglycemia; hypochloremic alkalosis.
Musculoskeletal: arthralgia, myalgia.
Respiratory: cough.

Interactions

Drug-drug. *Cholestyramine:* Decreases absorption of torsemide. Separate administration times by at least 3 hours.
Digoxin: Decreases torsemide clearance. Dosage adjustments not needed.
Indomethacin: Decreases diuretic effectiveness in sodium-restricted patients. Avoid using together.
Lithium, ototoxic drugs (such as aminoglycosides, ethacrynic acid): Possible increased toxicity of these drugs. Avoid using together.
NSAIDs: May potentiate nephrotoxicity of NSAIDs. Use together cautiously.
Probenecid: Decreases diuretic effectiveness. Avoid using together.
Salicylates: Decreases excretion, possibly leading to salicylate toxicity. Avoid using together.
Spironolactone: Decreases renal clearance of spironolactone. Dosage adjustments not needed.
Drug-herb. *Licorice:* Potential for rapid potassium loss. Discourage using together.

Effects on lab test results

- May increase glucose, BUN, creatinine, cholesterol, and uric acid levels. May decrease calcium, potassium, and magnesium levels.

Pharmacokinetics

Absorption: Some.
Distribution: Extensively bound to plasma protein.
Metabolism: Little first-pass metabolism.
Excretion: 22% to 34% excreted unchanged in urine.

Route	Onset	Peak	Duration
P.O.	1 hr	1-2 hr	6-8 hr
I.V.	≤ 10 min	≤ 1 hr	6-8 hr

Pharmacodynamics

Chemical effect: Enhances excretion of sodium, chloride, and water by acting on ascending portion of loop of Henle.
Therapeutic effect: Promotes water and sodium excretion and lowers blood pressure.

Available forms

Injection: 10 mg/ml
Tablets: 5 mg, 10 mg, 20 mg, 100 mg

NURSING PROCESS

Assessment

- Assess patient's condition before therapy and regularly thereafter.
- Monitor geriatric patients, who are especially susceptible to excessive diuresis, with potential for circulatory collapse and thromboembolic complications.
- Monitor fluid intake and output, electrolyte levels, blood pressure, weight, and pulse rate during rapid diuresis and routinely with long-

term use. Drug can cause profound diuresis and water and electrolyte depletion.
- Watch for signs of hypokalemia, such as muscle weakness and cramps.
- Be alert for adverse reactions and drug interactions.
- Evaluate patient's and family's knowledge of drug therapy.

Nursing diagnoses
- Excess fluid volume related to presence of edema
- Risk for injury related to presence of hypertension
- Deficient knowledge related to drug therapy

Planning and implementation
- **P.O. use:** Give drug in morning to prevent nocturia.
- **I.V. use:** Switch to oral form as soon as possible.

– Drug may be given by direct injection over at least 2 minutes. Rapid injection may cause ototoxicity. Don't give more than 200 mg at a time.
- Consult prescriber and dietitian to provide high-potassium diet. Foods rich in potassium include citrus fruits, tomatoes, bananas, dates, and apricots.

ALERT: Don't confuse torsemide with furosemide.

Patient teaching
- Tell patient to take drug in morning to prevent sleep interruption.
- Advise patient to change position slowly to prevent dizziness and to limit alcohol intake and strenuous exercise in hot weather to prevent orthostatic hypotension.
- Advise patient to immediately report ringing in ears because it may indicate toxicity.
- Tell patient to check with prescriber or pharmacist before taking OTC drugs.

Evaluation
- Patient shows no signs of edema.
- Patient's blood pressure is normal.
- Patient and family state understanding of drug therapy.

trace elements
(trays EL-uh-ments)

chromium (chromic chloride)
(KROH-mee-um)
Chroma-Pak, Chromic Chloride

copper (cupric sulfate)
(KAH-per)
Cupric Sulfate

iodine (sodium iodide)
(IGH-oh-dighn)
Iodopen

manganese (manganese chloride, manganese sulfate)
(MAN-geh-nees)

selenium (selenious acid)
(seh-LEHN-ee-um)
Sele-Pak, Selepen

zinc (zinc chloride, zinc sulfate)
(zink)
Zinca-Pak

Pharmacologic class: trace elements
Therapeutic class: nutritional agents
Pregnancy risk category: C

Indications and dosages
▶ **Prevention of individual trace element deficiencies in patients receiving long-term total parenteral nutrition (TPN).**
chromium. *Adults:* 10 to 15 mcg I.V. daily. *Children:* 0.14 to 0.20 mcg/kg I.V. daily.
copper. *Adults:* 0.5 to 1.5 mg I.V. daily. *Children:* 20 mcg/kg I.V. daily.
iodine. *Adults:* 1 to 2 mcg/kg I.V. daily. *Children:* 2 to 3 mcg/kg I.V. daily.
manganese. *Adults:* 0.15 to 0.8 mg I.V. daily. *Children:* 2 to 10 mcg/kg I.V. daily.
selenium. *Adults:* 20 to 40 mcg I.V. daily. *Children:* 3 mcg/kg I.V. daily.
zinc. *Adults:* 2.5 to 4 mg I.V. daily. *Children ages 5 and younger:* 100 mcg/kg I.V. daily. *Neonates:* 300 mcg/kg/I.V. daily.

Contraindications and precautions

• No known contraindications.
Lifespan: In pregnant women, use cautiously.

Adverse reactions

GI: nausea, vomiting.

Interactions

None significant.

Effects on lab test results

None reported.

Pharmacokinetics

Absorption: Administered I.V.
Distribution: Unknown.
Metabolism: Unknown.
Excretion: Unknown.

Route	Onset	Peak	Duration
I.V.	Immediate	Immediate	Unknown

Pharmacodynamics

Chemical effect: Participates in synthesis and stabilization of proteins and nucleic acids in subcellular and membrane transport systems.
Therapeutic effect: Restores normal body levels of trace elements.

Available forms

chromium
Injection: 4 mcg/ml, 20 mcg/ml
copper
Injection: 0.4 mg/ml, 2 mg/ml
iodine
Injection: 100 mcg/ml
manganese
Injection: 0.1 mg/ml
selenium
Injection: 40 mcg/ml
zinc
Injection: 1 mg/ml, 5 mg/ml

NURSING PROCESS

Assessment

• Obtain history of patient's underlying trace element deficiency before therapy and reassess regularly thereafter. Normal serum levels are 0.85 ng/ml chromium; 0.07 to 0.15 mg/ml copper; 4 to 20 mcg/dl manganese; 0.1 to 0.19 mcg/ml selenium; and 0.05 to 0.15 mg/dl zinc.
• Check levels of trace elements in patients who have received TPN for 2 months or longer. Call prescriber's attention to low serum levels of these elements because supplement may be needed.
• Evaluate patient's and family's knowledge of drug therapy.

Nursing diagnoses

• Imbalanced nutrition: less than body requirements related to presence of deficiency of trace elements
• Deficient knowledge related to drug therapy

Planning and implementation

• Cautiously infuse diluted solution through patent I.V. line over ordered duration.
ALERT: Don't give undiluted because of potential for phlebitis.
• Solutions of trace elements are compounded by pharmacy for addition to TPN solutions according to various formulas. One common trace element solution is Shils solution, which contains copper 1 mg/ml, iodide 0.06 mg/ml, manganese 0.4 mg/ml, and zinc 2 mg/ml.

Patient teaching
• Inform patient and family of need for trace elements.

Evaluation

• Patient regains normal levels of trace elements.
• Patient and family state understanding of drug therapy.

tramadol hydrochloride

(TRAM-uh-dohl high-droh-KLOR-ighd)
Ultram

Pharmacologic class: synthetic analgesic
Therapeutic class: analgesic
Pregnancy risk category: C

Indications and dosages

▶ **Moderate-to-moderately severe pain.**
Adults: 50 to 100 mg P.O. q 4 to 6 hours, p.r.n. Maximum dose is 400 mg daily. Maximum dose in patients older than 75 is 300 mg.

Contraindications and precautions

- Contraindicated in patients hypersensitive to drug and in those with acute intoxication from alcohol, hypnotics, centrally acting analgesics, opioids, or psychotropic drugs.
- Use cautiously in patients at risk for seizures or respiratory depression; patients with increased intracranial pressure or head injury, acute abdominal conditions, or renal or hepatic impairment; and patients physically dependent on opioids.

Lifespan: In pregnant women and children, safety hasn't been established. In breast-feeding women, drug isn't recommended.

Adverse reactions

CNS: *dizziness, vertigo, headache, somnolence, CNS stimulation, asthenia,* anxiety, confusion, coordination disturbance, malaise, euphoria, nervousness, sleep disorder, ***seizures.***
CV: vasodilation.
EENT: visual disturbances.
GI: *nausea, constipation, vomiting,* dyspepsia, dry mouth, diarrhea, abdominal pain, anorexia, flatulence.
GU: urine retention, urinary frequency, menopausal symptoms.
Musculoskeletal: hypertonia.
Respiratory: ***respiratory depression.***
Skin: *pruritus,* sweating, rash.

Interactions

Drug-drug. *Carbamazepine:* Increases tramadol metabolism. Patients receiving long-term carbamazepine therapy at dosage of up to 800 mg daily may require up to twice recommended dose of tramadol.
CNS depressants: May have additive effects. Use together cautiously. Dosage of tramadol may need to be reduced.
MAO inhibitors, neuroleptics: Increases risk of seizures. Monitor patient closely.
Drug-herb. *5-hydroxytryptophan (5-HTP), SAMe, St John's wort:* Increases serotonin levels. Discourage using together.

Effects on lab test results

- May increase liver enzyme levels.
- May decrease hemoglobin and hematocrit.

Pharmacokinetics

Absorption: Rapid and almost complete.
Distribution: About 20% bound to plasma proteins.
Metabolism: Extensively metabolized.
Excretion: 30% excreted in urine as unchanged drug and 60% as metabolites. *Half-life:* 6 to 7 hours.

Route	Onset	Peak	Duration
P.O.	Unknown	2 hr	Unknown

Pharmacodynamics

Chemical effect: Unknown; centrally acting synthetic analgesic compound not chemically related to opioids that is thought to bind to opioid receptors and inhibit reuptake of norepinephrine and serotonin.
Therapeutic effect: Relieves pain.

Available forms

Tablets: 50 mg

NURSING PROCESS

Assessment

- Assess patient's pain before therapy and regularly thereafter.
- Monitor CV and respiratory status.

ALERT: Closely monitor patient at risk for seizures. Drug has been reported to reduce seizure threshold.

- Monitor patient for drug dependence. Tramadol can produce dependence similar to that of codeine or dextropropoxyphene and thus has potential to be abused.
- Be alert for adverse reactions and drug interactions.
- Evaluate patient's and family's knowledge of drug therapy.

Nursing diagnoses

- Acute pain related to underlying condition
- Risk for constipation related to drug-induced adverse GI reactions
- Deficient knowledge related to drug therapy

Planning and implementation

- For better analgesic effect, drug should be given before onset of intense pain.
- Withhold dose and notify prescriber if respiratory rate decreases or falls below 12 breaths/minute.
- Because constipation is a common adverse effect, anticipate need for laxative therapy.

• Reduce dosage in patients with renal or hepatic impairment.

ALERT: Don't confuse tramadol with trazodone or trandolapril.

Patient teaching

• Instruct patient to take drug only as prescribed and not to increase dosage or dosage interval unless instructed by prescriber.

• Caution ambulatory patient to be careful when getting out of bed and walking. Warn outpatient to refrain from driving and performing other potentially hazardous activities that require mental alertness until drug's CNS effects are known.

• Advise patient to check with prescriber before taking OTC drugs; drug interactions can occur.

Evaluation

• Patient is free from pain.

• Patient regains normal bowel pattern.

• Patient and family state understanding of drug therapy.

trandolapril

(tran-DOH-luh-pril)

Mavik

Pharmacologic class: ACE inhibitor
Therapeutic class: antihypertensive
Pregnancy risk category: C (D in second and third trimesters)

Indications and dosages

▶ **Hypertension.** *Adults:* For patient not receiving a diuretic, initially 1 mg for a nonblack patient and 2 mg for a black patient P.O. once daily. If response isn't adequate, dosage may be increased at intervals of at least 1 week. Maintenance dose is from 2 to 4 mg daily for most patients. Some patients receiving 4-mg once-daily doses may need b.i.d. doses. For patient also receiving diuretic, initial dose is 0.5 mg P.O. once daily. Subsequent dosages adjusted based on blood pressure response.

▶ **Heart failure or left ventricular dysfunction after acute MI.** *Adults:* Initiate therapy 3 to 5 days after MI with 1 mg P.O. daily. Adjust as tolerated to target dose of 4 mg daily.

Contraindications and precautions

• Contraindicated in patients hypersensitive to drug, and patients with a history of angioedema with previous treatment with ACE inhibitor.

• Use cautiously in patients with impaired renal function, heart failure, or renal artery stenosis.

Lifespan: In pregnant women, drug is contraindicated.

Adverse reactions

CNS: dizziness, headache, fatigue, drowsiness, insomnia, paresthesia, vertigo, anxiety.
CV: chest pain, first-degree AV block, ***bradycardia,*** edema, flushing, hypotension, palpitations.
EENT: epistaxis, throat irritation.
GI: diarrhea, dyspepsia, abdominal distention, abdominal pain or cramps, constipation, vomiting, ***pancreatitis.***
GU: urinary frequency, impotence.
Hematologic: ***neutropenia, leukopenia.***
Metabolic: ***hyperkalemia,*** hyponatremia.
Respiratory: dry, persistent, tickling, nonproductive cough; dyspnea; upper respiratory tract infection.
Skin: rash, pruritus, pemphigus.
Other: ***anaphylaxis, angioedema,*** decreased libido.

Interactions

Drug-drug. *Diuretics:* Increases risk of excessive hypotension. Monitor blood pressure closely.
Lithium: Increases lithium level and lithium toxicity. Avoid using together; monitor lithium level.
Potassium-sparing diuretics, potassium supplements: Increases risk of hyperkalemia. Monitor potassium level closely.
Drug-herb. *Licorice:* May increase sodium retention and blood pressure. Discourage using together.
Drug-food. *Salt substitutes containing potassium:* Increases risk of hyperkalemia. Monitor potassium level closely.

Effects on lab test results

• May increase BUN, creatinine, potassium, and liver enzyme levels. May decrease sodium level.

• May decrease neutrophil and WBC counts.

Pharmacokinetics

Absorption: Food slows absorption.
Distribution: Unknown.
Metabolism: Metabolized in liver.
Excretion: Excreted in urine and feces.

Route	Onset	Peak	Duration
P.O.	Unknown	1 hr	Unknown (drug); 4-10 hr (metabolite)

Pharmacodynamics

Chemical effect: Inhibits circulating and tissue ACE activity, thus reducing angiotensin II formation, decreasing vasoconstriction, decreasing aldosterone secretion, and increasing plasma renin.
Therapeutic effect: Decreases aldosterone secretion, leading to diuresis, natriuresis, and small increase in serum potassium.

Available forms

Tablets: 1 mg, 2 mg, 4 mg

NURSING PROCESS

Assessment

- Monitor patient's blood pressure and potassium level before and during drug therapy.
- Monitor patient for hypotension. If possible, stop diuretic therapy 2 to 3 days before starting drug.
- Monitor patient for jaundice and alert prescriber immediately if occurs.
- Monitor patient's compliance with treatment.
- Evaluate patient's and family's knowledge of drug therapy.

Nursing diagnoses

- Risk for injury related to hypertension
- Deficient knowledge related to drug therapy

Planning and implementation

- Take steps to prevent or minimize orthostatic hypotension.
- Maintain patient's nondrug therapies, such as sodium restriction, stress management, smoking cessation, and exercise program.

ALERT: Angioedema with involvement of the tongue, glottis, or larynx may be fatal because of airway obstruction. Appropriate therapy should be ordered, including epinephrine 1:1,000 (0.3 to 0.5 ml) S.C.; have resuscitation equipment for maintaining a patent airway readily available.

Patient teaching

- Advise patient to report infection and other adverse reactions.
- Tell patient to avoid salt substitutes.
- Tell patient to use caution in hot weather and during exercise.
- Tell woman to report suspected pregnancy immediately.
- Advise patient about to undergo surgery or anesthesia to inform prescriber about use of this drug.

Evaluation

- Patient's blood pressure is normal.
- Patient and family state understanding of drug therapy.

tranylcypromine sulfate

(tran-il-SIGH-proh-meen SUL-fayt)
Parnate

Pharmacologic class: MAO inhibitor
Therapeutic class: antidepressant
Pregnancy risk category: C

Indications and dosages

▶ **Depression.** *Adults:* 10 mg P.O. t.i.d. Increase by 10 mg daily at 1- to 3-week intervals to maximum of 60 mg daily, if needed, after 2 weeks of initial therapy.

Contraindications and precautions

- Contraindicated in patients receiving MAO inhibitors or dibenzazepine derivatives; sympathomimetics (including amphetamines); some CNS depressants (including alcohol); some serotonin reuptake inhibitors; antihypertensive, diuretic, antihistaminic, sedative, or anesthetic drugs; bupropion hydrochloride, buspirone hydrochloride, dextromethorphan, meperidine; foods high in tyramine or tryptophan; or excessive quantities of caffeine.
- Contraindicated in patients with confirmed or suspected cerebrovascular defect, CV disease, hypertension, or history of headache and in those undergoing elective surgery.

• Use cautiously with antiparkinsonians or spinal anesthetics; in patients with renal disease, diabetes, seizure disorder, Parkinson's disease, or hyperthyroidism; and in patients at risk for suicide.

Lifespan: In pregnant women, drug isn't recommended. In breast-feeding women and children, safety of drug hasn't been established.

Adverse reactions

CNS: *dizziness, vertigo, headache,* anxiety, agitation, drowsiness, weakness, numbness, paresthesia, tremor, jitters, confusion.
CV: *orthostatic hypotension, tachycardia,* ***paradoxical hypertension,*** palpitations, *edema.*
EENT: blurred vision, tinnitus.
GI: dry mouth, *anorexia,* nausea, diarrhea, constipation, abdominal pain.
GU: impotence, urine retention, impaired ejaculation.
Hematologic: anemia, ***leukopenia, agranulocytosis, thrombocytopenia.***
Hepatic: ***hepatitis.***
Musculoskeletal: muscle spasm, myoclonic jerks.
Skin: rash.
Other: SIADH, chills.

Interactions

Drug-drug. *Amphetamines, antihistamines, ephedrine, levodopa, meperidine, metaraminol, methylphenidate, phenylephrine, sympathomimetics:* Enhances pressor effects of these drugs. Avoid using together.
Antiparkinsonians, barbiturates, dextromethorphan, methotrimeprazine, narcotics, other sedatives, selective serotonin reuptake inhibitors (SSRIs), tricyclic antidepressants: Enhances adverse CNS effects. Use with caution and in reduced dosage.
Buspirone: May elevate blood pressure. Monitor patient's blood pressure closely.
Insulin, oral antidiabetics: Increases risk of hypoglycemia. Use cautiously and in reduced dosages; monitor patient's glucose level.
Drug-herb. *Cacao tree:* May have potential vasopressor effects. Discourage using together.
Ginseng: May cause headache, tremors, mania. Discourage using together.
Green tea: Contains caffeine. Discourage using together.
Scotch broom: Contains high levels of tyramine. Discourage using together.
St. John's wort: Has properties similar to those of SSRIs. Discourage using together.
Drug-food. *Foods high in tryptophan, tyramine, caffeine:* May cause hypertensive crisis. Discourage using together.
Drug-lifestyle. *Alcohol use:* Enhances adverse CNS effects. Discourage using together.

Effects on lab test results

• May increase ALT and AST levels.
• May decrease hemoglobin, hematocrit, and WBC, granulocyte, and platelet counts.

Pharmacokinetics

Absorption: Rapid and complete.
Distribution: Unknown.
Metabolism: Metabolized in liver.
Excretion: Excreted primarily in urine; some excreted in feces. *Half-life:* 2½ hours.

Route	Onset	Peak	Duration
P.O.	Unknown	1-3.5 hr	≤ 10 days after therapy stopped

Pharmacodynamics

Chemical effect: Unknown; probably promotes accumulation of neurotransmitters by inhibiting MAO.
Therapeutic effect: Relieves depression.

Available forms

Tablets: 10 mg

NURSING PROCESS

Assessment

• Assess patient's condition before therapy and regularly thereafter.
• Assess patient for risk of self-harm.
• Obtain baseline blood pressure, heart rate, CBC, and liver function test results before beginning therapy; monitor throughout treatment.
• Be alert for adverse reactions and drug interactions.
• Evaluate patient's and family's knowledge of drug therapy.

Nursing diagnoses

• Disturbed thought processes related to presence of depression

• Risk for injury related to drug-induced adverse CNS reactions
• Deficient knowledge related to drug therapy

Planning and implementation

• Dosage usually is reduced to maintenance level as soon as possible.
ALERT: Don't withdraw drug abruptly.
• In most patients, discontinue MAO inhibitors 14 days before elective surgery to avoid drug interactions that may occur during anesthetic procedure.
• If patient develops symptoms of overdose (palpitations, severe hypotension, or frequent headaches), withhold dose and notify prescriber.
ALERT: Have phentolamine available to combat severe hypertension.
• Continue precautions for 10 days after stopping drug because it has long-lasting effects.

Patient teaching

• Warn patient to avoid foods high in tyramine or tryptophan and large amounts of caffeine. Tranylcypromine is the MAO inhibitor most often reported to cause hypertensive crisis with ingestion of foods high in tyramine, such as aged cheese, Chianti wine, beer, avocados, chicken livers, chocolate, bananas, soy sauce, meat tenderizers, salami, and bologna.
• Tell patient to avoid alcohol during drug therapy.
• Instruct patient to sit up for 1 minute before getting out of bed to avoid dizziness.
• Warn patient to avoid overexertion because MAO inhibitors may suppress angina.
• Advise patient to consult prescriber before taking other prescription or OTC drugs. Severe adverse effects can occur if MAO inhibitors are taken with OTC cold, hay fever, or diet aids.
• Warn patient not to stop drug suddenly.

Evaluation

• Patient's behavior and communication exhibit improved thought processes.
• Patient doesn't experience injury from adverse CNS reactions.
• Patient and family state understanding of drug therapy.

trastuzumab
(trahs-TOO-zuh-mab)
Herceptin

Pharmacologic class: monoclonal antibody
Therapeutic class: antineoplastic
Pregnancy risk category: B

Indications and dosages

▶ **Single-drug treatment of patients with metastatic breast cancer whose tumors overexpress the human epidermal growth factor receptor 2 (HER2) protein and who have received one or more chemotherapy regimens for their metastatic disease; or with paclitaxel for metastatic breast cancer in patients whose tumors overexpress the HER2 protein and who haven't received chemotherapy for their metastatic disease.** *Adults:* Initial loading dose of 4 mg/kg I.V. over 90 minutes. Maintenance dosage is 2 mg/kg I.V. weekly as a 30-minute I.V. infusion if the initial loading dose was well tolerated.

Contraindications and precautions

• Use cautiously in patients with cardiac dysfunction and patients hypersensitive to drug or its components.
Lifespan: Breast-feeding women should discontinue breast-feeding during drug therapy and for 6 months after last dose. In children, safety and effectiveness haven't been established. In geriatric patients, use cautiously.

Adverse reactions

CNS: *pain, fever, headache, asthenia, insomnia, dizziness,* paresthesia, depression, peripheral neuritis, neuropathy.
CV: tachycardia, ***heart failure,*** *peripheral edema,* edema.
EENT: *rhinitis, pharyngitis,* sinusitis.
GI: *nausea, diarrhea, vomiting, anorexia, abdominal pain.*
GU: urinary tract infection.
Hematologic: anemia, ***leukopenia.***
Musculoskeletal: bone pain, arthralgia, *back pain.*
Respiratory: *cough, dyspnea.*
Skin: *rash,* acne.
Other: *chills, infection, flulike syndrome,* allergic reaction, herpes simplex.

Interactions

Drug-drug. *Anthracyclines:* Increases potential for cardiotoxic effects. Monitor patient closely.

Paclitaxel: Decreases clearance of trastuzumab. Monitor patient closely when used together.

Effects on lab test results

- May decrease hemoglobin, hematocrit, and WBC count.

Pharmacokinetics

Absorption: Administered I.V.
Distribution: Volume is 44 ml/kg.
Metabolism: Unknown.
Excretion: Unknown. *Half-life:* 5.8 days (range 1 to 32 days).

Route	Onset	Peak	Duration
I.V.	Unknown	Unknown	Unknown

Pharmacodynamics

Chemical effect: Recombinant DNA–derived monoclonal antibody that selectively binds to HER2. Shown to inhibit the proliferation of human tumor cells that overexpress HER2.
Therapeutic effect: Hinders function of specific breast cancer tumor cells that overexpress HER2.

Available forms

Injection: lyophilized sterile powder containing 440 mg per vial

NURSING PROCESS

Assessment

- Before beginning therapy, patient should undergo thorough baseline cardiac assessment, including history and physical examination and appropriate evaluation methods to identify those at risk of developing cardiotoxicity.
- Drug should be used only in patients with metastatic breast cancer whose tumors have HER2 protein overexpression.
- Assess patient for chills and fever, especially during the first infusion.
- Monitor patient closely for signs and symptoms of cardiac dysfunction, especially if also receiving anthracyclines and cyclophosphamide.
- Monitor patient for dyspnea, increased cough, paroxysmal nocturnal dyspnea, peripheral edema, and S3 gallop. Patients also receiving chemotherapy should be monitored closely for cardiac dysfunction or failure, anemia, leukopenia, diarrhea, and infection.
- Evaluate patient's and family's understanding of drug therapy.

Nursing diagnoses

- Imbalanced nutrition: less than body requirements related to drug-induced GI adverse effects
- Decreased cardiac output related to drug-induced decreased left ventricular function
- Deficient knowledge related to drug therapy

Planning and implementation

- Treat first infusion-related symptoms with acetaminophen, diphenhydramine, and meperidine (with or without reducing the rate of infusion).
- Notify prescriber if patient develops a clinically significant decrease in cardiac function.
- Reconstitute drug in each vial with 20 ml of bacteriostatic water for injection, USP, 1.1% benzyl alcohol preserved, as supplied, to yield a multidose solution containing 21 mg/ml. Immediately after reconstitution, label vial for drug expiration 28 days from date of reconstitution.

ALERT: If patient is hypersensitive to benzyl alcohol, drug must be reconstituted with sterile water for injection. Drug reconstituted with sterile water for injection must be used immediately; unused portion must be discarded. Avoid other reconstitution diluents.

ALERT: Don't give as an I.V. push or bolus.

- Determine dose (mg) of trastuzumab needed, based on loading dose of 4 mg/kg or maintenance dose of 2 mg/kg. Calculate volume of 21 mg/ml solution and withdraw amount from vial; add it to an infusion bag containing 250 ml of normal saline solution. D_5W solution shouldn't be used.
- Don't mix or dilute trastuzumab with other drugs.
- Vials of drug are stable at 36° to 46° F (2° to 8° C) before reconstitution. Discard reconstituted solution after 28 days. Store trastuzumab solution diluted in normal saline solution for injection at 36° to 46° F before use; it's stable for up to 24 hours.

Patient teaching
- Tell patient about possibility of first-dose, infusion-related adverse effects.
- Instruct patient to notify prescriber immediately if signs and symptoms of cardiac dysfunction develop, such as shortness of breath, increased cough, or peripheral edema.
- Instruct patient to report adverse effects to prescriber.

Evaluation
- Patient doesn't experience adverse GI effects (nausea, vomiting, diarrhea).
- Patient doesn't exhibit dyspnea, increased cough, paroxysmal nocturnal dyspnea, peripheral edema, or S3 gallop as result of drug-induced cardiac dysfunction.
- Patient and family state understanding of drug therapy.

travoprost
(TRA-voe-prost)
Travatan

Pharmacologic class: prostaglandin analogue
Therapeutic class: antiglaucoma agent, ocular antihypertensive
Pregnancy risk category: C

Indications and dosages

▶ **Reduction of elevated intraocular pressure (IOP) in patients with open-angle glaucoma or ocular hypertension who are intolerant of other IOP-lowering drugs, or in patients who have had insufficient responses to other IOP-lowering drugs.** *Adults:* 1 gtt in conjunctival sac of affected eye once daily in evening.

Contraindications and precautions

- Contraindicated in patients hypersensitive to travoprost, benzalkonium chloride, or other components.
- Use cautiously in patients with renal or hepatic impairment, active intraocular inflammation (iritis, uveitis), or risk factors for macular edema.
- Use cautiously in aphakic patients and pseudophakic patients with a torn posterior lens capsule.
- Don't use in patients with angle-closure glaucoma or inflammatory or neovascular glaucoma.

Lifespan: In pregnant women or in women attempting to become pregnant, drug isn't recommended. In breast-feeding women, use cautiously. In children, safety and efficacy haven't been established.

Adverse reactions

CNS: anxiety, depression, headache, pain.
CV: angina pectoris, ***bradycardia,*** chest pain, hypertension, hypotension.
EENT: *ocular hyperemia, decreased visual acuity, eye discomfort, foreign body sensation, eye pain, eye pruritus,* conjunctival hyperemia, abnormal vision, blepharitis, blurred vision, cataracts, conjunctivitis, dry eyes, eye disorders, iris discoloration, keratitis, lid margin crusting, photophobia, subconjunctival hemorrhage, tearing, sinusitis.
GI: dyspepsia, GI disorder.
GU: prostate disorder, urinary incontinence, urinary tract infection.
Metabolic: hypercholesterolemia.
Respiratory: bronchitis.
Musculoskeletal: arthritis, back pain.
Other: accidental injury, cold syndrome, infection.

Interactions

Drug-herb. *Areca, jaborandi:* Possible additive effects. Avoid use together.

Effects on lab test results

- May increase cholesterol level.

Pharmacokinetics

Absorption: Absorbed through the cornea.
Distribution: Levels peak within 30 minutes.
Metabolism: Drug is an isopropyl ester prodrug, which is hydrolyzed by esterases in the cornea to its biologically active free acid. The liver primarily metabolizes the active acid of drug reaching the systemic circulation.
Excretion: After ocular administration, travoprost free acid is rapidly eliminated from plasma within 1 hour.

Route	Onset	Peak	Duration
Ophthalmic	Unknown	30 min	Unknown

Pharmacodynamics

Chemical effect: Unknown; thought to increase uveoscleral outflow.
Therapeutic effect: Reduces IOP.

Available forms

Ophthalmic solution: 0.004%

NURSING PROCESS

Assessment

- Assess underlying condition before therapy and reassess regularly throughout therapy.
- If a pregnant woman or a woman attempting to become pregnant accidentally comes in contact with drug, thoroughly cleanse the exposed area with soap and water immediately.
- Evaluate patient's and family's knowledge of travoprost therapy.

Nursing diagnoses

- Acute pain related to adverse EENT effects of drug
- Risk for activity intolerance related to decreased visual acuity
- Deficient knowledge related to travoprost therapy

Planning and implementation

- Patient should remove contact lenses before administration of drug. Lenses may be reinserted 15 minutes after administration.
- If more than one ophthalmic drug is being used, the drugs should be given at least 5 minutes apart.
- Temporary or permanent increased pigmentation of the iris and eyelid may occur as well as increased pigmentation and growth of the eyelashes.

Patient teaching

- Teach patient to instill drops and advise him to wash hands before and after instilling solution. Warn him not to touch dropper or tip to eye or surrounding tissue.
- Tell patient receiving treatment in only one eye about the potential for increased brown pigmentation of the iris, eyelid skin darkening, and increased length, thickness, pigmentation, or number of lashes in the treated eye.
- Tell patient that, if eye trauma or infection occurs or if eye surgery is needed, he should seek medical advice before continuing to use the multidose container.
- Advise patient to immediately report conjunctivitis or lid reactions.
- Advise patient to apply light pressure on lacrimal sac for 1 minute after instillation to minimize systemic absorption of drug.
- Tell patient to remove contact lenses before administration of solution and that he can reinsert them 15 minutes after administration.
- Advise patient that, if more than one ophthalmic drug is being used, the drugs should be given at least 5 minutes apart.
- Stress importance of compliance with recommended therapy.
- Tell patient to discard container within 6 weeks of removing it from the sealed pouch.
- Tell a pregnant woman or a woman attempting to become pregnant that, if she accidentally comes in contact with drug, she should thoroughly cleanse the exposed area with soap and water immediately.

Evaluation

- Patient denies pain.
- Patient's activity level improves.
- Patient and family state understanding of travoprost therapy.

trazodone hydrochloride

(TRAYZ-oh-dohn high-droh-KLOR-ighd)
Desyrel

Pharmacologic class: triazolopyridine derivative
Therapeutic class: antidepressant
Pregnancy risk category: C

Indications and dosages

▶ **Depression.** *Adults:* Initially, 150 mg P.O. daily in divided doses. Increased by 50 mg daily q 3 to 4 days, p.r.n. Average daily dose ranges from 150 to 400 mg. Maximum daily dose is 600 mg for inpatients or 400 mg for outpatients.

▶ **Aggressive behavior‡.** *Adults:* 50 mg P.O. b.i.d.

▶ **Panic disorder‡.** *Adults:* 300 mg P.O. daily.

Contraindications and precautions

- Contraindicated in patients in initial recovery phase of MI and in patients hypersensitive to drug.
- Use cautiously in patients with cardiac disease and in those at risk for suicide.

Lifespan: In pregnant and breast-feeding women and in children, safety of drug hasn't been established.

Adverse reactions

CNS: *drowsiness, dizziness,* nervousness, fatigue, confusion, tremor, weakness, hostility, syncope, anger, nightmares, vivid dreams, headache, insomnia.
CV: orthostatic hypotension, tachycardia, hypertension, shortness of breath.
EENT: blurred vision, tinnitus, nasal congestion.
GI: dry mouth, dysgeusia, constipation, nausea, vomiting, anorexia.
GU: urine retention; priapism, possibly leading to impotence; hematuria.
Hematologic: anemia.
Skin: rash, urticaria, diaphoresis.
Other: decreased libido.

Interactions

Drug-drug. *Antihypertensives:* Increases hypotensive effect of trazodone. Monitor blood pressure; antihypertensive dosage may have to be decreased.
Carbamazepine: May decrease plasma levels of trazodone. Monitor decreased therapeutic effect.
Clonidine, CNS depressants: Enhances CNS depression. Avoid using together.
Digoxin, phenytoin: May increase serum levels of these drugs. Monitor patient for toxicity.
MAO inhibitors: No clinical experience. Use together with extreme caution.
Phenothiazines: May increase trazodone serum level. Monitor toxic effects.
Venlafaxine, selective serotonin reuptake inhibitors (SSRIs): May cause serotonin syndrome. Don't use together.
Drug-herb. *St. John's wort:* Serotonin syndrome may occur. Discourage using together.
Drug-lifestyle. *Alcohol use:* Enhances CNS depression. Discourage using together.

Effects on lab test results

- May increase ALT and AST levels.
- May decrease hemoglobin and hematocrit.

Pharmacokinetics

Absorption: Well absorbed from GI tract. Food delays absorption but increases amount of drug absorbed by 20%.
Distribution: Distributed widely in body; isn't concentrated in any particular tissue.
Metabolism: Metabolized by liver.
Excretion: About 75% excreted in urine; remainder excreted in feces. *Half-life:* First phase, 3 to 6 hours; second phase, 5 to 9 hours.

Route	Onset	Peak	Duration
P.O.	Unknown	1-2 hr	Unknown

Pharmacodynamics

Chemical effect: Unknown, although it inhibits serotonin uptake in brain; not a tricyclic derivative.
Therapeutic effect: Relieves depression.

Available forms

Dividose tablets: 150 mg, 300 mg
Tablets (film coated): 50 mg, 100 mg

NURSING PROCESS

Assessment

- Assess patient's condition before therapy and regularly thereafter.
- Be alert for adverse reactions and drug interactions.
- Evaluate patient's and family's knowledge of drug therapy.

Nursing diagnoses

- Disturbed thought processes related to presence of depression
- Risk for injury related to drug-induced adverse CNS reactions
- Deficient knowledge related to drug therapy

Planning and implementation

- Give after meals or light snack for optimal absorption and to decrease risk of dizziness.
- Don't discontinue drug abruptly. However, it should be discontinued at least 48 hours before surgery.
- Notify prescriber if adverse reactions occur.

ALERT: Don't confuse trazodone with tramadol.

Patient teaching

- Instruct patient to take drug after meals or light snack.

ALERT: Inform male patients that priapism may occur. Advise him to notify prescriber immediately; surgical intervention may be needed.

- Warn patient to avoid activities that require alertness and good psychomotor coordination until CNS effects of drug are known. Drowsiness and dizziness usually subside after first few weeks.
- Teach patient's family how to recognize signs of suicidal tendency or suicidal ideation.

Evaluation

- Patient's behavior and communication exhibit improved thought processes.
- Patient doesn't experience adverse CNS reactions.
- Patient and family state understanding of drug therapy.

tretinoin

(TRET-ih-noyn)

Vesanoid

Pharmacologic class: retinoid
Therapeutic class: antineoplastic
Pregnancy risk category: D

Indications and dosages

▶ **Induction of remission in patients with acute promyelocytic leukemia (APL), French-American-British (FAB) classification M3 (including M3 variant), characterized by presence of the t(15,17) translocation or the PML/RAR alpha gene, who are refractory to or have relapsed from anthracycline chemotherapy or for whom anthracycline-based chemotherapy is contraindicated.** *Adults and children age 1 and older:* 45 mg/m² P.O. daily given as two evenly divided doses until complete remission is documented. Therapy should be discontinued 30 days after achievement of complete remission or after 90 days of treatment, whichever occurs first.

Contraindications and precautions

- Contraindicated in patients hypersensitive to retinoids or parabens, which are used as preservatives in the gelatin capsule.

Lifespan: Drug isn't recommended for pregnant or breast-feeding women.

Adverse reactions

CNS: *fever, pain,* hypothermia, weakness, fatigue, *malaise, headache,* dizziness, *paresthesia, anxiety, insomnia, depression, confusion,* ***cerebral hemorrhage, CVA, intracranial hypertension,*** agitation, hallucinations, abnormal gait, agnosia, aphasia, asterixis, cerebellar edema, cerebellar disorders, ***seizures, coma,*** CNS depression, dysarthria, ***encephalopathy,*** facial paralysis, hemiplegia, hyporeflexia, hypotaxia, no light reflex, neurologic reaction, spinal cord disorder, tremor, leg weakness, unconsciousness, dementia, forgetfulness, somnolence, slow speech.
CV: *chest discomfort,* **ARRHYTHMIAS,** *hypotension, hypertension, phlebitis, edema,* **HEART FAILURE, MI,** enlarged heart, heart murmur, ischemia, myocarditis, pericarditis, secondary cardiomyopathy, *pericardial effusions,* impaired myocardial contractility, facial edema, *peripheral edema, flushing.*
EENT: *earache, ear fullness,* changed visual acuity, laryngeal edema, visual field defects, hearing loss, *visual disturbances, ocular disorders.*
GI: **HEMORRHAGE,** *nausea, vomiting, anorexia, abdominal pain, GI disorders, diarrhea, constipation, dyspepsia, abdominal distention,* hepatosplenomegaly, ulcer.
GU: *renal insufficiency,* dysuria, ***acute renal failure,*** urinary frequency, renal tubular necrosis, enlarged prostate.
Hematologic: *leukocytosis,* **HEMORRHAGE,** ***disseminated intravascular coagulation.***
Hepatic: ***hepatitis,*** unspecified liver disorder, hypercholesterolemia, hypertriglyceridemia.
Metabolic: *weight changes,* fluid imbalance, ***acidosis.***
Musculoskeletal: *myalgia, bone pain,* flank pain, bone inflammation.
Respiratory: *pneumonia, upper respiratory tract disorders, dyspnea, respiratory insufficiency, pleural effusion, crackles, expiratory wheezing,* lower respiratory tract disorders, pulmonary infiltrates, bronchial asthma, ***pulmonary edema, progressive hypoxemia,*** un-

specified pulmonary disease, pulmonary hypertension.
Skin: *skin and mucous membrane dryness, pruritus, increased sweating, alopecia, skin changes, rash.*
Other: ***retinoic acid-APL syndrome,*** *infection, shivering, injection site reactions, mucositis,* ***septicemia, multi-organ failure,*** cellulitis, pallor, lymph disorder, ascites.

Interactions

Ketoconazole: May increase tretinoin plasma levels. Monitor toxicity.

Effects on lab test results

- May increase cholesterol and triglyceride levels.
- May increase WBC count and liver function test values.

Pharmacokinetics

Absorption: Absorbed from GI tract.
Distribution: About 95% protein-bound.
Metabolism: Drug induces its own metabolism.
Excretion: Excreted in urine and feces.

Route	Onset	Peak	Duration
P.O.	Unknown	1-2 hr	Unknown

Pharmacodynamics

Chemical effect: Unknown.
Therapeutic effect: Induces remission in selected patients with certain types of leukemia.

Available forms

Capsules: 10 mg

NURSING PROCESS

Assessment

- Assess patient's condition before therapy.
- Monitor CBC and platelet count regularly. Patient with elevated WBC counts at diagnosis has an increased risk of further rapid increase in WBC counts. Rapidly evolving leukocytosis is related to a higher risk of life-threatening complications.
- Monitor patient, especially a child, for signs and symptoms of pseudotumor cerebri. Early signs and symptoms include papilledema, headache, nausea, vomiting, and visual disturbances.
- Monitor cholesterol and triglyceride levels, coagulation profile, and liver function studies for abnormalities.
- Be alert for adverse reactions.
- Evaluate patient's knowledge of drug therapy.

Nursing diagnoses

- Ineffective health maintenance related to leukemia
- Risk for injury related to adverse reactions
- Deficient knowledge related to drug therapy

Planning and implementation

- Because patients with APL are at high risk in general and can have severe adverse reactions, drug should be given under supervision of a prescriber experienced in managing such patients and in a facility with laboratory and supportive services sufficient to monitor drug tolerance and to protect and maintain a patient compromised by toxicity.
- About 25% of patients treated during clinical studies have experienced a syndrome called retinoic acid-APL syndrome, which is characterized by fever, dyspnea, weight gain, radiographic pulmonary infiltrates, and pleural or pericardial effusion. Notify prescriber immediately if these signs and symptoms appear; this syndrome may be accompanied by impaired myocardial contractility and episodic hypotension with or without leukocytosis. Some patients have died of progressive hypoxemia and multiorgan failure. The syndrome generally occurs during the first month of therapy. Prompt treatment with high-dose steroids may reduce morbidity and mortality.
- Notify prescriber immediately if signs and symptoms of pseudotumor cerebri occur.
- Ensure that pregnancy testing and contraception counseling are repeated monthly throughout therapy and for 1 month after therapy.

ALERT: Don't confuse tretinoin with trientine.

Patient teaching

- Inform woman that a pregnancy test is required within 1 week before therapy. When possible, therapy is delayed until a negative result is obtained. Also advise her to use two forms of effective contraception simultaneously during therapy and for 1 month after discontinuation, even with a history of infertility or menopause (unless hysterectomy has been performed), unless abstinence is the chosen method. Tell her to alert prescriber immediately of suspected pregnancy.

- Instruct patient about infection-control and bleeding precautions. Tell him to notify prescriber of signs of infection (fever, sore throat, fatigue) or bleeding (easy bruising, nosebleeds, bleeding gums, melena) and to take temperature daily.

☑ Evaluation

- Patient responds well to therapy.
- Patient doesn't experience injury from adverse reactions.
- Patient and family state understanding of drug therapy.

triamcinolone

(trigh-am-SIN-oh-lohn)

Aristocort, Atolone, Kenacort**

triamcinolone acetonide

Kenaject-40, Kenalog-10, Kenalog-40, Tac-3, Tac-40, Triam-A, Triamonide 40, Tri-Kort, Trilog

triamcinolone diacetate

Amcort, Aristocort Forte, Aristocort Intralesional, Clinacort, Triam Forte, Trilone, Tristoject

triamcinolone hexacetonide

Aristospan Intra-Articular, Aristospan Intralesional

Pharmacologic class: glucocorticoid
Therapeutic class: anti-inflammatory, immunosuppressant
Pregnancy risk category: C

Indications and dosages

▶ **Severe inflammation or immunosuppression.** ***triamcinolone.*** *Adults:* 4 to 48 mg P.O. daily, in 1 to 4 divided doses.

triamcinolone acetonide. *Adults:* Initially, 2.5 to 60 mg I.M. Additional doses of 20 to 100 mg may be given, p.r.n., at 6-week intervals. Or, 2.5 to 15 mg intra-articularly, or up to 1 mg intralesionally, p.r.n.

triamcinolone diacetate. *Adults:* 40 mg I.M. weekly; or 5 to 48 mg by intralesional or sublesional injections (at 1- to 2-week intervals); or 2 to 40 mg by intra-articular, intrasynovial, or soft tissue injection (may repeat at 1- to 8-week intervals).

triamcinolone hexacetonide. *Adults:* Up to 0.5 mg/in^2 of affected skin intralesionally, or 2 to 20 mg intra-articularly q 3 to 4 weeks, p.r.n.

Contraindications and precautions

- Contraindicated in patients hypersensitive to drug or its components and in those with systemic fungal infections.
- Use cautiously in patients with GI ulcer, renal disease, hypertension, osteoporosis, diabetes mellitus, hypothyroidism, cirrhosis, diverticulitis, nonspecific ulcerative colitis, recent intestinal anastomoses, thromboembolic disorders, seizures, myasthenia gravis, heart failure, tuberculosis, ocular herpes simplex, emotional instability, or psychotic tendencies.

Lifespan: In pregnant or breast-feeding women, use cautiously.

Adverse reactions

CNS: *euphoria, insomnia,* psychotic behavior, pseudotumor cerebri, vertigo, headache, paresthesia, ***seizures.***
CV: ***heart failure,*** hypertension, edema, ***arrhythmias,*** thrombophlebitis, ***thromboembolism.***
EENT: cataracts, glaucoma.
GI: *peptic ulceration,* GI irritation, increased appetite, ***pancreatitis,*** nausea, vomiting.
GU: ***acute adrenal insufficiency*** may occur with increased stress (infection, surgery, or trauma) or abrupt withdrawal, menstrual irregularities.
Metabolic: hypokalemia, hyperglycemia, carbohydrate intolerance.
Musculoskeletal: muscular weakness, osteoporosis, growth suppression in children.
Skin: delayed wound healing, acne, various skin eruptions.
Other: susceptibility to infections, hirsutism, cushingoid state (moonface, buffalo hump, central obesity).

Interactions

Drug-drug. *Aspirin, indomethacin, other NSAIDs:* Increases risk of GI distress and bleeding. Give together cautiously.
Barbiturates, phenytoin, rifampin: Decreases corticosteroid effect. Increase corticosteroid.
Oral anticoagulants: Alters dosage requirements. Monitor PT closely.
Potassium-depleting drugs (such as thiazide diuretics): Enhances potassium-wasting effects of triamcinolone. Monitor potassium level.
Skin-test antigens: Decreases response. Defer skin testing.
Toxoids, vaccines: Decreases antibody response and increases risk of neurologic complications. Avoid using together.

Effects on lab test results

- May increase glucose and cholesterol levels. May decrease potassium and calcium levels.

Pharmacokinetics

Absorption: Absorbed readily after P.O. administration. Absorption is variable after other routes of administration, depending on whether drug is injected into intra-articular space or muscle and on blood supply to that muscle.
Distribution: Distributed to muscle, liver, skin, intestines, and kidneys. Drug is extensively bound to plasma proteins. Only unbound portion is active.
Metabolism: Metabolized in liver.
Excretion: Excreted in urine; insignificant quantities also excreted in feces. *Half-life:* 18 to 36 hours.

Route	Onset	Peak	Duration
P.O., I.M., intralesional, intra-articular, intrasynovial	Varies	Varies	Varies

Pharmacodynamics

Chemical effect: Not clearly defined; decreases inflammation, mainly by stabilizing leukocyte lysosomal membranes; suppresses immune response; stimulates bone marrow; and influences protein, fat, and carbohydrate metabolism.
Therapeutic effect: Relieves inflammation and suppresses immune system function.

Available forms

triamcinolone
Tablets: 4 mg, 8 mg
Syrup: 4 mg/5 ml
triamcinolone acetonide
Injection (suspension): 3 mg/ml, 10 mg/ml, 40 mg/ml
triamcinolone diacetate
Injection (suspension): 25 mg/ml, 40 mg/ml
triamcinolone hexacetonide
Injection (suspension): 5 mg/ml, 20 mg/ml

NURSING PROCESS

Assessment

- Assess patient before and after therapy; monitor weight, blood pressure, and serum electrolyte levels.
- Watch for adverse reactions, drug interactions, depression, or psychotic episodes, especially with high doses.
- Evaluate patient's and family's knowledge of drug therapy.

Nursing diagnoses

- Ineffective health maintenance related to underlying condition
- Risk for injury related to drug-induced adverse reactions
- Deficient knowledge related to drug therapy

Planning and implementation

- Drug isn't used for alternate-day therapy.
- Always adjust to lowest effective dose.
- For better results and less toxicity, give once-daily dose in morning.
- **P.O. use:** Give dose with food when possible to reduce GI irritation.
- **I.M. use:** Give I.M. injection deep into gluteal muscle. Rotate injection sites to prevent muscle atrophy.
  – Don't use 10 mg/ml strength for I.M. administration.
- **Intralesional, intra-articular, intrasynovial use:** Assist prescriber with administration, as directed.
  – Don't use 40 mg/ml strength for I.D. or intralesional administration.

ALERT: Parenteral form isn't for I.V. use. Different salt formulations aren't interchangeable.

- Don't use diluents that contain preservatives; flocculation may occur.

• Unless contraindicated, give low-sodium diet high in potassium and protein. Give potassium supplements, as needed.
• Gradually reduce drug dosage after long-term therapy. After abrupt withdrawal, patient may experience rebound inflammation, fatigue, weakness, arthralgia, fever, dizziness, lethargy, depression, fainting, orthostatic hypotension, dyspnea, anorexia, hypoglycemia; after prolonged use, sudden withdrawal may be fatal.
ALERT: Don't confuse triamcinolone with Triaminicin, Triaminic, or Triaminicol.

Patient teaching
• Tell patient not to discontinue drug abruptly or without prescriber's consent.
• Instruct patient to take oral drug with food.
• Teach patient signs of early adrenal insufficiency: fatigue, muscle weakness, joint pain, fever, anorexia, nausea, dyspnea, dizziness, and fainting.
• Instruct patient to wear or carry medical identification at all times.
• Warn patient receiving long-term therapy about cushingoid symptoms and tell him to report sudden weight gain and swelling to prescriber.
• Tell patient to report slow healing.
• Advise patient receiving long-term therapy to consider exercise or physical therapy. Also tell patient to ask prescriber about vitamin D or calcium supplements.

Evaluation
• Patient responds well to drug.
• Patient doesn't experience injury from adverse reactions.
• Patient and family state understanding of drug therapy.

triamcinolone acetonide
(trigh-am-SIN-oh-lohn as-EE-tuh-nighd)
Azmacort

Pharmacologic class: glucocorticoid
Therapeutic class: anti-inflammatory, immunosuppressant
Pregnancy risk category: C

Indications and dosages
▶ **Corticosteroid-dependent asthma.** *Adults:* 2 inhalations t.i.d. to q.i.d. Maximum dose is 16 inhalations daily. In some patients, maintenance can be accomplished when total daily dose is given b.i.d.
Children ages 6 to 12: 1 or 2 inhalations t.i.d. to q.i.d. or 2 to 4 inhalations b.i.d. Maximum dose is 12 inhalations daily.

Contraindications and precautions
• Contraindicated in patients hypersensitive to drug or its components and in those with status asthmaticus.
• Use with extreme caution, if at all, in patients with tuberculosis of respiratory tract; untreated fungal, bacterial, or systemic viral infections; or ocular herpes simplex.
• Use cautiously in patients receiving systemic corticosteroids.
Lifespan: In pregnant women, use cautiously. In breast-feeding women, drug isn't recommended.

Adverse reactions
EENT: dry or irritated nose or throat, hoarseness.
GI: *oral candidiasis,* dry or irritated tongue or mouth.
Respiratory: cough, wheezing.
Other: facial edema, ***hypothalamic-pituitary-adrenal function suppression,*** adrenal insufficiency.

Interactions
None significant.

Effects on lab test results
None reported.

Pharmacokinetics
Absorption: Absorbed slowly from lungs and GI tract.
Distribution: Without spacer, about 10% to 25% of inhaled dose is deposited in airways; remainder is deposited in mouth and throat and swallowed. A greater percentage of inhaled dose may reach lungs with use of spacer device.
Metabolism: Metabolized in liver. Some drug that reaches lungs may be metabolized locally.

Excretion: Excreted in urine and feces. *Half-life:* 18 to 36 hours.

Route	Onset	Peak	Duration
Inhalation	1-4 wk	Unknown	Unknown

Pharmacodynamics

Chemical effect: Unknown; probably decreases inflammation, mainly by stabilizing leukocyte lysosomal membranes.
Therapeutic effect: Improves breathing ability.

Available forms

Inhalation aerosol: 100 mcg/metered spray

NURSING PROCESS

Assessment

- Assess patient's asthma before therapy and regularly thereafter.
- Be alert for adverse reactions.
- Evaluate patient's and family's knowledge of drug therapy.

Nursing diagnoses

- Ineffective breathing pattern related to presence of asthma
- Impaired tissue integrity related to drug's adverse effect on oral mucosa
- Deficient knowledge related to drug therapy

Planning and implementation

- Patient who has recently been transferred to oral inhaled steroids from systemic administration of steroids may need to be placed back on systemic steroids during periods of stress or severe asthma attacks.
- Taper oral therapy slowly.
- If patient is also to receive bronchodilator by inhalation, give bronchodilator first, wait several minutes, then give triamcinolone.
- If more than one inhalation of triamcinolone is ordered for each dose, allow 1 minute to elapse before repeat inhalations.
- Store drug between 36° and 86° F (2° and 30° C).

ALERT: Don't confuse triamcinolone with Triaminicin, Triaminic, or Triaminicol.

Patient teaching

- Inform patient that inhaled steroids don't provide relief for emergency asthma attacks.
- Teach patient to use drug, even when feeling well.
- Advise patient to ensure delivery of proper dose by gently warming canister to room temperature before using. Patients can carry canister in pocket to keep it warm.
- Instruct patient requiring bronchodilator to use it several minutes before triamcinolone. Tell him to allow 1 minute to elapse before repeat inhalations and to hold breath for a few seconds to enhance drug action.
- Teach patient to check mucous membranes frequently for signs of fungal infection.
- Tell patient to prevent oral fungal infections by gargling or rinsing mouth with water after each use of inhaler but not to swallow water.
- Tell patient to keep inhaler clean and unobstructed by washing it with warm water and drying it thoroughly after use.
- Instruct patient to contact prescriber if response to therapy decreases; prescriber may need to adjust dosage. Tell patient not to exceed recommended dosage on his own.
- Instruct patient to wear or carry medical identification at all times.

Evaluation

- Patient exhibits improved breathing ability.
- Patient maintains normal oral mucosa integrity.
- Patient and family state understanding of drug therapy.

triamcinolone acetonide

(trigh-am-SIN-oh-lohn as-EE-tuh-nighd)
Nasacort Nasal Inhaler, Trinasal Spray, Nasacort AQ Nasal Spray

Pharmacologic class: glucocorticoid
Therapeutic class: anti-inflammatory
Pregnancy risk category: C

Indications and dosages

▶ **Rhinitis, allergic disorders, inflammatory conditions, nasal polyps.** *Nasacort. Adults:* 2 sprays in each nostril daily; may increase dose to maximum of 4 sprays per nostril daily, if needed.
Children ages 6 to 12: 2 sprays in each nostril daily.

Nasacort AQ. Adults: 2 sprays in each nostril daily; may decrease to 1 spray in each nostril daily for allergic disorders.
Children ages 6 to 12: 1 spray in each nostril daily. Maximum 2 sprays in each nostril daily.

Contraindications and precautions

- Contraindicated in patients hypersensitive to drug or its components.
- Use with extreme caution, if at all, in patients with active or quiescent tuberculosis infection of respiratory tract and in patients with untreated fungal, bacterial, or systemic viral infection or ocular herpes simplex.
- Use cautiously in patients already receiving systemic corticosteroids because of increased likelihood of hypothalamic-pituitary-adrenal suppression compared with therapeutic dosage of either one alone. Also use cautiously in patients with recent nasal septal ulcers, nasal surgery, or trauma because of inhibitory effect on wound healing.

Lifespan: In pregnant or breast-feeding women, use cautiously. In children younger than age 6, safety of drug hasn't been established.

Adverse reactions

CNS: *headache.*
EENT: *nasal irritation,* dry mucous membranes, nasal and sinus congestion, irritation, burning, stinging, throat discomfort, sneezing, epistaxis.

Interactions

None reported.

Effects on lab test results

None reported.

Pharmacokinetics

Absorption: Minimal.
Distribution: Local.
Metabolism: Metabolized in liver.
Excretion: Excreted primarily in feces. *Half-life:* 4 hours.

Route	Onset	Peak	Duration
Intranasal	≤ 12 hr	3-4 days	Several days after therapy is stopped

Pharmacodynamics

Chemical effect: Unknown.
Therapeutic effect: Relieves signs and symptoms of nasal inflammation.

Available forms

Nasal aerosol: 55 mcg/metered spray
Nasal solution: 50 mcg/metered spray
Nasal suspension: 55 mcg/metered spray

NURSING PROCESS

Assessment

- Assess patient's condition before therapy and regularly thereafter.
- Be alert for adverse reactions.
- Evaluate patient's and family's knowledge of drug therapy.

Nursing diagnoses

- Ineffective health maintenance related to presence of allergic rhinitis
- Impaired tissue integrity related to drug's adverse effect on nasal mucosa
- Deficient knowledge related to drug therapy

Planning and implementation

ALERT: When excessive doses are used, signs and symptoms of hyperadrenocorticism and adrenal suppression may occur; drug should be discontinued slowly.

- To give drug, shake canister before each use and have patient blow his nose. To instill drug, tilt patient's head forward slightly and insert nozzle into nostril, pointing it away from septum. Have patient hold other nostril closed and then inhale gently when drug is sprayed. Repeat procedure for other nostril after shaking canister.

ALERT: Don't confuse triamcinolone with Triaminicin, Triaminic, or Triaminicol.

Patient teaching

- Urge patient to read instruction sheet in package before using drug for first time.
- To instill, instruct patient to shake canister before using; to blow nose to clear nasal passages; and to tilt head slightly forward and insert nozzle into nostril, pointing away from septum. Tell him to hold other nostril closed and then to inhale gently and spray. Next, have patient shake canister again and repeat this procedure in other nostril.

• Tell patient to discard canister after 100 sprays.
• Stress importance of using drug on regular schedule because its effectiveness depends on regular use. Caution patient not to exceed dosage prescribed because serious adverse reactions may occur.
• Tell patient to notify prescriber if symptoms don't improve within 2 to 3 weeks or if condition worsens.
• Warn patient to avoid exposure to chickenpox or measles and, if exposed to either, to obtain medical advice.
• Instruct patient to watch for signs and symptoms of nasal infection. If symptoms occur, tell patient to notify prescriber because drug may need to be discontinued and appropriate local therapy given.
• Advise patient not to break or incinerate canister or store it in extreme heat; contents are under pressure and may explode.

☑ Evaluation

• Patient's allergic rhinitis is visibly improved.
• Patient maintains normal tissue integrity in nasal passages.
• Patient and family state understanding of drug therapy.

triamterene

(trigh-AM-tuh-reen)
Dyrenium

Pharmacologic class: potassium-sparing diuretic
Therapeutic class: diuretic
Pregnancy risk category: B

Indications and dosages

▶ **Edema.** *Adults:* Initially, 100 mg P.O. b.i.d. after meals. Total dose shouldn't exceed 300 mg daily.

Contraindications and precautions

• Contraindicated in patients hypersensitive to drug and those with anuria, severe or progressive renal disease or dysfunction, severe hepatic disease, or hyperkalemia.
• Use cautiously in patients with impaired liver function or diabetes mellitus, and in debilitated patients.

Lifespan: In pregnant women, use cautiously. In breast-feeding women, safety of drug hasn't been established. In geriatric patients, use cautiously.

Adverse reactions

CNS: dizziness, weakness, fatigue, headache.
CV: hypotension.
GI: dry mouth, nausea, vomiting, diarrhea.
GU: interstitial nephritis, nephrolithiasis.
Hematologic: megaloblastic anemia related to low folic acid levels, ***thrombocytopenia, agranulocytosis.***
Hepatic: jaundice.
Metabolic: HYPERKALEMIA, ***acidosis,*** hypokalemia, hyponatremia, hyperglycemia, azotemia.
Musculoskeletal: muscle cramps.
Skin: photosensitivity reactions, rash.
Other: ***anaphylaxis.***

Interactions

Drug-drug. *ACE inhibitors, potassium supplements:* Increases risk of hyperkalemia. Don't use together.
Amantadine: Increases risk of amantadine toxicity. Don't use together.
Lithium: Decreases lithium clearance, increasing risk of lithium toxicity. Monitor lithium level.
NSAIDs (indomethacin): May enhance risk of nephrotoxicity. Avoid using together.
Quinidine: May interfere with some laboratory tests that measure quinidine level. Inform laboratory that patient is taking triamterene.
Drug-food. *Potassium-containing salt substitutes, potassium-rich foods:* Increases risk of hyperkalemia. Discourage using together.
Drug-lifestyle. *Sun exposure:* Photosensitivity reactions may occur. Urge patient to avoid prolonged or unprotected exposure to sunlight.

Effects on lab test results

• May increase BUN, creatinine, glucose, and uric acid levels. May decrease sodium levels. May increase or decrease potassium level.
• May increase liver function test values. May decrease hemoglobin, hematocrit, and RBC, granulocyte, and platelet counts.

Pharmacokinetics

Absorption: Rapid; extent varies.
Distribution: About 67% protein-bound.

Metabolism: Metabolized by hydroxylation and sulfation.

Excretion: Excreted in urine. *Half-life:* 100 to 150 minutes.

Route	Onset	Peak	Duration
P.O.	2-4 hr	6-8 hr	7-9 hr

Pharmacodynamics

Chemical effect: Inhibits sodium reabsorption and potassium and hydrogen excretion by direct action on distal tubule.

Therapeutic effect: Promotes water and sodium excretion.

Available forms

Capsules: 50 mg, 100 mg

NURSING PROCESS

Assessment

- Obtain history of patient's edema before therapy and reassess regularly thereafter. Full effect of triamterene is delayed 2 to 3 days when used alone.
- Monitor blood pressure and BUN and electrolyte levels.
- Watch for blood dyscrasia.
- Be alert for adverse reactions and drug interactions.
- Evaluate patient's and family's knowledge of drug therapy.

Nursing diagnoses

- Excess fluid volume related to underlying condition
- Ineffective health maintenance related to drug-induced hyperkalemia
- Deficient knowledge related to drug therapy

Planning and implementation

- Give drug after meals to minimize nausea.

ALERT: Withdraw drug gradually to minimize excessive rebound potassium excretion.

- Drug is less potent than thiazides and loop diuretics and is useful as adjunct to other diuretic therapy. Triamterene is usually used with potassium-wasting diuretics.
- When used with other diuretics, the initial dose of each drug should be lowered and then adjusted to individual requirements.

ALERT: Don't confuse triamterene with trimipramine.

Patient teaching

- Tell patient to take drug after meals.

ALERT: Warn patient to avoid excessive ingestion of potassium-rich foods, potassium-containing salt substitutes, and potassium supplements to prevent serious hyperkalemia.

- Teach patient to avoid direct sunlight, wear protective clothing, and use sunblock to prevent photosensitivity reactions.

Evaluation

- Patient exhibits no signs of edema.
- Patient's serum potassium level is normal.
- Patient and family state understanding of drug therapy.

triazolam

(trigh-AH-zoh-lam)

Alti-Triazolam ♦, Apo-Triazo ♦, Halcion, Novo-Triolam ♦

Pharmacologic class: benzodiazepine
Therapeutic class: sedative-hypnotic
Pregnancy risk category: X
Controlled substance schedule: IV

Indications and dosages

▶ **Insomnia.** *Adults:* 0.125 to 0.5 mg P.O. h.s. *Adults older than age 65:* 0.125 mg P.O. h.s.; increased, p.r.n., to 0.25 mg P.O. h.s.

Contraindications and precautions

- Contraindicated in patients hypersensitive to benzodiazepines.
- Use cautiously in patients with impaired liver or kidney function, chronic pulmonary insufficiency, sleep apnea, depression, suicidal tendencies, or history of drug abuse.

Lifespan: In pregnant women, drug is contraindicated. In breast-feeding women, drug isn't recommended. In children, safety hasn't been established.

Adverse reactions

CNS: *drowsiness, dizziness, headache,* rebound insomnia, amnesia, light-headedness, lack of coordination, confusion, depression, nervousness, ataxia.

GI: nausea, vomiting.

Other: physical or psychological abuse.

Interactions

Drug-drug. *Cimetidine, contraceptives, erythromycin, isoniazid, ranitidine:* May cause prolonged triazolam blood levels. Monitor patient for increased sedation.
Other CNS depressants, including narcotic analgesics, other psychotropic drugs, anticonvulsants, antihistamines: May cause excessive CNS depression. Use together cautiously.
Potent CYP 3A inhibitors (itraconazole, ketoconazole, nefazodone): Decreases clearance of triazolam. Don't use together.
Drug-herb. *Ashwagandha, calendula, catnip, hops, lady's slipper, lemon balm, passion flower, sassafras, skullcap, valerian, yerba maté:* Potential for increased sedative effects. Monitor patient closely if used together.
Kava: May cause excessive sedation. Discourage using together.
Drug-food. *Grapefruit juice:* Increases serum levels. Don't give drug with grapefruit juice.
Drug-lifestyle. *Alcohol use:* May cause excessive CNS depression. Discourage using together.

Effects on lab test results

- May increase liver function test values.

Pharmacokinetics

Absorption: Well absorbed through GI tract.
Distribution: Distributed widely throughout body; 90% protein-bound.
Metabolism: Metabolized in liver.
Excretion: Excreted in urine. *Half-life:* 1½ to 5½ hours.

Route	Onset	Peak	Duration
P.O.	Unknown	1-2 hr	Unknown

Pharmacodynamics

Chemical effect: Unknown; probably acts on limbic system, thalamus, and hypothalamus of CNS to produce hypnotic effects.
Therapeutic effect: Promotes sleep.

Available forms

Tablets: 0.125 mg, 0.25 mg

NURSING PROCESS

Assessment

- Assess patient's condition before therapy and regularly thereafter.
- Assess mental status before starting therapy. Geriatric patients are more sensitive to drug's CNS effects.
- Be alert for adverse reactions and drug interactions.
- Evaluate patient's and family's knowledge of drug therapy.

Nursing diagnoses

- Disturbed sleep pattern related to underlying disorder
- Risk for injury related to drug-induced adverse CNS reactions
- Deficient knowledge related to drug therapy

Planning and implementation

- Take precautions to prevent hoarding or intentional overdosing by patients who are depressed, suicidal, or drug-dependent, or who have a history of drug abuse.
- Store drug in cool, dry place away from light.
- Institute safety precautions once drug has been given.

ALERT: Don't confuse Halcion with Haldol or halcinonide.

Patient teaching

- Warn patient not to take more than prescribed amount because overdose can occur at total daily dosage of 2 mg (or four times the highest recommended amount).
- Caution patient about performing activities that require mental alertness or physical coordination. For inpatient, supervise walking and raise bed rails, particularly for geriatric patient.
- Inform patient that drug is very short-acting and therefore has less tendency to cause morning drowsiness.
- Tell patient that rebound insomnia may develop for 1 or 2 nights after stopping therapy.

Evaluation

- Patient states that drug produces sleep.
- Patient doesn't experience injury from adverse CNS reactions.
- Patient and family state understanding of drug therapy.

trifluoperazine hydrochloride

(trigh-floo-oh-PER-eh-zeen high-droh-KLOR-ighd)

Apo-Trifluoperazine ♦, Novo-Flurazine ♦, PMS Trifluoperazine ♦, Stelazine, Stelazine Concentrate

Pharmacologic class: phenothiazine (piperazine derivative)
Therapeutic class: antipsychotic, antiemetic
Pregnancy risk category: C

Indications and dosages

▶ **Anxiety.** *Adults:* 1 to 2 mg P.O. b.i.d. Maximum daily dose is 6 mg. Drug shouldn't be used for longer than 12 weeks for anxiety.

▶ **Schizophrenia and other psychotic disorders.** *Adult outpatients:* 1 to 2 mg P.O. b.i.d., increased as needed. Or 1 to 2 mg deep I.M. q 4 to 6 hours, p.r.n.
Adult inpatients: 2 to 5 mg P.O. b.i.d.; may increase gradually to 40 mg daily.
Children ages 6 to 12 (hospitalized or under close supervision): 1 mg P.O. daily or b.i.d.; may increase gradually to 15 mg daily, if needed.

Contraindications and precautions

- Contraindicated in patients hypersensitive to phenothiazines or in patients experiencing coma, CNS depression, bone marrow suppression, or liver damage.
- Use cautiously in debilitated patients and in patients with CV disease (may cause drop in blood pressure), exposure to extreme heat, seizure disorder, glaucoma, or prostatic hyperplasia.

Lifespan: In pregnant or breast-feeding women and in children younger than age 6, safety of drug hasn't been established. In geriatric patients, use cautiously.

Adverse reactions

CNS: *extrapyramidal reactions, tardive dyskinesia,* pseudoparkinsonism, dizziness, drowsiness, insomnia, fatigue, headache, ***neuroleptic malignant syndrome.***
CV: *orthostatic hypotension,* tachycardia, ECG changes.
EENT: ocular changes, *blurred vision.*
GI: *dry mouth, constipation,* nausea.
GU: *urine retention,* menstrual irregularities, inhibited lactation.
Hematologic: ***transient leukopenia, agranulocytosis.***
Hepatic: cholestatic jaundice.
Metabolic: weight gain.
Skin: *photosensitivity reactions,* sterile abscesses, rash.
Other: allergic reaction, pain at I.M. injection site, gynecomastia.

Interactions

Drug-drug. *Antacids:* Inhibits absorption of oral phenothiazines. Separate doses by at least 2 hours.
Barbiturates, lithium: May decrease phenothiazine effect. Monitor patient.
Centrally acting antihypertensives: Decreases antihypertensive effect. Monitor blood pressure.
CNS depressants: Increases CNS depression. Use together cautiously.
Propranolol: Increases levels of both propranolol and trifluoperazine. Monitor patient closely.
Warfarin: Decreases effect of oral anticoagulants. Monitor PT and INR.
Drug-herb. *Dong quai, St. John's wort:* Increases photosensitivity reactions. Discourage using together.
Ginkgo: Potential decreased adverse effects of thioridazine. Monitor patient.
Kava: Increases risk of dystonic reactions. Discourage using together.
Milk thistle: Decreases liver toxicity caused by phenothiazines. Discourage using together; monitor liver enzymes if used together.
Yohimbe: Increases risk for yohimbe toxicity when used together. Discourage using together.
Drug-lifestyle. *Alcohol use:* Increases CNS depression. Discourage using together.

Effects on lab test results

- May increase liver enzyme levels.
- May decrease WBC and granulocyte counts.

Pharmacokinetics

Absorption: Variable with P.O. administration; rapid after I.M. use.
Distribution: Distributed widely in body; 91% to 99% protein-bound.
Metabolism: Metabolized extensively by liver.

Excretion: Excreted primarily in urine; some excreted in feces.

Route	Onset	Peak	Duration
P.O., I.M.	Up to several wk	Unknown	Unknown

Pharmacodynamics

Chemical effect: Unknown; probably blocks postsynaptic dopamine receptors in brain.
Therapeutic effect: Relieves anxiety and signs and symptoms of psychotic disorders.

Available forms

Injection: 2 mg/ml
Oral concentrate: 10 mg/ml
Tablets (regular and film-coated): 1 mg, 2 mg, 5 mg, 10 mg

NURSING PROCESS

Assessment

• Assess patient's condition before therapy and regularly thereafter.
• Watch for orthostatic hypotension, especially with parenteral use.
• Monitor patient for tardive dyskinesia, which may occur after prolonged use. It may not appear until months or years later and may disappear spontaneously or persist for life, despite discontinuation of drug.
• Monitor therapy with weekly bilirubin tests during first month; periodic blood tests (CBC and liver function); and ophthalmologic tests (long-term use).
ALERT: Monitor patient for symptoms of neuroleptic malignant syndrome (extrapyramidal effects, hyperthermia, autonomic disturbance), which is rare but can be fatal. It isn't necessarily related to length of drug use or type of neuroleptic; however, more than 60% of patients are men.
• Be alert for adverse reactions and drug interactions.
• Evaluate patient's and family's knowledge of drug therapy.

Nursing diagnoses

• Anxiety related to underlying condition
• Disturbed thought processes related to underlying psychotic disorder
• Deficient knowledge related to drug therapy

Planning and implementation

• Although there is little likelihood of contact dermatitis, people with known sensitivity to phenothiazine drugs should avoid direct contact. Wear gloves when preparing liquid forms.
• **P.O. use:** Dilute liquid concentrate with 60 ml of tomato or fruit juice, carbonated beverage, coffee, tea, milk, water, or semisolid food.
• **I.M. use:** Give deep I.M. only in upper outer quadrant of buttocks. Massage slowly afterward to prevent sterile abscess. Injection may sting.
– Protect drug from light. Slight yellowing of injection or concentrate is common; it doesn't affect potency. Discard markedly discolored solutions.
• Keep patient supine for 1 hour after drug administration, and advise him to change position slowly.
• Don't withdraw drug abruptly unless severe adverse reactions occur. Abrupt withdrawal of long-term therapy may cause gastritis, nausea, vomiting, dizziness, tremor, feeling of warmth or cold, diaphoresis, tachycardia, headache, insomnia, anorexia, muscle rigidity, altered mental status, or evidence of autonomic instability.
• Withhold dose and notify prescriber if patient develops jaundice, symptoms of blood dyscrasia (fever, sore throat, infection, cellulitis, weakness), or persistent extrapyramidal reactions (longer than a few hours), especially in pregnant woman or in child.
• Acute dystonic reactions may be treated with diphenhydramine.
ALERT: Don't confuse trifluoperazine with triflupromazine.

Patient teaching

• Teach patient or caregiver how to prepare oral form of drug.
• Warn patient to avoid activities that require alertness or good psychomotor coordination until CNS effects of drug are known. Drowsiness and dizziness usually subside after a few weeks.
• Tell patient to avoid alcohol during drug therapy.
• Instruct patient to report urine retention or constipation.
• Tell patient to use sun block and to wear protective clothing to avoid photosensitivity reactions.

• Tell patient to relieve dry mouth with sugarless gum or hard candy.

Evaluation
• Patient's anxiety is reduced.
• Patient's behavior and communication exhibit improved thought processes.
• Patient and family state understanding of drug therapy.

trihexyphenidyl hydrochloride
(trigh-heks-eh-FEEN-ih-dil high-droh-KLOR-ighd)
Apo-Trihex♦, Artane*, Artane Sequels, Trihexy-2, Trihexy-5

Pharmacologic class: anticholinergic
Therapeutic class: antiparkinsonian
Pregnancy risk category: C

Indications and dosages
▶ **All forms of parkinsonism and adjunct treatment to levodopa in management of parkinsonism.** *Adults:* 1 mg P.O. first day, then increased by 2 mg q 3 to 5 days until total of 6 to 10 mg is given daily. Usually given t.i.d. with meals. Sometimes given q.i.d. (last dose h.s.). Postencephalitic parkinsonism may require total daily dosage of 12 to 15 mg. Once stabilized, may switch to sustained release capsules on a mg per mg basis; give as a single dose after breakfast or in 2 divided doses 12 hours apart.
▶ **Drug-induced extrapyramidal reactions.** *Adults:* 5 to 15 mg P.O. daily. Initial dose of 1 mg may control some reactions.

Contraindications and precautions
• Contraindicated in patients hypersensitive to drug.
• Use cautiously in patients with glaucoma; cardiac, hepatic, or renal disorders; obstructive disease of GI and GU tracts; or prostatic hyperplasia.
Lifespan: In pregnant women, safety of drug hasn't been established. In breast-feeding women, drug isn't recommended. In children, safety of drug hasn't been established. In geriatric patients, monitor for mental confusion or disorientation.

Adverse reactions
CNS: nervousness, dizziness, headache, hallucinations, drowsiness, weakness.
CV: tachycardia.
EENT: blurred vision, mydriasis, increased intraocular pressure.
GI: *dry mouth,* constipation, *nausea,* vomiting.
GU: urinary hesitancy, urine retention.

Interactions
Drug-drug. *Amantadine:* May have additive anticholinergic reactions, such as confusion and hallucinations. Reduce dosage of trihexyphenidyl before giving.
Levodopa: Increases drug effect. May require lower doses of both drugs.
Drug-lifestyle. *Alcohol use:* Increases sedative effects. Discourage using together.

Effects on lab test results
None reported.

Pharmacokinetics
Absorption: Readily absorbed from GI tract.
Distribution: Unknown; crosses blood-brain barrier.
Metabolism: Unknown.
Excretion: Excreted in urine.

Route	Onset	Peak	Duration
P.O.	≤ 1 hr	2-3 hr	6-12 hr

Pharmacodynamics
Chemical effect: Unknown; blocks central cholinergic receptors, helping to balance cholinergic activity in basal ganglia.
Therapeutic effect: Improves physical mobility in patients with parkinsonism.

Available forms
Capsules (sustained-release): 5 mg
Elixir: 2 mg/5 ml
Tablets: 2 mg, 5 mg

NURSING PROCESS

Assessment
• Assess patient's condition before therapy and regularly thereafter.
ALERT: Gonioscopic ocular evaluation and monitoring of intraocular pressure are needed, especially in patients older than age 40.

• Be alert for adverse reactions and drug interactions. Adverse reactions are dose-related and usually transient.
• Evaluate patient's and family's knowledge of drug therapy.

Nursing diagnoses

• Impaired physical mobility related to presence of parkinsonism
• Risk for injury related to drug-induced adverse CNS reactions
• Deficient knowledge related to drug therapy

Planning and implementation

• Dosage may need to be gradually increased in patient who develops tolerance to drug.
• Give drug with meals.

ALERT: Don't confuse Artane with Anturane or Altace.

Patient teaching

• Warn patient that drug may cause nausea if taken before meals.
• Tell patient to avoid activities that require alertness until CNS effects of drug are known.
• Advise patient to report urinary hesitancy or urine retention.
• Tell patient to relieve dry mouth with cool drinks, ice chips, sugarless gum, or hard candy.

Evaluation

• Patient exhibits improved physical mobility.
• Patient doesn't experience injury from adverse reactions.
• Patient and family state understanding of drug therapy.

trimethobenzamide hydrochloride

(trigh-meth-oh-BEN-zuh-mighd high-droh-KLOR-ighd)

Tebamide, T-Gen, Ticon, Tigan, Triban, Trimazide

Pharmacologic class: ethanolamine-related antihistamine
Therapeutic class: antiemetic
Pregnancy risk category: NR

Indications and dosages

▶ **Nausea, vomiting.** *Adults:* 250 mg P.O. t.i.d. or q.i.d.; or 200 mg I.M. or P.R. t.i.d. or q.i.d.

▶ **Prevention of postoperative nausea and vomiting.** *Adults:* 200 mg I.M. or P.R. as single dose before or during surgery; if needed, repeat 3 hours after termination of anesthesia. Limit use to prolonged vomiting from known cause.
Children weighing 13 to 40 kg (28 to 88 lb): 100 to 200 mg P.O. or P.R. t.i.d. or q.i.d.
Children weighing less than 13 kg: 100 mg P.R. t.i.d. or q.i.d. Don't use in premature or newborn infants.

Contraindications and precautions

• Contraindicated in patients hypersensitive to drug. Suppositories are contraindicated in patients hypersensitive to benzocaine hydrochloride or similar local anesthetics.

Lifespan: In pregnant or breast-feeding women, safety of drug hasn't been established. In children, use cautiously. In children with viral illness, drug isn't recommended because it may contribute to development of Reye's syndrome.

Adverse reactions

CNS: *drowsiness,* dizziness, headache, disorientation, depression, Parkinsonian-like symptoms, ***coma, seizures.***
CV: hypotension.
EENT: blurred vision.
GI: diarrhea.
Hepatic: jaundice.
Musculoskeletal: muscle cramps.
Skin: hypersensitivity reaction (pain, stinging, burning, redness, swelling at I.M. injection site).

Interactions

Drug-drug. *CNS depressants:* May cause additive CNS depression. Avoid using together.
Drug-lifestyle. *Alcohol use:* May cause additive CNS depression. Discourage using together.

Effects on lab test results

None reported.

Pharmacokinetics

Absorption: About 60% after P.O. administration; unknown after P.R. or I.M. administration.
Distribution: Unknown.
Metabolism: About 50% to 70% metabolized, probably in liver.
Excretion: Excreted in urine and feces.

Route	Onset	Peak	Duration
P.O.	10-20 min	Unknown	3-4 hr
I.M.	15-30 min	Unknown	2-3 hr
P.R.	Unknown	Unknown	Unknown

Pharmacodynamics

Chemical effect: Unknown; probably acts on chemoreceptor trigger zone to inhibit nausea and vomiting.
Therapeutic effect: Prevents or relieves nausea and vomiting.

Available forms

Capsules: 100 mg, 250 mg
Injection: 100 mg/ml
Suppositories: 100 mg, 200 mg

NURSING PROCESS

Assessment

- Assess patient's condition before therapy and regularly thereafter.
- Be alert for adverse reactions and drug interactions.
- Evaluate patient's and family's knowledge of drug therapy.

Nursing diagnoses

- Risk for deficient fluid volume related to potential for or presence of nausea and vomiting
- Diarrhea related to drug-induced adverse GI reactions
- Deficient knowledge related to drug therapy

Planning and implementation

- **P.O. use:** Follow normal protocol.
- **I.M. use:** Inject deep into upper outer quadrant of gluteal region to reduce pain and local irritation.
- **P.R. use:** Refrigerate suppositories.
- Withhold drug if skin hypersensitivity reaction occurs.

ALERT: Don't confuse Tigan with Ticar.

Patient teaching

- Advise patient of possibility of drowsiness and dizziness, and caution against driving or performing other activities requiring alertness until CNS effects of drug are known.
- Warn patient that I.M. administration of drug may be painful.
- If patient will be using suppositories, instruct him to remove foil and, if needed, moisten suppository with water for 10 to 30 seconds before inserting. Tell him to store suppositories in refrigerator.

Evaluation

- Patient maintains adequate hydration with cessation of nausea and vomiting.
- Patient maintains normal bowel pattern.
- Patient and family state understanding of drug therapy.

trimethoprim

(trigh-METH-uh-prim)
Alprim◇, Primsol, Proloprim, Trimpex, Triprim◇

Pharmacologic class: synthetic folate antagonist
Therapeutic class: antibiotic
Pregnancy risk category: C

Indications and dosages

▶ **Acute otitis media caused by susceptible strains of *S. pneumoniae* and *H. influenzae*.** *Children age 6 months and older:* 10 mg/kg of Primsol daily in divided doses q 12 hours for 10 days.

▶ **Uncomplicated urinary tract infections caused by *E. coli, P. mirabilis, Klebsiella pneumoniae, Enterobacter* species, coagulase-negative *Staphylococcus* species (including *S. saprophyticus*).** *Adults:* 100 mg (10 ml) q 12 hours, or 200 mg (20 ml) daily for 10 days.

▶ **Prophylaxis of chronic and recurrent urinary tract infections‡.** *Adults:* 100 mg P.O. h.s. for 6 weeks to 6 months.

▶ **Traveler's diarrhea‡.** *Adults:* 200 mg P.O. b.i.d. for 3 to 5 days.

▶ ***Pneumocystis carinii* pneumonia‡.** *Adults:* 5 mg/kg P.O. t.i.d. with dapsone 100 mg daily for 21 days.

Patients with renal impairment: If creatinine clearance is 15 to 30 ml/minute, give half of the recommended dose q 12 hours; if less than 15 ml/minute, don't use drug.

Contraindications and precautions

• Contraindicated in patients hypersensitive to drug and in those with documented megaloblastic anemia caused by folate deficiency.
• Use cautiously in patients with impaired liver function. Dosage should be decreased in patients with severely impaired kidney function.
Lifespan: In pregnant women, use cautiously. In breast-feeding women, drug isn't recommended. In children younger than age 12, safety of drug hasn't been established.

Adverse reactions

CNS: fever.
GI: epigastric distress, nausea, vomiting, diarrhea, glossitis.
Hematologic: ***thrombocytopenia, leukopenia,*** megaloblastic anemia, ***methemoglobinemia.***
Skin: *rash, pruritus,* exfoliative dermatitis.

Interactions

Drug-drug. *Phenytoin:* May decrease phenytoin metabolism and increase its serum level. Monitor patient for toxicity.

Effects on lab test results

• May increase BUN, creatinine, bilirubin, and aminotransferase levels.
• May decrease hemoglobin, hematocrit, and platelet and WBC counts.

Pharmacokinetics

Absorption: Quick and complete.
Distribution: Wide; about 42% to 46% protein-bound.
Metabolism: Less than 20% metabolized in liver.
Excretion: Mostly excreted in urine. *Half-life:* 8 to 11 hours.

Route	Onset	Peak	Duration
P.O.	Unknown	1-4 hr	Unknown

Pharmacodynamics

Chemical effect: Interferes with action of dihydrofolate reductase, inhibiting bacterial synthesis of folic acid.
Therapeutic effect: Inhibits certain bacteria, including many gram-positive and gram-negative organisms, such as most enterobacteriaceae organisms (except *Pseudomonas*), *E. coli, Klebsiella,* and *P. mirabilis.*

Available forms

Oral solution: 50 mg/5 ml
Tablets: 100 mg, 200 mg

NURSING PROCESS

Assessment

• Assess patient's infection before therapy and regularly thereafter.
• Obtain urine specimen for culture and sensitivity tests before giving first dose. Therapy may begin pending results.
ALERT: Monitor CBC routinely. Signs and symptoms such as sore throat, fever, pallor, and purpura may be early indications of serious blood disorders. Prolonged use of trimethoprim at high doses may cause bone marrow suppression.
• Be alert for adverse reactions and drug interactions.
• Monitor patient's hydration status if adverse GI reactions occur.
• Evaluate patient's and family's knowledge of drug therapy.

Nursing diagnoses

• Infection related to presence of susceptible bacteria
• Risk for deficient fluid volume related to drug-induced adverse GI reactions
• Deficient knowledge related to drug therapy

Planning and implementation

• Because resistance to trimethoprim develops rapidly when given alone, it's usually given with other drugs.
ALERT: Trimethoprim is also used with sulfamethoxazole; don't confuse the two products.
• Use isn't recommended in patients with impaired renal function with a creatinine clearance of less than 15 ml/minute. Patients with a creatinine clearance of 15 to 30 ml/minute should receive half the dose recommended for patients of the same age with normal renal function.

Patient teaching
• Instruct patient to take drug as prescribed, even if he feels better.

Evaluation
• Patient is free from infection.
• Patient maintains adequate hydration.
• Patient and family state understanding of drug therapy.

triptorelin pamoate
(trip-TOE-reh-lin PAM-o-eight)
Trelstar Depot, Trelstar LA

Pharmacologic class: synthetic luteinizing hormone–releasing hormone (LHRH) analog
Therapeutic class: antineoplastic
Pregnancy risk category: X

Indications and dosages
▶ **Palliative treatment of advanced prostate cancer.** *Adults:* 3.75 mg I.M. given monthly as a single injection of Trelstar Depot, or 11.25 mg I.M q 12 weeks as Trelstar LA.

Contraindications and precautions
• Contraindicated in patients hypersensitive to triptorelin, its components, other LHRH agonists, or LHRH.
• Use cautiously in patients with metastatic vertebral lesions or upper or lower urinary tract obstruction during the first few weeks of therapy.
Lifespan: In women who are or may become pregnant, drug is contraindicated. If drug is used during pregnancy or if the patient becomes pregnant while she is taking it, she should be informed of the risks to fetus. In breast-feeding women, drug isn't indicated. In children, safety and efficacy haven't been studied; clinical studies have been conducted mainly in patients age 65 and older.

Adverse reactions
CNS: pain, headache, dizziness, *hot flushes,* fatigue, insomnia, emotional lability.
CV: hypertension.
GI: diarrhea, vomiting.
GU: urine retention, urinary tract infection, impotence.
Hematologic: anemia.
Musculoskeletal: *skeletal pain,* leg pain.
Skin: pruritus, pain at injection site.

Interactions
Drug-drug. *Hyperprolactinemic drugs:* Decreases pituitary gonadotropin-releasing hormone (GnRH) receptors. Don't use together.

Effects on lab test results
• May increase glucose, BUN, AST, ALT, and alkaline phosphatase. May transiently increase testosterone level.
• May decrease hemoglobin and hematocrit.

Pharmacokinetics
Absorption: I.M. injection provides plasma levels over a period of a month.
Distribution: No evidence of protein-binding.
Metabolism: Unknown, but is unlikely to involve hepatic microsomal enzymes; no metabolites have been identified.
Excretion: Eliminated by both liver and kidneys.

Route	Onset	Peak	Duration
I.M.	Unknown	Unknown	1 mo

Pharmacodynamics
Chemical effect: Triptorelin is a potent inhibitor of gonadotropin secretion. After the first dose, levels of luteinizing hormone (LH), follicle-stimulating hormone (FSH), testosterone, and estradiol surge transiently. After long-term continuous administration, LH and FSH secretion steadily declines and testicular and ovarian steroidogenesis decreases. In men, testosterone declines to a level typically seen in surgically castrated men. As a result, tissues and functions that depend on these hormones become quiescent.
Therapeutic effect: Decreases effects of sex hormones on tumor growth in the prostate gland.

Available forms
Injection: 3.75 mg, 11.25 mg

NURSING PROCESS

Assessment
• Assess underlying condition before therapy and reassess regularly throughout therapy.

• Monitor testosterone and prostate-specific antigen levels.
• Patients with renal or hepatic impairment have a twofold to fourfold higher risk of adverse effects than young healthy males. The clinical consequence of this increase, as well as the potential need for dose adjustment, is unknown.
• Evaluate patient's and family's knowledge of triptorelin therapy.

Nursing diagnoses
• Ineffective health maintenance related to underlying condition
• Acute pain related to adverse drug effects
• Deficient knowledge related to drug therapy

Planning and implementation
• Give drug only under the supervision of a prescriber.
• Change the injection site periodically.
• Monitor patients with metastatic vertebral lesions or upper or lower urinary tract obstruction during the first few weeks of therapy.
• Initially, triptorelin causes a transient increase in testosterone levels. As a result, signs and symptoms of prostate cancer may worsen during the first few weeks of treatment.
• Patients may experience worsening of symptoms or onset of new symptoms, including bone pain, neuropathy, hematuria, or urethral or bladder outlet obstruction.
• Spinal cord compression, which can lead to paralysis and possibly death, may occur. If spinal cord compression or renal impairment develops, standard treatment should be given. In extreme cases, immediate orchiectomy is considered.
• If patient has a hypersensitivity reaction, stop drug immediately and give supportive and symptomatic care.
• Diagnostic tests of pituitary-gonadal function conducted during and after therapy may be misleading.
• **I.M. use:** Reconstitute powder with 2 ml sterile water, using a 20-gauge needle.

Patient teaching
• Inform the patient about adverse reactions.
• Tell patient that symptoms (including bone pain, neuropathy, hematuria, or urethral or bladder outlet obstruction) may worsen during the first few weeks of therapy.
• Inform patient that a blood test will be used to monitor response to therapy.

Evaluation
• Patient responds well to drug.
• Patient denies pain.
• Patient and family state understanding of drug therapy.

tromethamine
(troh-METH-eh-meen)
Tham

Pharmacologic class: sodium-free organic amine
Therapeutic class: systemic alkalinizer
Pregnancy risk category: C

Indications and dosages
▶ **Metabolic acidosis linked to cardiac bypass surgery or cardiac arrest.** *Adults:* Dosage depends on bicarbonate deficit. Calculate as follows:

Each ml of 0.3 M tromethamine solution required = body weight (kg) × base deficit (mEq/L) × 1.1

Contraindications and precautions
• Contraindicated in patients with anuria, uremia, or chronic respiratory acidosis.
• Use cautiously in patients with renal disease and poor urine output.
Lifespan: In pregnant women, drug is contraindicated, except in acute, life-threatening situations.

Adverse reactions
CNS: fever.
CV: venospasm, I.V. thrombosis.
Hepatic: ***hemorrhagic hepatic necrosis.***
Metabolic: ***hypoglycemia, hyperkalemia*** (with decreased urine output).
Respiratory: ***respiratory depression.***
Other: inflammation, necrosis, sloughing (if extravasation occurs).

Interactions
None significant.

Effects on lab test results

- May increase potassium levels. May decrease glucose levels. May alter liver enzyme levels.

Pharmacokinetics

Absorption: Administered I.V.
Distribution: At pH of 7.4, about 25% of drug is not ionized; this portion may enter cells to neutralize acidic ions of intracellular fluid.
Metabolism: None.
Excretion: Rapidly excreted in urine as bicarbonate salt. *Half-life:* 7 to 40 minutes.

Route	Onset	Peak	Duration
I.V.	Immediate	Immediate	Unknown

Pharmacodynamics

Chemical effect: Combines with hydrogen ions and associated acid anions; resulting salts are excreted. Drug also has osmotic diuretic effect.
Therapeutic effect: Restores normal acid-base balance in body.

Available forms

Injection: 18 g/500 ml

NURSING PROCESS

Assessment

- Assess patient's condition before therapy and regularly thereafter.
- Monitor ECG and serum potassium level in patient with renal disease and poor urine output.
- Make the following determinations before, during, and after therapy: blood pH; carbon dioxide tension; bicarbonate, glucose, and electrolyte levels.
- Be alert for adverse reactions.
- Evaluate patient's and family's knowledge of drug therapy.

Nursing diagnoses

- Ineffective health maintenance related to presence of acid-base imbalance
- Impaired tissue integrity related to tromethamine extravasation
- Deficient knowledge related to drug therapy

Planning and implementation

- Give slowly through 18G to 20G needle into largest antecubital vein or by indwelling I.V. catheter.
- Total dose should be given over at least 1 hour and shouldn't exceed 500 mg/kg. Additional therapy is based on serial determinations of existing bicarbonate deficit.

ALERT: Drug shouldn't be used longer than 1 day except in life-threatening situations.

- Have mechanical ventilation available for patients with associated respiratory acidosis.
- To prevent blood pH from rising above normal, be prepared to adjust dosage carefully.
- If extravasation occurs, infiltrate area with 1% procaine and 150 units hyaluronidase; this may reduce vasospasm and dilute remaining drug locally.

Patient teaching

- Inform patient and family of need for drug, and be prepared to answer their questions.

Evaluation

- Patient regains normal acid-base balance.
- Patient doesn't exhibit signs and symptoms of extravasation.
- Patient and family state understanding of drug therapy.

tubocurarine chloride

(too-boh-kyoo-RAH-reen KLOR-ighd)
Tubarine ◆

Pharmacologic class: nondepolarizing neuromuscular blocker
Therapeutic class: skeletal muscle relaxant
Pregnancy risk category: C

Indications and dosages

▶ **Adjunct to general anesthesia.** Dosage depends on anesthetic used, individual needs, and response. *Adults:* 1 unit/kg or 0.165 mg/kg I.V. slowly over 60 to 90 seconds. Average dose is initially 6 to 9 mg I.V. or I.M., followed by 3 to 4.5 mg in 3 to 5 minutes, if needed. Additional doses of 3 mg may be given if needed during prolonged anesthesia.
Children: 0.6 mg/kg I.V or I.M.
Neonates: 0.3 mg/kg I.V. or I.M.

▶ **To assist with mechanical ventilation.** *Adults and children:* Initially, 0.0165 mg/kg I.V. (average 1 mg), then adjust subsequent doses to patient response.

▶ **To lessen muscle contractions in pharmacologically or electrically induced seizures.** *Adults and children:* 1 unit/kg or 0.165 mg/kg I.V. over 60 to 90 seconds. Initial dose is 3 mg less than calculated dose.

▶ **Diagnosis of myasthenia gravis.** *Adults:* 0.004 to 0.033 mg/kg as single I.V. or I.M. dose.

Contraindications and precautions

- Contraindicated in patients hypersensitive to drug and in those for whom histamine release is hazardous (such as asthmatic patients).
- Use cautiously in debilitated patients and in those with hepatic or pulmonary impairment, hypothermia, respiratory depression, myasthenia gravis, myasthenic syndrome of lung cancer or bronchogenic carcinoma, dehydration, thyroid disorders, collagen diseases, porphyria, electrolyte disturbances, fractures, or muscle spasms.

Lifespan: In women undergoing cesarean delivery and in breast-feeding women, use large doses cautiously. In geriatric patients, use cautiously.

Adverse reactions

CV: hypotension, ***arrhythmias, bradycardia, cardiac arrest.***
GI: increased salivation.
Musculoskeletal: profound and prolonged muscle relaxation, residual muscle weakness.
Respiratory: ***respiratory depression or apnea, bronchospasm.***
Other: ***hypersensitivity reactions, anaphylaxis.***

Interactions

Drug-drug. *Aminoglycoside antibiotics (including amikacin, gentamicin, kanamycin, neomycin, streptomycin), general anesthetics (such as enflurane, halothane, isoflurane), polymyxin antibiotics (colistin, polymyxin B sulfate):* Potentiates neuromuscular blockade, leading to increased skeletal muscle relaxation and potentiation of effect. Use cautiously during surgical and postoperative periods.
Amphotericin B, ethacrynic acid, furosemide, methotrimeprazine, opioid analgesics, propranolol, thiazide diuretics: Potentiates neuromuscular blockade, leading to increased skeletal muscle relaxation and, possibly, respiratory paralysis. Use with extreme caution during surgical and postoperative periods.
Quinidine: Prolongs neuromuscular blockade. Use together cautiously. Monitor patient closely.

Effects on lab test results

None reported.

Pharmacokinetics

Absorption: Unknown.
Distribution: Distributed in extracellular fluid and rapidly reaches its site of action; about 50% bound to plasma proteins, mainly globulins.
Metabolism: Undergoes *N*-demethylation in liver.
Excretion: About 33% to 75% excreted unchanged in urine in 24 hours; up to 11% excreted in bile.

Route	Onset	Peak	Duration
I.V., I.M.	≤ 1 min	2-5 min	20-40 min

Pharmacodynamics

Chemical effect: Prevents acetylcholine from binding to receptors on muscle end plate, thus blocking depolarization.
Therapeutic effect: Relaxes skeletal muscles; diagnostic aid for myasthenia gravis.

Available forms

Injection: 3 mg (20 units)/ml

NURSING PROCESS

Assessment

- Assess patient's condition before therapy and regularly thereafter.
- Monitor baseline electrolyte determinations (imbalance can potentiate neuromuscular blocking effects).
- Check vital signs every 15 minutes.
- Measure fluid intake and output; renal dysfunction prolongs duration of action because much of drug is unchanged before excretion.
- Monitor respiratory rate closely until patient is fully recovered from neuromuscular blockade, as evidenced by tests of muscle strength (hand grip, head lift, and ability to cough).
- Be alert for adverse reactions and drug interactions.

• Evaluate patient's and family's knowledge of drug therapy.

Nursing diagnoses

• Ineffective health maintenance related to underlying condition
• Ineffective breathing pattern related to drug-induced respiratory depression
• Deficient knowledge related to drug therapy

Planning and implementation

• Allow succinylcholine effects to subside before giving tubocurarine.
• Give sedatives or general anesthetics before neuromuscular blockers. Neuromuscular blockers don't obtund consciousness or alter pain threshold.
• Only personnel skilled in airway management should give tubocurarine.
• Keep airway clear. Have emergency respiratory support equipment immediately available.
• **I.V. use:** Give drug I.V. over 60 to 90 seconds.
– Don't mix drug with barbiturates (precipitate will form). Use only fresh solutions and discard if discolored.
• **I.M. use:** Follow normal protocol.
• Notify prescriber at once if changes in vital signs occur.
ALERT: Nerve stimulator and train-of-four monitoring are recommended to confirm antagonism of neuromuscular blockade and recovery of muscle strength. Before attempting pharmacologic reversal with neostigmine, some evidence of spontaneous recovery should be evident.
• Give analgesics.
ALERT: Careful drug calculation is essential. Do not confuse units with mg. Always verify dosage with another health care professional.

Patient teaching

• Explain all events and happenings to patient because he still can hear.
• Reassure patient that he is being monitored at all times.

Evaluation

• Patient responds well to drug.
• Patient maintains adequate breathing patterns with or without mechanical assistance.
• Patient and family state understanding of drug therapy.

U

unoprostone isopropyl

(yoo-noh-PROST-ohn igh-soh-PROH-pul)
Rescula

Pharmacologic class: docosanoid
Therapeutic class: antiglaucoma agent, ocular antihypertensive
Pregnancy risk category: C

Indications and dosages

▶ **Reduction of intraocular pressure (IOP) in patients with open-angle glaucoma or ocular hypertension who can't tolerate or who respond inadequately to other IOP-lowering drugs.** *Adults:* 1 gtt in the affected eye b.i.d.

Contraindications and precautions

• Contraindicated in patients hypersensitive to unoprostone isopropyl, benzalkonium chloride, or other ingredients in product.
• Use cautiously in patients with active intraocular inflammation (uveitis) or with angle-closure, inflammatory, or neovascular glaucoma.
• Use cautiously in patients with renal or hepatic impairment.
Lifespan: In pregnant women, weigh risks and benefits before giving drug. In breast-feeding women, effects of drug are unknown.

Adverse reactions

CNS: dizziness, headache, insomnia, pain.
CV: hypertension.
EENT: abnormal vision, blepharitis, cataracts, conjunctivitis, corneal lesion, *dry eyes,* eye discharge, *eye burning or stinging,* eye discomfort, eye irritation, eye hemorrhage, decreased length of eyelashes, *increased length of eyelashes,* eyelid disorder, foreign body sensation, keratitis, lacrimal disorder, pharyngitis, photophobia, rhinitis, sinusitis, vitreous disorder, *eye itching, injection of eye.*
Metabolic: diabetes mellitus.
Musculoskeletal: back pain.
Respiratory: bronchitis, increased cough.

Other: accidental injury, allergic reaction, flu-like syndrome.

Interactions

None reported.

Effects on lab test results

None reported.

Pharmacokinetics

Absorption: Absorbed through the cornea and conjunctival epithelium. Systemic absorption is minimal.
Distribution: Unknown.
Metabolism: Hydrolyzed by esterases to form unoprostone free acid.
Elimination: Rapid. Metabolites are excreted mainly in urine. *Half-life:* 14 minutes.

Route	Onset	Peak	Duration
Ophthalmic	Unknown	Unknown	Unknown

Pharmacodynamics

Chemical effect: Unknown. Thought to increase the outflow of aqueous humor.
Therapeutic effect: Reduces IOP.

Available forms

Ophthalmic solution: 0.15% (1.5 mg/ml)

NURSING PROCESS

Assessment

- Assess underlying condition before therapy and reassess regularly throughout therapy.
- Evaluate whether patient is wearing contact lenses. Don't use drug while patient is wearing contact lenses because drug contains benzalkonium chloride, which may be absorbed by the lenses. Have patient remove his contact lenses before giving drug. Lenses may be reinserted 15 minutes after administration.
- Assess solution carefully before instilling. Serious eye damage and blindness may result from using contaminated solutions.
- Evaluate patient's and family's knowledge of drug therapy.

Nursing diagnoses

- Noncompliance related to long-term therapy
- Risk for injury related to adverse EENT effects of drug
- Deficient knowledge related to drug therapy

Planning and implementation

- Avoid touching the tip of the container to the eye because this could cause infection.
- When giving an additional ophthalmic drug, separate administration of the drugs by 5 minutes.
- Store drug at room temperature (36° to 77° F).

Patient teaching

- Instruct patient to avoid touching the tip of the container to the eye because this could contaminate the tip and cause an eye infection. Serious eye damage and blindness may result from using contaminated solutions.
- Urge patient not to instill drops while wearing contact lenses. Tell patient to remove contact lenses before using drug and to wait 15 minutes before reinserting them.
- Tell patient that drug may permanently change eye color. Change may be gradual, over months to years.
- Instruct patient to report adverse effects, especially conjunctivitis (pink eye) or eyelid reactions.
- Before continuing to use a multidose container, tell patient to notify health care provider if eye trauma or infection occur or if ocular surgery is planned.
- Tell patient that drug may be used with other ocular drugs, but that doses should be separated by 5 minutes.
- Warn patient not to use if he's allergic to this drug, benzalkonium chloride, or any other ingredient in the product.
- Instruct patient to notify prescriber if she becomes pregnant or intends to breast-feed while taking drug.

Evaluation

- Patient is compliant with drug therapy.
- Patient sustains no injury.
- Patient and family state understanding of drug therapy.

urea (carbamide)

(yoo-REE-eh)
Ureaphil

Pharmacologic class: carbonic acid salt
Therapeutic class: osmotic diuretic
Pregnancy risk category: C

Indications and dosages

▶ **Elevated intracranial or intraocular pressure.** *Adults:* 1 to 1.5 g/kg as 30% solution by slow I.V. infusion over 1 to 2½ hours. Maximum dose is 120 g daily.
Children older than age 2: 0.5 to 1.5 g/kg slow I.V. infusion or 35 g/m² in 24 hours. Children younger than age 2 may receive as little as 0.1 g/kg slow I.V. infusion.
▶ **SIADH‡.** *Adults:* 80 g as a 30% solution I.V. over 6 hours.
▶ **Diuresis‡.** *Adults and children older than age 2:* 500 mg to 1.5 g/kg as a 30% solution given by slow I.V. infusion over 30 minutes to 2 hours.
Children age 2 and younger: 100 mg to 1.5 g/kg as a 30% solution given by slow I.V. infusion over 30 minutes to 2 hours.

Contraindications and precautions

- Contraindicated in patients with severely impaired kidney function, marked dehydration, frank hepatic failure, active intracranial bleeding, or sickle cell disease with CNS involvement.
- Use cautiously in patients with cardiac disease or hepatic or renal impairment.

Lifespan: In pregnant or breast-feeding women, use cautiously.

Adverse reactions

CNS: *headache,* syncope, disorientation, dizziness.
CV: hypotension, tachycardia, ECG changes.
GI: *nausea, vomiting.*
Metabolic: hyponatremia, hypokalemia, fluid overload.
Other: irritation, necrotic sloughing (with extravasation), hemolysis (with rapid administration).

Interactions

Drug-drug. *Lithium:* Increases lithium clearance and decreases lithium effectiveness. Monitor lithium level.

Effects on lab test results

- May decrease potassium and sodium levels.

Pharmacokinetics

Absorption: Administered I.V.
Distribution: Distributed in intracellular and extracellular fluid, including lymph, bile, and CSF.
Metabolism: Hydrolyzed in GI tract by bacterial uridase.
Excretion: Excreted by kidneys.

Route	Onset	Peak	Duration
I.V.	30-45 min	1-2 hr	3-10 hr

Pharmacodynamics

Chemical effect: Increases osmotic pressure of glomerular filtrate, inhibiting tubular reabsorption of water and electrolytes. Drug also elevates blood plasma osmolality, resulting in enhanced water flow into extracellular fluid.
Therapeutic effect: Promotes water excretion, which in turn reduces intracranial and intraocular pressure.

Available forms

Injection: 40 g/150 ml

NURSING PROCESS

Assessment

- Assess patient's condition before therapy and regularly thereafter.
- Assess breath sounds for crackles, indicating pulmonary edema.
- Watch for signs of hyponatremia (nausea, vomiting, tachycardia) or hypokalemia (muscle weakness, lethargy); they may indicate electrolyte depletion before levels are reduced.
- Monitor blood pressure, fluid intake and output, and electrolyte levels.
- In patient with renal disease, monitor BUN level.
- Be alert for adverse reactions and drug interactions.
- Evaluate patient's and family's knowledge of drug therapy.

Nursing diagnoses

- Excess fluid volume related to presence of water retention
- Acute pain related to drug-induced headache
- Deficient knowledge related to drug therapy

Planning and implementation

- To prepare 135 ml of 30% solution, mix contents of 40-g vial of urea with 105 ml of D_5W or dextrose 10% in water or 10% invert sugar

in water. Each ml of 30% solution provides 300 mg of urea.
• Use only freshly reconstituted urea for I.V. infusion; solution becomes ammonia on standing. Use within minutes of reconstitution and discard within 24 hours.
ALERT: Avoid rapid I.V. infusion; it may cause hemolysis or increased capillary bleeding. Maximum infusion rate is 4 ml/minute. Watch for irritation and infiltration; extravasation can cause tissue damage and necrosis.
• Don't give drug through same infusion set as blood or blood derivatives.
• Don't infuse drug into leg veins; doing so may cause phlebitis or thrombosis, especially in geriatric patients.
• Maintain adequate hydration.
• To ensure bladder emptying in comatose patient, use indwelling urinary catheter. Use hourly urometer collection bag for accurate evaluation of diuresis.
• If satisfactory diuresis doesn't occur in 6 to 12 hours, urea should be discontinued and kidney function reevaluated.
• Give mild analgesic if drug-induced headache occurs.

Patient teaching
• Inform patient and family of need for urea therapy, and answer any questions.

Evaluation
• Patient exhibits decreased intracranial or intraocular pressure.
• Patient states that drug-induced headache is relieved with mild analgesic.
• Patient and family state understanding of drug therapy.

urokinase
(yoo-roh-KIGH-nays)
Abbokinase

Pharmacologic class: thrombolytic enzyme
Therapeutic class: thrombolytic enzyme
Pregnancy risk category: B

Indications and dosages
▶ **Lysis of acute massive pulmonary emboli and pulmonary emboli accompanied by unstable hemodynamics.** *Adults:* For I.V. infusion only by constant infusion pump; priming dose: 4,400 IU/kg over 10 minutes, followed with 4,400 IU/kg per hour for 12 hours.
▶ **Coronary artery thrombosis‡.** *Adults:* 6,000 IU/minute intra-arterially via a coronary artery catheter until artery is maximally opened, usually within 15 to 30 minutes; however, drug may be administered for up to 2 hours. Average total dose, 5,000 IU.
▶ **Venous catheter occlusion‡.** *Adults:* Instill 5,000 IU into occluded line.

Contraindications and precautions
• Contraindicated in patients with active internal bleeding; history of CVA; aneurysm; arteriovenous malformation; bleeding diathesis; recent trauma with possible internal injuries; visceral or intracranial cancer; ulcerative colitis; diverticulitis; severe hypertension; hemostatic defects, including those secondary to severe hepatic or renal insufficiency; uncontrolled hypocoagulation; subacute bacterial endocarditis or rheumatic valvular disease; or recent cerebral embolism, thrombosis, or hemorrhage.
• Also contraindicated within 10 days after intra-arterial diagnostic procedure or surgery (liver or kidney biopsy, lumbar puncture, thoracentesis, paracentesis, or extensive or multiple cutdowns); and within 2 months after intracranial or intraspinal surgery.
• I.M. injections and other invasive procedures are contraindicated during urokinase therapy.
Lifespan: In pregnant women, drug is contraindicated. Also contraindicated during the first 10 days postpartum. In children, safety of drug hasn't been established.

Adverse reactions
CNS: fever.
CV: ***reperfusion arrhythmias,*** hypotension.
Hematologic: ***bleeding.***
GI: nausea, vomiting.
Respiratory: ***bronchospasm,*** minor breathing difficulties.
Other: phlebitis at injection site, hypersensitivity reactions, ***anaphylaxis,*** chills.

Interactions
Drug-drug. *Anticoagulants:* Increases risk of bleeding. Monitor patient closely.
Aspirin, dipyridamole, indomethacin, phenylbutazone, other drugs affecting platelet activi-

ty: Increases risk of bleeding. Monitor patient closely.

Effects on lab test results

- May increase PT, PTT, and INR. May decrease hemoglobin and hematocrit.

Pharmacokinetics

Absorption: Administered I.V.
Distribution: Rapidly cleared from circulation; most of drug accumulates in kidneys and liver.
Metabolism: Rapidly metabolized in liver.
Excretion: Small amount excreted in urine and bile. *Half-life:* 10 to 20 minutes.

Route	Onset	Peak	Duration
I.V.	Immediate	20 min-2 hr	About 4 hr

Pharmacodynamics

Chemical effect: Activates plasminogen by directly cleaving peptide bonds at two sites.
Therapeutic effect: Dissolves blood clots in lungs, coronary arteries, and venous catheters.

Available forms

Injection: 250,000-IU vial

NURSING PROCESS

Assessment

- Assess patient's condition before therapy and regularly thereafter.
- Assess patient for any contraindications to the therapy.
- Monitor patient for excessive bleeding every 15 minutes for first hour; every 30 minutes for second through eighth hours; then once every shift. Pretreatment with drugs affecting platelets places patient at high risk for bleeding.
- Monitor pulse rates and color and sensation of limbs every hour.
- Although risk of hypersensitivity is low, watch for signs of reaction.
- Keep laboratory flow sheet on patient's chart to monitor PTT, PT, INR, hemoglobin, and hematocrit.
- Monitor vital signs.
- Be alert for adverse reactions and drug interactions.
- Evaluate patient's and family's knowledge of drug therapy.

Nursing diagnoses

- Ineffective tissue perfusion (cardiopulmonary, peripheral) related to presence of blood clot(s)
- Ineffective protection related to drug-induced bleeding
- Deficient knowledge related to drug therapy

Planning and implementation

- Have typed and crossmatched RBCs, whole blood, and aminocaproic acid available to treat bleeding, and corticosteroids to treat allergic reactions.
- Add 5 ml of sterile water for injection to vial. Dilute further with normal saline solution or D_5W solution before infusion. Total volume of fluid administered shouldn't exceed 200 ml. Don't use bacteriostatic water for injection to reconstitute; it contains preservatives. Urokinase solutions may be filtered through 0.45-mcg or smaller cellulose membrane filter before administration. Give by infusion pump.
- Keep venipuncture sites to a minimum; use pressure dressing on puncture sites for at least 15 minutes.
- Keep limb being treated in straight alignment to prevent bleeding from infusion site.
- Avoid unnecessary handling of patient; pad side rails. Bruising is more likely during therapy.
- To prevent recurrent thrombosis, heparin by continuous infusion should be started when patient's thrombin time has decreased to less than twice the normal control value after urokinase has been stopped.

Patient teaching

- Instruct patient to report symptoms of bleeding and other adverse reactions.

Evaluation

- Patient regains normal tissue perfusion with dissolution of blood clots.
- Patient doesn't experience serious complications from drug-induced bleeding.
- Patient and family state understanding of drug therapy.

ursodiol

(ur-sih-DIGH-al)
Actigall

Pharmacologic class: bile acid
Therapeutic class: gallstone-solubilizing agent
Pregnancy risk category: B

Indications and dosages

▶ **Dissolution of gallstones smaller than 20 mm in diameter in patients who are poor candidates for surgery or who refuse surgery.** *Adults:* 8 to 10 mg/kg P.O. daily in two or three divided doses.

Contraindications and precautions

- Contraindicated in patients hypersensitive to ursodiol or other bile acids.
- Contraindicated in patients with chronic hepatic disease, unremitting acute cholecystitis, cholangitis, biliary obstruction, gallstone-induced pancreatitis, or biliary fistula.

Lifespan: In pregnant or breast-feeding women, use cautiously. In children, safety of drug hasn't been established.

Adverse reactions

CNS: *headache,* fatigue, anxiety, depression, *dizziness,* sleep disorders.
EENT: rhinitis.
GI: *nausea, vomiting, dyspepsia,* metallic taste, *abdominal pain,* biliary pain, cholecystitis, *diarrhea, constipation,* stomatitis, flatulence.
GU: urinary tract infection.
Musculoskeletal: arthralgia, myalgia, back pain.
Respiratory: cough.
Skin: pruritus, rash, dry skin, urticaria, hair thinning, diaphoresis.

Interactions

Drug-drug. *Antacids that contain aluminum, cholestyramine, colestipol:* Binds ursodiol and prevents its absorption. Avoid using together.
Clofibrate, estrogens, oral contraceptives: Increases hepatic cholesterol secretion; may counteract effects of ursodiol. Avoid using together.

Effects on lab test results

- May increase liver enzyme levels.

Pharmacokinetics

Absorption: About 90%.
Distribution: After absorption, ursodiol enters portal vein and is extracted from portal blood by liver (first-pass effect), where it's conjugated and then secreted into hepatic bile ducts. Ursodiol in bile is concentrated in gallbladder and expelled into duodenum in gallbladder bile. A small amount appears in systemic circulation.
Metabolism: Metabolized in liver. A small amount undergoes bacterial degradation with each cycle of enterohepatic circulation.
Excretion: Excreted primarily in feces. A very small amount is excreted in urine. Reabsorbed free ursodiol is reconjugated by liver.

Route	Onset	Peak	Duration
P.O.	Unknown	1-3 hr	Unknown

Pharmacodynamics

Chemical effect: Unknown; probably suppresses hepatic synthesis and secretion of cholesterol as well as intestinal cholesterol absorption. After long-term administration, ursodiol can solubilize cholesterol from gallstones.
Therapeutic effect: Dissolves cholesterol gallstones.

Available forms

Capsules: 300 mg

NURSING PROCESS

Assessment

- Assess patient's condition before therapy and regularly thereafter.
- Usually therapy is long-term and requires ultrasound images of gallbladder taken at 6-month intervals. If partial stone dissolution doesn't occur within 12 months, eventual success is unlikely. Safety of use for longer than 24 months hasn't been established.

ALERT: Monitor liver function test results, including AST and ALT levels, at beginning of therapy, after 1 month, after 3 months, and then every 6 months during ursodiol therapy. Abnormal test results may indicate worsening of disease. A hepatotoxic metabolite of ursodiol may form in some patients.

- Be alert for adverse reactions and drug interactions.
- Monitor patient's hydration status if adverse GI reactions occur.
- Evaluate patient's and family's knowledge of drug therapy.

Nursing diagnoses

- Risk for injury related to presence of gallstones
- Risk for deficient fluid volume related to drug-induced adverse GI reactions
- Deficient knowledge related to drug therapy

Planning and implementation

- Drug won't dissolve calcified cholesterol stones, radiolucent bile pigment stones, or radiopaque stones.

Patient teaching

- Tell patient about alternative therapies, including watchful waiting (no intervention) and cholecystectomy because relapse rate after bile acid therapy may be as high as 50% after 5 years.

Evaluation

- Patient is free from gallstones.
- Patient maintains adequate hydration.
- Patient and family state understanding of drug therapy.

V

valacyclovir hydrochloride

(val-ay-SIGH-kloh-veer high-droh-KLOR-ighd)

Valtrex

Pharmacologic class: synthetic purine nucleoside

Therapeutic class: antiviral

Pregnancy risk category: B

Indications and dosages

▶ **Treatment of herpes zoster (shingles) in immunocompetent patients.** *Adults:* 1 g P.O. t.i.d. daily for 7 days. Dosage is adjusted for patients with impaired kidney function, based on creatinine clearance.

▶ **Treatment of initial episodes of genital herpes in immunocompetent adults.** *Adults:* 1 g P.O. b.i.d. for 10 days.

▶ **Recurrent genital herpes in immunocompetent patients.** *Adults:* 500 mg P.O. b.i.d. for 3 days.

▶ **Chronic suppressive therapy of recurrent genital herpes.** *Adults:* 1 g P.O. once daily. In patients with a history of nine or fewer recurrences per year, may give 500 mg once daily.

Patients with renal impairment: Dosage adjustments necessary.

Contraindications and precautions

- Contraindicated in patients hypersensitive to or intolerant of valacyclovir, acyclovir, or components of their formulations.
- Drug isn't recommended for immunocompromised patients. Thrombotic thrombocytopenic purpura and hemolytic uremic syndrome have been fatal in some patients with advanced HIV disease and in bone marrow transplant and renal transplant recipients.
- Use cautiously in patients with renal impairment and in those receiving other nephrotoxic drugs.

Lifespan: In pregnant women, drug should be given only if potential benefits outweigh risk to the fetus. In breast-feeding women and in children, safety and efficacy haven't been established.

Adverse reactions

CNS: *headache,* dizziness, depression.
GI: *nausea,* vomiting, diarrhea, abdominal pain.
GU: dysmenorrhea.
Musculoskeletal: arthralgia.

Interactions

Drug-drug. *Cimetidine, probenecid:* Reduces rate (but not extent) of conversion from valacyclovir to acyclovir and reduces renal clearance of acyclovir, thereby increasing acyclovir blood levels. Monitor patient for possible toxicity.

Effects on lab test results

- May increase AST, ALT, alkaline phosphatase, and creatinine levels.

• May decrease hemoglobin and WBC and platelet counts.

Pharmacokinetics

Absorption: Rapid; absolute bioavailability of about 54.5%.
Distribution: Protein-binding ranges from 13.5% to 17.9%.
Metabolism: Rapidly and nearly completely converted to acyclovir and L-valine by first-pass intestinal or hepatic metabolism.
Excretion: Excreted in urine and feces. *Half-life:* Averages 2.5 to 3.3 hours.

Route	Onset	Peak	Duration
P.O.	30 min	Unknown	Unknown

Pharmacodynamics

Chemical effect: Rapidly converted to acyclovir, which becomes incorporated into viral DNA and inhibits viral DNA polymerase, thereby inhibiting viral replication.
Therapeutic effect: Inhibits susceptible viral growth of herpes zoster.

Available forms

Caplets: 500 mg, 1,000 mg

NURSING PROCESS

Assessment

• Assess patient's infection before therapy.
• Evaluate patient's and family's knowledge of drug therapy.

Nursing diagnoses

• Risk for infection related to herpes zoster
• Deficient fluid volume related to adverse GI reactions
• Deficient knowledge related to drug therapy

Planning and implementation

• Follow-up studies haven't shown an increased risk of birth defects for infants born to patients exposed to the drug during pregnancy.
• Dosage adjustment may be needed in geriatric patient, depending on underlying renal status.
• Although overdose hasn't been reported, precipitation of acyclovir in renal tubules may occur when solubility (2.5 mg/ml) is exceeded in the intratubular fluid. In the event of acute renal failure and anuria, the patient may benefit from hemodialysis until kidney function is restored.
ALERT: Don't confuse valacyclovir with valganciclovir.

Patient teaching

• Inform patient that drug may be taken without regard to meals.
• Review signs and symptoms of herpes infection (rash, tingling, itching, and pain), and advise patient to notify prescriber immediately if they occur. Treatment should begin as soon as possible after symptoms appear, preferably within 48 hours.

Evaluation

• Patient is free from infection.
• Patient maintains adequate hydration.
• Patient and family state understanding of drug therapy.

valdecoxib

(val-da-COX-ibb)
Bextra

Pharmacologic class: COX-2 inhibitor
Therapeutic class: nonsteroidal anti-inflammatory drug (NSAID)
Pregnancy risk category: C

Indications and dosages

▶ **Osteoarthritis, rheumatoid arthritis.** *Adults:* 10 mg P.O. once daily.
▶ **Primary dysmenorrhea.** *Adults:* 20 mg P.O. b.i.d.

Contraindications and precautions

• Contraindicated in patients hypersensitive to this drug or sulfonamides. Contraindicated in those with aspirin sensitivity that results in aspirin-induced asthma. Don't give to patients who have experienced asthma, urticaria, or allergic-type reactions after taking aspirin or NSAIDs. Don't use in patients with advanced renal or hepatic disease.
• Use with extreme caution in patients with a history of GI bleeding or peptic ulcer disease.
• Use cautiously in geriatric and debilitated patients, and in patients with conditions or on therapies that may increase the risk of GI bleeding, such as treatment with oral cortico-

steroids or anticoagulants, longer duration of NSAID therapy, smoking, alcoholism, and poor general health.
• Use cautiously in patients with impaired renal function, heart failure, hypertension, and preexisting asthma, and in those taking diuretics or ACE inhibitors. Also use cautiously in dehydrated patients and in patients with fluid retention or mild-to-moderate hepatic impairment.
Lifespan: In early pregnancy, use only if benefits outweigh risks. In late pregnancy, don't use drug; it may cause premature closure of the ductus arteriosus. In breast-feeding women, discontinue drug or breast-feeding, taking into account the importance of the drug to the mother; it isn't known whether drug appears in breast milk. In children, safety and effectiveness of drug haven't been established.

Adverse reactions

CNS: dizziness, headache, ***cerebrovascular disorder.***
CV: hypertension, angina pectoris, ***arrhythmias, heart failure, aneurysm,*** peripheral edema.
EENT: sinusitis.
GI: abdominal fullness, abdominal pain, diarrhea, dyspepsia, flatulence, nausea.
Hematologic: ***thrombocytopenia, leukopenia.***
Hepatic: ***hepatitis.***
Musculoskeletal: back pain, myalgia.
Respiratory: upper respiratory tract infection, ***bronchospasm.***
Skin: rash, ***Stevens-Johnson syndome.***
Other: flulike syndrome, accidental injury, ***hypersensitivity reactions.***

Interactions

Drug-drug. *Aspirin:* Increases risk of GI ulceration. Use together cautiously.
ACE inhibitors: May diminish antihypertensive effect. Monitor blood pressure carefully.
Furosemide, thiazide diuretics: May reduce natriuretic effect. Monitor patient carefully.
Dextromethorphan: Increases levels of dextromethorphan. Monitor patient carefully.
Lithium: Delays lithium clearance. Monitor lithium levels.
Warfarin: May increase anticoagulant activity. Monitor INR closely.
Fluconazole, ketoconazole: Enhances valdecoxib effects. Monitor patient closely.

Effects on lab test results

• May increase ALT, AST, alkaline phosphatase, BUN, creatine phosphokinase, creatinine clearance, cholesterol, glucose, potassium, lipid, uric acid, and LDH levels. May decrease calcium and potassium levels.
• May decrease hemoglobin, hematocrit, and platelet and WBC counts.

Pharmacokinetics

Absorption: Maximal plasma concentrations achieved in 3 hours.
Distribution: 98% protein-bound.
Metabolism: Extensive hepatic metabolism via P-450 and non–P-450 pathways.
Excretion: Eliminated predominantly via hepatic metabolism. Less than 5% of dose is excreted unchanged in urine and feces; 70% of dose is excreted via urine as metabolites.

Route	Onset	Peak	Duration
P.O.	Unknown	3 hr	Unknown

Pharmacodynamics

Chemical effect: May inhibit prostaglandin synthesis primarily through inhibition of cyclooxygenase-2 (COX-2). COX-1 doesn't appear to be inhibited at human therapeutic concentrations.
Therapeutic effect: Decreases pain, inflammation, and fever.

Available forms

Tablets: 10 mg, 20 mg

NURSING PROCESS

Assessment

• Assess underlying condition before therapy and reassess regularly throughout therapy.
• Assess volume status before therapy. Dehydrated patients should be rehydrated before treatment starts.
• Monitor kidney function if used in advanced kidney disease.
• Monitor patient carefully for signs and symptoms of GI toxicity, such as bleeding or ulceration.
• Monitor patient for signs and symptoms of anemia.
• Monitor hemoglobin and hematocrit in patients on long-term therapy.

• Evaluate patient's and family's knowledge of drug therapy.

Nursing diagnoses

• Chronic pain related to underlying condition
• Impaired physical mobility related to underlying condition
• Deficient knowledge related to valdecoxib therapy

Planning and implementation

• GI toxicity, as indicated by bleeding, ulceration, or perforation of the stomach, small intestine, or large intestine, can occur without warning. Risk increases with longer duration of treatment.
• Anaphylactoid reactions may occur in patients who have never before been exposed to the drug.
• Taper corticosteroid therapy slowly if discontinuing therapy.
• Liver function test results may be elevated, and there may be progression to more serious hepatic abnormalities.
• Stop drug if hepatic disease is suspected or if systemic symptoms such as eosinophilia or rash occur.

ALERT: Stop drug at the first sign of a skin rash or a hypersensitivity reaction and immediately notify the prescriber.

• Symptoms of overdose may include lethargy, drowsiness, nausea, vomiting, and epigastric pain. These are usually reversible with supportive treatment. GI bleeding, hypertension, acute renal failure, respiratory depression, and coma may occur. Anaphylactoid reactions also may occur. Treatment is symptomatic and supportive. No antidote exists.

ALERT: Don't confuse Bextra with Arixtra.

Patient teaching

• Advise patient to notify prescriber if signs or symptoms of GI bleeding and ulceration, weight gain, edema, skin rash, or liver toxicity (nausea, fatigue, lethargy, jaundice, right upper quadrant tenderness, flulike symptoms) occur.
• Advise patient to seek emergency attention if he has trouble breathing, especially if he has a history of aspirin sensitivity.

Evaluation

• Patient is free from pain.
• Patient states that physical mobility has improved.
• Patient and family state understanding of drug therapy.

valganciclovir

(val-gan-SYE-kloh-veer)
Valcyte

Pharmacologic class: synthetic nucleoside
Therapeutic class: antiviral drug
Pregnancy risk category: C

Indications and dosages

▶ **Active cytomegalovirus (CMV) retinitis in patients with AIDS.** *Adults:* 900 mg (two 450-mg tablets) P.O. b.i.d. with food for 21 days; maintenance dose: 900 mg (two 450-mg tablets) P.O. once daily with food.
▶ **Inactive CMV retinitis.** *Adults:* 900 mg (two 450-mg tablets) P.O. once daily with food.

Contraindications and precautions

• Contraindicated in patients hypersensitive to valganciclovir or ganciclovir.
• Don't use in patients receiving hemodialysis.
• Use cautiously in patients with preexisting cytopenias and in those who have received immunosuppressants or radiation.

Lifespan: In breast-feeding women, don't use drug; it's unknown whether drug appears in breast milk and there may be serious adverse reactions in infants who are breast-fed. In children, safety and effectiveness haven't been established.

Adverse reactions

CNS: *pyrexia, headache, insomnia,* peripheral neuropathy, paresthesia, ***seizures,*** psychosis, hallucinations, confusion, agitation.
EENT: *retinal detachment.*
GI: *diarrhea, nausea, vomiting, abdominal pain.*
Hematologic: NEUTROPENIA, *anemia,* ***thrombocytopenia, pancytopenia, bone marrow depression, aplastic anemia.***
Other: catheter-related infection, ***sepsis,*** local or systemic infections, ***hypersensitivity reactions.***

Interactions

Drug-drug. *Didanosine:* Possible increased absorption of didanosine. Monitor patient closely for didanosine toxicity.
Immunosuppressants, zidovudine: Possible enhanced neutropenia, anemia, thrombocytopenia, and bone marrow depression when used together. Monitor CBC.
Mycophenolate mofetil: Possible increased levels of both drugs in renally impaired patients. Use together carefully.
Probenecid: Decreases renal clearance of ganciclovir. Monitor patient for ganciclovir toxicity.
Drug-food. *Any food:* Increases absorption of drug. Give drug with food.

Effects on lab test results

- May increase creatinine levels.
- May decrease hemoglobin, hematocrit, and RBC, WBC, neutrophil, and platelet counts.

Pharmacokinetics

Absorption: Well absorbed from GI tract. Higher when taken with food.
Distribution: Minimal binding to plasma proteins.
Metabolism: Metabolized in intestinal wall and liver to ganciclovir.
Excretion: Eliminated renally.

Route	Onset	Peak	Duration
P.O.	Unknown	1-3 hr	Unknown

Pharmacodynamics

Chemical effect: Drug is a prodrug that is converted to ganciclovir, which inhibits replication of viral DNA synthesis of CMV.
Therapeutic effect: Inhibits CMV.

Available forms

Tablets: 450 mg

NURSING PROCESS

Assessment

- Assess underlying condition before therapy and reassess regularly throughout therapy.
- Obtain baseline laboratory studies before beginning therapy and reassess regularly.
- Evaluate patient's and family's knowledge of drug therapy.

Nursing diagnoses

- Risk for imbalanced fluid volume related to adverse GI effects
- Ineffective protection related to adverse hematologic reactions
- Deficient knowledge related to valganciclovir therapy

Planning and implementation

- Patients with impaired renal function may need reduced dosage.
- Overdose may cause severe, fatal bone marrow depression and renal toxicity. Treatment should include maintenance of adequate hydration and consideration of hematopoietic growth factors. Dialysis may be useful in reducing serum levels.
- Make sure to adhere to dosing guidelines for valganciclovir because ganciclovir and valganciclovir aren't interchangeable, and overdose may occur.
- Cytopenia may occur at any time during treatment and may increase with continued dosing. Cell counts usually recover 3 to 7 days after stopping drug.
- No drug interaction studies have been conducted with valganciclovir; however, because drug is converted to ganciclovir, it can be assumed that drug interactions would be similar.
- Drug may cause temporary or permanent inhibition of spermatogenesis.
- Women of childbearing age must use contraception during treatment. Men should use barrier contraception during and for 90 days after treatment.
- Clinical toxicities include severe leukopenia, neutropenia, anemia, pancytopenia, bone marrow depression, aplastic anemia and thrombocytopenia. Don't use if patient's ANC is less than 500 cells/mm^3, platelets are less than 25,000/mm^3, or hemoglobin is less than 8 g/dl.
- Monitor CBC, platelet counts, and creatinine levels or creatinine clearance values frequently during treatment.

ALERT: Don't confuse valganciclovir with valacyclovir.

Patient teaching

- Tell patient to use contraception during treatment.
- Instruct patient about infection control and bleeding precautions.
- Tell patient to take drug with food.

☑ Evaluation

- Patient remains well hydrated throughout therapy.
- Patient has no serious adverse hematologic reactions.
- Patient and family state understanding of drug therapy.

valproate sodium

(val-PROH-ayt SOH-dee-um)

Depacon, Depakene, Epilim ◇, Valpro ◇

valproic acid

Depakene

divalproex sodium

Depakote, Depakote ER, Depakote Sprinkle, Epival ♦

Pharmacologic class: carboxylic acid derivative
Therapeutic class: anticonvulsant
Pregnancy risk category: D

Indications and dosages

▶ **Complex partial seizures, simple and complex absence seizures, mixed seizure types (including absence seizures).** *Adults and children age 10 and older:* Initially, 15 mg/kg P.O. daily; then increased by 5 to 10 mg/kg daily at weekly intervals up to maximum of 60 mg/kg daily. When dose exceeds 250 mg daily, drug should be divided into two or more equal doses. Or, 10 to 15 mg/kg I.V. daily, increased by 5 to 10 mg/kg/week to clinical response. Maximum daily I.V. dose is 60 mg/kg.

▶ **Mania.** ***divalproex sodium delayed-release.*** *Adults:* Initially, 750 mg P.O. daily in divided doses. Maximum daily dose is 60 mg/kg.

▶ **Migraine prophylaxis.** ***divalproex sodium delayed-release.*** *Adults:* 250 mg P.O. b.i.d.; may increase up to 1,000 mg daily. Or, 500 mg of extended-release tablets P.O. once daily for 1 week; then may increase to 1 g once daily.

▶ **Status epilepticus refractory to I.V. diazepam‡.** *Adults:* 400 to 600 mg P.R. q 6 hours.

Contraindications and precautions

- Contraindicated in patients hypersensitive to drug and patients with hepatic dysfunction or urea cycle disorder (UCD).

Lifespan: In pregnant or breast-feeding women, drug isn't recommended. In elderly patients, start at lower dose.

Adverse reactions

CNS: *sedation,* emotional upset, depression, psychosis, aggressiveness, hyperactivity, behavioral deterioration, muscle weakness, tremor, ataxia, headache, dizziness, incoordination.
EENT: nystagmus, diplopia.
GI: *nausea, vomiting, indigestion,* diarrhea, abdominal cramps, constipation, increased appetite and weight gain, anorexia, ***pancreatitis.***
Hematologic: petechiae, bruising, eosinophilia, ***hemorrhage, leukopenia, bone marrow suppression, thrombocytopenia,*** increased bleeding time.
Hepatic: ***toxic hepatitis, hepatotoxicity.***
Skin: rash, alopecia, pruritus, photosensitivity reactions, ***erythema multiforme.***

Interactions

Drug-drug. *Aspirin, chlorpromazine, cimetidine, felbamate:* May cause valproic acid toxicity. Use together cautiously and monitor levels.
Benzodiazepines, other CNS depressants: May cause excessive CNS depression. Avoid using together.
Carbamazepine: May result in carbamazepine CNS toxicity (acute psychotic reaction). Carefully monitor drug levels.
Cholestyramine: Decreases valproate level. Monitor patient for decreased effect.
Erythromycin: Increases valproate level. Monitor patient for toxicity.
Lamotrigine: Inhibits lamotrigine metabolism. Decrease lamotrigine dosage when valproic acid therapy is initiated.
Phenobarbital: Increases phenobarbital levels. Monitor patient closely.
Phenytoin: Increases or decreases phenytoin level and increases metabolism of valproic acid. Monitor patient closely.
Rifampin: May decrease valproate levels. Monitor levels.

Warfarin: Valproic acid may displace warfarin from binding sites. Monitor PT and INR.
Drug-herb. *Glutamine:* Increases risk of seizures. Discourage using together.
White willow: Herb contains substances similar to aspirin. Discourage using together.
Drug-lifestyle. *Alcohol use:* May cause excessive CNS depression. Discourage using together.

Effects on lab test results

- May increase ALT, AST, and bilirubin levels.
- May increase eosinophil count and bleeding time. May decrease platelet and WBC counts.

Pharmacokinetics

Absorption: Valproate sodium and divalproex sodium quickly convert to valproic acid after administration. Valproic acid is then quickly and almost completely absorbed from the GI tract.
Distribution: Distributed rapidly throughout body; 80% to 95% protein-bound.
Metabolism: Metabolized by liver.
Excretion: Excreted primarily in urine; some excreted in feces and exhaled air. *Half-life:* 6 to 16 hours (may be considerably longer in patient with liver function impairment, in geriatric patient, and in child up to age 18 months; may be considerably shorter in patient receiving hepatic enzyme-inducing anticonvulsants).

Route	Onset	Peak	Duration
P.O.	Unknown	1-4 hr	Unknown
I.V., P.R.	Unknown	Unknown	Unknown

Pharmacodynamics

Chemical effect: Unknown; probably increases brain levels of gamma-aminobutyric acid, which transmits inhibitory nerve impulses in CNS.
Therapeutic effect: Prevents and treats certain types of seizure activity.

Available forms

valproate sodium
Injection: 100 mg/ml
Syrup: 250 mg/ml
valproic acid
Capsules: 250 mg
Tablets (crushable): 100 mg ◇
Tablets (enteric-coated): 200 mg ◇, 500 mg ◇
Syrup: 200 mg/5 ml ◇
divalproex sodium
Capsules (containing coated particles): 125 mg
Tablets (delayed-release): 125 mg, 250 mg, 500 mg
Tablets (extendeded-release): 500 mg

NURSING PROCESS

Assessment

- Assess patient's condition before therapy and regularly thereafter.
- Monitor level. Therapeutic blood level is 50 to 100 mcg/ml.
- Monitor liver function studies, platelet counts, and PT before starting drug and periodically thereafter.
- Be alert for adverse reactions and drug interactions.
- Evaluate patient's and family's knowledge of drug therapy.

Nursing diagnoses

- Risk for trauma related to seizure activity
- Disturbed thought processes related to drug-induced adverse CNS reactions
- Deficient knowledge related to drug therapy

Planning and implementation

- **P.O. use:** Don't give syrup to patient who needs sodium restriction. Check with prescriber.
– Give drug with food or milk to minimize adverse GI reactions.
- **I.V. use:** Dilute with at least 50 ml of a compatible diluent (D_5W, saline solution, lactated Ringer's injection) and give I.V. over 1 hour. Don't exceed 20 mg/minute.
- Sudden withdrawal may worsen seizures. Call prescriber at once if adverse reactions develop.

ALERT: Serious or fatal hepatotoxicity may follow nonspecific symptoms, such as malaise, fever, and lethargy. Notify prescriber at once if patient has suspected or apparently substantial hepatic dysfunction because drug will need to be discontinued.

- Patients at high risk for developing hepatotoxicity include those with congenital metabolic disorders, mental retardation, or organic brain disease; those taking other anticonvulsants; and children younger than age 2.

• Divalproex sodium carries a lower risk of adverse GI effects than other drug forms.
• Notify prescriber if tremors occur. Dosage may need to be reduced.
• Drug may produce false-positive test results for ketones in urine.
ALERT: Hyperammonemic encephalopathy, sometimes fatal, may occur following initiation of valproate therapy in patients with UCDs, a group of uncommon genetic abnormalities, particularly ornithine transcarbamylase deficiency. Evaluate patients with risk factors linked to UCDs before initiation of valproate therapy. Patients who develop symptoms of unexplained hyperammonemic encephalopathy during valproate therapy should have drug discontinued, undergo prompt appropriate treatment, and be evaluated for underlying UCD.

Patient teaching
• Tell patient that drug may be taken with food or milk to reduce adverse GI effects.
• Advise patient not to chew capsules and not to crush or chew extended-release tablets.
• Tell patient and parents that syrup shouldn't be mixed with carbonated beverages.
• Tell patient and parents to keep drug out of children's reach.
• Warn patient and parents not to stop drug therapy abruptly.
• Advise patient to refrain from driving or performing other potentially hazardous activities that require mental alertness until drug's CNS effects are known.

✓ Evaluation
• Patient is free from seizure activity.
• Patient maintains normal thought processes.
• Patient and family state understanding of drug therapy.

valrubicin
(val-ROO-buh-sin)
Valstar

Pharmacologic class: anthracycline
Therapeutic class: antineoplastic
Pregnancy risk category: C

Indications and dosages
▶ **Intravesical therapy of BCG-refractory carcinoma in situ of the urinary bladder in patients for whom immediate cystectomy would be linked to unacceptable morbidity or mortality.** *Adults:* 800 mg intravesically once weekly for 6 weeks.

Contraindications and precautions
• Contraindicated in patients hypersensitive to drug, other anthracyclines, or Cremophor EL (polyoxyethyleneglycol triricinoleate). Also contraindicated in patients with urinary tract infections, patients with a small bladder capacity (unable to tolerate a 75-ml instillation), patients with a perforated bladder, or those in whom the integrity of the bladder mucosa has been compromised.
• Use cautiously in patients with severe irritable bladder symptoms.
Lifespan: In breast-feeding women, don't use. In children, safety and effectiveness haven't been established.

Adverse reactions
CNS: asthenia, headache, malaise, dizziness, fever.
CV: vasodilation, chest pain, peripheral edema.
GI: diarrhea, flatulence, nausea, vomiting, abdominal pain.
GU: urine retention, *urinary tract infection, urinary frequency, dysuria, urinary urgency, bladder spasm, hematuria, bladder pain, urinary incontinence,* pelvic pain, urethral pain, nocturia, *cystitis,* local burning.
Hematologic: anemia.
Metabolic: hyperglycemia.
Musculoskeletal: myalgia, back pain.
Respiratory: pneumonia.
Skin: rash.

Interactions
None reported.

Effects on lab test results
• May increase glucose level.
• May decrease hemoglobin and hematocrit.

Pharmacokinetics
Absorption: Unknown.
Distribution: Penetrates into the bladder wall after intravesical administration. Systemic ex-

posure depends on the condition of the bladder wall.

Metabolism: Metabolites found in the blood.

Excretion: Drug is almost completely excreted by voiding the solution.

Route	Onset	Peak	Duration
Intravesical	Unknown	Unknown	Unknown

Pharmacodynamics

Chemical effect: Drug is an anthracycline that exerts cytotoxic activity by penetrating into cells, inhibiting the incorporation of nucleosides into nucleic acids, causing extensive chromosomal damage, and arresting the cell cycle in G_2. It also interferes with the normal DNA breaking-resealing action of DNA topoisomerase II, thereby inhibiting DNA synthesis.

Therapeutic effect: Kills certain cancer cells.

Available forms

Solution for intravesical instillation: 200 mg/5 ml

NURSING PROCESS

Assessment

- Obtain history of patient's underlying condition before therapy and reassess regularly thereafter.
- For patients undergoing transurethral resection of the bladder, evaluate the status of the bladder before intravesical instillation of drug in order to avoid dangerous systemic exposure. For bladder perforation, delay administration until bladder integrity has been restored.
- Monitor patient for myelosuppression, which begins during the first week, with the nadir by the second week and recovery by the third week.
- Monitor patient closely for disease recurrence or progression by cystoscopy, biopsy, and urine cytology every 3 months.
- Monitor CBC every 3 weeks if valrubicin is given when bladder rupture or perforation is suspected.
- Evaluate patient's and family's knowledge about drug therapy.

Nursing diagnoses

- Impaired urinary elimination related to drug-induced adverse effects
- Imbalanced nutrition: less than body requirements related to drug-induced adverse GI effects
- Deficient knowledge related to drug therapy

Planning and implementation

- Procedures for proper handling and disposal of antineoplastic drugs should be used.
- Use caution when handling and preparing solution. Use gloves during dose preparation and administration. Prepare and store solution in glass, polypropylene, or polyolefin containers and tubing, and use polyethylene-lined administration sets. Don't use polyvinyl chloride I.V. bags and tubing.
- Use aseptic techniques during administration to avoid introducing contaminants into the urinary tract or traumatizing the urinary mucosa.
- To prepare, slowly warm four vials of the drug to room temperature. Withdraw a total of 20 ml from the four vials (200 mg valrubicin in each 5-ml vial), and dilute with 55 ml of normal saline solution for injection, providing 75 ml of a diluted valrubicin solution.
- Refrigerate unopened vials at 2° to 8° C (36° to 46° F). Diluted valrubicin is stable for 12 hours at temperatures up to 25° C (77° F).

ALERT: Don't mix valrubicin with other drugs because compatibility is unknown.

ALERT: Drug should be given intravesically only under the supervision of clinicians experienced in the use of intravesical antineoplastic drugs. Don't give I.V. or I.M.

- To give drug, first drain the bladder by inserting a urethral catheter into the patient's bladder under aseptic conditions. Then, instill the solution slowly via gravity flow over a period of several minutes. Withdraw the catheter. The patient should retain the drug for 2 hours before voiding. At the end of 2 hours, have the patient void. (Some patients will be unable to retain the drug for the full 2 hours.)
- In patients with severe irritable bladder symptoms, bladder spasm and spontaneous discharge of the intravesical instillate may occur. Clamping of the urinary catheter isn't advised and, if performed, should be executed cautiously under medical supervision.
- If carcinoma in situ (CIS) doesn't show a complete response to valrubicin treatment after 3 months, or if it recurs, cystectomy must be

reconsidered because, if delayed, the patient could develop metastatic bladder cancer.

Patient teaching

- Inform patient that drug has been shown to induce complete response in only about 1 in 5 patients with refractory CIS. If there isn't a complete response of CIS to treatment after 3 months, or if CIS recurs, tell patient to discuss with prescriber the risks of cystectomy versus the risks of metastatic bladder cancer.
- Advise patient to retain the drug for 2 hours before voiding, if possible. Instruct patient to void at the end of 2 hours.
- Instruct patient to maintain adequate hydration following treatment.
- Inform patient that the major adverse reactions are related to irritable bladder symptoms that may occur during instillation and retention of the drug and for a limited period following voiding. For the first 24 hours following administration, red-tinged urine is typical. Tell patient to immediately report prolonged irritable bladder symptoms or prolonged passage of red-colored urine.
- Advise women of childbearing age to avoid pregnancy during treatment. Effective contraception should be used by all patients, including men, during the treatment period.

☑ Evaluation

- Patient maintains adequate urinary elimination.
- Patient doesn't experience adverse GI effects.
- Patient and family state understanding of drug therapy.

valsartan

(val-SAR-tin)
Diovan

Pharmacologic class: angiotensin II receptor blocker
Therapeutic class: antihypertensive
Pregnancy risk category: C (D in second and third trimesters)

Indications and dosages

▶ **Hypertension, used alone or with other antihypertensives.** *Adults:* Initially, 80 mg P.O. once daily. Expect a reduction in blood pressure in 2 to 4 weeks. If additional antihypertensive effect is needed, dose may be increased to 160 or 320 mg daily, or a diuretic may be added. (Addition of a diuretic has a greater effect than dose increases above 80 mg.) Usual dose range is 80 to 320 mg daily.

▶ **Heart failure (New York Heart Association classes II to IV) in patients who are intolerant of angiotensin converting enzyme (ACE) inhibitors.** *Adults:* Initially, 40 mg P.O. b.i.d. Increase as tolerated to 80 mg b.i.d. Maximum dosage is 160 mg b.i.d.

Contraindications and precautions

- Contraindicated in patients hypersensitive to drug.

Lifespan: During second or third trimester of pregnancy or in breast-feeding women, don't give drug. In children, safety and effectiveness haven't been established.

Adverse reactions

CNS: headache, *dizziness,* fatigue.
CV: edema.
EENT: rhinitis, sinusitis, pharyngitis.
GI: abdominal pain, diarrhea, nausea.
Hematologic: ***neutropenia.***
Metabolic: ***hyperkalemia.***
Musculoskeletal: arthralgia.
Respiratory: upper respiratory tract infection, cough.
Other: viral infections, ***angioedema.***

Interactions

Drug-drug. *Other angiotensin II blockers, potassium sparing diuretics, potassium supplements:* Increases potassium level. Avoid using together.

Drug-food. *Salt substitutes containing potassium:* Increases potassium levels. Discourage using together.

Effects on lab test results

- May increase potassium level.
- May decrease neutrophil count.

Pharmacokinetics

Absorption: Bioavailability about 25%; food decreases absorption.
Distribution: Not distributed into tissues extensively; 95% bound to serum proteins.
Metabolism: Metabolized in liver and kidneys.

Excretion: Excreted in urine and feces.

Route	Onset	Peak	Duration
P.O.	Within 2 hr	2-4 hr	24 hr

Pharmacodynamics

Chemical effect: Blocks binding of angiotensin II to receptor sites in vascular smooth muscle and adrenal gland.
Therapeutic effect: Inhibits pressor effects of renin-angiotensin system.

Available forms

Tablets: 80 mg, 160 mg, 320 mg

NURSING PROCESS

Assessment
- Use cautiously in patients with severe renal or hepatic disease.
- Monitor patient for hypotension. Correct volume and sodium depletions before starting drug therapy.

Nursing diagnoses
- Risk for injury related to presence of hypertension
- Deficient knowledge related to drug therapy

Planning and implementation
- Drug can be given without regard to meals.

Patient teaching
- Tell woman to notify prescriber if she becomes pregnant.
- Teach patient other means of reducing blood pressure, including proper diet, exercise, smoking cessation, and decreasing stress.

Evaluation
- Patient's blood pressure becomes normal.
- Patient and family state understanding of drug therapy.

vancomycin hydrochloride
(van-koh-MIGH-sin high-droh-KLOR-ighd)
Vancocin, Vancoled

Pharmacologic class: glycopeptide
Therapeutic class: antibiotic
Pregnancy risk category: C

Indications and dosages

▶ **Severe staphylococcal infections when other antibiotics are ineffective or contraindicated.** *Adults:* 500 mg I.V. q 6 hours, or 1 g q 12 hours.
Children: 40 mg/kg I.V. daily in divided doses q 6 hours.
Neonates: Initially, 15 mg/kg; then 10 mg/kg I.V. daily, divided q 12 hours for first week after birth; then q 8 hours up to age 1 month.
Patients with renal impairment: Dosage adjustment necessary.

▶ **Antibiotic-related pseudomembranous and staphylococcal enterocolitis.** *Adults:* 125 to 500 mg P.O. q 6 hours for 7 to 10 days.
Children: 40 mg/kg P.O. daily in divided doses q 6 to 8 hours for 7 to 10 days. Maximum, 2 g daily.
Patients with renal impairment: Dosage adjustment necessary.

▶ **Endocarditis prophylaxis for dental procedures.** *Adults:* 1 g I.V. slowly over 1 hour, starting 1 hour before procedure.
Children: 20 mg/kg I.V. over 1 hour, starting 1 hour before procedure.
Patients with renal impairment: Dosage adjustment necessary.

Contraindications and precautions

- Contraindicated in patients hypersensitive to drug.
- Use cautiously in patients receiving other neurotoxic, nephrotoxic, or ototoxic drugs; patients older than age 60; and those with impaired liver or kidney function, hearing loss, or allergies to other antibiotics.

Lifespan: In pregnant women, use cautiously. In breast-feeding women, safety of drug hasn't been established.

Adverse reactions

CNS: fever, pain.
CV: hypotension.
EENT: tinnitus, ototoxicity.
GI: nausea.
GU: ***nephrotoxicity, pseudomembranous colitis.***
Hematologic: eosinophilia, ***leukopenia.***
Respiratory: wheezing, dyspnea.
Skin: "red-neck" or "red-man" syndrome (maculopapular rash on face, neck, trunk, and limbs with rapid I.V. infusion; pruritus and hypotension with histamine release).

Other: chills, ***anaphylaxis,*** superinfection, thrombophlebitis at injection site.

Interactions

Drug-drug. *Aminoglycosides, amphotericin B, cisplatin, pentamidine:* Increases risk of nephrotoxicity and ototoxicity. Monitor patient closely.

Effects on lab test results

- May increase BUN and creatinine levels.
- May increase eosinophil counts. May decrease neutrophil and WBC counts.

Pharmacokinetics

Absorption: Minimal systemic absorption with P.O. administration. (Drug may accumulate in patients with colitis or renal failure.)
Distribution: Distributed in body fluids; achieves therapeutic levels in CSF if meninges inflamed.
Metabolism: Unknown.
Excretion: Excreted in urine with parenteral administration; excreted in feces with P.O. administration. *Half-life:* 6 hours.

Route	Onset	Peak	Duration
P.O.	Unknown	Unknown	Unknown
I.V.	Immediate	Immediate	Unknown

Pharmacodynamics

Chemical effect: Hinders bacterial cell wall synthesis, damaging bacterial plasma membrane and making cell more vulnerable to osmotic pressure.
Therapeutic effect: Kills susceptible bacteria, including many gram-positive organisms, including those resistant to other antibiotics. It's useful for *Staphylococcus epidermidis,* methicillin-resistant *Staphylococcus aureus,* and penicillin-resistant *Streptococcus pneumoniae.*

Available forms

Capsules: 125 mg, 250 mg
Powder for injection: 500-mg, 1-g vials
Powder for oral solution: 1-g, 10-g bottles

NURSING PROCESS

Assessment

- Assess patient's infection before therapy and regularly thereafter.
- Obtain urine specimen for culture and sensitivity tests before giving first dose. Therapy may begin pending test results.
- Obtain hearing evaluation and kidney function studies before therapy and repeat during therapy.
- Check serum levels regularly, especially in geriatric patients, premature infants, and those with decreased renal function.
- Be alert for adverse reactions and drug interactions.
- Evaluate patient's and family's knowledge of drug therapy.

Nursing diagnoses

- Risk for infection related to presence of susceptible bacteria
- Risk for injury related to drug-induced adverse reactions
- Deficient knowledge related to drug therapy

Planning and implementation

- Patient with renal dysfunction needs dosage adjustment.

ALERT: Oral administration is ineffective for systemic infections, and I.V. administration is ineffective for pseudomembranous (*Clostridium difficile*) diarrhea.

- **P.O. use:** Oral form is stable for 2 weeks if refrigerated.
- **I.V. use:** For I.V. infusion, dilute in 200 ml of saline solution injection or D_5W and infuse over 60 minutes.
  - Check site daily for phlebitis and irritation. Report pain at infusion site. Watch for irritation and infiltration; extravasation can cause tissue damage and necrosis.
  - If red-neck or red-man syndrome occurs because drug is infused too rapidly, stop infusion and report to prescriber.
  - Refrigerate I.V. solution after reconstitution and use within 96 hours.
- Don't give drug I.M.
- When using drug to treat staphylococcal endocarditis, give for at least 4 weeks.

Patient teaching

- Tell patient to take entire amount of drug exactly as directed, even after he feels better.
- Tell patient to stop drug immediately and report adverse reactions, especially fullness or ringing in ears.

Evaluation

- Patient is free from infection.
- Patient doesn't experience injury from adverse reactions.
- Patient and family state understanding of drug therapy.

vasopressin (ADH)

(VAY-soh-preh-sin)
Pitressin

Pharmacologic class: posterior pituitary hormone
Therapeutic class: ADH, peristaltic stimulant
Pregnancy risk category: C

Indications and dosages

▶ **Neurogenic diabetes insipidus.** *Adults:* 5 to 10 units I.M. or S.C. b.i.d. to q.i.d., p.r.n. Or, intranasally (aqueous solution used as spray or applied to cotton balls) in individualized doses, based on response.
Children: 2.5 to 10 units I.M. or S.C. b.i.d. to q.i.d., p.r.n. Or, intranasally (aqueous solution used as spray or applied to cotton balls) in individualized doses.
▶ **Postoperative abdominal distention.** *Adults:* Initially, 5 units (aqueous) I.M.; then q 3 to 4 hours, dose increased to 10 units, if needed. Dose reduced proportionately for children.
▶ **To expel gas before abdominal X-ray.** *Adults:* 10 units S.C. 2 hours before X-ray; then again 30 minutes later.

Contraindications and precautions

- Contraindicated in patients with chronic nephritis accompanied by nitrogen retention.
- Use cautiously in preoperative and postoperative polyuric patients, and those with seizure disorders, migraine headache, asthma, CV disease, heart failure, renal disease, goiter with cardiac complications, arteriosclerosis, or fluid overload.

Lifespan: In pregnant or breast-feeding women, children, and geriatric patients, use cautiously.

Adverse reactions

CNS: tremor, vertigo, headache.
CV: angina in patients with vascular disease, vasoconstriction, ***arrhythmias, cardiac arrest,*** myocardial ischemia, circumoral pallor, decreased cardiac output.
GI: abdominal cramps, nausea, vomiting, flatulence.
Skin: cutaneous gangrene, diaphoresis.
Other: water intoxication (drowsiness, listlessness, headache, confusion, weight gain, ***seizures, coma***), ***hypersensitivity reactions*** (urticaria, ***angioedema, bronchoconstriction, anaphylaxis***).

Interactions

Drug-drug. *Carbamazepine, chlorpropamide, clofibrate, fludrocortisone, tricyclic antidepressants:* Increases antidiuretic response. Use together cautiously.
Demeclocycline, heparin, lithium, norepinephrine: Reduces antidiuretic activity. Use together cautiously.
Drug-lifestyle. *Alcohol use:* Reduces antidiuretic activity. Discourage using together.

Effects on lab test results

None reported.

Pharmacokinetics

Absorption: Unknown.
Distribution: Distributed throughout extracellular fluid without evidence of protein-binding.
Metabolism: Most of drug is destroyed rapidly in liver and kidneys.
Excretion: Excreted in urine. *Half-life:* 10 to 20 minutes.

Route	Onset	Peak	Duration
S.C., I.M., intranasal	Unknown	Unknown	2-8 hr

Pharmacodynamics

Chemical effect: Increases permeability of renal tubular epithelium to adenosine monophosphate and water; epithelium promotes reabsorption of water and produces concentrated urine (ADH effect).
Therapeutic effect: Promotes water reabsorption and stimulates GI motility.

Available forms

Injection: 0.5-, 1-, and 10-ml ampules (20 units/ml)

NURSING PROCESS

Assessment
- Assess patient's condition before therapy and regularly thereafter.
- Monitor specific gravity of urine and fluid intake and output to aid evaluation of drug effectiveness.
- To prevent possible seizures, coma, and death, observe patient closely for early signs of water intoxication.
- Monitor blood pressure of patient on vasopressin frequently. Watch for excessively elevated blood pressure or lack of response to drug, which may be indicated by hypotension. Also monitor daily weight.
- Be alert for adverse reactions and drug interactions.
- Evaluate patient's and family's knowledge of drug therapy.

Nursing diagnoses
- Risk for deficient fluid volume related to polyuria from diabetes insipidus
- Diarrhea related to drug-induced increased GI motility
- Deficient knowledge related to drug therapy

Planning and implementation
- Drug may be used for transient polyuria resulting from ADH deficiency related to neurosurgery or head injury.
- Minimum effective dosage should be used to reduce adverse reactions.
- Give drug with one to two glasses of water to reduce adverse reactions and to improve therapeutic response.
- A rectal tube facilitates gas expulsion after vasopressin injection.
- **I.M. and S.C. use:** Follow normal protocol.

ALERT: Never inject during first stage of labor; doing so may cause uterus to rupture.
- **Intranasal use:** Aqueous solution can be used as a spray or applied to cotton balls. Follow manufacturer's guidelines for intranasal use.

ALERT: Don't confuse vasopressin with desmopressin.

Patient teaching
- Instruct patient how to give drug. Tell patient taking drug S.C. to rotate injection sites to prevent tissue damage.
- Stress importance of monitoring fluid intake and output.
- Tell patient to notify prescriber immediately if adverse reactions occur.

Evaluation
- Patient maintains adequate hydration.
- Patient doesn't experience diarrhea.
- Patient and family state understanding of drug therapy.

vecuronium bromide
(veh-kyoo-ROH-nee-um BROH-mighd)
Norcuron

Pharmacologic class: nondepolarizing neuromuscular blocker
Therapeutic class: skeletal muscle relaxant
Pregnancy risk category: C

Indications and dosages

▶ **Adjunct to general anesthesia; to facilitate endotracheal intubation; to provide skeletal muscle relaxation during surgery or mechanical ventilation.** Dosage depends on anesthetic used, individual needs, and response. Dosages are representative and must be adjusted.
Adults and children age 10 and older: Initially, 0.08 to 0.1 mg/kg I.V. bolus. Maintenance doses of 0.01 to 0.015 mg/kg within 25 to 40 minutes of initial dose should be given during prolonged surgical procedures. Maintenance doses may be given q 12 to 15 minutes in patients receiving balanced anesthesia. Or, drug may be given by continuous I.V. infusion of 1 mcg/kg/minute initially, then 0.8 to 1.2 mcg/kg/minute.
Children younger than age 10: May require slightly higher initial dose as well as supplementation slightly more often than adults.

Contraindications and precautions
- Contraindicated in patients hypersensitive to bromides.
- Use cautiously in patients with altered circulation caused by CV disease and edematous states, and in patients with hepatic disease, severe obesity, bronchogenic carcinoma, electrolyte disturbances, or neuromuscular disease.

Lifespan: In pregnant or breast-feeding women and geriatric patients, use cautiously.

Adverse reactions

Musculoskeletal: skeletal muscle weakness.
Respiratory: ***prolonged, dose-related respiratory insufficiency or apnea.***

Interactions

Drug-drug. *Aminoglycoside antibiotics, including amikacin, gentamicin, kanamycin, neomycin, streptomycin; bacitracin; clindamycin; general anesthetics, such as enflurane, halothane, isoflurane; other skeletal muscle relaxants; polymyxin antibiotics such as colistin, polymyxin B sulfate; quinidine; tetracyclines:* Potentiates neuromuscular blockade, leading to increased skeletal muscle relaxation and potentiation of effect. Use cautiously during surgical and postoperative periods.

Effects on lab test results

None reported.

Pharmacokinetics

Absorption: Administered I.V.
Distribution: Distributed in extracellular fluid and rapidly reaches its site of action (skeletal muscles); 60% to 90% plasma protein–bound.
Metabolism: Undergoes rapid and extensive hepatic metabolism.
Excretion: Excreted in feces and urine. *Half-life:* 20 minutes.

Route	Onset	Peak	Duration
I.V.	≤ 1 min	3-5 min	25-30 min

Pharmacodynamics

Chemical effect: Prevents acetylcholine from binding to receptors on motor end plate, thus blocking depolarization.
Therapeutic effect: Relaxes skeletal muscle.

Available forms

Injection: 10 mg/vial, 20 mg/vial

NURSING PROCESS

Assessment

- Assess patient's condition before therapy and regularly thereafter.
- Monitor respiratory rate closely until patient is fully recovered from neuromuscular blockade as evidenced by tests of muscle strength (hand grip, head lift, and ability to cough).
- Be alert for adverse reactions and drug interactions.
- Evaluate patient's and family's knowledge of drug therapy.

Nursing diagnoses

- Ineffective health maintenance related to underlying condition
- Ineffective breathing pattern related to drug's effect on respiratory muscles
- Deficient knowledge related to drug therapy

Planning and implementation

- Keep airway clear. Have emergency respiratory support equipment available immediately.
- Drug should be used only by personnel skilled in airway management.
- Previous administration of succinylcholine may enhance neuromuscular blocking effect and duration of action.
- Give sedatives or general anesthetics before neuromuscular blockers. Neuromuscular blockers don't obtund consciousness or alter pain threshold.
- Give drug by rapid I.V. injection. Or, 10 to 20 mg may be added to 100 ml of compatible solution and given by I.V. infusion. Compatible solutions include D_5W, normal saline solution for injection, dextrose 5% in normal saline solution for injection, and lactated Ringer's injection.
- Don't mix drug with alkaline solutions.
- Store reconstituted solution in refrigerator. Discard after 24 hours.
- Give analgesics for pain.
- Nerve stimulator and train-of-four monitoring are recommended to confirm antagonism of neuromuscular blockade and recovery of muscle strength. Before attempting pharmacologic reversal with neostigmine, some evidence of spontaneous recovery should be seen.

ALERT: Careful dosage calculation is essential. Always verify with another health care professional.

Patient teaching

- Explain all events and happenings to patient because he can still hear.
- Reassure patient that he is being monitored at all times.

Evaluation

- Patient responds well to drug.

• Patient maintains effective breathing pattern with mechanical assistance.
• Patient and family state understanding of drug therapy.

venlafaxine hydrochloride
(ven-leh-FAKS-een high-droh-KLOR-ighd)
Effexor, Effexor XR

Pharmacologic class: neuronal serotonin, norepinephrine, and dopamine reuptake inhibitor
Therapeutic class: antidepressant
Pregnancy risk category: C

Indications and dosages

▶ **Depression.** *Adults:* Initially, 75 mg P.O. daily in two or three divided doses or 1 single dose if given as extended-release form with food. Dosage increased as tolerated and needed in increments of 75 mg daily at intervals of no less than 4 days. For moderately depressed outpatients, usual maximum daily dosage is 225 mg; in certain severely depressed patients, dosage may be as high as 350 mg daily.
▶ **Generalized or social anxiety disorder.** *Adults:* 75 mg P.O. once daily as extended-release capsule. May increase p.r.n. in increments of 75 mg daily at intervals of no less than 4 days to maximum of 225 mg daily.

Contraindications and precautions

• Contraindicated in patients hypersensitive to drug and those who took an MAO inhibitor within 14 days.
• Use cautiously in patients with renal impairment or diseases, those with conditions that could affect hemodynamic responses or metabolism, and those with a history of mania or seizures.
Lifespan: In pregnant or breast-feeding women, use cautiously. In children, safety of drug hasn't been established.

Adverse reactions

CNS: *asthenia, headache, somnolence, dizziness, nervousness, insomnia,* anxiety, tremor, abnormal dreams, paresthesia, agitation.
CV: hypertension.
EENT: blurred vision.
GI: *nausea, constipation,* vomiting, *dry mouth, anorexia,* diarrhea, dyspepsia, flatulence.
GU: *abnormal ejaculation,* impotence, urinary frequency, impaired urination.
Metabolic: weight loss.
Skin: *diaphoresis,* rash.
Other: yawning, chills, infection.

Interactions

Drug-drug. *Haloperidol:* Increases haloperidol levels. Use together cautiously.
MAO inhibitors: May precipitate syndrome similar to neuroleptic malignant syndrome (myoclonus, hyperthermia, seizures, and death). Don't start venlafaxine within 14 days of stopping an MAO inhibitor, and don't start MAO inhibitor within 7 days of stopping venlafaxine.
Trazodone: May cause serotonin syndrome. Avoid using together.
Drug-herb. *St. John's wort:* Increases sedative-hypnotic effects. Discourage using together.
Yohimbe: May cause additive stimulation. Discourage using together.

Effects on lab test results

None reported.

Pharmacokinetics

Absorption: About 92%.
Distribution: About 25% to 29% protein-bound in plasma.
Metabolism: Extensively metabolized in liver.
Excretion: Excreted in urine.

Route	Onset	Peak	Duration
P.O.	Unknown	Unknown	Unknown

Pharmacodynamics

Chemical effect: Blocks reuptake of norepinephrine and serotonin into neurons in CNS.
Therapeutic effect: Relieves depression.

Available forms

Capsules (extended-release): 37.5 mg, 75 mg, 150 mg
Tablets: 25 mg, 37.5 mg, 50 mg, 75 mg, 100 mg

NURSING PROCESS

Assessment

• Assess patient's depression before therapy and regularly thereafter.

• Carefully monitor blood pressure. Venlafaxine therapy is linked to sustained, dose-dependent increases in blood pressure. Greatest increases (averaging about 7 mm Hg above baseline) occur in patients taking 375 mg daily.
• Be alert for adverse reactions and drug interactions.
• Evaluate patient's and family's knowledge of drug therapy.

Nursing diagnoses
• Disturbed thought processes related to presence of depression
• Risk for injury related to drug-induced adverse CNS reactions
• Deficient knowledge related to drug therapy

Planning and implementation
• Total daily dose should be reduced by 50% in patient with hepatic impairment. In patient with moderate renal impairment (GFR of 10 to 70 ml/minute), reduce total daily dose by 25% as directed. In patient undergoing hemodialysis, dose should be withheld until dialysis session is completed; reduce daily dose by 50%.
• Give drug with food.
ALERT: Don't discontinue drug abruptly if given for 6 weeks or more. Stop drug by tapering dosage over a 2-week period.

Patient teaching
• Instruct patient to take drug with food.
• Caution patient to avoid hazardous activities until full effects of drug are known.
• Tell patient it may take several weeks before the full antidepressant effect is seen.
• Tell patient to avoid alcohol while taking drug and to notify prescriber before taking other medications, including OTC preparations, because of possible interactions.
• Instruct patient to notify prescriber if adverse reactions occur.

Evaluation
• Patient's behavior and communication exhibit improved thought processes.
• Patient doesn't experience injury from adverse CNS reactions.
• Patient and family state understanding of drug therapy.

verapamil hydrochloride
(veh-RAP-uh-mil high-droh-KLOR-ighd)
Anpec◇, Anpec SR◇, Apo-Verap♦, Calan, Calan SR, Cordilox◇, Cordilox SR◇, Covera-HS, Isoptin◇, Isoptin SR, Novo-Veramil♦, Nu-Verap♦, Veracaps SR◇, Verahexal◇, Verelan, Verelan PM

Pharmacologic class: calcium channel blocker
Therapeutic class: antianginal, antihypertensive, antiarrhythmic
Pregnancy risk category: C

Indications and dosages
▶ **Vasospastic angina; classic chronic, stable angina pectoris; unstable angina; chronic atrial fibrillation.** *Adults:* Starting dose is 80 mg P.O. q 6 to 8 hours. Increase at weekly intervals, as needed. Some patients may need up to 480 mg daily.
▶ **Supraventricular arrhythmias.** *Adults:* 0.075 to 0.15 mg/kg (5 to 10 mg) by I.V. push over 2 minutes with ECG and blood pressure monitoring. If no response occurs, give a second dose of 10 mg (0.15 mg/kg) 15 to 30 minutes after the initial dose.
Children ages 1 to 15: 0.1 to 0.3 mg/kg as I.V. bolus over 2 minutes. Repeat in 30 minutes if no response.
Children younger than age 1: 0.1 to 0.2 mg/kg as I.V. bolus over 2 minutes with continuous ECG monitoring. Repeat in 30 minutes if no response.
▶ **Hypertension.** *Adults:* Start therapy with sustained-release capsules at 180 mg (240 mg for Verelan) P.O. daily in the morning. Adjust dosage based on clinical effectiveness 24 hours after dosing. Increase in increments of 120 mg daily to a maximum daily dose of 480 mg.

Contraindications and precautions
• Contraindicated in patients hypersensitive to drug and those with severe left ventricular dysfunction; cardiogenic shock; second- or third-degree AV block or sick sinus syndrome, except in presence of functioning pacemaker; atrial flutter or fibrillation and accessory bypass tract syndrome; severe heart failure (unless secondary to verapamil therapy); or severe hypotension. I.V. verapamil contraindicated in

patients with ventricular tachycardia and in those receiving I.V. beta blockers.
- Use cautiously in patients with increased intracranial pressure or hepatic or renal disease.

Lifespan: In pregnant women and geriatric patients, use cautiously. In breast-feeding women, drug isn't recommended.

Adverse reactions

CNS: dizziness, headache, asthenia.
CV: transient hypotension, ***heart failure, bradycardia, AV block, ventricular asystole, ventricular fibrillation,*** peripheral edema.
GI: constipation, nausea.
Respiratory: ***pulmonary edema.***
Skin: rash.

Interactions

Drug-drug. *Antihypertensives, quinidine:* May cause hypotension. Monitor blood pressure.
Carbamazepine, cardiac glycosides: May increase serum levels of these drugs. Monitor patient for toxicity.
Cyclosporine: May increase cyclosporine level. Monitor cyclosporine level.
Disopyramide, flecainide, propranolol, other beta blockers: May cause heart failure. Use together cautiously.
Lithium: May decrease lithium level. Monitor patient closely.
Rifampin: May decrease oral bioavailability of verapamil. Monitor patient for lack of effect.
Drug-herb. *Black catechu:* May cause additive effects. Tell patient to use together cautiously.
Yerba maté: May decrease clearance of yerba maté methylxanthines and cause toxicity. Tell patient to use together cautiously.
Drug-food. *Any food:* Increases drug absorption. Tell patient to take drug with food.
Drug-lifestyle. *Alcohol use:* May enhance effects of alcohol. Discourage using together.

Effects on lab test results

- May increase ALT, AST, alkaline phosphatase, and bilirubin levels.

Pharmacokinetics

Absorption: Rapid and complete from GI tract after P.O. administration; only about 20% to 35% reaches systemic circulation.
Distribution: About 90% of circulating drug is bound to plasma proteins.
Metabolism: Metabolized in liver.
Excretion: Excreted in urine as unchanged drug and active metabolites. *Half-life:* 6 to 12 hours.

Route	Onset	Peak	Duration
P.O.	1-2 hr	1-9 hr	8-24 hr
I.V.	Rapid	Immediate	1-6 hr

Pharmacodynamics

Chemical effect: Not clearly defined; inhibits calcium ion influx across cardiac and smooth-muscle cells, thus decreasing myocardial contractility and oxygen demand. Drug also dilates coronary arteries and arterioles.
Therapeutic effect: Relieves angina, lowers blood pressure, and restores normal sinus rhythm.

Available forms

Capsules (extended-release): 120 mg, 180 mg, 240 mg
Capsules (sustained-release): 120 mg, 160 mg ◇, 180 mg, 200 mg, 240 mg, 360 mg
Injection: 2.5 mg/ml
Tablets: 40 mg, 80 mg, 120 mg, 160 mg ◇
Tablets (extended-release): 100 mg, 120 mg, 180 mg, 200 mg, 240mg, 300 mg
Tablets (sustained-release): 120 mg, 180 mg, 240 mg

NURSING PROCESS

Assessment

- Assess patient's condition before therapy and regularly thereafter.
- All patients receiving I.V. verapamil should receive cardiac monitoring. Monitor R-R interval.
- Monitor blood pressure at start of therapy and during dosage adjustments.
- Monitor liver function studies during prolonged treatment.
- Be alert for adverse reactions and drug interactions.
- Evaluate patient's and family's knowledge of drug therapy.

Nursing diagnoses

- Acute pain related to presence of angina
- Decreased cardiac output related to presence of arrhythmia
- Deficient knowledge related to drug therapy

Planning and implementation

- Patient with severely compromised cardiac function or patient taking beta blockers should receive lower doses of verapamil.
- **P.O. use:** Drug should be taken with food, but keep in mind that taking extended-release tablets with food may decrease rate and extent of absorption. It also produces smaller fluctuations of peak and trough blood levels.
- **I.V. use:** Give drug by direct injection into vein or into tubing of free-flowing, compatible I.V. solution. Compatible solutions include D_5W, half-normal and normal saline solutions, and Ringer's and lactated Ringer's solutions.
  – Give I.V. doses slowly over at least 2 minutes (3 minutes for geriatric patients) to minimize risk of adverse reactions.
  – Perform continuous ECG and blood pressure monitoring during administration.
- If verapamil is being used to terminate supraventricular tachycardia, prescriber may have patient perform vagal maneuvers after receiving drug.
- Assist patient with walking because dizziness may occur.
- Notify prescriber if patient has signs of heart failure, such as swelling of hands and feet or shortness of breath.

ALERT: Don't confuse Isoptin with Intropin; don't confuse Verelan with Vivarin, Voltaren, Ferralyn, or Virilon.

Patient teaching

- Instruct patient to take drug with food.
- If patient is kept on nitrate therapy during adjustment of oral verapamil dosage, urge continued compliance. S.L. nitroglycerin, especially, may be taken as needed when angina is acute.
- Encourage patient to increase fluid and fiber intake to combat constipation. Give stool softener.
- Instruct patient to report adverse reactions, especially swelling of hands and feet and shortness of breath.

Evaluation

- Patient has reduced severity or frequency of angina.
- Patient regains normal cardiac output with restoration of normal sinus rhythm.
- Patient and family state understanding of drug therapy.

vinblastine sulfate (VLB)

(vin-BLAH-steen SUL-fayt)
Velban, Velbe ♦ ◇

Pharmacologic class: vinca alkaloid (specific to M phase of cell cycle)
Therapeutic class: antineoplastic
Pregnancy risk category: D

Indications and dosages

▶ **Breast or testicular cancer, Hodgkin's and non-Hodgkin's lymphoma, choriocarcinoma, lymphosarcoma, mycosis fungoides, Kaposi's sarcoma, histiocytosis.** *Adults:* 0.1 mg/kg or 3.7 mg/m² I.V. weekly or q 2 weeks. May be increased to maximum dose of 0.5 mg/kg or 18.5 mg/m² weekly according to response. Dose shouldn't be repeated if WBC count is less than 4,000/mm³.
Children: 2.5 mg/m² I.V. as a single dose every week, increased weekly in increments of 1.25 mg/m² to a maximum of 7.5 mg/m².

Contraindications and precautions

- Contraindicated in patients with severe leukopenia or bacterial infection.
- Use cautiously in patients with hepatic dysfunction.

Lifespan: In pregnant or breast-feeding women, drug isn't recommended.

Adverse reactions

CNS: depression, *paresthesia, peripheral neuropathy and neuritis, numbness, loss of deep tendon reflexes,* ***seizures, CVA,*** headache.
CV: hypertension, ***MI,*** *phlebitis.*
EENT: pharyngitis.
GI: *nausea, vomiting,* ulcer, ***bleeding,*** *constipation, ileus, anorexia,* diarrhea, abdominal pain, *stomatitis.*
GU: oligospermia, aspermia, urine retention.
Hematologic: anemia, ***leukopenia*** (nadir on days 4 to 10; lasts another 7 to 14 days), ***thrombocytopenia.***
Metabolic: hyperuricemia, *weight loss.*
Musculoskeletal: uric acid nephropathy, *muscle pain and weakness.*
Respiratory: ***acute bronchospasm,*** shortness of breath.
Skin: reversible alopecia, vesiculation, cellulitis, necrosis with extravasation.

Interactions

Drug-drug. *Erythromycin, other drugs that inhibit cytochrome P-450 pathway:* May increase toxicity of vinblastine. Monitor patient closely. *Mitomycin:* Increases risk of bronchospasm and shortness of breath. Monitor patient closely. *Phenytoin:* Decreases plasma phenytoin level. Monitor patient closely.

Effects on lab test results

- May increase uric acid level.
- May decrease hemoglobin, hematocrit, and WBC and platelet counts.

Pharmacokinetics

Absorption: Administered I.V.
Distribution: Distributed widely in body tissues; crosses blood-brain barrier but doesn't achieve therapeutic levels in CSF.
Metabolism: Metabolized partially in liver to active metabolite.
Excretion: Excreted primarily in bile as unchanged drug; smaller portion excreted in urine. *Half-life:* Alpha phase, 3.7 minutes; beta phase, 1.6 hours; terminal phase, 25 hours.

Route	Onset	Peak	Duration
I.V.	Unknown	Unknown	Unknown

Pharmacodynamics

Chemical effect: Arrests mitosis in metaphase, blocking cell division.
Therapeutic effect: Inhibits replication of certain cancer cells.

Available forms

Injection: 10-mg vials (lyophilized powder), 1 mg/ml in 10-ml vials

NURSING PROCESS

Assessment

- Assess patient's condition before therapy and regularly thereafter.

ALERT: After giving drug, monitor patient for development of life-threatening acute bronchospasm. Reaction is most likely if patient also receives mitomycin.

- Be alert for adverse reactions and drug interactions.
- Assess for numbness and tingling in hands and feet. Assess gait for early evidence of footdrop. Drug is less neurotoxic than vincristine.
- Evaluate patient's and family's knowledge of drug therapy.

Nursing diagnoses

- Ineffective health maintenance related to presence of neoplastic disease
- Ineffective protection related to drug-induced adverse hematologic reactions
- Deficient knowledge related to drug therapy

Planning and implementation

- Give antiemetic before giving drug.
- Follow facility policy to reduce risks. Preparation and administration of parenteral form are linked to carcinogenic, mutagenic, and teratogenic risks for personnel.
- Reconstitute drug in 10-mg vial with 10 ml of saline solution injection or sterile water. This yields 1 mg/ml. Refrigerate reconstituted solution. Discard after 30 days.
- Inject drug directly into vein or running I.V. line over 1 minute. Drug also may be given in 50 ml of D_5W or normal saline solution infused over 15 minutes.
- If extravasation occurs, stop infusion immediately and notify prescriber. Manufacturer recommends that moderate heat be applied to area of leakage. Local injection of hyaluronidase may help disperse drug. Some clinicians prefer to apply ice packs on and off every 2 hours for 24 hours, with local injection of hydrocortisone or normal saline solution.
- Don't give drug into limb with compromised circulation.

ALERT: Drug is fatal if given intrathecally; it's for I.V. use only.

- If acute bronchospasm occurs after administration, notify prescriber immediately.
- Make sure patient maintains adequate fluid intake to facilitate excretion of uric acid.
- Be prepared to stop drug and notify prescriber if stomatitis occurs.
- Dosage shouldn't be repeated more frequently than every 7 days or severe leukopenia will develop.

ALERT: Don't confuse vinblastine with vincristine or vindesine.

- Anticipate decrease in dosage by 50% if bilirubin level is greater than 3 mg/dl.

Patient teaching

- Teach patient about infection-control and bleeding precautions.

- Warn patient that alopecia may occur, but that it's usually reversible.
- Tell patient to report adverse reactions promptly.
- Encourage adequate fluid intake to increase urine output and facilitate excretion of uric acid.

☑ Evaluation

- Patient responds well to drug.
- Patient doesn't develop serious complications from adverse hematologic reactions.
- Patient and family state understanding of drug therapy.

vincristine sulfate

(vin-KRIH-steen SUL-fayt)
Oncovin, Vincasar PFS

Pharmacologic class: vinca alkaloid (specific to M phase of cell cycle)
Therapeutic class: antineoplastic
Pregnancy risk category: D

Indications and dosages

▶ **Breast cancer‡, acute lymphoblastic and other leukemias, Hodgkin's disease, non-Hodgkin's lymphoma, neuroblastoma, rhabdomyosarcoma, Wilms' tumor.** *Adults:* 1.4 mg/m^2 I.V. weekly. Maximum weekly dose is 2 mg.
Children weighing more than 10 kg (22 lb): 2 mg/m^2 I.V. weekly. Maximum single dose is 2 mg.
Children weighing 10 kg and less: 0.05 mg/kg I.V. once weekly.

Contraindications and precautions

- Contraindicated in patients hypersensitive to drug and in those with demyelinating form of Charcot-Marie-Tooth syndrome. Don't give drug to patients who are concurrently receiving radiation therapy through ports that include liver.
- Use cautiously in patients with hepatic dysfunction, neuromuscular disease, or infection.

Lifespan: In pregnant or breast-feeding women, drug isn't recommended.

Adverse reactions

CNS: fever, *peripheral neuropathy,* sensory loss, *loss of deep tendon reflexes, paresthesia, wristdrop and footdrop,* headache, ataxia, cranial nerve palsies, *jaw pain,* hoarseness, vocal cord paralysis, ***seizures, coma,*** permanent neurotoxicity.
CV: hypotension, hypertension, *phlebitis.*
EENT: visual disturbances, diplopia, optic and extraocular neuropathy, ptosis.
GI: diarrhea, *constipation, cramps,* ileus that mimics surgical abdomen, *nausea, vomiting,* anorexia, dysphagia, ***intestinal necrosis, stomatitis.***
GU: urine retention, dysuria, acute uric acid neuropathy, polyuria.
Hematologic: anemia, ***leukopenia, thrombocytopenia.***
Metabolic: hyponatremia, hyperuricemia, weight loss.
Musculoskeletal: *muscle weakness and cramps.*
Respiratory: ***acute bronchospasm.***
Skin: rash, *reversible alopecia,* cellulitis at injection site, severe local reaction with extravasation.
Other: SIADH.

Interactions

Drug-drug. *Asparaginase:* Decreases hepatic clearance of vincristine. Monitor patient closely for toxicity.
Calcium channel blockers: Enhances vincristine accumulation. Monitor patient for toxicity.
Digoxin: Decreases digoxin effects. Monitor digoxin level.
Mitomycin: Possible increased frequency of bronchospasm and acute pulmonary reactions. Monitor patient closely.
Phenytoin: May reduce phenytoin level. Monitor patient closely.

Effects on lab test results

- May increase uric acid level. May decrease sodium level.
- May decrease hemoglobin, hematocrit, and WBC and platelet counts.

Pharmacokinetics

Absorption: Administered I.V.
Distribution: Distributed widely in body tissues and bound to erythrocytes and platelets; crosses blood-brain barrier but doesn't achieve therapeutic levels in CSF.
Metabolism: Metabolized extensively in liver.

Excretion: Excreted primarily in bile; smaller portion excreted in urine. *Half-life:* First phase, 4 minutes; second phase, 2¼ hours; terminal phase, 85 hours.

Route	Onset	Peak	Duration
I.V.	Unknown	Unknown	Unknown

Pharmacodynamics

Chemical effect: Arrests mitosis in metaphase, blocking cell division.
Therapeutic effect: Inhibits replication of certain cancer cells.

Available forms

Injection: 1 mg/ml in 1-, 2-, and 5-ml multiple-dose vials; 1 mg/ml in 1- and 2-ml preservative-free vials

NURSING PROCESS

Assessment

- Assess patient's condition before therapy and regularly thereafter.

ALERT: After giving drug, monitor patient for development of life-threatening acute bronchospasm. Reaction is most likely to occur if patient also receives mitomycin.

- Monitor patient for hyperuricemia, especially if he has leukemia or lymphoma.
- Be alert for adverse reactions and drug interactions.
- Check for depression of Achilles tendon reflex, numbness, tingling, footdrop or wristdrop, difficulty in walking, ataxia, and slapping gait. Also check ability to walk on heels.
- Monitor bowel function. Constipation may be early sign of neurotoxicity.
- Evaluate patient's and family's knowledge of drug therapy.

Nursing diagnoses

- Ineffective health maintenance related to presence of neoplastic disease
- Ineffective protection related to drug-induced adverse hematologic reactions
- Deficient knowledge related to drug therapy

Planning and implementation

- Give antiemetic before drug.
- All vials (1-, 2-, and 5-mg) contain 1 mg/ml solution and should be refrigerated.
- Follow facility policy to reduce risks. Preparation and administration of parenteral form are linked to carcinogenic, mutagenic, and teratogenic risks for personnel.
- Inject drug directly into vein or running I.V. line slowly over 1 minute. Drug also may be given in 50 ml of D_5W or normal saline solution infused over 15 minutes.
- If drug extravasates, stop infusion immediately and notify prescriber. Apply heat on and off every 2 hours for 24 hours. Give 150 units of hyaluronidase to area of infiltrate.
- Don't give drug to one patient as single dose. The 5-mg vials are for multiple-dose use.

ALERT: Drug is fatal if given intrathecally; it's for I.V. use only.

- Because of risk of neurotoxicity, drug shouldn't be given more than once a week. Children are more resistant to neurotoxicity than adults. Neurotoxicity is dose-related and usually reversible.
- If acute bronchospasm occurs after administration, notify prescriber immediately.
- Maintain good hydration and give allopurinol to prevent uric acid nephropathy.
- Fluid restriction may be needed if SIADH develops.
- Give stool softener, laxative, or water before dosing to help prevent constipation.

ALERT: Don't confuse vincristine with vinblastine or vindesine.

Patient teaching

- Instruct patient on infection control and bleeding precautions.
- Warn patient that alopecia may occur, but that it's usually reversible.
- Tell patient to report adverse reactions promptly.
- Encourage fluid intake to facilitate excretion of uric acid.
- Advise woman of childbearing age to avoid becoming pregnant during therapy. Also recommend that she consult with prescriber before becoming pregnant.

Evaluation

- Patient responds well to drug.
- Patient doesn't develop serious complications from adverse hematologic reactions.
- Patient and family state understanding of drug therapy.

vinorelbine tartrate
(vin-oh-REL-been TAR-trayt)
Navelbine

Pharmacologic class: semisynthetic vinca alkaloid
Therapeutic class: antineoplastic
Pregnancy risk category: D

Indications and dosages

▶ **Alone or as adjunct therapy with cisplatin for first-line treatment of ambulatory patients with nonresectable advanced non–small-cell lung cancer; alone or with cisplatin in stage IV of non–small-cell lung cancer; with cisplatin in stage III of non–small-cell lung cancer.** *Adults:* 30 mg/m^2 I.V. weekly. In combination treatment, same dosage used along with 120 mg/m^2 of cisplatin, given on days 1 and 29, and then q 6 weeks.

Contraindications and precautions

- Contraindicated in patients with pretreatment granulocyte counts below 1,000 cells/mm^3.
- Use with extreme caution in patients whose bone marrow may have been compromised by previous exposure to radiation therapy or chemotherapy or whose bone marrow is still recovering from previous chemotherapy.
- Use cautiously in patients with hepatic impairment.

Lifespan: In pregnant or breast-feeding women, drug isn't recommended. In children, safety of drug hasn't been established.

Adverse reactions

CNS: *peripheral neuropathy, asthenia, fatigue.*
GI: *nausea, vomiting, anorexia, diarrhea, constipation, stomatitis.*
Hematologic: ***bone marrow suppression (agranulocytosis,*** **LEUKOPENIA,** ***thrombocytopenia,*** anemia).
Hepatic: *bilirubinemia.*
Musculoskeletal: jaw pain, chest pain, myalgia, arthralgia, loss of deep tendon reflexes.
Respiratory: dyspnea.
Skin: *alopecia,* rash, *injection site pain or reaction.*
Other: SIADH.

Interactions

Drug-drug. *Cisplatin:* Increases risk of bone marrow suppression when given with cisplatin. Monitor patient's hematologic status closely.
Mitomycin: May cause pulmonary reactions. Monitor patient's respiratory status closely.

Effects on lab test results

- May increase bilirubin level.
- May decrease liver function test values, hemoglobin, hematocrit, and granulocyte, WBC, and platelet counts.

Pharmacokinetics

Absorption: Administered I.V.
Distribution: Distributed widely in body tissues and bound to lymphocytes and platelets.
Metabolism: Metabolized extensively in liver.
Excretion: Excreted primarily in bile; smaller portion excreted in urine. *Half-life:* 27.7 to 43.6 hours.

Route	Onset	Peak	Duration
I.V.	Unknown	Unknown	Unknown

Pharmacodynamics

Chemical effect: Arrests mitosis in metaphase, blocking cell division.
Therapeutic effect: Inhibits replication of selected cancer cells.

Available forms

Injection: 10 mg/ml, 50 mg/5 ml

NURSING PROCESS

Assessment

- Assess patient's condition before therapy and regularly thereafter.
- Monitor patient closely for hypersensitivity reactions.
- To judge effects of therapy, monitor patient's peripheral blood count and bone marrow.
- Be alert for adverse reactions and drug interactions.
- Assess for numbness and tingling in hands and feet. Assess gait for early evidence of footdrop.

ALERT: Monitor patient's deep tendon reflexes; loss may indicate cumulative toxicity.

- Evaluate patient's and family's knowledge of drug therapy.

Nursing diagnoses
- Ineffective health maintenance related to presence of neoplastic disease
- Ineffective protection related to drug-induced adverse hematologic reactions
- Deficient knowledge related to drug therapy

Planning and implementation
- Give antiemetic before giving drug.
- Check patient's granulocyte count before administration. It should be 1,000 cells/mm^3 or more for drug to be given. Withhold drug and notify prescriber if count is less.
- Drug must be diluted before giving. Give drug I.V. over 6 to 10 minutes into side port of free-flowing I.V. line that is closest to I.V. bag. Afterward, flush with 75 to 125 ml of D_5W or normal saline solution.
- Take care to avoid extravasation during administration because drug can cause considerable irritation, localized tissue necrosis, and thrombophlebitis. If extravasation occurs, stop drug immediately and inject remaining portion of dose into a different vein.

ALERT: Drug is fatal if given intrathecally; it's for I.V. use only.
- Dosage adjustments are made according to hematologic toxicity or hepatic insufficiency, whichever results in lower dosage. Expect dosage to be halved if patient's granulocyte count falls between 1,000 and 1,500 cells/mm^3. If three consecutive doses are skipped because of agranulocytosis, discontinue vinorelbine, as directed.
- Drug may be a contact irritant, and solution must be handled and given with care. Gloves are recommended. Avoid inhaling vapors and allowing drug to contact skin or mucous membranes, especially those of eyes. In case of contact, wash with copious amounts of water for at least 15 minutes.

Patient teaching
- Instruct patient on infection control and bleeding precautions.
- Warn patient that alopecia may occur, but that it's usually reversible.
- Instruct patient not to take other drugs, including OTC preparations, unless approved by prescriber.
- Instruct patient to tell prescriber about signs and symptoms of infection (fever, chills, malaise) because drug may have immunosuppressant activity.

Evaluation
- Patient responds well to drug.
- Patient doesn't develop serious complications from adverse hematologic reactions.
- Patient and family state understanding of drug therapy.

vitamin A (retinol)
(VIGH-tuh-min ay)
Aquasol A, Palmitate-A 5000

Pharmacologic class: fat-soluble vitamin
Therapeutic class: vitamin
Pregnancy risk category: A (C at higher-than-recommended doses)

Indications and dosages
▶ **RDA.** RDAs have been converted to retinol equivalents (RE). One RE has activity of 1 mcg of all-trans retinol, 6 mcg of beta carotene, or 12 mcg of carotenoid provitamins.
Men older than age 11: 1,000 mcg RE or 5,000 IU
Pregnant women and women older than age 11: 800 mcg RE or 4,000 IU
Breast-feeding women (first 6 months): 1,300 mcg RE or 6,500 IU
Breast-feeding women (second 6 months): 1,200 mcg RE or 6,000 IU
Children ages 7 to 10: 700 mcg RE or 3,500 IU
Children ages 4 to 6: 500 mcg RE or 2,500 IU
Children ages 1 to 3: 400 mcg RE or 2,000 IU
Neonates and infants younger than age 1: 375 mcg RE or 1,875 IU
▶ **Severe vitamin A deficiency.** *Adults and children older than age 8:* 100,000 IU I.M. or P.O. daily for 3 days, followed by 50,000 IU I.M. or P.O. daily for 2 weeks; then 10,000 to 20,000 IU P.O. daily for 2 months. Follow with adequate dietary nutrition and RE vitamin A supplements.
Children ages 1 to 8: 17,500 to 35,000 IU I.M. daily for 10 days.
Infants under age 1: 7,500 to 15,000 IU I.M. daily for 10 days.
▶ **Maintenance dosage to prevent recurrence of vitamin A deficiency.** *Children ages 1 to 8:* 5,000 to 10,000 IU P.O. daily for 2

months; then adequate dietary nutrition and RE vitamin A supplements.

Contraindications and precautions

• Contraindicated for oral administration in patients with malabsorption syndrome; if malabsorption is from inadequate bile secretion, oral route may be used with concurrent administration of bile salts (dehydrocholic acid). Also contraindicated in patients hypersensitive to other ingredients in product and in those with hypervitaminosis A.

• I.V. administration contraindicated except for special water-miscible forms intended for infusion with large parenteral volumes. I.V. push of vitamin A of any type is also contraindicated (anaphylaxis or anaphylactoid reactions and death have resulted).

Lifespan: In pregnant or breast-feeding women, use cautiously, avoiding doses exceeding RE.

Adverse reactions

CNS: irritability, headache, ***increased intracranial pressure,*** fatigue, lethargy, malaise.
EENT: papilledema, exophthalmos.
GI: anorexia, epigastric pain, vomiting, polydipsia.
GU: hypomenorrhea, polyuria.
Hepatic: jaundice, hepatomegaly, ***cirrhosis.***
Metabolic: slow growth, decalcification of bone, hypercalcemia, periostitis, premature closure of epiphyses, migratory arthralgia, cortical thickening over radius and tibia.
Skin: alopecia; dry, cracked, scaly skin; pruritus; lip fissures; erythema; inflamed tongue, lips, and gums; massive desquamation; increased pigmentation; night sweats.
Other: splenomegaly, ***anaphylactic shock.***

Interactions

Drug-drug. *Cholestyramine resin, mineral oil:* Reduces GI absorption of fat-soluble vitamins. If needed, give mineral oil at bedtime.
Isotretinoin, multivitamins containing vitamin A: Increases risk of toxicity. Avoid using together.
Neomycin (oral): Decreases vitamin A absorption. Avoid using together.
Oral contraceptives: May increase plasma vitamin A levels. Monitor patient.
Warfarin: Increases risk of bleeding. Monitor PT and INR closely; monitor patient for bleeding.

Effects on lab test results

• May increase liver enzyme and calcium levels.

Pharmacokinetics

Absorption: In normal doses, absorbed readily and completely if fat absorption is normal; larger doses or regular dose in patients with fat malabsorption, low protein intake, or hepatic or pancreatic disease may be absorbed incompletely. Because vitamin A is fat-soluble, absorption requires bile salts, pancreatic lipase, and dietary fat.
Distribution: Stored (primarily as palmitate) in Kupffer's cells of liver. Normal adult liver stores are sufficient to provide vitamin A requirements for 2 years. Lesser amounts of retinyl palmitate are stored in kidneys, lungs, adrenal glands, retinas, and intraperitoneal fat. Vitamin A circulates bound to specific alpha1 protein, retinol-binding protein.
Metabolism: Metabolized in liver.
Excretion: Retinol (fat-soluble) combines with glucuronic acid and is metabolized to retinal and retinoic acid. Retinoic acid undergoes biliary excretion in feces. Retinal, retinoic acid, and other water-soluble metabolites are excreted in urine and feces.

Route	Onset	Peak	Duration
P.O., I.M.	Unknown	3-5 hr	Unknown

Pharmacodynamics

Chemical effect: Stimulates retinal function, bone growth, reproduction, and integrity of epithelial and mucosal tissues.
Therapeutic effect: Raises vitamin A levels in body.

Available forms

Capsules: 10,000 IU, 15,000 IU, 25,000 IU, 50,000 IU
Drops: 30 ml with dropper (50,000 IU/0.1 ml)
Injection: 2-ml vials (50,000 IU/ml with 0.5% chlorobutanol, polysorbate 80, butylated hydroxyanisole, and butylated hydroxytoluene)
Tablets: 5,000 IU, 10,000 IU

NURSING PROCESS

Assessment
• Assess patient's vitamin A intake from fortified foods, dietary supplements, self-administered drugs, and prescription drug sources before therapy and reassess regularly thereafter.
• Be alert for adverse reactions (if dose is high). Acute toxicity has resulted from single doses of 25,000 IU/kg; 350,000 IU in infants and over 2 million IU in adults also have proved acutely toxic. Doses that don't exceed RE are usually nontoxic.
• Chronic toxicity in infants (age 3 to 6 months) has resulted from doses of 18,500 IU daily for 1 to 3 months. In adults, chronic toxicity has resulted from doses of 50,000 IU daily for more than 18 months; 500,000 IU daily for 2 months, and 1 million IU daily for 3 days.
• Be alert for drug interactions.
• Evaluate patient's and family's knowledge of drug therapy.

Nursing diagnoses
• Imbalanced nutrition: less than body requirements related to inadequate intake
• Ineffective health maintenance related to vitamin A toxicity caused by excessive intake
• Deficient knowledge related to drug therapy

Planning and implementation
• Adequate vitamin A absorption requires suitable protein, vitamin E, zinc intake, and bile secretion; give supplemental salts, if necessary and as ordered. Zinc supplements may be necessary in patient receiving long-term total parenteral nutrition.
• **P.O. use:** Follow normal protocol.
– Liquid preparations available if NG administration is necessary. They may be mixed with cereal or fruit juice.
• **I.M. use:** Absorption is fastest and most complete with aqueous preparations, intermediate with emulsions, and slowest with oil suspensions.
ALERT: Give parenteral form by I.M. route or continuous I.V infusion in total parenteral nutrition. Never give as I.V. bolus.
• Protect drug from light.

Patient teaching
• Warn patient against taking megadoses of vitamins without specific indications. Also stress that he not share prescribed vitamins with others.
• Explain importance of avoiding prolonged use of mineral oil while taking this drug because mineral oil reduces vitamin A absorption.
• Review the signs and symptoms of vitamin A toxicity, and tell patient to report them immediately.
• Advise patient to consume adequate protein, vitamin E, and zinc, which, along with bile, are necessary for vitamin A absorption.
• Instruct patient to store vitamin A in tight, light-resistant container.

Evaluation
• Patient regains normal vitamin A levels.
• Patient doesn't exhibit signs and symptoms of vitamin A toxicity.
• Patient and family state understanding of drug therapy.

vitamin C (ascorbic acid)
(VIGH-tuh-min see)
Ascorbicap†, Cebid Timecelles†, Cecon†, Cenolate†, Cetane†, Cevalin†, Cevi-Bid, Ce-Vi-Sol*, Dull-C†, Flavorcee†, N'ice Vitamin C Drops†, Penta-Vite◇, Redoxon♦, Vita-C†

Pharmacologic class: water-soluble vitamin
Therapeutic class: vitamin
Pregnancy risk category: A (C at higher-than-recommended doses)

Indications and dosages
▶ **RDA.** *Adults and children age 15 and older:* 60 mg.
Pregnant women: 70 mg.
Breast-feeding women (first 6 months): 95 mg.
Breast-feeding women (second 6 months): 90 mg.
Children ages 11 to 14: 50 mg.
Children ages 4 to 10: 45 mg.
Children ages 1 to 3: 40 mg.
Infants ages 6 months to 1 year: 35 mg.
Neonates and infants younger than age 6 months: 30 mg.

▶ **Frank and subclinical scurvy.** *Adults:* Depending on severity, 300 mg to 1 g P.O., S.C., I.M., or I.V. daily; then at least 50 mg daily for maintenance.
Children: Depending on severity, 100 to 300 mg P.O., S.C., I.M., or I.V. daily, then at least 30 mg daily for maintenance.
Premature infants: 75 to 100 mg P.O., I.M., I.V., or S.C. daily.

▶ **Extensive burns, delayed fracture or wound healing, postoperative wound healing, severe febrile or chronic disease states.** *Adults:* 300 to 500 mg P.O., S.C., I.M., or I.V. daily for 7 to 10 days. For extensive burns, 1 to 2 g daily.
Children: 100 to 200 mg P.O., S.C., I.M., or I.V. daily.

▶ **Prevention of vitamin C deficiency in patients with poor nutritional habits or increased requirements.** *Adults:* 70 to 150 mg P.O., S.C., I.M., or I.V. daily.
Pregnant or breast-feeding women: 70 to 150 mg P.O., S.C., I.M., or I.V. daily.
Children: at least 40 mg P.O., S.C., I.M., or I.V. daily.
Infants: at least 35 mg P.O., S.C., I.M., or I.V. daily.

▶ **Potentiation of methenamine in urine acidification.** *Adults:* 4 to 12 g P.O. daily in divided doses.

Contraindications and precautions

- No known contraindications.

Lifespan: In pregnant women, give if clearly needed. In breast-feeding women, give cautiously.

Adverse reactions

CNS: faintness, dizziness with rapid I.V. administration.
GI: diarrhea.
GU: acid urine, oxaluria, renal calculi.
Other: discomfort at injection site.

Interactions

Drug-drug. *Aspirin (high doses):* Increases risk of ascorbic acid deficiency. Monitor patient closely.
Contraceptives, estrogen: Increases serum levels of estrogen. Monitor patient.
Oral iron supplements: Increases iron absorption. A beneficial drug interaction. Encourage using together.
Warfarin: Decreases anticoagulant effect. Monitor patient closely.
Drug-herb. *Bearberry:* Inactivates bearberry in urine. Caution patient about lack of effect.

Effects on lab test results

None reported.

Pharmacokinetics

Absorption: After P.O. administration, ascorbic acid is absorbed readily from GI tract. After very large doses, absorption may be limited because absorption is an active process. Absorption also may be reduced in patients with diarrhea or GI diseases. Degree of absorption unknown after I.M. or S.C. administration.
Distribution: Distributed widely in body with high levels found in liver, leukocytes, platelets, glandular tissues, and lens of eyes. Protein-binding is low.
Metabolism: Metabolized in liver.
Excretion: Excreted in urine. Renal excretion is directly proportional to blood concentrations.

Route	Onset	Peak	Duration
P.O., I.V., I.M., S.C.	Unknown	Unknown	Unknown

Pharmacodynamics

Chemical effect: Stimulates collagen formation and tissue repair; involved in oxidation-reduction reactions throughout body.
Therapeutic effect: Raises vitamin C level in body.

Available forms

Capsules (timed-release): 500 mg†
Crystals: 100 g (4 g/tsp)†, 500 g (4 g/tsp)†
Injection: 100 mg/ml; 250 mg/ml; 500 mg/ml
Lozenges: 60 mg†
Oral liquid: 50 ml (35 mg/0.6 ml)*†
Oral solution: 60 mg/ml†, 100 mg/ml†
Powder: 100 g (4 g/tsp)†, 500 g (4 g/tsp)†
Syrup: 20 mg/ml in 120 ml†, 480 ml†; 500 mg/5 ml in 5 ml†, 120 ml†, 480 ml†
Tablets: 25 mg†, 50 mg†, 100 mg†, 250 mg†, 500 mg†, 1,000 mg†
Tablets (chewable): 50 mg, 100 mg†, 250 mg†, 500 mg†, 1,000 mg†
Tablets (effervescent): 1,000 mg sugar-free†
Tablets (timed-release): 500 mg†, 1,000 mg†, 1,500 mg

NURSING PROCESS

Assessment
- Assess patient's condition before therapy and regularly thereafter.
- When giving for urine acidification, check urine pH to ensure efficacy.
- Be alert for adverse reactions and drug interactions.
- Monitor patient's hydration status if adverse GI reactions occur.
- Evaluate patient's and family's knowledge of drug therapy.

Nursing diagnoses
- Imbalanced nutrition: less than body requirements related to inadequate intake
- Risk for deficient fluid volume related to drug-induced adverse GI reactions
- Deficient knowledge related to drug therapy

Planning and implementation
- **P.O. use:** Give P.O. solution directly into mouth or mix with food.
  – Effervescent tablets should be dissolved in glass of water immediately before ingestion.
- **I.V. use:** Give I.V. infusion cautiously in patients with renal insufficiency.

ALERT: Avoid rapid I.V. administration. It may cause faintness or dizziness.
- **I.M. use:** Utilization of vitamin may be better with I.M. route, the preferred parenteral route.
- **S.C. use:** Follow normal protocol.
- Protect solution from light, and refrigerate ampules.

Patient teaching
- Stress proper nutritional habits to prevent recurrence of deficiency.
- Advise patient with vitamin C deficiency to decrease or stop smoking.

Evaluation
- Patient regains normal vitamin C levels.
- Patient maintains adequate hydration.
- Patient and family state understanding of drug therapy.

vitamin D

cholecalciferol (vitamin D_3)
(koh-lih-kal-SIF-eh-rol)
Delta-D , Vitamin D_3

ergocalciferol (vitamin D_2)
(er-goh-kal-SIF-er-ohl)
Calciferol, Drisdol, Radiostol Forte ♦, Vitamin D

Pharmacologic class: fat-soluble vitamin
Therapeutic class: vitamin
Pregnancy risk category: C

Indications and dosages

▶ **RDA for cholecalciferol.** *Adults age 25 and older:* 200 IU.
Pregnant or breast-feeding women: 400 IU.
Adults younger than age 25 and children age 6 months and older: 400 IU.
Neonates and infants younger than age 6 months: 300 IU.

▶ **Rickets and other vitamin D deficiency diseases.** *Adults:* Initially, 12,000 IU P.O. or I.M. daily, usually increased according to response up to 500,000 IU daily. After correction of deficiency, maintenance includes adequate diet and RDA supplements.

▶ **Hypoparathyroidism.** *Adults and children:* 50,000 to 200,000 IU P.O. or I.M. daily with calcium supplement.

▶ **Familial hypophosphatemia.** *Adults:* 10,000 to 80,000 IU P.O. or I.M. daily with phosphorus supplement.

Contraindications and precautions

- Contraindicated in patients with hypercalcemia, hypervitaminosis A, or renal osteodystrophy with hyperphosphatemia.
- Give ergocalciferol with extreme caution, if at all, to patients with impaired kidney function, heart disease, renal calculi, or arteriosclerosis.
- Use cautiously in cardiac patients, especially those receiving cardiac glycosides; and patients with increased sensitivity to these drugs.

Lifespan: In pregnant and breast-feeding women, give cautiously.

Adverse reactions

Adverse reactions listed are usually seen only in vitamin D toxicity.
CNS: headache, weakness, somnolence, overt psychosis, irritability.
CV: ***calcifications of soft tissues including heart, arrhythmias;*** hypertension.
EENT: rhinorrhea, conjunctivitis (calcific), photophobia.
GI: anorexia, nausea, vomiting, constipation, dry mouth, metallic taste, polydipsia.
GU: polyuria, albuminuria, hypercalciuria, nocturia, impaired kidney function, reversible azotemia.
Metabolic: hypercalcemia, hyperthermia, weight loss.
Musculoskeletal: bone and muscle pain, bone demineralization.
Skin: pruritus.
Other: decreased libido.

Interactions

Drug-drug. *Cardiac glycosides:* Increases risk of arrhythmias. Monitor calcium level.
Cholestyramine resin, mineral oil: Inhibits GI absorption of oral vitamin D. Space doses. Use together cautiously.
Corticosteroids: Antagonizes effect of vitamin D. Monitor vitamin D level closely.
Phenobarbital, phenytoin: Increases vitamin D metabolism, which decreases half-life as well as drug's effectiveness. Monitor patient closely.
Thiazide diuretics: May cause hypercalcemia in patients with hypoparathyroidism. Monitor patient closely.
Verapamil: Atrial fibrillation has occurred because of increased calcium. Monitor patient closely.

Effects on lab test results

- May increase BUN, creatinine, AST, ALT, urine urea, albumin, calcium, and cholesterol levels.

Pharmacokinetics

Absorption: Absorbed from small intestine with P.O. administration; unknown for I.M. administration.
Distribution: Widely distributed throughout body; bound to proteins stored in liver.
Metabolism: Metabolized in liver and kidneys.
Excretion: Excreted primarily in bile; small amount excreted in urine. *Half-life:* 24 hours.

Route	Onset	Peak	Duration
P.O., I.M.	2-24 hr	3-12 hr	Varies

Pharmacodynamics

Chemical effect: Promotes absorption and utilization of calcium and phosphate, helping to regulate calcium homeostasis.
Therapeutic effect: Helps to maintain normal calcium and phosphate levels in body.

Available forms

Capsules: 1.25 mg (50,000 IU)
Injection: 12.5 mg (500,000 IU)/ml
Oral liquid: 8,000 IU/ml in 60-ml dropper bottle
Tablets: 400 IU, 1,000 IU

NURSING PROCESS

Assessment

- Assess patient's condition before therapy and regularly thereafter.

ALERT: Monitor patient's eating and bowel habits; dry mouth, nausea, vomiting, metallic taste, and constipation may be early evidence of toxicity.

- Monitor serum and urine calcium, potassium, and urea levels when high therapeutic dosages are used.
- Be alert for adverse reactions and drug interactions.
- Evaluate patient's and family's knowledge of drug therapy.

Nursing diagnoses

- Imbalanced nutrition: less than body requirements related to inadequate intake
- Ineffective health maintenance related to vitamin D toxicity
- Deficient knowledge related to drug therapy

Planning and implementation

- **P.O. use:** Follow normal protocol.
- **I.M. use:** Use I.M. injection of vitamin D dispersed in oil for patient unable to absorb P.O. form.
- Dosages of 60,000 IU/day can cause hypercalcemia.

• Malabsorption from inadequate bile or hepatic dysfunction may require addition of exogenous bile salts with oral form.
• Patient with hyperphosphatemia requires dietary phosphate restrictions and binding agents to avoid metastatic calcifications and renal calculus formation.

Patient teaching
• Warn patient of dangers of increasing dosage without consulting prescriber. Vitamin D is fat-soluble.
• Tell patient taking vitamin D to restrict his intake of magnesium-containing antacids.

Evaluation
• Patient regains normal vitamin D level.
• Patient doesn't develop vitamin D toxicity.
• Patient and family state understanding of drug therapy.

vitamin E (tocopherol)

(VIGH-tuh-min ee)

Amino-Opti-E†, Aquasol E Drops†, Aquavit-E, d'ALPHA E 400 Softgels, d'ALPHA E 1000 Softgels, Dry E 400, E-Complex-600†, E-200 I.U. Softgels†, E-400 I.U. Softgels†, E-Vitamin Succinate†, Mixed E 400 Softgels, Mixed E 1000 Softgels, Vitamin E with Mixed Tocopherols, Vita-Plus E Softgels†

Pharmacologic class: fat-soluble vitamin
Therapeutic class: vitamin
Pregnancy risk category: A

Indications and dosages

▶ **RDA.** RDAs for vitamin E have been converted to α-tocopherol equivalents (α-TE). One α-TE equals 1 mg of D-α tocopherol or 1.49 IU
Men and boys age 11 and older: 10 α-TE or 15 IU
Women and girls age 11 and older: 8 α-TE or 12 IU
Pregnant women: 10 α-TE or 15 IU
Breast-feeding women (first 6 months): 12 α-TE or 18 IU
Breast-feeding women (second 6 months): 11 α-TE or 16 IU
Children ages 4 to 10: 7 α-TE or 10 IU
Children ages 1 to 3: 6 α-TE or 9 IU
Infants ages 6 months to 1 year: 4 α-TE or 6 IU
Neonates and infants younger than age 6 months: 3 α-TE or 4 IU

▶ **Vitamin E deficiency in adults and in children with malabsorption syndrome.**
Adults: Depending on severity, 60 to 75 IU P.O. daily.
Children: 1 IU/kg P.O. daily.

Contraindications and precautions

• No known contraindications.
Lifespan: None reported.

Adverse reactions

None reported with recommended dosages.

Interactions

Drug-drug. *Cholestyramine resin, mineral oil:* Inhibits GI absorption of oral vitamin E. Space doses. Use together cautiously.
Iron: May catalyze oxidation and increase daily requirements. Give separately.
Oral anticoagulants: Hypoprothrombinemic effects may be increased, possibly causing bleeding. Monitor patient closely.
Vitamin K: Antagonizes effects of vitamin K possible with large doses of vitamin E. Avoid using together.

Effects on lab test results

None reported.

Pharmacokinetics

Absorption: GI absorption depends on presence of bile. Only 20% to 60% of vitamin obtained from dietary sources is absorbed. As dosage increases, fraction of vitamin E absorbed decreases.
Distribution: Distributed to all tissues and stored in adipose tissues.
Metabolism: Metabolized in liver.
Excretion: Excreted primarily in bile; small amount excreted in urine.

Route	Onset	Peak	Duration
P.O.	Unknown	Unknown	Unknown

Pharmacodynamics

Chemical effect: Unknown; thought to act as an antioxidant and protect RBC membranes against hemolysis.
Therapeutic effect: Raises vitamin E level in body.

Available forms

Capsules: 100 IU, 200 IU†, 400 IU†, 600 IU†, 1,000 IU†
Drops: 15 IU/0.3 ml
Liquid: 15 IU/30 ml
Oral Solution: 50 IU/ml
Tablets (chewable): 100 IU, 200 IU†, 400 IU†, 500 IU, 600 IU, 800 IU, 1000 IU

NURSING PROCESS

Assessment

- Assess patient's condition before therapy and regularly thereafter.
- Monitor patient with liver or gallbladder disease for response to therapy. Adequate bile is essential for vitamin E absorption.
- Be alert for drug interactions.
- Evaluate patient's and family's knowledge of drug therapy.

Nursing diagnoses

- Imbalanced nutrition: less than body requirements related to inadequate intake
- Deficient knowledge related to drug therapy

Planning and implementation

- Requirements increase with rise in dietary polyunsaturated acids.
- Make sure patient swallows tablets or capsules whole.
- Store drug in tightly closed light-resistant container.
- Vitamin E should be given with bile salts if patient has malabsorption caused by lack of bile.
- Hypervitaminosis E symptoms include fatigue, weakness, nausea, headache, blurred vision, flatulence, diarrhea.

Patient teaching

- Tell patient not to crush tablets or open capsules. An oral solution and chewable tablets are commercially available.
- Discourage patient from taking megadoses, which can cause thrombophlebitis. Vitamin E is fat-soluble.

Evaluation

- Patient regains normal vitamin E level.
- Patient and family state understanding of drug therapy.

W

warfarin sodium

(WAR-feh-rin SOH-dee-um)
Coumadin, Warfilone ♦

Pharmacologic class: coumarin derivative
Therapeutic class: anticoagulant
Pregnancy risk category: X

Indications and dosages

▶ **Pulmonary embolism related to deep vein thrombosis, MI, rheumatic heart disease with heart valve damage, prosthetic heart valves, chronic atrial fibrillation.** *Adults:* Initially, 2 to 5 mg P.O. or I.V daily for 2 to 4 days. PT and INR determinations then can be used to establish optimal dose. Usual maintenance dose is 2 to 10 mg daily.

Contraindications and precautions

- Contraindicated in patients with bleeding or hemorrhagic tendencies, GI ulcerations, severe hepatic or renal disease, severe uncontrolled hypertension, subacute bacterial endocarditis, polycythemia vera, or vitamin K deficiency; and in patients who have had recent eye, brain, or spinal cord surgery.
- Use cautiously in patients with diverticulitis, colitis, mild-or-moderate hypertension, mild-or-moderate hepatic or renal disease, drainage tubes in any orifice, or regional or lumbar block anesthesia. Also use cautiously if patient has any condition that increases the risk of hemorrhage.

Lifespan: In pregnant women, drug is contraindicated. In breast-feeding women, use cautiously. Infants, especially neonates, may be more susceptible to anticoagulants because of vitamin K deficiency. Geriatric patients have an increased risk of bleeding and usually receive lower dosages.

Adverse reactions

CNS: headache, *fever.*
GI: anorexia, nausea, vomiting, cramps, *diarrhea,* mouth ulcerations, sore mouth, melena.

GU: hematuria, excessive menstrual bleeding.
Hematologic: ***hemorrhage*** with excessive dosage.
Hepatic: ***hepatitis,*** jaundice.
Skin: dermatitis, urticaria, necrosis, gangrene, alopecia, *rash.*

Interactions

Drug-drug. *Acetaminophen:* May increase bleeding with prolonged therapy (more than 2 weeks) with high doses (more than 2 g/day) of acetaminophen. Monitor patient carefully.
Allopurinol, amiodarone, anabolic steroids, cephalosporins, chloramphenicol, cimetidine, ciprofloxacin, clofibrate, danazol, diazoxide, diflunisal, disulfiram, erythromycin, ethacrynic acid, fenoprofen calcium, fluoroquinolones, glucagon, heparin, ibuprofen, influenza virus vaccine, isoniazid, ketoprofen, lovastatin, meclofenamate, methimazole, methylthiouracil, metronidazole, miconazole, nalidixic acid, neomycin (oral), pentoxifylline, propafenone, propoxyphene, propylthiouracil, quinidine, streptokinase, sulfinpyrazone, sulfonamides, sulindac, tamoxifen, tetracyclines, thiazides, thyroid drugs, tricyclic antidepressants, urokinase, vitamin E: Increases PT. Monitor patient for bleeding. Reduce anticoagulant dosage.
Anticonvulsants: Increases serum levels of phenytoin and phenobarbital. Monitor patient for toxicity.
Barbiturates, carbamazepine, corticosteroids, corticotropin, ethchlorvynol, griseofulvin, mercaptopurine, methaqualone, nafcillin, oral contraceptives containing estrogen, rifampin, spironolactone, sucralfate, trazodone: Decreases PT with reduced anticoagulant effect. Monitor patient carefully.
Chloral hydrate, glutethimide, propylthiouracil, sulfinpyrazone: May increase or decrease PT. Avoid use, if possible. Monitor patient carefully.
Cholestyramine: Decreases response when given too close together. Give 6 hours after oral anticoagulants.
NSAIDs, salicylates: Increases PT and ulcerogenic effects. Don't use together.
Sulfonylureas (oral antidiabetics): Increases hypoglycemic response. Monitor glucose level.
Drug-herb. *Angelica:* Significantly prolongs PT when used together. Discourage using together.
Motherwort, red clover: May increase risk of bleeding. Discourage using together.
Drug-food. *Foods or enteral products containing vitamin K:* May impair anticoagulation. Tell patient to maintain consistent daily intake of leafy green vegetables.
Drug-lifestyle. *Alcohol use:* Enhances anticoagulant effects. Discourage alcohol intake; however, one or two drinks daily are unlikely to affect warfarin response.

Effects on lab test results

- May increase ALT and AST levels.
- May increase INR, PT, and PTT.

Pharmacokinetics

Absorption: Rapid and complete.
Distribution: Highly bound to plasma proteins, especially albumin.
Metabolism: Metabolized in liver.
Excretion: Metabolites reabsorbed from bile and excreted in urine. *Half-life:* 1 to 3 days.

Route	Onset	Peak	Duration
P.O.	12-72 hr	Unknown	2-5 days
I.V.	Unknown	Unknown	2-5 days

Pharmacodynamics

Chemical effect: Inhibits vitamin K–dependent activation of clotting factors II, VII, IX, and X, formed in liver.
Therapeutic effect: Reduces ability of blood to clot.

Available forms

Powder for injection: 2 mg
Tablets: 1 mg, 2 mg, 2.5 mg, 3 mg, 4 mg, 5 mg, 6 mg, 7.5 mg, 10 mg

NURSING PROCESS

Assessment

- Assess patient's condition before therapy and regularly thereafter.
- Draw blood to establish baseline coagulation parameters before therapy.

ALERT: INR determinations are essential for proper control. Clinicians typically try to maintain INR at 2 to 3 times normal; risk of bleeding is high when INR exceeds 6 times normal.

- Be alert for adverse reactions and drug interactions. Elderly patients and patients with renal

or hepatic failure are especially sensitive to warfarin effect.
- Regularly inspect patient for bleeding gums, bruises on arms or legs, petechiae, nosebleeds, melena, tarry stools, hematuria, and hematemesis.
- Observe breast-feeding infant for unexpected bleeding if infant's mother takes drug.
- Evaluate patient's and family's knowledge of drug therapy.

Nursing diagnoses

- Risk for injury related to potential for blood clot formation from underlying condition
- Ineffective protection related to increased risk of bleeding
- Deficient knowledge related to drug therapy

Planning and implementation

- Give drug at same time daily.
- I.V. form may be obtained from manufacturer for rare patient who can't have oral therapy. Follow guidelines carefully for preparation and administration.
- Because onset of action is delayed, heparin sodium is commonly given during first few days of treatment. When heparin is being given simultaneously, blood for PT shouldn't be drawn within 5 hours of intermittent I.V. heparin administration. However, blood for PT may be drawn at any time during continuous heparin infusion.

ALERT: Withhold drug and call prescriber immediately if fever and rash occur; they may signal severe adverse reactions.

- The drug's anticoagulant effect can be neutralized by vitamin K injections.
- Drug is best oral anticoagulant for patient taking antacids or phenytoin.

Patient teaching

- Stress importance of compliance with prescribed dosage and follow-up appointments. Patient should wear or carry medical identification that indicates his increased risk of bleeding.
- Instruct patient and family to watch for signs of bleeding and to notify prescriber immediately if they occur.
- Warn patient to avoid OTC products containing aspirin, other salicylates, or drugs that may interact with warfarin.
- Tell patient to notify prescriber if menses are heavier than usual; dosage adjustment may be necessary.
- Tell patient to use electric razor when shaving to avoid scratching skin and to use soft toothbrush.
- Caution patient to read food labels. Food and enteral feedings that contain vitamin K may impair anticoagulation.
- Tell patient to eat a daily, consistent amount of leafy green vegetables that contain vitamin K. Eating varying amounts may alter anticoagulant effects.

Evaluation

- Patient doesn't develop blood clots.
- Patient states appropriate bleeding precautions to take.
- Patient and family state understanding of drug therapy.

X-Y

xylometazoline hydrochloride

(zigh-loh-met-uh-ZOH-leen high-droh-KLOR-ighd)
Otrivin

Pharmacologic class: sympathomimetic
Therapeutic class: decongestant, vasoconstrictor
Pregnancy risk category: NR

Indications and dosages

▶ **Nasal congestion.** *Adults and children age 12 and older:* 2 to 3 gtt or sprays of 0.1% solution in each nostril q 8 to 10 hours.
Children ages 6 months to 12 years: 2 to 3 gtt of 0.05% solution in each nostril q 8 to 10 hours.
Children younger than age 6 months: 1 gtt of 0.05% solution in each nostril q 6 hours, p.r.n. Drug shouldn't be used for more than 3 to 5 days.

Contraindications and precautions

- Contraindicated in patients hypersensitive to drug and in those with angle-closure glaucoma.

• Use cautiously in patients with hyperthyroidism, cardiac disease, hypertension, diabetes mellitus, or advanced arteriosclerosis.

Lifespan: In pregnant and breast-feeding women, safety of drug hasn't been established.

Adverse reactions

EENT: transient burning, stinging; dryness or ulceration of nasal mucosa; sneezing; rebound nasal congestion or irritation (with excessive or long-term use).

Interactions

None significant.

Effects on lab test results

None reported.

Pharmacokinetics

Absorption: Intranasal. Enough may be absorbed to produce systemic effects.
Distribution: Unknown.
Metabolism: Unknown.
Excretion: Unknown.

Route	Onset	Peak	Duration
Intranasal	5-10 min	Unknown	5-6 hr

Pharmacodynamics

Chemical effect: Unknown; thought to cause local vasoconstriction of dilated arterioles, reducing blood flow and nasal congestion.
Therapeutic effect: Relieves nasal congestion.

Available forms

Nasal solution: 0.05%, 0.1%.

NURSING PROCESS

Assessment

• Assess patient's condition before therapy and regularly thereafter.

• Be alert for adverse reactions.

• Evaluate patient's and family's knowledge of drug therapy.

Nursing diagnoses

• Ineffective health maintenance related to presence of nasal congestion

• Impaired tissue integrity related to drug's adverse effect on nasal mucosa

• Deficient knowledge related to drug therapy

Planning and implementation

• When giving more than one spray, allow 3 to 5 minutes to elapse between sprays. Have patient clear his nose before each spray.

Patient teaching

• Teach patient how to use drug. Have him hold his head upright to minimize swallowing of the drug; tell him to sniff spray briskly. Instruct him to wait 3 to 5 minutes between sprays and to clear his nose before each spray.

• Tell patient not to share drug to prevent spread of infection.

• Tell patient not to exceed recommended dosage, to use only as needed, and to use for only 3 to 5 days.

Evaluation

• Patient's nasal congestion is eliminated.

• Patient maintains normal intranasal mucosa.

• Patient and family state understanding of drug therapy.

Z

zafirlukast

(zay-FEER-loo-kast)
Accolate

Pharmacologic class: synthetic, selective peptide leukotriene receptor antagonist
Therapeutic class: antiasthmatic, bronchodilator
Pregnancy risk category: B

Indications and dosages

▶ **Prophylaxis and long-term treatment of chronic asthma.** *Adults and children age 12 and older:* 20 mg P.O. b.i.d. taken 1 hour before or 2 hours after meals.
Children ages 5 to 11: 10 mg P.O. b.i.d.

▶ **Prophylaxis for seasonal allergic rhinitis.** *Adults:* 20 to 40 mg P.O. as a single dose before exposure to allergen.

Contraindications and precautions

• Contraindicated in patients hypersensitive to drug.

Lifespan: In pregnant women, drug should be used only if clearly needed. In breast-feeding women, drug shouldn't be given. In patients younger than age 5, safety and effectiveness haven't been established. In geriatric patients, use cautiously.

Adverse reactions

CNS: *headache,* asthenia, dizziness, pain, fever.
GI: nausea, diarrhea, abdominal pain, vomiting, dyspepsia.
Musculoskeletal: myalgia, back pain.
Other: infection, accidental injury.

Interactions

Drug-drug. *Aspirin:* Increases zafirlukast level. Monitor patient.
Erythromycin, theophylline: Decreases zafirlukast level. Monitor patient.
Warfarin: Increases PT. Monitor PT and INR levels, and adjust dosage of anticoagulant.
Drug-food. *Any food:* Reduces rate and extent of drug absorption. Give drug 1 hour before or 2 hours after meals.

Effects on lab test results

- May increase liver enzyme levels.

Pharmacokinetics

Absorption: Rapid.
Distribution: Unknown.
Metabolism: Extensively metabolized.
Excretion: Excreted in feces; 10% in urine.

Route	Onset	Peak	Duration
P.O.	Unknown	3 hr	Unknown

Pharmacodynamics

Chemical effect: Selectively competes for leukotriene receptor sites.
Therapeutic effect: Blocks inflammatory action, inhibits bronchoconstriction, improves breathing.

Available forms

Tablets: 10 mg, 20 mg

NURSING PROCESS

Assessment

- Use cautiously in patients with hepatic impairment.
- Evaluate patient's and family's understanding of drug therapy.

Nursing diagnoses

- Impaired gas exchange related to bronchospasm
- Deficient knowledge related to drug therapy

Planning and implementation

ALERT: Don't use drug for reversing bronchospasm in acute asthma attack.
ALERT: Reduction in oral steroid dose has been followed in rare cases by eosinophilia, vasculitic rash, worsening pulmonary symptoms, cardiac complications, or neuropathy, sometimes presenting as Churg-Strauss syndrome.

Patient teaching

- Tell patient to keep taking drug even if symptoms disappear.
- Advise patient to continue taking other antiasthmatics.
- Instruct patient to take drug 1 hour before or 2 hours after meals.

Evaluation

- Patient demonstrates improved gas exchange.
- Patient and family state understanding of drug therapy.

zalcitabine (ddC, dideoxycytidine)

(zal-SIGH-tuh-been)
Hivid

Pharmacologic class: nucleoside analogue
Therapeutic class: antiviral
Pregnancy risk category: C

Indications and dosages

▶ **Advanced HIV infection (CD4+ T-cell count below 300 cells/mm³) in patients with significant clinical or immunologic deterioration.** *Adults and children age 13 and older weighing at least 30 kg (66 lb):* 0.75 mg P.O. q 8 hours given with other antiretrovirals.

Contraindications and precautions

- Contraindicated in patients hypersensitive to drug or its components.
- Use with extreme caution in patients with peripheral neuropathy.

• Use cautiously in patients with creatinine clearance less than 55 ml/minute because they may be at increased risk for toxicity.
• Use cautiously in patients with hepatic failure. Drug regimen (zalcitabine and zidovudine) may worsen hepatic dysfunction in patients with hepatic impairment.
• Use cautiously in patients with history of pancreatitis. Rarely, pancreatitis is fatal in patients receiving zalcitabine.
• Use cautiously in patients with baseline cardiomyopathy or history of heart failure.
Lifespan: In pregnant women and in children younger than age 13, safety of drug hasn't been established.

Adverse reactions

CNS: *peripheral neuropathy, headache, fatigue,* dizziness, confusion, ***seizures,*** impaired concentration, amnesia, insomnia, depression, tremor, hypertonia, asthenia, agitation, abnormal thinking, anxiety, *fever.*
CV: ***cardiomyopathy, heart failure,*** chest pain.
EENT: pharyngitis, ocular pain, abnormal vision, ototoxicity, nasal discharge.
GI: nausea, vomiting, diarrhea, abdominal pain, anorexia, constipation, stomatitis, esophageal ulcer, glossitis, ***pancreatitis.***
Hematologic: anemia, ***neutropenia, leukopenia, thrombocytopenia.***
Respiratory: cough.
Musculoskeletal: myalgia, arthralgia.
Skin: pruritus; night sweats; *erythematous, maculopapular, or follicular rash;* urticaria.

Interactions

Drug-drug. *Aminoglycosides, amphotericin B, foscarnet, other drugs that may impair kidney function:* Increases risk of nephrotoxicity. Avoid using together.
Antacids containing aluminum or magnesium: Decreases absorption of zalcitabine. Separate administration times.
Chloramphenicol, cisplatin, dapsone, disulfiram, ethionamide, glutethimide, gold salts, hydralazine, iodoquinol, isoniazid, metronidazole, nitrofurantoin, phenytoin, ribavirin, vincristine, and other drugs that can cause peripheral neuropathy: Increases risk of peripheral neuropathy. Avoid using together.
Cimetidine, probenecid: Increases zalcitabine level. Monitor patient carefully.
Pentamidine: Increases risk of pancreatitis. Avoid using together.
Drug-food. *Any food:* Decreases rate of drug absorption. Give drug on empty stomach.

Effects on lab test results

• May increase alkaline phosphatase, ALT, and AST levels. May alter glucose level.
• May decrease hemoglobin, hematocrit, and neutrophil, WBC, and platelet counts.

Pharmacokinetics

Absorption: Mean absolute bioavailability is above 80%. Administering drug with food decreases rate and extent of absorption.
Distribution: Enters CNS.
Metabolism: Doesn't appear to undergo significant hepatic metabolism; phosphorylation to active form occurs within cells.
Excretion: Excreted primarily in urine. *Half-life:* 2 hours.

Route	Onset	Peak	Duration
P.O.	Unknown	1-2 hr	Unknown

Pharmacodynamics

Chemical effect: Inhibits replication of HIV by blocking viral DNA synthesis.
Therapeutic effect: Reduces symptoms linked to advanced HIV infection.

Available forms

Tablets: 0.375 mg, 0.75 mg

NURSING PROCESS

Assessment

• Assess patient's condition before therapy and regularly thereafter.
• Assess patient for signs of peripheral neuropathy, characterized by numbness and burning in limbs.
• Be alert for adverse reactions and drug interactions.
• Evaluate patient's and family's knowledge of drug therapy.

Nursing diagnoses

• Risk for infection related to presence of HIV
• Disturbed sensory perceptions (tactile) related to drug-induced peripheral neuropathy
• Deficient knowledge related to drug therapy

Planning and implementation

- Dosage adjustments are necessary in patient with moderate-to-severe renal failure.
- Don't give drug with food because it decreases rate and extent of absorption.
- Notify prescriber if signs and symptoms of peripheral neuropathy occur. If patient experiences symptoms that resemble peripheral neuropathy, prepare to withdraw drug. Drug should be discontinued if symptoms are bilateral and persist beyond 72 hours. If symptoms persist or worsen beyond 1 week, drug should be permanently discontinued. If all findings relevant to peripheral neuropathy have resolved to minor symptoms, drug may be reintroduced at 0.375 mg P.O. q 8 hours. If drug isn't withdrawn, peripheral neuropathy can progress to sharp, shooting pain or severe continuous burning pain requiring opioid analgesics. It may or may not be reversible.
- If zalcitabine is discontinued because of toxicity, patient should resume recommended dose for zidovudine (100 mg q 4 hours).

ALERT: Don't confuse drug with other antivirals that use initials for identification.

Patient teaching

- Make sure patient understands that drug doesn't cure HIV infection and that opportunistic infections may occur despite continued use. Review safe sex practices with patient.
- Inform patient that peripheral neuropathy is the major toxicity linked to this drug and that pancreatitis is the major life-threatening toxicity. Review signs and symptoms of these adverse reactions, and instruct patient to call prescriber promptly if they appear.
- Instruct woman of childbearing age to use effective contraceptive during drug therapy.

Evaluation

- Patient responds well to drug.
- Patient doesn't develop peripheral neuropathy.
- Patient and family state understanding of drug therapy.

zaleplon

(ZAL-eh-plon)

Sonata

Pharmacologic class: pyrazolopyrimidine
Therapeutic class: hypnotic
Pregnancy risk category: C
Controlled substance schedule: IV

Indications and dosages

▶ **Short-term treatment of insomnia.** *Adults:* 10 mg P.O. h.s.; may increase dose to 20 mg if needed. Low-weight adults may respond to 5-mg dose.

Elderly and debilitated patients: Initially, 5 mg P.O. h.s.; doses over 10 mg aren't recommended.

Contraindications and precautions

- Don't use in patients with severe hepatic impairment.
- Use cautiously in debilitated patients, in those with compromised respiratory function, and in those with signs and symptoms of depression.

Lifespan: In elderly patients, use cautiously.

Adverse reactions

CNS: *headache,* amnesia, dizziness, somnolence, depression, hypertonia, nervousness, depersonalization, hallucinations, vertigo, difficulty concentrating, anxiety, paresthesia, hypesthesia, tremor, asthenia, migraine, malaise, fever.
CV: chest pain, peripheral edema.
EENT: abnormal vision, conjunctivitis, eye pain, ear pain, hyperacusis, epistaxis, parosmia.
GI: constipation, dry mouth, anorexia, dyspepsia, nausea, abdominal pain, colitis.
GU: dysmenorrhea.
Musculoskeletal: arthritis, myalgia, back pain.
Respiratory: bronchitis.
Skin: pruritus, rash, photosensitivity reactions.

Interactions

Drug-drug. *Carbamazepine, phenobarbital, phenytoin, rifampin, other drugs that induce CYP 3A4:* May reduce bioavailability and peak levels of zaleplon by about 80%. Consider a different hypnotic.

CNS depressants (imipramine, thioridazine): May produce additive CNS effects. Use cautiously together.
Cimetidine: Increases zaleplon bioavailability and peak levels by 85%. For patient taking cimetidine, use an initial zaleplon dose of 5 mg.
Drug-food. *High-fat foods, heavy meals:* Prolongs absorption, delaying peak zaleplon levels by about 2 hours; sleep onset may be delayed. Separate administration from meals.
Drug-lifestyle. *Alcohol use:* May increase CNS effects. Discourage using together.

Effects on lab test results

None reported.

Pharmacokinetics

Absorption: Rapid and almost complete. Levels peak within 1 hour. Dosing after a high-fat or heavy meal delays peak levels by about 2 hours.
Distribution: Substantially distributed into extravascular tissues. Protein-binding is about 60%.
Metabolism: Extensively metabolized, primarily by aldehyde oxidase and, to a lesser extent, CYP 3A4 to inactive metabolites. Less than 1% of dose is excreted unchanged in urine.
Excretion: Rapidly excreted. *Half-life:* 1 hour.

Route	Onset	Peak	Duration
P.O.	1 hr	1 hr	3-4 hr

Pharmacodynamics

Chemical effect: Although zaleplon is a hypnotic with a chemical structure unrelated to benzodiazepines, it interacts with the gamma-aminobutyric acid/benzodiazepine receptor complex in the CNS. Modulation of this complex is hypothesized to be responsible for sedative, anxiolytic, muscle relaxant, and anticonvulsant effects of benzodiazepines.
Therapeutic effect: Promotes sleep.

Available forms

Capsules: 5 mg, 10 mg

NURSING PROCESS

Assessment

- Careful patient evaluation is necessary because sleep disturbances may be a symptom of an underlying physical or psychiatric disorder.
- Closely monitor elderly or debilitated patients and patients with compromised respiratory function because of illness.
- Monitor patient for drug abuse and dependence.
- Evaluate patient's and family's knowledge about drug therapy.

Nursing diagnoses

- Disturbed sleep pattern related to presence of insomnia
- Risk for injury related to drug-induced adverse CNS reactions
- Deficient knowledge related to drug therapy

Planning and implementation

- Don't give drug with or following a high-fat or heavy meal.
- Because zaleplon works rapidly, it should only be taken immediately before bedtime or after patient has been unable to sleep.
- Adverse reactions are usually dose-related. The lowest effective dose should be given.
- Limit hypnotic use to 7 to 10 days. Patient should be reevaluated by a prescriber if hypnotics will be taken for more than 3 weeks.
- The potential for drug abuse and dependence exists. Zaleplon shouldn't be given as more than a 1-month supply.
- Patients with mild-to-moderate hepatic failure or those also taking cimetidine should take 5 mg P.O. every day at bedtime.

Patient teaching

- Advise patient that zaleplon works rapidly and should be taken immediately before bedtime or after trying to sleep but being unable to.
- Advise patient to take drug only if he can sleep undisturbed for at least 4 hours.
- Caution patient that drowsiness, dizziness, light-headedness, and difficulty with coordination occur most often within 1 hour after taking drug.
- Advise patient to avoid performing activities that require mental alertness until CNS effects of drug are known.
- Advise patient to avoid alcohol while taking drug and to notify prescriber before taking any prescription or OTC drugs.
- Tell patient not to take drug after a high-fat or heavy meal.

• Advise patient to report any continued sleep problems despite use of drug.
• Notify patient that dependence can occur, and that drug is recommended for short-term use only.
• Warn patient not to abruptly discontinue drug because withdrawal symptoms, including unpleasant feelings, stomach and muscle cramps, vomiting, sweating, shakiness, and seizures, may occur.
• Notify patient that insomnia may recur for a few nights after stopping drug, but should resolve on its own.
• Advise patient that zaleplon may cause changes in behavior and thinking, including outgoing or aggressive behavior, loss of personal identity, confusion, strange behavior, agitation, hallucinations, worsening of depression, or suicidal thoughts. Tell patient to notify prescriber immediately if any of these symptoms occur.

Evaluation

• Patient states that drug effectively promotes sleep.
• Patient doesn't experience injury as a result of drug-induced adverse CNS reactions.
• Patient and family state understanding of drug therapy.

zanamivir

(zah-NAM-ah-veer)
Relenza

Pharmacologic class: neuraminidase inhibitor
Therapeutic class: antiviral
Pregnancy risk category: C

Indications and dosages

▶ **Treatment of uncomplicated acute illness caused by influenza A and B virus in patients who have been symptomatic for no more than 2 days.** *Adults and children age 7 and older:* 2 oral inhalations (one 5-mg blister per inhalation for a total dose of 10 mg) b.i.d. using the Diskhaler inhalation device for 5 days. Two doses should be taken on the first day of treatment provided there is at least 2 hours between doses. Subsequent doses should be about 12 hours apart (in the morning and evening) at about the same time each day.

Contraindications and precautions

• Contraindicated in patients hypersensitive to zanamivir or its components. Use cautiously in patients with severe or decompensated COPD, asthma, or other underlying respiratory disease.
Lifespan: In breast-feeding women, use cautiously. In children younger than age 7, safety and effectiveness haven't been established.

Adverse reactions

CNS: headache, dizziness.
EENT: nasal signs and symptoms; sinusitis; ear, nose, and throat infections.
GI: diarrhea, nausea, vomiting.
Respiratory: bronchitis, cough.

Interactions

None reported.

Effects on lab test results

None reported.

Pharmacokinetics

Absorption: About 4% to 17%, with peak serum levels occurring 1 to 2 hours following a 10-mg dose.
Distribution: Less than 10%protein binding.
Metabolism: Not metabolized.
Excretion: Excreted unchanged in the urine within 24 hours. Unabsorbed drug is excreted in the feces. *Half-life:* 2½ to 5¼ hours.

Route	Onset	Peak	Duration
Inhalation	Unknown	1-2 hr	Unknown

Pharmacodynamics

Chemical effect: Zanamivir most likely inhibits neuraminidase on the surface of the influenza virus, possibly altering virus particle aggregation and release. With the inhibition of neuraminidase, the virus can't escape from its host cell to attack others, thereby inhibiting the process of viral proliferation.
Therapeutic effect: Lessens the symptoms of influenza.

Available forms

Powder for inhalation: 5 mg per blister

NURSING PROCESS

Assessment
- Obtain accurate patient medical history before starting therapy.
- Lymphopenia, neutropenia, and a rise in liver enzyme and CK levels may occur during treatment. Monitor patient appropriately.
- Monitor patient for bronchospasm and decline in lung function. Stop the drug in such situations.
- Evaluate patient's and family's understanding of drug therapy.

Nursing diagnoses
- Risk for infection related to influenza virus
- Imbalanced nutrition: less than body requirements related to drug's adverse GI effects
- Deficient knowledge related to drug therapy

Planning and implementation
- Have patient exhale fully before putting the mouthpiece in his mouth. Then, keeping the Diskhaler level, have patient close his lips around the mouthpiece, and have him breathe in steadily and deeply. Advise patient to hold his breath for a few seconds after inhaling to help zanamivir stay in the lungs.
- Patients with underlying respiratory disease should have a fast-acting bronchodilator available in case of wheezing while taking zanamivir. Patients scheduled to use an inhaled bronchodilator for asthma should use their bronchodilator before taking zanamivir.
- Safety and efficacy of zanamivir haven't been established for influenza prophylaxis. Use of zanamivir shouldn't affect the evaluation of patients for their annual influenza vaccination.
- No data are available to support safety and efficacy of zanamivir in patients who begin treatment after 48 hours of symptoms.

Patient teaching
- Tell patient to carefully read the instructions regarding how to use the Diskhaler inhalation device properly to administer zanamivir.
- Advise patient to keep the Diskhaler level when loading and inhaling zanamivir. Tell patient to always check inside the mouthpiece of the Diskhaler before each use to make sure it's free of foreign objects.
- Tell patient to exhale fully before putting the mouthpiece in his mouth, then, keeping the Diskhaler level, to close his lips around the mouthpiece and breathe in steadily and deeply. Advise patient to hold his breath for a few seconds after inhaling to help zanamivir stay in the lungs.
- Advise patient who has an impending scheduled dose of inhaled bronchodilator to take it before taking zanamivir. Tell patient to have a fast-acting bronchodilator available in case of wheezing while taking zanamivir.
- Advise patient that it's important to finish the entire 5-day course of treatment even if he starts to feel better and symptoms improve before the fifth day.
- Advise patient that the use of zanamivir hasn't been shown to reduce the risk of transmission of influenza virus to others.

Evaluation
- Patient recovers from influenza.
- Patient doesn't experience adverse GI effects.
- Patient and family state understanding of drug therapy.

zidovudine (azidothymidine, AZT)
(zigh-DOH-vyoo-deen)
Apo-Zidovudine ♦, Novo-AZT ♦, Retrovir

Pharmacologic class: thymidine analogue
Therapeutic class: antiviral
Pregnancy risk category: C

Indications and dosages
▶ **Treatment of HIV infection.** *Adults:* 600 mg daily in divided doses given with other antiretroviral agents.
Children age 6 weeks to 12 years: 160 mg/m^2 q 8 hours (480 mg/m^2 daily up to a maximum of 200 mg q 8 hours) given with other antiretroviral agents.
▶ **Prevention of maternal–fetal HIV transmission.** *Pregnant women past 14 weeks' gestation:* 100 mg P.O. 5 times daily until the start of labor. Then, 2 mg/kg I.V. over 1 hour followed by a continuous I.V. infusion of 1 mg/kg/hour until the umbilical cord is clamped.
Neonates: 2 mg/kg P.O. q 6 hours starting within 12 hours after birth and continuing until age 6 weeks. Or, give 1.5 mg/kg via I.V. infusion over 30 minutes q 6 hours.

Patients on hemodialysis or peritoneal dialysis: Administer 100 mg P.O. q 6 to 8 hours.
Patients with mild-to-moderate hepatic dysfunction or liver cirrhosis: Reduce daily dose.

Contraindications and precautions

- Contraindicated in patients hypersensitive to drug.
- Use cautiously and with close monitoring in patients with advanced symptomatic HIV infection and in those with severe bone marrow depression.
- Use cautiously in patients with hepatomegaly, hepatitis, or other known risk factors for hepatic disease.

Lifespan: In breast-feeding women, drug shouldn't be used. In geriatric patients, use cautiously.

Adverse reactions

CNS: *asthenia, headache,* ***seizures,*** paresthesia, *malaise,* insomnia, *dizziness,* somnolence, *fever.*
GI: *nausea, anorexia, abdominal pain, vomiting,* constipation, *diarrhea,* dyspepsia, taste perversion.
Hematologic: ***severe bone marrow suppression (resulting in anemia), agranulocytosis, thrombocytopenia.***
Metabolic: ***lactic acidosis.***
Musculoskeletal: myalgia.
Skin: *rash,* diaphoresis.

Interactions

Drug-drug. *Atovaquone, fluconazole, methadone, probenecid, valproic acid:* Increased bioavailability of zidovudine. Dosage adjustment may be needed.
Doxorubicin, ribavirin, stavudine: In vitro, these drugs, when used with zidovudine, have been shown to be antagonists. Avoid using together.
Ganciclovir, interferon-alpha, and other bone-marrow–suppressive or cytotoxic agents: May increase hematologic toxicity of zidovudine. Use cautiously as with other reverse transcriptase inhibitors.
Nelfinavir, rifampin, ritonavir: Decreased bioavailability of zidovudine may occur. Dosage adjustment isn't needed.
Phenytoin: Altered phenytoin level and 30% decrease in zidovudine clearance. Monitor patient closely.

Effects on lab test results

- May increase ALT, AST, alkaline phosphatase, and LDH levels.
- May decrease hemoglobin, hematocrit, and granulocyte and platelet counts.

Pharmacokinetics

Absorption: Rapid.
Distribution: Preliminary data reveal good CSF penetration; about 36% plasma protein-bound.
Metabolism: Metabolized rapidly to inactive compound.
Excretion: Excreted in urine. *Half-life:* 1 hour.

Route	Onset	Peak	Duration
P.O.	Unknown	30 to 90 min	Unknown
I.V.	Immediate	30 to 90 min	Unknown

Pharmacodynamics

Chemical effect: Prevents replication of HIV by inhibiting the enzyme reverse transcriptase.
Therapeutic effect: Reduces symptoms of HIV infection.

Available forms

Capsules: 100 mg
Injection: 10 mg/ml
Syrup: 50 mg/5 ml
Tablets: 300 mg

NURSING PROCESS

Assessment

- Assess patient's condition before therapy and regularly thereafter.
- Monitor blood studies every 2 weeks to detect anemia or agranulocytosis.
- Be alert for adverse reactions and drug interactions.
- Evaluate patient's and family's knowledge of drug therapy.

Nursing diagnoses

- Infection related to presence of HIV
- Ineffective protection related to drug-induced adverse hematologic reactions
- Deficient knowledge related to drug therapy

Planning and implementation

- Zidovudine temporarily decreases morbidity and mortality in certain patients with AIDS or AIDS-related complex.

• Optimum duration of treatment and optimum dosage for effectiveness with minimum toxicity aren't yet known.
• **P.O. use:** Follow normal protocol.
• **I.V. use:** Dilute drug before use. Remove calculated dose from vial; add to D_5W to yield no more than 4 mg/ml.
– Infuse drug over 1 hour at constant rate; give every 4 hours around the clock. Avoid rapid infusion or bolus injection.
– Adding mixture to biological or colloidal fluids (such as blood products and protein solutions) isn't recommended.
– After drug is diluted, solution is physically and chemically stable for 24 hours at room temperature and for 48 hours if refrigerated at 36° to 46° F (2° to 8° C). Store undiluted vials at 59° to 77° F (15° to 25° C) and protect them from light.
• Notify prescriber of abnormal hematologic study results. Significant anemia (hemoglobin of less than 7.5 g/dl or reduction of more than 25% of baseline) or significant neutropenia (granulocyte count of less than 750 cells/mm^3 or reduction of more than 50% from baseline) may require a dose interruption until evidence of marrow recovery is observed.

Patient teaching
• Advise patient that blood transfusions may be needed during treatment. Drug often causes low RBC count.
• Stress importance of compliance with every-4-hour dosage schedule. Suggest ways to avoid missing doses, perhaps by using an alarm clock.
• Warn patient not to take other drugs for AIDS (especially street drugs) unless approved by prescriber. Some supposed AIDS cures may interfere with drug's effectiveness.
• Advise pregnant HIV-infected women that drug therapy only reduces risk of HIV transmission to neonates. Long-term risks to infants are unknown.
• Advise health care worker considering zidovudine prophylaxis after occupational exposure (such as after needle-stick injury) that drug's safety and efficacy haven't been proven.

☑ Evaluation
• Patient exhibits reduced severity and frequency of symptoms linked to HIV infection.
• Patient doesn't develop complications from therapy.
• Patient and family state understanding of drug therapy.

ziprasidone
(zi-PRAY-si-done)
Geodon

Pharmacologic class: atypical antipsychotic
Therapeutic class: psychotropic
Pregnancy risk category: C

Indications and dosage
▶ **Symptomatic treatment of schizophrenia.** *Adults:* Initially, 20 mg b.i.d. with food. Dosages are highly individualized. Dosage adjustments should occur no sooner than every 2 days, but to allow for lowest possible doses, the interval should be several weeks. Effective dose range is usually 20 to 80 mg b.i.d. Maximum recommended dose is 100 mg b.i.d.
▶ **Rapid control of acute agitation in schizophrenic patients.** *Adults:* 10 to 20 mg I.M. as required up to a maximum dose of 40 mg daily. Doses of 10 mg may be given q 2 hours; doses of 20 mg may be given q 4 hours.

Contraindications and precautions
• Contraindicated in patients who are hypersensitive to the drug. Contraindicated in patients taking drugs that prolong QT interval and in patients who have a QTc interval longer than 500 msec. Contraindicated in patients with a history of QT-interval prolongation, congenital QT-interval syndrome, recent MI, and uncompensated heart failure.
• Use cautiously in patients with acute diarrhea and in patients with a history of bradycardia, hypokalemia, seizures, aspiration pneumonia, or hypomagnesemia.
• Patients with impaired renal function should be given I.M. ziprasidone with caution.
Lifespan: Breast-feeding women shouldn't take ziprasidone.

Adverse reactions
CNS: *somnolence,* akathesia, dizziness, extrapyramidal symptoms, hypertonia, asthenia; dystonia (P.O. only); *headache, dizziness,* anxiety, insomnia, agitation, cogwheel rigidity,

paresthesia, personality disorder, psychosis, speech disorders (I.M. only), ***suicide attempt.***
CV: orthostatic hypotension; tachycardia (P.O. only); hypertension, ***bradycardia,*** vasodilation (I.M. only).
EENT: rhinitis; abnormal vision (P.O.).
GI: *nausea,* constipation, dyspepsia, diarrhea, dry mouth, anorexia; abdominal pain, rectal hemorrhage, vomiting, dyspepsia.
GU: dysmenorrhea, priapism (I.M.).
Musculoskeletal: myalgia (P.O.); back pain (I.M.)
Respiratory: cough (P.O.).
Skin: rash (P.O.); injection site pain, furunculosis, sweating (I.M.).
Other: flulike syndrome (I.M.), tooth disorder (I.M.).

Interactions

Drug-drug. *Antihypertensives:* May enhance hypotensive effects. Monitor blood pressure.
Carbamazepine: May decrease levels of ziprasidone. Higher doses of ziprasidone may be needed to achieve desired effect.
Drugs that increase dopamine level, such as levodopa and dopamine agonists: May have antagonistic effect on ziprasidone. Use cautiously together.
Drugs that lower potassium and magnesium levels, such as diuretics: May increase risk of arrhythmias. Monitor potassium and magnesium levels if giving together.
Drugs that prolong QT interval, including arsenic trioxide, chlorpromazine, dofetilide, dolasetron mesylate, droperidol, gatifloxacin, halofantrine, levomethadyl acetate, mefloquine, mesoridazine, moxifloxacin, pentamidine, pimozide, probucol, quinidine, sotalol, sparfloxacin, tacrolimus, thioridazine, or other class Ia and III antiarrhythmics: May increase risk of arrhythmias when used together. Don't give together.
Itraconazole, ketoconazole: May increase ziprasidone level. Lower doses of ziprasidone may be needed to achieve desired effect.

Effects on lab test results

None reported.

Pharmacokinetics

Absorption: Doubled when taken with food, which is recommended. Peak serum concentrations reached in about 6 to 8 hours.
Distribution: Highly protein bound.
Metabolism: Hepatic metabolism; no active metabolites. Less than one-third of the drug is metabolized through the cytochrome P450 system. CYP3A4 (major) and CYP1A2 (minor) are the pathways involving the cytochrome P-450 system.
Excretion: *Half-life:* 7 hours.

Route	Onset	Peak	Duration
P.O.	1-3 days	6-8 hr	12 hr
I.M.	Unknown	1 hour	Unknown

Pharmacodynamics

Chemical effect: Unknown. Thought to work through dopamine and serotonin antagonism. These two neurotransmitters are generally targeted for treatment of positive and negative symptoms of schizophrenia. Blocking these neurotransmitters allows symptomatic improvement with minimal adverse effects in the extrapyramidal system.
Therapeutic effect: Relieves psychotic signs and symptoms of schizophrenia.

Available forms

Capsules: 20 mg, 40 mg, 60 mg, 80 mg
Injection: 20 mg/ml single-dose vials (after reconstitution)

NURSING PROCESS

Assessment

- Assess underlying condition before therapy and reassess regularly throughout therapy.
- Patients who experience dizziness, palpitations, or syncope should undergo further evaluation and monitoring.
- Drug may prolong QT interval. Other antipsychotics should be considered in patients with a history of QT interval prolongation, acute MI, congenital QT interval syndrome, and other conditions that place the patient at risk for life-threatening arrhythmias.
- Other drugs that prolong the QT interval shouldn't be prescribed with ziprasidone. Patients taking antipsychotics are at risk for developing neuroleptic malignant syndrome or tardive dyskinesia.
- Electrolyte disturbances, such as hypokalemia or hypomagnesemia, increase the risk of arrhythmias. Monitor potassium and magne-

sium levels before starting therapy and correct imbalances.
• Evaluate patient's and family's knowledge of drug therapy.

Nursing diagnoses
• Disturbed thought processes related to underlying condition
• Risk for fall related to adverse CNS effects of drug
• Deficient knowledge related to ziprasidone therapy

Planning and implementation
• Dosage adjustment shouldn't be performed any sooner than every 2 days. Longer intervals may be necessary because symptom response may not be seen for up to 4 to 6 weeks.
• Monitor patient for prolonged QT interval during therapy. Patients with symptoms of arrhythmias should undergo further monitoring. Stop drug if QTc interval is greater than 500 msec.
• Immediately treat patients with symptoms of neuroleptic malignant syndrome, which can be life-threatening.
• Monitor patient for tardive dyskinesia.
• If long-term therapy of ziprasidone is indicated, switch to P.O. as soon as possible. Effect of I.M. administration for more than 3 consecutive days isn't known.
• Don't give ziprasidone I.M. to schizophrenic patients already taking ziprasidone P.O.
• **P.O. use:** Give with food, which increases the effect.
• **I.M. use:** Add 1.2 ml of sterile water for injection to vial and shake vigorously until entire drug is dissolved.
– Don't mix injection with other medicinal products or solvents other than sterile water for injection.
– Inspect for particulate matter and discoloration before administration, whenever solution and container permit.
– Store dry form, 15° to 30°C (59° to 86°F). Protect from light. Store reconstituted form for up to 24 hours at 15° to 30°C or up to 7 days refrigerated, 2° to 8°C (36° to 46°F). Protect from light.

Patient teaching
• Tell patient to take drug with food.
• Tell patient to immediately report to prescriber symptoms of dizziness, fainting, irregular heart beat, or relevant cardiac problems.
• Advise patient to report to prescriber any recent episodes of diarrhea.
• Advise patient to report to prescriber abnormal movements.
• Tell patient to report to prescriber sudden fever, muscle rigidity, or change in mental status.

Evaluation
• Patient demonstrates reduced psychotic symptoms with drug therapy.
• Patient doesn't fall.
• Patient and family state understanding of drug therapy.

zoledronic acid
(zoe-LEH-druh-nick ASS-id)
Zometa

Pharmacologic class: bisphosphonate
Therapeutic class: antihypercalcemic
Pregnancy risk category: D

Indications and dosages
▶ **Hypercalcemia related to malignancy.** *Adults:* 4 mg by I.V. infusion over at least 15 minutes. If albumin-corrected calcium level doesn't return to normal, consider retreatment with 4 mg. Allow at least 7 days to pass before retreatment to allow a full response to the initial dose.
▶ **Multiple myeloma and bone metastases of solid tumors given with standard antineoplastic therapy. Prostate cancer should have progressed after treatment with at least one hormonal therapy.** *Adults:* 4 mg infused over 15 minutes q 3 or 4 weeks. Duration of treatment in the clinical studies was 15 months for prostate cancer, 12 months for breast cancer and multiple myeloma, and 9 months for other solid tumors.

Contraindications and precautions
• Contraindicated in patients with significant hypersensitivity to drug, other bisphosphonates, or ingredients in formulation.

• Not recommended in patients with hypercalcemia of malignancy with severe renal impairment (creatinine greater than 4.5 mg/dl).
• Use cautiously in patients with aspirin-sensitive asthma because other bisphosphonates have been linked to bronchoconstriction in these patients.
• Not recommended in patients with bone metastases with severe renal impairment (creatinine greater than 3.0 mg/dl).
Lifespan: In breast-feeding women, give cautiously; it isn't known whether drug appears in breast milk. In children, safety and effectiveness haven't been established. In geriatric patients, give cautiously.

Adverse reactions

Hypercalcemia
CNS: headache, somnolence, *anxiety,* confusion, agitation, *insomnia, fever.*
CV: ***hypotension.***
GI: *nausea, constipation, diarrhea, abdominal pain, vomiting,* anorexia, dysphagia.
GU: *urinary tract infection, candidiasis.*
Hematologic: *anemia,* ***granulocytopenia, thrombocytopenia, pancytopenia.***
Metabolic: dehydration.
Musculoskeletal: *skeletal pain,* arthralgia.
Respiratory: *dyspnea, cough,* pleural effusion.
Other: **PROGRESSION OF CANCER,** infection.
Bone metastases
CNS: *headache,* anxiety, *insomnia, depression, paresthesia, hypesthesia, fatigue, weakness, dizziness, fever.*
CV: ***hypotension,*** *leg edema.*
GI: *nausea, constipation, diarrhea, abdominal pain, vomiting, anorexia, increased appetite.*
GU: *urinary tract infection.*
Hematologic: *anemia,* ***neutropenia.***
Metabolic: *dehydration, weight loss.*
Musculoskeletal: *skeletal pain, arthralgia, myalgia, back pain.*
Respiratory: *dyspnea, cough.*
Skin: alopecia, dermatitis.
Other: **PROGRESSION OF CANCER**, rigors, infection.

Interactions

Drug-drug. *Aminoglycosides, loop diuretics:* May have additive effects to lower calcium level. Give together cautiously, and monitor calcium level.
Thalidomide: In multiple myeloma patients, the risk of renal dysfunction may be increased. Use together cautiously.

Effects on lab test results

• May increase creatinine level. May decrease calcium, phosphorus, magnesium, and potassium levels.
• May decrease hemoglobin, hematocrit, and RBC, WBC, and platelet counts.

Pharmacokinetics

Absorption: Administered I.V.
Distribution: Protein binding of about 22%. Post-infusion decline of level is consistent with a triphasic process: Low level observed up to 28 days after a dose.
Metabolism: Doesn't inhibit the P-450 enzymes or undergo biotransformation in vivo.
Excretion: Primarily excreted via the kidneys. *Half-life:* Alpha is 0.23 hours; beta is 1.75 hours for early distribution. *Terminal half-life:* 167 hours.

Route	Onset	Peak	Duration
I.V.	Unknown	Unknown	7-28 days

Pharmacodynamics

Chemical effect: Inhibits bone resorption, probably by inhibiting osteoclast activity and osteoclastic resorption of mineralized bone and cartilage, decreasing calcium release induced by the stimulatory factors produced by tumors.
Therapeutic effect: Lowers calcium level in malignant disease.

Available forms

Injection: 4 mg zoledronic acid, 220 mg mannitol, and 24 mg sodium citrate

NURSING PROCESS

Assessment

• Assess underlying condition before therapy and reassess regularly throughout therapy.
• Assess kidney function before therapy and during therapy because drug is excreted mainly via the kidneys. The risk of adverse reactions may be greater in patients with impaired renal function. If patient has renal impairment, give drug only if benefits outweigh risks and at an adjusted dosage.

- Measure creatinine level before each dose.
- Make sure patient is adequately hydrated before giving drug; urine output should be about 2 liters daily.
- Evaluate patient's and family's knowledge of drug therapy.

Nursing diagnoses

- Ineffective protection related to adverse hematologic effects
- Ineffective health maintenance related to underlying condition
- Deficient knowledge related to drug therapy

Planning and implementation

ALERT: A significant decline in renal function could progress to renal failure; single doses shouldn't exceed 4 mg and infusion should last at least 15 minutes.

ALERT: Monitor renal function and calcium, phosphate, magnesium, and creatinine levels carefully after giving drug.

- Other bisphosphonates have been linked to bronchoconstriction in patients with asthma and aspirin sensitivity.
- Reconstitute by adding 5 ml of sterile water to each vial. Powder must be completely dissolved.
- Withdraw 4 mg of drug and mix in 100 ml of normal saline solution or D_5W.
- The drug must be given as an I.V. infusion over at least 15 minutes.
- If not used immediately reconstituted, solution must be refrigerated and given within 24 hours.
- Inspect solution for particulate matter and discoloration before giving it.
- Give drug as a single I.V. solution in a line separate from all other drugs.

ALERT: Don't mix drug with solutions that contain calcium (such as lactated Ringer's solution).

- Patients should also be given an oral calcium supplement of 500 mg and a multiple vitamin containing 400 IU of vitamin D daily.

Patient teaching

- Review the use and administration of drug with patient and family.
- Instruct patient to report adverse effects promptly.
- Explain the importance of periodic laboratory tests to monitor therapy and renal function.
- Advise patient to alert prescriber if she is pregnant.

Evaluation

- Patient has no adverse hematologic reactions.
- Patient shows improvement in condition.
- Patient and family state understanding of drug therapy.

zolmitriptan

(zohl-muh-TRIP-tan)

Zomig, Zomig-ZMT

Pharmacologic class: selective 5-hydroxytryptamine receptor agonist
Therapeutic class: antimigraine agent
Pregnancy risk category: C

Indications and dosages

▶ **Treatment of acute migraine headaches.** *Adults:* Initially, 2.5 mg or less P.O. increased to 5 mg per dose, p.r.n. If headache returns after initial dose, second dose may be given after 2 hours. Maximum dose is 10 mg in 24-hour period. Or, give 2.5 mg P.O. of orally disintegrating tablets. Don't break tablets in half. If headache returns after initial dose, a second dose may be given after 2 hours. Maximum dose is 10 mg in 24-hour period.
Patients with liver disease: Use doses under 2.5 mg. Don't use orally disintegrating tablets.

Contraindications and precautions

- Contraindicated in patients hypersensitive to drug and in those with ischemic heart disease or other significant heart disease (including Wolff-Parkinson-White syndrome) or uncontrolled hypertension. Don't give drug within 24 hours of 5-HT1 agonists, ergot-containing drugs, or ergot-type drugs. Use of zolmitriptan with MAO inhibitor or within 2 weeks of MAO inhibitor therapy also is contraindicated.
- Use cautiously in patients with liver disease.
- Drug isn't intended for preventing migraine headaches or treating hemiplegic or basilar migraines.
- Safety of drug hasn't been established for cluster headaches.

Lifespan: In pregnant and breast-feeding women, drug is contraindicated.

Adverse reactions

CNS: somnolence, vertigo, *dizziness,* syncope, hyperesthesia, paresthesia, warm or cold sensations, asthenia.
CV: pain or heaviness in chest, ***arrhythmias,*** hypertension, *pain, tightness, or pressure in the neck, throat, or jaw.*
GI: dry mouth, dyspepsia, dysphagia, nausea.
Musculoskeletal: myalgia.
Skin: sweating.

Interactions

Drug-drug. *Cimetidine:* Doubles half-life of zolmitriptan. Monitor patient.
Ergot-type or ergot-containing drugs, 5-HT_1 agonists: May cause additive vasospastic reactions. Avoid using together.
Fluoxetine, fluvoxamine, paroxetine, sertraline: May cause weakness, hyperreflexia, and incoordination. Use cautiously.
MAO inhibitors: Increases effects of zolmitriptan. Avoid using together.

Effects on lab test results

- May increase glucose level.

Pharmacokinetics

Absorption: Well absorbed following P.O. administration with an absolute bioavailability of 40%.
Distribution: 25% bound to plasma protein.
Metabolism: Converted to active N-desmethyl metabolite.
Excretion: About 65% of dose is recovered in urine (8% unchanged) and 30% in feces. *Half-life:* 3 hours.

Route	Onset	Peak	Duration
P.O.	Unknown	2 hr	3 hr
P.O. (orally disintegrating)	Unknown	2 hr	Unknown

Pharmacodynamics

Chemical effect: Selective serotonin receptor agonist causes constriction of cranial blood vessels and inhibits proinflammatory neuropeptide release.
Therapeutic effect: Relieves migraine headache pain.

Available forms

Tablets: 2.5 mg, 5 mg
Tablets (orally disintegrating): 2.5 mg, 5 mg

NURSING PROCESS

Assessment

- Assess patient's history of migraine headaches and drug's effectiveness.
- Assess patient for history of known coronary artery disease, hypertension, arrhythmias, or presence of risk factors for coronary artery disease.
- Monitor liver function test results before starting drug therapy, and report abnormalities.
- Drug should be used only when a clear diagnosis of migraine has been established.
- Evaluate patient's and family's knowledge of drug therapy.

Nursing diagnoses

- Acute pain related to presence of migraine headache
- Impaired cardiopulmonary tissue perfusion related to drug-induced adverse cardiac events
- Deficient knowledge related to drug therapy

Planning and implementation

- Use a lower dose in patients with moderate-to-severe hepatic impairment; don't give them orally disintegrating tablets because those tablets can't be broken in half.
- Don't give drug to prevent migraine headaches or to treat hemiplegic migraines, basilar migraines, or cluster headaches.

ALERT: Don't give drug within 24 hours of ergot-containing drugs or within 2 weeks of MAO inhibitor.

Patient teaching

- Tell patient that drug is intended to relieve the symptoms of migraines, not to prevent them.
- Advise patient to take drug as prescribed. Caution against taking a second dose unless instructed by prescriber. Tell patient that if a second dose is indicated and permitted, he should take it at least 2 hours after initial dose.
- Advise patient to immediately report pain or tightness in chest or throat, heart throbbing, rash, skin lumps, or swelling of face, lips, or eyelids.

• Tell woman not to take drug if she plans or suspects pregnancy.
• Instruct patient to not release the orally disintegrating tablets from their blister pack until just before administration. Open the pack and dissolve on tongue.
• Advise patient not to break the orally disintegrating tablets in half.

Evaluation
• Patient has relief from migraine headache.
• Patient doesn't experience pain or tightness in the chest or throat, arrhythmias, increases in blood pressure, or MI.
• Patient and family state understanding of drug therapy.

zolpidem tartrate
(ZOHL-peh-dim TAR-trayt)
Ambien

Pharmacologic class: imidazopyridine
Therapeutic class: hypnotic
Pregnancy risk category: B
Controlled substance schedule: IV

Indications and dosages
▶ **Short-term management of insomnia.** *Adults:* 10 mg P.O. h.s.
Elderly or debilitated patients and patients with hepatic insufficiency: 5 mg P.O. h.s. Maximum daily dose is 10 mg.

Contraindications and precautions
• Use cautiously in patients with conditions that could affect metabolism or hemodynamic responses and in those with compromised respiratory status, because hypnotics may depress respiratory drive. Also use cautiously in patients with depression or history of alcohol or drug abuse.
Lifespan: In pregnant women, use cautiously. In breast-feeding women, drug isn't recommended. In children, safety of drug hasn't been established.

Adverse reactions
CNS: daytime drowsiness, light-headedness, abnormal dreams, amnesia, dizziness, *headache,* hangover effect, sleep disorder, lethargy, depression.
CV: palpitations.
EENT: sinusitis, pharyngitis.
GI: nausea, vomiting, diarrhea, dyspepsia, constipation, abdominal pain, dry mouth.
Musculoskeletal: back or chest pain, myalgia, arthralgia.
Skin: rash.
Other: flulike syndrome, hypersensitivity reactions.

Interactions
Drug-drug. *CNS depressants:* Enhances CNS depression. Use together cautiously.
Drug-food. *Any food:* Decreases rate and extent of absorption. Take drug on an empty stomach.
Drug-lifestyle. *Alcohol use:* May cause excessive CNS depression. Discourage using together.

Effects on lab test results
None reported.

Pharmacokinetics
Absorption: Rapid. Food delays drug absorption.
Distribution: Protein-binding is about 92.5%.
Metabolism: Metabolized in liver.
Excretion: Excreted primarily in urine. *Half-life:* 2½ hours.

Route	Onset	Peak	Duration
P.O.	Rapid	30 min-2 hr	Unknown

Pharmacodynamics
Chemical effect: Interacts with one of three identified GABA-benzodiazepine receptor complexes but isn't a benzodiazepine. It exhibits hypnotic activity but no muscle relaxant or anticonvulsant properties.
Therapeutic effect: Promotes sleep.

Available forms
Tablets: 5 mg, 10 mg

NURSING PROCESS

Assessment
• Assess patient's condition before therapy and regularly thereafter.
• Be alert for adverse reactions and drug interactions.

• Evaluate patient's and family's knowledge of drug therapy.

Nursing diagnoses
• Disturbed sleep pattern related to presence of insomnia
• Risk for injury related to drug-induced adverse CNS reactions
• Deficient knowledge related to drug therapy

Planning and implementation
• Drug has a rapid onset of action and should be given when patient is ready to go to bed.
• Hypnotics should be used only for short-term management of insomnia, usually 7 to 10 days. Persistent insomnia may indicate primary psychiatric or medical disorder.
• Because most adverse reactions are dose-related, smallest effective dose should be used in all patients, especially those who are elderly or debilitated.
• Give drug at least 1 hour before meals or 2 hours after meals.
ALERT: Don't confuse Ambien with Amen.

Patient teaching
• Tell patient to take drug immediately before going to bed.
• For faster onset, instruct patient not to take drug with or immediately after meals. Food decreases drug's absorption.
• Caution patient about performing activities that require mental alertness or physical coordination. For inpatient, supervise walking and raise bed rails, particularly for geriatric patient.

Evaluation
• Patient states that drug effectively promotes sleep.
• Patient doesn't experience injury from adverse CNS reactions.
• Patient and family state understanding of drug therapy.

zonisamide
(zon-ISS-a-mide)
Zonegran

Pharmacologic class: sulfonamide
Therapeutic class: anticonvulsant
Pregnancy risk category: C

Indications and dosages
▶ **Adjunct therapy for partial seizures in adults with epilepsy.** *Adults:* Initially, 100 mg P.O. as a single daily dose for 2 weeks. After 2 weeks, the dose may be increased to 200 mg daily for at least 2 weeks. It can be increased to 300 mg and 400 mg P.O. daily, with the dose stable for at least 2 weeks to achieve steady state at each level. Doses larger than 100 mg can be divided. Can be taken with or without food.

Contraindications and precautions
• Contraindicated in patients hypersensitive to sulfonamides or zonisamide.
• Rarely, patients receiving sulfonamides have died because of severe reactions such as Stevens-Johnson syndrome, fulminant hepatic necrosis, aplastic anemia, otherwise unexplained rashes, and agranulocytosis. If signs of hypersensitivity or other serious reactions occur, discontinue zonisamide immediately.
• Use cautiously in patients with renal and hepatic dysfunction. If GFR is less than 50 ml/minute, don't use drug. If patient develops acute renal failure or a clinically significant sustained increase in creatinine or BUN levels, the drug should be discontinued.
• Caution should be used when zonisamide is prescribed with other drugs that predispose patients to heat-related disorders (such as carbonic anhydrase inhibitors and anticholinergics).
Lifespan: In children, safety and effectiveness have not been established.

Adverse reactions
CNS: *headache, dizziness,* ataxia, nystagmus, paresthesia, confusion, difficulties in concentration and memory, mental slowing, agitation, irritability, depression, insomnia, anxiety, nervousness, schizophrenic or schizophreniform behavior, *somnolence,* fatigue, speech abnormalities, difficulties in verbal expression.
EENT: diplopia, rhinitis.
GI: *anorexia,* nausea, diarrhea, dyspepsia, constipation, dry mouth, taste perversion, abdominal pain.
Metabolic: weight loss.
Skin: ecchymoses, *rash.*
Other: flulike symptoms.

Interactions

Drug-drug. *Drugs that induce or inhibit CYP 3A4:* Alters zonisamide level. Zonisamide clearance is increased by phenytoin, carbamazepine, phenobarbital, and valproate. Monitor patient closely.

Effects on lab test results

- May increase BUN and creatinine levels.

Pharmacokinetics

Absorption: Level peaks in 2 to 6 hours; food delays but doesn't affect bioavailability.
Distribution: Extensively binds to erythrocytes. Drug is about 40% bound to plasma proteins. Protein-binding is unaffected in the presence of therapeutic levels of phenytoin, phenobarbital, or carbamazepine.
Metabolism: Metabolized by cytochrome P-450 3A4. Drug clearance increases in patients who are also taking enzyme-inducing drugs.
Excretion: Excreted primarily in urine as parent drug and as glucuronide of a metabolite. *Half-life:* About 63 hours.

Route	Onset	Peak	Duration
P.O.	Unknown	Unknown	Unknown

Pharmacodynamics

Chemical effect: The exact mechanism of action is unknown, but it's thought to produce antiseizure effects through action at the sodium and calcium channels, thereby stabilizing neuronal membranes and suppressing neuronal hypersynchronization. Other models suggest that synaptically driven electrical activity is suppressed without potentiation of GABA synaptic activity. The drug also may facilitate dopaminergic and serotonergic neurotransmission.
Therapeutic effect: Prevents and stops seizure activity.

Available forms

Capsules: 100 mg

NURSING PROCESS

Assessment

- Obtain history of patient's underlying condition before therapy, and reassess regularly thereafter.
- Monitor patient for symptoms of hypersensitivity.
- Monitor body temperature, especially in summer, because decreased sweating may occur (especially in children age 17 and younger), resulting in heatstroke and dehydration.
- Monitor renal function periodically.
- Evaluate patient's and family's knowledge about drug therapy.

Nursing diagnoses

- Risk for trauma related to seizures
- Risk for injury related to drug-induced adverse CNS effects
- Deficient knowledge related to drug therapy

Planning and implementation

- Drug may be taken with or without food. Don't bite or break the capsule.
- Use cautiously in patients with hepatic and renal disease; may need slower adjustment and more frequent monitoring. If GFR is less than 50 ml/minute, don't use drug.
- Abrupt zonisamide withdrawal may cause increased frequency of seizures or status epilepticus; reduce dose or discontinue drug gradually.
- Increase fluid intake and urine output to help prevent renal calculi, especially in patients with predisposing factors.
- Pediatric patients appear to be at an increased risk for zonisamide-associated oligohidrosis and hyperthermia. Patients, especially children, treated with zonisamide should be monitored closely for evidence of decreased sweating and increased body temperature, especially in warm or hot weather.

Patient teaching

- Tell patient to take medication with or without food. Caution against biting or breaking the capsule.
- Instruct patient to contact prescriber immediately if a skin rash develops or seizures worsen.
- Tell patient to contact prescriber immediately if he develops sudden back pain, abdominal pain, pain when urinating, bloody or dark urine, fever, sore throat, mouth sores, easy bruising, decreased sweating, increased body temperature, depression, or speech or language problems.

- Tell patient to drink 6 to 8 glasses of water a day.
- Tell patient to avoid hazardous activities until full effects of drug are known. It may cause drowsiness.
- Tell patient to not stop taking drug without prescriber's approval.
- Tell patient to notify prescriber about planned, suspected, or known pregnancy. Also tell her to notify prescriber if she's breast-feeding.
- Advise woman of childbearing age to use contraception while taking drug.

☑ Evaluation

- Patient is free from seizure activity.
- Patient doesn't experience adverse CNS effects.
- Patient and family state understanding of drug therapy.

Herbal Medicines

aloe

(AH-loh)

aloe vera, Barbados aloe, Cape aloe, Curacao aloe, lily of the desert

Reported uses

Used externally as a topical gel for minor burns, sunburn, cuts, frostbite, skin irritation, and other wounds and abrasions.

Used internally as a stimulant laxative. Also used to treat amenorrhea, asthma, colds, seizures, bleeding, and ulcers.

Aloe preparations also are used to treat acne, AIDS, arthritis, asthma, blindness, bursitis, cancer, colitis, depression, diabetes, glaucoma, hemorrhoids, multiple sclerosis, peptic ulcers, and varicose veins.

Dosages

▶ **Pruritus, skin irritation, burns, and other wounds (external forms).** Apply liberally, p.r.n. Although internal use isn't recommended, some sources suggest 100 to 200 mg aloe or 50 to 100 mg aloe extract P.O., taken in the evening. Information about dosages for aloe juice is inadequate.

Cautions

- External aloe preparations contraindicated in patients hypersensitive to aloe and in those with history of allergic reactions to plants in the Liliaceae family (such as garlic, onions, and tulips).
- Oral use is contraindicated in patients with cardiac or kidney disease (because of risk of hypokalemia and disturbance of cardiac rhythm); in those with intestinal obstruction; in those with Crohn's disease, ulcerative colitis, appendicitis, or abdominal pain of unknown origin; in women who are pregnant or breast-feeding; and in children.

Adverse reactions

CV: ***arrhythmias.***
GI: painful intestinal spasms, damage to intestinal mucosa, harmless brown discoloration of intestinal mucous membranes, ***severe hemorrhagic diarrhea.***
GU: kidney damage, red discoloration of urine, reflex stimulation of uterine musculature causing miscarriage or premature birth.
Metabolic: fluid and electrolyte loss, hypokalemia.
Musculoskeletal: muscle weakness, accelerated bone deterioration.
Skin: contact dermatitis, delayed healing of deep wounds.

Interactions

Herb-drug. *Antiarrhythmics, cardiac glycosides such as digoxin:* Oral aloe may lead to toxic reaction. Monitor patient closely.
Corticosteroids, diuretics: Increases potassium loss. Monitor patient for signs of hypokalemia.
Disulfiram: Tincture contains alcohol and could precipitate a disulfiram reaction. Discourage using together.
Herb-herb. *Licorice:* Increases risk of potassium deficiency. Discourage using together.

Actions

When taken internally, aloin produces a metabolite that irritates the large intestine and stimulates colonic activity. It also causes active secretion of fluids and electrolytes and inhibits reabsorption of fluids from the colon, resulting in a feeling of distention and increased peristalsis. The cathartic effect occurs 8 to 12 hours after ingestion.

When taken externally, besides acting as a moisturizer on burns and other wounds, aloe reduces inflammation. Its antipruritic effect may result from blockage of the conversion of histidine to histamine. Wound healing may result from increased blood flow to the wound area.

Common forms

In capsules or as cream, hair conditioner, jelly, juice, liniment, lotion, ointment, shampoo, skin cream, soap, sunscreen, and in facial tissues. Also as an ingredient in Benzoin Compound Tincture.
Capsules: 75 mg, 100 mg, 200 mg aloe vera extract or aloe vera powder.
Gel: 98%, 99.5%, 99.6% aloe vera gel.
Juice: 99.6%, 99.7% aloe vera juice.
Tincture*: 1:10, 50% alcohol.

*Liquid may contain alcohol.

NURSING CONSIDERATIONS

- Oral use can cause severe abdominal discomfort and serious hypokalemia and electrolyte imbalance.
- Studies on the use of aloe vera injections for cancer have shown a link to death.
- Use of injectable aloe vera preparations or chemical constituents of aloe vera isn't recommended.

Patient teaching

- Caution patient against use of aloe vera gel or aloe vera juice for internal use.
- Advise patient to consult prescriber before using an herbal preparation because another treatment may be available.
- Tell patient that when filling a new prescription he should inform pharmacist of any herbal or dietary supplement he's taking.
- Tell patient that if he uses aloe and delays in seeking medical diagnosis and treatment, his condition could worsen.
- Warn patient not to take aloe without medical advice if he's also taking digoxin, another drug to control his heart rate, a diuretic, or a corticosteroid.
- Aloe may cause feelings of dehydration, weakness, and confusion, especially if used for a prolonged period. Caution patient to seek medical help immediately if any of these signs or symptoms appear.

angelica

(an-JEL-ih-kah)

angelica root, angelique, dong quai, garden angelica, tang-kuei, wild angelica

Reported uses

Used to treat gynecologic disorders, postmenopausal symptoms, menstrual discomfort, regulation of the menstrual cycle, and anemia. Also used to treat headaches and backaches, improve circulation in the limbs, and relieve osteoporosis, hay fever, asthma, and eczema.

Dosages

No consensus exists.

Cautions

- Contraindicated in pregnant or breastfeeding women because of potential stimulant effects on the uterus.
- Urge caution in diabetic patients because various species of this plant contain polysaccharides that may disrupt glucose-level control.

Adverse reactions

CV: hypotension.
Skin: photodermatitis, phototoxicity.

Interactions

Herb-drug. *Antacids, H_2-receptor antagonists, proton pump inhibitors, sucralfate:* Angelica may increase acid production in the stomach and may interfere with absorption of these drugs. Discourage using together.
Anticoagulants: Potentiates effects with excessive doses of angelica. Monitor patient for bleeding.
Herb-lifestyle. *Sun exposure:* Photosensitivity reaction may occur. Advise patient to avoid unprotected or prolonged exposure to sunlight.

Actions

Root extracts may have antitumor properties; also may have anti-inflammatory and analgesic actions.

Isolated substances extracted from the root inhibit platelet aggregation, exert antimicrobial action, and decrease myocardial injury and the risk of PVCs and arrhythmias induced by myocardial reperfusion.

Improved pulmonary function and decreased mean arterial pulmonary pressures may occur when compounds are used with nifedipine in patient with chronic obstructive pulmonary disease and pulmonary hypertension.

Common forms

Fluid extract, tincture, essential oil, and cut, dried, and powdered root.

NURSING CONSIDERATIONS

- Monitor patients taking angelica for signs of bleeding—especially those already taking anticoagulants.
- Find out why patient is using the herb.

• Monitor patient for persistent diarrhea, which may be a sign of something more serious.
• Monitor patient for dermatologic reaction.
• Photodermatosis is possible after contact with the plant juice or plant extract.

Patient teaching

• Tell patient to remind the pharmacist of any herbal or dietary supplement he's taking when filling a new prescription.
• Warn patient not to treat symptoms with angelica before seeking appropriate medical evaluation because doing so may delay diagnosis of a potentially serious medical condition.
• Advise patient not to take angelica if pregnant or if taking an acid blocker or blood-thinning drug.
• Advise patient to report skin rash.

bilberry

(BIL-beh-ree)

bilberries, bog bilberries, European blueberries, huckleberries, whortleberries

Reported uses

Used to treat visual and circulatory problems, glaucoma, cataracts, diabetic retinopathy, macular degeneration, varicose veins, and hemorrhoids. Also used to improve night vision.

Dosages

Suggested dosages vary considerably. Most herbalists recommend using standardized products consisting of 25% anthocyanoside content.

▶ **Improve night vision.** 60 to 120 mg of bilberry extract P.O. daily.

▶ **Visual and circulatory problems.** 240 to 480 mg P.O. daily in two or three divided doses.

Cautions

• Contraindicated in pregnant and breast-feeding women.
• Urge caution in patients taking anticoagulants. Herb may be unsuitable for those with a bleeding disorder.

Adverse reactions

Other: *toxic reaction.*

Interactions

Herb-drug. *Anticoagulants, other antiplatelet drugs:* Inhibits platelet aggregation, possibly increasing the risk of bleeding. Monitor patient.

Disulfiram: May cause disulfiram reaction if herb preparation contains alcohol. Advise patient to avoid using together.

Actions

May reduce vascular permeability and tissue edema. Also may aid blood flow. Exerts potent antioxidant effects and a protective effect on low-density lipoproteins.

Chemical components of bilberry may exert changes in the retina, allowing better adaptation to darkness and light, decrease excessive platelet aggregation, and exert preventive and curative antiulcer actions.

Common forms

Capsules: 60 mg, 80 mg, 120 mg, 450 mg. Also available in liquid, tincture, fluid extract, and dried root, leaves, and berries.

NURSING CONSIDERATIONS

ALERT: Long-term consumption of large doses of bilberry leaves can be poisonous. Doses of 1.5 g/kg or more in a day may be fatal.
• Herb may reduce glucose level in diabetics. Dosage may need to be adjusted in those taking antidiabetic drugs.
• For treatment of vascular and ocular conditions, consistent dosing is required.

Patient teaching

• Tell patient to remind the pharmacist of any herbal or dietary supplement he's taking when filling a new prescription.
• Warn patient not to treat symptoms with bilberry before seeking appropriate medical evaluation because doing so may delay diagnosis of a potentially serious medical condition.
• Bilberry may be taken without regard to meals or food.
• Advise any patient using the dried fruit to take each dose with a full glass of water.

*Liquid may contain alcohol.

capsicum
(KAP-sih-kem)
bell pepper, capsaicin, cayenne pepper, chili pepper, hot pepper, paprika, red pepper, Tabasco pepper

Reported uses
Used to treat bowel disorders, chronic laryngitis, and peripheral vascular disease. Various preparations of capsicum are applied topically as counterirritants and external analgesics. The FDA has approved topical capsaicin for temporary relief of pain from rheumatoid arthritis, osteoarthritis, postherpetic neuralgia (shingles), and diabetic neuropathy. It's being tested for treatment of psoriasis, intractable pruritus, vitiligo, phantom limb pain, mastectomy pain, Guillain-Barré syndrome, neurogenic bladder, vulvar vestibulitis, apocrine chromhidrosis, and reflex sympathetic dystrophy. It's also used in personal defense sprays and to treat refractory pruritus and pruritus caused by renal failure.

Dosages
Topical preparations range from 0.025% to 0.25%. Most effective when applied t.i.d. or q.i.d.; duration of action is about 4 to 6 hours. Less frequent applications typically produce incomplete analgesia.

Cautions
• Contraindicated in patients hypersensitive to capsicum or chili pepper products.
• Also contraindicated in pregnant women because of possible uterine stimulant effects. Patients with irritable bowel syndrome should avoid use because capsicum has irritant and peristaltic effects. Patients with asthma who use capsicum may experience more bronchospasms.

Adverse reactions
EENT: blepharospasm, extreme burning pain, lacrimation, conjunctival edema, hyperemia, burning pain in nose, sneezing, serous discharge.
GI: oral burning, diarrhea, gingival irritation, bleeding gums.
Respiratory: ***bronchospasm,*** cough, retrosternal discomfort.
Skin: transient skin irritation, itching, stinging, erythema without vesicular eruption, contact dermatitis.

Interactions
Herb-drug. *ACE inhibitors:* Increases risk of cough when applied topically. Monitor patient closely.
Anticoagulants: May alter anticoagulant effects. Monitor PT and INR closely; tell patient to avoid using together.
Antiplatelet drugs, heparin and low–molecular-weight heparin, warfarin: Increases risk of bleeding. Advise patient to avoid using together. If they must be used together, monitor patient for bleeding.
Aspirin, salicylic acid compounds: Reduces bioavailability of these drugs. Discourage using together.
Theophylline: Increases absorption when given with capsicum. Discourage using together.
Herb-herb. *Feverfew, garlic, ginger, ginkgo, ginseng:* Increases anticoagulant effects of capsicum, and increases risk of bleeding. Discourage using together; if these herbs must be used together, monitor patient closely for bleeding.

Actions
Topical capsicum produces an extremely intense irritation at the contact point. Initial dose causes profound pain; however, repeated applications cause desensitization, with analgesic and anti-inflammatory effects.

Juices from the fruits may have antibacterial properties in vitro.

Common forms
Cream: 0.025%, 0.075%, 0.25%.
Gel: 0.025%.
Lotion: 0.025%, 0.075%.
Roll-on: 0.075%.
Self-defense spray: 5%, 10%.
Also available as the vegetable, pepper.

NURSING CONSIDERATIONS
• Find out why patient is using the herb.
• Topical product shouldn't be used on broken or irritated skin or covered with a tight bandage.
• Washing the area thoroughly with soap and water treats adverse skin reaction to topically applied capsicum. Soaking the area in vegetable oil after washing provides a slower on-

Bold italic type indicates that reaction may be life-threatening.

set but longer duration of relief than cold water. Vinegar water irrigation is moderately successful. Rubbing alcohol also may help.
- EMLA, an emulsion of lidocaine and prilocaine, provides pain relief in about 1 hour to skin that has been severely irritated by capsicum.
- Capsicum shouldn't be taken orally for more than 2 days and shouldn't be used again for 2 weeks.
- After topical application, relief may occur in 3 days but may take as long as 14 to 28 days, depending on the condition requiring analgesia.

Patient teaching

- Tell patient to avoid contact with eyes, mucous membranes, and broken skin.
- If patient is using capsicum topically, instruct him to wash his hands before and immediately after applying it. Advise contact lens wearers to wash hands and to use gloves or an applicator if handling lenses after applying capsicum.
- If incidental contact occurs, inform patient to flush exposed area with cool running water for as long as necessary.
- Caution patient taking MAO inhibitors or centrally acting adrenergics not to use of this herb.

cat's claw

(KATS klaw)

life-giving vine of Peru, samento, una de gato

Reported uses

Used to treat GI problems, including Crohn's disease, colitis, inflammatory bowel disease, diverticulitis, gastritis, dysentery, ulcerations and hemorrhoids, and to enhance immunity. Used to treat systemic inflammatory diseases (such as arthritis and rheumatism). Used by cancer patients for its antimutagenic effects. Used with zidovudine to stimulate the immune system by patients with HIV infection. Used as a contraceptive.

Dosages

No consensus exists. Herbal literature suggests 500 to 1,000 mg P.O. t.i.d. Other sources suggest different dosages depending on condition and form of herbal product.

Capsules: 2 capsules (175 mg/capsule) P.O. daily or 3 capsules P.O. t.i.d.; dosage varies by manufacturer.
Decoction: 2 to 3 cups/day made from 10 to 30 g inner stalk bark or root in 1 qt (1 L) of water for 30 to 60 minutes.
Extract (alcohol-free): 7 to 10 gtt t.i.d. up to 15 gtt five times a day.
Liquid or alcohol extract*: 10 to 15 gtt b.i.d. to t.i.d., to 1 to 3 ml t.i.d.
Powdered extract: 1 to 3 capsules (500 mg/capsule) P.O. b.i.d. to q.i.d.

Cautions

- Pregnant or breast-feeding women, patients who have had transplant surgery, and patients who have autoimmune disease, multiple sclerosis, or tuberculosis should avoid use.
- Patients with coagulation disorders or receiving anticoagulants should avoid use.
- Those with a history of peptic ulcer disease or gallstones should use caution when taking this herb because it stimulates stomach acid secretion.

Adverse reactions

CV: hypotension.

Interactions

Herb-drug. *Antihypertensives:* May potentiate hypotensive effects. Discourage using together. *Immunosuppressants:* May counteract the therapeutic effects because herb has immunostimulant properties. Discourage using together.
Herb-food. *Food:* Enhances absorption of herb. Patient can take herb with food.

Actions

Some chemical components stimulate immune system function and exert antitumor activity. Other components may inhibit platelet aggregation and the sympathetic nervous system, reduce the heart rate, decrease peripheral vascular resistance, and lower blood pressure. They also may exhibit antiviral activity and antioxidant properties in vitro. One component has weak diuretic properties.

Common forms

In tablets and capsules; as teas and tinctures; as cut, dried, and powdered bark, roots, and leaves.

*Liquid may contain alcohol.

Tablets, capsules: 25 mg, 150 mg, 175 mg, 300 mg, 350 mg (standard extract); 400 mg, 500 mg, 800 mg, 1 g, 5 g (raw herb).

NURSING CONSIDERATIONS

- Find out why patient is using the herb.
- Some liquid extracts contain alcohol and may be unsuitable for children or patients with liver disease.
- This herb and its contents vary from manufacturer to manufacturer; the alkaloid concentration varies from season to season.

Patient teaching

- Tell patient to remind the pharmacist of any herbal or dietary supplement he's taking when filling a new prescription.
- Inform patient that herb shouldn't be used for more than 8 weeks without a 2- to 3-week rest period from the herb.
- Instruct patient to promptly report adverse reactions and new signs or symptoms.
- Recommend another method of contraception if herb is being used for this purpose.
- Tell patient to rise slowly from a sitting or lying position to avoid dizziness from possible hypotension.
- Advise patient to watch for signs of bleeding, especially if anticoagulants are also being taken.

chamomile

(KAH-meh-mighl)

common chamomile, English chamomile, German chamomile, Hungarian chamomile, sweet false chamomile

Reported uses

Used to treat stomach disorders, such as GI spasms, and other GI inflammatory conditions. Used to treat insomnia. Used to treat menstrual disorders, migraine, epidermolysis bullosa, eczema, eye irritation, throat discomfort, and hemorrhoids. Used as a topical bacteriostat and mouthwash. Teas are mainly used for sedation or relaxation.

Dosages

Usually taken as a tea, prepared by adding 1 tbsp (3 g) of the flower head to hot water and steeping for 10 to 15 minutes; it is then taken up to q.i.d.

Cautions

- Discourage use by pregnant or breast-feeding women. Chamomile is believed to be an abortifacient, and some of its components may have teratogenic effects.
- Urge caution in patients hypersensitive to components of volatile oils and in those at risk for contact dermatitis. Chamomile shouldn't be used in teething babies or in children younger than age 2.
- Safety in patients with liver or kidney disorders hasn't been established, so these patients should avoid use.

Adverse reactions

EENT: conjunctivitis, eyelid angioedema.
GI: nausea, vomiting.
Skin: eczema, contact dermatitis.
Other: ***anaphylaxis.***

Interactions

Herb-drug. *Anticoagulants:* May potentiate effects. Discourage using together.
Other drugs: Potential for decreased absorption of drugs because of antispasmodic activity of chamomile in the GI tract. Discourage using together.

Actions

Exhibits anti-inflammatory, antiallergenic, antidiuretic, sedative, antibacterial, and antifungal properties. May lower urea level. Some compounds may stimulate liver regeneration after oral use; others have in vitro antitumor activity. One component may have antiulcer effects.

Common forms

As capsules, liquid, and tea, and as an ingredient in many cosmetic products.
Capsules: 354 mg, 360 mg

NURSING CONSIDERATIONS

- Find out why patient is using the herb.

ALERT: People sensitive to ragweed and chrysanthemums or other Compositae family members (arnica, yarrow, feverfew, tansy,

Bold italic type indicates that reaction may be life-threatening.

artemisia) may be more susceptible to contact allergies and anaphylaxis. Those with hay fever or bronchial asthma caused by pollens are more susceptible to anaphylactic reaction.
• Signs and symptoms of anaphylaxis include shortness of breath, swelling of the tongue, rash, tachycardia, and hypotension.

Patient teaching

• Advise patient to consult prescriber before using an herbal preparation because a treatment with proven efficacy may be available.
• Tell patient to remind the pharmacist of any herbal or dietary supplement he's taking when filling a new prescription.
• If patient is pregnant or is planning pregnancy, advise her not to use chamomile.
• If patient is taking an anticoagulant, advise him not to use chamomile because of possibly enhanced anticoagulant effects.
• Advise patient that chamomile may enhance an allergic reaction or make existing symptoms worse in susceptible individuals.
• Instruct parent not to give chamomile to child before checking with a knowledgeable practitioner.

echinacea

(eh-kih-NAY-zyah)

American cone flower, black sampson, black susans, coneflower, echinacea care liquid, Indian head

Reported uses

Used as a wound-healing agent for abscesses, burns, eczema, varicose ulcers of the leg and other skin wounds, and as a nonspecific immunostimulant for the supportive treatment of upper respiratory tract infections, the common cold, and urinary tract infections.

Dosages

Capsules containing powdered herb: Equivalent to 900 mg to 1 g P.O. t.i.d.; doses can vary.
Expressed juice: 6 to 9 ml P.O. daily.
Tea: 2 teaspoons (4 g) of coarsely powdered herb simmered in 1 cup (240 ml) of boiling water for 10 minutes. Avoid this method of administration because some active compounds are water-insoluble.
Tincture: 0.75 to 1.5 ml (15 to 30 gtt) P.O. two to five times daily. The tincture may be given as 60 gtt P.O. t.i.d.

Cautions

• Contraindicated in patients with severe illnesses, such as HIV infection, collagen disease, leukosis, multiple sclerosis, and tuberculosis or other autoimmune diseases.
• Discourage use of herb by pregnant or breast-feeding women; effects are unknown.

Adverse reactions

CNS: fever.
GI: nausea, vomiting, unpleasant taste, minor GI symptoms.
GU: diuresis.
Other: tachyphylaxis, allergic reaction in patients allergic to plants belonging to the daisy family.

Interactions

Herb-drug. *Disulfiram, metronidazole:* Herbal products that contain alcohol may cause a disulfiram reaction. Discourage using together. *Immunosuppressants such as cyclosporine:* Decreases effectiveness of these drugs. Discourage using together.
Herb-lifestyle. *Alcohol:* Echinacea preparations containing alcohol may enhance CNS depression. Discourage using together.

Actions

Extract stimulates the immune system and reduces growth of bacteria responsible for vaginal infections. Components may exert local anesthetic effects and anti-inflammatory activities. Essential oil components produce a tingling sensation on the tongue. Some compounds also exhibit direct antitumor activity and insecticidal activity. Conjugates in the plant activate adrenal cortex activity. The fresh-pressed juice of the aerial portion and the extract of the roots may inhibit influenza, herpes infections, and vesicular stomatitis virus.

Common forms

Capsules and tablets; also as hydroalcoholic extracts, fresh-pressed juice, glycerite, lozenges, and tinctures.
Capsules: 125 mg, 355 mg (85 mg herbal extract powder), 500 mg.
Tablets: 335 mg.

*Liquid may contain alcohol.

NURSING CONSIDERATIONS

- Daily dose depends on the preparation and potency.
- Echinacea shouldn't be taken for more than 8 weeks.
- Echinacea is considered supportive treatment for infection; it shouldn't be used in place of antibiotic therapy.
- Echinacea is usually taken at the first sign of illness and continued for up to 14 days. Regular prophylactic use isn't recommended.
- Herbalists recommend using liquid preparations because it's believed that echinacea functions in the mouth and should have direct contact with the lymph tissues at the back of the throat.
- Some tinctures contain 15% to 90% alcohol, which may be unsuitable for children and adolescents, alcoholics, and patients with hepatic disease.

Patient teaching

- Tell patient to remind the pharmacist of any herbal or dietary supplement he's taking when filling a new prescription.
- Advise patient not to delay seeking appropriate medical evaluation for a prolonged illness.

ALERT: Advise patient taking herb for prolonged time that overstimulation of the immune system and possible immune suppression may occur.

- Advise woman to avoid use of herb during pregnancy and when breast-feeding.

eucalyptus

(yoo-kah-LIP-tes)

fevertree, gum tree, Tasmanian blue gum

Reported uses

Used internally and externally as an expectorant. Used to treat infections and fevers. Also used topically to treat sore muscles and rheumatism.

Dosages

Essential oil: Oil is used in massage blends for sore muscles and in foot baths or saunas, steam inhalations, chest rubs, room sprays, bath blends, and air diffusions. For external use only.

Leaf: Average daily dose is 4 to 16 g P.O. divided every 3 to 4 hours.

Oil: For internal use, average dose is 0.3 to 0.6 g P.O. daily. For external use, oil with 5% to 20% concentration or a semisolid preparation with 5% to 10% concentration.

Tea: Prepared using one of two methods. For the infusion method, 6 oz (180 ml) of dried herb is steeped in boiling water for 2 to 3 minutes, and then strained. For the decoction method, 6 to 8 oz (180 to 240 ml) of dried herb is placed in boiling water, boiled for 3 to 5 minutes and then strained.

Tincture: 3 to 4 g P.O. daily.

Cautions

- Patients who have had an allergic reaction to eucalyptus or its vapors should avoid use.
- Patients who are pregnant or breast-feeding, have liver disease, or have intestinal tract inflammation should avoid use.
- Essential oil preparations shouldn't be applied to an infant's or child's face because of risk of severe bronchial spasm.

Adverse reactions

CNS: delirium, dizziness, ***seizures.***
EENT: miosis.
GI: epigastric burning, nausea, vomiting.
Musculoskeletal: muscular weakness.
Respiratory: ***asthma-like attacks.***

Interactions

Herb-drug. *Antidiabetics:* Enhances effects. Discourage using together, except under direct medical supervision.
Other drugs: Eucalyptus oil induces detoxication enzyme systems in the liver; therefore, the oil may affect any drug metabolized in liver. Monitor patient for effect and toxic reaction.

Herb-herb. *Other herbs that cause hypoglycemia (basil, Glucomannan, Queen Anne's lace):* Decreases glucose level. Monitor patient for effect and advise caution.

Actions

Produces a stimulant effect on nasal cold receptors. Acts as a counterirritant and causes an increase in cutaneous blood flow. Also exhibits antimicrobial, antifungal, and anti-inflammatory effects.

Common forms

As an oil and a lotion.

NURSING CONSIDERATIONS

- In susceptible patients, particularly infants and children, application of eucalyptus to the face or the inhalation of vapors can cause asthma-like attacks.
- Monitor glucose level in diabetic patient taking eucalyptus.

ALERT: The oil shouldn't be taken internally unless it has been diluted. As little as a few drops of oil for children and 4 to 5 ml of oil for adults can cause poisoning. Signs include hypotension, circulatory dysfunction, and cardiac and respiratory failure.

- If poisoning or overdose occurs, don't induce vomiting because of risk of aspiration. Administer activated charcoal and treat symptomatically.

Patient teaching

- Tell patient to remind the pharmacist of any herbal or dietary supplement he's taking when filling a new prescription.
- Advise the patient to stop taking eucalyptus immediately and to check with his prescriber if he has hives, skin rash, or trouble breathing.
- Inform patient of potential adverse effects.
- Instruct caregiver not to apply to the face of a child or infant, especially around the nose.

fennel

(FEN-el)

bitter fennel, carosella, common fennel, fenchel, fenouil, fenouille, sweet fennel

Reported uses

Used to increase milk secretion, promote menses, facilitate birth, and increase libido. Used as an expectorant to manage cough and bronchitis. Also used to treat mild spastic disorders of the GI tract, feelings of fullness, and flatulence. Fennel syrup has been used to treat upper respiratory tract infections in children.

Dosages

▶ **GI complaints.** Herbalists recommend 0.1 to 0.6 ml P.O. of the oil daily, or 5 to 7 g of the fruit daily.

Cautions

- Urge caution in patients allergic to other members of the Umbelliferae family, such as celery, carrots, or mugwort.
- Discourage use by pregnant women and those with a history of seizures.

Adverse reactions

CNS: *seizures,* hallucinations.
GI: nausea, vomiting.
Respiratory: ***pulmonary edema.***
Skin: photodermatitis, contact dermatitis.
Other: allergic reaction.

Interactions

Herb-drug. *Drugs that lower the seizure threshold, anticonvulsants:* Increases risk of seizure. Monitor patient very closely.
Herb-lifestyle. *Sun exposure:* Increases risk of photosensitivity reactions. Advise patient to wear protective clothing and sunscreen and to limit exposure to direct sunlight.

Actions

May exhibit stimulant and antiflatulent properties. Fennel oil with methylparaben inhibits the growth of *Salmonella enteritidis* and, to a lesser extent, *Listeria monocytogenes*.

Common forms

Volatile oil in water: 2% (sweet fennel), 4% (bitter fennel)

NURSING CONSIDERATIONS

- Find out why patient is using the herb.
- Verify that the patient doesn't have an allergic response to celery, fennel, or similar spices and herbs.

Patient teaching

- Inform patient that herb can't be recommended for any use because of insufficient evidence.
- Tell patient to remind the pharmacist of any herbal or dietary supplement he's taking when filling a new prescription.

*Liquid may contain alcohol.

ALERT: Don't mistake poison hemlock for fennel. Hemlock can cause vomiting, paralysis, and death. Know the source of preparation before taking fennel.
- Tell patient to stop taking this herb and contact prescriber immediately if he experiences hives, rash, or difficulty breathing.
- Advise patient to avoid sun exposure if photodermatitis occurs.

feverfew

(FEE-ver-fyoo)

altamisa, bachelors' button, chamomile grande, featherfew, featherfoil, midsummer daisy

Reported uses

Used as an antipyretic and to treat psoriasis, toothache, insect bites, rheumatism, asthma, stomachache, menstrual problems, and threatened miscarriage. Also used for migraine prophylaxis.

Dosages

Infusion: Prepared by steeping 2 tsp of feverfew in a cup of water for 15 minutes. For stronger infusion, double the amount of feverfew and allow it to steep for 25 minutes. Infusion dose in folk medicine is 1 cup (240 ml) t.i.d.; stronger infusions are used for washes.
Powder: Daily dose recommended by herbalists is 50 mg to 1.2 g.

▶ **Migraine treatment.** Average dose of 543 mcg P.O. parthenolide (a component of feverfew) daily.

▶ **Migraine prophylaxis.** 25 mg of freeze-dried leaf extract P.O. daily, or 50 mg of leaf P.O. daily with food, or 50 to 200 mg of aerial parts of plant P.O. daily.

Cautions

- Pregnant women should avoid use because of herb's potential abortifacient properties; breast-feeding women also should avoid use.
- Patients allergic to members of the daisy, or Asteraceae, family—including yarrow, southernwood, wormwood, chamomile, marigold, goldenrod, coltsfoot, and dandelion—and patients who have had previous reactions to feverfew shouldn't take it internally.
- Feverfew shouldn't be used in children.
- Those taking anticoagulants such as warfarin and heparin should use cautiously.

Adverse reactions

CNS: dizziness.
CV: tachycardia.
GI: GI upset, mouth ulcerations.
Skin: contact dermatitis.

Interactions

Herb-drug. *Anticoagulants, antiplatelet drugs including aspirin and thrombolytics:* Feverfew inhibits prostaglandin synthesis and platelet aggregation. Monitor patient for increased bleeding.

Actions

Main active ingredients may inhibit serotonin release by platelets. Extracts of feverfew contain chemicals that inhibit activation of leukocytes and the synthesis of leukotrienes and prostaglandins.

Common forms

As capsules, dried leaves, liquid, powder, seeds, and tablets.
Capsules: 250 mg (leaf extract), 380 mg (pure leaf).

NURSING CONSIDERATIONS

- Find out why patient is using the herb.
- Rash or contact dermatitis may indicate sensitivity to feverfew. Patient should discontinue use immediately.
- Potency is often based on the parthenolide content in the preparation, which varies.

Patient teaching

- Assure patient that several other strategies for migraine treatment and prophylaxis exist and that these should be attempted before taking products with unknown benefits and risks.
- Instruct patient not to withdraw herb abruptly, but to taper its use gradually because of risk of post-feverfew syndrome. Symptoms include tension headaches, insomnia, joint stiffness and pain, and lethargy.
- Remind patient to report promptly unusual signs and symptoms, such as mouth sores or skin ulcerations.

• Tell patient to remind the pharmacist of any herbal or dietary supplement he's taking when filling a new prescription.
• Educate patient about risk of increased bleeding when combining herb with an anticoagulant, such as warfarin or heparin, or an antiplatelet, such as aspirin or an NSAID.
• Caution patient that a rash or abnormal skin condition may indicate an allergy to feverfew. Instruct patient to stop taking the herb if a rash appears.

flax

(flaks)

flaxseed, linseed, lint bells, linum

Reported uses

Used to treat constipation, functional disorders of the colon resulting from laxative abuse, irritable bowel syndrome, and diverticulitis. Also used as a supplement to decrease the risk of hypercholesterolemia and atherosclerosis. Externally, flax has been made into a poultice and used to treat areas of local inflammation.

Dosages

▶ **For all systemic uses.** 1 to 2 tbsp (2 to 4 ml) of oil or mature seeds daily in two or three divided doses. Average dose is 1 oz (30 ml) of oil or 1 oz. mature seeds daily.

▶ **For topical use.** 30 to 50 g of flax meal applied as a hot, moist poultice or compress, as needed.

Cautions

• Those with an ileus, those with esophageal strictures, and those experiencing an acute inflammatory illness of the GI tract should avoid use.
• Pregnant and breast-feeding patients and those planning to become pregnant also should avoid use.

Adverse reactions

GI: diarrhea, flatulence, nausea.

Interactions

Herb-drug. *Laxatives, stool softeners:* Possible increase in laxative actions of flax. Discourage using together.

Oral medications: Because of its fibrous content and binding potential, drug absorption may be altered or prevented. Advise patient to avoid using flax within 2 hours of a drug.

Actions

Decreases total cholesterol and low-density lipoprotein levels. May decrease thrombin-mediated platelet aggregation. Flax contains lignins, which may have weak estrogenic, antiestrogenic, and steroid-like activity. Diets high in flax may lower the risk of breast and other hormone-dependent cancers. Linolenic acid supplement, derived from flax, arginine, and yeast RNA, may improve weight gain in some patients with HIV.

Common forms

As a powder, capsules, softgel capsules, and an oil.

Softgel capsules: 1,000 mg.

NURSING CONSIDERATIONS

• Find out why patient is using the herb.

ALERT: Immature seedpods are especially poisonous. Overdose symptoms include, but aren't limited to, shortness of breath, tachypnea, cyanosis, weakness, and unstable gait, progressing to paralysis and seizures.

Patient teaching

• Encourage patient to drink plenty of fluids to minimize flatulence.
• Instruct patient to refrigerate flaxseed oil to prevent breakdown of essential fatty acids.
• Remind patient that other cholesterol-lowering therapies exist that have been proven to improve survival and lower the risk of cardiac disease; flax has no such clinical support.
• Warn patient not to treat chronic constipation, other GI disturbances, or ophthalmic injury with flax before seeking appropriate medical evaluation, because doing so may delay diagnosis of a potentially serious medical condition.
• Instruct patient never to ingest immature seeds and to keep flax away from children and pets.
• Tell patient to report decreased effects of other drugs being taken if patient continues to use the herb.

*Liquid may contain alcohol.

garlic

(GAR-lik)

allium, camphor of the poor, da-suan, la-suan, nectar of the gods, poor man's treacle, stinking rose

Reported uses

Used most commonly to decrease total cholesterol level, decrease triglyceride level, and increase high-density lipoprotein cholesterol level. Also used to help prevent atherosclerosis because of its effect on blood pressure and platelet aggregation. Used to decrease the risk of cancer, especially cancer of the GI tract. Used to decrease the risk of CVA and MI and to treat cough, colds, fevers, and sore throats.

Used to treat asthma, diabetes, inflammation, heavy metal poisoning, constipation, and athlete's foot. Also used as an antimicrobial and to reduce symptoms in patients with AIDS.

Dosages

▶ **Lower cholesterol level.** 600 to 900 mg of dried power, 2 to 5 mg of allicin, or 2 to 5 g of fresh clove. Average dose is 4 g of fresh garlic or 8 mg of essential oil daily.

Cautions

- Contraindicated in patients sensitive to garlic or other members of the Lilaceae family and in those with GI disorders, such as peptic ulcer or reflux disease.
- Also contraindicated in pregnant women because of its oxytocic effects.

Adverse reactions

CNS: dizziness.
GI: halitosis; irritation of mouth, esophagus, and stomach; nausea; vomiting.
Hematologic: decreased hemoglobin production and lysis of RBCs (with long-term use or excessive dosages).
Skin: contact dermatitis, diaphoresis.
Other: allergic reaction, ***anaphylaxis,*** garlic odor.

Interactions

Herb-drug. *Anticoagulants, NSAIDs, prostacyclin:* May increase bleeding time. Discourage using together.
Antidiabetics: Glucose level may be further decreased. Advise caution if using together, and tell patient to monitor glucose level closely.
Drugs metabolized by the enzyme cytochrome P-2E1, a member of the cytochrome P-450 system (such as acetaminophen): Decreases metabolism of these drugs. Monitor patient for clinical effects and toxic reaction.
Herb-herb. *Herbs with anticoagulant effects:* Increases bleeding time. Discourage using together.
Herbs with antihyperglycemic effects: Glucose level may be further decreased. Tell patient to use caution and to monitor glucose level closely.

Actions

May exhibit antithrombotic, lipid-lowering, cholesterol-lowering, antitumor, and antimicrobial effects. May have hypoglycemic activity and hypotensive properties, as well as antibacterial, antifungal, larvicidal, insecticidal, amebicidal, and antiviral activities. A component in garlic oil may inhibit adenosine diphosphate-induced platelet aggregation. Also may decrease a type of carcinogen and nitrite accumulation.

Common forms

In tablets; also as fresh bulb, antiseptic oil, fresh extract, powdered, freeze-dried garlic powder, and garlic oil (essential oil).
Dried powder: 400 to 1,200 mg.
Fresh bulb: 2 to 5 g.
Tablets (allicin total potential): 2 to 5 mg.
Tablets (garlic extract): 100 mg, 320 mg, 400 mg, 600 mg.

NURSING CONSIDERATIONS

- Garlic isn't recommended for patients with diabetes, insomnia, pemphigus, organ transplants, or rheumatoid arthritis, or in postsurgical patients.
- Garlic may lower glucose level. If patient is taking an antihyperglycemic, watch for signs and symptoms of hypoglycemia and monitor his glucose level.

Patient teaching

- Advise patient that cholesterol-lowering drugs are commonly used for hypercholesterolemia because of their proven survival data

__Bold italic type__ indicates that reaction may be life-threatening.

and ability to lower cholesterol levels more effectively than garlic.

- Instruct patient to watch for signs of bleeding (bleeding gums, easy bruising, tarry stools, petechiae) if garlic supplements are taken with antiplatelet agents.
- Tell patient to remind the pharmacist of any herbal or dietary supplement he's taking when filling a new prescription.
- Advise patient not to delay seeking appropriate medical evaluation because doing so may delay diagnosis of a potentially serious medical condition.
- Discourage heavy use of garlic before surgery.
- If patient is using garlic to lower his cholesterol level, advise him to notify his prescriber and to have his cholesterol level monitored.
- If patient is using garlic as a topical antiseptic, tell him to avoid prolonged exposure to the skin because burns can occur.

ginger

(JIN-jer)
zingiber

Reported uses

Used as an antiemetic, GI protectant, anti-inflammatory agent useful for arthritis treatment, CV stimulant, antitumor agent, antioxidant, and as therapy for microbial and parasitic infestations. Also used to treat seasickness, morning or motion sickness, and postoperative nausea and vomiting, and to provide relief from pain and swelling caused by rheumatoid arthritis, osteoarthritis, or muscular discomfort.

Dosages

Infusion: Prepared by steeping 0.5 to 1 g of herb in boiling water and then straining after 5 minutes. (1 tsp is equal to 3 g of drug.)

Dosage forms and strengths vary with the condition.

▶ **As an antiemetic.** 500 to 1,000 mg powdered ginger P.O., or 1,000 mg fresh ginger root P.O.

▶ **Arthritis.** 1 to 2 g daily.

▶ **Nausea caused by chemotherapy.** 1 g before chemotherapy.

▶ **Migraine headache or arthritis.** Up to 2 g daily.

▶ **Motion sickness.** 1 g P.O. 30 minutes before travel, then 0.5 to 1 g q 4 hours. Also could begin 1 to 2 days before trip.

Cautions

- Patients with gallstones or with an allergy to ginger should avoid use.
- Pregnant women and those with bleeding disorders should avoid using large amounts of ginger.
- Patients taking a CNS depressant or an antiarrhythmic should use cautiously.

Adverse reactions

CNS: CNS depression.
CV: ***arrhythmias,*** increased bleeding time.
GI: heartburn.

Interactions

Herb-drug. *Anticoagulants and other drugs that can increase bleeding time:* May further increase bleeding time. Discourage using together.

Herb-herb. *Herbs that may increase bleeding time:* May further increase bleeding time. Discourage using together.

Actions

Inhibits platelet aggregation induced by adenosine diphosphate and epinephrine. May exhibit anti-inflammatory and positive inotropic effects. Specific components of ginger produce varying CV effects.

Common forms

As root, extract, liquid, powder, capsules, tablets, and teas.

Extract: 250 mg.
Liquid, powder, capsules: 100 mg, 465 mg.
Root: 530 mg.
Tablets (chewable): 67.5 mg.

NURSING CONSIDERATIONS

- Find out why patient is using the herb.
- Ginger may interfere with the intended therapeutic effect of conventional drugs.
- If overdose occurs, monitor patient for arrhythmias and CNS depression.

*Liquid may contain alcohol.

Patient teaching

- Advise patient to consult prescriber before using an herbal preparation because a treatment with proven efficacy may be available.
- Tell patient to remind the pharmacist of any herbal or dietary supplement he's taking when filling a new prescription.
- Advise pregnant patient to consult with a knowledgeable practitioner before using ginger medicinally.
- Educate patients to look for signs and symptoms of bleeding, such as nosebleeds or excessive bruising.

ginkgo

(GIN-koh)

EGB 761, GBE, GBE 24, GBX, ginkgo biloba, ginkogink, LI 1370, rokan, sophium, tanakan, tebonin

Reported uses

Primarily used to manage cerebral insufficiency, dementia, and circulatory disorders such as intermittent claudication. Also used to treat headaches, asthma, colitis, impotence, depression, altitude sickness, tinnitus, cochlear deafness, vertigo, premenstrual syndrome, macular degeneration, diabetic retinopathy, and allergies.

Used as an adjunctive treatment for pancreatic cancer and schizophrenia. Also used in addition to physical therapy for Fontaine stage IIb peripheral arterial disease to decrease pain during ambulation with a minimum of 6 weeks of treatment.

In Germany, standardized ginkgo extracts are required to contain 22% to 27% ginkgo flavonoids and 5% to 7% terpenoids.

Dosages

▶ **Dementia syndromes.** 120 to 240 mg P.O. daily in two or three divided doses.

▶ **Peripheral arterial disease, vertigo, and tinnitus.** 120 to 160 mg P.O. daily in two or three divided doses.

Cautions

- Patient with a history of an allergic reaction to gingko or any of its components should avoid use, as should patient with increased risk of intracranial hemorrhage (hypertension, diabetes).
- Patient receiving an antiplatelet or an anticoagulant should avoid use because of the increased risk of bleeding.
- Herb should be avoided in the perioperative period and before childbirth.

Adverse reactions

CNS: headache, ***seizures, subarachnoid hemorrhage.***

GI: diarrhea, flatulence, nausea, vomiting.

Skin: contact hypersensitivity reaction, dermatitis.

Interactions

Herb-drug. *Anticoagulants, antiplatelets, high-dose vitamin E:* May increase the risk of bleeding. Discourage using together.

MAO inhibitors: Theoretically, ginkgo can potentiate the activity of these drugs. Advise patient to stop taking herb.

Selective serotonin reuptake inhibitors: Ginkgo extracts may reverse the sexual dysfunction caused by these drugs. Urge patient to consult prescriber before using together.

Warfarin: Possibly increases INR when taken together. Monitor INR.

Herb-herb. *Garlic and other herbs that increase bleeding time:* Potentiates anticoagulant effects. Advise patient to use together cautiously.

Actions

Produces arterial and venous vasoactive changes that increase tissue perfusion and cerebral blood flow. Also produces arterial vasodilation, inhibits arterial spasms, decreases capillary permeability, reduces capillary fragility, decreases blood viscosity, and reduces erythrocyte aggregation. Ginkgo biloba extract acts as an antioxidant, and ginkgolide B (a component of gingko) may be a potent inhibitor of platelet activating factor.

Common forms

As ginkgo biloba extract in capsules, tablets, and sublingual sprays (standardized to contain 24% flavone glycosides and 6% terpenes) and as concentrated alcoholic extract of fresh leaf.

Capsules: 30 mg, 40 mg, 60 mg, 120 mg, 260 mg, 420 mg.

Bold italic type indicates that reaction may be life-threatening.

Capsules (ginkgo biloba extract [24% standardized extract] bound to phosphatidylcholine): 80 mg.
S.L. sprays: 15 mg/spray, 40 mg/spray.
Tablets: 30 mg, 40 mg, 60 mg, 120 mg, 260 mg, 420 mg.

NURSING CONSIDERATIONS

- Ginkgo extracts are considered standardized if they contain 24% ginkgo flavonoid glycosides and 6% terpene lactones.
- Treatment period ranges from 6 to 8 weeks, but therapy beyond 3 months isn't recommended.

ALERT: Seizures may occur in children after ingestion of more than 50 seeds.

- Patients must be monitored for possible adverse reactions such as GI problems, headaches, dizziness, allergic reaction, and serious bleeding.

Patient teaching

- Inform patient that the therapeutic and toxic components of gingko can vary significantly from product to product. Advise him to obtain gingko from a reliable source.
- Advise patient to discontinue use at least 2 weeks before surgery.
- Advise patient to report unusual bleeding or bruising.
- Instruct patient to keep seeds out of reach of children because of potential risk of seizures with ingestion.
- Advise patient to avoid contact with the fruit pulp or seed coats because of the risk of contact dermatitis. More potent preparations may cause irritation or blistering of skin or mucous membranes if applied externally.

ginseng
(JIN-sehng)
American ginseng, Asiatic ginseng, Chinese ginseng, G115, Japanese ginseng, jintsam, Korean ginseng

Reported uses

Used to minimize or reduce the activity of the thymus gland. Also used as a sedative, demulcent (soothes irritated or inflamed internal tissues or organs), aphrodisiac, antidepressant, sleep aid, and diuretic. May be used to improve stamina, concentration, healing, stress-resistance, vigilance, and work efficiency and to improve well-being in geriatric patients with debilitated or degenerative conditions.

Also used to decrease fasting blood glucose and hemoglobin A1c in diabetic and nondiabetic patients, and to treat hyperlipidemia, hepatic dysfunction, and impaired cognitive function.

Dosages

Dosages vary with the disease state; usually, 0.5 to 2 g dry ginseng root daily or 200 to 600 mg ginseng extract daily, in one or two equal doses.

▶ **Improved well-being in debilitated geriatric patients.** 0.4 to 0.8 g root P.O. daily on a continual basis.

Cautions

- Urge caution in patients with CV disease, hypertension, hypotension, or diabetes, and in those receiving steroid therapy.
- Discourage use by pregnant or breast-feeding women; effects are unknown.

Adverse reactions

CNS: headache, insomnia, nervousness.
CV: chest pain, palpitations, hypertension.
EENT: epistaxis.
GI: diarrhea, nausea, vomiting.
GU: impotence, vaginal bleeding.
Skin: pruritus, skin eruptions (with ginseng abuse).
Other: breast pain.

Interactions

Herb-drug. *Anticoagulants, antiplatelet drugs:* May decrease the effects of these drugs. Monitor PT and INR.
Antidiabetics, insulin: Increases hypoglycemic effects. Monitor glucose level.
Drugs metabolized by CYP 3A4: Ginseng may inhibit this enzyme system. Monitor patient for clinical effects and toxicity.
Phenelzine, other MAO inhibitors: May cause headache, irritability, visual hallucinations, and other interactions. Discourage using together.
Warfarin: Ginseng may decrease warfarin effect. Discourage using herbal drug.

*Liquid may contain alcohol.

Actions

Ginseng compounds may exert opposing effects. For example, one compound has CNS-depressant, anticonvulsant, analgesic, and antipsychotic effects and stress-ulcer–preventing action. Another compound has CNS-stimulating, antifatigue, hypertensive, and stress-ulcer–aggravating effects. Some components enhance cardiac performance, whereas others depress cardiac function.

Oral ginseng may reduce cholesterol and triglycerides, decrease platelet adhesiveness, impair coagulation, and increase fibrinolysis. It may also reduce stress by acting on the adrenal gland.

Extracts of ginseng may exhibit antioxidant activity.

Common forms

As capsules, teas, extract, root powder, whole root (by the pound), and oil.
Capsules: 100 mg, 250 mg, 500 mg.
Extract*: 2 oz root extract (in alcohol base).
Root powder: 1 oz, 4 oz.
Tea bags: 1,500 mg ginseng root.

NURSING CONSIDERATIONS

- Some debate exists concerning a possible ginseng abuse syndrome. It reportedly occurs when large doses of the herb are taken with other psychomotor stimulants, such as tea and coffee; symptoms include diarrhea, hypertension, restlessness, insomnia, skin eruptions, depression, appetite suppression, euphoria, and edema. However, some reputable herbal sources discredit such reports.
- Considering the high level of bioactivity for ginseng components, ginseng may not be safe for patients with a serious or chronic medical condition.
- Monitor diabetic patient for signs and symptoms of hypoglycemia.

Patient teaching

- Tell patient with medical conditions to check with prescriber before taking ginseng.
- Advise diabetic patient to check glucose level closely until effects are known.
- Instruct patient to watch for unusual symptoms (nervousness, insomnia, palpitations, diarrhea) because of risk of ginseng toxicity.
- Inform patient that the therapeutic and toxic components of ginseng can vary significantly from product to product. Advise him to obtain ginseng from a reliable source.

goldenseal

(GOHL-den-seel)

eye balm, eye root, goldsiegel, ground raspberry, Indian dye, Indian turmeric, jaundice root

Reported uses

Used to treat GI disorders, gastritis, peptic ulceration, anorexia, postpartum hemorrhage, dysmenorrhea, eczema, pruritus, tuberculosis, cancer, mouth ulcerations, otorrhea, tinnitus, and conjunctivitis; also used as a wound antiseptic, diuretic, laxative, and anti-inflammatory agent.

Used to shorten the duration of acute *Vibrio cholera* diarrhea and diarrhea caused by some species of *Giardia, Salmonella, Shigella,* and some *Enterobacteriaceae*. May be used to improve biliary secretion and function in patients with hepatic cirrhosis.

Dosages

Alcohol and water extract: 250 mg P.O. t.i.d.
Dried rhizome: 0.5 to 1 g t.i.d.

Cautions

- Patients with hypertension, heart failure, and arrhythmias should avoid use.
- Pregnant and breast-feeding patients and those with severe renal or hepatic disease should avoid use.
- Goldenseal shouldn't be given to infants.

Adverse reactions

CNS: sedation, reduced mental alertness, hallucinations, delirium, paresthesia, paralysis.
CV: hypotension, hypertension, ***asystole, heart block.***
GI: nausea, vomiting, diarrhea, GI cramping, mouth ulcerations.
Hematologic: megaloblastic anemia from decreased vitamin B absorption, ***leukopenia.***
Respiratory: ***respiratory depression.***
Skin: contact dermatitis.

Interactions

Herb-drug. *Anticoagulants:* May reduce anticoagulant effect. Discourage using together. *Antidiabetics, insulin:* Increases hypoglycemic effects. Discourage using together; advise patient to monitor glucose levels closely. *Antihypertensives:* May reduce or enhance hypotensive effect. Discourage using together. *Beta blockers, calcium channel blockers, digoxin:* May interfere or enhance cardiac effects. Discourage using together. *CNS depressants such as benzodiazepines:* May enhance sedative effects. Discourage using together. *Cephalosporins, disulfiram, metronidazole:* May cause disulfiram-like reaction when taken with liquid herbal preparations. Discourage using together.
Herb-lifestyle. *Alcohol use:* May enhance sedative effects. Discourage using together.

Actions

May have astringent, anti-inflammatory, oxytocic, antihemorrhagic, and laxative properties. Inhibits muscular contractions.

Decreases the anticoagulant effect of heparin and acts as a cardiac stimulant (at lower dosages), increases coronary perfusion, and inhibits cardiac activity (at higher dosages). May exhibit antipyretic activity (greater than aspirin) and antimuscarinic, antihistaminic, antitumor, antimicrobial, antiparasitic, and hypotensive effects.

Causes vasoconstriction and produces significant changes in blood pressure.

Common forms

In capsules and tablets; also as alcohol and water extracts, dried ground root powder, tinctures, and teas.
Capsules, tablets: 250 mg, 350 mg, 400 mg, 404 mg, 470 mg, 500 mg, 535 mg, 540 mg.

NURSING CONSIDERATIONS

- German Commission E hasn't endorsed the use of goldenseal for any condition because of its potential toxicity and lack of well-documented efficacy.
- Berberine, a chemical constitute of goldenseal, increases bilirubin levels in infants and thus shouldn't be given to them.
- Monitor patient for signs and symptoms of vitamin B deficiency such as megaloblastic anemia, paresthesia, seizures, cheilosis, glossitis, and seborrheic dermatitis.
- Monitor patient for adverse CV, respiratory, and neurologic effects. If patient has a toxic reaction, induce vomiting and perform gastric lavage. After lavage, instill activated charcoal and treat symptomatically.

Patient teaching

- Tell patient to remind the pharmacist of any herbal or dietary supplement he's taking when filling a new prescription.
- Advise patient not to use goldenseal because of its toxicity and lack of documented efficacy, especially if the patient has CV disease.

ALERT: High doses may lead to vomiting, bradycardia, hypertension, respiratory depression, exaggerated reflexes, seizures, and death.

grapeseed, pinebark

(GRAYP-seed; PIGHN-bahrk)
muskat, *Pinus maritima, Pinus nigra, Vitis coignetiae, Vitis vinifera*

Reported uses

Used as an antioxidant to treat circulatory disorders (hypoxia from atherosclerosis, inflammation, and cardiac or cerebral infarction). Also used to treat pain, limb heaviness, and swelling in patients with peripheral circulatory disorders and to treat inflammatory conditions, varicose veins, and cancer.

Dosages

Tablets, capsules: 25 to 300 mg P.O. daily for up to 3 weeks; maintenance dosage of 40 to 80 mg P.O. once daily.

Cautions

- Patients with liver dysfunction should use cautiously.

Adverse reactions

Hepatic: ***hepatotoxicity.***

Interactions

None reported.

*Liquid may contain alcohol.

Actions

Demonstrates antilipoperoxidant activity and xanthine oxidase inhibition. Inhibits enzymes responsible for skin turnover. Extract exhibits therapeutic effects in Ehrlich ascites carcinoma and inhibits growth of *Streptococcus mutans*.

Common forms

Tablets, capsules: 25 mg to 300 mg.

NURSING CONSIDERATIONS

- Grapeseed may interfere with the intended therapeutic effect of conventional drugs.
- Grapeseed extract may have antiplatelet effects. If a patient is having elective surgery, it may be prudent to stop the supplement 2 to 3 days before surgery. Monitor PT and INR.

Patient teaching

- Warn patient not to treat symptoms of venous insufficiency or circulatory disorders before seeking appropriate medical evaluation because doing so may delay diagnosis of a potentially serious medical condition.
- Tell the patient to remind the pharmacist of any herbal or dietary supplement he's taking when filling a new prescription.

kava

(KAH-veh)

ava, awa, kava-kava, kawa, kew, sakau, tonga, yagona

Reported uses

Used to treat nervous anxiety, stress, and restlessness. Used orally as a sedative, to promote wound healing, and to treat headaches, seizure disorders, the common cold, respiratory tract infection, tuberculosis, and rheumatism. Also used to treat urogenital infections, including chronic cystitis, venereal disease, uterine inflammation, menstrual problems, and vaginal prolapse. Some herbal practitioners consider kava an aphrodisiac. Kava juice is used to treat skin diseases, including leprosy. Also used as a poultice for intestinal problems, otitis, and abscesses.

Dosages

▶ **Anxiety.** 50 to 70 mg purified kava lactones t.i.d., equivalent to 100 to 250 mg of dried kava root extract per dose. (By comparison, the traditional bowl of raw kava beverage contains about 250 mg of kava lactones.)

▶ **Restlessness.** 180 to 210 mg of kava lactones taken as a tea 1 hour before bedtime. The typical dose in this form is 1 cup t.i.d. Prepare by simmering 2 to 4 g of the root in 5 oz boiling water for 5 to 10 minutes and then straining.

Cautions

- Patients hypersensitive to kava or any of its components should avoid this herb. Depressed patients should avoid the herb because of possible sedative activity; those with endogenous depression should avoid it because of possible increased risk of suicide. Pregnant women should avoid the herb because of possible loss of uterine tone; those who are breast-feeding also should avoid it. Children shouldn't use this herb.
- Patients with renal disease, thrombocytopenia, or neutropenia should use cautiously.

Adverse reactions

CNS: mild euphoric changes characterized by feelings of happiness, fluent and lively speech, and increased sensitivity to sounds; morning fatigue.
EENT: visual accommodation disorders, pupil dilation, and disorders of oculomotor equilibrium.
GI: reduced levels of albumin, total protein, bilirubin and urea; increased HDL cholesterol, mild GI disturbances, mouth numbness.
GU: hematuria.
Hematologic: increased RBC count, decreased platelets and lymphocytes.
Respiratory: pulmonary hypertension.
Skin: scaly rash.

Interactions

Herb-drug. *Antiplatelet drugs, MAO-type B inhibitors:* Possible additive effects. Monitor patient closely.
Barbiturates, benzodiazepines: Kava lactones potentiate the effects of CNS depressants, leading to toxicity. Discourage using together.
Levodopa: Possible reduced effectiveness of levodopa therapy in patients with Parkinson's

disease, apparently because of dopamine antagonism. Advise patient to use cautiously.

Herb-herb. *Calamus, calendula, California poppy, capsicum, catnip, celery, couch grass, elecampane, German chamomile, goldenseal, gotu kola, hops, Jamaican dogwood, lemon balm, sage, sassafras, shepherd's purse, Siberian ginseng, skullcap, stinging nettle, St. John's wort, valerian, wild lettuce, yerba maté:* Additive sedative effects may occur. Monitor patient closely.

Herb-lifestyle. *Alcohol:* Increases risk of CNS depression and liver damage. Discourage using together.

Actions

Components of the root may cause local anesthetic activity that is similar to cocaine but lasts longer than benzocaine. Some components show fungistatic properties against several fungi.

Induces muscular relaxation and inhibits the limbic system, an effect linked to suppression of emotional excitability and mood enhancement. Produces mild euphoria with no effect on thoughts and memory during the intoxication. Other effects include analgesia, sedation, hyporeflexia, impaired gait, and pupil dilation.

Common forms

A drink from pulverized roots, tablets, capsules, or extract.

NURSING CONSIDERATIONS

- Heavy kava users are more likely to complain of poor health. About 20% are underweight with reduced levels of albumin, total protein, bilirubin, urea, platelets, and lymphocytes; increased HDL cholesterol and RBCs; hematuria; puffy faces; scaly rashes; and some evidence of pulmonary hypertension. These symptoms resolve several weeks after the herb is stopped. Toxic doses can cause progressive ataxia, muscle weakness, and ascending paralysis, all of which resolve when herb is stopped. Extreme use (more than 300 g/week) may increase gamma-glutamyl transferase levels.
- Patient shouldn't use kava with conventional sedative-hypnotics, anxiolytics, MAO inhibitors, other psychopharmacologic drugs, levodopa, or antiplatelet drugs without first consulting prescriber.
- Adverse effects of kava may occur at start of therapy but are usually transient.

Patient teaching

ALERT: Tell patient to report jaundice, dark urine, easy bruising, and abdominal pain. Kava has been linked to liver damage including cirrhosis, hepatitis, and liver failure.

- Advise patient that usual doses can affect motor function; caution against performing hazardous activities.
- Warn patient to avoid taking herb with alcohol because of increased risk of CNS depression and liver damage.
- Tell patient to remind the pharmacist of any herbal or dietary supplement he's taking when filling a new prescription.

milk thistle

(MILK THIH-sel)

Carduus marianus L., Cnicus marianus, holy thistle, Lady's thistle, Marian thistle, Mary thistle, St. Mary thistle

Reported uses

Used to treat dyspepsia, liver damage from chemicals, *Amanita* mushroom poisoning, supportive therapy for inflammatory liver disease and cirrhosis, loss of appetite, and gallbladder and spleen disorders. It's also used as a liver protectant.

Dosages

Dried fruit or seed: 12 to 15 g P.O. daily.

Oral: Doses of milk thistle extract vary from 200 to 400 mg of silibinin (70% silymarin extract) P.O. daily.

Tea: 3 to 5 g freshly crushed fruit or seed steeped in 5 oz (148 ml) of boiling water for 10 to 15 minutes. One cup of tea P.O. t.i.d. to q.i.d., 30 minutes before meals.

Cautions

- Milk thistle shouldn't be used by women who are pregnant or breast-feeding or by patients hypersensitive to it or to plants in the Asteraceae family. Use in decompensated cirrhosis isn't recommended.

*Liquid may contain alcohol.

Adverse reactions

GI: nausea, vomiting, diarrhea.

Interactions

Herb-drug. *Aspirin:* Herb may improve aspirin metabolism in patients with liver cirrhosis. Advise patient to consult prescriber before use.
Cisplatin: Herb may prevent kidney damage by cisplatin. Advise patient to consult prescriber before use.
Disulfiram: Products that contain alcohol may cause a disulfiram-like reaction. Discourage using together.
Hepatotoxic drugs: May prevent liver damage from butyrophenones, phenothiazines, phenytoin, acetaminophen, and halothane. Advise patient to consult prescriber before use.
Tacrine: Silymarin reduces adverse cholinergic effects when given together. Advise patient to consult prescriber before use.

Actions

Exerts hepatoprotective and antihepatotoxic actions over liver toxins by altering the outer liver membrane cell structure so that toxins cannot enter the cell. Also leads to activation of the regenerative capacity of the liver through cell development.

Common forms

As capsules, tablets, and extract.
Capsules: 50 mg, 100 mg, 175 mg, 200 mg, 505 mg.
Tablets: 85 mg (standardized to contain 80% silymarin with the flavonoid silibinin).

NURSING CONSIDERATIONS

- Warn patient not to take herb for liver inflammation or cirrhosis before seeking appropriate medical evaluation because doing so may delay diagnosis of a potentially serious medical condition.
- Mild allergic reaction may occur, especially in people allergic to members of the Asteraceae family, including ragweed, chrysanthemums, marigolds, and daisies.
- Don't confuse milk thistle seeds or fruit with other parts of the plant or with blessed thistle *(Cnictus benedictus)*.
- Silymarin has poor water solubility; therefore, efficacy when prepared as a tea is questionable.

Patient teaching

- Tell patient to remind the pharmacist of any herbal or dietary supplement he's taking when filling a new prescription.
- Although no chemical interactions have been reported in clinical studies, advise patient that herb may interfere with therapeutic effect of conventional drugs.
- Warn patient not to take this herb while pregnant or breast-feeding.
- Tell patient to stay alert for possible allergic reaction, especially if allergic to ragweed, chrysanthemums, marigolds, or daisies.

nettle

(NEH-tel)

common nettle, greater nettle, stinging nettle

Reported uses

Used to treat allergic rhinitis, osteoarthritis, rheumatoid arthritis, kidney stones, asthma, and BPH. Also used as a diuretic, an expectorant, a general health tonic, a blood builder and purifier, a pain reliever and anti-inflammatory, and a lung tonic for ex-smokers. Also used for eczema, hives, bursitis, tendinitis, laryngitis, sciatica, and premenstrual syndrome. Nettle is being investigated for treatment of hay fever and irrigation of the urinary tract.

Dosages

▶ **Allergic rhinitis.** 600 mg freeze-dried leaf P.O. at onset of symptoms.
▶ **BPH.** 4 g root extract P.O. daily, or 600 to 1,200 mg P.O. encapsulated extract daily.
Fresh juice: 5 to 10 ml P.O. t.i.d.
Infusion: 1.5 g powdered nettle in cold water; heated to boiling for 1 minute, then steeped covered for 10 minutes and strained (1 tsp is equal to 1.3 g herb).
Liquid extract (1:1 in 25% alcohol)*: 2 to 6 ml P.O. t.i.d.
▶ **Osteoarthritis.** 1 leaf applied to affected area daily.
▶ **Rheumatoid arthritis.** 8 to 12 g leaf extract P.O. daily.
Tea: 1 tbsp fresh young plant steeped in 1 cup (240 ml) boiled water for 15 minutes. Three or more cups taken daily.

Tincture (1:5 in 45% alcohol)*: 2 to 6 ml P.O. t.i.d.

Cautions

- Contraindicated in pregnant and breast-feeding women because of its diuretic and uterine stimulation properties.
- Also contraindicated in children.

Adverse reactions

CV: edema.
GI: gastric irritation, gingivostomatitis.
GU: decreased urine formation; oliguria; increased diuresis in patients with arthritic conditions and those with myocardial or chronic venous insufficiency.
Skin: topical irritation, burning sensation.

Interactions

Herb-drug. *Disulfiram:* Possible adverse reaction if taken with liquid extract or tincture. Discourage using together.
Herb-lifestyle. *Alcohol:* Possible additive effect from liquid extract and tincture. Discourage alcohol use.

Actions

Acts primarily as a diuretic by increasing urine volume and decreasing systolic blood pressure. May stimulate uterine contractions. Extract reduces urine flow, nocturia, and residual urine.

Common forms

As capsules, dried leaf, root extract, and tincture.
Capsules: 150 mg, 300 mg.

NURSING CONSIDERATIONS

- Nettle is reported to be an abortifacient and may affect the menstrual cycle.
- Internal adverse effects are rare and allergic in nature.

Patient teaching

- Advise patient to consult prescriber before using an herbal preparation because a treatment with proven efficacy may be available.
- Tell patient to remind the pharmacist of any herbal or dietary supplement he's taking when filling a new prescription.
- Recommend caution if patient takes an antihypertensive or antidiabetic.
- Warn patient that external adverse effects result from skin contact and include burning and stinging that may persist for 12 hours or more.
- Advise patient to eat foods high in potassium, such as bananas and fresh vegetables, to replenish electrolytes lost through diuresis.
- Caution patient against using nettle for BPH or to relieve fluid accumulation caused by heart failure without medical approval and supervision.
- Tell patient to wash thoroughly with soap and water, use antihistamines and steroid creams, and wear heavy gloves if plant will be handled. If rubbed against the skin, nettles can cause intense burning for 12 hours or more.

passion flower

(PAH-shen FLOW-er)

apricot vine, granadilla, Jamaican honeysuckle, maypop, passion fruit, water lemon

Reported uses

Used as a sedative, a hypnotic, an analgesic, and an antispasmodic for treating muscle spasms caused by indigestion, menstrual cramping, pain, or migraines. Also used for neuralgia, generalized seizures, hysteria, nervous agitation, and insomnia. Crushed leaves and flowers are used topically for cuts and bruises.

Dosages

Dried herb: 250 mg to 1 g P.O., two to three 100-mg capsules P.O. b.i.d., or one 400-mg capsule P.O. daily.
Extract in vegetable glycerin base (alcohol-free): 10 to 15 gtt P.O., b.i.d. or t.i.d.
▶ **Cuts and bruises.** Crushed leaves and flowers are applied topically, p.r.n.
▶ **Hemorrhoids.** Prepare by soaking 20 g dried herb in 200 ml of simmering water, straining, then cooling before use. Apply topically, as indicated.
Infusion: 150 ml of hot water poured over 1 tsp of herb. Strain after standing for 10 minutes. Take b.i.d. or t.i.d., with a final dose about 30 minutes before h.s.

*Liquid may contain alcohol.

Liquid extract (1:1 in 25% alcohol)*: 0.5 to 1 ml P.O. t.i.d.
Solid extract: Taken in doses of 150 to 300 mg/day P.O.
Tincture (1:8 in 45% alcohol)*: 0.5 to 2 ml (½ to 1 tsp) P.O. t.i.d.
▶ **Parkinson's disease.** 10 to 30 gtt P.O. (0.7% flavonoids) t.i.d.
Dried herb: 0.25 to 1 g P.O. t.i.d.
Liquid extract: 0.5 to 1 ml P.O. t.i.d.
Tea: 4 to 8 g (3 to 6 tsp) daily in divided doses.
Tincture: 0.5 to 2 ml P.O. t.i.d.

Cautions

- Excessive doses may cause sedation and may potentiate MAO inhibitor therapy.
- Pregnant and breast-feeding women shouldn't take this herb.
- Those with liver disease or a history of alcoholism should avoid products that contain alcohol.

Adverse reactions

CNS: drowsiness, headache, flushing, agitation, confusion, psychosis.
CV: tachycardia, hypotension, ***ventricular arrhythmias.***
GI: nausea, vomiting.
Respiratory: asthma.
Other: allergic reaction, ***shock.***

Interactions

Herb-drug. *Disulfiram, metronidazole:* Herbal products that contain alcohol may cause a disulfiram-like reaction. Discourage using together.
Hexobarbital: Increases sleeping time and other barbiturate effects may be potentiated. Monitor patient's level of consciousness carefully.
Isocarboxazid, moclobemide, phenelzine, selegiline, and tranylcypromine: Actions can be potentiated by passion flower. Discourage using together.

Actions

Obtained from leaves, fruits, and flowers of *Passiflora incarnata*. Contains indole alkaloids, including harman and harmine, flavonoids, and maltol. Indole alkaloids are the basis of many biologically active substances, such as serotonin and tryptophan. Exact effect of these alkaloids is unknown; however, they can cause CNS stimulation via MAO inhibition, thereby decreasing intracellular metabolism of norepinephrine, serotonin, and other biogenic amines. Flavonoids can reduce capillary permeability and fragility. Maltol can cause sedative effects and potentiate hexobarbital and anticonvulsive activity.

Common forms

As liquid extract, crude extract, tincture, dried herb, and in several homeopathic remedies.
Liquid extract*: 1:1 in 25% alcohol.
Tincture*: 1:8 in 45% alcohol, or containing 0.7% flavonoids.

NURSING CONSIDERATIONS

- Monitor patient for possible adverse CNS effects.
- A disulfiram-like reaction may produce nausea, vomiting, flushing, headache, hypotension, tachycardia, and possibly ventricular arrhythmias and shock, leading to death.
- Patients with liver disease or alcoholism shouldn't use herbal products that contain alcohol.

Patient teaching

- Warn patient not to take herb for chronic pain or insomnia before seeking medical attention because doing so may delay diagnosis of a potentially serious medical condition.
- Tell patient to remind the pharmacist of any herbal or dietary supplement he's taking when filling a new prescription.
- Caution patient to avoid activities that require alertness and coordination until CNS effects are known.

primrose, evening
(PRIHM-rohz, EEV-ning)
king's-cure-all

Reported uses

Infusion used for sedative and astringent properties. Used to treat asthmatic coughs, GI disorders, whooping cough, psoriasis, multiple sclerosis, asthma, Raynaud's disease, and Sjögren's syndrome. Poultices made with evening primrose oil may be used to speed wound healing.

Bold italic type indicates that reaction may be life-threatening.

Used to treat pruritic symptoms of atopic dermatitis and eczema, breast pain and tenderness from premenstrual syndrome, benign breast disease, and diabetic neuropathy.

Used in rheumatoid arthritis to improve patients' symptoms and reduce the need for pain medication; also used to lower serum cholesterol, improve hypertension, and decrease platelet aggregation.

Also may be used to calm hyperactive children and to reduce mammary tumors from baseline size.

Dosages

The following dosages are based on a standardized gamma linoleic acid content of 8%.

▶ **Eczema.** *Adults:* 320 mg to 8 g P.O. daily. *Children ages 1 to 12:* 160 mg to 4 g P.O. daily for 3 months.

▶ **Breast pain.** 3 to 4 g P.O. daily.

No consensus exists for all other disorders.

Cautions

- Discourage use of herb by pregnant women; effects are unknown.
- Urge caution or discourage use in schizophrenic patients or in those taking antiseizure drugs

Adverse reactions

CNS: headache, temporal lobe epilepsy.
CV: thrombosis.
GI: nausea.
Skin: rash.
Other: inflammation, ***immunosuppression.***

Interactions

Herb-drug. *Phenothiazines:* May increase risk of seizures. Discourage using together.

Actions

Aids prostaglandin synthesis.

Common forms

Capsules: 50 mg, 500 mg, 1,300 mg.
Gelcaps: 500 mg, 1,300 mg.

NURSING CONSIDERATIONS

- Find out why patient is using the herb.
- Monitor patient for adverse effects, especially with long-term use.

Patient teaching

- Instruct patient with seizure disorders to reconsider need to use herb.
- Caution parents to use herb for a hyperactive child only under medical supervision.

Saint John's wort

(SAYNT JAHNS WART)

amber, devil's scourge, goatweed, grace of God, Hypericum, klamath weed, St. John's wort

Reported uses

Used to treat depression, bronchial inflammation, burns, cancer, enuresis, gastritis, hemorrhoids, hypothyroidism, insect bites and stings, insomnia, kidney disorders, and scabies, and has been used as a wound-healing agent. Saint John's wort can be used to treat HIV infection; also can be used topically for phototherapy of skin diseases, including psoriasis, cutaneous T-cell lymphoma, warts, and Kaposi's sarcoma.

Dosages

▶ **Depression.** 300 mg standardized extract preparations (standardized to 0.3% hypericin) P.O. t.i.d. for 4 to 6 weeks; or 2 to 4 g tea that has been steeped in 1 to 2 cups (240 to 480 ml) of water for about 10 minutes and taken P.O. daily for 4 to 6 weeks.

▶ **Burns and skin lesions.** Cream applied topically; strength isn't standardized.

Cautions

- Pregnant women and both men and women planning pregnancy shouldn't take St. John's wort because of mutagenic risk to sperm cells and oocytes and adverse effects on reproductive cells. Transplant patients maintained on cyclosporine therapy should avoid this herb because of the risk of organ rejection.

Adverse reactions

CNS: fatigue, neuropathy, restlessness, headache.
GI: digestive complaints, fullness sensation, constipation, diarrhea, nausea, abdominal pain, dry mouth.
Skin: photosensitivity reactions, pruritus.
Other: delayed hypersensitivity.

*Liquid may contain alcohol.

Interactions

Herb-drug. *Amitriptyline, chemotherapy drugs, cyclosporine, digoxin, drugs metabolized by the cytochrome P-450 enzyme system, oral contraceptives, protease inhibitors, theophylline, and warfarin:* Decreases effectiveness of these drugs. May require drug dosage adjustment. Monitor patient closely; discourage using together.
Barbiturates: Decreases sedative effects. Monitor patient closely.
Indinavir: Substantially reduces drug level, causing loss of therapeutic effects. Discourage using together.
MAO inhibitors, including phenelzine and tranylcypromine: May increase effects and cause toxicity and hypertensive crisis. Discourage using together.
Narcotics: Increases sedative effects. Discourage using together.
Reserpine: Antagonizes effects of reserpine. Discourage using together.
Selective serotonin reuptake inhibitors (SSRIs), such as citalopram, fluoxetine, paroxetine, sertraline: Increases risk of serotonin syndrome. Discourage using together.
Herb-herb. *Herbs with sedative effects, such as calamus, calendula, California poppy, capsicum, catnip, celery, couch grass, elecampane, German chamomile, goldenseal, gotu kola, Jamaican dogwood, kava, lemon balm, sage, sassafras, shepherd's purse, Siberian ginseng, skullcap, stinging nettle, valerian, wild carrot, and wild lettuce:* Possible enhanced effects of herbs. Monitor patient closely; discourage using together.
Herb-food. *Tyramine-containing foods such as beer, cheese, dried meats, fava beans, liver, wine, and yeast:* May cause hypertensive crisis when used together. Advise patient to separate administration times.
Herb-lifestyle. *Alcohol use:* May increase sedative effects. Discourage using together.
Sun exposure: Increases risk of photosensitivity reaction. Advise patient to avoid unprotected or prolonged exposure to sunlight.

Actions

Inhibits stress-induced increase in corticotropin-releasing hormone, corticotropin, and cortisol. Also has antiviral activity, including action against retroviruses.

Common forms

As capsules, sublingual capsules, and liquid tinctures.
Capsules: 100 mg, 300 mg, 500 mg (standardized to 0.3% hypericin); 250 mg (standardized to 0.14% hypericin).

NURSING CONSIDERATIONS

- Monitor patient for response to herbal therapy, as evidenced by improved mood and lessened depression.
- By using standardized extracts, patient can better control the dosage. Clinical studies have used formulations of standardized 0.3% hypericin as well as hyperforin-stabilized version of the extract.
- St. John's wort interacts with many other products; they must be considered before patient takes it with other prescription or OTC products.
- Signs and symptoms of serotonin syndrome include dizziness, nausea, vomiting, headache, epigastric pain, anxiety, confusion, restlessness, and irritability.
- Because St. John's wort decreases the effect of certain prescription drugs, watch for signs of drug toxicity if patient stops herb. Drug dosage may need reduction.

Patient teaching

- Tell patient to remind the pharmacist of any herbal or dietary supplement he's taking when filling a new prescription.
- Instruct patient to consult a health care provider for a thorough medical evaluation before using St. John's wort.
- If patient takes St. John's wort for mild-to-moderate depression, explain that several weeks may pass before effects occur. Tell patient that a new therapy may be needed if no improvement occurs in 4 to 6 weeks.

ALERT: If patient wants to switch from an SSRI to St. John's wort, tell him he may need to wait a few weeks for the SSRI to leave his system before it's safe to start taking the herb. The exact time required depends on which SSRI he's taking.

- Inform patient that St. John's wort interacts with many other prescription and OTC products.

saw palmetto

(SAW pal-MEH-toh)

American dwarf palm tree, cabbage palm, IDS 89, LSESR, sabal

Reported uses

Used as a mild diuretic; also used to treat such GU problems as BPH and to increase sperm production, breast size, and sexual vigor.

Dosages

▶ **BPH.** 320 mg P.O. daily in two divided doses for 3 months. Other recommendations include 1 to 2 g fresh saw palmetto berries or 0.5 to 1 g dried berry in decoction P.O. t.i.d.

Cautions

- Pregnant or breast-feeding women and women of childbearing age shouldn't use this herb.
- Adults and children with hormone-dependent illnesses other than BPH or breast cancer should avoid this herb.

Adverse reactions

CNS: headache.
CV: hypertension.
GI: abdominal pain, constipation, diarrhea, nausea.
GU: dysuria, impotence, urine retention.
Musculoskeletal: back pain.
Other: decreased libido.

Interactions

Herb-drug. *Adrenergics, hormones, hormone-like drugs:* Possible estrogen, androgen, and alpha-blocking effects. Drug dosages may need adjustment if patient takes this herb. Monitor patient closely.

Actions

Has an anti-inflammatory effect and inhibits prolactin and growth-factor–induced prostatic cell proliferation. May inhibit hormonally induced prostate enlargement.

Common forms

As tablets, capsules, teas, berries (fresh or dried), and liquid extract.

NURSING CONSIDERATIONS

- Find out why patient is using the herb.
- Herb should be used cautiously for conditions other than BPH because data about its effectiveness in other conditions is lacking.
- Obtain a baseline prostate-specific antigen (PSA) test before patient starts taking herb because it may cause a false-negative PSA result.
- Saw palmetto may not alter prostate size.

Patient teaching

- Tell patient to remind the pharmacist of any herbal or dietary supplement he's taking when filling a new prescription.
- Warn patient not to take herb for bladder or prostate problems before seeking medical attention because doing so could delay diagnosis of a potentially serious medical condition.
- Tell patient to take herb with food to minimize GI effects.

valerian

(veh-LEHR-ee-ehn)

all heal, amantilla, herba benedicta, katzenwurzel, phu germanicum, phu parvum

Reported uses

Used to treat menstrual cramps, restlessness and sleep disorders from nervous conditions, and other symptoms of psychological stress, such as anxiety, nervous headaches, and gastric spasms. Used topically as a bath additive for restlessness and sleep disorders.
Standardized tinctures: 2% essential oil.

Dosages

Bath additive: 100 g of root mixed with 2 L of hot water and added to one full bath.
Tea: 1 cup (240 ml) P.O. b.i.d. to t.i.d., and h.s.
Tincture (1:5 in 45% to 50% alcohol)*: 15 to 20 gtt in water several times daily.

▶ **Hastening sleep and improving sleep quality.** 400 to 800 mg root P.O. up to 2 hours before h.s. Some patients need 2 to 4 weeks of use for significant improvement. Maximum, 15 g daily.

▶ **Restlessness.** 220 mg of extract P.O. t.i.d.

*Liquid may contain alcohol.

Cautions

- Patients with history of allergy to valerian shouldn't use this herb.
- Patients with hepatic impairment shouldn't use this herb because of the risk of hepatotoxicity.
- Pregnant or breast-feeding women should avoid this herb; effects are unknown.
- Patients with acute or major skin injuries, fever, infectious diseases, cardiac insufficiency, or hypertonia shouldn't bathe with valerian products.

Adverse reactions

CNS: excitability, headache, insomnia.
CV: cardiac disturbance.
EENT: blurred vision.
GI: nausea.
Other: hypersensitivity reaction.

Interactions

Herb-drug. *Barbiturates, benzodiazepines:* Possible additive effects. Monitor patient closely.
CNS depressants: Potential additive effects. Discourage using together.
Disulfiram: Disulfiram reaction may occur if herbal extract or tincture contains alcohol. Discourage using together.
Herb-herb. *Herbs with sedative effects, such as catnip, hops, kava, passion flower, skullcap:* May potentiate sedative effects. Monitor patient closely.
Herb-lifestyle. *Alcohol use:* May potentiate sedative effects. Advise patient to avoid using together.

Actions

May exhibit a sedative effect and weak anticonvulsant and antidepressant properties. Also has antispasmodic effects on GI smooth muscle, produces coronary dilation, and has antiarrhythmic activity.

Common forms

As standardized capsules, tablets, and tinctures; also as tinctures and teas containing crude dried herb and in combination with other dietary supplements.
Standardized capsules, tablets (0.8% valerenic acid): 250 mg, 400 mg, 450 mg, 493 mg, 530 mg, 550 mg.

NURSING CONSIDERATIONS

- Valerian seems to have a more pronounced effect on those with disturbed sleep or sleep disorders.
- Evidence of valerian toxicity includes difficulty walking, hypothermia, and increased muscle relaxation.
- Withdrawal symptoms, such as increased agitation and decreased sleep, can occur if valerian is abruptly stopped after prolonged use.

Patient teaching

- Warn patient not to take herb for insomnia before seeking medical attention because doing so may delay diagnosis of a potentially serious medical condition.
- Tell patient to remind the pharmacist of any herbal or dietary supplement he's taking when filling a new prescription.
- If patient takes valerian, explain that herb may take 2 to 4 weeks to take effect.
- Inform patient that many extract products contain 40% to 60% alcohol and may not be appropriate for all patients.
- Inform patient that most adverse effects occur only after long-term use.

Appendices and Index

Glossary

Agranulocytosis: an abnormal blood condition, characterized by a severe reduction in the number of granulocytes, (basophils, eosinophils, and neutrophils), resulting in high fever, exhaustion, and bleeding ulcers of the throat, mucus membranes and GI tract. It is an acute disease and may be an adverse reaction to drug or radiation therapy.

Angioedema: a potentially life-threatening condition characterized by sudden swelling of tissue involving the face, neck, lips, tongue, throat, hands, feet, genitals, or intestine.

Aplastic anemia: a deficiency of all of the formed elements of the blood related to bone marrow failure. It may be caused by neoplastic bone marrow disease or by destruction of the bone marrow by exposure to toxic chemicals, radiation, or certain medications. Also known as pancytopenia.

Arthralgia: any pain that affects a joint.

Azotemia: a toxic condition caused by renal insufficiency and subsequent retention of urea in the blood. Also called uremia.

Cushing's syndrome: a metabolic disorder caused by an increased production of adrenocorticoptropic hormone from a tumor of the adrenal cortex or of the anterior lobe of the pituitary gland, or by excessive intake of glucocorticoids. It is characterized by central obesity, "moon face," glucose intolerance, growth suppression in children, and weakening of the muscles.

Disseminated intravascular coagulation (DIC): a life-threatening coagulopathy resulting from overstimulation of the body's clotting and anticlotting processes in response to disease, septicemia, neoplasms, obstetric emergencies, severe trauma, prolonged surgery, and hemorrhage.

Eosinophilia: an increase in the number of eosinophils in the blood accompanying many inflammatory conditions. Substantial increases are considered a reflection of an allergic response.

Erythema: redness of the skin caused by dilatation and congestion of the superficial capillaries, often a sign of inflammation or infection.

Gray baby syndrome: a possibly fatal condition that can occur in newborns (especially premature babies) who are given chloramphenicol for a bacterial infection, like meningitis. Symptoms usually appear 2 to 9 days after therapy has been initiated. They include vomiting, loose green stools, refusal to suck, hypotension, cyanosis, low body temperature, and cardiovascular collapse. The baby becomes limp and has a gray coloring.

Hemolytic anemia: a disorder characterized by the premature destruction of red blood cells. Anemia may be minimal or absent, reflecting the ability of the bone marrow to increase production of red blood cells.

Hirsutism: excessive growth of dark, coarse body hair, distributed in a male characteristic pattern.

Hypercalcemia: greater-than-normal amounts of calcium in the blood. Signs and symptoms include confusion, anorexia, abdominal pain, muscle pain, and weakness.

Hyperglycemia: greater-than-normal amounts of glucose in the blood. Classic signs and symptoms include excessive hunger, thirst, and frequent urination. Others include fatigue, weight loss, blurred vision, and poor wound healing.

Hyperkalemia: greater-than-normal amounts of potassium in the blood. Signs and symptoms include nausea, fatigue, weakness, and palpitations or irregular pulse.

Hypermagnesemia: greater-than-normal amounts of magnesium in the blood. Toxic levels in the blood may cause cardiac arrhythmias and may depress deep tendon reflexes and respiration.

Hypernatremia: greater-than-normal amounts of sodium in the blood. Signs and symptoms include confusion, seizures, coma, dysrhythmic muscle twitching, lethargy, tachycardia, and irritability.

Hyperplasia: an increase in the number of cells.

Hypocalcemia: less-than-normal amounts of calcium in the blood. Signs and symptoms of severe hypocalcemia include cardiac arrhythmias and muscle cramping and twitching as well as numbness and tingling of the hands, feet, lips, and tongue.

Hypoglycemia: less-than-normal amounts of glucose in the blood. Signs and symptoms include weakness, drowsiness, confusion, hunger, and dizziness. Patients may be pale, irritable, shaky, sweaty, and have a cold, clammy feeling and complain of headache and a rapid heart beat. Left untreated, delirium, coma, and death may occur.

Hypokalemia: less-than-normal amounts of potassium in the blood. Signs and symptoms include palpitations, muscle weakness or cramping, paresthesias, GI complaints such as constipation, nausea or vomiting, and abdominal cramping. Patient may also experience frequent urination, delirium, and depression.

Hypomagnesemia: less-than-normal amounts of magnesium in the blood. Signs and symptoms include nausea, vomiting, muscle weakness, tremors, tetany, and lethargy.

Hyponatremia: less-than-normal amounts of sodium in the blood. Signs and symptoms may range from mild anorexia, headache, or muscle cramps, to obtundation, coma, or seizures.

Leukocytosis: an abnormal increase in the number of circulating white blood cells. Kinds of leukocytosis include basophilia, eosinophilia, and neutrophilia.

Leukopenia: an abnormal decrease in the number of white blood cells to fewer than 5,000 cells/mm^3.

Myalgia: diffuse muscle pain, usually associated with malaise.

Nephrotic syndrome: an abnormal kidney condition characterized by marked proteinuria, hypoalbuminemia, and edema.

Neuroleptic malignant syndrome: the rarest and most serious of the neuroleptic-induced movement disorders. It is a neurologic emergency in most cases. Signs and symptoms include fever, rigidity, and tremor. Mental status changes such as drowsiness and confusion can progress to stupor and coma. Other symptoms may include seizures and cardiac arrhythmias.

Neutropenia: an abnormal decrease in the number of circulating neutrophils in the blood.

Pancytopenia: a deficiency of all of the formed elements of the blood related to bone marrow failure. It may be caused by neoplastic bone marrow disease or by destruction of the bone marrow after exposure to toxic chemicals, radiation, or certain medications. Also known as aplastic anemia.

Pharmacodynamics: the study of drug action in the body at the tissue site including uptake, movement, binding, and interactions.

Pharmacokinetics: the study of the action of drugs within the body, including the routes and mechanisms of absorption and excretion, the rate at which a drug's action begins and the duration of the effect, the biotransformation of the substance in the body, and the effects and routes of excretions of the metabolites of the drug.

Pseudomembranous colitis: a complication of antibiotic therapy that causes severe local tissue inflammation of the colon. Signs and symptoms include watery diarrhea, abdominal pain or cramping, and low-grade fever.

Pseudotumor cerebri: benign intracranial hypertension, most common in women between the ages of 20 and 50, caused by increased pressure within the brain. Symptoms include headache, dizziness, nausea, vomiting, and ringing or rushing sound in the ears.

Pruritus: itching

Reye's syndrome: an encephalopathy that affects children of all ages. While the cause and cure are unknown, research has established a link between the use of aspirin and other salicylate-containing medications, as well as other causes. The syndrome may follow an upper respiratory infection or chicken pox. Its onset is rapid, usually starting with irritable, combative behavior and vomiting, and progressing to semiconsciousness, seizures, coma, and possibly death.

Serotonin syndrome: a typically mild, yet potentially serious drug-related condition most often reported in patients taking two or more medications that increase CNS serotonin levels. The most common drug combinations associated with serotonin syndrome involve the monamine oxidase inhibitors (MAOIs), selective serotonin reuptake inhibitors (SSRIs), and the tricyclic antidepressants. Signs and symptoms include confusion, agitation, restlessness, rapid heart rate, muscle rigidity or twitching, tremors, and nausea.

Syncope: a brief loss of consciousness caused by oxygen deficiency to the brain. Often preceded by a feeling of dizziness, having the patient lie down or place his head between his knees may prevent it.

Thrombocytopenia: an abnormal decrease in the number of platelets in the blood, predisposing the patient to bleeding disorders.

Thrombocytopenic purpura: a bleeding disorder characterized by a marked decrease in the number of platelets, causing multiple bruises, petechiae, and hemorrhage into the tissues.

Tinnitus: a sound in one ear or both ears, such as buzzing, ringing, or whistling, occurring without external stimuli. It may be due to an ear infection, the use of certain drugs, a blocked auditory tube or canal, or head trauma.

Urticaria: an itchy skin condition characterized by pale wheals with well-defined red edges. This may be the result of an allergic response to insect bites, food, or drugs.

Look-alike and sound-alike drug names

Many drugs have similar-looking and similar-sounding generic and trade names. The list below will help you to eliminate confusion and errors by becoming familiar with some common drugs with similar names.

abciximab and infliximab

acetazolamide and acetohexamide

acetylcholine and acetylcysteine

acetylcysteine and acetylcholine

Aciphex and Aricept

Actidose and Actos

Aggrastat and argatroban

albuterol and atenolol or Albutein

Aldactone and Aldactazide

Aldomet and Aldoril or Anzemet

alitretinoin and tretinoin

alprazolam and alprostadil

amantadine and rimantadine

Ambien and Amen

Amicar and Amikin

Amikin and Amicar

amiloride and amiodarone

aminophylline and amitriptyline or ampicillin

Aminosyn and amikacin

amiodarone and amiloride

amitriptyline and nortriptyline or aminophylline

amlodipine and amiloride

amoxapine and amoxicillin

amoxicillin and amoxapine

Anafranil and enalapril, nafarelin, or alfentanil

anakinra and amikacin

anistreplase and alteplase

Antabuse and Anturane

Anturane and Accutane, or Artane

Anzemet and Aldomet

Apresoline and Apresazide

Aquasol A and AquaMEPHYTON

Aricept and Ascriptin

Artane and Anturane or Altace

Asacol and Os-Cal

Asendin and aspirin

atenolol and timolol or albuterol

Atropisol and Aplisol

Atrovent and Alupent

Avinza and Invanz

azathioprine and azidothymidine, Azulfidine, or azatadine

bacitracin and Bactroban

baclofen and Bactroban

BCG intravesical and BCG vaccine

Benadryl and Bentyl, or Benylin

Benemid and Beminal

Bentyl and Aventyl or Benadryl

benztropine and bromocriptine or brimonidine

bepridil and Prepidil

Betagan and BetaGen or Betapen

Bumex and Buprenex

bupropion and buspirone

calcifediol and calcitriol

captopril and Capitrol

Carbatrol and carvedilol

carboplatin and cisplatin

Cardene and Cardura or codeine

Cardizem SR and Cardene SR

Cardura and Coumadin, K-Dur, Cardene, or Cordarone

Catapres and Cetapred or Combipres

Celebrex and Cerebyx or Celexa

Celexa and Celebrex or Cerebyx

Cerebyx and Cerezyme, Celexa, or Celebrex

Chloromycetin and chlorambucil

chlorpromazine and chlorpropamide

Ciloxan and Cytoxan or cinoxacin

cimetidine and simethicone

Citrucel and Citracal

clomiphene and clomipramine or clonidine

clonidine and quinidine or clomiphene

clorazepate and clofibrate

clotrimazole and co-trimoxazole

clozapine and Cloxapen, clofazimine, or Klonopin

codeine and Cardene, Lodine, or Cordran

combination products and sulfamethoxazole alone

combination products and sulfisoxazole alone

Copaxone and Compazine

corticotropin and cosyntropin

Cozaar and Zocor

cyclosporine and cycloserine

cyproheptadine and cyclobenzaprine

dacarbazine and Dicarbosil or procarbazine

Dalmane and Dialume or Demulen

Dantrium and Daraprim

Demerol and Demulen, Dymelor, or Temaril

desipramine and disopyramide or imipramine

desmopressin and vasopressin

desonide and Desogen or Desoxyn

Desoxyn and digoxin or digitoxin

dexamethasone and desoximetasone

Dexedrine and dextran or Excedrin

diazepam and diazoxide

diazoxide and Dyazide

diclofenac and Diflucan or Duphalac

dicyclomine and dyclonine or doxycycline

different iron salts; elemental content may vary

digoxin and doxepin, Desoxyn, or digitoxin

Dilantin and Dilaudid

dimenhydrinate and diphenhydramine

Diprivan and Ditropan

dipyridamole and disopyramide

disopyramide and desipramine or dipyridamole

Ditropan and diazepam

dobutamine and dopamine

Don't confuse antivirals that use abbreviations for identification

doxapram and doxorubicin, doxepin, or doxazosin

doxepin and doxazosin, digoxin, doxapram, or Doxidan

doxycycline, doxylamine, and dicyclomine

d-penicillamine and penicillin

dronabinol and droperidol

droperidol and dronabinol

DynaCirc and Dynacin

Elavil and Equanil or Mellaril

Eldepryl and enalapril

enalapril and Anafranil or Eldepryl

Endep and Depen

ephedrine and epinephrine

epinephrine and ephedrine or norepinephrine

epinephrine and ephedrine

Epogen and Neupogen

Estratab and Estratest

Ethmozine and Erythrocin

ethosuximide and methsuximide

etidronate and etretinate, etidocaine, or etomidate

Eurax and Serax or Urex

Femara and Femhrt

fentanyl and alfentanil

Flexeril and Floxin or Flaxedil

Flomax and Fosamax

floxuridine and fludarabine or flucytosine

flunisolide and fluocinonide

fluorouracil and fludarabine, flucytosine, or floxuridine

fluoxetine and fluvoxamine or fluvastatin

fluticasone and fluconazole

fluvastatin and fluoxetine

folic acid and folinic acid

Foradil and Toradol

fosinopril and lisinopril

furosemide and torsemide

glimepiride and glyburide or glipizide

glucagon and Glaucon
guanabenz and guanadrel or guanfacine
guaifenesin and guanfacine
Haldol and Halcion or Halog
hydralazine and hydroxyzine
hydrocortisone and hydroxychloroquine
hydromorphone and morphine
hydroxyzine and hydroxyurea or hydralazine
HyperHep and Hyperstat or Hyper-Tet
Hyperstat and Nitrostat
idarubicin and daunorubicin
ifosfamide and cyclophosphamide
imipramine and desipramine
Imodium and Ionamin
Imuran and Inderal
Inderal and Inderide, Isordil, Adderall, or Imuran
Isoptin and Intropin
Isordil and Isuprel or Inderal
K-Phos-Neutral and Neutra-Phos-K
Lamictal and Lamisil
lamotrigine and lamivudine
Lantus and Lente
Levatol or Lipitor
levothyroxine and liothyronine or liotrix
Lithobid and Levbid
Lithonate and Lithostat
Lithotabs and Lithobid or Lithostat
Lodine and codeine, iodine, or Iopidine
Lorabid and Lortab
lorazepam and alprazolam
Lotensin and Loniten or lovastatin
Luvox and Lasix
magnesium sulfate and manganese sulfate
Maxidex and Maxzide
Mellaril and Elavil
melphalan and Mephyton
Mestinon and Mesantoin or Metatensin
metaproterenol and metoprolol or metipranolol
methicillin and mezlocillin
methimazole and mebendazole or methazolamide
methocarbamol and mephobarbital
methylprednisolone and medroxyprogesterone
methyltestosterone and medroxyprogesterone
metipranolol and metaproterenol
metoprolol and metaproterenol or metolazone
Mevacor and Mivacron
Micronor and Micro-K or Micronase
Miltown and Milontin
Minocin, niacin, and Mithracin
mitomycin and mithramycin
Monopril and Monurol
Nalfon and Naldecon
naloxone and naltrexone
Navane and Nubain or Norvasc
nelfinavir and nevirapine
Nicoderm and Nitro-Dur
Nicorette and Nordette
nifedipine and nimodipine or nicardipine
Nitro-Bid and Nicobid
nitroglycerin and nitroprusside
norepinephrine and epinephrine
Noroxin and Neurontin
nortriptyline and amitriptyline
Nubain and Navane
nystatin and Nitrostat
Ocuflox and Ocufen
olsalazine and olanzapine
opium tincture and camphorated opium tincture
oxaprozin and oxazepam
oxymorphone and oxymetholone
pancuronium and pipecuronium
Parlodel and pindolol
paroxetine and paclitaxel
Paxil and Doxil, paclitaxel, or Taxol
pemoline and Pelamine
penicillin G benzathine and Polycillin, penicillamine, or other types of penicillin

penicillin G potassium and Polycillin, penicillamine, or other types of penicillin

penicillin G procaine and Polycillin, penicillamine, or other types of penicillin

penicillin G sodium and Polycillin, penicillamine, or other types of penicillin

penicillin V potassium and Polycillin, penicillamine, or other types of penicillin

pentobarbital and phenobarbital

pentostatin and Pentostam

Persantine and Periactin

phentermine and phentolamine

phenytoin and mephenytoin

pindolol and Parlodel, Panadol, or Plendil

pioglitazone and rosiglitazone

Pitocin and Pitressin

Plendil and pindolol

pralidoxime and pramoxine or pyridoxine

Pravachol and Prevacid or propranolol

prednisolone and prednisone

Premarin and Primaxin

Prilosec and Prozac, or Prinivil

primidone and prednisone

Prinivil and Proventil or Prilosec

ProAmatine and protamine

probenecid and Procanbid

procainamide and probenecid

promethazine and promazine

propranolol and Pravachol

ProSom and Proscar, Prozac, or Psorcon

protamine and Protopam or Protropin

Prozac and Proscar, Prilosec, or ProSom

pyridoxine and pralidoxime or Pyridium

Questran and Quarzan

quinidine and quinine or clonidine

ranitidine and ritodrine or rimantadine

Reminyl and Robinul

Restoril and Vistaril

riboflavin and ribavirin

rifabutin, rifampin, and rifapentine

Rifater, Rifadin, and Rifamate

risperidone and reserpine

Ritalin and Rifadin

ritodrine and ranitidine

Sandimmune and Sandoglobulin or Sandostatin

saquinavir and saquinavir mesylate The dosages are different

selegiline and Stelazine

Serentil and Serevent or Aventyl

Serzone and Seroquel

simethicone and cimetidine

Sinequan and saquinavir

Solu-Cortef and Solu-Medrol

somatropin and somatrem, or sumatriptan

sotalol and Statrol or Stadol

streptozocin and streptomycin

sufentanil and alfentanil or fentanyl

sulfadiazine and sulfasalazine

sulfamethoxazole and sulfamethizole

sulfasalazine and sulfisoxazole, salsalate, or sulfadiazine

sulfisoxazole and sulfasalazine

sulfonamide drugs

sumatriptan and somatropin

Survanta and Sufenta

Tegretol and Toradol

Tenex and Xanax, Entex, or Ten-K

terbinafine and terbutaline

terbutaline and tolbutamide or terbinafine

terconazole and tioconazole

Testoderm and Estraderm

testosterone and testolactone

thiamine and Thorazine

thioridazine and Thorazine

Ticlid and Tequin

Tigan and Ticar

timolol and atenolol

Timoptic and Viroptic

tobramycin and Trobicin

Tobrex and Tobradex

tolnaftate and Tornalate

Toradol and Tegretol

Trandate and Trental

Trental and Trendar or Trandate

tretinoin and trientine

triamcinolone and Triaminicin or Triaminicol

triamterene and trimipramine

trifluoperazine and triflupromazine

trimipramine and triamterene or trimeprazine

Ultracet and Ultracef

Urispas and Urised

valacyclovir and valganciclovir

Vancenase and Vanceril

Vanceril and Vansil

Verelan and Vivarin, Ferralyn, or Virilon

Versed and VePesid

vidarabine and cytarabine

vinblastine and vincristine, vindesine, or vinorelbine

Visine and Visken

Voltaren and Ventolin or Verelan

Wellbutrin and Wellcovorin or Wellferon

Xanax and Zantac or Tenex

Xenical and Xeloda

Zarontin and Zaroxolyn

Zaroxolyn and Zarontin

Zebeta and DiaBeta

Zestril and Zostrix

Zofran and Zosyn, Zantac, or Zoloft

Zyloprim and ZORprin

Zyprexa and Zyrtec

Zyrtec and Zyprexa

Drugs that shouldn't be crushed

Many drug forms, such as slow-release, enteric-coated, encapsulated beads, wax-matrix, sublingual, and buccal forms, are made to release their active ingredients over a certain period of time or at preset points after administration. The disruptions caused by crushing these drug forms can dramatically affect the absorption rate and increase the risk of adverse reactions.

Other reasons not to crush these drug forms include such considerations as taste, tissue irritation, and unusual formulation—for example, a capsule within a capsule, a liquid within a capsule, or a multiple-compressed tablet. Avoid crushing the following drugs, listed by brand name, for the reasons noted beside them.

Accutane (irritant)
Aciphex (delayed release)
Adalat CC (sustained release)
Aggrenox (extended release)
Allegra-D (extended release)
Artane Sequels (slow release)
Arthrotec (delayed release)
Asacol (delayed release)
Azulfidine EN-tabs (enteric coated)
Bellergal-S (slow release)
Bisacodyl (enteric coated)
Bontril Slow-Release (slow release)
Breonesin (liquid filled)
Brexin L.A. (slow release)
Bromfed (slow release)
Bromfed-PD (slow release)
Bromphen (slow release)
Calan SR (slow release)
Carbatrol (extended release)
Carbiset-TR (slow release)
Cardizem CD, SR (slow release)
Ceclor CD (extended release)
Ceftin (taste)
Charcoal Plus DS (enteric coated)
Chloral Hydrate (liquid within a capsule, taste)
Chlor-Trimeton Allergy 8-hour and 12-hour (slow release)
Choledyl SA (slow release)
Chromagen (taste)
Cipro (taste)
Claritin-D (extended release)
Claritin-D 24 (extended release)
Colace (liquid within a capsule, taste)
Colazal (taste)
Colestid (protective coating)
Comhist LA (slow release)
Compazine Spansules (slow release)
Concerta (extended release)
Congess SR (sustained release)
Contac 12 Hour, Maximum Strength 12 Hour (slow release)
Cotazym-S (enteric coated)
Covera HS (extended release)
Creon (enteric coated)
Cytovene (irritant)
Dallergy (slow release)
Deconamine SR (slow release)
Deconsal, Sprinkle Capsules (slow release)
Demazin Repetabs (sustained release)
Depakene (slow release, mucous membrane irritant)
Depakote (enteric coated)
Desoxyn Gradumets (slow release)
Dexedrine Spansule (extended release)
Desyrel (taste)
Diamox Sequels (slow release)
Dilacor XR (slow release)
Dilatrate-SR (slow release)
Disobrom (slow release)
Ditropan XL (extended release)
Dolobid (irritant)
Donnatal Extentabs (slow release)

Donnazyme (slow release)
Drisdol (liquid filled)
Dristan 12 hour (extended release)
Drixoral (slow release)
Drixoral Plus
Drixoral SA
Drixoral Sinus (slow release)
Drize (slow release)
Dulcolax (enteric coated)
Duravent (extended release)
Duravent DA (extended release)
Duravent A (extended release)
Dynacirc CR (extended release)
Ecotrin (enteric coated)
Ecotrin Maximum Strength (enteric coated)
E.E.S. 400 Filmtab (enteric coated)
Effexor XR (extended release)
E-Mycin (enteric coated)
Endafed (slow release)
Entex DSE
Entex LA (slow release)
Equanil (taste)
Eryc (enteric coated)
Ery-Tab (enteric coated)
Erythrocin Stearate (enteric coated)
Erythromycin Base (enteric coated)
Eskalith CR (slow release)
Extendryl JR (extended release)
Extendryl SR (extended release)
Fedahist Gyrocaps, Timecaps (slow release)
Feldene (mucous membrane irritant)
Feocyte (slow release)
Feosol (enteric coated)
Feosol Spansules (slow release)
Feratab (enteric coated)
Fergon (slow release)
Fero-Folic 500 (slow release)
Fero-Grad-500 (slow release)
Ferro-Sequel (slow release)
Feverall Children's Capsules, Sprinkle (taste)
Flomax (extended release)
Fumatinic (slow release)
Geocillin (taste)
Glucotrol XL (extended release)
Gris-PEG (crushing may cause precipitation of larger particles)
Guaifed (slow release)
Guaifed-PD (slow release)
Guaifenex LA, PPA, PSE (extended release)
Humibid Sprinkle, DM, DM Sprinkle, LA (slow release)
Hydergine LC (liquid within a capsule)
Hytakerol (liquid filled)
Iberet (slow release)
Iberet-500 (slow release)
ICAPS Plus (slow release)
ICAPS Time Release (slow release)
Ilotycin (enteric coated)
Imdur (extended release)
Inderal LA (slow release)
Inderide LA (slow release)
Indocin SR (slow release)
Ionamin (slow release)
Isoptin SR (slow release)
Isordil Sublingual (sublingual)
Isordil Tembids (slow release)
Isosorbide Dinitrate Sublingual (sublingual)
Isuprel Glossets (sublingual)
Kaon-Cl (slow release)
K-Dur (slow release)
Klor-Con (slow release)
Klotrix (slow release)
K-Tab (slow release)
Levbid (extended release)
Levsinex Timecaps (slow release)
Lithobid (slow release)
Macrobid (extended release)
Mestinon Timespans (slow release)
Methylin ER (extended release)
Micro-K (slow release)

Micro-K Extencaps (slow release)
Motrin (taste)
MS Contin (slow release)
Naprelan (extended release)
Nia-Bid (extended release)
Niaspan (extended release)
Nexium (sustained release)
Nitro-Bid (slow release)
Nitroglyn (slow release)
Nitrong (sublingual)
Nitrostat (sublingual)
Noctec (liquid-filled capsule)
Nolamine (slow release)
Norflex (slow release)
Norpace CR (slow release)
Novafed A (slow release)
Oramorph SR (slow release)
Ornade Spansules (slow release)
Oruvail (extended release)
OxyContin (extended release)
Pancrease (enteric coated)
Pancrease MT (enteric coated)
PCE (slow release)
Pentasa (controlled release)
Perdiem (wax coated)
Phazyme (slow release)
Phazyme 95 (slow release)
Phenergan (taste)
Phyllocontin (slow release)
Placidyl (extended release)
Plendil (slow release)
Polaramine Repetabs (slow release)
Prelu-2 (slow release)
Prevacid (delayed release)
Prilosec (slow release)
Pro-Banthine (taste)
Procainamide HCl SR (slow release)
Procanbid (extended release)
Procan SR (extended release)
Procardia (delayed absorption)
Procardia XL (slow release)
Pronestyl-SR (slow release)
Protonix (delayed release)
Proventil Repetabs (slow release)
Prozac (slow release)
Quibron-T/SR (slow release)
Quinaglute Dura-Tabs (slow release)
Quinidex Extentabs (slow release)
Respaire SR (slow release)
Respbid (slow release)
Ritalin SR (slow release)
Rondec-TR (slow release)
Roxanol SR (sustained release)
Ru-Tuss (slow release)
Ru-Tuss DE, II (slow release)
Sinemet CR (slow release)
Slo-bid Gyrocaps (slow release)
Slo-Niacin (slow release)
Slo-Phyllin GG, Gyrocaps (slow release)
Slow FE (slow release)
Slow-K (slow release)
Slow-Mag (slow release)
Sorbitrate SA (slow release)
Sparine (taste)
Sudafed 12 Hour (slow release)
Sular (extended release)
Sustaire (slow release)
Tamine S.R. (slow release)
Tavist-D (multiple compressed tablet)
Tegretol-XR (extended release)
Teldrin (slow release)
Teldrin Spansules (slow release)
Ten-K (slow release)
Tenuate Dospan (slow release)
Tessalon Perles (slow release)
Theobid Duracaps (slow release)
Theochron (slow release)
Theoclear LA (slow release)
Theo-Dur (slow release)
Theolair-SR (slow release)

Theo-Sav (slow release)
Theospan-SR (slow release)
Theo-24 (slow release)
Theovent (slow release)
Theo-X (slow release)
Thorazine Spansules (slow release)
Tiazac (extended release)
Topamax (bitter taste)
Toprol XL (slow release)
T-Phyl (slow release)
Tranxene-SD (slow release)
Trental (slow release)
Triaminic (slow release)
Triaminic TR (slow release)
Triaminic-12 (slow release)
Trilafon Repetabs (slow release)
Trinalin Repetabs (slow release)
Triptone Caplets (slow release)
Tuss-LA (slow release)
Tuss-Ornade Spansules (slow release)
Tylenol Extended Relief (slow release)
ULR-LA (slow release)
Uniphyl (slow release)
Vantin (taste)
Verelan (slow release)
Volmax (extended release)
Voltaren (enteric coated)
Voltaren-XR (enteric coated)
Wellbutrin SR (sustained release)
Wygesic (taste)
ZORprin (slow release)
Zyban (slow release)
Zymase (enteric coated)

Dialyzable drugs

The amount of a drug removed by dialysis differs among patients and depends on several factors, including the patient's condition, the drug's properties, length of dialysis and dialysate used, rate of blood flow or dwell time, and purpose of dialysis. This table indicates the effect of hemodialysis on selected drugs.

Drug	Level reduced by hemodialysis?
acetaminophen	Yes (may not influence toxicity)
acetazolamide	No
acyclovir	Yes
allopurinol	Yes
alprazolam	No
amikacin	Yes
amiodarone	No
amitriptyline	No
amlodipine	No
amoxicillin	Yes
amoxicillin and clavulanate potassium	Yes
amphotericin B	No
ampicillin	Yes
ampicillin and sulbactam sodium	Yes
aspirin	Yes
atenolol	Yes
azathioprine	Yes
aztreonam	Yes
captopril	Yes
carbamazepine	No
carbenicillin	Yes
carmustine	No
cefaclor	Yes
cefadroxil	Yes
cefamandole	Yes
cefazolin	Yes
cefepime	Yes
cefonicid	Yes (only by 20%)
cefoperazone	Yes

Drug	Level reduced by hemodialysis?
cefotaxime	Yes
cefotetan	Yes (only by 20%)
cefoxitin	Yes
cefpodoxime	Yes
ceftazidime	Yes
ceftibuten	Yes
ceftizoxime	Yes
ceftriaxone	No
cefuroxime	Yes
cephalexin	Yes
cephalothin	Yes
cephradine	Yes
chloral hydrate	Yes
chlorambucil	No
chloramphenicol	Yes (very small amount)
chlordiazepoxide	No
chloroquine	No
chlorpheniramine	No
chlorpromazine	No
chlorthalidone	No
cimetidine	Yes
ciprofloxacin	Yes (only by 20%)
cisplatin	No
clindamycin	No
clofibrate	No
clonazepam	No
clonidine	No
clorazepate	No
cloxacillin	No
codeine	No

(continued)

Drug	Level reduced by hemodialysis?
colchicine	No
cortisone	No
co-trimoxazole	Yes
cyclophosphamide	Yes
diazepam	No
diazoxide	No
diclofenac	No
dicloxacillin	No
didanosine	Yes
digoxin	No
diltiazem	No
diphenhydramine	No
dipyridamole	No
disopyramide	Yes
doxazosin	No
doxepin	No
doxorubicin	No
doxycycline	No
enalapril	Yes
erythromycin	Yes (only by 20%)
ethacrynic acid	No
ethambutol	Yes (only by 20%)
ethchlorvynol	Yes
ethosuximide	Yes
famciclovir	Yes
famotidine	No
fenoprofen	No
flecainide	No
fluconazole	Yes
flucytosine	Yes
fluorouracil	Yes
fluoxetine	No
flurazepam	No
foscarnet	Yes
fosinopril	No
furosemide	No

Drug	Level reduced by hemodialysis?
gabapentin	Yes
ganciclovir	Yes
gemfibrozil	No
gentamicin	Yes
glipizide	No
glutethimide	Yes
glyburide	No
guanfacine	No
haloperidol	No
heparin	No
hydralazine	No
hydrochlorothiazide	No
hydroxyzine	No
ibuprofen	No
imipenem and cilastatin	Yes
imipramine	No
indapamide	No
indomethacin	No
insulin	No
irbesartan	No
iron dextran	No
isoniazid	Yes
isosorbide	No
isradipine	No
kanamycin	Yes
ketoconazole	No
ketoprofen	Yes
labetalol	No
levofloxacin	No
lidocaine	No
lisinopril	Yes
lithium	Yes
lomefloxacin	No
lomustine	No
loracarbef	Yes
loratadine	No

Drug	Level reduced by hemodialysis?
lorazepam	No
mechlorethamine	No
mefenamic acid	No
meperidine	No
mercaptopurine	Yes
meropenem	Yes
methadone	No
methicillin	No
methotrexate	Yes
methyldopa	Yes
methylprednisolone	No
metoclopramide	No
metolazone	No
metoprolol	No
metronidazole	Yes
mexiletine	Yes
mezlocillin	Yes
miconazole	No
midazolam	No
minocycline	No
minoxidil	Yes
misoprostol	No
morphine	No
nabumetone	No
nadolol	Yes
nafcillin	No
naproxen	No
nelfinavir	Yes
netilmicin	Yes
nifedipine	No
nimodipine	No
nitrofurantoin	Yes
nitroglycerin	No
nitroprusside	Yes
nizatidine	No
norfloxacin	No

Drug	Level reduced by hemodialysis?
nortriptyline	No
ofloxacin	Yes
olanzapine	No
omeprazole	No
oxacillin	No
oxazepam	No
paroxetine	No
penicillin G	Yes
pentamidine	No
pentazocine	Yes
perindopril	Yes
phenobarbital	Yes
phenylbutazone	No
phenytoin	No
piperacillin	Yes
piperacillin and tazobactam	Yes
piroxicam	No
prazosin	No
prednisone	No
primidone	Yes
procainamide	Yes
promethazine	No
propoxyphene	No
propranolol	No
protriptyline	No
pyridoxine	Yes
quinapril	No
quinidine	Yes
quinine	Yes
ranitidine	Yes
rifampin	No
rofecoxib	No
sertraline	No
sotalol	Yes
stavudine	Yes

(continued)

Drug	Level reduced by hemodialysis?
streptomycin	Yes
sucralfate	No
sulbactam	Yes
sulfamethoxazole	Yes
sulindac	No
temazepam	No
theophylline	Yes
ticarcillin	Yes
ticarcillin and clavulanate	Yes
timolol	No
tobramycin	Yes
tocainide	Yes
tolbutamide	No
topiramate	Yes
trazodone	No
triazolam	No
trimethoprim	Yes
valacyclovir	Yes
valproic acid	No
valsartan	No
vancomycin	No
verapamil	No
warfarin	No

Selected nonnarcotic analgesic combination products

Many common analgesics are combinations of two or more generic drugs. This table reviews common nonnarcotic analgesics.

Trade names	Generic drugs	Indications and adult dosages
Alka-Seltzer Plus Cold & Sinus Caplets, Allerest No-Drowsiness Tablets, Coldrine, Ornex No Drowsiness Tablets, Sinus-Relief Tablets, Sinutab Without Drowsiness	• acetaminophen 325 mg • pseudoephedrine hydrochloride 30 mg	For common cold, nasal congestion, sinus congestion, sinus pain. Give 2 tablets q 6 hours. Maximum, 8 tablets in 24 hours.
Esgic, Femcet, Fioricet, Fiorpap, Isocet, Repan, Triad	• acetaminophen 325 mg • caffeine 40 mg • butalbital 50 mg	For headache, mild to moderate pain, migraine. Give 1–2 tablets or capsules q 4 hours. Maximum, 6 tablets or capsules in 24 hours.
Anacin, Gensan, P-A-C Analgesic Tablets	• aspirin 400 mg • caffeine 32 mg	For headache, mild pain, myalgia. Give 2 tablets q 6 hours. Maximum, 8 tablets in 24 hours.
Ascriptin, Magnaprin	• aspirin 325 mg • magnesium hydroxide 50 mg • aluminum hydroxide 50 mg • calcium carbonate 50 mg	For fever, mild to moderate pain. Give 1–2 tablets q 4 hours.
Ascriptin A/D, Magnaprin Arthritis Strength Caplets	• aspirin 325 mg • magnesium hydroxide 75 mg • aluminum hydroxide 75 mg • calcium carbonate 75 mg	For mild to moderate pain. Give 1–2 tablets q 4 hours.
Aspirin-free Anacin PM, Excedrine P.M., Extra Strength Tylenol P.M., Sominex Pain Relief	• acetaminophen 500 mg • diphenhydramine 25 mg	For allergic rhinitis, headache, insomnia from pain or pruritus. Give 1 tablet at bedtime.
Axocet, Bucet, Butex Forte, Phrenilin Forte, Tencon	• acetaminophen 650 mg • butalbital 50 mg	For headache, mild to moderate pain. Give 1 tablet or capsule q 4 hours. Maximum, 4 tablets or capsules in 24 hours.
Bayer Select Head Cold Caplets, Dristan Cold Caplets, Sudafed Severe Cold Formula, Sinus Excedrin Extra Strength	• acetaminophen 500 mg • pseudoephedrine hydrochloride 30 mg	For common cold, nasal and sinus congestion, sinus pain. Give 2 tablets q 6 hours. Maximum, 8 tablets in 24 hours.
Bufferin Nitetime, Excedrin P.M. Caplets, Excedrin P.M. Geltabs, Excedrin P.M. Tablets	• acetaminophen 500 mg • diphenhydramine citrate 38 mg	For insomnia from pain or pruritus. Give 1 tablet at bedtime.
Cama Arthritis Pain Reliever	• aspirin 500 mg • magnesium oxide 150 mg • aluminum hydroxide 150 mg	For mild to moderate pain. Give 1–2 tablets q 4 hours. Maximum, 8 tablets in 24 hours.

(continued)

* Available in Canada only

Trade names	Generic drugs	Indications and adult dosages
Comtrex Allergy-Sinus, Sine-Off Medicine Caplets, Sine-Off Tablets, Sine-Off Allergy/Sinus Maximum Strength, Sinutab Maximum Strength	• acetaminophen 500 mg • pseudoephedrine hydrochloride 30 mg • chlorpheniramine maleate 2 mg	For allergic rhinitis, common cold, flu symptoms. Give 2 tablets q 4 hours. Maximum, 8 tablets in 24 hours.
Esgic-Plus	• acetaminophen 500 mg • caffeine 40 mg • butalbital 50 mg	For headache, migraine, mild to moderate pain. Give 1–2 tablets or capsules q 4 hours. Maximum, 6 tablets or capsules in 24 hours.
Excedrin Extra Strength, Excedrin Migraine	• aspirin 250 mg • acetaminophen 250 mg • caffeine 65 mg	For headache, migraine. Give 2 tablets q 4 hours. Maximum, 8 tablets in 24 hours.
Fiorinal, Fiortal, Lanorinal	• aspirin 325 mg • caffeine 40 mg • butalbital 50 mg	For headache, mild to moderate pain. Give 1–2 tablets or capsules q 4 hours. Maximum, 6 tablets or capsules in 24 hours.
Phrenilin	• acetaminophen 325 mg • butalbital 50 mg	For headache, mild to moderate pain. Give 1–2 tablets q 4 hours. Maximum, 6 tablets in 24 hours.
Midrin	• isometheptene mucate 65 mg • dichloralphenazone 100 mg • acetaminophen 325 mg	For migraine, tension headache. For migraine, give 2 capsules initially; then 1 capsule q 1 hour to a maximum of 5 capsules in 12 hours. For tension headache, give 1–2 capsules q 4 hours to a maximum of 8 capsules in 24 hours.
Sinutab	• acetaminophen 325 mg • chlorpheniramine 2 mg • pseudoephedrine hydrochloride 30 mg	For allergic rhinitis, common cold, flu symptoms. Give 2 tablets q 6 hours. Maximum, 8 tablets in 24 hours.
Tecnal*	• aspirin 330 mg • caffeine 40 mg • butalbital 50 mg	For headache, mild to moderate pain. Give 1–2 tablets or capsules q 4 hours. Maximum, 6 tablets or capsules in 24 hours.
Vanquish	• aspirin 227 mg • acetaminophen 194 mg • caffeine 33 mg • aluminum hydroxide 25 mg • magnesium hydroxide 50 mg	For minor aches and pains. Give 2 caplets q 4 hours. Maximum, 12 caplets in 24 hours.

* Available in Canada only

Selected narcotic analgesic combination products

Many common analgesics are combinations of two or more generic drugs. This table reviews common narcotic analgesics.

Trade names and controlled substance schedule (CSS)	Generic drugs	Indications and adult dosages
Aceta with Codeine, Tylenol with Codeine No. 3 *CSS III*	• acetminophen 300 mg • codeine phosphate 30 mg	For fever, mild to moderate pain. Give 1–2 tablets q 4 hours. Maximum, 12 tablets in 24 hours.
Alor 5/500 Tablets, Azdone, Damason-P, Lortab ASA, Panasal 5/500 *CSS III*	• aspirin 500 mg • hydrodocone bitartrate 5 mg	For moderate to moderately severe pain. Give 1–2 tablets q 4 hours. Maximum, 8 tablets in 24 hours.
Anexsia 7.5/650, Lorcet Plus *CSS III*	• acetaminophen 650 mg • hydrocodone bitartrate 7.5 mg	For arthralgia, bone pain, dental pain, headache, migraine, moderate pain. Give 1–2 tablets q 4 hours. Maximum, 6 tablets in 24 hours.
Capital with Codeine, Suspension, Tylenol with Codeine Elixir *CSS V*	• acetaminophen 120 mg • codeine phosphate 12 mg/5 ml	For mild to moderate pain. Give 15 ml q 4 hours.
Darvocet-N 50 *CSS IV*	• acetaminophen 325 mg • propoxyphene napsylate 50 mg	For mild to moderate pain. Give 1–2 tablets q 4 hours. Maximum, 12 tablets in 24 hours.
Darvocet-N 100, Propacet 100 *CSS IV*	• acetaminophen 650 mg • propoxyphene napsylate 100 mg	For mild to moderate pain. Give 1 tablet q 4 hours. Maximum, 6 tablets in 24 hours.
Empirin with Codeine No. 3 *CSS III*	• aspirin 325 mg • codeine phosphate 30 mg	For fever, mild to moderate pain. Give 1–2 tablets q 4 hours. Maximum, 12 tablets in 24 hours.
Empirin with Codeine No. 4 *CSS III*	• aspirin 325 mg • codeine phosphate 60 mg	For fever, mild to moderate pain. Give 1 tablet q 4 hours. Maximum, 6 tablets in 24 hours.
Fioricet with Codeine *CSS III*	• acetaminophen 325 mg • butalbital 50 mg • caffeine 40 mg • codeine phosphate 30 mg	For headache, mild to moderate pain. Give 1–2 capsules q 4 hours. Maximum, 6 capsules in 24 hours.
Fiorinal with Codeine *CSS III*	• aspirin 325 mg • butalbital 50 mg • caffeine 40 mg • codeine phosphate 30 mg	For headache, mild to moderate pain. Give 1–2 tablets or capsules q 4 hours. Maximum, 6 tablets or capsules in 24 hours.
Lorcet 10/650 CSS III	• acetaminophen 650 mg • hydrocodone bitartrate 10 mg	For moderate to moderately severe pain. Give 1 tablet q 4 hours. Maximum, 6 tablets in 24 hours.

(continued)

Trade names and controlled substance schedule (CSS)	Generic drugs	Indications and adult dosages
Lortab 2.5/500 *CSS III*	• acetaminophen 500 mg • hydrocodone bitartrate 2.5 mg	For moderate to moderately severe pain. Give 1–2 tablets q 4 hours. Maximum, 8 tablets in 24 hours.
Lortab 5/500 *CSS III*	• acetaminophen 500 mg • hydrocodone bitartrate 5 mg	For moderate to moderately severe pain. Give 1–2 tablets q 4 hours. Maximum, 8 tablets in 24 hours.
Lortab 7.5/500 *CSS III*	• acetaminophen 500 mgc • hydrocodone bitartrate 7.5 mg	For moderate to moderately severe pain. Give 1 tablet q 4 hours. Maximum, 8 tablets in 24 hours.
Lortab 10/500 *CSS III*	• acetaminophen 500 mg • hydrocodone bitartrate 10 mg	For moderate to moderately severe pain. Give 1 tablet q 4-6 hours. Maximum, 6 tablets in 24 hours.
Percocet 2.5/325 *CSS II*	• acetaminophen 325 mg • oxycodone hydrochloride 2.5 mg	For moderate to moderately severe pain. Give 1–2 tablets q 4-6 hours. Maximum, 12 tablets in 24 hours.
Percocet, Roxicet *CSS II*	• acetaminophen 325 mg • oxycodone hydrochloride 5 mg	For moderate to moderately severe pain. Give 1–2 tablets q 4 hours. Maximum, 12 tablets in 24 hours.
Percocet 7.5/500 *CSS II*	• acetaminophen 500 mg • oxycodone hydrochloride 7.5 mg	For moderate to moderately severe pain. Give 1–2 tablets q 4-6 hours. Maximum, 8 tablets in 24 hours.
Percocet 10/650 *CSS II*	• acetaminophen 650 mg • oxycodone hydrochloride 10 mg	For moderate to moderately severe pain. Give 1–2 tablets q 4-6 hours. Maximum, 6 tablets in 24 hours.
Percodan-Demi *CSS II*	• aspirin 325 mg • oxycodone hydrochloride 2.25 mg • oxycodone terephthalate 0.19 mg	For moderate to moderately severe pain. Give 1–2 tablets q 6 hours. Maximum, 8 tablets in 24 hours.
Percodan, Roxiprin *CSS II*	• aspirin 325 mg • oxycodone hydrochloride 4.5 mg • oxycodone terephthalate 0.38 mg	For moderate to moderately severe pain. Give 1 tablet q 6 hours. Maximum, 4 tablets in 24 hours.
Phenaphen/Codeine No. 3 *CSS III*	• acetaminophen 325 mg • codeine phosphate 30 mg	For fever, mild to moderate pain. Give 1–2 tablets q 4 hours. Maximum, 12 tablets in 24 hours.
Phenaphen/Codeine No. 4 *CSS III*	• acetaminophen 325 mg • codeine phosphate 60 mg	For fever, mild to moderate pain. Give 1 tablet q 4 hours. Maximum, 6 tablets in 24 hours.
Propoxyphene Napsylate/ Acetaminophen *CSS IV*	• acetaminophen 650 mg • propoxyphene napsylate 100 mg	For mild to moderate pain. Give 1 tablet q 4 hours. Maximum, 6 tablets in 24 hours.
Roxicet, Percocet *CSS II*	• acetaminophen 325 mg • oxycodone hydrochloride 5 mg	For moderate to moderately severe pain. Give 1–2 tablets q 4 hours. Maximum, 12 tablets in 24 hours.

Trade names and controlled substance schedule (CSS)	Generic drugs	Indications and adult dosages
Roxicet 5/500, Roxilox, Tylox *CSS II*	• acetaminophen 500 mg • oxycodone hydrochloride 5 mg	For moderate to moderately severe pain. Give 1–2 tablets q 4-6 hours. Maximum, 8 tablets in 24 hours.
Roxicet Oral Solution *CSS II*	• acetaminophen 325 mg • oxycodone hydrochloride 5 mg/5 ml	For moderate to moderately severe pain. Give 5–10 ml q 4-6 hours. Maximum, 60 ml in 24 hours.
Talacen *CSS IV*	• acetaminophen 650 mg • pentazocine hydrochloride 25 mg	For mild to moderate pain. Give 1 tablet q 4 hours. Maximum, 6 tablets in 24 hours.
Talwin Compound *CSS IV*	• aspirin 325 mg • pentazocine hydrochloride 12.5 mg	For moderate pain. Give 2 tablets q 6 hours. Maximum, 8 tablets in 24 hours.
Tylenol with Codeine No. 2 *CSS III*	• acetaminophen 300 mg • codeine phosphate 15 mg	For fever, mild to moderate pain. Give 1–2 tablets q 4 hours. Maximum, 12 tablets in 24 hours.
Tylenol with Codeine No. 3 *CSS III*	• acetaminophen 300 mg • codeine phosphate 30 mg	For fever, mild to moderate pain. Give 1–2 tablets q 4 hours. Maximum, 12 tablets in 24 hours.
Tylenol with Codeine No. 4 *CSS III*	• acetaminophen 300 mg • codeine phosphate 60 mg	For fever, mild to moderate pain. Give 1 tablet q 4 hours. Maximum, 6 tablets in 24 hours.
Tylox *CSS II*	• acetaminophen 500 mg • oxycodone hydrochloride 5 mg	For moderate to moderately severe pain. Give 1–2 tablets q 4 hours. Maximum, 12 tablets in 24 hours.
Vicodin *CSS III*	• acetaminophen 500 mg • hydrocodone bitartrate 5 mg	For moderate to moderately severe pain. Give 1–2 tablets q 4 hours. Maximum, 8 tablets in 24 hours.
Vicodin ES, *CSS III*	• acetaminophen 750 mg • hydrocodone bitartrate 7.5 mg	For moderate to moderately severe pain. Give 1 tablet q 4–6 hours. Maximum, 5 tablets in 24 hours.
Vicodin HP *CSS III*	• acetaminophen 660 mg • hydrocodone bitartrate 10 mg	For mild to moderate pain. Give 1 tablet q 4 hours. Maximum, 6 tablets in 24 hours.
Wygesic *CSS IV*	• acetaminophen 650 mg • propoxyphene napsylate 65 mg	For moderate to moderately severe pain. Give 1 tablet q 4–6 hours. Maximum, 6 tablets in 24 hours
Zydone *CSS III*	• acetaminophen 400 mg • hydrocodone bitartrate 5 mg	For moderate to moderately severe pain. Give 1 tablet q 4–6 hours. Maximum, 6 tablets in 24 hours.
Zydone 7.5 *CSS III*	• acetaminophen 400 mg • hydrocodone bitartrate 7.5 mg	For moderate to moderately severe pain. Give 1 tablet q 4–6 hours. Maximum, 6 tablets in 24 hours
Zydone 10 *CSS III*	• acetaminophen 400 mg • hydrocodone bitartrate 10 mg	For moderate to moderately severe pain. Give 1 tablet q 4–6 hours. Maximum, 6 tablets in 24 hours

Pregnancy risk categories

The Food and Drug Administration has assigned a pregnancy risk category to each systemically absorbed drug based on available clinical and preclinical information. The five categories (A, B, C, D, and X) reflect a drug's potential to cause birth defects. Although drugs are best avoided during pregnancy, this rating system permits rapid assessment of the risk-benefit ratio should drug administration to a pregnant woman become necessary. Drugs in category A are generally considered safe to use in pregnancy; drugs in category X are generally contraindicated.

- A: Adequate studies in pregnant women have failed to show a risk to fetus.
- B: Animal studies haven't shown a risk to fetus, but controlled studies haven't been conducted in pregnant women; or animal studies have shown an adverse effect on fetus, but adequate studies in pregnant women haven't shown a risk to fetus.
- C: Animal studies have shown an adverse effect on fetus, but adequate studies haven't been conducted in humans. The benefits from use in pregnant women may be acceptable despite potential risks.
- D: The drug may cause risk to human fetus, but the potential benefits of use in pregnant women may be acceptable despite the risks (such as in a life-threatening situation or a serious disease for which safer drugs can't be used or are ineffective).
- X: Studies in animals or humans show fetal abnormalities, or adverse-reaction reports indicate evidence of fetal risk. The risks involved clearly outweigh potential benefits.
- NR: Not rated.

Controlled substance schedules

Drugs regulated under the jurisdiction of the Controlled Substances Act of 1970 are divided into the following groups or schedules:

- Schedule I (C-I): High abuse potential and no accepted medical use. Examples include heroin, marijuana, and LSD.
- Schedule II (C-II): High abuse potential with severe dependence liability. Examples include narcotics, amphetamines, dronabinol, and some barbiturates.
- Schedule III (C-III): Less abuse potential than schedule II drugs and moderate dependence liability. Examples include nonbarbiturate sedatives, nonamphetamine stimulants, anabolic steroids, and limited amounts of certain narcotics.
- Schedule IV (C-IV): Less abuse potential than schedule III drugs and limited dependence liability. Examples include some sedatives, anxiolytics, and nonnarcotic analgesics.
- Schedule V (C-V): Limited abuse potential. This category includes mainly small amounts of narcotics, such as codeine, used as antitussives or antidiarrheals. Under federal law, limited quantities of certain C-V drugs may be purchased without a prescription directly from a pharmacist if allowed under specific state statutes. The purchaser must be at least age 18 and must furnish suitable identification. All such transactions must be recorded by the dispensing pharmacist.

Table of equivalents

Metric system equivalents

Metric weight

1 kilogram (kg or Kg)	=	1,000 grams (g or gm)
1 gram	=	1,000 milligrams (mg)
1 milligram	=	1,000 micrograms (mcg)
0.6 g	=	600 mg
0.3 g	=	300 mg
0.1 g	=	100 mg
0.06 g	=	60 mg
0.03 g	=	30 mg
0.015 g	=	15 mg
0.001 g	=	1 mg

Metric volume

1 liter (l or L)	=	1,000 milliliters (ml)*
1 milliliter	=	1,000 microliters (mcl)
Household		**Metric**
1 teaspoon (tsp)	=	5 ml
1 tablespoon (T or tbs)	=	15 ml
2 tablespoons	=	30 ml
8 ounces	=	240 ml
1 pint (pt)	=	473 ml
1 quart (qt)	=	946 ml
1 gallon (gal)	=	3,785 ml

Weight conversions

1 oz = 30 g

1 lb = 453.6 g

2.2 lb = 1 kg

Temperature conversions

Fahrenheit degrees	Centigrade degrees	Fahrenheit degrees	Centigrade degrees	Fahrenheit degrees	Centigrade degrees
106.0	41.1	100.6	38.1	95.2	35.1
105.8	41.0	100.4	38.0	95.0	35.0
105.6	40.9	100.2	37.9	94.8	34.9
105.4	40.8	100.0	37.8	94.6	34.8
105.2	40.7	99.8	37.7	94.4	34.7
105.0	40.6	99.6	37.6	94.2	34.6
104.8	40.4	99.4	37.4	94.0	34.4
104.6	40.3	99.2	37.3	93.8	34.3
104.4	40.2	99.0	37.2	93.6	34.2
104.2	40.1	98.8	37.1	93.4	34.1
104.0	40.0	98.6	37.0	93.2	34.0
103.8	39.9	98.4	36.9	93.0	33.9
103.6	39.8	98.2	36.8	92.8	33.8
103.4	39.7	98.0	36.7	92.6	33.7
103.2	39.6	97.8	36.5	92.4	33.6
103.0	39.4	97.6	36.4	92.2	33.4
102.8	39.3	97.4	36.3	92.0	33.3
102.6	39.2	97.2	36.2	91.8	33.2
102.4	39.1	97.0	36.1	91.6	33.1
102.2	39.0	96.8	36.0	91.4	33.0
102.0	38.9	96.6	35.9	91.2	32.9
101.8	38.8	96.4	35.8	91.0	32.8
101.6	38.7	96.2	35.7	90.8	32.7
101.4	38.6	96.0	35.6	90.6	32.6
101.2	38.4	95.8	35.4	90.4	32.4
101.0	38.3	95.6	35.3	90.2	32.3
100.8	38.2	95.4	35.2	90.0	32.2

*1 ml = 1 cubic centimeter (cc); however, ml is the preferred measurement term.

Normal laboratory test values

Hematology

Activated partial thromboplastin time
25 to 36 seconds

Hematocrit
Men: 42% to 54%
Women: 38% to 46%

Hemoglobin, total
Men: 14 to 18 g/dl
Women: 12 to 16 g/dl

Platelet count
140,000 to 400,000/mm^3

Prothrombin time
10 to 14 seconds
INR-DVT prophylaxis for major orthopedic surgery range 2 to 3

Red blood cell (RBC) count
Men: 4.5 to 6.2 million/mm^3
Women: 4.2 to 5.4 million/mm^3

RBC indices
MCH: 26 to 32 picograms/cell
MCHC: 32 to 36 g/dl
MCV: 84 to 99 femtoliters

Reticulocyte count
0.5% to 2% of total RBC count

White blood cell (WBC) count
4,100 to 10,900/mm^3

WBC differential, blood
Basophils: 0.3% to 2%
Eosinophils: 0.3% to 7%
Lymphocytes: 16.2% to 43%
Monocytes: 4% to 10%
Neutrophils: 47.6% to 76.8%

Blood chemistry

Alanine aminotransferase
Men: 10 to 35 units/L
Women: 9 to 24 units/L

Alkaline phosphatase
Adults: 39 to 117 units/L

Amylase
60 to 180 units/L

Arterial blood gases
HCO_3^-: 22 to 26 mEq/L
Pao_2: 75 to 100 mm Hg
$Paco_2$: 35 to 45 mm Hg
pH: 7.35 to 7.45
Sao_2: 94% to 100%

Aspartate aminotransferase
Men: 8 to 20 units/L
Women: 5 to 40 units/L

Bilirubin
Adults: direct, 0.1 to 0.3 mg/dl; indirect, 0.2 to 0.7 mg/dl

BUN
8 to 20 mg/dl

Calcium
Men ≥ age 22, women ≥ age 19: 8.9 to 10.1 mg/dl

Carbon dioxide, total, blood
22 to 34 mEq/L

Chloride
100 to 108 mEq/L

Creatine kinase (CK)
Total: Men ≥ age 18, 52 to 170 units/L; women ≥ age 18, 38 to 135 units/L
CK-BB: 0%
CK-MB: 0% to 7%
CK-MM: 96% to 100%

Creatinine
Men: 0.8 to 1.2 mg/dl
Women: 0.6 to 1.1 mg/dl

Glucose, fasting, plasma
70 to 100 mg/dl

Lactate dehydrogenase (LDH)
Total: 48 to 115 IU/L
LDH_1: 14% to 26%
LDH_2: 29% to 39%
LDH_3: 20% to 26%
LDH_4: 8% to 16%
LDH_5: 6% to 16%

Magnesium
1.5 to 2.5 mEq/L

Phosphorus
2.5 to 4.5 mg/dl

Potassium
3.8 to 5.5 mEq/L

Protein, total
6.4 to 8 g/dl
Albumin fraction: 3.3 to 4.5 g/dl

Sodium
135 to 145 mEq/L

Uric acid
Men: 2.5 to 8 mg/dl
Women: 1.5 to 6 mg/dl

Acknowledgments

We would like to thank the following companies for granting us permission to include their drugs in the full-color photoguide.

Abbott Laboratories
Depakote®
Hytrin®

AstraZeneca LP
Prilosec®
Tenormin®
Toprol-XL®

Aventis Pharmaceuticals
DiaBeta®
Lasix®

Bayer Corporation
Cipro®

Biovail Corporation
Cardizem®
Vasotec®

Bristol-Myers Squibb Company
Capoten®
Coumadin®
Glucophage®
Glucophage XR®
Monopril®
Pravachol®
Serzone®

Elan Pharmaceuticals, Inc.
Frova®

Forest Pharmaceuticals, Inc.
Celexa®

GlaxoSmithKline
Amoxil®
Augmentin®
Avandia®
Ceftin®
Compazine®
Coreg®
Lanoxin®
Paxil®
Relafen®
Wellbutrin SR®

Janssen Pharmaceutica, Inc.
Risperdal®

King Pharmaceuticals, Inc.
Levoxyl®

Eli Lilly and Company
Prozac®

Mallinckrodt, Inc.
Pamelor®

Merck & Co., Inc.
Cozaar®
Fosamax®
Mevacor®
Pepcid®
Prinivil®
Singulair®
Vioxx®
Zocor®

Novartis Corporation
Ritalin®
Ritalin SR®

Ortho-McNeil Pharmaceutical
Levaquin®

Parke-Davis
Accupril®
Dilantin® Kapseals®
Lipitor®
Neurontin®

Pfizer, Inc.
Celebrex®
Diflucan®
Glucotrol®
Glucotrol XL®
Norvasc®
Procardia XL®
Viagra®
Zantac®
Zithromax®
Zoloft®

Pharmacia Corporation
Bextra®
Micronase®
Provera®
Xanax®

Procter & Gamble Pharmaceuticals, Inc.
Actonel®

Purdue Pharma L.P.
OxyContin®

Roche Laboratories, Inc.
Ticlid®
Valium®

Sanofi-Synthelabo, Inc.
Ambien®

Schering Corporation and Key Pharmaceuticals, Inc.
Clarinex®
Claritin®
K-Dur®

Tap Pharmaceuticals, Inc.
Prevacid®

Warner Chilcott laboratories, Inc.
Duricef®
Eryc®
Estrace®
Ovcon® 35

Wyeth Pharmaceuticals
Effexor XR®
Phenergan®
Premarin®

Index

♦ Canada ◇ Australia

t refers to a table; **boldface** refers to the drug's monograph, ***boldface italic*** refers to full-color photograph

♦ Canada ◇ Australia

C

♦ Canada ◇ Australia

D

◆ Canada ◇ Australia

t refers to a table; **boldface** refers to the drug's monograph, ***boldface italic*** refers to full-color photograph

♦ Canada ◇ Australia

t refers to a table; **boldface** refers to the drug's monograph, ***boldface italic*** refers to full-color photograph

G

♦ Canada ◇ Australia

I

t refers to a table; **boldface** refers to the drug's monograph, ***boldface italic*** refers to full-color photograph

J

K

t refers to a table; **boldface** refers to the drug's monograph, ***boldface italic*** refers to full-color photograph

t refers to a table; **boldface** refers to the drug's monograph, ***boldface italic*** refers to full-color photograph

M

t refers to a table; **boldface** refers to the drug's monograph, ***boldface italic*** refers to full-color photograph

♦ Canada ◇ Australia

P

t refers to a table; **boldface** refers to the drug's monograph, ***boldface italic*** refers to full-color photograph

♦ Canada ◇ Australia

t refers to a table; **boldface** refers to the drug's monograph, ***boldface italic*** refers to full-color photograph

♦ Canada ◇ Australia

Q

R

S

♦ Canada ◇ Australia

t refers to a table; **boldface** refers to the drug's monograph, ***boldface italic*** refers to full-color photograph

W

t refers to a table; **boldface** refers to the drug's monograph, ***boldface italic*** refers to full-color photograph

THE SKY'S THE LIMIT
Nursing Students
■ Career Planning
■ Educational Programs
■ Involvement in Activities
■ Benefits and Money-Saving Programs
■ Leadership Opportunities
■ Networking
Nursing students in associate degree, diploma, baccalaureate,* generic masters, generic doctoral, or pre-nursing programs are invited to join the National Student Nurses' Association (NSNA), a pre-professional organization for nursing students. Over 30,000 nursing students are already taking advantage of the many programs, benefits, and leadership opportunities that NSNA has to offer: discounts on products and services, representation in the annual House of Delegates, opportunities to run for state and national office, a chance to win contests and prizes, and an opportunity to influence nursing practice in the future. "The Sky's the Limit." Join NSNA today!
*RNs in degree completion programs are also eligible for membership.
For more information contact:
NATIONAL STUDENT NURSES' ASSOCIATION, INC (NSNA).
45 Main Street, Suite 606
Brooklyn, NY 11201
Tel: (718) 210-0705 • Fax: (718) 210-0710
e-mail: nsna@nsna.org • Website: www.nsna.org
Earn academic credit; visit nsnaleadershipu.org
VISIT THE NSNA WEBSITE
http://www.nsna.org
NSNA
National Student Nurses' Association, Inc.

Visit eDrugInfo.com

This Web site gives you:

- updates on recently approved drugs, new indications, and new warnings
- patient-teaching aids on new drugs, administration techniques, and supportive measures
- news summaries on recent drug developments
- information on herbal medicines
- links to pharmaceutical companies and government agencies
- a drug information bookstore.

About PharmDisk 5.0

PharmDisk 5.0 mini-CD contains:

- a Pharmacology Self-Test—a self-paced test complete with rationales for correct and incorrect answers
- a Match Game—an engaging game that helps you learn to identify drug classes
- a direct link to **eDrugInfo.com** for drug updates and important drug news.

Windows system requirements

- Windows 98 or higher
- Pentium 166 or higher
- 64 MB RAM
- 30 MB free hard-disk space
- SVGA monitor with High Color (16-bit) and Small Fonts
- CD-ROM drive and mouse

CAUTION: Do not attempt to use this mini-CD in a floppy disk drive, Zip drive, certain slot drives, or a car stereo. Do not insert the mini-CD into a CD-ROM drive that requires the mini-CD to be in a vertical position. Placing the CD into such a drive may result in jamming.

Before installing this program, make sure your monitor is set to the minimum display requirements. If it isn't, consult your user's manual for instructions about changing the display settings.

To install on Windows 98 or higher:

- Place the mini-CD on the inner ring of the CD-ROM drive tray. Close the tray.
- In a few moments, the CD should automatically start. Once it starts, click the "Install" button to install on your computer.
- Click "Start" and select "Run" if the CD doesn't start automatically.
- Type **d:\setup** (where **d** is the letter of your CD-ROM drive), and click *OK*. Follow on-screen instructions for installing the CD.

Special note: Before using *PharmDisk 5.0*, read the file *Readme.txt* for important information about operating the program.

For technical support, call toll free 1-800-638-3030, Monday through Friday, 8:30 am to 5 pm Eastern Time.